Washington
Information Directory
2014–2015

Washington Information Directory 2014–2015

Los Angeles | London | New Delhi
Singapore | Washington DC

Los Angeles | London | New Delhi
Singapore | Washington DC

FOR INFORMATION:

CQ Press
An Imprint of SAGE Publications, Inc.
2455 Teller Road
Thousand Oaks, California 91320
E-mail: order@sagepub.com

SAGE Publications Ltd.
1 Oliver's Yard
55 City Road
London, EC1Y 1SP
United Kingdom

SAGE Publications India Pvt. Ltd.
B 1/I 1 Mohan Cooperative Industrial Area
Mathura Road, New Delhi 110 044
India

SAGE Publications Asia-Pacific Pte. Ltd.
3 Church Street
#10-04 Samsung Hub
Singapore 049483

Assistant Editor: Laura Notton
Research Editor: Catherine Farley
Editorial Assistant: Jordan Enobakhare
Researchers: Lisa Bhattacharji, Diane Goldenberg-
    Hart, Vicki Heitsch, Carol Horn, Mary Hunter,
    Frances Kerr, Ginger McCarthy, Sarah
    McGunnigle, Susie Ruth, Rebecca Stadd,
    Kate Stern, Ronald Stouffer
Production Editor: David C. Felts
Typesetter: Hurix Systems Pvt. Ltd., India
Proofreaders: Ellen Howard, Gretchen Treadwell
Indexers: Hurix Systems Pvt. Ltd., India; Wendy Allex
Cover Designer: Michael Dubowe
Marketing Manager: Carmel Schrire

Printed in the United States of America

Cover photos: iStockphoto.com; Corbis.

Library of Congress Cataloging-in-Publication Data

The Library of Congress catalogued the first edition of this title as follows:

Washington information directory. 1975/76—
    Washington. Congressional Quarterly Inc.
    1. Washington, D.C.—Directories.
    2. Washington metropolitan area—Directories.
    3. United States—Executive departments—
    Directories. I. Congressional Quarterly Inc.
F192.3.W33   975.3'0025   75-646321

ISBN: 978-1-4833-4792-9
ISSN: 0887-8064

This book is printed on acid-free paper.

14 15 16 17 18 10 9 8 7 6 5 4 3 2 1

Contents

Reference Boxes and Organization Charts

Each chapter also features a box listing the relevant committee and subcommittee resources in Congress.

Preface

Since 1975, *Washington Information Directory* has been the essential resource for locating information on governmental and nongovernmental organizations in the national capital region. This trusted and user-friendly directory helps researchers find the right contact at the right organization, whether their interest is consumer product and food safety, equal employment opportunities, finance and investments, housing, immigration, terrorism, or a wealth of other timely topics. The directory allows the user to locate accurate, complete, and current information quickly and easily in a way that free Internet searches cannot.

In updating *Washington Information Directory* every year, we research each existing organization entry to provide current addresses; phone, fax, TTY, and toll-free numbers; email and Web addresses; and key officers and descriptions. Our team which obtains this information, led by Catherine Farley, calls each organization and speaks with a member of its Washington office. In directory listings, we include contacts' direct lines whenever possible (many organizations do not publish these numbers on their Web sites in an attempt to channel all calls through an operator or answering service). When a federal department reorganizes, we assess the new divisions and directorates and reorganize the book, along with providing updated organization charts. Each year we add new government agencies and new nongovernmental organizations, which comprise national organizations and international organizations with Washington offices. Entries are arranged by topic, subtopic, and organization type. The result is an indispensable reference engine that makes finding up-to-date information easy, whether you are using the print edition or navigating the online edition.

Readers will find a comprehensive listing of the members of the 113th Congress as well as a handy "Resources in Congress" box at the beginning of each chapter listing relevant committees and subcommittees for that chapter's topic, along with their Web site and phone number. Readers may also turn to the first appendix, which offers a complete listing of each 113th Congress committee for which information is available and includes full contact information, leadership, membership, and jurisdictions.

Every new edition of the *Washington Information Directory* brings something altogether new. The 2014–2015 edition includes new federal organizations such as the Defense Department's Defense Health Agency (DHA). Arising from the 2013 Defense Authorization Act and established on October 1, 2013, the DHA is designed to integrate information technology, medical research, and budgeting to improve and administer TRICARE and the delivery of medical, dental, and pharmacy services provided to service members, retirees, and their families. Also new is the office of Educational Technology under the Education Department, which develops national educational policy and advocates for the transition from print-based to digital learning. Additionally, one of several initiatives announced by President Obama in the wake of the NSA scandal was the creation of the Civil Liberties and Privacy office under the arm of the Defense Dept. to advise the NSA director and ensure that privacy and civil liberties protections are intrinsic in national security decision-making. Among new nongovernmental organizations is nonpartisan think tank The Constitution Project (TCP), which brings together policy experts and legal practitioners across the ideological and political spectrum to tackle constitutional challenges. TCP recently made headlines with its report criticizing the U.S.'s anti-terrorism response and use of torture post 9/11. Readers will also find useful the addition of email addresses for foreign embassies and chancery offices.

The fully updated chapters of *Washington Information Directory* are supplemented by two appendices comprising a guide to the members and committees of the 113th Congress; a directory of government Web sites; a list of governors and other state officials; a list of foreign diplomats and embassies, U.S. ambassadors, and State Department country offices; and current information on the Freedom of Information Act and legislation and recent Supreme Court cases related to privacy. Readers will also find useful the addition of email addresses for foreign embassies and chancery offices. Also in the congressional delegation section, we have included Facebook and Twitter information in the members' profiles wherever available. Print readers can also search and cross-search across the edition in three ways: through the name index, the organization index, or the subject index.

CQ Press seeks to continue *Washington Information Directory*'s reputation as an invaluable, comprehensive, and authoritative reference of its kind. We welcome feedback related to the book's quality and functionality, as well as suggestions for future editions.

Laura Notton
Assistant Editor

How to Use This Directory

Washington Information Directory is designed to make your search for information quick and easy.

Each chapter covers a broad topic, and within the chapters, information is divided into more specific subject areas. This arrangement allows you to find in one place the departments and agencies of the federal government, congressional committees, and nongovernmental organizations that have the information you need.

The directory divides information sources into three main categories: (1) agencies, (2) Congress, and (3) nongovernmental organizations. There is also a small international organizations category. Each entry includes the name, address, and telephone and fax numbers of the organization; the name and title of the director or the best person to contact for information; press, hotline, and TTY numbers and Internet addresses whenever available; and a description of the work performed by the organization. Congressional committees and subcommittees appear in a box at the beginning of each chapter; a full entry for each committee appears in the first appendix.

HOW INFORMATION IS PRESENTED

The following examples represent the three main categories of entries and the other resources provided in the directory. The examples are drawn from the History and Preservation section in Chapter 4, Culture and Religion. (To read the mailing addresses, check the abbreviations at the end of this guide.)

Agencies

In the first category, government agencies are listed. For example, the National Park Service and its acronym appear in bold type. Next, in parentheses, is the name of its parent organization, the Interior Department. Entries may also include the name of an office within the agency, in this case the Office of Cultural Resources.

National Park Service (NPS), *(Interior Dept.),* *Cultural Resources, 1849 C St. N.W., #3128 20240-0001; (202) 208-7625. Fax, (202) 273-3237. Stephanie Toothman, Associate Director. Web, www.cr.nps.gov*

Oversees preservation of federal historic sites and administration of buildings programs. Programs include the National Register of Historic Places, National Historic and National Landmark

Programs, Historic American Building Survey, Historic American Engineering Record, Archeology and Antiquities Act Program, and Technical Preservation Services. Gives grant and aid assistance and tax benefit information to properties listed in the National Register of Historic Places.

Congress

Congressional committees and subcommittees relevant to each chapter are listed in a box in the beginning of each chapter. Each committee's phone number and Web site are listed here. For a complete listing of congressional committees, including their full contact information, leadership, memberships, and jurisdictions, please refer to the first appendix. Entries that appear under the "Congress" heading within each chapter are agencies under congressional authority, such as the Government Accountability Office or the Library of Congress. Each entry includes a description of the agency's activities relating to the section in which it appears.

Senate Office of Conservation and Preservation, *S416 CAP 20510; (202) 224-4550. Vacant, Director.*

Develops and coordinates programs related to the conservation and preservation of Senate records and materials for the secretary of the Senate.

Nongovernmental

Thousands of nongovernmental groups have headquarters or legislative offices in or near Washington. Their staffs are often excellent information sources, and these organizations frequently maintain special libraries or information centers. Here is an example of a group with an interest in the preservation of historic sites:

Civil War Trust, *1156 15th St. N.W., #900 20005; (202) 367-1861. Fax, (202) 367-1865. O. James Lighthizer, President. General email, info@civilwar.org Web, www.civilwar.org*

Membership: preservation professionals, historians, conservation activists, and citizens. Preserves endangered Civil War battlefields throughout the United States. Conducts preservation conferences and workshops. Advises local preservation groups. Monitors legislation and regulations at the federal, state, and local levels.

How *Washington Information Directory* Works

Washington Information Directory (WID) directs your search more efficiently and effectively than any other print or online search. This resource does the hard work of pinpointing the information you need. Here is an example of how to use it to find information on the preservation of historic sites and materials:

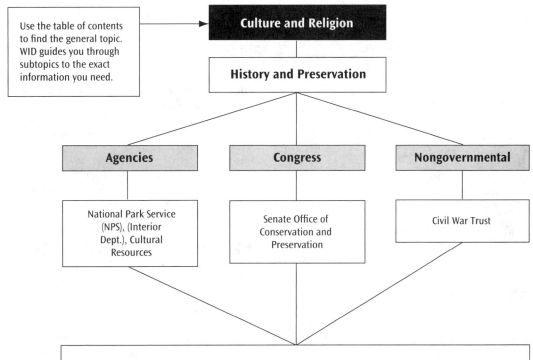

Charts and Boxes

This directory includes organization charts to make the hierarchy of federal departments and agencies easy to grasp, as well as reference boxes that provide essential agency contacts and other information. On the topic of historic sites, you can locate the National Park Service within the Interior Department (see chart on p. 276) or consult a list of sites administered by the National Park Service (see box on p. 135). The National Park Service's organization chart appears on page 533. The general organization chart for the federal government appears on page 848.

REFERENCE RESOURCES

Tables of Contents

The table of contents (p. v) lists the directory's chapters and their major subheadings. A list of reference boxes and organization charts within the chapters is provided on page vii. Each chapter opens with a detailed table of contents, including the boxes and charts that appear in the chapter.

Congressional Information

A section on the 113th Congress, beginning on page 724, provides extensive information about members and committees:

State Delegations. Here (p. 725) you can locate senators, representatives, and delegates by state (or territory) and congressional district.

Committees. These sections list the jurisdictions and memberships of committees and subcommittees of the House (p. 730) and Senate (p. 809), as well as the joint committees of Congress (p. 807). Also included are party leaderships and partisan committees of the House (p. 730) and Senate (p. 809).

Members' Offices. For the House (p. 750) and Senate (p. 823), we provide each member's Capitol Hill office

Map of Capitol Hill

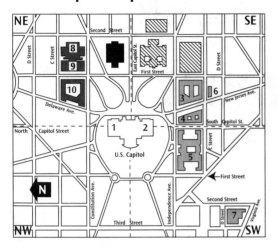

U.S. Capitol, Washington, DC 20510 or 20515*
1. Senate Wing   2. House Wing

House Office Buildings, Washington, DC 20515
3. Cannon   4. Longworth
5. Rayburn   6. O'Neill
7. Ford

Senate Office Buildings, Washington, DC 20510
8. Hart   9. Dirksen
10. Russell

Supreme Court, Washington, DC 20543

Library of Congress, Washington, DC 20540

* Mail sent to the U.S. Capitol should bear the zip code of the chamber to which it is addressed.

Note: Dashed lines indicate the city's quadrants, which are noted in the corners of the map.

address, telephone and fax numbers, Internet address, social media (if available), key professional aide, committee assignments, and district office contact information.

Ready Reference

A section of reference lists, beginning on page 843, provides information on the following subjects:

Government Information on the Internet. Organized by branch of government, this section (p. 845) lists Web addresses for locating information and social media on the White House, cabinet departments, Congress, and the judiciary.

State Government. The list of state officials (p. 850) provides the name, address, and telephone number for each governor, lieutenant governor, secretary of state, attorney general, and state treasurer. It includes a press contact for the governor and, where applicable, the governor's office representative in Washington, DC.

Diplomats. The foreign embassies section (p. 861) gives the names, official addresses, and telephone numbers of foreign diplomats in Washington; the names of ranking U.S. diplomatic officials abroad; and the phone numbers for State Department country desk offices.

Federal Laws on Information. This section presents current information on the Freedom of Information Act (p. 875) and privacy legislation (p. 878).

Indexes

Use the name index (p. 881) to look up any person listed in the directory. Use the organization index (p. 919) to find a specific organization or agency. Use the subject index (p. 967) to locate a particular area of interest. If you need information on a specific topic but do not know a particular source, the index has entries for chapter subsections to help you find where that topic is covered. For example, on the subject of equal employment for women, you can find index entries under Equal Employment Opportunity as well as under Women.

REACHING YOUR INFORMATION SOURCE

Phoning and Faxing

Call information or toll-free numbers first. Often you can get the answer you need without searching any further. If not, an explanation of your query should put you in touch with the person who can answer your question. Rarely will you need to talk to the top administrator.

Offer to fax your query if it is difficult to explain over the phone, but make sure that the person helping you knows to expect your fax. Faxing promptly and limiting your transmission to a single page brings the best results.

Remember that publications and documents are often available from a special office (for federal agencies, see p. 94) and, increasingly, on Web sites. Ask what is the fastest way to receive the information you need.

Keep in mind the agency or organization, not the name of the director. Personnel changes are common, but for most inquiries you will want to stay within the organization you call, rather than track down a person who may have moved on to a new job.

Concerning congressional questions, first contact one of your members of Congress; representatives have staff assigned to answer questions from constituents. Contact a committee only if you have a technical question that cannot be answered elsewhere.

Writing

Address letters to the director of an office or organization—the contact person listed. Your letter will be directed to the person who can answer your question. Be prepared to follow up by phone.

Using the Internet

Most agencies and governmental organizations have sites on the Internet (for federal departments and agencies, see pp. 99, 845–847) and an email address for general inquiries. Information available from these sources is expanding and is usually free once you are online. However, this approach is not always faster or better than a phone call—Internet connections can be slow, site menus can be complex or confusing, and information can be incomplete or out of date. The office also may be able to alert you to any upcoming changes.

As with faxing, reserve email for inquiries that may be too complex for a phone call, but phone first to establish that someone is ready to help.

ADDRESSES AND AREA CODES

Listings in the directory include full contact information, including telephone area code and, when available, room or suite number and nine-digit zip code. If an office prefers a mailing address that is different from the physical location, we provide both.

Washington, D.C., Addresses

For brevity, entries for agencies, organizations, and congressional offices in the District of Columbia (area code 202) do not include the city as part of the address. Here is the beginning of a typical Washington entry:

Equal Employment Opportunity Commission (EEOC), *131 M St., N.E. 20507; (202) 663-4001.*

To complete the mailing address, add "Washington, DC" before the zip code.

Building Addresses

Departments and agencies generally have their own zip codes. Updates to our directory reflect the increasing use of street addresses by the federal government. Federal offices at the following locations are listed by building name or abbreviation:

The White House. Located at 1600 Pennsylvania Ave. N.W. 20500.

Dwight D. Eisenhower Executive Office Building. Located at 17th St. and Pennsylvania Ave. N.W. 20500.

New Executive Office Building. Located at 725 17th St. N.W. 20503.

Main State Department Building. Located at 2201 C St. N.W. 20520.

The Pentagon. Located in Arlington, Virginia, but has a Washington mailing address and different zip codes for each branch of the military.

Navy Annex. Located at Columbia Pike and Southgate Rd., Arlington, VA 20370, but most offices use a Washington mailing address.

U.S. Capitol. Abbreviated as CAP; the letters *H* and *S* before the room number indicate the House or Senate side of the building. Zip codes are 20510 for the Senate, 20515 for the House.

Senate Office Buildings. Mail for delivery to Senate office buildings does not require a street address. The zip code is 20510. Abbreviations, building names, and street locations are as follows:

SDOB	Dirksen Senate Office Bldg., Constitution Ave. between 1st and 2nd Sts. N.E.
SHOB	Hart Senate Office Bldg., 2nd St. and Constitution Ave. N.E.
SROB	Russell Senate Office Bldg., Constitution Ave. between Delaware Ave. and 1st St. N.E.

House Office Buildings. Mail for delivery to House office buildings does not require a street address. The zip code is 20515. Abbreviations, building names, and street locations are as follows:

CHOB	Cannon House Office Bldg., Independence Ave. between New Jersey Ave. and 1st St. S.E.
FHOB	Ford House Office Bldg., 2nd and D Sts. S.W.
LHOB	Longworth House Office Bldg., Independence Ave. between S. Capitol St. and New Jersey Ave. S.E.
OHOB	O'Neill House Office Bldg., 300 New Jersey Ave. S.E.
RHOB	Rayburn House Office Bldg., Independence Ave. between S. Capitol and 1st Sts. S.W.

John Adams Building. Abbreviated as Adams Bldg.; located at 110 2nd St. S.E.

1 Agriculture, Food, and Nutrition

GENERAL POLICY AND ANALYSIS

Basic Resources

▶ AGENCIES

Agricultural Marketing Service (AMS) *(Agriculture Dept.)*, 1400 Independence Ave. S.W., #3933S, MS 0201 20250-0201; (202) 720-5115. Fax, (202) 720-8477. David R. Shipman, Administrator. Public Affairs, (202) 720-8998.
Web, www.ams.usda.gov

Provides domestic and international marketing services to the agricultural industry. Administers marketing, standardization, grading, inspection, and regulatory programs; maintains a market news service to inform producers of price changes; conducts agricultural marketing research and development programs; studies agricultural transportation issues.

Agriculture Dept. (USDA), 1400 Independence Ave. S.W., #200A 20250-0002; (202) 720-3631. Fax, (202) 720-2166. Thomas J. Vilsack, Secretary; Krysta Harden, Deputy Secretary. Press, (202) 720-4623. Locator, (202) 720-8732.
Web, www.usda.gov

Serves as principal adviser to the president on agricultural policy; works to increase and maintain farm income and to develop markets abroad for U.S. agricultural products.

Agriculture Dept. (USDA), *Advocacy and Outreach*, 1400 Independence Ave. S.W., 526-A Whitten Bldg. 20250; (202) 720-6350. Fax, (202) 720-7136. Carolyn Parker, Director. Toll-free, (800) 880-4183.
General email, outreachandadvocacy@usda.gov

Develops, manages, and supports programs that provide information, training, and technical assistance to socially disadvantaged farmers and ranchers and small and beginning farmers and ranchers. Administers the Small Farmer Outreach, Training, and Technical Assistance Program and the USDA Farm Worker Initiative. Provides policy guidance and feedback to the Agriculture Dept. on all outreach-related activities and functions.

Agriculture Dept. (USDA), *Chief Economist*, 1400 Independence Ave. S.W., #112A, Whitten Bldg. 20250-3810; (202) 720-4164. Fax, (202) 690-4915. Joseph W. Glauber, Chief Economist. Alternate phone, (202) 720-5955.
Web, www.usda.gov/oce

Prepares economic and statistical analyses used to plan and evaluate short- and intermediate-range agricultural policy. Evaluates Agriculture Dept. policy, proposals, and legislation for their impact on the agricultural economy. Administers Agriculture Dept. economic agencies, including the Office of Risk Assessment and Cost-Benefit Analysis, the Office of Energy Policy and New Uses, the Global Change Program Office, and the World Agricultural Outlook Board.

Agriculture Dept. (USDA), *Food, Nutrition, and Consumer Services*, 1400 Independence Ave. S.W., #216E 20250-0106; (202) 720-7711. Fax, (202) 690-3100. Kevin W. Concannon, Under Secretary.
Web, www.fns.usda.gov

Oversees the Food and Nutrition Service and the Center for Nutrition Policy and Promotion.

Farm Service Agency (FSA) *(Agriculture Dept.)*, 1400 Independence Ave. S.W., #3086 South Bldg., MS 0501 20250-0506; (202) 720-3467. Fax, (202) 720-9105. Juan M. Garcia, Administrator. Press, (202) 720-7807.
Web, www.fsa.usda.gov

Oversees farm commodity programs that provide crop loans and purchases. Administers price support programs that provide crop payments when market prices fall below specified levels; conducts programs to help obtain adequate farm and commercial storage and drying equipment for farm products; directs conservation and environmental cost-sharing projects and programs to assist farmers during natural disasters and other emergencies.

▶ CONGRESS

For a listing of relevant congressional committees and subcommittees, please see page 3 or the Appendix.

Government Accountability Office (GAO), *Natural Resources and Environment*, 441 G St. N.W., #2057 20548 (mailing address: 441 G St. N.W., #2T23A, Washington, DC 20548); (202) 512-3841. Fax, (202) 512-8774. Mark Gaffigan, Managing Director.
Web, www.gao.gov

Independent, nonpartisan agency in the legislative branch that audits the Agriculture Dept. and analyzes and reports on its handling of agriculture issues and food safety.

▶ NONGOVERNMENTAL

American Farm Bureau Federation (AFBF), *Washington Office*, 600 Maryland Ave. S.W., #1000W 20024-2520; (202) 406-3600. Fax, (202) 406-3606. Bob Stallman, President.
General email, reception@fb.org
Web, www.fb.org

Federation of state farm bureaus in fifty states and Puerto Rico. Promotes agricultural research. Interests include commodity programs, domestic production, marketing, education, research, financial assistance to the farmer, foreign assistance programs, rural development, the world food shortage, and inspection and certification of food.

National Assn. of State Departments of Agriculture, 4350 N. Fairfax Dr., #910, Arlington, VA 22203; (202) 296-9680. Fax, (703) 880-0509. Stephen Haterius, Chief Executive Officer.
General email, nasda@nasda.org
Web, www.nasda.org

AGRICULTURE RESOURCES IN CONGRESS

For a complete listing of Congress committees, including their full contact information, leadership, membership, and jurisdictions, please refer to the Appendix on pages 724–842.

HOUSE:

House Agriculture Committee, (202) 225-2171.
Web, agriculture.house.gov or democrats.agriculture
.house.gov
  **Subcommittee on Conservation, Energy, and
    Forestry,** (202) 225-2171.
  **Subcommittee on Department Operations,
    Oversight, and Nutrition,** (202) 225-2171.
  **Subcommittee on General Farm Commodities
    and Risk Management,** (202) 225-2171.
  **Subcommittee on Horticulture, Research,
    Biotechnology, and Foreign Agriculture,**
    (202) 225-2171.
  **Subcommittee on Livestock, Rural Development,
    and Credit,** (202) 225-2171.
House Appropriations Committee, (202) 225-2771.
Web, appropriations.house.gov or
democrats.appropriations.house.gov
  **Subcommittee on Agriculture, Rural
    Development, FDA, and Related Agencies,**
    (202) 225-2638.
House Education and the Workforce Committee,
  (202) 225-4527.
Web, edworkforce.house.gov or
democrats.edworkforce.house.gov
  **Subcommittee on Early Childhood,
    Elementary, and Secondary Education,**
    (202) 225-4527.
House Energy and Commerce Committee,
  (202) 225-2927.
Web, energycommerce.house.gov or
democrats.energycommerce.house.gov
  Subcommittee on Health, (202) 225-2927.
House Foreign Affairs Committee, (202) 225-5021.
Web, foreignaffairs.house.gov or
democrats.foreignaffairs.house.gov
**House Oversight and Government Reform
  Committee,** (202) 225-5074.
Web, oversight.house.gov or
democrats.oversight.house.gov
  **Subcommittee on Economic Growth, Job
    Creation, and Regulatory Affairs,**
    (202) 225-5074.
House Science, Space, and Technology Committee,
  (202) 225-6371.
Web, science.house.gov or democrats.science.house.gov
  Subcommittee on Research and Technology,
    (202) 225-7858.

House Small Business Committee, (202) 225-5821.
Web, smallbusiness.house.gov or
democrats.smallbusiness.house.gov
  **Subcommittee on Agriculture, Energy, and
    Trade,** (202) 225-5821.

SENATE:

**Senate Agriculture, Nutrition, and Forestry
  Committee,** (202) 224-2035.
Web, ag.senate.gov
  **Subcommittee on Commodities, Markets, Trade,
    and Risk Management,** (202) 224-2035.
  **Subcommittee on Conservation, Forestry, and
    Natural Resources,** (202) 224-2035.
  **Subcommittee on Jobs, Rural Economic Growth,
    and Energy Innovation,** (202) 224-2035.
  **Subcommittee on Livestock, Dairy, Poultry,
    Marketing and Agriculture Security,**
    (202) 224-2035.
  **Subcommittee on Nutrition, Specialty Crops,
    Food, and Agricultural Research,**
    (202) 224-2035.
Senate Appropriations Committee, (202) 224-7363.
Web, appropriations.senate.gov
  **Subcommittee on Agriculture, Rural
    Development, FDA, and Related Agencies,**
    (202) 224-8090.
**Senate Banking, Housing, and Urban Affairs
  Committee,** (202) 224-7391.
Web, banking.senate.gov
**Senate Commerce, Science, and Transportation
  Committee,** (202) 224-0411.
Web, commerce.senate.gov
  **Subcommittee on Consumer Protection, Product
    Safety, and Insurance,** (202) 224-1270.
Senate Environment and Public Works Committee,
  (202) 224-8832.
Web, epw.senate.gov
  **Subcommittee on Superfund, Toxics and
    Environmental Health,** (202) 224-8832.
Senate Finance Committee, (202) 224-4515.
Web, finance.senate.gov
**Senate Health, Education, Labor, and Pensions
  Committee,** (202) 224-5375.
Web, help.senate.gov
**Senate Small Business and Entrepreneurship
  Committee,** (202) 224-5175.
Web, sbc.senate.gov

Membership: commissioners, secretaries, and directors of agriculture from the fifty states, Puerto Rico, Guam, American Samoa, and the Virgin Islands. Serves as liaison between federal agencies and state governments to coordinate agricultural policies and laws. Provides data collection, emergency planning, and training. Seeks to protect consumers and the environment. Monitors legislation and regulations.

National Council of Agricultural Employers (NCAE), *8233 Old Courthouse Rd., #200, Vienna, VA 22182; (703) 790-9039. Fax, (703) 790-0845. Frank A. Gasperini Jr., Executive Vice President.*
General email, info@ncaeonline.org
Web, www.ncaeonline.org

Membership: employers of agricultural labor. Encourages establishment and maintenance of conditions conducive to an adequate supply of domestic and foreign farm labor.

National Farmers Union *(Farmers Educational and Cooperative Union of America), Washington Office, 20 F St. N.W., #300 20001-1560; (202) 554-1600. Fax, (202) 554-1654. Roger Johnson, President.*
General email, nationalfarmersunion@gmail.com
Web, www.nfu.org

Membership: family farmers belonging to state affiliates. Interests include commodity programs, domestic production, marketing, education, research, energy and natural resources, financial assistance to farmers, Social Security for farmers, foreign programs, rural development, world food issues, and inspection and certification of food. (Headquarters in Greenwood Village, Colo.)

National Grange, *1616 H St. N.W., 10th Floor 20006-4999; (202) 628-3507. Fax, (202) 347-1091. Edward L. Luttrell, President. Toll-free, (888) 447-2643.*
General email, info@nationalgrange.org
Web, www.nationalgrange.org

Membership: farmers and others involved in agricultural production and rural community service activities. Coordinates community service programs with state grange organizations.

National Sustainable Agriculture Coalition, *110 Maryland Ave. N.E., #209 20002-5622; (202) 547-5754. Fax, (202) 547-1837. Ferd Hoefner, Policy Director; Jeremy Emmi, Managing Director.*
General email, info@sustainableagriculture.net
Web, www.sustainableagriculturecoalition.org

National alliance of farm, rural, and conservation organizations. Advocates federal policies that promote environmentally sustainable agriculture, natural resources management, and rural community development. Monitors legislation and regulations.

Rural Coalition, *1029 Vermont Ave., #601 20005; (202) 628-7160. Fax, (202) 393-1816. Lorette Picciano, Executive Director.*
General email, ruralco@ruralco.org
Web, www.ruralco.org

Alliance of organizations that develop public policies benefiting rural communities. Collaborates with community-based groups on agriculture and rural development issues, including health and the environment, minority farmers, farm workers, Native Americans' rights, and rural community development. Provides rural groups with technical assistance.

Union of Concerned Scientists, *Food and Environment Program, Washington Office, 1825 K St. N.W., #800 20006-1232; (202) 223-6133. Fax, (202) 223-6162. Justin Tatham, Washington Representative.*
General email, ucs@ucsusa.org
Web, www.ucsusa.org

Promotes a food system that encourages innovative and environmentally sustainable ways of producing high-quality, safe, and affordable food. Focuses on reducing the unnecessary use of antibiotics and strengthening federal oversight of genetically engineered products for food and agriculture and promoting climate-friendly agricultural practices. (Headquarters in Cambridge, Mass.)

Agricultural Research, Education

▶**AGENCIES**

Agricultural Research Service *(Agriculture Dept.), 1400 Independence Ave. S.W., #302A, MS 0300 20250-0300; (202) 720-3656. Fax, (202) 720-5427. Vacant, Administrator.*
Web, www.ars.usda.gov

Conducts research on crops, livestock, poultry, soil and water conservation, agricultural engineering, and control of insects and other pests; develops new uses for farm commodities.

Agriculture Dept. (USDA), *National Agricultural Statistics Service, Census and Survey, 1400 Independence Ave. S.W., #6306, MS 2020 20250-2020; (202) 720-4557. Fax, (202) 720-8738. Renee Picanso, Director.*
General email, nass@nass.usda.gov
Web, www.nass.usda.gov

Conducts a quinquennial agricultural census that provides data on crops, livestock, operator characteristics, land use, farm production expenditures, machinery and equipment, and irrigation for counties, states, regions, and the nation.

Agriculture Dept. (USDA), *Research, Education, and Economics, 1400 Independence Ave. S.W., #214W, MS 0110 20250-0110; (202) 720-5923. Fax, (202) 690-2842. Catherine E. Woteki, Under Secretary.*
Web, www.ree.usda.gov

Coordinates agricultural research, extension, and teaching programs in the food and agricultural sciences, including human nutrition, home economics, consumer services, agricultural economics, environmental quality, natural and renewable resources, forestry and range management, animal and plant production and protection, aquaculture, and the processing, distribution, marketing,

Agriculture Department

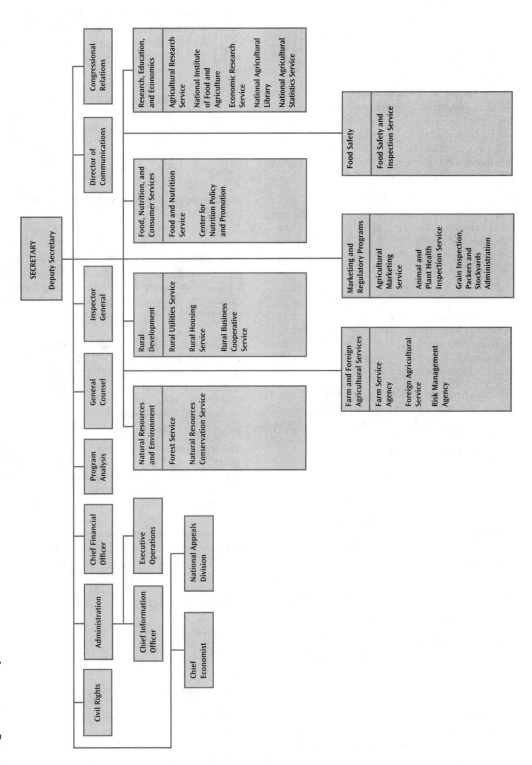

and utilization of food and agricultural products. Oversees the Agricultural Research Service, the National Institute of Food and Agriculture, the Economic Research Service, and the National Agricultural Statistics Service.

Agriculture Dept. (USDA), *Small and Disadvantaged Business Utilization (OSDBU), 1400 Independence Ave. S.W., #1085-S, Ag Stop 9501 20250-9501; (202) 720-7117. Fax, (202) 720-3001. Carmen Jones, Director, Acting. Web, www.usda.gov/osdbu*

Provides guidance and technical assistance to small businesses seeking to do business with the USDA; monitors the development and implementation of contracting policies to prevent barriers to small-business participation; works with other federal agencies and public/private partners to increase the number of small-businesses participating in the contracting arena.

Bureau of Labor Statistics (BLS) *(Labor Dept.), Industrial Prices and Price Index, 2 Massachusetts Ave. N.E., #3840 20212-0001; (202) 691-7700. Fax, (202) 691-7754. Alaric Brown, Manager, Agriculture, Food, Tobacco, and Paper Team; David M. Friedman, Assistant Commissioner. General email, ppi-info@bls.gov Web, www.bls.gov/ppi*

Compiles statistics on energy for the Producer Price Index; analyzes movement of prices for natural gas, petroleum, coal, and electric power in the primary commercial and industrial markets. Records changes over time in the prices domestic producers receive.

Economic Research Service *(Agriculture Dept.), 355 E St. S.W. 20024-8221; (202) 694-5000. Fax, (202) 245-4846. Mary Bohman, Administrator; Greg Pompelli, Associate Administrator. General email, service@ers.usda.gov Web, www.ers.usda.gov*

Conducts research on economic and policy issues involving food, natural resources, and rural development.

Foreign Agricultural Service (FAS) *(Agriculture Dept.), Global Analysis, 1400 Independence Ave. S.W., #4083S 20250; (202) 720-6301. Fax, (202) 690-0727. Patrick Packnett, Deputy Administrator. Web, www.fas.usda.gov/oga.asp*

Conducts research relevant to USDA's trade initiatives. Develops and maintains USDA's data on agricultural production, supply, and demand.

National Agricultural Library *(Agriculture Dept.), 10301 Baltimore Ave., Beltsville, MD 20705-2351; (301) 504-5248. Fax, (301) 504-7042. Simon Y. Liu, Library Director. Reference desk, (301) 504-5755, 8:30 a.m.–4:30 p.m. General email, circinfo@nal.usda.gov Web, www.nal.usda.gov*

Principal source of agricultural information in the United States. Makes significant information available to researchers, educators, policymakers, and the public; coordinates with state land-grant and Agriculture Dept. field libraries; promotes international cooperation and exchange of information. Deeper interests include food production, food safety, human nutrition, animal welfare, water quality, rural development, and invasive species.

National Agricultural Library *(Agriculture Dept.), Alternative Farming Systems Information Center (AFSIC), 10301 Baltimore Ave., #123, Beltsville, MD 20705-2351; (301) 504-6559. Fax, (301) 504-6927. William (Bill) Thomas, Coordinator. Web, http://afsic.nal.usda.gov*

Serves individuals and agencies seeking information on sustainability in agriculture, alternative plants and crops, farm energy options, grazing systems and alternative livestock breeds, alternative marketing and business practices, organic production, ecological pest management, and soil and water management.

National Agricultural Library *(Agriculture Dept.), Water Quality Information Center, 10301 Baltimore Ave., 1st Floor, Beltsville, MD 20705-2351; (301) 504-6077. Fax, (301) 504-5181. Joe Makuch, Coordinator. Web, http://wqic.nal.usda.gov*

Serves individuals and agencies seeking information on water quality and agriculture. Special subject areas include agricultural environmental management, irrigation, water availability, and water quality.

National Agricultural Statistics Service *(Agriculture Dept.), 1400 Independence Ave. S.W., #5041, MS 2001 20250-2001; (202) 720-2707. Fax, (202) 720-9013. Cynthia Clark, Administrator. Information, (800) 727-9540. Print reports, (800) 999-6779. General email, nass@nass.usda.gov Web, www.nass.usda.gov*

Prepares estimates and reports on production, supply, prices, and other items relating to the U.S. agricultural economy. Reports include statistics on field crops, fruits and vegetables, cattle, hogs, poultry, and related products. Prepares quinquennial national census of agriculture.

National Institute of Food and Agriculture (NIFA) *(Agriculture Dept.), Jaime L. Whitten Bldg., #305A, 800 9th St. S.W. 20024 (mailing address: 1400 Independence Ave. S.W., MS 2201, Washington, DC 20250-2201); (202) 720-4423. Fax, (202) 720-8987. Sonny Ramaswamy, Director. Press, (202) 720-8188. Information, (202) 720-4651. Web, www.nifa.usda.gov*

Supports research, education, and extension of issues pertaining to agricultural production, nutrition, food safety, energy independence, and the sustainability of natural resources. Partners with and funds scientists at land-grant universities and in private industry, addressing critical issues, including global food security and hunger, climate change, sustainable energy, childhood obesity, and food safety. Collaborates with historical black colleges and universities, Hispanic-serving institutions, and tribal colleges. Partners with agricultural extension offices in all counties, states, and territories.

National Institute of Food and Agriculture (NIFA) *(Agriculture Dept.), Institute of Bioenergy, Climate, and Environment, 800 9th St. S.W., #3700 20024 (mailing address: 1400 Independence Ave. S.W., MS 2210, Washington, DC 20250-2215); (202) 720-0740. Fax, (202) 720-7803. Bradley Rein, Assistant Director, Acting. Web, http://nifa.usda.gov/about/pdfs/factsheets/inst_fs_ibce.pdf*

Administers programs to address national science priorities that advance energy independence and help agricultural/forest/range production systems adapt to climate change variables. Provides grants to support the development of sustainable bioenergy production systems, agricultural production systems, and natural resource management activities that are adapted to climate variation and activities that otherwise support sustainable natural resource use.

National Institute of Food and Agriculture (NIFA) *(Agriculture Dept.), Institute of Food Production and Sustainability, 800 9th St. S.W., #3305 20024 (mailing address: 1400 Independence Ave. S.W., MS 2240, Washington, DC 20250-2240); (202) 401-5024. Fax, (202) 401-1782. Vacant, Assistant Director. Web, www.nifa.usda.gov/about/pdfs/fact_sheets/inst_fs_ifps.pdf*

Enhances food security through productive and sustainable agricultural systems. Includes divisions of Animal Safety, Plant Systems, Protection, Plant Systems Production, and Agriculture Systems.

National Institute of Food and Agriculture (NIFA) *(Agriculture Dept.), Institute of Youth, Family, and Community, 800 9th St. S.W., #4330, MS 2250 20024 (mailing address: 1400 Independence Ave. S.W., #2225, Washington, DC 20250-2225); (202) 720-5305. Fax, (202) 720-9366. Muquarrab Qureshi, Assistant Director. Web, www.nifa.usda.gov/about/pdfs/fact_sheets/inst_fs_iyfc.pdf*

Provides grants and programmatic training to support youth and family development; partners with county governments, the private sector, and state land-grant universities. Program areas include food and agricultural science education, particularly in minority-serving institutions; childhood nutrition; community food projects; and community service. Includes divisions of Community Education, Family and Consumer Sciences, and Youth and 4-H.

Office of Science and Technology Policy (OSTP) *(Executive Office of the President), Eisenhower Executive Office Bldg., 1650 Pennsylvania Ave. N.W. 20504; (202) 456-7116. Fax, (202) 456-6021. John P. Holdren, Director. Press, (202) 456-6124. General email, info@ostp.gov Web, www.ostp.gov*

Provides the president with policy analysis on scientific and technological matters, including energy policy and technology issues; coordinates executive office and federal agency responses to these issues; evaluates the effectiveness of scientific and technological programs.

Rural Development *(Agriculture Dept.), Business and Cooperative Programs, Business Programs, 1400 Independence Ave. S.W., #5813-S 20250-3220; (202) 720-7287. Fax, (202) 690-0097. Chad Parker, Deputy Administrator. Web, www.rurdev.usda.gov/LP_businessprograms.html*

Conducts economic research and provides financial assistance and business planning to help farmers market their products and purchase supplies.

Rural Development *(Agriculture Dept.), Business and Cooperative Programs, Cooperative Programs, 1400 Independence Ave. S.W., #4016-S 20250-3250; (202) 720-7558. Fax, (202) 720-4641. Andrew Jermolowicz, Deputy Administrator, Acting. Web, www.rurdev.usda.gov/LP_coopprograms.html*

Conducts economic research and helps people living in rural areas obtain business services through cooperatives.

▶ **NONGOVERNMENTAL**

National Council of Farmer Cooperatives (NCFC), *50 F St. N.W., #900 20001-1530; (202) 626-8700. Fax, (202) 626-8722. Charles F. Conner, President. General email, info@ncfc.org Web, www.ncfc.org*

Membership: cooperative businesses owned and operated by farmers. Conducts educational programs and encourages research on agricultural cooperatives; provides statistics and analyzes trends; presents awards for research papers.

National Ecological Observatory Network (NEON Inc.), *Washington Office, 1100 Jefferson Dr. S.W., #3123, MRC 705 20560-0001; (202) 370-7891. Fax, (202) 204-0128. Brian Wee, Chief of External Affairs; Russell Lea, Chief Executive Officer (in Boulder, Colo.). Press, (720) 746-4936. General email, bwee@neoninc.org Web, www.neoninc.org*

Collects data across the United States on the impact of climate change, land use change, and invasive species on natural resources and biodiversity, with the goal of detecting and forecasting ecological change on a continental scale over multiple decades. Working with various government agencies to develop standards for environmental observations and data interoperability; expected to become fully operational by 2016. Funded by the National Science Foundation in partnership with Neon, Inc. (Visitors note: Co-located in the Smithsonian's S. Dillon Ripley Center.) (Headquarters in Boulder, Colo.)

National FFA Organization, *Washington Office, 1410 King St., #400, Alexandria, VA 22314-2749; (703) 838-5889. Fax, (703) 838-5888. Steve A. Brown, National FFA Advisor, (202) 245-6078. Web, www.ffa.org*

Membership: local chapters of high school students enrolled in agricultural, food, and natural resources sciences education and agribusiness programs. Coordinates leadership training and other activities with local chapters across the United States. Formerly known as the Future Farmers of America. (Business Center in Indianapolis, Ind.)

National 4-H Council, *7100 Connecticut Ave., Chevy Chase, MD 20815-4999; (301) 961-2800. Fax, (301) 961-2894. Jennifer L. Sirangelo, President, (301) 961-2820. Press, (301) 961-2972.*
Web, www.4-h.org

4-H membership: young people across the United States engaged in hands-on learning activities in leadership, citizenship, life skills, science, healthy living, and food security. National 4-H Council is a national, private-sector partner of the 4-H Youth Development Program and its parent, the Cooperative Extension System of the United States Department of Agriculture. In the United States, 4-H programs are implemented by 109 land-grant universities and more than 3,000 cooperative extension offices. Outside the United States, 4-H programs operate through independent, country-led organizations in more than 50 countries.

Fertilizer and Pesticides

▶**AGENCIES**

Agriculture Dept. (USDA), *Natural Resources Conservation Service, Pest Management, 1400 Independence Ave. S.W., #5103 20250; (202) 720-4525. Fax, (202) 720-2646. Jason Weller, Chief.*
General email, jason.weller@usda.gov
Web, www.nrcs.usda.gov

Formulates and recommends agency policy in coordination with the Environmental Protection Agency and other USDA agencies for the establishment of standards, procedures, and management of agronomic, forest, and horticultural use of pesticides.

Environmental Protection Agency (EPA), *Chemical Safety and Pollution Prevention (OCSPP), 1201 Constitution Ave. N.W., #3130 EPA-E, MS 7101M 20460-7101; (202) 564-2902. Fax, (202) 564-0801. James J. Jones, Assistant Administrator. Pollution prevention and toxic substances, (202) 564-3810. Pesticide programs, (703) 305-7090.*
Web, www.epa.gov/aboutepa/about-office-chemical-safety-and-pollution-prevention-ocspp

Studies and makes recommendations for regulating chemical substances under the Toxic Substances Control Act; compiles list of chemical substances subject to the act; registers, controls, and regulates use of pesticides and toxic substances; manages the Endocrine Disruptor Screening Program.

Environmental Protection Agency (EPA), *Pesticide Programs, 1 Potomac Yard, 2777 S. Crystal Dr., Arlington, VA 22202 (mailing address: Ariel Rios Building, 1200 Pennsylvania Ave. N.W., MS 7501P, Washington, DC 20460-7101); (703) 305-7090. Fax, (703) 308-4776.*

Steven Bradbury, Director. National Pesticide Information Center, (800) 858-7378.
Web, www.epa.gov/pesticides/contacts

Evaluates data to determine the risks and benefits of pesticides; sets standards for safe use of pesticides, including those for use on foods. Develops rules that govern labeling and literature accompanying pesticide products. Administers the Integrated Pest Management in Schools and the Pesticide Environmental Stewardship programs.

▶**NONGOVERNMENTAL**

Beyond Pesticides, *701 E St. S.E., #200 20003; (202) 543-5450. Fax, (202) 543-4791. Jay Feldman, Executive Director.*
General email, info@beyondpesticides.org
Web, www.beyondpesticides.org

Coalition of family farmers, farm workers, consumers, home gardeners, physicians, lawyers, and others concerned about pesticide hazards and safety. Issues information to increase public awareness of environmental, public health, and economic problems caused by pesticide abuse; promotes alternatives to pesticide use, such as organic pest management program.

Croplife America, *1156 15th St. N.W., #400 20005-1752; (202) 296-1585. Fax, (202) 463-0474. Jay J. Vroom, President.*
General email, agriesser@croplifeamerica.org
Web, www.croplifeamerica.org

Membership: pesticide manufacturers. Provides information on pesticide safety, development, and use. Monitors legislation and regulations. (Formerly the American Crop Protection Assn.)

Entomological Society of America, *3 Park Pl., #307, Annapolis, MD 21401-3722; (301) 731-4535. Fax, (301) 731-4538. C. David Gammel, Executive Director.*
General email, esa@entsoc.org
Web, www.entsoc.org

Scientific association that promotes the science of entomology and the interests of professionals in the field, with branches throughout the United States. Advises on crop protection, food chain, and individual and urban health matters dealing with insect pests.

Fertilizer Institute, *Capitol View, 425 3rd St. S.W., #950 20024; (202) 962-0490. Fax, (202) 962-0577. Chris Jahn, President, (202) 515-2700.*
General email, info@tfi.org
Web, www.tfi.org

Membership: manufacturers, dealers, and distributors of fertilizer. Provides statistical data and other information concerning the effects of fertilizer and its relationship to world food production, food supply, and the environment.

Migrant Legal Action Program, *1001 Connecticut Ave. N.W., #915 20036-5524; (202) 775-7780. Fax, (202) 775-7784. Roger C. Rosenthal, Executive Director.*
General email, mlap@mlap.org
Web, www.mlap.org

Assists local legal services groups and private attorneys representing farm workers. Monitors legislation, regulations, and enforcement activities of the Environmental Protection Agency and the Occupational Safety and Health Administration in the area of pesticide use as it affects the health of migrant farm workers. Litigates cases concerning living and working conditions experienced by migrant farm workers. Works with local groups on implementation of Medicaid block grants.

National Agricultural Aviation Assn., *1440 Duke St., Alexandria, VA 22314; (202) 546-5722. Fax, (202) 546-5726. Andrew D. Moore, Executive Director.*
General email, information@agaviation.org
Web, www.agaviation.org

Membership: agricultural pilots; operating companies that seed, fertilize, and spray land by air; and allied industries. Monitors legislation and regulations. (Affiliated with National Agricultural Aviation Research and Education Foundation.)

National Pest Management Assn., *Government Affairs, 10460 North St., Fairfax, VA 22030; (703) 352-6762. Fax, (703) 352-3031. Robert M. Rosenberg, Executive Vice President. Toll-free, (800) 678-6722.*
Web, www.npmapestworld.org

Membership: pest control operators. Monitors federal regulations that affect pesticide use; provides members with technical information.

Horticulture and Gardening

▶AGENCIES

National Arboretum *(Agriculture Dept.), 3501 New York Ave. N.E. 20002-1958; (202) 245-2726. Fax, (202) 245-4575. Colien Hefferan, Director.*
Web, www.usna.usda.gov

Maintains public display of plants on 446 acres; provides information and makes referrals concerning cultivated plants (exclusive of field crops and fruits); conducts plant breeding and research; maintains herbarium.

Smithsonian Institution, *Botany and Horticulture Library, 10th St. and Constitution Ave. N.W., #W422 20560-0166 (mailing address: P.O. Box 37012, MRC 154, Washington, DC 20013-7012); (202) 633-1685. Robin Everly, Branch Librarian.*
General email, askalibrarian@si.edu
Web, www.library.si.edu/libraries/botany

Collection includes books, periodicals, and videotapes on horticulture, garden history, and landscape design. Specializes in American gardens and gardening of the late nineteenth and early twentieth centuries. Open to the public by appointment 10:00 a.m.–4:00 p.m. (Housed at the National Museum of Natural History.)

U.S. Botanic Garden, *100 Maryland Ave. S.W. 20001 (mailing address: 245 1st St. S.W., Washington, DC 20024); (202) 225-8333. Fax, (202) 225-1561. Ari Novy, Acting Executive Director. Horticulture hotline, (202) 226-4785. Program registration information, (202) 225-1116. Special events, (202) 226-7674. Tour line, (202) 226-2055.*
General email, usbg@aoc.gov
Web, www.usbg.gov

Collects, cultivates, and grows various plants for public display and study; identifies botanic specimens and furnishes information on proper growing methods. Conducts horticultural classes and tours.

▶NONGOVERNMENTAL

AmericanHort, *1200 G St. N.W., #800 20005; (202) 789-2900. Fax, (202) 789-1893. Michael Geary, Executive Vice President.*
General email, hello@AmericanHort.org
Web, www.AmericanHort.org

Membership: wholesale growers, garden center retailers, landscape firms, and suppliers to the horticultural community. Monitors legislation and regulations on agricultural, environmental, and small-business issues; conducts educational seminars on business management for members.

American Horticultural Society, *River Farm, 7931 E. Boulevard Dr., Alexandria, VA 22308-1300; (703) 768-5700, ext. 119. Fax, (703) 768-8700. Tom Underwood, Executive Director, (703) 768-5700, ext. 123. Toll-free, (800) 777-7931.*
Web, www.ahs.org

Promotes the expansion of horticulture in the United States through educational programs for amateur and professional horticulturists. Publishes gardening magazine. Oversees historic house and farm once owned by George Washington, with gardens maintained by staff; house and grounds are rented for special occasions.

American Society for Horticultural Science (ASHS), *1018 Duke St., Alexandria, VA 22314; (703) 836-4606. Fax, (703) 836-2024. Michael W. Neff, Executive Director, ext. 106.*
General email, webmaster@ashs.org
Web, www.ashs.org

Membership: educators, government workers, firms, associations, and individuals interested in horticultural science. Promotes scientific research and education in horticulture, including international exchange of information.

Society of American Florists, *1601 Duke St., Alexandria, VA 22314-3406; (703) 836-8700. Fax, (703) 836-8705. Peter J. Moran, Chief Executive Officer. Toll-free, (800) 336-4743.*
General email, pmoran@safnow.org
Web, www.safnow.org

Membership: growers, wholesalers, and retailers in the floriculture and ornamental horticulture industries. Interests include labor, pesticides, the environment, international trade, and toxicity of plants. Mediates industry problems.

Soil and Watershed Conservation

▶**AGENCIES**

Farm Service Agency (FSA) *(Agriculture Dept.),*
Conservation and Environmental Programs, *1400
Independence Ave. S.W., MS 0513 20250-0513; (202) 720-
6221. Fax, (202) 720-4619. Matthew Ponish, Deputy
Director, Acting.
Web, www.fsa.usda.gov*

Directs conservation and environmental projects and
programs to help farmers and ranchers prevent soil erosion and contamination of natural resources.

Interior Dept. (DOI), *Bird Habitat Conservation, 4501
N. Fairfax Dr., Arlington, VA 22203 (mailing address: 4401
N. Fairfax Dr., MBSP 4075, Arlington, VA 22203); (703)
358-1784. Fax, (703) 358-2282. Cyndi Perry, Chief;
Rachel F. Levin, Communications Coordinator, (703) 358-
2405.
General email, dbhc@fws.gov*

Web, www.fws.gov/birdhabitat

Membership: government and private-sector conservation experts. Works to protect, restore, and manage wetlands and other habitats for migratory birds and other
animals and to maintain migratory bird and waterfowl
populations.

Natural Resources Conservation Service *(Agriculture
Dept.), 1400 Independence Ave. S.W., #5105AS 20250
(mailing address: P.O. Box 2890, Washington, DC 20013-
2890); (202) 720-4525. Fax, (202) 720-7690. Jason Weller,
Chief, (202) 720-7246. Chief's Office, (202) 720-7246.
Public Affairs, (202) 720-0693.
Web, www.nrcs.usda.gov*

Responsible for soil and water conservation programs,
including watershed protection, flood prevention, river
basin surveys, and resource conservation and development. Provides landowners, operators, state and local
units of government, and community groups with technical assistance in carrying out local programs. Inventories
and monitors soil, water, and related resource data and
resource use trends. Provides information about soil surveys, farmlands, and other natural resources.

▶**NONGOVERNMENTAL**

American Farmland Trust (AFT), *1150 Connecticut Ave.
N.W., #600 20036; (202) 331-7300. Fax, (202) 659-8339.
Andrew McElwaine, President. Toll-free, (800) 886-5170.
General email, info@farmland.org*

Web, www.farmland.org

Works to protect farmland, promote sound farming
practices, and keep farmers on the land through local,
regional, and national efforts. Works to help farmers
implement practices that protect water quality. Conducts
independent analyses of policies that affect farmland, and
advocates for government policies that support farmland
conservation and keep farms economically viable.

Irrigation Assn., *6540 Arlington Blvd., Falls Church, VA
22042-6638; (703) 536-7080. Fax, (703) 536-7019.
Deborah Hamlin, Executive Director.
General email, info@irrigation.org*

Web, www.irrigation.org

Membership: companies and individuals involved in
irrigation, drainage, and erosion control worldwide. Promotes efficient and effective water management through
training, education, and certification programs. Interests
include economic development and environmental enhancement.

National Assn. of Conservation Districts (NACD), *509
Capitol Court N.E. 20002-4937; (202) 547-6223. Fax, (202)
547-6450. John Larson, Chief Executive Officer.
General email, bethany-shively@nacdet.org*

Web, www.nacdnet.org

Membership: conservation districts (local subdivisions
of state government). Works to promote the conservation
of land, forests, and other natural resources. Interests
include erosion and sediment control; water quality; forestry, water, flood plain, and range management; rural
development; and urban and community conservation.

Winrock International, *Washington Office, 2121 Crystal
Dr., #500, Arlington, VA 22202; (703) 302-6500. Fax, (703)
302-6512. Rodney Ferguson, President.
General email, information@winrock.org*

Web, www.winrock.org

Works globally to increase economic opportunity, sustain natural resources, and protect the environment.
Matches local individuals and communities with new
ideas and technologies. (Headquarters in Little Rock, Ark.)

COMMODITIES, FARM PRODUCE

General

▶**AGENCIES**

Agricultural Marketing Service (AMS) *(Agriculture
Dept.), Transportation and Marketing Programs, 1400
Independence Ave. S.W., #4543, MS 0266 20250-0264;
(202) 720-8317. Fax, (202) 690-0338. Arthur Neal, Deputy
Administrator; Bruce Blanton, Director, Transportation
Services Division, (202) 690-0435; Douglas Keeler, Director,
Marketing Services Division, (202) 720-8317.
Web, www.ams.usda.gov*

Promotes efficient, cost-effective marketing and transportation for U.S. agricultural products; sets standards for
domestic and international marketing of organic products.
Provides exporters with market information, educational
services, and regulatory representation.

Agricultural Research Service *(Agriculture Dept.),
National Plant Germplasm System, 5601 Sunnyside Ave.,
#4-2212, Beltsville, MD 20705-5139; (301) 504-5541.*

Fax, (301) 504-6191. Peter Bretting, National Program Leader.
Web, www.ars-grin.gov

Network of federal and state gene banks that preserve samples of all major field crops and horticultural crops. Collects, preserves, evaluates, and catalogs germplasm and distributes it for specific purposes.

Agriculture Dept. (USDA), *Marketing and Regulatory Programs, 1400 Independence Ave. S.W., #228W, MS 0109 20250-0109; (202) 720-4256. Fax, (202) 720-5775. Edward M. Avalos, Under Secretary.*
Web, www.usda.gov/mrp

Administers inspection and grading services and regulatory programs for agricultural commodities through the Agricultural Marketing Service; Animal and Plant Health Inspection Service; and Grain Inspection, Packers and Stockyards Administration.

Animal and Plant Health Inspection Service (APHIS) *(Agriculture Dept.), 1400 Independence Ave. S.W., #312E, MS 3401 20250-3401; (202) 799-7030. Fax, (202) 720-3054. Kevin A. Shea, Administrator. Press, (301) 851-4100. Veterinary Services, (301) 851-3300. Plants and Plant Products, (877) 770-5990.*
Web, www.aphis.usda.gov

Administers programs in cooperation with the states to prevent the spread of pests and plant diseases; certifies that U.S. exports are free of pests and disease.

Commodity Credit Corp. *(Agriculture Dept.), 1400 Independence Ave. S.W., MS 0599 20250-0571; (202) 720-0402. Fax, (202) 720-5398. Monique B. Randolph, Assistant Secretary, Acting.*
General email, steve.mikkelson@wdc.usda.gov
Web, www.fsa.usda.gov/ccc

Finances commodity stabilization programs, domestic and export surplus commodity disposal, foreign assistance, storage activities, and related programs.

Commodity Futures Trading Commission, *3 Lafayette Centre, 1155 21st St. N.W. 20581-0001; (202) 418-5000. Fax, (202) 418-5521. Mark P. Wetjen, Chair, Acting, (202) 418-5010; Anthony C. (Tony) Thompson, Executive Director, (202) 418-5697.*
General email, questions@cftc.gov
Web, www.cftc.gov

Oversees the Commodity Exchange Act, which regulates all commodity futures and options to prevent fraudulent trade practices.

Farm Service Agency (FSA) *(Agriculture Dept.), 1400 Independence Ave. S.W., #3086 South Bldg., MS 0501 20250-0506; (202) 720-3467. Fax, (202) 720-9105. Juan M. Garcia, Administrator. Press, (202) 720-7807.*
Web, www.fsa.usda.gov

Administers farm commodity programs providing crop loans and purchases; provides crop payments when market prices fall below specified levels; sets acreage allotments and marketing quotas; assists farmers in areas affected by natural disasters.

Foreign Agricultural Service (FAS) *(Agriculture Dept.), 1400 Independence Ave. S.W., #5071S, MS 1001 20250-1001; (202) 720-3935. Fax, (202) 690-2159. Philip (Phil) Karsting, Administrator. Public Affairs, (202) 720-3448.*
Web, www.fas.usda.gov

Promotes exports of U.S. commodities and assists with trade negotiations; coordinates activities of U.S. representatives in foreign countries who report on crop and market conditions; sponsors trade fairs in foreign countries to promote export of U.S. agricultural products; analyzes world demand and production of various commodities; administers food aid programs; monitors sales by private exporters; provides technical assistance and trade capacity building programs.

Foreign Agricultural Service (FAS) *(Agriculture Dept.), Trade Programs, 1400 Independence Ave. S.W., MS 1020 20250-1020; (202) 720-9516. Fax, (202) 401-0135. Christian Foster, Deputy Administrator.*
Web, www.fas.usda.gov/OTP.asp

Administers market development, export credit guarantee, dairy export incentive programs, and import programs for sugar, dairy, and trade adjustment assistance.

Rural Development *(Agriculture Dept.), Business and Cooperative Programs, Business Programs, 1400 Independence Ave. S.W., #5813-S 20250-3220; (202) 720-7287. Fax, (202) 690-0097. Chad Parker, Deputy Administrator.*
Web, www.rurdev.usda.gov/LP_businessprograms.html

Conducts economic research and provides financial assistance and business planning to help farmers market their products and purchase supplies.

State Dept., *Agriculture, Biotechnology, and Textile Trade Affairs, 2201 C St. N.W., #4470 20520-0002; (202) 647-3090. Fax, (202) 647-1894. Edward Kaska, Director.*
Web, www.state.gov/e/eeb/tpp/abt

Develops agricultural trade policy; handles questions pertaining to international negotiations on all agricultural products covered by the World Trade Organization (WTO) and bilateral trade agreements. Negotiates bilateral textile trade agreements with foreign governments concerning cotton, wool, and synthetic textile and apparel products. Oversees the distribution of biotechnology outreach funds to promote international acceptance of the technology.

► **CONGRESS**

For a listing of relevant congressional committees and subcommittees, please see page 3 or the Appendix.

► **NONGOVERNMENTAL**

American Seed Trade Assn., *1701 Duke St., #275, Alexandria, VA 22314-2878; (703) 837-8140. Fax, (703) 837-9365. Andrew W. LaVigne, President.*
Web, www.amseed.org

Membership: producers and merchandisers of seeds. Conducts seminars on research developments in corn, sorghum, soybean, garden seeds, and other farm seeds; promotes overseas seed market development.

Commodity Markets Council (CMC), *1300 L St. N.W., #1020 20005-4166; (202) 842-0400. Fax, (202) 789-7223. Gregg Doud, President.*
Web, http://commoditymkts.org

Federation of commodity futures exchanges, boards of trade, and industry stakeholders including commodity merchandisers, processors, and refiners; futures commission merchants; food and beverage manufacturers; transportation companies; and financial institutions. Combines members' expertise to formulate positions on market, policy, and contracting issues involving commodities, with an overall goal of facilitating growth in liquidity and transparency in cash and derivative markets. Monitors legislation and regulations. (Formerly the National Grain Trade Council.)

Global Cold Chain Alliance, *1500 King St., #201, Alexandria, VA 22314-2730; (703) 373-4300. Fax, (703) 373-4301. J. William Hudson, President, ext. 205.*
General email, email@gcca.org
Web, www.gcca.org

Membership: owners and operators of public refrigerated warehouses. Interests include labor, transportation, taxes, environment, safety, regulatory compliance, and food distribution. Monitors legislation and regulations. (Affiliated with the International Refrigerated Transportation Assn., the International Assn. for Cold Storage Construction, and the World Food Logistics Assn.)

National Cooperative Business Assn., *1401 New York Ave. N.W., #1100 20005-2160; (202) 638-6222. Fax, (202) 638-1374. Michael Bealle, President.*
General email, info@ncba.coop
Web, www.ncba.coop and Twitter, @NCBACLUSA

Alliance of cooperatives, businesses, and state cooperative associations. Provides information about starting and managing agricultural cooperatives in the United States and in developing nations. Monitors legislation and regulations.

National Council of Farmer Cooperatives (NCFC), *50 F St. N.W., #900 20001-1530; (202) 626-8700. Fax, (202) 626-8722. Charles F. Conner, President.*
General email, info@ncfc.org
Web, www.ncfc.org

Membership: cooperative businesses owned and operated by farmers. Encourages research on agricultural cooperatives; provides statistics and analyzes trends. Monitors legislation and regulations on agricultural trade, transportation, energy, and tax issues.

U.S. Agricultural Export Development Council, *8233 Old Courthouse Rd., #200, Vienna, VA 22182; (703) 556-9290. Fax, (703) 790-0845. Annie Durbin, Executive Director.*
General email, adurbin@usaedc.org
Web, www.usaedc.org

Membership: agricultural growers and processors, commodity trade associations, farmer cooperatives, and state regional trade groups. Works with the Foreign Agricultural Service on projects to create, expand, and maintain agricultural markets abroad. Sponsors seminars and workshops.

Cotton

Agricultural Marketing Service (AMS) *(Agriculture Dept.), Cotton and Tobacco Programs, 1400 Independence Ave. S.W., #2641S, MS 0224 20250-0224; (202) 720-2145. Fax, (202) 690-1718. Darryl W. Earnest, Deputy Administrator.*
Web, www.ams.usda.gov/cotton/index.htm

Administers cotton marketing programs; sets cotton and tobacco grading standards and conducts quality inspections based on those standards. Maintains market news service to inform producers of daily price changes.

Farm Service Agency (FSA) *(Agriculture Dept.), Fibers, Peanuts, and Tobacco Analysis, 1400 Independence Ave. S.W., #37605, MS 0515 20250-0515; (202) 720-3392. Fax, (202) 690-2186. Scott Sanford, Director.*
Web, www.fsa.usda.gov

Develops production adjustment and price support programs to balance supply and demand for cotton, peanuts, and tobacco.

▶INTERNATIONAL ORGANIZATIONS

International Cotton Advisory Committee, *1629 K St. N.W., #702 20006-1636; (202) 463-6660. Fax, (202) 463-6950. José Sette, Executive Director, ext. 116.*
General email, secretariat@icac.org
Web, www.icac.org

Membership: cotton producing and consuming countries. Provides information on cotton production, trade, consumption, stocks, and prices.

▶NONGOVERNMENTAL

Cotton Council International, *Washington Office, 1521 New Hampshire Ave. N.W. 20036-1203; (202) 745-7805. Fax, (202) 483-4040. Kevin Latner, Executive Director.*
General email, cottonusa@cotton.org
Web, www.cottonusa.org

Division of National Cotton Council of America. Promotes U.S. raw cotton and cotton-product exports. (Headquarters in Memphis, Tenn.)

Cotton Warehouse Assn. of America, *316 Pennsylvania Ave., #401 20003; (202) 544-5875. Fax, (202) 544-5874. Larry Combest, Executive Vice President.*
General email, cwaa@cottonwarehouse.org
Web, www.cottonwarehouse.org

Membership: cotton compress and warehouse operators. Serves as a liaison between members and government agencies; monitors legislation and regulations.

National Cotton Council of America, *Washington Office*, *1521 New Hampshire Ave. N.W. 20036-1205; (202) 745-7805. Fax, (202) 483-4040. A. John Maguire, Senior Vice President.*
Web, www.cotton.org

Membership: all segments of the U.S. cotton industry. Provides statistics and information on such topics as cotton history and processing. (Headquarters in Memphis, Tenn.)

Dairy Products and Eggs

▶**AGENCIES**

Agricultural Marketing Service (AMS) *(Agriculture Dept.), Livestock, Poultry, and Seed, 1400 Independence Ave. S.W., #2092S, MS 0249 20250-0249; (202) 720-5705. Fax, (202) 720-3499. Craig Morris, Deputy Administrator.*
Web, www.ams.usda.gov/lsprogram

Sets poultry and egg grading standards. Provides promotion and market news services for domestic and international markets.

Agricultural Marketing Service (AMS) *(Agriculture Dept.), Dairy Programs, 1400 Independence Ave. S.W., #2968 20250-0225; (202) 720-4392. Fax, (202) 690-3410. Dana H. Coale, Deputy Administrator.*
Web, www.ams.usda.gov/dairy/index.htm

Administers dairy product marketing and promotion programs; grades dairy products; maintains market news service on daily price changes; sets minimum price that farmers receive for milk.

Farm Service Agency (FSA) *(Agriculture Dept.), Dairy and Sweeteners Analysis, 1400 Independence Ave. S.W., #3752, MS 0516 20250-0516; (202) 690-0734. Fax, (202) 690-2186. Daniel Colacicco, Group Director.*
Web, www.fsa.usda.gov

Develops production adjustment and price support programs to balance supply and demand for certain commodities, including dairy products, sugar, and honey.

▶**NONGOVERNMENTAL**

American Butter Institute (ABI), *2101 Wilson Blvd., #400, Arlington, VA 22201-3062; (703) 243-5630. Fax, (703) 841-9328. Annja Miner, Executive Director.*
General email, AMiner@nmpf.org
Web, www.nmpf.org/abi

Membership: butter manufacturers, packagers, and distributors. Interests include dairy price supports and programs, packaging and labeling, and imports. Monitors legislation and regulations.

Humane Farm Animal Care, *P.O. Box 727, Herndon, VA 20172-0727; (703) 435-3883. Fax, (703) 435-3981. Adele Douglass, Chief Executive Officer.*
General email, info@certifiedhumane.org
Web, www.certifiedhumane.org

Seeks to improve the welfare of farm animals by providing viable, duly monitored standards for humane food production. Administers the Certified Humane Raised and Handled program for meat, poultry, eggs, and dairy products.

International Dairy Foods Assn., *1250 H St. N.W., #900 20005-3952; (202) 737-4332. Fax, (202) 331-7820. Constance E. (Connie) Tipton, President.*
Web, www.idfa.org

Membership: processors, manufacturers, marketers, and distributors of dairy foods in the United States and abroad. Provides members with marketing, public relations, training, and management services. Monitors legislation and regulations. (Affiliated with the Milk Industry Foundation, the National Cheese Institute, and the International Ice Cream Assn.)

National Milk Producers Federation, *2101 Wilson Blvd., #400, Arlington, VA 22201-3062; (703) 243-6111. Fax, (703) 841-9328. Jim Mulhern, Chief Executive Officer.*
General email, info@nmpf.org
Web, www.nmpf.org

Membership: dairy farmer cooperatives. Provides information on development and modification of sanitary regulations, product standards, and marketing procedures for dairy products.

United Egg Producers, *Government Relations, 300 Independence Ave. S.E. 20003; (202) 448-9500. Randy Green, Vice President of Government Relations.*
General email, lperry@cgagroup.com
Web, www.unitedegg.org

Membership: egg marketing cooperatives and egg producers. Monitors legislation and regulations. (Headquarters in Atlanta, Ga.)

Fruits and Vegetables

▶**AGENCIES**

Agricultural Marketing Service (AMS) *(Agriculture Dept.), Fruit and Vegetable Program, 1400 Independence Ave. S.W., #2077-S, MS 0235 20250-0235; (202) 720-4722. Fax, (202) 720-0016. Charles Parrott, Deputy Administrator.*
Web, www.ams.usda.gov/fv/index.htm

Administers research, marketing, promotional, and regulatory programs for fruits, vegetables, nuts, ornamental plants, and other specialty crops; focus includes international markets. Sets grading standards for fresh and processed fruits and vegetables; conducts quality inspections; maintains market news service to inform producers of price changes.

Economic Research Service *(Agriculture Dept.)*, 355 E St. S.W. 20024-8221; (202) 694-5000. Fax, (202) 245-4846. *Mary Bohman, Administrator; Greg Pompelli, Associate Administrator.*
General email, service@ers.usda.gov

Web, www.ers.usda.gov

Conducts market research; studies and forecasts domestic supply-and-demand trends for fruits and vegetables.

▶NONGOVERNMENTAL

United Fresh Produce Assn., *1901 Pennsylvania Ave. N.W., #1100 20006; (202) 303-3400. Fax, (202) 303-3433. Tom Stenzel, President.*
General email, united@unitedfresh.org

Web, www.unitedfresh.org

Membership: growers, shippers, wholesalers, retailers, food service operators, importers, and exporters involved in producing and marketing fresh fruits and vegetables. Represents the industry before the government and the public sector. (Formerly the United Fresh Fruit and Vegetable Assn.; name changed upon merging with the International Fresh-Cut Assn.)

U.S. Apple Assn., *8233 Old Courthouse Rd., #200, Vienna, VA 22182; (703) 442-8850. Fax, (703) 790-0845. James (Jim) Bair, President.*
General email, info@usapple.org

Web, www.usapple.org

Membership: U.S. commercial apple growers and processors, distributors, exporters, importers, and retailers of apples. Promotes nutrition research and marketing; provides information about apples and nutrition to educators. Monitors legislation and regulations.

Wine Institute, *Federal Relations, 601 13th St. N.W., #330 South 20005-3866; (202) 408-0870. Fax, (202) 371-0061. Charles Jefferson, Vice President; Linda Ulrich, Vice President.*
Web, www.wineinstitute.org

Membership: California wineries and affiliated businesses. Seeks international recognition for California wines; conducts promotional campaigns in other countries. Monitors legislation and regulations. (Headquarters in San Francisco, Calif.)

Grains and Oilseeds

▶AGENCIES

Agricultural Marketing Service (AMS) *(Agriculture Dept.), Livestock, Poultry, and Seed, 1400 Independence Ave. S.W., #2092S, MS 0249 20250-0249; (202) 720-5705. Fax, (202) 720-3499. Craig Morris, Deputy Administrator.*
Web, www.ams.usda.gov/lsprogram

Administers programs for marketing grain, including rice; maintains market news service to inform producers of grain market situation and daily price changes.

Farm Service Agency (FSA) *(Agriculture Dept.), Feed Grains and Oilseeds Analysis, 1400 Independence Ave. S.W., #3740S, MS 0532 20250-0532; (202) 720-3451. Fax, (202) 690-2186. Philip Sronce, Group Director.*
Web, www.fsa.usda.gov

Develops, analyzes, and implements domestic farm policy focusing on corn, soybeans, and other feed grains and oilseeds. Develops production adjustment and price support programs to balance supply and demand for these commodities.

Farm Service Agency (FSA) *(Agriculture Dept.), Food Grains, 1400 Independence Ave. S.W., MS 0518 20250-0532; (202) 720-2891. Fax, (202) 690-2186. Thomas F. Tice, Director.*
Web, www.fsa.usda.gov

Develops marketing loan and contract crop programs in support of food grain commodities, including wheat, rice, and pulse crops.

Grain Inspection, Packers and Stockyards Administration *(Agriculture Dept.), 1400 Independence Ave. S.W., #2055, South Bldg., MS 3601 20250-3601; (202) 720-0219. Fax, (202) 205-9237. Larry Mitchell, Administrator. Toll-free, (800) 455-3447.*
General email, larry.mitchell@gipsa.usda.gov

Web, www.gipsa.usda.gov

Administers inspection and weighing program for grain, soybeans, rice, sunflower seeds, and other processed commodities; conducts quality inspections based on established standards.

▶NONGOVERNMENTAL

American Feed Industry Assn. (AFIA), *2101 Wilson Blvd., #916, Arlington, VA 22201; (703) 524-0810. Fax, (703) 524-1921. Joel Newman, President.*
General email, afia@afia.org

Web, www.afia.org

Membership: more than 5,000 feed manufacturers, pharmaceutical companies, and ingredient suppliers and integrators. Conducts seminars on feed grain production, marketing, advertising, and quality control; interests include international trade.

American Soybean Assn., *Washington Office, 600 Pennsylvania Ave. S.E., #320 20003-6300; (202) 969-7040. John Gordley, Washington Representative.*
Web, www.soygrowers.com

Membership: soybean farmers. Promotes expanded world markets and research for the benefit of soybean growers; maintains a network of state and international offices. Monitors legislation and regulations. (Headquarters in St. Louis, Mo.)

Corn Refiners Assn., *1701 Pennsylvania Ave. N.W., #950 20006-5805; (202) 331-1634. Fax, (202) 331-2054. John Bode, Chief Executive Officer; David Knowles, Communications, (202) 534-3494.*
General email, comments@corn.org

Web, www.corn.org

Promotes research on technical aspects of corn refining and product development; acts as a clearinghouse for members who award research grants to colleges and universities. Monitors legislation and regulations.

National Assn. of Wheat Growers, *415 2nd St. N.E., #300 20002-4993; (202) 547-7800. Fax, (202) 546-2638. Jim Palmer, Chief Executive Officer.*
General email, wheatworld@wheatworld.org

Web, www.wheatworld.org

Federation of state wheat grower associations. Monitors legislation and regulations.

National Corn Growers Assn., *Public Policy,* *20 F St. N.W., #600 20001; (202) 628-7001. Fax, (202) 628-1933. Jon Doggett, Vice President, Public Policy.*
General email, corninfo@ncga.com

Web, www.ncga.com

Represents the interests of U.S. corn farmers, including in international trade; promotes the use, marketing, and efficient production of corn; conducts research and educational activities; monitors legislation and regulations. (Headquarters in St. Louis, Mo.)

National Grain and Feed Assn., *1250 Eye St. N.W., #1003 20005-3939; (202) 289-0873. Fax, (202) 289-5388. Randall C. Gordon, President.*
General email, ngfa@ngfa.org

Web, www.ngfa.org

Membership: firms that process U.S. grains and oilseeds for domestic and export markets. Arbitration panel resolves disputes over trade and commercial regulations.

National Institute of Oilseed Products, *750 National Press Bldg., 529 14th St. N.W. 20045; (202) 591-2461. Fax, (202) 223-9741. Lauren Newberry, Washington Representative.*
General email, niop@kellencompany.com

Web, www.niop.org

Membership: companies and individuals involved in manufacturing and trading oilseed products. Maintains standards for trading and transport of vegetable oils and oilseeds worldwide.

National Oilseed Processors Assn., *1300 L St. N.W., #1020 20005-4168; (202) 842-0463. Fax, (202) 842-9126. Thomas A. Hammer, President.*
Web, www.nopa.org

Provides information on oilseed crops, products, processing, and commodity programs; interests include international trade.

North American Export Grain Assn. (NAEGA), *1250 Eye St. N.W., #1003 20005-3939; (202) 682-4030. Fax, (202) 682-4033. Gary C. Martin, President.*
General email, info@naega.org

Web, www.naega.org

Membership: grain exporting firms and others interested in the grain export industry. Provides information on grain export and contracting; sponsors foreign seminars.

Monitors domestic and international legislation and regulations.

North American Millers' Assn., *600 Maryland Ave. S.W., #825W 20024-2573; (202) 484-2200. Fax, (202) 488-7416. James A. McCarthy, President.*
General email, generalinfo@namamillers.org

Web, www.namamillers.org

Trade association representing the dry corn, wheat, oats, and rye milling industry. Seeks to inform the public, the industry, and government about issues affecting the domestic milling industry. Monitors legislation and regulations.

USA Rice Federation, *2101 Wilson Blvd., #610, Arlington, VA 22201; (703) 236-2300. Fax, (703) 236-2301. Betsy Ward, Chief Executive Officer. Toll-free, (800) 888-7423.*
General email, riceinfo@usarice.com

Web, www.usarice.com

Membership: rice producers, millers, merchants, and related firms. Provides U.S. and foreign rice trade and industry information; assists in establishing quality standards for rice production and milling. Monitors legislation and regulations.

U.S. Grains Council, *20 F St. N.W. 20001; (202) 789-0789. Fax, (202) 898-0522. Thomas Sleight, President.*
General email, grains@grains.org

Web, www.grains.org

Membership: barley, corn, and sorghum producers and exporters; chemical, machinery, malting, and seed companies interested in feed grain exports. Promotes development of U.S. feed grain markets overseas.

U.S. Wheat Associates, *3103 10th St. North, #300, Arlington, VA 22201; (202) 463-0999. Fax, (703) 524-4399. Alan Tracy, President.*
General email, info@uswheat.org

Web, www.uswheat.org

Membership: wheat farmers. Develops export markets for the U.S. wheat industry; provides information on wheat production and marketing. Interests include trade policy, food aid, and biotechnology.

Sugar

▶ **AGENCIES**

Economic Research Service *(Agriculture Dept.),* *355 E St. S.W. 20024-8221; (202) 694-5000. Fax, (202) 245-4846. Mary Bohman, Administrator; Greg Pompelli, Associate Administrator.*
General email, service@ers.usda.gov

Web, www.ers.usda.gov

Conducts market research; studies and forecasts domestic supply-and-demand trends for sugar and other sweeteners.

Farm Service Agency (FSA) *(Agriculture Dept.), Dairy and Sweeteners Analysis, 1400 Independence Ave. S.W., #3752, MS 0516 20250-0516; (202) 690-0734. Fax, (202) 690-2186. Daniel Colacicco, Group Director.*
Web, www.fsa.usda.gov

Develops production adjustment and price support programs to balance supply and demand for certain commodities, including dairy products, sugar, and honey.

▶**NONGOVERNMENTAL**

American Sugar Alliance, *2111 Wilson Blvd., #600, Arlington, VA 22201-3051; (703) 351-5055. Fax, (703) 351-6698. Vickie R. Myers, Executive Director.*
General email, info@sugaralliance.org
Web, www.sugaralliance.org

National coalition of sugarcane and sugarbeet farmers, processors, refiners, suppliers, workers, and others dedicated to preserving a strong domestic sweetener industry. Monitors legislation and regulations.

American Sugarbeet Growers Assn., *1156 15th St. N.W., #1101 20005-1756; (202) 833-2398. Fax, (240) 235-4291. Luther Markwart, Executive Vice President.*
General email, info@americansugarbeet.org
Web, www.americansugarbeet.org

Membership: sugarbeet growers associations. Serves as liaison to U.S. government agencies, including the Agriculture Dept. and the U.S. Trade Representative; interests include international trade. Monitors legislation and regulations.

National Confectioners Assn., *1101 30th St. N.W., #200 20007; (202) 534-1440. Fax, (202) 357-0637. Lawrence T. Graham, President.*
General email, info@candyusa.com
Web, www.candyusa.com

Membership: confectionery manufacturers and suppliers. Provides information on confectionery consumption and nutrition; sponsors educational programs and research on candy technology. Monitors legislation and regulations.

Sugar Assn., *1300 L St. N.W., #1001 20005-4263; (202) 785-1122. Fax, (202) 785-5019. Andrew Briscoe, President.*
General email, sugar@sugar.org
Web, www.sugar.org

Membership: sugar processors, growers, refiners, and planters. Provides nutritional information, public education, and research on sugar.

U.S. Beet Sugar Assn., *1156 15th St. N.W., #1019 20005-1704; (202) 296-4820. Fax, (202) 331-2065. James W. Johnson Jr., President.*
General email, beetsugar@aol.com
Web, www.beetsugar.org

Membership: beet sugar processors. Library open to the public by appointment. Monitors legislation and regulations.

Tobacco and Peanuts

▶**AGENCIES**

Agricultural Marketing Service (AMS) *(Agriculture Dept.), Cotton and Tobacco Programs, 1400 Independence Ave. S.W., #2641S, MS 0224 20250-0224; (202) 720-2145. Fax, (202) 690-1718. Darryl W. Earnest, Deputy Administrator.*
Web, www.ams.usda.gov/cotton/index.htm

Administers cotton marketing programs; sets cotton and tobacco grading standards and conducts quality inspections based on those standards. Maintains market news service to inform producers of daily price changes.

Economic Research Service *(Agriculture Dept.), 355 E St. S.W. 20024-8221; (202) 694-5000. Fax, (202) 245-4846. Mary Bohman, Administrator; Greg Pompelli, Associate Administrator.*
General email, service@ers.usda.gov
Web, www.ers.usda.gov

Conducts market research; studies and forecasts domestic supply-and-demand trends for tobacco.

Farm Service Agency (FSA) *(Agriculture Dept.), Farm Programs, 1400 Independence Ave. S.W., MS 0510 20250-0510; (202) 720-3175. Fax, (202) 720-4726. J. Michael Schmidt, Deputy Administrator. Press, (202) 720-7807.*
Web, www.fsa.usda.gov

Administers and manages aid programs for farmers, including conservation efforts, disaster relief, loans, subsidies, and the Tobacco Transition Payment program. Operates through county offices spread throughout the continental United States, Hawaii, and several American territories.

Farm Service Agency (FSA) *(Agriculture Dept.), Fibers, Peanuts, and Tobacco Analysis, 1400 Independence Ave. S.W., #37605, MS 0515 20250-0515; (202) 720-3392. Fax, (202) 690-2186. Scott Sanford, Director.*
Web, www.fsa.usda.gov

Develops production adjustment and price support programs to balance supply and demand for cotton, peanuts, and tobacco.

▶**NONGOVERNMENTAL**

American Peanut Council, *1500 King St., #301, Alexandria, VA 22314-2737; (703) 838-9500. Fax, (703) 838-9508. Patrick Archer, President.*
General email, info@peanutsusa.com
Web, www.peanutsusa.com

Membership: peanut growers, shellers, brokers, and manufacturers, as well as allied domestic and international companies. Provides information on economic and nutritional value of peanuts; coordinates research; promotes U.S. peanut exports, domestic production, and market development.

Cigar Assn. of America, *1100 G St. N.W., #1050 20005-7405; (202) 223-8204. Fax, (202) 833-0379. Craig P. Williamson, President. General email, nsharp@cigarassociation.org*

Web, www.cigarassociation.org

Membership: growers and suppliers of cigar leaf tobacco; manufacturers, packagers, importers, distributors of cigars; and suppliers to the cigar industry. Monitors legislation and regulations.

Tobacco Associates, Inc., Washington Office, *8452 Holly Leaf Dr., McLean, VA 22102; (703) 821-1255. Fax, (703) 821-1511. Clyde N. (Kirk) Wayne, President. General email, taw@tobaccoassociatesinc.org*

Web, www.tobaccoassociatesinc.org

Membership: U.S. producers of flue-cured tobacco. Promotes exports; provides information to encourage overseas market development. (Headquarters in Raleigh, N.C.)

FARM LOANS, INSURANCE, AND SUBSIDIES

General

▶ **AGENCIES**

Commodity Credit Corp. *(Agriculture Dept.), 1400 Independence Ave. S.W., MS 0599 20250-0571; (202) 720-0402. Fax, (202) 720-5398. Monique B. Randolph, Assistant Secretary, Acting. General email, steve.mikkelson@wdc.usda.gov*

Web, www.fsa.usda.gov/ccc

Administers and finances the commodity stabilization program through loans, purchases, and supplemental payments; sells through domestic and export markets commodities acquired by the government under this program; administers some aspects of foreign food aid through the Food for Peace program; provides storage facilities.

Farm Credit Administration, *1501 Farm Credit Dr., McLean, VA 22102-5090; (703) 883-4056. Fax, (703) 790-3260. Jill Long Thompson, Chair, (703) 883-4006. General email, info-line@fca.gov*

Web, www.fca.gov

Examines and regulates the cooperative Farm Credit System, which comprises farm credit banks, one agricultural credit bank, agricultural credit associations, and federal land credit associations. Oversees credit programs and related services for farmers, ranchers, producers and harvesters of aquatic products, farm-related service businesses, rural homeowners, agricultural and aquatic cooperatives, and rural utilities.

Farm Credit Administration, Examination, *1501 Farm Credit Dr., McLean, VA 22102-5090; (703) 883-4160. Fax, (703) 893-2978. S. Robert Coleman, Chief Examiner, (703) 883-4246.*

General email, info-line@fca.gov

Web, www.fca.gov/about/offices/offices.html

Enforces and oversees compliance with the Farm Credit Act. Monitors cooperatively owned member banks' and associations' compliance with laws prohibiting discrimination in credit transactions.

Farm Service Agency (FSA) *(Agriculture Dept.), 1400 Independence Ave. S.W., #3086 South Bldg., MS 0501 20250-0506; (202) 720-3467. Fax, (202) 720-9105. Juan M. Garcia, Administrator. Press, (202) 720-7807. Web, www.fsa.usda.gov*

Administers farm commodity programs providing crop loans and purchases; provides crop payments when market prices fall below specified levels; sets acreage allotments and marketing quotas; assists farmers in areas affected by natural disasters.

Farm Service Agency (FSA) *(Agriculture Dept.), Farm Loan Programs, 1400 Independence Ave. S.W., #3605S, MS 0520 20250-0520; (202) 720-4671. Fax, (202) 690-3573. Chris Beyerhelm, Deputy Administrator, (202) 720-7597. Web, www.fsa.usda.gov*

Provides services and loans to beginning farmers and ranchers and administers emergency farm and ranch loan programs.

Farm Service Agency (FSA) *(Agriculture Dept.), Minority and Socially Disadvantaged Farmers Assistance, 1400 Independence Ave. S.W., MS 0503 20250-0503; (202) 690-1098. Fax, (202) 690-4727. J. Latrice Hill, Director, Outreach. General email, oasdfr@osec.usda.gov*

Web, www.fsa.usda.gov

Works with minority and socially disadvantaged farmers who have concerns and questions about loan applications filed with local offices or other Farm Service Agency programs.

Farmer Mac, *1999 K St. N.W., 4th Floor 20036; (202) 872-7700. Fax, (202) 872-7713. Timothy Buzby, President. Toll-free, (800) 879-3276.*

Web, www.farmermac.com

Private corporation chartered by Congress to provide a secondary mortgage market for farm and rural housing loans. Guarantees principal and interest repayment on securities backed by farm and rural housing loans. (Farmer Mac stands for Federal Agricultural Mortgage Corp.)

Risk Management Agency *(Agriculture Dept.), 1400 Independence Ave. S.W., #6092S, MS 0801 20250-0801; (202) 690-2803. Fax, (202) 690-2818. Brandon C. Willis, Administrator. Information, (202) 690-0437. General email, rma.cco@rma.usda.gov*

Web, www.rma.usda.gov

Provides farmers with insurance against crops lost because of bad weather, insects, disease, and other natural causes.

Rural Development *(Agriculture Dept.), Civil Rights, 1400 Independence Ave. S.W., #1341, MS 0703 20250;*

(202) 692-0090. Fax, (202) 692-0279. Vacant, Director.
Toll-free, (800) 669-9777.
Web, www.rurdev.usda.gov/rd_civilrights.html

Processes Equal Employment Opportunity complaints for Rural Development employees, former employees, and applicants. Enforces compliance with the Equal Credit Opportunity Act, which prohibits discrimination on the basis of sex, marital status, race, color, religion, disability, or age in rural housing, utilities, and business programs. Provides civil rights training to Rural Development's national, state, and field staffs.

▶**CONGRESS**

For a listing of relevant congressional committees and sub-committees, please see page 3 or the Appendix.

▶**NONGOVERNMENTAL**

Environmental Working Group, *1436 U St. N.W., #100 20009-3987; (202) 667-6982. Fax, (202) 232-2592. Kenneth A. Cook, President.*
General email, generalinfo@ewg.org
Web, www.ewg.org

Research and advocacy group that studies and publishes reports on a wide range of agricultural and environmental issues, including farm subsidies and industrial pollution. Monitors legislation and regulations.

Farm Credit Council, *50 F St. N.W., #900 20001-1530; (202) 626-8710. Fax, (202) 626-8718. Ken Auer, President, (202) 879-0843.*
General email, auer@fccouncil.com
Web, www.fccouncil.com

Represents the Farm Credit System, a national financial cooperative that makes loans to agricultural producers, rural homebuyers, farmer cooperatives, and rural utilities. Finances the export of U.S. agricultural commodities.

FOOD AND NUTRITION

General

▶**AGENCIES**

Agricultural Marketing Service (AMS) *(Agriculture Dept.), Science and Technology, 1400 Independence Ave. S.W., #3533 20250-0003; (202) 720-5231. Fax, (202) 720-6496. Ruihong Guo, Deputy Administrator, (202) 720-8556.*
Web, www.ams.usda.gov/science/index.htm

Provides analytical testing to AMS community programs, federal and state agencies, and the private sector food industry; participates in international food safety organizations. Tests commodities traded with specific countries and regions, including butter, honey, eggs, nuts, poultry, and meat; analyzes nutritional value of U.S. military rations.

Agricultural Research Service *(Agriculture Dept.), 1400 Independence Ave. S.W., #302A, MS 0300 20250-0300; (202) 720-3656. Fax, (202) 720-5427. Vacant, Administrator.*
Web, www.ars.usda.gov

Conducts studies on agricultural problems of domestic and international concern through nationwide network of research centers. Studies include research on human nutrition; livestock production and protection; crop production, protection, and processing; postharvest technology; and food distribution and market value.

Agriculture Dept. (USDA), *Food, Nutrition, and Consumer Services, 1400 Independence Ave. S.W., #216E 20250-0106; (202) 720-7711. Fax, (202) 690-3100. Kevin W. Concannon, Under Secretary; Janey Thornton, Deputy Under Secretary.*
Web, www.fns.usda.gov

Oversees the Food and Nutrition Service and the Center for Nutrition Policy and Promotion.

Animal and Plant Health Inspection Service (APHIS) *(Agriculture Dept.), 1400 Independence Ave. S.W., #312E, MS 3401 20250-3401; (202) 799-7030. Fax, (202) 720-3054. Kevin A. Shea, Administrator. Press, (301) 851-4100. Veterinary Services, (301) 851-3300. Plants and Plant Products, (877) 770-5990.*
Web, www.aphis.usda.gov

Administers animal disease control programs in cooperation with states; inspects imported animals, flowers, and plants; licenses the manufacture and marketing of veterinary biologics to ensure purity and effectiveness.

Food and Drug Administration (FDA) *(Health and Human Services Dept.), Center for Food Safety and Applied Nutrition, 5100 Paint Branch Pkwy., College Park, MD 20740-3835; (240) 402-1600. Fax, (301) 436-2668. Michael M. Landa, Director.*
General email, consumer@fda.gov
Web, www.fda.gov

Develops standards of composition and quality of foods (except meat and poultry but including fish); develops safety regulations for food and color additives for foods, cosmetics, and drugs; monitors pesticide residues in foods; conducts food safety and nutrition research; develops analytical methods for measuring food additives, nutrients, pesticides, and chemical and microbiological contaminants; recommends action to Justice Dept.

Food and Drug Administration (FDA) *(Health and Human Services Dept.), Nutrition, Labeling, and Dietary Supplements, 5100 Paint Branch Pkwy., CPK-1 Bldg. #4C-095, College Park, MD 20740-3835; (240) 402-2373. Fax, (301) 436-2639. Philip Stiller, Director.*
Web, www.cfsan.fda.gov

Scientific and technical component of the Center for Food Safety and Applied Nutrition. Conducts research on nutrients; develops regulations and labeling requirements on infant formulas, medical foods, and dietary supplements, including herbs.

Food and Nutrition Service *(Agriculture Dept.), 3101 Park Center Dr., #906, Alexandria, VA 22302-1500; (703) 305-2060. Fax, (703) 305-2908. Audrey Rowe, Administrator. Information, (703) 305-2286.*
Web, www.fns.usda.gov

Administers all Agriculture Dept. domestic food assistance, including the distribution of funds and food for school breakfast and lunch programs (preschool through secondary) to public and nonprofit private schools; the Supplemental Nutrition Assistance Program (SNAP, formerly the food stamp program); and a supplemental nutrition program for women, infants, and children (WIC).

Food and Nutrition Service *(Agriculture Dept.), Child Nutrition, 3101 Park Center Dr., #640, Alexandria, VA 22302-1500; (703) 305-2590. Fax, (703) 305-2879. Cindy Long, Director, (703) 305-2054. Press, (703) 305-2281.*
General email, cndinternet@fns.usda.gov
Web, www.fns.usda.gov/cnd

Administers the transfer of funds to state agencies for the National School Lunch Program; the School Breakfast Program; the Special Milk Program, which helps schools and institutions provide children who do not have access to full meals under other child nutrition programs with fluid milk; the Child and Adult Care Food Program, which provides children in nonresidential child-care centers and family day-care homes with year-round meal service; and the Summer Food Service Program, which provides children from low-income areas with meals during the summer months.

Food and Nutrition Service *(Agriculture Dept.), Food Distribution, 3101 Park Center Dr., #504, Alexandria, VA 22302-1500; (703) 305-2680. Fax, (703) 305-2964. Laura Castro, Director.*
General email, fdd-pst@fns.usda.gov
Web, www.fns.usda.gov/fdd

Provides food for the National School Lunch Program, the Summer Food Service Program, and the Child and Adult Care Food Program. Administers the Commodity Supplemental Food Program for low-income pregnant and breastfeeding women, new mothers, infants, children, and the elderly. Supplies food to relief organizations for distribution following disasters. Makes commodity food and cash available through the Nutrition Services Incentive Program (formerly the Nutrition Program for the Elderly). Administers the Emergency Food Assistance Program through soup kitchens and food banks and the Food Distribution Program on Indian reservations and to Indian households elsewhere.

Food and Nutrition Service *(Agriculture Dept.), Research and Analysis, 3101 Park Center Dr., #1014, Alexandria, VA 22302-1500; (703) 305-2017. Fax, (703) 305-2576. Richard (Rich) Lucas, Associate Administrator, Acting.*
General email, oaneweb@fns.usda.gov
Web, www.fns.usda.gov/ora

Evaluates federal nutrition assistance programs; provides results to policymakers and program administrators. Funds demonstration grants for state and local nutrition assistance projects.

Food and Nutrition Service *(Agriculture Dept.), Supplemental Food Programs, 3101 Park Center Dr., #528, Alexandria, VA 22302-1594; (703) 305-2746. Fax, (703) 305-2196. Debra Whitford, Director.*
Web, www.fns.usda.gov/wic

Provides health departments and agencies with federal funding for food supplements and administrative expenses to make food, nutrition education, and health services available to infants, young children, and pregnant, nursing, and postpartum women.

Food and Nutrition Service *(Agriculture Dept.), Supplemental Nutrition Assistance Program (SNAP), 3101 Park Center Dr., #808, Alexandria, VA 22302-1500; (703) 305-2026. Fax, (703) 305-2454. Jessica Shahin, Associate Administrator, (703) 305-2022.*
Web, www.fns.usda.gov

Administers SNAP through state welfare agencies to provide needy persons with Electronic Benefit Transfer cards to increase food purchasing power. Provides matching funds to cover half the cost of EBT card issuance.

Food Safety and Inspection Service *(Agriculture Dept.), 1400 Independence Ave. S.W., #331E 20250-3700; (202) 720-7025. Fax, (202) 690-0550. Alfred (Al) Amanza, Administrator. Press, (202) 720-9113. Consumer inquiries, (800) 535-4555.*
Web, www.usda.gov/fsis

Inspects meat, poultry, and egg products moving in interstate commerce for use as human food to ensure that they are safe, wholesome, and accurately labeled. Provides safe handling and labeling guidelines.

Health and Human Services Dept. (HHS), *President's Council on Fitness, Sports, and Nutrition, 1101 Wootton Pkwy., #560, Tower Bldg., Rockville, MD 20852; (240) 276-9567. Fax, (240) 276-9860. Shellie Pfohl, Executive Director.*
General email, fitness@hhs.gov
Web, www.fitness.gov and www.presidentschallenge.org

Provides schools, state and local governments, recreation agencies, and employers with information on designing and implementing physical fitness and nutrition programs; conducts award programs for children and adults and for schools, clubs, and other institutions.

National Agricultural Library *(Agriculture Dept.), Food and Nutrition Information Center, 10301 Baltimore Ave., #108, Beltsville, MD 20705-2351; (301) 504-5414. Fax, (301) 504-6409. Vacant, Nutrition and Food Safety Program Leader.*
General email, fnic@nal.usda.gov
Web, http://fnic.nal.usda.gov/

Serves primarily educators, health professionals, and consumers seeking information about nutrition assistance programs and general nutrition. Serves as an online provider of science-based information about food and nutrition and links to such information. Lends books and audiovisual materials for educational purposes through inter-library loan; maintains a database of food and nutrition software and multimedia programs; provides reference services; develops resource lists of health and nutrition publications. Library open to the public.

National Agricultural Library *(Agriculture Dept.), Food Safety Information Center, 10301 Baltimore Ave., #304B, Beltsville, MD 20705-2351; (301) 504-5515. Fax, (301) 504-7680. Tara Smith, Manager.*
General email, fsic@ars.usda.gov
Web, http://fsrio.nal.usda.gov

Provides food safety information to educators, industry, researchers, and the general public. Special subject areas include pathogens and contaminants, sanitation and quality standards, food preparation and handling, and food processing and technology. The center includes the Food Safety Research Information Office, which focuses on providing information and reference services to the research community and the general public.

National Institute of Diabetes and Digestive and Kidney Diseases *(National Institutes of Health), Nutrition Research Coordination, 6707 Democracy Blvd., #624, MSC-5461, Bethesda, MD 20892-5450; (301) 594-8822. Fax, (301) 480-3768. Dr. Van S. Hubbard, Chief, (301) 594-8827.*
General email, DNRC@nih.hhs.gov
Web, www.dnrc.nih.gov

Supports research on nutritional requirements, dietary fiber, obesity, eating disorders, energy regulation, clinical nutrition, trace minerals, and basic nutrient functions.

National Institute of Food and Agriculture (NIFA) *(Agriculture Dept.), Jaime L. Whitten Bldg., #305A, 800 9th St. S.W. 20024 (mailing address: 1400 Independence Ave. S.W., MS 2201, Washington, DC 20250-2201); (202) 720-4423. Fax, (202) 720-8987. Sonny Ramaswamy, Director. Press, (202) 720-8188. Information, (202) 720-4651.*
Web, www.nifa.usda.gov

Supports research, education, and extension of issues pertaining to agricultural production, nutrition, food safety, energy independence, and the sustainability of natural resources. Partners with and funds scientists at land-grant universities and in private industry, addressing critical issues, including global food security and hunger, climate change, sustainable energy, childhood obesity, and food safety. Collaborates with historical black colleges and universities, Hispanic-serving institutions, and tribal colleges. Partners with agricultural extension offices in all counties, states, and territories.

National Institute of Food and Agriculture (NIFA) *(Agriculture Dept.), Institute of Food Safety and Nutrition, 1400 Independence Ave. S.W., MS 2225 20250-2225; (202) 720-5004. Fax, (202) 401-4888. Robert Holland, Assistant Director.*
Web, www.nifa.usda.gov/about/pdfs/fact_sheets/inst_fs_fsn.pdf

Works toward safe food supply by reducing food-borne illness. Addresses causes of microbial contamination and antimicrobial resistance; educates consumer and food safety professionals; and develops food processing technologies. Promotes programs to improve citizens' health through better nutrition, reducing childhood obesity, and improving food quality.

National Oceanic and Atmospheric Administration (NOAA) *(Commerce Dept.), Seafood Inspection Program, 1315 East-West Hwy., #9519, Silver Spring, MD 20910; (301) 713-2355. Fax, (301) 713-1081. Timothy Hansen, Director. Toll-free, (800) 422-2750.*
General email, nmfs.seafood.services@noaa.gov
Web, http://seafood.nmfs.noaa.gov

Administers voluntary inspection program for fish products and fish processing plants; certifies fish for wholesomeness, safety, and condition; grades for quality. Conducts training and workshops to help U.S. importers and foreign suppliers comply with food regulations.

►CONGRESS

For a listing of relevant congressional committees and sub-committees, please see page 3 or the Appendix.

►INTERNATIONAL ORGANIZATIONS

Codex Alimentarius Commission, U.S. Codex Office, *Washington Office, 1400 Independence Ave. S.W., South Bldg., #4861 20250-3700; (202) 205-7760. Fax, (202) 720-3157. Mary Frances Lowe, U.S. Codex Manager; Paulo Almeida, U.S. Associate Manager. Press, (202) 720-9113. Meat and Poultry Hotline, (888) 674-6854.*
General email, uscodex@fsis.usda.gov
Web, www.fsis.usda.gov/codex

Operates within the Food and Agricultural Organization (FAO) and the World Health Organization (WHO) to establish international food and food safety standards and to ensure fair trade practices. Convenes committees in member countries to address specific commodities and issues including labeling, additives in food and veterinary drugs, pesticide residues and other contaminants, and systems for food inspection. (Located in the USDA Food Safety and Inspection Service; international headquarters in Rome at the UN's Food and Agricultural Organization.)

►NONGOVERNMENTAL

Academy of Nutrition and Dietetics, *Washington Office, 1120 Connecticut Ave. N.W., #480 20036-3989; (202) 775-8277. Fax, (202) 775-8284. Jeanne Blankenship, Vice President. Toll-free, (800) 877-0877.*
General email, govaffairs@eatright.org and media@eatright.org
Web, www.eatright.org

Membership: dietitians and other nutrition professionals. Promotes public health and nutrition; accredits academic programs in clinical nutrition and food service management; sets standards of professional practice. Sponsors the National Center for Nutrition and Dietetics. (Headquarters in Chicago, Ill.)

American Herbal Products Assn., *8630 Fenton St., #918, Silver Spring, MD 20910; (301) 588-1171. Fax, (301) 588-1174. Michael McGuffin, President.*
General email, ahpa@ahpa.org

Web, www.ahpa.org

Membership: U.S. companies and individuals that grow, manufacture, and distribute botanicals and herbal products, including foods, beverages, dietary supplements, and personal care products; associates in education, law, media, and medicine. Supports research; promotes quality standards, consumer access, and self-regulation in the industry. Monitors legislation and regulations.

American Society for Nutrition, *9650 Rockville Pike, #5000, Bethesda, MD 20814-3990; (301) 634-7050. Fax, (301) 634-7894. John Courtney, Executive Officer.*
General email, info@nutrition.org

Web, www.nutrition.org

Membership: nutritional research scientists and practioners, including clinical nutritionists. Supports and advocates research on the role of human nutrition in health and disease; encourages undergraduate and graduate nutrition education; offers awards for research. (Merger of the American Society for Clinical Nutrition and the American Society for Nutritional Sciences.)

American Society for Parenteral and Enteral Nutrition (ASPEN), *8630 Fenton St., #412, Silver Spring, MD 20910-3805; (301) 587-6315. Fax, (301) 587-2365. Debra BenAvram, Executive Director. Toll-free, (800) 727-4567.*
General email, aspen@nutr.org

Web, www.nutritioncare.org

Membership: health care professionals who provide patients with intravenous nutritional support during hospitalization and rehabilitation at home. Develops nutrition guidelines; provides educational materials; conducts annual meetings.

Center for Science in the Public Interest, *1220 L St. N.W., #300 20005; (202) 332-9110. Fax, (202) 265-4954. Michael F. Jacobson, Executive Director.*
General email, cspi@cspinet.org

Web, www.cspinet.org

Conducts research on food and nutrition. Interests include eating habits, food safety regulations, food additives, organically produced foods, and links between diet and disease. Publishes *Nutrition Action* health letter. Monitors U.S. and international policy.

Congressional Hunger Center, *Hall of the States Bldg., 400 N. Capitol St. N.W., #G100 20001-1592; (202) 547-7022. Fax, (202) 547-7575. Edward M. Cooney, Executive Director.*
Web, www.hungercenter.org

Works to increase public awareness of hunger in the United States and abroad. Develops strategies and trains leaders to combat hunger and facilitates collaborative efforts between organizations.

Council for Responsible Nutrition (CRN), *1828 L St. N.W., #510 20036-5114; (202) 204-7700. Fax, (202) 204-7701. Steven Mister, President.*
General email, nstewart@crnus.org

Web, www.crnusa.org

Membership: manufacturers, distributors, and ingredient suppliers of dietary supplements. Provides information to members; monitors Food and Drug Administration, Federal Trade Commission, and Consumer Product Safety Commission regulations.

Food & Water Watch, *1616 P St. N.W., #300 20036; (202) 683-2500. Fax, (202) 683-2501. Wenonah Hauter, Executive Director.*
General email, info@fwwatch.org

Web, www.foodandwaterwatch.org

Consumer organization that advocates for stricter water and food safety regulations. Organizes public awareness campaigns and lobbies Congress. Publishes studies of agricultural, food preparation, and drinking water sanitation practices. Chapters in fifteen states and international chapter in Brussels, Belgium.

Food Allergy Research and Education (FARE), *7925 Jones Branch Dr., #1100, McLean, VA 22102; (703) 691-3179. Fax, (703) 691-2713. John Lehr, Chief Executive Officer. Toll-free, (800) 929-4040.*
General email, faan@foodallergy.org

Web, www.foodallergy.org

Membership: dieticians, nurses, physicians, school staff, government representatives, members of the food and pharmaceutical industries, and food-allergy patients and their families. Provides information and educational resources on food allergies and allergic reactions. Offers research grants.

Food Research and Action Center (FRAC), *1200 18th St. N.W., #400 20036; (202) 986-2200. Fax, (202) 986-2525. James D. Weill, President.*
General email, comments@frac.org

Web, www.frac.org

Public interest advocacy center that works to end hunger and undernutrition in the United States. Offers organizational aid, training, and information to groups seeking to improve or expand federal food programs, including food stamp, child nutrition, and WIC (women, infants, and children) programs; conducts studies relating to hunger and poverty; coordinates network of antihunger organizations. Monitors legislation and regulations.

International Food Information Council, *1100 Connecticut Ave. N.W., #430 20036-4120; (202) 296-6540. Fax, (202) 296-6547. David B. Schmidt, President.*
General email, info@foodinsight.org

Web, www.foodinsight.org

Food Safety Resources and Contacts

AGENCIES

Center for Food Safety and Applied Nutrition, Food and Drug Administration (FDA), (Health and Human Services Department),
Michael M. Landa, Director (Acting), (888) 723-3366
Office of Food Additive Safety, Dr. Dennis M. Keefe, Director, (240) 402-1200
Office of Food Defense, Communication and Emergency Response, Faye Feldstein, Director, (301) 436-2428
Office of Food Safety, Dr. Nega Beru, Director, (240) 402-1700
Office of Nutritional Products, Labeling and Dietary Supplements, Philip Spiller, Director (Acting), (240) 402-2373

Food Safety and Inspection Service (FSIS), (Agriculture Department),
Alfred V. Almanza, Administrator, (202) 720-7025
Office of Data Integration and Food Protection, Terri Nintemann, Assistant Administrator, (202) 690-6486

Food Safety Information Center (FSIC), National Agricultural Library, (Agriculture Department),
Simon Y. Liu, Director, (301) 504-5248

Office of Ground Water and Drinking Water, Environmental Protection Agency,
Peter Grevatt, Director, (202) 564-8954

Seafood Inspection Program, National Oceanic and Atmospheric Administration (NOAA), (Commerce Department),
Tim Hansen, Director, (301) 427-8300

ORGANIZATIONS

Center for Food Safety,
Andrew Kimbrell, Executive Director, (202) 547-9359

Center for Science in the Public Interest,
Michael F. Jacobson, Executive Director, (202) 332-9110

Food and Water Watch,
Wenonah Hauter, Executive Director, (202) 683-2500

International Food Information Council,
David B. Schmidt, President, (202) 296-6540

HOTLINES

24-Hour Emergency Number: (866) 395-9701
www.fsis.usda.gov

FDA Center for Food Safety and Applied Nutrition, (888) SAFEFOOD, (888) 723-3366
www.fda.gov/aboutfda/centersoffices/officeoffoods/cfsan/default.htm

Gateway to Government Food Safety Information,
www.foodsafety.gov; www.facebook.com/FoodSafety.gov

Safe Drinking Water Hotline, (800) 426-4791
water.epa.gov/drink

USDA Meat and Poultry Hotline, (888) MPHOTLINE; , (888) 674-6854
mphotline.fsis@usda.gov

Membership: food and beverage companies and manufacturers of food ingredients. Provides the media, health professionals, and consumers with science-based information about food safety, health, and nutrition. Interests include harmonization of international food safety standards.

International Life Sciences Institute (ILSI), *North America, 1156 15th St. N.W., #200 20005-5802; (202) 659-0074. Fax, (202) 659-3859. Eric J. Hentges, Executive Director; Sharon Weiss, Deputy Executive Director.*
General email, info@ilsi.org

Web, www.ilsi.org

Acts as liaison among scientists from international government agencies, concerned industries, research institutes, and universities regarding the safety of foods and chemical ingredients. Conducts research on caffeine, food coloring, oral health, human nutrition, and other food issues. Promotes international cooperation among scientists.

Physicians Committee for Responsible Medicine (PCRM), *5100 Wisconsin Ave. N.W., #400 20016; (202) 686-2210. Fax, (202) 686-2216. Neal Barnard, President.*

General email, pcrm@pcrm.org

Web, www.pcrm.org

Membership: health care professionals, medical students, and laypersons interested in preventive medicine, nutrition, and higher standards in research. Conducts clinical research, educational programs, and public information campaigns; advocates for more effective and compassionate health-related policies in government and in public and private institutions.

Public Citizen, *Health Research Group, 1600 20th St. N.W. 20009-1001; (202) 588-1000. Fax, (202) 588-7796. Michael Carome, Director.*
General email, hrg@citizen.org

Web, www.citizen.org

Citizens' interest group that studies and reports on unsafe foods; monitors and petitions the Food and Drug Administration.

United Food and Commercial Workers International Union (UFCW), *1775 K St. N.W. 20006-1598; (202) 223-3111. Fax, (202) 466-1562. Joseph T. Hansen, President.*
Web, www.ufcw.org and Twitter, https://twitter.com/ufcw

Membership: approximately 1.3 million workers primarily in the retail, meatpacking, food processing, and poultry industries. Interests include health care reform, living wages, retirement security, safe working conditions, and the right to unionize. Monitors legislation and regulations.

Vegetarian Resource Group, *P.O. Box 1463, Baltimore, MD 21203-1463; (410) 366-8343. Fax, (410) 366-8804. Charles Stahler, Co-Director; Debra Wasserman, Co-Director.*
General email, vrg@vrg.org
Web, www.vrg.org

Works to educate the public on vegetarianism and issues of health, nutrition, ecology, ethics, and world hunger.

Vegetarian Union of North America, *c/o Vegetarian Society of DC, P.O. Box 4921 20008-0121; (202) 362-8349, option 3. Fax, (888) 445-9891. Saurabh Dalal, President.*
General email, vuna@vsdc.org
Web, www.ivu.org/vuna

Builds a network of vegetarian groups throughout the United States and Canada. Serves as a liaison with the worldwide vegetarian movement. (Affiliated with the International Vegetarian Union and the Vegetarian Society of DC.)

Beverages

▶ AGENCIES

Alcohol and Tobacco Tax and Trade Bureau (TTB) *(Treasury Dept.), 1310 G St. N.W., #300E 20220; (202) 453-2000. John J. Manfreda, Administrator. Press, (202) 453-2134.*
General email, info@ttb.gov
Web, www.ttb.gov

Regulates the advertising and labeling of alcohol beverages, including the size of containers; enforces federal taxation of alcohol and tobacco. Authorized to refer violations to the Justice Dept. for criminal prosecution.

Substance Abuse and Mental Health Services Administration *(Health and Human Services Dept.),* **Center for Substance Abuse Prevention,** *1 Choke Cherry Rd., #4-1057, Rockville, MD 20857; (240) 276-2420. Fax, (240) 276-2430. Frances M. Harding, Director. Workplace Helpline, (800) WORKPLACE; (800) 967-5752. Information, (877) 726-4727.*
Web, www.samhsa.gov/about/csap.aspx

Demonstrates, evaluates, and disseminates strategies to prevent alcohol and drug abuse. Operates the National Clearinghouse for Alcohol and Drug Information, which provides information, publications, and grant applications for programs to prevent substance abuse. (Clearinghouse address: http://ncadi.samhsa.gov, or P.O. Box 2345, Rockville, MD 20847; toll-free phone, [877] 726-4727.)

Substance Abuse and Mental Health Services Administration *(Health and Human Services Dept.),* **Center for Substance Abuse Treatment,** *1 Choke Cherry Rd., #5-1015, Rockville, MD 20857; (240) 276-1660. Fax, (240) 276-1670. Dr. H. Westley Clark, Director. Treatment referral, (800) 662-4357. Publications, (800) 729-6686. Information, (877) 726-4727.*
Web, www.samhsa.gov/about/csat.aspx

Develops and supports policies and programs that improve and expand treatment services for alcoholism, substance abuse, and addiction. Administers grants that support private and public addiction prevention and treatment services. Evaluates alcohol treatment programs and other drug treatment programs and delivery systems.

▶ NONGOVERNMENTAL

American Beverage Assn., *1101 16th St. N.W. 20036-6396; (202) 463-6732. Fax, (202) 659-5349. Susan Neely, President. Press, (202) 463-6770.*
General email, info@ameribev.org
Web, www.ameribev.org

Membership: companies engaged in producing or distributing carbonated and noncarbonated soft drinks and bottled water. Acts as industry liaison with government and the public. (Formerly the National Soft Drink Assn.)

American Beverage Institute, *1090 Vermont Ave. N.W., #800 20005; (202) 463-7110. Fax, (202) 463-7107. Sarah Longwell, Managing Director.*
General email, info@abionline.org
Web, www.abionline.org

Promotes responsible alcohol consumption in restaurants and bars. Opposes restrictions on alcohol use. Monitors legislation and regulations.

American Beverage Licensees (ABL), *5101 River Rd., #108, Bethesda, MD 20816-1560; (301) 656-1494. Fax, (301) 656-7539. John D. Bodnovich, Executive Director.*
General email, info@ablusa.org
Web, www.ablusa.org

Membership: state associations of on- and off-premise beverage alcohol licensees. Monitors legislation and regulations affecting the alcohol beverage industry. (Formerly National Assn. of Beverage Retailers and National Licensed Beverage Assn.)

Beer Institute, *122 C St. N.W., #350 20001-2150; (202) 737-2337. Fax, (202) 737-7004. Vacant, President.*
General email, info@beerinstitute.org
Web, www.beerinstitute.org

Membership: domestic brewers and beer importers and suppliers to the domestic brewing industry. Monitors legislation and regulations.

Distilled Spirits Council of the United States, *1250 Eye St. N.W., #400 20005-3998; (202) 628-3544. Fax, (202) 682-8888. Peter H. Cressy, President.*
Web, www.discus.org

Membership: manufacturers and marketers of distilled spirits sold in the United States. Provides consumer information on alcohol-related issues and topics. Monitors legislation and regulations.

International Bottled Water Assn. (IBWA), *1700 Diagonal Rd., #650, Alexandria, VA 22314-2864; (703) 683-5213. Fax, (703) 683-4074. Joseph K. Doss, President, (703) 647-4605. Information, 800-WATER-11. Press, (703) 647-4609.*
General email, info@bottledwater.org
Web, www.bottledwater.org

Serves as a clearinghouse for industry-related consumer, regulatory, and technical information; interests include international trade. Monitors state and federal legislation and regulations.

Mothers Against Drunk Driving (MADD), *Public Policy Office, Washington Office, 1025 Connecticut Ave. N.W., #1210 20036-5415; (202) 688-1193. Fax, (972) 869-2206. J. T. Griffin, Chief; Frank Harris, State Legislative Affairs Manager, (202) 688-1194. Toll-free, (877) 275-6233. 24-hr Helpline, 877-MADD-HELP.*
General email, madd@madd.org
Web, www.madd.org

Advocacy group that seeks to stop drunk driving and prevent underage drinking. Monitors legislation and regulations. (Headquarters in Irving, Texas.)

National Alcohol Beverage Control Assn. (NABCA), *4401 Ford Ave., #700, Alexandria, VA 22302; (703) 578-4200. Fax, (703) 820-3551. James M. Sgueo, President.*
General email, nabcainfo@nabca.org
Web, www.nabca.org

Membership: distilleries, importers, brokers, trade associations, and state agencies that control the purchase, distribution, and sale of alcohol beverages. Promotes responsible sale and consumption of these beverages. Serves as an information clearinghouse. Monitors legislation and regulations.

National Assn. of State Alcohol and Drug Abuse Directors (NASADAD), *1025 Connecticut Ave. N.W., #605 20036-5430; (202) 293-0090. Fax, (202) 293-1250. Rob Morrison, Executive Director, ext. 106.*
General email, dcoffice@nasadad.org
Web, www.nasadad.org

Provides information on drug abuse treatment and prevention; contracts with federal and state agencies for design of programs to fight and prevent drug abuse.

National Beer Wholesalers Assn., *1101 King St., #600, Alexandria, VA 22314-2965; (703) 683-4300. Fax, (703) 683-8965. Craig A. Purser, President. Toll-free, (800) 300-6417.*
General email, info@nbwa.org
Web, www.nbwa.org

Works to enhance the independent beer wholesale industry. Advocates before government and the public; encourages responsible consumption of beer; sponsors programs and services to benefit members; monitors legislation and regulations.

Wine and Spirits Wholesalers of America (WSWA), *805 15th St. N.W., #430 20005-2273; (202) 371-9792. Fax, (202) 789-2405. Craig Wolf, President.*
General email, info@wswa.org
Web, www.wswa.org

Trade association of wholesale distributors of domestic and imported wine and distilled spirits. Provides information on drinking awareness. Represents members' interests before Congress and federal agencies.

Wine Institute, *Federal Relations, 601 13th St. N.W., #330 South 20005-3866; (202) 408-0870. Fax, (202) 371-0061. Charles Jefferson, Vice President; Linda Ulrich, Vice President.*
Web, www.wineinstitute.org

Membership: California wineries and affiliated businesses. Seeks international recognition for California wines; conducts promotional campaigns in other countries. Monitors legislation and regulations. (Headquarters in San Francisco, Calif.)

Food Industries

▶ **NONGOVERNMENTAL**

American Bakers Assn. (ABA), *1300 Eye St. N.W., #700W 20005-7203; (202) 789-0300. Fax, (202) 898-1164. Robb MacKie, President.*
General email, info@americanbakers.org
Web, www.americanbakers.org

Membership: wholesale baking companies and their suppliers. Promotes increased consumption of baked goods; provides consumers with nutritional information; conducts conventions. Monitors legislation and regulations.

American Frozen Food Institute, *2000 Corporate Ridge Blvd., #1000, McLean, VA 22102-7862; (703) 821-0770. Fax, (703) 821-1350. Kraig Naasz, President.*
General email, info@affi.com
Web, www.affi.org

Membership: frozen food packers, distributors, and suppliers. Testifies before Congress and federal agencies.

American Meat Institute, *1150 Connecticut Ave. N.W., 12th Floor 20036; (202) 587-4200. Fax, (202) 587-4300. James Hodges, President, Interim.*
Web, www.meatami.com

Membership: national and international meat and poultry packers, suppliers, and processors. Provides statistics on meat production and exports. Funds research projects and consumer education programs. Monitors legislation and regulations.

Bakery, Confectionery, Tobacco Workers, and Grain Millers International Union, *10401 Connecticut Ave., Kensington, MD 20895-3940; (301) 933-8600. Fax, (301) 946-8452. David B. Durkee, President.*
Web, www.bctgm.org

Membership: approximately 120,000 workers from the bakery, confectionery, grain miller, and tobacco industries. Helps members negotiate pay, benefits, and better working conditions; conducts training programs and workshops. Monitors legislation and regulations. (Affiliated with the AFL-CIO.)

Biscuit and Cracker Manufacturers' Assn., *6325 Woodside Court, #125, Columbia, MD 21046-3215; (443) 545-1645. Fax, (410) 290-8585. Stacey Sharpless, President. Web, www.thebcma.org*

Membership: companies in the cookie and cracker industry. Provides multimedia educational materials to members.

Food Marketing Institute (FMI), *2345 Crystal Dr., #800, Arlington, VA 22202-4813; (202) 452-8444. Fax, (202) 429-4519. Leslie G. Sarasin, President. General email, feedback@fmi.org*

Web, www.fmi.org

Trade association of food retailers and wholesalers. Conducts programs in research, education, industry relations, and public affairs; participates in international conferences. Library open to the public by appointment.

Food Processing Suppliers Assn. (FPSA), *1451 Dolley Madison Blvd., #101, McLean, VA 22101-3850; (703) 761-2600. Fax, (703) 761-4334. David Seckman, President, (703) 663-1200.*

General email, info@fpsa.org

Web, www.fpsa.org

Membership: equipment and ingredient manufacturers, suppliers, and servicers for the food, dairy, and beverage processing industry. Sponsors food engineering scholarships and the bi-annual Process Expo. (Merger of the International Assn. of Food Industry Suppliers and the Food Processing Machinery Assn.)

Grocery Manufacturers Assn. (GMA), *1350 Eye St. N.W., #300 20005-3377; (202) 639-5900. Fax, (202) 639-5932. Pamela Bailey, President. Press, (202) 295-3938. General email, info@gmaonline.org*

Web, www.gmaonline.org

Membership: manufacturers of food, beverage, and consumer packaged goods sold through the retail grocery trade. Interests include holistic waste management solutions, nutritional labeling, and the safety and security of the food supply. Supplies industry information to members. Monitors legislation and regulations.

International Foodservice Distributors Assn., *1410 Spring Hill Rd., #210, McLean, VA 22102; (703) 532-9400. Fax, (703) 538-4673. Mark S. Allen, President. General email, info@ifdaonline.org*

Web, www.ifdaonline.org

Trade association of foodservice distribution companies that advocates the interests of members in government and industry affairs through research, education, and communication.

National Assn. of Convenience Stores (NACS), *1600 Duke St., #700, Alexandria, VA 22314-3421; (703) 684-3600. Fax, (703) 836-4564. Henry Armour, President. Toll-free, (800) 966-6227.*

General email, nacs@nacsonline.com

Web, www.nacsonline.com

Membership: convenience store retailers and industry suppliers. Advocates industry position on labor, tax, environment, alcohol, and food-related issues; conducts research and training programs. Monitors legislation and regulations.

National Automatic Merchandising Assn. (NAMA), *Washington Office, 1600 Wilson Blvd., #650, Arlington, VA 22209; (571) 346-1900. Fax, (703) 836-8262. Carla Balakgie, President, (312) 346-0370; Eric Dell, Senior Vice President, Government Affairs. Press, (301) 987-7113. Web, www.vending.org*

Membership: service companies, equipment manufacturers, and product suppliers for the food and refreshment vending, coffee service, and foodservice management industries. Seeks to advance and promote the automatic merchandising and coffee service industries, provide administrative, logistical, and financial assistance to its members. (Headquarters in Chicago, Ill.)

National Council of Chain Restaurants (NCCR), *1101 New York Ave. N.W., #1200 20005; (202) 626-8183. Fax, (202) 737-2849. Robert (Rob) Green, Executive Director. Toll-free, (800) 673-4692.*

General email, purviss@nccr.net

Web, www.nccr.net

Trade association representing chain restaurant companies. Affiliated with the National Retail Federation. Monitors legislation and regulations.

National Grocers Assn., *1005 N. Glebe Rd., #250, Arlington, VA 22201-5758; (703) 516-0700. Fax, (703) 516-0115. Peter Larkin, President. General email, feedback@nationalgrocers.org*

Web, www.nationalgrocers.org

Trade association that represents independent retail and wholesale grocers. Membership also includes affiliated associations, manufacturers, and service suppliers. Provides members with educational materials through a Web site, publications, and conferences. Monitors legislation and regulations.

National Pasta Assn. (NPA), *750 National Press Bldg., 529 14th St. N.W. 20045-1806; (202) 637-5888. Fax, (202) 223-9741. Carol Freysinger, Executive Director. General email, info@ilovepasta.org*

Web, www.ilovepasta.org

Membership: U.S. pasta manufacturers, related suppliers, and allied industry representatives. Represents the industry on public policy issues; monitors and addresses technical issues; and organizes events and seminars for the industry.

National Restaurant Assn., *2055 L St. N.W., #700 20036; (202) 331-5900. Fax, (202) 331-2429. Dawn Sweeney, Chief Executive Officer. Toll-free, (800) 424-5156.*
General email, info@restaurant.org

Web, www.restaurant.org

Membership: restaurants, cafeterias, clubs, contract feeders, caterers, institutional food services, and other members of the food industry. Supports food service education and research. Monitors legislation and regulations.

Snack Food Assn. (SFA), *1600 Wilson Blvd., #650, Arlington, VA 22209-2510; (703) 836-4500. Fax, (703) 836-8262. Thomas Dempsey Jr., President. Toll-free, (800) 628-1334.*
General email, sfa@sfa.org

Web, www.sfa.org

Membership: snack food manufacturers and suppliers. Promotes industry sales; compiles statistics; conducts research and surveys; assists members with training and education; provides consumers with industry information. Monitors legislation and regulations.

Soyfoods Assn. of North America, *1050 17th St. N.W., #600 20036-5570; (202) 659-3520. Fax, (202) 659-3522. Nancy Chapman, Executive Director.*
General email, info@soyfoods.org

Web, www.soyfoods.org

Membership: large and small soyfood companies, growers and suppliers of soybeans, nutritionists, equipment representatives, food scientists, and retailers. Promotes soybean consumption. Helps establish standards for soyfoods. Monitors legislation and regulations.

Tortilla Industry Assn., *1600 Wilson Blvd., #650, Arlington, VA 22209; (800) 944-6099. Fax, (800) 944-6177. Jim Kabbani, Executive Director, (703) 819-9550.*
General email, jkabbaani@tortilla-info.com

Web, www.tortilla-info.com

Membership: tortilla manufacturers, industry suppliers, and distributors. Promotes tortilla consumption. Provides market research and other industry-related information to its members. Sponsors conferences, seminars, and educational events for the industry.

UNITE HERE, Washington Office, *1775 K St. N.W., #620 20006-1530; (202) 393-4373. Fax, (202) 223-6213. Tom Snyder, Political Director; John W. Wilhelm, President.*
Web, www.unitehere.org

Membership: more than 270,000 workers in the United States and Canada who work in the hospitality, gaming, food service, manufacturing, textile, laundry, and airport industries. Helps members negotiate pay, benefits, and better working conditions; conducts training programs and workshops. Monitors legislation and regulations. (Headquarters in New York. Formed by the merger of the former Union of Needletrades, Textiles and Industrial Employees and the Hotel Employees and Restaurant Employees International Union.)

World Cocoa Foundation, *1411 K St. N.W., #502 20005; (202) 737-7870. Fax, (202) 737-7832. William Guyton, President.*
General email, wcf@worldcocoa.org

Web, www.worldcocoafoundation.org

Promotes a sustainable cocoa economy through economic and social development and environmental conservation in cocoa-growing communities. Helps raise funds for cocoa farmers and increases their access to modern farming practices.

Vegetarianism

▶NONGOVERNMENTAL

Farm Animal Rights Movement (FARM), *10101 Ashburton Lane, Bethesda, MD 20817-1729; (301) 530-1737. Fax, (301) 530-5683. Alex Hershaft, President. Toll-free, 888-FARM-USA.*
General email, info@farmusa.org

Web, www.farmusa.org and www.livevegan.org

Works to end use of animals for food. Interests include animal protection, consumer health, agricultural resources, and environmental quality. Conducts national educational campaigns, including World Farm Animals Day, the Live Vegan program, and the Great American Meatout. Monitors legislation and regulations.

Great American Meatout, *10101 Ashburton Lane, Bethesda, MD 20817-1729; (800) 632-8688. Fax, (301) 530-5683. Alex Hershaft, President.*
General email, info@farmusa.org

Web, www.meatout.org

Promotes the dietary elimination of meat. Facilitates vegan-diet information tables, exhibits, cooking demonstrations, and festivals nationwide. (Affiliated with Farm Animal Rights Movement.)

Vegetarian Resource Group, *P.O. Box 1463, Baltimore, MD 21203-1463; (410) 366-8343. Fax, (410) 366-8804. Charles Stahler, Co-Director; Debra Wasserman, Co-Director.*
General email, vrg@vrg.org

Web, www.vrg.org

Works to educate the public on vegetarianism and issues of health, nutrition, ecology, ethics, and world hunger.

Vegetarian Union of North America, *c/o Vegetarian Society of DC, P.O. Box 4921 20008-0121; (202) 362-8349, option 3. Fax, (888) 445-9891. Saurabh Dalal, President.*
General email, vuna@vsdc.org

Web, www.ivu.org/vuna

Builds a network of vegetarian groups throughout the United States and Canada. Serves as a liaison with the worldwide vegetarian movement. (Affiliated with the International Vegetarian Union and the Vegetarian Society of DC.)

World Food Assistance

►AGENCIES

Foreign Agricultural Service (FAS) *(Agriculture Dept.),* *Capacity Building and Development,* 1400 Independence Ave. S.W., #3008S, MS 1030 20250-1030; (202) 720-6887. Fax, (202) 720-0069. Roger Mireles, Deputy Administrator, Acting.
Web, www.fas.usda.gov

Operates food aid programs, trade, science, and regulatory capacity-building projects, including training and technical assistance programs, and supports USDA's post-conflict and postdisaster reconstruction efforts.

World Agricultural Outlook Board *(Agriculture Dept.),* 1400 Independence Ave. S.W., #4419S 20250-3812; (202) 720-6030. Fax, (202) 720-4043. Gerald A. Bange, Chair; Brenda Chapin, Information Officer, (202) 720-5447.
Web, www.usda.gov/oce/commodity

Reports to the USDA chief economist. Coordinates the department's commodity forecasting program, which develops the official prognosis of supply, utilization, and prices for commodities worldwide. Works with the National Weather Service to monitor the impact of global weather on agriculture.

►INTERNATIONAL ORGANIZATIONS

Food and Agriculture Organization of the United Nations (FAO), *Liaison Office in Washington,* 2121 K St. N.W., #800B 20037-0001; (202) 653-2400. Fax, (202) 653-5760. Nicholas Nelson, Director. Press, (202) 653-0011.
General email, faolow@fao.org
Web, www.fao.org/north_america/en/ and *www.worldfooddayusa.org*

Offers development assistance; collects, analyzes, and disseminates information; provides policy and planning advice to governments; acts as an international forum for debate on food and agricultural issues, including animal health and production, fisheries, and forestry; encourages sustainable agricultural development and a long-term strategy for the conservation and management of natural resources. Coordinates World Food Day. (International headquarters in Rome.)

International Fund for Agricultural Development (IFAD), *North American Liaison Office,* 1775 K St. N.W., #410 20006-1502; (202) 331-9099. Fax, (202) 331-9366. Cheryl Morden, Director.
General email, c.morden@ifad.org
Web, www.ifad.org

Specialized agency of the United Nations that provides the rural poor of developing nations with cost-effective ways of overcoming hunger, poverty, and malnutrition. Advocates a community-based approach to reducing rural poverty. (International headquarters in Rome.)

►NONGOVERNMENTAL

ACDI/VOCA, 50 F St. N.W., #1075 20001-1530; (202) 469-6000. Fax, (202) 469-6257. William Polidoro, President.
General email, webmaster@acdivoca.org
Web, www.acdivoca.org

Promotes agribusiness systems that improve production and link farmers to national, regional, and international markets. Partners with farm supply, processing, and marketing cooperatives; farm credit banks; national farmer organizations; and insurance cooperatives. Provides cooperatives with training and technical, management, and marketing assistance; supports farm credit systems, agribusiness, and government agencies in developing countries. (Merger of Agricultural Cooperative Development International and Volunteers in Overseas Cooperative Assistance. Affiliated with the National Council of Farmer Cooperatives.)

American Red Cross, *National Headquarters,* 2025 E St. N.W. 20006-5009; (202) 303-5000. Gail J. McGovern, President. Press, (202) 303-5551. Toll-free, 800-RED-CROSS.
Web, www.redcross.org

Humanitarian relief and health education organization chartered by Congress. Provides food and supplies to assist in major disaster and refugee situations worldwide. U.S. delegate of the international Red Cross and Red Crescent Societies in international response efforts.

Bread for the World/Bread for the World Institute, 425 3rd St. S.W., #1200 20024; (202) 639-9400. Fax, (202) 639-9401. David Beckmann, President. Information, (800) 822-7323.
General email, bread@bread.org
Web, www.bread.org

Christian citizens' movement that works to eradicate world hunger. Organizes and coordinates political action on issues and public policy affecting the causes of hunger.

CARE, *Washington Office,* 1825 Eye St. N.W., #301 20006-1611; (202) 595-2800. Fax, (202) 296-8695. David Ray, Head of Policy and Advocacy. Toll-free, (800) 422-7385.
General email, info@care.org
Web, www.care.org

Assists the developing world's poor through emergency assistance and community self-help programs that focus on sustainable development, agriculture, agroforestry, water and sanitation, health, family planning, and income generation. Community-based efforts are centered on providing resources to poor women. (U.S. headquarters in Atlanta, Ga.; international headquarters in Geneva.)

International Food Policy Research Institute (IFPRI), 2033 K St. N.W., #400 20006-1002; (202) 862-5600. Fax, (202) 467-4439. Shenggen Fan, Director General. Library, (202) 862-5614.
General email, ifpri@cgiar.org
Web, www.ifpri.org

Research organization that analyzes the world food situation and suggests ways of making food more available in developing countries. Provides various governments with information on national and international food policy. Sponsors conferences and seminars; publishes research reports. Library open to the public by appointment.

National Center for Food and Agricultural Policy, *1616 P St. N.W., #100 20036; (202) 328-5183. Fax, (202) 328-5133. Joe Dunn, Chief Executive Officer.*
General email, ncfap@ncfap.org

Web, www.ncfap.org

Research and educational organization concerned with domestic and international food and agricultural issues. Examines public policy concerning agriculture, food safety and quality, natural resources, and the environment.

Oxfam America, *Policy, 1100 15th St. N.W. #600 20005-1759; (202) 496-1180. Fax, (202) 496-1190. Raymond C. Offenheiser, President; Paul O'Brien, Vice President for Policy and Campaigns. Information, (800) 776-9326. Press, (202) 496-1169.*
General email, info@oxfamamerica.org

Web, www.oxfamamerica.org

Funds disaster relief and long-term development programs internationally. Organizes grassroots support in the United States for issues affecting global poverty, including climate change, aid reform, and corporate transparency. (Headquarters in Boston, Mass.)

RESULTS, *1101 14th St. N.W., #1200 20005; (202) 783-7100. Fax, (202) 783-2818. Joanne Carter, Executive Director.*
General email, results@results.org

Web, www.results.org

Works to end hunger and poverty nationally and worldwide; encourages grassroots and legislative support of programs and proposals dealing with hunger and hunger-related issues. Monitors legislation and regulations.

Winrock International, *Washington Office, 2121 Crystal Dr., #500, Arlington, VA 22202; (703) 302-6500. Fax, (703) 302-6512. Rodney Ferguson, President.*
General email, information@winrock.org

Web, www.winrock.org

Works to increase economic opportunity; sustain natural resources; protect the environment; and increase long-term productivity, equity, and responsible resource management to benefit the world's poor and disadvantaged communities. Matches innovative approaches in agriculture, natural resources management, clean energy, and leadership development with the unique needs of its partners. Links local individuals and communities with new ideas and technology. (Headquarters in Little Rock, Ark.)

Worldwatch Institute, *1400 16th St. N.W., #430 20036; (202) 745-8092. Fax, (202) 478-2534. Robert Engelman, President.*
General email, worldwatch@worldwatch.org

Web, www.worldwatch.org

Environmental thinktank that studies the environmental, political, and economic links to world population growth and health trends. Interests include food and sustainable agriculture.

LIVESTOCK AND POULTRY

General

▶AGENCIES

Agricultural Marketing Service (AMS) *(Agriculture Dept.), Livestock, Poultry, and Seed, 1400 Independence Ave. S.W., #2092S, MS 0249 20250-0249; (202) 720-5705. Fax, (202) 720-3499. Craig Morris, Deputy Administrator.*
Web, www.ams.usda.gov/lsprogram

Administers meat marketing program; maintains market news service to inform producers of meat market situation and daily price changes; develops, establishes, and revises U.S. standards for classes and grades of livestock and meat; grades, examines, and certifies meat and meat products.

Food Safety and Inspection Service *(Agriculture Dept.), 1400 Independence Ave. S.W., #331E 20250-3700; (202) 720-7025. Fax, (202) 690-0550. Alfred (Al) Amanza, Administrator. Press, (202) 720-9113. Consumer inquiries, (800) 535-4555.*
Web, www.usda.gov/fsis

Inspects meat and poultry products and provides safe handling and labeling guidelines.

Grain Inspection, Packers and Stockyards Administration *(Agriculture Dept.), 1400 Independence Ave. S.W., #2055, South Bldg., MS 3601 20250-3601; (202) 720-0219. Fax, (202) 205-9237. Larry Mitchell, Administrator. Toll-free, (800) 455-3447.*
General email, larry.mitchell@gipsa.usda.gov

Web, www.gipsa.usda.gov

Maintains competition in the marketing of livestock, poultry, grain, and meat by prohibiting deceptive and monopolistic marketing practices; tests market scales and conducts check weighings for accuracy.

▶CONGRESS

For a listing of relevant congressional committees and subcommittees, please see page 3 or the Appendix.

▶NONGOVERNMENTAL

American Meat Institute, *1150 Connecticut Ave. N.W., 12th Floor 20036; (202) 587-4200. Fax, (202) 587-4300. James Hodges, President, Interim.*
Web, www.meatami.com

Membership: national and international meat and poultry packers and processors. Provides statistics on meat production and consumption, livestock, and feed grains. Funds meat research projects and consumer education programs; sponsors conferences and correspondence courses on meat production and processing. Monitors legislation and regulations.

Animal Health Institute, *1325 G St. N.W., #700 20005-3104; (202) 637-2440. Fax, (202) 393-1667. Alexander S. Mathews, President.*
Web, www.ahi.org

Membership: manufacturers of drugs and other products (including vaccines, pesticides, and vitamins) for pets and food-producing animals. Interests include pet health, livestock health, and disease outbreak prevention. Monitors legislation and regulations.

Farm Animal Rights Movement (FARM), *10101 Ashburton Lane, Bethesda, MD 20817-1729; (301) 530-1737. Fax, (301) 530-5683. Alex Hershaft, President. Toll-free, 888-FARM-USA.*
General email, info@farmusa.org
Web, www.farmusa.org and www.livevegan.org

Works to end use of animals for food. Interests include animal protection, consumer health, agricultural resources, and environmental quality. Conducts national educational campaigns, including World Farm Animals Day, the Live Vegan program, and the Great American Meatout. Monitors legislation and regulations.

Humane Farm Animal Care, *P.O. Box 727, Herndon, VA 20172-0727; (703) 435-3883. Fax, (703) 435-3981. Adele Douglass, Chief Executive Officer.*
General email, info@certifiedhumane.org
Web, www.certifiedhumane.org

Seeks to improve the welfare of farm animals by providing viable, duly monitored standards for humane food production. Administers the Certified Humane Raised and Handled program for meat, poultry, eggs, and dairy products.

National Cattlemen's Beef Assn., Government Affairs, *1301 Pennsylvania Ave. N.W., #300 20004-1701; (202) 347-0228. Fax, (202) 638-0607. Colin Woodall, Vice President.*
Web, www.beefusa.org

Membership: individual cattlemen, state cattlemen's groups, and breed associations. Provides information on beef research, agricultural labor, beef grading, foreign trade, taxes, marketing, cattle economics, branding, animal health, and environmental management. (Headquarters in Denver, Colo.)

National Chicken Council, *1152 15th St. N.W., #430 20005-2622; (202) 296-2622. Fax, (202) 293-4005. Mike Brown, President.*
General email, ncc@chickenusa.org
Web, www.nationalchickencouncil.com

Trade association that represents the vertically integrated producers of 95 percent of the chickens raised and processed for meat in the United States. Monitors domestic and international legislation and regulations.

National Pork Producers Council, *Washington Office, 122 C St. N.W., #875 20001; (202) 347-3600. Fax, (202) 347-5265. Audrey Adamson, Vice President of Domestic Issues.*
General email, pork@nppc.org
Web, www.nppc.org

Membership: pork producers and state pork producer organizations. Interests include pork production, food safety, the environment, trade, and federal regulations. Monitors legislation and regulations. (Headquarters in Des Moines, Iowa.)

National Renderers Assn., *500 Montgomery St., #310, Alexandria, VA 22314; (703) 683-0155. Fax, (571) 970-2279. Nancy Foster, President.*
General email, renderers@nationalrenderers.com
Web, http://nationalrenderers.org

Membership: manufacturers of meat meal and tallow. Compiles industry statistics; sponsors research; conducts seminars and workshops. Monitors legislation and regulations.

National Turkey Federation, *1225 New York Ave. N.W., #400 20005-6404; (202) 898-0100. Fax, (202) 898-0203. Joel Brandenberger, President.*
General email, info@turkeyfed.org
Web, www.eatturkey.com

Membership: turkey growers, hatcheries, breeders, and processors. Promotes turkey consumption. Monitors legislation and regulations.

North American Meat Assn. (NAMA), *1707 L St. N.W., #200 20036; (202) 640-5333. Fax, (202) 318-4078. Philip H. Kimball, Executive Director, ext. 102. Toll-free, (800) 368-3043.*
General email, sabrina@meatassociation.com
Web, www.meatassociation.com

Membership: meat and poultry companies specializing in the food service and retail industries. Conducts seminars; interests include quality standards and procedures for handling meat and poultry. Publishes the *Meat Buyers Guide.*

Shelf-Stable Food Processors Assn. (SFPA), *1150 Connecticut Ave. N.W., 12th Floor 20036; (202) 587-4200. Fax, (202) 587-4300. James Hodges, President, (202) 587-4231.*
General email, sfpa@meatami.com
Web, www.meatami.com

Membership: shelf-stable food manufacturers and their suppliers. Provides information on the shelf-stable industry, particularly as it pertains to meat products. (Subsidiary of the American Meat Institute.)

U.S. Hide, Skin, and Leather Assn. (USHSLA), *1150 Connecticut Ave. N.W., 12th Floor 20036; (202) 587-4250. Fax, (202) 587-4300. Stephen Sothmann, President.*
Web, www.ushsla.org

Membership: meatpackers, brokers, dealers, processors, and exporters of hides and skins. Maintains liaison with allied trade associations and participates in programs on export statistics, hide price reporting, and freight rates; conducts seminars and consumer information programs. (Division of American Meat Institute.)

2

Business and Economics

GENERAL POLICY AND ANALYSIS

Basic Resources

▶AGENCIES

Census Bureau *(Commerce Dept.), Economic Programs,* 4600 Silver Hill Rd., #8H132, Suitland, MD 20746 (mailing address: change city, state, and zip code to Washington, DC 20233-6000); (301) 763-8842. Fax, (301) 763-8150. William G. Bostic Jr., Associate Director.
Web, www.census.gov/econ/

Compiles comprehensive statistics on the level and structure of U.S. economic activity and the characteristics of industrial and business establishments at the national, state, and local levels; collects and publishes foreign trade statistics.

Commerce Dept., 1401 Constitution Ave. N.W. 20230; (202) 482-2000. Fax, (202) 482-5168. Penny Pritzker, Secretary, Acting. Press, (202) 482-4883. Library, (202) 482-1154.
Web, www.commerce.gov

Acts as a principal adviser to the president on federal policy affecting industry and commerce; promotes job creation, national economic growth and development, competitiveness, international trade, and technological development; provides business and government with economic statistics, research, and analysis; encourages minority business; promotes tourism.

Commerce Dept., *Business Liaison,* 1401 Constitution Ave. N.W., #5062 20230; (202) 482-1360. Fax, (202) 482-4054. Matthew T. McGuire, Director.
General email, businessliaison@doc.gov
Web, www.commerce.gov/office-secretary/office-business-liaison

Serves as the federal government's central office for business assistance. Handles requests for information and services as well as complaints and suggestions from businesses; provides a forum for businesses to comment on federal regulations; initiates meetings on policy issues with industry groups, business organizations, trade and small-business associations, and the corporate community.

Consumer Product Safety Commission (CPSC), *Economic Analysis,* 4330 East-West Hwy., Bethesda, MD 20814; (301) 504-7705. Fax, (301) 504-0109. Gregory B. Rodgers, Associate Executive Director, (301) 504-7702.
Web, www.cpsc.gov/about/offices.html

Conducts studies to determine the impact of CPSC's regulations on consumers, the economy, industry, and production. Studies the potential environmental effects of commission actions.

Council of Economic Advisers *(Executive Office of the President),* 725 17th St. N.W. 20502; (202) 395-5062. Fax, (202) 395-5630. Jason Furman, Chair; Jessica Schumer, Chief of Staff.
Web, www.whitehouse.gov/administration/eop/cea

Advisory body consisting of three members and supporting staff of economists. Monitors and analyzes the economy and advises the president on economic developments, trends, and policies and on the economic implications of other policy initiatives. Prepares the annual *Economic Report of the President* for Congress. Assesses economic implications of international policy.

Economics and Statistics Administration *(Commerce Dept.),* 1401 Constitution Ave. N.W., #4848 20230; (202) 482-3727. Fax, (202) 482-0432. Rebecca M. Blank, Deputy Secretary.
General email, esa@doc.gov
Web, www.esa.doc.gov

Advises the secretary on economic policy matters, including consumer and capital spending, inventory status, and the short- and long-term outlook in output and unemployment. Seeks to improve economic productivity and growth. Serves as departmental liaison with the Council of Economic Advisers and other government agencies concerned with economic policy. Supervises and sets policy for the Census Bureau and the Bureau of Economic Analysis.

Federal Deposit Insurance Corps (FDIC), *Complex Financial Institutions,* 1776 F St. N.W., #F-3080 20429; (202) 898-6993. Arthur J. Murton, Director.
Web, www.fdic.gov/about/contact/directory/#OCFI

Reviews and oversees large bank holding companies and non-bank financial companies designated as systemically important by the Financial Stability Oversight Council. Implements orderly liquidations of such companies that fail.

Federal Reserve System, *Board of Governors,* 20th St. and Constitution Ave., N.W. 20551; (202) 452-3000. Fax, (202) 452-3819. Ben S. Bernanke, Chair; Vacant, Vice Chair. Information (meetings), (202) 452-3204. Public Affairs, (202) 452-2955. Congressional Liaison, (202) 452-3003. Publications, (202) 452-3245.
General email, eric.j.kollig@frb.gov
Web, www.federalreserve.gov

Sets U.S. monetary policy. Supervises the Federal Reserve System and influences credit conditions through the buying and selling of Treasury securities in the open market, by fixing the amount of reserves depository institutions must maintain, and by determining discount rates.

Federal Reserve System, *Financial Stability Policy and Research,* 20th and C Sts. N.W., #B2046 20551; (202) 452-2918. Fax, (202) 263-4852. John W. Schindler, Chief, Financial Stability Assessment; J. Nellie Liang, Director, Program Direction.
Web, www.federalreserve.gov/econresdata/fsprstaff.htm

Identifies and analyzes potential threats to financial stability; monitors financial markets, institutions, and structures; and assesses and recommends policy alternatives to address these threats. Conducts long-term research in banking, finance, and macroeconomics.

BUSINESS AND ECONOMICS RESOURCES IN CONGRESS

For a complete listing of Congress committees, including their full contact information, leadership, membership, and jurisdictions, please refer to the Appendix on pages 724–842.

HOUSE:

House Agriculture Committee, (202) 225-2171.
Web, agriculture.house.gov or
democrats.agriculture.house.gov
    Subcommittee on Livestock, Rural Development, and Credit, (202) 225-2171.
House Appropriations Committee, (202) 225-2771.
Web, appropriations.house.gov or
democrats.appropriations.house.gov
    Subcommittee on Commerce, Justice, Science, and Related Agencies, (202) 225-3351.
    Subcommittee on Financial Services and General Government, (202) 225-7245.
    Subcommittee on Transportation, HUD, and Related Agencies, (202) 225-2141.
House Budget Committee, (202) 226-7270.
Web, budget.house.gov or democrats.budget.house.gov
House Energy and Commerce Committee, (202) 225-2927.
Web, energycommerce.house.gov or
democrats.energycommerce.house.gov
    Subcommittee on Commerce, Manufacturing, and Trade, (202) 225-2927.
    Subcommittee on Energy and Power, (202) 225-2927.
    Subcommittee on Environment and the Economy, (202) 225-2927.
    Subcommittee on Health, (202) 225-2927.
House Financial Services Committee, (202) 225-7502.
Web, financialservices.house.gov or
democrats.financialservices.house.gov
    Subcommittee on Housing and Insurance, (202) 225-7502.
House Foreign Affairs Committee, (202) 225-5021.
Web, foreignaffairs.house.gov or
democrats.foreignaffairs.house.gov
    Subcommittee on Terrorism, Nonproliferation and Trade, (202) 226-1500.

House Judiciary Committee, (202) 225-3951.
Web, judiciary.house.gov or
democrats.judiciary.house.gov
    Subcommittee on Courts, Intellectual Property, and the Internet, (202) 225-5741.
    Subcommittee on Regulatory Reform, Commercial and Antitrust Law, (202) 226-7680.
House Oversight and Government Reform Committee, (202) 225-5074.
Web, oversight.house.gov or
democrats.oversight.house.gov
    Subcommittee on Economic Growth, Job Creation, and Regulatory Affairs, (202) 225-5074.
House Science, Space, and Technology Committee, (202) 225-6371.
Web, science.house.gov or
democrats.science.house.gov
    Subcommittee on Research and Technology, (202) 225-6371.
House Small Business Committee, (202) 225-5821.
Web, smallbusiness.house.gov or
democrats.smallbusiness.house.gov
    Subcommittee on Agriculture, Energy, and Trade, (202) 225-5821.
    Subcommittee on Contracting and Workforce, (202) 225-5821.
    Subcommittee on Economic Growth, Tax, and Capital Access, (202) 225-5821.
    Subcommittee on Health and Technology, (202) 225-5821.
    Subcommittee on Investigations, Oversight, and Regulations, (202) 225-5821.
House Ways and Means Committee, (202) 225-3625.
Web, waysandmeans.house.gov or
democrats.waysandmeans.house.gov
    Subcommittee on Trade, (202) 225-6649.

Federal Trade Commission (FTC), *600 Pennsylvania Ave. N.W., #340 20580; (202) 326-2222. Edith Ramirez, Chair; David B. Robbins, Executive Director. Press, (202) 326-2180. Library, (202) 326-2395. Congressional Relations, (202) 326-2195. Identity theft hotline, (877) 438-4338.*
Web, www.ftc.gov

Promotes policies designed to maintain strong competitive enterprise and consumer protection within the U.S. economic system. Monitors trade practices and investigates cases involving monopoly, unfair restraints, or deceptive practices. Enforces Truth in Lending and Fair Credit Reporting acts. Library open to the public.

Federal Trade Commission (FTC), *Economics, 600 Pennsylvania Ave. N.W. 20580; (202) 326-3429. Fax, (202) 326-2380. Martin Gaynor, Director.*
Web, www.ftc.gov/ftc/economic.htm

Provides economic analyses for consumer protection and antitrust investigations, cases, and rulemakings; advises the commission on the effect of government regulations on competition and consumers in various industries; develops special reports on competition, consumer protection, and regulatory issues.

National Economic Council *(Executive Office of the President), The White House 20502; (202) 456-2800.*

JOINT:

Joint Committee on Taxation, (202) 225-3621.
Web, www.jct.gov
Joint Economic Committee, (202) 224-5171.
Web, www.jec.senate.gov/public/ or
   www.jec.senate.gov/republicans/public/

SENATE:

**Senate Agriculture, Nutrition, and Forestry
   Committee,** (202) 224-2035.
Web, ag.senate.gov
   **Subcommittee on Commodities, Markets, Trade,
      and Risk Management,** (202) 224-2035.
Senate Appropriations Committee, (202) 224-7363.
Web, appropriations.senate.gov
   **Subcommittee on Commerce, Justice, Science,
      and Related Agencies,** (202) 224-5202.
   **Subcommittee on Labor, Health and Human
      Services, Education, and Related Agencies,**
      (202) 224-9145.
**Senate Banking, Housing, and Urban Affairs
   Committee,** (202) 224-7391.
Web, banking.senate.gov
   Subcommittee on Economic Policy,
      (202) 224-3753.
   **Subcommittee on Financial Institutions and
      Consumer Protection,** (202) 224-2315.
   **Subcommittee on Securities, Insurance, and
      Investment,** (202) 224-4642.
   **Subcommittee on National Security and
      International Trade and Finance,**
      (202) 224-2023.
Senate Budget Committee, (202) 224-0642.
Web, www.budget.senate.gov/democratic/ or
   www.budget.senate.gov/republican/public/
**Senate Commerce, Science, and Transportation
   Committee,** (202) 224-0411.
Web, commerce.senate.gov

**Subcommittee on Competitiveness, Innovation,
   and Export Promotion,** (202) 224-1270.
**Subcommittee on Consumer Protection, Product
   Safety, and Insurance,** (202) 224-1270.
Senate Environment and Public Works Committee,
   (202) 224-8832.
Web, epw.senate.gov
   **Subcommittee on Green Jobs and the New
      Economy,** (202) 224-8832.
Senate Finance Committee, (202) 224-4515.
Web, finance.senate.gov
   **Subcommittee on Energy, Natural Resources, and
      Infrastructure,** (202) 224-4515.
   **Subcommittee on Fiscal Responsibility and
      Economic Growth,** (202) 224-4515.
   Subcommittee on Health Care, (202) 224-4515.
   **Subcommittee on International Trade,
      Customs, and Global Competitiveness,**
      (202) 224-4515.
   **Subcommittee on Social Security, Pensions and
      Family Policy,** (202) 224-4515.
   Subcommittee on Taxation and IRS Oversight,
      (202) 224-4515.
**Senate Health, Education, Labor, and Pensions
   Committee,** (202) 224-5375.
Web, help.senate.gov
**Senate Homeland Security and Governmental Affairs
   Committee,** (202) 224-2627.
Web, hsgac.senate.gov
   Permanent Subcommittee on Investigations,
      (202) 224-9505.
Senate Judiciary Committee, (202) 224-7703.
Web, judiciary.senate.gov
   **Subcommittee on Antitrust, Competition
      Policy, and Consumer Rights,**
      (202) 224-7703.
   Subcommittee on Bankruptcy and the Courts,
      (202) 224-7703.

Fax, (202) 456-2223. *Gene B. Sperling, Assistant to the
President for Economic Policy.*
Web, www.whitehouse.gov/nec

   Comprised of cabinet members and other high-ranking
executive branch officials. Coordinates domestic and international economic policy making, provides economic
policy advice to the president, ensures that policy decisions and programs are consistent with the president's
economic goals, and monitors the implementation of the
president's economic agenda.

National Institute of Standards and Technology (NIST)
(Commerce Dept.), Baldrige Performance Excellence

*Program, 100 Bureau Dr., MS 1020, Gaithersburg, MD
20899; (301) 975-2036. Fax, (301) 948-3716. Robert
Fangmeyer, Director.*
General email, nqp@nist.gov
Web, www.nist.gov/baldrige/index.cfm

   Public-private partnership that educates business, education, and organization leaders on industry-specific best-
practices management. Offers organizational assessment
tools and criteria.

National Institute of Standards and Technology (NIST)
(Commerce Dept.), Standards Services, 100 Bureau Dr.,

Commerce Department

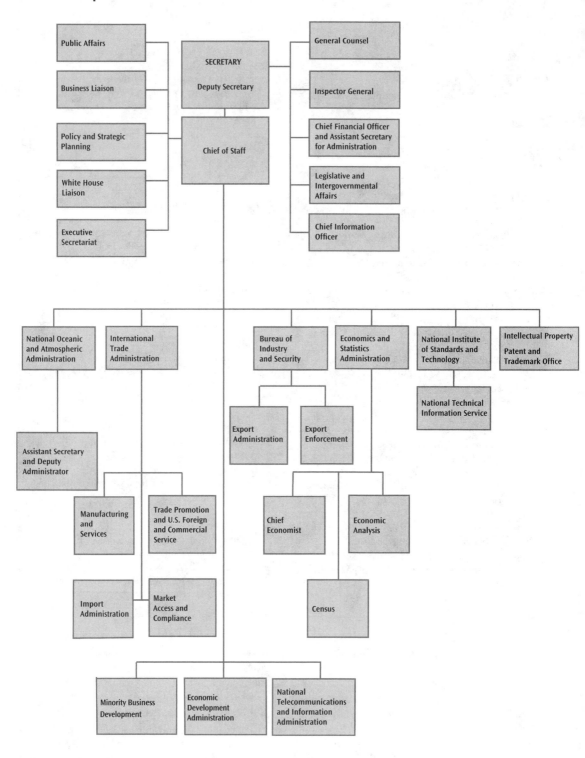

Federal Trade Commission

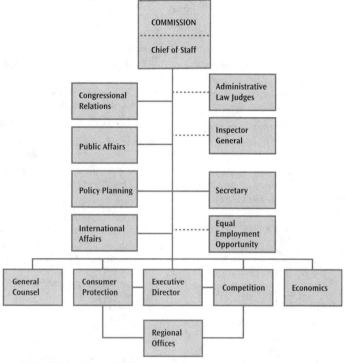

---- Denotes independent operation within the agency

MS 2100, Gaithersburg, MD 20899; (301) 975-8046.
Fax, (301) 975-4715. Gordon Gillerman, Director.
General email, gsi@nist.gov

Web, http://gsi.nist.gov/global/index.cfm

Monitors and participates in industries' development
of standards and standard-enforcement mechanisms.
Conducts standards-related research and holds workshops for domestic and international audiences. Provides
information on industry standards and specifications, conformity assessment, test methods, domestic and international
technical regulations, codes, and recommended practices.

National Institute of Standards and Technology (NIST)
(Commerce Dept.), Weights and Measures, Laws and
Metric Group, 100 Bureau Dr., MS 2600, Gaithersburg,
MD 20899-2600; (301) 975-4004. Fax, (301) 975-8091.
Kenneth S. Butcher, Group Leader.
General email, owm@nist.gov

Web, www.nist.gov/metric

Coordinates federal metric conversion transition to
ensure consistency in the interpretation and enforcement
of packaging, labeling, net content, and other laws; provides the public with technical and general information
about the metric system; assists state and local governments,
businesses, and educators with metric conversion activities.

National Women's Business Council, *409 3rd St. S.W.,*
#210 20416; (202) 205-3850. Fax, (202) 205-6825. Anie
Borja, Executive Director.

General email, info@nwbc.gov

Web, www.nwbc.gov

Independent, congressionally mandated council established by the Women's Business Ownership Act of 1988.
Reviews the status of women-owned businesses nationwide and makes policy recommendations to the president,
Congress, and the Small Business Administration. Assesses
the role of the federal government in aiding and promoting
women-owned businesses.

Small Business Administration (SBA), *409 3rd St. S.W.,*
#7000 20416-7000; (202) 205-6605. Maria
Contreras-Sweet, Administrator; Vacant, Deputy
Administrator. Toll-free information (Answer Desk), (800)
827-5722. Locator, (202) 205-6600.
General email, answerdesk@sba.gov

Web, www.sba.gov

Maintains and strengthens the nation's economy by
aiding, counseling, assisting, and protecting the interests
of small businesses and by helping families and businesses
recover from natural disasters.

Treasury Dept., *1500 Pennsylvania Ave. N.W., #3330*
20220; (202) 622-2000. Fax, (202) 622-0073. Jacob J. Lew,
Secretary, (202) 622-1100; Vacant, Deputy Secretary.
Information, (202) 622-5500. Library, (202) 622-0990.
Press, (202) 622-2960.
Web, www.treasury.gov

Serves as chief financial officer of the government and adviser to the president on economic policy. Formulates and recommends domestic and international financial, economic, tax, and broad fiscal policies; manages the public debt; collects monies owed to the U.S. government; supervises national banks and thrifts. Library open to the public by appointment.

Treasury Dept., *Bureau of Fiscal Service,* 401 14th St. S.W., #545 20227; (202) 874-7000. Fax, (202) 874-6743. *David A. Lebryk, Commissioner. Public Affairs,* (202) 874-6750. *Press,* (202) 504-3502. *Savings bonds,* (800) 553-2663. *Web, www.fms.treas.gov and www.treasurydirect.gov*

Serves as the government's central financial manager, responsible for cash management and investment of government trust funds, credit administration, and debt collection. Handles central accounting for government fiscal activities; promotes sound financial management practices and increased use of automated payments, collections, accounting, and reporting systems.

Treasury Dept., *Economic Policy,* 1500 Pennsylvania Ave. N.W., #3454 20220; (202) 622-2200. Fax, (202) 622-2633. *Vacant, Assistant Secretary.* *Web, www.treasury.gov/about/organizational-structure/ offices/Pages/Economic-Policy.aspx*

Assists and advises the Treasury secretary in the formulation and execution of domestic and international economic policies and programs; helps prepare economic forecasts for the federal budget.

▶CONGRESS

For a listing of relevant congressional committees and subcommittees, please see pages 32–33 or the Appendix.

Government Accountability Office (GAO), 441 G St. N.W. 20548; (202) 512-5500. Fax, (202) 512-5507. *Gene L. Dodaro, Comptroller General. Information,* (202) 512-3000. *Publications and Documents,* (202) 512-6000. *Congressional Relations,* (202) 512-4400. *Web, www.gao.gov*

Independent, nonpartisan agency in the legislative branch. Serves as the investigating agency for Congress; carries out legal, accounting, auditing, and claims settlement functions; makes recommendations for more effective government operations; publishes monthly lists of reports available to the public.

▶NONGOVERNMENTAL

American Business Conference, 1828 L St. N.W., #280 20036; (202) 822-9300. Fax, (202) 467-4070. *John Endean, President.* *General email, abc@americanbusinessconference.org* *Web, www.americanbusinessconference.org*

Membership: chief executive officers of midsize, high-growth companies. Seeks a public policy role for growth companies. Studies capital formation, tax policy, regulatory reform, and international trade.

American Chamber of Commerce Executives, 1330 *Braddock Pl., #300, Alexandria, VA 22314; (703) 998-0072. Fax, (888) 577-9883. Michael Fleming, President, (703) 998-3553.* *General email, info@acce.org* *Web, www.acce.org*

Membership: executives of local, state, and international chambers of commerce. Conducts for members educational programs and conferences on topics of interest, including economic development, government relations, management symposiums, and membership drives. Assembles special interest committees for members.

American Council for Capital Formation (ACCF), 1750 K *St. N.W., #400 20006; (202) 293-5811. Fax, (202) 785-8165. Mark A. Bloomfield, President. Press, (202) 420-9361.* *General email, info@accf.org* *Web, www.accf.org*

Advocates tax, trade, and environmental policies conducive to saving, investment, and economic growth. Affiliated with the ACCF Center for Policy Research, which conducts and funds research on capital formation topics.

American Enterprise Institute (AEI), 1150 17th St. N.W. *20036; (202) 862-5800. Fax, (202) 862-7177. Arthur C. Brooks, President. Press, (202) 862-4871.* *Web, www.aei.org*

Conducts research. Sponsors events. Interests include monetary, tax, trade, financial services, regulatory policy, labor, Social Security issues, and retirement.

American Management Assn. International, *Washington Office,* 2345 Crystal Dr., #200, Arlington, VA *22202-4807; (571) 481-2200. Fax, (571) 481-2211. Richard Nusbaum, Center Manager.* *Web, www.amanet.org*

Membership: managers and other corporate professionals. Offers training and education programs to members. (Headquarters in New York.)

Americans for Prosperity, 2111 Wilson Blvd., #350, *Arlington, VA 22201; (703) 224-3200. Fax, (703) 224-3201. Tim Phillips, President. Toll-free, (866) 730-0150.* *General email, info@AFPhq.org* *Web, www.americansforprosperity.org*

Grassroots organization that seeks to educate citizens about economic policy and encourage their participation in the public policy process. Supports limited government and free markets on the local, state, and federal levels. Specific interests include Social Security, trade, and taxes. Monitors legislation and regulations.

American Society of Assn. Executives (ASAE), 1575 Eye *St. N.W., #1100 20005-1103; (202) 371-2723. Fax, (202) 371-8315. John H. Graham IV, President. Press, (202) 326-9505.* *General email, pr@asaecenter.org* *Web, www.asaecenter.org*

Membership: managers of trade associations, membership societies, and volunteer organizations. Conducts research and provides educational programs on association management, trends, and developments. Library open to the public.

Aspen Institute, *1 Dupont Circle N.W., #700 20036-7133; (202) 736-5800. Fax, (202) 467-0790. Walter Isaacson, President. Press, (202) 736-3849.*
General email, info@aspeninstitute.org
Web, www.aspeninstitute.org

Educational and policy studies organization. Promotes consideration of the public good in a wide variety of policy areas, including business management and economic development. Working with international partners, offers educational seminars, nonpartisan policy forums, public conferences and events, and leadership development initiatives.

The Brookings Institution, *Economic Studies Program, 1775 Massachusetts Ave. N.W. 20036-2188; (202) 797-6000. Fax, (202) 797-6181. Ted Gayer, Director. Press, (202) 797-6105.*
General email, escomment@brookings.edu
Web, www.brookings.edu/economics

Sponsors economic research and publishes studies on domestic and international economics, worldwide economic growth and stability, public finance, industrial organization and regulation, labor economics, social policy, and the economics of human resources.

The Business Council, *45575 Shepard Dr., Sterling, VA 20164 (mailing address: P.O. Box 20147, Washington, DC 20041); (202) 298-7650. Fax, (202) 785-0296. Marlene Colucci, Executive Director.*
Web, www.businesscouncil.com

Membership: current and former chief executive officers of major corporations. Serves as a forum for business and government to exchange views and explore public policy as it affects U.S. business interests.

Business–Higher Education Forum, *2025 M St. N.W., #800 20036; (202) 367-1189. Fax, (202) 367-2100. Brian K. Fitzgerald, Chief Executive Officer.*
General email, info@bhef.com
Web, www.bhef.com

Membership: chief executive officers of major corporations, foundations, colleges, and universities. Develops and promotes policy positions to enhance U.S. competitiveness. Interests include improving student achievement and readiness for college and work; and strengthening higher education, particularly in the fields of science, technology, engineering, and math.

The Business Roundtable, *300 New Jersey Ave. N.W., #800 20001; (202) 872-1260. Fax, (202) 466-3509. Gov. John Engler, President. Press, (202) 496-3269.*
General email, info@brt.org
Web, www.businessroundtable.org

Membership: chief executives of the nation's largest corporations. Examines issues of taxation, antitrust law, corporate governance, international trade, employment policy, and the federal budget. Monitors legislation and regulations.

Center for Economic and Policy Research (CEPR), *1611 Connecticut Ave. N.W., #400 20009; (202) 293-5380. Fax, (202) 588-1356. Dean Baker, Co-Director; Mark Weisbrot, Co-Director.*
General email, cepr@cepr.net
Web, www.cepr.net

Researches economic and social issues and the impact of related public policies. Presents findings to the public with the goal of better preparing citizens to choose among various policy options. Promotes democratic debate and voter education. Areas of interest include health care, trade, financial reform, Social Security, taxes, housing, and the labor market.

Center for Study of Public Choice *(George Mason University), Carow Hall, MS 1D3, 4400 University Dr., Fairfax, VA 22030-4444; (703) 993-2330. Fax, (703) 993-2323. Alexander Tabarrok, Director.*
Web, www.gmu.edu/centers/publicchoice

Promotes research in public choice, an interdisciplinary approach to the study of the relationship between economic and political institutions. Interests include constitutional economics, public finance, federalism and local government, econometrics, and trade protection and regulation. Sponsors conferences and seminars. Library open to the public.

Committee for Economic Development, *2000 L St. N.W., #700 20036; (202) 296-5860. Fax, (202) 223-0776. Steve Odland, Chief Executive Officer; Joseph J. Minarik, Senior Vice President of Research. Toll-free, (800) 676-7353.*
General email, info@ced.org; email addresses are first.last@ced.org
Web, www.ced.org

Nonpartisan, business-led public-policy organization that offers research and analysis. Interests include tax and health care reform, corporate governance and the role of women as administrators, education, immigration, older workers, and international trade.

Competitive Enterprise Institute, *1899 L St. N.W., 12th Floor 20036; (202) 331-1010. Fax, (202) 331-0640. Lawson Bader, President. Press, (202) 331-2258.*
General email, info@cei.org
Web, www.cei.org

Advocates free enterprise and limited government. Produces policy analyses on tax, budget, financial services, antitrust, biotechnological, and environmental issues. Monitors legislation and litigates against restrictive regulations through its Free Market Legal Program.

Council for Social and Economic Studies, *1133 13th St. N.W., #C2 20005-4297; (202) 371-2700. Fax, (202) 371-1523. Roger Pearson, Executive Director.*
General email, socecon@aol.com
Web, www.jspes.org

Conducts research on domestic and international economic, social, and political issues. Publishes the *Journal of*

Social, Political, and Economic Studies; and Mankind Quarterly.

Council on Competitiveness, 1500 K St. N.W., #850 20005; (202) 682-4292. Fax, (202) 682-5150. Deborah Wince-Smith, President.
General email, communications@compete.org
Web, www.compete.org

Membership: chief executives from business, education, and labor. Seeks increased public awareness of issues related to economic competitiveness. Works to set a national action agenda for U.S. competitiveness in global markets.

Economic Policy Institute, 1333 H St. N.W., #300 East Tower 20005-4707; (202) 775-8810. Fax, (202) 775-0819. Lawrence Mishel, President.
General email, epi@epi.org
Web, www.epi.org

Research and educational organization that publishes analyses on economics, economic development, competitiveness, income distribution, industrial competitiveness, and investment. Conducts public conferences and seminars.

Ethics Resource Center, 2345 Crystal Dr., #201, Arlington, VA 22202; (703) 647-2185. Fax, (703) 647-2180. Patricia J. Harned, President. Information, (800) 777-1285.
General email, ethics@ethics.org
Web, www.ethics.org

Nonpartisan research organization that fosters ethical practices among individuals and institutions. Interests include research, knowledge building, education, and advocacy.

Financial Executives International, Washington Office, 1825 K St. N.W., #510 20006; (202) 626-7801. Fax, (973) 843-1119. Robert Kramer, Vice President, Government Affairs, (202) 626-7804.
General email, rkramer@financialexecutives.org
Web, www.financialexecutives.org

Membership: chief financial officers, treasurers, controllers, and other corporate financial managers involved in policy making. Offers professional development opportunities through peer networking, career management services, conferences, teleconferences, and publications. Provides regulatory updates and continuing education on financial management and reporting, including Sarbanes-Oxley Act compliance. (Headquarters in Morristown, N.J.)

Good Jobs First, 1616 P St. N.W., #210 20036; (202) 232-1616. Greg LeRoy, Executive Director.
General email, info@goodjobsfirst.org
Web, www.goodjobsfirst.org

Promotes corporate and government accountability in economic development and job growth. Provides information on state and local job subsidies. Monitors legislation and regulations.

Greater Washington Board of Trade, 1725 Eye St. N.W. 20006; (202) 857-5900. Fax, (202) 223-2648. James C. (Jim) Dinegar, President.
General email, info@bot.org and danielflores@bot.org
Web, www.bot.org

Promotes and plans economic growth for the capital region. Supports business-government partnerships, technological training, and transportation planning; promotes international trade; works to increase economic viability of the city of Washington. Monitors legislation and regulations at local, state, and federal levels.

Institute for Credentialing Excellence, 2025 M St. N.W., #800 20036-3309; (202) 367-1165. Fax, (202) 367-2165. Denise Roosendaal, Executive Director.
General email, info@credentialingexcellence.org
Web, www.credentialingexcellence.org

Membership: certifying agencies and other groups that issue credentials for professions and occupations. Promotes public understanding of competency assurance certification programs. Oversees commission that establishes certification program standards. Monitors regulations.

International Business Ethics Institute, 1776 Eye St. N.W., 9th Floor 20006; (202) 296-6936. Fax, (202) 296-5897. Lori Tansey Martens, President.
General email, info@business-ethics.org
Web, www.business-ethics.org

Nonpartisan educational organization that promotes business ethics and corporate responsibility. Works to increase public awareness and dialogue about international business ethics issues through various educational resources and activities. Works with companies to assist them in establishing effective international ethics programs.

Mercatus Center (George Mason University), 3434 Washington Blvd., 4th Floor, Arlington, VA 22201; (703) 993-4930. Fax, (703) 993-4935. Tyler Cowen, Director. Information, (800) 815-5711.
General email, mercatus@mercatus.gmu.edu
Web, www.mercatus.org

Research center that studies sustained prosperity in societies and the conditions that contribute to economic success. Interests include the drivers of social, political, and economic change; international and domestic economic development; entrepreneurship and the institutions that enable it; the benefits and costs of regulatory policy; government performance and transparency; and good governance practices. Also studies the benefits of market-oriented systems using market process analysis.

National Assn. of Corporate Directors, 2001 Pennsylvania Ave. N.W., #500 20006; (202) 775-0509. Fax, (202) 775-4857. Kenneth Daly, President.
General email, join@nacdonline.org
Web, www.nacdonline.org

Membership: executives of public, private, and non-profit companies. Serves as a clearinghouse on corporate governance and current board practices. Sponsors seminars, peer forums, research, publications, and board development programs.

National Assn. of Manufacturers (NAM), *733 10th St. N.W., #700 20001; (202) 637-3000. Fax, (202) 637-3182. Jay Timmons, President. Toll-free, (800) 814-8468. General email, manufacturing@nam.org*

Web, www.nam.org

Membership: public and private manufacturing companies. Interests include manufacturing technology, economic growth, international trade, national security, taxation, corporate finance and governance, labor relations, occupational safety, workforce education, health care, energy and natural resources, transportation, and environmental quality. Monitors legislation and regulations.

National Assn. of State Auditors, *Comptrollers, and Treasurers, Washington Office, 444 N. Capitol St. N.W., #234 20001; (202) 624-5451. Fax, (202) 624-5473. Cornelia Chebinou, Washington Director. General email, chebinou@nasact.org*

Web, www.nasact.org

Membership: elected and appointed state and territorial officials who deal with the financial management of state government. Provides information on financial best practices and research. Monitors legislation and regulations. (Headquarters in Lexington, Ky.)

National Assn. of State Budget Officers, *444 N. Capitol St. N.W., #642 20001-1501; (202) 624-5382. Fax, (202) 624-7745. Scott D. Pattison, Executive Director. General email, nasbo-direct@nasbo.org*

Web, www.nasbo.org

Membership: state budget and financial officers. Publishes research reports on budget-related issues; shares best practices; provides training and technical assistance. (Affiliate of the National Governors Assn.)

National Chamber Litigation Center, *1615 H St. N.W. 20062-2000; (202) 463-5337. Fax, (202) 463-5346. Lily Fu Claffee, Executive Vice President. General email, nclc@uschamber.com*

Web, www.chamberlitigation.com/nclc

Public policy law firm of the U.S. Chamber of Commerce. Advocates businesses' positions in court on such issues as employment, environmental, and constitutional law. Provides businesses with legal assistance and amicus support in legal proceedings before federal courts and agencies.

National Cooperative Business Assn., *1401 New York Ave. N.W., #1100 20005-2160; (202) 638-6222. Fax, (202) 638-1374. Michael Bealle, President. General email, info@ncba.coop*

Web, www.ncba.coop and Twitter, @NCBACLUSA

Alliance of cooperatives, businesses, and state cooperative associations. Supports development of cooperative businesses; promotes and develops trade among domestic and international cooperatives. Monitors legislation and regulations.

National Economists Club, *P.O. Box 19281 20036; (703) 493-8824. Jaime Narbon, President. General email, info@national-economists.org*

Web, www.thenationaleconomistsclub.shuttlepod.org

Provides venues for scholars, policymakers, business leaders, and public figures to present and defend their views on timely economic topics. Offers members employment and networking opportunities.

National Retail Federation, *325 7th St. N.W., #1100 20004-2802; (202) 783-7971. Fax, (202) 737-2849. Matthew R. Shay, President; David French, Senior Vice President, Government Relations. Toll-free, (800) 673-4692. Web, www.nrf.com*

Membership: international, national, and state associations of retailers and major retail corporations. Concerned with federal regulatory activities and legislation that affect retailers, including tax, employment, trade, and credit issues. Provides information on retailing through seminars, conferences, and publications.

National Venture Capital Assn., *1655 Fort Myer Dr., #850, Arlington, VA 22209; (703) 524-2549. Fax, (703) 524-3940. Bobby Franklin, President, ext. 113. General email, info@nvca.org*

Web, www.nvca.org

Membership: venture capital organizations and individuals and corporate financiers. Promotes understanding of venture capital investment. Facilitates networking opportunities and provides research data on equity investment in emerging growth companies. Monitors legislation.

Partnership for Public Service, *1100 New York Ave. N.W., #200E 20005; (202) 775-9111. Fax, (202) 775-8885. Max Stier, President. Web, www.ourpublicservice.org*

Membership: large corporations and private businesses, including financial and information technology organizations. Seeks to improve government efficiency, productivity, and management through a cooperative effort of the public and private sectors.

Private Equity Gross Capital Council (PEGCC), *950 F St. N.W., #550 20004; (202) 465-7700. Fax, (202) 639-0209. Steve Judge, President; Kenneth P. (Ken) Spain, Vice President of Public Affairs. General email, info@pegcc.org*

Web, www.pegcc.org

Advocacy, communications, and research organization and resource center that develops, analyzes, and distributes information about the private equity industry and its contributions to the national and global economy.

U.S. Business and Industry Council (USBIC), *512 C St. N.E. 20002; (202) 266-3980. Fax, (202) 266-3981. Kevin L. Kearns, President.*

General email, council@usbusiness.org

Web, www.americaneconomicalert.org

Membership: owners of privately held manufacturing, farming, processing, and fabricating companies. Advocates energy independence, reindustrialization, and effective use of natural resources and manufacturing capacity. Interests include business tax reduction, the liability crisis, defense and other federal spending, and the trade deficit. Media network distributes op-ed pieces to newspapers and radio stations. (Affiliated with AmericanEconomicAlert .org.)

U.S. Chamber of Commerce, *1615 H St. N.W. 20062-2000; (202) 659-6000. Fax, (202) 463-5327. Thomas J. Donohue, Chief Executive Officer. Press, (202) 463-5682. Customer Service, (800) 638-6582.*

Web, www.uschamber.com

Federation of businesses, trade and professional associations, state and local chambers of commerce, and American chambers of commerce abroad. Sponsors programs on management, business confidence, small business, consumer affairs, economic policy, minority business, and tax policy. Monitors legislation and regulations.

U.S. Chamber of Commerce, *Congressional and Public Affairs, 1615 H St. N.W. 20062-2000; (202) 463-5600. Fax, (202) 544-4157. Jack Howard, Senior Vice President.*

Web, www.uschamber.com

Advocates businesses' position on government and regulatory affairs. Monitors legislation and regulations on antitrust and corporate policy, product liability, and business-consumer relations.

U.S. Chamber of Commerce, *Economic Policy, 1615 H St. N.W. 20062-2000; (202) 463-5620. Fax, (202) 463-3174. Martin A. Regalia, Chief Economist.*

Web, www.uschamber.com/issues/econtax/economic-tax-and-tax-policy

Represents the business community's views on economic policy, including government spending, the federal budget, and tax issues. Forecasts the economy of the United States and other industrialized nations and projects the impact of major policy changes. Studies economic trends and analyzes their effect on the business community.

Coins and Currency

▶**AGENCIES**

Bureau of Engraving and Printing (BEP) *(Treasury Dept.), 14th and C Sts. S.W. 20228; (202) 874-4000. Fax, (202) 874-3177. Larry R. Felix, Director. Information, (877) 874-4114. Tours, (202) 874-2330.*

Web, www.moneyfactory.gov

Designs, engraves, and prints Federal Reserve notes, military certificates, White House invitations, presidential portraits, and special security documents for the federal government. Provides information on history, design, and engraving of currency; offers public tours; maintains reading room where materials are brought for special research (for appointment, write to the BEP's Historical Resource Center).

Bureau of Engraving and Printing (BEP) *(Treasury Dept.), Mutilated Currency Division, 14th and C Sts. S.W. 20018 (mailing address: BEP/MCD, #344A, P.O. Box 37048, Washington, DC 20013); (202) 874-2141. Fax, (202) 874-4082. Tiyonna White, Head, (202) 874-2131. Toll-free, (866) 575-2361.*

General email, mcdstatus@bep.gov

Web, www.moneyfactory.gov

Redeems U.S. currency that has been mutilated.

Federal Reserve System, *Board of Governors, 20th St. and Constitution Ave., N.W. 20551; (202) 452-3000. Fax, (202) 452-3819. Ben S. Bernanke, Chair; Vacant, Vice Chair. Information (meetings), (202) 452-3204. Public Affairs, (202) 452-2955. Congressional Liaison, (202) 452-3003. Publications, (202) 452-3245.*

General email, eric.j.kollig@frb.gov

Web, www.federalreserve.gov

Influences the availability of money as part of its responsibility for monetary policy; maintains reading room for inspection of records that are available to the public.

National Museum of American History *(Smithsonian Institution), National Numismatic Collection, 14th St. and Constitution Ave. N.W. 20013 (mailing address: P.O. Box 37012, MRC609, Washington, DC 20013-7012); (202) 633-3829. Vacant, Senior Curator; Karen Lee, Numismatic Curator.*

General email, leek@si.edu

Web, http://americanhistory.si.edu/collections/ numismatics

Develops and maintains collections of ancient, medieval, modern, U.S., and world coins; U.S. and world currencies; tokens; medals; orders and decorations; and traditional exchange media. Conducts research and responds to public inquiries.

Treasury Dept., *1500 Pennsylvania Ave. N.W., #3330 20220; (202) 622-2000. Fax, (202) 622-0073. Jacob J. Lew, Secretary, (202) 622-1100; Vacant, Deputy Secretary. Information, (202) 622-5500. Library, (202) 622-0990. Press, (202) 622-2960.*

Web, www.treasury.gov

Oversees the manufacture of U.S. coins and currency; submits to Congress final reports on the minting of coins or any changes in currency. Library open to the public by appointment.

Treasury Dept., *Bureau of Fiscal Service, 401 14th St. S.W., #545 20227; (202) 874-7000. Fax, (202) 874-6743. David A. Lebryk, Commissioner. Public Affairs, (202) 874-6750. Press, (202) 504-3502. Savings bonds, (800) 553-2663.*

Web, www.fms.treas.gov and www.treasurydirect.gov

Prepares and publishes for the president, Congress, and the public monthly, quarterly, and annual statements of government financial transactions, including reports on U.S. currency and coins in circulation.

Treasury Dept., *Treasurer of the United States, 1500 Pennsylvania Ave. N.W., #2134 20220; (202) 622-0100. Rosie G. Rios, Treasurer.*
Web, www.treasury.gov/about/organizational-structure/ offices/Pages/Office-of-the-Treasurer-of-the-United-States. aspx

Advises the secretary of the Treasury on matters relating to coinage, currency, and the production of other instruments issued by the United States. Serves as the national honorary director of the Savings Bond Program. Represents the department in public engagement efforts.

U.S. Mint *(Treasury Dept.), 801 9th St. N.W., 8th Floor 20220; (202) 354-7200. Fax, (202) 756-6160. Richard L. Peterson, Deputy Director, (202) 756-6468. Information, (202) 354-7227. Press, (202) 354-7222. Customer Service, (800) 872-6468.*
Web, www.usmint.gov

Manufactures and distributes all domestic coins; safeguards the government's holdings of precious metals; manufactures and sells commemorative coins and medals of historic interest. Maintains a sales area at Union Station in Washington, D.C., and a kiosk at its main building.

Federal Budget

▶**AGENCIES**

Federal Financing Bank *(Treasury Dept.), 1500 Pennsylvania Ave. N.W. 20220; (202) 622-2470. Fax, (202) 622-0707. Gary H. Burner, Chief Financial Officer.*
General email, ffb@do.treas.gov
Web, www.treasury.gov/ffb

Coordinates federal agency borrowing by purchasing securities issued or guaranteed by federal agencies; funds its operations by borrowing from the Treasury.

Office of Management and Budget (OMB) *(Executive Office of the President), Eisenhower Executive Office Bldg., #208 20503; (202) 395-4840. Sylvia Burwell, Director. Press, (202) 395-7254.*
Web, www.whitehouse.gov/omb

Prepares president's annual budget; works with the Council of Economic Advisers and the Treasury Dept. to develop the federal government's fiscal program; oversees administration of the budget; reviews government regulations; coordinates administration procurement and management policy.

Treasury Dept., *Bureau of Fiscal Service, 401 14th St. S.W., #545 20227; (202) 874-7000. Fax, (202) 874-6743. David A. Lebryk, Commissioner. Public Affairs, (202) 874-6750. Press, (202) 504-3502. Savings bonds, (800) 553-2663.*
Web, www.fms.treas.gov and www.treasurydirect.gov

Borrows to finance federal government operations by selling public debt securities, Treasury notes, and bonds; maintains all records on series EE and HH savings bonds.

Treasury Dept., *Debt Management, 1500 Pennsylvania Ave. N.W., #2417 20220; (202) 622-1885. Fax, (202) 622-0244. Fred Tietrangeli, Director.*
General email, Debt.Management@do.treas.gov
Web, www.treasury.gov/about/organizational-structure/ offices/Pages/-Debt-Management.aspx

Provides financial and economic analysis on government financing and Treasury debt management. Coordinates, analyzes, and reviews government borrowing, lending, and investment activities. Determines interest rates for government borrowing and lending programs.

Treasury Dept., *Financial Market Policy, 1500 Pennsylvania Ave. N.W., #5011 20220; (202) 622-2692. Fax, (202) 622-0974. Heidilynne Schultheiss, Director.*
Web, www.treasury.gov/about/organizational-structure/ offices/Pages/-Financial-Market-Policy.aspx

Provides analyses and policy recommendations on financial markets, government financing, and securities, tax implications, and related regulations.

Treasury Dept., *Policy and Legislative Review, 1120 Vermont Ave. N.W., #916B 20005; (202) 622-2450. Fax, (202) 622-0427. Paula Farrell, Director.*
General email, policyandlegislativereview@do.treas.gov
Web, www.treasury.gov/about/organizational-structure/ offices/Pages/-Office-of-Policy-and-Legislative-Review.aspx

Analyzes federal credit program principles and standards, legislation, and proposals related to government borrowing, lending, and investment. Furnishes actuarial and mathematical analysis required for Treasury market financing, the Federal Financing Bank, and other government agencies.

▶**CONGRESS**

For a listing of relevant congressional committees and subcommittees, please see pages 32–33 or the Appendix.

Congressional Budget Office, *402 FHOB 20515; (202) 226-2700. Fax, (202) 225-7509. Douglas W. Elmendorf, Director. Information, (202) 226-2600. Publications, (202) 226-2809.*
Web, www.cbo.gov

Nonpartisan office that provides the House and Senate with analyses needed for economic and budget decisions, and with the information and estimates required for the congressional budget process.

▶**NONGOVERNMENTAL**

Center for Effective Government, *2040 S St. N.W. 20009; (202) 234-8494. Fax, (202) 234-8584. Katherine McFate, President.*
General email, ombwatch@ombwatch.org
Web, www.foreffectivegov.org

Research and advocacy organization that promotes improved access to governmental decision makers, including

Treasury Department

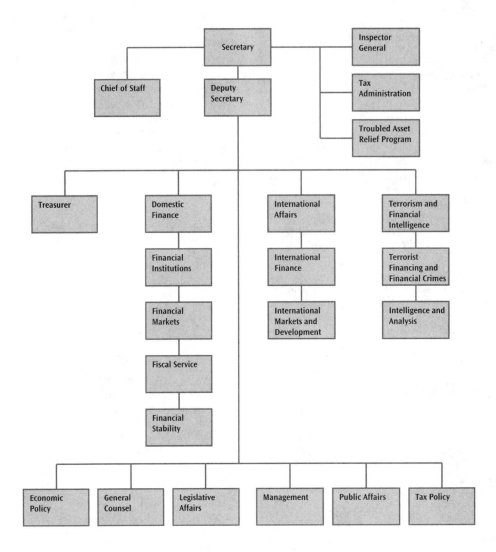

those in the Office of Management and Budget. Promotes a just, equitable, and accountable government as well as a politically active electorate. Specific interests include the federal budget, taxes, information access, and regulatory policy. (Formerly OMB Watch.)

Concord Coalition, *1011 Arlington Blvd., #300, Arlington, VA 22209; (703) 894-6222. Fax, (703) 894-6231. Robert L. Bixby, Executive Director.*
General email, concordcoalition@concordcoalition.org

Web, www.concordcoalition.org

Nonpartisan grassroots organization advocating fiscal responsibility and ensuring Social Security, Medicare, and Medicaid are secure for all generations.

Institute for Policy Studies, *Foreign Policy in Focus, 1112 16th St., #600 20036; (202) 234-9382. Fax, (202) 387-7915. John Feffer, Co-Director; Emira Woods, Co-Director.*

General email, fpif@ips-dc.org

Web, www.fpif.org

Think tank that provides analysis of U.S. foreign policy and international affairs and recommends progressive policy alternatives. Publishes reports; organizes briefings for the public, media, and policymakers. Interests include climate change, global poverty, nuclear weapons, terrorism, and military conflict.

Statistics, Economic Projections

▶**AGENCIES**

Bureau of Economic Analysis *(Commerce Dept.),* *1441 L St. N.W., #6006 20230; (202) 606-9900. Fax, (202) 606-5311. J. Steven Landefeld, Director.*
Web, www.bea.gov

Compiles, analyzes, and publishes data on measures of aggregate U.S. economic activity, including gross domestic product; prices by type of expenditure; personal income and outlays; personal savings; corporate profits; capital stock; U.S. international transactions; and foreign investment. Provides statistics of personal income and employment by industry for regions, states, metropolitan areas, and counties. Refers specific inquiries to economic specialists in the field.

Bureau of Labor Statistics (BLS) *(Labor Dept.), 2 Massachusetts Ave. N.E., #4040 20212-0001; (202) 691-5200. Fax, (202) 691-7890. Erica Lynn Groshen, Commissioner, Acting, (202) 691-7800. Press, (202) 691-5902.*
General email, blsdata_staff@bls.gov
Web, www.bls.gov

Provides statistical data on labor economics, including labor force, employment and unemployment, hours of work, wages, employee compensation, prices, living conditions, labor-management relations, productivity, technological developments, occupational safety and health, and structure and growth of the economy. Publishes reports on these statistical trends including the Consumer Price Index, Producer Price Index, and Employment and Earnings.

Census Bureau *(Commerce Dept.), Economic Programs, 4600 Silver Hill Rd., #8H132, Suitland, MD 20746 (mailing address: change city, state, and zip code to Washington, DC 20233-6000); (301) 763-8842. Fax, (301) 763-8150. William G. Bostic Jr., Associate Director.*
Web, www.census.gov/econ/

Provides data and explains proper use of data on county business patterns, classification of industries and commodities, and business statistics. Compiles quarterly reports listing financial data for corporations in certain industrial sectors.

Census Bureau *(Commerce Dept.), Governments, 4600 Silver Hill Rd., #5K156, Suitland, MD 20746 (mailing address: change city, state, and zip code to Washington, DC 20233-6800); (301) 763-1489. Fax, (301) 763-6792. Vacant, Chief.*
Web, www.census.gov/govs

Provides data and explains proper use of data concerning state and local governments, employment, finance, governmental organization, and taxation.

Census Bureau *(Commerce Dept.), Manufacturing and Construction, 4600 Silver Hill Rd., #7K154, Suitland, MD 20746-4600 (mailing address: change city, state, and zip code to Washington, DC 20233-6900); (301) 763-4593. Fax, (301) 763-7783. Mendel D. Gayle, Division Chief.*
Web, www.census.gov/mcd

Collects and distributes manufacturing, construction, and mineral industry data. Reports are organized by commodity, industry, and geographic area.

Census Bureau *(Commerce Dept.), Service Sector Statistics, 4700 Silver Hill Rd., #8K154, Suitland, MD* 20746-2401 *(mailing address: change city, state, and zip code Washington, DC 20233-6500); (301) 763-5170. Fax, (301) 763-6843. Vacant, Chief.*
Web, www.census.gov/econ/services.html

Provides data of five-year census programs on retail, wholesale, and service industries. Conducts periodic monthly or annual surveys for specific items within these industries.

Census Bureau *(Commerce Dept.), Manufacturing and Construction, Construction and Minerals, 4600 Silver Hill Rd., 7th Floor, Suitland, MD 20746 (mailing address: change city, state, and zip code to Washington, DC 20233); (301) 763-4680. Fax, (301) 763-8398. Mary Susan Bucci, Chief.*
Web, www.census.gov/mcd

Collects, tabulates, and publishes statistics for the mining and construction sectors of the Economic Census; collects and tabulates data for the Manufacturing Energy Consumption Survey for the Energy Dept. concerning combustible and noncombustible energy sources for the U.S. manufacturing sector.

Council of Economic Advisers *(Executive Office of the President), Statistical Office, 725 17th St. N.W. 20502; (202) 395-5062. Fax, (202) 395-5630. Adreanne Pilot, Director.*
Web, www.whitehouse.gov/administration/eop/cea

Compiles and reports aggregate economic data, including national income and expenditures, employment, wages, productivity, production and business activity, prices, money stock, credit, finance, government finance, corporate profits and finance, agriculture, and international statistics, including balance of payments and import-export levels by commodity and area.

Economic Research Service *(Agriculture Dept.), 355 E St. S.W. 20024-8221; (202) 694-5000. Fax, (202) 245-4846. Mary Bohman, Administrator; Greg Pompelli, Associate Administrator.*
General email, service@ers.usda.gov
Web, www.ers.usda.gov

Conducts market research; studies and forecasts domestic supply-and-demand trends for fruits and vegetables.

Federal Reserve System, *Monetary Affairs, 20th and C Sts. N.W., #B3022B 20551; (202) 452-3327. Fax, (202) 452-2301. William B. English, Director.*
Web, www.federalreserve.gov/research/mastaff.htm

Assists the Federal Reserve Board and the Federal Open Market Committee in the conduct of monetary policy, especially in the areas of finance, money and banking, and monetary policy design and implementation. Provides expertise on open-market operations, discount window policy, and reserve markets.

Federal Reserve System, *Research and Statistics, 20th and C Sts. N.W., #B3048 20551; (202) 452-3301. Fax, (202) 452-5296. David W. Wilcox, Director.*
Web, www.federalreserve.gov/econresdata/rsstaff.htm

Publishes statistical data and analyses on business finance, real estate credit, consumer credit, industrial production, construction, and flow of funds.

Internal Revenue Service (IRS) *(Treasury Dept.),* **Statistics of Income,** *77 K St. N.E., #4112 20002 (mailing address: P.O. Box 2608, Washington, DC 20013-2608); (202) 874-0410. Fax, (202) 874-0964. Susan Boehmer, Director. Publications, (202) 874-0410.*
Web, www.irs.ustreas.gov/prod/tax_stats

Provides the public and the Treasury Dept. with statistical information on tax laws. Prepares statistical information for the Commerce Dept. to use in formulating the gross national product (GNP). Publishes *Statistics of Income,* a series available at cost to the public.

International Trade Administration (ITA) *(Commerce Dept.),* **Industry and Analysis, Trade Policy and Analysis,** *1401 Constitution Ave. N.W., #2128 20230; (202) 482-3177. Fax, (202) 482-4614. Praveen Dixit, Deputy Assistant Secretary, (202) 482-6232.*
Web, www.trade.gov/index.asp

Analyzes international and domestic competitiveness of U.S. industry and component sectors. Assesses impact of regulations on competitive positions. Produces and disseminates U.S. foreign trade and related economic data. Supports U.S. international trade negotiations initiative.

National Agricultural Statistics Service *(Agriculture Dept.),* *1400 Independence Ave. S.W., #5041, MS 2001 20250-2001; (202) 720-2707. Fax, (202) 720-9013. Cynthia Clark, Administrator. Information, (800) 727-9540. Print reports, (800) 999-6779.*
General email, nass@nass.usda.gov
Web, www.nass.usda.gov

Prepares estimates and reports on production, supply, prices, and other items relating to the U.S. agricultural economy. Reports include statistics on field crops, fruits and vegetables, cattle, hogs, poultry, and related products. Prepares quinquennial national census of agriculture.

Office of Management and Budget (OMB) *(Executive Office of the President),* **Statistical and Science Policy,** *New Executive Office Bldg., 725 17th St. N.W., #10201 20503; (202) 395-3093. Fax, (202) 395-7245. Katherine K. Wallman, Chief.*
Web, www.whitehouse.gov/omb

Carries out the statistical policy and coordination functions under the Paperwork Reduction Act of 1995; develops long-range plans for improving federal statistical programs; develops policy standards and guidelines for statistical data collection, classification, and publication; evaluates statistical programs and agency performance.

Securities and Exchange Commission (SEC), *Economic and Risk Analysis, 100 F St. N.E. 20549; (202) 551-6600. Fax, (202) 756-0505. Craig M. Lewis, Director. Information, (202) 942-8088.*
General email, RiskFin@sec.gov
Web, www.sec.gov/dera#.ux9TeoXfmaQ

Advises the SEC and its staff on economic issues as they pertain to the commission's regulatory activities. Publishes data on trading volume of the stock exchanges; compiles statistics on financial reports of brokerage firms.

U.S. International Trade Commission, *Industries, 500 E St. S.W., #504-A 20436; (202) 205-2023. Fax, (202) 205-3161. Karen Laney, Director. Press, (202) 205-1819. Web, www.usitc.gov/research_and_analysis/office_ industry.htm*

Identifies, analyzes, and develops data on economic and technical matters related to the competitive position of the United States in domestic and world markets in agriculture and forest production, chemicals, textiles, energy, electronics, transportation, services and investments, minerals, metals, and machinery.

▶**NONGOVERNMENTAL**

American Statistical Assn., *732 N. Washington St., Alexandria, VA 22314-1943; (703) 684-1221. Fax, (703) 684-2037. Ronald Wasserstein, Executive Director. Toll-free, (888) 231-3473.*
General email, asainfo@amstat.org
Web, www.amstat.org

Membership: statistical practitioners in industry, government, and academia. Supports excellence in the development, application, and dissemination of statistical science through meetings, publications, membership services, education, accreditation, and advocacy.

Taxes and Tax Reform

▶**AGENCIES**

Alcohol and Tobacco Tax and Trade Bureau (TTB) *(Treasury Dept.), 1310 G St. N.W., #300E 20220; (202) 453-2000. John J. Manfreda, Administrator. Press, (202) 453-2134.*
General email, info@ttb.gov
Web, www.ttb.gov

Enforces and administers revenue laws relating to firearms, explosives, alcohol, and tobacco.

Internal Revenue Service (IRS) *(Treasury Dept.), 1111 Constitution Ave. N.W. 20224 (mailing address from outside the U.S.: IRS International Accounts, Philadelphia, PA 19255-0725); (202) 622-5000. John A. Koskinen, Commissioner. Information and assistance, (800) 829-1040. Press, (202) 622-4000. National taxpayer advocates helpline, (877) 777-4778. Identity theft hotline, (800) 908-4490. Phone from outside the U.S., (267) 941-1000. Fax from outside the U.S., (267) 941-1055. Information for businesses, (800) 829-4933.*
Web, www.irs.gov

Administers and enforces internal revenue laws and related statutes (except those relating to firearms, explosives, alcohol, and tobacco).

Internal Revenue Service (IRS) *(Treasury Dept.), Art Advisory Panel,* 999 N. Capitol St. N.E., #739 20002; (202) 317-8853. Ruth Vriend, Chair.
Web, www.irs.gov/individuals/Art-Appraisal-Services

Panel of twenty-five art professionals that assists the IRS by reviewing and evaluating taxpayers' appraisals on works of art valued at $50,000 or more involved in federal income, estate, and gift taxes.

Internal Revenue Service (IRS) *(Treasury Dept.), Taxpayer Advocate,* 1111 Constitution Ave. N.W., #3031 20224; (202) 622-6100. Fax, (202) 622-7854. Nina E. Olson, National Taxpayer Advocate. Toll-free, (877) 777-4778.
Web, www.irs.gov/Taxpayer-Advocate-Service-At-a-Glance

Helps taxpayers resolve problems with the IRS and recommends changes to prevent the problems. Represents taxpayers' interests in the formulation of policies and procedures.

Justice Dept. (DOJ), *Tax Division,* 950 Pennsylvania Ave. N.W., #4141 20530; (202) 514-2901. Fax, (202) 514-5479. Kathryn Keneally, Assistant Attorney General, (202) 307-3366.
General email, tax.mail@usdoj.gov
Web, www.usdoj.gov/tax

Acts as counsel for the Internal Revenue Service (IRS) in court litigation between the government and taxpayers (other than those handled by the IRS in the U.S. Tax Court).

Multistate Tax Commission, 444 N. Capitol St. N.W., #425 20001-1538; (202) 650-0300. Joe Huddleston, Executive Director.
General email, mtc@mtc.gov
Web, www.mtc.gov

Membership: state governments that have enacted the Multistate Tax Compact. Promotes fair, effective, and efficient state tax systems for interstate and international commerce; works to preserve state tax sovereignty. Encourages uniform state tax laws and regulations for multistate and multinational enterprises. Maintains three regional audit offices that monitor compliance with state tax laws and encourage uniformity in taxpayer treatment. Administers program to identify businesses that do not file tax returns with states.

Treasury Dept., *Tax Policy,* 1500 Pennsylvania Ave. N.W., #3120 20220; (202) 622-0050. Fax, (202) 622-0605. Mark J. Mazur, Assistant Secretary.
Web, www.treasury.gov/about/organizational-structure/offices/Pages/Tax-Policy.aspx

Formulates and implements domestic and international tax policies and programs; conducts analyses of proposed tax legislation and programs; participates in international tax treaty negotiations; responsible for receipts estimates for the annual budget of the United States.

▶JUDICIARY

U.S. Tax Court, 400 2nd St. N.W., #134 20217; (202) 521-0700. Michael B. Thornton, Chief Judge, (202) 521-0777.
Web, www.ustaxcourt.gov

Tries and adjudicates disputes involving income, estate, and gift taxes and personal holding company surtaxes in cases in which deficiencies have been determined by the Internal Revenue Service.

▶NONGOVERNMENTAL

American Enterprise Institute (AEI), *Economic Policy Studies,* 1150 17th St. N.W., #1100 20036; (202) 862-5800. Fax, (202) 862-7177. Kevin Hassett, Director.
Web, www.aei.org

Conducts research on fiscal policy and taxes. Sponsors events.

Americans for Tax Reform, 722 12th St. N.W., 4th Floor 20005; (202) 785-0266. Fax, (202) 785-0261. Grover G. Norquist, President.
General email, info@atr.org
Web, www.atr.org

Advocates reduction of federal and state taxes; encourages candidates for public office to pledge their opposition to income tax increases through a national pledge campaign.

Center on Budget and Policy Priorities, 820 1st St. N.E., #510 20002; (202) 408-1080. Fax, (202) 408-1056. Robert Greenstein, President.
General email, center@cbpp.org
Web, www.cbpp.org

Research group that analyzes changes in federal and state programs, such as tax credits, Medicaid coverage, and food stamps, and their effect on low- and moderate-income households.

Citizens Against Government Waste, 1301 Pennsylvania Ave. N.W., #1075 20004; (202) 467-5300. Fax, (202) 467-4253. Thomas A. Schatz, President.
General email, membership@cagw.org
Web, www.cagw.org

Taxpayer watchdog group that monitors government spending to identify how waste, mismanagement, and inefficiency in government can be eliminated. Has created criteria to identify pork-barrel spending. Publishes the annual *Congressional Pig Book*, which lists the names of politicians and their pet pork-barrel projects. Monitors legislation and regulations.

Citizens for Tax Justice, *Institute on Taxation and Economic Policy,* 1616 P St. N.W., #200 20036; (202) 299-1066. Fax, (202) 299-1065. Matthew Gardner, Executive Director.
General email, ctj@ctj.org; itep@itep.org
Web, www.ctj.org; www.itep.org

Research and advocacy organization that works for progressive taxes at the federal, state, and local levels.

Federation of Tax Administrators, *444 N. Capitol St. N.W., #348 20001; (202) 624-5890. Fax, (202) 624-7888. Gale Garriott, Executive Director.*
Web, www.taxadmin.org

Membership: tax agencies in the fifty states, plus New York City and the District of Columbia. Provides information upon written request on tax-related issues, including court decisions and legislation. Conducts research and sponsors workshops.

FreedomWorks, *400 N. Capitol St. N.W., #765 20001; (202) 783-3870. Fax, (202) 942-7649. Matt Kibbe, President. Toll-free, (888) 564-6273.*
Web, www.freedomworks.org

Recruits, educates, trains, and mobilizes citizens to promote lower taxes, less government, and greater economic freedom. Maintains scorecards on members of the Senate and House based on adherence to FreedomWorks positions.

National Assn. of Manufacturers (NAM), *Tax and Domestic Economic Policy, 733 10th St. N.W., #700 20001; (202) 637-3096. Fax, (202) 637-3182. Dorothy B. Coleman, Vice President, (202) 637-3077.*
Web, www.nam.org

Represents and advocates for manufacturers on federal tax and budget policies; acts as a spokesperson for manufacturers on fiscal issues in the media; works with the broader business community to advance pro-growth, pro-competitiveness tax policy; conducts conferences. Monitors legislation and regulations.

National Tax Assn., *725 15th St. N.W., #600 20005-2109; (202) 737-3325. Fax, (202) 737-7308. J. Fred Giertz, Executive Director, (217) 244-4822; Charmaine Wright, Associate Director.*
General email, natltax@aol.com
Web, www.ntanet.org

Membership: tax lawyers and accountants, academics, legislators, and students. Seeks to advance understanding of tax theory, practice, and policy, as well as other aspects of public finance. Holds conferences and symposiums, including the Annual Conference on Taxation. Publishes the *National Tax Journal.*

National Taxpayers Union, *Communications, 108 N. Alfred St., Alexandria, VA 22314; (703) 683-5700. Fax, (703) 683-5722. Peter Sepp, Executive Vice President; Duane Parde, President.*
General email, ntu@ntu.org
Web, www.ntu.org

Citizens' interest group that promotes tax and spending reduction at all levels of government. Supports constitutional amendments to balance the federal budget and limit taxes.

Tax Analysts, *400 S. Maple Ave., #400, Falls Church, VA 22046; (703) 533-4400. Fax, (703) 533-4444. Christopher Bergin, President. Customer Service, (800) 955-3444.*

General email, cservice@tax.org
Web, www.taxanalysts.com

Nonpartisan publisher of state, federal, and international tax news and analysis. Advocates tax reforms to develop tax systems that are fair, simple, and efficient. Provides publications to educate tax professionals and the public about tax reform.

The Tax Council, *1301 K St. N.W., #800W 20005; (202) 822-8062. Fax, (202) 315-3413. Lynda K. Walker, Executive Director.*
General email, general@thetaxcouncil.org
Web, www.thetaxcouncil.org

Organization of corporations concerned with tax policy and legislation. Interests include tax rate, capital formation, capital gains, foreign source income, and capital cost recovery. (Affiliated with the Tax Council Policy Institute [TCPI].)

Tax Executives Institute, *1200 G St. N.W., #300 20005-3814; (202) 638-5601. Fax, (202) 638-5607. Eli J. Dicker, Executive Director.*
Web, www.tei.org

Membership: accountants, lawyers, and other corporate and business employees dealing with tax issues. Sponsors seminars and conferences on federal, state, local, and international tax issues. Develops and monitors tax legislation, regulations, and administrative procedures.

Tax Foundation, *529 14th St. N.W., #420 20045-1000; (202) 464-6200. Scott A. Hodge, President.*
General email, tf@taxfoundation.org
Web, www.taxfoundation.org

Membership: individuals and businesses interested in federal, state, and local fiscal matters. Conducts research and analysis and prepares reports on taxes and government expenditures. Advocates for a simple, transparent, neutral, and stable tax policy.

Urban-Brookings Tax Policy Center, *2100 M St. N.W. 20037; (202) 833-7200. Fax, (202) 728-0232. Donald B. Marron, Director.*
Web, www.taxpolicycenter.org

Provides analysis of current and pending tax issues to policymakers, journalists, researchers, and citizens. (Joint venture of the Urban Institute and the Brookings Institution.)

U.S. Conference of Mayors, *1620 Eye St. N.W., #400 20006; (202) 293-7330. Fax, (202) 293-2352. J. Thomas Cochran, Executive Director.*
General email, info@usmayors.org
Web, www.usmayors.org

Membership: mayors of cities with populations of 30,000 or more. Monitors tax policy and legislation. (Approximately 1,400 U.S. cities.)

Consumer Product Safety Commission

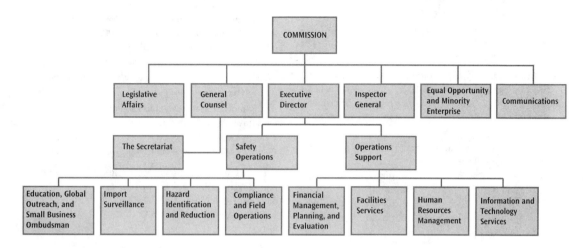

CONSUMER PROTECTION

General

Consumer Product Safety Commission (CPSC), *4330 East-West Hwy., #820, Bethesda, MD 20814; (301) 504-7923. Fax, (301) 504-0124. Robert S. (Bob) Adler, Chair, Acting; Elliott Kaye, Executive Director, (301) 504-7881. Congressional Relations, (301) 504-7660. Product safety hotline, (800) 638-2772. National Injury Information Clearinghouse, (301) 504-7921.*
General email, info@cpsc.gov

Web, www.cpsc.gov/about/offices.html

Establishes and enforces product safety standards; collects data; studies the causes and prevention of product-related injuries; identifies hazardous products, including imports, and recalls them from the marketplace.

Consumer Product Safety Commission (CPSC), *Education, Global Outreach, and Small Business Ombudsman, 4330 East-West Hwy., Bethesda, MD 20814; (301) 504-7054. Fax, (301) 504-0407. Robert J. (Jay) Howell, Director, Acting.*
Web, www.cpsc.gov

Coordinates international and intergovernmental efforts to improve consumer product safety standards development, harmonization efforts, inspection and enforcement coordination, consumer education, and information transfer about best manufacturing practices across industries.

Consumer Product Safety Commission (CPSC), *Hazard Identification and Reduction, 4330 East-West Hwy., #611, Bethesda, MD 20814-4408; (301) 987-2472. Fax, (301) 504-0533. George Berlase, Associate Executive Director.*
Web, www.cpsc.gov

Establishes labeling and packaging regulations. Develops standards in accordance with the Poison Prevention Packaging Act, the Federal Hazardous Substances Act, the Consumer Products Safety Act, and the Consumer Products Safety Improvement Act.

Federal Trade Commission (FTC), *Consumer Response Center, 600 Pennsylvania Ave. N.W., #240 20580; (202) 326-2830. Fax, (202) 326-2012. David Torok, Director. Identity fraud report line, (877) ID-THEFT. Toll-free, (877) FTC-HELP. Do-Not-Call Registry, (888) 382-1222.*
Web, www.ftc.gov

Handles complaints about regulations dealing with unfair or deceptive business practices in advertising, credit, marketing, and service industries; educates consumers and businesses about these regulations.

Federal Trade Commission (FTC), *Enforcement, 600 Pennsylvania Ave. N.W. 20580; (202) 326-2156. Fax, (202) 326-2558. James A. Kohm, Associate Director.*
Web, www.ftc.gov

Enforces consumer protection, including advertising and financial practices, data security, high-tech fraud, and telemarketing and other scams. Coordinates FTC actions with criminal law enforcement agencies; litigates civil actions against those who defraud consumers; and develops, reviews, and enforces a variety of consumer protection rules.

General Services Administration (GSA), *Federal Citizen Information Center, 1800 F St. N.W. 20405; (202) 501-1794. Fax, (202) 357-0078. Beverly Godwin, Director.*
Web, www.publications.usa.gov and www.gobiernoUSA.gov

Manages the portal site to U.S. government information, www.usa.gov. Manages kids.gov, a resource that provides government information to younger Americans. Distributes free and low-cost federal publications of consumer interest via the Internet at www.publications.usa

.gov, or by calling (888) 878-3256 for a catalog. Publishes the *Consumer Action Handbook,* a free resource that can be used online at http://consumeraction.gov or obtained by calling 888-8-PUEBLO. Assists people with questions about American government agencies, programs, and services via telephone, 800-FED-INFO ([800] 333-4636), or Web site, http://answers.usa.gov.

Securities and Exchange Commission (SEC), *Investor Education and Advocacy,* 100 F St. N.E. 20549-0213; (202) 551-6500. Fax, (202) 772-9295. Rick Fleming, Director; Frank White, Assistant to the Director, (202) 551-4310.
Web, www.sec.gov/investor

Assists individual consumers in investing wisely and avoiding fraud. Provides a variety of services and tools, including publications on mutual funds and annuities, studies and recommendations concerning the evaluation of brokers and advisors, online calculators, and explanations about fees and expenses. Information is also available in Spanish.

▶**AGENCY AND DEPARTMENT CONSUMER CONTACTS**

Commission on Civil Rights, *Public Affairs and Congressional Affairs Office,* 1331 Pennsylvania Ave. N.W., #1150 20425; (202) 376-8591. Fax, (202) 376-7672. Lenore Ostrowsky, Chief, Acting.
General email, publicaffairs@usccr.gov
Web, www.usccr.gov

Comptroller of the Currency *(Treasury Dept.),* **Ombudsman,** 400 7th St. S.W., Constitution Center 20024; (202) 649-5530. Fax, (202) 649-5727. Larry L. Hattix, Senior Deputy Comptroller for Enterprise Governance.
Web, www.occ.gov

Ensures that bank customers and the banks the agency supervises receive fair and expeditious resolution of their concerns.

Consumer Product Safety Commission (CPSC), *Public Affairs,* 4330 East-West Hwy., #519C, Bethesda, MD 20814-4408; (301) 504-7051. Fax, (301) 504-0862. Scott J. Wolfson, Director, (301) 504-7051. Product safety hotline, (800) 638-2772.
General email, info@cpsc.gov
Web, www.cpsc.gov

Provides information concerning consumer product safety; works with local and state governments, school systems, and private groups to develop product safety information and education programs. Toll-free hotline accepts consumer complaints on hazardous products and injuries associated with a product and offers recorded information on product recalls and CPSC safety recommendations.

Education Dept., *Legislative and Congressional Affairs,* 400 Maryland Ave. S.W., #6W315 20202-3500; (202) 401-0020. Fax, (202) 401-1438. Gabriella C. Gomez, Assistant Secretary.
General email, olca@ed.gov
Web, www2.ed.gov/about/offices/list/olca

Directs and supervises all legislative activities of the Education Dept. Participates on legislation and regulation

development teams within the department and provides legislative history behind the current law.

Energy Dept. (DOE), *Congressional and Intergovernmental Affairs,* 1000 Independence Ave. S.W., #7B138 20585; (202) 586-5450. Fax, (202) 586-4891. Brad Cowell, Assistant Secretary. Toll-free, (800) 342-5363.
General email, robert.tuttle@hq.doe.gov
Web, www.energy.gov/congressional/office-congressional-and-intergovernmental-affairs

Promotes Energy Dept. policies, programs, and initiatives through communications with Congress; state, tribal, city, and county governments; other federal agencies; stakeholders; and the general public.

Federal Communications Commission (FCC), *Consumer and Governmental Affairs Bureau,* 445 12th St. S.W., #5C758 20554; (202) 418-1400. Fax, (202) 418-2839. Kris A. Monteith, Chief, Acting.
General email, fccinfo@fcc.gov
Web, www.fcc.gov/consumer-governmental-affairs-bureau

Develops and implements FCC policies, including disability access. Operates a consumer center that responds to consumer inquiries and complaints. Partners with state, local, and tribal governments in areas of emergency preparedness and implementation of new technologies.

Federal Deposit Insurance Corp. (FDIC), *Depositor and Consumer Protection, Consumer and Community Affairs,* 1310 Court House Rd., #11060, Arlington, VA 22201; (703) 254-1043. Fax, (703) 254-0222. Elizabeth Ortiz, Deputy Director. Information, 877-ASK-FDIC.
General email, consumer@fdic.gov
Web, www.fdic.gov/about/contact/directory/index.html#DDCP

Coordinates and monitors complaints filed by consumers against federally insured state banks that are not members of the Federal Reserve System; handles complaints concerning truth-in-lending and other fair credit provisions, including charges of discrimination on the basis of sex or marital status; responds to general banking inquiries; answers questions on deposit insurance coverage.

Federal Maritime Commission (FMC), *Consumer Affairs and Dispute Resolution Services,* 800 N. Capitol St. N.W., #939 20573; (202) 523-5807. Fax, (202) 275-0059. Rebecca A. Fenneman, Deputy Director. Toll-free, (866) 448-9586.
General email, complaints@fmc.gov
Web, www.fmc.gov/bureaus_offices/consumer_affairs_and_dispute_resolution_services.aspx

Provides ombuds, mediation, facilitation, small claims adjudication, and arbitration services to assist shippers, carriers, marine terminal operators, and the shipping public to resolve commercial cargo shipping disputes. Provides assistance to cruise passengers to resolve disputes with cruise operators for cruises between the United States and international ports.

Federal Reserve System, *Consumer and Community Affairs,* 1709 New York Ave. N.W. 20006; (202) 785-6032.

Fax, (202) 452-3849. Vacant, Director. Complaints, (888) 851-1920.

Web, www.federalreserve.gov/econresdata/ccastaff.htm

Food and Drug Administration (FDA) *(Health and Human Services Dept.), External Affairs,* 10903 New Hampshire Ave., #5322, Silver Spring, MD 20993; (301) 796-8641. Fax, (301) 827-8030. Patricia Kuntze, Senior Advisor for Consumer Affairs; Steven Immergut, Associate Commissioner, Acting. Consumer inquiries, (888) 463-6332.
General email, patricia.kuntze@fda.hhs.gov

Web, www.fda.gov

Responds to inquiries on issues related to the FDA. Conducts consumer health education programs for specific groups, including women, older adults, and the educationally and economically disadvantaged. Serves as liaison with national health and consumer organizations.

Food and Nutrition Service *(Agriculture Dept.),* **Communications and Governmental Affairs,** 3101 Park Center Dr., #926, Alexandria, VA 22302; (703) 305-2281. Fax, (703) 305-2312. Bruce Alexander, Director; Vacant, Chief Communications Officer.
Web, www.fns.usda.gov/cga

Provides information concerning the Food and Nutrition Service and its fifteen nutrition assistance programs to the media, program participants, advocates, members of Congress, and the general public. Monitors and analyzes relevant legislation; prepares congressional testimony.

General Services Administration (GSA), *Federal Citizen Information Center,* 1800 F St. N.W. 20405; (202) 501-1794. Fax, (202) 357-0078. Beverly Godwin, Director.
Web, www.publications.usa.gov and
www.gobiernoUSA.gov

Manages the portal site to U.S. government information, www.usa.gov. Manages kids.gov, a resource that provides government information to younger Americans. Distributes free and low-cost federal publications of consumer interest via the Internet at www.publications.usa.gov, or by calling (888) 878-3256 for a catalog. Publishes the Consumer Action Handbook, a free resource that can be used online at http://consumeraction.gov or obtained by calling 888-8-PUEBLO. Assists people with questions about American government agencies, programs, and services via telephone, 800-FED-INFO ([800] 333-4636), or Web site, http://answers.usa.gov.

Interior Dept. (DOI), *Communications,* 1849 C St. N.W., #6312 20240; (202) 208-6416. Fax, (202) 208-5133. Kate Kelly, Director. Employee Directory, (202) 208-3100.
General email, interior_news@ios.doi.gov

Web, http://doi.gov/news/index.cfm

Issues press releases about Interior Dept. events. Provides information to the general public, tourists, businesses, Native Americans, governments, and others.

Justice Dept. (DOJ), *Civil Division, Consumer Protection,* 450 5th St. N.W., #6400 20001; (202) 616-0295. Fax, (202) 514-8742. Michael Blume, Director.
Web, www.usdoj.gov

Files suits to enforce the Truth-in-Lending Act and other federal statutes protecting consumers, generally upon referral by client agencies.

Merit Systems Protection Board, 1615 M St. N.W., 5th Floor 20419; (202) 653-7200. Fax, (202) 653-7130. Susan Swafford, Chair; William Spencer, Clerk of the Board. Toll-free, (800) 209-8960. MSPB Inspector General hotline, (800) 424-9121.
General email, mspb@mspb.gov

Web, www.mspb.gov

Independent quasi-judicial agency that handles hearings and appeals involving federal employees; protects the integrity of federal merit systems and ensures adequate protection for employees against abuses by agency management. Library open to the public by appointment.

National Institute of Standards and Technology (NIST) *(Commerce Dept.), Inquiries,* 100 Bureau Dr., Stop 1070, Gaithersburg, MD 20899-1070; (301) 975-6478. Fax, (301) 926-1630. Sharon Seide, Head.
General email, inquiries@nist.gov

Web, www.nist.gov

Responds to inquiries concerning NIST.

Nuclear Regulatory Commission, *Public Affairs,* 11555 Rockville Pike, MS 016D3, Rockville, MD 20852-2738; (301) 415-8200. Fax, (301) 415-3716. Eliot B. Brenner, Director.
General email, opa.resource@nrc.gov

Web, www.nrc.gov/about-nrc/organization/opafuncdesc.html

Provides the public and the news media with information about the Nuclear Regulatory Commission's programs, policy decisions, and activities, primarily through social media and by issuing news releases and distributing commission speeches, fact sheets, and brochures. Follows news coverage of the agency and responds to media and public inquiries.

Postal Regulatory Commission, *Public Affairs and Government Relations (PAGR),* 901 New York Ave. N.W., #200 20268; (202) 789-6800. Fax, (202) 789-6891. Ann C. Fisher, Director.
General email, prc-pagr@prc.gov

Web, www.prc.gov/prc-pages/about/offices/office.aspx?office=pagr

Supports public outreach and education and media relations and acts as liaison with Congress, the U.S. Postal Service, and other government agencies. Provides information for consumers and responds to their inquiries. Informal complaints regarding individual rate and service inquiries are referred to the Consumer Advocate of the Postal Service.

Small Business Administration (SBA), *Capital Access,* 409 3rd St. S.W., #8200 20416; (202) 205-6657. Fax, (202) 205-7230. Ann Marie Mehlum, Associate Administrator.
Web, www.sba.gov/about-offices-content/1/2458

Provides financial assistance to small business, including microloans, surety bond guarantees, investment, and international trade.

State Dept., *Commercial and Business Affairs, 2201 C St. N.W., #5820 20520-5820; (202) 647-1625. Fax, (202) 647-3953. Lorraine J. Hariton, Special Representative for Commercial and Business Affairs.*
General email, cbaweb@state.gov

Web, www.state.gov/e/eb/cba

Serves as primary contact in the State Dept. for U.S. businesses. Coordinates efforts to facilitate U.S. business interests abroad, ensures that U.S. business interests are given sufficient consideration in foreign policy, and provides assistance to firms with problems overseas (such as claims and trade complaints). Works with agencies in the Export Promotion Coordinating Committee to support U.S. business interests overseas.

Transportation Dept. (DOT), *Aviation Consumer Protection, 1200 New Jersey Ave. S.E. 20590; (202) 366-2220. Norman Strickman, Director, (202) 366-5960. Disability-Related Problems, (800) 778-4838. TTY, (202) 366-0511.*
Web, www.dot.gov/airconsumer

Processes consumer complaints; advises the secretary on consumer issues; investigates air travel consumer rule violations; educates the public about air travel via reports and Web site.

Transportation Security Administration (TSA) *(Homeland Security Dept.), Contact Center, 601 S. 12th St., 7th Floor, Arlington, VA 20598; (866) 289-9673. Michelle Cartagena, Program Manager.*
General email, tsa-contactcenter@dhs.gov

Web, www.tsa.gov

Answers questions and collects concerns from the public regarding travel security.

Treasury Dept., *Public Affairs, 1500 Pennsylvania Ave. N.W., #3442 20220; (202) 622-2960. Fax, (202) 622-2808. Natalie Earnest, Assistant Secretary.*
Web, www.treasury.gov/about/organizational-structure/offices/Pages/Public-Affairs.aspx

Serves as the department's liaison to the media and public.

U.S. Postal Service (USPS), *Office of the Consumer Advocate, 475 L'Enfant Plaza S.W., #4012 20260-0004; (202) 268-6308. Fax, (202) 636-5344. James A. Nemec, Vice President and Consumer Advocate, (202) 268-2681. Inquiries, (800) ASK-USPS or (800) 275-8777.*
General email, usps_ca_response@usps.gov

Web, www.usps.com

Handles consumer complaints; oversees investigations into consumer problems; intercedes in local areas when problems are not adequately resolved; provides information on specific products and services; represents consumers' viewpoint before postal management bodies; initiates projects to improve the U.S. Postal Service.

Veterans Affairs Dept. (VA), *Consumer Affairs, 810 Vermont Ave. N.W., #915 20420; (202) 461-7383. Fax, (202) 273-5716. Shirley Williams, Program Assistant, (202) 461-7088; Gabe Gough, Program Specialist, (202) 461-0746.*
Web, www.va.gov

Responds to veterans' complaints concerning VA benefits and services. Answers questions about policy and makes referrals to other VA offices, as appropriate.

▶**CONGRESS**

For a listing of relevant congressional committees and subcommittees, please see pages 32–33 or the Appendix.

▶**NONGOVERNMENTAL**

Call for Action, *11820 Parklawn Dr., #340, Rockville, MD 20852; (240) 747-0229. Shirley Rooker, President; Eduard Bartholme, Executive Director.*
Web, www.callforaction.org

International network of consumer hotlines affiliated with local broadcast partners. Helps consumers resolve problems with businesses, government agencies, and other organizations through mediation. Provides information on privacy concerns.

Center for Auto Safety, *1825 Connecticut Ave. N.W., #330 20009-5708; (202) 328-7700. Fax, (202) 387-0140. Clarence Ditlow, Executive Director.*
General email, accounts@autosafety.org

Web, www.autosafety.org

Public interest organization that receives written consumer complaints against auto manufacturers; monitors federal agencies responsible for regulating and enforcing auto and highway safety rules.

Center for Consumer Freedom, *P.O. Box 34557 20043; (202) 463-7112. Richard Berman, Executive Director.*
General email, info2consumerfreedom.com

Web, www.consumerfreedom.com

Membership: restaurants, food companies, and consumers. Seeks to promote personal freedom and protect consumer choices in lifestyle- and health-related areas such as diet and exercise. Monitors legislation and regulations.

Consumer Federation of America, *1620 Eye St. N.W., #200 20006; (202) 387-6121. Fax, (202) 265-7989. Stephen Brobeck, Executive Director. Press, (202) 737-0766.*
General email, cfa@consumerfed.org

Web, www.consumerfed.org

Federation of national, regional, state, and local pro-consumer organizations. Promotes consumer interests in banking, credit, and insurance; telecommunications; housing; food, drugs, and medical care; safety; and energy and natural resources development.

Consumers Union of the United States, *Washington Office, 1101 17th St. N.W., #500 20036; (202) 462-6262. Fax, (202) 265-9548. James A. Guest, President; Ellen Bloom, Director, Washington Office.*
Web, www.consumersunion.org

Consumer advocacy group that represents consumer interests before Congress and regulatory agencies and litigates consumer affairs cases involving the government. Interests include consumer impact of world trade.

Consumer Financial Protection Bureau

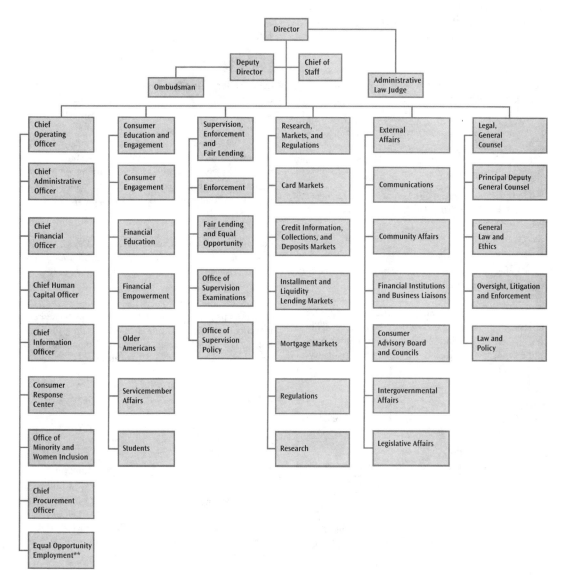

**Position has direct report responsibilities to the Director

Publishes *Consumer Reports* magazine. (Headquarters in Yonkers, N.Y.)

Council of Better Business Bureaus, *3033 Wilson Blvd., #600, Arlington, VA 22201-3843; (703) 276-0100. Fax, (703) 525-8277. Carrie Hurt, President, Interim.*
Web, www.bbb.org

Membership: businesses and Better Business Bureaus in the United States and Canada. Promotes ethical business practices and truth in national advertising; mediates disputes between consumers and businesses.

National Assn. of Consumer Advocates, *1730 Rhode Island Ave. N.W., #710 20036; (202) 452-1989. Fax, (202) 452-0099. Ira J. Rheingold, Executive Director.*

General email, info@naca.net

Web, www.naca.net

Membership: consumer advocate attorneys. Seeks to protect the rights of consumers from fraudulent, abusive, and predatory business practices. Provides consumer law training through conferences and publications. Monitors legislation and regulations on banking, credit, and housing laws.

National Consumers League, *1701 K St. N.W., #1200 20006; (202) 835-3323. Fax, (202) 835-0747. Sally Greenberg, Executive Director.*
General email, info@nclnet.org

Web, www.nclnet.org

Advocacy group that engages in research and educational activities related to consumer and worker issues. Interests include fraud, privacy, child labor, product safety, and food and drug safety. Web resources include fieldsofhope.org, fraud.org, lifesmarts.org, sosrx.org, and stop childlabor.org.

Public Citizen, *1600 20th St. N.W. 20009; (202) 588-1000. Fax, (202) 588-7798. Robert Weissman, President. General email, pcmail@citizen.org*

Web, www.citizen.org

Public interest consumer advocacy organization comprising the following programs: Congress Watch, Health Research Group, Energy Program, Litigation Group, and Global Trade Watch.

Public Justice Foundation, *1825 K St. N.W., #200 20006; (202) 797-8600. Fax, (202) 232-7203. Arthur H. Bryant, Executive Director. General email, publicjustice@publicjustice.net*

Web, www.publicjustice.net

Membership: consumer activists, trial lawyers, and public interest lawyers. Litigates to influence corporate and government decisions about products or activities adversely affecting health or safety. Interests include toxic torts, environmental protection, civil rights and civil liberties, workers' safety, consumer protection, and the preservation of the civil justice system. (Formerly Trial Lawyers for Public Justice.)

SAFE KIDS Worldwide, *1301 Pennsylvania Ave. N.W., #1000 20004-1707; (202) 662-0600. Fax, (202) 393-2072. John H. Claster, Chair; Kate Carr, Chief Executive Officer. General email, info@safekids.org*

Web, www.safekids.org

Promotes awareness among adults that unintentional injury is the leading cause of death among children ages nineteen and under. Conducts educational programs on childhood injury prevention. (Affiliated with SAFE KIDS USA.)

U.S. Chamber of Commerce, *Congressional and Public Affairs, 1615 H St. N.W. 20062-2000; (202) 463-5600. Fax, (202) 544-4157. Jack Howard, Senior Vice President. Web, www.uschamber.com*

Monitors legislation and regulations regarding business and consumer issues, including legislation and policies affecting the Federal Trade Commission, the Consumer Product Safety Commission, and other agencies.

U.S. Public Interest Research Group (USPIRG), *Washington Office, 218 D St. S.E. 20003; (202) 546-9707. Fax, (202) 543-6489. Andre Delattre, Executive Director (in Boston), (312) 544-4436; Michael (Mike) Russo, Director, (202) 461-3823. General email, uspirg@pirg.org*

Web, www.uspirg.org

Conducts research and advocacy on consumer and environmental issues, including telephone rates, banking practices, insurance, campaign finance reform, product safety, toxic and solid waste; monitors private and governmental actions affecting consumers; supports efforts to challenge consumer fraud and illegal business practices. Serves as national office for state groups.

Credit Practices

▶**AGENCIES**

Comptroller of the Currency *(Treasury Dept.),* **Chief Counsel,** *400 7th St. S.W., Constitution Center 20024; (202) 649-5400. Fax, (202) 649-6077. Amy S. Friend, Senior Deputy Comptroller and Chief Counsel. Web, www.occ.gov*

Enforces and oversees compliance by nationally chartered banks with laws prohibiting discrimination in credit transactions on the basis of sex or marital status. Enforces regulations concerning bank advertising; may issue cease-and-desist orders.

Comptroller of the Currency *(Treasury Dept.),* **Compliance Policy,** *400 7th St. S.W., Constitution Center 20024; (202) 649-5470. Grovetta Gardineer, Deputy Comptroller. Web, www.occ.treas.gov*

Develops policy for enforcing consumer laws and regulations that affect national banks, including the Bank Secrecy (BSA/AML), Truth-in-Lending, Community Reinvestment, and Equal Credit Opportunity acts.

Comptroller of the Currency *(Treasury Dept.),* **Public Affairs,** *400 7th St. S.W., Constitution Center 20024; (202) 649-6870. Fax, (202) 874-5678. Paul M. Nash, Chief of Staff; Robert M. Garsson, Deputy Comptroller for Public Affairs. Congressional Affairs, (202) 649-6440. General email, publicaffairs3@occ.treas.gov*

Web, www.occ.gov and http://helpwithmybank.gov

Advises the comptroller on relations with the media and the banking industry.

Consumer Financial Protection Bureau (CFPB), *1700 G St. N.W. 20552; (202) 435-7000. Richard Cordray, Director. RESPA enquiries, (855) 411-2372. General email, info@consumerfinance.gov*

Web, www.consumerfinance.gov

An independent government agency created per the Dodd-Frank Act of 2010. Functions will include implementing and enforcing federal laws pertaining to mortgages, credit cards, and other consumer financial products and services. Current tasks of the implementation team include gathering data on the needs and concerns of consumers and financial services companies; collecting information about the risks and benefits of existing products and services; and developing a consumer hotline. Administers the Real Estate Settlement Procedures Act (RESPA) and Interstate Land Sales Full Disclosure Act

Federal Deposit Insurance Corp. (FDIC), *Depositor and Consumer Protection, 1776 F St. N.W., #F6074 20429; (202) 898-7088. Fax, (202) 898-3909. Mark Pearce, Director.*

*Web, www.fdic.gov/about/contact/directory/index
.html#DDCP*

Examines and supervises federally insured state banks that are not members of the Federal Reserve System to ascertain their safety and soundness.

Federal Deposit Insurance Corp. (FDIC), *Depositor and Consumer Protection, Consumer and Community Affairs, 1310 Court House Rd., #11060, Arlington, VA 22201; (703) 254-1043. Fax, (703) 254-0222. Elizabeth Ortiz, Deputy Director. Information, 877-ASK-FDIC. General email, consumer@fdic.gov*

*Web, www.fdic.gov/about/contact/directory/index
.html#DDCP*

Coordinates and monitors complaints filed by consumers against federally insured state banks that are not members of the Federal Reserve System; handles complaints concerning truth-in-lending and other fair credit provisions, including charges of discrimination on the basis of sex or marital status; responds to general banking inquiries; answers questions on deposit insurance coverage.

Federal Deposit Insurance Corp. (FDIC), *Risk Management Supervision, 550 17th St. N.W., #5028 20429; (202) 898-6519. Fax, (202) 898-3638. Doreen R. Eberly, Director. Web, www.fdic.gov/about/contact/#HQDSC*

Federal Reserve System, *Consumer and Community Affairs, 1709 New York Ave. N.W. 20006; (202) 785-6032. Fax, (202) 452-3849. Vacant, Director. Complaints, (888) 851-1920. Web, www.federalreserve.gov/econresdata/ccastaff.htm*

Receives consumer complaints concerning truth-in-lending, fair credit billing, equal credit opportunity, electronic fund transfer, home mortgage disclosure, consumer leasing, and advertising; receives complaints about unregulated practices; refers complaints to district banks. The Federal Reserve monitors enforcement of fair lending laws with regard to state-chartered banks that are members of the Federal Reserve System.

Federal Trade Commission (FTC), *Consumer Protection, Financial Practices, 600 Pennsylvania Ave. N.W., MS 3158 20580; (202) 326-3224. Fax, (202) 326-3768. Reilly Dolan, Associate Director. Web, www.ftc.gov*

Challenges unfair or deceptive financial practices, including those involving lending, loan servicing, debt negotiation, and debt collection. Enforces specific consumer credit statutes, including the Fair Debt Collection Practices Act, Equal Credit Opportunity Act, Truth-in-Lending Act, Credit Repair Organization Act, Home Ownership and Equity Protection Act, Electronic Fund Transfer Act, Consumer Leasing Act, Holder-In-Due-Course Rule, and Credit Practices Rule.

Justice Dept. (DOJ), *Civil Division, Consumer Protection, 450 5th St. N.W., #6400 20001; (202) 616-0295. Fax, (202) 514-8742. Michael Blume, Director. Web, www.usdoj.gov*

Files suits to enforce the Truth-in-Lending Act and other federal statutes protecting consumers, generally upon referral by client agencies.

National Credit Union Administration, *Examination and Insurance, 1775 Duke St., Alexandria, VA 22314-3428; (703) 518-6360. Fax, (703) 518-6499. Larry D. Fazio, Director. Toll-free investment hotline, (800) 755-5999. General email, eimail@ncua.gov*

Web, www.ncua.gov

Oversees and enforces compliance by federally chartered credit unions with the Truth-in-Lending Act, the Equal Credit Opportunity Act, and other federal statutes protecting consumers.

Small Business Administration (SBA), *Diversity, Inclusion, and Civil Rights, 409 3rd St. S.W., #6800 20416; (202) 205-6750. Fax, (202) 205-7580. Tinisha Agramonte, Associate Administrator.*

Web, www.sba.gov/about-offices-content/1/2900

Reviews complaints based on disability against the Small Business Administration by recipients of its assistance in cases of alleged discrimination in credit transactions; monitors recipients for civil rights compliance.

▶ NONGOVERNMENTAL

American Bankers Assn. (ABA), *Communications, 1120 Connecticut Ave. N.W., 8th Floor 20036; (202) 663-5315. Fax, (202) 663-7578. Stephanie M. O'Keefe, Executive Vice President.*

Web, www.aba.com

Provides information on a wide range of banking issues and financial management.

American Financial Services Assn. (AFSA), *919 18th St. N.W., #300 20006-5517; (202) 296-5544. Fax, (202) 223-0321. Chris Stinebert, President. General email, info@afsamail.org*

Web, www.afsaonline.org

Trade association for the consumer credit industry. Focus includes government relations and consumer education. Monitors legislation and regulations.

National Assn. of Consumer Advocates, *1730 Rhode Island Ave. N.W., #710 20036; (202) 452-1989. Fax, (202) 452-0099. Ira J. Rheingold, Executive Director. General email, info@naca.net*

Web, www.naca.net

Membership: consumer advocate attorneys. Seeks to protect the rights of consumers from fraudulent, abusive, and predatory business practices. Provides consumer law training through conferences and publications. Monitors legislation and regulations on banking, credit, and housing laws.

National Retail Federation, *325 7th St. N.W., #1100 20004-2802; (202) 783-7971. Fax, (202) 737-2849. Matthew R. Shay, President; David French, Senior Vice President, Government Relations. Toll-free, (800) 673-4692. Web, www.nrf.com*

Membership: national and state associations of retailers and major retail corporations. Provides information on credit, truth-in-lending laws, and other fair credit practices.

Product Safety, Testing

Consumer Product Safety Commission (CPSC), *4330 East-West Hwy., #820, Bethesda, MD 20814; (301) 504-7923. Fax, (301) 504-0124. Robert S. (Bob) Adler, Chair, Acting; Elliott Kaye, Executive Director, (301) 504-7881. Congressional Relations, (301) 504-7660. Product safety hotline, (800) 638-2772. National Injury Information Clearinghouse, (301) 504-7921.*
General email, info@cpsc.gov
Web, www.cpsc.gov/about/offices.html

Establishes and enforces product safety standards; collects data; studies the causes and prevention of product-related injuries; identifies hazardous products, including imports, and recalls them from the marketplace.

Consumer Product Safety Commission (CPSC), *Compliance and Field Operations, 4330 East-West Hwy., #610, Bethesda, MD 20814; Ray Aragon, Associate Executive Director; Marc Schoem, Deputy Director, (301) 504-7520.*
Web, www.cpsc.gov/about/offices.html

Identifies and acts on defective consumer products; enforces industry compliance with safety standards for domestic and imported products; conducts enforcement litigation. Monitors recall of defective products and issues warnings to consumers.

Consumer Product Safety Commission (CPSC), *Engineering Sciences, 4330 East-West Hwy., #611, Bethesda, MD 20814-4408; (301) 987-2472. Fax, (301) 504-0533. George A. Borlase, Associate Executive Director.*
Web, www.cpsc.gov

Develops and evaluates consumer product safety standards, test methods, performance criteria, design specifications, and quality standards; conducts and evaluates engineering tests. Collects scientific and technical data to determine potential hazards of consumer products.

Consumer Product Safety Commission (CPSC), *Epidemiology, 4330 East-West Hwy., Bethesda, MD 20814-4408; (301) 504-7416. Fax, (301) 504-0081. Kathleen Stralka, Associate Executive Director, (301) 504-0038.*
Web, www.cpsc.gov

Collects data on consumer product-related hazards and potential hazards; determines the frequency, severity, and distribution of the various types of injuries and investigates their causes; and assesses the effects of product safety standards and programs on consumer injuries. Conducts epidemiological studies and research in the fields of consumer-related injuries.

Consumer Product Safety Commission (CPSC), *Health Sciences, 4330 East-West Hwy., #600, Bethesda, MD 20814-4408; (301) 504-7919. Fax, (301) 504-0079. Mary Ann Danello, Associate Executive Director.*
Web, www.cpsc.gov

Evaluates potential health effects and hazards of consumer products and their foreseeable uses, and performs exposure and risk assessments for product-related hazards.

Consumer Product Safety Commission (CPSC), *Laboratory Sciences, Five Research Place, Rockville, MD 20850; (301) 987-2037. Fax, (301) 413-7107. Andrew Stadnik, Associate Executive Director.*
Web, www.cpsc.gov

Conducts engineering analyses and testing of consumer products, supports the development of voluntary and mandatory standards, and supports the agency's compliance activities through product safety assessments.

National Injury Information Clearinghouse *(Consumer Product Safety Commission), 4330 East-West Hwy., #820, Bethesda, MD 20814; (301) 504-7923. Fax, (301) 504-0127. Shoma Ramaswamy, Program Analyst. To report consumer product-related accidents or injuries, (800) 638-2772.*
General email, clearinghouse@cpsc.gov
Web, www.cpsc.gov/en/research–statistics/NEISS-Injury-Data

Analyzes types and frequency of injuries resulting from consumer and recreational products. Collects injury information from consumer complaints, investigations, coroners' reports, death certificates, newspaper clippings, and statistically selected hospital emergency rooms nationwide.

American Academy of Pediatrics, *Federal Affairs, 601 13th St. N.W., #400N 20005; (202) 347-8600. Fax, (202) 393-6137. Mark Del Monte, Director. Information, (800) 336-5475.*
General email, kids1st@aap.org
Web, www.aap.org

Promotes legislation and regulations concerning child health and safety. Committee on Injury and Poison Prevention drafts policy statements and publishes information on toy safety, poisons, and other issues that affect children and adolescents. (Headquarters in Elk Grove Village, Ill.)

Cosmetic Ingredient Review, *1620 L St. N.W., #1200 20036; (202) 331-0651. Fax, (202) 331-0088. Lillian Gill, Director.*
General email, cirinfo@cir-safety.org
Web, www.cir-safety.org

Voluntary self-regulatory program funded by the Personal Products Council. Reviews and evaluates published and unpublished data to assess the safety of cosmetic ingredients.

Federal Deposit Insurance Corporation

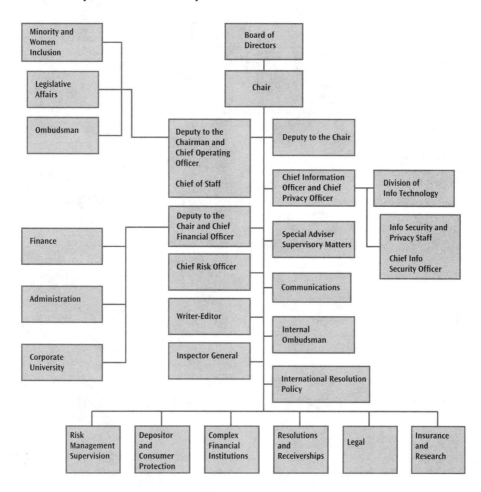

Tobacco

Alcohol and Tobacco Tax and Trade Bureau (TTB)
(Treasury Dept.), 1310 G St. N.W., #300E 20220; (202) 453-2000. John J. Manfreda, Administrator. Press, (202) 453-2134.
General email, info@ttb.gov

Web, www.ttb.gov

Enforces and administers existing federal laws and tax code provisions relating to the production and taxation of alcohol and tobacco.

Centers for Disease Control and Prevention *(Health and Human Services Dept.), Office of Smoking and Health (OSH), 395 E St. S.W., #9100 20201; (202) 245-0550. Fax, (202) 245-0554. Simon McNabb, Lead Public Health Analyst. Information, (800) 232-4636.*
General email, tobaccoinfo@cdc.gov

Web, www.cdc.gov/tobacco

Funds tobacco prevention and control programs administered by state health departments. Programs focus on tobacco use prevention, cessation, smoke-free environments, and tobacco-related disparities. Provides strategic direction, current science, and technical assistance to partner organizations to advance evidence-based interventions at the state and local levels.

Food and Drug Administration (FDA) *(Health and Human Services Dept.), Center for Tobacco Products, 9200 Corporate Blvd., Rockville, MD 20850-3229; (240) 276-1717. Mitch Zeller, Director. Toll-free, (877) 287-1373.*
General email, askctp@fda.hhs.gov

Web, www.fda.gov/tobaccoproducts

Regulates the manufacture, distribution, and marketing of tobacco products.

Action on Smoking and Health (ASH), *701 4th St. N.W. 20001; (202) 659-4310. Fax, (202) 289-7166. Laurent Huber, Executive Director.*
General email, info@ash.org

Web, www.ash.org

Federal Reserve System

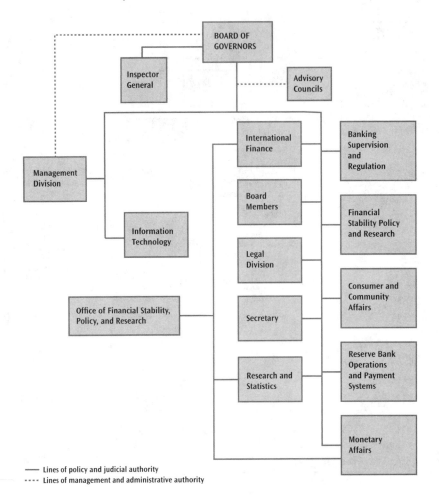

— Lines of policy and judicial authority
···· Lines of management and administrative authority

Educational and legal organization that works to protect nonsmokers from cigarette smoking; provides information about smoking hazards and nonsmokers' rights.

Bakery, Confectionery, Tobacco Workers, and Grain Millers International Union, *10401 Connecticut Ave., Kensington, MD 20895-3940; (301) 933-8600. Fax, (301) 946-8452. David B. Durkee, President.*
Web, www.bctgm.org

Membership: approximately 120,000 workers from the bakery, confectionery, grain miller, and tobacco industries. Helps members negotiate pay, benefits, and better working conditions; conducts training programs and workshops. Monitors legislation and regulations. (Affiliated with the AFL-CIO.)

National Campaign for Tobacco-Free Kids, *1400 Eye St. N.W., #1200 20005; (202) 296-5469. Fax, (202) 296-5427. Matthew Myers, President. Information, (800) 803-7178. Web, www.tobaccofreekids.org*

Seeks to reduce tobacco use by children through public policy change and educational programs. Provides technical assistance to state and local programs.

FINANCE AND INVESTMENTS

Banking

▶AGENCIES

Antitrust Division *(Justice Dept.),* **Networks and Technology Enforcement,** *450 5th St. N.W., #7100 20530; (202) 307-6200. Fax, (202) 616-8544. James J. Tierney, Chief. Web, www.justice.gov/atr/about/ntes.html*

Investigates and litigates certain antitrust cases involving financial institutions, including securities, commodity futures, computer software, professional associations, and insurance; participates in agency proceedings and rulemaking in these areas; monitors and analyzes legislation.

Comptroller of the Currency *(Treasury Dept.),* *400 7th St. S.W., Constitution Center 20024; (202) 649-6400. Thomas J. Curry, Comptroller, Acting. Press, (202) 649-6870.*
General email, publicaffairs3@occ.gov
Web, www.occ.treas.gov

Charters and examines operations of national banks, federal savings associations, and U.S. operations of foreign-owned banks; establishes guidelines for bank examinations; handles mergers of national banks with regard to antitrust law. Ensures that national banks and savings associations operate in a safe and sound manner, provide fair access to financial services, treat customers fairly, and comply with applicable laws and regulations.

Comptroller of the Currency *(Treasury Dept.),*
Licensing, 400 7th St. S.W., Constitution Center 20024; (202) 649-6260. Fax, (202) 649-5728. Stephen A. Lybarger, Deputy Comptroller.
Web, www.occ.gov

Advises the comptroller on policy matters and programs related to bank corporate activities and is the primary decision maker on national bank corporate applications, including charters, mergers and acquisitions, conversions, and operating subsidiaries.

Comptroller of the Currency *(Treasury Dept.),*
Ombudsman, 400 7th St. S.W., Constitution Center 20024; (202) 649-5530. Fax, (202) 649-5727. Larry L. Hattix, Senior Deputy Comptroller for Enterprise Governance.
Web, www.occ.gov

Ensures that bank customers and the banks the agency supervises receive fair and expeditious resolution of their concerns.

Federal Deposit Insurance Corp. (FDIC), 550 17th St. N.W. 20429; (703) 562-2222. Fax, (202) 898-3543. Martin J. Gruenberg, Chair. Toll-free Information, (877) 275-3342. Press, (202) 898-6993.
Web, www.fdic.gov

Insures deposits in national banks and state banks. Conducts examinations of insured state banks that are not members of the Federal Reserve System.

Federal Deposit Insurance Corp. (FDIC), *Ombudsman,*
3501 N. Fairfax Dr., Arlington, VA 22226; (703) 562-6049. Fax, (703) 562-6057. Cottrell L. Webster, Director.
Web, www.fdic.gov/about/contact/directory/#HQOO

An independent, neutral, and confidential source of assistance for the public. Provides answers to the public in the areas of depositor concerns, loan questions, asset information, bank closing issues, and any FDIC regulation or policy.

Federal Deposit Insurance Corp. (FDIC), *Resolutions and Receiverships,* 1776 F St. N.W., #F-8076 20429; (202) 898-6525. Fax, (202) 898-6528. Bret Edwards, Director.
Web, www.fdic.gov/about/contact/directory/#HQDRR

Plans, executes, and monitors the orderly and least cost resolution of failing FDIC-insured institutions. Manages remaining liability of the federal savings and deposit insurance funds.

Federal Deposit Insurance Corp. (FDIC), *Risk Management Supervision,* 550 17th St. N.W., #5028 20429; (202) 898-6519. Fax, (202) 898-3638. Doreen R. Eberly, Director.
Web, www.fdic.gov/about/contact/#HQDSC

Serves as the federal regulator and supervisor of insured state banks that are not members of the Federal Reserve System. Conducts regular examinations and investigations of banks under the jurisdiction of FDIC; advises bank managers on improving policies and practices. Administers the Bank Insurance Fund, which insures deposits in commercial and savings banks, and the Savings Assn. Insurance Fund, which insures deposits in savings and loan institutions.

Federal Housing Finance Agency (FHFA), 400 7th St. 20024; (202) 649-3800. Fax, (202) 649-1071. Edward J. DeMarco, Director, Acting.
General email, fhfainfo@fhfa.gov
Web, www.fhfa.gov

Regulates and works to ensure the financial soundness of Fannie Mae (Federal National Mortgage Assn.), Freddie Mac (Federal Home Loan Mortgage Corp.), and the twelve Federal Home Loan banks. FHFA was formed by a legislative merger of the Office of Federal Housing Enterprise Oversight (OFHEO), the Federal Housing Finance Board, and HUD's Government-Sponsored Enterprise (GSE) mission team.

Federal Reserve System, *Banking Supervision and Regulation,* 20th St. and Constitution Ave. N.W. 20551; (202) 452-2774. Michael Gibson, Director.
Web, www.federalreserve.gov/econresdata/brstaff.htm

Supervises and regulates state banks that are members of the Federal Reserve System; supervises and inspects all bank holding companies; monitors banking practices; approves bank mergers, consolidations, and other changes in bank structure.

Federal Reserve System, *Board of Governors,* 20th St. and Constitution Ave., N.W. 20551; (202) 452-3000. Fax, (202) 452-3819. Ben S. Bernanke, Chair; Vacant, Vice Chair. Information (meetings), (202) 452-3204. Public Affairs, (202) 452-2955. Congressional Liaison, (202) 452-3003. Publications, (202) 452-3245.
General email, eric.j.kollig@frb.gov
Web, www.federalreserve.gov

Serves as the central bank and fiscal agent for the government. Examines Federal Reserve banks and state member banks; supervises bank holding companies. Controls wire system transfer operations and supplies currency for depository institutions.

Federal Reserve System, *Reserve Bank Operations and Payment Systems,* 20th and C Sts. N.W., MS 190 20551; (202) 452-2789. Fax, (202) 452-2746. Louise L. Roseman, Director.
Web, www.federalreserve.gov/econresdata/rbopsstaff.htm

Oversees the Federal Reserve banks' provision of financial services to depository institutions and fiscal agency services to the Treasury Dept. and other federal agencies; provides support, such as information technology and financial cost accounting. Develops policies and regulations to foster the efficiency and integrity of U.S. payment systems; works with other central banks and international organizations to improve payment systems more broadly; and conducts research on payment issues.

National Credit Union Administration, *1775 Duke St., Alexandria, VA 22314-3428; (703) 518-6300. Fax, (703) 518-6319. Deborah Matz, Chair. Information, (703) 518-6440. Media, (703) 518-6336.*
General email, consumerassistance@ncua.gov
Web, www.ncua.gov

Administers the National Credit Union Share Insurance Fund, which, with the backing of the full faith and credit of the U.S. government, operates and manages the National Credit Union, which insures the deposits of nearly 96 million account holders. Regulates all federally chartered credit unions; charters new credit unions; supervises and examines federal credit unions and insures their member accounts up to $250,000. Insures state-chartered credit unions that apply and are eligible. Manages the Central Liquidity Facility, which supplies emergency short-term loans to members. Conducts research on economic trends and their effect on credit unions and advises the administration's board on economic and financial policy and regulations.

Office of Management and Budget (OMB) *(Executive Office of the President),* **Housing, Treasury, and Commerce,** *New Executive Office Bldg., #9201 20503; (202) 395-4516. Fax, (202) 395-6889. Mark Weatherly, Chief.*
Web, www.whitehouse.gov/omb

Monitors the financial condition of deposit insurance funds including the Bank Insurance Fund, the Savings Assn. Insurance Fund, and the Federal Savings and Loan Insurance Corp. (FSLIC) Resolution Fund. Monitors the Securities and Exchange Commission. Has limited oversight over the Federal Housing Finance Board and the Federal Home Loan Bank System.

Securities and Exchange Commission (SEC), *Corporation Finance, 100 F St. N.E., MS 4553 20549; (202) 551-3100. Fax, (202) 772-9215. Keith F. Higgins, Director, (202) 551-3110.*
Web, www.sec.gov/corpfin#.ux83y4xfmaq

Receives and examines disclosure statements and other information from publicly held companies, including bank holding companies.

Securities and Exchange Commission (SEC), *Economic and Risk Analysis, 100 F St. N.E. 20549; (202) 551-6600. Fax, (202) 756-0505. Craig M. Lewis, Director. Information, (202) 942-8088.*
General email, RiskFin@sec.gov
Web, www.sec.gov/dera#.ux9TeoXfmaQ

Provides the commission with economic analyses of proposed rule and policy changes and other information to guide the SEC in influencing capital markets. Evaluates the effect of policy and other factors on competition within the securities industry and among competing securities markets; compiles financial statistics on capital formation and the securities industry.

Treasury Dept., *Financial Institutions, 1500 Pennsylvania Ave. N.W., #2326 20220; (202) 622-2610. Fax, (202) 622-4774. Cyrus Amir-Mokri, Assistant Secretary.*
Web, www.treasury.gov/about/organizational-structure/offices/Pages/Financial-Institutions.aspx

Advises the under secretary for domestic finance and the Treasury secretary on financial institutions, banks, and thrifts.

Treasury Dept., *Financial Stability, 1500 Pennsylvania Ave. N.W., #2428 20220; (202) 622-5800. Fax, (202) 622-4161. Timothy G. Massad, Assistant Secretary.*
Web, www.financialstability.gov

Seeks to normalize lending. Provides eligible financial institutions with capital assistance; administers mortgage modification programs. Manages the Troubled Asset Relief Program (TARP).

Treasury Dept., *Special Inspector General for the Troubled Asset Relief Program (SIGTARP), 1801 L St. N.W. 20220; (202) 622-1419. Fax, (202) 622-4559. Christy L. Romero, Special Inspector General. Fraud, waste, and abuse hotline, 877-SIG-2009. Press, (202) 927-8940.*
Web, www.sigtarp.gov

Conducts, supervises, and coordinates audits and investigations of the purchase, management, and sale of assets under the Troubled Asset Relief Program (TARP).

►**CONGRESS**

For a listing of relevant congressional committees and subcommittees, please see pages 32–33 or the Appendix.

►**NONGOVERNMENTAL**

American Bankers Assn. (ABA), *1120 Connecticut Ave. N.W. 20036; (202) 663-5000. Fax, (202) 663-7578. Frank Keating, President. Information, 800-BANKERS.*
General email, custserv@aba.com
Web, www.aba.com

Membership: commercial banks. Operates schools to train banking personnel; conducts conferences; formulates government relations policies for the banking community.

American Council of State Savings Supervisors, *1129 20th St. N.W., 9th Floor 20036; (202) 728-5757. Ed Smith, Executive Director.*
Web, www.acsss.org

Membership: supervisors and regulators of state-chartered savings associations; associate members include state-chartered savings associations and state savings banks. Trains state financial regulatory examiners. Monitors legislation and regulations affecting the state-chartered thrift industry.

American Institute of Certified Public Accountants, *Washington Office, 1455 Pennsylvania Ave. N.W., 10th Floor 20004-1081; (202) 737-6600. Fax, (202) 638-4512. Mark Peterson, Vice President of Congressional and Public Affairs. Press, (202) 434-9266.*
Web, www.aicpa.org

Establishes voluntary professional and ethical regulations for the profession; sponsors conferences and training workshops. Answers technical auditing and accounting questions. (Headquarters in Durham, N.C.)

Assn. for Financial Professionals, *4520 East-West Hwy., #750, Bethesda, MD 20814; (301) 907-2862. Fax, (301) 907-2864. James A. Kaitz, President.*
Web, www.afponline.org

Membership: more than 16,000 members from a wide range of industries throughout all stages of their careers in various aspects of treasury and financial management. Acts as a resource for continuing education, financial tools and publications, career development, certifications, research, representation to legislators and regulators, and the development of industry standards.

BAFT, *1120 Connecticut Ave. N.W., 5th Floor 20036-3902; (202) 663-7575. Fax, (202) 663-5538. Tod R. Burwell, Chief Executive Officer.*
General email, info@baft-ifsa.com
Web, www.baft.org

Membership: international financial services providers, including U.S. and non-U.S. commercial banks, financial services companies, and suppliers with major international operations. Interests include international trade, trade finance, payments, compliance, asset servicing, and transaction banking. Monitors and advocates globally on activities that affect the business of commercial and international banks and nonfinancial companies. (Formerly Bankers' Assn. for Financial Trade.)

Conference of State Bank Supervisors, *1129 20th St. N.W., 9th Floor 20036; (202) 296-2840. Fax, (202) 296-1928. John Ryan, President, (202) 728-5724.*
Web, www.csbs.org

Membership: state officials responsible for supervision of state-chartered banking institutions. Conducts educational programs. Monitors legislation.

Consumer Bankers Assn., *1225 Eye St. N.W., #550 20005; (202) 552-6382. Richard Hunt, President. Media, (703) 869-1246.*
Web, www.cbanet.org

Membership: federally insured financial institutions. Provides information on retail banking, including industry trends. Operates the Graduate School of Retail Bank Management to train banking personnel; conducts research and analysis on retail banking trends; sponsors conferences.

Consumer Data Industry Assn., *1090 Vermont Ave. N.W., #200 20005-4905; (202) 371-0910. Fax, (202) 371-0134. Stuart Pratt, President. Press, (202) 408-7406.*
General email, cdia@cdiaonline.org
Web, www.cdiaonline.org

Membership: credit reporting, mortgage reporting, and collection service companies. Provides information about credit rights to consumers. Monitors legislation and regulations.

Credit Union National Assn., *Washington Office, 601 Pennsylvania Ave. N.W., South Bldg. 20004-2601; (202) 638-5777. Fax, (202) 638-7734. Bill Cheney, President.*
Web, www.cuna.org

Confederation of credit unions from every state, the District of Columbia, and Puerto Rico. Represents federal and state chartered credit unions. Monitors legislation and regulations. (Headquarters in Madison, Wis.)

Electronic Funds Transfer Assn., *4000 Legato Rd., #1100, Fairfax, VA 22033; (571) 318-5556. Fax, (571) 318-5557. Kurt Helwig, President, (571) 318-5555.*
Web, www.efta.org

Membership: financial institutions, electronic funds transfer hardware and software providers, automatic teller machine networks, and others engaged in electronic commerce. Promotes electronic payments and commerce technologies; sponsors industry analysis. Monitors legislation and regulations.

Employee Benefit Research Institute, *1100 13th St. N.W., #878 20005; (202) 659-0670. Fax, (202) 775-6312. Dallas L. Salisbury, President.*
General email, info@ebri.org
Web, www.ebri.org

Research institute that focuses on economic security and employee benefit issues. Seeks to raise public awareness about long-term personal financial independence and encourage retirement savings. Does not lobby and does not take public policy positions.

Financial Services Roundtable, *1001 Pennsylvania Ave., N.W., #500S 20004; (202) 289-4322. Fax, (202) 628-2507. Tim Pawlenty, Chief Executive Officer; Eric Hoplin, Executive Director.*
General email, info@fsroundtable.org
Web, www.fsroundtable.org

Membership: one hundred integrated financial services companies. Provides banking, insurance, investment products, and services to American consumers.

Independent Community Bankers of America, *1615 L St. N.W., #900 20036; (202) 659-8111. Fax, (202) 659-9216. Camden Fine, President. Information, (800) 422-8439.*
General email, info@icba.org
Web, www.icba.org

Membership: medium-sized and smaller community banks. Interests include farm credit, deregulation, interstate banking, deposit insurance, and financial industry standards.

Mortgage Bankers Assn., *1919 M St. N.W., 5th Floor 20036; (202) 557-2700. Fax, (202) 408-4961. David Stevens, President.*
Web, www.mba.org

Membership: institutions involved in real estate finance. Maintains School of Mortgage Banking and sponsors educational seminars; collects statistics on the industry.

Securities and Exchange Commission

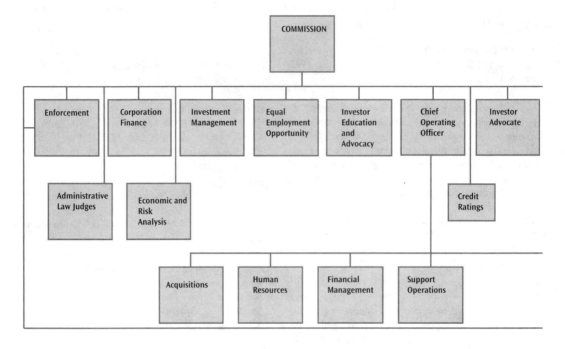

NACHA–Electronic Payments Assn., *13450 Sunrise Valley Dr., #100, Herndon, VA 20171; (703) 561-1100. Fax, (703) 787-0996. Jan Estep, President.*
General email, info@nacha.org
Web, www.nacha.org

Membership: ACH Network participants. Supports ACH Network growth by managing its development, administration, and governance. Facilitates the expansion and diversification of electronic payments, supporting Direct Deposit and Direct Payment via ACH transactions, including credit and debit transactions; recurring and one-time payments; government, consumer, and business-to-business transactions; international payments; and payments plus payment-related information. Develops operating rules and business practices through its collaborative, self-regulatory model. Sponsors workshops and seminars. (Formerly the National Automated Clearing House Assn.)

National Assn. of Federal Credit Unions (NAFCU), *3138 10th St. North, Arlington, VA 22201-2149; (703) 842-2240. Fax, (703) 522-2734. Dan Berger, President.*
Web, www.nafcu.org

Membership: federally chartered credit unions. Issues legislative and regulatory alerts for members and consumers. Sponsors briefings on current financial trends, legislation and regulations, and management techniques.

National Assn. of State Credit Union Supervisors, *1655 N. Fort Myer Dr., #650, Arlington, VA 22209-3113; (703) 528-8351. Fax, (703) 528-3248. Mary Martha Fortney, Chief Executive Officer.*
General email, offices@nascus.org
Web, www.nascus.org

Membership: state credit union supervisors, state-chartered credit unions, and credit union leagues. Interests include state regulatory systems; conducts educational programs for examiners.

National Bankers Assn., *1513 P St. N.W. 20005; (202) 588-5432. Fax, (202) 588-5443. Michael A. Grant, President.*
General email, mgrant@nationalbankers.org
Web, www.nationalbankers.org

Membership: minority- and women-owned financial institutions. Monitors legislation and regulations.

National Society of Accountants, *1010 N. Fairfax St., Alexandria, VA 22314-1574; (703) 549-6400. Fax, (703) 549-2984. John G. Ams, Executive Vice President, ext. 1313. Toll-free, (800) 966-6679.*
General email, members@nsacct.org
Web, www.nsacct.org

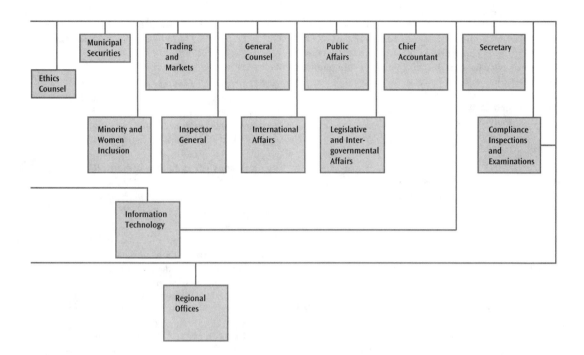

Seeks to improve the accounting profession and to enhance the status of individual practitioners. Sponsors seminars and correspondence courses on accounting, auditing, business law, and estate planning; monitors legislation and regulations affecting accountants and their small-business clients.

Transparency International USA, *1023 15th St. N.W., #300 20005; (202) 589-1616. Fax, (202) 589-1512. Claudia J. Damas, President.*
General email, administration@transparency-usa.org

Web, www.transparency-usa.org

Seeks to curb corruption in international transactions. Promotes reform of government, business, and development assistance transactions through effective anticorruption laws and policies. (Headquarters in Berlin, Germany.)

Stocks, Bonds, and Securities

▶**AGENCIES**

Bureau of the Fiscal Service *(Treasury Dept.),* **Legislative and Public Affairs,** *401 14th St. S.W., 5th Floor 20227; (202) 504-3502. Fax, (202) 874-7016. Joyce Harris, Director.*
Web, www.treasurydirect.gov

Plans, develops, and implements communication regarding Treasury securities.

Federal Reserve System, *Board of Governors, 20th St. and Constitution Ave., N.W. 20551; (202) 452-3000. Fax, (202) 452-3819. Ben S. Bernanke, Chair; Vacant, Vice Chair. Information (meetings), (202) 452-3204. Public Affairs, (202) 452-2955. Congressional Liaison, (202) 452-3003. Publications, (202) 452-3245.*
General email, eric.j.kollig@frb.gov

Web, www.federalreserve.gov

Regulates amount of credit that may be extended and maintained on certain securities in order to prevent excessive use of credit for purchase or carrying of securities.

Securities and Exchange Commission (SEC), *100 F St. N.E. 20549; (202) 551-2100. Fax, (202) 772-9200. Mary Jo White, Chair. Press, (202) 551-4120. Investor Education and Advocacy, (202) 551-6500. Toll-free, (800) 732-0330. Locator, (202) 551-6000. Legislative and Intergovernmental Affairs, (202) 551-2010. Information, (888) 732-6585. Library, (202) 551-5450.*
Web, www.sec.gov

Requires public disclosure of financial and other information about companies whose securities are offered for public sale, traded on exchanges, or traded over the counter; issues and enforces regulations to prevent fraud in securities markets and investigates securities frauds and violations; supervises operations of stock exchanges and activities of securities dealers, investment advisers, and investment companies; regulates purchase and sale of securities; participates in bankruptcy proceedings involving publicly held companies; has some jurisdiction over municipal securities trading. Public Reference Section makes available corporation reports and statements filed with the SEC. The information is available via the Web (www.sec.gov/edgar.shtml). Library open to the public by appointment.

Securities and Exchange Commission (SEC), *Economic and Risk Analysis,* *100 F St. N.E. 20549; (202) 551-6600. Fax, (202) 756-0505. Craig M. Lewis, Director. Information, (202) 942-8088.*
General email, RiskFin@sec.gov
Web, www.sec.gov/dera#.ux9TeoXfmaQ

Provides the commission with economic analyses of proposed rule and policy changes and other information to guide the SEC in influencing capital markets. Evaluates the effect of policy and other factors on competition within the securities industry and among competing securities markets; compiles financial statistics on capital formation and the securities industry.

Securities and Exchange Commission (SEC), *Office of the Whistleblower,* *100 F St. N.E., MS 5971 20549; (202) 551-4790. Fax, (703) 813-9322. Sean McKessy, Chief.*
Web, www.sec.gov/whistleblower

Receives information about possible securities law violations and provides information about the whistleblower program.

Securities and Exchange Commission (SEC), *Trading and Markets,* *100 F St. N.E. 20549; (202) 551-5500. Fax, (202) 772-9273. Stephen Luparaello, Director.*
General email, tradingandmarkets@sec.gov
Web, www.sec.gov/tm#.ux9uQixfmaQ

Oversees and regulates the operations of securities exchanges, the Financial Industry Regulatory Authority (FINRA), nationally recognized statistical rating organizations, brokers-dealers, clearing agencies, transfer agents, alternative trading systems, large traders, security-based swap dealers, security futures product exchanges, and securities information processors. Promotes the establishment of a national system for clearing and settling securities transactions. Facilitates the development of a national market system.

Treasury Dept., *Financial Institutions Policy,* *1500 Pennsylvania Ave. N.W., #1310 20220; (202) 622-2730. Fax, (202) 622-0256. Katheryn Rosen, Deputy Assistant Secretary.*
General email, ofip@do.treas.gov/offices/domestic-finance/financial-institution
Web, www.treasury.gov/about/organizational-structure/offices/Pages/–Office-of-Financial-Institutions-Policy.aspx

Coordinates department efforts on all legislation and regulations affecting financial institutions. Develops department policy on all matters relating to agencies responsible for supervising financial institutions and financial markets.

▶**NONGOVERNMENTAL**

Council of Institutional Investors, *888 17th St. N.W., #500 20006; (202) 822-0800. Fax, (202) 822-0801. Ann Yerger, Executive Director.*
Web, www.cii.org

Membership: pension funds and other employee benefit funds, foundations, and endowments. Studies investment issues that affect pension plan assets. Focuses on corporate governance and shareholder rights. Monitors legislation and regulations.

Financial Industry Regulatory Authority (FINRA), *1735 K St. N.W. 20006-1506; (202) 728-8000. Fax, (202) 728-8075. Richard G. Ketchum, Chair. Member services, (301) 590-6500. Public disclosure, (800) 289-9999.*
Web, www.finra.org

Membership: investment brokers and dealers authorized to conduct transactions of the investment banking and securities business under federal and state laws. Serves as the self-regulatory mechanism in the over-the-counter securities market. Operates speakers bureau. (Formerly the National Assn. of Securities Dealers.)

Futures Industry Assn., *2001 Pennsylvania Ave. N.W., #600 20006; (202) 466-5460. Fax, (202) 296-3184. Walter L. Lukken, President.*
General email, info@futuresindustry.org
Web, www.futuresindustry.org

Membership: futures commission merchants, introducing brokers, exchanges, clearinghouses, and others interested in derivative markets. Serves as a forum for discussion of industry issues; engages in regulatory and legislative advocacy; provides market information and statistical data; offers educational programs; works to establish professional and ethical standards for members.

Intercontinental Exchange, *Washington Office, 801 Pennsylvania Ave. N.W., #630 20004-2685; (202) 347-4300. Fax, (202) 347-4372. Alex Albert, Vice President.*
Web, www.nyse.com

Provides limited information on operations of the New York Stock Exchange; Washington office monitors legislation and regulations. (Formerly listed as New York Stock Exchange; headquarters in New York.)

Investment Company Institute, *1401 H St. N.W., #1200 20005-2148; (202) 326-5800. Fax, (202) 326-5899. Paul Schott Stevens, President.*
General email, ianthe.zabel@ici.org
Web, www.ici.org

Membership: mutual funds, exchange-traded funds, and closed-end funds registered under the Investment Company Act of 1940 (including investment advisers to and underwriters of such companies) and the unit investment trust industry. Conducts research and disseminates information on issues affecting mutual funds.

Investor Protection Trust, *919 18th St. N.W., #300 20006-5517; (202) 775-2112. Don M. Blandin, President.*
General email, iptinfo@investorprotection.org
Web, www.investorprotection.org

Provides noncommercial investment information to consumers to help them make informed investment decisions. Serves as an independent source of noncommercial investor education materials. Operates programs under its own auspices and uses grants to underwrite important initiatives carried out by other organizations.

Municipal Securities Rulemaking Board, *1900 Duke St., #600, Alexandria, VA 22314; (703) 797-6600. Fax, (703) 797-6700. Lynnette Kelly, Executive Director.*
Web, www.msrb.org

Congressionally chartered self-regulatory organization for the municipal securities market. Regulates municipal securities dealers and municipal advisers and seeks to provide market transparency through the Electronic Municipal Market Access Web site. Conducts education and outreach. Subject to oversight by the Securities and Exchange Commission.

National Assn. of Bond Lawyers, *601 13th St., #800-S 20005-3875; (202) 503-3300. Fax, (202) 637-0217. Linda H. Wyman, Chief Operating Officer.*
General email, bdaly@nabl.org
Web, www.nabl.org

Membership: state and municipal finance lawyers. Educates members and others on the law relating to state and municipal bonds and other obligations. Provides advice and comment at the federal, state, and local levels on legislation, regulations, rulings, and court and administrative proceedings regarding public obligations.

National Assn. of Real Estate Investment Trusts, *1875 Eye St. N.W., #600 20006-5413; (202) 739-9400. Fax, (202) 739-9401. Steven Wechsler, President. Toll-free, (800) 362-7348.*
Web, www.reit.com

Membership: real estate investment trusts and corporations, partnerships, and individuals interested in real estate securities and the industry. Interests include federal taxation, securities regulation, financial standards and reporting standards and ethics, and housing and education; compiles industry statistics. Monitors federal and state legislation and regulations.

National Investor Relations Institute, *225 Reinekers Lane, #560, Alexandria, VA 22314; (703) 562-7700. Fax, (703) 562-7701. Jeffrey D. Morgan, President, ext. 7676.*
Web, www.niri.org

Membership: executives engaged in investor relations and financial communications. Provides publications, educational training sessions, and research on investor relations for members; offers conferences and workshops;

maintains job placement and referral services for members.

North American Securities Administrators Assn., *750 1st St. N.E., #1140 20002; (202) 737-0900. Fax, (202) 783-3571. Russel Iuculano, Executive Director.*
Web, www.nasaa.org

Membership: state, provincial, and territorial securities administrators of the United States, Canada, and Mexico. Serves as the national representative of the state agencies responsible for investor protection. Works to prevent fraud in securities markets and provides a national forum to increase the efficiency and uniformity of state regulation of capital markets. Operates the Central Registration Depository, a nationwide computer link for agent registration and transfers, in conjunction with the National Assn. of Securities Dealers. Monitors legislation and regulations.

Public Company Accounting Oversight Board, *1666 K St. N.W., #800 20006-2803; (202) 207-9100. Fax, (202) 862-8430. James R. Doty, Chair; Suzanne Kinzer, Chief Administrative Officer, ext. 2139.*
General email, info@pcaobus.org
Web, www.pcaobus.org

Established by Congress to oversee the audits of public companies in order to protect the interests of investors and the public. Also oversees the audits of broker-dealers, including compliance reports filed pursuant to federal securities laws.

Securities Industry and Financial Markets Assn.
(SIFMA), *Washington Office, 1101 New York Ave. N.W., 8th Floor 20005; (202) 962-7300. Fax, (202) 962-7305. Kenneth Bentsen Jr., Chief Executive Officer; David Oxner, Managing Director, Federal Government Affairs.*
General email, inquiry@sifma.org
Web, www.sifma.org

Represents securities firms, banks, and asset managers. Focuses on enhancing the public's trust in markets. Provides educational resources for professionals and investors in the industry. Monitors legislation and regulations. (Headquarters in New York. Merger of the Securities Industry Assn. and the Bond Market Assn.)

Securities Investor Protection Corp. (SIPC), *805 15th St. N.W., #800 20005-2215; (202) 371-8300. Fax, (202) 371-6728. Stephen P. Harbeck, Chief Executive Officer; Ailes Aaron Wolf, Media, (703) 276-3265.*
General email, asksipc@sipc.org
Web, www.sipc.org

Private corporation established by Congress to administer the Securities Investor Protection Act. Acts as a trustee or works with an independent, court-appointed trustee to recover funds in brokerage insolvency cases.

Small Business Investor Alliance, *1100 H St. N.W., #610 20005; (202) 628-5055. Brett Palmer, President.*
General email, info@sbia.org
Web, www.sbia.org

Membership: private equity, venture capital, and middle market funds that invest in small businesses. Provides training to fund managers and holds industry networking events. Monitors legislation and regulations.

US-SIF: The Forum for Sustainable and Responsible Investment, *910 17th St. N.W., #1000 20006; (202) 872-5361. Fax, (202) 775-8686. Lisa Woll, Chief Executive Officer.*
Web, www.ussif.org

Membership association promoting sustainable and socially responsible investing. Conducts research, events, and courses on investments considering environmental, social, and corporate governance criteria. Monitors legislation and regulations. (Formerly Social Investment Forum.)

Tangible Assets

▶**AGENCIES**

Commodity Futures Trading Commission, *Three Lafayette Centre, 1155 21st St. N.W. 20581-0001; (202) 418-5000. Fax, (202) 418-5521. Mark P. Wetjen, Chair, Acting, (202) 418-5010; Anthony C. (Tony) Thompson, Executive Director, (202) 418-5697.*
General email, questions@cftc.gov
Web, www.cftc.gov

Enforces federal statutes relating to commodity futures and options, including gold and silver futures and options. Monitors and regulates gold and silver leverage contracts, which provide for deferred delivery of the commodity and the payment of an agreed portion of the purchase price on margin.

Defense Logistics Agency *(Defense Dept.),* **Strategic Materials,** *8725 John Jay Kingman Rd., #3229, Fort Belvoir, VA 22060-6223; (703) 767-5500. Fax, (703) 767-3316. Ronnie Favors, Administrator; Paula Stead, Deputy Administrator. Press, (703) 767-4430.*
Web, https://www.dnsc.dla.mil

Manages the national defense stockpile of strategic and critical materials. Purchases strategic materials, including beryllium and newly developed high-tech alloys. Disposes of excess materials, including tin, silver, industrial diamond stones, tungsten, and vegetable tannin.

U.S. Geological Survey (USGS) *(Interior Dept.),* **Global Minerals Analysis,** *12201 Sunrise Valley Dr., MS 989, Reston, VA 20192-0002; (703) 648-4976. Fax, (703) 648-4995. Steven D. Textoris, Chief.*
Web, http://minerals.usgs.gov/minerals

Collects, analyzes, and disseminates information on ferrous and nonferrous metals, including gold, silver, platinum group metals, iron, iron ore, steel, chromium, and nickel.

U.S. Mint *(Treasury Dept.),* *801 9th St. N.W., 8th Floor 20220; (202) 354-7200. Fax, (202) 756-6160. Richard L. Peterson, Deputy Director, (202) 756-6468. Information, (202) 354-7227. Press, (202) 354-7222. Customer Service, (800) 872-6468.*
Web, www.usmint.gov

Produces and distributes the national coinage so that the nation can conduct trade and commerce. Produces gold, silver, and platinum coins for sale to investors.

▶**NONGOVERNMENTAL**

Silver Institute, *1400 Eye St. N.W., #550 20005; (202) 835-0185. Fax, (202) 835-0155. Michael DiRienzo, Executive Director.*
General email, info@silverinstitute.org
Web, www.silverinstitute.org

Membership: companies that mine, refine, fabricate, or manufacture silver or silver-containing products. Conducts research on new technological and industrial uses for silver. Compiles statistics on mining; coinage; and the production, distribution, and use of refined silver.

Silver Users Assn., *3930 Walnut St., Fairfax, VA 22030; (703) 383-1330. Fax, (703) 383-1332. Bill LeRoy, President.*
General email, pmiller@mwcapitol.com
Web, www.silverusersassociation.org

Membership: users of silver, including the photographic industry, silversmiths, and other manufacturers. Conducts research on the silver market; monitors government activities in silver; analyzes government statistics on silver consumption and production. Monitors legislation and regulations.

INDUSTRIAL PRODUCTION, MANUFACTURING

General

▶**AGENCIES**

Bureau of Industry and Security *(Commerce Dept.),* *14th St. and Constitution Ave. N.W., #3898 20230; (202) 482-1455. Fax, (202) 482-6216. Eric L. Hirschhorn, Under Secretary. Press, (202) 482-2721. Export licensing information, (202) 482-4811.*
Web, www.bis.doc.gov

Assists in providing for an adequate supply of strategic and critical materials for defense activities and civilian needs, including military requirements, and other domestic energy supplies; develops plans for industry to meet national emergencies. Studies the effect of imports on national security and recommends actions. Manages the nation's dual-use export control laws and regulations.

Bureau of Labor Statistics (BLS) *(Labor Dept.),* **Industrial Prices and Price Index,** *2 Massachusetts Ave. N.E., #3840 20212-0001; (202) 691-7700. Fax, (202) 691-7754. Nicholas Johnson, Manager, Apparel, Pharmaceuticals, Printing, and Construction Materials Team; David M. Friedman, Assistant Commissioner.*
General email, ppi-info@bls.gov
Web, www.bls.gov/ppi

Compiles statistics on apparel, pharmaceuticals, printing, construction materials, and all U.S. products for the Producer Price Index.

Census Bureau *(Commerce Dept.), Manufacturing and Construction, 4600 Silver Hill Rd., #7K154, Suitland, MD 20746-4600 (mailing address: change city, state, and zip code to Washington, DC 20233-6900); (301) 763-4593. Fax, (301) 763-7783. Mendel D. Gayle, Division Chief.*
Web, www.census.gov/mcd

Collects and distributes manufacturing, construction, and mineral industry data. Reports are organized by commodity, industry, and geographic area.

Economic Development Administration *(Commerce Dept.), 1401 Constitution Ave. N.W., #78006 20230; (202) 482-5081. Fax, (202) 273-4781. Mark Doms, Under Secretary.*
Web, www.eda.gov

Assists U.S. firms in increasing their competitiveness against foreign imports. Certifies eligibility and provides domestic firms and industries adversely affected by increased imports with technical assistance under provisions of the Trade Act of 1974. Administers eleven regional Trade Adjustment Assistance Centers that offer services to eligible U.S. firms.

International Trade Administration (ITA) *(Commerce Dept.), Industry and Analysis, 1401 Constitution Ave. N.W., #3832 20230; (202) 482-1465. Fax, (202) 482-5697. Maureen Smith, Assistant Secretary, Acting; Maureen Smith, Deputy Assistant Secretary.*
General email, tdwebmaster@ita.doc.gov
Web, www.ita.doc.gov/td and www.trade.gov/industry

Conducts industry trade analysis. Shapes U.S. trade policy. Participates in trade negotiations. Organizes trade capacity building programs. Evaluates the impact of domestic and international economic and regulatory policies on U.S. manufacturers and service industries.

Manufacturing Extension Partnership, managed by National Institute of Standards and Technology *(Commerce Dept.), 100 Bureau Dr., MS 4800, Gaithersburg, MD 20899-4800; (301) 975-5020. Fax, (301) 963-6556. Roger D. Kilmer, Director, (301) 975-4676.*
General email, mfg@nist.gov
Web, www.nist.gov/mep

Network of nonprofit centers that assist manufacturers with such issues as process improvements, worker training, sound business practices, and technology transfer.

National Institute of Standards and Technology (NIST) *(Commerce Dept.), Hollings Manufacturing Extension Partnership, 100 Bureau Dr., MS 4800, Gaithersburg, MD 20899-4800; (301) 975-5020. Phillip Singerman, Director, Acting.*
General email, mfg@nist.gov
Web, www.nist.gov/mep/index.cfm

Collaborates with and advises private manufacturers in the United States on innovation strategies, process improvements, green manufacturing, and market diversification.

National Institute of Standards and Technology (NIST) *(Commerce Dept.), Weights and Measures, 100 Bureau Dr., MS 2600, Gaithersburg, MD 20899-2600; (301) 975-4004. Fax, (301) 975-8091. Carol Hockert, Chief.*
General email, owm@nist.gov
Web, www.nist.gov/pml/wmd

Promotes uniform standards among the states for packaging and labeling products and for measuring devices, including scales and commercial measurement instruments; advises manufacturers on labeling and packaging laws and on measuring device standards. Partners with the National Conference on Weights and Measures to develop standards.

▶NONGOVERNMENTAL

American National Standards Institute (ANSI), *1899 L St. N.W., 11th Floor 20036; (202) 293-8020. Fax, (202) 293-9287. Joe Bhatia, President.*
Web, www.ansi.org

Administers and coordinates the voluntary U.S. private sector–led voluntary consensus standards and conformity assessment system. Serves as the official U.S. representative to the International Organization of Standardization (ISO) and, via the U.S. National Committee, the International Electrotechnical Commission (IEC); and is a U.S. representative to the International Accreditation Forum (IAF).

Assn. for Manufacturing Technology, *7901 Westpark Dr., McLean, VA 22102-4206; (703) 893-2900. Fax, (703) 893-1151. Douglas Woods, President.*
General email, amt@amtonline.org
Web, www.amtonline.org

Supports the U.S. manufacturing industry; sponsors workshops and seminars; fosters safety and technical standards. Monitors legislation and regulations.

Can Manufacturers Institute, *1730 Rhode Island Ave. N.W., #1000 20036; (202) 232-4677. Fax, (202) 232-5756. Robert Budway, President.*
Web, www.cancentral.com

Represents can manufacturers and suppliers; promotes the use of the can as a form of food and beverage packaging. Conducts market research. Monitors legislation and regulations.

Envelope Manufacturers Assn., *500 Montgomery St., #550, Alexandria, VA 22314-1565; (703) 739-2200. Fax, (703) 739-2209. Maynard H. Benjamin, President.*
General email, mhbenjamin@envelope.org
Web, www.envelope.org

Membership: envelope manufacturers and suppliers. Monitors legislation and regulations.

Flexible Packaging Assn., *971 Corporate Blvd., #403, Linthicum, MD 21090-2211; (410) 694-0800. Fax, (410) 694-0900. Marla Donahue, President.*

General email, fpa@flexpack.org

Web, www.flexpack.org

Membership: companies that supply or manufacture flexible packaging. Researches packaging trends and technical developments. Compiles industry statistics. Monitors legislation and regulations.

Glass Packaging Institute, *1000 N. Fairfax St., #301A, Alexandria, VA 22314; (703) 684-6359. Fax, (703) 546-0588. Lynn Bragg, President.*

General email, info@gpi.org

Web, www.gpi.org

Membership: manufacturers of glass containers and their suppliers. Promotes industry policies to protect the environment, conserve natural resources, and reduce energy consumption; conducts research; monitors legislation affecting the industry. Interests include glass recycling.

Independent Lubricant Manufacturers Assn., *400 North Columbus St., #201, Alexandria, VA 22314; (703) 684-5574. Fax, (703) 836-8503. Celeste Powers, Executive Director.*

General email, ilma@ilma.org

Web, www.ilma.org

Membership: U.S. and international companies that manufacture automotive, industrial, and metalworking lubricants; associates include suppliers and related businesses. Conducts two workshops and conferences annually; compiles statistics. Monitors legislation and regulations.

Independent Office Products and Furniture Dealers Assn., *3601 E. Joppa Rd., Baltimore, MD 21234; (410) 931-8100. Fax, (410) 931-8111. Michael Tucker, President.*

Web, www.iopfda.org

Membership: independent dealers of office products and office furniture. Serves independent dealers and works with their trading partners to develop programs and opportunities that help strengthen the dealer position in the marketplace.

Industrial Designers Society of America, *555 Grove St., #200, Herndon, VA 20170; (703) 707-6000. Fax, (703) 787-8501. Daniel Martinage, Chief Executive Officer.*

General email, idsa@idsa.org

Web, www.idsa.org

Membership: designers of products, equipment, instruments, furniture, transportation, packages, exhibits, information services, and related services, and educators of industrial design. Provides the Bureau of Labor Statistics with industry information. Monitors legislation and regulations.

Industrial Energy Consumers of America, *1155 15th St. N.W., #500 20005; (202) 223-1420. Fax, (202) 530-0659. Paul N. Cicio, President.*

Web, www.ieca-us.com

National trade association that represents the manufacturing industry and advocates on energy, environmental, and public policy issues. Advocates for greater diversity of and lower costs for energy. Monitors legislation and regulations.

Industrial Research Institute Inc., *2300 Clarendon Blvd., #400, Arlington, VA 22201; (703) 647-2580. Fax, (703) 647-2581. Edward Bernstein, President.*

Web, www.iriweb.org

Membership: companies that maintain laboratories for industrial research. Seeks to improve the process of industrial research by promoting cooperative efforts among companies, between the academic and research communities, and between industry and the government. Monitors legislation and regulations concerning technology, industry, and national competitiveness.

International Sleep Products Assn., *501 Wythe St., Alexandria, VA 22314-1917; (703) 683-8371. Fax, (703) 683-4503. Ryan Trainer, President.*

General email, info@sleepproducts.org

Web, www.sleepproducts.org

Membership: manufacturers of bedding and mattresses. Compiles statistics on the industry. (Affiliated with Sleep Products Safety Council and the Better Sleep Council.)

Clothing and Textiles

► **AGENCIES**

American Fiber Manufacturers Assn., *1530 Wilson Blvd., #690, Arlington, VA 22209; (703) 875-0432. Fax, (703) 875-0907. Paul T. O'Day, President.*

General email, feb@afma.org

Web, www.fibersource.com

Membership: U.S. manufacturers of synthetic and cellulosic fibers, filaments, and yarns. Interests include international trade, education, and environmental and technical services. Monitors legislation and regulations.

International Trade Administration (ITA) *(Commerce Dept.), Industry and Analysis, Textiles and Apparel, 1401 Constitution Ave. N.W., #3001 20230; (202) 482-5078. Fax, (202) 482-2331. Kimberley (Kim) Glas, Deputy Assistant Secretary, (202) 482-3737; Janet Heinzen, Director.*

General email, otexa@trade.gov

Web, http://otexa.ita.doc.gov

Participates in negotiating bilateral textile and apparel import restraint agreements; responsible for export expansion programs and reduction of nontariff barriers for textile and apparel goods; provides data on economic conditions in the domestic textile and apparel markets, including impact of imports.

► **NONGOVERNMENTAL**

American Apparel and Footwear Assn. (AAFA), *1601 N. Kent St., #1200, Arlington, VA 22209; (703) 524-1864. Fax, (703) 522-6741. Steven E. Lamar, President. Toll-free, (800) 520-2262.*

Web, www.apparelandfootwear.org

Membership: manufacturers of apparel, sewn products, footwear and their suppliers, importers, and distributors. Provides members with information on the industry, including import and export data. Interests include product flammability and trade promotion. Monitors legislation and regulations.

American Fiber Manufacturers Assn., *1530 Wilson Blvd., #690, Arlington, VA 22209; (703) 875-0432. Fax, (703) 875-0907. Paul T. O'Day, President.*
General email, feb@afma.org
Web, www.fibersource.com

Membership: U.S. manufacturers of synthetic and cellulosic fibers, filaments, and yarns. Interests include international trade, education, and environmental and technical services. Monitors legislation and regulations.

American Textile Machinery Assn., *201 Park Washington Court, Falls Church, VA 22046-4527; (703) 538-1789. Fax, (703) 241-5603. Clay D. Tyeryar, President.*
General email, info@atmanet.org
Web, www.atmanet.org

Membership: U.S.-based manufacturers of textile machinery and related parts and accessories. Interests include competitiveness and expansion of foreign markets. Monitors legislation and regulations.

Dry Cleaning and Laundry Institute, *14700 Sweitzer Lane, Laurel, MD 20707; (301) 622-1900. Fax, (240) 295-0865. Mary Scalco, Chief Executive Officer. Toll-free, (800) 638-2627.*
General email, techline@dlionline.org
Web, www.dlionline.org

Membership: dry cleaners and launderers. Conducts research and provides information on products and services. Monitors legislation and regulations.

Footwear Distributors and Retailers of America, *1319 F St. N.W., #700 20004-1179; (202) 737-5660. Fax, (202) 645-0789. Richard (Matt) Priest, President.*
General email, info@fdra.org
Web, www.fdra.org

Membership: companies that operate shoe retail outlets and wholesale footwear companies with U.S. and global brands. Provides business support and government relations to members. Interests include intellectual property rights, ocean shipping rates, trade with China, and labeling regulations.

National Cotton Council of America, *Washington Office, 1521 New Hampshire Ave. N.W. 20036-1205; (202) 745-7805. Fax, (202) 483-4040. A. John Maguire, Senior Vice President.*
Web, www.cotton.org

Membership: all segments of the U.S. cotton industry. Formulates positions on trade policy and negotiations; seeks to improve competitiveness of U.S. exports; sponsors programs to educate the public about flammable fabrics. (Headquarters in Memphis, Tenn.)

National Council of Textile Organizations, *1001 Connecticut Ave. N.W., #315 20036; (202) 822-8028. Fax, (202) 822-8029. Augustine Tantillo, President.*
Web, www.ncto.org

Membership: U.S. companies that spin, weave, knit, or finish textiles from natural fibers, and associate members from affiliated industries. Interests include domestic and world markets. Monitors legislation and regulations.

UNITE HERE, *Washington Office, 1775 K St. N.W., #620 20006-1530; (202) 393-4373. Fax, (202) 223-6213. Tom Snyder, Political Director; John W. Wilhelm, President.*
Web, www.unitehere.org

Membership: more than 270,000 workers in the United States and Canada who work in the hospitality, gaming, food service, manufacturing, textile, laundry, and airport industries. Assists members with contract negotiation and grievances; conducts training programs and workshops. Monitors legislation and regulations. (Headquarters in New York. Formed by the merger of the former Union of Needletrades, Textiles and Industrial Employees and the Hotel Employees and Restaurant Employees International Union.)

Electronics and Appliances

▶**NONGOVERNMENTAL**

AHRI (Air-Conditioning, Heating, and Refrigeration Institute), *2111 Wilson Blvd., #500, Arlington, VA 22201; (703) 524-8800. Fax, (703) 562-1942. Stephen R. Yurek, President.*
General email, ahri@ahrinet.org
Web, www.ari.org

Membership: manufacturers of gas appliances and equipment for residential and commercial use and related industries. Advocates product improvement; provides market statistics. Monitors legislation and regulations. (Merger of the Air-Conditioning and Refrigeration Institute [ARI] and the Gas Appliance Manufacturers Assn. [GAMA].)

Assn. of Electrical and Medical Imaging Equipment Manufacturers (NEMA), *1300 N. 17th St., #900, Rosslyn, VA 22209-3801; (703) 841-3200. Fax, (703) 841-5900. Evan Gaddis, President. Press, (703) 841-3241.*
Web, www.nema.org

Membership: manufacturers of products used in the generation, transmission, distribution, control, and end-use of electricity, including manufacturers of medical diagnostic imaging equipment. Develops technical standards; collects, analyzes, and disseminates industry data. Interests include Smart Grid, high-performance building, carbon footprint, energy storage, and an intelligence portal. Monitors legislation, regulations, and international trade activities.

Consumer Electronics Assn., *1919 S. Eads St., Arlington, VA 22202; (703) 907-7600. Fax, (703) 907-7675. Gary*

Shapiro, President. Toll-free, (866) 858-1555. Press, (703) 907-7650.
General email, cea@ce.org
Web, www.ce.org

Membership: 2,000 U.S. consumer electronics companies. Promotes the industry; sponsors seminars and conferences; conducts research; consults with member companies. Monitors legislation and regulations. (Affiliated with Electronic Industries Alliance.)

Electronic Components Industry Association, 2214 Rock Hill Rd., #170, Herndon, VA 20170; (571) 323-0294. Fax, (571) 323-0245. John Denslinger, President.
Web, www.eciaonline.org

Membership: manufacturers, distributors, and manufacturer representatives of electronic components and semiconductor products. Provides information and data on industry trends; advocates for the authorized sale of electronics components to prevent counterfeit product moving through the supply chain. Monitors legislation and regulations.

National Electrical Contractors Assn., 3 Bethesda Metro Center, #1100, Bethesda, MD 20814; (301) 657-3110. Fax, (301) 215-4500. John Grau, Chief Executive Officer.
Web, www.necanet.org

Membership: electrical contractors who build and service electrical wiring and equipment, including high-voltage construction and service. Represents members in collective bargaining with union workers; sponsors research and educational programs.

Optoelectronics Industry Development Assn., 2010 Massachusetts Ave. N.W. 20036; (202) 416-1982. Fax, (202) 416-1408. Claudio Mazzali, Chair.
General email, oidainfo@oida.org
Web, www.oida.org

Membership: optoelectronics components and systems providers, businesses, and research institutions in North America. Activities include workshops and conferences, industry reports, and advocacy. Monitors legislation and regulations. (Affiliated with the Optical Society.)

Steel, Metalworking, Machinery

▶ **NONGOVERNMENTAL**

American Boiler Manufacturers Assn., 8221 Old Courthouse Rd., #202, Vienna, VA 22182; (703) 356-7172. Fax, (703) 356-4543. Diana McClung, Director, Interim; Kevin Hoey, Chair.
Web, www.abma.com

Membership: manufacturers of boiler systems and boiler-related products, including fuel-burning systems. Interests include energy and environmental issues.

American Gear Manufacturers Assn., 1001 N. Fairfax St., #500, Alexandria, VA 22314; (703) 684-0211. Fax, (703) 684-0242. Joe T. Franklin Jr., President.

General email, agma@agma.org
Web, www.agma.org

Membership: gear manufacturers, suppliers, and industry consultants. Conducts workshops, seminars, and conferences; develops industry standards; sponsors research. Monitors legislation and regulations.

American Institute for International Steel, 701 W. Broad St., #301, Falls Church, VA 22046; (703) 245-8075. Fax, (703) 610-0215. Richard Chriss, President, ext. 301.
General email, chriss@aiis.org
Web, www.aiis.org

Membership: importers and exporters of steel, logistics companies, and port authorities. Conducts research and provides analysis on steel market and importing and exporting. Holds annual conferences.

American Wire Producers Assn., 7011 A Manchester Blvd., #178, Alexandria, VA 22314-3202; (703) 299-4434. Fax, (703) 299-9233. Kimberly A. Korbel, Executive Director.
General email, info@awpa.org
Web, www.awpa.org

Membership: companies that produce carbon, alloy, and stainless steel wire and wire products in the United States, Canada, and Mexico. Interests include imports of rod, wire, and wire products. Publishes survey of the domestic wire industry. Monitors legislation and regulations.

International Assn. of Bridge, Structural, Ornamental, and Reinforcing Iron Workers, 1750 New York Ave. N.W., #400 20006; (202) 383-4800. Fax, (202) 638-4856. Walter W. Wise, President.
General email, iwmagazine@iwintl.org
Web, www.ironworkers.org

Membership: approximately 140,000 iron workers. Helps members negotiate pay, benefits, and better working conditions; conducts training programs and workshops. Monitors legislation and regulations. (Affiliated with the AFL-CIO.)

International Assn. of Machinists and Aerospace Workers, 9000 Machinists Pl., Upper Marlboro, MD 20772-2687; (301) 967-4500. Fax, (301) 967-4588. R. Thomas Buffenbarger, International President. Information, (301) 967-4520.
General email, websteward@iamaw.org
Web, www.goiam.org

Membership: machinists in more than 200 industries. Helps members negotiate pay, benefits, and better working conditions; conducts training programs and workshops. Monitors legislation and regulations. (Affiliated with the AFL-CIO, the Canadian Labour Congress, the International Metalworkers Federation, the International Transport Workers' Federation, and the Railway Labor Executives Assn.)

Machinery Dealers National Assn., 315 S. Patrick St., Alexandria, VA 22314; (703) 836-9300. Fax, (703)

836-9303. *Mark Robinson, Executive Vice President.*
Toll-free, (800) 872-7807.
General email, office@mdna.org
Web, www.mdna.org

Membership: companies that buy and sell used capital equipment. Establishes a code of ethics for members; publishes a buyer's guide that lists members by types of machinery they sell.

Outdoor Power Equipment Institute, *341 S. Patrick St., Alexandria, VA 22314; (703) 549-7600. Fax, (703) 549-7604. Kris Kiser, President.*
General email, info@opei.org
Web, www.opei.org

Membership: manufacturers of powered lawn and garden maintenance products, components, and attachments, and their suppliers. Promotes safe use of outdoor power equipment; keeps statistics on the industry; fosters exchange of information. Monitors legislation and regulations.

Packaging Machinery Manufacturers Institute, *11911 Freedom Dr., #600, Reston, VA 20190; (703) 243-8555. Fax, (703) 243-8556. Charles D. Yuska, President.*
General email, communications@pmmi.org
Web, www.pmmi.org

Membership: manufacturers of packaging, machinery, packaging-related converting machinery, components, processing materials, and containers. Provides industry information and statistics; offers educational programs to members.

Sheet Metal Workers International Assn., *1750 New York Ave. N.W., 6th Floor 20006; (202) 783-5880. Fax, (202) 662-0880. Joseph J. Nigro, General President.*
Web, www.smwia.org

Membership: U.S., Puerto Rican, and Canadian workers in the building and construction trades, manufacturing, and the railroad and shipyard industries. Assists members with contract negotiation and grievances; conducts training programs and workshops. Monitors legislation and regulations. (Affiliated with the Sheet Metal and Air Conditioning Contractors' Assn., the AFL-CIO, and the Canadian Labour Congress.)

Specialty Steel Industry of North America, *3050 K St. N.W., #400 20007; (202) 342-8630. Fax, (202) 342-8451. Carl R. Moulton, Chair. Toll-free, (800) 982-0355.*
Web, www.ssina.com

Membership: manufacturers of products in stainless and other specialty steels. Establishes manufacturing techniques and issues technical guides; operates a hotline for technical questions.

Steel Manufacturers Assn., *1150 Connecticut Ave. N.W., #715 20036-3101; (202) 296-1515. Fax, (202) 296-2506. Phil Bell, President.*
General email, webmail@steelnet.org
Web, www.steelnet.org

Membership: steel producers and their vendors in North America. Helps members exchange information on technical matters; provides information on the steel industry to the public and government. Monitors legislation and regulations.

United Steelworkers, Paper & Forestry, Rubber, Manufacturing, *Allied Indust. & Service Workers International Union, Washington Office, 1155 Connecticut Ave. N.W., #500 20036; (202) 778-4384. Fax, (202) 419-1486. Holly Hart, Legislative Director.*
Web, www.usw.org

Membership: more than 850,000 workers in the steel, paper, rubber, energy, chemical, pharmaceutical, and allied industries. Helps members negotiate pay, benefits, and better working conditions; conducts training programs and workshops. Monitors legislation and regulations. (Headquarters in Pittsburgh, Pa.; affiliated with the AFL-CIO.)

INSURANCE

General

▶**AGENCIES**

Federal Emergency Management Agency (FEMA) (Homeland Security Dept.), *Federal Insurance and Mitigation Administration, 1800 S. Bell St., MS 3020, Arlington, VA 22202; (202) 646-2781. Fax, (202) 646-7970. David L. Miller, Associate Administrator.*
Web, www.fema.gov/what-mitigation/federal-insurance-mitigation-administration

Administers federal flood insurance programs, including the National Flood Insurance Program. Makes low-cost flood insurance available to eligible homeowners.

Small Business Administration (SBA), *Disaster Assistance, 409 3rd St. S.W., #6050 20416; (202) 205-6734. Fax, (202) 205-7728. James Rivera, Associate Administrator. Call center, (800) 659-2955.*
Web, www.sba.gov/about-offices-content/1/2462

Provides victims of physical disasters with disaster and economic injury loans for homes, businesses, and personal property. Lends funds for uncompensated losses incurred from any disaster declared by the president of the United States or the administrator of the SBA. Lends funds to individual homeowners, business concerns of all sizes, and nonprofit institutions to repair or replace damaged structures and furnishings, business machinery, equipment, and inventory. Provides economic injury loans to small businesses for losses to meet necessary operating expenses, provided the business could have paid these expenses prior to the disaster.

▶**CONGRESS**

For a listing of relevant congressional committees and subcommittees, please see pages 32–33 or the Appendix.

▶NONGOVERNMENTAL

American Academy of Actuaries, *1850 M St. N.W., #300 20036; (202) 223-8196. Fax, (202) 872-1948. Mary Downs, Executive Director.*
Web, www.actuary.org

Membership: professional actuaries practicing in the areas of life, health, liability, property, and casualty insurance; pensions; government insurance plans; and general consulting. Provides information on actuarial matters, including insurance and pensions; develops professional standards; advises public policymakers.

American Assn. for Justice, *777 6th St. N.W., #200 20001; (202) 965-3500. Fax, (202) 342-5484. Linda Lipsen, Chief Executive Officer. Toll-free, (800) 424-2725.*
General email, aaj@justice.org
Web, www.justice.org

Membership: attorneys, judges, law professors, and students. Interests include aspects of legal and legislative activity relating to the adversary system and trial by jury, including property and casualty insurance. (Formerly the Assn. of Trial Lawyers of America.)

American Council of Life Insurers, *101 Constitution Ave. N.W., #700 20001-2133; (202) 624-2000. Fax, (202) 624-2319. Dirk A. Kempthorne, President.*
Web, www.acli.com

Membership: life insurance companies authorized to do business in the United States. Conducts research and compiles statistics at state and federal levels. Monitors legislation and regulations.

American Insurance Assn., *2101 L St. N.W., #400 20037; (202) 828-7100. Fax, (202) 293-1219. Leigh Ann Pusey, President.*
General email, info@aiadc.org
Web, www.aiadc.org

Membership: companies providing property and casualty insurance. Conducts public relations and educational activities; provides information on issues related to property and casualty insurance.

American Society of Pension Professionals and Actuaries, *4245 N. Fairfax Dr., #750, Arlington, VA 22203-1648; (703) 516-9300. Fax, (703) 516-9308. Brian Graff, Executive Director.*
General email, asppa@asppa.org
Web, www.asppa.org

Membership: administrators, actuaries, advisers, lawyers, accountants, and other financial services professionals who provide consulting and administrative services for employee-based retirement plans. Sponsors educational conferences, webcasts, and credentialing programs for retirement professionals. Monitors legislation and regulations.

Assn. for Advanced Life Underwriting, *11921 Freedom Dr., #1100, Reston, VA 20190; 101 Constitution Ave., Suite 703 East 20001; (703) 641-9400. Fax, (703) 641-9885.*

David J. Stertzer, Chief Executive Officer. Toll-free, (888) 275-0092.
General email, info@aalu.org
Web, www.aalu.org

Membership: specialized underwriters in the fields of estate analysis, charitable planning, business insurance, pension planning, and employee benefit plans. Monitors legislation and regulations on small-business taxes and capital formation. (Maintains an additional office in Washington, D.C.)

Consumer Federation of America, *1620 Eye St. N.W., #200 20006; (202) 387-6121. Fax, (202) 265-7989. Stephen Brobeck, Executive Director. Press, (202) 737-0766.*
General email, cfa@consumerfed.org
Web, www.consumerfed.org

Federation of national, regional, state, and local pro-consumer organizations. Promotes consumer interests in banking, credit, and insurance; telecommunications; housing; food, drugs, and medical care; safety; and energy and natural resources development.

Council of Insurance Agents and Brokers, *701 Pennsylvania Ave. N.W., #750 20004; (202) 783-4400. Fax, (202) 783-4410. Ken A. Crerar, President.*
General email, ciab@ciab.com
Web, www.ciab.com

Represents commercial property and casualty insurance agencies and brokerage firms. Members offer insurance products and risk management services to business, government, and the public.

ERISA Industry Committee, *1400 L St. N.W., #350 20005; (202) 789-1400. Fax, (202) 789-1120. Scott Macey, President, (202) 627-1910.*
General email, eric@eric.org
Web, www.eric.org

Membership: major U.S. employers. Advocates members' positions on employee retirement, health care coverage, and welfare benefit plans. Monitors legislation and regulations.

GAMA International, *2901 Telestar Court, #140, Falls Church, VA 22042-1205; (571) 499-4300. Fax, (571) 499-4302. Jeffrey R. (Jeff) Hughes, Chief Executive Officer. Information, (800) 345-2687.*
General email, info@gamaweb.com
Web, www.gamaweb.com

Membership: general agents and managers who provide life insurance and related financial products and services. Provides information, education, and training for members.

Independent Insurance Agents and Brokers of America, *127 S. Peyton St., Alexandria, VA 22314; (703) 683-4422. Fax, (703) 683-7556. Robert Rusbuldt, President. Toll-free, (800) 221-7917.*
General email, info@iiaba.net
Web, www.independentagent.com

Provides educational and advisory services; researches issues pertaining to auto, home, business, life, and health insurance; offers cooperative advertising program to members. Political action committee monitors legislation and regulations.

National Assn. of Independent Life Brokerage Agencies, *11325 Random Hills Rd., #110, Fairfax, VA 22030; (703) 383-3081. Fax, (703) 383-6942. Jack Chiasson, Executive Director.*
Web, www.nailba.org

Membership: owners of independent life insurance agencies. Fosters the responsible and effective distribution of life and health insurance and related financial services; provides a forum for exchange of information among members. Monitors legislation and regulations.

National Assn. of Insurance and Financial Advisors, *2901 Telestar Court, Falls Church, VA 22042-1205; (703) 770-8100. Susan Waters, Chief Executive Officer. Toll-free, (877) 866-2432.*
General email, membersupport@naifa.org
Web, www.naifa.org

Federation of state and local life underwriters, agents, and financial advisers. Provides information on life and health insurance and other financial services; sponsors education and training programs.

National Assn. of Insurance Commissioners, *Washington Office, 444 N. Capitol St. N.W., #701 20001-1509; (202) 471-3990. Fax, (816) 460-7493. Hon. Ben Nelson, Chief Executive Officer.*
Web, www.naic.org

Membership: state insurance commissioners, directors, and supervisors. Provides members with information on legal and market conduct, and financial services; publishes research and statistics on the insurance industry. Monitors legislation and regulations. (Affiliated with the Center for Insurance Policy and Research. Headquarters in Kansas City, Mo.)

National Assn. of Professional Insurance Agents, *400 N. Washington St., Alexandria, VA 22314-2353; (703) 836-9340. Fax, (703) 836-1279. Mike Becker, Executive Vice President; Jon Gentile, Assistant Vice President, Federal Affairs, (703) 518-1365. Information, (800) 742-6900. Press, (703) 518-1352.*
General email, web@pianet.org
Web, www.pianet.com

Membership: independent insurance agents and brokers. Provides basic and continuing education for agents through courses, seminars, and educational materials. Monitors legislation and regulations.

Nonprofit Risk Management Center, *15 N. King St., #203, Leesburg, VA 20176; (202) 785-3891. Fax, (703) 443-1990. Melanie L. Herman, Executive Director.*
General email, info@nonprofitrisk.org
Web, www.nonprofitrisk.org

Provides information on insurance and risk management issues through conferences, consulting, online tools, and publications for nonprofit organizations.

Property Casualty Insurers Assn. of America, *Washington Office, 444 N. Capitol St., #801 20001; (202) 639-0490. Fax, (202) 639-0494. David A. Sampson, Chief Executive Officer.*
Web, www.pciaa.net

Membership: companies providing property and casualty insurance. Monitors legislation and compiles statistics; interests include personal and commercial property and casualty insurance. (Headquarters in Chicago, Ill.)

Reinsurance Assn. of America, *1445 New York Ave. N.W., 7th Floor 20005; (202) 638-3690. Fax, (202) 638-0936. Franklin W. Nutter, President.*
General email, infobox@reinsurance.org
Web, www.reinsurance.org

Membership: companies writing property and casualty reinsurance. Monitors legislation and regulations.

PATENTS, COPYRIGHTS, AND TRADEMARKS

General

▶**AGENCIES**

Justice Dept. (DOJ), *Civil Division, Intellectual Property, 1100 L St. N.W., #11116 20005; (202) 514-7223. Fax, (202) 307-0345. John Fargo, Director.*
General email, john.fargo@usdoj.gov
Web, www.justice.gov/civil/commercial/intellectual/c-ip.html

Represents the United States in patent, copyright, and trademark cases. Includes the defense of patent infringement suits; legal proceedings to establish government priority of invention; defense of administrative acts of the Register of Copyrights; and actions on behalf of the government involving the use of trademarks.

Patent and Trademark Office *(Commerce Dept.), 600 Dulany St., Madison West Bldg., #10-D44, Alexandria, VA 22314 (mailing address: P.O. Box 1450, Alexandria, VA 22313-1450); (571) 272-1000. Fax, (571) 273-8300. Vacant, Under Secretary; Michelle Lee, Deputy Director. Customer support, (800) 786-9199. Press, (571) 272-8400. Patent search library, (571) 272-3275.*
Web, www.uspto.gov

Grants patents, registers trademarks, and provides patent and trademark information. Library and search file of U.S. and foreign patents available for public use.

State Dept., *Intellectual Property Enforcement, 2201 C St. N.W., #4931 20520-4931; (202) 647-3251. Fax, (202) 647-1537. Jean A. Bonilla, Director.*
Web, www.state.gov

Handles multilateral and bilateral policy formulation involving patents, copyrights, and trademarks, and international industrial property of U.S. nationals.

U.S. Customs and Border Protection *(Homeland Security Dept.), Intellectual Property Rights and Restrictions,* 1300 Pennsylvania Ave. N.W., Mint Annex 20229; (202) 325-0020. Fax, (202) 572-8744. Charles Stewart, Chief.
General email, hqiprbranch@dhs.gov
Web, www.cbp.gov

Responsible for customs recordation of registered trademarks and copyrights. Enforces rules and regulations pertaining to intellectual property rights. Coordinates enforcement of International Trade Commission exclusion orders against unfairly competing goods. Determines admissibility of restricted merchandise and cultural properties. Provides support to and coordinates with international organizations and the Office of the U.S. Trade Representative.

►CONGRESS

For a listing of relevant congressional committees and subcommittees, please see pages 32–33 or the Appendix.

Library of Congress, *Copyright Office,* 101 Independence Ave. S.E., #403 20540; (202) 707-8350. Maria A. Pallante, Register of Copyrights. Information, (202) 707-3000; (877) 476-0778. Forms and publications hotline, (202) 707-9100.
Web, www.copyright.gov

Provides information on copyright registration procedures and requirements, copyright law, and international copyrights; registers copyright claims and maintains public records of copyright registrations. Copyright record searches conducted on an hourly fee basis. Files open to public for research during weekday business hours. Does not give legal advice on copyright matters.

►JUDICIARY

U.S. Court of Appeals for the Federal Circuit, 717 Madison Pl. N.W. 20439; (202) 275-8000. Fax, (202) 275-8036. Randall R. Rader, Chief Judge, (202) 633-6297; Jan Horbaly, Clerk, (202) 312-5520. Helpdesk, (202) 275-8040; (855) 860-8240. Mediation, (202) 275-8120.
Web, www.cafc.uscourts.gov

Reviews decisions of U.S. Patent and Trademark Office on applications and interferences regarding patents and trademarks; hears appeals on patent infringement cases from district courts.

►NONGOVERNMENTAL

American Intellectual Property Law Assn., 241 18th St. South, #700, Arlington, VA 22202; (703) 415-0780. Fax, (703) 415-0786. Q. Todd Dickinson, Executive Director; Judy Curvan, Assistant, (703) 412-4349.
General email, aipla@aipla.org
Web, www.aipla.org

Membership: lawyers practicing in the field of patents, trademarks, and copyrights (intellectual property law). Holds continuing legal education conferences.

Assn. of American Publishers, *Government Affairs,* 455 Massachusetts Ave. N.W., #700 20001; (202) 347-3375. Fax, (202) 347-3690. Allan R. Adler, Vice President, Legal and Government Affairs.
General email, info@publishers.org
Web, www.publishers.org

Represents U.S. book and journal publishing industry priorities on policy, legislation, and regulatory issues regionally, nationally, and worldwide. Interests include intellectual property rights, worldwide copyright enforcement, digital and new technology issues, tax and trade, and First Amendment rights.

Intellectual Property Owners Assn., 1501 M St. N.W., #1150 20005; (202) 507-4500. Fax, (202) 507-4501. Herbert C. Wamsley, Executive Director; Samantha Garner Jakhelln, Director of Government Relations.
General email, info@ipo.org
Web, www.ipo.org

Monitors and advocates for intellectual property legislation. Conducts educational programs to protect intellectual property through patents, trademarks, copyrights, and trade secret laws.

International Anticounterfeiting Coalition, 1730 M St. N.W., #1020 20036; (202) 223-6667. Fax, (202) 223-6668. Robert Barchiesi, President.
General email, meghang@iacc.org
Web, www.iacc.org

Works to combat counterfeiting and piracy by promoting laws, regulations, and directives to render theft of intellectual property unprofitable. Oversees anticounterfeiting programs that increase patent, trademark, copyright, service mark, trade dress, and trade secret protection. Provides information and training to law enforcement officials to help identify counterfeit and pirate products.

International Intellectual Property Alliance, 1818 N St. N.W., 8th Floor 20036; (202) 355-7900. Fax, (202) 355-7899. Michael Schlesinger, Counsel.
General email, info@iipa.com
Web, www.iipa.com

Represents U.S. copyright-based industries in efforts to improve international protection of copyrighted materials. Monitors legislation domestically and abroad; promotes enforcement reform abroad.

National Assn. of Manufacturers (NAM), *Technology Policy,* 733 10th St. N.W., #700 20001; (202) 637-3096. Fax, (202) 637-3182. Bryan Raymond, Director, (202) 637-3072.
Web, www.nam.org

Represents manufacturers in government and the media, advocating pro-manufacturing positions on technology policy issues, including cybersecurity, telecommunication,

R&D funding, and intellectual property protection; develops policy and legislation on patents, copyrights, trademarks, and trade secrets; works with the broader business community to advance pro-growth, pro-competitiveness technology policy

National Music Publishers' Assn., *975 F St. N.W., #375 20004; (202) 393-6672. Fax, (202) 393-6673. David M. Israelite, President. General email, pr@nmpa.org*

Web, www.nmpa.org

Works to enforce music copyrights. Sponsors litigation against copyright violators. Monitors and interprets legislation and regulations.

National School Boards Assn., *1680 Duke St., Alexandria, VA 22314; (703) 838-6722. Fax, (703) 549-7590. Thomas Gentzel, Executive Director, (703) 838-6700; Francisco Negron, General Counsel, (703) 838-6710. General email, info@nsba.org*

Web, www.nsba.org

Promotes a broad interpretation of copyright law to permit legitimate scholarly use of published and musical works, videotaped programs, and materials for computer-assisted instruction.

U.S. Chamber of Commerce, *Congressional and Public Affairs, 1615 H St. N.W. 20062-2000; (202) 463-5600. Fax, (202) 544-4157. Jack Howard, Senior Vice President. Web, www.uschamber.com*

Monitors legislation and regulations on patents, copyrights, and trademarks.

SALES AND SERVICES

General

▶AGENCIES

Bureau of Labor Statistics (BLS) *(Labor Dept.), Prices and Living Conditions, 2 Massachusetts Ave. N.E., #3120 20212-0001; (202) 691-6960. Fax, (202) 691-7080. Michael W. Horrigan, Associate Commissioner. Information, (202) 691-7000. Web, www.bls.gov/cpi*

Collects, processes, analyzes, and disseminates data relating to prices and consumer expenditures; maintains the Consumer Price Index.

Census Bureau *(Commerce Dept.), Service Sector Statistics, 4700 Silver Hill Rd., #8K154, Suitland, MD 20746-2401 (mailing address: change city, state, and zip code Washington, DC 20233-6500); (301) 763-5170. Fax, (301) 763-6843. Vacant, Chief. Web, www.census.gov/econ/services.html*

Provides data of five-year census programs on retail, wholesale, and service industries. Conducts periodic monthly or annual surveys for specific items within these industries.

▶NONGOVERNMENTAL

American Wholesale Marketers Assn., *2750 Prosperity Ave., #530, Fairfax, VA 22031; (703) 208-3358. Fax, (703) 573-5738. Scott Ramminger, President. General email, info@awmanet.org*

Web, www.awmanet.org

Membership: wholesalers, manufacturers, retailers, and brokers who sell or distribute convenience products. Conducts educational programs. Monitors legislation and regulations.

ASIS International, *1625 Prince St., Alexandria, VA 22314-2818; (703) 519-6200. Fax, (703) 519-6299. Michael J. Stack, Chief Executive Officer. General email, asis@asisonline.org*

Web, www.asisonline.org

Membership: security administrators who oversee physical and logistical security for private and public organizations, including law enforcement and the military. Develops security standards; offers educational programs and materials on general and industry-specific practices; and administers certification programs.

Council of Better Business Bureaus, *3033 Wilson Blvd., #600, Arlington, VA 22201-3843; (703) 276-0100. Fax, (703) 525-8277. Carrie Hurt, President, Interim. Web, www.bbb.org*

Membership: businesses and Better Business Bureaus in the United States and Canada. Promotes ethical business practices and truth in national advertising; mediates disputes between consumers and businesses.

Equipment Leasing and Finance Assn., *1825 K St. N.W., #900 20006; (202) 238-3400. Fax, (202) 238-3401. William G. Sutton, President. General email, wsutton@elfaonline.org*

Web, www.elfaonline.org

Membership: independent leasing companies, banks, financial service companies, and independent brokers and suppliers to the leasing industry. Promotes the interests of the equipment leasing and finance industry; assists in the resolution of industry problems; encourages standards. Monitors legislation and regulations.

Grocery Manufacturers Assn. (GMA), *1350 Eye St. N.W., #300 20005-3377; (202) 639-5900. Fax, (202) 639-5932. Pamela Bailey, President. Press, (202) 295-3938. General email, info@gmaonline.org*

Web, www.gmaonline.org

Membership: sales and marketing agents and retail merchandisers of food and consumer products worldwide. Sponsors research, training, and educational programs for members and their trading partners. Monitors legislation and regulations.

International Cemetery, Cremation, and Funeral Assn., *107 Carpenter Dr., #100, Sterling, VA 20164; (703) 391-8400. Fax, (703) 391-8416. Robert M. Fells, Executive Director, ext. 1212. Information, (800) 645-7700.*

General email, rfells@iccfa.com

Web, www.iccfa.com

Membership: owners and operators of cemeteries, crematories, funeral homes, mausoleums, and columbariums. Promotes the building and proper maintenance of modern interment places; promotes high ethical standards in the industry; encourages pre-arrangement of funerals.

International Council of Shopping Centers, *Global Public Policy,* *555 12th St. N.W., #660 20004; (202) 626-1400. Fax, (202) 626-1418. Betsy Laird, Senior Vice President; Christopher Gerlach, Director, Public Policy Research, (202) 626-1413.*

General email, gpp@icsc.org

Web, www.icsc.org

Membership: shopping center owners, developers, managers, retailers, contractors, and others in the industry worldwide. Provides information, including research data. Monitors legislation and regulations. (Headquarters in New York.)

International Franchise Assn., *1501 K St. N.W., #350 20005; (202) 628-8000. Fax, (202) 628-0812. Stephen J. Caldeira, President.*

General email, ifa@franchise.org

Web, www.franchise.org

Membership: national and international franchisers. Sponsors seminars, workshops, trade shows, and conferences. Monitors legislation and regulations.

National Assn. of Convenience Stores (NACS), *1600 Duke St., #700, Alexandria, VA 22314-3421; (703) 684-3600. Fax, (703) 836-4564. Henry Armour, President. Toll-free, (800) 966-6227.*

General email, nacs@nacsonline.com

Web, www.nacsonline.com

Membership: convenience store retailers and industry suppliers. Advocates industry position on labor, tax, environment, alcohol, and food-related issues; conducts research and training programs. Monitors legislation and regulations.

National Assn. of Wholesaler-Distributors, *1325 G St. N.W., #1000 20005-3100; (202) 872-0885. Fax, (202) 785-0586. Dirk Van Dongen, President.*

General email, naw@nawd.org

Web, www.naw.org

Membership: wholesale distributors and trade associations, product sellers, manufacturers, and their insurers. Provides members and government policymakers with research, education, and government relations information. Promotes federal product liability tort reform. Monitors legislation and regulations.

National Retail Federation, *325 7th St. N.W., #1100 20004-2802; (202) 783-7971. Fax, (202) 737-2849. Matthew R. Shay, President; David French, Senior Vice President, Government Relations. Toll-free, (800) 673-4692.*

Web, www.nrf.com

Membership: international, national, and state associations of retailers and major retail corporations. Concerned with federal regulatory activities and legislation that affect retailers, including tax, employment, trade, and credit issues. Provides information on retailing through seminars, conferences, and publications.

Personal Care Products Council, *1620 L St. N.W., #1200 20036; (202) 331-1770. Fax, (202) 331-1969. Lezlee Westine, President.*

Web, www.personalcarecouncil.org; www.cosmeticsinfo.org

Membership: manufacturers and distributors of finished personal care products. Conducts product safety research and advocacy. Represents the industry at the local, state, and national levels. Interests include legal issues, international trade, legislation, and regulatory policy. (Formerly Cosmetic, Toiletry, and Fragrance Assn.)

Retail Industry Leaders Assn., *1700 N. Moore St., #2250, Arlington, VA 22209-1998; (703) 841-2300. Fax, (703) 841-1184. Sandra (Sandy) Kennedy, President.*

Web, www.rila.org

Membership: retailers, consumer product manufacturers, and service suppliers in the United States and abroad. Interests include supply chain, trade, finance, asset protection, and workforce issues, and energy. Monitors legislation and regulations. (Formerly International Mass Retail Assn.)

Security Industry Assn., *8405 Colesville Rd., #500, Silver Spring, MD 20910; (301) 804-4700. Fax, (301) 804-4761. Donald Erickson, Chief Executive Officer, (301) 804-4747. Toll-free, (866) 817-8888.*

General email, info@siaonline.org

Web, www.siaonline.org

Membership: manufacturers, service providers, and integrators of electronic security equipment. Sponsors trade shows, develops industry standards, supports educational programs and job training, and publishes statistical research. Monitors legislation and regulations.

Service Station Dealers of America and Allied Trades, *1532 Pointer Ridge Pl., Suite E, Bowie, MD 20716; (301) 390-4405. Fax, (301) 390-3161. Marta Gates, Executive Vice President, Acting.*

General email, mgates@wmda.net

Membership: state associations of gasoline retailers, repair facilities, car washes, and convenience stores. Interests include environmental issues, retail marketing, oil allocation, imports and exports, prices, and taxation. Monitors legislation and regulations.

Society of Consumer Affairs Professionals in Business (SOCAP International), *625 N. Washington St., #304, Alexandria, VA 22314; (703) 519-3700. Fax, (703) 549-4886. Matthew R. D'Uva, President, ext. 10.*

General email, socap@socap.org

Web, www.socap.org

Membership: managers and supervisors who are responsible for consumer affairs, customer service, market research, and sales and marketing operations. Provides information on customer service techniques, market trends, and industry statistics; sponsors seminars and conferences. Monitors legislation and regulations.

Advertising

▶AGENCIES

Federal Highway Administration (FHWA)
(Transportation Dept.), Planning, Environment, and Realty, 1200 New Jersey Ave. S.E., #E76-306 20590; (202) 366-0116. Fax, (202) 366-3713. Gloria M. Shepherd, Associate Administrator.
Web, www.fhwa.dot.gov/realestate

Administers laws concerning outdoor advertising along interstate and federally aided primary highways.

Federal Trade Commission (FTC), *Consumer Protection, Advertising Practices,* 601 New Jersey Ave. N.W., #3223 20001 (mailing address: 600 Pennsylvania Ave. N.W., Washington, DC 20580); (202) 326-3090. Fax, (202) 326-3259. Mary Engle, Associate Director.
Web, www.ftc.gov/bcp/bcpap.shtm

Protects consumers from deceptive and unsubstantiated advertising through law enforcement, public reports, and industry outreach. Focuses on national advertising campaigns for food, dietary supplements, and over-the-counter drugs, particularly advertising that makes claims difficult for consumers to evaluate. Monitors alcohol advertising for unfair practices; issues reports on alcohol labeling, advertising, and promotion. Issues reports on the marketing to children of violent movies, video games, and music recordings.

Food and Drug Administration (FDA) *(Health and Human Services Dept.), Prescription Drug Promotion,* 10903 New Hampshire Ave., Bldg. 51, #3314, Silver Spring, MD 20903-0002; (301) 796-1200. Fax, (301) 847-8444. Thomas W. Abrams, Director.
Web, www.fda.gov/drugs

Monitors prescription drug advertising and labeling; investigates complaints; conducts market research on health care communications and drug issues.

▶NONGOVERNMENTAL

American Advertising Federation, *1101 Vermont Ave. N.W., #500 20005; (202) 898-0089. Fax, (202) 898-0159. James Edmund Datri, President. Toll-free, (800) 999-2231.*
General email, aaf@aaf.org
Web, www.aaf.org

Membership: advertising companies (ad agencies, advertisers, media, and services), clubs, associations, and college chapters. A founder of the National Advertising Review Board, a self-regulatory body. Sponsors annual awards for outstanding advertising.

American Assn. of Advertising Agencies, *Washington Office,* 1707 L St. N.W., #600 20036; (202) 331-7345. Fax, (202) 857-3675. Richard (Dick) O'Brien, Executive Vice President.
General email, wash@aaaadc.org
Web, www.aaaa.org

Co-sponsors the National Advertising Review Board (a self-regulatory body), the Advertising Council, and the Media/Advertising Partnership for a Drug Free America. Monitors legislation and regulations at the federal, state, and local level to protect the agency business and the advertising industry as a whole. (Headquarters in New York.)

Color Marketing Group, *1908 Mount Vernon Ave., Alexandria, VA 22301; (703) 329-8500. Fax, (703) 535-3190. Mark Woodman, President; Sharon Griffis, Executive Director.*
General email, sgriffis@colormarketing.org
Web, www.colormarketing.org

Provides a forum for the exchange of noncompetitive information by color design professionals; seeks to create color forecast information for design and marketing. Holds meetings; sponsors special events in the United States as well as abroad.

Direct Marketing Assn., *Washington Office,* 1615 L St. N.W., #1100 20036-5624; (202) 955-5030. Fax, (202) 955-0085. Linda A. Woolley, Chief Executive Officer.
General email, info@the-dma.org
Web, www.the-dma.org

Membership: businesses and nonprofit organizations using and supporting direct marketing tools. Advocates standards for marketing, focusing on relevance to consumers. Provides research, education, and networking opportunities to members. Operates a service that removes consumer names from unwanted mailing lists. Monitors legislation and regulations. (Headquarters in New York.)

International Sign Assn., *1001 N. Fairfax St., #301, Alexandria, VA 22314; (703) 836-4012. Fax, (703) 836-8353. Lori Anderson, President, ext. 116.*
General email, info@signs.org
Web, www.signs.org

Membership: manufacturers and distributors of signs. Promotes the sign industry; conducts workshops and seminars; sponsors annual competition.

Outdoor Advertising Assn. of America, *1850 M St. N.W., #1040 20036; (202) 833-5566. Fax, (202) 833-1522. Nancy Fletcher, President.*
General email, info@oaaa.org
Web, www.oaaa.org

Membership: outdoor advertising companies, operators, suppliers, and affiliates. Serves as a clearinghouse for public service advertising campaigns. Monitors legislation and regulations.

Small Business Administration

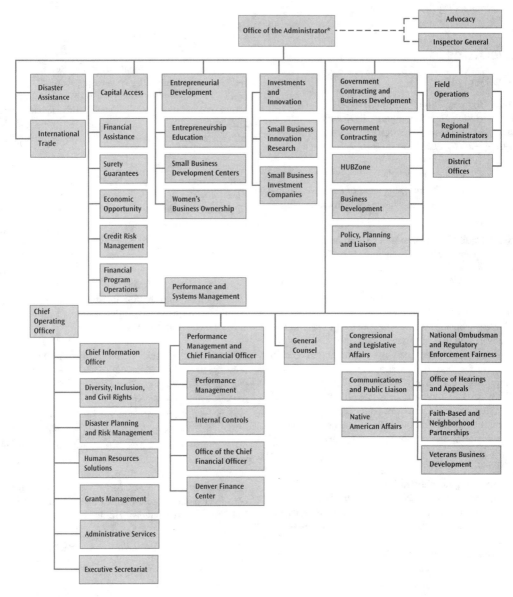

*Includes Administrator, Deputy Administrator, Chief of Staff

– – – Denotes offices that do not report directly to the administrator but operate independently

SMALL AND DISADVANTAGED BUSINESS

General

▶AGENCIES

Agency for International Development (USAID), *Small and Disadvantaged Business Utilization (OSDBU),* 1300 Pennsylvania Ave. N.W., #5.8-C 20523-5800; (202) 567-4730. Mauricio Vera, Director, (202) 567-4730.

Web, www.usaid.gov/who-we-are/organization/ independent-offices/office-small-and-disadvantaged- business-utilization

Counsels small and minority-owned businesses on how to do business with USAID. Identifies opportunities for small businesses in subcontracting with the agency.

Commerce Dept., *Business Liaison,* 1401 Constitution Ave. N.W., #5062 20230; (202) 482-1360. Fax, (202) 482-4054. Matthew T. McGuire, Director.

General email, businessliaison@doc.gov

Web, www.commerce.gov/office-secretary/office-business-liaison

Serves as the federal government's central office for business assistance. Handles requests for information and services as well as complaints and suggestions from businesses; provides a forum for businesses to comment on federal regulations; initiates meetings on policy issues with industry groups, business organizations, trade and small business associations, and the corporate community.

Commerce Dept., *Office of Small and Disadvantaged Business Utilization, 1401 Constitution Ave. N.W. 20230; (202) 482-1472. LaJuene Desmukes, Director.*
General email, osdbu@doc.gov

Web, www.osec.doc.gov/osdbu

An advocacy and advisory office that works toward increasing Commerce Dept. contract awards to small, disadvantaged, women-owned, veteran-owned, and HUB-Zone small businesses.

Consumer Product Safety Commission (CPSC), *Small Business Ombudsman, 4330 East-West Hwy., Bethesda, MD 20814; (888) 531-9070. Fax, (301) 504-0121. Neal S. Cohen, Ombudsman, (301) 504-7504.*
General email, sbo@cpsc.gov

Web, www.cpsc.gov/businfo/smbus.html

Provides guidance and advice to small businesses and small batch manufacturers about compliance with CPSC laws and regulations as well as technical assistance in resolving problems.

Education Dept., *White House Initiative on Asian Americans and Pacific Islanders, 550 12th St. S.W., 10th Floor 20202; (202) 453-7277. Fax, (202) 453-6238. Kiran Ahuja, Executive Director. Press, (202) 453-6566.*
General email, http://whitehouseaapi@ed.gov

Web, www.whitehouse.gov/aapi and Twitter, @whitehouseAAPI

Works to increase Asian American and Pacific Islander participation in federal business and economic development programs.

Farm Service Agency (FSA) *(Agriculture Dept.), Minority and Socially Disadvantaged Farmers Assistance, 1400 Independence Ave. S.W., MS 0503 20250-0503; (202) 690-1098. Fax, (202) 690-4727. J. Latrice Hill, Director, Outreach.*
General email, oasdfr@osec.usda.gov

Web, www.fsa.usda.gov

Works with minority and socially disadvantaged farmers who have concerns and questions about loan applications filed with local offices or other Farm Service Agency programs.

Federal Emergency Management Agency (FEMA) *(Homeland Security Dept.), Federal Insurance and Mitigation Administration, 1800 S. Bell St., MS 3020, Arlington, VA 22202; (202) 646-2781. Fax, (202) 646-7970. David L. Miller, Associate Administrator.*
Web, www.fema.gov/what-mitigation/federal-insurance-mitigation-administration

---

Small and Disadvantaged Business Contacts at Federal Departments and Agencies

DEPARTMENTS

Agriculture, Dexter L. Pearson (Acting), (202) 720-7117

Commerce, LaJuene Desmukes, (202) 482-1472

Defense, Andre Gudger, (571) 372-6191

   Air Force, John Caporal (Acting), (571) 256-8052

   Army, Tracey L. Pinson, (703) 697-2868

   Navy, Sean Crean, (202) 685-6490

Education, Kristi Wilson, (202) 245-6300

Energy, William Valdez, (202) 586-7377

Health and Human Services, Teresa Lewis, (202) 690-7300

Homeland Security, Kevin Boshears, (202) 447-5555

   Coast Guard, Nauman Ansari, (202) 475-5786

Housing and Urban Development, Sharman Lancefield, (202) 402-5477

Interior, Mark Oliver, (202) 208-3493

Justice, Bob Connolly, (202) 616-0523

Labor, Sonya Carrion, (202) 693-7299

State, Shapleigh Driscko, (703) 875-6822

Transportation, Brandon Neal, (202) 366-1930

Treasury, Dan Tangherlini, (202) 622-2826

Veterans Affairs, Tom Leney, (202) 461-4300

AGENCIES

Agency for International Development, Mauricio Vera, (202) 712-1500

Consumer Product Safety Commission, Neal S. Cohen, (888) 531-9070

Environmental Protection Agency, Jeanette L. Brown, (202) 566-2075

General Services Administration, Jiyoung C. Park, (202) 208-5938

National Aeronautics and Space Administration, Glenn Delgado, (202) 358-2088

Nuclear Regulatory Commission, Corenthis Kelley, (301) 415-7380

Social Security Administration, Wayne McDonald, (410) 965-7467

Administers federal crime and flood insurance programs. Makes low-cost flood and crime insurance available to eligible small businesses.

General Services Administration (GSA), *Small Business Utilization, 1275 1st St. N.E. 20417; (202) 501-1021. Fax, (202) 501-2590. Jiyoung C. Park, Associate Administrator. Toll-free, (855) 672-8472.*
General email, smallbusiness@gsa.gov

Web, www.gsa.gov/osbu

Works to increase small business access to government contract procurement opportunities. Provides policy guidance and direction for GSA Regional Small Business Offices, which offer advice and assistance to businesses interested in government procurement.

Minority Business Development Agency *(Commerce Dept.),* 1401 Constitution Ave. N.W., #5053 20230; (202) 482-2332. Fax, (202) 501-4698. Alejandra Castillo, Director. Information, (888) 324-1551.
Web, www.mbda.gov

Assists minority business owners in obtaining federal loans and contract awards; produces an annual report on federal agencies' performance in procuring from minority-owned businesses. Assists minority entrepreneurs one-on-one with financial planning, marketing, management, and technical assistance. Focuses on promoting wealth in minority communities.

National Science Foundation (NSF), *Industrial Innovation and Partnerships, Small Business Innovation Research/Small Business Technology Transfer Programs,* 4201 Wilson Blvd., #590N, Arlington, VA 22230; (703) 292-2214. Fax, (703) 292-9057. Grace Wang, Director, (703) 292-7076; Joseph Hennessey, Senior Adviser, (703) 292-7069.
General email, sbir@nsf.gov
Web, www.nsf.gov/eng/iip/sttr/index.jsp

Serves as liaison between the small-business community and NSF offices; awards grants and contracts. Administers the Small Business Innovation Research and Small Business Technology Transfer Programs, which fund research proposals from small science/high technology firms; offers incentives for commercial development, including NSF-funded research.

National Women's Business Council, 409 3rd St. S.W., #210 20416; (202) 205-3850. Fax, (202) 205-6825. Anie Borja, Executive Director.
General email, info@nwbc.gov
Web, www.nwbc.gov

Independent, congressionally mandated council established by the Women's Business Ownership Act of 1988. Reviews the status of women-owned businesses nationwide and makes policy recommendations to the president, Congress, and the Small Business Administration. Assesses the role of the federal government in aiding and promoting women-owned businesses.

Securities and Exchange Commission (SEC), *Economic and Risk Analysis,* 100 F St. N.E. 20549; (202) 551-6600. Fax, (202) 756-0505. Craig M. Lewis, Director. Information, (202) 942-8088.
General email, RiskFin@sec.gov
Web, www.sec.gov/dera#.ux9TeoXfmaQ

Provides the commission with economic analyses of proposed rule and policy changes and other information to guide the SEC in influencing capital markets. Evaluates the effect of policy and other factors on competition within the securities industry and among competing securities markets; compiles financial statistics on capital formation and the securities industry.

Small Business Administration (SBA), *409 3rd St. S.W., #7000 20416-7000; (202) 205-6605. Maria Contreras-Sweet, Administrator; Vacant, Deputy Administrator. Toll-free information (Answer Desk), (800) 827-5722. Locator, (202) 205-6600.*
General email, answerdesk@sba.gov
Web, www.sba.gov

Provides small businesses with financial and management assistance; offers loans to victims of floods, natural disasters, and other catastrophes; licenses, regulates, and guarantees some financing of small-business investment companies; conducts economic and statistical research on small businesses. SBA Answer Desk is an information and referral service. District or regional offices can be contacted for specific loan information.

Small Business Administration (SBA), *Advocacy,* 409 3rd St. S.W., #7800 20416; (202) 205-6533. Fax, (202) 205-6928. Winslow L. Sargeant, Chief Counsel.
General email, advocacy@sba.gov
Web, www.sba.gov/about-offices-content/1/28

Acts as an advocate for small business viewpoints in regulatory and legislative proceedings. Economic Research Office analyzes the effects of government policies on small businesses and documents the contributions of small business to the economy.

Small Business Administration (SBA), *Business Development,* 409 3rd St. S.W., 8th Floor 20416; (202) 205-5852. Fax, (202) 205-7259. Darryl K. Hairston, Associate Administrator.
General email, 8abd@sba.gov
Web, www.sba.gov/about-offices-content/1/2896

Coordinates the services provided by private industry, banks, the SBA, and other government agencies–such as business development and management and technical assistance–to increase the number of small businesses owned by socially and economically disadvantaged Americans.

Small Business Administration (SBA), *Capital Access,* 409 3rd St. S.W., #8200 20416; (202) 205-6657. Fax, (202) 205-7230. Ann Marie Mehlum, Associate Administrator.
Web, www.sba.gov/about-offices-content/1/2458

Provides financial assistance to small business, including microloans, surety bond guarantees, investment, and international trade.

Small Business Administration (SBA), *Entrepreneurial Development,* 409 3rd St. S.W., #6200 20416; (202) 205-6239. Fax, (202) 205-6903. Tameka Montgomery, Associate Administrator.
Web, www.sba.gov/about-offices-content/1/2463

Responsible for business development programs of the offices of the Small Business Development Centers and the offices of Business Initiatives and Women's Business Ownership.

Small Business Administration (SBA), *Entrepreneurship Education,* 409 3rd St. S.W., #6200 20416; (202) 205-6665.

Fax, (202) 205-6093. Ellen M. Thrasher, Associate Administrator.
Web, www.sba.gov/about-offices-content/1/2893

Outreach and education arm of SBA. Provides small businesses with instruction and counseling in marketing, accounting, product analysis, production methods, research and development, and management problems. Provides in-person as well as online training and specialized services for underserved markets.

Small Business Administration (SBA), *Financial Assistance*, 409 3rd St. S.W., #8300 20416; (202) 205-6843. Fax, (202) 481-7722. Grady Hedgespeth, Director, Acting, (202) 205-7562.
Web, www.sba.gov/about-offices-content/1/2888

Makes available guaranteed loans, intellectual property, and federal research funds to aid in developing small businesses.

Small Business Administration (SBA), *Women's Business Ownership*, 409 3rd St. S.W., 6th Floor 20416; (202) 205-6673. Fax, (202) 205-7287. Erin Andrew, Assistant Administrator.
Web, www.sba.gov/about-offices-content/1/2895

Advocates for current and potential women business owners throughout the federal government and in the private sector. Provides training, counseling, and mentoring through a nationwide network of women's business centers; offers information on national and local resources, including SBA small business programs.

►CONGRESS

For a listing of relevant congressional committees and subcommittees, please see pages 32–33 or the Appendix.

►NONGOVERNMENTAL

AHHA: The Voice of Hispanic Marketing, *8280 Willow Oaks Corporate Dr., #600, Fairfax, VA 22031; (703) 610-9014. Horacio Gavilan, Executive Director, (703) 256-5069.*
General email, info@ahaa.org
Web, www.ahaa.org

Works to grow, strengthen, and protect the Hispanic marketing and advertising industry. Strives to increase Hispanics' awareness of market opportunities and enhance professionalism of the industry. (Formerly the Assn. of Hispanic Advertising Agencies.)

Capital Region Minority Supplier Development Council, *10750 Columbia Pike, 2nd Floor, Silver Spring, MD 20901; (301) 593-5860. Fax, (301) 593-1364. Tracey Jeter, President.*
General email, info@mddcmsdc.org
Web, www.mddcmsdc.org

Certifies minority (Asian, African American, Hispanic, and Native American) business enterprises. Refers corporate buyers to minority suppliers and supports the development, expansion, and promotion of corporate minority supplier development programs. Offers networking opportunities and gives awards. Disseminates statistics and information. Provides consultation services, educational seminars, technical assistance, and training opportunities. (Regional council of the National Minority Supplier Development Council.)

Enterprise Development Group (EDG), *901 S. Highland St., Arlington, VA 22204; (703) 685-0510. Fax, (703) 685-4200. Kevin Kelly, Managing Director.*
General email, edg-loan@ecdcus.org
Web, www.entdevgroup.org

Provides microloans to clients in the Washington metropolitan area with low-to-moderate income in order to promote new business enterprises and individual self-sufficiency. Offers business training and pre- and post-loan technical assistance to entrepreneurs. Operates a matched savings program for low-income refugees and a car loan program for those with inadequate transportation. An independent subsidiary of the Ethiopian Community Development Council.

National Assn. of Investment Companies, *1300 Pennsylvania Ave. N.W., #700 20005; (202) 204-3001. Fax, (202) 204-3022. Ed Dandridge, President.*
General email, info@naicpe.com
Web, www.naicvc.com

Membership: investment companies that provide minority-owned businesses with venture capital and management guidance. Provides technical assistance; monitors legislation and regulations.

National Assn. of Negro Business and Professional Women's Clubs Inc., *1806 New Hampshire Ave. N.W. 20009; (202) 483-4206. Fax, (202) 462-7253. Jennifer Bryant, Executive Director.*
General email, executivedirector@nanbpwc.org
Web, www.nanbpwc.org

Promotes opportunities for African American women in business; sponsors workshops and scholarships; maintains a job bank. Monitors legislation and regulations.

National Assn. of Women Business Owners, *601 Pennsylvania Ave. N.W., South Bldg., #900 20004; (202) 609-9817. Fax, (202) 403-3788. Vacant, Chief Executive Officer. Toll-free, (800) 556-2926.*
General email, national@nawbo.org
Web, www.nawbo.org

Promotes the economic, social, and political interests of women business owners through networking, leadership and business development training, and advocacy.

National Black Chamber of Commerce, *4400 Jenifer St. N.W., #331 20015; (202) 466-6888. Fax, (202) 466-4918. Harry C. Alford, President.*
General email, info@nationalbcc.org
Web, www.nationalbcc.org

Membership: African American–owned businesses. Educates and trains the African American community in entrepreneurship and other economic areas. Monitors legislation and regulations.

National Federation of Independent Business (NFIB), *Washington Office*, *1201 F St. N.W., #200 20004-1221; (202) 314-2000. Fax, (202) 554-0496. Dan Danner, President; Caitlin McDevitt, Legislative Services Representative. Toll-free, (800) 634-2669. Press, (202) 554-9800.*
General email, media@nfib.com

Web, www.nfib.com

Membership: independent businesses. Monitors public policy issues and legislation affecting small and independent businesses, including taxation, government regulation, labor-management relations, and liability insurance. (Headquarters in Nashville, Tenn.)

National Gay and Lesbian Chamber of Commerce, *729 15th St. N.W., 9th Floor 20005; (202) 234-9181. Fax, (202) 234-9185. Justin Nelson, President.*
General email, info@nglcc.org

Web, www.nglcc.org

Communicates ideas and information for and between businesses and organizations. Works with state and local chambers of commerce and business groups on various issues. Advocates on behalf of lesbian, gay, bisexual, and transgender owned businesses; professionals; students of business; and corporations.

National Small Business Assn., *1156 15th St. N.W., #1100 20005; (202) 293-8830. Fax, (202) 872-8543. Todd McCracken, President. Toll-free, (800) 345-6728.*
General email, nsba@nsba.biz

Web, www.nsba.biz

Membership: manufacturing, wholesale, retail, service, exporting, and other small business firms and regional small-business organizations. Represents the interests of small business before Congress, the administration, and federal agencies. Services to members include a toll-free legislative hotline and group insurance.

SCORE Assn., *1175 Herndon Pkwy., #900, Herndon, VA 20170; (703) 487-3612. Fax, (703) 487-3066. W. Kenneth (Ken) Yancey Jr., Chief Executive Officer. Information, (800) 634-0245.*
General email, contactus@score.org

Web, www.score.org

Independent volunteer organization funded by the Small Business Administration through which retired, semiretired, and active business executives use their knowledge and experience to counsel small businesses. (Formerly Service Corps of Retired Executives Assn.)

Small Business and Entrepreneurship Council *(SBE Council), 301 Maple Ave. West, Vienna, VA 22180; (703) 242-5840. Fax, (703) 242-5841. Karen Kerrigan, President.*
General email, info@sbecouncil.org

Web, www.sbecouncil.org

Membership: U.S. entrepreneurs and business owners. Seeks to protect small business and promotes entrepreneurship. Provides networking opportunities, educational

resources, and market intelligence for its members. Monitors legislation and regulations.

Small Business Legislative Council, *1100 H St. N.W., #540 20005-5476; (202) 639-8500. Fax, (202) 296-5333. John S. Satagaj, President; Paul Stalknecht, Chair.*
General email, email@sblc.org

Web, www.sblc.org

Membership: trade associations that represent small businesses in the manufacturing, retail, professional, service, and technical services, and the agricultural, transportation, tourism, and construction sectors. Monitors and proposes legislation and regulations to benefit small businesses.

U.S. Chamber of Commerce, *Small Business Policy, 1615 H St. N.W. 20062-2000; (202) 463-5498. Fax, (202) 463-3174. Giovanni Coratolo, Vice President.*
Web, www.uschambersmallbusinessnation.com

Seeks to enhance visibility of small businesses within the national chamber and the U.S. business community. Provides members with information on national small business programs and legislative issues.

U.S. Hispanic Chamber of Commerce, *1424 K St. N.W., #401 20015; (202) 842-1212. Fax, (202) 842-3221. Javier Palomarez, President. Toll-free, (800) 874-8866.*
General email, info@ushcc.com

Web, www.ushcc.com

Membership: Hispanic Chambers of Commerce and business organizations. Monitors legislation. Provides technical assistance to Hispanic business associations and owners. Promotes public policies that enhance the economic development of its members, trade between Hispanic businesses in the United States and Latin America, and partnerships with the larger business community.

U.S. Pan Asian American Chamber of Commerce, *1329 18th St. N.W. 20036; (202) 296-5221. Fax, (202) 296-5225. Susan Au Allen, President, (202) 378-1130. Toll-free, (800) 696-7818.*
General email, info@uspaacc.com

Web, www.uspaacc.com

Helps Asian American–owned businesses gain access to government and corporate contracts.

U.S. Women's Chamber of Commerce, *700 12th St. N.W., #700 20005; (888) 418-7922. Margot Dorfman, Chief Executive Officer.*
General email, notify@uswcc.org

Web, www.uswcc.org

Provides services and career opportunities to women in business, including networking, leadership training, political advocacy, access to government procurement markets, and technical expertise. Monitors legislation and regulations.

3

Communications
and the Media

GENERAL POLICY AND ANALYSIS

Basic Resources

▶AGENCIES

Access Board, *1331 F St. N.W., #1000 20004-1111; (202) 272-0080. Fax, (202) 272-0081. David M. Capozzi, Executive Director, (202) 272-0010. TTY toll-free, (800) 993-2822. Toll-free technical assistance, (800) 872-2253. General email, info@access-board.gov*

Web, www.access-board.gov

Develops and maintains accessibility requirements for buildings, transit vehicles, telecommunications equipment, medical diagnostic equipment, and electronic and information technology. Provides technical assistance and training on these guidelines and standards. Enforces access standards for federally funded facilities through the Architectural Barriers Act.

Federal Communications Commission (FCC), *445 12th St. S.W. 20554; (202) 418-1000. Fax, (202) 418-2801. Tom Wheeler, Chair. Toll-free, (888) 825-5322. Toll-free fax, (866) 418-0232. National Call Center, (888) 225-5322. Reference Information Center, (202) 418-0270. Media Relations, (202) 418-0500. Consumer and Government Affairs, (202) 418-1400. Legislative Affairs, (202) 418-1900. General email, fccinfo@fcc.gov*

Web, www.fcc.gov

Regulates interstate and foreign communications by radio, television, wire, cable, microwave, and satellite; consults with other government agencies and departments on national and international matters involving wire and radio telecommunications and with state regulatory commissions on telegraph and telephone matters; reviews applications for construction permits and licenses for such services. Reference Information Center open to the public (except under high-alert status of orange and higher).

Federal Communications Commission (FCC), *Media Bureau, Policy Division, 445 12th St. S.W. 20554; (202) 418-2120. Fax, (202) 418-1069. Mary Beth Murphy, Chief. Web, www.fcc.gov/encyclopedia/policy-division-media-bureau*

Conducts proceedings concerning broadcast, cable, and postlicensing Direct Broadcast Satellite issues. Facilitates competition in the multichannel video programming marketplace by resolving carriage and other complaints involving access to facilities. Administers FCC's programs for political broadcasting and equal opportunity matters.

National Telecommunications and Information Administration (NTIA) *(Commerce Dept.), 1401 Constitution Ave. N.W., #4898 20230; (202) 482-1840. Fax, (202) 501-0536. Lawrence E. Strickling, Assistant Secretary. Press, (202) 482-7002. Web, www.ntia.doc.gov*

Develops domestic and international telecommunications policy for the executive branch; manages federal use of radio spectrum; conducts research on radiowave transmissions and other aspects of telecommunications; serves as information source for federal and state agencies on the efficient use of telecommunications resources.

▶CONGRESS

For a listing of relevant congressional committees and subcommittees, please see page 84 or the Appendix.

Legislative Resource Center, *Office of the Clerk, House of Representatives, B106 CHOB 20515; (202) 226-5200. Fax, (202) 226-5208. Ronald (Dale) Thomas, Chief. Bill status, (202) 225-1772. General email, info.clerkweb@mail.house.gov*

Web, http://clerk.house.gov/about/offices_lrc.aspx

Records, stores, and provides legislative status information on all bills and resolutions pending in Congress. Print publications include a biographical directory, a guide to research collection of former House members, and books on African Americans and women who have served in Congress.

Library of Congress, *Copyright Office, Licensing, 101 Independence Ave. S.E., #LM504 20557; (202) 707-8150. Fax, (202) 707-0905. James Enzinna, Chief. Information, (202) 707-3000. Web, www.copyright.gov/licensing*

Licenses cable television companies and satellite carriers; collects and distributes royalty payments under the copyright law. Distributes licenses for making and distributing digital audio recording products and for use of certain noncommercial broadcasting. Administers Section 115 licensing for making and distributing phonorecords.

▶INTERNATIONAL ORGANIZATIONS

Inter-American Telecommunication Commission (CITEL) *(Organization of American States), 1889 F St. N.W., 6th Floor 20006; (202) 458-3004. Fax, (202) 458-6854. Clovis Baptista Neto, Executive Secretary. General email, citel@oas.org*

Web, www.citel.oas.org

Works with the public and private sectors to facilitate the development of universal telecommunications in the Americas.

▶NONGOVERNMENTAL

Accuracy in Media (AIM), *4350 East-West Hwy., #555, Bethesda, MD 20814; (202) 364-4401. Donald K. Irvine, Chair. General email, info@aim.org*

Web, www.aim.org

Analyzes print and electronic news media for bias, omissions, and errors in news; approaches media with complaints. Maintains a speakers bureau and a library on political and media topics.

Alliance for Telecommunications Industry Solutions (ATIS), *1200 G St. N.W., #500 20005; (202) 628-6380.*

Fax, (202) 393-5453. Susan M. Miller, President, (202) 434-8828.

General email, atispr@atis.org

Web, www.atis.org

Develops and promotes the worldwide technical and operations standards for information, entertainment, and communications technologies. Sponsors industry forums; serves as an information clearinghouse. Member of the Inter-American Telecommunication Commission (CITEL). Monitors legislation and regulations.

Center for Media and Public Affairs (CMPA), 933 N. Kenmore St., #405, Arlington, VA 22201; (571) 319-0029. Fax, (571) 319-0034. S. Robert Lichter, President.

General email, mail@cmpa.com

Web, www.cmpa.com

Nonpartisan research and educational organization that studies media coverage of social and political issues and campaigns, specifically information about health risks, scientific matters, and presidential campaigns. Conducts surveys; publishes materials and reports. (Affiliated with George Mason University.)

Computer and Communications Industry Assn. (CCIA), 900 17th St. N.W., #1100 20006; (202) 783-0070. Fax, (202) 783-0534. Edward J. Black, President; Heather Greenfield, Director of Communications.

General email, hgreenfield@ccianet.org

Web, www.ccianet.org

Membership: Internet service providers, software providers, and manufacturers and suppliers of computer data processing and communications-related products and services. Interests include Internet freedom, privacy and neutrality, government electronic surveillance, telecommunications policy, tax policy, federal procurement policy, communications and computer industry standards, intellectual property policies, encryption, international trade, and antitrust reform.

Free Press, *Washington Office*, 1025 Connecticut Ave. N.W., #1110 20036; (202) 265-1490. Fax, (202) 265-1489. Craig Aaron, President.

General email, info@freepress.net

Web, www.freepress.net

Seeks to engage the public in media policy making. Advocates policies for more competitive and public interest–oriented media. (Headquarters in Northhampton, Mass.)

Info Comm International, 11242 Waples Mill Rd., #200, Fairfax, VA 22030; (703) 273-7200. Fax, (703) 278-8082. David Labuskes, Executive Director. Information, (800) 659-7469.

Web, www.infocomm.org

Membership: video and audiovisual dealers, manufacturers and producers, and individuals. Promotes the professional AV communications industry and seeks to enhance members' ability to conduct business successfully through tradeshows, education, certification, market research, and government relations. Interests include small

business issues, intellectual property, sustainable buildings, e-waste, and standards. Monitors legislation and regulations. (Formerly the International Communications Industries Assn.)

Institute for Public Representation, 600 New Jersey Ave. N.W., #312 20001; (202) 662-9535. Fax, (202) 662-9634. Hope Babcock, Co-Director; Angela Campbell, Co-Director; Brian Wolfman, Co-Director.

General email, gulcipr@law.georgetown.edu

Web, www.law.georgetown.edu/academics/academic-programs/clinical-programs/our-clinics/ipr/index.cfm and Blog, instituteforpublicrepresentation.org

Public interest law firm and clinical education program founded by Georgetown University Law Center. Attorneys act as counsel for groups and individuals unable to obtain effective legal representation in the areas of First Amendment and media law, environmental law, civil rights, and general public interest matters. Gives graduate fellows an opportunity to work on unique, large-scale projects.

Media Institute, 2300 Clarendon Blvd., #602, Arlington, VA 22201; (703) 243-5700. Fax, (703) 243-8808. Patrick D. Maines, President.

General email, info@mediainstitute.org

Web, www.mediainstitute.org

Research foundation that conducts conferences, files court briefs and regulatory comments, and sponsors programs on communications topics. Advocates a competitive media and communications industry and free-speech rights for individuals, media, and corporate speakers.

Media Matters for America, P.O. Box 52155 20091; (202) 756-4100. Fax, (202) 756-4101. Bradley Beychok, President.

Web, http://mediamatters.org

Web-based research and information center concerned with monitoring and analyzing print, broadcast, cable, radio, and Internet media for inaccurate news and commentary. Seeks to inform journalists and the general public about specific instances of misinformation and provide resources for taking action against false claims.

Media Research Center, 1900 Campus Commons Dr., #600, Reston, VA 20191; (571) 267-3500. Fax, (571) 375-0099. L. Brent Bozell III, President; David Martin, Executive Vice President.

General email, mrc@mediaresearch.org

Web, www.mrc.org

Media-watch organization working for balanced and responsible news coverage of political issues. Records and analyzes network news programs; analyzes print media; maintains profiles of media executives and library of recordings.

National Assn. of Broadcasters (NAB), 1771 N St. N.W. 20036; (202) 429-5300. Fax, (202) 429-5406. Gordon Smith, President. Communications, (202) 429-5350.

General email, nab@nab.org

Web, www.nab.org

Membership: radio and television broadcast stations and broadcast networks holding an FCC license or

COMMUNICATIONS AND THE MEDIA RESOURCES IN CONGRESS

For a complete listing of Congress committees, including their full contact information, leadership, membership, and jurisdictions, please refer to the Appendix on pages 724–842.

HOUSE:

House Administration Committee, (202) 225-8281.
Web, cha.house.gov or democrats.cha.house.gov

House Appropriations Committee, (202) 225-2771.
Web, appropriations.house.gov or
democrats.appropriations.house.gov
**Subcommittee on Labor, Health and Human
Services, Education, and Related Agencies,**
(202) 225-3508.

House Energy and Commerce Committee,
(202) 225-2927.
Web, energycommerce.house.gov or
democrats.energycommerce.house.gov
**Subcommittee on Communications and
Technology,** (202) 225-2927.

House Judiciary Committee, (202) 225-3951.
Web, judiciary.house.gov or
democrats.judiciary.house.gov
**Subcommittee on the Constitution and Civil
Justice,** (202) 225-2825.
**Subcommittee on Courts, Intellectual
Property, and the Internet,**
(202) 225-5741.

**House Oversight and Government Reform
Committee,** (202) 225-5074.
Web, oversight.house.gov or
democrats.oversight.house.gov
**Subcommittee on Economic Growth, Job
Creation, and Regulatory Affairs,**
(202) 225-5074.

House Science, Space, and Technology Committee,
(202) 225-6371.
Web, science.house.gov or
democrats.science.house.gov
Subcommittee on Research and Technology,
(202) 225-6371.

House Small Business Committee,
(202) 225-5821.
Web, smallbusiness.house.gov or
democrats.smallbusiness.house.gov
Subcommittee on Health and Technology,
(202) 225-5821.

JOINT:

Joint Committee on the Library of Congress,
(202) 225-8281.
Web, cha.house.gov/jointcommittees/joint-committee-
library
Joint Committee on Printing, (202) 225-8281.
Web, cha.house.gov/jointcommittees/joint-committee-
on-printing

SENATE:

**Senate Agriculture, Nutrition, and Forestry
Committee,** (202) 224-2035.
Web, ag.senate.gov
**Subcommittee on Jobs, Rural Economic Growth,
and Energy Innovation,** (202) 224-2035.

Senate Appropriations Committee, (202) 224-7363.
Web, appropriations.senate.gov
**Subcommittee on Labor, Health and Human
Services, Education, and Related Agencies,**
(202) 224-9145.

**Senate Commerce, Science, and Transportation
Committee,** (202) 224-0411.
Web, commerce.senate.gov
**Subcommittee on Communications, Technology,
and the Internet,** (202) 224-9340.

Senate Foreign Relations Committee, (202) 224-4651.
Web, foreign.senate.gov
**Subcommittee on International Operations and
Organizations, Human Rights, Democracy,
and Global Women's Issues,** (202) 224-4651.

Senate Judiciary Committee, (202) 224-7703.
Web, judiciary.senate.gov
**Subcommittee on Antitrust, Competition Policy,
and Consumer Rights,** 202-224-7703
(202) 224-7703.
**Subcommittee on the Constitution, Civil Rights,
and Human Rights,** (202) 224-1158.
Subcommittee on Crime and Terrorism,
(202) 228-3740.

Senate Rules and Administration Committee,
(202) 224-6352.
Web, rules.senate.gov

---

construction permit; associate members include producers of equipment and programs. Assists members in areas of management, engineering, and research. Monitors legislation and regulations.

National Assn. of Regulatory Utility Commissioners,
1101 Vermont Ave. N.W., #200 20005-3521; (202) 898-2200. Fax, (202) 898-2213. Charles D. Gray, Executive Director. General email, admin@naruc.org

Web, www.naruc.org

Membership: members of federal, state, municipal, and international regulatory commissions that have jurisdiction over utilities and carriers of transportation services. Interests include telecommunications, energy, and water regulation.

National Captioning Institute, *3725 Concorde Pkwy., #100, Chantilly, VA 20151; (703) 917-7600. Fax, (703) 917-9853. Gene Chao, President. Phone/TTY, (703) 917-7600. Main phone is voice and TTY accessible.*

Federal Communications Commission

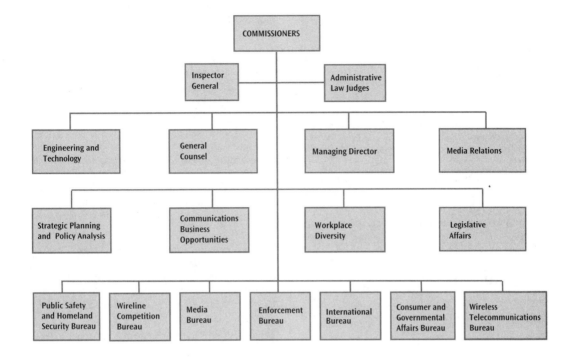

General email, mail@ncicap.org

Web, www.ncicap.org

Captions television programs for the deaf and hard of hearing and produces audio descriptions for the blind on behalf of public and commercial broadcast television networks, cable networks, syndicators, program producers, government agencies, advertisers, and home video distributors. Produces and disseminates information about the national closed-captioning service and audio description services.

Pew Research Center for the People and the Press, *1615 L St. N.W., #700 20036; (202) 419-4350. Fax, (202) 419-4399. Carroll Doherty, Director, (202) 419-4363.*

General email, info@people-press.org

Web, http://people-press.org

Studies attitudes toward media, politics, and public policy issues through public opinion research. Conducts national surveys measuring public attentiveness to major news stories; charts trends in values and political and social attitudes. Makes survey results available online, free of charge.

TDI, *8630 Fenton St., #121, Silver Spring, MD 20910-3803; (301) 563-9112. Claude L. Stout, Executive Director. Phone (voice/video), (301) 563-9112.*

General email, info@TDIforaccess.org

Web, www.TDIforaccess.org

Membership: individuals, organizations, and businesses that advocate for equal access to telecommunications, media, and information technologies for Americans who are deaf and hard of hearing. Interests include closed captioning for television, movies, DVDs, and online videos; emergency access (911); and TTY and Telecommunications Relays Services. Publishes a quarterly magazine and an annual resource directory. Monitors legislation and regulations. (Formerly Telecommunications for the Deaf and Hard of Hearing.)

Telecommunications Industry Assn. (TIA), *1320 N. Courthouse Rd., #200, Arlington, VA 222014; (703) 907-7700. Fax, (703) 907-7727. Grant Seiffert, President; Danielle Coffey, Vice President, Government Affairs, (703) 907-7734.*

General email, tia@tiaonline.org

Web, www.tiaonline.org

Trade association for the information and communications technology industry, including broadband, mobile wireless, information technology, networks, cable, satellite, and unified communications. Develops standards; provides market intelligence; analyzes environmental regulations; hosts trade shows and facilitates business opportunities for members. Monitors legislation and regulations.

Cable Services

▶**AGENCIES**

Federal Communications Commission (FCC), *Media Bureau, 445 12th St. S.W., 3rd Floor 20554; (202) 418-7200. Fax, (202) 418-2376. William T. Lake, Chief;*

Janice Wise, Director of Media Relations, (202) 418-8165. Press, (202) 418-0503.
General email, mweb@fcc.gov
Web, www.fcc.gov/office-media-relations

Makes, recommends, and enforces rules governing cable television and other video distribution services; promotes industry growth, competition, and availability to the public; ensures reasonable rates for consumers in areas that do not have competition in cable service.

Federal Communications Commission (FCC), *Media Bureau, Engineering, 445 12th St. S.W., #4-C838 20554; (202) 418-7000. Fax, (202) 418-1189. John Wong, Chief, (202) 418-7012.*
Web, www.fcc.gov/encyclopedia/engineering-division-media-bureau

Provides technical advice for digital television (DTV) transition, latest cable technologies, and spectrum and broadband policies. Oversees the processing of routine cable applications.

▶**NONGOVERNMENTAL**

CTAM, *120 Waterfront St. #200, National Harbor, MD 20745; (301) 485-8900. Fax, (301) 560-4964. John F. Lansing, President, (301) 485-8920.*
General email, info@ctam.com
Web, www.ctam.com

Promotes innovation in the cable and related industries in areas of marketing, research, management, and new product development. Sponsors annual marketing and research conferences; interests include international markets. CTAM stands for Cable and Telecommunications Assn. for Marketing.

National Cable Telecommunications Assn., *25 Massachusetts Ave. N.W., #100 20001-1413; (202) 222-2300. Fax, (202) 222-2411. Michael K. Powell, President. Press, (202) 222-2350. Government Relations, (202) 222-2410.*
General email, webmaster@ncta.com
Web, www.ncta.com and Twitter, @NCTAcable

Membership: companies that operate cable television systems, cable television programmers, and manufacturers and suppliers of hardware and software for the industry. Represents the industry before federal regulatory agencies and Congress and in the courts; provides management and promotional aids and information on legal, legislative, and regulatory matters.

Enforcement, Judicial, and Legal Actions

▶**AGENCIES**

Antitrust Division *(Justice Dept.), Networks and Technology Enforcement, 450 5th St. N.W., #7100 20530; (202) 307-6200. Fax, (202) 616-8544. James J. Tierney, Chief.*
Web, www.justice.gov/atr/about/ntes.html

Reviews mergers in the areas of information technology, Internet-related businesses, computer hardware and software, high-technology components, manufacturing, professional associations, financial services, and the securities industry.

Antitrust Division *(Justice Dept.), Telecommunications and Media Enforcement, 450 5th St. N.W., #7000 20530; (202) 514-5621. Fax, (202) 514-6381. Scott Scheele, Chief. Press, (202) 514-2007.*
Web, www.justice.gov/atr/about/tel.html

Investigates and litigates antitrust cases dealing with communications and media, including mobile wireless services, broadband Internet, satellite communications services, and voice communication services. Participates in agency proceedings and rulemaking concerning communications and media; monitors and analyzes legislation.

Federal Bureau of Investigation (FBI) *(Justice Dept.), CALEA Implementation Unit, FBI Quantico Engineering Research Facility (ERF) Building, #27958A, Quantico, VA 22135; (540) 361-4600. Fax, (540) 361-7082. Maribeth Paglino, Unit Chief, (540) 361-2300. Toll-free, (800) 551-0336.*
Web, http://askcalea.fbi.gov

Administers enforcement of the Communications Assistance for Law Enforcement Act (CALEA). Sets standards for telecommunications carriers concerning the development and deployment of electronic suveillance technologies. Promotes cooperation between the telecommunications industry, government entities, and law enforcement officials to develop intercept capabilities required by law enforcement.

Federal Communications Commission (FCC), *Administrative Law Judges, 445 12th St. S.W., #1C768 20554; (202) 418-2280. Fax, (202) 418-0195. Richard L. Sippel, Chief Judge; Mary Gosse, Administrative Officer.*
Web, www.fcc.gov/office-administrative-law-judges

Presides over hearings and issues initial decisions in disputes concerning FCC adjudication proceedings and applications for licensing.

Federal Communications Commission (FCC), *Enforcement Bureau, 445 12th St. S.W., 3rd Floor, #7C723 20554; (202) 418-7450. P. Michele Ellison, Chief, Enforcement Bureau. Toll-free fax, (888) 418-0232. Media Relations, (202) 418-0500.*
Web, www.fcc.gov/enforcement-bureau

Commission's primary enforcement organization responsible for compliance with the Communications Act of 1934, the FCC's rules, Commission orders, and the terms of licenses and other authorizations. Promotes competition under the Telecommunications Act of 1996 and related regulations and ensures access to communications by the disabled. Houses the FCC's Office of Homeland Security.

► NONGOVERNMENTAL

Federal Communications Bar Assn., *1020 19th St. N.W.,*
#325 20036-6101; (202) 293-4000. Fax, (202) 293-4317.
Stanley Zenor, Executive Director.
General email, fcba@fcba.org
Web, www.fcba.org

Membership: attorneys, nonattorneys, and law students
in communications law who practice before the Federal
Communications Commission, the courts, and state and
local regulatory agencies. Cooperates with the FCC and
other members of the bar on legal aspects of communications issues.

International and Satellite Communications

► AGENCIES

Federal Communications Commission (FCC),
International Bureau, 445 12th St. S.W., 6th Floor 20554;
(202) 418-0437. Fax, (202) 418-2818. Mindel De La Torre,
Chief.
General email, contact_ib@fcc.gov
Web, www.fcc.gov/international-bureau

Coordinates the FCC's international policy activities;
represents the FCC in international forums. Licenses
international telecommunications carriers, undersea cables,
international short-wave broadcasters, and satellite facilities. Coordinates the FCC's collection and dissemination
of information on communications and telecommunications policy, regulation, and market developments in other
countries and the policies and regulations of international
organizations.

Federal Communications Commission (FCC), *Media*
Bureau, Policy Division, 445 12th St. S.W. 20554; (202)
418-2120. Fax, (202) 418-1069. Mary Beth Murphy, Chief.
Web, www.fcc.gov/encyclopedia/policy-division-media-
bureau

Conducts proceedings and drafts policy on postlicensing Direct Broadcast Satellite issues. Enforces the Satellite
Home Viewer Improvement Act.

Federal Communications Commission (FCC), *Wireline*
Competition Bureau, 445 12th St. S.W., #5C343 20554;
(202) 418-1500. Fax, (202) 418-2825. Julie Veach, Chief.
Web, www.fcc.gov/wireline-competition-bureau

Develops and recommends FCC policies involving
common carriers (wireline facilities that furnish interstate
communications services for hire). Interests include deregulation, pricing policy, economic and technical aspects,
numbering resources, and competition in telecommunications markets.

National Telecommunications and Information
Administration (NTIA) *(Commerce Dept.), 1401*
Constitution Ave. N.W., #4898 20230; (202) 482-1840.

Fax, (202) 501-0536. Lawrence E. Strickling, Assistant
Secretary. Press, (202) 482-7002.
Web, www.ntia.doc.gov

Represents the U.S. telecommunications sector (along
with the State Department) in negotiating international
agreements, including conferences with the International
Telecommunication Union.

State Dept., *International Communications and*
Information Policy, 2201 C St. N.W., #4634, MC EEB/CIP
20520-5820; (202) 647-5212. Fax, (202) 647-5957.
Daniel A. Sepulveda, U.S. Coordinator.
Web, www.state.gov/e/eeb/cip

Coordinates U.S. government international communication and information policy. Acts as a liaison for other
federal agencies and the private sector in international
communications issues. Promotes advancement of information and communication technology with expanded
access and improved efficiency and security; the creation
of business opportunities at home and abroad in this sector; resolution of telecommunications trade issues in conjunction with the Office of the U.S. Trade Representative;
and the expansion of access to this technology globally.

► INTERNATIONAL ORGANIZATIONS

Intelsat, *Washington Office, 3400 International Dr. N.W.*
20008-3006; (202) 944-6800. Fax, (202) 944-7898.
David McGlade, Chief Executive Officer.
Web, www.intelsat.com

Owns and operates a global satellite communications
system and complementary terrestrial network. Helps service providers, broadcasters, corporations, and governments transmit information and content internationally.
(Headquarters in Luxembourg.)

► NONGOVERNMENTAL

Satellite Broadcasting and Communications Assn.
(SBCA), *1100 17th St. N.W., #1150 20036; (202) 349-3620.*
Fax, (202) 349-3621. Joseph Widoff, Executive Director,
(202) 349-3656. Toll-free, (800) 541-5981.
General email, info@sbca.org
Web, www.sbca.org

Membership: owners, operators, manufacturers, dealers, and distributors of satellite receiving stations, software
and program suppliers, and others in the satellite services
industry. Promotes use of satellite technology for broadcast delivery of video, audio, voice, broadband, and interactive services and as part of the national and global
information infrastructure. Monitors legislation and regulations.

Satellite Industry Association (SIA), *1200 18th St. N.W.,*
#1001 20036; (202) 503-1560. Fax, (202) 503-1590.
Patricia Cooper, President.
General email, info@sia.org
Web, www.sia.org

Trade association representing global satellite operators, service providers, manufacturers, launch services

providers, and ground equipment suppliers. Promotes the benefits and uses of commercial satellite technology. Monitors legislation and regulations, domestically and abroad.

Radio and Television

Corporation for Public Broadcasting, *401 9th St. N.W. 20004-2129; (202) 879-9600. Fax, (202) 879-9700. Patricia de Stacy Harrison, Chief Executive Officer; Anne Brachman, Press Contact. Press, (202) 879-9836. Comments, (800) 272-2190.*
General email, press@cpb.org
Web, www.cpb.org

Private corporation chartered by Congress under the Public Broadcasting Act of 1967 and funded by the federal government. Supports public media through grants for public radio and television stations; provides general support for national program production and operation, including content for underserved communities; helps fund projects on U.S. and international news, education, arts, culture, history, and natural history; invests in emerging technologies, such as cable and satellite transmission, the Internet and broadband communication networks, for possible use by public telecommunications; supports training activities.

Federal Communications Commission (FCC),
Enforcement Bureau, 445 12th St. S.W., 3rd Floor, #7C723 20554; (202) 418-7450. P. Michele Ellison, Chief, Enforcement Bureau. Toll-free fax, (888) 418-0232. Media Relations, (202) 418-0500.
Web, www.fcc.gov/enforcement-bureau

Monitors the radio spectrum and inspects broadcast stations; ensures that U.S. radio laws and FCC rules are observed. Develops activities to inform, assist, and educate licensees; provides presentations and information. Manages the Emergency Alert System. Operates the National Call Center in Gettysburg, Pa.

Federal Communications Commission (FCC),
Engineering and Technology, 445 12th St. S.W., 7th Floor 20554; (202) 418-2470. Fax, (202) 418-1944. Julius Knapp, Chief.
General email, oetinfo@fcc.gov
Web, www.fcc.gov/office-eengineering-technology

Advises the FCC on technical and spectrum matters and assists in developing U.S. telecommunications policy. Identifies and reviews developments in telecommunications and related technologies. Studies characteristics of radio frequency spectrum. Certifies radios and other electronic equipment to meet FCC standards.

National Endowment for the Arts (NEA), *Media, Arts Design, and Visual Arts, 400 7th St. S.W., Constitution Center 20024; (202) 682-5452. Fax, (202) 682-5721. Jason Schupbach, Director, Design, (202) 682-5786; Vacant, Director, Media Arts; Wendy Clark, Director, Museums and Visual Arts, Acting, (202) 682-5555.*
Web, www.arts.gov

Awards grants to nonprofit organizations for film, video, and radio productions; supports arts programming broadcast nationally on public television and radio.

National Assn. of Broadcasters (NAB), *1771 N St. N.W. 20036; (202) 429-5300. Fax, (202) 429-5406. Gordon Smith, President. Communications, (202) 429-5350. General email, nab@nab.org*
Web, www.nab.org

Membership: radio and television broadcast stations and broadcast networks holding an FCC license or construction permit; associate members include producers of equipment and programs. Assists members in areas of management, engineering, and research. Monitors legislation and regulations.

National Public Radio, *1111 N. Capitol Street N.E. 20002; (202) 513-2000. Fax, (202) 513-3329. Paul G. Haaga, President, Acting. Press, (202) 513-2300. General email, ombudsman@npr.org*
Web, www.npr.org

Multimedia news organization composed of 849 member stations operated by 269 member organizations nationwide that are locally owned and operated. Produces and distributes news, music, and entertainment programming in all 50 states. Provides program distribution service via satellite. Represents member stations before Congress, the FCC, and other regulatory agencies. Supported by member station programming fee (about 40 percent of funding); corporate sponsorships; and institutional grants.

Public Broadcasting Service, *2100 Crystal Dr., Arlington, VA 22202; (703) 739-5000. Fax, (703) 739-0775. Paula Kerger, President; Michael Getler, Ombudsman, (703) 739-5768.*
General email, pbs@pbs.org
Web, www.pbs.org

Membership: public television stations nationwide. Selects, schedules, promotes, and distributes national programs; provides public television stations with educational, instructional, and cultural programming; also provides news and public affairs, science and nature, and children's programming. Assists members with technology development and fundraising.

Telephone and Telegraph

For cellular telephones, see Wireless Telecommunications.

Federal Communications Commission (FCC), *Wireline Competition Bureau, 445 12th St. S.W., #5C343 20554; (202) 418-1500. Fax, (202) 418-2825. Julie Veach, Chief.*
Web, www.fcc.gov/wireline-competition-bureau

Develops and recommends FCC policies involving common carriers (wireline facilities that furnish interstate communications services for hire). Interests include deregulation, pricing policy, economic and technical aspects, numbering resources, and competition in telecommunications markets.

General Services Administration (GSA), *Federal Relay Service (FedRelay), 10304 Eaton Pl., Fairfax, VA 22030; (703) 306-6308. Vacant, Program Manager. Customer service, (800) 877-0996 (Voice/TTY, ASCII, Spanish). Toll-free, (800) 877-8339 (TTY/ASCII). VCO (Voice Carry Over), (877) 877-6280. Speech-to-Speech, (877) 877-8982. Voice, (866) 377-8642. TeleBraille, (866) 893-8340.*
General email, ed.smith@gsa.gov

Web, www.gsa.gov/fedrelay and http://ITCSC@gsa.gov

Provides telecommunications services for conducting official business with and within the federal government to individuals who are deaf, hard of hearing, or have speech disabilities. Federal Relay Service features are: Voice, TTY, HCO, Speech-to-Speech, Spanish, Telebraille, Captioned Telephone Service (CTS), IP Relay, Video Relay Service (VRS), Internet Relay (FRSO), and Relay Conference Captioning (RCC). For those with limited English proficiency, contact fas.car@gsa.gov, as services are available in Spanish, Vietnamese, Russian, Portuguese, Polish, Haitian, Creole, and Arabic.

▶**NONGOVERNMENTAL**

COMPTEL, *900 17th St. N.W., #400 20006; (202) 296-6650. Fax, (202) 296-7585. Chip Pickering, Chief Executive Officer.*
Web, www.comptel.org

Membership: providers of voice, video, and data offerings and the developers and providers of IP-based networks and services. Advocates for the competitive telecommunications industry before Congress, the FCC, and state regulatory agencies; sponsors trade shows and conferences. Monitors legislation and regulations.

National Telecommunications Cooperative Assn. (NTCA), *4121 Wilson Blvd., #1000, Arlington, VA 22203-1801; (703) 351-2000. Fax, (703) 351-2001. Shirley Bloomfield, Chief Executive Officer.*
General email, pubrelations@ntca.org

Web, www.ntca.org

Membership: locally owned and controlled telecommunications cooperatives and companies serving rural and small-town areas. Offers educational seminars, workshops, publications, technical assistance, and various employee benefits programs to members. Monitors legislation and regulations.

U.S. Telecom Assn. (USTA), *607 14th St. N.W., #400 20005; (202) 326-7300. Fax, (202) 315-3603. Walter B. McCormick Jr., President.*
General email, policy@ustelecom.org

Web, www.ustelecom.org

Membership: broadband telecommunication service providers and manufacturers and suppliers for these companies. Provides members with information on the industry; conducts webinars; participates in FCC regulatory proceedings.

Wireless Telecommunications

▶**AGENCIES**

Federal Communications Commission (FCC), *Wireless Telecommunications Bureau, 445 12th St. S.W., #6408 20554; (202) 418-0600. Fax, (202) 418-0787. Roger C. Sherman, Chief, Acting.*
Web, www.fcc.gov/wireless-telecommunications-bureau

Regulates domestic wireless communications, including cellular telephone, paging, personal communications services, public safety, air and maritime navigation, and other commercial and private radio services. Responsible for implementing the competitive bidding authority for spectrum auctions. Assesses new uses of wireless technologies, including electronic commerce. (Gettysburg office handles all licensing: FCC Wireless Telecommunications Bureau, Spectrum Management Resources and Technologies Division, 1270 Fairfield Rd., Gettysburg, PA 17325; (717) 338-2510.)

U.S. Secret Service *(Homeland Security Dept.),* **Criminal** *Investigative Division, 950 H St. N.W., #5000 20223; (202) 406-9330. Fax, (202) 406-5016. Edward Lowery, Special Agent in Charge.*
Web, www.secretservice.gov/criminal.shtml

Plans, reviews, and coordinates criminal investigations involving reports of bank fraud, credit fraud, telecommunications and computer crimes, fraudulent securities, and electronic funds transfer fraud.

▶**NONGOVERNMENTAL**

CTIA—The Wireless Assn., *1400 16th St. N.W., #600 20036; (202) 736-3200. Fax, (202) 785-0721. Steve Largent, President.*
General email, ctiaadministration@ctia.org

Web, www.ctia.org

Membership: system operators, equipment manufacturers, engineering firms, and others engaged in the cellular telephone and mobile communications industry in domestic and world markets. Monitors legislation and regulations.

Enterprise Wireless Alliance, *2121 Cooperative Way, #225, Herdon, VA 20171; (703) 528-5115. Fax, (703) 524-1074. Mark E. Crosby, Chief Executive Officer. Toll-free, (800) 482-8282.*
General email, customerservice@enterprisewireless.org

Web, www.ita-relay.com

Membership: enterprise wireless companies, dealers, and trade associations. Serves as an information source on radio frequencies, licensing, new products and technology, and market conditions. Monitors legislation and regulations.

PCIA—The Wireless Infrastructure Assn., *500 Montgomery St., #500, Alexandria, VA 22314; (703) 739-0300. Fax, (703) 836-1608. Jonathan Adelstein, President. Information, (800) 759-0300. Press, (703) 535-7424. Web, www.pcia.com*

Represents companies that make up the wireless telecommunications infrastructure industry. Supports wireless communications and information infrastructure.

Utilities Telecom Council (UTC), *1129 20th St. N.W., #350 20036; (202) 872-0030. Fax, (202) 872-1331. Connie Durcsak, President, (202) 833-6801. General email, utcadmin@utc.org*

Web, www.utc.org

Membership: companies that own, manage, or provide critical telecommunications systems in support of their core business, including energy, gas, and water utility companies, pipeline companies, and radio and international critical infrastructure organizations. Participates in FCC rulemaking proceedings. Interests include fiber security; radio spectrum for fixed and mobile wireless communication; and technological, legislative, and regulatory developments affecting telecommunications operations of energy utilities.

GOVERNMENT INFORMATION

General

▶ **AGENCIES**

General Services Administration (GSA), *National Contact Center, 1275 1st St. N.E. 20417; (800) 333-4636. Mary Ann Monroe, Division Director, (202) 501-4179. Chat and email options (8:00 a.m.–8:00 p.m. Eastern time), answers.usa.gov*

Web, www.usa.gov

Operates a contact center to provide information in English or Spanish on all federal government agencies, programs, and services via toll-free telephone, email, and chat. Operated under contract by Sykes in Pennsylvania and Florida.

National Archives and Records Administration (NARA), *700 Pennsylvania Ave. N.W. 20408; (866) 272-6272. Fax, (301) 837-0483. David S. Ferriero, Archivist of the United States. Press, (202) 357-5300. Public affairs, (202) 357-5300.*

Web, www.archives.gov

Identifies, preserves, and makes available federal government documents of historic value; administers a network of regional storage centers and archives and operates the presidential library system. Collections include photographs, graphic materials, films, and maps; holdings include records generated by foreign governments (especially in wartime) and by international conferences, commissions, and exhibitions.

National Archives and Records Administration (NARA), *Agency Services, 8601 Adelphi Rd., #3600, College Park, MD 20740-6001; (301) 837-3064. Fax, (301) 837-1617. Jay A. Trainer, Executive, Acting.*

Web, www.archives.gov

Manages the federal record centers throughout the country. Works with the record managers to feed records into the National Archives. Oversees the National Declassification Center and Office of Government Information Services.

National Archives and Records Administration (NARA), *Center for Legislative Archives, 700 Pennsylvania Ave. N.W., #8E 20408; (202) 357-5350. Fax, (202) 357-5911. Richard H. Hunt, Director.*

Web, www.archives.gov/legislative

Collects and maintains records of congressional committees and legislative files from 1789 to the present. Publishes inventories and guides to these records.

National Archives and Records Administration (NARA), *Electronic Records Division, 8601 Adelphi Rd., #5320, College Park, MD 20740-6001; (301) 837-3420. Fax, (301) 837-3681. Theodore J. Hull, Director, (301) 837-1824. General email, cer@nara.gov*

Web, www.archives.gov/research/electronic-records

Preserves, maintains, and makes available electronic records of the U.S. government in all subject areas. Provides researchers with magnetic tape, CD, DVD, and other copies of electronic records on a cost-recovery basis. Offers direct downloads and searches of selected holdings.

National Archives and Records Administration (NARA), *Federal Register, 800 N. Capitol St. N.W., #700 20001 (mailing address: FP, 8601 Adelphi Rd., College Park, MD 20740-6001); (202) 741-6000. Fax, (202) 741-6012. Charley Barth, Director. Public Laws Update Service (PLUS), (202) 741-6043. General email, fedreg.info@nara.gov*

Web, www.archives.gov/federal_register

Informs citizens of their rights and obligations by providing access to the official texts of federal laws, presidential documents, administrative regulations and notices, and descriptions of federal organizations, programs, and activities. Provides online and in-person access to documents on file before their publication. Administers the Electoral College and the constitutional amendment process. Publications available from the U.S. Government Printing Office, (301) 317-3953, http://bookstore.gpo.gov.

National Archives and Records Administration (NARA), *Modern Records Program, 8601 Adelphi Rd., #2100, College Park, MD 20740; (301) 837-3570. Fax, (301) 837-3697. Paul M. Wester Jr., Director, (301) 837-3120. General email, rmcommunications@nara.gov*

Web, www.archives.gov

Administers programs that establish standards, guidelines, and procedures for agency records administration. Manages training programs; inspects records management

Chief Information Officers for Federal Departments and Agencies

DEPARTMENTS

Agriculture, Cheryl Cook, (202) 720-8833

Commerce, Simon Szykman, (202) 482-4797

Defense, Teresa M. Takai, (703) 695-0348

  Air Force, Lt. Gen. Michael Basla, (703) 695-6829

  Army, Lt. Susan S. Lawrence, (703) 695-4366

  Navy, Terry Halvorsen, (703) 695-1840

Education, Danny Harris, (202) 245-6252

Energy, Robert Brese, (202) 586-0166

Health and Human Services, Frank Baitman, (202) 690-6162

Homeland Security, Luke McCormack, (202) 514-0507

Housing and Urban Development, Kevin R. Cooke, (202) 708-0306

Interior, Bernard J. Mazer, (202) 208-6194

Justice, Kevin Deeley, (202) 514-0507

Labor, Michael Kerr, (202) 693-4040

State, Steven C. Taylor, (202) 647-2889

Transportation, Richard McKinney, (202) 366-9201

Treasury, Robyn East, (202) 622-1200

Veterans Affairs, Stephen Warren (Acting), (202) 461-6910

AGENCIES

Environmental Protection Agency, Renee P. Wynn, (202) 564-6665

Federal Emergency Management Agency, Adrian Gardner, (202) 646-3006

Federal Trade Commission, Bajinder Paul, (202) 326-2979

General Services Administration, Sonny Hashmi, (202) 501-1000

National Aeronautics and Space Administration, Larry N. Sweet, (202) 358-1824

National Archives and Records Administration, Michael Wash, (301) 837-1992

National Science Foundation, Amy Northcutt, (703) 292-8100

Nuclear Regulatory Commission, Darren Ash, (301) 415-7443

Office of Personnel Management, Donna Seymour, (202) 606-2150

Office of the Director of National Intelligence, Al Tarasiuk, (703) 275-2008

Office of Management and Budget, Steven VanRoekel, (202) 395-3018

Securities and Exchange Commission, Thomas A. Bayer, (202) 551-8800

Small Business Administration, Renee Macklin, (202) 205-6708

Social Security Administration, William Zielinski (Acting), (800) 772-1213

practices; monitors certain records not contained in National Archives depositories.

National Archives and Records Administration (NARA), *Presidential Libraries, 8601 Adelphi Rd., #2200F, College Park, MD 20740-6001; (301) 837-3250. Fax, (301) 837-3199. Susan K. Donius, Director, (301) 837-1662. Web, www.archives.gov/presidential-libraries*

Administers thirteen presidential libraries. Directs all programs relating to acquisition, preservation, and research use of materials in presidential libraries; conducts oral history projects; publishes finding aids for research sources; provides reference service, including information from and about documentary holdings. Conducts community outreach; oversees museum exhibition programming.

National Archives and Records Administration (NARA), *Reference Services, 8601 Adelphi Rd., #2400, College Park, MD 20740-6001; (301) 837-3510. Fax, (301) 837-1752. Timothy K. Nenninger, Branch Chief. Web, www.archives.gov/research/order/textual-records-dc .html*

Provides reference service for unpublished civil and military federal government records. Maintains central catalog of all archival materials. Compiles comprehensive bibliographies of materials related to archival administration and records management. Permits research in American history, archival science, and records management.

Maintains collections of the papers of the Continental Congress (1774–1789), U.S. State Dept. diplomatic correspondence (1789–1963), and general records of the U.S. government.

National Archives and Records Administration (NARA), *Research Services, 8601 Adelphi Rd., #3400, College Park, MD 20740-6001; (301) 837-1893. Fax, (301) 837-3633. William A. Mayer, Executive. Web, www.archives.gov/locations/archival-research.html*

Preserves and makes available federal records at fifteen National Archives facilities across the country.

National Security Staff (NSS) *(Executive Office of the President), Office of Strategic Communications and Speechwriting, Dwight D. Eisenhower Executive Office Bldg., #302 20500; (202) 456-9271. Fax, (202) 456-9270. Benjamin J. (Ben) Rhodes, Deputy National Security Adviser. Administrative office, (202) 456-9301. Web, www.whitehouse.gov/administration/eop/nsc*

Advises U.S. government agencies on the direction and theme of the president's message. Assists in the development and coordination of communications programs that disseminate consistent and accurate messages about the U.S. government and policies to the global audience.

National Technical Information Service (NTIS) *(Commerce Dept.), 5301 Shawnee Rd., Alexandria, VA*

22312; (703) 605-6000. Fax, (703) 605-6900.
Bruce Borzino, Director, (703) 605-6400. Toll-free, (800)
553-6847. Bookstore, (703) 605-6040. Customer support,
(703) 605-6050. Toll-free customer support, (888) 584-8332.
General email, info@ntis.gov

Web, www.ntis.gov

Collects and organizes technical, scientific, engineering, and business-related information generated by U.S.
and foreign governments and makes it available for
commercial use in the private sector. Makes available
approximately three million works covering research and
development, current events, business and management
studies, translations of foreign open source reports, foreign and domestic trade, general statistics, environment
and energy, health and social sciences, and hundreds of
other areas. Provides computer software and computerized data files in a variety of formats, including Internet
downloads. Houses the Homeland Security Information
Center, a centralized source on major security concerns
for health and medicine, food and agriculture, and bio-
chemical war.

State Dept., *International Information Programs,* 2200
C St. N.W., #05G12 20522; (202) 632-9942. Fax, (202) 632-
9901. Robert M. (Macon) Phillips, Coordinator.
General email, iip.pd@state.gov

Web, www.state.gov/r/iip

Implements strategic communications programs—
including Internet and print publications, traveling and
electronically transmitted speaker programs, and information resource services—that reach key international audiences and support department initiatives. Explains U.S.
foreign policy. Develops governmentwide technology policies that help disseminate this information.

▶ CONGRESS

*For a listing of relevant congressional committees and sub-
committees, please see page 84 or the Appendix.*

Government Accountability Office (GAO), *Publications
and Dissemination,* 441 G St. N.W., #1T61B 20548; (202)
512-3992. Leo Barbour, Director.
General email, info@gao.gov

Web, www.gao.gov

Provides information to the public on federal programs, reports, and testimonies. GAO publications and
information about GAO publications are available upon
request in print or online.

Government Printing Office (GPO), 732 N. Capitol St.
N.W. 20401; (202) 512-0000. Fax, (202) 512-2104.
Davita E. Vance-Cooks, Public Printer of the United States.
Public Relations, (202) 512-1957. Congressional
documents, (202) 512-1808. To order government
publications, (202) 512-1800.
General email, contactcenter@gpo.gov

Web, www.gpo.gov

Prints, distributes, and sells selected publications of
the U.S. Congress, government agencies, and executive

departments. Provides personal assistance in locating and
using government information. Makes available, for a fee,
the *Monthly Catalog of U.S. Government Publications,*
a comprehensive listing of all publications issued by the
various departments and agencies each month. Publications are distributed to GPO Regional Depository Libraries; some titles also may be purchased at the Washington,
D.C., GPO bookstore. GPO Access provides free electronic
access to government publications through the federal
digital system at www.fdsys.gov.

Legislative Resource Center, *Office of the Clerk, House
of Representatives,* B106 CHOB 20515; (202) 226-5200.
Fax, (202) 226-5208. Ronald (Dale) Thomas, Chief. Bill
status, (202) 225-1772.
General email, info.clerkweb@mail.house.gov

Web, http://clerk.house.gov/about/offices_lrc.aspx

Provides legislative information, records and registration, historical information, and library services to the
House and the public. Reading room contains computer
terminals where collections may be viewed or printed out.
Collections include House and Senate journals (1st Congress to present); Congressional Record and its predeces-
sors (1st Congress to present); House reports, documents,
bills, resolutions, and hearings; Senate reports and documents; U.S. statutes, treaties, the Federal Register, U.S.
codes, and numerous other documents. (See Web site or
call for a complete list of collections.)

Library of Congress, *Federal Library and Information
Network (FEDLINK),* 101 Independence Ave. S.E., #LA217
20540; (202) 707-4800. Fax, (202) 707-4818.
Kathryn Mendenhall, Executive Director, Interim;
Robin Harvey, Editor-in-Chief, (202) 707-4820. FEDLINK
Hotline, (202) 707-4900.
General email, flicc@loc.gov

Web, www.loc.gov/flicc

Promotes better utilization of federal library and information resources by seeking to provide the most cost-
effective and efficient administrative mechanisms for
providing services and materials to federal libraries and
information centers; serves as a forum for discussion of
federal library and information policies, programs, and
procedures; helps inform Congress, federal agencies,
and others concerned with libraries and information
centers.

Library of Congress, *Federal Research Division, Adams
Bldg.,* 101 Independence Ave. S.E., #LA5281 20540-4840;
(202) 707-3900. Fax, (202) 707-3920.
Roberta W. Goldblatt, Chief, Acting.
General email, frds@loc.gov

Web, www.loc.gov/rr/frd

Provides research and analytical support to federal
agencies

Library of Congress, *Serial and Government
Publications,* 101 Independence Ave. S.E., #LM133 20540;
(202) 707-5690. Teri Sierra, Assistant Chief. Reference

Desk, (202) 707-5208. *Current Periodical Reading Room*, (202) 707-5690.
Web, www.loc.gov/rr/news

Operates Newspaper and Current Periodical Reading Room; maintains library's collection of domestic and foreign newspapers, current periodicals, comic books, and current serially issued publications of federal, state, and foreign governments; maintains a selective U.S. federal government publication depository since 1979, a United Nations document collection, and a Federal Advisory Committee (FAC) collection. Responds to written or telephone requests for information on newspapers, periodicals, or government publications, or online through Ask a Librarian. Lends some microfilm through interlibrary loans.

Office of Art and Archives, *Office of the Clerk, House of Representatives, B53 CHOB 20515; (202) 226-1300. Fax, (202) 226-4635. Farar P. Elliott, Chief, Art and Archives.*
Web, http://clerk.house.gov

Works with the Office of the Historian to provide access to published documents and historical records of the House. Advises members on the disposition of their records and papers; maintains information on manuscript collections of former members; maintains biographical files on former members; houses photographs and artifacts of former members. Produces publications on Congress and its members.

Office of the Historian, *Office of the Clerk, U.S. House of Representatives, B56 CHOB 20515; (202) 226-5525. Fax, (202) 226-2931. Matthew A. Wasniewski, House Historian.*
Web, http://clerk.house.gov

Works with the Office of Art and Archives to provide access to published documents and historical records of the House. Conducts historical research. Advises members on the disposition of their records and papers; maintains information on manuscript collections of former members; maintains biographical files on former members. Produces publications on Congress and its members.

Senate Historical Office, *SH-201 20510; (202) 224-6900. Donald A. Ritchie, Historian.*
General email, historian@sec.senate.gov
Web, www.senate.gov

Serves as an information clearinghouse on Senate history, traditions, and members. Collects, organizes, and distributes to the public unpublished Senate documents; collects and preserves photographs and pictures related to Senate history; conducts an oral history program; advises senators and Senate committees on the disposition of their noncurrent papers and records. Produces publications on the history of the Senate.

Freedom of Information

▶AGENCIES

Justice Dept. (DOJ), *Information Policy, 1425 New York Ave. N.W., #11050 20530; (202) 514-3642. Fax, (202) 514-1009. Melanie Ann Pustay, Director. Information, (202) 514-2000.*
General email, doj.oip.foia@usdoj.gov
Web, www.justice.gov/oip/index.html

Provides federal agencies with advice and policy guidance on matters related to implementing and interpreting the Freedom of Information Act (FOIA). Litigates selected FOIA and Privacy Act cases; adjudicates administrative appeals from Justice Dept. denials of public requests for access to documents; conducts FOIA training for government agencies.

National Archives and Records Administration (NARA), *Information Security Oversight (ISOO), 700 Pennsylvania Ave. N.W., #100 20408-0001; (202) 357-5250. Fax, (202) 357-5907. John P. Fitzpatrick, Director, (202) 357-5205.*
General email, isoo@nara.gov
Web, www.archives.gov/isoo

Receiving guidance from the National Security Council, ISOO oversees policy on security classification/declassification on documents and programs for the federal government and industry; it also develops policies and procedures for sensitive unclassified information.

National Archives and Records Administration (NARA), *National Declassification Center, 8601 Adelphi Rd., #6350, College Park, MD 20740; (301) 837-0585. Fax, (301) 837-0346. Sheryl Shenberger, Director.*
General email, ndc@nara.gov
Web, www.archives.gov

Directs the review and declassification of records and security-classified materials in the National Archives in accordance with Executive Order 13526 and the Freedom of Information Act; assists other federal archival agencies in declassifying security-classified documents in their holdings.

▶NONGOVERNMENTAL

American Civil Liberties Union (ACLU), *Washington Legislative Office, 915 15th St. N.W. 20005; (202) 544-1681. Fax, (202) 546-0738. Laura W. Murphy, Director. Press, (202) 417-7547.*
General email, media@dcaclu.org
Web, www.aclu.org/legiupdate

Advocates for legislation to guarantee constitutional rights and civil liberties. Monitors agency compliance with the Privacy Act and other access statutes. Produces publications. (Headquarters in New York maintains docket of cases.)

Publications Contacts at Federal Departments and Agencies

GENERAL

Government Printing Office (GPO), (202) 512-1800, Toll-free, (866) 512-1800, Fax, (202) 512-2104; www.gpo.gov

National Technical Information Service (NTIS), (703) 605-6000 or (888) 584-8332; www.ntis.gov/products/publications.aspx

DEPARTMENTS

Agriculture, Information, (202) 694-5050; Orders (via NTIS); www.usda.gov/wps/portal/usda/usdahome?navid=USDA_PUBS

Commerce, Orders (via NTIS)

Defense, Orders (via NTIS); www.defense.gov/pubs

Education, Orders, (877) 433-7827, TTY, (877) 576-7734, Fax orders, (301) 470-1244; http://www2.ed.gov/about/pubs/intro/index.html?src=gu

Energy, Orders (via NTIS and GPO); www1.eere.energy.gov/library or www.osti.gov

Health and Human Services, Toll-free, (877) 696-6775; www.hhs.gov/about/infoguid.html

Housing and Urban Development, Orders, (800) 767-7468, Fax orders, (202) 708-2313; www.huduser.org/portal/publications/titlesatoz.html

Justice, Orders, (800) 851-3420; www.justice.gov/publications/publications_a.html

Labor, Statistic orders, (202) 691-5200; Employee benefits, (866) 444-3272; Web; www.dol.gov/ebsa/publications or www.dol.gov/odep/topics/OrderPublications.htm or www.dol.gov/dol/topic/statistics/publications.htm

State, Orders (via GPO); www.state.gov/r/pa/ei/rls

Transportation, Orders, (301) 322-5377, Fax orders, (301) 386-5394. Orders also via NTIS; www.fhwa.dot.gov/research/publications/periodicals.cfm

Treasury, Orders (via NTIS and GPO); www.treasury.gov/tigta/publications.shtml

Veterans Affairs, www.va.gov/opa/publications

AGENCIES

Census Bureau, Orders, (301) 763-4400; www.census.gov/prod/www

Commission on Civil Rights, Orders, (202) 376-8128; www.usccr.gov/pubs

Consumer Product Safety Commission, Orders, (301) 504-7921; www.cpsc.gov/en/Safety-Education/Safety-Guides/General-Information/Publications-Listing/

Corporation for National and Community Service (AmeriCorps), Orders, (800) 942-2677; https://pubs.nationalservice.gov

Energy Information Administration, Orders, (202) 586-8800; www.eia.gov/reports/

Environmental Protection Agency, Orders, (800) 490-9198; http://www.epa.gov/nscep/

Equal Employment Opportunity Commission, Orders, (800) 669-3362, TTY, (800) 800-3302; www1.eeoc.gov/eeoc/publications

Federal Election Commission, Orders, (800) 424-9530; www.fec.gov/info/publications.shtml

American Society of Access Professionals, *1444 Eye St. N.W., #700 20005; (202) 712-9054. Fax, (202) 216-9646. Claire Shanley, Executive Director. General email, asap@bostrom.com*

Web, www.accesspro.org

Membership: federal employees, attorneys, journalists, and others working with or interested in access-to-information laws. Seeks to improve the administration of the Freedom of Information Act, the Privacy Act, and other access statutes.

Center for National Security Studies, *1730 Pennsylvania Ave. N.W., 7th Floor 20006; (202) 721-5650. Fax, (202) 530-0128. Kate A. Martin, Director. General email, cnss@cnss.org*

Web, www.cnss.org

Human rights and civil liberties organization specializing in national security, access to government information, government secrecy, government surveillance, intelligence oversight, and detentions.

Radio Television Digital News Assn., *529 14th St. N.W., #1240 20045; (202) 659-6510. Fax, (202) 223-4007. Mike Cavender, Executive Director, (770) 622-7011.*

General email, rtdna@rtdna.org

Web, www.rtdna.org

Membership: electronic journalists in radio, television, and all digital media. Sponsors and promotes education and advocacy concerning First Amendment issues, freedom of information, and government secrecy issues; ethics in reporting; improving coverage; implementing technology; and other news industry issues. Radio and Television News Directors Foundation (RTNDF) is the educational arm of the association.

INTERNET AND RELATED TECHNOLOGIES

General

▶ **AGENCIES**

Criminal Division *(Justice Dept.), Computer Crime and Intellectual Property, 1301 New York Ave. N.W., #600 20530; (202) 514-1026. Fax, (202) 514-6113. John Lynch, Chief. Web, www.justice.gov/criminal/cybercrime*

Federal Emergency Management Agency, Toll-free, (800) 480-2520, Fax orders, (301) 362-5335; http://www.fema.gov/publications-archive or www.ready.gov/publications

Federal Reserve System, Orders, (202) 452-3245, Fax orders, (202) 728-5886; www.federalreserve.gov/pubs/order.htm

Federal Trade Commission, Orders, (877) 382-4357; https://bulkorder.ftc.gov

General Services Administration, (GAO), Orders, (800) 488-3111; www.gsa.gov/portal/content/101674

Government Accountability Office, Orders, (202) 512-6000, Toll-free, (866) 801-7077, TTY, (202) 512-2537; www.gao.gov/ordering.htm

International Bank for Reconstruction and Development (World Bank), Orders, (703) 661-1580, Toll-free, (800) 645-7247, Fax, (703) 661-1501; http://publications.worldbank.org

International Trade Administration, Information, (202) 482-5487; Orders via NTIS and GPO; http://trade.gov/publications

National Archives and Records Administration, Orders, (202) 357-5332, Toll-free, (866) 325-7208; www.archives.gov/publications

National Endowment for the Humanities, Orders, (202) 606-8435

National Park Service, Information on brochures, (202) 208-4747; www.nps.gov/aboutus/publications.htm; Orders by mail only

National Science Foundation, Orders, (703) 292-7827; www.nsf.gov/publications

National Transportation Safety Board, Information, (202) 314-6551; www.ntsb.gov/Info/gils/Publications.html; Postpublication orders via NTIS.

Nuclear Regulatory Commission, Orders, (301) 415-4737 or (800) 397-4209; Orders also from GPO; www.nrc.gov/reading-rm/pdr.html

Occupational Safety and Health Administration, Orders, (202) 693-1888, Fax, (202) 693-2498; www.osha.gov/pls/publications/publication.html

Office of Personnel Management, Orders (via GPO); Retirement and insurance information, (202) 606-1800; http://apps.opm.gov/publications

Peace Corps, Toll-free hotline, (855) 855-1961; http://collection.peacecorps.gov/cdm/landingpage/collection/p15105coll3

Securities and Exchange Commission, Orders, (202) 551-4040; Public documents, (202) 551-8090; www.sec.gov/investor/pubs.shtml

Social Security Administration, Orders, (410) 965-2039 or Fax, (410) 965-2037; www.ssa.gov/pubs

U.S. Fish and Wildlife Service, Orders, (800) 344-WILD; Orders via NTIS; www.fws.gov/external-affairs/dpps/visualmedia/printingandpublishing/index.html?OrgCode=97130

U.S. Geological Survey, Orders, (888) ASK-USGS; http://store.usgs.gov

U.S. Institute of Peace, Book orders, (800) 868-8064, Fax orders, (703) 661-1501; http://bookstore.usip.org

---

Investigates and litigates criminal cases involving computers, intellectual property, and the Internet. Administers the Computer Crime Initiative, a program designed to combat electronic penetrations, data theft, and cyberattacks on critical information systems. Provides specialized technical and legal assistance to other Justice Dept. divisions; coordinates international efforts; formulates policies and proposes legislation on computer crime and intellectual property issues.

Cyber Crimes Center (C3) *(Homeland Security Dept.),* 500 12th St. S.W. 20536; (703) 293-8005. Fax, (703) 293-9127. Ian Quinn, Deputy Assistant Director, (703) 293-9558. Press, (202) 732-4242.
Web, www.ice.gov/cyber-crimes

Focuses on the investigation of international Internet crimes, such as money laundering, financing of terrorist activities, child sexual exploitation, human smuggling and trafficking, intellectual property rights violations, identity and document fraud, illegal arms trafficking, and drug trafficking.

Defense Advanced Research Projects Agency *(Defense Dept.),* 675 N. Randolph St., Arlington, VA 22203-2114;

(703) 696-2400. Fax, (703) 696-2209. Arati Prabhakar, Director; Eric Mazzacone, External Relations, (703) 526-4758.
Web, www.darpa.mil

Develops technologically advanced research ideas, assesses technical feasibility, and develops prototypes.

Federal Bureau of Investigation (FBI) *(Justice Dept.), Asset Forfeiture/Money Laundering Unit,* 935 Pennsylvania Ave. N.W., #3901 20535; (202) 324-8628. Fax, (202) 324-6248. Crosby Brackett, Chief, Acting.
Web, www.fbi.gov

Investigates crimes of fraud, theft, or embezzlement within or against financial institutions. Priorities include identity theft, mortgage and credit card fraud, asset forfeiture, and money laundering.

Federal Communications Commission (FCC), *Strategic Planning and Policy Analysis,* 445 12th St. S.W., #7-C347 20554; (202) 418-2030. Fax, (202) 418-2807. Jonathan Chambers, Chief, Acting.
Web, www.fcc.gov/office-strategic-planning-policy-analysis

Public Affairs Contacts at Federal Departments and Agencies

DEPARTMENTS

Agriculture, Carol Blake, (202) 720-3884

Commerce, Jim Hock, (202) 482-4883

Defense, George E. Little, (703) 697-5131

  Air Force, Brig. Gen. Les Kodlick, (703) 697-6061

  Army, Brig. Gen. Gary Volesky, (703) 693-4723

  Marine Corps, Brig. Gen. Paul Kennedy, (703) 614-4309

  Navy, Rear Adm. John Kirby, (703) 697-5342

Education, Massie Ritsch, (202) 401-2000

Energy, Dan Leistikow, (202) 586-4940

Health and Human Services, Dori Salcido (Acting), (202) 205-4347

Homeland Security, Clark Stevens, (202) 282-8010

Housing and Urban Development, Melanie Roussell, (202) 708-0980

Interior, Kate Kelly, (202) 208-6416

Justice, Brian Fallon, (202) 514-2007

Labor, Carl Fillichio, (202) 693-4676

State, Michael A. Hammer, (202) 647-6575

Transportation, Sasha Johnson, (202) 366-4000

Treasury, Natalie Wyeth Earnest, (202) 622-2960

Veterans Affairs, Michael S. Galloucis, (202) 461-7500

AGENCIES

Agency for International Development, T. Charles Cooper, (202) 712-4320

Commission on Civil Rights, Lenore Ostrowsky (Acting), (202) 376-8591

Commodity Futures Trading Commission, Steven Adamske, (202) 418-5080

Consumer Product Safety Commission, Scott Wolfson, (301) 504-7051

Corporation for National and Community Service, Jacqueline Aker, (202) 606-6722

Environmental Protection Agency, Donna Heron (Acting), (215) 814-5113

Equal Employment Opportunity Commission, Kimberly Smith Brown, (202) 663-4950

Export-Import Bank, Phil Cogan, (202) 565-3203

Farm Credit Administration, Michael A. Stokke, (703) 883-4056

Federal Communications Commission, Shannon Gilson, (202) 418-0503

Federal Deposit Insurance Corporation, Andrew Gray, (877) 275-3342

Federal Election Commission, Patricia K. Young, (202) 694-1120

Federal Emergency Management Agency, Lars Anderson, (202) 646-4600

Federal Labor Relations Authority, Sarah Whittle Spooner, (202) 218-7791

Federal Mediation and Conciliation Service, John Arnold, (202) 606-5442

Monitors developments in expansion of the global Internet and the communications industry. Reviews legal trends in intellectual property law and e-commerce issues.

General Services Administration (GSA), *Government-wide Policy, Information, Integrity, and Access,* 1275 1st St. N.E. 20417; (202) 501-0161. Fax, (202) 357-0044. *Angela Smith, Senior Technical Advisor.*
Web, www.gsa.gov/portal/category/21399

Develops, coordinates, and defines ways that electronic and information technology business strategies can assist the Office of Management and Budget and other federal agencies to enhance access to and delivery of information and services.

National Science Foundation (NSF), *Computer and Information Science and Engineering (CISE),* 4201 Wilson Blvd., #1105N, Arlington, VA 22230; (703) 292-8900. Fax, (703) 292-9074. *Farnam Jahanian, Assistant Director.* Web, www.nsf.gov/div/index.jsp?org=cise

Supports investigator-initiated research in computer science and engineering. Promotes the use of advanced computing, communications, and information systems. Provides grants for research and education.

National Telecommunications and Information Administration (NTIA) *(Commerce Dept.),* 1401 Constitution Ave. N.W., #4898 20230; (202) 482-1840. Fax, (202) 501-0536. Lawrence E. Strickling, Assistant Secretary. Press, (202) 482-7002.
Web, www.ntia.doc.gov

Responsible for oversight of the technical management of the Internet domain name system (DNS).

Office of Management and Budget (OMB) *(Executive Office of the President), Information and Regulatory Affairs,* New Executive Office Bldg., #10236 20503; (202) 395-3785. Fax, (202) 395-5167. Boris Bershteyn, Administrator, Acting.
Web, www.whitehouse.gov/omb/inforeg_infopoltech

Oversees implementation and policy development under the Information Technology Reform Act of 1996 and the Paperwork Reduction Act of 1995; focuses on information technology management and substantive information policy, including records management, privacy and computer security, and the Freedom of Information Act.

▶ CONGRESS

Government Accountability Office (GAO), *Applied Research and Methods,* 441 G St. N.W., #6419 20548; (202) 512-2700. Fax, (202) 512-3938. Nancy Kingsbury, Managing Director.
Web, www.gao.gov

Federal Reserve System, Lucretia M. Boyer, (202) 452-2955

Federal Trade Commission, Justin Cole, (202) 326-2180

General Services Administration, Betsaida Alcantara, (202) 590-6075

Government Accountability Office, Chuck Young, (202) 512-4800

Government Printing Office, Gary Somerset, (202) 512-1957

Institute of Museum and Library Services, Mamie Bittner, (202) 653-4757

National Aeronautics and Space Administration, Michael Cabbage, (212) 678-5516

National Archives and Records Administration, Chris Isleib, (202) 357-5328

National Capital Planning Commission, Stephen Staudigl, (202) 482-7279

National Credit Union Administration, Todd Harper, (703) 518-6330

National Endowment for the Arts, Elizabeth Auclair, Sally Gifford, (202) 682-5570

National Endowment for the Humanities, Judy Havemann, (202) 606-8355

National Labor Relations Board, Gregory J. King, (202) 273-0222

National Science Foundation, Noreen M. Hecmanczuk, (703) 292-7414

National Transportation Safety Board, Kelly A. Nantel, (202) 314-6100

Nuclear Regulatory Commission, Diane P. Screnci, (610) 337-5330

Occupational Safety and Health Review Administration, Melik Ahmir-Abdul, (202) 606-5370

Office of Personnel Management, Edmund D. Byrnes, (202) 606-2402

Office of Special Counsel, Ann O'Hanlon, (202) 254-3631

Pension Benefit Guaranty Corporation, Jioni Palmer (Acting), (202) 326-4010

Securities and Exchange Commission, John Nester, (202) 551-4120

Selective Service System, Richard S. Flahaven, (703) 605-4100

Small Business Administration, Fred Baldassaro, (202) 205-7085

Social Security Administration, LaVenia J. LaVelle, (410) 965-8904

U.S. International Trade Commission, Peg O'Laughlin, (202) 205-1819

U.S. Postal Service, Toni DeLancey, (202) 268-6915

Assesses the quality of the nation's major statistical databases and helps adapt the government's dissemination of information to a new technological environment. Conducts congressional studies that entail specialized analysis.

Government Accountability Office (GAO), *Information Technology,* 441 G St. N.W., #4T21 20548; (202) 512-6408. Joel C. Willemssen, Managing Director. Web, www.gao.gov

Seeks to make the federal government more effective in its information management by improving performance and reducing costs. Assesses best practices in the public and private sectors; makes recommendations to government agencies. Interests include information security.

▶**NONGOVERNMENTAL**

American Library Assn., *Office for Information Technology Policy,* 1615 New Hampshire Ave. N.W., 1st Floor 20009-2520; (202) 628-8410. Fax, (202) 628-8419. Alan Inouye, Director. General email, oitp@alawash.org Web, www.ala.org/offices/oitp

Provides policy research and analysis of developments in technology and telecommunications as they affect libraries and library users. Interests include information

policy, law, and regulations; free expression on the Internet; equitable access to electronic information resources; and treaty negotiations of the United Nations World Intellectual Property Organization.

Assn. for Information Science and Technology (ASIS&T), 8555 16th St., #850, Silver Spring, MD 20910; (301) 495-0900. Fax, (301) 495-0810. Richard Hill, Executive Director. General email, asis@asis.org Web, www.asis.org

Membership: information specialists from such fields as computer science, linguistics, management, librarianship, engineering, law, medicine, chemistry, and education. Advocates research and development in basic and applied information science. Offers continuing education programs.

Assn. for Competitive Technology (ACT), 1401 K St. N.W., #502 20005; (202) 331-2130. Fax, (202) 331-2139. Jonathan Zuck, President. General email, info@actonline.org Web, www.actonline.org

Membership: businesses that engage in or support the information technology industry. International education and advocacy organization for information technology

Freedom of Information Contacts at Federal Departments and Agencies

DEPARTMENTS

Agriculture, Ravoyne Peyton, (202) 260-2657

Commerce, Brenda Dolan, (202) 482-3258

Defense, Jim Hogan, (866) 574-4970

  Air Force, Anh Trinh, (703) 614-8500

  Army, Alecia Bolling, (703) 428-7128

  Marine Corps, Sally Hughes, (703) 614-4008

  Navy, Robin Patterson, (202) 685-0412

Education, Elise Cook, (202) 401-8365

Energy, Kevin T. Hagerty, (202) 586-5955

Health and Human Services, Michael Bell (Acting), (202) 690-7453

Homeland Security, Sabrina Burroughs, (202) 325-0150

Housing and Urban Development, Vicky J. Lewis, (202) 708-3054

Interior, Clarice Julka, (202) 565-1076

Justice, Michael Clay, (202) 514-0217

Labor, Thomas G. Hicks Sr., (202) 693-5427

State, Marianne Manheim, (202) 261-8484

Transportation, Fern Kaufman, (202) 366-8067

Treasury, Hugh Gilmore, (202) 622-0876

Veterans Affairs, Laurie Karnay, (202) 632-7465

AGENCIES

Agency for International Development, Alecia S. Sillah, (202) 712-0960

Central Intelligence Agency, Scott Koch, (703) 613-1287

Commission on Civil Rights, Lenore Ostrowsky, (202) 376-8591

Commodity Futures Trading Commission, Linda Mauldin, (202) 418-5497

Consumer Product Safety Commission, Deborah Acosta, (301) 504-6890

Council on Environmental Quality, Vacant, (202) 456-4327

Environmental Protection Agency, Larry F. Gottesman, (202) 566-1667

Equal Employment Opportunity Commission, Stephanie Garner, (202) 663-4634

Export-Import Bank, Dawn R. Kral, (202) 565-3248

Farm Credit Administration, Christine D. Quinn, (703) 883-4108

Federal Communications Commission, Stephanie Kost, (202) 418-1379

Federal Deposit Insurance Corp., Cottrell L. Webster, (703) 562-6040

Federal Election Commission, Kate Higginbothom, (202) 694-1650

Federal Emergency Management Agency, Terry Cochran, (202) 646-3323

Federal Labor Relations Authority, Gina Grippando, (202) 218-7776

Federal Maritime Commission, Karen Gregory, (202) 523-5725

Federal Reserve, Jeanne McLaughlin, (202) 452-3236

Federal Trade Commission, Richard Gold, (202) 326-3355

General Services Administration, Ralph Boldt, (202) 501-3094

Legal Services Corp., Cheryl DuHart, (202) 295-1500

Merit Systems Protection Board, Bernard Parker, (202) 254-4475

National Aeronautics and Space Administration, Miriam Brown-Lam, (202) 358-0718

National Archives and Records Administration, Gary Stern, (301) 837-2024

National Credit Union Administration, Linda Dent, (703) 518-6450

National Endowment for the Humanities, Lisette Voyatzis, (202) 606-8322

National Labor Relations Board, Jayme Sophir, (202) 273-3800

National Mediation Board, Susanne Parker, (202) 692-5040

National Science Foundation, Sandra Evans, (703) 292-8060

National Transportation Safety Board, Melba D. Moye, (202) 314-6540

Nuclear Regulatory Commission, Mark H. Graff (Acting), (301) 415-7169

Office of Government Ethics, Arthur A. Lopez, (202) 482-9316

Office of Management and Budget, Lauren Wright, (202) 395-3642

Office of National Drug Control Policy, Daniel Petersen, (202) 395-6745

Office of Personnel Management, Trina Porter, (202) 606-4417

Office of Science and Technology Policy, Rachael Leonard, (202) 456-6125

Office of the U.S. Trade Representative, Jacqueline B. Caldwell, (202) 395-3419

Peace Corps, Denore Miller, (202) 692-1236

Pension Benefit Guaranty Corp., Michelle Y. Chase, (202) 326-4040

Securities and Exchange Commission, John Livornese, (202) 551-7900

Selective Service, Paula A. Sweeney, (703) 605-4100

Small Business Administration, Lisa Babcock, (202) 401-8203

Social Security Administration, Dawn S. Wiggins, (410) 965-1727

U.S. International Trade Commission, Jacqueline N. Gross, (202) 205-1816

U.S. Postal Service, Jane Eyre, (202) 268-2608

Federal Government Web Sites

CONGRESS
Government Accountability Office, www.gao.gov

House of Representatives, www.house.gov

Library of Congress, www.loc.gov

Senate, www.senate.gov

WHITE HOUSE
General Information, www.whitehouse.gov

DEPARTMENTS
Agriculture, www.usda.gov

Commerce, www.commerce.gov

Defense, www.defense.mil

  Air Force, www.af.mil

  Army, www.army.mil

  Marine Corps, www.marines.mil

  Navy, www.navy.mil

Education, www2.ed.gov

Energy, www.energy.gov

Health and Human Services, www.hhs.gov

Homeland Security, www.dhs.gov

  Coast Guard, www.uscg.mil

Housing and Urban Development, www.hud.gov

Interior, www.doi.gov

Justice, www.justice.gov

Labor, www.dol.gov

State, www.state.gov

Transportation, www.dot.gov

Treasury, www.ustreas.gov

Veterans Affairs, www.va.gov

AGENCIES
Consumer Product Safety Commission, www.cpsc.gov

Corporation for Public Broadcasting, www.cpb.org

Drug Enforcement Administration, www.justice.gov/dea

Environmental Protection Agency, www.epa.gov

Export-Import Bank, www.exim.gov

Federal Aviation Administration, www.faa.gov

Federal Bureau of Investigation, www.fbi.gov

Federal Communications Commission, www.fcc.gov

Federal Deposit Insurance Corporation, www.fdic.gov

Federal Election Commission, www.fec.gov

Federal Emergency Management Agency, www.fema.gov

Federal Energy Regulatory Commission, www.ferc.gov

Federal Reserve System, www.federalreserve.gov

Federal Trade Commission, www.ftc.gov

Food and Drug Administration, www.fda.gov

General Services Administration, www.gsa.gov

Government Printing Office, www.gpo.gov

Internal Revenue Service, www.irs.gov

National Aeronautics and Space Administration, www.nasa.gov

National Archives and Records Administration, www.archives.gov

National Institute of Standards and Technology, www.nist.gov

National Institutes of Health, www.nih.gov

National Oceanic and Atmospheric Administration, www.noaa.gov; www.climate.gov

National Park Service, www.nps.gov

National Railroad Passenger Corporation (Amtrak), www.amtrak.com

National Science Foundation, www.nsf.gov

National Technical Information Service, www.ntis.gov

National Transportation Safety Board, www.ntsb.gov

Nuclear Regulatory Commission, www.nrc.gov

Occupational Safety and Health Administration, www.osha.gov

Patent and Trademark Office, www.uspto.gov

Peace Corps, www.peacecorps.gov

Pension Benefit Guaranty Corporation, www.pbgc.gov

Securities and Exchange Commission, www.sec.gov

Small Business Administration, www.sba.gov

Smithsonian Institution, www.si.edu

Social Security Administration, www.ssa.gov

U.S. Fish and Wildlife Service, www.fws.gov

U.S. Geological Survey, www.usgs.gov

U.S. International Trade Commission, www.usitc.gov

U.S. Postal Service, www.usps.com

companies worldwide. Interests include intellectual property, international trade, e-commerce, privacy, tax policy, antitrust, and commercial piracy issues. Focuses predominantly on the interests of small and midsized entrepreneurial technology companies. Monitors legislation and regulations.

Assn. of Research Libraries (ARL), *21 Dupont Circle N.W., #800 20036-1118; (202) 296-2296. Fax, (202) 872-0884. Elliott Shore, Executive Director.*
General email, webmgr@arl.org
Web, www.arl.org

Federation of 126 research and academic libraries in the United States and Canada. Interests include public access to federally funded research; federal, state, and international copyright and intellectual property laws; information technology and telecommunications policies; appropriations for selected federal and congressional agencies, national libraries, and agency programs and initiatives; scholarly communication, including publication and dissemination systems; the library's role in the transformation of research, teaching, and learning; and library performance assessment.

Business Software Alliance (BSA), *20 F St. N.W., #800 20001; (202) 872-5500. Fax, (202) 872-5501. Victoria Espinel, President. Toll-free, (888) 667-4722.*
General email, info@bsa.org
Web, www.bsa.org

Membership: personal and business computer software publishing companies. Promotes growth of the software industry worldwide; helps develop electronic commerce. Investigates claims of software theft within corporations, financial institutions, academia, state and local governments, and nonprofit organizations. Provides legal counsel and initiates litigation on behalf of members.

Center for Democracy and Technology, *1634 Eye St. N.W., #1100 20006; (202) 637-9800. Fax, (202) 637-0968. Nuala O'Connor, President.*
General email, info@cdt.org
Web, www.cdt.org

Promotes and defends privacy and civil liberties on the Internet. Interests include free expression, social networking and access to the Internet, consumer protection, health information privacy and technology, and government surveillance.

Center for Digital Democracy, *1621 Connecticut Ave. N.W., #550 20005; (202) 986-2220. Jeffrey Chester, Executive Director, (202) 494-7100.*
General email, jeff@democraticmedia.org
Web, www.democraticmedia.org

Seeks to ensure that the public interest is a fundamental part of the digital communications landscape. Conducts public education designed to protect consumer privacy and works to ensure competition in the new media industries, especially at the Federal Trade Commission and the Justice Dept. Tracks and analyzes the online advertising market, including areas affecting public health, news and

information, children and adolescents, and financial industries.

Coalition for Networked Information, *21 Dupont Circle N.W., #800 20036; (202) 296-5098. Fax, (202) 872-0884. Clifford A. Lynch, Executive Director.*
General email, info@cni.org
Web, www.cni.org

Membership: higher education, publishing, network and telecommunications, information technology, and libraries and library organizations, as well as government agencies and foundations. Promotes networked information technology, scholarly communication, intellectual productivity, and education.

Computer and Communications Industry Assn. (CCIA), *900 17th St. N.W., #1100 20006; (202) 783-0070. Fax, (202) 783-0534. Edward J. Black, President; Heather Greenfield, Director of Communications.*
General email, hgreenfield@ccianet.org
Web, www.ccianet.org

Membership: Internet service providers, software providers, and manufacturers and suppliers of computer data processing and communications-related products and services. Interests include Internet freedom, privacy and neutrality, government electronic surveillance, telecommunications policy, tax policy, federal procurement policy, communications and computer industry standards, intellectual property policies, encryption, international trade, and antitrust reform.

Cyber Security Policy and Research Institute, *George Washington University, 707 22nd St. N.W., #304A 20052; (202) 994-5613. Fax, (202) 994-4875. Lance J. Hoffman, Director.*
General email, cspri@gwu.edu
Web, www.cspri.seas.gwu.edu

Promotes education, research, and policy analysis in the areas of computer security and privacy, computer networks, electronic commerce, e-government, and the cultural aspects of cyberspace. (Affiliated with George Washington University.)

Data Interchange Standards Assn. (DISA), *8300 Greensboro Dr., #800, McLean, VA 22102; (703) 970-4480. Fax, (703) 970-4488. Jerry C. Connors, President.*
General email, info@disa.org
Web, www.disa.org

Promotes the development of cross-industry interchange standards in electronic commerce that help organizations improve business methods, lower costs, and increase productivity. Provides administrative and technical support to ASC X12.

Electronic Privacy Information Center (EPIC), *1718 Connecticut Ave. N.W., #200 20009; (202) 483-1140. Fax, (202) 483-1248. Marc Rotenberg, Executive Director.*
General email, info@epic.org
Web, www.epic.org

Public interest research center. Conducts research and conferences on domestic and international civil liberties issues, including privacy, free speech, information access, computer security, and encryption; litigates cases. Monitors legislation and regulations.

Entertainment Software Assn. (ESA), *575 7th St. N.W., #300 20004; (202) 223-2400. Fax, (202) 223-2401. Michael D. (Mike) Gallagher, President. General email, esa@theesa.com*

Web, www.theesa.com

Membership: publishers of interactive entertainment software. Distributes marketing statistics and information. Administers a worldwide antipiracy program. Established an independent rating system for entertainment software. Monitors legislation and regulations. Interests include First Amendment and intellectual property protection efforts.

Family Online Safety Institute, *400 7th St. N.W., #306 20004; (202) 775-0131. Stephen (Steve) Balkam, Chief Executive Officer. Press, (202) 775-0158. General email, fosi@fosi.org*

Web, www.fosi.org

Membership: Internet safety advocates in business, government, academia, the media, and the general public. Identifies risks to children on the Internet; develops and promotes solutions to keep children safe while protecting free speech. Issues reports on online trends among young people; hosts conferences and other educational events; monitors legislation and regulations internationally.

IDEAlliance, *1600 Duke St., #420, Alexandria, VA 22314; (703) 837-1070. Fax, (703) 837-1072. David J. Steinhardt, President, (703) 837-1066. General email, registrar@idealliance.org*

Web, www.idealliance.org

Membership: firms and customers in printing, publishing, and information technology. Helps set industry standards for electronic and Web commerce and conducts studies on new information technologies.

Info Comm International, *11242 Waples Mill Rd., #200, Fairfax, VA 22030; (703) 273-7200. Fax, (703) 278-8082. David Labuskes, Executive Director. Information, (800) 659-7469.*

Web, www.infocomm.org

Membership: video and audiovisual dealers, manufacturers and producers, and individuals. Promotes the professional AV communications industry and seeks to enhance members' ability to conduct business successfully through tradeshows, education, certification, market research, and government relations. Interests include small business issues, intellectual property, sustainable buildings, e-waste, and standards. Monitors legislation and regulations. (Formerly the International Communications Industries Assn.)

Information Sciences Institute - East, *Washington Office, 3811 N. Fairfax Dr., #200, Arlington, VA 22203; (703) 812-3700. Fax, (703) 812-3712. Joseph Sullivan, Associate Director, (310) 448-8206.*

Web, www.isi.edu

Conducts basic and applied research in advanced computer, communications, and information processing technologies. Works with public- and private-sector customers to develop diverse information technologies for civilian and military uses, often bridging multiple technology disciplines. Projects include advanced communications and network research; distributed databases and pattern recognition with applications in law enforcement, inspection systems, and threat detection; and computing architectures and devices. (Headquarters in Marina del Rey, Calif.; part of the University of Southern California.)

Information Technology Industry Council (ITI), *1101 K St. N.W., #610 20005; (202) 737-8888. Fax, (202) 638-4922. Dean C. Garfield, President. Press, (202) 626-5725. General email, info@itic.org*

Web, www.itic.org

Membership: providers of information and communications technology products and services. Advocates for member companies in three main areas: environment and sustainability, global policy, and government relations. Interests include international tax reform, telecommunications, STEM education, trade, accessibility, voluntary standards, and sustainability.

Internet Alliance, *1615 L St. N.W., #1100 20036; (202) 861-2407. Tammy Cota, Executive Director. General email, tammyc@internetalliance.org*

Web, www.internetalliance.org

Membership: companies involved in the online industry, including marketing agencies, consulting and research organizations, entrepreneurs, financial institutions, interactive service providers, software vendors, telecommunications companies, and service bureaus. Promotes consumer confidence and trust in the Internet and monitors the effect of public policy on the Internet and its users with a focus on privacy, taxation, intellectual property, online security, unsolicited email, and content regulation.

Internet Education Foundation, *1634 Eye St. N.W., #1100 20006; (202) 638-4370. Fax, (202) 637-0968. Tim Lordan, Executive Director. General email, info@neted.org*

Web, www.neted.org

Sponsors educational initiatives promoting the Internet as a valuable medium for democratic participation, communications, and commerce. Funds the Congressional Internet Caucus Advisory Committee, which works to inform Congress of important Internet-related policy issues. Monitors legislation and regulations.

Internet Engineering Task Force (IETF), *c/o Internet Society (ISOC), 1775 Wiehle Ave., #201, Reston, VA 20190-5108; (703) 439-2133. Fax, (703) 326-9881. Ray Pelletier, Administrative Director. General email, ietf@ietf.org*

Web, www.ietf.org

Membership: network designers, operators, vendors, and researchers from around the world who are concerned with the evolution, smooth operation, and continuing development of the Internet. Establishes working groups to address technical concerns. IETF is an organized activity of the Internet Society. (Headquarters in Fremont, Calif.)

Internet Society (ISOC), *1775 Wiehle Ave., #201, Reston, VA 20190-5108; (703) 439-2120. Fax, (703) 326-9881. Katy Brown, President.*
General email, media@isoc.org

Web, www.internetsociety.org

Membership: individuals, corporations, nonprofit organizations, and government agencies. Promotes development and availability of the Internet and its associated technologies and applications; publishes international standards. Conducts research and educational programs; assists technologically developing countries in achieving Internet usage; provides information about the Internet.

Pew Internet and American Life Project, *1615 L St. N.W., #700 20036; (202) 419-4500. Fax, (202) 419-4505. Lee Rainie, Director.*
General email, info@pewinternet.org

Web, www.pewinternet.org

Conducts research, surveys, and analyses to explore the impact of the Internet on families, communities, teens, health care, mobile technologies, and civic and political life. Makes its reports available online for public and academic use. (A project of the Pew Research Center.)

Public Knowledge, *1818 N St. N.W., #410 20036; (202) 861-0020. Fax, (202) 861-0040. Gene Kimmelman, President.*
General email, pk@publicknowledge.org

Web, www.publicknowledge.org

Coalition of libraries, educators, scientists, artists, musicians, journalists, lawyers, and consumers interested in intellectual property law and technology policy as it pertains to the Internet and electronic information. Encourages openness, access, and competition in the digital age. Supports U.S. laws and policies that provide incentives to innovators as well as ensure a free flow of information and ideas to the public.

Software and Information Industry Assn. (SIIA), *1090 Vermont Ave. N.W., 6th Floor 20005; (202) 289-7442. Fax, (202) 289-7097. Kenneth (Ken) Wasch, President, (202) 789-4440.*
Web, www.siia.net

Membership: software and digital content companies. Promotes the industry worldwide; conducts antipiracy program and other intellectual property initiatives; sponsors conferences, seminars, and other events. Monitors legislation and regulations.

TechAmerica, *Government Affairs Office, 601 Pennsylvania Ave. N.W., North Bldg., #600 20004; (202) 682-9110. Fax, (202) 682-9111. Shawn Osborne, President; Michael (Mike) Hettinger, Senior Vice President, Public Sector and Federal Government Affairs; Shawn Osborne, Chief Executive Officer. Press, (202) 682-4443.*

General email, csc@techamerica.org

Web, www.techamerica.org

Trade association for technology companies offering hardware, software, electronics, telecommunications, and information technology products and services. Offers business services and networking programs to members. Monitors legislation and regulations.

Technology CEO Council, *1341 G St. N.W., #1100 20005; (202) 585-0258. Fax, (202) 393-3031. Bruce Mehlman, Executive Director.*
General email, info@techceocouncil.org

Web, www.techceocouncil.org

Membership: chief executive officers from U.S. information technology companies. Monitors legislation and regulations on technology and trade issues. Interests include health care information technology, telecommunications, international trade, innovation, digital rights management, export and knowledge controls, and privacy. (Formerly the Computer Systems Policy Project.)

The Telework Coalition (TelCoa), *204 E. St. N.E. 20002; (202) 266-0046. Fax, (202) 465-3776. Chuck Wilsker, President.*
General email, info@telcoa.org

Web, www.telcoa.org

Promotes telework and access to broadband services to increase productivity and provide employment opportunities for disabled, rural, and older workers, while reducing vehicular travel and energy use. Monitors legislation and regulations.

MEDIA PROFESSIONS AND RESOURCES

General

▶**AGENCIES**

Federal Communications Commission (FCC), *Communications Business Opportunities, 445 12th St. S.W., #4A624 20554; (202) 418-0990. Fax, (202) 418-0235. Thomas Reed, Director.*
General email, ocbo@fcc.gov

Web, www.fcc.gov/office-communications-business-opportunities

Provides technical and legal guidance and assistance to the small, minority, and female business communities in the telecommunications industry. Advises the FCC chair on small, minority, and female business issues. Serves as liaison between federal agencies, state and local governments, and trade associations representing small, minority, and female enterprises concerning FCC policies, procedures, rulemaking activities, and increased ownership and employment opportunities.

Federal Communications Commission (FCC), *Media Bureau, Equal Employment Opportunity, 445 12th St.*

S.W., #3A738 20554; (202) 418-1450. Fax, (202) 418-1797. Lewis Pulley, Assistant Chief, Policy Division, EEO, (202) 418-2120.
Web, www.fcc.gov/encyclopedia/equal_employment_ opportunity_0

Responsible for the annual certification of cable television equal employment opportunity compliance. Oversees broadcast employment practices.

▶NONGOVERNMENTAL

American News Women's Club, 1607 22nd St. N.W. 20008; (202) 332-6770. Fax, (202) 265-6092. Claire Sanders Swift, President.
General email, anwclub@comcast.net
Web, www.anwc.org

Membership: women in communications. Promotes the advancement of women in all media. Sponsors professional receptions and lectures.

Communications Workers of America (CWA), 501 3rd St. N.W. 20001; (202) 434-1100. Fax, (202) 434-1279. Larry Cohen, President.
General email, cwaweb@cwa-union.org
Web, www.cwa-union.org

Membership: approximately 700,000 workers in telecommunications, journalism, publishing, cable television, electronics, and other fields. Interests include workplace democracy and restoring bargaining rights. Represents members in contract negotiations and grievances; conducts training programs and workshops. Monitors legislation and regulations. (Affiliated with the AFL-CIO.)

Freedom Forum, 555 Pennsylvania Ave. N.W. 20001; (202) 292-6100. James C. Duff, Chief Executive Officer. Toll-free inquiries, (888) 639-7386.
General email, news@freedomforum.org
Web, www.freedomforum.org

Sponsors training and research that promote free press, free speech, and freedom of information. Interests include the First Amendment and newsroom diversity. Primary funder for the Newseum, an interactive museum of news.

Fund for Investigative Journalism, 529 14th St. N.W., 13th Floor 20045; (202) 662-7564. Sandy Bergo, Executive Director.
General email, fundfij@gmail.com
Web, www.fij.org

Provides investigative reporters working outside the protection and backing of major news organizations with grants to cover the expenses of investigative pieces involving corruption, malfeasance, incompetence, and domestic and international societal ills.

International Center for Journalists (ICFJ), 2000 M St. N.W., #250 20036; (202) 737-3700. Fax, (202) 737-0530. Joyce Barnathan, President. Press, (202) 349-7624.
General email, editor@icfj.org
Web, www.icfj.org

Fosters international freedom of the press through hands-on training, workshops, seminars, online courses, fellowships, and international exchanges. Offers online mentoring and consulting; publishes media training manuals in various languages.

International Women's Media Foundation (IWMF), 1625 K St. N.W., #1275 20006; (202) 496-1992. Fax, (202) 496-1977. Elisa Lees Munoz, Executive Director.
General email, info@iwmf.org
Web, http://iwmf.org

Researches the role of women journalists. Conducts training on career development and leadership, free press, and the media business. Publishes media training guide. Facilitates networking among women journalists.

J-Lab: The Institute for Interactive Journalism, American University School of Communication, McKinley 317, 4400 Massachusetts Ave. 20016; (202) 885-8100. Fax, (202) 885-2019. Jan Schaffer, Executive Director.
General email, news@j-lab.org
Web, www.j-lab.org and Twitter, @jlab

Funds and researches new ideas to help journalists and citizens engage in public life. Projects include community news startups, innovations in journalism, news entrepreneurship, participatory and civic journalism, training, and publications.

Minority Media and Telecommunications Council (MMTC), 3636 16th St. N.W., #B-366 20010; (202) 332-0500. Fax, (202) 332-0503. David Honig, President.
General email, info@mmtconline.org
Web, www.mmtconline.org

Membership: lawyers, engineers, broadcasters, cablecasters, telecommunicators, and scholars. Provides pro bono services to the civil rights community on communication policy matters. Represents civil rights groups before the FCC on issues concerning equal opportunity and diversity. Promotes equal opportunity and civil rights in the mass media and telecommunications industries. Operates nonprofit media brokerage and offers fellowships for lawyers and law students interested in FCC practice.

National Assn. of Black Journalists (NABJ), 1100 Knight Hall, #3100, College Park, MD 20742; (301) 405-0248. Fax, (301) 314-1714. Darryl R. Matthews, Executive Director.
General email, sberry@nabj.org
Web, www.nabj.org

Membership: African American students and media professionals. Works to increase recognition and career advancement of minority journalists, to expand opportunities for minority students entering the field, and to promote balanced coverage of the African American community. Sponsors scholarships, internship program, and annual convention.

National Assn. of Government Communicators (NAGC), 201 Park Washington Ct., Falls Church, VA 22046-4527; (703) 538-1787. Fax, (703) 241-5603. Elizabeth B. Armstrong, Executive Director.

Media Contacts in Washington, D.C.

MAGAZINES

CQ Weekly, 77 K St. N.E., 20002-4681;
(202) 650-6500

National Journal, 600 New Hampshire Ave. N.W., 20037;
(202) 739-8400

Time, 1130 Connecticut Ave. N.W., Suite 900 20036;
(202) 861-4000

U.S. News & World Report, 1050 Thomas Jefferson St.
N.W., 20007; (202) 955-2155

NEWSPAPERS

New York Times, 1627 Eye St. N.W., #700 20006;
(202) 862-0300

USA Today, 1575 Eye St. N.W., #350 20005;
(202) 464-8150

Wall Street Journal, 1025 Connecticut Ave. N.W., #800
20036; (202) 862-9200

Washington City Paper, 1400 Eye St. N.W., #900 20005;
(202) 332-2100

Washington Post, 1150 15th St. N.W., 20071;
(202) 334-6000

Washington Times, 3600 New York Ave. N.E., 20002;
(202) 636-3000

NEWS SERVICES

Agence France-Presse, 1500 K St. N.W., #600 20005;
(202) 289-0700

Associated Press, 1100 13th St. N.W., #700 20005;
(202) 641-9000

McClatchy, 700 12th St. N.W., #1000 20005;
(202) 383-6080

Reuters, 1333 H St. N.W., #410E 20005; (202) 898-8333

Scripps-Howard Newspapers, 1090 Vermont Ave. N.W.,
20005; (202) 408-1484

United Press International, 1133 19th St. N.W.,
#9 20036; (202) 898-8000

Washington Post News Services, 1150 15th St. N.W.,
#4 20071; (202) 334-6375

TELEVISION/RADIO NETWORKS

ABC News, 1400 Pentagon Pedestrian Tunnel, 20301;
(703) 979-4587

CBS News, 2020 M St. N.W., 20036; (202) 457-4321

CNN, 820 1st St. N.E., 20002; (202) 898-7900

C-SPAN, 400 N. Capitol St. N.W., #650 20001;
(202) 737-3220

Fox News, 400 N. Capitol St. N.W., #550 20001;
(202) 824-6300

National Public Radio, 1111 North Capitol St. NE, 20002;
(202) 216-9242

NBC News, 4001 Nebraska Ave. N.W., 20016;
(202) 885-4111

Public Broadcasting Service, 2100 Crystal Dr, Alexandria,
VA 22202; (703) 739-5000

General email, info@nagconline.org

Web, www.nagconline.org

National network of federal, state, and local government communications employees. Provides professional development through public meetings, exhibitions, workshops, and formal courses of instruction. Promotes high standards for the government communications profession and recognizes noteworthy service.

National Assn. of Hispanic Journalists (NAHJ), *1050 Connecticut Ave., 10th Floor 20036; (202) 662-7145. Fax, (202) 662-7144. Anna Lopez-Buck, Executive Director.* General email, nahj@nahj.org

Web, www.nahj.org

Membership: professional journalists, educators, students, and others interested in encouraging and supporting the study and practice of journalism and communications by Hispanics. Promotes fair representation and treatment of Hispanics by the media. Provides professional development and computerized job referral service; compiles and updates national directory of Hispanics in the media; sponsors national high school essay contest, journalism awards, and scholarships.

National Federation of Press Women (NFPW), *P.O. Box 5556, Arlington, VA 22205; (703) 237-9804. Fax, (703)*

237-9808. *Carol Pierce, Executive Director, ext. 102.*
Toll-free, (800) 780-2715.
General email, presswomen@aol.com
Web, www.nfpw.org

Membership: communications professionals, both men and women. Provides professional development opportunities for members, including an annual conference. Advocates freedom of the press. Provides cost-effective libel insurance. Monitors legislation and regulations.

National Hispanic Foundation for the Arts (NHFA), *Washington Square, 1050 Connecticut Ave. N.W., 10th Floor 20036; (202) 293-8330. Fax, (202) 772-3101. Felix Sanchez, Chair.* General email, info@hispanicarts.org

Web, www.hispanicarts.org

Strives to increase the presence of Hispanics in the media, telecommunications, entertainment industries, and performing arts, and to increase programming for the U.S. Latino community. Provides scholarships for Hispanic students to pursue graduate study in the arts.

National Lesbian and Gay Journalists Assn. (NLGJA), *2120 L St. N.W., #850 20037; (202) 588-9888. Fax, (202) 588-1818. Michael Tune, Executive Director.* General email, info@nlgja.org

Web, www.nlgja.org

Congressional News Media Galleries

The congressional news media galleries serve as liaisons between members of Congress and their staffs and accredited newspaper, magazine, and broadcasting correspondents. The galleries provide facilities to cover activities of Congress, and gallery staff members ensure that congressional press releases reach appropriate correspondents. Independent committees of correspondents working through the press galleries are responsible for accreditation of correspondents.

House Periodical Press Gallery, H-304 CAP, Washington, DC 20515; (202) 225-2941. Robert M. Zatkowski, Director.

House Press Gallery, H-315 CAP, Washington, DC 20515; (202) 225-3945. Annie Tin, Superintendent.

House Radio and Television Gallery, H-320 CAP, Washington, DC 20515; (202) 225-5214. Olga Ramirez Kornacki, Director.

Press Photographers Gallery, S-317 CAP, Washington, DC 20510; (202) 224-6548. Jeffrey S. Kent, Director.

Senate Periodical Press Gallery, S-320 CAP, Washington, DC 20510; (202) 224-0265. Heather Rothman, Chair.

Senate Press Gallery, S-316 CAP, Washington, DC 20510; (202) 224-0241. Laura Lytle, Director.

Senate Radio and Television Gallery, S-325 CAP, Washington, DC 20510; (202) 224-6421. Michael Mastrian, Director.

Works within the journalism industry to foster fair and accurate coverage of lesbian, gay, bisexual, and transgender issues. Opposes workplace bias against all minorities and provides professional development for its members.

National Press Club, *529 14th St. N.W., 13th Floor 20045; (202) 662-7500. Fax, (202) 879-6725. Myron Belkind, President. Library and Research Center, (202) 662-7523.*
General email, info@press.org
Web, www.press.org

Membership: reporters, editors, writers, publishers, cartoonists, producers, librarians, and teachers of journalism at all levels. Interests include advancement of professional standards and skills and the promotion of free expression. Provides networking opportunities and manages an online job listing site for members. Library available to members for research.

National Press Foundation (NPF), *1211 Connecticut Ave. N.W., #310 20036; (202) 663-7280. Fax, (202) 530-2855. Bob Meyers, President.*
General email, npf@nationalpress.org
Web, www.nationalpress.org

Works to enhance the professional competence of journalists through in-career education projects. Sponsors conferences, seminars, fellowships, and awards; conducts public forums and international exchanges. Supports the National Press Club library.

The Newspaper Guild–CWA, *501 3rd St. N.W., 6th Floor 20001-2797; (202) 434-7177. Fax, (202) 434-1472. Bernard J. Lunzer, President.*
General email, guild@cwa-union.org
Web, www.newsguild.org

Membership: journalists, sales and media professionals. Advocates for higher standards in journalism; equal employment opportunity in the print, broadcast, wire, and Web media industries; and advancement of members' economic interests. (Affiliated with Communications Workers of America and the AFL-CIO.)

Pew Research Center Journalism Project, *1615 L St. N.W., #700 20036; (202) 419-3650. Fax, (202) 419-3699. Amy Mitchell, Director.*
General email, journalism@pewresearch.org
Web, www.journalism.org

Evaluates and studies the performance of the press, particularly content analysis using empirical research to quantify what is occurring in the press. Tracks key industry trends. Publishes a daily digest of media news and an annual report on American journalism. (Formerly Project for Excellence in Journalism.)

Society for Technical Communication (STC), *9401 Lee Hwy., #300, Fairfax, VA 22031; (703) 522-4114. Fax, (703) 522-2075. Chris Lyons, Executive Director; Lloyd Tucker, Education Director.*
General email, stc@stc.org
Web, www.stc.org

Membership: writers, publishers, educators, editors, illustrators, and others involved in technical communication. Encourages research and develops training programs; aids educational institutions in devising curricula; awards scholarships.

Statistical Assessment Service (STATS), *933 N. Kenmore St., #405, Arlington, VA 22201; (571) 319-0029. Fax, (202) 872-4014. S. Robert Lichter, President.*
Web, www.stats.org

Research and resource organization. Interests include improving the quality of scientific and statistical information in public discourse. Acts as a resource for journalists and policymakers on scientific issues and controversies. (Affiliated with George Mason University.)

UNITY: Journalists of Color Inc., *7950 Jones Branch Dr., McLean, VA 22107; (703) 854-3585. Fax, (703) 854-3586. Eloiza Altoro, Executive Director.*
General email, info@unityjournalists.org
Web, www.unityjournalists.org

Alliance of Asian American Journalists Assn., National Lesbian and Gay Journalists Assn., National Assn. of Hispanic Journalists, and Native American Journalists Association. Fosters representative media leadership and fair promotion practices for minority journalists. Educates the industry about the accurate representation of diverse populations in coverage. Encourages diversity in newsrooms.

Washington Press Club Foundation, *National Press Bldg.,* 529 14th St. N.W., #1115 20045; (202) 393-0613. Fax, (202) 662-7040. *Suzanne Pierron, Executive Director; David Meyers, President.*
General email, wpcf@wpcf.org
Web, www.wpcf.org

Seeks to advance professionalism in journalism. Sponsors programs and events to educate students and the public on the role of a free press. Awards paid internships for minorities in D.C.-area newsrooms. Administers an oral history of women in journalism. Sponsors annual Congressional Dinner in February to welcome Congress back into session.

White House Correspondents' Assn., 600 New Hampshire Ave., #800 20037; (202) 266-7453. Fax, (202) 266-7454. *Julia Whiston, Executive Director.*
General email, whca@starpower.net
Web, www.whca.net

Membership: reporters with permanent White House press credentials. Acts as a liaison between reporters and White House staff. Sponsors annual WHCA Journalism Awards and Scholarships fundraising dinner.

Women's Institute for Freedom of the Press, 1940 Calvert St. N.W. 20009-1502; (202) 656-0893. *Martha Allen, President.*
General email, allen@wifp.org
Web, www.wifp.org

Conducts research and publishes in areas of communications and the media that are of particular interest to women. Promotes freedom of the press. Publishes a free online directory of media produced by and for women.

Accreditation in Washington

▶ **AGENCIES**

Defense Dept. (DoD), *Public Affairs,* The Pentagon, #2D961 20301-1400; (703) 571-3343. Fax, (703) 697-3501. *Bryan G. Whitman, Assistant Secretary, Acting,* (703) 697-9312. Press, (703) 697-5131.
Web, www.defense.gov/news

Selects staff of accredited Washington-based media organizations by lottery for rotating assignments with the National Media Pool. Correspondents must be familiar with U.S. military affairs, be available on short notice to deploy to the site of military operations, and adhere to pool ground rules. Issues Pentagon press passes to members of the press regularly covering the Pentagon.

Foreign Press Center *(State Dept.),* 529 14th St. N.W., #800 20045; (202) 504-6300. Fax, (202) 504-6334. *Margot Carrington, Director, Foreign Press Centers,* (202) 504-6320; *Cynthia Brown, Director, Washington FPC,* (202) 504-6317.
General email, carringtonmj@fpc.state.gov
Web, http://fpc.state.gov

Provides foreign journalists with access to news sources, including wire services and daily briefings from the White House, State Dept., and Pentagon. Holds live news conferences. Foreign journalists wishing to use the center should check the Web site for information on what documents to present for admission.

Metropolitan Police Dept., *Police Public Information,* 300 Indiana Ave. N.W., #5124 20001; (202) 727-4383. Fax, (202) 727-4822. *Gwendolyn Crump, Director.*
General email, mpd@dc.gov
Web, www.mpdc.dc.gov

Serves as connection between the media and the police department. Provides application forms and issues press passes required for crossing police lines within the city of Washington. Passes are issued on a yearly basis; applicants should allow four to six weeks for processing of passes.

National Park Service (NPS) *(Interior Dept.),* **National Capital Region,** 1100 Ohio Dr. S.W. 20242; (202) 619-7174. *Steven Whitesell, Regional Director.* Permits, (202) 245-4715.
Web, www.nps.gov/ncro

Regional office that administers national parks, monuments, historic sites, and recreation areas in the Washington metropolitan area. Issues special permits required for commercial filming on public park lands. News media representatives covering public events that take place on park lands must notify the Office of Public Affairs and Tourism in advance. A White House, Capitol Hill, metropolitan police, or other policy-agency-issued press pass is required in some circumstances. Commercial filming on park lands requires a special-use permit.

State Dept., *Public Affairs Press Office,* 2201 C St. N.W., #2109 20520-6180; (202) 647-2492. Fax, (202) 647-0244. *Jeff Raghke, Director.*
General email, pressduty@state.gov
Web, www.state.gov/press

Each U.S. journalist seeking a building pass must apply in person with a letter from his or her editor or publisher, two application forms (available from the press office), and a passport-size photograph. In addition, foreign correspondents need a letter from the embassy of the country in which their organization is based. Proof of citizenship is required of all applicants. All journalists must cover the State Dept.'s daily briefing on a regular basis, and thus reside in the Washington, D.C., area. Applicants should allow three months for security clearance. Members of the press wishing to attend an individual briefing should request clearance from the press office.

White House, *Press Office,* 1600 Pennsylvania Ave. N.W. 20500; (202) 456-2580. Fax, (202) 456-3347. *James F. (Jay) Carney, Press Secretary.* Comments and information, (202) 456-1111.
General email, press@who.eop.gov
Web, www.whitehouse.gov and http://whitehouse.gov/briefing-room

Journalists seeking permanent accreditation must meet four criteria. The journalist must be a designated White House correspondent and expected to cover the White House daily; must be accredited by the House and Senate press galleries; must be a resident of the Washington, D.C., area; and must be willing to undergo the required Secret Service background investigation. A journalist's editor, publisher, or employer must write to the press office requesting accreditation. Freelance journalists, camera operators, or technicians wishing temporary accreditation must send letters from at least two news organizations indicating the above criteria.

▶ **CONGRESS**

House Periodical Press Gallery, *H304 CAP 20515; (202) 225-2941. Robert M. Zatkowski, Director.*
General email, periodical.press@mail.house.gov
Web, http://periodical.house.gov

Open by application to periodical correspondents whose chief occupation is gathering and reporting news for periodicals not affiliated with lobbying or membership organizations. Accreditation with the House Gallery covers accreditation with the Senate Gallery.

▶ **JUDICIARY**

Supreme Court of the United States, *1 1st St. N.E. 20543; (202) 479-3000. John G. Roberts Jr., Chief Justice; Kathleen Arberg, Public Information Officer, (202) 479-3211.*
Web, www.supremecourtus.gov

Journalists seeking to cover the Court should be accredited by either the White House or the House or Senate press galleries, but others may apply by submitting a letter from their editors. Contact the public information office to make arrangements.

Broadcasting

▶ **AGENCIES**

Federal Communications Commission (FCC), *Media Bureau, Policy Division, 445 12th St. S.W. 20554; (202) 418-2120. Fax, (202) 418-1069. Mary Beth Murphy, Chief.*
Web, www.fcc.gov/encyclopedia/policy-division-media-bureau

Handles complaints and inquiries concerning the equal time rule, which requires equal broadcast opportunities for all legally qualified candidates for the same office, and other political broadcast, cable, and satellite rules. Interprets and enforces related Communications Act provisions, including the requirement for sponsorship identification of all paid political broadcast, cable, and satellite announcements and the requirement for broadcasters to furnish federal candidates with reasonable access to broadcast time for political advertising. Administers Equal Employment Opportunity (EEO) matters.

▶ **NONGOVERNMENTAL**

Alliance for Women in Media Information, *1760 Old Meadow Rd., #500, McLean, VA 22102; (703) 506-3290. Fax, (703) 506-3266. Sylvia Strobel, President.*
Web, www.allwomeninmedia.org

Membership: professionals in the electronic media and full-time students in accredited colleges and universities. Promotes industry cooperation and advancement of women. Maintains foundation supporting educational programs, charitable activities, public service campaigns, and scholarships.

Broadcast Education Assn. (BEA), *1771 N St. N.W. 20036-2891; (202) 429-3935. Fax, (202) 775-2981. Heather Birks, Executive Director.*
General email, BEAMemberServices@nab.org
Web, www.beaweb.org

Membership: universities, colleges, and faculty members offering specialized training in the radio, television, and electronic media industries. Promotes improvement of curriculum and teaching methods. Fosters working relationships among academics, students, and professionals in the industry. Interests include documentaries, international business and regulatory practices, gender issues, interactive media and emerging technologies, and electronic media law and policy. Administers scholarships in the field.

National Academy of Television Arts and Sciences (NATAS), *National Capital Chesapeake Bay Chapter Office, 9405 Russell Rd., Silver Spring, MD 20910-1445; (301) 587-3993. Fax, (301) 587-3993. Dianne E. Bruno, Administrator.*
General email, capitalemmys@aol.com
Web, www.capitalemmys.tv

Membership: professionals in television and related fields and students in communications. Serves the Virginia, Maryland, and Washington, D.C., television community. Works to upgrade television programming; awards scholarships to junior, senior, or graduate students in communications. Sponsors annual Emmy Awards. (Headquarters in New York.)

National Assn. of Black Owned Broadcasters (NABOB), *1201 Connecticut Ave. N.W., #200 20036; (202) 463-8970. Fax, (202) 429-0657. James L. Winston, Executive Director.*
General email, nabobinfo@nabob.org
Web, www.nabob.org

Membership: minority owners and employees of radio and television stations and telecommunications properties. Provides members and the public with information on the broadcast industry and the FCC. Provides members with legal and advertising research facilities. Monitors legislation and regulations.

National Assn. of Broadcast Employees and Technicians (NABET-CWA), *501 3rd St. N.W., 6th Floor*

20001; (202) 434-1254. Fax, (202) 434-1426. James Joyce, President.
Web, www.nabetcwa.org

Membership: approximately 10,000 commercial broadcast and cable television and radio personnel. Helps members negotiate pay, benefits, and better working conditions; conducts training programs and workshops. Monitors legislation and regulations. (Broadcast and Cable Television Workers Sector of the Communications Workers of America.)

National Assn. of Broadcasters (NAB), *1771 N St. N.W. 20036; (202) 429-5300. Fax, (202) 429-5406. Gordon Smith, President. Communications, (202) 429-5350.*
General email, nab@nab.org
Web, www.nab.org

Membership: radio and television broadcast stations and broadcast networks holding an FCC license or construction permit; associate members include producers of equipment and programs. Assists members in areas of management, engineering, and research. Monitors legislation and regulations.

Radio Television Digital News Assn., *529 14th St. N.W., #1240 20045; (202) 659-6510. Fax, (202) 223-4007. Mike Cavender, Executive Director, (770) 622-7011.*
General email, rtdna@rtdna.org
Web, www.rtdna.org

Membership: local and network news executives in broadcasting, cable, and other electronic media in more than thirty countries. Serves as information source for members; provides advice on legislative, political, and judicial problems of electronic journalism; conducts international exchanges.

Senate Radio-Television Gallery, *S-325 CAP 20515; (202) 224-6421. Fax, (202) 224-4882. Michael Mastrian, Director.*
General email, senatetvg@saa.senate.gov
Web, www.senate.gov/galleries/radiotv

Membership: broadcast correspondents who cover Congress. Sponsors annual dinner. Officers also serve on the executive committee of the Congressional Radio-Television Galleries and determine eligibility for broadcast media credentials in Congress. Acts as a liaison between congressional offices and members of the media, and facilitates broadcast coverage of Senate activities. (Formerly the Radio and Television Correspondents Assn.)

Press Freedom

▶**NONGOVERNMENTAL**

Reporters Committee for Freedom of the Press, *1101 Wilson Blvd., #1100, Arlington, VA 22209; (703) 807-2100. Fax, (703) 807-2109. Bruce D. Brown, Executive Director. Legal defense hotline, (800) 336-4243.*
General email, info@rcfp.org
Web, www.rcfp.org

Committee of reporters and editors that provides journalists and media lawyers with a twenty-four-hour hotline for media law and freedom of information questions. Provides assistance to journalists and media lawyers in media law court cases, and to student journalists. Produces publications on newsgathering legal issues. Interests include freedom of speech abroad, primarily as it affects U.S. citizens in the press.

Reporters Without Borders (Reporters Sans Frontières), *Washington Office, 1500 K St. N.W., #600 20005; (202) 256-5613. Delphine Halgand, Director.*
General email, delphine@rsf.org
Web, www.rsf.org

Defends journalists who have been imprisoned or persecuted while conducting their work. Works to improve the safety of journalists. Advocates for freedom of the press internationally through its offices in eleven countries. Sponsors annual events and awards. (Headquarters in Paris, France.)

Student Press Law Center, *1101 Wilson Blvd., #1100, Arlington, VA 22209-2275; (703) 807-1904. Fax, (703) 807-2109. Frank LoMonte, Executive Director.*
General email, admin@splc.org
Web, www.splc.org

Collects, analyzes, and distributes information on free expression and freedom of information rights of student journalists (print, online, and broadcast) and on violations of those rights in high schools and colleges. Provides free legal advice and referrals to students and faculty advisers experiencing censorship. (Affiliated with the Reporters Committee for Freedom of the Press.)

Print and Online Media

▶**NONGOVERNMENTAL**

American Press Institute (API), *4401 Wilson Blvd., #900, Arlington, VA 22203; (571) 366-1200. Fax, (703) 620-5814. Thomas (Tom) Rosenstiel, Executive Director, (571) 366-1035.*
General email, info@americanpressinstitute.org
Web, www.americanpressinstitute.org

Conducts research and training for journalists. Interests include sustaining a free press and understanding changing audiences, new revenue models, and best practices for journalism in the digital age.

Assn. of American Publishers, *Government Affairs, 455 Massachusetts Ave. N.W., #700 20001; (202) 347-3375. Fax, (202) 347-3690. Allan R. Adler, Vice President, Legal and Government Affairs.*
General email, info@publishers.org
Web, www.publishers.org

Membership: U.S. publishers of books, scholarly journals, and multiplatform K–12 and higher education course materials. Represents industry priorities on policy, legislation, and regulatory issues regionally, nationally, and worldwide. Interests include intellectual property rights and copyright protection, tax and trade, new technology, educational and library funding, and First Amendment rights.

Assn. Media and Publishing, *12100 Sunset Hills Rd., #130, Reston, VA 20190; (703) 234-4063. Fax, (703) 435-4390. Sarah Patterson, Executive Director. General email, info@associationmediaandpublishing.com*
Web, www.associationmediaandpublishing.org

Membership: association publishers and communications professionals. Works to develop high standards for editorial and advertising content in members' publications. Compiles statistics; bestows editorial and graphics awards; monitors postal regulations. (Formerly Society of National Assn. Publications.)

Essential Information, *1530 P St. N.W. 20005 (mailing address: P.O. Box 19405, Washington, DC 20036); (202) 387-8030. Fax, (202) 234-5176. John Richard, Executive Director.*
General email, info@essential.org
Web, www.essential.org

Provides writers and the public with information on public policy matters; awards grants to investigative reporters; sponsors conference on investigative journalism. Interests include activities of multinational corporations in developing countries.

Graphic Communications Conference of the International Brotherhood of Teamsters (GCC/IBT), *25 Louisiana Ave. N.W. 20001; (202) 508-6660. Fax, (202) 624-8145. George Tedeschi, President.*
General email, webmessenger@gciu.org
Web, www.gciu.org

Membership: approximately 60,000 members of the print and publishing industries, including lithographers, photoengravers, and bookbinders. Assists members with contract negotiation and grievances; conducts training programs and workshops. Monitors legislation and regulations.

IDEAlliance, *1600 Duke St., #420, Alexandria, VA 22314; (703) 837-1070. Fax, (703) 837-1072. David J. Steinhardt, President, (703) 837-1066.*
General email, registrar@idealliance.org
Web, www.idealliance.org

Membership: firms and customers in printing, publishing, and related industries. Assists members in production of color graphics and conducts studies on print media management methods.

Magazine Publishers of America (MPA), *Government Affairs, 1211 Connecticut Ave. N.W., #610 20036; (202) 296-7277. Fax, (202) 296-0343. James Cregan, Executive Vice President.*
Web, www.magazine.org/advocacy

Membership: publishers of consumer magazines. Washington office represents members in all aspects of government relations in Washington and state capitals. Interests include intellectual property, the First Amendment,

consumer protection, advertising, and postal, environmental, and tax policy. (Headquarters in New York.)

National Newspaper Assn. (NNA), *200 Little Falls Rd., #405, Falls Church, VA 22046; (703) 237-9802. Fax, (703) 237-9808. Tonda Rush, Chief Executive Officer. Toll-free, (800) 429-4662.*
Web, www.nnaweb.org

Membership: community, weekly, and daily newspapers. Provides members with advisory services; informs members of legislation and regulations that affect their business. Educational arm, the National Newspaper Foundation, conducts management seminars and conferences. (Headquarters in Columbia, Mo.)

National Newspaper Publishers Assn. (NNPA), *1816 12th St. N.W., 2nd Floor 20009; (202) 588-8764. Fax, (202) 588-8960. Bill Tompkins, President.*
General email, info@nnpa.org
Web, www.nnpa.org

Membership: newspapers owned by African Americans serving an African American audience. Assists in improving management and quality of the African American press through workshops and merit awards. Sponsors NNPA Media Services, a print and Web advertising-placement and press release distribution service.

Newspaper Assn. of America, *4401 Wilson Blvd., #900, Arlington, VA 22203-1867; (571) 366-1000. Fax, (571) 366-1195. Caroline Little, President, (571) 366-1100; Kathryn Mason, Vice President, Government Affairs, (571) 366-1152.*
Web, www.naa.org

Membership: daily and weekly newspapers, other papers, and online products published in the United States, Canada, other parts of the Western Hemisphere, and Europe. Conducts research and disseminates information on newspaper publishing, including labor relations, legal matters, government relations, technical problems and innovations, telecommunications, economic and statistical data, marketing, and training programs.

NPES: The Assn. for Suppliers of Printing, Publishing, and Converting Technologies, *1899 Preston White Dr., Reston, VA 20191-4367; (703) 264-7200. Fax, (703) 620-0994. Ralph J. Nappi, President.*
General email, npes@npes.org
Web, www.npes.org

Trade association representing companies that manufacture and distribute equipment, supplies, systems, software, and services for printing, publishing, and converting.

Print Communications Professionals International Inc. (PCPI), *2100 N. Potomac St., Arlington, VA 22205; (703) 534-9305. Fax, (703) 534-1858. Suzanne Morgan, President.*
General email, smorgan@pcpi.org
Web, www.pcpi.org

Membership: print buyers, communications professionals, and other purchasers of printing services. Educates members about best practices in the industry.

Printing Industries of America (PIA), *Washington Office,*
601 13th St., #350S 20005-3807; (202) 730-7970. Fax, (202)
730-7987. Julie Riccio, Vice President. Governmental
affairs, (202) 744-6251.
General email, llyons@printing.org

Web, www.printing.org

Membership: printing firms and businesses that service printing industries. Represents members before Congress and regulatory agencies. Assists members with labor
relations, human resources management, and other business management issues. Sponsors graphic arts competition. Monitors legislation and regulations. (Headquarters
in Sewickley, Pa.)

Specialized Information Publishers Assn. (SIPA), *1090*
Vermont Ave. N.W., 6th Floor 20005; (202) 289-7442.
Fax, (202) 289-7097. Louis Hernandez, Vice President.
General email, sipa@sipaonline.com

Web, www.sipaonline.com

Membership: newsletter publishers, specialized information services, and vendors to that market. Serves as
an information clearinghouse and provides educational
resources in the field. Monitors legislation and regulations.
Library open to the public. (Division of SIIA; formerly the
Newsletter and Electronic Publishers Assn.)

Specialty Graphic Imaging Assn., *10015 Main St.,*
Fairfax, VA 22031-3489; (703) 385-1335. Fax, (703) 273-
0456. Michael E. Robertson, President. Toll-free, (888) 385-
3588.
General email, sgia@sgia.org

Web, www.sgia.org

Provides screen printers, graphic imagers, digital imagers, suppliers, manufacturers, and educators with technical guidebooks, training videos, managerial support, and
guidelines for safety programs. Monitors legislation and
regulations.

4

Culture and Religion

ARTS AND HUMANITIES

General

▶ AGENCIES

General Services Administration (GSA), *Design and Construction, Office of the Chief Architect, 1800 F St. N.W. 20405; (202) 501-1888. Fax, (202) 501-3393. Leslie Shepherd, Director, (202) 501-2289. General email, les.shepherd@gsa.gov*
Web, www.gsa.gov

Administers the Art in Architecture Program, which commissions publicly scaled works of art for government buildings and landscapes, and the Fine Arts Program, which manages the GSA's collection of fine artwork that has been commissioned for use in government buildings.

John F. Kennedy Center for the Performing Arts, *2700 F St. N.W. 20566-0001; (202) 416-8000. Michael Kaiser, President, (202) 416-8011; David M. Rubenstein, Chair. Performance and ticket information, (202) 467-4600. Toll-free, (800) 444-1324. TTY, (202) 416-8524. Web, www.kennedy-center.org*

National cultural center created by Congress that operates independently; funded in part by federal dollars but primarily through private gifts and sales. Sponsors educational programs; presents American and international performances in theater, music, dance, and film; sponsors the John F. Kennedy Center Education Program, which produces the annual American College Theater Festival; and presents and subsidizes events for young people. The Kennedy Center stages free daily performances open to the public 365 days a year on its Millennium Stage in the Grand Foyer.

National Endowment for the Arts (NEA), *400 7th St. S.W., Constitution Center 20024; (202) 682-5400. Fax, (202) 682-5611. Joan Shigekawa, Senior Deputy Chair. Press, (202) 682-5570.*
General email, webmgr@arts.gov
Web, www.arts.gov

Independent grant-making agency. Awards grants to support artistic excellence, creativity, and innovation for the benefit of individuals and communities. Works through partnerships with state arts agencies, local leaders, other federal agencies, and the philanthropic sector. Main funding categories include: Art Works (replaces Access to Artistic Excellence and Learning in the Arts for Children and Youth); Challenge America Fast-Track (for art projects in underserved communities); and Our Town (for art projects that contribute to the livability of communities).

National Endowment for the Humanities (NEH), *400 7th St. S.W., Constitution Center 20024; (202) 606-8310. Fax, (202) 606-8588. Vacant, Chair; Donna McClish, Librarian; Andrea Anderson, Director, Challenge Grants, Acting. Information, (202) 606-8400. Toll-free, 800-NEH-1121. Library, (202) 606-8244. Public Affairs, (202) 606-8446. TTY Toll-free, (866) 372-2930.*

General email, info@neh.gov
Web, www.neh.gov

Independent federal grant-making agency. Awards grants to individuals and institutions for research, scholarship, and educational and public programs (including broadcasts, museum exhibitions, lectures, and symposia) in the humanities (defined as study of archaeology; history; jurisprudence; language; linguistics; literature; philosophy; comparative religion; ethics; history, criticism, and theory of the arts; and humanistic aspects of the social sciences). Funds preservation of books, newspapers, historical documents, and photographs. Library open by appointment only.

President's Committee on the Arts and the Humanities, *1100 Pennsylvania Ave. N.W., #526 20506; (202) 682-5409. Fax, (202) 682-5668. Rachel Goslins, Executive Director; Margo Lion, Co-Chair; George Stevens Jr., Co-Chair.*
General email, pcah@pcah.gov
Web, www.pcah.gov

Helps to incorporate the arts and humanities into White House objectives. Bridges federal agencies and the private sector. Recognizes cultural excellence, engages in research, initiates special projects, and stimulates private funding.

U.S. Commission of Fine Arts, *401 F St. N.W., #312 20001-2728; (202) 504-2200. Fax, (202) 504-2195. Earl A. Powell III, Chair; Thomas Luebke, Secretary.*
General email, cfastaff@cfa.gov
Web, www.cfa.gov

Advises the federal and D.C. governments on matters of art and architecture that affect the appearance of the nation's capital.

▶ CONGRESS

For a listing of relevant congressional committees and subcommittees, please see page 113 or the Appendix.

▶ NONGOVERNMENTAL

Americans for the Arts, *1000 Vermont Ave. N.W., 6th Floor 20005; (202) 371-2830. Fax, (202) 371-0424. Robert L. Lynch, President.*
General email, info@artsusa.org
Web, www.americansforthearts.org

Membership: groups and individuals promoting advancement of the arts and culture in U.S. communities. Provides information on programs, activities, and administration of local arts agencies; on funding sources and guidelines; and on government policies and programs. Conducts, sponsors, and disseminates research on the social, educational, and economic benefits of arts programs. Monitors legislation and regulations.

Assn. of Performing Arts Presenters, *1211 Connecticut Ave. N.W., #200 20036; (202) 833-2787. Fax, (202) 833-1543. Mario Gracia Durham, President.*

CULTURE AND RELIGION RESOURCES IN CONGRESS

For a complete listing of Congress committees, including their full contact information, leadership, membership, and jurisdictions, please refer to the Appendix on pages 724–842.

HOUSE:

House Administration Committee, (202) 225-8281.
Web, cha.house.gov or democrats.cha.house.gov
House Agriculture Committee, (202) 225-2171.
Web, agriculture.house.gov or
democrats.agriculture.house.gov
House Appropriations Committee, (202) 225-2771.
Web, appropriations.house.gov or
democrats.appropriations.house.gov
   **Subcommittee on Interior, Environment, and
Related Agencies,** (202) 225-3081.
   **Subcommittee on Labor, Health and Human
Services, Education, and Related Agencies,**
(202) 225-3508.
   Subcommittee on Legislative Branch,
(202) 226-7252.
House Education and the Workforce Committee,
(202) 225-4527.
Web, edworkforce.house.gov or
democrats.edworkforce.house.gov
   **Subcommittee on Early Childhood, Elementary,
and Secondary Education,** (202) 225-4527.
   **Subcommittee on Higher Education, and
Workforce Training,** (202) 225-4527.
House Energy and Commerce Committee,
(202) 225-2927.
Web, energycommerce.house.gov or
democrats.energycommerce.house.gov
   **Subcommittee on Commerce, Manufacturing,
and Trade,** (202) 225-2927.
   **Subcommittee on Communications and
Technology,** (202) 225-2927.
House Judiciary Committee, (202) 225-3951.
Web, judiciary.house.gov or
democrats.judiciary.house.gov
   **Subcommittee on the Constitution and Civil
Justice,** (202) 225-2825.
House Natural Resources Committee,
(202) 225-2761.
Web, naturalresources.house.gov or
democrats.naturalresources.house.gov
   **Subcommittee on Public Lands and
Environmental Regulation,** (202) 226-7736.
House Science, Space, and Technology Committee,
(202) 225-6371.
Web, science.house.gov or democrats.science.house.gov
   Subcommittee on Research and Technology,
(202) 225-6371.
House Ways and Means Committee, (202) 225-3625.
Web, waysandmeans.house.gov or
democrats.waysandmeans.house.gov

JOINT:

Joint Committee on the Library of Congress,
(202) 225-8281.
Web, cha.house.gov/jointcommittees/joint-committee-library

SENATE:

**Senate Agriculture, Nutrition, and Forestry
Committee,** (202) 224-2035.
Web, ag.senate.gov
   **Subcommittee on Nutrition, Specialty Crops,
Food, and Agricultural Research,**
(202) 224-2035.
Senate Appropriations Committee,
(202) 224-7363.
Web, appropriations.senate.gov
   **Subcommittee on Interior, Environment, and
Related Agencies,** (202) 228-0774.
   **Subcommittee on Labor, Health and Human
Services, Education, and Related Agencies,**
(202) 224-7363.
**Senate Banking, Housing, and Urban Affairs
Committee,** (202) 224-7391.
Web, banking.senate.gov
**Senate Commerce, Science, and Transportation
Committee,** (202) 224-0411.
Web, commerce.senate.gov
   **Subcommittee on Competitiveness,
Innovation, and Export Promotion,**
(202) 224-1270.
   Subcommittee on Science and Space,
(202) 224-0415.
Senate Energy and Natural Resources Committee,
(202) 224-4971.
Web, energy.senate.gov
   Subcommittee on National Parks,
(202) 224-4971.
Senate Finance Committee, (202) 224-4515.
Web, finance.senate.gov
**Senate Health, Education, Labor, and Pensions
Committee,** (202) 224-5375.
Web, help.senate.gov
   Subcommittee on Children and Families,
(202) 224-5375.
Senate Indian Affairs Committee, (202) 224-2251.
Web, indian.senate.gov
Senate Judiciary Committee, (202) 224-7703.
Web, judiciary.senate.gov
Senate Rules and Administration Committee,
(202) 224-6352.
Web, rules.senate.gov

General email, info@artspresenters.org

Web, www.artspresenters.org

Connects performing artists to audiences and communities around the world. Facilitates the work of presenters, artist managers, and consultants through continuing education, regranting programs, and legislative advocacy.

Federation of State Humanities Councils, *1600 Wilson Blvd., #902, Arlington, VA 22209-2511; (703) 908-9700. Fax, (703) 908-9706. Esther Mackintosh, President. General email, info@statehumanities.org*

Web, www.statehumanities.org

Membership: humanities councils from U.S. states and territories. Provides members with information; forms partnerships with other organizations and with the private sector to promote the humanities. Monitors legislation and regulations.

National Assembly of State Arts Agencies, *1029 Vermont Ave. N.W., 2nd Floor 20005; (202) 347-6352. Fax, (202) 737-0526. Jonathan Katz, Chief Executive Officer. General email, nasaa@nasaa-arts.org*

Web, www.nasaa-arts.org

Membership: state and territorial arts agencies. Provides members with information, resources, and representation. Interests include arts programs for rural and underserved populations and the arts as a catalyst for economic development. Monitors legislation and regulations.

National Humanities Alliance, *21 Dupont Circle N.W., #800 20036; (202) 296-4994. Fax, (202) 872-0884. Stephen Kidd, Executive Director, ext. 149.*

Web, www.nhalliance.org

Represents scholarly and professional humanities associations; associations of museums, libraries, and historical societies; higher education institutions; state humanities councils; and independent and university-based research centers. Promotes the interests of individuals engaged in research, writing, and teaching.

National League of American Pen Women, *1300 17th St. N.W. 20036-1973; (202) 785-1997. Fax, (202) 452-6868. Sharyn Bowman Greberman, National President. General email, contact@nlapw.org*

Web, www.nlapw.org

Promotes the development of the creative talents of professional women in the fields of art, letters, and music composition. Conducts and promotes literary, educational, and charitable activities. Offers scholarships, workshops, and discussion groups.

Performing Arts Alliance, *1211 Connecticut Ave. N.W., #200 20036; (202) 207-3850. Fax, (202) 833-1543. Cristine Davis, Manager. General email, info@theperformingartsalliance.org*

Web, www.theperformingartsalliance.org

Membership: organizations of the professional, non-profit performing arts and presenting fields. Through legislative and grassroots activities, advocates policies favorable to the performing arts and presenting fields.

Provisions Library Resource Center for Arts and Social Change, *Art and Design Bldg., #L002, George Mason University, Fairfax, VA 22030; (202) 670-7768. Donald H. Russell, Executive Director. General email, provisionslibrary@gmail.com*

Web, www.provisionslibrary.com

Library collection on politics and culture open to the public by appointment. Offers educational and arts programs concerning social change and social justice.

Wolf Trap Foundation for the Performing Arts, *1645 Trap Rd., Vienna, VA 22182-2064; (703) 255-1900. Fax, (703) 255-1905. Arvind Manocha, President. Press, (703) 255-4096. Tickets, (877) 965-3872. General email, wolftrap@wolftrap.org*

Web, www.wolftrap.org

Established by Congress; operates as a public-private partnership between the National Park Service, which maintains the grounds, and the Wolf Trap Foundation, which sponsors performances in theater, music, and dance. Conducts educational programs for children, internships for college students, career-entry programs for young singers, and professional training for teachers and performers.

Education

▶**AGENCIES**

Education Dept., *Office of Innovation and Improvement, Arts in Education Model Development and Dissemination, 400 Maryland Ave. S.W., #4W210 20202-5950; (202) 260-1280. Fax, (202) 205-5630. Anna Hinton, Director, Acting. General email, artsdemo@ed.gov/programs/artsedmodel/index.html*

Web, www2.ed.gov

Supports the development of innovative model programs that integrate and strengthen the arts into core elementary and middle school curricula and that strengthen arts instruction in those grades. Provides grants to local education agencies and nonprofit art organizations.

Education Dept., *Office of Innovation and Improvement, Professional Development for Arts Educators, 400 Maryland Ave. S.W., #4W246A 20202-5950; (202) 260-2072. Fax, (202) 205-5630. Michelle Johnson Armstrong, Program Manager, (202) 205-1729. General email, artspd@ed.gov*

Web, www2.ed.gov/programs/artsedprofdev/index.html

Supports the implementation of high-quality professional development model programs in elementary and secondary education for music, dance, drama, and visual arts educators in high-poverty schools. Funds support innovative instructional methods, especially those linked to scientifically based research.

John F. Kennedy Center for the Performing Arts, *Education,* 2700 F St. N.W. 20566-0001; (202) 416-8854. *Darrell Ayers, Vice President of Education. Press, (202) 416-8447.*
Web, www.kennedy-center.org/education

Establishes and supports state committees to encourage arts education in schools; promotes community partnerships between performing arts centers and school systems (Partners in Education); provides teachers, artists, and school and arts administrators with professional development classes; offers in-house and touring performances for students, teachers, families, and the general public; arranges artist and company residencies in schools; sponsors the National Symphony Orchestra education program; presents lectures, demonstrations, and classes in the performing arts for the general public; offers internships in arts management and fellowships for visiting artists; and produces annually the Kennedy Center American College Theater Festival.

John F. Kennedy Center for the Performing Arts, *National Partnerships,* 2700 F St. N.W. 20566-0001; (202) 416-8854. *Barbara Shepherd, Director. Press, (202) 416-8447.*
Web, www.kennedy-center.org/education/partners

Supports community-based educational partnerships and state alliances by providing professional development, technical support, resource development, and project grants through the Kennedy Center Alliance for Arts Education Network (KCAAEN) and the Partners in Education program. These two national networks provide communities with such services as teacher professional development, policy and research formation, and arts education programming.

National Endowment for the Arts (NEA), *Literature and Arts Education,* 400 7th St. S.W., Constitution Center 20024; (202) 682-5707. Fax, (202) 682-5481. *Ayanna N. Hudson, Director.*
General email, webmgr@arts.gov
Web, www.arts.gov

Provides grants for curriculum-based arts education for children and youth (generally between ages five and eighteen) in schools or other community-based settings. Projects must provide participatory learning that engages students with accomplished artists and teachers, align with national or state arts education standards, and include assessments of participant learning. Also provides funding to support professional development opportunities for teachers, teaching artists, and other educators.

National Endowment for the Humanities (NEH), *Digital Humanities,* 400 7th St. S.W., Constitution Center 20024; (202) 606-8401. Fax, (202) 606-8411. *Brett Bobley, Director.*
General email, odh@neh.gov
Web, www.neh.gov/divisions/odh

Encourages and supports projects that utilize or study the impact of digital technology on research, education, preservation, access, and public programming in the humanities.

National Endowment for the Humanities (NEH), *Education Programs,* 400 7th St. S.W., Constitution Center 20024; (202) 606-8500. Fax, (202) 606-8394. *William Craig Rice, Director, (202) 606-8286.*
General email, education@neh.gov
Web, www.neh.gov/divisions/education

Supports the improvement of education in the humanities. Supports classroom resources and faculty training and development.

National Endowment for the Humanities (NEH), *Research Programs,* 400 7th St. S.W., Constitution Center 20024; (202) 606-8200. Fax, (202) 606-8558. *Jane Aikin, Director, (202) 606-8212.*
General email, research@neh.gov
Web, www.neh.gov/divisions/research

Sponsors fellowship programs for humanities scholars, including summer stipend programs. Provides support to libraries, museums, and independent centers for advanced study.

National Gallery of Art, *Education,* 4th St. and Constitution Ave. N.W. 20565 (mailing address: 2000B S. Club Dr., Landover, MD 20785); (202) 842-6246. Fax, (202) 842-6935. *Lynn Russell, Head.*
General email, EdResources@nga.gov
Web, www.nga.gov/education

Serves as an educational arm of the gallery by providing free programs for schools, families, and adults. Lends audiovisual educational materials free of charge to schools, colleges, community groups, libraries, and individuals. Provides answers to written and telephone inquiries about European and American art.

Smithsonian Center for Learning and Digital Access, 600 Maryland Ave. S.W., #105W 20024 (mailing address: P.O. Box 37012, MRC 508, Washington, DC 20013-7012); (202) 633-5330. Fax, (202) 633-5489. *Stephanie Norby, Director.*
General email, learning@si.edu
Web, www.smithsonianeducation.org

Serves as the Smithsonian's central education office. Provides elementary and secondary teachers with programs, publications, audiovisual materials, regional workshops, and summer courses on using museums and primary source materials as teaching tools. Publishes books and other educational materials for teachers.

Smithsonian Institution, *Smithsonian Resident Associates,* 1100 Jefferson Dr. S.W., #3077 20560 (mailing address: P.O. Box 23293, Washington, DC 20026-3293); (202) 633-3030. Fax, (202) 786-2034. *Frederica Adelman, Director.*
General email, customerservice@smithsonianassociates.org
Web, http://smithsonianassociates.org

National cultural and educational membership organization that offers courses and lectures for adults and young people. Presents films and offers study tours on arts-, humanities-, and science-related subjects; sponsors performances, studio arts workshops, and research.

▶ **NONGOVERNMENTAL**

National Art Education Assn., *1806 Robert Fulton Dr., #300, Reston, VA 20191; (703) 860-8000. Fax, (703) 860-2960. Deborah Reeve, Executive Director. Toll-free, (800) 299-8321.*
General email, info@arteducators.org
Web, www.arteducators.org

Membership: art teachers (pre-K through university), school administrators, museum staff, and manufacturers and suppliers of art materials. Issues publications on art education theory and practice, research, and current trends; provides technical assistance to art educators. Sponsors awards.

National Assn. of Schools of Art and Design, *11250 Roger Bacon Dr., #21, Reston, VA 20190-5248; (703) 437-0700. Fax, (703) 437-6312. Karen Moynahan, Executive Director.*
General email, info@arts-accredit.org
Web, http://nasad.arts-accredit.org

Specialized professional accrediting agency for post-secondary programs in art and design. Conducts and shares research and analysis on topics pertinent to art and design programs and to fields of art and design. Offers professional development opportunities for executives of art and design programs.

Film, Photography, and Broadcasting

▶ **AGENCIES**

American Film Institute (AFI), *Silver Theatre and Cultural Center, 8633 Colesville Rd., Silver Spring, MD 20910-3916; (301) 495-6720. Fax, (301) 495-6777. Ray Barry, Director. Recorded information, (301) 495-6700.*
General email, silverinfo@afi.com
Web, www.afi.com/silver

Shows films of historical and artistic importance. AFI theater open to the public.

National Archives and Records Administration (NARA), *Motion Picture, Sound, and Video Branch, 8601 Adelphi Rd., #3360, College Park, MD 20740-6001; (301) 837-0526. Fax, (301) 837-3620. Daniel Rooney, Chief.*
General email, mopix@nara.gov
Web, www.archives.gov

Selects and preserves audiovisual records produced or acquired by federal agencies; maintains collections from the private sector, including newsreels. Research room open to the public.

National Archives and Records Administration (NARA), *Still Picture Branch, 8601 Adelphi Rd., NWCS #5360, College Park, MD 20740-6001; (301) 837-3530. Fax, (301)*
837-3621. Deborah Lelamski, Director, Acting. Reference desk, (301) 837-0561.
General email, stillpix@nara.gov
Web, www.archives.gov/dc-metro/college-park/photographs-dc.html

Provides the public with access to and copies of still picture and poster records created or acquired by the federal government; supplies research assistance (both offsite and onsite), finding aids and guides to these materials. Records include still pictures and posters from more than 200 federal agencies, from the mid-nineteenth century to the present.

National Endowment for the Arts (NEA), *Media, Arts Design, and Visual Arts, 400 7th St. S.W., Constitution Center 20024; (202) 682-5452. Fax, (202) 682-5721. Wendy Clark, Director, Museums and Visual Arts, Acting, (202) 682-5555.*
Web, www.arts.gov

Awards grants to nonprofit organizations for film, video, and radio productions; supports film and video exhibitions and workshops.

National Endowment for the Humanities (NEH), *Public Programs, 400 7th St. S.W., Constitution Center 20024; (202) 606-8269. Fax, (202) 606-8557. Karen Mittelman, Director, (202) 606-8631.*
General email, publicpgms@neh.gov
Web, www.neh.gov/divisions/public

Awards grants to libraries, museums, special projects, and media for projects that enhance public appreciation and understanding of the humanities through books and other resources in American library collections. Projects include conferences, exhibitions, essays, documentaries, radio programs, and lecture series.

▶ **CONGRESS**

For a listing of relevant congressional committees and sub-committees, please see page 113 or the Appendix.

Library of Congress, *Motion Picture, Broadcasting, and Recorded Sound Division, 101 Independence Ave. S.E. 20540; (202) 707-5840. Fax, (202) 707-8464. Gregory Lukow, Chief. Recorded sound reference center, #LM113, (202) 707-7833. Fax for recorded sound reference center, #LM113, (202) 707-8572. Fax for motion picture and television reading room, #338.*
Web, www.loc.gov/rr/mopic

Collections include archives of representative motion pictures (1942–present); historic films (1894–1915); early American films (1898–1926); German, Italian, and Japanese features, newsreels, and documentary films (1930–1945); and a selected collection of stills, newspaper reviews, and U.S. government productions. Collection also includes television programs of all types (1948–present), radio broadcasts (1924–present), and sound recordings (1890–present). Tapes the library's concert series and other musical events for radio broadcast; produces recordings of music and poetry for sale to the public. American Film

Institute film archives are interfiled with the division's collections. Use of collections restricted to scholars and researchers; reading room open to the public.

Library of Congress, *National Film Preservation Board,* *19053 Mount Pony Rd., Culpeper, VA 22701-7551; (202) 707-5912. Fax, (202) 707-2371. Steve Leggett, Staff Coordinator.*
Web, www.loc.gov/film

Administers the National Film Preservation Plan. Establishes guidelines and receives nominations for the annual selection of twenty-five films of cultural, historical, or aesthetic significance; selections are entered in the National Film Registry to ensure archival preservation in their original form.

Library of Congress, *Prints and Photographs Division,* *101 Independence Ave. S.E., #LM 339 20540; (202) 707-6394. Fax, (202) 707-6647. Helena Zinkham, Chief.*
Web, www.loc.gov/rr/print

Maintains the Library of Congress's collection of pictorial material not in book format, totaling more than 13.5 million items. U.S. and international collections include artists' prints; historical prints, posters, and drawings; photographs (chiefly documentary); political and social cartoons; and architectural plans, drawings, prints, and photographs. Reference service provided in the Prints and Photographs Reading Room. Reproductions of nonrestricted material available through the Library of Congress's Photoduplication Service; prints and photographs may be borrowed through the Exhibits Office for exhibits by qualified institutions. A portion of the collections and an overview of reference services are available on the World Wide Web.

▶ **NONGOVERNMENTAL**

CINE (Council on International Nontheatrical Events), *4641 Montgomery Ave., #512, Bethesda, MD 20814; (301) 652-8714. Fax, (301) 652-8713. Jon Gann, Executive Director.*
General email, info@cine.org
Web, www.cine.org

Serves as peer group for emerging and established film, television, and new media professionals. Sponsors semi-annual competition for film, television, and new media; holds annual showcase and awards ceremonies.

Motion Picture Assn. of America, *1600 Eye St. N.W. 20006; (202) 293-1966. Fax, (202) 296-7410. Christopher J. Dodd, President. Anti-piracy hotline, (800) 662-6797.*
Web, www.mpaa.org

Membership: motion picture producers and distributors. Advises state and federal governments on copyrights, censorship, cable broadcasting, and other topics; administers volunteer rating system for motion pictures; works to prevent video piracy.

Special Collections in Mass Media and Culture, *3210 Hornbake Library, University of Maryland, College Park,* *MD 20742-7011; (301) 405-9160. Fax, (301) 314-2634. Chuck Howell, Curator.*
General email, labcast@umd.edu
Web, www.lib.umd.edu/special

Maintains library and archives on the history of radio and television. Houses the National Public Broadcasting Archives. Open to the public. (Formerly Library of American Broadcasting.)

Language and Literature

▶ **AGENCIES**

National Endowment for the Arts (NEA), *Literature,* *400 7th St. S.W., Constitution Center 20024; (202) 682-5707. Fax, (202) 682-5481. Amy Stolls, Literature Director, Acting.*
Web, www.arts.gov

Awards grants to published writers, poets, and translators of prose and poetry; awards grants to nonprofit presses, literary magazines, and literature organizations that publish poetry and fiction.

▶ **CONGRESS**

For a listing of relevant congressional committees and subcommittees, please see page 113 or the Appendix.

Library of Congress, *Center for the Book,* *101 Independence Ave. S.E., #LM 650 20540; (202) 707-5221. Fax, (202) 707-0269. John Y. Cole, Director.*
General email, cfbook@loc.gov
Web, www.read.gov/cfb

Seeks to broaden public appreciation of books, reading, literacy, and libraries; sponsors lectures and conferences on the educational and cultural role of the book worldwide, including the history of books and printing, television and the printed word, and the publishing and production of books; cooperates with state centers and with other organizations. Projects and programs are privately funded except for basic administrative support from the Library of Congress.

Library of Congress, *Children's Literature Center,* *101 Independence Ave. S.E., #LJ129 20540; (202) 707-5535. Sybille A. Jagusch, Chief.*
General email, childref@loc.gov
Web, www.loc.gov/rr/child

Provides reference and information services by telephone, by correspondence, and in person; maintains reference materials on all aspects of the study of children's literature. Serves children indirectly through assistance given to teachers, librarians, and others who work with youth.

Library of Congress, *Poetry and Literature Center,* *101 Independence Ave. S.E., #A102 20540; (202) 707-5394. Fax, (202) 707-9946. Robert Casper, Head; Natasha Trethewey, Poet Laureate.*

General email, criz@loc.gov

Web, www.loc.gov/poetry

Advises the library on public literary programs and on the acquisition of literary materials. Sponsors public poetry and fiction readings, lectures, symposia, occasional dramatic performances, and other literary events. Arranges for poets to record readings of their work for the library's tape archive. The poet laureate is appointed annually by the Librarian of Congress on the basis of literary distinction.

▶ **NONGOVERNMENTAL**

Alliance Française de Washington, *2142 Wyoming Ave. N.W. 20008-3906; (202) 234-7911. Fax, (202) 234-0125. Sarah Diligenti, Executive Director.*
General email, alliance@francedc.org

Web, www.francedc.org

Offers courses in French language and literature; presents lectures and cultural events; maintains library of French-language publications for members; offers language programs, including on-site corporate language programs.

American Councils for International Education: ACTR/ ACCELS, *1828 L. St. N.W., #1200 20036; (202) 833-7522. Fax, (202) 833-7523. Dan E. Davidson, President.*
General email, general@americancouncils.org

Web, www.americancouncils.org

Advances education and research worldwide through international programs focused on academic exchange, professional training, distance learning, curriculum and test development, delivery of technical assistance, research, evaluation, and institution building. Conducts educational exchanges for high school, university, and graduate school students as well as scholars with the countries of Africa, eastern Europe, Eurasia, southeast Europe, and the Middle East.

Center for Applied Linguistics, *4646 40th St. N.W., #200 20016-1859; (202) 362-0700. Fax, (202) 362-3740. Terrence Wiley, President.*
General email, info@cal.org

Web, www.cal.org

Research and technical assistance organization that serves as a clearinghouse on application of linguistics to practical language problems. Interests include English as a second language (ESL), teacher training and material development, language education, language proficiency test development, bilingual education, and sociolinguistics.

English First, *8001 Forbes Pl., #102, Springfield, VA 22151-2205; (703) 321-8818. Fax, (703) 321-7636. Frank McGlynn, Executive Director.*
Web, www.englishfirst.org

Seeks to make English the official language of the United States. Advocates policies that make English education available to all children. Monitors legislation and regulations. Opposes multilingual education and governmental policies, including Clinton Executive Order 13166.

Folger Shakespeare Library, *201 E. Capitol St. S.E. 20003-1004; (202) 544-4600. Fax, (202) 544-4623. Michael Witmore, Director, (202) 675-0301. Press, (202) 675-0342. Box Office, (202) 544-7077.*
Web, www.folger.edu

Maintains major Shakespearean and Renaissance materials; awards fellowships for postdoctoral research; presents concerts, theater performances, poetry and fiction readings, exhibits, and other public events. Offers educational programs for elementary, secondary, high school, college, and graduate school students and teachers. Publishes the New Folger Library Shakespeare editions and, in association with the George Washington University, *Shakespeare Quarterly.*

Japan-America Society of Washington, *1819 L St. N.W., Level B2 20036-3807; (202) 833-2210. Fax, (202) 833-2456. Amb. John R. Malott, President.*
General email, jaswdc@us-japan.org

Web, www.jaswdc.org

Offers lectures and films on Japan; operates a Japanese-language school and an annual nationwide language competition for high school students; partner of the National Cherry Blossom Festival. Maintains library for members.

Joint National Committee for Languages/National Council for Languages and International Studies, *4600 Waverly Ave. 20016 (mailing address: P.O. Box 386, Garrett Park, MD 20896); (202) 580-8684. William Rivers, Executive Director.*
General email, info@languagepolicy.org

Web, www.languagepolicy.org

Coalition of professional organizations in teaching, translation, interpreting, testing, and research. Supports a national policy on language study and international education. Provides forum and clearinghouse for professional language and international education associations. National Council for Languages and International Studies is the political arm.

Linguistic Society of America, *1325 18th St. N.W., #211 20036; (202) 835-1714. Fax, (202) 835-1717. Alyson Reed, Executive Director.*
General email, lsa@lsadc.org

Web, www.linguisticsociety.org

Membership: individuals and institutions interested in the scientific analysis of language. Holds linguistic institutes every other year and an annual meeting.

Malice Domestic Ltd., *P.O. Box 8007, Gaithersburg, MD 20898-8007; (301) 730-1675. Verena Rose, Chair; Shawn Reilly Simmons, Public Relations.*
General email, malicedomesticPR@gmail.com

Web, www.malicedomestic.org

Membership: authors and readers of traditional mysteries. Sponsors annual Agatha Awards and an annual convention. Awards grants to unpublished writers in the genre.

National Foreign Language Center *(University of Maryland),* 5700 Rivertech Court, #250, Riverdale, MD 20737 (mailing address: Mail Services, Bldg. #343, P.O. Box 93, College Park, MD 20742); (301) 405-9828. Fax, (301) 405-9829. Catherine Ingold, Director.
General email, inquiries@nflc.org
Web, www.nflc.org

Research and policy organization that develops new strategies to strengthen foreign language competence in the United States. Conducts research on national language needs and assists policymakers in identifying priorities, allocating resources, and designing programs. Interests include the role of foreign language in higher education, national competence in critical languages, ethnic language maintenance, and K–12 and postsecondary language programs.

PEN/Faulkner Foundation, 201 E. Capitol St. S.E. 20003-1094; (202) 898-9063. Fax, (202) 544-4623. Emma Snyder, Executive Director.
Web, www.penfaulkner.org

Sponsors an annual juried award for American fiction. Brings authors to visit public schools to discuss their work. Holds readings by noted authors of American fiction.

U.S. English, 2000 L St. N.W., #702 20036; (202) 833-0100. Fax, (202) 833-0108. Mauro E. Mujica, Chair. Toll-free, (800) 787-8216.
General email, info@usenglish.org
Web, www.usenglish.org

Advocates English as the official language of federal and state government. Affiliate U.S. English Foundation promotes English language education for immigrants.

The Writer's Center, 4508 Walsh St., Bethesda, MD 20815; (301) 654-8664. Fax, (240) 223-0458. Sally Mott Freeman, Chair.
General email, post.master@writer.org
Web, www.writer.org

Membership: writers, editors, and interested individuals. Supports the creation, publication, presentation, and dissemination of literary texts. Sponsors workshops in writing. Presents author readings. Maintains a book gallery.

Museums

▶ **AGENCIES**

Anacostia Community Museum *(Smithsonian Institution),* 1901 Fort Place S.E. 20020 (mailing address: P.O. Box 37012, MRC 0777, Washington, DC 20013-7012); (202) 633-4820. Fax, (202) 287-3183. Camille Akeju, Director. Press, (202) 633-4876. Public affairs, (202) 633-4869. Public programs, (202) 633-4844. Special events, (202) 633-4867. Recorded Information, (202) 633-1000.
General email, ACMinfo@si.edu
Web, http://anacostia.si.edu

Explores, documents, and interprets social and cultural issues that impact contemporary urban communities. Presents changing exhibits and programs.

Federal Council on the Arts and the Humanities, 1100 Pennsylvania Ave. N.W. 20506-0001; (202) 682-5541. Fax, (202) 682-5721. Patricia Loiko, Indemnity Administrator.
Web, http://arts.gov/artistic-fields/museums/arts-and-artifacts-indemnity-program-domestic-indemnity and http://arts.gov/artistic-fields/museums/arts-and-artifacts-indemnity-program-international-indemnity

Membership: leaders of federal agencies sponsoring arts-related activities. Administers the Arts and Artifacts Indemnity Act, which helps museums reduce the costs of commercial insurance for traveling exhibits.

Ford's Theatre National Historic Site, 511 10th St. N.W. 20004; (202) 426-6924. Fax, (202) 426-1845. William Cheek, Site Manager. Recorded ticket information, (202) 638-2941.
General email, NACC_FOTH_Interpretation@nps.gov
Web, www.nps.gov/foth

Administered by the National Park Service, which manages Ford's Theatre, Ford's Theatre Museum, and the Peterson House (house where Lincoln died). Presents interpretive talks, exhibits, and tours. Research library open by appointment. Functions as working stage for theatrical productions.

Frederick Douglass National Historic Site, 1411 W St. S.E. 20020; (202) 426-5961. Fax, (202) 426-0880. Julie A. Kutruff, District Manager; Ka'mal McClarin, Site Curator. Reservations, (877) 444-6777.
General email, julie_kutruff@nps.gov
Web, www.nps.gov/frdo

Administered by the National Park Service. Museum of the life and work of abolitionist Frederick Douglass and his family. Offers tours of the home and special programs, such as documentary films, videos, and slide presentations; maintains visitors center and bookstore. Reservations are required for parties of more than ten. Online reservations can be made at www.recreation.gov.

Freer Gallery of Art and Arthur M. Sackler Gallery *(Smithsonian Institution),* 1050 Independence Ave. S.W. 20560 (mailing address: P.O. Box 37012, MRC 707, Washington, DC 20013-7012); (202) 633-4880. Fax, (202) 357-4911. Julian Raby, Director. Press, (202) 633-0519. Public programs, (202) 633-1000 (recording). Library, (202) 633-0477. Education, (202) 633-0457.
General email, publicaffairsasia@si.edu
Web, www.asia.si.edu

Exhibits ancient and contemporary Asian art from the Mediterranean to Japan and late nineteenth- and early twentieth-century American art from its permanent collection, including works by James McNeill Whistler. Presents films, lectures, and concerts. Library open to the public Monday through Friday, 10:00 a.m.–5:00 p.m.

Museum Education Programs

Alexandria Archaeology, (703) 746-4399

American Alliance of Museums, Museum Assessment Program, (202) 289-1818

Arlington Arts Center, (703) 248-6800

Assn. of Science-Technology Centers, (202) 783-7200

B'nai B'rith Klutznick Museum, (202) 857-6600

C & O Canal, (301) 739-4200

Corcoran Gallery of Art, (202) 639-1700

Daughters of the American Revolution (DAR) Museum, (202) 628-1776

Decatur House, (202) 842-0917

Dumbarton Oaks, (202) 339-6401

Federal Reserve Board Fine Arts Program, (202) 452-3324

Folger Shakespeare Library, (202) 544-4600

Gadsby's Tavern Museum, (703) 746-4242

Institute of Museum and Library Services, (202) 653-4657

J.F.K. Center for the Performing Arts, (202) 416-8800

The Lyceum: Alexandria's History Museum, (703) 838-4994

Mount Vernon, (703) 780-2000

National Arboretum, (202) 245-2726

National Archives, (866) 272-6272

National Building Museum, (202) 272-2448

National Gallery of Art, (202) 737-4215

National Museum of Women in the Arts, (202) 783-5000

Navy Museum, (202) 433-6826

Octagon Museum, (202) 626-7439

Phillips Collection, (202) 387-2151

Smithsonian Institution, (202) 633-1000

  Anacostia Community Museum, (202) 633-4820

  Arthur M. Sackler Gallery, (202) 633-0457

  Center for Learning and Digital Access, (202) 633-5330

  Freer Gallery of Art, (202) 633-0457

  Hirshhorn Museum and Sculpture Garden, (202) 633-3382

  National Air and Space Museum, (202) 633-2540

  National Museum of African Art, (202) 633-4633

  National Museum of American Art, (202) 633-7970

  National Museum of American History, (202) 633-3717

  National Museum of the American Indian, (202) 633-6900

  National Museum of Natural History, (202) 633-1077

  National Portrait Gallery, (202) 633-8500

  Renwick Gallery, (202) 633-2850

Textile Museum, (202) 667-0441

Woodrow Wilson House, (202) 387-4062

Hirshhorn Museum and Sculpture Garden *(Smithsonian Institution),* 7th St. and Independence Ave. S.W. 20560 *(mailing address: P.O. Box 37012, HMSG, MRC 350, Washington, DC 20013-7012); (202) 633-4674. Fax, (202) 633-8835. Kerry Brougher, Director, Acting, (202) 633-4674. Press, (202) 633-2822.*
General email, hmsginquiries@si.edu

Web, www.hirshhorn.si.edu

Preserves and exhibits modern and contemporary art. Offers films, lectures, and tours of the collection.

Institute of Museum and Library Services, *1800 M St. N.W., 9th Floor 20036-5802; (202) 653-4657. Fax, (202) 653-4600. Susan Hildreth, Director, (202) 653-4711. Main IMLS office, (202) 653-4657. Library Services, (202) 653-4700. Museum Services, (202) 653-4789. Communications and government affairs, (202) 653-4757.*
General email, imlsinfo@imls.gov

Web, www.imls.gov and Twitter, @US_IMLS

Independent federal agency established by Congress to assist museums and libraries in increasing and improving their services. Awards grants for the professional development of museum and library staff, conservation projects, and creation of new tools, services, practices, and alliances. Also funds research, conferences, and publications.

National Archives and Records Administration (NARA), *National Archives Museum, 700 Pennsylvania Ave. N.W., #G9 20408; (202) 357-5210. Fax, (202) 357-5926.*

Lisa Royce, Director, Acting. Information, (202) 357-5000. Press, (202) 357-5300.
General email, inquire@nara.gov

Web, www.archives.gov

Plans and directs activities to acquaint the public with the mission and holdings of the National Archives; conducts behind-the-scenes tours; presents hands-on workshops; develops both traditional and interactive exhibits; produces publications, including teaching packets that feature historic documents and online educational tools.

National Cryptologic Museum *(National Security Agency),* 9800 Savage Rd., Fort Meade, MD 20755 *(mailing address: 8290 Colony Seven Rd., Annapolis Junction, MD 20701); (301) 688-5849. Fax, (301) 688-5847.*
Patrick Weadon, Curator. NSA Public and Media Affairs, (301) 688-6524.
General email, crypto_museum@nsa.gov

Web, www.nsa.gov/about/cryptologic_heritage/museum

Documents the history of the cryptologic profession.

National Endowment for the Arts (NEA), *Media, Arts Design, and Visual Arts,* 400 7th St. S.W., Constitution Center 20024; (202) 682-5452. Fax, (202) 682-5721. *Jason Schupbach, Director, Design, (202) 682-5786; Vacant, Director, Media Arts; Wendy Clark, Director, Museums and Visual Arts, Acting, (202) 682-5555.*
Web, www.arts.gov

Awards grants to museums for installing and cataloging permanent and special collections; conducts traveling exhibits; trains museum professionals; conserves and preserves museum collections; and develops arts-related educational programs.

National Gallery of Art, 4th St. and Constitution Ave. N.W. 20565 (mailing address: 2000B S. Club Dr., Landover, MD 20785); (202) 737-4215. Fax, (202) 842-2356. Earl A. Powell III, Director. Press, (202) 842-6353. Visitor services, (202) 842-6954. Library, (202) 842-6511. Web, www.nga.gov

Created by a joint resolution of Congress, the museum is a public-private partnership that preserves and exhibits European and American paintings, sculpture, and decorative and graphic arts. Offers concerts, demonstrations, lectures, symposia, films, tours, and teachers' workshops to enhance exhibitions, the permanent collection, and related topics. Lends art to museums in all fifty states and abroad through the National Lending Service. Publishes a bimonthly calendar of events.

National Museum of African Art (Smithsonian Institution), 950 Independence Ave. S.W. 20560 (mailing address: P.O. Box 37012, MRC 708, Washington, DC 20013-7012); (202) 633-4600. Fax, (202) 357-4879. Johnnetta Cole, Director. Press, (202) 633-4649. General Smithsonian Information, (202) 633-1000. General email, nmafaweb@nmafa.si.edu

Web, http://africa.si.edu

Collects, studies, and exhibits traditional and contemporary arts of Africa. Exhibits feature objects from the permanent collection and from private and public collections worldwide. Library and photo archive open to the public by appointment.

National Museum of American History (Smithsonian Institution), 14th St. and Constitution Ave. N.W., #4260, MRC 622 20560-0630 (mailing address: P.O. Box 37012, Washington, DC 20013); (202) 633-3435. Fax, (202) 786-2624. John Gray, Director. Library, (202) 633-3865. Press, (202) 633-3129. General Smithsonian Information, (202) 633-1000. General email, info@si.edu

Web, http://americanhistory.si.edu

Collects and exhibits objects representative of American cultural history, applied arts, industry, national and military history, and science and technology. Library open to the public by appointment.

National Museum of the American Indian (Smithsonian Institution), 4th St. and Independence Ave. S.W. 20560; (202) 633-6803. Fax, (202) 633-6920. Kevin Gover, Director. Group reservations, (202) 633-6644. General Smithsonian Information, (202) 633-1000. General email, nmaiweb@si.edu

Web, www.americanindian.si.edu

Collects, exhibits, preserves, and studies American Indian languages, literature, history, art, and culture. Operates ImagiNations activity center, open to the public. (Affiliated with the George Gustav Heye Ctr., 1 Bowling Green, New York, NY 10004 and the Cultural Resource Center, 4220 Silver Hill Rd., Suitland, MD.)

National Museum of Health and Medicine (Defense Dept.), 2500 Linden Lane, Silver Spring, MD 20910 (mailing address: 2460 Linden Lane, Bldg. 2500, Silver Spring, MD 20910); (301) 319-3300. Fax, (301) 319-3373. Dr. Adrianne Noe, Director. General email, usarmy.detrick.medcom-usamrmc.list.medical-museum@mail.mil

Web, http://medicalmuseum.mil and Twitter, @medicalmuseum

Collects and exhibits medical models, tools, and pathological specimens. Maintains exhibits on military medicine and surgery. Open to the public 10:00 a.m. to 5:30 p.m., seven days a week. Study collection available to scholars by appointment.

National Portrait Gallery (Smithsonian Institution), 800 F St. N.W. 20001 (mailing address: P.O. Box 37012, Victor Bldg., MRC 973, Washington, DC 20013-7012); (202) 633-8300. Fax, (202) 633-8243. Kim Sajet, Director; Nik Apostolides, Associate Director; Brandon Fortune, Chief Curator. Library, (202) 633-8230. Press, (202) 633-8293. General Smithsonian information, (202) 633-1000. General email, npgnews@si.edu

Web, www.npg.si.edu

Exhibits paintings, photographs, sculpture, drawings, and prints of individuals who have made significant contributions to the history, development, and culture of the United States. Library open to the public.

National Postal Museum (Smithsonian Institution), 2 Massachusetts Ave. N.E. 20013 (mailing address: P.O. Box 37012, Washington, DC 20013); (202) 633-5555. Fax, (202) 633-9393. Allen Kane, Director. Tours, (202) 633-5534. Press, (202) 633-5518. Web, http://postalmuseum.si.edu

Exhibits postal history and stamp collections; provides information on world postal and stamp history.

Naval History and Heritage Command (Navy Dept.), Navy Art Collection, 822 Sicard St. S.E., Washington Navy Yard, Bldg. 67 20374 (mailing address: 805 Kidder Breese St. S.E., Washington Navy Yard, DC 20374); (202) 433-3815. Gale Munro, Head. General email, NavyArt@navy.mil

Web, www.history.navy.mil

Holdings include more than 18,000 paintings, prints, drawings, and sculptures. Artworks depict naval ships, personnel, and action from all eras of U.S. naval history, especially the eras of World War II, the Korean War, and Desert Shield/Storm. Open to the public. Visitors without Defense Dept. or military identification must call in advance. Photo identification required.

Renwick Gallery of the Smithsonian American Art Museum (Smithsonian Institution), 17th St. and Pennsylvania Ave. N.W. 20006 (mailing address: Renwick Gallery, MRC 510, P.O. Box 37012, Washington, DC

20013-7012); (202) 633-8530. *Robyn Kennedy, Chief. Press,*
(202) 633-8530.
General email, americanartinfo@si.edu
Web, www.americanart.si.edu

Curatorial department of the Smithsonian American
Art Museum. Exhibits contemporary American crafts and
decorative arts. (Currently closed for renovation.)

Smithsonian American Art Museum *(Smithsonian*
Institution), 8th and F Sts. N.W. 20004
(mailing address: P.O. Box 37012, MRC 970, Washington,
DC 20013-7012); (202) 633-7970. Fax, (202) 633-8424.
Elizabeth Broun, Director. Library, (202) 633-8230. Press,
(202) 633-8530.
General email, americanartinfo@si.edu
Web, www.americanart.si.edu

Exhibits and interprets American painting, sculpture,
photographs, folk art, and graphic art in the permanent
collection and temporary exhibition galleries. Library open
to the public. (Includes the Renwick Gallery.)

Smithsonian Center for Learning and Digital Access,
600 Maryland Ave. S.W., #105W 20024 (mailing address:
P.O. Box 37012, MRC 508, Washington, DC 20013-7012);
(202) 633-5330. Fax, (202) 633-5489. Stephanie Norby,
Director.
General email, learning@si.edu
Web, www.smithsonianeducation.org

Serves as the Smithsonian's central education office.
Provides elementary and secondary teachers with programs, publications, audiovisual materials, regional workshops, and summer courses on using museums and
primary source materials as teaching tools. Publishes
books and other educational materials for teachers.

Smithsonian Institution, *1000 Jefferson Dr. S.W. 20560*
(mailing address: P.O. Box 37012, SIB 153, MRC 010,
Washington, DC 20013-7012); (202) 633-1000.
G. Wayne Clough, Secretary; Eva J. Pell, Under Secretary
for Science; Richard Kurin, Under Secretary for Art,
History, and Culture; Albert Horvath, Under Secretary
for Finance and Administration. Information, (202) 633-
1000. Library, (202) 633-1700. Press (journalists only),
(202) 633-2400.
General email, info@si.edu
Web, www.si.edu

Conducts research; publishes results of studies, explorations, and investigations; presents study and reference collections on science, culture, and history; presents
exhibitions in the arts, American history, technology, aeronautics and space exploration, and natural history. Smithsonian Institution sites in Washington, D.C., include the
Anacostia Community Museum, Archives of American
Art, Arthur M. Sackler Gallery, Arts and Industries Building, Freer Gallery of Art, Hirshhorn Museum and Sculpture Garden, National Air and Space Museum, National
Museum of African Art, Renwick Gallery, Smithsonian
American Art Museum, National Museum of American
History, National Museum of the American Indian,
National Museum of Natural History, National Portrait

Gallery, National Postal Museum, National Zoological
Park, S. Dillon Ripley Center, and Smithsonian Institution
Building. Libraries open to the public by appointment;
library catalogs are available on the Web. Affiliated with
more than 175 organizations in 41 states, Panama, and
Puerto Rico. Autonomous organizations affiliated with the
Smithsonian Institution include the John F. Kennedy Cen-
ter for the Performing Arts, National Gallery of Art, and
Woodrow Wilson International Center for Scholars.

Smithsonian Institution, *International Relations, 1100*
Jefferson Dr. S.W., #3123 20560 (mailing address: P.O. Box
37012, Quad MRC 705, Washington, DC 20013-7012); (202)
633-4795. Fax, (202) 786-2557. Molly Fannon, Director.
General email, global@si.edu
Web, www.si.edu/intrel

Fosters the development and coordinates the international aspects of Smithsonian cultural activities; facilitates
basic research in history and art and encourages international collaboration among individuals and institutions.

Smithsonian Institution, *Office of Fellowships and*
Internships, 470 L'Enfant Plaza S.W., #7102 20013
(mailing address: P.O. Box 37012, MRC 902, Washington,
DC 20013-7012); (202) 633-7070. Fax, (202) 633-7069.
Eric Woodard, Director.
General email, siofg@si.edu
Web, www.smithsonianofi.com

Provides fellowships to students and scholars for independent research projects in association with members of
the Smithsonian professional research staff. Provides central management for all Smithsonian research fellowship
programs. Facilitates the Smithsonian's scholarly interactions with universities, museums, and research institutions around the world.

Smithsonian Institution, *Smithsonian Museum Support*
Center, 4210 Silver Hill Rd., MRC 534, Suitland, MD
20746-2863; (301) 238-1026. Fax, (301) 238-3661.
Elizabeth Dietrich, Management Officer, (301) 238-1010.
General email, libmail@si.edu
Web, www.mnh.si.edu

Museum collections management facility dedicated to
collections, storage, research, and conservation. Library
serves Smithsonian staff, other government agencies, and
researchers. Open to the public by appointment.

Steven F. Udvar-Hazy Center *(Smithsonian Institution),*
National Air and Space Museum, 14390 Air and Space
Museum Pkwy., Chantilly, VA 20151; (703) 572-4118.
Gen. John R. Dailey (USMC, Ret.), Director. Public Affairs,
(703) 572-4040.
General email, nasm-visitorservices@si.edu
Web, www.airandspace.si.edu/visit/udvar-hazy-center

Displays and preserves a collection of historical aviation and space artifacts, including the B-29 Superfortress,
Enola Gay, the Lockheed SR-71 Blackbird, the prototype
of the Boeing 707, the space shuttle *Discovery*, and the
Concord. Provides a center for research into the history,
science, and technology of aviation and space flight.

Open to the public daily 10:00 a.m.–5:30 p.m., except December 25.

U.S. Botanic Garden, *100 Maryland Ave. S.W. 20001 (mailing address: 245 1st St. S.W., Washington, DC 20024); (202) 225-8333. Fax, (202) 225-1561. Ari Novy, Acting Executive Director. Horticulture hotline, (202) 226-4785. Program registration information, (202) 225-1116. Special events, (202) 226-7674. Tour line, (202) 226-2055.*
General email, usbg@aoc.gov
Web, www.usbg.gov

Educates the public on the aesthetic, cultural, economic, therapeutic, and ecological importance of plants to the well-being of humankind.

U.S. Navy Museum *(Naval Historical Center), Bldg. 76, 805 Kidder Breese St. S.E. 20374-5060; (202) 433-4882. Fax, (202) 433-8200. Karin Hill, Director, Education and Public Programs; James H. Bruns, Director of Museum; Capt. Henry J. Hendrix II, Director of Naval History. Tours, (202) 433-6826. Internships, (202) 433-6901.*
General email, navymuseum@navy.mil
Web, www.history.navy.mil/branches/org8-1.htm

Collects, preserves, displays, and interprets historic naval artifacts and artwork. Presents a complete overview of U.S. naval history. Open to the public. Photo identification required.

►CONGRESS

For a listing of relevant congressional committees and subcommittees, please see page 113 or the Appendix.

Library of Congress, *Interpretive Programs, 101 Independence Ave. S.E., #LA G25 20540; (202) 707-5223. Fax, (202) 707-9063. William Jacobs, Interpretive Programs Officer. Information, (202) 707-4604.*
Web, www.loc.gov/exhibits

Handles exhibits within the Library of Congress; establishes and coordinates traveling exhibits; handles loans of library material.

►NONGOVERNMENTAL

American Alliance of Museums, *1575 Eye St. N.W., #400 20005-1105; (202) 289-1818. Fax, (202) 289-6578. Ford W. Bell, President.*
General email, infocenter@aam-us.org
Web, www.aam-us.org

Membership: individuals, institutions, museums, and museum professionals. Accredits museums; conducts educational programs; promotes international professional exchanges.

Art Services International, *1319 Powhatan St., Alexandria, VA 22314; (703) 548-4554. Fax, (703) 548-3305. Lynn K. Rogerson, Director.*
General email, asi@asiexhibitions.org
Web, www.asiexhibitions.org

Develops, organizes, and circulates fine arts exhibitions throughout the world.

Corcoran Contemporary, *National Gallery of Art, 500 17th St. N.W. 20006-4804; (202) 639-1700. Fax, (202) 639-1768. Peggy Loar, President, Interim. College, (202) 639-1800.*
General email, museum@corcoran.org
Web, www.corcoran.org

Exhibits paintings, sculpture, and drawings, primarily American. Collections include European art and works of local Washington artists. The affiliated Corcoran College of Art and Design offers BFA, MFA, and MA degrees and a continuing education program. Library open to the public by appointment. (Affiliated with George Washington University.)

Dumbarton Oaks, *1703 32nd St. N.W. 20007-2961; (202) 339-6400. Fax, (202) 625-0280. Jan M. Ziolkowski, Director. Information, (202) 339-6400.*
General email, directorsoffice2011@doaks.org
Web, www.doaks.org

Exhibits Byzantine and pre-Columbian art and artifacts; conducts advanced research and maintains publication programs and library collections in Byzantine and pre-Columbian studies and garden and landscape studies. Gardens open to the public Tuesday through Sunday 2:00–6:00 p.m. in summer, and 2:00–5:00 p.m. in winter (except during inclement weather and on federal holidays; fee charged March 15 through October 31); library open to qualified scholars by advance application. Administered by the trustees for Harvard University.

Fondo Del Sol Visual Arts Center, *2112 R St. N.W. 20008; (202) 483-2777. Marc Zuver, Director.*
General email, info@fondodelsol.org
Web, www.fondodelsol.org

Bilingual museum exhibiting pre-Columbian, Santero, and twentieth-century Latino and Caribbean art, as well as select Afro-American works. Collection includes paintings, prints, drawings, photographs, objects, and a film and video archive. Offers bilingual educational programs; internships in art, history, and language; workshop spaces; and art consultation services.

Hillwood Estate, *Museum, and Gardens, 4155 Linnean Ave. N.W. 20008-3806; (202) 686-5807. Fax, (202) 966-7846. Kate Markert, Director, (202) 243-3900. Press, (202) 243-3975.*
General email, info@hillwoodmuseum.org
Web, www.hillwoodmuseum.org

Former residence of Marjorie Merriweather Post. Maintains and exhibits collection of Russian imperial art, including Fabergé eggs, and eighteenth-century French decorative arts; includes twelve acres of formal gardens. Gardens and museum open to the public Tuesday through Saturday, 10:00 a.m.–5:00 p.m., and select Sundays 1:00 p.m.–5:00 p.m.; reservations required for large groups.

International Spy Museum, *800 F St. N.W. 20004; (202) 393-7798. Fax, (202) 393-7797. Peter Earnest, Executive Director. Toll-free, (866) 779-6873.*

General email, other@spymuseum.org

Web, www.spymuseum.org

Educates the public about espionage, particularly human intelligence, by examining its role in and effect on current and historical events. (Affiliated with the Malrite Company.)

Marian Koshland Science Museum *(National Academy of Sciences), 525 E St. N.W., 20001 (mailing address: 500 5th St. N.W., Washington, DC 20001); (202) 334-1201. Fax, (202) 334-1548. Patrice Legro, Director. Toll-free, (888) 567-4526.*

General email, ksm@nas.edu

Web, www.koshland-science-museum.org and Twitter, @koshlandscience

Encourages teenagers and adults to use science to solve problems in their communities through exhibits, public events, and educational programs. Provides information aimed at stimulating discussion and insight into how science supports decision-making.

National Building Museum, *401 F St. N.W. 20001-2637; (202) 272-2448. Fax, (202) 272-2564. Chase W. Rynd, President. Press, (202) 272-2448 ext. 3109.*

Web, www.nbm.org

Celebrates achievements in building, architecture, urban planning, engineering, and historic preservation through educational programs, exhibitions, tours, lectures, workshops, and publications.

National Children's Museum, *151 St. George Blvd., National Harbor, MD 20745; (301) 392-2400. Fax, (301) 392-2440. Wendy Blackwell, Executive Director.*

General email, info@ncm.museum

Web, www.ncm.museum

A cultural and educational institution serving children and families onsite and through national partners and programs. Exhibits and activities focus on the arts, civic engagement, the environment, global citizenship, health and well-being, and play. Open Tuesday–Saturday, 10:00 a.m. to 4:00 p.m. and Sunday 12:00 p.m. to 4:00 p.m. Closed Mondays. (Affiliated with the Association of Children's Museums [ACM] Reciprocal Network.)

National Geographic Museum, *1145 17th St. N.W. 20036-4688; (202) 857-7588. Kathryn Keane, Vice President, Exhibitions. Information, (202) 857-7588.*

Web, www.ngmuseum.org

Maintains self-guided exhibits about past and current expeditions, scientific research, and other themes in history and culture. Admission is free; some special exhibitions require ticket purchase.

National Guard Memorial Museum, *1 Massachusetts Ave. N.W. 20001; (202) 789-0031. Fax, (202) 682-9358. Anne Armstrong, Deputy Director, (202) 408-5890. Toll-free, (888) 226-4287.*

General email, ngef@ngaus.org

Web, www.ngef.org

Features six core exhibit areas that explore the National Guard from colonial times through the world wars and the cold war to the modern era through timelines, photographs, artifacts, light, and sound.

National Museum of Civil War Medicine, *48 East Patrick St., Frederick, MD 21705 (mailing address: P.O. Box 470, Frederick, MD 21705); (301) 695-1864. Fax, (301) 695-6823. George Wunderlich, Executive Director.*

General email, info@civilwarmed.org

Web, www.civilwarmed.org

Maintains artifacts and exhibits pertaining to general and wartime medicine in the 1800s, including dentistry, veterinary medicine, and medical evacuation. Presents information about individual soldiers, surgeons, medics, and nurses. Research department assists with questions about individuals injured in the Civil War.

National Museum of Crime and Punishment, *575 7th St. N.W. 20004; (202) 393-1099. Fax, (202) 621-5568. Janine Vaccarello, Chief Operating Officer. Information, (202) 621-5550.*

General email, info@crimemuseum.org

Web, www.crimemuseum.org

Presents artifacts, interactive exhibits, and programs pertaining to crime and law enforcement.

National Museum of Women in the Arts, *1250 New York Ave. N.W. 20005-3970; (202) 783-5000. Fax, (202) 393-3234. Susan Fisher Sterling, Director. Information, (800) 222-7270. Library, (202) 783-7338. Press, (202) 783-7373.*

Web, www.nmwa.org

Acquires, researches, and presents the works of women artists from the Renaissance to the present. Promotes greater representation and awareness of women in the arts. Library open for research to the public by appointment.

Newseum, *555 Pennsylvania Ave. N.W. 20001; (202) 292-6100. James C. Duff, Chief Executive Officer; Peter S. Prichard, Chair. Press, (202) 292-6200. Toll-free, (888) 639-7386.*

General email, info@newseum.org

Web, www.newseum.org

World's only interactive museum of news. Collects items related to the history of news coverage; offers multimedia presentations and exhibits on the past, present, and future of news coverage; emphasizes the importance of the First Amendment to news coverage. (Affiliated with Freedom Forum.)

Octagon Museum, *1799 New York Ave. N.W. 20006-5207; (202) 626-7439. Fax, (202) 626-7426. Erica Gees, Executive Director.*

General email, octagonmuseum@aia.org

Web, www.theoctagon.org

Federal period historic residence open to the public for tours; served as the executive mansion during the War of 1812. Sponsors exhibits, lectures, publications, and educational programs. (Owned by the AIA Foundation [American

Institute of Architects].) Group tours available by appointment. Call for hours.

Phillips Collection, *1600 21st St. N.W. 20009; (202) 387-2151. Fax, (202) 387-2436. Dorothy Kosinski, Director. Press, (202) 387-2151, ext. 220. Membership, (202) 387-3036. Shop, (202) 387-2151, ext. 239.*
General email, communications@phillipscollection.org
Web, www.phillipscollection.org

Maintains permanent collection of European and American paintings, primarily of the nineteenth through twenty-first centuries, and holds special exhibitions from the same periods. Sponsors lectures, gallery talks, and special events, including Sunday concerts (October–May). Library open to researchers and members by appointment.

Sewall-Belmont House and Museum, *144 Constitution Ave. N.E. 20002-5608; (202) 546-1210. Fax, (202) 546-3997. Page Harrington, Executive Director. Press, (202) 546-1210, ext. 12.*
General email, info@sewallbelmont.org
Web, www.sewallbelmont.org

Maintains archives and artifacts documenting women's equality under the law. Interests include the suffragists, the National Women's Party, and the Equal Rights Amendment campaign.

Textile Museum, *2320 S St. N.W. 20008-4088; (202) 667-0441. Fax, (202) 483-0994. John Wetenhall, Director. Press, (202) 667-0441, ext. 78.*
General email, tmatgw@gwu.edu
Web, www.textilemuseum.org

Exhibits historic and handmade textiles and carpets with the goal of expanding appreciation of the artistic and cultural importance of the world's textiles. Exhibitions draw from loans and the permanent collection, specializing in the Eastern Hemisphere. Offers annual Fall Symposium, Celebration of Textiles festival, and other programs. Library open to the public during restricted hours Wednesdays and Saturdays.

Tudor Place, *1644 31st St. N.W. 20007; (202) 965-0400. Fax, (202) 965-0164. Leslie Buhler, Executive Director.*
General email, info@tudorplace.org
Web, www.tudorplace.org

Operates a historic property, home of Martha Washington's granddaughter and six generations of Custis-Peter family descendants. Seeks to educate the public about American history and culture, focusing on the capitol region from the 18th century. Maintains and displays artifacts, maintains a manuscript collection, conducts guided tours, and sponsors educational programs for students and teachers.

U.S. Holocaust Memorial Museum, *100 Raoul Wallenberg Pl. S.W. 20024-2126; (202) 488-0400. Fax, (202) 488-2690. Sara J. Bloomfield, Director. Library, (202) 479-9717. Press, (202) 488-6133. Toll-free, (866) 998-7466.*
General email, info@ushmm.org
Web, www.ushmm.org

Preserves documentation about the Holocaust and works to prevent genocide worldwide. Hosts exhibitions and Web site; conducts public programs, educational outreach, leadership training programs, and Holocaust commemorations; operates the Center for Advanced Holocaust Studies and the Academy for Genocide Prevention. Library and archives are open to the public.

Woodrow Wilson House *(National Trust for Historic Preservation), 2340 S St. N.W. 20008-4016; (202) 387-4062. Fax, (202) 483-1466. Robert A. Enholm, Executive Director; Nancy A. Bliss, Chair, ext. 41224.*
General email, sandrews@woodrowwilsonhouse.org
Web, www.woodrowwilsonhouse.org

Georgian Revival home that exhibits state gifts, furnishings, and memorabilia from President Woodrow Wilson's political and postpresidential years.

Music

► **AGENCIES**

National Museum of American History *(Smithsonian Institution), Culture and the Arts, 12th St. and Constitution Ave. N.W. 20560-0616 (mailing address: P.O. Box 37012, MRC 616, Washington, DC 20013-7012); (202) 633-1707. Fax, (202) 786-2883. Stacey Kluck, Chair. Press, (202) 633-3129.*
General email, info@si.edu
Web, www.americanhistory.si.edu/about/departments/culture-and-the-arts

Preserves American culture and heritage through collections, research, exhibitions, publications, teaching and lectures, and broadcasts. Sponsors Jazz Appreciation Month and a chamber music program. Research areas are open by appointment.

National Symphony Orchestra *(John F. Kennedy Center for the Performing Arts), 2700 F St. N.W. 20566-0004; (202) 416-8100. Fax, (202) 416-8105. Christoph Eschenbach, Music Director; Steven Reineke, Principal Pops Conductor. Information and reservations, (202) 467-4600. Toll-free, (800) 444-1324. TTY, (202) 416-8524. Tours, (202) 416-8340. Tour accessibility, (202) 416-8727. Tour accessibility TTY, (202) 416-8728.*
Web, www.nationalsymphony.org

Year-round orchestra that presents a full range of symphonic activities: classical, pops, and educational events; national and international tours; recordings; and special events.

National Symphony Orchestra Education Dept. *(John F. Kennedy Center for the Performing Arts), 2700 F St. N.W. 20566-0004 (mailing address: P.O. Box 101510, Arlington, VA 22210); (202) 416-8820. Carole J. Wysocki, Director, (202) 416-8828.*
General email, kced@kennedy-center.org
Web, www.kennedy-center.org/nso

Presents wide range of activities: concerts for students and families; fellowship program for talented high school musicians and a young associates program for high school students interested in arts management and professional music careers; annual soloist competition open to high school and college pianists, and orchestral instrumentalists; and Youth Orchestra Day for area youth orchestra members selected by their conductors.

▶ CONGRESS

For a listing of relevant congressional committees and subcommittees, please see page 113 or the Appendix.

Library of Congress, *Motion Picture, Broadcasting, and Recorded Sound Division,* *101 Independence Ave. S.E. 20540; (202) 707-5840. Fax, (202) 707-8464. Gregory Lukow, Chief. Recorded sound reference center, #LM113, (202) 707-7833. Fax for recorded sound reference center, #LM113, (202) 707-8572. Fax for motion picture and television reading room, #338.*
Web, www.loc.gov/rr/mopic

Maintains library's collection of musical and vocal recordings; tapes the library's concert series and other musical events for radio broadcast; produces recordings of music and poetry for sale to the public. Collection also includes sound recordings (1890–present). Reading room open to the public Monday through Friday, 8:30 a.m. to 5:00 p.m.; listening and viewing by appointment only.

Library of Congress, *Music Division,* *101 Independence Ave. S.E., #LM 113 20540; (202) 707-5503. Fax, (202) 707-0621. Susan H. Vita, Chief. Concert information, (202) 707-5502. Performing Arts Reading Room, (202) 707-5507. Web, www.loc.gov/rr/perform*

Maintains and services, through the Performing Arts Reading Room, the library's collection of music manuscripts, sheet music, books, and instruments. Coordinates the library's chamber music concert series; produces radio broadcasts and, for sale to the public, recordings of concerts sponsored by the division; issues publications relating to the field of music and to division collections.

▶ NONGOVERNMENTAL

American Music Therapy Assn., *8455 Colesville Rd., #1000, Silver Spring, MD 20910; (301) 589-3300. Fax, (301) 589-5175. Andrea Farbman, Executive Director. General email, info@musictherapy.org*
Web, www.musictherapy.org

Promotes the therapeutic use of music by approving degree programs and clinical training sites, establishing professional competencies and clinical practice standards for music therapists, and conducting research in the music therapy field.

Future of Music Coalition, *1615 L St. N.W., #520 20036; (202) 822-2051. Casey Rae, Executive Director, Interim. General email, suggestions@futureofmusic.org*
Web, www.futureofmusic.org

Seeks to educate the media, policymakers, and the public on music technology issues. Identifies and promotes innovative business models that will help musicians and citizens benefit from new technologies.

League of American Orchestras, *Advocacy and Government, Washington Office,* *910 17th St. N.W., #800 20006; (202) 776-0215. Fax, (202) 776-0224. Heather Noonan, Vice President for Advocacy. General email, league@americanorchestras.org*
Web, www.americanorchestras.org/advocacy-government .html

Service and educational organization dedicated to strengthening orchestras. Provides information and analysis on subjects of interest to orchestras through reports, seminars, and other educational forums. Seeks to improve policies that increase public access to orchestral music. Monitors legislation and regulations. (Headquarters in New York.)

National Assn. for Music Education, *1806 Robert Fulton Dr., Reston, VA 20191-4348; (703) 860-4000. Fax, (703) 860-1531. Michael Butera, Executive Director. Information, (800) 336-3768. General email, hain@nafme.org*
Web, www.nafme.org

Membership: music educators (preschool through university). Holds biennial conference. Publishes books and teaching aids for music educators.

National Assn. of Schools of Music, *11250 Roger Bacon Dr., #21, Reston, VA 20190-5248; (703) 437-0700. Fax, (703) 437-6312. Karen Moynahan, Executive Director. General email, info@arts-accredit.org*
Web, http://nasm.arts-accredit.org

Specialized professional accrediting agency for postsecondary programs in music. Conducts and shares research and analysis on topics pertinent to music programs and to the field of music. Offers professional development opportunities for executives of music programs.

Recording Industry Assn. of America, *1025 F St. N.W., 10th Floor 20004; (202) 775-0101. Fax, (202) 775-7253. Cary Sherman, Chief Executive Officer. Web, www.riaa.com*

Membership: creators, manufacturers, and marketers of sound recordings. Educates members about new technology in the music industry. Advocates copyright protection and opposes censorship. Works to prevent recording piracy, counterfeiting, bootlegging, and unauthorized rental and imports. Certifies gold, platinum, and multiplatinum recordings. Publishes statistics on the recording industry.

Washington Area Music Assn., *6263 Occoquan Forest Dr., Manassas, VA 20112-3011; (703) 368-3300. Fax, (703) 393-1028. Mike Schreibman, Executive Director. Information, (703) 368-3300. General email, dcmusic@wamadc.com*
Web, www.wamadc.com

Membership: musicians, concert promoters, lawyers, recording engineers, managers, contractors, and other music industry professionals. Sponsors workshops on industry-related topics. Represents professionals from all musical genres. Serves as a liaison between the Washington-area music community and music communities nationwide.

Theater and Dance

▶AGENCIES

Ford's Theatre National Historic Site, *511 10th St. N.W. 20004; (202) 426-6924. Fax, (202) 426-1845. William Cheek, Site Manager. Recorded ticket information, (202) 638-2941. General email, NACC_FOTH_Interpretation@nps.gov*

Web, www.nps.gov/foth

Administered by the National Park Service, which manages Ford's Theatre, Ford's Theatre Museum, and the Peterson House (house where Lincoln died). Presents interpretive talks, exhibits, and tours. Research library open by appointment. Functions as working stage for theatrical productions.

National Endowment for the Arts (NEA), *Performing Arts, 400 7th St. S.W., Constitution Center 20024; (202) 682-5438. Fax, (202) 682-5612. Douglas Sonntag, Director of Performing Arts, Acting, (202) 682-5791. General email, webmgr@arts.gov*

Web, www.arts.gov

Awards grants to dance companies and presenters for projects of all sizes and many styles, including ballet, modern dance, jazz, folkloric, tap, hip-hop, and other contemporary forms.

Smithsonian Institution, *Discovery Theater, 1100 Jefferson Dr. S.W. 20024 (mailing address: Discovery Theater, P.O. Box 23293, Washington, DC 20026-3293); (202) 633-8700. Fax, (202) 633-1322. Roberta Gasbarre, Director. General email, info@discoverytheater.org*

Web, www.discoverytheater.org

Presents live theatrical performances, including storytelling, dance, music, puppetry, and plays, for young people and their families.

▶NONGOVERNMENTAL

Dance/USA, *1111 16th St. N.W. 20036; (202) 833-1717. Fax, (202) 833-2686. Amy Fitterer, Executive Director. General email, danceusa@danceusa.org*

Web, www.danceusa.org

Membership: professional dance companies, artists, artist managers, presenters, service organizations, educators, libraries, businesses, and individuals. Advances the art form by addressing the needs, concerns, and interests of the professional dance community through public communications, research and information services, professional development, advocacy, re-granting initiatives, and other projects.

National Assn. of Schools of Dance, *11250 Roger Bacon Dr., #21, Reston, VA 20190-5248; (703) 437-0700. Fax, (703) 437-6312. Karen Moynahan, Executive Director. General email, info@arts-accredit.org*

Web, http://nasd.arts-accredit.org

Specialized professional accrediting agency for postsecondary programs in dance. Conducts and shares research and analysis on topics pertinent to dance programs and the field of dance. Offers professional development opportunities for executives of dance programs.

National Assn. of Schools of Theatre, *11250 Roger Bacon Dr., #21, Reston, VA 20190-5248; (703) 437-0700. Fax, (703) 437-6312. Karen Moynahan, Executive Director. General email, info@arts-accredit.org*

Web, http://nast.arts-accredit.org

Specialized professional accrediting agency for postsecondary programs in theatre. Conducts and shares research and analysis on topics pertinent to theatre programs and the field of theatre. Offers professional development opportunities for executives of theatre programs.

National Conservatory of Dramatic Arts, *1556 Wisconsin Ave. N.W. 20007; (202) 333-2202. Fax, (202) 333-1753. Nan Ficca, Director of Admissions; Raymond G. (Ray) Ficca, President. General email, nficca@theconservatory.org*

Web, www.theconservatory.org

Offers an accredited two-year program in postsecondary professional actor training and a one-year program in advanced professional training. Emphasizes both physical and mental preparedness for acting in the professional entertainment industry.

Shakespeare Theatre Company, *Lansburgh Theatre, 450 7th St. N.W., and Sidney Harmon Hall, 610 F St., N.W. 20004 (mailing address: 516 8th St. S.E., Washington, DC 20003-2834); (202) 547-3230. Fax, (202) 547-0226. Michael Kahn, Artistic Director; Chris Jennings, Managing Director; Michael R. Klein, Chair. Toll-free, (877) 487-8849. Box office, (202) 547-1122. Educational programs, (202) 547-5688.*

Web, www.shakespearetheatre.org

Professional resident theater that presents Shakespearean and other classical plays. Offers actor training program for youths, adults, and professional actors. Produces free outdoor summer Shakespeare plays and free Shakespeare plays for schools.

Visual Arts

▶AGENCIES

National Endowment for the Arts (NEA), *Media, Arts Design, and Visual Arts, 400 7th St. S.W., Constitution Center 20024; (202) 682-5452. Fax, (202) 682-5721. Jason Schupbach, Director, Design, (202) 682-5786; Vacant, Director, Media Arts; Wendy Clark, Director, Museums and Visual Arts, Acting, (202) 682-5555. Web, www.arts.gov*

Awards grants to nonprofit organizations for creative works and programs in the visual arts, including painting, sculpture, crafts, video, photography, printmaking, drawing, artists' books, and performance art.

State Dept., *Art in Embassies, M-OBO-OM-ART, Dept. of State 20552; (703) 875-4202. Fax, (703) 875-4182. Owen Susman, Director, Acting. Web, http://art.state.gov*

Exhibits American art in U.S. ambassadorial residences. Borrows artworks from artists, collectors, galleries, and museums.

►CONGRESS

For a listing of relevant congressional committees and subcommittees, please see page 113 or the Appendix.

Library of Congress, *Prints and Photographs Division, 101 Independence Ave. S.E., #LM 339 20540; (202) 707-6394. Fax, (202) 707-6647. Helena Zinkham, Chief. Web, www.loc.gov/rr/print*

Maintains Library of Congress's collection of pictorial material not in book format, totaling more than 13.5 million items. U.S. and international collections include artists' prints; historical prints, posters, and drawings; photographs (chiefly documentary); political and social cartoons; and architectural plans, drawings, prints, and photographs. Reference service provided in the Prints and Photographs Reading Room. Reproductions of nonrestricted material available through the Library of Congress's Photoduplication Service; prints and photographs may be borrowed through the Exhibits Office for exhibits by qualified institutions. A portion of the collections and an overview of reference services are available on the World Wide Web.

►NONGOVERNMENTAL

American Institute of Architects, *1735 New York Ave. N.W. 20006-5292; (202) 626-7300. Fax, (202) 626-7547. Robert Ivy, Chief Executive Officer. Press, (202) 626-7467. Toll-free, (800) 242-3837. Government advocacy, (202) 626-7507. General email, infocentral@aia.org Web, www.aia.org*

Membership: licensed American architects, interns, architecture faculty, engineers, planners, and those in government, manufacturing, or other fields in a capacity related to architecture. Works to advance the standards of architectural education, training, and practice. Promotes the aesthetic, scientific, and practical efficiency of architecture, urban design, and planning; monitors international developments. Offers continuing and professional education programs; sponsors scholarships, internships, and awards. Houses archival collection, including documents and drawings of American architects and architecture. Library open to the public by appointment. Monitors legislation and regulations.

Foundation for Art and Preservation in Embassies (FAPE), *1725 Eye St. N.W., #300 20006-2423; (202) 349-3724. Fax, (202) 349-3727. Jennifer A. Duncan, Director. General email, info@fapeglobal.org Web, www.fapeglobal.org*

Works with the State Dept. to contribute fine art for placement in U.S. embassies worldwide.

National Assn. of Schools of Art and Design, *11250 Roger Bacon Dr., #21, Reston, VA 20190-5248; (703) 437-0700. Fax, (703) 437-6312. Karen Moynahan, Executive Director. General email, info@arts-accredit.org Web, http://nasad.arts-accredit.org*

Specialized professional accrediting agency for postsecondary programs in art and design. Conducts and shares research and analysis on topics pertinent to art and design programs and fields of art and design. Offers professional development opportunities for executives of art and design programs.

HISTORY AND PRESERVATION

General

►AGENCIES

Advisory Council on Historic Preservation, *1100 Pennsylvania Ave. N.W., #803 20004; (202) 606-8503. Fax, (202) 606-8647. John M. Fowler, Executive Director; Milford W. Donaldson, Chair. General email, achp@achp.gov Web, www.achp.gov*

Advises the president and Congress on historic preservation; reviews and comments on federal projects and programs affecting historic, architectural, archaeological, and cultural resources.

Bureau of Land Management (BLM) *(Interior Dept.), Cultural, Paleontological Resources, and Tribal Consultation, 20 M St. S.E. 20003 (mailing address: 1849 C St. N.W., Washington, DC 20240); (202) 912-7208. Fax, (202) 245-0015. Byron Loosle, Division Chief. Web, www.blm.gov/wo/st/en/prog/more/CRM.html*

Develops bureau policy on historic preservation, archaeological resource protection, consultation with Native Americans, curation of artifacts and records, heritage education, and paleontological resource management.

General Services Administration (GSA), *Urban Development/Good Neighbor Program, 18th St. N.W., #3341 20405-0001; (202) 501-1856. Frank Giblin, Program Manager, (202) 501-3393. General email, giblin@gsa.gov Web, www.gsa.gov/goodneighbor*

Advises on locations, designs, and renovations of federal facilities in central business areas, historic districts, and local redevelopment areas where they can anchor or promote community development. Collaborates with local and national civic and other organizations. Serves as clearinghouse for good practices.

International Cultural Property Protection *(State Dept.), Bureau of Education and Cultural Affairs,* Cultural Heritage Center, 2200 C St. N.W., SA-5, 5th Floor 20037; (202) 632-6445. Carmen G. Cantor, Executive Director; Evan Ryan, Assistant Secretary.
General email, culprop@state.gov
Web, http://exchanges.state.gov/us

Reviews country requests for import restrictions on archaeological or ethnological artifacts and makes recommendations on them to the State Department.

National Archives and Records Administration (NARA), *Cartographic and Architectural Unit,* 8601 Adelphi Rd., #3320, College Park, MD 20740-6001; (301) 837-3200. Fax, (301) 837-3622. Deborah Lelansky, Cartographic Supervisor, (301) 837-1911.
General email, carto@nara.gov
Web, www.archives.gov/dc-metro/college-park/researcher-info.html#cartographic

Preserves and makes available historical records of federal agencies, including maps, charts, aerial photographs, architectural engineering drawings, patents, lighthouse plans, and ships' plans. Research room open to the public. Records are available for reproduction.

National Archives and Records Administration (NARA), *Preservation Programs,* 8601 Adelphi Rd., #2800, College Park, MD 20740-6001; (301) 837-1785. Fax, (301) 837-3701. Doris A. Hamburg, Director. Toll-free, (866) 272-6272.
General email, preservation@nara.gov
Web, www.archives.gov/preservation

Manages the preservation program for the forty-four National Archives facilities across the country. Develops preservation policy, regulations, and planning. Responsible for conserving and reformatting archival holdings. Ensures that the storage environments are designed and maintained to prolong the life of records. Manages records emergency preparedness and response for the agency; advises other federal agencies in event of need. Conducts research and testing for materials purchased by and used in the archives, as well as deterioration and preservation processes. Monitors and maintains the condition of the Charters of Freedom.

National Capital Planning Commission, 401 9th St. N.W., North Lobby, #500 20004; (202) 482-7200. Fax, (202) 482-7272. Marcel Acosta, Executive Director.
General email, info@ncpc.gov
Web, www.ncpc.gov

Central planning agency for the federal government in the national capital region, which includes the District of Columbia and suburban Maryland and Virginia. Reviews and approves plans for the preservation of certain historic and environmental features in the national capital region, including the annual federal capital improvement plan.

National Endowment for the Arts (NEA), *Multidisciplinary Arts,* 400 7th St. S.W., Constitution Center 20024; (202) 682-5428. Fax, (202) 682-5669. Michael Orlove, Director of Presenting and Multidisciplinary Works; Barry Bergey, Director of Folk and Traditional Arts.
Web, www.arts.gov

Awards grants to artist communities, folk and traditional arts organizations, and presenting organizations.

National Endowment for the Humanities (NEH), *Preservation and Access,* 400 7th St. S.W., Constitution Center 20024; (202) 606-8570. Fax, (202) 606-8639. Nadina Gardner, Director, (202) 606-8442.
General email, preservation@neh.gov
Web, www.neh.gov/divisions/preservation

Sponsors preservation and access projects, the stabilization and documentation of material culture collections, and the National Digital Newspaper program.

National Museum of American History *(Smithsonian Institution), Culture and the Arts,* 12th St. and Constitution Ave. N.W. 20560-0616 (mailing address: P.O. Box 37012, MRC 616, Washington, DC 20013-7012); (202) 633-1707. Fax, (202) 786-2883. Stacey Kluck, Chair. Press, (202) 633-3129.
General email, info@si.edu
Web, www.americanhistory.si.edu/about/departments/culture-and-the-arts

Collects and preserves artifacts related to U.S. cultural heritage; supports research, exhibits, performances, and educational programs. Areas of focus include sports, recreation, and leisure; popular culture; music and dance; theater, film, broadcast media, graphic arts, printing, and photographic history.

National Park Service (NPS) *(Interior Dept.), Cultural Resources,* 1849 C St. N.W., #3128, MIB 20240-0001; (202) 208-7625. Fax, (202) 273-3237. Stephanie Toothman, Associate Director.
Web, www.cr.nps.gov

Oversees preservation of federal historic sites and administration of buildings programs. Programs include the National Register of Historic Places, National Historic and National Landmark Programs, Historic American Building Survey, Historic American Engineering Record, Archeology and Antiquities Act Program, and Technical Preservation Services. Gives grant and aid assistance and tax benefit information to properties listed in the National Register of Historic Places.

▶ CONGRESS

For a listing of relevant congressional committees and subcommittees, please see page 113 or the Appendix.

Senate Office of Conservation and Preservation, S416 CAP 20510; (202) 224-4550. Vacant, Director.

Develops and coordinates programs related to the conservation and preservation of Senate records and materials for the secretary of the Senate.

▶**NONGOVERNMENTAL**

American Historical Assn., *400 A St. S.E. 20003; (202) 544-2422. Fax, (202) 544-8307. James Grossman, Executive Director.*
General email, info@historians.org
Web, www.historians.org

Membership: university academics, colleges, museums, historical organizations, libraries and archives, independent historians, students, K-12 teachers, government and business professionals, and individuals interested in history. Interests include academic freedom, professional standards, publication, teaching, professional development, networking, and advocacy. Supports public access to government information; publishes original historical research, journals, bibliographies, historical directories, and a job placement bulletin.

American Institute for Conservation of Historic and Artistic Works, *1156 15th St. N.W., #320 20005-1714; (202) 452-9545. Fax, (202) 452-9328. Eryl P. Wentworth, Executive Director.*
General email, info@conservation-US.org
Web, www.conservation-US.org

Membership: professional conservators, scientists, students, administrators, cultural institutions, collection care professionals, and others. Promotes the knowledge and practice of the conservation of cultural property; supports research; and disseminates information on conservation.

American Studies Assn., *1120 19th St. N.W., #301 20036-3614; (202) 467-4783. Fax, (202) 467-4786. John F. Stephens, Executive Director.*
General email, asastaff@theasa.net
Web, www.theasa.net

Fosters the interdisciplinary exchange of ideas about American culture and history in local and global contexts; awards annual prizes for contributions to American studies; provides curriculum resources.

Civil War Trust, *1156 15th St. N.W., #900 20005; (202) 367-1861. Fax, (202) 367-1865. James Lighthizer, President.*
General email, info@civilwar.org
Web, www.civilwar.org

Membership: preservation professionals, historians, conservation activists, and citizens. Preserves endangered Civil War battlefields throughout the United States. Conducts preservation conferences and workshops. Advises local preservation groups. Monitors legislation and regulations at the federal, state, and local levels.

Colonial Dames XVII Century, *National Society, 1300 New Hampshire Ave. N.W. 20036-1502; (202) 293-1700. Fax, (202) 466-6099. Lillie Frances Harrington Davis, President General.*
General email, cd17th@verizon.net
Web, www.colonialdames17c.org

Membership: American women who are lineal descendants of persons who rendered civil or military service and lived in America or one of the British colonies before 1701. Preserves records and shrines; encourages historical research; awards scholarships to undergraduate and graduate students and scholarships in medicine to persons of Native American descent.

Colonial Dames of America, *National Society, 2715 Que St. N.W. 20007-3071; (202) 337-2288. Fax, (202) 337-0348. Karen L. Daly, Executive Director.*
General email, info@dumbartonhouse.org
Web, www.nscda.org

Membership: descendants of colonists in America before 1750. Conducts historical and educational activities; maintains Dumbarton House, a museum open to the public Tuesday–Saturday; and offers lectures and concerts.

Daughters of the American Revolution, *National Society, 1776 D St. N.W. 20006-5303; (202) 628-1776. Fax, (202) 347-4712. Merry Ann Thompson Wright, President General.*
Web, www.dar.org

Membership: women descended from American Revolutionary War patriots. Conducts historical, educational, and patriotic activities; maintains a genealogical library, fine arts museum, and documentary collection antedating 1830. Library open to the public (nonmembers charged fee for use).

David S. Wyman Institute for Holocaust Studies, *1200 G St. N.W., #800 20005; (202) 434-8994. Rafael Medoff, Director.*
General email, rafaelmedoff@aol.com
Web, www.wymaninstitute.org

Educates the public about U.S. response to Nazism and the Holocaust through scholarly research, public events and exhibits, publications, conferences, and educational programs.

Heritage Preservation, *1012 14th St. N.W., #1200 20005-3408; (202) 233-0800. Fax, (202) 233-0807. Lawrence L. (Larry) Reger, President. Information, (888) 388-6789.*
General email, info@heritagepreservation.org
Web, www.heritagepreservation.org

Membership: museums, libraries, archives, historic preservation organizations, historical societies, and conservation groups. Advocates the conservation and preservation of works of art, anthropological artifacts, documents, historic objects, architecture, and natural science specimens. Programs include Save Outdoor Sculpture, which works to inventory all U.S. outdoor sculpture; the Conservation Assessment Program, which administers grants to museums for conservation surveys of their collections; the Heritage Health Index, which documents the condition of U.S. collections; the Heritage Emergency Task Force, which helps institutions protect their collections from disasters and emergencies; Rescue Public Murals, which aids in the conservation of public murals throughout the United States; and the Collections Connections Online Community, which allows smaller museums, libraries, archives, and historical societies to get answers to collections care questions, quickly locate reliable preservation resources, and network with colleagues.

National Conference of State Historic Preservation Officers, *444 N. Capitol St. N.W., #342 20001-1512; (202) 624-5465. Fax, (202) 624-5419. Erik Hein, Executive Director.*
Web, www.ncshpo.org

Membership: state and territorial historic preservation officers and deputy officers. Compiles statistics on programs; monitors legislation and regulations.

National Park Trust, *401 E. Jefferson St., #203, Rockville, MD 20850; (301) 279-7275. Fax, (301) 279-7211. Grace K. Lee, Executive Director.*
General email, npt@parktrust.org
Web, www.parktrust.org

Protects national parks, wildlife refuges, and historic monuments. Uses funds to purchase private land within or adjacent to existing parks and land suitable for new parks; works with preservation organizations to manage acquired resources.

National Preservation Institute, *P.O. Box 1702, Alexandria, VA 22313; (703) 765-0100. Fax, (703) 768-9350. Jere Gibber, Executive Director; Kathleen McLaughlin, President.*
General email, info@npi.org
Web, www.npi.org

Conducts seminars in historic preservation and cultural resource management for those involved in the management, preservation, and stewardship of historic and cultural resources.

National Society of the Children of the American Revolution, *1776 D St. N.W., #224 20006-5303; (202) 638-3153. Fax, (202) 737-3162. Hans E. Jackson, Senior National President.*
General email, hq@nscar.org
Web, www.nscar.org

Membership: descendants, age twenty-two years and under, of American soldiers and patriots of the American Revolution. Conducts historical, educational, and patriotic activities; preserves places of historical interest.

National Trust for Historic Preservation, *2600 Virginia Ave. N.W., #1000 20037; (202) 588-6000. Fax, (202) 588-6038. Stephanie Meeks, President. Press, (202) 588-6141.*
General email, feedback@savingplaces.org
Web, www.preservationnation.org

Conducts seminars, workshops, and conferences on topics related to preservation, including neighborhood conservation, main street revitalization, rural conservation, and preservation law; offers financial assistance through loan and grant programs; provides advisory services; operates historic house sites, which are open to the public; and publishes quarterly magazine and e-newsletters.

Preservation Action, *1307 New Hampshire Ave. N.W. 20036; (202) 463-0970. Fax, (202) 463-1299. Darlene R. Taylor, President.*
General email, mail@preservationaction.org
Web, www.preservationaction.org

Monitors legislation affecting historic preservation and neighborhood conservation. Maintains a nationwide database of activists. Promotes adequate funding for historic preservation programs and policies that support historic resource protection.

Society for American Archaeology, *1111 14th St. N.W., #800 20005-5622; (202) 789-8200. Fax, (202) 789-0284. Tobi Brimsek, Executive Director.*
General email, headquarters@saa.org
Web, www.saa.org

Promotes greater awareness, understanding, and research of archaeology on the American continents; works to preserve and publish results of scientific data and research; serves as information clearinghouse for members.

Archives and Manuscripts

▶AGENCIES

National Archives and Records Administration (NARA), *700 Pennsylvania Ave. N.W. 20408; (866) 272-6272. Fax, (301) 837-0483. David S. Ferriero, Archivist of the United States. Press, (202) 357-5300. Public affairs, (202) 357-5300.*
Web, www.archives.gov

Identifies, preserves, and makes available federal government documents of historic value; administers a network of regional storage centers and archives and operates the presidential library system. Collections include photographs, graphic materials, films, and maps; holdings include records generated by foreign governments (especially in wartime) and by international conferences, commissions, and exhibitions.

National Archives and Records Administration (NARA), *Center for Legislative Archives, 700 Pennsylvania Ave. N.W., #8E 20408; (202) 357-5350. Fax, (202) 357-5911. Richard H. Hunt, Director.*
Web, www.archives.gov/legislative

Collects and maintains records of congressional committees and legislative files from 1789 to the present. Publishes inventories and guides to these records.

National Archives and Records Administration (NARA), *Presidential Libraries, 8601 Adelphi Rd., #2200F, College Park, MD 20740-6001; (301) 837-3250. Fax, (301) 837-3199. Susan K. Donius, Director, (301) 837-1662.*
Web, www.archives.gov/presidential-libraries

Administers thirteen presidential libraries. Directs all programs relating to acquisition, preservation, and research use of materials in presidential libraries; conducts oral history projects; publishes finding aids for research sources; provides reference service, including information from and about documentary holdings. Conducts community outreach; oversees museum exhibition programming.

National Historical Publications and Records Commission *(National Archives and Records Administration), 700 Pennsylvania Ave. N.W., #106 20408-0001; (202) 357-5010. Fax, (202) 357-5914. Kathleen Williams, Executive Director. Toll-free, (866) 272-6272.*
General email, nhprc@nara.gov
Web, www.archives.gov/nhprc

Awards grants to nonprofit institutions, educational institutions, and local and state governments to preserve and make accessible historical records, including the papers of nationally significant Americans. Helps preserve electronic records and digitize and publish online collections.

National Museum of American History *(Smithsonian Institution), Archives Center, 12th St. and Constitution Ave. N.W., #1100 20560-0601 (mailing address: P.O. Box 37012, NMAH MRC 601, Washington, DC 20013-7012); (202) 633-3270. Fax, (202) 786-2453. Wendy Shay, Chair, Acting. Press, (202) 633-3129.*
General email, archivescenter@si.edu
Web, www.americanhistory.si.edu/archives

Acquires, organizes, preserves, and makes available for research the museum's archival and documentary materials relating to American history and culture. Three-dimensional objects and closely related documents are in the care of curatorial divisions. Research areas are open by appointment.

Smithsonian Institution, *Archives of American Art, 750 9th St. N.W., #2200 20001 (mailing address: P.O. Box 37012, Victor Bldg., MRC 937, Washington, DC 20013-7012); (202) 633-7940. Fax, (202) 633-7994. Katie Haw, Director. Reference desk, (202) 633-7950.*
Web, www.aaa.si.edu

Collects and preserves manuscript items, such as notebooks, sketchbooks, letters, and journals; photos of artists and works of art; tape-recorded interviews with artists, dealers, and collectors; exhibition catalogs; directories; and biographies on the history of visual arts in the United States. Library open to scholars and researchers. Reference centers that maintain microfilm copies of a selection of the Archives' collection include New York; Boston; San Francisco; and San Marino, Calif.

▶ **CONGRESS**

For a listing of relevant congressional committees and subcommittees, please see page 113 or the Appendix.

Library of Congress, *Manuscript Division, 101 Independence Ave. S.E., #LM 102 20540; (202) 707-5383. Fax, (202) 707-7791. James H. Hutson, Chief. Reading room, (202) 707-5387.*
Web, www.loc.gov/rr/mss

Maintains, describes, and provides reference service on the library's manuscript collections, including the papers of U.S. presidents and other eminent Americans. Manuscript Reading Room primarily serves serious scholars and researchers; historians and reference librarians are available for consultation.

Library of Congress, *Microform and Electronic Resources Center, 101 Independence Ave. S.E., #LJ139B 20540-4660; (202) 707-3399. Fax, (202) 707-1957. Barbara R. Morland, Head, Acting.*
Web, www.loc.gov/rr/main/ccc.html and www.loc.gov/rr/microform/

Has custody of and services the library's general microform collection. Provides work stations for searching the library's online catalog and accessing the Internet. Open to the public, hours posted on the Web site.

Library of Congress, *Rare Book and Special Collections Division, 101 Independence Ave. S.E., #LJ 239 20540; (202) 707-3448. Fax, (202) 707-4142. Mark G. Dimunation, Chief.*
Web, www.loc.gov/rr/rarebook

Maintains collections of incunabula (books printed before 1501) and other early printed books; early imprints of American history and literature; illustrated books; early Spanish American, Russian, and Bulgarian imprints; Confederate states imprints; libraries of famous personalities (including Thomas Jefferson, Woodrow Wilson, and Oliver Wendell Holmes); special format collections (miniature books, broadsides, almanacs, and pre-1870 copyright records); special interest collections; and special provenance collections. Reference assistance is provided in the Rare Book and Special Collections Reading Room.

Office of Art and Archives, *Office of the Clerk, House of Representatives, B53 CHOB 20515; (202) 226-1300. Fax, (202) 226-4635. Farar P. Elliott, Chief, Art and Archives.*
Web, http://clerk.house.gov

Works with the Office of the Historian to provide access to published documents and historical records of the House. Advises members on the disposition of their records and papers; maintains information on manuscript collections of former members; maintains biographical files on former members; houses photographs and artifacts of former members. Produces publications on Congress and its members.

Office of the Historian, *Office of the Clerk, U.S. House of Representatives, B56 CHOB 20515; (202) 226-5525. Fax, (202) 226-2931. Matthew A. Wasniewski, House Historian.*
Web, http://clerk.house.gov

Works with the Office of Art and Archives to provide access to published documents and historical records of the House. Conducts historical research. Advises members on the disposition of their records and papers; maintains information on manuscript collections of former members; maintains biographical files on former members. Produces publications on Congress and its members.

Senate Historical Office, *SH-201 20510; (202) 224-6900. Donald A. Ritchie, Historian.*

General email, historian@sec.senate.gov

Web, www.senate.gov

Serves as an information clearinghouse on Senate history, traditions, and members. Collects, organizes, and distributes to the public unpublished Senate documents; collects and preserves photographs and pictures related to Senate history; conducts an oral history program; advises senators and Senate committees on the disposition of their noncurrent papers and records. Produces publications on the history of the Senate.

▶ NONGOVERNMENTAL

Assassination Archives and Research Center, *962 Wayne Ave., #910, Silver Spring, MD 20910; (301) 565-0249. James Lesar, President.*

General email, jhlesar@gmail.com

Web, www.aarclibrary.org

Acquires, preserves, and disseminates information on political assassinations. Materials and information available on Web site and by request through mail. On-site access available to the public by appointment only.

Moorland-Spingarn Research Center (MSRC) *(Howard University),* *500 Howard Pl. N.W., #129 20059; (202) 806-7239. Fax, (202) 806-6405. Dr. Howard Dodson, Director. Library, (202) 806-7266.*

Web, www.howard.edu/msrc

Comprehensive repository for the documentation of the history and culture of people of African descent in Africa, the Americas, and other parts of the world; collects, preserves, and makes available for research a wide range of resources chronicling the black experience.

Genealogy

▶ AGENCIES

National Archives and Records Administration (NARA), *Archives 1, Research Support Branch,* *700 Pennsylvania Ave. N.W., #G13 20408; (202) 357-5400. Fax, (202) 357-5934. Trevor Plante, Branch Chief, Acting.*

General email, inquire@nara.gov

Web, www.archives.gov

Assists individuals interested in researching record holdings of the National Archives, including genealogical records; issues research cards to researchers who present photo identification. Users must be at least fourteen years of age.

National Archives and Records Administration (NARA), *National Archives Museum,* *700 Pennsylvania Ave. N.W., #G9 20408; (202) 357-5210. Fax, (202) 357-5926. Lisa Royce, Director, Acting. Information, (202) 357-5000. Press, (202) 357-5300.*

General email, inquire@nara.gov

Web, www.archives.gov

Plans and directs activities to acquaint the public with the mission and holdings of the National Archives; conducts behind-the-scenes tours; presents hands-on workshops; develops both traditional and interactive exhibits; produces publications, including teaching packets that feature historic documents and online educational tools.

National Archives and Records Administration (NARA), *Research Services,* *8601 Adelphi Rd., #3400, College Park, MD 20740-6001; (301) 837-1893. Fax, (301) 837-3633. William A. Mayer, Executive.*

Web, www.archives.gov/locations/archival-research.html

Preserves and makes available federal records at fifteen National Archives facilities across the country.

▶ CONGRESS

For a listing of relevant congressional committees and subcommittees, please see page 113 or the Appendix.

Library of Congress, *Local History and Genealogy Reading Room,* *101 Independence Ave. S.E., #LJ-100 20540; (202) 707-5537. Fax, (202) 707-1957. James P. Sweany, Head.*

Web, www.loc.gov/rr/genealogy

Provides reference and referral service on topics related to local history, genealogy, and heraldry throughout the United States.

▶ NONGOVERNMENTAL

Daughters of the American Revolution, *National Society,* *1776 D St. N.W. 20006-5303; (202) 628-1776. Fax, (202) 347-4712. Merry Ann Thompson Wright, President General.*

Web, www.dar.org

Membership: women descended from American Revolutionary War patriots. Maintains a genealogical library, which is open to the public (nonmembers charged fee for use).

National Genealogical Society, *3108 Columbia Pike, #300, Arlington, VA 22204-4370; (703) 525-0050. Fax, (703) 525-0052. Jordan Jones, President. Toll-free, (800) 473-0060.*

General email, ngs@ngsgenealogy.org

Web, www.ngsgenealogy.org

Encourages study of genealogy and publication of all records that are of genealogical interest. Provides online courses and an in-depth home study program; holds an annual conference.

National Museum of Civil War Medicine, *48 East Patrick St., Frederick, MD 21705 (mailing address: P.O. Box 470, Frederick, MD 21705); (301) 695-1864. Fax, (301) 695-6823. George Wunderlich, Executive Director.*

General email, info@civilwarmed.org

Web, www.civilwarmed.org

Assists individuals with questions about ancestors injured in the Civil War.

National Society, *Daughters of the American Colonists,* 2205 Massachusetts Ave. N.W. 20008-2813; (202) 667-3076. Fax, (202) 667-0571. Carole L. Rambo Holt, President.
Web, www.nsdac.org

Membership: women descended from men and women who were resident in or gave civil or military service to the colonies prior to the Revolutionary War. Maintains library of colonial and genealogical records, open to the public by appointment.

Washington DC Family History Center, *Church of Jesus Christ of Latter-Day Saints,* 10000 Stoneybrook Dr., Kensington, MD 20895 (mailing address: P.O. Box 49, Kensington, MD 20895); (301) 587-0042.
Linda Christenson, Director.
General email, DC_Washington@ldsmail.net

Web, www.wdcfhc.org and https://familysearch.org/learn/wiki/en/washington_dc_family_history_center

Maintains genealogical library for research. Collection includes international genealogical index, family group record archives, microfiche registers, and the Family Search Computer Program (www.familysearch.org). Library open to the public. (Sponsored by the Church of Jesus Christ of Latter-Day Saints.)

Specific Cultures

▶AGENCIES

Interior Dept. (DOI), *Indian Arts and Crafts Board,* 1849 C St. N.W., #2528 20240-0001; (888) 278-3253. Fax, (202) 208-5196. Meridith Z. Stanton, Director.
General email, iacb@ios.doi.gov

Web, www.doi.gov/iacb

Advises Native American artisans and craft guilds; produces a source directory on arts and crafts of Native Americans (including Alaska Natives); maintains museums of native crafts in Montana, South Dakota, and Oklahoma; provides information on the Indian Arts and Crafts Act.

National Museum of American History *(Smithsonian Institution),* *Curatorial Affairs,* 12th St. and Constitution Ave. N.W. 20560 (mailing address: P.O. Box 37012, MRC 664, Washington, DC 20013-7012); (202) 633-3497. Fax, (202) 633-4284. David Allison, Associate Director.
General email, info@si.edu

Web, www.americanhistory.si.edu/about/departments

Conducts research, develops collections, and creates exhibits on American social and public history, based on collections of folk and popular arts, ethnic and craft objects, textiles, coins, costumes and jewelry, ceramics and glass, graphic arts, musical instruments, photographs, technological innovations, appliances, and machines. Research areas are open by appointment.

Smithsonian Institution, *Center for Folklife and Cultural Heritage,* 600 Maryland Ave. S.W., #2001 20024 (mailing address: P.O. Box 37012, MRC 520, Washington, DC 20013-7012); (202) 633-6440. Fax, (202) 633-6474. Michael Atwood Mason, Director. Press, (202) 633-5183.
General email, folklife-info@si.edu

Web, www.folklife.si.edu

Promotes and conducts research into traditional U.S. cultures and foreign folklife traditions; produces folkways recordings, films, videos, and educational programs; presents annual Smithsonian Folklife Festival in Washington, D.C.

▶CONGRESS

For a listing of relevant congressional committees and sub-committees, please see page 113 or the Appendix.

Library of Congress, *American Folklife Center,* 101 Independence Ave. S.E., #LJ G49 20540; (202) 707-5510. Fax, (202) 707-2076. Elizabeth (Betsy) Peterson, Director. Reading room, (202) 707-5510.
General email, folklife@loc.gov

Web, www.loc.gov/folklife

Coordinates national, regional, state and local government, and private folklife activities; contracts with individuals and groups for research and field studies in American folklife and for exhibits and workshops; maintains the National Archive of Folk Culture (an ethnographic collection of American and international folklore, grassroots oral histories, and ethnomusicology) and the Veterans History Project (a collection of oral histories and documentary materials from veterans of World Wars I and II and the Korean, Vietnam, and Persian Gulf wars). Conducts internships at the archive; lectures; sponsors year-round concerts of traditional and ethnic music.

▶NONGOVERNMENTAL

National Council for the Traditional Arts, 8757 Georgia Ave., #450, Silver Spring, MD 20910; (301) 565-0654. Fax, (301) 565-0472. Julia Olin, Executive Director.
General email, info@ncta.net

Web, www.ncta.net

Seeks to celebrate and honor arts of cultural and ethnic significance, including music, crafts, stories, and dance. Promotes artistic authenticity in festivals, national and international tours, concerts, radio and television programs, CD recordings, and films. Works with national parks and other institutions to create, plan, and present cultural events, exhibits, and other programs. Sponsors the annual National Folk Festival.

National Hispanic Foundation for the Arts (NHFA), Washington Square, 1050 Connecticut Ave. N.W., 10th Floor 20036; (202) 293-8330. Fax, (202) 772-3101. Felix Sanchez, Chair.
General email, info@hispanicarts.org

Web, www.hispanicarts.org

Strives to increase the presence of Hispanics in the media, telecommunications, entertainment industries, and performing arts and to increase programming for the U.S.

National Park Service Sites in the Capital Region

The National Park Service administers most parks, circles, and monuments in the District of Columbia, as well as sites in nearby Maryland, Virginia, and West Virginia. For information on facilities not listed here, visit www.nps.gov/parks.html.

Go to www.recreation.gov for information on visiting and making reservations at federal recreation sites nationwide.

Antietam National Battlefield, (301) 432-5124

Arlington House, Robert E. Lee Memorial, (703) 235-1530

C & O Canal National Historical Park, (301) 739-4200

  Great Falls Area (C & O Canal Maryland), (301) 767-3714

Catoctin Mountain Park, (301) 663-9330

Clara Barton National Historic Site, (301) 320-1410

Ford's Theatre National Historic Site, (202) 426-6924

Fort Washington Park, (301) 763-4600 (includes Piscataway Park)

Frederick Douglass National Historic Site, (202) 426-5961

George Washington Memorial Parkway, (703) 289-2500 (includes memorials to Theodore Roosevelt, Lyndon Johnson, and U.S. Marine Corps)

Glen Echo Park, (703) 289-2500

Great Falls Park, (703) 285-2965

Greenbelt Park, (301) 344-3948

Harpers Ferry National Historical Park, (304) 535-6029

Manassas National Battlefield Park, (703) 754-1861

Mary McLeod Bethune Council House National Historic Site, (202) 673-2402

Monocacy National Battlefield, (301) 662-3515

National Mall, (202) 426-6841 (includes presidential and war memorials and Pennsylvania Avenue National Historic Site)

Prince William Forest Park, (703) 221-4706

Rock Creek Park, (202) 895-6000

Thomas Stone National Historic Site, (301) 392-1776

White House, (202) 456-7041

Wolf Trap National Park for the Performing Arts, (703) 255-1800

Latino community. Provides scholarships for Hispanic students to pursue graduate study in the arts.

National Italian American Foundation, *1860 19th St. N.W. 20009; (202) 387-0600. Fax, (202) 387-0800. John Viola, Chief Operating Officer, (202) 939-3115. General email, info@niaf.org*

Web, www.niaf.org

Membership: U.S. citizens of Italian ancestry. Promotes recognition of Italian American contributions to American society. Funds cultural events, educational symposia, antidefamation programs, and grants and scholarships. Represents the interests of Italian Americans before Congress. Serves as an umbrella organization for local Italian American clubs throughout the United States.

Washington Area

▶AGENCIES

National Park Service (NPS) *(Interior Dept.), National Capital Region, 1100 Ohio Dr. S.W. 20242; (202) 619-7174. Steven Whitesell, Regional Director. Permits, (202) 245-4715.*

Web, www.nps.gov/ncro

Provides visitors with information on Washington-area parks, monuments, and Civil War battlefields; offers press services for the media and processes special-event applications and permits.

White House Visitor Center *(President's Park), 1450 Pennsylvania Ave. N.W. 20230; (202) 208-1631. Fax, (202) 208-1643. Peter Lonsway, Park Manager; Kathy Langley, Manager, Visitor Center; John Stanwich, National Park Service Liaison, Acting, (202) 619-6344.*

General email, whho_presidents_park@nps.gov

Web, www.nps.gov/whho

Administered by the National Park Service. Educates visitors about the White House through videos, exhibits, and historical artifacts. Public tours of the White House are available by submitting requests to one's member of Congress and are accepted up to 90 days in advance. (Temporary Visitor Center at the Ellipse Visitor Pavillon, just west of the intersection of 15th and E Streets N.W.)

▶CONGRESS

For a listing of relevant congressional committees and sub-committees, please see page 113 or the Appendix.

Architect of the Capitol, *Office of the Curator, S411 CAP 20515; (202) 224-2955. Melinda K. Smith, Curator. General email, curator@sec.senate.gov*

Web, www.aoc.gov

Preserves artwork; maintains collection of drawings, photographs, and manuscripts on and about the Capitol and the House and Senate office buildings. Maintains records of the Architect of the Capitol. Library open to the public.

Senate Commission on Art, *S-411 CAP 20510; (202) 224-2955. Melinda K. Smith, Curator of the Senate. General email, curator@sec.senate.gov*

Web, www.senate.gov/pagelayout/art/one_item_and_ teasers/Explore_Senate_Art.htm

Accepts artwork and historical objects for display in Senate office buildings and the Senate wing of the Capitol.

Maintains and exhibits Senate collections (paintings, sculptures, furniture, and manuscripts); oversees and maintains old Senate and Supreme Court chambers.

▶**NONGOVERNMENTAL**

Assn. for Preservation of Historic Congressional Cemetery, *1801 E St. S.E. 20003-2499; (202) 543-0539. Fax, (202) 449-8364. Paul Williams, President. General email, staff@congressionalcemetery.org*

Web, www.congressionalcemetery.org

Administers and maintains the Washington Parish Burial Ground (commonly known as the Congressional Cemetery). Tours available Saturdays at 11:00 am in warm weather. See Web site for tour information.

Historical Society of Washington, D.C., *801 K St. N.W., 2nd Floor 20001-3746; (202) 249-3955. Fax, (202) 417-3823. John Suau, Executive Director; Anne McDonough, Library Director. Library, (202) 249-3954. General email, info@historydc.org*

Web, www.historydc.org

Maintains research collections on the District of Columbia. Publishes *Washington History* magazine. Library open to the public by appointment for researchers involved in projects about Washington, D.C. Museum open Monday and Wednesday, 10:00 a.m.–4:00 p.m, Thursday 10:00 a.m.–6:00 p.m.

Martin Luther King Jr. Memorial Library,
Washingtoniana Division, *901 G St. N.W., #307 20001-1443; (202) 727-1213. Kimberly Zablud, Manager, Special Collections.*

General email, wash.dcpl@dc.gov

Web, www.dclibrary.org/research/collections

Maintains reference collections of District of Columbia current laws and regulations, history, and culture. Collections include biographies; travel books; memoirs and diaries; family, church, government, and institutional histories; maps (1612–present); plat books; city, telephone, and real estate directories (1822–present); census schedules; newspapers (1800–present), including the *Washington Star* microfilm (1852–1981) and microfilm of several other historic newspapers dating back to 1800, and a collection of clippings and photographs (1940–1981); periodicals; photographs; and oral history materials on local neighborhoods, ethnic groups, and businesses.

National Coalition to Save Our Mall, *9507 Overlea Dr., Rockville, MD 20850 (mailing address: P.O. Box 4709, Rockville, MD 20849); (301) 340-3938. Fax, (301) 340-3947. Judy Scott Feldman, President. General email, jfeldman@savethemall.org*

Web, www.savethemall.org

Coalition of professional and civic organizations and concerned artists, historians, and citizens promoting the protection and long-range vision planning of the National Mall in Washington, D.C.

Supreme Court Historical Society, *224 E. Capitol St. N.E. 20003; (202) 543-0400. Fax, (202) 547-7730. David T. Pride, Executive Director.*

Web, www.supremecourthistory.org

Acquires, preserves, and displays historic items associated with the Court; conducts and publishes scholarly research. Conducts lecture programs; promotes and supports educational activities about the Court.

U.S. Capitol Historical Society, *200 Maryland Ave. N.E. 20002; (202) 543-8919. Fax, (202) 544-8244. Ronald A. Sarasin, President; Donald R. Kennon, Vice President for Scholarship and Education (historian). Information, (800) 887-9318. General email, uschs@uschs.org*

Web, www.uschs.org

Membership: members of Congress, individuals, and organizations interested in the preservation of the history and traditions of the U.S. Capitol. Conducts historical research; offers tours, lectures, workshops, and films; holds events involving members of Congress; publishes an annual historical calendar.

White House Historical Assn., *740 Jackson Pl. N.W. 20006 (mailing address: P.O. Box 27624, Washington, DC 20038-7624); (202) 737-8292. Fax, (202) 789-0440. Neil W. Horstman, President. Toll-free for purchases, (800) 555-2451.*

webmaster@whha.org,

Web, www.whitehousehistory.org

Seeks to enhance the understanding and appreciation of the White House. Publishes books on the White House, its inhabitants, its artworks, its furnishings, and its history. Net proceeds from book sales, videos and DVDs, traveling exhibits, the museum shop (located in the Commerce Dept.), and gift shop go toward the purchase of historic items for the White House permanent collection.

PHILANTHROPY, PUBLIC SERVICE, AND VOLUNTEERISM

General

▶**AGENCIES**

Agency for International Development (USAID),
Volunteers for Prosperity (VfP), *1300 Pennsylvania Ave. N.W. 20523-8600; (202) 712-0076. Fax, (202) 712-0077. Kathleen Hunt, Director, Acting. General email, volunteersforprosperity@usaid.gov*

Web, www.volunteersforprosperity.gov

Links U.S.-based companies and nonprofit organizations deployed in foreign assistance with skilled American professionals in volunteer opportunities that support the strategic development goals of the U.S. government.

AmeriCorps *(Corporation for National and Community Service),* *1201 New York Ave. N.W. 20525; (202) 606-5000.*

Fax, (202) 606-3475. Wendy M. Spencer, Chief Executive Officer. Volunteer recruiting information, (800) 942-2677. TTY, (800) 833-3722. Local TTY, (202) 606-3472.
General email, info@cns.gov
Web, www.nationalservice.gov

Provides Americans age seventeen and older with opportunities to serve their communities on a full- or part-time basis. Participants work in the areas of education, public safety, human needs, and the environment, and earn education awards for college or vocational training.

AmeriCorps (*Corporation for National and Community Service*), *National Civilian Community Corps*, 1201 New York Ave. N.W. 20525; (202) 606-5000. Fax, (202) 606-3462. Kate Raftery, Director, (202) 606-6706. Alternate phone, (202) 606-6798. Volunteer recruiting information, (800) 942-2677. TTY, (800) 833-3722. Local TTY, (202) 565-2799.
General email, info@cns.gov
Web, www.nationalservice.gov/programs/americorps/americorps-nccc

Provides a ten-month residential service and leadership program for men and women ages eighteen to twenty-four of all social, economic, and educational backgrounds. Works to restore and preserve the environment. Working in teams of eight to ten, members provide disaster relief, fight forest fires, restore homes and habitats after natural disasters, and work in a variety of other service projects in every state.

AmeriCorps (*Corporation for National and Community Service*), *State and National Program*, 1201 New York Ave. N.W. 20525; (202) 606-5000. John Gomperts, Director, (202) 606-6790. Alternate phone, (202) 606-6790. Information, (800) 942-2677. TTY, (800) 833-3722.
General email, questions@americorps.gov
Web, www.nationalservice.gov/programs/americorps/americorps-state-and-national

AmeriCorps State administers and oversees AmeriCorps funding distributed to governor-appointed state commissions, which distribute grants to local organizations and to such national organizations as Habitat for Humanity. AmeriCorps National provides grants directly to national public and nonprofit organizations that sponsor service programs, Indian tribes, and consortia formed across two or more states, including faith-based and community organizations, higher education institutions, and public agencies.

AmeriCorps (*Corporation for National and Community Service*), *Volunteers in Service to America (VISTA)*, 1201 New York Ave. N.W. 20525; (202) 606-5000. Fax, (202) 565-2789. Mary Strasser, Director, (202) 606-6943. Volunteer recruiting information, (800) 942-2677. TTY, (800) 833-3722.
General email, questions@americorps.gov
Web, www.americorps.gov/programs/americorps/americorps-vista

Assigns full-time volunteers to public and private nonprofit organizations for one year to alleviate poverty in local communities. Volunteers receive a living allowance, health care, and other benefits and their choice of a postservice stipend or education award.

Corporation for National and Community Service, 1201 New York Ave. N.W. 20525; (202) 606-5000. Fax, (202) 606-3460. Wendy M. Spencer, Chief Executive Officer, (202) 606-5000, ext. 6735. Press, (202) 606-6944. Volunteer recruiting information, (800) 942-2677.
General email, info@cns.gov
Web, www.nationalservice.gov

Partners people of all ages with national and community-based organizations, schools, faith-based groups, and local agencies to assist with community needs in education, the environment, public safety, homeland security, and other areas. Programs include AmeriCorps-VISTA (Volunteers in Service to America), AmeriCorps-NCCC (National Civilian Community Corps), Learn and Serve America, and the Senior Corps.

Federal Emergency Management Agency (FEMA) (*Homeland Security Dept.*), *Individual and Community Preparedness (ICPD)*, *Techworld Bldg.*, 800 K St. N.W., #5127 20472-3630; (202) 786-9557. Karen Marsh, Director, Acting.
General email, citizencorps@dhs.gov
Web, www.citizencorps.gov and www.ready.gov/research

Conducts research on individual, business, and community preparedness. Administers Citizen Corps, a national network of state, territory, tribal, and local councils that coordinate with local first responders to develop community-specific public education, outreach, training, and volunteer opportunities that address community preparedness and resiliency.

Peace Corps, 1111 20th St. N.W. 20526; (202) 692-2100. Fax, (202) 692-2101. Carolyn Hessler-Radelet, Director, Acting. Information, (855) 855-1961. Press, (202) 692-2230.
Web, www.peacecorps.gov and Twitter, @PeaceCorps

Promotes world peace, friendship, and mutual understanding between the United States and developing nations. Administers volunteer programs to assist developing countries in education, the environment, health (particularly HIV awareness and prevention), small business development, agriculture, and urban youth development.

Senior Corps (*Corporation for National and Community Service*), *Retired and Senior Volunteer Program, Foster Grandparent Program, and Senior Companion Program,* 1201 New York Ave. N.W. 20525; (202) 606-5000. Erwin Tan, Director, (202) 606-3237. National service information hotline, (800) 942-2677. TTY, (800) 833-3722.
General email, info@cns.gov
Web, www.seniorcorps.gov

Network of programs that help older Americans find service opportunities in their communities, including the Retired and Senior Volunteer Program, which encourages older citizens to use their talents and experience in community service; the Foster Grandparent Program, which gives older citizens opportunities to work with exceptional children and children with special needs; and the Senior Companion Program, which recruits older citizens to help homebound adults, especially seniors, with special needs.

▶CONGRESS

For a listing of relevant congressional committees and subcommittees, please see page 113 or the Appendix.

Government Accountability Office (GAO), *Education, Workforce, and Income Security,* 441 G St. N.W., #5928 20548; (202) 512-7215. Barbara D. Bovbjerg, Managing Director.
Web, www.gao.gov

Independent, nonpartisan agency in the legislative branch. Audits, analyzes, and evaluates programs of the Corporation for National and Community Service; makes reports available to the public.

▶NONGOVERNMENTAL

Arca Foundation, 1308 19th St. N.W. 20036; (202) 822-9193. Fax, (202) 785-1446. Anna Lefer Kuhn, Executive Director.
General email, proposals@arcafoundation.org
Web, www.arcafoundation.org

Awards grants to nonprofit organizations in the areas of social equity and justice. Interests include corporate accountability, and civic participation domestically and internationally.

Assn. of Fundraising Professionals (AFP), 4300 Wilson Blvd., #300, Arlington, VA 22203-4168; (703) 684-0410. Fax, (703) 684-0540. Andrew Watt, President. Information, (800) 666-3863.
General email, afp@afpnet.org
Web, www.afpnet.org

Membership: individuals who serve as fundraising executives for nonprofit institutions or as members of counseling firms engaged in fundraising management. Promotes ethical standards; offers workshops; provides resources for member certification; monitors legislation and regulations. AFP Foundation promotes philanthropy and volunteerism. Library open to the public by appointment.

Assn. of Small Foundations (ASF), 1720 N St. N.W. 20036; (202) 580-6560. Fax, (202) 580-6579. Henry L. Berman, Chief Executive Officer. Toll-free, (888) 212-9922.
General email, asf@smallfoundations.org
Web, www.smallfoundations.org

Membership: donors, trustees, consultants, and employees of philanthropic foundations that have few or no staff. Offers educational programs and publications, referrals, networking opportunities, and liability insurance to members.

BoardSource, 750 9th St. N.W., #650 20001; (202) 349-2500. Fax, (202) 349-2599. Anne Wallestad, Chief Executive Officer. Toll-free, (877) 892-6273.
Web, www.boardsource.org

Works to improve the effectiveness of nonprofit organizations by strengthening their boards of directors. Operates an information clearinghouse; publishes materials on governing nonprofit organizations; assists organizations in conducting training programs, workshops, and conferences for board members and chief executives.

Capital Research Center, 1513 16th St. N.W. 20036; (202) 483-6900. Fax, (202) 483-6990. Terrence M. Scanlon, President.
General email, contact@capitalresearch.org
Web, www.capitalresearch.org

Conservative think tank that researches funding sources of public interest and advocacy groups. Analyzes the impact these groups have on public policy. Publishes findings in newsletters and reports.

Caring Institute, 228 7th St. S.E. 20003; (202) 547-4273. Fax, (202) 547-6137. Kathleen Brennan, President.
General email, info@caringinstitute.org
Web, www.caring.org

Promotes selflessness and public service. Recognizes the achievements of individuals who have demonstrated a commitment to serving others. Operates the Frederick Douglass Museum and Hall of Fame for Caring Americans. Sponsors the National Caring Award and offers internships to high school and college students.

The Congressional Award, 379 FHOB 20515 (mailing address: P.O. Box 77440, Washington, DC 20013-7440); (202) 226-0130. Fax, (202) 226-0131. Erica Wheelan Heyse, National Director. Toll-free, (888) 802-9273.
General email, information@congressionalaward.org
Web, www.congressionalaward.org

Noncompetitive program established by Congress that recognizes the achievements of young people ages thirteen and one-half to twenty-three. Participants are awarded certificates or medals for setting and achieving goals in four areas: volunteer public service, personal development, physical fitness, and expeditions and exploration.

Council of Better Business Bureaus, *Wise Giving Alliance,* 3033 Wilson Blvd., #600, Arlington, VA 22201-3843; (703) 276-0100. Fax, (703) 525-8277. H. Art Taylor, President.
General email, charities@cbbb.bbb.org
Web, www.give.org

Serves as a donor information service on national charities. Evaluates charities in relation to Better Business Bureau standards for charitable solicitation, which address charity finances, solicitations, fundraising practices, and governance. Produces quarterly guide that summarizes these findings.

Council on Foundations, 2121 Crystal Drive, Ste. 700, Arlington, VA 22202; (800) 673-9036. Vikki N. Spruill, President.
General email, info@cof.org
Web, www.cof.org

Membership: independent community, family, and public- and company-sponsored foundations; corporate giving programs; and foundations in other countries. Promotes responsible and effective philanthropy through educational programs, publications, government relations, and promulgation of a set of principles and practices for effective grant making.

Earth Share, *7735 Old Georgetown Rd., #900, Bethesda, MD 20814; (240) 333-0300. Fax, (240) 333-0301. Kalman Stein, President. Information, (800) 875-3863.*
General email, info@earthshare.org

Web, www.earthshare.org

Federation of environmental and conservation organizations. Works with government and private payroll contribution programs to solicit contributions to member organizations for environmental research, education, and community programs. Provides information on establishing environmental giving options in the workplace.

Evangelical Council for Financial Accountability, *440 W. Jubal Early Dr., #100, Winchester, VA 22601-6319; (540) 535-0103. Fax, (540) 535-0533. Dan Busby, President. Information, (800) 323-9473.*
General email, information@ecfa.org

Web, www.ecfa.org

Membership: charitable, religious, international relief, and educational nonprofit U.S.-based organizations committed to evangelical Christianity. Assists members in making appropriate public disclosure of their financial practices and accomplishments. Certifies organizations that conform to standards of financial integrity and Christian ethics.

Foundation Center, *Washington Office, 1627 K St. N.W., 3rd Floor 20006-1708; (202) 331-1400. Fax, (202) 331-1739. Patricia Pasqual, Director.*
General email, jzr@foundationcenter.org

Web, www.foundationcenter.org/washington and *http://grantspace.org*

Publishes foundation guides. Serves as a clearinghouse on foundations and corporate giving, nonprofit management, fundraising, and grants for individuals. Provides training and seminars on fundraising and grant writing. Operates libraries in Atlanta, Cleveland, New York, San Francisco, and Washington, D.C; library catalog available on the Web site. Libraries open to the public. (Headquarters in New York.)

General Federation of Women's Clubs, *1734 N St. N.W. 20036-2990; (202) 347-3168. Fax, (202) 835-0246. Michele Mount, Executive Director, Interim. Toll-free, (800) 443-4392.*
General email, gfwc@gfwc.org

Web, www.gfwc.org

Nondenominational, nonpartisan international organization of women volunteers. Interests include conservation, education, international and public affairs, and the arts.

Good360, *1330 Braddock Pl., #600, Alexandria, VA 22314; (703) 836-2121. Fax, (877) 798-3192. Cindy Hallberlin, President.*
General email, serviceteam@good360.org

Web, www.good360.org

Online product donation marketplace that seeks to meet the needs of nonprofit organizations by encouraging corporations to donate newly manufactured products to domestic and international charities. Works with companies to develop in-kind programs, coordinates the distribution of gifts to nonprofit agencies, collects tax documentation from recipients, and conducts community-wide public relations activities to encourage product giving. Serves schools and health, recreational, housing, arts, and environmental groups. (Formerly Gifts in Kind International.)

Grantmakers in Health, *1100 Connecticut Ave. N.W., #1200 20036; (202) 452-8331. Fax, (202) 452-8340. Faith Mitchell, President.*
General email, info@gih.org

Web, www.gih.org

Seeks to increase the capacity of private sector grantmakers to enhance public health. Fosters information exchange among grantmakers. Publications include a bulletin on current news in health and human services.

Habitat for Humanity International, *Government Relations and Advocacy, 1424 K St. N.W., #600 20005; (202) 628-9171. Fax, (202) 628-9169. Elizabeth Blake, Senior Vice President for Legal, Government Relations, and General Counsel.*
General email, advocacy@habitat.org

Web, www.habitat.org

Christian ministry that seeks to eliminate poverty housing. Builds and sells homes to low-income families. Monitors legislation and regulations.

Independent Sector, *1602 L St. N.W., #900 20036; (202) 467-6100. Fax, (202) 467-6101. Diana Aviv, President.*
General email, info@independentsector.org

Web, www.independentsector.org

Membership: corporations, foundations, and national voluntary, charitable, and philanthropic organizations. Encourages volunteering, giving, and not-for-profit nonpartisan initiatives by the private sector for public causes.

Institute for Justice, *901 N. Glebe Rd., #900, Arlington, VA 22203; (703) 682-9320. Fax, (703) 682-9321. William (Chip) Mellor, President.*
General email, general@ij.org

Web, www.ij.org

Sponsors seminars to train law students, grassroots activists, and practicing lawyers in applying advocacy strategies in public interest litigation. Seeks to protect individuals from arbitrary government interference in free speech, private property rights, parental school choice, and economic liberty. Litigates cases.

Institute for Sustainable Communities, *Washington Office,* 888 17th St. N.W., #610 20006; (202) 777-7575. Fax, (202) 777-7577. *George Hamilton, President; Debra Perry, Senior Program Manager, U.S. General email, isc@iscvt.org*
Web, www.iscvt.org

Public interest organization that offers mentoring and training in advocacy skills and strategies to nonprofit and international groups interested in such issues as civil and human rights, public health, arms control, and environmental and consumer affairs. Aids groups in making better use of resources, such as access to the media and coalition building. (Headquarters in Montpelier, Vt.)

Lutheran Volunteer Corps, *1226 Vermont Ave. N.W. 20005; (202) 387-3222. Fax, (202) 667-0037. Sam Collins, President.*
General email, staff@lutheranvolunteercorps.org
Web, www.lutheranvolunteercorps.org and *Twitter, @LVCorps*

Administers volunteer program in selected U.S. cities; coordinates activities with health and social service agencies, educational institutions, and environmental groups. Places volunteers in full-time positions in direct service, community organizing, advocacy, and public policy.

Mars Foundation, *6885 Elm St., McLean, VA 22101; (703) 821-4900. Fax, (703) 448-9678. Sue Martin, Assistant Secretary; O. O. Otih, Secretary-Treasurer.*

Awards grants in education, arts, health care concerns, animal wildlife, environment, and history.

National Committee for Responsive Philanthropy, *1331 H St. N.W., #200 20005; (202) 387-9177. Fax, (202) 332-5084. Aaron Dorfman, Executive Director.*
General email, info@ncrp.org
Web, www.ncrp.org

Directs philanthropic giving to benefit the socially, economically, and politically disenfranchised; advocates for groups that represent the poor, minorities, and women. Conducts research; organizes local coalitions. Monitors legislation and regulations.

National Human Services Assembly, *1101 14th St. N.W., #600 20005; (202) 347-2080. Fax, (202) 393-4517. Irv Katz, President.*
General email, nassembly@nassembly.org
Web, www.nassembly.org

Membership: national voluntary health and human service organizations. Provides collective leadership in the areas of health and human service. Provides members' professional staff and volunteers with a forum to share information. Supports public policies, programs, and resources that advance the effectiveness of health and human service organizations and their service delivery. (Formerly the National Assembly of Health and Human Services Organizations.)

Philanthropy Roundtable, *1730 M St. N.W., #601 20036; (202) 822-8333. Fax, (202) 822-8325. Adam Meyerson, President.*

General email, main@philanthropyroundtable.org
Web, www.philanthropyroundtable.org

Membership: individual donors, foundation trustees and staff, and corporate giving officers. Helps donors achieve their charitable objectives by offering counsel and peer-to-peer exchange opportunities.

Points of Light Institute, *1625 K St. N.W., #500 20006; (202) 979-2900. Fax, (202) 979-2901. Julie Murphy, Director of Government Relations. Media, (202) 352-3232. General email, info@pointsoflight.org*
Web, www.pointsoflight.org

Promotes mobilization of people for volunteer community service aimed at solving social problems. Through HandsOn Network regional centers, offers technical assistance, training, and information services to nonprofit organizations, public agencies, corporations, and others interested in volunteering. (Headquarters in Atlanta, Ga.)

United Way Worldwide, *701 N. Fairfax St., Alexandria, VA 22314-2045; (703) 836-7112. Fax, (703) 519-0097. Brian A. Gallagher, President.*
General email, worldwide@unitedway.org
Web, http://worldwide.unitedway.org

Membership: independent United Way organizations in 40 countries and territories, including 1,300 in the United States. Provides staff training; fundraising, planning, and communications assistance; resource management; and national public service advertising. Activities support education, financial stability, and health.

Urban Institute, *Center on Nonprofits and Philanthropy,* 2100 M St. N.W. 20037; (202) 833-7200. Fax, (202) 833-6231. *Elizabeth Boris, Director.*
Web, www.urban.org/center/cnp/index.cfm

Conducts and disseminates research on the role and impact of nonprofit organizations and philanthropy.

Volunteers of America, *1660 Duke St., Alexandria, VA 22314; (703) 341-5000. Fax, (703) 341-7000. Michael King, President. Toll-free, (800) 899-0089.*
General email, communications@voa.org
Web, www.voa.org

Faith-based organization that promotes local human services and outreach programs. Facilitates individual and community involvement. Focuses on children at risk, abused and neglected children, older adults, homeless individuals, people with disabilities, and others.

W. O'Neil Foundation, *5454 Wisconsin Ave., #730, Chevy Chase, MD 20815; (301) 656-5848. Helene O'Neil Shere, President.*

Awards grants primarily to Roman Catholic organizations providing programs and basic needs of the poor, such as food, clothing, shelter, and basic medical care, both nationally and internationally.

Youth Service America, *1101 15th St. N.W., #200 20005; (202) 296-2992. Fax, (202) 296-4030. Steven A. Culbertson, President.*

General email, info@ysa.org

Web, www.ysa.org

Advocates youth service at national, state, and local levels. Promotes opportunities for young people to be engaged in community service. Sponsors Global Youth Service Day. Hosts database of U.S. volunteer opportunities.

Washington Area

►NONGOVERNMENTAL

D.C. Preservation League, *1221 Connecticut Ave. N.W., #5A 20036; (202) 783-5144. Fax, (202) 783-5596. Rebecca A. Miller, Executive Director.*
General email, info@dcpreservation.org

Web, www.dcpreservation.org

Participates in planning and preserving buildings and sites in Washington, D.C. Programs include protection and enhancement of the city's landmarks; educational lectures, tours, and seminars; and technical assistance to neighborhood groups. Monitors legislation and regulations.

Eugene and Agnes E. Meyer Foundation, *1250 Connecticut Ave. N.W., #800 20036; (202) 483-8294. Fax, (202) 328-6850. Julie L. Rogers, President.*
General email, meyer@meyerfdn.org

Web, www.meyerfoundation.org

Seeks to improve the quality of life in Washington, D.C. Awards grants to nonprofit organizations in four program areas: education, health communities, economic security, and a strong nonprofit sector.

Eugene B. Casey Foundation, *800 S. Frederick Ave., #100, Gaithersburg, MD 20877-4150; (301) 948-6500. Betty Brown Casey, Chair.*

Philanthropic organization that supports the arts, education, and social services in the metropolitan Washington area.

Junior League of Washington, *3039 M St. N.W. 20007; (202) 337-2001. Fax, (202) 342-3148. Shiela Corley, President. General email, office@jlw.org*

Web, www.jlw.org

Educational and charitable women's organization that promotes volunteerism and works for community improvement through leadership of trained volunteers. Interests include promoting volunteerism and developing the potential of women. Current emphasis is on literacy. (Assn. of Junior Leagues International headquarters in New York.)

Morris and Gwendolyn Cafritz Foundation, *1825 K St. N.W., #1400 20006; (202) 223-3100. Fax, (202) 296-7567. Calvin Cafritz, Chair; Rose Ann Cleveland, Executive Director.*
General email, info@cafritzfoundation.org

Web, www.cafritzfoundation.org

Awards grants to educational, arts, and social services institutions in the metropolitan Washington area.

Washington Regional Assn. of Grantmakers, *1400 16th St. N.W., #740 20036; (202) 939-3440. Fax, (202) 939-3442. Tamara Lucas Copeland, President, (202) 939-3441. General email, info@washingtongrantmakers.org*

Web, www.washingtongrantmakers.org

Network of funders that partners with agencies and nongovernmental organizations in the Washington, D.C., region. Identifies and implements new and innovative forms of philanthropy. Shares best practices. Advocates for collective philanthropic community in the region and publishes a biweekly newsletter.

RECREATION AND SPORT

General

►AGENCIES

Health and Human Services Dept. (HHS), *President's Council on Fitness, Sports, and Nutrition, 1101 Wootton Pkwy., #560, Tower Bldg., Rockville, MD 20852; (240) 276-9567. Fax, (240) 276-9860. Shellie Pfohl, Executive Director.*
General email, fitness@hhs.gov

Web, www.fitness.gov and www.presidentschallenge.org

Provides schools, state and local governments, recreation agencies, and employers with information on designing and implementing physical fitness and nutrition programs; conducts award programs for children and adults and for schools, clubs, and other institutions.

►NONGOVERNMENTAL

American Alliance for Health, *Physical Education, Recreation, and Dance, 1900 Association Dr., Reston, VA 20191-1598; (703) 476-3400. Fax, (703) 476-9527. Paul Roetert, Chief Executive Officer. Toll-free, (800) 213-7193. Press, (703) 476-3461.*
General email, info@aahperd.org

Web, www.aahperd.org

Membership: teachers and others who work with school health, physical education, athletics, recreation, dance, and safety education programs (kindergarten through postsecondary levels). Member associations are National Assn. for Girls and Women in Sport, American Assn. for Health Education, National Dance Assn., National Assn. for Sport and Physical Education, and American Assn. for Physical Activity and Recreation.

American Canoe Assn., *503 Sophia St., #100, Fredericksburg, VA 22401; (540) 907-4460. Fax, (888) 229-3792. Wade Blackwood, Executive Director.*
General email, aca@americancanoe.org

Web, www.americancanoe.org

Membership: individuals and organizations interested in the promotion of canoeing, kayaking, and other paddle sports. Works to preserve the nation's recreational waterways. Sponsors programs in safety education, competition, recreation, public awareness, conservation, and public policy. Monitors legislation and regulations.

American Gaming Assn., *1299 Pennsylvania Ave. N.W., #1175 20004; (202) 552-2675. Fax, (202) 552-2676. Geoff Freeman, President.*
General email, info@americangaming.org
Web, www.americangaming.org

Membership: casinos, casino and gaming equipment manufacturers, and financial services companies. Compiles statistics and serves as an information clearinghouse on the gaming industry. Administers a task force to study gambling addiction, raise public awareness of the condition, and develop assistance programs for it. Monitors legislation and regulations.

American Hiking Society, *1422 Fenwick Lane, Silver Spring, MD 20910-3328; (301) 565-6704. Fax, (301) 565-6714. Gregory Miller, President. Toll-free, (800) 972-8608.*
General email, info@americanhiking.org
Web, www.americanhiking.org

Membership: individuals and clubs interested in preserving America's trail system and protecting the interests of hikers and other trail users. Sponsors research on trail construction and a trail maintenance summer program. Provides information on outdoor volunteer opportunities on public lands.

American Medical Athletic Assn., *4405 East-West Hwy., #405, Bethesda, MD 20814-4535; (301) 913-9517. Fax, (301) 913-9520. David Watt, Executive Director, ext. 13. Information, (800) 776-2732.*
General email, amaa@americanrunning.org
Web, www.amaasportsmed.org

Membership: sports medicine and allied health professionals. Assists members in promoting running and physical fitness to their patients and in developing their own physical fitness programs. Promotes and reports on sports medicine research and discussion. (Sister organization to American Running Assn.)

American Recreation Coalition, *1200 G St. N.W., #650 20005; (202) 682-9530. Fax, (202) 682-9529. Derrick A. Crandall, President.*
General email, arc@funoutdoors.com
Web, www.funoutdoors.com

Membership: recreation industry associations, recreation enthusiast groups, and leading corporations in the recreation products and services sectors. Promotes health and well-being through recreation.

American Resort Development Assn., *1201 15th St. N.W., #400 20005; (202) 371-6700. Fax, (202) 289-8544. Howard Nusbaum, President.*
Web, www.arda.org

Membership: U.S. and international developers, builders, financiers, marketing companies, and others involved in resort, recreational, and community development. Serves as an information clearinghouse; monitors federal and state legislation affecting land, time share, and community development industries.

American Running Assn., *4405 East-West Hwy., #405, Bethesda, MD 20814-4535; (301) 913-9517. Fax, (301) 913-9520. David Watt, Executive Director, ext. 13. Information, (800) 776-2732.*
General email, milerun@americanrunning.org
Web, www.americanrunning.org

Membership: athletes, health clubs, physicians, businesses, and individuals. Promotes proper nutrition and regular exercise. Provides members with medical advice and referrals, fitness information, and assistance in developing fitness programs. (Sister organization to American Medical Athletic Assn.)

American Sportfishing Assn., *1001 N. Fairfax St., #501, Alexandria, VA 22314; (703) 519-9691. Fax, (703) 519-1872. Michael Nussman, President.*
General email, info@asafishing.org
Web, www.asafishing.org

Works to ensure healthy and sustainable fisheries resources and to expand market growth for its members through increased participation in sportfishing. Programs include "Keep America Fishing" and the Fish America Foundation.

Assn. of Pool and Spa Professionals, *2111 Eisenhower Ave., #500, Alexandria, VA 22314-4698; (703) 838-0083. Fax, (703) 549-0493. Rich Gottwald, President.*
General email, MemberServices@apsp.org
Web, www.apsp.org

Membership: manufacturers, dealers and retailers, service companies, builders, and distributors of pools, spas, and hot tubs. Promotes the industry; provides educational programs for industry professionals; establishes standards for construction and safety. Monitors legislation and regulations.

Boat Owners Assn. of the United States (Boat U.S.), *880 S. Pickett St., Alexandria, VA 22304-4695; (703) 461-2864. Fax, (703) 461-2847. Margaret Podlich, President.*
General email, govtaffairs@boatus.com
Web, www.boatus.com

Membership: owners of recreational boats. Represents boat-owner interests before the federal, state, and local governments.

Club Managers Assn. of America, *1733 King St., Alexandria, VA 22314; (703) 739-9500. Fax, (703) 739-0124. James Singerling, Chief Executive Officer.*
General email, cmaa@cmaa.org
Web, www.cmaa.org

Membership: managers of membership clubs. Promotes the profession of club management through education and other assistance.

Disabled Sports USA, *451 Hungerford Dr., #100, Rockville, MD 20850; (301) 217-0960. Fax, (301) 217-0968. Kirk M. Bauer, Executive Director, (301) 217-9838.*

General email, info@dsusa.org

Web, www.dsusa.org and www.disabledsportsusa.org

Offers nationwide sports rehabilitation programs in more than forty summer and winter sports; promotes independence, confidence, and fitness through programs for people with permanent disabilities, including wounded service personnel; conducts workshops and competitions through community-based chapters; participates in world championships.

FishAmerica Foundation, *1001 N. Fairfax St., #501, Alexandria, VA 22314; (703) 519-9691. Fax, (703) 519-1872. Gordon Robertson, Vice President, American Sportfishing Assn.; Ruth Jackson, Grants Manager.*

General email, fishamerica@asafishing.org

Web, www.fishamerica.org

Invests in local communities to restore habitat, improve water quality, and advance fisheries research to increase sportfish populations and sportfishing opportunities. (Affiliated with the American Sportfishing Assn.)

National Aeronautic Assn., *Reagan National Airport, Hangar 7, #202 20001-6015; (703) 416-4888. Fax, (703) 416-4877. Jonathan Gaffney, President.*

General email, naa@naa.aero

Web, www.naa.aero

Membership: persons interested in development of general and sporting aviation, including skydiving, commercial and military aircraft, and spaceflight. Supervises sporting aviation competitions; administers awards in aviation; oversees and approves official U.S. aircraft, aeronautics, and space records. Serves as U.S. representative to the International Aeronautical Federation in Lausanne, Switzerland.

National Club Assn., *1201 15th St. N.W., #450 20005; (202) 822-9822. Fax, (202) 822-9808. Susanne R. Wegrzyn, President.*

General email, info@nationalclub.org

Web, www.nationalclub.org

Promotes the interests of private, social, and recreational clubs. Monitors legislation and regulations.

National Collegiate Athletic Assn. (NCAA), *Government Relations, 1 Dupont Circle N.W., #310 20036-1139; (202) 293-3050. Fax, (202) 293-3075. Abe L. Frank, Director, ext. 2122.*

Web, www.ncaa.org

Membership: colleges and universities, conferences, and organizations interested in the administration of intercollegiate athletics. Certifies institutions' athletic programs; compiles records and statistics; produces publications and television programs; administers youth development programs; awards student athletes with postgraduate scholarships and degree-completion grants. (Headquarters in Indianapolis, Ind.)

National Football League Players Assn., *1133 20th St. N.W., #600 20036; (202) 463-2200. Fax, (202) 756-9310. DeMaurice Smith, Executive Director. Toll-free, (800) 372-2000.*

Web, www.nflplayers.com

Membership: professional football players. Represents members in matters concerning wages, hours, and working conditions. Provides assistance to charitable and community organizations. Sponsors programs and events to promote the image of professional football and its players.

National Indian Gaming Assn. (NIGA), *224 2nd St. S.E. 20003; (202) 546-7711. Fax, (202) 546-1755. Jason Giles, Executive Director.*

General email, info@indiangaming.org

Web, www.indiangaming.org

Membership: more than 180 Indian nations as well as other organizations, tribes, and businesses engaged in gaming enterprises. Operates as a clearinghouse for tribes, policymakers, and the public on Indian gaming issues and tribal community development.

National Recreation and Park Assn., *22377 Belmont Ridge Rd., Ashburn, VA 20148-4501; (703) 858-0784. Fax, (703) 858-0794. Barbara Tulipane, Chief Executive Officer, (703) 858-2144. Toll-free, (800) 626-6772.*

General email, customerservice@nrpa.org

Web, www.nrpa.org

Membership: park and recreation professionals and interested citizens. Promotes support and awareness of park, recreation, and leisure services; advances environmental and conservation efforts; facilitates development, expansion, and management of resources; provides technical assistance for park and recreational programs; and provides professional development to members. Monitors legislation and regulations.

Poker Players Alliance, *1325 G St. N.W., #500 20005; (202) 552-7429. Fax, (202) 552-7423. John A. Pappas, Executive Director. Toll-free, (888) 448-4772.*

General email, email@theppa.org

Web, www.theppa.org

Membership: poker players and enthusiasts. Seeks to promote the game and protect players' rights. Monitors legislation and regulations.

Project for Public Spaces, *1612 K St. N.W., #802 20006; (202) 223-3621. Mark Plotz, Vice President.*

General email, info@bikewalk.org

Web, www.bikewalk.org

Promotes bicycle use; conducts research, planning, and training projects; develops safety education and public information materials; offers consulting services for long-range planning and policy analysis. Works to increase public awareness of the benefits and opportunities of bicycling and walking. (Formerly National Center for Bicycling and Walking. Headquarters in New York.)

Road Runners Club of America, *1501 Lee Hwy., #140, Arlington, VA 22209; (703) 525-3890. Fax, (703) 525-3891. Jean Knaack, Executive Director.*

General email, office@rrca.org

Web, www.rrca.org

Develops and promotes road races and fitness programs, including the Children's Running Development

Program and the Women's Distance Festival. Issues guidelines on road races concerning safety, legal issues, and runners with disabilities. Facilitates communication between clubs.

SnowSports Industries America, *8377-B Greensboro Dr., McLean, VA 22102-3587; (703) 556-9020. Fax, (703) 821-8276. David Ingemie, President.*
General email, siamail@snowsports.org
Web, www.snowsports.org

Membership: manufacturers and distributors of ski and other outdoor sports equipment, apparel, and accessories. Interests include international markets and reducing global warming. Monitors legislation and regulations.

Special Olympics International Inc., *1133 19th St. N.W. 20036-3604; (202) 628-3630. Fax, (202) 824-0200. Janet Froetscher, Chief Executive Officer; Timothy P. Shriver, Chair. Toll-free, (800) 700-8585.*
General email, info@specialolympics.org
Web, www.specialolympics.org

Offers individuals with intellectual disabilities opportunities for year-round sports training; sponsors athletic competition for 4 million athletes worldwide in twenty-two individual and team sports.

StopPredatoryGambling.org, *100 Maryland Ave. N.E., #311 20002; (202) 567-6996. Les Bernal, Executive Director, (202) 567-6996, ext. 1. Toll-free and fax, (800) 664-2680.*
General email, mail@stoppredatorygambling.org
Web, www.stoppredatorygambling.org

Seeks to end government support of exploitive forms of gambling. Compiles information on the personal, social, economic, and public health impacts of gambling and disseminates it to citizens and policymakers at the local, state, and national levels. Monitors legislation and regulations.

U.S. Eventing Assn. (USEA), *525 Old Waterford Rd. N.W., Leesburg, VA 20176-2050; (703) 779-0440. Fax, (703) 779-0550. Jo Whitehouse, Chief Executive Officer, (703) 669-9999.*
General email, info@useventing.com
Web, www.useventing.com

Membership: individuals interested in eventing, an Olympic-recognized equestrian sport featuring dressage, cross-country, and show jumping. Registers all national events to ensure that they meet the standards set by the U.S. Equestrian Federation. Sponsors three-day events for members from beginner novice to Olympic levels. Provides educational materials on competition, riding, and care of horses.

U.S. Olympic Committee, *Government Relations, 1100 H St. N.W., #600 20005; (202) 466-3399. Fax, (202) 466-5068. Desiree Filippone, Director; Karen Irish, Associate Director.*
General email, communications@usoc.org
Web, www.teamusa.org

Responsible for training, entering, and underwriting U.S. teams in the Olympic, Paralympic, Pan American,

---

Faith-Based and Neighborhood Partnerships Contacts at Federal Departments and Agencies

White House Office of Faith-Based and Neighborhood Partnerships, Melissa Rogers (202) 456-3394
www.whitehouse.gov/administration/eop/ofbnp

DEPARTMENTS

Agriculture, Max Finberg (202) 720-2032;
www.usda.gov/partnerships

Commerce, Josh Dickson (202) 482-2770;
www.commerce.gov/office-secretary/center-faith-based-and-neighborhood-partnerships

Education, Rev. Brenda Girton-Mitchell (202) 401-1876;
www2.ed.gov/about/inits/list/fbci/index.html

Health and Human Services, Acacia Salatti (Acting) (202) 358-3595; www.hhs.gov/partnerships

Homeland Security, David L. Myers (202) 646-3487;
www.dhs.gov/fbci

Housing and Urban Development, Paula Lincoln (202) 708-2404; www.hud.gov/offices/fbci

Justice, Eugene Schneeberg (202) 305-7462;
www.justice.gov/fbci

Labor, Rev. Phil Tom (202) 693-6017; www.dol.gov/cfbnp

Veterans Affairs, Rev. E. Terri LaVelle (202) 461-7689;
www.va.gov/cfbnpartnerships

AGENCIES

Agency for International Development, J. Mark Brinkmoeller (202) 712-4080; www.usaid.gov/work-usaid/partnership-opportunities/faith-based-community-organizations

Corporation for National and Community Service, John Kelly (202) 606-6743; www.nationalservice.gov/for_organizations/faith/index.asp

Small Business Administration, Sarah Bard (202) 205-6677; www.sba.gov/fbci

---

and Parapan Games. Supports the bid of U.S. cities to host the Games; recognizes the national governing body of each sport in these games. Promotes international athletic competition. (Headquarters in Colorado Springs, Colo.)

U.S. Parachute Assn., *5401 Southpoint Centre Blvd., Fredericksburg, VA 22407-2612; (540) 604-9740. Fax, (540) 604-9741. Edward Scott, Executive Director.*
General email, uspa@uspa.org
Web, www.uspa.org

Membership: individuals and organizations interested in skydiving. Develops safety procedures; maintains training programs; issues skydiving licenses and ratings; certifies skydiving instructors; sanctions national competitions; and documents record attempts. Offers liability insurance to members. Monitors legislation and regulations.

RELIGION

General

▶ **NONGOVERNMENTAL**

American Assn. of Pastoral Counselors, *9504A Lee Hwy., Fairfax, VA 22031-2303; (703) 385-6967. Fax, (703) 352-7725. Douglas M. Ronsheim, Executive Director.*
General email, info@aapc.org
Web, www.aapc.org

Membership: mental health professionals with training in both religion and the behavioral sciences. Nonsectarian organization that accredits pastoral counseling centers, certifies pastoral counselors, and approves training programs.

American Friends Service Committee (AFSC), *Public Policy, Washington Office, 1822 R St. N.W. 20009-1604; (202) 483-3341. Fax, (202) 232-3197. Aura Kanegis, Director.*
General email, WashOfficeInfo@afsc.org
Web, www.afsc.org/locations/dc

Education, outreach, and advocacy office for the AFSC, an independent organization affiliated with the Religious Society of Friends (Quakers) in America. Sponsors domestic and international service, development, justice, and peace programs. Priorities include Iraq, Israel/Palestine, civil rights and liberties, and economic justice in the United States. Interests include peace education; arms control and disarmament; social and economic justice; gay and lesbian rights, racism, sexism, and civil rights; refugees and immigration policy; crisis response and relief efforts; and international development efforts, especially in Central America, the Middle East, and southern Africa. (Headquarters in Philadelphia, Pa.)

American Humanist Assn., *1777 T St. N.W. 20009-7125; (202) 238-9088. Fax, (202) 238-9003. Rebecca Hale, President. Toll-free, (800) 837-3792.*
General email, aha@americanhumanist.org
Web, www.americanhumanist.org

Seeks to educate the public about Humanism and bring Humanists together for mutual support and action. Defends the civil liberties and constitutional freedoms of Humanists and leads both local and national Humanist organizations toward progressive societal change.

American Islamic Congress, *1718 M St. N.W., #243 20036; (202) 595-3160. Fax, (202) 621-6005. Zainab Al-Suwaij, Executive Director.*
General email, info@aicongress.org
Web, www.aicongress.org

Independent, nonpartisan initiative of American Muslims challenging negative perceptions of Muslims by advocating interethnic and interfaith understanding. Promotes open multicultural society and civil liberties; advocates for women's equality, free expression, and

nonviolence. Encourages the denouncement of terrorism, extremism, and hate speech within the Muslim community.

American Jewish Committee, *Government and International Affairs, 1156 15th St. N.W. 20005; (202) 785-4200. Fax, (202) 785-4115. Melanie Maron Pell, Washington Regional Director.*
Web, www.ajc.org

Human relations agency devoted to protecting civil and religious rights for all people. Interests include church-state issues, research on energy security, Israel and the Middle East, the security and well-being of Jewish diasporic communities worldwide, immigration, social discrimination, civil and women's rights, education, and international cooperation for peace and human rights. (Headquarters in New York.)

Americans United for Separation of Church and State, *1301 K St. N.W., #850E 20005; (202) 466-3234. Fax, (202) 466-2587. Barry W. Lynn, Executive Director.*
General email, americansunited@au.org
Web, www.au.org

Citizens' interest group. Opposes federal and state aid to parochial schools; works to ensure religious neutrality in public schools; supports free religious exercise; initiates litigation; maintains speakers bureau. Monitors legislation and regulations.

Baptist Joint Committee for Religious Liberty, *200 Maryland Ave. N.E., 3rd Floor 20002; (202) 544-4226. Fax, (202) 544-2094. J. Brent Walker, Executive Director.*
General email, bjc@bjconline.org
Web, www.bjconline.org

Membership: Baptist conventions and conferences. Conducts research and operates an information service. Interests include religious liberty, separation of church and state, First Amendment religious issues, and government regulation of religious institutions.

Baptist World Alliance, *405 N. Washington St., Falls Church, VA 22046; (703) 790-8980. Fax, (703) 893-5160. Neville Callam, General Secretary.*
General email, bwa@bwanet.org
Web, www.bwanet.org

International Baptist organization. Conducts religious teaching and works to create a better understanding among nations. Organizes development efforts and disaster relief worldwide. Interests include human rights and religious liberty.

Becket Fund for Religious Liberty, *3000 K St. N.W., #220 20007; (202) 955-0095. Fax, (202) 955-0090. William Mumma, President; Kristina Arriaga de Bucholz, Executive Director. Press, (202) 349-7224.*
Web, www.becketfund.org

Public interest law firm that promotes freedom of expression for people of all faiths. Works to ensure that people and institutions of all faiths, domestically and abroad, are entitled to a voice in public affairs.

B'nai B'rith International, *2020 K St. N.W., 7th Floor 20006; (202) 857-6600. Fax, (202) 857-2700. Allan J. Jacobs, President; Daniel S. Mariaschin, Executive Vice President. Toll-free, (888) 388-4224.*
General email, info@bnaibrith.org
Web, www.bnaibrith.org

International Jewish organization that promotes the security and continuity of the Jewish people and the State of Israel; defends human rights; combats anti-Semitism; and promotes Jewish identity through cultural activities. Interests include strengthening family life and the education and training of youth, providing broad-based services for the benefit of senior citizens, and advocacy on behalf of Jews throughout the world.

Catholic Charities USA, *2050 Ballenger Ave., Alexandria, VA 22314; (703) 549-1390. Fax, (703) 549-1656. Rev. Larry Snyder, President, (703) 236-2600.*
General email, info@catholiccharitiesusa.org
Web, www.catholiccharitiesusa.org

Member agencies and institutions provide assistance to persons of all backgrounds; community-based services include day care, counseling, food, and housing. National office provides members with advocacy and professional support, including networking, training and consulting, program development, and financial benefits. Represents the Catholic community in times of domestic disaster.

Catholic Information Center, *1501 K St. N.W., #175 20005; (202) 783-2062. Fax, (202) 783-6667. Rev. Arne Panula, Director.*
General email, contract@cicdc.org
Web, www.cicdc.org

Provides information on Roman Catholicism and the Catholic Church. Offers free counseling services. Includes Catholic bookstore and chapel.

Center for Islamic Pluralism, *1718 M St. N.W., #260 20036; (415) 956-9296. Fax, (866) 792-9439. Stephen Schwartz, Executive Director.*
General email, schwartz@islamicpluralism.org
Web, www.islamicpluralism.org

Think tank that opposes the radicalization of Islam in America and promotes integration of moderate Muslims into the American interfaith environment. Seeks to educate the public about moderate Islam. Activities include media releases, conferences, and publications.

Center for Law and Religious Freedom, *8001 Braddock Rd., #300, Springfield, VA 22151; (703) 642-1070, ext. 4. Fax, (703) 642-1075. Kimberlee W. Colby, Director.*
Web, www.clsnet.org/center

Provides legal assistance and advocacy on anti-abortion and religious-freedom issues. Monitors legislation and regulations. (Affiliated with the Christian Legal Society.)

Center for the Study of Islam and Democracy, *1625 Massachusetts Ave. N.W., #601 20036; (202) 265-1200. Fax, (202) 265-1222. Radwan Masmoudi, President.*

General email, feedback@islam-democracy.org
Web, www.csidonline.org

Strives to merge Islamic and democratic political thought into a modern Islamic democratic discourse and improve understanding of Islam's approach to civil rights and political pluralism.

Chaplain Alliance for Religious Liberty, *P.O. Box 151353, Alexandria, VA 22315; (571) 293-2427. Fax, (910) 221-2226. Col. Ron Crews (USAR, Ret.), Executive Director; Chaplain Brig. Gen. Doug Lee (USA, Ret.), President.*
General email, info@chaplainalliance.org
Web, http://chaplainalliance.org

Membership: military chaplains and others who support orthodox Christian doctrines. Seeks to ensure that all chaplains and those they serve may exercise their religious liberties without fear of reprisal. Interests include the conflict between official protection for gays in the military and orthodox Christian teachings. Issues press releases; grants media interviews; monitors legislation and regulations.

Christian Science Committee on Publication, *Federal Office, 1660 L St. N.W., #216 20036; (202) 296-2190. Fax, (202) 296-2426. Gary Jones, Manager.*
General email, federal@christianscience.com
Web, http://christianscience.com/member-resources/for-churches/committee-on-publications/US-federal-office

Public service organization that provides information on the religious convictions and practices of Christian Scientists; works with Congress and regulatory agencies to ensure that Christian Science practitioners are not adversely affected by law or regulations.

Conference of Major Superiors of Men (CMSM), *8808 Cameron St., Silver Spring, MD 20910; (301) 588-4030. Fax, (301) 587-4575. John A. Pavlik, Executive Director.*
General email, postmaster@cmsm.org
Web, www.cmsm.org

National representative body for more than 19,000 men in 210 religious and apostolic communities in the United States, as well as foreign missionaries. Collaborates with U.S. bishops and other key groups and organizations that serve church and society.

Council on American-Islamic Relations, *453 New Jersey Ave. S.E. 20003-4034; (202) 488-8787. Fax, (202) 488-0833. Nihad Awad, National Executive Director; Ibrahim Hooper, Communications, (202) 744-7726.*
General email, info@cair.com
Web, www.cair.com

Promotes the understanding of Islam to the American public. Seeks to empower the Muslim community in the United States and protect civil liberties through political and social activism.

Episcopal Church, *Government Relations, 110 Maryland Ave. N.E., #309 20002; (202) 547-7300. Fax, (202) 547-4457. Alexander Baumgarten, Director. Toll-free, (800) 228-0515.*
Web, www.episcopalchurch.org/eppn

Informs Congress, the executive branch, and governmental agencies about the actions and resolutions of the Episcopal Church. Monitors legislation and regulations. (Denominational headquarters in New York.)

Ethics and Public Policy Center, *1730 M St. N.W., #910 20036; (202) 682-1200. Fax, (202) 408-0632. M. Edward Whelan III, President. General email, ethics@eppc.org*

Web, www.eppc.org

Considers implications of Judeo-Christian moral tradition for domestic and foreign policy making.

Evangelical Lutheran Church in America, *Washington Office, 122 C St. N.W., #125 20001; (202) 626-7938. Fax, (202) 783-7502. Stacy Martin, Director. General email, washingtonoffice@elca.org*

Web, www.elca.org/advocacy

Represents the church's ministries, relationships, projects, and relief efforts on behalf of underrepresented people in order to effect policy change. Monitors and responds to proposed legislation and regulations. (Headquarters in Chicago, Ill.)

Faith in Public Life, *1111 14th St. N.W., #900 20005; (202) 499-4095. Fax, (202) 315-0469. Rev. Jennifer Butler, Executive Director. Press, (202) 459-8625. General email, press@faithinpubliclife.org*

Web, www.faithinpubliclife.org

Provides organizing and communications support to diverse faith leaders and organizations working to further justice and the common good in public policy; designs and implements coalitions and initiatives to promote faith as a force for the common good.

Friends Committee on National Legislation (FCNL), *245 2nd St. N.E. 20002-5795; (202) 547-6000. Fax, (202) 547-6019. Diane Randall, Executive Secretary. Toll-free, (800) 630-1330. Recorded information, (202) 547-4343. General email, fcnl@fcnl.org*

Web, www.fcnl.org

Advocates for economic justice, world disarmament, international cooperation, and religious rights. Advocates on behalf of Native Americans in such areas as treaty rights, self-determination, and U.S. trust responsibilities. Conducts research and educational activities through the FCNL Education Fund. Opposes the death penalty. Monitors national legislation and policy. (Affiliated with the Religious Society of Friends [Quakers].)

General Board of Church and Society of the United Methodist Church, *100 Maryland Ave. N.E. 20002; (202) 488-5600. Fax, (202) 488-5619. Rev. Susan Henry-Crowe, General Secretary, (202) 488-5620. Press, (202) 488-5630. General email, gbcs@umc-gbcs.org*

Web, www.umc-gbcs.org

One of four international general program boards of the United Methodist Church. Provides training and educational resources to member churches on social concerns.

Monitors legislation and regulations. (Has offices at the Church Center for the United Nations.)

General Conference of Seventh-day Adventists, *12501 Old Columbia Pike, Silver Spring, MD 20904-6600; (301) 680-6000. Ted N.C. Wilson, President; Williams Costa Jr., Director, Communications. General email, info@gcadventist.org*

Web, www.adventist.org

World headquarters of the Seventh-day Adventist Church. Interests include education, health care, humanitarian relief, and development. Supplies educational tools for the blind and the hard of hearing. Operates schools worldwide. Organizes community service–oriented youth groups.

Institute on Religion and Democracy, *1023 15th St. N.W., #601 20005-2601; (202) 682-4131. Fax, (202) 682-4136. Mark Tooley, President. General email, info@theird.org*

Web, www.theird.org

Interdenominational bipartisan organization that supports democratic and constitutional forms of government consistent with the values of Christianity. Serves as a resource center to promote Christian perspectives on U.S. foreign policy questions. Interests include international conflicts, religious liberties, and the promotion of democratic forms of government in the United States and worldwide.

Interfaith Alliance, *1250 24th St. N.W., #300 20037; (202) 466-0567. Fax, (202) 466-0502. Rev. Dr. C. Welton Gaddy, President. General email, info@interfaithalliance.org*

Web, www.interfaithalliance.org

Membership: seventy-five faith traditions, including Protestant, Catholic, Jewish, and Muslim clergy, laity, and others who favor a positive, nonpartisan role for religious faith in public life. Advocates mainstream religious values; promotes tolerance and social opportunity; opposes the use of religion to promote political extremism at national, state, and local levels. Monitors legislation and regulations.

International Religious Liberty Assn., *12501 Old Columbia Pike, Silver Spring, MD 20904-6600; (301) 680-6686. Fax, (301) 680-6695. Robert Seiple, President. General email, info@iria.org*

Web, www.irla.org

Seeks to preserve and expand religious liberty and freedom of conscience; advocates separation of church and state; sponsors international and domestic meetings and congresses.

Islamic Society of North America (ISNA), *Office of Interfaith and Community Alliances, Washington Office, 110 Maryland Ave. N.E., #304 20002; (202) 544-5656. Fax, (202) 544-6636. Sayyid M. Syeed, National Director. General email, info@isna.net*

Web, www.isna.net

Conducts outreach to grassroots organizations and engages in joint programs with other religious organizations, including the National Council of Churches, the United States Conference of Catholic Bishops, and the Union for Reform Judaism. Seeks to promote a positive image of Islam and Muslims to national political leaders and strong relationships with U.S. congressional staff and federal government officials. Serves as an outreach resource to the American Muslim community. (Headquarters in Plainfield, Ind.)

Jesuit Conference, *Social and International Ministries,* *1016 16th St. N.W., 4th Floor 20036; (202) 462-0400.* *Fax, (202) 328-9212. Shaina Aber, Policy Director;* *Thomas P. Greene S.J., Secretary.* *General email, usjc@jesuit.org*

Web, www.jesuitsocialapostolate.org/node/201

Information and advocacy organization of Jesuits and laypersons concerned with peace and social justice issues. Interests include peace and disarmament, domestic poverty, socially responsible investing, and migration and immigration.

Jewish Federations of North America, *Washington Office, 1720 Eye St. N.W., #800 20006; (202) 785-5900.* *Fax, (202) 785-4937. William Daroff, Director.* *General email, dc@JewishFederations.org*

Web, www.jewishfederations.org

Advocates for the 153 Jewish federations across the United States on issues of concern, including long-term care, families at risk, and naturally occurring retirement communities. Offers marketing, communications, and public relations support; coordinates a speakers bureau. (Formerly United Jewish Communities [UJC].Headquarters in New York.)

Leadership Conference of Women Religious, *8808 Cameron St., Silver Spring, MD 20910; (301) 588-4955.* *Fax, (301) 587-4575. Janet Mock, Executive Director.* *Web, www.lcwr.org*

Membership: Roman Catholic women who are the principal administrators of their congregations in the United States and around the world. Offers programs and support to members; conducts research; serves as an information clearinghouse.

Loyola Foundation, *10335 Democracy Lane, #202, Fairfax, VA 22030; (571) 435-9401. Fax, (571) 435-9402.* *A. Gregory McCarthy IV, Executive Director.* *General email, info@loyolafoundation.org*

Web, www.loyolafoundation.org

Assists overseas Catholic mission activities. Awards grants to international missionaries and Catholic dioceses for vehicle and equipment purchase and construction.

Maryknoll Office for Global Concerns *(Catholic Foreign Mission Society of America), Washington Office, 200 New York Ave. N.W. 20001; (202) 832-1780. Fax, (202) 832-5195. Gerry Lee, Director, Interim.* *General email, ogc@maryknoll.org*

Web, www.maryknollogc.org

Conducts education and advocacy for international policies that promote peace, social justice, and ecological integrity. (Headquarters in Maryknoll, N.Y.)

Mennonite Central Committee, *Washington Office, 920 Pennsylvania Ave. S.E. 20003; (202) 544-6564. Fax, (202) 544-2820. Rachelle Lyndaker Schlabach, Director.* *General email, mccwash@mcc.org*

Web, http://washington.mcc.org

Christian organization engaged in service and development projects. Monitors legislation and regulations affecting issues of interest to Mennonite and Brethren in Christ churches. Interests include human rights in developing countries, military spending, the environment, world hunger, poverty, and civil and religious liberties. (Headquarters in Akron, Pa.)

Muslim Public Affairs Council, *Washington Office, 1020 16th St. N.W. 20036; (202) 547-7701. Fax, (202) 547-7704.* *Salam Al-Marayati, National President; Haris Tarin, Director.* *General email, haris@mpac.org*

Web, www.mpac.org and Twitter, @mpac_national

Promotes the civil rights of American Muslims and the integration of Islam into American pluralism. Seeks an accurate portrayal of Islam and Muslims in the media and popular culture. (Headquarters in Los Angeles, Calif.)

National Assn. of Evangelicals, *701 G St. S.W. 20024 (mailing address: P.O. Box 23269, Washington, DC 20026); (202) 789-1011. Fax, (202) 842-0392. Leith Anderson, President.* *General email, info@nae.net*

Web, www.nae.net

Represents Christian evangelical denominations. Interests include religious liberty; economic policy; church-state relations; public health issues, including HIV and AIDS; immigration and refugee policy; and world relief efforts. Provides networking opportunities and commissions chaplains. Monitors legislation and regulations.

National Clergy Council, *109 2nd St. N.E. 20002; (202) 546-8329. Fax, (202) 546-6864. Rev. Rob Schenck, President; Peggy Nienaber, Chief of Programs.* *General email, info@faithandaction.org*

Web, www.faithandaction.org

Informal network of conservative and traditional Christian clergy and heads of religious organizations and societies. Advocates interjecting religious morality into public policy debates. Monitors legislation and regulations.

National Council of Catholic Women, *200 N. Glebe Rd., #725, Arlington, VA 22203; (703) 224-0990. Fax, (703) 224-0991. Vacant, Executive Director. Toll-free, (800) 506-9407.* *General email, nccw01@nccw.org*

Web, www.nccw.org

Roman Catholic women's organization. Provides education and information to Catholic women regarding social issues. Interests include women and poverty, employment, family life, abortion, care for older adults, day care, world hunger, global water supplies, genetic engineering research, pornography legislation, and substance abuse. Special programs include volunteer respite care, leadership training for women, mentoring of mothers, and drug and alcohol abuse education. Monitors legislation and regulations.

National Council of Churches, *Washington Office*, 110 *Maryland Ave. N.E., #108 20002-5603; Jim Winkler, President.*
General email, info@nationalcouncilofchurches.us
Web, www.nationalcouncilofchurches.us

Membership: thirty-seven Protestant, Anglican, and Orthodox denominations. Interests include interreligious relations, racial and social equality; social welfare, economic justice, environmental justice, peace, and international issues, with a focus on peacemaking and mass incarceration issues; and church-state relations. (Headquarters in New York.)

National Council of Jewish Women, *Public Policy, Washington Office*, *1707 L St. N.W., #950 20036-4206; (202) 296-2588. Fax, (202) 331-7792. Sammie Moshenberg, Director.*
General email, action@ncjwdc.org
Web, www.ncjw.org

Progressive Jewish women's membership organization. Activities include education, community service, and advocacy. Interests include women's issues; reproductive, civil, and constitutional rights; child care; judicial nominations; religion-state separation; and human needs funding issues. (Headquarters in New York.)

NCSJ: Advocates on Behalf of Jews in Russia, Ukraine, the Baltic States and Eurasia, *2020 K St. N.W., #7800 20006; (202) 898-2500. Fax, (202) 898-0822. Mark B. Levin, Executive Director; Stephen M. Greenberg, Chair.*
General email, ncsj@ncsj.org
Web, www.ncsj.org

Advocacy group promoting political and religious freedom on behalf of Jews in Russia, Ukraine, the Baltic states, and Eurasia. Works with community and government leadership in the United States and in the former Soviet Union addressing issues of anti-Semitism, community relations, and promotion of democracy, tolerance, and U.S. engagement in the region.

NETWORK, *25 E St. N.W., #200 20001; (202) 347-9797. Fax, (202) 347-9864. Sr. Simone Campbell, Executive Director.*
General email, networkupdate@networklobby.org
Web, www.networklobby.org

Catholic social justice lobby that coordinates political activity and promotes economic and social justice. Monitors legislation and regulations.

Orthodox Union, *OU Institute for Public Affairs, Washington Office*, *800 8th St. N.W., #318 20001; (202) 513-6484. Fax, (202) 289-8936. Nathan Diament, Executive Director.*

General email, info@ouadvocacy.org
Web, www.ou.org/public_affairs

Works to protect Jewish interests and freedoms through dissemination of policy briefings to government officials. Encourages Jewish law and a traditional perspective on public policy issues. Coordinates grassroots activities. (Headquarters in New York.)

Pew Forum on Religion and Public Life, *1615 L St. N.W., #700 20036; (202) 419-4550. Fax, (202) 419-4559. Alan Cooperman, Director. Media, (202) 419-4562.*
General email, religion@pewresearch.org
Web, www.pewforum.org

Nonpartisan organization that seeks to explore the impact of religion on public affairs, political behavior, the law, domestic policy, and international affairs. Conducts polling and independent research; serves as a clearinghouse and forum on these issues. Delivers findings to journalists, government officials, and other interested groups.

Presbyterian Mission (U.S.A.), *Office of Public Witness*, *100 Maryland Ave. N.E., #410 20002; (202) 543-1126. Fax, (202) 543-7755. Rev. J. Herbert Nelson II, Director. Toll-free, (800) 728-7228, ext. 5580.*
General email, ga_washington_office@pcusa.org
Web, www.presbyterianmission/ministries/washington

Provides information on the views of the general assembly of the Presbyterian Church on public policy issues; monitors legislation affecting issues of concern. Interests include budget priorities, foreign policy, arms control, civil rights, religious liberty, church-state relations, economic justice, environmental justice, and public policy issues affecting women. (Headquarters in Louisville, Ky.)

Progressive National Baptist Convention Inc., *601 50th St. N.E. 20019; (202) 396-0558. Fax, (202) 398-4998. Rev. Carroll A. Baltimore Sr., President. Toll-free, (800) 876-7622.*
General email, fmccraw@pnbc.org
Web, www.pnbc.org

Baptist denomination that supports missionaries, implements education programs, and advocates for civil and human rights.

Sojourners, *3333 14th St. N.W., #200 20010; (202) 328-8842. Fax, (202) 328-8757. Jim Wallis, Chief Executive Officer; Lisa Sharon Harper, Director of Mobilizing. Toll-free, (800) 714-7474. Press, (202) 328-8842.*
General email, sojourners@sojo.net
Web, www.sojo.net

Membership: Catholics, Protestants, Evangelicals, and other interested Christians. Grassroots network that focuses on social injustices and the intersection of faith, politics, and culture. (Merger of Sojourners and Call to Renewal.)

Union for Reform Judaism, *Religious Action Center of Reform Judaism*, *2027 Massachusetts Ave. N.W. 20036;*

(202) 387-2800. Fax, (202) 667-9070.
Rabbi David Saperstein, Director.
General email, rac@urj.org
Web, www.rac.org

Religious and educational organization that mobilizes the American Jewish community on legislative and social concerns. Interests include economic justice, civil rights, religious liberty, and international peace.

United Church of Christ, Washington Office, *100 Maryland Ave. N.E., #330 20002; (202) 543-1517. Fax, (202) 543-5994. Sandra (Sandy) Sorensen, Director.*
General email, sorenses@ucc.org
Web, www.ucc.org

Studies public policy issues and promotes church policy on these issues; organizes legislative advocacy to address church views. Interests include health care, international peace, economic justice, the environment, climate change, civil rights, and immigration. (Headquarters in Cleveland, Ohio.)

U.S. Conference of Catholic Bishops (USCCB), *3211 4th St. N.E. 20017; (202) 541-3000. Fax, (202) 541-3173. Sr. Mary Ann Walsh, Director, Media Relations, (202) 541-3200; Helen Osman, Secretary of Communications, (202) 241-3320. Toll-free, (800) 235-8722.*
Web, www.usccb.org

Serves as a forum for bishops to exchange ideas, debate concerns of the church, and draft responses to religious and social issues. Provides information on doctrine and policies of the Roman Catholic Church; develops religious education and training programs; formulates policy positions on social issues, including the economy, employment, federal budget priorities, voting rights, energy, health, housing, rural affairs, international military and political matters, human rights, the arms race, global economics, and immigration and refugee policy.

Washington Ethical Society, *7750 16th St. N.W. 20012; (202) 882-6650. Christine Parcelli, Administrator.*
General email, wes@ethicalsociety.org
Web, www.ethicalsociety.org

A humanistic religious community that sets standards, distributes ethical culture materials, trains leaders, awards grants, publishes statements on moral issues and public policy, and coordinates national projects such as youth programs. (Affiliated with the American Ethical Union and the Unitarian Universalist Assn.)

Women's Alliance for Theology, Ethics, and Ritual (WATER), *8121 Georgia Ave., #310, Silver Spring, MD 20910; (301) 589-2509. Fax, (301) 589-3150. Diann L. Neu, Co-Director; Mary E. Hunt, Co-Director.*
General email, water@hers.com
Web, www.waterwomensalliance.org

Feminist theological organization that focuses on issues concerning women and religion. Interests include social issues; work skills for women with disabilities; human rights in Latin America; and liturgies, rituals, counseling, and research.

TRAVEL AND TOURISM

General

► **AGENCIES**

International Trade Administration (ITA) *(Commerce Dept.), Industry and Analysis, Travel and Tourism Industries, 1401 Constitution Ave. N.W., #1003 20230-0001; (202) 482-0140. Fax, (202) 482-2887. Vacant, Director.*
General email, info@tinet.ita.doc.gov
Web, http://travel.gov/about/index.html

Fosters international tourism trade development, including public-private partnerships; represents the United States in tourism-related meetings with foreign government officials. Assembles, analyzes, and disseminates data and statistics on travel and tourism to and from the United States.

National Park Service (NPS) *(Interior Dept.), Sustainable Tourism, 1201 Eye St. N.W., #933 20005; (202) 354-6986. Fax, (202) 371-5179. Dean T. Reeder, Chief.*
General email, dean_reeder@nps.gov
Web, www.nps.gov/tourism

Directs and supports the National Park Service's tourism program. Acts as liaison to government departments and agencies on tourism issues. Serves as the primary contact for national and international travel and tourism industry officials and professionals.

State Dept., *Consular Affairs, Special Issuance Agency, 600 19th St. N.W., #3200 20006; (202) 485-9202. Fax, (202) 955-0182. Michael D. Thomas, Director. National passport information, (877) 487-2778.*
Web, http://travel.state.gov

Administers passport laws and issues passports. (Most branches of the U.S. Postal Service and most U.S. district and state courts are authorized to accept applications and payment for passports and to administer the required oath to U.S. citizens. Completed applications are sent from the post office or court to the nearest State Dept. regional passport office for processing.) Maintains a variety of records received from the Overseas Citizens Services, including consular certificates of witness to marriage and reports of birth and death. (Individuals wishing to apply for a U.S. passport may seek additional information via the phone number or Web address listed above.)

► **CONGRESS**

For a listing of relevant congressional committees and subcommittees, please see page 113 or the Appendix.

► **INTERNATIONAL ORGANIZATIONS**

Organization of American States (OAS), *Economic and Social Development, 1889 F St. N.W., #750 20006; (202) 370-9953. Fax, (202) 458-3561. Maurice Roberts, Director.*

General email, mrobert@oas.org

Web, www.oas.org/en/sedi/dedtt/about/asp

Responsible for matters related to economic development in the hemisphere. Works for sustainable tourism development and safety and security; promotes cooperation among international, regional, and subregional tourism offices.

▶ **NONGOVERNMENTAL**

American Hotel and Lodging Assn., *1201 New York Ave. N.W., #600 20005-3931; (202) 289-3100. Fax, (202) 289-3199. Katherine Lugar, President; John Fitzpatrick, Chair, (202) 289-3112.*

General email, info@ahla.com

Web, www.ahla.com

Membership: state and city partner lodging associations. Provides operations, technical, educational, marketing, and communications services to members. Monitors legislation and regulations.

American Society of Travel Agents, *1101 King St., #200, Alexandria, VA 22314-2963; (703) 739-2782. Fax, (703) 739-3268. Zane Kerby, President.*

General email, askasta@asta.org

Web, www.asta.org

Membership: representatives of the travel industry. Works to safeguard the traveling public against fraud, misrepresentation, and other unethical practices. Offers training programs for travel agents. Consumer affairs department offers help for anyone with a travel complaint against a member of the association.

Center for Responsible Travel, *1333 H St. N.W., #300 East Tower 20005; (202) 347-9203, ext. 417. Fax, (202) 775-0819. Martha Honey, Director.*

General email, staff@responsibletravel.org

Web, www.responsibletravel.org

Designs, monitors, evaluates, and seeks to improve ecotourism and sustainable tourism principles and practices. (Affiliated with Stanford University.)

Cruise Lines International Assn., *2111 Wilson Blvd., 8th Floor, Arlington, VA 22201; (703) 522-8463. Fax, (703) 522-3811. Christine Duffy, President.*

General email, info@cruising.org

Web, www.cruising.org

Membership: chief executives of twenty-six cruise lines and other cruise industry professionals. Advises domestic and international regulatory organizations on shipping policy. Works with U.S. and international agencies to promote safety, public health, security, medical facilities, environmental awareness, and passenger protection. Monitors legislation and regulations. (Formerly the International Council of Cruise Lines.)

Destination Marketing Assn. International, *2025 M St. N.W., #500 20036-3309; (202) 296-7888. Fax, (202) 296-7889. Michael Gehrisch, President.*

General email, info@destinationmarketing.org

Web, www.destinationmarketing.org

Membership: travel- and tourism-related businesses, convention and meeting professionals, and tour operators. Encourages business travelers and tourists to visit local historic, cultural, and recreational areas; assists in meeting preparations. Monitors legislation and regulations.

Global Business Travel Assn., *123 N. Pitt St., 1st Floor, Alexandria, VA 22314; (703) 684-0836. Fax, (703) 342-4324. Michael (Mike) McCormick, Executive Director, (703) 236-1129.*

General email, info@gbta.org

Web, www.gbta.org

Membership: corporate travel managers and travel service suppliers. Promotes educational advancement of members and provides a forum for exchange of information on U.S. and international travel. Monitors legislation and regulations.

Hostelling International—American Youth Hostels, *8401 Colesville Rd., #600, Silver Spring, MD 20910-9663; (301) 495-1240. Fax, (240) 650-2094. Russell Hedge, Executive Director.*

General email, members@hiusa.org

Web, www.hiusa.org

Seeks to improve cultural understanding through a nationwide network of hostels and travel-based programs. Provides opportunities for outdoor recreation and inexpensive educational travel and accommodations through hostelling. Member of the International Youth Hostel Federation.

International Assn. of Amusement Parks and Attractions, *1448 Duke St., Alexandria, VA 22314; (703) 836-4800. Fax, (703) 836-4801. Paul Noland, President, ext. 769. Press, (703) 299-5127.*

General email, iaapa@iaapa.org

Web, www.iaapa.org

Membership: companies from around the world in the amusement parks and attractions industry. Conducts an international exchange program for members. Monitors legislation and regulations.

International Ecotourism Society, *P.O. Box 96503, #34145 20090-6503; (202) 506-5033. Fax, (202) 789-7279. Kelly Bricker, Chair.*

General email, info@ecotourism.org

Web, www.ecotourism.org

Promotes tourism practices that conserve the environment and improve the situation of local peoples. Sponsors meetings and workshops for ecotourism professionals; publishes guide for travelers.

Passenger Vessel Assn., *103 Oronoco St., #200, Alexandria, VA 22314; (703) 518-5005. Fax, (703) 518-5151. John R. Groundwater, Executive Director. Toll-free, (800) 807-8360.*

General email, pvainfo@passengervessel.com

Web, www.passengervessel.com

Membership: owners, operators, and suppliers for U.S. and Canadian passenger vessels and international vessel companies. Interests include insurance, safety and security, and U.S. congressional impact upon dinner and excursion boats, car and passenger ferries, overnight cruise ships, and riverboat casinos. Monitors legislation and regulations.

UNITE HERE, *Washington Office*, 1775 K St. N.W., #620 20006-1530; (202) 393-4373. Fax, (202) 223-6213. *Tom Snyder, Political Director; John W. Wilhelm, President.*
Web, www.unitehere.org

Membership: more than 270,000 workers in the United States and Canada who work in the hospitality, gaming, food service, manufacturing, textile, laundry, and airport industries. Helps members negotiate pay, benefits, and better working conditions; conducts training programs and workshops. Monitors legislation and regulations. (Headquarters in New York. Formed by the merger of the former Union of Needletrades, Textiles and Industrial Employees and the Hotel Employees and Restaurant Employees International Union.)

U.S. Travel Assn., *1100 New York Ave. N.W., #450 20005-3934; (202) 408-8422. Fax, (202) 408-1255. Roger Dow, President.*
General email, feedback@ustravel.org
Web, www.USTravel.org and www.traveleffect.com

Membership: travel-related companies and associations, state tourism offices, convention and visitors bureaus. Advocates for increased travel to and within the United States; conducts research, provides marketing, and hosts trade shows. Monitors legislation and regulations. (Merger of the Travel Industry Assn. and the Travel Business Roundtable.)

U.S. Virgin Islands Department of Tourism, *Washington Office, 444 N. Capitol St. N.W., #305 20001; (202) 624-3590. Fax, (202) 624-3594. Gerda Sebastian, Director of Administration and Management; Beverly Nicholson Doty, Commissioner. Toll-free, (800) 372-8784.*
General email, info@usvitourism.vi
Web, www.visitusvi.com

Provides information about the U.S. Virgin Islands; promotes tourism. (Headquarters in St. Thomas.)

5

Education

GENERAL POLICY AND ANALYSIS

Basic Resources

▶AGENCIES

Educational Resources Information Center (ERIC)
(Education Dept.), 400 Maryland Ave. S.W., #BE101 20202-5950; (800) 538-3742. Fax, (202) 401-0547. Erin Pollard, Program Director, (202) 219-3400. General email, ericacq@csc.com

Web, http://eric.ed.gov

Coordinates an online national information system of education literature and resources. Provides a centralized bibliographic and full-text database of journal articles and other published and unpublished materials. Available at no charge to educators worldwide. Managed by the Computer Sciences Corporation.

Education Dept., *400 Maryland Ave. S.W., #7W301 20202-0001; (202) 401-3000. Fax, (202) 260-7867. Arne Duncan, Secretary; James H. Shelton III, Deputy Secretary, Acting, (201) 401-9965; Philip H. Rosenfelt, General Counsel, Acting, (202) 401-6000. Federal Student Aid Information Center, (800) 433-3243. Information Resource Center, (202) 401-2000. Toll-free, (800) 872-5327. Press, (202) 401-1576.*

Web, www2.ed.gov

Establishes education policy and acts as principal adviser to the president on education matters; administers and coordinates most federal assistance programs on education.

Education Dept., *Educational Technology, 400 Maryland Ave., S.W., #5W114 20202; (202) 453-6381. Richard Culatta, Director.*

Web, www2.ed.gov/edblogs/technology

Develops national educational policy and advocates for the transition from print-based to digital learning.

Education Dept., *International Affairs, 400 Maryland Ave. S.W., #6W118 20202-0001; (202) 401-0430. Fax, (202) 401-2508. Maureen McLaughlin, Director, (202) 401-8964. General email, international.affairs@ed.gov*

Web, www2.ed.gov/edblogs/international

Responsible for the overall coordination of the Education Dept.'s international presence. Works with department program offices, support units, and senior leadership as well as with external partners, including other federal agencies, state and local agencies, foreign governments, international organizations, and the private sector.

Education Dept., *Legislative and Congressional Affairs, 400 Maryland Ave. S.W., #6W315 20202-3500; (202) 401-0020. Fax, (202) 401-1438. Gabriella C. Gomez, Assistant Secretary.*

General email, olca@ed.gov

Web, www2.ed.gov/about/offices/list/olca

Directs and supervises all legislative activities of the Education Dept. Participates on legislation and regulation

development teams within the department and provides legislative history behind the current law.

Education Dept., *Office of Innovation and Improvement, 400 Maryland Ave. S.W., #4W300 20202-0001; (202) 205-4500. Fax, (202) 205-4123. Nadya Chinoy Dabby, Assistant Deputy Secretary, Acting. Web, www2.ed.gov/edblogs/oii*

Provides grants for innovative K–12 educational practices in areas such as alternative routes to teacher certification, traditional teaching of American history, financial literacy and economic education, and arts in education. Supports the establishment of charter schools, magnet schools, and other public and nonpublic education alternatives. Serves as liaison and resource to the nonpublic education community.

Education Dept., *School Support and REAP Programs, 400 Maryland Ave. S.W., #3W205 20202-6400; (202) 401-0039. Fax, (202) 205-5870. Jenelle Leonard, Director. Web, www2.ed.gov/programs/edtech*

Provides a coordinated strategy to focus federal resources on supporting improvements in schools; promotes development and implementation of comprehensive improvement plans that direct resources toward improved achievement for all students.

▶CONGRESS

For a listing of relevant congressional committees and subcommittees, please see page 155 or the Appendix.

Government Accountability Office (GAO), *Education, Workforce, and Income Security, 441 G St. N.W., #5928 20548; (202) 512-7215. Barbara D. Bovbjerg, Managing Director.*

Web, www.gao.gov

Independent, nonpartisan agency in the legislative branch. Audits, analyzes, and evaluates Education Dept. programs; makes reports available to the public.

▶NONGOVERNMENTAL

APPA—Leadership in Educational Facilities, *1643 Prince St., Alexandria, VA 22314-2818; (703) 684-1446. Fax, (703) 549-2772. E. Lander Medlin, Executive Vice President. General email, info@appa.org*

Web, www.appa.org

Membership: professionals involved in the administration, maintenance, planning, and development of buildings and facilities used by colleges and universities, K–12 private and public schools, museums, libraries, and other educational institutions. Interests include maintenance and upkeep of housing facilities. Provides information on campus energy management programs and campus accessibility for people with disabilities. (Formerly the Assn. of Higher Education Facilities Officers.)

Aspen Institute, *1 Dupont Circle N.W., #700 20036-7133; (202) 736-5800. Fax, (202) 467-0790. Walter Isaacson, President. Press, (202) 736-3849.*

EDUCATION RESOURCES IN CONGRESS

For a complete listing of Congress committees, including their full contact information, leadership, membership, and jurisdictions, please refer to the Appendix on pages 724–842.

HOUSE:

House Administration Committee, (202) 225-8281. Web, cha.house.gov or democrats.cha.house.gov

House Agriculture Committee, (202) 225-2171. Web, agriculture.house.gov or democrats.agriculture.house.gov

 Subcommittee on Horticulture, Research, Biotechnology, and Foreign Agriculture, (202) 225-2171.

House Appropriations Committee, (202) 225-2771. Web, appropriations.house.gov or democrats.appropriations.house.gov

 Subcommittee on Interior, Environment, and Related Agencies, (202) 225-3081.

 Subcommittee on Labor, Health and Human Services, Education, and Related Agencies, (202) 225-3508.

 Subcommittee on Legislative Branch, (202) 226-7252.

House Armed Services Committee, (202) 225-4151. Web, armedservices.house.gov or democrats.armedservices.house.gov

 Subcommittee on Military Personnel, (202) 225-4151.

House Education and the Workforce Committee, (202) 225-4527. Web, edworkforce.house.gov or democrats.edworkforce.house.gov

 Subcommittee on Early Childhood, Elementary, and Secondary Education, (202) 225-4527.

 Subcommittee on Higher Education, and Workforce Training, (202) 225-4527.

House Natural Resources Committee, (202) 225-2761. Web, naturalresources.house.gov or democrats.naturalresources.house.gov

House Oversight and Government Reform Committee, (202) 225-5074. Web, oversight.house.gov or democrats.oversight.house.gov

 Subcommittee on Economic Growth, Job Creation, and Regulatory Affairs, (202) 225-5074.

House Science, Space, and Technology Committee, (202) 225-6371. Web, science.house.gov or democrats.science.house.gov

 Subcommittee on Research and Technology, (202) 225-6371.

JOINT:

Joint Committee on the Library of Congress, (202) 225-8281. Web, cha.house.gov/jointcommittees/joint-committee-library

SENATE:

Senate Agriculture, Nutrition, and Forestry Committee, (202) 224-2035. Web, ag.senate.gov

 Subcommittee on Nutrition, Specialty Crops, Food, and Agricultural Research, (202) 224-2035.

Senate Appropriations Committee, (202) 224-7363. Web, appropriations.senate.gov

 Subcommittee on Interior, Environment, and Related Agencies, (202) 228-0774.

 Subcommittee on Labor, Health and Human Services, Education, and Related Agencies, (202) 224-9145.

 Subcommittee on Legislative Branch, (202) 224-7256.

Senate Armed Services Committee, (202) 224-3871. Web, armed-services.senate.gov

 Subcommittee on Personnel, (202) 224-3871.

Senate Banking, Housing, and Urban Affairs Committee, (202) 224-7391. Web, banking.senate.gov

Senate Commerce, Science, and Transportation Committee, (202) 224-0411. Web, commerce.senate.gov

 Subcommittee on Science and Space, (202) 224-0415.

Senate Health, Education, Labor, and Pensions Committee, (202) 224-5375. Web, help.senate.gov

 Subcommittee on Children and Families, (202) 224-5375.

Senate Indian Affairs Committee, (202) 224-2251. Web, indian.senate.gov

Senate Rules and Administration Committee, (202) 224-6352. Web, rules.senate.gov

Education Department

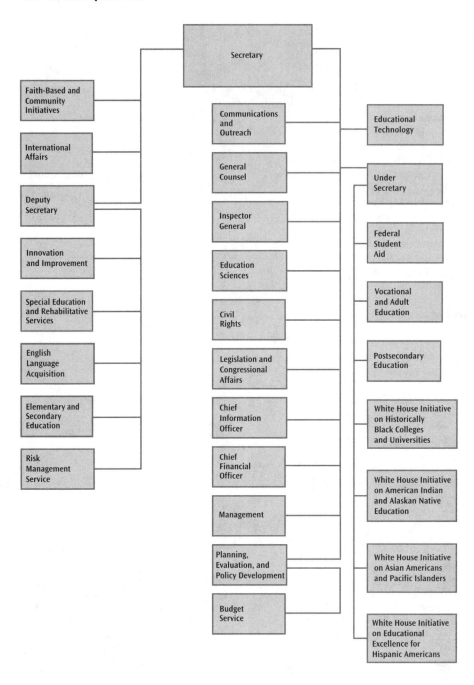

General email, info@aspeninstitute.org

Web, www.aspeninstitute.org

Educational and policy studies organization. Promotes consideration of the public good in a wide variety of policy areas, including education. Working with international partners, offers educational seminars, nonpartisan policy forums, public conferences and events, and leadership development initiatives.

Center for Education Reform, *910 17th St. N.W., #1120 20006; (301) 986-8088. Fax, (301) 986-1826. Kara Kerwin, President. Toll-free, (800) 521-2118.*
General email, cer@edreform.com

Web, www.edreform.com

Research and informational organization that promotes education reform through grassroots advocacy. Interests include charter school laws, school choice programs, teacher qualifications, and educational standards. Web site serves as a networking forum for parents, educators, policymakers, and others interested in education reform, providing news reports and information on education seminars throughout the country.

Center for Law and Education, *Washington Office, 1875 Connecticut Ave. N.W., #510 20009-5728; (202) 986-3000. Fax, (202) 986-6648. Paul Weckstein, Co-Director, (202) 986-3000, ext. 101; Kathleen Boundy, Co-Director (located in Boston).*
General email, cle@cleweb.org
Web, www.cleweb.org

Works to advance the right of all students, and low-income students in particular, to a high-quality education. Interests include testing and tracking; bilingual education; discriminatory discipline; special education; special needs for Native Americans, migrants, and Hispanics; parent, community, and student participation in education; and vocational and compensatory education. (Headquarters in Boston, Mass.)

Charles F. Kettering Foundation, *Washington Office, 444 N. Capitol St. N.W., #434 20001-1512; (202) 393-4478. Fax, (202) 393-7644. David Mathews, President.*
Web, www.kettering.org

Works to improve the domestic policy-making process through citizen deliberation. Supports international programs focusing on unofficial, citizen-to-citizen diplomacy. Encourages greater citizen involvement in formation of public policy. Interests include public education and at-risk youths. (Headquarters in Dayton, Ohio.)

Council for Advancement and Support of Education, *1307 New York Ave. N.W., #1000 20005-4701; (202) 328-2273. Fax, (202) 387-4973. John Lippincott, President.*
General email, memberservicecenter@case.org
Web, www.case.org

Membership: two- and four-year colleges, universities, and independent schools. Offers professional education and training programs to members; advises members on institutional advancement issues, including fundraising, public relations programs, government relations, and management. Library open to professional members by appointment.

DECA Inc., *1908 Association Dr., Reston, VA 20191-1594; (703) 860-5000. Fax, (703) 860-4013. Edward L. Davis, Executive Director.*
General email, info@deca.org
Web, www.deca.org

Educational organization that helps high school and college students develop skills in marketing, management, and entrepreneurship. Promotes business and education partnerships.

Ethics Resource Center, *2345 Crystal Dr., #201, Arlington, VA 22202; (703) 647-2185. Fax, (703) 647-2180. Patricia J. Harned, President. Information, (800) 777-1285.*
General email, ethics@ethics.org
Web, www.ethics.org

Nonpartisan research organization that fosters ethical practices among individuals and institutions. Interests include research, knowledge building, education, and advocacy.

Institute for Educational Leadership, *4301 Connecticut Ave. N.W., #100 20008; (202) 822-8405. Fax, (202) 872-4050. Martin Blank, President.*
General email, iel@iel.org
Web, www.iel.org

Works with educators, human services personnel, government officials, and association executives to improve educational opportunities for youths; conducts research on education issues.

National Assn. of State Boards of Education, *2121 Crystal Dr., #350, Arlington, VA 22202; (703) 684-4000. Fax, (703) 836-2313. Kristen Amundson, Executive Director. Toll-free, (800) 368-5023.*
General email, boards@nasbe.org
Web, www.nasbe.org

Membership: members of state boards of education, state board attorneys, and executives to state boards. Works to strengthen state boards as the preeminent educational policy-making bodies for students and citizens.

National Center on Education and the Economy (NCEE), *2000 Pennsylvania Ave. N.W., #5300 20006; (202) 379-1800. Fax, (202) 293-1560. Marc S. Tucker, President.*
General email, info@ncee.org
Web, www.ncee.org

Provides research, analysis, advocacy, tools, and technical assistance to improve the nation's school systems and student performances. (Administers the National Institute for School Leadership.)

National Children's Museum, *151 St. George Blvd., National Harbor, MD 20745; (301) 392-2400. Fax, (301) 392-2440. Wendy Blackwell, Executive Director.*
General email, info@ncm.museum
Web, www.ncm.museum

A cultural and educational institution serving children and families onsite and through national partners and programs. Exhibits and activities focus on the arts, civic engagement, the environment, global citizenship, health and well-being, and play. Open Tuesday through Saturday, 10:00 a.m. to 4:00 p.m., and Sunday, 12:00 p.m. to 4:00 p.m. Closed Mondays. (Affiliated with the Association of Children's Museums [ACM] Reciprocal Network.)

National Humanities Institute (NHI), *P.O. Box 1387, Bowie, MD 20718-1387; (301) 464-4277. Joseph Baldacchino, President.*
General email, mail@nhinet.org
Web, www.nhinet.org

Promotes research, publishing, and teaching in the humanities. Interests include the effect of the humanities on society.

National Institute for School Leadership, Inc. (NISL), *2000 Pennsylvania Ave. N.W., #5300 20006; (202) 449-5060. Fax, (202) 293-1560. Felicia Cumings Smith, President.*
General email, nislinfo@ncee.org

Web, www.nisl.net

Offers research-based professional development programs designed to give principals the knowledge and skills they need to be instructional leaders and improve student achievement in their schools. (For-profit subsidiary of National Center on Education and the Economy [NCEE].)

National School Public Relations Assn., *15948 Derwood Rd., Rockville, MD 20855; (301) 519-0496. Fax, (301) 519-0494. Richard D. Bagin, Executive Director.*
General email, nspra@nspra.org

Web, www.nspra.org

Membership: educators and individuals interested in improving communications in education. Works to improve communication between educators and the public on the needs of schools. Provides educators with information on public relations and policy developments.

Pearson School Improvement Services, *1919 M St. N.W., #600 20036; (202) 783-3668. Fax, (202) 783-3672. Vacant, President. Toll-free, (877) 530-2716.*
General email, schoolimprovementus@pearson.com

Web, www.pearsonsschoolimprovement.com

Provides school improvement services, including professional development for educators and schoolwide solutions for federal, state, and local standards implementation, with the goals of increasing student achievement and college and career readiness. Fee for services. (Formerly Pearson's School Achievement Services.)

Internships, Fellowships, Grants

▶**AGENCIES**

Harry S. Truman Scholarship Foundation, *712 Jackson Pl. N.W., 3rd Floor 20006-4901; (202) 395-4831. Fax, (202) 395-6995. Andrew Rich, Executive Secretary.*
General email, office@truman.gov

Web, www.truman.gov

Memorial to Harry S. Truman established by Congress. Provides students preparing for careers in public service with graduate school scholarship funding. (Candidates are nominated by their respective colleges or universities while in their third year of undergraduate study.)

National Endowment for the Arts (NEA), *400 7th St. S.W., Constitution Center 20024; (202) 682-5400. Fax, (202) 682-5611. Joan Shigekawa, Senior Deputy Chair. Press, (202) 682-5570.*
General email, webmgr@arts.gov

Web, www.arts.gov

Independent grant-making agency. Awards grants to support artistic excellence, creativity, and innovation for the benefit of individuals and communities. Works through partnerships with state arts agencies, local leaders,

other federal agencies, and the philanthropic sector. Main funding categories include: Art Works (replaces Access to Artistic Excellence and Learning in the Arts for Children and Youth); Challenge America Fast-Track (for art projects in underserved communities); and Our Town (for art projects that contribute to the livability of communities).

National Endowment for the Humanities (NEH), *400 7th St. S.W., Constitution Center 20024; (202) 606-8310. Fax, (202) 606-8588. Vacant, Chair; Donna McClish, Librarian; Andrea Anderson, Director, Challenge Grants, Acting. Information, (202) 606-8400. Toll-free, 800-NEH-1121. Library, (202) 606-8244. Public Affairs, (202) 606-8446. TTY Toll-free, (866) 372-2930.*
General email, info@neh.gov

Web, www.neh.gov

Independent federal grant-making agency. Awards grants to individuals and institutions for research, scholarship, and educational and public programs (including broadcasts, museum exhibitions, lectures, and symposia) in the humanities (defined as study of archaeology; history; jurisprudence; language; linguistics; literature; philosophy; comparative religion; ethics; history, criticism, and theory of the arts; and humanistic aspects of the social sciences). Funds preservation of books, newspapers, historical documents, and photographs. Library open by appointment only.

National Endowment for the Humanities (NEH), *Education Programs, 400 7th St. S.W., Constitution Center 20024; (202) 606-8500. Fax, (202) 606-8394. William Craig Rice, Director, (202) 606-8286.*
General email, education@neh.gov

Web, www.neh.gov/divisions/education

Offers seminars and institutes for higher education faculty, school teachers, and independent scholars. Promotes research and development.

National Institute of Food and Agriculture (NIFA) (Agriculture Dept.), Institute of Youth, Family, and Community, *800 9th St. S.W., #4330, MS2250 20024 (mailing address: 1400 Independence Ave. S.W., #2225, Washington, DC 20250-2225); (202) 720-5305. Fax, (202) 720-9366. Muquarrab Qureshi, Assistant Director.*
Web, www.nifa.usda.gov/about/pdfs/fact_sheets/inst_fs_iyfc.pdf

Provides grants and programmatic training to support youth and family development; partners with county governments, the private sector, and state land-grant universities. Program areas include food and agricultural science education, particularly in minority-serving institutions; childhood nutrition; community food projects; and community service. Includes divisions of Community Education, Family and Consumer Sciences, and Youth and 4-H.

National Science Foundation (NSF), *Graduate Education, 4201 Wilson Blvd., #875S, Arlington, VA 22230; (703) 292-8630. Fax, (703) 292-9048. James H. Lightbourne, Division Director, (703) 292-4628.*
Web, www.nsf.gov/div/index.jsp?div=dge

Supports activities to strengthen the education of research scientists and engineers; promotes career development; offers predoctoral fellowships and traineeships for study and research.

President's Commission on White House Fellowships, *712 Jackson Pl. N.W. 20503; (202) 395-4522. Fax, (202) 395-6179. Cindy Moelis, Director.*
Web, www.whitehouse.gov/about/fellows

Nonpartisan commission that provides professionals from all sectors of national life with the opportunity to observe firsthand the processes of the federal government. Fellows work for one year as special assistants to cabinet members or to principal members of the White House staff. Qualified applicants have demonstrated superior accomplishments early in their careers and have a commitment to leadership and public service.

Smithsonian Institution, *Office of Fellowships and Internships, 470 L'Enfant Plaza S.W., #7102 20013 (mailing address: P.O. Box 37012, MRC 902, Washington, DC 20013-7012); (202) 633-7070. Fax, (202) 633-7069. Eric Woodard, Director.*
General email, siofg@si.edu
Web, www.smithsonianofi.com

Administers internships and fellowships in residence for study and research at the Smithsonian Institution in history of science and technology, American and cultural history, history of art, anthropology, evolutionary and systematic biology, environmental sciences, astrophysics and astronomy, earth sciences, and tropical biology.

Woodrow Wilson International Center for Scholars, *1300 Pennsylvania Ave. N.W. 20004-3027; (202) 691-4000. Fax, (202) 691-4001. Jane Harman, President, (202) 691-4202; Blair A. Ruble, Vice President for Programs.*
General email, fellowships@wilsoncenter.org
Web, www.wilsoncenter.org

Supports research in the social studies and humanities. Awards fellowships to individuals from a wide variety of backgrounds, including academia, government, the nonprofit sector, the corporate world, and the professions. Hosts public policy and senior scholars, who conduct research and write in a variety of disciplines. Offers grant competitions through regional programs: the Asia Program, the Kennan Institute, East European Studies, and the Canada Institute.

▶ **NONGOVERNMENTAL**

American Architectural Foundation, *2102 L St. N.W., #670 20037; (202) 787-1001. Fax, (202) 787-1002. Ronald E. Bogle, President.*
General email, info@archfoundation.org
Web, www.archfoundation.org

Seeks to advance the quality of American architecture. Works to increase public awareness and understanding and to apply new technology to create more humane environments. Acts as liaison between the profession and the public. Awards grants for architecture-oriented projects. Operates the historic Octagon Museum.

American Assn. of University Women (AAUW), *1111 16th St. N.W. 20036-4873; (202) 785-7700. Fax, (202) 872-1425. Linda D. Hallman, Executive Director. Toll-free, (800) 326-2289.*
General email, connect@aauw.org
Web, www.aauw.org

Awards fellowships and grants to women for various areas of study and educational pursuit. Offers fellowships to foreign women coming to the United States for one year of graduate study. Awards grants to women returning to school for postbaccalaureate education or professional development.

American Political Science Assn. (APSA), *Congressional Fellowship Program, 1527 New Hampshire Ave. N.W. 20036-1206; (202) 483-2512. Fax, (202) 483-2657. Jeffrey C. Biggs, Program Director, ext. 521.*
General email, cfp@apsanet.org
Web, www.apsanet.org/cfp

Places mid-career political scientists, journalists, faculty of medical schools (Robert Wood Johnson Fellowships, Health and Aging Policy Fellowships), and federal executives in congressional offices and committees for nine-month fellowships. Individual government agencies nominate federal executive participants.

Center for the Study of the Presidency and Congress, *1020 19th St. N.W., #250 20036; (202) 872-9800. Fax, (202) 872-9811. Maximillian Angerholtzer III, President.*
General email, ann.packo@thepresidency.org
Web, www.thepresidency.org

Membership: college students, government officials, and business leaders interested in the presidency, government, and politics. Conducts conferences, lectures, and symposiums on domestic, economic, and foreign policy issues. Publishes papers, essays, books, and reports on various aspects of the presidency and Congress.

Congressional Black Caucus Foundation, *1720 Massachusetts Ave. N.W. 20036-1903; (202) 263-2800. Fax, (202) 775-0773. A. Shuanise Washington, President.*
General email, info@cbcfinc.org
Web, www.cbcfinc.org

Conducts public policy research on issues of concern to African Americans. Sponsors fellowship programs in which professionals and academic candidates work on congressional committees and subcommittees. Sponsors internship, scholarship, and fellowship programs.

Council for International Exchange of Scholars, *1400 K St. N.W., #700 20005; (202) 686-4000. Fax, (202) 686-4029. Gary Sayed, Executive Director; Debra Egan, Director, Scholarly Academic Partnerships, (202) 686-6230.*
General email, scholars@iie.org
Web, www.cies.org

Cooperates with the U.S. government in administering Fulbright grants for university teaching and advanced research abroad. (A division of the Institute of International Education.)

Council on Foundations, *2121 Crystal Drive, Ste. 700, Arlington, VA 22202; (800) 673-9036. Vikki N. Spruill, President.*
General email, info@cof.org
Web, www.cof.org

Membership: independent community, family, and public- and company-sponsored foundations; corporate giving programs; and foundations in other countries. Promotes responsible and effective philanthropy through educational programs, publications, government relations, and promulgation of a set of principles and practices for effective grant making.

Education Trust, *1250 H St. N.W., #700 20005; (202) 293-1217. Fax, (202) 293-2605. Kati Haycock, President.*
General email, bmann@edtrust.org
Web, www.edtrust.org

Researches and disseminates data on student achievement. Provides assistance to school districts, colleges, and other organizations to raise student achievement, especially among poor and minority students. Monitors legislation and regulations.

Foundation Center, *Washington Office, 1627 K St. N.W., 3rd Floor 20006-1708; (202) 331-1400. Fax, (202) 331-1739. Patricia Pasqual, Director.*
General email, jzr@foundationcenter.org
Web, www.foundationcenter.org/washington and http://grantspace.org

Publishes foundation guides. Serves as a clearinghouse on foundations and corporate giving, nonprofit management, fundraising, and grants for individuals. Provides training and seminars on fundraising and grant writing. Operates libraries in Atlanta, Cleveland, New York, San Francisco, and Washington, D.C.; library catalog available on the web site. Libraries open to the public. (Headquarters in New York.)

The Fund for American Studies (TFAS), *1706 New Hampshire Ave. N.W. 20009; (202) 986-0384. Fax, (202) 986-0390. Roger R. Ream, President.*
General email, info@tfas.org
Web, www.tfas.org

Sponsors internships for college students on comparative political and economic systems, business and government affairs, political journalism, philanthropy, and voluntary service; grants scholarships. Interests include political and economic freedoms.

Institute of International Education, *National Security Education Program, 1400 K St. N.W., 7th Floor 20005-2403 (mailing address: P.O. Box 20010, Arlington, VA 22209); (703) 696-1991. Fax, (703) 696-5667. Michael Nugent, Director. Information, (800) 618-6737.*

General email, nsep@nsep.gov
Web, www.nsep.gov

Administers Boren Awards and Language Flagship programs; provides scholarships, fellowships, and institutional grants to students and academics with an interest in foreign affairs and national security.

National Journalism Center, *529 14th St. N.W., #1145 20045; (202) 628-1490. Fax, (202) 628-1491. Kirby Wilbur, Executive Director.*
Web, www.nationaljournalismcenter.org

Sponsors a comprehensive internship program in journalism composed of a series of training seminars that enhance students' knowledge of policy reporting in the areas of economics, education, and business. (Affiliated with the Young America's Foundation.)

The Washington Center for Internships and Academic Seminars, *1333 16th St. N.W. 20036-2205; (202) 238-7900. Fax, (202) 238-7700. Michael B. Smith, President. Information, (800) 486-8921.*
General email, info@twc.edu
Web, www.twc.edu

Arranges congressional, agency, and public service internships for college undergraduate students for credit. Sponsors classes and lectures as part of the internship program. Scholarships and stipends available. Fee for internship and housing assistance.

Washington Center for Politics and Journalism, *600 Pennsylvania Ave. S.E. 20003 (mailing address: P.O. Box 15603, Washington, DC 20003-0603); (202) 296-8455. Terry Michael, Executive Director.*
General email, terrymichael@wcpj.org
Web, www.wcpj.org

Offers internships in political journalism to undergraduate and graduate students and recent graduates; provides a $3,000 stipend for living expenses. The Politics & Journalism Semester provides for free sixteen-week fall and winter/spring sessions, which include full-time work in Washington news bureaus and twice weekly seminars in campaign, governance, and interest group politics for future political reporters.

Women's Research and Education Institute (WREI), *3808 Brighton Ct., Alexandria, VA 22305; (703) 837-1977. Susan Scanlan, President.*
General email, wrei@wrei.org
Web, www.wrei.org

Provides data and analysis of issues affecting women and their families to policymakers, the press, and the public. Sponsors Congressional Fellowships on Women and Public Policy for graduate students who are placed in congressional offices from January through August to work on policy issues affecting women. Its Women in the Military project advocates on policy issues affecting women in uniform through publications and conferences.

Professional Interests and Benefits

▶NONGOVERNMENTAL

American Assn. of Colleges for Teacher Education, *1307 New York Ave. N.W., #300 20005-4701; (202) 293-2450. Fax, (202) 457-8095. Sharon P. Robinson, President, (202) 478-4505.*
General email, aacte@aacte.org
Web, www.aacte.org

Membership: colleges and universities with teacher education programs. Informs members about state and federal policies affecting teacher education and about professional issues such as accreditation, certification, and assessment. Collects and analyzes information on education.

American Assn. of School Administrators, *1615 Duke St., Alexandria, VA 22314; (703) 528-0700. Fax, (703) 841-1543. Daniel Domenech, Executive Director.*
General email, info@aasa.org
Web, www.aasa.org

Membership: more than 13,000 educational leaders, including superintendents, chief executive officers, senior-level school administrators, and professors, as well as aspiring school system leaders. Seeks to support and develop effective school system leaders through publications and professional development workshops.

American Federation of School Administrators, *1101 17th St. N.W., #408 20036-4704; (202) 986-4209. Fax, (202) 986-4211. Diann Woodard, President.*
General email, afsa@afsaadmin.org
Web, www.afsaadmin.org

Membership: approximately 20,000 school administrators, including principals, vice principals, directors, and supervisors in the United States, Puerto Rico, and U.S. Virgin Islands. Helps members negotiate pay, benefits, and better working conditions; conducts training programs and workshops. Monitors legislation and regulations. (Affiliated with the AFL-CIO.)

American Federation of Teachers (AFT), *555 New Jersey Ave. N.W. 20001-2079; (202) 879-4400. Fax, (202) 879-4556. Randi Weingarten, President.*
General email, online@aft.org
Web, www.aft.org

Membership: 1.5 million public school teachers and staff, higher education faculty and staff, state and local government employees, and nurses and health care professionals. Assists members with contract negotiation and grievances; conducts training programs and workshops. Monitors legislation and regulations. (Affiliated with the AFL-CIO.)

American Political Science Assn. (APSA), *1527 New Hampshire Ave. N.W. 20036-1206; (202) 483-2512. Fax, (202) 483-2657. Steven Rathgeb Smith, Executive Director.*
General email, apsa@apsanet.org
Web, www.apsanet.org

Membership: political scientists, primarily college and university professors. Promotes scholarly inquiry into all aspects of political science, including international affairs and comparative government. Works to increase public understanding of politics; provides services to facilitate and enhance research, teaching, and professional development of its members. Acts as liaison with federal agencies, Congress, and the public. Seeks to improve the status of women and minorities in the profession. Offers congressional fellowships, workshops, and awards. Provides information on political science issues.

Assn. of School Business Officials International, *11401 N. Shore Dr., Reston, VA 20190-4232; (703) 478-0405. Fax, (703) 478-0205. John Musso, Executive Director. Toll-free, (866) 682-2729.*
General email, asboreq@asbointl.org
Web, www.asbointl.org

Membership: administrators, directors, and others involved in school business management. Provides news and information concerning management best practices and the effective use of educational resources. Hosts conferences; sponsors research; monitors legislation and regulations.

Assn. of Teacher Educators, *11350 Random Hills Rd., #800, Fairfax, VA 22030 (mailing address: P.O. Box 793, Manassas, VA 20113); (703) 659-1708. Fax, (703) 595-4792. David A. Ritchey, Executive Director.*
General email, info@ate1.org
Web, www.ate1.org

Membership: individuals and public and private agencies involved with teacher education. Seeks to improve teacher education at all levels; conducts workshops and conferences; produces and disseminates publications.

Council for the Accreditation of Education Preparation, *2010 Massachusetts Ave. N.W., #500 20036-1023; (202) 223-0077. Fax, (202) 296-6620. James G. (Jim) Cibulka, President.*
General email, ncate@ncate.org
Web, www.ncate.org

Evaluates and accredits schools and departments of education at colleges and universities. Publishes list of accredited institutions and standards for accreditation. (Formerly National Council for Accreditation of Teacher Education.)

Council of Chief State School Officers, *1 Massachusetts Ave. N.W., #700 20001-1431; (202) 336-7000. Fax, (202) 408-8072. Chris Minnich, Executive Director. Press, (202) 336-7034.*
General email, info@ccsso.org
Web, www.ccsso.org

Membership: the public officials who head departments of elementary and secondary education in the states, the District of Columbia, the Department of Defense Education Activity, and five U.S. extra-state jurisdictions.

Provides leadership, advocacy, and technical assistance on major educational issues. Seeks member consensus on major educational issues and advocates issue positions to civic and professional organizations, federal agencies, Congress, and the public.

Federal Education Assn., *1201 16th St. N.W., #117 20036; (202) 822-7850. Fax, (202) 822-7867. Chuck McCarter, President.*
General email, fea@feaonline.org
Web, www.feaonline.org

Membership: teachers and personnel of Defense Dept. schools for military dependents in the United States and abroad. Helps members negotiate pay, benefits, and better working conditions. Provides professional development through workshops and publications. Monitors legislation and regulations.

International Test and Evaluation Assn., *4400 Fair Lakes Court, #104, Fairfax, VA 22033-3801; (703) 631-6220. Fax, (703) 631-6221. James M. Gaidry, Executive Director, ext. 204.*
General email, info@itea.org
Web, www.itea.org

Membership: engineers, scientists, managers, and other industry, government, and academic professionals interested in testing and evaluating products and complex systems. Provides a forum for information exchange; monitors international research.

National Assn. of Biology Teachers, *12100 Sunset Hills Rd., #130, Reston, VA 20190; (703) 264-9696. Fax, (703) 435-4390. Jaclyn Reeves-Pepin, Executive Director. Information, (888) 501-6228.*
General email, office@nabt.org
Web, www.nabt.org

Membership: biology teachers and others interested in life sciences education at the elementary, secondary, and collegiate levels. Provides professional development opportunities through its publication program, summer workshops, conventions, and national award programs. Interests include teaching standards, science curriculum, and issues affecting biology and life sciences education.

National Business Education Assn., *1914 Association Dr., Reston, VA 20191-1596; (703) 860-8300. Fax, (703) 620-4483. Janet M. Treichel, Executive Director.*
General email, nbea@nbea.org
Web, www.nbea.org

Membership: business education teachers and others interested in the field. Provides information on business education; offers teaching materials; sponsors conferences. Monitors legislation and regulations affecting business education.

National Council for the Social Studies (NCSS), *8555 16th St., #500, Silver Spring, MD 20910; (301) 588-1800. Fax, (301) 588-2049. Susan Griffin, Executive Director, ext. 103. Publications, (800) 683-0812.*
General email, information@ncss.org
Web, www.socialstudies.org

Membership: curriculum developers, educational administrators, state supervisors, and social studies educators, including K–12 classroom teachers and university professors of history, political science, geography, economics, civics, psychology, sociology, and anthropology. Promotes the teaching of social studies; encourages research; sponsors publications; works with other organizations to advance social studies education.

National Council of Teachers of Mathematics, *1906 Association Dr., Reston, VA 20191-1502; (703) 620-9840. Fax, (703) 476-2970. Robert M. Doucette, Executive Director. Toll-free, (800) 235-7566.*
General email, nctm@nctm.org
Web, www.nctm.org

Membership: teachers of mathematics in elementary and secondary schools and two-year colleges; university teacher education faculty; students; and other interested persons. Works for the improvement of classroom instruction at all levels. Serves as forum and information clearinghouse on issues related to mathematics education. Offers educational materials and conferences. Monitors legislation and regulations.

National Education Assn. (NEA), *1201 16th St. N.W. 20036-3290; (202) 833-4000. Fax, (202) 822-7974. Dennis Van Roekel, President; John C. Stocks, Executive Director.*
Web, www.nea.org

Membership: more than 3.2 million educators from preschool to university graduate programs. Promotes the interest of the profession of teaching and the cause of education in the United States. Monitors legislation and regulations at state and national levels.

National Science Teachers Assn., *1840 Wilson Blvd., Arlington, VA 22201-3000; (703) 243-7100. Fax, (703) 243-7177. David L. Evans, Executive Director.*
Web, www.nsta.org

Membership: science teachers from elementary through college levels. Seeks to improve science education; provides forum for exchange of information. Monitors legislation and regulations.

NEA Foundation, *1201 16th St. N.W., #416 20036-3207; (202) 822-7840. Fax, (202) 822-7779. Harriet Sanford, President.*
General email, foundation_info@nea.org
Web, www.neafoundation.org

Offers grants and programs to public educators to improve teaching techniques, increase classroom innovations, and otherwise further professional development. Grant areas include science, technology, engineering, and mathematics teaching and learning, with a current special emphasis on "green" grants. Program specialties include strategies for improving achievement rates for poor and minority students.

NRTA: AARP's Educator Community, *601 E St. N.W. 20049; (202) 434-2380. Fax, (202) 434-3439. Bara L. Dann, Vice President. Information, (888) 687-2277.*

General email, gruiz@aarp.org

Web, www.aarp.org/nrta

Membership: active and retired teachers and other school personnel (elementary through postsecondary) over age fifty. Provides members with information on relevant national issues. Provides state associations of retired school personnel with technical assistance. (Formerly the National Retired Teachers Assn.)

Smithsonian Science Education Center, *901 D St. S.W., #704-B 20024; (202) 633-2972. Fax, (202) 287-7309. Thomas A. Emrick, Executive Director, (202) 633-2966.*

General email, ssecinfo@si.edu

Web, www.nsrconline.org; bakern@si.edu

Works to establish effective science programs for all students. Disseminates research information; develops curriculum materials; seeks to increase public support for change of science education through the development of strategic partnerships. (Formerly National Science Resources Center.)

Teachers of English to Speakers of Other Languages Inc. (TESOL), *1925 Ballenger Ave., #550, Alexandria, VA 22314-6820; (703) 836-0774. Fax, (703) 836-7864. Rosa Aronson, Executive Director. Information, (888) 547-3369.*

General email, info@tesol.org

Web, www.tesol.org

Provides professional development programs and career services for teachers of English to speakers of other languages. Sponsors professional development programs and provides career management services.

Research

▶ **AGENCIES**

Education Dept., *Institute of Education Sciences (IES),* *400 Maryland Ave. S.W. 20202; 555 New Jersey Ave. N.W., #600 20208-5500; (202) 219-1385. Fax, (202) 219-1466. John Q. Easton, Director. Library, (202) 205-4945.*

General email, contact.ies@ed.gov

Web, www2.ed.gov/about/offices/list/ies/index.html

Provides evidence on which to ground education practice and policy through the work of four centers dealing with education research, education statistics, education evaluation and regional assistance, and special education research. Funds studies on ways to improve academic achievement, conducts large-scale evaluations of federal education programs, and reports a wide array of statistics on the condition of education.

Education Dept., *National Center for Education Evaluation and Regional Assistance (NCEE),* *555 New Jersey Ave. N.W. 20208-5500; (202) 208-1200. Ruth Neild, Commissioner.*

Web, www2.ies.ed.gov/ncee

Conducts large-scale evaluations of education programs and practices supported by federal funds; provides research-based technical assistance to educators and policymakers; and supports the synthesis and dissemination of the results of research and evaluation.

Education Dept., *National Center for Education Research,* *555 New Jersey Ave. N.W. 20208; (202) 219-2006. Fax, (202) 219-1402. Thomas W. Brock, Commissioner.*

Web, http://ncer.ed.gov

Supports research that addresses the nation's education needs, from early childhood to adult education.

Education Dept., *National Center for Education Statistics (NCES),* *1990 K St. N.W., #9000 20006; (202) 502-7300. Fax, (202) 502-7466. John Q. Easton, Commissioner, Acting.*

Web, www2.nces.ed.gov

Primary federal entity for collecting and analyzing data related to education. Administers the National Assessment of Educational Progress (NAEP), the "Nation's Report Card."

Education Dept., *National Center for Special Education Research (NCSER),* *555 New Jersey Ave. N.W. 20208-5500; (202) 219-1309. Fax, (202) 219-1402. Joan McLaughlin, Commissioner, Acting.*

Web, http://ies.ed.gov/ncser

Sponsors a comprehensive program of special education research designed to expand the knowledge and understanding of infants, toddlers, and children with disabilities.

Education Dept., *National Library of Education,* *400 Maryland Ave. S.W. 20202-5721; (202) 205-5019. Fax, (202) 401-0547. Pamela Tripp-Melby, Director, (202) 453-6536. Information, (800) 424-1616.*

General email, askalibrarian@ed.gov

Web, http://ies.ed.gov/ncee/projects/nle

Federal government's main resource center for education information. Provides information, statistical, and referral services to the Education Dept. and other government agencies, the education community, and the public. Collection focuses on education research, but also includes fields such as law, public policy, economics, urban affairs, and sociology. Includes current and historical Education Dept. publications. Provides information and answers questions on education statistics and research.

Education Dept., *Special Education and Rehabilitation Services, National Institute on Disability and Rehabilitation Research,* *550 12th St. S.W. 20202-7100 (mailing address: 400 Maryland Ave. S.W., MS 2700, Washington, DC 20202-7100); (202) 245-7640. Fax, (202) 245-7323. K. Charlie Lakin, Director. Main number is TTY enabled.*

General email, nidrr-mailbox@ed.gov

Web, www3.ed.gov/about/offices/list/osers/nidrr/index.html

Supports applied research, training, and development to improve the lives of individuals with disabilities. Generates new knowledge and promotes its effective use to improve the abilities of people with disabilities to perform activities of their choice in the community, and also to expand society's capacity to provide full opportunities and accommodations for its citizens with disabilities.

▶**NONGOVERNMENTAL**

American Educational Research Assn., *1430 K St. N.W., #1200 20005; (202) 238-3200. Fax, (202) 238-3250. Felice J. Levine, Executive Director. General email, members@aera.net*

Web, www.aera.net

Membership: educational researchers affiliated with universities and colleges, school systems, think tanks, and federal and state agencies. Publishes original research in education; sponsors publication of reference works in educational research; conducts continuing education programs; studies status of women and minorities in the education field.

American Institutes for Research, *1000 Thomas Jefferson St. N.W. 20007; (202) 403-5000. Fax, (202) 403-5001. David Myers, President. General email, inquiry@air.org*

Web, www.air.org

Conducts research on educational evaluation and improvement. Develops and implements assessment and testing services that improve student education as well as meet the requirements set forth by state and federally mandated programs.

Council on Governmental Relations, *1200 New York Ave. N.W., #750 20005; (202) 289-6655. Fax, (202) 289-6698. Anthony DeCrappeo, President. Web, www.cogr.edu*

Membership: research universities, institutes, and medical colleges maintaining federally supported programs. Advises members and makes recommendations to government agencies regarding policies and regulations affecting federally funded university research.

Knowledge Alliance, *20 F St. N.W., #700 20001; (202) 507-6370. Michele McLaughlin, President. General email, waters@knowledgeall.net*

Web, www.knowledgeall.net

Membership: university-based educational research and development organizations, educational entrepreneurs, and technical assistance providers. Promotes use of scientifically based solutions for improving teaching and learning. (Formerly the National Education Knowledge Industry Assn.)

National Assn. of Independent Colleges and Universities, *1025 Connecticut Ave. N.W., #700 20036-5405; (202) 785-8866. Fax, (202) 835-0003. David L. Warren, President. General email, webmaster@naicu.edu*

Web, www.naicu.edu

Membership: liberal arts colleges, research universities, church- and faith-related institutions, historically black

colleges and universities, women's colleges, performing and visual arts institutions, two-year colleges; graduate schools of law, medicine, engineering, business, and other professions. Tracks campus trends, conducts research, analyzes higher education issues, and helps coordinate state-level activities. Interests include federal policies that affect student aid, taxation, and government regulation. Monitors legislation and regulations.

Pew Research Center, *1615 L St. N.W., #700 20036; (202) 419-4300. Fax, (202) 419-4349. Alan Murray, President. General email, info@pewresearch.org*

Web, www.pewresearch.org

Nonpartisan research organization that studies issues of public interest in America and around the world. Conducts public opinion polling and social science research; reports news; analyzes news coverage; and holds forums and briefings.

RAND Corporation, *Washington Office, 1200 S. Hayes St., Arlington, VA 22202-5050; (703) 413-1100. Fax, (703) 413-8111. Lynn E. Davis, Director, ext. 5399; Debra Knopman, Director, Justice, Infrastructure, and Environment. Web, www.rand.org*

Research organization partially funded by federal agencies. Conducts research on education policy. (Headquarters in Santa Monica, Calif.)

LIBRARIES AND EDUCATIONAL MEDIA

General

▶**AGENCIES**

Institute of Museum and Library Services, *1800 M St. N.W., 9th Floor 20036-5802; (202) 653-4657. Fax, (202) 653-4600. Susan Hildreth, Director, (202) 653-4711. Main IMLS office, (202) 653-4657. Library Services, (202) 653-4700. Museum Services, (202) 653-4789. Communications and Government Affairs, (202) 653-4757. General email, imlsinfo@imls.gov*

Web, www.imls.gov and Twitter, @US_IMLS

Awards federal grants to support learning experiences in all types of libraries and all types of museums, including opportunities for formal and informal learning, 21st-century skills development, STEM (science, technology, engineering, and math), and early learning. Promotes access to information through electronic networks, links between libraries, and services to individuals having difficulty using a library. Provides federal grants for improved care of museum collections and increased professional development, including the training and development of library students, librarians, and museum professionals. Provides museum grants for African American history and culture, and funding for improved library services to Native American tribal communities, Alaska Native villages, and Native Hawaiian library users.

Libraries at Federal Departments and Agencies

DEPARTMENTS

Agriculture, (301) 504-5248

Commerce, (202) 482-1154

Defense, (703) 695-1992

Education, (202) 205-5015

Energy (Main), (202) 586-2886

Energy (Law), (202) 586-4849

Health and Human Services (Law), (202) 619-0190

Housing and Urban Development, (202) 402-4531

Interior, (202) 208-5815

Justice, (202) 532-4895

Labor, (202) 693-6600

State, (202) 647-1099

Transportation, (800) 853-1351

Treasury, (202) 874-4722

Veterans Affairs, (202) 461-8182

AGENCIES

Agency for International Development, (202) 712-0579

Commission on Civil Rights, (202) 376-8110

Commodity Futures Trading Commission, (202) 418-5254

Consumer Product Safety Commission, (301) 504-7923

Drug Enforcement Administration, (202) 307-8932

Environmental Protection Agency, (202) 566-0556

Equal Employment Opportunity Commission, (202) 663-4630

Export-Import Bank, (202) 565-3980

Federal Communications Commission, (202) 418-0450 or (202) 418-2805

Federal Deposit Insurance Corporation, (202) 898-3631

Federal Election Commission, (202) 694-1516

Federal Labor Relations Authority, (202) 218-7798

Federal Maritime Commission, (202) 523-5762

Federal Reserve Board, (202) 452-3283

Federal Trade Commission, (202) 326-2395

Government Accountability Office (Law), (202) 512-5941

International Bank for Reconstruction and Development (World Bank)/International Monetary Fund, (202) 623-7054

Merit Systems Protection Board, (202) 653-6772 ext. 1212

National Aeronautics and Space Administration, (202) 358-0168

National Credit Union Administration (Law), (703) 518-6540

National Endowment for the Humanities, (202) 606-8244

National Institutes of Health, (301) 496-1080 or (301) 496-5611

National Labor Relations Board, (202) 273-3720

National Library of Medicine, (301) 594-5983

National Science Foundation, (703) 292-7830

Nuclear Regulatory Commission, (301) 415-6239

Occupational Safety and Health Review Commission, (202) 606-5729

Overseas Private Investment Corporation, (202) 336-8566

Peace Corps, http://collection.peacecorps.gov/cdm

Postal Regulatory Commission, (202) 789-6800

Securities and Exchange Commission, (202) 551-5450

Small Business Administration Law Library, (202) 205-6849

Smithsonian Institution, (202) 633-2240

Social Security Administration, (410) 965-6107

U.S. International Trade Commission,

Law, (202) 205-3287

Main Library, (202) 205-2630

U.S. Postal Service, (202) 268-2904

National Archives and Records Administration (NARA), *Presidential Libraries, 8601 Adelphi Rd., #2200F, College Park, MD 20740-6001; (301) 837-3250. Fax, (301) 837-3199. Susan K. Donius, Director, (301) 837-1662. Web, www.archives.gov/presidential-libraries*

Administers thirteen presidential libraries. Directs all programs relating to acquisition, preservation, and research use of materials in presidential libraries; conducts oral history projects; publishes finding aids for research sources; provides reference service, including information from and about documentary holdings. Conducts community outreach; oversees museum exhibition programming.

National Endowment for the Humanities (NEH), *Digital Humanities, 400 7th St. S.W., Constitution Center 20024; (202) 606-8401. Fax, (202) 606-8411. Brett Bobley, Director.*

Library of Congress Divisions and Programs

African and Middle Eastern Division, (202) 707-7937

American Folklife Center, (202) 707-5510

Asian Division, (202) 707-5420

Business Enterprises, (202) 707-3156

Cataloging Distribution Service, (202) 707-6100

Center for the Book, (202) 707-5221

Children's Literature Center, (202) 707-5535

Computer Catalog Center, (202) 707-3370

Copyright Office, (202) 707-3000 or (202) 707-9100

European Division, (202) 707-4515

Federal Library and Information Center Committee, (202) 707-4800

Geography and Map Division, (202) 707-6277

Hispanic Division, (202) 707-5397

Humanities and Social Science Division, (202) 707-3399

Interlibrary Loan Division (CALM), (202) 707-5444

Interpretive Programs, (202) 707-5223

Law Library, (202) 707-5079

Law Library Reading Room, (202) 707-5080

Local History and Genealogy Reading Room, (202) 707-5537

Manuscript Division, (202) 707-5383

Mary Pickford Theater, (202) 707-5677

Microform Reading Room, (202) 707-5471

Motion Picture, Broadcasting, and Recorded Sound Division, (202) 707-5840 or (202) 707-8572

Music Reference, (202) 707-5507

National Library Service for the Blind and Physically Handicapped, (202) 707-5100

Poetry and Literature Center, (202) 707-5394

Preservation Directorate, (202) 707-2598

Prints and Photographs Division, (202) 707-6394

Rare Book and Special Collections Division, (202) 707-3448

Science, Technology, and Business Division, (202) 707-5639

Serial and Government Publications Division, (202) 707-5691

General email, odh@neh.gov

Web, www.neh.gov/divisions/odh

Encourages and supports projects that utilize or study the impact of digital technology on research, education, preservation, access, and public programming in the humanities.

National Endowment for the Humanities (NEH), *Public Programs, 400 7th St. S.W., Constitution Center 20024; (202) 606-8269. Fax, (202) 606-8557. Karen Mittelman, Director, (202) 606-8631.*
General email, publicpgms@neh.gov
Web, www.neh.gov/divisions/public

Awards grants to libraries, museums, special projects, and media for projects that enhance public appreciation and understanding of the humanities through books and other resources in American library collections. Projects include conferences, exhibitions, essays, documentaries, radio programs, and lecture series.

Smithsonian Institution, *Office of the Director, Libraries, 10th St. and Constitution Ave. N.W., National Museum of Natural History 20560 (mailing address: P.O. Box 37012, MRC 154, Washington, DC 20013-7012); (202) 633-2240. Fax, (202) 633-4315. Nancy E. Gwinn, Director.*
Web, http://library.si.edu

Unites twenty libraries into one system supported by an online catalog of the combined collections. Maintains collection of general reference, biographical, and interdisciplinary materials; serves as an information resource on institution libraries and museum studies. Open to the public by appointment.

▶ **CONGRESS**

For a listing of relevant congressional committees and subcommittees, please see page 155 or the Appendix.

Library of Congress, *101 Independence Ave. S.E. 20540; (202) 707-5000. Fax, (202) 707-1714. James H. Billington, Librarian of Congress. Visitor Information, (202) 707-8000. Public Affairs, (202) 707-2905. General reference, (202) 707-3399. Copyright information, (202) 707-3000.*
Web, www.loc.gov and General reference, www.loc.gov//rr/askalib

The nation's library.

Library of Congress, *Center for the Book, 101 Independence Ave. S.E., #LM 650 20540; (202) 707-5221. Fax, (202) 707-0269. John Y. Cole, Director.*
General email, cfbook@loc.gov
Web, www.read.gov/cfb

Seeks to broaden public appreciation of books, reading, literacy, and libraries; sponsors lectures and conferences on the educational and cultural role of the book worldwide, including the history of books and printing, television and the printed word, and the publishing and production of books; cooperates with state centers and with other organizations. Projects and programs are privately funded except for basic administrative support from the Library of Congress.

Library of Congress, *Federal Library and Information Network (FEDLINK),* 101 Independence Ave. S.E., #LA217 20540; (202) 707-4800. Fax, (202) 707-4818. *Kathryn Mendenhall, Executive Director, Interim; Robin Harvey, Editor-in-Chief, (202) 707-4820. FEDLINK Hotline, (202) 707-4900.* *General email, flicc@loc.gov* *Web, www.loc.gov/flicc*

Promotes better utilization of federal library and information resources by seeking to provide the most cost-effective and efficient administrative mechanisms for providing services and materials to federal libraries and information centers; serves as a forum for discussion of federal library and information policies, programs, and procedures; helps inform Congress, federal agencies, and others concerned with libraries and information centers.

Library of Congress, *Federal Research Division, Adams Bldg.,* 101 Independence Ave. S.E., #LA5281 20540-4840; (202) 707-3900. Fax, (202) 707-3920. *Roberta W. Goldblatt, Chief, Acting.* *General email, frds@loc.gov* *Web, www.loc.gov/rr/frd*

Provides research and analytical support to federal agencies

Library of Congress, *Preservation Directorate,* 101 Independence Ave. S.E. 20540; (202) 707-2958. *Mark Sweeney, Director.* *General email, preserve@loc.gov* *Web, www.loc.gov/preservation*

Responsible for preserving book and paper materials in the library's collections.

▶ **NONGOVERNMENTAL**

American Library Assn., *Washington Office,* 1615 New Hampshire Ave. N.W., 1st Floor 20009-2520; (202) 628-8410. Fax, (202) 628-8419. Emily Sheketoff, Executive Director. Information, (800) 941-8478. *General email, alawash@alawash.org* *Web, www.ala.org/offices/wo*

Educational organization of librarians, trustees, and educators. Washington office monitors legislation and regulations on libraries and information science. (Headquarters in Chicago, Ill.)

Assn. for Information and Image Management (AIIM), 1100 Wayne Ave., #1100, Silver Spring, MD 20910; (301) 587-8202. Fax, (301) 587-2711. John F. Mancini, President. Information, (800) 477-2446. *General email, aiim@aiim.org* *Web, www.aiim.org*

Membership: manufacturers and users of image-based information systems. Works to advance the profession of information management; develops training standards on information management and document formats.

Assn. for Information Science and Technology (ASIS&T), 8555 16th St., #850, Silver Spring, MD 20910; (301) 495-0900. Fax, (301) 495-0810. Richard Hill, Executive Director. *General email, asis@asis.org* *Web, www.asis.org*

Membership: information specialists from such fields as computer science, linguistics, management, librarianship, engineering, law, medicine, chemistry, and education. Advocates research and development in basic and applied information science. Offers continuing education programs.

Assn. of Research Libraries (ARL), 21 Dupont Circle N.W., #800 20036-1118; (202) 296-2296. Fax, (202) 872-0884. Elliott Shore, Executive Director. *General email, webmgr@arl.org* *Web, www.arl.org*

Membership: major research libraries, mainly at universities, in the United States and Canada. Interests include development of library resources in all formats, subjects, and languages; computer information systems and other bibliographic tools; management of research libraries; preservation of library materials; worldwide information policy; and publishing and scholarly communication.

Council on Library and Information Resources, 1707 L St. N.W., #650 20036; (202) 939-4750. Fax, (202) 939-4765. Charles Henry, President. *Web, www.clir.org*

Acts on behalf of the nation's libraries, archives, and universities to develop and encourage collaborative strategies for preserving the nation's intellectual heritage; seeks to strengthen its information systems and learning environments.

Gallaudet University, *Library,* 800 Florida Ave. N.E. 20002-3695; (202) 651-5217. Sarah Hamrick, Director, Library Public Services; Michael (Mike) Olson, Director, Archives Preservation Specialist. Video phone, (202) 250-2384. *General email, library.help@gallaudet.edu* *Web, http://library.gallaudet.edu*

Maintains extensive special collection on deafness, including archival materials relating to deaf cultural history and Gallaudet University.

Info Comm International, 11242 Waples Mill Rd., #200, Fairfax, VA 22030; (703) 273-7200. Fax, (703) 278-8082. David Labuskes, Executive Director. Information, (800) 659-7469. *Web, www.infocomm.org*

Membership: manufacturers, dealers, and specialists in educational communications products. Provides educators with information on federal funding for audiovisual, video, and computer equipment and materials; monitors trends in educational technology; conducts audiovisual trade shows worldwide. (Formerly the International Communications Industries Assn.)

Society for Imaging Science and Technology, *7003 Kilworth Lane, Springfield, VA 22151; (703) 642-9090. Fax, (703) 642-9094. Suzanne E. Grinnan, Executive Director.*
General email, info@imaging.org
Web, www.imaging.org

Membership: individuals and companies worldwide in fields of imaging science and technology, including digital printing, electronic imaging, color science, image preservation, photo finishing, pre-press technology, hybrid imaging, and silver halide. Gathers and disseminates technical information; fosters professional development.

Special Libraries Assn., *331 S. Patrick St., Alexandria, VA 22314-3501; (703) 647-4900. Fax, (703) 647-4901. Janice R. Lachance, Chief Executive Officer.*
General email, sla@sla.org
Web, www.sla.org

Membership: librarians and information managers serving institutions that use or produce information in specialized areas, including business, engineering, law, the arts and sciences, government, museums, and universities. Conducts professional development programs, research projects, and an annual conference. Monitors legislation and regulations.

POSTSECONDARY EDUCATION

General

▶AGENCIES

Education Dept., *Fund for the Improvement of Postsecondary Education, 1990 K St. N.W., 6th Floor 20006-8544; (202) 502-7500. Fax, (202) 502-7877. Ralph Hines, Director, (202) 502-7618.*
Web, www2.ed.gov/FIPSE

Works to improve postsecondary education by administering grant competitions.

Education Dept., *Office of Postsecondary Education (OPE), 1990 K St. N.W., 7th Floor 20006; (202) 502-7750. Fax, (202) 502-7677. Brenda Dann-Messier, Assistant Secretary.*
Web, www2.ed.gov/about/offices/list/ope/index.html

Formulates federal postsecondary education policy. Administers federal assistance programs for public and private postsecondary institutions; provides financial support for faculty development, construction of facilities, and improvement of graduate, continuing, cooperative, and international education; awards grants and loans for financial assistance to eligible students.

Education Dept., *Office of Postsecondary Education (OPE), Higher Education Programs, 1990 K St. N.W., 6th Floor 20006; (202) 502-7812. James Minor, Deputy Assistant Secretary, (202) 219-7555.*
Web, www2.ed.gov/about/offices/list/ope/hep.html

Administers programs to increase access to postsecondary education for low-income, first-generation students and students with disabilities. Supports higher education facilities and programs through financial support to eligible institutions, and management of programs that recruit and prepare low-income students for successful completion of college. Programs include eight TRIO programs, institutional development programs for minority-serving institutions, and the Fund for the Improvement of Postsecondary Education.

▶CONGRESS

For a listing of relevant congressional committees and subcommittees, please see page 155 or the Appendix.

▶NONGOVERNMENTAL

Accuracy in Academia, *4350 East-West Hwy., #555, Bethesda, MD 20814; (202) 364-4401. Malcolm A. Kline, Executive Director.*
General email, info@academia.org
Web, www.academia.org

Seeks to eliminate political bias in university education, particularly discrimination against students, faculty, or administrators on the basis of political beliefs. Publishes a monthly newsletter.

ACT Inc. *(American College Testing), Washington Office, 1 Dupont Circle N.W., #220 20036-1170; (202) 223-2318. Fax, (202) 293-2223. Tom Lindsley, Director of Federal Advocacy. TTY, (319) 337-1701.*
Web, www.act.org

Administers ACT assessment planning and examination for colleges and universities. Provides more than one hundred assessment, research, information, and program management services in the areas of education and workforce development to elementary and secondary schools, colleges, professional associations, businesses, and government agencies. (Headquarters in Iowa City, Iowa.)

American Assn. of Colleges of Pharmacy, *1727 King St., Alexandria, VA 22314-2700; (703) 739-2330. Fax, (703) 836-8982. Lucinda L. Maine, Executive Vice President.*
General email, mail@aacp.org
Web, www.aacp.org

Represents and advocates for pharmacists in the academic community. Conducts programs and activities in cooperation with other national health and higher education associations.

American Assn. of Collegiate Registrars and Admissions Officers, *1 Dupont Circle N.W., #520 20036-1135; (202) 293-9161. Fax, (202) 872-8857. Michael Reilly, Executive Director.*
General email, info@aacrao.org
Web, www.aacrao.org

Membership: degree-granting postsecondary institutions, government agencies, higher education coordinating boards, private education organizations, and education-oriented businesses. Promotes higher education and contributes to the professional development of members working in admissions, enrollment management, financial aid, institutional research, records, and registration.

American Assn. of Community Colleges, *1 Dupont Circle N.W., #410 20036-1176; (202) 728-0200. Fax, (202) 833-2467. Walter G. Bumphus, President.*
Web, www.aacc.nche.edu

Membership: accredited two-year community technical and junior colleges, corporate foundations, international associates, and institutional affiliates. Studies include policies for lifelong education, workforce training programs and partnerships, international curricula, enrollment trends, and cooperative programs with public schools and communities. (Affiliated with the Council for Resource Development.)

American Assn. of State Colleges and Universities, *1307 New York Ave. N.W., 5th Floor 20005; (202) 293-7070. Fax, (202) 296-5819. Muriel Howard, President, (202) 478-4647.*
General email, info@aascu.org
Web, www.aascu.org

Membership: presidents and chancellors of state colleges and universities. Promotes equity in education and fosters information exchange among members. Interests include student financial aid, international education programs, academic affairs, teacher education, and higher education access and affordability. Monitors legislation and regulations.

American Assn. of University Professors (AAUP), *1133 19th St. N.W., #200 20036; (202) 737-5900. Fax, (202) 737-5526. Julie Schmid, Executive Director.*
General email, aaup@aaup.org
Web, www.aaup.org

Membership: college and university faculty members. Defends faculties' and professional staffs' academic freedom and tenure; advocates collegial governance; assists in the development of policies ensuring due process. Conducts workshops and education programs. Monitors legislation and regulations.

American Conference of Academic Deans, *1818 R St. N.W. 20009; (202) 884-7419. Fax, (202) 265-9532. Laura A. Rzepka, Executive Director.*
General email, info@acad-edu.org
Web, www.acad-edu.org

Membership: academic administrators of two- and four-year accredited colleges, universities, and community colleges (private and public). Fosters information exchange among members on college curricular and administrative issues.

American Council of Trustees and Alumni, *1726 M St. N.W., #802 20036-4525; (202) 467-6787. Fax, (202) 467-6784. Anne D. Neal, President. Toll-free, (800) 258-6648.*
General email, info@goacta.org
Web, www.goacta.org

Membership: college and university alumni and trustees interested in promoting academic freedom and excellence. Seeks to help alumni and trustees direct their financial contributions to programs that will raise educational standards at their alma maters. Promotes the role of alumni and trustees in shaping higher education policies.

American Council on Education (ACE), *1 Dupont Circle N.W., #800 20036-1193; (202) 939-9300. Fax, (202) 833-4762. Molly Corbett Broad, President. Press, (202) 939-9365.*
General email, comments@acenet.edu
Web, www.acenet.edu

Membership: presidents of universities and other education institutions. Conducts and publishes research; maintains offices dealing with government relations, women and minorities in higher education, management of higher education institutions, adult learning and educational credentials (academic credit for nontraditional learning, especially in the armed forces), leadership development, and international education.

ASCD (Assn. for Supervision and Curriculum Development), *1703 N. Beauregard St., Alexandria, VA 22311-1714; (703) 578-9600. Fax, (703) 575-5400. Gene R. Carter, Executive Director. Information, (800) 933-2723.*
General email, member@ascd.org
Web, www.ascd.org

Membership: approximately 140,000 professional educators internationally, including superintendents, supervisors, principals, teachers, professors of education, and school board members. Develops programs, products, and services for educators.

Assn. of American Colleges and Universities (AACU), *1818 R St. N.W. 20009; (202) 387-3760. Fax, (202) 265-9532. Carol Geary Schneider, President.*
Web, www.aacu.org

Membership: two- and four-year public and private colleges, universities, and postsecondary consortia. Works to develop effective academic programs and improve undergraduate curricula and services. Seeks to encourage, enhance, and support student achievement through liberal education for all students, regardless of academic specialization or intended career.

Assn. of American Law Schools, *1614 20th St. N.W. 20009-1001; (202) 296-8851. Fax, (202) 296-8869. Judith Areem, Executive Director.*
General email, aals@aals.org
Web, www.aals.org

Membership: law schools, subject to approval. Membership criteria include high-quality academic programs, faculty, scholarship, and students; academic freedom; diversity of people and viewpoints; and emphasis on public service. Hosts meetings and workshops; publishes a directory of law teachers. Advocates on behalf of legal education; monitors legislation and judicial decisions.

Colleges and Universities in the Washington Metropolitan Area

Agriculture Dept. Graduate School, 600 Maryland Ave. S.W., 20024. Switchboard: (888) 744-4723. Interim President: Elaine Ryan, (202) 314-3300

American University, 4400 Massachusetts Ave. N.W., 20016. Switchboard: (202) 885-1000. President: Cornelius Kerwin, (202) 885-2121

Catholic University of America, 620 Michigan Ave. N.E., 20064. Switchboard: (202) 319-5000. President: John Garvey, (202) 319-5100

Corcoran College of Art and Design, 500 17th St. N.W., 20006. Switchboard: (202) 639-1800. Provost: Catherine Armour, (202) 639-1803

Gallaudet University, 800 Florida Ave. N.E., 20002. Switchboard: (202) 651-5000 (voice and TTY). President: T. Alan Hurwitz, (202) 651-5005 (voice and TTY)

George Mason University, 4400 University Dr., Fairfax, VA 22030. Switchboard: (703) 993-1000. President: Ángel Cabrera, (703) 993-8700

George Washington University, 2121 Eye St. N.W., 20052. Switchboard: (202) 994-1000. President: Steven Knapp, (202) 994-6500

George Washington University at Mount Vernon Campus, 2100 Foxhall Rd. N.W., 20007. Switchboard: (202) 242-6673. Associate Vice President: Frederic A. Siegel, (202) 242-6609

Georgetown University, 3700 O St. N.W., 20057. Switchboard: (202) 687-0100. President: John J. DeGioia, (202) 687-4134

Howard University, 2400 6th St. N.W., 20059. Switchboard: (202) 806-6100. Interim President: Wayne A.I. Frederick, (202) 806-2500

Marymount University, 2807 N. Glebe Rd., Arlington, VA 22207. Switchboard: (703) 522-5600. President: Matthew D. Shank, (703) 284-1598

Paul H. Nitze School of Advanced International Studies (SAIS), Johns Hopkins University, 1740 Massachusetts Ave. N.W., 20036. Switchboard: (202) 663-5600 Dean: Vali R. Nasr, (202) 663-5624

Trinity Washington University, 125 Michigan Ave. N.E., 20017. Switchboard: (202) 884-9000. President: Patricia A. McGuire, (202) 884-9050

University of Maryland, College Park, MD 20742. Switchboard: (301) 405-1000. President: Wallace D. Loh, (301) 314-9560

University of the District of Columbia, 4200 Connecticut Ave. N.W., 20008. Switchboard: (202) 274-5000. President: James E. Lyons, (202) 274-5100

University of Virginia (Northern Virginia Center), 7054 Haycock Rd., Falls Church, VA 22043. Switchboard: (703) 536-1100. Vice Provost for Academic Outreach: Billy Cannaday, (434) 924-3728

Virginia Tech (Northern Virginia Center), 7054 Haycock Rd., Falls Church, VA 22043 Switchboard: (703) 538-8310. Director of Northern Virginia Campus: Sherry J. Fontaine, (703) 538-8310

Virginia Theological Seminary, 3737 Seminary Rd., Alexandria, VA 22304. Switchboard: (703) 370-6600. Dean: The Very Rev. Ian S. Markham, (703) 461-1701

Washington Adventist University, 7600 Flower Ave., Takoma Park, MD 20912. Switchboard: (301) 891-4000. President: Weymouth Spence, (301) 891-4128

Assn. of American Universities, *1200 New York Ave. N.W., #550 20005; (202) 408-7500. Fax, (202) 408-8184. Hunter R. Rawlings III, President. Web, www.aau.edu*

Membership: public and private universities with emphasis on graduate and professional education and research. Fosters information exchange among presidents of member institutions.

Assn. of Catholic Colleges and Universities, *1 Dupont Circle N.W., #650 20036; (202) 457-0650. Fax, (202) 728-0977. Michael Galligan-Stierle, President. General email, accu@accunet.org Web, www.accunet.org*

Membership: regionally accredited American Catholic colleges and universities. Offers affiliated status for selected international Catholic universities. Acts as a clearinghouse for information on Catholic institutions of higher education.

Assn. of Community College Trustees, *1233 20th St. N.W., #301 20036; (202) 775-4667. Fax, (202) 223-1297. J. Noah Brown, President.*

General email, acctinfo@acct.org Web, www.acct.org

Provides members of community college governing boards with training in educational programs and services. Monitors federal education programs and advocates on behalf of community colleges and their trustees.

Assn. of Governing Boards of Universities and Colleges, *1133 20th St. N.W., #300 20036; (202) 296-8400. Fax, (202) 223-7053. Richard D. Legon, President. Toll-free, (800) 356-6317. Web, www.agb.org*

Membership: presidents, boards of trustees, regents, commissions, and other groups governing colleges, universities, and institutionally related foundations. Interests include the relationship between the president and board of trustees and other subjects relating to governance.

Assn. of Jesuit Colleges and Universities, *1 Dupont Circle N.W., #405 20036-1140; (202) 862-9893. Fax, (202) 862-8523. Rev. Michael J. Sheeran, President. General email, dhowes@ajcunet.edu Web, www.ajcunet.edu*

Membership: American Jesuit colleges and universities. Monitors government regulatory and policy-making activities affecting higher education. Publishes the *AJCU Directory* and a monthly newsletter. Promotes national and international cooperation among Jesuit higher education institutions.

Assn. of Private Sector Colleges and Universities, *1101 Connecticut Ave. N.W., #900 20036; (202) 336-6700. Fax, (202) 336-6828. Steve Gunderson, President.*
General email, cca@career.org

Web, www.career.org

Membership: private postsecondary colleges and career schools in the United States. Works to expand the accessibility of postsecondary career education and to improve the quality of education offered by member schools. (Formerly Career College Assn.)

Assn. of Public and Land-Grant Universities, *1307 New York Ave. N.W., #400 20005-4722; (202) 478-6040. Fax, (202) 478-6046. M. Peter McPherson, President.*
Web, www.aplu.org

Membership: land-grant colleges; state and public research universities. Serves as clearinghouse on issues of public higher education.

Business–Higher Education Forum, *2025 M St. N.W., #800 20036; (202) 367-1189. Fax, (202) 367-2100. Brian K. Fitzgerald, Chief Executive Officer.*
General email, info@bhef.com

Web, www.bhef.com

Membership: chief executive officers of major corporations, foundations, colleges, and universities. Develops and promotes policy positions to enhance U.S. competitiveness. Interests include improving student achievement and readiness for college and work, and strengthening higher education, particularly in the fields of science, technology, engineering, and math.

College Board, *Advocacy, Government Relations, and Development, 1233 20th St. N.W., #600 20036-2304; (202) 741-4700. Fax, (202) 741-4743. Tom Rudin, Senior Vice President.*
General email, govrelations@collegeboard.org

Web, www.collegeboard.org

Membership: colleges and universities, secondary schools, school systems, and education associations. Provides direct student support programs and professional development for educators; conducts policy analysis and research; and advocates public policy positions that support educational excellence and promote student access to higher education. (Headquarters in New York.)

Council for Christian Colleges & Universities, *321 8th St. N.E. 20002; (202) 546-8713. Fax, (202) 546-8913. Willliam P. Robinson, President.*
General email, council@cccu.org

Web, www.cccu.org

Membership: accredited four-year Christian liberal arts colleges. Offers faculty development conferences on faith and the academic disciplines. Coordinates annual gathering of college administrators. Sponsors internship/seminar programs for students at member colleges. Promotes Christian-affiliated higher education. Interests include religious and educational freedom.

Council for Resource Development, *8720 Georgia Ave., #700, Silver Spring, MD 20910; (202) 822-0750. Shelly Connor, President.*
General email, info@crdnet.org

Web, www.crdnet.org

Membership: college presidents, administrators, fundraisers, grant writers, and development officers at two-year colleges. Educates members on how to secure resources for their institution; conducts workshops and training programs. Monitors legislation and regulations. (Affiliated with the American Assn. of Community Colleges.)

Council of Graduate Schools, *1 Dupont Circle N.W., #230 20036-1173; (202) 223-3791. Fax, (202) 331-7157. Debra W. Stewart, President.*
General email, general_inquiries@cgs.nche.edu

Web, www.cgsnet.org

Membership: private and public colleges and universities with significant involvement in graduate education, research, and scholarship. Produces publications and information about graduate education; provides a forum for member schools to exchange information and ideas.

Council of Independent Colleges, *1 Dupont Circle N.W., #320 20036-1142; (202) 466-7230. Fax, (202) 466-7238. Richard Ekman, President.*
General email, cic@cic.nche.edu

Web, www.cic.edu

Membership: independent liberal arts colleges and universities, and higher education affiliates and organizations. Sponsors development programs for college presidents, deans, and faculty members and communications officers on topics such as leadership, financial management, academic quality, visibility, and other issues crucial to high-quality education and independent liberal arts colleges. Holds workshops and annual meetings, conducts research, and produces publications.

Council on Social Work Education, *1701 Duke St., #200, Alexandria, VA 22314-3457; (703) 683-8080. Fax, (703) 683-8099. Darla Spence Coffey, Executive Director.*
General email, info@cswe.org

Web, www.cswe.org

Membership: educational and professional institutions, social welfare agencies, and private citizens. Promotes high-quality education in social work. Accredits social work programs.

Educational Testing Service (ETS), *Communications and Public Affairs, Washington Office, 1800 K St. N.W., #900 20006-2202; (202) 659-0616. Fax, (202) 659-8075. Kurt Landgraf, President.*
General email, etsinfo@ets.org

Web, www.ets.org

Administers examinations for admission to educational programs and for graduate and licensing purposes; conducts instructional programs in testing, evaluation, and research in education fields. Washington office handles government and professional relations. Fee for services. (Headquarters in Princeton, N.J.)

NASPA–Student Affairs Administrators in Higher Education, *111 K St. N.E., 10th Floor 20002; (202) 265-7500. Fax, (202) 898-5737. Kevin Kruger, President.*
General email, office@naspa.org
Web, www.naspa.org and Twitter, @NASPAtweets

Membership: student affairs administrators, deans, faculty, and graduate and undergraduate students at 2,100 campuses, representing 25 countries. Seeks to develop leadership and improve practices in student affairs administration. Initiates and supports programs and legislation to improve student affairs administration.

National Assn. for College Admission Counseling, *1050 N. Highland St., #400, Arlington, VA 22201; (703) 836-2222. Fax, (703) 243-9375. Joyce Smith, Chief Executive Officer. Information, (800) 822-6285.*
General email, info@nacacnet.com
Web, www.nacac.net.org

Membership: high school guidance counselors, independent counselors, college and university admissions officers, and financial aid officers. Promotes and funds research on admission counseling and on the transition from high school to college. Advocates for student rights in college admissions. Sponsors national college fairs and continuing education for members.

National Assn. of College and University Attorneys, *1 Dupont Circle N.W., #620 20036-1182; (202) 833-8390. Fax, (202) 296-8379. Kathleen Curry Santora, Chief Executive Officer.*
General email, nacua@nacua.org
Web, www.nacua.org

Provides information on legal developments affecting postsecondary education. Operates a clearinghouse through which in-house and external legal counselors are able to network with their counterparts on current legal problems.

National Assn. of College and University Business Officers, *1110 Vermont Ave. N.W., #800 20005; (202) 861-2500. Fax, (202) 861-2583. John D. Walda, President. Toll-free, (800) 462-4916.*
General email, support@nacubo.org
Web, www.nacubo.org

Membership: chief business officers at higher education institutions. Provides members with information on financial management, federal regulations, and other subjects related to the business administration of universities and colleges; conducts workshops on issues such as student aid, institutional budgeting, and accounting.

National Assn. of Independent Colleges and Universities, *1025 Connecticut Ave. N.W., #700 20036-5405; (202) 785-8866. Fax, (202) 835-0003. David L. Warren, President.*
General email, webmaster@naicu.edu
Web, www.naicu.edu

Membership: liberal arts colleges, research universities, church- and faith-related institutions, historically black colleges and universities, women's colleges, performing and visual arts institutions, two-year colleges; graduate schools of law, medicine, engineering, business, and other professions. Tracks campus trends, conducts research, analyzes higher education issues, and helps coordinate state-level activities. Interests include federal policies that affect student aid, taxation, and government regulation. Monitors legislation and regulations.

National Council of University Research Administrators, *1015 18th St. N.W., #901 20036; (202) 466-3894. Fax, (202) 223-5573. Kathleen Larmett, Executive Director.*
General email, info@ncura.edu
Web, www.ncura.edu

Membership: individuals involved in grant administration at colleges, universities, and teaching hospitals. Encourages development of effective policies and procedures in the administration of these programs.

U.S. Student Assn., *1211 Connecticut Ave. N.W., #406 20036; (202) 640-6570. Fax, (202) 223-4005. Sophia Zaman, Operations Manager.*
General email, manager@usstudents.org
Web, www.usstudents.org

Represents postsecondary students, student government associations, and state student lobby associations. Monitors legislation and regulations. Organizes students to participate in the political process through congressional testimony, letter-writing campaigns, and lobbying visits. Represents students in various coalitions, including the Committee for Education Funding, the Student Aid Alliance, the Generational Alliance, and the Leadership Conference on Civil Rights.

Washington Higher Education Secretariat, *1 Dupont Circle N.W., #800 20036-1110; (202) 939-9410. Fax, (202) 833-4760. Molly Corbett Broad, Chair.*
General email, whes@ace.nche.edu
Web, www.whes.org

Membership: national higher education association chief executives representing the different sectors and functions in postsecondary institutions. Provides forum for discussion on national and local education issues. (Coordinated by the president of the American Council on Education.)

College Accreditation

Many college- or university-based independent postsecondary education programs are accredited by member associations. See specific headings and associations within the chapter.

►AGENCIES

Education Dept., *Accreditation Group, 1990 K St. N.W., #8065 20006-8509; (202) 219-7011. Herman Bounds, Director.*
Web, www2.ed.gov

Reviews accrediting agencies and state approval agencies that seek initial or renewed recognition by the secretary; provides the National Advisory Committee on Institutional Quality and Integrity with staff support.

►NONGOVERNMENTAL

Accrediting Council for Independent Colleges and Schools (ACICS), *750 1st St. N.E., #980 20002-4241; (202) 336-6780. Fax, (202) 842-2593. Albert C. Gray, Executive Director.*
General email, info@acics.org
Web, www.acics.org

Accredits postsecondary institutions offering programs of study through the master's degree level that are designed to train and educate persons for careers or professions where business applications and concepts constitute or support the career or professional activity. Promotes educational excellence and ethical business practices in its member schools.

American Academy for Liberal Education (AALE), *127 S. Peyton St., #210, Alexandria, VA 22314; (703) 717-9719. Charles Butterworth, President.*
General email, aaleinfo@aale.org
Web, www.aale.org

Accredits colleges, universities, and charter schools whose general education program in the liberal arts meets the academy's accreditation requirements. Provides support for institutions that maintain substantial liberal arts programs and desire to raise requirements to meet AALE standards.

Council for Higher Education Accreditation, *1 Dupont Circle N.W., #510 20036; (202) 955-6126. Fax, (202) 955-6129. Judith S. Eaton, President.*
General email, ciqq@cheainternational.org
Web, www.chea.org and www.cheainternational.org

Advocates voluntary self-regulation of colleges and universities through accreditation; conducts recognition processes for accrediting organizations; coordinates research, debate, and processes that improve accreditation; mediates disputes and fosters communications among accrediting bodies and the higher education community.

Financial Aid to Students

►AGENCIES

Education Dept., *Federal Student Aid, 830 1st St. N.E. 20202; (202) 377-3000. Fax, (202) 275-5000. James Runcie, Chief Operating Officer. Student Aid Information Center, (800) 433-3243.*
Web, www2.ed.gov

Administers federal loan, grant, and work-study programs for postsecondary education to eligible individuals. Administers the Pell Grant Program, the Perkins Loan Program, the Stafford Student Loan Program (Guaranteed Student Loan)/PLUS Program, the College Work-Study Program, the Supplemental Loans for Students (SLS), and the Supplemental Educational Opportunity Grant Program.

►NONGOVERNMENTAL

College Board, *Advocacy, Government Relations, and Development, 1233 20th St. N.W., #600 20036-2304; (202) 741-4700. Fax, (202) 741-4743. Tom Rudin, Senior Vice President.*
General email, govrelations@collegeboard.org
Web, www.collegeboard.org

Membership: colleges and universities, secondary schools, school systems, and education associations. Provides direct student support programs and professional development for educators; conducts policy analysis and research; and advocates public policy positions that support educational excellence and promote student access to higher education. (Headquarters in New York.)

Education Finance Council, *1850 M St. N.W., #920 20036; (202) 955-5510. Fax, (202) 955-5530. Vincent Sampson, President.*
General email, samanthad@efc.org
Web, www.efc.org

Membership: state-based student loan secondary market organizations. Participates in the Federal Family Education Loan Program (FFELP). Works to maintain and expand student access to higher education through tax-exempt funding for loans.

National Assn. of Student Financial Aid Administrators, *1101 Connecticut Ave. N.W., #1100 20036-4303; (202) 785-0453. Fax, (202) 785-1487. Justin Draeger, President.*
General email, ask@nasfaa.org
Web, www.nasfaa.org and Twitter, @nasfaa

Membership: more than 20,000 financial aid professionals at nearly 3,000 colleges, universities, and career schools. Interests include student aid legislation, regulatory analysis, and training for financial aid administrators.

National Council of Higher Education Resources, *1100 Connecticut Ave. N.W., #1200 20036-4110; (202) 822-2106. Fax, (202) 822-2142. Sheldon (Shelly) Repp, President.*
General email, info@nchelp.org
Web, www.ncher.us

Membership: agencies and organizations involved in servicing and collecting federal student loans and to providing debt management, financial literacy, student loan counseling, and other college access and success services. Fosters information exchange among members.

Student Aid Alliance, *1 Dupont Circle N.W., #800 20036-1193; (202) 939-9355. Fax, (202) 833-4762.*

Molly Corbett Broad, President, ACE; David L. Warren, President, NAICU.
Web, studentaidalliance.org

Membership: more than seventy organizations representing students, administrators, and faculty members from all sectors of higher education. Seeks to ensure adequate funding of federal aid programs. Monitors legislation and regulations. (Co-chaired by the National Assn. of Independent Colleges and Universities and the American Council on Education.)

PRESCHOOL, ELEMENTARY, SECONDARY EDUCATION

General

▶**AGENCIES**

Education Dept., *Elementary and Secondary Education,* *400 Maryland Ave. S.W., #3W315 20202; (202) 401-0113. Fax, (202) 205-0310. Deborah S. Delisle, Assistant Secretary.*
General email, oese@ed.gov
Web, www2.ed.gov/about/offices/list/oese/index.html

Administers federal assistance programs for preschool, elementary, and secondary education (both public and private). Program divisions include Student Achievement and School Accountability (including Title I aid for disadvantaged children); School Turnaround; Migrant Education; Impact Aid; School Support and Rural Programs; Early Learning; Sage and Healthy Students; and Academic Improvement and Teacher Quality Programs.

Education Dept., *Elementary and Secondary Education,* *Academic Improvement and Teacher Quality Programs (AITQ), 400 Maryland Ave. S.W. 20202; (202) 260-2551. Fax, (202) 260-8969. Sylvia Lyles, Director.*
Web, www2.ed.gov/about/offices/list/oese/aitq/index.html

Provides financial assistance to state and local educational agencies, community and faith-based organizations, and other entities to support activities to recruit and retain high-quality teaching staff and to strengthen the quality of elementary and secondary education. Divided into four program groups: the Academic Improvement Program, the High School Programs, the Teacher Quality Program, and Literacy Programs; implements programs providing support for reopening and rebuilding schools in areas impacted by natural disasters; implements the 21st Century Community Learning Centers, which provide academic enrichment opportunities during nonschool hours for students attending high-poverty and low-performing schools.

Education Dept., *Elementary and Secondary Education,* *Academic Improvement and Teacher Quality (AITQ),* *Early Childhood Reading Group, 9400 Maryland Ave. S.W., #3E314 20202-6132; (202) 260-2551. Fax, (202) 260-8969. Sylvia Lyles, Group Leader.*

Administers formula and discretionary grants that support family literacy programs that provide early childhood, adult literacy, and parenting education to low-income families (Even Start); enhance early childhood literacy instruction for children in the two years before kindergarten (Early Reading First); and support partnerships between institutions of higher education and other entities to improve the professional development of early childhood instructors (Early Childhood Educator Professional Development).

Education Dept., *Impact Aid, 400 Maryland Ave. S.W., #3E105 20202-6244; (202) 260-3858. Fax, (202) 205-0088. Alfred Lott, Director. Toll-free:, (866) 799-1272.*
General email, impact.aid@ed.gov
Web, www2.ed.gov/about/offices/list/oese/impactaid

Provides funds for elementary and secondary educational activities to school districts in federally impacted areas (where federal activities such as military bases enlarge staff and reduce taxable property).

Education Dept., *Office of English Language Acquisition (OELA), 400 Maryland Ave. S.W., #5E106 20202-6510; (202) 401-4300. Fax, (202) 205-1229. Libia Gil, Assistant Deputy Secretary.*
Web, www2.ed.gov/about/offices/list/oela/index.html

Provides grants for the professional development of teachers of English learners and administers the Native American/Alaska-Native Children in School Program and National Professional Development Discretionary Grant Programs. (Formerly the Office of Bilingual Education and Minority Language Affairs.)

Education Dept., *Safe and Healthy Students, 400 Maryland Ave. S.W., LBJ Bldg. 20202-6135; (202) 453-6722. Fax, (202) 205-4921. David Esquith, Director.*
General email, osdfs.safeschl@ed.gov
Web, www2.ed.gov/about/offices/list/oese/oshs

Develops policy for the department's drug and violence prevention initiatives for students in elementary and secondary schools and institutions of higher education. Provides financial assistance for drug and violence prevention activities. Coordinates education efforts in drug and violence prevention with those of other federal departments and agencies.

Environmental Protection Agency (EPA), *Pollution Prevention and Toxics (OPPT), 1200 Pennsylvania Ave. N.W., #4146, MC 7401M 20460; (202) 564-3810. Fax, (202) 564-0575. Wendy Cleland-Hamnett, Director. Toxic substance hotline, (202) 554-1404.*
Web, www.epa.gov/oppt/index.htm and www.epa.gov/aboutepa/ocspp.html

Manages programs on pollution prevention and new and existing chemicals in the marketplace such as asbestos, lead, mercury, formaldehyde, PFOAs, and PCBs. Programs include the High Production Volume Challenge Program, Sustainable Futures, the Green Chemistry Program, Green Suppliers Network, the High Production Volume Challenge Program, Design for the Environment, and the Chemical Right-to-Know Initiative.

Health and Human Services Dept. (HHS), *Head Start,* *1250 Maryland Ave. S.W., 8th Floor 20024; (202) 205-8573. Fax, (202) 205-9721. Ann M. Linehan, Director, Acting.* *Web, http://transition.acf.hhs.gov/programs/ohs*

Awards grants to nonprofit and for-profit organizations and local governments for operating community Head Start programs (comprehensive development programs for children, ages three to five, of low-income families); manages a limited number of parent and child centers for families with children up to age five. Conducts research and manages demonstration programs, including those under the Comprehensive Child Care Development Act of 1988; administers the Child Development Associate scholarship program, which trains individuals for careers in child development, often as Head Start teachers.

Health and Human Services Dept. (HHS), *President's Council on Fitness, Sports, and Nutrition, 1101 Wootton Pkwy., #560, Tower Bldg., Rockville, MD 20852; (240) 276-9567. Fax, (240) 276-9860. Shellie Pfohl, Executive Director.* *General email, fitness@hhs.gov* *Web, www.fitness.gov and www.presidentschallenge.org*

Provides schools, state and local governments, recreation agencies, and employers with information on designing and implementing physical fitness and nutrition programs; conducts award programs for children and adults and for schools, clubs, and other institutions.

National Agricultural Library *(Agriculture Dept.),* *Food and Nutrition Information Center, 10301 Baltimore Ave., #108, Beltsville, MD 20705-2351; (301) 504-5414. Fax, (301) 504-6409. Vacant, Nutrition and Food Safety Program Leader.* *General email, fnic@nal.usda.gov* *Web, http://fnic.nal.usda.gov/*

Serves as a resource center for school and child nutrition program personnel who need information on food service management and nutrition education. Library open to the public.

National Assessment Governing Board, *800 N. Capitol St. N.W., #825 20002-4233; (202) 357-6938. Fax, (202) 357-6945. Cornelia S. Orr, Executive Director. Toll-free, (877) 977-6938.* *General email, nagb@ed.gov* *Web, www.nagb.org*

Independent board of local, state, and federal officials, educators, and others appointed by the secretary of education and funded under the National Assessment of Educational Progress (NAEP) program. Sets policy for NAEP, a series of tests measuring achievements of U.S. students since 1969.

United States Presidential Scholars Program *(Education Dept.),* *400 Maryland Ave. S.W., #5E228 20202-8173; (202) 401-0961. Fax, (202) 260-7465. Simone M. Olson, Executive Director.* *General email, Presidential.Scholars@ed.gov* *Web, www2.ed.gov/programs*

Honorary recognition program that selects high school seniors of outstanding achievement in academics, community service, artistic ability, and leadership to receive the Presidential Scholars Award. Scholars travel to Washington during national recognition week to receive the award.

► **CONGRESS**

For a listing of relevant congressional committees and subcommittees, please see page 155 or the Appendix.

► **NONGOVERNMENTAL**

Achieve, Inc., *1400 16th St. N.W., #510 20036; (202) 419-1540. Fax, (202) 828-0911. Michael Cohen, President.* *Web, www.achieve.org*

Bipartisan organization that seeks to raise academic standards, improve performance assessments, and strengthen personal accountability among young people. Encourages high school graduates to pursue postsecondary education and rewarding careers. Monitors legislation and regulations.

Alliance for Excellent Education, *1201 Connecticut Ave. N.W., #901 20036; (202) 828-0828. Fax, (202) 828-0821. Bob Wise, President.* *Web, www.all4ed.org*

Policy and advocacy organization that promotes secondary education reform, with a focus on the most at-risk students. Works to increase public awareness through conferences, reports, and press releases. Monitors legislation and regulations.

American Coal Foundation, *101 Constitution Ave. N.W., #500 East 20001-2133; (202) 463-9785. Fax, (202) 463-9786. Alma Paty, Executive Director.* *General email, info@teachcoal.org* *Web, www.teachcoal.org*

Provides coal-related educational materials designed for elementary school teachers and students via the Internet at www.teachcoal.org. Web site provides free coal sample kits. Supported by coal producers and manufacturers of mining equipment and supplies.

ASCD (Assn. for Supervision and Curriculum Development), *1703 N. Beauregard St., Alexandria, VA 22311-1714; (703) 578-9600. Fax, (703) 575-5400. Gene R. Carter, Executive Director. Information, (800) 933-2723.* *General email, member@ascd.org* *Web, www.ascd.org*

Membership: approximately 140,000 professional educators internationally, including superintendents, supervisors, principals, teachers, professors of education, and school board members. Develops programs, products, and services for educators.

Assn. for Childhood Education International, *1101 16th St. N.W., #300 20036; (202) 372-9986. Fax, (202) 372-9989. Diane Whitehead, Executive Director. Information, (800) 423-3563.*

General email, headquarters@acei.org

Web, www.acei.org

Membership: educators, parents, and professionals who work with children (infancy to adolescence). Works to promote the rights, education, and well-being of children worldwide. Holds annual conference.

Center for Inspired Teaching, *1436 U St. N.W., #400 20009; (202) 462-1956. Fax, (202) 462-1905. Aleta Margolis, Executive Director.*

General email, info@inspiredteaching.org

Web, www.inspiredteaching.org

Promotes teaching skills that make the most of children's innate desire to learn. Provides professional development through course, mentoring, new teacher certification and residency programs, school partnerships, and a demonstration charter school.

Center on Education Policy, *2140 Pennsylvania Ave. N.W., #103 20037; (202) 994-9050. Fax, (202) 994-8859. Maria Voles Ferguson, Executive Director.*

General email, cep-dc@cep-dc.org

Web, www.cep-dc.org

Advocates for public education. Interests include the federal role in education and the status and effects of state high school exit examinations. Provides expert advice upon request. Works with many other education, business, state, and civic organizations. Monitors local, state, and federal legislation and regulations.

Council of the Great City Schools, *1301 Pennsylvania Ave. N.W., #702 20004-1758; (202) 393-2427. Fax, (202) 393-2400. Mike Casserly, Executive Director.*

Web, www.cgcs.org

Membership: superintendents and school board members of large urban school districts. Provides research, legislative, and support services for members; interests include elementary and secondary education and school finance.

Editorial Projects in Education, Inc., *6935 Arlington Rd., #100, Bethesda, MD 20814-5233; (301) 280-3100. Fax, (301) 280-3200. Virginia Edwards, President. Toll-free, (800) 346-1834.*

General email, gined@epe.org

Web, www.edweek.org

Promotes awareness of important issues in K–12 education among professionals and the public. Publishes books and special reports on topics of interest to educators.

National Assn. for College Admission Counseling, *1050 N. Highland St., #400, Arlington, VA 22201; (703) 836-2222. Fax, (703) 243-9375. Joyce Smith, Chief Executive Officer. Information, (800) 822-6285.*

General email, info@nacacnet.com

Web, www.nacac.net.org

Membership: high school guidance counselors, independent counselors, college and university admissions officers, and financial aid officers. Promotes and funds research on admission counseling and on the transition from high school to college. Advocates for student rights in college admissions. Sponsors national college fairs and continuing education for members.

National Assn. for the Education of Young Children, *1313 L St. N.W., #500 20005; (202) 232-8777. Fax, (202) 328-1846. Rhian Allvin, Executive Director. Information, (800) 424-2460.*

General email, naeyc@naeyc.org

Web, www.naeyc.org

Membership: early childhood teachers, administrators, college faculty, and directors of early childhood programs at the state and local levels. Works to improve the education of and the quality of services to children from birth through age eight. Sponsors professional development opportunities for early childhood educators. Offers an accreditation program and conducts two conferences annually; issues publications.

National Assn. of Elementary School Principals, *1615 Duke St., Alexandria, VA 22314; (703) 684-3345. Fax, (703) 549-5568. Gail Connelly, Executive Director. Toll-free, (800) 386-2377.*

General email, naesp@naesp.org

Web, www.naesp.org

Membership: elementary school and middle school principals. Conducts workshops for members on federal and state policies and programs and on professional development. Offers assistance in contract negotiations.

National Assn. of Secondary School Principals, *1904 Association Dr., Reston, VA 20191-1537; (703) 860-0200. Fax, (703) 476-5432. JoAnn Bartoletti, Executive Director.*

Web, www.principals.org

Membership: principals and assistant principals of middle schools and senior high schools, both public and private, and college-level teachers of secondary education. Conducts training programs for members; serves as clearinghouse for information on secondary school administration. Student activities office provides student councils, student activity advisers, and national and junior honor societies with information on national associations.

National Head Start Assn., *1651 Prince St., Alexandria, VA 22314; (703) 739-0875. Fax, (703) 739-0878. Yasmina Vinci, Executive Director; Vanessa Rich, Chair. Toll-free, (866) 677-8724.*

Web, www.nhsa.org

Membership: organizations that represent Head Start children, families, and staff. Recommends strategies on issues affecting Head Start programs; provides training and professional development opportunities. Monitors legislation and regulations.

National PTA, *1250 N. Pitt St., Alexandria, VA 22314; (703) 518-1200. Fax, (703) 836-0942. Joanne Dunne, Executive Director, Acting. Toll-free, (800) 307-4782.*

General email, info@pta.org

Web, www.pta.org

Membership: parent-teacher associations at the preschool, elementary, and secondary levels. Washington office represents members' interests on education, funding for education, parent involvement, child protection and safety, comprehensive health care for children, AIDS, the environment, children's television and educational technology, child care, and nutrition. (Formerly the National Congress of Parents and Teachers.)

National School Boards Assn., *1680 Duke St., Alexandria, VA 22314; (703) 838-6722. Fax, (703) 549-7590. Thomas Gentzel, Executive Director, (703) 838-6700; Francisco Negron, General Counsel, (703) 838-6710. General email, info@nsba.org*

Web, www.nsba.org

Federation of state school board associations. Interests include funding of public education, local governance, and quality of education programs. Sponsors seminars, an annual conference, and an information center. Publishes a monthly journal and various newsletters. Monitors legislation and regulations. Library open to the public by appointment.

Reading Is Fundamental, *1730 Rhode Island Ave. N.W., 11th Floor 20036 (mailing address: P.O. Box 33728, Washington, DC 20033); (202) 536-3400. Fax, (202) 536-3518. Carol H. Rasco, President. Information, 877-RIF-READ. Press, (202) 536-3441. General email, contactus@rif.org*

Web, www.rif.org

Conducts programs and workshops to motivate young people to read. Provides young people in low-income neighborhoods with free books and parents with services to encourage reading at home.

School Nutrition Assn., *120 Waterfront St., #300, National Harbor, MD 20745; (301) 686-3100. Fax, (301) 686-3115. Patricia Montague, Chief Executive Officer. Information, (800) 877-8822. General email, servicecenter@schoolnutrition.org*

Web, www.schoolnutrition.org

Membership: state and national food service workers and supervisors, school cafeteria managers, nutrition educators, industry members, and others interested in school food programs and child nutrition. Offers credentialing and sponsors National School Lunch Week and National School Breakfast Week. (Formerly the American School Food Service Assn.)

Teach for America, *Washington Office, 1411 K St. N.W., 12th Floor 20005; (202) 552-2400. Fax, (202) 371-9272. Matt Kramer, Co-Chief Executive Officer; Elisa Villanuera-Beard, Co-Chief Executive Officer. Information, (800) 832-1230. General email, admissions@teachforamerica.org*

Web, www.teachforamerica.org

A national teacher corps of recent college graduates who teach in underfunded urban and rural public schools. Promotes outstanding teaching methodologies

and educational equity. Monitors legislation and regulations. (Headquarters in New York.)

Private, Parochial, and Home Schooling

►AGENCIES

Education Dept., Non-Public *Education, 400 Maryland Ave. S.W., #4W341 20202-5940; (202) 401-1365. Fax, (202) 401-1368. Maureen Dowling, Director, (202) 260-7820. General email, onpee@ed.gov*

Web, www2.ed.gov/about/offices/list/oii/nonpublic/index.html

Acts as ombudsman for interests of teachers and students in non-public schools (elementary and secondary levels); reports to the secretary of education on matters relating to non-public education.

►NONGOVERNMENTAL

Americans United for Separation of Church and State, *1301 K St. N.W., #850E 20005; (202) 466-3234. Fax, (202) 466-2587. Barry W. Lynn, Executive Director. General email, americansunited@au.org*

Web, www.au.org

Citizens' interest group. Opposes federal and state aid to parochial schools; works to ensure religious neutrality in public schools; supports free religious exercise; initiates litigation; maintains speakers bureau. Monitors legislation and regulations.

Council for American Private Education, *13017 Wisteria Dr., #457, Germantown, MD 20874; (301) 916-8460. Fax, (301) 916-8485. Joe McTighe, Executive Director. General email, cape@capenet.org*

Web, www.capenet.org

Coalition of national private school associations serving private elementary and secondary schools. Acts as a liaison between private education and government, other educational organizations, the media, and the public. Seeks greater access to private schools for all families. Monitors legislation and regulations.

Home School Legal Defense Assn., *1 Patrick Henry Circle, Purcellville, VA 20132 (mailing address: P.O. Box 3000, Purcellville, VA 20134-9000); (540) 338-5600. Fax, (540) 338-2733. J. Michael Smith, President. General email, info@hslda.org*

Web, www.hslda.org

Membership: families who practice home schooling. Provides members with legal consultation and defense. Initiates civil rights litigation on behalf of members. Monitors legislation and regulations.

National Assn. of Independent Schools, *Government Relations, 1129 20th St. N.W., #800 20036; (202) 973-9700. Fax, (888) 316-3862. John Chubb, President. Press, (202) 973-9717.*

General email, info@nais.org

Web, www.nais.org

Membership: independent elementary and secondary schools in the United States and abroad. Provides statistical and educational information to members. Monitors legislation and regulations.

National Catholic Educational Assn., *1005 N. Glebe Rd., #525, Arlington, VA 22201; (571) 257-0010. Fax, (703) 243-0025. Brother Robert Bimonte, President. Toll-free, (800) 711-6232.*

General email, ncea@ncea.org

Web, www.ncea.org

Membership: Catholic schools (preschool through college and seminary) and school administrators. Provides consultation services to members for administration, curriculum, continuing education, religious education, campus ministry, boards of education, and union and personnel negotiations; conducts workshops and conferences; supports federal aid for private education. (Affiliated with the Assn. of Catholic Colleges and Universities.)

National PTA, *1250 N. Pitt St., Alexandria, VA 22314; (703) 518-1200. Fax, (703) 836-0942. Joanne Dunne, Executive Director, Acting. Toll-free, (800) 307-4782.*

General email, info@pta.org

Web, www.pta.org

Membership: parent-teacher associations at the preschool, elementary, and secondary levels. Coordinates the National Coalition for Public Education, which opposes tuition tax credits and vouchers for private education. (Formerly the National Congress of Parents and Teachers.)

U.S. Conference of Catholic Bishops (USCCB), *Secretariat of Catholic Education, 3211 4th St. N.E. 20017-1194; (202) 541-3132. Fax, (202) 541-3390. Sr. John Mary Fleming, Executive Director.*

Web, www.usccb.org/beliefs-and-teachings/how-we-teach/catholic-education/index.cfm

Represents Catholic bishops in the United States in public policy educational issues.

SPECIAL GROUPS IN EDUCATION

Gifted and Talented

▶**NONGOVERNMENTAL**

Council for Exceptional Children (CEC), *2900 Crystal Dr., #1000, Arlington, VA 22202; (703) 620-3660. Fax, (703) 264-9494. Mikki Garcia, Executive Director. Toll-free, (888) 232-7733.*

General email, service@cec.sped.org

Web, www.cec.sped.org

Membership association that advocates on behalf of children with disabilities and gifts and talents as well as special educators. Sets professional standards for the field;

publishes books, journals, newsletters, and other resources; and offers professional development for teachers and administrators, including an annual convention. Sponsors the Yes I Can! Awards for children with disabilities who excel. Monitors legislation and regulations.

National Assn. for Gifted Children, *1330 H St. N.W., #1001 20005; (202) 785-4268. Fax, (202) 785-4248. Nancy Green, Executive Director.*

General email, nagc@nagc.org

Web, www.nagc.org

Membership: teachers, administrators, state coordinators, and parents. Advocates for increased federal support for intellectually and creatively gifted children in public and private schools. Produces publications and conducts training for educators and parents.

Learning and Physically Disabled

▶**AGENCIES**

Education Dept., *National Center for Special Education Research (NCSER), 555 New Jersey Ave. N.W. 20208-5500; (202) 219-1309. Fax, (202) 219-1402. Joan McLaughlin, Commissioner, Acting.*

Web, http://ies.ed.gov/ncser

Sponsors a comprehensive program of special education research designed to expand the knowledge and understanding of infants, toddlers, and children with disabilities.

Education Dept., *Special Education and Rehabilitative Services, 550 12th St. S.W., 5th Floor 20202 (mailing address: 400 Maryland Ave. S.W., Washington, DC 20202-7000); (202) 245-6496. Fax, (202) 245-7638. Michael Yudin, Assistant Secretary, Acting.*

Web, www2.ed.gov/about/offices/list/osers

Administers federal assistance programs for the education and rehabilitation of people with disabilities through the National Institute of Disability and Rehabilitation Research, the Office of Special Education Programs, and the Rehabilitation Services Administration; maintains a national information clearinghouse for people with disabilities.

Education Dept., *Special Education and Rehabilitation Services, Special Education Programs, 550 12th St. S.W., 4th Floor 20202-3600; (202) 245-7459. Fax, (202) 245-7614. Melody Musgrove, Director.*

Web, www2.ed.gov/about/offices/list/osers/osep/about.html

Responsible for special education programs and services designed to meet the needs and develop the full potential of children from infancy through age 21. Programs include support for training of teachers and other professional personnel; grants for research; financial aid to help states initiate and improve their resources; and media services and captioned films for hearing impaired persons.

John F. Kennedy Center for the Performing Arts, *Dept. of VSA and Accessibility,* *2700 F St. N.W. 20566 (mailing address: P.O. Box 10150, Arlington, VA 22210); (202) 416-8898. Fax, (202) 416-8802. Betty Siegel, Director.*
General email, access@kennedy-center.org

Web, www.vsarts.org

Initiates and supports research and program development providing arts training and programming for persons with disabilities to make classrooms and communities more inclusive. Provides technical assistance and training to VSA Arts state organizations; acts as an information clearinghouse for arts and persons with disabilities.

Office of Personnel Management (OPM), *Veterans Services,* *1900 E St. N.W., #7439 20415; (202) 606-3602. Fax, (202) 606-6017. Hakeem Basheerud-Deen, Director.*
Web, www.opm.gov/policy-data-oversight/veterans-services

Provides outreach to colleges and universities on Schedule A hiring authorities for people with disabilities.

Smithsonian Institution, *Accessibility Program,* *14th St. and Constitution Ave. N.W., #1050, NMAH, MRC 607 20013-7012; (202) 633-2921. Fax, (202) 633-4352. Elizabeth Ziebarth, Director. Information, (888) 783-0001.*
General email, ziebarth@si.edu

Web, www.si.edu/accessibility

Coordinates the Smithsonian's efforts to improve accessibility of its programs and facilities to visitors and staff with disabilities. Serves as a resource for museums and individuals nationwide.

►CONGRESS

For a listing of relevant congressional committees and sub-committees, please see page 155 or the Appendix.

Library of Congress, *National Library Service for the Blind and Physically Handicapped,* *1291 Taylor St. N.W. 20542 (mailing address: Library of Congress, Washington, DC 20542); (202) 707-5100. Fax, (202) 707-0712. Karen Keninger, Director. Toll-free, (800) 424-8567.*
General email, nls@loc.gov

Web, www.loc.gov/nls

Administers a national program of free library services for persons with physical disabilities in cooperation with regional and subregional libraries. Produces and distributes full-length books and magazines in recorded form and in Braille. Reference section answers questions relating to blindness and physical disabilities and on library services available to persons with disabilities.

►NONGOVERNMENTAL

Assn. for Education and Rehabilitation of the Blind and Visually Impaired, *1703 N. Beauregard St., #440, Alexandria, VA 22311; (703) 671-4500. Fax, (703) 671-6391. Louis M. Tutt, Executive Director. Toll-free, (877) 492-2708.*

General email, aer@aerbvi.org

Web, www.aerbvi.org

Membership: professionals who work in all phases of education and rehabilitation of children and adults who are blind and visually impaired. Provides support and professional development opportunities through conferences, continuing education, and publications. Issues professional recognition awards and student scholarships. Monitors legislation and regulations.

Assn. of University Centers on Disabilities (AUCD), *1100 Wayne Ave., #1000, Silver Spring, MD 20910; (301) 588-8252. Fax, (301) 588-2842. Andrew J. Imparato, Executive Director.*
General email, aucdinfo@aucd.org

Web, www.aucd.org

Network of facilities that diagnose and treat the developmentally disabled. Trains graduate students and professionals in the field; helps state and local agencies develop services. Interests include interdisciplinary training and services, early screening to prevent developmental disabilities, and development of equipment and programs to serve persons with disabilities.

Council for Exceptional Children (CEC), *2900 Crystal Dr., #1000, Arlington, VA 22202; (703) 620-3660. Fax, (703) 264-9494. Mikki Garcia, Executive Director. Toll-free, (888) 232-7733.*
General email, service@cec.sped.org

Web, www.cec.sped.org

Membership association that advocates on behalf of children with disabilities and gifts and talents as well as special educators. Sets professional standards for the field; publishes books, journals, newsletters, and other resources; and offers professional development for teachers and administrators, including an annual convention. Sponsors the Yes I Can! Awards for children with disabilities who excel. Monitors legislation and regulations.

Gallaudet University, *800 Florida Ave. N.E. 20002-3695; (202) 651-5000. Fax, (202) 651-5508. T. Alan Horowitz, President, (202) 651-5005. Video phone, (202) 651-5866 (or IP address, 134.231.18.170). Toll-free, (866) 563-8896.*
Web, www.gallaudet.edu

Offers undergraduate, graduate, and doctoral degree programs for deaf, hard of hearing, and hearing students. Conducts research; maintains the Laurent Clerc National Deaf Education Center and demonstration preschool, elementary (Kendall Demonstration Elementary School), and secondary (Model Secondary School for the Deaf) programs. Sponsors the Center for Global Education, National Deaf Education Network and Clearinghouse, and the Cochlear Implant Education Center.

National Assn. of Private Special Education Centers, *601 Pennsylvania Ave. N.W., South Bldg., #900 20004; (202) 434-8225. Fax, (202) 434-8224. Sherry L. Kolbe, Executive Director.*
General email, napsec@aol.com

Web, www.napsec.org

Membership: private special education programs at the preschool, elementary, and secondary levels. Advocates for greater education opportunities for children, youth, and adults with disabilities.

National Assn. of State Directors of Special Education, *225 Reinkers Lane, #420, Alexandria, VA 22314; (703) 519-3800. Fax, (703) 519-3808. Bill East, Executive Director.*
General email, nasdse@nasdse.org
Web, www.nasdse.org

Membership: state directors of special education and others interested in special education policy. Monitors legislation, regulations, policy, and research affecting special education.

Minorities and Women

▶**AGENCIES**

Bureau of Indian Education (BIE) *(Interior Dept.),* *1849 C St. N.W., MS 3609, MIB 20240; (202) 208-6123. Fax, (202) 208-3312. Charles M. Roessel, Director.*
Web, www.bie.edu

Operates schools and promotes school improvement for Native Americans, including people with disabilities. Provides assistance to Native American pupils in public schools. Aids Native American college students. Sponsors adult education programs designed specifically for Native Americans.

Commission on Civil Rights, *Civil Rights Evaluation,* *1331 Pennsylvania Ave. N.W., #1150 20425; (202) 376-7700. Fax, (202) 376-7754. Margaret Butler, Chief, Acting.*
Web, www.usccr.gov

Researches federal policy on education, including desegregation. Library open to the public.

Education Dept., *Civil Rights,* *400 Maryland Ave. S.W. 20202-1100; (202) 453-5900. Fax, (202) 453-6012. Catherine Lhamon, Assistant Secretary, (202) 453-7240. Hotline, (800) 421-3481.*
General email, ocr@ed.gov
Web, www2.ed.gov/ocr

Enforces laws prohibiting use of federal funds for education programs or activities that discriminate on the basis of race, color, sex, national origin, age, or disability; authorized to discontinue funding.

Education Dept., *Federal TRIO Programs,* *1990 K St. N.W., 7th Floor 20006-8510; (202) 502-7600. Fax, (202) 502-7857. Linda Byrd-Johnson, Director.*
Web, www2.ed.gov/about/offices/list/ope/trio/index.html

Administers programs for low-income, potential first-generation middle school to postbaccalaureate college students, including Educational Opportunity Centers, Upward Bound, Upward Bound Math and Science, Talent Search, Student Support Services, Ronald E. McNair Post-Baccalaureate Achievement Program, TRIO training program, and Veterans Upward Bound.

Education Dept., *Indian Education Programs,* *400 Maryland Ave. S.W., #3E205 20202-6335; (202) 260-3774. Fax, (202) 260-7779. Joyce Silverthorne, Director, (202) 401-0767.*
General email, indian.education@ed.gov
Web, www2.ed.gov/about/offices/list/oese/oie/index.html

Aids local school districts with programs for Native American and Alaska Native students.

Education Dept., *Migrant Education,* *400 Maryland Ave. S.W., #3E317, LBJ 20202-6135; (202) 260-1164. Fax, (202) 205-0089. Lisa Ramirez, Director.*
Web, www2.ed.gov/programs/mep/index.html

Administers programs that fund education (preschool through postsecondary) for children of migrant workers.

Education Dept., *Office of Postsecondary Education (OPE), Higher Education Programs, Institutional Service,* *1990 K St. N.W., 6th Floor 20006; (202) 502-7510. Fax, (202) 502-7677. Leonard L. Haynes III, PhD, Director, (202) 502-7549.*
General email, OPE_Institutional_Development@ed.gov
Web, www2.ed.gov/about/offices/list/OPE/idues/index.html

Provides financial and administrative support for postsecondary programs serving minority and financially disadvantaged students. Areas include Title III programs American Indian Tribally Controlled Colleges, predominately black institutions, HBCU Capital Financing Program and Alaska Native- and Native Hawaii-serving institutions; programs serving Hispanic and other low-income students; the Robert C. Byrd Honors Scholarship Program; and programs under Part J of the College Cost Reduction and Access Act of 2007 for minority-serving institutions.

Education Dept., *Student Achievement and School Accountability,* *400 Maryland Ave. S.W. 20202-6132; (202) 260-0826. Fax, (202) 260-7764. Monique Chism, Director, (202) 260-1824.*
Web, www2.ed.gov/oese

Administers the Title I and Title III federal assistance programs for education of educationally deprived children (preschool through secondary), including homeless children, neglected children, delinquents, and residents in state institutions.

Education Dept., *White House Initiative on American Indian and Alaska Natives,* *400 Maryland Ave. S.W., #4W116 20202; (202) 453-6600. Fax, (202) 453-5635. William Mendoza, Executive Director, (202) 260-0513.*
Web, www2.ed.gov/whiaiane

Supports activities that expand and improve educational opportunities for American Indians and Alaska Native students. Interests include reducing the student dropout rate, strengthening tribal colleges and universities, and helping students acquire industry-recognized credentials for job attainment and advancement. Supports teaching native languages and histories at all educational levels.

Education Dept., *White House Initiative on Asian Americans and Pacific Islanders,* 550 12th St. S.W., 10th Floor 20202; (202) 453-7277. Fax, (202) 453-6238. Kiran Ahuja, Executive Director. Press, (202) 453-6566.
General email, http://whitehouseaapi@ed.gov

Web, www.whitehouse.gov/aapi and Twitter, @whitehouseAAPI

Works to increase Asian American and Pacific Islander participation in federal education programs. Supports institutions of higher education through two-year grants to improve academic programs, institutional management, and fiscal stability.

Education Dept., *White House Initiative on Educational Excellence for Hispanics,* 400 Maryland Ave. S.W., #4W108 20202-3601; (202) 401-1411. Fax, (202) 401-8377. Alejandra (Alex) Ceja, Executive Director, Acting.
General email, whieeh@ed.gov

Web, www2.ed.gov/edblogs/hispanic-initiative

Promotes high-quality education for Hispanic communities and the participation of Hispanics in federal education programs. Disseminates information on educational resources. Promotes parental involvement, engagement of the business community, early learning programs, and enrollment in college. Works directly with communities nationwide in public-private partnerships.

Education Dept., *White House Initiative on Historically Black Colleges and Universities,* 400 Maryland Ave. S.W., #4C120 20202; (202) 453-5634. Fax, (202) 453-5632. George Cooper, Executive Director.
General email, oswhi-hbcu@ed.gov

Web, www2.ed.gov/about/inits/list/whhbcu/edlite-index.html

Seeks to expand the participation of the black college community in the programs of the federal government and to engage the private sector to help achieve this objective. Hosts annual conference. Provides information about federal contracts, grants, scholarships, fellowships, and other resources available to historically black colleges and universities.

Justice Dept. (DOJ), *Civil Rights Division, Educational Opportunities,* 601 D St. N.W., #4300 20530; (202) 514-4092. Fax, (202) 514-8337. Anurima Bhargava, Chief. Toll-free, (877) 292-3804.
General email, education@usdoj.gov

Web, www.justice.gov/crt/about/edu

Initiates litigation to ensure equal opportunities in public education; enforces laws dealing with civil rights in public education.

► **CONGRESS**

For a listing of relevant congressional committees and subcommittees, please see page 155 or the Appendix.

► **NONGOVERNMENTAL**

American Assn. of University Women (AAUW), 1111 16th St. N.W. 20036-4873; (202) 785-7700. Fax, (202) 872-1425.

Linda D. Hallman, Executive Director. Toll-free, (800) 326-2289.
General email, connect@aauw.org

Web, www.aauw.org

Membership: graduates of accredited colleges, universities, and recognized foreign institutions. Interests include equity for women and girls in education, the workplace, health care, and the family.

American Indian Higher Education Consortium, 121 Oronoco St., Alexandria, VA 22314; (703) 838-0400, ext. 101. Fax, (703) 838-0388. Carrie L. Billy, President.
General email, info@aihec.org

Web, www.aihec.org

Membership: tribal colleges and universities (TCUs). Objectives include increased financial support for TCUs, equitable participation in the land-grant system, expanded technology programs in Indian Country, and development of an accrediting body for postsecondary institutions that serve Native Americans.

Assn. of American Colleges and Universities (AACU), 1818 R St. N.W. 20009; (202) 387-3760. Fax, (202) 265-9532. Carol Geary Schneider, President.
Web, www.aacu.org

Serves as clearinghouse for information on women professionals in higher education. Interests include women's studies, women's centers, and women's leadership and professional development.

Assn. of Public and Land-Grant Universities, *Office for Access and Success: The Advancement of Public Black Colleges and Hispanic Serving Institutions,* 1307 New York Ave. N.W., #400 20005-4722; (202) 478-6056. Fax, (202) 478-6046. John Michael Lee Jr., Vice President.
Web, www.aplu.org

Seeks to improve equity, access, and successful outcomes at all public and land-grant universities with a special focus on underserved students and minority-serving institutions. Conducts research, provides advocacy, implements programs, and provides capacity-building for such institutions; acts as a liaison between these institutions, the federal government, and private associations. Monitors legislation and regulations.

Clare Booth Luce Policy Institute, 112 Elden St., Suite P, Herndon, VA 20170; (703) 318-0730. Fax, (703) 318-8867. Michelle Easton, President. Toll-free, (888) 891-4288.
General email, info@cblpi.org

Web, www.cblpi.org

Seeks to engage young women through student programs promoting conservative values and leadership. Offers mentoring, internship, and networking opportunities for young women.

Council for Opportunity in Education, 1025 Vermont Ave. N.W., #900 20005-3516; (202) 347-7430. Fax, (202) 347-0786. Maureen Hoyler, President.
General email, beth.hogan@coenet.us

Web, www.coenet.us

Represents institutions of higher learning, administrators, counselors, teachers, and others committed to advancing equal educational opportunity in colleges and universities. Works to sustain and improve educational opportunity programs such as the federally funded TRIO programs, designed to help low-income, first-generation immigrant, physically disabled students, and veterans enroll in and graduate from college.

Hispanic Assn. of Colleges and Universities,
Washington Office, 1 Dupont Circle N.W., #430 20036; (202) 833-8361. Fax, (202) 261-5082. Antonio R. Flores, President.
General email, govrel@hacu.net
Web, www.hacu.net

Membership: Hispanic-serving institutions (HSIs) and other higher education institutions committed to improving the quality of schools for Hispanics in the United States, Puerto Rico, Latin America, and Spain. Focuses on increased federal funding for HSIs; partnerships with government agencies and industry; faculty development and research; technological assistance; and financial aid and internships for Hispanic students. (Headquarters in San Antonio, Texas.)

League of United Latin American Citizens, *1133 19th St. N.W., #1000 20036; (202) 833-6130. Fax, (202) 833-6135. Brent Wilkes, Executive Director. Toll-free, (877) LULAC-01.*
General email, info@lulac.org
Web, www.lulac.org

Seeks to increase the number of minorities, especially Hispanics, attending postsecondary schools; supports legislation to increase educational opportunities for Hispanics and other minorities; provides scholarship funds and educational and career counseling.

The Links Inc., *1200 Massachusetts Ave. N.W. 20005-4501; (202) 842-8686. Fax, (202) 842-4020.*
Margot James Copeland, President; Eris T. Sims, Executive Director.
Web, www.linksinc.org

Predominantly African American women's service organization that works with the educationally disadvantaged and culturally deprived; focuses on arts, services for youth, and national and international trends and services.

NAACP Legal Defense and Educational Fund, Inc.,
Washington Office, 1444 Eye St. N.W., 10th Floor 20005; (202) 682-1300. Fax, (202) 682-1312. Leslie M. Proll, Director.
Web, www.naacpldf.org

Civil rights litigation group that provides legal information about civil rights and advice on educational discrimination against women and minorities; monitors federal enforcement of civil rights laws. Not affiliated with the NAACP. (Headquarters in New York.)

National Alliance of Black School Educators, *310 Pennsylvania Ave. S.E. 20003; (202) 608-6310. Fax, (202) 608-6319. Bernard Hamilton, Executive Director, Acting. Toll-free, (800) 221-2654.*

Web, www.nabse.org

Seeks to increase the academic achievement of all children, in particular those of African American descent, by developing and recommending educational policy. Provides professional development, networking, advocacy, and research and development opportunities for educators and school administrators, including workshops and conferences. Disseminates new instructional and learning strategies.

National Assn. for Equal Opportunity in Higher Education (NAFEO), *209 3rd St. S.E. 20003; (202) 552-3300. Fax, (202) 552-3330. Lezli Baskerville, President.*
Web, www.nafeo.org

Membership: historically and predominantly black colleges and universities, including public, private, land-grant, two-year, four-year, graduate, and professional schools. Represents and advocates on behalf of its member institutions and the students, faculty, and alumni they serve. Operates a national research and resource center on blacks in higher education.

National Assn. for the Advancement of Colored People (NAACP), *Washington Bureau, 1156 15th St. N.W., #915 20005; (202) 463-2940. Fax, (202) 463-2953. Hilary O. Shelton, Director.*
General email, washingtonbureau@naacpnet.org
Web, www.naacp.org

Membership: persons interested in civil rights for all minorities. Works for equal opportunity for minorities in all areas, including education; seeks to ensure a high-quality, desegregated education for all through litigation and legislation. (Headquarters in Baltimore, Md.)

National Assn. of Colored Women's and Youth Clubs Inc. (NACWYC), *1601 R St. N.W. 20009-6420; (202) 667-4080. Fax, (202) 667-2574. Evelyn J. Rising, President.*
General email, erising@usw.edu
Web, www.nacwc.org

Seeks to promote education; protect and enforce civil rights; raise the standard of family living; promote interracial understanding; and enhance leadership development. Awards scholarships; conducts programs in education, social service, and philanthropy.

National Clearinghouse for English Language Acquisition (NCELA), *Language Instruction Educational Programs, 8757 Georgia Ave., #460, Silver Spring, MD 20910; (866) 347-6864. Joel Gomez, Principal Investigator.*
General email, askncela@leedmci.com
Web, www.ncela.us

Collects, analyzes, and disseminates information relating to the effective education of linguistically and culturally diverse learners in the United States. Focuses on K–12 English learners, Title III, bilingual programs, and ESL programs' accountability. Other interests include foreign language programs, Head Start, Title I, migrant education, and adult education programs. (Funded by the Department of Education.)

National Council of La Raza, *1126 16th St. N.W., #600 20036-4845; Janet Murguia, President.*
General email, comments@nclr.org

Web, www.nclr.org

Provides research, policy analysis, and advocacy on educational status and needs of Hispanics; promotes education reform benefiting Hispanics; develops and tests community-based models for helping Hispanic students succeed in school. Interests include counseling, testing, and bilingual, vocational, preschool through postsecondary, and migrant education.

National Council of Women's Organizations, *714 G St. S.E., #200 20003; (202) 293-4505. Fax, (202) 293-4507. Susan Scanlan, Chair.*
General email, ncwo@ncwo-online.org

Web, www.womensorganizations.org

Membership: local and national women's organizations. Engages in policy work and grassroots activism to address issues of concern to women, including workplace and economic equity, education and job training, affirmative action, Social Security, child care, reproductive freedom, health, and global women's equality. Monitors legislation and regulations.

National Hispanic Foundation for the Arts (NHFA), *Washington Square, 1050 Connecticut Ave. N.W., 10th Floor 20036; (202) 293-8330. Fax, (202) 772-3101. Felix Sanchez, Chair.*
General email, info@hispanicarts.org

Web, www.hispanicarts.org

Strives to increase the presence of Hispanics in the media, telecommunications, entertainment industries, and performing arts, and to increase programming for the U.S. Latino community. Provides scholarships for Hispanic students to pursue graduate study in the arts.

National Indian Education Assn. (NIEA), *1514 P St. N.W., Suite B 20005; (202) 544-7290. Fax, (202) 544-7293. Ahniwake Rose, Executive Director.*
General email, niea@niea.org

Web, www.niea.org

Represents American Indian, Alaska Native, and Native Hawaiian educators and students. Seeks to improve educational opportunities and resources for those groups nationwide while preserving their traditional cultures and values. Monitors legislation and regulations.

National Society of Black Engineers, *205 Daingerfield Rd., Alexandria, VA 22314; (703) 549-2207. Fax, (703) 683-5312. Virginia Womack, Executive Director, Acting.*
General email, info@nsbe.org

Web, www.nsbe.org

Membership: college students studying engineering. Offers academic excellence programs, scholarships, leadership training, and professional and career development opportunities. Activities include tutorial programs, group study sessions, high school/junior high outreach programs, technical seminars and workshops, career fairs, and an annual convention.

National Women's Law Center, *11 Dupont Circle N.W., #800 20036; (202) 588-5180. Fax, (202) 588-5185. Nancy Duff Campbell, Co-President; Marcia D. Greenberger, Co-President.*
General email, info@nwlc.org

Web, www.nwlc.org

Works to protect and advance the rights of women and girls at work, in school, and beyond. Maintains programs that focus on enforcing Title IX's provisions for equal treatment in education and narrowing the gender gap in athletics and the technology-oriented workplace. Other interests include equal pay and benefits, sexual harassment laws, the right to family leave, child care and early learning, poverty and income support, and the preservation of diversity in the workplace.

UNCF (United Negro College Fund), *1805 7th St. N.W. 20001 (mailing address: P.O. Box 10444, Fairfax, VA 22031-0444); (202) 810-0200. Fax, (703) 205-3575. Michael L. Lomax, President. Toll-free, (800) 331-2244.*
Web, www.uncf.org

Membership: private colleges and universities with historically black enrollment. Raises money for member institutions; monitors legislation and regulations.

Younger Women's Task Force, *1111 16th St. N.W. 20036; (202) 785-7700. Fax, (202) 833-1112. LaToya Millet, Executive Director, (202) 785-7713. Toll-free, (800) 326-2289.*
General email, ywtf@aauw.org

Web, www.ywtf.org

Grassroots organization that encourages young women to engage in political activism on issues directly affecting them. Provides leadership training and a local and national network for peer mentoring; runs financial literacy programs. (Sponsored by the American Assn. of University Women.)

SPECIAL TOPICS IN EDUCATION

Bilingual and Multicultural

▶**AGENCIES**

Education Dept., *Office of English Language Acquisition (OELA), 400 Maryland Ave. S.W., #5E106 20202-6510; (202) 401-4300. Fax, (202) 205-1229. Libia Gil, Assistant Deputy Secretary.*
Web, www2.ed.gov/about/offices/list/oela/index.html

Provides grants for the professional development of teachers of English learners and administers the Native American/Alaska-Native Children in School Program and National Professional Development Discretionary Grant Programs. (Formerly the Office of Bilingual Education and Minority Language Affairs.)

Education Dept., *Office of Postsecondary Education (OPE), International and Foreign Language Education (IFLE), 1990 K St. N.W., 6th Floor 20006; (202) 502-7514.*

Lenore Yaffee Garcia, Senior Director, Acting, (202) 502-7576.

Web, www2.ed.gov/about/offices/list/ope/iegps/index.html

Advises the Assistant Secretary for Postsecondary Education on matters affecting postsecondary, international, and foreign language education. Responsible for encouraging and promoting the study of foreign languages and cultures of other countries at the elementary, secondary, and postsecondary levels in the United States. Administers programs that increase expertise in foreign languages and area or international studies, and coordinates with related international and foreign language education programs of other federal agencies.

▶**NONGOVERNMENTAL**

National Assn. for Bilingual Education, *8701 Georgia Ave., #700, Silver Spring, MD 20910; (240) 450-3700. Fax, (240) 450-3799. Eudes Budhai, President.*

General email, nabe@nabe.org

Web, www.nabe.org

Membership: educators, policymakers, paraprofessionals, parents, personnel, students, and researchers. Works to strengthen educational programs for non-English-speaking students and to promote foreign language education among American students. Conducts annual conference and workshops; publishes research.

Teachers of English to Speakers of Other Languages Inc. (TESOL), *1925 Ballenger Ave., #550, Alexandria, VA 22314-6820; (703) 836-0774. Fax, (703) 836-7864. Rosa Aronson, Executive Director. Information, (888) 547-3369.*

General email, info@tesol.org

Web, www.tesol.org

Provides professional development programs and career services for teachers of English to speakers of other languages. Sponsors professional development programs and provides career management services.

World Learning, *International Exchange Programs, 1015 15th St. N.W., 7th Floor 20005-2065; (202) 408-5420. Fax, (202) 408-5397. Carol Jenkins, Senior Vice President, International Development and Exchange Programs, (202) 464-6643. Toll-free, (800) 858-0292.*

General email, carol.jenkins@worldlearning.org

Web, www.worldlearning.org

Partners with government agencies, educational institutions, and communities to remove barriers to education and improve educational quality. Works with universities and training institutions to design and deliver higher- and vocational education programs. Provides training for English language teachers and other education professionals. Increases access to and the quality of basic education. Administered by World Learning's Division of International Development and Exchange Programs. Administers field-based study abroad programs, which offer semester and summer programs for high school, college, and graduate students.

Citizenship Education

▶**NONGOVERNMENTAL**

American Press Institute (API), *4401 Wilson Blvd., #900, Arlington, VA 22203; (571) 366-1200. Fax, (703) 620-5814. Thomas (Tom) Rosenstiel, Executive Director, (571) 366-1035.*

General email, info@americanpressinstitute.org

Web, www.americanpressinstitute.org

Supports student programs that focus on newspaper readership and an appreciation of the First Amendment as ways of developing engaged and literate citizens.

Close Up Foundation, *1330 Braddock Pl., #400, Alexandria, VA 22314-1952; (703) 706-3300. Fax, (703) 706-0001. Timothy S. Davis, President. Toll-free, (800) 256-7387.*

General email, info@closeup.org

Web, www.closeup.org

Sponsors week-long programs on American government in Washington, D.C., for middle and high school students.

Horatio Alger Assn. of Distinguished Americans, *99 Canal Center Plaza, #320, Alexandria, VA 22314; (703) 684-9444. Fax, (703) 548-3822. Terrence J. Giroux, Executive Director.*

General email, association@horatioalger.org

Web, www.horatioalger.org

Educates young people about the economic and personal opportunities available in the American free enterprise system. Conducts seminars on careers in public and community service; operates internship program. Presents the Horatio Alger Youth Award to outstanding high school students and the Horatio Alger Award to professionals who have overcome adversity to achieve success in their respective fields. Awards college scholarships to individuals who have overcome adversity.

League of Women Voters Education Fund (LWV), *1730 M St. N.W., #1000 20036; (202) 429-1965. Fax, (202) 429-4343. Nancy E. Tate, Executive Director.*

General email, lwv@lwv.org

Web, www.lwv.org/education-fund

Education and research organization established by the League of Women Voters of the United States. Promotes citizen knowledge of and involvement in representative government; conducts citizen education on current public policy issues; seeks to increase voter registration and turnout; sponsors candidate forums and debates.

National 4-H Council, *7100 Connecticut Ave., Chevy Chase, MD 20815-4999; (301) 961-2800. Fax, (301) 961-2894. Jennifer L. Sirangelo, President, (301) 961-2820. Press, (301) 961-2972.*

Web, www.4-h.org

4-H membership: young people across America learning leadership, citizenship, and life skills. National 4-H Council strengthens and complements the 4-H youth development program of the U.S. Dept. of Agriculture's cooperative extension system of state land-grant universities. Interests include 4-H afterschool; healthy lifestyle; science, engineering, and technology; food security, and citizenship in governance.

Washington Workshops Foundation, *1250 24th St. N.W., #300 20037; (202) 965-3434. Fax, (202) 965-1018. Tom Crossan, Executive Director. Information, (800) 368-5688.*
General email, info@workshops.org
Web, www.workshops.org

Educational foundation that provides introductory seminars on American government and politics to junior and senior high school students, including the congressional seminars for high school students.

Consumer Education

▶**AGENCIES**

Agriculture Dept. (USDA), *Research, Education, and Economics, 1400 Independence Ave. S.W., #214W, MS 0110 20250-0110; (202) 720-5923. Fax, (202) 690-2842. Catherine E. Woteki, Under Secretary.*
Web, www.ree.usda.gov

Coordinates agricultural research, extension, and teaching programs in the food and agricultural sciences, including human nutrition, home economics, consumer services, agricultural economics, environmental quality, natural and renewable resources, forestry and range management, animal and plant production and protection, aquaculture, and the production, distribution, and utilization of food and agricultural products. Oversees the National Institute of Food and Agriculture.

Consumer Product Safety Commission (CPSC), *Public Affairs, 4330 East-West Hwy., #519C, Bethesda, MD 20814-4408; (301) 504-7051. Fax, (301) 504-0862. Scott J. Wolfson, Director, (301) 504-7051. Product safety hotline, (800) 638-2772.*
General email, info@cpsc.gov
Web, www.cpsc.gov

Provides information concerning consumer product safety; works with local and state governments, school systems, and private groups to develop product safety information and education programs. Toll-free hotline accepts consumer complaints on hazardous products and injuries associated with a product and offers recorded information on product recalls and CPSC safety recommendations.

Federal Trade Commission (FTC), *Consumer Protection, Consumer and Business Education, 600 Pennsylvania Ave. N.W. 20580; (202) 326-3650. Fax, (202) 326-3574. Carolyn Shanoff, Associate Director. Consumer Response Center, (877) FTC-HELP.*
Web, www.business.ftc.gov

Develops educational material about FTC activities in order to inform consumers about their rights and to alert businesses about their compliance responsibilities.

Food and Drug Administration (FDA) *(Health and Human Services Dept.), External Affairs, 10903 New Hampshire Ave., #5322, Silver Spring, MD 20993; (301) 796-8641. Fax, (301) 827-8030. Patricia Kuntze, Senior Advisor for Consumer Affairs; Steven Immergut, Associate Commissioner, Acting. Consumer inquiries, (888) 463-6332.*
General email, patricia.kuntze@fda.hhs.gov
Web, www.fda.gov

Responds to inquiries on issues related to the FDA. Conducts consumer health education programs for specific groups, including women, older adults, and the educationally and economically disadvantaged. Serves as liaison with national health and consumer organizations.

Food Safety and Inspection Service *(Agriculture Dept.), 1400 Independence Ave. S.W., #331E 20250-3700; (202) 720-7025. Fax, (202) 690-0550. Alfred (Al) Amanza, Administrator. Press, (202) 720-9113. Consumer inquiries, (800) 535-4555.*
Web, www.usda.gov/fsis

Sponsors food safety educational programs to inform the public about measures to prevent foodborne illnesses; sponsors lectures, publications, and public service advertising campaigns. Toll-free hotline answers food safety questions.

▶**NONGOVERNMENTAL**

American Assn. of Family and Consumer Sciences, *400 N. Columbus St., #202, Alexandria, VA 22314; (703) 706-4600. Fax, (703) 706-4663. Carolyn W. Jackson, Executive Director. Toll-free, (800) 424-8080.*
General email, staff@aafcs.org
Web, www.aafcs.org

Membership: professional home economists. Supports family and consumer sciences education; develops accrediting standards for undergraduate family and consumer science programs; trains and certifies family and consumer science professionals. Monitors legislation and regulations concerning family and consumer issues.

Family, Career, and Community Leaders of America, *1910 Association Dr., Reston, VA 20191-1584; (703) 476-4900. Fax, (703) 860-2713. Sandy Spavone, Executive Director. Toll-free, (800) 234-4425.*
General email, natlhdqtrs@fcclainc.org
Web, www.fcclainc.org

National vocational student organization that helps young men and women address personal, family, work, and social issues through family and consumer sciences education.

Literacy, Basic Skills

▶**AGENCIES**

AmeriCorps *(Corporation for National and Community Service), Volunteers in Service to America (VISTA), 1201 New York Ave. N.W. 20525; (202) 606-5000. Fax, (202)*

565-2789. *Mary Strasser, Director, (202) 606-6943.*
Volunteer recruiting information, (800) 942-2677. TTY,
(800) 833-3722.
General email, questions@americorps.gov
Web, www.americorps.gov/programs/americorps/
americorps-vista

Assigns volunteers to local and state education departments, to public agencies, and to private nonprofit organizations that have literacy programs. Other activities include tutor recruitment and training and the organization and expansion of local literacy councils, workplace literacy programs, and intergenerational literacy programs.

Education Dept., *Office of Vocational and Adult*
Education (OVAE), Adult Education and Literacy, 550
12th St. S.W., 11th Floor 20202-7100 (mailing address: 400
Maryland Ave. S.W., P-OVAE, DAEL, Washington, DC
20202); (202) 245-7700. Fax, (202) 245-7838.
Cheryl L. Keenan, Director.
Web, www2.ed.gov/about/offices/list/ovae/pi/AdultEd/
index.html

Provides state and local education agencies and the general public with information on establishing, expanding, improving, and operating adult education and literacy programs. Emphasizes basic and life skills attainment, English literacy, and high school completion. Awards grants to state education agencies for adult education and literacy programs, including workplace and family literacy.

▶**CONGRESS**

For a listing of relevant congressional committees and subcommittees, please see page 155 or the Appendix.

Library of Congress, *Center for the Book, 101*
Independence Ave. S.E., #LM 650 20540; (202) 707-5221.
Fax, (202) 707-0269. John Y. Cole, Director.
General email, cfbook@loc.gov
Web, www.read.gov/cfb

Promotes family and adult literacy; encourages the study of books and stimulates public interest in books, reading, and libraries; sponsors publication of a directory describing national organizations that administer literacy programs. Affiliated state centers sponsor projects and hold events that call attention to the importance of literacy.

▶**NONGOVERNMENTAL**

AFL-CIO Working for America Institute, *815 16th St.*
N.W. 20006; (202) 508-3717. Fax, (202) 508-3719.
Jeff Rickert, Deputy Director, (202) 508-3725. Office Manager, (202) 637-5251.
General email, info@workingforamerica.org
Web, www.workingforamerica.org

Provides labor unions, employers, education agencies, and community groups with technical assistance for workplace education programs focusing on adult literacy, basic skills, and job training. Interests include new technologies and workplace innovations.

American Society for Training and Development
(ASTD), *1640 King St., 3rd Floor, Box 1443, Alexandria, VA*
22313-2043; (703) 683-8100. Fax, (703) 683-1523.
Tony Bingham, Chief Executive Officer.
General email, customercare@astd.org
Web, www.astd.org

Membership: trainers and human resource development specialists. Publishes information on workplace literacy.

Center for Applied Linguistics, *4646 40th St. N.W., #200*
20016-1859; (202) 362-0700. Fax, (202) 362-3740.
Terrence Wiley, President.
General email, info@cal.org
Web, www.cal.org

Research and technical assistance organization that serves as a clearinghouse on application of linguistics to practical language problems. Interests include English as a second language (ESL), teacher training and material development, language education, language proficiency test development, bilingual education, and sociolinguistics.

First Book, *1319 F St. N.W., #1000 20004-1155; (202) 393-*
1222. Fax, (202) 628-1258. Kyle Zimmer, President.
Toll-free, (866) 732-3669.
General email, staff@firstbook.org
Web, www.firstbook.org

Donates and sells books to programs serving children of low-income families. Organizes fundraisers to support and promote literacy programs.

General Federation of Women's Clubs, *1734 N St. N.W.*
20036-2990; (202) 347-3168. Fax, (202) 835-0246.
Michele Mount, Executive Director, Interim. Toll-free,
(800) 443-4392.
General email, gfwc@gfwc.org
Web, www.gfwc.org

Nondenominational, nonpartisan international organization of women volunteers. Develops literacy projects in response to community needs; sponsors tutoring.

National Coalition for Literacy, *P.O. Box 2932 20013-*
2932; (484) 443-8457. Marty Finsterbusch, Chair.
General email, ncl@ncladvocacy.org
Web, www.national-coalition-literacy.org

Members: national organizations concerned with adult education. Promotes adult education, family literacy, and English language acquisition in the United States.

Reading Is Fundamental, *1730 Rhode Island Ave. N.W.,*
11th Floor 20036 (mailing address: P.O. Box 33728,
Washington, DC 20033); (202) 536-3400. Fax, (202) 536-
3518. Carol H. Rasco, President. Information, 877-RIF-
READ. Press, (202) 536-3441.
General email, contactus@rif.org
Web, www.rif.org

Conducts programs and workshops to motivate young people to read. Provides young people in low-income neighborhoods with free books and parents with services to encourage reading at home.

Science and Mathematics Education

►AGENCIES

Education Dept., *Office of Postsecondary Education (OPE), Institutional Service: Minority Science and Engineering Improvement,* 1990 K St. N.W., 6th Floor 20006-8512; (202) 502-7520. Fax, (202) 502-7861. *John Clement, Director, Acting.*
General email, OPE.MSEIP@ed.gov
Web, www2.ed.gov/programs/iduesmsi/index.html

Provides grants to effect long-range improvement in science and engineering education at predominantly minority institutions and to increase the flow of underrepresented ethnic minorities, particularly minority women, into science and engineering careers.

National Aeronautics and Space Administration (NASA), *Education,* 300 E St. S.W., #5G15 20546; (202) 358-0103. Fax, (202) 358-7097. *Roosevelt Johnson, Associate Administrator, Acting.*
General email, education@nasa.gov
Web, http://education.nasa.gov

Coordinates NASA's education programs and activities to meet national educational needs and ensure a sufficient talent pool to preserve U.S. leadership in aeronautical technology and space science.

National Institute of Biomedical Imaging and Bioengineering *(National Institutes of Health),* 9000 Rockville Pike, Bldg. 31, #1C14, Bethesda, MD 20892; (301) 496-8859. Fax, (301) 480-0679. *Dr. Roderic I. Pettigrew, Director. Public Liaison,* (301) 402-1374.
General email, info@nibib.nih.gov
Web, www.nibib.nih.gov

Offers multidisciplinary training programs for scientists and engineers at all stages of their careers in bioimaging and bioengineering.

National Oceanic and Atmospheric Administration (NOAA) *(Commerce Dept.),* *National Sea Grant College Program,* 1315 East-West Hwy., SSMC-3, 11th Floor, Silver Spring, MD 20910; (301) 734-1066. Fax, (301) 713-1031. *Leon M. Cammen, Director.*
General email, oar.hq.sg@noaa.gov
Web, www.seagrant.noaa.gov

Provides grants, primarily to colleges and universities, for marine resource development; sponsors undergraduate and graduate education and the training of technicians at the college level.

National Science Foundation (NSF), *Education and Human Resources,* 4201 Wilson Blvd., #805N, Arlington, VA 22230; (703) 292-8600. Fax, (703) 292-9179. *Joan E. Ferrini-Mundy, Assistant Director.*
Web, www.nsf.gov/div/index.jsp?org=ehr

Develops and supports programs to strengthen science and mathematics education. Provides fellowships and grants for graduate research and teacher education, instructional materials, and studies on the quality of existing science and mathematics programs. Participates in international studies.

National Science Foundation (NSF), *National Center for Science and Engineering Statistics,* 4201 Wilson Blvd., #965S, Arlington, VA 22230; (703) 292-8780. Fax, (703) 292-9092. *John R. Gawalt, Director*(703) 292-7776.
Web, www.nsf.gov/statistics

Develops and analyzes U.S. and international statistics on training, use, and characteristics of scientists, engineers, and technicians.

Office of Science and Technology Policy (OSTP) *(Executive Office of the President),* *Science,* Eisenhower Executive Office Bldg., 1650 Pennsylvania Ave. N.W. 20504; (202) 456-4444. Fax, (202) 456-6027. *Vacant, Associate Director; Philip Rubin, Principal Assistant Director for Science.*
General email, info@ostp.gov
Web, www.ostp.gov

Advises the president and others within the EOP on the impact of science and technology on domestic and international affairs; coordinates executive office and federal agency actions related to these issues. Evaluates the effectiveness of science education programs, which include environment; life sciences; physical sciences and engineering; and social, behavioral, and educational sciences. Provides technical support to Homeland Security Dept.

►NONGOVERNMENTAL

American Assn. for the Advancement of Science (AAAS), *Education and Human Resources Programs,* 1200 New York Ave. N.W. 20005; (202) 326-6680. Fax, (202) 682-1630. *Shirley M. Malcom, Head,* (202) 326-6720.
General email, ehr@aaas.org
Web, www.aaas.org/program/education-and-human-resources

Membership: scientists, scientific organizations, and others interested in science and technology education. Works to increase and provide information on the status of women, minorities, and people with disabilities in the sciences and in engineering; focuses on expanding science education opportunities for women, minorities, and people with disabilities.

American Assn. of Physics Teachers, 1 Physics Ellipse, College Park, MD 20740-3845; (301) 209-3311. Fax, (301) 209-0845. *Beth Cunningham, Executive Officer,* (301) 209-3310.
General email, eo@aapt.org
Web, www.aapt.org

Membership: physics teachers and others interested in physics education. Seeks to advance the institutional and cultural role of physics education. Sponsors seminars and conferences; provides educational information and materials. (Affiliated with the American Institute of Physics.)

American Society for Engineering Education, *1818 N St. N.W., #600 20036-2479; (202) 331-3500. Fax, (202) 265-8504. Norman L. Fortenberry, Executive Director. Press, (202) 331-3537.*
Web, www.asee.org

Membership: engineering faculty and administrators, professional engineers, and government agencies; engineering colleges, corporations, and professional societies. Conducts research, conferences, and workshops on engineering education. Monitors legislation and regulations.

Assn. of Science-Technology Centers, *818 Connecticut Ave. N.W., 7th Floor 20006-2734; (202) 783-7200. Fax, (202) 783-7207. Anthony F. Rock, Executive Director.*
General email, info@astc.org
Web, www.astc.org

Membership: more than 600 science centers, science museums, and similar operations in forty-seven countries. Strives to enhance the ability of its members to engage visitors in science activities and explorations of scientific phenomena. Sponsors conferences and informational exchanges on interactive exhibits, hands-on science experiences, and educational programs for children, families, teachers, and older audiences; publishes journal; compiles statistics; provides technical assistance for museums; speaks for science centers before Congress and federal agencies.

Challenger Center for Space Science Education, *422 1st St. S.E., 3rd Floor 20003; (202) 827-1580. Fax, (202) 827-0031. Lance Bush, President. Toll-free, (800) 969-5747.*
General email, info@challenger.org
Web, www.challenger.org

Educational organization designed to stimulate interest in science, math, and technology among middle school and elementary school students. Students participate in interactive mission simulations that require training and classroom preparation. Sponsors Challenger Learning Centers across the United States, Canada, the United Kingdom, and Korea.

Entomological Society of America, *3 Park Pl., #307, Annapolis, MD 21401-3722; (301) 731-4535. Fax, (301) 731-4538. C. David Gammel, Executive Director.*
General email, esa@entsoc.org
Web, www.entsoc.org

Scientific association that promotes the science of entomology and the interests of professionals in the field, with branches throughout the United States. Advises on crop protection, food chain, and individual and urban health matters dealing with insect pests.

Mathematical Assn. of America, *1529 18th St. N.W. 20036-1358; (202) 387-5200. Fax, (202) 265-2384. Michael Pearson, Executive Director. Information, (800) 741-9415.*

General email, maahq@maa.org
Web, www.maa.org

Membership: mathematics professors and individuals worldwide with a professional interest in mathematics. Seeks to improve the teaching of collegiate mathematics. Conducts professional development programs.

National Assn. of Biology Teachers, *12100 Sunset Hills Rd., #130, Reston, VA 20190; (703) 264-9696. Fax, (703) 435-4390. Jaclyn Reeves-Pepin, Executive Director. Information, (888) 501-6228.*
General email, office@nabt.org
Web, www.nabt.org

Membership: biology teachers and others interested in life sciences education at the elementary, secondary, and collegiate levels. Provides professional development opportunities through its publication program, summer workshops, conventions, and national award programs. Interests include teaching standards, science curriculum, and issues affecting biology and life sciences education.

National Council of Teachers of Mathematics, *1906 Association Dr., Reston, VA 20191-1502; (703) 620-9840. Fax, (703) 476-2970. Robert M. Doucette, Executive Director. Toll-free, (800) 235-7566.*
General email, nctm@nctm.org
Web, www.nctm.org

Membership: teachers of mathematics in elementary and secondary schools and two-year colleges; university teacher education faculty; students; and other interested persons. Works for the improvement of classroom instruction at all levels. Serves as forum and information clearinghouse on issues related to mathematics education. Offers educational materials and conferences. Monitors legislation and regulations.

National Geographic Society, *1145 17th St. N.W. 20036-4688; (202) 857-7000. Fax, (202) 775-6141. John M. Fahey, President. Information, (800) 647-5463. Library, (202) 857-7783. Press, (202) 857-7027.*
Web, www.nationalgeographic.com

Educational and scientific organization. Publishes *National Geographic, National Geographic Adventure, National Geographic Traveler, National Geographic Kids,* and *National Geographic Little Kids* magazines; produces maps, books, and films; maintains a museum; offers film-lecture series; produces television specials and the National Geographic Channel. Library open to the public.

National Science Teachers Assn., *1840 Wilson Blvd., Arlington, VA 22201-3000; (703) 243-7100. Fax, (703) 243-7177. David L. Evans, Executive Director.*
Web, www.nsta.org

Membership: science teachers from elementary through college levels. Seeks to improve science education; provides forum for exchange of information. Monitors legislation and regulations.

Smithsonian Science Education Center, *901 D St. S.W., #704-B 20024; (202) 633-2972. Fax, (202) 287-7309. Thomas A. Emrick, Executive Director, (202) 633-2966.*

General email, ssecinfo@si.edu

Web, www.nsrconline.org; bakern@si.edu

Works to establish effective science programs for all students. Disseminates research information; develops curriculum materials; seeks to increase public support for change of science education through the development of strategic partnerships. (Formerly National Science Resources Center.)

Society for Science & the Public, *1719 N Street, N.W. 20036; (202) 785-2255. Fax, (202) 785-3751. Rick Bates, Chief Executive Officer, Interim.*

Web, www.societyforscience.org/

Promotes understanding and appreciation of science and the role it plays in human advancement. Sponsors science competitions and other science education programs in schools; awards scholarships. Publishes *Science News* and *Science News for Kids.* Provides funds and training to select U.S. science and math teachers who serve under-resourced students.

World Future Society, *7910 Woodmont Ave., #450, Bethesda, MD 20814; (301) 656-8274. Fax, (301) 951-0394. Timothy C. Mack, President. Toll-free, (800) 989-8279. General email, info@wfs.org*

Web, www.wfs.org

Scientific and educational organization interested in future social and technological developments on a global scale. Publishes books, a magazine, and a journal.

Vocational and Adult

▶AGENCIES

Education Dept., *Office of Vocational and Adult Education (OVAE), 550 12th St. S.W., 11th Floor 20202-7100 (mailing address: 400 Maryland Ave. S.W., P-OVAE, Washington, DC 20202-7100); (202) 245-7700. Fax, (202) 245-7838. Brenda Dann-Messier, Assistant Secretary, (202) 245-7898.*

General email, ovae@ed.gov

Web, www2.ed.gov/ovae

Administers programs pertaining to adult education and literacy, career and technical education, and community colleges.

Education Dept., *Office of Vocational and Adult Education (OVAE), Academic and Technical Education, 550 12th St. S.W., #11059 20202-7100 (mailing address: 400 Maryland Ave. S.W., P-OVAE, DATE, Washington, DC 20202-7100); (202) 245-7700. Fax, (202) 245-7838. Sharon Miller, Director.*

Web, www2.ed.gov/about/offices/list/ovae/pi/cte/index .html

Establishes national initiatives that help states implement career and technical education programs. Administers state formula and discretionary grant programs under the Carl D. Perkins Career and Technical Education Act.

▶NONGOVERNMENTAL

ACCET-Accrediting Council for Continuing Education and Training, *1722 N St. N.W. 20036; (202) 955-1113. Fax, (202) 955-1118. William B. Larkin, Executive Director. General email, info@accet.org*

Web, www.accet.org

Peer-reviewed accrediting agency for noncollegiate continuing education and training institutions. Seeks to identify, evaluate, and enhance the delivery of continuing education and training programs. Offers professional development through workshops, conferences, and Webinars.

Accrediting Commission of Career Schools and Colleges, *2101 Wilson Blvd., #302, Arlington, VA 22201; (703) 247-4212. Fax, (703) 247-4533. Michale S. McComis, Executive Director.*

General email, info@accsc.org

Web, www.accsc.org

Serves as the national accrediting agency for private postsecondary institutions offering occupational and vocational programs. Sponsors workshops and meetings on academic excellence and ethical practices in career education.

American Assn. for Adult and Continuing Education (AAACE), *10111 Martin Luther King Jr. Hwy., #200C, Bowie, MD 20720; (301) 459-6261. Fax, (301) 459-6241. Cle Anderson, Association Manager.*

General email, office@aaace.org

Web, www.aaace.org

Membership: adult and continuing education professionals. Acts as an information clearinghouse; evaluates adult and continuing education programs; sponsors conferences, seminars, and workshops.

Assn. for Career and Technical Education (ACTE), *1410 King St., Alexandria, VA 22314; (703) 683-3111. Fax, (703) 683-7424. LeAnn Wilson, Executive Director. Information, (800) 826-9972.*

General email, acte@acteonline.org

Web, www.acteonline.org

Membership: teachers, students, supervisors, administrators, and others working or interested in career and technical education (middle school through postgraduate). Interests include the impact of high school graduation requirements on career and technical education; private sector initiatives; and the improvement of the quality and image of career and technical education. Offers an annual convention and other professional development opportunities. Monitors legislation and regulations.

Assn. of Private Sector Colleges and Universities, *1101 Connecticut Ave. N.W., #900 20036; (202) 336-6700. Fax, (202) 336-6828. Steve Gunderson, President. General email, cca@career.org*

Web, www.career.org

Acts as an information clearinghouse on trade and technical schools. (Formerly Career College Assn.)

Distance Education and Training Council (DETC), *1601 18th St. N.W., #2 20009; (202) 234-5100. Fax, (202) 332-1386. Leah K. Matthews, Executive Director.*
General email, info@detc.org
Web, www.detc.org

Membership: accredited distance education and online schools. Accredits distance education and online institutions, many of which offer vocational training.

International Assn. for Continuing Education and Training (IACET), *1760 Old Meadow Rd., #500, McLean, VA 22102; (703) 506-3275. Fax, (703) 506-3266. Sara Meier, Executive Director.*
General email, iacet@iacet.org
Web, www.iacet.org

Membership: education and training organizations and individuals who use the Continuing Education Unit. (The C.E.U. is defined as ten contact hours of participation in an organized continuing education program that is non-credit.) Authorizes organizations that issue the C.E.U.; develops criteria and guidelines for use of the C.E.U.

International Technology and Engineering Educators Assn., *1914 Association Dr., #201, Reston, VA 20191-1539; (703) 860-2100. Fax, (703) 860-0353. Steven A. Barbato, Executive Director.*
General email, iteea@iteea.org
Web, www.iteea.org

Membership: technology education teachers, supervisors, teacher educators, and individuals studying to be technology education teachers (elementary school through university level). Technology education includes the curriculum areas of manufacturing, construction, communications, transportation, robotics, energy, design, and engineering.

National Assn. of State Directors of Career Technical Education Consortium, *8484 Georgia Ave., #320, Silver Spring, MD 20910; (301) 588-9630. Fax, (301) 588-9631. Kimberly A. Green, Executive Director.*
General email, info@careertech.org
Web, www.careertech.org

Membership: state career education agency heads, senior staff, and business, labor, and other education officials. Advocates state and national policy to strengthen career technical education and workforce development. Monitors legislation and regulations.

SkillsUSA, *14001 SkillsUSA Way, Leesburg, VA 20176; (703) 777-8810. Fax, (703) 777-8999. Timothy W. Lawrence, Executive Director, ext. 601. Web, www.skillsusa.org*

Membership: students, teachers, and administrators of trade, industrial, technical, and health occupations programs at public high schools, vocational schools, and two-year and four-year colleges. Promotes strong work skills, workplace ethics, understanding of free enterprise, and lifelong education. (Formerly Vocational Industrial Clubs of America.)

University Professional & Continuing Education Assn. (UPCEA), *1 Dupont Circle N.W., #615 20036; (202) 659-3130. Fax, (202) 785-0374. Robert J. Hansen, Executive Director.*
Web, www.upcea.edu

Membership: higher education institutions and non-profit organizations involved in postsecondary continuing education. Prepares statistical analyses and produces data reports for members; recognizes accomplishments in the field. Monitors legislation and regulations.

6 Employment and Labor

GENERAL POLICY AND ANALYSIS

Basic Resources

▶ AGENCIES

Labor Dept. (DOL), *200 Constitution Ave. N.W. 20210;* (202) 693-6000. Fax, (202) 693-6111. Thomas E. Perez, Secretary; M. Patricia Smith, Deputy Secretary, Acting. Library, (202) 693-6600. Toll-free, (866) 487-2365.
Web, www.dol.gov

Promotes and develops the welfare of U.S. wage earners; administers federal labor laws; acts as principal adviser to the president on policies relating to wage earners, working conditions, and employment opportunities. Library open to the public, 8:15 a.m.–4:45 p.m.

Labor Dept. (DOL), *Administrative Law Judges, 800 K St. N.W., #400N 20001-8002; (202) 693-7300. Fax, (202) 693-7365. Stephen L. Purcell, Chief Administrative Law Judge, (202) 693-7542; Yvonne Washington, Chief Docket Clerk.*
General email, OALJ-Questions@dol.gov
Web, www.oalj.dol.gov

Presides over formal hearings to determine violations of minimum wage requirements, overtime payments, compensation benefits, employee discrimination, grant performance, alien certification, employee protection, the Sarbanes-Oxley Act, and health and safety regulations set forth under numerous statutes, executive orders, and regulations. With few exceptions, hearings are required to be conducted in accordance with the Administrative Procedure Act.

Labor Dept. (DOL), *Administrative Review Board, 200 Constitution Ave. N.W., #S-5220 20210; (202) 693-6200. Fax, (202) 693-6220. Paul M. Igasaki, Chair, (202) 693-6222.*
Web, www.dol.gov/arb

Issues final decisions for the secretary of labor on appeals from decisions of the administrator of the Wage and Hour Division and the Office of Administrative Law Judges under a broad range of federal labor laws, including nuclear, environmental, safety and security, financial, and transportation whistle-blower protection provisions; contract compliance laws; child labor laws; immigration laws; migrant and seasonal agricultural worker protection laws; the McNamara O'Hara Service Contract Act; and the Davis-Bacon Act.

Office of Personnel Management (OPM), *Agency and Veterans Support, Work/Life Wellness, 1900 E St. N.W., #7456 20415-2000; (202) 606-0416. Ingrid Buford, Manager, Acting.*
General email, worklife@opm.gov
Web, www.opm.gov/employment_and_benefits/worklife

Sets policy and guidelines for federal agencies in establishing and maintaining programs on the federal telework program, employee assistance programs, the Federal Child Care Subsidy Program, and health and wellness.

▶ CONGRESS

For a listing of relevant congressional committees and subcommittees, please see page 193 or the Appendix.

Government Accountability Office (GAO), *Education, Workforce, and Income Security, 441 G St. N.W., #5928 20548; (202) 512-7215. Barbara D. Bovbjerg, Managing Director.*
Web, www.gao.gov

Independent, nonpartisan agency in the legislative branch. Audits, analyzes, and evaluates Education Dept. programs; makes reports available to the public.

▶ NONGOVERNMENTAL

AFL-CIO (American Federation of Labor-Congress of Industrial Organizations), *815 16th St. N.W. 20006; (202) 637-5000. Fax, (202) 637-5058. Richard L. Trumka, President.*
Web, www.aflcio.org

Voluntary federation of national and international labor unions in the United States. Represents members before Congress and other branches of government. Each member union conducts its own contract negotiations. Library (located in Silver Spring, Md.) open to the public.

American Civil Liberties Union (ACLU), *National Capital Area, 4301 Connecticut Ave. N.W., #434 20008-2368; (202) 457-0800. Monica Hopkins, Executive Director.*
Web, www.aclu-nca.org

Seeks to protect the civil liberties of the citizens, including federal employees, of the District of Columbia. Interests include First Amendment rights, privacy, and due process.

American Enterprise Institute (AEI), *1150 17th St. N.W. 20036; (202) 862-5800. Fax, (202) 862-7177. Arthur C. Brooks, President. Press, (202) 862-4871.*
Web, www.aei.org

Research and educational organization that studies trends in employment, earnings, the environment, health care, and income in the United States.

American Staffing Assn., *277 S. Washington St., #200, Alexandria, VA 22314-3675; (703) 253-2020. Fax, (703) 253-2053. Richard A. Wahlquist, President.*
General email, asa@americanstaffing.net
Web, www.americanstaffing.net

Membership: companies supplying other companies with workers on a temporary or permanent basis, with outsourcing, with human resources, and with professional employer organizations (PEOs) arrangements. Monitors legislation and regulations. Encourages the maintenance of high ethical standards and provides public relations and educational support to members.

Campaign for America's Future, *1825 K St. N.W., #400 20006; (202) 955-5665. Fax, (202) 955-5606. Robert L. Borosage, Co-Director; Roger Hickey, Co-Director.*
Web, www.ourfuture.org

EMPLOYMENT AND LABOR RESOURCES IN CONGRESS

For a complete listing of Congress committees, including their full contact information, leadership, membership, and jurisdictions, please refer to the Appendix on pages 724–842.

HOUSE:

House Appropriations Committee, (202) 225-2771.
Web, appropriations.house.gov or
democrats.appropriations.house.gov
  Subcommittee on Labor, Health and Human Services, Education, and Related Agencies, (202) 225-3508.
House Armed Services Committee, (202) 225-4151.
Web, armedservices.house.gov or
democrats.armedservices.house.gov
  Subcommittee on Military Personnel, (202) 225-7560.
House Education and the Workforce Committee, (202) 225-4527.
Web, edworkforce.house.gov or
democrats.edworkforce.house.gov
  Subcommittee on Health, Employment, Labor, and Pensions, (202) 225-4527.
  Subcommittee on Higher Education, and Workforce Training, (202) 225-4527.
  Subcommittee on Workforce Protections, (202) 225-4527.
House Judiciary Committee, (202) 225-3951.
Web, judiciary.house.gov or
democrats.judiciary.house.gov
  Subcommittee on Immigration and Border Security, (202) 225-3926.
House Oversight and Government Reform Committee, (202) 225-5074.
Web, oversight.house.gov or
democrats.oversight.house.gov
  Subcommittee on Federal Workforce, U.S. Postal Service, and the Census, (202) 225-5074.
House Small Business Committee, (202) 225-5821.
Web, smallbusiness.house.gov or
democrats.smallbusiness.house.gov
  Subcommittee on Contracting and Workforce, (202) 225-5821.
House Veterans' Affairs Committee, (202) 225-3527.
Web, veterans.house.gov or
democrats.veterans.house.gov
  Subcommittee on Economic Opportunity, (202) 226-5491.
House Ways and Means Committee, (202) 225-3625.
Web, waysandmeans.house.gov or
democrats.waysandmeans.house.gov
  Subcommittee on Human Resources, (202) 225-1025.
  Subcommittee on Social Security, (202) 225-9263.

JOINT:

Joint Economic Committee, (202) 224-5171.
Web, jec.senate.gov/public or
jec.senate.gov/republicans/public

SENATE:

Senate Agriculture, Nutrition, and Forestry Committee, (202) 224-2035.
Web, ag.senate.gov
  Subcommittee on Jobs, Rural Economic Growth and Energy Innovation, (202) 224-2035.
Senate Appropriations Committee, (202) 224-7363.
Web, appropriations.senate.gov
  Subcommittee on Labor, Health and Human Services, Education, and Related Agencies, (202) 224-9145.
Senate Environment and Public Works Committee, (202) 224-8832.
Web, epw.senate.gov
  Subcommittee on Green Jobs and the New Economy, (202) 224-8832.
Senate Finance Committee, (202) 224-4515.
Web, finance.senate.gov
  Subcommittee on International Trade, Customs, and Global Competitiveness, (202) 224-4515.
  Subcommittee on Social Security, Pensions and Family Policy, (202) 224-4515.
  Subcommittee on Taxation and IRS Oversight, (202) 224-4515.
Senate Health, Education, Labor, and Pensions Committee, (202) 224-5375.
Web, help.senate.gov
  Subcommittee on Employment and Workplace Safety, (202) 228-1455.
  Subcommittee on Primary Health and Aging, (202) 224-5480.
Senate Homeland Security and Governmental Affairs Committee, (202) 224-2627.
Web, hsgac.senate.gov
  Permanent Subcommittee on Investigations, (202) 224-9505.
  Subcommittee on Efficiency and Effectiveness of Federal Programs and the Federal Workforce, (202) 224-2627.
Senate Judiciary Committee, (202) 224-7703.
Web, judiciary.senate.gov
  Subcommittee on Immigration, Refugees, and Border Security, (202) 224-6498.
Senate Small Business and Entrepreneurship Committee, (202) 224-5175.
Web, sbc.senate.gov
Senate Special Committee on Aging, (202) 224-5364.
Web, aging.senate.gov

Operates the Campaign for America's Future and the Institute for America's Future. Advocates policies to help working people. Supports improved employee benefits, including health care, child care, and paid family leave; promotes lifelong education and training of workers. Seeks full employment, higher wages, and increased productivity. Monitors legislation and regulations.

Center for Economic and Policy Research (CEPR), *1611 Connecticut Ave. N.W., #400 20009; (202) 293-5380. Fax, (202) 588-1356. Dean Baker, Co-Director; Mark Weisbrot, Co-Director.*
General email, cepr@cepr.net
Web, www.cepr.net

Researches economic and social issues and the impact of related public policies. Presents findings to the public with the goal of better preparing citizens to choose among various policy options. Promotes democratic debate and voter education. Areas of interest include health care, trade, financial reform, Social Security, taxes, housing, and the labor market.

Employment Policies Institute, *1090 Vermont Ave. N.W., #800 20005-4605; (202) 463-7650. Fax, (202) 463-7107. Richard Berman, Executive Director.*
General email, info@epionline.org
Web, www.epionline.org

Sponsors and conducts research on public policy and employment. Opposes raising the minimum wage. Monitors legislation and regulations.

Good Jobs First, *1616 P St. N.W., #210 20036; (202) 232-1616. Greg LeRoy, Executive Director.*
General email, info@goodjobsfirst.org
Web, www.goodjobsfirst.org

Promotes corporate and government accountability in economic development and job growth. Provides information on state and local job subsidies. Monitors legislation and regulations.

HR Policy Assn., *1100 13th St. N.W., #850 20005-4090; (202) 789-8670. Fax, (202) 789-0064. Daniel V. Yager, President.*
General email, info@hrpolicy.org
Web, www.hrpolicy.org

Membership: corporate vice presidents in charge of employee relations. Promotes research in employee relations, particularly in federal employment policy and implementation. Interests include international labor issues, including immigration and child labor.

Institute for Credentialing Excellence, *2025 M St. N.W., #800 20036-3309; (202) 367-1165. Fax, (202) 367-2165. Denise Roosendaal, Executive Director.*
General email, info@credentialingexcellence.org
Web, www.credentialingexcellence.org

Membership: certifying agencies and other groups that issue credentials for professions and occupations. Promotes public understanding of competency assurance certification programs. Oversees commission that establishes certification program standards. Monitors regulations.

National Assn. of Professional Employer Organizations, *707 N. Saint Asaph St., Alexandria, VA 22314; (703) 836-0466. Fax, (703) 836-0976. Pat Cleary, President.*
General email, info@napeo.org
Web, www.napeo.org

Membership: professional employer organizations. Provides code of ethics. Conducts research; sponsors seminars and conferences for members. Monitors legislation and regulations.

Society for Human Resource Management, *1800 Duke St., Alexandria, VA 22314-3499; (703) 548-3440. Fax, (703) 535-6490. Henry G. (Hank) Jackson, President, (703) 548-3440. Information, (800) 283-7476. Press, (703) 535-6273.*
General email, shrm@shrm.org
Web, www.shrm.org

Membership: human resource management professionals. Monitors legislation and regulations concerning recruitment, training, and employment practices; occupational safety and health; compensation and benefits; employee and labor relations; and equal employment opportunity. Sponsors seminars and conferences.

Urban Institute, *Center on Labor, Human Services, and Population,* *2100 M St. N.W. 20037; (202) 833-7200. Fax, (202) 463-8522. Elizabeth Peters, Director.*
Web, www.urban.org/center/lhp/index.cfm

Analyzes employment and income trends, studies how the U.S. population is growing, and evaluates programs dealing with homelessness, child welfare, and job training. Other areas of interest include immigration, mortality, sexual and reproductive health, adolescent risk behavior, child care, domestic violence, and youth development.

U.S. Chamber of Commerce, *Economic Policy,* *1615 H St. N.W. 20062-2000; (202) 463-5620. Fax, (202) 463-3174. Martin A. Regalia, Chief Economist.*
Web, www.uschamber.com/issues/econtax/economic-tax-and-tax-policy

Monitors legislation and regulations affecting the business community, including employee benefits, health care, legal and regulatory affairs, transportation and telecommunications infrastructure, defense conversion, and equal employment opportunity.

International Issues

▶**AGENCIES**

Bureau of Labor Statistics (BLS) *(Labor Dept.),* *International Labor Comparison,* *2 Massachusetts Ave. N.E., #2120 20212-0001; (202) 691-5200. Fax, (202) 691-5679. Chris Bart, Division Chief, Acting.*
General email, ilchelp@bls.gov
Web, www.bls.gov/ilc

Labor Department

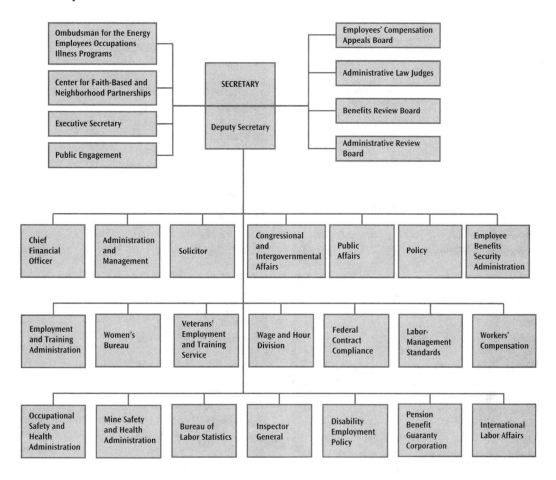

Issues statistical reports on labor force, productivity, employment and unemployment, prices, unit labor costs, hourly compensation costs, and GDP per capita and per hour figures in foreign countries adjusted to U.S. concepts.

Employment and Training Administration *(Labor Dept.), Trade Adjustment Assistance, 200 Constitution Ave. N.W., #C5321 20210; (202) 693-3560. Fax, (202) 693-3584. Norris T. Tyler III, Administrator, Acting. Toll-free, (888) 365-6822.*
Web, www.doleta.gov/tradeact

Assists American workers who are totally or partially unemployed because of increased imports or a shift in production; offers training, job search and relocation assistance, weekly benefits at state unemployment insurance levels, and other reemployment services.

Labor Dept. (DOL), *International Labor Affairs, 200 Constitution Ave. N.W., #C4325 20210; (202) 693-4770. Fax, (202) 693-4780. Christopher P. Lu, Deputy Secretary; Carol Pier, Deputy Under Secretary; Mark A. Mittelhauser, Associate Deputy Under Secretary.*
General email, Contact-ILAB@dol.gov
Web, www.dol.gov/ilab

Assists in formulating international economic and trade policies affecting American workers. Represents the United States in trade negotiations. Helps administer the United States labor attaché program. Carries out overseas technical assistance projects. Represents the United States in various international organizations. Houses the Office of Trade Agreement Implementation, which is responsible for overseeing the implementation of the labor provisions of free trade agreements.

Labor Dept. (DOL), *International Labor Affairs, Office of Trade and Labor Affairs, 200 Constitution Ave. N.W., #S5317 20210; (202) 693-4887. Fax, (202) 693-4851. Gregory Schoepfle, Director.*
General email, contact-OTLAC@dol.gov
Web, www.dol.gov/ilab

Coordinates international technical cooperation in support of the labor provisions in free trade agreements. Provides services, information, expertise, and technical cooperation programs that support the Labor Dept.'s foreign policy objectives. Administers the U.S. government's responsibilities under the North American Free Trade Agreement on Labor Cooperation and labor chapters of U.S. regional and bilateral free trade agreements. Provides technical assistance for postconflict reconstruction and reintegration activities in countries key to U.S. security. Provides technical assistance globally to help countries observe international labor standards. Supports HIV/AIDS workplace preventive education in countries around the world.

Labor Dept. (DOL), *International Relations, 200 Constitution Ave. N.W., #S5317 20210; (202) 693-4855. Fax, (202) 693-4860. Robert B. Shepard, Director.*
General email, Contact-OIR@dol.gov
Web, www.dol.gov/ilab/programs/oir

Provides administrative support for U.S. participation in the International Labor Organization (ILO) and Asian Pacific Economic Cooperation (APEC), and at the Paris-based Organization for Economic Cooperation and Development (OECD). Provides research on labor and employment in other countries. Facilitates information-sharing between Labor Dept. and other countries.

Labor Dept. (DOL), *U.S. Foreign Visitors Program, 200 Constitution Ave. N.W., #S5303 20210; (202) 693-4793. Fax, (202) 693-4784. Patricia Butler, International Program Specialist.*
General email, butler.patricia@dol.gov
Web, www.dol.gov/ilab/programs/oir/fvp.htm

Works with the State Dept., the Agency for International Development, and other agencies in arranging visits and training programs for foreign officials interested in U.S. labor and trade unions.

President's Committee on the International Labor Organization *(Labor Dept.), 200 Constitution Ave. N.W., #S5004 20210; (202) 693-4808. Fax, (202) 693-4860. Thomas E. Perez, Secretary of Labor; Carol Pier, Deputy Under Secretary for International Affairs.*
Web, www.dol.gov/ilab/diplomacy/ilo.htm

Advisory committee that directs U.S. participation in the International Labor Organization. Composed of government, employer, and worker representatives, including secretaries of labor, commerce, and state; the president's national security adviser; the president's national economic adviser; and the presidents of the AFL-CIO and the U.S. Council of International Business. Formulates and coordinates policy on the International Labor Organization (ILO); advises the president and the secretary of labor.

State Dept., *International Labor Affairs, 1800 G St. N.W., #2422 20006; (202) 312-9763. Fax, (202) 216-5895. Bruce Levine, Director, (202) 216-5886.*
Web, www.state.gov/g/drl/lbr

Works with organized labor, nongovernmental organizations, international organizations, and corporations to monitor and promote worker rights throughout the world. Contributes to U.S. foreign policy goals related to democracy promotion, trade, development, and human rights.

State Dept., *International Organization Affairs, 2201 C St. N.W., #6323 20520-6319; (202) 647-9600. Fax, (202) 736-4116. H. Dean Pittman, Assistant Secretary, Acting. Press, (202) 647-6899.*
General email, io-bureau@state.gov
Web, www.state.gov

Coordinates and develops policy guidelines for U.S. participation in the United Nations and in other international organizations and conferences.

► **CONGRESS**

For a listing of relevant congressional committees and sub-committees, please see page 193 or the Appendix.

► **INTERNATIONAL ORGANIZATIONS**

International Labor Organization (ILO), *Washington Office, 1808 Eye St. N.W., 9th Floor 20006; (202) 617-3952. Fax, (202) 617-3960. Nancy A. Donaldson, Director.*
General email, washington@ilo.org
Web, www.ilo.org/washington

Works toward advancing social justice through the promotion of international labor standards, employment, social protection, and social dialogue. Carries out research and technical cooperation and advisory services under these four major themes and related subthemes, including labor statistics, wages, occupational safety and health and other working conditions, Social Security, eradication of child labor and forced labor, equality of treatment in employment and occupation, freedom of association, and bargaining rights. Liaison office for the United States and multilateral organizations in Washington, D.C. (Headquarters in Geneva.)

► **NONGOVERNMENTAL**

Immigration Works USA, *737 8th St. S.E., #201 20003; (202) 506-4541. Fax, (202) 595-8962. Tamar Jacoby, President.*
General email, info@immigrationworksusa.org
Web, www.immigrationworksusa.org

Coalition of business owners that seeks to educate the public about the benefits of immigration and build support for bringing immigration policy in line with the country's labor needs. Monitors legislation and regulations.

International Labor Rights Forum, *1634 Eye St. N.W., #1001 20006; (202) 347-4100. Fax, (202) 347-4885. Judy Gearheart, Executive Director, ext. 106.*
General email, laborrights@ilrf.org
Web, www.laborrights.org

Promotes the enforcement of international labor rights through policy advocacy; advocates for better protection of workers. Concerns include child labor, sweatshops, and exploited workers. Monitors legislation and regulations on national and international levels.

NumbersUSA, *Capitol Hill Office,* 310 6th St. S.E., #310 20003; 1601 N. Kent St., #1100, Arlington, VA 22209; (703) 816-8820. Fax, (202) 543-3147. Roy Beck, Executive Director.
General email, info@numbersusa.com
Web, www.numbersusa.com

Public policy organization that favors immigration reduction as a way of promoting economic justice for American workers. Monitors legislation and regulations.

Solidarity Center, 888 16th St. N.W., #400 20006; (202) 974-8383. Fax, (202) 974-8384. Shawna Bader-Blau, Executive Director.
General email, information@solidaritycenter.org
Web, www.solidaritycenter.org

Provides assistance to free and democratic trade unions worldwide. Provides trade union leadership courses in collective bargaining, union organization, trade integration, labor-management cooperation, union administration, and political theories. Sponsors social and community development projects; focus includes child labor, human and worker rights, and the role of women in labor unions. (Affiliated with the AFL-CIO.)

U.S. Chamber of Commerce, *Labor, Immigration, and Employee Benefits,* 1615 H St. N.W. 20062-2000; (202) 463-5522. Fax, (202) 463-3194. Randel K. Johnson, Senior Vice President; Amy Nice, Executive Director for Immigration Policy.
Web, www.uschamber.com/labor-immigration-and-employee benefits

Formulates and analyzes Chamber policy in the areas of labor law, immigration, pension, and health care. Monitors legislation and regulations affecting labor-management relations, employee benefits, and immigration issues.

Labor Standards and Practices

▶ **AGENCIES**

Bureau of Labor Statistics (BLS) *(Labor Dept.),* *Compensation and Working Conditions,* 2 Massachusetts Ave. N.E., #4130 20212; (202) 691-6300. Fax, (202) 691-6310. William J. Wiatrowski, Associate Commissioner.
Web, www.bls.gov/bls/proghome.htm#ocwc

Conducts annual area wage surveys to determine occupational pay information in individual labor markets. Conducts industry wage surveys, which provide wage and employee benefit information; collects data on labor costs, job injuries and illnesses, and work stoppages.

Housing and Urban Development Dept. (HUD), *Office of Labor Relations,* 451 7th St. S.W., #2124 20410; (202) 708-0370. Fax, (202) 401-8898. Jackie Roundtree, Executive Director, Acting.
Web, www.hud.gov/offices/olr

Seeks to ensure that laborers on HUD-assisted construction projects are paid prevailing wages by contractors. Administers and enforces labor standards provisions within the Davis-Bacon and related acts, the Copeland Act, and Contract Work Hours and Safety Standards Act, and the maintenance wage requirements of the U.S. Housing Act of 1937.

Labor Dept. (DOL), *Federal Contract Compliance Programs,* 200 Constitution Ave. N.W., #C3325 20210; (202) 693-0101. Fax, (202) 693-1304. Patricia A. Shiu, Director; Les Jin, Deputy Director. Toll-free, (800) 397-6251.
General email, OFCCP-Public@dol.gov
Web, www.dol.gov/ofccp

Monitors and enforces government contractors' compliance with federal laws and regulations on equal employment opportunities and affirmative action, including employment rights of minorities, women, persons with disabilities, and disabled and Vietnam-era veterans.

Labor Dept. (DOL), *Wage and Hour Division,* 200 Constitution Ave. N.W., #S3502 20210; (202) 693-0051. Fax, (202) 693-1406. Vacant, Administrator; Laura A. Fortman, Principal Deputy Administrator. Toll-free, (866) 487-9243. Press, (202) 693-4676.
Web, www.dol.gov/whd

Enforces the minimum-wage, overtime pay, record-keeping, and child labor requirements of the Fair Labor Standards Act, the Migrant and Seasonal Agricultural Worker Protection Act, the Employee Polygraph Protection Act, the Family and Medical Leave Act, and a number of employment standards and worker protections as provided in several immigration-related statutes. Also enforces the wage garnishment provisions of the Consumer Credit Protection Act; and the prevailing wage requirements of the Davis-Bacon Act, the Service Contract Act, and other statutes applicable to federal contracts for construction and the provision of goods and services.

Wage and Hour *(Labor Dept.),* *Enforcement Policy, Child Labor and Fair Labor Standards Act Enforcement,* 200 Constitution Ave. N.W., #S3510 20210; (202) 693-0051. Fax, (202) 693-1387. Derrick Witherspoon, Branch Chief. Press, (202) 693-4659.
Web, www.dol.gov

Issues interpretations and rulings of the Fair Labor Standards Act of 1938.

Wage and Hour *(Labor Dept.),* *Enforcement Policy, Family and Medical Leave,* 200 Constitution Ave. N.W., #S3510 20210; (202) 693-0066. Fax, (202) 693-1387. Diane Dawson, Branch Chief. Press, (202) 693-4676.
Web, www.dol.gov/whd

Authorizes subminimum wages under the Fair Labor Standards Act for certain categories of workers, including full-time students, student learners, and workers with disabilities. Administers the Fair Labor Standards Act restrictions on working at home in certain industries and enforces child labor laws.

Wage and Hour *(Labor Dept.), Enforcement Policy, Farm and Labor and Immigration Team,* 200 Constitution Ave. N.W., #S3510 20210; (202) 693-0070. Fax, (202) 693-1387. James Kessler, Branch Chief, (202) 693-0071. Toll-free, (866) 487-9243.
Web, www.dol.gov/whd

Enforces certain provisions under the Immigration and Nationality Act (INA), including labor standards protections for certain temporary nonimmigrant workers and inspection for compliance with the employment eligibility record keeping requirements.

Wage and Hour *(Labor Dept.), Enforcement Policy, Government Contracts Enforcement,* 200 Constitution Ave. N.W., #S3006 20210; (202) 693-0064. Fax, (202) 693-1087. Timothy Helm, Branch Chief.
General email, whdpwc@dol.gov
Web, www.dol.gov/whd

Enforces the Davis-Bacon Act, the Walsh-Healey Public Contracts Act, the Contract Work Hours and Safety Standards Act, the Service Contract Act, and other related government contract labor standards statutes.

Wage and Hour *(Labor Dept.), Wage Determination, Service Contracts,* 200 Constitution Ave. N.W., #S3028 20210; (202) 693-0073. Fax, (202) 693-1425. Sandra W. Hamlett, Branch Chief, (202) 693-0571.
Web, www.dol.gov/whd

Issues prevailing wage determinations under the Service Contract Act of 1965 and other regulations pertaining to wage determination.

▶ CONGRESS

For a listing of relevant congressional committees and subcommittees, please see page 193 or the Appendix.

▶ NONGOVERNMENTAL

Fair Labor Assn. (FLA), 1111 19th St. N.W., #401 20036; (202) 898-1000. Fax, (202) 898-9050. Jorge Perez-Lopez, Executive Director.
General email, info@fairlabor.org
Web, www.fairlabor.org

Membership: consumer, human, and labor rights groups; apparel and footwear manufacturers and retailers; and colleges and universities. Seeks to protect the rights of workers in the United States and worldwide. Concerns include sweatshop practices, forced labor, child labor, and worker health and benefits. Monitors workplace conditions and reports findings to the public. Develops capacity for sustainable labor compliance.

Statistics and Information

▶ AGENCIES

Bureau of Labor Statistics (BLS) *(Labor Dept.),* 2 Massachusetts Ave. N.E., #4040 20212-0001; (202) 691-5200. Fax, (202) 691-7890. Erica Lynn Groshen,

Commissioner, Acting, (202) 691-7800. Press, (202) 691-5902.
General email, blsdata_staff@bls.gov
Web, www.bls.gov

Collects, analyzes, and publishes data on labor economics, including employment, unemployment, hours of work, wages, employee compensation, prices, consumer expenditures, labor-management relations, productivity, technological developments, occupational safety and health, and structure and growth of the economy. Publishes reports on these statistical trends, including the Consumer Price Index, the Producer Price Index, and Employment and Earnings.

Bureau of Labor Statistics (BLS) *(Labor Dept.), Compensation Levels and Trends,* 2 Massachusetts Ave. N.E., #4175 20212; (202) 691-6200. Fax, (202) 691-6647. Philip M. Doyle, Assistant Commissioner.
Web, www.bls.gov/ncs

Compiles data on wages and benefits. Develops the National Compensation Survey. Analyzes, distributes, and disseminates information on occupational earnings, benefits, and compensation trends.

Bureau of Labor Statistics (BLS) *(Labor Dept.), Current Employment Statistics, National,* 2 Massachusetts Ave. N.E., #4860 20212; (202) 691-5473. Fax, (202) 691-6641. Julie Hatch Maxfield, Chief.
General email, cesinfo@bls.gov
Web, www.bls.gov/ces/home.htm

Surveys business and government agencies and publishes detailed industry data on employment, hours, and earnings of workers on nonfarm payrolls. Estimates are produced for the nation.

Bureau of Labor Statistics (BLS) *(Labor Dept.), Current Employment Statistics, State and Area,* 2 Massachusetts Ave. N.E., #4860 20212; (202) 691-6538. Chris Manning, Chief.
Web, www.bls.gov/sae

Surveys business agencies and publishes detailed industry data on employment, hours, and earnings of workers on nonfarm payrolls. Estimates are produced for states and selected metropolitan areas.

Bureau of Labor Statistics (BLS) *(Labor Dept.), Current Employment Status,* 2 Massachusetts Ave. N.E., #4675 20212; (202) 691-6405. Fax, (202) 691-6459. Sandra L. (Sandi) Mason, Assistant Commissioner. Press, (202) 691-5902.
General email, lausinfo@bls.gov
Web, www.bls.gov/lau

Issues labor force and unemployment statistics for states, counties, metropolitan statistical areas, and cities with populations of 25,000 or more.

Bureau of Labor Statistics (BLS) *(Labor Dept.), Employment and Unemployment Statistics,* 2 Massachusetts Ave. N.E., #4945 20212-0022; (202)

691-6400. Fax, (202) 691-6425. Vacant, Associate Commissioner. Press, (202) 691-5907.
General email, labstathelpdesk@bls.gov
Web, www.bls.gov/bls/employment.htm

Monitors employment and unemployment trends on national and local levels; compiles data on worker and industry employment and earnings.

Bureau of Labor Statistics (BLS) *(Labor Dept.), Industry Employment Statistics, 2 Massachusetts Ave. N.E., #2135 20212; (202) 691-5440. Fax, (202) 691-5745.*
Kenneth W. Robertson, Assistant Commissioner.
General email, ep-info@bls.gov
Web, www.bls.gov/emp

Produces occupational employment and wage estimates for states, metropolitan and nonmetropolitan areas, and for the nation by industry. Prepares long-term projections for the labor force, the overall economy, industry output and employment, and occupational employment. Develops career guidance material.

Bureau of Labor Statistics (BLS) *(Labor Dept.), International Labor Comparison, 2 Massachusetts Ave. N.E., #2120 20212-0001; (202) 691-5200. Fax, (202) 691-5679.* Chris Bart, Division Chief, Acting.
General email, ilchelp@bls.gov
Web, www.bls.gov/ilc

Issues statistical reports on labor force, productivity, employment and unemployment, prices, unit labor costs, hourly compensation costs, and GDP per capita and per hour figures in foreign countries adjusted to U.S. concepts.

Bureau of Labor Statistics (BLS) *(Labor Dept.), Productivity and Technology, 2 Massachusetts Ave. N.E., #2150 20212-0001; (202) 691-6304. Fax, (202) 691-5664.* John W. Ruser, Associate Commissioner.
General email, dipsweb@bls.gov
Web, www.bls.gov/bls/productivity.htm

Develops and analyzes productivity measures for the U.S. business economy and industries, conducts research on factors affecting productivity, and provides international comparisons of productivity measures and other statistical data.

Employment and Training Administration *(Labor Dept.), Unemployment Insurance, 200 Constitution Ave. N.W., #S4524 20210; (202) 693-3029. Fax, (202) 693-3229.* Gay M. Gilbert, Administrator.
Web, www.ows.doleta.gov/unemploy

Provides guidance and oversight with respect to federal and state unemployment compensation. Compiles statistics on state unemployment insurance programs. Studies unemployment issues related to benefits.

Occupational Safety and Health Administration (OSHA) *(Labor Dept.), Statistical Analysis, 200 Constitution Ave.* N.W., #N3507 20210; (202) 693-1702. Fax, (202) 693-1631. Dave Schmidt, Director, (202) 693-1886.
Web, www.osha.gov/dop/index.html

Compiles and provides all statistical data for OSHA, such as occupational injury and illness records, which are used in setting standards and making policy.

►**CONGRESS**

For a listing of relevant congressional committees and subcommittees, please see page 193 or the Appendix.

Unemployment Benefits

►**AGENCIES**

Employment and Training Administration *(Labor Dept.), Trade Adjustment Assistance, 200 Constitution Ave. N.W., #C5321 20210; (202) 693-3560. Fax, (202) 693-3584.* Norris T. Tyler III, Administrator, Acting. Toll-free, (888) 365-6822.
Web, www.doleta.gov/tradeact

Assists American workers who are totally or partially unemployed because of increased imports or a shift in production; offers training, job search and relocation assistance, weekly benefits at state unemployment insurance levels, and other reemployment services.

Employment and Training Administration *(Labor Dept.), Unemployment Insurance, 200 Constitution Ave. N.W., #S4524 20210; (202) 693-3029. Fax, (202) 693-3229.* Gay M. Gilbert, Administrator.
Web, www.ows.doleta.gov/unemploy

Directs and reviews the state-administered system that provides income support for unemployed workers nationwide; advises state and federal employment security agencies on wage-loss, worker dislocation, and adjustment assistance compensation programs.

►**CONGRESS**

For a listing of relevant congressional committees and subcommittees, please see page 193 or the Appendix.

►**NONGOVERNMENTAL**

National Assn. of State Workforce Agencies, *444 N. Capitol St. N.W., #142 20001; (202) 434-8020. Fax, (202) 434-8033.* Richard A. Hobbie, Executive Director. Press, (202) 434-8023.
General email, mkatz@naswa.org
Web, www.naswa.org

Membership: state workforce agency administrators. Informs members of employment training programs, unemployment insurance programs, employment services, labor market information, and legislation. Provides unemployment insurance and workforce development professionals with opportunities for networking and information exchange.

Personnel Offices at Federal Departments and Agencies

Job seekers interested in additional information can explore federal government career opportunities through the government's official employment information system: (703) 724-1850; Web site, www.usajobs.opm.gov

DEPARTMENTS

Agriculture, (202) 720-8732

Commerce, (202) 482-4807

Defense Logistics Agency, (703) 767-4012

Education, (202) 606-1579

Energy, (202) 586-8734

Health and Human Services, (202) 690-6191

   Food and Drug Administration, (240) 402-4500

   Health Resources and Services Administration, (888) 275-4772

   National Institutes of Health, (301) 496-2404

Homeland Security,

   Coast Guard, (703) 872-6338

   Federal Emergency Management Agency, (202) 646-4006

   Transportation Security Administration, (877) 872-7990

Housing and Urban Development, (202) 708-2000

Interior, (202) 208-1738; recording, (800) 336-4562

Justice, (202) 514-4350

Labor, (202) 693-7600

State, (202) 647-9898

Transportation, (202) 366-1298

Treasury, (202) 622-0341

Veterans Affairs, (202) 461-7750

AGENCIES

Administrative Office of the U.S. Courts, (202) 502-2600

Commodity Futures Trading Commission, (202) 418-5009

Consumer Product Safety Commission, (301) 504-7925

Corporation for National and Community Service, (202) 606-5000

Environmental Protection Agency, (202) 564-4606

Equal Employment Opportunity Commission, (202) 663-4306

Export-Import Bank, (202) 565-3300

Farm Credit Administration, (703) 883-4200

Federal Communications Commission, (202) 418-0130

Federal Deposit Insurance Corporation, (877) 275-3342

Federal Election Commission, (202) 694-1080

Federal Labor Relations Authority, (202) 218-7979

Federal Mediation and Conciliation Service, (202) 606-5460

Federal Reserve Board, (202) 452-3880

Federal Trade Commission, (202) 326-3633

General Services Administration, (202) 501-0370

Government Accountability Office, (202) 512-3522

Government Printing Office, (202) 512-1308

National Aeronautics and Space Administration, (202) 358-1998

National Archives and Records Administration, (301) 837-3710

National Credit Union Administration, (703) 518-6510

National Endowment for the Arts, (202) 682-5405

National Endowment for the Humanities, (202) 606-8415

National Labor Relations Board, (202) 273-3900

National Mediation Board, (202) 692-5010

National Science Foundation, (703) 292-8180

National Transportation Safety Board, (202) 314-6230; recording, (800) 573-0937

Nuclear Regulatory Commission, (301) 415-7400

Office of Personnel Management, (202) 606-1800

Securities and Exchange Commission, (202) 551-5400

Small Business Administration, (202) 205-6600

Smithsonian Institution, (202) 633-6370

Social Security Administration, (800) 772-1213

U.S. International Trade Commission, (202) 205-2651

U.S. Postal Service, (877) 477-3273

EMPLOYMENT AND TRAINING PROGRAMS

General

►AGENCIES

Education Dept., *Office of Vocational and Adult Education (OVAE), Academic and Technical Education,* *550 12th St. S.W., #11059 20202-7100 (mailing address: 400 Maryland Ave. S.W., P-OVAE, DATE, Washington, DC 20202-7100); (202) 245-7700. Fax, (202) 245-7838. Sharon Miller, Director.*
Web, www2.ed.gov/about/offices/list/ovae/pi/cte/index .html

Establishes national initiatives that help states implement career and technical education programs. Administers state formula and discretionary grant programs under the Carl D. Perkins Career and Technical Education Act.

Employment and Training Administration *(Labor Dept.), 200 Constitution Ave. N.W., #S2307 20210; (202) 693-2700. Fax, (202) 693-2726. Eric Seleznow, Assistant Secretary, Acting. Press, (202) 693-4650. Toll-free employment and training hotline, (877) US2-JOBS. Web, www.doleta.gov*

Administers federal government job training and worker dislocation programs, federal grants to states for public employment service programs, and unemployment insurance benefits, primarily through state and local workforce development systems.

Employment and Training Administration *(Labor Dept.), Adult Services, 200 Constitution Ave. N.W., #S4209 20210; (202) 693-3046. Fax, (202) 693-3817. Robert Kight, Chief.*
Web, www.doleta.gov/etainfo/wrksys/WIAdultServices.cfm

Responsible for adult training and services for dislocated workers funded under the Workforce Investment Act; examines training initiatives. Provides targeted job training services for migrant and seasonal farm workers, Native Americans, older workers, and the disabled.

Employment and Training Administration *(Labor Dept.), Division of Strategic Investment, 200 Constitution Ave. N.W., #C4518 20210; (202) 693-3949. Fax, (202) 693-3890. Robin Fernkas, Division Chief.*
General email, divisionofstrategicinvestment@dol.gov
Web, www.doleta.gov/etainfo/wrksysldinap.cfm#DSI

Serves as liaison between business and industry and the workforce investment system, a network of state and local resources that connects workers to job opportunities and helps businesses recruit, train, and maintain a skilled workforce. Manages the High Growth Job Training Initiative with the goal of preparing workers for high-growth and high-demand jobs. Targeted industries include advanced manufacturing, aerospace, biotechnology, health care, and information technology, construction, hospitality, transportation, and energy.

Employment and Training Administration *(Labor Dept.), National Programs, Tools, and Technical Assistance, 200 Constitution Ave. N.W., #C4510 20210-3945; (202) 693-3045. Fax, (202) 693-3015. Kim Vitelli, Chief, (202) 693-3639.*
Web, www.doleta.gov/etainfo/wrksys/dinap.cfm#DNPTTA

Oversees and provides support for implementation of employment and training services to targeted populations, including National Farmworker Jobs Program; migrant and seasonal farmworker Monitor Advocate activities; and services for individuals with disabilities, including the Disability Employment Initiative; Work Opportunity Tax Credit; and Senior Community Service Employment Program. Provides workers and businesses with labor market information to help connect skilled workers to businesses. Oversees and provides support for grants to states to produce labor market information; oversees the agency's technical assistance platform for use by workforce development professionals, www.workforce3one.org.

Employment and Training Administration *(Labor Dept.), Workforce Investment, 200 Constitution Ave. N.W., #C4526 20210; (202) 693-3980. Fax, (202) 693-3981. Amanda Ahlstrand, Administrator.*
Web, www.doleta.gov/etainfo/WrkSys/WIOffice.cfm

Oversees federal employment and training programs under the Workforce Investment Act for adults, dislocated workers, and youths and Wagner-Peyser employment services as delivered through the one-stop delivery system nationwide.

Housing and Urban Development Dept. (HUD), *Office of Labor Relations, 451 7th St. S.W., #2124 20410; (202) 708-0370. Fax, (202) 401-8898. Jackie Roundtree, Executive Director, Acting.*
Web, www.hud.gov/offices/olr

Partnership between HUD and the Labor Dept. that assists low-income housing residents in obtaining job training and employment.

►CONGRESS

For a listing of relevant congressional committees and subcommittees, please see page 193 or the Appendix.

►NONGOVERNMENTAL

AFL-CIO Working America, *815 16th St. N.W. 20006; (202) 637-5137. Fax, (202) 508-6900. Karen Nussbaum, Executive Director.*
General email, info@workingamerica.org
Web, www.workingamerica.org

Advocates on behalf of nonunion workers at the community, state, and national levels. Seeks to secure better jobs, health care, education, and retirement benefits for these workers. Monitors legislation and regulations. (A community affiliate of the AFL-CIO.)

AFL-CIO Working for America Institute, *815 16th St. N.W. 20006; (202) 508-3717. Fax, (202) 508-3719. Jeff Rickert, Deputy Director, (202) 508-3725. Office Manager, (202) 637-5251.*

General email, info@workingforamerica.org

Web, www.workingforamerica.org

Provides technical assistance to labor unions, employers, education agencies, and community groups for workplace programs focusing on dislocated workers, economically disadvantaged workers, and skill upgrading. Interests include new technologies and workplace innovations.

American Society for Training and Development (ASTD), *1640 King St., 3rd Floor, Box 1443, Alexandria, VA 22313-2043; (703) 683-8100. Fax, (703) 683-1523. Tony Bingham, Chief Executive Officer.*

General email, customercare@astd.org

Web, www.astd.org

Membership: trainers and human resource development specialists. Promotes workplace training programs and human resource development. Interests include productivity, leadership development, and employee retraining and performance improvement. Holds conferences; publishes information about employee learning and development; provides online training.

Graduate School, *Center for Leadership Management, 600 Maryland Ave. S.W. 20024-2520; (202) 314-3300. Fax, (202) 479-6813. Kimberley Robinson, Director. Toll-free, (866) 329-4723.*

General email, customersupport@graduateschool.edu

Web, www.graduateschool.edu

Trains federal employees with managerial potential for executive positions in the government. Leadership programs serve employees at levels from GS4 through SES.

National Assn. of State Workforce Agencies, *444 N. Capitol St. N.W., #142 20001; (202) 434-8020. Fax, (202) 434-8033. Richard A. Hobbie, Executive Director. Press, (202) 434-8023.*

General email, mkatz@naswa.org

Web, www.naswa.org

Membership: state employment security administrators. Informs members of federal legislation on job placement, veterans' affairs, and employment and training programs. Distributes labor market information; trains new state administrators and executive staff. Provides employment and training professionals with opportunities for networking and information exchange.

National Assn. of Workforce Boards (NAWB), *1133 19th St. N.W., #400 20036; (202) 857-7900. Fax, (202) 857-7955. Ron Painter, Chief Executive Officer.*

General email, nawb@nawb.org

Web, www.nawb.org

Membership: private industry councils and state job training coordinating councils established under the Job Training Partnership Act of 1982 (renamed Workforce Boards under the Workforce Investment Act). Interests include job training opportunities for youth and unemployed, economically disadvantaged, and dislocated workers; and private sector involvement in federal employment and training policy. Provides members with technical assistance; holds conferences and seminars.

National Assn. of Workforce Development Professionals (NAWDP), *1133 19th St. N.W., 4th Floor 20036; (202) 589-1790. Fax, (202) 589-1799. Bridget Brown, Executive Director.*

General email, info@nawdp.org

Web, www.nawdp.org

Membership: professionals and policymakers in the employment and training field. Promotes professionalism, information exchange, networking, and professional growth in the workforce development field.

National Center on Education and the Economy (NCEE), *2000 Pennsylvania Ave. N.W., #5300 20006; (202) 379-1800. Fax, (202) 293-1560. Marc S. Tucker, President.*

General email, info@ncee.org

Web, www.ncee.org

Partnership of states, school districts, corporations, foundations, and nonprofit organizations that provides tools and technical assistance for school districts to improve education and training for the workplace.

National Governors Assn. (NGA), *Center for Best Practices, Workforce Development Programs, 444 N. Capitol St. N.W., #267 20001-1512; (202) 624-5345. Fax, (202) 624-7829. Martin Simon, Director.*

Web, www.nga.org/cms/center/ehsw

Provides information and technical assistance to members participating in federal job training programs, including programs authorized under the federal workforce development programs; informs members of related legislation. Provides technical assistance to members in areas of work and welfare programs, youth programs, employment services, dislocated workers, and dropout prevention.

The Telework Coalition (TelCoa), *204 E. St. N.E. 20002; (202) 266-0046. Fax, (202) 465-3776. Chuck Wilsker, President.*

General email, info@telcoa.org

Web, www.telcoa.org

Promotes telework and access to broadband services to increase productivity and provide employment opportunities for disabled, rural, and older workers, while reducing vehicular travel and energy use. Monitors legislation and regulations.

U.S. Chamber of Commerce, *Institute for a Competitive Workforce, 1615 H St. N.W. 20062-2000; (202) 463-5525. Fax, (202) 887-3424. Cheryl A. Oldham, Vice President.*

General email, education@uschamber.com

Web, www.education.uschamber.com

Works with U.S. Chamber of Commerce members on workforce development issues, including educational reform, human resources, and job training.

U.S. Conference of Mayors, *Workforce Development Council, 1620 Eye St. N.W., #400 20006; (202) 293-7330. Fax, (202) 293-2352. Kathleen (Kathy) Wiggins, Assistant Executive Director for Jobs, Education, and the Workforce Development Council, (202) 861-6724; Ida Mukendi, Administrative Assistant.*

Web, www.usmayors.org/workforce

Offers technical assistance to members participating in federal job training programs; monitors related legislation; acts as an information clearinghouse on employment and training programs.

Worldwide ERC *(Employee Relocation Council),* *4401 Wilson Blvd., #510, Arlington, VA 22203; (703) 842-3400. Fax, (703) 527-1552. Peggy Smith, Chief Executive Officer, (703) 842-3407.*
General email, webmaster@worldwideerc.org
Web, www.worldwideerc.org

Membership: corporations that relocate employees and moving, real estate, and relocation management companies. Researches and recommends policies that provide a smooth transition for relocated employees and their families. Holds conferences and issues publications on employee relocation issues.

Aliens

▶**AGENCIES**

Administration for Children and Families (ACF) *(Health and Human Services Dept.), Refugee Resettlement, 901 D St. S.W., 8th Floor West 20447; (202) 401-9246. Fax, (202) 401-0981. Eskinder Negash, Director.*
Web, www.acf.hhs.gov/programs/orr

Directs a domestic resettlement program for refugees; reimburses states for costs incurred in giving refugees monetary and medical assistance; awards funds to voluntary resettlement agencies for providing refugees with monetary assistance and case management; provides states and nonprofit agencies with grants for social services such as English and employment training.

Employment and Training Administration *(Labor Dept.), Foreign Labor Certification, 200 Constitution Ave. N.W., #C4312 20210; (202) 693-3010. Fax, (202) 693-2768. William Carlson, Administrator.*
Web, www.foreignlaborcert.doleta.gov

Sets national policies and guidelines to carry out the responsibilities of the secretary of labor pursuant to the Immigration and Nationality Act regarding the admission of foreign workers to the United States for both temporary and permanent employment; certifies whether U.S. workers are available for positions for which admission of foreign workers is sought and whether employment of foreign nationals will adversely affect the wages and working conditions of similarly employed U.S. citizens.

Apprenticeship Programs

▶**AGENCIES**

Employment and Training Administration *(Labor Dept.), National Office of Apprenticeship, 200 Constitution Ave. N.W., #N5311 20210-0001; (202) 693-2796. Fax, (202) 693-3799. John V. Ladd, Administrator.*
Web, www.doleta.gov/oa

Advises the secretary of labor on the role of apprenticeship programs in employment training and on safety standards for those programs; encourages sponsors to include these standards in planning apprenticeship programs. Promotes establishment of apprenticeship programs in private industry and the public sector.

Employment and Training Administration *(Labor Dept.), Youth Services, 200 Constitution Ave. N.W., #N4508 20210; (202) 693-3030. Fax, (202) 693-3861. Jen Troke, Director.*
General email, youthservices@dol.gov
Web, www.doleta.gov/youth_services

Administers youth grant programs designed to enhance youth education, encourage school completion, and provide career and apprenticeship opportunities. Oversees the Going Home: Serious and Violent Offender Reentry Initiative.

Dislocated Workers

▶**AGENCIES**

Employment and Training Administration *(Labor Dept.), Adult Services, 200 Constitution Ave. N.W., #S4209 20210; (202) 693-3046. Fax, (202) 693-3817. Robert Kight, Chief.*
Web, www.doleta.gov/etainfo/wrksys/WIAdultServices.cfm

Responsible for adult training and services for dislocated workers funded under the Workforce Investment Act; examines training initiatives. Provides targeted job training services for migrant and seasonal farm workers, Native Americans, older workers, and the disabled.

▶**NONGOVERNMENTAL**

National Assn. of Workforce Boards (NAWB), *1133 19th St. N.W., #400 20036; (202) 857-7900. Fax, (202) 857-7955. Ron Painter, Chief Executive Officer.*
General email, nawb@nawb.org
Web, www.nawb.org

Membership: private industry councils and state job training coordinating councils established under the Job Training Partnership Act of 1982 (renamed Workforce Boards under the Workforce Investment Act). Interests include job training opportunities for youth and unemployed, economically disadvantaged, and dislocated workers; and private sector involvement in federal employment and training policy. Provides members with technical assistance; holds conferences and seminars.

National Governors Assn. (NGA), *Center for Best Practices, Workforce Development Programs, 444 N. Capitol St. N.W., #267 20001-1512; (202) 624-5345. Fax, (202) 624-7829. Martin Simon, Director.*
Web, www.nga.org/cms/center/ehsw

Provides technical assistance to members participating in employment and training activities for dislocated workers.

Selected Internships and Other Opportunities in the Washington Metropolitan Area

For congressional internships, contact members' offices. For opportunities at federal agencies, visit www.usajobs.gov/studentjobs. For information on changes to the federal internship program, see http://www.opm.gov/HiringReform/Pathways/program/interns.

American Assn. for the Advancement of Science, Joan Abdallah (202) 326-6673; www.aaas.org

American Civil Liberties Union, Adina Ellis (202) 544-1681; www.aclu.org

American Farm Bureau Federation, Marty Tatman (202) 406-3682; www.fb.org

American Federation of Teachers, Intern Coordinator, (202) 879-4439; www.aft.org

American Red Cross, Internship Coordinator, (202) 303-5214; www.redcross.org

Americans for the Arts, Intern Coordinator, (202) 371-2830; www.americansforthearts.org

Amnesty International, Internship Coordinator, (202) 544-0200; www.amnestyusa.org

B'nai B'rith International, (202) 857-6507; www.bnaibrith.org

Carnegie Institution of Washington, Cady Canapp (202) 939-1113; www.carnegiescience.edu

Center for Responsive Politics, Internship Coordinator, (202) 857-0044; www.opensecrets.org

Center for Science in the Public Interest, Intern Coordinator, (202) 332-9110; www.cspinet.org

Children's Defense Fund, Internship Coordinator, (202) 662-3507; www.childrensdefense.org

Common Cause, Tracy Leatherberry (202) 736-5710; www.commoncause.org

Council on Hemispheric Affairs, Larry Birns (202) 223-4975; www.coha.org

C-SPAN, (202) 737-3220; www.cspan.org

Democratic National Committee, Dana Berardi (202) 863-8000; www.democrats.org

Friends of the Earth, (202) 783-7400; www.foe.org

Inter-American Dialogue, (202) 822-9002; www.thedialogue.org

International Assn. of Chief of Police, Ryan Daugirda (800) 843-4227, ext.851; www.theiacp.org

Middle East Institute, Alex BetGeorge (202) 785-1141, ext. 206; www.mei.edu

Motion Picture Assn. of America, Internship Coordinator, (202) 293-1966; www.mpaa.org

Migrant and Seasonal Farm Workers

▶**AGENCIES**

Employment and Training Administration *(Labor Dept.), National Farmworker Jobs Program, 200 Constitution Ave. N.W., #C4311 20210-3945; (202) 693-3045. Fax, (202) 693-3015. Amy Young, Program Manager. General email, NFJP@dol.gov*

Web, www.doleta.gov/msfw

Provides funds for programs that help migrant and seasonal farm workers and their families find better jobs in agriculture and other areas. Services include occupational training, education, and job development and placement.

Wage and Hour *(Labor Dept.), Enforcement Policy, Farm and Labor and Immigration Team, 200 Constitution Ave. N.W., #S3510 20210; (202) 693-0070. Fax, (202) 693-1387. James Kessler, Branch Chief, (202) 693-0071. Toll-free, (866) 487-9243. Web, www.dol.gov/whd*

Administers and enforces the Migrant and Seasonal Agricultural Worker Protection Act, which protects migrant and seasonal agricultural workers from substandard labor practices by farm labor contractors, agricultural employers, and agricultural associations. Also enforces the provisions of the Immigration and Nationality Act that pertain to the employment of H-2A visa workers and U.S. workers in corresponding employment; the temporary labor camp and field sanitation standards of the Occupational Safety and Health Act; and the standards pertaining to employment in agriculture of the Fair Labor Standards Act.

▶**NONGOVERNMENTAL**

Assn. of Farmworker Opportunity Programs, *1726 M St. N.W., #602 20036; (202) 828-6006. Fax, (202) 828-6005. Daniel Sheehan, Executive Director. General email, nguyen@afop.org*

Web, www.afop.org

Represents state-level organizations that provide job training and other services and support to migrant and seasonal farm workers. Monitors legislation and conducts research.

Migrant Legal Action Program, *1001 Connecticut Ave. N.W., #915 20036-5524; (202) 775-7780. Fax, (202) 775-7784. Roger C. Rosenthal, Executive Director. General email, mlap@mlap.org*

Web, www.mlap.org

Supports and assists local legal services, migrant education, migrant health issues, and other organizations and private attorneys with respect to issues involving the living

National Academy of Sciences, (202) 334-2000; www.nasonline.org

National Assn. for Equal Opportunity in Higher Education, Intern Coordinator, (202) 552-3300; www.nafeo.org

National Assn. for the Advancement of Colored People, (202) 463-2940; www.naacpdc.org

National Assn. of Broadcasters, (202) 429-3928; www.nab.org

National Center for Missing and Exploited Children, Intern Coordinator, (877) 446-2632, ext. 6240; www.missingkids.com

National Geographic Society, Karen Gibbs (202) 775-6715; www.nationalgeographic.com

National Governors Assn., Deborah Lately (202) 624-5300; www.nga.org

National Head Start Assn., Julie Antoniou (703) 739-0875; www.nhsa.org

National Law Center on Homelessness and Poverty, Louise Weissman (202) 638-2535; www.nlchp.org

National Organization for Women, Intern/Volunteer Coordinator, (202) 628-8669; www.now.org

National Public Radio, (202) 513-2000; www.npr.org

National Trust for Historic Preservation, (202) 588-6000; www.preservationnation.org

National Wildlife Federation, Courtney Cochran (703) 438-6265; www.nwf.org

The Nature Conservancy, Front Desk (703) 841-5300; www.nature.org

Points of Light Institute, Joselyn Cassidy (404) 979-2913; www.pointsoflight.org

Radio Free Europe/Radio Liberty, (202) 457-6900; www.rferl.org

Republican National Committee, Intern Coordinator, (202) 863-8630; www.gop.com

Special Olympics International, Andrea Cahn (202) 628-3630; www.specialolympics.org

United Negro College Fund, Internship/Scholarship Info, (800) 331-2244; www.uncf.org

U.S. Chamber of Commerce, (202) 659-6000; www.uschamber.com

and working conditions of migrant farm workers. Monitors legislation and regulations.

Older Workers

▶ AGENCIES

Employment and Training Administration *(Labor Dept.), Senior Community Service Employment Program, 200 Constitution Ave. N.W., #S4209 20210; (202) 693-3761. Fax, (202) 693-3817. Karen Davis, Federal Program Officer for the Washington D.C. Area, (202) 693-3938.* Web, www.doleta.gov/seniors

Provides funds for part-time, community service work-training programs; the programs pay minimum wage and are operated by national sponsoring organizations and state and territorial governments. The program is aimed at unemployed economically disadvantaged persons age fifty-five and over.

▶ NONGOVERNMENTAL

AARP, *601 E St. N.W. 20049; (202) 434-2277. Fax, (202) 434-2320. A. Barry Rand, Chief Executive Officer. Press, (202) 434-2560. Library, (202) 434-6233. Toll-free, (888) 687-2277. Membership, (202) 434-3525.* General email, member@aarp.org

Web, www.aarp.org

Researches and testifies on private, federal, and other government employee pension legislation and regulations; conducts seminars; provides information on preretirement preparation.

Experience Works, Inc., *4401 Wilson Blvd., #1100, Arlington, VA 22203; (703) 522-7272. Fax, (703) 522-0141. Sarah Biggery, Executive Director. Toll-free, (866) 397-9757.* Web, www.experienceworks.org

Trains and places older adults in the workforce. Seeks to increase awareness of issues affecting older workers and build support for policies and legislation benefiting older adults. Maintains a help line for those unemployed who are 55 and older.

National Council on the Aging, *Senior Community Service Employment Program, 1901 L St. N.W., 4th Floor 20036; (202) 479-1200. Fax, (202) 479-0735. Tim Hamre, Director.* General email, info@ncoa.org

Web, www.ncoa.org/enhance-economic-security/mature-workers/senior-community-service-employment-program-scsep/

Operates a grant through funding from the U.S. Labor Dept. under the authority of the Older Americans Act to provide workers age fifty-five and over with community service employment and training opportunities in their resident communities.

Workers with Disabilities

Education Dept., *Special Education and Rehabilitative Services, Rehabilitation Services Administration,* 400 Maryland Ave. S.W. 20202-7100; (202) 245-7468. Janet L. Labreck, Commissioner.
Web, www2.ed.gov/about/offices/list/osers/rsa/index.html

Provides leadership and fiscal resources to state and other agencies to provide vocational rehabilitation, independent living, and other services to individuals with disabilities.

Equal Employment Opportunity Commission (EEOC), *131 M St. N.E. 20507; (202) 663-4001. Fax, (202) 663-4110. Jacqueline A. Berrien, Chair.*
General email, info@eeoc.gov

Web, www.eeoc.gov

Works for increased employment of persons with disabilities, affirmative action by the federal government, and an equitable work environment for employees with mental and physical disabilities.

Office of Disability Employment Policy *(Labor Dept.),* 200 Constitution Ave. N.W., #S1303 20210; (202) 693-7880. Fax, (202) 693-7888. Kathleen Martinez, Assistant Secretary. Toll-free, 866-ODEP-DOL (633-7365).
General email, odep@dol.gov

Web, www.dol.gov/odep

Influences disability employment policy by developing and promoting the use of evidence-based disability employment policies and practices, building collaborative partnerships, and delivering data on employment of people with disabilities.

Office of Personnel Management (OPM), *Veterans Services,* 1900 E St. N.W., #7439 20415; (202) 606-3602. Fax, (202) 606-6017. Hakeem Basheerud-Deen, Director.
Web, www.opm.gov/policy-data-oversight/veterans-services

Provides federal employees and transitioning military service members and their families, federal human resources professionals, and hiring managers with information on employment opportunities with the federal government. Administers the Disabled Veterans Affirmative Action Program.

Rehabilitation Services Administration *(Education Dept.),* 400 Maryland Ave. S.W. 20202-7100; (202) 245-7468. Fax, (202) 245-7591. Janet L. Labreck, Commissioner.
Web, www2.ed.gov/about/offices/list/osers/rsa/index.html

Coordinates and directs federal services for eligible persons with physical or mental disabilities, with emphasis on programs that promote employment opportunities. Provides vocational training and job placement; supports projects with private industry; administers grants for the establishment of supported-employment programs.

U.S. AbilityOne Commission, 1401 S. Clark St., Arlington, VA 22202; 1421 Jefferson Davis Hwy., #10800, Arlington, VA 22202-3259; (703) 603-7740. Fax, (703) 603-0655. Tina Ballard, Executive Director.
General email, info@abilityone.gov

Web, www.abilityone.gov

Presidentially appointed committee. Determines which products and services are suitable for federal procurement from qualified nonprofit agencies that employ people who are blind or have other significant disabilities; seeks to increase employment opportunities for these individuals. (Formerly Committee for Purchase from People Who Are Blind or Severely Disabled.)

Wage and Hour *(Labor Dept.), Enforcement Policy, Family and Medical Leave,* 200 Constitution Ave. N.W., #S3510 20210; (202) 693-0066. Fax, (202) 693-1387. Diane Dawson, Branch Chief. Press, (202) 693-4676. Web, www.dol.gov/whd

Administers certification of special lower minimum wage rates for workers with disabilities and impaired earning capacity; wage applies in industry, sheltered workshops, hospitals, institutions, and group homes.

Youth

Employment and Training Administration *(Labor Dept.), Youth Services,* 200 Constitution Ave. N.W., #N4508 20210; (202) 693-3030. Fax, (202) 693-3861. Jen Troke, Director.
General email, youthservices@dol.gov

Web, www.doleta.gov/youth_services

Administers youth grant programs designed to enhance youth education, encourage school completion, and provide career and apprenticeship opportunities. Oversees the Going Home: Serious and Violent Offender Reentry Initiative.

Forest Service *(Agriculture Dept.), Youth Conservation Corps,* 1621 N. Kent St., Arlington, VA 22209 (mailing address: 1400 Independence Ave. S.W., MS 1125, Washington, DC 20250-1125); (202) 205-0650. Fax, (703) 605-5131. Merlene Mazyck, Program Manager. Toll-free, (800) 832-1355.
General email, mmazyck@fs.fed.us

Web, www.fs.fed.us/recreation/programs/ycc/index.shtml

Administers with the National Park Service and the Fish and Wildlife Service the Youth Conservation Corps, a summer employment and training public works program for youths ages fifteen to eighteen. The program is conducted in national parks, in national forests, and on national wildlife refuges.

Labor Dept. (DOL), *Job Corps,* 200 Constitution Ave. N.W., #N4463 20210; (202) 693-3000. Fax, (202) 693-2767. Grace Kilbane, Administrator. Information, (800) 733-5627.
General email, national_office@jobcorps.gov

Web, http://jobcorps.doleta.gov

Equal Employment Opportunity Commission

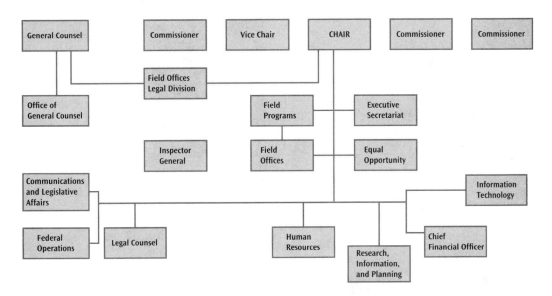

Provides job training for disadvantaged youth at residential centers. Most of the centers are managed and operated by corporations and nonprofit organizations.

Wage and Hour *(Labor Dept.), Enforcement Policy, Child Labor and Fair Labor Standards Act Enforcement,* *200 Constitution Ave. N.W., #S3510 20210; (202) 693-0051. Fax, (202) 693-1387. Derrick Witherspoon, Branch Chief. Press, (202) 693-4659.*
Web, www.dol.gov

Administers and enforces child labor, special minimum wage, and other provisions of Section 14 of the Fair Labor Standards Act.

▶ **NONGOVERNMENTAL**

The Corps Network, *1100 G St. N.W., #1000 20005; (202) 737-6272. Fax, (202) 737-6277. Mary Ellen Ardouny, President.*
Web, www.corpsnetwork.org

Membership: youth corps programs. Produces publications and workshops on starting and operating youth corps and offers technical assistance programs. Holds annual conference. Monitors legislation and regulations.

EQUAL EMPLOYMENT OPPORTUNITY

General

▶ **AGENCIES**

Commission on Civil Rights, *Civil Rights Evaluation,* *1331 Pennsylvania Ave. N.W., #1150 20425; (202) 376-7700. Fax, (202) 376-7754. Margaret Butler, Chief, Acting.*
Web, www.usccr.gov

Researches federal policy in areas of equal employment and job discrimination; monitors the economic status of minorities and women, including their employment and earnings. Library open to the public.

Equal Employment Opportunity Commission (EEOC), *131 M St. N.E. 20507; (202) 663-4001. Fax, (202) 663-4110. Jacqueline A. Berrien, Chair.*
General email, info@eeoc.gov
Web, www.eeoc.gov

Works to end job discrimination by private and government employers based on race, color, religion, sex, national origin, disability, or age. Works to protect employees against reprisal for protest of employment practices alleged to be unlawful in hiring, promotion, firing, wages, and other terms and conditions of employment. Works for increased employment of persons with disabilities, affirmative action by the federal government, and an equitable work environment for employees with mental and physical disabilities. Enforces Title VII of the Civil Rights Act of 1964, as amended, which includes the Pregnancy Discrimination Act; Americans with Disabilities Act; Age Discrimination in Employment Act; Equal Pay Act; and, in the federal sector, rehabilitation laws. Receives charges of discrimination; attempts conciliation or settlement; can bring court action to force compliance; has review and appeals responsibility in the federal sector. Library open to the public by appointment only.

Equal Employment Opportunity Commission (EEOC), *Field Programs, 131 M St. N.E., 5th Floor 20507; (202) 663-4801. Fax, (202) 663-7190. Nicholas Inzeo, Director.*
Web, www.eeoc.gov/field/index.cfm

Provides guidance and technical assistance through 15 district offices to employees who suspect discrimination and to employers who are working to comply with equal employment laws.

Equal Employment Opportunity Contacts at Federal Departments and Agencies

DEPARTMENTS

Agriculture, Joe Leonard Jr., (202) 720-3808

Commerce, Suzan J. Aramaki, (202) 482-0625

Defense, Clarence A. Johnson, (703) 571-9319

  Air Force, Cyrus Salazar, (240) 612-4357

  Army, James Braxton Sr., (202) 761-8706

  Marine Corps, Paula E. Bedford, (703) 784-2946

  Navy, Laura Molsen, (202) 685-6466

Education, Selina Lee, (202) 205-0518

Energy, Dot Harris, (202) 586-8383

Health and Human Services, Arlene E. Austin, (410) 786-5110

Homeland Security, Tamara Kessler, (202) 254-8200

  Coast Guard, Terri Dickerson, (202) 372-4500

Housing and Urban Development, Vacant, (202) 708-3362

Interior, Sharon Eller, (202) 208-5693

Justice, Thomas E. Perez, (202) 514-4609

Labor, Vacant, (202) 693-6500

State, John M. Robinson, (202) 647-9295

Transportation, Camille Hazeur, (202) 366-4648

Treasury, Mariam G. Harvey, (202) 622-0316

Veterans Affairs, Georgia Coffey, (202) 461-4131

AGENCIES

Commission on Civil Rights, Martin R. Castro, (202) 376-7700

Commodity Futures Trading Commission, Sarah Summerville, (202) 418-5257

Consumer Product Safety Commission, Kathy Buttrey, (301) 504-7923

Corporation for National and Community Service, Elizabeth Honnoll, (202) 606-6913

Environmental Protection Agency, Bob Perciasepe, (202) 564-4711

Equal Employment Opportunity Commission, Jacqueline A. Berrien, (202) 663-4900

Export-Import Bank, Patrease Jones-Brown, (202) 565-3591

Farm Credit Administration, Thais Burlew, (703) 883-4390

Federal Communications Commission, Linda Miller, (202) 418-0581

Federal Deposit Insurance Corporation, Anthony Pagano, (703) 562-6062

Federal Election Commission, Kevin Salley, (202) 694-1229

Federal Emergency Management Agency, Pauline Campbell, (202) 646-4122

Federal Energy Regulatory Commission (FERC), Madeline H. Lewis, (202) 502-8120

Federal Labor Relations Authority, Bridget Sisson, (202) 218-7919

Federal Maritime Commission, Keith I. Gilmore, (202) 523-5859

Federal Mediation and Conciliation Service, Adam Ramsey, (202) 606-5460

Federal Reserve Board, Sheila Clark, (202) 452-2883

Federal Trade Commission, Kevin Williams, (202) 326-2196

General Services Administration, Madeline Caliendo, (202) 501-0767

Merit Systems Protection Board, Jerry Beat, (202) 254-4405

National Aeronautics and Space Administration, Frederick Dalton, (202) 358-0941

National Credit Union Administration, S. Denise Hendricks, (703) 518-6326

National Endowment for the Humanities, Anthony Mitchell, (202) 606-8415

National Labor Relations Board, Debra Brown, (202) 273-3891

National Science Foundation, Claudia Postell, (703) 292-8020

National Transportation Safety Board, Fara Guest, (202) 314-6190

Nuclear Regulatory Commission, Lori Suto-Goldbsy, (301) 415-0590

Occupational Safety and Health Review Commission, Anthony Pellegrino, (202) 606-5390

Office of Personnel Management, Lorna Lewis, (202) 606-2460

Peace Corps, Janet Bernal, (202) 692-2113

Securities and Exchange Commission, Pamela A. Gibbs, (202) 551-6046

Small Business Administration, Sandra Winston, (202) 205-7156

Smithsonian Institution, Era Marshall, (202) 633-6430

Social Security Administration, Karen W. Ames, (410) 965-7185

U.S. International Trade Commission, Jacqueline Waters, (202) 205-2240

U.S. Postal Service, Eloise Lance, (202) 268-3820

Justice Dept. (DOJ), *Civil Rights Division, Employment Litigation, 601 D St. N.W., #4040 20579; (202) 514-3831. Fax, (202) 514-1005. Delora L. Kennebrew, Chief. Library, (202) 514-3775.*

Web, www.justice.gov/crt/about/emp

Investigates, negotiates, and litigates allegations of employment discrimination by public schools, universities, state and local governments, and federally funded employers; has enforcement power. Enforces the Uniform Services Employment and Reemployment Rights Act. Members of the public are asked to contact the library with questions about access.

Labor Dept. (DOL), *Federal Contract Compliance Programs, 200 Constitution Ave. N.W., #C3325 20210; (202) 693-0101. Fax, (202) 693-1304. Patricia A. Shiu, Director; Les Jin, Deputy Director. Toll-free, (800) 397-6251. General email, OFCCP-Public@dol.gov*

Web, www.dol.gov/ofccp

Monitors and enforces government contractors' compliance with federal laws and regulations on equal employment opportunities and affirmative action, including employment rights of minorities, women, persons with disabilities, and disabled and Vietnam-era veterans.

Office of Personnel Management (OPM), *Veterans Services, 1900 E St. N.W., #7439 20415; (202) 606-3602. Fax, (202) 606-6017. Hakeem Basheerud-Deen, Director. Web, www.opm.gov/policy-data-oversight/veterans-services*

Administers the Disabled Veterans Affirmative Action Program.

► CONGRESS

For a listing of relevant congressional committees and sub-committees, please see page 193 or the Appendix.

► NONGOVERNMENTAL

Center for Equal Opportunity, *7700 Leesburg Pike, #231, Falls Church, VA 22043; (703) 442-0066. Fax, (703) 442-0449. Roger Clegg, President; Linda Chavez, Chair. General email, comment@ceousa.org*

Web, www.ceousa.org

Research organization concerned with issues of race, ethnicity, and assimilation; opposes racial preferences in employment or education, contracting, and other areas. Monitors legislation and regulations.

Equal Employment Advisory Council, *1501 M St. N.W., #400 20005; (202) 629-5650. Fax, (202) 629-5651. Joseph S. Lakis, President. General email, info@eeac.org*

Web, www.eeac.org

Membership: principal equal employment officers and lawyers. Files amicus curiae (friend of the court) briefs; conducts research and provides information on equal employment law and policy. Monitors legislation and regulations.

NAACP Legal Defense and Educational Fund, Inc., *Washington Office, 1444 Eye St. N.W., 10th Floor 20005; (202) 682-1300. Fax, (202) 682-1312. Leslie M. Proll, Director.*

Web, www.naacpldf.org

Civil rights litigation group that provides legal information about civil rights legislation and advice on employment discrimination against women and minorities; monitors federal enforcement of equal opportunity rights laws. Not affiliated with the NAACP. (Headquarters in New York.)

Minorities

► AGENCIES

Bureau of Indian Affairs (BIA) *(Interior Dept.), Indian Energy and Economic Development, 1951 Constitution Ave. N.W., MS-20, 20245; (202) 219-0740. Fax, (202) 208-4564. Karen J. Atkinson, Director.*

Web, www.bia.gov

Develops policies and programs to promote the achievement of economic goals for members of federally recognized tribes who live on or near reservations. Provides job training; assists those who have completed job training programs in finding employment; provides loan guarantees; enhances contracting opportunities for individuals and tribes; assists with environmentally responsible exploration, development, and management of energy and mineral resources to generate new jobs.

Education Dept., *White House Initiative on Asian Americans and Pacific Islanders, 550 12th St. S.W., 10th Floor 20202; (202) 453-7277. Fax, (202) 453-6238. Kiran Ahuja, Executive Director. Press, (202) 453-6566. General email, http://whitehouseaapi@ed.gov*

Web, www.whitehouse.gov/aapi

Works to expand Asian American and Pacific Islander federal employment opportunities. Ensures that workers' rights are protected and upheld.

Employment and Training Administration *(Labor Dept.), Indian and Native American Programs, 200 Constitution Ave. N.W., #S4209 20210; (202) 693-3949. Fax, (202) 693-3890. Evangeline Campbell, Program Manager, (202) 693-3737.*

Web, www.doleta.gov/dinap

Administers grants for training and employment-related programs to promote employment opportunity; provides unemployed, underemployed, and economically disadvantaged Native Americans and Alaska and Hawaiian Natives with funds for training, job placement, and support services.

► NONGOVERNMENTAL

American Assn. for Affirmative Action, *888 16th St. N.W., #800 20006; (202) 349-9855. Fax, (202) 355-1399. Shirley J. Wilcher, Executive Director. Toll-free, (800) 252-8952.*

General email, execdir@affirmativeaction.org

Web, www.affirmativeaction.org

Membership: professional managers in the areas of affirmative action, equal opportunity, diversity, and human resources. Sponsors education, research, and training programs. Acts as a liaison with government agencies involved in equal opportunity compliance. Maintains ethical standards for the profession.

Coalition of Black Trade Unionists, *1150 17th St. N.W., #300 20036 (mailing address: P.O. Box 66268, Washington, DC 20035); (202) 778-3318. Fax, (202) 293-5308. Terrence L. Melvin, President.*

General email, cbtul@hotmail.com

Web, www.cbtu.org

Monitors legislation affecting African American and other minority trade unionists. Focuses on equal employment opportunity, unemployment, and voter education and registration.

Labor Council for Latin American Advancement, *815 16th St. N.W., 3rd Floor 20006; (202) 508-6919. Fax, (202) 508-6922. Hector Sanchez, Executive Director.*

General email, headquarters@lclaa.org

Web, www.lclaa.org

Membership: Hispanic trade unionists. Encourages equal employment opportunity, voter registration, and participation in the political process. (Affiliated with the AFL-CIO and the Change to Win Federation.)

Mexican American Legal Defense and Educational Fund, *Washington Office, 1016 16th St. N.W., #100 20036; (202) 293-2828. James Ferg-Cadima, Regional Counsel. Web, www.maldef.org/about/offices/washington_dc/index.html*

Provides Mexican Americans and other Hispanics with high-impact litigation in the areas of employment, education, immigration rights, and voting rights. Monitors legislation and regulations. (Headquarters in Los Angeles, Calif.)

National Assn. for the Advancement of Colored People (NAACP), *Washington Bureau, 1156 15th St. N.W., #915 20005; (202) 463-2940. Fax, (202) 463-2953. Hilary O. Shelton, Director.*

General email, washingtonbureau@naacpnet.org

Web, www.naacp.org

Membership: persons interested in civil rights for all minorities. Advises individuals with employment discrimination complaints. Seeks to eliminate job discrimination and to bring about full employment for all Americans through legislation and litigation. (Headquarters in Baltimore, Md.)

National Assn. of Hispanic Federal Executives, Inc., *P.O. Box 23270 20026-3270; (202) 315-3942. Al Gallegos, National President.*

General email, president@nahfe.org

Web, www.nahfe.org

Works to ensure that the needs of the Hispanic American community are addressed in the policy-making levels of the federal government by promoting career opportunities for qualified Hispanics in the federal GS/GM-12/15 grade levels and the Senior Executive Service policy-making positions.

National Assn. of Negro Business and Professional Women's Clubs Inc., *1806 New Hampshire Ave. N.W. 20009; (202) 483-4206. Fax, (202) 462-7253. Jennifer Bryant, Executive Director.*

General email, executivedirector@nanbpwc.org

Web, www.nanbpwc.org

Promotes opportunities for African American women in business; sponsors workshops and scholarships; maintains a job bank. Monitors legislation and regulations.

National Council of La Raza, *1126 16th St. N.W., #600 20036-4845; (202) 785-1670. Fax, (202) 776-1792. Janet Murguia, President.*

General email, comments@nclr.org

Web, www.nclr.org

Provides research, policy analysis, and advocacy on Hispanic employment status and programs; provides Hispanic community-based groups with technical assistance to help develop effective employment programs with strong educational components. Works to promote understanding of Hispanic employment needs in the private sector. Interests include women in the workplace, affirmative action, equal opportunity employment, and youth employment. Monitors federal employment legislation and regulations.

National Urban League, *Washington Bureau, 1805 7th St. N.W., #520 20001; (202) 898-1604. Chanelle Hardy, Executive Director.*

Web, www.nulwb.iamempowered.com

Federal advocacy division of social service organization concerned with the social welfare of African Americans and other minorities. Testifies before congressional committees and federal agencies on equal employment; studies and evaluates federal enforcement of equal employment laws and regulations. (Headquarters in New York.)

Society of American Indian Government Employees, *P.O. Box 7715 20044-7715; (202) 378-8346. Susan Johnson, Chair; Fredericka Joseph, Vice Chair.*

General email, chair@saige.org

Web, www.saige.org

Fosters the recruitment, development, and advancement of American Indians and Alaska Natives in the government workforce. Promotes communication among its members. Serves as an information clearinghouse. Coordinates training and conferences for government employees on issues concerning American Indians and Alaska Natives. Monitors legislation and policies.

Women

▶AGENCIES

Labor Dept. (DOL), *Women's Bureau, 200 Constitution Ave. N.W., #S3002 20210; (202) 693-6710. Fax, (202) 693-6725. Loctifa Lyles, Director, Acting. Information, (800) 827-5335.* General email, Women'sBureauNetwork@dol.gov

Web, www.dol.gov/wb

Monitors women's employment issues. Promotes employment opportunities for women; sponsors workshops, job fairs, symposia, demonstrations, and pilot projects. Offers technical assistance; conducts research and provides publications on issues that affect working women; represents working women in international forums.

▶NONGOVERNMENTAL

Business and Professional Women's Foundation, *1718 M St. N.W., #148 20036; (202) 293-1100. Fax, (202) 861-0298. Deborah Frett, Chief Executive Officer.* General email, foundation@bpwfoundation.org

Web, www.bpwfoundation.org

Works to eliminate barriers to the full participation of women in the workplace. Interests include pay equity, work-life balance, women veterans, and green jobs for women. Conducts research; provides issue briefs and other publications; monitors legislation and regulations.

Federally Employed Women, *455 Massachusetts Ave. N.W., #306 20001; (202) 898-0994. Fax, (202) 898-1535. Michelle Crockett, President.* General email, few@few.org

Web, www.few.org

Membership: women and men who work for the federal government. Works to eliminate sex discrimination in government employment and to increase job opportunities for women; offers training programs. Monitors legislation and regulations.

Institute for Women's Policy Research (IWPR), *1200 18th St. N.W., #301 20036; (202) 785-5100. Fax, (202) 833-4362. Heidi Hartmann, President.* General email, iwpr@iwpr.org

Web, www.iwpr.org

Public policy research organization that focuses on women's issues, including welfare reform, family and work policies, employment and wages, and discrimination based on gender, race, or ethnicity.

National Assn. of Women Business Owners, *601 Pennsylvania Ave. N.W., South Bldg., #900 20004; (202) 609-9817. Fax, (202) 403-3788. Vacant, Chief Executive Officer. Toll-free, (800) 556-2926.* General email, national@nawbo.org

Web, www.nawbo.org

Promotes the economic, social, and political interests of women business owners through networking, leadership and business development training, and advocacy.

National Council of Women's Organizations, *714 G St. S.E., #200 20003; (202) 293-4505. Fax, (202) 293-4507. Susan Scanlan, Chair.* General email, ncwo@ncwo-online.org

Web, www.womensorganizations.org

Membership: local and national women's organizations. Engages in policy work and grassroots activism to address issues of concern to women, including workplace and economic equity, education and job training, affirmative action, Social Security, child care, reproductive freedom, health, and global women's equality. Monitors legislation and regulations.

National Women's Law Center, *11 Dupont Circle N.W., #800 20036; (202) 588-5180. Fax, (202) 588-5185. Nancy Duff Campbell, Co-President; Marcia D. Greenberger, Co-President.* General email, info@nwlc.org

Web, www.nwlc.org

Works to protect and advance the rights of women and girls at work, in school, and beyond. Maintains programs that focus on enforcing Title IX's provisions for equal treatment in education and narrowing the gender gap in athletics and the technology-oriented workplace. Other interests include equal pay and benefits, sexual harassment laws, the right to family leave, child care and early learning, poverty and income support, and the preservation of diversity in the workplace.

Wider Opportunities for Women, *1001 Connecticut Ave. N.W., #930 20036-5504; (202) 464-1596. Fax, (202) 464-1660. Shawn McMahon, Chief Executive Officer, Acting.* General email, info@WOWonline.org

Web, www.WOWonline.org

Promotes equal employment opportunities for women through equal access to jobs and training, equal incomes, and an equitable workplace. Monitors public policy relating to jobs, affirmative action, vocational education, training opportunities, and welfare reform.

LABOR-MANAGEMENT OPPORTUNITY

General

▶AGENCIES

Bureau of Labor Statistics (BLS) *(Labor Dept.),* ***Compensation and Working Conditions,*** *2 Massachusetts Ave. N.E., #4130 20212; (202) 691-6300. Fax, (202) 691-6310. William J. Wiatrowski, Associate Commissioner.* Web, www.bls.gov/bls/proghome.htm#ocwc

Compiles data on wages and benefits, work stoppages, and workplace injuries, illnesses, and fatalities. Compiles data for Employment Cost Index, published quarterly.

Criminal Division *(Justice Dept.),* ***Organized Crime and Gang Section,*** *1301 New York Ave. N.W., #700 20005;*

National Labor Relations Board

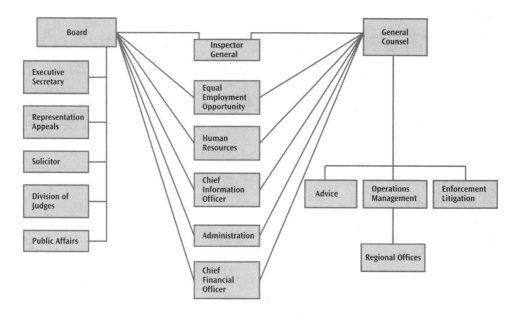

(202) 514-3594. Fax, (202) 514-3601. James Trusty, Chief. Press, (202) 353-4542.

General email, criminaldivision@us.doj.gov

Reviews and advises on prosecutions of criminal violations involving labor-management relations, the operation of employee pension and health care plans, and internal affairs of labor unions.

Defense Dept. (DoD), *National Committee for Employer Support of the Guard and Reserve (ESGR),* 4800 Mark Center Dr., #03E25, Arlington, VA 22350-1200; (703) 882-3747. Ronald Young, Executive Director. Toll-free, (800) 336-4590. Media, (571) 372-0705.
General email, USERRA@osd.mil

Web, www.esgr.mil

Works to gain and maintain employer support for National Guard and Reserve service by recognizing outstanding support and providing service members and employers with information on applicable laws. Volunteers provide free education, consultation, and, if necessary, mediation between employers and National Guard and Reserve service members.

Federal Mediation and Conciliation Service, 2100 K St. N.W. 20427; (202) 606-8100. Fax, (202) 606-4251.
George H. Cohen, Director.
Web, www.fmcs.gov

Assists labor and management representatives in resolving disputes in collective bargaining contract negotiation through voluntary mediation and arbitration services; awards competitive grants to joint labor-management initiatives; trains other federal agencies in mediating administrative disputes and formulating rules and regulations under the Administrative Dispute Resolution Act

of 1996 and the Negotiated Rulemaking Act of 1996; provides training to unions and management in cooperative processes. Operates 60 field offices.

Labor Dept. (DOL), *Labor-Management Standards,* 200 Constitution Ave. N.W., #N1519 20210; (202) 693-0122. Fax, (202) 693-1206. Michael J. Hayes, Director. Press, (202) 693-4676. Information, (202) 693-0123.
General email, olms-public@dol.gov

Web, www.dol.gov/olms

Administers and enforces the Labor-Management Reporting and Disclosure Act of 1959 (Landrum-Griffin Act), which guarantees union members certain rights; sets rules for electing union officers, handling union funds, and using trusteeships; requires unions, union officers and employees, employers, and labor consultants to file financial and other reports with the Labor Dept. Administers relevant sections of the Civil Service Reform Act of 1980 and the Foreign Service Act of 1980. Administers the employee protection provisions of the Federal Transit law.

National Labor Relations Board (NLRB), 1099 14th St. N.W. 20570-0001; (202) 273-1000. Fax, (202) 273-1789. Mark G. Pearce, Chair; Richard F. Griffin Jr., General Counsel. Library, (202) 273-3720. Press and public information, (202) 273-1991. Toll-free, (866) 667-6572. Web, www.nlrb.gov

Administers the National Labor Relations Act. Works to prevent and remedy unfair labor practices by employers and labor unions; conducts elections among employees to determine whether they wish to be represented by a labor union for collective bargaining purposes. Complaints may be filed in field offices by calling the toll-free line. Library open to the public.

National Mediation Board, *1301 K St. N.W., #250E 20005; (202) 692-5000. Fax, (202) 692-5080. Harry R. Hoglander, Chair. Information, (202) 692-5050.*
General email, infoline@nmb.gov
Web, www.nmb.gov

Mediates labor disputes in the railroad and airline industries; determines and certifies labor representatives for those industries. Library open by appointment.

▶**CONGRESS**

For a listing of relevant congressional committees and sub-committees, please see page 193 or the Appendix.

▶**NONGOVERNMENTAL**

AFL-CIO (American Federation of Labor–Congress of Industrial Organizations), *815 16th St. N.W. 20006; (202) 637-5000. Fax, (202) 637-5058. Richard L. Trumka, President.*
Web, www.aflcio.org

Voluntary federation of national and international labor unions in the United States. Represents members before Congress and other branches of government. Each member union conducts its own contract negotiations. Library (located in Silver Spring, Md.) open to the public.

American Arbitration Assn., *Government Relations, Washington Office, Regional Office, 1776 Eye St. N.W., #850 20006; (202) 739-8280. Fax, (202) 223-7095. Pierre Paret, Vice President.*
General email, paretp@adr.org
Web, www.adr.org

Provides alternative dispute resolution services to governments and the private sector. (Headquarters in New York.)

American Federation of Musicians, *Government Relations, 5335 Wisconsin Ave. N.W., #440 20015; (202) 274-4756. Fax, (202) 274-4759. Alfonso Pollard, Director.*
General email, apollard@afm.org
Web, www.afm.org

Seeks to improve the working conditions and salary of musicians. Monitors legislation and regulations affecting musicians and the arts. (Headquarters in New York.)

American Foreign Service Assn. (AFSA), *2101 E St. N.W. 20037; (202) 338-4045. Fax, (202) 338-6820. Ian Houston, Executive Director. Press, (202) 944-5501. Toll-free (within the U.S.), (800) 704-2372.*
General email, member@afsa.org
Web, www.afsa.org

Membership: active and retired foreign service employees of federal agencies. Represents active duty foreign service personnel in labor-management negotiations; seeks to ensure adequate resources for foreign service operations and personnel. Monitors legislation and regulations related to foreign service personnel and retirees.

The Center for Union Facts, *1090 Vermont Ave. N.W., #800 20005 (mailing address: P.O. Box 34507, Washington,*

AFL-CIO

DEPARTMENTS
Civil, Human, and Women's Rights, Rosalyn Pelles, Director, (202) 637-5270
Government Affairs, William Samuel, Director, (202) 637-5320
International Affairs, Cathy Feingold, Director, (202) 637-5050
Legal Dept., Lynn Rhinehart, General Counsel, (202) 637-5053
Office of the President, Richard L. Trumka, President, (202) 637-5231
Organizing, Mary Bunn, Director, (202) 639-6200
Political, Michael Podhorzer, Director, (202) 637-5101
Public Affairs, Denise Mitchell, Assistant to the President, (202) 637-5340
Safety and Health, Margaret Seminario, Director, (202) 637-5366

TRADE AND INDUSTRIAL SECTORS
Building and Construction Trades, Sean McGarvey, President, (202) 347-1461
Maritime Trades, Michael Sacco, President, (202) 628-6300
Metal Trades, Ronald Ault, President, (202) 508-3705
Professional Employees, Paul E. Almeida, President, (202) 638-0320
Transportation Trades, Edward Wytkind, President, (202) 628-9262
Union Label and Service Trades, Richard Kline, President, (202) 508-3700

DC 20043); (202) 463-7106. Fax, (202) 463-7107. Richard Berman, Executive Director.
General email, info@unionfacts.com
Web, www.unionfacts.com

Seeks to educate businesses, union members, and the public about the labor movement's political activities, specifically those of union officials. Interests include management of union dues. Monitors legislation and regulations.

Coalition of Black Trade Unionists, *1150 17th St. N.W., #300 20036 (mailing address: P.O. Box 66268, Washington, DC 20035); (202) 778-3318. Fax, (202) 293-5308. Terrence L. Melvin, President.*
General email, cbtul@hotmail.com
Web, www.cbtu.org

Monitors legislation affecting African American and other minority trade unionists. Focuses on equal employment opportunity, unemployment, and voter education and registration.

Coalition of Labor Union Women, *815 16th St. N.W., 2nd Floor South 20006-1119; (202) 508-6969. Fax, (202) 508-6968. Connie Leak, President; Carol S. Rosenblatt, Executive Director.*
General email, getinfo@cluw.org

Web, www.cluw.org

Seeks to make unions more responsive to the needs of women in the workplace; advocates affirmative action and the active participation of women in unions. Monitors legislation and regulations.

International Brotherhood of Teamsters, *25 Louisiana Ave. N.W. 20001-2198; (202) 624-6800. Fax, (202) 624-6918. James P. Hoffa, General President; Fred McLuckie, Director, Federal Legislation and Regulation, (202) 624-8741. Press, (202) 624-6911.*
General email, feedback@teamster.org

Web, www.teamster.org

Membership: more than 1.4 million workers in the transportation and construction industries, factories, offices, hospitals, warehouses, and other workplaces. Helps members negotiate pay, benefits, and better working conditions; conducts training programs and workshops. Monitors legislation and regulations.

Labor Council for Latin American Advancement, *815 16th St. N.W., 3rd Floor 20006; (202) 508-6919. Fax, (202) 508-6922. Hector Sanchez, Executive Director.*
General email, headquarters@lclaa.org

Web, www.lclaa.org

Membership: Hispanic trade unionists. Encourages equal employment opportunity, voter registration, and participation in the political process. (Affiliated with the AFL-CIO and the Change to Win Federation.)

Laborers' International Union of North America, *905 16th St. N.W. 20006-1765; (202) 737-8320. Fax, (202) 737-2754. Terence O'Sullivan, President.*
Web, www.liuna.org

Membership: more than 500,000 construction workers; federal, state, and local government employees; health care professionals; mail handlers; custodial service personnel; shipbuilders; and hazardous waste handlers. Helps members negotiate pay, benefits, and better working conditions; conducts training programs and workshops. Monitors legislation and regulations. (Affiliated with the AFL-CIO.)

National Assn. of Manufacturers (NAM), *Human Resources Policy, 733 10th St. N.W., #700 20001; (202) 637-3127. Fax, (202) 637-3182. Joe Trauger, Vice President. Alternate phone, (202) 637-3000.*
Web, www.nam.org

Provides information on corporate industrial relations, including collective bargaining, labor standards, international labor relations, productivity, employee benefits, health care, and other current labor issues; monitors legislation and regulations.

National Labor College, *10000 New Hampshire Ave., Silver Spring, MD 20903-1706; (301) 431-6400. Fax, (301)*
431-5411. Paula E. Peinovich, President, (301) 431-5401. Toll-free, (888) 427-8100.
Web, www.nlc.edu

Accredited college that offers a bachelor of arts in labor studies disciplines and union skills. Offers graduate opportunities through programs with George Mason University and the University of Baltimore.

National Right to Work Committee, *8001 Braddock Rd., #500, Springfield, VA 22160; (703) 321-9820. Fax, (703) 321-7342. Mark Mix, President. Information, (800) 325-7892.*
General email, info@nrtwc.org

Web, www.nrtwc.org

Citizens' organization opposed to compulsory union membership. Supports right-to-work legislation.

National Right to Work Legal Defense Foundation, *8001 Braddock Rd., #600, Springfield, VA 22160; (703) 321-8510. Fax, (703) 321-9613. Mark Mix, President. Toll-free, (800) 336-3600.*
General email, info@nrtw.org

Web, www.nrtw.org

Provides free legal aid for employees in cases of compulsory union membership abuses.

Public Service Research Foundation, *320 D Maple Ave. East, Vienna, VA 22180-4747; (703) 242-3575. Fax, (703) 242-3579. David Y. Denholm, President.*
General email, info@psrf.org

Web, www.psrf.org

Independent, nonpartisan research and educational organization. Studies labor unions and labor issues with emphasis on employment in the public sector. Sponsors conferences and seminars. Library open to the public by appointment.

Service Employees International Union, *1800 Massachusetts Ave. N.W. 20036; (202) 730-7000. Fax, (202) 429-5563. Mary Kay Henry, President. Press, (202) 730-7162. Toll-free, (800) 424-8592.*
General email, media@seiu.org

Web, www.seiu.org

Membership: approximately 2.2 million members in Canada, the United States, and Puerto Rico among health care, public services, and property services employees. Promotes better wages, health care, and job security for workers. Monitors legislation and regulations.

UNITE HERE, *Washington Office, 1775 K St. N.W., #620 20006-1530; (202) 393-4373. Fax, (202) 223-6213. Tom Snyder, Political Director; John W. Wilhelm, President.*
Web, www.unitehere.org

Membership: more than 270,000 workers in the United States and Canada who work in the hospitality, gaming, food service, manufacturing, textile, laundry, and airport industries. Helps members negotiate pay, benefits, and better working conditions; conducts training programs and workshops. Monitors legislation and regulations. (Headquarters in New York. Formed by the merger of the former Union of Needletrades, Textiles, and Industrial Employees and the Hotel Employees and Restaurant Employees International Union.)

United Auto Workers, *Washington Office, 1757 N St. N.W. 20036; (202) 828-8500. Fax, (202) 293-3457. Josh Nassar, Legislative Director.*
Web, www.uaw.org

Membership: approximately 750,000 active and 600,000 retired North American workers in aerospace, automotive, defense, manufacturing, steel, technical, and other industries. Assists members with contract negotiations and grievances; conducts training programs and workshops. Monitors legislation and regulations. (Headquarters in Detroit, Mich.)

United Electrical, Radio and Machine Workers of America, *P.O. Box 10031, Alexandria, VA 22310-0031; (703) 341-9446. Chris Townsend, Political Action Director. Information, (412) 471-8919.*
General email, uewashingtonoffice@gmail.com
Web, www.ueunion.org

Represents over 35,000 workers in electrical, metal working, and plastic manufacturing public sector and private nonprofit sector jobs. Membership: manufacturing assembly workers, plastic injection molders, tool and die makers, sheet metal workers, truck drivers, warehouse workers, custodians, clerical workers, graduate instructors, graduate researchers, scientists, librarians, social workers, and day care workers. (National headquarters in Pittsburgh, Pa.)

U.S. Chamber of Commerce, *Labor, Immigration, and Employee Benefits, 1615 H St. N.W. 20062-2000; (202) 463-5522. Fax, (202) 463-3194. Randel K. Johnson, Senior Vice President; Amy Nice, Executive Director for Immigration Policy.*
Web, www.uschamber.com/labor-immigration-and-employee benefits

Formulates and analyzes Chamber policy in the areas of labor law, immigration, pension, and health care. Monitors legislation and regulations affecting labor-management relations, employee benefits, and immigration issues.

PENSIONS AND BENEFITS

General

▶ **AGENCIES**

Advisory Council on Employee Welfare and Pension Benefit Plans *(ERISA Advisory Council), (Labor Dept.), 200 Constitution Ave. N.W., #N5623 20210; (202) 693-8668. Fax, (202) 219-8141. Larry Good, Executive Secretary.*
Web, www.dol.gov/ebsa

Advises and makes recommendations to the secretary of labor under the Employee Retirement Income Security Act of 1974 (ERISA).

Bureau of Labor Statistics (BLS) *(Labor Dept.), Compensation and Working Conditions, 2 Massachusetts Ave. N.E., #4130 20212; (202) 691-6300. Fax, (202) 691-6310. William J. Wiatrowski, Associate Commissioner.*
Web, www.bls.gov/bls/proghome.htm#ocwc

Compiles data on wages and benefits, work stoppages, and workplace injuries, illnesses, and fatalities. Compiles data for Employment Cost Index, published quarterly.

Bureau of Labor Statistics (BLS) *(Labor Dept.), Compensation Levels and Trends, 2 Massachusetts Ave. N.E., #4175 20212; (202) 691-6200. Fax, (202) 691-6647. Philip M. Doyle, Assistant Commissioner.*
Web, www.bls.gov/ncs

Compiles data on wages and benefits. Develops the National Compensation Survey. Analyzes, distributes, and disseminates information on occupational earnings, benefits, and compensation trends.

Criminal Division *(Justice Dept.), Organized Crime and Gang Section, 1301 New York Ave. N.W., #700 20005; (202) 514-3594. Fax, (202) 514-3601. James Trusty, Chief. Press, (202) 353-4542.*
General email, criminaldivision@us.doj.gov

Reviews and advises on prosecutions of criminal violations concerning the operation of employee benefit plans in the private sector.

Employee Benefits Security Administration *(Labor Dept.), 200 Constitution Ave. N.W., #S2524 20210; (202) 693-8300. Fax, (202) 219-5526. Phyllis C. Borzi, Assistant Secretary.*
Web, www.dol.gov/ebsa

Administers, regulates, and enforces private employee benefit plan standards established by the Employee Retirement Income Security Act of 1974 (ERISA), with particular emphasis on fiduciary obligations; receives and maintains required reports from employee benefit plan administrators pursuant to ERISA.

Federal Retirement Thrift Investment Board, *77 K St. N.W., #1000 20005; (202) 942-1600. Fax, (202) 639-4428. Gregory T. Long, Executive Director. Toll-free, (877) 968-3778.*
Web, www.frtib.gov

Administers the Thrift Savings Plan, a tax-deferred, defined contribution plan that permits federal employees and members of the uniformed services to save for additional retirement security under a program similar to private 401(k) plans.

Joint Board for the Enrollment of Actuaries, *1111 Constitution Ave. N.W., SE: RPO, Internal Revenue Service 20224; (202) 622-8229. Fax, (202) 622-8300. Patrick McDonough, Executive Director, (202) 622-8225.*
General email, nhqjbea@irs.gov
Web, www.irs.gov/taxpros/actuaries/index.html

Joint board, with members from the Departments of Labor and Treasury and the Pension Benefit Guaranty Corp., established under the Employee Retirement Income Security Act of 1974 (ERISA). Promulgates regulations for the enrollment of pension actuaries; examines applicants and grants certificates of enrollment; disciplines enrolled actuaries who have engaged in misconduct in the discharge of duties under ERISA.

Office of Personnel Management (OPM), *Retirement Operations, 1900 E St. N.W., #3305 20415-1000; (202) 606-0300. Fax, (202) 606-0145. Nick Ashendon, Deputy Associate Director, (724) 794-2005, ext. 3214. Toll-free, (888) 767-6738.*
General email, retire@opm.gov

Web, www.opm.gov/retire

Provides civil servants with information and assistance on federal retirement payments.

Pension Benefit Guaranty Corp., *1200 K St. N.W., #12000 20005-4026 (mailing address: P.O. Box 151750, Alexandria, VA 22315-1750); (202) 326-4000. Fax, (202) 326-4047. Joshua Gotbaum, Director. General Legal Inquiries, (202) 326-4020. Locator, (202) 326-4110. Customer Service, (800) 400-7242.*
Web, www.pbgc.gov

Self-financed U.S. government corporation. Insures private-sector defined benefit pension plans; guarantees payment of retirement benefits subject to certain limitations established in the Employee Retirement Income Security Act of 1974 (ERISA). Provides insolvent multiemployer pension plans with financial assistance to enable them to pay guaranteed retirement benefits.

►CONGRESS

For a listing of relevant congressional committees and subcommittees, please see page 193 or the Appendix.

Government Accountability Office (GAO), *Education, Workforce, and Income Security, 441 G St. N.W., #5928 20548; (202) 512-7215. Barbara D. Bovbjerg, Managing Director.*
Web, www.gao.gov

Independent, nonpartisan agency in the legislative branch. Audits, analyzes, and evaluates federal agency and private sector pension programs; makes reports available to the public.

►NONGOVERNMENTAL

AARP, *601 E St. N.W. 20049; (202) 434-2277. Fax, (202) 434-2320. A. Barry Rand, Chief Executive Officer. Press, (202) 434-2560. Library, (202) 434-6233. Toll-free, (888) 687-2277. Membership, (202) 434-3525.*
General email, member@aarp.org

Web, www.aarp.org

Researches and testifies on private, federal, and other government employee pension legislation and regulations; conducts seminars; provides information on preretirement preparation.

American Academy of Actuaries, *1850 M St. N.W., #300 20036; (202) 223-8196. Fax, (202) 872-1948. Mary Downs, Executive Director.*
Web, www.actuary.org

Membership: professional actuaries practicing in the areas of life, health, liability, property, and casualty insurance; pensions; government insurance plans; and general consulting. Provides information on actuarial matters, including insurance and pensions; develops professional standards; advises public policymakers.

American Benefits Council, *1501 M St. N.W., #600 20005; (202) 289-6700. Fax, (202) 289-4582. James A. Klein, President.*
General email, info@abcstaff.org

Web, www.americanbenefitscouncil.org

Membership: employers, consultants, banks, and service organizations. Informs members of employee benefits, including private pension benefits, health benefits, and compensation.

American Society of Pension Professionals and Actuaries, *4245 N. Fairfax Dr., #750, Arlington, VA 22203-1648; (703) 516-9300. Fax, (703) 516-9308. Brian Graff, Executive Director.*
General email, asppa@asppa.org

Web, www.asppa.org

Membership: administrators, actuaries, advisers, lawyers, accountants, and other financial services professionals who provide consulting and administrative services for employee-based retirement plans. Sponsors educational conferences, webcasts, and credentialing programs for retirement professionals. Monitors legislation and regulations.

Coalition to Preserve Retirement Security, *112 S. Pitt St., Alexandria, VA 22314; (703) 684-5236. Fax, (703) 684-3417. Thomas Lussier, Administrator.*
General email, tlussier@lgva.net

Web, www.retirementsecurity.org

Coalition of current public employees and retirees. Supports the voluntary participation of state and local employees in the Social Security system. Opposes all legislation that would compel public employees into participation in the system.

Employee Benefit Research Institute, *1100 13th St. N.W., #878 20005; (202) 659-0670. Fax, (202) 775-6312. Dallas L. Salisbury, President.*
General email, info@ebri.org

Web, www.ebri.org

Research organization serving as an employee benefits information source on health, welfare, and retirement issues. Does not lobby and does not take public policy positions.

Employers Council on Flexible Compensation, *1444 Eye St. N.W., #700 20005; (202) 659-4300. Fax, (202) 216-9646. Natasha Rankin, Executive Director.*
General email, info@ecfc.org

Web, www.ecfc.org

Advocates for tax-advantaged, private employer benefit programs. Supports the preservation and expansion of employee choice in savings and pension plans. Monitors legislation and regulations. Interests include cafeteria plans and 401(k) plans.

ERISA Industry Committee, *1400 L St. N.W., #350 20005; (202) 789-1400. Fax, (202) 789-1120. Scott Macey, President, (202) 627-1910.*
General email, eric@eric.org
Web, www.eric.org

Membership: major U.S. employers. Advocates members' positions on employee retirement, health care coverage, and welfare benefit plans. Monitors legislation and regulations.

National Assn. of Manufacturers (NAM), *Human Resources Policy, 733 10th St. N.W., #700 20001; (202) 637-3127. Fax, (202) 637-3182. Joe Trauger, Vice President. Alternate phone, (202) 637-3000.*
Web, www.nam.org

Interests include health care, cost containment, mandated benefits, Medicare, and other federal programs that affect employers. Opposed to government involvement in health care and proposed expansion of health care liability.

Pension Rights Center, *1350 Connecticut Ave. N.W., #206 20036; (202) 296-3776. Fax, (202) 833-2472. Karen W. Ferguson, Director. Toll-free, (888) 420-6550.*
General email, kgarrett@pensionrights.org
Web, www.pensionrights.org

Works to preserve and expand pension rights; provides information and technical assistance on pension law.

Plan Sponsor Council of America, *Washington Office, 1155 F St. N.W., #1050 20004; (202) 641-7671. Edward Ferrigno, Vice President of Washington Affairs.*
General email, ferrigno@401k.org
Web, www.psca.org

Encourages the use of profit sharing, 401(k) accounts, and related savings and incentive programs to strengthen free-enterprise systems. Provides assistance and information to member companies about the design, administration, compliance, investment, communication, and motivation practices associated with such programs. (Headquarters in Chicago.)

Society of Professional Benefit Administrators, *2 Wisconsin Circle, #670, Chevy Chase, MD 20815; (301) 718-7722. Fax, (301) 718-9440. Anne Lennan, President.*
General email, info@spbatpa.org
Web, www.spbatpa.org

Membership: third-party administration firms that manage outside claims and benefit plans for client employers. Monitors government compliance requirements. Interests include pensions and retirement policy and funding, health funding, and the Employee Retirement Income Security Act of 1974 (ERISA).

United Mine Workers of America Health and Retirement Funds, *2121 K St. N.W., #350 20037-1801; (202) 521-2200. Fax, (202) 521-2394. Lorraine Lewis, Executive Director. Call center, (800) 291-1425.*
General email, health1@umwafunds.org
Web, www.umwafunds.org

Labor/management trust fund that provides health and retirement benefits to coal miners. Health benefits are provided to pensioners, their dependents, and, in some cases, their survivors.

Urban Institute, *The Income and Benefits Policy Center, 2100 M St. N.W. 20037; (202) 833-7200. Fax, (202) 833-4388. Gregory Acf, Director.*
Web, www.urban.org/center/ibp

Studies how public policy influences behavior and the economic well-being of families, particularly the disabled, the elderly, and those with low incomes.

Women's Institute for a Secure Retirement (WISER), *1140 19th St. N.W., #550 20036; (202) 393-5452. Fax, (202) 393-5890. Cindy Hounsell, President.*
General email, info@wiserwomen.org
Web, www.wiserwomen.org

Provides information on women's retirement issues. Monitors legislation and regulations.

WORKPLACE SAFETY AND HEALTH

General

▶ **AGENCIES**

Bureau of Labor Statistics (BLS) *(Labor Dept.),* **Compensation and Working Conditions,** *2 Massachusetts Ave. N.E., #4130 20212; (202) 691-6300. Fax, (202) 691-6310. William J. Wiatrowski, Associate Commissioner.*
Web, www.bls.gov/bls/proghome.htm#ocwc

Compiles data on occupational safety and health.

Federal Mine Safety and Health Review Commission, *1331 Pennsylvania Ave., N.W., #520N 20004-1710; (202) 434-9905. Fax, (202) 434-9906. Lisa Boyd, Executive Director; Mary L. Jordan, Chair.*
General email, fmshrc@fmshrc.gov
Web, www.fmshrc.gov

Independent agency established by the Federal Mine Safety and Health Act of 1977. Holds fact-finding hearings and issues orders affirming, modifying, or vacating the labor secretary's enforcement actions regarding mine safety and health. Reading room open to the public by appointment.

Health, Safety, and Security *(Energy Dept.),* *1000 Independence Ave. S.W., #7G040 20585; (301) 903-3777. Fax, (202) 586-7960. Glenn S. Podonsky, Chief Officer, (202) 586-0271.*
General email, HSSusersupport@hq.doe.gov
Web, www.hss.energy.gov

Develops policy and establishes standards to ensure safety and health protection in all department activities.

Occupational Safety and Health Administration

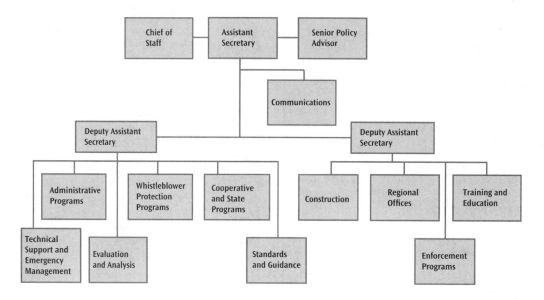

Mine Safety and Health Administration *(Labor Dept.),* *1100 Wilson Blvd., #2322, Arlington, VA 22209-3939; (202) 693-9899. Fax, (202) 693-9801. Joseph A. Main, Assistant Secretary.*
General email, ASKMSHA@dol.gov

Web, www.msha.gov

Administers and enforces the health and safety provisions of the Federal Mine Safety and Health Act of 1977.

National Institute for Occupational Safety and Health (NIOSH) *(Centers for Disease Control and Prevention),* *395 E St. S.W., Patriots Plaza 1, #9200 20201; (202) 245-0625. John Howard, Director. Information, (800) 232-4636.*
General email, cdcinfo@cdc.gov

Web, www.cdc.gov/niosh

Entity within the Centers for Disease Control and Prevention in Atlanta. Supports and conducts research on occupational safety and health issues; provides technical assistance and training; develops recommendations for the Labor Dept. Operates an occupational safety and health bibliographic database (mailing address: NIOSH Clearinghouse for Occupational Safety and Health Information, 4676 Columbia Pkwy., Cincinnati, OH 45226).

Occupational Safety and Health Administration (OSHA) *(Labor Dept.), 200 Constitution Ave. N.W., #S2315 20210; (202) 693-2000. Fax, (202) 693-1659. David M. Michaels, Assistant Secretary. Hotline, (800) 321-6742.*
Web, www.osha.gov

Sets and enforces rules and regulations for workplace safety and health. Implements the Occupational Safety and Health Act of 1970. Provides federal agencies and private industries with compliance guidance and assistance.

Occupational Safety and Health Administration (OSHA) *(Labor Dept.), Communications, 200 Constitution Ave. N.W., #N3647 20210; (202) 693-1999. Fax, (202) 693-1635. Francis Meilinger, Director. Emergency hotline, (800) 321-OSHA.*
Web, www.osha.gov/as/index.html

Develops strategies, products, and materials to promote public understanding of OSHA standards, regulations, guidelines, policies, and activities to improve the safety and health of employees.

Occupational Safety and Health Administration (OSHA) *(Labor Dept.), Construction, 200 Constitution Ave. N.W., #N3468 20210; (202) 693-2020. Fax, (202) 693-1689. Jim Maddux, Director.*
Web, www.osha.gov/doc

Provides technical expertise to OSHA's enforcement personnel; initiates studies to determine causes of construction accidents; works with the private sector to promote construction safety and training and to identify, reduce, and eliminate construction-related hazards.

Occupational Safety and Health Administration (OSHA) *(Labor Dept.), Cooperative and State Programs, 200 Constitution Ave. N.W., #N3700 20210; (202) 693-2200. Fax, (202) 693-1671. Douglas Kalinowski, Director.*
Web, www.osha.gov/dcsp

Implements OSHA's cooperative programs, coordinates the agency's compliance assistance and outreach activities, and coordinates the agency's relations with state plan states.

Occupational Safety and Health Administration (OSHA) *(Labor Dept.), Enforcement Programs, 200 Constitution*

Ave. N.W., #N3119 20210; (202) 693-2100. Fax, (202) 693-1681. Thomas Galassi, Director.
Web, www.osha.gov/dep/enforcement/dep_offices.html

Interprets compliance safety standards for agency field personnel and private employees and employers.

Occupational Safety and Health Administration (OSHA) (Labor Dept.), Standards and Guidance, 200 Constitution Ave. N.W., #N3718 20210; (202) 693-1950. Fax, (202) 693-1678. Bill Perry, Director, Acting. Press, (202) 693-1950.
Web, www.osha.gov/dsg/index.html

Develops new or revised occupational health standards for toxic, hazardous, and carcinogenic substances; biological and safety hazards; or other harmful physical agents, such as vibration, noise, and radiation.

Occupational Safety and Health Review Commission, 1120 20th St. N.W., 9th Floor 20036-3457; (202) 606-5100. Fax, (202) 606-5050. Thomasina V. Rogers, Chair, (202) 606-5370.
Web, www.oshrc.gov

Independent executive branch agency that adjudicates disputes between private employers and the Occupational Safety and Health Administration arising under the Occupational Safety and Health Act of 1970.

▶CONGRESS

For a listing of relevant congressional committees and subcommittees, please see page 193 or the Appendix.

▶NONGOVERNMENTAL

American Industrial Hygiene Assn., 3141 Fairview Park Dr., #777, Falls Church, VA 20042-4507; (703) 849-8888, ext. 0. Fax, (703) 207-3561. Peter O'Neil, Executive Director, ext. 760.
General email, infonet@aiha.org
Web, www.aiha.org

Membership: scientists and engineers who practice industrial hygiene in government, labor, academic institutions, and independent organizations. Promotes health and safety standards in the workplace and the community; conducts research to identify potential dangers; educates workers about job-related risks; monitors safety regulations. Interests include international standards and information exchange.

Fair Labor Assn. (FLA), 1111 19th St. N.W., #401 20036; (202) 898-1000. Fax, (202) 898-9050. Jorge Perez-Lopez, Executive Director.
General email, info@fairlabor.org
Web, www.fairlabor.org

Membership: consumer, human, and labor rights groups; apparel and footwear manufacturers and retailers; and colleges and universities. Seeks to protect the rights of workers in the United States and worldwide. Concerns include sweatshop practices, forced labor, child labor, and worker health and benefits. Monitors workplace conditions and

reports findings to the public. Develops capacity for sustainable labor compliance.

Institute for a Drug-Free Workplace, 10701 Parkridge Blvd., #300, Reston, VA 20191; (703) 391-7222. Fax, (703) 391-7223. Mark A. de Bernardo, Executive Director.
General email, institute@drugfreeworkplace.org
Web, www.drugfreeworkplace.org

Coalition of businesses, business organizations, and individuals. Seeks to increase productivity, improve safety, and control insurance costs through detection and treatment of drug and alcohol abuse. Promotes fair and consistent implementation of drug abuse prevention programs; supports the right of employers to test for drugs. Monitors legislation and regulations.

ISEA—International Safety Equipment Assn., 1901 N. Moore St., #808, Arlington, VA 22209-1702; (703) 525-1695. Fax, (703) 528-2148. Daniel K. Shipp, President.
General email, isea@safetyequipment.org
Web, www.safetyequipment.org

Trade organization that drafts industry standards for employees' and emergency responders' personal safety and protective equipment; encourages development and use of proper equipment to deal with workplace hazards; participates in international standards activities, especially in North America. Monitors legislation and regulations.

National Assn. of Manufacturers (NAM), Human Resources Policy, 733 10th St. N.W., #700 20001; (202) 637-3127. Fax, (202) 637-3182. Joe Trauger, Vice President. Alternate phone, (202) 637-3000.
Web, www.nam.org

Conducts research, develops policy, and informs members of toxic injury compensation systems, and occupational safety and health legislation, regulations, and standards internationally. Offers mediation service to business members.

Public Citizen, Health Research Group, 1600 20th St. N.W. 20009-1001; (202) 588-1000. Fax, (202) 588-7796. Michael Carome, Director.
General email, hrg@citizen.org
Web, www.citizen.org

Citizens' interest group that studies and reports on occupational diseases; monitors the Occupational Safety and Health Administration and participates in OSHA enforcement proceedings.

Workers' Compensation

▶AGENCIES

Bureau of Labor Statistics (BLS) (Labor Dept.), Safety, Health, and Working Conditions, 2 Massachusetts Ave. N.E., #3180 20212-0001; (202) 691-5184. Fax, (202) 691-6196. Hilery Simpson, Assistant Commissioner.
General email, iif-staff@bls.gov
Web, www.bls.gov/iif

Compiles and publishes statistics on occupational injuries, illnesses, and fatalities.

Labor Dept. (DOL), *Benefits Review Board,* 200 Constitution Ave. N.W., #N5101 20210 (mailing address: P.O. Box 37601, Washington, DC 20013-7601); (202) 693-6300. Fax, (202) 693-6310. Nancy S. Dolder, Chair. Web, www.dol.gov/brb

Reviews appeals of workers seeking benefits under the Longshore and Harbor Workers' Compensation Act and its extensions, including the District of Columbia Workers' Compensation Act, and Title IV (Black Lung Benefits Act) of the Federal Coal Mine Health and Safety Act.

Labor Dept. (DOL), *Employees' Compensation Appeals Board,* 200 Constitution Ave. N.W., #S-5220 20210; (202) 693-6420. Fax, (202) 693-6367. Richard J. Daschbach, Chair, (202) 693-6374. Case Inquiries, (866) 487-2365. Web, www.dol.gov/appeals

Reviews and determines appeals of final determinations of benefit claims made by the Office of Workers' Compensation Programs under the Federal Employees' Compensation Act.

Labor Dept. (DOL), *Workers' Compensation Programs (OWCP),* 200 Constitution Ave. N.W., #S3524 20210; (202) 693-0031. Fax, (202) 693-1378. Gary A. Steinberg, Director, Acting. Web, www.dol.gov/owcp

Administers four federal workers' compensation programs: the Federal Employees' Compensation Program, the Longshore and Harbor Workers' Compensation Program, the Black Lung Benefits Program, and the Energy Employees Occupational Illness Compensation Program.

Workers Compensation (OWCP) *(Labor Dept.),* *Coal Mine Workers' Compensation,* 200 Constitution Ave. N.W., #C3524 20210; (202) 693-0036. Fax, (202) 693-1378. Michael A. Chance, Director, Acting, (202) 693-0046. Toll-free, (800) 638-7072. Web, www.dol.gov/owcp/dcmwc/index.htm

Provides direction for administration of the black lung benefits program. Adjudicates all black lung claims; certifies benefit payments and maintains black lung beneficiary rolls.

▶NONGOVERNMENTAL

American Insurance Assn., 2101 L St. N.W., #400 20037; (202) 828-7100. Fax, (202) 293-1219. Leigh Ann Pusey, President. General email, info@aiadc.org Web, www.aiadc.org

Membership: companies providing property and casualty insurance. Offers information on workers' compensation legislation and regulations; conducts educational activities.

National Assn. of Manufacturers (NAM), *Human Resources Policy,* 733 10th St. N.W., #700 20001; (202) 637-3127. Fax, (202) 637-3182. Joe Trauger, Vice President. Alternate phone, (202) 637-3000. Web, www.nam.org

Conducts research, develops policy, and informs members of workers' compensation law; provides feedback to government agencies.

7 🔆

Energy

GENERAL POLICY AND ANALYSIS

Basic Resources

▶**AGENCIES**

Bureau of Land Management (BLM) *(Interior Dept.),*
Minerals and Realty Management, 1849 C St. N.W.,
#5625 20240; (202) 208-4201. Fax, (202) 208-4800.
Mike Nedd, Assistant Director.
General email, mnedd@blm.gov
Web, www.blm.gov/wo/st/en/info/directory.html

Evaluates and classifies onshore oil, natural gas, geothermal resources, and all solid energy and mineral resources, including coal and uranium, on federal lands. Develops and administers regulations for fluid and solid mineral leasing on national lands and on the subsurface of land where fluid and solid mineral rights have been reserved for the federal government.

Defense Logistics Agency *(Defense Dept.), Energy, 8725*
John Jay Kingman Rd., #4950, Fort Belvoir, VA 22060-
6222; (703) 767-9706. Fax, (703) 767-1338. Brig.
Gen. Giovanni K. Tuck, Commander. Toll-free, (877) 352-
2255. Public Affairs, (703) 767-4108.
Web, www.energy.dla.mil

Provides the Defense Dept. and other federal agencies with products and services to meet energy-related needs; facilitates the cycle of storage and deployment of fuels and other energy sources, including petroleum, electricity, water and natural gas, as well as space and missile propellants. Provides information on alternative fuels and renewable energy and serves as the executive agent for the Defense Dept.'s bulk petroleum supply chain.

Energy Dept. (DOE), *Advanced Manufacturing, 1000*
Independence Ave. S.W., #5F065 20585-0121; (202) 586-
9488. Fax, (202) 586-9234. Mark Johnson, Director.
Web, www1.eere.energy.gov/manufacturing

Offers financial and technical support to small businesses and individual inventors for establishing technical performance and conducting early development of innovative ideas and inventions that have a significant energy saving impact and future commercial market potential.

Energy Dept. (DOE), *Advanced Research Projects Agency,*
1000 Independence Ave. S.W., 20585; (202) 287-1005, Press,
Fax, (202) 287-6405. Dr. Cheryl Martin, Director (acting).
General email, ARPA-E@hq.doe.gov
Web, www.arpa-e.energy.gov

Seeks to advance energy technologies that are too early for private-sector investment yet have the potential to radically improve U.S. economic prosperity, national security, and environmental well-being. Provides energy researchers with funding, technical assistance, and market readiness through a competitive project selection process and active program management.

Energy Dept. (DOE), *Deputy Secretary, 1000*
Independence Ave. S.W., #7B252 20585; (202) 586-5500.
Fax, (202) 586-7210. Daniel B. Poneman, Deputy
Secretary. Press, (202) 586-4940. Locator, (202) 586-5000.
Web, www.energy.gov

Serves as chief operations officer. Manages departmental programs in conservation and renewable energy, fossil energy, energy research, the Energy Information Administration, nuclear energy, civilian radioactive waste management, and the power marketing administrations.

Energy Dept. (DOE), *Economic Impact and Diversity,*
1000 Independence Ave. S.W., #5B110 20585; (202) 586-
8383. Fax, (202) 586-3075. Dot Harris, Director.
Web, www.doe.gov/diversity

Advises the secretary on the impacts of energy policies, programs, regulations, and other departmental actions on underrepresented communities; minority educational institutions; and minority, small, and women-owned business enterprises.

Energy Dept. (DOE), *Energy Policy and Systems Analysis,*
1000 Independence Ave. S.W., #7C016 20585; (202) 586-
9045. Melanie Kenderdine, Director.
Web, www.energy.gov/epsa

Principal energy policy adviser to the secretary and deputy secretary on domestic energy policy development and implementation, as well as Energy Dept. policy analysis and activities. Supports the Energy Dept. White House interagency process, providing data collection, analysis, stakeholder engagement, and data synthesis.

Energy Dept. (DOE), *National Nuclear Security*
Administration, Emergency Operations, 1000
Independence Ave. S.W., #GH060 20585; (202) 586-9892.
Fax, (202) 586-3904. Joseph J. Krol Jr., Associate
Administrator.
Web, www.nnsa.energy.gov/aboutus/ourprograms/
emergencyoperationscounterterrorism

Works to ensure coordinated Energy Dept. responses to energy-related emergencies. Recommends policies to mitigate the effects of energy supply crises on the United States; recommends government responses to energy emergencies.

Energy Dept. (DOE), *Secretary, 1000 Independence Ave.*
S.W., #7A257 20585; (202) 586-6210. Fax, (202) 586-1441.
Ernest J. Moniz, Secretary. Press, (202) 586-4940. Locator,
(202) 586-5000.
General email, thesecretary@hq.doe.gov
Web, www.energy.gov

Decides major energy policy issues and acts as principal adviser to the president on energy matters, including strategic reserves and nuclear power; acts as principal spokesperson for the department.

Energy Dept. (DOE), *Under Secretary for Management*
and Performance, 1000 Independence Ave. S.W., #7A219
20585; (202) 586-7700. Fax, (202) 586-0148. David Klaus,
Deputy Under Secretary. Press, (202) 586-4940. Locator,
(202) 586-5000.
Web, www.energy.gov

Responsible for all administration and management matters and for regulatory and information programs.

Energy Dept. (DOE), *Under Secretary for Science and Energy,* 1000 Independence Ave. S.W. 20585; (202) 586-0505. Vacant, Under Secretary for Science and Energy; Michael Knotek, Deputy Under Secretary for Science and Energy. Web, http://energy.gov/office-under-secretary-science-and-energy

Responsible for driving transformative science and technology solutions through planning and management oversight of the department's science and energy programs.

Energy Information Administration (EIA) *(Energy Dept.),* 1000 Independence Ave. S.W., #2H027 20585; (202) 586-4361. Fax, (202) 586-0329. Adam E. Sieminski, Administrator. Information, (202) 586-8800.
General email, infoctr@eia.doe.gov

Web, www.eia.gov

Collects and publishes data on national and international energy reserves, financial status of energy-producing companies, production, demand, consumption, and other areas; provides long- and short-term analyses of energy trends and data.

Energy Information Administration (EIA) *(Energy Dept.), Energy Analysis,* 1000 Independence Ave. S.W., #2H-073 20585; (202) 586-2222. Fax, (202) 586-3045. John J. Conti, Assistant Administrator.
Web, www.eia.gov

Analyzes and forecasts alternative energy futures. Develops, applies, and maintains modeling systems for analyzing the interactions of demand, conversion, and supply for all energy sources and their economic and environmental impacts. Concerned with emerging energy markets and U.S. dependence on petroleum imports.

Energy Information Administration (EIA) *(Energy Dept.), Energy Consumption and Efficiency Statistics,* 1000 Independence Ave. S.W., #2F-073 20585; (202) 586-3548. Fax, (202) 586-9739. Thomas Leckey, Director.
Web, www.eia.gov

Conducts national energy consumption surveys and publishes energy consumption data and analysis.

Energy Information Administration (EIA) *(Energy Dept.), Energy Statistics,* 1000 Independence Ave. S.W., #2G024 20585; (202) 586-6012. Stephen J. Harvey, Assistant Administrator.
General email, infoctr@eia.doe.gov

Web, www.eia.gov

Conducts survey, statistical methods, and integration activities related to energy consumption and efficiency; electricity; nuclear and renewable energy; oil, gas, and coal supply; and petroleum and biofuels. Manages EIA data collection program and the quality control for statistical reports.

Federal Energy Regulatory Commission (FERC) *(Energy Dept.),* 888 1st St. N.E., #11A 20426; (202) 502-6088. Fax, (202) 502-8612. Cheryl A. LaFleur, Chair, Acting. Toll-free, (866) 208-3372. Press, (202) 502-8680. eLibrary questions, (202) 502-6652. Enforcement hotline, (202) 502-8390. Enforcement toll-free, (888) 889-8030.
General email, customer@ferc.gov

Web, www.ferc.gov

Independent agency that regulates the interstate transmission of electricity, natural gas, and oil, including approving rates and charges. Reviews proposals to build liquefied natural gas terminals and interstate natural gas pipelines and approves siting. Licenses and inspects non-federal hydroelectric projects. Regulates the sale of natural gas for resale in interstate commerce and wholesale interstate sales of electricity. Ensures the reliability of high-voltage interstate transmission systems. Establishes accounting and financial reporting requirements for regulated utilities. Studies and recommends policies and regulations.

Health, Safety, and Security *(Energy Dept.),* 1000 Independence Ave. S.W., #7G040 20585; (301) 903-3777. Fax, (202) 586-7960. Glenn S. Podonsky, Chief Officer, (202) 586-0271.
General email, HSSusersupport@hq.doe.gov

Web, www.hss.energy.gov

Develops policy and establishes standards to ensure safety and health protection in all department activities.

Interior Dept. (DOI), *Land and Minerals Management,* 1849 C St. N.W. 20240; (202) 208-6734. Fax, (202) 208-3619. Tommy P. Beaudreau, Assistant Secretary, Acting.
Web, www.doi.gov

Directs and supervises the Bureau of Land Management; the Bureau of Ocean Energy Management, Regulation, and Enforcement; and the Office of Surface Mining and Reclamation Enforcement. Supervises programs associated with land-use planning, onshore and offshore minerals, surface mining reclamation and enforcement, and Outer Continental Shelf minerals management.

Office of Management and Budget (OMB) *(Executive Office of the President), Energy, Science, and Water,* New Executive Office Bldg., #8002 20503; (202) 395-3404. Fax, (202) 395-3049. John Pasquantino, Deputy Associate Director. Press, (202) 395-7254.
Web, www.whitehouse.gov/omb

Advises and assists the president in preparing the budget for energy programs; coordinates OMB energy policy and programs.

Office of Science *(Energy Dept.),* 1000 Independence Ave. S.W., #7B058 20585; (202) 586-5430. Fax, (202) 586-4120. Patricia M. Dehmer, Director, Acting; Patricia Dehmer, Deputy Director of Science Programs.
Web, www.science.energy.gov

Advises the secretary on the department's physical science research and energy research and development programs; the use of multipurpose laboratories (except weapons laboratories); and education and training for basic and applied research activities. Manages the department's high-energy and nuclear physics programs and the fusion energy program. Conducts environmental and health-related research and development programs, including studies of energy-related pollutants and hazardous materials.

Office of Science and Technology Policy (OSTP) *(Executive Office of the President),* Eisenhower Executive Office Bldg., 1650 Pennsylvania Ave. N.W. 20504; (202)

ENERGY RESOURCES IN CONGRESS

For a complete listing of Congress committees, including their full contact information, leadership, membership, and jurisdictions, please refer to the Appendix on pages 724–842.

HOUSE:

House Agriculture Committee, (202) 225-2171.
Web, agriculture.house.gov or
democrats.agriculture.house.gov
   Subcommittee on Conservation, Energy, and Forestry, (202) 225-2171.
House Appropriations Committee, (202) 225-2771.
Web, appropriations.house.gov or
democrats.appropriations.house.gov
   Subcommittee on Energy and Water Development, and Related Agencies, (202) 225-3421.
   Subcommittee on Interior, Environment, and Related Agencies, (202) 225-3081.
House Armed Services Committee, (202) 225-4151.
Web, armedservices.house.gov or
democrats.armedservices.house.gov
   Subcommittee on Readiness, (202) 226-8979.
House Education and the Workforce Committee, (202) 225-4527.
Web, edworkforce.house.gov or
· democrats.edworkforce.house.gov
   Subcommittee on Workforce Protections, (202) 225-4527.
House Energy and Commerce Committee, (202) 225-2927.
Web, energycommerce.house.gov or
democrats.energycommerce.house.gov
   Subcommittee on Commerce, Manufacturing, and Trade, (202) 225-2927.
   Subcommittee on Energy and Power, (202) 225-2927.

House Foreign Affairs Committee, (202) 225-5021.
Web, foreignaffairs.house.gov or
democrats.foreignaffairs.house.gov
House Natural Resources Committee, (202) 225-2761.
Web, naturalresources.house.gov or
democrats.naturalresources.house.gov
   Subcommittee on Energy and Mineral Resources, (202) 225-9297.
   Subcommittee on Public Lands and Environmental Regulation, (202) 226-7736.
   Subcommittee on Water and Power, (202) 225-8331.
House Oversight and Government Reform Committee, (202) 225-5074.
Web, oversight.house.gov or
democrats.oversight.house.gov
   Subcommittee on Energy Policy, Health Care, and Entitlements, (202) 225-5074.
House Science, Space, and Technology Committee, (202) 225-6371.
Web, science.house.gov or democrats.science.house.gov
   Subcommittee on Energy, (202) 225-6371.
House Small Business Committee, (202) 225-5821.
Web, smallbusiness.house.gov or
democrats.smallbusiness.house.gov
   Subcommittee on Agriculture, Energy, and Trade, (202) 225-5821.
House Transportation and Infrastructure Committee, (202) 225-9446.
Web, transportation.house.gov or
democrats.transportation.house.gov

456-7116. Fax, (202) 456-6021. John P. Holdren, Director. Press, (202) 456-6124.
General email, info@ostp.gov
Web, www.ostp.gov

Advises the president on science and technology matters as they affect national security; coordinates science and technology initiatives at the interagency level. Interests include nuclear materials, security, nuclear arms reduction, and counterterrorism.

Treasury Dept., *Business and International Taxation,* 1500 Pennsylvania Ave. N.W., #4116 20220; (202) 622-1782. Fax, (202) 622-2969. William Randolph, Director. Web, www.treasury.gov/about/organizational-structure/offices/Pages/Tax-Policy.aspx

Analyzes tax policies affecting businesses and international taxation. Negotiates tax treaties with foreign governments and participates in meetings of international organizations. Develops legislative proposals and regulations.

▶CONGRESS

For a listing of relevant congressional committees and subcommittees, please see the above box or the Appendix.

Government Accountability Office (GAO), *Natural Resources and Environment,* 441 G St. N.W., #2057 20548 (mailing address: 441 G St. N.W., #2T23A, Washington, DC 20548); (202) 512-3841. Fax, (202) 512-8774. Mark Gaffigan, Managing Director.
Web, www.gao.gov

Independent, nonpartisan agency in the legislative branch. Audits, analyzes, and reports on efficiency and effectiveness of the Defense, Energy, and Interior Depts. Addresses governmentwide science issues and the production, regulation, and consumption of energy.

▶NONGOVERNMENTAL

American Assn. of Blacks in Energy (AABE), 1625 K St. N.W., #405 20006; (202) 371-9530. Fax, (202) 371-9218.

Subcommittee on Railroads, Pipelines, and Hazardous Materials, (202) 226-0727.
Subcommittee on Water Resources and Environment, (202) 225-4360.
House Ways and Means Committee, (202) 225-3625.
Web, waysandmeans.house.gov or democrats.waysandmeans.house.gov
Subcommittee on Trade, (202) 225-6649.

JOINT:

Joint Committee on Taxation,
Web, www.jct.gov
Joint Economic Committee,
Web, jec.senate.gov/public or jec.senate.gov/republicans/public

SENATE:

Senate Agriculture, Nutrition, and Forestry Committee, (202) 224-2035.
Web, ag.senate.gov
Subcommittee on Jobs, Rural Economic Growth, and Energy Innovation, (202) 224-2035.
Senate Appropriations Committee, (202) 224-7363.
Web, appropriations.senate.gov
Subcommittee on Energy and Water Development, (202) 224-8119.
Subcommittee on Interior, Environment, and Related Agencies, (202) 228-0774.
Senate Commerce, Science, and Transportation Committee, (202) 224-0411.
Web, commerce.senate.gov
Subcommittee on Oceans, Atmosphere, Fisheries and the Coast Guard, (202) 224-4912.

Subcommittee on Science and Space, (202) 224-0415.
Senate Energy and Natural Resources Committee, (202) 224-4971.
Web, energy.senate.gov
Subcommittee on Energy, (202) 224-4971.
Subcommittee on Water and Power, (202) 224-4971.
Senate Environment and Public Works Committee, (202) 224-8832.
Web, epw.senate.gov
Subcommittee on Clean Air and Nuclear Safety, (202) 224-8832.
Subcommittee on Public Lands, Forests, and Mining, (202) 224-8832.
Subcommittee on Water and Wildlife, (202) 224-8832.
Senate Finance Committee, (202) 224-4515.
Web, finance.senate.gov
Subcommittee on Energy, Natural Resources, and Infrastructure, (202) 224-4515.
Senate Foreign Relations Committee, (202) 224-4651.
Web, foreign.senate.gov
Senate Health, Education, Labor, and Pensions Committee, (202) 224-5375.
Web, help.senate.gov
Subcommittee on Employment and Workplace Safety, (202) 228-1455.
Senate Homeland Security and Governmental Affairs Committee, (202) 224-2627.
Web, hsgac.senate.gov

Paula Jackson, President.
General email, info@aabe.org
Web, www.aabe.org

Encourages participation of African Americans and other minorities in energy research and in formulating energy policy. Provides financial aid and scholarships to African American students who pursue careers in energy-related fields. Promotes greater awareness in private and public sectors of the impacts of energy policy on minority communities.

American Boiler Manufacturers Assn., 8221 Old Courthouse Rd., #202, Vienna, VA 22182; (703) 356-7172. Fax, (703) 356-4543. Diana McClung, Director, Interim; Kevin Hoey, Chair.
Web, www.abma.com

Membership: manufacturers of boiler systems and boiler-related products, including fuel-burning systems. Interests include energy and environmental issues.

Aspen Institute, 1 Dupont Circle N.W., #700 20036-7133; (202) 736-5800. Fax, (202) 467-0790. Walter Isaacson, President. Press, (202) 736-3849.
General email, info@aspeninstitute.org
Web, www.aspeninstitute.org

Educational and policy studies organization. Promotes consideration of the public good in a wide variety of policy areas, including energy, the environment, international relations, and homeland security. Working with international partners, offers educational seminars, nonpartisan policy forums, public conferences and events, and leadership development initiatives.

CECA Solutions, 2737 Devonshire Pl., #102 20008; (202) 468-8440. Fax, (703) 690-5920. Ellen Berman, Chief Executive Officer.
General email, info@cecarf.org
Web, www.cecarf.org

Analyzes economic and social effects of energy policies and advances interests of residential and small business

Energy Department

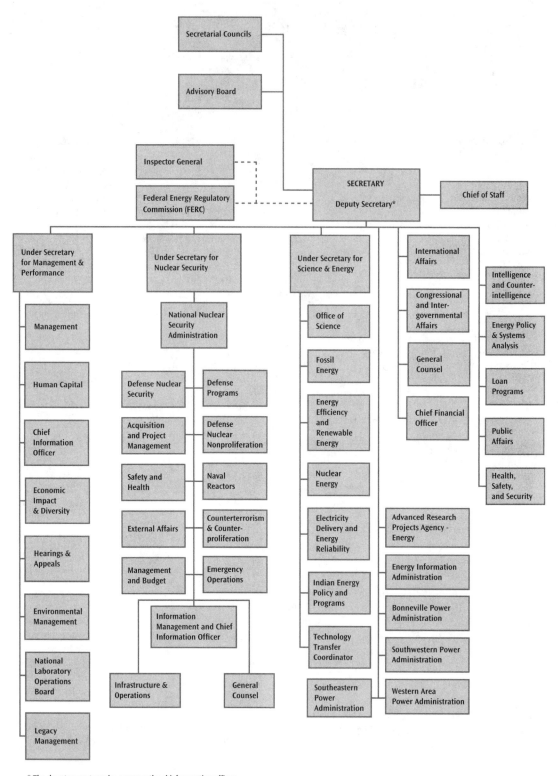

* The deputy secretary also serves as the chief operating officer.
  The FERC is an independent regulatory agency within the Dept. of Energy.

– – – – – – Indicates a support or advisory relationship with the unit rather than a direct reporting relationship

consumers. Builds consensus on energy policy issues among public- and private-sector organizations, state and local groups, businesses, utilities, consumers, environmentalists, government agencies, and others. Interests include clean and sustainable fuels, distributed generation of electricity, and reliable electric systems. Conducts consumer education campaigns concerning fuel choices, energy conservation, and legislative and regulatory developments. (Formerly the Consumer Energy Council of America.)

Diesel Technology Forum, *5291 Corporate Drive, #102, Frederick, MD 21703-2875; (301) 668-7230. Fax, (301) 668-7234. Allen Schaeffer, Executive Director.*
General email, dtf@dieselforum.org
Web, www.dieselforum.org

Represents diesel interests, with a focus on environmental protection. Advocates use of diesel engines. Supports energy research and advises policymakers. Monitors legislation and regulations.

Energy Bar Assn., *2000 M St. N.W., #715 20036; (202) 223-5625. Fax, (202) 833-5596. Adrienne E. Clair, President.*
General email, admin@eba-net.org
Web, www.eba-net.org

Membership: lawyers interested in all areas of energy law. Interests include administration of laws covering production, development, conservation, transmission, and economic regulation of energy.

Energy Future Coalition, *1750 Pennsylvania Ave. N.W., #300 20006; (202) 463-1947. Fax, (202) 650-5350. Reid Detchon, Executive Director.*
General email, info@energyfuturecoalition.org
Web, www.energyfuturecoalition.org

Seeks to bridge the differences among business, labor, and environmental groups and identify energy policy options with broad political support. Interests include development of a national electricity transmission plan to bring renewable resources to market and reduction of energy waste.

Industrial Energy Consumers of America, *1155 15th St. N.W., #500 20005; (202) 223-1420. Fax, (202) 530-0659. Paul N. Cicio, President.*
Web, www.ieca-us.com

National trade association that represents the manufacturing industry and advocates on energy, environmental, and public policy issues. Advocates for greater diversity of and lower costs for energy. Monitors legislation and regulations.

National Assn. of Energy Service Companies, *1615 M St. N.W., #800 20036-3213; (202) 822-0950. Fax, (202) 822-0955. Terry E. Singer, Executive Director.*
General email, info@naesco.org
Web, www.naesco.org

Membership: companies that design, manufacture, finance, and install energy efficiency and renewable energy equipment; energy efficiency and renewable energy services companies; and government officials. Advocates and serves as a clearinghouse on energy efficiency strategies. Monitors legislation and regulations.

National Assn. of Regulatory Utility Commissioners, *1101 Vermont Ave. N.W., #200 20005-3521; (202) 898-2200. Fax, (202) 898-2213. Charles D. Gray, Executive Director.*
General email, admin@naruc.org
Web, www.naruc.org

Membership: members of federal, state, municipal, and international regulatory commissions that have jurisdiction over utilities and carriers. Interests include electricity, natural gas, and nuclear power.

National Assn. of State Energy Officials (NASEO), *2107 Wilson Blvd., #850, Arlington, VA 22201; (703) 299-8800. Fax, (703) 299-6208. David Terry, Executive Director.*
General email, energy@naseo.org
Web, www.naseo.org

Represents governor-designated energy officials from each state and territory. Seeks to improve energy programs, provide policy analysis, and act as an information clearinghouse. Interests include efficiency, renewables, building codes, emergency preparedness, and fuel production and distribution.

National Governors Assn. (NGA), *Center for Best Practices, Environment, Energy, and Transportation, 444 N. Capitol St. N.W., #267 20001-1512; (202) 624-5300. Fax, (202) 624-7829. Sue Gander, Director.*
General email, webmaster@nga.org
Web, www.nga.org/cms/center/eet

Identifies best practices for energy, land-use, environment, and transportation issues, and shares these with the states.

National Governors Assn. (NGA), *Natural Resources Committee, 444 N. Capitol St. N.W., #267 20001-1512; (202) 624-5300. Fax, (202) 624-7814. Alex Whitaker, Director.*
General email, webmaster@nga.org
Web, www.nga.org/cms/center/eet

Monitors legislation and regulations and makes recommendations on agriculture, energy, environment, and natural resource issues to ensure governors' views and priorities are represented in federal policies and regulations.

RAND Corporation, *Washington Office, 1200 S. Hayes St., Arlington, VA 22202-5050; (703) 413-1100. Fax, (703) 413-8111. Lynn E. Davis, Director, ext. 5399; Debra Knopman, Director, Justice, Infrastructure, and Environment.*
Web, www.rand.org

Analyzes the effects of existing and proposed energy policies on the environment. (Headquarters in Santa Monica, Calif.)

U.S. Chamber of Commerce, *Environment, Technology, and Regulatory Affairs, 1615 H St. N.W. 20062-2000; (202) 463-5533. Fax, (202) 887-3445. William L. Kovacs, Senior Vice President.*
General email, environment@uschamber.com
Web, www.uschamber.com/issues/etra

Develops policy on all issues affecting energy, including alternative energy, emerging technologies, regulatory affairs, energy taxes, telecommunications, and on- and offshore mining of energy resources.

U.S. Conference of Mayors, *Municipal Waste Management Assn.,* 1620 Eye St. N.W., #400 20006; (202) 293-7330. Fax, (202) 429-2352. Jubi Headley, Managing Director, (202) 861-6798; Judy Sheahan, Assistant Executive Director for Environmental Policy, (202) 861-6775. General email, info@usmayors.org

Web, www.usmayors.org/mwma

Membership: mayors of cities with populations of 30,000 or more. Interests include solid waste management, Superfund, brownfields, air and water quality, and waste-to-energy technologies.

Utility Workers Union of America, 815 16th St. N.W. 20006; (202) 974-8200. Fax, (202) 974-8201. Ed Good, Legislative Director, (740) 676-5650; Gary Ruffner, National Secretary-Treasurer. General email, webmaster@uwua.net

Web, www.uwua.net

Labor union representing approximately 50,000 workers in utilities and related industries. Helps members negotiate pay, benefits, and better working conditions; conducts training programs and workshops. Monitors legislation and regulations. (Affiliated with the AFL-CIO.)

Energy Conservation

▶ **AGENCIES**

Energy Efficiency and Renewable Energy *(Energy Dept.),* 1000 Independence Ave. S.W., #6A013 20585; (202) 586-9220. Fax, (202) 586-9260. David Danielson, Assistant Secretary. Information, (877) 337-3463. Press, (202) 586-4940. General email, eereic@ee.doe.gov

Web, www.eere.energy.gov

Develops and manages programs to improve markets for renewable energy sources including solar, biomass, wind, geothermal, and hydropower and to increase efficiency of energy use among residential, commercial, transportation, utility, and industrial users. Administers financial and technical assistance for state energy programs, weatherization for low-income households, and implementation of energy conservation measures by schools, hospitals, local governments, and public care institutions and federal facilities.

Energy Efficiency and Renewable Energy *(Energy Dept.),* **Advanced Manufacturing, Research, and Development,** 1000 Independence Ave. S.W., #5F065, EE5A 20585; (202) 586-9488. Fax, (202) 586-9234. Mark Johnson, Director. Web, www.eere.energy.gov/industry

Conducts research and disseminates information to increase energy end-use efficiency, promote renewable energy use and industrial applications, and reduce the volume of industrial and municipal waste.

Energy Efficiency and Renewable Energy *(Energy Dept.),* **Building Technologies (BTP),** 1000 Independence Ave. S.W., MSEE-5B 20585; (202) 586-9127. Fax, (202) 586-4617. Roland Risser, Program Manager. Web, www.eere.energy.gov/buildings

Funds research to reduce commercial and residential building energy use. Programs include research and development, equipment standards and analysis, and technology validation and market introduction.

Energy Efficiency and Renewable Energy *(Energy Dept.),* **Federal Energy Management Program (FEMP),** 1000 Independence Ave. S.W., MSEE2L 20585; (202) 586-5772. Fax, (202) 586-3000. Timothy Unruh, Program Manager. Web, http://energy.gov/eere/femp/federal-energy-management-program

Provides federal agencies with information and technology services to implement energy conservation measures. Areas include finance and contract assistance, purchase of energy-efficient products, design and operation of buildings, and vehicle fleet management.

Energy Efficiency and Renewable Energy *(Energy Dept.),* **Vehicle Technologies,** 1000 Independence Ave. S.W., #5G030 20585; (202) 586-8055. Fax, (202) 586-7409. Patrick Davis, Program Manager. Web, www1.eere.energy.gov/vehiclesandfuels

Works with the motor vehicle industry to develop technologies for improved vehicle fuel efficiency and cleaner fuels.

Energy Efficiency and Renewable Energy *(Energy Dept.),* **Weatherization and Intergovernmental Programs,** 1000 Independence Ave. S.W., #MSEE-2K 20585; (202) 586-1510. Fax, (202) 586-1233. Anna Garcia, Director, (202) 287-1858. Web, www.eere.energy.gov/wip

Supports private and government efforts to improve the energy efficiency of buildings and transportation. Promotes accelerated market penetration of energy efficiency and renewable energy technologies. Provides funding and technical assistance to state and local governments and Indian tribes. Administers weatherization assistance program that assists elderly and low-income persons to make their homes energy efficient. Reviews building codes that promote energy efficiency in buildings.

Energy Information Administration (EIA) *(Energy Dept.),* **Energy Consumption and Efficiency Analysis,** 1000 Independence Ave. S.W. 20585; (202) 586-1762. James Turnure, Director. Web, www.eia.gov

Collects and provides data on energy consumption in the residential, commercial, and industrial sectors. Prepares analyses on energy consumption by sector and fuel type, including the impact of conservation measures.

Housing and Urban Development Dept. (HUD), *Environment and Energy,* 451 7th St. S.W. 20410; (202)

708-2894. Fax, (202) 708-3363. Danielle Schopp, Director, (202) 402-4442.
Web, www.hud.gov/offices/cpd/environment

Develops policies promoting energy efficiency, conservation, and renewable sources of supply in housing and community development programs.

National Institute of Standards and Technology (NIST) (Commerce Dept.), Engineering Laboratory, 100 Bureau Dr., MS 8600, Gaithersburg, MD 20899-8600; (301) 975-5900. Fax, (301) 975-4032. Howard H. Harary, Director, Acting.
General email, el@nist.gov
Web, www.nist.gov/el

Develops measurement techniques, test methods, and mathematical models to encourage energy conservation in large buildings. Interests include refrigeration, lighting, infiltration and ventilation, heating and air conditioning, indoor air quality, and heat transfer in the building envelope.

► **CONGRESS**

For a listing of relevant congressional committees and subcommittees, please see pages 224–225 or the Appendix.

► **NONGOVERNMENTAL**

Alliance to Save Energy, 1850 M St. N.W., #600 20036; (202) 857-0666. Fax, (202) 331-9588. Kateri Callahan, President.
General email, info@ase.org
Web, www.ase.org

Coalition of business, government, environmental, and consumer leaders who promote the efficient and clean use of energy to benefit consumers, the environment, the economy, and national security. Conducts programs addressing energy efficiency in commercial and residential buildings, utilities, appliances, and equipment, industry, and education. International programs provide technical and financial assistance to national and local partners.

American Council for an Energy-Efficient Economy (ACEEE), 529 14th St. N.W., #600 20045-1000; (202) 507-4000. Fax, (202) 429-2248. Steven Nadel, Executive Director, (202) 507-4011.
General email, aceeeinfo@aceee.org
Web, www.aceee.org

Independent research organization concerned with energy policy, technologies, and conservation. Interests include consumer information, energy efficiency in buildings and appliances, improved transportation efficiency, industrial efficiency, utility issues, and conservation in developing countries.

Environmental Defense Fund, Washington Office, 1875 Connecticut Ave. N.W., #600 20009-5728; (202) 387-3500. Fax, (202) 234-6049. Diane Regas, Senior Vice President. Information, (800) 684-3322. Press, (202) 572-3396.
Web, www.edf.org

Citizens' interest group staffed by lawyers, economists, and scientists. Provides information on energy issues and advocates energy conservation measures. Interests include China and the Amazon rain forest. Provides utilities and environmental organizations with research and guidance on energy conservation. (Headquarters in New York.)

Friends of the Earth (FOE), Washington Office, 1100 15th St. N.W., 11th Floor 20005; (202) 783-7400. Fax, (202) 783-0444. Erich Pica, President. Toll-free, (877) 843-8687.
General email, foe@foe.org
Web, www.foe.org

Environmental advocacy group. Interests include global warming, conservation, renewable energy resources, and air and water pollution. Specializes in federal budget and tax issues related to the environment, including the Keystone XL pipeline, and World Bank and International Monetary Fund reform.

National Insulation Assn. (NIA), 12100 Sunset Hills Rd., #330, Reston, VA 20190-3233; (703) 464-6422. Fax, (703) 464-5896. Michele M. Jones, Executive Vice President, ext. 119.
General email, niainfo@insulation.org
Web, www.insulation.org

Membership: open-shop and union contractors, distributors, laminators, fabricators, and manufacturers that provide thermal insulation, insulation accessories, and components to the commercial, mechanical, and industrial markets. Provides information to members on industry trends and technologies. Monitors legislation and regulations.

North American Insulation Manufacturers Assn., 11 Canal Center Plaza, #103, Alexandria, VA 22314; (703) 684-0084. Fax, (703) 684-0427. Angus Crane, President.
General email, insulation@naima.org
Web, www.naima.org

Membership: manufacturers of insulation products for use in homes, commercial buildings, and industrial facilities. Provides information on the use of insulation for thermal efficiency, sound control, and fire safety; monitors research in the industry. Interests include energy efficiency and sustainability. Monitors legislation and regulations.

Resources for the Future, 1616 P St. N.W. 20036-1400; (202) 328-5000. Fax, (202) 939-3460. Philip R. Sharp, President, (202) 328-5077. Library, (202) 328-5089. Press, (202) 328-5019.
General email, info@rff.org
Web, www.rff.org

Research organization that conducts independent studies on economic and policy aspects of energy, environment, conservation, and natural resource management issues worldwide. Interests include climate change, energy, natural resource issues in developing countries, and public health.

Sierra Club, Washington Office, 50 F St. N.W., 8th Floor 20001; (202) 547-1141. Fax, (202) 547-6009. Debbie Sease, Legislative Director; Bob Bingaman, National Field

Director, (202) 675-7904; Shanice Penn, Operations Manager. Press, (202) 675-6698.
General email, information@sierraclub.org
Web, www.sierraclub.org

Citizens' interest group that promotes protection and responsible use of the Earth's ecosystems and its natural resources. Focuses on combating global warming/greenhouse effect through energy conservation, efficient use of renewable energy resources, auto efficiency, and constraints on deforestation. Monitors federal, state, and local legislation relating to the environment and natural resources. (Headquarters in San Francisco, Calif.)

Union of Concerned Scientists, *Strategy and Policy, Washington Office*, 1825 K St., N.W., #800 20006-1232; (202) 223-6133. Fax, (202) 223-6162. Kathleen M. Rest, Executive Director.
General email, ucs@ucsusa.org
Web, www.ucsusa.org

Independent group of scientists and citizens that advocate safe and sustainable international, national, and state energy policies. Conducts research, advocacy, and educational outreach focusing on market-based strategies for developing renewable energy and alternative fuels, transportation policy, climate change policy, and energy efficiency. (Headquarters in Cambridge, Mass.)

Worldwatch Institute, 1400 16th St. N.W., #430 20036; (202) 745-8092. Fax, (202) 478-2534. Robert Engelman, President.
General email, worldwatch@worldwatch.org
Web, www.worldwatch.org

Focuses on an interdisciplinary approach to solving global environmental problems. Interests include energy conservation, renewable resources, solar power, and energy use in developing countries.

International Trade and Cooperation

▶ AGENCIES

Census Bureau *(Commerce Dept.), Foreign Trade*, 4600 Silver Hill Rd., #6K032, Suitland, MD 20746 (mailing address: change city, state, and zip code to Washington, DC 20233-6700); (301) 763-2255. Fax, (301) 763-6638. Nick Orsini, Chief. Toll-free Information, (800) 549-0595.
Web, www.census.gov/trade

Provides detailed statistics on all U.S. imports and exports, including petroleum, advanced technology products, and agricultural products; organizes this information by commodity, country, state, district, and port. Compiles information for 240 trading partners, including China, Japan, and Mexico, through all U.S. states and ports. Publishes the monthly economic indicator, *U.S. International Trade in Goods and Services*, in conjunction with the U.S. Bureau of Economic Analysis.

Commerce Dept., *Bureau of Economic Analysis, Balance of Payments*, 1441 L St. N.W. 20230; (202) 606-9900. Fax, (202) 606-5314. Paul Farello, Chief. Press, (202) 606-2649.
General email, customerservice@bea.gov
Web, www.bea.gov/international

Provides statistics on U.S. balance of trade, including figures on energy commodities. Produces monthly joint release with the U.S. Census.

Energy Dept. (DOE), *International Affairs*, 1000 Independence Ave. S.W., #7C016, IA-1 20585; (202) 586-5800. Fax, (202) 586-0861. Jonathan Elkind, Assistant Secretary, Acting.
Web, www.pi.energy.gov

Advises the Energy Dept. leadership in the development of a national policy concerning domestic and international energy matters. Coordinates the varied interests of the department's divisions and other government organizations. Negotiates and manages international energy agreements.

Energy Dept. (DOE), *National Nuclear Security Administration, Emergency Operations*, 1000 Independence Ave. S.W., #GH060 20585; (202) 586-9892. Fax, (202) 586-3904. Joseph J. Krol Jr., Associate Administrator.
Web, www.nnsa.energy.gov/aboutus/ourprograms/emergencyoperationscounterterrorism

Monitors international energy situations as they affect domestic market conditions; recommends policies on and government responses to energy emergencies; represents the United States in the International Energy Agency's emergency programs and NATO civil emergency preparedness activities.

Energy Dept. (DOE), *National Nuclear Security Administration, Nuclear Nonproliferation and International Security*, 1000 Independence Ave. S.W., #7A175 20585; (202) 586-0645. Fax, (202) 586-0862. Anne M. Harrington, Deputy Administrator.
Web, www.nnsa.energy.gov/aboutus/ourprograms/dnn

Provides U.S. government agencies and departments with technical and operational expertise on foreign nuclear and energy issues. Oversees programs to prevent the spread of nuclear, chemical, and biological weapons and missiles for their delivery. Partners with Russia and other former Soviet states to secure weapons of mass destruction materials and expertise; works to strengthen legal and institutional nonproliferation norms; builds technologies to detect proliferation activities; and promotes the safe use of nuclear power.

Energy Dept. (DOE), *Policy, Policy Analysis*, 1000 Independence Ave. S.W., #7D034, PI-40 20585; (202) 586-8436. Carmine Difiglio, Deputy Director for Energy Security.
Web, www.pi.energy.gov

Advises the assistant secretary and Energy Dept. leadership on energy demand and supply, energy efficiency, energy research and development, and the environment, including air quality and climate. Provides analysis for the development of domestic and international energy policy. Responds to energy market disruptions and emergencies. Recommends science and technology policies.

Energy Information Administration (EIA) *(Energy Dept.), Integrated and International Energy Analysis,* 1000 Independence Ave. S.W., MSEI-35 20585; (202) 586-1284. Fax, (202) 586-3045. Paul D. Holtberg, Team Leader. Web, www.eia.gov

Compiles, interprets, and reports international energy statistics and U.S. energy data for international energy organizations. Analyzes international energy markets; makes projections concerning world prices and trade for energy sources, including oil, natural gas, coal, and electricity; monitors world petroleum market to determine U.S. vulnerability.

Fossil Energy *(Energy Dept.), International,* 19901 Germantown Rd., Germantown, MD 20874 (mailing address: 1000 Independence Ave. S.W., Washington, DC 20585); (301) 903-3820. Jonathan Elkind, Assistant Secretary, Acting. Phone (Maryland), (301) 903-3820. Phone (DC), (202) 586-8660. Web, http://energy.gov/ia/office-international-affairs

Coordinates all international clean coal activities within the Office of Fossil Energy. Fosters international opportunities for U.S. energy firms. Develops and promotes international partnerships for deployment of greenhouse gas abatement technologies.

International Trade Administration (ITA) *(Commerce Dept.), Industry and Analysis, Energy and Environmental Industries,* 1400 Constitution Ave. N.W., #4053 20230; (202) 482-5225. Fax, (202) 482-5665. Adam O'Malley, Director, (202) 482-4850. Web, www.environment.ita.doc.gov and www.trade.gov/td/energy

Promotes global competitiveness of U.S. energy and environmental companies. Conducts analyses of these two sectors and of overseas trade and investment opportunities and trade barriers affecting them. Develops strategies to remove foreign trade barriers and improve investment conditions. Organizes conferences and workshops.

Nuclear Regulatory Commission, *International Programs,* 11555 Rockville Pike, MS04E21, Rockville, MD 20852; (301) 415-2344. Fax, (301) 415-2400. Nader Marnesh, Director, (301) 415-1780. Web, www.nrc.gov/about-nrc/organization/oipfuncdesc.html

Coordinates application review process for exports and imports of nuclear materials, facilities, and components. Makes recommendations on export-import licensing upon completion of review process. Conducts related policy reviews.

Office of Science *(Energy Dept.),* 1000 Independence Ave. S.W., #7B058 20585; (202) 586-5430. Fax, (202) 586-4120. Patricia M. Dehmer, Director, Acting; Patricia Dehmer, Deputy Director of Science Programs. Web, www.science.energy.gov

Coordinates energy research, science, and technology programs among producing and consuming nations; analyzes existing international research and development activities; pursues international collaboration in research and in the design, development, construction, and operation of new facilities and major scientific experiments; participates in negotiations for international cooperation activities.

State Dept., *Energy Bureau, Policy Analysis and Public Diplomacy,* 2201 C St. N.W., #4805 20520; (202) 647-2879. Fax, (202) 647-7431. Richard Westerdale, Director. Web, www.state.gov

Seeks to put energy security interests at the forefront of U.S. foreign policy. Objectives include increasing energy diplomacy with major producers and consumers; stimulating market forces toward energy development and reconstruction, with an emphasis on alternative energies and electricity; and promoting good governance and increased transparency to improve commercially viable and environmentally sustainable access to people without energy services.

State Dept., *Nuclear Energy, Safety, and Security Affairs,* 2201 C St. N.W., #3320 20520; (202) 647-4413. Fax, (202) 647-0775. Richard J.K. Stratford, Director. Web, www.state.gov

Coordinates and supervises international nuclear energy policy for the State Dept. Advises the secretary on policy matters relating to nonproliferation and export controls, nuclear technology and safeguards, and nuclear safety. Promotes adherence to technical conventions regarding peaceful uses of nuclear energy.

Treasury Dept., International Affairs, Middle East and North Africa (MENA), 1500 Pennsylvania Ave. N.W., #5012 20220; (202) 622-2129. Fax, (202) 622-0431. Andrew Baukol, Deputy Assistant Secretary. Web, www.treasury.gov/about/organizational-structure/offices/Pages/-Middle-East-and-North-Africa.aspx

Represents the department in the World Bank, International Monetary Fund, and other international institutions that address economic, financial, development, and energy matters. Provides economic analyses of the Middle East (including Turkey) and North Africa.

U.S. International Trade Commission, *Natural Resources and Energy,* 500 E St. S.W., #511J 20436; (202) 205-3348. Fax, (202) 205-2217. Robert Carr, Chief, (202) 205-2007. General email, cynthia.foreso@usitc.gov Web, www.usitc.gov

Advisory fact-finding agency on tariffs, commercial policy, and foreign trade matters. Analyzes data on oil, crude petroleum, petroleum products, natural gas and its products, and coal and its products (including all forms of coke) traded internationally; investigates effects of tariffs on certain chemical and energy imports.

U.S. Trade Representative *(Executive Office of the President),* 600 17th St. N.W., #205 20508; (202) 395-6890.

Fax, (202) 395-4549. Amb. Michael Froman, U.S. Trade Representative. Press, (202) 395-3230.
General email, correspondence@ustr.eop.gov
Web, www.ustr.gov

Serves as principal adviser to the president and primary trade negotiator on international trade policy. Develops and coordinates energy trade matters among government agencies.

► CONGRESS

For a listing of relevant congressional committees and subcommittees, please see pages 224–225 or the Appendix.

► INTERNATIONAL ORGANIZATIONS

European Union, *Delegation to the United States of America,* 2175 K St. N.W., #800 20037-1400; (202) 862-9500. Fax, (202) 429-1766. João Vale de Almeida, Ambassador.
General email, delegation-usa-info@eeas.europa.eu
Web, www.eurunion.org

Provides information on European Union energy policy, initiatives, research activities, and selected statistics. (Headquarters in Brussels.)

International Energy Agency *(Organization for Economic Cooperation and Development),* Washington Office, 2001 L St. N.W., #650 20036-4922; (202) 785-6323. Fax, (202) 785-0350. Vacant, Head of Center; Kathleen DeBoer, Deputy Head of Center; Maria Josephina Arnoldina van der Hoeven, Executive Director.
General email, washington.contact@oecd.org
Web, www.iea.org

Promotes cooperation in energy research among developed nations; assists developing countries in negotiations with energy-producing nations; prepares plans for international emergency energy allocation. Publishes statistics and analyses on most aspects of energy. Washington Center maintains reference library open to the public. (Headquarters in Paris.)

► NONGOVERNMENTAL

Atlantic Council, *Energy and Environment Program,* 1101 15th St. N.W., 11th Floor 20005-5003; (202) 463-7226. Fax, (202) 463-4590. John Lyman, Director. Press, (202) 778-4967.
General email, mcarstei@atlanticcouncil.org
Web, www.atlanticcouncil.org/programs/energy-and-environment

Seeks to create common understanding of critical energy and environmental issues through nonpartisan policy analysis and recommendations. Studies and makes policy recommendations on the economic, political, and security aspects of energy supply and international environment issues.

U.S. Energy Assn., 1300 Pennsylvania Ave. N.W., #550, Mailbox 142 20004-3022; (202) 312-1230. Fax, (202) 682-1682. Barry K. Worthington, Executive Director.

General email, reply@usea.org
Web, www.usea.org

Membership: energy-related organizations, including professional, trade, and government groups. Participates in the World Energy Council (headquartered in London). Sponsors seminars and conferences on energy resources, policy management, technology, utilization, and conservation.

Statistics

► AGENCIES

Bureau of Labor Statistics (BLS) *(Labor Dept.),* *Industrial Prices and Price Index,* 2 Massachusetts Ave. N.E., #3840 20212-0001; (202) 691-7700. Fax, (202) 691-7754. Jayson Pollock, Manager, Energy and Chemical Team; David M. Friedman, Assistant Commissioner.
General email, ppi-info@bls.gov
Web, www.bls.gov/ppi

Compiles statistics on energy for the Producer Price Index; analyzes movement of prices for natural gas, petroleum, coal, and electric power in the primary commercial and industrial markets. Records changes over time in the prices domestic producers receive.

Energy Information Administration (EIA) *(Energy Dept.),* *National Energy Information Center,* 1000 Independence Ave. S.W., #1E210, EI-30 20585; (202) 586-6537. Fax, (202) 586-0114. Gina Pearson, Director.
General email, infoctr@eia.doe.gov
Web, www.eia.gov/neic/neicservices.htm

Serves as the information point of contact for federal, state, and local governments; academia, businesses, and industry; foreign governments and international organizations; the news media; and the public. Manages and oversees the Energy Information Administration's public Web site, printed publications, and a customer contact center.

► NONGOVERNMENTAL

American Gas Assn., *Statistics,* 400 N. Capitol St. N.W., #450 20001-1535; (202) 824-7133. Fax, (202) 824-7115. Paul Pierson, Manager.
Web, www.aga.org

Issues statistics on the gas utility industry, including supply and reserves.

American Petroleum Institute, *Statistics,* 1220 L St. N.W. 20005-4070; (202) 682-8000. Fax, (202) 962-4730. Hazem Arafa, Director. Information, (202) 682-8520.
General email, statistics@api.org
Web, www.api.org

Provides basic statistical information on petroleum industry operations, market conditions, and environmental, health, and safety performance. Includes data on supply and demand of crude oil and petroleum products, exports and imports, refinery operations, drilling activities and costs, environmental expenditures, injuries, illnesses and fatalities, oil spills, and emissions.

Edison Electric Institute, *Business Information, 701 Pennsylvania Ave. N.W. 20004-2696; (202) 508-5000. Fax, (202) 508-5599. Christopher Eisenbrey, Manager; Dave K. Owens, Executive Vice President, Business Operations. Press, (202) 508-5659.*
General email, ceisenbrey@eei.org

Web, www.eei.org

Provides statistics on electric utility operations, including the *Statistical Yearbook of the Electric Utility Industry,* which contains data on the capacity, generation, sales, customers, revenue, and finances of the electric utility industry.

National Mining Assn., *Communications, 101 Constitution Ave. N.W., #500E 20001-2133; (202) 463-2600. Fax, (202) 463-2666. Nancy Gravett, Senior Vice President.*
Web, www.nma.org

Collects, analyzes, and distributes statistics on the mining industry, including statistics on the production, transportation, and consumption of coal and hard rock minerals.

ELECTRICITY

General

▶AGENCIES

Energy Dept. (DOE), *Power Marketing Liaison Office, 1000 Independence Ave. S.W., #8G037 20585; (202) 586-5581. Fax, (202) 586-6261. Michael D. McElhany, Assistant Administrator.*
Web, www.wapa.gov

Serves as a liaison among the Southeastern, Southwestern, and Western area power administrations; other federal agencies; and Congress. Coordinates marketing of electric power from federally owned hydropower projects.

Energy Information Administration (EIA) *(Energy Dept.), Electricity, Coal, Nuclear, and Renewable Analysis, 1000 Independence Ave. S.W., #2H073, EI-50 20585; (202) 586-2432. Jim Diefenderfer, Director.*
Web, www.eia.gov

Prepares analyses and forecasts on electric power supplies, including the effects of government policies and regulatory actions on capacity, consumption, finances, and rates. Publishes statistics on electric power industry.

National Institute of Standards and Technology (NIST) *(Commerce Dept.), Smart Grid, 100 Bureau Dr., MS 8200, Gaithersburg, MD 20899-8200; (301) 975-2232. Fax, (301) 975-4091. David Wollman, Director.*
General email, smartgrid@nist.gov

Web, www.nist.gov/smartgrid

Develops interoperable standards to govern operations and future growth of the national Smart Grid, a planned electricity system that will add digital technology to electricity grids throughout the United States to channel their electric currents at an anticipated lower cost and higher efficiency. Works with manufacturers, consumers, energy providers, and regulators to ensure cohesion throughout the Smart Grid infrastructure.

Tennessee Valley Authority, *Government Affairs, 1 Massachusetts Ave. N.W., #300 20444; (202) 898-2999. Fax, (202) 898-2998. Nick Pearson, Director.*
General email, latootle@tva.gov

Web, www.tva.gov

Federal corporation that coordinates resource conservation, development, and land-use programs in the Tennessee River Valley. Uses fossil fuel, nuclear, and hydropower sources to generate and supply wholesale power to municipal and cooperative electric systems, federal installations, and some industries. (Headquarters in Knoxville, Tenn.)

▶CONGRESS

For a listing of relevant congressional committees and subcommittees, please see pages 224–225 or the Appendix.

▶NONGOVERNMENTAL

American Coalition for Clean Coal Electricity, *1152 15th St. N.W., #400 20005; (202) 459-4800. Fax, (202) 459-4897. Robert M. Duncan, President.*
General email, info@cleancoalusa.org

Web, www.cleancoalusa.org

Membership: coal, railroad, and electric utility companies and suppliers. Educates the public and policymakers about economic, technological, and scientific research on energy resources employed in generating electricity. Promotes the use of coal in generating electricity and supports development of carbon-sequestration and clean-coal technologies for minimizing coal's environmental impacts.

Assn. of Electrical and Medical Imaging Equipment Manufacturers (NEMA), *1300 N. 17th St., #900, Rosslyn, VA 22209-3801; (703) 841-3200. Fax, (703) 841-5900. Evan Gaddis, President. Press, (703) 841-3241.*
Web, www.nema.org

Membership: manufacturers of products used in the generation, transmission, distribution, control, and end-use of electricity, including manufacturers of medical diagnostic imaging equipment. Develops technical standards; collects, analyzes, and disseminates industry data. Interests include Smart Grid, high-performance building, carbon footprint, energy storage, and an intelligence portal. Monitors legislation, regulations, and international trade activities.

Electric Power Supply Assn., *1401 New York Ave., #1230 20005; (202) 628-8200. Fax, (202) 628-8260. John Shelk, President.*
Web, www.epsa.org

Federal Energy Regulatory Commission

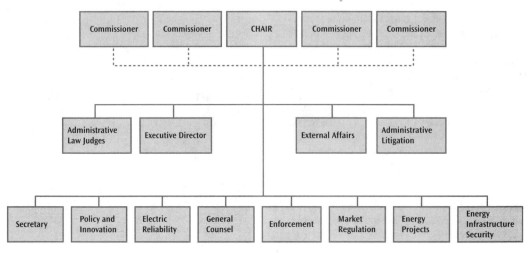

```
                    [Commissioner] [Commissioner] [CHAIR] [Commissioner] [Commissioner]

        [Administrative    [Executive Director]          [External Affairs]  [Administrative
         Law Judges]                                                           Litigation]

[Secretary] [Policy and    [Electric      [General   [Enforcement]  [Market      [Energy    [Energy
             Innovation]    Reliability]   Counsel]                  Regulation]  Projects]  Infrastructure
                                                                                             Security]
```

- - - - - - - Signifies members of the governing body

Membership: power generators active in U.S. and global markets, power marketers, and suppliers of goods and services to the industry. Promotes competition in the delivery of electricity to consumers.

Electricity Consumers Resource Council (ELCON), *1101 K St. N.W., #700 20005; (202) 682-1390. John Anderson, President.*
General email, elcon@elcon.org

Web, www.elcon.org

Membership: large industrial users of electricity. Promotes development of coordinated federal, state, and local policies concerning electrical supply for industrial users; studies rate structures and their impact on consumers.

National Electrical Contractors Assn., *3 Bethesda Metro Center, #1100, Bethesda, MD 20814; (301) 657-3110. Fax, (301) 215-4500. John Grau, Chief Executive Officer.*
Web, www.necanet.org

Membership: electrical contractors who build and service electrical wiring and equipment, including high-voltage construction and service. Represents members in collective bargaining with union workers; sponsors research and educational programs.

National Hydropower Assn., *25 Massachusetts Ave. N.W., #450 20001; (202) 682-1700. Fax, (202) 682-9478. Linda Church Ciocci, Executive Director.*
General email, help@hydro.org

Web, www.hydro.org

Membership: investor-owned utilities and municipal and independent companies that generate hydroelectric power and power from new water technologies; consulting, engineering, and law firms; and equipment suppliers and manufacturers. Focus includes regulatory relief, public affairs, and coalition building. Monitors legislation and regulations.

Public Utilities

▶**AGENCIES**

Federal Energy Regulatory Commission (FERC) *(Energy Dept.), Electric Reliability, 888 1st St. N.E., #9M-01 20426; (202) 502-8600. Fax, (202) 219-2836. Michael A. Bardee, Office Director.*
Web, www.ferc.gov/about/offices/oer.asp

Oversees the reliability and security of the nation's bulk power system. Establishes and ensures compliance with reliability and security standards for users, owners, and operators of the bulk power system.

Federal Energy Regulatory Commission (FERC) *(Energy Dept.), Energy Market Regulation, 888 1st St. N.E., #8A-01 20426; (202) 502-6700. Fax, (202) 219-2836. Michael C. McLaughlin, Director.*
Web, www.ferc.gov/about/offices/oemr.asp

Advises the Commission and processes caseloads related to the economic regulation of the electric utility, natural gas, and oil industries. Concerns include energy markets, tariffs, and pipeline rates relating to electric utility and natural gas and oil pipeline facilities and services. Analyzes applications for electric public utility corporate transactions, including public utility mergers, issuance of securities, or the assumption of liabilities, to determine if the proposed transactions are consistent with the public interest.

Federal Energy Regulatory Commission (FERC) *(Energy Dept.), Energy Projects, 888 1st St. N.E., #6A01 20426; (202) 502-8700. Fax, (202) 219-0205. Jeff Wright, Director.*
Web, www.ferc.gov/about/offices/oep.asp

Focuses on the engineering and environmental aspects of siting and development of new gas pipeline projects;

authorizes and monitors hydroelectric projects for compliance and to safeguard the public.

Rural Development *(Agriculture Dept.), Rural Utilities Service, 1400 Independence Ave. S.W., #5135-S, MS 1510 20250-1510; (202) 720-9540. Fax, (202) 720-1725. John Chas Padalino, Administrator. Information, (202) 720-1255.*
Web, www.rurdeve.usda.gov/utilities_assistance.html and www.rurdeve.usda.gov/utilities_LP.html

Makes loans and loan guarantees to provide electricity, telecommunication systems, and water and waste disposal services to rural areas.

▶ **NONGOVERNMENTAL**

American Public Power Assn., *1875 Connecticut Ave. N.W., #1200 20009-5715; (202) 467-2900. Fax, (202) 467-2910. Mark Crisson, President.*
Web, www.publicpower.org

Membership: local, municipally owned electric utilities nationwide. Represents industry interests before Congress, federal agencies, and the courts; provides educational programs; collects and disseminates information; funds energy research and development projects.

Edison Electric Institute, *701 Pennsylvania Ave. N.W. 20004-2696; (202) 508-5000. Fax, (202) 508-5096. Thomas R. Kuhn, President. Library, (202) 508-5623. General email, feedback@eei.org*
Web, www.eei.org

Membership: investor-owned electric power companies. Interests include electric utility operation and concerns, including conservation and energy management, energy analysis, generation and transmission facilities, fuel resources, the environment, cogeneration and renewable energy resources, safety, reliability, taxes, and regulation matters. Provides information and statistics relating to electric energy; aids member companies in generating and selling electric energy; and conducts information forums. Library open to the public by appointment.

National Assn. of Regulatory Utility Commissioners, *1101 Vermont Ave. N.W., #200 20005-3521; (202) 898-2200. Fax, (202) 898-2213. Charles D. Gray, Executive Director.*
General email, admin@naruc.org
Web, www.naruc.org

Membership: members of federal, state, municipal, and international regulatory commissions that have jurisdiction over utilities. Interests include electric utilities.

National Assn. of State Utility Consumer Advocates (NASUCA), *8380 Colesville Rd., #101, Silver Spring, MD 20910-6267; (301) 589-6313. Fax, (301) 589-6380. Charles A. (Charlie) Acquard, Executive Director.*
General email, nasuca@nasuca.org
Web, www.nasuca.org

Membership: public advocate offices authorized by states to represent ratepayer interests before state and federal utility regulatory commissions. Monitors legislation and regulatory agencies with jurisdiction over electric utilities, telecommunications, natural gas, and water; conducts conferences.

National Rural Electric Cooperative Assn. (NRECA), *4301 Wilson Blvd., Arlington, VA 22203-1860; (703) 907-5500. Fax, (703) 907-5511. Jo Ann Emerson, Chief Executive Officer; Tracy Ward, Media Relations, (703) 907-5746. Web, www.nreca.org*

Membership: rural electric cooperative systems and public power and utility districts. Provides members with legislative, legal, and regulatory services. Supports energy and environmental research and offers technical advice and assistance to developing countries.

Research and Development

▶ **AGENCIES**

Energy Dept. (DOE), *Office of Science, Fusion Energy Sciences, SC-24/Germantown Bldg., 19901 Germantown Rd., Germantown, MD 20874; (301) 903-4941. Fax, (301) 903-8584. Edmund J. Synakowski, Associate Director.*
Web, http://science.energy.gov/fes

Conducts research and development on fusion energy for electric power generation.

National Institute of Standards and Technology (NIST) *(Commerce Dept.), Quantum Measurement Division, 100 Bureau Dr., MS 8420, Gaithersburg, MD 20899-8420; (301) 975-3200. Fax, (301) 926-3972. Carl J. Williams, Chief.*
Web, www.nist.gov/pml/div684/facilities.cfm

Conducts research to characterize and define performance parameters of electrical/electronic systems, components, and materials; applies research to advance measurement instrumentation and the efficiency of electric power transmission and distribution; develops and maintains national electrical reference standards, primarily for power, energy, and related measurements, to assist in the development of new products and promote international competitiveness.

▶ **NONGOVERNMENTAL**

Electric Power Research Institute (EPRI), *Washington Office, 2000 L St. N.W., #805 20036-4913; (202) 872-9222. Fax, (202) 296-5436. Barbara Bauman Tyran, Director.*
Web, www.epri.com

Membership: investor- and municipally owned electric utilities and rural cooperatives. Conducts research and development in power generation and delivery technologies, including fossil fuel, nuclear, and renewable energy sources used by electric utilities. Studies energy management and utilization, including conservation and environmental issues. (Headquarters in Palo Alto, Calif.)

FOSSIL FUELS

General

▶AGENCIES

Energy Information Administration (EIA) *(Energy Dept.), Oil, Gas, and Coal Supply, Statistics,* 1000 *Independence Ave. S.W., #BE072 20585; (202) 586-9646. Fax, (202) 586-1076. James M. Kendell, Director. General email, infoctr@eia.doe.gov*
Web, www.eia.gov

Collects and publishes weekly, monthly, and annual estimates of domestic natural gas, coal, and upstream oil. Performs analyses of the natural gas, coal, and upstream oil industries, including consumption, prices, and storage levels.

Fossil Energy *(Energy Dept.),* 1000 *Independence Ave. S.W., #4G084 20585-1290; (202) 586-6660. Fax, (202) 586-7847. Vacant, Assistant Secretary; Christopher A. Smith, Principal Deputy.*
Web, www.fe.doe.gov and http://energy.gov/fe/office-fossil-energy

Responsible for policy and management of high-risk, long-term research and development in recovering, converting, and using fossil energy, including coal, petroleum, oil shale, and unconventional sources of natural gas. Handles the petroleum reserve and the naval petroleum and oil shale reserve programs; oversees the Clean Coal Program to design and construct environmentally clean coal-burning facilities.

U.S. Geological Survey (USGS) *(Interior Dept.), Energy Resources Program,* 12201 *Sunrise Valley Dr., MS913, Reston, VA 20192 (mailing address: 913 National Center, Reston, VA 20192); (703) 648-6470. Fax, (703) 648-5464. Brenda S. Pierce, Program Coordinator.*
General email, gd-energyprogram@usgs.gov
Web, http://energy.usgs.gov and Twitter, @usgs.gov

Conducts research on geologically based energy resources of the United States and the world, including assessments of the quality, quantity, and geographic locations of natural gas, oil, gas hydrates, geothermal, and coal resources. Estimates energy resource availability and recoverability, including hydraulic fracturing ("fracking"); and conducts research on the deleterious environmental impacts of energy resource occurence and use.

▶CONGRESS

For a listing of relevant congressional committees and subcommittees, please see pages 224–225 or the Appendix.

Coal

▶AGENCIES

Bureau of Land Management (BLM) *(Interior Dept.), Solid Minerals,* 20 *M St. S.E. 20003 (mailing address: 1849 C St. N.W., Washington, DC 20240); (202) 912-7300. Fax, (202) 912-7193. Mitchell Leverette, Chief. General email, mitchell_leverette@blm.gov*
Web, www.blm.gov/wo/st/en/info/directory/WO-320_dir .html

Evaluates and classifies coal resources on federal lands; develops and administers leasing programs. Supervises coal mining operations on federal lands; oversees pre- and postlease operations, including production phases of coal development. Oversees implementation of the Mining Law of 1872 and the Mineral Materials Act of 1955.

Energy Information Administration (EIA) *(Energy Dept.), Electricity, Coal, Nuclear, and Renewable Analysis,* 1000 *Independence Ave. S.W., #2H073, EI-50 20585; (202) 586-2432. Jim Diefenderfer, Director.*
Web, www.eia.gov

Collects data, compiles statistics, and prepares analyses and forecasts on domestic coal supply, including availability, production, costs, processing, transportation, and distribution. Publishes data on the export and import of coal; makes forecasts and provides analyses on coal imports and exports.

Federal Mine Safety and Health Review Commission, 1331 *Pennsylvania Ave., N.W., #520N 20004-1710; (202) 434-9905. Fax, (202) 434-9906. Lisa Boyd, Executive Director; Mary L. Jordan, Chair.*
General email, fmshrc@fmshrc.gov
Web, www.fmshrc.gov

Independent agency established by the Federal Mine Safety and Health Act of 1977. Holds fact-finding hearings and issues orders affirming, modifying, or vacating the labor secretary's enforcement actions regarding mine safety and health. Reading room open to the public by appointment.

Interior Dept. (DOI), *Surface Mining Reclamation and Enforcement,* 1951 *Constitution Ave. N.W., #233 20240; (202) 208-4006. Fax, (202) 219-3106. Joseph G. Pizarchik, Director. Press, (202) 208-2565.*
General email, getinfo@osmre.gov
Web, www.osmre.gov

Administers the Surface Mining Control and Reclamation Act of 1977. Establishes and enforces national standards for the regulation and reclamation of surface coal mining and the surface effects of underground coal mining; oversees state implementation of these standards.

Mine Safety and Health Administration *(Labor Dept.),* 1100 *Wilson Blvd., #2322, Arlington, VA 22209-3939; (202) 693-9899. Fax, (202) 693-9801. Joseph A. Main, Assistant Secretary.*
General email, ASKMSHA@dol.gov
Web, www.msha.gov

Administers and enforces the health and safety provisions of the Federal Mine Safety and Health Act of 1977. Monitors underground mining and processing operations of minerals, including minerals used in construction materials; produces educational materials in engineering; and assists with rescue operations following mining accidents.

▶NONGOVERNMENTAL

American Coal Foundation, *101 Constitution Ave. N.W., #500 East 20001-2133; (202) 463-9785. Fax, (202) 463-9786. Alma Paty, Executive Director.*
General email, info@teachcoal.org
Web, www.teachcoal.org

Provides coal-related educational materials designed for elementary school teachers and students via the Internet at www.teachcoal.org. Web site provides free coal sample kits. Supported by coal producers and manufacturers of mining equipment and supplies.

American Coke and Coal Chemicals Institute, *25 Massachusetts Ave. N.W., #800 20001; (202) 452-7198. Fax, (202) 463-6573. Bruce A. Steiner, President.*
General email, information@accci.org
Web, www.accci.org

Membership: producers of metallurgical coke and coal; tar distillers and coal chemical producers; coke and coal brokers; equipment, materials, and service suppliers to the coke industry; builders of coke ovens and coke byproduct plants. Maintains committees on coke, coal chemicals, manufacturing, environment, safety and health, human resources, quality, governmental relations, and international affairs.

Assn. of Bituminous Contractors, *1250 Eye St. N.W., #650 20005-5976; (202) 522-8700. Fax, (202) 331-8049. William H. Howe, General Counsel.*

Membership: independent and general contractors that build coal mines. Represents members before the Federal Mine Safety and Health Review Commission and in collective bargaining with the United Mine Workers of America.

Bituminous Coal Operators' Assn., *801 Pennsylvania Ave. 20004; (202) 783-3195. Michael O. McKown, President.*

Membership: firms that mine bituminous coal. Represents members in collective bargaining with the United Mine Workers of America.

Coal Technologies Associates, *12548 Granite Ridge Dr., North Potomac, MD 20878; (301) 330-2256. Barbara A. Sakkestad, President.*
General email, barbarasak@aol.com
Web, www.coaltechnologies.com

Membership: business professionals interested in energy (coal technology), economic, and environmental policies and regulations. Seeks to improve coal utilization technologies and to develop coal cleaning technologies. Facilitates the exchange of technical information on coal technologies through annual international conference.

National Coal Council, *1730 M St. N.W., #907 20036-4512; (202) 223-1191. Fax, (202) 223-9031. Janet Gellici, Executive Vice President.*
General email, jgellici@ncc1.org
Web, www.nationalcoalcouncil.org

Membership: individuals appointed by the secretary of energy. Represents coal consumers and producers, transporters, engineering firms, equipment and supply

vendors, academics, consultants, NGOs, and public officials. Monitors federal policies.

National Mining Assn., *101 Constitution Ave. N.W., #500 East 20001-2133; (202) 463-2600. Fax, (202) 463-2666. Harold P. Quinn Jr., President. Press, (202) 463-2667.*
General email, webmaster@nma.org
Web, www.nma.org

Membership: coal producers, coal sales and transportation companies, equipment manufacturers, consulting firms, coal resource developers and exporters, coal-burning electric utility companies, and other energy companies. Collects, analyzes, and distributes industry statistics; conducts special studies of competitive fuels, coal markets, production and consumption forecasts, and industry planning. Interests include exports, coal leasing programs, coal transportation, environmental issues, health and safety, national energy policy, slurry pipelines, and research and development, including synthetic fuels. Monitors legislation and regulation. (Merged with Coal Exporters Assn. of the United States.)

United Mine Workers of America, *18354 Quantico Gateway Dr., #200, Triangle, VA 22172-1779; (703) 291-2400. Cecil E. Roberts, President.*
Web, www.umwa.org

Membership: coal miners and other mining workers. Represents members in collective bargaining with industry. Conducts educational, housing, and health and safety training programs; monitors federal coal mining safety programs.

Oil and Natural Gas

▶AGENCIES

Bureau of Land Management (BLM) *(Interior Dept.), Fluid Minerals, 20 M St. S.E. 20003 (mailing address: 1849 C St. N.W., Washington, DC 20240); (202) 912-7162. Fax, (202) 912-7194. Steven Wells, Division Chief.*
Web, www.blm.gov/wo/st/en/info/directory/WO-310_dir.html

Evaluates and classifies oil, natural gas, and geothermal resources on federal lands; develops and administers leasing programs. Supervises extraction of oil (including from oil shale deposits), natural gas, and geothermal energy resources on federal lands; oversees pre- and postlease operations, including production phases of oil and natural gas development; oversees federal land-leasing reforms.

Bureau of Ocean Energy Management (BOEM) *(Interior Dept.), Strategic Resources, 1849 C St. N.W. 20240; (202) 208-6474. Fax, (202) 219-0726. L. Renee Orr, Chief, (202) 208-3515.*
General email, boempublicaffairs@boem.gov
Web, www.boem.gov

Develops and administers the Five-Year Outer Continental Shelf (OCS) Oil and Natural Gas Leasing Program; oversees assessments of the oil, gas, and other mineral resource potential of the OCS; inventories oil and gas reserves and develops production projections; conducts economic evaluations that ensure fair market value for OCS leases. Oversees marine mineral program and all marine cadastre.

Bureau of Safety and Environmental Enforcement (BSEE) *(Interior Dept.)*, 1849 C St. N.W., MS DM 5438 20240-0001; (202) 208-3985. Fax, (202) 208-3968. *Brian Salerno, Director.*
General email, bseepublicaffairs@bsee.gov
Web, www.bsee.gov

Responsible for inspections, enforcement, and safety of offshore oil and gas operations. Functions include the development and enforcement of safety and environmental regulations, research, inspections, offshore regulatory and compliance programs, oil spill response, and training of inspectors and industry professionals.

Bureau of Safety and Environmental Enforcement (BSEE) *(Interior Dept.)*, *Offshore Regulatory Programs,* 1849 C St. N.W., MS DM 5438 20240-0001; (202) 208-3985. Fax, (202) 208-3968. *Douglas Morris, Chief.*
General email, bseepublicaffairs@bsee.gov
Web, www.bsee.gov

Develops standards, regulations, and compliance programs governing Outer Continental Shelf oil, gas, and minerals exploration and operations. Purview includes safety management programs, safety and pollution prevention research, technology assessments, standards for inspections and enforcement policies, and accident investigation practices.

Energy Information Administration (EIA) *(Energy Dept.)*, *Petroleum and Biofuel Statistics,* 1000 Independence Ave. S.W., #BG041 20585; (202) 586-1831. Fax, (202) 586-3873. *Douglas M. MacIntyre, Director.*
General email, infoctr@eia.doe.gov
Web, www.eia.gov

Collects, compiles, interprets, and publishes data on domestic production, distribution, and prices of crude oil and refined petroleum products; analyzes and projects availability of petroleum supplies.

Fossil Energy *(Energy Dept.)*, *Oil and Natural Gas,* 1000 Independence Ave. S.W., #3E028 20585; (202) 586-5600. Fax, (202) 586-6221. *Paula Gant, Deputy Assistant Secretary.*
Web, www.fe.doe.gov

Responsible for research and development programs in oil and gas exploration, production, processing, and storage; studies ways to improve efficiency of oil recovery in depleted reservoirs; coordinates and evaluates research and development among government, universities, and industrial research organizations.

Fossil Energy *(Energy Dept.)*, *Petroleum Reserves,* Forrestal Bldg., 1000 Independence Ave. S.W., FE-40 20585; (202) 586-4733. *Robert Corbin, Deputy Assistant Secretary.*
Web, www.fossil.energy.gov

Manages programs that provide the United States with strategic and economic protection against disruptions in oil supplies, including the Strategic Petroleum Reserves, the Northeast Home Heating Oil Reserve, and the Naval Petroleum and Oil Shale Reserves.

Internal Revenue Service (IRS) *(Treasury Dept.)*, *Passthroughs and Special Industries, Excise Tax Branch,* 1111 Constitution Ave. N.W., #5314 20224; (202) 317-3100. *Frank Boland, Chief.*
Web, www.irs.gov

Administers excise tax programs, including taxes on diesel, gasoline, and special fuels. Advises district offices, internal IRS offices, and general inquirers on tax policy, rules, and regulations.

▶ NONGOVERNMENTAL

AHRI (Air-Conditioning, Heating, and Refrigeration Institute), 2111 Wilson Blvd., #500, Arlington, VA 22201; (703) 524-8800. Fax, (703) 562-1942. *Stephen R. Yurek, President.*
General email, ahri@ahrinet.org
Web, www.ari.org

Membership: manufacturers of gas appliances and equipment for residential and commercial use and related industries. Advocates product improvement; provides market statistics. Monitors legislation and regulations. (Merger of the Air-Conditioning and Refrigeration Institute [ARI] and the Gas Appliance Manufacturers Assn. [GAMA].)

American Fuel and Petrochemical Manufacturers, 1667 K St. N.W., #700 20006-1605; (202) 457-0480. Fax, (202) 457-0486. *Charles T. Drevna, President.*
General email, info@afpm.org
Web, www.afpm.org

Membership: petroleum, petrochemical, and refining companies. Interests include allocation, imports, refining technology, petrochemicals, and environmental regulations. (Formerly the National Petrochemical and Refiners Assn. [NPRA].)

American Gas Assn., 400 N. Capitol St. N.W., #450 20001-1535; (202) 824-7000. Fax, (202) 824-7115. *Dave McCurdy, President. Press, (202) 824-7027.*
Web, www.aga.org

Membership: natural gas utilities and pipeline companies. Interests include all technical and operational aspects of the gas industry. Publishes comprehensive statistical record of the gas industry; conducts national standard testing for gas appliances. Advocates for policies that are favorable to increased supplies and lower prices. Monitors legislation and regulations.

American Petroleum Institute, 1220 L St. N.W., 12th Floor 20005-4070; (202) 682-8000. Fax, (202) 682-8110. *Jack N. Gerard, President. Press, (202) 682-8114.*
Web, www.api.org

Membership: producers, refiners, marketers, pipeline operators, and transporters of oil, natural gas, and related products such as gasoline. Provides information on the industry, including data on exports and imports, taxation, transportation, weekly refinery operations and inventories, and drilling activity and costs; conducts research on petroleum and publishes statistical and drilling reports. Develops equipment and operating standards. Certifies compliance of equipment manufacturing and of environmental and occupational safety and health management systems.

American Public Gas Assn. (APGA), *201 Massachusetts Ave. N.E., #C4 20002-4988; (202) 464-2742. Fax, (202) 464-0246. Bert Kalisch, President.*
General email, apga@apga.org
Web, www.apga.org

Membership: municipally owned gas distribution systems. Provides information on federal developments affecting natural gas. Promotes efficiency and works to protect the interests of public gas systems. Sponsors workshops and conferences.

Center for Liquefied Natural Gas, *1620 Eye St. N.W., #700 20006; (202) 289-2253. Fax, (202) 962-4753. Bill Cooper, President. Press, (202) 962-4752.*
Web, www.LNGfacts.org

Membership: liquefied natural gas producers, shippers, terminal operators and developers, and energy trade associations. Provides general and technical information on liquefied natural gas. Monitors legislation and regulations.

Compressed Gas Assn., *14501 George Carter Way, #103, Chantilly, VA 20151; (703) 788-2700. Fax, (703) 961-1831. Michael Tiller, President.*
General email, cga@cganet.com
Web, www.cganet.com

Membership: all segments of the compressed gas industry, including producers and distributors of compressed and liquefied gases. Promotes and coordinates technical development and standardization of the industry. Monitors legislation and regulations.

Gas Technology Institute (GTI), *Policy and Regulatory Affairs, 655 15th St. N.W., #420 20005-3355; (202) 661-8650. Fax, (202) 661-8651. Richard Kaelin, Executive Director, Washington Operations. Alternate phone, (847) 768-0511.*
General email, washingtonops@gastechnology.org
Web, www.gastechnology.org

Membership: all segments of the natural gas industry, including producers, pipelines, and distributors. Conducts research and develops new technology for gas customers and the industry. (Headquarters in Des Plaines, Ill.)

Independent Petroleum Assn. of America, *1201 15th St. N.W., #300 20005-2842; (202) 857-4722. Fax, (202) 857-4799. Barry Russell, President.*
Web, www.ipaa.org

Membership: independent oil and gas producers; land and royalty owners; and others with interests in domestic exploration, development, and production of oil and natural gas. Interests include leasing, prices and taxation, foreign trade, environmental restrictions, and improved recovery methods.

International Assn. of Drilling Contractors (IADC), *Government and Regulatory Affairs, 1667 K St. N.W., #420 20006; (202) 293-0670. Fax, (202) 872-0047. Bill Taner, Executive Vice President.*
General email, info@iadc.org
Web, www.iadc.org

Membership: drilling contractors, oil and gas producers, and others in the industry worldwide. Promotes safe exploration and production of hydrocarbons, advances in drilling technology, and preservation of the environment. Monitors legislation and regulations. (Headquarters in Houston, Texas.)

International Liquid Terminals Assn. (ILTA), *1005 N. Glebe Rd., #600, Arlington, VA 22201; (703) 875-2011. Fax, (703) 875-2018. Melinda Whitney, President.*
General email, info@ilta.org
Web, www.ilta.org

Membership: commercial operators of for-hire bulk liquid terminals and tank storage facilities, including those for crude oil and petroleum. Promotes the safe and efficient handling of various types of bulk liquid commodities. Sponsors workshops and seminars and publishes directories. Monitors legislation and regulations.

National Ocean Industries Assn., *1120 G St. N.W., #900 20005; (202) 347-6900. Fax, (202) 347-8650. Randall Luthi, President.*
General email, noia@noia.org
Web, www.noia.org

Membership: manufacturers, producers, suppliers, and support and service companies involved in marine, offshore, and ocean work. Interests include offshore oil and gas supply and production, pursuit of offshore renewable-energy opportunities, environmental safeguards, equipment supply, gas transmission, navigation, research and technology, and shipyards.

National Petroleum Council, *1625 K St. N.W., #600 20006-1656; (202) 393-6100. Fax, (202) 331-8539. Marshall W. Nichols, Executive Director; James T. Hackett, Chair.*
General email, info@npc.org
Web, www.npc.org

Advisory committee to the secretary of energy on matters relating to the petroleum industry, including oil and natural gas. Publishes reports concerning technical aspects of the oil and gas industries.

National Propane Gas Assn., *1899 L St. N.W., #350 20036-4623; (202) 466-7200. Fax, (202) 466-7205. Richard R. Roldan, President.*
General email, info@npga.org
Web, www.npga.org

Membership: retail marketers, producers, wholesale distributors, appliance and equipment manufacturers, equipment fabricators, and distributors and transporters of liquefied petroleum gas. Conducts research, safety, and educational programs; provides statistics on the industry.

Natural Gas Supply Assn., *1620 Eye St. N.W., #700 20006; (202) 326-9300. Fax, (202) 326-9308. Dena Wiggins, President.*
Web, www.ngsa.org

Membership: major and independent producers of domestic natural gas. Interests include the production, consumption, marketing, and regulation of natural gas. Monitors legislation and regulations.

NGVAmerica (Natural Gas Vehicles for America), *400 N. Capitol St. N.W. 20001; (202) 824-7366. Fax, (202) 824-9160. Richard R. Kolodziej, President; Paul Kerkhoven, Director, Government Affairs, (202) 824-7363.*
General email, pkerkhoven@ngvamerica.org
Web, www.ngvamerica.org

Membership: natural gas distributors and producers; automobile and engine manufacturers; natural gas vehicle product and service suppliers; research and development organizations; and state and local government agencies. Advocates installation of natural gas and biomethane fuel stations and development of industry standards. Helps market new products and equipment related to natural gas– and biomethane-powered vehicles. (Formerly known as the Natural Gas Vehicle Coalition.)

Petroleum Marketers Assn. of America (PMAA), *1901 N. Fort Myer Dr., #500, Arlington, VA 22209-1604; (703) 351-8000. Fax, (703) 351-9160. Daniel F. Gilligan, President.*
General email, info@pmaa.org
Web, www.pmaa.org

Membership: state and regional associations representing independent branded and nonbranded marketers of petroleum products. Provides information on all aspects of petroleum marketing. Monitors legislation and regulations.

Service Station Dealers of America and Allied Trades, *1532 Pointer Ridge Pl., Suite E, Bowie, MD 20716; (301) 390-4405. Fax, (301) 390-3161. Marta Gates, Executive Vice President, Acting.*
General email, mgates@wmda.net

Membership: state associations of gasoline retailers, repair facilities, car washes, and convenience stores. Interests include environmental issues, retail marketing, oil allocation, imports and exports, prices, and taxation. Monitors legislation and regulations.

SIGMA (Society of Independent Gasoline Marketers of America), *3930 Pender Dr., #340, Fairfax, VA 22030-0985; (703) 709-7000. Fax, (703) 709-7007. Kenneth A. Doyle, Executive Vice President.*
General email, sigma@sigma.org
Web, www.sigma.org

Membership: marketers and wholesalers of brand and nonbrand gasoline. Seeks to ensure adequate supplies of gasoline at competitive prices. Monitors legislation and regulations affecting gasoline supply and price.

Pipelines

▶AGENCIES

Federal Energy Regulatory Commission (FERC) *(Energy Dept.), Energy Market Regulation, 888 1st St. N.E., #8A-01 20426; (202) 502-6700. Fax, (202) 219-2836. Michael C. McLaughlin, Director.*
Web, www.ferc.gov/about/offices/oemr.asp

Establishes and enforces maximum rates and charges for oil and natural gas pipelines; establishes oil pipeline–operating rules; issues certificates for and regulates construction, sale, and acquisition of natural gas pipeline facilities. Ensures compliance with the Natural Gas Policy Act, the Natural Gas Act, and other statutes.

National Transportation Safety Board, *Railroad, Pipeline, and Hazardous Materials Investigations, 490 L'Enfant Plaza East, SW 20594; (202) 314-6000. Fax, (202) 314-6482. Robert Hall, Director. Press, (202) 314-6100.*
Web, www.ntsb.gov

Investigates hazardous materials and petroleum pipeline accidents.

Pipeline and Hazardous Materials Safety Administration *(Transportation Dept.), Hazardous Materials Safety, 1200 New Jersey Ave. S.E., E21-317 20590; (202) 366-0656. Fax, (202) 366-5713. Magdy A. El-Sibaie, Associate Administrator. Hazardous Materials Information Center, (800) 467-4922.*
General email, phmsa.hmhazmatsafety@dot.gov
Web, http://hazmat.dot.gov

Designates fuels, chemicals, and other substances as hazardous materials and regulates their transportation in interstate commerce. Provides technical assistance on hazardous waste materials transportation safety and security to state and local governments. Gathers and analyzes incident data from carriers transporting hazardous materials.

Pipeline and Hazardous Materials Safety Administration *(Transportation Dept.), Pipeline Safety, 1200 New Jersey Ave. S.E., E22-321 20590; (202) 366-4595. Fax, (202) 493-2311. Jeffery D. Wiese, Associate Administrator.*
General email, phmsa.pipelinesafety@dot.gov
Web, http://phmsa.dot.gov

Issues and enforces federal regulations for oil, natural gas, and petroleum products pipeline safety. Inspects pipelines and oversees risk management by pipeline operators.

▶NONGOVERNMENTAL

Assn. of Oil Pipe Lines (AOPL), *1808 Eye St., N.W., #300 20006; (202) 408-7970. Fax, (202) 280-1949. Andrew J. Black, President.*
General email, aopl@aopl.org
Web, www.aopl.org

Membership: owners and operators of oil pipelines. Analyzes industry statistics. Monitors legislation and regulations.

Interstate Natural Gas Assn. of America, *20 F St. N.W., #450 20001; (202) 216-5900. Donald F. Santa Jr., President. Press, (202) 216-5913.*
Web, www.ingaa.org

Membership: U.S. interstate, Canadian, and Mexican interprovincial natural gas pipeline companies. Commissions studies and provides information on the natural gas pipeline industry.

NUCLEAR ENERGY

General

▶AGENCIES

Energy Information Administration (EIA) *(Energy Dept.), Electricity, Coal, Nuclear, and Renewable Analysis, 1000 Independence Ave. S.W., #2H073, EI-50 20585; (202) 586-2432. Jim Diefenderfer, Director.*
Web, www.eia.gov

Prepares analyses and forecasts on the availability, production, prices, processing, transportation, and distribution of nuclear energy, both domestically and internationally. Collects and publishes data concerning the uranium supply and market.

Nuclear Energy *(Energy Dept.), International Nuclear Energy Policy and Cooperation, 1000 Independence Ave. S.W., #5A-143 20585; (202) 586-5253. Fax, (202) 586-8353. Edward G. McGinnis, Deputy Assistant Secretary.*
Web, www.nuclear.energy.gov/ne/international-energy-policy-and-cooperation

Responsible for the Energy Dept.'s international civilian nuclear energy activities, including research, development and demonstration cooperation, international framework and partnership development, and international nuclear energy policy.

Nuclear Regulatory Commission, *11555 Rockville Pike, MS 016G4, Rockville, MD 20852; (301) 415-1750. Fax, (301) 415-3504. Mark A. Satorius, Chair; R. William Borchardt, Executive Director; Annette Vietti-Cook, Secretary, (301) 415-1969. Press, (301) 415-8200. Toll-free, (800) 368-5642. Public Document Room, (301) 397-4737.*
General email, opa@nrc.gov
Web, www.nrc.gov

Regulates commercial uses of nuclear energy; responsibilities include licensing, inspection, and enforcement; monitors and regulates the imports and exports of nuclear material and equipment.

Tennessee Valley Authority, *Government Affairs, 1 Massachusetts Ave. N.W., #300 20444; (202) 898-2999. Fax, (202) 898-2998. Nick Pearson, Director.*
General email, latootle@tva.gov
Web, www.tva.gov

Coordinates resource conservation, development, and land-use programs in the Tennessee River Valley. Produces and supplies wholesale power to municipal and cooperative electric systems, federal installations, and some industries; interests include nuclear power generation.

▶CONGRESS

For a listing of relevant congressional committees and subcommittees, please see pages 224–225 or the Appendix.

▶NONGOVERNMENTAL

American Physical Society, *Washington Office, 529 14th St. N.W., #1050 20045-2065; (202) 662-8700. Fax, (202) 662-8711. Michael Lubell, Director, Public Affairs. Press Secretary, (202) 662-8702.*
General email, opa@aps.org
Web, www.aps.org

Scientific and educational society of educators, students, citizens, and scientists, including industrial scientists. Sponsors studies on issues of public concern related to physics, such as reactor safety and energy use. Informs members of national and international developments. (Headquarters in College Park, Md.)

Nuclear Energy Institute, *1201 F. St. N.W., #1100 20004; (202) 739-8000. Fax, (202) 785-4019. Marvin Fertel, President.*
General email, media@nei.org
Web, www.nei.org

Membership: utilities; industries; labor, service, and research organizations; law firms; universities; and government agencies interested in peaceful uses of nuclear energy, including the generation of electricity. Acts as a spokesperson for the nuclear power industry; provides information on licensing and plant siting, research and development, safety and security, waste disposal, and legislative and policy issues.

Nuclear Information and Resource Service, *6930 Carroll Ave., #340, Takoma Park, MD 20912-4446; (301) 270-6477. Fax, (301) 270-4291. Michael Mariotte, Executive Director.*
General email, nirsnet@nirs.org
Web, www.nirs.org

Information and networking clearinghouse for environmental activists and other individuals concerned about nuclear power plants, radioactive waste, and radiation and sustainable energy issues. Initiates large-scale organizing and public education campaigns and provides technical and strategic expertise to environmental groups. Library open to the public by appointment.

Public Citizen, *Energy Program, 215 Pennsylvania Ave. S.E. 20003-1155; (202) 546-4996. Fax, (202) 546-5562. Tyson Slocum, Director.*
General email, energy@citizen.org
Web, www.citizen.org/cmep

Nuclear Regulatory Commission

— — — Indicates a support or advisory relationship with the unit rather than a direct reporting relationship

Public interest group that promotes energy efficiency and renewable energy technologies; opposes nuclear energy. Interests include nuclear plant safety and energy policy issues.

Union of Concerned Scientists, *Global Security, Washington Office, 1825 K St., N.W., #800 20006-1232; (202) 223-6133. Fax, (202) 223-6162. Stephen Young, Senior Washington Representative; Vacant, Nuclear Energy and Climate Change Project Manager.*
General email, ucs@ucsusa.org

Web, www.ucsusa.org

An independent public interest group of scientists and citizens concerned with U.S. energy policy, including nuclear energy economics and power plant safety and security. Monitors the performance of nuclear power plants and their regulators; evaluates the economics

of nuclear power relative to other low-carbon energy resources. (Headquarters in Cambridge, Mass.)

Licensing and Plant Siting

► **AGENCIES**

Federal Emergency Management Agency (FEMA) *(Homeland Security Dept.), National Preparedness, Technological Hazards, 1800 S. Bell St., MS 3025, Arlington, VA 22202; (202) 646-3158. Fax, (703) 308-0324. Andrew Mitchell, Director, (202) 646-2618.*
Web, www.fema.gov/technological-hazards-division

Reviews off-site preparedness for commercial nuclear power facilities; evaluates emergency plans before plant licensing and submits findings to the Nuclear Regulatory Commission.

Nuclear Regulatory Commission, *New Reactors,* 11555 *Rockville Pike, MS T6F15, Rockville, MD 20852; (301) 415-1897. Fax, (301) 415-6323. Glenn M. Tracy, Director. Web, www.nrc.gov/about-nrc/organization/nrofuncdesc .html*

Licenses and regulates nuclear power plants that use new designs; approves siting of new plants.

Nuclear Regulatory Commission, *Nuclear Material Safety and Safeguards, 11601 Landsdown St., N. Bethesda, MD 20852; (301) 287-9243. Fax, (301) 287-0500. Catherine Haney, Director. Web, www.nrc.gov/about-nrc/organization/nmssfuncdesc .html*

Licenses all nuclear facilities and materials except power reactors; directs principal licensing and regulation activities for the management of nuclear waste.

Nuclear Regulatory Commission, *Nuclear Reactor Regulation, 11555 Rockville Pike, MS O13H16M, Rockville, MD 20852; (301) 415-1270. Fax, (301) 415-8333. Eric J. Leeds, Director. Web, www.nrc.gov/about-nrc/organization/nrrfuncdesc .html*

Licenses nuclear power plants and operators.

Research and Development

▶**AGENCIES**

Energy Dept. (DOE), *Office of Science, Fusion Energy Sciences, SC-24/Germantown Bldg., 19901 Germantown Rd., Germantown, MD 20874; (301) 903-4941. Fax, (301) 903-8584. Edmund J. Synakowski, Associate Director. Web, http://science.energy.gov/fes*

Conducts research and development on fusion energy for electric power generation.

Nuclear Energy *(Energy Dept.), 1000 Independence Ave. S.W., #5A143, E-1 20585; (202) 586-6630. Fax, (202) 586-0544. Peter B. Lyons, Assistant Secretary. Web, www.nuclear.energy.gov*

Responsible for nuclear technology research and development, management of the Energy Dept.'s nuclear technology infrastructure, uranium activities, and fuel cycle issues. Supports nuclear education, including university reactor instrumentation and equipment upgrades and general support to nuclear engineering programs at U.S. universities. Leads U.S. participation in the Global Nuclear Energy Partnership, which seeks to demonstrate a more proliferation-resistant closed fuel cycle and increase the safety and security of nuclear energy.

Nuclear Regulatory Commission, *Nuclear Regulatory Research, 21 Church St., MS C6D20M, Rockville, MD 20852-2746; (301) 251-7400. Fax, (301) 251-7426. Brian W. Sheron, Director. Web, www.nrc.gov/about-nrc/organization/resfuncdesc .html*

Plans, recommends, and implements nuclear regulatory research, standards development, and resolution of safety issues for nuclear power plants and other facilities regulated by the Nuclear Regulatory Commission; develops and promulgates all technical regulations.

Safety, Security, and Waste Disposal

▶**AGENCIES**

Defense Nuclear Facilities Safety Board, *625 Indiana Ave. N.W., #700 20004-2901; (202) 694-7080. Fax, (202) 208-6518. Peter S. Winokur, Chair. Information, (202) 694-7000. General email, mailbox@dnfsb.gov Web, www.dnfsb.gov*

Independent board created by Congress and appointed by the president to provide external oversight of Energy Dept. defense nuclear weapons production facilities and make recommendations to the secretary of energy regarding public health and safety.

Energy Information Administration (EIA) *(Energy Dept.), Electricity, Coal, Nuclear, and Renewable Analysis, 1000 Independence Ave. S.W., #2H073, EI-50 20585; (202) 586-2432. Jim Diefenderfer, Director. Web, www.eia.gov*

Directs collection of spent fuel data and validation of spent nuclear fuel discharge data for the Civilian Radioactive Waste Management Office.

Environmental Management *(Energy Dept.), Disposal Operations, 1000 Independence Ave. S.W., #EM-31 20585; (301) 903-7212. Fax, (301) 903-7238. Douglas Tonkay, Director. General email, douglas.tonkay.em.does.gov Web, www.em.doe.gov*

Manages Energy Dept. programs that treat, stabilize, and dispose of radioactive waste, including that generated from the decontamination and decommissioning of Energy Dept. facilities and sites. Works to develop a reliable national system for low-level waste management and techniques for treatment and immobilization of waste from former nuclear weapons complex sites. Provides technical assistance to states and Regional Disposal Compacts on the safe and effective management of commercially generated wastes.

Environmental Protection Agency (EPA), *Radiation and Indoor Air (ORIA), 1310 L St. N.W., 4th Floor, MC 6601J 20005; (202) 343-9320. Fax, (202) 343-2395. Michael P. Flynn, Director. Web, www2.epa.gov/aboutepa/about-office-air-and-radiation-oar#oria*

Establishes standards to regulate the amount of radiation discharged into the environment from uranium mining and milling projects, and other activities that result in radioactive emissions; and to ensure the safe disposal of radioactive waste. Fields a Radiological Emergency Response Team to respond to radiological incidents. Oversees the

National Air and Radiation Environmental Laboratory in Montgomery, Ala.

Federal Emergency Management Agency (FEMA) *(Homeland Security Dept.),* 500 C St. S.W. 20472; (202) 646-3900. Fax, (202) 646-3930. W. Craig Fugate, Administrator. Press, (202) 646-3272. Locator, (202) 646-2500. Disaster assistance, (800) 621-3362. Toll-free, 800-621-FEMA.
General email, femaopa@dhs.gov
Web, www.fema.gov

Assists state and local governments responding to and recovering from natural, technological, and attack-related emergencies, including in communities where accidents at nuclear power facilities have occurred and communities surrounding accidents involving transportation of radioactive materials; operates the National Emergency Training Center. Coordinates emergency preparedness, mitigation, response, and recovery activities, and planning for all federal agencies and departments.

Health, Safety, and Security *(Energy Dept.),* 1000 Independence Ave. S.W., #7G040 20585; (301) 903-3777. Fax, (202) 586-7960. Glenn S. Podonsky, Chief Officer, (202) 586-0271.
General email, HSSusersupport@hq.doe.gov
Web, www.hss.energy.gov

Develops policy and establishes standards to ensure safety and health protection in all department activities.

Health, Safety, and Security *(Energy Dept.),* **Health and Safety,** 1000 Independence Ave. S.W., HS-10-GTN 20585; (301) 903-5926. Fax, (301) 903-3445.
Patricia R. Worthington, Director.
Web, http://energy.gov/hss/office-health-safety-and-security

Establishes hazardous material worker safety and health requirements and expectations for the Energy Dept. and assists in their implementation. Conducts and supports domestic and international hazardous material health studies and programs. Supports the Labor Dept. in the implementation of the Energy Employees Occupational Illness Compensation Program Act (EEOICPA).

Health, Safety, and Security *(Energy Dept.),* **HS20 Environmental Protection, Sustainability Support, and Corporate Safety Analysis,** 1000 Independence Ave. S.W., #6B-128 20585; (202) 586-5680. Fax, (202) 586-7330. Andrew C. Lawrence, Director.
Web, www.hss.doe.gov/sesa

Establishes policies and guidance for environmental protection and compliance; provides technical assistance to departmental program and field offices in complying with environmental requirements.

National Transportation Safety Board, *Railroad, Pipeline, and Hazardous Materials Investigations,* 490 L'Enfant Plaza East, SW 20594; (202) 314-6000. Fax, (202) 314-6482. Robert Hall, Director. Press, (202) 314-6100.
Web, www.ntsb.gov

Investigates accidents involving the transportation of hazardous materials.

Nuclear Energy *(Energy Dept.),* **Fuel Cycle Research and Development,** 1000 Independence Ave. S.W., #5A-107 20585; (202) 586-6692. Fax, (202) 586-0541. Monica Regalbuto, Deputy Assistant Secretary.
Web, www.ne.doe.gov/fuelcycle/neFuelCycle.html

Develops and administers research and development focused on nuclear fuel recycling and waste management.

Nuclear Regulatory Commission, *Advisory Committee on Reactor Safeguards,* 11545 Rockville Pike, Rockville, MD 20852 (mailing address: Nuclear Regulatory Commission, MS T2E26, Washington, DC 20555-0001); (301) 415-7360. Fax, (301) 415-5589. Edwin M. Hackett, Executive Director, (301) 415-7360.
Web, www.nrc.gov/about-nrc/organization/acrsfuncdesc.html

Advises the commission on the licensing and operation of production and utilization facilities and related safety issues, the adequacy of proposed reactor safety standards, and technical and policy issues related to the licensing of evolutionary and passive plant designs. Reports on the NRC Safety Research Program. Reviews Energy Dept. nuclear activities and facilities and provides technical advice to the Energy Dept.'s Nuclear Safety Board upon request.

Nuclear Regulatory Commission, *Enforcement,* 11555 Rockville Pike, MS O4A 15A, Rockville, MD 20852; (301) 415-2741. Fax, (301) 415-3431. Roy P. Zimmerman, Director.
Web, www.nrc.gov/about-nrc/organization/oefuncdesc.html

Oversees the development and implementation of policies and programs that enforce the commission's procedures concerning public health and safety. Identifies and takes action against violators.

Nuclear Regulatory Commission, *Federal and State Materials and Environmental Management Programs,* 11545 Rockville Pike, MS T8D22, Rockville, MD 20852-2746; (301) 415-7197. Brian E. Holian, Director, Acting.
Web, www.nrc.gov/about-nrc/organization/fsmefuncdesc.html

Implements rules and guidance in providing for the safe, environmentally sound, and secure uses and disposal of nuclear materials and the decommissioning of regulated facilities.

Nuclear Regulatory Commission, *Investigations,* 11555 Rockville Pike, MS O3F1, Rockville, MD 20852; (301) 415-2373. Fax, (301) 415-2370. Cheryl L. McCrary, Director.
Web, www.nrc.gov/about-nrc/organization/oifuncdesc.html

Develops policy, procedures, and standards for investigations of licensees, applicants, and their contractors or vendors concerning wrongdoing. Refers substantiated criminal cases to the Justice Dept. Informs the commission's leadership about investigations concerning public health and safety.

Nuclear Regulatory Commission, *Nuclear Material Safety and Safeguards,* 11601 Landsdown St., N. Bethesda, MD 20852; (301) 287-9243. Fax, (301) 287-0500. Catherine Haney, Director.
Web, www.nrc.gov/about-nrc/organization/nmssfuncdesc .html

Develops and implements safeguards programs; directs licensing and regulation activities for the management and disposal of nuclear waste.

Nuclear Regulatory Commission, *Nuclear Reactor Regulation,* 11555 Rockville Pike, MS O13H16M, Rockville, MD 20852; (301) 415-1270. Fax, (301) 415-8333. Eric J. Leeds, Director.
Web, www.nrc.gov/about-nrc/organization/nrrfuncdesc .html

Conducts safety inspections of nuclear reactors. Regulates nuclear materials used or produced at nuclear power plants.

Nuclear Regulatory Commission, *Nuclear Regulatory Research,* 21 Church St., MS C6D20M, Rockville, MD 20852-2746; (301) 251-7400. Fax, (301) 251-7426. Brian W. Sheron, Director.
Web, www.nrc.gov/about-nrc/organization/resfuncdesc .html

Plans, recommends, and implements resolution of safety issues for nuclear power plants and other facilities regulated by the Nuclear Regulatory Commission.

Nuclear Regulatory Commission, *Nuclear Security and Incident Response,* 11601 Landsdown St., #3WFN09D20, N. Bethesda, MD 20852; (301) 287-3734. Fax, (301) 287-9351. James T. Wiggins, Director. Emergency, (301) 816-5100. Nonemergency, (800) 695-7403.
Web, www.nrc.gov/about-nrc/organization/nsirfuncdesc .html

Evaluates technical issues concerning security at nuclear facilities. Develops and directs the commission's response to incidents. Serves as point of contact with Homeland Security Dept., Energy Dept., Federal Emergency Management Agency, and intelligence and law enforcement offices and other agencies.

Nuclear Waste Technical Review Board, 2300 Clarendon Blvd., #1300, Arlington, VA 22201-3367; (703) 235-4473. Fax, (703) 235-4495. Nigel Mote, Executive Director.
General email, info@nwtrb.gov
Web, www.nwtrb.gov

Independent board of scientists and engineers nominated by the Academy of Sciences and appointed by the president to review, evaluate, and report on Energy Dept. development of waste disposal systems and repositories for spent fuel and high-level radioactive waste. Oversees siting, packaging, and transportation of waste, in accordance with the amendments to the Nuclear Waste Policy Act of 1987.

Pipeline and Hazardous Materials Safety Administration *(Transportation Dept.), Hazardous Materials Safety,* 1200 New Jersey Ave. S.E., E21-317 20590; (202) 366-0656. Fax, (202) 366-5713. Magdy A. El-Sibaie, Associate Administrator. Hazardous Materials Information Center, (800) 467-4922.
General email, phmsa.hmhazmatsafety@dot.gov
Web, http://hazmat.dot.gov

Issues safety regulations and exemptions for the transportation of hazardous materials; works with the International Atomic Energy Agency on standards for international shipments of radioactive materials.

RENEWABLE ENERGIES, ALTERNATIVE FUELS

General

►AGENCIES

Energy Efficiency and Renewable Energy *(Energy Dept.),* 1000 Independence Ave. S.W., #6A013 20585; (202) 586-9220. Fax, (202) 586-9260. David Danielson, Assistant Secretary. Information, (877) 337-3463. Press, (202) 586-4940.
General email, eereic@ee.doe.gov
Web, www.eere.energy.gov

Develops and manages programs to improve markets for renewable energy sources including solar, biomass, wind, geothermal, and hydropower and to increase efficiency of energy use among residential, commercial, transportation, utility, and industrial users. Administers financial and technical assistance for state energy programs, weatherization for low-income households, and implementation of energy conservation measures by schools, hospitals, local governments, and public care institutions and federal facilities.

Energy Information Administration (EIA) *(Energy Dept.), Electricity, Coal, Nuclear, and Renewable Analysis,* 1000 Independence Ave. S.W., #2H073, EI-50 20585; (202) 586-2432. Jim Diefenderfer, Director.
Web, www.eia.gov

Prepares analyses on the availability, production, costs, processing, transportation, and distribution of uranium and alternative energy supplies, including biomass, solar, wind, waste, wood, and alcohol.

►CONGRESS

For a listing of relevant congressional committees and subcommittees, please see pages 224–225 or the Appendix.

►NONGOVERNMENTAL

Biomass Thermal Energy Council (BTEC), 1211 Connecticut Ave. N.W., #600 20036; (202) 596-3974. Fax, (202) 223-5537. Joseph Seymour, Executive Director.

General email, info@biomassthermal.org

Web, www.biomassthermal.org

Membership: biomass fuel producers, appliance manufacturers and distributors, supply chain companies, and nonprofit organizations that seek to advance the use of biomass for heat and other thermal energy applications. Conducts research, public education, and advocacy for the biomass thermal energy industry. Monitors legislation and regulations.

Bipartisan Policy Center/Commission on Energy Policy, 1225 Eye St. N.W., #1000 20005-5977; (202) 204-2400. Fax, (202) 637-9220. Jason S. Grumet, President; Julie Anderson, Executive Director.
General email, info@energycommission.org

Web, www.energycommission.org

Researches and advocates for a reduction of oil consumption in the United States. Evaluates policy options and makes recommendations to lawmakers. Monitors legislation and regulations.

Electric Power Supply Assn., 1401 New York Ave., #1230 20005; (202) 628-8200. Fax, (202) 628-8260. John Shelk, President.
Web, www.epsa.org

Membership: companies that generate electricity, steam, and other forms of energy using a broad spectrum of fossil fuel–fired and renewable technologies.

Fuel Cell and Hydrogen Energy Assn., 1211 Connecticut Ave. N.W., #600 20036; (202) 261-1331. Morry Markowitz, President.
General email, mmarkowitz@fchea.org

Web, www.fchea.org

Membership: industry, small businesses, universities, government agencies, and nonprofit organizations. Promotes use of hydrogen as an energy carrier; fosters the development and application of fuel cell and hydrogen technologies.

Institute for the Analysis of Global Security, 7811 Montrose Rd., #505, Potomac, MD 20854-3363; (866) 713-7527. Gal Luft, Co-Director; Anne Korin, Co-Director; Johanna Rose, Co-Director. Toll-free, (866) 713-7527.
General email, info@iags.org

Web, www.iags.org

Seeks to promote public awareness of the link between energy and security; explores options to strengthen the world's energy security, including approaches to reducing the strategic importance of oil. Conducts and publishes research; hosts conferences; monitors legislation and regulations.

SRI International, *Washington Office,* 1100 Wilson Blvd., #2800, Arlington, VA 22209; (703) 524-2053. Fax, (703) 247-8569. Jerry Harrison, Vice President, Government Business Development, (703) 247-8569.
Web, www.sri.com

Conducts energy-related research and development. Interests include power generation, fuel and solar cells,

clean energy storage, and advanced batteries. (Headquarters in Menlo Park, Calif.)

Biofuels

►AGENCIES

Alcohol and Tobacco Tax and Trade Bureau (TTB) *(Treasury Dept.), Regulations and Rulings,* 1310 G St. N.W., #200 East, Box 12 20005; (202) 453-2265. Rochelle Stern, Director.
General email, ttbquestions@ttb.treas.gov

Web, www.ttb.gov

Develops guidelines for regional offices responsible for issuing permits for producing gasohol and other ethyl alcohol fuels, whose uses include heating and operating machinery. Writes and interprets regulations for distilleries that produce ethyl alcohol fuels.

Energy Efficiency and Renewable Energy *(Energy Dept.), Fuel Cells Technologies,* 1000 Independence Ave. S.W., #5G082 20585; (202) 586-3388. Fax, (202) 586-2373. Sunita Satyapal, Program Manager, (202) 586-2336.
General email, fuelcells@ee.doe.gov

Web, www1.eere.energy.gov/hydrogenandfuelcells

Works with industry, academia, nonprofit institutions, national labs, government agencies, and other Energy Dept. offices to promote the use of fuel cells and related technologies.

Energy Information Administration (EIA) *(Energy Dept.), Petroleum and Biofuel Statistics,* 1000 Independence Ave. S.W., #BG041 20585; (202) 586-1831. Fax, (202) 586-3873. Douglas M. MacIntyre, Director.
General email, infoctr@eia.doe.gov

Web, www.eia.gov

Collects, compiles, interprets, and publishes data on domestic production, distribution, and prices of crude oil and refined petroleum products; analyzes and projects availability of petroleum supplies.

National Institute of Food and Agriculture (NIFA) *(Agriculture Dept.), Institute of Bioenergy, Climate, and Environment,* 800 9th St. S.W., #3700 20024 *(mailing address: 1400 Independence Ave. S.W., MS 2210, Washington, DC 20250-2215);* (202) 720-0740. Fax, (202) 720-7803. Bradley Rein, Assistant Director, Acting.
Web, http://nifa.usda.gov/about/pdfs/factsheets/inst_fs_ibce.pdf

Administers programs to address national science priorities that advance energy independence and help agricultural/forest/range production systems adapt to climate change variables. Provides grants to support the development of sustainable bioenergy production systems, agricultural production systems, and natural resource management activities that are adapted to climate variation and activities that otherwise support sustainable natural resource use.

Rural Development *(Agriculture Dept.), Business and Cooperative Programs, Business Programs,* 1400 Independence Ave. S.W., #5813-S 20250-3220; (202) 720-7287. Fax, (202) 690-0097. Chad Parker, Deputy Administrator.
Web, www.rurdev.usda.gov/LP_businessprograms.html

Makes loan guarantees to rural businesses, including those seeking to develop alcohol fuels production facilities.

▶**NONGOVERNMENTAL**

Biomass Thermal Energy Council (BTEC), *1211 Connecticut Ave. N.W., #600 20036; (202) 596-3974. Fax, (202) 223-5537. Joseph Seymour, Executive Director.*
General email, info@biomassthermal.org
Web, www.biomassthermal.org

Membership: biomass fuel producers, appliance manufacturers and distributors, supply chain companies, and nonprofit organizations that seek to advance the use of biomass for heat and other thermal energy applications. Conducts research, public education, and advocacy for the biomass thermal energy industry. Monitors legislation and regulations.

Coalition of Northeastern Governors (CONEG), *Policy Research Center, Inc.,* 400 N. Capitol St. N.W., #382 20001; (202) 624-8450. Fax, (202) 624-8463. Anne D. Stubbs, Executive Director.
General email, coneg@sso.org
Web, www.coneg.org

Membership: governors of seven northeastern states (Connecticut, Maine, Massachusetts, New Hampshire, New York, Rhode Island, and Vermont). Addresses common issues of concern such as energy, economic development, transportation, and the environment; serves as an information clearinghouse and liaison among member states and with the federal government. Administers the Northeast Regional Biomass Program, a public-private cooperative initiative among eleven northeastern states, the federal government, regional and national organizations, and key industries to advance the development and use of biomass resources and technologies in the Northeast.

Hearth, Patio, and Barbecue Assn. (HPBA), *1901 N. Moore St., #600, Arlington, VA 22209-1708; (703) 522-0086. Fax, (703) 522-0548. Jack Goldman, President.*
General email, hpbamail@hpba.org
Web, www.hpba.org

Membership: all sectors of the hearth products industry. Provides industry training programs to its members on the safe and efficient use of alternative fuels and appliances. Works with the Hearth Education Foundation, which certifies gas hearth, fireplace, pellet stove, and wood stove appliances and venting design specialists.

Methanol Institute, *124 South West St., #203, Alexandria, VA 22314; (703) 248-3636. Fax, (703) 248-3997. Greg Dolan, Chief Executive Officer.*
General email, mi@methanol.org
Web, www.methanol.org

Membership: global methanol producers and related industries. Encourages use of methanol fuels and development of chemical-derivative markets. Monitors legislation and regulations.

Renewable Fuels Assn., *425 3rd St. S.W., #1150 20024; (202) 289-3835. Fax, (202) 289-7519. Bob Dinneen, President.*
General email, info@ethanolrfa.org
Web, www.ethanolrfa.org

Membership: companies and state governments involved in developing the domestic ethanol industry. Distributes publications on ethanol performance. Monitors legislation and regulations.

Geothermal Energy

▶**AGENCIES**

Energy Efficiency and Renewable Energy *(Energy Dept.), Geothermal Technologies,* 1000 Independence Ave. S.W., #BH039, MS EE-2C 20585-0121; (202) 287-1818. Doug Hollett, Program Manager.
General email, geothermal@ee.doe.gov
Web, www1.eere.energy.gov/geothermal

Responsible for research and technology development of geothermal energy resources. Conducts outreach to state energy offices and consumers.

U.S. Geological Survey (USGS) *(Interior Dept.), Volcano Hazards,* 12201 Sunrise Valley Dr., MS 904, Reston, VA 20192 (mailing address: 904 National Center, Reston, VA 20192); (703) 648-6711. Fax, (703) 648-5483. Charles W. Mandeville, Program Coordinator.
General email, vhpweb@usgs.gov
Web, http://volcanoes.usgs.gov

Provides staff support to the U.S. Geological Survey through programs in volcano hazards.

Solar, Ocean, and Wind Energy

▶**AGENCIES**

Bureau of Ocean Energy Management (BOEM) *(Interior Dept.), Renewable Energy Programs,* 381 Elden St., MS 1328, Herndon, VA 20170-4817; (703) 787-1300. Fax, (703) 787-1708. Maureen A. Bornholdt, Chief.
General email, boempublicaffairs@boem.gov
Web, www.boem.gov

Grants leases, easements, and rights-of-way for orderly, safe, and environmentally responsible renewable energy development activities on the Outer Continental Shelf, including offshore wind and hydrokinetic projects.

Energy Efficiency and Renewable Energy *(Energy Dept.), Solar Energy Technologies, SunShot Initiative,* 950 L'Enfant Plaza, 6th Floor 20585 (mailing address: 1000 Independence Ave. S.W., Washington, DC 20585); (202)

287-1862. Fax, (202) 586-8148. Minh Le, Program Manager.

General email, solar@ee.doe.gov

Web, www1.eere.energy.gov/solar

Supports research and development of solar technologies of all types through national laboratories and partnerships with industries and universities. Seeks to make solar energy cost-effective through research, manufacturing, and market solutions.

Energy Efficiency and Renewable Energy *(Energy Dept.), Wind and Water Power Technologies, 1000 Independence Ave. S.W., #5H072, MS EE-2B 20585; (202) 586-5348. Fax, (202) 586-5124. Jose Zayas, Director.*

Web, www1.eere.energy.gov/wind/newsletter/detail.cfm/articlel=43

Conducts research on wind and water power technologies. Works with U.S. industries to develop hydropower and wind technologies.

National Oceanic and Atmospheric Administration (NOAA) *(Commerce Dept.), Ocean and Coastal Resource Management, 1305 East-West Hwy., 10th Floor, SSMC4, Silver Spring, MD 20910; (301) 713-3155. Fax, (301) 713-4012. Margaret Davidson, Director, Acting.*

Web, http://coastalmanagement.noaa.gov

Administers the Coastal Zone Management Act and the National Estuarine Research Reserve System to carry out NOAA's goals for preservation, conservation, and restoration management of the ocean and coastal environment.

▶**CONGRESS**

For a listing of relevant congressional committees and subcommittees, please see pages 224–225 or the Appendix.

▶**NONGOVERNMENTAL**

American Wind Energy Assn., *1501 M St. N.W., #1000 20005-1700; (202) 383-2500. Fax, (202) 383-2505. Tom Kieman, Chief Executive Officer.*

General email, windmail@awea.org

Web, www.awea.org

Membership: manufacturers, developers, operators, and distributors of wind machines; utility companies; and others interested in wind energy. Advocates wind energy as an alternative energy source; makes industry data available to the public and to federal and state legislators. Promotes export of wind energy technology.

National Ocean Industries Assn., *1120 G St. N.W., #900 20005; (202) 347-6900. Fax, (202) 347-8650. Randall Luthi, President.*

General email, noia@noia.org

Web, www.noia.org

Membership: manufacturers, producers, suppliers, and support and service companies involved in marine, off-shore, and ocean work. Interests include ocean thermal energy and new energy sources.

Solar Electric Light Fund, *1612 K St. N.W., #300 20006; (202) 234-7265. Fax, (202) 328-9512. Robert A. Freling, Executive Director.*

General email, info@self.org

Web, http://self.org

Promotes and develops solar rural electrification and energy self-sufficiency in developing countries. Assists developing world communities and governments in acquiring and installing decentralized household and community solar electric systems.

Solar Energy Industries Assn., *505 9th St. N.W., #800 20004; (202) 682-0556. Fax, (202) 682-0559. Rhone Resch, Chief Executive Officer; Heather Whitpan, Government Affairs. Press, (202) 556-2885.*

General email, info@seia.org

Web, www.seia.org

Membership: industries with interests in the production and use of solar energy. Promotes growth of U.S. and international markets. Interests include photovoltaic, solar thermal power, and concentrating solar power. Conducts conferences. Monitors legislation and regulations.

Sustainable Buildings Industry Council, *1090 Vermont Ave. N.W., #700 20005-4950; (202) 289-7800. Fax, (202) 289-1092. Ryan Colker, Director.*

General email, rcolker@nibs.org

Web, www.nibs.org/?page=sbic

Membership: building industry associations, corporations, small businesses, and independent professionals. Provides information on sustainable design and construction. Interests include passive solar industry and related legislation, regulations, and programs. (Affiliated with the National Institute of Building Sciences.)

8

Environment and Natural Resources

GENERAL POLICY AND ANALYSIS

Basic Resources

▶ AGENCIES

Agriculture Dept. (USDA), *Natural Resources and Environment,* 1400 Independence Ave. S.W., #240E 20250-0108; (202) 720-7173. Fax, (202) 720-0632. Robert Bonnie, Under Secretary.
Web, www.usda.gov

Formulates and promulgates policy relating to environmental activities and management of natural resources. Oversees the Forest Service and the Natural Resources Conservation Service.

Council on Environmental Quality *(Executive Office of the President),* 730 Jackson Pl. N.W. 20503; (202) 395-5750. Fax, (202) 456-6546. Nancy Sutley, Chair.
Web, www.whitehouse.gov/administration/eop/ceq

Develops environmental priorities; advises and assists the president on national and international environmental policy; evaluates, coordinates, and mediates federal activities on the environment; prepares the president's yearly environmental quality report to Congress.

Environmental Protection Agency (EPA), 1200 Pennsylvania Ave. N.W., #3000, MC 1101A 20460; (202) 564-4700. Fax, (202) 501-1450. Gina McCarthy, Administrator, Acting; Robert Perciasepe, Deputy Administrator. Information, (202) 272-0167. Press, (202) 564-4355.
Web, www.epa.gov/aboutepa/ao.html

Administers federal environmental policies, research, and regulations; provides information on environmental subjects, including water pollution, pollution prevention, hazardous and solid waste disposal, air and noise pollution, pesticides and toxic substances, and radiation.

Environmental Protection Agency (EPA), *Children's Health Protection (OCHP),* 1200 Pennsylvania Ave. N.W., #2512, MC 1107T 20460; (202) 564-2188. Fax, (202) 564-2733. Jackie Mosby, Director, Acting.
Web, www.epa.gov/aboutepa/iaq/childrenshealth.html and *http://yosemite.epa.gov/ochp/ochpweb.nsf/content/whatwe.htm*

Supports and facilitates the EPA's efforts to protect children's health from environmental risks, both domestically and internationally; provides leadership on interagency Healthy Homes Work Group and Healthy School Environments Initiative; offers grants through the Office of Children's Health Protection and Environmental Education (OCHPEE).

Environmental Protection Agency (EPA), *National Center for Environmental Assessment,* 2 Potomac Yard, North Bldg., 7th Floor, 273 S. Crystal Dr., Arlington, VA 22202 (mailing address: 1200 Pennsylvania Ave. N.W., MC 8601 P, Washington, DC 20004); (703) 347-8600. Fax, (703) 347-8699. Debra Walsh, Director, Acting.

General email, deener.kathleen@epa.gov
Web, www.epa.gov/ncea/basicinfo.htm

Evaluates animal and human health data to define environmental health hazards and estimate risk to humans.

Environmental Protection Agency (EPA), *Policy,* 1200 Pennsylvania Ave. N.W., #3513, MC 1804A 20460; (202) 564-4332. Fax, (202) 501-1688. Michael Goo, Associate Administrator.
General email, policyoffice@epa.gov
Web, www.epa.gov/aboutepa/about-office-policy-op

Coordinates agency policy development and standard-setting activities through four divisions: Regulatory Policy and Management (ORPM), the National Center for Environmental Economics (NCEE), Strategic Environmental Management (OSEM), and Sustainable Communities (OSC).

Environmental Protection Agency (EPA), *Research and Development (ORD),* 1200 Pennsylvania Ave. N.W., #41222, MC 8101R 20460; (202) 564-6620. Fax, (202) 565-2430. Vacant, Assistant Administrator.
Web, www2.epa.gov/aboutepa/about-office-research-and-development-ord

Develops scientific data and methods to support EPA standards and regulations; conducts exposure and risk assessments; researches applied and long-term technologies to reduce risks from pollution.

Environmental Protection Agency (EPA), *Science Advisory Board,* 1300 Pennsylvania Ave. N.W., #31150 20004 (mailing address: 1200 Pennsylvania Ave. N.W., MC 1400R, Washington, DC 20460); (202) 564-2221. Fax, (202) 565-2098. Angela Nugent, Designated Federal Officer, (202) 564-2218.
General email, sab@epa.gov
Web, www.epa.gov/sab

Coordinates nongovernment scientists and engineers who advise the administrator on scientific and technical aspects of environmental problems and issues. Evaluates EPA research projects, the technical basis of regulations and standards, and policy statements.

Federal Highway Administration (FHWA) (Transportation Dept.), *Planning, Environment, and Realty,* 1200 New Jersey Ave. S.E., #E76-306 20590; (202) 366-0116. Fax, (202) 366-3713. Gloria M. Shepherd, Associate Administrator.
Web, www.fhwa.dot.gov/realestate

Works with developers and municipalities to ensure conformity with the National Environmental Policy Act (NEPA) project development process.

Housing and Urban Development Dept. (HUD), *Environment and Energy,* 451 7th St. S.W. 20410; (202) 708-2894. Fax, (202) 708-3363. Danielle Schopp, Director, (202) 402-4442.
Web, www.hud.gov/offices/cpd/environment

Issues policies and sets standards for environmental and land-use planning and environmental management practices. Oversees HUD implementation of requirements on environment, historic preservation, archaeology, flood plain management, wetlands protection, environmental justice (ensuring that the environment and human health are fairly protected for all people/Executive Order 12898), coastal zone management, sole source aquifers, farmland protection, endangered species, airport clear zones, explosive hazards, and noise.

Interior Dept. (DOI), *1849 C St. N.W. 20240; (202) 208-7351. Fax, (202) 208-6956. Hon. Sally Jewell, Secretary; Vacant, Deputy Secretary. Information, (202) 208-3100. Library, (202) 208-5815. Press, (202) 208-6416.*
General email, feedback@ios.doi.gov
Web, www.doi.gov

Principal U.S. conservation agency. Manages most federal land; responsible for conservation and development of mineral and water resources; responsible for conservation, development, and use of fish and wildlife resources; operates recreation programs for federal parks, refuges, and public lands; preserves and administers the nation's scenic and historic areas; reclaims arid lands in the West through irrigation; administers Native American lands and develops relationships with tribal governments.

Interior Dept. (DOI), *Policy Analysis, 1849 C St. N.W., MS 3530 20240; (202) 208-5978. Fax, (202) 208-4867. Joel Clement, Director.*
Web, www.doi.gov/ppa

Analyzes how policies affect the department; makes recommendations and develops policy options for resolving natural resource problems.

Justice Dept. (DOJ), *Environment and Natural Resources, 950 Pennsylvania Ave. N.W., #2143 20530-0001; (202) 514-2701. Fax, (202) 514-0557. Robert G. Dreher, Assistant Attorney General, Acting. Press, (202) 514-2008.*
Web, www.justice.gov/enrd

Handles civil suits involving the federal government in all areas of the environment and natural resources; handles some criminal suits involving pollution control, wildlife protection, stewardship of public lands, and natural resources.

National Institute of Environmental Health Sciences *(National Institutes of Health), Washington Office, 31 Center Dr., #B1C02, MSC 2256, Bethesda, MD 20892-2256; (301) 496-3511. Fax, (301) 480-2978. Dr. Linda S. Birnbaum, Director. Information, (919) 541-4794.*
General email, webcenter@niehs.nih.gov
Web, www.niehs.nih.gov

Conducts and supports research on the human effects of various environmental exposures, expanding the scientific basis for making public health decisions based on the potential toxicity of environmental agents. (Most operations located in Research Triangle, N.C.)

National Oceanic and Atmospheric Administration *(NOAA) (Commerce Dept.), 1401 Constitution Ave. N.W., #5128 20230; (202) 482-3436. Fax, (202) 408-9674. Kathryn D. Sullivan, Under Secretary. Library, (301) 713-2600. Press, (202) 482-6090.*
Web, www.noaa.gov

Conducts research in marine and atmospheric sciences; issues weather forecasts and warnings vital to public safety and the national economy; surveys resources of the sea; analyzes economic aspects of fisheries operations; develops and implements policies on international fisheries; provides states with grants to conserve coastal zone areas; protects marine mammals; maintains a national environmental center with data from satellite observations and other sources, including meteorological, oceanic, geodetic, and seismological data centers; provides colleges and universities with grants for research, education, and marine advisory services; prepares and provides nautical and aeronautical charts and maps.

National Oceanic and Atmospheric Administration *(NOAA) (Commerce Dept.), National Environmental Satellite, Data, and Information Service, 1335 East-West Hwy., SSMC1, 8th Floor, Silver Spring, MD 20910; (301) 713-3578. Fax, (301) 713-1249. Mary E. Kicza, Assistant Administrator.*
Web, www.nesdis.noaa.gov

Provides satellite observations of the environment by operating polar orbiting and geostationary satellites; develops satellite techniques; increases the utilization of satellite data in environmental services.

National Oceanic and Atmospheric Administration *(NOAA) (Commerce Dept.), Program, Planning, and Integration, 1315 East-West Hwy., SSMC3, Silver Spring, MD 20910; (301) 713-1632. Fax, (301) 713-0585. Patricia A. Montanio, Assistant Administrator.*
General email, strategic.planning@noaa.gov
Web, www.ppi.noaa.gov

Develops NOAA's strategic plan. Manages designated programs and fosters strategic management throughout NOAA offices and advisory panels.

Office of Science and Technology Policy (OSTP) *(Executive Office of the President), Eisenhower Executive Office Bldg., 1650 Pennsylvania Ave. N.W. 20504; (202) 456-7116. Fax, (202) 456-6021. John P. Holdren, Director. Press, (202) 456-6124.*
General email, info@ostp.gov
Web, www.ostp.gov

Advises the president on science and technology matters as they affect national security; coordinates science and technology initiatives at the interagency level. Interests include nuclear materials, security, nuclear arms reduction, and counterterrorism.

Office of Science and Technology Policy (OSTP) *(Executive Office of the President), National Science and Technology Council (NSTC), Eisenhower Executive Office Bldg., 1650 Pennsylvania Ave. N.W. 20504; (202) 456-4444. Fax, (202) 456-6021. Jayne Morrow, Executive Director.*
General email, info@ostp.gov
Web, www.ostp.gov

Coordinates research and development activities and programs that involve more than one federal agency. Activities concern earth sciences, materials, forestry research, and radiation policy.

ENVIRONMENTAL RESOURCES IN CONGRESS

For a complete listing of Congress committees, including their full contact information, leadership, membership, and jurisdictions, please refer to the Appendix on pages 724–842.

HOUSE:

House Agriculture Committee, (202) 225-2171.
Web, agriculture.house.gov or
democrats.agriculture.house.gov
> **Subcommittee on Conservation, Energy, and Forestry,** (202) 225-2171.
> **Subcommittee on Horticulture, Research, Biotechnology, and Foreign Agriculture,** (202) 225-2171.
> **Subcommittee on Livestock, Rural Development, and Credit,** (202) 225-2171.

House Appropriations Committee, (202) 225-2771.
Web, appropriations.house.gov or
democrats.appropriations.house.gov
> **Subcommittee on Agriculture, Rural Development, FDA, and Related Agencies,** (202) 225-2638.
> **Subcommittee on Commerce, Justice, Science, and Related Agencies,** (202) 225-3351.
> **Subcommittee on Energy and Water Development, and Related Agencies,** (202) 225-3421.
> **Subcommittee on Interior, Environment, and Related Agencies,** (202) 225-3081.

House Energy and Commerce Committee, (202) 225-2927.
Web, energycommerce.house.gov or
democrats.energycommerce.house.gov
> **Subcommittee on Environment and the Economy,** (202) 225-2927.

House Natural Resources Committee, (202) 225-2761.
Web, naturalresources.house.gov or
democrats.naturalresources.house.gov
> **Subcommittee on Energy and Mineral Resources,** (202) 225-9297.
> **Subcommittee on Fisheries, Wildlife, Oceans, and Insular Affairs,** (202) 226-0200.
> **Subcommittee on Public Lands and Environmental Regulation,** (202) 226-7736.
> **Subcommittee on Water and Power,** (202) 225-8331.

House Science, Space, and Technology Committee, (202) 225-6371.
Web, science.house.gov or democrats.science.house.gov
> **Subcommittee on Environment,** (202) 225-6371.
> **Subcommittee on Research and Technology,** (202) 225-6371.

House Small Business Committee, (202) 225-5821.
Web, smallbusiness.house.gov or
democrats.smallbusiness.house.gov

House Transportation and Infrastructure Committee, (202) 225-9446.
Web, transportation.house.gov or
democrats.transportation.house.gov
> **Subcommittee on Coast Guard and Maritime Transportation,** (202) 226-3552.
> **Subcommittee on Railroads, Pipelines, and Hazardous Materials,** (202) 226-0727.
> **Subcommittee on Water Resources and Environment,** (202) 225-4360.

U.S. Geological Survey (USGS) *(Interior Dept.), 12201 Sunrise Valley Dr., MS 100, Reston, VA 20192-0002; (703) 648-4000. Fax, (703) 648-4454. Suzette M. Kimball, Director, Acting, (703) 648-7412. Information, 888-ASK-USGS. Library, (703) 648-4301. Press, (703) 648-4460. General email, suzette_kimball@usgs.gov*

Web, www.usgs.gov

Provides reports, maps, and databases that describe and analyze water, energy, biological, and mineral resources; the land surface; and the underlying geological structure and dynamic processes of the Earth.

► **CONGRESS**

For a listing of relevant congressional committees and subcommittees, please see pages 252–253 or the Appendix.

Government Accountability Office (GAO), *Natural Resources and Environment, 441 G St. N.W., #2057 20548*

(mailing address: 441 G St. N.W., #2T23A, Washington, DC 20548); (202) 512-3841. Fax, (202) 512-8774. Mark Gaffigan, Managing Director.
Web, www.gao.gov

Independent, nonpartisan agency in the legislative branch that audits the Agriculture Dept. and analyzes and reports on its handling of agriculture issues and food safety.

► **NONGOVERNMENTAL**

Aspen Institute, *1 Dupont Circle N.W., #700 20036-7133; (202) 736-5800. Fax, (202) 467-0790. Walter Isaacson, President. Press, (202) 736-3849.*
General email, info@aspeninstitute.org
Web, www.aspeninstitute.org

Educational and policy studies organization. Promotes consideration of the public good in a wide variety of policy

SENATE:

Senate Agriculture, Nutrition, and Forestry Committee, (202) 224-2035.
Web, ag.senate.gov

Subcommittee on Conservation, Forestry, and Natural Resources, (202) 224-2035.

Subcommittee on Jobs, Rural Economic Growth, and Energy Innovation, (202) 224-2035.

Subcommittee on Livestock, Dairy, Poultry, Marketing and Agriculture Security, (202) 224-2035.

Senate Appropriations Committee, (202) 224-7363.
Web, appropriations.senate.gov

Subcommittee on Agriculture, Rural Development, FDA, and Related Agencies, (202) 224-8090.

Subcommittee on Commerce, Justice, Science, and Related Agencies, (202) 224-5202.

Subcommittee on Energy and Water Development, (202) 224-8119.

Subcommittee on Interior, Environment, and Related Agencies, (202) 228-0774.

Senate Commerce, Science, and Transportation Committee, (202) 224-0411.
Web, commerce.senate.gov

Subcommittee on Oceans, Atmosphere, Fisheries and the Coast Guard, (202) 224-4912.

Senate Energy and Natural Resources Committee, (202) 224-4971.
Web, energy.senate.gov

Subcommittee on Energy, (202) 224-4971.

Subcommittee on National Parks, (202) 224-4971.

Subcommittee on Public Lands, Forests, and Mining, (202) 224-4971.

Subcommittee on Water and Power, (202) 224-4971.

Senate Environment and Public Works Committee, (202) 224-8832.
Web, epw.senate.gov

Subcommittee on Clean Air and Nuclear Safety, (202) 224-8832.

Subcommittee on Green Jobs and the New Economy, (202) 224-8832.

Subcommittee on Oversight, (202) 224-8832.

Subcommittee on Superfund, Toxics and Environmental Health, (202) 224-8832.

Subcommittee on Transportation and Infrastructure, (202) 224-8832.

Subcommittee on Water and Wildlife, (202) 224-8832.

Senate Finance Committee, (202) 224-4515.
Web, finance.senate.gov

Subcommittee on Energy, Natural Resources, and Infrastructure, (202) 224-4515.

Senate Foreign Relations Committee, (202) 224-4651.
Web, foreign.senate.gov

Subcommittee on International Development and Foreign Assistance, Economic Affairs, International Environmental Protection, and Peace Corps, (202) 224-4651.

Senate Indian Affairs Committee, (202) 224-2251.
Web, indian.senate.gov

Senate Small Business and Entrepreneurship Committee, (202) 224-5175.
Web, sbc.senate.gov

---

areas, including energy and the environment. Working with international partners, offers educational seminars, nonpartisan policy forums, public conferences and events, and leadership development initiatives.

The Conservation Fund, *1655 N. Fort Myer Dr., #1300, Arlington, VA 22209-3199; (703) 525-6300. Fax, (703) 525-4610. Lawrence A. Selzer, President.*
General email, webmaster@conservationfund.org
Web, www.conservationfund.org

Creates partnerships with the private sector, nonprofit organizations, and public agencies to promote land and water conservation. Operates land trusts, identifies real estate for conservation, and runs loan programs.

Earth Share, *7735 Old Georgetown Rd., #900, Bethesda, MD 20814; (240) 333-0300. Fax, (240) 333-0301. Kalman Stein, President. Information, (800) 875-3863.*
General email, info@earthshare.org
Web, www.earthshare.org

Federation of environmental and conservation organizations. Works with government and private payroll contribution programs to solicit contributions to member organizations for environmental research, education, and community programs. Provides information on establishing environmental giving options in the workplace.

Edison Electric Institute, *701 Pennsylvania Ave. N.W. 20004-2696; (202) 508-5000. Fax, (202) 508-5096. Thomas R. Kuhn, President. Library, (202) 508-5623.*
General email, feedback@eei.org
Web, www.eei.org

Membership: investor-owned electric power companies. Interests include electric utility operation and concerns, including conservation and energy management, energy analysis, resources and environment, cogeneration

Environmental Protection Agency

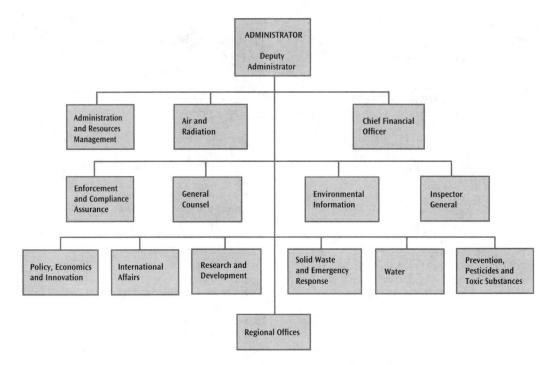

and renewable energy resources, safety, reliability, taxes, and regulation matters. Library open to the public by appointment.

Environment America, *Federal Advocacy Office, 218 D St. S.E., 2nd Floor 20003; (202) 683-1250. Fax, (202) 546-2461. Anna Aurilio, Director, ext. 317.*
Web, www.environmentamerica.org

Coordinates grassroots efforts to advance environmental and consumer protection laws; conducts research on environmental issues, including global warming, clean energy, preservation and conservation, clean water and air, and toxic pollution; compiles reports and disseminates information on such issues; drafts and monitors environmental laws; testifies on behalf of proposed environmental legislation. (Headquarters in Boston.)

Environmental and Energy Study Institute (EESI), *1112 16th St. N.W., #300 20036-4819; (202) 628-1400. Fax, (202) 204-5244. Carol Werner, Executive Director, (202) 662-1881.*
General email, eesi@eesi.org
Web, www.eesi.org

Nonpartisan policy education and analysis group established by members of Congress to foster informed debate on environmental and energy issues. Interests include policies for sustainable development, energy, sustainable bioenergy, climate change, agriculture, transportation, and fiscal policy reform.

Environmental Council of the States, *50 F St. N.W., #350 20001; (202) 266-4920. Fax, (202) 266-4937.*
Alexandra Dapolito Dunn, Executive Director.

General email, ecos@ecos.org
Web, www.ecos.org

Works to improve the environment by providing for the exchange of ideas and experiences among states and territories; fosters cooperation and coordination among environmental management professionals.

Environmental Defense Fund, *Washington Office, 1875 Connecticut Ave. N.W., #600 20009-5728; (202) 387-3500. Fax, (202) 234-6049. Diane Regas, Senior Vice President. Information, (800) 684-3322. Press, (202) 572-3396.*
Web, www.edf.org

Citizens' interest group staffed by lawyers, economists, and scientists. Takes legal action on environmental issues; provides information on pollution prevention, environmental health, wetlands, toxic substances, acid rain, tropical rain forests, and litigation of water pollution standards. (Headquarters in New York.)

Environmental Law Institute, *2000 L St. N.W., #620 20036; (202) 939-3800. Fax, (202) 939-3868. John C. Cruden, President, (202) 939-3824.*
General email, law@eli.org
Web, www.eli.org

Conducts policy studies on the environment and sustainability. Publishes materials on environmental issues, sponsors education and training courses and conferences on environmental law, issues policy recommendations, and provides technical assistance in the United States and abroad.

Environmental Working Group, *1436 U St. N.W., #100 20009-3987; (202) 667-6982. Fax, (202) 232-2592. Kenneth A. Cook, President.*
General email, generalinfo@ewg.org
Web, www.ewg.org

Research and advocacy organization that studies and reports on the presence of herbicides and pesticides in food and drinking water. Monitors legislation and regulations.

Friends of the Earth (FOE), *Washington Office, 1100 15th St. N.W., 11th Floor 20005; (202) 783-7400. Fax, (202) 783-0444. Erich Pica, President. Toll-free, (877) 843-8687.*
General email, foe@foe.org
Web, www.foe.org

Environmental advocacy group. Interests include climate and energy, oceans and water, food and emerging technology, and economic drivers of environmental degradation. Specializes in federal budget and tax issues related to the environment, ozone layer and groundwater protection, and World Bank and International Monetary Fund reform.

Green America, *1612 K St. N.W., #600 20006; (202) 872-5307. Fax, (202) 331-8166. Alisa Gravitz, President. Information, (800) 584-7336. Press, (202) 872-5310.*
General email, info@greenamerica.org
Web, www.greenamerica.org

Educates consumers and businesses about social and environmental responsibility. Publishes a directory of environmentally and socially responsible businesses and a financial planning guide for investment.

Izaak Walton League of America, *707 Conservation Lane, Gaithersburg, MD 20878-2983; (301) 548-0150. Fax, (301) 548-0146. Scott Kovarovics, Executive Director. Toll-free, (800) 453-5463.*
General email, info@iwla.org
Web, www.iwla.org

Grassroots organization that promotes conservation of natural resources and the environment. Interests include air and water pollution, farmland conservation, clean and renewable energy, wildlife habitat protection, and instilling conservation ethics in outdoor recreationists.

League of Conservation Voters (LCV), *1920 L St. N.W., #800 20036; (202) 785-8683. Fax, (202) 835-0491. Gene Karpinski, President.*
Web, www.lcv.org

Supports the environmental movement by advocating for sound environmental policies and helping elect environmentally concerned candidates to public office. Publishes the National Environmental Scorecard and Presidential Report Card.

National Assn. of Conservation Districts (NACD), *509 Capitol Court N.E. 20002-4937; (202) 547-6223. Fax, (202) 547-6450. John Larson, Chief Executive Officer.*
General email, bethany-shively@nacdet.org
Web, www.nacdnet.org

Membership: conservation districts (local subdivisions of state government). Works to promote the conservation of land, forests, and other natural resources. Interests include erosion and sediment control; water quality; forestry, water, flood plain, and range management; rural development; and urban and community conservation.

National Audubon Society, *Public Policy, 1200 18th St. N.W., #500 20036; (202) 861-2242. Fax, (202) 861-4290. Mike Daulton, Vice President, Government Relations, (202) 861-2242, ext. 3030.*
General email, audubonaction@audubon.org
Web, www.audubon.org and Twitter, @audobonsociety

Citizens' interest group that promotes environmental conservation and education, focusing on birds and their habitats. Provides information on bird science, water resources, public lands, rangelands, forests, parks, wildlife conservation, and the National Wildlife Refuge System. Operates state offices, local chapters, and nature centers nationwide. (Headquarters in New York.)

National Ecological Observatory Network (NEON, Inc.), *Washington Office, 1100 Jefferson Dr. S.W., #3123, MRC 705 20560-0001; (202) 370-7891. Fax, (202) 204-0128. Brian Wee, Chief of External Affairs; Russell Lea, Chief Executive Officer (in Boulder). Press, (720) 746-4936.*
General email, bwee@neoninc.org
Web, www.neoninc.org

Collects data across the United States on the impact of climate change, land-use change, and invasive species on natural resources and biodiversity, with the goal of detecting and forecasting ecological change on a continental scale over multiple decades. Working with various government agencies to develop standards for environmental observations and data interoperability; expected to become fully operational by 2016. Funded by the National Science Foundation in partnership with Neon, Inc. (Visitors note: co-located in the Smithsonian's S. Dillon Ripley Center.) (Headquarters in Boulder, Colo.)

National Governors Assn. (NGA), *Center for Best Practices, Environment, Energy, and Transportation, 444 N. Capitol St. N.W., #267 20001-1512; (202) 624-5300. Fax, (202) 624-7829. Sue Gander, Director.*
General email, webmaster@nga.org
Web, www.nga.org/cms/center/eet

Identifies best practices for energy, land-use, environment, and transportation issues and shares these with the states.

National Governors Assn. (NGA), *Natural Resources Committee, 444 N. Capitol St. N.W., #267 20001-1512; (202) 624-5300. Fax, (202) 624-7814. Alex Whitaker, Director.*
General email, webmaster@nga.org
Web, www.nga.org/cms/center/eet

Monitors legislation and regulations and makes recommendations on agriculture, energy, environment, and natural resource issues to ensure governors' views and priorities are represented in federal policies and regulations.

National Sustainable Agriculture Coalition, *110 Maryland Ave. N.E., #209 20002-5622; (202) 547-5754.*

Fax, (202) 547-1837. Ferd Hoefner, Policy Director; Jeremy Emmi, Managing Director.
General email, info@sustainableagriculture.net
Web, www.sustainableagriculturecoalition.org

National alliance of farm, rural, and conservation organizations. Advocates federal policies that promote environmentally sustainable agriculture, natural resources management, and rural community development. Monitors legislation and regulations.

National Wildlife Federation, 11100 Wildlife Center Dr., Reston, VA 20190-5362; (703) 438-6000. Fax, (703) 438-3570. Larry J. Schweiger, President. Information, (800) 822-9919.
General email, info@nwf.org
Web, www.nwf.org

Promotes conservation of natural resources; provides information on the environment and resource management; takes legal action on environmental issues.

Natural Resources Defense Council, Washington Office, 1152 15th St. N.W., #300 20005; (202) 289-6868. Fax, (202) 289-0622. Wesley Warren, Director of Policy Advocacy; Ed Chen, Director of Federal Communications.
General email, nrdcinfo@nrdc.org
Web, www.nrdc.org

Environmental organization staffed by lawyers and scientists who conduct litigation and research. Interests include air, water, land use, forests, toxic materials, natural resources management and conservation, preservation of endangered plant species, and ozone pollution. (Headquarters in New York.)

Nature Conservancy, 4245 N. Fairfax Dr., #100, Arlington, VA 22203-1606; (703) 841-5300. Fax, (703) 841-1283. Mark Tercek, President; Bill Ginn, Executive Vice President of Global Conservation Initiatives. Information, (800) 628-6860. Press, (703) 841-3939.
General email, comment@tnc.org
Web, www.nature.org

Maintains an international system of natural sanctuaries; acquires land to protect endangered species and habitats. Collaborates with other conservation organizations, country and local governments, corporations, indigenous peoples and communities, and individuals such as fishermen, ranchers, and farmers to create management plans for natural areas.

Pew Environment Group, 901 E St. N.W. 20004-2008; (202) 552-2000. Fax, (202) 552-2299. Josh Reichert, Executive Vice President.
General email, info@pewenvironment.org
Web, www.pewenvironment.org

Identifies and publicizes environmental issues at the international, national, and local levels, with the goal of strengthening environmental policies and practices. Interests include climate change, clean air, endangered species, global warming, hazardous chemicals, national park pollution, and campaign finance reform. Opposes efforts to weaken environmental laws. Monitors legislation and regulations.

Public Employees for Environmental Responsibility (PEER), 2000 P St. N.W., #240 20036; (202) 265-7337. Fax, (202) 265-4192. Jeff Ruch, Executive Director.
General email, info@peer.org
Web, www.peer.org

Service organization for public citizens and employees of federal, state, and local resource management agencies. Defends legal rights of public employees who speak out concerning natural resource management and environmental protection issues. Monitors enforcement of environmental protection laws.

Resources for the Future, 1616 P St. N.W. 20036-1400; (202) 328-5000. Fax, (202) 939-3460. Philip R. Sharp, President, (202) 328-5077. Library, (202) 328-5089. Press, (202) 328-5019.
General email, info@rff.org
Web, www.rff.org

Engages in research and education on environmental and natural resource issues, including forestry, multiple use of public lands, costs and benefits of pollution control, endangered species, environmental risk management, energy and national security, and climate resources. Interests include hazardous waste, the Superfund, and biodiversity. Publishes research findings; offers academic fellowships. Library open to the public by appointment.

Science Communication Network, 4833 West Lane, Bethesda, MD 20814; (301) 654-6665. Amy Kostant, Executive Director.
General email, www.emily@sciencecom.org
Web, www.sciencecommunicationnetwork.org

Conducts educational workshops to give scientists and other health professionals the media tools to enable their work to be accurately reported to the public. Focuses on environmental health science, green chemistry, and science integrity issues.

Sierra Club, Washington Office, 50 F St. N.W., 8th Floor 20001; (202) 547-1141. Fax, (202) 547-6009. Debbie Sease, Legislative Director; Bob Bingaman, National Field Director, (202) 675-7904; Shanice Penn, Operations Manager. Press, (202) 675-6698.
General email, information@sierraclub.org
Web, www.sierraclub.org

Citizens' interest group that promotes protection of natural resources. Interests include the Clean Air Act; the Arctic National Wildlife Refuge; protection of national forests, parks, and wilderness; toxins; global warming; promotion of responsible international trade; and international development lending reform. Monitors legislation and regulations. (Headquarters in San Francisco, Calif.)

Union of Concerned Scientists, Strategy and Policy, Washington Office, 1825 K St., N.W., #800 20006-1232; (202) 223-6133. Fax, (202) 223-6162. Kathleen M. Rest, Executive Director.
General email, ucs@ucsusa.org
Web, www.ucsusa.org

Membership: scientists and citizens who advocate a comprehensive approach to resolving global environmental and resource issues. Educates and mobilizes citizens on the linkages between resource depletion, environmental degradation, climate changes, and consumption patterns. (Headquarters in Cambridge, Mass.)

U.S. Chamber of Commerce, *Environment, Technology, and Regulatory Affairs,* 1615 H St. N.W. 20062-2000; (202) 463-5533. Fax, (202) 887-3445. William L. Kovacs, Senior Vice President.
General email, environment@uschamber.com
Web, www.uschamber.com/issues/etra

Monitors operations of federal departments and agencies responsible for environmental programs, policies, regulatory issues, and food safety. Analyzes and evaluates legislation and regulations that affect the environment.

The Wilderness Society, 1615 M St. N.W., #100 20036; (202) 833-2300. Fax, (202) 429-3958. Jamie Williams, President. Toll-free, (800) 843-9453.
General email, action@tws.org
Web, www.wilderness.org

Promotes preservation of wilderness and the responsible management of federal lands, including national parks and forests, wilderness areas, wildlife refuges, and land administered by the Interior Dept.'s Bureau of Land Management.

Global Warming and Climate Change

▶AGENCIES

Economic Research Service *(Agriculture Dept.),* 355 E St. S.W. 20024-8221; (202) 694-5000. Fax, (202) 245-4846. Mary Bohman, Administrator; Greg Pompelli, Associate Administrator.
General email, service@ers.usda.gov
Web, www.ers.usda.gov

Provides research and economic information to the USDA. Interests include economic and policy issues involving food, farm practices and management, natural resources, and rural development. Web site offers a briefing room on global climate change and other environmental topics.

Environmental Protection Agency (EPA), *Atmospheric Programs, Climate Change Division,* 1200 Pennsylvania Ave. N.W., MC 6207J 20460; (202) 343-9876. Fax, (202) 343-2202. Paul M. Gunning, Director.
General email, hargrove.anne@epa.gov
Web, www.epa.gov/aboutepa/oar.html#oap and *www.epa.gov/climatechange*

Works to address global climate change and the associated risks to human health and the environment. Implements voluntary programs to reduce non–carbon dioxide emissions; analyzes greenhouse gas emissions and reduction options; educates the public on climate change and

provides climate analysis and strategies to policymakers, experts, and U.S. climate negotiators.

U.S. Geological Survey (USGS) *(Interior Dept.), Climate and Land Use Change,* 12201 Sunrise Valley Dr., MS 409, Reston, VA 20192; (703) 648-5215. Fax, (703) 648-7031. Matthew C. Larsen, Associate Director for Climate and Land Use Change.
Web, www.usgs.gov/climate_landuse

Researches the effects of climate and land use change on natural resources. Methods include monitoring, modeling, and forecasting. Operates the Landsat satellites. Provides coordination, technical support, and funding for existing research programs. Provides research products to policymakers, natural resources managers, and the general public.

▶CONGRESS

For a listing of relevant congressional committees and subcommittees, please see pages 252–253 or the Appendix.

▶NONGOVERNMENTAL

Climate Institute, 900 17th St. N.W., #700 20006; (202) 552-4723. Fax, (202) 737-6410. John C. Topping, President.
General email, info@climate.org
Web, www.climate.org

Educates the public and policymakers on climate change (greenhouse effect, or global warming) and on the depletion of the ozone layer. Assesses climate change risks and develops strategies on mitigating climate change in developing countries and in North America.

Competitive Enterprise Institute, 1899 L St. N.W., 12th Floor 20036; (202) 331-1010. Fax, (202) 331-0640. Lawson Bader, President. Press, (202) 331-2258.
General email, info@cei.org
Web, www.cei.org

Advocates free enterprise and limited government. Produces policy analyses on tax, budget, financial services, antitrust, biotechnological, and environmental issues. Monitors legislation and litigates against restrictive regulations through its Free Market Legal Program.

George C. Marshall Institute, 1601 N. Kent St., #802, Arlington, VA 22209; (571) 970-3180. William O'Keefe, Chief Executive Officer.
General email, info@marshall.org
Web, www.marshall.org

Analyzes the technical and scientific aspects of public policy and defense issues; produces publications on environmental science, space, national security, energy issues, and technology policy. Interests include climate change, space, and defense policy.

Global Green USA, *Washington Office,* 1100 15th St. N.W., 11th Floor 20005; (202) 222-0700. Mary Luévano, Executive Director, Interim.

General email, ggusa@globalgreen.org

Web, www.globalgreen.org

Offers research and community-based projects to educate people about the environment and encourage improved environmental policy. Interests include climate change solutions, green building for affordable housing and schools, energy efficiency, and clean energy, as well as security and nonproliferation of weapons of mass destruction, protection of natural resources, and recycling. (Headquarters in Santa Monica, Calif.) (U.S. national affiliate of Mikhail Gorbachev's Green Cross International.)

National Council for Science and the Environment, *1101 17th St. N.W., #250 20036; (202) 530-5810. Fax, (202) 628-4311. Peter Saundry, Executive Director, (202) 207-0002.*

General email, ncse@ncseonline.org

Web, www.ncseonline.org

Coordinates programs that bring together individuals, institutions, and communities to discuss environmental education, research, and public policy decisions affecting the environment.

National Ecological Observatory Network (NEON, Inc.), *Washington Office, 1100 Jefferson Dr. S.W., #3123, MRC 705 20560-0001; (202) 370-7891. Fax, (202) 204-0128. Brian Wee, Chief of External Affairs; Russell Lea, Chief Executive Officer (in Boulder). Press, (720) 746-4936.*

General email, bwee@neoninc.org

Web, www.neoninc.org

Collects data across the United States on the impact of climate change, land-use change, and invasive species on natural resources and biodiversity, with the goal of detecting and forecasting ecological change on a continental scale over multiple decades. Working with various government agencies to develop standards for environmental observations and data interoperability; expected to become fully operational by 2016. Funded by the National Science Foundation in partnership with Neon, Inc. (Visitors note: Co-located in the Smithsonian's S. Dillon Ripley Center.) (Headquarters in Boulder, Colo.)

Resources for the Future, *1616 P St. N.W. 20036-1400; (202) 328-5000. Fax, (202) 939-3460. Philip R. Sharp, President, (202) 328-5077. Library, (202) 328-5089. Press, (202) 328-5019.*

General email, info@rff.org

Web, www.rff.org

Research organization that conducts independent studies on economic and policy aspects of energy, environment, conservation, and natural resource management issues worldwide. Interests include climate change, energy, natural resource issues in developing countries, and public health.

Science and Environmental Policy Project (SEPP), *1600 S. Eads St., #712-S, Arlington, VA 22202-2907; (703) 920-2744. S. Fred Singer, President.*

General email, info@sepp.org

Web, www.sepp.org

Works to clarify environmental problems and provide effective, economical solutions. Encourages use of scientific knowledge when making health or environmental public policy decisions. Disseminates research and policy papers by skeptics of global warming.

Union of Concerned Scientists, *Strategy and Policy, Washington Office, 1825 K St., N.W., #800 20006-1232; (202) 223-6133. Fax, (202) 223-6162. Kathleen M. Rest, Executive Director.*

General email, ucs@ucsusa.org

Web, www.ucsusa.org

Membership: scientists and citizens who advocate a comprehensive approach to resolving global environmental and resource issues. Educates and mobilizes citizens on the linkages between resource depletion, environmental degradation, climate changes, and consumption patterns. (Headquarters in Cambridge, Mass.)

International Issues

▶**AGENCIES**

Environmental Protection Agency (EPA), *International Affairs, 1200 Pennsylvania Ave. N.W., #31106, MC 2610R 20460; (202) 564-6600. Fax, (202) 565-2407. Jane Nishida, Assistant Administrator.*

General email, oiainternet-comments@epa.gov

Web, www2.epa.gov/aboutepa/about-office-international-and-tribal-affairs-oita

Coordinates the agency's work on international environmental issues and programs, including management of bilateral agreements and participation in multilateral organizations and negotiations. Works to strengthen public health and environmental programs on tribal lands, emphasizing helping tribes administer their own environment programs.

International Trade Administration (ITA) *(Commerce Dept.), Industry and Analysis, Energy and Environmental Industries, 1400 Constitution Ave. N.W., #4053 20230; (202) 482-5225. Fax, (202) 482-5665. Adam O'Malley, Director, (202) 482-4850.*

Web, www.environment.ita.doc.gov and www.trade.gov/td/energy

Works to facilitate and increase export of U.S. environmental technologies, including goods and services. Conducts market analysis, business counseling, and trade promotion.

State Dept., *Ecology and Conservation, 2201 C St. N.W., #2657 20520; (202) 647-3367. Fax, (202) 736-7351. Christine Dawson, Director.*

Web, www.state.gov

Represents the United States in international affairs relating to ecology and conservation issues. Interests include wildlife, tropical forests, and biological diversity.

State Dept., *Environmental Policy, 2201 C St. N.W., #2726 20520; (202) 647-9266. Fax, (202) 647-1052. Deborah E. Klepp, Director.*
Web, www.state.gov/e/oes/env

Advances U.S. interests internationally regarding multilateral environmental organizations, chemical waste and other pollutants, and bilateral and regional environmental policies.

State Dept., *Oceans and International Environmental Scientific Affairs, 2201 C St. N.W., #3880 20520-7818; (202) 647-1554. Fax, (202) 647-0217. Kerri-Ann Jones, Assistant Secretary. Press, (202) 647-3486.*
Web, www.state.gov/e/oes

Concerned with foreign policy as it affects natural resources and the environment, human health, the global climate, energy production, and oceans and fisheries.

▶CONGRESS

For a listing of relevant congressional committees and subcommittees, please see pages 252–253 or the Appendix.

▶INTERNATIONAL ORGANIZATIONS

International Joint Commission, United States and Canada, U.S. Section, *2000 L St. N.W., #615 20036; (202) 736-9000. Fax, (202) 632-2007. Frank Bevacqua, Public Information Officer, (202) 736-9024.*
General email, bevacquaf@washington.ijc.org
Web, www.ijc.org

Prevents and resolves disputes between the United States and Canada on transboundary water and air resources. Investigates issues upon request of the governments of the United States and Canada. Reviews applications for water resource projects. (Canadian section in Ottawa; Great Lakes regional office in Windsor, Ontario.)

International Union for the Conservation of Nature, U.S. Office, *1630 Connecticut Ave. N.W., 3rd Floor 20009; (202) 387-4826. Fax, (202) 387-4823. Frank Hawkis, Director.*
General email, deborah.good@iucn.org
Web, www.iucn.org/usa

Membership: world governments, their environmental agencies, and nongovernmental organizations. Studies conservation issues from local to global levels. Interests include protected areas, forests, oceans, polar regions, biodiversity, species survival, environmental law, sustainable use of resources, and the impact of trade on the environment. (Headquarters in Gland, Switzerland.)

Organization of American States (OAS), *Sustainable Development, 1889 F St. N.W., #710 20006; (202) 370-9084. Fax, (202) 458-3560. Cletus Springer, Director.*
Web, www.oas.org/en/sedi/dsd

Promotes integrated and sustainable development of natural resources in OAS member states through the design and implementation of policies, programs, and partnerships. Interests include integrated management of shared water resources, hazard risk management, sustainable cities, biodiversity protection, sustainable energy, and environmental law.

▶NONGOVERNMENTAL

Antarctic and Southern Ocean Coalition, *1630 Connecticut Ave. N.W., 3rd Floor 20009; (202) 234-2480. Fax, (202) 387-4823. James N. Barnes, Executive Director.*
General email, secretariat@asoc.org
Web, www.asoc.org

Promotes effective implementation of the Antarctic Treaty System; works to protect the fragile environment and biodiversity of the Antarctic continent and promote responsible sustainable fisheries, including krill conservation, in the Southern Ocean.

Conservation International, *2011 Crystal Dr., #500, Arlington, VA 22202; (703) 341-2400. Fax, (703) 553-0654. Peter Seligmann, Chief Executive Officer; Russell Mittermeier, President. Toll-free, (800) 429-5660.*
Web, www.conservation.org

Works to conserve tropical rain forests through economic development; promotes exchange of debt relief for conservation programs that involve local people and organizations. Interests include fresh water, food, biodiversity, climate, health, and cultural services. Provides private groups and governments with information and technical advice on conservation efforts and collaborates with business and government in these efforts; supports conservation data gathering in the Americas, Europe, Africa, Asia, and the Caribbean, as well as the oceans.

Environmental Investigation Agency (EIA), *Washington Office, P.O. Box 53343 20009; (202) 483-6621. Fax, (202) 986-8626. Alexander (Sascha) von Bismarck, Director.*
General email, usinfo@eia-global.org
Web, www.eia-global.org

Works to expose international environmental crime, including illegal trade of wildlife, illegal logging, and sale of ozone-depleting substances. Monitors legislation and regulations. Also maintains an office in London.

Greenpeace USA, *Washington Office, 702 H St. N.W., #300 20001; (202) 462-1177. Fax, (202) 462-4507. Phil Radford, Executive Director.*
General email, info@wdc.greenpeace.org
Web, www.greenpeace.org

Seeks to expose global environmental problems and to promote solutions through nonviolent direct action, lobbying, and creative communication. Interests include forests, oceans, toxins, global warming, nuclear energy, disarmament, and genetic engineering. (International office in Amsterdam, Netherlands.)

Pinchot Institute for Conservation, *1616 P St. N.W., #100 20036; (202) 797-6580. Fax, (202) 797-6583. V. Alaric Sample, President. General email, pinchot@pinchot.org*

Web, www.pinchot.org

Seeks to advance forest conservation and sustainable natural resources management nationally through research and analysis, education and technical assistance, and development of conservation leaders.

Winrock International, *Washington Office, 2121 Crystal Dr., #500, Arlington, VA 22202; (703) 302-6500. Fax, (703) 302-6512. Rodney Ferguson, President. General email, information@winrock.org*

Web, www.winrock.org

Works to sustain natural resources and protect the environment. Matches innovative approaches in agriculture, natural resource management, clean energy, and leadership development with the unique needs of its partners. (Headquarters in Little Rock, Ark.)

World Resources Institute, *10 G St. N.E., #800 20002; (202) 729-7600. Fax, (202) 729-7610. Andrew Steer, President. Press, (202) 729-7639. General email, fdesk@wri.org*

Web, www.wri.org

Conducts research on environmental problems and studies the interrelationships of natural resources, economic growth, and human needs. Interests include forestry and land use, renewable energy, fisheries, and sustainable agriculture. Assesses environmental policies of aid agencies.

Worldwatch Institute, *1400 16th St. N.W., #430 20036; (202) 745-8092. Fax, (202) 478-2534. Robert Engelman, President. General email, worldwatch@worldwatch.org*

Web, www.worldwatch.org

Focuses on an interdisciplinary approach to solving global environmental problems. Interests include energy conservation, renewable resources, solar power, and energy use in developing countries.

World Wildlife Fund (WWF), *1250 24th St. N.W. 20037-1193 (mailing address: P.O. Box 97180, Washington, DC 20090-7180); (202) 293-4800. Fax, (202) 293-9211. Carter S. Roberts, President. Web, www.worldwildlife.org*

Conducts scientific research and analyzes policy on environmental and conservation issues, including pollution reduction, land use, forestry and wetlands management, parks, soil conservation, and sustainable development. Supports projects to promote biological diversity and to save endangered species and their habitats, including tropical forests in Latin America, Asia, and Africa. Awards grants and provides technical assistance to local conservation groups.

ANIMALS AND PLANTS

General

▶**AGENCIES**

Animal and Plant Health Inspection Service (APHIS) *(Agriculture Dept.), Investigative and Enforcement Services, 4700 River Rd., Unit 85, Riverdale, MD 20737-1234; (301) 851-2948. Fax, (301) 734-4328. Bernadette Juarez, Director. Web, www.aphis.usda.gov/ies*

Provides investigative and enforcement services and leadership, direction, and support for compliance activities within the service.

Animal and Plant Health Inspection Service (APHIS) *(Agriculture Dept.), Plant Protection and Quarantine, 1400 Independence Ave. S.W., #302E 20250; (202) 799-7163. Fax, (202) 690-0472. Osama El-Lissy, Deputy Administrator. Antismuggling hotline, (800) 877-3835. General email, aphis.web@aphis.usda.gov*

Web, www.aphis.usda.gov/plant_health

Encourages compliance with regulations that safeguard agriculture and natural resources from the risks associated with the entry, establishment, or spread of animal and plant pests and noxious weeds. Methods include requirements for the import and export of plants and plant products; partnership agreements with industry groups, community organizations, and government entities; and public education and outreach.

Food and Drug Administration (FDA) *(Health and Human Services Dept.), Center for Veterinary Medicine, 7519 Standish Pl., Rockville, MD 20855-0001; (240) 276-9000. Fax, (240) 276-9001. Dr. Bernadette Dunham, Director. General email, askcvm@fda.hhs.gov*

Web, www.fda.gov/animalveterinary

Regulates the manufacture and distribution of drugs, food additives, feed, and devices for livestock and pets. Conducts research; works to ensure animal health and the safety of food derived from animals.

National Zoological Park *(Smithsonian Institution), 3001 Connecticut Ave. N.W. 20008 (mailing address: DEVS, P.O. Box 37012, MRC 5516, Washington, DC 20013-7012); (202) 633-4888. Fax, (202) 673-4836. Dennis W. Kelly, Executive Director. Phone (recorded information line), (202) 633-4888. Library, (202) 633-1031. Press, (202) 633-3055. Friends of the Zoo, (202) 633-2922. Friends of the Zoo Press, (202) 633-4333. Zoo police, (202) 633-4111. Web, www.nationalzoo.si.edu*

Maintains a public zoo. Conducts research on animal behavior, ecology, nutrition, reproductive physiology, pathology, and veterinary medicine; operates an annex near Front Royal, Va., for the propagation and study of endangered species. Houses a unit of the Smithsonian

Institution library open to qualified researchers by appointment. Interlibrary loans available.

U.S. Customs and Border Protection *(Homeland Security Dept.), Agricultural Program and Trade Liaison Office,* 1300 Pennsylvania Ave. N.W., #2.5B 20229; (202) 344-3298. Fax, (202) 344-1442. Kevin Harriger, Executive Director.
Web, www.cbp.gov

Responsible for safeguarding the nation's animal and natural resources from pests and disease through inspections at ports of entry and beyond.

►**CONGRESS**

For a listing of relevant congressional committees and subcommittees, please see pages 252–253 or the Appendix.

►**NONGOVERNMENTAL**

American Herbal Products Assn., 8630 Fenton St., #918, Silver Spring, MD 20910; (301) 588-1171. Fax, (301) 588-1174. Michael McGuffin, President.
General email, ahpa@ahpa.org
Web, www.ahpa.org

Membership: U.S. companies and individuals that grow, manufacture, and distribute botanicals and herbal products, including foods, beverages, dietary supplements, and personal care products; associates in education, law, media, and medicine. Supports research; promotes quality standards, consumer access, and self-regulation in the industry. Monitors legislation and regulations.

American Veterinary Medical Assn., *Governmental Relations,* 1910 Sunderland Pl. N.W. 20036-1642; (202) 789-0007. Fax, (202) 842-4360. Dr. Mark Lutschaunig, Director. Toll-free, (800) 321-1473.
General email, avmagrd@avma.org
Web, www.avma.org

Monitors legislation and regulations that influence animal and human health and advance the veterinary medical profession. (Headquarters in Schaumburg, Ill.)

Animal Health Institute, 1325 G St. N.W., #700 20005-3104; (202) 637-2440. Fax, (202) 393-1667. Alexander S. Mathews, President.
Web, www.ahi.org

Membership: manufacturers of drugs and other products (including vaccines, pesticides, and vitamins) for pets and food-producing animals. Interests include pet health, livestock health, and disease outbreak prevention. Monitors legislation and regulations.

Assn. of American Veterinary Medical Colleges (AAVMC), 1101 Vermont Ave. N.W., #301 20005-3536; (202) 371-9195. Fax, (202) 842-0773. Andrew T. Maccabe, Executive Director.
Web, www.aavmc.org

Membership: U.S., Canadian, and international schools and colleges of veterinary medicine, departments of comparative medicine, and departments of veterinary science in agricultural colleges. Produces veterinary reports, provides information about scholarships and continuing education programs, and sponsors conferences on veterinary medical issues.

Animal Rights and Welfare

►**AGENCIES**

Animal and Plant Health Inspection Service (APHIS) *(Agriculture Dept.), Animal Care,* 4700 River Rd., Unit 84, Riverdale, MD 20737-1234; (301) 851-3751. Fax, (301) 734-4978. Chester A. Gipson, Deputy Administrator.
General email, ace@aphis.usda.gov
Web, www.aphis.usda.gov/animal_welfare/index.shtml

Administers laws for the breeding, exhibition, and care of animals raised for sale and research and transported commercially.

National Agricultural Library *(Agriculture Dept.), Animal Welfare Information Center,* 10301 Baltimore Ave., #118, Beltsville, MD 20705; (301) 504-6212. Fax, (301) 504-5181. Vacant, Coordinator.
General email, awic@ars.usda.gov
Web, http://awic.nal.usda.gov

Provides information for improved animal care and use in research, testing, teaching, and exhibition.

National Institutes of Health (NIH) *(Health and Human Services Dept.), Animal Care and Use,* 31 Center Dr., Bldg. 31, #B1C37, MSC-2252, Bethesda, MD 20892-2252; (301) 496-5424. Fax, (301) 480-8298. Terri Clark, Director.
General email, secoacu@od.nih.gov
Web, http://oacu.od.nih.gov

Provides guidance for the humane care and use of animals in the intramural research program at NIH.

National Institutes of Health (NIH) *(Health and Human Services Dept.), Laboratory Animal Welfare,* 6705 Rockledge Dr., RLK1, #360, MSC 7982, Bethesda, MD 20892-7982; (301) 496-7163. Fax, (301) 402-7065. Patricia Brown, Director.
General email, olaw@od.nih.gov
Web, http://grants.nih.gov/grants/olaw/olaw.htm

Develops and monitors policy on the humane care and use of animals in research conducted by any public health service entity.

►**CONGRESS**

For a listing of relevant congressional committees and subcommittees, please see pages 252–253 or the Appendix.

►**NONGOVERNMENTAL**

Alley Cat Allies, 7920 Norfolk Avenue, #600, Bethesda, MD 20814-2525; (240) 482-1980. Fax, (240) 482-1990. Becky Robinson, President.

General email, info@alleycat.org

Web, www.alleycat.org

Clearinghouse for information on feral and stray cats. Advocates the trap-neuter-return method to reduce feral cat populations.

American Horse Protection Assn., *1000 29th St. N.W., #T100 20007; (202) 965-0500. Fax, (202) 965-9621. Robin C. Lohnes, Executive Director.*
General email, info@ahpa.us

Membership: individuals, corporations, and foundations interested in protecting wild and domestic horses.

Americans for Medical Progress Educational Foundation, *526 King St., #201, Alexandria, VA 22314; (703) 836-9595. Fax, (703) 836-9594. Jacqueline Calnan, President.*
General email, amp@amprogress.org

Web, www.amprogress.org

Promotes and protects animal-based medical research. Serves as a media resource by fact-checking claims of animal rights groups. Conducts public education campaigns on the link between animal research and medical advances.

Animal Welfare Institute, *900 Pennsylvania Ave. S.E. 20003 (mailing address: P.O. Box 3650, Washington, DC 20027); (202) 337-2332. Fax, (202) 446-2131. Cathy Liss, President.*
General email, awi@awionline.org

Web, www.awionline.org

Works to improve conditions for animals in laboratories, on farms, in commerce, in homes, and in the wild. Promotes efforts to end horse slaughter. Monitors legislation and regulations. (Merged with the Society for Animal Protective Legislation.)

Compassion Over Killing, *6930 Carroll Ave., #910, Tacoma Park, MD 20912 (mailing address: P.O. Box 9773, Washington, DC 20016); (301) 891-2458. Fax, (301) 891-6815. Erica Meier, Executive Director.*
General email, info@cok.net

Web, www.cok.net

Animal rights organization that focuses primarily on cruelty to animals in agriculture. Promotes vegetarianism.

Council on Humane Giving, *5100 Wisconsin Ave. N.W., #400 20016; (202) 527-7307. Fax, (202) 686-2216. Greg Mazur, Research and Education Program Specialist; Neal Barnard, President.*
General email, gmazur@pcrm.org

Web, www.humaneseal.org

Supports charities that conduct health-related research using nonanimal methods; sponsors the Humane Charity Seal of Approval program. Administered by the Physicians Committee for Responsible Medicine.

Doris Day Animal League, *2100 L St. N.W. 20037; (202) 452-1100. Holly Hazard, Executive Director.*

General email, info@ddal.org

Web, www.ddal.org

Seeks to reduce the inhumane treatment of animals through legislative initiatives, education, and programs. Works with all levels of government to pass new protection laws and strengthen existing ones. (Affiliated with the Humane Society of the United States.)

Farm Animal Rights Movement (FARM), *10101 Ashburton Lane, Bethesda, MD 20817-1729; (301) 530-1737. Fax, (301) 530-5683. Alex Hershaft, President. Toll-free, 888-FARM-USA.*
General email, info@farmusa.org

Web, www.farmusa.org and www.livevegan.org

Works to end use of animals for food. Interests include animal protection, consumer health, agricultural resources, and environmental quality. Conducts national educational campaigns, including World Farm Animals Day, the Live Vegan program, and the Great American Meatout. Monitors legislation and regulations.

Humane Farm Animal Care, *P.O. Box 727, Herndon, VA 20172-0727; (703) 435-3883. Fax, (703) 435-3981. Adele Douglass, Chief Executive Officer.*
General email, info@certifiedhumane.org

Web, www.certifiedhumane.org

Seeks to improve the welfare of farm animals by providing viable, duly monitored standards for humane food production. Administers the Certified Humane Raised and Handled program for meat, poultry, eggs, and dairy products.

Humane Society Legislative Fund, *2100 L St. N.W., #310 20037; (202) 676-2314. Fax, (202) 676-2300. Michael Markarian, President. Press, (301) 548-7778.*
General email, humanesociety@hslf.org

Web, www.hslf.org

Works to pass state and federal laws protecting animals from cruelty and suffering. (Lobbying arm of the Humane Society of the United States.)

Humane Society of the United States, *2100 L St. N.W. 20037; (202) 452-1100. Fax, (202) 778-6132. Wayne Pacelle, President.*
Web, www.humanesociety.org

Citizens' interest group that sponsors programs in pet and equine protection, disaster preparedness and response, wildlife and habitat protection, animals in research, and farm animal welfare. Interests include legislation to protect pets, provide more humane treatment for farm animals, strengthen penalties for illegal animal fighting, and curb abusive sport-hunting practices such as trophy hunting, baiting, and hounding.

National Assn. for Biomedical Research, *818 Connecticut Ave. N.W., #900 20006; (202) 857-0540. Fax, (202) 659-1902. Frankie L. Trull, President.*
General email, info@nabr.org

Web, www.nabr.org

Membership: scientific and medical professional societies, academic institutions, and research-oriented corporations involved in the use of animals in biomedical research. Supports the humane use of animals in medical research, education, and product-safety assessment. Monitors legislation and regulations.

National Research Council (NRC), *Earth and Life Studies, Institute for Laboratory Animal Research,* 500 5th St. N.W., Keck 645 20001; (202) 334-2187. Fax, (202) 334-1687. Fran Sharples, Director, Acting; Fran Sharples, Managing Editor.
Web, www.dels.nas.edu/ilar

Physicians Committee for Responsible Medicine (PCRM), 5100 Wisconsin Ave. N.W., #400 20016; (202) 686-2210. Fax, (202) 686-2216. Neal Barnard, President.
General email, pcrm@pcrm.org
Web, www.pcrm.org

Membership: health care professionals, medical students, and laypersons interested in preventive medicine, nutrition, and higher standards in research. Investigates alternatives to animal use in medical research experimentation, product testing, and education.

Fish

▶**AGENCIES**

Atlantic States Marine Fisheries Commission, 1050 N. Highland St., #200 A-N, Arlington, VA 22201; (703) 842-0740. Fax, (703) 842-0741. Robert E. Beal, Executive Director.
General email, info@asmfc.org
Web, www.asmfc.org

Interstate compact commission of marine fisheries representatives from fifteen states along the Atlantic seaboard. Assists states in developing joint fisheries programs; works with other fisheries organizations and the federal government on environmental, natural resource, and conservation issues.

Interior Dept. (DOI), *Fish, Wildlife, and Parks,* 1849 C St. N.W., #3156 20240; (202) 208-4416. Fax, (202) 208-4684. Rachel L. Jacobson, Principal Assistant Secretary.
Web, www.doi.gov

Responsible for programs associated with the development, conservation, and use of fish, wildlife, recreational, historical, and national park system resources. Coordinates marine environmental quality and biological resources programs with other federal agencies.

Justice Dept. (DOJ), *Environmental Crimes,* 601 D St. N.W., 2nd Floor 20004 (mailing address: P.O. Box 7611, Washington, DC 20044); (202) 305-0321. Fax, (202) 305-0396. Stacey H. Mitchell, Chief.
Web, www.justice.gov/enrd/ENRD_ecs.html

Supervises criminal cases under federal maritime law and other laws protecting marine fish and mammals.

Focuses on smugglers and black market dealers of protected wildlife.

Justice Dept. (DOJ), *Wildlife and Marine Resources,* 601 D St. N.W., 3rd Floor 20004 (mailing address: P.O. Box 7415, Ben Franklin Station, Washington, DC 20044-7369); (202) 305-0210. Fax, (202) 305-0275. Seth M. Barsky, Section Chief.
Web, www.justice.gov/enrd/ENRD_wmrs.html

Supervises civil cases under federal maritime law and other laws protecting marine fish and mammals.

National Oceanic and Atmospheric Administration (NOAA) *(Commerce Dept.), National Marine Fisheries Service,* 1315 East-West Hwy., SSMC3, Silver Spring, MD 20910; (301) 427-8000. Fax, (301) 713-1940. Eileen Sobeck, Assistant Administrator. Press, (301) 427-8003.
Web, www.nmfs.noaa.gov

Administers marine fishing regulations, including offshore fishing rights and international agreements; conducts marine resources research; studies use and management of these resources; administers the Magnuson-Stevens Fishery Conservation and Management Act; manages and protects marine resources, especially endangered species and marine mammals, within the exclusive economic zone.

U.S. Fish and Wildlife Service *(Interior Dept.),* 1849 C St. N.W., #3358 20240; (202) 208-4717. Fax, (202) 208-6965. Daniel M. Ashe, Director. Press, (202) 208-5634. Toll-free, (800) 344-9453.
Web, www.fws.gov

Works with federal and state agencies and nonprofits to conserve, protect, and enhance fish and wildlife and their habitats for the continuing benefit of the American people.

U.S. Fish and Wildlife Service *(Interior Dept.), Endangered Species,* 1849 C St. N.W., #3345 20240; (202) 208-4646. Fax, (202) 208-5618. Gary Frazer, Assistant Director.
Web, www.fws.gov/endangered

Administers federal policy on fish and wildlife under the Endangered Species Act, Marine Mammal Protection Act, Fish and Wildlife Coordination Act, Oil Pollution Act, and other environmental laws. Reviews all federal and federally licensed projects to determine environmental effects on fish and wildlife. Responsible for maintaining the endangered species list and for protecting and restoring species to healthy numbers.

U.S. Fish and Wildlife Service *(Interior Dept.), Fisheries and Habitat Conservation,* 1849 C St. N.W., #3347 20240; 4401 N. Fairfax Dr., MS-ARLSQ880, Arlington, VA 22203; (202) 208-6393. Fax, (202) 208-5618. Jeff Underwood, Assistant Director, Acting.
Web, www.fws.gov/fisheries

Develops, manages, and protects interstate and international fisheries, including fisheries of the Great Lakes, fisheries on federal lands, aquatic ecosystems, endangered species of fish, and anadromous species. Administers the National Fish Hatchery System and the National Fish and

Wildlife Resource Management Offices, as well as the Habitat and Conservation and Environmental Quality Divisions.

U.S. Geological Survey (USGS) *(Interior Dept.),* *Ecosystems, 12201 Sunrise Valley Dr., MS 300, Reston, VA 20192; (703) 648-4050. Fax, (703) 648-7031. Anne E. Kinsinger, Associate Director, (703) 648-4051. Web, www.usgs.gov/ecosystems*

Conducts research and monitoring to develop and convey an understanding of ecosystem function and distributions, physical and biological components, and trophic dynamics for freshwater, terrestrial, and marine ecosystems and the human and fish and wildlife communities they support. Subject areas include invasive species, endangered species and habitats, genetics and genomics, and microbiology.

►CONGRESS

For a listing of relevant congressional committees and subcommittees, please see pages 252–253 or the Appendix.

►NONGOVERNMENTAL

American Fisheries Society (AFS), *5410 Grosvenor Lane, #110, Bethesda, MD 20814-2199; (301) 897-8616. Fax, (301) 897-8096. Douglas Austen, Executive Director. General email, main@fisheries.org*

Web, www.fisheries.org

Membership: biologists and other scientists interested in fisheries. Promotes the fisheries profession, the advancement of fisheries science, and conservation of renewable aquatic resources. Monitors legislation and regulations.

Assn. of Fish and Wildlife Agencies, *444 N. Capitol St. N.W., #725 20001; (202) 624-7890. Fax, (202) 624-7891. Ron Regan, Executive Director. General email, info@fishwildlife.org*

Web, www.fishwildlife.org

Membership: federal, state, and provincial fish and wildlife management agencies in the United States, Canada, and Mexico. Encourages balanced, research-based fish and wildlife resource management. Monitors legislation and regulations.

Grocery Manufacturers Assn. (GMA), *1350 Eye St. N.W., #300 20005-3377; (202) 639-5900. Fax, (202) 639-5932. Pamela Bailey, President. Press, (202) 295-3938. General email, info@gmaonline.org*

Web, www.gmaonline.org

Membership: manufacturers and suppliers of processed and packaged food, drinks, and juice. Serves as industry liaison between seafood processors and the federal government.

Marine Fish Conservation Network, *1920 L St. N.W., #800 20003; (202) 466-3061. Robert C. Vandermark, Executive Director. Web, www.conservefish.org*

Membership: commercial and recreational fishing associations, aquaria, national and regional conservation groups, and marine science organizations. Advocates policies that promote healthy oceans and productive fisheries.

National Fisheries Institute, *7918 Jones Branch Dr., #700, McLean, VA 22102; (703) 752-8882. Fax, (703) 752-7583. John Connelly, President. Press, (703) 752-8891. General email, contact@nfi.org*

Web, www.aboutseafood.com

Membership: vessel owners and distributors, processors, wholesalers, importers, traders, and brokers of fish and shellfish. Monitors legislation and regulations on fisheries. Advocates eating seafood for health benefits.

Ocean Conservancy, *1300 19th St. N.W., 8th Floor 20036; (202) 429-5609. Fax, (202) 872-0619. Andreas Merkl, President. Toll-free, (800) 519-1541. General email, membership@oceanconservancy.org*

Web, www.oceanconservancy.org

Works to prevent the overexploitation of living marine resources, including fisheries, and to restore depleted marine wildlife populations through research, education, and science-based advocacy.

Trout Unlimited, *1300 N. 17th St., #500, Arlington, VA 22209-2404; (703) 522-0200. Fax, (703) 284-9400. Chris Wood, President. Toll-free, (800) 834-2419. General email, trout@tu.org*

Web, www.tu.org

Membership: individuals interested in the protection and restoration of cold-water fish and their habitat. Sponsors research projects with federal and state fisheries agencies; administers programs for water-quality surveillance and cleanup of streams and lakes. Monitors legislation and regulations.

Wildlife and Marine Mammals

►AGENCIES

Animal and Plant Health Inspection Service (APHIS) *(Agriculture Dept.), Wildlife Services, 1400 Independence Ave. S.W., #1624S 20250-3402; 4700 River Road, Riverdale, MD 20737; (202) 799-7095. Fax, (202) 690-0053. William H. Clay, Deputy Administrator. Hotline, (866) 487-3297.*

Web, www.aphis.usda.gov/wildlife_damage

Works to minimize damage caused by wildlife to crops and livestock, natural resources, and human health and safety. Removes or eliminates predators and nuisance birds. Interests include aviation safety and coexistence of people and wildlife in suburban areas. Oversees the National Wildlife Research Center in Ft. Collins, Colo.

Forest Service *(Agriculture Dept.), Watershed, Fish, Wildlife, Air, and Rare Plants, 1621 N. Kent St., Arlington, VA 22209; (202) 205-1167. Fax, (703) 605-1544. Anne J. Zimmermann, Director, (202) 205-1205.*

General email, switt01@fs.fed.us

Web, www.fs.fed.us

Provides national policy direction and management for watershed, fish, wildlife, air, and rare plants programs on lands managed by the Forest Service.

Interior Dept. (DOI), *Bird Habitat Conservation,* 4501 N. Fairfax Dr., Arlington, VA 22203 (mailing address: 4401 N. Fairfax Dr., MBSP 4075, Arlington, VA 22203); (703) 358-1784. Fax, (703) 358-2282. Cyndi Perry, Chief; Rachel F. Levin, Communications Coordinator, (703) 358-2405.

General email, dbhc@fws.gov

Web, www.fws.gov/birdhabitat

Membership: government and private-sector conservation experts. Works to protect, restore, and manage wetlands and other habitats for migratory birds and other animals and to maintain migratory bird and waterfowl populations.

Interior Dept. (DOI), *Fish, Wildlife, and Parks,* 1849 C St. N.W., #3156 20240; (202) 208-4416. Fax, (202) 208-4684. Rachel L. Jacobson, Principal Assistant Secretary.

Web, www.doi.gov

Responsible for programs associated with the development, conservation, and use of fish, wildlife, recreational, historical, and national park system resources. Coordinates marine environmental quality and biological resources programs with other federal agencies.

Justice Dept. (DOJ), *Wildlife and Marine Resources,* 601 D St. N.W., 3rd Floor 20004 (mailing address: P.O. Box 7415, Ben Franklin Station, Washington, DC 20044-7369); (202) 305-0210. Fax, (202) 305-0275. Seth M. Barsky, Section Chief.

Web, www.justice.gov/enrd/ENRD_wmrs.html

Responsible for criminal enforcement and civil litigation under federal fish and wildlife conservation statutes, including protection of wildlife, fish, and plant resources within U.S. jurisdiction, and management and restoration of Florida Everglades. Monitors interstate and foreign commerce of these resources.

Marine Mammal Commission, 4340 East-West Hwy., #700, Bethesda, MD 20814; (301) 504-0087. Fax, (301) 504-0099. Rebecca Lent, Executive Director.

General email, mmc@mmc.gov

Web, www.mmc.gov

Established by Congress to ensure protection and conservation of marine mammals and the ecosystems of which they are a part. Supports research and makes recommendations to federal agencies to ensure that their activities are consistent with the provisions of the Marine Mammal Protection Act.

Migratory Bird Conservation Commission, 4401 N. Fairfax Dr., #622, MS ARLSQ622, Arlington, VA 22203-1610; (703) 358-1716. Fax, (703) 358-2223. Eric Alvarez, Secretary.

Web, www.fws.gov/refuges/realty/mbcc.html

Established by the Migratory Bird Conservation Act of 1929. Decides which areas to purchase for use as migratory bird refuges and the price at which they are acquired.

National Oceanic and Atmospheric Administration (NOAA) *(Commerce Dept.), Protected Resources,* 1315 East-West Hwy., 13th Floor, Silver Spring, MD 20910; (301) 427-8400. Fax, (301) 713-0376. Donna Wieting, Director.

General email, pr.webmaster@noaa.gov

Web, www.nmfs.noaa.gov/pr

Administers the Endangered Species Act and the Marine Mammal Protection Act. Provides guidance on the conservation and protection of marine mammals, threatened and endangered marine and anadromous species, and their habitat. Develops national guidelines and policies for the implementation of the Acts, including recovery of protected species, review and issuance of permits and authorization under the Acts, and consultations with other agencies on federal actions that may affect protected species or their habitat. Prepares and reviews management and recovery plans and environmental impact analysis.

U.S. Fish and Wildlife Service *(Interior Dept.),* 1849 C St. N.W., #3358 20240; (202) 208-4717. Fax, (202) 208-6965. Daniel M. Ashe, Director. Press, (202) 208-5634. Toll-free, (800) 344-9453.

Web, www.fws.gov

Works with federal and state agencies and nonprofits to conserve, protect, and enhance fish and wildlife and their habitats for the continuing benefit of the American people.

U.S. Fish and Wildlife Service *(Interior Dept.), Bird Habitat Conservation,* 4401 N. Fairfax Dr., MS-ARLSQ, 4075, Arlington, VA 22203; (703) 358-1784. Fax, (703) 358-2282. Michael Kreger, Deputy Chief, (703) 358-2432.

General email, cyndi_perry@fws.gov

Web, www.fws.gov/birdhabitat

Coordinates U.S. activities with Canada and Mexico to protect waterfowl habitats, restore waterfowl populations, and set research priorities under the North American Waterfowl Management Plan.

U.S. Fish and Wildlife Service *(Interior Dept.), Endangered Species,* 1849 C St. N.W., #3345 20240; (202) 208-4646. Fax, (202) 208-5618. Gary Frazer, Assistant Director.

Web, www.fws.gov/endangered

Administers federal policy on fish and wildlife under the Endangered Species Act, Marine Mammal Protection Act, Fish and Wildlife Coordination Act, Oil Pollution Act, and other environmental laws. Reviews all federal and federally licensed projects to determine environmental effects on fish and wildlife. Responsible for maintaining the endangered species list and for protecting and restoring species to healthy numbers.

U.S. Fish and Wildlife Service *(Interior Dept.), National Wildlife Refuge System,* 1849 C St. N.W., #3349 20240;

(202) 208-5333. Fax, (202) 208-3082. James W. Kurth, Chief.
Web, www.fws.gov/refuges

Determines policy for the management of wildlife. Manages the National Wildlife Refuge System and land acquisition for wildlife refuges.

U.S. Geological Survey (USGS) *(Interior Dept.),*
Ecosystems, 12201 Sunrise Valley Dr., MS 300, Reston, VA 20192; (703) 648-4050. Fax, (703) 648-7031.
Anne E. Kinsinger, Associate Director, (703) 648-4051.
Web, www.usgs.gov/ecosystems

▶ **CONGRESS**

For a listing of relevant congressional committees and sub-committees, please see pages 252–253 or the Appendix.

▶ **NONGOVERNMENTAL**

Animal Welfare Institute, *900 Pennsylvania Ave. S.E. 20003 (mailing address: P.O. Box 3650, Washington, DC 20027); (202) 337-2332. Fax, (202) 446-2131. Cathy Liss, President.*
General email, awi@awionline.org
Web, www.awionline.org

Works to preserve species threatened with extinction and protect wildlife from inhumane means of capture. Promotes efforts to end whaling and shark finning. Programs include preserving American wild horses and promoting nonlethal wildlife management solutions. Monitors legislation and regulations. (Merged with the Society for Animal Protective Legislation.)

Assn. of Fish and Wildlife Agencies, *444 N. Capitol St. N.W., #725 20001; (202) 624-7890. Fax, (202) 624-7891. Ron Regan, Executive Director.*
General email, info@fishwildlife.org
Web, www.fishwildlife.org

Membership: federal, state, and provincial fish and wildlife management agencies in the United States, Canada, and Mexico. Encourages balanced, research-based fish and wildlife resource management. Monitors legislation and regulations.

Defenders of Wildlife, *1130 17th St. N.W. 20036; (202) 682-9400. Fax, (202) 682-1331. Jamie Rappaport Clark, President. Toll-free, (800) 385-9712.*
General email, defenders@mail.defenders.org
Web, www.defenders.org

Advocacy group that works to protect wild animals, marine life, and plant life in their natural communities. Interests include endangered species and biodiversity. Monitors legislation and regulations.

Ducks Unlimited, *Governmental Affairs, 1301 Pennsylvania Ave. N.W., #402 20004; (202) 347-1530. Fax, (202) 347-1533. Gary Taylor, Director.*
Web, www.ducks.org

Promotes waterfowl and other wildlife conservation through activities aimed at developing and restoring natural nesting and migration habitats. (Headquarters in Memphis, Tenn.)

Humane Society of the United States, *2100 L St. N.W. 20037; (202) 452-1100. Fax, (202) 778-6132. Wayne Pacelle, President.*
Web, www.humanesociety.org

Works for the humane treatment and protection of animals. Interests include protecting endangered wildlife and marine mammals and their habitats and ending inhumane or cruel conditions in zoos.

Jane Goodall Institute, *1595 Spring Hill Rd., #550, Vienna, VA 22182; (703) 682-9220. Fax, (703) 682-9312. Mary Humphrey, Chief Operating Officer.*
Web, www.janegoodall.org

Seeks to increase primate habitat conservation, expand noninvasive primate research, and promote activities that ensure the well-being of primates. (Affiliated with Jane Goodall Institutes in Canada, Europe, Asia, and Africa.)

National Fish and Wildlife Foundation, *1133 15th St. N.W., #1100 20005; (202) 857-0166. Fax, (202) 857-0162. Jeff Trandahl, Executive Director.*
General email, info@nfwf.org
Web, www.nfwf.org

Forges partnerships between the public and private sectors in support of national and international conservation activities that identify and root out causes of environmental problems that affect fish, wildlife, and plants.

National Wildlife Federation, *11100 Wildlife Center Dr., Reston, VA 20190-5362; (703) 438-6000. Fax, (703) 438-3570. Larry J. Schweiger, President. Information, (800) 822-9919.*
General email, info@nwf.org
Web, www.nwf.org

Promotes conservation of natural resources; provides information on the environment and resource management; takes legal action on environmental issues.

National Wildlife Refuge Assn., *1001 Connecticut Ave. N.W., #905 20036; (202) 417-3803. David Houghton, President, ext. 12.*
General email, nwra@refugeassociation.org
Web, www.refugeassociation.org

Works to improve management and protection of the National Wildlife Refuge System by providing information to administrators, Congress, and the public. Advocates adequate funding and improved policy guidance for the Refuge System; assists individual refuges with particular needs.

Nature Conservancy, *4245 N. Fairfax Dr., #100, Arlington, VA 22203-1606; (703) 841-5300. Fax, (703) 841-1283. Mark Tercek, President; Bill Ginn, Executive Vice*

President of Global Conservation Initiatives. *Information*, (800) 628-6860. *Press*, (703) 841-3939.
General email, comment@tnc.org

Web, www.nature.org

Maintains an international system of natural sanctuaries; acquires land to protect endangered species and habitats. Collaborates with other conservation organizations, country and local governments, corporations, indigenous peoples and communities, and individuals such as fishermen, ranchers, and farmers to create management plans for natural areas.

Ocean Conservancy, *1300 19th St. N.W., 8th Floor 20036; (202) 429-5609. Fax, (202) 872-0619. Andreas Merkl, President. Toll-free, (800) 519-1541.*
General email, membership@oceanconservancy.org

Web, www.oceanconservancy.org

Works to conserve the diversity and abundance of life in the oceans and coastal areas, to prevent the overexploitation of living marine resources and the degradation of marine ecosystems, and to restore depleted marine wildlife populations and their ecosystems.

Wildlife Habitat Council, *8737 Colesville Rd., #800, Silver Spring, MD 20910; (301) 588-8994. Fax, (301) 588-4629. Margaret O'Gorman, President.*
General email, whc@wildlifehc.org

Web, www.wildlifehc.org

Membership: corporations, conservation groups, local governments, and academic institutions. Seeks to increase the quality and amount of wildlife habitat on corporate, private, and public lands. Builds partnerships between corporations and conservation groups to find solutions that balance economic growth with a healthy, biodiverse, and sustainable environment. Provides technical assistance and educational programs; fosters collaboration among members.

The Wildlife Society, *5410 Grosvenor Lane, #200, Bethesda, MD 20814-2144; (301) 897-9770. Fax, (301) 530-2471. Kenneth Williams, Executive Director.*
General email, tws@wildlife.org

Web, www.wildlife.org

Membership: wildlife biologists and resource management specialists. Provides information on management techniques, sponsors conferences, maintains list of job opportunities for members.

World Wildlife Fund (WWF), *1250 24th St. N.W. 20037-1193 (mailing address: P.O. Box 97180, Washington, DC 20090-7180); (202) 293-4800. Fax, (202) 293-9211. Carter S. Roberts, President.*
Web, www.worldwildlife.org

International conservation organization that supports and conducts scientific research and conservation projects to promote biological diversity and to save endangered species and their habitats. Awards grants for habitat protection.

POLLUTION AND TOXINS

General

▶AGENCIES

Environmental Protection Agency (EPA), *Enforcement and Compliance Assurance (OECA), 1200 Pennsylvania Ave. N.W., #3204, MC 2201A 20460; (202) 564-2440. Fax, (202) 501-3842. Cynthia J. Giles, Assistant Administrator.*
Web, www2.epa.gov/aboutepa/about-office-enforcement-oeca

Enforces laws that protect public health and the environment from hazardous materials, pesticides, and toxic substances.

Justice Dept. (DOJ), *Environmental Crimes, 601 D St. N.W., 2nd Floor 20004 (mailing address: P.O. Box 7611, Washington, DC 20044); (202) 305-0321. Fax, (202) 305-0396. Stacey H. Mitchell, Chief.*
Web, www.justice.gov/enrd/ENRD_ecs.html

Conducts criminal enforcement actions on behalf of the United States for all environmental protection statutes, including air, water, pesticides, hazardous waste, wetland matters investigated by the Environmental Protection Agency, and other criminal environmental enforcement.

Justice Dept. (DOJ), *Environmental Defense, 601 D St. N.W., #8000 20004 (mailing address: P.O. Box 23986, Washington, DC 20026-3986); (202) 514-2219. Fax, (202) 514-8865. Letitia J. Grishaw, Chief.*
Web, www.justice.gov/enrd/ENRD_eds.html

Conducts litigation on air, water, noise, pesticides, solid waste, toxic substances, Superfund, and wetlands in cooperation with the Environmental Protection Agency; represents the EPA in suits involving judicial review of EPA actions; represents the U.S. Army Corps of Engineers in cases involving dredge-and-fill activity in navigable waters and adjacent wetlands; represents the Coast Guard in oil and hazardous spill cases; defends all federal agencies in environmental litigation.

Justice Dept. (DOJ), *Environmental Enforcement, 601 D St. N.W., #2121 20004 (mailing address: P.O. Box 7611, Ben Franklin Station, Washington, DC 20044-7611); (202) 514-2750. Fax, (202) 514-0097. W. Benjamin Fisherow, Chief.*
Web, www.justice.gov/enrd

Conducts civil enforcement actions on behalf of the United States for all environmental protection statutes, including air, water, pesticides, hazardous waste, wetland matters investigated by the Environmental Protection Agency, and other civil environmental enforcement.

▶CONGRESS

For a listing of relevant congressional committees and subcommittees, please see pages 252–253 or the Appendix.

▶ NONGOVERNMENTAL

American Academy of Environmental Engineers & Scientists, *147 Old Solomons Rd., #303, Annapolis, MD 20141; (410) 266-3311. Fax, (410) 266-7653. Burk Kalweit, Executive Director.*
General email, info@aaee.net
Web, www.aaee.net

Membership: state-licensed environmental engineers and scientists who have passed examinations in environmental engineering and/or science specialties, including general environment, air pollution control, solid waste management, hazardous waste management, industrial hygiene, radiation protection, water supply, environmental sustainability, and wastewater.

National Waste and Recycling Assn., *4301 Connecticut Ave. N.W., #300 20008-2304; (202) 244-4700. Fax, (202) 966-4824. Sharon H. Kneiss, President, (202) 364-3730. Toll-free, (800) 424-2869.*
General email, skneiss@wasterecycling.org
Web, https://wasterecycling.org/

Membership: trade associations from the waste services and environmental technology industries. A merger of Environmental Industry Assns. and its sub-associations, the National Solid Waste Management Assn. and the Waste Equipment Technology Assn. (Formerly Environmental Industry Assns. [EIA].)

Air Pollution

▶ AGENCIES

Environmental Protection Agency (EPA), *Air and Radiation (OAR),* *1200 Pennsylvania Ave. N.W., #5426, MC 6101A 20460; (202) 564-7400. Fax, (202) 501-0986. Janet McCabe, Assistant Administrator, Acting, (202) 564-7404; Elizabeth Shaw, Deputy Assistant Administrator.*
Web, www.epa.gov/aboutepa/about-office-air-and-radiation-oar

Administers air quality standards and planning programs of the Clean Air Act Amendment of 1990; operates the Air and Radiation Docket and Information Center. Supervises the Office of Air Quality Planning and Standards in Durham, N.C., which develops air quality standards and provides information on air pollution control issues, including industrial air pollution. Administers the Air Pollution Technical Information Center in Research in Triangle Park, N.C., which collects and provides technical literature on air pollution. Administers the National Center for Advanced Technology and the National Vehicle Fuel Emissions Laboratory in Ann Arbor, Mich.

Environmental Protection Agency (EPA), *Atmospheric Programs (OAP),* *1310 L St. N.W., 10th Floor, MC 6201J 20005; (202) 343-9140. Fax, (202) 343-2210. Sarah W. Dunham, Director.*
Web, www.epa.gov/aboutepa/about-office-air-and-radiation-oar#oap

Responsible for acid rain and global protection programs; examines strategies for preventing atmospheric pollution and mitigating climate change. Administers public-private partnerships, such as ENERGY STAR.

Environmental Protection Agency (EPA), *Monitoring Assistance and Media Programs,* *1200 Pennsylvania Ave. N.W., #7138, MC 2223A 20460; (202) 564-1191. Fax, (202) 564-0050. Edward Messina, Director; Rafael Sánchez, EPA Contact, (202) 564-7028.*
Web, www.epa.gov/aboutepa/oeca.html#oc

Responsible for development and implementation of a national program of compliance concerning lead regulations and matters related to the Clean Air Act, Clean Water Act, Resource Conservation and Recovery Act, and Oil Pollution Act.

Federal Aviation Administration (FAA) *(Transportation Dept.),* *Environment and Energy,* *800 Independence Ave. S.W., #900W 20591; (202) 267-3576. Fax, (202) 267-5594. Lourdes Maurice, Director.*
Web, www.faa.gov/about/office_org/headquarters_offices/apl/research

Develops government standards for aircraft noise and emissions.

U.S. Geological Survey (USGS) *(Interior Dept.),* *Energy Resources Program,* *12201 Sunrise Valley Dr., MS913, Reston, VA 20192 (mailing address: 913 National Center, Reston, VA 20192); (703) 648-6470. Fax, (703) 648-5464. Brenda S. Pierce, Program Coordinator.*
General email, gd-energyprogram@usgs.gov
Web, http://energy.usgs.gov and Twitter, @usgs.gov

Conducts research on geologically based energy resources of the United States and the world; estimates energy resource availability and recoverability; anticipates and mitigates deleterious environmental impacts of energy resource extraction and use.

▶ NONGOVERNMENTAL

Alliance for Responsible Atmospheric Policy, *2111 Wilson Blvd., #850, Arlington, VA 22201; (703) 243-0344. Fax, (703) 243-2874. Stephen Van Maren, Executive Director.*
General email, info@arap.org
Web, www.arap.org

Coalition of users and producers of chlorofluorocarbons (CFCs). Seeks further study of the ozone depletion theory.

American Lung Assn., *1301 Pennsylvania Ave. N.W., #800 20004-1725; (202) 785-3355. Fax, (202) 452-1805. Harold Wimmer, President; Paul Billings, Vice President of Advocacy and Education.*
Web, www.lung.org

Promotes improved lung health and the prevention of lung disease through research, education, and advocacy. Interests include antismoking campaigns; lung-related biomedical research; air pollution; and all lung diseases, including asthma, COPD, and lung cancer.

Asbestos Information Assn./North America, *P.O. Box 2227, Arlington, VA 22202-9227; (703) 560-2980. Fax, (703) 560-2981. B. J. Pigg, President. General email, aiabjpigg@aol.com*

Membership: firms that manufacture, sell, and use products containing asbestos fiber and those that mine, mill, and sell asbestos. Provides information on asbestos and health and on industry efforts to eliminate problems associated with asbestos dust; serves as liaison between the industry and federal and state governments.

Center for Auto Safety, *1825 Connecticut Ave. N.W., #330 20009-5708; (202) 328-7700. Fax, (202) 387-0140. Clarence Ditlow, Executive Director. General email, accounts@autosafety.org*

Web, www.autosafety.org

Public interest organization that conducts research on air pollution caused by auto emissions; monitors fuel economy regulations.

Center for Clean Air Policy, *750 1st St. N.E., #940 20002; (202) 408-9260. Fax, (202) 408-8896. Ned Helme, President. General email, general@ccap.org or tassistant@ccap.org*

Web, www.ccap.org

Membership: international policymakers, climate negotiators, corporations, environmentalists, and academicians. Analyzes economic and environmental effects of air pollution and related environmental problems. Serves as a liaison among government, corporate, community, and environmental groups.

Center for Climate and Energy Solutions, *2101 Wilson Blvd., #550, Arlington, VA 22201; (703) 516-4146. Fax, (703) 516-9551. Eileen Claussen, President. Web, www.c2es.org*

Independent organization that issues information and promotes discussion by policymakers on the science, economics, and policy of climate change. (Formerly Pew Center on Global Climate Change.)

Climate Institute, *900 17th St. N.W., #700 20006; (202) 552-4723. Fax, (202) 737-6410. John C. Topping, President. General email, info@climate.org*

Web, www.climate.org

Educates the public and policymakers on climate change (greenhouse effect, or global warming) and on the depletion of the ozone layer. Assesses climate change risks and develops strategies on mitigating climate change in developing countries and in North America.

Environmental Defense Fund, *Washington Office, 1875 Connecticut Ave. N.W., #600 20009-5728; (202) 387-3500. Fax, (202) 234-6049. Diane Regas, Senior Vice President. Information, (800) 684-3322. Press, (202) 572-3396. Web, www.edf.org*

Citizens' interest group staffed by lawyers, economists, and scientists. Conducts research and provides information on pollution prevention, environmental health, and the Clean Air Act. (Headquarters in New York.)

Manufacturers of Emission Controls Assn., *2200 Wilson Blvd., #310, Arlington, VA 22201; (202) 296-4797. Joseph Kubsh, Executive Director. Web, www.meca.org*

Membership: manufacturers of motor vehicle emission control equipment. Provides information on emission technology and industry capabilities.

National Assn. of Clean Air Agencies (NACAA), *444 North Capitol St. N.W., #307 20001; (202) 624-7864. Fax, (202) 624-7863. Bill Becker, Executive Director. General email, 4cleanair@4cleanair.org*

Web, www.4cleanair.org

Membership: air pollution control agencies nationwide. Seeks to improve effective management of air resources by encouraging the exchange of information among air pollution control officials. Develops software tools to better analyze various air pollution control scenarios; monitors federal regulation; publishes reports and analyses; develops model rules for states and localities.

Hazardous Materials

►AGENCIES

Agency for Toxic Substances and Disease Registry (Health and Human Services Dept.), Washington Office, *395 E St. S.W., #9100 20201; (202) 245-0600. Fax, (202) 245-0602. Barbara A. Rogers, Associate Administrator. Press, (770) 488-0700. Web, www.cdc.gov/washingtonoffice*

Works with federal, state, and local agencies to minimize or eliminate adverse effects of exposure to toxic substances at spill and waste disposal sites. Maintains a registry of persons exposed to hazardous substances and of diseases and illnesses resulting from exposure to hazardous or toxic substances. Maintains inventory of hazardous substances and registry of sites closed or restricted because of contamination by hazardous material. (Headquarters in Atlanta, Ga.)

Defense Dept. (DOD), *Installations and Environment, 3400 Defense Pentagon, #3B856A 20301-3400; (703) 695-2880. Fax, (703) 693-7011. John Conger, Deputy Under Secretary, Acting. Web, www.acq.osd.mil/ie*

Oversees and offers policy guidance for all Defense Dept. installations and environmental programs.

Environmental Protection Agency (EPA), *Chemical Safety and Pollution Prevention (OCSPP), 1201 Constitution Ave. N.W., #3130 EPA-E, MS 7101M 20460-7101; (202) 564-2902. Fax, (202) 564-0801. James J. Jones, Assistant Administrator. Pollution prevention and toxic substances, (202) 564-3810. Pesticide programs, (703) 305-7090. Web, www.epa.gov/aboutepa/about-office-chemical-safety-and-pollution-prevention-ocspp*

Studies and makes recommendations for regulating chemical substances under the Toxic Substances Control Act; compiles list of chemical substances subject to the act;

registers, controls, and regulates use of pesticides and toxic substances; manages the Endocrine Disruptor Screening Program.

Environmental Protection Agency (EPA), *Emergency Management,* 1200 Pennsylvania Ave. N.W., #1448, MC 5104A 20460; (202) 564-8600. Fax, (202) 564-8222. *Lawrence M. Stanton, Director; Dana S. Tulis, Deputy Director. Toll-free call center, (800) 424-9346.* Web, www.epa.gov/aboutepa/osweroe1

Develops and administers chemical emergency preparedness and prevention programs; reviews effectiveness of programs; prepares community right-to-know regulations. Provides guidance materials, technical assistance, and training. Implements the preparedness and community right-to-know provisions of the Superfund Amendments and Reauthorization Act of 1986.

Environmental Protection Agency (EPA), *Enforcement and Compliance Assurance (OECA),* 1200 Pennsylvania Ave. N.W., #3204, MC 2201A 20460; (202) 564-2440. Fax, (202) 501-3842. Cynthia J. Giles, Assistant Administrator. Web, www2.epa.gov/aboutepa/about-office-enforcement-oeca

Enforces laws that protect public health and the environment from hazardous materials, pesticides, and toxic substances.

Environmental Protection Agency (EPA), *Pollution Prevention and Toxics (OPPT),* 1200 Pennsylvania Ave. N.W., #4146, MC 7401M 20460; (202) 564-3810. Fax, (202) 564-0575. Wendy Cleland-Hamnett, Director. Toxic substance hotline, (202) 554-1404.
Web, www.epa.gov/oppt/index.htm and www.epa.gov/aboutepa/ocspp.html

Assesses the health and environmental hazards of existing chemical substances and mixtures; collects information on chemical use, exposure, and effects; maintains inventory of existing chemical substances; reviews new chemicals and regulates the manufacture, distribution, use, and disposal of harmful chemicals. Implements the Toxic Substances Control Act and the Pollution Prevention Act.

Environmental Protection Agency (EPA), *Solid Waste and Emergency Response (OSWER),* 1200 Pennsylvania Ave. N.W., MC 5101T 20460; (202) 566-0200. Fax, (202) 566-0207. Mathy V. Stanislaus, Assistant Administrator. Superfund/Resource conservation and recovery hotline, (800) 424-9346. Hotline for reporting oil or chemical spills, (800) 424-8802. local, (703) 412-9810. TTY, (800) 553-7672. Web, www2.epa.gov/aboutepa/about-office-solid-waste-and-emergency-response.oswer

Administers and enforces the Superfund act; manages the handling, cleanup, and disposal of hazardous wastes.

Housing and Urban Development Dept. (HUD), *Healthy Homes and Lead Hazard Control,* 451 7th St. S.W., #8236 20410; (202) 708-0310. Fax, (202) 708-0014. Jon L. Gant, Director.
Web, www.hud.gov/offices/lead

Advises HUD offices, other agencies, health authorities, and the housing industry on lead poisoning prevention. Develops regulations for lead-based paint; conducts research; makes grants to state and local governments for lead hazard reduction and inspection of housing.

Justice Dept. (DOJ), *Environmental Enforcement,* 601 D St. N.W., #2121 20004 (mailing address: P.O. Box 7611, Ben Franklin Station, Washington, DC 20044-7611); (202) 514-2750. Fax, (202) 514-0097. W. Benjamin Fisherow, Chief. Web, www.justice.gov/enrd

Represents the United States in civil cases under environmental laws that involve the handling, storage, treatment, transportation, and disposal of hazardous waste. Recovers federal money spent to clean up hazardous waste sites or sues defendants to clean up sites under Superfund.

National Response Center *(Homeland Security Dept.),* 2100 2nd St. S.W., #2111B 20593-0001; (202) 267-2180. Fax, (202) 267-1322. Syed M. Qadir, Director, (202) 372-2440. TTY, (202) 267-4477. Hotline, (800) 424-8802. local, (202) 267-2675.
General email, hqs-dg-lst-nrcinfo@comdt.uscg.mil
Web, www.nrc.uscg.mil

Maintains twenty-four-hour hotline for reporting oil spills, hazardous materials accidents, and chemical releases. Notifies appropriate federal officials to reduce the effects of accidents.

Pipeline and Hazardous Materials Safety Administration *(Transportation Dept.),* 1200 New Jersey Ave. S.E., #E27-300 20590; (202) 366-4433. Fax, (202) 366-3666. Cynthia L. Quarterman, Administrator. Hazardous Materials Information Center, (800) 467-4922. To report an incident, (800) 424-8802.
Web, www.phmsa.dot.gov and
Twitter, PHMSA@PHMSA_DOT

Oversees the safe and secure movement of hazardous materials to industry and consumers by all modes of transportation, including pipelines. Works to eliminate transportation-related deaths and injuries. Promotes transportation solutions to protect communities and the environment.

Pipeline and Hazardous Materials Safety Administration *(Transportation Dept.),* **Hazardous Materials Safety,** 1200 New Jersey Ave. S.E., E 21-317 20590; (202) 366-0656. Fax, (202) 366-5713. Magdy A. El-Sibaie, Associate Administrator. Hazardous Materials Information Center, (800) 467-4922.
General email, phmsa.hmhazmatsafety@dot.gov
Web, http://hazmat.dot.gov

Designates substances as hazardous materials and regulates their transportation in interstate commerce; coordinates international standards regulations.

Pipeline and Hazardous Materials Safety Administration *(Transportation Dept.),* **Pipeline Safety,** 1200 New Jersey Ave. S.E., E22-321 20590; (202) 366-4595. Fax, (202) 493-2311. Jeffery D. Wiese, Associate Administrator.
General email, phmsa.pipelinesafety@dot.gov
Web, http://phmsa.dot.gov

Issues and enforces federal regulations for hazardous liquids pipeline safety.

State Dept., *Environmental Policy, 2201 C St. N.W., #2726 20520; (202) 647-9266. Fax, (202) 647-1052. Deborah E. Klepp, Director. Web, www.state.gov/e/oes/env*

Advances U.S. interests internationally regarding multilateral environmental organizations, chemical waste and other pollutants, and bilateral and regional environmental policies.

►CONGRESS

For a listing of relevant congressional committees and subcommittees, please see pages 252–253 or the Appendix.

►NONGOVERNMENTAL

Alliance of Hazardous Materials Professionals, *9650 Rockville Pike, Bethesda, MD 20814; (301) 634-7430. Fax, (301) 634-7431. A. Cedric Calhoun, Executive Director. Toll-free, (800) 437-0137. General email, info@ahmpnet.org Web, www.ahmpnet.org*

Membership: professionals who work with hazardous materials and environmental, health, and safety issues. Offers professional development and networking opportunities to members. Members must be certified by the Institute of Hazardous Materials Management (IHMM).

Center for Health, Environment, and Justice, *150 S. Washington St., #300, Falls Church, VA 22046-2921 (mailing address: P.O. Box 6806, Falls Church, VA 22040-6806); (703) 237-2249. Fax, (703) 237-8389. Lois Marie Gibbs, Executive Director. General email, chej@chej.org Web, www.chej.org*

Provides citizens' groups, individuals, and municipalities with support and information on solid and hazardous waste. Sponsors workshops, a speakers bureau, leadership development conference, and convention. Operates a toxicity data bank on the environmental and health effects of common chemical compounds; maintains a registry of technical experts to assist in solid and hazardous waste problems; gathers information on polluting corporations.

Chlorine Institute Inc., *1300 Wilson Blvd., #525, Arlington, VA 22209; (703) 894-4140. Fax, (703) 894-4130. Frank Reiner, President. General email, info@cl2.com Web, www.chlorineinstitute.org*

Safety, health, and environmental protection center of the chlor-alkali (chlorine, caustic soda, caustic potash, and hydrogen chloride) industry. Interests include employee health and safety, resource conservation and pollution abatement, control of chlorine emergencies, product specifications, and public and community relations. Publishes technical pamphlets and drawings.

Consumer Specialty Products Assn., *1667 K St. N.W., #300 20006; (202) 872-8110. Fax, (202) 223-2636. Christopher Cathcart, President.*

General email, info@cspa.org Web, www.cspa.org

Membership: manufacturers, marketers, packagers, and suppliers in the chemical specialties industry. Focus includes cleaning products and detergents, nonagricultural pesticides, disinfectants, automotive and industrial products, polishes and floor finishes, antimicrobials, air care products and candles, and aerosol products. Monitors scientific developments; conducts surveys and research; provides chemical safety information and consumer education programs; sponsors National Inhalants and Poisons Awareness and Aerosol Education Bureau. Monitors legislation and regulations.

Dangerous Goods Advisory Council, *1100 H St. N.W., #740 20005; (202) 289-4550. Fax, (202) 289-4074. Vaughn Arthur, President. General email, info@dgac.org Web, www.dgac.org*

Membership: shippers, carriers, container manufacturers and conditioners, emergency response and spill cleanup companies, and trade associations. Promotes safety in the domestic and international transportation of hazardous materials. Provides information and educational services; sponsors conferences, workshops, and seminars. Advocates uniform hazardous materials regulations. (Formerly the Hazardous Materials Advisory Council.)

Environmental Technology Council, *1112 16th St. N.W., #420 20036; (202) 783-0870. Fax, (202) 737-2038. David R. Case, Executive Director. Press, (202) 783-0870, ext. 202. General email, mail@etc.org Web, www.etc.org*

Membership: environmental service firms. Interests include the recycling, detoxification, and disposal of hazardous and industrial waste and cleanup of contaminated industrial sites; works to encourage permanent and technology-based solutions to environmental problems. Provides the public with information.

Institute of Hazardous Materials Management (IHMM), *11900 Parklawn Dr., #450, Rockville, MD 20852; (301) 984-8969. Fax, (301) 984-1516. Jeffrey Greenwald, Executive Director. General email, info@ihmm.org Web, www.ihmm.org*

Seeks to educate professionals and the general public about proper handling of hazardous materials; issues certifications. Administers the Certified Hazardous Materials Manager program and the Certified Hazardous Materials Practitioner program.

International Assn. of Heat and Frost Insulators and Allied Workers, *9602 Martin Luther King Hwy., Lanham, MD 20706-1839; (301) 731-9101. Fax, (301) 731-5058. James A. Grogan, General President. General email, hfi@insulators.org Web, www.insulators.org*

Membership: approximately 18,000 workers in insulation industries. Helps members negotiate pay, benefits, and better working conditions; conducts training programs and workshops. Monitors legislation and regulations. (Affiliated with the AFL-CIO.)

National Insulation Assn. (NIA), *12100 Sunset Hills Rd., #330, Reston, VA 20190-3233; (703) 464-6422. Fax, (703) 464-5896. Michele M. Jones, Executive Vice President, ext. 119.*
General email, niainfo@insulation.org
Web, www.insulation.org

Membership: open-shop and union contractors, distributors, laminators, fabricators, and manufacturers that provide thermal insulation, insulation accessories, and components to the commercial, mechanical, and industrial markets. Provides information to members on industry trends and technologies. Monitors legislation and regulations.

Rachel Carson Council Inc., *P.O. Box 714, Laurel, MD 20725-0714; (240) 456-0009. Dr. Robert Musil, President, (301) 493-4571.*
General email, office@rachelcarsoncouncil.org
Web, www.rachelcarsoncouncil.org

Acts as a clearinghouse for information on pesticides and alternatives to their use; maintains extensive data on toxicity and the effects of pesticides on humans, domestic animals, and wildlife. Library open to the public by appointment.

Radiation Protection

▶AGENCIES

Armed Forces Radiobiology Research Institute *(Defense Dept.), 8901 Wisconsin Ave., Bldg. 42, Bethesda, MD 20889-5603; (301) 295-1210. Fax, (301) 295-4967. Col. Lester Huff USAF, MC, Director. Public Affairs, (301) 295-1214.*
Web, www.afrri.usuhs.mil

Serves as the principal ionizing radiation radiobiology research laboratory under the jurisdiction of the Uniformed Services of the Health Sciences. Participates in international conferences and projects.

Environmental Protection Agency (EPA), *Radiation and Indoor Air (ORIA), 1310 L St. N.W., 4th Floor, MC 6601J 20005; (202) 343-9320. Fax, (202) 343-2395. Michael P. Flynn, Director.*
Web, www2.epa.gov/aboutepa/about-office-air-and-radiation-oar#oria

Establishes standards to regulate the amount of radiation discharged into the environment from uranium mining and milling projects and other activities that result in radioactive emissions; and to ensure safe disposal of radioactive waste. Fields a Radiological Emergency Response Team. Administers the nationwide Environmental Radiation Ambient Monitoring System (RadNet), which analyzes environmental radioactive contamination. Oversees

the National Air and Radiation Environmental Laboratory in Montgomery, Ala.

Food and Drug Administration (FDA) *(Health and Human Services Dept.), Center for Devices and Radiological Health, 10903 New Hampshire Ave., #5429, Silver Spring, MD 20993; (301) 796-5900. Fax, (301) 847-8510. Jeffrey E. Shuren, Director.*
General email, jeff.shuren@fda.hhs.gov
Web, www.fda.gov/medicaldevices

Administers national programs to control exposure to radiation; establishes standards for emissions from consumer and medical products; conducts factory inspections. Accredits and certifies mammography facilities and personnel; provides physicians and consumers with guidelines on radiation-emitting products. Conducts research, training, and educational programs.

▶NONGOVERNMENTAL

Institute for Science and International Security, *236 Massachusetts Ave. N.E., #305 20002; (202) 547-3633. Fax, (202) 547-3634. David Albright, President.*
General email, isis@isis-online.org
Web, www.isis-online.org

Analyzes scientific and policy issues affecting national and international security, including the problems of war, regional and global arms races, the spread of nuclear weapons, and the environmental, health, and safety hazards of nuclear weapons production.

National Council on Radiation Protection and Measurements (NCRP), *7910 Woodmont Ave., #400, Bethesda, MD 20814-3095; (301) 657-2652. Fax, (301) 907-8768. James Cassata, Executive Director; John D. Boice, President.*
General email, ncrp@ncrponline.org
Web, www.ncrponline.org; for publications, www.ncrppublications.org

Nonprofit organization chartered by Congress that collects and analyzes information and provides recommendations on radiation protection and measurement. Studies radiation emissions from household items and from office and medical equipment. Holds annual conference; publishes reports on radiation protection and measurement.

Recycling and Solid Waste

▶AGENCIES

Environmental Protection Agency (EPA), *Solid Waste and Emergency Response (OSWER), 1200 Pennsylvania Ave. N.W., MC 5101T 20460; (202) 566-0200. Fax, (202) 566-0207. Mathy V. Stanislaus, Assistant Administrator. Superfund/Resource conservation and recovery hotline, (800) 424-9346. Hotline for reporting oil or chemical spills, (800) 424-8802. local, (703) 412-9810. TTY, (800) 553-7672.*
Web, www2.epa.gov/aboutepa/about-office-solid-waste-and-emergency-response.oswer

Administers and enforces the Resource Conservation and Recovery Act and the Brownfields Program and Superfund.

▶CONGRESS

For a listing of relevant congressional committees and sub-committees, please see pages 252–253 or the Appendix.

▶NONGOVERNMENTAL

Alliance of Foam Packaging Recyclers (AFPR), *1298 Cronson Blvd., #201, Crofton, MD 21114; (410) 451-8340. Fax, (410) 451-8343. Betsy Steiner, Executive Director. Toll-free, (800) 607-3772.*
General email, info@epspackaging.org
Web, www.epspackaging.org

Membership: companies that recycle foam packaging material. Coordinates national network of collection centers for postconsumer foam packaging products; helps to establish new collection centers.

American Chemistry Council, *700 2nd St. N.E. 20002; (202) 249-7000. Fax, (202) 249-6100. Calvin M. (Cal) Dooley, President.*
Web, www.americanchemistry.com

Seeks to increase plastics recycling; conducts research on disposal of plastic products; sponsors research on waste-handling methods, incineration, and degradation; supports programs that test alternative waste management technologies. Monitors legislation and regulations. (Merged with Plastic Foodservice Packaging Group.)

Assn. of State and Territorial Solid Waste Management Officials, *1101 17th St. N.W., #707 20036; (202) 640-1060. Dania Rodriguez, Executive Director.*
Web, www.astswmo.org

Membership: state and territorial solid waste management officials. Works with the Environmental Protection Agency to develop policy affecting waste, materials management, and remediation.

Energy Recovery Council, *1730 Rhode Island Ave. N.W., #700 20036; (202) 467-6240. Edward (Ted) Michaels, President.*
General email, tmichaels@energyrecoverycouncil.org
Web, www.energyrecoverycouncil.org

Membership: companies that design, build, and operate resource recovery facilities. Promotes integrated solutions to municipal solid waste management issues. Encourages the use of waste-to-energy technology.

Foodservice Packaging Institute (FPI), *201 Park Washington Court, Falls Church, VA 22046; (703) 538-3550. Fax, (703) 241-5603. Lynn Dyer, President, (703) 538-3551.*
General email, fpi@fpi.org
Web, www.fpi.org

Membership: manufacturers, suppliers, and distributors of disposable products used in food service, packaging, and consumer products. Promotes the use of disposables for commercial and home use.

Glass Packaging Institute, *1000 N. Fairfax St., #301A, Alexandria, VA 22314; (703) 684-6359. Fax, (703) 546-0588. Lynn Bragg, President.*
General email, info@gpi.org
Web, www.gpi.org

Membership: manufacturers of glass containers and their suppliers. Promotes industry policies to protect the environment, conserve natural resources, and reduce energy consumption; conducts research; monitors legislation affecting the industry. Interests include glass recycling.

Institute for Local Self-Reliance, *2001 S St. N.W., #570 20009; (202) 898-1610. Fax, (202) 898-1612. Neil N. Seldman, President.*
General email, info@ilsr.org
Web, www.ilsr.org

Conducts research and provides technical assistance on environmentally sound economic development for government, small businesses, and community organizations. Advocates the development of a materials policy at local, state, and regional levels to reduce per capita consumption of raw materials and to shift from dependence on fossil fuels to reliance on renewable resources.

Institute of Scrap Recycling Industries, Inc., *1615 L St. N.W., #600 20036-5610; (202) 662-8500. Fax, (202) 626-0900. Robin K. Wiener, Staff Liaison.*
General email, isri@isri.org
Web, www.isri.org

Represents processors, brokers, and consumers of scrap and recyclable paper, glass, plastic, textiles, rubber, ferrous and nonferrous metals, and electronics.

National Recycling Coalition, Inc., *1220 L St. N.W., #100-155 20005; (202) 618-2107. Mark Lichtenstein, President; Lisa Ruggero, Communications.*
General email, info@nrcrecycles.org
Web, http://nrcrecycles.org

Membership: public officials; community recycling groups; local, state, and national agencies; environmentalists; waste haulers; solid waste disposal consultants; and private recycling companies. Encourages recycling to reduce waste, preserve resources, and promote economic development.

National Waste and Recycling Assn., *4301 Connecticut Ave. N.W., #300 20008-2304; (202) 244-4700. Fax, (202) 966-4824. Sharon H. Kneiss, President, (202) 364-3730. Toll-free, (800) 424-2869.*
General email, skneiss@wasterecycling.org
Web, https://wasterecycling.org/

Membership: organizations engaged in refuse collection, processing, and disposal. Provides information on solid and hazardous waste recycling and waste equipment, organics and composting, waste-based energy, and emerging technologies; sponsors workshops. A merger of Environmental Industry Assns. and its sub-associations, the National Solid Waste Management Assn. and the Waste Equipment Technology Assn. (Formerly Environmental Industry Assns. [EIA].)

Secondary Materials and Recycled Textiles Assn. (SMART), *2105 Laurel Bush Rd., #200, Bel Air, MD 21015; (443) 640-1050, ext. 112. Fax, (443) 640-1086. Jackie King, Executive Director, ext. 105.*
General email, casey@ksgroup.org
Web, www.smartasn.org

Membership: organizations and individuals involved in producing, shipping, and distributing recycled textiles and other textile products. Sponsors educational programs; publishes newsletters. Monitors legislation and regulations.

Solid Waste Assn. of North America (SWANA), *1100 Wayne Ave., #650, Silver Spring, MD 20910-7219; (301) 585-2898. Fax, (301) 589-7068. John H. Skinner, Chief Executive Officer, (240) 494-2254. Toll-free, (800) 467-9262.*
Web, www.swana.org

Membership: government and private industry officials who manage municipal solid waste programs. Interests include waste reduction, collection, recycling (including of electronics), combustion, and disposal. Conducts training and certification programs. Operates solid waste information clearinghouse. Monitors legislation and regulations.

U.S. Conference of Mayors, *Municipal Waste Management Assn., 1620 Eye St. N.W., #400 20006; (202) 293-7330. Fax, (202) 429-2352. Jubi Headley, Managing Director, (202) 861-6798; Judy Sheahan, Assistant Executive Director for Environmental Policy, (202) 861-6775.*
General email, info@usmayors.org
Web, www.usmayors.org/mwma

Organization of local governments and private companies involved in planning and developing solid waste management programs, including pollution prevention, waste-to-energy, and recycling. Assists communities with financing, environmental assessments, and associated policy implementation.

Water Pollution

▶ **AGENCIES**

Bureau of Safety and Environmental Enforcement (BSEE) *(Interior Dept.), Offshore Regulatory Programs, 1849 C St. N.W., MS DM 5438 20240-0001; (202) 208-3985. Fax, (202) 208-3968. Douglas Morris, Chief.*
General email, bseepublicaffairs@bsee.gov
Web, www.bsee.gov

Develops standards, regulations, and compliance programs governing Outer Continental Shelf oil, gas, and minerals exploration and operations. Purview includes safety management programs, safety and pollution prevention research, technology assessments, standards for inspections and enforcement policies, and accident investigation practices.

Environmental Protection Agency (EPA), *Ground Water and Drinking Water, 1200 Pennsylvania Ave. N.W., #2104, EPA East, MC 4601M 20460; (202) 564-3750. Fax, (202) 564-3753. Peter C. Grevatt, Director, (202) 564-8954. Toll-free hotline, (800) 426-4791. Local and international, (703) 412-3330.*
General email, ogwdw.web@epa.gov
Web, www2.epa.gov/aboutepa/about-office-water#ground

Develops standards for the quality of drinking water supply systems; regulates underground injection of waste and protection of groundwater wellhead areas under the Safe Drinking Water Act; provides information on public water supply systems.

Environmental Protection Agency (EPA), *Municipal Support, 1200 Pennsylvania Ave. N.W., #7119A EPA East, MC 4204M 20460; (202) 564-0749. Fax, (202) 501-2346. Bill Anderson, Deputy Director.*
Web, www2.epa.gov/aboutepa/about-office-water#wastewater

Directs programs to assist in the design and construction of municipal sewage systems; develops programs to ensure efficient operation and maintenance of municipal wastewater treatment facilities; implements programs for prevention of water pollution.

Environmental Protection Agency (EPA), *Science and Technology, 1200 Pennsylvania Ave. N.W., #5231 EPA West, MC 4301T 20460; (202) 566-0430. Fax, (202) 566-0441. Elizabeth Southerland, Director.*
General email, ost.comments@epa.gov
Web, www2.epa.gov/aboutepa/about-office-water#science

Develops and coordinates water pollution control programs for the Environmental Protection Agency; assists state and regional agencies in establishing water quality standards and planning local water resources management; develops guidelines for industrial and municipal wastewater discharge; provides grants for water quality monitoring and swimming advisories at recreational coastal and Great Lakes beaches; formulates shellfish protection policies and issues fish advisories.

Environmental Protection Agency (EPA), *Wastewater Management, 1200 Pennsylvania Ave. N.W., #7116A EPA East, MC 4201M 20460; (202) 564-0748. Fax, (202) 501-2338. Andrew Sawyers, Director.*
General email, owm.comments@epa.gov
Web, http://epa.gov/polwaste/wastewater

Oversees the issuance of water permits. Responsible for the Pretreatment Program regulating industrial discharges to local sewage treatment. Oversees the State Revolving Funds Program, which provides assistance for the construction of wastewater treatment plants.

National Drinking Water Advisory Council, *1200 Pennsylvania Ave. N.W., #4100T, MC4606M 20460; (202) 564-3868. Fax, (202) 564-3753. Roy Simon, Designated Federal Officer.*
Web, http://water.epa.gov/drink/ndwac/index.cfm

Membership: members of the general public, state and local agencies, and private groups. Advises the EPA administrator on activities, functions, and policies relating to implementation of the Safe Drinking Water Act.

National Oceanic and Atmospheric Administration (NOAA) *(Commerce Dept.), Office of Response and Restoration,* 1305 East-West Hwy., 10th Floor, Bldg. 4, Silver Spring, MD 20910; (301) 713-4248. Fax, (301) 713-4389. David Westerholm, Director.
Web, http://response.restoration.noaa.gov

Provides information on damage to marine ecosystems caused by pollution. Offers information on spill trajectory projections and chemical hazard analyses. Researches trends of toxic contamination on U.S. coastal regions.

U.S. Coast Guard (USCG) *(Homeland Security Dept.), Marine Environmental Response Policy,* CG-533, 2703 Martin Luther King Jr. Ave. S.E. 20593; (202) 372-2234. Fax, (202) 372-2905. Edward Bock, Chief.
Web, http://homeport.uscg.mil

Oversees cleanup operations after spills of oil and other hazardous substances in U.S. waters, on the Outer Continental Shelf, and in international waters. Reviews coastal zone management and enforces international standards for pollution prevention and response.

U.S. Coast Guard (USCG) *(Homeland Security Dept.), National Pollution Funds Center,* 4200 Wilson Blvd., #1000, MS 7100, Arlington, VA 20598-7100; (703) 872-6000. Fax, (703) 872-6900. Craig A. Bennett, Director.
Web, www.uscg.mil/npfc

Certifies pollution liability coverage for vessels and companies involved in oil exploration and transportation in U.S. waters and on the Outer Continental Shelf. Ensures adequacy of funds to respond to oil spills and deters future spills by managing the Oil Spill Liability Trust Fund.

▶**CONGRESS**

For a listing of relevant congressional committees and subcommittees, please see pages 252–253 or the Appendix.

▶**NONGOVERNMENTAL**

Assn. of Clean Water Administrators, 1221 Connecticut Ave. N.W., 2nd Floor 20036; (202) 756-0600. Fax, (202) 756-0605. Alexandra Dapolito Dunn, Executive Director.
General email, memberservices@acwa-us.org
Web, www.acwa-us.org

Membership: state and interstate water quality regulators. Represents the states' concerns on implementation, funding, and reauthorization of the Clean Water Act. Monitors legislation and regulations.

Clean Water Action, 1444 Eye St. N.W., #400 20005; (202) 895-0420. Fax, (202) 895-0438. Robert (Bob) Wendelgass, Chief Executive Officer.
General email, cwa@cleanwater.org
Web, www.cleanwateraction.org

Citizens' organization interested in clean, safe, and affordable water. Works to influence public policy through education, technical assistance, and grassroots organizing. Interests include toxins and pollution, drinking water, water conservation, sewage treatment, pesticides, mass burn incineration, bay and estuary protection, and consumer water issues. Monitors legislation and regulations.

Ocean Conservancy, 1300 19th St. N.W., 8th Floor 20036; (202) 429-5609. Fax, (202) 872-0619. Andreas Merkl, President. Toll-free, (800) 519-1541.
General email, membership@oceanconservancy.org
Web, www.oceanconservancy.org

Works to protect the health of oceans and seas. Advocates policies that restrict discharge of pollutants harmful to marine ecosystems.

Water Environment Federation, 601 Wythe St., Alexandria, VA 22314-1994; (703) 684-2400. Fax, (703) 684-2492. Eileen O'Neill, Executive Director, Interim. Toll-free, (800) 666-0206.
General email, inquiry@wef.org
Web, www.wef.org

Membership: civil and environmental engineers, wastewater treatment plant operators, scientists, government officials, and others concerned with water quality. Works to preserve and improve water quality worldwide. Provides the public with technical information and educational materials. Monitors legislation and regulations.

RESOURCES MANAGEMENT

General

▶**AGENCIES**

Bureau of Land Management (BLM) *(Interior Dept.), Renewable Resources and Planning,* 1849 C St. N.W., #5644 20240; (202) 208-4896. Fax, (202) 208-5010. Edwin Roberson, Assistant Director.
General email, woinfo@blm.gov
Web, www.blm.gov/wo/st/en/info/directory.html

Develops and implements natural resource programs for renewable resources use and protection, including management of forested land, rangeland, wild horses and burros, wildlife habitats, endangered species, soil and water quality, recreation, and cultural programs.

Bureau of Safety and Environmental Enforcement (BSEE) *(Interior Dept.),* 1849 C St. N.W., MS DM 5438 20240-0001; (202) 208-3985. Fax, (202) 208-3968. Brian Salerno, Director.
General email, bseepublicaffairs@bsee.gov
Web, www.bsee.gov

Responsible for inspections, enforcement, and safety of offshore oil and gas operations. Functions include the development and enforcement of safety and environmental regulations, research, inspections, offshore regulatory

Interior Department

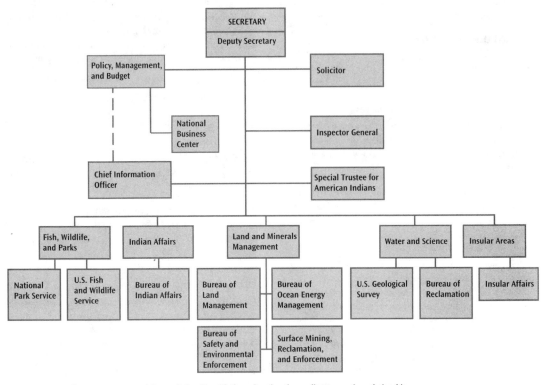

SECRETARY
Deputy Secretary

Policy, Management, and Budget

Solicitor

National Business Center

Inspector General

Chief Information Officer

Special Trustee for American Indians

Fish, Wildlife, and Parks | Indian Affairs | Land and Minerals Management | Water and Science | Insular Areas

National Park Service | U.S. Fish and Wildlife Service | Bureau of Indian Affairs | Bureau of Land Management | Bureau of Ocean Energy Management | U.S. Geological Survey | Bureau of Reclamation | Insular Affairs

Bureau of Safety and Environmental Enforcement | Surface Mining, Reclamation, and Enforcement

— — — Indicates a support or advisory relationship with the unit rather than a direct reporting relationship

and compliance programs, oil spill response, and training of inspectors and industry professionals.

Interior Dept. (DOI), *1849 C St. N.W. 20240; (202) 208-7351. Fax, (202) 208-6956. Hon. Sally Jewell, Secretary; Vacant, Deputy Secretary. Information, (202) 208-3100. Library, (202) 208-5815. Press, (202) 208-6416.*
General email, feedback@ios.doi.gov
Web, www.doi.gov

Manages most federal land through its component agencies. Responsible for conservation and development of mineral, water, and fish and wildlife resources. Operates recreation programs for federal parks, refuges, and public lands. Preserves and administers scenic and historic areas. Administers Native American lands and develops relationships with tribal governments.

Tennessee Valley Authority, *Government Affairs, 1 Massachusetts Ave. N.W., #300 20444; (202) 898-2999. Fax, (202) 898-2998. Nick Pearson, Director.*
General email, latootle@tva.gov
Web, www.tva.gov

Coordinates resource conservation, development, and land-use programs in the Tennessee River Valley. Activities include forestry and wildlife development.

▶ **NONGOVERNMENTAL**

National Assn. of Conservation Districts (NACD), *509 Capitol Court N.E. 20002-4937; (202) 547-6223. Fax, (202) 547-6450. John Larson, Chief Executive Officer.*
General email, bethany-shively@nacdet.org
Web, www.nacdnet.org

Membership: conservation districts (local subdivisions of state government). Works to promote the conservation of land, forests, and other natural resources. Interests include erosion and sediment control; water quality; forestry, water, flood plain, and range management; rural development; and urban and community conservation.

Renewable Natural Resources Foundation, *5430 Grosvenor Lane, #220, Bethesda, MD 20814-2142; (301) 493-9101. Fax, (301) 493-6148. Robert D. Day, Executive Director.*
General email, info@rnrf.org
Web, www.rnrf.org

Consortium of professional, scientific, and education organizations working to advance scientific and public education in renewable natural resources. Encourages the application of sound scientific practices to resource management and conservation. Fosters interdisciplinary cooperation among its member organizations.

U.S. Chamber of Commerce, *Environment, Technology, and Regulatory Affairs, 1615 H St. N.W. 20062-2000; (202) 463-5533. Fax, (202) 887-3445. William L. Kovacs, Senior Vice President.*
General email, environment@uschamber.com
Web, www.uschamber.com/issues/etra

Develops policy on all issues affecting the production, use, and conservation of natural resources, including fuel and nonfuel minerals, timber, water, public lands, on- and offshore energy, wetlands, and endangered species.

Forests and Rangelands

▶AGENCIES

Forest Service *(Agriculture Dept.), 1621 N. Kent St., Arlington, VA 22209 (mailing address: 1400 Independence Ave. S.W., MS 1144, Washington, DC 20250-1144); (202) 205-1661. Fax, (202) 205-1765. Tom Tidwell, Chief, (202) 205-8439. Press, (202) 205-8333.*
Web, www.fs.fed.us

Manages national forests and grasslands for outdoor recreation and sustained yield of renewable natural resources, including timber, water, forage, fish, and wildlife. Cooperates with state and private foresters; conducts forestry research.

Forest Service *(Agriculture Dept.), International Programs, 1 Thomas Circle, #400 20005; (202) 273-4695. Fax, (202) 273-4750. Valdis E. Mezainis, Director, (202) 644-4621.*
Web, www.fs.fed.us/global

Responsible for the Forest Service's involvement in international forest conservation efforts. Analyzes international resource issues; promotes information exchange; provides planning and technical assistance. Interests include tropical forests and sustainable forest management.

Forest Service *(Agriculture Dept.), National Forest System, 1621 N. Kent St., Arlington, VA 22209 (mailing address: 1400 Independence Ave. S.W., MS 1106, Washington, DC 20250-1106); (202) 205-1689. Fax, (202) 205-1758. Leslie A.C. Weldon, Deputy Chief, (202) 205-1523.*
Web, www.fs.fed.us

Manages 193 million acres of forests and rangelands. Products and services from these lands include timber, water, forage, wildlife, minerals, and recreation.

Forest Service *(Agriculture Dept.), Research and Development, 201 14th St. S.W., #1NW, MS1120 20250; (202) 205-1665. Fax, (202) 205-1530. Jim Reaves, Deputy Chief.*
Web, www.fs.fed.us

Conducts biological, physical, and economic research related to forestry, including studies on harvesting methods, acid deposition, international forestry, the effects of global climate changes on forests, and forest products. Provides information on the establishment, improvement, and growth of trees, grasses, and other forest vegetation. Works to protect forest resources from fire, insects, diseases, and animal pests. Examines the effect of forest use activities on water quality, soil erosion, and sediment production. Conducts continuous forest survey and analyzes outlook for future supply and demand.

Forest Service *(Agriculture Dept.), State and Private Forestry, 1621 N. Kent St., Arlington, VA 22209 (mailing address: 1400 Independence Ave. S.W., MS 1109, Washington, DC 20250-1109); (202) 205-1657. Fax, (202) 205-1174. James E. Hubbard, Deputy Chief.*
Web, www.fs.fed.us

Assists state and private forest owners with the protection and management of 574 million acres of forest and associated watershed lands. Assistance includes fire control, protecting forests from insects and diseases, land-use planning, developing multiple-use management, and improving practices in harvesting, processing, and marketing of forest products.

Forest Service *(Agriculture Dept.), Youth Conservation Corps, 1621 N. Kent St., Arlington, VA 22209 (mailing address: 1400 Independence Ave. S.W., MS 1125, Washington, DC 20250-1125); (202) 205-0650. Fax, (703) 605-5131. Merlene Mazyck, Program Manager. Toll-free, (800) 832-1355.*
General email, mmazyck@fs.fed.us
Web, www.fs.fed.us/recreation/programs/ycc/index.shtml
and *http://youthgo.gov*

Administers with the National Park Service and the Fish and Wildlife Service the Youth Conservation Corps, a summer employment and training public works program for youths ages fifteen to eighteen. The program is conducted in national parks, in national forests, and on national wildlife refuges.

▶CONGRESS

For a listing of relevant congressional committees and subcommittees, please see pages 252–253 or the Appendix.

▶NONGOVERNMENTAL

American Forest and Paper Assn., *Government Affairs, 1101 K St. N.W., #700 20005; (202) 463-2700. Fax, (202) 463-2471. Elizabeth Bartheld, Vice President, Government Affairs; Donna Harman, President.*
General email, info@afandpa.org
Web, www.afandpa.org

Membership: pulp, paper, and paper-based product manufacturers and those in related associations. Interests include tax, housing, environmental, international trade, sustainability, and land-use issues that affect the forest products industry.

American Forests, *1220 L St. N.W., #750 20005; (202) 737-1944. Fax, (202) 737-2457. Scott Steen, Chief Executive Officer.*
General email, info@amfor.org
Web, www.americanforests.org

Citizens' interest group that promotes protection and responsible management of forests and natural resources. Provides information on conservation, public land policy, and urban forestry. Promotes an international tree-planting campaign to help mitigate global warming.

Forest Resources Assn., *1901 Pennsylvania Ave. N.W., #303 20006; (202) 296-3937. Fax, (202) 296-0562. Deb Hawkinson, President.*
General email, fra@forestresources.org
Web, www.forestresources.org

Membership: suppliers, brokers, transporters, and consumers of unprocessed wood products, as well as businesses that serve the forest products supply chain. Provides information on the safe, efficient, and sustainable harvest of forest products and their transport from woods to mill; works to ensure continued access to the timberland base. Monitors legislation and regulations.

International Wood Products Assn., *4214 King St. West, Alexandria, VA 22302; (703) 820-6696. Fax, (703) 820-8550. Cindy L. Squire, Executive Director.*
General email, info@iwpawood.org
Web, www.iwpawood.org

Membership: companies that handle imported wood products. Encourages environmentally responsible forest management and international trade in wood products. Sponsors research and environmental education on tropical forestry. (Affiliated with the Tropical Forest Foundation.)

National Assn. of State Foresters, *444 N. Capitol St. N.W., #540 20001; (202) 624-5415. Fax, (202) 624-5407. Jay Farrell, Executive Director.*
General email, nasf@stateforesters.org
Web, www.stateforesters.org

Membership: directors of state forestry agencies from all states, the District of Columbia, and U.S. territories. Interests include forest management, employment generated by forestry and forest products, and climate change. Monitors legislation and regulations.

National Lumber and Building Material Dealers Assn., *2025 M St. N.W., #800 20036-3309; (202) 367-1169. Fax, (202) 367-2169. Michael O'Brien, President.*
General email, info@dealer.org
Web, www.dealer.org

Membership: federated associations of retailers in the lumber and building material industries. Provides statistics training and networking opportunities to members. Monitors legislation and regulations.

Save America's Forests, *4 Library Court S.E. 20003; (202) 544-9219. Fax, (202) 544-7462. Carl Ross, Executive Director.*
General email, forests@saveamericasforests.org
Web, www.saveamericasforests.org

Coalition of environmental and public interest groups, scientists, businesses, and individuals. Advocates comprehensive nationwide laws and international policies to prevent deforestation and to protect forest ecosystems and indigenous rights.

Society of American Foresters, *5400 Grosvenor Lane, Bethesda, MD 20814-2198; (301) 897-8720. Fax, (301) 897-3690. Louise Murgia, Executive Vice President, Interim. Toll-free, (866) 897-8720.*
General email, safweb@safnet.org
Web, www.safnet.org

Association of forestry professionals. Provides technical information on forestry, accredits forestry programs in universities and colleges, and publishes scientific forestry journals.

Sustainable Forestry Initiative, *900 17th St. N.W., #700 20006; (202) 596-3450. Fax, (202) 596-3451. Kathy Abusow, President.*
Web, www.sfiprogram.org

Works to ensure protection of forests while continuing to produce wood and paper products as needed by the economy. Encourages perpetual growing and harvesting of trees and protection of wildlife, plants, soil, water, and air quality. Seeks to mitigate illegal logging. Interests include the economic, environmental, cultural, and legal issues related to forestry.

Land Resources

▶**AGENCIES**

Bureau of Land Management (BLM) *(Interior Dept.), 1849 C St. N.W., #5665 20240; (202) 208-3801. Fax, (202) 208-5242. Neil Kornze, Deputy Director. Press, (202) 208-6913.*
General email, director@blm.gov
Web, www.blm.gov

Manages public lands and federally owned mineral resources, including oil, gas, and coal. Resources managed and leased include wildlife habitats, timber, minerals, open space, wilderness areas, forage, and recreational resources. Surveys federal lands and maintains public land records.

Bureau of Land Management (BLM) *(Interior Dept.), Lands, Realty, and Cadastral Survey, 20 M St. S.E. 20003 (mailing address: 1849 C St. N.W., Washington, DC 20240); (202) 912-7300. Fax, (202) 912-7199. Robyn Shoop, Division Chief, Acting.*
Web, www.blm.gov/wo/st/en/info/directory/WO-350_dir.html

Oversees use, acquisition, and disposal of public lands. Conducts the Public Lands Survey; authorizes rights-of-way on public lands for uses that include roads, power lines, and wind and solar facilities.

Bureau of Reclamation *(Interior Dept.), 1849 C St. N.W., #7654, 7069 MIB 20240-0001; (202) 513-0501. Fax, (202) 513-0309. Michael L. Connor, Commissioner. Press, (202) 513-0575.*
Web, www.usbr.gov

Manages, develops, and protects water and related resources in seventeen western states, in partnership with states, tribes, and water and power customers. Water resource development projects include dams, power plants, and canals.

Interior Dept. (DOI), *Board of Land Appeals, 801 N. Quincy St., #300, Arlington, VA 22203; (703) 235-3750. Fax, (703) 235-3750. James S. Roberts, Chief Administrative Judge, Acting.*
Web, www.doi.gov/oha/ibla

Adjunct office of the interior secretary that decides appeals from decisions rendered by the Bureau of Land Management; the Bureau of Ocean Energy Management, Regulation, and Enforcement; the Office of Surface Mining and Reclamation Enforcement; and the Bureau of Indian Affairs concerning the use and disposition of public lands and minerals. Issues final decisions concerning the Surface Mining Control and Reclamation Act of 1977. Is separate and independent from bureaus and offices whose decisions it reviews.

Interior Dept. (DOI), *Land and Minerals Management, 1849 C St. N.W. 20240; (202) 208-6734. Fax, (202) 208-3619. Tommy P. Beaudreau, Assistant Secretary, Acting.*
Web, www.doi.gov

Directs and supervises the Bureau of Land Management; the Bureau of Ocean Energy Management, Regulation, and Enforcement; and the Office of Surface Mining and Reclamation Enforcement. Supervises programs associated with land-use planning, onshore and offshore minerals, surface mining reclamation and enforcement, and Outer Continental Shelf minerals management.

Interior Dept. (DOI), *Surface Mining Reclamation and Enforcement, 1951 Constitution Ave. N.W., #233 20240; (202) 208-4006. Fax, (202) 219-3106. Joseph G. Pizarchik, Director. Press, (202) 208-2565.*
General email, getinfo@osmre.gov
Web, www.osmre.gov

Regulates surface mining of coal and surface effects of underground coal mining. Responsible for reclamation of abandoned coal mine lands.

Natural Resources Conservation Service *(Agriculture Dept.), 1400 Independence Ave. S.W., #5105AS 20250 (mailing address: P.O. Box 2890, Washington, DC 20013-2890); (202) 720-4525. Fax, (202) 720-7690. Jason Weller, Chief, (202) 720-7246. Chief's Office, (202) 720-7246. Public Affairs, (202) 720-0693.*
Web, www.nrcs.usda.gov

Responsible for soil and water conservation programs, including watershed protection, flood prevention, river basin surveys, and resource conservation and development. Provides landowners, operators, state and local units of government, and community groups with technical assistance in carrying out local programs.

Tennessee Valley Authority, *Government Affairs, 1 Massachusetts Ave. N.W., #300 20444; (202) 898-2999. Fax, (202) 898-2998. Nick Pearson, Director.*

General email, latootle@tva.gov
Web, www.tva.gov

Coordinates resource conservation, development, and land-use programs in the Tennessee River Valley. Provides information on land usage in the region.

▶**CONGRESS**

For a listing of relevant congressional committees and subcommittees, please see pages 252–253 or the Appendix.

▶**NONGOVERNMENTAL**

American Geosciences Institute, *4220 King St., Alexandria, VA 22302-1502; (703) 379-2480. Fax, (703) 379-7563. P. Patrick Leahy, Executive Director.*
General email, agi@agiweb.org
Web, www.agiweb.org

Membership: earth science societies and associations. Provides education and outreach. Maintains computerized database of the world's geoscience literature (available to the public for a fee).

American Resort Development Assn., *1201 15th St. N.W., #400 20005; (202) 371-6700. Fax, (202) 289-8544. Howard Nusbaum, President.*
Web, www.arda.org

Membership: U.S. and international developers, builders, financiers, marketing companies, and others involved in resort, recreational, and community development. Serves as an information clearinghouse; monitors federal and state legislation affecting land, time share, and community development industries.

Land Trust Alliance, *1660 L St. N.W., #1100 20036; (202) 638-4725. Fax, (202) 638-4730. Rand Wentworth, President, (202) 800-2249.*
General email, info@lta.org
Web, www.landtrustalliance.org and Twitter, @italliance

Membership: organizations and individuals who work to conserve land resources. Serves as a forum for the exchange of information; conducts research and public education programs. Monitors legislation and regulations.

National Assn. of Conservation Districts (NACD), *509 Capitol Court N.E. 20002-4937; (202) 547-6223. Fax, (202) 547-6450. John Larson, Chief Executive Officer.*
General email, bethany-shively@nacdet.org
Web, www.nacdnet.org

Membership: conservation districts (local subdivisions of state government). Works to promote the conservation of land, forests, and other natural resources. Interests include erosion and sediment control; water quality; forestry, water, flood plain, and range management; rural development; and urban and community conservation.

Public Lands Council, *1301 Pennsylvania Ave. N.W., #300 20004-1701; (202) 347-0228. Fax, (202) 638-0607. Dustin Van Liew, Executive Director.*
Web, www.publiclandscouncil.org

Membership: cattle and sheep ranchers who hold permits and leases to graze livestock on public lands. (Affiliated with the National Cattlemen's Beef Association and the American Sheep Industry.)

Scenic America, *1307 New Hampshire Ave. N.W. 20036; (202) 463-1294. Fax, (202) 463-1299. Mary Tracy, President.*
General email, ashburn@scenic.org

Web, www.scenic.org

Membership: national, state, and local groups concerned with land-use control, growth management, and landscape protection. Works to enhance the scenic quality of America's communities and countryside. Provides information and technical assistance on scenic byways, tree preservation, economics of aesthetic regulation, billboard and sign control, scenic areas preservation, and growth management.

Wallace Genetic Foundation, *4910 Massachusetts Ave. N.W., #221 20016; (202) 966-2932. Fax, (202) 966-3370. Patricia M. Lee, Co-Executive Director; Carolyn H. Sand, Co-Executive Director.*
General email, info@wallacegenetic.org

Web, www.wallacegenetic.org

Supports national and international nonprofits in the areas of agricultural research, preservation of farmland, reduction of environmental toxins, conservation, biodiversity protection, global climate issues, and sustainable development.

Metals and Minerals

▶**AGENCIES**

Bureau of Land Management (BLM) *(Interior Dept.), Minerals and Realty Management, 1849 C St. N.W., #5625 20240; (202) 208-4201. Fax, (202) 208-4800. Mike Nedd, Assistant Director.*
General email, mnedd@blm.gov

Web, www.blm.gov/wo/st/en/info/directory.html

Evaluates and classifies onshore oil, natural gas, geothermal resources, and all solid energy and mineral resources, including coal and uranium, on federal lands. Develops and administers regulations for fluid and solid mineral leasing on national lands and on the subsurface of land where fluid and solid mineral rights have been reserved for the federal government.

Bureau of Safety and Environmental Enforcement (BSEE) *(Interior Dept.), Offshore Regulatory Programs, 1849 C St. N.W., MS DM 5438 20240-0001; (202) 208-3985. Fax, (202) 208-3968. Douglas Morris, Chief.*
General email, bseepublicaffairs@bsee.gov

Web, www.bsee.gov

Develops standards, regulations, and compliance programs governing Outer Continental Shelf oil, gas, and minerals exploration and operations. Purview includes safety management programs, safety and pollution prevention research, technology assessments, standards for inspections and enforcement policies, and accident investigation practices.

Interior Dept. (DOI), *Board of Land Appeals, 801 N. Quincy St., #300, Arlington, VA 22203; (703) 235-3750. Fax, (703) 235-3750. James S. Roberts, Chief Administrative Judge, Acting.*
Web, www.doi.gov/oha/ibla

Adjunct office of the interior secretary that decides appeals from decisions rendered by the Bureau of Land Management; the Bureau of Ocean Energy Management, Regulation, and Enforcement; the Office of Surface Mining and Reclamation Enforcement; and the Bureau of Indian Affairs concerning the use and disposition of public lands and minerals. Issues final decisions concerning the Surface Mining Control and Reclamation Act of 1977. Is separate and independent from bureaus and offices whose decisions it reviews.

Interior Dept. (DOI), *Land and Minerals Management, 1849 C St. N.W. 20240; (202) 208-6734. Fax, (202) 208-3619. Tommy P. Beaudreau, Assistant Secretary, Acting.*
Web, www.doi.gov

Directs and supervises the Bureau of Land Management; the Bureau of Ocean Energy Management, Regulation, and Enforcement; and the Office of Surface Mining and Reclamation Enforcement. Supervises programs associated with land-use planning, onshore and offshore minerals, surface mining reclamation and enforcement, and Outer Continental Shelf minerals management.

Interior Dept. (DOI), *Natural Resources Revenue, Washington Office, 1849 C St. N.W., MS4209 20240; (202) 513-0603. Fax, (202) 513-0682. Gregory J. (Greg) Gould, Director. Press, (303) 231-3162.*
Web, www.onrr.gov

Manages revenues associated with federal offshore and federal and American Indian onshore mineral leases, as well as revenues received through offshore renewable energy efforts. Collects and disburses all natural resources revenues.

Interior Dept. (DOI), *Water and Science, 1849 C St. N.W., #6657, MS 6640 20240; (202) 208-3186. Fax, (202) 208-6948. Anne Castle, Assistant Secretary.*
Web, www.doi.gov

Administers departmental water, scientific, and research activities. Directs and supervises the Bureau of Reclamation and the U.S. Geological Survey.

State Dept., *Energy Bureau, Policy Analysis and Public Diplomacy, 2201 C St. N.W., #4805 20520; (202) 647-2879. Fax, (202) 647-7431. Richard Westerdale, Director.*
Web, www.state.gov

Seeks to put energy security interests at the forefront of U.S. foreign policy. Objectives include increasing energy diplomacy with major producers and consumers; stimulating market forces toward energy development and reconstruction, with an emphasis on alternative energies and electricity; and promoting good governance and increased transparency to improve commercially viable and environmentally sustainable access to people without energy services.

U.S. Geological Survey (USGS) *(Interior Dept.)*, *Mineral Resources Program*, *913 National Center, Reston, VA 20192 (mailing address: 12201 Sunrise Valley Dr., #4A324, MS 913, Reston, VA 20192); (703) 648-6110. Fax, (703) 648-6057. Lawrence Meinert, Program Coordinator, (703) 648-6100.*
Web, www.minerals.usgs.gov

Coordinates mineral resource activities for the Geological Survey, including research and information on U.S. and international mineral resources, baseline information on earth materials, and geochemical and geophysical instrumentation and applications.

▶**CONGRESS**

For a listing of relevant congressional committees and subcommittees, please see pages 252–253 or the Appendix.

▶**NONGOVERNMENTAL**

Aluminum Assn., *1525 Wilson Blvd., #600, Arlington, VA 22209; (703) 358-2960. Fax, (703) 358-2961.*
Heidi Biggs Brock, President, (703) 358-2977. Press, (703) 358-2966.
Web, www.aluminum.org

Represents the aluminum industry. Develops voluntary standards and technical data; compiles statistics concerning the industry. Monitors legislation and regulations.

American Iron and Steel Institute (AISI), *Washington Office*, *25 Massachusetts Ave. N.W., #800 20001; (202) 452-7100. Fax, (202) 463-6573. Thomas Gibson, President. Press, (202) 452-7116.*
General email, steelnews@steel.org
Web, www.steel.org

Represents the iron and steel industry. Publishes statistics on iron and steel production; promotes the use of steel; conducts research. Monitors legislation and regulations. (Maintains offices in Southfields, Mich., and Pittsburgh, Pa.)

Mineralogical Society of America, *3635 Concorde Pkwy., #500, Chantilly, VA 20151-1125; (703) 652-9950. Fax, (703) 652-9951. David J. Vaughan, President.*
General email, business@minsocam.org
Web, www.minsocam.org

Membership: mineralogists, petrologists, crystallographers, geochemists, educators, students, and others interested in mineralogy. Conducts research; sponsors educational programs; promotes industrial application of mineral studies.

National Mining Assn., *101 Constitution Ave. N.W., #500 East 20001-2133; (202) 463-2600. Fax, (202) 463-2666. Harold P. Quinn Jr., President. Press, (202) 463-2667.*
General email, webmaster@nma.org
Web, www.nma.org

Membership: domestic producers of coal and industrial-agricultural minerals and metals; manufacturers of mining equipment; engineering and consulting firms; and financial institutions. Interests include mine-leasing programs, mine health and safety, research and development, public lands, and minerals availability. Monitors legislation and regulations.

Salt Institute, *700 N. Fairfax St., #600, Alexandria, VA 22314-2040; (703) 549-4648. Fax, (703) 548-2194.*
Lori Roman, President.
General email, info@saltinstitute.org
Web, www.saltinstitute.org

Membership: North American salt companies and overseas companies that produce dry salt for use in food, animal feed, highway de-icing, water softening, and chemicals. Monitors legislation and regulations.

Native American Trust Resources

▶**AGENCIES**

Bureau of Indian Affairs (BIA) *(Interior Dept.)*, *Trust Services*, *1849 C St. N.W., MS 4620-MIB 20240; (202) 208-5831. Fax, (202) 219-1255. Bryan Rice, Deputy Bureau Director.*
Web, www.bia.gov/WhoWeAre/BIA/OTS/index.htm

Assists in developing and managing bureau programs involving Native American trust resources (agriculture, forestry, wildlife, water, irrigation, real property management probate, and title records.)

Interior Dept. (DOI), *Natural Resources Revenue, Washington Office, 1849 C St. N.W., MS4209 20240; (202) 513-0603. Fax, (202) 513-0682. Gregory J. (Greg) Gould, Director. Press, (303) 231-3162.*
Web, www.onrr.gov

Manages revenues associated with federal offshore and federal and American Indian onshore mineral leases, as well as revenues received through offshore renewable energy efforts. Collects and disburses all natural resources revenues.

Interior Dept. (DOI), *Office of the Solicitor, Indian Affairs, 1849 C St. N.W., MS 6511 20240; (202) 208-3401. Fax, (202) 219-1791. Michael Berrigan, Associate Solicitor.*
Web, www.doi.gov

Advises the Bureau of Indian Affairs and the secretary of the interior on all legal matters, including its trust responsibilities toward Native Americans and their natural resources.

Justice Dept. (DOJ), *Indian Resources, 601 D St. N.W., #3507 20004 (mailing address: P.O. Box 7611, L'Enfant Plaza, Washington, DC 20044); (202) 305-0269. Fax, (202) 305-0271. S. Craig Alexander, Chief.*
Web, www.justice.gov/enrd/ENRD_irs.html

Represents the United States in suits, including trust violations, brought on behalf of individual Native Americans and Native American tribes against the government.

Also represents the United States as trustee for Native Americans in court actions involving protection of Native American land and resources.

► CONGRESS

For a listing of relevant congressional committees and subcommittees, please see pages 252–253 or the Appendix.

► NONGOVERNMENTAL

Native American Rights Fund, *Washington Office, 1514 P St. N.W., Suite D 20005; (202) 785-4166. Fax, (202) 822-0068. John E. Echohawk, Executive Director; Richard Guest, Managing Attorney.*
Web, www.narf.org

Provides Native Americans and Alaska Natives with legal assistance in land claims, water rights, hunting, and other areas. Practices federal Indian law. (Headquarters in Boulder, Colo.)

Ocean Resources

► AGENCIES

National Oceanic and Atmospheric Administration (NOAA) *(Commerce Dept.), Marine and Aviation Operations, 8403 Colesville Rd., #500, Silver Spring, MD 20910-3282; (301) 713-1045. Fax, (301) 713-1541. Rear Adm. David A. Score, Director. Press, (301) 713-7671.*
Web, www.omao.noaa.gov

Uniformed service of the Commerce Dept. that operates and manages NOAA's fleet of atmospheric, hydrographic, oceanographic, and fisheries research ships and aircraft. Supports NOAA's scientific programs.

National Oceanic and Atmospheric Administration (NOAA) *(Commerce Dept.), National Environmental Satellite, Data, and Information Service, 1335 East-West Hwy., SSMC1, 8th Floor, Silver Spring, MD 20910; (301) 713-3578. Fax, (301) 713-1249. Mary E. Kicza, Assistant Administrator.*
Web, www.nesdis.noaa.gov

Disseminates worldwide environmental data through a system of meteorological, oceanographic, geophysical, and solar-terrestrial data centers.

National Oceanic and Atmospheric Administration (NOAA) *(Commerce Dept.), National Marine Sanctuaries, 1305 East-West Hwy., 11th Floor, Silver Spring, MD 20910; (301) 713-3125. Fax, (301) 713-0404. Daniel J. Basta, Director.*
General email, sanctuaries@noaa.gov
Web, www.sanctuaries.noaa.gov and Twitter, @santuaries

Administers the National Marine Sanctuary Program, which seeks to protect the ecology and the recreational and cultural resources of marine and Great Lakes waters.

National Oceanic and Atmospheric Administration (NOAA) *(Commerce Dept.), National Sea Grant College Program, 1315 East-West Hwy., SSMC-3, 11th Floor, Silver Spring, MD 20910; (301) 734-1066. Fax, (301) 713-1031. Leon M. Cammen, Director.*
General email, oar.hq.sg@noaa.gov
Web, www.seagrant.noaa.gov

Provides institutions with grants for marine research, education, and advisory services; provides marine environmental information.

National Oceanic and Atmospheric Administration (NOAA) *(Commerce Dept.), Ocean and Coastal Resource Management, 1305 East-West Hwy., 10th Floor, SSMC4, Silver Spring, MD 20910; (301) 713-3155. Fax, (301) 713-4012. Margaret Davidson, Director, Acting.*
Web, http://coastalmanagement.noaa.gov

Administers the Coastal Zone Management Act and the National Estuarine Research Reserve System to carry out NOAA's goals for preservation, conservation, and restoration management of the ocean and coastal environment.

National Oceanic and Atmospheric Administration (NOAA) *(Commerce Dept.), Special Projects, 1305 East-West Hwy., Silver Spring, MD 20910; (301) 713-3000, ext. 111. Fax, (301) 713-4384. Brent Ache, Chief.*
Web, http://specialprojects.nos.noaa.gov

Conducts national studies and develops policies on ocean management and use along the U.S. coastline and the exclusive economic zone.

U.S. Geological Survey (USGS) *(Interior Dept.), Coastal and Marine Geology Program, 12201 Sunrise Valley Dr., Reston, VA 20192 (mailing address: USGS National Center, MS 915, Reston, VA 20192); (703) 648-6422. Fax, (703) 648-5464. John W. Haines, Program Coordinator.*
Web, http://marine.usgs.gov

Handles resource assessment, exploration research, and marine geologic and environmental studies on U.S. coastal regions and the Outer Continental Shelf.

► CONGRESS

For a listing of relevant congressional committees and subcommittees, please see pages 252–253 or the Appendix.

► NONGOVERNMENTAL

Blue Frontier Campaign, *1530 P St. N.W. 20005 (mailing address: P.O. Box 19367, Washington, DC 20036); (202) 387-8030. Fax, (202) 234-5176. David Helvarg, Executive Director.*
General email, info@bluefront.org
Web, www.bluefront.org

Promotes ocean conservation. Seeks to strengthen unity among ocean conservationists and encourage public awareness at the local, regional, and national levels.

Coastal States Organization, *444 N. Capitol St. N.W., #638 20001; (202) 508-3860. Fax, (202) 508-3843. Mary Munson, Executive Director.*
General email, cso@coastalstates.org
Web, www.coastalstates.org

Nonpartisan organization that represents governors of thirty-five U.S. coastal states, territories, and commonwealths on management of coastal, Great Lakes, and marine resources. Interests include ocean dumping, coastal pollution, wetlands preservation and restoration, national oceans policy, and the Outer Continental Shelf. Gathers and analyzes data to assess state coastal needs; sponsors and participates in conferences and workshops.

Joint Ocean Commission Initiative, *c/o Meridian Institute, 1920 L St. N.W., #500 20036; (202) 354-6444. Fax, (202) 354-6441. Laura Cantral, Director.*
General email, lcantral@merid.org
Web, www.jointoceancommission.org

Provides policy information on ocean conservation and releases Ocean Policy Report Cards that analyze the effectiveness of policy initiatives on ocean and coast protection. (Formed by the U.S. Commission on Ocean Policy and the Pew Oceans Commission.)

Marine Technology Society, *1100 H St. N.W., #LL-100 20005; (202) 717-8705. Fax, (202) 347-4302. Richard Lawson, Executive Director.*
General email, membership@mtsociety.org
Web, www.mtsociety.org

Membership: scientists, engineers, technologists, and others interested in marine science and technology. Provides information on marine science, technology, and education.

National Ocean Industries Assn., *1120 G St. N.W., #900 20005; (202) 347-6900. Fax, (202) 347-8650. Randall Luthi, President.*
General email, noia@noia.org
Web, www.noia.org

Membership: manufacturers, producers, suppliers, and support and service companies involved in marine, offshore, and ocean work. Interests include offshore oil and gas supply and production, deep-sea mining, ocean thermal energy, and new energy sources.

Oceana, *1350 Connecticut Ave. N.W., #500 20036; (202) 833-3900. Fax, (202) 833-2070. Andrew F. Sharpless, Chief Executive Officer. Toll-free, (877) 7-OCEANA.*
General email, info@oceana.org
Web, www.oceana.org

Promotes ocean conservation both nationally and internationally; pursues policy changes to reduce pollution and protect fish, marine mammals, and other forms of sea life. Conducts specific two- to five-year scientific, legal, policy, and advocacy campaigns. Monitors legislation and regulations.

Parks and Recreation Areas

▶ AGENCIES

Bureau of Land Management (BLM) *(Interior Dept.), Cultural, Paleontological Resources, and Tribal Consultation, 20 M St. S.E. 20003 (mailing address: 1849 C St. N.W., Washington, DC 20240); (202) 912-7208. Fax, (202) 245-0015. Byron Loosle, Division Chief.*
Web, www.blm.gov/wo/st/en/prog/more/CRM.html

Identifies and manages cultural heritage and recreation programs on public lands.

Bureau of Land Management (BLM) *(Interior Dept.), Recreation, Heritage, and Visitor Services, 20 M St. S.E., 6th Floor 20003 (mailing address: 1849 C St. N.W., Washington, DC 20240); (202) 912-7256. Fax, (202) 912-7362. Robn Morgan, Director, Acting, (202) 912-7094.*
Web, www.blm.gov/wo/st/en/info/directory/WO-250_dir .html

Develops recreation opportunities on public lands.

Bureau of Reclamation *(Interior Dept.), 1849 C St. N.W., #7654, 7069 MIB 20240-0001; (202) 513-0501. Fax, (202) 513-0309. Michael L. Connor, Commissioner. Press, (202) 513-0575.*
Web, www.usbr.gov

Responsible for acquisition, administration, management, and disposal of lands in seventeen western states associated with bureau water resource development projects. Provides overall policy guidance for land-use, including agreements with public agencies for outdoor recreation, fish and wildlife enhancement, and land-use authorizations such as leases, licenses, permits, and rights of way. Interests include increasing water-based outdoor recreation facilities and opportunities.

Forest Service *(Agriculture Dept.), Recreation, Heritage, and Volunteer Resources, 1621 N. Kent St., Arlington, VA 22209; (202) 205-1240. Fax, (703) 605-5105. Robn Morgan, Director, Acting, (202) 205-1145.*
Web, www.fs.fed.us/recreation

Develops policy and sets guidelines on administering national forests and grasslands for recreational purposes. (The Forest Service administers some of the lands designated as national recreation areas.)

Interior Dept. (DOI), *Fish, Wildlife, and Parks, 1849 C St. N.W., #3156 20240; (202) 208-4416. Fax, (202) 208-4684. Rachel L. Jacobson, Principal Assistant Secretary.*
Web, www.doi.gov

Responsible for programs associated with the development, conservation, and use of fish, wildlife, recreational, historical, and national park system resources. Coordinates marine environmental quality and biological resources programs with other federal agencies.

National Park Service (NPS) *(Interior Dept.), 1849 C St. N.W., #3115 20240; (202) 208-4621. Fax, (202) 208-7889. Jonathan B. Jarvis, Director. Press, (202) 208-6843.*

General email, asknps@nps.gov

Web, www.nps.gov and Twitter, @NatlParkService

Administers national parks, monuments, historic sites, and recreation areas. Oversees coordination, planning, and financing of public outdoor recreation programs at all levels of government. Conducts recreation research surveys; administers financial assistance program to states for planning and development of outdoor recreation programs. (Some lands designated as national recreation areas are not under NPS jurisdiction.)

National Park Service (NPS) *(Interior Dept.), Policy,* 1201 Eye St. N.W., 12th Floor 20005 (mailing address: 1849 C St. N.W., Washington, DC 20240); (202) 354-3950. Fax, (202) 371-5189. Alma Ripps, Chief.
Web, www.nps.gov/policy

Researches and develops management policy on matters relating to the National Park Service; makes recommendations on the historical significance of national trails and landmarks.

Tennessee Valley Authority, *Government Affairs,* 1 Massachusetts Ave. N.W., #300 20444; (202) 898-2999. Fax, (202) 898-2998. Nick Pearson, Director.
General email, latootle@tva.gov

Web, www.tva.gov

Operates Land Between the Lakes, a national recreation and environmental education area located in western Kentucky and Tennessee.

U.S. Fish and Wildlife Service *(Interior Dept.), National Wildlife Refuge System,* 1849 C St. N.W., #3349 20240; (202) 208-5333. Fax, (202) 208-3082. James W. Kurth, Chief.
Web, www.fws.gov/refuges

Manages the National Wildlife Refuge System. Most refuges are open to public use; activities include bird and wildlife watching, fishing, hunting, and environmental education.

▶ **CONGRESS**

For a listing of relevant congressional committees and subcommittees, please see pages 252–253 or the Appendix.

▶ **NONGOVERNMENTAL**

American Hiking Society, 1422 Fenwick Lane, Silver Spring, MD 20910-3328; (301) 565-6704. Fax, (301) 565-6714. Gregory Miller, President. Toll-free, (800) 972-8608.
General email, info@americanhiking.org

Web, www.americanhiking.org

Membership: individuals and clubs interested in preserving America's trail system and protecting the interests of trail users. Provides information on outdoor volunteer opportunities on public lands.

American Recreation Coalition, 1200 G St. N.W., #650 20005; (202) 682-9530. Fax, (202) 682-9529. Derrick A. Crandall, President.

General email, arc@funoutdoors.com

Web, www.funoutdoors.com

Membership: recreation industry associations, recreation enthusiast groups, and leading corporations in the recreation products and services sectors. Promotes health and well-being through recreation.

National Park Foundation, 1201 Eye St. N.W., #550B 20005; (202) 354-6460. Fax, (202) 371-2066. Neil Mulholland, President; Hon. Sally Jewell, Chair.
General email, ask-npf@nationalparks.org

Web, www.nationalparks.org

Encourages private sector support of the national park system; provides grants and sponsors educational and cultural activities. Chartered by Congress and chaired by the interior secretary.

National Parks Conservation Assn., 777 6th St. N.W., #700 20001-3723; (202) 223-6722. Fax, (202) 454-3333. Clark Bunting, President. Information, (800) 628-7275.
General email, npca@npca.org

Web, www.npca.org

Citizens' interest group that seeks to protect national parks and other park system areas.

National Park Trust, 401 E. Jefferson St., #203, Rockville, MD 20850; (301) 279-7275. Fax, (301) 279-7211. Grace K. Lee, Executive Director.
General email, npt@parktrust.org

Web, www.parktrust.org

Protects national parks, wildlife refuges, and historic monuments. Uses funds to purchase private land within or adjacent to existing parks and land suitable for new parks; works with preservation organizations to manage acquired resources.

National Recreation and Park Assn., 22377 Belmont Ridge Rd., Ashburn, VA 20148-4501; (703) 858-0784. Fax, (703) 858-0794. Barbara Tulipane, Chief Executive Officer, (703) 858-2144. Toll-free, (800) 626-6772.
General email, customerservice@nrpa.org

Web, www.nrpa.org

Membership: park and recreation professionals and interested citizens. Promotes support and awareness of park, recreation, and leisure services; advances environmental and conservation efforts; facilitates development, expansion, and management of resources; provides technical assistance for park and recreational programs; and provides professional development to members. Monitors legislation and regulations.

Rails-to-Trails Conservancy, 2121 Ward Court N.W., 5th Floor 20037; (202) 331-9696. Fax, (202) 223-9257. Keith Laughlin, President.
General email, info@railtrails.org

Web, www.railstotrails.org

Promotes the conversion of abandoned railroad corridors into hiking and biking trails for public use. Provides public education programs and technical and legal assistance. Publishes trail guides. Monitors legislation and regulations.

Scenic America, *1307 New Hampshire Ave. N.W. 20036; (202) 463-1294. Fax, (202) 463-1299. Mary Tracy, President.*
General email, ashburn@scenic.org
Web, www.scenic.org

Membership: national, state, and local groups concerned with land-use control, growth management, and landscape protection. Works to enhance the scenic quality of America's communities and countryside. Provides information and technical assistance on scenic byways, tree preservation, economics of aesthetic regulation, billboard and sign control, scenic areas preservation, and growth management.

Student Conservation Assn., *Washington Office, 4245 N. Fairfax Dr., #825, Arlington, VA 22203; (703) 524-2441. Dale Penny, President.*
General email, DCinfo@thesca.org
Web, www.thesca.org

Service organization that provides youth and adults with opportunities for training and work experience in natural resource management and conservation. Volunteers serve in national parks, forests, wildlife refuges, and other public lands.

World Wildlife Fund (WWF), *1250 24th St. N.W. 20037-1193 (mailing address: P.O. Box 97180, Washington, DC 20090-7180); (202) 293-4800. Fax, (202) 293-9211. Carter S. Roberts, President.*
Web, www.worldwildlife.org

International conservation organization that provides funds and technical assistance for establishing and maintaining parks.

Water Resources

▶**AGENCIES**

Army Corps of Engineers *(Defense Dept.), 441 G St. N.W., #3K05 20314-1000; (202) 761-0001. Fax, (202) 761-4463. Lt. Gen. Thomas Bostick, Chief of Engineers.*
General email, hq-publicaffairs@usace.army.mil
Web, www.usace.army.mil

Provides local governments with disaster relief, flood control, navigation, and hydroelectric power services.

Bureau of Reclamation *(Interior Dept.), 1849 C St. N.W., #7654, 7069 MIB 20240-0001; (202) 513-0501. Fax, (202) 513-0309. Michael L. Connor, Commissioner. Press, (202) 513-0575.*
Web, www.usbr.gov

Administers federal programs for water and power resource development and management in seventeen western states; oversees municipal and industrial water supplies, hydroelectric power generation, irrigation, flood control, water quality improvement, river regulation, fish and wildlife enhancement, and outdoor recreation.

Environmental Protection Agency (EPA), *Wetlands, Oceans, and Watersheds, 1200 Pennsylvania Ave. N.W.,* *#7231A, MC 4502T 20460; Fax, (202) 566-1349. Benita Best-Wong, Director, (202) 566-1146; Jim Pendergast, Director, Wetlands, Acting, (202) 566-1348; Tom Wall, Director, Assessment and Watershed Protection, (202) 566-1155; Paul F. Cough, Director, Oceans and Coastal Protection, (202) 566-1200.*
General email, ow-owow-internet-comments@epa.gov
Web, www2.epa.gov/aboutepa/about-office-water#wetlands

Coordinates federal policies affecting marine and freshwater ecosystems, including watersheds, coastal ecosystems, and wetlands. Regulates and monitors ocean dumping; seeks to minimize polluted runoff and restore impaired waters. Manages dredge-and-fill program under section 404 of the Clean Water Act. Promotes public awareness of resource preservation and management.

Interstate Commission on the Potomac River Basin, *30 W. Gude Dr., #450, Rockville, MD 20850; (301) 984-1908. Fax, (301) 984-5841. Carlton Haywood, Executive Director.*
General email, info@icprb.org
Web, www.potomacriver.org

Nonregulatory interstate compact commission established by Congress to control and reduce water pollution and to restore and protect living resources in the Potomac River and its tributaries. Monitors water quality; assists metropolitan water utilities; seeks innovative methods to solve water supply and land resource problems. Provides information and educational materials on the Potomac River basin.

Office of Management and Budget (OMB) *(Executive Office of the President), Water and Power, New Executive Office Bldg., #8002 20503; (202) 395-4590. Fax, (202) 395-4817. Kelly Colyar, Chief.*
Web, www.whitehouse.gov/omb

Reviews all plans and budgets related to federal or federally assisted water power and related land resource projects.

Rural Development *(Agriculture Dept.), Rural Utilities Service, 1400 Independence Ave. S.W., #5135-S, MS 1510 20250-1510; (202) 720-9540. Fax, (202) 720-1725. John Chas Padalino, Administrator. Information, (202) 720-1255.*
Web, www.rurdeve.usda.gov/utilities_assistance.html and www.rurdeve.usda.gov/utilities_LP.html

Makes loans and provides technical assistance for development, repair, and replacement of water and waste disposal systems in rural areas.

Smithsonian Environmental Research Center *(Smithsonian Institution), 647 Contees Wharf Rd., Edgewater, MD 21037 (mailing address: P.O. Box 28, Edgewater, MD 21037-0028); (443) 482-2200. Fax, (443) 482-2380. Anson H. Hines, Director. Press, (443) 482-2325.*
Web, www.serc.si.edu

Serves as a research center on water ecosystems in the coastal zone.

Tennessee Valley Authority, *Government Affairs,*
1 Massachusetts Ave. N.W., #300 20444; (202) 898-2999.
Fax, (202) 898-2998. Nick Pearson, Director.
General email, latootle@tva.gov
Web, www.tva.gov

Coordinates resource conservation, development, and land-use programs in the Tennessee River Valley. Operates the river control system; projects include flood control, navigation development, and multiple-use reservoirs.

U.S. Geological Survey (USGS) *(Interior Dept.), Water,*
12201 Sunrise Valley Dr., MS 150, Reston, VA 20192; (703) 648-4557. Fax, (703) 648-4588. Jerad Bales, Associate Director, Acting, (703) 648-5044.
Web, http://water.usgs.gov

Administers the Water Resources Research Act of 1990. Monitors and assesses the quantity and quality of the nation's freshwater resources; collects, analyzes, and disseminates data on water use and the effect of human activity and natural phenomena on hydrologic systems; assesses sources and behavior of contaminants in the water environment, and develops tools to improve management and understanding of water resources. Provides federal agencies, state and local governments, international organizations, and foreign governments with scientific and technical assistance.

▶ **CONGRESS**

For a listing of relevant congressional committees and subcommittees, please see pages 252–253 or the Appendix.

▶ **NONGOVERNMENTAL**

American Rivers, *1101 14th St. N.W., #1400 20005; (202) 347-7550. Fax, (202) 347-9240. William Robert (Bob) Irvin, President.*
General email, outreach@americanrivers.org
Web, www.americanrivers.org

Works to preserve and protect the nation's river systems through public information and advocacy. Collaborates with grassroots river and watershed groups, other conservation groups, sporting and recreation groups, businesses, local citizens, and various federal, state, and tribal agencies. Monitors legislation and regulations.

American Water Works Assn., *Washington Office, 1300 Eye St. N.W., #701W 20005; (202) 628-8303. Fax, (202) 628-2846. Tom Curtis, Deputy Executive Director.*
Web, www.awwa.org

Membership: municipal water utilities, manufacturers of equipment for water industries, water treatment companies, and individuals. Provides information on drinking water treatment and trends and issues affecting water safety; publishes voluntary standards for the water industry; issues policy statements on water supply matters. Monitors legislation and regulations. (Headquarters in Denver, Colo.)

Assn. of State Drinking Water Administrators (ASDWA),
1401 Wilson Blvd., #1225, Arlington, VA 22209; (703) 812-9505. Fax, (703) 812-9506. James D. Taft, Executive Director.
General email, info@asdwa.org
Web, www.asdwa.org

Membership: state officials responsible for the drinking water supply and enforcement of safety standards. Monitors legislation and regulations.

Environmental Defense Fund, *Washington Office, 1875 Connecticut Ave. N.W., #600 20009-5728; (202) 387-3500. Fax, (202) 234-6049. Diane Regas, Senior Vice President. Information, (800) 684-3322. Press, (202) 572-3396.*
Web, www.edf.org

Citizens' interest group staffed by lawyers, economists, and scientists. Takes legal action on environmental issues; provides information on pollution prevention, environmental health, water resources, and water marketing. (Headquarters in New York.)

Irrigation Assn., *6540 Arlington Blvd., Falls Church, VA 22042-6638; (703) 536-7080. Fax, (703) 536-7019. Deborah Hamlin, Executive Director.*
General email, info@irrigation.org
Web, www.irrigation.org

Membership: companies and individuals involved in irrigation, drainage, and erosion control worldwide. Promotes efficient and effective water management through training, education, and certification programs. Interests include economic development and environmental enhancement.

Izaak Walton League of America, *707 Conservation Lane, Gaithersburg, MD 20878-2983; (301) 548-0150. Fax, (301) 548-0146. Scott Kovarovics, Executive Director. Toll-free, (800) 453-5463.*
General email, info@iwla.org
Web, www.iwla.org

Grassroots organization that promotes conservation of natural resources and the environment. Coordinates a citizen action program to monitor and improve the condition of local streams.

National Assn. of Conservation Districts (NACD), *509 Capitol Court N.E. 20002-4937; (202) 547-6223. Fax, (202) 547-6450. John Larson, Chief Executive Officer.*
General email, bethany-shively@nacdet.org
Web, www.nacdnet.org

Membership: conservation districts (local subdivisions of state government). Develops national policies and works to promote the conservation of water resources. Interests include erosion and sediment control and control of nonpoint source pollution.

National Assn. of Flood and Stormwater Management Agencies (NAFSMA), *1333 H St. N.W., West Tower, 10th Floor 20005 (mailing address: P.O. Box 56764, Washington, DC 20040); (202) 289-8625. Fax, (202) 530-3389. Susan Gilson, Executive Director.*

General email, sgilson@nafsma.org

Web, www.nafsma.org

Membership: state, county, and local governments, and special flood management districts concerned with management of water resources. Interests include stormwater management, disaster assistance, flood insurance, and federal flood management policy. Monitors legislation and regulations.

National Assn. of Regulatory Utility Commissioners, *1101 Vermont Ave. N.W., #200 20005-3521; (202) 898-2200. Fax, (202) 898-2213. Charles D. Gray, Executive Director.*

General email, admin@naruc.org

Web, www.naruc.org

Membership: members of federal, state, municipal, and international regulatory commissions that have jurisdiction over utilities. Interests include water.

National Assn. of Water Companies (NAWC), *2001 L St. N.W., #850 20036; (202) 833-8383. Fax, (202) 331-7442. Michael Deane, Executive Director.*

General email, info@nawc.com

Web, www.nawc.org

Membership: privately owned, regulated water companies. Provides members with information on legislative and regulatory issues and other subjects.

National Utility Contractors Assn. (NUCA), *3925 Chain Bridge Rd., Fairfax, VA 22030; (703) 358-9300. Fax, (703) 358-9307. Bill Hillman, Chief Executive Officer.*

Web, www.nuca.com

Membership: contractors who perform water, sewer, and other underground utility construction. Sponsors conferences; conducts surveys. Monitors public works legislation and regulations.

National Water Resources Assn. (NWRA), *4 E St. S.E. 20003; (202) 698-0693. Fax, (202) 698-0694. Tom Myrum, President; Robert Johnson, Executive Vice President.*

General email, nwra@nwra.org

Web, http://nwra.org

Membership: conservation and irrigation districts, municipalities, and others interested in water resources. Works for the development and maintenance of water resources and a sustainable water supply. Represents interests of members before Congress and regulatory agencies.

Rural Community Assistance Partnership (RCAP), *1701 K St. N.W., #700 20006; (202) 408-1273. Fax, (202) 408-8165. Robert Stewart, Executive Director. Toll-free, (800) 321-7227.*

General email, info@rcap.org

Web, www.rcap.org

Provides expertise to rural communities on wastewater disposal, protection of groundwater supply, and access to safe drinking water. Targets communities with predominantly low-income or minority populations. Offers outreach policy analysis, training, and technical assistance to elected officials and other community leaders, utility owners and operators, and residents.

9 🏛

Government Operations

GENERAL POLICY AND ANALYSIS

Basic Resources

▶AGENCIES

Domestic Policy Council *(Executive Office of the President), The White House 20502; (202) 456-5594. Fax, (202) 456-3213. Cecilia Muñoz, Director.*
Web, www.whitehouse.gov/dpc

Comprised of cabinet officials and staff members. Coordinates the domestic policy-making process to facilitate the implementation of the president's domestic agenda throughout federal agencies in such major domestic policy areas as agriculture, education, energy, environment, health, housing, labor, and veterans affairs.

Executive Office of the President, *Public Engagement, Dwight D. Eisenhower Executive Office Bldg., #110 20502; (202) 456-1097. Fax, (202) 456-1641. Stephanie Valencia, Director, Acting.*
Web, www.whitehouse.gov/engage

Promotes presidential priorities through outreach to concerned constituencies and public interest groups.

Federal Bureau of Investigation (FBI) *(Justice Dept.), Congressional Affairs, 935 Pennsylvania Ave. N.W., #7240 20535; (202) 324-5051. Fax, (202) 324-6490. Stephen D. Kelly, Assistant Director.*
Web, www.fbi.gov

Provides information to Congress about FBI activities.

General Services Administration (GSA), *1800 F St. N.W. 20405; (202) 501-0800. Daniel M. Tangherlini, Administrator; Denise Turner Roth, Deputy Administrator; Brian D. Miller, Inspector General, (202) 501-0450. Press, (202) 501-1231.*
Web, www.gsa.gov and Twitter, @DanGSA

Establishes policies for managing federal government property, including construction and operation of buildings and procurement and distribution of supplies and equipment; manages transportation and telecommunications. Manages disposal of surplus federal property. Responsible for www.USA.gov.

General Services Administration (GSA), *Citizen Services and Innovative Technologies, 1275 1st St. N.E. 20417; (202) 501-0705. Fax, (202) 357-0077. David L. McClure, Associate Administrator.*
Web, www.gsa.gov

Identifies and applies new technologies to improve the way the federal government provides the public with access to information and services. Administers the Web site www.USA.gov, a comprehensive search engine of government information; call (800) FED-INFO for information by phone.

General Services Administration (GSA), *Government-wide Policy, 1275 1st St. N.E., 6th Floor 20417; (202) 501-8880. Fax, (202) 208-1224. Anne E. Rung, Associate Administrator.*
Web, www.gsa.gov/ogp

Coordinates GSA policy-making activities, including areas of personal and real property, travel and transportation, acquisition (internal GSA and governmentwide), information technology, regulatory information, and use of federal advisory committees; promotes collaboration between government and the private sector in developing policy and management techniques; works to integrate acquisition, management, and disposal of government property.

General Services Administration (GSA), *Government-wide Policy, Acquisition Policy, 1275 1st St. N.E. 20417; (202) 501-0692. Fax, (202) 357-0038. Jeffrey A. (Jeff) Koses, Senior Procurement Executive.*
General email, askacquisition@gsa.gov
Web, www.gsa.gov/chiefacquisitionofficer

Develops and implements federal government acquisition policies and procedures; administers Federal Acquisition Regulation (FAR) for civilian agencies. Manages several GSA-specific and governmentwide acquisition database systems. Conducts pre-award and post-award contract reviews; suspends and debars contractors for unsatisfactory performance; coordinates and promotes governmentwide career management and training programs for contracting personnel.

General Services Administration (GSA), *National Contact Center, 1275 1st St. N.E. 20417; (800) 333-4636. Mary Ann Monroe, Division Director, (202) 501-4179. Chat and email options (8:00 a.m.–8:00 p.m. Eastern time), answers.usa.gov*
Web, www.usa.gov

Responds to inquiries about federal programs and services. Gives information about or referrals to appropriate offices.

National Archives and Records Administration (NARA), *Federal Register, 800 N. Capitol St. N.W., #700 20001 (mailing address: FP, 8601 Adelphi Rd., College Park, MD 20740-6001); (202) 741-6000. Fax, (202) 741-6012. Charley Barth, Director. Public Laws Update Service (PLUS), (202) 741-6043.*
General email, fedreg.info@nara.gov
Web, www.archives.gov/federal_register

Informs citizens of their rights and obligations by providing access to the official texts of federal laws; presidential documents; administrative regulations and notices; and descriptions of federal organizations, programs, and activities. Provides online and in-person access to documents on file before their publication. Administers the Electoral College and the constitutional amendment process. Publications available from the U.S. Government Printing Office, (301) 317-3953, http://bookstore.gpo.gov.

Office of Administration *(Executive Office of the President), 725 17th St. N.W., #240 20503; (202) 456-2861. Elizabeth (Beth) Jones, Director.*
Web, www.whitehouse.gov/oa

Provides administrative support services to the Executive Office of the President, including financial management and information technology support, human resources

GOVERNMENT OPERATIONS RESOURCES IN CONGRESS

For a complete listing of Congress committees, including their full contact information, leadership, membership, and jurisdictions, please refer to the Appendix on pages 724–842.

HOUSE:

House Administration Committee, (202) 225-8281.
Web, cha.house.gov or democrats.cha.house.gov

House Agriculture Committee, (202) 225-2171.
Web, agriculture.house.gov or
  democrats.agriculture.house.gov
  Subcommittee on Department Operations,
    Oversight, and Nutrition, (202) 225-2171.

House Appropriations Committee, (202) 225-2771.
Web, appropriations.house.gov or
  democrats.appropriations.house.gov
  Subcommittee on Commerce, Justice, Science,
    and Related Agencies, (202) 225-3351.
  Subcommittee on Financial Services and General
    Government, (202) 225-7245.
  Subcommittee on Legislative Branch,
    (202) 226-7252.

House Budget Committee, (202) 226-7270.
Web, budget.house.gov or
  democrats.budget.house.gov

House Education and the Workforce Committee,
  (202) 225-4527.
Web, edworkforce.house.gov or
  democrats.edworkforce.house.gov
  Subcommittee on Workforce Protections,
    (202) 225-4527.

House Energy and Commerce Committee,
  (202) 225-2927.
Web, energycommerce.house.gov or
  democrats.energycommerce.house.gov
  Subcommittee on Oversight and Investigations,
    (202) 225-2927.

House Ethics Committee, (202) 225-7103.
Web, ethics.house.gov

House Financial Services Committee, (202) 225-7502.
Web, financialservices.house.gov or
  democrats.financialservices.house.gov
  Subcommittee on Oversight and Investigations,
    (202) 225-7502.

House Homeland Security Committee, (202) 226-8417.
Web, homeland.house.gov or chsdemocrats.house.gov
  Subcommittee on Oversight and Management
    Efficiency, (202) 226-8417.

House Judiciary Committee, (202) 225-3951.
Web, judiciary.house.gov or
  democrats.judiciary.house.gov
  Subcommittee on the Constitution and Civil
    Justice, (202) 225-2825.

House Oversight and Government Reform
  Committee, (202) 225-5074.
Web, oversight.house.gov or
  democrats.oversight.house.gov
  Subcommittee on Energy Policy, Health Care,
    and Entitlements, (202) 225-5074.
  Subcommittee on Federal Workforce, U.S. Postal
    Service, and the Census, (202) 225-5074.
  Subcommittee on Government Operations,
    (202) 225-5074.

House Rules Committee, (202) 225-9191.
Web, rules.house.gov or democrats.rules.house.gov

House Science, Space, and Technology Committee,
  (202) 225-6371.
Web, science.house.gov or democrats.science.house.gov
  Subcommittee on Oversight, (202) 225-6371.

---

management, library and research assistance, facilities management, procurement, printing and graphics support, security, and mail and messenger operations.

Office of Management and Budget (OMB) *(Executive Office of the President), Eisenhower Executive Office Bldg., #208 20503; (202) 395-4840. Sylvia Burwell, Director. Press, (202) 395-7254.*
Web, www.whitehouse.gov/omb

Works with other federal agencies to develop and maintain the Web site ExpectMore.gov, which uses the Program Assessment Rating Tool (PART) to gauge the effectiveness of federal programs. Holds programs accountable for improving their performance and management.

Office of Management and Budget (OMB) *(Executive Office of the President), Federal Procurement Policy, New Executive Office Bldg., #9013 20503; (202) 395-5802. Fax, (202) 395-5105. Lesley A. Field, Administrator, Acting.*
Web, www.whitehouse.gov/omb/procurement

Oversees and coordinates government procurement policies, regulations, and procedures. Responsible for cost accounting rules governing federal contractors and subcontractors. Interests include effective use of competition, cost effective contracting for vehicles, and managing a useful information technology system for federal procurement managers.

Office of Management and Budget (OMB) *(Executive Office of the President), Information and Regulatory Affairs, New Executive Office Bldg., #10236 20503; (202) 395-3785. Fax, (202) 395-5167. Boris Bershteyn, Administrator, Acting.*
Web, www.whitehouse.gov/omb/inforeg_infopoltech

Oversees development of federal regulatory programs. Supervises agency information management activities in accordance with the Paperwork Reduction Act of 1995, as amended; reviews agency analyses of the effect of government regulatory activities on the U.S. economy.

House Small Business Committee, (202) 225-5821.
Web, smallbusiness.house.gov or
democrats.smallbusiness.house.gov
   Subcommittee on Investigations, Oversight, and
Regulations, (202) 225-5821.
House Veterans' Affairs Committee,
(202) 225-3527.
Web, veterans.house.gov or
democrats.veterans.house.gov
   Subcommittee on Oversight and Investigations,
(202) 225-3569.
House Ways and Means Committee, (202) 225-3625.
Web, waysandmeans.house.gov or
democrats.waysandmeans.house.gov
   Subcommittee on Oversight, (202) 225-5522.

SENATE:

Senate Appropriations Committee, (202) 224-7363.
Web, appropriations.senate.gov
   Subcommittee on Commerce, Justice,
Science, and Related Agencies,
(202) 224-5202.
   Subcommittee on Financial Services and General
Government, (202) 224-1133.
   Subcommittee on Legislative Branch,
(202) 224-7256.
Senate Budget Committee, (202) 224-0642.
Web, www.budget.senate.gov/democratic/ or
www.budget.senate.gov/republican/public/
Senate Environment and Public Works Committee,
(202) 224-8832.
Web, epw.senate.gov

   Subcommittee on Oversight, (202) 224-8832.
   Subcommittee on Transportation and
Infrastructure, (202) 224-8832.
Senate Finance Committee, (202) 224-4515.
Web, finance.senate.gov
   Subcommittee on Fiscal Responsibility and
Economic Growth, (202) 224-4515.
Senate Homeland Security and Governmental Affairs
Committee, (202) 224-2627.
Web, hsgac.senate.gov
   Permanent Subcommittee on Investigations,
(202) 224-9505.
   Subcommittee on Efficiency and Effectiveness of
Federal Programs and the Federal Workforce,
(202) 224-2627.
   Subcommittee on Emergency Management,
Intergovernmental Relations, and the District
of Columbia, (202) 224-2627.
   Subcommittee on Financial and Contracting
Oversight, (202) 224-4462.
Senate Judiciary Committee, (202) 224-7703.
Web, judiciary.senate.gov
   Subcommittee on Oversight, Federal Rights, and
Agency Actions, (202) 224-7703.
Senate Rules and Administration Committee,
(202) 224-6352.
Web, rules.senate.gov
Senate Select Committee on Ethics, (202) 224-2981.
Web, ethics.senate.gov
Senate Small Business and Entrepreneurship
Committee, (202) 224-5175.
Web, sbc.senate.gov

Office of Management and Budget (OMB) *(Executive Office of the President), Performance and Personnel Management,* New Executive Office Bldg., 725 17th St. N.W., #7236 20503; (202) 395-5017. Fax, (202) 395-5738. *Dustin Brown, Deputy Assistant Director.*
Web, www.whitehouse.gov/omb/performance

Examines, evaluates, and suggests improvements for agencies and programs within the Office of Personnel Management and the Executive Office of the President.

Regulatory Information Service Center *(General Services Administration),* 1275 1st St. N.E., 6th Floor 20417; (202) 482-7340. Fax, (202) 482-7360. *John C. Thomas, Director.*
General email, risc@gsa.gov

Web, www.gsa.gov/risc

Provides the president, Congress, and the public with information on federal regulatory policies and their effects on society; recommends ways to make regulatory

information more accessible to government officials and the public. Publishes the *Unified Agenda of Federal Regulatory and Deregulatory Actions.* See www.reginfo.gov for information about government regulations.

▶ **CONGRESS**

For a listing of relevant congressional committees and subcommittees, please see pages 290–291 or the Appendix.

Government Accountability Office (GAO), 441 G St. N.W. 20548; (202) 512-5500. Fax, (202) 512-5507. *Gene L. Dodaro, Comptroller General. Information, (202) 512-3000. Publications and Documents, (202) 512-6000. Congressional Relations, (202) 512-4400.*
Web, www.gao.gov

Independent, nonpartisan agency in the legislative branch. Serves as the investigating agency for Congress; carries out legal, accounting, auditing, and claims settlement

White House Offices

OFFICE OF THE PRESIDENT

President, Barack Obama

> 1600 Pennsylvania Ave. N.W., 20500; (202) 456-1414,
> Fax (202) 456-2461
> Web, www.whitehouse.gov
> Email, president@whitehouse.gov

Chief of Staff, Denis McDonough, (202) 456-1414.
Deputy Chiefs of Staff Rob Nabors and
Alyssa Mastromonaco, (202) 456-1414

Advance and Operations, David I. Cusack, Director,
(202) 456-4709

Cabinet Secretary, Christopher Lu, Director, (202) 456-2572

Communications, Daniel Pfeiffer, Director, (202) 456-1414

Correspondence, Elizabeth Olson, Director, Recording and
voice mail, (202) 456-1414

Counsel, Peter Rouse, White House Counsel,
(202) 456-1414

Faith-Based and Neighborhood Partnerships,
Joshua DuBois, Director, (202) 456-3394

House Liaison, David Agnew, Deputy Assistant to the
President, (202) 456-6620

Intergovernmental Affairs and Public Engagement,
Valerie B. Jarrett, Assistant to the President,
(202) 456-1414

Legislative Affairs, Katie Beirne Fallon, Assistant to the
President, (202) 456-1414

Management and Administration, Katy Kale,
Assistant to the President, (202) 456-5400

Media Affairs, Christina Reynolds, Director, (202) 456-6238

National AIDS Policy, Grant Colfax, Director,
(202) 456-7320

National Intelligence, James R. Clapper, Director,
(703) 733-8600

National Security Advisor, Susan Rice, (202) 456-9491

New Media, Leigh Heyman, Director, (202) 456-6238

Presidential Personnel, Jonathan McBride, Assistant to the
President, (202) 456-9713

Press Secretary, Jay Carney, Press Secretary, (202) 456-2580

Public Engagement, Paulette Aniskoff, Director,
(202) 456-1414

Scheduling and Advance, (Vacant), (202) 456-5325

Speechwriting, Cody Keenan, Director, (202) 456-1414

Staff Secretary, Doug Cramer, (202) 456-2702

U.S. Secret Service (Homeland Security), Julia Pierson,
Director, (202) 406-5708

White House Fellows, Cindy Moelis, (202) 395-4522

White House Military Office, George Mulligan Jr., Director,
(202) 757-2151

OFFICE OF THE FIRST LADY

First Lady, Michelle Obama

> 1600 Pennsylvania Ave. N.W., 20500;
> (202) 456-7064; www.whitehouse.gov firstlady/
> first.lady@whitehouse.gov

Chief of Staff, Christina Tchen, Chief of Staff,
(202) 456-7064

Communications, Maria Cristina González, Director.
Hannah August, Press Secretary, (202) 456-6313

OFFICE OF THE VICE PRESIDENT

Vice President, Joseph R. Biden Jr.

> 1600 Pennsylvania Ave. N.W., 20500;
> www.whitehouse.gov
> vicepresidentvice.president@whitehouse.gov

Chief of Staff, Steve Ricchetti, Chief of Staff, (202) 456-2423

Communications, Shailagh Murray, Director,
(202) 456-1414

Wife of the Vice President, Dr. Jill Biden, (202) 456-1414

---

functions; makes recommendations for more effective government operations; publishes monthly lists of reports available to the public.

▶ **NONGOVERNMENTAL**

The Brookings Institution, *Governance Studies, 1755 Massachusetts Ave. N.W. 20036; (202) 797-6090. Fax, (202) 797-6144. Darrell M. West, Director, (202) 797-6481. Information, (202) 797-6000. Press, (202) 797-6105. Web, www.brookings.edu/governance.aspx*

Explores the formal and informal political institutions of democratic governments to assess how they govern, how their practices compare, and how citizens and government servants can advance sound government.

Center for Plain Language, *3315 Longwood Dr., Falls Church, VA 22041; (301) 219-1731. Rebecca Gholson, Executive Director. General email, centerforplainlanguage@gmail.com Web, www.centerforplainlanguage.org*

Advocates plain-language/reader-focused writing through education and training within government, the private sector, and academia.

Center for Regulatory Effectiveness (CRE), *1601 Connecticut Ave. N.W., #500 20009; (202) 265-2383. Fax, (202) 939-6969. James J. Tozzi, Executive Director. General email, comments@thecre.com Web, www.thecre.com*

Clearinghouse for methods to improve the federal regulatory process and public access to data and information

The Cabinet of Barack Obama

The president's cabinet includes the vice president and the heads of fifteen executive departments. In addition, every president has discretion to elevate any number of other government officials to cabinet-rank status. The cabinet is primarily an advisory group.

VICE PRESIDENT

Joseph R. Biden Jr., Vice President (202) 456-1414; Web, www.whitehouse.gov/vicepresident; Email, vice.president@whitehouse.gov

EXECUTIVE DEPT. CABINET MEMBERS

Agriculture Dept., Thomas J. Vilsack, Secretary (202) 720-3631; Web, www.usda.gov;

Commerce Dept., Penny Pritzker, Secretary (202) 482-2000; Web, www.commerce.gov; Email, TheSec@doc.gov

Defense Dept., Chuck Hagel, Secretary (703) 571-3343; Web, www.defense.gov

Education Dept., Arne Duncan, Secretary (202) 401-3000; Web, www2.ed.gov

Energy Dept., Ernest Moniz, Secretary (202) 586-6210; Web, www.energy.gov

Health and Human Services Dept., Vacant, Secretary (202) 690-7000; Web, www.hhs.gov

Homeland Security Dept., Jeh Johnson, Secretary (202) 282-8000; Web, www.dhs.gov

Housing and Urban Development Dept., Shaun L.S. Donovan, Secretary (202) 708-0417; Web, www.hud.gov

Interior Dept., Sally Jewell, Secretary (202) 208-3100; Web, www.doi.gov

Justice Dept., Eric H. Holder Jr., Attorney General (202) 514-2000; Web, www.justice.gov

Labor Dept., Thomas E. Perez, Secretary (202) 693-6000; Web, www.dol.gov

State Dept., John Kerry, Secretary (202) 647-5291; Web, www.state.gov

Transportation, Anthony Foxx, Secretary (202) 366-9201; Web, www.dot.gov

Treasury Dept., Jack Lew, Secretary (202) 622-2000; Web, www.treasury.gov

Veterans Affairs Dept., Sloan Gibson, Acting Secretary (202) 461-4800; Web, www.va.gov

OTHER CABINET-RANK OFFICIALS

Council of Economic Advisors, Jason Furman, Chair (202) 456-1414; Web, www.whitehouse.gov/cea

Environmental Protection Agency, Gina McCarthy, Administrator (202) 564-4700; Web, www.epa.gov

Office of Management and Budget, Sylvia Burwell, Director (202) 395-3080; Web, www.whitehouse.gov/omb

United States Mission to the United Nations, Samantha Power, Ambassador, (212) 415-4050

U.S. Trade Representative, Michael Froman, Ambassador (202) 395-6890; Web, www.ustr.gov

Office of the White House Chief of Staff, Denis McDonough, Chief of Staff (202) 456-1414; Web, www.whitehouse.gov

---

used to develop federal regulations. Conducts analyses of the activities of the OMB Office of Information and Regulatory Affairs and serves as a regulatory watchdog over executive branch agencies. Advocates on regulatory issues.

Center for the Study of the Presidency and Congress, *1020 19th St. N.W., #250 20036; (202) 872-9800. Fax, (202) 872-9811. Maximillian Angerholtzer III, President. General email, ann.packo@thepresidency.org*

Web, www.thepresidency.org

Membership: college students, government officials, and business leaders interested in the presidency, government, and politics. Conducts conferences, lectures, and symposiums on domestic, economic, and foreign policy issues. Publishes papers, essays, books, and reports on various aspects of the presidency and Congress.

Federal Managers Assn., *1641 Prince St., Alexandria, VA 22314-2818; (703) 683-8700. Fax, (703) 683-8707. Patricia J. Niehaus, National President; Todd Wells, Executive Director.*

General email, info@fedmanagers.org

Web, www.fedmanagers.org

Seeks to improve the effectiveness of federal supervisors and managers and the operations of the federal government. Interests include cost-effective government restructuring, competitive civil service pay and benefits, and maintaining the core values of the civil service.

Partnership for Public Service, *1100 New York Ave. N.W., #200E 20005; (202) 775-9111. Fax, (202) 775-8885. Max Stier, President.*

Web, www.ourpublicservice.org

Membership: large corporations and private businesses, including financial and information technology organizations. Seeks to improve government efficiency, productivity, and management through a cooperative effort of the public and private sectors.

Project on Government Secrecy, *Federation of American Scientists (FAS), 1725 DeSales St. N.W., 6th Floor 20036; (202) 546-3300. Fax, (202) 675-1010. Steven Aftergood, Project Director. Press, (202) 454-4694.*

Government Accountability Office

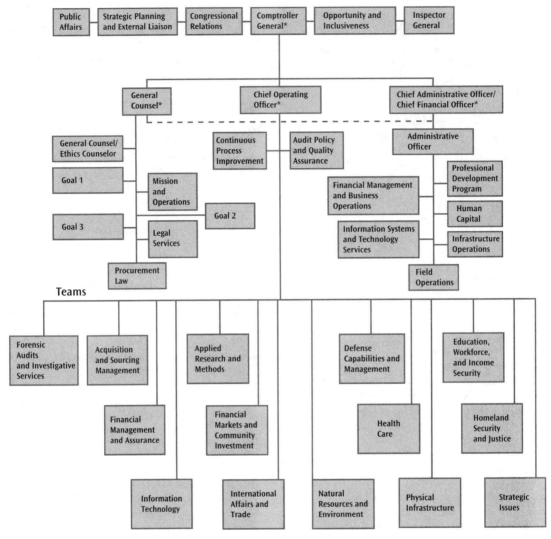

– – – – Indicates a support or advisory relationship with the teams/units rather than a direct reporting relationship
*The Executive Committee

General email, fas@fas.org

Web, www.fas.org/programs/ssp/govsec/index.html

Promotes public access to government information and fosters development of rational information security policies. Works to reduce the scope of government secrecy, including national security classification and declassification policies. Publishes hard-to-find government documents online.

Understanding Government, *1312 18th St. N.W., #510 20036; (202) 775-8080. Ned Hodgman, Executive Director. General email, info@understandinggov.org*

Web, www.understandinggov.org

Seeks to stimulate more informed reporting and analyses of executive branch activities. Funds investigations of government programs; operates news Web site and blog.

Buildings and Services

▶**AGENCIES**

Federal Protective Service (FPS) *(Homeland Security Dept.), 800 N. Capitol St., 5th Floor 20002; (202) 282-8000. Fax, (202) 732-8109. L. Eric Patterson, Director. Switchboard, (202) 282-8000. National hotline, (866) 347-2423.*

Web, www.dhs.gov/about-federal-protective-service

Works to ensure that appropriate levels of security are in place in General Services Administration–managed facilities throughout the United States. Conducts assessments on all GSA-controlled facilities to evaluate threats and tailor appropriate security countermeasures. Has enforcement capability to detain and arrest people, seize goods or conveyances, obtain arrest and search warrants, respond to incidents and emergency situations, provide protection during demonstrations or civil unrest, and to be deputized for law enforcement response in special situations.

General Services Administration (GSA), *Asset and Travel, Transportation Management,* *1275 1st St. N.E. 20417; (202) 501-1777. Fax, (202) 208-6601. Carolyn Austin-Diggs, Principal Deputy Administrator, (202) 208-6601.*
Web, www.gsa.gov/transportationpolicy

Seeks to improve the management and control of procured transportation services governmentwide, promoting regulatory flexibility and business incentives and tools.

General Services Administration (GSA), *Federal Acquisition Institute,* *9830 Flagler Rd., Bldg. 270, Ft. Belvoir, VA 22060-5565; (703) 805-2333. Fax, (703) 805-2111. Donna Jenkins, Director.*
General email, contact@fai.gov
Web, www.fai.gov

Fosters development of a professional acquisition workforce governmentwide; collects and analyzes acquisition workforce data; helps agencies identify and recruit candidates for the acquisitions field; develops instructional materials; evaluates training and career development programs.

General Services Administration (GSA), *Federal Acquisition Service,* *2200 Crystal Dr., 11th Floor, Arlington, VA 22202; (703) 605-5400. Fax, (703) 605-9955. Thomas A. Sharpe Jr., Commissioner. National Customer Service Center (NCSC), (800) 488-3111 and NCSCcustomer.service@gsa.gov.*
General email, contactfas@gsa.gov
Web, www.gsa.gov/fas

Responsible for providing federal agencies with common-use goods and nonpersonal services and for procurement and supply, transportation and travel management, and disposal of surplus personal property.

General Services Administration (GSA), *National Capital Region,* *301 7th St. S.W., #7022 20407; (202) 708-9100. Fax, (202) 708-9966. Julia E. Hudson, Regional Administrator.*
Web, www.gsa.gov/ncr

Provides federal agencies with office space and property management services, supplies, telecommunications, transportation, construction services, energy conservation and recycling services, and information technology support; has equal status with regional offices.

General Services Administration (GSA), *Portfolio Management,* *1800 F St. N.W., #7300 20405-0001; (202) 501-0638. Fax, (202) 208-0033. Martha Benson, Assistant Commissioner, (202) 208-7176.*
Web, www.gsa.gov

Develops, promotes, and assesses compliance with management policies and regulations for the effective and efficient stewardship of federal real property assets and alternative workplaces. Provides oversight and guidance for governmentwide real property asset management plans and related activities, including the use and disposal of excess real property.

General Services Administration (GSA), *Public Buildings Service,* *1800 F St. N.W., #1344 20405; (202) 501-1100. Fax, (202) 219-0856. Dorothy Robyn, Commissioner.*
Web, www.gsa.gov/pbs

Administers the acquisition, construction, maintenance, and operation of buildings owned or leased by the federal government. Manages and disposes of federal real estate.

General Services Administration (GSA), *Public Buildings Service, Organizational Resources,* *1800 F St. N.W., #3002 20405; (202) 501-0971. Fax, (202) 501-3296. Erika Dinnie, Assistant Commissioner, (202) 494-2144.*
Web, www.gsa.gov/pbs

Oversees operations of federal buildings, including facility management, safety programs, personnel hiring and training, purchasing and divesting of equipment, and contracting of services and vendors.

Ethics in Government

▶**AGENCIES**

Office of Government Ethics, *1201 New York Ave. N.W., #500 20005-3917; (202) 482-9300. Fax, (202) 482-9237. Walter M. Shaub Jr., Director.*
General email, contactoge@oge.gov
Web, www.oge.gov

Ensures that executive branch ethics programs are in compliance with applicable ethics laws and regulations. Administers executive branch policies relating to financial disclosure, employee conduct, and conflict-of-interest laws. Works to prevent conflicts of interest on the part of federal employees, and to resolve those that do occur. Provides educational materials and training; conducts outreach to the general public, the private sector, and civil society; shares model practices with and provides technical assistance to state, local, and foreign governments and international organizationsl; manages email list service to notify federal ethics officials of changes in law and regulations.

U.S. Office of Special Counsel, *1730 M St. N.W., #218 20036-4505; (202) 254-3600. Fax, (202) 254-3711. Carolyn N. Lerner, Associate Special Counsel; Adam Miles, Director of Policy and Congressional Affairs; Ann O'Hanlon, Director of Press and Public Affairs; Catherine McMullen, Chief, Disclosure Unit. Issues relating to the Hatch Act, (800) 854-2824. Prohibited personnel practices, (800) 872-9855. Whistleblower disclosure hotline, (800) 572-2249 and (202) 254-3640.*
Web, www.osc.gov

Investigates allegations of prohibited personnel practices and prosecutes individuals who violate federal statutes and regulations governing federal employees, military veterans, and reservists. Receives and refers federal employee disclosures of waste, fraud, inefficiency, mismanagement, and other violations in the federal government. Enforces the Hatch Act, which limits political activity by most federal and District of Columbia employees.

►CONGRESS

For a listing of relevant congressional committees and sub-committees, please see pages 290–291 or the Appendix.

►NONGOVERNMENTAL

Center for Public Integrity, *910 17th St. N.W., #700 20006; (202) 466-1300. Fax, (202) 466-1102. Bill Buzenberg, Executive Director. Web, www.publicintegrity.org*

Nonpartisan organization that seeks to produce original investigative journalism on significant issues in the United States and around the world. Organizes and supports investigative journalists committed to transparent and comprehensive reporting. Interests include the environment, public health, public accountability, federal and state lobbying, war profiteering, and financial disclosure.

Citizens for Responsibility and Ethics in Washington, *1400 Eye St. N.W., #450 20005; (202) 408-5565. Fax, (202) 588-5020. Melanie Sloan, Executive Director. General email, info@citizensforethics.org*

Web, www.citizensforethics.org

Promotes ethics and accountability in government and public life. Investigates, reports, and litigates government misconduct. Seeks to enforce government disclosure of information.

Fund for Constitutional Government (FCG), *122 Maryland Ave. N.E. 20002; (202) 546-3799. Fax, (202) 543-3156. Conrad Martin, Executive Director. General email, info@fcgonline.org*

Web, www.fcgonline.org

Promotes an open and accountable government. Seeks to expose and correct corruption in the federal government and private sector through research and public education. Sponsors the Electronic Privacy Information Center, the Government Accountability Project, the Project on Government Oversight, and OpenTheGovernment.org.

Government Accountability Project, *1612 K St. N.W., #1100 20006; (202) 457-0034. Fax, (202) 457-0059. Beatrice Edwards, Executive Director and International Director; Louis Clark, President. General email, info@whistleblower.org*

Web, www.whistleblower.org

Membership: federal employees, union members, professionals, and interested citizens. Provides legal and strategic counsel to employees in the public and private sectors who seek to expose corporate and government actions that are illegal, wasteful, or repressive; aids such employees in personnel action taken against them; assists

grassroots organizations investigating corporate wrongdoing, government inaction, or corruption. Promotes policy and legal reforms of whistle-blower laws. (Formerly the National Whistleblower Center.)

Project on Government Oversight, *1100 G St. N.W., #500 20005-3806; (202) 347-1122. Fax, (202) 347-1116. Danielle Brian, Executive Director. General email, info@pogo.org*

Web, www.pogo.org

Public interest organization that works to expose waste, fraud, abuse, and conflicts of interest in all aspects of federal spending.

Sunlight Foundation, *1818 N St. N.W., #300 20036; (202) 742-1520. Fax, (202) 742-1524. Ellen S. Miller, Executive Director. Web, www.sunlightfoundation.com*

Utilizes new information technology to make government more transparent and accountable. Projects include Sunlight Labs, Sunlight Reporting Group, http://Political PartyTime.org, and http://influenceexplorer.com. Offers "OpenGov grants" for innovative projects that liberate or use municipal government data and tutorials for media and citizens on the role of money in politics.

Executive Reorganization

►AGENCIES

Office of Management and Budget (OMB) *(Executive Office of the President), President's Management Council,* *Dwight D. Eisenhower Executive Office Bldg., #216 20503; (202) 395-5020. Fax, (202) 395-6102. Jeffrey D. Zients, Chair. Web, www.whitehouse.gov/omb and www.qsa.gov/portal/content/1338811*

Membership: chief operating officers of federal government departments and agencies. Responsible for implementing the management improvement initiatives of the administration. Develops and oversees improved governmentwide management and administrative systems; formulates long-range plans to promote these systems; works to resolve interagency management problems and to implement reforms.

►CONGRESS

For a listing of relevant congressional committees and sub-committees, please see pages 290–291 or the Appendix.

Government Accountability Office (GAO), *Information Technology,* *441 G St. N.W., #4T21 20548; (202) 512-6408. Joel C. Willemssen, Managing Director. Web, www.gao.gov*

Seeks to make the federal government more effective in its information management by improving performance and reducing costs. Assesses best practices in the public and private sectors; makes recommendations to government agencies. Interests include information security.

CENSUS, POPULATION DATA

General

▶**AGENCIES**

Census Bureau *(Commerce Dept.),* *4600 Silver Hill Rd., #8H001, Suitland, MD 20746 (mailing address: change city, state, and zip code to Washington, DC 20233-0100); (301) 763-2135. Fax, (301) 763-3761. John H. Thompson, Director. Information, (800) 923-8282. Press, (301) 763-3030. Library, (301) 763-2511.*
General email, pio@census.gov
Web, www.census.gov

Conducts surveys and censuses (including the decennial census of population, the American Community Survey, the economic census, and census of governments); collects and analyzes demographic, social, economic, housing, agricultural, foreign trade, and data on governmental data; publishes statistics for use by federal, state, and local governments, Congress, businesses, planners, and the public. Provides online resources and data analysis tools. Library open to the public Monday through Friday, 9:30 a.m.–3:30 p.m.

Census Bureau *(Commerce Dept.), Decennial Census, 4600 Silver Hill Rd., #8H122, Suitland, MD 20746 (mailing address: Washington, DC 20233-7000); (301) 763-2069. Fax, (301) 763-8867. Frank A. Vitrano, Associate Director.*
Web, www.census.gov

Provides data from the decennial census (including general plans and procedures); economic, demographic, and population statistics; and information on trends. Conducts preparation for the next census.

Census Bureau *(Commerce Dept.), Population, 4600 Silver Hill Rd., #5H174, Suitland, MD 20746 (mailing address: change city, state, and zip code to Washington, DC 20233-8800); (301) 763-2071. Fax, (301) 763-2516. Victoria A. Velkoff, Division Chief.*
General email, pop@census.gov
Web, www.census.gov/popest

Prepares population estimates and projections for national, state, and local areas and congressional districts. Provides data on demographic and social statistics in the following areas: families and households, marital status and living arrangements, farm population, migration and mobility, population distribution, ancestry, fertility, child care, race and ethnicity, language patterns, school enrollment, educational attainment, and voting.

Census Bureau *(Commerce Dept.), Social, Economic, and Housing Statistics, 4600 Silver Hill Rd., #7H174, Suitland, MD 20746 (mailing address: change city, state, and zip code to Washington, DC 20233-8500); (301) 763-3234. Fax, (301) 763-3232. David S. Johnson, Chief.*
Web, www.census.gov/housing

Develops statistical programs for the decennial census, the American Community Survey, and for other surveys on housing, income, poverty, and the labor force. Collects and explains the proper use of economic, social, and demographic data. Responsible for the technical planning, analysis, and publication of data from current surveys, including the decennial census, the American Community Survey, the American Housing Survey, the Current Population Survey, and the Survey of Income and Program Participation.

▶**CONGRESS**

For a listing of relevant congressional committees and subcommittees, please see pages 290–291 or the Appendix.

▶**NONGOVERNMENTAL**

Population Assn. of America, *8630 Fenton St., #722, Silver Spring, MD 20910; (301) 565-6710. Fax, (301) 565-7850. Stephanie Dudley, Executive Director; Robert A. Moffitt, President.*
General email, membersvc@popassoc.org
Web, www.popassoc.org

Membership: university, government, and industry researchers in demography. Publishes newsletters, monitors legislation and related government activities, and supports collaboration of demographers. Holds annual technical sessions to present papers on domestic and international population issues and statistics.

Population Reference Bureau, *1875 Connecticut Ave. N.W., #520 20009-5728; (202) 483-1100. Fax, (202) 328-3937. James Scott, President, Acting. Toll-free, (800) 877-9881.*
General email, popref@prb.org
Web, www.prb.org

Educational organization engaged in information dissemination, training, and policy analysis on domestic and international population trends and issues. Interests include international development and family planning programs, the environment, and U.S. social and economic policy. Library open to the public.

CIVIL SERVICE

General

▶**AGENCIES**

National Archives and Records Administration (NARA), *Information Security Oversight (ISOO), 700 Pennsylvania Ave. N.W., #100 20408-0001; (202) 357-5250. Fax, (202) 357-5907. John P. Fitzpatrick, Director, (202) 357-5205.*
General email, isoo@nara.gov
Web, www.archives.gov/isoo

Receiving guidance from the National Security Council, oversees policy on security classification on documents for the federal government and industry; monitors performance of all security classification/declassification

Financial Officers for Federal Departments and Agencies

DEPARTMENTS

Agriculture, Jon Holladay (Acting), (202) 720-5539

  Coast Guard, Rear Adm. Stephen P. Metruck, (202) 372-3470

Commerce, Ellen Herbst, (202) 482-4951

Defense, Robert F. Hale, (703) 571-3343

  Air Force, Jamie M. Morin, (703) 571-3343

  Army, Robert M. Speer, (703) 614-4356

  Navy, Susan J. Rabern, (703) 697-2325

Education, Thomas Skelly, (202) 401-0287

Energy, Allison Doone (Deputy), (202) 586-4171

Health and Human Services, Sheila Conley, (202) 690-6396

Homeland Security, Peggy Sherry, (202) 447-5751

Housing and Urban Development, David P. Sidari (Deputy), (202) 402-3899

Interior, Rhea S. Suh, (202) 208-4246

Justice, Leigh Benda, (202) 307-0623

Labor, James L. Taylor, (202) 693-6800

State, James L. Millette, (202) 647-4000

Transportation, Sylvia I. Garcia, (202) 366-9191

Treasury, Chief Financial Officer, Daniel M. Tangherlini, (202) 622-0410. Comptroller of the Currency, Thomas Curry, (202) 649-6400

Veterans Affairs, Vacant, (202) 461-6703

AGENCIES

Advisory Council on Historic Preservation, Ralston Cox, (202) 606-8528

Agency for International Development, Angelique Crumbly, (202) 712-1200

Central Intelligence Agency, Vacant, (703) 482-1100

Commission on Civil Rights, (202) 376-7700

Commodity Futures Trading Commission, Mary Jean Buhler, (202) 418-5477

Consumer Product Safety Commission, Jay Hoffman, (301) 504-7207

Corporation for National and Community Service, David Rebich, (202) 606-6649

Corporation for Public Broadcasting, Bill Tayman, (202) 879-9600

Environmental Protection Agency, Maryann Froehlich, (202) 564-1151

Equal Employment Opportunity Commission, (800) 669-4000

Export-Import Bank, Nathalie Herman, (202) 565-3952

Farm Credit Administration, Stephen Smith, (703) 883-4200

Federal Bureau of Investigation, Richard L. Haley II, (202) 324-3000

Federal Communications Commission, Mark Stephens (Acting), (202) 418-0817

Federal Deposit Insurance Corporation, Steven O. App, (202) 898-8732

Federal Election Commission, Judy Berning, (202) 694-1315

Federal Emergency Management Agency, Edward Johnson, (800) 621-3362

Federal Energy Regulatory Commission, William Douglas Foster Jr., (202) 502-6118

Federal Home Loan Mortgage Corporation (Freddie Mac), James G. Mackey, (703) 903-2000

Federal Maritime Commission, Karon E. Douglass, (202) 523-5770

programs for the federal government and industry; develops policies and procedures for sensitive unclassified information. Evaluates implementation, advises department and agency heads of corrective actions, and prepares an annual report to the president.

Office of Personnel Management (OPM), *1900 E St. N.W., #5A09 20415-0001; (202) 606-1000. Fax, (202) 606-2573. Katherine Archuleta, Director. Press, (202) 606-2402.*
Web, www.opm.gov

Administers civil service rules and regulations; sets policy for personnel management, labor-management relations, workforce effectiveness, and employment within the executive branch; manages federal personnel activities, including recruitment, pay comparability, and benefit programs.

Office of Personnel Management (OPM), *Planning and Policy Analysis, Data Analysis Group, 1900 E St. N.W., #2449 20415-0001; (202) 606-1449. Fax, (202) 606-1719. Gary A. Lukowski, Group Manager.*
General email, fedstats@opm.gov
Web, www.opm.gov/feddata

Official government source of statistics on the government workforce. Produces information and analyses for the Office of Personnel Management, Congress, and the public on statistical aspects of the federal civilian workforce, including trends in composition, grade levels, minority employment, sizes of agencies, and salaries.

Office of Personnel Management (OPM), *Veterans Services, 1900 E St. N.W., #7439 20415; (202) 606-3602. Fax, (202) 606-6017. Hakeem Basheerud-Deen, Director.*
Web, www.opm.gov/policy-data-oversight/veterans-services

Federal Mediation and Conciliation Service, Fran Leonard, (202) 606-3661

Federal National Mortgage Association (Fannie Mae), David Benson, (202) 752-7000

Federal Trade Commission, Steven A. Fisher, (202) 326-2116

General Services Administration, Michael Casella, (202) 501-1721

Government Accountability Office, Karl Maschino, (202) 512-5800

International Bank for Reconstruction and Development (World Bank), Bertrand Badré, (202) 473-1000

John F. Kennedy Center for the Performing Arts, Lynne Pratt, (202) 416-8000

Merit Systems Protection Board, Kevin J. Nash, (202) 653-7263

National Academy of Sciences, Mary Didi Salmon, (202) 334-2000

National Aeronautics and Space Administration, Elizabeth Robinson, (202) 358-0001

National Archives and Records Administration, Micah Cheatham, (301) 837-2992

National Credit Union Administration, Mary Ann Woodson, (703) 518-6570

National Endowment for the Arts, Winona Varnon (Deputy), (202) 682-5534

National Endowment for the Humanities, John Gleason, (202) 606-8336

National Labor Relations Board, Ronald E. Crupi, (202) 273-3884

National Mediation Board, June D.W. King, (202) 692-5010

National Railroad Passenger Corporation (Amtrak), Gerald Sokol Jr., (202) 906-3369

National Science Foundation, Martha A. Rubenstein, (703) 292-8200

National Transportation Safety Board, Steven Goldberg, (202) 314-6210

Nuclear Regulatory Commission, James Dyer, (301) 415-7322

Occupational Safety and Health Review Commission, Thomasina V. Roger, (202) 606-5370

Office of Management and Budget, Sylvia Mathews Burwell, (202) 395-3080

Office of Personnel Management, Dennis Coleman, (202) 606-1918

Overseas Private Investment Corporation, Allan Villabroza, (202) 336-8400

Peace Corps, Joseph Hepp, (202) 692-1606

Pension Benefit Guaranty Corporation, Patricia Kelly, (202) 326-4008

Postal Regulatory Commission, (202) 789-6840

Securities and Exchange Commission, Paul Beswick, (202) 551-5300

Small Business Administration, Jonathan Carver, (202) 205-6449

Smithsonian Institution, Albert Horvath, (202) 633-5225

Social Security Administration, Peter D. Spencer, (410) 965-3148

U.S. International Trade Commission, John Ascienzo, (202) 205-3175

U.S. Postal Service, Joseph R. Corbett, (202) 268-5272

Monitors federal agencies' personnel practices and develops policies and programs for veterans.

U.S. Office of Special Counsel, *1730 M St. N.W., #218 20036-4505; (202) 254-3600. Fax, (202) 254-3711. Carolyn N. Lerner, Associate Special Counsel; Adam Miles, Director of Policy and Congressional Affairs; Ann O'Hanlon, Director of Press and Public Affairs; Catherine McMullen, Chief, Disclosure Unit. Issues relating to the Hatch Act, (800) 854-2824. Prohibited personnel practices, (800) 872-9855. Whistleblower disclosure hotline, (800) 572-2249 and (202) 254-3640.*
Web, www.osc.gov

Interprets federal laws, including the Hatch Act, concerning political activities allowed by certain federal employees; investigates allegations of Hatch Act violations and conducts prosecutions. Investigates and prosecutes complaints under the Whistleblower Protection Act.

► **CONGRESS**

For a listing of relevant congressional committees and subcommittees, please see pages 290–291 or the Appendix.

► **NONGOVERNMENTAL**

American Federation of Government Employees (AFGE), *80 F St. N.W. 20001; (202) 737-8700. Fax, (202) 639-6490. J. David Cox, President. Press, (202) 639-6419. Membership, (202) 639-6410. General email, comments@afge.org*
Web, www.afge.org

Membership: approximately 670,000 federal and District of Columbia government employees. Provides legal services to members; assists members with contract negotiations and grievances. Monitors legislation and regulations. (Affiliated with the AFL-CIO.)

Blacks in Government, *3005 Georgia Ave. N.W. 20001-3807; (202) 667-3280. Fax, (202) 667-3705. Darlene H. Young, President.*
General email, bignational@bignet.org
Web, www.bignet.org

Advocacy organization for public employees. Promotes equal opportunity and career advancement for African American government employees; provides career development information; seeks to eliminate racism in the federal workforce; sponsors programs, business meetings, and social gatherings; represents interests of African American government workers to Congress and the executive branch; promotes voter education and registration.

Federally Employed Women, *455 Massachusetts Ave. N.W., #306 20001; (202) 898-0994. Fax, (202) 898-1535. Michelle Crockett, President.*
General email, few@few.org
Web, www.few.org

Membership: women and men who work for the federal government. Works to eliminate sex discrimination in government employment and to increase job opportunities for women; offers training programs. Monitors legislation and regulations.

Federal Managers Assn., *1641 Prince St., Alexandria, VA 22314-2818; (703) 683-8700. Fax, (703) 683-8707. Patricia J. Niehaus, National President; Todd Wells, Executive Director.*
General email, info@fedmanagers.org
Web, www.fedmanagers.org

Seeks to improve the effectiveness of federal supervisors and managers and the operations of the federal government. Interests include cost-effective government restructuring, competitive civil service pay and benefits, and maintaining the core values of the civil service.

Senior Executives Assn., *77 K St. N.E., #2600 20002; (202) 927-7000. Fax, (202) 971-3317. Carol A. Bonosaro, President.*
General email, action@seniorexecs.org
Web, www.seniorexecs.org

Professional association representing Senior Executive Service members and other federal career executives. Sponsors professional education. Interests include management improvement. Monitors legislation and regulations.

Dismissals and Disputes

▶**AGENCIES**

Merit Systems Protection Board, *1615 M St. N.W., 5th Floor 20419; (202) 653-7200. Fax, (202) 653-7130. Susan Swafford, Chair; William Spencer, Clerk of the Board. Toll-free, (800) 209-8960. MSPB Inspector General hotline, (800) 424-9121.*
General email, mspb@mspb.gov
Web, www.mspb.gov

Independent quasi-judicial agency that handles hearings and appeals involving federal employees; protects the integrity of federal merit systems and ensures adequate protection for employees against abuses by agency management. Library open to the public by appointment.

Merit Systems Protection Board, *Appeals Counsel, 1615 M St. N.W. 20419; (202) 653-7200. Fax, (202) 653-7130. Susan Swafford, Director.*
General email, settlement@mspb.gov
Web, www.mspb.gov

Analyzes and processes petitions for review of appeals decisions from the regional offices; prepares opinions and orders for board consideration; analyzes and processes cases that are reopened and prepares proposed depositions.

Merit Systems Protection Board, *Policy and Evaluations, 1615 M St. N.W. 20419; (202) 653-7200. Fax, (202) 653-7211. James Tsuwaga, Director. Information, (800) 209-8960, option 2.*
General email, studies@mspb.gov
Web, www.mspb.gov

Conducts studies on the civil service and other executive branch merit systems; reports to the president and Congress on whether federal employees are adequately protected against political abuses and prohibited personnel practices. Conducts annual oversight review of the Office of Personnel Management.

Merit Systems Protection Board, *Washington Regional Office, 1901 S. Ball St., #950, Arlington, VA 22202; (703) 756-6250. Fax, (703) 756-7112. Jeremiah Cassidy, Regional Director.*
General email, washingtonregion@mspb.gov
Web, www.mspb.gov

Hears and decides appeals of adverse personnel actions (such as removals, suspensions for more than fourteen days, and reductions in grade or pay), retirement, and performance-related actions for federal civilian employees who work in the Washington area, Virginia, North Carolina, or in overseas areas not covered by other regional board offices. Federal civilian employees who work outside Washington should contact the Merit Systems Protection Board regional office in their area.

Office of Personnel Management (OPM), *General Counsel, 1900 E St. N.W., #7347 20415-0001; (202) 606-1700. Fax, (202) 606-2609. Kamala Srinivasagam, General Counsel.*
Web, www.opm.gov/about-us/our-people-organization/office-of-the-general-counsel

Represents the federal government before the Merit Systems Protection Board, other administrative tribunals, and the courts.

Office of Personnel Management (OPM), *Partnership and Labor Relations, Employee Accountability, 1900 E St. N.W., #7H28H 20415-0001; (202) 606-2580. Fax, (202) 606-2613. Debra Buford, Manager.*

Inspectors General for Federal Departments and Agencies

Departmental and agency inspectors general are responsible for identifying and reporting program fraud and abuse, criminal activity, and unethical conduct in the federal government. The legislative branch the Government Accountability Office also has a fraud and abuse hotline: (202) 512-7470. Check www.ignet.gov for additional listings.

DEPARTMENTS

Agriculture, Phyllis Fong, (202) 720-8001;
Hotline, (800) 424-9121; (202) 690-1622, Washington area

Commerce, Todd J. Zinser, (202) 482-4661;
Hotline, (800) 482-5197; (202) 482-2495, Washington area

Defense, Jon T. Rymer, (703) 604-8300;
Hotline, (800) 424-9098

Education, Kathleen Tighe, (202) 245-6900;
Hotline, (800) 647-8733

Energy, Gregory H. Friedman, (202) 586-4393;
Hotline, (800) 541-1625; (202) 586-4073, Washington area

Health and Human Services, Daniel Levinson, (202) 619-3148;
Hotline, (800) 447-8477

Homeland Security and FEMA, Vacant, (202) 254-4100;
Hotline, (800) 323-8603

Housing and Urban Development, David A. Montoya, (202) 708-0430;
Hotline, (800) 347-3735

Interior, Mary L. Kendall (Acting) (202) 208-5745;
Hotline, (800) 424-5081; (202) 208-5300, Washington area

Justice, Michael E. Horowitz, (202) 514-3435;
Hotline, (800) 869-4499

Labor, Scott Dahl, (202) 693-5100;
Hotline, (800) 347-3756; (202) 693-6999, Washington area

State, Steve Linick, (202) 663-0340;
Hotline, (800) 409-9926

Transportation, Calvin L. Scovel III, (202) 366-1959;
Hotline, (800) 424-9071

Treasury, Eric M. Thorson, (202) 622-1090;
Hotline, (800) 359-3898

Veterans Affairs, Richard J. Griffin, (202) 461-4720;
Hotline, (800) 488-8244

AGENCIES

Agency for International Development, Michael G. Carroll (Acting) (202) 712-1150;
Hotline, (202) 712-1023

Central Intelligence Agency, David Buckley, (703) 874-2553;
Hotline, (703) 874-2600

Environmental Protection Agency, Arthur A. Elkins Jr., (202) 566-0847;
Hotline, (888) 546-8740; (202) 566-2476, Washington area

Federal Deposit Insurance Corporation, Fred W. Gibson, (703) 562-2166;
Hotline, (800) 964-3342

Federal Labor Relations Authority, Dana Rooney-Fisher, (202) 218-7744;
Hotline, (800) 331-3572

General Services Administration, Brian D. Miller, (202) 501-0450;
Hotline, (800) 424-5210; (202) 501-1780, Washington area

National Aeronautics and Space Administration, Paul K. Martin, (202) 358-1220;
Hotline, (800) 424-9183

National Science Foundation, Allison Lerner, (703) 292-7100;
Hotline, (800) 428-2189

Nuclear Regulatory Commission, Hubert T. Bell, (301) 415-5930;
Hotline, (800) 233-3497

Office of Personnel Management, Patrick E. McFarland, (202) 606-1200;
Hotline, (202) 418-3300

Small Business Administration, Peggy E. Gustafson, (202) 205-6586;
Hotline, (800) 767-0385

Social Security Administration, Patrick P. O'Carroll, (410) 966-8385;
Hotline (800) 269-0271

U.S. Postal Service, David Williams, (703) 248-2300;
Hotline, (888) 877-7644

General email, er@opm.gov

Web, www.opm.gov/er

Develops, implements, and interprets policy on governmentwide employee relations. Intervenes in or seeks reconsideration of erroneous third-party decisions.

U.S. Office of Special Counsel, *1730 M St. N.W., #218 20036-4505; (202) 254-3600. Fax, (202) 254-3711. Carolyn N. Lerner, Associate Special Counsel; Adam Miles, Director of Policy and Congressional Affairs; Ann O'Hanlon, Director of Press and Public Affairs; Catherine McMullen, Chief, Disclosure Unit. Issues relating to the Hatch Act, (800) 854-2824. Prohibited personnel practices, (800) 872-9855. Whistleblower Disclosure Hotline, (800) 572-2249 and (202) 254-3640.*

Web, www.osc.gov

Investigates allegations of prohibited personnel practices, including reprisals against whistleblowers (federal employees who disclose waste, fraud, inefficiency, and wrongdoing by supervisors of federal departments and agencies). Initiates necessary corrective or disciplinary action. Enforces the Hatch Act, which limits political activity by most federal and District of Columbia employees.

▶JUDICIARY

U.S. Court of Appeals for the Federal Circuit, *717 Madison Pl. N.W. 20439; (202) 275-8000. Fax, (202) 275-8036. Randall R. Rader, Chief Judge, (202) 633-6297; Jan Horbaly, Clerk, (202) 312-5520. Helpdesk, (202) 275-8040; (855) 860-8240. Mediation, (202) 275-8120.*

Web, www.cafc.uscourts.gov

Reviews decisions of the Merit Systems Protection Board.

Hiring, Recruitment, and Training

▶AGENCIES

Office of Personnel Management (OPM), *Federal Investigative Services, 1900 E St. N.W., #2H31 20415-0001; (202) 606-1042. Fax, (202) 606-2390. Merton W. Miller, Associate Director.*

Web, www.opm.gov/investigate

Initiates and conducts investigations of new federal employees.

Office of Personnel Management (OPM), *Human Resources Solutions, 1900 E St. N.W., #2469F 20415-1000; (202) 606-0900. Fax, (202) 606-9200. Joseph S. Kennedy, Associate Director.*

Web, www.opm.gov/about-us/our-people-organization/program-divisions/human-resources-solutions

Manages federal human resources policy, including staffing, compensation, benefits, labor relations, and position classification.

Office of Personnel Management (OPM), *Merit System Accountability and Compliance, 1900 E St. N.W., #6484*

20415-5100; (202) 606-2980. Fax, (202) 606-5056. Mark W. Lambert, Associate Director.

Web, www.opm.gov/about-us/our-people-organization/program-divisions/merit-system-accountability-and-compliance

Responsible for training and curriculum development programs for government executives and supervisors.

Office of Personnel Management (OPM), *Recruitment and Hiring, Classification and Assessment Policy, 1900 E St. N.W., #6500 20415-0001; (202) 606-3600. Fax, (202) 606-4891. April Davis, Manager, (202) 606-3590.*

General email, fedclass@opm.gov

Web, www.opm.gov/fedclass

Develops job classification standards for occupations in the general schedule and federal wage system.

Office of Personnel Management (OPM), *Veterans Services, 1900 E St. N.W., #7439 20415; (202) 606-3602. Fax, (202) 606-6017. Hakeem Basheerud-Deen, Director.*

Web, www.opm.gov/policy-data-oversight/veterans-services

Provides federal employees and transitioning military service members and their families, federal human resources professionals, and hiring managers with information on employment opportunities with the federal government.

Office of Personnel Management (OPM), *Veterans Services, Intergovernmental Personnel Act Mobility Program, 1900 E St. N.W., #6544 20415-0001; (202) 606-1730. Fax, (202) 606-4430. Gregory Snowden, Program Head.*

General email, ipa@opm.gov

Web, www.opm.gov/programs/ipa

Implements temporary personnel exchanges between federal agencies and nonfederal entities, including state and local governments, institutions of higher education, and other organizations.

Labor-Management Relations

▶AGENCIES

Federal Labor Relations Authority, *1400 K St. N.W. 20424-0001; (202) 218-7770. Fax, (202) 482-6526. Carol Waller Pope, Chair; Sarah Whittle Spooner, Executive Director.*

Web, www.flra.gov

Oversees the federal labor-management relations program; administers the law that protects the right of nonpostal federal employees to organize, bargain collectively, and participate through labor organizations of their own choosing.

Federal Service Impasses Panel *(Federal Labor Relations Authority), 1400 K St. N.W., #200 20424-0001; (202) 218-7790. Fax, (202) 482-6674. H. Joseph Schimansky, Executive Director; Mary E. Jacksteit, Chair.*

Web, www.flra.gov/fsip

Assists in resolving contract negotiation impasses over conditions of employment between federal agencies and labor organizations representing federal employees.

Office of Personnel Management (OPM), *Employee Services, Partnership and Labor Relations, 1900 E St. N.W., #7H28 20415-0001; (202) 606-2584. Fax, (202) 606-2613. Tim F. Curry, Deputy Associate Director.*
Web, www.opm.gov/about-us/our-people-organization/program-divisions/employee-services

Develops policy for government agencies and unions regarding employee- and labor-management relations.

Office of Personnel Management (OPM), *General Counsel, 1900 E St. N.W., #7347 20415-0001; (202) 606-1700. Fax, (202) 606-2609. Kamala Srinivasagam, General Counsel.*
Web, www.opm.gov/about-us/our-people-organization/office-of-the-general-counsel

Advises the government on law and legal policy relating to federal labor-management relations; represents the government before the Merit Systems Protection Board.

▶**NONGOVERNMENTAL**

National Alliance of Postal and Federal Employees (NAPFE), *1628 11th St. N.W. 20001; (202) 939-6325. Fax, (202) 939-6389. James M. McGee, President.*
General email, headquarters@napfe.org
Web, www.napfe.com

Membership: approximately 70,000 postal and federal employees. Helps members negotiate pay, benefits, equal opportunity, and better working conditions; conducts training programs and workshops. Monitors legislation and regulations.

National Assn. of Government Employees (NAGE), *Washington Office, 901 N. Pitt St., #100, Alexandria, VA 22314; (703) 519-0300. Fax, (703) 519-0311. David J. Holway, National President. Toll-free, (866) 412-7790.*
Web, www.nage.org

Membership: approximately 200,000 federal government employees. Helps members negotiate pay, benefits, and better working conditions; conducts training programs and workshops. Monitors legislation and regulations. (Affiliated with Service Employees International Union. Headquarters in Quincy, Mass.)

National Federation of Federal Employees, *805 15th St. N.W., #500 20005; (202) 216-4420. Fax, (202) 898-1861. William R. Dougan, National President.*
General email, cbythrow@nffe.org
Web, www.nffe.org

Membership: approximately 100,000 employees throughout various agencies within the federal government. Helps members negotiate pay, benefits, and better working conditions; conducts training programs and workshops. Monitors legislation and regulations.

National Treasury Employees Union (NTEU), *1750 H St. N.W. 20006; (202) 572-5500. Fax, (202) 572-5644. Colleen Kelly, President, (202) 572-5641.*
General email, nteu-pr@nteu.org
Web, www.nteu.org

Membership: approximately 150,000 employees from the Treasury Dept. and thirty-two other federal agencies and departments. Helps members negotiate pay, benefits, and better working conditions; conducts training programs and workshops. Monitors legislation and regulations.

Public Service Research Foundation, *320 D Maple Ave. East, Vienna, VA 22180-4747; (703) 242-3575. Fax, (703) 242-3579. David Y. Denholm, President.*
General email, info@psrf.org
Web, www.psrf.org

Independent, nonpartisan research and educational organization. Studies labor unions and labor issues with emphasis on employment in the public sector. Sponsors conferences and seminars. Library open to the public by appointment.

Pay and Employee Benefits

▶**AGENCIES**

Labor Dept. (DOL), *Federal Employees' Compensation, 200 Constitution Ave. N.W., #S3229 20210; (202) 693-0040. Fax, (202) 693-1497. Douglas C. Fitzgerald, Director. Toll-free, (866) 692-7487 (customers should contact their district office first, www.dol.gov/esa/owcp/contacts/fecacont.htm).*
Web, www.dol.gov/owcp/dfec

Administers the Federal Employees Compensation Act, which provides disability compensation for federal employees, including wage replacement benefits, medical treatment, vocational rehabilitation, and other benefits.

Office of Personnel Management (OPM), *Employee Services, 1900 E St. N.W., #7460 MM 20415; (202) 606-2520. Mark D. Reinhold, Associate Director, Acting, (202) 606-0388. Vacant, Principal Deputy Associate Director.*
Web, www.opm.gov/about-us/our-people-organization/program-divisions/employee-services

Develops federal human resource systems for pay and leave, employee development, staffing, recruiting, hiring, Factor Evaluation System (FES) policy, and labor and employee relations, senior executive services, veterans' services, and performance management.

Office of Personnel Management (OPM), *Federal Prevailing Rate Advisory Committee, 1900 E St. N.W., #5H27 20415; (202) 606-9400. Fax, (202) 606-2573. Sheldon Friedman, Chair, (202) 606-1712.*
Web, www.opm.gov/policy-data-oversight/pay-leave/pay-systems/federal-wage-system#url=Ffprac

Advises OPM on the governmentwide administration of Federal Wage System employees.

Office of Personnel Management (OPM), *Healthcare and Insurance, Federal Employee Insurance Operations,* *1900 E St. N.W., #3425 20415; (202) 606-1234. Fax, (202) 606-4640. Lloyd Williams, Deputy Assistant Director.* *Web, www.opm.gov/insure*

Administers group life insurance for federal employees and retirees; negotiates rates and benefits with health insurance carriers; settles disputed claims. Administers the Federal Employees' Health Benefits (FEHB), the Federal Employees' Group Life Insurance (FEGLI), the Federal Long Term Care Insurance (FLTCIP), Federal Employee Dental and Vision Benefits (FEDVIP), and the Flexible Spending Accounts (FSA) programs.

Office of Personnel Management (OPM), *Pay and Leave,* *1900 E St. N.W., #7H31 20415; (202) 606-2858. Fax, (202) 606-4264. Vacant, Deputy Associate Director.* *General email, pay-leave-policy@opm.gov*

Web, www.opm.gov/policy-data-oversight/pay-leave

Develops and maintains governmentwide agency regulations pertaining to pay and leave. Responsible for the General Schedule and locality pay adjustment process for white-collar federal workers. Supports the Federal Salary Council and the president's "pay agent" (composed of the directors of OPM and the Office of Management and Budget and the secretary of labor). Annual report of the pay agent and General Schedule pay rates are available on OPM's Web site. Supports the Federal Prevailing Rate Advisory Committee and provides regulations and policies for the administration of the federal wage system for blue-collar federal employees.

Office of Personnel Management (OPM), *Retirement Operations, 1900 E St. N.W., #3305 20415-1000; (202) 606-0300. Fax, (202) 606-0145. Nick Ashendon, Deputy Associate Director, (724) 794-2005, ext. 3214. Toll-free, (888) 767-6738. General email, retire@opm.gov*

Web, www.opm.gov/retire

Administers the civil service and federal employees' retirement systems; responsible for monthly annuity payments and other benefits; organizes and maintains retirement records; distributes information on retirement and on insurance programs for annuitants.

Office of Personnel Management (OPM), *Retirement Services, 1900 E St. N.W., #4312 20415; (202) 606-0462. Fax, (724) 794-4323. Kenneth J. Zawodny Jr., Associate Director, (202) 606-3582. Toll-free, (888) 767-6738. General email, retire@opm.gov*

Web, www.opm.gov/retire; Forms, www.opm.gov/forms/html/ri.asp

Implements federal policy and regulations on retirement benefits.

▶**NONGOVERNMENTAL**

National Active and Retired Federal Employees Assn. (NARFE), *606 N. Washington St., Alexandria, VA 22314; (703) 838-7760. Fax, (703) 838-7785. Joseph Beaudoin, President. Member relations, (800) 456-8410.*

General email, hq@narfe.org

Web, www.narfe.org

Works to preserve the integrity of the federal employee retirement systems. Provides members with information about benefits for retired federal employees and for survivors of deceased federal employees. Monitors legislation and regulations.

FEDERAL CONTRACTS AND PROCUREMENT

General

▶**AGENCIES**

Defense Health Agency (DHA) *(Defense Dept.),* **Small** *Business Programs, 7700 Arlington Blvd., #5101, Falls Church, VA 22042-5101; (703) 681-4614. Cassandra W. Martin, Director.* *Web, http://www.tricare.mil/tma/ams/smallbusiness/default.aspx*

Seeks to ensure that small businesses have a fair opportunity to compete and be selected for DHA contracts, both at the prime and subcontract levels. Provides information on agency purchases and the contracting process through forums, mentoring programs, and written materials.

General Services Administration (GSA), *Civilian Board of Contract Appeals, 1800 F St. N.W. 20405; (202) 606-8820. Fax, (202) 606-0019. Stephen M. Daniels, Chair, (202) 606-8800. For filings, (202) 606-8800. General email, stephendaniels@cbca.gov*

Web, www.cbca.gov

Hears and decides contract disputes between government contractors and agencies and certain federal employee claims concerning expense reimbursement, excluding the Departments of Defense, Army, Navy, and Air Force; the National Aeronautics and Space Administration; the U.S. Postal Service; the Postal Regulatory Commission; and the Tennessee Valley Authority. Provides alternative dispute resolution services on contract-related matters to executive agencies when jointly requested by the agency and its contractor.

General Services Administration (GSA), *Federal Procurement Data System–Next Generation (FPDS-NG), 10780 Parkridge Blvd., Reston, VA 20191; (703) 390-5360. Mary Searcy, Director; Praveen Chinnam, Program Manager, Serendipity Now. Help Desk, (703) 390-5360. General email, fpdssupport@serendipitynow.com*

Web, www.fpds.gov

Service contracted out by GSA that collects procurement data from all federal government contracts and disseminates these data via the Internet. Reports include agency identification, products or services purchased, dollar obligation, principal place of performance, and contractor identification; also provides socioeconomic indicators such as business size and business ownership type.

Office of Personnel Management

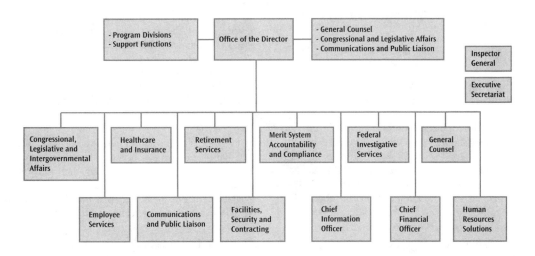

General Services Administration (GSA), *Government-wide Policy,* 1275 1st St. N.E., 6th Floor 20417; (202) 501-8880. Fax, (202) 208-1224. Anne E. Rung, Associate Administrator. Web, www.gsa.gov/ogp

Coordinates GSA policy-making activities, including areas of personal and real property, travel and transportation, acquisition (internal GSA and governmentwide), information technology, regulatory information, and use of federal advisory committees; promotes collaboration between government and the private sector in developing policy and management techniques; works to integrate acquisition, management, and disposal of government property.

General Services Administration (GSA), *Government-wide Policy, Acquisition Policy,* 1275 1st St. N.E. 20417; (202) 501-0692. Fax, (202) 357-0038. Jeffrey A. (Jeff) Koses, Senior Procurement Executive.
General email, askacquisition@gsa.gov

Web, www.gsa.gov/chiefacquisitionofficer

Develops and implements federal government acquisition policies and procedures; administers Federal Acquisition Regulation (FAR) for civilian agencies. Manages several GSA-specific and governmentwide acquisition database systems. Conducts pre-award and post-award contract reviews; suspends and debars contractors for unsatisfactory performance; coordinates and promotes governmentwide career management and training programs for contracting personnel.

General Services Administration (GSA), *Small Business Utilization,* 1275 1st St. N.E. 20417; (202) 501-1021. Fax, (202) 501-2590. Jiyoung C. Park, Associate Administrator. Toll-free, (855) 672-8472.
General email, smallbusiness@gsa.gov

Web, www.gsa.gov/osbu

Works to increase small business access to government contract procurement opportunities. Provides policy guidance and direction for GSA Regional Small Business Offices, which offer advice and assistance to businesses interested in government procurement.

Minority Business Development Agency *(Commerce Dept.),* 1401 Constitution Ave. N.W., #5053 20230; (202) 482-2332. Fax, (202) 501-4698. Alejandra Castillo, Director. Information, (888) 324-1551.
Web, www.mbda.gov

Assists minority business owners in obtaining federal loans and contract awards; produces an annual report on federal agencies' performance in procuring from minority-owned businesses. Assists minority entrepreneurs one-on-one with financial planning, marketing, management, and technical assistance. Focuses on promoting wealth in minority communities.

U.S. AbilityOne Commission, 1401 S. Clark St., Arlington, VA 22202; 1421 Jefferson Davis Hwy., #10800, Arlington, VA 22202-3259; (703) 603-7740. Fax, (703) 603-0655. Tina Ballard, Executive Director.
General email, info@abilityone.gov

Web, www.abilityone.gov

Presidentially appointed committee. Determines which products and services are suitable for federal procurement from qualified nonprofit agencies that employ people who are blind or have other significant disabilities; seeks to increase employment opportunities for these individuals. (Formerly Committee for Purchase from People Who Are Blind or Severely Disabled.)

► CONGRESS

For a listing of relevant congressional committees and subcommittees, please see pages 290–291 or the Appendix.

Government Accountability Office (GAO), *Procurement Law Division,* 441 G St. N.W., #7494 20548; (202) 512-8278. Fax, (202) 512-9749. Ralph O. White, Managing Associate General Counsel.
Web, www.gao.gov

Considers and rules on the proposed or actual award of a government contract upon receipt of a written protest.

▶NONGOVERNMENTAL

Coalition for Government Procurement, *1990 M St. N.W., #450 20036; (202) 331-0975. Fax, (202) 822-9788. Roger D. Waldron, President. General email, info@thecgp.org*

Web, www.thecgp.org

Alliance of business firms that sell to the federal government. Seeks equal opportunities for businesses to sell to the government; monitors practices of the General Services Administration and government procurement legislation and regulations.

National Contract Management Assn. (NCMA), *21740 Beaumeade Circle, #125, Ashburn, VA 20147; (571) 382-0082. Fax, (703) 448-0939. Michael Fischetti, Executive Director, (571) 382-1123. Toll-free, (800) 344-8096. General email, memberservices@ncmahq.org*

Web, www.ncmahq.org

Membership: individuals concerned with administering, procuring, negotiating, and managing government and commercial contracts and subcontracts. Sponsors the Certified Professional Contracts Manager Program and various educational and professional programs.

NIGP (The Institute for Public Procurement), *151 Spring St., Herndon, VA 20170-5223; (703) 736-8900. Fax, (703) 736-2818. Rick Grimm, Chief Executive Officer, ext. 240. Information, (800) 367-6447.*

Web, www.nigp.org

Membership: governmental purchasing departments, agencies, and organizations at the federal, state, and local levels in the United States, Canada, and internationally. Provides public procurement officers with technical assistance and information, training seminars, and professional certification. (Formerly the National Institute of Governmental Purchasing.)

Professional Services Council (PSC), *4401 Wilson Blvd., #1110, Arlington, VA 22203; (703) 875-8059. Fax, (703) 875-8922. Stan Z. Soloway, President.*

Web, www.pscouncil.org

Membership: associations and firms that provide local, state, federal, and international governments with professional, engineering, and technical services. Analyzes the process by which the government awards contracts to private firms. Monitors legislation and regulations. (Merged with Contract Services Assn. of America.)

POSTAL SERVICE

General

▶AGENCIES

U.S. Postal Service (USPS), *475 L'Enfant Plaza S.W. 20260-0001; (202) 268-2000. Fax, (202) 268-5211. Patrick R. Donahoe, Postmaster General. Library, (202) 268-2906. Press, (202) 268-2155. Locator, (202) 268-2000.*

General inquiries, (800) 275-8777. Web, www.usps.com

Offers postal service throughout the country as an independent establishment of the executive branch. Library open to the public by appointment.

U.S. Postal Service (USPS), *Inspection Service, 475 L'Enfant Plaza S.W., #3100 20260-2100; (202) 268-4264. Fax, (202) 268-7316. Guy Cottrell, Chief Postal Inspector. Fraud and abuse hotline, (877) 876-2455. Web, http://postalinspectors.uspis.gov*

Investigates criminal violations of postal laws, such as theft of mail or posted valuables, assaults on postal employees, organized crime in postal-related matters, and prohibited mailings. Conducts internal audits; investigates postal activities to determine effectiveness of procedures; monitors compliance of individual post offices with postal regulations.

▶CONGRESS

For a listing of relevant congressional committees and subcommittees, please see pages 290–291 or the Appendix.

Consumer Services

▶AGENCIES

U.S. Postal Service (USPS), *Consumer and Industry Affairs, 475 L'Enfant Plaza S.W. 20260; (202) 268-4910. Fax, (202) 268-6251. James A. Nemec, Vice President, Consumer and Industry Affairs.*

Web, www.usps.com

Develops policies, plans, and programs for commercial mailers to improve customer satisfaction. Directs the Business Partners program. Activities include local postal customer councils, the National Postal Forum, and the Mailers' Technical Advisory Committee.

U.S. Postal Service (USPS), *Office of the Consumer Advocate, 475 L'Enfant Plaza S.W., #4012 20260-0004; (202) 268-6308. Fax, (202) 636-5344. James A. Nemec, Vice President and Consumer Advocate, (202) 268-2681. Inquiries, (800) ASK-USPS or (800) 275-8777. General email, usps_ca_response@usps.gov*

Web, www.usps.com

Provides information to consumers on USPS services and products. Receives and attempts to settle consumer grievances.

Employee and Labor Relations

▶AGENCIES

U.S. Postal Service (USPS), *Employee Resource Management, 475 L'Enfant Plaza S.W., #9840 20260-4200; (202) 268-3783. Fax, (202) 268-5605. Rosemarie Fernandez, Vice President.*

Web, www.usps.com

Drafts and implements employment policies and practices and safety and health guidelines.

Procurement Officers for Federal Departments and Agencies

DEPARTMENTS

Agriculture, Lisa M. Wilusz, (202) 720-9448

Commerce, Barry Berkowitz, (202) 482-4248

Defense, Shay D. Assad, (703) 695-7145

Education, James Ropelewski, (202) 245-6221

Energy, Paul Bosco, (202) 586-3524

Health and Human Services, Nancy Gunderson, (202) 690-8554

Homeland Security, Nick Nayak, (202) 447-5300

Housing and Urban Development, Jemine A. Bryon, (202) 708-0600

Interior, Debra E. Sonderman, (202) 254-5501

Justice, Michael H. Allen, (202) 514-3101

Labor, Edward Hugler, (202) 693-4040

State, Corey Rindner, (703) 516-1689

Transportation, Willie Smith, (202) 366-5613

Treasury, Cathy Higginbothem, (202) 622-1039

Veterans Affairs, Jan R. Frye, (202) 461-6920

AGENCIES

Consumer Product Safety Commission, Donna M. Hutton, (301) 504-7009

Corporation for National and Community Service, William Anderson, (202) 606-6980

Environmental Protection Agency, John Bashista, (202) 564-4310

Export-Import Bank, Mark Pitra, (202) 565-3338

Farm Credit Administration, Philip J. Shebest, (703) 883-4378

Federal Communications Commission, Joseph Giuliani, (202) 418-0152

Federal Deposit Insurance Corporation, Michael J. Rubino, (703) 562-2192

Federal Emergency Management Agency, Francis Spampinato, (202) 646-3355

Federal Maritime Commission, Michael Kilby, (202) 523-5900

Federal Mediation and Conciliation Service, Vacant, (202) 606-5477

Federal Reserve System, Vacant, (202) 452-2767

Federal Trade Commission, John Isgrigg III, (202) 326-2307

General Services Administration, Houston Taylor, (703) 605-2759

National Aeronautics and Space Administration, William P. McNally, (202) 358-2090

National Labor Relations Board, Gloria Joseph, (202) 273-3890

National Mediation Board, June D.W. King, (202) 692-5010

National Science Foundation, Jeffery Lupis, (703) 292-7944

Nuclear Regulatory Commission, Kathryn O. Greene, (301) 492-3500

Office of Personnel Management, Tina McGuire, (202) 606-2200

Securities and Exchange Commission, Julie Basile, (202) 551-8699

Small Business Administration, LeAnn Delaney, (202) 205-6731

Social Security Administration, Pete Spencer, (410) 965-2475

U.S. International Trade Commission, Celeste H. Rueffert, (202) 205-2252

U.S. Postal Service, Susan Brownell, (202) 268-4040

U.S. Postal Service (USPS), *Labor Relations, 475 L'Enfant Plaza S.W., #9014 20260-4100; (202) 268-7447. Fax, (202) 268-3074. Douglas A. Tulino, Vice President. Web, www.usps.com*

Handles collective bargaining and contract administration for the U.S. Postal Service.

▶ **NONGOVERNMENTAL**

American Postal Workers Union (APWU), AFL-CIO, *1300 L St. N.W. 20005; (202) 842-4200. Fax, (202) 842-4297. Mark Dimondstein, President. Web, www.apwu.org*

Membership: approximately 330,000 postal employees, including clerks, motor vehicle operators, maintenance operators, and retirees. Assists members with contract negotiation and grievances; conducts training programs and workshops. Monitors legislation and regulations.

(Affiliated with the Postal, Telegraph, and Telephone International and the AFL-CIO.)

National Alliance of Postal and Federal Employees (NAPFE), *1628 11th St. N.W. 20001; (202) 939-6325. Fax, (202) 939-6389. James M. McGee, President. General email, headquarters@napfe.org Web, www.napfe.com*

Membership: approximately 70,000 postal and federal employees. Helps members negotiate pay, benefits, equal opportunity, and better working conditions; conducts training programs and workshops. Monitors legislation and regulations.

National Assn. of Letter Carriers, AFL-CIO, *100 Indiana Ave. N.W. 20001-2144; (202) 393-4695. Fax, (202) 737-1540. Fredric V. Rolando, President. Information, (202) 662-2850. Web, www.nalc.org*

Membership: approximately 300,000 city letter carriers working for, or retired from, the U.S. Postal Service. Assists members with contract negotiation and grievances; conducts training programs and workshops. Monitors legislation and regulations. (Affiliated with the AFL-CIO and the Union Network International.)

National Assn. of Postal Supervisors, *1727 King St., #400, Alexandria, VA 22314-2753; (703) 836-9660. Fax, (703) 836-9665. Louis Atkins, President.*
General email, napshq@naps.org
Web, www.naps.org

Membership: more than 35,000 present and retired postal supervisors, managers, and postmasters. Management association that cooperates with other postal management associations, unions, and the U.S. Postal Service to improve the efficiency of the postal service; promotes favorable working conditions and broader career opportunities for all postal employees; provides members with information on current functions and legislative issues of the postal service.

National Assn. of Postmasters of the United States, *8 Herbert St., Alexandria, VA 22305-2600; (703) 683-9027. Fax, (703) 683-6820. David Ravenelle, Executive Director.*
General email, napusinfo@napus.org
Web, www.napus.org

Membership: present and former postmasters of the United States. Promotes the postal service and the welfare of its members. Assists postmasters facing discipline or other adverse actions. Monitors legislation and regulations.

National League of Postmasters, *1 Beltway Center, 5904 Richmond Hwy., #500, Alexandria, VA 22303-1864; (703) 329-4550. Fax, (703) 329-0466. Mark Strong, President, ext. 19.*
General email, information@postmasters.org
Web, www.postmasters.org

Represents postmasters in labor negotiations with the U.S. Postal Service and in legislative matters of concern. Works to improve the salaries, working hours, and working conditions of postmasters.

National Rural Letter Carriers' Assn., *1630 Duke St., Alexandria, VA 22314-3467; (703) 684-5545. Fax, (703) 518-0677. Jeanette P. Dwyer, President.*
Web, www.nrlca.org

Membership: more than 100,000 rural letter carriers working for, or retired from, the U.S. Postal Service. Seeks to improve rural mail delivery. Negotiates labor agreements affecting members; conducts training programs and workshops. Monitors legislation and regulations.

National Star Route Mail Contractors Assn., *324 E. Capitol St. N.E. 20003-3897; (202) 543-1661. Fax, (202) 543-8863. John V. Maraney, Executive Director.*
General email, info@starroutecontractors.org
Web, www.starroutecontractors.org

Membership: contractors for highway mail transport and selected rural route deliverers. Acts as liaison between contractors and the U.S. Postal Service, the Transportation Dept., the Labor Dept., and Congress concerning contracts, wages, and other issues. Monitors legislation and regulations.

Mail Rates and Classification

►AGENCIES

Postal Regulatory Commission, *901 New York Ave. N.W., #200 20268-0001; (202) 789-6800. Fax, (202) 789-6891. Ruth Y. Goldway, Chair.*
General email, ann.fisher@prc.gov
Web, www.prc.gov

Independent agency with regulatory oversight over the U.S. Postal Service. Develops and maintains regulations concerning postal rates; consults with the Postal Service on delivery service standards and performance measures; consults with the State Dept. on international postal policies; prevents anticompetitive postal practices; and adjudicates complaints.

U.S. Postal Service (USPS), *Mail Entry, 475 L'Enfant Plaza S.W., #2P836 20260; (202) 268-8081. Fax, (202) 268-8273. Diane Smith, Manager, (202) 268-8091.*
Web, General web site, www.usps.com and
Business services, www.usps.com/business

Implements policies governing the acceptance and verification of business mail by the U.S. Postal Service.

U.S. Postal Service (USPS), *Pricing, 475 L'Enfant Plaza S.W., #4100 20260-5014; (202) 268-8116. Fax, (202) 268-6251. Cynthia Sanchez-Hernandez, Vice President.*
Web, www.usps.com

Sets prices for U.S. Postal Service product lines using competitive pricing methods.

U.S. Postal Service (USPS), *Product Classification, 475 L'Enfant Plaza S.W., #4446 20260-5015; (202) 268-3789. Fax, (202) 268-3888. Lizbeth (Liz) Dobbins, Manager.*
Web, www.usps.com

Issues policy statements on domestic mail classification matters. Ensures the accuracy of policies developed by the Postal Regulatory Commission with respect to domestic mail classification schedules.

►NONGOVERNMENTAL

Alliance of Nonprofit Mailers, *1211 Connecticut Ave. N.W., #610 20036-2705; (202) 462-5132. Fax, (202) 462-0423. Stephen Kearney, Executive Director.*
General email, alliance@nonprofitmailers.org
Web, www.nonprofitmailers.org

Works to maintain reasonable mail rates for nonprofit organizations. Represents member organizations before Congress, the U.S. Postal Service, the Postal Regulatory Commission, and the courts on nonprofit postal rate and mail classification issues.

Assn. of Marketing Service Providers (AMSP), *1800 Diagonal Rd., #320, Alexandria, VA 22314-2806; (703) 836-9200. Fax, (703) 548-8204. Ken Garner, President. General email, amsp@amsp.org*

Web, www.amsp.org

Membership: direct mail advertising services, order-fulfillment businesses, and their suppliers. Serves as a clearinghouse for members on improving methods of using the mail for advertising. Sponsors workshops and conferences; accredits fulfillment companies. (Formerly Mailing and Fulfillment Service Assn.)

Assn. for Postal Commerce (POSTCOM), *1800 Diagonal Rd., #320, Alexandria, VA 22314-2862; (703) 524-0096. Fax, (703) 997-2414. Gene A. Del Polito, President. General email, info@postcom.org*

Web, www.postcom.org

Membership: companies and organizations interested in mail as a medium for advertising and product delivery. Provides members with information about postal news worldwide, postal policy, postal rates, and legislation regarding postal regulations. Monitors legislation and regulations.

DMA Nonprofit Federation, *1615 L St. N.W., #1100 20036; (202) 861-2498. Fax, (202) 628-4383. Xenia Boone, Senior Vice President. Alternate phone, (202) 861-2427. General email, aosgood@the-dma.org*

Web, www.nonprofitfederation.org

Membership: nonprofit organizations and their suppliers that rely on nonprofit mail and other marketing channels, including digital, email, and telephone, to reach donors. Serves as a liaison between members and the U.S. Postal Service; represents members' interests before regulatory agencies; monitors legislation and regulations. Hosts conferences on fundraising across marketing channels.

Parcel Shippers Assn. (PSA), *1800 Diagonal Rd., #320, Alexandria, VA 22314; (571) 257-7617. Fax, (571) 257-7613. Richard Porras, President. General email, psa@parcelshippers.org*

Web, www.parcelshippers.org

Voluntary organization of business firms concerned with the shipment of parcels. Works to improve parcel post rates and service; represents members before the Postal Regulatory Commission in matters regarding parcel post rates. Monitors legislation and regulations.

Stamps, Postal History

▶AGENCIES

National Postal Museum *(Smithsonian Institution),* *2 Massachusetts Ave. N.E. 20013 (mailing address: P.O. Box 37012, Washington, DC 20013); (202) 633-5555. Fax, (202) 633-9393. Allen Kane, Director. Tours, (202) 633-5534. Press, (202) 633-5518. Web, http://postalmuseum.si.edu*

Exhibits postal history and stamp collections; provides information on world postal and stamp history.

U.S. Postal Service (USPS), *Citizens' Stamp Advisory Committee, 475 L'Enfant Plaza, S.W., #3300 20260-3501; (202) 268-3875. Fax, (202) 268-4965. Janet Klug, Chair. Web, http://about.usps.com/who-we-are/leadership/stamp-advisory-committee.htm*

Reviews stamp subject nominations, which are open to the public. Develops the annual Stamp Program and makes subject and design recommendations to the Postmaster General.

U.S. Postal Service (USPS), *Stamp Development, 475 L'Enfant Plaza, S.W., #3300 20260-3501; (202) 268-5141. Fax, (202) 268-4965. Mary Anne Penner, Manager, Acting. Web, www.usps.com*

Manages the stamp selection function; develops the basic stamp preproduction design; manages relationship with stamp collecting community.

PUBLIC ADMINISTRATION

General

▶AGENCIES

Office of Management and Budget (OMB) *(Executive Office of the President), President's Management Council, Dwight D. Eisenhower Executive Office Bldg., #216 20503; (202) 395-5020. Fax, (202) 395-6102. Jeffrey D. Zients, Chair. Web, www.whitehouse.gov/omb and www.qsa.gov/portal/content/1338811*

Membership: chief operating officers of federal government departments and agencies. Responsible for implementing the management improvement initiatives of the administration. Develops and oversees improved governmentwide management and administrative systems; formulates long-range plans to promote these systems; works to resolve interagency management problems and to implement reforms.

President's Commission on White House Fellowships, *712 Jackson Place N.W. 20503; (202) 395-4522. Fax, (202) 395-6179. Cindy Moelis, Director. Web, www.whitehouse.gov/about/fellows*

Nonpartisan commission that provides professionals from all sectors of national life with the opportunity to observe firsthand the processes of the federal government. Fellows work for one year as special assistants to cabinet members or to principal members of the White House staff. Qualified applicants have demonstrated superior accomplishments early in their careers and have a commitment to leadership and public service.

▶CONGRESS

For a listing of relevant congressional committees and subcommittees, please see pages 290–291 or the Appendix.

Government Accountability Office (GAO), *Education, Workforce, and Income Security, 441 G St. N.W., #5928 20548; (202) 512-7215. Barbara D. Bovbjerg, Managing Director.*
Web, www.gao.gov

Independent, nonpartisan agency in the legislative branch. Responsible for intergovernmental relations activities. Reviews the effects of federal grants and regulations on state and local governments. Works to reduce intergovernmental conflicts and costs. Seeks to improve the allocation and targeting of federal funds to state and local governments through changes in federal funding formulas.

▶**NONGOVERNMENTAL**

American Society for Public Administration, *1301 Pennsylvania Ave. N.W., #700 20004; (202) 393-7878. Fax, (202) 638-4952. William P. Shields Jr., Executive Director.*
General email, info@aspanet.org
Web, www.aspanet.org

Membership: government administrators, public officials, educators, researchers, and others interested in public administration. Presents awards to distinguished professionals in the field; sponsors workshops and conferences; disseminates information about public administration. Promotes high ethical standards for public service.

Assn. of Government Accountants, *2208 Mount Vernon Ave., Alexandria, VA 22301; (703) 684-6931. Fax, (703) 548-9367. Relmond Van Daniker, Executive Director. Toll-free, (800) 242-7211.*
General email, agamembers@agacgfm.org
Web, www.agacgfm.org

Membership: professionals engaged in government accounting, auditing, budgeting, and information systems. Sponsors education, research, and conferences; administers certification program.

Federally Employed Women, *455 Massachusetts Ave. N.W., #306 20001; (202) 898-0994. Fax, (202) 898-1535. Michelle Crockett, President.*
General email, few@few.org
Web, www.few.org

Membership: women and men who work for the federal government. Works to eliminate sex discrimination in government employment and to increase job opportunities for women; offers training programs. Monitors legislation and regulations.

International City/County Management Assn. (ICMA), *777 N. Capitol St. N.E., #500 20002-4201; (202) 289-4262. Fax, (202) 962-3500. Robert J. O'Neill, Executive Director, ext. 3610. Member services and information, (202) 962-3680. Toll-free, (800) 745-8780.*
General email, customercontact@icma.org
Web, www.icma.org

Membership: appointed managers and administrators of cities, towns, counties, and other local governments around the world; local government employees; academics; and citizens. Provides technical assistance to local governments in the United States and abroad to develop professional practices and ethical, transparent government. Services include research and development, performance measurement, and consulting. Sponsors workshops and conferences. Publishes resources for local government management professionals.

International Public Management Assn. for Human Resources (IPMA-HR), *1617 Duke St., Alexandria, VA 22314; (703) 549-7100. Fax, (703) 684-0948. Neil Reichenberg, Executive Director.*
General email, ipma@ipma-hr.org
Web, www.ipma-hr.org

Membership: personnel professionals from federal, state, and local governments. Provides information on training procedures, management techniques, and legislative developments on the federal, state, and local levels.

National Academy of Public Administration, *1600 K St. N.W., #400 20006; (202) 347-3190. Fax, (202) 223-0823. Dan G. Blair, President.*
General email, academy@napawash.org
Web, www.napawash.org

Membership: scholars and administrators in public management. Chartered by Congress to assist federal, state, and local government agencies, public officials, and foundations on government and management challenges.

National Foundation for Women Legislators, *1727 King St., #300, Alexandria, VA 22314; (703) 518-7931. Jody Thomas, Executive Director.*
General email, nfwl@womenlegislators.org
Web, www.womenlegislators.org

Provides leadership development and networking resources to women leaders at the city, state, and federal levels of government.

National Women's Political Caucus, *110 H St. N.W., #300 20005 (mailing address: P.O. Box 50476, Washington, DC 20091); (202) 785-1100. Fax, (202) 370-6306. Linda Young, President; Bettina M. Hager, Program Director.*
General email, info@nwpc.org
Web, www.nwpc.org

Seeks to increase the number of women in policy-making positions in federal, state, and local government. Identifies, recruits, trains, and supports pro-choice women candidates for public office. Monitors agencies and provides names of qualified women for high- and mid-level appointments.

Network of Schools of Public Policy, Affairs, and Administration (NASPAA), *1029 Vermont Ave. N.W., #1100 20005-3517; (202) 628-8965. Fax, (202) 626-4978. Laurel McFarland, Executive Director.*
General email, naspaa@naspaa.org
Web, www.naspaa.org

Membership: universities involved in education, research, and training in public management in the United

States and internationally. Serves as a clearinghouse for information on education in public administration, public policy, and public affairs programs in colleges and universities. Accredits master's degree programs in public affairs, public policy, and public administration. (Formerly National Assn. of Schools of Public Affairs and Administration.)

Women in Government Relations, *8400 Westpark Dr., McLean, VA 22102; (703) 299-8546. Fax, (703) 299-9233. Emily Bardach, Executive Director.*
General email, info@wgr.org

Web, www.wgr.org

Membership: professionals in business, trade associations, and government whose jobs involve governmental relations at the federal, state, or local level. Serves as a forum for exchange of information among its members.

STATE AND LOCAL GOVERNMENT

General

▶ **AGENCIES**

Census Bureau *(Commerce Dept.),* **Governments,** *4600 Silver Hill Rd., #5K156, Suitland, MD 20746 (mailing address: change city, state, and zip code to Washington, DC 20233-6800); (301) 763-1489. Fax, (301) 763-6792. Vacant, Chief.*
Web, www.census.gov/govs

Collects data from all state and local government organization units every five years; surveys government functions and activities, public employment, and government finances. Releases data by level of government, type of government, and category of activity.

General Services Administration (GSA), *Catalog of Federal Domestic Assistance (CFDA), 2200 Crystal City Dr., Crystal Park 1, Arlington, VA 22202; (703) 605-3427. Priscilla Owens, Director, (703) 605-3408. Help desk, (866) 606-8220.*
General email, priscilla.owens@gsa.gov

Web, www.cfda.gov

Disseminates information on federal domestic assistance programs through the CFDA Web site. Information includes all types of federal aid and explains types of assistance, eligibility requirements, application processes, and suggestions for writing proposals. Catalog may be downloaded from the CFDA Web site. Printed version may be ordered from the Superintendent of Documents, U.S. Government Printing Office, Washington, DC 20402; (202) 512-1800, or toll-free, (866) 512-1800; or online at http://bookstore.gpo.gov.

Housing and Urban Development Dept. (HUD), *Policy Development and Research, 451 7th St. S.W., #8100 20410-6000; (202) 708-1600. Fax, (202) 619-8000. Vacant, Assistant Secretary.*
Web, www.huduser.org

Assesses and maintains information on housing needs, market conditions, and programs; conducts research on housing and community development issues such as building technology, economic development, and urban planning.

Multistate Tax Commission, *444 N. Capitol St. N.W., #425 20001-1538; (202) 650-0300. Joe Huddleston, Executive Director.*
General email, mtc@mtc.gov
Web, www.mtc.gov

Membership: state governments that have enacted the Multistate Tax Compact. Promotes fair, effective, and efficient state tax systems for interstate and international commerce; works to preserve state tax sovereignty. Encourages uniform state tax laws and regulations for multistate and multinational enterprises. Maintains three regional audit offices that monitor compliance with state tax laws and encourage uniformity in taxpayer treatment. Administers program to identify businesses that do not file tax returns with states.

Office of Management and Budget (OMB) *(Executive Office of the President),* **Federal Financial Management,** *New Executive Office Bldg., #6025 20503; (202) 395-3895. Fax, (202) 395-3952. Daniel I. (Danny) Werfel, Controller.*
Web, www.whitehouse.gov/omb/financial_default

Facilitates exchange of information on financial management standards, techniques, and processes among officers of state and local governments.

▶ **CONGRESS**

For a listing of relevant congressional committees and subcommittees, please see pages 290–291 or the Appendix.

▶ **NONGOVERNMENTAL**

American Legislative Exchange Council (ALEC), *2900 Crystal Dr., #600, Arlington, VA 22202; (703) 373-0933. Fax, (703) 373-0927. Ron Scheberle, Executive Director.*
General email, membership@alec.org

Web, www.alec.org

Nonpartisan educational and research organization for state legislators. Conducts research and provides information and model state legislation on public policy issues. Supports the development of state policies to limit government, expand free markets, promote economic growth, and preserve individual liberty.

Coalition of Northeastern Governors (CONEG), *Policy Research Center, Inc., 400 N. Capitol St. N.W., #382 20001; (202) 624-8450. Fax, (202) 624-8463. Anne D. Stubbs, Executive Director.*
General email, coneg@sso.org

Web, www.coneg.org

Membership: governors of seven northeastern states (Connecticut, Maine, Massachusetts, New Hampshire, New York, Rhode Island, and Vermont). Addresses common issues of concern such as energy, economic development, transportation, and the environment; serves as an information clearinghouse and liaison among member states and with the federal government. Administers the Northeast Regional Biomass Program, a public-private cooperative initiative among eleven northeastern states, the federal government, regional and national organizations, and key industries to advance the development and use of biomass resources and technologies in the Northeast.

Council of State Governments (CSG), *Washington Office,* *444 N. Capitol St. N.W., #401 20001; (202) 624-5460. Fax, (202) 624-5452. David Adkins, Executive Director (Ky.); Vacant, Director. Media, (859) 244-8246.*
General email, staterecovery@csg.org

Web, www.csg.org and www.csgdc.org

Membership: governing bodies of states, commonwealths, and territories, and various affiliated national organizations of state officials. Promotes interstate, federal-state, and state-local cooperation; interests include education, transportation, human services, housing, natural resources, and economic development. Provides services to affiliates and associated organizations, including the National Assn. of State Treasurers, National Assn. of Government Labor Officials, and other state administrative organizations in specific fields. Monitors legislation and executive policy. (Headquarters in Lexington, Ky.)

Government Finance Officers Assn. (GFOA), *Federal Liaison Center, 1301 Pennsylvania Ave., #309 20004-1714; (202) 393-8020. Fax, (202) 393-0780. Dustin McDonald, Director.*
General email, federalliaison@gfoa.org

Web, www.gfoa.org

Membership: state and local government finance managers. Offers training and publications in public financial management. Conducts research in public fiscal management, design and financing of government programs, and formulation and analysis of government fiscal policy. (Headquarters in Chicago, Ill.)

International Municipal Lawyers Assn. (IMLA), *7910 Woodmont Ave., #1440, Bethesda, MD 20814; (202) 466-5424. Fax, (202) 785-0152. Chuck Thompson, General Counsel, ext. 7110.*
General email, info@imla.org

Web, www.imla.org

Membership: local government attorneys and public law practitioners. Acts as a research service for members in all areas of municipal law; participates in litigation of municipal and constitutional law issues.

National Assn. of Bond Lawyers, *601 13th St., #800-S 20005-3875; (202) 503-3300. Fax, (202) 637-0217. Linda H. Wyman, Chief Operating Officer.*
General email, bdaly@nabl.org

Web, www.nabl.org

Membership: state and municipal finance lawyers. Educates members and others on the law relating to state and municipal bonds and other obligations. Provides advice and comment at the federal, state, and local levels on legislation, regulations, rulings, and court and administrative proceedings regarding public obligations.

National Assn. of Clean Water Agencies, *1816 Jefferson Pl. N.W. 20036; (202) 833-2672. Fax, (888) 267-9505. Ken Kirk, Executive Director, (202) 833-4653.*
General email, info@nacwa.org

Web, www.nacwa.org

Represents public wastewater treatment works, public and private organizations, law firms representing public clean water agencies, and nonprofit or academic organizations. Interests include water quality and watershed management. Sponsors conferences. Monitors legislation and regulations.

National Assn. of Counties (NACo), *25 Massachusetts Ave. N.W., #500 20001-2028; (202) 393-6226. Fax, (202) 393-2630. Matthew D. Chase, Executive Director. Press, (202) 942-4220. Toll-free, (888) 407-6226.*
Web, www.naco.org

Membership: county governments and county officials and their staffs through NACo's affiliates. Conducts research, supplies information, and provides technical and public affairs assistance on issues affecting counties. Interests include homeland security, drug abuse, access to health care, and public-private partnerships. Monitors legislation and regulations.

National Assn. of Regional Councils, *777 N. Capitol St. N.E., #305 20002; (202) 986-1032. Fax, (202) 986-1038. Fred Abousleman, Executive Director.*
Web, www.narc.org

Membership: regional councils of local governments, councils of government, and metropolitan planning organizations. Works to improve local governments' intergovernmental planning and coordination at the regional level. Interests include housing, urban and rural planning, transportation, the environment, homeland security and emergency preparedness, workforce development, economic and community development, and aging.

National Assn. of Secretaries of State, *444 N. Capitol St. N.W., #401 20001; (202) 624-3525. Fax, (202) 624-3527. Leslie Reynolds, Executive Director.*
General email, nass@sso.org

Web, www.nass.org

Organization of secretaries of state and lieutenant governors or other comparable state officials from the fifty states, the District of Columbia, Guam, Puerto Rico, and the U.S. Virgin Islands. Interests include budget and finance, elections and voting, state business services and licensing, e-government, and state heritage, including a digital archives initiative.

National Assn. of State Budget Officers, *444 N. Capitol St. N.W., #642 20001-1501; (202) 624-5382. Fax, (202) 624-7745. Scott D. Pattison, Executive Director.*
General email, nasbo-direct@nasbo.org

Web, www.nasbo.org

Membership: state budget and financial officers. Publishes research reports on budget-related issues; shares best practices; provides training and technical assistance. (Affiliate of the National Governors Assn.)

National Assn. of Towns and Townships (NATaT), *1130 Connecticut Ave. N.W., #300 20036; (202) 454-3954. Fax, (202) 331-1598. Jennifer Imo, Federal Director. Toll-free, (866) 830-0008.*
General email, info@natat.org
Web, www.natat.org

Membership: towns, townships, small communities, and others interested in supporting small town government. Provides local government officials from small jurisdictions with technical assistance, educational services, and public policy support; conducts research and coordinates training for local government officials nationwide. Interests include tax benefits for local public service volunteers, local economic development, water and wastewater infrastructure, transportation improvements, and allocation of federal resources. (Affiliated with National Center for Small Communities.)

National Black Caucus of Local Elected Officials (NBC/ LEO), *c/o National League of Cities, 1301 Pennsylvania Ave. N.W. 20004-1763; (202) 626-3169. Adam McFadden, President. Press, (202) 626-3015.*
General email, constituencygroup@nlc.org
Web, www.nlc.org

Membership: African American elected officials at the local level and other interested individuals. Seeks to increase African American participation on the National League of Cities' steering and policy committees. Informs members on issues, and plans strategies to achieve objectives through legislation and direct action. Interests include cultural diversity, local government and community participation, housing, economics, job training, the family, and human rights.

National Black Caucus of State Legislators, *444 N. Capitol St. N.W., #622 20001; (202) 624-5457. Fax, (202) 508-3826. LaKimba DeSadier, Executive Director.*
Web, www.nbcsl.org

Membership: African American state legislators. Promotes effective leadership among African American state legislators through education, research, and training; serves as an information network and clearinghouse for members.

National Conference of State Legislatures, *Washington Office, 444 N. Capitol St. N.W., #515 20001; (202) 624-5400. Fax, (202) 737-1069. Neal Osten, Director; Molly Ramsdell, Director.*
General email, info@ncsl.org
Web, www.ncsl.org

Coordinates and represents state legislatures at the federal level; conducts research, produces videos, and publishes reports in areas of interest to state legislatures; conducts an information exchange program on intergovernmental relations; sponsors seminars for state legislators and their staffs. Interests include unfunded federal mandates, state-federal law conflict, and fiscal integrity.

Monitors legislation and regulations. (Headquarters in Denver, Colo.)

National Foundation for Women Legislators, *1727 King St., #300, Alexandria, VA 22314; (703) 518-7931. Jody Thomas, Executive Director.*
General email, nfwl@womenlegislators.org
Web, www.womenlegislators.org

Provides leadership development and networking resources to women leaders at the city, state, and federal levels of government.

National Governors Assn. (NGA), *444 N. Capitol St. N.W., #267 20001-1512; (202) 624-5300. Dan L. Crippen, Executive Director. Press, (202) 624-5301.*
General email, webmaster@nga.org
Web, www.nga.org

Membership: governors of states, commonwealths, and territories. Provides members with policy and technical assistance. Makes policy recommendations to Congress and the president on community and economic development; education; international trade and foreign relations; energy and the environment; health care and welfare reform; agriculture; transportation, commerce, and technology; communications; criminal justice; public safety; and workforce development.

National League of Cities, *1301 Pennsylvania Ave. N.W., #550 20004; (202) 626-3000. Fax, (202) 626-3043. Clarence Anthony, Executive Director.*
General email, info@nlc.org
Web, www.nlc.org

Membership: cities and state municipal leagues. Provides city leaders with training, technical assistance, and publications; investigates needs of local governments in implementing federal programs that affect cities. Holds two annual conferences; conducts research; sponsors awards. Monitors legislation and regulations. (Affiliates include National Black Caucus of Local Elected Officials.)

NIGP (The Institute for Public Procurement), *151 Spring St., Herndon, VA 20170-5223; (703) 736-8900. Fax, (703) 736-2818. Rick Grimm, Chief Executive Officer, ext. 240. Information, (800) 367-6447.*
Web, www.nigp.org

Membership: governmental purchasing departments, agencies, and organizations at the federal, state, and local levels in the United States, Canada, and internationally. Provides public procurement officers with technical assistance and information, training seminars, and professional certification. (Formerly the National Institute of Governmental Purchasing.)

Public Risk Management Assn. (PRIMA), *700 S. Washington St., #218, Alexandria, VA 22314; (703) 528-7701. Fax, (703) 739-0200. Marshall W. Davies, Executive Director, (703) 253-1265.*
General email, info@primacentral.org
Web, www.primacentral.org

Membership: state and local governments and their risk management practitioners, including benefits and insurance managers, and private sector organizations. Develops and teaches cost-effective management techniques for handling public liability issues; promotes professional development of its members. Gathers and disseminates information about risk management to public and private sectors.

Public Technology Institute (PTI), *1420 Prince St., #200, Alexandria, VA 22314-2815; (202) 626-2400.*
Alan R. Shark, Executive Director. Press, (202) 626-2432.
General email, info@pti.org

Web, www.pti.org

Cooperative research, development, and technology-transfer organization of cities and counties in North America. Assists local governments in increasing efficiency, reducing costs, improving services, and developing public enterprise programs to help local officials create revenues and serve citizens. Participates in international conferences.

Southern Governors' Assn., *444 N. Capitol St. N.W., #200 20001-1585; (202) 624-5897. Fax, (202) 624-7797.*
Diane Duff, Executive Director.
General email, sga@sso.org

Web, www.southerngovernors.org

Membership: governors of sixteen southern states, plus the territories of Puerto Rico and the U.S. Virgin Islands, and corporate affiliates. Provides a regional, bipartisan forum for governors to help formulate and implement national policy; works to enhance the region's competitiveness nationally and internationally, to explore common problems, and to coordinate regional initiatives.

Stateline.org, *901 E St. N.W., 8th Floor 20004; (202) 552-2000. Fax, (202) 552-2299. Sandy Johnson, Project Director.*
General email, editor@stateline.org

Web, www.stateline.org

Independent online news site and forum. Encourages debate on state-level issues such as health care, tax and budget policy, the environment, and immigration. (Part of the Pew Charitable Trust.)

U.S. Conference of Mayors, *1620 Eye St. N.W., #400 20006; (202) 293-7330. Fax, (202) 293-2352.*
J. Thomas Cochran, Executive Director.
General email, info@usmayors.org

Web, www.usmayors.org

Membership: mayors of cities with populations of 30,000 or more. Promotes city-federal cooperation; publishes reports and conducts meetings on federal programs, policies, and initiatives that affect urban and suburban interests. Serves as a clearinghouse for information on urban and suburban problems. (Approximately 1,400 U.S. cities.)

Western Governors' Assn., *Washington Office, 400 N. Capitol St. N.W., #376 20001; (202) 624-5402. Fax, (202) 624-7707. James (Jim) Ogsbury, Executive Director.*
Web, www.westgov.org

Local Government in the Washington Metropolitan Area

DISTRICT OF COLUMBIA

Executive Office of the Mayor,
Vincent C. Gray, Mayor
John A. Wilson Building
1350 Pennsylvania Ave. N.W., # 316, 20004;
   (202) 727-6300, Fax: (202) 727-0505
Email, eom@dc.gov
Web, major.dc.gov

MARYLAND

Montgomery County,
Ike Leggett, County Executive
101 Monroe St., 2nd Floor, Rockville, MD 20850;
   (240) 777-0311, Fax: (240) 777-2544;
Email, countyexecutive@co.pg.md.us or
ocemail@montgomerycountymd.gov
Web, www.montgomerycountymd.gov/exec/

Prince George's County,
Rushern L. Baker III, County Executive
14741 Gov. Oden Bowie Dr., Upper Marlboro, MD 20772;
   (301) 952-4131, Fax: (301) 952-5148
Email, countyexecutive@co.pg.md.us
Web, www.princegeorgescountymd.gov

VIRGINIA

City of Alexandria,
William D. Euille, Mayor
301 King St., Rm. 1900, Alexandria, VA 22314;
   (703) 746-4357, Fax: (703) 838-6426
Email, alexvamayor@aol.com
Web, www.alexandriava.gov

Arlington County,
Barbara Donnellan, County Manager
2100 Clarendon Blvd., Arlington, VA 22201;
   (703) 228-3120, Fax: (703) 228-4611
Email, countymanager@arlingtonva.us
Web, www.arlingtonva.us

Fairfax County,
Edward L. Long Jr., County Executive
12000 Government Center Pkwy., #552, Fairfax, VA 22035;
   (703) 324-2531, Fax: (703) 324-3956
Email, coexec@fairfaxcounty.gov
Web, www.fairfaxcounty.gov

City of Falls Church,
Wyatt Shields, City Manager
300 Park Ave., #303E, Falls Church, VA 22046;
   (703) 248-5004, Fax: (703) 248-5146
Email, city-manager@fallschurchva.gov
Web, www.fallschurchva.gov

Independent, nonpartisan organization of governors from nineteen western states, two Pacific territories, and one commonwealth. Identifies and addresses key policy and governance issues in natural resources, clean energy and alternative transportation fuels, the environment, radioactive waste transportation, human services, economic development, international relations, and public management. (Headquarters in Denver, Colo.)

Women In Government, *1319 F St. N.W., #710 20004; (202) 333-0825. Fax, (202) 333-0875. Dyan Alexander, Executive Director, Interim.*
General email, wig@womeningovernment.org
Web, www.womeningovernment.org

Membership: women state legislators. Seeks to enhance the leadership role of women policymakers by providing issue education and leadership training. Sponsors seminars and conducts educational research.

Washington Area

►CONGRESS

For a listing of relevant congressional committees and subcommittees, please see pages 290–291 or the Appendix.

►NONGOVERNMENTAL

Metropolitan Washington Council of Governments,
777 N. Capitol St. N.E., #300 20002-4239; (202) 962-3200. Fax, (202) 962-3203. Chuck Bean, Executive Director. Press, (202) 962-3250.
General email, ccogdtp@mwcog.org
Web, www.mwcog.org

Membership: local governments in the Washington area, plus members of the Maryland and Virginia legislatures and the U.S. Congress. Analyzes and develops regional responses to issues such as the environment, affordable housing, economic development, health, population growth, human and social services, public safety, and transportation.

Walter E. Washington Convention Center Authority, *801 Mt. Vernon Pl. N.W. 20001; (202) 249-3000. Fax, (202) 249-3133. Gregory A. O'Dell, Chief Executive Officer. Information, (800) 368-9000. Press, (202) 249-3217.*
Web, www.dcconvention.com

Promotes national and international conventions, meetings, and trade shows; hosts sports, entertainment, and special events; fosters redevelopment of downtown Washington.

10 Health

GENERAL POLICY AND ANALYSIS

Basic Resources

▶ **AGENCIES**

Agency for Health Care Research and Quality *(Health and Human Services Dept.), Office of Communication and Knowledge Transfer,* 540 Gaither Rd., Rockville, MD 20850; (301) 427-1364. Fax, (301) 427-1873. Howard Holland, Director, (301) 427-1857. Public inquiries, (301) 427-1104.
General email, info@ahrq.gov

Web, www.ahrq.gov/about/ockt/ocktmiss.htm

Works to improve the quality, safety, effectiveness, and efficiency of health care in the United States. Promotes improvements in clinical practices and in organizing, financing, and delivering health care services. Conducts and supports comparative effectiveness research, demonstration projects, evaluations, and training; disseminates information on a wide range of activities.

Assistant Secretary for Health *(Health and Human Services Dept.),* 200 Independence Ave. S.W., #701H 20201 *(mailing address: Tower Bldg., Plaza Level 1, #100, 1101 Wooton Pkwy., Rockville, MD 20852);* (240) 276-8853. Fax, (240) 453-6141. Dr. Howard K. Koh, Assistant Secretary, Acting; Dr. Boris D. Lushniak, Surgeon General, Acting.
Web, www.surgeongeneral.gov

Directs activities of the Office of the Assistant Secretary for Health. Serves as the secretary's principal adviser on health concerns; exercises specialized responsibilities in various health areas, including domestic and global health. Advises the public on smoking, AIDS, immunization, diet, nutrition, disease prevention, and other general health issues, including responses to bioterrorism. Oversees activities of all members of the Public Health Service Commissioned Corps. For information on avian and pandemic flu, go to PandemicFlu.gov.

Assistant Secretary for Health *(Health and Human Services Dept.), Disease Prevention and Health Promotion,* 1101 Wootton Pkwy., #LL100, Rockville, MD 20852; (240) 453-8280. Fax, (240) 453-8282. Donald Wright, Director. Alternate phone, (240) 453-8250.
Web, www.odphp.osophs.dhhs.gov

Develops national policies for disease prevention, clinical preventive services, and health promotion; assists the private sector and agencies with disease prevention, clinical preventive services, and health promotion activities.

Assistant Secretary for Health *(Health and Human Services Dept.), National Health Information Center,* 1100 Wooton Pkwy., #LL100, Rockville, MD 20852 *(mailing address: P.O. Box 1133, Washington, DC 20013-1133);* (240) 453-8280. Fax, (301) 984-4256. Donald Wright, Project Manager. Information, (800) 336-4797.
General email, healthfinder@nhic.org

Web, www.health.gov/nhic and www.healthfinder.gov

A project of the Office of Disease Prevention and Health Promotion; provides referrals on health topics and resources.

Centers for Disease Control and Prevention (CDC) *(Health and Human Services Dept.), Washington Office,* 395 E St. S.W., #9100 20201; (202) 245-0600. Fax, (202) 245-0602. Dr. Thomas R. Frieden, Director; Edward Hunter, Director of Washington Office *(Congressional Affairs).* Public inquiries, (800) 232-4636. General email, cdinfo@cdc.gov

Web, www.cdc.gov/washington

Collaborates with state and local health departments to further health promotion; prevention of disease, injury, and disability; and preparedness for new health threats. Monitors the health of individuals, detects and investigates health problems, conducts research to enhance prevention, develops and advocates public health policies, implements prevention strategies, promotes healthy behaviors, fosters safe and healthful environments, and provides leadership and training. (Headquarters in Atlanta, Ga.: 1600 Clifton Rd. N.E. 30333.)

Federal Trade Commission (FTC), *Consumer Protection, Advertising Practices,* 601 New Jersey Ave. N.W., #3223 20001 *(mailing address: 600 Pennsylvania Ave. N.W., Washington, DC 20580);* (202) 326-3090. Fax, (202) 326-3259. Mary Engle, Associate Director.
Web, www.ftc.gov/bcp/bcpap.shtm

Protects consumers from deceptive and unsubstantiated advertising through law enforcement, public reports, and industry outreach. Evaluates the nutritional and health benefits of foods and the effectiveness of dietary supplements, drugs, and medical devices, particularly as they relate to weight loss.

Food and Drug Administration (FDA) *(Health and Human Services Dept.),* 10903 New Hampshire Ave., Silver Spring, MD 20993; (888) 463-6332. Fax, (301) 847-3536. Margaret A. Hamburg, Commissioner. Main Library *(White Oak in Silver Spring),* (301) 796-2039. Press, (301) 796-4540.
Web, www.fda.gov

Protects public health by assessing the safety, effectiveness, and security of human and veterinary drugs, vaccines, and other biological products. Protects the safety and security of the nation's food supply, cosmetics, diet supplements, and products emitting radiation. Regulates tobacco products. Develops labeling and packaging standards; conducts inspections of manufacturers; issues orders to companies to recall and/or cease selling or producing hazardous products; enforces rulings and recommends action to Justice Dept. when necessary. Libraries open to the public; 24-hour advance appointment required.

Food and Drug Administration (FDA) *(Health and Human Services Dept.), International Programs,* 10903 New Hampshire Ave., Bldg. 31/32, Silver Spring, MD 20993; (301) 796-8400. Fax, (301) 595-5063. Mary Lou Valdez, Associate Commissioner.
Web, www.fda.gov/internationalprograms

HEALTH RESOURCES IN CONGRESS

For a complete listing of Congress committees, including their full contact information, leadership, membership, and jurisdictions, please refer to the Appendix on pages 724–842.

HOUSE:

House Agriculture Committee, (202) 225-2171.
Web, agriculture.house.gov or
democrats.agriculture.house.gov
  Subcommittee on Department Operations, Oversight, and Nutrition, (202) 225-2171.
House Appropriations Committee, (202) 225-2771.
Web, appropriations.house.gov or
democrats.appropriations.house.gov
  Subcommittee on Agriculture, Rural Development, FDA, and Related Agencies, (202) 225-2638.
  Subcommittee on Labor, Health and Human Services, Education, and Related Agencies, (202) 225-3508.
House Armed Services Committee, (202) 225-4151.
Web, armedservices.house.gov or
democrats.armedservices.house.gov
  Subcommittee on Military Personnel, (202) 225-7560.
House Budget Committee, (202) 226-7270.
Web, budget.house.gov or
democrats.budget.house.gov
House Education and the Workforce Committee, (202) 225-4527.
Web, edworkforce.house.gov or
democrats.edworkforce.house.gov
  Subcommittee on Health, Employment, Labor, and Pensions, (202) 225-4527.
  Subcommittee on Workforce Protections, (202) 225-4527.
House Energy and Commerce Committee, (202) 225-2927.

Web, energycommerce.house.gov or
democrats.energycommerce.house.gov
  Subcommittee on Environment and the Economy, (202) 225-2927.
  Subcommittee on Health, (202) 225-2927.
House Foreign Affairs Committee, (202) 225-5021.
Web, foreignaffairs.house.gov or
democrats.foreignaffairs.house.gov
  Subcommittee on Africa, Global Health, Global Human Rights, and International Organizations, (202) 226-7812.
House Natural Resources Committee, (202) 225-2761.
Web, naturalresources.house.gov or
democrats.naturalresources.house.gov
House Oversight and Government Reform Committee, (202) 225-5074.
Web, oversight.house.gov or
democrats.oversight.house.gov
  Subcommittee on Energy Policy, Health Care, and Entitlements, (202) 225-5074.
House Science, Space, and Technology Committee, (202) 225-6371.
Web, science.house.gov or democrats.science.house.gov
  Subcommittee on Research and Technology, (202) 225-6371.
House Small Business Committee, (202) 225-5821.
Web, smallbusiness.house.gov or
democrats.smallbusiness.house.gov
  Subcommittee on Health and Technology, (202) 225-5821.
House Veterans' Affairs Committee, (202) 225-3527.
Web, veterans.house.gov or democrats.veterans.house.gov
  Subcommittee on Health, (202) 225-9154.

Serves as FDA's liaison with foreign counterpoint agencies, international organizations, and the U.S. diplomatic corps. Gathers and assesses information to inform decisions about FDA-regulated product imports. Seeks to advance global public health through distribution of health information, coordination of public health strategies, and promotion of public safety. Seeks to harmonize regulatory standards. Provides technical assistance.

Food and Drug Administration (FDA) *(Health and Human Services Dept.), Regulatory Affairs, 5600 Fishers Lane, #14101, #HFC01, Rockville, MD 20857; (301) 796-8800. Fax, (301) 595-7943. Melinda K. Plaisier, Associate Commissioner.*
Web, www.fda.gov/ora

Directs and coordinates the FDA's compliance activities; manages field offices; advises FDA commissioner on domestic and international regulatory policies.

Health and Human Services Dept. (HHS), *200 Independence Ave. S.W. 20201; (202) 690-7000. Fax, (202) 690-7203. Vacant, Secretary; William V. Corr, Deputy Secretary, (202) 690-6133. Press, (202) 690-6343. Press, (202) 690-6139. Toll-free, (877) 696-6775.*
Web, www.hhs.gov

Acts as principal adviser to the president on health and welfare plans, policies, and programs of the federal government. Encompasses the Centers for Medicare and Medicaid Services, the Administration for Children and Families, the Public Health Service, and the Centers for Disease Control and Prevention.

Health and Human Services Dept. (HHS), *National Committee on Vital and Health Statistics, 3311 Toledo Rd., #2339, Hyattsville, MD 20782; (301) 458-4614. Fax, (301) 458-4022. Debbie Jackson, Executive Secretary, Acting.*
Web, www.ncvhs.hhs.gov

House Ways and Means Committee, (202) 225-3625.
Web, waysandmeans.house.gov or
democrats.waysandmeans.house.gov
Subcommittee on Health, (202) 225-3943.

SENATE:

Senate Agriculture, Nutrition, and Forestry
Committee, (202) 224-2035.
Web, ag.senate.gov
Subcommittee on Jobs, Rural Economic Growth,
and Energy Innovation, (202) 224-2035.
Subcommittee on Nutrition, Specialty Crops,
Food, and Agricultural Research,
(202) 224-2035.
Senate Appropriations Committee, (202) 224-7363.
Web, appropriations.senate.gov
Subcommittee on Agriculture, Rural
Development, FDA, and Related Agencies,
(202) 224-8090.
Subcommittee on Labor, Health and Human
Services, Education, and Related Agencies,
(202) 224-7363.
Senate Armed Services Committee, (202) 224-3871.
Web, armed-services.senate.gov
Subcommittee on Personnel, (202) 224-3871.
Senate Banking, Housing, and Urban Affairs
Committee, (202) 224-7391.
Web, banking.senate.gov
Senate Budget Committee, (202) 224-0642.
Web, budget.senate.gov
Senate Commerce, Science, and Transportation
Committee, (202) 224-0411.
Web, commerce.senate.gov
Subcommittee on Science and Space,
(202) 224-0415.

Senate Environment and Public Works Committee,
(202) 224-8832.
Web, epw.senate.gov
Subcommittee on Clean Air and Nuclear Safety,
(202) 224-8832.
Subcommittee on Superfund, Toxics and
Environmental Health, (202) 224-8832.
Subcommittee on Transportation and
Infrastructure, (202) 224-8832.
Senate Finance Committee, (202) 224-4515.
Web, finance.senate.gov
Subcommittee on Health Care,
(202) 224-4515.
Senate Health, Education, Labor, and Pensions
Committee, (202) 224-5375.
Web, help.senate.gov
Subcommittee on Children and Families,
(202) 224-5375.
Subcommittee on Employment and Workplace
Safety, (202) 228-1455.
Subcommittee on Primary Health and Aging,
(202) 224-5480.
Senate Indian Affairs Committee,
(202) 224-2251.
Web, indian.senate.gov
Senate Judiciary Committee, (202) 224-7703.
Web, judiciary.senate.gov
Subcommittee on Crime and Terrorism,
(202) 228-3740.
Senate Small Business and Entrepreneurship
Committee, (202) 224-5175.
Web, sbc.senate.gov
Senate Special Committee on Aging,
(202) 224-5364.
Web, aging.senate.gov

Statutory public advisory body on health data statistics and national health information policy. Serves as a national forum on health data. Aims to accelerate the evolution of public and private health information systems toward more uniform, shared data standards within the context of privacy and security concerns.

Health and Human Services Dept. (HHS), *Office of the National Coordinator for Health Information Technology, 200 Independence Ave. S.W., #729-D 20201; (202) 690-7151. Fax, (202) 690-6079. Dr. Karen de Salvo, National Coordinator.*
General email, onc.request@hhs.gov
Web, http://healthit.hhs.gov

Coordinates nationwide efforts to implement information technology that allows for electronic use and exchange of health information. Goals include ensuring security for

patient health information, improving health care quality, and reducing health care costs.

Health and Human Services Dept. (HHS), *Planning and Evaluation, 200 Independence Ave. S.W., #415F 20201; (202) 690-7858. Fax, (202) 690-7383. Rima Cohen, Assistant Secretary, Acting.*
Web, www.hhs.gov/aspe

Advises the secretary on policy development in health, disability, human services, data, and science, and provides advice and analysis on economic policy. Manages strategic and legislative planning and reviews regulations. Conducts research and evaluation studies, develops policy analyses, and estimates the cost and benefits of policy alternatives under consideration by the department or Congress.

Health and Human Services Dept. (HHS), *Preparedness and Response (ASPR), 200 Independence Ave. S.W.,*

#638-G 20201; (202) 205-2882. Nicole Lurie, Assistant Secretary.
Web, www.phe.gov

Serves as the secretary's principal adviser on matters relating to bioterrorism and public health emergencies. Directs activities of HHS relating to the protection of the civilian population from acts of bioterrorism and other public health emergencies.

Health and Human Services Dept. (HHS), President's Commission for the Study of Bioethical Issues, 1425 New York Ave. N.W., #C100 20005; (202) 233-3960. Fax, (202) 233-3990. Amy Gutmann, Chair; Lisa M. Lee, Executive Director.
General email, info@bioethics.gov
Web, www.bioethics.gov

Advises the president on ethical issues related to advances in biomedical science and technology, including stem cell research, assisted reproduction, cloning, end of life care, and the protection of human subjects in research.

Health Resources and Services Administration (Health and Human Services Dept.), 5600 Fishers Lane, #1471, Rockville, MD 20857; (301) 443-2216. Fax, (301) 443-1246. Mary Wakefield, Administrator. Information, (301) 443-3376. Toll-free, (888) 275-4772.
General email, askhrsa.gov
Web, www.hrsa.gov

Administers federal health service programs related to access, quality, equity, and cost of health care. Supports state and community efforts to deliver care to underserved areas and groups with special health needs.

Health Resources and Services Administration (Health and Human Services Dept.), Rural Health Policy, 5600 Fishers Lane, #5A05, Rockville, MD 20857; (301) 443-0835. Fax, (301) 443-2803. Tom Morris, Associate Administrator.
General email, tmorris@hrsa.gov
Web, www.ruralhealth.hrsa.gov

Works with federal agencies, states, and the private sector to develop solutions to health care problems in rural communities. Administers grants to rural communities and supports rural health services research. Studies the effects of Medicare and Medicaid programs on rural access to health care.

National Center for Health Statistics (Centers for Disease Control and Prevention), 3311 Toledo Rd., #7204, Hyattsville, MD 20782; (301) 458-4500. Fax, (301) 458-4020. Charles J. Rothwell, Director. Information, (800) 232-4636.
Web, www.cdc.gov/nchs

Compiles, analyzes, and disseminates national statistics on population health characteristics, health facilities and human resources, health costs and expenditures, and health hazards. Interests include international health statistics.

National Institute of Food and Agriculture (NIFA) (Agriculture Dept.), Institute of Food Safety and Nutrition, 1400 Independence Ave. S.W., MS 2225 20250-2225; (202) 720-5004. Fax, (202) 401-4888. Robert Holland, Assistant Director.

Web, www.nifa.usda.gov/about/pdfs/fact_sheets/inst_fs_fsn.pdf

Works toward safe food supply by reducing food-borne illness. Addresses causes of microbial contamination and antimicrobial resistance; educates consumer and food safety professionals; and develops food processing technologies. Promotes programs to improve citizens' health through better nutrition, reducing childhood obesity, and improving food quality.

National Institute for Occupational Safety and Health (NIOSH) (Centers for Disease Control and Prevention), 395 E St. S.W., Patriots Plaza 1, #9200 20201; (202) 245-0625. John Howard, Director. Information, (800) 232-4636.
General email, cdcinfo@cdc.gov
Web, www.cdc.gov/niosh

Supports and conducts research on occupational safety and health issues; provides technical assistance and training; organizes international conferences and symposia; develops recommendations for the Labor Dept. Operates occupational safety and health bibliographic databases; publishes documents on occupational safety and health.

National Institutes of Health (NIH) (Health and Human Services Dept.), 1 Center Dr., Bldg. 1, #344, MSC-0188, Bethesda, MD 20892-0148; (301) 496-4000. Fax, (301) 496-0017. Francis S. Collins, Director; Dr. Lawrence A. Tabak, Deputy Director. Press, (301) 496-5787.
Web, www.nih.gov

Supports and conducts biomedical research into the causes and prevention of diseases and furnishes information to health professionals and the public. Comprises research institutes and other components (the National Library of Medicine, the National Center for Advancing Translational Sciences, the John E. Fogarty International Center, and 27 institutes, including the National Cancer Institute; the National Institute of Allergy and Infectious Diseases; the National Heart, Lung, and Blood Institute; and the National Institute of Diabetes and Digestive and Kidney Diseases). All institutes are located in Bethesda, except the National Institute of Environmental Health Sciences, P.O. Box 12233, Research Triangle Park, N.C. 27709.

► CONGRESS

Government Accountability Office (GAO), Health Care, 441 G St. N.W., #5A14 20548; (202) 512-7114. Cynthia A. Bascetta, Managing Director.
Web, www.gao.gov

Independent, nonpartisan agency in the legislative branch. Audits all federal government health programs, including those administered by the departments of Defense, Health and Human Services, and Veterans Affairs.

► CONGRESS

For a listing of relevant congressional committees and subcommittees, please see pages 318–319 or the Appendix.

►INTERNATIONAL ORGANIZATIONS

International Bank for Reconstruction and Development *(World Bank), Human Development Network, 1818 H St. N.W. 20433; (202) 473-1000. Elizabeth King, Vice President, Acting; Carolyn Reynolds, Media Contact, (202) 473-0049.*
Web, www.worldbank.org

Provides member countries with support for initiatives to eradicate extreme poverty and hunger, achieve universal primary education, promote gender equality, reduce child mortality, combat HIV/AIDS, and ensure environmental sustainability.

Pan American Health Organization, *525 23rd St. N.W. 20037; (202) 974-3000. Fax, (202) 974-3663. Dr. Carissa F. Etienne, Director.*
Web, www.paho.org

Works to extend health services to underserved populations of its member countries and to control or eradicate communicable diseases; promotes cooperation among governments to solve public health problems. (Regional Office for the Americas of the World Health Organization, which is headquartered in Geneva.)

►NONGOVERNMENTAL

American Clinical Laboratory Assn., *1100 New York Ave. N.W., #725 West 20005; (202) 637-9466. Fax, (202) 637-2050. Alan Mertz, President.*
General email, info@acla.com
Web, www.acla.com

Membership: laboratories and laboratory service companies. Advocates laws and regulations that recognize the role of laboratory services in cost-effective health care. Works to ensure the confidentiality of patient test results. Provides education, information, and research materials to members.

American Public Health Assn., *800 Eye St. N.W. 20001-3710; (202) 777-2430. Fax, (202) 777-2534. Dr. Georges Benjamin, Executive Director.*
General email, comments@apha.org
Web, www.apha.org

Membership: health providers, educators, environmentalists, policymakers, and health officials at all levels working both within and outside of governmental organizations and educational institutions. Works to protect communities from serious, preventable health threats. Strives to ensure that community-based health promotion and disease prevention activities and preventive health services are universally accessible in the United States. Develops standards for scientific procedures in public health.

Assn. of State and Territorial Health Officials, *2231 Crystal Dr., #450, Arlington, VA 22202; (202) 371-9090. Fax, (571) 527-3189. Dr. Paul Jarris, Executive Director.*
Web, www.astho.org

Membership: executive officers of state and territorial health departments. Serves as legislative review agency and information source for members. Alternate Web site: www.statepublichealth.org.

The Brookings Institution, *Economic Studies Program, 1775 Massachusetts Ave. N.W. 20036-2188; (202) 797-6000. Fax, (202) 797-6181. Ted Gayer, Director. Press, (202) 797-6105.*
General email, escomment@brookings.edu
Web, www.brookings.edu/economics

Studies federal health care issues and health programs, including Medicare, Medicaid, and long-term care.

Center for Economic and Policy Research (CEPR), *1611 Connecticut Ave. N.W., #400 20009; (202) 293-5380. Fax, (202) 588-1356. Dean Baker, Co-Director; Mark Weisbrot, Co-Director.*
General email, cepr@cepr.net
Web, www.cepr.net

Researches economic and social issues and the impact of related public policies. Presents findings to the public with the goal of better preparing citizens to choose among various policy options. Promotes democratic debate and voter education. Areas of interest include health care, trade, financial reform, Social Security, taxes, housing, and the labor market.

Global Health Council, *1199 N. Fairfax St., #300, Alexandria, VA 22314; 1120 20th St. N.W., #500 20036; (703) 717-5200. Fax, (703) 717-5215. Christina Sow, Chair; Scott Jackson, Chief Executive Officer.*
General email, membership@globalhealth.org
Web, www.globalhealth.org

Membership: health care professionals, NGOs, foundations, corporations, government agencies, and academic institutions. Works to secure the information and resources for improved global health.

Grantmakers in Health, *1100 Connecticut Ave. N.W., #1200 20036; (202) 452-8331. Fax, (202) 452-8340. Faith Mitchell, President.*
General email, info@gih.org
Web, www.gih.org

Seeks to increase the capacity of private sector grantmakers to enhance public health. Fosters information exchange among grantmakers. Publications include a bulletin on current news in health and human services.

Healthcare Leadership Council, *750 9th St. N.W., #500 20001; (202) 452-8700. Fax, (202) 296-9561. Mary R. Grealy, President; Michael Freeman, Executive Vice President.*
General email, mfreeman@hlc.org
Web, www.hlc.org

Membership: health care leaders who examine major health issues, including access and affordability. Works to implement new public policies.

Health and Human Services Department

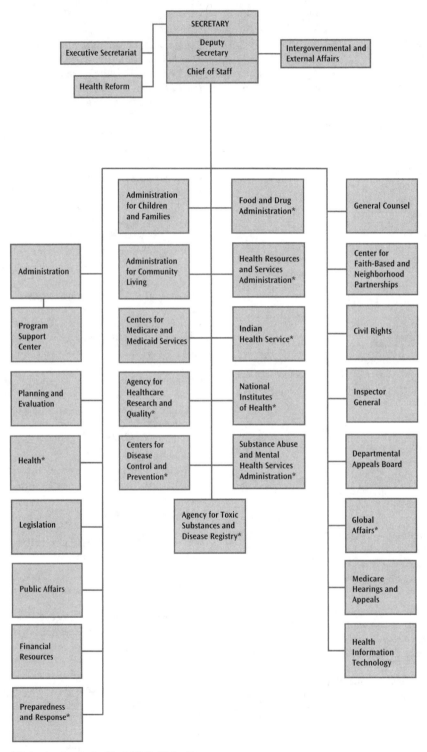

SECRETARY

Deputy Secretary

Chief of Staff

Executive Secretariat

Health Reform

Intergovernmental and External Affairs

Administration

Program Support Center

Planning and Evaluation

Health*

Legislation

Public Affairs

Financial Resources

Preparedness and Response*

Administration for Children and Families

Administration for Community Living

Centers for Medicare and Medicaid Services

Agency for Healthcare Research and Quality*

Centers for Disease Control and Prevention*

Agency for Toxic Substances and Disease Registry*

Food and Drug Administration*

Health Resources and Services Administration*

Indian Health Service*

National Institutes of Health*

Substance Abuse and Mental Health Services Administration*

General Counsel

Center for Faith-Based and Neighborhood Partnerships

Civil Rights

Inspector General

Departmental Appeals Board

Global Affairs*

Medicare Hearings and Appeals

Health Information Technology

* Designates components of the Public Health Service

Health Policy Institute, 3300 Whitehaven St. N.W., #5000, Box 571444, 20057-1485; (202) 687-0880. Fax, (202) 687-3110. Toni McRae, Administrative Assistant.
Web, http://ihcrp.georgetown.edu

Research branch of Georgetown University's Public Policy Institute. Interests include quality of care, cost effectiveness, outcomes research, structure and impact of managed care, health privacy, and access to care.

Henry J. Kaiser Family Foundation, *Washington Office*, 1330 G St. N.W. 20005; (202) 347-5270. Fax, (202) 347-5274. Drew Altman, President.
Web, www.kff.org

Offers information on major health care issues. Conducts research and communications programs. Monitors legislation and regulations. (Headquarters in Menlo Park, Calif. Not affiliated with Kaiser Permanente or Kaiser Industries.)

International Epidemiology Institute, 1455 Research Blvd., #550, Rockville, MD 20850; (301) 424-1054. Fax, (301) 424-1053. William J. Blot, Chief Executive Officer; Joseph K. McLaughlin, President.
General email, info@iei.ws
Web, www.iei.us

Investigates biomedical problems and environmental health issues for the public and private sectors, universities, and other institutions. Conducts studies and clinical trials. Helps identify potential risks and benefits associated with new medicines and new medical devices, including implants. (Affiliated with Vanderbilt University in Nashville, Tenn.)

National Assn. of Counties (NACo), 25 Massachusetts Ave. N.W., #500 20001-2028; (202) 393-6226. Fax, (202) 393-2630. Matthew D. Chase, Executive Director. Press, (202) 942-4220. Toll-free, (888) 407-6226.
Web, www.naco.org

Promotes federal understanding of county governments' role in providing, funding, and overseeing health services at the local level. Interests include indigent health care, Medicaid and Medicare, prevention of and services for HIV infection and AIDS, long-term care, mental health, maternal and child health, and traditional public health programs conducted by local health departments. Monitors legislation and regulations.

National Assn. of County and City Health Officials, 1100 17th St. N.W., 7th Floor 20036; (202) 783-5550. Fax, (202) 783-1583. Robert M. Pestronk, Executive Director.
General email, info@naccho.org
Web, www.naccho.org

Represents the nation's approximately 3,000 local health departments. Develops resources and programs to support local public health practices and systems. Submits health policy proposals to the federal government.

National Governors Assn. (NGA), *Health Division,* 444 N. Capitol St. N.W., #267 20001-1512; (202) 624-5343. Fax, (202) 624-7825. Frederick Isasi, Director. Information, (202) 624-5300.

General email, knolan@nga.org
Web, www.nga.org/cms/center/health

Provides technical assistance regarding the Title 21 Program, state oversight of managed care, public/private efforts to improve health care quality, and long-term care services.

National Health Council, 1730 M St. N.W., #500 20036-4561; (202) 785-3910. Fax, (202) 785-5923. Myrl Weinberg, President, ext. 546.
General email, info@nhcouncil.org
Web, www.nationalhealthcouncil.org

Membership: voluntary health agencies, associations, and business, insurance, and government groups interested in health. Conducts research on health and health-related issues. Monitors legislation and regulations.

National Health Policy Forum, 2131 K St. N.W., #500 20037; (202) 872-1390. Fax, (202) 862-9837. Judith Miller Jones, Director.
General email, nhpf@gwu.edu
Web, www.nhpf.org

Nonpartisan policy analysis and research organization that provides executive branch and congressional staff with information on financing and delivery of health care services. Affiliated with George Washington University.

National Quality Forum, 1030 15th St. N.W., #800 20005; (202) 783-1300. Fax, (202) 783-3434. Christine Castle, President. Press, (202) 478-9326.
General email, info@qualityforum.org
Web, www.qualityforum.org

Works to improve the quality of health care in the United States by setting national priorities and goals for performance improvement, endorsing national consensus standards for measuring and publicly reporting on performances, and promoting the attainment of national goals through education and outreach programs.

National Vaccine Information Center, 21525 Ridgetop Circle, #100, Sterling, VA 20166; (703) 938-0342. Fax, (571) 313-1268. Barbara Loe Fisher, President, (703) 938-0342.
General email, contactnvic@gmail.com
Web, www.nvic.org

Educational organization that supports informed vaccination decisions, including the option to forgo vaccination. Provides assistance to parents of children who have experienced vaccine reactions and publishes information on diseases and vaccines. Monitors vaccine research, legislation, and regulations.

Partnership for Prevention, 1015 18th St. N.W., #300 20036; (202) 833-0009. Fax, (202) 833-0113. Elissa Matulis Meyers, Executive Director.
General email, info@prevent.org
Web, www.prevent.org

Seeks to make prevention a priority in national health policy and practice. Coordinates the prevention-oriented efforts of federal health agencies, corporations, states, and nonprofit organizations in order to achieve the Healthy People 2020 national prevention goals.

Physicians for Human Rights, *Washington Office, 1730 Pennsylvania Ave. N.W., 7th Floor 20006; 1110 Vermont Ave. N.W. 20005; (202) 728-5335. Fax, (202) 728-3053. Andrea Gittleman, Interim Director, U.S. Policy; Vacant, Washington Director.*
General email, phrusa@phrusa.org
Web, www.physiciansforhumanrights.org

Mobilizes doctors, nurses, health specialists, scientists, and others to promote health and human rights globally. Investigates and seeks to end human rights abuses. Issues reports and press releases; conducts training programs on health and human rights issues; advocates to policymakers. (Headquarters in New York City.)

Public Citizen, *Health Research Group, 1600 20th St. N.W. 20009-1001; (202) 588-1000. Fax, (202) 588-7796. Michael Carome, Director.*
General email, hrg@citizen.org
Web, www.citizen.org

Citizens' interest group that conducts policy-oriented research on health care issues. Interests include hospital quality and costs, doctors' fees, physician discipline and malpractice, state administration of Medicare programs, workplace safety and health, unnecessary surgery, comprehensive health planning, dangerous drugs, carcinogens, and medical devices. Favors a single-payer (Canadian-style), comprehensive health program.

RAND Corporation, *Health Unit, Washington Office, 1200 S. Hayes St., Arlington, VA 22202-5050; (703) 413-1100. Fax, (703) 413-8111. C. Ross Anthony, Leader, Global Health Initiative, ext. 5265; Jeffrey Wasserman, Director, Health, (310) 393-0411. Media Relations, (703) 414-4795.*
General email, globalhealth@rand.org
Web, www.rand.org/health

Research organization that assesses health issues, including alternative reimbursement schemes for health care. Interests include health care costs and quality, military health, obesity, chronic disease prevention, and public health preparedness. Monitors national and international trends. (Headquarters in Santa Monica, Calif.)

Regulatory Affairs Professionals Society, *5635 Fishers Lane, #550, Rockville, MD 20852; (301) 770-2920. Fax, (301) 770-2924. Sherry Keramidas, Executive Director.*
General email, raps@raps.org
Web, www.raps.org

Membership: regulatory professionals in the medical device, pharmaceutical, and biotechnology product sectors worldwide. Promotes the safety and effectiveness of health care products. Supports the regulatory profession with resources, including education and certification. Monitors legislation and regulations.

Urban Institute, *The Health Policy Center, 2100 M St. N.W. 20037; (202) 833-7200. Fax, (202) 223-1149. Genevieve Kenney, Director; Stephen Zuckerman, Director. General email, uihealthpolicy@urban.org*
Web, http://healthpolicycenter.org

Analyzes trends and underlying causes of changes in health insurance, coverage access to care, and use of health care services by the U.S. population. Researches and analyzes select health issues, including private insurance; the uninsured; Medicaid, Medicare, and the State Children's Health Insurance Program (SCHIP); disability and long-term care; vulnerable populations; and health care reform.

Health Insurance, Managed Care

▶AGENCIES

Centers for Medicare and Medicaid Services (CMS) *(Health and Human Services Dept.), Center for Consumer Information and Insurance Oversight, 200 Independence Ave. S.W., #739H 20001; (202) 260-6085. Fax, (202) 690-6518. Gary Cohen, Director.*
Web, http://cciio.cms.gov

Assists states in reviewing insurance rates, including oversight of administrative costs as a percentage of expenditures for medical care (medical loss ratio); provides guidance and oversight for state-based insurance exchanges; administers the preexisting condition insurance plan, the temporary high-risk pool program, and the early retiree reinsurance program; compiles and maintains data for an Internet portal providing information on insurance options.

Centers for Medicare and Medicaid Services (CMS) *(Health and Human Services Dept.), Center for Medicare, 7500 Security Blvd., C5-01-07, Baltimore, MD 21244; (410) 786-0552. Fax, (410) 786-0192. Elizabeth Richter, Deputy Director. Information, (410) 786-3000.*
Web, www.cms.gov/medicare/medicare.html

Manages the traditional fee-for-service Medicare program, which includes the development of payment policy and management of Medicare fee-for-service contractors.

▶CONGRESS

For a listing of relevant congressional committees and subcommittees, please see pages 318–319 or the Appendix.

Congressional Budget Office, *Retirement and Long-Term Analysis, 419 FHOB 20515; (202) 226-2666. Fax, (202) 225-3149. Linda Bilheimer, Assistant Director. Web, www.cbo.gov*

Analyzes federal programs and policies concerning health care and retirement, including Medicare, Medicaid, subsidies to be provided through health insurance exchanges, and Social Security. Responsible for long-term budget protection and analyses of long-term effects of proposed legislation. Prepares reports to Congress.

▶NONGOVERNMENTAL

Alliance for Health Reform, *1444 Eye St. N.W., #910 20005-6573; (202) 789-2300. Fax, (202) 789-2233. Edward F. Howard, Executive Vice President. General email, info@allhealth.org*

Web, www.allhealth.org

Nonpartisan organization that advocates health care reform, including cost containment and coverage for all. Sponsors conferences and seminars for journalists, business leaders, policymakers, and the public.

American Medical Assn. (AMA), *Government Relations, 25 Massachusetts Ave. N.W., #600 20001-7400; (202) 789-7400. Fax, (202) 789-7485. Richard Deem, Senior Vice President of Advocacy.*

Web, www.ama-assn.org

Membership: physicians, residents, and medical students. Interests include the cost, quality, and access to health care; and physician payment and delivery innovation. Monitors legislation and regulations. (Headquarters in Chicago, Ill.)

America's Health Insurance Plans, *601 Pennsylvania Ave., South Bldg. N.W., #500 20004; (202) 778-3200. Fax, (202) 331-7487. Karen Ignagni, President. Press, (202) 778-8494.*

General email, ahip@ahip.org

Web, www.ahip.org

Membership: companies providing medical expense, long-term care, disability income, dental, supplemental, and stop-loss insurance and reinsurance to consumers, employers, and public purchasers. Advocates evidence-based medicine; targeted strategies to give all Americans access to health care; and health care cost savings through regulatory, legal, and other reforms. Provides educational programs and legal counsel. Monitors legislation and regulations. (Merger of the American Assn. of Health Plans and Health Insurance Assn. of America.)

Blue Cross and Blue Shield Assn., *Washington Office, 1310 G St. N.W. 20005; (202) 626-4780. Fax, (202) 626-4833. Scott Serota, President. Press, (202) 626-8625.*

Web, www.bcbs.com

Owns the Blue Cross and Blue Shield names and marks (brands) and grants several types of licenses to use them; also conducts trade association activities and operates businesses to support its license holders. (Headquarters in Chicago, Ill.)

Council for Affordable Health Insurance, *127 S. Peyton St., #210, Alexandria, VA 22314; (703) 836-6200. Fax, (866) 439-1657. Marianne Eterno, Executive Director. General email, mail@cahi.org*

Web, www.cahi.org

Membership: insurance carriers in the small group, individual, and senior markets, business groups, doctors, actuaries, and insurance brokers. Research and advocacy organization devoted to free-market solutions to America's health care problems. Promotes reform measures, including health savings accounts, tax equity, universal access, medical price disclosure prior to treatment, and caps on malpractice awards. Serves as a liaison with businesses, provider organizations, and public interest groups. Monitors legislation and regulations at state and federal levels.

Employee Benefit Research Institute, *1100 13th St. N.W., #878 20005; (202) 659-0670. Fax, (202) 775-6312. Dallas L. Salisbury, President. General email, info@ebri.org*

Web, www.ebri.org

Research organization serving as an employee benefits information source on health, welfare, and retirement issues. Does not lobby and does not take public policy positions.

Employers Council on Flexible Compensation, *1444 Eye St. N.W., #700 20005; (202) 659-4300. Fax, (202) 216-9646. Natasha Rankin, Executive Director. General email, info@ecfc.org*

Web, www.ecfc.org

Represents employers who have or are considering flexible compensation plans. Supports the preservation and expansion of employee choice in health insurance coverage. Monitors legislation and regulations.

Galen Institute, *P.O. Box 320010, Alexandria, VA 22320; (703) 299-8900. Fax, (703) 299-0721. Grace-Marie Turner, President. General email, galen@galen.org*

Web, www.galen.org

Provides ideas and information on health care financing, and the use of tax policy to advance consumer choice. Advocates for health savings accounts, competition among private plans in Medicare, and other free-market health reform ideas.

National Academy of Social Insurance, *1776 Massachusetts Ave. N.W., #400 20036-1904; (202) 452-8097. Fax, (202) 452-8111. Pamela J. Larson, Executive Vice President. General email, nasi@nasi.org*

Web, www.nasi.org

Promotes research and education on Social Security, Medicare, health care financing, and related public and private programs; assesses social insurance programs and their relationship to other programs; supports research and leadership development. Acts as a clearinghouse for social insurance information.

National Assn. of Health Underwriters, *1212 New York Ave. N.W., #1100 20005; (202) 552-5060. Fax, (202) 747-6820. Janet Trautwein, Executive Vice President. Press, (202) 595-0724. General email, info@nahu.org*

Web, www.nahu.org

Membership: licensed health insurance agents, brokers, consultants, and benefit professionals. Offers continuing education programs as well as business-development tools. Promotes private sector health insurance. Monitors legislation and regulations.

National Assn. of Manufacturers (NAM), *Human Resources Policy, 733 10th St. N.W., #700 20001; (202) 637-3127. Fax, (202) 637-3182. Joe Trauger, Vice President. Alternate phone, (202) 637-3000.*
Web, www.nam.org

Interests include health care, Social Security, employee benefits, cost containment, mandated benefits, Medicare, and other federal programs that affect employers. Opposed to government involvement in health care.

National Business Group on Health, *20 F St. N.W., #200 20001-6700; (202) 558-3000. Fax, (202) 628-9244. Helen Darling, President, (202) 558-3005.*
General email, info@businessgrouphealth.org
Web, www.businessgrouphealth.org

Membership: large corporations with an interest in health care benefits. Interests include reimbursement policies, disease prevention and health promotion, hospital cost containment, health care planning, corporate education, Medicare, and retiree medical costs. Monitors legislation and regulations.

National Coalition on Health Care, *1825 K St. N.W., #411 20005; (202) 638-7151. Fax, (202) 318-8509. John Rother, Chief Executive Officer.*
General email, bbeauregard@nchc.org
Web, www.nchc.org

Membership: insurers, labor organizations, large and small businesses, consumer groups, and health care providers. Advocates for improved access to affordable health care coverage and improved quality of care. Monitors legislation and regulations.

National Health Care Anti-Fraud Assn., *1201 New York Ave. N.W., #1120 20005; (202) 659-5955. Fax, (202) 785-6764. Louis Saccoccio, Chief Executive Officer.*
General email, nhcaa@nhcaa.org
Web, www.nhcaa.org

Membership: health insurance companies and regulatory and law enforcement agencies. Members work to identify, investigate, and prosecute individuals and groups defrauding health care reimbursement systems. Offers education and training for fraud investigators, including medical identity theft. Sponsors the Institute for Health Care Fraud Prevention.

Society of Professional Benefit Administrators,
2 Wisconsin Circle, #670, Chevy Chase, MD 20815; (301) 718-7722. Fax, (301) 718-9440. Anne Lennan, President.
General email, info@spbatpa.org
Web, www.spbatpa.org

Membership: third-party administration firms that manage employee benefit plans for client employers. Interests include health care regulations, employee benefits, revision of Medicare programs, and health care cost containment. Monitors industry trends, government compliance requirements, and developments in health care financing.

Hospitals

▶**AGENCIES**

Centers for Medicare and Medicaid Services (CMS) *(Health and Human Services Dept.), Survey and Certification Group, 7500 Security Blvd., C2-21-16, Baltimore, MD 21244-1850; (410) 786-9493. Fax, (410) 786-0194. Thomas Hamilton, Director; Jan Tarantino, Deputy Director, (410) 786-0905.*
Web, www.cms.gov/medicare/medicare.html

Enforces health care and safety standards for hospitals, nursing homes, and other health care facilities.

NIH Clinical Center *(National Institutes of Health), 10 Center Dr., #6-2551, Bethesda, MD 20892-1504; (301) 496-4114. Fax, (301) 402-0244. Dr. John I. Gallin, Director. Communications, (301) 496-2563.*
Web, www.cc.nih.gov

Serves as a clinical research center for the NIH; patients are referred by physicians and self-referred throughout the United States and overseas.

▶**CONGRESS**

For a listing of relevant congressional committees and subcommittees, please see pages 318–319 or the Appendix.

▶**NONGOVERNMENTAL**

American Hospital Assn., Washington Office, *325 7th St. N.W., #700 20004-2802; (202) 638-1100. Fax, (202) 626-2303. Richard Umbdenstock, President, (202) 626-2363. Information, (800) 424-4301.*
Web, www.aha.org

Membership: hospitals, other inpatient care facilities, outpatient centers, Blue Cross plans, areawide planning agencies, regional medical programs, hospital schools of nursing, and individuals. Conducts research and education projects in such areas as provision of comprehensive care, hospital economics, hospital facilities and design, and community relations; participates with other health care associations in establishing hospital care standards. Monitors legislation and regulations. (Headquarters in Chicago, Ill.)

America's Essential Hospitals, *1301 Pennsylvania Ave. N.W., #950 20004-1712; (202) 585-0100. Fax, (202) 585-0101. Dr. Bruce Siegel, Chief Executive Officer.*
General email, info@essentialhospitals.org
Web, www.essentialhospitals.org

Membership: city and county public hospitals, state universities, and hospital districts and authorities. Interests include Medicaid patients and vulnerable populations, including AIDS patients, the homeless, the mentally ill, and non–English-speaking patients. Holds annual regional meetings. Monitors legislation and regulations. (Formerly National Assn. of Public Hospitals and Health Systems.)

Assn. of Academic Health Centers, *1400 16th St. N.W., #720 20036; (202) 265-9600. Fax, (202) 265-7514. Dr. Steven Wartman, President. Web, www.aahcdc.org*

Membership: academic health centers (composed of a medical school, a teaching hospital, and at least one other health professional school or program). Participates in studies and public debates on health professionals' training and education, patient care, and biomedical research.

Children's Hospital Association, *401 Wythe St., Alexandria, VA 22314; (703) 684-1355. Fax, (703) 684-1589. Mark Weitecha, President. Web, www.childrenshospitals.net and www.facebook.com/childrenshospitals*

Membership: more than 220 children's hospitals nationwide. Acts as a resource for pediatric data and analytics for clinical and operational performance. Monitors state and federal issues on clinical care, education, research, and advocacy. (Merger of the Child Health Corporation of America, National Assn. of Children's Hospitals and Related Institutions, and National Assn. of Children's Hospitals.)

Federation of American Hospitals, *750 9th St. N.W., #600 20001-4524; (202) 624-1500. Fax, (202) 737-6462. Charles N. Kahn III, President. Web, www.fah.org*

Membership: investor-owned or federally owned or managed community hospitals and health systems. Interests include national health care issues, such as cost containment, Medicare and Medicaid, the tax code, and the hospital workforce. Monitors legislation and regulations.

Medicaid and Medicare

▶**AGENCIES**

Centers for Medicare and Medicaid Services (CMS) *(Health and Human Services Dept.), 200 Independence Ave. S.W., #314G 20201; (202) 690-6726. Fax, (202) 690-6262. Marilyn Tavenner, Administrator; Aryana C. Khalid, Chief of Staff. Information, (410) 786-3000. Web, www.cms.gov*

Administers Medicare (a health insurance program for persons with disabilities or age sixty-five or older who are eligible to participate) and Medicaid (a health insurance program for persons judged unable to pay for health services).

Centers for Medicare and Medicaid Services (CMS) *(Health and Human Services Dept.), Center for Medicaid and CHIP Services, 7500 Security Blvd., #C5-21-17, Baltimore, MD 21244; (410) 786-3871. Fax, (410) 786-0025. Cynthia (Cindy) Mann, Director; Penny Thompson, Deputy Director. Web, www.cms.gov and www.medicaid.gov*

Administers and monitors Medicaid programs to ensure program quality and financial integrity; promotes beneficiary awareness and access to services.

Centers for Medicare and Medicaid Services (CMS) *(Health and Human Services Dept.), Center for Medicare, 7500 Security Blvd., C5-01-07, Baltimore, MD 21244; (410) 786-0552. Fax, (410) 786-0192. Elizabeth Richter, Deputy Director. Information, (410) 786-3000. Web, www.cms.gov/medicare/medicare.html*

Manages the contractual framework for the Medicare program; establishes and enforces performance standards for contractors who process and pay Medicare claims. Issues regulations and guidelines for administration of the Medicare program.

Centers for Medicare and Medicaid Services (CMS) *(Health and Human Services Dept.), Center for Medicare and Medicaid Innovation, 7500 Security Blvd., S3-13-17, Baltimore, MD 21244; (410) 786-3316. Patrick Conway, Deputy Administrator. CMS Press, (410) 786-3316. General email, innovate@cms.hhs.gov Web, www.innovations.cms.gov*

Established pursuant to the Affordable Care Act of 2010 to explore innovative approaches to Medicare, Medicaid, and CHIP health care delivery and administration, with the goal of improving health outcomes and lowering costs. Solicits input from health care providers, the business community, patients and families, and other interested parties in order to indentify best practices. Funds state demonstration projects to evaluate integrated care and payment approaches.

Centers for Medicare and Medicaid Services (CMS) *(Health and Human Services Dept.), Chronic Care Management, 7500 Security Blvd., C5-05-27, Baltimore, MD 21244; (410) 786-4533. Fax, (410) 786-0765. Janet P. Samen, Director, (410) 786-4533. Web, www.cms.gov/medicare/medicare.html*

Administers coverage policy and payment for Medicare patients with end-stage renal disease and psychiatric inpatient and outpatient services for the severely mentally ill.

Centers for Medicare and Medicaid Services (CMS) *(Health and Human Services Dept.), Clinical Standards and Quality, 7500 Security Blvd., S3-26-17, Baltimore, MD 21244; (410) 786-6841. Fax, (410) 786-6857. Patrick Conway, Deputy Administrator. Web, www.cms.gov*

Develops, establishes, and enforces standards that regulate the quality of care of hospitals and other health care facilities under Medicare and Medicaid programs. Administers operations of survey and peer review organizations that enforce health care standards, primarily for institutional care.

Centers for Medicare and Medicaid Services (CMS) *(Health and Human Services Dept.), Disabled and Elderly Health Group, 7500 Security Blvd., S2-14-26, Baltimore, MD 21244; (410) 786-0325. Fax, (410) 786-9004. Barbara Edwards, Director. Web, www.medicaid.gov*

Centers for Medicare and Medicaid Services

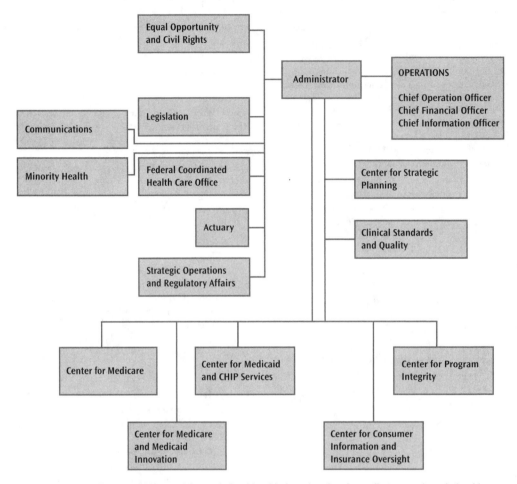

– – – – Indicates a support or advisory relationship with the unit rather than a direct reporting relationship

Reviews all benefit and pharmacy state plan amendments for all Medicaid populations, Medicaid managed-care delivery systems, home- and community-based services, and long-term services. Supports transformation grant programs, including Money Follows the Person and the Balancing Incentive Program.

Centers for Medicare and Medicaid Services (CMS) *(Health and Human Services Dept.), Information Services,* 7500 Security Blvd., N3-14-17, Baltimore, MD 21244; (410) 786-5246. Fax, (410) 786-1810. David Nelson, Director.
Web, www.cms.gov

Serves as primary federal statistical office for disseminating economic data on Medicare and Medicaid.

Health Resources and Services Administration *(Health and Human Services Dept.), Rural Health Policy,* 5600 Fishers Lane, #5A05, Rockville, MD 20857; (301) 443-0835. Fax, (301) 443-2803. Tom Morris, Associate Administrator.

General email, tmorris@hrsa.gov
Web, www.ruralhealth.hrsa.gov

Studies the effects of Medicare and Medicaid programs on rural access to health care.

▶ NONGOVERNMENTAL

Federation of American Hospitals, 750 9th St. N.W., #600 20001-4524; (202) 624-1500. Fax, (202) 737-6462. Charles N. Kahn III, President.
Web, www.fah.org

Membership: investor-owned, for-profit hospitals and health care systems. Studies Medicaid and Medicare reforms. Maintains speakers bureau; compiles statistics on investor-owned hospitals. Monitors legislation and regulations.

National Committee to Preserve Social Security and Medicare, 10 G St. N.E., #600 20002-4215; (202) 216-0420. Fax, (202) 216-0446. May Richtman, President. Press, (202)

216-8378. Senior hotline/Legislative updates, (800) 998-0180.

Web, www.ncpssm.org

Educational and advocacy organization that focuses on Social Security and Medicare programs and on related income security and health issues. Interests include retirement income protection, health care reform, and the quality of life of seniors. Monitors legislation and regulations.

Medical Devices and Technology

▶AGENCIES

Access Board, 1331 F St. N.W., #1000 20004-1111; (202) 272-0080. Fax, (202) 272-0081. David M. Capozzi, Executive Director, (202) 272-0010. TTY toll-free, (800) 993-2822. Toll-free technical assistance, (800) 872-2253.
General email, info@access-board.gov

Web, www.access-board.gov

Develops and maintains accessibility requirements for buildings, transit vehicles, telecommunications equipment, medical diagnostic equipment, and electronic and information technology. Provides technical assistance and training on these guidelines and standards. Enforces access standards for federally funded facilities through the Architectural Barriers Act.

Food and Drug Administration (FDA) *(Health and Human Services Dept.), Center for Devices and Radiological Health,* 10903 New Hampshire Ave., #5429, Silver Spring, MD 20993; (301) 796-5900. Fax, (301) 847-8510. Jeffrey E. Shuren, Director.
General email, jeff.shuren@fda.hhs.gov

Web, www.fda.gov/medicaldevices

Evaluates safety, efficacy, and labeling of medical devices; classifies devices; establishes performance standards; assists in legal actions concerning medical devices; coordinates research and testing; conducts training and educational programs. Maintains an international reference system to facilitate trade in devices. Library open to the public.

Food and Drug Administration (FDA) *(Health and Human Services Dept.), Combination Products,* W032 Hub/Mail Room #5129, 10903 New Hampshire Ave., Silver Spring, MD 20993; (301) 796-8930. Fax, (301) 847-8619. Thinh X. Nguyen, Director.
General email, combination@fda.gov

Web, www.fda.gov/oc/combination

Seeks to streamline the processing of complex drug-device, drug-biologic, and device-biologic combination products. Responsibilities cover the entire regulatory life cycle of combination products, including jurisdiction decisions as well as the timeliness and effectiveness of premarket review, and the consistency and appropriateness of postmarket regulation. Responsible for the classification of medical or biological products.

Lister Hill National Center for Biomedical Communications *(National Library of Medicine),* 8600 Rockville Pike, Bldg. 38A, #07N707, Bethesda, MD 20894; (301) 496-4441. Fax, (301) 402-0118. Dr. Clement McDonald, Director. Visitor's Center, (301) 496-7771.
Web, http://lhncbc.nlm.nih.gov

A research and development division of the National Library of Medicine. Conducts and supports research and development in the dissemination of high-quality imagery, medical language processing, high-speed access to biomedical information, intelligent database systems development, multimedia visualization, knowledge management, data mining, and machine-assisted indexing.

National Institute of Biomedical Imaging and Bioengineering *(National Institutes of Health),* 9000 Rockville Pike, Bldg. 31, #1C14, Bethesda, MD 20892; (301) 496-8859. Fax, (301) 480-0679. Dr. Roderic I. Pettigrew, Director. Public Liaison, (301) 402-1374.
General email, info@nibib.nih.gov

Web, www.nibib.nih.gov

Conducts and supports research and development of biomedical imaging and bioengineering techniques and devices to improve the prevention, detection, and treatment of disease.

▶NONGOVERNMENTAL

Advanced Medical Technology Assn., 701 Pennsylvania Ave. N.W., #800 20004-2654; (202) 783-8700. Fax, (202) 783-8750. Stephen J. Ubl, President.
General email, info@advamed.org

Web, www.advamed.org

Membership: manufacturers of medical devices, diagnostic products, and health care information systems. Interests include safe and effective medical devices; conducts educational seminars. Monitors legislation, regulations, and international issues. (Formerly Health Industry Manufacturers Assn.)

American Assn. for Homecare, 1707 L St. N.W., #350 20036; (202) 372-0107. Fax, (202) 835-8306. Thomas Ryan, President. Toll-free, (866) 289-0492.
General email, info@aahomecare.org

Web, www.aahomecare.org

Membership: home medical equipment manufacturers and home health care service providers. Works to serve the medical needs of Americans who require oxygen equipment and therapy, mobility assistive technologies, medical supplies, inhalation drug therapy, home infusion, and other home medical services. Provides members with education, training, and information about industry trends. Monitors legislation and regulations.

American College of Radiology, Washington Office, 505 9th St. N.W., #910 20004; 1891 Preston White Dr., Reston, VA 20191-4326; (703) 648-8900. Fax, (703) 295-6773. Joshua Cooper, Senior Director, Government Relations, (202) 223-1670; Dr. Harvey L. Neiman, Chief Executive Officer. Toll-free, (800) 227-5463.

General email, info@acr.org

Web, www.acr.org

Membership: certified radiologists and medical physicists in the United States and Canada. Develops programs in radiation protection, technologist training, practice standards, and health care insurance; maintains a placement service for radiologists; participates in international conferences.

American Institute of Ultrasound in Medicine, *14750 Sweitzer Lane, #100, Laurel, MD 20707-5906; (301) 498-4100. Fax, (301) 498-4450. Carmine Valente, Chief Executive Officer. Toll-free, (800) 638-5352.*

General email, admin@aium.org

Web, www.aium.org

Membership: medical professionals who use ultrasound technology in their practices. Promotes multidisciplinary research and education on safe and effective use of diagnostic ultrasound through conventions and educational programs. Develops guidelines for accreditation. Monitors international research.

American Medical Informatics Assn., *4720 Montgomery Lane, #500, Bethesda, MD 20814; (301) 657-1291. Fax, (301) 657-1296. Vacant, President; Karen Greenwood, Chief Operating Officer.*

General email, mail@amia.org

Web, www.amia.org

Membership: medical professionals and students interested in informatics. Studies and pursues effective uses of biomedical data, information, and knowledge for scientific inquiry, problem solving, and decision making to improve human health. Applications include basic and applied research, clinical services, consumer services, and public health.

American Orthotic and Prosthetic Assn., *330 John Carlyle St., #200, Alexandria, VA 22314-5760; (571) 431-0876. Fax, (571) 431-0899. Tom Fise, Executive Director.*

Web, www.aopanet.org

Membership: companies that manufacture or supply artificial limbs and braces, and patient care professionals who fit and supervise their use.

American Roentgen Ray Society, *44211 Slatestone Court, Leesburg, VA 20176-5109; (703) 729-3353. Fax, (703) 729-4839. Susan B. Cappitelli, Executive Director. Toll-free, (866) 940-2777.*

General email, info@arrs.org

Web, www.arrs.org

Membership: physicians and researchers in radiology and allied sciences. Publishes research; conducts conferences; presents scholarships and awards; monitors international research.

Health Industry Distributors Assn., *310 Montgomery St., Alexandria, VA 22314-1516; (703) 549-4432. Fax, (703) 549-6495. Matthew Rowan, President.*

General email, hida@hida.org

Web, www.hida.org

Membership: medical products distributors. Sponsors and conducts trade shows and training seminars. Monitors legislation and regulations.

Optical Society, *2010 Massachusetts Ave. N.W. 20036; (202) 223-8130. Fax, (202) 223-1096. Elizabeth Rogan, Chief Executive Officer.*

General email, info@osa.org

Web, www.osa.org

Membership: global optics and photonic scientists, engineers, educators, students, technicians, business professionals, and others interested in optics and photonics worldwide. Promotes research and information exchange; conducts conferences; publishes a scientific journal; sponsors technical groups and programming, and outreach and educational activities.

Program for Appropriate Technology in Health (PATH), *Washington Office, 455 Massachusetts Ave. N.W., #1000 20001; (202) 822-0033. Fax, (202) 457-1466. Steve Davis, President.*

General email, info@path.org

Web, www.path.org

Develops, tests, and implements health technologies and strategies for low-resource countries. Works with community groups, other nongovernmental organizations, governments, companies, and United Nations agencies to expand the most successful programs. Interests include reproductive health, immunization, maternal-child health, emerging and epidemic diseases, and nutrition. (Headquarters in Seattle, Wash.)

Nursing Homes and Hospices

▶**AGENCIES**

Centers for Medicare and Medicaid Services (CMS) *(Health and Human Services Dept.), Continuing Care Providers, 7500 Security Blvd., C2-21-16, Baltimore, MD 21244-1850; (410) 786-4857. Fax, (410) 786-0194. Martin Kennedy, Director, (410) 786-0784; Peggye Wilkerson, Deputy Director, (410) 786-4857.*

Web, www.cms.gov

Monitors compliance with government standards of psychiatric hospitals and long-term and intermediate care facilities, including residential treatment facilities, community mental health centers, intermediate care facilities for mental retardation, outpatient rehabilitation facilities, home health care, hospice care, portable X-ray units, dialysis facilities, and outpatient physical, language, and speech therapy facilities. Focus includes quality of care, environmental conditions, and participation in Medicaid and Medicare programs. Coordinates health care programs for the mentally challenged.

Centers for Medicare and Medicaid Services (CMS) *(Health and Human Services Dept.), Nursing Homes, 7500 Security Blvd., Baltimore, MD 21244; (410) 786-6782. Fax, (410) 786-0194. Karen Tritz, Director.*

Web, www.cms.gov

Monitors compliance of nursing homes with government standards. Focus includes quality of care, environmental conditions, and participation in Medicaid and Medicare programs.

Centers for Medicare and Medicaid Services (CMS) (Health and Human Services Dept.), Survey and Certification Group, 7500 Security Blvd., C2-21-16, Baltimore, MD 21244-1850; (410) 786-9493. Fax, (410) 786-0194. Thomas Hamilton, Director; Jan Tarantino, Deputy Director, (410) 786-0905.
Web, www.cms.gov/medicare/medicare.html

Enforces health care and safety standards for nursing homes and other long-term care facilities.

▶ NONGOVERNMENTAL

AARP, Federal Affairs Health and Family, 601 E St. N.W. 20049; (202) 434-3770. Fax, (202) 434-3745. Ariel Gonzalez, Director of Health and Family Advocacy. Main switchboard, (202) 434-2277.
Web, www.aarp.org

Maintains the Legal Counsel for the Elderly, which advocates on behalf of older residents of the District of Columbia who reside in nursing homes and board and care homes. Monitors legislation and regulations.

American College of Health Care Administrators, 1321 Duke St., #400, Alexandria, VA 22314; (202) 536-5120. Fax, (866) 874-1585. Marianna Kern Grachek, President.
General email, info@achca.org

Web, www.achca.org

Membership: administrators of long-term health care organizations and facilities, including home health care programs, hospices, day care centers for the elderly, nursing and hospital facilities, retirement communities, assisted living communities, and mental health care centers. Conducts research on statistical characteristics of nursing home and other medical administrators; conducts seminars and workshops; offers education courses; provides certification for administrators.

American Health Care Assn., 1201 L St. N.W. 20005; (202) 842-4444. Fax, (202) 842-3860. Mark Parkinson, President. Publication orders, (800) 321-0343.
Web, www.ahcancal.org

Association of facility-based long-term and post-acute care providers and affiliates of state health organizations. Advocates for high-quality care and services for frail, elderly, and disabled Americans to government, business leaders, and the general public. Provides information, education, and administrative tools. Monitors legislation and regulations.

Assisted Living Federation of America, 1650 King St., #602, Alexandria, VA 22314; (703) 894-1805. Fax, (703) 894-1831. Richard Grimes, President. Press, (703) 562-1185.
General email, info@alfa.org

Web, www.alfa.org

Represents operators of communities for seniors, including independent-living, assisted-living, and Alzheimer's care facilities, but not including nursing homes or hospices. Promotes the development of standards and increased awareness for the senior living industry. Provides members with information on policy, funding access, and quality of care. Interests include informed choice, safe environments, caring and competent staff, and funding alternatives to increase accessibility to senior communities. Monitors legislation and regulations.

Consumer Consortium on Assisted Living, 2342 Oak St., Falls Church, VA 22046; (703) 533-3225. Jackie Pinkowitz, Chair.
General email, info@ccal.org

Web, www.ccal.org

Educates consumers, trains professionals, and advocates for assisted living issues, and home and community services.

Hospice Foundation of America, 1710 Rhode Island Ave. N.W., #400 20036; (202) 457-5811. Fax, (202) 457-5815. Amy Tucci, President. Toll-free, (800) 854-3402.
General email, hfaoffice@hospicefoundation.org

Web, www.hospicefoundation.org

Acts as an advocate for the hospice style of health care through ongoing programs of public education and training, information dissemination, and research.

National Assn. for Home Care and Hospice, 228 7th St. S.E. 20003; (202) 547-7424. Fax, (202) 547-3540. Val J. Halamandaris, President.
General email, info@nahc.org

Web, www.nahc.org

Membership: hospice, home care, and private-duty providers and other community service organizations assisting those with chronic health problems or life-threatening illness. Works to educate and provide information for the public on hospice and home care. Interests include Medicare, Medicaid, and other insurance for home care and hospice. Monitors legislation and regulations.

National Center for Assisted Living, 1201 L St. N.W. 20005; (202) 842-4444. Fax, (202) 842-3860. Vacant, Senior Director for Assisted Living Policy; Lindsay Schwartz, Director, Workforce and Quality Improvement Programs. Public Affairs, (202) 898-2825.
General email, lgluckstern@ncal.org

Web, www.ncal.org

Membership: assisted living professionals. Provides networking opportunities and professional development; hosts educational seminars and an annual convention. Provides free resources for consumers looking into assisted living and other long-term care resources. Monitors legislation and regulations. (Affiliated with American Health Care Assn.)

National Consumer Voice for Quality Long-Term Care (NCCNHR), 1001 Connecticut Ave. N.W., #425 20036; (202) 332-2275. Fax, (866) 230-9789. Richard Gelula, Executive

Director; Lori O. Smetanka, Director, National Long-Term Care Ombudsmen Resource Center.
General email, info@theconsumervoice.org
Web, www.theconsumervoice.org

Advocates for high-quality care and quality of life for consumers in all long-term care settings. Promotes citizen participation in all aspects of nursing homes; acts as clearinghouse for nursing home advocacy. Hosts National Long-Term Care Ombudsmen Resource Center.

National Hospice and Palliative Care Organization,
1731 King St., Alexandria, VA 22314; (703) 837-1500.
Fax, (703) 837-1233. J. Donald (Don) Schumacher, President. Press, (703) 837-3139. Toll-free consumer information and referral helpline, (800) 658-8898.
General email, nhpco_info@nhpco.org
Web, www.nhpco.org

Membership: institutions and individuals providing hospice and palliative care and other interested organizations and individuals. Promotes supportive care for the terminally ill and their families; sets hospice program standards; provides information on hospices. Monitors legislation and regulations. Consumer Web site can be found at www.caringinfo.org.

National Long-Term Care Ombudsman Resource Center,
1001 Connecticut Ave. N.W., #425 20036; (202) 332-2275.
Fax, (202) 332-2949. Lori O. Smetanka, Director.
General email, info@theconsumervoice.org
Web, www.ltcombudsman.org

Provides technical assistance, management guidance, policy analysis, and program development information on behalf of state and substate ombudsman programs. (Affiliate of the National Consumer Voice for Quality Long-Term Care.)

Pharmaceuticals

▶**AGENCIES**

Assistant Secretary for Health (Health and Human Services Dept.), Orphan Products Development, 10903 New Hampshire Ave., Bldg. 32, #5271, Silver Spring, MD 20993; (301) 796-8660. Fax, (301) 847-8621.
Gayatri R. Rao, Director.
Web, www.fda.hhs.gov/orphan

Promotes the development of drugs, devices, and alternative medical food therapies for rare diseases or conditions. Coordinates activities on the development of orphan drugs among federal agencies, manufacturers, and organizations representing patients.

Federal Trade Commission (FTC), Consumer Protection, Advertising Practices, 601 New Jersey Ave. N.W., #3223 20001 (mailing address: 600 Pennsylvania Ave. N.W., Washington, DC 20580); (202) 326-3090. Fax, (202) 326-3259. Mary Engle, Associate Director.
Web, www.ftc.gov/bcp/bcpap.shtm

Protects consumers from deceptive and unsubstantiated advertising through law enforcement, public reports, and industry outreach. Evaluates the nutritional and health benefits of foods and the effectiveness of dietary supplements, drugs, and medical devices, particularly as they relate to weight loss.

Food and Drug Administration (FDA) (Health and Human Services Dept.), Center for Drug Evaluation and Research, 10903 New Hampshire Ave., Silver Spring, MD 20993; (301) 796-5400. Fax, (301) 847-8752.
Dr. Janet Woodcock, Director. Press, (301) 796-4540.
Web, www.fda.gov/drugs

Reviews and approves applications to investigate and market new drugs; monitors prescription drug advertising; works to harmonize drug approval internationally.

Food and Drug Administration (FDA) (Health and Human Services Dept.), Center for Drug Evaluation and Research, Generic Drugs, 7519 Standish Pl., MPN 4, #3020, Rockville, MD 20855; (240) 276-9310. Fax, (240) 276-9327. Kathleen Uhl, Director, Acting.
Web, www.fda.gov/aboutfda/centersoffices/officeofmedicalproductsandtobacco/cder/ucm119100.htm

Oversees generic drug review process to ensure the safety and effectiveness of approved drugs.

Food and Drug Administration (FDA) (Health and Human Services Dept.), Center for Drug Evaluation and Research, Pharmaceutical Science Office, New Drug Quality Assessment, 10903 New Hampshire Ave., WO Bldg. 21, #2626, Silver Spring, MD 20993; (301) 796-1900. Fax, (301) 796-9745. Christine Moore, Director, Acting.
Web, www.fda.gov/drugs

Reviews the critical quality attributes and manufacturing processes of new drugs, establishes quality standards to ensure safety and efficacy, and facilitates new drug development.

Food and Drug Administration (FDA) (Health and Human Services Dept.), Prescription Drug Promotion, 10903 New Hampshire Ave., Bldg. 51, #3314, Silver Spring, MD 20903-0002; (301) 796-1200. Fax, (301) 847-8444.
Thomas W. Abrams, Director.
Web, www.fda.gov/drugs

Monitors prescription drug advertising and labeling; investigates complaints; conducts market research on health care communications and drug issues.

National Institutes of Health (NIH) (Health and Human Services Dept.), Dietary Supplements, 6100 Executive Blvd., #3B01, MSC-7517, Bethesda, MD 20892-7517; (301) 435-2920. Fax, (301) 480-1845. Paul M. Coates, Director.
General email, ods@nih.gov
Web, http://ods.od.nih.gov

Reviews scientific evidence on the safety and efficacy of dietary supplements. Conducts, promotes, and coordinates scientific research within the NIH relating to dietary supplements. Conducts and supports conferences, workshops, and symposia and publishes research results on scientific topics related to dietary supplements.

►NONGOVERNMENTAL

American Assn. of Colleges of Pharmacy, *1727 King St., Alexandria, VA 22314-2700; (703) 739-2330. Fax, (703) 836-8982. Lucinda L. Maine, Executive Vice President. General email, mail@aacp.org*

Web, www.aacp.org

Represents and advocates for pharmacists in the academic community. Conducts programs and activities in cooperation with other national health and higher education associations.

American Assn. of Pharmaceutical Scientists, *2107 Wilson Blvd., #700, Arlington, VA 22201-3042; (703) 243-2800. Fax, (703) 243-9650. John Lisack Jr., Executive Director. Public Relations, (703) 248-4740. General email, aaps@aaps.org*

Web, www.aaps.org

Membership: pharmaceutical scientists from biomedical, biotechnological, and health care fields. Promotes pharmaceutical sciences as an industry. Represents scientific interests within academia and public and private institutions. Provides forums for scientists to engage in dialogue, networking, and career development. Monitors legislation and regulations.

American Pharmacists Assn., *2215 Constitution Ave. N.W. 20037-2985; (202) 628-4410. Fax, (202) 783-2351. Thomas Menighan, Chief Executive Officer. Information, (800) 237-2742. Library, (202) 429-7524.*

Web, www.pharmacist.com

Membership: practicing pharmacists, pharmaceutical scientists, and pharmacy students. Promotes professional education and training; publishes scientific journals and handbooks on nonprescription drugs; monitors international research. Library open to the public by appointment.

American Society for Pharmacology and Experimental Therapeutics, *9650 Rockville Pike, Bethesda, MD 20814-3995; (301) 634-7060. Fax, (301) 634-7061. Ashlee Laughlin, Executive Officer. General email, info@aspet.org*

Web, www.aspet.org

Membership: researchers and teachers involved in basic and clinical pharmacology primarily in the United States and Canada.

American Society of Health-System Pharmacists, *7272 Wisconsin Ave., Bethesda, MD 20814; (301) 657-3000. Fax, (301) 657-1251. Paul W. Abramowitz, Chief Executive Officer.*

Web, www.ashp.org

Membership: pharmacists who practice in organized health care settings such as hospitals, health maintenance organizations, and long-term care facilities. Publishes reference materials and provides educational programs and conferences. Accredits pharmacy residency and pharmacy technician training programs. Monitors legislation and regulations.

Consumer Healthcare Products Assn., *900 19th St. N.W., #700 20006; (202) 429-9260. Fax, (202) 223-6835. James J. Mackey, Chair; Scott Melville, President. Web, www.chpa-info.org*

Membership: manufacturers and distributors of nonprescription medicines and nutritional supplements; associate members include suppliers, advertising agencies, research and testing laboratories, and others. Promotes the role of self-medication in health care. Monitors legislation and regulations.

Drug Policy Alliance, *Washington Office, 925 15th St. N.W., 2nd Floor 20005; (202) 683-2030. Fax, (202) 216-0803. Ethan Nadelmann, Director. General email, dc@drugpolicy.org*

Web, www.drugpolicy.org

Seeks to broaden debate on drug policy to include considering alternatives to incarceration, expanding maintenance therapies, and restoring constitutional protections. Studies drug policy in other countries. Monitors legislation and regulations. (Headquarters in New York.)

Generic Pharmaceutical Assn., *777 6th St. N.W., #510 20001; (202) 249-7100. Fax, (202) 249-7105. Ralph G. Neas, President. General email, info@gphaonline.org*

Web, www.gphaonline.org

Membership: manufacturers and distributors of generic pharmaceuticals and pharmaceutical chemicals and suppliers of goods and services to the generic pharmaceutical industry. Monitors legislation and regulations. Attempts to increase availability and public awareness of safe, effective generic medicines.

Healthcare Distribution Management Assn., *901 N. Glebe Rd., #1000, Arlington, VA 22203; (703) 787-0000. Fax, (703) 812-5282. John Gray, President. Web, www.healthcaredistribution.org*

Membership: distributors of pharmaceutical and health-related products and information. Serves as a forum on major industry issues. Researches and disseminates information on distribution issues and management practices. Monitors legislation and regulations. (Formerly the National Wholesale Druggists' Assn.)

National Assn. of Chain Drug Stores, *1776 Wilson Blvd., #200, Arlington, VA 22209 (mailing address: P.O. Box 1417-D49, Alexandria, VA 22314); (703) 549-3001. Fax, (703) 836-4869. Steven Anderson, President. General email, contactus@nacds.org*

Web, www.nacds.org

Membership: chain drug retailers; associate members include manufacturers, suppliers, publishers, and advertising agencies. Provides information on the pharmacy profession, community pharmacy practice, and retail prescription drug economics. Monitors legislation and regulations.

National Community Pharmacists Assn., *100 Daingerfield Rd., Alexandria, VA 22314; (703) 683-8200. Fax, (703) 683-3619. Douglas Hoey, Chief Executive Officer, ext. 2648. Toll-free, (800) 544-7447.*

Food and Drug Administration

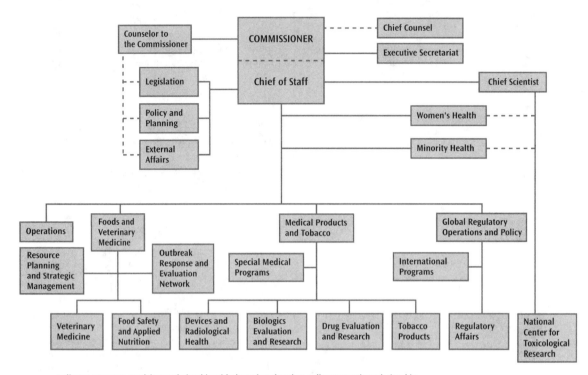

- - - - - Indicates a support or advisory relationship with the unit rather than a direct reporting relationship

General email, info@ncpanet.org

Web, www.ncpanet.org

Membership: independent pharmacy owners, including independent pharmacies, independent pharmacy franchises, and independent chains. Promotes the interests of independent community pharmacists to compete in the health care market. Monitors legislation and regulations.

National Council on Patient Information and Education, *200-A Monroe St., #212, Rockville, MD 20850-4448; (301) 340-3940. Fax, (301) 340-3944. W. Ray Bullman, Executive Vice President.*
General email, ncpie@ncpie.info

Web, www.talkaboutrx.org

Membership: organizations of health care professionals, pharmaceutical manufacturers, federal agencies, voluntary health organizations, and consumer groups. Works to improve communication between health care professionals and patients about the appropriate use of medicines; produces educational resources; conducts public affairs programs; sponsors awards program. Additional information can be found at www.bemedwise.org and www.mustforseniors.org (medication use safety training for seniors).

National Pharmaceutical Council, *Washington Office, 1717 Pennsylvania Ave., #800 20006; (202) 827-2100.*

Fax, (202) 827-0314. Dan Leonard, President, (202) 827-2080.
General email, info@npcnow.org

Web, www.npcnow.org

Membership: pharmaceutical manufacturers that research and produce trade-name prescription medication and other pharmaceutical products. Sponsors and conducts scientific analyses of the use of pharmaceuticals and the clinical and economic value of innovation.

Parenteral Drug Assn. (PDA), *4350 East-West Hwy., #150, Bethesda, MD 20814; (301) 656-5900. Fax, (301) 986-0296. Richard Johnson, President.*
General email, info@pda.org

Web, www.pda.org

Membership: scientists involved in the development, manufacture, quality control, and regulation of pharmaceuticals/biopharmaceuticals and related products. Provides science, technology, and regulatory information and education to the pharmaceutical and biopharmaceutical community. Influences FDA regulatory process.

Pharmaceutical Care Management Assn.,
601 Pennsylvania Ave. N.W., 7th Floor 20004; (202) 207-3610. Fax, (202) 207-3623. Mark Merritt, President.

General email, info@pcmanet.org

Web, www.pcmanet.org

Membership: companies providing managed care pharmacy and pharmacy benefits management. Promotes legislation, research, education, and practice standards that foster high-quality, affordable pharmaceutical care.

Pharmaceutical Research and Manufacturers of America, *950 F St. N.W., #300 20004; (202) 835-3400. John J. Castellani, President. Web, www.phrma.org*

Membership: research-based pharmaceutical and biotechnology companies that orginate, develop, and manufacture prescription drugs. Advocates public policies that encourage discovery of new medicines. Provides consumer information on drug abuse, the safe and effective use of prescription medicines, and developments in important areas, including the treatment of HIV/AIDS.

U.S. Pharmacopeial Convention, *Washington Office, 12601 Twinbrook Pkwy., Rockville, MD 20852-1790; (301) 881-0666. Fax, (301) 816-8299. Ronald Piervincenzi, Chief Executive Officer. Toll-free, (800) 227-8772. General email, usp@usp.org*

Web, www.usp.org

Establishes and revises standards for drug strength, quality, purity, packaging, labeling, and storage of prescription and over-the-counter medications. Publishes drug use information, official drug quality standards, patient education materials, and consumer drug references. Interests include international standards. (Offices in Switzerland, India, China, and Brazil.)

HEALTH PROFESSIONS

General

▶**AGENCIES**

Assistant Secretary for Health *(Health and Human Services Dept.), Commissioned Corps of the U.S. Public Health Service, Office of the Surgeon General (OSG), Division of Commissioned Corps Personnel and Readiness (DCCPR), 1101 Wootton Pkwy., Plaza Level, #100, Rockville, MD 20852; (240) 453-6161. Fax, (240) 453-6109. Capt. Paul Jung, Director, Acting. General information, (877) 463-6327. Application information, (800) 279-1605. General email, OCCFMHelpdesk@hhs.gov*

Web, www.usphs.gov

Responsible for the overall force management, operations, and deployment readiness and response of the Commissioned Corps of the U.S. Public Health Service, uniformed service health professionals with a wide range of specialties who respond to emergencies, conduct research, and care for patients in underserved communities through federal agencies such as the National Institutes of Health, the Centers for Disease Control and Prevention, the Indian Health Service, and the Bureau of Prisons.

Centers for Medicare and Medicaid Services (CMS) *(Health and Human Services Dept.), Clinical Standards and Quality, 7500 Security Blvd., S3-26-17, Baltimore, MD 21244; (410) 786-6841. Fax, (410) 786-6857. Patrick Conway, Deputy Administrator. Web, www.cms.gov*

Oversees professional review and other medical review programs; establishes guidelines; prepares issue papers relating to legal aspects of professional review and quality assurance.

Clinician Recruitment and Services *(Health and Human Services Dept.), National Health Service Corps, 5600 Fishers Lane, Rockville, MD 20857; (301) 594-4400. Fax, (301) 594-4981. Mary Wakefield, Director. Toll-free, (800) 221-9393. Web, www.nhsc.hrsa.gov*

Supplies communities experiencing a shortage of health care personnel with doctors and other medical professionals. Provides educational financial aid incentives for service.

Health Resources and Services Administration *(Health and Human Services Dept.), Health Education Assistance Loan Branch, 5600 Fishers Lane, #9-105, Parklawn Bldg., Rockville, MD 20857; (301) 443-9396. Fax, (301) 443-0795. Kae Mason Brickerd, Branch Chief. To speak with a HEAL representative, (301) 443-1540. Web, http://bhpr.hrsa.gov/scholarshiploans/index.html*

Insures loans provided by private lenders to students attending eligible health professions schools under the Public Health Service Act. New loans to student borrowers have been discontinued. Refinancing has been terminated.

Health Resources and Services Administration *(Health and Human Services Dept.), Health Professions, 5600 Fishers Lane, #905, Rockville, MD 20857; (301) 443-5794. Fax, (301) 443-2111. Rebecca Spitzgo, Associate Administrator. Web, www.bhpr.hrsa.gov*

Supports primary care and public health education and practice. Supports recruitment of health care professionals, including nursing and allied health professionals, for underserved populations. Administers categorical training programs, scholarship and loan programs, and minority and disadvantaged assistance programs. Oversees National Practitioner Data Bank.

Health Resources and Services Administration *(Health and Human Services Dept.), National Health Services Corps, 5600 Fishers Lane, #8-05, Rockville, MD 20857; (301) 594-4130. Fax, (301) 443-2080. Kimberly Kleine, Associate Administrator, Acting. Toll-free, (800) 221-9393. Web, www.nhsc.hrsa.gov*

Supplies communities experiencing a shortage of health care personnel with doctors and other medical professionals.

Health Resources and Services Administration *(Health and Human Services Dept.)*, **National Practitioner Data Bank**, *4094 Majestic Lane, PMB-332, Fairfax, VA 22033; (703) 802-9380. Fax, (703) 803-1964. Ernia Hughes, Division Director, Acting, (301) 443-2300. Information, (800) 767-6732.*
General email, help@npdb-hipdb.hrsa.gov
Web, www.npdb-hipdb.hrsa.gov

Provides information on reports of malpractice payments, adverse state licensure, clinical privileges, and society membership actions (only to eligible state licensing boards, hospitals, and other health care entities) about physicians, dentists, and other licensed health care practitioners.

National Institute of Biomedical Imaging and Bioengineering *(National Institutes of Health)*, *9000 Rockville Pike, Bldg. 31, #1C14, Bethesda, MD 20892; (301) 496-8859. Fax, (301) 480-0679. Dr. Roderic I. Pettigrew, Director. Public Liaison, (301) 402-1374.*
General email, info@nibib.nih.gov
Web, www.nibib.nih.gov

Offers multidisciplinary training programs for scientists and engineers at all stages of their careers in bioimaging and bioengineering.

National Institutes of Health (NIH) *(Health and Human Services Dept.)*, **Minority Opportunities in Research**, *45 Center Dr., Bldg. 45, #2AS37, MSC-6200, Bethesda, MD 20892-6200; (301) 594-3900. Fax, (301) 480-2753. Dr. Alison Hall, Director, Acting.*
Web, www.nigms.nih.gov/minority

Administers research and research training programs aimed at increasing the number of minority biomedical scientists. Funds grants, fellowships, faculty development awards, and development of research facilities.

▶**CONGRESS**

For a listing of relevant congressional committees and subcommittees, please see pages 318–319 or the Appendix.

▶**NONGOVERNMENTAL**

AFT Healthcare, *555 New Jersey Ave. N.W. 20001; (202) 879-4400. Fax, (202) 879-4545. Randi Weingarten, President.*
General email, afthealthcare@aft.org
Web, www.aft.org/healthcare

Membership: teachers, public employees, and nurses and other health care workers. Assists members with contract negotiation and grievances; conducts training programs and workshops. Monitors legislation and regulations. (Division of the American Federation of Teachers.)

Alliance for Academic Internal Medicine, *330 John Carlyle St., #610, Alexandria, VA 22314; (703) 341-4540. Fax, (703) 519-1893. Bergitta E. Smith, Executive Vice President.*
General email, apm@im.org
Web, www.im.org

Membership: program directors, clerkship directors, administrators, and chairs of internal medicine departments at all U.S. medical schools and several affiliated teaching hospitals. Provides services, training, and educational opportunities for leaders in internal medicine departments. Monitors legislation and regulations.

American Assn. of Colleges of Pharmacy, *1727 King St., Alexandria, VA 22314-2700; (703) 739-2330. Fax, (703) 836-8982. Lucinda L. Maine, Executive Vice President.*
General email, mail@aacp.org
Web, www.aacp.org

Membership: teachers and administrators representing colleges of pharmacy accredited by the American Council on Pharmaceutical Education. Sponsors educational programs; conducts research; provides career information; helps administer the Pharmacy College Admissions Test.

American College of Health Care Administrators, *1321 Duke St., #400, Alexandria, VA 22314; (202) 536-5120. Fax, (866) 874-1585. Marianna Kern Grachek, President.*
General email, info@achca.org
Web, www.achca.org

Membership: administrators of long-term health care organizations and facilities, including home health care programs, hospices, day care centers for the elderly, nursing and hospital facilities, retirement communities, assisted living communities, and mental health care centers. Conducts research on statistical characteristics of nursing home and other medical administrators; conducts seminars and workshops; offers education courses; provides certification for administrators.

American Health Lawyers Assn., *1620 Eye St. N.W., 6th Floor 20006-4010; (202) 833-1100. Fax, (202) 833-1105. Peter Leibold, Chief Executive Officer.*
General email, info@healthlawyers.org
Web, www.healthlawyers.org

Membership: corporate, institutional, and government lawyers interested in the health field; law students; and health professionals. Serves as an information clearinghouse on health law; sponsors health law educational programs and seminars.

American Institute of Ultrasound in Medicine, *14750 Sweitzer Lane, #100, Laurel, MD 20707-5906; (301) 498-4100. Fax, (301) 498-4450. Carmine Valente, Chief Executive Officer. Toll-free, (800) 638-5352.*
General email, admin@aium.org
Web, www.aium.org

Membership: medical professionals who use ultrasound technology in their practices. Promotes multidisciplinary research and education on safe and effective use of diagnostic ultrasound through conventions and educational programs. Develops guidelines for accreditation. Monitors international research.

American Medical Athletic Assn., *4405 East-West Hwy., #405, Bethesda, MD 20814-4535; (301) 913-9517. Fax, (301) 913-9520. David Watt, Executive Director, ext. 13. Information, (800) 776-2732.*
General email, amaa@americanrunning.org

Web, www.amaasportsmed.org

Membership: sports medicine and allied health professionals. Assists members in promoting running and physical fitness to their patients and in developing their own physical fitness programs. Promotes and reports on sports medicine research and discussion. (Sister organization to American Running Assn.)

American Medical Group Assn., *1 Prince St., Alexandria, VA 22314-3318; (703) 838-0033. Fax, (703) 548-1890. Donald W. Fisher, President.*
Web, www.amga.org

Membership: medical group and health system organizations. Compiles statistics on group practice and clinical best practices. Sponsors a foundation for research and education programs. Advocates the multispecialty group practice model of health care delivery. Provides educational and networking programs and publications, benchmarking data services, and financial and operations assistance. Monitors legislation and regulations.

American Roentgen Ray Society, *44211 Slatestone Court, Leesburg, VA 20176-5109; (703) 729-3353. Fax, (703) 729-4839. Susan B. Cappitelli, Executive Director. Toll-free, (866) 940-2777.*
General email, info@arrs.org

Web, www.arrs.org

Membership: physicians and researchers in radiology and allied sciences. Publishes research; conducts conferences; presents scholarships and awards; monitors international research.

American Running Assn., *4405 East-West Hwy., #405, Bethesda, MD 20814-4535; (301) 913-9517. Fax, (301) 913-9520. David Watt, Executive Director, ext. 13. Information, (800) 776-2732.*
General email, milerun@americanrunning.org

Web, www.americanrunning.org

Membership: athletes, health clubs, physicians, businesses, and individuals. Promotes proper nutrition and regular exercise. Provides members with medical advice and referrals, fitness information, and assistance in developing fitness programs. (Sister organization to American Medical Athletic Assn.)

American Society of Consultant Pharmacists, *1321 Duke St., 4th Floor, Alexandria, VA 22314-3563; (703) 739-1300. Fax, (703) 739-1321. Vacant, Executive Director. Toll-free phone, (800) 355-2727. Toll-free fax, (800) 220-1321.*
General email, info@ascp.com

Web, www.ascp.com

Membership: dispensing and clinical pharmacists with expertise in therapeutic medication management for geriatric patients; provides services to long-term care facilities, institutions, and hospices as well as older adults in assisted living and home-based care. Monitors legislation and regulations.

American Speech-Language-Hearing Assn. (ASHA), *2200 Research Blvd., Rockville, MD 20850-3289; (301) 296-5700. Fax, (301) 296-8580. Arlene Pietranton, Executive Director. Press, (301) 296-8732. Toll-free hotline (except Alaska, Hawaii, and Maryland), (800) 638-8255 (voice and TTY accessible).*
General email, actioncenter@asha.org

Web, www.asha.org

Membership: specialists in speech-language pathology and audiology. Sponsors professional education programs; acts as accrediting agent for graduate programs; certifies audiologists and speech-language pathologists. Advocates the rights of the communicatively disabled; provides information on speech, hearing, and language problems. Provides referrals to speech-language pathologists and audiologists. Interests include national and international standards for bioacoustics and noise.

Assn. for Healthcare Philanthropy, *313 Park Ave., #400, Falls Church, VA 22046; (703) 532-6243. Fax, (703) 532-7170. William C. McGinly, President.*
General email, ahp@ahp.org

Web, www.ahp.org

Membership: hospital and health care executives who manage fundraising activities and organizations and individuals who provide consulting services for such activities. Acts as a clearinghouse on philanthropy and offers programs, services, and publications and e-communications to members.

Assn. for Prevention Teaching and Research, *1001 Connecticut Ave. N.W., #610 20036; (202) 463-0550. Fax, (202) 463-0555. Allison L. Lewis, Executive Director. Toll-free, (866) 520-2787.*
General email, info@aptrweb.org

Web, www.aptrweb.org

Membership: faculty, researchers, residents, and students within schools of medicine, schools of public health, schools of nursing, schools of pharmacy, physician assistant programs, graduate programs for public health, and health agencies. Works to advance population-based and public health education, research, and service by linking supporting members from the academic prevention community. Develops curricular resources and professional development programs. (Formerly the Assn. of Teachers of Preventive Medicine.)

Assn. of Reproductive Health Professionals, *1901 L St. N.W., #300 20036; (202) 466-3825. Fax, (202) 466-3826. Wayne C. Shields, President.*
General email, arhp@arhp.org

Web, www.arhp.org

Membership: obstetricians, gynecologists, other physicians, researchers, clinicians, and educators. Educates health professionals and the public on reproductive health issues, including family planning, contraception, HIV/AIDS and other sexually transmitted diseases, abortion, menopause, infertility, and cancer prevention and detection. Monitors legislation and regulations.

Assn. of Schools of Allied Health Professions, *122 C St. N.W., #650 20001; (202) 237-6481. Fax, (202) 237-6485. John Colbert, Executive Director.*
General email, thomas@asahp.org
Web, www.asahp.org

Membership: two- and four-year colleges and academic health science centers with allied health professional training programs; administrators, educators, and practitioners; and professional societies. Serves as information resource; works with the Health and Human Services Dept. to conduct surveys of allied health education programs. Interests include health promotion and disease prevention, ethics in health care, and the participation of women and persons with disabilities in allied health. Monitors legislation and regulations.

Assn. of Schools and Programs of Public Health, *1900 M St. N.W., #710 20036; (202) 296-1099. Fax, (202) 296-1252. Dr. Harrison C. Spencer, President.*
General email, info@aspph.org
Web, www.aspph.org

Membership: deans, faculty, and students of accredited graduate schools of public health. Promotes improved education and training of professional public health personnel; interests include disease prevention, health promotion, and international health.

Assn. of State and Territorial Health Officials, *2231 Crystal Dr., #450, Arlington, VA 22202; (202) 371-9090. Fax, (571) 527-3189. Dr. Paul Jarris, Executive Director.*
Web, www.astho.org

Membership: executive officers of state and territorial health departments. Serves as legislative review agency and information source for members. Alternate Web site: www.statepublichealth.org.

Assn. of University Programs in Health Administration, *2000 14th St. North, #780, Arlington, VA 22201; (703) 894-0940. Fax, (703) 894-0941. Kristi Donovan, Senior Director of Professional Affairs, (703) 894-0940, ext. 113.*
General email, aupha@aupha.org
Web, www.aupha.org

Membership: university-based educational programs, faculty, practitioners, and provider organizations. Works to improve the field of health care management and practice by educating entry-level professional managers.

Council on Education for Public Health, *1010 Wayne Ave., #220, Silver Spring, MD 20910; (202) 789-1050. Fax, (202) 789-1895. Laura Rasar King, Executive Director.*
Web, www.ceph.org

Accredits schools of public health and graduate programs in public health. Works to strengthen public health programs through research and other means.

Healthcare Financial Management Assn., *Washington Office, 1825 K St. N.W., #900 20006; (202) 296-2920.*

Fax, (202) 238-3456. Richard Gundling, Vice President. Information, (800) 252-4362.
Web, www.hfma.org

Membership: health care financial management specialists. Offers educational programs; provides information on financial management of health care. (Headquarters in Westchester, Ill.)

Hispanic-Serving Health Professions Schools, *2639 Connecticut Ave. N.W., #203 20008; (202) 290-1186. Fax, (202) 290-1339. Dr. Valerie Romero-Leggott, President.*
General email, hshps@hshps.org
Web, www.hshps.org

Seeks to increase representation of Hispanics in all health care professions through academic development, initiatives, and training. Monitors legislation and regulations.

National Assn. of County and City Health Officials, *1100 17th St. N.W., 7th Floor 20036; (202) 783-5550. Fax, (202) 783-1583. Robert M. Pestronk, Executive Director.*
General email, info@naccho.org
Web, www.naccho.org

Membership: city, county, and district health officers. Provides members with information on national, state, and local health developments. Works to develop the technical competence, managerial capacity, and leadership potential of local public health officials.

National Assn. of Healthcare Access Management, *2025 M St. N.W., #800 20036-3309; (202) 367-1125. Fax, (202) 367-2125. Mike Copps, Executive Director.*
General email, info@naham.org
Web, www.naham.org

Promotes professional growth and recognition of health care patient access managers, who handle hospital patient admissions, registration, finance, and patient relations; provides instructional videotapes; sponsors educational programs.

National Center for Homeopathy, *1760 Old Meadow Rd., #500, McLean, VA 22102; (703) 506-7667. Fax, (703) 506-3266. Alison Teitelbaum, Executive Director.*
General email, info@nationalcenterforhomeopathy.org
Web, www.nationalcenterforhomeopathy.org and Twitter, @NCHHomeopathy

Educational organization for professionals, groups, associations, and individuals interested in homeopathy. Promotes health through homeopathy; conducts education programs; holds annual conference; publishes quarterly magazine and monthly newsletter.

Society of Health and Physical Educators (SHAPE) America, *1900 Association Dr., Reston, VA 20191-1599; (703) 476-3410. Fax, (703) 391-0607. Cheryl Richardson, Executive Director.*
General email, programming@aahperd.org
Web, www.aahperd.org/aahe

Membership: health educators and allied health professionals in community and volunteer health agencies, educational institutions, and businesses. Develops health education programs; monitors legislation. (Formerly American Assn. for Health Education.)

Chiropractors

▶NONGOVERNMENTAL

American Chiropractic Assn., *1701 Clarendon Blvd., 2nd Floor, Arlington, VA 22209; (703) 276-8800. Fax, (703) 243-2593. Jim Potter, Executive Vice President, (703) 812-0219. Toll-free, (800) 986-4636.*
General email, memberinfo@amerchiro.org
Web, www.acatoday.org

Association of chiropractic physicians. Promotes standards of care. Interests include health care coverage, sports injuries, physical fitness, internal disorders, and orthopedics. Supports foundation for chiropractic education and research. Maintains a legal action fund to sue on behalf of patients whose insurers deny them coverage of chiropractic services. Monitors legislation and regulations.

Foundation for the Advancement of Chiropractic Tenets and Science, *6400 Arlington Blvd., #800, Falls Church, VA 22042; (703) 528-5000. Fax, (703) 528-5023. Michael McLean, President. Toll-free, (800) 423-4690.*
General email, chiro@chiropractic.org
Web, www.chiropractic.org

Offers financial aid for education and research programs in colleges and independent institutions; studies chiropractic services in the United States; provides international relief and development programs. (Affiliate of the International Chiropractors Assn.)

International Chiropractors Assn., *6400 Arlington Blvd., #800, Falls Church, VA 22042; (703) 528-5000. Fax, (703) 528-5023. Don Reno, Executive Director. Toll-free, (800) 423-4690.*
General email, chiro@chiropractic.org
Web, www.chiropractic.org

Membership: chiropractors, students, educators, and laypersons. Seeks to increase public awareness of chiropractic care. Supports research on health issues; administers scholarship program; monitors legislation and regulations.

Dental Care

▶AGENCIES

National Institute of Dental and Craniofacial Research *(National Institutes of Health), 31 Center Dr., MSC-2190, Bldg. 31, #2C39, Bethesda, MD 20892-2190; (301) 496-4261. Fax, (301) 480-4098. Martha J. Somerman, Director. Toll-free, (866) 232-4528.*
General email, nidcrinfo@mail.nih.gov
Web, www.nidcr.nih.gov

Conducts and funds clinical research and promotes training and career development in oral, dental, and craniofacial health. Monitors international research and evaluates its implications for public policy.

▶NONGOVERNMENTAL

American College of Dentists, *839 Quince Orchard Blvd., Suite J, Gaithersburg, MD 20878-1614; (301) 977-3223. Fax, (301) 977-3330. Stephen A. Ralls, Executive Director.*
General email, office@acd.org
Web, www.acd.org

Honorary society of dentists. Fellows are elected based on their contributions to education, research, dentistry, and community and civic organizations. Organizes ethics seminars, award programs, online courses on leadership and dental ethics, and speaker series.

American Dental Assn. (ADA), *Government Relations, 1111 14th St. N.W., #1100 20005; (202) 898-2400. Fax, (202) 898-2437. Michael Graham, Managing Director.*
General email, govtpol@ada.org
Web, www.ada.org

Conducts research, provides dental education materials, compiles statistics on dentistry and dental care. Monitors legislation and regulations. (Headquarters in Chicago, Ill.)

American Dental Education Assn., *1400 K St., #1100 20005; (202) 289-7201. Fax, (202) 289-7204. Dr. Richard W. Valachovic, President.*
General email, adea@adea.org
Web, www.adea.org

Membership: U.S. and Canadian dental schools; advanced, hospital, and allied dental education programs; corporations; and faculty and students. Works to influence education, research, and the delivery of oral health care for the improvement of public health. Provides information on dental teaching and research and on admission requirements of U.S. dental schools; publishes a monthly journal and newsletter.

Dental Trade Alliance, *4350 N. Fairfax Dr., #220, Arlington, VA 22203; (703) 379-7755. Fax, (703) 931-9429. Gary W. Price, Chief Executive Officer.*
General email, info@dentaltradealliance.org
Web, www.dentaltradealliance.org

Membership: dental laboratories and distributors and manufacturers of dental equipment and supplies. Collects and disseminates statistical and management information; conducts studies, programs, and projects of interest to the industry; acts as liaison with government agencies. (Formerly the American Dental Trade Assn.)

International Assn. for Dental Research, *1619 Duke St., Alexandria, VA 22314-3406; (703) 548-0066. Fax, (703) 548-1883. Dr. Christopher H. Fox, Executive Director.*
General email, research@iadr.org
Web, www.dentalresearch.org

Membership: professionals engaged in dental research worldwide. Conducts annual convention, conferences, and symposia.

National Dental Assn., *3517 16th St. N.W. 20010; (202) 588-1697. Fax, (202) 588-1244. Robert S. Johns, Executive Director.*

Web, www.ndaonline.org

Promotes the interests of ethnic minority dentists through recruitment, educational and financial services, and federal legislation and programs.

Medical Researchers

▶**AGENCIES**

National Institutes of Health (NIH) *(Health and Human Services Dept.), Office of Intramural Training and Education, 2 Center Dr., Bldg. 2, #2E04, MSC 0230, Bethesda, MD 20892-0240; (301) 496-2427. Fax, (301) 594-9606. Sharon Milgram, Director.*

General email, trainingwww@mail.nih.gov

Web, www.training.nih.gov

Administers programs and initiatives to recruit and develop individuals who participate in research training activities on the NIH's campuses. Maintains an interactive Web site for the various research training programs. Supports the training mission of the NIH Intramural Research Program through placement, retention, support, and tracking of trainees at all levels, as well as program delivery and evaluation. Administers the NIH Academy, the Summer Internship Program, the Undergraduate Scholarship Program, the Graduate Partnerships Program, and the Postbac and Technical Intramural Research Training Award programs.

▶**NONGOVERNMENTAL**

Alliance for Regenerative Medicine, *525 2nd St. N.E. 20002; (202) 568-6240. Michael Werner, President; Robert Margolin, Vice President, Communications.*

General email, info@alliancerm.org

Web, www.alliancerm.org

Membership: nationally recognized patient advocacy organizations, academic research institutions, companies, health insurers, financial institutions, foundations, and individuals with life-threatening illnesses and disorders. Advocates for research and technologies in regenerative medicine, including stem cell research and somatic cell nuclear transfer; seeks to increase public understanding. (Formerly Coalition for the Advancement of Medical Research.)

American Assn. for Clinical Chemistry, *1850 K St. N.W., #625 20006-2215; (202) 857-0717. Fax, (202) 887-5093. Janet Kreizman, Chief Executive Officer. Toll-free, (800) 892-1400.*

General email, info@aacc.org

Web, www.aacc.org

International society of chemists, physicians, and other scientists specializing in clinical chemistry. Provides educational and professional development services; presents awards for outstanding achievement. Monitors legislation and regulations.

American Assn. of Immunologists, *9650 Rockville Pike, Bethesda, MD 20814-3994; (301) 634-7178. Fax, (301) 634-7887. M. Michele Hogan, Executive Director.*

General email, infoaai@aai.org

Web, www.aai.org

Membership: scientists working in virology, bacteriology, biochemistry, genetics, immunology, and related disciplines. Conducts training courses and workshops; compiles statistics; participates in international conferences; publishes *The Journal of Immunology.* Monitors legislation and regulations.

American Medical Writers Assn., *30 W. Gude Dr., #525, Rockville, MD 20850-1161; (301) 294-5303. Fax, (301) 294-9006. Susan Krug, Executive Director.*

General email, amwa@amwa.org

Web, www.amwa.org

Provides professional education and additional services to writers, editors, and others in the field of biomedical communication.

American Society for Clinical Laboratory Science, *1861 International Dr., #200, Tysons Corner, VA 22102; (571) 748-3770. Elissa Passiment, Executive Vice President.*

General email, ascls@ascls.org

Web, www.ascls.org

Membership: clinical laboratory scientists. Conducts continuing education programs for clinical laboratory scientists and laboratory practitioners. Monitors legislation and regulations.

American Society for Clinical Pathology, *Washington Office, 1225 New York Ave. N.W., #350 20005-6156; (202) 347-4450. Fax, (202) 347-4453. Jeff Jacobs, Senior Vice President. Information, (800) 267-2727.*

General email, info@ascp.org

Web, www.ascp.org

Membership: pathologists, residents, and other physicians; clinical scientists; registered certified medical technologists; and technicians. Promotes continuing education, educational standards, and research in pathology. Monitors legislation, regulations, and international research. (Headquarters in Chicago, Ill.)

Assn. of Public Health Laboratories, *8515 Georgia Ave., 7th Floor, Silver Spring, MD 20910; (240) 485-2745. Fax, (240) 485-2700. Scott Becker, Executive Director, (240) 485-2742. Press, (240) 485-2793.*

General email, info@aphl.org

Web, www.aphl.org

Membership: state and local public health, environmental, and agricultural laboratories. Acts as a liaison to the Centers for Disease Control and Prevention. Interests include disease detection and surveillance, including response to health crises. Sponsors educational programs for public health and clinical laboratory practitioners; develops national systems for electronic exchange of laboratory data; develops laboratory systems in under-resourced countries, including strategic planning, informatics, training, and technical assistance to build lab testing capability and capacity.

Society of Toxicology, *1821 Michael Faraday Dr., #300, Reston, VA 20190; (703) 438-3115. Fax, (703) 438-3113. Shawn Douglas Lamb, Executive Director.*
General email, sothq@toxicology.org

Web, www.toxicology.org

Membership: scientists from academic institutions, government, and industry worldwide who work in toxicology. Promotes professional development, exchange of information, and research to advance toxicological science.

Nurses and Physician Assistants

►AGENCIES

National Institute of Nursing Research *(National Institutes of Health), 31 Center Dr., Bldg. 31, #5B10, MSC 2178, Bethesda, MD 20892-2178; (301) 496-0207. Fax, (301) 496-8845. Dr. Patricia A. Grady, Director, (301) 496-8230.*
Web, www.ninr.nih.gov

Provides grants and awards for nursing research and research training. Research focus includes health promotion and disease prevention, quality of life, health disparities, and end-of-life issues.

►NONGOVERNMENTAL

AFT Healthcare, *555 New Jersey Ave. N.W. 20001; (202) 879-4400. Fax, (202) 879-4545. Randi Weingarten, President.*
General email, afthealthcare@aft.org

Web, www.aft.org/healthcare

Membership: teachers, public employees, and nurses and other health care workers. Assists members with contract negotiation and grievances; conducts training programs and workshops. Monitors legislation and regulations. (Division of the American Federation of Teachers.)

American Academy of Physician Assistants (AAPA), *2318 Mill Rd., #1300, Alexandria, VA 22314-1552; (703) 836-2272. Fax, (703) 684-1924. Jenna Dorn, Chief Executive Officer.*
General email, aapa@aapa.org

Web, www.aapa.org

Membership: physician assistants and physician assistant students. Sponsors continuing medical education programs for recertification of physician assistants; offers malpractice insurance. Interests include health care reform, quality of care, research, and laws and regulations

affecting physician assistant practice and patients. Monitors legislation and regulations.

American Assn. of Colleges of Nursing, *1 Dupont Circle N.W., #530 20036-1120; (202) 463-6930. Fax, (202) 785-8320. Jennifer Butlin, Executive Director.*
General email, info@aacn.nche.edu

Web, www.aacn.nche.edu

Promotes high-quality baccalaureate and graduate nursing education; works to secure federal support of nursing education, nursing research, and student financial assistance; operates databank providing information on enrollments, graduations, salaries, and other conditions in nursing higher education. Interests include international practices.

American College of Nurse-Midwives, *8403 Colesville Rd., #1550, Silver Spring, MD 20910-6374; (240) 485-1800. Fax, (240) 485-1818. Lorrie Kaplan, Chief Executive Officer, (240) 485-1810. Press, (240) 485-1826.*
General email, info@acnm.org

Web, www.midwife.org

Membership: certified nurse-midwives and certified midwives who preside at deliveries and provide postnatal care or primary gynecological care. Establishes clinical practice studies. Interests include preventive health care for women.

American Nurses Assn., *8515 Georgia Ave., #400, Silver Spring, MD 20910; (301) 628-5000. Fax, (301) 628-5001. Marla Weston, Chief Executive Officer. Toll-free, (800) 274-4262.*
General email, info@ana.org

Web, www.nursingworld.org

Membership: registered nurses. Promotes high standards of nursing practice, the rights of nurses in the workplace, and a positive and realistic view of nursing. Affiliated organizations include the American Nurses Foundation, the American Academy of Nursing, and the American Nurses Credentialing Center. Monitors legislation and regulations.

National Assn. of Nurse Practitioners in Women's Health, *505 C St. N.E. 20002; (202) 543-9693. Fax, (202) 543-9858. Gay Johnson, Chief Executive Officer.*
General email, info@npwh.org

Web, www.npwh.org

Develops standards for nurse practitioner training and practices. Sponsors and provides accreditation of women's health nurse practitioner continuing education programs. Provides the public and government with information on nurse practitioner education, practice, and women's health issues.

National Black Nurses Assn., *8630 Fenton St., #330, Silver Spring, MD 20910-3803; (301) 589-3200. Fax, (301) 589-3223. Millicent Gorham, Executive Director.*
General email, info@nbna.org

Web, www.nbna.org

Membership: African American nurses from the United States, the eastern Caribbean, and Africa. Fosters improvement in the level of care available to minorities, conducts continuing education programs, and builds relationships with public and private agencies and organizations to exert influence on laws and programs. Conducts and publishes research.

Physical and Occupational Therapy

▶ NONGOVERNMENTAL

American Occupational Therapy Assn., *4720 Montgomery Lane, Bethesda, MD 20814; (301) 652-2682. Fax, (301) 652-7711. Fred Somers, Executive Director. Web, www.aota.org*

Membership: registered occupational therapists, certified occupational therapy assistants, and students. Associate members include businesses and organizations supportive of occupational therapy. Accredits educational programs and credentials occupational therapists. Supports research and sponsors scholarships, grants, and fellowships. Library is open to the public by appointment.

American Physical Therapy Assn., *1111 N. Fairfax St., Alexandria, VA 22314-1488; (703) 684-2782. Fax, (703) 684-7343. Michael Bowers, Chief Executive Officer. Information, (800) 999-2782. General email, memberservices@apta.org*

Web, www.apta.org

Membership: physical therapists, assistants, and students. Establishes professional standards and accredits physical therapy programs; seeks to improve physical therapy education, practice, and research.

Physicians

▶ NONGOVERNMENTAL

American Academy of Dermatology, *Government Affairs, 1445 New York Ave. N.W., #800 20005; (202) 842-3555. Fax, (202) 842-4355. Barbara Greenan, Senior Director. Web, www.aad.org*

Membership: practicing dermatologists. Promotes the science and art of medicine and surgery related to the skin, hair, and nails. Advocates for high-quality dermatologic care and for higher standards of care. Monitors legislation and regulations.

American Academy of Family Physicians, *Washington Office, 1133 Connecticut Ave. N.W., #1100 20036-4342; (202) 232-9033. Fax, (202) 232-9044. R. Shawn Martin, Vice President for Practice Advancement and Advocacy. Toll-free, (888) 794-7481. General email, fp@aafp.org*

Web, www.aafp.org

Membership: family physicians, family practice residents, and medical students. Sponsors continuing medical education programs; promotes family practice residency programs. Monitors legislation and regulations. (Headquarters in Leawood, Kan.)

American Academy of Otolaryngology—Head and Neck Surgery, *1650 Diagonal Rd., Alexandria, VA 22314-2857; (703) 836-4444. Fax, (703) 683-5100. Brenda Hargett, Chief Operating Officer. Press, (703) 535-3762. Web, www.entnet.org*

Membership: otolaryngologists—head and neck surgeons. Supports the advancement of scientific medical research. Provides continuing medical education for members. Monitors legislation, regulations, and international research.

American Assn. of Colleges of Osteopathic Medicine, *5550 Friendship Blvd., #310, Chevy Chase, MD 20815-7231; (301) 968-4100. Fax, (301) 968-4101. Stephen C. Shannon, President. Web, www.aacom.org*

Administers a centralized application service for osteopathic medical colleges; supports an increase in the number of minority and economically disadvantaged students in osteopathic colleges; maintains an information database; sponsors recruitment programs. Monitors legislation and regulations.

American Assn. of Naturopathic Physicians, *818 18th St. N.W., #250 20006; (202) 237-8150. Fax, (202) 237-8152. Jud Richland, Chief Executive Officer. Toll-free, (866) 538-2267. General email, member.services@naturopathic.org*

Web, www.naturopathic.org

Promotes naturopathic physician education and acceptance of naturopathic medicine in the nation's health care system.

American College of Cardiology, *2400 N St. N.W. 20037; (202) 375-6000. Fax, (202) 375-7000. Shalom Jacobovitz, Chief Executive Officer. Press, (202) 375-6476. Toll-free, (800) 253-4636. General email, resource@acc.org*

Web, www.acc.org

Membership: physicians, surgeons, and scientists specializing in cardiovascular health care. Sponsors programs in continuing medical education; collaborates with national and international cardiovascular organizations.

American College of Emergency Physicians, *Public Affairs, Washington Office, 2121 K St. N.W., #325 20037-1801; (202) 728-0610, ext. 3011. Fax, (202) 728-0617. Dean Wilkerson, Executive Director. General email, pr@acep.org*

Web, www.acep.org

Membership: physicians, residents, and interns. Interests include health care reform, Medicare and Medicaid legislation and regulations, medical liability, overcrowding in emergency departments, access to emergency care, bioterrorism and terrorism preparedness, managed care, and adult and pediatric emergencies. Disseminates public education materials. (Headquarters in Dallas, Texas.)

American College of Obstetricians and Gynecologists, *409 12th St. S.W. 20024-2188 (mailing address: P.O. Box 70620, Washington, DC 20024-9998); (202) 638-5577. Fax, (202) 488-3983. Dr. Hal C. Lawrence III, Executive Vice President. Press, (202) 484-3321. Toll-free, (800) 673-8444.*
Web, www.acog.org

Membership: medical specialists in obstetrics and gynecology. Disseminates standards of clinical practice and promotes patient involvement in medical care. Monitors legislation, regulations, and international research on maternal and child health care.

American College of Osteopathic Surgeons, *123 N. Henry St., Alexandria, VA 22314-2903; (703) 684-0416. Fax, (703) 684-3280. Linda Ayers, Executive Director. Toll-free, (800) 888-1312.*
General email, info@facos.org
Web, www.facos.org

Membership: osteopathic surgeons in disciplines of neurosurgery, thoracic surgery, cardiovascular surgery, urology, plastic surgery, and general surgery. Offers members continuing surgical education programs and use of the ACOS-sponsored coding and reimbursement online database. Monitors legislation and regulations.

American College of Preventive Medicine, *455 Massachusetts Ave. N.W., #200 20001; (202) 466-2044. Fax, (202) 466-2662. Michael Barry, Executive Director.*
General email, info@acpm.org
Web, www.acpm.org

Membership: physicians in general preventive medicine, public health, international health, occupational medicine, and aerospace medicine. Provides educational opportunities; advocates public policies consistent with scientific principles of the discipline; supports the investigation and analysis of issues relevant to the field.

American College of Radiology, *Washington Office, 505 9th St. N.W., #910 20004; 1891 Preston White Dr., Reston, VA 20191-4326; (703) 648-8900. Fax, (703) 295-6773. Joshua Cooper, Senior Director, Government Relations, (202) 223-1670; Dr. Harvey L. Neiman, Chief Executive Officer. Toll-free, (800) 227-5463.*
General email, info@acr.org
Web, www.acr.org

Membership: certified radiologists and medical physicists in the United States and Canada. Develops programs in radiation protection, technologist training, practice standards, and health care insurance; maintains a placement service for radiologists; participates in international conferences.

American College of Surgeons, *Washington Office, 20 F St. N.W., #1000 20001; (202) 337-2701. Fax, (202) 337-4271. Christian Shalgian, Director, Advocacy and Health Policy, (202) 337-2701.*
General email, cshalgian@facs.org
Web, www.facs.org

Monitors legislation and regulations concerning surgery; conducts continuing education programs and sponsors scholarships for graduate medical education. Interests include hospital cancer programs, trauma care, hospital accreditation, and international research. (Headquarters in Chicago, Ill.)

American Health Quality Assn., *1776 Eye St. N.W., 9th Floor 20006; (202) 331-5790. Todd D. Ketch, Executive Director.*
General email, info@ahqa.org
Web, www.ahqa.org

National network of private Quality Improvement Organizations (QIOs) that seek to improve health care provider performance through quality improvement, technical assistance, provider performance measurement feedback, teaching self-assessment techniques, responding to consumer complaints and appeals, and initiating community-based quality improvement programs. Monitors legislation and regulations.

American Medical Assn. (AMA), *Government Relations, 25 Massachusetts Ave. N.W., #600 20001-7400; (202) 789-7400. Fax, (202) 789-7485. Richard Deem, Senior Vice President of Advocacy.*
Web, www.ama-assn.org

Membership: physicians, residents, and medical students. Provides information on the medical profession and health care; cooperates in setting standards for medical schools and hospital intern and residency training programs; offers physician placement service and counseling on management practices; provides continuing medical education. Interests include international research and peer review. Monitors legislation and regulations. (Headquarters in Chicago, Ill.)

American Osteopathic Assn., *Washington Office, 1090 Vermont Ave. N.W., #500 20005; (202) 414-0140. Adrienne White-Faines, Executive Director, Government Relations. Information, (800) 962-9008.*
General email, info@osteopathic.org
Web, www.osteopathic.org

Membership: osteopathic physicians. Promotes public health, education, and research; accredits osteopathic educational institutions. Monitors legislation and regulations. (Headquarters in Chicago, Ill.)

American Podiatric Medical Assn., *9312 Old Georgetown Rd., Bethesda, MD 20814; (301) 581-9200. Fax, (301) 530-2752. Dr. Glenn Gastwirth, Executive Director.*
Web, www.apma.org

Membership: podiatrists in affiliated and related societies. Interests include advocacy in legislative affairs, health policy and practice, scientific meetings, and public education.

American Psychiatric Assn., *1000 Wilson Blvd., #1825, Arlington, VA 22209-3901; (703) 907-7300. Fax, (703) 907-1085. Dr. Saul Levin, Medical Director. Press, (703) 907-8640. Publishing, (703) 907-7322.*

General email, apa@psych.org

Web, www.psychiatry.org

Membership: psychiatrists. Promotes availability of high-quality psychiatric care; provides the public with information; assists state and local agencies; conducts educational programs for professionals and students in the field; participates in international meetings and research. Library open to members.

American Society of Addiction Medicine, *4601 N. Park Ave., Upper Arcade, #101, Chevy Chase, MD 20815-4520; (301) 656-3920. Fax, (301) 656-3815. Penny Mills, Executive Vice President.*

General email, email@asam.org

Web, www.asam.org

Membership: physicians and medical students. Supports the study and provision of effective treatment and care for people with alcohol and drug dependencies; educates physicians. Monitors legislation and regulations.

American Society of Nuclear Cardiology, *4340 East-West Hwy., #1120, Bethesda, MD 20814; (301) 215-7575. Fax, (301) 215-7113. Kathleen Flood, Chief Executive Officer.*

General email, info@asnc.org

Web, www.asnc.org

Membership: physicians, scientists, technologists, and other professionals engaged in nuclear cardiology practice or research. Provides professional education programs; establishes standards and guidelines for training and practice; promotes research worldwide. Works with agreement states to monitor user-licensing requirements of the Nuclear Regulatory Commission.

American Society of Transplant Surgeons, *2461 S. Clark St., #640, Arlington, VA 22202; (703) 414-7870. Fax, (703) 414-7874. Kim Gifford, Executive Director.*

General email, asts@asts.org

Web, www.asts.org

Promotes education and research of organ and tissue transplantation for patients with end stage organ failure. Provides information for policy decisions affecting the practice of transplantation. Offers professional development for transplant colleagues.

Assn. of American Medical Colleges (AAMC), *2450 N St. N.W. 20037-1126; (202) 828-0400. Fax, (202) 828-1125. Dr. Darrell G. Kirch, President.*

General email, aacas@aamc.org

Web, www.aamc.org

Membership: accredited U.S. and Canadian schools of medicine, teaching hospitals, health systems, academic and scientific societies, medical students and faculty, and residents and resident physicians. Administers Medical College Admission Test.

Clerkship Directors in Internal Medicine, *330 John Carlyle St., #610, Alexandria, VA 22314; (703) 341-4540. Fax, (703) 519-1893. Bergitta E. Smith, Executive Vice President.*

General email, aaim@im.org

Web, www.im.org/cdim

Membership: directors of third- and fourth-year internal medicine clerkships at U.S. and Canadian medical schools. (Affiliated with Alliance for Academic Internal Medicine.)

College of American Pathologists, *Advocacy Division, 1350 Eye St. N.W., #590 20005-3305; (202) 354-7100. Fax, (202) 354-8101. John Scott, Vice President. Information, (800) 392-9994.*

Web, www.cap.org

Membership: physicians who are board certified in clinical or anatomic pathology. Accredits laboratories and provides them with proficiency testing programs; promotes the practice of pathology and laboratory medicine worldwide. Monitors legislation and regulations. (Headquarters in Northfield, Ill.)

National Medical Assn., *8403 Colesville Rd., #820, Silver Spring, MD 20910; (202) 347-1895. Fax, (301) 495-0359. Vacant, Executive Director.*

Web, www.nmanet.org

Membership: minority physicians. Supports increased participation of minorities in the health professions, especially medicine.

Vision Care

▶**AGENCIES**

National Eye Institute *(National Institutes of Health), 31 Center Dr., #6A32, MSC 2510, Bethesda, MD 20892-2510; (301) 496-5248. Fax, (301) 402-1065. Dr. Paul A. Sieving, Director. Information, (301) 496-5248.*

General email, 2020@nei.nih.gov

Web, www.nei.nih.gov

Conducts and supports research, training, health information dissemination, and other programs with respect to blinding eye diseases, visual disorders, mechanisms of visual function, preservation of sight, and the special health problems and requirements of the blind.

▶**NONGOVERNMENTAL**

American Academy of Ophthalmology, *Governmental Affairs, 20 F St. N.W., #400 20001-6701; (202) 737-6662. Fax, (202) 737-7061. Cathy G. Cohen, Vice President.*

General email, politicalaffairs@aaodc.org

Web, www.aao.org

Membership: eye physicians and surgeons. Provides information on eye diseases. Monitors legislation, regulations, and international research. (Headquarters in San Francisco, Calif.)

American Board of Opticianry and National Contact Lens Examiners Board, *6506 Loisdale Rd., #209, Springfield, VA 22150; (703) 719-5800. Fax, (703)*

719-9144. James Morris, Executive Director. Toll-free, (800) 296-1379.

General email, mail@abo-ncle.org

Web, www.abo-ncle.org

Establishes standards for opticians who dispense eyeglasses and contact lenses. Administers voluntary professional exams and awards certification to opticians and ophthalmic professionals; maintains registry of certified eyeglass and contact lens dispensers. Adopts and enforces continuing education requirements; assists state licensing boards; approves educational offerings for recertification requirements.

American Optometric Assn., *Washington Office*, 1505 Prince St., #300, Alexandria, VA 22314-2874; (703) 739-9200. Fax, (703) 739-9497. Jon Hymes, Deputy Executive Director. Information, (800) 365-2219.

General email, jfhymes@aoa.org

Web, www.aoa.org

Membership: optometrists, optometry students, and paraoptometric assistants and technicians in a federation of state, student, and armed forces optometric associations. Sets professional standards and provides research and information on eye care to the public. Monitors legislation and regulations and acts as liaison with international optometric groups and government optometrists; conducts continuing education programs for optometrists and provides information on eye care. (Headquarters in St. Louis, Mo.)

American Society of Cataract and Refractive Surgery, 4000 Legato Rd., #700, Fairfax, VA 22033; (703) 591-2220. Fax, (703) 591-0614. David Karcher, Executive Director.

Web, www.ascrs.org

Membership: more than 9,000 ophthalmologists who specialize in cataract and refractive surgery. Offers educational programs and services to its members. Monitors regulations affecting ophthalmic practices. Sponsors independent research. Maintains a foundation dedicated to improving public understanding of ophthalmology and providing eye care to underserved parts of the world.

Assn. for Research in Vision and Ophthalmology (ARVO), 1801 Rockville Pike, #400, Rockville, MD 20852-5622; (240) 221-2900. Fax, (240) 221-0370. Iris M. Rush, Executive Director, Interim.

General email, arvo@arvo.org

Web, www.arvo.org

Promotes eye and vision research; issues awards for significant research and administers research grant program.

Assn. of Schools and Colleges of Optometry, 6110 Executive Blvd., #420, Rockville, MD 20852; (301) 231-5944. Fax, (301) 770-1828. Martin A. Wall, Executive Director.

General email, cdoyle@opted.org

Web, www.opted.org

Membership: U.S. and Puerto Rican optometry schools and colleges and foreign affiliates. Provides information about the Optometry College Admission Test to students. Supports the international development of optometric education. Monitors legislation and regulations.

Eye Bank Assn. of America, 1015 18th St. N.W., #1010 20036-5504; (202) 775-4999. Fax, (202) 429-6036. Kevin P. Corcoran, President.

General email, info@restoresight.org

Web, www.restoresight.org

Membership: eye banks in Brazil, Canada, England, Japan, Saudi Arabia, Taiwan, and the United States. Sets and enforces medical standards for eye banking; seeks to increase donations to eye, tissue, and organ banks; conducts training and certification programs for eye bank technicians; compiles statistics; accredits eye banks.

International Eye Foundation, 10801 Connecticut Ave., Kensington, MD 20895; (240) 290-0263. Fax, (240) 290-0269. Victoria M. Sheffield, President.

General email, ief@iefusa.org

Web, www.iefusa.org

Operates blindness prevention programs focusing on cataracts, trachoma, "river blindness," and childhood blindness, including vitamin A deficiency. Provides affordable ophthalmic instruments, equipment, and supplies to eye hospitals in developing countries to help lower surgical costs. Works to strengthen management and financial sustainability of eye hospitals and clinics in developing countries. Works with the World Health Organization, ministries of health, and international and indigenous organizations in Africa, Asia, Latin America, and eastern Europe to promote eye care.

Optical Laboratories Division, 225 Reinekers Lane, #700, Alexandria, VA 22314; (703) 548-6619. Fax, (703) 548-4580. R. Michael Daley, Lab Division Liaison; Ed Green, Chief Executive Officer. Toll-free, (800) 477-5652.

General email, info@thevisioncouncil.org

Web, www.ola-labs.org

Membership: optical laboratories. Promotes the eyewear industry; sponsors conferences. Monitors legislation and regulations. (Affiliated with the Vision Council.)

Vision Council, 225 Reinekers Lane, #700, Alexandria, VA 22314; (703) 548-4560. Fax, (703) 548-4580. Ed Greene, Chief Executive Officer. Toll-free, (866) 826-0290.

General email, info@thevisioncouncil.org

Web, www.thevisioncouncil.org

Sponsors trade shows and public relations programs for the ophthalmic industry. Educates the public on developments in the optical industry. Represents manufacturers and distributors of optical products and equipment.

HEALTH SERVICES FOR SPECIAL GROUPS

General

▶**AGENCIES**

Administration for Children and Families (ACF) *(Health and Human Services Dept.)*, *901 D St. S.W., #600 20447; (202) 401-2337. Fax, (202) 401-4678 (mailing address: 370 L'Enfant Promenade S.W., Washington, DC 20447); Mark Greenberg, Assistant Secretary, Acting. Public Affairs, (202) 401-9215.*
Web, www.acf.hhs.gov

Administers and funds programs for Native Americans, children, youth, low-income families, and those with intellectual and developmental disabilities. Responsible for Social Services Block Grants to the states. Provides agencies with technical assistance; administers Head Start program; funds the National Runaway Switchboard, (800) RUNAWAY (786-2929), the Domestic Violence Hotline, (800) 799-7233, the National Teen Dating Abuse Help Line, (866) 331-9474, and programs for abused children.

Assistant Secretary for Health *(Health and Human Services Dept.)*, *Minority Health, 1101 Wootton Pkwy., #600, Rockville, MD 20852; (240) 453-2882. Fax, (240) 453-2883. J. Nadine Gracia, Deputy Assistant Secretary, Acting. Information, (800) 444-6472.*
General email, info@minorityhealth.gov
Web, http://minorityhealth.hhs.gov

Oversees the implementation of the secretary's Task Force on Black and Minority Health and legislative mandates; develops programs to meet the health care needs of minorities; awards grants to coalitions of minority community organizations and to minority AIDS education and prevention projects.

Centers for Medicare and Medicaid Services (CMS) *(Health and Human Services Dept.)*, *Continuing Care Providers, 7500 Security Blvd., C2-21-16, Baltimore, MD 21244-1850; (410) 786-4857. Fax, (410) 786-0194. Martin Kennedy, Director, (410) 786-0784; Peggye Wilkerson, Deputy Director, (410) 786-4857.*
Web, www.cms.gov

Monitors compliance with government standards of psychiatric hospitals and long-term and intermediate care facilities, including residential treatment facilities, community mental health centers, intermediate care facilities for mental retardation, outpatient rehabilitation facilities, home health care, hospice care, portable X-ray units, dialysis facilities, and outpatient physical, language, and speech therapy facilities. Focus includes quality of care, environmental conditions, and participation in Medicaid and Medicare programs. Coordinates health care programs for the mentally challenged.

Centers for Medicare and Medicaid Services (CMS) *(Health and Human Services Dept.)*, *Nursing Homes, 7500 Security Blvd., Baltimore, MD 21244; (410) 786-6782. Fax, (410) 786-0194. Karen Tritz, Director.*
Web, www.cms.gov

Monitors compliance of nursing homes with government standards. Focus includes quality of care, environmental conditions, and participation in Medicaid and Medicare programs.

Eunice Kennedy Shriver National Institute of Child Health and Human Development *(National Institutes of Health)*, *National Center for Medical Rehabilitation Research, 6100 Executive Blvd., Bldg. 6100, #2A-03, MSC 7510, Bethesda, MD 20892; (301) 402-2242. Fax, (301) 402-0832. Ralph Nitkin, Director, (301) 402-4201.*
General email, RN21E@nih.gov
Web, www.nichd.nih.gov/about/org/ncmrr

Fosters the development of scientific knowledge needed to enhance the health, productivity, independence, and quality of life of persons with disabilities. Supports a program of basic and applied research promoting tissue plasticity, assistive technology and devices, improved outcomes, and increased patient participation.

Health Resources and Services Administration *(Health and Human Services Dept.)*, *Bureau of Primary Health Care, 5600 Fishers Lane, #17-105, Rockville, MD 20857; (301) 594-4110. Fax, (301) 594-4072. James Macrae, Associate Administrator.*
Web, www.bphc.hrsa.gov

Advocates to improve the health of racial and ethnic minority populations and others who experience difficulty in accessing health care, through the development of health policies and programs that will increase access and eliminate health disparities. Advises the associate administrator for primary care on public health activities affecting ethnic, racial, and other minority groups, including migrant and seasonal farmworkers, homeless persons, persons living in public housing, older adults, and women.

Health Resources and Services Administration *(Health and Human Services Dept.)*, *Policy Program and Development, 5600 Fishers Lane, #17C-26, Rockville, MD 20857; (301) 594-4300. Fax, (301) 594-4997. Jennifer Jones, Director.*
Web, www.bphc.hrsa.gov

Awards grants to public and nonprofit migrant, community, and health care centers to provide direct health care services in areas that are medically underserved. Provides staff support for National Advisory Council on Migrant Health. Administers Consolidated Health Centers Program and other bureau-funded programs.

Immigration and Customs Enforcement (ICE) *(Homeland Security Dept.)*, *ICE Health Service Corps, 500 12th St. S.W., 2nd Floor 20536; (202) 732-4600. Jon R. Krohmer, Assistant Director, (202) 732-3047.*
Web, www.ice.gov/about/offices/enforcement-removal-operations/ihs

Consists of U.S. Public Health Service commissioned officers, federal civil servants, and contract support staff. Administers ICE's detainee health care program, providing direct care to detained aliens at designated facilities and overseeing medical care at other detention facilities.

Indian Health Service *(Health and Human Services Dept.),* 801 Thompson Ave., #440, Rockville, MD 20852; (301) 443-1083. Fax, (301) 443-4794. Yvette Roubideaux, Director. Information, (301) 443-3593.
Web, www.ihs.gov

Acts as the health advocate for and operates hospitals and health centers that provide preventive, curative, and community health care for Native Americans and Alaska Natives. Provides and improves sanitation and water supply systems in Native American and Alaska Native communities.

National Institute on Deafness and Other Communication Disorders *(National Institutes of Health),* 31 Center Dr., #3C02, MSC-2320, Bethesda, MD 20892-2320; (301) 402-0900. Fax, (301) 402-1590. Dr. James F. Battey Jr., Director. Information Toll-free, (800) 241-1044.
General email, nidcdinfo@nidcd.nih.gov
Web, www.nidcd.nih.gov

Conducts and supports research and research training and disseminates information on hearing disorders and other communication processes, including diseases that affect hearing, balance, smell, taste, voice, speech, and language. Monitors international research.

Rehabilitation Services Administration *(Education Dept.),* 400 Maryland Ave. S.W. 20202-7100; (202) 245-7468. Fax, (202) 245-7591. Janet L. Labreck, Commissioner.
Web, www2.ed.gov/about/offices/list/osers/rsa/index.html

Allocates funds to state agencies and nonprofit organizations for programs serving eligible physically and mentally disabled persons; services provided by these funds include medical and psychological treatment as well as establishment of supported-employment and independent-living programs.

▶**CONGRESS**

For a listing of relevant congressional committees and subcommittees, please see pages 318–319 or the Appendix.

▶**NONGOVERNMENTAL**

Assn. of Clinicians for the Underserved (ACU), 1420 Spring Hill Rd., #600, Tysons Corner, VA 22102; (703) 442-5318. Fax, (703) 562-8801. Craig Kennedy, Executive Director.
General email, acu@clinicians.org
Web, www.clinicians.org

Membership: clinicians, advocates, and health care organizations. Works to improve the health of underserved populations and eliminate health disparities in the United States. Educates and supports health care clinicians serving these populations. Interests include health care access, transdisciplinary approaches to health care, workforce development and diversity, pharmaceutical access, and health information technology.

Catholic Health Assn. of the United States, 1875 Eye St. N.W., #1000 20006; (202) 296-3993. Fax, (202) 296-3997. Sister Carol Keehan, President.
Web, www.chausa.org

Concerned with the health care needs of the poor and disadvantaged. Promotes health care reform, including universal insurance coverage, and more cost-effective, affordable health care.

Easter Seals, *Greater Washington–Baltimore Region Office,* 1420 Spring Street, Silver Spring, MD 20910; (301) 588-8700. Fax, (301) 920-9770. Lisa Reeves, Executive Officer. Toll-free, (800) 886-3771.
Web, www.gwbr.easterseals.com

Promotes equal opportunity for people with disabilities or special needs. Interests include child development, early childhood education, adult day services, and services aimed to aid military veterans and their families as they reenter their communities. (Headquarters in Chicago, Ill.)

National Assn. of Community Health Centers, 7501 Wisconsin Ave., #1100W, Bethesda, MD 20814; (301) 347-0400. Fax, (301) 347-0459. Tom Van Coverden, President.
General email, fsmuck@nachc.com
Web, www.nachc.com

Membership: community, migrant, public housing, and homeless health centers. Represents America's federally qualified health centers. Seeks to ensure the continued development of community health care programs through policy analysis, research, technical assistance, publications, education, and training.

National Health Law Program, *Washington Office,* 1444 Eye St. N.W., #1105 20005; (202) 289-7661. Fax, (202) 289-7724. Emily Spitzer, Executive Director.
General email, nhelpdc@healthlaw.org
Web, www.healthlaw.org

Organization of lawyers representing the economically disadvantaged, minorities, and older adults on issues concerning federal, state, and local health care programs. Offers technical assistance, workshops, seminars, and training for health law specialists. (Headquarters in Los Angeles, Calif.)

Older Adults

▶**AGENCIES**

National Institute on Aging *(National Institutes of Health),* 31 Center Dr., Bldg. 31, #5C35, MSC-2292, Bethesda, MD 20892-2292; (301) 496-9265. Fax, (301) 496-2525. Dr. Richard J. Hodes, Director. Communications and Public Liaison, (301) 496-1752. Information Center, (800) 222-2225. Alzheimer's Disease Education and Referral Center, (800) 438-4380.
General email, niaic@nih.gov
Web, www.nia.nih.gov

Conducts and supports biomedical, social, and behavioral research and training related to the aging process and the diseases and special problems of the aged. Manages the Alzheimer's Disease Education and Referral Center (www .alzheimers.nia.nih.gov).

▶NONGOVERNMENTAL

AARP, *601 E St. N.W. 20049; (202) 434-2277. Fax, (202) 434-2320. A. Barry Rand, Chief Executive Officer. Press, (202) 434-2560. Library, (202) 434-6233. Toll-free, (888) 687-2277. Membership, (202) 434-3525.*
General email, member@aarp.org
Web, www.aarp.org

Membership: people fifty years of age and older. Conducts educational and counseling programs in areas concerning older adults, such as widowed persons' services, health promotion, housing, and consumer protection.

AARP, *Federal Affairs Health and Family, 601 E St. N.W. 20049; (202) 434-3770. Fax, (202) 434-3745. Ariel Gonzalez, Director of Health and Family Advocacy. Main switchboard, (202) 434-2277.*
Web, www.aarp.org

Maintains the Legal Counsel for the Elderly, which advocates on behalf of older residents of the District of Columbia who reside in nursing homes and board and care homes. Monitors legislation and regulations.

AARP Foundation, *601 E St. N.W. 20049; (202) 434-6200. Fax, (202) 434-6593. Jo Ann C. Jenkins, Executive Director. Press, (202) 434-2560. Toll-free, (888) 687-2277.*
General email, foundation@aarp.org
Web, www.aarp.org/foundation

Seeks to educate the public on aging issues; sponsors conferences and produces publications on age-related concerns. Interests include aging and living environments for older persons. Funds age-related research, educational grants, legal hotlines, senior employment programs, and reverse mortgage projects. (Affiliated with AARP.)

Alliance for Aging Research, *1700 K St. N.W., #740 20006; (202) 293-2856. Fax, (202) 955-8394. Daniel P. Perry, Executive Director.*
General email, info@agingresearch.org
Web, www.agingresearch.org

Membership: senior corporate and foundation executives, science leaders, and congressional representatives. Citizen advocacy organization that seeks to improve the health and independence of older Americans through public and private research.

Alliance for Retired Americans, *815 16th St. N.W., 4th Floor North 20006-4104; (202) 637-5399. Fax, (202) 637-5398. Barbara J. Esterling, President. Membership, (800) 333-7212.*
Web, www.retiredamericans.org

Supports expansion of Medicare, improved health programs, national health care, and reduced cost of drugs. Nursing Home Information Service provides information on nursing home standards and regulations. Monitors legislation and regulations. (Affiliate of the AFL-CIO.)

Alzheimer's Assn., *Public Policy, 1212 New York Ave., #800 20005-6105; (202) 393-7737. Fax, (866) 865-0270. Robert J. Egge, Senior Vice President. Toll-free, (800) 272-3900.*
General email, advocate@alz.org
Web, www.alz.org

Offers family support services and educates the public about Alzheimer's disease, a neurological disorder mainly affecting the brain tissue in older adults. Promotes research and long-term care protection; maintains liaison with Alzheimer's associations abroad. Monitors legislation and regulations. (Headquarters in Chicago, Ill.)

American Assn. for Geriatric Psychiatry, *7910 Woodmont Ave., #1050, Bethesda, MD 20814-3004; (301) 654-7850. Fax, (301) 654-4137. Christine deVries, Chief Executive Officer, (301) 654-7850, ext. 103.*
General email, main@aagponline.org
Web, www.aagponline.org

Works to improve the practice of geriatric psychiatry and knowledge about it through education, research, and advocacy. Monitors legislation and regulations.

Gerontological Society of America, *1220 L St. N.W., #901 20005-4018; (202) 842-1275. Fax, (202) 842-1150. James Appleby, Executive Director, (202) 587-2821.*
General email, geron@geron.org
Web, www.geron.org

Scientific organization of researchers, educators, and professionals in the field of aging. Promotes the study of aging and the application of research to public policy. Interests include health and civic engagement.

Leading Age, *2519 Connecticut Ave. N.W. 20008-1520; (202) 783-2242. Fax, (202) 783-2255. William L. (Larry) Minnix, Chief Executive Officer.*
General email, info@leadingage.org
Web, www.leadingage.org

Membership: nonprofit nursing homes, housing, and health-related facilities for the elderly sponsored by religious, fraternal, labor, private, and governmental organizations. Conducts research on long-term care for the elderly; sponsors institutes and workshops on accreditation, financing, and institutional life. Monitors legislation and regulations. (Formerly the American Assn. of Homes and Services for the Aging.)

National Assn. for Home Care and Hospice, *228 7th St. S.E. 20003; (202) 547-7424. Fax, (202) 547-3540. Val J. Halamandaris, President.*
General email, info@nahc.org
Web, www.nahc.org

Membership: hospice, home care, and private-duty providers. Advocates the rights of the aged, disabled, and ill to remain independent in their own homes as long as possible. Monitors legislation and regulations.

National Consumer Voice for Quality Long-Term Care (NCCNHR), *1001 Connecticut Ave. N.W., #425 20036; (202) 332-2275. Fax, (866) 230-9789. Richard Gelula, Executive*

Director; Lori O. Smetanka, Director, National Long-Term Care Ombudsmen Resource Center.
General email, info@theconsumervoice.org

Web, www.theconsumervoice.org

Advocates for high-quality care and quality of life for consumers in all long-term care settings. Promotes citizen participation in all aspects of nursing homes; acts as clearinghouse for nursing home advocacy. Hosts National Long-Term Care Ombudsmen Resource Center.

National Council on the Aging, 1901 L St. N.W., 4th Floor 20036; (202) 479-1200. Fax, (202) 479-0735.
James P. Firman, President. Press, (202) 600-3131.
Eldercare Locator, (800) 677-1116.
General email, info@ncoa.org

Web, www.ncoa.org

Promotes the physical, mental, and emotional health of older persons and studies adult day care and community-based long-term care. Monitors legislation and regulations.

National Hispanic Council on Aging, 734 15th St. N.W., #1050 20005; (202) 347-9733. Fax, (202) 347-9735.
Yanira Cruz, President.
General email, nhcoa@nhcoa.org

Web, www.nhcoa.org

Membership: senior citizens, health care workers, professionals in the field of aging, and others in the United States and Puerto Rico who are interested in topics related to Hispanics and aging. Provides research training, policy analysis, consulting, and technical assistance; sponsors seminars, workshops, and management internships.

National Long-Term Care Ombudsman Resource Center, 1001 Connecticut Ave. N.W., #425 20036; (202) 332-2275. Fax, (202) 332-2949. Lori O. Smetanka, Director.
General email, info@theconsumervoice.org

Web, www.ltcombudsman.org

Provides technical assistance, management guidance, policy analysis, and program development information on behalf of state and substate ombudsman programs. (Affiliate of the National Consumer Voice for Quality Long-Term Care.)

National Osteoporosis Foundation, 1150 17th St. N.W., #850 20036-4641; (202) 223-2226. Fax, (202) 223-2237. Amy Porter, Executive Director. Toll-free, (800) 231-4222.
General email, www.nof.org/request-information

Web, www.nof.org

Volunteer health organization that seeks to prevent osteoporosis and related bone fractures, to promote life-long bone health, to improve the lives of those affected by osteoporosis, and to find a cure through programs of awareness, advocacy, and public health education and research. Monitors legislation and international research.

Prenatal, Maternal, and Child Health Care

▶ AGENCIES

Centers for Medicare and Medicaid Services (CMS) *(Health and Human Services Dept.), Center for Medicaid and CHIP Services,* 7500 Security Blvd., #C5-21-17, Baltimore, MD 21244; (410) 786-3871. Fax, (410) 786-0025. Cynthia (Cindy) Mann, Director; Penny Thompson, Deputy Director.
Web, www.cms.gov and www.medicaid.gov

Develops health care policies and programs for needy children under Medicaid; works with the Public Health Service and other related agencies to coordinate the department's child health resources.

Environmental Protection Agency (EPA), *Children's Health Protection (OCHP),* 1200 Pennsylvania Ave. N.W., #2512, MC 1107T 20460; (202) 564-2188. Fax, (202) 564-2733. Jackie Mosby, Director, Acting.
Web, www.epa.gov/aboutepa/iaq/childrenshealth.html and http://yosemite.epa.gov/ochp/ochpweb.nsf/content/whatwe.htm

Supports and facilitates the EPA's efforts to protect children's health from environmental risks, both domestically and internationally; provides leadership on interagency Healthy Homes Work Group and Healthy School Environments Initiative; offers grants through the Office of Children's Health Protection and Environmental Education (OCHPEE).

Eunice Kennedy Shriver National Institute of Child Health and Human Development *(National Institutes of Health),* 31 Center Dr., Bldg. 31, #2A32, MSC-2425, Bethesda, MD 20892-2425 (mailing address: NICHD Information Resource Center, P.O. Box 3006, Rockville, MD 20847); (301) 496-3454. Fax, (301) 402-1104. Alan E. Guttmacher, Director. Toll-free, (800) 370-2943. Toll-free fax, (866) 760-5947. Information, (301) 496-5133.
General email, nichdinformationresourcescenter@mail.nih.gov

Web, www.nichd.nih.gov

Supports and conducts clinical and translational research in biomedical, behavioral, and social sciences related to child and maternal health; in medical rehabilitation; and in the reproductive sciences. Interests include health education, sudden infant death syndrome (SIDS), media and how they impact decisions on nutrition and physical activity, and environmental effects on child health and development. Information available in both English and Spanish.

Eunice Kennedy Shriver National Institute of Child Health and Human Development *(National Institutes of Health), Division of Extramural Research (DER), Developmental Biology and Structural Variation Branch (DSVB),* Dr. Arthur Tyl Hewitt, Branch Chief.
Web, www.nichd.nih.gov/about/org/der/branches/dsvb/Pages/overview.aspx

Supports basic and clinical research on normal and abnormal development that relates to the causes and prevention of structural birth defects, as well as research training in relevant academic and medical areas. Research focuses on elucidating the biochemical, molecular biologic, genetic, and cellular mechanisms of embryonic development.

Health Resources and Services Administration *(Health and Human Services Dept.), National Vaccine Injury Compensation Program,* 5600 Fishers Lane, Parklawn Bldg., #11C-26, Rockville, MD 20857; (301) 443-6593. Fax, (301) 443-8196. Vito Caserta, Director, Acting. Toll-free hotline, (800) 338-2382.
Web, www.hrsa.gov/vaccinecompensation

Provides no-fault compensation to individuals thought to be injured by certain childhood vaccines, including rotavirus vaccine; diphtheria and tetanus toxoids and pertussis vaccine; measles, mumps, and rubella vaccine; varicella, hepatitis A and B, HiB vaccine; oral polio and inactivated polio vaccines; and influenza, pneumococcal conjugate, meningococcal, and human papillomavirus vaccines.

▶ **NONGOVERNMENTAL**

Advocates for Youth, 2000 M St. N.W., #750 20036; (202) 419-3420. Fax, (202) 419-1448. Debra Hauser, President. General email, information@advocatesforyouth.org
Web, www.advocatesforyouth.org

Seeks to reduce the incidence of unintended teenage pregnancy and AIDS through public education, training and technical assistance, research, and media programs.

American Academy of Child and Adolescent Psychiatry, 3615 Wisconsin Ave. N.W. 20016-3007; (202) 966-7300. Fax, (202) 966-2891. Dr. Paramjit T. Joshi, President. Web, www.aacap.org

Membership: child and adolescent psychiatrists trained to promote healthy development and to evaluate, diagnose, and treat children, adolescents, and families affected by mental illness. Sponsors annual meeting and review for medical board examinations. Provides information on child and adolescent development and mental illnesses. Monitors international research and U.S. legislation concerning children with mental illness.

American Academy of Pediatrics, *Federal Affairs,* 601 13th St. N.W., #400N 20005; (202) 347-8600. Fax, (202) 393-6137. Mark Del Monte, Director. Information, (800) 336-5475.
General email, kids1st@aap.org
Web, www.aap.org

Advocates for maternal and child health legislation and regulations. Interests include increased access and coverage for persons under age twenty-one, immunizations, injury prevention, environmental hazards, child abuse, emergency medical services, biomedical research, Medicaid, disabilities, pediatric AIDS, substance abuse, and nutrition. (Headquarters in Elk Grove Village, Ill.)

American College of Nurse-Midwives, 8403 Colesville Rd., #1550, Silver Spring, MD 20910-6374; (240) 485-1800. Fax, (240) 485-1818. Lorrie Kaplan, Chief Executive Officer, (240) 485-1810. Press, (240) 485-1826. General email, info@acnm.org
Web, www.midwife.org

Membership: certified nurse-midwives and certified midwives who preside at deliveries and provide postnatal care or primary gynecological care. Establishes clinical practice studies. Interests include preventive health care for women.

American College of Obstetricians and Gynecologists, 409 12th St. S.W. 20024-2188 (mailing address: P.O. Box 70620, Washington, DC 20024-9998); (202) 638-5577. Fax, (202) 488-3983. Dr. Hal C. Lawrence III, Executive Vice President. Press, (202) 484-3321. Toll-free, (800) 673-8444.
Web, www.acog.org

Membership: medical specialists in obstetrics and gynecology. Disseminates standards of clinical practice and promotes patient involvement in medical care. Monitors legislation, regulations, and international research on maternal and child health care.

Assn. of Maternal and Child Health Programs (AMCHP), 2030 M St. N.W., #350 20036; (202) 775-0436. Fax, (202) 775-0061. Barbara Laur, Chief Executive Officer, Interim. General email, info@amchp.org
Web, www.amchp.org

Membership: state public health leaders and others. Works to improve the health and well-being of women, children, and youth, including those with special health care needs and their families.

Assn. of Women's Health, Obstetric, and Neonatal Nurses, 2000 L St. N.W., #740 20036; (202) 261-2400. Fax, (202) 728-0575. Kathy Ivory, President. Toll-free, (800) 673-8499.
General email, customerservice@awhonn
Web, www.awhonn.org

Promotes the health of women and newborns. Provides nurses with information and support. Produces educational materials and legislative programs.

Children's Defense Fund, 25 E St. N.W. 20001; (202) 628-8787. Fax, (202) 662-3510. Marian Wright Edelman, President. Toll-free, (800) 233-1200.
General email, cdfinfo@childrensdefense.org
Web, www.childrensdefense.org

Advocacy group concerned with programs for children and youth. Assesses adequacy of the Early and Periodic Screening, Diagnosis, and Treatment Program for Medicaid-eligible children. Promotes adequate prenatal care for adolescent and lower-income women; works to prevent adolescent pregnancy.

Children's Hospital Association, 401 Wythe St., Alexandria, VA 22314; (703) 684-1355. Fax, (703) 684-1589. Mark Weitecha, President.

Web, *www.childrenshospitals.net* and
www.facebook.com/childrenshospitals

Membership: more than 220 children's hospitals nationwide. Acts as a resource for pediatric data and analytics for clinical and operational performance. Monitors state and federal issues on clinical care, education, research, and advocacy. (Merger of the Child Health Corporation of America, National Assn. of Children's Hospitals and Related Institutions, and National Assn. of Children's Hospitals.)

Guttmacher Institute, *Public Policy, 1301 Connecticut Ave. N.W., #700 20036-3902; (202) 296-4012. Fax, (202) 223-5756. Rachel Benson Gold, Vice President for Public Policy, Acting; Susan Cohen, Vice President for Public Policy, Acting. Toll-free, (877) 823-0262.*
General email, *policyinfo@guttmacher.org*

Web, *www.guttmacher.org*

Conducts research, policy analysis, and public education in reproductive health issues, including maternal and child health. (Headquarters in New York.)

Healthy Teen Network, *1501 St. Paul St., #124, Baltimore, MD 21202; (410) 685-0410. Fax, (410) 685-0481. Pat Paluzzi, Executive Director.*
General email, *info@healthyteennetwork.org*

Web, *www.healthyteennetwork.org*

Membership: health and social work professionals, community and state leaders, and individuals. Promotes services to prevent and resolve problems associated with adolescent sexuality, pregnancy, and parenting. Helps to develop stable and supportive family relationships through program support and evaluation. Monitors legislation and regulations.

Lamaze International, *2025 M St. N.W., #800 20036-3309; (202) 367-1128. Fax, (202) 367-2128. Linda Harmon, Executive Director. Information, (800) 368-4404.*
General email, *info@lamaze.org*

Web, *www.lamaze.org* and *Twitter, @LamazeOnline*

Membership: supporters of the Lamaze philosophy of childbirth, including parents, physicians, childbirth educators, and other health professionals. Trains and certifies Lamaze educators. Provides referral service for parents seeking Lamaze classes.

March of Dimes, *Government Affairs, 1401 K St., N.W., 9th Floor 20005; (202) 659-1800. Fax, (202) 296-2964. Cynthia Pelligrini, Senior Vice President for Public Policy and Government Affairs.*
Web, *www.marchofdimes.com/advocacy-and-government-affairs-issues-and-advocacy-priorities.aspx*

Works to prevent birth defects, low birth weight, and infant mortality. Awards grants for research and provides funds for treatment of birth defects. Medical services grantees provide prenatal counseling. Monitors legislation and regulations. (Headquarters in White Plains, N.Y.)

National Assn. of School Psychologists, *4340 East-West Hwy., Bethesda, MD 20814; (301) 657-0270. Fax, (301)* 657-0275. Susan Gorin, Executive Director, (301) 347-1640. Toll-free, (866) 331-6277.
General email, *kcowan@naspweb.org*

Web, *www.nasponline.org*

Membership: school psychologists, supervisors of school psychological services, and others who provide mental health services for children in school settings. Provides professional education and development to members. Provides school safety and crisis response direct services. Fosters information exchange; advises local, state, and federal policymakers and agencies that develop children's mental health educational services. Develops professional ethics and standards.

National Center for Education in Maternal and Child Health, *2115 Wisconsin Ave. N.W., #601 20007-2292 (mailing address: Georgetown University, Box 571272, Washington, DC 20057-1272); (202) 784-9770. Fax, (202) 784-9777. Rochelle Mayer, Director; Olivia Pickett, Director of Library Services. Toll-free, (877) 624-1935.*
General email, *mchgroup@georgetown.edu*

Web, *www.ncemch.org* and *Twitter, @MCH_Library*

Collects and disseminates information about maternal and child health to health professionals and the general public. Carries out special projects for the U.S. Maternal and Child Health Bureau. Library open to the public by appointment. (Affiliated with Georgetown University, Public Policy Institute.)

National Organization on Fetal Alcohol Syndrome, *1200 Eton Court N.W., 3rd Floor 20007; (202) 785-4585. Fax, (202) 466-6456. Tom Donaldson, President, ext. 100. Information, (800) 666-6327.*
General email, *information@nofas.org*

Web, *www.nofas.org*

Works to eradicate fetal alcohol syndrome and alcohol-related birth defects through public education, conferences, medical school curricula, and partnerships with federal programs interested in fetal alcohol syndrome.

Pediatric/Adolescent Gastroesophageal Reflux Assn. (PAGER), *404 Wheaton Pl., Suite C, Catonsville, MD 21228; (301) 601-9541. Beth Anderson, Director. Message Center, (301) 601-9541.*
General email, *gergroup@aol.com*

Web, *www.reflux.org* and
Web site in Spanish, *www.ReflujoEnNinos.org*

Promotes public awareness of pediatric gastroesophageal reflux (GER) and provides support for those who suffer from it. Researches GER and acts as a clearinghouse for information on the disorder.

Zero to Three: National Center for Infants, Toddlers, and Families, *1255 23rd St. N.W., #350 20037; (202) 638-1144. Fax, (202) 638-0851. Matthew Melmed, Executive Director. Publications, (800) 899-4301.*
General email, *0to3@zerotothree.org*

Web, *www.zerotothree.org*

Works to improve infant health, mental health, and development. Sponsors training programs for professionals;

offers fellowships; and publishes books, curricula, assessment tools, videos, and practical guidebooks. Provides private and government organizations with information on early childhood development issues.

HEALTH TOPICS: RESEARCH AND ADVOCACY

General

▶**AGENCIES**

Armed Forces Radiobiology Research Institute *(Defense Dept.),* 8901 Wisconsin Ave., Bldg. 42, Bethesda, MD 20889-5603; (301) 295-1210. Fax, (301) 295-4967. Col. Lester Huff USAF, MC, Director. Public Affairs, (301) 295-1214.
Web, www.afrri.usuhs.mil

Serves as the principal ionizing radiation radiobiology research laboratory under the jurisdiction of the Uniformed Services of the Health Sciences. Participates in international conferences and projects.

Eunice Kennedy Shriver National Institute of Child Health and Human Development *(National Institutes of Health), Division of Extramural Research (DER),*
Dr. Catherine Yvonne Spong, Director.
Web, www.nichd.nih.gov/about/org/der/Pages/index.aspx

Develops, implements, and coordinates cross-cutting, multidisciplinary research activities that focus on demography, social sciences, and population dynamics; male and female fertility and infertility; developing and evaluating contraceptive methods; improving the safety and efficacy of pharmaceuticals for use in pregnant women, infants, and children; HIV infection and transmission, AIDS, and associated infections; pediatric growth and endocrine research; child development and behavior; developmental biology and typical and atypical development; intellectual and developmental disabilities; gynecologic health conditions, including pelvic floor disorders; and childhood injury and critical illness. Coordinates research and training grant programs.

Fogarty International Center *(National Institutes of Health),* NIH, 31 Center Dr., MSC 2220, Bethesda, MD 20892-2220; (301) 496-1415. Fax, (301) 402-2173.
Dr. Roger I. Glass, Director.
General email, ficinfo@nih.gov
Web, www.fic.nih.gov

Promotes and supports international scientific research and training to reduce disparities in global health. Leads formulation and implementation of international biomedical research and policy. Supports the conduct of research in high-priority global health areas, including infectious diseases such as HIV/AIDS, and helps build research capacity in the developing world.

Health and Human Services Dept. (HHS), *Human Research Protections,* 1101 Wootton Pkwy., The Tower

Bldg., #200, Rockville, MD 20852; (240) 453-6900. Fax, (240) 453-6909. Dr. Jerry Menikoff, Director.
General email, ohrp@hhs.gov
Web, www.hhs.gov/ohrp

Promotes the rights, welfare, and well-being of subjects involved in research conducted or supported by the Health and Human Services Dept.; helps to ensure that research is carried out in accordance with federal regulations by providing clarification and guidance, developing educational programs and materials, and maintaining regulatory oversight.

Health Resources and Services Administration *(Health and Human Services Dept.), Health Care Systems Bureau, Transplantation,* 5600 Fishers Lane, #12C-06, Rockville, MD 20857; (301) 443-4861. Fax, (301) 594-6095. Robert Walsh, Director.
Web, www.organdonor.gov

Implements provisions of the National Organ Transplant Act. Provides information on federal, state, and private programs involved in transplantation; supports a national computerized network for organ procurement and matching; maintains information on transplant recipients; awards grants to organ procurement organizations. Administers the C.W. Bill Young Cell Transplantation Program and the National Cord Blood Inventory.

Mark O. Hatfield Clinical Research Center *(National Institutes of Health),* 10 Center Dr., Bethesda, MD 20892; (301) 496-4000. Dr. John I. Gallin, Director. Patient Recruitment, (800) 411-1222. Admissions, (301) 496-3315.
Web, http://clinicalcenter.nih.gov

Provides in-patient and out-patient care and conducts clinical research. Promotes the application of scientific laboratory research to benefit patient health and medical care. With the Warren Grant Magnuson Clinical Center, forms the NIH Clinical Center.

National Heart, Lung, and Blood Institute *(National Institutes of Health),* 31 Center Dr., Bldg. 31, #5A48, MSC-2486, Bethesda, MD 20892-2486; (301) 592-8573.
Fax, (301) 592-8563. Gary H. Gibbons, Director, (301) 496-5166. Press, (301) 496-4236.
General email, nhlbiinfo@nhlbi.nih.gov
Web, www.nhlbi.nih.gov

Collects and disseminates information on diseases of the heart, lungs, and blood, with an emphasis on disease prevention. Works with patients, families, health care professionals, scientists, community organizations, and the media to promote the application of research results to address public health needs. Promotes international collaboration in its educational programs for scientists and clinicians.

National Heart, Lung, and Blood Institute *(National Institutes of Health), Lung Diseases, National Center on Sleep Disorders Research (NCSDR),* 6701 Rockledge Dr., #10170, MS 7952, Bethesda, MD 20892; (301) 435-0199. Fax, (301) 480-3451. Michael J. Twery, Director.
Web, www.nhlbi.nih.gov/about/ncsdr

National Institutes of Health

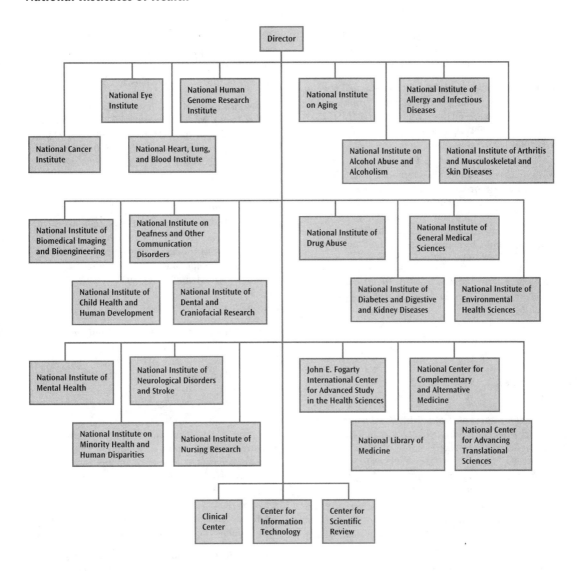

Supports research, health education, and research training related to sleep-disordered breathing and circadian rhythms. Areas of interest include respiratory neurobiology and effects of sleep deprivation. Facilitates sleep research across NIH and with other federal agencies and outside organizations.

National Institute of Diabetes and Digestive and Kidney Diseases *(National Institutes of Health)*, 31 Center Dr., Bldg. 31, #9A52, MSC-2560, Bethesda, MD 20892-2560; (301) 496-5877. Fax, (301) 402-2125. Dr. Griffin P. Rodgers, Director. Press, (301) 496-3583. Web, www.niddk.nih.gov

Conducts and supports basic and clinical research and research training on diabetes and other endocrine and metabolic diseases, digestive diseases, nutrition, obesity, and kidney, urologic, and hematologic diseases. Web site provides evidence-based health information.

National Institute of General Medical Sciences *(National Institutes of Health)*, 45 Center Dr., #3AN32, MSC-6200, Bethesda, MD 20892-6200; (301) 496-7301. Fax, (301) 402-0224. Jon Lorsch, Director. General email, info@nigms.nih.gov

Web, www.nigms.nih.gov

Primarily supports basic biomedical research and training that lays the foundation for advances in disease diagnosis, treatment, and prevention. Areas of special interest include bioinformatics, cell biology, developmental biology, physiology, biological chemistry genetics, and computational biology. Major initiatives include the Pharmacogenetics Research Network, the Protein Structure Initiative, and the Models of Infectious Diseases Study.

National Institutes of Health (NIH) *(Health and Human Services Dept.)*, 1 Center Dr., Bldg. 1, #344, MSC-0188, Bethesda, MD 20892-0148; (301) 496-4000. Fax, (301)

496-0017. *Francis S. Collins, Director; Dr. Lawrence A. Tabak, Deputy Director. Press, (301) 496-5787.*
Web, www.nih.gov

Supports and conducts biomedical research on the causes and prevention of diseases; furnishes health professionals and the public with information.

National Institutes of Health (NIH) *(Health and Human Services Dept.), Center for Information Technology,* *10401 Fernwood Rd., Bethesda, MD 20817; (301) 496-5703. Fax, (301) 402-1754. Andrea Norris, Director.*
Web, http://cit.nih.gov

Responsible for incorporating computers into biomedical research information, technology, security, and administrative procedures of the NIH. Serves as the primary scientific and technological resource for the NIH in the areas of high performance computing, database applications, mathematics, statistics, laboratory automation, engineering, computer science and technology, telecommunications, and information resources management.

National Institutes of Health (NIH) *(Health and Human Services Dept.), Center for Scientific Review, 6701 Rockledge Dr., #3030, MSC-7776, Bethesda, MD 20892-7776; (301) 435-1114. Fax, (301) 480-3965. Richard K. Nakamura, Director.*
Web, www.csr.nih.gov

Conducts scientific merit review of research grant and fellowship applications submitted to the NIH. Participates in formulating grant and award policies.

National Institutes of Health (NIH) *(Health and Human Services Dept.), Minority Opportunities in Research, 45 Center Dr., Bldg. 45, #2AS37, MSC-6200, Bethesda, MD 20892-6200; (301) 594-3900. Fax, (301) 480-2753. Dr. Alison Hall, Director, Acting.*
Web, www.nigms.nih.gov/minority

Administers research and research training programs aimed at increasing the number of minority biomedical scientists. Funds grants, fellowships, faculty development awards, and development of research facilities.

National Institutes of Health (NIH) *(Health and Human Services Dept.), National Center for Advancing Translational Sciences, One Democracy Plaza, 9th Floor, #900, 6701 Democracy Blvd., MSC 4874, Bethesda, MD 20892-4874 (mailing address: Use zip code 20817 for express mail.); (301) 496-5793. Fax, (301) 402-0006. Christopher P. Austin, Director. Information, (301) 435-0888.*
General email, info@ncats.nih.gov
Web, www.ncats.nih.gov

Works in partnership with regulatory, academic, nonprofit, and private sectors to identify and overcome hurdles that slow the development of effective treatments and cures.

National Institutes of Health (NIH) *(Health and Human Services Dept.), National Center for Complementary and Alternative Medicine, 31 Center Dr., Bldg. 31, #2B11, MSC-2182, Bethesda, MD 20892-2182; (301) 435-6826.*

Fax, (301) 435-6549. Dr. Josephine Briggs, Director. Information, (888) 644-6226.
General email, nccam-info@nccam.nih.gov
Web, www.nccam.nih.gov

Conducts and supports research on complementary and alternative medicine; trains researchers and disseminates information to practitioners and the public.

National Institutes of Health (NIH) *(Health and Human Services Dept.), National Institute on Minority Health and Health Disparities (NIMHD), 2 Democracy Plaza, 6707 Democracy Blvd., #800, MSC-5465, Bethesda, MD 20892-5465; (301) 402-1366. Fax, (301) 480-4049. John Ruffin, Director.*
General email, nimhdinfor@nimhd.nih.gov
Web, www.ncmhd.nih.gov

Promotes minority health and leads, coordinates, supports, and assesses the NIH's effort to eliminate health disparities. Conducts and supports basic clinical, social, and behavioral research; promotes research infrastructure and training; fosters emerging programs; disseminates information; and reaches out to minority and other communities suffering from health disparities.

National Institutes of Health (NIH) *(Health and Human Services Dept.), Science Policy, 6705 Rockledge Dr., MSC-7985, Bethesda, MD 20892-7985; (301) 496-9838. Fax, (301) 402-1759. Dr. Amy Patterson, Associate Director.*
General email, osp@od.nih.gov
Web, http://osp.od.nih.gov

Advises the NIH director on science policy issues affecting the medical research community. Participates in the development of new policy and program initiatives. Monitors and coordinates agency planning and evaluation activities. Plans and implements a comprehensive science education program. Develops and implements NIH policies and procedures for the safe conduct of recombinant DNA and other biotechnology activities.

National Institutes of Health (NIH) *(Health and Human Services Dept.), Stem Cell Task Force, 9000 Rockville Pike, 31 Center Dr., Bldg. 31, #8A52, MSC2540, Bethesda, MD 20892-2540; (301) 496-9746. Fax, (301) 496-0296. Dr. Story Landis, Chair.*
General email, stemcell@mail.nih.gov
Web, http://stemcells.nih.gov

The federal government's primary source for stem cell research, policy, and funding. Enables and speeds the pace of stem cell research by identifying resources and developing measures to enhance such resources. Seeks the advice of scientific leaders in stem cell research about the challenges to advancing the stem cell research agenda and strategies to overcome them.

National Library of Medicine *(National Institutes of Health), 8600 Rockville Pike, Bldg. 38, #2E17, MSC-3808, Bethesda, MD 20894; (301) 496-6308. Fax, (301) 402-1384. Dr. Donald A.B. Lindberg, Director. Local and international, (301) 594-5983.*

General email, custserv@nlm.nih.gov

Web, www.nlm.nih.gov and
PubMed Central, www.ncbi.nlm.nih.gov/pmc

Offers medical library services and computer-based reference service to the public, health professionals, libraries in medical schools and hospitals, and research institutions. Operates a toxicology information service for the scientific community, industry, and federal agencies. Assists medical libraries through the National Network of Libraries of Medicines. Assists in the improvement of basic library resources. Reading room open to the public Monday through Friday, 8:30 a.m.–5:00 p.m.

National Library of Medicine *(National Institutes of Health), Health Information Programs Development, 8600 Rockville Pike, Bldg. 38, #2S20, MSC-12, Bethesda, MD 20894; (301) 496-2311. Fax, (301) 496-4450. Michael F. Huerta, Director.*
General email, custserv@nlm.nih.gov

Web, www.nlm.nih.gov

Facilitates worldwide use of the library's medical databases through agreements with individual nations, international organizations, and commercial vendors. Helps the library acquire and share international biomedical literature.

National Library of Medicine *(National Institutes of Health), National Center for Biotechnology Information, 8600 Rockville Pike, Bldg. 38A, 8th Floor, Bethesda, MD 20892; (301) 496-2475. Fax, (301) 480-4559. Dr. David J. Lipman, Director.*
General email, info@ncbi.nlm.nih.gov

Web, www.ncbi.nlm.nih.gov and
www.pubmedcentral.nih.gov

Creates automated systems for storing and analyzing knowledge of molecular biology and genetics. Develops new information technologies to aid in understanding the molecular processes that control human health and disease. Conducts basic research in computational molecular biology. Sponsors PubMed Central, a publicly accessible digital archive of life sciences journal literature.

Naval Medical Research Center *(Defense Dept.), 503 Robert Grant Ave., #1W28, Silver Spring, MD 20910-7500; (301) 319-9646. Fax, (301) 319-7410. Capt. John W. Sanders, Commanding Officer.*
General email, svc.pao.nmrc@med.navy.mil

Web, www.med.navy.mil/sites/nmrc

Performs basic and applied biomedical research in areas of military importance, including infectious diseases, hyperbaric medicine, wound repair enhancement, environmental stress, and immunobiology. Provides support to field laboratories and naval hospitals; monitors research internationally.

NIH Clinical Center *(National Institutes of Health), 10 Center Dr., #6-2551, Bethesda, MD 20892-1504; (301) 496-4114. Fax, (301) 402-0244. Dr. John I. Gallin, Director. Communications, (301) 496-2563.*
Web, www.cc.nih.gov

Serves as a clinical research center for the NIH; patients are referred by physicians and self-referred throughout the United States and overseas.

Walter Reed Army Institute of Research *(Defense Dept.), 503 Robert Grant Ave., Silver Spring, MD 20910-7500; (301) 319-9100. Fax, (301) 319-9549. Col. Steven Braverman M.D., Commander. Public Affairs Officer, (301) 319-9471. Reference Librarian, (301) 319-7157.*
General email, wrair.publicaffairs@amedd.army.mil

Web, www.wrair.army.mil

Provides research, education, and training in support of the Defense Dept.'s health care system. Develops vaccines and drugs to prevent and treat infectious diseases. Other research efforts include surveillance of naturally occurring infectious diseases of military importance and study of combat casualty care (blood loss, resuscitation, and brain and other organ system trauma), battle casualties, operational stress, sleep deprivation, and medical countermeasures against biological and chemical agents.

▶CONGRESS

For a listing of relevant congressional committees and subcommittees, please see pages 318–319 or the Appendix.

▶NONGOVERNMENTAL

AcademyHealth, *1150 17th St. N.W., #600 20036; (202) 292-6700. Fax, (202) 292-6800. Dr. Lisa A. Simpson, Chief Executive Officer.*
Web, www.academyhealth.org

Membership: individuals and organizations with an interest in health services research, including health policymakers, universities, private research organizations, professional associations, consulting firms, advocacy organizations, insurers, managed care companies, health care systems, and pharmaceutical companies. Serves as an information clearinghouse on health services research and policy; communicates with policymakers concerning state and federal health policies; works to increase public and private funding for health services research, including comparative effectiveness and public health systems and services research. Offers professional development and training programs for health services researchers and policymakers. Monitors legislation and regulations. (Formerly Academy for Health Services Research and Health Policy.)

American Physiological Society, *9650 Rockville Pike, 4th Floor, Bethesda, MD 20814-3991; (301) 634-7164. Fax, (301) 634-7245. Martin Frank, Executive Director.*
Web, www.the-aps.org

Researches how the body and its organ systems function. Promotes scientific research, education, and dissemination of information through publication of peer-reviewed journals; monitors international research. Offers travel fellowships for scientific meetings; encourages minority participation in physiological research. Works to establish standards for the humane care and use of laboratory animals. Publishes fourteen scientific journals and a newsletter.

American Public Health Assn., *800 Eye St. N.W. 20001-3710; (202) 777-2430. Fax, (202) 777-2534. Dr. Georges Benjamin, Executive Director. General email, comments@apha.org*

Web, www.apha.org

Membership: health providers, educators, environmentalists, policymakers, and health officials at all levels working both within and outside of governmental organizations and educational institutions. Works to protect communities from serious, preventable health threats. Strives to ensure that community-based health promotion and disease prevention activities and preventive health services are universally accessible in the United States. Develops standards for scientific procedures in public health.

American Trauma Society, *201 Park Washington Court, Falls Church, VA 22046; (703) 538-3544. Fax, (703) 241-5603. Ian Weston, Executive Director. Toll-free, (800) 556-7890. General email, info@amtrauma.org*

Web, www.amtrauma.org

Seeks to prevent trauma and improve its treatment. Coordinates programs aimed at reducing the incidence and severity of trauma; sponsors research; provides training to nurses and others involved in the trauma field. Provides support to trauma survivors. Monitors legislation and regulations.

Center for Applied Proteomics and Molecular Medicine *(George Mason University), Bull Run Hall, #325, MSN 1A9, 10900 University Blvd., Manassas, VA 20110; (703) 993-9526. Fax, (703) 993-8606. Lance Liotta, Co-Director; Emanuel Petricoin III, Co-Director. General email, phackett@gmu.edu*

Web, http://capmm.gmu.edu

Researches blood-based protein biomarker discovery and molecular analysis of tissue in order to tailor treatment to individual patients. Participates in clinical trials.

Foundation for the National Institutes of Health, *9650 Rockville Pike, Bethesda, MD 20814-3999; (301) 402-5311. Fax, (301) 480-2752. Maria C. Freire, President, (301) 443-1811. General email, foundation@fnih.org*

Web, www.fnih.org

Established by Congress to support the NIH's mission of developing new knowledge through biomedical research. Works to foster collaborative relationships in education, research, and related activities between the NIH, industry, academia, and nonprofit organizations; supports basic and clinical research to advance medical knowledge; supports training and advanced education programs for future researchers; and invests in educational programs related to medical research.

Howard Hughes Medical Institute, *4000 Jones Bridge Rd., Chevy Chase, MD 20815-6789; (301) 215-8500. Fax, (301) 215-8863. Robert Tjian, President.*

Web, www.hhmi.org

Conducts biomedical research programs in major academic medical centers, hospitals, and universities. Areas of research include cell biology, computational biology, genetics, immunology, neuroscience, and structural biology. Maintains a grants program in science education, including precollege, undergraduate, graduate, and postgraduate levels. Supports selected biomedical researchers in foreign countries.

Institute for Alternative Futures (IAF), *100 N. Pitt St., #307, Alexandria, VA 22314-3134; (703) 684-5880. Fax, (703) 684-0640. Jonathan Peck, President. General email, futurist@altfutures.org*

Web, www.altfutures.org

Research and educational organization that explores the implications of future developments in various fields and facilitates planning efforts. Works with state and local governments, Congress, international organizations, federal government, and regional associations; conducts seminars. Interests include pharmaceutical research, health care, telecommunications, artificial intelligence, energy, the environment, and sustainability.

Institute of Medicine, *500 5th St. N.W. 20001; (202) 334-2352. Fax, (202) 334-3851. Harvey V. Fineberg, President, (202) 334-3300. Library, (202) 334-2125. Press, (202) 334-2138. General email, iomwww@nas.edu*

Web, www.iom.edu

Seeks to improve health nationally; provides evidence-based advice to policymakers, health professionals, the private sector, and the public. National Academy of Sciences George E. Brown Jr. Library open to the public by appointment.

Johns Hopkins University Applied Physics Laboratory, *Research and Exploratory Development, 11100 Johns Hopkins Rd., Laurel, MD 20723-6099; (240) 228-5000. Sezin Palmer, Business Area Executive, Acting.*

Web, www.jhuapl.edu/ourwork/red/

Research and development laboratory that seeks to improve warfighter survivability, sustainment, and performance through battlefield trauma prevention and mitigation, along with medical device evaluation and development. Programs include improvement of soldier protection equipment, the development of a neurally integrated upper extremity prosthetic, and blast-related traumatic brain injury research.

National Center for Healthy Housing, *10320 Little Patuxent Pkwy., #500, Columbia, MD 21044; (410) 992-0712. Fax, (443) 539-4150. Rebecca Morley, Executive Director. General email, info@nchh.org*

Web, www.nchh.org

Collects, analyzes, and distributes information on creating and maintaining safe and healthful housing. Provides technical assistance and training to public health, housing, and environmental professionals. Interests include radon, allergens, pest management, and lead poisoning.

National Institute of Environmental Health Sciences *(National Institutes of Health), Washington Office,* *31 Center Dr., #B1C02, MSC 2256, Bethesda, MD 20892-2256; (301) 496-3511. Fax, (301) 480-2978. Dr. Linda S. Birnbaum, Director. Information, (919) 541-4794.* *General email, webcenter@niehs.nih.gov*

Web, www.niehs.nih.gov

Conducts and supports research on the human effects of various environmental exposures, expanding the scientific basis for making public health decisions based on the potential toxicity of environmental agents. (Most operations located in Research Triangle, N.C.)

National Sleep Foundation, *1010 N. Glebe Rd., #310, Arlington, VA 22201; (703) 243-1697. Fax, (202) 347-3472. David Cloud, Chief Executive Officer.* *General email, nsf@sleepfoundation.org*

Web, www.sleepfoundation.org

Supports sleep-related public education and research to understand sleep problems and sleep disorders, including insomnia, sleep apnea, and narcolepsy. Works to prevent sleep-related accidents, especially those that involve driving. Monitors legislation and regulations related to sleep, alertness, and safety, such as hours-of-service rules for commercial drivers.

Obesity Society, *8757 Georgia Ave., #1320, Silver Spring, MD 20910; (301) 563-6526. Fax, (301) 563-6595. Francesca Dea, Executive Director. Toll-free, (800) 974-3084.* *Web, www.obesity.org*

Promotes research, education, and advocacy to better understand, prevent, and treat obesity. Informs the medical community and the public of new advances.

Research!America, *1101 King St., #520, Alexandria, VA 22314-2960; (703) 739-2577. Fax, (703) 739-2372. Mary Woolley, President. Information, (800) 366-2873.* *General email, info@researchamerica.org*

Web, www.researchamerica.org

Membership: academic institutions, professional societies, voluntary health organizations, corporations, and individuals interested in promoting medical research. Provides information on the benefits of medical and health research and seeks to increase funding for research.

SRI International, *Washington Office, 1100 Wilson Blvd., #2800, Arlington, VA 22209; (703) 524-2053. Fax, (703) 247-8569. Jerry Harrison, Vice President, Government Business Development, (703) 247-8569.* *Web, www.sri.com*

Research and consulting organization. Conducts studies on biotechnology, genetic engineering, drug metabolism, cancer, toxicology, disease control systems, and other areas of basic and applied research; monitors international research. (Headquarters in Menlo Park, Calif.)

Alternative Medicine

►AGENCIES

Food and Drug Administration (FDA) *(Health and Human Services Dept.), Center for Food Safety and Applied Nutrition, 5100 Paint Branch Pkwy., College Park, MD 20740-3835; (240) 402-1600. Fax, (301) 436-2668. Michael M. Landa, Director.* *General email, consumer@fda.gov*

Web, www.fda.gov

Develops standards for dietary supplements taken as part of alternative medicine treatments. Conducts research about dietary supplements and nutrition in general.

National Institutes of Health (NIH) *(Health and Human Services Dept.), National Center for Complementary and Alternative Medicine, 31 Center Dr., Bldg. 31, #2B11, MSC-2182, Bethesda, MD 20892-2182; (301) 435-6826. Fax, (301) 435-6549. Dr. Josephine Briggs, Director. Information, (888) 644-6226.* *General email, nccam-info@nccam.nih.gov*

Web, www.nccam.nih.gov

Works with the Food and Drug Administration (FDA) to develop regulations for the research and use of alternative medicine.

►NONGOVERNMENTAL

Alliance for Natural Health USA, *6931 Arlington Rd., #304, Bethesda, MD 20814; (202) 467-1985. Fax, (202) 315-5837. Gretchen DuBeau, Executive and Legal Director. Toll-free, (800) 230-2762. Press, (202) 803-5123.* *General email, office@anh-usa.org*

Web, www.anh-usa.org

Advocates on behalf of natural healthcare consumers and practitioners, and the dietary supplements industry. Promotes an integrative approach to health and natural healthcare choices for both physicians and patients. Monitors legislation and regulations. (The American Assn. for Health Freedom merged with the Alliance for Natural Health in December 2009.)

American Assn. of Naturopathic Physicians, *818 18th St. N.W., #250 20006; (202) 237-8150. Fax, (202) 237-8152. Jud Richland, Chief Executive Officer. Toll-free, (866) 538-2267.* *General email, member.services@naturopathic.org*

Web, www.naturopathic.org

Membership: naturopathic physicians who are licensed as primary health care providers. Promotes the combination of modern medicine and natural and traditional therapies, including therapeutic nutrition, botanical medicine, homeopathy, and natural childbirth.

American Music Therapy Assn., *8455 Colesville Rd., #1000, Silver Spring, MD 20910; (301) 589-3300. Fax, (301) 589-5175. Andrea Farbman, Executive Director.* *General email, info@musictherapy.org*

Web, www.musictherapy.org

Promotes the therapeutic use of music by approving degree programs and clinical training sites, establishing professional competencies and clinical practice standards for music therapists, and conducting research in the music therapy field.

National Center for Homeopathy, *1760 Old Meadow Rd., #500, McLean, VA 22102; (703) 506-7667. Fax, (703) 506-3266. Alison Teitelbaum, Executive Director.*
General email, info@nationalcenterforhomeopathy.org

Web, www.nationalcenterforhomeopathy.org and Twitter, @NCHHomeopathy

Promotes health through homeopathy. Seeks to educate the public about homeopathic medicine and increase its availability in the United States.

Arthritis

▶**AGENCIES**

National Institute of Arthritis and Musculoskeletal and Skin Diseases *(National Institutes of Health), 31 Center Dr., Bldg. 31, #4C32, MSC-2350, Bethesda, MD 20892-2350; (301) 496-4353. Fax, (301) 402-3607.*
Dr. Stephen I. Katz, Director. Information, (301) 496-8190. Health information, (877) 225-4267.
General email, niamsinfo@mail.nih.gov

Web, www.niams.nih.gov

Conducts and funds research on arthritis, rheumatic, skin, muscle, and bone diseases and musculoskeletal disorders. Funds national arthritis centers.

National Institute of Arthritis and Musculoskeletal and Skin Diseases *(National Institutes of Health), Information Clearinghouse, 1 AMS Circle, Bethesda, MD 20892-3675; (301) 495-4484. Fax, (301) 718-6366.*
Dr. Stephen I. Katz, Project Manager. Toll-free, (877) 226-4267.
General email, niamsinfo@mail.nih.gov

Web, www.niams.nih.gov

Supports medical research into the causes, treatment, and prevention of diseases of the bones, muscles, joints, and skin. Provides general information on health conditions and referrals to organizations.

Blood and Bone Marrow

▶**AGENCIES**

Health Resources and Services Administration *(Health and Human Services Dept.), Health Care Systems Bureau, Transplantation, 5600 Fishers Lane, #12C-06, Rockville, MD 20857; (301) 443-4861. Fax, (301) 594-6095.*
Robert Walsh, Director.
Web, www.organdonor.gov

Administers the National Marrow Donor Program, which maintains a registry of potential unrelated bone marrow donors.

National Heart, Lung, and Blood Institute *(National Institutes of Health), Blood Diseases and Resources, 6701 Rockledge Dr., #9030, MSC-7950, Bethesda, MD 20892-7950; (301) 435-0080. Fax, (301) 480-0867.*
Dr. W. Keith Hoots, Director. Public Affairs, (301) 496-4236.
Web, www.nhlbi.nih.gov/about/dbdr

Supports research and training on the causes, diagnosis, treatment, and prevention of non-malignant blood diseases and research in transfusion medicine and blood banking, stem cell biology, and blood supply adequacy and safety. Provides biospecimens and cellular resources to the scientific community.

National Heart, Lung, and Blood Institute *(National Institutes of Health), Blood Diseases and Resources, Transfusion Medicine and Cellular Therapeutic Branch, 6701 Rockledge Dr., #9142, MSC-7950, Bethesda, MD 20892-7950; (301) 435-0075. Fax, (301) 480-0867.*
Dr. Simone Glynn, Branch Chief.
Web, www.nhlbi.nih.gov/about/dbdr

Supports research and research training in transfusion medicine, stem cell biology and disease, clinical cellular medicine, and blood supply adequacy and safety. Collaborates with governmental, private-sector, and international organizations to improve the safety and availability of the global supply of blood and blood components.

National Heart, Lung, and Blood Institute *(National Institutes of Health), Health Information Center, 31 Center Dr., Bldg. 31, Bethesda, MD 20892-2480 (mailing address: P.O. Box 30105, Bethesda, MD 20824-0105); (301) 592-8573. Ann Taubenheim, Director.*
General email, nhlbInfo@nhlbi.nih.gov

Web, www.nhlbi.nih.gov/health/infoctr

Provides public and patient education materials on the prevention and treatment of heart, lung, and blood diseases.

National Institute of Diabetes and Digestive and Kidney Diseases *(National Institutes of Health), Kidney, Urologic, and Hematologic Diseases, 6707 Democracy Blvd., #654, #MSC 5458, Bethesda, MD 20892; (301) 594-7717. Fax, (301) 480-3510. Dr. Robert Star, Director, (301) 496-6325. Press, (301) 496-3583.*
Web, www.niddk.nih.gov

Funds research on the prevention, diagnosis, and treatment of renal disorders. Conducts research and reviews grant proposals concerning maintenance therapy for persons with chronic kidney, urologic, and renal diseases.

Warren Grant Magnuson Clinical Center *(National Institutes of Health), Transfusion Medicine, 10 Center Dr., Bldg. 10, #1C711, MSC-1184, Bethesda, MD 20892-1184; (301) 496-9702. Fax, (301) 402-1360.*
Dr. Harvey G. Klein, Chief. Alternate phone, (301) 496-4506. Information, (301) 496-4506. Press, (301) 496-2563.
Web, www.cc.nih.gov/dtm/index.html

Supplies blood and blood components for research and patient care. Provides training programs and conducts research in the preparation and transfusion of blood and blood products. Research topics include hepatitis, automated cell separation, immunohematology, and AIDS transmittal through transfusions.

AABB, *8101 Glenbrook Rd., Bethesda, MD 20814-2749; (301) 907-6977. Fax, (301) 907-6895.*
Miriam A. Markowitz, Chief Executive Officer. Press, (301) 215-6526.
General email, aabb@aabb.org
Web, www.aabb.org

Membership: hospital and community blood centers, transfusion and transplantation services, and individuals involved in transfusion and transplantation medicine and related biological therapies. Develops and implements standards, accreditation and educational programs, and services that optimize patient and donor care and safety. Encourages the voluntary donation of blood and other tissues and organs through education and public information. (Formerly the American Assn. of Blood Banks.)

American Red Cross, *National Headquarters, 2025 E St. N.W. 20006-5009; (202) 303-5000. Gail J. McGovern, President. Press, (202) 303-5551. Toll-free, 800-RED-CROSS.*
Web, www.redcross.org

Humanitarian relief and health education organization chartered by Congress; provides services in the United States and internationally, when requested. Collects blood and maintains blood centers; conducts research; operates the national bone marrow registry and a rare-donor registry. Serves as U.S. member of the International Federation of Red Cross and Red Crescent Societies, headquartered in Geneva, Switzerland.

Cancer

National Cancer Institute *(National Institutes of Health), 31 Center Dr., Bldg. 31, #11A48, Bethesda, MD 20892; (301) 496-5615. Fax, (301) 402-0338.*
Harold Varmus, Director. Press, (301) 496-6641. Toll-free, (800) 422-6237.
Web, www.cancer.gov

Conducts and funds research on the causes, diagnosis, treatment, prevention, control, and biology of cancer and the rehabilitation of cancer patients; administers the National Cancer Program; coordinates international research activities. Sponsors regional and national cancer information services.

National Cancer Institute *(National Institutes of Health), Communications and Education, 9609 Medical Center Dr., #2E-532, Bethesda, MD 20892-9760; (240) 276-6600. Fax, (240) 276-7680. Nelvis Castro, Director, Acting.*
General email, ncioce@mail.nih.gov
Web, www.cancer.gov.aboutnci/organization/oce

Collects and disseminates scientific information on cancer biology, etiology, screening, prevention, treatment, and supportive care. Evaluates and develops new media formats for cancer information.

National Cancer Institute *(National Institutes of Health), Cancer Prevention, 9609 Medical Center Dr., Rockville, MD 20850; 9609 Medical Center Dr, Bethesda, MD 20892; (240) 276-7120. Barnett S. (Barry) Kramer, Director.*
Web, http://prevention.cancer.gov

Seeks to plan, direct, implement, and monitor cancer research focused on early detection, cancer risk, chemoprevention, and supportive care. Focuses on intervention in the process of carcinogenesis to prevent development into invasive cancer. Supports various approaches, from preclinical discovery and development of biomarkers and chemoprevention agents, including pharmaceuticals and micronutrients, to Phase III clinical testing. Programs are carried out with other National Cancer Institute divisions, NIH institutes, and federal and state agencies.

National Cancer Institute *(National Institutes of Health), Translational Research Program, 9609 Medical Center Dr, Bethesda, MD 20892; (240) 276-5730. Fax, (240) 276-7881. Dr. Toby T. Hecht, Associate Director.*
General email, ncitrp-r@mail.nih.gov
Web, http://trp.cancer.gov

Administers SPORE grants (the Specialized Programs of Research Excellence). Encourages the study of organ-specific cancers, blood malignancies, and other cancers. Promotes and funds interdisciplinary research and information exchange between basic and clinical science to move basic research findings from the laboratory to applied settings involving patients and populations. Encourages laboratory and clinical scientists to work collaboratively to plan, design, and implement research programs on cancer prevention, detection, diagnosis, treatment, and control.

President's Cancer Panel, *c/o National Cancer Institute, 9000 Rockville Pike, Bldg. 31, B2-B37, MSC 2590, Bethesda, MD 20892; (301) 451-9399. Fax, (301) 451-5909.*
Dr. Abby Sandler, Executive Secretary.
General email, pcp-r@mail.nih.gov
Web, http://deainfo.nci.nih.gov/advisory/pcp

Presidentially appointed committee that monitors and evaluates the National Cancer Program; reports to the president and Congress.

American Cancer Society, *Cancer Action Network, Washington Office, 555 11th St. N.W., #300 20004; (202) 661-5700. Fax, (202) 661-5750. Christopher W. Hansen, President.*
Web, www.acscan.org

Supports evidence-based policy and legislation designed to eliminate cancer as a major health problem; works to encourage elected officials and candidates to make cancer a top national priority. Monitors legislation and regulations. (Headquarters in Atlanta, Ga.)

American Childhood Cancer Organization, *10920 Connecticut Ave., Suite A, Kensington, MD 20895 (mailing address: P.O. Box 498, Kensington, MD 20895-0498); (301) 962-3520. Fax, (301) 962-3521. Ruth I. Hoffman, Executive Director. Information, (855) 858-2226.*
General email, staff@acco.org
Web, www.acco.org

Membership: families of children with cancer, survivors of childhood cancer, and health and education professionals. Serves as an information and educational network; sponsors self-help groups for parents of children and adolescents with cancer. Monitors legislation and regulations.

American Institute for Cancer Research, *1759 R St. N.W. 20009-2583; (202) 328-7744. Fax, (202) 328-7226. Marilyn Gentry, Executive Director. Information, (800) 843-8114.*
General email, aicrweb@aicr.org
Web, www.aicr.org

Funds research on relationship of nutrition, physical activity, and weight management to cancer risk. Interprets scientific literature; sponsors education programs on cancer prevention.

American Society for Radiation Oncology (ASTRO), *8280 Willow Oaks Corporate Dr., #500, Fairfax, VA 22031; (703) 502-1550. Fax, (703) 502-7852. Laura Thevenot, Chief Executive Officer. Toll-free, (800) 962-7876.*
General email, information@astro.org
Web, www.astro.org

Radiation oncology, biology, and physics organization that seeks to improve patient care through education, clinical practice, the advancement of science, and advocacy.

American Society of Clinical Oncology, *2318 Mill Rd., #800, Alexandria, VA 22314; (571) 483-1300. Fax, (571) 366-9590. Dr. A. Hudis Clifford, President.*
General email, asco@asco.org
Web, www.asco.org

Membership: physicians and scientists specializing in cancer prevention, treatment, education, and research. Promotes exchange of information in clinical research and patient care relating to all stages of cancer; monitors international research.

Assn. of Community Cancer Centers, *11600 Nebel St., #201, Rockville, MD 20852-2557; (301) 984-9496. Fax, (301) 770-1949. Christian Downs, Executive Director.*
Web, www.accc-cancer.org

Membership: individuals from community hospitals involved in multidisciplinary cancer programs, including physicians, administrators, nurses, medical directors, pharmacists, and other members of the cancer care team.

Supports comprehensive cancer care for all. Monitors legislation and regulations.

Leukemia and Lymphoma Society, *National Capital Area Chapter, 5845 Richmond Hwy., #800, Alexandria, VA 22303; (703) 399-2900. Fax, (703) 399-2901. Beth Gorman, Executive Director. Information, (800) 955-4572.*
Web, www.lls.org

Voluntary health organization that funds blood cancer research, education, and patient services. Seeks to find cures for leukemia, lymphoma, Hodgkin's disease, and myeloma, and to improve the quality of life of patients and their families. Local chapters provide blood cancer patients with disease and treatment information, financial assistance, counseling, and referrals. (Headquarters in White Plains, New York.)

National Breast Cancer Coalition, *1101 17th St., N.W., #1300 20036; (202) 296-7477. Fax, (202) 265-6854. Frances M. Visco, President. Toll-free, (800) 622-2838. Press, (202) 973-0593.*
General email, info@breastcancerdeadline2020.org
Web, www.breastcancerdeadline2020.org

Membership: organizations, local coalitions, and individuals. Supports increasing funding for breast cancer research; monitors how funds are spent; seeks to expand access to quality health care for all; and ensures that trained advocates influence all decision making that impacts breast cancer.

National Coalition for Cancer Survivorship, *1010 Wayne Ave., #315, Silver Spring, MD 20910-5600; (301) 650-9127. Fax, (301) 565-9670. Shelley Fuld Nasso, Chief Executive Officer; Michael L. Kappel, Chair. Toll-free information and publications, (888) 650-9127.*
General email, info@canceradvocacy.org
Web, www.canceradvocacy.org

Membership: survivors of cancer (newly diagnosed, in treatment, and living beyond cancer), their families and friends, health care providers, and support organizations. Distributes information, including the Cancer Survival Toolbox, about living with cancer diagnosis and treatment; offers free publications and resources that help enable individuals to take charge of their own care or the care of others.

Ovarian Cancer National Alliance, *901 E St. N.W., #405 20004; (202) 331-1332. Fax, (202) 331-2292. Calaneet Balas, Chief Executive Officer. Toll-free, (866) 399-6262.*
General email, ocna@ovariancancer.org
Web, www.ovariancancer.org

Advocates at the federal and state levels for adequate and sustained funding for ovarian cancer research and awareness programs. Promotes legislation that would improve the quality of life and access to care for all cancer patients.

Diabetes, Digestive Diseases

▶AGENCIES

National Diabetes Information Clearinghouse
(National Institutes of Health), 1 Information Way, Bethesda, MD 20892-3560; (800) 860-8747. Fax, (703) 738-4929. Griffin P. Rodgers, Director; April Boughman, Senior Information Specialist.
General email, ndic@info.niddk.nih.gov
Web, www.diabetes.niddk.nih.gov

Provides health professionals and the public with information on the symptoms, causes, treatments, and general nature of diabetes.

National Digestive Diseases Information Clearinghouse
(National Institutes of Health), 2 Information Way, Bethesda, MD 20892-3570; (800) 891-5389. Fax, (703) 738-4929. Griffin P. Rodgers, Director; Vacant, Senior Information Specialist.
General email, nddic@info.niddk.nih.gov
Web, www.digestive.niddk.nih.gov

Provides health professionals and the public with information on the symptoms, causes, treatments, and general nature of digestive diseases and ailments.

National Institute of Diabetes and Digestive and Kidney Diseases *(National Institutes of Health), Diabetes, Endocrinology, and Metabolic Diseases,* 6707 Democracy Blvd., MSC 5640, Bethesda, MD 20892; (301) 496-7348. Fax, (301) 480-3503. Judith E. Fradkin, Director, (301) 496-7349. Press, (301) 496-3585.
Web, www.niddk.nih.gov

Provides research funding and support for basic and clinical research in the areas of type 1 and type 2 diabetes and other metabolic disorders, including cystic fibrosis; endocrinology and endocrine disorders; obesity, neuroendocrinology, and energy balance; and development, metabolism, and basic biology of liver, fat, and endocrine tissues.

National Institute of Diabetes and Digestive and Kidney Diseases *(National Institutes of Health), Digestive Diseases and Nutrition,* 2 Democracy Plaza, 6707 Democracy Blvd., #677, MSC 5450, Bethesda, MD 20892-5450; (301) 594-7680. Fax, (301) 480-8300. Stephen James, Director, (301) 594-7680. Press, (301) 496-3583.
Web, www.niddk.nih.gov/about-niddk/offices-divisions/division-digestive-diseases-nutrition/pages/default.aspx

Awards grants and contracts to support basic and clinical related to digestive diseases and nutrition, as well as training and career development. Conducts and supports research concerning liver and biliary diseases; pancreatic diseases; gastrointestinal disease, including neuroendocrinology, motility, immunology, absorption, and transport in the gastrointestinal tract; nutrient metabolism; obesity; and eating disorders.

▶NONGOVERNMENTAL

American Diabetes Assn. (ADA),
1701 N. Beauregard St., Alexandria, VA 22311; (703) 549-1500. Fax, (703) 549-5995. Larry Hausner, Chief Executive Officer. Toll-free, (800) 342-2383.
Web, www.diabetes.org

Works to improve access to quality care and to eliminate discrimination against people because of their diabetes. Provides local affiliates with education, information, and referral services. Conducts and funds research on diabetes. Monitors international research. Monitors legislation and regulations.

American Gastroenterological Assn.,
4930 Del Ray Ave., Bethesda, MD 20814; (301) 654-2055. Fax, (301) 654-5920. Lynn P. Robinson, Co-Executive Vice President; Tom Serena, Co-Executive Vice President. Press, (301) 941-2620.
General email, member@gastro.org
Web, www.gastro.org

Membership: 17,000 gastroenterology clinicians, scientists, health care professionals, and educators. Sponsors scientific research on digestive diseases; disseminates information on new methods of prevention and treatment. Monitors legislation and regulations. (Affiliated with the Foundation of Digestive Health and Nutrition.)

Endocrine Society,
2055 L St. N.W. 20036; (202) 971-3636. Teresa K. Woodruff, President.
Web, www.endo-society.org

Membership: scientists, doctors, health care educators, clinicians, nurses, and others interested in endocrine glands and their disorders. Promotes endocrinology research and clinical practice; sponsors seminars and conferences; gives awards and travel grants.

JDRF, Governmental Relations,
1400 K St. N.W., #1212 20005; (202) 371-9746. Fax, (202) 371-2760. Cynthia Rice, Vice President. Toll-free, (800) 533-1868.
General email, advocacy@jdrf.org
Web, www.jdrf.org

Conducts research, education, and public awareness programs aimed at improving the lives of people with type 1 (juvenile) diabetes and finding a cure for diabetes and its related complications. Monitors legislation and regulations. (Formerly the Juvenile Diabetes Research Foundation.) (Headquarters in New York.)

Pediatric/Adolescent Gastroesophageal Reflux Assn. (PAGER),
404 Wheaton Pl., Suite C, Catonsville, MD 21228; (301) 601-9541. Beth Anderson, Director. Message Center, (301) 601-9541.
General email, gergroup@aol.com
Web, www.reflux.org and
Web site in Spanish, www.ReflujoEnNinos.org

Promotes public awareness of pediatric gastroesophageal reflux (GER) and provides support for those who suffer from it. Researches GER and acts as a clearinghouse for information on the disorder.

Family Planning and Population

►AGENCIES

Agency for International Development (USAID), *Global Health, Population and Reproductive Health, 1300 Pennsylvania Ave. N.W., #3.06-011 20523-3600; (202) 712-4120. Fax, (202) 216-3485. Ellen Starbird, Director. Press, (202) 712-4328.*
pi@usaid.gov,
Web, www.usaid.gov/what-we-do/global-health/family-planning

Advances and supports family planning and reproductive health programs in more than 45 countries.

Assistant Secretary for Health *(Health and Human Services Dept.), Population Affairs, 1101 Wootton Pkwy., #700, Rockville, MD 20852; (240) 453-2800. Fax, (240) 453-8823. Marylyn J. Keefe, Deputy Assistant Secretary.*
General email, opa@hhs.gov
Web, www.hhs.gov/opa

Responsible for Title X Family Planning Program, which provides family planning services, health screening services, and screening for STDs (including HIV) to all who want and need them, with priority given to low-income persons; the Title XX Adolescent Family Life Program, including demonstration projects to develop, implement, and evaluate program interventions to promote abstinence from sexual activity among adolescents and to provide comprehensive health care, education, and social services to pregnant and parenting adolescents; and for planning, monitoring, and evaluating population research.

Census Bureau *(Commerce Dept.), Fertility and Family Statistics, 4600 Silver Hill Rd., #7H484, Suitland, MD 20746-8500 (mailing address: change city, state, and zip code to Washington, DC 20233); (301) 763-2416. Fax, (301) 763-3232. Rose Kreider, Branch Chief.*
Web, www.census.gov/hhes/fertility and www.census.gov/hhes/families

Provides data and statistics on fertility and family composition. Conducts census and survey research on the number of children, household composition and living arrangements of women in the United States, especially working mothers. Conducts studies on child care and child well-being.

Eunice Kennedy Shriver National Institute of Child Health and Human Development *(National Institutes of Health), Division of Extramural Research (DER), Contraceptive Discovery and Development Branch (CDDB), Dr. Trent Mackay, Medical Officer, (301) 435-6988.*
Web, http://www.nichd.nih.gov/about/org/der/branches/cddb/Pages/overview.aspx

Develops and supports research and research training programs in contraceptive development, pelvic floor disorders, and other areas of reproductive health. Major research areas include new contraceptive methods; mechanisms of action and effects of contraceptive and reproductive hormones, drugs, devices, and procedures; as well as optimal formulations and dosages of contraceptive agents and spermicidal microbicides.

Eunice Kennedy Shriver National Institute of Child Health and Human Development *(National Institutes of Health), Division of Extramural Research (DER), Fertility and Infertility (FI) Branch, Dr. Louis DePaolo, Branch Chief.*
Web, www.nichd.nih.gov/about/org/der/branches/fi/Pages/overview.aspx

Encourages, enables, and supports scientific research aimed at alleviating human infertility, discovering new ways to control fertility, and expanding knowledge of processes that underlie human reproduction. Provides funds for basic, clinical, and tranlational studies that enhance understanding of normal reproduction and reproductive pathophysiology, as well as enable the development of more effective strategies for the diagnosis, management, and prevention of conditions that compromise fertility.

►INTERNATIONAL ORGANIZATIONS

International Bank for Reconstruction and Development *(World Bank), Human Development Network, 1818 H St. N.W. 20433; (202) 473-1000. Elizabeth King, Vice President, Acting; Carolyn Reynolds, Media Contact, (202) 473-0049.*
Web, www.worldbank.org

Provides member countries with support for initiatives to eradicate extreme poverty and hunger, achieve universal primary education, promote gender equality, reduce child mortality, combat HIV/AIDS, and ensure environmental sustainability.

►NONGOVERNMENTAL

Advocates for Youth, *2000 M St. N.W., #750 20036; (202) 419-3420. Fax, (202) 419-1448. Debra Hauser, President.*
General email, information@advocatesforyouth.org
Web, www.advocatesforyouth.org

Seeks to reduce the incidence of unintended teenage pregnancy and AIDS through public education, training and technical assistance, research, and media programs.

American Society for Reproductive Medicine, *J. Benjamin Younger Office of Public Affairs, 409 12th St. S.W. 20024-2188; (202) 863-2494. Sean B. Tipton, Public Affairs Director.*
General email, advocacy@asrm.dc.org
Web, www.asrm.org

Membership: obstetrician/gynecologists, urologists, reproductive endocrinologists, embryologists, mental health professionals, internists, nurses, practice administrators, laboratory technicians, pediatricians, research scientists, and veterinarians. Seeks to educate health care professionals, policymakers, and the public on the science and practice of reproductive medicine and associated legal and ethical issues. Monitors legislation and regulations. (Headquarters in Birmingham, Ala.).

Guttmacher Institute, *Public Policy,* 1301 Connecticut Ave. N.W., #700 20036-3902; (202) 296-4012. Fax, (202) 223-5756. Rachel Benson Gold, Vice President for Public Policy, Acting; Susan Cohen, Vice President for Public Policy, Acting. Toll-free, (877) 823-0262.
General email, policyinfo@guttmacher.org

Web, www.guttmacher.org

Conducts research, policy analysis, and public education in reproductive health, fertility regulation, population, and related areas of U.S. and international health. (Headquarters in New York.)

National Abortion Federation (NAF), 1660 L St. N.W., #450 20036; (202) 667-5881. Fax, (202) 667-5890. Vicki Saporta, President. NAF Hotline, (800) 772-9100.
General email, naf@prochoice.org

Web, www.prochoice.org

Professional association of abortion providers in the United States, Canada, and Mexico City. Offers information on medical, legal, and social aspects of abortion; sets quality standards for abortion care. Conducts training and accredited continuing medical education. Runs a toll-free hotline for women seeking information or referrals. Monitors legislation and regulations.

National Family Planning and Reproductive Health Assn., 1627 K St. N.W., 12th Floor 20006-1702; (202) 293-3114. Fax, (202) 293-1990. Clare Coleman, President.
General email, info@nfprha.org

Web, www.nfprha.org

Represents family planning providers, including nurses, nurse practitioners, administrators, and other health care professionals nationwide. Provides advocacy, education, and training for those in the family planning and reproductive health care field. Interests include family planning for the low-income and uninsured, and reducing rates of unintended pregnancy.

Planned Parenthood Federation of America, *Public Policy,* 1110 Vermont Ave. N.W., #300 20005; (202) 973-4800. Fax, (202) 296-3242. Amy Taylor Marshall, President. Media, (202) 261-4433.
Web, www.plannedparenthood.org

Educational, research, and medical services organization. Washington office conducts research and monitors legislation on health care topics, including reproductive health, women's health, contraception, family planning, abortion, and global health. (Headquarters in New York accredits affiliated local centers, which offer medical services, birth control, and family planning information.)

Population Action International, 1300 19th St. N.W., #200 20036; (202) 557-3400. Fax, (202) 728-4177. Suzanne Ehlers, President.
General email, pai@popact.org

Web, www.populationaction.org

Promotes population stabilization through public education and universal access to voluntary family planning. Library open to the public by appointment.

Population Connection, 2120 L St. N.W., #500 20037; (202) 332-2200. Fax, (202) 332-2302. John Seager, President. Toll-free, (800) 757-1956.
General email, info@populationconnection.org

Web, www.populationconnection.org

Membership: persons interested in sustainable world populations. Promotes the expansion of domestic and international family planning programs; supports a voluntary population stabilization policy and women's access to abortion and family planning services; works to protect the earth's resources and environment. (Formerly Zero Population Growth.)

Population Institute, 107 2nd St. N.E. 20002; (202) 544-3300. Fax, (202) 544-0068. Robert Walker, President.
General email, info@populationinstitute.org

Web, www.populationinstitute.org

Promotes voluntary family planning and reproductive health services. Seeks to increase public awareness of social, economic, and environmental consequences of rapid population growth. Advocates a balance between global population and natural resources to policymakers in developing and industrialized nations. Recruits and trains population activists.

Population Reference Bureau, 1875 Connecticut Ave. N.W., #520 20009-5728; (202) 483-1100. Fax, (202) 328-3937. James Scott, President, Acting. Toll-free, (800) 877-9881.
General email, popref@prb.org

Web, www.prb.org

Educational organization engaged in information dissemination, training, and policy analysis on domestic and international population trends and issues. Interests include international development and family planning programs, the environment, and U.S. social and economic policy. Library open to the public.

Genetic Disorders

▶**AGENCIES**

Health Resources and Services Administration *(Health and Human Services Dept.),* **Genetic Services, Maternal and Child Health,** 5600 Fishers Lane, #18A19, Rockville, MD 20857; (301) 443-1080. Fax, (301) 480-1312. Joan Scott, Chief; Michael Lu, Associate Administrator.
Web, www.mchb.hrsa.gov

Awards funds, including demonstration grants, to develop or enhance regional, local, and state genetic screening, diagnostic, counseling, and follow-up programs; assists states in their newborn screening programs; provides funding for regional hemophilia treatment centers; and supports comprehensive care for individuals and families with Cooley's anemia, and those with sickle cell anemia identified through newborn screening.

National Heart, Lung, and Blood Institute *(National Institutes of Health),* **Blood Diseases and Resources, Blood Diseases Program,** 6701 Rockledge Dr., #90930,

Bethesda, MD 20892-7950; (301) 435-0050. Fax, (301) 480-0867. Dr. Harvey Luksenburg, Branch Chief, Acting. Press, (301) 496-4236.

Web, www.nhlbi.nih.gov/about/dbdr

Supports outcomes-related research and research training in blood diseases, including sickle cell disease (SCD) and other aplastic anemias and malaria. Areas of emphasis include genetics, hemoglobin synthesis, fetal hemoglobin production, transplantation, and gene therapy.

National Human Genome Research Institute (National Institutes of Health), 31 Center Dr., Bldg. 31, #4B09, MSC-2152, Bethesda, MD 20892-2152; (301) 496-0844. Fax, (301) 402-0837. Eric D. Green, Director. Information, (301) 496-0844.

Web, www.genome.gov

Conducts and funds a broad range of studies aimed at understanding the structure and function of the human genome and its role in health and disease. Supports the development of resources and technology that will accelerate genome research and its application to human health. Studies the ethical, legal, and social implications of genome research, and supports the training of investigators, as well as the dissemination of genome information to the public and to health professionals.

National Institute of Allergy and Infectious Diseases (National Institutes of Health), Allergy, Immunology, and Transplantation, 6610 Rockledge Dr., #6124, Bethesda, MD 20892-6601; (301) 496-1886. Fax, (301) 402-0175. Dr. Daniel Rotrosen, Director.

Web, www.niaid.nih.gov/about/organization/dait

Supports extramural basic and clinical research to increase understanding of the causes and mechanisms that lead to the development of immunologic diseases and to expand knowledge that can be applied to developing improved techniques of diagnosis, treatment, and prevention. Interests include lupus; allergic diseases, such as asthma, hay fever, and contact dermatitis; and acute and chronic inflammatory disorders.

National Institute of Diabetes and Digestive and Kidney Diseases (National Institutes of Health), Kidney, Urologic, and Hematologic Diseases, 6707 Democracy Blvd., #654, #MSC 5458, Bethesda, MD 20892; (301) 594-7717. Fax, (301) 480-3510. Dr. Robert Star, Director, (301) 496-6325. Press, (301) 496-3583.

Web, www.niddk.nih.gov

Funds research on the prevention, diagnosis, and treatment of renal disorders. Conducts research and reviews grant proposals concerning maintenance therapy for persons with chronic kidney, urologic, and renal diseases.

National Institute of General Medical Sciences (National Institutes of Health), Genetics and Developmental Biology, 45 Center Dr., #2AS25N, MSC 6200, Bethesda, MD 20892-6200; (301) 594-0943. Fax, (301) 480-2228. Judith H. Greenberg, Director.

Web, www.nigms.nih.gov/about/overview/gdb.htm

Supports research and research training in genetics. Maintains Human Genetic Cell Repository; distributes cell lines and DNA samples to research scientists.

National Institutes of Health (NIH) (Health and Human Services Dept.), Biotechnology Activities, 6705 Rockledge Dr., #750, MSC-7985, Bethesda, MD 20892-7985; (301) 496-9838. Fax, (301) 402-1759. Dr. Jacqueline Corrigan-Curay, Director, Acting.

General email, oba-osp@od.nih.gov

Web, http://oba.od.nih.gov/oba

Reviews requests submitted to the NIH involving genetic testing, recombinant DNA technology, xenotransplantation, and biosecurity; develops and implements research guidelines for safe conduct of DNA-related research. Monitors scientific progress in human genetics.

▶ **NONGOVERNMENTAL**

Center for Sickle Cell Disease (Howard University), 1840 7th St. N.W. 20001; (202) 865-8292. Fax, (202) 232-6719. Juan Saloman Andonie, Director.

Web, www.sicklecell.howard.edu

Screens and tests for sickle cell disease; conducts research; promotes public education and community involvement; provides counseling and patient care.

Cystic Fibrosis Foundation, 6931 Arlington Rd., #200, Bethesda, MD 20814; (301) 951-4422. Fax, (301) 951-6378. Robert J. Beall, President. Information, (800) 344-4823.

General email, info@cff.org

Web, www.cff.org

Conducts research on cystic fibrosis, a genetic disease affecting the respiratory and digestive systems. Focuses on medical research to identify a cure and to improve quality of life for those living with cystic fibrosis.

Genetic Alliance, 4301 Connecticut Ave. N.W., #404 20008-2369; (202) 966-5557. Fax, (202) 966-8553. Sharon Terry, President.

General email, info@geneticalliance.org

Web, www.geneticalliance.org

Coalition of government, industry, advocacy organizations, and private groups that seeks to advance genetic research and its applications. Promotes increased funding for research, improved access to services, and greater support for emerging technologies, tests, and treatments. Advocates on behalf of individuals and families living with genetic conditions.

Genetics Society of America, 9650 Rockville Pike, Bethesda, MD 20814-3998; (301) 634-7300. Fax, (301) 634-7079. Adam Fagen, Executive Director. Toll-free, (866) 486-4363.

General email, society@genetics-gsa.org

Web, www.genetics-gsa.org

Facilitates professional cooperation among persons conducting research in and teaching genetics. Advocates for research funding; sponsors meetings; and publishes scholarly research journals.

Kennedy Institute of Ethics *(Georgetown University),* *Healy Hall, 37th and O Sts. N.W., 4th Floor 20057; (202) 687-8099. Fax, (202) 687-8089. Margaret Little, Director. Library, (202) 687-3885. Toll-free, United States and Canada, (888) 246-3849 and (888) 633-3849.* *General email, kennedyinstitute@georgetown.edu* *Web, http://kennedyinstitute.georgetown.edu*

Carries out teaching and research on medical ethics, including legal and ethical definitions of death, allocation of health resources, and recombinant DNA and human gene therapy. Sponsors the annual Intensive Bioethics Course. Conducts international programs. Serves as the home of the Bioethics Research Library at Georgetown University (http://bioethics.georgetown.edu) and the National Information Resource on Ethics and Human Genetics (http://genthx.georgetown.edu). Provides free reference assistance and bibliographic databases covering all ethical issues in health care, genetics, and biomedical research. Library open to the public.

March of Dimes, *Government Affairs, 1401 K St., N.W., 9th Floor 20005; (202) 659-1800. Fax, (202) 296-2964. Cynthia Pelligrini, Senior Vice President for Public Policy and Government Affairs.* *Web, www.marchofdimes.com/advocacy-and-government-issues-and-advocacy-priorities.aspx*

Works to prevent and treat birth defects. Awards grants for research and provides funds for treatment of birth defects. Monitors legislation and regulations. (Headquarters in White Plains, N.Y.)

Heart Disease, Strokes

▶**AGENCIES**

National Heart, Lung, and Blood Institute *(National Institutes of Health), Cardiovascular Sciences, 6701 Rockledge Dr., #8128, Bethesda, MD 20892; (301) 435-0422. Fax, (301) 480-7971. Michael Lauer, Director. Press, (301) 496-4236.* *General email, lauerm@nhlbi.nih.gov* *Web, www.nhlbi.nih.gov/about/dcvd/index.htm*

Supports basic, clinical, population, and health services research on the causes, prevention, and treatment of cardiovascular disease and technology development. Interests include disease and risk factor patterns in populations; clinical trials of interventions; and genetic, behavioral, sociocultural, environmental, and health-systems factors of disease risk and outcomes.

National Heart, Lung, and Blood Institute *(National Institutes of Health), Health Information Center,* *31 Center Dr., Bldg. 31, Bethesda, MD 20892-2480 (mailing address: P.O. Box 30105, Bethesda, MD 20824-0105); (301) 592-8573. Ann Taubenheim, Director.* *General email, nhlbInfo@nhlbi.nih.gov* *Web, www.nhlbi.nih.gov/health/infoctr*

Acquires, maintains, and disseminates information on cholesterol, high blood pressure, heart attack awareness, and asthma to the public and health professionals.

National Institute of Neurological Disorders and Stroke *(National Institutes of Health), 31 Center Dr., Bldg. 31, #8A52, P.O. Box 5801, Bethesda, MD 20824; (301) 496-5924. Fax, (301) 402-2186. Story Landis, Director. Information, (301) 496-5751. Toll-free, (800) 352-9424.* *Web, www.ninds.nih.gov*

Conducts research and disseminates information on the causes, prevention, diagnosis, and treatment of neurological disorders and stroke; supports basic and clinical research in related scientific areas. Provides research grants to public and private institutions and individuals. Operates a program of contracts for the funding of research and research-support efforts.

▶**NONGOVERNMENTAL**

American Heart Assn., *Washington Office, 1150 Connecticut Ave. N.W., #300 20036; (202) 785-7900. Fax, (202) 785-7955. Retha Sherrod, Director, Media Advocacy.* *Web, www.heart.org*

Membership: physicians, scientists, and other interested individuals. Supports research, patient advocacy, treatment, and community service programs that provide information about heart disease and stroke; participates in international conferences and research. Monitors legislation and regulations. (Headquarters in Dallas, Texas.)

WomenHeart: National Coalition for Women With Heart Disease, *818 18th St. N.W., #1000 20006; (202) 728-7199. Fax, (202) 728-7238. Lisa M. Tate, Chief Executive Officer.* *General email, mail@womenheart.org* *Web, www.womenheart.org*

Patient-centered organization that seeks to advance women's heart health through advocacy, community education, and patient support. Comprised of patients and their families, health care providers, advocates, and interested consumers.

HIV and AIDS

▶**AGENCIES**

Assistant Secretary for Health *(Health and Human Services Dept.), HIV/AIDS Policy, 200 Independence Ave. S.W., #730E 20201; (202) 690-5560. Fax, (202) 690-7560. Ronald O. Valdiserri, Director. HIV/AIDS information, http://aids.gov.* *Web, www.hhs.gov/oash/ohaidp*

Coordinates national AIDS policy, sets priorities, recommends funding, and helps implement all Public Health Service HIV programs. Monitors progress of prevention and control programs; serves as a liaison with governmental and private organizations.

Assistant Secretary for Health *(Health and Human Services Dept.), Minority Health, 1101 Wootton Pkwy., #600, Rockville, MD 20852; (240) 453-2882. Fax, (240) 453-2883. J. Nadine Gracia, Deputy Assistant Secretary, Acting. Information, (800) 444-6472.*
General email, info@minorityhealth.gov
Web, http://minorityhealth.hhs.gov

Oversees the implementation of the secretary's Task Force on Black and Minority Health and legislative mandates; develops programs to meet the health care needs of minorities; awards grants to coalitions of minority community organizations and to minority AIDS education and prevention projects.

Centers for Disease Control and Prevention (CDC) *(Health and Human Services Dept.), Washington Office, 395 E St. S.W., #9100 20201; (202) 245-0600. Fax, (202) 245-0602. Dr. Thomas R. Frieden, Director; Edward Hunter, Director of Washington Office (Congressional Affairs). Public inquiries, (800) 232-4636.*
General email, cdinfo@cdc.gov
Web, www.cdc.gov/washington

Conducts research to prevent and control acquired immune deficiency syndrome (AIDS); promotes public awareness through guidelines for health care workers, educational packets for schools, and monthly reports on incidences of AIDS. (Headquarters in Atlanta, Ga.: 1600 Clifton Rd. N.E. Atlanta, GA 30333.)

Food and Drug Administration (FDA) *(Health and Human Services Dept.), Center for Biologics Evaluation and Research, 1401 Rockville Pike, #200 North, Rockville, MD 20852-1448 (mailing address: 5515 Security Lane, #7100, Rockville, MD 20852); (301) 827-0372. Fax, (301) 827-0440. Karen Midthun, Director. Press and publications, (301) 827-2000.*
General email, karen.midthun@fda.gov
Web, www.fda.gov/cber

Develops testing standards for vaccines, blood supply, and blood products and derivatives to prevent transmission of the human immunodeficiency virus (HIV); regulates biological therapeutics; helps formulate international standards. Serves as the focus for AIDS activities within the FDA.

Food and Drug Administration (FDA) *(Health and Human Services Dept.), Center for Drug Evaluation and Research, 10903 New Hampshire Ave., Silver Spring, MD 20993; (301) 796-5400. Fax, (301) 847-8752. Dr. Janet Woodcock, Director. Press, (301) 796-4540.*
Web, www.fda.gov/drugs

Approves new drugs for AIDS and AIDS-related diseases. Reviews and approves applications to investigate and market new drugs; works to harmonize drug approval internationally.

Health Resources and Services Administration *(Health and Human Services Dept.), HIV/AIDS Bureau, 5600 Fishers Lane, #705, Rockville, MD 20857; (301) 443-1993. Laura Cheever, Associate Administrator.*
Web, www.hab.hrsa.gov

Administers grants to support health care programs for AIDS patients, including those that reimburse low-income patients for drug expenses. Provides patients with AIDS and HIV-related disorders with ambulatory and community-based care. Conducts AIDS/HIV education and training activities for health professionals.

National Institute of Allergy and Infectious Diseases *(National Institutes of Health), HIV/AIDS, 6700-B Rockledge Dr., #4142, Bethesda, MD 20892-7620; (301) 496-0545. Fax, (301) 402-1505. Dr. Carl W. Dieffenbach, Director.*
Web, www.niaid.nih.gov/about/organization/daids/pages/default.aspx

Supports extramural basic and clinical research to better understand HIV and how it causes disease; find new tools to prevent HIV infection, including a preventative vaccine; develop new and more effective treatments for people infected with HIV; and work toward a cure.

National Institutes of Health (NIH) *(Health and Human Services Dept.), Office of AIDS Research, 5635 Fishers Lane, #4000, MSC 9310, Rockville, MD 20892-9310; (301) 496-0357. Fax, (301) 496-2119. Jack E. Whitescarver, Director.*
General email, oartemp1@od31em1.od.nih.gov
Web, www.oar.nih.gov

Responsible for the scientific, budgetary, legislative, and policy elements of the NIH AIDS research program. Plans, coordinates, evaluates, and funds all NIH AIDS research.

State Dept., U.S. Global AIDS Coordinator, *2100 Pennsylvania Ave. N.W., Bldg. SA-29, #200 20037 (mailing address: 2201 C St. N.W., Washington, DC 20520); (202) 663-2440. Fax, (202) 663-2979. Dr. Deborah L. Birx, Ambassador. Press, (202) 663-2708.*
General email, SGAC_Public_Affairs@state.gov
Web, www.pepfar.gov

Oversees and coordinates all U.S. international HIV/AIDS activities, including implementation of the President's Emergency Plan for AIDS Relief.

Walter Reed Army Institute of Research *(Defense Dept.), U.S. Military HIV Research Program, 6720A Rockledge Dr., Bethesda, MD 20817; (301) 500-3660. Fax, (301) 500-3666. Col. Nelson L. Michael, Director. Public affairs, (301) 251-5070.*
General email, info@hivresearch.org
Web, www.hivresearch.org

Conducts HIV research, encompassing vaccine development, prevention, disease surveillance, and care and treatment options.

Warren Grant Magnuson Clinical Center *(National Institutes of Health), Transfusion Medicine, 10 Center Dr., Bldg. 10, #1C711, MSC-1184, Bethesda, MD 20892-1184; (301) 496-9702. Fax, (301) 402-1360. Dr. Harvey G. Klein, Chief. Alternate phone, (301) 496-4506. Information, (301) 496-4506. Press, (301) 496-2563.*
Web, www.cc.nih.gov/dtm/index.html

Supplies blood and blood components for patient care and research. Conducts research on diseases transmissible by blood, primarily AIDS and hepatitis.

▶ **NONGOVERNMENTAL**

AIDS Alliance for Children, *Youth, and Families,* *1705 DeSales St. N.W. 20036; (202) 835-8373. Fax, (202) 835-8368. Michael Ruppal, Executive Director.*
General email, info@aids-alliance.org
Web, www.aids-alliance.org

Conducts research and disseminates information on health care and HIV issues. Develops and promotes policy aimed at improving the health and welfare of children, youth, and families affected by HIV. Provides training and technical assistance to health care providers and consumers. (Part of AIDS Institute.)

American Red Cross, *National Headquarters,* *2025 E St. N.W. 20006-5009; (202) 303-5000. Gail J. McGovern, President. Press, (202) 303-5551. Toll-free, 800-RED-CROSS.*
Web, www.redcross.org

Humanitarian relief and health education organization chartered by Congress. Conducts public education campaigns on HIV/AIDS. Operates worldwide vaccination program. Serves as U.S. member of the international Red Cross and Red Crescent Societies, headquartered in Geneva, Switzerland.

Children's AIDS Fund, *1329 Shepard Dr., #7, Sterling, VA 20164 (mailing address: P.O. Box 16433, Washington, DC 20041); (703) 433-1560. Fax, (703) 433-1561. Anita M. Smith, President.*
General email, info@childrensaidsfund.org
Web, www.childrensaidsfund.org

Provides care, services, resources, referrals, and education to children and their families affected by HIV disease. Focuses on children from birth through age 24 who are infected with, are orphaned by, or will potentially be orphaned by HIV.

The Foundation for AIDS Research (amfAR), *Public Policy, Washington Office*, *1150 17th St. N.W., #406 20036-4622; (202) 331-8600. Fax, (202) 331-8606. Chris Collins, Vice President.*
Web, www.amfar.org

Supports funding for basic biomedical and clinical AIDS research; promotes AIDS prevention education worldwide; advocates effective AIDS-related public policy. Monitors legislation, regulations, and international research. (Headquarters in New York.)

Human Rights Campaign (HRC), *1640 Rhode Island Ave. N.W. 20036; (202) 628-4160. Fax, (202) 347-5323. Chad Griffin, President. Toll-free, (800) 777-4723.*
General email, hrc@hrc.org
Web, www.hrc.org

Promotes legislation to fund AIDS research.

AIDS United, *1424 K St. N.W., #200 20005; (202) 408-4848. Fax, (202) 408-1818. Michael Kaplan, President; Donna Crews, Director, Government Affairs.*
General email, aidsaction@aidsaction.org
Web, www.aidsunited.org

Channels resources to community-based organizations to fight HIV/AIDS at the local level. Provides grants and other support to nearly 400 organizations, principally for prevention efforts.

National Minority AIDS Council, *1931 13th St. N.W. 20009-4432; (202) 483-6622. Fax, (202) 483-1135. Paul A. Kawata, Executive Director.*
General email, info@nmac.org
Web, www.nmac.org

Works to build the capacity of small faith- and community-based organizations delivering HIV/AIDS services in communities of color. Holds national conferences; administers treatment and research programs and training; disseminates electronic and printed resource materials; conducts public policy advocacy.

Infectious Diseases, Allergies

▶ **AGENCIES**

National Institute of Allergy and Infectious Diseases *(National Institutes of Health),* *6610 Rockledge Dr., #2400, MSC 6612, Bethesda, MD 20892-6612; (301) 496-5717. Fax, (301) 402-3573. Dr. Anthony S. Fauci, Director. Toll-free, health and research information, (866) 284-4107. TTY, health and research information, (800) 877-8339. Press, (301) 402-1663.*
Web, www.niaid.nih.gov

Conducts research and supports research worldwide on the causes of infectious and immune-mediated diseases to develop better means of prevention, diagnosis, and treatment.

National Institute of Allergy and Infectious Diseases *(National Institutes of Health), Microbiology and Infectious Diseases,* *6610 Rockledge Dr., #4126, Bethesda, MD 20892-6603; (301) 496-1884. Carole A. Heilman, Director.*
Web, www.niaid.nih.gov/about/organization/dmid/pages/default.aspx

Supports extramural basic and clinical research to control and prevent diseases caused by virtually all human infectious agents except HIV by providing funding and resources for researchers.

▶ **NONGOVERNMENTAL**

Allergy and Asthma Network Mothers of Asthmatics, *8229 Boone Blvd., #260, Vienna, VA 22182-2661; (703) 641-9595. Fax, (703) 288-5271. Tonya Winders, President. Information, (800) 878-4403.*
Web, www.aanma.org

Membership: families dealing with asthma and allergies. Works to eliminate suffering and death due to asthma, allergies, and related conditions through education, advocacy, and community outreach.

Asthma and Allergy Foundation of America, *8201 Corporate Dr., #1000, Landover, MD 20785; (202) 466-7643. Fax, (202) 466-8940. Vacant, President. Information, (800) 727-8462.*
General email, info@aafa.org
Web, www.aafa.org

Provides information on asthma and allergies; awards research grants to asthma and allergic disease professionals; offers in-service training to allied health professionals, child care providers, and others.

Food Allergy Research and Education (FARE), *7925 Jones Branch Dr., #1100, McLean, VA 22102; (703) 691-3179. Fax, (703) 691-2713. John Lehr, Chief Executive Officer. Toll-free, (800) 929-4040.*
General email, faan@foodallergy.org
Web, www.foodallergy.org

Membership: dieticians, nurses, physicians, school staff, government representatives, members of the food and pharmaceutical industries, and food-allergy patients and their families. Provides information and educational resources on food allergies and allergic reactions. Offers research grants.

National Center for Biodefense and Infectious Diseases *(George Mason University), 10650 Pyramid Pl., Manassas, VA 20110; (703) 993-4271. Fax, (703) 993-4280. Charles Bailey, Executive Director.*
General email, cbailey@gmu.edu
Web, http://ncbid.gmu.edu and http://cos.gmu.edu

Researches and develops diagnostics and treatments for emerging infectious diseases as well as those pathogens that could be used as terrorist weapons that require special containment. Manages a graduate education program.

Kidney Disease

Centers for Medicare and Medicaid Services (CMS) *(Health and Human Services Dept.), Chronic Care Management, 7500 Security Blvd., C5-05-27, Baltimore, MD 21244; (410) 786-4533. Fax, (410) 786-0765. Janet P. Samen, Director, (410) 786-4533.*
Web, www.cms.gov/medicare/medicare.html

Administers coverage policy and payment for Medicare patients with end-stage renal disease and psychiatric inpatient and outpatient services for the severely mentally ill.

National Institute of Allergy and Infectious Diseases *(National Institutes of Health), Allergy, Immunology, and Transplantation, 6610 Rockledge Dr., #6124,*

Bethesda, MD 20892-6601; (301) 496-1886. Fax, (301) 402-0175. Dr. Daniel Rotrosen, Director.
Web, www.niaid.nih.gov/about/organization/dait

Supports extramural basic and clinical research to increase understanding of the causes and mechanisms that lead to the development of immunologic diseases and to expand knowledge that can be applied to developing improved techniques of diagnosis, treatment, and prevention. Interests include lupus; allergic diseases, such as asthma, hay fever, and contact dermatitis; and acute and chronic inflammatory disorders.

National Institute of Diabetes and Digestive and Kidney Diseases *(National Institutes of Health), Kidney, Urologic, and Hematologic Diseases, 6707 Democracy Blvd., #654, #MSC 5458, Bethesda, MD 20892; (301) 594-7717. Fax, (301) 480-3510. Dr. Robert Star, Director, (301) 496-6325. Press, (301) 496-3583.*
Web, www.niddk.nih.gov

Funds research on the prevention, diagnosis, and treatment of renal disorders. Conducts research and reviews grant proposals concerning maintenance therapy for persons with chronic kidney, urologic, and renal diseases.

National Institute of Diabetes and Digestive and Kidney Diseases *(National Institutes of Health), National Kidney and Urologic Diseases Information Clearinghouse, 3 Information Way, Bethesda, MD 20892-3580; (301) 654-4415. Fax, (703) 738-4929. Jody Nurik, Project Manager. Information, (800) 891-5390. Press, (301) 496-3583.*
General email, nkudic@info.niddk.nih.gov
Web, http://kidney.niddk.nih.gov

Supplies health care providers and the public with information on the symptoms, causes, treatments, and general nature of kidney and urologic diseases.

American Kidney Fund, *11921 Rockville Pike, #300, Rockville, MD 20852; (301) 881-3052. Fax, (240) 514-3510. LaVarne A. Burton, Chief Executive Officer. Information, (800) 638-8299. Helpline, (866) 300-2900.*
General email, helpline@kidneyfund.org
Web, www.kidneyfund.org

Provides direct financial support to dialysis and kidney transplant patients in need; supports health education and kidney disease prevention efforts.

National Kidney Foundation, *Government Relations, Washington Office, 5335 Wisconsin Ave. N.W., #300 20015-2078; (202) 244-7900. Fax, (202) 244-7405. Troy Zimmerman, Director. Information, (888) 543-6398.*
General email, info@kidneywdc.org
Web, www.kidney.org; www.kidneywdc.org

Supports funding for kidney dialysis and other forms of treatment for kidney disease; provides information on detection and screening of kidney diseases; supports organ transplantation programs. Monitors legislation, regulations, and international research. (Headquarters in New York.)

Lung Disease

▶AGENCIES

National Heart, Lung, and Blood Institute *(National Institutes of Health)*, *Health Information Center,* 31 Center Dr., Bldg. 31, Bethesda, MD 20892-2480 *(mailing address: P.O. Box 30105, Bethesda, MD 20824-0105); (301) 592-8573. Ann Taubenheim, Director.*
General email, nhlbIInfo@nhlbi.nih.gov
Web, www.nhlbi.nih.gov/health/infoctr

Acquires, maintains, and disseminates information on asthma and other lung ailments.

National Heart, Lung, and Blood Institute *(National Institutes of Health)*, *Lung Diseases,* 2 Rockledge Center, 6701 Rockledge Dr., #10042, MS 7952, Bethesda, MD 20892; (301) 435-0233. Fax, (301) 480-3547. James P. Kiley, Director.*
Web, www.nhlbi.nih.gov/about/dld

Plans, implements, and monitors research and training programs in lung diseases and sleep disorders, including research on causes, diagnosis, treatments, prevention, and health education. Interests include COPD, genetics, cystic fibrosis, asthma, bronchopulmonary dysplasia, immunology, respiratory neurobiology, sleep-disordered breathing, critical care and acute lung injury, developmental biology and pediatric pulmonary diseases, immunologic and fibrotic pulmonary disease, rare lung disorders, pulmonary vascular disease, and pulmonary complications of AIDS and tuberculosis.

▶NONGOVERNMENTAL

American Lung Assn., 1301 Pennsylvania Ave. N.W., #800 20004-1725; (202) 785-3355. Fax, (202) 452-1805. *Harold Wimmer, President; Paul Billings, Vice President of Advocacy and Education.*
Web, www.lung.org

Promotes improved lung health and the prevention of lung disease through research, education, and advocacy. Interests include antismoking campaigns; lung-related biomedical research; air pollution; and all lung diseases, including asthma, COPD, and lung cancer.

Cystic Fibrosis Foundation, 6931 Arlington Rd., #200, Bethesda, MD 20814; (301) 951-4422. Fax, (301) 951-6378. *Robert J. Beall, President. Information, (800) 344-4823.*
General email, info@cff.org
Web, www.cff.org

Conducts research on cystic fibrosis, a genetic disease affecting the respiratory and digestive systems. Focuses on medical research to identify a cure and to improve quality of life for those living with cystic fibrosis.

Minority Health

▶AGENCIES

Agency for Health Care Research and Quality *(Health and Human Services Dept.)*, *Office of Communication and Knowledge Transfer,* 540 Gaither Rd., Rockville, MD 20850; (301) 427-1364. Fax, (301) 427-1873. *Howard Holland, Director, (301) 427-1857. Public inquiries, (301) 427-1104.*
General email, info@ahrq.gov
Web, www.ahrq.gov/about/ockt/ocktmiss.htm

Researches health care quality among minorities. Identifies and devises solutions for disparities in access to care, diagnosis, and treatment of illness. Provides health care professionals with research on minority health.

Assistant Secretary for Health *(Health and Human Services Dept.)*, *Minority Health,* 1101 Wootton Pkwy., #600, Rockville, MD 20852; (240) 453-2882. Fax, (240) 453-2883. J. Nadine Gracia, Deputy Assistant Secretary, Acting. Information, (800) 444-6472.*
General email, info@minorityhealth.gov
Web, http://minorityhealth.hhs.gov

Oversees the implementation of the secretary's Task Force on Black and Minority Health and legislative mandates; develops programs to meet the health care needs of minorities; awards grants to coalitions of minority community organizations and to minority AIDS education and prevention projects.

Centers for Medicare and Medicaid Services (CMS) *(Health and Human Services Dept.)*, *Minority Health,* 7500 Security Blvd., Baltimore, MD 21244; (410) 786-6884. *Cara V. James, Director.*
Web, http://minorityhealth.hhs.gov/templates/content .aspx?1&lvlid=45&ID=9353

Seeks to reduce inequalities in health outcomes of racial and ethnic minority populations. Manages disparities data and evaluates impact; coordinates minority health initiatives within the agency; serves as the liaison to other agency offices of minority health.

Education Dept., *White House Initiative on Asian Americans and Pacific Islanders,* 550 12th St. S.W., 10th Floor 20202; (202) 453-7277. Fax, (202) 453-6238. *Kiran Ahuja, Executive Director. Press, (202) 453-6566.*
General email, http://whitehouseaapi@ed.gov
Web, www.whitehouse.gov/aapi and
Twitter, @whitehouseAAPI

Works to increase Asian American and Pacific Islander participation in federal health programs. Interests include reducing health risks, improving assess to high-quality health care, and promoting healthy living.

Health and Human Services Dept. (HHS), *Civil Rights,* 200 Independence Ave. S.W., #515F 20201; (202) 619-0403. Fax, (202) 619-3437. Leon Rodriguez, Director.*
General email, OCRMail@hhs.gov
Web, www.hhs.gov/ocr

Administers and enforces laws prohibiting discrimination on the basis of race, color, sex, national origin, religion, age, or disability in programs receiving federal funds from the department; authorized to discontinue funding. Responsible for health information privacy under the Health Insurance Portability and Accountability Act.

Health and Human Services Dept. (HHS), *Minority Health,* *1101 Wootton Pkwy., #600, Rockville, MD 20852; (240) 453-2882. Fax, (240) 453-2883. Dr. Nadine Gracia, Deputy Assistant Secretary. Information, (800) 444-6472.*
General email, info@omhrc.gov
Web, http://minorityhealth.hhs.gov

Promotes improved health among racial and ethnic minority populations. Advises the secretary and the Office of Public Health and Science on public health program activities affecting American Indian and Alaska Native, African American, Asian American and Pacific Islander, and Hispanic populations. Awards grants to minority AIDS education and prevention projects to administer health promotion, education, and disease prevention programs.

Health and Human Services Dept. (HHS), *Minority Health Resource Center,* *8400 Corporate Dr., #500, Landover, MD 20785 (mailing address: P.O. Box 37337, Washington, DC 20013-7337); (301) 251-1797. Fax, (301) 251-2160. Michelle Loosli, Director. Information, (800) 444-6472.*
General email, info@minorityhealth.hhs.gov
Web, www.minorityhealth.hhs.gov

Serves as a national resource and referral service on minority health issues. Distributes information on health topics such as substance abuse, cancer, heart disease, violence, diabetes, HIV/AIDS, and infant mortality. Provides free services, including customized database searches, publications, mailing lists, and referrals regarding American Indian and Alaska Native, African American, Asian American and Pacific Islander, and Hispanic populations.

Health Resources and Services Administration *(Health and Human Services Dept.),* **Health Equity,** *5600 Fishers Lane, #1270, Rockville, MD 20857; (301) 443-2964. Fax, (301) 443-7853. Michelle Allender-Smith, Director.*
General email, ask@hrsa.gov
Web, www.hrsa.gov

Sponsors programs and activities that address the special health needs of racial and ethnic minorities. Advises the administrator on minority health issues affecting the Health Resources and Services Administration (HRSA) and policy development; collects data on minority health activities within HRSA; represents HRSA programs affecting the health of racial and ethnic minorities to the health community and organizations in the public, private, and international sectors.

Indian Health Service *(Health and Human Services Dept.),* *801 Thompson Ave., #440, Rockville, MD 20852; (301) 443-1083. Fax, (301) 443-4794. Yvette Roubideaux, Director. Information, (301) 443-3593.*
Web, www.ihs.gov

Acts as the health advocate for and operates hospitals and health centers that provide preventive, curative, and community health care for Native Americans and Alaska Natives. Provides and improves sanitation and water supply systems in Native American and Alaska Native communities.

National Institutes of Health (NIH) *(Health and Human Services Dept.),* **National Institute on Minority Health and Health Disparities (NIMHD),** *2 Democracy Plaza, 6707 Democracy Blvd., #800, MSC-5465, Bethesda, MD 20892-5465; (301) 402-1366. Fax, (301) 480-4049. John Ruffin, Director.*
General email, nimhdinfor@nimhd.nih.gov
Web, www.ncmhd.nih.gov

Promotes minority health and leads, coordinates, supports, and assesses the NIH's effort to eliminate health disparities. Conducts and supports basic clinical, social, and behavioral research; promotes research infrastructure and training; fosters emerging programs; disseminates information; and reaches out to minority and other communities suffering from health disparities.

▶ NONGOVERNMENTAL

Asian and Pacific Islander American Health Forum, *Washington Office,* *1629 K St. N.W., #400 20036; (202) 466-7772. Fax, (202) 296-0610. Priscilla Huang, Policy Director.*
General email, healthinfo@apiahf.org
Web, www.apiahf.org

Works to improve the health status of and access to care by Asian Americans and Pacific Islanders and to address health disparities, including disability and mental health, HIV/AIDS, smoking, and cancer. Monitors legislation in the areas of health, politics, and social and economic issues that affect Asian Americans, native Hawaiians, and Pacific Islanders.

National Alliance for Hispanic Health, *1501 16th St. N.W. 20036-1401; (202) 387-5000. Fax, (202) 797-4353. Dr. Jane L. Delgado, Chief Executive Officer. Toll-free, (866) 783-2645. Toll-free in Spanish, (866) 783-2645.*
General email, alliance@hispanichealth.org
Web, www.hispanichealth.org

Advocates and conducts research to improve the health of Hispanics; promotes research and philanthropy; develops capacity of community-based health and social service organizations. Educates consumers on family and prenatal health, diabetes, depression, ADHD, immunization, HIV/AIDS, women's health, osteoporosis, tobacco control, and environmental health.

National Council of Urban Indian Health, *924 Pennsylvania Ave. S.E. 20003; (202) 544-0344. Fax, (202) 544-9394. Jay Stiener, Executive Director, Acting.*
General email, jstiener@ncuih.org
Web, www.ncuih.org

Membership: Indian health care providers. Supports accessible, high-quality health care programs for American

Indians and Alaska Natives living in urban communities. Provides education and training. Monitors legislation and funding.

National Hispanic Medical Assn., *1920 L St. N.W., #725 20036; (202) 628-5895. Fax, (202) 628-5898. Elena V. Rios, President.*
General email, nhma@nhmamd.org
Web, www.nhmamd.org

Provides policymakers and health care providers with information and support to strengthen the delivery of health care to Hispanic communities in the United States. Areas of interest include high-quality care and increased opportunities in medical education for Latinos. Works with federal officials, other Hispanic advocacy groups, and Congress to eliminate disparities in health care for minorities.

National Minority AIDS Council, *1931 13th St. N.W. 20009-4432; (202) 483-6622. Fax, (202) 483-1135. Paul A. Kawata, Executive Director.*
General email, info@nmac.org
Web, www.nmac.org

Works to build the capacity of small faith- and community-based organizations delivering HIV/AIDS services in communities of color. Holds national conferences; administers treatment and research programs and training; disseminates electronic and printed resource materials; conducts public policy advocacy.

Neurological and Muscular Disorders

▶AGENCIES

National Institute of Neurological Disorders and Stroke *(National Institutes of Health), 31 Center Dr., Bldg. 31, #8A52, P.O. Box 5801, Bethesda, MD 20824; (301) 496-5924. Fax, (301) 402-2186. Story Landis, Director. Information, (301) 496-5751. Toll-free, (800) 352-9424. Web, www.ninds.nih.gov*

Conducts research and disseminates information on the causes, prevention, diagnosis, and treatment of neurological disorders and stroke; supports basic and clinical research in related scientific areas. Provides research grants to public and private institutions and individuals. Operates a program of contracts for the funding of research and research-support efforts.

▶NONGOVERNMENTAL

Alzheimer's Assn., Public Policy, *1212 New York Ave., #800 20005-6105; (202) 393-7737. Fax, (866) 865-0270. Robert J. Egge, Senior Vice President. Toll-free, (800) 272-3900.*
General email, advocate@alz.org
Web, www.alz.org

Offers family support services and educates the public about Alzheimer's disease, a neurological disorder mainly affecting the brain tissue in older adults. Promotes research and long-term care protection; maintains liaison with Alzheimer's associations abroad. Monitors legislation and regulations. (Headquarters in Chicago, Ill.)

Brain Injury Assn. of America, *1608 Spring Hill Rd., #110, Vienna, VA 22182; (703) 761-0750. Fax, (703) 761-0755. Susan H. Connors, President. Information, (800) 444-6443.*
General email, info@biausa.org
Web, www.biausa.org

Works to improve the quality of life for persons with traumatic brain injuries and for their families. Promotes the prevention of head injuries through public awareness and education programs. Offers state-level support services for individuals and their families. Monitors legislation and regulations.

Epilepsy Foundation, *8301 Professional Pl. East, #200, Landover, MD 20785-7223; (301) 459-3700. Fax, (301) 577-2684. Phillip Gattone, Chief Executive Officer. Information, (800) 332-1000. Library, (800) 332-4050. Spanish language, (866) 748-8008.*
General email, contactus@efa.org
Web, www.epilepsyfoundation.org

Promotes research and treatment of epilepsy; makes research grants; disseminates information and educational materials. Affiliates provide direct services for people with epilepsy and make referrals when necessary. Library open to the public by appointment.

Foundation for the Advancement of Chiropractic Tenets and Science, *6400 Arlington Blvd., #800, Falls Church, VA 22042; (703) 528-5000. Fax, (703) 528-5023. Michael McLean, President. Toll-free, (800) 423-4690.*
General email, chiro@chiropractic.org
Web, www.chiropractic.org

Offers financial aid for education and research programs in colleges and independent institutions; studies chiropractic services in the United States; provides international relief and development programs. (Affiliate of the International Chiropractors Assn.)

National Multiple Sclerosis Society, *Washington Chapter, 1800 M St. N.W., #750 South 20036; (202) 296-5363. Fax, (202) 296-3425. Christopher Broullire, Chapter President. Toll-free, (800) 344-4867.*
General email, information@msandyou.org
Web, www.msandyou.org

Seeks to advance medical knowledge of multiple sclerosis, a disease of the central nervous system; disseminates information worldwide. Patient services include individual and family counseling, exercise programs, equipment loans, medical and social service referrals, transportation assistance, back-to-work training programs, and in-service training seminars for nurses, homemakers, and physical and occupational therapists. (Headquarters in New York.)

Society for Neuroscience, *1121 14th St. N.W., #1010 20005; (202) 962-4000. Fax, (202) 962-4941. Marty Saggese, Executive Director. General email, info@sfn.org*

Web, www.sfn.org

Membership: scientists and physicians worldwide who research the brain, spinal cord, and nervous system. Interests include the molecular and cellular levels of the nervous system; systems within the brain, such as vision and hearing; and behavior produced by the brain. Promotes education in the neurosciences and the application of research to treat nervous system disorders.

Spina Bifida Assn., *1600 Wilson Blvd., #800, Arlington, VA 22209 (mailing address: P.O. Box 17427, Arlington, VA 22216); (202) 944-3285. Fax, (202) 944-3295. Sara Struwe, Chief Executive Officer, Interim. Information, (800) 621-3141. General email, sbaa@sbaa.org*

Web, www.spinabifidaassociation.org

Membership: individuals with spina bifida, their supporters, and concerned professionals. Offers educational programs, scholarships, and support services; acts as a clearinghouse; provides referrals and information about treatment and prevention. Serves as U.S. member of the International Federation for Hydrocephalus and Spina Bifida, which is headquartered in Geneva. Monitors legislation and regulations.

United Cerebral Palsy Assns., *1825 K St. N.W., #600 20006; (202) 776-0406. Fax, (202) 776-0414. Stephen Bennett, President. Information, (800) 872-5827. General email, info@ucp.org*

Web, www.ucp.org

National network of state and local affiliates that assists individuals with cerebral palsy and other developmental disabilities and their families. Provides parent education, early intervention, employment services, family support and respite programs, therapy, assistive technology, and vocational training. Promotes research on cerebral palsy; supports the use of assistive technology and community-based living arrangements for persons with cerebral palsy and other developmental disabilities.

Skin Disorders

▶**AGENCIES**

National Institute of Arthritis and Musculoskeletal and Skin Diseases *(National Institutes of Health), 31 Center Dr., Bldg. 31, #4C32, MSC-2350, Bethesda, MD 20892-2350; (301) 496-4353. Fax, (301) 402-3607. Dr. Stephen I. Katz, Director. Information, (301) 496-8190. Health information, (877) 225-4267. General email, niamsinfo@mail.nih.gov*

Web, www.niams.nih.gov

Supports research on the causes and treatment of skin diseases, including psoriasis, eczema, and acne.

▶**NONGOVERNMENTAL**

American Academy of Facial Plastic and Reconstructive Surgery, *310 S. Henry St., Alexandria, VA 22314; (703) 299-9291. Fax, (703) 299-8898. Dr. Edward H. Farrior, President. General email, info@aafprs.org*

Web, www.aafprs.org

Membership: facial plastic and reconstructive surgeons and other board-certified surgeons whose focus is surgery of the face, head, and neck. Promotes research and study in the field. Helps train residents in facial plastic and reconstructive surgery; offers continuing medical education. Sponsors scientific and medical meetings, international symposia, fellowship training program, seminars, and workshops. Provides videotapes on facial plastic and reconstructive surgery.

Substance Abuse

▶**AGENCIES**

Education Dept., *Safe and Healthy Students, 400 Maryland Ave. S.W., LBJ Bldg. 20202-6135; (202) 453-6722. Fax, (202) 205-4921. David Esquith, Director. General email, osdfs.safeschl@ed.gov*

Web, www2.ed.gov/about/offices/list/oese/oshs

Develops policy for the department's drug and violence prevention initiatives for students in elementary and secondary schools and institutions of higher education. Provides financial assistance for drug and violence prevention activities. Coordinates education efforts in drug and violence prevention with those of other federal departments and agencies.

Health Resources and Services Administration *(Health and Human Services Dept.), Policy Program and Development, 5600 Fishers Lane, #17C-26, Rockville, MD 20857; (301) 594-4300. Fax, (301) 594-4997. Jennifer Jones, Director.*

Web, www.bphc.hrsa.gov

Provides grants to health centers to expand services to include behavioral health and substance abuse services.

National Institute on Drug Abuse *(National Institutes of Health), 6001 Executive Blvd., #5274, MSC-9581, Bethesda, MD 20892-9581; (301) 443-1124. Fax, (301) 443-9127. Dr. Nora Volkow, Director. Press, (301) 443-6245.*

Web, www.nida.nih.gov

Conducts and sponsors research on the prevention, effects, and treatment of drug abuse. Monitors international policy and research.

Office of National Drug Control Policy (ONDCP) *(Executive Office of the President), 750 17th St. N.W. 20503; (202) 395-6700. Fax, (202) 395-6680. R. Gil Kerlikowske, Director. Drug Policy Information Clearinghouse, (800) 666-3332.*

Web, www.whitehouse.gov/ondcp

Establishes policies and oversees the implementation of a national drug control strategy with the goal of reducing illicit drug use, manufacturing, trafficking, and drug-related crimes, violence, and health consequences. Coordinates the international and domestic anti-drug efforts of executive branch agencies and ensures that such efforts sustain and complement state and local anti-drug activities. Advises the president and the National Security Council on drug control policy. (Clearinghouse address: P.O. Box 6000, Rockville, MD 20849-6000.)

Substance Abuse and Mental Health Services Administration *(Health and Human Services Dept.),* *1 Choke Cherry Rd., #8-1065, Rockville, MD 20857; (240) 276-2000. Fax, (240) 276-2010. Pamela S. Hyde, Administrator. Information, (800) 789-2647. General email, samhsainfo@samhsa.hhs.gov*

Web, www.samhsa.gov

Provides and manages block grants and special programmatic funding aimed at reducing the impact of substance abuse and mental illness on communities. Provides states, providers, communities, and the public with information about behavioral health issues and prevention/treatment approaches. Administers substance abuse and mental health treatment referral service: (800) 662-4357 or www.samhsa.gov/treatment. Offers behavioral health publications and other resources: http://store.samhsa.gov/home or P.O. Box 2345, Rockville, MD 20847.

Substance Abuse and Mental Health Services Administration *(Health and Human Services Dept.),* *Center for Substance Abuse Prevention, 1 Choke Cherry Rd., #4-1057, Rockville, MD 20857; (240) 276-2420. Fax, (240) 276-2430. Frances M. Harding, Director. Workplace Helpline, (800) WORKPLACE; (800) 967-5752. Information, (877) 726-4727. Web, www.samhsa.gov/about/csap.aspx*

Demonstrates, evaluates, and disseminates strategies to prevent alcohol and drug abuse. Operates the National Clearinghouse for Alcohol and Drug Information, which provides information, publications, and grant applications for programs to prevent substance abuse. (Clearinghouse address: http://ncadi.samhsa.gov or P.O. Box 2345, Rockville, MD 20847; toll-free phone, (877) 726-4727.)

Substance Abuse and Mental Health Services Administration *(Health and Human Services Dept.),* *Center for Substance Abuse Treatment, 1 Choke Cherry Rd., #5-1015, Rockville, MD 20857; (240) 276-1660. Fax, (240) 276-1670. Dr. H. Westley Clark, Director. Treatment referral, (800) 662-4357. Publications, (800) 729-6686. Information, (877) 726-4727. Web, www.samhsa.gov/about/csat.aspx*

Develops and supports policies and programs that improve and expand treatment services for alcoholism, substance abuse, and addiction. Administers grants that support private and public addiction prevention and treatment services. Evaluates alcohol treatment programs and other drug treatment programs and delivery systems.

▶ **INTERNATIONAL ORGANIZATIONS**

International Commission for the Prevention of Alcoholism and Drug Dependency, *12501 Old Columbia Pike, Silver Spring, MD 20904; (301) 680-6719. Fax, (301) 680-6707. Dr. Peter N. Landless, Executive Director; Katia Reinart, Director, North American Region, (301) 680-6833. General email, the_icpa@hotmail.com*

Web, http://icpaworld.org

Membership: health officials, physicians, educators, clergy, and judges worldwide. Promotes scientific research on prevention of alcohol and drug dependencies; provides information about medical effects of alcohol and drugs; conducts world congresses. (Health Ministries Dept. of the General Conference of Seventh-Day Adventists.)

▶ **NONGOVERNMENTAL**

American Legacy Foundation, *1724 Massachusetts Ave. N.W. 20036; (202) 454-5555. Fax, (202) 454-5599. Robin Koval, President. General email, info@legacyforhealth.org*

Web, www.legacyforhealth.org

Develops programs to disseminate information on the health effects of tobacco. Provides prevention and cessation services through grants, technical training and assistance, youth activism, partnerships, and community outreach.

American Society of Addiction Medicine, *4601 N. Park Ave., Upper Arcade, #101, Chevy Chase, MD 20815-4520; (301) 656-3920. Fax, (301) 656-3815. Penny Mills, Executive Vice President. General email, email@asam.org*

Web, www.asam.org

Membership: physicians and medical students. Supports the study and provision of effective treatment and care for people with alcohol and drug dependencies; educates physicians. Monitors legislation and regulations.

Assn. for Addiction Professionals (NAADAC), *1001 N. Fairfax St., #201, Alexandria, VA 22314; (703) 741-7686. Fax, (703) 741-7698. Cynthia Moreno Tuohy, Executive Director. Information, (800) 548-0497. General email, naadac2@naadac.org*

Web, www.naadac.org

Membership: professionals in the addiction field. Supports professional development by providing educational resources, certification programs, workshops, and conferences for treatment professionals. (Formerly National Assn. of Alcoholism and Drug Abuse Counselors.)

Employee Assistance Professionals Assn., *4350 N. Fairfax Dr., #740, Arlington, VA 22203; (703) 387-1000. Fax, (703) 522-4585. Steven Haught, President. General email, info@eapassn.org*

Web, www.eapassn.org

Membership: professionals in the workplace who assist employees and their family members with personal and behavioral problems, including health, marital, family,

Information Sources on Women's Health

AIDSinfo (NIH), (800) 448-0440, TTY, (888) 480-3739;
http://aidsinfo.nih.gov

American College of Nurse-Midwives, (240) 485-1800;
www.midwife.org

**American College Of Obstetricians and Gynecologists,
Public Information,** (202) 638-5577; www.acog.org

**American Society of Reproductive Medicine, Office of
Public Affairs,** (202) 863-4985; www.asrm.org

Assn. of Maternal and Child Health Programs,
(202) 775-0436; www.amchp.org

Assn. of Reproductive Health Professionals,
(202) 466-3825; www.arhp.org

**Assn. of Women's Health, Obstetric, and Neonatal
Nurses,** (202) 261-2400, Toll-free, (800) 673-8499;
www.awhonn.org

Breast Cancer Network of Strength, (414) 977-1780;
www.abcdbreastcancersupport.org

Guttmacher Institute, (202) 296-4012, Toll-free,
(877) 823-0262; www.guttmacher.org

Healthfinder (HHS), www.healthfinder.gov

**Health Resources and Services Administration
(HRSA), Maternal and Child Health (HHS),**
(888) 275-4772, Prenatal services, (800) 311-2229;
www.mchb.hrsa.gov

Lamaze International, (202) 367-1128, Toll-free,
(800) 368-4404; www.lamaze.org

Medem Network, (877) 599-5123;
www.medfusion.net/ihealth

Medline (NIH), www.nlm.nih.gov/medlineplus/
women.html

National Abortion Federation, (202) 667-5881;
Hotline, (800) 772-9100; www.prochoice.org

National Breast Cancer Coalition, (202) 296-7477,
Toll-free, (800) 622-2838; www.stopbreastcancer.org

National Cancer Institute (NIH), (800) 422-6237;
www.cancer.gov

**National Center for Education in Maternal and Child
Health (Georgetown Univ.),** (202) 784-9770;
www.ncemch.org

National Coalition for Women With Heart Disease,
(202) 728-7199; www.womenheart.org

**National Family Planning and Reproductive Health
Assn.,** (202) 293-3114; www.nationalfamilyplanning.org

National Institute of Aging (NIH), Information Center,
(800) 222-2225, TTY, (800) 222-4225;
www.nia.nih.gov

**National Institute of Allergy and Infectious Diseases
(NIH), AIDS,** (301) 496-5717, Toll-free hotline,
(866) 284-4107; www.niaid.nih.gov

**National Institute of Child Health and Human
Development (NIH), Program and Public Liaison,**
(800) 370-2943; www.nichd.nih.gov

National Osteoporosis Foundation, (202) 223-2226,
Toll-free, (800) 231-4222; www.nof.org

National Research Center for Women and Families,
(202) 223-4000; www.center4research.org

National Women's Health Information Center (HHS),
(800) 994-9662; www.womenshealth.gov;
www.girlshealth.gov

National Women's Health Network, (202) 682-2640;
www.nwhn.org

Office of Research on Women's Health (NIH),
(301) 402-1770; http://orwh.od.nih.gov

Planned Parenthood Federation of America,
(202) 973-4800; www.plannedparenthood.org

Society for Women's Health Research, (202) 223-8224;
www.womenshealthresearch.org

**United States National Library of Medicine (NIH),
Communications,** (301) 594-5983; www.nlm.nih.gov

**Women's Mental Health Consortium, National Institute
of Mental Health (NIH),** (866) 615-6464;
www.nimh.nih.gov; www.wmhcnyc.org

---

financial, alcohol, drug, legal, emotional, stress, or other personal problems that adversely affect employee job performance and productivity.

**National Assn. of State Alcohol and Drug Abuse
Directors (NASADAD),** *1025 Connecticut Ave. N.W., #605
20036-5430; (202) 293-0090. Fax, (202) 293-1250.
Rob Morrison, Executive Director, ext. 106.
General email, dcoffice@nasadad.org*

Web, www.nasadad.org

Provides information on drug abuse treatment and prevention; contracts with federal and state agencies for design of programs to fight and prevent drug abuse.

Treatment Communities of America (TCA), *1776 Eye St.
N.W., 9th Floor, #937 20006; (202) 296-3503. Fax, (202)
518-5475. Patricia Beauchemin, Executive Director.*

General email, tca.office@verizon.net

Web, www.treatmentcommunitiesofamerica.org

Membership: nonprofit organizations that provide substance abuse and mental health treatment and rehabilitation. Provides policy analysis and educates the public on substance abuse and treatment issues. Promotes the interests of therapeutic communities, their clients, and staffs. Monitors legislation and regulations.

Women's Health

▶**AGENCIES**

Assistant Secretary for Health *(Health and Human
Services Dept.), Women's Health, 200 Independence Ave.
S.W., #712E 20201; (202) 690-7650. Fax, (202) 401-4005.*

Marsha B. Henderson, Deputy Assistant Secretary.
Information, (800) 994-9662.
Web, www.womenshealth.gov/owh or
www.womenshealth.gov and www.girlshealth.gov

Promotes better health for girls and women as well as health equity through sex/gender-specific approaches. Methods include educating health professionals and motivating behavior change in consumers through the dissemination of health information.

Eunice Kennedy Shriver National Institute of Child Health and Human Development (National Institutes of Health), Division of Extramural Research (DER), Gynecologic Health and Disease Branch (GHDB),

Dr. Trent Mackay, Medical Officer.
Web, www.nichd.nih.gov/about/org/der/branches/ghdb/Pages/overview.aspx

Supports and promotes basic science, translational, and clinical research, and research training programs related to gynecologic health in women and adolescent girls. Promotes research in gynecological health through grants, cooperative agreements, and contracts. Emphasizes studies of the menstrual cycle, uterine fibroids, endometriosis, polycystic ovary syndrome, pelvic floor disorders, and menopause transition/perimenopause, as well as studies of the mechanisms underlying chronic pelvic pain, vulvodynia, and dysmenorrhea. Supports research training and career development programs of investigators interested in women's reproductive health.

Food and Drug Administration (FDA) (Health and Human Services Dept.), Women's Health, 10903 New Hampshire Ave., W032-2333, Silver Spring, MD 20993; (301) 796-9440. Fax, (301) 847-8604.

Marsha B. Henderson, Assistant Commissioner, (202) 796-9439.
General email, marsha.henderson@fda.hhs.gov
Web, www.fda.gov/AboutFDA/CentersOffices/OC/OfficeofWomensHealth

Supports scientific research on women's health and collaborates with other government agencies and national organizations to sponsor scientific and consumer outreach on women's health issues. Interests include breast cancer, cardiovascular disease, diabetes, pregnancy, menopause, and the safe use of medications.

National Heart, Lung, and Blood Institute (National Institutes of Health), Cardiovascular Sciences, Women's Health Initiative, 2 Rockledge Center, 6701 Rockledge Dr., #9192, MS 7913, Bethesda, MD 20892-7935; (301) 435-6669. Fax, (301) 480-5158. Dr. Jacques Rossouw, Chief.

Information, (301) 592-8573. Press, (301) 496-4236.
General email, nm9o@nih.gov
Web, www.nhlbi.nih.gov/whi

Supports clinical trials and observational studies to improve understanding of the causes and prevention of major diseases affecting the health of women. Interests include cardiovascular disease, cancer, fractures, and hormone therapy.

National Institutes of Health (NIH) (Health and Human Services Dept.), Office of Research on Women's Health, 6707 Democracy Blvd., #400, MSC-5484, Bethesda, MD 20892-5484; (301) 402-1770. Fax, (301) 402-1798.

Janine Austin Clayton, Director.
Web, http://orwh.od.nih.gov

Collaborates with NIH institutes and centers to establish NIH goals and policies for research related to women's health and sex- or gender-based studies of the differences between women and men. Supports expansion of research on diseases, conditions, and disorders that affect women; monitors inclusion of women and minorities in clinical research; develops opportunities and support for recruitment and advancement of women in biomedical careers.

▶ NONGOVERNMENTAL

Black Women's Health Imperative, 1726 M St. N.W., #300 20036; (202) 548-4000. Fax, (202) 543-9743.

Linda Blount, President.
General email, imperative@blackwomenshealth.org
Web, www.blackwomenshealth.org

Provides the tools and information for African American women to prevent health problems, to recognize symptoms and early warning signs, and to understand all of the options available for their specific health situations. Achieves these ends through community outreach, advocacy, resources and research, and education. (Formerly the National Black Women's Health Project.)

Eating Disorders Coalition for Research, Policy, and Action, 720 7th St. N.W., #300 20001; (202) 543-9570. Fax, (646) 417-6378. David Jaffe, Executive Director.

General email, manager@eatingdisorderscoalition.org
Web, www.eatingdisorderscoalition.org

Seeks greater national and federal recognition of eating disorders. Promotes recognition of eating disorders as a public health priority and the implementation of more accessible treatment and more effective prevention programs. Monitors legislation and regulations.

Institute for Women's Policy Research (IWPR), 1200 18th St. N.W., #301 20036; (202) 785-5100. Fax, (202) 833-4362.

Heidi Hartmann, President.
General email, iwpr@iwpr.org
Web, www.iwpr.org

Public policy research organization that focuses on women's issues, including health care and comprehensive family and medical leave programs.

National Research Center for Women and Families, 1001 Connecticut Ave. N.W., #1100 20036; (202) 223-4000. Fax, (202) 223-4242. Diana Zuckerman, President;

Paul Brown, Government Relations.
General email, info@center4research.org
Web, www.center4research.org

Utilizes scientific and medical research to improve the quality of women's lives and the lives of family members. Seeks to educate policymakers about medical and scientific research through hearings, meetings, and publications.

National Women's Health Network, *1413 K St. N.W., 4th Floor 20005; (202) 682-2640. Fax, (202) 682-2648. Cynthia Pearson, Executive Director. Health information requests, (202) 682-2646.*
General email, nwhn@nwhn.org
Web, www.nwhn.org

Acts as an information clearinghouse on women's health issues; monitors federal health policies and legislation. Interests include older women's health issues, sexual and reproductive health, contraception, menopause, abortion, unsafe drugs, AIDS, breast cancer, and universal health.

Society for Women's Health Research, *1025 Connecticut Ave. N.W., #601 20036; (202) 223-8224. Fax, (202) 833-3472. Phyllis Greenberger, President.*
General email, info@swhr.org
Web, www.womenshealthresearch.org

Promotes public and private funding for women's health research and changes in public policies affecting women's health. Seeks to advance women as leaders in the health professions and to inform policymakers, educators, and the public of research outcomes. Sponsors meetings; produces reports; conducts educational campaigns.

WomenHeart: National Coalition for Women With Heart Disease, *818 18th St. N.W., #1000 20006; (202) 728-7199. Fax, (202) 728-7238. Lisa M. Tate, Chief Executive Officer.*
General email, mail@womenheart.org
Web, www.womenheart.org

Patient-centered organization that seeks to advance women's heart health through advocacy, community education, and patient support. Comprised of patients and their families, health care providers, advocates, and interested consumers.

MENTAL HEALTH

General

▶ **AGENCIES**

National Institute of Mental Health *(National Institutes of Health), 6001 Executive Blvd., #6200, MSC 9663, Bethesda, MD 20892-9663; (301) 443-4513. Fax, (301) 443-4279. Dr. Thomas R. Insel, Director. Toll-free, (866) 615-6464. Toll-free TTY, (866) 415-8051.*
General email, nimhinfo@nih.gov
Web, www.nimh.nih.gov

Conducts research on the cause, diagnosis, treatment, and prevention of mental disorders; provides information on mental health problems and programs. Participates in international research.

National Institute of Mental Health *(National Institutes of Health), Developmental Translational Research, 6001*

Executive Blvd., #7177, MSC 9617, Bethesda, MD 20892; (301) 443-5944. Fax, (301) 480-4415. Kathleen Anderson, Director.
Web, www.nimh.nih.gov/about/organization/ddtr/index .shtml

Promotes research programs and training aimed at the prevention and cure of mental disorders that originate in childhood and adolescence and the promotion of mental health. Interests include mood disorders, schizophrenia, conduct disorder, OCD, autism, ADHD, eating disorders, anxiety, and Tourette syndrome.

National Institute of Mental Health *(National Institutes of Health), Neuroscience and Basic Behavioral Science, 6001 Executive Blvd., #7204, MSC 9645, Rockville, MD 20892; (301) 443-3563. Fax, (301) 443-1731. Linda S. Brady, Director.*
Web, www.nimh.nih.gov/about/organization/dnbbs/index .shtml

Supports research programs in the areas of basic neuroscience, genetics, basic behavioral science, research training, resource development, drug discovery, and research dissemination. Responsible for ensuring that relevant basic science knowledge is generated to create improved diagnosis, treatment, and prevention of mental and behavioral disorders.

National Institute of Mental Health *(National Institutes of Health), Research on Disparities and Global Mental Health (ORDGMH), 6001 Executive Blvd., #6127, MSC 9659, Bethesda, MD 20892; (301) 443-2847. Fax, (301) 443-8552. Pamela Y. Collins, Director.*
Web, www.nimh.nih.gov/about/organization/od/office-for-research-on-disparities-and-global-mental-health-ordgmh .shtml

Funds and oversees research to identify trends and gaps in the areas of mental health disparities, women's mental health, and global mental health. Supports research training for minorities in the mental health field; supports development of the mental health research workforce in low- and middle-income countries.

National Institutes of Health (NIH) *(Health and Human Services Dept.), Behavioral and Social Sciences Research, 31 Center Dr., Bldg. 31, #B1C19, Bethesda, MD 20892-0183; (301) 402-1146. Fax, (301) 402-1150. Robert M. Kaplan, Director.*
Web, http://obssr.od.nih.gov

Works to advance behavioral and social sciences training, to integrate a biobehavioral perspective across the NIH, and to improve communication among scientists and with the public. Develops funding initiatives for research and training. Sets priorities for research. Provides training and career development opportunities for behavioral and social scientists. Links minority students with mentors. Organizes cultural workshops and lectures.

Substance Abuse and Mental Health Services Administration *(Health and Human Services Dept.), 1 Choke Cherry Rd., #8-1065, Rockville, MD 20857; (240)*

276-2000. Fax, (240) 276-2010. Pamela S. Hyde, Administrator. Information, (800) 789-2647.
General email, samhsainfo@samhsa.hhs.gov
Web, www.samhsa.gov

Provides and manages block grants and special programmatic funding aimed at reducing the impact of substance abuse and mental illness on communities. Provides states, providers, communities, and the public with information about behavioral health issues and prevention/treatment approaches. Administers substance abuse and mental health treatment referral service: (800) 662-4357 or www.samhsa.gov/treatment. Offers behavioral health publications and other resources: http://store.samhsa.gov/home or P.O. Box 2345, Rockville, MD 20847.

Substance Abuse and Mental Health Services Administration *(Health and Human Services Dept.), Center for Mental Health Services, 1 Choke Cherry Rd., #6-1057, Rockville, MD 20857; (240) 276-1310. Fax, (240) 276-1320. Paolo del Vecchio, Director. Information, (877) 726-4727. Treatment referral, (800) 662-4357.*
Web, www.samhsa.gov/about/cmhs.aspx

Works with federal agencies, tribal entities and territories, and state and local governments to demonstrate, evaluate, and disseminate service delivery models to treat mental illness, promote mental health, and prevent the developing or worsening of mental illness. Operates the National Mental Health Information Center.

►CONGRESS

For a listing of relevant congressional committees and subcommittees, please see pages 318–319 or the Appendix.

►NONGOVERNMENTAL

American Academy of Child and Adolescent Psychiatry, *3615 Wisconsin Ave. N.W. 20016-3007; (202) 966-7300. Fax, (202) 966-2891. Dr. Paramjit T. Joshi, President.*
Web, www.aacap.org

Membership: child and adolescent psychiatrists trained to promote healthy development and to evaluate, diagnose, and treat children, adolescents, and families affected by mental illness. Sponsors annual meeting and review for medical board examinations. Provides information on child and adolescent development and mental illnesses. Monitors international research and U.S. legislation concerning children with mental illness.

American Assn. of Pastoral Counselors, *9504A Lee Hwy., Fairfax, VA 22031-2303; (703) 385-6967. Fax, (703) 352-7725. Douglas M. Ronsheim, Executive Director.*
General email, info@aapc.org
Web, www.aapc.org

Membership: mental health professionals with training in both religion and the behavioral sciences. Nonsectarian organization that accredits pastoral counseling centers, certifies pastoral counselors, and approves training programs.

American Assn. of Suicidology, *5221 Wisconsin Ave. N.W. 20015; (202) 237-2280. Fax, (202) 237-2282. Alan Berman, Executive Director.*
General email, info@suicidology.org
Web, www.suicidology.org

Membership: educators, researchers, suicide prevention centers, school districts, volunteers, and survivors affected by suicide. Works to understand and prevent suicide; provides suicide prevention training, serves as an information clearinghouse.

American Bar Assn. (ABA), *Commission on Disability Rights, 1050 Connecticut Ave. N.W., #400 20036; (202) 662-1570. Fax, (202) 442-3439. Amy Allbright, Director.*
General email, cdr@americanbar.org
Web, www.americanbar.org/disability

Promotes the rule of law for persons with mental, physical, and sensory disabilities and their full and equal participation in the legal profession. Offers online resources, publications, and continuing education opportunities on disability law topics and engages in national initiatives to remove barriers to the education, employment, and advancement of lawyers with disabilities.

American Foundation for Suicide Prevention, *1010 Vermont Ave. N.W., #408 20005; (202) 449-3600. Fax, (202) 449-3601. John Madigan, Senior Director of Public Policy. National Suicide Prevention Lifeline, (800) 273-8255.*
General email, jmadigan@afsp.org
Web, www.afsp.org

Seeks to understand and prevent suicide through research, education, and advocacy. Provides programs and resources for survivors of suicide loss and people at risk, funds scientific research, offers educational programs for professionals, educates the public about mood disorders and suicide prevention, and promotes policies that impact suicide and prevention. Monitors legislation and regulations. (Headquarters in New York, NY.)

American Mental Health Counselors Assn., *801 N. Fairfax St., #304, Alexandria, VA 22314; (703) 548-6002. Fax, (703) 548-4775. Joel Miller, Executive Director. Toll-free, (800) 326-2642.*
Web, www.amhca.org

Membership: professional counselors and graduate students in the mental health field. Sponsors leadership training and continuing education programs for professionals in the field of mental health counseling; holds annual conference. Monitors legislation and regulations.

American Psychiatric Assn., *1000 Wilson Blvd., #1825, Arlington, VA 22209-3901; (703) 907-7300. Fax, (703) 907-1085. Dr. Saul Levin, Medical Director. Press, (703) 907-8640. Publishing, (703) 907-7322.*
General email, apa@psych.org
Web, www.psychiatry.org

Membership: psychiatrists. Promotes availability of high-quality psychiatric care; provides the public with information; assists state and local agencies; conducts educational programs for professionals and students in the field; participates in international meetings and research. Library open to members.

American Psychological Assn., *750 1st St. N.E. 20002-4242; (202) 336-5500. Fax, (202) 336-5502. Norman B. Anderson, Chief Executive Officer. Library, (202) 336-5640. Toll-free, (800) 374-2721.*
Web, www.apa.org

Membership: professional psychologists, educators, and behavioral research scientists. Supports research, training, and professional services; works toward improving the qualifications, competence, and training programs of psychologists. Monitors international research and U.S. legislation on mental health.

American Psychosomatic Society, *6728 Old McLean Village Dr., McLean, VA 22101-3906; (703) 556-9222. Fax, (703) 556-8729. George K. Degnon, Executive Director.*
General email, info@psychosomatic.org
Web, www.psychosomatic.org

Advances and disseminates scientific understanding of relationships among biological, psychological, social, and behavioral factors in health and disease through publications, annual meetings, conferences, and interest groups.

Anxiety and Depression Assn. of America, *8701 Georgia Ave., #412, Silver Spring, MD 20910; (240) 485-1001. Fax, (240) 485-1035. Alies Muskin, Executive Director. Press, (240) 485-1016.*
Web, www.adaa.org

Membership: clinicians and researchers who treat and study anxiety and depression disorders; individuals with these disorders and their families; and other interested individuals. Promotes prevention, treatment, and cure of anxiety and depression disorders by disseminating information, linking individuals to treatment, and encouraging research and advancement of scientific knowledge.

Assn. of Black Psychologists, *7119 Allentown Rd., #203Ft. Washington, MD 20744; (301) 449-3082. Fax, (301) 449-3084. Anisha N. Lewis, Executive Director.*
General email, abpsi@abpsi.org
Web, www.abpsi.org

Membership: psychologists, psychology students, and others in the mental health field. Develops policies and resources to foster mental health in the African American community; holds annual convention.

Bazelon Center for Mental Health Law, *1101 15th St. N.W., #1212 20005; (202) 467-5730. Fax, (202) 223-0409. Robert Bernstein, President.*
General email, communications@bazelon.org
Web, www.bazelon.org

Public interest law firm. Works to establish and advance the legal rights of children and adults with mental disabilities and ensure their equal access to services and resources needed for full participation in community life. Provides technical support to lawyers and other advocates. Conducts test case litigation to defend rights of persons with mental disabilities. Conducts policy analysis, builds coalitions, issues advocacy alerts, publishes handbooks, and maintains advocacy resources online. Monitors legislation and regulations.

Mental Health America, *2000 N. Beauregard St., 6th Floor, Alexandria, VA 22311; (703) 684-7722. Fax, (703) 684-5968. David L. Shern, President, Acting. Information, (800) 969-6642.*
General email, infoctr@nmha.org
Web, www.mentalhealthamerica.net

Works to increase accessible and appropriate care for adults and children with mental disorders. Informs and educates public about mental illnesses and available treatment. Supports research on illnesses and services.

National Alliance on Mental Illness (NAMI), *3803 N. Fairfax Dr., #100, Arlington, VA 22203; (703) 524-7600. Fax, (703) 524-9094. Mary Giliberti, Executive Director. Toll-free, (800) 950-6264.*
General email, info@nami.org
Web, www.nami.org

Membership: mentally ill individuals and their families and caregivers. Works to eradicate mental illness and improve the lives of those affected by brain disorders; sponsors public education and advocacy. Monitors legislation and regulations.

National Assn. of Psychiatric Health Systems, *900 17th St. N.W., #420 20006-2507; (202) 393-6700. Fax, (202) 783-6041. Mark Covall, President.*
General email, naphs@naphs.org
Web, www.naphs.org

Membership: behavioral health care systems that provide in-patient, residential, and out-patient treatment and prevention and care programs for children, adolescents, adults, and older adults with mental and substance use disorders.

National Assn. of School Psychologists, *4340 East-West Hwy., Bethesda, MD 20814; (301) 657-0270. Fax, (301) 657-0275. Susan Gorin, Executive Director, (301) 347-1640. Toll-free, (866) 331-6277.*
General email, kcowan@naspweb.org
Web, www.nasponline.org

Membership: school psychologists, supervisors of school psychological services, and others who provide mental health services for children in school settings. Provides professional education and development to members. Provides school safety and crisis response direct services. Fosters information exchange; advises local, state, and federal policymakers and agencies that develop children's mental health educational services. Develops professional ethics and standards.

National Assn. of State Mental Health Program Directors, *66 Canal Center Plaza, #302, Alexandria, VA 22314-1591; (703) 739-9333. Fax, (703) 548-9517. Robert W. Glover, Executive Director.*
Web, www.nasmhpd.org

Membership: officials in charge of state mental health agencies. Compiles data on state mental health programs. Fosters collaboration among members; provides technical assistance and consultation. Maintains research institute. Operates under a cooperative agreement with the National Governors Association. (Affiliated with NASMHPD Research Institute, Inc., Falls Church, Va.

National Council for Behavioral Healthcare, *1701 K St. N.W., #400 20006; (202) 684-7457. Fax, (202) 386-9391. Linda Rosenberg, President.*
General email, communications@thenationalcouncil.org
Web, www.TheNationalCouncil.org

Membership: community mental health agencies and state community mental health associations. Conducts research on community mental health activities; provides information, technical assistance, and referrals. Operates a job bank; publishes newsletters and a membership directory. Monitors legislation and regulations affecting community mental health facilities. (Formerly National Council for Community Behavioral Healthcare.)

Psychiatric Rehabilitation Assn., *1760 Old Meadow Rd., #500, McLean, VA 22102; (703) 442-2075. Fax, (703) 506-3266. Tom Gibson, Chief Executive Officer, Interim.*
General email, info@uspra.org
Web, www.uspra.org

Membership: agencies, mental health practitioners, researchers, policymakers, family groups, and consumer organizations. Supports the community adjustment of persons with psychiatric disabilities. Promotes the role of rehabilitation in mental health systems; opposes discrimination based on mental disability. Certifies psychosocial rehabilitation practitioners.

The Treatment Advocacy Center, *200 N. Glebe Rd., #730, Arlington, VA 22203; (703) 294-6001. Fax, (703) 294-6010. Doris A. Fuller, Executive Director. Press, (703) 294-6003.*
General email, info@treatmentadvocacycenter.org
Web, www.treatmentadvocacycenter.org

Works to eliminate legal and other barriers to treatment of severe mental illness.

11 Housing and Development

GENERAL POLICY AND ANALYSIS

Basic Resources

▶AGENCIES

Economic Development Administration *(Commerce Dept.)*, 1401 Constitution Ave. N.W., #78006 20230; (202) 482-5081. Fax, (202) 273-4781. Mark Doms, Under Secretary.
Web, www.eda.gov

Advises the commerce secretary on domestic economic development. Administers development assistance programs that provide financial and technical aid to economically distressed areas to stimulate economic growth and create jobs. Awards public works and technical assistance grants to public institutions, nonprofit organizations, and Native American tribes; assists state and local governments with economic adjustment problems caused by long-term or sudden economic dislocation.

General Services Administration (GSA), *Catalog of Federal Domestic Assistance (CFDA)*, 2200 Crystal City Dr., Crystal Park 1, Arlington, VA 22202; (703) 605-3427. Priscilla Owens, Director, (703) 605-3408. Help desk, (866) 606-8220.
General email, priscilla.owens@gsa.gov
Web, www.cfda.gov

Disseminates information on federal domestic assistance programs through the CFDA Web site. Information includes all types of federal aid and explains types of assistance, eligibility requirements, application processes, and suggestions for writing proposals. Catalog may be downloaded from the CFDA Web site. Printed version may be ordered from the Superintendent of Documents, U.S. Government Printing Office, Washington, DC 20402; (202) 512-1800, or toll-free, (866) 512-1800; or online at http://bookstore.gpo.gov.

Housing and Urban Development Dept. (HUD), 451 7th St. S.W., #10000 20410; (202) 708-0417. Fax, (202) 619-8257. Shaun Donovan, Secretary; Maurice Jones, Deputy Secretary, (202) 708-0123. Information, (202) 708-1112. Congressional and Intergovernmental Relations, (202) 708-0005. Locator, (202) 401-0388.
Web, www.hud.gov

Responsible for federal programs concerned with housing needs, fair housing opportunities, and improving and developing the nation's urban and rural communities. Administers mortgage insurance, rent subsidy, preservation, rehabilitation, and antidiscrimination in housing programs. Advises the president on federal policy and makes legislative recommendations on housing and community development issues.

Housing and Urban Development Dept. (HUD), *HUD USER*, P.O. Box 23268 20026-3268; (800) 245-2691. Fax, (703) 742-7889. Jennie Bray, Project Manager, (703) 742-7881, ext. 211.

General email, helpdesk@huduser.org
Web, www.huduser.org

Research information service and clearinghouse for HUD research reports. Provides information on past and current HUD research; maintains HUD USER, an in-house database. Extensive collection of publications and documents available online.

Housing and Urban Development Dept. (HUD), *Policy Development and Research*, 451 7th St. S.W., #8100 20410-6000; (202) 708-1600. Fax, (202) 619-8000. Vacant, Assistant Secretary.
Web, www.huduser.org

Studies ways to improve the effectiveness and equity of HUD programs; analyzes housing and urban issues, including national housing goals, the operation of housing financial markets, the management of housing assistance programs, and statistics on federal and housing insurance programs; conducts the American Housing Survey; develops policy recommendations to improve federal housing programs. Works to increase the affordability of rehabilitated and newly constructed housing through technological and regulatory improvements.

Housing and Urban Development Dept. (HUD), *Program Evaluation*, 451 7th St. S.W., #8120 20410; (202) 402-6139. Carol S. Star, Director.
General email, carol.s.star@hud.gov
Web, www.hud.gov

Conducts research, program evaluations, and demonstrations for all HUD housing, community development, and fair housing and equal opportunity programs.

Office of Management and Budget (OMB) *(Executive Office of the President)*, *Housing*, New Executive Office Bldg., #9226 20503; (202) 395-4610. Fax, (202) 395-1307. Michelle Enger, Chief.
Web, www.whitehouse.gov/omb

Assists and advises the OMB director in budget preparation, reorganizations, and evaluations of Housing and Urban Development Dept. programs.

▶CONGRESS

For a listing of relevant congressional committees and subcommittees, please see page 382 or the Appendix.

▶NONGOVERNMENTAL

APPA—Leadership in Educational Facilities, 1643 Prince St., Alexandria, VA 22314-2818; (703) 684-1446. Fax, (703) 549-2772. E. Lander Medlin, Executive Vice President.
General email, info@appa.org
Web, www.appa.org

Membership: professionals involved in the administration, maintenance, planning, and development of buildings and facilities used by colleges and universities, K–12 private and public schools, museums, libraries, and other educational institutions. Interests include maintenance and upkeep of housing facilities. Provides information

HOUSING AND DEVELOPMENT RESOURCES IN CONGRESS

For a complete listing of Congress committees, including their full contact information, leadership, membership, and jurisdictions, please refer to the Appendix on pages 724–842.

HOUSE:

House Agriculture Committee, (202) 225-2171.
Web, agriculture.house.gov or
democrats.agriculture.house.gov
  Subcommittee on Conservation, Energy, and Forestry, (202) 225-2171.
  Subcommittee on Livestock, Rural Development, and Credit, (202) 225-2171.
House Appropriations Committee, (202) 225-2771.
Web, appropriations.house.gov or
democrats.appropriations.house.gov
  Subcommittee on Agriculture, Rural Development, FDA, and Related Agencies, (202) 225-2638.
  Subcommittee on Financial Services and General Government, (202) 225-7245.
  Subcommittee on Transportation, HUD, and Related Agencies, (202) 225-2141.
House Budget Committee, (202) 226-7270.
Web, budget.house.gov or democrats.budget.house.gov
House Financial Services Committee, (202) 225-7502.
Web, financialservices.house.gov or
democrats.financialservices.house.gov
  Subcommittee on Capital Markets, and Government Sponsored Enterprises, (202) 225-7502.
  Subcommittee on Monetary Policy and Trade, (202) 225-7502.
  Subcommittee on Financial Institutions and Consumer Credit, (202) 225-7502.
  Subcommittee on Housing and Insurance, (202) 225-7502.
  Subcommittee on Monetary Policy and Trade, (202) 225-7502.
  Subcommittee on Oversight and Investigations, (202) 225-7502.
House Small Business Committee, (202) 225-5821.
Web, smallbusiness.house.gov or
democrats.smallbusiness.house.gov
  Subcommittee on Agriculture, Energy, and Trade, (202) 225-5821.
House Transportation and Infrastructure Committee, (202) 225-9446.
Web, transportation.house.gov or
democrats.transportation.house.gov
  Subcommittee on Economic Development, Public Buildings, and Emergency Management, (202) 225-3014.
House Ways and Means Committee, (202) 225-3625.
Web, waysandmeans.house.gov or
democrats.waysandmeans.house.gov
  Subcommittee on Oversight, (202) 225-5522.

SENATE:

Senate Agriculture, Nutrition, and Forestry Committee, (202) 224-2035.
Web, ag.senate.gov
  Subcommittee on Jobs, Rural Economic Growth, and Energy Innovation, (202) 224-2035.
Senate Appropriations Committee, (202) 224-7363.
Web, appropriations.senate.gov
  Subcommittee on Agriculture, Rural Development, FDA, and Related Agencies, (202) 224-8090.
  Subcommittee on Financial Services and General Government, (202) 224-1133.
  Subcommittee on Transportation, HUD, and Related Agencies, (202) 224-7281.
Senate Banking, Housing, and Urban Affairs Committee, (202) 224-7391.
Web, banking.senate.gov
  Subcommittee on Economic Policy, (202) 224-3753.
  Subcommittee on Financial Institutions and Consumer Protection, (202) 224-2315.
  Subcommittee on Housing, Transportation and Community Development, (202) 224-4744.
  Subcommittee on Securities, Insurance, and Investment, (202) 224-4642.
Senate Budget Committee, (202) 224-0642.
Web, budget.senate.gov
Senate Environment and Public Works Committee, (202) 224-8832.
Web, epw.senate.gov
Senate Finance Committee, (202) 224-4515.
Web, finance.senate.gov
Senate Homeland Security and Governmental Affairs Committee, (202) 224-2627.
Web, hsgac.senate.gov
Senate Indian Affairs Committee, (202) 224-2251.
Web, indian.senate.gov
Senate Judiciary Committee, (202) 224-7703.
Web, judiciary.senate.gov
  Subcommittee on the Constitution, Civil Rights, and Human Rights, (202) 224-1158.
Senate Small Business and Entrepreneurship Committee, (202) 224-5175.
Web, sbc.senate.gov
Senate Special Committee on Aging, (202) 224-5364.
Web, aging.senate.gov

Housing and Urban Development Department

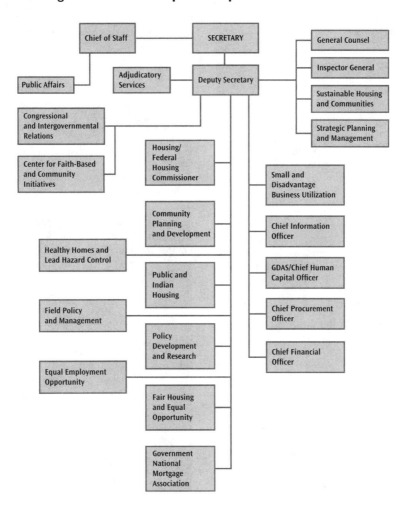

on campus energy management programs and campus accessibility for people with disabilities. (Formerly the Assn. of Higher Education Facilities Officers.)

Center for Economic and Policy Research (CEPR), *1611 Connecticut Ave. N.W., #400 20009; (202) 293-5380. Fax, (202) 588-1356. Dean Baker, Co-Director; Mark Weisbrot, Co-Director.*
General email, cepr@cepr.net
Web, www.cepr.net

Researches economic and social issues and the impact of related public policies. Presents findings to the public with the goal of better preparing citizens to choose among various policy options. Promotes democratic debate and voter education. Areas of interest include health care, trade, financial reform, Social Security, taxes, housing, and the labor market.

Center for Housing Policy, *1900 M St. N.W., #200 20036; (202) 466-2121. Fax, (202) 466-2122. Lisa Sturtevant, Executive Director.*

General email, nhc@nhc.org
Web, www.nhc.org

Researches and develops fundamentals of housing policy. Seeks to create new policies that integrate housing into overall social and economic goals. Sponsors educational forums and publishes reports (available online). (Research affiliate of the National Housing Conference.)

Housing and Development Law Institute, *630 Eye St. N.W. 20001-3736; (202) 289-3400. Fax, (202) 289-3401. Lisa L. Walker, Executive Director.*
General email, hdli@hdli.org
Web, www.hdli.org

Membership organization that assists agencies and developers in public and affordable housing and community development in addressing common legal concerns and problems; publishes a quarterly compilation of nationwide case law affecting housing agencies; conducts seminars on legal issues and practices in the housing and community development field.

Institute for Local Self-Reliance, *2001 S St. N.W., #570 20009; (202) 898-1610. Fax, (202) 898-1612. Neil N. Seldman, President. General email, info@ilsr.org*

Web, www.ilsr.org

Conducts research and provides technical assistance on environmentally sound economic development for government, small businesses, and community organizations.

National Assn. of Housing and Redevelopment Officials, *630 Eye St. N.W. 20001-3736; (202) 289-3500. Fax, (202) 289-8181. Saul N. Ramirez Jr., Chief Executive. Toll-free, (877) 866-2476. General email, nahro@nahro.org*

Web, www.nahro.org

Membership: housing, community, and urban development practitioners and organizations, and state and local government agencies and personnel. Works with federal government agencies to improve community development and affordable and public housing programs; conducts training programs.

National Center for Healthy Housing, *10320 Little Patuxent Pkwy., #500, Columbia, MD 21044; (410) 992-0712. Fax, (443) 539-4150. Rebecca Morley, Executive Director. General email, info@nchh.org*

Web, www.nchh.org

Collects, analyzes, and distributes information on creating and maintaining safe and healthful housing. Provides technical assistance and training to public health, housing, and environmental professionals. Interests include radon, allergens, pest management, and lead poisoning.

Statistics

▶**AGENCIES**

Census Bureau *(Commerce Dept.), Manufacturing and Construction, 4600 Silver Hill Rd., #7K154, Suitland, MD 20746-4600 (mailing address: change city, state, and zip code to Washington, DC 20233-6900); (301) 763-4593. Fax, (301) 763-7783. Mendel D. Gayle, Division Chief. Web, www.census.gov/mcd*

Publishes statistics on the value of construction put in place; housing starts, sales, and completions; building permits; price index of single-family homes sold; characteristics of new housing; and expenditures for residential improvements. Conducts a census of construction industries every five years.

Census Bureau *(Commerce Dept.), Social, Economic, and Housing Statistics, 4600 Silver Hill Rd., #7H174, Suitland, MD 20746 (mailing address: change city, state, and zip code to Washington, DC 20233-8500); (301) 763-3234. Fax, (301) 763-3232. David S. Johnson, Chief. Web, www.census.gov/housing*

Publishes decennial census of housing and the American Housing Survey, which describe housing inventory characteristics. Also publishes a quarterly survey of market absorption. Survey on housing vacancy is available on the Web site.

Housing and Urban Development Dept. (HUD), *Economic Affairs, 451 7th St. S.W., #8204 20410-6000; (202) 708-2770. Fax, (202) 708-1159. Kurt Usowski, Deputy Assistant Secretary. Web, www.hud.gov*

Directs research in public finance and urban economic development; assembles data on housing markets; conducts annual housing surveys; analyzes financial instruments used in housing.

International Trade Administration (ITA) *(Commerce Dept.), Industry and Analysis, Manufacturing, 1401 Constitution Ave. N.W., #2800A 20230; (202) 482-1872. Fax, (202) 482-0856. Chandra Brown, Deputy Assistant Secretary, Acting. Web, www.trade.gov/td/manufacturing and www.manufacturing.gov*

Analyzes and maintains data on international construction and engineering. Monitors production costs, prices, financial and labor conditions, technological changes, distribution, markets, trade patterns, and other aspects of these industries. Promotes international trade, develops competitive assessments, and assists engineering and construction companies in obtaining overseas construction projects.

COMMUNITY AND REGIONAL DEVELOPMENT

General

▶**AGENCIES**

Administration for Children and Families (ACF) *(Health and Human Services Dept.), Office of Community Services, 370 L'Enfant Promenade S.W., 5th Floor 20447; (202) 401-9333. Fax, (202) 401-4694. Jeannie Chaffin, Director. Web, www.acf.hhs.gov*

Administers the Community Services Block Grant and Discretionary Grant programs and the Low-Income Home Energy Assistance Block Grant Program for heating, cooling, and weatherizing low-income households.

Administration for Native Americans *(Health and Human Services Dept.), 370 L'Enfant Promenade S.W., 2nd Floor, West Aerospace Center 20447-0002; (202) 690-7776. Fax, (202) 690-7441. Lillian A. Sparks, Commissioner. Toll-free, (877) 922-9262. General email, ana@acf.hhs.gov*

Web, www.acf.hhs.gov/programs/ana

Awards grants for locally determined social and economic development strategies; promotes Native American economic and social self-sufficiency; funds tribes and Native American and Native Hawaiian organizations. Commissioner chairs the Intradepartmental Council on Indian Affairs, which coordinates Native American–related programs.

Army Corps of Engineers *(Defense Dept.),* *441 G St. N.W., #3K05 20314-1000; (202) 761-0001. Fax, (202) 761-4463. Lt. Gen. Thomas Bostick, Chief of Engineers. General email, hq-publicaffairs@usace.army.mil*
Web, www.usace.army.mil

Provides local governments with disaster relief, flood control, navigation, and hydroelectric power services.

Community Development Financial Institutions Fund *(Treasury Dept.), 1801 L St. N.W., 6th Floor 20036 (mailing address: 1500 Pennsylvania Ave. N.W., Washington, DC 20220); (202) 653-0300. Fax, (202) 453-2466. Vacant, Director. Help Desk, (202) 653-0421. General email, cdfihelp@cdfi.treas.gov*
Web, www.cdfifund.gov

Provides funds and tax credits to financial institutions to build private markets, create healthy local tax revenues, and expand the availability of credit, investment capital, affordable housing, and financial services in low-income urban, rural, and Native communities.

Defense Dept. (DoD), *Office of Economic Adjustment, 2231 Crystal Dr., #520, Arlington, VA 22202-4704; (703) 697-2130. Fax, (703) 607-0170. Patrick J. O'Brien, Director. Web, www.oea.gov*

Civilian office that helps community officials develop strategies and coordinate plans to alleviate the economic effect of major defense program changes, including base closings (BRAC) and contract cutbacks. Assists communities where defense activities are being expanded. Serves as the staff for the Economic Adjustment Committee, an interagency group that coordinates federal technical and financial transition assistance to localities.

Education Dept., *White House Initiative on Asian Americans and Pacific Islanders, 550 12th St. S.W., 10th Floor 20202; (202) 453-7277. Fax, (202) 453-6238. Kiran Ahuja, Executive Director. Press, (202) 453-6566. General email, http://whitehouseaapi@ed.gov*
Web, www.whitehouse.gov/aapi and Twitter, @whitehouseAAPI

Works to increase Asian American and Pacific Islander participation in federal housing and community development programs. Interests include creating sustainable communities by connecting housing to jobs and helping to build clean energy communities.

Housing and Urban Development Dept. (HUD), *Block Grant Assistance, 451 7th St. S.W., #7286 20410; (202) 708-3587. Fax, (202) 401-2044. Stan Gimont, Director. Press, (202) 708-1577.*

Web, http://portal.hud.gov/offices/cpd/hudportal/HUD?src=/program_offices/comm_planning/communitydevelopment/programs

Provides grants on a formula basis to states, cities, and urban counties to be used for a wide range of eligible activities selected by the grantee.

Housing and Urban Development Dept. (HUD), *Community Planning and Development, 451 7th St. S.W., #7100 20410; (202) 708-2690. Fax, (202) 708-3336. Mark Johnston, Assistant Secretary, Acting; Clifford Taffet, General Deputy Assistant Secretary. Web, www.hud.gov/offices/cpd*

Provides cities and states with community and economic development and housing assistance, including community development block grants. Encourages public-private partnerships in urban development and private sector initiatives. Oversees enterprise zone development program.

Housing and Urban Development Dept. (HUD), *Environment and Energy, 451 7th St. S.W. 20410; (202) 708-2894. Fax, (202) 708-3363. Danielle Schopp, Director, (202) 402-4442. Web, www.hud.gov/offices/cpd/environment*

Issues policies and sets standards for environmental and land-use planning and for environmental management practices. Develops policies promoting energy efficiency, conservation, and renewable sources of supply in housing and community development programs.

Housing and Urban Development Dept. (HUD), *Field Policy and Management, 451 7th St. S.W., #7108 20410; (202) 708-2426. Fax, (202) 708-1558. Mary McBride, Deputy Assistant Secretary. Web, www.hud.gov*

Acts as liaison and coordinates all activities between the Office of Community Planning and Development and regional and field offices; evaluates the performance of regional and field offices. Conducts policy analyses and evaluations of community planning and development programs, including the Community Development Block Grant Program, the Empowerment Zones/Enterprise Communities Program, and the McKinney Act programs.

Housing and Urban Development Dept. (HUD), *States Division, 451 7th St. S.W., #7184 20410; (202) 708-1322. Fax, (202) 401-2044. Steve Rhodeside, Director. Web, www.hud.gov/offices/cpd/communitydevelopment/programs/index.cfm*

Provides states with grants for distribution to small cities (fewer than 50,000 persons) and counties (fewer than 200,000 persons) that do not receive funding through the Entitlement Community Development Block Grant Program. Funds benefit low- and moderate-income persons, eliminate slums and blighted conditions, or meet other urgent community development needs. All states (except Hawaii), plus Puerto Rico, receive State Community Development Block Grant (CDBG) program funding. In Hawaii, HUD provides funding directly to the local governments. A separate program also provides funding to the Insular Areas.

Housing and Urban Development Dept. (HUD),
Sustainable Housing and Communities, 451 7th St. S.W., #10180 20410; (202) 402-6045. Fax, (202) 708-0465. Salin Geevarghese, Director, Acting.
Web, www.hud.gov/sustainability

Works to connect housing to jobs, helping to build a clean energy economy. Fosters local innovation and coordinated federal housing and transportation. Awards grants for affordable housing development and transportation-related issues, as well as green and sustainable energy practices.

Housing and Urban Development Dept. (HUD),
Technical Assistance, 451 7th St. S.W., #7216 20410; (202) 708-3176. David Enzel, Director.
Web, www.hud.gov/offices/cpd

Develops program policies and designs and implements technical assistance plans for state and local governments for use in community planning and development programs.

▶**CONGRESS**

For a listing of relevant congressional committees and subcommittees, please see page 382 or the Appendix.

▶**NONGOVERNMENTAL**

American Planning Assn., *1030 15th St. N.W., #750W 20005; (202) 872-0611. Fax, (202) 872-0643. W. Paul Farmer, Chief Executive Officer; Jason Jordan, Director of Governmental Affairs.*
Web, www.planning.org

Membership: professional planners and others interested in urban, suburban, and rural planning. Serves as a clearinghouse for planners. Sponsors professional development workshops conducted by the American Institute of Certified Planners. Prepares studies and technical reports; conducts seminars and conferences.

American Resort Development Assn., *1201 15th St. N.W., #400 20005; (202) 371-6700. Fax, (202) 289-8544. Howard Nusbaum, President.*
Web, www.arda.org

Membership: U.S. and international developers, builders, financiers, marketing companies, and others involved in resort, recreational, and community development. Serves as an information clearinghouse; monitors federal and state legislation affecting land, time share, and community development industries.

Center for Community Change, *1536 U St. N.W. 20009; (202) 339-9300. Fax, (202) 387-4892. Deepak Bhargava, Executive Director.*
General email, info@communitychange.org
Web, www.communitychange.org

Works to strengthen grassroots organizations that help low-income people, working-class people, and minorities develop skills and resources to improve their communities and change the policies and institutions that affect their lives. Monitors legislation and regulations.

Corporation for Enterprise Development (CFED), *1200 G St. N.W., #400 20005; (202) 408-9788. Fax, (202) 408-9793. Andrea Levere, President.*
General email, info@cfed.org
Web, www.cfed.org

Works to alleviate poverty by expanding economic opportunity and participation, bringing together community practice, public policy, and private markets in new and effective ways.

Council of State Community Development Agencies, *1825 K St. N.W., #515 20006; (202) 293-5820. Fax, (202) 293-2820. Dianne E. Taylor, Executive Director.*
General email, info@coscda.org
Web, www.coscda.org

Membership: directors and staff of state community development agencies. Promotes common interests among the states, including community and economic development, housing, homelessness, infrastructure, and state and local planning.

Institute for Sustainable Communities, *Washington Office, 888 17th St. N.W., #610 20006; (202) 777-7575. Fax, (202) 777-7577. George Hamilton, President; Debra Perry, Senior Program Manager, U.S..*
General email, isc@iscvt.org
Web, www.iscvt.org

Provides training and technical assistance to communities to engage citizens in developing and implementing plans for a sustainable future. (Headquarters in Montpelier, Vt.)

International Institute of Site Planning (InSitu), *715 G St. S.E. 20003; (202) 546-2322. Fax, (202) 546-2722. Beatriz de Winthuysen Coffin, Director.*
General email, iisitep@aol.com
Web, www.iisp-insitu.com

Directs research and provides information on site planning development and design of sites and buildings; conducts study and travel programs.

Land Trust Alliance, *1660 L St. N.W., #1100 20036; (202) 638-4725. Fax, (202) 638-4730. Rand Wentworth, President, (202) 800-2249.*
General email, info@lta.org
Web, www.landtrustalliance.org and Twitter, @italliance

Membership: organizations and individuals who work to conserve land resources. Serves as a forum for the exchange of information; conducts research and public education programs. Monitors legislation and regulations.

Local Initiatives Support Corp., *Washington Office, 1825 K St. N.W., #1100 20006; (202) 739-9284. Fax, (202) 785-4850. Ornamenta Newsome, Executive Director; Matt Josephs, Senior Vice President, Policy.*
Web, www.lisc.org/washington_dc

Provides community development corporations and nonprofit organizations with financial and technical assistance to build affordable housing and revitalize distressed neighborhoods. (Headquarters in New York.)

National Assn. of Conservation Districts (NACD), 509 Capitol Court N.E. 20002-4937; (202) 547-6223. Fax, (202) 547-6450. John Larson, Chief Executive Officer.
General email, bethany-shively@nacdet.org
Web, www.nacdnet.org

Membership: conservation districts (local subdivisions of state government). Works to promote the conservation of land, forests, and other natural resources. Interests include erosion and sediment control; water quality; forestry, water, flood plain, and range management; rural development; and urban and community conservation.

National Assn. of Counties (NACo), *Community and Economic Development,* 25 Massachusetts Ave. N.W., 5th Floor 20001; (202) 393-6226. Fax, (202) 942-4281. Daria Daniel, Associate Legislative Director.
Web, www.naco.org/programs/csd/pages/communityeconomicdevelopment.aspx

Membership: county governments. Conducts research and provides information on community development block grants, assisted low-income housing, and other housing and economic development programs. Monitors legislation and regulations.

National Assn. of Development Organizations, 400 N. Capitol St. N.W., #390 20001; (202) 624-7806. Fax, (202) 624-8813. Joe McKinney, Executive Director, (202) 624-5947.
General email, info@nado.org
Web, www.nado.org

Membership: organizations interested in regional, local, and rural economic development. Provides information on federal, state, and local development programs and revolving loan funds; sponsors conferences and training.

National Assn. of Regional Councils, 777 N. Capitol St. N.E., #305 20002; (202) 986-1032. Fax, (202) 986-1038. Fred Abousleman, Executive Director.
Web, www.narc.org

Membership: regional councils of local governments and metropolitan planning organizations. Works with member local governments to encourage areawide economic growth and cooperation between public and private sectors, with emphasis on community development.

National Community Development Assn., 522 21st St. N.W., #120 20006; (202) 293-7587. Fax, (202) 887-5546. Cardell Cooper, Executive Director.
Web, www.ncdaonline.org

Membership: local governments that administer federally supported community and economic development, housing, and human service programs.

National Trust for Historic Preservation, 2600 Virginia Ave. N.W., #1000 20037; (202) 588-6000. Fax, (202) 588-6038. Stephanie Meeks, President. Press, (202) 588-6141.

General email, feedback@savingplaces.org
Web, www.preservationnation.org

Conducts seminars, workshops, and conferences on topics related to preservation, including neighborhood conservation, main street revitalization, rural conservation, and preservation law; offers financial assistance through loan and grant programs; provides advisory services; operates historic house sites, which are open to the public; and publishes quarterly magazine and e-newsletters.

Partners for Livable Communities, 1429 21st St. N.W. 20036; (202) 887-5990. Robert H. McNulty, President.
General email, livability@livable.org
Web, www.livable.org

Promotes working partnerships among public, private, and governmental sectors to improve the quality of life and economic development at local and regional levels. Conducts conferences and workshops; maintains referral clearinghouse; provides technical assistance.

Scenic America, 1307 New Hampshire Ave. N.W. 20036; (202) 463-1294. Fax, (202) 463-1299. Mary Tracy, President.
General email, ashburn@scenic.org
Web, www.scenic.org

Membership: national, state, and local groups concerned with land-use control, growth management, and landscape protection. Works to enhance the scenic quality of America's communities and countryside. Provides information and technical assistance on scenic byways, tree preservation, economics of aesthetic regulation, billboard and sign control, scenic areas preservation, and growth management.

Smart Growth America, 1707 L St. N.W., #250 20036; (202) 207-3355. Fax, (202) 207-3349. Geoffrey Anderson, President.
General email, info@smartgrowthamerica.org
Web, www.smartgrowthamerica.org

Coalition of advocacy groups that supports citizen-driven planning that coordinates development, transportation, revitalization of older areas, and preservation of open space and the environment.

Rural Areas

►**AGENCIES**

Agriculture Dept. (USDA), *Rural Development,* 1400 Independence Ave. S.W., #205W 20250-0107; (202) 720-4581. Fax, (202) 720-2080. Vacant, Under Secretary; Doug O'Brien, Deputy Under Secretary.
Web, www.rurdev.usda.gov

Acts as chief adviser to the secretary on agricultural credit and related matters; coordinates rural development policies and programs throughout the federal government; supervises the Rural Utilities Service, Rural Housing Service, and Rural Business-Cooperative Service.

Farm Service Agency (FSA) *(Agriculture Dept.), Farm Loan Programs,* 1400 Independence Ave. S.W., #3605S, MS 0520 20250-0520; (202) 720-4671. Fax, (202) 690-3573. Chris Beyerhelm, Deputy Administrator, (202) 720-7597. Web, www.fsa.usda.gov

Supports rural development through farm program loans, including real estate, farm production, and emergency loans.

National Agricultural Library *(Agriculture Dept.), Rural Information Center,* 10301 Baltimore Ave., #123, Beltsville, MD 20705-2351; (800) 633-7701. Fax, (301) 504-5181. William Thomas, Coordinator. General email, rice@ars.usda.gov Web, http://ric.nal.usda.gov

Provides services for rural communities, local officials, organizations, businesses, and rural citizens in the interest of maintaining rural areas. Interests include community development, tourism promotion, water quality, recycling, and technology transfer.

Rural Development *(Agriculture Dept.), Business and Cooperative Programs, Business Programs,* 1400 Independence Ave. S.W., #5813-S 20250-3220; (202) 720-7287. Fax, (202) 690-0097. Chad Parker, Deputy Administrator. Web, www.rurdev.usda.gov/LP_businessprograms.html

Promotes rural economic development by providing financial assistance and business planning to community businesses.

Rural Development *(Agriculture Dept.), Rural Utilities Service,* 1400 Independence Ave. S.W., #5135-S, MS 1510 20250-1510; (202) 720-9540. Fax, (202) 720-1725. John Chas Padalino, Administrator. Information, (202) 720-1255. Web, www.rurdeve.usda.gov/utilities_assistance.html and www.rurdeve.usda.gov/utilities_LP.html

Makes loans and loan guarantees to provide electricity, telecommunication systems, and water and waste disposal services to rural areas.

Rural Development *(Agriculture Dept.), Rural Utilities Service,* 1400 Independence Ave. S.W., #5135-S, MS 1510 20250-1510; (202) 720-9540. Fax, (202) 720-1725. John Chas Padalino, Administrator. Information, (202) 720-1255. Web, www.rurdeve.usda.gov/utilities_assistance.html and www.rurdeve.usda.gov/utilities_LP.html

Makes loans and loan guarantees to rural electric and telephone companies providing service in rural areas. Administers the Rural Telephone Bank, which provides supplemental financing from federal sources. Makes loans for economic development and creation of jobs in rural areas, for water and waste disposal, and for distance learning and telemedicine.

Rural Housing Service *(Agriculture Dept.), Housing Programs,* 1400 Independence Ave. S.W., #501, MS 0701 20250-0780; (202) 690-1533. Fax, (202) 690-0500. Richard A. Davis, Administrator, Acting. Web, www.rurdev.usda.gov/rhs

Offers financial assistance to apartment dwellers and homeowners in rural areas; provides funds to construct or improve single-family and multi-family housing and community facilities.

▶ **CONGRESS**

For a listing of relevant congressional committees and subcommittees, please see page 382 or the Appendix.

▶ **NONGOVERNMENTAL**

Farm Credit Council, 50 F St. N.W., #900 20001-1530; (202) 626-8710. Fax, (202) 626-8718. Ken Auer, President, (202) 879-0843. General email, auer@fccouncil.com Web, www.fccouncil.com

Represents the Farm Credit System, a national financial cooperative that makes loans to agricultural producers, rural homebuyers, farmer cooperatives, and rural utilities. Finances the export of U.S. agricultural commodities.

Housing Assistance Council, 1025 Vermont Ave. N.W., #606 20005-3516; (202) 842-8600. Fax, (202) 347-3441. Moises Loza, Executive Director. General email, hac@ruralhome.org Web, www.ruralhome.org

Provides low-income housing development groups in rural areas with seed money loans and technical assistance; assesses programs designed to respond to rural housing needs; makes recommendations for federal and state involvement; publishes technical guides and reports on rural housing issues.

Irrigation Assn., 6540 Arlington Blvd., Falls Church, VA 22042-6638; (703) 536-7080. Fax, (703) 536-7019. Deborah Hamlin, Executive Director. General email, info@irrigation.org Web, www.irrigation.org

Membership: companies and individuals involved in irrigation, drainage, and erosion control worldwide. Promotes efficient and effective water management through training, education, and certification programs. Interests include economic development and environmental enhancement.

National Cooperative Business Assn., 1401 New York Ave. N.W., #1100 20005-2160; (202) 638-6222. Fax, (202) 638-1374. Michael Bealle, President. General email, info@ncba.coop Web, www.ncba.coop and Twitter, @NCBACLUSA

Alliance of cooperatives, businesses, and state cooperative associations. Provides information about starting and managing agricultural cooperatives in the United States and in developing nations. Monitors legislation and regulations.

National Council of Farmer Cooperatives (NCFC), *50 F St. N.W., #900 20001-1530; (202) 626-8700. Fax, (202) 626-8722. Charles F. Conner, President.*
General email, info@ncfc.org
Web, www.ncfc.org

Membership: cooperative businesses owned and operated by farmers. Encourages research on agricultural cooperatives; provides statistics and analyzes trends. Monitors legislation and regulations on agricultural trade, transportation, energy, and tax issues.

National Rural Electric Cooperative Assn. (NRECA), *4301 Wilson Blvd., Arlington, VA 22203-1860; (703) 907-5500. Fax, (703) 907-5511. Jo Ann Emerson, Chief Executive Officer; Tracy Ward, Media Relations, (703) 907-5746.*
Web, www.nreca.org

Membership: rural electric cooperative systems and public power and utility districts. Provides members with legislative, legal, and regulatory services. Supports energy and environmental research and offers technical advice and assistance to developing countries.

National Telecommunications Cooperative Assn. (NTCA), *4121 Wilson Blvd., #1000, Arlington, VA 22203-1801; (703) 351-2000. Fax, (703) 351•2001. Shirley Bloomfield, Chief Executive Officer.*
General email, pubrelations@ntca.org
Web, www.ntca.org

Membership: locally owned and controlled telecommunications cooperatives and companies serving rural and small-town areas. Offers educational seminars, workshops, publications, technical assistance, and various employee benefits programs to members. Monitors legislation and regulations.

Rural Coalition, *1029 Vermont Ave., #601 20005; (202) 628-7160. Fax, (202) 393-1816. Lorette Picciano, Executive Director.*
General email, ruralco@ruralco.org
Web, www.ruralco.org

Alliance of organizations that develop public policies benefiting rural communities. Collaborates with community-based groups on agriculture and rural development issues, including health and the environment, minority farmers, farm workers, Native Americans' rights, and rural community development. Provides rural groups with technical assistance.

Rural Community Assistance Partnership (RCAP), *1701 K St. N.W., #700 20006; (202) 408-1273. Fax, (202) 408-8165. Robert Stewart, Executive Director. Toll-free, (800) 321-7227.*
General email, info@rcap.org
Web, www.rcap.org

Provides expertise to rural communities on wastewater disposal, protection of groundwater supply, and access to safe drinking water. Targets communities with predominantly low-income or minority populations. Offers outreach policy analysis, training, and technical assistance

to elected officials and other community leaders, utility owners and operators, and residents.

Specific Regions

▶**AGENCIES**

Appalachian Regional Commission, *1666 Connecticut Ave. N.W., #700 20009-1068; (202) 884-7700. Fax, (202) 884-7691. Thomas M. Hunter, Executive Director; Earl F. Gohl, Federal Co-Chair. Press, (202) 884-7771.*
General email, info@arc.gov and thunter@arc.gov
Web, www.arc.gov

Federal-state-local partnership for economic development of the region including West Virginia and parts of Alabama, Georgia, Kentucky, Maryland, Mississippi, New York, North Carolina, Ohio, Pennsylvania, South Carolina, Tennessee, and Virginia. Plans and provides technical and financial assistance and coordinates federal and state efforts for economic development of Appalachia.

Bureau of Reclamation *(Interior Dept.), 1849 C St. N.W., #7654, 7069 MIB 20240-0001; (202) 513-0501. Fax, (202) 513-0309. Michael L. Connor, Commissioner. Press, (202) 513-0575.*
Web, www.usbr.gov

Administers federal programs for water and power resource development and management in seventeen western states; oversees municipal and industrial water supplies, hydroelectric power generation, irrigation, flood control, water quality improvement, river regulation, fish and wildlife enhancement, and outdoor recreation.

Interstate Commission on the Potomac River Basin, *30 W. Gude Dr., #450, Rockville, MD 20850; (301) 984-1908. Fax, (301) 984-5841. Carlton Haywood, Executive Director.*
General email, info@icprb.org
Web, www.potomacriver.org

Nonregulatory interstate compact commission established by Congress to control and reduce water pollution and to restore and protect living resources in the Potomac River and its tributaries. Monitors water quality; assists metropolitan water utilities; seeks innovative methods to solve water supply and land resource problems. Provides information and educational materials on the Potomac River basin.

National Capital Planning Commission, *401 9th St. N.W., North Lobby, #500 20004; (202) 482-7200. Fax, (202) 482-7272. Marcel Acosta, Executive Director.*
General email, info@ncpc.gov
Web, www.ncpc.gov

Central planning agency for the federal government in the national capital region, which includes the District of Columbia and suburban Maryland and Virginia. Reviews and approves plans for the physical growth and development of the national capital area, using environmental, historic, and land-use criteria.

Tennessee Valley Authority, *Government Affairs,* 1 Massachusetts Ave. N.W., #300 20444; (202) 898-2999. Fax, (202) 898-2998. Nick Pearson, Director.
General email, latootle@tva.gov

Web, www.tva.gov

Federal corporation that coordinates resource conservation, development, and land-use programs in the Tennessee River Valley. Uses fossil fuel, nuclear, and hydropower sources to generate and supply wholesale power to municipal and cooperative electric systems, federal installations, and some industries. (Headquarters in Knoxville, Tenn.)

▶**NONGOVERNMENTAL**

Greater Washington Board of Trade, 1725 Eye St. N.W. 20006; (202) 857-5900. Fax, (202) 223-2648. James C. (Jim) Dinegar, President.
General email, info@bot.org and danielflores@bot.org

Web, www.bot.org

Promotes and plans economic growth for the capital region. Supports business-government partnerships, technological training, and transportation planning; promotes international trade; works to increase economic viability of the city of Washington. Monitors legislation and regulations at local, state, and federal levels.

New England Council, *Washington Office,* 331 Constitution Ave. N.E. 20002; (202) 547-0048. Fax, (202) 547-9149. James T. Brett, President; Peter Phipps, Director of Federal Affairs.
General email, dcoffice@newenglandcouncil.com

Web, www.newenglandcouncil.com

Provides information on business and economic issues concerning New England; serves as liaison between the New England congressional delegations and business community. (Headquarters in Boston, Mass.)

Northeast-Midwest Congressional Coalition, 1519 LHOB 20515-2308; (202) 226-6106. Rep. Mike Kelly, Co-Chair; Rep. James P. McGovern, Co-Chair; Samuel Breene, Legislative Director.

Develops public policies emphasizing regional equity, manufacturing efficiency, and sustainable development; looks into such issues as manufacturing, energy, transportation, and the environment.

Urban Areas

▶**AGENCIES**

General Services Administration (GSA), *Urban Development/Good Neighbor Program,* 18th St. N.W., #3341 20405-0001; (202) 501-1856. Frank Giblin, Program Manager, (202) 501-3393.
General email, giblin@gsa.gov

Web, www.gsa.gov/goodneighbor

Advises on locations, designs, and renovations of federal facilities in central business areas, historic districts, and local redevelopment areas where they can anchor or promote community development. Collaborates with local and national civic and other organizations. Serves as clearinghouse for good practices.

Housing and Urban Development Dept. (HUD), *Affordable Housing Programs,* 451 7th St. S.W., #7164 20410; (202) 708-2684. Fax, (202) 708-1744. Virginia Sardone, Director, Acting.
Web, www.hud.gov/hudportal/HUD?src=/program_offices/comm_planning/affordablehousing

Coordinates with cities to convey publicly owned, abandoned property to low-income families in exchange for their commitment to repair, occupy, and maintain the property.

Housing and Urban Development Dept. (HUD), *Economic Development,* 451 7th St. S.W., #7136 20410; (202) 708-4091. Fax, (202) 401-2231. Valerie Piper, Deputy Assistant Secretary, (202) 402-4445.
Web, www.hud.gov/hudportal/HUD?src=/contact/principal_directory

Manages economic development programs, including Empowerment Zones/Renewal Communities, Rural Housing and Economic Development, and Brownfields Economic Development Initiatives. Encourages private-public partnerships for development through neighborhood development corporations. Formulates policies and legislative proposals on economic development.

NeighborWorks America, 999 N. Capitol St. N.E., #900 20002; (202) 760-4000. Eileen M. Fitzgerald, Chief Executive Officer.
Web, www.nw.org

Chartered by Congress to assist localities in developing and operating local neighborhood-based programs designed to reverse decline in urban residential neighborhoods and rural communities. Oversees the National NeighborWorks Network, an association of local nonprofit organizations concerned with urban and rural development. (Formerly the Neighborhood Reinvestment Corp.)

▶**NONGOVERNMENTAL**

The Brookings Institution, *Metropolitan Policy Program,* 1755 Massachusetts Ave. N.W. 20036; (202) 797-6000. Fax, (202) 797-2965. Bruce Katz, Co-Director; Amy Liu, Co-Director. Press, (202) 797-6105.
General email, metro@brookings.edu

Web, www.brookings.edu/metro.aspx

Helps U.S. cities and metropolitan areas study and reform their economic, fiscal, and social policies. Conducts research at the national, state, and local levels.

Center for Neighborhood Enterprise, 1625 K St. N.W., #1200 20006; (202) 518-6500. Fax, (202) 588-0314. Robert L. Woodson Sr., President. Information, (866) 518-1263.
General email, info@cneonline.org

Web, www.cneonline.org

Provides community and faith-based organizations with training, technical assistance, and additional sources of support. Addresses homelessness and deteriorating neighborhoods.

International Downtown Assn., *1025 Thomas Jefferson St. N.W., #500W 20007; (202) 393-6801. Fax, (202) 393-6869. David T. Downey, President, (202) 624-7111.*
General email, question@ida-downtown.org
Web, www.ida-downtown.org

Membership: organizations, corporations, public agencies, and individuals interested in the development and management of city downtown areas. Supports cooperative efforts between the public and private sectors to revitalize downtowns and adjacent neighborhoods; provides members with information, technical assistance, and advice.

International Economic Development Council, *734 15th St. N.W., #900 20005; (202) 223-7800. Fax, (202) 223-4745. Jeffrey Finkle, President; Erin Way, Press. Press, (703) 942-9474.*
General email, mail@iedconline.org
Web, www.iedconline.org

Membership: public economic development directors, chamber of commerce staff, utility executives, academicians, and others who design and implement development programs. Provides information to members on job creation, attraction, and retention.

Milton S. Eisenhower Foundation, *1875 Connecticut Ave. N.W., #410 20009-5728; (202) 234-8104. Fax, (202) 234-8484. Alan Curtis, President.*
General email, hr@eisenhowerfoundation.org
Web, www.eisenhowerfoundation.org

Strives to help urban communities combat violence by supporting programs with proven records of success. Provides funding, technical assistance, evaluation, and supervision to communities wishing to replicate successful programs.

National Assn. for the Advancement of Colored People (NAACP), *Washington Bureau, 1156 15th St. N.W., #915 20005; (202) 463-2940. Fax, (202) 463-2953. Hilary O. Shelton, Director.*
General email, washingtonbureau@naacpnet.org
Web, www.naacp.org

Membership: persons interested in civil rights for all minorities. Works to eliminate discrimination in housing and urban affairs. Interests include programs for urban redevelopment, urban homesteading, and low-income housing. Supports programs that make affordable rental housing available to minorities and that maintain African American ownership of urban and rural land. (Headquarters in Baltimore, Md.)

National Assn. of Neighborhoods, *1300 Pennsylvania Ave. N.W., #700 20004; (202) 332-7766. Fax, (202) 789-7349. Ricardo C. Byrd, Executive Director.*
General email, info@nanworld.org
Web, www.nanworld.org

Federation of neighborhood groups that provides technical assistance to local governments, neighborhood groups, and businesses. Seeks to increase influence of grassroots groups on decisions affecting neighborhoods; sponsors training workshops promoting neighborhood awareness.

National League of Cities, *1301 Pennsylvania Ave. N.W., #550 20004; (202) 626-3000. Fax, (202) 626-3043. Clarence Anthony, Executive Director.*
General email, info@nlc.org
Web, www.nlc.org

Membership: cities and state municipal leagues. Aids city leaders in developing programs; investigates needs of local governments in implementing federal community development programs.

National Urban League, *Washington Bureau, 1805 7th St. N.W., #520 20001; (202) 898-1604. Chanelle Hardy, Executive Director.*
Web, www.nulwb.iamempowered.com

Federal advocacy division of social service organization concerned with the social welfare of African Americans and other minorities. Conducts legislative and policy analysis on housing and urban affairs. Operates a job bank. (Headquarters in New York.)

Urban Institute, *Metropolitan Housing and Communities Policy Center, 2100 M St. N.W. 20037; (202) 833-7200. Fax, (202) 872-8154. Rolf Pendall, Director.*
General email, publicaffairs@urban.org
Web, www.urban.org/center/met

Research center that deals with urban problems. Researches federal, state, and local policies; focus includes community development block grants, neighborhood rehabilitation programs, and housing issues.

Urban Land Institute, *1025 Thomas Jefferson St. N.W., #500W 20007-5201; (202) 624-7000. Patrick L. Phillips, President. Information, (800) 321-5011. Library, (202) 624-7137.*
Web, www.uli.org

Membership: land developers, planners, state and federal agencies, financial institutions, home builders, consultants, and realtors. Provides responsible leadership in the use of land to enhance the total environment; monitors trends in new community development. Library open to the public by appointment for a fee.

U.S. Conference of Mayors, *1620 Eye St. N.W., #400 20006; (202) 293-7330. Fax, (202) 293-2352. J. Thomas Cochran, Executive Director.*
General email, info@usmayors.org
Web, www.usmayors.org

Membership: mayors of cities with populations of 30,000 or more. Promotes city-federal cooperation; publishes reports and conducts meetings on federal programs, policies, and initiatives that affect urban and suburban interests. Serves as a clearinghouse for information on urban and suburban problems. (Approximately 1,400 U.S. cities.)

CONSTRUCTION

General

►AGENCIES

Census Bureau *(Commerce Dept.), Manufacturing and Construction*, 4600 Silver Hill Rd., #7K154, Suitland, MD 20746-4600 (mailing address: change city, state, and zip code to Washington, DC 20233-6900); (301) 763-4593. Fax, (301) 763-7783. Mendel D. Gayle, Division Chief. Web, www.census.gov/mcd

Publishes statistics on the value of construction put in place; housing starts, sales, and completions; building permits; price index of single-family homes sold; characteristics of new housing; and expenditures for residential improvements. Conducts a census of construction industries every five years.

General Services Administration (GSA), *Public Buildings Service*, 1800 F St. N.W., #1344 20405; (202) 501-1100. Fax, (202) 219-0856. Dorothy Robyn, Commissioner. Web, www.gsa.gov/pbs

Administers the acquisition, construction, maintenance, and operation of buildings owned or leased by the federal government. Manages and disposes of federal real estate.

International Trade Administration (ITA) *(Commerce Dept.), Industry and Analysis, Manufacturing*, 1401 Constitution Ave. N.W., #2800A 20230; (202) 482-1872. Fax, (202) 482-0856. Chandra Brown, Deputy Assistant Secretary, Acting. Web, www.trade.gov/td/manufacturing and www.manufacturing.gov

Analyzes and maintains data on international construction and engineering. Monitors production costs, prices, financial and labor conditions, technological changes, distribution, markets, trade patterns, and other aspects of these industries. Promotes international trade, develops competitive assessments, and assists engineering and construction companies in obtaining overseas construction projects.

►NONGOVERNMENTAL

American Public Works Assn., *Washington Office*, 1275 K St. N.W., #750 20005; (202) 408-9541. Fax, (202) 408-9542. Peter B. King, Executive Director. General email, apwa.dc@apwa.net
Web, www.apwa.net

Membership: engineers, architects, and others who maintain and manage public works facilities and services. Conducts research and education and promotes exchange of information on transportation and infrastructure-related issues. (Headquarters in Kansas City, Mo.)

American Subcontractors Assn., 1004 Duke St., Alexandria, VA 22314-3588; (703) 684-3450. Fax, (703) 836-3482. Colette Nelson, Chief Advocacy Officer.

General email, asaoffice@asa-hq.com
Web, www.asaonline.com

Membership: construction subcontractors, specialty contractors, and their suppliers. Addresses business, contract, and payment issues affecting all subcontractors. Interests include procurement laws, payment practices, and lien laws. Monitors legislation and regulations.

Associated Builders and Contractors, 440 1st St. N.W., #200 20001; (202) 595-1636. Michael Bellaman, President. General email, gotquestion@abc.org
Web, www.abc.org

Membership: construction contractors engaged primarily in nonresidential construction, subcontractors, and suppliers. Sponsors apprenticeship, safety, and training programs. Provides labor relations information; compiles statistics. Monitors legislation and regulations.

Associated General Contractors of America, 2300 Wilson Blvd., #400, Arlington, VA 22201; (703) 548-3118. Fax, (703) 548-3119. Stephen E. Sandherr, Chief Executive Officer. General email, info@agc.org
Web, www.agc.org

Membership: general contractors engaged primarily in nonresidential construction; subcontractors; suppliers; accounting; insurance and bonding; and law firms. Conducts training programs, conferences, seminars, and market development activities for members. Produces position papers on construction issues. Monitors legislation and regulations.

Construction Management Assn. of America, 7926 Jones Branch Dr., #800, McLean, VA 22102-3303; (703) 356-2622. Fax, (703) 356-6388. Bruce D'Agostino, President. General email, info@cmaanet.org
Web, www.cmaanet.org

Promotes the development of construction management as a profession through publications, education, a certification program, and an information network. Serves as an advocate for construction management in the legislative, executive, and judicial branches of government.

Construction Specifications Institute, 110 S. Union St., #100, Alexandria, VA 22314; (800) 689-2900. Fax, (703) 236-4600. Walter T. Marlowe, Executive Director. General email, csi@csinet.org
Web, http://csinet.org

Membership: architects, engineers, contractors, and others in the construction industry. Promotes construction technology; publishes reference materials to help individuals prepare construction documents; sponsors certification programs for construction specifiers and manufacturing representatives.

Mechanical Contractors Assn. of America, 1385 Piccard Dr., Rockville, MD 20850; (301) 869-5800. Fax, (301) 990-9690. John R. Gentille, Executive Vice President. Web, www.mcaa.org

Membership: mechanical contractors and members of related professions. Seeks to improve building standards and codes. Provides information, publications, and training programs; conducts seminars and annual convention. Monitors legislation and regulations.

National Assn. of Home Builders (NAHB), *1201 15th St. N.W. 20005-2800; (202) 266-8409. Fax, (202) 266-8400. Gerald M. Howard, Chief Executive Officer. Press, (202) 266-8254. Toll-free, (800) 368-5242.*
Web, www.nahb.org

Membership: contractors, builders, architects, engineers, mortgage lenders, and others interested in home building and residential real estate construction. Participates in updating and developing building codes and standards; offers technical information. Interests include policies to stimulate the housing market; taxation, financing, environmental, and land usage policies. Monitors legislation and regulations.

National Assn. of Minority Contractors, *910 17th St. N.W., #413 20006; (202) 296-1600. Fax, (202) 296-1644. Robert Brewer, National Executive Director.*
General email, info@namcnational.org
Web, www.namcnational.org

Membership: minority businesses and related firms, associations, and individuals serving those businesses in the construction industry. Advises members on commercial and government business; develops resources for technical assistance and industry-specific training; provides bid information on government contracts. Monitors legislation and regulations.

National Assn. of Plumbing-Heating-Cooling Contractors, *180 S. Washington St., #100, Falls Church, VA 22046 (mailing address: P.O. Box 6808, Falls Church, VA 22046); (703) 237-8100. Fax, (703) 237-7442. Gererd Kennedy, Executive Vice President. Information, (800) 533-7694.*
General email, naphcc@naphcc.org
Web, www.phccweb.org

Provides education and training for plumbing, heating, and cooling contractors and their employees. Offers career information, internships, and scholarship programs for business and engineering students to encourage careers in the plumbing and mechanical contracting field.

National Electrical Contractors Assn., *3 Bethesda Metro Center, #1100, Bethesda, MD 20814; (301) 657-3110. Fax, (301) 215-4500. John Grau, Chief Executive Officer. Web, www.necanet.org*

Membership: electrical contractors who build and service electrical wiring and equipment, including high-voltage construction and service. Represents members in collective bargaining with union workers; sponsors research and educational programs.

National Utility Contractors Assn. (NUCA), *3925 Chain Bridge Rd., Fairfax, VA 22030; (703) 358-9300. Fax, (703) 358-9307. Bill Hillman, Chief Executive Officer. Web, www.nuca.com*

Membership: contractors who perform water, sewer, and other underground utility construction. Sponsors conferences; conducts surveys. Monitors public works legislation and regulations.

Sheet Metal and Air Conditioning Contractors' National Assn., *4201 Lafayette Center Dr., Chantilly, VA 20151-1219; (703) 803-2980. Fax, (703) 803-3732. Vincent R. Sandusky, Chief Executive Officer.*
General email, info@smacna.org
Web, www.smacna.org

Membership: unionized sheet metal and air conditioning contractors. Provides information on standards and installation and fabrication methods. Interests include energy efficiency and sustainability.

Society for Marketing Professional Services, *123 N. Pitt St., #400, Alexandria, VA 22314; (703) 549-6117. Fax, (703) 549-2498. Ronald D. Worth, Chief Executive Officer. Information, (800) 292-7677.*
General email, info@smps.org
Web, www.smps.org

Membership: individuals who provide professional services to the building industry. Assists individuals who market design services in the areas of architecture, engineering, planning, interior design, landscape architecture, and construction management. Provides seminars, workshops, and publications for members. Maintains job banks.

Sustainable Buildings Industry Council, *1090 Vermont Ave. N.W., #700 20005-4950; (202) 289-7800. Fax, (202) 289-1092. Ryan Colker, Director.*
General email, rcolker@nibs.org
Web, www.nibs.org/?page=sbic

Provides information on all aspects of sustainable design and construction: energy efficiency, renewable technologies, daylighting, healthy indoor environments, sustainable building materials and products, and resource conservation. (Affiliated with the National Institute of Building Sciences.)

U.S. Green Building Council, *2101 L St. N.W., #500 20037; (202) 742-3792. Fax, (202) 828-5110. S. Richard Fedrizzi, President. Toll-free, (800) 795-1747.*
General email, LEEDinfo@usgbc.org
Web, www.usgbc.org

Promotes buildings that are environmentally responsible, profitable, and healthy. Rates green buildings in order to accelerate implementation of environmentally friendly design practices.

Architecture and Design

▶**AGENCIES**

General Services Administration (GSA), *Design and Construction, Office of the Chief Architect, 1800 F St. N.W. 20405; (202) 501-1888. Fax, (202) 501-3393. Leslie Shepherd, Director, (202) 501-2289.*

General email, les.shepherd@gsa.gov

Web, www.gsa.gov

Administers the Art in Architecture Program, which commissions publicly scaled works of art for government buildings and landscapes, and the Fine Arts Program, which manages the GSA's collection of fine artwork that has been commissioned for use in government buildings.

▶ **NONGOVERNMENTAL**

AmericanHort, 1200 G St. N.W., #800 20005; (202) 789-2900. Fax, (202) 789-1893. Michael Geary, Executive Vice President.

General email, hello@AmericanHort.org

Web, www.AmericanHort.org

Serves as an information clearinghouse on the technical aspects of nursery and landscape business and design.

American Institute of Architects, 1735 New York Ave. N.W. 20006-5292; (202) 626-7300. Fax, (202) 626-7547. Robert Ivy, Chief Executive Officer. Press, (202) 626-7467. Toll-free, (800) 242-3837. Government Advocacy, (202) 626-7507.

General email, infocentral@aia.org

Web, www.aia.org

Membership: licensed American architects, interns, architecture faculty, engineers, planners, and those in government, manufacturing, or other fields in a capacity related to architecture. Works to advance the standards of architectural education, training, and practice. Promotes the aesthetic, scientific, and practical efficiency of architecture, urban design, and planning; monitors international developments. Offers continuing and professional education programs; sponsors scholarships, internships, and awards. Houses archival collection, including documents and drawings of American architects and architecture. Library open to the public by appointment. Monitors legislation and regulations.

American Society of Interior Designers, 608 Massachusetts Ave. N.E. 20002-6006; (202) 546-3480. Fax, (202) 546-3240. Randy Fiser, Chief Executive Officer.

General email, asid@asid.org

Web, www.asid.org

Offers certified professional development courses addressing the technical, professional, and business needs of designers; bestows annual scholarships, fellowships, and awards; supports licensing efforts at the state level.

American Society of Landscape Architects, 636 Eye St. N.W. 20001-3736; (202) 898-2444. Fax, (202) 898-1185. Nancy Somerville, Executive Vice President. Toll-free, (888) 999-2752.

General email, info@asla.org

Web, www.asla.org

Membership: professional landscape architects. Advises government agencies on land-use policy and environmental matters. Accredits university-level programs in landscape architecture; conducts professional education seminars for members.

Assn. of Collegiate Schools of Architecture, 1735 New York Ave. N.W., 3rd Floor 20006; (202) 785-2324. Fax, (202) 628-0448. Michael J. Monti, Executive Director.

General email, info@acsa-arch.org

Web, www.acsa-arch.org

Membership: U.S. and Canadian institutions that offer at least one accredited architecture degree program. Conducts workshops and seminars for architecture school faculty; presents awards for student and faculty excellence in architecture; publishes a guide to architecture schools in North America.

Industrial Designers Society of America, 555 Grove St., #200, Herndon, VA 20170; (703) 707-6000. Fax, (703) 787-8501. Daniel Martinage, Chief Executive Officer.

General email, idsa@idsa.org

Web, www.idsa.org

Membership: designers of products, equipment, instruments, furniture, transportation, packages, exhibits, information services, and related services, and educators of industrial design. Provides the Bureau of Labor Statistics with industry information. Monitors legislation and regulations.

Landscape Architecture Foundation, 1129 20th St. N.W., #202 20036; (202) 331-7070. Fax, (202) 331-7079. Barbara Deutsch, Executive Director.

General email, ededad@lafoundation.org

Web, www.lafoundation.org

Conducts research and provides educational and scientific information on sustainable land design and development and related fields. Awards scholarships and fellowships.

National Architectural Accrediting Board Inc., 1101 Connecticut Ave. N.W., #410 20036; (202) 783-2007. Fax, (202) 783-2822. Andrea S. Rutledge, Executive Director.

General email, info@naab.org

Web, www.naab.org

Accredits Bachelor, Master, and Doctor of Architecture degree programs in the United States; assists organizations in other countries to develop accreditation standards.

National Assn. of Schools of Art and Design, 11250 Roger Bacon Dr., #21, Reston, VA 20190-5248; (703) 437-0700. Fax, (703) 437-6312. Karen Moynahan, Executive Director.

General email, info@arts-accredit.org

Web, http://nasad.arts-accredit.org

Specialized professional accrediting agency for postsecondary programs in art and design. Conducts and shares research and analysis on topics pertinent to art and design programs, and fields of art and design. Offers professional development opportunities for executives of art and design programs.

National Council of Architectural Registration Boards (NCARB), 1801 K St. N.W., #700-K 20006-1310; (202)

783-6500. *Fax, (202) 783-0290. Michael J. Armstrong, Chief Executive Officer. Customer Service, (202) 879-0520.*
Web, www.ncarb.org

Membership: state architectural registration boards. Develops examinations used in U.S. states and territories for licensing architects; certifies architects.

PLANET (Professional Landcare Network), *950 Herndon Pkwy., #450, Herndon, VA 20170; (703) 736-9666. Fax, (703) 736-9668. Sabeena Hickman, Chief Executive Officer. Toll-free, (800) 395-2522.*
General email, info@landcarenetwork.org
Web, www.landcarenetwork.org

Membership: lawn care professionals, exterior maintenance contractors, installation/design/building professionals, and interiorscapers. Provides members with education, business management and marketing tools, and networking opportunities. Offers certification program. Focus is the green industry. Monitors legislation.

Codes, Standards, and Research

▶**AGENCIES**

Access Board, *1331 F St. N.W., #1000 20004-1111; (202) 272-0080. Fax, (202) 272-0081. David M. Capozzi, Executive Director, (202) 272-0010. TTY toll-free, (800) 993-2822. Toll-free technical assistance, (800) 872-2253.*
General email, info@access-board.gov
Web, www.access-board.gov

Develops and maintains accessibility requirements for buildings, transit vehicles, telecommunications equipment, medical diagnostic equipment, and electronic and information technology. Provides technical assistance and training on these guidelines and standards. Enforces access standards for federally funded facilities through the Architectural Barriers Act.

Energy Efficiency and Renewable Energy *(Energy Dept.), Building Technologies (BTP), 1000 Independence Ave. S.W., MSEE-5B 20585; (202) 586-9127. Fax, (202) 586-4617. Roland Risser, Program Manager.*
Web, www.eere.energy.gov/buildings

Funds research to reduce commercial and residential building energy use. Programs include research and development, equipment standards and analysis, and technology validation and market introduction.

Environmental Protection Agency (EPA), *Radiation and Indoor Air (ORIA), 1310 L St. N.W., 4th Floor, MC 6601J 20005; (202) 343-9320. Fax, (202) 343-2395. Michael P. Flynn, Director.*
Web, www2.epa.gov/aboutepa/about-office-air-and-radiation-oar#oria

Establishes standards for measuring radon; develops model building codes for state and local governments; provides states and building contractors with technical assistance and training on radon detection and mitigation.

Oversees the Radiation and Indoor Environments Laboratory in Las Vegas, Nev.

Federal Housing Administration (FHA) *(Housing and Urban Development Dept.), Manufactured Housing Programs, 451 7th St. S.W., #9168 20410-8000; (202) 708-6409. Fax, (202) 708-4213. Henry S. Czauski, Deputy Administrator, Acting. Consumer complaints, (800) 927-2891.*
General email, mhs@hud.gov
Web, http://portal.hud.gov/hudportal/HUD?src=/ program_offices/housing/rmra/mhs/mhshome

Establishes and maintains standards for selection of new materials and methods of construction; evaluates technical suitability of products and materials; develops uniform, preemptive, and mandatory national standards for manufactured housing; enforces standards through design review and quality control inspection of factories; administers a national consumer protection program. Handles dispute resolution.

Housing and Urban Development Dept. (HUD), *Healthy Homes and Lead Hazard Control, 451 7th St. S.W., #8236 20410; (202) 708-0310. Fax, (202) 708-0014. Jon L. Gant, Director.*
Web, www.hud.gov/offices/lead

Advises HUD offices, other agencies, health authorities, and the housing industry on lead poisoning prevention. Develops regulations for lead-based paint; conducts research; makes grants to state and local governments for lead hazard reduction and inspection of housing.

National Institute of Building Sciences, *1090 Vermont Ave. N.W., #700 20005-4950; (202) 289-7800. Fax, (202) 289-1092. Henry L. Green, President.*
General email, nibs@nibs.org
Web, www.nibs.org

Public-private partnership authorized by Congress to improve the regulation of building construction, facilitate the safe introduction of innovative building technology, and disseminate performance criteria and other technical information.

National Institute of Standards and Technology (NIST) *(Commerce Dept.), Engineering Laboratory, 100 Bureau Dr., MS 8600, Gaithersburg, MD 20899-8600; (301) 975-5900. Fax, (301) 975-4032. Howard H. Harary, Director, Acting.*
General email, el@nist.gov
Web, www.nist.gov/el

Performs analytical, laboratory, and field research in the area of building technology and its applications for building usefulness, safety, and economy; produces performance criteria and evaluation, test, and measurement methods for building owners, occupants, designers, manufacturers, builders, and federal, state, and local regulatory authorities.

U.S. Fire Administration *(Homeland Security Dept.), 16825 S. Seton Ave., Emmitsburg, MD 21727; (301) 447-1000. Fax, (301) 447-1270. Ernest Mitchell Jr., Administrator, (202) 646-4223.*
Web, www.usfa.fema.gov

Conducts research and collects, analyzes, and disseminates data on combustion, fire prevention, firefighter safety, and the management of fire prevention organizations; studies and develops arson prevention programs and fire prevention codes; maintains the National Fire Data System.

▶ **NONGOVERNMENTAL**

American Society of Civil Engineers (ASCE), *1801 Alexander Bell Dr., Reston, VA 20191-4400;* ***Washington Office****, 101 Constitution Ave., #375E 20001; (202) 789-7850. Fax, (202) 789-7859. Patrick Natale, Executive Director. Toll-free, (800) 548-2723. Government Relations, (202) 789-7850. Press, (703) 295-6406.*
Web, www.asce.org

Membership: professionals and students in civil engineering. Develops standards by consensus for construction documents and building codes, and standards for civil engineering education, licensure, and ethics. Organizes international conferences; maintains technical and professional reference materials; hosts e-learning sites. Advocates for improvements in public infrastructure; monitors legislation and regulations.

American Society of Heating, *Refrigerating, and Air Conditioning Engineers, Government Affairs, 1828 L St. N.W., #810 20036-5104; (202) 833-1830. Fax, (202) 833-0118. Douglas E. (Doug) Read, Director; Mark Ames, Manager.*
General email, washdc@ashrae.org
Web, www.ashrae.org

Membership: engineers and other involved with the heating, ventilation, air conditioning, and refrigeration industry in the United States and abroad, including students. Sponsors research, meetings, and educational activities. Develops industry standards; publishes technical data. Monitors legislation and regulations.

Assn. of Pool and Spa Professionals, *2111 Eisenhower Ave., #500, Alexandria, VA 22314-4698; (703) 838-0083. Fax, (703) 549-0493. Rich Gottwald, President.*
General email, MemberServices@apsp.org
Web, www.apsp.org

Membership: manufacturers, dealers and retailers, service companies, builders, and distributors of pools, spas, and hot tubs. Promotes the industry; provides educational programs for industry professionals; establishes standards for construction and safety. Monitors legislation and regulations.

Center for Auto Safety, *1825 Connecticut Ave. N.W., #330 20009-5708; (202) 328-7700. Fax, (202) 387-0140. Clarence Ditlow, Executive Director.*
General email, accounts@autosafety.org
Web, www.autosafety.org

Monitors Federal Trade Commission warranty regulations and HUD implementation of federal safety and construction standards for manufactured mobile homes.

Home Innovation Research Labs, *400 Prince George's Blvd., Upper Marlboro, MD 20774; (301) 249-4000. Fax, (301) 430-6180. Michael Luzier, President. Toll-free, (800) 638-8556.*
Web, www.homeinnovation.com

Conducts contract research and product labeling and certification for U.S. industry, government, and trade associations related to home building and light commercial industrial building. Interests include energy conservation, new technologies, international research, public health issues, affordable housing, special needs housing for the elderly and persons with disabilities, building codes and standards, land development, and environmental issues. (Independent subsidiary of the National Assn. of Home Builders [NAHB].)

International Code Council, *500 New Jersey Ave. N.W., 6th Floor 20001-2070; (202) 370-1800. Fax, (202) 783-2348. Dominic Sims, Chief Executive Officer. Toll-free, (888) 422-7233.*
Web, www.iccsafe.org

Membership association dedicated to building safety and sustainability. Develops codes used to construct residential and commercial buildings, including homes and schools. Offers "green" standards accreditation for businesses providing energy-efficient and sustainable infrastructure.

National Fire Protection Assn., *Government Affairs, 1401 K St. N.W., #500 20005; (202) 898-0222. Fax, (202) 898-0044. Gregory B. Cade, Director.*
General email, wdc@nfpa.org
Web, www.nfpa.org

Membership: individuals and organizations interested in fire protection. Develops and updates fire protection codes and standards; sponsors technical assistance programs; collects fire data statistics. Monitors legislation and regulations. (Headquarters in Quincy, Mass.)

Materials and Labor

▶ **NONGOVERNMENTAL**

American Coatings Assn., *1500 Rhode Island Ave. N.W. 20005; (202) 462-6272. Fax, (202) 462-8549. J. Andrew Doyle, President, (202) 462-3932.*
General email, aca@paint.org
Web, www.paint.org

Membership: paint and coatings manufacturers, raw materials suppliers, distributors, and other industry professionals. Provides educational and public outreach programs for the industry; interests include health, safety, and the environment. Monitors legislation and regulations.

American Forest and Paper Assn., *Government Affairs, 1101 K St. N.W., #700 20005; (202) 463-2700. Fax, (202) 463-2471. Elizabeth Bartheld, Vice President, Government Affairs; Donna Harman, President.*

General email, info@afandpa.org

Web, www.afandpa.org

Membership: wood and specialty products manufacturers and those in related associations. Interests include tax, housing, environmental, international trade, natural resources, and land-use issues that affect the wood and paper products industry.

Architectural Woodwork Institute, 46179 Westlake Dr., #120, Potomac Falls, VA 20165-5874; (571) 323-3636. Fax, (571) 323-3630. Philip Duvic, Executive Vice President.

General email, info@awinet.org

Web, www.awinet.org

Membership: architectoral woodworkers, suppliers, design professionals, and students. Promotes the use of architectural woodworking; establishes industry standards; conducts seminars and workshops.

Asbestos Information Assn./North America, P.O. Box 2227, Arlington, VA 22202-9227; (703) 560-2980. Fax, (703) 560-2981. B.J. Pigg, President.

General email, aiabjpigg@aol.com

Membership: firms that manufacture, sell, and use products containing asbestos fiber and those that mine, mill, and sell asbestos. Provides information on asbestos and health and on industry efforts to eliminate problems associated with asbestos dust; serves as liaison between the industry and federal and state governments.

Asphalt Roofing Manufacturers Assn., 529 14th St. N.W., #750 20045; (202) 591-2450. Fax, (202) 591-2445. Reed Hitchcock, Executive Vice President.

General email, arma@kellencompany.com

Web, www.asphaltroofing.org

Membership: manufacturers of bitumen-based roofing products. Assists in developing local building codes and standards for asphalt roofing products. Provides technical information; supports research. Monitors legislation and regulations.

Assn. of the Wall and Ceiling Industries, 513 W. Broad St., #210, Falls Church, VA 22046-3257; (703) 538-1600. Fax, (703) 534-8307. Steven A. Etkin, Executive Vice President.

Web, www.awci.org

Membership: contractors and suppliers working in the wall and ceiling industries. Sponsors conferences and seminars. Monitors legislation and regulations.

Brick Industry Assn., 1850 Centennial Park Dr., #301, Reston, VA 20191-1542; (703) 620-0010. Fax, (703) 620-3928. Raymond W. Leonhard, President, (703) 674-1537.

General email, brickinfo@bia.org

Web, www.gobrick.com

Membership: manufacturers and distributors of clay brick. Provides technical expertise and assistance; promotes bricklaying vocational education programs; maintains collection of technical publications on brick masonry construction. Monitors legislation and regulations.

Building Systems Councils of the National Assn. of Home Builders, 1201 15th St. N.W., 7th Floor 20005-2800; (202) 266-8357. Fax, (202) 266-8141. Donna Peak, Executive Director. Toll-free, (800) 368-5242, ext. 8357.

Web, www.nahb.org/buildingsystems

Membership: manufacturers and suppliers of home building products and services. Represents all segments of the industry. Assists in developing National Assn. of Home Builders policies regarding building codes, legislation, and government regulations affecting manufacturers of model-code-complying, factory-built housing (includes concrete, log, modular, and panelized); sponsors educational programs; conducts plant tours of member operations.

Composite Panel Assn., 19465 Deerfield Ave., #306, Leesburg, VA 20176; (703) 724-1128. Fax, (703) 724-1588. Thomas A. Julia, President; Chad Campbell, Director of Communications.

General email, ccampbell@cpamail.org

Web, www.pbmdf.com

Membership: manufacturers of particleboard, medium-density fiberboard, and hardboard in North America. Promotes use of these materials; conducts industry education; offers a certification program for recycled and low emitting products (Environmentally Preferable Products). Monitors legislation and regulations.

Door and Hardware Institute, 14150 Newbrook Dr., #200, Chantilly, VA 20151-2232; (703) 222-2010. Fax, (703) 222-2410. Jerry S. Heppes, Chief Executive Officer.

General email, info@dhi.org

Web, www.dhi.org

Membership: companies and individuals that manufacture or distribute doors and related fittings. Promotes the industry. Interests include building security, life safety and exit devices, and compliance with the Americans with Disabilities Act. Monitors legislation and regulations.

Gypsum Assn., 6525 Belcrest Rd., #480, Hyattsville, MD 20782; (301) 277-8686. Fax, (301) 277-8747. Michael A. Gardner, Executive Director.

General email, info@gypsum.org

Web, www.gypsum.org

Membership: manufacturers of gypsum wallboard and plaster. Assists members, code officials, builders, designers, and others with technical problems and building code questions; publishes Fire Resistance Design Manual referenced by major building codes; conducts safety programs for member companies. Monitors legislation and regulations.

Hardwood, Plywood, and Veneer Assn., 1825 Michael Faraday Dr., Reston, VA 20190-5350; (703) 435-2900. Fax, (703) 435-2537. Clifford (Kip) Howlett, President.

General email, hpva@hpva.org

Web, www.hpva.org

Membership: manufacturers, distributors, wholesalers, suppliers, and sales agents of hardwood, plywood, veneer, and laminated wood floor. Disseminates business information; sponsors workshops and seminars; issues certifications; conducts research.

International Assn. of Bridge, Structural, Ornamental, and Reinforcing Iron Workers, *1750 New York Ave. N.W., #400 20006; (202) 383-4800. Fax, (202) 638-4856. Walter W. Wise, President.*
General email, iwmagazine@iwintl.org

Web, www.ironworkers.org

Membership: approximately 140,000 iron workers. Helps members negotiate pay, benefits, and better working conditions; conducts training programs and workshops. Monitors legislation and regulations. (Affiliated with the AFL-CIO.)

International Assn. of Heat and Frost Insulators and Allied Workers, *9602 Martin Luther King Hwy., Lanham, MD 20706-1839; (301) 731-9101. Fax, (301) 731-5058. James A. Grogan, General President.*
General email, hfi@insulators.org

Web, www.insulators.org

Membership: approximately 18,000 workers in insulation industries. Helps members negotiate pay, benefits, and better working conditions; conducts training programs and workshops. Monitors legislation and regulations. (Affiliated with the AFL-CIO.)

International Brotherhood of Boilermakers, Iron Ship Builders, Blacksmiths, Forgers, and Helpers, Government Affairs, *1750 New York Ave. N.W., #335 20006; (202) 756-2868. Fax, (202) 756-2869. Bridget P. Martin, Director, Political Affairs; Cecile Conroy, Director, Legislative Affairs.*
General email, bmartin@boilermakers.org

Web, www.boilermakers.org

Membership: approximately 80,000 workers in construction, repair, maintenance, manufacturing, and related industries in the United States and Canada. Helps members negotiate pay, benefits, and better working conditions; conducts training programs and workshops. Monitors legislation and regulations. (Headquarters in Kansas City, Kan.; affiliated with the AFL-CIO.)

International Brotherhood of Electrical Workers (IBEW), *900 7th St. N.W. 20001; (202) 833-7000. Fax, (202) 728-7676. Edwin D. Hill, President; Salvatore J. Chilia, Secretary-Treasurer.*
General email, web@ibew.org

Web, www.ibew.org

Helps members negotiate pay, benefits, and better working conditions; conducts training programs and workshops. Monitors legislation and regulations. (Affiliated with the AFL-CIO.)

International Brotherhood of Teamsters, *25 Louisiana Ave. N.W. 20001-2198; (202) 624-6800. Fax, (202) 624-6918. James P. Hoffa, General President; Fred McLuckie, Director, Federal Legislation and Regulation, (202) 624-8741. Press, (202) 624-6911.*

General email, feedback@teamster.org

Web, www.teamster.org

Membership: more than 1.4 million workers in the transportation and construction industries, factories, offices, hospitals, warehouses, and other workplaces. Helps members negotiate pay, benefits, and better working conditions; conducts training programs and workshops. Monitors legislation and regulations.

International Union of Bricklayers and Allied Craftworkers, *620 F St. N.W. 20004; (202) 783-3788. Fax, (202) 393-0219. James Boland, President. Toll-free, (888) 880-8222.*
General email, askbac@bacweb.org

Web, www.bacweb.org

Membership: bricklayers, stonemasons, and other skilled craftworkers in the building industry. Helps members negotiate pay, benefits, and better working conditions; conducts training programs and workshops. Monitors legislation and regulations. (Affiliated with the AFL-CIO and the International Masonry Institute.)

International Union of Operating Engineers, *1125 17th St. N.W. 20036; (202) 429-9100. Fax, (202) 778-2613. James T. Callahan, General President.*
Web, www.iuoe.org

Membership: approximately 400,000 operating engineers, including heavy equipment operators, mechanics, and surveyors in the construction industry, and stationary engineers, including operations and building maintenance staff. Helps members negotiate pay, benefits, and better working conditions; conducts training programs and workshops. Monitors legislation and regulations. (Affiliated with the AFL-CIO.)

International Union of Painters and Allied Trades, *7234 Parkway Dr., Hanover, MD 21076; (410) 564-5900. Fax, (866) 656-4160. Kenneth Rigmaiden, General President.*
General email, mail@iupat.org

Web, www.iupat.org

Membership: more than 140,000 painters, glaziers, floor covering installers, signmakers, show decorators, and workers in allied trades in the United States and Canada. Helps members negotiate pay, benefits, and better working conditions; conducts training programs and workshops. Monitors legislation and regulations. (Affiliated with the AFL-CIO.)

Kitchen Cabinet Manufacturers Assn., *1899 Preston White Dr., Reston, VA 20191-5435; (703) 264-1690. Fax, (703) 620-6530. C. Richard Titus, Executive Vice President.*
General email, info@kcma.org

Web, www.kcma.org

Represents cabinet manufacturers and suppliers to the industry. Provides government relations, management statistics, marketing information, and plant tours. Administers cabinet testing and certification programs.

National Concrete Masonry Assn., *13750 Sunrise Valley Dr., Herndon, VA 20171-4662; (703) 713-1900. Fax, (703) 713-1910. Robert D. Thomas, President.*
General email, ncma@ncma.org
Web, www.ncma.org

Membership: producers of concrete masonry and suppliers of related goods and services. Conducts research; provides members with technical, marketing, government relations, and communications assistance.

National Glass Assn. (NGA), *1945 Old Gallows Rd., #750, Vienna, VA 22182; (703) 442-4890. Fax, (703) 442-0630. Philip J. James, President. Toll-free, (866) 342-5642.*
Web, www.glass.org

Membership: companies in flat (architectural and automotive) glass industry. Provides education and training programs to promote quality workmanship, ethics, and safety standards in the architectural, automotive, and window and door glass industries. Acts as a clearinghouse for information and links professionals with job listings, suppliers, and technical support. Monitors legislation and regulations.

National Insulation Assn. (NIA), *12100 Sunset Hills Rd., #330, Reston, VA 20190-3233; (703) 464-6422. Fax, (703) 464-5896. Michele M. Jones, Executive Vice President, ext. 119.*
General email, niainfo@insulation.org
Web, www.insulation.org

Membership: open-shop and union contractors, distributors, laminators, fabricators, and manufacturers that provide thermal insulation, insulation accessories, and components to the commercial, mechanical, and industrial markets. Provides information to members on industry trends and technologies. Monitors legislation and regulations.

National Lumber and Building Material Dealers Assn., *2025 M St. N.W., #800 20036-3309; (202) 367-1169. Fax, (202) 367-2169. Michael O'Brien, President.*
General email, info@dealer.org
Web, www.dealer.org

Membership: federated associations of retailers in the lumber and building material industries. Provides statistics training and networking opportunities to members. Monitors legislation and regulations.

North American Insulation Manufacturers Assn., *11 Canal Center Plaza, #103, Alexandria, VA 22314; (703) 684-0084. Fax, (703) 684-0427. Angus Crane, President.*
General email, insulation@naima.org
Web, www.naima.org

Membership: manufacturers of insulation products for use in homes, commercial buildings, and industrial facilities. Provides information on the use of insulation for thermal efficiency, sound control, and fire safety; monitors research in the industry. Interests include energy efficiency and sustainability. Monitors legislation and regulations.

Operative Plasterers' and Cement Masons' International Assn. of the United States and Canada, *11720 Beltsville Dr., #700, Beltsville, MD 20705; (301) 623-1000. Fax, (301) 623-1032. Patrick D. Finley, President.*

General email, opcmiaintel@opcmia.org
Web, www.opcmia.org

Membership: approximately 58,000 cement masons and plasterers. Helps members negotiate pay, benefits, and better working conditions; conducts training programs and workshops. Monitors legislation and regulations. (Affiliated with the AFL-CIO.)

Portland Cement Assn., *500 New Jersey Ave. N.W., 7th Floor 20001-2066; (202) 408-9494. Fax, (202) 408-0877. Gregory M. (Greg) Scott, President.*
Web, www.cement.org

Membership: producers of portland cement. Monitors legislation and regulations.

Roof Coatings Manufacturers Assn., *529 14th St. N.W., #750 20045; (202) 591-2452. Fax, (202) 591-2445. John Ferraro, Executive Director, (202) 207-0919.*
General email, questions@roofcoatings.org
Web, www.roofcoatings.org

Represents the manufacturers of cold-applied protective roof coatings, cements, and systems, and the suppliers of products, equipment, and services to and for the roof coating manufacturing industry, including energy-efficient roofing.

Sheet Metal Workers International Assn., *1750 New York Ave. N.W., 6th Floor 20006; (202) 783-5880. Fax, (202) 662-0880. Joseph J. Nigro, General President.*
Web, www.smwia.org

Membership: U.S., Puerto Rican, and Canadian workers in the building and construction trades, manufacturing, and the railroad and shipyard industries. Assists members with contract negotiation and grievances; conducts training programs and workshops. Monitors legislation and regulations. (Affiliated with the Sheet Metal and Air Conditioning Contractors' Assn., the AFL-CIO, and the Canadian Labour Congress.)

FIRE PREVENTION AND CONTROL

General

▶**AGENCIES**

Consumer Product Safety Commission (CPSC), *Hazard Identification and Reduction, 4330 East-West Hwy., #611, Bethesda, MD 20814-4408; (301) 987-2472. Fax, (301) 504-0533. George Berlase, Associate Executive Director.*
Web, www.cpsc.gov

Proposes, evaluates, and develops standards and test procedures for safety of consumer products. Reports injuries resulting from use of products.

Forest Service *(Agriculture Dept.), Fire and Aviation Management, 1621 N. Kent St., Arlington, VA 22209 (mailing address: 1400 Independence Ave. S.W., MS 1107, Washington, DC 20250-0003); (202) 205-1483. Fax, (202) 205-1401. Tom Harbour, Director.*
Web, www.fs.fed.us/fire

Responsible for aviation and fire management programs, including fire control planning and prevention, suppression of fires, and the use of prescribed fires. Provides state foresters with financial and technical assistance for fire protection in forests and on rural lands.

National Institute of Standards and Technology (NIST) *(Commerce Dept.), Engineering Laboratory, 100 Bureau Dr., MS 8600, Gaithersburg, MD 20899-8600; (301) 975-5900. Fax, (301) 975-4032. Howard H. Harary, Director, Acting.*
General email, el@nist.gov
Web, www.nist.gov/el

Conducts basic and applied research on fire and fire resistance of construction materials; develops testing methods, standards, design concepts, and technologies for fire protection and prevention.

U.S. Fire Administration *(Homeland Security Dept.), 16825 S. Seton Ave., Emmitsburg, MD 21727; (301) 447-1000. Fax, (301) 447-1270. Ernest Mitchell Jr., Administrator, (202) 646-4223.*
Web, www.usfa.fema.gov

Conducts research and collects, analyzes, and disseminates data on combustion, fire prevention, firefighter safety, and the management of fire prevention organizations; studies and develops arson prevention programs and fire prevention codes; maintains the National Fire Data System.

U.S. Fire Administration *(Homeland Security Dept.), National Fire Academy, 16825 S. Seton Ave., Emmitsburg, MD 21727-8998; (301) 447-1117. Fax, (301) 447-1173. Denis Onieal, Superintendent.*
Web, www.usfa.dhs.gov/nfa

Trains fire officials and related professionals in fire prevention and management, current firefighting technologies, and the administration of fire prevention organizations.

International Assn. of Fire Chiefs, *4025 Fair Ridge Dr., #300, Fairfax, VA 22033-2868; (703) 273-0911. Fax, (703) 273-9363. Mark Light, Executive Director, (703) 537-4808.*
Web, www.iafc.org

Membership: fire service chiefs and chief officers. Conducts research on fire control; testifies before congressional committees. Monitors legislation and regulations affecting fire safety codes.

International Assn. of Fire Fighters, *1750 New York Ave. N.W., #300 20006-5395; (202) 737-8484. Fax, (202) 737-8418. Harold A. Schaitberger, General President.*
General email, pr@iaff.org
Web, www.iaff.org

Membership: more than 298,000 professional firefighters and emergency medical personnel. Assists members with contract negotiation and grievances; conducts training programs and workshops. Monitors legislation and regulations. (Affiliated with the AFL-CIO and the Canadian Labour Congress.)

National Fire Protection Assn., *Government Affairs, 1401 K St. N.W., #500 20005; (202) 898-0222. Fax, (202) 898-0044. Gregory B. Cade, Director.*
General email, wdc@nfpa.org
Web, www.nfpa.org

Membership: individuals and organizations interested in fire protection. Develops and updates fire protection codes and standards; sponsors technical assistance programs; collects fire data statistics. Monitors legislation and regulations. (Headquarters in Quincy, Mass.)

HOUSING

General

Federal Housing Administration (FHA) *(Housing and Urban Development Dept.), Housing Assistance and Grant Administration, 451 7th St. S.W., #6134 20410-8000; (202) 708-3000. Fax, (202) 708-3104. Catherine Brennan, Director.*
Web, http://portal.hud.gov/hudportal/HUD?src=/program_offices/housing/mfh/hsgmfbus/abouthaga

Directs and oversees the housing assistance and grant programs, including project-based Section 8 housing assistance, Section 202/811 capital advance and project rental assistance programs, the Assisted-Living Conversion Program (ALCP), rent supplements, service coordinator, and congregate housing services grant programs.

Federal Housing Administration (FHA) *(Housing and Urban Development Dept.), Housing Assistance Contract Administration Oversight, 451 7th St. S.W., #6151 20410-8000; (202) 708-2677. Fax, (202) 708-1300. Kerry Hickman, Director; Lewis Suiter, Deputy Director.*
Web, http://portal.hud.gov/hudportal/HUD?src=/program_offices/housing/mfh/hsgmfbus/abouthacao

Administers Section 8 contracts and other rental subsidy programs. Ensures that Section 8 subsidized properties meet the department's goal of providing decent, safe, and sanitary housing to low-income families.

Federal Housing Administration (FHA) *(Housing and Urban Development Dept.), Multifamily Housing, 451 7th St. S.W., #6106 20410; (202) 708-2495. Fax, (202) 708-2583. Benjamin T. Metcalf, Deputy Assistant Secretary.*
Web, http://portal.hud.gov/hudportal/HUD?src=/program_offices/housing/mfh/hsgmfbus/aboutdas

Determines risk and administers programs associated with government-insured mortgage programs, architectural procedures, and land development programs for multifamily housing. Administers the Rural Rental Housing Program and the development of congregate housing facilities that provide affordable housing, adequate space for meals, and supportive services.

Federal Housing Administration (FHA) *(Housing and Urban Development Dept.), Single Family Housing,* 451 7th St. S.W., #9282 20410; (202) 708-3175. Fax, (202) 708-2582. Charles S. Coulter, Deputy Assistant Secretary.
Web, http://portal.hud.gov/hudportal/HUD?src=/program_offices/housing/sfh/hsgsingle

Determines risk and administers programs associated with government-insured mortgage programs for single family housing. Administers requirements to obtain and maintain federal government approval of mortgages.

Housing and Urban Development Dept. (HUD), *Entitlement Communities,* 451 7th St. S.W., #7282 20410; (202) 708-1577. Fax, (202) 401-2044. Steve Johnson, Director.
Web, www.hud.gov

Provides entitled cities and counties with block grants to provide housing, community, revitalization, and economic opportunity for low- and moderate-income people.

Housing and Urban Development Dept. (HUD), *Housing,* 451 7th St. S.W., #9100 20410; (202) 708-2601. Fax, (202) 708-1403. Carol J. Galante, Assistant Secretary.
Web, www.hud.gov/offices/hsg/index.cfm

Administers housing programs, including the production, financing, and management of housing; directs preservation and rehabilitation of the housing stock; manages regulatory programs.

Rural Housing Service *(Agriculture Dept.), Housing Programs,* 1400 Independence Ave. S.W., #501, MS 0701 20250-0780; (202) 690-1533. Fax, (202) 690-0500. Richard A. Davis, Administrator, Acting.
Web, www.rurdev.usda.gov/rhs

Makes loans and grants in rural communities (population under 20,000) to low-income borrowers, including the elderly and persons with disabilities, for buying, building, or improving single-family houses. Makes grants to communities for rehabilitating single-family homes.

► **CONGRESS**

For a listing of relevant congressional committees and subcommittees, please see page 382 or the Appendix.

► **NONGOVERNMENTAL**

Center for Housing Policy, 1900 M St. N.W., #200 20036; (202) 466-2121. Fax, (202) 466-2122. Lisa Sturtevant, Executive Director.
General email, nhc@nhc.org
Web, www.nhc.org

Researches and develops fundamentals of housing policy. Seeks to create new policies that integrate housing into overall social and economic goals. Sponsors educational forums and publishes reports (available online). (Research affiliate of the National Housing Conference.)

Enterprise Community Partners, 10227 Wincopin Circle, Columbia, MD 21044; (410) 964-1230. Fax, (410) 964-1376. Terry L. Ludwig, Chief Executive Officer. Toll-free, (800) 624-4298.
Web, www.enterprisecommunity.org

Works with local groups to help provide decent, affordable housing for low-income individuals and families, including green affordable housing. Works to link public transit to affordable housing.

Habitat for Humanity International, *Government Relations and Advocacy,* 1424 K St. N.W., #600 20005; (202) 628-9171. Fax, (202) 628-9169. Elizabeth Blake, Senior Vice President for Legal, Government Relations, and General Counsel.
General email, advocacy@habitat.org
Web, www.habitat.org

Christian ministry that seeks to eliminate poverty housing. Builds and sells homes to low-income families. Monitors legislation and regulations.

Housing Assistance Council, 1025 Vermont Ave. N.W., #606 20005-3516; (202) 842-8600. Fax, (202) 347-3441. Moises Loza, Executive Director.
General email, hac@ruralhome.org
Web, www.ruralhome.org

Operates in rural areas and in cities of fewer than 25,000 citizens. Advises low-income and minority groups seeking federal assistance for improving rural housing and community facilities; studies and makes recommendations for state and local housing policies; makes low-interest loans for housing programs for low-income and minority groups living in rural areas, including Native Americans and farm workers.

National Housing and Rehabilitation Assn., *HousingOnline.com,* 1400 16th St. N.W., #420 20036; (202) 939-1750. Fax, (202) 265-4435. Peter H. Bell, President, (202) 939-1741; Thom Amdur, Executive Director, (202) 939-1753.
General email, info@housingonline.com
Web, www.housingonline.com

Membership: historic rehabilitation businesses, development firms and organizations and city, state, and local agencies concerned with affordable multifamily housing. Monitors government policies affecting multifamily development and rehabilitation.

National Housing Conference (NHC), 1900 M St. N.W., #200 20036; (202) 466-2121. Fax, (202) 466-2122. Chris Estes, President; Lisa Sturtevant, Executive Director, Center.
General email, nhc@nhc.org
Web, www.nhc.org

Membership: state and local housing officials, community development specialists, builders, bankers, lawyers, civic leaders, tenants, architects and planners, labor and religious groups, and national housing and housing-related organizations. Mobilizes public support for community development and affordable housing programs; conducts educational sessions. Supports the Center for Housing Policy, NHC's research affiliate.

National Leased Housing Assn., *1900 L St. N.W., #300 20036; (202) 785-8888. Fax, (202) 785-2008. Denise B. Muha, Executive Director. General email, info@hudnlha.com*

Web, www.hudnlha.com

Membership: public and private organizations and individuals concerned with multifamily, government-assisted housing programs. Conducts training seminars. Monitors legislation and regulations.

National Low Income Housing Coalition, *727 15th St. N.W., 6th Floor 20005; (202) 662-1530. Fax, (202) 393-1973. Sheila Crowley, President, ext. 224. General email, info@nlihc.org*

Web, www.nlihc.org

Membership: organizations and individuals that support low-income housing. Works to end the affordable housing crisis in America. Interests include the needs of the lowest-income people and those who are homeless. Monitors legislation.

National Rural Housing Coalition, *1331 G St. N.W., 10th Floor 20005; (202) 393-5229. Fax, (202) 393-3034. Robert A. Rapoza, Executive Secretary. General email, nrhc@ruralhousingcoalitions.org*

Web, www.ruralhousingcoalition.org

Advocates improved housing for low-income rural families; works to increase public awareness of rural housing problems. Monitors legislation.

Fair Housing, Special Groups

Federal Housing Administration (FHA) *(Housing and Urban Development Dept.), Asset Management, 451 7th St. S.W., #6160 20410; (202) 708-3730. Fax, (202) 401-5978. Mark Van Kirk, Director. Web, http://portal.hud.gov/hudportal/HUD?src=/ program_offices/housing/mfh/hsgmfbus/aboutam*

Oversees HUD management, ownership, and sale of properties, which HUD owns by virtue of default and foreclosure or for which HUD is mortgagee-in-possession.

Housing and Urban Development Dept. (HUD), *Fair Housing and Equal Opportunity, 451 7th St. S.W., #5100 20410-2000; (202) 708-4252. Fax, (202) 708-4483. Bryan Greene, Assistant Secretary, Acting. Housing discrimination hotline, (800) 669-9777. Web, www.hud.gov/offices/fheo/index.cfm*

Monitors compliance with legislation requiring equal opportunities in housing for minorities, persons with disabilities, and families with children. Monitors compliance with construction codes to accommodate people with disabilities in multifamily dwellings. Hotline answers inquiries about housing discrimination.

Housing and Urban Development Dept. (HUD), *Fair Housing Initiative Programs (FHIP), 451 7th St. S.W.,*

#5222 20410; (202) 402-7095. Fax, (202) 708-4886. Myron P. Newry, Director. Web, www.hud.gov

Awards grants to public and private organizations and to state and local agencies. Funds projects that educate the public about fair housing rights; programs are designed to prevent or eliminate discriminatory housing practices; investigates housing discrimination complaints. Administers the Fair Housing Initiative Programs (FHIP).

Justice Dept. (DOJ), *Civil Rights Division, 950 Pennsylvania Ave. N.W., #5643 20530; (202) 514-4609. Fax, (202) 514-0293. Jocelyn Samuels, Assistant Attorney General, Acting, (202) 514-2151. Press, (202) 514-2007. Web, www.justice.gov/crt*

Enforces federal civil rights laws prohibiting discrimination on the basis of race, color, religion, sex, disability, age, or national origin in housing, public accommodations and facilities, and credit and federally assisted programs.

Public and Indian Housing *(Housing and Urban Development Dept.), Native American Programs, 451 7th St. S.W., #4126 20410-5000; (202) 401-7914. Fax, (202) 401-7909. Rodger J. Boyd, Deputy Assistant Secretary, (202) 402-4141. Web, http://portal.hud.gov/hudportal/HUD?src=/ program_offices/public_indian_housing/ih*

Administers federal assistance for Native American tribes. Assistance programs focus on housing and community and economic development through competitive and formula grants. Funds for approved activities are provided directly to tribes or Alaska Native villages or to a tribally designated housing authority.

Rural Development *(Agriculture Dept.), Civil Rights, 1400 Independence Ave. S.W., #1341, MS 0703 20250; (202) 692-0090. Fax, (202) 692-0279. Vacant, Director. Toll-free, (800) 669-9777. Web, www.rurdev.usda.gov/rd_civilrights.html*

Enforces compliance with laws prohibiting discrimination in credit transactions on the basis of sex, marital status, race, color, religion, age, or disability. Ensures equal opportunity in granting Rural Economic and Community Development housing, farm ownership, and operating loans and a variety of community and business program loans.

Leading Age, *2519 Connecticut Ave. N.W. 20008-1520; (202) 783-2242. Fax, (202) 783-2255. William L. (Larry) Minnix, Chief Executive Officer. General email, info@leadingage.org*

Web, www.leadingage.org

Membership: nonprofit nursing homes, housing, and health-related facilities for the elderly. Provides research and technical assistance on housing and long-term care for the elderly. Monitors legislation and regulations. (Formerly the American Assn. of Homes and Services for the Aging.)

B'nai B'rith International, *Center for Senior Services,* *2020 K St. N.W., 7th Floor 20006; (202) 857-6535.* *Fax, (202) 857-2782. Mark D. Olshan, Director.* *General email, seniors@bnaibrith.org*

Web, www.bnaibrith.org

Advocates on behalf of the aging population in America. Works with local groups to sponsor federally assisted housing for independent low-income senior citizens and persons with disabilities, regardless of race or religion.

Center for Community Change, *1536 U St. N.W. 20009; (202) 339-9300. Fax, (202) 387-4892. Deepak Bhargava, Executive Director.* *General email, info@communitychange.org*

Web, www.communitychange.org

Works to strengthen grassroots organizations that help low-income people, working-class people, and minorities develop skills and resources to improve their communities and change the policies and institutions that affect their lives. Monitors legislation and regulations.

National American Indian Housing Council, *900 2nd St. N.E., #107 20002; (202) 789-1754. Fax, (202) 789-1758. David Sanborn, Executive Director. Toll-free, (800) 284-9165.* *General email, info@naihc.net*

Web, www.naihc.net

Membership: Native American housing authorities. Clearinghouse for information on Native American housing issues; works for safe and sanitary dwellings for Native American and Alaska Native communities; monitors policies of the Housing and Urban Development Dept. and housing legislation; provides members with training and technical assistance in managing housing assistance programs.

National Assn. for the Advancement of Colored People (NAACP), *Washington Bureau, 1156 15th St. N.W., #915 20005; (202) 463-2940. Fax, (202) 463-2953. Hilary O. Shelton, Director.* *General email, washingtonbureau@naacpnet.org*

Web, www.naacp.org

Membership: persons interested in civil rights for all minorities. Works to eliminate discrimination in housing and urban affairs. Supports programs that make affordable rental housing available to minorities and that maintain African American ownership of land. (Headquarters in Baltimore, Md.)

National Assn. of Real Estate Brokers, *9831 Greenbelt Rd., #309, Lanham, MD 20706; (301) 552-9340. Fax, (301) 552-9216. Donnell Spivey, President; Michelle Savoy, Executive Assistant.* *General email, nareb3@comcast.net*

Web, www.nareb.com

Membership: minority real estate brokers, appraisers, contractors, property managers, and salespersons. Works to prevent discrimination in housing policies and practices; conducts seminars on contracting and federal policy.

National Council of La Raza, *1126 16th St. N.W., #600 20036-4845; (202) 785-1670. Fax, (202) 776-1792. Janet Murguia, President.* *General email, comments@nclr.org*

Web, www.nclr.org

Helps Hispanic community-based groups obtain funds, develop and build low-income housing and community facilities, and develop and finance community economic development projects; conducts research and provides policy analysis on the housing status and needs of Hispanics; monitors legislation on fair housing and government funding for low-income housing.

National Council on the Aging, *1901 L St. N.W., 4th Floor 20036; (202) 479-1200. Fax, (202) 479-0735. James P. Firman, President. Press, (202) 600-3131. Eldercare Locator, (800) 677-1116.* *General email, info@ncoa.org*

Web, www.ncoa.org

Serves as an information clearinghouse on aging. Works to ensure quality housing for older persons. Monitors legislation and regulations.

Public and Subsidized Housing

▶**AGENCIES**

Public and Indian Housing, *(Housing and Urban Development Dept.), 451 7th St. S.W., #4100 20410-0800; (202) 402-4100. Fax, (202) 619-8478. Sandra B. Henriquez, Assistant Secretary.* *General email, daniella.d.mungo@hud.gov*

Web, http://portal.hud.gov/hudportal/HUD?src=/ program_offices/public_indian_housing

Seeks to ensure that safe, decent, and affordable housing is available to low-income and Native American families, the elderly, and persons with disabilities.

Public and Indian Housing *(Housing and Urban Development Dept.), Housing Voucher Management and Operations, 451 7th St. S.W., #4208 20410; (202) 708-0477. Fax, (202) 708-0690. Milan Ozdinec, Deputy Assistant Secretary.* *Web, http://portal.hud.gov/hudportal/HUD?src=/ program_offices/public_indian_housing*

Administers certificate and housing voucher programs and moderate rehabilitation authorized by Section 8 of the Housing Act of 1937, as amended. Provides rental subsidies to lower-income families.

Public and Indian Housing *(Housing and Urban Development Dept.), Public Housing and Voucher Programs, 451 7th St. S.W., #4204 20410-5000; (202) 708-2815. Fax, (202) 708-0690. Milan M. Ozdinec, Deputy Assistant Secretary, (202) 708-1380. Section 8, (202) 708-0477. Information Service, (202) 708-0744.* *Web, http://portal.hud.gov/hudportal/HUD?src=/ program_offices/public_indian_housing*

Establishes policies and procedures for low-income public housing and rental assistance programs, including special needs for the elderly and disabled, standards for rental and occupancy, utilities and maintenance engineering, and financial management.

Public and Indian Housing *(Housing and Urban Development Dept.), Public Housing Investments, 451 7th St. S.W., #4130 20410-0050; (202) 401-8812. Fax, (202) 401-7910. Dominique Blom, Deputy Assistant Secretary.*
Web, http://portal.hud.gov/hudportal/HUD?src=/ program_offices/public_indian_housing

Establishes development policies and procedures for low-income housing programs, including criteria for site approval and construction standards; oversees administration of the Capital Fund for modernizing existing public housing and the Choice Neighborhood Program. Administers the HOPE VI Program.

▶ NONGOVERNMENTAL

Council of Large Public Housing Authorities, *455 Massachusetts Ave. N.W., #425 20001; (202) 638-1300. Fax, (202) 638-2364. Sunia Zaterman, Executive Director. General email, clpha@clpha.org*
Web, www.clpha.org

Works to preserve and improve public housing through advocacy, research, policy analysis, and public education.

Public Housing Authorities Directors Assn., *511 Capitol Court N.E., #200 20002-4937; (202) 546-5445. Fax, (202) 546-2280. Timothy G. Kaiser, Executive Director. Web, www.phada.org*

Membership: executive directors of public housing authorities. Serves as liaison between members and the Housing and Urban Development Dept. and Congress; conducts educational seminars and conferences. Monitors legislation and regulations.

Urban Institute, *Metropolitan Housing and Communities Policy Center, 2100 M St. N.W. 20037; (202) 833-7200. Fax, (202) 872-8154. Rolf Pendall, Director. General email, publicaffairs@urban.org*
Web, www.urban.org/center/met

Research center that deals with urban problems. Researches housing policy problems, including housing management, public housing programs, finance, and rent control.

REAL ESTATE

General

▶ AGENCIES

Federal Emergency Management Agency (FEMA) *(Homeland Security Dept.), Federal Insurance and Mitigation Administration, 1800 S. Bell St., MS 3020,*

Arlington, VA 22202; (202) 646-2781. Fax, (202) 646-7970. David L. Miller, Associate Administrator.
Web, www.fema.gov/what-mitigation/federal-insurance-mitigation-administration

Administers federal flood insurance programs, including the National Flood Insurance Program. Makes low-cost flood insurance available to eligible homeowners.

Federal Highway Administration (FHWA) *(Transportation Dept.), Planning, Environment, and Realty, 1200 New Jersey Ave. S.E., #E76-306 20590; (202) 366-0116. Fax, (202) 366-3713. Gloria M. Shepherd, Associate Administrator.*
Web, www.fhwa.dot.gov/realestate

Works with developers and municipalities to ensure conformity with the National Environmental Policy Act (NEPA) project development process.

General Services Administration (GSA), *Public Buildings Service, 1800 F St. N.W., #1344 20405; (202) 501-1100. Fax, (202) 219-0856. Dorothy Robyn, Commissioner.*
Web, www.gsa.gov/pbs

Administers the acquisition, construction, maintenance, and operation of buildings owned or leased by the federal government. Manages and disposes of federal real estate.

Housing and Urban Development Dept. (HUD), *Affordable Housing Programs, 451 7th St. S.W., #7164 20410; (202) 708-2684. Fax, (202) 708-1744. Virginia Sardone, Director, Acting.*
Web, www.hud.gov/hudportal/HUD?src=/program_offices/comm_planning/affordablehousing

HOME program helps to expand the supply of decent, affordable housing for low- and very low–income families by providing grants to states and local governments to help renters, new homebuyers, or existing homeowners. SHOP program provides funds for nonprofit organizations to purchase home sites and develop or improve the infrastructure needed to facilitate sweat equity and volunteer-based homeownership programs for low-income families.

Small Business Administration (SBA), *Disaster Assistance, 409 3rd St. S.W., #6050 20416; (202) 205-6734. Fax, (202) 205-7728. James Rivera, Associate Administrator. Call center, (800) 659-2955.*
Web, www.sba.gov/about-offices-content/1/2462

Provides victims of physical disasters with disaster and economic injury loans for homes, businesses, and personal property. Lends funds for uncompensated losses incurred from any disaster declared by the president of the United States or the administrator of the SBA. Lends funds to individual homeowners, business concerns of all sizes, and nonprofit institutions to repair or replace damaged structures and furnishings, business machinery, equipment, and inventory. Provides economic injury loans to small businesses for losses to meet necessary operating expenses, provided the business could have paid these expenses prior to the disaster.

▶ CONGRESS

For a listing of relevant congressional committees and sub-committees, please see page 382 or the Appendix.

▶ NONGOVERNMENTAL

American Land Title Assn., *1828 L St. N.W., #705 20036-5104; (202) 296-3671. Fax, (202) 223-5843. Michelle L. Korsmo, Chief Executive Officer. General email, service@alta.org*

Web, www.alta.org

Membership: land title insurance underwriting companies, abstracters, lawyers, and title insurance agents. Searches, reviews, and insures land titles to protect real estate investors, including home buyers and mortgage lenders; provides industry information. Monitors legislation and regulations.

American Resort Development Assn., *1201 15th St. N.W., #400 20005; (202) 371-6700. Fax, (202) 289-8544. Howard Nusbaum, President.*

Web, www.arda.org

Membership: U.S. and international developers, builders, financiers, marketing companies, and others involved in resort, recreational, and community development. Serves as an information clearinghouse; monitors federal and state legislation.

American Society of Appraisers (ASA), *11107 Sunset Hills Rd., #310, Reston, VA 20190; (703) 478-2228. Fax, (703) 742-8471. Jim Hirt, Executive Vice President. Toll-free, (800) 272-8258.*

General email, asainfo@appraisers.org

Web, www.appraisers.org

Membership: accredited appraisers of real property, including land, houses, and commercial buildings; business valuation; machinery and technical specialties; yachts; aircraft; public utilities; personal property, including antiques, fine art, residential contents; gems and jewelry. Affiliate members include students and professionals interested in appraising. Provides technical information; accredits appraisers; provides consumer information programs.

Appraisal Foundation, *1155 15th St. N.W., #1111 20005; (202) 347-7722. Fax, (202) 347-7727. David S. Bunton, President.*

General email, info@appraisalfoundation.org

Web, www.appraisalfoundation.org

Ensures that appraisers are qualified to offer their services by promoting uniform appraisal standards and establishing education, experience, and examination requirements.

Appraisal Institute, *External Affairs, 122 C St. N.W., #360 20001; (202) 298-6449. Fax, (202) 298-5547. William (Bill) Garber, Director of Government and External Relations.*

General email, insidethebeltway@appraisalinstitute.org

Web, www.appraisalinstitute.org

Provides Congress, regulatory agencies, and the executive branch with information on appraisal matters. (Headquarters in Chicago, Ill.)

Assn. of Foreign Investors in Real Estate, *1300 Pennsylvania Ave. N.W. 20004-3020; (202) 312-1400. Fax, (202) 312-1401. James A. Fetgatter, Chief Executive.*

General email, afireinfo@afire.org

Web, www.afire.org

Represents foreign institutions that are interested in the laws, regulations, and economic trends affecting the U.S. real estate market. Informs the public and the government of the contributions foreign investment makes to the U.S. economy. Examines current issues and organizes seminars for members.

International Real Estate Federation (FIABCI), *U.S. Chapter, 1050 Connecticut Ave. N.W., #1000 20036; (202) 772-3308. Bill Endsley, President.*

General email, info@fiabci-usa.com

Web, www.fiabci.com

Membership: real estate professionals in the fields of appraisal, brokerage, counseling, development, financing, and property management. Sponsors seminars, workshops, and conferences. (International headquarters in Paris.)

Manufactured Housing Institute, *1655 N. Ft. Meyer Dr., #104, Arlington, VA 22209; (703) 558-0400. Fax, (703) 558-0401. Richard A. Jennison, President.*

General email, info@mfghome.org

Web, www.manufacturedhousing.org

Represents community owners and developers, financial lenders, and builders, suppliers, and retailers of manufactured and modular homes. Provides information on manufactured and modular home construction standards, finance, site development, property management, and marketing.

National Assn. of Home Builders (NAHB), *1201 15th St. N.W. 20005-2800; (202) 266-8409. Fax, (202) 266-8400. Gerald M. Howard, Chief Executive Officer. Press, (202) 266-8254. Toll-free, (800) 368-5242.*

Web, www.nahb.org

Membership: contractors, builders, architects, engineers, mortgage lenders, and others interested in home building and residential real estate construction. Offers educational programs and information on housing policy and mortgage finance in the United States.

National Assn. of Real Estate Brokers, *9831 Greenbelt Rd., #309, Lanham, MD 20706; (301) 552-9340. Fax, (301) 552-9216. Donnell Spivey, President; Michelle Savoy, Executive Assistant.*

General email, nareb3@comcast.net

Web, www.nareb.com

Membership: minority real estate brokers, appraisers, contractors, property managers, and salespersons. Works to prevent discrimination in housing policies and practices; conducts seminars on contracting and federal policy.

National Assn. of Real Estate Investment Trusts, *1875 Eye St. N.W., #600 20006-5413; (202) 739-9400. Fax, (202) 739-9401. Steven Wechsler, President. Toll-free, (800) 362-7348.*
Web, www.reit.com

Membership: real estate investment trusts and corporations, partnerships, and individuals interested in real estate securities and the industry. Interests include federal taxation, securities regulation, financial standards and reporting standards and ethics, and housing and education; compiles industry statistics. Monitors federal and state legislation and regulations.

National Assn. of Realtors, *Government Affairs, 500 New Jersey Ave. N.W. 20001-2020; (202) 383-1000. Fax, (202) 383-7580. Jerry Giovaniello, Senior Vice President. Toll-free, (800) 874-6500.*
Web, www.realtor.org

Sets professional standards, trademark regulations, and code of ethics for the real estate business; promotes education, research, and exchange of information. Interests include housing markets, property rights, and federal housing finance and insurance programs and agencies. Monitors legislation and regulations. (Headquarters in Chicago, Ill.)

The Real Estate Roundtable, *801 Pennsylvania Ave. N.W., #720 20004; (202) 639-8400. Fax, (202) 639-8442. Jeffrey D. DeBoer, President.*
General email, info@rer.org
Web, www.rer.org

Membership: real estate owners, advisers, builders, investors, lenders, and managers. Serves as forum for public policy issues, including taxes, energy, homeland security, the environment, capital, credit, and investments.

Society of Industrial and Office Realtors, *1201 New York Ave., #350 20005-6126; (202) 449-8200. Fax, (202) 216-9325. Richard Hollander, Executive Vice President.*
General email, admin@sior.com
Web, www.sior.com

Membership: commercial and industrial real estate brokers worldwide. Certifies brokers; sponsors seminars and conferences; mediates and arbitrates business disputes for members; sponsors a speakers bureau. (Affiliated with the National Assn. of Realtors.)

Mortgages and Finance

▶**AGENCIES**

Comptroller of the Currency *(Treasury Dept.), Chief Counsel, 400 7th St. S.W., Constitution Center 20024;*

(202) 649-5400. Fax, (202) 649-6077. Amy S. Friend, Senior Deputy Comptroller and Chief Counsel.
Web, www.occ.gov

Enforces and oversees compliance by nationally chartered banks with laws prohibiting discrimination in credit transactions on the basis of sex or marital status. Enforces regulations concerning bank advertising; may issue cease-and-desist orders.

Consumer Financial Protection Bureau (CFPB), *1700 G St. N.W. 20552; (202) 435-7000. Richard Cordray, Director. RESPA enquiries, (855) 411-2372.*
General email, info@consumerfinance.gov
Web, www.consumerfinance.gov

Responsible for helping home buyers become better shoppers for settlement services and eliminating kickbacks and referral fees that unnecessarily increase the costs of certain settlement services. Administers the Interstate Land Sales Full Disclosure Act, which requires land developers who sell undeveloped land through interstate commerce or the mail to disclose required information about the land to the purchaser prior to signing a sales contract and to file information with the federal government.

Fannie Mae *(Federal Housing Finance Agency), 3900 Wisconsin Ave. N.W. 20016-2892; (202) 752-7000. Fax, (202) 649-1071. Timothy J. Mayopoulos, Chief Executive Officer. Information for consumers, (800) 732-6643. Press, (202) 752-7351.*
General email, andrew_j_wilson@fanniemae.com
Web, www.fanniemae.com and www.fhfa.gov

Congressionally chartered, shareholder-owned corporation under conservatorship of the Federal Housing Finance Agency. Makes mortgage funds available by buying conventional and government-insured mortgages in the secondary mortgage market; raises capital through sale of short- and long-term obligations, mortgages, and stock; issues and guarantees mortgage-backed securities; administers the mortgage fraud program. (Fannie Mae stands for Federal National Mortgage Assn.)

Farmer Mac, *1999 K St. N.W., 4th Floor 20036; (202) 872-7700. Fax, (202) 872-7713. Timothy Buzby, President. Toll-free, (800) 879-3276.*
Web, www.farmermac.com

Private corporation chartered by Congress to provide a secondary mortgage market for farm and rural housing loans. Guarantees principal and interest repayment on securities backed by farm and rural housing loans. (Farmer Mac stands for Federal Agricultural Mortgage Corp.)

Federal Housing Administration (FHA) *(Housing and Urban Development Dept.), Multifamily Housing Development, 451 7th St. S.W., #6136 20410-8000; (202) 708-1142. Fax, (202) 708-3104. Theodore K. Toon, Director.*
Web, http://portal.hud.gov/hudportal/HUD?src=/program_offices/housing/mfh/hsgmfbus/aboutmfd

Federal Housing Finance Agency

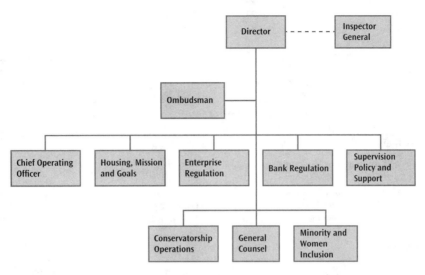

- - - - - Indicates a support or advisory relationship with the unit rather than a direct reporting relationship

Establishes procedures for the origination of FHA-insured mortgages for multifamily housing. Administers the mortgage insurance programs for rental, cooperative, and condominium housing, nursing homes, and assisted living systems.

Federal Housing Administration (FHA) *(Housing and Urban Development Dept.), Single Family Program Development, 451 7th St. S.W., #9278 20410-8000; (202) 708-2121. Fax, (202) 401-9713. Karen Hill, Director.*
Web, http://portal.hud.gov/hudportal/HUD?src=/ program_offices/housing/dirhousi

Establishes procedures for mortgage insurance programs related to the purchase or rehabilitation of single family homes.

Federal Housing Administration (FHA) *(Housing and Urban Development Dept.), Title I Insurance, 451 7th St. S.W., #9266 20410; (202) 708-2121. Fax, (202) 708-4308. Arlene Nunes, Director.*
Web, http://portal.hud.gov/hudportal/HUD?src=/ program_offices/housing/sfh/title/ti_home

Sets policy for Title I loans on manufactured home and property improvement loans. Provides information to borrowers and lenders on policy issues.

Federal Housing Finance Agency (FHFA), *400 7th St. 20024; (202) 649-3800. Fax, (202) 649-1071. Edward J. DeMarco, Director, Acting.*
General email, fhfainfo@fhfa.gov
Web, www.fhfa.gov

Regulates and works to ensure the financial soundness of Fannie Mae (Federal National Mortgage Assn.), Freddie Mac (Federal Home Loan Mortgage Corp.), and the twelve Federal Home Loan banks. FHFA was formed by a legislative merger of the Office of Federal Housing Enterprise Oversight (OFHEO), the Federal Housing Finance Board, and HUD's Government-sponsored Enterprise (GSE) mission team.

Federal Housing Finance Agency (FHFA), *Enterprise Regulation, 400 7th St. 20024; (202) 649-3809. Fax, (202) 649-1609. Jon D. Greenlee, Deputy Director.*
General email, DeputyDirector-Enterprises@FHFA.gov
Web, www.fhfa.gov

Responsible for ensuring that Fannie Mae and Freddie Mac are adequately capitalized and operate in a safe and sound manner. Supervision includes programs for accounting and disclosure, capital adequacy, examination, financial analysis, and supervision infrastructure.

Federal Housing Finance Agency (FHFA), *Federal Home Loan Bank Registration (FHLBank Regulation), 400 7th St. 20024; (202) 649-3808. Fax, (202) 649-1608. Fred Graham, Deputy Director.*
General email, DeputyDirector-FHLBanks@FHFA.gov
Web, www.fhfa.gov/webfiles/2654/ 2.1overviewoftheFHLbanksystem_1.pdf

Responsible for ensuring that the Federal Home Loan Banks operate in a fiscally sound manner, have adequate capital, and are able to raise funds in capital markets. Conducts safety and soundness examinations, Affordable Housing Program examinations, examination and supervisory policy and program development, FHLBank analysis, risk modeling, risk monitoring and information management, and risk analysis and research.

Freddie Mac *(Federal Housing Finance Agency)*, *8200 Jones Branch Dr., McLean, VA 22102-3100; (703) 903-2000. Fax, (703) 903-3495. Donald H. Layton, Chief Executive Officer. Press, (703) 903-3933. Homeowners hotline, (888) 995-4673.*
Web, www.freddiemac.com and www.fhfa.gov

Chartered by Congress to support homeownership and rental housing by increasing the flow of funds for residential mortgages and mortgage-related securities. Issues mortgage passthrough securities and debt instruments in capital markets toward this end. (Freddie Mac stands for Federal Home Loan Mortgage Corp.)

Ginnie Mae *(Housing and Urban Development Dept.)*, *550 12th St. S.W., 3rd Floor 20024 (mailing address: 451 7th St. S.W., #B-133, Washington, DC 20410); (202) 708-0926. Fax, (202) 485-0206. Theodore W. Tozer, President; Mary K. Kinney, Executive Vice President. Hotline, (888) 446-6434.*
Web, www.ginniemae.gov

Supports government housing objectives by establishing secondary markets for multi- and single-family residential, hospital, and nursing home mortgages. Serves as a vehicle for channeling funds from the capital markets into the mortgage market through mortgage-backed securities programs and helps to increase the supply of credit available for housing. Guarantees privately issued securities backed by Federal Housing Administration, Veterans Affairs Dept., Farmers Home Administration, USDA Rural Development, and HUD's Office of Public and Indian Housing mortgages. (Ginnie Mae stands for Government National Mortgage Assn.)

Housing and Urban Development Dept. (HUD), *Housing, 451 7th St. S.W., #9100 20410; (202) 708-2601. Fax, (202) 708-1403. Carol J. Galante, Assistant Secretary.*
Web, www.hud.gov/offices/hsg/index.cfm

Administers all Federal Housing Administration (FHA) mortgage insurance programs; approves and monitors all lending institutions that conduct business with HUD.

▶**CONGRESS**

For a listing of relevant congressional committees and subcommittees, please see page 382 or the Appendix.

▶**NONGOVERNMENTAL**

American Bankers Assn. (ABA), *1120 Connecticut Ave. N.W. 20036; (202) 663-5000. Fax, (202) 663-7578. Frank Keating, President. Information, 800-BANKERS.*
General email, custserv@aba.com
Web, www.aba.com

Membership: insured depository institutions involved in finance, including community banking. Provides information on issues that affect the industry. Monitors economic issues affecting savings institutions; publishes real estate lending survey. Monitors legislation and regulations. (America's Community Bankers merged with the American Banking Assn.)

Center for Responsible Lending, *Washington Office, 910 17th St. N.W., #500 20006; (202) 349-1850. Fax, (202) 289-9009. Michael Calhoun, President.*
Web, www.responsiblelending.org

Seeks to protect homeownership and family wealth by working to eliminate abusive financial practices. Conducts studies on lending practices, assists consumer attorneys, and provides information to policymakers. Provides a Web-based archive of information for public use. Monitors legislation and regulations at state and federal levels.

Mortgage Bankers Assn., *1919 M St. N.W., 5th Floor 20036; (202) 557-2700. Fax, (202) 408-4961. David Stevens, President.*
Web, www.mba.org

Membership: institutions involved in real estate finance. Maintains School of Mortgage Banking; collects statistics on the industry. Conducts seminars and workshops in specialized areas of mortgage finance. Monitors legislation and regulations.

National Assn. of Affordable Housing Lenders, *1667 K St. N.W., #210 20006; (202) 293-9850. Fax, (202) 293-9852. Judith A. Kennedy, President.*
General email, naahl@naahl.org
Web, www.naahl.org

Membership: lenders who specialize in providing private capital for affordable housing and community development in low- and moderate-income areas. Serves as an information clearinghouse; provides education, training, and direct technical assistance. Monitors legislation and regulations.

National Assn. of Consumer Advocates, *1730 Rhode Island Ave. N.W., #710 20036; (202) 452-1989. Fax, (202) 452-0099. Ira J. Rheingold, Executive Director.*
General email, info@naca.net
Web, www.naca.net

Membership: consumer advocate attorneys. Seeks to protect the rights of consumers from fraudulent, abusive, and predatory business practices. Provides consumer law training through conferences and publications. Monitors legislation and regulations on banking, credit, and housing laws.

National Assn. of Local Housing Finance Agencies, *2025 M St. N.W., #800 20036-3309; (202) 367-1197. Fax, (202) 367-2197. John C. Murphy, Executive Director.*
General email, info@nalhfa.org
Web, www.nalhfa.org

Membership: professionals of city and county governments that finance affordable housing. Provides professional development programs in new housing finance and other areas. Monitors legislation and regulations.

National Council of State Housing Agencies, *444 N. Capitol St. N.W., #438 20001; (202) 624-7710. Fax, (202) 624-5899. Barbara J. Thompson, Executive Director.*
General email, info@ncsha.org
Web, www.ncsha.org

Resources for Mortgage Financing and Other Housing Assistance

The following agencies and organizations offer consumer information pertaining to mortgages and other housing issues.

Center for Responsible Lending, Washington office, (202) 349-1850; www.responsiblelending.org

Center on Budget and Policy Priorities, (202) 408-1080; www.cbpp.org

Consumer Federation of America, (202) 387-6121; www.consumerfed.org

Council for Affordable and Rural Housing, (703) 837-9001; www.carh.org

Fannie Mae, (202) 752-7000; www.fanniemae.com

The Finance Project, Economic Success Clearinghouse, (202) 628-4200; www.financeproject.org

Freddie Mac, (703) 903-2000; www.freddiemac.com

Housing and Urban Development Dept., (202) 708-1112; www.hud.gov

Housing Assistance Council, (202) 842-8600; www.ruralhome.org

Mortgage Bankers Assn., (202) 557-2700; www.mbaa.org

National Assn. of Development Companies, (202) 349-0070; www.nadco.org

National Assn. of Home Builders, (202) 266-8200; www.nahb.org

National Assn. of Local Housing Finance Agencies, (202) 367-1197; www.nalhfa.org

National Assn. of Realtors, (800) 874-6500; www.realtor.org

National Council of State Housing Agencies, (202) 624-7710; www.ncsha.org

National Housing Conference, (202) 466-2121; www.nhc.org

National Housing Trust, (202) 333-8931; www.nhtinc.org

National Leased Housing Assn., (202) 785-8888; www.hudnlha.com

National Low Income Housing Coalition, (202) 662-1530; www.nlihc.org

National Reverse Mortgage Lenders Assn., (202) 939-1760; www.reversemortgage.org or www.nrmla.org

NeighborhoodWorks America, (202) 760-4000; www.nw.org

Smart Growth America, (202) 207-3355; www.smartgrowthamerica.org

Urban Institute, (202) 833-7200; www.urban.org

Membership: state housing finance agencies. Promotes greater opportunities for lower-income people to rent or buy affordable housing.

National Reverse Mortgage Lenders Assn., *1400 16th St. N.W., #420 20036; (202) 939-1760. Fax, (202) 265-4435. Peter H. Bell, President, (202) 939-1741. Web, www.nrmlaonline.org*

National trade association for firms that originate, service, and invest in reverse mortgages. Monitors legislation and regulations.

Property Management

▶ **AGENCIES**

Bureau of Land Management (BLM) *(Interior Dept.), Lands, Realty, and Cadastral Survey, 20 M St. S.E. 20003 (mailing address: 1849 C St. N.W., Washington, DC 20240); (202) 912-7300. Fax, (202) 912-7199. Robyn Shoop, Division Chief, Acting. Web, www.blm.gov/wo/st/en/info/directory/WO-350_dir.html*

Oversees use, acquisition, and disposal of public lands. Conducts the Public Lands Survey; authorizes rights-of-

way on public lands for uses that include roads, power lines, and wind and solar facilities.

Federal Housing Administration (FHA) *(Housing and Urban Development Dept.), Asset Management, 451 7th St. S.W., #6160 20410; (202) 708-3730. Fax, (202) 401-5978. Mark Van Kirk, Director. Web, http://portal.hud.gov/hudportal/HUD?src=/program_offices/housing/mfh/hsgmfbus/aboutam*

Oversees HUD management, ownership, and sale of properties, which HUD owns by virtue of default and foreclosure or for which HUD is mortgagee-in-possession.

Federal Housing Administration (FHA) *(Housing and Urban Development Dept.), Procurement Management, 451 7th St. S.W., #2222 20410; (202) 708-4466. Fax, (202) 708-3698. Amelia McCormick, Director. Web, http://portal.hud.gov/hudportal/HUD?src=/program_offices/public_indian_housing/programs/ph/am/prcrmnt*

Develops and implements policies and procedures and conducts contract administration for the Office of Housing and the Federal Housing Administration headquarters' procurement actions.

Real Estate Assessment Center *(Housing and Urban Development Dept.), 550 12th St. S.W., #100 20410; (202)*

475-7949. Fax, (202) 485-0286. Donald J. Lavoy, Deputy Assistant Secretary. Toll-free, (888) 245-4860.
General email, reac_tac@hud.gov
Web, www.hud.gov/reac

Conducts physical inspections and surveys of resident satisfaction in publicly owned, insured, or subsidized housing. Assesses financial condition and management operations of public housing agencies.

►NONGOVERNMENTAL

Building Owners and Managers Assn. International,
1101 15th St. N.W., #800 20005; (202) 408-2662. Fax, (202) 326-6377. Henry Chamberlain, President.
General email, info@boma.org
Web, www.boma.org

Membership: office building owners and managers. Reviews changes in model codes and building standards; conducts seminars and workshops on building operation and maintenance issues; sponsors educational and training programs. Monitors legislation and regulations.

Community Associations Institute, 6402 Arlington Blvd., #500, Falls Church, VA 22042; (703) 970-9220. Fax, (703) 970-9558. Tom Skiva, Chief Executive Officer. Toll-free, (888) 224-4321.
Web, www.caionline.org

Membership: homeowner associations, builders, lenders, owners, managers, realtors, insurance companies, and public officials. Provides members with information on creating, financing, and maintaining common facilities and services in condominiums and other planned developments.

NAIOP Commercial Real Estate Development Assn.,
2201 Cooperative Way, #300, Herndon, VA 20171-3034; (703) 904-7100. Fax, (703) 904-7942.
Thomas J. Bisacquino, President.
Web, www.naiop.org

Membership: developers, planners, designers, builders, financiers, and managers of industrial and office properties. Provides research and continuing education programs. Monitors legislation and regulations on capital gains, real estate taxes, impact fees, growth management, environmental issues, and hazardous waste liability.

National Apartment Assn., 4300 Wilson Blvd., #400, Arlington, VA 22203; (703) 797-0600. Fax, (703) 248-9440.
Doug Culkin, President.
General email, webmaster@naahq.org
Web, www.naahq.org

Membership: state and local associations of owners, managers, investors, developers, and builders of apartment houses or other rental properties. Conducts educational and professional certification programs. Monitors legislation and regulations.

National Assn. of Home Builders (NAHB), 1201 15th St. N.W. 20005-2800; (202) 266-8409. Fax, (202) 266-8400.

Gerald M. Howard, Chief Executive Officer. Press, (202) 266-8254. Toll-free, (800) 368-5242.
Web, www.nahb.org

Membership: contractors, builders, architects, engineers, mortgage lenders, and others interested in home building and residential real estate construction.

National Assn. of Housing and Redevelopment Officials, 630 Eye St. N.W. 20001-3736; (202) 289-3500. Fax, (202) 289-8181. Saul N. Ramirez Jr., Chief Executive. Toll-free, (877) 866-2476.
General email, nahro@nahro.org
Web, www.nahro.org

Membership: housing, community, and urban development practitioners and organizations, and state and local government agencies and personnel. Conducts studies and provides training and certification in the operation and management of rental housing.

National Assn. of Housing Cooperatives, 1444 Eye St. N.W., #700 20005-6542; (202) 737-0797. Fax, (202) 216-9646. Mitch Dvorak, Executive Director.
General email, info@nahc.coop
Web, www.coophousing.org

Membership: housing cooperative professionals and organizations that provide services to housing cooperatives. Promotes housing cooperatives; provides technical assistance in all phases of cooperative housing; sponsors educational programs and on-site training; provides legal service referrals; monitors legislation; maintains an information clearinghouse on housing cooperatives. Online resources include a directory of financial, legal, and management services experts in the housing cooperative community.

National Center for Housing Management, 1801 Old Reston Ave., #203, Reston, VA 20190; (703) 435-9393. Fax, (703) 435-9775. W. Glenn Stevens, President. Toll-free, (800) 368-5625.
General email, service@nchm.org
Web, www.nchm.org

Private corporation created by executive order to meet housing management and training needs. Conducts research, demonstrations, and educational and training programs in all types of multifamily housing management. Develops and implements certification systems for housing management programs.

National Cooperative Business Assn., 1401 New York Ave. N.W., #1100 20005-2160; (202) 638-6222. Fax, (202) 638-1374. Michael Bealle, President.
General email, info@ncba.coop
Web, www.ncba.coop and Twitter, @NCBACLUSA

Alliance of cooperatives, businesses, and state cooperative associations. Provides information about starting and managing housing cooperatives. Monitors legislation and regulations.

National Multi Housing Council, 1850 M St. N.W., #540 20036-5803; (202) 974-2300. Fax, (202) 775-0112.
Douglas Bibby, President.

General email, info@nmhc.org

Web, www.nmhc.org

Membership: owners, financiers, managers, and developers of multifamily housing. Advocates policies and programs at the federal, state, and local levels to increase the supply and quality of multifamily units in the United States; serves as a clearinghouse on rent control, condominium conversion, taxes, fair housing, and environmental issues.

Property Management Assn., *7508 Wisconsin Ave., 4th Floor, Bethesda, MD 20814; (301) 657-9200. Fax, (301) 907-9326. Carole Worley, Executive Director.*

General email, info@pma-dc.org

Web, www.pma-dc.org

Membership: property managers and firms that offer products and services needed in the property management field. Promotes information exchange on property management practices.

12 International Affairs

GENERAL POLICY AND ANALYSIS

Basic Resources

▶AGENCIES

Agency for International Development (USAID), *Conflict Management and Mitigation,* 1300 Pennsylvania Ave. N.W., #7.7131 20523; (202) 712-0121. Neil Levine, Director.
General email, conflict@usaid.gov
Web, http://transition.usaid.gov/our_work/cross-cutting_programs/conflict/about/index.html

Supports USAID's work as it relates to conflict management, fragility, political instability, and extremism. Applies best practices of conflict management to areas such as democracy and governance, economic growth, natural resource management, and peace-building efforts.

Defense Dept. (DoD), *International Security Affairs,* The Pentagon, #3C889 20301-2400; (703) 697-2788. Fax, (703) 697-3279. Derek H. Chollet, Assistant Secretary.
Web, www.defense.gov

Advises the secretary of defense and recommends policies on regional security issues in the Middle East, Africa, Russia/Eurasia, and Europe/NATO.

National Security Staff (NSS) *(Executive Office of the President), International Economic Affairs,* The White House 20504; (202) 456-9281. Fax, (202) 456-9280. Caroline Atkinson, Deputy National Security Adviser.
Web, www.whitehouse.gov/administration/eop/nsc

Advises the president, the National Security Council, and the National Economic Council on all aspects of U.S. foreign policy dealing with U.S. international economic policies.

National Security Staff (NSS) *(Executive Office of the President), Office of Strategic Communications and Speechwriting,* Dwight D. Eisenhower Executive Office Bldg., #302 20500; (202) 456-9271. Fax, (202) 456-9270. Benjamin J. (Ben) Rhodes, Deputy National Security Adviser. Administrative office, (202) 456-9301.
Web, www.whitehouse.gov/administration/eop/nsc

Advises U.S. government agencies on the direction and theme of the president's message. Assists in the development and coordination of communications programs that disseminate consistent and accurate messages about the U.S. government and policies to the global audience.

President's Foreign Intelligence Advisory Board *(Executive Office of the President),* New Executive Office Bldg., #5020 20502; (202) 456-2352. Fax, (202) 395-3403. Chuck Hagel, Chair; Stefanie R. Osburn, Executive Director.
Web, www.whitehouse.gov/administration/eop/piab

Members appointed by the president. Assesses the quality, quantity, and adequacy of foreign intelligence collection and of counterintelligence activities by all government agencies; advises the president on matters concerning intelligence and national security.

State Dept., 2201 C St. N.W. 20520; (202) 647-4000. Fax, (202) 647-3344. John F. Kerry, Secretary, (202) 647-5291; William J. Burns, Deputy Secretary. Press, (202) 647-2492.
Web, www.state.gov

Directs and coordinates U.S. foreign relations and interdepartmental activities of the U.S. government overseas.

State Dept., *Civilian Security, Democracy, and Human Rights,* 2201 C St. N.W., #7261 20520; (202) 647-6240. Fax, (202) 647-0753. Vacant, Under Secretary.
Web, www.state.gov

Advises the secretary on transnational issues. Divisions include Democracy, Human Rights, and Labor; International Narcotics and Law Enforcement; Conflict and Stabilization Operations; Population, Refugees, and Migration; Counter-terrorism; Global Criminal Justice; Monitor and Combat Trafficking in Persons; and Global Youth Issues.

State Dept., *Consular Affairs,* 2201 C St. N.W., #6826 20520-4818; (202) 647-9576. Fax, (202) 647-9622. Janice L. Jacobs, Assistant Secretary. National Passport Information Center (fees are charged for calls to this number), (877) 487-2778 with credit card. Assistance to U.S. citizens overseas, (888) 407-4747 during business hours or (202) 647-5225 after hours.
Web, http://travel.state.gov

Issues passports to U.S. citizens and visas to immigrants and nonimmigrants seeking to enter the United States. Provides protection, assistance, and documentation for U.S. citizens abroad.

State Dept., *Intelligence and Research,* 2201 C St. N.W., #6468 20520-6531; (202) 647-9177. Fax, (202) 736-4688. Philip S. Goldberg, Assistant Secretary.
Web, www.state.gov

Coordinates foreign policy–related research, analysis, and intelligence programs for the State Dept. and other federal agencies.

State Dept., *International Conferences,* 2201 C St. N.W., SA-1, Room H-436 20520-6319; (202) 663-1026. Fax, (202) 663-1042. Richard Weston, Director.
Web, www.state.gov

Coordinates U.S. participation in multilateral conferences and accredits delegations.

State Dept., *International Organization Affairs,* 2201 C St. N.W., #6323 20520-6319; (202) 647-9600. Fax, (202) 736-4116. H. Dean Pittman, Assistant Secretary, Acting. Press, (202) 647-6899.
General email, io-bureau@state.gov
Web, www.state.gov

Coordinates and develops policy guidelines for U.S. participation in the United Nations and in other international organizations and conferences.

INTERNATIONAL AFFAIRS RESOURCES IN CONGRESS

For a complete listing of Congress committees, including their full contact information, leadership, membership, and jurisdictions, please refer to the Appendix on pages 724–842.

HOUSE:

House Agriculture Committee, (202) 225-2171.

Web, agriculture.house.gov or democrats.agriculture.house.gov

Subcommittee on Horticulture, Research, Biotechnology, and Foreign Agriculture, (202) 225-2171.

House Armed Services Committee, (202) 225-4151.

Web, armedservices.house.gov or democrats.armedservices.house.gov

Subcommittee on Strategic Forces, (202) 225-1967.

House Appropriations Committee, (202) 225-2771.

Web, appropriations.house.gov or democrats.appropriations.house.gov

Subcommittee on Commerce, Justice, Science, and Related Agencies, (202) 225-3351.

Subcommittee on Interior, Environment, and Related Agencies, (202) 225-3081.

Subcommittee on State, Foreign Operations, and Related Programs, (202) 225-2041.

House Energy and Commerce Committee, (202) 225-2927.

Web, energycommerce.house.gov or democrats.energycommerce.house.gov

Subcommittee on Commerce, Manufacturing, and Trade, (202) 225-2927.

House Financial Services Committee, (202) 225-7502.

Web, financialservices.house.gov or democrats.financialservices.house.gov

Subcommittee on Monetary Policy and Trade, (202) 225-7502.

House Foreign Affairs Committee, (202) 225-5021.

Web, foreignaffairs.house.gov or democrats.foreignaffairs.house.gov

Tom Lantos Human Rights Commission, (202) 226-3599.

Subcommittee on Africa, Global Health, Global Human Rights, and International Organizations, (202) 226-7812.

Subcommittee on Asia and the Pacific, (202) 226-7825.

Subcommittee on Europe, Eurasia, and Emerging Threats, (202) 226-6434.

Subcommittee on the Middle East and North Africa, (202) 225-3345.

Subcommittee on Terrorism, Nonproliferation and Trade, (202) 226-1500.

Subcommittee on the Western Hemisphere, (202) 226-9980.

House Homeland Security Committee, (202) 226-8417.

Web, homeland.house.gov or chsdemocrats.house.gov

Subcommittee on Border and Maritime Security, (202) 226-8417.

House Judiciary Committee, (202) 225-3951.

Web, judiciary.house.gov or democrats.judiciary.house.gov

Subcommittee on Crime, Terrorism and Homeland Security, and Investigations, (202) 225-5727.

Subcommittee on Immigration and Border Security, (202) 225-3926.

House Natural Resources Committee, (202) 225-2761.

Web, naturalresources.house.gov or democrats.naturalresources.house.gov

Subcommittee on Fisheries, Wildlife, Oceans, and Insular Affairs, (202) 226-0200.

House Oversight and Government Reform Committee, (202) 225-5074.

Web, oversight.house.gov or democrats.oversight.house.gov

Subcommittee on National Security, (202) 225-5074.

House Science, Space, and Technology Committee, (202) 225-6371.

Web, science.house.gov or democrats.science.house.gov

Subcommittee on Research and Technology, (202) 225-6371.

Subcommittee on Space, (202) 225-6371.

House Small Business Committee, (202) 225-5821.

Web, smallbusiness.house.gov or democrats.smallbusiness.house.gov

Subcommittee on Agriculture, Energy, and Trade, (202) 225-5821.

Subcommittee on Economic Growth, Tax, and Capital Access, (202) 225-5821.

House Permanent Select Committee on Intelligence, (202) 225-4121.
Web, intelligence.house.gov
House Transportation and Infrastructure Committee, (202) 225-9446.
Web, transportation.house.gov or democrats.transportation.house.gov
Subcommittee on Coast Guard and Maritime Transportation, (202) 226-3552.
House Ways and Means Committee, (202) 225-3625.
Web, waysandmeans.house.gov or democrats.waysandmeans.house.gov
Subcommittee on Trade, (202) 225-6649.

JOINT:
Joint Economic Committee, (202) 224-5171.
Web, jec.senate.gov/public/ or jec.senate.gov/republicans/public/

SENATE:
Senate Agriculture, Nutrition, and Forestry Committee, (202) 224-2035.
Web, ag.senate.gov
Subcommittee on Commodities, Markets, Trade, and Risk Management, (202) 224-2035.
Subcommittee on Nutrition, Specialty Crops, Food, and Agricultural Research, (202) 224-2035.
Senate Appropriations Committee, (202) 224-7363.
Web, appropriations.senate.gov
Subcommittee on Commerce, Justice, Science, and Related Agencies, (202) 224-5202.
Subcommittee on Interior, Environment, and Related Agencies, (202) 228-0774.
Subcommittee on State, Foreign Operations, and Related Programs, (202) 224-7363.
Senate Armed Services Committee, (202) 224-3871.
Web, armed-services.senate.gov
Subcommittee on Seapower, (202) 224-3871.
Senate Banking, Housing, and Urban Affairs Committee, (202) 224-7391.
Web, banking.senate.gov
Subcommittee on National Security and International Trade and Finance, (202) 224-2023.
Senate Commerce, Science, and Transportation Committee, (202) 224-0411.
Web, commerce.senate.gov

Subcommittee on Oceans, Atmosphere, Fisheries and the Coast Guard, (202) 224-4912.
Senate Energy and Natural Resources Committee, (202) 224-4971.
Web, energy.senate.gov
Senate Finance Committee, (202) 224-4515.
Web, finance.senate.gov
Subcommittee on International Trade, Customs, and Global Competitiveness, (202) 224-4515.
Senate Foreign Relations Committee, (202) 224-4651.
Web, foreign.senate.gov
Subcommittee on African Affairs, (202) 224-4651.
Subcommittee on East Asian and Pacific Affairs, (202) 224-4651.
Subcommittee on European Affairs, (202) 224-4651.
Subcommittee on International Development and Foreign Assistance, Economic Affairs, International Environmental Protection, and Peace Corps, (202) 224-4651.
Subcommittee on International Operations and Organizations, Human Rights, Democracy, and Global Women's Issues, (202) 224-4651.
Subcommittee on Near Eastern and South and Central Asian Affairs, (202) 224-4651.
Subcommittee on Western Hemisphere and Global Narcotics Affairs, (202) 224-4651.
Senate Homeland Security and Governmental Affairs Committee, (202) 224-2627.
Web, hsgac.senate.gov
Permanent Subcommittee on Investigations, (202) 224-9505.
Senate Judiciary Committee, (202) 224-7703.
Web, judiciary.senate.gov
Subcommittee on Crime and Terrorism, (202) 228-3740.
Subcommittee on Immigration, Refugees, and Border Security, (202) 224-6498.
Subcommittee on Privacy, Technology, and the Law, (202) 228-3177.
Senate Small Business and Entrepreneurship Committee, (202) 224-5175.
Web, sbc.senate.gov

State Dept., *Management,* 2201 C St. N.W., #7207 20520; (202) 647-1500. Fax, (202) 647-0168. Patrick F. Kennedy, Under Secretary.
Web, www.state.gov

Serves as principal adviser to the secretary on management matters, including budgetary, administrative, and personnel policies of the department and the Foreign Service.

State Dept., *Policy Planning Staff,* 2201 C St. N.W., #7311 20520; (202) 647-2972. Fax, (202) 647-0844. David McKean, Director.
Web, www.state.gov

Advises the secretary and other State Dept. officials on foreign policy matters.

State Dept., *Political Affairs,* 2201 C St. N.W., #7250 20520; (202) 647-0995. Fax, (202) 647-4780. Wendy R. Sherman, Under Secretary.
Web, www.state.gov

Assists in the formulation and conduct of foreign policy and in the overall direction of the department; coordinates interdepartmental activities of the U.S. government abroad.

State Dept., *Public Diplomacy and Public Affairs,* 2201 C St. N.W., #5932 20520; (202) 647-9199. Fax, (202) 647-9140. Richard Stengel, Under Secretary.
Web, www.state.gov

Seeks to broaden public affairs discussion on foreign policy with U.S. citizens, media, and institutions. Provides cultural and educational exchange opportunities and international information programs to people in the United States and abroad.

State Dept., *Public Diplomacy and Public Affairs, Bureau of Educational and Cultural Affairs,* 2200 C St. N.W., SA-5 20522; (202) 632-6445. Fax, (202) 632-2701. Carmen G. Cantor, Executive Director.
Web, www.state.gov

Seeks to promote mutual understanding between the people of the United States and other countries through international educational and training programs. Promotes personal, professional, and institutional ties between private citizens and organizations in the United States and abroad; presents U.S. history, society, art, and culture to overseas audiences.

U.S. Institute of Peace, 2301 Constitution Ave. N.W. 20037; (202) 457-1700. Fax, (202) 429-6063. Stephen J. Hadley, Chair; Kristin Lord, President, Acting. Press, (202) 429-4725.
General email, info@usip.org
Web, www.usip.org

Independent, nonpartisan institution established by Congress. Aims to prevent and resolve violent international conflicts, promote postconflict stability, and increase peace-building capacity, tools, and intellectual capital worldwide.

► **CONGRESS**

For a listing of relevant congressional committees and subcommittees, please see pages 414–415 or the Appendix.

Government Accountability Office (GAO), *International Affairs and Trade,* 441 G St. N.W., #4T21 20548; (202) 512-4128. Loren Yager, Managing Director.
Web, www.gao.gov

Independent, nonpartisan agency in the legislative branch. Audits, analyzes, and evaluates international programs; makes unclassified reports available to the public.

House Democracy Partnership Commission, 227 CHOB 20515; (202) 225-4561. Fax, (202) 225-1166. Rep. Peter Roskam, Chair; Mike Dankler, Staff Director, (202) 225-5021.
General email, democracy@mail.house.gov
Web, http://hdac.house.gov

Provides advice to members and staff of parliaments of select countries that have established or are developing democratic governments.

Library of Congress, *Serial and Government Publications,* 101 Independence Ave. S.E., #LM133 20540; (202) 707-5690. Teri Sierra, Assistant Chief. Reference Desk, (202) 707-5208. Current periodical reading room, (202) 707-5690.
Web, www.loc.gov/rr/news

Collects and maintains information on governmental and nongovernmental organizations that are domestically or internationally based, financed, and sponsored. Responds to written or telephone requests to provide information on the history, structure, operation, and activities of these organizations. Collects and maintains domestic and foreign newspapers and periodicals. Some microfilm materials are available for interlibrary loan through the Library of Congress CALM Division.

► **INTERNATIONAL ORGANIZATIONS**

European Parliament Liaison Office, 2175 K St. N.W., 6th Floor 20037; (202) 862-4730. Antione Ripoll, Director.
General email, epwashington@ep.europarl.eu
Web, www.europarl.europa.eu/us

Acts as the contact point between the European Parliament and the U.S. government. Seeks to intensify working relations between the European Parliament and the U.S. Congress at all levels, particularly between corresponding committees of jurisdiction, and between European Parliament lawmakers and U.S. regulators. Represents the Parliament's viewpoint to the U.S. administration and Congress.

European Union, *Delegation to the United States of America,* 2175 K St. N.W., #800 20037-1400; (202) 862-9500. Fax, (202) 429-1766. João Vale de Almeida, Ambassador.
General email, delegation-usa-info@eeas.europa.eu
Web, www.eurunion.org

State Department

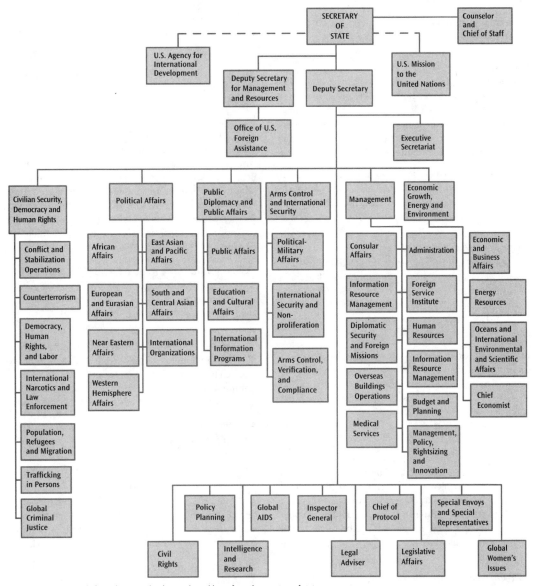

— — — Denotes independent agencies that receive guidance from the secretary of state

Provides information on European Union energy policy, initiatives, research activities, and selected statistics. (Headquarters in Brussels.)

International Bank for Reconstruction and Development *(World Bank), 1818 H St. N.W. 20433; (202) 473-1000. Fax, (202) 477-6391. Hon. KimJim Yong, President; Vacant, U.S. Executive Director. Press, (202) 473-7660. Bookstore, (202) 458-4500. Anticorruption hotline, (800) 831-0463.*
General email, gchopra@worldbank.org

Web, www.worldbank.org

International development institution funded by government membership subscriptions and borrowings on private capital markets. Encourages the flow of public and private foreign investments into developing countries through loans, grants, and technical assistance. Finances foreign economic development projects in agriculture, environmental protection, education, public utilities, telecommunications, water supply, sewerage, public health, and other areas.

International Crisis Group, *Washington Office, 1629 K St. N.W., #450 20006; (202) 785-1601. Fax, (202) 785-1630. Mark L. Schneider, Senior Vice President.*
General email, washington@crisisgroup.org

Web, www.crisisgroup.org

Private, multinational organization that seeks to prevent international conflict. Writes and distributes reports and raises funds. (Headquarters in Brussels.)

International Monetary Fund (IMF), *700 19th St. N.W. 20431; (202) 623-7000. Fax, (202) 623-4661. Christine Lagarde, Managing Director; Meg Lundsager, U.S. Executive Director.*
Web, www.imf.org

International organization of 187 member countries that promotes policies for financial stability and economic growth, works to prevent financial crises, and helps members solve balance-of-payments problems through loans funded by member contributions.

Organisation for Economic Co-operation and Development (OECD), *Washington Center, 2001 L St. N.W., #650 20036-4922; (202) 785-6323. Fax, (202) 312-2508. Jill A. Schuker, Deputy, Washington Office.*
General email, washington.contact@oecd.org
Web, www.oecd.org

Membership: thirty-four nations, including Australia, Canada, Japan, Mexico, New Zealand, the United States, and western European nations. Serves as a forum for government officials to exchange information on their countries' policies. The Washington Center maintains a reference library open to the public. (Headquarters in Paris.)

Organization of American States (OAS), *17th St. and Constitution Ave. N.W. 20006 (mailing address: 1889 F St. N.W., Washington, DC 20006); (202) 458-3000. Fax, (202) 458-3967. José Miguel Insulza, Secretary General. Library, (202) 458-6041.*
General email, ai@oas.org
Web, www.oas.org

Membership: the United States, Canada, and all independent Latin American and Caribbean countries. Funded by quotas paid by member states and by contributions to special multilateral funds. Works to promote democracy, eliminate poverty, and resolve disputes among member nations. Provides member states with technical and advisory services in cultural, educational, scientific, social, and economic areas. Library open to the public.

United Nations Information Centre, *1775 K St. N.W., #400 20006-1500; (202) 331-8670. Fax, (202) 331-9191. Rodney Bent, Director.*
General email, unicdc@unic.org
Web, www.unicwash.org

Lead United Nations (UN) office in Washington. Serves as a resource for information and materials about the United Nations. Houses a collection of UN official documents (which includes General Assembly, Economic & Social Council, and Security Council documents), which can be accessed on a case-by-case basis by contacting the office.

▶ **NONGOVERNMENTAL**

American Enterprise Institute (AEI), *Foreign and Defense Policy Studies, 1150 17th St. N.W., #1100 20036;*
(202) 862-5800. Fax, (202) 862-7177. Danielle Pletka, Vice President.
Web, www.aei.org

Research and educational organization that conducts conferences, seminars, and debates and sponsors research on international affairs.

Aspen Institute, *1 Dupont Circle N.W., #700 20036-7133; (202) 736-5800. Fax, (202) 467-0790. Walter Isaacson, President. Press, (202) 736-3849.*
General email, info@aspeninstitute.org
Web, www.aspeninstitute.org

Educational and policy studies organization. Promotes consideration of the public good in a wide variety of policy areas, including international relations and homeland security, business and economic development, education, energy, and the environment. Working with international partners, offers educational seminars, nonpartisan policy forums, public conferences and events, and leadership development initiatives.

Assn. on Third World Affairs, Inc., *1717 K St. N.W., #600 20036; (202) 973-0157. Fax, (202) 775-7465. Lorna Hahn, Executive Director.*
General email, info@atwa.org
Web, www.atwa.org

Membership: individuals and groups interested in developing nations and nations in transition. Promotes research projects; arranges lectures and conferences; holds Capitol Hill conference series featuring ambassadors, members of Congress, and other distinguished persons.

Atlantic Council, *1030 15th St. N.W., 12th Floor 20005; (202) 463-7226. Fax, (202) 463-4590. Frederick Kempe, President.*
General email, info@atlanticcouncil.org
Web, www.atlanticcouncil.org

Conducts studies and makes policy recommendations on U.S. foreign security and international economic policies in the Atlantic and Pacific communities; sponsors conferences and educational exchanges.

The Brookings Institution, *Foreign Policy Studies, 1775 Massachusetts Ave. N.W. 20036; (202) 797-6000. Fax, (202) 797-6004. Ted Piccone, Director. Press, (202) 797-6105.*
Web, www.brookings.edu/foreign-policy.aspx

Conducts studies on foreign policy, national security, regional and global affairs, and economic policies. Includes four policy centers: Saban Center for Middle East Policy, the Center for Northeast Asian Policy Studies, the Center on the United States and Europe, and the John L. Thornton China Center.

Carnegie Endowment for International Peace, *Washington Office, 1779 Massachusetts Ave. N.W. 20036; (202) 483-7600. Fax, (202) 483-1840. Jessica T. Mathews, President.*
General email, info@carnegieendowment.org
Web, www.carnegieendowment.org

Global network of policy research centers in Russia, China, Europe, the Middle East, and the United States. Conducts research on international affairs and U.S. foreign policy. Program activities cover a broad range of military, political, and economic issues; sponsors panel discussions.

Center for Strategic and International Studies, *1616 Rhode Island Ave. N.W., 20036; (202) 887-0200. Fax, (202) 775-3199. John J. Hamre, Chief Executive Officer. Publications, (800) 462-6420.*
Web, www.csis.org

A bipartisan organization that seeks to advance global security and prosperity by providing strategic insights and practical policy solutions to decision makers. Expertise includes defense and international security, emerging global issues, and regional transformation.

Center for the Advanced Study of Language *(University of Maryland), 7005 52nd Ave., College Park, MD 20742; (301) 226-8900. Fax, (301) 226-8811. Amy Weinberg, Executive Director.*
General email, info@casl.umd.edu
Web, www.casl.umd.edu

Works to improve the performance of foreign language professionals in the federal government. Joint venture with the National Security Agency; collaborates with government agencies. Conducts research, conferences, and workshops on topics such as Arabic media and detecting deception in language and cultural context.

Center for the National Interest, *1025 Connecticut Ave. N.W., #1200 20036-5651; (202) 887-1000. Fax, (202) 887-5222. Dimitri K. Simes, President; Paul J. Saunders, Executive Director.*
General email, mail@nixoncenter.org
Web, www.cftni.org

Works to develop new principles for U.S. global engagement and security; energy security and climate change; immigration and national security; and U.S. relations with China, Japan, Mexico, and Russia. Publishes a bimonthly magazine. (Formerly the Nixon Center; affiliated with the Richard Nixon Library and Birthplace Foundation.)

Center of Concern, *1225 Otis St. N.E. 20017; (202) 635-2757. Fax, (202) 832-9494. Lester A. Myers, President, (202) 421-1181.*
General email, coc@coc.org
Web, www.coc.org

Independent, interdisciplinary organization that conducts social analysis, theological reflection, policy advocacy, and public education on issues of international justice and peace.

Charles F. Kettering Foundation, *Washington Office, 444 N. Capitol St. N.W., #434 20001-1512; (202) 393-4478. Fax, (202) 393-7644. David Mathews, President.*
Web, www.kettering.org

Works to improve the domestic policy-making process through citizen deliberation. Supports international programs focusing on unofficial, citizen-to-citizen diplomacy. Encourages greater citizen involvement in formation of

public policy. Interests include public education and at-risk youths. (Headquarters in Dayton, Ohio.)

Citizens Network for Foreign Affairs (CNFA), *1828 L St. N.W., #710 20036; (202) 296-3920. Fax, (202) 296-3948. John H. Costello, President.*
General email, info@cnfa.org
Web, www.cnfa.org

Public policy and education organization that works to involve Americans in the foreign policy process. Advocates a more collaborative partnership between the public and private sectors to promote global economic growth.

Council on Foreign Relations, *Washington Office, 1777 F St. N.W. 20006; (202) 509-8400. Fax, (202) 509-8490. Richard Haass, President.*
General email, communications@cfr.org
Web, www.cfr.org

Promotes understanding of U.S. foreign policy and international affairs. Awards research grants through its International Affairs Fellowship Program. (Headquarters in New York.)

David S. Wyman Institute for Holocaust Studies, *1200 G St. N.W., #800 20005; (202) 434-8994. Rafael Medoff, Director.*
General email, rafaelmedoff@aol.com
Web, www.wymaninstitute.org

Educates the public about U.S. response to Nazism and the Holocaust through scholarly research, public events and exhibits, publications, conferences, and educational programs.

Eisenhower Institute, *818 Connecticut Ave. N.W., 8th Floor 20006; (202) 628-4444. Fax, (202) 628-4445. Jeffrey M. Blavatt, Executive Director; Susan Eisenhower, Chair Emeritus.*
General email, ei@eisenhowerinstitute.org
Web, www.eisenhowerinstitute.org

Nonpartisan research and educational organization modeled on President Eisenhower's legacy of public policy formation and leadership, stressing pursuit of facts, respectful dialogue, and a focus on the future. Provides scholarships, fellowships, internships, and other sponsored opportunities for students to participate in dialogue with prominent figures and to pursue study of public policy and related fields. (Affiliated with Gettysburg College in Gettysburg, Pa.)

Freedom House, *1301 Connecticut Ave. N.W., 6th Floor 20036; (202) 296-5101. Fax, (202) 293-2840. David J. Kramer, President.*
General email, info@freedomhouse.org
Web, www.freedomhouse.org

Promotes civil society; democratic governance; women's rights; LGBTI rights; elections; intergovernmental bodies; free markets; the rule of law; independent media, including Internet freedom; and U.S. engagement in international affairs through education, advocacy, and training initiatives. Collects and analyzes data on political rights and civil liberties worldwide; publishes comparative surveys and reports; sponsors conferences and training programs.

Friends Committee on National Legislation (FCNL), *245 2nd St. N.E. 20002-5795; (202) 547-6000. Fax, (202) 547-6019. Diane Randall, Executive Secretary. Toll-free, (800) 630-1330. Recorded information, (202) 547-4343.*
General email, fcnl@fcnl.org
Web, www.fcnl.org

Seeks to broaden public interest and affect legislation and policy concerning regional and global institutions, peace processes, international development, and the work of the United Nations. (Affiliated with the Religious Society of Friends [Quakers].)

Global Solutions.org, *420 7th St. S.E. 20003; (202) 546-3950. Don Kraus, Chief Executive Officer, (202) 330-4103.*
General email, info@globalsolutions.org
Web, www.globalsolutions.org

Encourages U.S. global engagement on a broad range of foreign policy issues, including UN reform, international law and justice, health and the environment, international institutions, and peace and security.

International Foundation for Electoral Systems (IFES), *1850 K St. N.W., 5th Floor 20006; (202) 350-6700. Fax, (202) 350-6701. William R. (Bill) Sweeney, President.*
General email, media@ifes.org
Web, www.ifes.org

Nonpartisan organization providing professional support to electoral democracies, both emerging and mature. Through field work and applied research and advocacy, strives to promote citizen participation, transparency, and accountability in political life and civil society.

Institute for Foreign Policy Analysis, *1725 DeSales St. N.W., #402 20036; (202) 463-7942. Fax, (202) 785-2785. Robert L. Pfaltzgraff Jr., President.*
General email, dcmail@ifpa.org
Web, www.ifpa.org

Trains policy analysts in the fields of foreign policy and national security. Sponsors research and workshops.

Institute for Policy Studies, *1112 16th St. N.W., #600 20036; (202) 234-9382. Fax, (202) 387-7915. John Cavanagh, Director.*
General email, info@ips-dc.org
Web, www.ips-dc.org

Research and educational organization. Interests include foreign policy, peace, the economy, and the environment.

Institute of International Education, *National Security Education Program, 1400 K St. N.W., 7th Floor 20005-2403 (mailing address: P.O. Box 20010, Arlington, VA 22209); (703) 696-1991. Fax, (703) 696-5667. Michael Nugent, Director. Information, (800) 618-6737.*
General email, nsep@nsep.gov
Web, www.nsep.gov

Administers Boren Awards and Language Flagship programs; provides scholarships, fellowships, and institutional grants to students and academics with an interest in foreign affairs and national security.

Institute of World Politics, *1521 16th St. N.W. 20036-1464; (202) 462-2101. Fax, (202) 464-0335. John Lenczowski, President. Toll-free, (888) 566-9497.*
General email, info@iwp.edu
Web, www.iwp.edu

Offers master's degree in national security, international affairs, foreign policy, methods of statecraft, and comparative political culture.

International Center, *1001 North Carolina Ave. S.E. 20003 (mailing address: P.O. Box 41720, Arlington, VA 22204); (202) 285-4328. Virginia Foote, President.*
General email, theinternationalcenter@theintlcenter.org
Web, www.theintlcenter.org

Research, advocacy, and aid organization concerned with U.S. foreign policy in developing countries. Project arms include trade and investment between the United States and Vietnam, reforestation and agroforestry training in Central America and the Caribbean, rehabilitation services and equipment for Cambodians with disabilities, landmine clearance and school upgrades in Vietnam, and youth sports exchange programs.

International Republican Institute (IRI), *1225 Eye St. N.W., #700 20005-3987; (202) 408-9450. Fax, (202) 408-9462. Mark Green, President.*
General email, info@iri.org
Web, www.iri.org

Created under the National Endowment for Democracy Act. Fosters democratic self-rule through closer ties and cooperative programs with political parties and other nongovernmental institutions overseas.

National Democratic Institute for International Affairs (NDI), *455 Massachusetts Ave. N.W., 8th Floor 20001-2621; (202) 728-5500. Kenneth Wollack, President. Toll-free fax, (888) 875-2887.*
General email, contactndi@ndi.org
Web, www.ndi.org

Conducts nonpartisan international programs to help maintain and strengthen democratic institutions worldwide. Focuses on party building, governance, and electoral systems.

National Endowment for Democracy, *1025 F St. N.W., #800 20004; (202) 378-9700. Fax, (202) 378-9407. Carl Gershman, President; J. William (Bill) Leonard, Chief Operating Officer.*
General email, info@ned.org
Web, www.ned.org

Grant-making organization that receives funding from Congress. Awards grants to private organizations involved in democratic development abroad, including the areas of democratic political processes; pluralism; and education, culture, and communications.

National Security Archive, *Gelman Library, George Washington University, 2130 H St. N.W., #701 20037; (202) 994-7000. Fax, (202) 994-7005. Thomas Blanton, Director.*
General email, nsarchiv@gwu.edu
Web, www.nsarchive.org

Research institute and library that provides information on U.S. foreign and economic policy and national security affairs. Maintains and publishes collection of declassified and unclassified documents obtained through the Freedom of Information Act. Archive open to the public by appointment.

Paul H. Nitze School of Advanced International Studies, *1740 Massachusetts Ave. N.W. 20036; (202) 663-5600. Fax, (202) 663-5656. Vali Nasr, Dean. Press, (202) 663-5626.*
Web, www.sais-jhu.edu

Offers graduate and nondegree programs in international relations, economics, public policy, regional and functional studies, and foreign languages. Sponsors the Johns Hopkins Foreign Policy Institute and several other research centers. (Affiliated with Johns Hopkins University.)

Pew Global Attitudes Project, *1615 L St. N.W., #700 20036; (202) 419-4400. Fax, (202) 419-4399. Andrew Kohut, Director.*
General email, info@pewglobal.org
Web, www.pewglobal.org

Conducts public opinion surveys about world affairs and makes results available to journalists, academics, policymakers, and the public. Attempts to gauge attitudes in every region of the world toward globalization, democracy, trade, and other key issues. (A Pew Research Center project.)

U.S. Conference of Catholic Bishops (USCCB), *International Justice and Peace, 3211 4th St. N.E. 20017-1194; (202) 541-3160. Fax, (202) 541-3339. Stephen Colecchi, Director.*
General email, jphdmail@usccb.org
Web, www.usccb.org/about/international-justice-and-peace/

Works with the U.S. State Dept., foreign government offices, and international organizations on issues of peace, justice, and human rights.

Women in International Security, *c/o SIPRI North America, 1111 19th St. N.W., 12th Floor 20036; (202) 552-5401. Chantal de Jonge Oudraat, President.*
General email, info@wiisglobal.org
Web, www.wiisglobal.org

Seeks to advance the role of women in international relations and international peace and security. Maintains a database of women foreign and defense policy specialists worldwide; organizes conferences in the United States and elsewhere; disseminates information on jobs, internships, and fellowships. Has chapters in the United States and international affiliates. (Affiliated with SIPRI North America.)

Women's Foreign Policy Group, *1615 M St. N.W., #210 20036; (202) 429-2692. Fax, (202) 429-2630. Patricia Ellis, President.*
General email, programs@wfpg.org
Web, www.wfpg.org

Promotes women's leadership and women's interests in international affairs professions. Conducts policy programs, mentoring, and research.

Diplomats and Foreign Agents

▶**AGENCIES**

Foreign Service Institute *(State Dept.), 4000 Arlington Blvd., Arlington, VA 22204-1500 (mailing address: U.S. Department of State, Washington, DC 20522-4201); (703) 302-6729. Fax, (703) 302-7227. Nancy McEldowney, Director. Student messages and course information, (703) 302-7144.*
Web, www.state.gov/m/fsi

Provides training for U.S. government personnel involved in foreign affairs agencies, including employees of the State Dept., the Agency for International Development, and the Defense Dept. Includes the Schools of Applied Information Technology, Language Studies, Leadership and Management, and Professional and Area Studies as well as the Transition Center and the Assn. for Diplomatic Studies and Training.

Justice Dept. (DOJ), *Foreign Agents Registration Unit, 600 E St. N.W., #1301 20004; (202) 233-0776. Fax, (202) 233-2147. Heather H. Hunt, Chief.*
General email, fara.public@usdoj.gov
Web, www.fara.gov

Receives and maintains the registration of agents representing foreign countries, companies, organizations, and individuals. Compiles semi-annual report on foreign agent registrations. Foreign agent registration files are open for public inspection.

State Dept., *Career Development and Assignments, 2121 Virginia Ave. N.W., #4100 20007 (mailing address: HR/CDA, Washington, DC 20520-6258); (202) 663-0779. Fax, (202) 647-0277. Kenneth Gross, Director.*
Web, www.state.gov

Coordinates programs related to the professional development of American members of the Foreign Service, including career development and assignment counseling programs, training, and presidential appointments and resignations.

State Dept., *Diplomatic Security Bureau, 2201 C St. N.W., #6316 20520; (202) 647-1493. Fax, (202) 647-0953. Gregory B. Starr, Assistant Secretary.*
General email, DSPublicAffairs@state.gov
Web, www.state.gov

Provides a secure environment for conducting U.S. diplomacy and promoting American interests abroad and in the United States.

State Dept., *Family Liaison,* *2201 C St. N.W., #1239 20520-0108; (202) 647-1076. Fax, (202) 647-1670. Susan Frost, Director. General email, flo@state.gov Web, www.state.gov/m/dghr/flo*

Works to improve the quality of life of U.S. government employees and their family members assigned to, or returning from, a U.S. embassy or consulate abroad. Areas of interest are education and youth, family member employment, and support services for personal and past crises, including evacuations. Manages the worldwide Community Liaison Office program.

State Dept., *Foreign Missions,* *2201 C St. N.W., #2236 20520; (202) 647-3417. Fax, (202) 736-4145. Frederick Ketchem, Deputy Assistant Secretary, Acting. General email, ofminfo@state.gov Web, www.state.gov/ofm*

Regulates the benefits, privileges, and immunities granted to foreign missions and their personnel in the United States on the basis of the treatment accorded U.S. missions abroad and considerations of national security and public safety.

State Dept., *Human Resources,* *2201 C St. N.W., #6218 20520; (202) 647-9898. Fax, (202) 647-5080. Hans G. Klemm, Director General of the Foreign Service and Director of Human Resources, Interim. Web, http://careers.state.gov*

Directs human resource policies of the State Dept. and Foreign Service.

State Dept., *Medical Services,* *2401 E St. N.W., #L218 20522-0102; (202) 663-1649. Fax, (202) 663-1613. Dr. Gary D. Penner, Medical Director. Web, www.state.gov*

Operates a worldwide primary health care system for U.S. citizen employees, and eligible family members, of participating U.S. government agencies. Conducts physical examinations of Foreign Service officers and candidates; provides clinical services; assists with medical evacuation of patients overseas.

State Dept., *Overseas Schools,* *2401 E St. N.W., #H328 20037; (202) 261-8200. Fax, (202) 261-8224. Keith D. Miller, Director. General email, OverseasSchools@state.gov Web, www.state.gov/m/a/os*

Promotes high-quality educational opportunities at the elementary and secondary school levels for dependents of American citizens carrying out the programs and interests of the U.S. government abroad.

State Dept., *Protocol,* *2201 C St. N.W., #1238 20520; (202) 647-4543. Fax, (202) 647-3980. Vacant, Chief. Press, (202) 647-2681. Web, www.state.gov*

Serves as principal adviser to the president, vice president, the secretary, and other high-ranking government officials on matters of diplomatic procedure governed by law or international customs and practice.

▶CONGRESS

For a listing of relevant congressional committees and subcommittees, please see pages 414–415 or the Appendix.

▶NONGOVERNMENTAL

American Foreign Service Assn. (AFSA), *2101 E St. N.W. 20037; (202) 338-4045. Fax, (202) 338-6820. Ian Houston, Executive Director. Press, (202) 944-5501. Toll-free (within the U.S.), (800) 704-2372. General email, member@afsa.org Web, www.afsa.org*

Membership: active and retired foreign service employees of the State Dept., International Broadcasting Board, Agency for International Development, Foreign Commercial Service, and the Foreign Agricultural Service. Offers scholarship programs; maintains club for members; represents active duty foreign service personnel in labor-management negotiations. Seeks to ensure adequate resources for foreign service operations and personnel. Conducts outreach programs to educate the public on diplomacy. Interests include business-government collaboration and international trade. Monitors legislation and regulations related to foreign service personnel and retirees.

Council of American Ambassadors, *888 17th St. N.W., #306 20006-3312; (202) 296-3757. Fax, (202) 296-0926. Timothy A. Chorba, President; Carolyn M. Gretzinger, Executive Director. General email, council@americanambassadors.org Web, www.americanambassadors.org*

Membership: U.S. ambassadors. Seeks to educate the public on foreign policy issues affecting the national interest. Hosts discussions, lectures, and conferences. Offers fellowships for students and foreign service personnel.

Executive Council on Diplomacy, *818 Connecticut Ave. N.W., #1200 20006-2702; (202) 872-8181. Fax, (202) 872-8696. Solveig Spielmann, Executive Director. Web, www.ibgc.com/secretariat.htm*

Brings foreign diplomats from international organizations such as the United Nations and World Bank into contact with their U.S. counterparts. Provides a forum for discussion on issues such as agriculture, international trade, education, and the arts.

Institute for the Study of Diplomacy *(Georgetown University), 1316 36th St. N.W. 20007; (202) 965-5735. Fax, (202) 965-5652. James P. Seevers, Director, Interim. Web, http://isd.georgetown.edu*

Part of the Edmund A. Walsh School of Foreign Service. Focuses on the practical implementation of foreign policy objectives; draws on academic research and the concrete experience of diplomats and other members of the policy community.

Humanitarian Aid

►AGENCIES

Administration for Children and Families (ACF) *(Health and Human Services Dept.), Refugee Resettlement,* 901 D St. S.W., 8th Floor West 20447; (202) 401-9246. Fax, (202) 401-0981. Eskinder Negash, Director.
Web, www.acf.hhs.gov/programs/orr

Directs a domestic resettlement program for refugees; reimburses states for costs incurred in giving refugees monetary and medical assistance; awards funds to voluntary resettlement agencies for providing refugees with monetary assistance and case management; provides states and nonprofit agencies with grants for social services such as English and employment training.

Agency for International Development (USAID), *Democracy, Conflict, and Humanitarian Assistance,* 1300 Pennsylvania Ave. N.W., #8.6-84 20523-8601; (202) 712-0100. Nancy E. Lindborg, Assistant Administrator.
Web, www.usaid.gov/who-we-are/organization/bureaus/bureau-democracy-conflict-and-humanitarian-assistance

Manages U.S. foreign disaster assistance, emergency and developmental food aid, democracy programs, conflict management programs, and programs to assist countries transitioning out of crises. Assists U.S. voluntary organizations, schools, and hospitals abroad. Serves as USAID's liaison to the U.S. military.

Agency for International Development (USAID), *Global Health,* 1300 Pennsylvania Ave. N.W., #3.64 20523-3100; (202) 712-4120. Fax, (202) 216-3485. Ariel Pablos-Méndez, Assistant Administrator.
Web, www.usaid.gov/who-we-are/organization/bureaus/bureau-global-health

Participates in global efforts to stabilize world population growth and support women's reproductive rights. Focus includes family planning; reproductive health care; infant, child, and maternal health; and prevention of sexually transmitted diseases, especially AIDS. Conducts demographic and health surveys; educates girls and women.

Agency for International Development (USAID), *U.S. Foreign Disaster Assistance,* 1300 Pennsylvania Ave. N.W., 8th Floor 20523-8602; (202) 712-0841. Fax, (202) 216-3191. Carol Chan, Director, Acting.
Web, www.usaid.gov/who-we-are/organization/bureaus/bureau-democracy-conflict-and-humanitarian-assistance

Office within the Democracy, Conflict, and Humanitarian Assistance Bureau. Administers disaster relief and preparedness assistance to foreign countries to save lives and alleviate human suffering. Aids displaced persons in disaster situations and helps other countries manage natural disasters and complex emergencies.

Agency for International Development (USAID), *Volunteers for Prosperity (VfP),* 1300 Pennsylvania Ave. N.W. 20523-8600; (202) 712-0076. Fax, (202) 712-0077. Kathleen Hunt, Director, Acting.

General email, volunteersforprosperity@usaid.gov
Web, www.volunteersforprosperity.gov

Links U.S.-based companies and nonprofit organizations deployed in foreign assistance with skilled American professionals in volunteer opportunities that support the strategic development goals of the U.S. government.

Assistant Secretary for Health *(Health and Human Services Dept.), Global Health Affairs,* 200 Independence Ave. S.W., #639H 20201; (202) 690-6174. Fax, (202) 690-7127. Nils Daulaire, Assistant Secretary.
General email, globalhealth@hhs.gov
Web, www.globalhealth.gov

Represents the Health and Human Services Dept. before other governments, U.S. government agencies, international organizations, and the private sector on international and refugee health issues. Promotes international cooperation; provides health-related humanitarian and developmental assistance.

State Dept., *Conflict and Stabilization Operations,* 2121 Virginia Ave. N.W., 7th Floor 20037; (202) 663-0323. Fax, (202) 663-0327. Amb. Rick Barton, Assistant Secretary.
General email, csopublic@state.gov
Web, www.state.gov/j/cso/

Advances U.S. national security by working with partners in select countries to mitigate and prevent violent conflict. Conducts conflict analysis to identify factors contributing to mass violence or instability; develops prioritized strategies to address these factors; provides experienced leadership and technical experts to operationalize U.S. government and host-nation plans. Provides funding and training.

State Dept., *Population, Refugees, and Migration,* 2201 C St. N.W., #6825 20520-5824; (202) 647-7360. Fax, (202) 647-8162. Anne C. Richard, Assistant Secretary.
Web, www.state.gov/j/prm

Develops and implements policies and programs on matters relating to international refugees, internally displaced persons, and victims of conflict, including repatriation and resettlement programs; funds and monitors overseas relief, assistance, and repatriation programs; manages refugee admission to the United States.

►CONGRESS

For a listing of relevant congressional committees and subcommittees, please see pages 414–415 or the Appendix.

►INTERNATIONAL ORGANIZATIONS

International Committee of the Red Cross (ICRC), *Washington Office,* 1100 Connecticut Ave. N.W., #500 20036; (202) 587-4600. Fax, (202) 587-4696. François Stamm, Head, U.S. and Canadian Delegation. Press, (202) 587-4604.
General email, washington_was@icrc.org
Web, www.icrc.org

International Disaster Relief Organizations

Action Against Hunger, (877) 777-1420; www.actionagainsthunger.org

American Jewish Joint Distribution Committee, (212) 687-6200; www.jdc.org

American Red Cross, (800) 733-2767 or (202) 303-5214; www.redcross.org

AmeriCares, (800) 486-4357; www.americares.org

CARE, (800) 521-2273 or (202) 595-2800; www.care.org

Catholic Relief Services, (888) 277-7575; www.catholicrelief.org

Child Fund, (800) 776-6767; www.childfund.org

Church World Service, (800) 297-1516 or (202) 544-2350; www.cwsglobal.org

Direct Relief International, (805) 964-4767; www.directrelief.org

Episcopal Relief and Development, (855) 312-4325; www.er-d.org

Health Right International, (212) 226-9890; www.healthright.org

InterAction, (202) 667-8227; www.interaction.org

International Federation of Red Cross/Red Crescent, (212) 338-0161; www.ifrc.org

International Medical Corps, (800) 481-4462 or (202) 828-5155; www.internationalmedicalcorps.org

International Rescue Committee, (301) 562-8633; www.rescue.org

Islamic Relief USA, (855) 447-1001; www.irw.org

Lutheran World Relief, (800) 597-5972; www.lwr.org

Mercy Corps, (800) 292-3355; www.mercycorps.org

Operation USA, (800) 678-7255; www.opusa.org

Oxfam America, (800) 776-9326; www.oxfamamerica.org

Pan American Health Organization, (202) 974-3000; www.paho.org/disasters

Save the Children, (800) 728-3843 or (202) 640-6600; www.savethechildren.org

UNICEF, (800) 486-4233; www.unicefusa.org

World Food Programme (UN), (202) 653-0010; www.wfp.org

World Vision, (888) 511-6443; www.worldvision.org

Serves as the ICRC's main point of contact with U.S. authorities on issues concerning operations and international humanitarian law. Supports efforts internationally. Visits people held by the U.S. government in Guantanamo Bay, Cuba. (Headquarters in Geneva.)

International Organization for Migration (IOM), *Washington Office, 1752 N St. N.W., #700 20036; (202) 862-1826. Fax, (202) 862-1879. Luca Dall'Oglio, Chief of Mission, ext. 229; William Lacy Swing, Director General. General email, RMFWashingtonRMF@iom.int*

Web, www.iom.int/unitedstates

Nonpartisan organization that plans and operates resource mobilization functions (RMF), including refugee resettlement, national migration, and humanitarian assistance programs at the request of its member governments. Recruits skilled professionals for developing countries. (Headquarters in Geneva.)

Pan American Health Organization, *525 23rd St. N.W. 20037; (202) 974-3000. Fax, (202) 974-3663. Dr. Carissa F. Etienne, Director. Web, www.paho.org*

Works to extend health services to underserved populations of its member countries and to control or eradicate communicable diseases; promotes cooperation among governments to solve public health problems. (Regional Office for the Americas of the World Health Organization, which is headquartered in Geneva.)

United Nations High Commissioner for Refugees, *Washington Office, 1775 K St. N.W., #300 20006-1502;*

(202) 296-5191. Fax, (202) 296-5660. Shelly Pitterman, Regional Representative. General email, usawa@unhcr.org Web, www.unhcrwashington.org

Works with governments and voluntary organizations to protect and assist refugees worldwide. Promotes long-term alternatives to refugee camps, including voluntary repatriation, local integration, and resettlement overseas. (Headquarters in Geneva.)

U.S. Fund for the United Nations Children's Fund (UNICEF), *Public Policy and Advocacy, 1775 K St. N.W., #360 20006; (202) 296-4242. Fax, (202) 296-4060. Martin S. Rendón, Vice President; Mark Engman, Director, ext. 16. General email, OPPA@unicefusa.org Web, www.unicefusa.org/campaigns/public-policy-advocacy/*

Serves as information reference service on UNICEF; advocates policies to advance the well-being of the world's children. Interests include international humanitarian assistance, U.S. volunteerism, child survival, and international health. (Headquarters in New York.)

▶ **NONGOVERNMENTAL**

American Red Cross, *National Headquarters, 2025 E St. N.W. 20006-5009; (202) 303-5000. Gail J. McGovern, President. Press, (202) 303-5551. Toll-free, 800-RED-CROSS. Web, www.redcross.org*

Humanitarian organization chartered by Congress to provide domestic and international disaster relief and to act as a medium of communication between the U.S. armed forces and their families in time of war and personnel emergencies. Provides shelter, food, emotional support, supplies, funds, and technical assistance for relief in domestic and major international with disasters through the International Federation of Red Cross and Red Crescent Societies, headquartered in Geneva.

Bikes for the World, *3108 17th St. North, Arlington, VA 22201; (703) 740-7856. Fax, (703) 525-0931. Keith Oberg, Director.*
General email, office@bikesfortheworld.org
Web, www.bikesfortheworld.org

Collects unwanted bicycles and related paraphernalia in the United States and delivers them to low-cost community development programs assisting the poor in developing countries.

Center for Civilians in Conflict, *1210 18th St. N.W., 4th Floor 20036; (202) 558-6958. Sarah Holewinski, Executive Director.*
General email, info@civicworldwide.org
Web, www.civicworldwide.org

Advocates to national governments and militaries for recognition, compensation, and other assistance to civilians they have harmed in armed conflicts.

ChildFund International, *Washington Office, 1413 K St. N.W., #1200 20005; (202) 682-3482. Fax, (202) 682-3481. Anne Lynam Goddard, Director; Sarah Bouchie, Vice President of Program Development. Toll-free, (800) 776-6767.*
General email, washington@childfund.org
Web, www.childfund.org

Nonsectarian international humanitarian organization that promotes improved child welfare standards and services worldwide by supporting long-term sustainable development. Provides children in emergency situations brought on by war, natural disaster, and other circumstances with education, medical care, food, clothing, and shelter. Provides aid and promotes the development potential of children of all backgrounds. (Headquarters in Richmond, Va.)

Disability Rights International, *1166 Connecticut Ave. N.W., #325 20009; (202) 296-0800. Fax, (202) 697-5422. Eric Rosenthal, Executive Director.*
General email, info@disabilityrightsintl.org
Web, www.disabilityrightsintl.org

Challenges discrimination of and abuse faced by people with disabilities worldwide, with special attention to protecting the rights of children with mental disabilities. Documents conditions, publishes reports, and trains grassroots advocates.

Health Volunteers Overseas, *1900 L St. N.W., #310 20036; (202) 296-0928. Fax, (202) 296-8018. Nancy A. Kelly, Executive Director.*
General email, info@hvousa.org
Web, www.hvousa.org

Operates training programs in developing countries for health professionals who wish to teach low-cost health care delivery practices.

International Rescue Committee, *Public Policy and Advocacy, 1730 M St. N.W., #505 20036; (202) 822-0166. Fax, (202) 822-0089. Sharon Waxman, Vice President.*
General email, advocacy@theIRC.org
Web, www.rescue.org

Provides worldwide emergency aid, protection, resettlement services, educational support, and advocacy for refugees, displaced persons, and victims of oppression and violent conflict; recruits volunteers. (Headquarters in New York.)

Jesuit Refugee Service/USA, *Washington Office, 1016 16th St. N.W., #500 20036; (202) 462-0400. Fax, (202) 328-9212. Mitzi Schroeder, Director for Policy; Armando Borja, National Director.*
General email, jrsusa@jesuit.org
Web, www.jrsusa.org

U.S. Jesuit organization that aids refugees and other forcibly displaced persons worldwide, through accompaniment, advocacy, and service. Mobilizes the U.S. Jesuit response to force displacement; provides advocacy and funding support to programs throughout the world. Monitors refugee- and immigration-related legislation. (International headquarters in Rome.)

Latino Resource and Justice Center (CARECEN), *1460 Columbia Rd. N.W., #C-1 20009; (202) 328-9799. Fax, (202) 328-7894. Abel Nuñez, Executive Director.*
General email, info@carecendc.org
Web, http://carecendc.org

Helps Central American and Latino immigrants obtain and maintain legal status. Seeks to address the legal and social service needs of Latinos in the Washington area; to facilitate Latinos' transition to life in the United States; and to provide Latinos with the resources and leadership skills necessary to promote the community's development. Works closely with other community-based agencies.

National Council of Churches, *Washington Office, 110 Maryland Ave. N.E., #108 20002-5603; (202) 544-2350. Fax, (202) 543-1297. Jim Winkler, President.*
General email, info@nationalcouncilofchurches.us
Web, www.nationalcouncilofchurches.us

Works to foster cooperation among Christian congregations across the nation in programs concerning poverty, racism, family, environment, and international humanitarian objectives. (Headquarters in New York.)

Oxfam America, *Policy, 1100 15th St. N.W. #600 20005-1759; (202) 496-1180. Fax, (202) 496-1190. Raymond C. Offenheiser, President; Paul O'Brien, Vice President for Policy and Campaigns. Information, (800) 776-9326. Press, (202) 496-1169.*
General email, info@oxfamamerica.org
Web, www.oxfamamerica.org

Funds disaster relief and long-term development programs internationally. Organizes grassroots support in the United States for issues affecting global poverty, including climate change, aid reform, and corporate transparency. (Headquarters in Boston, Mass.)

Program for Appropriate Technology in Health (PATH), *Washington Office, 455 Massachusetts Ave. N.W., #1000 20001; (202) 822-0033. Fax, (202) 457-1466. Steve Davis, President.*
General email, info@path.org
Web, www.path.org

Develops, tests, and implements health technologies and strategies for low-resource countries. Works with community groups, other nongovernmental organizations, governments, companies, and United Nations agencies to expand the most successful programs. Interests include reproductive health, immunization, maternal-child health, emerging and epidemic diseases, and nutrition. (Headquarters in Seattle, Wash.)

Refugees International, *2001 S St. N.W., #700 20009; (202) 828-0110. Fax, (202) 828-0819. Michel Gabaudan, President. Toll-free, (800) 733-8433.*
General email, ri@refugeesinternational.org
Web, www.refugeesinternational.org

Advocates for assistance and protection for displaced people worldwide. Conducts field studies to identify basic needs and makes recommendations to policymakers and aid agencies.

The Salvation Army Disaster Service, *2626 Pennsylvania Ave. N.W. 20037-1618; (202) 756-2600. Fax, (202) 464-7203. Maj. Andrew Wiley, Divisional Secretary.*
Web, www.salvationarmyusa.org

Provides U.S. and international disaster victims and rescuers with emergency support, including food, clothing, and counseling services.

Southeast Asia Resource Action Center (SEARAC), *1628 16th St. N.W., 3rd Floor 20009; (202) 601-2960. Fax, (202) 667-6449. Quyen Dinh, Executive Director.*
General email, searac@searac.org
Web, www.searac.org

Works to advance Cambodian, Laotian, and Vietnamese rights through leadership and advocacy training. Collects and analyzes data on Southeast Asian Americans; publishes reports.

Unitarian Universalist Service Committee, *Washington Office, 1100 G St. N.W., #800 20005; (202) 393-2255, ext. 24. Fax, (202) 393-5494. Shelley Moskowitz, Manager of Public Policy.*
General email, smoskowitz@uusc.org
Web, www.uusc.org

Secular human rights organization fighting race, gender, environmental, and economic injustice worldwide. Partners with organizations defending right to water, workers' rights, and the democratic process. Responds to disasters. Provides education through travel and service. (Headquarters in Cambridge, MA.)

U.S. Committee for Refugees and Immigrants, *2231 Crystal Dr., #350, Arlington, VA 22202-3711; (703) 310-1130. Fax, (703) 769-4241. Lavinia Limón, President. Press, (703) 310-1166.*
General email, uscri@uscridc.org
Web, www.refugees.org

Defends rights of refugees in the United States and abroad. Helps immigrants and refugees adjust to American society; assists in resettling recently arrived immigrants and refugees; offers information, counseling services, and temporary living accommodations through its member agencies nationwide; issues publications on refugees and refugee resettlement; collects and disseminates information on refugee issues. Monitors legislation and regulations.

U.S. Conference of Catholic Bishops (USCCB), *3211 4th St. N.E. 20017; (202) 541-3000. Fax, (202) 541-3173. Sr. Mary Ann Walsh, Director, Media Relations, (202) 541-3200; Helen Osman, Secretary of Communications, (202) 241-3320. Toll-free, (800) 235-8722.*
Web, www.usccb.org

Serves as a forum for bishops to exchange ideas, debate concerns of the church, and draft responses to religious and social issues. Provides information on doctrine and policies of the Roman Catholic Church; develops religious education and training programs; formulates policy positions on social issues, including the economy, employment, federal budget priorities, voting rights, energy, health, housing, rural affairs, international military and political matters, human rights, the arms race, global economics, and immigration and refugee policy.

U.S. Conference of Catholic Bishops (USCCB), *Migration and Refugee Services, 3211 4th St. N.E. 20017; (202) 541-3352. Fax, (202) 541-3399. Johnny Young, Executive Director, (202) 541-3169.*
General email, mrs@usccb.org
Web, www.usccb.org/mrs

Advocates for immigrants, refugees, migrants, and victims of human trafficking. Works with legislative and executive branches of the U.S. government and with national and international organizations such as the U.N. High Commissioner for Refugees to promote fair and responsive immigration and refugee policy.

Women for Women International, *2000 M St. N.W., #200 20036; (202) 737-7705. Fax, (202) 737-7709. Afshan Khan, Chief Executive Officer.*
General email, general@womenforwomen.org
Web, www.womenforwomen.org

Helps women in war-torn regions rebuild their lives through financial and emotional support, job skills training, rights education, access to capital, and assistance for small business development.

World Vision, *Washington Office, 300 Eye St. N.E. 20002; (202) 572-6300. Fax, (202) 572-6479. Kent R. Hill, Senior Vice President, International Programs. Press, (202) 572-6595.*

General email, info@worlddivision.org

Web, www.worldvision.org

Christian humanitarian and development organization that works with children, their families, and their communities worldwide. Interests include social injustice and the causes of poverty. Provides emergency disaster relief and long-term development programs domestically and abroad. (Headquarters in Seattle, Wash.)

Information and Exchange Programs

▶ AGENCIES

Broadcasting Board of Governors, *330 Independence Ave. S.W., #3360 20237; (202) 203-4545. Fax, (202) 203-4585. Suzie Carroll, Executive Director. Press, (202) 203-4400.*
General email, publicaffairs@bbg.gov

Web, www.bbg.gov

Established by Congress to supervise all U.S. government nonmilitary international broadcasting, including Voice of America, Radio and TV Marti, Radio Free Europe/Radio Liberty, Radio Free Asia, and the Middle East Broadcasting Networks (MBN). Assesses the quality and effectiveness of broadcasts with regard to U.S. foreign policy objectives; reports annually to the president and to Congress.

Voice of America *(International Broadcasting Bureau), 330 Independence Ave. S.W., #3300 20237; (202) 203-4500. Fax, (202) 203-4960. David Ensor, Director. Information, (202) 203-4959. Press, (202) 203-4959.*
General email, askvoa@voahews.com

Web, www.voanews.com

A multimedia international broadcasting service funded by the U.S. government through the Broadcasting Board of Governors. Broadcasts news, information, educational, and cultural programming to an estimated worldwide audience of more than 134 million people weekly. Programs are produced in forty-five languages.

▶ NONGOVERNMENTAL

Alliance for International Educational and Cultural Exchange, *1828 L St. N.W., #1150 20036; (202) 293-6141. Fax, (202) 293-6144. Michael McCarry, Executive Director.*
General email, merber@alliance-exchange.org

Web, www.alliance-exchange.org

Promotes public policies that support the growth of international exchange between the United States and other countries. Provides professional representation, resource materials, publications, and public policy research for those involved in international exchanges.

American Bar Assn. (ABA), *International Legal Exchange Program (ILEX), 1050 Connecticut Ave. N.W., #400 20036; (202) 662-1660. Fax, (202) 662-1669. Christina Heid, Director, (202) 662-1034.*

General email, intilex@staff.abanet.org

Web, www.americanbar.org/groups/international_law

Facilitates entry into the United States for foreign lawyers offered training in U.S. law firms. Serves as designated U.S. government overseer for the J-1 visa and accepts applications from foreign lawyers. Houses the International Legal Resource Center.

American Council of Young Political Leaders, *2131 K St. N.W., #400 20037; (202) 857-0999. Fax, (202) 857-0027. Linda Rotunno, Chief Executive Officer.*
General email, lrotunno@acypl.org

Web, www.acypl.org

Bipartisan political education organization that promotes understanding among young elected leaders and political professionals around the world. Designs and manages international educational exchanges.

Business–Higher Education Forum, *2025 M St. N.W., #800 20036; (202) 367-1189. Fax, (202) 367-2100. Brian K. Fitzgerald, Chief Executive Officer.*
General email, info@bhef.com

Web, www.bhef.com

Membership: chief executive officers of major corporations, museums, colleges, and universities. Promotes the development of industry-university alliances around the world. Provides countries in central and eastern Europe with technical assistance in enterprise development, management training, market economics, education, and infrastructure development.

Center for Intercultural Education and Development, *330 Whitehaven St. N.W., #1000 20007 (mailing address: P.O. Box 579400, Georgetown University, Washington, DC 20057-9400); (202) 687-1400. Fax, (202) 687-2555. Chantal Santelices, Director.*
Web, http://cied.georgetown.edu

Designs and administers programs aimed at improving the quality of life of economically disadvantaged people; provides technical education, job training, leadership skills development, and business management training; runs programs in Central America, the Caribbean, Central Europe, and Southeast Asia.

Council for International Exchange of Scholars, *1400 K St. N.W., #700 20005; (202) 686-4000. Fax, (202) 686-4029. Gary Sayed, Executive Director; Debra Egan, Director, Scholarly Academic Partnerships, (202) 686-6230.*
General email, scholars@iie.org

Web, www.cies.org

Cooperates with the U.S. government in administering Fulbright grants for university teaching and advanced research abroad. (A division of the Institute of International Education.)

English-Speaking Union, *Washington Office, 4000 Cathedral Ave., #152B 20016; (202) 333-8258. Fax, 333-8258. Frederic Schwartz, President.*
General email, agdawn@msn.com

Web, www.esuus.org

International educational and cultural organization that promotes exchange programs with countries in which English is a major language; presents programs on the culture and history of the English-speaking world; sponsors annual Shakespeare competition among Washington metropolitan area schools. (National headquarters in New York.)

Global Ties U.S., *1420 K St. N.W., #800 20005-2401; (202) 842-1414. Fax, (202) 289-4625. Jennifer Clinton, President.*
General email, info@globalties.org
Web, www.globalties.org

Members coordinate international exchange programs and bring international visitors to communities throughout the United States. Provides its members, from 44 states and 13 countries, with connections, leadership development, and professional resources. (Formerly National Council for International Visitors.)

Graduate School USA, *International Institute, 600 Maryland Ave. S.W., #320 20024-2520; (202) 314-3500. Fax, (202) 479-6806. David Simpson, Director. Toll-free, (866) 329-4723.*
General email, intlinst@graduateschool.edu
Web, www.graduateschool.edu/ii

Offers professional training and educational services to the public, including employees of foreign governments, international organizations, nongovernmental agencies, and employees of U.S. agencies engaged in international activities. Provides tailored programs in the areas of capacity building, professional and educational exchanges, governance, and health.

Institute of International Education, *Washington Office, 1400 K St. N.W., #700 20005-2403; (202) 898-0600. Fax, (202) 326-7754. Allan Goodman, President.*
Web, www.iie.org

Educational exchange, technical assistance, and training organization that arranges professional programs for international visitors; conducts training courses in energy, environment, journalism, human resource development, educational policy and administration, and business-related fields; provides developing countries with short- and long-term technical assistance in human resource development; arranges professional training and support for staff of human rights organizations; sponsors fellowships and applied internships for midcareer professionals from developing countries; manages programs sending U.S. teachers, undergraduate and graduate students, and professionals abroad; implements contracts and cooperative agreements for the State Dept., the U.S. Agency for International Development, foreign governments, philanthropic foundations, multilateral banks, and other organizations. (Headquarters in New York.)

International Research and Exchanges Board (IREX), *1275 K St. N.W., #600 20005; (202) 628-8188. Fax, (202) 628-8189. W. Robert Pearson, President.*
General email, irex@irex.org
Web, www.irex.org

Provides programs, grants, and consulting expertise in more than 100 countries to improve the quality of education, strengthen independent media, and foster pluralistic civil society development.

Meridian International Center, *1630 Crescent Pl. N.W. 20009; (202) 667-6800. Fax, (202) 667-1475. Amb. Stuart Holliday, President. Toll-free, (800) 424-2974.*
General email, info@meridian.org
Web, www.meridian.org

Conducts international educational and cultural programs; provides foreign visitors and diplomats in the United States with services, including cultural orientation, seminars, and language assistance. Offers international exhibitions for Americans.

NAFSA: Assn. of International Educators, *1307 New York Ave. N.W., 8th Floor 20005-4701; (202) 737-3699. Fax, (202) 737-3657. Marlene M. Johnson, Executive Director. Publications, (866) 538-1927.*
General email, inbox@nafsa.org
Web, www.nafsa.org

Membership: individuals engaged in the field of international education and exchange at the postsecondary level. Promotes educational opportunities across national boundaries. Sets and upholds standards of good practice and provides professional education and training.

Radio Free Europe/Radio Liberty, *Washington Office, 1201 Connecticut Ave. N.W., 4th Floor 20036; (202) 457-6900. Fax, (202) 457-6992. John Giambalvo, Manager, Interim; Nejad Pejic, Manager, Interim. Press, (202) 457-6917.*
General email, rferlcomms@rferl.org
Web, www.rferl.org

Independent radio, Internet, and television service funded by federal grants to promote and support democracy. Broadcasts programs to Russia, Afghanistan, Pakistan, Iraq, Iran, and the republics of Central Asia; programming includes news, analysis, and specials on political developments, as well as cultural programs. Research materials available to the public by appointment. (Headquarters in Prague, Czech Republic.)

Sister Cities International, *915 15th St. N.W., 4th Floor 20005; (202) 347-8630. Fax, (202) 393-6524. Mary D. Kane, President.*
General email, info@sister-cities.org
Web, www.sister-cities.org

A network of 2,000 partnerships between U.S. and foreign cities. Promotes global cooperation at the municipal level, cultural understanding, and economic stimulation through exchanges of citizens, ideas, and materials. Serves as information clearinghouse for economic and sustainability issues and as program coordinator for trade missions. Sponsors youth programs.

World Learning, *International Exchange Programs, 1015 15th St. N.W., 7th Floor 20005-2065; (202) 408-5420. Fax, (202) 408-5397. Carol Jenkins, Senior Vice President,*

International Development and Exchange Programs, (202) 464-6643. Toll-free, (800) 858-0292.
General email, carol.jenkins@worldlearning.org
Web, www.worldlearning.org

Assists public and private organizations engaged in international cooperation and business. Works with governments and private counterparts to support foreign professional exchanges. Develops tailored technical training programs for mid-career professionals. Provides technical expertise, management support, travel, and business development services. Administers programs that place international exchange students in U.S. colleges and universities. Implements youth exchanges focused on leadership, current issues, and peacebuilding. Administered by World Learning's Division of International Development and Exchange Programs. Administers field-based study abroad programs, which offer semester and summer programs for high school, college, and graduate students.

Youth for Understanding USA, *6400 Goldsboro Rd., #100, Bethesda, MD 20817; (240) 235-2100. Fax, (240) 235-2104. Michael E. Hill, President. Teen Information, (800) 833-6243.*
General email, admissions@yfu.org
Web, www.yfuusa.org

Educational organization that administers international exchange programs, primarily for high school students. Administers scholarship programs that sponsor student exchanges.

War, Conflict, and Peacekeeping

▶AGENCIES

State Dept., *Policy Planning Staff, 2201 C St. N.W., #7311 20520; (202) 647-2972. Fax, (202) 647-0844. David McKean, Director.*
Web, www.state.gov

Advises the secretary and other State Dept. officials on foreign policy matters, including international peacekeeping and peace enforcement operations.

U.S. Institute of Peace, *2301 Constitution Ave. N.W. 20037; (202) 457-1700. Fax, (202) 429-6063. Stephen J. Hadley, Chair; Kristin Lord, President, Acting. Press, (202) 429-4725.*
General email, info@usip.org
Web, www.usip.org

Independent, nonpartisan institution established by Congress. Aims to prevent and resolve violent international conflicts, promote postconflict stability, and increase peace-building capacity, tools, and intellectual capital worldwide.

▶CONGRESS

For a listing of relevant congressional committees and subcommittees, please see pages 414–415 or the Appendix.

▶NONGOVERNMENTAL

Act Now to Stop War and End Racism (ANSWER) Coalition, *617 Florida Ave. N.W., Lower Level 20001; (202) 265-1948. Fax, (202) 280-1022. Sarah Sloan, National Staff Coordinator. Press, (202) 265-1948.*
General email, info@answercoalition.org
Web, www.answercoalition.org

Works to end war and conflict, with current emphasis on ending the occupation in Iraq, Afghanistan, and Pakistan. Conducts demonstrations with other peace and antiwar groups, especially ethnic and cultural identity groups concerned with ending racism.

Fourth Freedom Forum, *Washington Office, 1101 14th St. N.W., #900 20036; (202) 464-6009. Fax, (202) 238-9604. Alistair Millar, President.*
General email, amillar@fourthfreedom.org
Web, www.fourthfreedom.org

Conducts research and training to advance global cooperation to address transnational threats, including terrorism, nuclear proliferation, and drug trafficking. (Headquarters in Goshen, Ind.)

International Stability Operations Assn. (ISOA), *8221 Old Courthouse Rd., #200, Tysons Corner, VA 22182; (703) 596-7417. Fax, (571) 282-4800. Ado Machida, President.*
General email, isoa@stability-operations.org
Web, www.stability-operations.org

Membership: private-sector service companies involved in all sectors of peace and stability operations around the world, including mine clearance, logistics, security, training, and emergency humanitarian aid. Works to institute standards and codes of conduct. Monitors legislation.

Just Foreign Policy, *4410 Massachusetts Ave. N.W., #290 20016; (202) 448-2898. Robert Naiman, Policy Director.*
General email, info@justforeignpolicy.org
Web, www.justforeignpolicy.org

Nonpartisan membership organization that seeks to influence U.S. foreign policy through education, organization, and mobilization of citizens. Advocates cooperation, international law, and diplomacy as means to achieve a just foreign policy.

Refugees International, *2001 S St. N.W., #700 20009; (202) 828-0110. Fax, (202) 828-0819. Michel Gabaudan, President. Toll-free, (800) 733-8433.*
General email, ri@refugeesinternational.org
Web, www.refugeesinternational.org

Advocates for assistance and protection for displaced people worldwide. Conducts field studies to identify basic needs and makes recommendations to policymakers and aid agencies.

United to End Genocide, *1100 17th St. N.W., #500 20036; (202) 556-2100. Fax, (202) 833-1479. Thomas H. (Tom) Andrews, President.*
General email, info@endgenocide.org
Web, www.endgenocide.org

Seeks to prevent and end genocide and mass atrocities by advocacy to elected officials and civil society leaders worldwide. Goals include accountability for perpetrators and justice for victims. Monitors warning signs of genocide. Organizes Diaspora and human rights advocates. Promotes grassroots actions. Monitors legislation. (Formerly the Save Darfur Coalition/Genocide Awareness Network.)

Win Without War, *2000 M St. N.W., #720 20036; (202) 232-3317. Fax, (202) 232-3440. Thomas H. (Tom) Andrews, National Director.*
General email, info@winwithoutwarus.org
Web, www.winwithoutwar.org

Coalition of national organizations promoting international cooperation and agreements as the best means for securing peace. Encourages U.S. foreign policies of counterterrorism and weapons nonproliferation, but opposes unilateral military preemption. (Affiliated with the Center for National Policy.)

IMMIGRATION AND NATURALIZATION

General

▶**AGENCIES**

Administration for Children and Families (ACF) *(Health and Human Services Dept.), Refugee Resettlement, 901 D St. S.W., 8th Floor West 20447; (202) 401-9246. Fax, (202) 401-0981. Eskinder Negash, Director.*
Web, www.acf.hhs.gov/programs/orr

Directs a domestic resettlement program for refugees; reimburses states for costs incurred in giving refugees monetary and medical assistance; awards funds to voluntary resettlement agencies for providing refugees with monetary assistance and case management; provides states and nonprofit agencies with grants for social services such as English and employment training.

Justice Dept. (DOJ), *Civil Division, Immigration Litigation, 450 5th St. N.W. 20539 (mailing address: P.O. Box 878, Ben Franklin Station, Washington, DC 20044); (202) 616-4881. Fax, (202) 307-8837. David M. McConnell, Director.*
Web, www.justice.gov/civil/oil/oil_home.html

Handles most civil litigation arising under immigration and nationality laws.

Justice Dept. (DOJ), *Executive Office for Immigration Review, 5107 Leesburg Pike, #2600, Falls Church, VA 22041; (703) 305-0169. Fax, (703) 305-0985. Juan P. Osuna, Director. Legislative and Public Affairs, (703) 305-0289. Case Information System, (800) 898-7180. Employer Sanctions and Antidiscrimination Cases, (800) 305-0864.*
Web, www.justice.gov/eoir

Quasi-judicial body that includes the Board of Immigration Appeals and offices of the chief immigration judge and the chief administration hearing officer. Interprets immigration laws; conducts hearings and hears appeals on immigration issues.

Justice Dept. (DOJ), *Human Rights and Special Prosecutions, 1301 New York Ave. N.W., John C. Keeney Bldg., #200 20530; (202) 616-2492. Fax, (202) 616-2491. Teresa McHenry, Chief; Eli M. Rosenbaum, Director, Strategy and Policy.*
Web, www.justice.gov

Tracks war criminals within the United States with connections to world genocidal conflicts. Handles legal action to ensure denaturalization and/or deportation.

State Dept., *Visa Services, 2401 E St. N.W., #703 20522-0106; (202) 647-9584. Edward J. Ramotwski, Deputy Assistant Secretary, (202) 647-6544. National Visa Center, (603) 334-0700.*
Web, http://travel.state.gov/visa/visa

Supervises visa issuance system, which is administered by U.S. consular offices abroad.

U.S. Citizenship and Immigration Services (USCIS) *(Homeland Security Dept.), 20 Massachusetts Ave. N.W. 20529; (800) 375-5283. Lori L. Scialabba, Director, Acting. Press, (202) 272-1200.*
Web, www.uscis.gov

Responsible for the administration of immigration and naturalization adjudication functions and establishing immigration services policies and priorities.

▶**CONGRESS**

For a listing of relevant congressional committees and subcommittees, please see pages 414–415 or the Appendix.

▶**INTERNATIONAL ORGANIZATIONS**

International Catholic Migration Commission (ICMC), *Washington Office, 3211 4th St. N.E., #453-A 20017-1194; (202) 541-3389. Johan Ketelers, Secretary General; Jane Bloom, U.S. Liaison Officer.*
General email, bloom@icmc.net
Web, www.icmc.net

Supports ICMC's worldwide programs by liaising with the U.S. government, nongovernmental organizations, and the American public. Works with refugees, internally displaced persons, forced migrants, and trafficking victims. Responds to refugees' immediate needs while working for return to and reintegration in their home country, local integration, or resettlement in a third country. (Headquarters in Geneva.)

International Organization for Migration (IOM), *Washington Office, 1752 N St. N.W., #700 20036; (202) 862-1826. Fax, (202) 862-1879. Luca Dall'Oglio, Chief of Mission, ext. 229; William Lacy Swing, Director General.*

General email, RMFWashingtonRMF@iom.int

Web, www.iom.int/unitedstates

Nonpartisan organization that plans and operates resource mobilization functions (RMF), including refugee resettlement, national migration, and humanitarian assistance programs at the request of its member governments. Recruits skilled professionals for developing countries. (Headquarters in Geneva.)

▶ **NONGOVERNMENTAL**

American Immigration Lawyers Assn., *1331 G St. N.W., #300 20005-3142; (202) 507-7600. Fax, (202) 783-7853. Crystal Williams, Executive Director.*

Web, www.aila.org

Association for lawyers interested in immigration law. Provides information and continuing education programs on immigration law and policy; offers workshops and conferences. Monitors legislation and regulations.

Center for Immigration Studies, *1629 K St. N.W., #600 20005; (202) 466-8185. Fax, (202) 466-8076. Mark Krikorian, Executive Director.*

General email, center@cis.org

Web, www.cis.org

Nonpartisan organization that conducts research and policy analysis of the economic, social, demographic, and environmental impact of immigration on the United States. Sponsors symposiums.

Ethiopian Community Development Council, Inc., *901 S. Highland St., Arlington, VA 22204; (703) 685-0510. Fax, (703) 685-0529. Tsehaye Teferra, President.*

General email, contact_us@ecdus.org

Web, www.ecdcinternational.org

Seeks to improve quality of life for African immigrants and refugees in the United States through local and national programs. Interests include the resettlement and acculturation of refugees, health education, and cultural outreach for communities. Also provides business loans and management training for minority- and women-owned businesses in the Washington metropolitan area.

Federation for American Immigration Reform (FAIR), *25 Massachusetts Ave. N.W., #330 20001; (202) 328-7004. Fax, (202) 387-3447. Daniel A. Stein, President. Toll-free, (877) 627-3247.*

General email, fair@fairus.org

Web, www.fairus.org

Organization of individuals interested in immigration reform. Monitors immigration laws and policies.

Immigration Works USA, *737 8th St. S.E., #201 20003; (202) 506-4541. Fax, (202) 595-8962. Tamar Jacoby, President.*

General email, info@immigrationworksusa.org

Web, www.immigrationworksusa.org

Coalition of business owners that seeks to educate the public about the benefits of immigration and build support for bringing immigration policy in line with the country's labor needs. Monitors legislation and regulations.

Lutheran Immigration and Refugee Service, *Advocacy, Washington Office, 122 C St. N.W., #125 20001-2172; (202) 626-7907. Fax, (202) 783-7502. Brittney Nystrom, Director of Advocacy.*

General email, dc@lirs.org

Web, www.lirs.org

Resettles refugees and provides them with case management, job training, English language, and legal assistance. Provides specialized foster care services for unaccompanied refugee youth and facilitates the reunification of unaccompanied immigrant children in federal custody with their parents or relatives. Funds and provides technical assistance to local projects that offer social and legal services to immigrants and refugees, particularly those in immigration detention. (Headquarters in Baltimore, Md.)

Migration Policy Institute, *1400 16th St. N.W., #300 20036; (202) 266-1940. Fax, (202) 266-1900. Demetrios G. Papademetriou, President.*

General email, info@migrationpolicy.org

Web, www.migrationpolicy.org

Nonpartisan think tank that studies the movement of people within the United States and worldwide. Provides analysis, development, and evaluation of migration, integration, and refugee policies at local, national, and international levels.

National Council of La Raza, *1126 16th St. N.W., #600 20036-4845; (202) 785-1670. Fax, (202) 776-1792. Janet Murguia, President.*

General email, comments@nclr.org

Web, www.nclr.org

Provides research, policy analysis, and advocacy relating to immigration policy and programs. Monitors federal legislation on immigration, legalization, employer sanctions, employment discrimination, and eligibility of immigrants for federal benefit programs. Assists community-based groups involved in immigration and education services and educates employers about immigration laws.

National Immigration Forum, *50 F St. N.W., #300 20001; (202) 347-0040. Fax, (202) 347-0058. Ali Noorani, Executive Director. Press, (202) 383-5987.*

General email, media@immigrationforum.org

Web, www.immigrationforum.org

Pro-immigration advocacy organization that provides policy analysis, research, and updates on immigration policy developments to members and allies across the country. Monitors legislation and regulations related to immigrants and immigration. Works in coalition with broad cross-section of immigrant advocacy, immigrant-serving, religious, business, and labor organizations to advance policies welcoming to immigrants.

NumbersUSA, *Capitol Hill Office, 310 6th St. S.E., #310 20003; 1601 N. Kent St., #1100, Arlington, VA 22209; (703) 816-8820. Fax, (202) 543-3147. Roy Beck, Executive Director.*

General email, info@numbersusa.com

Web, www.numbersusa.com

Public policy organization that favors immigration reduction as a way of promoting economic justice for American workers. Monitors legislation and regulations.

Pew Hispanic Center, *1615 L St. N.W., #700 20036; (202) 419-3600. Fax, (202) 419-3608. Mark Lopez, Director. Information, (202) 419-3606. Press, (202) 419-4372. General email, hispanic@pewresearch.org*

Web, www.pewhispanic.org

Seeks to improve understanding of the U.S. Hispanic population and its impact on the nation, as well as explore Latino views on a range of social matters and public policy issues. Conducts public opinion surveys and other studies that are made available to the public. (A project of the Pew Research Center.)

Pew Research Center Social and Demographic Trends Project, *1615 L St. N.W., #700 20036; (202) 419-4374. Fax, (202) 419-4349. Kim Parker, Director of Social Trends Research. Media inquiries, (202) 419-4372. General email, info@socialtrends.org*

Web, www.pewsocialtrends.org

Studies behaviors and attitudes of Americans in key realms of their daily lives, using original survey research and analysis of government data. Topics of study include immigration, population geography, and demographics

U.S. Border Control, *8001 Forbes Pl., #102, Springfield, VA 22151; (703) 740-8668. Fax, (202) 740-9755. Edward I. Nelson, Chair. General email, info@usbc.org*

Web, www.usbc.org

Seeks to end illegal immigration by securing borders and reforming immigration policies. Monitors legislation and regulations.

U.S. Committee for Refugees and Immigrants, *2231 Crystal Dr., #350, Arlington, VA 22202-3711; (703) 310-1130. Fax, (703) 769-4241. Lavinia Limón, President. Press, (703) 310-1166. General email, uscri@uscridc.org*

Web, www.refugees.org

Defends rights of refugees in the United States and abroad. Helps immigrants and refugees adjust to American society; assists in resettling recently arrived immigrants and refugees; offers information, counseling services, and temporary living accommodations through its member agencies nationwide; issues publications on refugees and refugee resettlement; collects and disseminates information on refugee issues. Monitors legislation and regulations.

U.S. Conference of Catholic Bishops (USCCB), *3211 4th St. N.E. 20017; (202) 541-3000. Fax, (202) 541-3173. Sr. Mary Ann Walsh, Director, Media Relations, (202) 541-3200; Helen Osman, Secretary of Communications, (202) 241-3320. Toll-free, (800) 235-8722. Web, www.usccb.org*

Serves as a forum for bishops to exchange ideas, debate concerns of the church, and draft responses to religious and social issues. Provides information on doctrine and policies of the Roman Catholic Church; develops religious education and training programs; formulates policy positions on social issues, including the economy, employment, federal budget priorities, voting rights, energy, health, housing, rural affairs, international military and political matters, human rights, the arms race, global economics, and immigration and refugee policy.

INTERNATIONAL LAW AND AGREEMENTS

General

▶**AGENCIES**

Commission on Security and Cooperation in Europe (Helsinki Commission), *234 FHOB 20515; (202) 225-1901. Fax, (202) 226-4199. Sen. Benjamin L. Cardin, Chair; Rep. Christopher H. Smith, Co-Chair; Fred Turner, Chief of Staff. General email, info@csce.gov*

Web, www.csce.gov

Independent agency created by Congress. Membership includes individuals from the executive and legislative branches. Monitors and encourages compliance with the Helsinki Accords, a series of agreements with provisions on security, economic, environmental, human rights, and humanitarian issues; conducts hearings; serves as an information clearinghouse for issues in eastern and western Europe, Canada, and the United States relating to the Helsinki Accords.

Federal Bureau of Investigation (FBI) (Justice Dept.), International Operations, *935 Pennsylvania Ave. N.W., #7825 20535; (202) 324-5904. Fax, (202) 324-5292. Michael S. Welch, Assistant Director. Web, www.fbi.gov/about-us/international_operations*

Supports FBI involvement in international investigations; oversees liaison offices in U.S. embassies abroad. Maintains contacts with other federal agencies; Interpol; foreign police and security officers based in Washington, D.C.; and national law enforcement associations.

Securities and Exchange Commission (SEC), International Affairs, *100 F St. N.E., MS 1004 20549; (202) 551-6690. Fax, (202) 772-9281. Robert M. Fisher, Director, Acting. Web, www.sec.gov/oia#.ux83foxfmar*

Promotes investor protection, cross-border securities transactions, and fair, efficient, and transparent markets by advancing international regulatory and enforcement cooperation, promoting the adoption of high regulatory standards worldwide, and formulating technical assistance programs to strengthen the regulatory structure in global finance markets. Works with a global network of securities regulators and law enforcement authorities to facilitate cross-border regulatory compliance and help ensure that international borders are not used to escape detection and prosecution of fraudulent securities activities. Provides the commission and SEC staff with advice and assistance in international enforcement and regulatory efforts.

State Dept., *Global Criminal Justice, 2201 C St. N.W., #7419A 20520; (202) 647-5072. Fax, (202) 736-4495. Stephen J. Rapp, Director.*
Web, www.state.gov/s/wci

Oversees U.S. stance on the creation of courts and other judicial mechanisms to bring perpetrators of crimes under international law to justice. Engages in diplomacy with foreign governments whose nationals have been captured in the war on terrorism. Has primary responsibility for policy on Iraqi war crimes.

State Dept., *International Claims and Investment Disputes, 2430 E St. N.W., #203 20037-2800; (202) 776-8360. Fax, (202) 776-8389. Lisa J. Grosh, Assistant Legal Adviser.*
Web, www.state.gov

Handles claims by foreign governments and their nationals against the U.S. government, as well as claims against the State Dept. for negligence under the Federal Tort Claims Act. Administers the Iranian claims program and negotiates agreements with other foreign governments on claims settlements.

State Dept., *Law Enforcement and Intelligence, 2201 C St. N.W., #5419 20520; (202) 647-7324. Fax, (202) 647-4802. Thomas Heinemann, Assistant Legal Adviser.*
Web, www.state.gov

Negotiates extradition treaties, legal assistance treaties in criminal matters, and other agreements relating to international criminal matters.

State Dept., *Legal Adviser, 2201 C St. N.W., #6421 20520-6310; (202) 647-9598. Fax, (202) 647-7096. Mary McLeud, Legal Adviser, Acting.*
Web, www.state.gov/s/l

Provides the secretary and the department with legal advice on domestic and international problems; participates in international negotiations; represents the U.S. government in international litigation and in international conferences related to legal issues.

State Dept., *Political-Military Affairs, 2201 C St. N.W., #6212 20520; (202) 647-9022. Fax, (202) 736-4779. Puneet Talwar, Assistant Secretary.*
Web, www.state.gov

Principal link between State Dept. and Defense Dept. Provides policy direction in the areas of international security, security assistance, military operations, defense strategy and policy, military use of space, and defense trade.

State Dept., *Treaty Affairs, 2201 C St. N.W., #5420 20520; (202) 647-1345. Fax, (202) 647-9844. Paul B. Dean, Assistant Legal Adviser for Treaty Affairs.*

General email, treatyoffice@state.gov
Web, www.state.gov/s/l/treaty

Provides legal advice on treaties and other international agreements, including constitutional questions, drafting, negotiation, and interpretation of treaties; maintains records of treaties and executive agreements.

Transportation Dept. (DOT), *International Aviation, 1200 New Jersey Ave. S.E., #W86-316 20590; (202) 366-2423. Fax, (202) 366-3694. Paul L. Gretch, Director.*
Web, www.dot.gov/policy/aviation-policy/office-international-aviation

Responsible for international aviation regulation and negotiations, including fares, tariffs, and foreign licenses; represents the United States at international aviation meetings.

► **CONGRESS**

For a listing of relevant congressional committees and subcommittees, please see pages 414–415 or the Appendix.

► **INTERNATIONAL ORGANIZATIONS**

INTERPOL, *Washington Office, U.S. National Central Bureau, 145 N St. N.E. 20002 (mailing address: INTERPOL Washington, U.S. Dept. of Justice, Washington, DC 20530-0001); (202) 616-9000. Fax, (202) 616-8400. Shawn A. Bray, Director.*
Web, www.justice.gov/usncb

U.S. representative to INTERPOL; participates in international investigations on behalf of U.S. police; coordinates the exchange of investigative information on crimes, including drug trafficking, counterfeiting, missing persons, and terrorism. Coordinates law enforcement requests for investigative assistance in the United States and abroad. Assists with extradition processes. Serves as liaison between foreign and U.S. law enforcement agencies at federal, state, and local levels. (Headquarters in Lyons, France.)

► **NONGOVERNMENTAL**

American Arbitration Assn., *Government Relations, Regional Office, 1776 Eye St. N.W., #850 20006; (202) 739-8280. Fax, (202) 223-7095. Pierre Paret, Vice President.*
General email, paretp@adr.org
Web, www.adr.org

Provides dispute resolution services and information. Administers international arbitration and mediation systems. (Headquarters in New York.)

American Bar Assn. (ABA), *International Law, 1050 Connecticut Ave. N.W. 20036; (202) 662-1660. Fax, (202) 662-1669. Leanne Pfautz, Section Director, (202) 662-1661.*
General email, intlaw@americanbar.org
Web, www.americanbar.org/intlaw

Monitors and makes recommendations concerning developments in the practice of international law that affect ABA members and the public. Conducts programs, including International Legal Exchange, and produces publications covering the practice of international law.

American Society of International Law, *2223 Massachusetts Ave. N.W. 20008-2864; (202) 939-6000. Fax, (202) 797-7133. Elizabeth Andersen, Executive Director.*
Web, www.asil.org

Membership: lawyers, academics, corporate counsel, judges, representatives of government and nongovernmental organizations, international civil servants, students, and others interested in international law. Conducts research and study programs on international law. Holds an annual meeting on current issues in international law. Library open to the public, 9:00 a.m.–4:00 p.m.

Antarctic and Southern Ocean Coalition, *1630 Connecticut Ave. N.W., 3rd Floor 20009; (202) 234-2480. Fax, (202) 387-4823. James N. Barnes, Executive Director. General email, secretariat@asoc.org*
Web, www.asoc.org

Promotes effective implementation of the Antarctic Treaty System; works to protect the fragile environment and biodiversity of the Antarctic continent and promote responsible sustainable fisheries, including krill conservation, in the Southern Ocean.

Codex Alimentarius Commission, *U.S. Codex Office, 1400 Independence Ave. S.W., South Bldg., #4861 20250-3700; (202) 205-7760. Fax, (202) 720-3157. Mary Frances Lowe, U.S. Codex Manager; Paulo Almeida, U.S. Associate Manager. Press, (202) 720-9113. Meat and Poultry Hotline, (888) 674-6854. General email, uscodex@fsis.usda.gov*
Web, www.fsis.usda.gov/codex

Operates within the Food and Agricultural Organization (FAO) and the World Health Organization (WHO) to establish international food and food safety standards and to ensure fair trade practices. Convenes committees in member countries to address specific commodities and issues including labeling, additives in food and veterinary drugs, pesticide residues and other contaminants, and systems for food inspection. (Located in the USDA Food Safety and Inspection Service; international headquarters in Rome at the UN's Food and Agricultural Organization.)

Inter-American Bar Assn., *1211 Connecticut Ave. N.W., #202 20036; (202) 466-5944. Fax, (202) 466-5946. Henry S. Dahl, Secretary General. General email, iaba@iaba.org*
Web, www.iaba.org

Membership: lawyers and bar associations in the Western Hemisphere with associate members in Europe. Works to promote uniformity of national and international laws; holds conferences; makes recommendations to national governments and organizations. Library open to the public.

World Jurist Assn., *7910 Woodmont Ave., #1440, Bethesda, MD 20814; (202) 466-5428. Fax, (202) 452-8540.*

Sona Pancholy, Executive Vice President; Garry E. Hunter, General Counsel. General email, wja@worldjurist.org
Web, www.worldjurist.org

Membership: lawyers, law professors, judges, law students, and nonlegal professionals worldwide. Conducts research; promotes world peace through adherence to international law; holds annual conference and biennial congresses. (Affiliates, at same address, include World Assn. of Judges, World Assn. of Law Professors, World Assn. of Lawyers, and World Business Assn.)

Americans Abroad

▶**AGENCIES**

Administration for Children and Families (ACF) *(Health and Human Services Dept.), Refugee Resettlement, 901 D St. S.W., 8th Floor West 20447; (202) 401-9246. Fax, (202) 401-0981. Eskinder Negash, Director.*
Web, www.acf.hhs.gov/programs/orr

Provides benefits and services to refugees, Cuban and Haitian entrants, asylees, trafficking and torture victims, repatriated U.S. citizens, and unaccompanied alien children. Seeks to help individuals achieve economic self-sufficiency and social adjustment within the shortest time possible following arrival to the United States.

Foreign Claims Settlement Commission of the United States *(Justice Dept.), 600 E St. N.W., #6002 20579; (202) 616-6975. Fax, (202) 616-6993. Anuj C. Desai, Commissioner; Sylvia Becker, Commissioner. General email, info.fcsc@usdoj.gov*
Web, www.justice.gov/fcsc/

Processes claims by U.S. nationals against foreign governments for property losses sustained.

National Security Division *(Justice Dept.), Justice for Victims of Overseas Terrorism, 950 Pennsylvania Ave. N.W. 20530; (202) 514-1057. Fax, (202) 514-8714. Heather L. Cartwright, Director. General email, nsd.public@usdoj.gov*
Web, www.justice.gov/nsd

Monitors the investigation and prosecution of terrorist attacks against U.S. citizens abroad; works with other Justice Dept. offices to ensure that the rights of victims are respected. Responsible for establishing a Joint Task Force with the State Dept. in the event of a terrorist incident against U.S. citizens overseas. Responds to congressional and citizens' inquiries on the department's response to such attacks.

State Dept., *Children's Issues, 2201 C St. N.W., SA-17, 9th Floor 20520-2818; (202) 501-4444. Beth Payne, Director. Toll-free, (888) 407-4747.*
Web, http://travel.state.gov/abduction/abduction_580.html

Assists with consular aspects of children's services and fulfills U.S. treaty obligations relating to the abduction of children. Advises foreign service posts on international parental child abduction and intercountry adoption.

State Dept., *Consular Affairs, Special Issuance Agency,* *600 19th St. N.W., #3200 20006; (202) 485-9202. Fax, (202) 955-0182. Michael D. Thomas, Director. National passport information, (877) 487-2778.*
Web, http://travel.state.gov

Administers passport laws and issues passports. (Most branches of the U.S. Postal Service and most U.S. district and state courts are authorized to accept applications and payment for passports and to administer the required oath to U.S. citizens. Completed applications are sent from the post office or court to the nearest State Dept. regional passport office for processing.) Maintains a variety of records received from the Overseas Citizens Services, including consular certificates of witness to marriage and reports of birth and death. (Individuals wishing to apply for a U.S. passport may seek additional information via the phone number or Web address listed above.)

State Dept., *International Claims and Investment Disputes, 2430 E St. N.W., #203 20037-2800; (202) 776-8360. Fax, (202) 776-8389. Lisa J. Grosh, Assistant Legal Adviser.*
Web, www.state.gov

Handles claims by U.S. government and citizens against foreign governments; handles claims by owners of U.S. flag vessels for reimbursements of fines, fees, licenses, and other direct payments for illegal seizures by foreign governments in international waters under the Fishermen's Protective Act.

State Dept., *Overseas Citizens Services (OCS), 19th St. N.W., SA-17, 10th Floor 20431; (888) 407-4747. Fax, (202) 647-3732. Michelle Bernier-Toth, Director. From overseas, (1) (202) 501-4444.*
Web, http://travel.state.gov

Handles matters involving protective services for Americans abroad, including arrests, assistance in death cases, loans, medical emergencies, welfare and whereabouts inquiries, travel warnings and consular information, nationality and citizenship determination, document issuance, judicial and notarial services, estates, property claims, third-country representation, and disaster assistance.

State Dept., *Overseas Citizens Services (OCS), Office of Legal Affairs, 600 19th St. N.W., SA-17A 20037; (202) 485-6079. Fax, (202) 485-8033. Edward A. Betancourt, Director of Legal Affairs. Recorded consular information, (202) 647-5225. Toll-free, (888) 407-4747.*
General email, ask-ocs-l-attyreplies@state.gov
Web, www.state.gov

Offers guidance concerning the administration and enforcement of laws on citizenship and on the appropriate documentation of Americans traveling and residing abroad; gives advice on legislative matters, including implementation of new laws, and on treaties and agreements; reconsiders the acquisition and loss of U.S. citizenship in complex

cases; and administers the overseas federal benefits program.

Boundaries

▶AGENCIES

Saint Lawrence Seaway Development Corp. *(Transportation Dept.), 1200 New Jersey Ave. S.E., #W32-300 20590; (202) 366-0091. Fax, (202) 366-7147. Betty Sutton, Administrator. Toll-free, (800) 785-2779.*
Web, www.greatlakes-seaway.com

Operates and maintains the Saint Lawrence Seaway within U.S. territorial limits; conducts development programs and coordinates activities with its Canadian counterpart.

State Dept., *Mexican Affairs, 2201 C St. N.W., #3909 20520-6258; (202) 647-8113. Fax, (202) 647-5752. Kevin O'Reilly, Director.*
Web, www.state.gov

Advises the secretary on Mexican affairs. Acts as liaison between the United States and Mexico in international boundary and water matters as defined by binational treaties and agreements. Also involved with border health and environmental issues, new border crossings, and significant modifications to existing crossings.

▶INTERNATIONAL ORGANIZATIONS

International Boundary Commission, United States and Canada, U.S. Section, *2000 L St. N.W., #615 20036; (202) 736-9102. Fax, (202) 632-2008. Kyle K. Hipsley, Commissioner, Acting, (202) 736-9102.*
General email, hipsleyk@ibcusca.org
Web, www.internationalboundarycommission.org

Defines and maintains the international boundary line between the United States and Canada. Rules on applications for approval of projects affecting boundary or transboundary waters. Assists the United States and Canada in protecting the transboundary environment. Alerts the governments to emerging issues that may give rise to bilateral disputes. Commissioners represent only the commission, not the government that appointed them. (Canadian section in Ottawa.)

International Joint Commission, United States and Canada, U.S. Section, *2000 L St. N.W., #615 20036; (202) 736-9000. Fax, (202) 632-2007. Frank Bevacqua, Public Information Officer, (202) 736-9024.*
General email, bevacquaf@washington.ijc.org
Web, www.ijc.org

Handles disputes concerning the use of boundary waters; negotiates questions dealing with the rights, obligations, and interests of the United States and Canada along the border; establishes procedures for the adjustment and settlement of questions. (Canadian section in Ottawa; Great Lakes regional office in Windsor, Ontario.)

Extradition

►AGENCIES

Justice Dept. (DOJ), *International Affairs, 1301 New York Ave. N.W., #800 20005 (mailing address: P.O. Box 27330, Washington, DC 20038-7330); (202) 514-0000. Fax, (202) 514-0080. Mary E. (Molly) Warlow, Director, (202) 514-0008. Citizen Phoneline, (202) 353-4641.*
General email, criminal.division@usdoj.gov
Web, www.justice.gov/criminal/about/oia.html

Performs investigations necessary for extradition of fugitives from the United States and other nations. Handles U.S. and foreign government requests for mutual legal assistance, including documentary evidence.

State Dept., *Law Enforcement and Intelligence, 2201 C St. N.W., #5419 20520; (202) 647-7324. Fax, (202) 647-4802. Thomas Heinemann, Assistant Legal Adviser.*
Web, www.state.gov

Negotiates and approves extradition of fugitives between the United States and other nations.

►NONGOVERNMENTAL

Center for National Security Studies, *1730 Pennsylvania Ave. N.W., 7th Floor 20006; (202) 721-5650. Fax, (202) 530-0128. Kate A. Martin, Director.*
General email, cnss@cnss.org
Web, www.cnss.org

Monitors and conducts research on extradition, intelligence, national security, and civil liberties.

Fishing, Law of the Sea

►AGENCIES

National Oceanic and Atmospheric Administration (NOAA) *(Commerce Dept.),* **National Marine Fisheries Service,** *1315 East-West Hwy., SSMC3, Silver Spring, MD 20910; (301) 427-8000. Fax, (301) 713-1940. Eileen Sobeck, Assistant Administrator. Press, (301) 427-8003.*
Web, www.nmfs.noaa.gov

Administers marine fishing regulations, including offshore fishing rights and international agreements.

►CONGRESS

For a listing of relevant congressional committees and subcommittees, please see pages 414–415 or the Appendix.

Human Rights

►AGENCIES

Commission on Security and Cooperation in Europe (Helsinki Commission), *234 FHOB 20515; (202) 225-1901. Fax, (202) 226-4199. Sen. Benjamin L. Cardin, Chair;*

Rep. Christopher H. Smith, Co-Chair; Fred Turner, Chief of Staff.
General email, info@csce.gov
Web, www.csce.gov

Independent agency created by Congress. Membership includes individuals from the executive and legislative branches. Monitors and encourages compliance with the human rights provisions of the Helsinki Accords; conducts hearings; serves as an information clearinghouse for human rights issues in eastern and western Europe, Canada, and the United States relating to the Helsinki Accords.

Congressional–Executive Commission on China, *243 FHOB 20515; (202) 226-3766. Fax, (202) 226-3804. Sen. Sherrod Brown, Co-Chair; Rep. Christopher H. Smith, Co-Chair; Lawrence T. Liu, Staff Director, (202) 226-3821; Paul B. Protic, Deputy Staff Director, (202) 226-3798.*
General email, infocecc@mail.house.gov
Web, www.cecc.gov

Independent agency created by Congress. Membership includes individuals from the executive and legislative branches. Monitors human rights and the development of the rule of law in the People's Republic of China. Submits an annual report to the president and Congress.

State Dept., *Democracy, Human Rights, and Labor, 2201 C St. N.W., #7827 20520-7812; (202) 647-2126. Fax, (202) 647-5283. Tom Malinowski, Assistant Secretary, Acting.*
Web, www.state.gov/g/drl

Implements U.S. policies relating to human rights, labor, and religious freedom; prepares annual review of human rights worldwide; provides the U.S. Citizenship and Immigration Services with advisory opinions regarding asylum petitions.

State Dept., *Global Women's Issues, 2201 C St. N.W., #7532 20520; (202) 647-7285. Fax, (202) 647-7288. Catherine M. Russell, Ambassador at Large for Global Women's Issues.*
Web, www.state.gov/s/gwi

Works to promote the human rights of women within U.S. foreign policy. Participates in international organizations and conferences; advises other U.S. agencies; disseminates information.

State Dept., *International Labor Affairs, 1800 G St. N.W., #2422 20006; (202) 312-9763. Fax, (202) 216-5895. Bruce Levine, Director, (202) 216-5886.*
Web, www.state.gov/g/drl/lbr

Works with organized labor, nongovernmental organizations, international organizations, and corporations to monitor and promote worker rights throughout the world. Contributes to U.S. foreign policy goals related to democracy promotion, trade, development, and human rights.

State Dept., *Monitor and Combat Trafficking in Persons, 1800 G St. N.W., #2201 20520; (202) 312-9639. Fax, (202) 312-9637. Amb. Louis C. deBaca, Director.*

General email, tipoutreach@state.gov

Web, www.state.gov/g/tip

Combats trafficking in persons domestically and internationally. Publishes annual Trafficking in Persons Report, which assesses the progress of other governments, analyzes best practices and new data, and summarizes U.S. efforts to combat human trafficking at home.

State Dept., *Multilateral and Global Affairs, Business and Human Rights Team,* 2201 C St. N.W., #7822 20520; (202) 647-1385. Jason Tielemeier, Section Chief.

General email, BHR@state.gov

Web, www.humanrights.gov

Works with companies, nongovernmental organizations, and governments to provide corporate contributions to global prosperity while ensuring companies operate in a manner that protects against human rights abuses.

U.S. Commission on International Religious Freedom, 732 N. Capitol St. N.W., #A714 20401; (202) 523-3240. Fax, (202) 523-5020. Jackie Wokott, Executive Director.

General email, communications@uscirf.gov

Web, www.uscirf.gov

Agency created by the International Religious Freedom Act of 1998 to monitor religious freedom worldwide and to advise the president, the secretary of state, and Congress on how best to promote it.

▶ CONGRESS

For a listing of relevant congressional committees and subcommittees, please see pages 414–415 or the Appendix.

▶ NONGOVERNMENTAL

Amnesty International USA, *Washington Office,* 600 Pennsylvania Ave. S.E., 5th Floor 20003; (202) 544-0200. Fax, (202) 546-7142. Frank S. Jannuzi, Managing Director. Toll-free, (866) 273-4466.

General email, aiusa@aiusa.org

Web, www.amnestyusa.org

International organization that investigates, exposes, and responds to human rights abuses. Works for the release of men and women imprisoned anywhere in the world for their beliefs, political affiliation, color, ethnic origin, sex, language, or religion, provided they have neither used nor advocated violence. Opposes torture and the death penalty; urges fair and prompt trials for all political prisoners. (U.S. headquarters in New York.)

Center for Human Rights and Humanitarian Law, 4910 Massachusetts Ave., #16 20016 (mailing address: 4801 Massachusetts Ave. N.W., Washington, DC 20016-8181); (202) 274-4180. Fax, (202) 274-0783. Hadar Harris, Executive Director.

General email, humlaw@wcl.american.edu

Web, www.wclcenterforhr.org

Seeks to promote human rights and humanitarian law. Establishes training programs for judges, lawyers, and law schools; assists emerging democracies and other nations

in developing laws and institutions that protect human rights; organizes conferences with public and private institutions. (Affiliated with the Washington College of Law at American University.)

Free the Slaves, 1320 19th St. N.W., #600 20036; (202) 775-7480. Fax, (202) 775-7485. Maurice Middleberg, Executive Director.

General email, info@freetheslaves.net

Web, http://freetheslaves.net

Researches modern slavery and funds the work of grassroots antislavery organizations. Partners with concerned businesses and nongovernmental organizations to remove slavery from product supply chains and build a consumer movement that chooses slave-free goods. Maintains a video library, holds public presentations, and distributes educational materials. Monitors legislation and regulations.

Genocide Watch, P.O. Box 809 20044 (mailing address: School of Conflict Analysis and Resolution, George Mason University, 3331 Fairfax Dr., MS 403, Arlington, VA 22201); (703) 448-0222. Fax, (703) 993-1302. Gregory Stanton, President.

General email, communications@genocidewatch.org

Web, www.genocidewatch.org

Educates the public and policymakers about the causes, processes, and warning signs of genocide; seeks to create the institutions and the political will to prevent and stop genocide and to bring perpetrators of genocide to justice. (Coordinator of the International Alliance to End Genocide.)

Global Rights, 1200 18th St. N.W., #602 20036; (202) 822-4600. Fax, (202) 822-4606. Susan Farnsworth, Executive Director.

General email, info@globalrights.org

Web, www.globalrights.org

Public interest law center concerned with promoting and protecting international human rights. Conducts educational programs and conferences; provides legal and paralegal services; conducts community outreach and mobilization; monitors the electoral and judicial process in several countries.

GoodWeave USA, 2001 S St. N.W., #510 20009; (202) 234-9050. Fax, (202) 234-9056. Nina Smith, Executive Director.

General email, info@goodweave.org

Web, www.goodweave.org

International human rights organization working to end child labor in Indian, Nepalese, and Afghanistani handmade carpet industries. Inspects and certifies workplace conditions. Runs schools and rehabilitation centers for former child workers.

Human Rights First, *Washington Office,* 805 15th St. N.W., #900 20005; (202) 547-5692. Fax, (202) 543-5999. Elisa Massimino, President. Press, (202) 370-3323.

General email, perezsantiago@humanrightsfirst.org

Web, www.humanrightsfirst.org

Promotes human rights as guaranteed by the International Bill of Human Rights. Mobilizes activists and the legal community to pressure the U.S. government and private companies to respect human rights and the rule of the law. Advocates for American leadership to secure core freedoms worldwide.

Human Rights Watch, *Washington Office,* 1630 *Connecticut Ave. N.W., #500 20009; (202) 612-4321. Fax, (202) 612-4333. Kenneth Roth, Executive Director, U.S. Foreign Policy.*
General email, hrwdc@hrw.org

Web, www.hrw.org

International, nonpartisan human rights organization that monitors human rights violations worldwide. Subdivided into six regional concentrations–Africa, Americas, Asia, Europe and Central Asia, Middle East and North Africa, and South Asia. Coordinates thematic projects on women's rights, arms sales, and prisons. Sponsors fact-finding missions to various countries; publicizes violations and encourages international protests; maintains file on human rights violations. (Headquarters in New York.)

International Assn. of Official Human Rights Agencies (IAOHRA), *444 N. Capitol St. N.W., #536 20001; (202) 624-5410. Fax, (202) 624-8185. Jean M. Keller, President; Shannon Bennett, Director, Acting.*
General email, iaohra@sso.org

Web, www.iaohra.org

Works with government and human rights agencies worldwide to promote civil and human rights, including elimination of unlawful discrimination in employment, housing, education, and public accommodations. Offers management training for human rights executives and civil rights workshops for criminal justice agencies; develops training programs in investigative techniques, settlement and conciliation, and legal theory. Serves as an information clearinghouse on human rights laws and enforcement.

International Justice Mission, *P.O. Box 58147 20037-8147; (703) 465-5495. Fax, (703) 465-5499. Gary A. Haugen, President.*
General email, contact@ijm.org

Web, www.ijm.org

Seeks to help people suffering injustice and oppression who cannot rely on local authorities for relief. Documents and monitors conditions of abuse and oppression, educates churches and the public about abuses, and mobilizes intervention on behalf of victims.

Jubilee Campaign USA, *9689-C Main St., Fairfax, VA 22031; (703) 503-0791. Ann Buwalda, Executive Director.*
General email, jubilee@jubileecampaign.org

Web, www.jubileecampaign.org

Promotes human rights and religious liberty for ethnic and religious minorities in countries that oppress them. Advocates the release of prisoners of conscience and revising laws to achieve this. Especially interested in ending the exploitation of children.

Physicians for Human Rights, *Washington Office,* 1730 *Pennsylvania Ave. N.W., 7th Floor 20006; 1110 Vermont Ave. N.W. 20005; (202) 728-5335. Fax, (202) 728-3053. Andrea Gittleman, Interim Director, U.S. Policy; Vacant, Washington Director.*
General email, phrusa@phrusa.org

Web, www.physiciansforhumanrights.org

Mobilizes doctors, nurses, health specialists, scientists, and others to promote health and human rights globally. Investigates and seeks to end human rights abuses. Issues reports and press releases; conducts training programs on health and human rights issues; advocates to policymakers. (Headquarters in New York City.)

Polaris Project, *P.O. Box 65323 20035; (202) 745-1001. Fax, (202) 745-1119. Bradley Myles, Executive Director. 24-hour hotline, (888) 373-7888.*
General email, info@polarisproject.org

Web, www.polarisproject.org

Fights human trafficking at the local, national, and international levels with an emphasis on policy advocacy and survivor support. Operates the 24-hour National Human Trafficking Resource Center Hotline for victims, law enforcement agencies, and others.

Robert F. Kennedy Center for Justice and Human Rights, *1300 19th St. N.W., #750 20036-1651; (202) 463-7575. Fax, (202) 463-6606. Lynn Delaney, Executive Director; Kerry Kennedy, President.*
General email, info@rfkcenter.org

Web, www.rfkcenter.org

Presents annual book, journalism, and human rights awards and carries out programs that support the work of the human rights award laureates in their countries. Investigates and reports on human rights; campaigns to heighten awareness of these issues, stop abuses, and encourage governments, international organizations, and corporations to adopt policies that ensure respect for human rights.

Torture Abolition and Survivors Support Coalition International (TASSC), *4121 Harewood Rd. N.E., Suite B 20017-1597; (202) 529-2991. Fax, (202) 529-8334. Gizachew Emiru, Director.*
General email, info@tassc.org

Web, www.tassc.org

Coalition of torture survivors seeking to end torture through public education and political advocacy. Provides resources and information to survivors of torture and their families.

Unitarian Universalist Service Committee, *Washington Office,* 1100 G St. N.W., #800 20005; (202) 393-2255, ext. 24. Fax, (202) 393-5494. Shelley Moskowitz, Manager of Public Policy.*
General email, smoskowitz@uusc.org

Web, www.uusc.org

Secular human rights organization fighting race, gender, environmental, and economic injustice worldwide. Partners with organizations defending right to water, workers' rights, and the democratic process. Responds to disasters. Provides education through travel and service. (Headquarters in Cambridge, MA.)

Narcotics Trafficking

▶AGENCIES

Defense Dept. (DoD), *Counternarcotics and Global Threats,* 2500 Defense Pentagon, #5C653 20301-1510; (703) 697-7202. Fax, (703) 692-6947. Caryn Hollis, Deputy Assistant Secretary.
Web, http://policy.defense.gov/solic/cgnt

Coordinates and monitors Defense Dept. support of civilian drug law enforcement agencies and interagency efforts to detect and monitor the maritime and aerial transit of illegal drugs into the United States. Represents the secretary on drug control matters outside the department.

Drug Enforcement Administration (DEA) *(Justice Dept.),* 700 Army-Navy Dr., Arlington, VA 22202 (mailing address: 8701 Morrissette Dr., MS AES, Springfield, VA 22152); (202) 307-8000. Fax, (202) 307-4540. Michele Leonhart, Administrator. Phone (Command Center), (202) 307-8000. Press, (202) 307-7977. General information, (202) 307-1000.
Web, www.justice.gov/dea

Assists foreign narcotics agents; cooperates with the State Dept., embassies, the Agency for International Development, and international organizations to strengthen narcotics law enforcement and to reduce supply and demand in developing countries; trains and advises narcotics enforcement officers in developing nations.

State Dept., *International Narcotics and Law Enforcement Affairs,* 2201 C St. N.W., #7826 20520-7512; (202) 647-8464. William R. Brownfield, Assistant Secretary. General email, samuelcm@state.gov
Web, www.state.gov/j/inl

Coordinates efforts to establish and facilitate stable criminal justice systems in order to strengthen international law enforcement and judicial effectiveness, bolster cooperation in legal affairs, and support the rule of law, while respecting human rights. Seeks to disrupt the overseas production and trafficking of illicit drugs by means of counter-drug and anti-crime assistance and coordination with foreign nations and international organizations.

U.S. Coast Guard (USCG) *(Homeland Security Dept.),* Law Enforcement, CG-MLE, 2703 Martin Luther King Jr. Ave. S.E., MS 7516 20593-7516; (202) 372-2183. Capt. Phil Welzant, Chief.
Web, www.uscg.mil/hq/cg5/cg531

Oversees enforcement of federal laws and treaties and other international agreements to which the United States is party on, over, and under the high seas and waters subject to the jurisdiction of the United States; jurisdiction includes narcotics, alien migration interdiction, and fisheries.

U.S. Customs and Border Protection *(Homeland Security Dept.),* Border Patrol, 1300 Pennsylvania Ave. N.W., #6.5E 20229; (202) 344-2050. Fax, (202) 344-3140. Michael J. Fisher, Chief.
Web, www.cbp.gov/xp/cgov/border_security/border_patrol

Mobile uniformed law enforcement arm of the Homeland Security Dept. Primary mission is to detect and prevent the illegal trafficking of people and contraband across U.S. borders.

U.S. Customs and Border Protection *(Homeland Security Dept.),* Field Operations, 1300 Pennsylvania Ave. N.W., #2.4A 20229; (202) 344-1620. Fax, (202) 344-2777. Susan T. Mitchell, Assistant Commissioner, Acting. Press, (202) 344-1700. Hotline to report suspicious activity, (800) BE-ALERT; (800) 232-5378.
Web, www.cbp.gov/xp/cgov/about/organization/assist_comm_off/field_operations.xml

Interdicts and seizes contraband, including narcotics and other drugs, at the U.S. border.

INTERNATIONAL TRADE AND DEVELOPMENT

General

▶AGENCIES

Antitrust Division *(Justice Dept.),* Foreign Commerce, 450 5th St. N.W., #1100 20530; (202) 514-2464. Fax, (202) 514-4508. Edward T. Hand, Chief.
Web, www.justice.gov/atr

Acts as the division's liaison with foreign governments and international organizations including the European Union, regarding antitrust enforcement and competition issues. Works with the State Dept. to exchange information with foreign governments concerning investigations involving foreign corporations and nationals.

Bureau of Economic Analysis *(Commerce Dept.),* International Economics, 1441 L St. N.W., #6063 20230; (202) 606-9604. Fax, (202) 606-5311. Sarahelen (Sally) Thompson, Associate Director, (202) 606-9660. General email, internationalaccounts@bea.gov
Web, www.bea.gov

Compiles statistics under the International Investment and Trade in Services Survey Act for an ongoing study of foreign direct investment in the United States and direct investment abroad by the United States.

Bureau of Industry and Security *(Commerce Dept.),* 14th St. and Constitution Ave. N.W., #3898 20230; (202) 482-1455. Fax, (202) 482-6216. Eric L. Hirschhorn, Under Secretary. Press, (202) 482-2721. Export licensing information, (202) 482-4811.
Web, www.bis.doc.gov

U.S. Customs and Border Protection

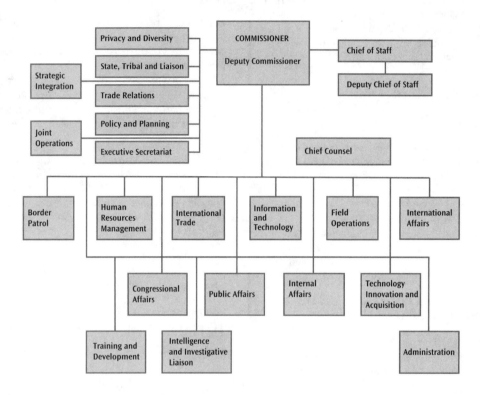

Administers Export Administration Act; coordinates export administration programs of federal departments and agencies; maintains control lists and performs export licensing for the purposes of national security, foreign policy, and short supply. Monitors impact of foreign boycotts on the United States; ensures availability of goods and services essential to industrial performance on contracts for national defense. Assesses availability of foreign products and technology to maintain control lists and licensing.

Census Bureau *(Commerce Dept.), Foreign Trade, 4600 Silver Hill Rd., #6K032, Suitland, MD 20746 (mailing address: change city, state, and zip code to Washington, DC 20233-6700); (301) 763-2255. Fax, (301) 763-6638. Nick Orsini, Chief. Toll-free Information, (800) 549-0595. Web, www.census.gov/trade*

Provides data on all aspects of foreign trade in commodities.

Committee on Foreign Investment in the United States *(Treasury Dept.), 1500 Pennsylvania Ave. N.W., #5221 20220; (202) 622-1860. Fax, (202) 622-0391. Stephen (Steve) Hanson, Staff Chair. General email, cfius@treasury.gov Web, www.treasury.gov/cfius*

Reviews foreign acquisition of U.S. companies and determines whether they pose national security threats. Conducts investigations into such acquisitions.

Consumer Product Safety Commission (CPSC), *Education, Global Outreach, and Small Business Ombudsman, 4330 East-West Hwy., Bethesda, MD 20814; (301) 504-7054. Fax, (301) 504-0407. Robert J. (Jay) Howell, Director, Acting. Web, www.cpsc.gov*

Coordinates international and intergovernmental efforts to improve consumer product safety standards development, harmonization efforts, inspection and enforcement coordination, consumer education, and information transfer about best manufacturing practices across industries.

Export-Import Bank of the United States, *811 Vermont Ave. N.W., #417 20571; (202) 565-3946. Fax, (202) 565-3380. Fred P. Hochberg, Chair. Press, (202) 565-3200. Toll-free hotline, (800) 565-3946. Web, www.exim.gov*

Independent agency of the U.S. government with 12 regional offices. Aids in financing exports of U.S. goods and services; offers direct credit to borrowers outside the United States; guarantees export loans made by commercial lenders, working capital guarantees, and export credit insurance; conducts an intermediary loan program. Hotline advises businesses in using U.S. government export programs.

Federal Trade Commission (FTC), *International Affairs, 600 Pennsylvania Ave. N.W., #H494 20580; (202) 326-3051. Fax, (202) 326-2873. Randolph W. Tritell, Director. Web, www.ftc.gov*

International Trade Administration

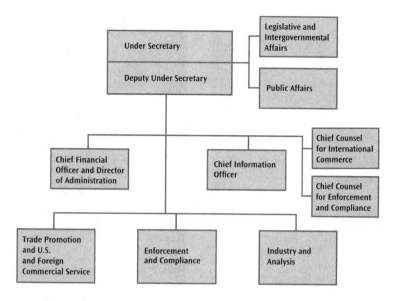

Assists in the enforcement of antitrust laws and consumer protection by arranging appropriate cooperation and coordination with foreign governments in international cases. Negotiates bilateral and multilateral antitrust and consumer protection agreements and represents the United States in international antitrust policy forums. Assists developing countries in moving toward market-based economies.

International Trade Administration (ITA) *(Commerce Dept.),* *1401 Constitution Ave. N.W., #3850 20230; (202) 482-2867. Fax, (202) 482-4821. Kenneth E. Hyatt, Under Secretary, Acting. Press, (202) 482-3809. Publications, (202) 482-5487. Trade information, (800) 872-8723.*
Web, www.trade.gov

Seeks to strengthen the competitiveness of U.S. industry, promote trade and investment, and ensure fair trade and compliance with trade law and agreements.

International Trade Administration (ITA) *(Commerce Dept.), Enforcement and Compliance, 1401 Constitution Ave. N.W., #3099B 20230; (202) 482-1780. Fax, (202) 482-0947. Paul Piquado, Assistant Secretary; Ronald K. Lorentzen, Deputy Assistant Secretary.*
Web, http://trade.gov/enforcement

Enforces antidumping and countervailing duty statutes if foreign goods are subsidized or sold at less than fair market value. Evaluates and processes applications by U.S. international air- and seaport communities seeking to establish limited duty-free zones. Administers the Statutory Import Program, which governs specific tariff schedules and imports and determines whether property left abroad by U.S. agencies may be imported back into the United States.

International Trade Administration (ITA) *(Commerce Dept.), Global Markets, North and Central America, 1401 Constitution Ave. N.W., #3024 20230; (202) 482-6452. Fax, (202) 482-5865. Geri Word, Director.*
Web, www.trade.gov/markets

Coordinates Commerce Dept. activities and assists U.S. business regarding export to Mexico, Canada, Central America, and the Caribbean. Helps negotiate and ensures compliance with U.S. free-trade agreements, including NAFTA (North American Free Trade Agreement) and the Dominican Republic–Central American Free Trade Agreement (CAFTA-DR).

International Trade Administration (ITA) *(Commerce Dept.), Global Markets, SelectUSA, 1401 Constitution Ave. N.W., #1038 20230-0001; (202) 482-5199. Fax, (202) 482-3643. Vinai K. Thummalapally, Executive Director; Aaron Brickman, Deputy Executive Director, (202) 482-1889. Call center, (202) 482-6800.*
General email, info@selectusa.gov
Web, http://selectusa.gov

Manages foreign direct investment promotion and encourages U.S. companies to expand, add new facilities, and bring back jobs from abroad. Facilitates investor inquiries, conducts outreach to foreign investors, provides support for state and local governments' investment promotion efforts, and serves as an ombudsman in Washington, D.C., for the international investment community. Web site available in eight languages.

International Trade Administration (ITA) *(Commerce Dept.), Industry and Analysis, 1401 Constitution Ave. N.W., #3832 20230; (202) 482-1465. Fax, (202) 482-5697. Maureen Smith, Assistant Secretary, Acting; Maureen Smith, Deputy Assistant Secretary.*

General email, tdwebmaster@ita.doc.gov

Web, www.ita.doc.gov/td and www.trade.gov/industry

Seeks to strengthen the international competitiveness of U.S. businesses; coordinates export promotion programs and trade missions; compiles and analyzes trade data. Divisions focus on basic industries, service industries and finance, technology and aerospace, consumer goods, tourism, and environmental technologies exports.

International Trade Administration (ITA) *(Commerce Dept.), Industry and Analysis, Trade Policy and Analysis, 1401 Constitution Ave. N.W., #2128 20230; (202) 482-3177. Fax, (202) 482-4614. Praveen Dixit, Deputy Assistant Secretary, (202) 482-6232.*
Web, www.trade.gov/index.asp

Monitors and analyzes U.S. international trade and competitive performance, foreign direct investment in the United States, and international economic factors affecting U.S. trade; identifies future trends and problems. Annual reports include *U.S. Industrial Trade Outlook* and *Foreign Direct Investment in the United States: Transactions.* Foreign Trade Reference Room open to the public.

International Trade Administration (ITA) *(Commerce Dept.), Industry and Analysis, Trade Promotion Programs, Ronald Reagan Bldg., 1401 Constitution Ave. N.W., #800-RRB 20230; (202) 482-0691. Fax, (202) 482-7800. Gary Rand, Director, International Buyer Program.*
Web, www.export.gov/ibp

Promotes and directs programs to expand exports abroad; manages overseas trade missions; conducts trade fair certification programs. Participates in trade fairs and technology seminars to introduce American products abroad. Provides the business community with sales and trade information through an automated system, which allows a direct connection between U.S. and overseas offices.

International Trade Administration (ITA) *(Commerce Dept.), Trade Promotion, Global Markets, 1401 Constitution Ave. N.W., #3868A 20230; (202) 482-3022. Fax, (202) 482-5444. John M. Andersen, Deputy Assistant Secretary, (202) 482-5341.*
Web, www.trade.gov/markets

Develops and implements trade and investment policies affecting countries, regions, or international organizations to improve U.S. market access abroad. Provides information and analyses of foreign market barriers and economic conditions to the U.S. private sector; monitors foreign compliance with trade agreements signed with the United States.

International Trade Administration (ITA) *(Commerce Dept.), Trade Promotion and U.S. and Foreign Commercial Service, 1401 Constitution Ave. N.W., #3868 20230; (202) 482-5777. Judy Reinke, Assistant Secretary, Acting.*
Web, www.trade.gov

Promotes the export of U.S. goods and services; protects and advocates U.S. business interests abroad; provides counseling and information on overseas markets, international contacts, and trade promotion.

National Institute of Food and Agriculture (NIFA) *(Agriculture Dept.), Center for International Programs, 800 9th St. S.W., #2434 20024 (mailing address: 1400 Independence Ave. S.W., MS 2203, Washington, DC 20250-2203); (202) 720-3801. Fax, (202) 690-2355. Hiram Larew, Assistant Director.*
Web, www.nifa.usda.gov/about/background.html/about/pdfs/fact_sheets/inst_fs_intl.pdf

Promotes science education in developing economies and shares research to enhance food production and stabilize economies. Interests include agricultural extension, teaching, and research.

National Institute of Standards and Technology (NIST) *(Commerce Dept.), Standards Services, 100 Bureau Dr., MS 2100, Gaithersburg, MD 20899; (301) 975-8046. Fax, (301) 975-4715. Gordon Gillerman, Director.*
General email, gsi@nist.gov
Web, http://gsi.nist.gov/global/index.cfm

Monitors and participates in industries' development of standards and standard-enforcement mechanisms. Conducts standards-related research and holds workshops for domestic and international audiences. Provides information on industry standards and specifications, conformity assessment, test methods, domestic and international technical regulations, codes, and recommended practices.

Overseas Private Investment Corp., *1100 New York Ave. N.W. 20527; (202) 336-8400. Fax, (202) 336-7949. Elizabeth L. Littlefield, President. Press, (202) 312-2186. Anti-corruption hotline, (202) 312-2153.*
General email, info@opic.gov
Web, www.opic.gov

Provides assistance through political risk insurance, direct loans, and loan guarantees to qualified U.S. private investors to support their investments in emerging markets. Offers preinvestment information and counseling. Provides insurance against the risks of expropriation, political violence, and inconvertibility of local currency.

President's Export Council *(Commerce Dept.), 14th St. and Constitution Ave. N.W., #4043 20230; (202) 482-1124. Fax, (202) 482-4452. Tricia Van Orden, Executive Secretariat.*
Web, www.trade.gov/pec

Advises the president on all aspects of export trade, including export controls, promotion, and expansion. Composed of 28 private-sector leaders in business, agriculture, and federal, state, and local government.

Small Business Administration (SBA), *International Trade, 409 3rd St. S.W., #8500 20416; (202) 205-6720. Fax, (202) 205-7272. Luz A. Hopewell, Associate Administrator.*
Web, www.sba.gov/about-offices-content/1/2889

Offers instruction, assistance, and information on exporting through counseling and conferences. Helps businesses gain access to export financing through loan guarantee programs. Ensures interests of small businesses are considered and reflected in trade negotiations.

State Dept., *Commercial and Business Affairs,* 2201 C St. N.W., #5820 20520-5820; (202) 647-1625. Fax, (202) 647-3953. Lorraine J. Hariton, Special Representative for Commercial and Business Affairs.
General email, cbaweb@state.gov

Web, www.state.gov/e/eb/cba

Serves as primary contact in the State Dept. for U.S. businesses. Coordinates efforts to facilitate U.S. business interests abroad, ensures that U.S. business interests are given sufficient consideration in foreign policy, and provides assistance to firms with problems overseas (such as claims and trade complaints). Works with agencies in the Export Promotion Coordinating Committee to support U.S. business interests overseas.

State Dept., *Economic and Business Affairs,* 2201 C St. N.W., #4932 20520-5820; (202) 647-7971. Fax, (202) 647-5713. Charles H. Rivkin, Assistant Secretary.
Web, www.state.gov/e/eb

Formulates and implements policies related to U.S. economic relations with foreign countries, including international business practices, communications and information, trade, finance, investment, development, natural resources, energy, and transportation.

State Dept., *Growth, Energy, and the Environment,* 2201 C St. N.W., #7256 20520-7512; (202) 647-7575. Fax, (202) 647-9763. Catherine (Cathy) Novelli, Under Secretary.
Web, www.state.gov/e

Advises the secretary on formulation and conduct of foreign economic policies and programs, including international monetary and financial affairs, trade, telecommunications, energy, agriculture, commodities, investments, and international transportation issues. Coordinates economic summit meetings.

State Dept., *Investment Affairs,* 2201 C St. N.W., #4669 20520-5820; (202) 736-4762. Fax, (202) 647-0320. Michael Tracton, Director.
Web, www.state.gov

Develops U.S. investment policy. Makes policy recommendations regarding multinational enterprises and the expropriation of and compensation for U.S. property overseas. Negotiates bilateral and multilateral investment agreements. Coordinates the State Dept.'s position with respect to the Committee on Foreign Investments in the United States.

State Dept., *Sanctions Policy and Implementation,* 2201 C St. N.W., #4657 20520; (202) 647-7489. Fax, (202) 647-4064. Darnall Steuart, Director, (202) 647-7677.
Web, www.state.gov

Develops and implements U.S. economic sanctions of embargoed countries. Coordinates U.S. participation in multilateral strategic trade control and revisions related to the export of strategically critical high-technology goods. Cooperates with the Commerce, Defense, and Treasury Depts. regarding export controls.

State Dept., *Trade Policy and Programs,* 2201 C St. N.W., #4658, EB/TPP 20520-5820; (202) 647-4017. Fax, (202) 647-6540. Robert D. Manogue, Deputy Assistant Secretary, Acting.
General email, ebtpp@state.gov

Web, www.state.gov/e/eb/tpp

Develops and administers policies and programs on international trade, including trade negotiations and agreements, import relief, unfair trade practices, trade relations with developing countries, export development, and export controls (including controls imposed for national security or foreign policy purposes).

Trade Promotion Coordinating Committee, 14th St. and Constitution Ave. N.W., #31027 20230; (202) 482-5455. Fax, (202) 482-4137. Penny Pritzker, Secretary; Patrick Kirwan, Director.
Web, www.export.gov/advocacy/eg_main_022762.asp

Coordinates all export promotion and export financing activities of the U.S. government. Composed of heads of the departments of Commerce, State, Treasury, Defense, Homeland Security, Interior, Agriculture, Labor, Transportation, and Energy, OMB, U.S. Trade Representative, National Security Council/National Economic Council, EPA, Small Business Administration, AID, Export-Import Bank, Overseas Private Investment Corporation, and the U.S. Trade and Development Agency. Secretary of Commerce is the chair.

Treasury Dept., *Foreign Assets Control,* 1500 Pennsylvania Ave. N.W., OFAC 20220; (202) 622-2510. Fax, (202) 622-1657. Adam Szubin, Director. Fax-on-demand, (202) 622-0077. Hotline, (800) 540-6322.
General email, ofac_feedback@do.treas.gov

Web, www.ustreas.gov/offices/enforcement/ofac

Administers and enforces economic and trade sanctions against targeted foreign countries and regimes, terrorists, international narcotics traffickers, transnational criminal organizations, and those engaged in activities related to the proliferation of weapons of mass destruction. Acts under presidential wartime and national emergency powers, as well as under authority granted by specific legislation, to impose controls on transactions and freeze foreign assets under U.S. jurisdiction.

Treasury Dept., *International Trade,* 1500 Pennsylvania Ave. N.W., #5204 20220; (202) 622-1733. Fax, (202) 622-1731. Brad McDonald, Director.
Web, www.treasury.gov

Formulates Treasury Dept. foreign trade policies and coordinates them with other agencies through the U.S. Trade Representative.

Treasury Dept., *Investment Security,* 1500 Pennsylvania Ave. N.W., #5221 20220; (202) 622-1860. Fax, (202) 622-9212. Mark Jaskowiak, Deputy Assistant Secretary.
General email, cifius@do.treas.gov

Web, www.treasury.gov/about/organizational-structure/offices/International-Affairs/Pages/cfius-index.aspx

Oversees foreign investment and U.S. open investment policy.

U.S. Customs and Border Protection *(Homeland Security Dept.),* 1300 Pennsylvania Ave. N.W., #4.4A 20229; (202) 344-2001. Fax, (202) 344-1380. R. Gil Kerlikowske, Commissioner. Information, (877) 227-5511. Press, (202) 344-1700.
Web, www.cbp.gov

Assesses and collects duties and taxes on imported merchandise; processes persons and baggage entering the United States; collects import and export data for international trade statistics; controls export carriers and goods to prevent fraud and smuggling. Library open to the public by appointment.

U.S. Customs and Border Protection *(Homeland Security Dept.), Commercial Targeting and Enforcement,* 1300 Pennsylvania Ave. N.W., #L-14 20229; (202) 863-6550. Fax, (202) 863-6060. Jerry Malmo, Executive Director, Acting.
Web, www.cbp.gov

Enforces compliance with all commercial import requirements; collects import statistics.

U.S. Foreign Trade Zones Board *(Commerce Dept.),* 1401 Constitution Ave. N.W., #21013 20230; (202) 482-2862. Fax, (202) 482-0002. Andrew McGilvray, Executive Secretary.
Web, www.trade.gov/ftz

Authorizes public and private corporations to establish foreign trade zones to which foreign and domestic goods can be brought without being subject to customs duties.

U.S. International Trade Commission, 500 E St. S.W. 20436; (202) 205-2000. Fax, (202) 708-2431. Irving A. Williamson, Chair, (202) 205-2051. Reference Library, (202) 205-2630.
Web, www.usitc.gov

Provides Congress, the president, and the U.S. trade representative with technical information and advice on trade and tariff matters. Determines the impact of imports on U.S. industries in antidumping and countervailing duty investigations. Directs actions against certain unfair trade practices, such as intellectual property infringement. Investigates and reports on U.S. industries and the global trends that affect them. Publishes the Harmonized Tariff Schedule of the United States. Library open to the public.

U.S. Trade and Development Agency, 1000 Wilson Blvd., #1600, Arlington, VA 22209-3901; (703) 875-4357. Fax, (703) 875-4009. Leocadia I. Zak, Director.
General email, info@ustda.gov
Web, www.ustda.gov

Assists U.S. companies exporting to developing and middle-income countries. Provides grants for feasibility studies. Offers technical assistance and identifies commercial opportunities in these countries.

U.S. Trade Representative *(Executive Office of the President),* 600 17th St. N.W., #205 20508; (202) 395-6890.

Fax, (202) 395-4549. Amb. Michael Froman, U.S. Trade Representative. Press, (202) 395-3230.
General email, correspondence@ustr.eop.gov
Web, www.ustr.gov

Serves as principal adviser to the president and primary trade negotiator on international trade policy. Develops and coordinates U.S. trade policy, including commodity and direct investment matters, import remedies, East–West trade policy, U.S. export expansion policy, and the implementation of MTN (Multilateral Trade Negotiations) agreements. Conducts international trade negotiations and represents the United States in World Trade Organization (WTO) matters.

U.S. Trade Representative *(Executive Office of the President), Intergovernmental Affairs and Public Engagement (IAPE),* 600 17th St. N.W., #107 20508; (202) 395-6120. Fax, (202) 395-3692. Jewel James, Assistant U.S. Trade Representative.
Web, www.ustr.gov

Leads the U.S. Trade Representatives's public outreach efforts to state and local governments; business and agricultural communities; and labor, environmental, and consumer groups. Oversees the U.S. Trade Advisory Committee system.

► CONGRESS

For a listing of relevant congressional committees and subcommittees, please see pages 414–415 or the Appendix.

► INTERNATIONAL ORGANIZATIONS

Food and Agriculture Organization of the United Nations (FAO), *Liaison Office in Washington,* 2121 K St. N.W., #800B 20037-0001; (202) 653-2400. Fax, (202) 653-5760. Nicholas Nelson, Director. Press, (202) 653-0011.
General email, faolow@fao.org
Web, www.fao.org/north_america/en/ and *www.worldfooddayusa.org*

Offers development assistance; collects, analyzes, and disseminates information; provides policy and planning advice to governments; acts as an international forum for debate on food and agricultural issues, including animal health and production, fisheries, and forestry; encourages sustainable agricultural development and a long-term strategy for the conservation and management of natural resources. Coordinates World Food Day. (International headquarters in Rome.)

Inter-American Development Bank, 1300 New York Ave. N.W. 20577; (202) 623-1000. Fax, (202) 623-3096. Luis Alberto Moreno, President; Gustavo Arnavat, U.S. Executive Director. Library, (202) 623-3211. Press, (202) 623-1555.
Web, www.iadb.org

Promotes, through loans and technical assistance, the investment of public and private capital in member countries of Latin America and the Caribbean for social and economic development purposes. Facilitates economic integration of the Latin American region, operating the Inter-American Investment Corporation and the Multilateral Investment Fund. Library open to the public by appointment.

International Bank for Reconstruction and Development *(World Bank),* *1818 H St. N.W. 20433; (202) 473-1000. Fax, (202) 477-6391. Hon. KimJim Yong, President; Vacant, U.S. Executive Director. Press, (202) 473-7660. Bookstore, (202) 458-4500. Anticorruption hotline, (800) 831-0463.*
General email, gchopra@worldbank.org
Web, www.worldbank.org

International development institution funded by government membership subscriptions and borrowings on private capital markets. Encourages the flow of public and private foreign investment into developing countries through loans, grants, and technical assistance; collects data on selected economic indicators, world trade, and external public debt. Finances economic development projects in agriculture, environmental protection, education, public utilities, telecommunications, water supply, sewerage, public health, and other areas.

International Centre for Settlement of Investment Disputes (ICSID), *1818 H St. N.W., MS J2-200 20433; (202) 458-1534. Fax, (202) 522-2615. Meg Kinnear, Secretary General, (202) 473-5531.*
General email, ICSIDsecretariat@worldbank.org
Web, www.worldbank.org/icsid

Handles the conciliation and arbitration of investment disputes between contracting states and foreign investors. Has more than 140 member states and is affiliated with the World Bank.

International Development Assn., *1818 H St. N.W., #H3306 20433; (202) 473-1400. Fax, (202) 522-2515. Antonella Bassani, Director, (202) 473-1468.*
Web, www.worldbank.org/ida

Affiliate of the World Bank funded by membership contributions and transfers of funds from the World Bank. Provides long-term interest-free loans and grants to the poorest countries.

International Monetary Fund (IMF), *Statistics, 700 19th St. N.W. 20431; (202) 623-7123. Louis Marc Ducharme, Director. Publications, (202) 623-7430.*
General email, statisticsquery@imf.org
Web, www.elibrary-data.imf.org and www.imf.org/external/data.htm

Publishes monthly *International Financial Statistics (IFS),* which includes comprehensive financial data for most countries, and *Direction of Trade Statistics,* a quarterly publication, which includes the distribution of exports and imports for 1692 countries. Annual statistical publications include the *Balance of Payments Statistics Yearbook, Direction of Trade Statistics Yearbook,Government Finance Statistics Yearbook,* and *International Financial Statistics Yearbook.* Subscriptions available to the public. All four publications are available on CD-ROM and on the Web site.

Organisation for Economic Co-operation and Development (OECD), *Washington Center, 2001 L St. N.W., #650 20036-4922; (202) 785-6323. Fax, (202) 312-2508. Jill A. Schuker, Deputy, Washington Office.*
General email, washington.contact@oecd.org
Web, www.oecd.org

Membership: thirty-four nations, including Australia, Canada, Japan, Mexico, New Zealand, the United States, and western European nations. Funded by membership contributions. Serves as a forum for members to exchange information and coordinate their economic policies; compiles statistics. Washington Center sells OECD publications and software; maintains a reference library that is open to the public. (Headquarters in Paris.)

United Nations Information Centre *1775 K St. N.W., #400 20006-1500; (202) 331-8670. Fax, (202) 331-9191. Rodney Bent, Director.*
General email, unicdc@unic.org
Web, www.unicwash.org

► **JUDICIARY**

U.S. Court of Appeals for the Federal Circuit *717 Madison Pl. N.W. 20439; (202) 275-8000. Fax, (202) 275-8036. Randall R. Rader, Chief Judge, (202) 633-6297; Jan Horbaly, Clerk, (202) 312-5520. Helpdesk, (202) 275-8040; (855) 860-8240. Mediation, (202) 275-8120.*
Web, www.cafc.uscourts.gov

► **NONGOVERNMENTAL**

Assn. of Foreign Investors in Real Estate, *1300 Pennsylvania Ave. N.W. 20004-3020; (202) 312-1400. Fax, (202) 312-1401. James A. Fetgatter, Chief Executive.*
General email, afireinfo@afire.org
Web, www.afire.org

Represents foreign institutions that are interested in the laws, regulations, and economic trends affecting the U.S. real estate market. Informs the public and the government of the contributions foreign investment makes to the U.S. economy. Examines current issues and organizes seminars for members.

Assn. of Women in International Trade, *204 E St. N.E. 20002; (202) 293-2948. Fax, (202) 547-6348. Phyllis Derrick, President.*
General email, info@wiit.org
Web, www.wiit.org

Membership: women and men from all sectors concerned with international trade, including import-export firms, government, corporations, and nonprofit organizations. Provides members with opportunities for professional development. Maintains job bank and sponsors mentoring program.

Center for Global Development, *250 L St. N.W., #500 20036; (202) 416-4000. Fax, (202) 416-4050. Nancy Birdsall, President.*

General email, info@cgdev.org

Web, www.cgdev.org

Works to reduce global poverty and inequality through policy-oriented research and active engagement on development issues with policymakers and the public. Conducts independent research to develop practical ideas for global prosperity.

Center for International Private Enterprise, *1155 15th St. N.W., #700 20005-2706; (202) 721-9200. Fax, (202) 721-9250. Greg Lebedev, Chair; John D. Sullivan, Executive Director.*

General email, info@cipe.org

Web, www.cipe.org

Promotes global democratic development through private enterprise and market-oriented reform. Supported by the National Endowment for Democracy, works with business leaders, policymakers, and journalists to build civic institutions. Key program areas include anti-corruption, access to information, the informal sector and property rights, and women and youth. (Affiliated with the U.S. Chamber of Commerce.)

Coalition for Employment Through Exports, *1625 K St. N.W., #200 20006; (202) 296-6107. Fax, (202) 296-9709. John Hardy Jr., President.*

General email, info@usaexport.org

Web, www.usaexport.org

Membership: major U.S. exporters and banks. Works to ensure adequate lending authority for the Export-Import Bank and other trade finance facilities as well as aggressive export financing policies for the United States.

Economic Strategy Institute, *3050 K St. N.W., #220 20007; (202) 965-9484. Fax, (202) 339-0880. Clyde V. Prestowitz Jr., President.*

General email, info@econstrat.org

Web, www.econstrat.org

Works to increase U.S. economic competitiveness through research on domestic and international economic policies, industrial and technological developments, and global security issues. Testifies before Congress and government agencies.

Emergency Committee for American Trade, *900 17th St. N.W., #1150 20006; (202) 659-5147. Fax, (202) 659-1347. Calman J. Cohen, President.*

General email, ecattrade@ecattrade.com

Web, www.ecattrade.com

Membership: U.S. corporations interested in international trade and investment. Supports liberalized trade and investment and opposes restrictions on U.S. exports and imports.

Federation of International Trade Assns., *11654 Plaza America Dr., #120, Reston, VA 20190; (703) 929-3672. Kimberly Park, President.*

General email, info@fita.org

Web, www.fita.org

Membership: local, regional, and national trade associations throughout North America that have an international mission. Works to increase North American exports.

Global Business Dialogue, *1140 Connecticut Ave. N.W., #950 20036; (202) 463-5074. Fax, (202) 463-7075. R.K. Morris, President.*

General email, comments@gbdinc.org

Web, www.gbdinc.org

Promotes discussion of trade and investment within the global business community.

Institute for Sustainable Communities, *Washington Office, 888 17th St. N.W., #610 20006; (202) 777-7575. Fax, (202) 777-7577. George Hamilton, President; Debra Perry, Senior Program Manager, U.S..*

General email, isc@iscvt.org

Web, www.iscvt.org

Provides training and technical assistance to communities to engage citizens in developing and implementing plans for a sustainable future. (Headquarters in Montpelier, Vt.)

International Business Ethics Institute, *1776 Eye St. N.W., 9th Floor 20006; (202) 296-6936. Fax, (202) 296-5897. Lori Tansey Martens, President.*

General email, info@business-ethics.org

Web, www.business-ethics.org

Nonpartisan educational organization that promotes business ethics and corporate responsibility. Works to increase public awareness and dialogue about international business ethics issues through various educational resources and activities. Works with companies to assist them in establishing effective international ethics programs.

National Assn. of Manufacturers (NAM), *International Economic Affairs, 733 10th St. N.W., #700 20001; (202) 637-3144. Fax, (202) 637-3182. Linda Dempsey, Vice President.*

Web, www.nam.org

Represents manufacturing business interests on international economic issues, including trade, international investment, export financing, and export controls.

National Customs Brokers and Forwarders Assn. of America, *1200 18th St. N.W., #901 20036; (202) 466-0222. Fax, (202) 466-0226. Barbara Reilly, Executive Vice President.*

General email, staff@ncbfaa.org

Web, www.ncbfaa.org

Membership: customs brokers and freight forwarders in the United States. Fosters information exchange within the industry. Monitors legislation and regulations.

National Foreign Trade Council, *1625 K St. N.W., #200 20006-1604; (202) 887-0278. Fax, (202) 452-8160. William A. Reinsch, President.*

General email, nftcinformation@nftc.org

Web, www.nftc.org

Membership: U.S. companies engaged in international trade and investment. Advocates open international trading, export expansion, and policies to assist U.S. companies competing in international markets. Provides members with information on international trade topics. Sponsors seminars and conferences.

Organization for International Investment, *1225 19th St. N.W., #501 20036; (202) 659-1903. Fax, (202) 659-2293. Nancy McLernon, President.*
General email, johnsamford@offii.org

Web, www.ofii.org

Membership: U.S. subsidiaries of international companies. Provides data on international investment in the United States, including reports on exports, tax revenue, and job creation. Monitors legislation and regulations concerning the business operations of U.S. subsidiaries.

Peterson Institute for International Economics (IIE), *1750 Massachusetts Ave. N.W. 20036-1903; (202) 328-9000. Fax, (202) 659-3225. Adam Posen, Director.*
General email, comments@piie.com

Web, www.petersoninstitute.org

Conducts studies and makes policy recommendations on international economic issues, including monetary affairs, trade, investment, energy, exchange rates, commodities, and North–South and East–West economic relations.

United States Council for International Business, *Policy and Government Affairs, 1400 K St. N.W., #450 20005; (202) 371-1316. Fax, (202) 371-8249. Robert Mulligan, Senior Vice President.*
General email, info@uscib.org

Web, www.uscib.org

Membership: multinational corporations, service companies, law firms, and business associations. Represents U.S. business positions before intergovernmental bodies, foreign governments, and business communities. Promotes an open system of world trade, finance, and investment. (Headquarters in New York.)

Urban Institute, *Center on International Development and Governance, 2100 M St. N.W. 20037; (202) 261-5735. Fax, (202) 466-3982. Charles Cadwell, Director.*
General email, idginfo@urban.org

Web, www.urban.org/center/idg/index.cfm

Promotes economic and democratic development in developing and transition countries. Conducts research and works with government officials, international development agencies, and international financial institutions to provide technical assistance toward local governance, service delivery, and public finance.

U.S. Chamber of Commerce, *International Division, 1615 H St. N.W. 20062-2000; (202) 463-5460. Fax, (202) 463-3114. Myron Brilliant, Executive Vice President.*
Web, www.uschamber.com/international

Provides liaison with network of U.S. chambers of commerce abroad; administers bilateral business councils; responsible for international economic policy development;

informs members of developments in international affairs, business economics, and trade; sponsors seminars and conferences. Monitors legislation and regulations.

Washington International Trade Assn., *1300 Pennsylvania Ave. N.W., #400 20004-3014; (202) 312-1600. Fax, (202) 312-1601. Javiera Gallardo, Executive Director.*
General email, wita@wita.org

Web, www.wita.org

Membership: trade professionals. Conducts programs and provides neutral forums to discuss international trade issues. Monitors legislation and regulations.

Women Thrive Worldwide, *1726 M St. N.W., #1075 20036; (202) 999-4500. Fax, (202) 999-4455. Ritu Sharma, President.*
General email, thrive@womenthrive.org

Web, www.womenthrive.org

Advocates international economic policies and human rights that support women worldwide in ending poverty. Researches and develops economic trade policies that reduce poverty, illiteracy, illness, and violence in developing countries.

World Cocoa Foundation, *1411 K St. N.W., #502 20005; (202) 737-7870. Fax, (202) 737-7832. William Guyton, President.*
General email, wcf@worldcocoa.org

Web, www.worldcocoafoundation.org

Promotes a sustainable cocoa economy through economic and social development and environmental conservation in cocoa-growing communities. Helps raise funds for cocoa farmers and increases their access to modern farming practices.

World Shipping Council, *1156 15th St. N.W., #300 20005; (202) 589-1230. Fax, (202) 589-1231. Christopher L. Koch, President.*
General email, info@worldshipping.org

Web, www.worldshipping.org

Membership association representing the liner shipping industry. Works with policymakers and other industry groups interested in international transportation issues, including maritime security, regulatory policy, tax issues, safety, the environment, harbor dredging, and trade infrastructure. Monitors legislation and regulations.

Development Assistance

▶**AGENCIES**

Agency for International Development (USAID), *Education, 1300 Pennsylvania Ave. N.W., #3.9-37 20523-3901; (202) 712-1873. Fax, (202) 216-3229. Natasha DeMarcken, Director.*
Web, www.usaid.gov/who-we-are/organization/bureaus/ bureau-economic-growth-education-and-environment

Provides field support, technical leadership, and research to help foreign missions and countries manage and develop their human resources. Improves the means of basic and higher education as well as training. Administers the AID Participant Training Program, which provides students and midcareer professionals from developing countries with academic and technical training, and the Entrepreneur International Initiative, a short-term training/trade program that matches developing country entrepreneurs with American counterparts to familiarize them with American goods, services, and technology.

Agency for International Development (USAID),
Volunteers for Prosperity (VfP), 1300 Pennsylvania Ave. N.W. 20523-8600; (202) 712-0076. Fax, (202) 712-0077. Kathleen Hunt, Director, Acting.
General email, volunteersforprosperity@usaid.gov
Web, www.volunteersforprosperity.gov

Links U.S.-based companies and nonprofit organizations deployed in foreign assistance with skilled American professionals in volunteer opportunities that support the strategic development goals of the U.S. government.

Foreign Agricultural Service (FAS) *(Agriculture Dept.),*
1400 Independence Ave. S.W., #5071S, MS 1001 20250-1001; (202) 720-3935. Fax, (202) 690-2159. Philip (Phil) Karsting, Administrator. Public Affairs, (202) 720-3448.
Web, www.fas.usda.gov

Administers the U.S. foreign food aid program with the U.S. Agency for International Development. Responsible for the Food for Progress Program, and the McGovern-Dole International Food for Education and Child Nutrition Program.

Millennium Challenge Corp., *875 15th St. N.W. 20005; (202) 521-3600. Fax, (202) 521-3700. Daniel W. Yohannes, Chief Executive Officer.*
General email, web@mcc.gov
Web, www.mcc.gov

Government corporation that provides financial assistance to developing nations that encourage economic freedom. Funds are used for agricultural development, education, enterprise and private-sector development, governance, health, and building trade capacity. Monitors legislation and regulations.

Peace Corps, *1111 20th St. N.W. 20526; (202) 692-2100. Fax, (202) 692-2101. Carolyn Hessler-Radelet, Director, Acting. Information, (855) 855-1961. Press, (202) 692-2230.*
Web, www.peacecorps.gov and Twitter, @PeaceCorps

Promotes world peace, friendship, and mutual understanding between the United States and developing nations. Administers volunteer programs to assist developing countries in education, the environment, health (particularly HIV awareness and prevention), small business development, agriculture, and urban youth development.

Treasury Dept., *Development Policy and Debt, 1500 Pennsylvania Ave. N.W., #5417 20220; (202) 622-9124. Fax, (202) 622-0664. Karen Mathiasen, Deputy Assistant Secretary.*
Web, www.treasury.gov/about/organizational-structure/offices/Pages/Development-Policy-and-Debt.aspx

Leads economic growth and poverty reduction efforts in developing countries by providing funds to multilateral development banks; advises the department and the department banks on reforms and innovative financing proposals; formulates the U.S. position on issues facing debtor countries.

▶**INTERNATIONAL ORGANIZATIONS**

International Bank for Reconstruction and Development *(World Bank), Human Development Network, 1818 H St. N.W. 20433; (202) 473-1000. Elizabeth King, Vice President, Acting; Carolyn Reynolds, Media Contact, (202) 473-0049.*
Web, www.worldbank.org

Provides member countries with support for initiatives to eradicate extreme poverty and hunger, achieve universal primary education, promote gender equality, reduce child mortality, combat HIV/AIDS, and ensure environmental sustainability.

United Nations Development Programme (UNDP),
Washington Office, 1775 K St. N.W., #420 20006; (202) 331-9130. Fax, (202) 331-9363. Helen Clark, Administrator.
Web, www.undp.org

Funded by voluntary contributions from national governments. Administers United Nations' support for economic and social development in developing countries, democratic governance, poverty reduction, crisis prevention and recovery, energy and the environment, and HIV/AIDS. (Headquarters in New York.)

▶**NONGOVERNMENTAL**

ACDI/VOCA, *50 F St. N.W., #1075 20001-1530; (202) 469-6000. Fax, (202) 469-6257. William Polidoro, President.*
General email, webmaster@acdivoca.org
Web, www.acdivoca.org

Recruits professionals for voluntary, short-term technical assistance to cooperatives, environmental groups, and agricultural enterprises in developing countries and emerging democracies. Interests include poverty reduction, community stabilization, and market integration. Promotes rural finance for micro- to medium-sized enterprises. (ACDI/VOCA resulted from the 1997 merger of Agricultural Cooperative Development International and Volunteers in Overseas Cooperative Assistance.)

Adventist Development and Relief Agency, *12501 Old Columbia Pike, Silver Spring, MD 20904; (301) 680-6380. Fax, (301) 680-6370. Jonathan Duffy, President. Toll-free, (800) 424-2372.*
General email, response@adra.org
Web, www.adra.org

Worldwide humanitarian agency of the Seventh-day Adventist Church. Works to alleviate poverty in developing countries and responds to disasters. Sponsors activities that improve health, foster economic and social well-being, and build self-reliance.

American Jewish World Service, *Washington Office,*
1001 Connecticut Ave. N.W., #1200 20036-3405; (202) 379-
4300. Fax, (202) 379-4310. Timi Gerson, Director of
Advocacy. Information, (800) 889-7146.
Web, www.ajws.org

International development organization that works to
alleviate poverty, hunger, and disease. Provides grants to
grassroots organizations; offers volunteer services, advocacy, and education for society building, sustainable development, and protection of human rights. Promotes global
citizenship within the Jewish community. (Headquarters
in New York.)

Ashoka: Innovators for the Public, *1700 N. Moore St.,*
#2000, Arlington, VA 22209; (703) 527-8300. Fax, (703)
527-8383. Diana Wells, President.
General email, info@ashoka.org
Web, www.ashoka.org

Supports fellowships for individuals with ideas for
social change in sixty developing nations. Provides fellows
with research support, organizational networking, legal
counseling, economic support, and business consulting.
Seeks to educate the public about the developing world
and the work of its fellows.

CARE, *Washington Office, 1825 Eye St. N.W., #301 20006-*
1611; (202) 595-2800. Fax, (202) 296-8695. David Ray,
Head of Policy and Advocacy. Toll-free, (800) 422-7385.
General email, info@care.org
Web, www.care.org

Assists the developing world's poor through emergency assistance and community self-help programs that
focus on sustainable development, agriculture, agroforestry, water and sanitation, health, family planning, and
income generation. Community-based efforts are centered
on providing resources to poor women. (U.S. headquarters
in Atlanta, Ga.; international headquarters in Geneva.)

Center for Intercultural Education and Development,
330 Whitehaven St. N.W., #1000 20007 (mailing address:
P.O. Box 579400, Georgetown University, Washington, DC
20057-9400); (202) 687-1400. Fax, (202) 687-2555.
Chantal Santelices, Director.
Web, http://cied.georgetown.edu

Designs and administers programs aimed at improving the quality of life of economically disadvantaged people; provides technical education, job training, leadership
skills development, and business management training;
runs programs in Central America, the Caribbean, Central
Europe, and Southeast Asia.

Global Communities, *8601 Georgia Ave., #800, Silver*
Spring, MD 20910-3440; (301) 587-4700. Fax, (301) 587-
7315. David Weiss, President.
General email, mailbox@chfinternational.org
Web, www.globalcommunities.org

Works under contract with the Agency for International Development, United Nations, and World Bank
to strengthen local government housing departments
abroad.

InterAction, *1400 16th St. N.W., #210 20036; (202) 667-*
8227. Fax, (202) 667-8236. Samuel A. Worthington,
President. Communications, (202) 552-6561.
General email, ia@interaction.org
Web, www.interaction.org

Alliance of more than 190 U.S.-based international
development and humanitarian nongovernmental organizations. Provides a forum for exchange of information on
development assistance issues, including food aid and
other relief services, migration, and refugee affairs. Monitors legislation and regulations.

International Center for Research on Women, *1120 20th*
St. N.W., #500N 20036; (202) 797-0007. Fax, (202) 797-
0020. Sarah Degnan Kambou, President. Press, (202) 742-
1250.
General email, info@icrw.org
Web, www.icrw.org

Advances gender equality and human rights, fights
poverty, and promotes sustainable economic and social
development through research, publications, and media
outreach. Conducts empirical research and promotes
practical, evidence-based solutions that enable women to
control their own lives and fully participate in their societies.

National Peace Corps Assn., *1900 L St. N.W., #610 20036-*
5002; (202) 293-7728. Fax, (202) 293-7554. Anne Baker,
Vice President, ext. 19.
General email, news@peacecorpsconnect.org
Web, www.peacecorpsconnect.org

Membership: returned Peace Corps volunteers, staff,
and interested individuals. Promotes a global perspective
in the United States; seeks to educate the public about the
developing world; supports Peace Corps programs; maintains network of returned volunteers.

Oxfam America, *Policy, 1100 15th St. N.W. #600 20005-*
1759; (202) 496-1180. Fax, (202) 496-1190.
Raymond C. Offenheiser, President; Paul O'Brien, Vice
President for Policy and Campaigns. Information, (800)
776-9326. Press, (202) 496-1169.
General email, info@oxfamamerica.org
Web, www.oxfamamerica.org

Funds disaster relief and long-term development programs internationally. Organizes grassroots support in the
United States for issues affecting global poverty, including
climate change, aid reform, and corporate transparency.
(Headquarters in Boston, Mass.)

Partners for Livable Communities, *1429 21st St. N.W.*
20036; (202) 887-5990. Robert H. McNulty, President.
General email, livability@livable.org
Web, www.livable.org

Provides technical assistance, support services, and
information to assist communities in creating better living
environments. Works in the Caribbean, South America,
and Europe on public-private partnerships and resource
development to improve living environments. Conducts

conferences and workshops; maintains referral clearinghouse.

Pyxera Global, *1030 15th St. N.W. 20005; (202) 872-0933. Fax, (202) 872-0923. Deirdre White, Chief Executive Officer.*
General email, info@cdc.org
Web, www.cdc.org

Recruits and coordinates public, private, and volunteer resources to strengthen small and medium-sized businesses and the institutions, governments, and industries that drive economic growth in emerging markets through five practice areas: global citizenship and volunteerism, supply chain development, tourism development, security and economic recovery, and access to finance for development. (Formerly CDC Development Solutions.)

Salvation Army World Service Office, *615 Slaters Lane, Alexandria, VA 22314 (mailing address: P.O. Box 1428, Alexandria, VA 22313); (703) 684-5528. Fax, (703) 684-5536. Lt. Col. William Mackabee, Executive Director; Susan Davis, Development, (703) 519-5890.*
General email, sawso@usn.salvationarmy.org
Web, www.sawso.org

Works in Eastern Europe, Latin America, the Caribbean, Africa, Asia, and the South Pacific to provide technical assistance to local Salvation Army programs of health services, vocational and business training, literacy, microenterprise, and relief and reconstruction assistance. (International headquarters in London.)

United Way Worldwide, *701 N. Fairfax St., Alexandria, VA 22314-2045; (703) 836-7112. Fax, (703) 519-0097. Brian A. Gallagher, President.*
General email, worldwide@unitedway.org
Web, http://worldwide.unitedway.org

Membership: independent United Way organizations in 40 countries and territories, including 1,300 in the United States. Provides staff training; fundraising, planning, and communications assistance; resource management; and national public service advertising. Activities support education, financial stability, and health.

Vital Voices Global Partnership, *1625 Massachusetts Ave. N.W., #300 20036; (202) 861-2625. Fax, (202) 296-4142. Alyse Nelson, Chief Executive Officer.*
General email, info@vitalvoices.org
Web, www.vitalvoices.org

Worldwide organization of volunteers with governmental, corporate, or other leadership expertise that trains and mentors emerging women leaders in Asia, Africa, Eurasia, Latin America, and the Middle East. Seeks to expand women's political participation and representation, increase women's entrepreneurship and business leadership, and combat human rights violations affecting women.

World Learning, *International Exchange Programs, 1015 15th St. N.W., 7th Floor 20005-2065; (202) 408-5420. Fax, (202) 408-5397. Carol Jenkins, Senior Vice President,*

International Development and Exchange Programs, (202) 464-6643. Toll-free, (800) 858-0292.
General email, carol.jenkins@worldlearning.org
Web, www.worldlearning.org

Partners with nongovernmental organizations, government institutions, schools, universities, and others to strengthen local capacity and performance. Develops training programs that prepare local organizations to lead development initiatives. Provides technical assistance, mentoring, and small grant funding. Administered by World Learning's Division of International Development and Exchange Programs. Administers field-based study abroad programs, which offer semester and summer programs for high school, college, and graduate students.

Finance, Monetary Affairs

▶**AGENCIES**

Commerce Dept., *Bureau of Economic Analysis, Balance of Payments, 1441 L St. N.W. 20230; (202) 606-9900. Fax, (202) 606-5314. Paul Farello, Chief. Press, (202) 606-2649.*
General email, customerservice@bea.gov
Web, www.bea.gov/international

Compiles, analyzes, and publishes quarterly U.S. balance-of-payments figures, including international investment positions.

Federal Reserve System, *International Finance, 20th and C Sts. N.W., #B1242C 20551-0001; (202) 452-3770. Fax, (202) 452-6424. Steven B. Kamin, Director; Michelle Smith, Press Contact. Press, (202) 452-3799.*
Web, www.federalreserve.gov/econresdata/ifstaff.htm

Provides the Federal Reserve's board of governors with economic analyses of international developments. Compiles data on exchange rates.

State Dept., *International Finance and Development, 2201 C St. N.W., #4950 20520; (202) 647-9496. Fax, (202) 647-5713. William E. Craft, Principal Deputy Assistant Secretary.*
Web, www.state.gov

Formulates and implements policies related to multinational investment and insurance; activities of the World Bank and regional banks in the financial development of various countries; bilateral aid; international monetary reform; international antitrust cases; and international debt, banking, and taxation.

State Dept., *Monetary Affairs, 2201 C St. N.W., #4880 20520; (202) 647-9497. Fax, (202) 647-7453. Andrew Haviland, Director.*
Web, www.state.gov

Monitors global macroeconomic developments and identifies financial trends and potential crises in countries affecting U.S. interests. Formulates debt relief policies and negotiates debt relief agreements.

Treasury Dept., *International Affairs*, 1500 Pennsylvania Ave. N.W., #3432 20220; (202) 622-1270. Fax, (202) 622-0417. Vacant, Under Secretary. Press, (202) 622-2920. Web, www.treasury.gov/about/organizational-structure/ Pages/Office-of-International-Affairs.aspx

Coordinates and implements U.S. international economic and financial policy in cooperation with other government agencies. Works to improve the international monetary and investment system; monitors international gold and foreign exchange operations; coordinates development lending; coordinates Treasury Dept. participation in foreign investment in the United States; studies international monetary, economic, and financial issues; analyzes data on international transactions.

Treasury Dept., *Trade Finance and Investment Negotiations*, 1500 Pennsylvania Ave. N.W., #5419 20220; (202) 622-2120. Fax, (202) 622-0967. David Drysdale, Director.
Web, www.treasury.gov

Heads the U.S. delegation to the Participants and Working Party on Export Credits and Credit Guarantees of the Organisation for Economic Co-operation and Development, negotiating agreements to reduce subsidies in export credit support. Negotiates bilateral investment treaties (BITs) and the investment portion of free-trade agreements (FTAs) with foreign governments.

▶ CONGRESS

For a listing of relevant congressional committees and subcommittees, please see pages 414–415 or the Appendix.

▶ INTERNATIONAL ORGANIZATIONS

International Finance Corp., 2121 Pennsylvania Ave. N.W. 20433; (202) 473-3800. Jin-Yong Caj, Executive Vice President. Press, (202) 473-8764.
Web, www.ifc.org

World Bank affiliate that promotes private enterprise in developing countries through direct investments in projects that establish new businesses or expand, modify, or diversify existing businesses; provides its own financing or recruits financing from other sources. Gives developing countries technical assistance in capital market development, privatization, corporate restructuring, and foreign investment.

International Monetary Fund (IMF), 700 19th St. N.W. 20431; (202) 623-7000. Fax, (202) 623-4661. Christine Lagarde, Managing Director; Meg Lundsager, U.S. Executive Director.
Web, www.imf.org

International organization of 187 member countries that promotes policies for financial stability and economic growth, works to prevent financial crises, and helps members solve balance-of-payments problems through loans funded by member contributions.

Multilateral Investment Guarantee Agency, 1818 H St. N.W. 20433; (202) 458-4798. Fax, (202) 522-0316.

Keiko Hinda, Executive Vice President. Press, (202) 473-0844.
General email, migaenquiry@worldbank.org
Web, www.miga.org

World Bank affiliate that encourages foreign investment in developing countries. Provides guarantees against losses due to currency transfer, expropriation, war, civil disturbance, breach of contract, and the nonhonoring of a sovereign financial obligation. Provides dispute resolution services for guaranteed investments to prevent disruptions to developmentally beneficial projects. Membership open to World Bank member countries.

▶ NONGOVERNMENTAL

BAFT, 1120 Connecticut Ave. N.W., 5th Floor 20036-3902; (202) 663-7575. Fax, (202) 663-5538. Tod R. Burwell, Chief Executive Officer.
General email, info@baft-ifsa.com
Web, www.baft.org

Membership: international financial services providers, including U.S. and non-U.S. commercial banks, financial services companies, and suppliers with major international operations. Interests include international trade, trade finance, payments, compliance, asset servicing, and transaction banking. Monitors and advocates globally on activities that affect the business of commercial and international banks and non-financial companies. (Formerly Bankers' Assn. for Financial Trade.)

Bretton Woods Committee, 1726 M St. N.W., #200 20036; (202) 331-1616. Fax, (202) 785-9423. Randy Rodgers, Executive Director.
General email, info@brettonwoods.org
Web, www.brettonwoods.org

Works to increase public understanding of the World Bank, the regional development institutions, the International Monetary Fund, and the World Trade Organization.

Institute of International Finance, 1333 H St. N.W., #800 East 20005; (202) 857-3600. Fax, (202) 775-1430. Timothy D. Adams, President. Press, (202) 331-8183.
General email, info@iif.com
Web, www.iif.com

Global association of financial institutions. Provides analysis and research on emerging markets. Identifies and analyzes regulatory, financial, and economic policy issues. Promotes the development of sound financial systems, with particular emphasis on emerging markets.

Transparency International USA, *Washington Office*, 1023 15th St. N.W., #300 20005; (202) 589-1616. Fax, (202) 589-1512. Claudia J. Damas, President.
General email, administration@transparency-usa.org
Web, www.transparency-usa.org

Seeks to curb corruption in international transactions. Promotes reform of government, business, and development assistance transactions through effective anti-corruption laws and policies. (Headquarters in Berlin, Germany.)

REGIONAL AFFAIRS

See also Foreign Embassies, U.S. Ambassadors, and Country Desk Offices (Appendix).

Africa

For North Africa, see Near East and South Asia.

▶AGENCIES

African Development Foundation (ADF), *1400 Eye St. N.W., #1000 20005-2248; (202) 673-3916. Fax, (202) 673-3810. Shari Berenbach, President. Press, (202) 673-3916, ext. 8811.*
General email, info@usadf.gov
Web, www.usadf.gov

Established by Congress to work with and fund organizations and individuals involved in community-based development projects in Africa. Gives preference to projects involving extensive participation by local Africans. Work focuses on conflict and postconflict areas.

Agency for International Development (USAID), *Africa Bureau, 1300 Pennsylvania Ave. N.W., #4.08C 20523-4801; (202) 712-4810. Fax, (202) 216-3008. Erica Navarro, Senior Deputy Assistant Administrator, Acting. Press, (202) 712-4320.*
Web, www.usaid.gov/who-we-are/organization/bureaus/bureau-africa

Advises the AID administrator on U.S. policy toward developing countries in Africa.

Defense Dept. (DoD), *International Security Affairs, The Pentagon, #3C889 20301-2400; (703) 697-2788. Fax, (703) 697-3279. Derek H. Chollet, Assistant Secretary.*
Web, www.defense.gov

Advises the secretary of defense and recommends policies on regional security issues in the Middle East, Africa, Russia/Eurasia, and Europe/NATO.

State Dept., *Bureau of African Affairs, 2201 C St. N.W., #6234 20520-3430; (202) 647-4440. Fax, (202) 647-6301. Linda Thomas-Greenfield, Assistant Secretary.*
Web, www.state.gov

Advises the secretary on U.S. policy toward sub-Saharan Africa. Directors, assigned to different regions in Africa, aid the assistant secretary.

State Dept., *Central African Affairs, 2201 C St. N.W., #4244 20520-2902; (202) 647-4977. Fax, (202) 647-1726. Robin D. Meyer, Director.*
Web, www.state.gov

Includes Burundi, Cameroon, Central African Republic, Chad, the Democratic Republic of Congo, the Republic of Congo, Equatorial Guinea, Gabon, Rwanda, and São Tomé and Principe.

State Dept., *East African Affairs, 2201 C St. N.W., #5238 20520; (202) 647-8852. Fax, (202) 647-0810. Michael Morrow, Director.*
Web, www.state.gov

Includes Comoros, Djibouti, Eritrea, Ethiopia, Kenya, Madagascar, Mauritius, Seychelles, Somalia, Tanzania, and Uganda.

State Dept., *Southern African Affairs, 2201 C St. N.W., #4236 20520; (202) 647-9836. Fax, (202) 647-5007. Christine A. Elder, Director.*
Web, www.state.gov

Includes Angola, Botswana, Lesotho, Malawi, Mozambique, Namibia, South Africa, Swaziland, Zambia, and Zimbabwe.

State Dept., *Special Envoy for Sudan and South Sudan, 2201 C St. N.W., #5819 20520; (202) 647-4531. Fax, (202) 647-4553. Donald E. Booth, Special Envoy.*
Web, www.state.gov

Represents the U.S. government's interests in Sudan and Darfur/South Sudan.

State Dept., *West African Affairs, 2201 C St. N.W., #4246 20520-3430; (202) 647-3395. Fax, (202) 647-4855. Stephen M. Schwartz, Director.*
Web, www.state.gov

Includes Benin, Burkina Faso, Cape Verde, Côte d'Ivoire, the Gambia, Ghana, Guinea, Guinea-Bissau, Liberia, Mali, Mauritania, Niger, Nigeria, Senegal, Sierra Leone, and Togo.

▶CONGRESS

For a listing of relevant congressional committees and subcommittees, please see pages 414–415 or the Appendix.

Library of Congress, *African and Middle Eastern Division, 101 Independence Ave. S.E., #LJ220 20540; (202) 707-7937. Fax, (202) 252-3180. Mary-Jane Deeb, Chief. Reading room, (202) 707-4188.*
General email, amed@loc.gov
Web, www.loc.gov/rr/amed

Maintains collections of African, Near Eastern, and Hebraic material. Prepares bibliographies and special studies relating to Africa and the Middle East. Reference service and reading rooms available to the public. (Need reader's card to use.)

▶INTERNATIONAL ORGANIZATIONS

International Bank for Reconstruction and Development *(World Bank), Africa, 1818 H St. N.W. 20433; (202) 473-100. Diop Makhtar, Vice President; Phil Hay, Media Contact, (202) 473-1796.*
Web, www.worldbank.org

Works to fight poverty and improve the living standards of low- and middle-income people in the countries of sub-Saharan Africa by providing loans, grants, policy advice, technical assistance, and knowledge-sharing services. Areas of interest include finance, economic development, education, water supply, agriculture, public health, and environmental protection.

Africa Faith and Justice Network (AFJN), *3025 4th St. N.E., #122 20017; (202) 817-3670. Rev. Aniedi Okure OP, Executive Director.*
General email, afjn@afjn.org
Web, www.afjn.org

Advocates with Catholic missionary congregations and Africa-focused coalitions for U.S. economic and political policies that benefit Africa. Promotes the Catholic view of peace building, human rights, and social justice. Interests include ending armed conflict, equitable trade with and investment in Africa, and sustainable development.

Africare, *440 R St. N.W. 20001-1935; (202) 462-3614. Fax, (202) 464-0867. Darius Mans, President.*
General email, info@africare.org
Web, www.africare.org

Seeks to improve the quality of life in rural Africa through development of water resources, increased food production, and delivery of health services.

TransAfrica, *1718 M St. N.W., #370 20036; (202) 223-1960. Nicole C. Lee, President. Library, (202) 223-1960, ext. 137.*
General email, info@transafrica.org
Web, www.transafrica.org

Focuses on U.S. foreign policy toward African nations, the Caribbean, Latin America, and peoples of African descent. Provides members with information on foreign policy issues. The Arthur R. Ashe Foreign Policy Library is open to the public by appointment.

East Asia and Pacific

Agency for International Development (USAID), *Asia Bureau, 1300 Pennsylvania Ave. N.W. 20523-4900; (202) 712-0200. Fax, (202) 216-3386. Denise Rollins, Assistant Administrator.*
Web, www.usaid.gov/who-we-are/organization/bureaus/bureau-asia

Advises the AID administrator on U.S. economic development policy in Asia.

Defense Dept. (DoD), *Asian and Pacific Security Affairs, The Pentagon, #5D688 20301-2400 (mailing address: 2700 Defense Pentagon, Washington, DC 20301); (703) 695-4175. Peter R. Lavoy, Assistant Secretary, Acting; Vacant, Principal Deputy Assistant Secretary; John E. Kreul, Chief of Staff. Press, (703) 697-5131.*
Web, http://policy.defense.gov/OUSDPOffices/ASDforAsianandPacificSecurityAffairs.aspx

Advises the under secretary of defense on matters dealing with Asia and the Pacific.

Japan–United States Friendship Commission, *1201 15th St. N.W., #330 20005-2842; (202) 653-9800. Fax, (202) 653-9802. Paige Cottingham-Streater, Executive Director.*
General email, jusfc@jusfc.gov
Web, www.jusfc.gov

Independent agency established by Congress that makes grants and administers funds and programs promoting educational and cultural exchanges between Japan and the United States.

State Dept., *Australia, New Zealand, and Pacific Island Affairs, 2201 C St. N.W., #4318 20520; (202) 736-4741. Fax, (202) 647-0118. Dan Larsen, Director.*
Web, www.state.gov

State Dept., *Bureau of East Asian and Pacific Affairs, 2201 C St. N.W., #6205 20520-6205; (202) 647-6600. Fax, (202) 647-0971. Daniel Russel, Assistant Secretary, Acting. Press, (202) 647-2538.*
Web, www.state.gov/p/eap

Advises the secretary on U.S. policy toward East Asian and Pacific countries. Directors assigned to specific countries within the bureau aid the assistant secretary.

State Dept., *Chinese and Mongolian Affairs, 2201 C St. N.W., #4318 20520; (202) 647-6787. Fax, (202) 736-7809. Aubrey Carlson, Director.*
Web, www.state.gov

State Dept., *Japanese Affairs, 2201 C St. N.W., #4206 20520; (202) 647-2913. Fax, (202) 647-4402. Marc Knapper, Director.*
Web, www.state.gov

State Dept., *Korean Affairs, 2201 C St. N.W., #4206 20520; (202) 647-7700. Fax, (202) 647-7388. Robert G. Rapson, Director.*
Web, www.state.gov

State Dept., *Mainland Southeast Asia Affairs, 2201 C St. N.W., #5206 20520-6310; (202) 647-3132. Fax, (202) 647-3069. Howard V. (Ike) Reed, Director.*
Web, www.state.gov

Handles issues related to Americans missing in action in Indochina; serves as liaison with Congress, international organizations, and foreign governments on developments in these countries. Includes Thailand, Cambodia, Laos, Vietnam, and Burma.

State Dept., *Maritime Southeast Asia Affairs, 2201 C St. N.W., #5210 20520; (202) 647-1222. Fax, (202) 736-4559. Susan M. Sutton, Director.*
Web, www.state.gov

Includes the Philippines, Malaysia, Brunei, Indonesia, East Timor, and Singapore.

State Dept., *Taiwan Coordination, 2201 C St. N.W., #4312 20520; (202) 647-7711. Fax, (202) 736-7818. Christopher Beede, Director.*
Web, www.state.gov

U.S.-China Economic and Security Review Commission, *444 N. Capitol St. N.W., #602, Hall of the States 20001; (202) 624-1407. Fax, (202) 624-1406. Michael R. Danis, Executive Director.*
General email, contact@uscc.gov

Web, www.uscc.gov

Investigates the national security implications of the bilateral trade and economic relationship between China and the United States. Makes recommendations to Congress based on its findings.

►**CONGRESS**

For a listing of relevant congressional committees and subcommittees, please see pages 414–415 or the Appendix.

Library of Congress, *Asian Division, 101 Independence Ave. S.E., #LJ149 20540; (202) 707-3766. Fax, (202) 252-3336. Dongfang Shao, Chief. Reading room, (202) 707-5426.*
Web, www.loc.gov/rr/asian

Maintains collections of Asian-American Pacific, Chinese, Korean, Japanese, Southeast Asian, South Asian, and Tibetan and Mongolian material. Reference service is provided in the Asian Reading Room, room #150.

►**INTERNATIONAL ORGANIZATIONS**

International Bank for Reconstruction and Development *(World Bank), East Asia and Pacific, 1818 H St. N.W. 20433; (202) 473-1000. Ulrich Zachau, Vice President; Axel Van Trotsenburg, Media Contact, (202) 458-8087.*
Web, www.worldbank.org

Works to fight poverty and improve the living standards of low- and middle-income people in the countries of East Asia and the Pacific by providing loans, policy advice, technical assistance, and knowledge-sharing services. Areas of interest include finance, economic development, education, water supply, agriculture, public health, and environmental protection.

►**NONGOVERNMENTAL**

American Institute in Taiwan, *1700 N. Moore St., #1700, Arlington, VA 22209-1385; (703) 525-8474. Fax, (703) 841-1385. Joseph R. DonovanJr., Managing Director; Amb. Raymond Burghardt, Chair.*
Web, www.ait.org.tw

Chartered by Congress to coordinate commercial, cultural, and other activities between the people of the United States and Taiwan. Represents U.S. interests and maintains offices in Taiwan.

Asia Foundation, *Washington Office, 1779 Massachusetts Ave. N.W., #815 20036; (202) 588-9420. Fax, (202) 588-9409. Nancy Yuan, Director.*
General email, info@asiafound-dc.org

Web, www.asiafoundation.org

Provides grants and technical assistance in Asia and the Pacific Islands (excluding the Middle East). Seeks to strengthen legislatures, legal and judicial systems, market economies, the media, and nongovernmental organizations. (Headquarters in San Francisco, Calif.)

Asia Policy Point (APP), *1730 Rhode Island Ave. N.W., #414 20036; (202) 822-6040. Fax, (202) 822-6044. Mindy Kotler, Director.*
General email, access@jiaponline.org

Web, www.jiaponline.org and
Blog, http://newasiapolicypoint.blogspot.com

Studies Japanese and Northeast Asian security and public policies as they relate to the United States. Researches and analyzes issues affecting Japan's relationship with the West. (Formerly the Japan Information Access Project.)

Asia Society Washington Center, *Washington Office, 1526 New Hampshire Ave. N.W. 20036; (202) 833-2742. Fax, (202) 833-0189. Matt Stumpf, Director.*
General email, asiadc@asiasociety.org

Web, www.asiasociety.org/

Membership: individuals, organizations, and corporations interested in Asia and the Pacific (excluding the Middle East). Sponsors seminars and lectures on political, economic, and cultural issues. (Headquarters in New York.)

East–West Center Washington, *1819 L St. N.W., #600 20036; (202) 293-3995. Fax, (202) 293-1402. Satu P. Limaye, Director.*
General email, washington@eastwestcenter.org

Web, www.eastwestcenter.org

Promotes strengthening of relations and understanding among countries and peoples of Asia, the Pacific, and the United States. Plans to undertake substantive programming activities, including collaborative research, training, seminars, and outreach; publications; and congressional study groups. (Headquarters in Honolulu.)

Heritage Foundation, *Asian Studies Center, 214 Massachusetts Ave. N.E. 20002-4999; (202) 546-4400. Fax, (202) 675-1779. Walter Lohman, Director. Press, (202) 675-1761.*
General email, info@heritage.org

Web, www.heritage.org/about/staff/departments/asian-studies-center?ac=1

Conducts research and provides information on U.S. policies in Asia and the Pacific. Interests include economic and security issues in the Asia Pacific region. Hosts speakers and visiting foreign policy delegations; sponsors conferences.

Japan-America Society of Washington, *1819 L St. N.W., Level B2 20036-3807; (202) 833-2210. Fax, (202) 833-2456. Amb. John R. Malott, President.*
General email, jaswdc@us-japan.org

Web, www.jaswdc.org

Conducts programs on U.S.-Japan political, security, and economic issues. Cultural programs include lectures, a Japanese-language school, and assistance to Japanese performing artists. Maintains library for members. Participates in National Cherry Blossom Festival.

National Congress of Vietnamese Americans, *6433 Northanna Dr., Springfield, VA 22150-1335; (703) 971-9178. Fax, (703) 719-5764. Bich Nguyen, Chair.*
General email, nnb726.nguyen@aol.com
Web, www.ncvaonline.org

Advances the cause of Vietnamese Americans by encouraging them to actively participate in their communities as civic-minded citizens engaged in education, culture, and civic liberties.

Taipei Economic and Cultural Representative Office (TECRO), *4201 Wisconsin Ave. N.W. 20016; (202) 895-1800. Fax, (202) 966-0825. Pu-Tsung King, Representative. Press, (202) 895-1850.*
General email, tecroinfodc@tecro.org
Web, www.taiwanembassy.org/US

Represents political, economic, and cultural interests of the government of the Republic of China (Taiwan) in the United States.

United States Asia Pacific Council, *1819 L St. N.W., #600 20036; (202) 293-3995. Fax, (202) 293-1402. Satu P. Limaye, Director.*
General email, washington@eastwestcenter.org
Web, www.eastwestcenter.org

Membership: U.S. corporations and representatives from business, government, education, research, and journalism interested in the advancement of the U.S. relationship with Asian and Pacific nations. Works on practical government and business policy issues to increase trade, investment, and economic development in the region. (Formerly the Pacific Economic Cooperation Council. Affiliated with East–West Center.)

U.S.-Asia Institute, *232 E. Capitol St. N.E. 20003; (202) 544-3181. Fax, (202) 747-5889. Mary Sue Bissell, Executive Director.*
General email, usasiainstitute@verizon.net
Web, www.usasiainstitute.org

Organization of individuals interested in Asia. Encourages dialogue among political and business leaders in the United States and Asia. Interests include foreign policy, international trade, Asian and American cultures, education, and employment. Conducts research and sponsors conferences and workshops in cooperation with the State Dept. to promote greater understanding between the United States and Asian nations.

U.S.-China Business Council, *Washington Office, 1818 N St. N.W., #200 20036-2470; (202) 429-0340. Fax, (202) 775-2476. John Frisbie, President.*
General email, info@uschina.org
Web, www.uschina.org

Member-supported organization that represents U.S. companies engaged in business relations with the People's Republic of China. Participates in U.S. policy issues relating to China and other international trade. Publishes research reports. (Maintains offices in Beijing and Shanghai.)

Europe

(Includes the Baltic states)

Agency for International Development (USAID), *Europe and Eurasia Bureau, 301 4th St. S.W., #247 20523 (mailing address: 1300 Pennsylvania Ave. N.W., Washington, DC 20521); (202) 567-4020. Fax, (202) 567-4256. Paige Alexander, Assistant Administrator.*
Web, www.usaid.gov/who-we-are/organization/bureaus/bureau-europe-and-eurasia

Advises the AID administrator on U.S. economic development policy in Europe and Eurasia.

Defense Dept. (DoD), *European and NATO Policy, The Pentagon, #5B652 20301-2400; (703) 695-5553. Fax, (703) 571-9637. Jim Townsend, Deputy Assistant Secretary.*
Web, www.defense.gov

Advises the assistant secretary for international security affairs on matters dealing with Europe and NATO.

Defense Dept. (DoD), *International Security Affairs, The Pentagon, #3C889 20301-2400; (703) 697-2788. Fax, (703) 697-3279. Derek H. Chollet, Assistant Secretary.*
Web, www.defense.gov

Advises the secretary of defense and recommends policies on regional security issues in the Middle East, Africa, Russia/Eurasia, and Europe/NATO.

State Dept., *Bureau of European and Eurasian Affairs, 2201 C St. N.W., #6226 20520; (202) 647-9626. Fax, (202) 647-5575. Victoria Newland, Assistant Secretary. Press, (202) 647-6925.*
Web, www.state.gov

Advises the secretary on U.S. policy toward European and Eurasian countries. Directors assigned to specific countries within the bureau aid the assistant secretary.

State Dept., *Central European Affairs, 2201 C St. N.W., #4230 20520; (202) 647-1484. Fax, (202) 647-5117. Anne Hall, Director.*
Web, www.state.gov

Includes Austria, Bulgaria, Czech Republic, Hungary, Liechtenstein, Poland, Romania, Slovak Republic, Slovenia, and Switzerland.

State Dept., *European Security and Political Affairs, 2201 C St. N.W., #6511 20520; (202) 647-1358. Fax, (202) 647-1369. Richard Holtzapple, Director.*
Web, www.state.gov

Coordinates and advises, with the Defense Dept. and other agencies, the U.S. mission to NATO and the U.S. delegation to the Organization for Security and Cooperation in Europe regarding political, military, and arms control matters.

State Dept., *European Union and Regional Affairs*, 2201 C St. N.W., #5424 20520; (202) 647-2469. Fax, (202) 647-9959. Wendela Moore, Director, Acting.
Web, www.state.gov

Handles all matters concerning the European Union, the Council of Europe, and the Organisation for Economic Co-operation and Development, with emphasis on trade issues. Monitors export controls and economic activities for the North Atlantic Treaty Organization and the Organization for Security and Co-operation in Europe.

State Dept., *Nordic and Baltic Affairs*, 2201 C St. N.W., #5428 20520; (202) 647-5669. Fax, (202) 736-4170. Tara Erath, Director.
Web, www.state.gov

Includes Denmark, Estonia, Finland, Iceland, Latvia, Lithuania, Norway, and Sweden.

State Dept., *South Central European Affairs*, 2201 C St. N.W., #5227 20520; (202) 647-0608. Fax, (202) 647-1838. Jonathan M. Moore, Director.
Web, www.state.gov

Includes Albania, Bosnia-Herzegovina, Croatia, Kosovo, Macedonia, Serbia, and Montenegro.

State Dept., *Southern European Affairs*, 2201 C St. N.W., #5511 20520; (202) 647-6112. Fax, (202) 647-5087. Vivian S. Walker, Director.
Web, www.state.gov

Includes Cyprus, Greece, and Turkey.

State Dept., *Western European Affairs*, 2201 C St. N.W., #5218 20520; (202) 647-3072. Fax, (202) 647-3459. Nancy Pettit, Director.
Web, www.state.gov

Includes Andorra, Belgium, Bermuda, France, Ireland, Italy, Luxembourg, Malta, Monaco, the Netherlands, Portugal, San Marino, Spain, the United Kingdom, and the Vatican.

►CONGRESS

For a listing of relevant congressional committees and subcommittees, please see pages 414–415 or the Appendix.

Library of Congress, *European Division*, 101 Independence Ave. S.E., #LJ-249 20540; (202) 707-5414. Fax, (202) 707-8482. Georgette M. Dorn, Chief, Acting. Reference desk, (202) 707-4515.
Web, www.loc.gov/rr/european

Provides reference service on the library's European collections (except collections on Spain, Portugal, and the British Isles). Prepares bibliographies and special studies relating to European countries, including Russia and the other states of the former Soviet Union and eastern bloc. Maintains current unbound Slavic-language periodicals and newspapers, which are available at the European Reference Desk.

►INTERNATIONAL ORGANIZATIONS

European Union, *Delegation to the United States of America*, 2175 K St. N.W., #800 20037-1400; (202) 862-9500. Fax, (202) 429-1766. João Vale de Almeida, Ambassador.
General email, delegation-usa-info@eeas.europa.eu
Web, www.eurunion.org

Information and public affairs office in the United States for the European Union. Provides social policy data on the European Union and provides statistics and information on member countries, including those related to energy, economics, development and cooperation, commerce, agriculture, industry, and technology. (Headquarters in Brussels.)

International Bank for Reconstruction and Development *(World Bank)*, *Europe and Central Asia*, 1818 H St. N.W. 20433; (202) 473-1000. Laura Tuck, Vice President; Andrew Kircher, Media Contact, (202) 473-6313.
Web, www.worldbank.org

Works to fight poverty and improve the living standards of low- and middle-income people in the countries of eastern Europe by providing loans, policy advice, technical assistance, and knowledge-sharing services. Areas of interest include finance, economic development, education, water supply, agriculture, public health, and environmental protection.

►NONGOVERNMENTAL

American Bar Assn. (ABA), *Rule of Law Initiative*, 1050 Connecticut Ave. N.W., #450 20036; (202) 662-1950. Fax, (202) 662-1597. Rob Boone, Director.
General email, rol@americanbar.org
Web, www.americanbar.org/rol

Promotes the rule of law and specific legal reforms in developing countries throughout the world; recruits volunteer legal professionals from the United States and western Europe. Interests include human rights, anticorruption initiatives, criminal law, efforts against human trafficking, judicial reform, legal education reform, civic education, reforming the legal profession, and women's rights.

American Hellenic Institute, 1220 16th St. N.W. 20036-3202; (202) 785-8430. Fax, (202) 785-5178. Nick Larigakis, President.
General email, info@ahiworld.org
Web, www.ahiworld.org

Works to strengthen relations between Greece and Cyprus and the United States and within the American Hellenic community.

British-American Business Assn., P.O. Box 16482 20041; (202) 293-0010. Andrew Baker, President.
General email, info@babawashington.org
Web, www.babawashington.org

Organization dedicated to the development of business relations between the United Kingdom and the United States.

British American Security Information Council (BASIC), *1725 DeSales St. N.W., #600 20036; (202) 546-8055. Fax, (202) 546-8056. Paul Ingram, Executive Director.*
General email, basicus@basicint.org

Web, www.basicint.org

Independent analysis and advocacy organization that researches global security issues, including nuclear policies, military strategies, armaments, and disarmament. Assists in the development of global security policies, promotes public awareness, and facilitates exchange of information on both sides of the Atlantic.

European Institute, *1001 Connecticut Ave. N.W., #220 20036; (202) 895-1670. Fax, (202) 362-1088. Joelle Attinger, President.*
General email, info@europeaninstitute.org

Web, www.europeaninstitute.org

Membership: governments and multinational corporations. Provides an independent forum for business leaders, government officials, journalists, academics, and policy experts. Organizes seminars and conferences. Interests include international finance, economics, energy, telecommunications, defense and procurement policies, the integration of central Europe into the European Union and NATO, and relations with Asia and Latin America.

German American Business Council, *2000 M St. N.W., #335 20036; (202) 955-5595. Ulrich Gamerdinger, Executive Director.*
General email, info@gabcwashington.com

Web, http://gabcwashington.com

Promotes closer ties between Germany and the United States through improved communication between embassies, industry, governments, and academia.

German Marshall Fund of the United States, *1744 R St. N.W. 20009; (202) 683-2650. Fax, (202) 265-1662. Karen Donfried, President.*
General email, info@gmfus.org

Web, www.gmfus.org

American institution created by a gift from Germany as a permanent memorial to Marshall Plan aid. Seeks to stimulate exchange of ideas and promote transatlantic cooperation. Awards grants to promote the study of international and domestic policies; supports comparative research and debate on key issues.

Irish National Caucus, *P.O. Box 15128 20003-0849; (202) 544-0568. Fax, (202) 488-7537. Fr. Sean McManus, President.*
General email, reply@irishnationalcaucus.org

Web, www.irishnationalcaucus.org

Educational organization concerned with protecting human rights in Northern Ireland. Seeks to end anti-Catholic discrimination in Northern Ireland through implementation of the McBride Principles, initiated in 1984. Advocates nonviolence and supports the peace process in Northern Ireland. Monitors legislation and regulations.

Joint Baltic American National Committee (JBANC), *400 Hurley Ave., Rockville, MD 20850; (301) 340-1954. Karl Altau, Managing Director.*
General email, jbanc@jbanc.org

Web, www.jbanc.org and
Twitter, http://twitter.com/JBANCchatter

Washington representative of the Estonian, Latvian, and Lithuanian American communities in the United States; acts as a representative on issues affecting the Baltic states.

Transatlantic Business Council, *919 18th St. N.W., #220 20006; (202) 828-9104. Fax, (202) 828-9106. Tim Bennett, Director General.*
General email, dnunnery@transatlanticbusiness.org

Web, www.transatlanticbusiness.org

Membership: American companies with operations in Europe and European companies with operations in the United States. Promotes a barrier-free transatlantic market that contributes to economic growth, innovation, and security.

Latin America, Canada, and the Caribbean

▶**AGENCIES**

Agency for International Development (USAID), *Latin America and the Caribbean Bureau, 1300 Pennsylvania Ave. N.W., #5.09 20523-5900; (202) 712-4760. Fax, (202) 216-3012. Mark Feierstein, Assistant Administrator. Press, (202) 712-4793.*
Web, www.usaid.gov/who-we-are/organization/bureaus/ bureau-latin-america-and-caribbean

Advises the AID administrator on U.S. policy toward developing Latin American and Caribbean countries. Designs and implements assistance programs for developing nations.

Defense Dept. (DoD), *Western Hemisphere Policy, 2000 Defense Pentagon, #3E806 20301; (703) 697-7200. Fax, (703) 697-6602. Rebecca B. Chavez, Deputy Assistant Secretary.*
Web, www.defense.gov

Advises the assistant secretary for international security affairs on inter-American matters; aids in the development of U.S. policy toward Latin America.

Inter-American Foundation, *1331 Pennsylvania Ave. N.W., #1200 20004; (202) 360-4530. Robert N. Kaplan, President.*
General email, inquiries@iaf.gov

Web, www.iaf.gov

Supports small-scale Latin American and Caribbean social and economic development efforts through grassroots development programs, grants, and fellowships.

International Trade Administration (ITA) *(Commerce Dept.), Global Markets, North and Central America,* 1401 Constitution Ave. N.W., #3024 20230; (202) 482-6452. Fax, (202) 482-5865. Geri Word, Director.
Web, www.trade.gov/markets

Coordinates Commerce Dept. activities and assists U.S. business regarding export to Mexico, Canada, Central America, and the Caribbean. Helps negotiate and ensures compliance with U.S. free-trade agreements, including NAFTA (North American Free Trade Agreement) and the Dominican Republic–Central American Free Trade Agreement (CAFTA-DR).

State Dept., *Andean Affairs,* 2201 C St. N.W., #4915 20520; (202) 647-1715. Fax, (202) 647-2628. William Duncan, Director.
Web, www.state.gov

Includes Bolivia, Colombia, Ecuador, Peru, and Venezuela.

State Dept., *Brazilian, Southern Cone Affairs,* 2201 C St. N.W., #1330 20520; (202) 647-1929. Fax, (202) 736-7825. William Ostick, Director.
Web, www.state.gov

Includes Argentina, Brazil, Chile, Paraguay, and Uruguay.

State Dept., *Bureau of Western Hemisphere Affairs,* 2201 C St. N.W., #6262 20520; (202) 647-5780. Fax, (202) 647-0834. Roberta S. Jacobson, Assistant Secretary. Press, (202) 647-4252.
Web, www.state.gov

Advises the secretary on U.S. policy toward North, Central, and South America. Directors assigned to specific regions within the bureau aid the assistant secretary.

State Dept., *Canadian Affairs,* 2201 C St. N.W., #3918 20520; (202) 647-2170. Fax, (202) 647-4088. Susan E. Saarnio, Director.
Web, www.state.gov

State Dept., *Caribbean Affairs,* 2201 C St. N.W., #4262 20520-6258; (202) 647-5088. Fax, (202) 647-2901. Juan Alsace, Director.
Web, www.state.gov

Includes Antigua and Barbuda, Aruba, Bahamas, Barbados, Dominica, Dominican Republic, Grenada, Guyana, Jamaica, Netherlands Antilles, St. Kitts and Nevis, St. Lucia, St. Vincent and the Grenadines, Suriname, and Trinidad and Tobago.

State Dept., *Central American Affairs,* 2201 C St. N.W., #5906 20520; (202) 647-4087. Fax, (202) 647-2597. Scott Hamilton, Director.
Web, www.state.gov

Includes Belize, Costa Rica, El Salvador, Guatemala, Honduras, Nicaragua, and Panama.

State Dept., *Cuban Affairs,* 2201 C St. N.W., #3234 20520; (202) 647-9272. Fax, (202) 647-7095. Raymond McGraph, Coordinator.
Web, www.state.gov

State Dept., *Haiti Special Coordinator,* 2201 C St. N.W., 12B63 20520-6258; (202) 647-9510. Fax, (202) 647-8900. Thomas C. Adams, Special Coordinator for Haiti. General email, haitiofficecollective@state.gov
Web, www.state.gov

Coordinates assistance to Haiti. Oversees U.S. government engagement with Haiti, including implementation of a reconstruction strategy in partnership with the Haitian government.

State Dept., *Mexican Affairs,* 2201 C St. N.W., #3909 20520-6258; (202) 647-8113. Fax, (202) 647-5752. Kevin O'Reilly, Director.
Web, www.state.gov

Advises the secretary on Mexican affairs. Acts as liaison between the United States and Mexico in international boundary and water matters as defined by binational treaties and agreements. Also involved with border health and environmental issues, new border crossings, and significant modifications to existing crossings.

State Dept., *U.S. Mission to the Organization of American States,* 2201 C St. N.W., #5914 20520-6258; (202) 647-9376. Fax, (202) 647-0911. Carmen Lomellin, U.S. Permanent Representative.
Web, www.state.gov

Formulates U.S. policy and represents U.S. interests at the Organization of American States (OAS).

▶**CONGRESS**

For a listing of relevant congressional committees and subcommittees, please see pages 414–415 or the Appendix.

Library of Congress, *Hispanic Division,* 101 Independence Ave. S.E., #LJ240 20540; (202) 707-5400. Fax, (202) 707-2005. Georgette M. Dorn, Chief. Reference staff and reading room, (202) 707-5397.
Web, www.loc.gov/rr/hispanic

Orients researchers and scholars in the area of Iberian, Latin American, Caribbean, and U.S. Latino studies. Primary and secondary source materials are available in the library's general collections for the study of all periods, from pre-Columbian to the present, including recordings of 640 authors reading their own material. All major subject areas are represented with emphasis on history, literature, and the social sciences; the "Archive of Hispanic Literature on Tape" is available in the reading room.

▶**INTERNATIONAL ORGANIZATIONS**

Inter-American Development Bank, 1300 New York Ave. N.W. 20577; (202) 623-1000. Fax, (202) 623-3096. Luis Alberto Moreno, President; Gustavo Arnavat, U.S. Executive Director. Library, (202) 623-3211. Press, (202) 623-1555.
Web, www.iadb.org

Promotes, through loans and technical assistance, the investment of public and private capital in member countries of Latin America and the Caribbean for social and economic development purposes. Facilitates economic integration of the Latin American region, operating the Inter-American Investment Corporation and the Multilateral Investment Fund. Library open to the public by appointment.

International Bank for Reconstruction and Development *(World Bank), Latin America and the Caribbean, 1818 H St. N.W. 20433; (202) 473-1000. Hasan Tuluy, Vice President; Sergio Jellinek, Media Contact, (202) 458-2841.*
Web, www.worldbank.org

Works to fight poverty and improve the living standards of poor and middle-income people in the countries of Latin America and the Caribbean by providing loans, policy advice, technical assistance, and knowledge-sharing services. Areas of interest include finance, economic development, education, water supply, agriculture, public health, and environmental protection.

Organization of American States (OAS), *17th St. and Constitution Ave. N.W. 20006 (mailing address: 1889 F St. N.W., Washington, DC 20006); (202) 458-3000. Fax, (202) 458-3967. José Miguel Insulza, Secretary General. Library, (202) 458-6041.*
General email, ai@oas.org
Web, www.oas.org

Membership: the United States, Canada, and all independent Latin American and Caribbean countries. Funded by quotas paid by member states and by contributions to special multilateral funds. Works to promote democracy, eliminate poverty, and resolve disputes among member nations. Provides member states with technical and advisory services in cultural, educational, scientific, social, and economic areas. Library open to the public.

United Nations Economic Commission for Latin America and the Caribbean (CEPAL), *Washington Office, 1825 K St. N.W., #1120 20006-1210; (202) 955-5613. Fax, (202) 296-0826. Inés Bustillo, Chief.*
General email, ines.bustillo@cepal.org
Web, www.eclac.org

Membership: Latin American, Caribbean, and some industrially developed Western nations. Seeks to strengthen economic relations between countries both within and outside Latin America through research and analysis of socioeconomic problems, training programs, and advisory services to member governments. (Headquarters in Santiago, Chile.)

▶**NONGOVERNMENTAL**

Caribbean-Central American Action, *1300 Pennsylvania Ave. N.W., #700 20004; (202) 204-3050. Fax, (202) 789-7349. Sally Yearwood, Executive Director, Acting.*
General email, info@c-caa.org
Web, www.c-caa.org

Promotes trade and investment in Caribbean Basin countries; encourages democratic public policy in member countries and works to strengthen private initiatives.

Center for International Policy, *2000 M St. N.W., #720 20036; (202) 232-3317. Fax, (202) 232-3440. William Goodfellow, Executive Director.*
General email, cip@ciponline.org
Web, www.ciponline.org

Research and educational organization concerned with peace and security worldwide. Special interests include military spending; U.S. intelligence policy; and U.S. policy toward Asia, Colombia, and Cuba. Publishes the *International Policy Report.*

Council of the Americas, *Americas Society, Washington Office, 1615 L St. N.W., #250 20036; (202) 659-8989. Fax, (202) 659-7755. Susan Segal, President; Eric Farnsworth, Vice President.*
Web, www.counciloftheamericas.org

Membership: businesses with interests and investments in Latin America. Seeks to expand the role of private enterprise in development of the region. (Headquarters in New York.)

Council on Hemispheric Affairs, *1250 Connecticut Ave. N.W., #1C 20036; (202) 223-4975. Fax, (202) 223-4979. Larry R. Birns, Director.*
General email, coha@coha.org
Web, www.coha.org

Seeks to expand interest in inter-American relations and increase press coverage of Latin America and Canada. Monitors U.S., Latin American, and Canadian relations, with emphasis on human rights, trade, growth of democratic institutions, freedom of the press, and hemispheric economic and political developments; provides educational materials and analyzes issues. Issues annual survey on human rights and freedom of the press. Publishes a biweekly newsletter.

Guatemala Human Rights Commission/USA, *3321 12th St. N.E. 20017-4008; (202) 529-6599. Kelsey Alford-Jones, Director.*
General email, ghrc-usa@ghrc-usa.org
Web, www.ghrc-usa.org

Provides information and collects and makes available reports on human rights violations in Guatemala; publishes a quarterly report of documented cases of specific abuses. Takes on special projects and leads delegations to further sensitize the public and the international community to human rights abuses in Guatemala.

Inter-American Dialogue, *1211 Connecticut Ave. N.W., #510 20036-2701; (202) 822-9002. Fax, (202) 822-9553. Michael Shifter, President.*
General email, iad@thedialogue.org
Web, www.thedialogue.org

Serves as a forum for communication and exchange among leaders of the Americas. Provides analyses and policy recommendations on issues of hemispheric concern.

Interests include economic integration, trade, and the strengthening of democracy in Latin America. Hosts private and public exchanges; sponsors conferences and seminars; publishes daily newsletter, *Latin America Advisor.*

Latin America Working Group, *424 C St. N.E. 20002; (202) 546-7010. Fax, (202) 543-7647. Lisa Haugaard, Executive Director.*
General email, lawg@lawg.org
Web, www.lawg.org

Represents more than sixty organizations concerned with Latin America. Encourages U.S. policies toward Latin America that promote human rights, justice, peace, and sustainable development.

Pan American Development Foundation, *1889 F St. N.W., 2nd Floor 20006; (202) 458-3969. Fax, (202) 458-6316. John Sanbrailo, Executive Director.*
General email, padf-dc@padf.org
Web, www.padf.org

Works with the public and private sectors to improve the quality of life throughout the Caribbean and Latin America. Associated with the Organization of American States (OAS).

Partners of the Americas, *1424 K St. N.W., #700 20005-2410; (202) 628-3300. Fax, (202) 628-3306. Stephen Vetter, President.*
General email, info@partners.net
Web, www.partners.net

Membership: chapters, individuals and organizations in the United States, Latin America, Brazil, and the Caribbean. Sponsors technical assistance projects and cultural exchanges between the United States, Latin America, Brazil, and the Caribbean; supports self-help projects in food security and agricultural development, sport for development, youth and children, climate change and environmental protection, professional leadership exchanges, civil society and governance, and women and gender equality.

U.S.-Mexico Chamber of Commerce, *6800 Versar Center, #450, Springfield, VA 22151 (mailing address: P.O. Box 14414, Washington, DC 20044); (703) 752-4751. Fax, (703) 642-1088. Albert C. Zapanta, President.*
General email, info@usmcoc.org
Web, www.usmcoc.org

Promotes trade and investment between the United States and Mexico. Provides members with information and expertise on conducting business between the two countries as pertains to NAFTA. Serves as a clearinghouse for information.

Washington Office on Latin America, *1666 Connecticut Ave. N.W., #400 20009; (202) 797-2171. Fax, (202) 797-2172. Joy Olson, Executive Director.*
General email, wola@wola.org
Web, www.wola.org

Acts as a liaison between government policymakers and groups and individuals concerned with human rights and U.S. policy in Latin America and the Caribbean. Serves as an information resource center; monitors legislation.

Near East and South Asia

(Includes North Africa)

▶**AGENCIES**

Agency for International Development (USAID), *Asia Bureau, 1300 Pennsylvania Ave. N.W. 20523-4900; (202) 712-0200. Fax, (202) 216-3386. Denise Rollins, Assistant Administrator.*
Web, www.usaid.gov/who-we-are/organization/bureaus/bureau-asia

Advises the AID administrator on U.S. economic development policy in Asia.

Defense Dept. (DoD), *International Security Affairs, The Pentagon, #3C889 20301-2400; (703) 697-2788. Fax, (703) 697-3279. Derek H. Chollet, Assistant Secretary.*
Web, www.defense.gov

Advises the secretary of defense and recommends policies on regional security issues in the Middle East, Africa, Russia/Eurasia, and Europe/NATO.

State Dept., *Afghanistan Affairs, 2201 C St. N.W., #1880 20520-6258; (202) 647-5175. Fax, (202) 647-5505. David Rank, Director.*
Web, www.state.gov

State Dept., *Arabian Peninsula Affairs, 2201 C St. N.W., #4224 20520-6243; (202) 647-7521. Fax, (202) 736-4459. Donald Dlone, Director.*
General email, nea-arp-dl@state.gov
Web, www.state.gov

Includes Bahrain, Kuwait, Oman, Qatar, Saudi Arabia, United Arab Emirates, and Yemen.

State Dept., *Bureau of Near Eastern Asian Countries, 2201 C St. N.W., #6242 20520-6243; (202) 647-7209. Fax, (202) 736-4462. Anne W. Patterson, Assistant Secretary.*
Web, www.state.gov

Advises the secretary on U.S. policy toward countries of the Near East and North Africa. Directors assigned to specific countries within the bureau aid the assistant secretary.

State Dept., *Bureau of South and Central Asian Affairs, 2201 C St. N.W., #6254 20520-6258; (202) 736-4325. Fax, (202) 736-4333. Nisha Desai Biswal, Assistant Secretary.*
Web, www.state.gov

Advises the secretary on U.S. policy toward South and Central Asian countries. Directors assigned to specific countries within the bureau aid the assistant secretary.

State Dept., *Egypt and Levant Affairs,* *2201 C St. N.W.,*
#2808 20520-6243; (202) 647-2670. Fax, (202) 647-0989.
Joan A. Polaschik, Director.
Web, www.state.gov

Includes Egypt, Jordan, Lebanon, and Syria.

State Dept., *India Affairs,* *2201 C St. N.W., #5251 20520-*
6243; (202) 647-1114. Fax, (202) 736-4463. John Fennerty,
Director.
Web, www.state.gov

State Dept., *Iran Affairs,* *2201 C St. N.W., #1058 20520;*
(202) 647-2520. Leslie Tsou, Director.
Web, www.state.gov

Advises the secretary on Iranian affairs.

State Dept., *Iraq Affairs,* *2201 C St. N.W., #4827 20520;*
(202) 647-0459. Fax, (202) 736-4464. Anthony Godfrey,
Director.
Web, www.state.gov

State Dept., *Israeli-Palestinian Affairs,* *2201 C St. N.W.,*
#6251 20520; (202) 647-3672. Fax, (202) 736-4461.
Christopher Henzel, Director, Acting.
Web, www.state.gov

State Dept., *Middle East Partnership Initiative,* *2430 E*
St. N.W., 2nd Floor 20524; (202) 776-8500. Fax, (202) 776-
8445. Paul R. Sutphin, Director.
Web, http://mepi.state.gov

Funds programs that seek to advance democracy in the
Middle East. Encourages reform in the areas of politics,
economics, education, and women's rights.

State Dept., *Near Eastern Affairs and Maghreb Affairs,*
2201 C St. N.W., #2808 20520-6243; (202) 647-2365.
Fax, (202) 736-4460. Suzanne Cooper, Director.
Web, www.state.gov

Includes Algeria, Libya, Morocco, and Tunisia.

State Dept., *Nepal, Sri Lanka, Bangladesh, Bhutan, and*
Maldives Affairs (NSB Affairs), *2201 C St. N.W., #5250*
20520-6243; (202) 647-1613. Fax, (202) 647-1183.
Heather Variava, Director.
Web, www.state.gov

State Dept., *Pakistan Affairs,* *2201 C St. N.W., #1861*
20520-6258; (202) 647-9823. Fax, (202) 647-3001.
Jonathan Pratt, Director.
Web, www.state.gov

U.S.-China Economic and Security Review Commission,
444 N. Capitol St. N.W., #602, Hall of the States 20001;
(202) 624-1407. Fax, (202) 624-1406. Michael R. Danis,
Executive Director.
General email, contact@uscc.gov
Web, www.uscc.gov

Investigates the national security implications of the
bilateral trade and economic relationship between China
and the United States. Makes recommendations to Congress based on its findings.

►**CONGRESS**

For a listing of relevant congressional committees and sub-
committees, please see pages 414–415 or the Appendix.

Library of Congress, *African and Middle Eastern*
Division, *101 Independence Ave. S.E., #LJ220 20540; (202)*
707-7937. Fax, (202) 252-3180. Mary-Jane Deeb, Chief.
Reading room, (202) 707-4188.
General email, amed@loc.gov
Web, www.loc.gov/rr/amed

Maintains collections of African, Near Eastern, and
Hebraic material. Prepares bibliographies and special
studies relating to Africa and the Middle East. Reference
service and reading rooms available to the public. (Need
reader's card to use.)

Library of Congress, *Asian Division,* *101 Independence*
Ave. S.E., #LJ149 20540; (202) 707-3766. Fax, (202) 252-
3336. Dongfang Shao, Chief. Reading room, (202) 707-5426.
Web, www.loc.gov/rr/asian

Maintains collections of Asian-American Pacific, Chinese, Korean, Japanese, Southeast Asian, South Asian, and
Tibetan and Mongolian material. Reference service is
provided in the Asian Reading Room, room #150.

►**INTERNATIONAL ORGANIZATIONS**

International Bank for Reconstruction and
Development *(World Bank), Middle East and North*
Africa, 1818 H St. N.W. 20433; (202) 473-1000.
Inger Andersen, Vice President; Dale Lautenbach,
Media Contact, (202) 473-8177.
Web, www.worldbank.org

Works to fight poverty and improve the living standards of low- and middle-income people in the countries
of the Middle East and North Africa by providing loans,
policy advice, technical assistance, and knowledge-sharing
services. Areas of interest include finance, economic development, education, water supply, agriculture, public health,
and environmental protection.

International Bank for Reconstruction and
Development *(World Bank), South Asia, 1818 H St.*
N.W. 20433; (202) 473-1000. Philippe H. Le Houérou, Vice
President; Alex Ferguson, Media Contact, (202) 458-4953.
Web, www.worldbank.org

Works to fight poverty and improve the living standards of low- and middle-income people in the countries
of South Asia by providing loans, policy advice, technical
assistance, and knowledge-sharing services. Areas of interest include finance, economic development, education,
water supply, agriculture, public health, and environmental protection.

League of Arab States, *Washington Office, 1100 17th St.*
N.W., #602 20036; (202) 265-3210. Fax, (202) 331-1525.
Amb. Mohamed Al-Hussaini Al-Sharif, Director.
General email, arableague@aol.com
Web, www.arableague-us.org

Membership: Arab countries in the Near East, North Africa, and the Indian Ocean. Coordinates members' policies in political, cultural, economic, and social affairs; mediates disputes among members and between members and third parties. Washington office maintains the Arab Information Center. (Headquarters in Cairo.)

▶**NONGOVERNMENTAL**

American Israel Public Affairs Committee, *251 H St. N.W. 20001-2017; (202) 639-5200. Fax, (202) 347-4889. Howard Kohr, Executive Director.*
General email, information@aipac.org
Web, www.aipac.org

Works to maintain and improve relations between the United States and Israel.

American Kurdish Information Network (AKIN), *2722 Connecticut Ave. N.W., #42 20008-5366; (202) 483-6444. Kani Xulam, Director.*
General email, akin@kurdistan.org
Web, www.kurdistan.org

Membership: Americans of Kurdish origin, recent Kurdish immigrants and refugees, and others. Collects and disseminates information about the Kurds, an ethnic group living in parts of Turkey, Iran, Iraq, and Syria. Monitors human rights abuses against Kurds; promotes self-determination in Kurdish homelands; fosters Kurdish American friendship and understanding.

American Near East Refugee Aid (ANERA), *1111 14th St. N.W., #400 20005; (202) 266-9700. Fax, (202) 266-9701. William Corcoran, President.*
General email, anera@anera.org
Web, www.anera.org

Works with local institutions and partner organizations to provide sustainable development, health, education, and employment programs to Palestinian communities and impoverished families throughout the Middle East. Delivers humanitarian aid during emergencies. (Field offices in the West Bank, Gaza, and Lebanon.)

AMIDEAST, *1730 M St. N.W., #1100 20036-4505; (202) 776-9600. Fax, (202) 776-7011. Theodore H. Kattouf, President.*
General email, inquiries@amideast.org
Web, www.amideast.org

Promotes understanding and cooperation between Americans and the people of the Middle East and North Africa through education, information, and development programs in the region. Produces educational material to help improve teaching about the Middle East and North Africa in American schools and colleges.

Asia Society Washington Center, *Washington Office, 1526 New Hampshire Ave. N.W. 20036; (202) 833-2742. Fax, (202) 833-0189. Matt Stumpf, Director.*
General email, asiadc@asiasociety.org
Web, www.asiasociety.org/

Membership: individuals, organizations, and corporations interested in Asia and the Pacific (excluding the Middle East). Sponsors seminars and lectures on political, economic, and cultural issues. (Headquarters in New York.)

B'nai B'rith International, *2020 K St. N.W., 7th Floor 20006; (202) 857-6600. Fax, (202) 857-2700. Allan J. Jacobs, President; Daniel S. Mariaschin, Executive Vice President. Toll-free, (888) 388-4224.*
General email, info@bnaibrith.org
Web, www.bnaibrith.org

International Jewish organization that promotes the security and continuity of the Jewish people and the State of Israel; defends human rights; combats anti-Semitism; and promotes Jewish identity through cultural activities. Interests include strengthening family life and the education and training of youth, providing broad-based services for the benefit of senior citizens, and advocacy on behalf of Jews throughout the world.

Center for Contemporary Arab Studies *(Georgetown University), 241 Intercultural Center, 37th and O St. N.W. 20057-1020; (202) 687-5793. Fax, (202) 687-7001. Osama Abi-Mershod, Director.*
General email, ccasinfo@georgetown.edu
Web, http://ccas.georgetown.edu

Sponsors lecture series, seminars, and conferences. Conducts a community outreach program that assists secondary school teachers in the development of instructional materials on the Middle East; promotes the study of the Arabic language in area schools. Offers master's degree program in Arab studies.

Foundation for Democracy in Iran, *11140 Rockville Pike, #100, Rockville, MD 20852; (301) 946-2918. Fax, (301) 942-5341. Kenneth Timmerman, President.*
General email, exec@iran.org
Web, www.iran.org

Seeks to foster democracy in Iran. Acts as a clearinghouse for information pertaining to opposition efforts in Iran.

Foundation for Middle East Peace, *1761 N St. N.W. 20036-2801; (202) 835-3650. Fax, (202) 835-3651. Amb. Philip C. Wilcox Jr., President.*
General email, info@fmep.org
Web, www.fmep.org

Educational organization that seeks to promote understanding and resolution of the Israeli-Palestinian conflict. Publishes bimonthly Report on Israeli Settlement in the Occupied Territories; provides media with information; and awards grants to organizations and activities that contribute to the solution of the conflict.

Institute for Palestine Studies, *Washington Office, 3501 M St. N.W. 20007-2624; (202) 342-3990. Fax, (202) 342-3927. Michelle Esposito, Executive Director. Press, (202) 342-3990, ext. 11.*
General email, ipsdc@palestine-studies.org
Web, www.palestine-studies.org

Scholarly research institute that specializes in the history and development of the Palestine problem, the Arab-Israeli conflict, and their peaceful resolution.

Institute of Turkish Studies *(Georgetown University),* *Intercultural Center, Box 571033, #305R 20057-1033; (202) 687-0292. Fax, (202) 687-3780. Sinan Ciddi, Executive Director.*
General email, itsdirector@turkishstudies.org
Web, www.turkishstudies.org

Independent grant-making organization that supports and encourages the development of Turkish studies in American colleges and universities. Awards grants to individual scholars and educational institutions in the United States.

MEMRI (Middle East Media Research Institute), *P.O. Box 27837 20038-7837; (202) 955-9070. Fax, (202) 955-9077. Steven Stalinsky, Executive Director.*
General email, memri@memri.org
Web, www.memri.org

Explores the Middle East through the region's media. Seeks to inform the debate over U.S. policy in the Middle East.

Middle East Institute, *1761 N St. N.W. 20036-2882; (202) 785-1141. Fax, (202) 331-8861.*
Amb. Wendy J. Chamberlin, President. Library, (202) 785-1141, 222. Press, (202) 785-1141, 236. Language Dept., (202) 785-1141, ext. 211.
General email, info@mei.edu
Web, www.mei.edu

Membership: individuals interested in the Middle East. Seeks to broaden knowledge of the Middle East through research, conferences and seminars, language classes, lectures, and exhibits. Library open to members and the press Monday through Friday 10:00 a.m.–5:00 p.m.

Middle East Policy Council, *1730 M St. N.W., #512 20036-4505; (202) 296-6767. Fax, (202) 296-5791. Ford M. Fraker, President.*
General email, info@mepc.org
Web, www.mepc.org and Twitter, @MidEastPolicy

Encourages public discussion and understanding of issues affecting U.S. policy in the Middle East. Sponsors conferences for the policy community; conducts educational outreach program; publishes journal and an e-newsletter.

Middle East Research and Information Project, *1344 T St. N.W., #1 20009; (202) 223-3677. Fax, (202) 223-3604. Christopher J. Toensing, Executive Director.*
General email, subscriptions@merip.org
Web, www.merip.org

Works to educate the public about the contemporary Middle East. Focuses on U.S. policy in the region and issues of human rights and social justice; publishes quarterly journal and online news analysis.

National Council on U.S.-Arab Relations, *1730 M St. N.W., #503 20036; (202) 293-6466. Fax, (202) 293-7770. John Duke Anthony, President.*
General email, info@ncusar.org
Web, http://ncusar.org

Educational organization that works to improve mutual understanding between the United States and the Middle East and North Africa (MENA) region. Serves as a clearinghouse on Arab issues and maintains speakers bureau. Coordinates trips for U.S. professionals and congressional delegations to the MENA region.

National U.S.-Arab Chamber of Commerce, *1023 15th St. N.W., #400 20005; (202) 289-5920. Fax, (202) 289-5938. David Hamod, President.*
General email, info@nusacc.org
Web, www.nusacc.org

Promotes trade between the United States and the Middle East and North Africa (MENA) region. Offers members informational publications, research and certification services, and opportunities to meet with international delegations.

New Israel Fund, *Washington Office, 2100 M St. N.W., #619 20037; (202) 842-0900. Fax, (202) 842-0991. Karen Paul-Stern, Washington Regional Director; Daniel Sokatch, Chief Executive Officer. Press, (202) 513-7824.*
General email, info@nif.org
Web, www.nif.org

International philanthropic partnership of North Americans, Israelis, and Europeans. Supports activities that defend civil and human rights, promote Jewish-Arab equality and coexistence, advance the status of women, nurture tolerance, bridge social and economic gaps, encourage government accountability, and assist citizen efforts to protect the environment. Makes grants and provides capacity-building assistance to Israeli public interest groups; trains civil rights lawyers. (Headquarters in New York City.)

S. Daniel Abraham Center for Middle East Peace, *633 Pennsylvania Ave. N.W., 5th Floor 20004; (202) 624-0850. Fax, (202) 624-0855. S. Daniel Abraham, Chair.*
General email:, info@centerpeace.org
Web, www.centerpeace.org

Membership: Middle Eastern policymakers, U.S. government officials, and international business leaders. Serves as a mediator to encourage a peaceful resolution to the Arab-Israeli conflict; sponsors travel to the region, diplomatic exchanges, and conferences for Middle Eastern and U.S. leaders interested in the peace process.

United Palestinian Appeal (UPA), *1330 New Hampshire Ave. N.W., #104 20036-6350; (202) 659-5007. Fax, (202) 296-0224. Saleem F. Zaru, Executive Director.*
General email, contact@helpupa.org
Web, www.helpUPA.org

An American charitable organization dedicated to improving the quality of life for Palestinians in the Middle

East, particularly those in the West Bank, the Gaza Strip, and refugee camps. Provides funding for community development projects, health care, education, children's services, and emergency relief. Funded by private donations from individuals and foundations in the United States and the Middle East and North Africa (MENA) region.

Washington Institute for Near East Policy, *1828 L St. N.W., #1050 20036; (202) 452-0650. Fax, (202) 223-5364. Richard S. Abramson, President; Robert Satloff, Executive Director.*
Web, www.washingtoninstitute.org

Research and educational organization that seeks to improve the effectiveness of U.S. policy in the Middle East by promoting debate among policymakers, journalists, and scholars.

Washington Kurdish Institute, *1612 5th St. N.W., #2 20001; (202) 484-0140. Najmaldin O. Karim, President. General email, wki@kurd.org*
Web, www.kurd.org

Membership: scholars, human rights practitioners, Middle East and foreign policy experts, and Kurds from around the world.

Russia and New Independent States

For the Baltic states, see Europe.

►AGENCIES

Agency for International Development (USAID), *Europe and Eurasia Bureau, 301 4th St. S.W., #247 20523 (mailing address: 1300 Pennsylvania Ave. N.W., Washington, DC 20521); (202) 567-4020. Fax, (202) 567-4256. Paige Alexander, Assistant Administrator.*
Web, www.usaid.gov/who-we-are/organization/bureaus/bureau-europe-and-eurasia

Advises the AID administrator on U.S. economic development policy in Europe and Eurasia.

Defense Dept. (DoD), *International Security Affairs, The Pentagon, #3C889 20301-2400; (703) 697-2788. Fax, (703) 697-3279. Derek H. Chollet, Assistant Secretary.*
Web, www.defense.gov

Advises the secretary of defense and recommends policies on regional security issues in the Middle East, Africa, Russia/Eurasia, and Europe/NATO.

State Dept., *Caucasus Affairs and Regional Conflicts, 2201 C St. N.W., #4220 20520-7512; (202) 647-8741. Fax, (202) 736-7915. John M. Pommershein, Director.*
Web, www.state.gov

Includes Armenia, Azerbaijan, Georgia, and conflict regions.

State Dept., *Central Asian Affairs, 2201 C St. N.W., #1880 20520; (202) 647-9370. Fax, (202) 736-4650. Lesslie Viguerie, Director.*
Web, www.state.gov

Covers affairs of Kazakhstan, Kyrgyzstan, Tajikistan, Turkmenistan, and Uzbekistan.

State Dept., *Russian Affairs, 2201 C St. N.W., #4417 20520-7512; (202) 647-9806. Fax, (202) 647-8980. David J. Kostelancik, Director.*
Web, www.state.gov

State Dept., *Ukraine, Moldova, and Belarus Affairs, 2201 C St. N.W., #4427 20520-7512; (202) 647-8671. Fax, (202) 647-3506. Michael D. Scanlan, Director.*
Web, www.state.gov

►CONGRESS

For a listing of relevant congressional committees and subcommittees, please see pages 414–415 or the Appendix.

Library of Congress, *European Division, 101 Independence Ave. S.E., #LJ-249 20540; (202) 707-5414. Fax, (202) 707-8482. Georgette M. Dorn, Chief, Acting. Reference desk, (202) 707-4515.*
Web, www.loc.gov/rr/european

Provides reference service on the library's European collections (except collections on Spain, Portugal, and the British Isles). Prepares bibliographies and special studies relating to European countries, including Russia and the other states of the former Soviet Union and eastern bloc. Maintains current; unbound Slavic-language periodicals and newspapers, which are available at the European Reference Desk.

►INTERNATIONAL ORGANIZATIONS

International Bank for Reconstruction and Development *(World Bank), Europe and Central Asia, 1818 H St. N.W. 20433; (202) 473-1000. Laura Tuck, Vice President; Andrew Kircher, Media Contact, (202) 473-6313.*
Web, www.worldbank.org

Works to fight poverty and improve the living standards of low- and middle-income people in the countries of eastern Europe and central Asia, including states of the former Soviet Union, by providing loans, policy advice, technical assistance, and knowledge-sharing services. Interests include finance, economic development, education, water supply, agriculture, public health, and environmental protection.

►NONGOVERNMENTAL

American Bar Assn. (ABA), *Rule of Law Initiative, 1050 Connecticut Ave. N.W., #450 20036; (202) 662-1950. Fax, (202) 662-1597. Rob Boone, Director. General email, rol@americanbar.org*
Web, www.americanbar.org/rol

Promotes the rule of law and specific legal reforms in developing countries throughout the world; recruits volunteer legal professionals from the United States and western Europe. Interests include human rights, anti-corruption initiatives, criminal law, efforts against human trafficking, judicial reform, legal education reform, civic education, reforming the legal profession, and women's rights.

American Councils for International Education: ACTR/ ACCELS, *1828 L. St. N.W., #1200 20036; (202) 833-7522. Fax, (202) 833-7523. Dan E. Davidson, President.*
General email, general@americancouncils.org
Web, www.americancouncils.org

Advances education and research worldwide through international programs focused on academic exchange, professional training, distance learning, curriculum and test development, delivery of technical assistance, research, evaluation, and institution building. Conducts educational exchanges for high school, university, and graduate school students as well as scholars with the countries of Africa, eastern Europe, Eurasia, southeast Europe, and the Middle East.

Armenian Assembly of America, *1334 G St. N.W., #200 20005; (202) 393-3434. Fax, (202) 638-4904. Bryan Ardouny, Executive Director.*
General email, info@aaainc.org
Web, www.aaainc.org

Promotes public understanding and awareness of Armenian issues; advances research and data collection and disseminates information on the Armenian people; advocates greater Armenian American participation in the American democratic process; works to alleviate human suffering of Armenians.

Armenian National Committee of America (ANCA), *1711 N St. N.W. 20036; (202) 775-1918. Fax, (202) 775-5648. Kenneth V. Hachikian, Chair.*
General email, anca@anca.org
Web, www.anca.org

Armenian American grassroots political organization. Works to advance concerns of the Armenian American community. Interests include strengthening U.S.-Armenian relations.

Eurasia Foundation, *1350 Connecticut Ave. N.W., #1000 20036-1730; (202) 234-7370. Fax, (202) 234-7377. William Horton Beebe-Center, President.*
General email, eurasia@eurasia.org
Web, www.eurasia.org

Network of local foundations in Russia, Central Asia, the South Caucasus, Ukraine, and Moldova that works in partnership with the U.S. foundation, providing technical assistance and grants to further small business growth, the responsiveness of local governments, and the leadership skills of young people.

Institute for European, Russian, and Eurasian Studies *(George Washington University), 1957 E St. N.W., #412 20052-0001; (202) 994-6340. Fax, (202) 994-5436. Peter Rollberg, Director.*
General email, ieresgwu@gwu.edu
Web, www.ieres.org

Studies and researches European, Russian, and Eurasian affairs. Sponsors a master's program in European and Eurasian studies. (Affiliated with the George Washington University Elliott School of International Affairs.)

Jamestown Foundation, *1111 16th St. N.W., #320 20036; (202) 483-8888. Fax, (202) 483-8337. Glen E. Howard, President.*
General email, pubs@jamestown.org
Web, www.jamestown.org

Provides policymakers with information about events and trends in societies that are strategically or tactically important to the United States and that frequently restrict access to such information. Serves as an alternative source to official or intelligence channels, especially with regard to Eurasia and terrorism. Publishes the *Militant Leadership Monitor,* covering leaders of major insurgencies and militant movements.

Kennan Institute, *One Woodrow Wilson Plaza, 1300 Pennsylvania Ave. N.W. 20004-3027; (202) 691-4100. Fax, (202) 691-4247. Matthew Rojansky, Director.*
General email, kennan@wilsoncenter.org
Web, www.wilsoncenter.org/program/kennan-institute

Offers residential research scholarships to academic scholars and to specialists from government, media, and the private sector for studies to improve American knowledge about Russia, Central Asia, and the Caucasus. Sponsors lectures; publishes reports; promotes dialogue between academic specialists and policymakers. (Affiliated with the Woodrow Wilson International Center for Scholars.)

NCSJ: Advocates on Behalf of Jews in Russia, Ukraine, the Baltic States and Eurasia, *2020 K St. N.W., #7800 20006; (202) 898-2500. Fax, (202) 898-0822. Mark B. Levin, Executive Director; Stephen M. Greenberg, Chair.*
General email, ncsj@ncsj.org
Web, www.ncsj.org

Membership: national Jewish organizations and local federations. Coordinates efforts by members to aid Jews in the former Soviet Union.

Open Society Foundation, Eastern Europe/Former Soviet Union Project, *1730 Pennsylvania Ave. N.W., 7th Floor 20006; (202) 721-5600. Fax, (202) 530-0128. Stephen Rickard, Director, Washington Office.*
General email, info@osi-dc.org
Web, www.soros.org/initiatives/washington

Serves as a resource for government agencies, multilateral institutions, and nongovernmental organizations interested in the region. Promotes open societies in the region. Provides policy briefings and political analysis. Oversees OSI foundations established in the region. (Affiliated with the Soros Foundation Network.)

Ukrainian National Information Service, *Washington Office, 311 Massachusetts Ave. N.E., Lower Level 20002; (202) 547-0018. Fax, (202) 547-0019. Michael Sawkiw Jr., Director.*

General email, unis@ucca.org

Web, www.ucca.org

Information bureau of the Ukrainian Congress Committee of America in New York. Monitors U.S. policy and foreign assistance to Ukraine. Supports educational, cultural, and humanitarian activities in the Ukranian-American community. (Headquarters in New York.)

U.S.-Russia Business Council, *1110 Vermont Ave. N.W., #350 20005; (202) 739-9180. Fax, (202) 659-5920. Daniel A. Russell, President. Press, (202) 739-9182.*
General email, info@usrbc.org

Web, www.usrbc.org

Membership: U.S. companies involved in trade and investment in Russia. Promotes commercial ties between the United States and Russia; provides business services. Monitors legislation and regulations. (Maintains office in Moscow. Formerly Coalition for U.S.-Russia Trade.)

U.S.-Ukraine Foundation, *Washington Office, 1660 L St. N.W., #1000 20036-5634; (202) 524-6555. Fax, (202) 280-1989. Nadia K. McConnell, President.*
General email, info@usukraine.org

Web, www.usukraine.org

Encourages and facilitates democratic and human rights development and free market reform in the Ukraine. Creates and sustains communications channels between the United States and Ukraine. Manages the U.S.-Ukraine Community Partnerships Program. (Maintains office in Kiev, Ukraine.)

U.S. Territories and Associated States

▶ AGENCIES

Interior Dept. (DOI), *Insular Areas (U.S. Territories and Freely Associated States), 1849 C St. N.W., MS 2429 20240; (202) 208-4736. Fax, (202) 501-7759. Lori Faeth, Assistant Secretary, Acting, (202) 208-4709; Nikolao (Nik) Pula, Director.*
Web, www.doi.gov/oia

Promotes economic, social, and political development of U.S. territories (Guam, American Samoa, the Virgin Islands, and the Commonwealth of the Northern Mariana Islands). Supervises federal programs for the Freely Associated States (Federated States of Micronesia, Republic of the Marshall Islands, and Republic of Palau).

▶ CONGRESS

For a listing of relevant congressional committees and subcommittees, please see pages 414–415 or the Appendix.

American Samoa's Delegate to Congress, *2422 RHOB 20515; (202) 225-8577. Fax, (202) 225-8757. Del. Eni F. H. Faleomavaega.*

General email, Faleomavaega@mail.house.gov

Web, www.house.gov/faleomavaega

Represents American Samoa in Congress.

Guam's Delegate to Congress, *2441 RHOB 20515; (202) 225-1188. Fax, (202) 226-0341. Del. Madeleine Z. Bordallo.*
Web, www.house.gov/bordallo

Represents Guam in Congress.

Puerto Rican Resident Commissioner, *1213 LHOB 20515; (202) 225-2615. Fax, (202) 225-2154. Pedro Pierluisi, Resident Commissioner.*
Web, http://pierluisi.house.gov

Represents the Commonwealth of Puerto Rico in Congress.

Virgin Islands' Delegate to Congress, *1510 LHOB 20515; (202) 225-1790. Fax, (202) 225-5517. Del. Donna M. Christensen.*
Web, www.house.gov/christian-christensen

Represents the Virgin Islands in Congress.

▶ NONGOVERNMENTAL

Commonwealth of Puerto Rico Federal Affairs Administration, *1100 17th St. N.W., #800 20036; (202) 778-0710. Fax, (202) 778-0721. Juan E. Hernández, Executive Director.*
General email, info@prfaa.com

Web, www.prfaa.com

Represents the governor and the government of the Commonwealth of Puerto Rico before Congress and the executive branch; conducts research; serves as official press information center for the Commonwealth of Puerto Rico. Monitors legislation and regulations.

Private Equity Gross Capital Council (PEGCC), *950 F St. N.W., #550 20004; (202) 465-7700. Fax, (202) 639-0209. Steve Judge, President; Kenneth P. (Ken) Spain, Vice President of Public Affairs.*
General email, info@pegcc.org

Web, www.pegcc.org

Advocacy, communications, and research organization and resource center that develops, analyzes, and distributes information about the private equity industry and its contributions to the national and global economy.

U.S. Virgin Islands Department of Tourism, *Washington Office, 444 N. Capitol St. N.W., #305 20001; (202) 624-3590. Fax, (202) 624-3594. Gerda Sebastian, Director of Administration and Management; Beverly Nicholson Doty, Commissioner. Toll-free, (800) 372-8784.*
General email, info@usvitourism.vi

Web, www.visitusvi.com

Provides information about the U.S. Virgin Islands; promotes tourism. (Headquarters in St. Thomas.)

13 ⚖

Law and Justice

GENERAL POLICY AND ANALYSIS

Basic Resources

▶AGENCIES

Executive Office for U.S. Attorneys *(Justice Dept.),* *950 Pennsylvania Ave. N.W., #2242 20530-0001; (202) 252-1000. Fax, (202) 252-1309. H. Marshall Jarrett, Director.*
Web, www.justice.gov/usao/eousa/director.html

Provides the offices of U.S. attorneys with technical assistance and supervision in areas of legal counsel, personnel, and training. Publishes the *U.S. Attorneys' Manual* and *United States Attorneys' Bulletin.* Administers the Attorney General's Office of Legal Education, which conducts workshops and seminars to develop the litigation skills of the department's attorneys in criminal and civil trials. Develops and implements Justice Dept. procedures for collecting criminal fines.

Justice Dept. (DOJ), *950 Pennsylvania Ave. N.W. 20530-0001; (202) 514-2001. Fax, (202) 307-6777. Eric Holder, Attorney General; James M. Cole, Deputy Attorney General, (202) 514-2101; Tony West, Associate Attorney General, (202) 514-9500; Brian Fallon, Public Affairs, (202) 514-2007. Information and switchboard, (202) 514-2000. Public Affairs, (202) 514-2007. Library, (202) 514-3775. Public Comments, (202) 353-1555.*
General email, askdoj@usdoj.gov
Web, www.justice.gov

Serves as counsel for the U.S. government. Represents the government in enforcing the law in the public interest. Plays key role in protecting against criminals and subversion, in ensuring healthy competition of business in U.S. free enterprise system, in safeguarding the consumer, and in enforcing drug, immigration, and naturalization laws. Plays a significant role in protecting citizens through effective law enforcement, crime prevention, crime detection, and prosecution and rehabilitation of offenders. Conducts all suits in the Supreme Court in which the United States is concerned. Represents the government in legal matters generally, furnishing legal advice and opinions to the president, the cabinet, and to the heads of executive departments, as provided by law. Justice Dept. organization includes divisions on antitrust, civil law, civil rights, criminal law, environment and natural resources, and taxes, as well as the Bureau of Alcohol, Tobacco, Firearms, and Explosives; Drug Enforcement Administration; Executive Office for Immigration Review; Federal Bureau of Investigation; Federal Bureau of Prisons; Foreign Claims Settlement Commission; Office of Justice Programs; U.S. Attorneys; U.S. Marshals Service; U.S. Parole Commission; and U.S. Trustees.

Justice Dept. (DOJ), *Access to Justice Initiative, 950 Pennsylvania Ave. N.W., #3340 20530; (202) 514-5312. Fax, (202) 514-5326. Deborah Leff, Senior Counselor, Acting.*
Web, www.justice.gov/atj

Works to improve the availability and quality of legal defense for vulnerable populations, including immigrants, juveniles, the homeless, disabled veterans, and victims of domestic and sexual violence. Identifies areas of need and effective programs, and works collaboratively with local, state, tribal, and federal participants to implement solutions. Priorities include expanding community partnerships, promoting less court-intensive solutions, and increasing resources for defender programs.

Justice Dept. (DOJ), *Legal Policy, 950 Pennsylvania Ave. N.W., #4234 20530-0001; (202) 514-4601. Fax, (202) 514-2424. Elana J. Tyrangiel, Principal Deputy Assistant Attorney General.*
Web, www.justice.gov/olp

Develops and implements the Justice Dept.'s major policy initiatives, often with the cooperation of other offices within the department and among other agencies. Works with Office of Legislative Affairs to promote the department's policies in Congress.

Justice Dept. (DOJ), *Professional Responsibility, 950 Pennsylvania Ave. N.W., #3529 20530-0001; (202) 514-3365. Fax, (202) 514-5050. Robin C. Ashton, Counsel.*
Web, www.justice.gov/opr

Receives and reviews allegations of misconduct by Justice Dept. attorneys; refers cases that warrant further review to appropriate investigative agency or unit; makes recommendations to the attorney general for action on certain misconduct cases.

Justice Dept. (DOJ), *Solicitor General, 950 Pennsylvania Ave. N.W., #5143 20530-0001; (202) 514-2203. Fax, (202) 514-9769. Donald B. Verrilli Jr., Solicitor General. Information on pending cases, (202) 514-2218.*
Web, www.justice.gov/osg

Represents the federal government before the Supreme Court of the United States.

Legal Services Corp., *3333 K St. N.W., 3rd Floor 20007-3522; (202) 295-1500. Fax, (202) 337-6797. James J. Sandman, President, (202) 295-1575. Public reading room, (202) 295-1502.*
General email, campbellp@lsc.gov
Web, www.lsc.gov

Independent federal corporation established by Congress. Awards grants to local agencies that provide the poor with legal services. Library open to the public by appointment only.

Office of Justice Programs (OJP) *(Justice Dept.),* *810 7th St. N.W. 20531; (202) 307-5933. Fax, (202) 514-7805. Karol V. Mason, Assistant Attorney General, Acting. Press, (202) 307-0703.*
General email, askojp@ncjrs.gov
Web, www.ojp.usdoj.gov

Provides federal leadership, coordination, and assistance in developing the nation's capacity to prevent and control crime, administer justice, and assist crime victims. Includes the Bureau of Justice Assistance, which supports state and local criminal justice strategies; the Bureau of

Justice Statistics, which collects, analyzes, and disseminates criminal justice data; the National Institute of Justice, which is the primary research and development agency of the Justice Dept.; the Office of Juvenile Justice and Delinquency Prevention, which supports state and local efforts to combat juvenile crime and victimization; the Office of Victims of Crime, which provides support for crime victims and leadership to promote justice and healing for all crime victims; and the Community Capacity Development Office, which provides resources to support community-based anti-crime efforts.

State Justice Institute, *11951 Freedom Dr., #1020, Reston, VA 20190; (571) 313-8843. Fax, (571) 313-1173. Jonathan Mattiello, Executive Director. General email, contact@sji.gov*

Web, www.sji.gov

Awards grants to state courts and to state agencies for programs that improve state courts' judicial administration. Maintains judicial information clearinghouses and establishes technical resource centers; conducts educational programs; delivers technical assistance.

►CONGRESS

For a listing of relevant congressional committees and subcommittees, please see pages 470–471 or the Appendix.

Government Accountability Office (GAO), *Homeland Security and Justice, 441 G St. N.W., #6834 20548; (202) 512-8777. George A. Scott, Managing Director. Web, www.gao.gov*

Independent, nonpartisan agency in the legislative branch. Audits, analyzes, and evaluates federal administration of homeland security programs and activities; makes some reports available to the public.

►JUDICIARY

Administrative Office of the U.S. Courts, *1 Columbus Circle N.E. 20544-0001; (202) 502-2600. Thomas F. Hogan, Director, (202) 502-3000. Web, www.uscourts.gov/adminoff.html*

Provides administrative support to the federal courts, including the procurement of supplies and equipment; the administration of personnel, budget, and financial control services; and the compilation and publication of statistical data and reports on court business. Implements the policies of the Judicial Conference of the United States and supports its committees. Recommends plans and strategies to manage court business. Procures needed resources, legislation, and other assistance for the judiciary from Congress and the executive branch.

Federal Judicial Center, *1 Columbus Circle N.E. 20002-8003; (202) 502-4160. Fax, (202) 502-4099. Jeremy D. Fogel, Director. Room 6140. Library, (202) 502-4156. Public Affairs, (202) 502-4250. Web, www.fjc.gov*

Conducts research on the operations of the federal court system; develops and conducts continuing education and training programs for judges and judicial personnel; and makes recommendations to improve the administration of the courts.

Judicial Conference of the United States, *1 Columbus Circle N.E., #7-425 20544; (202) 502-2400. Fax, (202) 502-1144. John G. Roberts Jr., Chief Justice of the United States, Chair; Thomas F. Hogan, Secretary, (202) 502-3000. Web, www.uscourts.gov*

Serves as the policy-making and governing body for the administration of the federal judicial system; advises Congress on the creation of new federal judgeships. Interests include international judicial relations.

Supreme Court of the United States, *1 1st St. N.E. 20543; (202) 479-3000. John G. Roberts Jr., Chief Justice; Kathleen Arberg, Public Information Officer, (202) 479-3211. Web, www.supremecourtus.gov*

Highest appellate court in the federal judicial system. Interprets the U.S. Constitution, federal legislation, and treaties. Provides information on new cases filed, the status of pending cases, and admissions to the Supreme Court Bar. Library open to Supreme Court bar members only.

►NONGOVERNMENTAL

Alliance for Justice, *11 Dupont Circle N.W., 2nd Floor 20036-1213; (202) 822-6070. Fax, (202) 822-6068. Nan Aron, President. General email, alliance@afj.org*

Web, www.afj.org

Membership: public interest lawyers and advocacy, environmental, civil rights, and consumer organizations. Promotes reform of the legal system to ensure access to the courts; monitors selection of federal judges; works to preserve the rights of nonprofit organizations to advocate on behalf of their constituents.

American Assn. for Justice, *777 6th St. N.W., #200 20001; (202) 965-3500. Fax, (202) 342-5484. Linda Lipsen, Chief Executive Officer. Toll-free, (800) 424-2725. General email, aaj@justice.org*

Web, www.justice.org

Membership: attorneys, judges, law professors, and students. Works to strengthen the civil justice system and the right to trial by jury. Interests include victims' rights, property and casualty insurance, revisions of federal rules of evidence, criminal code, jurisdictions of courts, juries, and consumer law. (Formerly the Assn. of Trial Lawyers of America.)

American Bar Assn. (ABA), *Washington Office, 1050 Connecticut Ave. N.W., #400 20036; (202) 662-1000. Fax, (202) 662-1099. Jack Rives, Executive Director. Information, (800) 285-2221. Library, (202) 662-1011. Web, www.americanbar.org*

Composed of the Governmental Affairs Office, Public Services Division, Government and Public Sector Lawyers

LAW AND JUSTICE RESOURCES IN CONGRESS

For a complete listing of Congress committees, including their full contact information, leadership, membership, and jurisdictions, please refer to the Appendix on pages 724–842.

HOUSE:

House Administration Committee, (202) 225-8281.
Web, cha.house.gov or democrats.cha.house.gov

House Appropriations Committee, (202) 225-2771.
Web, appropriations.house.gov or
democrats.appropriations.house.gov
  Subcommittee on Commerce, Justice, Science, and Related Agencies, (202) 225-3351.
  Subcommittee on Homeland Security, (202) 225-5834.

House Education and the Workforce Committee, (202) 225-4527.
Web, edworkforce.house.gov or
democrats.edworkforce.house.gov
  Subcommittee on Workforce Protections, (202) 225-4527.

House Energy and Commerce Committee, (202) 225-2927.
Web, energycommerce.house.gov or
democrats.energycommerce.house.gov
  Subcommittee on Commerce, Manufacturing, and Trade, (202) 225-2927.
  Subcommittee on Energy and Power, (202) 225-2927.
  Subcommittee on Health, (202) 225-2927.

House Ethics Committee, (202) 225-7103.
Web, ethics.house.gov

House Financial Services Committee, (202) 225-7502.
Web, financialservices.house.gov or
democrats.financialservices.house.gov
  Subcommittee on Financial Institutions and Consumer Credit, (202) 225-7502.

House Homeland Security Committee, (202) 226-8417.
Web, homeland.house.gov or chsdemocrats.house.gov
  Subcommittee on Border and Maritime Security, (202) 226-8417.

House Judiciary Committee, (202) 225-3951.
Web, judiciary.house.gov or
democrats.judiciary.house.gov
  Subcommittee on the Constitution and Civil Justice, (202) 225-2825.
  Subcommittee on Courts, Intellectual Property, and the Internet, (202) 225-5741.
  Subcommittee on Crime, Terrorism and Homeland Security, and Investigations, (202) 225-5727.
  Subcommittee on Immigration and Border Security, (202) 225-3926.
  Subcommittee on Regulatory Reform, Commercial and Antitrust Law, (202) 226-7680.

House Natural Resources Committee, (202) 225-2761.
Web, naturalresources.house.gov or
democrats.naturalresources.house.gov
  Subcommittee on Energy and Mineral Resources, (202) 225-9297.

House Oversight and Government Reform Committee, (202) 225-5074.
Web, oversight.house.gov or
democrats.oversight.house.gov
  Subcommittee on Government Operations, (202) 225-5074.

House Small Business Committee, (202) 225-5821.
Web, smallbusiness.house.gov or
democrats.smallbusiness.house.gov
  Subcommittee on Health and Technology, (202) 225-5821.

House Ways and Means Committee, (202) 225-3625.
Web, waysandmeans.house.gov or
democrats.waysandmeans.house.gov
  Subcommittee on Human Resources, (202) 225-1025.

Division, International Law and Practice Section, Criminal Justice Section, Taxation Section, Individual Rights and Responsibilities Section, Dispute Resolution Section, Administrative Law and Regulatory Practice Section, Rule of Law Initiative, and others. (Headquarters in Chicago, Ill.)

American Bar Assn. (ABA), *Governmental Affairs, 1050 Connecticut Ave. N.W., #400 20036; (202) 662-1760. Fax, (202) 662-1762. Thomas M. Susman, Director, (202) 662-1765.*
General email, thomas.susman@americanbar.org
Web, www.americanbar.org/poladv

Advocates before Congress, the executive branch, and other governmental entities on issues of importance to the legal profession. Publishes the ABA Washington Letter, a monthly online legislative analysis, and ABA Washington Summary, a daily online publication.

American Constitution Society for Law and Policy, *1333 H St. N.W., 11th Floor 20005; (202) 393-6181. Fax, (202) 393-6189. Caroline Fredrickson, President.*
General email, info@acslaw.org
Web, www.acslaw.org

National association of lawyers, law students, judges, legal scholars, and policymakers that promotes a progressive vision of constitutional law and public policy. Produces issue briefs and publications. Organizes lectures, conferences, seminars, and two annual student competitions.

SENATE:

Senate Agriculture, Nutrition, and Forestry
   Committee, (202) 224-2035.
Web, ag.senate.gov
   Subcommittee on Livestock, Dairy, Poultry,
      Marketing and Agriculture Security,
      (202) 224-2035.
Senate Appropriations Committee, (202) 224-7363.
Web, appropriations.senate.gov
   Subcommittee on Commerce, Justice, Science,
      and Related Agencies, (202) 224-5202.
   Subcommittee on Homeland Security,
      (202) 224-7363.
Senate Commerce, Science, and Transportation
   Committee, (202) 224-0411.
Web, commerce.senate.gov
   Subcommittee on Consumer Protection,
      Product Safety, and Insurance,
      (202) 224-1270.
   Subcommittee on Oceans, Atmosphere, Fisheries
      and the Coast Guard, (202) 224-4912.
Senate Finance Committee, (202) 224-4515.
Web, finance.senate.gov
   Subcommittee on Taxation and IRS Oversight,
      (202) 224-4515.
Senate Foreign Relations Committee,
   (202) 224-4651.
Web, foreign.senate.gov
   Subcommittee on Western Hemisphere and
      Global Narcotics Affairs, (202) 224-4651.
Senate Health, Education, Labor, and Pensions
   Committee, (202) 224-5375.
Web, help.senate.gov
   Subcommittee on Children and Families,
      (202) 224-5375.
   Subcommittee on Employment and Workplace
      Safety, (202) 228-1455.

Senate Homeland Security and Governmental Affairs
   Committee, (202) 224-2627.
Web, hsgac.senate.gov
Permanent Subcommittee on Investigations,
   (202) 224-9505.
Senate Indian Affairs Committee, (202) 224-2251.
Web, indian.senate.gov
Senate Judiciary Committee, (202) 224-7703.
Web, judiciary.senate.gov
   Subcommittee on Antitrust, Competition
      Policy, and Consumer Rights,
      (202) 224-7703.
   Subcommittee on Bankruptcy and the Courts,
      (202) 224-7703.
   Subcommittee on the Constitution, Civil
      Rights, and Human Rights,
      (202) 224-1158.
   Subcommittee on Crime and Terrorism,
      (202) 228-3740.
   Subcommittee on Immigration, Refugees, and
      Border Security, (202) 224-6498.
   Subcommittee on Oversight, Federal Rights, and
      Agency Actions, (202) 224-7703.
   Subcommittee on Privacy, Technology, and the
      Law, (202) 228-3177.
Senate Rules and Administration Committee,
   (202) 224-6352.
Web, rules.senate.gov
Senate Select Committee on Ethics,
   (202) 224-2981.
Web, ethics.senate.gov
Senate Small Business and Entrepreneurship
   Committee, (202) 224-5175.
Web, sbc.senate.gov
Senate Special Committee on Aging,
   (202) 224-5364.
Web, aging.senate.gov

American Tort Reform Assn., *1101 Connecticut Ave.
N.W., #400 20036-4351; (202) 682-1163. Fax, (202) 682-
1022. Sherman Joyce, President.*
Web, www.atra.org

Membership: businesses, associations, trade groups,
professional societies, and individuals interested in reforming
the civil justice system in the United States. Develops model
state legislation and position papers on tort liability and
reform. Monitors legislation, regulations, and legal rulings.

Aspen Institute, *1 Dupont Circle N.W., #700 20036-7133;
(202) 736-5800. Fax, (202) 467-0790. Walter Isaacson,
President. Press, (202) 736-3849.*
General email, info@aspeninstitute.org
Web, www.aspeninstitute.org

Educational and policy studies organization. Brings
together individuals from diverse backgrounds to discuss
how to deal with longstanding philosophical disputes and
contemporary social challenges in law and justice.

Center for Study of Responsive Law, *1530 P St. N.W.
20005 (mailing address: P.O. Box 19367, Washington, DC
20036); (202) 387-8030. Fax, (202) 234-5176. John Richard,
Administrator.*
General email, info@csrl.org
Web, www.csrl.org

Consumer interest clearinghouse that conducts research
and holds conferences on public interest law. Interests
include white-collar crime, the environment, occupational
health and safety, the postal system, banking deregulation,

Justice Department

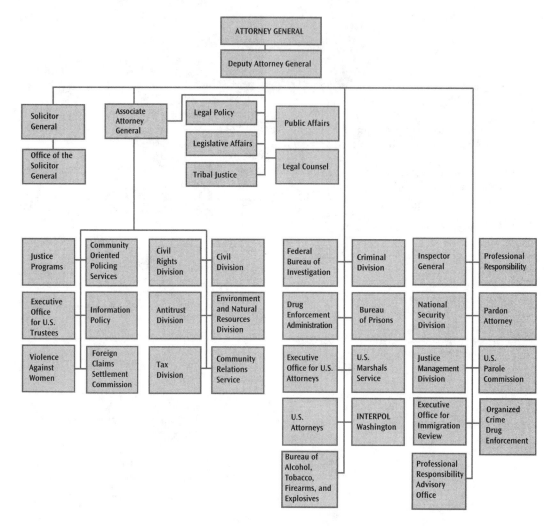

insurance, freedom of information policy, and broadcasting.

The Constitution Project (TCP), *1200 18th St. N.W., #1000 20036; (202) 580-6920. Fax, (202) 580-6929. Press, (202) 580-6922. Virginia E. Sloan, President; Scott Messinger, Chief Operating Officer.*
General email, info@constitutionproject.org

Web, www.constitutionproject.org

Think tank that brings together policy experts and legal practitioners from across the political and ideological spectrum to address current constitutional challenges. Interests include checks and balances, counterterrorism policies and practices, criminal discovery, data collection and privacy, the death penalty, DNA collection, government surveillance and searches, immigration, right to counsel, sentencing, and transparency and accountability. Hosts discussions and online forums; issues written reports and press releases.

Death Penalty Information Center, *1015 18th St. N.W., #704 20036; (202) 289-2275. Fax, (202) 289-7336.*

Richard Dieter, Executive Director.
General email, dpic@deathpenaltyinfo.org

Web, www.deathpenaltyinfo.org

Provides the media and public with analysis and information on issues concerning capital punishment. Conducts briefings for journalists; prepares reports; issues press releases.

Federal Bar Assn., *1220 N. Fillmore St., #444, Arlington, VA 22201; (571) 481-9100. Fax, (571) 481-9090. Karen Silberman, Executive Director.*
General email, fba@fedbar.org

Web, www.fedbar.org

Membership: attorneys employed by the federal government or practicing before federal courts or agencies. Conducts research and programs in fields that include tax, environment, veterans health, intellectual property, Social Security, transportation, Native American, antitrust, immigration, and international law; concerns include professional ethics, legal education (primarily continuing education), and legal services.

The Federalist Society, *1015 18th St. N.W., #425 20036; (202) 822-8138. Fax, (202) 296-8061. Eugene B. Meyer, President. General email, info@fed-soc.org*

Web, www.fed-soc.org

Promotes conservative and libertarian principles among lawyers, judges, law professors, law students, and the general public. Sponsors lectures, debates, seminars, fellowships, and awards programs.

Government Accountability Project, *1612 K St. N.W., #1100 20006; (202) 457-0034. Fax, (202) 457-0059. Beatrice Edwards, Executive Director and International Director; Louis Clark, President. General email, info@whistleblower.org*

Web, www.whistleblower.org

Membership: federal employees, union members, professionals, and interested citizens. Supports and represents employee whistleblowers. Works to ensure that whistleblower disclosures about improper government and industry actions that are harmful to the environment, public health, national security, food safety, the financial sector, and several other areas are defended and heard. Represents whistleblower clients in legal actions and operates attorney referral service through National Whistleblower Legal Defense and Education Fund. (Formerly the National Whistleblower Center.)

HALT—An Organization of Americans for Legal Reform, *1612 K St. N.W., #1102 20006-2802; (571) 403-1268. Fax, (202) 887-9699. Rodd M. Santomauro, Executive Director. Toll-free, (888) 367-4258. General email, halt@halt.org*

Web, www.halt.org

Public interest organization concerned with legal reform. Interests include freedom of information, small claims reform, lawyer accountability, and judicial integrity. Conducts research on alternative dispute resolution programs for delivery of legal services, including arbitration, legal clinics, and mediation services; provides educational and self-help manuals for consumers on the legal process.

Lawyers for Civil Justice, *1140 Connecticut Ave. N.W., #503 20036-4013; (202) 429-0045. Fax, (202) 429-6982. Barry Bauman, Executive Director. Web, www.lfcj.com*

Membership: defense lawyers and corporate counsel. Interests include tort reform, litigation cost containment, and tort and product liability. Monitors legislation and regulations affecting civil justice reform.

National Assn. for the Advancement of Colored People (NAACP), *Washington Bureau, 1156 15th St. N.W., #915 20005; (202) 463-2940. Fax, (202) 463-2953. Hilary O. Shelton, Director. General email, washingtonbureau@naacpnet.org*

Web, www.naacp.org

Membership: persons interested in civil rights for all minorities. Seeks, through litigation, to end discrimination in all areas, including discriminatory practices in the administration of justice. Studies and recommends policy on court administration and jury selection. Maintains branch offices in many state and federal prisons. (Headquarters in Baltimore, Md.)

National Bar Assn., *1225 11th St. N.W. 20001-4217; (202) 842-3900. Fax, (202) 289-6170. Alfreda Davis, Executive Director, Acting; Patricia Rosier, President. General email, nbapresident@nationalbar.org*

Web, www.nationalbar.net

Membership: primarily minority attorneys, legal professionals, judges, and law students. Interests include legal education and improvement of the judicial process. Sponsors legal education seminars in all states that require continuing legal education for lawyers.

National Center for State Courts, *Government Relations, Washington Office, 111 2nd St. N.E. 20002; (202) 684-2622. Fax, (202) 544-0978. Kay Farley, Executive Director. Toll-free, (866) 941-0229. General email, govrel@ncsc.org*

Web, www.ncsc.org

Works to improve state court systems through research, technical assistance, and training programs. Monitors legislation affecting court systems; interests include state-federal jurisdiction, family law, criminal justice, court administration, international agreements, and automated information systems. Serves as secretariat for eleven state court organizations, including the Conference of Chief Justices, Conference of State Court Administrators, American Judges Assn., and National Assn. for Court Management. (Headquarters in Williamsburg, Va.)

RAND Corporation, *Washington Office, 1200 S. Hayes St., Arlington, VA 22202-5050; (703) 413-1100. Fax, (703) 413-8111. Lynn E. Davis, Director, ext. 5399; Debra Knopman, Director, Justice, Infrastructure, and Environment. Web, www.rand.org*

Analyzes current problems of the American civil and criminal justice systems and evaluates recent and pending changes and reforms. (Headquarters in Santa Monica, Calif.)

Urban Institute, *The Justice Policy Center, 2100 M St. N.W. 20037; (202) 833-7200. Fax, (202) 659-8985. Nancy LaVigne, Director. Web, www.urban.org/center/jpc/index.cfm*

Conducts research and evaluation designed to improve justice and public safety policies and practices at the national, state, and local levels. Works with practitioners, public officials, and community groups to generate evidence on effectiveness of existing programs and to provide guidance on improvements.

U.S. Chamber of Commerce, *Congressional and Public Affairs, 1615 H St. N.W. 20062-2000; (202) 463-5600. Fax, (202) 544-4157. Jack Howard, Senior Vice President. Web, www.uschamber.com*

Federation of individuals; firms; corporations; trade and professional associations; and local, state, and regional chambers of commerce. Monitors legislation and regulations in administrative law, antitrust policy, civil justice reform, and product liability reform.

General Counsels for Federal Departments and Agencies

DEPARTMENTS

Agriculture, Ramona E. Romero, (202) 720-3351

Commerce, Justin Antonipillai, (202) 482-4772

Defense, Robert Taylor, (703) 695-3341

  Air Force, Joseph M. McDade Jr. (Principal Deputy), (703) 697-0941

  Army, Brad Carson, (703) 697-9235

  Navy, Paul L. Oostburg Sanz, (703) 614-1994

Education, Philip H. Rosenfelt, (202) 401-6000

Energy, Eric J. Fygi (Deputy), (202) 586-5281

Health and Human Services, William B. Schultz, (202) 690-7741

Homeland Security, Stevan E. Bunnell, (202) 282-9822

Housing and Urban Development, Helen R. Kanovsky, (202) 708-0123

Interior, Hilary Tompkins, (202) 208-4423

Justice, Jeff Rosenblum, (703) 305-0470

Labor, Patricia Smith, (202) 693-6300

State, Erich Hart, (202) 663-0383

Transportation, Kathryn B. Thomson (Acting), (202) 366-4702

Treasury, Christopher Meade, (202) 622-0283

Veterans Affairs, Will Gunn, (800) 488-8244

AGENCIES

Advisory Council on Historic Preservation, Javier Marques (Associate), (202) 606-8596

Agency for International Development, Douglas Kramer, (202) 712-0900

Central Intelligence Agency, Vacant, (703) 482-1100

Commission on Civil Rights, Todd Gaziano (Chief Legal Officer), (202) 376-7700

Commodity Futures Trading Commission, Jonathan L. Marcus, (202) 418-5120

Consumer Product Safety Commission, Stephanie Tsacoumis, (301) 504-0124

Corporation for National Service, Valerie Green, (202) 606-6677

Environmental Protection Agency, Avi Garbow, (202) 564-8040

Equal Employment Opportunity Commission, P. David Lopez, (202) 663-4702

Export-Import Bank, Angela M. Freyre, (202) 565-3451

Farm Credit Administration, Charles R. Rawls, (703) 883-4021

Federal Communications Commission, Jonathan Sallet (Acting), (202) 418-1700

Federal Deposit Insurance Corporation, Richard Osterman Jr. (Acting), (877) 275-3342

Federal Election Commission, Gregory R. Baker (Administration), Lisa J. Stevenson (Law), (202) 694-1650

Federal Emergency Management Agency, Brad Kieserman, (800) 621-3362

Federal Energy Regulatory Commission, David Morenoff (Acting), (202) 502-6000

Federal Labor Relations Authority, Julia Akins Clark, (202) 218-7910

U.S. Chamber of Commerce, *Institute for Legal Reform,* *1615 H St. N.W. 20062-2000; (202) 463-5724. Fax, (202) 463-5302. Lisa A. Rickard, President.*
General email, ilr@uschamber.com

Web, www.instituteforlegalreform.org

Works to reform state and federal civil justice systems. Strives to reduce excessive litigation. Hosts public forums on legal and tort reform.

Washington Legal Foundation, *2009 Massachusetts Ave. N.W. 20036; (202) 588-0302. Fax, (202) 588-0386. Constance Claffey Larcher, Executive Director.*
General email, info@wlf.org

Web, www.wlf.org

Public interest law and policy center. Seeks legal and regulatory environment supportive of free enterprise through litigation, publishing, and communications. Interests include environmental health, safety regulations, intellectual property rights, and commercial speech.

Women's Bar Assn., *2020 Pennsylvania Ave. N.W., #446 20006; (202) 639-8880. Fax, (202) 639-8889. Carol Montoya, Executive Director.*

General email, admin@wbadc.org

Web, www.wbadc.org

Membership: women and men who are judges, attorneys in the public and private sectors, law students, and lawyers at home who remain professionally active. Promotes appointment of members to positions in the judiciary and legislative policies that foster the advancement of women.

World Jurist Assn., *7910 Woodmont Ave., #1440, Bethesda, MD 20814; (202) 466-5428. Fax, (202) 452-8540. Sona Pancholy, Executive Vice President; Garry E. Hunter, General Counsel.*
General email, wja@worldjurist.org

Web, www.worldjurist.org

Membership: lawyers, law professors, judges, law students, and nonlegal professionals worldwide. Conducts research; promotes world peace through adherence to international law; holds annual conference and biennial congresses. (Affiliates, at same address, include World Assn. of Judges, World Assn. of Law Professors, World Assn. of Lawyers, and World Business Assn.)

Federal Maritime Commission, Tyler J. Wood (Deputy),
(202) 523-5740

Federal Mediation and Conciliation Service, Dawn Starr,
(202) 606-5444

Federal Reserve System, Scott G. Alvarez,
(202) 974-7008

Federal Trade Commission, Jonathan Nuechterlein,
(202) 326-2868

General Services Administration, Kris E. Durmer,
(202) 501-2200

**International Bank for Reconstruction and
Development (World Bank),** Rachel F. Robbins,
(202) 473-1000

Merit Systems Protection Board, Bryan Polisuk,
(202) 653-7171

National Aeronautics and Space Administration,
Michael C. Wholley, (202) 358-2440

National Credit Union Administration, Michael T.
McKenna, (703) 518-6540

National Endowment for Humanities, Michael McDonald,
(202) 606-8322

National Endowment for the Arts, India Pinkney,
(202) 682-5418

National Labor Relations Board, Richard F. Griffin Jr.,
(202) 273-3700

National Mediation Board, Mary L. Johnson,
(202) 692-5040

National Railroad Passenger Corporation (Amtrak),
Eleanor Acheson, (800) 872-7245

National Science Foundation, Lawrence Rudolph,
(703) 292-8060

National Transportation Safety Board, David Tochen,
(202) 314-6080

Nuclear Regulatory Commission, Margaret Doane,
(301) 415-1743

Occupational Safety and Health Review Commission,
Nadine Mancini, (202) 606-5410

Office of Personnel Management, Kamala Vasagam,
(202) 606-1700

Overseas Private Investment Corporation,
Don S. De Amicis, (202) 336-8400

Peace Corps, Bill Rubin, (202) 692-2150

Pension Benefit Guaranty Corporation, Judith Starr,
(202) 326-4400

Postal Regulatory Commission, Stephen Sharfman,
(202) 789-6820

Securities and Exchange Commission, Annie Small,
(202) 551-5100

Small Business Administration, Sara D. Lipscomb,
(202) 205-7425

Smithsonian Institution, Judith Leonard,
(202) 633-5115

Social Security Administration, David F. Black,
(404) 562-1182

U.S. International Trade Commission, Dominic Bianchi,
(202) 205-3061

U.S. Postal Service, Thomas J. Marshall, (202) 268-2950

Dispute Resolution

▶AGENCIES

Justice Dept. (DOJ), *Legal Policy, Interagency Alternative
Dispute Resolution Working Group, 950 Pennsylvania
Ave. N.W., #4529 20530-0001; (202) 616-9471. Fax, (202)
616-9570. Joanna L. Jacobs, Director, (202) 305-4439.
General email, ADRWeb@usdoj.gov*

Web, www.adr.gov

Division of the office of the associate attorney general.
Coordinates Justice Dept. activities related to dispute res-
olution. Responsible for alternative dispute resolution
(ADR) policy and training. Manages the Interagency ADR
Working Group.

▶NONGOVERNMENTAL

American Arbitration Assn., *Government Relations,
Washington Office, Regional Office, 1776 Eye St. N.W.,
#850 20006; (202) 739-8280. Fax, (202) 223-7095.
Pierre Paret, Vice President.
General email, paretp@adr.org*

Web, www.adr.org

Provides alternative dispute resolution services to governments and the private sector. (Headquarters in New York.)

American Bar Assn. (ABA), *Dispute Resolution, 1050
Connecticut Ave. N.W., #400 20036; (202) 662-1680. Fax, (202)
662-1683. David Moora, Section Director, (202) 662-1685.
General email, dispute@americanbar.org*

Web, www.americanbar.org/dispute

Provides training and resources to lawyers, law students, mediators, and arbitrators on dispute resolution.

Assn. for Conflict Resolution, *12100 Sunset Hills Rd.,
#130, Reston, VA 20190; (703) 234-4141. Fax, (703) 435-
4390. Suzanne Burnett, Director of Operations.
General email, membership@acrnet.org*

Web, www.acrnet.org

Membership: mediators, arbitrators, facilitators, and
others involved in conflict resolution and collaborative
decision making. Provides professional development and
educational opportunities for members and the public
through its conferences, publications, and Web site. Offers
referrals for mediation. (The Assn. for Conflict Resolution
is a merger of the Academy of Family Mediators, the

Conflict Resolution Education Network, and the Society of Professionals in Dispute Resolution.)

Center for Dispute Settlement, *1666 Connecticut Ave. N.W., #525 20009-1039; (202) 265-9572. Fax, (202) 332-3951. Linda R. Singer, President.*
General email, administration@cdsusa.org
Web, www.cdsusa.org

Designs, implements, and evaluates alternative and nonjudicial methods of dispute resolution. Mediates disputes. Provides training in dispute resolution for public and private institutions, individuals, and communities.

Council of Better Business Bureaus, *Dispute Resolution, 3033 Wilson Blvd., #600, Arlington, VA 22201-3843; (703) 276-0100. Rod Davis, Senior Vice President, Enterprise Programs.*
General email, contactdr@council.bbb.org
Web, www.bbb.org/council/programs-services/dispute-handling-and-resolution

Administers mediation and arbitration programs through Better Business Bureaus nationwide to assist in resolving disputes between businesses and consumers. Assists with unresolved disputes between car owners and automobile manufacturers. Maintains pools of certified arbitrators nationwide. Provides mediation training.

HALT—An Organization of Americans for Legal Reform, *1612 K St. N.W., #1102 20006-2802; (571) 403-1268. Fax, (202) 887-9699. Rodd M. Santomauro, Executive Director. Toll-free, (888) 367-4258.*
General email, halt@halt.org
Web, www.halt.org

Public interest organization concerned with legal reform. Interests include freedom of information, small claims reform, lawyer accountability, and judicial integrity. Conducts research on alternative dispute resolution programs for delivery of legal services, including arbitration, legal clinics, and mediation services; provides educational and self-help manuals for consumers on the legal process.

Judicial Appointments

▶**AGENCIES**

Justice Dept. (DOJ), *Legal Policy, 950 Pennsylvania Ave. N.W., #4234 20530-0001; (202) 514-4601. Fax, (202) 514-2424. Elana J. Tyrangiel, Principal Deputy Assistant Attorney General.*
Web, www.justice.gov/olp

Investigates and processes prospective candidates for presidential appointment (subject to Senate confirmation) to the federal judiciary.

▶**CONGRESS**

For a listing of relevant congressional committees and subcommittees, please see pages 470–471 or the Appendix.

▶**JUDICIARY**

Administrative Office of the U.S. Courts, *1 Columbus Circle N.E. 20544-0001; (202) 502-2600. Thomas F. Hogan,*

Director, (202) 502-3000.
Web, www.uscourts.gov/adminoff.html

Supervises all administrative matters of the federal court system, except the Supreme Court. Transmits to Congress the recommendations of the Judicial Conference of the United States concerning creation of federal judgeships and other legislative proposals.

Judicial Conference of the United States, *1 Columbus Circle N.E., #7-425 20544; (202) 502-2400. Fax, (202) 502-1144. John G. Roberts Jr., Chief Justice of the United States, Chair; Thomas F. Hogan, Secretary, (202) 502-3000.*
Web, www.uscourts.gov

Serves as the policy-making and governing body for the administration of the federal judicial system; advises Congress on the creation of new federal judgeships. Interests include international judicial relations.

▶**NONGOVERNMENTAL**

BUSINESS AND TAX LAW

Antitrust

▶**AGENCIES**

Antitrust Division *(Justice Dept.), 950 Pennsylvania Ave. N.W., #3109 20530-0001; (202) 514-2401. Fax, (202) 616-2645. William J. Baer, Assistant Attorney General. Press, (202) 514-2007.*
General email, antitrust.atr@usdoj.gov
Web, www.usdoj.gov/atr

Enforces antitrust laws to prevent monopolies and unlawful restraint of trade; has civil and criminal jurisdiction; coordinates activities with the Bureau of Competition of the Federal Trade Commission.

Antitrust Division *(Justice Dept.), Antitrust Documents Group, 450 6th St. N.W., #1024 20530; (202) 514-2481. Fax, (202) 514-3763. Janie M. Ingalls, Supervisor; SueAnn Slates, FOIA Chief.*
General email, atrdocsgrp@usdoj.gov
Web, www.justice.gov/atr

Maintains files and handles requests for information on federal civil and criminal antitrust cases; provides the president and Congress with copies of statutory reports prepared by the division on a variety of competition-related issues; issues opinion letters on whether certain business activity violates antitrust laws.

Antitrust Division *(Justice Dept.), Litigation I, 450 5th St. N.W., #4100 20530; (202) 307-0001. Fax, (202) 307-5802. Peter J. Mucchetti, Chief.*
General email, atr.personnel@usdoj.gov
Web, www.justice.gov/atr/about/lit1.html

Investigates and litigates cases involving health care, paper, pulp, timber, food products, cosmetics and hair care, bread, beer, appliances, and insurance.

Federal Maritime Commission

Commissioner

Commissioner

CHAIR

Commissioner

Commissioner

Equal Employment Opportunity

Inspector General

Managing Director

Human Resources

Budget and Finance

Management Services

Information Technology

Consumer Affairs and Dispute Resolution

Administrative Law Judges

General Counsel

Secretary

Enforcement

Certification and Licensing

Trade Analysis

Area Representatives

- - - · - Technical Direction

- - - - Administrative Direction

Antitrust Division *(Justice Dept.), Litigation II,* 450 5th St. N.W., #8700 20530; (202) 307-0924. Fax, (202) 514-9033. Maribeth Petrizzi, Chief.
Web, www.justice.gov/atr/about/lit2.html

Investigates and litigates cases involving defense, waste industries, aeronautics, road and highway construction, metals and mining, and banking.

Antitrust Division *(Justice Dept.), Litigation III,* 450 4th St. N.W., #4000 20530-0001; (202) 307-0468. Fax, (202) 514-7308. John R. Read, Chief.
General email, ATR.LitIII.Information@usdoj.gov
Web, www.justice.gov/atr/about/lit3.html

Investigates and litigates certain antitrust cases involving such commodities as movies, radio, TV, newspapers, performing arts, sports, toys, and credit and debit cards. Handles certain violations of antitrust laws that involve patents, copyrights, and trademarks. Deals with mergers and acquisitions.

Antitrust Division *(Justice Dept.), Networks and Technology Enforcement,* 450 5th St. N.W., #7100 20530; (202) 307-6200. Fax, (202) 616-8544. James J. Tierney, Chief.
Web, www.justice.gov/atr/about/ntes.html

Investigates and litigates certain antitrust cases involving financial services, including securities, commodity futures, and insurance firms; participates in agency proceedings and rulemaking in these areas.

Antitrust Division *(Justice Dept.), Transportation, Energy, and Agriculture,* 450 5th St. N.W., #8000 20530; (202) 307-6349. Fax, (202) 307-2784. William H. Stallings, Chief.
Web, www.justice.gov/atr/about/tea.html

Enforces antitrust laws in the airline, railroad, motor carrier, barge line, ocean carrier, and energy industries. Litigates antitrust cases pertaining to agriculture and agricultural biotechnology, fish and livestock, business and leisure travel, transportation, and energy. Participates in proceedings before the Federal Energy Regulatory Commission, Environmental Protection Agency, Agriculture Dept., Energy Dept., State Dept., Commerce Dept., Transportation Dept., and the Federal Maritime Commission.

Comptroller of the Currency *(Treasury Dept.),* 400 7th St. S.W., Constitution Center 20024; (202) 649-6400. Thomas J. Curry, Comptroller, Acting. Press, (202) 649-6870.
General email, publicaffairs3@occ.gov
Web, www.occ.treas.gov

Charters and examines operations of national banks, federal savings associations, and U.S. operations of foreign-owned banks; establishes guidelines for bank examinations; handles mergers of national banks with regard to antitrust law. Ensures that national banks and savings associations operate in a safe and sound manner, provide fair access to financial services, treat customers fairly, and comply with applicable laws and regulations.

Federal Communications Commission (FCC), *Wireline Competition Bureau,* 445 12th St. S.W., #5C343 20554; (202) 418-1500. Fax, (202) 418-2825. Julie Veach, Chief.
Web, www.fcc.gov/wireline-competition-bureau

Regulates mergers involving common carriers (wireline facilities that furnish interstate communications services).

Federal Deposit Insurance Corp. (FDIC), *Risk Management Supervision,* 550 17th St. N.W., #5028 20429; (202) 898-6519. Fax, (202) 898-3638. Doreen R. Eberly, Director.
Web, www.fdic.gov/about/contact/#HQDSC

Studies and analyzes applications for mergers, consolidations, acquisitions, and assumption transactions between insured banks.

Federal Energy Regulatory Commission (FERC) *(Energy Dept.),* 888 1st St. N.E., #11A 20426; (202) 502-6088. Fax, (202) 502-8612. Cheryl A. LaFleur, Chair, Acting. Toll-free, (866) 208-3372. Press, (202) 502-8680. eLibrary questions, (202) 502-6652. Enforcement hotline, (202) 502-8390. Enforcement toll-free, (888) 889-8030.
General email, customer@ferc.gov
Web, www.ferc.gov

Regulates mergers, consolidations, and acquisitions of electric utilities; regulates the acquisition of interstate natural gas pipeline facilities.

Federal Maritime Commission (FMC), 800 N. Capitol St. N.W. 20573-0001; (202) 523-5725. Fax, (202) 523-0014. Vern W. Hill, Managing Director; Mario Cordero, Chair. Library, (202) 523-5762.
General email, inquiries@fmc.gov
Web, www.fmc.gov

Regulates the foreign ocean shipping of the United States; reviews agreements (on rates, services, and other matters) filed by ocean common carriers for compliance with shipping statutes and grants limited antitrust immunity. Monitors the laws and practices of foreign governments that could have a discriminatory or otherwise adverse impact on shipping conditions in the United States. Enforces special regulatory requirements applicable to ocean common carriers owned or controlled by foreign governments (controlled carriers). Adjudicates claims filed by regulated entities and the shipping public. Library open to the public.

Federal Reserve System, *Banking Supervision and Regulation,* 20th St. and Constitution Ave. N.W. 20551; (202) 452-2774. Michael Gibson, Director.
Web, www.federalreserve.gov/econresdata/brstaff.htm

Approves bank mergers, consolidations, and other alterations in bank structure.

Federal Trade Commission (FTC), *Competition,* 600 Pennsylvania Ave. N.W., #374 20580; (202) 326-2555. Fax, (202) 326-2884. Deborah L. Feinstein, Director. Press, (202) 326-2555. Toll-free, (877) 382-4357.
General email, antitrust@ftc.gov
Web, www.ftc.gov/bc

Enforces antitrust laws and investigates possible violations, mergers and acquisitions, and anticompetitive practices; seeks voluntary compliance and pursues civil judicial remedies; reviews premerger filings; coordinates activities with the Antitrust Division of the Justice Dept.

Federal Trade Commission (FTC), *Competition, Anticompetitive Practices, 601 New Jersey Ave. N.W., #6264 20001 (mailing address: 600 Pennsylvania Ave. N.W., #7117, Washington, DC 20580); (202) 326-2641. Fax, (202) 326-3496. Geoffrey Green, Assistant Director. Toll-free, (877) 382-4357.*
General email, antitrust@ftc.gov
Web, www.ftc.gov/bc

Investigates nonmerger anticompetitive practices in real estate and a variety of other industries. Interests include intellectual property and professional and regulatory boards.

Federal Trade Commission (FTC), *Competition, Compliance, 601 New Jersey Ave. N.W., #5222 20580 (mailing address: 600 Pennsylvania Ave. N.W., Washington, DC 20580); (202) 326-2526. Fax, (202) 326-3396. Daniel P. Ducore, Assistant Director.*
General email, bccompliance@ftc.gov
Web, www.ftc.gov/bc

Monitors and enforces competition orders and oversees required remediations in company conduct. Investigates possible violations of the Hart-Scott-Rodino Act.

Federal Trade Commission (FTC), *Competition, Health Care Division, 600 Pennsylvania Ave. N.W 20580; (202) 326-3759. Fax, (202) 326-3384. Markus H. Meier, Assistant Director.*
General email, antitrust@ftc.gov
Web, www.ftc.gov/bc

Investigates and litigates nonmerger anticompetitive practices among physicians, hospitals, and health insurers in the health care industry, including the pharmaceutical industry. Works against pay-for-delay agreements among pharmaceutical companies that insulate brand-name drugs from competition with lower cost generic drugs.

Federal Trade Commission (FTC), *Competition, Honors Paralegal Program, 600 Pennsylvania Ave. N.W. 20580; (202) 326-2982. Fax, (202) 326-3496. Mari Hart, Coordinator, Acting.*
General email, honorsparalegals@ftc.gov
Web, www.ftc.gov/bc

Administers paralegal program for individuals considering a career in law, economics, business, or public service. Honors paralegals are given significant responsibility and hands-on experience while assisting attorneys and economists in the investigation and litigation of antitrust matters. Applicants are appointed for 14-month terms.

Federal Trade Commission (FTC), *Competition, Mergers I, 600 Pennsylvania Ave. N.W. 20580; (202) 326-3106. Fax, (202) 326-2655. Michael Moiseyev, Assistant Director.*
General email, antitrust@ftc.gov
Web, www.ftc.gov/bc

Investigates and litigates antitrust violations in mergers and acquisitions, primarily in the health care–related industries, including pharmaceutical manufacturing and distribution and medical devices. Also handles scientific, industrial, defense, and technology industries.

Federal Trade Commission (FTC), *Competition, Mergers II, 601 New Jersey Ave. N.W., #6120 20001 (mailing address: 600 Pennsylvania Ave. N.W., Washington, DC 20580); (202) 326-2749. Fax, (202) 326-2071. Catharine M. Moscatelli, Assistant Director.*
General email, antitrust@ftc.gov
Web, www.ftc.gov/bc

Investigates and litigates antitrust violations in mergers and acquisitions in the chemicals, coal mining, technology, entertainment, and computer hardware and software industries.

Federal Trade Commission (FTC), *Competition, Mergers III, 600 Pennsylvania Ave. N.W. 20580; (202) 326-2805. Fax, (202) 326-3383. Phillip Broyles, Assistant Director.*
General email, antitrust@ftc.gov
Web, www.ftc.gov/bc

Investigates and litigates antitrust violations in mergers and acquisitions concerning the oil and gas, ethanol, industrial spray equipment, and energy industries.

Federal Trade Commission (FTC), *Competition, Mergers IV, 601 New Jersey Ave. N.W., #5245 20001 (mailing address: 600 Pennsylvania Ave. N.W., Washington, DC 20580); (202) 326-2682. Fax, (202) 326-2286. Jeffrey Perry, Assistant Director.*
General email, antitrust@ftc.gov
Web, www.ftc.gov/bc

Investigates and litigates antitrust violations in mergers and acquisitions concerning hospitals, the grocery food product industry, the media, funeral homes, and consumer goods.

Federal Trade Commission (FTC), *Competition, Premerger Notification, 600 Pennsylvania Ave. N.W., #H-301 20580; (202) 326-3100. Fax, (202) 326-2624. Robert L. Jones, Deputy Assistant Director.*
General email, antitrust@ftc.gov
Web, www.ftc.gov/bc/hsr/hsrbook.shtm

Reviews premerger filings under the Hart-Scott-Rodino Act for the FTC and Justice Dept. Coordinates investigative work with federal and state agencies; participates in international projects.

Surface Transportation Board *(Transportation Dept.), 395 E St. S.W., #1220 20423-0001 (mailing address: 395 E St. S.W., Washington, DC 20024); (202) 245-0245. Fax, (202) 245-0458. Daniel R. Elliott III, Chair, (202) 245-0220. Library, (202) 245-0406. TTY, (800) 877-8339. Press, (202) 245-0234.*
Web, www.stb.dot.gov

Regulates rail rate disputes, railroad consolidations, rail line construction proposals, line abandonments, and rail car service. Library open to the public.

►CONGRESS

For a listing of relevant congressional committees and sub-committees, please see pages 470–471 or the Appendix.

►NONGOVERNMENTAL

American Antitrust Institute (AAI), *2919 Ellicott St. N.W., #1000 20008-1022; (202) 276-6002. Fax, (202) 966-8711. Albert A. (Bert) Foer, President. Press, (410) 897-7028.*
Web, www.antitrustinstitute.org

Pro-antitrust organization that provides research and policy analysis to journalists, academic researchers, lawyers, economists, businesspeople, government officials, courts, and the general public. Seeks to educate the public on the importance of fair competition. Monitors legislation and regulations on competition-oriented policies.

Assn. of Corporate Counsel, *1025 Connecticut Ave. N.W., #200 20036-5425; (202) 293-4103. Fax, (202) 293-4701. Veta T. Richardson, President.*
Web, www.acc.com

Membership: practicing lawyers in corporate law departments, associations, and in legal departments of other private-sector organizations. Provides information on corporate law issues, including securities, health and safety, the environment, intellectual property, litigation, international legal affairs, pro bono work, and labor benefits. Monitors legislation and regulations, with primary focus on issues affecting in-house attorneys' ability to practice law. (Formerly American Corporate Counsel Assn.)

The Business Roundtable, *300 New Jersey Ave. N.W., #800 20001; (202) 872-1260. Fax, (202) 466-3509. Gov. John Engler, President. Press, (202) 496-3269. General email, info@brt.org*
Web, www.businessroundtable.org

Membership: chief executives of the nation's largest corporations. Examines issues of concern to business, including antitrust law.

Bankruptcy

►AGENCIES

Executive Office for U.S. Trustees *(Justice Dept.), 441 G St. N.W., #6150 20530; (202) 307-1399. Fax, (202) 307-2397. Clifford J. White III, Director, (202) 307-1391. General email, ustrustee.program@usdoj.gov*
Web, www.justice.gov/ust

Handles the administration and oversight of bankruptcy and liquidation cases filed under the Bankruptcy Reform Act, including detecting and combating bankruptcy fraud. Provides individual U.S. trustee offices with administrative and management support.

Justice Dept. (DOJ), *Legal Policy, 950 Pennsylvania Ave. N.W., #4234 20530-0001; (202) 514-4601. Fax, (202) 514-2424. Elana J. Tyrangiel, Principal Deputy Assistant Attorney General.*
Web, www.justice.gov/olp

Studies and develops policy for improvement of the criminal and civil justice systems, including bankruptcy reform policy.

►CONGRESS

For a listing of relevant congressional committees and sub-committees, please see pages 470–471 or the Appendix.

►JUDICIARY

Administrative Office of the U.S. Courts, *Bankruptcy Judges Division, 1 Columbus Circle N.E., #4-250 20544-0001; (202) 502-1900. Fax, (202) 502-1988. Amanda L. Anderson, Chief.*
Web, www.uscourts.gov and www.uscourts.gov/bankruptcycourts.aspx

Provides administrative assistance and support in the operation of U.S. bankruptcy courts.

►NONGOVERNMENTAL

American Bankruptcy Institute, *66 Canal Center Plaza, #600, Alexandria, VA 22314-1592; (703) 739-0800. Fax, (703) 739-1060. Samuel Gerdano, Executive Director. General email, support@abiworld.org*
Web, www.abiworld.org

Membership: lawyers; federal and state legislators; and representatives of accounting and financial services firms, lending institutions, credit organizations, and consumer groups. Provides information and educational services on insolvency, reorganization, and bankruptcy issues; sponsors conferences, seminars, and workshops.

National Assn. of Consumer Bankruptcy Attorneys, *2300 M St. N.W., #800 20037; (216) 491-6770. Fax, (866) 571-3560. Maureen Thompson, Legislative Director; Vacant, Executive Director, (216) 491-6770. General email, admin@nacba.org*
Web, www.nacba.org

Advocates on behalf of consumer debtors and their attorneys. Files amicus briefs on behalf of parties in the U.S. courts of appeal and Supreme Court, and provides educational programs and workshops for attorneys. Monitors legislation and regulations.

Tax Violations

►AGENCIES

Internal Revenue Service (IRS) *(Treasury Dept.), Procedures and Administration, 1111 Constitution Ave. N.W., #5503 20224; (202) 622-3400. Fax, (202) 622-4914. Deborah Butler, Associate Chief Counsel. Press, (202) 622-4000.*
Web, www.irs.gov

Oversees field office litigation of civil cases that involve underpayment of taxes when the taxpayer chooses to challenge the determinations of the Internal Revenue Service

(IRS) in the U.S. Tax Court, or when the taxpayer chooses to pay the amount in question and sue the IRS for a refund. Reviews briefs and defense letters prepared by field offices for tax cases; drafts legal advice memos; prepares tax litigation advice memoranda; coordinates litigation strategy. Makes recommendations concerning appeal and certiorari. Prepares tax regulations, rulings, and other published guidance regarding the Internal Revenue Code, as enacted.

Justice Dept. (DOJ), *Tax Division,* 950 Pennsylvania Ave. N.W., #4141 20530; (202) 514-2901. Fax, (202) 514-5479. *Kathryn Keneally, Assistant Attorney General, (202) 307-3366. General email, tax.mail@usdoj.gov*

Web, www.usdoj.gov/tax

Authorizes prosecution of all criminal cases involving tax violations investigated and developed by the Internal Revenue Service (IRS); represents the IRS in civil litigation except in U.S. Tax Court proceedings; represents other agencies, including the departments of Defense and Interior, in cases with state or local tax authorities.

▶**CONGRESS**

For a listing of relevant congressional committees and subcommittees, please see pages 470–471 or the Appendix.

▶**JUDICIARY**

U.S. Tax Court, 400 2nd St. N.W., #134 20217; (202) 521-0700. *Michael B. Thornton, Chief Judge, (202) 521-0777. Web, www.ustaxcourt.gov*

Tries and adjudicates disputes involving income, estate, and gift taxes and personal holding company surtaxes in cases in which deficiencies have been determined by the Internal Revenue Service.

▶**NONGOVERNMENTAL**

American Bar Assn. (ABA), *Taxation Section,* 1050 Connecticut Ave. N.W., #400 20036; (202) 662-8670. Fax, (202) 662-8682. *Janet In, Director, (202) 662-8677. General email, tax@americanbar.org*

Web, www.americanbar.org/tax

Studies and recommends policies on taxation; provides information on tax issues; sponsors continuing legal education programs; monitors tax laws and legislation.

CIVIL RIGHTS

General

▶**AGENCIES**

Commission on Civil Rights, 1331 Pennsylvania Ave. N.W., #1150 20425; (202) 376-7700. Fax, (202) 376-7672. *Martin R. Castro, Chair; Marlene Sallo, Staff Director. Press, (202) 376-8591.*

General email, publiccomments@usccr.gov

Web, www.usccr.gov

Assesses federal laws, policies, and legal developments to determine the nature and extent of denial of equal protection under the law on the basis of race, color, religion, sex, national origin, age, or disability in employment, voting rights, education, administration of justice, and housing. Issues reports and makes recommendations to the president and Congress; serves as national clearinghouse for civil rights information; receives civil rights complaints and refers them to the appropriate federal agency for action. Library open to the public.

Education Dept., *Civil Rights,* 400 Maryland Ave. S.W. 20202-1100; (202) 453-5900. Fax, (202) 453-6012. *Catherine Lhamon, Assistant Secretary, (202) 453-7240. Hotline, (800) 421-3481. General email, ocr@ed.gov*

Web, www2.ed.gov/ocr

Enforces laws prohibiting use of federal funds for education programs or activities that discriminate on the basis of race, color, sex, national origin, age, or disability; authorized to discontinue funding.

Equal Employment Opportunity Commission (EEOC), 131 M St. N.E. 20507; (202) 663-4001. Fax, (202) 663-4110. *Jacqueline A. Berrien, Chair. General email, info@eeoc.gov*

Web, www.eeoc.gov

Works to end job discrimination by private and government employers based on race, color, religion, sex, national origin, disability, or age. Works to protect employees against reprisal for protest of employment practices alleged to be unlawful in hiring, promotion, firing, wages, and other terms and conditions of employment. Works for increased employment of persons with disabilities, affirmative action by the federal government, and an equitable work environment for employees with mental and physical disabilities. Enforces Title VII of the Civil Rights Act of 1964, as amended, which includes the Pregnancy Discrimination Act; Americans with Disabilities Act; Age Discrimination in Employment Act; Equal Pay Act; and, in the federal sector, rehabilitation laws. Receives charges of discrimination; attempts conciliation or settlement; can bring court action to force compliance; has review and appeals responsibility in the federal sector. Library open to the public by appointment only.

Health and Human Services Dept. (HHS), *Civil Rights,* 200 Independence Ave. S.W., #515F 20201; (202) 619-0403. Fax, (202) 619-3437. *Leon Rodriguez, Director. General email, OCRMail@hhs.gov*

Web, www.hhs.gov/ocr

Administers and enforces laws prohibiting discrimination on the basis of race, color, sex, national origin, religion, age, or disability in programs receiving federal funds from the department; authorized to discontinue funding. Responsible for health information privacy under the Health Insurance Portability and Accountability Act.

Selected Minorities-Related Resources

ADVOCACY AND ANTIDISCRIMINATION

American-Arab Anti Discrimination Committee, (202) 244-2990; www.adc.org

Anti-Defamation League, (212) 885-7700; www.adl.org

Arab American Institute, (202) 429-9210; www.aaiusa.org

Human Rights Campaign, (202) 628-4160; www.hrc.org

Japanese American Citizens League, (202) 223-1240; www.jacl.org

Mexican American Legal Defense and Education Fund, (202) 293-2828; www.maldef.org

NAACP (National Assn. For the Advancement of Colored People), (202) 463-2940; www.naacp.org

National Council of La Raza, (202) 785-1670; www.nclr.org

National Gay and Lesbian Task Force, (202) 393-5177; www.thetaskforce.org

National Organization for Women, (202) 628-8669; www.now.org

OCA (Organization of Asian Pacific Americans, formerly the Organization of Chinese Americans), (202) 223-5500; www.ocanational.org

Rainbow/PUSH Coalition, (202) 393-7874; www.rainbowpush.org

BUSINESS AND LABOR

Business and Professional Women USA, (202) 293-1100; www.bpwfoundation.org

Center for Women's Business Research, (212) 785-7335; www.ncrw.org

Council of Federal EEO and Civil Rights Executives, www.fedcivilrights.org

Minority Business Development Agency, (202) 482-2332; www.mbda.gov

National Assn. of Hispanic Federal Executives Inc., (202) 315-3942; www.nahfe.org

National Assn. of Minority Contractors, (202) 296-1600; www.namcnational.org

National Assn. of Women Business Owners, (800) 556-2926; www.nawbo.org

National Black Chamber of Commerce, (202) 466-6888; www.nationalbcc.org

National U.S.-Arab Chamber of Commerce, (202) 289-5920; www.nusacc.org

U.S. Hispanic Chamber of Commerce, (202) 842-1212; www.ushcc.com

U.S. Pan Asian American Chamber of Commerce, (202) 296-5221; www.uspaacc.com

EDUCATION

American Assn. for Affirmative Action, (202) 349-9855; www.affirmativeaction.org

American Indian Higher Education Consortium, (703) 838-0400; www.aihec.org

Assn. of American Colleges and Universities, (202) 387-3760; www.aacu.org

Assn. of Research Libraries, (202) 296-2296; www.arl.org/diversity

---

Justice Dept. (DOJ), *Civil Rights Division, 950 Pennsylvania Ave. N.W., #5643 20530; (202) 514-4609. Fax, (202) 514-0293. Jocelyn Samuels, Assistant Attorney General, Acting, (202) 514-2151. Press, (202) 514-2007. Web, www.justice.gov/crt*

Enforces federal civil rights laws prohibiting discrimination on the basis of race, color, religion, sex, disability, age, or national origin in voting, education, employment, credit, housing, public accommodations and facilities, and federally assisted programs.

Labor Dept. (DOL), *Civil Rights Center, 200 Constitution Ave. N.W., #N4123 20210; (202) 693-6500. Fax, (202) 693-6505. Naomi M. Barry-Perez, Director. Library, (202) 693-6613. General email, civilrightscenter@dol.gov Web, www.dol.gov/oasam/programs/crc*

Resolves complaints of discrimination on the basis of race, color, religion, sex, national origin, age, or disability in programs funded by the department. Library open to the public.

▶ **CONGRESS**

For a listing of relevant congressional committees and subcommittees, please see pages 470–471 or the Appendix.

▶ **NONGOVERNMENTAL**

American Assn. for Affirmative Action, *888 16th St. N.W., #800 20006; (202) 349-9855. Fax, (202) 355-1399. Shirley J. Wilcher, Executive Director. Toll-free, (800) 252-8952. General email, execdir@affirmativeaction.org Web, www.affirmativeaction.org*

Membership: professional managers in the areas of affirmative action, equal opportunity, diversity, and human resources. Sponsors education, research, and training programs. Acts as a liaison with government agencies involved in equal opportunity compliance. Maintains ethical standards for the profession.

Appleseed: A Network of Public Interest Justice Centers, *727 15th St. N.W., 11th Floor 20005; (202) 347-7960. Fax, (202) 347-7961. Betsy Cavendish, Director.*

National Assn. for Equal Opportunity in Higher Education, (202) 552-3300; www.nafeo.org

GOVERNMENT, LAW, AND PUBLIC POLICY

Asian American Justice Center, (202) 296-2300; www.advancingequality.org

Blacks in Government, (202) 667-3280; www.bignet.org

Congressional Black Caucus Foundation, Inc., (202) 263-2800; www.cbcfinc.org

Congressional Hispanic Caucus Institute, (202) 543-1771; www.chci.org

Council on American-Islamic Relations, (202) 488-8787; www.cair.com

Institute for Women's Policy Research, (202) 785-5100; www.iwpr.org

Joint Center for Political and Economic Studies, (202) 789-3500; www.jointcenter.org

Leadership Conference on Civil Rights, (202) 466-3311; www.civilrights.org

National Congress on American Indians, (202) 466-7767; www.ncai.org

National Women's Law Center, (202) 588-5180; www.nwlc.org

National Women's Political Caucus, (202) 785-1100; www.nwpc.org

Society of American Indian Government Employees, www.saige.org

HEALTH

Asian and Pacific Islander American Health Forum, (202) 466-7772; www.apiahf.org

National Alliance for Hispanic Health, (202) 387-5000; www.hispanichealth.org

National Black Nurses Assn., (301) 589-3200; www.nbna.org

National Council of Urban Indian Health, (202) 544-0344; www.ncuih.org

National Hispanic Medical Assn., (202) 628-5895; www.nhmamd.org

National Minority AIDS Council, (202) 483-6622; www.nmac.org

MEDIA

Center for Digital Democracy, (202) 986-2220; www.democraticmedia.org

International Women's Media Foundation, (202) 496-1992; www.iwmf.org

Minority Media and Telecommunications Council, (202) 332-0500; www.mmtconline.org

National Assn. of Black Owned Broadcasters, (202) 463-8970; www.nabob.org

National Assn. of Hispanic Journalists, (202) 662-7145; www.nahj.org

National Lesbian and Gay Journalists Assn., (202) 588-9888; www.nlgja.org

---

General email, appleseed@appleseednetwork.org

Web, www.appleseednetwork.org

Network of seventeen public interest justice centers in the United States and Mexico advocating for universal access to legal help through its pro bono network.

Center for Neighborhood Enterprise, *1625 K St. N.W., #1200 20006; (202) 518-6500. Fax, (202) 588-0314. Robert L. Woodson Sr., President. Information, (866) 518-1263. General email, info@cneonline.org*

Web, www.cneonline.org

Provides community and faith-based organizations with training, technical assistance, and additional sources of support. Addresses issues such as youth violence, substance abuse, teen pregnancy, homelessness, joblessness, poor education, and deteriorating neighborhoods.

Leadership Conference on Civil and Human Rights, *1629 K St. N.W., 10th Floor 20006; (202) 466-3311. Fax, (202) 466-3435. Wade Henderson, President. General email, info@civilrights.org*

Web, www.civilrights.org

Coalition of national organizations representing minorities, women, labor, older Americans, people with disabilities, and religious groups. Works for enactment and enforcement of civil rights, human rights, and social welfare legislation; acts as clearinghouse for information on civil rights legislation and regulations.

NAACP Legal Defense and Educational Fund, Inc., *Washington Office, 1444 Eye St. N.W., 10th Floor 20005; (202) 682-1300. Fax, (202) 682-1312. Leslie M. Proll, Director.*

Web, www.naacpldf.org

Civil rights litigation group that provides legal information on civil rights issues, including employment, housing, and educational discrimination; monitors federal enforcement of civil rights laws. Not affiliated with the NAACP. (Headquarters in New York.)

National Black Justice Coalition, *P.O. Box 71395 20024; (202) 319-1552. Fax, (202) 319-7365. Sharon J. Lettman-Hicks, Chief Executive Officer. General email, info@nbjc.org*

Web, www.nbjc.org

Seeks equality for black, lesbian, gay, bisexual, and transgender people by fighting racism and homophobia through education initiatives.

Poverty and Race Research Action Council, *1200 18th St. N.W., #200 20036; (202) 906-8023. Fax, (202) 842-2885. Philip Tegeler, Executive Director.*
General email, info@prrac.org

Web, www.prrac.org

Facilitates cooperative links between researchers and activists who work on race and poverty issues. Publishes bimonthly *Poverty and Race* and a civil rights history curriculum guide. Policy research areas include housing, education, and health disparities.

African Americans

▶NONGOVERNMENTAL

Blacks in Government, *3005 Georgia Ave. N.W. 20001-3807; (202) 667-3280. Fax, (202) 667-3705. Darlene H. Young, President.*
General email, bignational@bignet.org

Web, www.bignet.org

Advocacy organization for public employees. Promotes equal opportunity and career advancement for African American government employees; provides career development information; seeks to eliminate racism in the federal workforce; sponsors programs, business meetings, and social gatherings; represents interests of African American government workers to Congress and the executive branch; promotes voter education and registration.

Congressional Black Caucus Foundation, *1720 Massachusetts Ave. N.W. 20036-1903; (202) 263-2800. Fax, (202) 775-0773. A. Shuanise Washington, President.*
General email, info@cbcfinc.org

Web, www.cbcfinc.org

Conducts research and offers programs on public policy issues with the aim of improving the socioeconomic circumstances of African Americans and other underserved populations. Sponsors fellowship programs in which professionals and academic candidates work on congressional committees and subcommittees. Holds issue forums and leadership seminars. Provides elected officials, organizations, and researchers with statistical, demographic, public policy, and political information. Sponsors internship, scholarship, and fellowship programs.

Joint Center for Political and Economic Studies, *805 15th St. N.W., 2nd Floor 20005-4928; (202) 789-3500. Fax, (202) 789-6390. Spencer Overton, President, Acting.*
General email, general@jointcenter.org

Web, www.jointcenter.org

Documents and analyzes the political and economic status of African Americans and other minority populations, focusing on political participation, economic advancement, and health policy. Publishes an annual profile of African American elected officials in federal, state,

and local government; disseminates information through forums, conferences, publications, and the Internet.

Lincoln Institute for Research and Education, *P.O. Box 254, Great Falls, VA 22066; (703) 759-4278. Fax, (703) 759-4597. Jay Parker, President.*
General email, contactus@lincolnreview.com

Web, www.lincolnreview.com

Public policy research group that studies issues of interest to middle-class African Americans, including business, economics, employment, education, national defense, health, and culture. Files amicus curiae briefs. Sponsors seminars.

National Assn. for the Advancement of Colored People (NAACP), *Washington Bureau, 1156 15th St. N.W., #915 20005; (202) 463-2940. Fax, (202) 463-2953. Hilary O. Shelton, Director.*
General email, washingtonbureau@naacpnet.org

Web, www.naacp.org

Membership: persons interested in civil rights for all minorities. Works for the political, educational, social, and economic equality and empowerment of minorities through legal, legislative, and direct action. (Headquarters in Baltimore, Md.)

National Assn. of Colored Women's and Youth Clubs Inc. (NACWYC), *1601 R St. N.W. 20009-6420; (202) 667-4080. Fax, (202) 667-2574. Evelyn J. Rising, President.*
General email, erising@usw.edu

Web, www.nacwc.org

Seeks to promote education; protect and enforce civil rights; raise the standard of family living; promote interracial understanding; and enhance leadership development. Awards scholarships; conducts programs in education, social service, and philanthropy.

National Black Caucus of Local Elected Officials (NBC/LEO), *c/o National League of Cities, 1301 Pennsylvania Ave. N.W. 20004-1763; (202) 626-3169. Adam McFadden, President. Press, (202) 626-3015.*
General email, constituencygroup@nlc.org

Web, www.nlc.org

Membership: African American elected officials at the local level and other interested individuals. Seeks to increase African American participation on the National League of Cities' steering and policy committees. Informs members on issues, and plans strategies to achieve objectives through legislation and direct action. Interests include cultural diversity, local government and community participation, housing, economics, job training, the family, and human rights.

National Black Caucus of State Legislators, *444 N. Capitol St. N.W., #622 20001; (202) 624-5457. Fax, (202) 508-3826. LaKimba DeSadier, Executive Director.*
Web, www.nbcsl.org

Membership: African American state legislators. Promotes effective leadership among African American state legislators through education, research, and training; serves as an information network and clearinghouse for members.

National Council of Negro Women, *633 Pennsylvania Ave. N.W. 20004-2605; (202) 737-0120. Fax, (202) 737-0476. Ingrid Saunders Jones, Chair.*
General email, ncnwinfo@ncnw.org
Web, www.ncnw.org

Seeks to advance opportunities for African American women, their families, and communities through research, advocacy, and national and community-based programs in the United States and Africa.

National Urban League, *Washington Bureau, 1805 7th St. N.W., #520 20001; (202) 898-1604. Chanelle Hardy, Executive Director.*
Web, www.nulwb.iamempowered.com

Federal advocacy division of social service organization concerned with the social welfare of African Americans and other minorities. Seeks elimination of racial segregation and discrimination; monitors legislation, policies, and regulations to determine impact on minorities; interests include employment, health, welfare, education, housing, and community development. (Headquarters in New York.)

Project 21, National Center for Public Policy Research, *501 Capitol Ct. N.E., #200 20002; (202) 543-4110. Fax, (202) 543-5975. Horace Cooper, Co-Chair; Cherylyn LeBon, Co-Chair; David W. Almasi, Executive Director.*
General email, project21@nationalcenter.org
Web, www.nationalcenter.org/P21index.html

Emphasizes spirit of entrepreneurship, sense of family, and traditional values among African Americans.

Washington Government Relations Group, *1325 G St. N.W., #500 20005; (202) 449-7651. Fax, (202) 449-7701. Marcus Sebastian Mason, President.*
General email, info@wgrginc.org
Web, www.wgrginc.org

Works to enrich the careers and leadership abilities of African American government relations professionals working in business, financial institutions, law firms, trade associations, and nonprofit organizations. Increases dialogue between members and senior-level policymakers to produce public policy solutions.

Hispanics

▶**NONGOVERNMENTAL**

Congressional Hispanic Caucus Institute, *300 M St. S.E. 20003; (202) 543-1771. Fax, (202) 546-2143. Rep. Rubén Hinojosa, Chair, (202) 225-2531; Esther Aguilera, President.*
General email, chci@chci.org
Web, www.chci.org

Develops educational and leadership programs to familiarize Hispanic students with policy-related careers and to encourage their professional development. Aids in the developing of future Latino leaders. Provides scholarship, internship, and fellowship opportunities.

League of United Latin American Citizens, *1133 19th St. N.W., #1000 20036; (202) 833-6130. Fax, (202) 833-6135. Brent Wilkes, Executive Director. Toll-free, (877) LULAC-01.*
General email, info@lulac.org
Web, www.lulac.org

Seeks full social, political, economic, and educational rights for Hispanics in the United States. Programs include housing projects for the poor, employment and training for youth and women, and political advocacy on issues affecting Hispanics, including immigration. Operates National Educational Service Centers (LNESCs) and awards scholarships. Holds exposition open to the public.

Mexican American Legal Defense and Educational Fund, *Washington Office, 1016 16th St. N.W., #100 20036; (202) 293-2828. James Ferg-Cadima, Regional Counsel.*
Web, www.maldef.org/about/offices/washington_dc/index.html

Works with Congress and the White House to promote legislative advocacy for minority groups. Interests include equal employment, voting rights, bilingual education, immigration, and discrimination. Monitors legislation and regulations. (Headquarters in Los Angeles, Calif.)

National Council of La Raza, *1126 16th St. N.W., #600 20036-4845; (202) 785-1670. Fax, (202) 776-1792. Janet Murguia, President.*
General email, comments@nclr.org
Web, www.nclr.org

Seeks to reduce poverty of and discrimination against Hispanic Americans. Offers assistance to Hispanic community-based organizations. Conducts research and policy analysis. Interests include education, employment and training, asset development, immigration, language access issues, civil rights, and housing and community development. Monitors legislation and regulations.

National Puerto Rican Coalition, Inc., *1444 Eye St. N.W., #800 20005; (202) 223-3915. Fax, (202) 429-2223. Rafael A. Fantauzzi, President.*
General email, nprc@nprcinc.org
Web, www.nprcinc.org

Membership: Puerto Rican organizations and individuals. Analyzes and advocates for public policy that benefits Puerto Ricans; offers training and technical assistance to Puerto Rican organizations and individuals; develops national communication network for Puerto Rican community-based organizations and individuals.

U.S. Conference of Catholic Bishops (USCCB), *Cultural Diversity in the Church, Office of Hispanic Affairs, 3211 4th St. N.E. 20017-1194; (202) 541-3150. Fax, (202) 541-5417. Alejandro Aguilera-Titus, Assistant Director; Lorena G. Orellana, Staff Assistant.*

General email, cdha@usccb.org

Web, www.usccb.org/issues-and-action/cultural-diversity/hispanic-latino/

Acts as an information clearinghouse on communications and pastoral and liturgical activities; serves as liaison for other church institutions and government and private agencies concerned with Hispanics; provides information on legislation; acts as advocate for Hispanics within the National Conference of Catholic Bishops.

Lesbian, Gay, Bisexual, and Transgender People

▶**NONGOVERNMENTAL**

Dignity USA, *Washington Office, 721 8th St. S.E. 20003 (mailing address: P.O. Box 15279, Washington, DC 20003-0279); (202) 546-2235. Fax, (202) 521-3954. Daniel Barutta, President.*
General email, dignity@dignitywashington.org

Web, www.dignitywashington.org

Membership: gay, lesbian, bisexual, and transgender Catholics, their families, and friends. Works to promote spiritual development, social interaction, educational outreach, and acceptance within the Catholic community. Sponsors a Spanish language affiliate group, Grupo Latino. (Headquarters in Medford, Mass.)

Gay and Lesbian Activists Alliance of Washington (GLAA), *P.O. Box 75265 20013; (202) 667-5139. Richard J. (Rick) Rosendall, President.*
General email, equal@glaa.org

Web, www.glaa.org

Advances the rights of gays, lesbians, and transgender people within the Washington community.

Gay & Lesbian Victory Fund and Leadership Institute, *1133 15th St. N.W., #350 20005; (202) 842-8679. Fax, (202) 289-3863. Chuck Wolfe, President.*
General email, victory@victoryfund.org

Web, www.victoryfund.org

Supports the candidacy of openly gay and lesbian individuals in federal, state, and local elections.

Human Rights Campaign (HRC), *1640 Rhode Island Ave. N.W. 20036; (202) 628-4160. Fax, (202) 347-5323. Chad Griffin, President. Toll-free, (800) 777-4723.*
General email, hrc@hrc.org

Web, www.hrc.org

Provides campaign support and educates the public to ensure the rights of lesbian, gay, bisexual, and transgender people at home, work, school, and in the community. Works to prohibit workplace discrimination based on sexual orientation and gender identity, combat hate crimes, and fund AIDS research, care, and prevention.

Log Cabin Republicans, *1090 Vermont Ave. N.W., #850 20005; (202) 420-7873. Gregory T. Angelo, Executive Director.*

General email, info@logcabin.org

Web, www.logcabin.org

Membership: lesbian, gay, bisexual, transgender and allied Republicans. Educates conservative politicians and voters on LGBT issues; disseminates information; conducts seminars for members. Promotes conservative values among members of the gay community. Raises campaign funds. Monitors legislation and regulations.

National Center for Transgender Equality (NCTE), *1325 Massachusetts Ave. N.W., #700 20005; (202) 903-0112. Mara Keisling, Executive Director.*
General email, ncte@transequality.org

Web, www.transequality.org

Works to advance the equality of transgender people through advocacy, collaboration, and empowerment, and to make them safe from discrimination and violence. Provides resources to local efforts nationwide.

National Gay and Lesbian Task Force (NGLTF), *1325 Massachusetts Ave. N.W., #600 20005-4164; (202) 393-5177. Fax, (202) 393-2241. Rea Carey, Executive Director, rcarey@thetaskforce.org.*
General email, thetaskforce@thetaskforce.org

Web, www.thetaskforce.org

Works toward equal rights for the lesbian, gay, bisexual, and transgender community. Trains activists working at the state and local levels. Conducts research and public policy analysis. Monitors legislation.

National Lesbian and Gay Journalists Assn. (NLGJA), *2120 L St. N.W., #850 20037; (202) 588-9888. Fax, (202) 588-1818. Michael Tune, Executive Director.*
General email, info@nlgja.org

Web, www.nlgja.org

Works within the journalism industry to foster fair and accurate coverage of lesbian, gay, bisexual, and transgender issues. Opposes workplace bias against all minorities and provides professional development for its members.

National Organization for Women (NOW), *1100 H St. N.W., #300 20005; (202) 628-8669. Fax, (202) 785-8576. Terry O'Neill, President.*
General email, now@now.org

Web, www.now.org

Membership: women and men interested in feminist civil rights. Promotes the development and enforcement of legislation prohibiting discrimination on the basis of sexual orientation. Works toward achieving constitutional equality for women. Organizes membership and provides education. Monitors legislation and regulations.

OutServe-SLDN, *P.O. Box 65301 20035-5301; (202) 328-3244. Fax, (202) 797-1635. Allyson D. Robinson, Executive Director. Toll-free legal hotline, (800) 538-7418.*
General email, admin@outserve-sldn.org

Web, www.sldn.org

Seeks to secure equal opportunity, protection, and benefits, without threat of harassment or discrimination, for lesbian, gay, bisexual, and transgender military service members and veterans. Provides free legal services to LGBT service members and veterans; conducts media and outreach campaigns on matters relating to the service of LGBT personnel; provides networking opportunities; monitors legislation and regulations.

Parents, Families, and Friends of Lesbians and Gays (PFLAG), *1828 L St. N.W., #660 20036; (202) 467-8180. Fax, (202) 349-0788. Jody M. Huckaby, Executive Director.*
General email, info@pflag.org
Web, www.pflag.org

Promotes the health and well-being of gay, lesbian, transgender, and bisexual persons, their families, and their friends through support, education, and advocacy. Works to change public policies and attitudes toward gay, lesbian, transgender, and bisexual persons. Monitors legislation and regulations.

Supporting and Mentoring Youth Advocates and Leaders, *410 7th St. S.E. 20003-2707; (202) 546-5940. Fax, (202) 330-5839. Andrew Barnett, Executive Director, (202) 567-3151.*
General email, supporterinfo@smyal.org
Web, www.smyal.org

Provides support to youth who are lesbian, gay, bisexual, transgender, intersex, or who may be questioning their sexuality. Facilitates youth center and support groups; promotes HIV/AIDS awareness; coordinates public education programs about homophobia. (Formerly Sexual Minority Youth Assistance League [SMYAL].)

Native Americans

▶AGENCIES

Administration for Native Americans *(Health and Human Services Dept.),* *370 L'Enfant Promenade S.W., 2nd Floor, West Aerospace Center 20447-0002; (202) 690-7776. Fax, (202) 690-7441. Lillian A. Sparks, Commissioner. Toll-free, (877) 922-9262.*
General email, ana@acf.hhs.gov
Web, www.acf.hhs.gov/programs/ana

Awards grants for locally determined social and economic development strategies; promotes Native American economic and social self-sufficiency; funds tribes and Native American and Native Hawaiian organizations. Commissioner chairs the Intradepartmental Council on Indian Affairs, which coordinates Native American–related programs.

Bureau of Indian Affairs (BIA) *(Interior Dept.),* *1849 C St. N.W., MS 4640 20240; (202) 208-7163. Fax, (202) 208-6334. Kevin Washburn, Assistant Secretary. Press, (202) 219-4150.*
Web, www.bia.gov

Works with federally recognized Indian tribal governments and Alaska Native communities in a government-to-government relationship. Encourages and supports tribes' efforts to govern themselves and to provide needed

programs and services on the reservations. Manages land held in trust for Indian tribes and individuals. Funds educational benefits, road construction and maintenance, social services, police protection, economic development efforts, and special assistance to develop governmental and administrative skills.

▶CONGRESS

For a listing of relevant congressional committees and sub-committees, please see pages 470–471 or the Appendix.

▶JUDICIARY

U.S. Court of Federal Claims, *717 Madison Pl. N.W. 20005; (202) 357-6400. Fax, (202) 357-6401. Emily Clark Hewitt, Chief Judge, (202) 357-6483; Hazel Keahey, Clerk, (202) 357-6412.*
Web, www.uscfc.uscourts.gov

Deals with Native American tribal claims against the government that are founded upon the Constitution, congressional acts, government regulations, and contracts. Examples include congressional reference cases; patent cases; claims for land, water, and mineral rights; and the accounting of funds held for Native Americans under various treaties.

▶NONGOVERNMENTAL

National Congress of American Indians, *Embassy of Tribal Nations, 1516 P St. N.W. 20005; (202) 466-7767. Fax, (202) 466-7797. Jacqueline Johnson Pata, Executive Director.*
General email, ncai@ncai.org
Web, www.ncai.org

Membership: American Indian and Alaska Native tribal governments and individuals. Provides information and serves as general advocate for tribes. Monitors legislative and regulatory activities affecting Native American affairs.

Native American Rights Fund, *Washington Office, 1514 P St. N.W., Suite D 20005; (202) 785-4166. Fax, (202) 822-0068. John E. Echohawk, Executive Director; Richard Guest, Managing Attorney.*
Web, www.narf.org

Provides Native Americans and Alaska Natives with legal assistance in land claims, water rights, hunting, and other areas. Practices federal Indian law. (Headquarters in Boulder, Colo.)

Navajo Nation, *Washington Office, 750 1st St. N.E., #1010 20002; (202) 682-7390. Fax, (202) 682-7391. Clara Pratte, Executive Director.*
General email, info@nnwo.org
Web, www.nnwo.org

Monitors legislation and regulations affecting the Navajo people; serves as an information clearinghouse on the Navajo Nation. (Headquarters in Window Rock, Ariz.)

Older Adults

►AGENCIES

Administration for Community Living (ACL) *(Health and Human Services Dept.)*, *Administration on Aging (AoA)*, 1 Massachusetts Ave. N.W. 20201; (202) 619-0724. Fax, (202) 357-3555. Edwin L. Walker, Deputy Assistant Secretary, (202) 401-4634. Press, (202) 357-3507. Eldercare Locator, (800) 677-1116.
General email, aclinfo@acl.hhs.gov

Web, www.aoa.hhs.gov

Advocacy agency for older Americans and their concerns. Collaborates with tribal organizations, community and national organizations, and state and area agencies to implement grant programs and services designed to improve the quality of life for older Americans, such as information and referral, adult day care, elder abuse prevention, home-delivered meals, in-home care, transportation, and services for caregivers.

►CONGRESS

For a listing of relevant congressional committees and subcommittees, please see pages 470–471 or the Appendix.

►NONGOVERNMENTAL

AARP, 601 E St. N.W. 20049; (202) 434-2277. Fax, (202) 434-2320. A. Barry Rand, Chief Executive Officer. Press, (202) 434-2560. Library, (202) 434-6233. Toll-free, (888) 687-2277. Membership, (202) 434-3525.
General email, member@aarp.org

Web, www.aarp.org

Membership organization for persons age fifty and older. Provides members with training, employment information, and volunteer programs; offers financial services, including insurance, investment programs, and consumer discounts; makes grants through AARP Andrus Foundation for research on aging. Monitors legislation and regulations and disseminates information on issues affecting older Americans, including age discrimination, Social Security, Medicaid and Medicare, pensions and retirement, and consumer protection. (Formerly the American Assn. of Retired Persons.)

Alliance for Retired Americans, 815 16th St. N.W., 4th Floor North 20006-4104; (202) 637-5399. Fax, (202) 637-5398. Barbara J. Esterling, President. Membership, (800) 333-7212.
Web, www.retiredamericans.org

Alliance of retired members of unions affiliated with the AFL-CIO, senior citizen clubs, associations, councils, and other groups. Seeks to nationalize health care services and to strengthen benefits to older adults, including improved Social Security payments, increased employment, and education and health programs. Offers prescription drug program and vision care Medicare supplement. (Affiliate of the AFL-CIO.)

Gray Panthers, 10 G St. N.E., #600 20002-4215; (202) 737-6637. Sally Brown, Executive Director. Information, (800) 280-5362.
General email, info@graypanthers.org

Web, www.graypanthers.org

Intergenerational educational and advocacy organization that promotes peace and economic and social justice for all people; seeks universal health care, the preservation of Social Security, affordable housing, access to education, and jobs for all with a living wage.

National Caucus and Center for the Black Aged, Inc., 1220 L St. N.W., #800 20005-2407; (202) 637-8400. Fax, (202) 347-0895. Karyne Jones, President.
General email, support@ncba-aged.org

Web, www.ncba-aged.org

Concerned with issues that affect older African Americans and other minorities. Sponsors employment and housing programs for older adults and education and training for professionals in gerontology. Monitors legislation and regulations.

National Council on the Aging, 1901 L St. N.W., 4th Floor 20036; (202) 479-1200. Fax, (202) 479-0735. James P. Firman, President. Press, (202) 600-3131. Eldercare Locator, (800) 677-1116.
General email, info@ncoa.org

Web, www.ncoa.org

Serves as an information clearinghouse on training, technical assistance, advocacy, and research on every aspect of aging. Provides information on social services for older persons. Monitors legislation and regulations.

National Hispanic Council on Aging, 734 15th St. N.W., #1050 20005; (202) 347-9733. Fax, (202) 347-9735. Yanira Cruz, President.
General email, nhcoa@nhcoa.org

Web, www.nhcoa.org

Membership: senior citizens, health care workers, professionals in the field of aging, and others in the United States and Puerto Rico who are interested in topics related to Hispanics and aging. Provides research training, policy analysis, consulting, and technical assistance; sponsors seminars, workshops, and management internships.

National Senior Citizens Law Center, 1444 Eye St. N.W., #1100 20005; (202) 289-6976. Fax, (202) 289-7224. Kevin Prindiville, Executive Director.
General email, nsclc@nsclc.org

Web, www.nsclc.org

Provides training, technical assistance, and litigation for attorneys representing the elderly poor and persons with disabilities. Represents clients before Congress and federal departments and agencies. Focus includes Social Security, Medicare, Medicaid, long-term care residents' rights, home health care, pensions, and protective services. Funded by the Administration on Aging and various charitable foundations.

Seniors Coalition, *1250 Connecticut Ave. N.W., #200 20036; (202) 261-3594. Fax, (866) 728-5450. Joseph L. Bridges, Chief Executive Officer. Toll-free, (800) 325-9891.*

General email, tsc@senior.org

Web, www.senior.org

Seeks to protect the quality of life and economic well-being of older Americans. Interests include health care, Social Security, taxes, pharmaceutical issues, and Medicare. Conducts seminars and monitors legislation and regulations.

60 Plus, *515 King St., #315, Alexandria, VA 22314; (703) 807-2070. Fax, (703) 807-2073. James L. Martin, Chair.*

General email, info@60plus.org

Web, www.60plus.org

Advocates for the rights of senior citizens. Interests include free enterprise, less government regulation, and tax reform. Works to eliminate estate taxes. Publishes rating system of members of Congress. Monitors legislation and regulations.

Women

▶**NONGOVERNMENTAL**

Assn. for Women in Science, *1321 Duke St., #210, Alexandria, VA 22314; (703) 894-4490. Fax, (703) 894-4489. Janet Bandows Koster, Executive Director.*

General email, awis@awis.org

Web, www.awis.org

Promotes equal opportunity for women in scientific professions; provides career and funding information. Provides educational scholarships for women in science. Interests include international development.

Center for Women Policy Studies, *1420 North Park Ave., #302W, Chevy Chase, MD 20815; (202) 872-1770. Fax, (202) 296-8962. Leslie R. Wolfe, President.*

General email, cwps@centerwomenpolicy.org

Web, www.centerwomenpolicy.org

Policy and advocacy organization concerned with women's issues, including educational and employment equity for women, women and AIDS, violence against women, economic opportunity for low-income women, women's health, and reproductive laws.

Independent Women's Forum (IWF), *1875 Eye St. N.W., #500 20006; (202) 857-5201. Fax, (202) 429-9574. Sabrina Schaeffer, Executive Director.*

General email, info@iwf.org

Web, www.iwf.org

Membership: women and men interested in advancing limited government, equality under the law, property rights, free markets, strong families, and a powerful and effective national defense and foreign policy. Publishes policy papers; makes appearances on radio and television broadcasts; maintains speakers bureau. Interests include school choice, Social Security, health care reform, and

democracy promotion and women's human rights in the Middle East.

Jewish Women International, *1129 20th St. N.W., #801 20036; (202) 857-1300. Fax, (202) 857-1380. Loribeth Weinstein, Executive Director. Toll-free, (800) 343-2823.*

General email, jwi@jwi.org

Web, www.jwi.org

Organization of Jewish women in the United States. Interests include emotional health of children and youth, family violence, women's health care, civil and constitutional rights, community service, and anti-Semitism.

National Council of Women's Organizations, *714 G St. S.E., #200 20003; (202) 293-4505. Fax, (202) 293-4507. Susan Scanlan, Chair.*

General email, ncwo@ncwo-online.org

Web, www.womensorganizations.org

Membership: local and national women's organizations. Engages in policy work and grassroots activism to address issues of concern to women, including workplace and economic equity, education and job training, affirmative action, Social Security, child care, reproductive freedom, health, and global women's equality. Monitors legislation and regulations.

National Organization for Women (NOW), *1100 H St. N.W., #300 20005; (202) 628-8669. Fax, (202) 785-8576. Terry O'Neill, President.*

General email, now@now.org

Web, www.now.org

Membership: women and men interested in feminist civil rights. Uses traditional and nontraditional forms of political activism, including nonviolent civil disobedience, to improve the status of all women regardless of age, income, sexual orientation, or race. Maintains liaisons with counterpart organizations worldwide.

National Partnership for Women and Families, *1875 Connecticut Ave. N.W., #650 20009-5731; (202) 986-2600. Fax, (202) 986-2539. Debra L. Ness, President.*

General email, info@nationalpartnership.org

Web, www.nationalpartnership.org

Advocacy organization that promotes fairness in the workplace, access to high-quality health care, and policies that help women and men meet the demands of work and family. Publishes and disseminates information in print and on the Web to heighten awareness of work and family issues. Monitors legislative activity and pending Supreme Court cases and argues on behalf of family issues before Congress and in the courts.

National Women's Law Center, *11 Dupont Circle N.W., #800 20036; (202) 588-5180. Fax, (202) 588-5185. Nancy Duff Campbell, Co-President; Marcia D. Greenberger, Co-President.*

General email, info@nwlc.org

Web, www.nwlc.org

Works to expand and protect women's legal rights through advocacy and public education. Interests include reproductive rights, health, education, employment, income security, and family support.

OWL: The Voice of Midlife and Older Women, *1625 K St. N.W., #1275 20006; (202) 567-2606. Fax, (202) 332-2949. Bobbie A. Brinegar, Executive Director. General email, info@owl-national.org*

Web, www.owl-national.org

Grassroots organization concerned with the status and quality of life of middle-aged and older women. Interests include health care, Social Security, pension rights, housing, employment, women as caregivers, effects of budget cuts, and issues relating to health insurance and long-term care.

Quota International, *1420 21st St. N.W. 20036; (202) 331-9694. Fax, (202) 331-4395. Barbara Schreiber, Executive Director. General email, staff@quota.org*

Web, www.quota.org

International service organization that links members in twelve countries in a worldwide network of service and friendship. Interests include deaf, hard-of-hearing, and speech-impaired individuals and disadvantaged women and children. Maintains the We Share Foundation, a charitable organization.

Sewall-Belmont House & Museum, *144 Constitution Ave. N.E. 20002-5608; (202) 546-1210. Fax, (202) 546-3997. Page Harrington, Executive Director. Press, (202) 546-1210, ext. 12. General email, info@sewallbelmont.org*

Web, www.sewallbelmont.org

Maintains archives and artifacts documenting women's equality under the law. Interests include the suffragists, the National Women's Party, and the Equal Rights Amendment campaign.

Women's Action for New Directions (WAND), *Washington Office, 322 4th St. N.E. 20002; (202) 544-5055. Fax, (202) 544-7612. Maureen Campbell, WAND Senior Associate; Kathy Crandall Robinson, Director, Public Policy. General email, peace@wand.org*

Web, www.wand.org

Seeks to empower women to act politically to reduce violence and militarism and redirect excessive military resources toward unmet human and environmental needs. Monitors legislation on federal budget priorities. (Headquarters in Arlington, Mass.)

Women's Research and Education Institute (WREI), *3808 Brighton Ct., Alexandria, VA 22305; (703) 837-1977. Susan Scanlan, President. General email, wrei@wrei.org*

Web, www.wrei.org

Analyzes policy-relevant information on women's issues. Sponsors fellowships in congressional offices; educates the public through reports and conferences. Interests include women's employment and economic status; women

in nontraditional occupations; military women and veterans; older women; women's health issues; and women and immigration. Library open to the public.

YWCA of the USA *(YWCA USA), 2025 M St. N.W., #550 20036; (202) 467-0801. Fax, (202) 467-0802. Dara Richardson-Heron, Chief Executive Officer, (202) 835-2352. General email, info@ywca.org*

Web, www.ywca.org

Strives to empower women and girls and to eliminate racism. Provides services and programs concerning child care and youth development, economic empowerment, global awareness, health and fitness, housing and shelter, leadership development, racial justice and human rights, and violence prevention. (YWCA stands for Young Women's Christian Association.)

Other Minority Groups

▶**AGENCIES**

Education Dept., *White House Initiative on Asian Americans and Pacific Islanders, 550 12th St. S.W., 10th Floor 20202; (202) 453-7277. Fax, (202) 453-6238. Kiran Ahuja, Executive Director. Press, (202) 453-6566. General email, http://whitehouseaapi@ed.gov*

Web, www.whitehouse.gov/aapi and Twitter, @whitehouseAAPI

Ensures that Asian Americans and Pacific Islanders have equal access to federal programs and services. Methods include expanding language access and increasing enforcement efforts to combat discrimination.

▶**NONGOVERNMENTAL**

American-Arab Anti-Discrimination Committee (ADC), *1990 M St. N.W., #610 20036; (202) 244-2990. Fax, (202) 333-3980. Samer E. Khalaf, President. General email, adc@adc.org*

Web, www.adc.org

Nonpartisan and nonsectarian organization that promotes and seeks to protect the human rights and cultural heritage of Americans of Arab descent. Works to combat discrimination against Arab Americans in employment, education, and political life and to prevent stereotyping of Arabs in the media. Monitors legislation and regulations.

Anti-Defamation League, *Washington Office, 1100 Connecticut Ave. N.W., #1020 20036; (202) 452-8310. Fax, (202) 296-2371. David Friedman, Regional Director. General email, washington-dc@adl.org*

Web, www.adl.org

Seeks to combat anti-Semitism and other forms of bigotry. Interests include discrimination in employment, housing, voting, and education; U.S. foreign policy in the Middle East; and the treatment of Jews worldwide. Monitors legislation and regulations affecting Jewish interests and the civil rights of all Americans. (Headquarters in New York.)

U.S. Courts

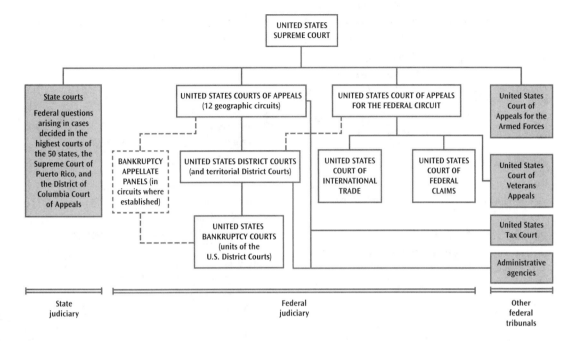

Asian American Justice Center (AAJC), *1140 Connecticut Ave. N.W., #1200 20036; (202) 296-2300. Fax, (202) 296-2318. Mee Moua, President.*
General email, information@advancingequality.org

Web, www.advancingequality.org

Works to advance the human and civil rights of Asian Americans and other minority groups through advocacy, public policy, public education, and litigation. Promotes civic engagement at the local, regional, and national levels. Interests include affirmative action, hate crimes, media diversity, census, broadband and telecommunications, youth advocacy, immigrant rights, language access, and voting rights.

Japanese American Citizens League, *Washington Office, 1629 K St. N.W., #400 20006; (202) 223-1240. Fax, (202) 296-8082. Priscilla Ouchida, Executive Director.*
General email, dc@jacl.org

Web, www.jacl.org

Monitors legislative and regulatory activities affecting the rights of Japanese Americans. Supports civil rights of all Americans, with a focus on Asian and Asian Pacific Americans. (Headquarters in San Francisco, Calif.)

OCA (Asian Pacific American Advocates), *1322 18th St. N.W. 20036-1803; (202) 223-5500. Fax, (202) 296-0540. Tom Lim Hayashi, Executive Director.*
General email, oca@ocanational.org

Web, www.ocanational.org

Advocacy group seeking to advance the social, political, and economic well-being of Asian Pacific Americans in the United States.

Organization of Chinese American Women, *4641 Montgomery Ave., #208, Bethesda, MD 20814 (mailing address: P.O. Box 815, Great Falls, VA 22066); (301) 907-3898. Fax, (301) 907-3899. Donna Byler, Executive Director.*
General email, info@ocawwomen.org

Web, www.ocawwomen.org

Promotes equal rights and opportunities for Chinese and other Asian Pacific American women in professional and nonprofessional fields. Provides members with leadership and skills training and newly arrived immigrants with career development.

CONSTITUTIONAL LAW AND CIVIL LIBERTIES

General

▶ AGENCIES

Commission on Civil Rights, *1331 Pennsylvania Ave. N.W., #1150 20425; (202) 376-7700. Fax, (202) 376-7672. Martin R. Castro, Chair; Marlene Sallo, Staff Director. Press, (202) 376-8591.*
General email, publiccomments@usccr.gov

Web, www.usccr.gov

Assesses federal laws, policies, and legal developments to determine the nature and extent of denial of equal protection under the law on the basis of race, color, religion, sex, national origin, age, or disability in employment, voting rights, education, administration of justice, and housing.

Issues reports and makes recommendations to the president and Congress; serves as national clearinghouse for civil rights information; receives civil rights complaints and refers them to the appropriate federal agency for action. Library open to the public.

Justice Dept. (DOJ), *Legal Counsel,* 950 Pennsylvania Ave. N.W., #5218 20530-0001; (202) 514-2051. Fax, (202) 514-0539. Caroline D. Krass, Assistant Attorney General, Acting. Web, www.justice.gov/olc/index.html

Advises the attorney general, the president, and executive agencies on questions regarding constitutional law.

►CONGRESS

For a listing of relevant congressional committees and subcommittees, please see pages 470–471 or the Appendix.

►JUDICIARY

Supreme Court of the United States, 1 1st St. N.E. 20543; (202) 479-3000. John G. Roberts Jr., Chief Justice; Kathleen Arberg, Public Information Officer, (202) 479-3211.
Web, www.supremecourtus.gov

Highest appellate court in the federal judicial system. Interprets the U.S. Constitution, federal legislation, and treaties. Provides information on new cases filed, the status of pending cases, and admissions to the Supreme Court Bar. Library open to Supreme Court bar members only.

►NONGOVERNMENTAL

American Civil Liberties Union (ACLU), *Washington Legislative Office,* 915 15th St. N.W. 20005; (202) 544-1681. Fax, (202) 546-0738. Laura W. Murphy, Director. Press, (202) 417-7547.
General email, media@dcaclu.org
Web, www.aclu.org/legiupdate

Focuses on constitutional rights and civil liberties, minority and women's rights, gay and lesbian rights, and privacy; supports legalized abortion, opposes government-sponsored school prayer and legislative restrictions on television content. Washington office monitors legislative and regulatory activities and public policy. Library open to the public by appointment. (Headquarters in New York maintains docket of cases.)

American Constitution Society for Law and Policy, 1333 H St. N.W., 11th Floor 20005; (202) 393-6181. Fax, (202) 393-6189. Caroline Fredrickson, President.
General email, info@acslaw.org
Web, www.acslaw.org

National association of lawyers, law students, judges, legal scholars, and policymakers that promotes a progressive vision of constitutional law and public policy. Produces issue briefs and publications. Organizes lectures, conferences, seminars, and two annual student competitions.

Supreme Court Justices

CHIEF JUSTICE
John G. Roberts Jr.
Appointed chief justice by President George W. Bush, sworn in Sept. 29, 2005.

ASSOCIATE JUSTICES
in order of appointment

Antonin Scalia
Appointed by President Reagan, sworn in Sept. 26, 1986.

Anthony M. Kennedy
Appointed by President Reagan, sworn in Feb. 18, 1988.

Clarence Thomas
Appointed by President George Bush, sworn in Oct. 23, 1991.

Ruth Bader Ginsburg
Appointed by President Clinton, sworn in Aug. 10, 1993.

Stephen G. Breyer
Appointed by President Clinton, sworn in Aug. 3, 1994.

Samuel A. Alito Jr.
Appointed by President George W. Bush, sworn in Jan. 31, 2006.

Sonia Sotomayor
Appointed by President Barack Obama, sworn in Aug. 8, 2009.

Elena Kagan
Appointed by President Barack Obama, sworn in Aug. 7, 2010.

Center for Individual Rights, 1233 20th St. N.W., #300 20036; (202) 833-8400. Fax, (202) 833-8410. Terence J. (Terry) Pell, President. Toll-free, (877) 426-2665.
General email, cir@cir-usa.org
Web, www.cir-usa.org

Public interest law firm that provides free representation to individuals who cannot afford adequate legal counsel in cases raising constitutional questions of individual rights. Interests include freedom of speech and religious expression, civil rights, and Congress's enumerated powers.

Ethics and Public Policy Center, 1730 M St. N.W., #910 20036; (202) 682-1200. Fax, (202) 408-0632. M. Edward Whelan III, President.
General email, ethics@eppc.org
Web, www.eppc.org

Examines current issues of jurisprudence, especially those relating to constitutional interpretation.

First Amendment Center, 555 Pennsylvania Ave. N.W. 20001; (202) 292-6288. Fax, (202) 292-6295.

Charles C. Haynes, Senior Scholar, (202) 292-6293; Ken Paulson, President, (615) 727-1302.
General email, info@fac.org
Web, www.firstamendmentcenter.org

Works to preserve and protect First Amendment freedoms through information and education. Serves as a nonpartisan forum for the study and exploration of free-expression issues, including freedom of speech, the press, religion, and the rights to assemble and to petition the government. Co-sponsors with the Newseum the Religious Freedom Education Project. The center is an operating program of the Freedom Forum and is associated with the Diversity Institute. Affiliated with Vanderbilt University through the Vanderbilt Institute for Public Policy Studies. Located in the Newseum.

Institute for Justice, *901 N. Glebe Rd., #900, Arlington, VA 22203; (703) 682-9320. Fax, (703) 682-9321. William (Chip) Mellor, President.*
General email, general@ij.org
Web, www.ij.org

Sponsors seminars to train law students, grassroots activists, and practicing lawyers in applying advocacy strategies in public interest litigation. Seeks to protect individuals from arbitrary government interference in free speech, private property rights, parental school choice, and economic liberty. Litigates cases.

National Organization for Women (NOW), *1100 H St. N.W., #300 20005; (202) 628-8669. Fax, (202) 785-8576. Terry O'Neill, President.*
General email, now@now.org
Web, www.now.org

Membership: women and men interested in civil rights for women. Works to end discrimination based on gender, to preserve abortion rights, and to pass an equal rights amendment to the Constitution.

OSI (Open Society Institute), *Washington Office, 1730 Pennsylvania Ave. N.W., 7th Floor 20006; (202) 721-5600. Fax, (202) 530-0128. Stephen Rickard, Director.*
General email, info@osi-dc.org
Web, www.soros.org/initiatives/washington

Addresses violations of civil liberties in the United States. Interests include criminal and civil justice reform, global economic policies, and women's rights. (Headquarters in New York. Affiliated with the Soros Foundation Network.)

Abortion and Reproductive Issues

▶ **NONGOVERNMENTAL**

Assn. of Reproductive Health Professionals, *1901 L St. N.W., #300 20036; (202) 466-3825. Fax, (202) 466-3826. Wayne C. Shields, President.*
General email, arhp@arhp.org
Web, www.arhp.org

Membership: obstetricians, gynecologists, other physicians, researchers, clinicians, and educators. Educates health professionals and the public on reproductive health issues, including family planning, contraception, HIV/AIDS and other sexually transmitted diseases, abortion, menopause, infertility, and cancer prevention and detection. Monitors legislation and regulations.

Catholics for Choice, *1436 U St. N.W., #301 20009-3997; (202) 986-6093. Fax, (202) 332-7995. Jon O'Brien, President.*
General email, cfc@catholicsforchoice.org
Web, www.catholicsforchoice.org

Works to change church positions and public policies that limit individual freedom, particularly those related to sexuality and reproduction. Provides the public, policymakers, and groups working for change with information and analysis.

Feminists for Life of America, *P.O. Box 320667, Alexandria, VA 22320; (703) 836-3354. Serrin M. Foster, President.*
General email, info@feministsforlife.org
Web, www.feministsforlife.org

Membership: women and men who are against abortion and in favor of feminism. Opposes abortion, euthanasia, and capital punishment; seeks to redress economic and social conditions that cause women to choose abortion.

March for Life Education and Defense Fund, *1317 8th St. N.W. 22201; (202) 234-3300. Fax, (202) 234-3350. Jeanne F. Monahan, President.*
General email, annconant@marchforlife.org
Web, www.marchforlife.org and Twitter, @March_for_Life

Membership: individuals and organizations that support government action prohibiting abortion. Sponsors annual march in Washington each January 22. Monitors legislation and regulations.

NARAL Pro-Choice America, *1156 15th St. N.W., #700 20005; (202) 973-3000. Fax, (202) 973-3096. Ilyse Hogue, President. Press, (202) 973-3032.*
Web, www.prochoiceamerica.org and Twitter, @NARAL

Membership: persons who support using the political process to guarantee women a range of reproductive choices, including preventing unintended pregnancy, bearing healthy children, and choosing legal abortion. (Formerly National Abortion and Reproductive Rights Action League.)

National Abortion Federation (NAF), *1660 L St. N.W., #450 20036; (202) 667-5881. Fax, (202) 667-5890. Vicki Saporta, President. NAF hotline, (800) 772-9100.*
General email, naf@prochoice.org
Web, www.prochoice.org

Membership: abortion providers. Seeks to ensure that abortion is safe, legal, and accessible.

National Committee for a Human Life Amendment, *1500 Massachusetts Ave. N.W., #24 20005; (202) 393-0703. Fax, (202) 347-1383. Michael A. Taylor, Executive Director.*

Privacy Resources

See government agencies' individual Web sites for their privacy policies and freedom of information procedures.

AGENCIES AND CONGRESS

Federal Trade Commission, ID Theft;
www.ftc.gov/idtheft; Identity Theft;
www.ftc.gov/privacy; Privacy Initiatives; Hotline,
(877) 438-4338

House Judiciary Committee, Subcommittee on the Constitution and Civil Justice, (202) 225-2825;
www.judiciary.house.gov

National Do-Not-Call Registry, toll-free, (888) 382-1222, TTY, (866) 290-4236; www.fcc.gov/encyclopedia/do-not-call-list

Office of Management and Budget (concerning the Privacy Act), (202) 395-3647;
www.whitehouse.gov/omb/inforeg_infopoltech#pg

Senate Judiciary Committee, (202) 224-7703 (Majority), (202) 224-5225 (Minority);
www.judiciary.senate.gov

U.S. Postal Service,
www.usps.com/privacyoffice

NONGOVERNMENTAL

American Bar Association, Lawyer Referral Service, (202) 662-1000; www.findlegalhelp.org

American Civil Liberties Union, (202) 544-1681;
www.aclu.org/technology-and-liberty

Call for Action, (240) 747-0229;
www.callforaction.org

Center for Democracy and Technology, (202) 637-9800;
www.cdt.org

Center for National Security Studies, (202) 721-5650;
www.cnss.org

Center for Study of Responsive Law, (202) 387-8030;
www.csrl.org

Consumer Data Industry Association, (202) 371-0910;
www.cdiaonline.org

Consumer Privacy Guide, www.consumerprivacyguide.org
Consumers Union of the United States, (202) 462-6262;
www.consumersunion.org

Direct Marketing Assn., Do-Not-Call Registry,
(202) 955-5030; www.the-dma.org

Electronic Privacy Information Center, (202) 483-1140;
www.epic.org

Health Privacy Project, www.healthprivacy.org

National Consumers League, (202) 835-3323;
www.nclnet.org

Privacy Site (EPIC), www.privacy.org

U.S. Postal Inspection Service, (877) 876-2455,
postalinspectors.uspis.gov

U.S. Public Interest Research Group (USPIRG),
(202) 546-9707; www.uspirg.org

General email, info@nchla.org

Web, www.nchla.org

Supports legislation and a constitutional amendment prohibiting abortion.

National Organization for Women (NOW), *1100 H St. N.W., #300 20005; (202) 628-8669. Fax, (202) 785-8576. Terry O'Neill, President.*
General email, now@now.org

Web, www.now.org

Membership: women and men interested in civil rights for women. Works to preserve abortion rights.

National Right to Life Committee, *512 10th St. N.W. 20004-1401; (202) 626-8800. Fax, (202) 737-9189. David N. O'Steen, Executive Director, ext. 114; Carol Tobias, President. Press, (202) 626-8825.*
General email, nrlc@nrlc.org; mediarelations@nrlc.org

Web, www.nrlc.org

Association of fifty state right-to-life organizations. Opposes abortion, infanticide, and euthanasia; supports legislation prohibiting abortion except when the life of the mother is endangered. Operates an information clearinghouse and speakers bureau. Monitors legislation and regulations.

National Women's Health Network, *1413 K St. N.W., 4th Floor 20005; (202) 682-2640. Fax, (202) 682-2648. Cynthia Pearson, Executive Director. Health information requests, (202) 682-2646.*
General email, nwhn@nwhn.org

Web, www.nwhn.org

Advocacy organization interested in women's health. Seeks to preserve legalized abortion; monitors legislation and regulations; testifies before Congress.

National Women's Political Caucus, *110 H St. N.W., #300 20005 (mailing address: P.O. Box 50476, Washington, DC 20091); (202) 785-1100. Fax, (202) 370-6306. Linda Young, President; Bettina M. Hager, Program Director.*
General email, info@nwpc.org

Web, www.nwpc.org

Advocacy group that seeks greater involvement of women in politics. Supports legalized abortion.

Religious Coalition for Reproductive Choice, *1413 K St. N.W., 14th Floor 20005; (202) 628-7700. Fax, (202) 628-7716. Rev. Harry Knox, President.*
General email, info@rcrc.org

Web, www.rcrc.org

Coalition of religious groups favoring birth control, sexuality education, and access to legal abortion. Opposes constitutional amendments and federal and state legislation restricting access to abortion services in most cases. Monitors legislation and regulations.

U.S. Conference of Catholic Bishops (USCCB), *Secretariat of Pro-Life Activities, 3211 4th St. N.E. 20017-1194; (202) 541-3070. Fax, (202) 541-3054. Tom Grenchik, Executive Director. Publications, (800) 235-8722.*
General email, prolife@usccb.org

Web, www.usccb.org/prolife

Provides information on the position of the Roman Catholic Church on abortion. Monitors legislation on abortion, embryonic stem-cell research, human cloning, and related issues. Promotes alternatives to abortion.

Claims Against the Government

▶ AGENCIES

Justice Dept. (DOJ), *Civil Division, National Courts, 1100 L St. N.W., #12124 20530; (202) 514-7300. Fax, (202) 307-0972. Bryant Snee, Director, Acting.*
Web, www.justice.gov/civil/commercial/national-courts/c-natcourts.html

Represents the United States in the U.S. Court of Federal Claims, except in cases involving taxes, lands, or Native American claims.

Justice Dept. (DOJ), *Environment and Natural Resources, 950 Pennsylvania Ave. N.W., #2143 20530-0001; (202) 514-2701. Fax, (202) 514-0557. Robert G. Dreher, Assistant Attorney General, Acting. Press, (202) 514-2008.*
Web, www.justice.gov/enrd

Represents the United States in the U.S. Court of Federal Claims in cases arising from acquisition of property, Indian rights and claims, and environmental challenges to federal programs and activities.

Justice Dept. (DOJ), *Tax Division, 950 Pennsylvania Ave. N.W., #4141 20530; (202) 514-2901. Fax, (202) 514-5479. Kathryn Keneally, Assistant Attorney General, (202) 307-3366.*
General email, tax.mail@usdoj.gov

Web, www.usdoj.gov/tax

Represents the United States and its officers in all civil and criminal litigation arising under the internal revenue laws, other than proceedings in the United States Tax Court.

State Dept., *International Claims and Investment Disputes, 2430 E St. N.W., #203 20037-2800; (202) 776-8360. Fax, (202) 776-8389. Lisa J. Grosh, Assistant Legal Adviser.*
Web, www.state.gov

Handles claims by U.S. government and citizens against foreign governments, as well as claims by foreign governments and their nationals against the U.S. government; negotiates international claims agreements. Handles claims against the State Dept. for negligence (under the Federal Tort Claims Act) and claims by owners of U.S. flag vessels due to illegal seizures by foreign governments in international waters (under the Fishermen's Protective Act).

▶ CONGRESS

For a listing of relevant congressional committees and subcommittees, please see pages 470–471 or the Appendix.

▶ JUDICIARY

U.S. Court of Federal Claims, *717 Madison Pl. N.W. 20005; (202) 357-6400. Fax, (202) 357-6401. Emily Clark Hewitt, Chief Judge, (202) 357-6483; Hazel Keahey, Clerk, (202) 357-6412.*
Web, www.uscfc.uscourts.gov

Renders judgment on any nontort claims for monetary damages against the United States founded upon the Constitution, statutes, government regulations, and government contracts. Examples include compensation for taking of property, claims arising under construction and supply contracts, certain patent cases, cases involving the refund of federal taxes, and statutory claims made by foreign governments against the United States. Hears cases involving Native American claims.

Privacy

▶ AGENCIES

Federal Trade Commission (FTC), *Consumer Protection, Financial Practices, 600 Pennsylvania Ave. N.W., MS3158 20580; (202) 326-3224. Fax, (202) 326-3768. Reilly Dolan, Associate Director.*
Web, www.ftc.gov

Enforces the Fair Credit Reporting Act, which requires credit bureaus to furnish correct and complete information to businesses evaluating credit, insurance, or job applications.

National Security Agency (NSA) *(Defense Dept.),* **Civil Liberties and Privacy,** *9800 Savage Rd., #6272, Fort Meade, MD 20755-6000; (301) 688-6524. Rebecca Richards, Civil Liberties and Privacy Officer.*
Web, http://www.nsa.gov/public_info/press_room/2014/civil_liberties_privacy_officer.shtml

Advises the director of the NSA to ensure that privacy and civil liberties protections are inherent in strategic decisions, particularly in the areas of technology and processes.

Office of Management and Budget (OMB) *(Executive Office of the President),* **Information and Regulatory Affairs,** *New Executive Office Bldg., #10236 20503; (202) 395-3785. Fax, (202) 395-5167. Boris Bershteyn, Administrator, Acting.*
Web, www.whitehouse.gov/omb/inforeg_infopoltech

Oversees implementation of the Privacy Act of 1974 and other privacy- and security-related statutes. Issues guidelines and regulations.

▶ CONGRESS

For a listing of relevant congressional committees and subcommittees, please see pages 470–471 or the Appendix.

▶NONGOVERNMENTAL

Assn. of Direct Response Fundraising Counsel, *1612 K St. N.W., #1102 20006-2849; (202) 293-9640. Fax, (202) 887-9699. Robert S. Tigner, General Counsel.*
General email, adrfco@msn.com
Web, www.adrfco.org

Membership: businesses in the direct response fundraising industry. Establishes standards of ethical practice in such areas as ownership of direct mail donor lists and mandatory disclosures by fundraising counsel. Educates nonprofit organizations and the public on direct response fundraising. Represents members' interests before the federal and state governments.

Call for Action, *11820 Parklawn Dr., #340, Rockville, MD 20852; (240) 747-0229. Shirley Rooker, President; Eduard Bartholme, Executive Director.*
Web, www.callforaction.org

International network of consumer hotlines affiliated with local broadcast partners. Helps consumers resolve problems with businesses, government agencies, and other organizations through mediation. Provides information on privacy concerns.

Center for Democracy and Technology, *1634 Eye St. N.W., #1100 20006; (202) 637-9800. Fax, (202) 637-0968. Nuala O'Connor, President.*
General email, info@cdt.org
Web, www.cdt.org

Promotes and defends privacy and civil liberties on the Internet. Interests include free expression, social networking and access to the Internet, consumer protection, health information privacy and technology, and government surveillance.

Communications Workers of America (CWA), *501 3rd St. N.W. 20001; (202) 434-1100. Fax, (202) 434-1279. Larry Cohen, President.*
General email, cwaweb@cwa-union.org
Web, www.cwa-union.org

Membership: telecommunications, broadcast, and printing and publishing workers. Opposes electronic monitoring of productivity, eavesdropping by employers, and misuse of drug and polygraph tests.

Consumers Union of the United States, *Washington Office, 1101 17th St. N.W., #500 20036; (202) 462-6262. Fax, (202) 265-9548. James A. Guest, President; Ellen Bloom, Director, Washington Office.*
Web, www.consumersunion.org

Consumer advocacy group active in protecting the privacy of consumers. Interests include credit report accuracy. (Headquarters in Yonkers, N.Y.)

Electronic Privacy Information Center (EPIC), *1718 Connecticut Ave. N.W., #200 20009; (202) 483-1140. Fax, (202) 483-1248. Marc Rotenberg, Executive Director.*
General email, info@epic.org
Web, www.epic.org

Public interest research center. Conducts research and conferences on domestic and international civil liberties issues, including privacy, free speech, information access, computer security, and encryption; litigates cases. Monitors legislation and regulations.

National Assn. of State Utility Consumer Advocates (NASUCA), *8380 Colesville Rd., #101, Silver Spring, MD 20910-6267; (301) 589-6313. Fax, (301) 589-6380. Charles A. (Charlie) Acquard, Executive Director.*
General email, nasuca@nasuca.org
Web, www.nasuca.org

Membership: public advocate offices authorized by states to represent ratepayer interests before state and federal utility regulatory commissions. Supports privacy protection for telephone customers.

National Consumers League, *1701 K St. N.W., #1200 20006; (202) 835-3323. Fax, (202) 835-0747. Sally Greenberg, Executive Director.*
General email, info@nclnet.org
Web, www.nclnet.org

Advocacy group concerned with privacy rights of consumers. Interests include credit and financial records, medical records, direct marketing, telecommunications, and workplace privacy.

U.S. Public Interest Research Group (USPIRG), *Washington Office, 218 D St. S.E. 20003; (202) 546-9707. Fax, (202) 543-6489. Andre Delattre, Executive Director (in Boston), (312) 544-4436; Michael (Mike) Russo, Director, (202) 461-3823.*
General email, uspirg@pirg.org
Web, www.uspirg.org

Coordinates grassroots efforts to advance consumer protection laws. Works for the protection of privacy rights, particularly in the area of fair credit reporting. (Headquarters in Boston.)

Religious Freedom

▶NONGOVERNMENTAL

Americans for Religious Liberty, *P.O. Box 6656, Silver Spring, MD 20916; (301) 460-1111. Edd Doerr, President.*
General email, arlinc@verizon.net
Web, www.arlinc.org

Educational organization concerned with issues involving the separation of church and state. Opposes government-sponsored school prayer and tax support for religious institutions; supports religious neutrality in public education; defends abortion rights. Provides legal services in litigation cases. Maintains speakers bureau.

Americans United for Separation of Church and State, *1301 K St. N.W., #850E 20005; (202) 466-3234. Fax, (202) 466-2587. Barry W. Lynn, Executive Director.*
General email, americansunited@au.org
Web, www.au.org

Citizens' interest group that opposes government-sponsored prayer in public schools and tax aid for parochial schools.

Chaplain Alliance for Religious Liberty, *P.O. Box 151353, Alexandria, VA 22315; (571) 293-2427. Fax, (910) 221-2226. Col. Ron Crews (USAR, Ret.), Executive Director; Chaplain Brig. Gen. Doug Lee (USA, Ret.), President. General email, info@chaplainalliance.org*

Web, http://chaplainalliance.org

Membership: military chaplains and others who support orthodox Christian doctrines. Seeks to ensure that all chaplains and those they serve may exercise their religious liberties without fear of reprisal. Interests include the conflict between official protection for gays in the military and orthodox Christian teachings. Issues press releases; grants media interviews; monitors legislation and regulations.

Christian Legal Society, *8001 Braddock Rd., #302, Springfield, VA 22151; (703) 642-1070. Fax, (703) 642-1075. David Nammo, Chief Executive Officer. General email, clshq@clsnet.org*

Web, www.clsnet.org

Membership: Christian lawyers, judges, paralegals, law professors, law students, and others. Interests include the defense of religious freedom and the provision of legal aid to the poor.

International Religious Liberty Assn., *12501 Old Columbia Pike, Silver Spring, MD 20904-6600; (301) 680-6686. Fax, (301) 680-6695. Robert Seiple, President. General email, info@iria.org*

Web, www.irla.org

Seeks to preserve and expand religious liberty and freedom of conscience; advocates separation of church and state; sponsors international and domestic meetings and congresses.

National Assn. of Evangelicals, *701 G St. S.W. 20024 (mailing address: P.O. Box 23269, Washington, DC 20026); (202) 789-1011. Fax, (202) 842-0392. Leith Anderson, President. General email, info@nae.net*

Web, www.nae.net

Membership: evangelical churches, organizations (including schools), and individuals. Supports religious freedom. Monitors legislation and regulations.

Separation of Powers

▶ NONGOVERNMENTAL

Public Citizen Litigation Group, *1600 20th St. N.W. 20009; (202) 588-1000. Allison Zieve, Director of Litigation. Press, (202) 588-7741. General email, litigation@citizen.org*

Web, www.citizen.org/litigation

Conducts litigation for Public Citizen, a citizens' interest group, in cases involving separation of powers; represents individuals and groups with similar interests.

CRIMINAL LAW

General

▶ AGENCIES

Criminal Division *(Justice Dept.), 950 Pennsylvania Ave. N.W., #2107 20530-0001; (202) 514-2601. Fax, (202) 514-9412. Mythili Raman, Assistant Attorney General, Acting. General email, Criminal.Division@usdoj.gov*

Web, www.justice.gov/criminal

Enforces all federal criminal laws except those specifically assigned to the antitrust, civil rights, environment and natural resources, and tax divisions of the Justice Dept. Supervises and directs U.S. attorneys in the field on criminal matters and litigation; supervises international extradition proceedings. Coordinates federal enforcement efforts against white-collar crime, fraud, and child pornography; handles civil actions under customs, liquor, narcotics, gambling, and firearms laws; coordinates enforcement activities against organized crime. Directs the National Asset Forfeiture Program for seizing the proceeds of criminal activity. Investigates and prosecutes criminal offenses involving public integrity and subversive activities, including treason, espionage, and sedition; Nazi war crimes; and related criminal offenses. Handles all civil cases relating to internal security and counsels federal departments and agencies regarding internal security matters. Drafts responses on proposed and pending criminal law legislation.

Criminal Division *(Justice Dept.), Enforcement Operations, International Prisoner Transfer Unit, 1301 New York Ave. N.W., John C. Keeney Bldg., 10th Floor 20005; (202) 514-3173. Fax, (202) 514-9003. Paula A. Wolff, Chief. Web, www.justice.gov/criminal/oeo*

Implements prisoner transfer treaties with foreign countries.

Criminal Division *(Justice Dept.), Organized Crime and Gang Section, 1301 New York Ave. N.W., #700 20005; (202) 514-3594. Fax, (202) 514-3601. James Trusty, Chief. Press, (202) 353-4542. General email, criminaldivision@us.doj.gov*

Investigates and prosecutes important gang cases. Formulates violent crime and gang prosecution policy. Maintains responsibility over all domestic violent crime and firearms-related statutes within the U.S. code. Works with law enforcement to target and dismantle the most serious gang-related threats nationwide and internationally.

Federal Bureau of Investigation (FBI) *(Justice Dept.), 935 Pennsylvania Ave. N.W., #7176 20535-0001; (202) 324-3000. James B. Comey, Director. Information, (202) 324-3000. Press, (202) 324-3691. Web, www.fbi.gov*

Investigates all violations of federal criminal laws except those assigned specifically to other federal agencies. Exceptions include alcohol, counterfeiting, and tobacco violations (Justice Dept. and Commerce Dept.); customs violations and illegal entry of aliens (Homeland Security Dept.); and postal violations (U.S. Postal Service). Priorities include protecting the United States against terror attacks; protecting civil rights; combating public corruption at all levels, transnational/national criminal organizations and enterprises, white-collar crime, and significant violent crime; and supporting federal, state, local, and international partners. Services to other law enforcement agencies include fingerprint identifications, laboratory services, police training, and access to the National Crime Information Center (a communications network among federal, state, and local police agencies).

Federal Bureau of Investigation (FBI) *(Justice Dept.),* *Victim Assistance, 935 Pennsylvania Ave. N.W., #3329* *20535; (202) 324-1339. Fax, (202) 324-2113.* *Kathryn McKay Turman, Program Director. Toll-free,* *(866) 828-5320.* *General email, victim.assistance@ic.fbi.gov*

Web, www.fbi.gov/stats-services/victim_assistance

Ensures that victims of crimes investigated by the FBI are identified, offered assistance, and given information about case events. Manages the Victim Assistance Program in the fifty-six FBI field offices as well as the FBI's international offices. Trains agents and personnel to work with victims. Coordinates resources and services to victims in cases of terrorism and crimes against citizens that occur outside the United States. Coordinates with other federal agencies on behalf of victims.

Office of Justice Programs (OJP) *(Justice Dept.), National* *Institute of Justice, 810 7th St. N.W., 7th Floor 20531;* *(202) 307-2942. Fax, (202) 307-6394. Greg Ridgeway,* *Director, Acting, (202) 307-5146. Press, (202) 307-0703.* *Web, www.nij.gov*

Conducts research on all aspects of criminal justice, including crime prevention, enforcement, adjudication, and corrections; evaluates programs; develops model programs using new techniques. Serves as an affiliated institute of the United Nations Crime Prevention and Criminal Justice Program (UNCPCJ); studies transnational issues, especially within the Western Hemisphere. Maintains the National Criminal Justice Reference Service, which provides information on criminal justice research: (800) 851-3420; in Maryland, (301) 519-5500; Web, www.ncjrs.gov. Sponsors the National Missing and Unidentified Persons System, a clearinghouse for missing persons and unidentified decedent records: http://NamUs.gov.

Office of Justice Programs (OJP) *(Justice Dept.), Victims* *of Crime, 810 7th St. N.W., 8th Floor 20531; (202) 307-* *5983. Fax, (202) 514-6383. Joye E. Frost, Director. Resource* *Center, (800) 851-3420 or TTY, (877) 947-8374. Victim* *hotline, (800) 331-0075 or TTY, (800) 833-6885.* *Web, www.ovc.gov*

Works to advance the rights of and improve services to the nation's crime victims. Supports programs and initiatives to assist other federal agencies, state and local governments, tribal governments, private nonprofit organizations, and the international community in their efforts to aid victims of violent and nonviolent crime. Provides emergency funding and services for victims of terrorism and mass violence and victims of human trafficking. Funds the development of training and technical assistance for victim service providers and other professionals through the Training and Technical Assistance Center, (866) 682-8822 or TTY, (866) 682-8880. Funds demonstration projects and coordinates annual observances of National Crime Victims' Rights Week.

►**CONGRESS**

For a listing of relevant congressional committees and sub- *committees, please see pages 470–471 or the Appendix.*

►**INTERNATIONAL ORGANIZATIONS**

INTERPOL, *Washington Office, U.S. National Central* *Bureau, 145 N St. N.E. 20002 (mailing address: INTERPOL* *Washington, U.S. Dept. of Justice, Washington, DC 20530-* *0001); (202) 616-9000. Fax, (202) 616-8400.* *Shawn A. Bray, Director.* *Web, www.justice.gov/usncb*

U.S. representative to INTERPOL; participates in international investigations on behalf of U.S. police; coordinates the exchange of investigative information on crimes, including drug trafficking, counterfeiting, missing persons, and terrorism. Coordinates law enforcement requests for investigative assistance in the United States and abroad. Assists with extradition processes. Serves as liaison between foreign and U.S. law enforcement agencies at federal, state, and local levels. (Headquarters in Lyons, France.)

►**NONGOVERNMENTAL**

American Bar Assn. (ABA), *Criminal Justice, Washington* *Office, 1050 Connecticut Ave. N.W., #400 20036; (202)* *662-1500. Fax, (202) 662-1501. Jane Messmer, Director,* *(202) 662-1511. Press, (202) 662-1090.* *General email, crimjustice@americanbar.org*

Web, www.americanbar.org/crimjust

Responsible for all matters pertaining to criminal law and procedure for the association. Studies and makes recommendations on all facets of the criminal and juvenile justice systems, including sentencing, juries, pretrial procedures, grand juries, and white-collar crime. (Headquarters in Chicago, Ill.)

Justice Policy Institute, *1012 14th St. N.W., #400 20005;* *(202) 558-7974. Fax, (202) 558-7978. Marc Schindler,* *Executive Director.* *General email, info@justicepolicy.org*

Web, www.justicepolicy.org

Research, advocacy, and policy development organization. Analyzes current and emerging adult and juvenile criminal justice problems; educates the public about criminal justice issues; provides technical assistance to communities seeking to reform incarceration policies. Interests include new prison construction, alternatives to incarceration, anti-gang legislation, and curfew laws.

National Assn. of Attorneys General, *2030 M St. N.W., 8th Floor 20036; (202) 326-6000. James McPherson, Executive Director. Press, (202) 326-6027.*
Web, www.naag.org

Membership: attorneys general of the states, territories, and commonwealths. Fosters interstate cooperation on legal and law enforcement issues, conducts policy research and analysis, and facilitates communication between members and all levels of government.

National Assn. of Crime Victim Compensation Boards, *P.O. Box 16003, Alexandria, VA 22302; (703) 780-3200. Dan Eddy, Executive Director.*
General email, dan.eddy@nacvcb.org
Web, www.nacvcb.org

Provides state compensation agencies with training and technical assistance. Provides public information on victim compensation.

National Assn. of Criminal Defense Lawyers, *1660 L St. N.W., 12th Floor 20036; (202) 872-8600. Fax, (202) 872-8690. Norman L. Reimer, Executive Director.*
General email, assist@nacdl.org
Web, www.nacdl.org

Volunteer bar association of criminal defense attorneys and their local, state, and international chapters. Provides members with continuing education, a brief bank, an ethics hotline, and specialized assistance in such areas as forensic science. Offers free legal assistance to members threatened with sanctions. Interests include eliminating mandatory minimum sentencing, forensic lab reform, death penalty reform, protection of privacy rights, indigent defense reform, overcriminalization, and civil liberties. Monitors legislation and regulations.

National Center for Missing and Exploited Children, *Charles B. Wang International Children's Building, 699 Prince St., Alexandria, VA 22314-3175; (703) 224-2150. Fax, (703) 224-2122. John Ryan, Chief Executive Officer. Toll-free hotline, (800) 843-5678.*
Web, www.missingkids.com

Private organization that assists parents and citizens' groups in locating and safely returning missing children; offers technical assistance to law enforcement agencies; coordinates public and private missing children programs; maintains database that coordinates information on missing children.

National Center for Victims of Crime, *2000 M St. N.W., #480 20036; (202) 467-8700. Fax, (202) 467-8701. Mai Fernandez, Executive Director.*
Web, www.ncvc.org

Works with victims' groups and criminal justice agencies to protect the rights of crime victims through state and federal statutes and policies. Promotes greater responsiveness to crime victims through training and education; provides research and technical assistance in the development of victim-related legislation.

National Crime Prevention Council, *20001 Jefferson Davis Hwy., #901, Arlington, VA 22202; (202) 466-6272.*

Fax, (202) 296-1356. Ann M. Harkins, President. Publications office, (800) 627-2911.
Web, www.ncpc.org

Educates public on crime prevention through media campaigns, supporting materials, and training workshops; sponsors McGruff public service campaign; runs demonstration programs in schools.

National District Attorneys Assn. (NDAA), *99 Canal Center Plaza, #330, Alexandria, VA 22314; (703) 549-9222. Fax, (703) 836-3195. Scott Burns, Executive Director. ·*
Web, www.ndaa.org

Membership: prosecutors. Sponsors conferences and workshops on such topics as criminal justice, district attorneys, the courts, child abuse, national traffic laws, community prosecution, violence against women, gun violence, and others. Conducts research; provides information, training, and technical assistance to prosecutors; and analyzes policies related to improvements in criminal prosecution.

National Organization for Victim Assistance, *510 King St., #424, Alexandria, VA 22314; (703) 535-6682. Fax, (703) 535-5500. Will Marling, Executive Director. Toll-free and referral line, (800) 879-6682.*
Web, www.trynova.org

Membership: persons involved with victim and witness assistance programs, criminal justice professionals, researchers, crime victims, and others interested in victims' rights. Monitors legislation; provides victims and victim support programs with technical assistance, referrals, and program support; provides information on victims' rights.

Child Abuse, Domestic Violence, and Sexual Assault

►AGENCIES

Administration for Children and Families (ACF) *(Health and Human Services Dept.), Family and Youth Services, 1250 Maryland Ave. S.W., 8th Floor 20024; (202) 205-8347. Fax, (202) 205-9721. Debbie Powell, Associate Commissioner, Acting.*
Web, www.acf.hhs.gov/programs/fysb

Administers federal discretionary grant programs for projects serving runaway and homeless youth and for projects that deter youth involvement in gangs. Provides youth service agencies with training and technical assistance. Monitors federal policies, programs, and legislation. Supports research on youth development issues, including gangs, runaways, and homeless youth. Operates national clearinghouse on families and youth. Issues grants and monitors abstinence education programs.

Criminal Division *(Justice Dept.), Child Exploitation and Obscenity, 1400 New York Ave. N.W., 6th Floor 20005; (202) 514-5780. Fax, (202) 514-1793. Andrew Oosterbaan, Chief.*
Web, www.justice.gov/criminal/ceos

Enforces federal child exploitation, obscenity, and pornography laws; prosecutes cases involving violations of these laws, including international trafficking and kidnapping. Maintains collection of briefs, pleadings, and other material for use by federal, state, and local prosecutors. Assists the U.S. Attorney's Office with investigations, trials, and appeals pertaining to these offenses. Advises and trains law enforcement personnel, federal prosecutors, and Justice Dept. officials.

Defense Dept. (DoD), *Sexual Assault Prevention and Response,* 4800 Mark Center Dr., #07G21, Alexandria, VA 22350; (571) 372-2657. Fax, (703) 696-9437. Maj. Gen. Jeffrey J. Snow, Director.
General email, SAPRO@sapr.mil

Web, www.sapr.mil and www.myduty.mil

Serves as the single point of accountability for the Defense Dept.'s sexual assault policy. Responsible for improving prevention, enhancing reporting and response, and holding perpetrators appropriately accountable.

Justice Dept. (DOJ), *Violence Against Women,* 145 N St. N.E., #10W.121 20530; (202) 307-6026. Fax, (202) 305-2589. Beatrice A. Hanson, Director, Acting, (202) 307-0728. National Domestic Violence Hotline, (800) 799-SAFE.
General email, ovwdirector@usdoj.gov

Web, www.ovw.usdoj.gov

Seeks more effective policies and services to combat domestic violence, sexual assault, stalking, and other crimes against women. Helps administer grants to states to fund shelters, crisis centers, and hotlines, and to hire law enforcement officers, prosecutors, and counselors specializing in cases of sexual violence and other violent crimes against women.

Office of Justice Programs (OJP) *(Justice Dept.),* National Institute of Justice, 810 7th St. N.W., 7th Floor 20531; (202) 307-2942. Fax, (202) 307-6394. Greg Ridgeway, Director, Acting, (202) 307-5146. Press, (202) 307-0703.
Web, www.nij.gov

Conducts research on all aspects of criminal justice, including AIDS issues for law enforcement officials. Studies on rape and domestic violence available from the National Criminal Justice Reference Service: (800) 851-3420; in Maryland, (301) 519-5500; Web, www.ncjrs.gov.

American Bar Assn. (ABA), *Center on Children and the Law,* 1050 Connecticut Ave. N.W., #400 20036; (202) 662-1720. Fax, (202) 662-1755. Howard Davidson, Director. Toll-free, (800) 285-2221.
General email, ctrchildlaw@americanbar.org

Web, www.americanbar.org/child

Provides state and private child welfare organizations with training and technical assistance. Interests include child abuse and neglect, adoption, foster care, and medical neglect.

Rape, Abuse, and Incest National Network (RAINN), 1220 L St. N.W., #505 20005; (202) 544-1034. Fax, (202) 544-3556. Scott Berkowitz, President. National Sexual Assault Hotline, (800) 656-4673.
General email, info@rainn.org

Web, www.rainn.org

Links sexual assault victims to confidential local services through national sexual assault hotline. Operates the Defense Dept.'s sexual assault helpline. Provides extensive public outreach and education programs nationwide on sexual assault prevention, prosecution, and recovery. Promotes national policy efforts to improve services to victims.

Drug Control

▶AGENCIES

Criminal Division *(Justice Dept.),* Narcotic and Dangerous Drugs, 145 N St. N.E. 20530; (202) 514-0917. Fax, (202) 514-6112. Arthur G. Wyatt, Chief; Wayne Raabe, Principal Deputy Chief. Press, (202) 514-2007.
Web, www.justice.gov/criminal

Investigates and prosecutes participants in criminal syndicates involved in the large-scale importation, manufacture, shipment, or distribution of illegal narcotics and other dangerous drugs. Trains agents and prosecutors in the techniques of major drug litigation.

The DEA Museum and Visitors Center *(Justice Dept.),* 700 Army Navy Dr., Arlington, VA 22202; (202) 307-3463. Fax, (202) 307-8956. Sean Fearns, Director.
Web, www.deamuseum.org

Seeks to educate the public on the role and impact of federal drug law enforcement through state-of-the-art exhibits, displays, interactive stations, and outreach programs. Admission is free; groups of fifteen or more should call ahead for reservations.

Defense Dept. (DoD), *Counternarcotics and Global Threats,* 2500 Defense Pentagon, #5C653 20301-1510; (703) 697-7202. Fax, (703) 692-6947. Caryn Hollis, Deputy Assistant Secretary.
Web, http://policy.defense.gov/solic/cgnt

Advises the secretary on Defense Dept. policies and programs in support of federal counternarcotics operations and the implementation of the president's national drug control policy.

Drug Enforcement Administration (DEA) *(Justice Dept.),* 700 Army-Navy Dr., Arlington, VA 22202 (mailing address: 8701 Morrissette Dr., MS AES, Springfield, VA 22152); (202) 307-8000. Fax, (202) 307-4540. Michele Leonhart, Administrator. Phone (Command Center), (202) 307-8000. Press, (202) 307-7977. General information, (202) 307-1000.
Web, www.justice.gov/dea

Enforces federal laws and statutes relating to narcotics and other dangerous drugs, including addictive drugs, depressants, stimulants, and hallucinogens; manages the

National Narcotics Intelligence System in cooperation with federal, state, and local officials; investigates violations and regulates legal trade in narcotics and dangerous drugs. Provides school and community officials with drug abuse policy guidelines. Provides information on drugs and drug abuse.

Federal Bureau of Investigation (FBI) *(Justice Dept.)*, 935 Pennsylvania Ave. N.W., #7176 20535-0001; (202) 324-3000. James B. Comey, Director. Information, (202) 324-3000. Press, (202) 324-3691.
Web, www.fbi.gov

Shares responsibility with the Drug Enforcement Administration for investigating violations of federal criminal drug laws; investigates organized crime involvement with illegal narcotics trafficking.

Food and Drug Administration (FDA) *(Health and Human Services Dept.)*, Center for Drug Evaluation and Research, 10903 New Hampshire Ave., Silver Spring, MD 20993; (301) 796-5400. Fax, (301) 847-8752.
Dr. Janet Woodcock, Director. Press, (301) 796-4540.
Web, www.fda.gov/drugs

Makes recommendations to the Justice Dept.'s Drug Enforcement Administration on narcotics and dangerous drugs to be controlled.

Interior Dept. (DOI), *Law Enforcement and Security: Drug Enforcement Coordination*, 1849 C St. N.W., MS 3409 MIB 20240; (202) 208-3759. Fax, (202) 219-1185.
Howard Huey Jr., National Drug Enforcement Coordinator.
Web, www.doi.gov/pmb/oles/law-enforcement.cfm

Facilitates the coordination of drug enforcement activities for law enforcement branches of DOI bureaus, including National Park Service, Bureau of Land Management, Fish and Wildlife Service, and Bureau of Indian Affairs on public lands. Coordinates drug enforcement on DOI lands with federal agencies, including the ONDCP and DEA. Develops and implements DOI counter-drug policy and strategy.

Office of Justice Programs (OJP) *(Justice Dept.)*, Justice Assistance, 810 7th St. N.W., 4th Floor 20531; (202) 616-6500. Fax, (202) 514-7805. Denise E. O'Donnell, Director.
General email, askbja@usdoj.gov
Web, www.bja.gov

Awards grants and provides eligible state, local, and tribal governments with training and technical assistance to enforce laws relating to narcotics and other dangerous drugs.

Office of National Drug Control Policy (ONDCP) *(Executive Office of the President)*, 750 17th St. N.W. 20503; (202) 395-6700. Fax, (202) 395-6680.
R. Gil Kerlikowske, Director. Drug Policy Information Clearinghouse, (800) 666-3332.
Web, www.whitehouse.gov/ondcp

Establishes policies and oversees the implementation of a national drug control strategy with the goal of reducing illicit drug use, manufacturing, trafficking, and drug-related crimes, violence, and health consequences. Coordinates the international and domestic anti-drug efforts of executive branch agencies and ensures that such efforts sustain and complement state and local anti-drug activities. Advises the president and the National Security Council on drug control policy. (Clearinghouse address: P.O. Box 6000, Rockville, MD 20849-6000.)

U.S. Coast Guard (USCG) *(Homeland Security Dept.)*, Law Enforcement, CG-MLE, 2703 Martin Luther King Jr. Ave. S.E., MS 7516 20593-7516; (202) 372-2183.
Capt. Phil Welzant, Chief.
Web, www.uscg.mil/hq/cg5/cg531

Combats smuggling of narcotics and other drugs into the United States via the Atlantic and Pacific Oceans and the Gulf of Mexico. Works with U.S. Customs and Border Protection on drug law enforcement; interdicts illegal migrants; enforces domestic fisheries laws and international fisheries agreements.

U.S. Customs and Border Protection *(Homeland Security Dept.)*, Border Patrol, 1300 Pennsylvania Ave. N.W., #6.5E 20229; (202) 344-2050. Fax, (202) 344-3140.
Michael J. Fisher, Chief.
Web, www.cbp.gov/xp/cgov/border_security/border_patrol

Mobile uniformed law enforcement arm of the Homeland Security Dept. Primary mission is to detect and prevent the illegal trafficking of people and contraband across U.S. borders.

U.S. Customs and Border Protection *(Homeland Security Dept.)*, Field Operations, 1300 Pennsylvania Ave. N.W., #2.4A 20229; (202) 344-1620. Fax, (202) 344-2777.
Susan T. Mitchell, Assistant Commissioner, Acting. Press, (202) 344-1700. Hotline to report suspicious activity, (800) BE-ALERT; (800) 232-5378.
Web, www.cbp.gov/xp/cgov/about/organization/assist_comm_off/field_operations.xml

Interdicts and seizes contraband, including narcotics and other drugs, at the U.S. border.

U.S. Immigration and Customs Enforcement (ICE) *(Homeland Security Dept.)*, 500 12th St. S.W. 20536; (202) 732-3000. Fax, (202) 732-3080. Vacant, Director. Press, (202) 732-4242. Hotline to report suspicious activity, (866) 347-2423.
Web, www.ice.gov

Investigates narcotics smuggling, including money laundering, document and identity fraud, and immigration enforcement; interdicts flow of narcotics into the United States.

►NONGOVERNMENTAL

Drug Policy Alliance, *Washington Office*, 925 15th St. N.W., 2nd Floor 20005; (202) 683-2030. Fax, (202) 216-0803. Ethan Nadelmann, Director.
General email, dc@drugpolicy.org
Web, www.drugpolicy.org

Supports reform of current drug control policy. Advocates medical treatment to control drug abuse; opposes random drug testing. Sponsors the biennial International Conference on Drug Policy Reform. (Headquarters in New York.)

Marijuana Policy Project, *P.O. Box 77492, Capital Hill 20013; (202) 462-5747. Fax, (202) 232-0442. Robert D. Kampia, Executive Director.*
General email, info@mpp.org

Web, www.mpp.org

Promotes reform of marijuana policies and regulations. Opposes the prohibition of responsible growing and use of marijuana by adults. Interests include allowing doctors to recommend marijuana to seriously ill patients and eliminating criminal penalties for marijuana use.

National Assn. of State Alcohol and Drug Abuse Directors (NASADAD), *1025 Connecticut Ave. N.W., #605 20036-5430; (202) 293-0090. Fax, (202) 293-1250. Rob Morrison, Executive Director, ext. 106.*
General email, dcoffice@nasadad.org

Web, www.nasadad.org

Provides information on drug abuse treatment and prevention; contracts with federal and state agencies for design of programs to fight and prevent drug abuse.

National Organization for the Reform of Marijuana Laws (NORML), *1100 H St. N.W., #830 20005; (202) 483-5500. Fax, (202) 483-0057. Allen St. Pierre, Executive Director; Mitch Earlywine, Chair.*
General email, norml@norml.org

Web, www.norml.org

Works to reform federal, state, and local marijuana laws and policies. Educates the public and conducts litigation on behalf of marijuana consumers. Monitors legislation and regulations.

RAND Corporation, *Drug Policy Research Center, Washington Office, 1200 S. Hayes St., Arlington, VA 22202-5050; (703) 413-1100. Fax, (703) 413-8111. Beau Kilmer, Co-Director; Rosalie Liccardo Pacula, Co-Director.*
General email, dprc@rand.org

Web, www.rand.org/multi/dprc

Studies and analyzes the nation's drug problems and policies. Emphasis on empirical research and policy recommendations; interests include international and local policy, trafficking, interdiction, modeling and forecasting, prevention, and treatment. Provides policymakers with information. (Headquarters in Santa Monica, Calif.)

Gun Control

▶**AGENCIES**

Bureau of Alcohol, Tobacco, Firearms, and Explosives (ATF) *(Justice Dept.), 99 New York Ave. N.E., #5S144 20226; (202) 648-7777. Fax, (202) 648-9762. B. Todd Jones, Director. Hotline, (800) 283-8477.*

General email, ATFTips@atf.gov

Web, www.atf.gov

Enforces and administers laws to eliminate illegal possession and use of firearms. Investigates criminal violations and regulates legal trade, including imports and exports. To report illegal firearms activity, (888) 283-4867; firearms theft hotline, (800) 930-9275; or email, ATFTips@atf.gov.

▶**NONGOVERNMENTAL**

Brady Center to Prevent Gun Violence, *840 1st St. N.E., #400 20002; (202) 370-8100. Fax, (202) 370-8102. Dan Gross, President.*
Web, www.bradycenter.org

Educational, research, and legal action organization that seeks to allay gun violence, especially among children. Library open to the public.

Coalition to Stop Gun Violence, *1805 15th St. 20005; (202) 408-0061. Fax, (888) 860-2477. Michael K. Beard, President Emeritus; Joshua Horwitz, Executive Director.*
General email, csgv@csgv.org

Web, www.csgv.org

Membership: 48 national organizations and individual supporters. Works to reduce gun violence by fostering effective community and national action.

Educational Fund to Stop Gun Violence, *805 15th St., #700 20005; (202) 408-0061. Fax, (888) 860-2477. Michael K. Beard, President Emeritus; Joshua Horwitz, Executive Director.*
Web, General email, efsgv@efsgv.org and www.efsgv.org

Coalition of national organizations, including faith-based groups, child welfare advocates, public health professionals, and social justice organizations that seeks to reduce gun violence through research and education. Monitors legislation and regulations. (Affiliated with the Coalition to Stop Gun Violence.)

Gun Owners of America, *8001 Forbes Pl., #102, Springfield, VA 22151; (703) 321-8585. Fax, (703) 321-8408. Lawrence D. Pratt, Executive Director.*
Web, www.gunowners.org

Seeks to preserve the right to bear arms and to protect the rights of law-abiding gun owners. Administers foundation that provides gun owners with legal assistance in suits against the federal government. Monitors legislation, regulations, and international agreements.

National Rifle Assn. of America (NRA), *11250 Waples Mill Rd., Fairfax, VA 22030; (703) 267-1000. Fax, (703) 267-3976. Wayne LaPierre, Executive Vice President. Press, (703) 267-3820. Toll-free, (800) 672-3888.*
Web, www.nra.org

Membership: target shooters, hunters, gun collectors, gunsmiths, police officers, and others interested in firearms. Promotes shooting sports and recreational shooting and safety; studies and makes recommendations on firearms laws. Opposes gun control legislation. (Affiliated with the Institute for Legislative Action, the NRA's lobbying arm.)

Juvenile Justice

► **AGENCIES**

Education Dept., *Student Achievement and School Accountability*, 400 Maryland Ave. S.W. 20202-6132; (202) 260-0826. Fax, (202) 260-7764. Monique Chism, Director, (202) 260-1824.
Web, www2.ed.gov/oese

Funds state and local institutions responsible for providing neglected or delinquent children with free public education.

Office of Justice Programs (OJP) *(Justice Dept.), Juvenile Justice and Delinquency Prevention*, 810 7th St. N.W. 20531; (202) 307-5911. Fax, (202) 514-7805. Robert L. Listenbee Jr., Administrator, Acting. Clearinghouse, (800) 851-3420.
Web, www.ojgdp.gov

Administers federal programs related to prevention and treatment of juvenile delinquency; missing and exploited children; child victimization; and training, technical assistance, and research and evaluation in these areas. Coordinates with youth programs of the departments of Agriculture, Education, Housing and Urban Development, Interior, and Labor, and the Health and Human Services Administration, including the Center for Studies of Crime and Delinquency. Operates the Juvenile Justice Clearinghouse.

► **NONGOVERNMENTAL**

Coalition for Juvenile Justice, 1319 F St. N.W., #402 20004; (202) 467-0864. Fax, (202) 887-0738. Marie Williams, Executive Director, ext. 113. General email, info@juvjustice.org
Web, www.juvjustice.org

Nationwide coalition of governor-appointed advisory groups, practitioners, and volunteers. Seeks to improve juvenile justice and to prevent children and youth from becoming involved in the courts. Issues include the removal of youth from adult jails and lockups and attention to the disproportionate number of youth of color in the juvenile justice system.

Organized Crime

► **AGENCIES**

Criminal Division *(Justice Dept.), Narcotic and Dangerous Drugs*, 145 N St. N.E. 20530; (202) 514-0917. Fax, (202) 514-6112. Arthur G. Wyatt, Chief; Wayne Raabe, Principal Deputy Chief. Press, (202) 514-2007.
Web, www.justice.gov/criminal

Investigates and prosecutes participants in criminal syndicates involved in the large-scale importation, manufacture, shipment, or distribution of illegal narcotics and other dangerous drugs. Trains agents and prosecutors in the techniques of major drug litigation.

Criminal Division *(Justice Dept.), Organized Crime and Gang Section*, 1301 New York Ave. N.W., #700 20005; (202) 514-3594. Fax, (202) 514-3601. James Trusty, Chief. Press, (202) 353-4542.
General email, criminaldivision@us.doj.gov

Enforces federal criminal laws when subjects under investigation are alleged racketeers or part of syndicated criminal operations; coordinates efforts of federal, state, and local law enforcement agencies against organized crime, including emerging international groups. Cases include extortion, murder, bribery, fraud, money laundering, narcotics, labor racketeering, and violence that disrupts the criminal justice process.

Federal Bureau of Investigation (FBI) *(Justice Dept.), Organized Crime*, 935 Pennsylvania Ave. N.W., #3352 20535-0001; (202) 324-5625. Fax, (202) 324-0880. Stewart Roberts, Section Chief, Acting.
Web, www.fbi.gov/about-us/investigate/organizedcrime

Coordinates all FBI organized crime investigations. Determines budget, training, and resource needs for investigations, including those related to international organized crime.

Other Violations

► **AGENCIES**

Bureau of Alcohol, Tobacco, Firearms, and Explosives (ATF) *(Justice Dept.)*, 99 New York Ave. N.E., #5S144 20226; (202) 648-7777. Fax, (202) 648-9762. B. Todd Jones, Director. Hotline, (800) 283-8477.
General email, ATFTips@atf.gov
Web, www.atf.gov

Performs law enforcement functions relating to alcohol (beer, wine, distilled spirits), tobacco, arson, explosives, and destructive devices; investigates criminal violations and regulates legal trade.

Criminal Division *(Justice Dept.), Asset Forfeiture and Money Laundering*, 1400 New York Ave. N.W., #10100 20005; (202) 514-1263. Fax, (202) 514-5522. Jaikumar Ramaswamy, Chief.
Web, www.justice.gov/criminal/afmls

Investigates and prosecutes money laundering and criminal and civil forfeiture offenses involving illegal transfer of funds within the United States and from the United States to other countries. Oversees and coordinates legislative policy proposals. Advises U.S. attorneys' offices in multidistrict money laundering and criminal and civil forfeiture prosecutions. Represents Justice Dept. in international anti–money laundering and criminal and civil forfeiture initiatives.

Criminal Division *(Justice Dept.), Fraud, 1400 New York Ave. N.W., #4100 20530; (202) 514-7023. Fax, (202) 514-7021. Jeffrey Knox, Chief.*
Web, www.justice.gov/criminal/fraud

Administers federal enforcement activities related to fraud and white-collar crime. Focuses on frauds against government programs, transnational and multidistrict fraud, and cases involving the security and commodity exchanges, banking practices, and consumer victimization.

Federal Bureau of Investigation (FBI) *(Justice Dept.), Counterintelligence, 935 Pennsylvania Ave. N.W., #4012 20535; (202) 324-4614. Fax, (202) 324-0848. Robert Anderson Jr., Assistant Director.*
Web, www.fbi.gov/about-us/investigate/counterintelligence

Provides centralized management and oversight of all foreign counterintelligence investigations. Integrates law enforcement with intelligence efforts to investigate violations of federal laws against espionage, including economic espionage. Seeks to prevent foreign acquisition of weapons of mass destruction, penetration of the U.S. intelligence community and government agencies and contractors, and compromise of U.S. critical national assets.

Federal Bureau of Investigation (FBI) *(Justice Dept.), Cyber Division, 935 Pennsylvania Ave. N.W., #5835 20535; (202) 324-7770. Fax, (202) 324-2840. Joseph M. Demarest Jr., Assistant Director.*
Web, www.fbi.gov/about-us/investigate/cyber

Coordinates the investigations of federal violations in which the Internet or computer networks are exploited for terrorist, foreign government–sponsored intelligence, or criminal activities, including copyright violations, fraud, pornography, child exploitation, and malicious computer intrusions.

Federal Bureau of Investigation (FBI) *(Justice Dept.), Economic Crimes, 935 Pennsylvania Ave. N.W., #3925 20535; (202) 324-6352. Fax, (202) 324-9147. Francine Gross, Chief. Press, (202) 324-3691.*
Web, www.fbi.gov

Investigates, reduces, and prevents significant financial crimes against individuals, businesses, and industries by safeguarding the integrity and credibility of corporations, securities and commodities markets, investment vehicles, and the insurance industry. Reinforces compliance in the corporate world and promotes investor confidence in the United States' financial markets. Categorizes the frauds it investigates into four separate classifications: corporate fraud, securities and commodities fraud, insurance fraud (non–health care related), and mass marketing fraud.

National Security Division *(Justice Dept.), 950 Pennsylvania Ave. N.W., #7339 20530; (202) 514-1057. Fax, (202) 514-8714. John P. Carlin, Assistant Attorney General, Acting. Press, (202) 514-2007.*
General email, nsd.public@usdoj.gov
Web, www.justice.gov/nsd

Coordinates the Justice Dept.'s intelligence, counterterrorism, counterespionage, and other national security activities. Offers support for victims of overseas terrorism; provides legal assistance and advice, in coordination with the Office of Legal Counsel as appropriate, to all branches of government on matters of national security law and policy.

National Security Division *(Justice Dept.), Counterespionage, 950 Pennsylvania Ave. N.W. 20530; (202) 514-1057. Fax, (202) 514-8714. John P. Carlin, Assistant Attorney General, Acting.*
General email, nsd.public@usdoj.gov
Web, www.justice.gov/nsd

Supervises the investigation and prosecution of cases affecting national security, foreign relations, and the export of military and strategic commodities and technology. Has executive responsibility for authorizing the prosecution of cases under criminal statutes relating to espionage, sabotage, neutrality, and atomic energy. Provides legal advice to U.S. Attorney's offices and investigates agencies on federal statutes concerning national security. Coordinates criminal cases involving the application of the Classified Information Procedures Act. Administers and enforces the Foreign Agents Registration Act of 1938 and related disclosure statutes.

National Security Division *(Justice Dept.), Counterterrorism, 950 Pennsylvania Ave. N.W. 20530; (202) 514-1057. Fax, (202) 514-8714. Michael J. Mullaney, Chief.*
General email, nsd.public@usdoj.gov
Web, www.justice.gov/nsd

Responsible for the design, implementation, and support of law enforcement efforts, legislative initiatives, policies, and strategies related to combating international and domestic terrorism. Seeks to assist, through investigation and prosecution, in preventing and disrupting acts of terrorism anywhere in the world that impact significant U.S. interests and persons.

National Security Division *(Justice Dept.), Law and Policy, 950 Pennsylvania Ave. N.W. 20530; (202) 514-1057. Brad Wiegmann, Deputy Assistant Attorney General.*
General email, nsd.justice@usdoj.gov
Web, www.justice.gov/nsd

Develops and implements Justice Dept. policies with regard to intelligence, counterterrorism, and other national security matters. Provides legal assistance and advice on matters of national security law.

Securities and Exchange Commission (SEC), *Office of the Whistleblower, 100 F St. N.E., MS 5971 20549; (202) 551-4790. Fax, (703) 813-9322. Sean McKessy, Chief.*
Web, www.sec.gov/whistleblower

Receives information about possible securities law violations and provides information about the whistleblower program.

U.S. Customs and Border Protection *(Homeland Security Dept.), Field Operations, 1300 Pennsylvania Ave. N.W., #2.4A 20229; (202) 344-1620. Fax, (202) 344-2777. Susan T. Mitchell, Assistant Commissioner, Acting. Press,*

(202) 344-1700. Hotline to report suspicious activity, (800) BE-ALERT; (800) 232-5378.
Web, www.cbp.gov/xp/cgov/about/organization/assist_comm_off/field_operations.xml

Combats smuggling of funds; enforces statutes relating to the processing and regulation of people, carriers, cargo, and mail into and out of the United States. Investigates counterfeiting, child pornography, commercial fraud, and Internet crimes.

U.S. Postal Service (USPS), Inspection Service, 475 L'Enfant Plaza S.W., #3100 20260-2100; (202) 268-4264. Fax, (202) 268-7316. Guy Cottrell, Chief Postal Inspector. Fraud and abuse hotline, (877) 876-2455.
Web, http://postalinspectors.uspis.gov

Protects mail, postal funds, and property from violations of postal laws, such as mail fraud or distribution of obscene materials.

U.S. Secret Service (Homeland Security Dept.), 950 H St. N.W., #8000 20223; (202) 406-5700. Fax, (202) 406-5246. Julia A. Pierson, Director. Information, (202) 406-5708. Press, (202) 406-5708.
Web, www.secretservice.gov

Protects the president and vice president of the United States and their immediate family members, foreign heads of state and their spouses, and other individuals as designated by the president. Investigates threats against these protectees; protects the White House, vice president's residence, and foreign missions; and plans and implements security designs for national special security events. Investigates violations of laws relating to counterfeiting of U.S. currency; financial crimes, including access device fraud, financial institution fraud, identity theft, and computer fraud; and computer-based attacks on the financial, banking, and telecommunications infrastructure.

International Anticounterfeiting Coalition, 1730 M St. N.W., #1020 20036; (202) 223-6667. Fax, (202) 223-6668. Robert Barchiesi, President.
General email, meghang@iacc.org
Web, www.iacc.org

Works to combat counterfeiting and piracy by promoting laws, regulations, and directives to render theft of intellectual property unprofitable. Oversees anticounterfeiting programs that increase patent, trademark, copyright, service mark, trade dress, and trade secret protection. Provides information and training to law enforcement officials to help identify counterfeit and pirate products.

Stalking Resource Center, 2000 M St. N.W., #480 20036; (202) 467-8700. Fax, (202) 467-8701. Michelle Garcia, Director.
General email, src@ncvc.org
Web, www.ncvc.org/src

Acts as an information clearinghouse on stalking. Works to raise public awareness of the dangers of stalking. Encourages the development and implementation of multidisciplinary responses to stalking in local communities. Offers practitioner training and technical assistance. (Affiliated with the National Center for Victims of Crime.)

Sentencing and Corrections

► AGENCIES

Federal Bureau of Prisons (Justice Dept.), 320 1st St. N.W. 20534; (202) 307-3198. Fax, (202) 514-6620. Charles E. Samuels Jr., Director, (202) 307-3250. Press, (202) 514-6551. Inmate locator service, (202) 307-3126.
Web, www.bop.gov

Supervises operations of federal correctional institutions, community treatment facilities, and commitment and management of federal inmates; oversees contracts with local institutions for confinement and support of federal prisoners. Regional offices are responsible for administration; central office in Washington coordinates operations and issues standards and policy guidelines. Central office includes Federal Prison Industries, a government corporation providing prison-manufactured goods and services for sale to federal agencies, and the National Institute of Corrections, an information and technical assistance center on state and local corrections programs.

Federal Bureau of Prisons (Justice Dept.), Health Services, 320 1st St. N.W., #1454 20534; (202) 307-3055. Fax, (202) 307-0826. Dr. Newton E. Kendig, Assistant Director.
Web, www.bop.gov/about/agency/organization.jsp

Administers health care and treatment programs for prisoners in federal institutions.

Federal Bureau of Prisons (Justice Dept.), Industries, Education, and Vocational Training—UNICOR, 400 1st St. N.W. 20534; (202) 305-3500. Fax, (202) 305-7340. Mary M. Mitchell, Assistant Director, (202) 305-3501. Customer Service, (800) 827-3168.
Web, www.unicor.gov and www.bop.gov/about/agency/org_ievt.jsp

Administers program whereby inmates in federal prisons produce goods and services that are sold to the federal government.

Federal Bureau of Prisons (Justice Dept.), National Institute of Corrections, 320 1st St. N.W., #5007 20534; (202) 307-3106. Fax, (202) 307-3361. Robert M. Brown Jr., Director, Acting. Toll-free, (800) 995-6423.
Web, www.nicic.org and www.bop.gov/about/agency/org_nic.jsp

Offers technical assistance and training for upgrading state and local corrections systems through staff development, research, and evaluation of correctional operations and programs. Acts as a clearinghouse on correctional information.

Justice Dept. (DOJ), *Pardon Attorney, 1425 New York Ave. N.W., #11000 20530; (202) 616-6070. Fax, (202) 616-6069. Ronald L. Rodgers, Pardon Attorney.*
Web, www.justice.gov/pardon

Receives and reviews petitions to the president for all forms of executive clemency, including pardons and sentence reductions; initiates investigations and prepares the deputy attorney general's recommendations to the president on petitions.

Office of Justice Programs (OJP) *(Justice Dept.),* **Justice Assistance,** *810 7th St. N.W., 4th Floor 20531; (202) 616-6500. Fax, (202) 514-7805. Denise E. O'Donnell, Director.*
General email, askbja@usdoj.gov
Web, www.bja.gov

Provides states and communities with funds and technical assistance for corrections demonstration projects.

Office of Justice Programs (OJP) *(Justice Dept.),* **National Institute of Justice,** *810 7th St. N.W., 7th Floor 20531; (202) 307-2942. Fax, (202) 307-6394. Greg Ridgeway, Director, Acting, (202) 307-5146. Press, (202) 307-0703.*
Web, www.nij.gov

Conducts research on all aspects of criminal justice, including crime prevention, enforcement, adjudication, and corrections. Maintains the National Criminal Justice Reference Service, which provides information on corrections research, (800) 851-3420; in Maryland, (301) 519-5500; Web, www.ncjrs.gov.

U.S. Parole Commission *(Justice Dept.), 90 K St. N.E., 3rd Floor 20530; (202) 346-7000. Fax, (202) 357-1085. Isaac Fulwood Jr., Chair.*
General email, publicinquiries@usdoj.gov
Web, www.justice.gov/uspc

Makes release and revocation decisions for all federal prisoners serving sentences of more than one year for offenses committed before November 1, 1987, and for D.C. Code offenders serving parolable offenses or subject to a term of supervised release.

U.S. Sentencing Commission, *1 Columbus Circle N.E., #2-500 South Lobby 20002-8002; (202) 502-4500. Fax, (202) 502-4699. Patti B. Saris, Chair. Press, (202) 502-4597.*
Web, www.ussc.gov

Establishes sentencing guidelines and policy for all federal courts, including guidelines prescribing the appropriate form and severity of punishment for those convicted of federal crimes. Provides training and research on sentencing-related issues. Serves as an information resource. Library open to the public.

▶ JUDICIARY

Administrative Office of the U.S. Courts, *1 Columbus Circle N.E. 20544-0001; (202) 502-2600. Thomas F. Hogan, Director, (202) 502-3000.*
Web, www.uscourts.gov/adminoff.html

Supervises all administrative matters of the federal court system, except the Supreme Court; collects statistical data on business of the courts.

Administrative Office of the U.S. Courts, *Probation and Pretrial Services, 1 Columbus Circle N.E., #4-300 20544-0001; (202) 502-1600. Fax, (202) 502-1677. Matthew Rowland, Assistant Director.*

Determines the resource and program requirements of the federal and pretrial services system. Provides policy guidance, program evaluation services, management and technical assistance, and training to probation and pretrial services officers.

▶ NONGOVERNMENTAL

American Bar Assn. (ABA), *Criminal Justice, Washington Office, 1050 Connecticut Ave. N.W., #400 20036; (202) 662-1500. Fax, (202) 662-1501. Jane Messmer, Director, (202) 662-1511. Press, (202) 662-1090.*
General email, crimjustice@americanbar.org
Web, www.americanbar.org/crimjust

Studies and makes recommendations on all aspects of the correctional system, including overcrowding in prisons and the privatization of prisons and correctional institutions. (Headquarters in Chicago, Ill.)

American Civil Liberties Union Foundation, *National Prison Project, 915 15th St. N.W., 7th Floor 20005; (202) 393-4930. Fax, (202) 393-4931. David Fathi, Director.*
Web, www.aclu.org/prison

Litigates on behalf of prisoners through class action suits. Seeks to improve prison conditions and the penal system; serves as resource center for prisoners' rights.

American Correctional Assn. (ACA), *206 N. Washington St., #200, Alexandria, VA 22314; (703) 224-0000. Fax, (703) 224-0009. James A. Gondles Jr., Executive Director. Information, (800) 222-5646.*
Web, www.aca.org

Membership: corrections professionals in all aspects of corrections, including juvenile and adult facilities, community facilities, and academia; affiliates include state and regional corrections associations in the United States and Canada. Conducts and publishes research; provides state and local governments with technical assistance; certifies corrections professionals. Offers professional development courses and accreditation programs. Monitors legislation and regulation. Interests include criminal justice issues, correctional standards, and accreditation programs. Library open to the public.

Amnesty International USA, *Washington Office, 600 Pennsylvania Ave. S.E., 5th Floor 20003; (202) 544-0200. Fax, (202) 546-7142. Frank S. Jannuzi, Managing Director. Toll-free, (866) 273-4466.*
General email, aiusa@aiusa.org
Web, www.amnestyusa.org

International organization that opposes retention or reinstitution of the death penalty; advocates humane treatment of all prisoners. (U.S. headquarters in New York.)

Families Against Mandatory Minimums, *1100 H St. N.W., #1000 20005; (202) 822-6700. Fax, (202) 822-6704. Julie Stewart, President.*

General email, famm@famm.org

Web, www.famm.org

Seeks to repeal statutory mandatory minimum prison sentences. Works to increase public awareness of inequity of mandatory minimum sentences through grassroots efforts and media outreach programs.

NAACP Legal Defense and Educational Fund, Inc., Washington Office, *1444 Eye St. N.W., 10th Floor 20005; (202) 682-1300. Fax, (202) 682-1312. Leslie M. Proll, Director.*

Web, www.naacpldf.org

Civil rights litigation group that supports abolition of capital punishment; assists attorneys representing prisoners on death row; focuses public attention on race discrimination in the application of the death penalty. Not affiliated with the NAACP. (Headquarters in New York.)

National Center on Institutions and Alternatives, *7222 Ambassador Rd., Baltimore, MD 21244; (443) 780-1300. Fax, (410) 597-9656. Herbert J. Hoelter, Chair.*

General email, hhoelter@ncianet.org

Web, www.ncianet.org

Seeks to reduce incarceration as primary form of punishment imposed by criminal justice system; advocates use of extended community service, work-release, and halfway house programs; operates youth and adult residential programs; provides defense attorneys and courts with specific recommendations for sentencing and parole. (Affiliated with the Augustus Institute. Headquarters in Baltimore, Md.)

National Coalition to Abolish the Death Penalty, *1620 L St. N.W., #250 20036; (202) 331-4090. Diann Rust-Tierney, Executive Director.*

General email, info@ncadp.org

Web, www.ncadp.org

Membership: organizations and individuals opposed to the death penalty. Maintains collection of death penalty research. Provides training, resources, and conferences. Works with families of murder victims; tracks execution dates. Monitors legislation and regulations.

Prison Fellowship Ministries, *44180 Riverside Pkwy., Lansdowne, VA 20176; (703) 478-0100. Fax, (703) 554-8608. Jim Liske, President. Toll-free, (800) 206-9764.*

Web, www.pfm.org

Religious organization that ministers to prisoners and ex-prisoners, victims, and the families involved. Offers counseling, seminars, and support for readjustment after release; works to increase the fairness and effectiveness of the criminal justice system.

The Sentencing Project, *1705 DeSales St. N.W., 8th Floor 20036; (202) 628-0871. Fax, (202) 628-1091. Marc Mauer, Executive Director.*

General email, staff@sentencingproject.org

Web, www.sentencingproject.org

Engages in research and advocacy on criminal justice policy issues, including sentencing, incarceration, juvenile justice, racial disparity, alternatives to incarceration, and felony disenfranchisement. Publishes research.

LAW ENFORCEMENT

General

▶AGENCIES

Criminal Division *(Justice Dept.)*, **Computer Crime and Intellectual Property**, *1301 New York Ave. N.W., #600 20530; (202) 514-1026. Fax, (202) 514-6113. John Lynch, Chief.*

Web, www.justice.gov/criminal/cybercrime

Investigates and litigates criminal cases involving computers, intellectual property, and the Internet. Administers the Computer Crime Initiative, a program designed to combat electronic penetrations, data theft, and cyberattacks on critical information systems. Provides specialized technical and legal assistance to other Justice Dept. divisions; coordinates international efforts; formulates policies and proposes legislation on computer crime and intellectual property issues.

Federal Bureau of Investigation (FBI) *(Justice Dept.)*, **Law Enforcement Coordination**, *935 Pennsylvania Ave. N.W., #7110 20535; (202) 324-7126. Fax, (202) 324-0920. Ronald C. Ruecker, Assistant Director.*

General email, olec@leo.gov

Web, www.fbi.gov/hq/olec/olec.htm

Advises FBI executives on the use of state and local law enforcement and resources in criminal, cyber, and counterterrorism investigations. Coordinates the bureau's intelligence-sharing and technological efforts with state and local law enforcement. Serves as a liaison with the Homeland Security Dept. and other federal entities.

Federal Law Enforcement Training Center *(Homeland Security Dept.)*, **Washington Operations**, *9000 Commo Rd., #32, Chelterham, MD 20623-5000; (202) 233-0260. Fax, (202) 233-0258. Connie Patrick, Director, (912) 267-2070.*

General email, FLETC-WashingtonOffice@dhs.gov

Web, www.fletc.gov

Trains federal law enforcement personnel. Provides services to state, local, tribal, and international law enforcement agencies. (Headquarters in Glynco, Ga.)

Interior Dept. (OLESEM), *Law Enforcement and Security, 1849 C St. N.W., MS 3428-MIB 20240; (202) 208-6319. Fax, (202) 208-1185. Kimberly (Kim) Thorsen, Deputy Assistant Secretary; Harry Hambert, Director. Watch Office, (202) 208-1067.*

Web, www.doi.gov/pmb/oles/index.cfm

Provides leadership, policy guidance, and oversight to the Interior Dept.'s law enforcement, homeland security, and security programs. Works to protect critical infrastructure facilities, national icons, and monuments; develops law enforcement staffing models; establishes departmental training requirements and monitors their implementation; oversees the hiring of key law enforcement and security personnel; and reviews law enforcement and security budgets.

Internal Revenue Service (IRS) *(Treasury Dept.),* **Criminal Investigation,** *1111 Constitution Ave. N.W., #2501 20224; (202) 317-3200. Richard Weber, Chief. Tax fraud hotline, (800) 829-0433.*
Web, www.irs.gov

Investigates money laundering and violations of the tax law. Lends support in counterterrorism and narcotics investigations conducted in conjunction with other law enforcement agencies, both foreign and domestic.

National Institute of Standards and Technology (NIST) *(Commerce Dept.),* **Law Enforcement Standards,** *100 Bureau Dr., Bldg. 220, #B208, MS-8102, Gaithersburg, MD 20899-8102; (301) 975-2756. Fax, (301) 948-0978. Mark Stolorow, Director.*
General email, oles@nist.gov
Web, www.nist.gov/oles

Answers inquiries and makes referrals concerning the application of science and technology to the criminal justice community; maintains information on standards and current research; prepares reports and formulates standards for the National Institute of Justice, the Defense Dept., the Homeland Security Dept., and other local, state, and federal agencies

Office of Justice Programs (OJP) *(Justice Dept.),* **Justice Assistance,** *810 7th St. N.W., 4th Floor 20531; (202) 616-6500. Fax, (202) 514-7805. Denise E. O'Donnell, Director.*
General email, askbja@usdoj.gov
Web, www.bja.gov

Provides funds to eligible state and local governments and to nonprofit organizations for criminal justice programs, primarily those that combat drug trafficking and other drug-related crime.

Transportation Security Administration (TSA) *(Homeland Security Dept.),* **Office of Law Enforcement, Federal Air Marshal Service,** *TSA-18, 601 S. 12th St., Arlington, VA 20598-6018; (703) 487-3400. Fax, (703) 487-3405. Robert S. Bray, Director.*
Web, www.tsa.gov/about-tsa/office-law-enforcement

Protects air security in the United States. Promotes public confidence in the U.S. civil aviation system. Deploys marshals on flights around the world to detect and deter hostile acts targeting U.S. air carriers, airports, passengers, and crews.

Treasury Dept., *Financial Crimes Enforcement Network, P.O. Box 39, Vienna, VA 22183-0039; (703) 905-3591. Fax, (703) 905-3690. Jennifer Shasky Calvery, Director. Press, (703) 905-3770.*
General email, frc@fincen.gov
Web, www.fincen.gov

Administers an information network in support of federal, state, and local law enforcement agencies in the prevention and detection of terrorist financing, money-laundering operations, and other financial crimes. Administers the Bank Secrecy Act.

U.S. Marshals Service *(Justice Dept.),* *CS-3 #1200, 2604 Jefferson Davis Hwy., Alexandria, VA 22301; (202) 307-9001. Fax, (703) 603-7021. Stacia A. Hylton, Director. Public Affairs, (202) 307-9065. Information, (202) 307-9100.*
General email, us.marshals@usdoj.gov
Web, www.usmarshals.gov

Acts as the enforcement arm of the federal courts and U.S. attorney general. Responsibilities include court and witness security, prisoner custody and transportation, prisoner support, maintenance and disposal of seized and forfeited property, and special operations. Administers the Federal Witness Security Program. Apprehends fugitives, including those wanted by foreign nations and believed to be in the United States; oversees the return of fugitives apprehended abroad and wanted by U.S. law enforcement. Carries out the provisions of the Adam Walsh Child Protection and Safety Act.

►CONGRESS

For a listing of relevant congressional committees and subcommittees, please see pages 470–471 or the Appendix.

►NONGOVERNMENTAL

Feminist Majority Foundation, *National Center for Women and Policing, 1600 Wilson Blvd., #801, Arlington, VA 22209; (703) 522-2214. Fax, (703) 522-2219. Eleanor Smeal, Director.*
Web, http://womenandpolicing.com

Seeks to increase the number of women at all ranks of policing and law enforcement. Sponsors conferences and training programs.

International Assn. of Chiefs of Police, *44 Canal Center Plaza, #200, Alexandria, VA 22314; (703) 836-6767. Fax, (703) 836-4543. Vince Talucci, Executive Director. Toll-free, (800) 843-4227.*
General email, information@theiacp.org
Web, www.theiacp.org

Membership: foreign and U.S. police executives and administrators at federal, state, and local levels. Consults and conducts research on all aspects of police activity; conducts training programs and develops educational aids; conducts public education programs.

National Criminal Justice Assn., *720 7th St. N.W., 3rd Floor 20001; (202) 628-8550. Fax, (202) 448-1723. Cabell C. Cropper, Executive Director. Press, (202) 448-1713.*
General email, info@ncja.org
Web, www.ncja.org

Membership: criminal justice organizations and professionals. Provides members and interested individuals with technical assistance and information.

National Organization of Black Law Enforcement Executives, *4609 Pinecrest Office Park Dr., #F, Alexandria, VA 22312-1442; (703) 658-1529. Fax, (703) 658-9479. Joseph Akers, Executive Director, Interim.*
General email, noble@noblenatl.org

Web, www.noblenational.org

Membership: African American police chiefs and senior law enforcement executives. Works to increase community involvement in the criminal justice system and to enhance the role of African Americans in law enforcement. Provides urban police departments with assistance in police operations, community relations, and devising strategies to sensitize the criminal justice system to the problems of the African American community.

National Sheriffs' Assn., *1450 Duke St., Alexandria, VA 22314-3490; (703) 836-7827. Fax, (703) 838-5349. Aaron D. Kennard, Executive Director. Toll-free, (800) 424-7827.*
General email, nsamail@sheriffs.org

Web, www.sheriffs.org

Membership: sheriffs and other municipal, state, and federal law enforcement officers. Conducts research and training programs for members in law enforcement, court procedures, and corrections. Publishes *Sheriff* magazine and an e-newsletter.

Police Executive Research Forum, *1120 Connecticut Ave. N.W., #930 20036; (202) 466-7820. Fax, (202) 466-7826. Chuck Wexler, Executive Director.*
General email, perf@policeforum.org

Web, www.policeforum.org

Membership: law enforcement executives. Conducts research on law enforcement issues and methods of disseminating criminal justice and law enforcement information.

Police Foundation, *1201 Connecticut Ave. N.W., #200 20036-2636; (202) 833-1460. Fax, (202) 659-9149. James Bueermann, President.*
General email, jspecht@policefoundation.org

Web, www.policefoundation.org

Research and education foundation that conducts studies to improve police procedures; provides technical assistance for innovative law enforcement strategies, including community-oriented policing.

LEGAL PROFESSIONS AND RESOURCES

General

▶ **NONGOVERNMENTAL**

American Assn. of Visually Impaired Attorneys, *2200 Wilson Blvd., #650, Arlington, VA 22201; (202) 467-5081. Fax, (703) 465-5085. Chris Prentice, President. Toll-free, (800) 424-8666.*

General email, info@acb.org

Web, www.visuallyimpairedattorneys.org

Membership: visually impaired lawyers and law students. Provides members with legal information; acts as an information clearinghouse on legal materials available in Braille, in large print, on computer disc, and on tape. (Formerly the American Blind Lawyers Assn. Affiliated with American Council of the Blind.)

American Bar Assn. (ABA), *International Law, 1050 Connecticut Ave. N.W. 20036; (202) 662-1660. Fax, (202) 662-1669. Leanne Pfautz, Section Director, (202) 662-1661.*
General email, intlaw@americanbar.org

Web, www.americanbar.org/intlaw

Monitors and makes recommendations concerning developments in the practice of international law that affect ABA members and the public. Conducts programs, including International Legal Exchange, and produces publications covering the practice of international law.

American Health Lawyers Assn., *1620 Eye St. N.W., 6th Floor 20006-4010; (202) 833-1100. Fax, (202) 833-1105. Peter Leibold, Chief Executive Officer.*
General email, info@healthlawyers.org

Web, www.healthlawyers.org

Membership: corporate, institutional, and government lawyers interested in the health field; law students; and health professionals. Serves as an information clearinghouse on health law; sponsors health law educational programs and seminars.

American Inns of Court Foundation, *225 Reinekers Lane, Alexandria, VA 22314; (703) 684-3590. Fax, (703) 684-3607. BG Malinda E. Dunn, Executive Director. Toll-free, (800) 233-3590.*
General email, info@innsofcourt.org

Web, www.innsofcourt.org

Promotes professionalism, ethics, civility, and legal skills of judges, lawyers, academicians, and law students in order to improve the quality and efficiency of the justice system.

Asian American Justice Center (AAJC), *1140 Connecticut Ave. N.W., #1200 20036; (202) 296-2300. Fax, (202) 296-2318. Mee Moua, President.*
General email, information@advancingequality.org

Web, www.advancingequality.org

Works to advance the human and civil rights of Asian Americans and other minority groups through advocacy, public policy, public education, and litigation. Promotes civic engagement at the local, regional, and national levels. Interests include affirmative action, hate crimes, media diversity, census, broadband and telecommunications, youth advocacy, immigrant rights, language access, and voting rights.

Assn. of American Law Schools, *1614 20th St. N.W. 20009-1001; (202) 296-8851. Fax, (202) 296-8869. Judith Areem, Executive Director.*

General email, aals@aals.org

Web, www.aals.org

Membership: law schools, subject to approval. Membership criteria include high-quality academic programs, faculty, scholarship, and students; academic freedom; diversity of people and viewpoints; and emphasis on public service. Hosts meetings and workshops; publishes a directory of law teachers. Advocates on behalf of legal education; monitors legislation and judicial decisions.

Federal Circuit Bar Assn., *1620 Eye St. N.W., #801 20006; (202) 466-3923. Fax, (202) 833-1061. James E. Brookshire, Executive Director, (202) 558-2421.*

General email, brookshire1@fedcirbar.org

Web, www.fedcirbar.org

Represents practitioners before the Court of Appeals for the Federal Circuit. Fosters discussion between different groups within the legal community; sponsors regional seminars; publishes a scholarly journal.

Hispanic National Bar Assn., *1900 L St. N.W., #700 20036; (202) 223-4777. Fax, (202) 503-3403. Miguel Alexander Poze, President; Alba Cruz Hacker, Chief Operating Officer.*

General email, info@hnba.com

Web, www.hnba.com

Membership: Hispanic American attorneys, judges, professors, paralegals, and law students. Seeks to increase professional opportunities in law for Hispanic Americans and to increase Hispanic American representation in law schools. (Affiliated with National Hispanic Leadership Agenda and the American Bar Assn.)

International Law Institute, *1055 Thomas Jefferson St. N.W., #M-100 20007; (202) 247-6006. Fax, (202) 247-6010. Kim Phan, Executive Director.*

General email, info@ili.org

Web, www.ili.org

Performs scholarly research, offers training programs, and provides technical assistance in the areas of international law and economic development. Sponsors international conferences.

National Consumer Law Center, *Washington Office, 1001 Connecticut Ave. N.W., #510 20036-5528; (202) 452-6252. Fax, (202) 463-9462. Lauren Saunders, Managing Attorney.*

General email, consumerlaw@nclc.org

Web, www.consumerlaw.org and www.nclc.org

Provides lawyers funded by the Legal Services Corp. with research and assistance; provides lawyers with training in consumer and energy law. (Headquarters in Boston, Mass.)

National Court Reporters Assn., *8224 Old Courthouse Rd., Vienna, VA 22182-3808; (703) 556-6272. Fax, (703) 556-6291. Jim Cudahy, Executive Director. Toll-free, (800) 272-6272.*

General email, msic@ncrahq.org

Web, www.ncra.org

Membership organization that offers certification and continuing education for court reporting and captioning. Acts as a clearinghouse on technology and information for and about court reporters; certifies legal video specialists. Monitors legislation and regulations.

Street Law, Inc., *1010 Wayne Ave., #870, Silver Spring, MD 20910; (301) 589-1130. Fax, (301) 589-1131. Lee Arbetman, Executive Director.*

Web, www.streetlaw.org

International educational organization that promotes public understanding of law, the legal system, democracy, and human rights. Provides curriculum materials, training, and technical assistance to secondary school systems, law schools, departments of corrections, juvenile justice systems, bar associations, community groups, and state, local, and foreign governments.

Data and Research

▶**AGENCIES**

Justice Dept. (DOJ), *Community Oriented Policing Services (COPS),* *145 N St. N.E. 20530 (mailing address: for overnight delivery, use zip code 20002); (202) 307-1480. Fax, (202) 616-2914. Ronald L. Davis, Director, (202) 616-2888. Phone for COPS program, (202) 307-1480. Congressional Relations, (202) 616-2888. Outside Washington, (202) 514-9079.*

General email, askCopsRC@usdoj.gov

Web, www.cops.usdoj.gov

Awards grants to tribal, state, and local law enforcement agencies to hire and train community policing professionals, acquire and deploy crime-fighting technologies, and develop and test policing strategies. Provides publications and other educational materials on a wide range of law enforcement concerns and community policing topics. Community policing emphasizes crime prevention through partnerships between law enforcement and citizen.

Office of Justice Programs (OJP) *(Justice Dept.), Bureau of Justice Statistics,* *810 7th St. N.W., 2nd Floor 20531; (202) 307-0765. Fax, (202) 307-5846. William J. Sabol, Director, Acting.*

General email, askbjs@usdoj.gov

Web, www.ojp.usdoj.gov/bjs

Collects, evaluates, publishes, and provides statistics on criminal justice. Data available from the National Criminal Justice Reference Service: P.O. Box 6000, Rockville, MD 20849-6000; toll-free, (800) 851-3420; international callers, (301) 519-5500; TTY, (877) 712-9279; and from the National Archive of Criminal Justice Data in Ann Arbor, MI, (800) 999-0960.

Office of Justice Programs (OJP) *(Justice Dept.), National Institute of Justice,* *810 7th St. N.W., 7th Floor 20531; (202) 307-2942. Fax, (202) 307-6394. Greg Ridgeway, Director, Acting, (202) 307-5146. Press, (202) 307-0703.*

Web, www.nij.gov

Conducts research on all aspects of criminal justice, including crime prevention, enforcement, adjudication, and corrections; evaluates programs; develops model programs using new techniques. Serves as an affiliated institute of the United Nations Crime Prevention and Criminal Justice Programme (UNCPCJ); studies transnational issues. Maintains the National Criminal Justice Reference Service, which provides information on criminal justice, including activities of the Office of National Drug Control Policy and law enforcement in Latin America: (800) 851-3420 or (301) 519-5500; Web, www.ncjrs.gov.

►**CONGRESS**

For a listing of relevant congressional committees and subcommittees, please see pages 470–471 or the Appendix.

Library of Congress, *Law Library, Madison Bldg.,* *101 Independence Ave. S.E., #LM240 20540; (202) 707-5065. Fax, (202) 707-1820. David S. Mao, Law Librarian. Reading room, (202) 707-5080. Reference information, (202) 707-5079.* *Web, www.loc.gov/law*

Maintains collections of foreign, international, and comparative law texts organized jurisdictionally by country; covers all legal systems–common, civil, Roman, canon, religious, and ancient and medieval law. Services include a public reading room; a microtext facility, with readers and printers for microfilm and microfiche; and foreign law/rare book reading areas. Staff of legal specialists is competent in approximately forty languages; does not provide advice on legal matters.

►**JUDICIARY**

Administrative Office of the U.S. Courts, *1 Columbus Circle N.E. 20544-0001; (202) 502-2600. Thomas F. Hogan, Director, (202) 502-3000.* *Web, www.uscourts.gov/adminoff.html*

Supervises all administrative matters of the federal court system, except the Supreme Court; prepares statistical data and reports on the business of the courts, including reports on juror utilization; caseloads of federal, public, and community defenders; and types of cases adjudicated.

Administrative Office of the U.S. Courts, *Statistics,* *1 Columbus Circle N.E., #2-250 20544; (202) 502-1440. Fax, (202) 502-1411. Catherine Whitaker, Chief. Press, (202) 502-2600.* *Web, www.uscourts.gov*

Compiles information and statistics from civil, criminal, appeals, and bankruptcy cases. Publishes statistical reports on court management; juror utilization; federal offenders; equal access to justice; the Financial Privacy Act; caseloads of federal, public, and community defenders; and types of cases adjudicated.

Supreme Court of the United States, *Library, 1 1st St. N.E. 20543; (202) 479-3037. Fax, (202) 479-3477. Linda Maslow, Librarian, (202) 479-3000.* *Web, www.supremecourtus.gov*

Maintains collection of Supreme Court documents dating from the mid-1800s. Records, briefs, and depository documents available for public use.

►**NONGOVERNMENTAL**

Justice Research and Statistics Assn., *720 7th St. N.W., 3rd Floor 20001; (202) 842-9330. Fax, (202) 448-1723. Joan C. Weiss, Executive Director.* *General email, cjinfo@jrsa.org* *Web, www.jrsa.info.org*

Provides information on the collection, analysis, dissemination, and use of data concerning crime and criminal justice at the state level; serves as liaison between the Justice Dept. Bureau of Justice Statistics and the states; develops standards for states on the collection, analysis, and use of statistics. Offers courses in criminal justice and in research and evaluation methodologies in conjunction with its annual conference.

PUBLIC INTEREST LAW

General

►**AGENCIES**

Justice Dept. (DOJ), *Access to Justice Initiative,* *950 Pennsylvania Ave. N.W., #3340 20530; (202) 514-5312. Fax, (202) 514-5326. Deborah Leff, Senior Counselor, Acting.* *Web, www.justice.gov/atj*

Works to improve the availability and quality of legal defense for vulnerable populations, including immigrants, juveniles, the homeless, disabled veterans, and victims of domestic and sexual violence. Identifies areas of need and effective programs, and works collaboratively with local, state, tribal, and federal participants to implement solutions. Priorities include expanding community partnerships, promoting less court-intensive solutions, and increasing resources for defender programs.

Legal Services Corp., *3333 K St. N.W., 3rd Floor 20007-3522; (202) 295-1500. Fax, (202) 337-6797. James J. Sandman, President, (202) 295-1575. Public reading room, (202) 295-1502.* *General email, campbellp@lsc.gov* *Web, www.lsc.gov*

Independent federal corporation established by Congress. Awards grants to local agencies that provide the poor with legal services. Library open to the public by appointment only.

►**CONGRESS**

For a listing of relevant congressional committees and subcommittees, please see pages 470–471 or the Appendix.

▶NONGOVERNMENTAL

Alliance for Justice, *11 Dupont Circle N.W., 2nd Floor 20036-1213; (202) 822-6070. Fax, (202) 822-6068. Nan Aron, President.*
General email, alliance@afj.org

Web, www.afj.org

Membership: public interest lawyers and advocacy, environmental, civil rights, and consumer organizations. Promotes reform of the legal system to ensure access to the courts; monitors selection of federal judges; works to preserve the rights of nonprofit organizations to advocate on behalf of their constituents.

American Bar Assn. (ABA), *Commission on Disability Rights, 1050 Connecticut Ave. N.W., #400 20036; (202) 662-1570. Fax, (202) 442-3439. Amy Allbright, Director.*
General email, cdr@americanbar.org

Web, www.americanbar.org/disability

Promotes the rule of law for persons with mental, physical, and sensory disabilities and their full and equal participation in the legal profession. Offers online resources, publications, and continuing education opportunities on disability law topics and engages in national initiatives to remove barriers to the education, employment, and advancement of lawyers with disabilities.

Bazelon Center for Mental Health Law, *1101 15th St. N.W., #1212 20005; (202) 467-5730. Fax, (202) 223-0409. Robert Bernstein, President.*
General email, communications@bazelon.org

Web, www.bazelon.org

Public interest law firm. Works to establish and advance the legal rights of children and adults with mental disabilities and ensure their equal access to services and resources needed for full participation in community life. Provides technical support to lawyers and other advocates. Conducts test case litigation to defend rights of persons with mental disabilities. Conducts policy analysis, builds coalitions, issues advocacy alerts, publishes handbooks, and maintains advocacy resources online. Monitors legislation and regulations.

Center for Law and Education, *Washington Office, 1875 Connecticut Ave. N.W., #510 20009-5728; (202) 986-3000. Fax, (202) 986-6648. Paul Weckstein, Co-Director, (202) 986-3000, ext. 101; Kathleen Boundy, Co-Director (located in Boston).*
General email, cle@cleweb.org

Web, www.cleweb.org

Assists local legal services programs in matters concerning education, civil rights, and provision of legal services to low-income persons; litigates some cases for low-income individuals. (Headquarters in Boston, Mass.)

Center for Law and Social Policy, *1200 18th St. N.W., #200 20036; (202) 906-8000. Fax, (202) 842-2885. Olivia Golden, Executive Director.*
General email, info@clasp.org

Web, www.clasp.org

Public policy organization with expertise in national, state, and local policy affecting low-income Americans. Seeks to improve the economic security and educational and workforce prospects of low-income children, youth, adults, and families.

Center for Study of Responsive Law, *1530 P St. N.W. 20005 (mailing address: P.O. Box 19367, Washington, DC 20036); (202) 387-8030. Fax, (202) 234-5176. John Richard, Administrator.*
General email, info@csrl.org

Web, www.csrl.org

Consumer interest clearinghouse that conducts research and holds conferences on public interest law. Interests include white-collar crime, the environment, occupational health and safety, the postal system, banking deregulation, insurance, freedom of information policy, and broadcasting.

Institute for Justice, *901 N. Glebe Rd., #900, Arlington, VA 22203; (703) 682-9320. Fax, (703) 682-9321. William (Chip) Mellor, President.*
General email, general@ij.org

Web, www.ij.org

Sponsors seminars to train law students, grassroots activists, and practicing lawyers in applying advocacy strategies in public interest litigation. Seeks to protect individuals from arbitrary government interference in free speech, private property rights, parental school choice, and economic liberty. Litigates cases.

Institute for Public Representation, *600 New Jersey Ave. N.W., #312 20001; (202) 662-9535. Fax, (202) 662-9634. Hope Babcock, Co-Director; Angela Campbell, Co-Director; Brian Wolfman, Co-Director.*
General email, gulcipr@law.georgetown.edu

Web, www.law.georgetown.edu/academics/academic-programs/clinical-programs/our-clinics/ipr/index.cfm and Blog, instituteforpublicrepresentation.org

Public interest law firm funded by Georgetown University Law Center that studies federal administrative law and federal court litigation. Interests include communications law, environmental protection, and disability rights.

Lawyers' Committee for Civil Rights Under Law, *1401 New York Ave. N.W., #400 20005-2124; (202) 662-8600. Fax, (202) 783-0857. Barbara R. Arnwine, Executive Director. Toll-free, (888) 299-5227.*
Web, www.lawyerscommittee.org

Provides minority groups and the poor with legal assistance in such areas as voting rights, employment discrimination, education, environment, and equal access to government services and benefits.

Migrant Legal Action Program, *1001 Connecticut Ave. N.W., #915 20036-5524; (202) 775-7780. Fax, (202) 775-7784. Roger C. Rosenthal, Executive Director.*
General email, mlap@mlap.org

Web, www.mlap.org

Provides both direct representation to farm workers and technical assistance and support to health, education, and legal services programs for migrants. Monitors legislation and regulations.

National Assn. of Consumer Bankruptcy Attorneys, *2300 M St. N.W., #800 20037; (216) 491-6770. Fax, (866) 571-3560. Maureen Thompson, Legislative Director; Vacant, Executive Director, (216) 491-6770.*
General email, admin@nacba.org

Web, www.nacba.org

Advocates on behalf of consumer debtors and their attorneys. Files amicus briefs on behalf of parties in the U.S. courts of appeal and Supreme Court, and provides educational programs and workshops for attorneys. Monitors legislation and regulations.

National Consumer Law Center, *Washington Office, 1001 Connecticut Ave. N.W., #510 20036-5528; (202) 452-6252. Fax, (202) 463-9462. Lauren Saunders, Managing Attorney.*
General email, consumerlaw@nclc.org

Web, www.consumerlaw.org and www.nclc.org

Provides lawyers funded by the Legal Services Corp. with research and assistance; researches problems of low-income consumers and develops alternative solutions. (Headquarters in Boston, Mass.)

National Health Law Program, *Washington Office, 1444 Eye St. N.W., #1105 20005; (202) 289-7661. Fax, (202) 289-7724. Emily Spitzer, Executive Director.*
General email, nhelpdc@healthlaw.org

Web, www.healthlaw.org

Organization of lawyers representing the economically disadvantaged, minorities, and older adults on issues concerning federal, state, and local health care programs. Offers technical assistance, workshops, seminars, and training for health law specialists. (Headquarters in Los Angeles, Calif.)

National Legal Aid and Defender Assn., *1140 Connecticut Ave. N.W., #900 20036; (202) 452-0620. Fax, (202) 872-1031. Jo-Ann Wallace, President.*
General email, info@nlada.org

Web, www.nlada.org

Membership: national organizations and individuals providing indigent clients, including prisoners, with legal aid and defender services. Serves as a clearinghouse for member organizations; provides training and support services.

Public Citizen Litigation Group, *1600 20th St. N.W. 20009; (202) 588-1000. Allison Zieve, Director of Litigation. Press, (202) 588-7741.*
General email, litigation@citizen.org

Web, www.citizen.org/litigation

Conducts litigation for Public Citizen, a consumer advocacy group, in the areas of consumer rights, access to courts, health and safety, government and corporate accountability, and separation of powers; represents other individuals and nonprofit groups with similar interests.

Public Justice Foundation, *1825 K St. N.W., #200 20006; (202) 797-8600. Fax, (202) 232-7203. Arthur H. Bryant, Executive Director.*
General email, publicjustice@publicjustice.net

Web, www.publicjustice.net

Membership: consumer activists, trial lawyers, and public interest lawyers. Litigates to influence corporate and government decisions about products or activities adversely affecting health or safety. Interests include toxic torts, environmental protection, civil rights and civil liberties, workers' safety, consumer protection, and the preservation of the civil justice system. (Formerly Trial Lawyers for Public Justice.)

14

Military Personnel and Veterans

GENERAL POLICY AND ANALYSIS

Basic Resources

▶AGENCIES

Air Force Dept. *(Defense Dept.), Force Management,* 1400 W. Perimeter Rd., #4710, Joint Base Andrews 20762; (240) 612-4040. Fax, (703) 604-1657. Col. Jerry Diaz, Chief. Web, www.afpc.af.mil

Military office that oversees Air Force retention policies for officers and enlisted personnel, and provides analytical support for personnel issues.

Air Force Dept. *(Defense Dept.), Manpower Personnel and Services,* 1040 Air Force Pentagon, #4E168 20330-1040; (703) 697-6088. Lt. Gen. Samuel D. Cox, Deputy Chief of Staff. Web, www.afpc.af.mil

Military office that coordinates military and civilian personnel policies of the Air Force Dept.

Army Dept. *(Defense Dept.), G-1,* 300 Army Pentagon, #2E446 20310-0300; (703) 697-8060. Fax, (703) 695-1377. Lt. Gen. Howard B. Bromberg, Deputy Chief of Staff, G-1. Web, www.army.mil

Military office that coordinates military and civilian personnel policies of the Army Dept.

Army Dept. *(Defense Dept.), Human Resources Policy Directorate,* 2530 Crystal Dr., #6000, Arlington, VA 22202; (703) 571-7243. Fax, (703) 601-0057. Brig. Gen. Henry L. Huntley, Director. Web, http://myarmybenefits.us.army.mil

Military office that coordinates military personnel policies of the Army Dept. Focus includes health promotion, equal opportunity, drug and alcohol abuse, retirement, suicide prevention, housing, uniform policy, and women in the army.

Army Dept. *(Defense Dept.), Manpower and Reserve Affairs,* 111 Army Pentagon, #2E460 20310-0111; (703) 697-9253. Fax, (703) 692-9000. Thomas R. Lamont, Assistant Secretary. Web, www.asamra.army.mil

Civilian office that reviews policies and programs for Army personnel and reserves; makes recommendations to the secretary of the Army. Oversees training, military preparedness, and mobilization for all civilians and active and reserve members of the Army.

Defense Dept. (DoD), *Community and Public Outreach,* 1400 Defense Pentagon, 2E984 20301-1400; (703) 693-2337. Fax, (703) 697-2577. Rene C. Bardorf, Deputy Assistant Secretary, (703) 693-2337. Toll-free (Military OneSource), (800) 342-9647. Public Affairs, (703) 571-3343. Web, www.ourmilitary.mil; www.defense.gov

Administers Pentagon tours; hosts Joint Civilian Orientation Conference (JCOC), enabling senior American business, education, and community leaders to engage with military personnel; replies to inquiries from the general public; serves as primary liaison to national veterans and military organizations.

Defense Dept. (DoD), *Military Personnel Policy,* 4000 Defense Pentagon, #5A678 20301-4000; (703) 571-0116. Fax, (703) 571-0120. Virginia S. Penrod, Deputy Assistant Secretary. Web, www.defenselink.mil/prhome/mpp.html

Military office that coordinates military personnel policies of the Defense Dept. and reviews military personnel policies of the individual services.

Defense Dept. (DoD), *Personnel and Readiness,* 4000 Defense Pentagon, #3E986 20301-4000; (703) 695-5254. Fax, (703) 571-5363. Jessica L. Wright, Under Secretary, Acting. Web, www.defense.gov

Coordinates civilian and military personnel policies of the Defense Dept. and reviews personnel policies of the individual services. Handles equal opportunity policies; serves as focal point for all readiness issues. Administers Military OneSource, a 24/7 toll-free information and referral telephone service for matters relating to education, financial aid, relocation, housing, child care, counseling, and other employee concerns. Military OneSource is available worldwide to military personnel and their families. Toll-free, (800) 342-9647; international, (800) 3429-6477; international collect, (484) 530-5908; www.militaryonesource.mil.

Defense Dept. (DoD), *Public Affairs,* The Pentagon, #2D961 20301-1400; (703) 571-3343. Fax, (703) 697-3501. Bryan G. Whitman, Assistant Secretary, Acting, (703) 697-9312. Press, (703) 697-5131. Web, www.defense.gov/news

Responds to public inquiries concering Defense Dept. mission, activities, policies, and personnel.

Navy Dept. *(Defense Dept.), Manpower and Reserve Affairs,* 1000 Navy Pentagon, #4E590 20350-1000; (703) 695-4333. Fax, (703) 614-4103. Juan M. Garcia III, Assistant Secretary. Web, www.navy.mil/local/oasnmra

Civilian office that reviews policies of the U.S. Naval Academy, Navy and Marine Corps service schools, and officer candidates' training and Reserve Officer Training Corps (ROTC) programs. Advises the secretary of the Navy on education matters, including voluntary education programs.

Navy Dept. *(Defense Dept.), Military Personnel, Plans, and Policy,* 701 S. Courthouse Rd., Arlington, VA 22204; (703) 604-6155. Fax, (703) 604-5943. Rear Adm. Frederick J. (Fritz) Roegge, Director. Web, www.navy.mil

Military office that coordinates naval personnel policies, including promotions, professional development, and compensation, for officers and enlisted personnel.

MILITARY PERSONNEL AND VETERANS RESOURCES IN CONGRESS

For a complete listing of Congress committees, including their full contact information, leadership, membership, and jurisdictions, please refer to the Appendix on pages 724–842.

HOUSE:

House Appropriations Committee, (202) 225-2771.
Web, appropriations.house.gov or
   democrats.appropriations.house.gov
   Subcommittee on Defense, (202) 225-2847.
   Subcommittee on Military Construction,
      Veterans Affairs, and Related Agencies,
      (202) 225-3047.
House Armed Services Committee, (202) 225-4151.
Web, armedservices.house.gov or
   democrats.armedservices.house.gov
   Subcommittee on Intelligence, Emerging
      Threats, and Capabilities,
      (202) 226-2843.
   Subcommittee on Military Personnel,
      (202) 225-7560.
   Subcommittee on Oversight and Investigations,
      (202) 226-5048.
   Subcommittee on Readiness, (202) 226-8979.
   Subcommittee on Seapower and Protection
      Forces, (202) 226-2211.
   Subcommittee on Strategic Forces,
      (202) 225-1967.
   Subcommittee on Tactical Air and Land Forces,
      (202) 225-4440.
House Financial Services Committee,
   (202) 225-7502.
Web, financialservices.house.gov or
   democrats.financialservices.house.gov
   Subcommittee on Financial Institutions and
      Consumer Credit, (202) 225-7502.
   Subcommittee on Housing and Insurance,
      (202) 225-7502.
   Subcommittee on Oversight and Investigations,
      (202) 225-7502.
House Foreign Affairs Committee,
   (202) 225-5021.
Web, foreignaffairs.house.gov or
   democrats.foreignaffairs.house.gov
House Oversight and Government Reform
   Committee, (202) 225-5074.
Web, oversight.house.gov or
   democrats.oversight.house.gov
   Subcommittee on National Security,
      (202) 225-5074.
House Transportation and Infrastructure
   Committee, (202) 225-9446.

Web, transportation.house.gov or
   democrats.transportation.house.gov
   Subcommittee on Coast Guard and Maritime
      Transportation, (202) 226-3552.
House Veterans' Affairs Committee,
   (202) 225-3527.
Web, veterans.house.gov or
   democrats.veterans.house.gov
   Subcommittee on Disability Assistance and
      Memorial Affairs, (202) 225-9164.
   Subcommittee on Economic Opportunity,
      (202) 226-5491.
   Subcommittee on Health, (202) 225-9154.
   Subcommittee on Oversight and Investigations,
      (202) 225-3569.

SENATE:

Senate Appropriations Committee, (202) 224-7363.
Web, appropriations.senate.gov
   Subcommittee on Defense, (202) 224-6688.
   Subcommittee on Military Construction,
      Veterans Affairs, and Related Agencies,
      (202) 224-8224.
Senate Armed Services Committee, (202) 224-3871.
Web, armed-services.senate.gov
   Subcommittee on Airland, (202) 224-3871.
   Subcommittee on Emerging Threats and
      Capabilities, (202) 224-3871.
   Subcommittee on Personnel, (202) 224-3871.
   Subcommittee on Readiness and Management
      Support, (202) 224-3871.
   Subcommittee on Seapower, (202) 224-3871.
   Subcommittee on Strategic Forces,
      (202) 224-3871.
Senate Banking, Housing, and Urban Affairs
   Committee, (202) 224-7391.
Web, banking.senate.gov
   Subcommittee on Financial Institutions and
      Consumer Protection, (202) 224-2315.
Senate Foreign Relations Committee,
   (202) 224-4651.
Web, foreign.senate.gov
Senate Homeland Security and Governmental Affairs
   Committee, (202) 224-2627.
Web, hsgac.senate.gov
Senate Veterans' Affairs Committee, (202) 224-9126.
Web, veterans.senate.gov

Navy Dept. *(Defense Dept.), Naval Personnel, 701 S. Courthouse Rd., Arlington, VA 22204; (703) 604-2863. Vice Adm. William F. Moran, Chief.*
Web, www.navy.mil/cnp/index.asp

Responsible for planning and programming of manpower and personnel resources, budgeting for Navy personnel, developing systems to manage total force manpower and personnel resources, and assignment of Navy personnel. (Office based in Millington, Tenn.)

Selective Service System, *1515 Wilson Blvd., Arlington, VA 22209-2425; (703) 605-4100. Fax, (703) 605-4106. Lawrence G. Romo, Director. Locator, (703) 605-4000. Toll-free, (888) 655-1825. TTY Espanol, (800) 845-6136.*
General email, information@sss.gov
Web, www.sss.gov

Supplies the armed forces with manpower when authorized; registers male citizens of the United States ages eighteen to twenty-five. In an emergency, would institute a draft and would provide alternative service assignments to men classified as conscientious objectors.

U.S. Coast Guard (USCG) *(Homeland Security Dept.), Human Resources Directorate, CG-1, MS 7907 2703 Martin Luther King Jr. Ave. S.E. 20593; (202) 475-5000. Rear Adm. Daniel A. Neptune, Assistant Commandant.*
Web, www.uscg.mil/hr

Responsible for hiring, recruiting, and training all military and nonmilitary Coast Guard personnel. Administers employee benefits.

▶CONGRESS

For a listing of relevant congressional committees and subcommittees, please see page 516 or the Appendix.

▶NONGOVERNMENTAL

Air Force Assn., *1501 Lee Hwy., Arlington, VA 22209-1198; (703) 247-5800. Fax, (703) 247-5853. Gen. Craig R. Mckinley (USAF, Ret.), President. Toll-free, (800) 727-3337. Press, (703) 247-5850.*
General email, membership@afa.org
Web, www.afa.org

Membership: civilians and active duty, reserve, retired, and cadet personnel of the Air Force. Informs members and the public of developments in the aerospace field. Monitors legislation and Defense Dept. policies. Library on aviation history open to the public by appointment.

Air Force Sergeants Assn., *5211 Auth Rd., Suitland, MD 20746; (301) 899-3500. Fax, (301) 899-8136. John R. "Doc" McCauslin, Executive Director. Toll-free, (800) 638-0594.*
General email, staff@hqafsa.org
Web, www.hqafsa.org

Membership: active duty, reserve, National Guard, and retired enlisted Air Force personnel. Monitors and advocates legislation and policies that promote quality of life benefits for its members.

Assn. of the United States Army, *2425 Wilson Blvd., Arlington, VA 22201; (703) 841-4300. Fax, (703) 525-9039. Gordon R. Sullivan, President. Information, (800) 336-4570.*
Web, www.ausa.org

Membership: civilians and active duty and retired members of the armed forces. Conducts symposia on defense issues and researches topics that affect the military.

Chaplain Alliance for Religious Liberty, *P.O. Box 151353, Alexandria, VA 22315; (571) 293-2427. Fax, (910) 221-2226. Col. Ron Crews (USAR, Ret.), Executive Director; Chaplain Brig. Gen. Doug Lee (USA, Ret.), President.*
General email, info@chaplainalliance.org
Web, http://chaplainalliance.org

Membership: military chaplains and others who support orthodox Christian doctrines. Seeks to ensure that all chaplains and those they serve may exercise their religious liberties without fear of reprisal. Interests include the conflict between official protection for gays in the military and orthodox Christian teachings. Issues press releases; grants media interviews; monitors legislation and regulations.

Enlisted Assn., Washington Office, *1001 N. Fairfax St., #102, Alexandria, VA 22314; (703) 684-1981. Fax, (703) 548-4876. Deirdre Parke Holleman, Executive Director. Toll-free, (800) 554-8732. VA Caregiver Support, (855) 260-3274.*
General email, dholleman@treadc.org
Web, www.trea.org

Membership: enlisted personnel of the armed forces, including active duty, reserve, guard, and retirees. Runs scholarship, legislative, and veterans service programs. (Formerly Retired Enlisted Assn.; headquarters in Aurora, Colo.)

Fleet Reserve Assn., *125 N. West St., Alexandria, VA 22314-2754; (703) 683-1400. Fax, (703) 549-6610. Thomas J. Snee, National Executive Director. Membership/ Customer Service, (800) 372-1924.*
General email, news-fra@fra.org
Web, www.fra.org

Membership: current and former enlisted members of the Navy, Marine Corps, and Coast Guard. Interests include health care, pay, benefits, and quality-of-life programs for sea services personnel. Recognized by the Veterans Affairs Dept. to assist veterans and widows of veterans with benefit claims. Monitors legislation and regulations.

Marine Corps League, *8626 Lee Hwy., #201, Fairfax, VA 22031-3070 (mailing address: P.O. Box 3070, Merrifield, VA 22116); (703) 207-9588. Fax, (703) 207-0047. Michael A. Blum, Executive Director. Toll-free, (800) 625-1775.*
Web, www.mcleague.org

Membership: active duty, retired, and reserve Marine Corps groups. Promotes the interests of the Marine Corps and works to preserve its traditions; assists veterans and their survivors. Monitors legislation and regulations.

Military Order of the World Wars, *435 N. Lee St., Alexandria, VA 22314-2301; (703) 683-4911. Fax, (703) 683-4501. Brig. Gen. Arthur B. Morrill III, Chief of Staff. Toll-free, (877) 320-3774.*

General email, mowwcs@comcast.net

Web, www.militaryorder.net

Membership: retired and active duty commissioned officers, warrant officers, and flight officers. Supports a strong national defense; supports patriotic education in schools; presents awards to outstanding Junior and Senior Reserve Officers Training Corps (ROTC) cadets, Boy Scouts, and Girl Scouts.

National Assn. for Uniformed Services, *5535 Hempstead Way, Springfield, VA 22151-4094; (703) 750-1342. Fax, (703) 354-4380. Lt. Gen. Jack Klimp (USMC, Ret.), President. Information, (800) 842-3451.*

General email, naus@naus.org

Web, www.naus.org

Membership: active duty, reserve, and retired officers and enlisted personnel of all uniformed services and their families and survivors. Interests include benefits of military retirees, veterans, active duty military families, and survivors. Monitors legislation and regulations. (Affiliated with the Society of Military Widows.)

Navy League of the United States, *2300 Wilson Blvd., #200, Arlington, VA 22201-5424; (703) 528-1775. Fax, (703) 528-2333. Bruce K. Butler, National Executive Director, ext. 1550. Toll-free, (800) 356-5760.*

General email, service@navyleague.org

Web, www.navyleague.org

Membership: retired and reserve military personnel and civilians interested in the U.S. Navy, Marine Corps, Coast Guard, and Merchant Marine. Distributes literature, provides speakers, and conducts seminars to promote interests of the sea services. Monitors legislation.

Noncommissioned Officers Assn., *National Capital Office, P.O. Box 3085, Oakton, VA 22124; (703) 549-0311. Fax, (703) 549-0245. H. Gene Overstreet, President; Jon Ostrowski, Executive Director for Government Affairs. Toll-free, (800) 662-2620.*

General email, rschneider@ncoadc.org

Web, www.ncoausa.org

Congressionally chartered fraternal organization of active duty, reserve, guard, and retired enlisted military personnel. Sponsors job fairs to assist members in finding employment. (Headquarters in Selma, Texas.)

OutServe-SLDN, *P.O. Box 65301 20035-5301; (202) 328-3244. Fax, (202) 797-1635. Allyson D. Robinson, Executive Director. Toll-free legal hotline, (800) 538-7418.*

General email, admin@outserve-sldn.org

Web, www.sldn.org

Seeks to secure equal opportunity, protection, and benefits, without threat of harassment or discrimination, for lesbian, gay, bisexual, and transgender military service members and veterans. Provides free legal services to LGBT service members and veterans; conducts media and outreach campaigns on matters relating to the service of LGBT personnel; provides networking opportunities; monitors legislation and regulations.

United Service Organizations (USO), *2111 Wilson Blvd., #1200, Arlington, VA 22201 (mailing address: P.O. Box 96322, Washington, DC 20090-6322); (703) 908-6400. Fax, (703) 908-6402. John I. Pray Jr., President. Toll-free, (888) 484-3876.*

Web, www.uso.org

Voluntary civilian organization chartered by Congress. Provides military personnel and their families in the United States and overseas with social, educational, and recreational programs.

U.S. Army Warrant Officers Assn., *462 Herndon Pkwy., #207, Herndon, VA 20170-5235; (703) 742-7727. Fax, (703) 742-7728. Jack DuTeil, Executive Director. Toll-free, (800) 587-2962.*

General email, usawoahq@verizon.net

Web, www.usawoa.org

Membership: active duty, guard, reserve, and retired and former warrant officers. Monitors and makes recommendations to Defense Dept., Army Dept., and Congress on policies and programs affecting Army warrant officers and their families. Provides professional development programs for members.

DEFENSE PERSONNEL

Chaplains

▶**AGENCIES**

Air Force Dept. *(Defense Dept.), Chief of Chaplains, 1380 Air Force Pentagon 20330; (571) 256-7729. Fax, (571) 256-7642. Maj. Gen. Howard D. Stendahl, Chief of Chaplains. General email, usaf.pentagon.af.hc.mbx.workflow@mail.mil*

Web, www.chaplaincorps.af.mil

Oversees chaplains and religious services within the Air Force; maintains liaison with religious denominations.

Armed Forces Chaplains Board *(Defense Dept.), OUSD (P&R) MPP-AFCB, 4000 Defense Pentagon, #2E341 20301-4000; (703) 697-9015. Fax, (703) 693-2280. Rear Adm. Mark L. Tidd, Chair; Col. Jerry Pitts, Executive Director.*

General email, afcb@osd.mil

Web, http://prhome.defense.gov/RFM/MPP/AFCB.aspx

Membership: chiefs and deputy chiefs of chaplains of the armed services; works to coordinate religious policies and services among the military branches.

Army Dept. *(Defense Dept.), Chief of Chaplains, 2700 Army Pentagon, #3E524 20310-2700; (703) 695-1133. Fax, (703) 695-9834. Maj. Gen. Donald L. Rutherford, Chief of Chaplains.*

Web, www.chapnet.army.mil

Oversees chaplains and religious services within the Army; maintains liaison with religious denominations.

Marine Corps *(Defense Dept.), Chaplain,* 3000 Navy Pentagon 20350; (703) 614-4627. Fax, (703) 695-3431. Rear Adm. Margaret Grunkibben, Chaplain.
Web, www.hqmc.marines.mil/Agencies/HeadquartersandServiceBattalion/chaplainoffice.aspx

Oversees chaplains and religious services within the Marine Corps; maintains liaison with religious denominations.

National Guard Bureau *(Defense Dept.), Chaplain Services,* 111 S. George Mason Dr., Arlington, VA 22204; (703) 607-8657. Fax, (703) 607-5295. Brig. Gen. Alphonse Stephenson, Director.
General email, chaplain@ngb.ang.af.mil
Web, http://chaplain.ng.mil

Represents the Chief National Guard Bureau on all aspects of the chaplains' mission. Directs and oversees the activities and policies of the National Guard Chaplain Services. Oversees chaplains and religious services within the National Guard; maintains liaison with religious denominations.

Navy Dept. *(Defense Dept.), Chief of Chaplains,* 1000 Navy Pentagon, #5E270 20350-1000; (703) 614-4043. Fax, (703) 693-2907. Rear Adm. Mark L. Tidd, Chief.
Web, www.navy.mil/local/crb

Oversees chaplains and religious services within the Navy; maintains liaison with religious denominations.

U.S. Coast Guard (USCG) *(Homeland Security Dept.), Chaplain,* CG-00A, 2703 Martin Luther King Jr. Ave. S.E. 20593; (202) 372-4434. Fax, (202) 372-4962. Capt. Gary P. Weeden, Chaplain; Cmdr. Steven Smith, Deputy Chaplain.
General email, Gregory.N.Todd@uscg.mil
Web, www.uscg.mil/hq/chaplain

Oversees chaplains and religious services within the Coast Guard; maintains liaison with religious denominations.

Military Chaplains Assn. of the United States of America, 5541 Lee Hwy., Arlington, VA 22207-7056 (mailing address: P.O. Box 7056, Arlington, VA 22207-7056); (703) 533-5890. Robert G. Certain, Executive Director.
General email, chaplains@mca-usa.org
Web, www.mca-usa.org

Membership: chaplains of all faiths in all branches of the armed services and chaplains of veterans affairs and civil air patrol. Provides training opportunities for chaplains and a referral service concerning chaplains and chaplaincy.

National Conference on Ministry to the Armed Forces, 7724 Silver Sage Ct., Springfield, VA 22153; (703) 608-2100. Jack Williamson, Executive Director.
General email, jack@ncmaf.org
Web, www.ncmaf.org

Offers support to the Armed Forces Chaplains Board, the chief of chaplains of each service, and chaplains

throughout the military and Veterans Affairs Dept.; disseminates information on matters affecting service personnel welfare.

Civilian Employees

►AGENCIES

Air Force Dept. *(Defense Dept.), Civilian Force Policy,* 1400 W. Perimeter Rd., #4770, Joint Base Andrews 20762; (240) 612-4022. Dana Crowe, Chief.
Web, www.afpc.af.mil/main/welcome.asp

Civilian office that monitors and reviews Air Force policies, benefits and entitlements, civilian pay, career programs, and external and internal placement of staff.

Air Force Dept. *(Defense Dept.), Personnel Policy,* 1040 Air Force Pentagon, #4D950 20330-1040; (703) 695-6770. Col. Brian Kelly, Director.
Web, www.afpc.af.mil

Implements and evaluates Air Force civilian personnel policies; serves as the principal adviser to the Air Force personnel director on civilian personnel matters and programs.

Army Dept. *(Defense Dept.), Civilian Personnel,* 300 Army Pentagon, #2C453 20310-0300; (703) 695-5701. Fax, (703) 695-6997. Jay D. Aronowitz, Assistant G-1 for Civilian Personnel.
Web, www.cpol.army.mil

Develops and reviews Army civilian personnel policies and advises the Army leadership on civilian personnel matters.

Army Dept. *(Defense Dept.), Diversity and Leadership,* 111 Army Pentagon, #2A332 20310-0111; (703) 614-5284. Fax, (703) 614-5332. Larry Stubblefield, Deputy Assistant Secretary.
Web, http://eeoa.army.pentagon.mil

Civilian office that administers equal employment opportunity and civil rights programs and policies for civilian employees of the Army.

Defense Dept. (DoD), *Staffing and Civilian Transition Programs,* 4800 Mark Center Dr., #05F16, SCTP Division, Alexandria, VA 22350-1100; (571) 372-1528. Fax, (571) 372-1704. William Mann, Chief of Staff.
Web, www.cpms.osd.mil/care

Manages workforce restructuring programs for Defense Dept. civilians, including downsizing, placement, voluntary early retirement, and transition assistance programs.

Marine Corps *(Defense Dept.), Human Resources and Organizational Management,* Headquarters, U.S. Marine Corps (HQMC), Code ARHM, 3000 Marine Corps Pentagon, #2C253 20350-3000; (703) 614-8371. William Whaley, Director.
Web, www.marines.mil/unit/hqmc/hr

Develops and implements personnel and equal employment opportunity programs for civilian employees of the Marine Corps headquarters.

Navy Dept. *(Defense Dept.), Civilian Human Resources,* *1000 Navy Pentagon, #4D548 20350-1000; (703) 695-2633. Fax, (703) 693-4959. Patricia C. Adams, Deputy Assistant Secretary.*
General email, patricia.c.adams@navy.mil
Web, www.donaa.navy.mil

Civilian office that develops and reviews Navy and Marine Corps civilian personnel and equal opportunity programs and policies.

U.S. Coast Guard (USCG) *(Homeland Security Dept.),* *Civil Rights Directorate, Commandant, CG-00H, 2703 Martin Luther King Jr. Ave. S.E. 20593-7000; (202) 372-4500. Terri A. Dickerson, Director.*
General email, OCR@uscg.mil
Web, www.uscg.mil/hq/cg00/cg00h

Manages military and civilian internal equal employment opportunity programs.

U.S. Coast Guard (USCG) *(Homeland Security Dept.),* *Human Resources Directorate, CG-1, MS 7907 2703 Martin Luther King Jr. Ave. S.E. 20593; (202) 475-5000. Rear Adm. Daniel A. Neptune, Assistant Commandant.*
Web, www.uscg.mil/hr

Responsible for hiring, recruiting, and training all military and nonmilitary Coast Guard personnel. Administers employee benefits.

Equal Opportunity

▶AGENCIES

Air Force Dept. *(Defense Dept.), Equal Opportunity,* *1602 California Ave., #217, Joint Base Andrews, NAF, MD 20762; (240) 612-4113. James Carlock, Program Director.*
Web, www.afpc.af.mil

Office that develops and administers Air Force equal opportunity programs and policies.

Army Dept. *(Defense Dept.), Diversity and Leadership,* *111 Army Pentagon, #2A332 20310-0111; (703) 614-5284. Fax, (703) 614-5332. Larry Stubblefield, Deputy Assistant Secretary.*
Web, http://eeoa.army.pentagon.mil

Develops policy and conducts program reviews for the Dept. of Army Civilian Equal Employment Opportunity and Affirmative Employment Programs.

Defense Dept. (DoD), *Defense Dept. Advisory Committee on Women in the Services, 4000 Defense Pentagon, #5A734 20301-4000; (703) 697-2122. Fax, (703) 614-6233. Col. Betty J. Yarbrough, Military Director.*
General email, dacowits@osd.mil
Web, www.dacowits.defense.gov

Provides the DoD with advice and recommendations on matters and policies relating to the recruitment and

retention, treatment, employment, integration, and well-being of highly qualified professional women in the armed forces.

Defense Dept. (DoD), *Diversity Management and Equal Opportunity, 4000 Defense Pentagon, #5D641 20301-4000; (703) 571-9321. Fax, (703) 571-9338. Clarence A. Johnson, Director.*
Web, http://diversity.defense.gov

Formulates equal employment opportunity policy for the Defense Dept. Evaluates civil rights complaints from military personnel, including issues of sexual harassment and recruitment.

Marine Corps *(Defense Dept.), Equal Opportunity and Diversity Management, HQUSMC, MNRA (MPE), 3280 Russell Rd., Quantico, VA 22134-5103; (703) 784-9371. Fax, (703) 784-9814. Col. Thomas Johnson, Head.*
Web, www.marines.mil

Military office that develops, monitors, and administers Marine Corps equal opportunity and diversity programs.

Navy Dept. *(Defense Dept.), Diversity Directorate,* *701 S. Courthouse Rd., #3R180, Arlington, VA 22204; (703) 604-5004. Fax, (703) 604-6957. Cmdr. Mery-Angela Katson, Director; Lt. Maura Betts, Women's Policy.*
Web, www.public.navy.mil/bupers-npc/support/diversity

Military office that develops and administers Navy diversity programs and policies.

U.S. Coast Guard (USCG) *(Homeland Security Dept.),* *Civil Rights Directorate, Commandant, CG-00H, 2703 Martin Luther King Jr. Ave. S.E. 20593-7000; (202) 372-4500. Terri A. Dickerson, Director.*
General email, OCR@uscg.mil
Web, www.uscg.mil/hq/cg00/cg00h

Administers equal opportunity regulations for Coast Guard military personnel.

▶NONGOVERNMENTAL

Human Rights Campaign (HRC), *1640 Rhode Island Ave. N.W. 20036; (202) 628-4160. Fax, (202) 347-5323. Chad Griffin, President. Toll-free, (800) 777-4723.*
General email, hrc@hrc.org
Web, www.hrc.org

Promotes legislation affirming the rights of lesbian, gay, bisexual, and transgender people. Focus includes discrimination in the military.

Minerva Center, *20 Granada Rd., Pasadena, MD 21122-2708; (410) 437-5379. Linda Grant DePauw, Director.*
General email, lgdepauw@gmail.com
Web, www.minervacenter.com

Encourages the study of women in war and women and the military. Focus includes current U.S. service-women; women veterans; women in war and the military abroad; and the preservation of artifacts, oral history, and first-hand accounts of women's experience in military service.

OutServe-SLDN, *P.O. Box 65301 20035-5301; (202) 328-3244. Fax, (202) 797-1635. Allyson D. Robinson, Executive Director. Toll-free legal hotline, (800) 538-7418.*
General email, admin@outserve-sldn.org
Web, www.sldn.org

Seeks to secure equal opportunity, protection, and benefits, without threat of harassment or discrimination, for lesbian, gay, bisexual, and transgender military service members and veterans. Provides free legal services to LGBT service members and veterans; conducts media and outreach campaigns on matters relating to the service of LGBT personnel; provides networking opportunities; monitors legislation and regulations.

Family Services

▶AGENCIES

Air Force Dept. *(Defense Dept.), Manpower Personnel and Services, 1040 Air Force Pentagon, #4E168 20330-1040; (703) 697-6088. Lt. Gen. Samuel D. Cox, Deputy Chief of Staff.*
Web, www.afpc.af.mil

Military office that responds to inquiries concerning deceased Air Force personnel and their beneficiaries; refers inquiries to the Military Personnel Center at Randolph Air Force Base in San Antonio, Texas.

Air Force Dept. *(Defense Dept.), Military and Family Support Center, 1191 Menoher Dr., Andrews AFB, MD 20762; (301) 981-7087. Fax, (301) 981-9215. Linda Logan, Chief.*
Web, www.afcrossroads.com

Military policy office that monitors and reviews services provided to Air Force families and civilian employees with family concerns; oversees Airmen and Family Readiness Centers.

Defense Dept. (DoD), *Education Activity, 4800 Mark Center Dr., Alexandria, VA 22350-1400; (571) 372-1885. Fax, (571) 372-5829. Andrian B. Talley, Director, Acting.*
General email, dodea.director@hq.dodea.edu
Web, www.dodea.edu

Civilian office that maintains school system for dependents of all military personnel and eligible civilians in the United States and abroad. Develops uniform curriculum and educational standards; monitors student performance and school accreditation.

Defense Dept. (DoD), *Resources and Oversight, 4000 Defense Pentagon, #2E319 20301-4000; (703) 697-7191. Fax, (703) 695-1977. Carolee Van Horn, Director.*
Web, www.defense.gov

Coordinates policies related to quality of life of military personnel and their families.

Marine Corps *(Defense Dept.), Casualty Section, HQUSMC, 2008 Elliott Rd., Quantico, VA 22134-5102; (703) 784-9512. Fax, (703) 784-4134. Gerald Castle, Head. Toll-free, (800) 847-1597.*
General email, casualtysection@usmc.mil
Web, www.marines.mil

Confirms beneficiaries of deceased Marine Corps personnel for benefits distribution.

Marine Corps *(Defense Dept.), Marine and Family Programs, HQUSMC, M and RA (MF), 3280 Russell Rd., Quantico, VA 22134-5103; (703) 784-9501. Fax, (703) 432-9269. Brig. Gen. Russell A. C. Sanborn, Director.*
Web, www.usmc-mccs.org

Sponsors family service centers located on major Marine Corps installations. Oversees the administration of policies affecting the quality of life of Marine Corps military families. Administers relocation assistance programs.

Navy Dept. *(Defense Dept.), Personnel Readiness and Community Support, 701 S. Courthouse Rd., Arlington, VA 22204; (703) 604-5045. Thomas Yavorski, Liaison.*
Web, www.npc.navy.mil

Acts as liaison between D.C. area and Navy quality of life programs located in Tenn., which provide naval personnel and families being sent overseas with information and support; addresses problems of abuse and sexual assault within families; helps Navy spouses find employment; facilitates communication between Navy families and Navy officials; and assists in relocating Navy families during transition from military to civilian life.

▶CONGRESS

For a listing of relevant congressional committees and subcommittees, please see page 516 or the Appendix.

▶NONGOVERNMENTAL

Air Force Aid Society Inc., *241 18th St. South, #202, Arlington, VA 22202-3409; (703) 607-3034. Fax, (703) 607-3022. Lt. Gen. John D. Hopper Jr. (USAF, Ret.), Chief Executive Officer. Toll-free, (800) 769-8951.*
General email, afas-hq@afas.org
Web, www.afas.org

Membership: Air Force active duty, reserve, and retired military personnel and their dependents. Provides active duty and retired Air Force military personnel with personal emergency loans for basic needs, travel, or dependents' health expenses; assists families of active duty, deceased, or retired Air Force personnel with postsecondary education grants.

American Red Cross, *Service to the Armed Forces, 2025 E St. N.W., 2nd Floor 20006-5009; (202) 303-5000, ext. 2. Fax, (202) 303-0216. Sherri L. Brown, Senior Vice President, (202) 303-8283. Emergency communication services, (877) 272-7337.*
Web, www.redcross.org

Provides emergency services for active duty armed forces personnel and their families, including verified communications, financial assistance, information and referral, and counseling. Mandated by Congress to contact military personnel in family emergencies; provides military personnel with verification of family situations for emergency leave applications.

Armed Forces Hostess Assn., *6604 Army Pentagon, #1E541 20310-6604; (703) 614-0350. Fax, (703) 697-5542. Tami Robinson, President. Alternate phone number, (703) 614-0485.*
General email, usarmy-pentagon.hqda-sptsvcs.mbx .afha@mail.mil
Web, www.facebook.com/AFHAVols

Volunteer office staffed by spouses of military personnel of all armed services. Serves as an information clearinghouse for military and civilian Defense Dept. families; maintains information on military bases in the United States and abroad; issues information handbook for families in the Washington area.

Army Distaff Foundation (Knollwood), *6200 Oregon Ave. N.W. 20015-1543; (202) 541-0149. Fax, (202) 364-2856. Maj. Gen. Stephen T. Rippe (USA, Ret.), Chief Executive Officer. Information, (800) 541-4255.*
General email, marketing@armydistaff.org
Web, www.armydistaff.org

Nonprofit continuing care retirement community for career military officers and their families. Provides retirement housing and health care services.

Army Emergency Relief, *200 Stovall St., #5S33, Alexandria, VA 22332; (703) 428-0000. Fax, (703) 325-7183. Lt. Gen. Robert F. Foley (USA, Ret.), Executive Director. Toll-free, (866) 878-6378.*
General email, aer@aerhq.org
Web, www.aerhq.org

Provides emergency financial assistance to retirees and to soldiers and family members of the U.S. Army, Army Reserves, and National Guard who are on extended active duty; provides scholarships to further the education of service members' spouses and dependents.

EX-POSE, Ex-Partners of Servicemembers for Equality, *P.O. Box 11191, Alexandria, VA 22312-0191; (703) 941-5844. Fax, (703) 212-6951. Nancy Davis, Manager.*
General email, ex-pose@juno.com
Web, www.ex-pose.org

Membership: current and former partners of military members, both officers and enlisted, and other interested parties. Educates current and former spouses about potential benefits that may be gained or lost through divorce, including retirement pay, survivors' benefits, and medical, commissary, and exchange benefits. Provides information concerning legal resources and related federal laws and regulations. Serves as an information clearinghouse. Open Tuesday through Thursday, 10:00 a.m.–3:00 p.m.

Federal Education Assn., *1201 16th St. N.W., #117 20036; (202) 822-7850. Fax, (202) 822-7867. Chuck McCarter, President.*
General email, fea@feaonline.org
Web, www.feaonline.org

Membership: teachers and personnel of Defense Dept. schools for military dependents in the United States and abroad. Helps members negotiate pay, benefits, and better working conditions. Provides professional development through workshops and publications. Monitors legislation and regulations.

Fisher House Foundation, *111 Rockville Pike, #420, Rockville, MD 20850; (301) 294-8560. Fax, (301) 294-8562. David A. Coker, President. Toll-free, (888) 294-8560.*
General email, info@fisherhouse.org
Web, www.fisherhouse.org and Twitter, @CokerDavid

Builds new houses on the grounds of major military and VA hospitals to enable families of hospitalized service members to stay within walking distance. Donates the Fisher Houses to the U.S. government. Administers the Hero Miles Program, which uses donated frequent flier miles to purchase airline tickets for hospitalized service members and their families. Provides scholarships for military children.

Freedom Alliance, *22570 Markey Court, #240, Dulles, VA 20166; (703) 444-7940. Fax, (703) 444-9893. Tom Kilgannon, President. Toll-free, (800) 475-6620.*
Web, www.freedomalliance.org

Promotes strong national defense and honors military service. Awards monetary grants to wounded troops; assists soldiers and their families with housing and travel expenses; provides active duty troops with meals, clothing, entertainment, and other comforts. Provides college scholarships to children of those killed or permanently disabled in an operations mission or training accident.

National Military Family Assn., *2500 N. Van Dorn St., #102, Alexandria, VA 22302-1601; (703) 931-6632. Fax, (703) 931-4600. Mary Scott, Chair; Joyce Raezer, Executive Director.*
General email, info@militaryfamily.org
Web, www.militaryfamily.org

Membership: active duty and retired military, National Guard, and reserve personnel of all U.S. uniformed services, civilian personnel, families, and other interested individuals. Works to improve the quality of life for military families.

Naval Services FamilyLine, *1043 Harwood St. S.E., #100, Bldg. 154 20374-5067; (202) 433-2333. Fax, (202) 433-4622. Beth Mulloy, Chair. Toll-free, (877) 673-7773.*
General email, nsfamline@aol.com
Web, www.nsfamilyline.org

Offers support services to spouses of Navy personnel; disseminates information on all aspects of military life; fosters sense of community among sea service personnel and their families.

Navy–Marine Corps Relief Society, *875 N. Randolph St., #225, Arlington, VA 22203-1977; (703) 696-4904. Fax, (703) 696-0144. Adm. Charles S. (Steve) Abbot (USN, Ret.), President.*
General email, communications@nmcrs.org
Web, www.nmcrs.org

Assists active duty and retired Navy and Marine Corps personnel and their families in times of need. Disburses interest-free loans and grants. Provides educational scholarships and loans; visiting nurse services; and other services, including combat casualty assistance, thrift shops, budget counseling, and volunteer training.

Our Military Kids, Inc., *6861 Elm St., #2-A, McLean, VA 22101; (703) 734-6654. Fax, (703) 734-6503. Linda Davidson, Executive Director. Toll-free, (866) 691-6654.*
General email, omkinquiry@ourmilitarykids.org
Web, www.ourmilitarykids.org

Provides grants for extracurricular activities for school-aged children of deployed and severely injured soldiers, including Reserve and National Guard military personnel.

Financial Services

▶**AGENCIES**

Air Force Dept. *(Defense Dept.),* **Financial Management and Comptroller,** *1130 Air Force Pentagon, #4E978 20330-1130; (703) 697-1974. Fax, (703) 695-8144. Marilyn M. Thomas, Principal Deputy Assistant Secretary.*
Web, www.saffm.hq.af.mil

Advises the secretary of the Air Force on policies relating to financial services for military and civilian personnel.

Defense Dept. (DoD), *Accounting and Finance Policy Analysis, 1100 Defense Pentagon, #3E769 20301-1100; (703) 602-0508. Donjette Gilmore, Director.*
Web, www.defense.gov

Develops accounting policy for the Defense Dept. federal management regulation.

▶**CONGRESS**

For a listing of relevant congressional committees and subcommittees, please see page 516 or the Appendix.

▶**NONGOVERNMENTAL**

Armed Forces Benefit Assn., *909 N. Washington St., Alexandria, VA 22314; (703) 549-4455. Fax, (703) 706-5961. Gen. Ralph E. Eberhart (USAF, Ret.), President. Toll-free, (800) 776-2322.*
General email, info@afba.com
Web, www.afba.com

Membership: active duty and retired personnel of the uniformed services, federal civilian employees, government contractors, first responders, and family members. Offers low-cost life, health, and long-term care insurance and financial, banking, and investment services worldwide.

Army and Air Force Mutual Aid Assn., *102 Sheridan Ave., Fort Myer, VA 22211-1110; (703) 707-4600. Fax, (703) 522-1336. Maj. Walt Lincoln (USA, Ret.), President.*
General email, info@aafmaa.com
Web, www.aafmaa.com

Private organization that offers member and family life insurance products and survivor assistance services to all ranks of Army, Air Force, Coast Guard, Marine Corps, and Navy who are active duty; Guard, Reserve, USAFA, USCGA, USMA, USMMA, and USNA cadets or midshipmen; ROTC contract/scholarship cadets; and retirees.

Army Emergency Relief, *200 Stovall St., #5S33, Alexandria, VA 22332; (703) 428-0000. Fax, (703) 325-7183. Lt. Gen. Robert F. Foley (USA, Ret.), Executive Director. Toll-free, (866) 878-6378.*
General email, aer@aerhq.org
Web, www.aerhq.org

Provides emergency financial assistance to retirees and to soldiers and family members of the U.S. Army, Army Reserves, and National Guard who are on extended active duty; provides scholarships to further the education of service members' spouses and dependents.

Defense Credit Union Council, *601 Pennsylvania Ave. N.W., South Bldg., #600 20004-2601; (202) 638-3950. Fax, (202) 638-3410. Roland Arteaga, President.*
General email, admin@dcuc.org
Web, www.dcuc.org

Trade association of credit unions serving the Defense Dept.'s military and civilian personnel. Works with the National Credit Union Administration to solve problems concerning the operation of credit unions for the military community; maintains liaison with the Defense Dept.

Health Care

▶**AGENCIES**

Air Force Dept. *(Defense Dept.),* **Surgeon General,** *1780 Air Force Pentagon, #4E114 20330-1780; (703) 692-6800. Lt. Gen. Thomas W. Travis, Surgeon General. Press, (703) 681-7921.*
Web, www.airforcemedicine.afms.mil

Directs the provision of medical and dental services for Air Force personnel and their beneficiaries.

Army Dept. *(Defense Dept.),* **Command Policy and Programs,** *2530 Crystal Dr., Arlington, VA 22202-3941; (703) 571-7229. Col. Linda Sheimo, Chief, (703) 571-7226.*
Web, www.armyg1.army.mil/hr/cpp.asp

Develops policies and initiatives to enhance soldiers' health, fitness, and morale, with the goal of improving personnel readiness and institutional strength of the army. Interests include weight control and suicide prevention.

Army Dept. *(Defense Dept.),* **Surgeon General,** *7700 Arlington Blvd., #4SW112, Falls Church, VA 22042-5140; (703) 681-3000. Fax, (703) 681-3167. Lt. Gen. Patricia D. Horoho, Surgeon General.*

General email, OTSGWebPublisher@amedd.army.mil

Web, www.armymedicine.army.mil

Directs the provision of medical and dental services for Army personnel and their dependents.

Army Dept. *(Defense Dept.), Warrior Transition Command, 200 Stovall Street, #7527, Alexandria, VA 22332; (703) 428-7118. Fax, (703) 325-0291. Brig. Gen. David J. Bishop, Commander, (202) 782-6746. Wounded soldier and family hotline, (800) 984-8523. Web, www.wtc.army.mil*

Provides leadership, command, and control for wounded soldiers' health and welfare, military administrative requirements, and readiness. Collaborates with medical providers in order to facilitate quality care, disposition, and transition. Supports the needs of wounded warriors and their families; supports the professional growth of all personnel.

Army Dept. *(Defense Dept.), Wounded Warrior Program (AW2), 200 Stovall St., #7N65, Alexandria, VA 22332-5000; (877) 393-9058. Fax, (703) 325-1516. Col. Johnny Davis, Director. Overseas, (312) 221-9113. General email, usarmy.pentagon.medcom-WTC.mbx .contact-center@mail.mil*

Web, http://wtc.army.mil/aw2

Incorporates several existing programs to provide holistic support services for severely disabled and ill soldiers and their families. Provides each soldier with a personal AW2 advocate. Tracks and monitors severely disabled soldiers beyond their medical retirement.

Defense Dept. (DoD), *Health Affairs, Clinical Program Policy, 1200 Defense Pentagon, #3E1082 20301-1200; (703) 681-1708. Fax, (703) 681-3655. Jack W. Smith, Director. Web, www.health.mil/about_MHS*

Develops policies for the medical benefits programs for active duty and retired military personnel and dependents in the Defense Dept.

Defense Dept. (DoD), *National Intrepid Center of Excellence, 8901 Wisconsin Ave., Bldg. 51, Bethesda, MD 20889; (301) 319-3600. Dr. James P. Kelly, Director. 24-hour help line, (301) 319-3600. Press, (301) 319-3619. General email, nicoe@health.mil*

Web, www.nicoe.capmed.mil

Provides evaluation, treatment planning, research, and education for service members and their families dealing with the interactions of mild traumatic brain injury and psychological health conditions. Primary patient population is active duty service members who are not responding to current therapy; provider-referral required.

Defense Health Agency (DHA) *(Defense Dept.), 7700 Arlington Blvd., #5101, Falls Church, VA 22042-5101; (703) 681-1730. Lt. Gen. (Dr.) Douglas J. Robb, (USAF), Director.*

Web, www.health.mil/About-MHS/Defense-Health-Agency

Combat support agency directing medical services for the Army, Navy, Air Force, and Marine Corps. Administers the TRICARE health plan providing medical, dental, and pharmacy programs worldwide to service members,

retirees, and their families. Manages inpatient facilities and associated clinics in the national capital region.

Marine Corps *(Defense Dept.), Marine and Family Programs, HQUSMC, M and RA (MF), 3280 Russell Rd., Quantico, VA 22134-5103; (703) 784-9501. Fax, (703) 432-9269. Brig. Gen. Russell A. C. Sanborn, Director. Web, www.usmc-mccs.org*

Military office that directs Marine Corps health care, family violence, and drug and alcohol abuse policies and programs.

Naval Medical Research Center *(Defense Dept.), 503 Robert Grant Ave., #1W28, Silver Spring, MD 20910-7500; (301) 319-9646. Fax, (301) 319-7410. Capt. John W. Sanders, Commanding Officer. General email, svc.pao.nmrc@med.navy.mil*

Web, www.med.navy.mil/sites/nmrc

Performs basic and applied biomedical research in areas of military importance, including infectious diseases, hyperbaric medicine, wound repair enhancement, environmental stress, and immunobiology. Provides support to field laboratories and naval hospitals; monitors research internationally.

Navy Dept. *(Defense Dept.), Manpower and Reserve Affairs, Health Affairs, 1000 Navy Pentagon, #4D548 20350-1000; (703) 693-0238. Fax, (703) 675-1211. Capt. Mike Bridges, Director. Web, www.navy.mil*

Reviews medical programs for Navy and Marine Corps military personnel and develops and reviews policies relating to these programs.

Navy Dept. *(Defense Dept.), Patient Administration/ TriCare Operations, 7700 Arlington Blvd., #5113, Falls Church, VA 22042; (703) 681-9025. Capt. Mary Jenkins, Director, Health Care Operations, (703) 681-5516; Lt. Cmdr. Noah Sperner, Patient Administration, (703) 681-9205; Capt. Clarence Thomas, TriCare Operations, (202) 702-3152. Web, www.med.navy.mil*

Military office that interprets and oversees the implementation of Navy health care policy. Assists in the development of eligibility policy for medical benefits programs for Navy and Marine Corps military personnel.

Navy Dept. *(Defense Dept.), Surgeon General, 7700 Arlington Blvd., #5113, Falls Church, VA 22042-5113; (703) 681-5200. Fax, (703) 681-9527. Vice Adm. Matthew L. Nathan, Surgeon General. Web, www.med.navy.mil*

Directs the provision of medical and dental services for Navy and Marine Corps personnel and their dependents; oversees the Navy's Bureau of Medicine and Surgery.

U.S. Coast Guard (USCG) *(Homeland Security Dept.), Health, Safety, and Work-Life, CG-11, 2703 Martin Luther King Jr. Ave. S.E. 20593; (202) 475-5130. Fax, (202) 372-8463. Maura Dollymore, Director. General email, germaine.y.jefferson@uscg.mil*

Web, www.uscg.mil/hq/cg1/cg11/default.asp

Oversees all health, safety, and work-life aspects of the Coast Guard, including the operation of medical and dental clinics and sick bays on ships. Investigates Coast Guard accidents, such as the grounding of ships and downing of aircraft. Oversees all work life–related programs, including health promotion, mess halls and galleys, and individual and family support programs.

Walter Reed Army Institute of Research *(Defense Dept.),* 503 Robert Grant Ave., Silver Spring, MD 20910-7500; (301) 319-9100. Fax, (301) 319-9549. Col. Steven Braverman M.D., Commander. Public Affairs Officer, (301) 319-9471. Reference Librarian, (301) 319-7157. General email, wrair.publicaffairs@amedd.army.mil

Web, www.wrair.army.mil

Provides research, education, and training in support of the Defense Dept.'s health care system. Develops vaccines and drugs to prevent and treat infectious diseases. Other research efforts include surveillance of naturally occurring infectious diseases of military importance and study of combat casualty care (blood loss, resuscitation, and brain and other organ system trauma), battle casualties, operational stress, sleep deprivation, and medical countermeasures against biological and chemical agents.

▶**NONGOVERNMENTAL**

Assn. of Military Surgeons of the United States (AMSUS), *Society of Federal Health Professionals,* 9320 Old Georgetown Rd., Bethesda, MD 20814-1653; (301) 897-8800. Fax, (301) 530-5446. Vice Adm. Michael L. Cowan (USN, Ret.), Executive Director. Toll-free, (800) 761-9320. General email, amsus@amsus.org

Web, www.amsus.org

Membership: health professionals, including nurses, dentists, pharmacists, and physicians, who work or have worked for the U.S. Public Health Service, the VA, or the Army, Navy, Air Force, Guard, and Reserves, and students. Works to improve all phases of federal health services.

CAUSE—Comfort for America's Uniformed Services, 4114 Legato Rd., Suite B, Fairfax, VA 22033; (703) 591-4965. Fax, (703) 591-4931. Chief Master Sgt. Pamela A. Derrow, Executive Director. General email, info@cause-usa.org

Web, www.cause-usa.org

Provides comfort items and organizes recreational programs for U.S. military service personnel undergoing medical treatment or recuperating in government hospitals or rehabilitation facilities.

Commissioned Officers Assn. of the U.S. Public Health Service, 8201 Corporate Dr., #200, Landover, MD 20785; (301) 731-9080. Fax, (301) 731-9084. Gerard M. Farrell, Executive Director. Toll-free, (866) 366-9593. Web, www.coausphs.org

Membership: commissioned officers of the U.S. Public Health Service. Supports improvements to public health, especially through the work of the PHS Commissioned Corps. Sponsors conferences and training workshops. Monitors legislation and regulations.

Injured Marine Semper Fi Fund, 715 Broadway St., Quantico, VA 22134 (mailing address: Wounded Warrior Center, Bldg. H49, Box 555193, Camp Pendleton, CA 92055-5193); (703) 640-0181. Fax, (703) 640-0192. Karen Guenther, Executive Director. General email, info@semperfifund.org

Web, www.semperfifund.org

Provides financial assistance to marines injured in combat and training, other service members injured while in direct support of marine units, and families of marines for expenses during hospitalization, rehabilitation, and recovery.

Missing in Action, Prisoners of War

▶**AGENCIES**

Air Force Dept. *(Defense Dept.), Manpower Personnel and Services,* 1040 Air Force Pentagon, #4E168 20330-1040; (703) 697-6088. Lt. Gen. Samuel D. Cox, Deputy Chief of Staff. Web, www.afpc.af.mil

Military office that responds to inquiries about missing in action (MIA) personnel for the Air Force; refers inquiries to the Military Personnel Center at Randolph Air Force Base in San Antonio, Texas.

Defense Dept. (DoD), *Defense Prisoners of War/Missing Personnel,* 241 18th St. South, #800, Arlington, VA 22202; (703) 699-1102. Fax, (703) 602-1890. W. Montague Winfield, Deputy Assistant Secretary. Press, (703) 699-1420. Web, www.dtic.mil/dpmo

Civilian office responsible for policy matters relating to prisoners of war and missing personnel issues. Represents the Defense Dept. before Congress, the media, veterans organizations, and prisoner of war and missing personnel families.

Defense Dept. (DoD), *Public Affairs,* The Pentagon, #2D961 20301-1400; (703) 571-3343. Fax, (703) 697-3501. Bryan G. Whitman, Assistant Secretary, Acting, (703) 697-9312. Press, (703) 697-5131. Web, www.defense.gov/news

Responds to public inquiries concerning Defense Dept. personnel.

Marine Corps *(Defense Dept.), Casualty Section,* HQUSMC, 2008 Elliott Rd., Quantico, VA 22134-5102; (703) 784-9512. Fax, (703) 784-4134. Gerald Castle, Head. Toll-free, (800) 847-1597. General email, casualtysection@usmc.mil

Web, www.marines.mil

Military office that responds to inquiries about missing in action (MIA) personnel for the Marine Corps and distributes information about Marine Corps MIAs to the next of kin.

Navy Dept. *(Defense Dept.), Naval Personnel,* 701 S. Courthouse Rd., Arlington, VA 22204; (703) 604-2863. Vice Adm. William F. Moran, Chief. Web, www.navy.mil/cnp/index.asp

Military office that responds to inquiries about missing in action (MIA) personnel for the Navy and distributes information about Navy MIAs. (Office based in Millington, Tenn.)

State Dept., *Mainland Southeast Asia Affairs, 2201 C St. N.W., #5206 20520-6310; (202) 647-3132. Fax, (202) 647-3069. Howard V. (Ike) Reed, Director.*
Web, www.state.gov

Handles issues related to Americans missing in action in Indochina; serves as liaison with Congress, international organizations, and foreign governments on developments in these countries. Includes Thailand, Cambodia, Laos, Vietnam, and Burma.

►**CONGRESS**

For a listing of relevant congressional committees and subcommittees, please see page 516 or the Appendix.

►**NONGOVERNMENTAL**

National League of Families of American Prisoners and Missing in Southeast Asia, *5673 Columbia Pike, #100, Falls Church, VA 22041; (703) 465-7432. Fax, (703) 465-7433. Ann Mills-Griffith, Chair; Lacy Rourke, National Coordinator.*
General email, powmiafam@aol.com
Web, www.pow-miafamilies.org

Membership: family members of MIAs and POWs and returned POWs of the Vietnam War are voting members; nonvoting associate members include veterans and other interested people. Works for the release of all prisoners of war, an accounting of the missing, and repatriation of the remains of those who have died serving their country in Southeast Asia. Works to raise public awareness of these issues; maintains regional and state coordinators.

Pay and Compensation

►**AGENCIES**

Air Force Dept. *(Defense Dept.), Manpower Personnel and Services (A1P), Compensation and Travel Policy, 1500 Perimeter Rd., #4790, Andrews AFB, MD 20762; (240) 612-4350. Jean Love, Chief.*
Web, www.afpc.af.mil

Military office that develops and administers Air Force military personnel pay and compensation policies.

Army Dept. *(Defense Dept.), Military Compensation and Entitlements, 111 Army Pentagon, #2E469 20310-0111; (703) 693-1909. Fax, (703) 693-7072. Lt. Col. Rodney Connor, Assistant Deputy.*
Web, www.asamra.army.mil

Military office that provides oversight of the development and administration of and compliance with Army military personnel pay and compensation policies.

Defense Dept. (DoD), *Military Compensation, 4000 Defense Pentagon, #3D1067 20301-4000; (703) 695-3177.*

Fax, (703) 697-0202. Jerilyn B. (Jeri) Busch, Director.
Web, http://militarypay.defense.gov

Promulgates military pay and compensation policies to the uniformed services and advises the secretary of defense on military compensation policy.

Marine Corps *(Defense Dept.), Military Manpower Policy, 3280 Russell Rd., Quantico, VA 22134-5105; (703) 784-9350. Fax, (703) 784-9812. Michael F. Applegate, Director; Lt. Col. Roberto Richards, Compensation/ Incentive Officer.*
Web, www.marines.mil

Military office that develops and administers Marine Corps personnel pay and compensation policies.

Navy Dept. *(Defense Dept.), Military Pay and Compensation Policy, 1000 Navy Pentagon 20350; (703) 604-4718. Matthew Busky, Deputy Dispensing Officer (located in Tennessee); David Haldeman, Branch Head (DC).*
General email, nxag_n130@navy.mil
Web, www.navy.mil

Military office that develops and administers Navy military pay, compensation, and personnel policies.

Recruitment

►**AGENCIES**

Air Force Dept. *(Defense Dept.), Force Management, 1400 W. Perimeter Rd., #4710, Joint Base Andrews 20762; (240) 612-4040. Fax, (703) 604-1657. Col Jerry Diaz, Chief.*
Web, www.afpc.af.mil

Military office that oversees Air Force retention policies for officers and enlisted personnel, and provides analytical support for personnel issues.

Defense Dept. (DoD), *Accession Policy, 4000 Defense Pentagon, #3D1066 20301-4000; (703) 695-5525. Jeffrey Mayo, Director.*
Web, http://prhome.defense.gov/rfm/mpp/accessionpolicy.html

Military office that monitors Defense Dept. recruiting programs and policies, including advertising, market research, and enlistment standards. Coordinates with the individual services on recruitment of military personnel.

Marine Corps *(Defense Dept.), Recruiting Command, 3280 Russell Rd., Quantico, VA 22134-5105; (703) 784-9400. Fax, (703) 784-9863. Maj. Gen. Mark A. Brilakis, Commanding General.*
Web, www.mcrc.marines.mil

Military office that administers and executes policies for Marine Corps officer and enlisted recruitment programs.

Retirement, Separation

►**AGENCIES**

Armed Forces Retirement Home—Washington, *140 Rock Creek Church Rd. N.W. 20011-8400 (mailing address: 3700 N. Capitol St. N.W., Washington, DC*

20011-8400); (800) 422-9988. Fax, (202) 541-7519. Steven G. McManus, Chief Operating Officer.
General email, admissions@afrh.gov

Web, www.afrh.gov

Gives domiciliary and medical care to retired members of the armed services or career service personnel unable to earn a livelihood. Formerly known as U.S. Soldiers' and Airmen's Home. (Armed Forces Retirement Home in Gulfport, Miss., reopened in 2010.)

Army Dept. (Defense Dept.), Retirement Services, Taylor Bldg., 2530 Crystal Dr., 6th Floor, Alexandria, VA 22202-3941; (703) 571-7232. Fax, (703) 601-0120. John W. Radke, Chief.
General email, armyechoes@mail.mil

Web, www.armyg1.army.mil/retirees.asp

Military office that makes retirement policy and oversees retirement programs for Army military personnel.

Defense Dept. (DoD), Military Compensation, 4000 Defense Pentagon, #3D1067 20301-4000; (703) 695-3177. Fax, (703) 697-0202. Jerilyn B. (Jeri) Busch, Director.
Web, http://militarypay.defense.gov

Develops retirement policies and reviews administration of retirement programs for all Defense Dept. military personnel.

Marine Corps (Defense Dept.), Retired Services, 3280 Russell Rd., Quantico, VA 22134-5103; (703) 784-9312. Fax, (703) 784-9834. Wesley R. Combs, Head. Toll-free, (800) 336-4649.
Web, www.marines.mil

Military office that administers retirement programs and benefits for Marine Corps retirees and the Marine Corps retirement community survivor benefit plan.

Marine Corps (Defense Dept.), Separation and Retirement, 3280 Russell Rd., Quantico, VA 22134-5103; (703) 784-9304. Fax, (703) 784-9834. Steven M. Hanscom, Head.
Web, www.marines.mil

Military office that processes Marine Corps military personnel retirements and separations but does not administer benefits.

▶NONGOVERNMENTAL

Army Distaff Foundation (Knollwood), 6200 Oregon Ave. N.W. 20015-1543; (202) 541-0149. Fax, (202) 364-2856. Maj. Gen. Stephen T. Rippe (USA, Ret.), Chief Executive Officer. Information, (800) 541-4255.
General email, marketing@armydistaff.org

Web, www.armydistaff.org

Nonprofit continuing care retirement community for career military officers and their families. Provides retirement housing and health care services.

MILITARY EDUCATION AND TRAINING

General

▶AGENCIES

Air Force Dept. (Defense Dept.), Force Management Integration, 1660 Air Force Pentagon, #5E818 20330-1660; (703) 614-4751. Fax, (703) 693-4244. Norma L. Inabinet, Deputy Assistant Secretary.

Civilian office that monitors and reviews education policies of the U.S. Air Force Academy at Colorado Springs and officer candidates' training and Reserve Officers Training Corps (ROTC) programs for the Air Force. Advises the secretary of the Air Force on education matters, including graduate education, voluntary education programs, and flight, specialized, and recruit training.

Air Force Dept. (Defense Dept.), Personnel Policy, 1040 Air Force Pentagon, #4D950 20330-1040; (703) 695-6770. Col. Brian Kelly, Director.
Web, www.afpc.af.mil

Supervises operations and policies of all professional military education, including continuing education programs. Oversees operations and policies of Air Force service schools, including technical training for newly enlisted Air Force personnel.

Army Dept. (Defense Dept.), Collective Training Division, 400 Army Pentagon, #2D623 20310-0450 (mailing address: CASC6M, G3, T&D, Bldg. 5020, 2221 Adams Ave., Fort Lee, VA 23801); (703) 692-8370. Fax, (703) 692-4093. Col. John Drago, Chief.
General email, usarmy.lee.tradoc.mbx.leee-cascom-doctrine@mail.mil

Web, www.army.mil

Military office that plans and monitors program resources for active duty and reserve unit training readiness programs.

Army Dept. (Defense Dept.), Military Personnel Management, 300 Army Pentagon, #1D429 20310-0300; (703) 695-5871. Fax, (703) 695-7978. Maj. Gen. Thomas C. Seamands, Director.
Web, www.hqda.army.mil

Military office that supervises operations and policies of the U.S. Military Academy and officer candidates' training and Reserve Officers Training Corps (ROTC) programs. Advises the chief of staff of the Army on academy and education matters.

Civil Air Patrol National Capital Wing, 200 McChord St. S.W., #111, Joint Base Anacostia-Bolling 20032; (202) 767-4405. Bruce Heinlein, Wing Commander.
General email, pa@natcapwg.cap.gov

Web, www.natcapwg.cap.gov and www.natcapwing.org

Official auxiliary of the U.S. Air Force. Sponsors a cadet training and education program for junior and senior high school age students. Conducts emergency services, homeland security missions, and an aerospace education program. (Headquarters at Maxwell Air Force Base, Ala.)

Defense Acquisition University *(Defense Dept.)*, *9820 Belvoir Rd., Fort Belvoir, VA 22060-5565; (703) 805-3360. Fax, (703) 805-2639. James P. Woolsey, President. Toll-free, (866) 568-6924. Registrar, (703) 805-5142.*
Web, www.dau.mil

Academic institution that offers courses to military and civilian personnel who specialize in acquisition and procurement. Conducts research to support and improve management of defense systems acquisition programs.

Defense Dept. (DoD), *Accession Policy, 4000 Defense Pentagon, #3D1066 20301-4000; (703) 695-5525. Jeffrey Mayo, Director.*
Web, http://prhome.defense.gov/rfm/mpp/accessionpolicy .html

Reviews and develops education policies of the service academies, service schools, graduate and voluntary education programs, education programs for active duty personnel, tuition assistance programs, and officer candidates' training and Reserve Officers Training Corps (ROTC) programs for the Defense Dept. Advises the secretary of defense on education matters.

Defense Dept. (DoD), *Training, Readiness, and Strategy, 4000 Defense Pentagon, #1E537 20301-4000; (703) 695-2618. Fax, (703) 692-2855. Frank C. DiGiovanni, Director.*
Web, http://prhome.defense.gov

Develops, reviews, and analyzes legislation, policies, plans, programs, resource levels, and budgets for the training of military personnel and military units. Develops the substantive-based framework, working collaboratively across the defense, federal, academic, and private sectors, for the global digital knowledge environment. Manages with other government agencies the sustainability and modernization of DoD training ranges.

Dwight D. Eisenhower School for National Security and Resource Strategy *(Defense Dept.)*, *Fort Lesley J. McNair, 408 4th Ave. S.W., Bldg. #59 20319-5062; (202) 685-4278. Fax, (202) 685-3920. Brig. Gen. Thomas A. Gorry (USMC), Commandant, Interim. Administration, (202) 685-4333. General email, university-registrar@ndu.edu*
Web, www.ndu.edu/ICAF

Division of National Defense University. Offers professional level courses for senior military officers and senior civilian government officials. Academic program focuses on management of national resources, mobilization, and industrial preparedness. (Formerly known as the Industrial College of the Armed Forces.)

Marine Corps *(Defense Dept.)*, *Alfred M. Gray Research Center, 2040 Broadway St., Quantico, VA 22134; (703) 784-2240. Fax, (703) 784-4306. Charles P. Neimeyer, Director. Library, (703) 784-4411. Archives, (703) 784-4685.*
Web, www.tecom.marines.mil/units/educationcommand/ libraryofthemarinecorpsresearchcenter.aspx

Supports the professional, military, educational, and academic needs of the students and faculty of the Marine Corps University. Acts as a central research facility for marines in operational units worldwide. Houses the library and archives of the Marine Corps.

Marine Corps *(Defense Dept.)*, *Training and Education Command, 1019 Elliot Rd., Quantico, VA 22134-5001; (703) 784-3730. Fax, (703) 784-0012. Maj. Gen. Thomas M. Murray, Commanding General.*
Web, www.marines.mil

Military office that develops and implements training and education programs for regular and reserve personnel and units.

National Defense University *(Defense Dept.)*, *Fort Lesley J. McNair, 300 5th Ave. 20319-5066; (202) 685-4700. Fax, (202) 685-3935. Maj. Gen. Gregg F. Martin, President. Help Desk, (202) 685-3824. Press, (202) 685-3140.*
Web, www.ndu.edu

Specialized university sponsored by the Joint Chiefs of Staff to prepare individuals for senior executive duties in the national security establishment. Offers master of science degrees in national resource strategy, national security strategy, joint campaign planning and strategy, and government information leadership; a master of arts degree in strategic security studies; and nondegree and certificate programs and courses.

National War College *(Defense Dept.)*, *Fort Lesley J. McNair, 300 D St. S.W., Bldg. #61 20319-5078; (202) 685-4342. Fax, (202) 685-3993. Brig. Gen. Guy (Tom) Consentino, Commandant. Information, (202) 685-3674. Press, (202) 685-3140.*
Web, www.ndu.edu/nwc

Division of National Defense University. Offers professional level courses for senior military officers, senior civilian government officials, and foreign officers. Academic program focuses on the formulation and implementation of national security policy and military strategy.

Navy Dept. *(Defense Dept.)*, *Manpower and Reserve Affairs, 1000 Navy Pentagon, #4E590 20350-1000; (703) 695-4333. Fax, (703) 614-4103. Juan M. Garcia III, Assistant Secretary.*
Web, www.navy.mil/local/oasnmra

Civilian office that reviews policies of the U.S. Naval Academy, Navy and Marine Corps service schools, and officer candidates' training and Reserve Officer Training Corps (ROTC) programs. Advises the secretary of the Navy on education matters, including voluntary education programs.

Uniformed Services University of the Health Sciences *(Defense Dept.)*, *4301 Jones Bridge Rd., Bethesda, MD 20814-4799; (301) 295-3013. Fax, (301) 295-1960. Dr. Charles L. Rice, President. Toll-free information, (800) 515-5257. Registrar, (301) 295-3199. General email, president@usuhs.edu*
Web, www.usuhs.mil

An accredited four-year medical and dental school under the auspices of the Defense Dept. Awards doctorates and master's degrees in health- and science-related fields. The Graduate School of Nursing awards a master of science and a doctoral degree in nursing.

U.S. Coast Guard (USCG) *(Homeland Security Dept.), Human Resources Directorate, CG-1, MS 7907 2703 Martin Luther King Jr. Ave. S.E. 20593; (202) 475-5000. Rear Adm. Daniel A. Neptune, Assistant Commandant.*
Web, www.uscg.mil/hr

Responsible for hiring, recruiting, and training all military and nonmilitary Coast Guard personnel. Administers employee benefits.

U.S. Naval Academy *(Defense Dept.), 121 Blake Rd., Annapolis, MD 21402-5000; (410) 293-1000. Fax, (410) 293-3133. Vice Adm. Michael H. Miller, Superintendent; Capt. Stephen B. Latta, Dean of Admissions; Capt. William D. Byrne Jr., Commandant of Midshipmen. Visitor information, (410) 293-8687. Admissions/ Candidate guidance, (410) 293-1858. Public Affairs, (410) 293-2291.*
General email, pao@usna.edu
Web, www.usna.edu and www.usna.edu/Admissions

Provides undergraduate education for young men and women who have been nominated by members of their state's congressional delegation or, in some cases, the president or vice president of the United States. Graduates receive bachelor of science degrees and are commissioned as either an ensign in the U.S. Navy or a second lieutenant in the U.S. Marine Corps.

▶CONGRESS

For a listing of relevant congressional committees and subcommittees, please see page 516 or the Appendix.

▶NONGOVERNMENTAL

Assn. of Military Colleges and Schools of the U.S., *12332 Washington Brice Rd., Fairfax, VA 22033; (703) 272-8406. Fax, (703) 280-1082. Col. Ray Rottman (USAF, Ret.), Executive Director.*
General email, amcsus@cox.net
Web, www.amcsus.org

Membership: nonfederal military colleges and universities, junior colleges, and preparatory secondary schools that emphasize character development, leadership, and knowledge. Interests include Reserve Officers Training Corps (ROTC). Publishes a newsletter; sponsors an annual meeting and outreach activities. Represents member schools before the Defense Dept., Education Dept., and the general public.

George and Carol Olmsted Foundation, *80 East Jefferson St., #300B, Falls Church, VA 22046; (703) 536-3500. Bruce K. Scott, President. Toll-free, (877) 656-7833.*

General email, scholars@olmstedfoundation.org
Web, www.olmstedfoundation.org

Administers grants for two years of graduate study overseas, including foreign language study, for selected officers of the armed forces.

Military Order of the World Wars, *435 N. Lee St., Alexandria, VA 22314-2301; (703) 683-4911. Fax, (703) 683-4501. Brig. Gen. Arthur B. Morrill III, Chief of Staff. Toll-free, (877) 320-3774.*
General email, mowwcs@comcast.net
Web, www.militaryorder.net

Membership: retired and active duty commissioned officers, warrant officers, and flight officers. Presents awards to outstanding Reserve Officers Training Corps (ROTC) cadets; gives awards to Boy Scouts and Girl Scouts; conducts youth leadership conferences.

Navy League of the United States, *2300 Wilson Blvd., #200, Arlington, VA 22201-5424; (703) 528-1775. Fax, (703) 528-2333. Bruce K. Butler, National Executive Director, ext. 1550. Toll-free, (800) 356-5760.*
General email, service@navyleague.org
Web, www.navyleague.org

Sponsors Naval Sea Cadet Corps and Navy League Sea Cadet Corps for young people ages eleven through eighteen years. Graduates are eligible to enter the Navy at advanced pay grades.

Servicemembers Opportunity Colleges, *1307 New York Ave. N.W., 5th Floor 20005-4701; (202) 667-0079. Fax, (202) 667-0622. Kathryn (Kathy) Snead, Director. Information, (800) 368-5622.*
General email, socmail@aascu.org
Web, www.soc.aascu.org

Partnership of higher education associations, educational institutions, the Defense Dept., and the military services. Offers courses for credit and degree programs to military personnel and their families stationed in the United States and around the world.

MILITARY GRIEVANCES AND DISCIPLINE

General

▶AGENCIES

Air Force Dept. *(Defense Dept.), Air Force Review Boards Agency, 1500 W. Perimeter Rd., #3700, Andrews AFB, MD 20762-7002; (240) 612-5400. Fax, (240) 612-6016. R. Philip Deavel, Director.*
Web, www.af.mil/information/factsheets/factsheet.asp

Civilian office that responds to complaints from Air Force military and civilian personnel and assists in seeking corrective action.

Air Force Dept. *(Defense Dept.), Complaints Resolution Directorate,* 5683 Castle Ave., Carpenter Bldg., Joint Base Anacostia-Bolling 20032; (202) 404-5262.
Lawrence Brundidge, Chief.
Web, www.af.mil/inspectorgeneralcomplaints.asp

Military office that handles complaints and requests for assistance from civilians and Air Force and other military personnel.

Army Dept. *(Defense Dept.), Army Review Boards Agency,* 251 18th St. South, 3rd Floor, Arlington, VA 22202-3523; (703) 545-6900. Fax, (703) 601-0703.
Francine Blackmon, Deputy Assistant Secretary.
Web, http://arba.army.pentagon.mil

Civilian office that administers boards reviewing appeals cases. Administers the Ad Hoc Board, Army Grade Determination Review Board, Army Board for Correction of Military Records, Army Active Duty Board, Disability Rating Review Board, Discharge Review Board, Elimination Review Board, Army Clemency and Parole Board, Physical Disability Review Board, and Physical Disability Appeals Board.

Army Dept. *(Defense Dept.), Human Resources Policy Directorate,* 2530 Crystal Dr., #6000, Arlington, VA 22202; (703) 571-7243. Fax, (703) 601-0057. Brig. Gen. Henry L. Huntley, Director.
Web, http://myarmybenefits.us.army.mil

Military office that receives complaints from Army military personnel and assists in seeking corrective action.

Defense Dept. (DoD), *Diversity Management and Equal Opportunity,* 4000 Defense Pentagon, #5D641 20301-4000; (703) 571-9321. Fax, (703) 571-9338. Clarence A. Johnson, Director.
Web, http://diversity.defense.gov

Formulates equal employment opportunity policy for the Defense Dept. Evaluates civil rights complaints from military personnel, including issues of sexual harassment and recruitment.

Defense Dept. (DoD), *Legal Policy,* 4000 Defense Pentagon, #5A668 20301-4000; (703) 697-3387.
Col. Paul Kantwill, Director; Maj. Ryan Oakley, Deputy Director.
Web, www.defense.gov

Coordinates policy in a variety of personnel-related areas, including the Members Civil Relief Act, legal assistance, political activities, and corrections.

Defense Dept. (DoD), *Sexual Assault Prevention and Response,* 4800 Mark Center Dr., #07G21, Alexandria, VA 22350; (571) 372-2657. Fax, (703) 696-9437. Maj. Gen. Jeffrey J. Snow, Director.
General email, SAPRO@sapr.mil
Web, www.sapr.mil and www.myduty.mil

Serves as the single point of accountability for the Defense Dept.'s sexual assault policy. Responsible for improving prevention, enhancing reporting and response, and holding perpetrators appropriately accountable.

Marine Corps *(Defense Dept.), Inspector General of the Marine Corps,* Headquarters, U.S. Marine Corps, Code IG 20380-1775; (703) 604-4661. Col. Carl E. Shelton Jr., Inspector General, Acting. Complaint Hotline, (866) 243-3887.
General email, ORGMB_IGMC_ADMIN@usmc.mil
Web, www.hqmc.marines.mil/igmc/unithome.aspx

Military office that investigates complaints from Marine Corps personnel and assists in seeking corrective action.

Navy Dept. *(Defense Dept.), Manpower and Reserve Affairs,* 1000 Navy Pentagon, #4E590 20350-1000; (703) 695-4333. Fax, (703) 614-4103. Juan M. Garcia III, Assistant Secretary.
Web, www.navy.mil/local/oasnmra

Civilian office that receives complaints from Navy and Marine Corps military personnel and assists in seeking corrective action.

►**CONGRESS**

For a listing of relevant congressional committees and subcommittees, please see page 516 or the Appendix.

►**NONGOVERNMENTAL**

OutServe-SLDN, P.O. Box 65301 20035-5301; (202) 328-3244. Fax, (202) 797-1635. Allyson D. Robinson, Executive Director. Toll-free legal hotline, (800) 538-7418.
General email, admin@outserve-sldn.org
Web, www.sldn.org

Seeks to secure equal opportunity, protection, and benefits, without threat of harassment or discrimination, for lesbian, gay, bisexual, and transgender military service members and veterans. Provides free legal services to LGBT service members and veterans; conducts media and outreach campaigns on matters relating to the service of LGBT personnel; provides networking opportunities; monitors legislation and regulations.

Correction of Military Records

►**AGENCIES**

Air Force Dept. *(Defense Dept.), Board for the Correction of Military Records,* SAF/MRBC, 1500 W. Perimeter, #3700 Joint Base Andrews, NAF, Washington 20762; (240) 612-5379. Fax, (240) 612-5619. Michael F. LoGrande, Executive Director.
Web, http://kb.defense.gov/app/answers/detail/a_id/386/~/boards-for-correction-of-military-records

Civilian board that reviews appeals for corrections to Air Force personnel records and makes recommendations to the secretary of the Air Force.

Army Dept. *(Defense Dept.), Board for the Correction of Military Records,* 251 18th St. South, 3rd Floor, Arlington,

VA 22202-3523; (703) 545-6900. Fax, (703) 601-0703. Sarah Bercaw, Director.

Web, http://arba.army.pentagon.mil

Civilian board that reviews appeals for corrections to Army personnel records and makes recommendations to the secretary of the Army under Section 1552 of Title 10 of the U.S. Code.

Defense Dept. (DoD), *Legal Policy,* *4000 Defense Pentagon, #5A668 20301-4000; (703) 697-3387. Col. Paul Kantwill, Director; Maj. Ryan Oakley, Deputy Director.*

Web, www.defense.gov

Coordinates policy for armed services boards charged with correcting military records.

Navy Dept. *(Defense Dept.),* **Board for Correction of Naval Records,** *701 S. Courthouse Rd., Bldg. 12, #1001, Arlington, VA 2204-2490; (703) 604-0814. Fax, (703) 604-3437. Robert Zsalman, Executive Director, Acting.*

General email, karen.clemons@navy.mil

Web, www.donhq.navy.mil/bcnr/bcnr.htm

Civilian board that reviews appeals for corrections to Navy and Marine Corps personnel records and makes recommendations to the secretary of the Navy.

U.S. Coast Guard (USCG) *(Homeland Security Dept.),* **Board for Correction of Military Records,** *245 Murray Lane, MS 485 20528; (202) 447-4099. Fax, (202) 447-3111. Julia Andrews, Chair.*

General email, cgbcmr@dhs.gov

Web, www.uscg.mil/legal/BCMR.asp

Civilian board (an adjunct to the U.S. Coast Guard) that reviews appeals for corrections to Coast Guard personnel records and makes recommendations to the general counsel of the Homeland Security Dept.

Legal Proceedings

▶ AGENCIES

Air Force Dept. *(Defense Dept.),* **Judge Advocate General,** *1420 Air Force Pentagon 20330-1420; (703) 614-5732. Vacant, Judge Advocate General.*

Web, www.afjag.af.mil

Military office that prosecutes and defends Air Force personnel during military legal proceedings. Gives legal advice and assistance to Air Force staff.

Army Dept. *(Defense Dept.),* **Army Clemency and Parole Board,** *Crystal Square 5, 251 18th St. South, #385, Arlington, VA 22202-3531; (703) 607-2309. Fax, (703) 601-0493. Steven L. Andraschko, Chair, (703) 571-0533.*

General email, army.arbainquiry@mail.mil

Web, http://arba.army.pentagon.mil/clemency-parole.cfm

Considers confined Army prisoners for clemency, parole, and mandatory supervised release.

Army Dept. *(Defense Dept.),* **Judge Advocate General,** *2200 Army Pentagon, #3E542 20310-2200; (703) 697-5151.*

Fax, (703) 697-1059. Lt. Gen. Flora D. Darpino, Judge Advocate General.

Web, www.jagcnet.army.mil

Military policy office for the field offices that prosecute and defend Army personnel during military legal proceedings. Serves as an administrative office for military appeals court, which hears legal proceedings involving Army personnel.

Defense Dept. (DoD), *Court of Appeals for the Armed Forces,* *450 E St. N.W. 20442-0001; (202) 761-1448. Fax, (202) 761-4672. William DeCicco, Clerk of the Court. Library, (202) 761-1466.*

Web, www.armfor.uscourts.gov

Serves as the appellate court for cases involving dishonorable or bad conduct discharges, confinement of a year or more, and the death penalty, and for cases certified to the court by the judge advocate general of an armed service. Less serious cases are reviewed by the individual armed services. Library open to the public.

Marine Corps *(Defense Dept.),* **Judge Advocate,** *3000 Marine Corps Pentagon, #4D558 20350-3000; (703) 614-8661. Fax, (703) 693-3208. Maj. Gen. Vaughan A. Ary, Staff Judge Advocate.*

Web, www.hqmc.marines.mil/sja/unithome.aspx

Military office that administers legal proceedings involving Marine Corps personnel.

Navy Dept. *(Defense Dept.),* **Judge Advocate General,** *1322 Patterson Ave. S.E., #3000 20374-5066; (703) 614-7420. Fax, (703) 697-4610. Vice Adm. Nanette M. DeRenzi, Judge Advocate General. Press, (202) 685-5394.*

Web, www.jag.navy.mil

Military office that administers the Judge Advocate General's Corps, which conducts legal proceedings involving Navy and Marine Corps personnel.

Military Police and Corrections

▶ AGENCIES

Army Dept. *(Defense Dept.),* **Provost Marshal General, Operations Division,** *2800 Army Pentagon, DAPM-MPO, #MF748 20310-2800; (703) 693-9478. Fax, (703) 693-6580. Lt. Col. Adolphus Weems, Chief, (703) 693-9478.*

Web, www.army.mil

Develops policies and supports military police and corrections programs in all branches of the U.S. Army. Operates the Military Police Management Information System (MPMIS), which automates incident reporting and tracks information on facilities, staff, and inmates, including enemy prisoners of war.

Defense Dept. (DoD), *Legal Policy,* *4000 Defense Pentagon, #5A668 20301-4000; (703) 697-3387. Col. Paul Kantwill, Director; Maj. Ryan Oakley, Deputy Director.*

Web, www.defense.gov

Coordinates and reviews Defense Dept. policies and programs relating to deserters.

MILITARY HISTORY AND HONORS

General

▶AGENCIES

Air Force Dept. *(Defense Dept.), Air Force History and Museum Programs, AF/HO, 1190 Air Force Pentagon, #4E284 20330-1190; (703) 697-5600. Fax, (703) 693-3496. Walter (Walt) Grudzinskas, Director. Reference, (202) 404-2264.*
Web, www.airforcehistory.af.mil

Publishes histories, studies, monographs, and reference works; directs worldwide Air Force History and Museums Program and provides guidance to the Air Force Historical Research Agency at Maxwell Air Force Base in Alabama; supports Air Force Air Staff agencies and responds to inquiries from the public and the U.S. government.

Army Dept. *(Defense Dept.), Institute of Heraldry, 9325 Gunston Rd., Bldg. 1466, #S112, Fort Belvoir, VA 22060-5579; (703) 806-4971. Fax, (703) 806-4964. Charles Mugno, Director.*
General email, TIOHWebmaster@us.army.mil
Web, www.tioh.hqda.pentagon.mil

Furnishes heraldic services to the armed forces and other U.S. government agencies, including the Executive Office of the President. Responsible for research, design, development, and standardization of official symbolic items, including seals, decorations, medals, insignias, badges, flags, and other items awarded to or authorized for official wear or display by government personnel and agencies. Limited research and information services on these items are provided to the general public.

Army Dept. *(Defense Dept.), U.S. Army Center of Military History, Fort Lesley J. McNair, Collins Hall, 102 4th Ave., Bldg. 35 20319-5060; (202) 685-2706. Fax, (202) 685-4570. Robert J. (Rob) Dalessandro, Director. Library, (202) 685-3573.*
Web, www.history.army.mil

Publishes the official history of the Army. Provides information on Army history; coordinates Army museum system and art program. Works with Army school system to ensure that history is included in curriculum. Sponsors professional appointments, fellowships, and awards. Library open to researchers for archival research Monday through Thursday, 8:00 a.m.–4:00 p.m., and Friday, 8:00 a.m.–12:00 noon; not a lending library.

Defense Dept. (DoD), *Historical Office, 1777 N. Kent St., #5000, Arlington, VA 22209; (703) 588-7890. Erin R. Mahan, Chief Historian.*
Web, http://osdhistory.defense.gov

Researches and writes historical accounts of the office of the secretary of defense; coordinates historical activities of the Defense Dept. and prepares special studies at the request of the secretary.

Defense Dept. (DoD), *Joint History Office, 9999 Defense Pentagon, #1A466 20318-9999; (703) 695-2114. Fax, (703) 614-6243. John F. Shortal, Director, (703) 695-2137.*
General email, john.f.shortal.civ@mail.mil
Web, www.defense.gov

Provides historical support services to the chair of the Joint Chiefs of Staff and the Joint Staff, including research; writes the official history of the Joint Chiefs. Supervises field programs encompassing nine Unified Commands.

Marine Corps *(Defense Dept.), History Division, Marine Corps University, 3078 Upshur Ave., Quantico, VA 22134; (703) 432-4877. Fax, (703) 432-5054. Charles P. Neimeyer, Director. Reference, (703) 432-4874.*
General email, history.division@usmc.mil
Web, www.marines.mil

Writes official histories of the corps for government agencies and the public; answers inquiries about Marine Corps history.

National Archives and Records Administration (NARA), *Reference Services, 8601 Adelphi Rd., #2400, College Park, MD 20740-6001; (301) 837-3510. Fax, (301) 837-1752. Timothy K. Nenninger, Branch Chief.*
Web, www.archives.gov/research/order/textual-records-dc .html

Contains Army records from the Revolutionary War to the Vietnam War, Navy records from the Revolutionary War to the Korean War, and Air Force records from 1947 to 1954. Handles records captured from enemy powers at the end of World War II and a small collection of records captured from the Vietnamese. Conducts research in response to specific inquiries; makes records available for reproduction or examination in research room.

National Museum of American History *(Smithsonian Institution), Division of Armed Forces History, 14th St. and Constitution Ave. N.W., NMAH-4032, MRC 620 20560-0620; (202) 633-3950. Jennifer Locke Jones, Chair.*
Web, http://americanhistory.si.edu/about/departments/ armed-forces-history

Maintains collections relating to the history of the U.S. armed forces, U.S. military technology, and the American flag; includes manuscripts, documents, correspondence, uniforms, small arms and weapons, and other personal memorabilia of armed forces personnel of all ranks. Research areas are open by appointment.

National Museum of Health and Medicine *(Defense Dept.), 2500 Linden Lane, Silver Spring, MD 20910 (mailing address: 2460 Linden Lane, Bldg. 2500, Silver Spring, MD 20910); (301) 319-3300. Fax, (301) 319-3373. Dr. Adrianne Noe, Director.*
General email, usarmy.detrick.medcom-usamrmc.list .medical-museum@mail.mil
Web, http://medicalmuseum.mil and Twitter, @medicalmuseum

Maintains exhibits related to pathology and the history of medicine, particularly military medicine during the Civil

National Park Service

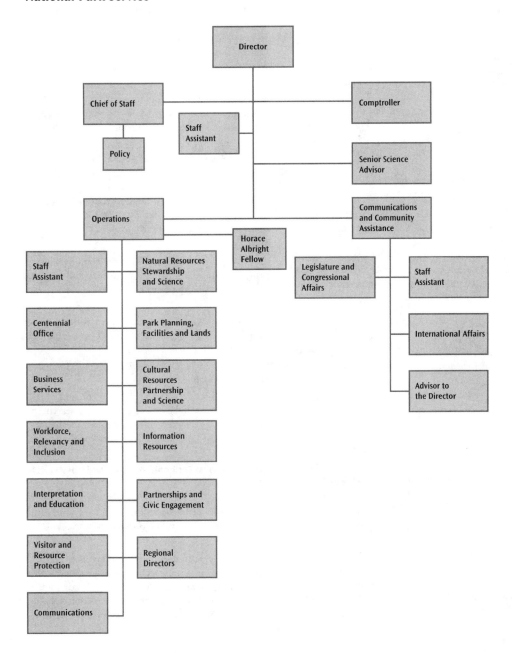

War. Open to the public 10:00 a.m. to 5:30 p.m., 7 days a week. Study collection available for scholars by appointment.

National Park Service (NPS) *(Interior Dept.), 1849 C St. N.W., #3115 20240; (202) 208-4621. Fax, (202) 208-7889. Jonathan B. Jarvis, Director. Press, (202) 208-6843. General email, asknps@nps.gov*

Web, www.nps.gov and Twitter, @NatlParkService

Administers national parks, monuments, historic sites, and recreation areas. Oversees coordination, planning, and financing of public outdoor recreation programs at all

levels of government. Conducts recreation research surveys; administers financial assistance program to states for planning and development of outdoor recreation programs. (Some lands designated as national recreation areas are not under NPS jurisdiction.)

Naval History and Heritage Command *(Navy Dept.), 805 Kidder Breese St. S.E. 20374-5060; (202) 433-2210. Fax, (202) 433-3593. Capt. Jerry Hendrix, Director, Acting. Library, (202) 433-4132. Museum, (202) 433-4882. Art Gallery, (202) 433-3815. Archives, (202) 433-3224. Press, (202) 433-7880.*

General email, NHHCPublicAffairs@navy.mil

Web, www.history.navy.mil

Produces publications on naval history. Maintains historical files on Navy ships, operations, shore installations, and aviation. Collects Navy art, artifacts, and photographs. Library, archives, museum, and gallery are open to the public. (Formerly the Naval Historical Center.)

Naval History and Heritage Command *(Navy Dept.),* *Navy Art Collection, 822 Sicard St. S.E., Washington Navy Yard, Bldg. 67 20374 (mailing address: 805 Kidder Breese St. S.E., Washington Navy Yard, DC 20374); (202) 433-3815. Gale Munro, Head.*

General email, NavyArt@navy.mil

Web, www.history.navy.mil

Holdings include more than 18,000 paintings, prints, drawings, and sculptures. Artworks depict naval ships, personnel, and action from all eras of U.S. naval history, especially the eras of World War II, the Korean War, and Desert Shield/Storm. Open to the public. Visitors without Defense Dept. or military identification must call in advance. Photo identification required.

U.S. Coast Guard (USCG) *(Homeland Security Dept.),* *Historian, CG-09224, 2703 Martin Luther King Jr. Ave. S.E. 20593; (202) 372-4651. Fax, (202) 372-4984. Robert M. Browning, Chief Historian.*

Web, www.uscg.mil/history

Collects and maintains Coast Guard historical artifacts and documents. Archives are available to the public by appointment only.

U.S. Navy Museum *(Naval Historical Center), Bldg. 76, 805 Kidder Breese St. S.E. 20374-5060; (202) 433-4882. Fax, (202) 433-8200. Karin Hill, Director, Education and Public Programs; James H. Bruns, Director of Museum; Capt. Henry J. Hendrix II, Director of Naval History. Tours, (202) 433-6826. Internships, (202) 433-6901.*

General email, navymuseum@navy.mil

Web, www.history.navy.mil/branches/org8-1.htm

Collects, preserves, displays, and interprets historic naval artifacts and artwork. Presents a complete overview of U.S. naval history. Open to the public. Photo identification required.

▶NONGOVERNMENTAL

Air Force Historical Foundation, *1500 W. Perimeter Rd., #2130, Joint Base Andrews, MD 20762-7002 (mailing address: P.O. Box 790, Clinton, MD 20735-0790); (301) 736-1959. Lt. Col. James Vertenten (USAF, Ret.), Executive Director, (240) 691-3323.*

General email, execdir@afhistoricalfoundation.org

Web, www.afhistoricalfoundation.org

Membership: individuals interested in the history of the U.S. Air Force and U.S. air power. Bestows awards on Air Force Academy and Air War College students and to other active duty personnel. Funds research and publishes books on aviation and Air Force history.

Marine Corps Heritage Foundation, *3800 Fettler Park Dr., #104, Dumfries, VA 22025; (703) 640-7965. Fax, (703) 640-9546. Lt. Gen. Robert R. Blackman Jr. (USMC, Ret.), President. Toll-free, (800) 397-7585.*

General email, info@marineheritage.org

Web, www.marineheritage.org

Preserves and promotes Marine Corps history through education, awards, and publications. Offers funding for the study of Marine Corps history. Funds the ongoing expansion of the National Museum of the Marine Corps.

National Guard Educational Foundation, *1 Massachusetts Ave. N.W. 20001; (202) 789-0031. Fax, (202) 682-9358. Anne Armstrong, Deputy Director, (202) 408-5890; Amelia Meyer, Archivist, (202) 408-5887. Library, (202) 408-5890. Toll-free, (888) 226-4287.*

General email, ngef@ngef.org

Web, www.ngef.org

Promotes public awareness of the National Guard by providing information about its history and traditions. Museum and library open to the public.

National Museum of American Jewish Military History, *1811 R St. N.W. 20009; (202) 265-6280. Fax, (202) 462-3192. Col. Herb Rosenbleeth, Director.*

General email, nmajmh@nmajmn.org

Web, www.nmajmh.org

Collects, preserves, and displays memorabilia of Jewish men and women in the military; conducts research; sponsors seminars; provides information on the history of Jewish participation in the U.S. armed forces.

Naval Historical Foundation, *1306 Dahlgren Ave. S.E. 20374-5055; (202) 678-4333. Fax, (202) 889-3565. Capt. Charles T. Creekman (USN, Ret.), Executive Director. Toll-free, (888) 880-0102.*

General email, nhfwny@navyhistory.org

Web, www.navyhistory.org

Collects private documents and artifacts relating to naval history; maintains collection on deposit with the Library of Congress for public reference; conducts oral history and heritage speakers programs; raises funds to support the Navy Museum and historical programs.

Cemeteries and Memorials

▶AGENCIES

American Battle Monuments Commission, *Courthouse Plaza 2, 2300 Clarendon Blvd., #500, Arlington, VA 22201-3367; (703) 696-6900. Fax, (703) 696-6666. Max Cleland, Secretary.*

General email, info@abmc.gov

Web, www.abmc.gov

Manages twenty-four military cemeteries overseas and certain memorials in the United States; provides next of kin with grave site and related information.

Army Dept. *(Defense Dept.), Arlington National Cemetery, Interment Services, Arlington, VA 22211; (877) 907-8585. Patrick K. Hallinan, Executive Director. Fax (for documents), (571) 256-3334-.*
Email (for documents), arlingtoncemetery.isb@mail.mil
Web, www.arlingtoncemetery.mil

Arranges interment services and provides eligibility information for burials at Arlington National Cemetery.

Veterans Affairs Dept. (VA), *National Cemetery Administration, 810 Vermont Ave. N.W., #400 20420; (202) 461-6112. Fax, (202) 273-6709. Steve L. Muro, Under Secretary for Memorial Affairs. Information on burial eligibility, (800) 827-1000.*
Web, www.cem.va.gov and www.gravelocator.cem.va.gov

Administers VA national cemeteries; furnishes markers and headstones for deceased veterans; administers state grants to establish, expand, and improve veterans' cemeteries. Provides presidential memorial certificates to next of kin.

▶**CONGRESS**

For a listing of relevant congressional committees and subcommittees, please see page 516 or the Appendix.

▶**NONGOVERNMENTAL**

Air Force Memorial Foundation, *1 Air Force Memorial Dr., Arlington, VA 22204; (703) 979-0674. Fax, (703) 979-0556. Col. Peter Lindquist, Managing Director.*
General email, afmf@airforcememorial.org
Web, www.airforcememorial.org

Oversees daily management of and directs event planning and fundraising in support of the Air Force Memorial.

U.S. Navy Memorial Foundation, *701 Pennsylvania Ave. N.W., #123 20004-2608; (202) 737-2300. Fax, (202) 737-2308. Vice Adm. John B. Totushek (USN, Ret.), President. Toll-free, (800) 821-8892.*
General email, cmccalip@navymemorial.org
Web, www.navymemorial.org

Educational foundation authorized by Congress. Focuses on U.S. naval history; built and supports the national Navy memorial to honor those who serve or have served in the sea services.

Women in Military Service for America Memorial Foundation, *200 N. Glebe Rd., #400, Arlington, VA 22203-3755 (mailing address: Dept. 560, Washington, DC 20042-0560); (703) 533-1155. Fax, (703) 931-4208. Brig. Gen. Wilma L. Vaught (USAF, Ret.), President; Ann Marie Sharratt, Executive Director. Information, (800) 222-2294.*
General email, hq@womensmemorial.org
Web, www.womensmemorial.org

Authorized by Congress to create, support, and build the national memorial to honor women who serve or have served in the U.S. armed forces from the Revolutionary War to the present. Mailing address is for donations.

Ceremonies, Military Bands

▶**AGENCIES**

Air Force Dept. *(Defense Dept.), Air Force Bands, 1690 Air Force Pentagon, #5D1068 20330; (703) 695-0019. Fax, (703) 693-9601. Lt. Col. Daniel Price, Chief of Music. Web, www.bands.af.mil*

Disseminates information to the public regarding various Air Force bands, including their schedules and performances. Oversees policy, training, and personnel assignments for Air Force bands.

Army Dept. *(Defense Dept.), Army Field Band, 4214 Field Band Dr., #5330, Fort Meade, MD 20755-7055; (301) 677-6231. Fax, (301) 677-6533. Col. Timothy J. Holtan, Commander.*
General email, field.band@usarmy.mil
Web, www.army.mil/fieldband and http://armyfieldband.com

Supports the Army by providing musical services for official military ceremonies and community events. Sponsors vocal and instrumental clinics for high school and college students.

Army Dept. *(Defense Dept.), Ceremonies and Special Events, Fort Lesley J. McNair, 103 3rd Ave., Bldg. 42 20319-5058; (202) 685-4937. Fax, (202) 685-3379. Phil Fowler, Director; Gary S. Davis, Ceremonies Chief; Tina Peck, Special Events Coordinator.*
Web, www.mdw.army.mil/ceremonialsupport

Coordinates and schedules public ceremonies and special events, including appearances of all armed forces bands and honor guards.

Army Dept. *(Defense Dept.), The U.S. Army Band, Attn: TUSAB, 400 McNair Rd., Fort Myer, VA 22211-1306; (703) 696-3718. Fax, (703) 696-0279. Col. Thomas H. Palmatier, Commander. Music Library, (703) 696-3648.*
Web, www.usarmyband.com

Supports the Army by providing musical services for official military ceremonies and community events.

Defense Dept. (DoD), *Community and Public Outreach, 1400 Defense Pentagon, 2E984 20301-1400; (703) 693-2337. Fax, (703) 697-2577. Rene C. Bardorf, Deputy Assistant Secretary, (703) 693-2337. Toll-free (Military OneSource), (800) 342-9647. Public Affairs, (703) 571-3343.*
Web, www.ourmilitary.mil; www.defense.gov

Administers requests for ceremonial bands and other military assets for public events.

Marine Corps *(Defense Dept.), Marine Band, Marine Barracks Annex, 7th St. and K St. S.E. 20003 (mailing address: Marine Barracks Washington, 8th St. and Eye St. S.E., Washington, DC 20390); (202) 433-5809. Fax, (202) 433-4752. Col. Michael J. Colburn, Director. Concert information line, (202) 433-4011.*
General email, marineband.publicaffairs@usmc.mil
Web, www.marineband.usmc.mil

Supports the Marine Corps by providing musical services for official military ceremonies and community events.

Navy Dept. *(Defense Dept.), Navy Band,* 617 Warrington Ave. S.E. 20374-5054; (202) 433-3676. Fax, (202) 433-4108. Capt. Brian O. Walden, Commanding Officer. Information, (202) 433-3366. Press, (202) 433-4777. General email, NavyBand.Public.Affairs@navy.mil

Web, www.navyband.navy.mil

Supports the Navy by providing musical services for official military ceremonies and community events.

U.S. Naval Academy *(Defense Dept.), Band,* 101 Buchanan Rd., Annapolis, MD 21402-1258; (410) 293-1257. Fax, (410) 293-2116. Lt. Cmdr. Bruce A. McDonald, Director; Vacant, Coordinator, Music Department, (410) 293-2439. Concert information, (410) 293-0263. Press, (410) 293-1262. Web, www.usna.edu/USNABand

The Navy's oldest continuing musical organization. Supports the Navy by providing musical services for official military ceremonies and community events.

U.S. Naval Academy *(Defense Dept.), Drum and Bugle Corps,* U.S. Naval Academy, Alumni Hall, 675 Decatur Rd., Annapolis, MD 21402-5086; (410) 293-3602. Fax, (410) 293-4508. Jeff Weir, Corps Director. General email, weir@usna.edu

Web, www.usna.edu/USNADB

One of the oldest drum and bugle corps in the United States. The all-midshipmen drum and bugle corps plays for Brigade of Midshipmen at sporting events, pep rallies, parades, and noon formations. Supports the Navy by providing musical services for official military ceremonies and community events.

RESERVES AND NATIONAL GUARD

General

▶**AGENCIES**

Air Force Dept. *(Defense Dept.), Air Force Reserve,* 1150 Air Force Pentagon, #4E138 20330-1150; (703) 695-9225. Fax, (703) 695-8959. Lt. Gen. James F. Jackson, Chief. Web, www.afrc.af.mil

Military office that coordinates and directs Air Force Reserve matters (excluding the Air National Guard).

Air Force Dept. *(Defense Dept.), Reserve Affairs,* 1660 Air Force Pentagon, #5D742 20330-1660; (703) 697-6375. Fax, (703) 695-2701. Vacant, Deputy Assistant Secretary. Web, www.af.mil

Civilian office that reviews and monitors Air Force Reserve and Air National Guard.

Army Dept. *(Defense Dept.), Army Reserve,* 2400 Army Pentagon, #3E562 20310-2400; (703) 695-0031. Lt. Gen. Jeffrey W. Talley, Chief. Web, www.usar.army.mil

Military office that coordinates and directs Army Reserve matters (excluding the Army National Guard).

Army Dept. *(Defense Dept.), Manpower and Reserve Affairs,* 111 Army Pentagon, #2E460 20310-0111; (703) 697-9253. Fax, (703) 692-9000. Thomas R. Lamont, Assistant Secretary. Web, www.asamra.army.mil

Civilian office that reviews policies and programs for Army personnel and reserves; makes recommendations to the secretary of the Army. Oversees training, military preparedness, and mobilization for all civilians and active and reserve members of the Army.

Defense Dept. (DoD), *Reserve Affairs,* 1500 Defense Pentagon, #2E556 20301-1500; (703) 697-6631. Fax, (703) 697-1682. Richard O. Wightman Jr., Principal Deputy Assistant Secretary. Web, http://ra.defense.gov

Civilian office that addresses all policy matters pertaining to the seven reserve components of the military services.

Marine Corps *(Defense Dept.), Reserve Affairs,* 3280 Russell Rd., Quantico, VA 22134-5103; (703) 784-9100. Fax, (703) 784-9805. Maj. Gen. Rex C. McMillian, Director. Web, www.marines.mil

Military office that coordinates and directs Marine Corps Reserve matters.

National Guard Bureau *(Defense Dept.),* 111 S. George Mason Dr., Arlington, VA 22204; (703) 614-3087. Fax, (703) 614-0274. Gen. (S) Frank J. Grass, Chief. Press, (703) 607-2584. Web, www.ngb.army.mil

Military office that oversees and coordinates activities of the Air National Guard and Army National Guard.

National Guard Bureau *(Defense Dept.), Air National Guard,* 1000 Airforce Pentagon, #4E126 20330; (703) 614-8033. Fax, (703) 692-9056. Lt. Gen. Stanley E. Clark, Director. Web, www.ang.af.mil

Military office that coordinates and directs Air National Guard matters.

National Guard Bureau *(Defense Dept.), Army National Guard,* 111 S. George Mason Dr., Arlington, VA 22204; (703) 607-7000. Fax, (703) 607-3686. Maj. Gen. Judd Lyons, Director, Acting. Public Affairs, (703) 601-6767. Web, www.nationalguard.mil

Military office that coordinates and directs Army National Guard matters.

National Guard Bureau *(Defense Dept.), Chaplain Services,* 111 S. George Mason Dr., Arlington, VA 22204; (703) 607-8657. Fax, (703) 607-5295. Brig. Gen. Alphonse Stephenson, Director. General email, chaplain@ngb.ang.af.mil

Web, http://chaplain.ng.mil

Veterans Affairs Department

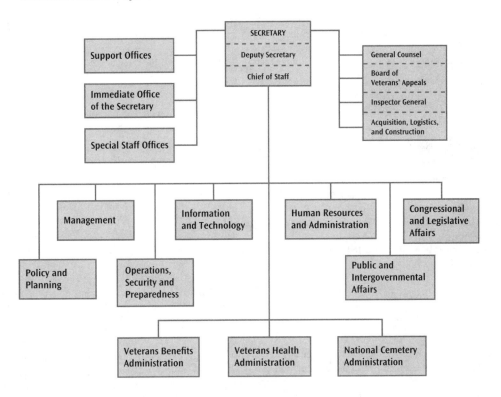

Represents the Chief National Guard Bureau on all aspects of the chaplains' mission. Directs and oversees the activities and policies of the National Guard Chaplain Services. Oversees chaplains and religious services within the National Guard; maintains liaison with religious denominations.

Navy Dept. *(Defense Dept.), Navy Reserve, 2000 Navy Pentagon, CNO-N095, #4E426 20350-2000; (703) 693-5757. Fax, (703) 693-5760. Vice Adm. (S) Robin R. Braun, Chief. Duty office, (757) 445-8506.*
Web, www.navy.mil

Military office that coordinates and directs Navy Reserve matters.

Navy Dept. *(Defense Dept.), Reserve Affairs, 1000 Navy Pentagon, #4D548 20350-1000; (703) 614-1327. Fax, (703) 693-4959. Dennis Biddick, Deputy Assistant Secretary.*
Web, www.navy.mil

Civilian office that reviews Navy and Marine Corps Reserve policies.

U.S. Coast Guard (USCG) *(Homeland Security Dept.), Reserve and Military Personnel, CG-13, USCG Stop 7907 2703 Martin Luther King Jr. Ave. S.E. 20593-7097; (202) 475-5420. Capt. Stephen B. Nye, Director, Acting.*
Web, www.uscg.mil/hq/cg1/cg13

Develops and oversees military personnel policy programs to recruit, train, and support all U.S. Coast Guard reserve and active duty forces.

▶ **NONGOVERNMENTAL**

Assn. of Civilian Technicians (ACT), *12620 Lake Ridge Dr., Lake Ridge, VA 22192-2354; (703) 494-4845. Fax, (703) 494-0961. Terry W. Garnett, National President.*
Web, www.actnat.com

Membership: federal civil service employees of the National Guard and Title 5 federal employees. Represents members before federal agencies and Congress.

Assn. of the U.S. Navy, *1619 King St., Alexandria, VA 22314-2793; (703) 548-5800. Fax, (703) 683-3647. Vice Adm. John B. Totushek (USN, Ret.), Executive Director. Toll-free, (877) 628-9411.*
Web, www.ausn.org

Membership: active duty, inactive, and retired Navy and Navy Reserve officers and their families. Supports and promotes U.S. military and naval policies, particularly the interests of the Navy and Navy Reserve. Offers education programs for naval reservists and potential naval commissioned officers and financial assistance for education of family members. Provides the public with information on national security issues. Assists members with Navy Reserve careers, military retirement, and veterans' benefits.

Enlisted Assn. of the National Guard of the United States, *3133 Mt. Vernon Ave., Alexandria, VA 22305-2640; (703) 519-3846. Fax, (703) 519-3849. Al Garver, Executive Director. Information, (800) 234-3264.*

General email, eangus@eangus.org

Web, www.eangus.org

Membership: active duty and retired enlisted members and veterans of the National Guard. Promotes a strong national defense and National Guard. Sponsors scholarships, conducts seminars, and provides information concerning members and their families.

National Guard Assn. of the United States,

1 Massachusetts Ave. N.W. 20001-1431; (202) 789-0031. Fax, (202) 682-9358. Maj. Gen. Gus Hargett (Ret.), President, (202) 408-5894.

General email, ngaus@ngaus.org

Web, www.ngaus.org

Membership: active duty and retired officers of the National Guard. Works to promote a strong national defense and to maintain a strong, ready National Guard.

Reserve Officers Assn. of the United States,

1 Constitution Ave. N.E. 20002-5618; (202) 479-2200. Fax, (202) 547-1641. Maj. Gen. Andrew Davis (USMC, Ret.), Executive Director, (202) 646-7706. Information, (800) 809-9448.

General email, info@roa.org

Web, www.roa.org

Membership: active duty and inactive commissioned and noncommissioned officers of all uniformed services. Supports continuation of a reserve force to enhance national security. Monitors legislation and regulations.

VETERANS

General

▶AGENCIES

Armed Forces Retirement Home—Washington,

140 Rock Creek Church Rd. N.W. 20011-8400 (mailing address: 3700 N. Capitol St. N.W., Washington, DC 20011-8400); (800) 422-9988. Fax, (202) 541-7519. Steven G. McManus, Chief Operating Officer.

General email, admissions@afrh.gov

Web, www.afrh.gov

Gives domiciliary and medical care to retired members of the armed services or career service personnel unable to earn a livelihood. Formerly known as U.S. Soldiers' and Airmen's Home. (Armed Forces Retirement Home in Gulfport, Miss., reopened in 2010.)

Center for Minority Veterans (Veterans Affairs Dept.),

810 Vermont Ave. N.W., #436, MC-00M 20420; (202) 461-6191. Fax, (202) 273-7092. Barbara Ward, Director.

Web, www.va.gov/centerforminorityveterans

Advises the secretary on adoption and implementation of policies and programs affecting minority veterans, specifically Pacific Islander, Asian American, African American, Hispanic/Latino, and Native American, including American Indian, Alaska Native, and Native Hawaiian, veterans.

Center for Women Veterans (Veterans Affairs Dept.),

810 Vermont Ave. N.W., #435, MC-00W 20420; (202) 461-6193. Fax, (202) 273-7092. Elisa Basnight, Director.

General email, oow@va.gov

Web, www.va.gov/womenvet

Advises the secretary and promotes research on matters related to women veterans; seeks to ensure that women veterans receive benefits and services on par with those of male veterans.

Veterans Affairs Dept. (VA), 810 Vermont Ave. N.W.,

MC-00 20420; (202) 461-4800. Fax, (202) 495-5463. Dr. Robert A. Petzel, Under Secretary; Jose D. (Joe) Riojas, Deputy Secretary; Sloan D. Gibson, Acting Secretary. Press, (202) 461-7500. Locator, (202) 273-5400. Crisis Line, (800) 273-8255, option 1. Health Care, (877) 222-8387. Benefits, (800) 827-1000.

Web, www.va.gov and

Information System (IRIS), https://iris.va.gov

Administers programs benefiting veterans, including disability compensation, pensions, education, home loans, insurance, vocational rehabilitation, medical care at veterans' hospitals and outpatient facilities, and burial benefits.

Veterans Affairs Dept. (VA), National Cemetery Administration,

810 Vermont Ave. N.W., #400 20420; (202) 461-6112. Fax, (202) 273-6709. Steve L. Muro, Under Secretary for Memorial Affairs. Information on burial eligibility, (800) 827-1000.

Web, www.cem.va.gov and www.gravelocator.cem.va.gov

Administers VA national cemeteries; furnishes markers and headstones for deceased veterans; administers state grants to establish, expand, and improve veterans' cemeteries. Provides presidential memorial certificates to next of kin.

Veterans Affairs Dept. (VA), Policy and Planning,

810 Vermont Ave. N.W., #300, MS 008 20420; (202) 461-5800. Fax, (202) 273-5993. Robert D. Snyder, Assistant Secretary, Acting.

General email, vacontactopp@va.gov

Web, www.va.gov

Serves as the single, departmentwide repository, clearinghouse, and publication source for veterans' demographic and statistical information. Provides advice and support to the secretary in the areas of strategic planning, policy development, program analysis and management, and data governance.

Veterans Benefits Administration (VBA) (Veterans Affairs Dept.),

1800 G St. N.W. 20223 (mailing address: 810 Vermont Ave. N.W., #520, Washington, DC 20420); (202) 461-9301. Fax, (202) 275-3591. Allison A. Hickey, Under Secretary. Toll-free insurance hotline, (800) 669-8477.

Web, www.vba.va.gov

Administers nonmedical benefits programs for veterans and their dependents and survivors. Benefits include veterans' compensation (including disability compensation) and pensions, survivors' benefits, education and rehabilitation assistance, home loan benefits, insurance coverage, and burials. (Directs benefits delivery nationwide through regional offices and veterans' insurance offices in Philadelphia and St. Paul.)

Veterans Benefits Administration (VBA) *(Veterans Affairs Dept.), Compensation Service, 810 Vermont Ave. N.W., #645, MS 21 20420; (202) 461-9700. Fax, (202) 275-5661. Thomas J. Murphy, Director. Toll-free, (800) 827-1000. Web, www.vba.va.gov/bln/21*

Administers disability payments; handles claims for burial and plot allowances by veterans' survivors. Provides information on and assistance with benefits legislated by Congress for veterans of active military, naval, or air service.

▶**CONGRESS**

For a listing of relevant congressional committees and subcommittees, please see page 516 or the Appendix.

▶**NONGOVERNMENTAL**

American Legion, *1608 K St. N.W. 20006; (202) 861-2700. Fax, (202) 861-2786. Peter Gaytan, Executive Director. Web, www.legion.org*

Membership: honorably discharged veterans who served on active duty during periods of declared military conflict. Chartered by Congress to assist veterans with claims for benefits; offers a large array of programs and services for veterans and their families.

American Red Cross, *Service to the Armed Forces, 2025 E St. N.W., 2nd Floor 20006-5009; (202) 303-5000, ext. 2. Fax, (202) 303-0216. Sherri L. Brown, Senior Vice President, (202) 303-8283. Emergency communication services, (877) 272-7337. Web, www.redcross.org*

Assists veterans and their dependents with claims for benefits on a limited basis; provides emergency services for active duty armed forces personnel and their families; supports medical care and rehabilitation services at military and veterans hospitals.

AMVETS (American Veterans), *5275 Leesburg Pike, #N-5000, Falls Church, VA 22041; (301) 459-9600. Fax, (301) 459-7924. Stewart M. Hickey, Executive Director. Toll-free, (877) 726-8387. General email, amvets@amvets.org Web, www.amvets.org*

Membership: those who served honorably in the military after September 15, 1940. Helps members obtain benefits and services; participates in community programs; operates a volunteer service that donates time to hospitalized veterans and warrior transition programs. Monitors legislation and regulations.

Blinded Veterans Assn., *477 H St. N.W. 20001-2694; (202) 371-8880. Fax, (202) 371-8258. Al Avina, Executive Director. Toll-free, (800) 669-7079. General email, bva@bva.org Web, www.bva.org*

Chartered by Congress to assist veterans with claims for benefits. Seeks out blinded veterans to make them aware of benefits and services available to them.

Catholic War Veterans U.S.A., *441 N. Lee St., Alexandria, VA 22314-2301; (703) 549-3622. Fax, (703) 684-5196. Dave Crum, Executive Director. Web, www.cwv.org*

Recognized by the Veterans Affairs Dept. to assist veterans with claims for benefits. Conducts community service programs; offers scholarships for children; supports benefits for Vietnam veterans commensurate with those received by World War II veterans.

Disabled American Veterans, *National Service and Legislative Headquarters, 807 Maine Ave. S.W. 20024-2410; (202) 554-3501. Fax, (202) 554-3581. J. Marc Burgess, National Adjutant; Joseph W. Johnston, National Commander. Web, www.dav.org*

Chartered by Congress to assist veterans with claims for benefits; represents veterans seeking to correct alleged errors in military records. Assists families of veterans with disabilities. (Headquarters in Cold Spring, Ky.)

Enlisted Assn., *Washington Office, 1001 N. Fairfax St., #102, Alexandria, VA 22314; (703) 684-1981. Fax, (703) 548-4876. Deirdre Parke Holleman, Executive Director. Toll-free, (800) 554-8732. VA Caregiver Support, (855) 260-3274. General email, dholleman@treadc.org Web, www.trea.org*

Membership: enlisted personnel of the armed forces, including active duty, reserve, guard, and retirees. Runs scholarship, legislative, and veterans service programs. (Formerly Retired Enlisted Assn.; headquarters in Aurora, Colo.)

Jewish War Veterans of the U.S.A., *1811 R St. N.W. 20009; (202) 265-6280. Fax, (202) 234-5662. Herb Rosenbleeth, National Executive Director. General email, jwv@jwv.org Web, www.jwv.org*

Recognized by the Veterans Affairs Dept. to assist veterans with claims for benefits. Offers programs in community relations and services, foreign affairs, national defense, and veterans' affairs. Monitors legislation and regulations that affect veterans.

Marine Corps League, *8626 Lee Hwy., #201, Fairfax, VA 22031-3070 (mailing address: P.O. Box 3070, Merrifield, VA 22116); (703) 207-9588. Fax, (703) 207-0047. Michael A. Blum, Executive Director. Toll-free, (800) 625-1775. Web, www.mcleague.org*

Membership: active duty, retired, and reserve Marine Corps groups. Chartered by Congress to assist veterans with claims for benefits. Operates a volunteer service program in VA hospitals.

Military Officers Assn. of America, *201 N. Washington St., Alexandria, VA 22314-2539; (703) 549-2311. Fax, (703) 838-8173. Vice Adm. Norbert R. Ryan Jr. (USN, Ret.), President. Information, (800) 234-6622.*
General email, msc@moaa.org

Web, www.moaa.org

Membership: officers, former officers, and surviving spouses of officers of the uniformed services. Assists members, their dependents, and survivors with military personnel matters, including service status and retirement problems; provides employment assistance. Monitors legislation affecting active duty officers, retirees, and veterans' affairs, health, and military compensation issues.

Military Order of the Purple Heart of the U.S.A., *5413-B Backlick Rd., Springfield, VA 22151-3960; (703) 642-5360. Fax, (703) 642-1841. David Jackson, National Adjutant. Toll-free, (888) 668-1656.*
General email, info@purpleheart.org

Web, www.purpleheart.org

Membership: veterans awarded the Purple Heart for combat wounds. Chartered by Congress to assist veterans and their families. Conducts service and welfare work on behalf of disabled and needy veterans and their families, especially those requiring claims assistance, those who are homeless, and those requiring employment assistance. Organizes volunteers to provide assistance to hospitalized veterans at VA medical facilities and State Veterans Homes.

National Coalition for Homeless Veterans, *333 1/2 Pennsylvania Ave. S.E. 20003-1148; (202) 546-1969. Fax, (202) 546-2063. John Driscoll, President. Toll-free, (800) VET-HELP. Toll-free fax, (888) 233-8582.*
General email, info@nchv.org

Web, www.nchv.org

Provides technical assistance to service providers; advocates on behalf of homeless veterans.

National Veterans Legal Services Program, *1600 K St. N.W., #500 20006 (mailing address: P.O. Box 65762, Washington, DC 20035); (202) 265-8305. Fax, (202) 328-0063. Ronald B. Abrams, Co-Executive Director; Barton F. Stichman, Co-Executive Director.*
General email, info@nvlsp.org

Web, www.nvlsp.org

Represents the interests of veterans through educational programs, advocacy, public policy programming, and litigation.

Noncommissioned Officers Assn., *National Capital Office, P.O. Box 3085, Oakton, VA 22124; (703) 549-0311. Fax, (703) 549-0245. H. Gene Overstreet, President; Jon Ostrowski, Executive Director for Government Affairs. Toll-free, (800) 662-2620.*
General email, rschneider@ncoadc.org

Web, www.ncoausa.org

Congressionally chartered and accredited by the Veterans Affairs Dept. to assist veterans and widows of veterans with claims for benefits. (Headquarters in Selma, Texas.)

Paralyzed Veterans of America, *801 18th St. N.W. 20006-3517; (202) 872-1300. Fax, (202) 416-7662.*
Homer Townsend, Executive Director. Information, (800) 424-8200.
General email, info@pva.org

Web, www.pva.org

Congressionally chartered veterans service organization that assists veterans with claims for benefits. Distributes information on special education for paralyzed veterans; advocates for high-quality care and supports and raises funds for medical research.

Veterans of Foreign Wars of the United States, *National Legislative Service, Washington Office, 200 Maryland Ave. N.E. 20002-5724; (202) 543-2239. Fax, (202) 543-6719. Robert E. Wallace, Executive Director; William L. Bradshaw, Director. Helpline, (800) 839-1899.*
General email, vfw@vfw.org

Web, www.vfw.org

Chartered by Congress to assist veterans with claims for benefits, including disability compensation, education, and pensions. Inspects VA health care facilities and cemeteries. Monitors medical updates and employment practices regarding veterans. (Headquarters in Kansas City, Mo.)

Veterans of Modern Warfare, *#33107, P.O. Box 96503 20090; (888) 445-9891. Fax, (202) 596-6779. Joseph F. Morgan, President. Toll-free, (888) 445-9891. Suicide hotline, (800) 273-8255.*
General email, info@vmwusa.org

Web, www.vmwusa.org

Chapter-based membership organization. Provides information and assistance in obtaining benefits to all veterans, including active duty and National Guard and Reserve components, as well as any veteran who has served in the U.S. Armed Forces since August 2, 1990. Advocates for veterans.

Vietnam Veterans of America, *8719 Colesville Rd., #100, Silver Spring, MD 20910-3710; (301) 585-4000. Fax, (301) 585-0519. John P. Rowan, President. Information, (800) 882-1316.*
General email, vva@vva.org

Web, www.vva.org

Congressionally chartered membership organization that provides information on legislation that affects Vietnam era veterans and their families. Engages in legislative and judicial advocacy in areas relevant to Vietnam era veterans. Provides information concerning benefits and initiates programs that ensure access to education and employment opportunities. Promotes full accounting of POWs and MIAs.

Appeals of VA Decisions

►AGENCIES

Defense Dept. (DoD), *Legal Policy, 4000 Defense Pentagon, #5A668 20301-4000; (703) 697-3387. Col. Paul Kantwill, Director; Maj. Ryan Oakley, Deputy Director. Web, www.defense.gov*

Coordinates policy in a variety of personnel-related areas, including the Members Civil Relief Act, legal assistance, political activities, and corrections.

Veterans Affairs Dept. (VA), *Board of Veterans' Appeals, 810 Vermont Ave. N.W., #845 20420; (800) 923-8387. Fax, (202) 343-1889. Steven L. Keller, Chair, Acting. Claims status, (202) 565-5436. Web, www.bva.va.gov*

Final appellate body within the department; reviews claims for veterans' benefits on appeal from agencies of original jurisdiction. Decisions of the board are subject to review by the U.S. Court of Appeals for Veterans Claims.

►JUDICIARY

U.S. Court of Appeals for the Federal Circuit, *717 Madison Pl. N.W. 20439; (202) 275-8000. Fax, (202) 275-8036. Randall R. Rader, Chief Judge, (202) 633-6297; Jan Horbaly, Clerk, (202) 312-5520. Helpdesk, (202) 275-8040; (855) 860-8240. Mediation, (202) 275-8120. Web, www.cafc.uscourts.gov*

Reviews decisions concerning the Veterans' Judicial Review Provisions.

U.S. Court of Appeals for Veterans Claims, *625 Indiana Ave. N.W., #900 20004-2950; (202) 501-5970. Fax, (202) 501-5848. Bruce E. Kasold, Chief Judge, (202) 501-5890; Gregory O. Block, Clerk. Web, www.uscourts.cavc.gov*

Independent court that reviews decisions of the VA's Board of Veterans' Appeals concerning benefits. Focuses primarily on disability benefits claims.

►NONGOVERNMENTAL

American Legion, *Claims Services, Veterans Affairs, and Rehabilitation Division, 1608 K St. N.W. 20006; (202) 861-2700. Fax, (202) 833-4452. Zack Hearn, Deputy Director. Web, www.legion.org*

Membership: honorably discharged veterans who served during declared military conflicts. Assists veterans with appeals before the Veterans Affairs Dept. for compensation and benefits claims.

American Legion, *Discharge Review and Correction Boards Unit, 1608 K St. N.W. 20006-2847; (202) 861-2700. Fax, (202) 861-0033. Ray Spencer, Supervisor. Web, www.legion.org*

Membership: honorably discharged veterans who served during declared military conflicts. Represents before the Defense Dept. former military personnel seeking to upgrade less-than-honorable discharges and to correct alleged errors in military records.

Disabled American Veterans, *National Service and Legislative Headquarters, 807 Maine Ave. S.W. 20024-2410; (202) 554-3501. Fax, (202) 554-3581. J. Marc Burgess, National Adjutant; Joseph W. Johnston, National Commander. Web, www.dav.org*

Oversees regional offices in assisting disabled veterans with claims, benefits, and appeals, including upgrading less-than-honorable discharges. Monitors legislation. (Headquarters in Cold Spring, Ky.)

National Veterans Legal Services Program, *1600 K St. N.W., #500 20006 (mailing address: P.O. Box 65762, Washington, DC 20035); (202) 265-8305. Fax, (202) 328-0063. Ronald B. Abrams, Co-Executive Director; Barton F. Stichman, Co-Executive Director. General email, info@nvlsp.org Web, www.nvlsp.org*

Represents the interests of veterans through educational programs, advocacy, public policy programming, and litigation.

Veterans of Foreign Wars of the United States, *National Legislative Service, 200 Maryland Ave. N.E. 20002-5724; (202) 543-2239. Fax, (202) 543-6719. Robert E. Wallace, Executive Director; William L. Bradshaw, Director. Helpline, (800) 839-1899. General email, vfw@vfw.org Web, www.vfw.org*

Assists veterans and their dependents and survivors with appeals before the Veterans Affairs Dept. for benefits claims. Assists with cases in the U.S. Court of Appeals for Veterans Claims.

Education, Economic Opportunity

►AGENCIES

Office of Personnel Management (OPM), *Veterans Services, 1900 E St. N.W., #7439 20415; (202) 606-3602. Fax, (202) 606-6017. Hakeem Basheerud-Deen, Director. Web, www.opm.gov/policy-data-oversight/veterans-services*

Provides federal employees and transitioning military service members and their families, federal human resources professionals, and hiring managers with information on employment opportunities with the federal government. Administers the Disabled Veterans Affirmative Action Program.

Small Business Administration (SBA), *Veterans Business Development, 409 3rd St. S.W., #5110 20416; (202) 205-6773. Fax, (202) 205-7292. Rhett Jeppson, Associate Administrator. Web, www.sba.gov/about-offices-content/1/2985*

Helps veterans use SBA loans through counseling, procurement, and training programs in entrepreneurship.

Veterans Benefits Administration (VBA) *(Veterans Affairs Dept.), Education Service, 1800 G St. N.W., #601 20006 (mailing address: 810 Vermont Ave. N.W., Washington, DC 20420); (202) 461-9800. Fax, (202) 275-1653. Maj. Gen. Robert M. Worley II (USAF, Ret.), Director. Bill information, (888) 442-4551.*
Web, www.gibill.va.gov

Administers VA's education program, including financial support for veterans' education and for spouses and dependent children of deceased and disabled veterans; provides eligible veterans and dependents with educational assistance under the G.I. Bill and Veterans Educational Assistance Program. Provides postsecondary institutions with funds, based on their enrollment of eligible veterans.

Veterans Benefits Administration (VBA) *(Veterans Affairs Dept.), Loan Guaranty Service, 810 Vermont Ave. N.W., #525 20420; (202) 632-8862. Fax, (202) 495-5798. Michael L. (Mike) Frueh, Director.*
Web, www.benefits.va.gov/homeloans

Guarantees private institutional financing of home loans (including manufactured home loans) for veterans; provides disabled veterans with direct loans and grants for specially adapted housing; administers a direct loan program for Native American veterans living on trust land.

Veterans Benefits Administration (VBA) *(Veterans Affairs Dept.), Vocational Rehabilitation and Employment Service, 810 Vermont Ave. N.W., MS 28 20420; (202) 461-9600. Fax, (202) 275-5122. Margarita Devlin, Director, Acting.*
Web, www.vba.va.gov/bln/vre

Administers VA's vocational rehabilitation and employment program, which provides service-disabled veterans with services and assistance; helps veterans to become employable and to obtain and maintain suitable employment.

Veterans' Employment and Training Service *(Labor Dept.), 200 Constitution Ave. N.W., #S1325 20210; (202) 693-4700. Fax, (202) 693-4754. Eric Seleznow, Assistant Secretary, Acting, (202) 693-2700. Toll-free, (800) 487-2365.*
Web, www.dol.gov/vets

Works with and monitors state employment offices to see that preference is given to veterans seeking jobs; advises the secretary on veterans' issues.

▶**CONGRESS**

For a listing of relevant congressional committees and subcommittees, please see page 516 or the Appendix.

▶**NONGOVERNMENTAL**

Blinded Veterans Assn., *477 H St. N.W. 20001-2694; (202) 371-8880. Fax, (202) 371-8258. Al Avina, Executive Director. Toll-free, (800) 669-7079.*

General email, bva@bva.org
Web, www.bva.org

Provides blind and disabled veterans with vocational rehabilitation.

National Assn. of State Workforce Agencies, *444 N. Capitol St. N.W., #142 20001; (202) 434-8020. Fax, (202) 434-8033. Richard A. Hobbie, Executive Director. Press, (202) 434-8023.*
General email, mkatz@naswa.org
Web, www.naswa.org

Membership: state employment security administrators. Provides veterans' employment and training professionals with opportunities for networking and information exchange. Monitors legislation and regulations that affect veterans' employment and training programs involving state employment security agencies.

Paralyzed Veterans of America, *801 18th St. N.W. 20006-3517; (202) 872-1300. Fax, (202) 416-7662. Homer Townsend, Executive Director. Information, (800) 424-8200.*
General email, info@pva.org
Web, www.pva.org

Congressionally chartered veterans service organization that assists veterans with claims for benefits. Promotes access to educational and public facilities and to public transportation for people with disabilities; seeks modification of workplaces.

Health Care, VA Hospitals

▶**AGENCIES**

Army Dept. *(Defense Dept.), Wounded Warrior Program (AW2), 200 Stovall St., #7N65, Alexandria, VA 22332-5000; (877) 393-9058. Fax, (703) 325-1516. Col. Johnny Davis, Director. Overseas, (312) 221-9113.*
General email, usarmy.pentagon.medcom-WTC.mbx .contact-center@mail.mil
Web, http://wtc.army.mil/aw2

Incorporates several existing programs to provide holistic support services for severely disabled and ill soldiers and their families. Provides each soldier with a personal AW2 advocate. Tracks and monitors severely disabled soldiers beyond their medical retirement.

Defense Dept. (DoD), *Force Health Protection and Readiness, 7700 Arlington Blvd., Falls Church, VA 22042; (703) 578-8599. Dr. Michael Kilpatrick, Deputy Director.*
General email, FHPR.communications@tma.osd.mil
Web, http://fhp.osd.mil

Advises the secretary of defense on measures to improve the health of deployed forces. Maintains communication between the Defense Dept., service members, veterans, and their families.

Veterans Affairs Dept. (VA), *Construction and Facilities Management, 425 Eye St., N.W., 6th Floor 20001 (mailing address: 810 Vermont Ave. N.W., MS003C, Washington, DC 20420); (202) 632-4607. Fax, (202) 632-5830. Stella S. Fiotes, Executive Director.*
General email, cfm@va.gov

Web, www.cfm.va.gov

Principal construction and real estate arm of the Veterans Administration.

Veterans Health Administration (VHA) *(Veterans Affairs Dept.), 810 Vermont Ave. N.W., #800 20420; (202) 461-7016. Fax, (202) 273-7090. Dr. Robert A. Petzel, Under Secretary. Toll-free, (877) 222-8387.*
Web, www.va.gov/health

Oversees all health care policies for all eligible veterans. Recommends policy and administers medical and hospital services for eligible veterans. Publishes guidelines on treatment of veterans exposed to Agent Orange.

Veterans Health Administration (VHA) *(Veterans Affairs Dept.), Academic Affiliations, 1800 G St. N.W., #870 20006; (202) 461-9490. Fax, (202) 461-9855.*
Dr. Malcolm Cox, Chief.
Web, www.va.gov/oaa

Administers education and training programs for health professionals, students, and residents through partnerships with affiliated academic institutions.

Veterans Health Administration (VHA) *(Veterans Affairs Dept.), Dentistry, 1722 Eye St. N.W. 20420; (202) 632-8342. Dr. Patricia Arola, Assistant Under Secretary.*
Web, www.va.gov/dental

Administers and coordinates VA oral health care programs; dental care delivered in a VA setting; administration of oral research, education, and training for VA oral health personnel; delivery of care to VA patients in private practice settings.

Veterans Health Administration (VHA) *(Veterans Affairs Dept.), Geriatrics and Extended Care, 810 Vermont Ave. N.W., #10P4G 20420; (202) 461-6750. Fax, (202) 273-9131. Richard Allman, Chief Consultant.*
Web, www.va.gov/geriatricsshg

Administers research, educational, and clinical health care programs in geriatrics at VA and community nursing homes, personal care homes, VA domiciliaries, state veterans' homes, and in home-based and other non-institutional care.

Veterans Health Administration (VHA) *(Veterans Affairs Dept.), Mental Health Services, 810 Vermont Ave. N.W., MS 10P4M 20420; (202) 461-4170. Fax, (202) 273-9069. Marsden McGuire, Chief Consultant; Vashtie Reedy, Management Program Analyst.*
Web, www.mentalhealth.va.gov

Develops ambulatory and inpatient psychiatry and psychology programs for the mentally ill and for drug and alcohol abusers; programs are offered in VA facilities and twenty-one Veterans Integrated Service Networks. Incorporates special programs for veterans suffering from posttraumatic stress disorders, serious mental illness, addictive disorders, and homelessness.

Veterans Health Administration (VHA) *(Veterans Affairs Dept.), Office of the Assistant Deputy Under Secretary for Health Policy and Planning, 810 Vermont Ave. N.W., 8th Floor 20420; (202) 461-7100. Fax, (202) 273-9030. Pat Vandenberg, Assistant Deputy Under Secretary.*
Web, www.va.gov

Coordinates and develops departmental planning to distribute funds to VA field facilities.

Veterans Health Administration (VHA) *(Veterans Affairs Dept.), Patient Care Services, 810 Vermont Ave. N.W., #994, MS 11 20420; (202) 461-7590. Fax, (202) 273-9274. Rajiv Jain, Chief Officer, (202) 461-7567.*
Web, www.va.gov

Manages clinical programs of the VA medical care system, including rehabilitation and recovery, diagnosis and therapy, palliative care, disease prevention, and health promotion.

Veterans Health Administration (VHA) *(Veterans Affairs Dept.), Readjustment Counseling Service, 810 Vermont Ave. N.W., #870 20420; (202) 461-6525. Fax, (202) 495-6206. Don Smith, Chief Officer, Acting.*
Web, www.vetcenter.va.gov and www.va.gov

Responsible for community-based centers for veterans nationwide. Provides outreach and counseling services for war-related psychological problems and transition to civilian life. Offers bereavement counseling to surviving family members.

Veterans Health Administration (VHA) *(Veterans Affairs Dept.), Research and Development, 810 Vermont Ave. N.W., 1st Floor, MS 10P9 20420; (202) 443-5600. Fax, (202) 495-6153. Timothy O'Leary, Chief, Acting, (202) 443-5602.*
Web, www.research.va.gov

Formulates and implements policy for the research and development program of the Veterans Health Administration; advises the under secretary for health on research-related matters and on management of the VA's health care system; represents the VA in interactions with external organizations in matters related to biomedical and health services research.

Veterans Health Administration (VHA) *(Veterans Affairs Dept.), Voluntary Service, 810 Vermont Ave. N.W., #10C2 20420; (202) 461-7300. Fax, (202) 495-6208. Sabrina Clark, Director.*
General email, VHAC010B2AStaff@va.gov

Web, www.volunteer.va.gov

Supervises volunteer programs in VA medical centers.

▶**CONGRESS**

For a listing of relevant congressional committees and subcommittees, please see page 516 or the Appendix.

▶**NONGOVERNMENTAL**

National Assn. of Veterans Affairs Physicians and Dentists, *P.O. Box 15418, Arlington, VA 22215-0418; (866) 836-3520. Fax, (540) 972-1728. Dr. Samuel V. Spagnolo, President.*
General email, opscoord@navapd.org
Web, www.navapd.org

Seeks to improve the quality of care and conditions at VA hospitals. Monitors legislation and regulations on veterans' health care.

National Conference on Ministry to the Armed Forces, *Endorsers Conference for Veterans Affairs Chaplaincy, 7724 Silver Sage Ct., Springfield, VA 22153; (703) 608-2100. Jack Williamson, Executive Director.*
General email, jack@ncmaf.org
Web, www.ncmaf.org

Encourages religious ministry to veterans in VA hospitals and centers and at the Defense Dept.

Paralyzed Veterans of America, *801 18th St. N.W. 20006-3517; (202) 872-1300. Fax, (202) 416-7662. Homer Townsend, Executive Director. Information, (800) 424-8200.*
General email, info@pva.org
Web, www.pva.org

Congressionally chartered veterans service organization. Consults with the Veterans Affairs Dept. on the establishment and operation of spinal cord injury treatment centers.

Vietnam Veterans of America, *Veterans Health Council, 8719 Colesville Rd., #100, Silver Spring, MD 20910-3710; (301) 585-4000, ext. 148. Fax, (301) 585-3180. Thomas J. (Tom) Berger, Executive Director.*
General email, vhc@veteranshealth.org
Web, www.veteranshealth.org

Health education and information network for veterans and their families.

Spouses, Dependents, Survivors

▶**AGENCIES**

Air Force Dept. *(Defense Dept.), Manpower Personnel and Services, 1040 Air Force Pentagon, #4E168 20330-1040; (703) 697-6088. Lt. Gen. Samuel D. Cox, Deputy Chief of Staff.*
Web, www.afpc.af.mil

Military office that responds to inquiries concerning deceased Air Force personnel and their beneficiaries; refers inquiries to the Military Personnel Center at Randolph Air Force Base in San Antonio, Texas.

Marine Corps *(Defense Dept.), Casualty Section, HQUSMC, 2008 Elliott Rd., Quantico, VA 22134-5102; (703) 784-9512. Fax, (703) 784-4134. Gerald Castle, Head. Toll-free, (800) 847-1597.*
General email, casualtysection@usmc.mil
Web, www.marines.mil

Confirms beneficiaries of deceased Marine Corps personnel for benefits distribution.

Veterans Health Administration (VHA) *(Veterans Affairs Dept.), Readjustment Counseling Service, Bereavement Counseling for Surviving Family Members, 810 Vermont Ave. N.W., #675, MS 15 20420; (1) (720) 874-1031. Fax, (303) 216-9074. Andrew Carraway, Chief Officer. Bereavement Center, (202) 461-6530.*
General email, vetcenter.bereavement@va.gov
Web, www.vetcenter.va.gov/Bereavement_Counseling.asp

Offers bereavement counseling to parents, spouses, siblings, and children of armed forces personnel who died in service to their country and to family members of reservists and those in the National Guard who died while federally activated. Services include outreach, counseling, and referrals. Counseling provided without cost at community-based Vet Centers.

▶**NONGOVERNMENTAL**

American Gold Star Mothers Inc., *2128 Leroy Pl. N.W. 20008-1893; (202) 265-0991. Barb Benard, National President.*
General email, goldstarmoms@yahoo.com
Web, www.goldstarmoms.com

Membership: mothers who have lost sons or daughters in military service. Members serve as volunteers in VA hospitals and around the country.

Army and Air Force Mutual Aid Assn., *102 Sheridan Ave., Fort Myer, VA 22211-1110; (703) 707-4600. Fax, (703) 522-1336. Maj. Walt Lincoln (USA, Ret.), President.*
General email, info@aafmaa.com
Web, www.aafmaa.com

Private service organization that offers member and family insurance services to U.S. armed forces personnel. Recognized by the Veterans Affairs Dept. to assist veterans and their survivors with claims for benefits.

Army Distaff Foundation (Knollwood), *6200 Oregon Ave. N.W. 20015-1543; (202) 541-0149. Fax, (202) 364-2856. Maj. Gen. Stephen T. Rippe (USA, Ret.), Chief Executive Officer. Information, (800) 541-4255.*
General email, marketing@armydistaff.org
Web, www.armydistaff.org

Nonprofit continuing care retirement community for career military officers and their families. Provides retirement housing and health care services.

EX-POSE, Ex-Partners of Servicemembers for Equality, *P.O. Box 11191, Alexandria, VA 22312-0191; (703) 941-5844. Fax, (703) 212-6951. Nancy Davis, Manager.*
General email, ex-pose@juno.com
Web, www.ex-pose.org

Membership: current and former partners of military members, both officers and enlisted, and other interested parties. Educates current and former spouses about potential benefits that may be gained or lost through divorce, including retirement pay, survivors' benefits, and medical, commissary, and exchange benefits. Provides information concerning legal resources and related federal laws and regulations. Serves as an information clearinghouse. Open Tuesday through Thursday, 10:00 a.m.–3:00 p.m.

Society of Military Widows, *5535 Hempstead Way, Springfield, VA 22151; (703) 750-1342, ext. 1009. Fax, (703) 354-4380. Etta Brown, President; Janet Snyder, Legislative Chair. Information, (800) 842-3451, ext. 1005. General email, pdshecter76@gmail.com*

Web, www.militarywidows.org

Membership: widows of active, reserve, or veteran military personnel. Serves the interests of widows of servicemen; provides support programs and information. Monitors legislation concerning military widows' benefits. (Affiliated with the National Assn. for Uniformed Services.)

Tragedy Assistance Program for Survivors (TAPS), *3033 Wilson Blvd., #630, Arlington, VA 22201; (202) 588-8277. Fax, (571) 385-2524. Bonnie Carroll, President. Toll-free 24-hr crisis intervention hotline, (800) 959-8277. General email, info@taps.org*

Web, www.taps.org

Offers emotional support to those who have lost a loved one in military service. Has caseworkers who act as liaisons to military and veterans agencies. Provides 24/7 resource and information help line. Hosts Good Grief camps for children, seminars for adults, and online and in-person support groups. Publishes a quarterly magazine on grief and loss.

15

National and Homeland Security

GENERAL POLICY AND ANALYSIS

Basic Resources

▶AGENCIES

Air Force Dept. *(Defense Dept.),* 1670 Air Force Pentagon, #4E878 20330-1670; (703) 697-7376. Fax, (703) 695-7791. Deborah Lee James, Secretary; Eric Fanning, Under Secretary, Acting. Press, (703) 695-0640.
Web, www.af.mil

Civilian office that develops and reviews Air Force national security policies in conjunction with the chief of staff of the Air Force and the secretary of defense.

Air Force Dept. *(Defense Dept.), Chief of Staff,* 1670 Air Force Pentagon 20330-1670; (703) 697-9225. Fax, (703) 693-9297. Gen. Mark A. Welch III, Chief of Staff.
Web, www.af.mil/information/csaf

Military office that develops and directs Air Force national security policies in conjunction with the secretary of the Air Force and the secretary of defense.

Army Dept. *(Defense Dept.),* 101 Army Pentagon, #3E700 20310-0101; (703) 695-1717. Fax, (703) 697-8036. John M. McHugh, Secretary.
Web, www.army.mil

Civilian office that develops and reviews Army national security policies in conjunction with the chief of staff of the Army and the secretary of defense.

Army Dept. *(Defense Dept.), Chief of Staff,* 200 Army Pentagon, #3E672 20310-0200; (703) 697-0900. Fax, (703) 614-5268. Gen. Raymond T. Odierno, Chief of Staff.
Web, www.army.mil

Military office that develops and administers Army national security policies in conjunction with the secretary of the Army and the secretary of defense.

Defense Dept. (DoD), 1000 Defense Pentagon, #3E880 20301-1000; (703) 692-7100. Fax, (703) 571-8951. Chuck Hagel, Secretary; Christine H. Fox, Deputy Secretary, Acting. Information, (703) 571-3343. Pentagon operator, (703) 545-6700. Press, (703) 697-5131. Tours, (703) 697-1776.
Web, www.defense.gov

Civilian office that develops national security policies and has overall responsibility for administering national defense; responds to public and congressional inquiries about national defense matters.

Defense Dept. (DoD), Global Strategic Affairs, 2900 Defense Pentagon, #3C852A 20301-2900; (703) 697-7728. Fax, (703) 614-2259. Madelyn R. Creedon, Assistant Secretary; Eric B. Rosenbach, Principal Deputy Assistant Secretary, Acting.
Web, www.defense.gov

Develops and coordinates national security and defense strategies and advises on the resources, forces, and contingency plans necessary to implement those strategies.

Ensures the integration of defense strategy into the department's resource allocation and force structure development. Evaluates the capability of forces to accomplish defense strategy.

Defense Dept. (DoD), Homeland Defense and America's Security Affairs, 2600 Defense Pentagon, #3C249 20301-2600; (703) 697-5664. Fax, (571) 256-8383. Todd Rosenbloom, Assistant Secretary, Acting.
Web, http://policy.defense.gov/hdasa

Serves as primary liaison between the Defense Dept. and the Homeland Security Dept. Supervises all Defense Dept. homeland defense activities.

Defense Dept. (DoD), Installations and Environment, 3400 Defense Pentagon, #3B856A 20301-3400; (703) 695-2880. Fax, (703) 693-7011. John Conger, Deputy Under Secretary, Acting.
Web, www.acq.osd.mil/ie

Oversees and offers policy guidance for all Defense Dept. installations and environmental programs.

Defense Dept. (DoD), Joint Chiefs of Staff, 9999 Defense Pentagon, #2E872 20318-9999; (703) 697-9121. Fax, (703) 697-6002. Gen. Martin E. Dempsey, Chair.
Web, www.jcs.mil

Joint military staff office that assists the president, the National Security Council, and the secretary of defense in developing national security policy and in coordinating operations of the individual armed services.

Defense Dept. (DoD), Policy, 2000 Defense Pentagon, #3E806 20301; (703) 697-7200. Fax, (703) 697-6602. Vacant, Under Secretary for Policy.
Web, http://policy.defense.gov

Civilian office responsible for policy matters relating to international security issues and political-military affairs. Oversees such areas as arms control, foreign military sales, intelligence collection and analysis, and NATO and regional security affairs.

Defense Dept. (DoD), Special Operations and Low-Intensity Conflict, 2500 Defense Pentagon, #3C852A 20301-2500; (703) 695-9667. Fax, (703) 693-6335. Michael D. Lumpkin, Assistant Secretary.
Web, www.defense.gov

Serves as special staff assistant and civilian adviser to the secretary of defense on matters related to special operations and international terrorism.

Defense Logistics Agency *(Defense Dept.), Energy,* 8725 John Jay Kingman Rd., #4950, Fort Belvoir, VA 22060-6222; (703) 767-9706. Fax, (703) 767-1338. Brig. Gen. Giovanni K. Tuck, Commander. Toll-free, (877) 352-2255. Public Affairs, (703) 767-4108.
Web, www.energy.dla.mil

Provides the Defense Dept. and other federal agencies with products and services to meet energy-related needs; facilitates the cycle of storage and deployment of fuels and other energy sources, including petroleum, electricity, water and natural gas, as well as space and missile propellants. Provides information on alternative fuels and

NATIONAL AND HOMELAND SECURITY RESOURCES IN CONGRESS

For a complete listing of Congress committees, including their full contact information, leadership, membership, and jurisdictions, please refer to the Appendix on pages 724–842.

HOUSE:

House Appropriations Committee, (202) 225-2771.
Web, appropriations.house.gov or
  democrats.appropriations.house.gov
  Subcommittee on Defense, (202) 225-2847.
  Subcommittee on Energy and Water
    Development, and Related Agencies,
    (202) 225-3421.
  Subcommittee on Financial Services and General
    Government, (202) 225-7245.
  Subcommittee on Homeland Security,
    (202) 225-5834.
  Subcommittee on Interior, Environment, and
    Related Agencies, (202) 225-3081.
  Subcommittee on Military Construction,
    Veterans Affairs, and Related Agencies,
    (202) 225-3047.
  Subcommittee on State, Foreign Operations, and
    Related Programs, (202) 225-2041.
House Armed Services Committee, (202) 225-4151.
Web, armedservices.house.gov or
  democrats.armedservices.house.gov
  Subcommittee on Intelligence, Emerging Threats,
    and Capabilities, (202) 226-2843.
  Subcommittee on Military Personnel,
    (202) 225-7560.
  Subcommittee on Readiness, (202) 226-8979.
  Subcommittee on Strategic Forces,
    (202) 225-1967.
  Subcommittee on Tactical Air and Land Forces,
    (202) 225-4440.
House Energy and Commerce Committee,
  (202) 225-2927.
Web, energycommerce.house.gov or
  democrats.energycommerce.house.gov
  Subcommittee on Health, (202) 225-2927.
House Financial Services Committee, (202) 225-7502.
Web, financialservices.house.gov or
  democrats.financialservices.house.gov
  Subcommittee on Housing and Insurance,
    (202) 225-7502.
House Foreign Affairs Committee, (202) 225-5021.
Web, foreignaffairs.house.gov or
  democrats.foreignaffairs.house.gov

  Subcommittee on Terrorism, Nonproliferation
    and Trade, (202) 226-1500.
House Homeland Security Committee,
  (202) 226-8417.
Web, homeland.house.gov or chsdemocrats.house.gov
  Subcommittee on Border and Maritime Security,
    (202) 226-8417.
  Subcommittee on Counterterrorism and
    Intelligence, (202) 226-8417.
  Subcommittee on Cybersecurity, Infrastructure
    Protection, and Security Technologies,
    (202) 226-8417.
  Subcommittee on Emergency Preparedness
    Response, and Communications,
    (202) 226-8417.
  Subcommittee on Oversight and Management
    Efficiency, (202) 226-8417.
  Subcommittee on Transportation Security,
    (202) 226-8417.
House Judiciary Committee, (202) 225-3951.
Web, judiciary.house.gov or
  democrats.judiciary.house.gov
  Subcommittee on the Constitution and Civil
    Justice, (202) 225-2825.
  Subcommittee on Crime, Terrorism and
    Homeland Security, and Investigations,
    (202) 225-5727.
  Subcommittee on Immigration and Border
    Security, (202) 225-3926.
House Oversight and Government Reform
  Committee, (202) 225-5074.
Web, oversight.house.gov or
  democrats.oversight.house.gov
  Subcommittee on National Security,
    (202) 225-5074.
House Permanent Select Committee on Intelligence,
  (202) 225-4121.
Web, intelligence.house.gov
  Subcommittee on Oversight, (202) 225-4121.
  Subcommittee on Technical and Tactical
    Intelligence, (202) 225-4121.
  Subcommittee on Terrorism, Human
    Intelligence, Analysis, and
    Counterintelligence, (202) 225-4121.

renewable energy and serves as the executive agent for the Defense Dept.'s bulk petroleum supply chain.

Homeland Security Dept. (DHS), *Nebraska Ave. Complex, 3801 Nebraska Ave. N.W. 20528; (202) 282-8000. Fax, (202) 282-8401. Joh Johnson, Secretary; Alejandro Mayorkas, Deputy Secretary. Press, (202)* *282-8010. Comments, (202) 282-8495. Web, www.dhs.gov*

Responsible for the development and coordination of a comprehensive national strategy to protect the United States against terrorist attacks and other threats and hazards. Coordinates the strategy of the executive branch with those of state and local governments and private

House Science, Space, and Technology Committee, (202) 225-6371.
Web, science.house.gov or democrats.science.house.gov
  Subcommittee on Research and Technology, (202) 225-6371.
House Transportation and Infrastructure Committee, (202) 225-9446.
Web, transportation.house.gov or democrats.transportation.house.gov
  Subcommittee on Economic Development, Public Buildings, and Emergency Management, (202) 225-3014.

SENATE:

Senate Appropriations Committee, (202) 224-7363.
Web, appropriations.senate.gov
  Subcommittee on Defense, (202) 224-6688.
  Subcommittee on Energy and Water Development, (202) 224-8119.
  Subcommittee on Financial Services and General Government, (202) 224-1133.
  Subcommittee on Homeland Security, (202) 224-8244.
  Subcommittee on Interior, Environment, and Related Agencies, (202) 228-0774.
  Subcommittee on Military Construction, Veterans Affairs, and Related Agencies, (202) 224-8224.
  Subcommittee on State, Foreign Operations, and Related Programs, (202) 224-7284.
Senate Armed Services Committee, (202) 224-3871.
Web, armed-services.senate.gov
  Subcommittee on Airland, (202) 224-3871.
  Subcommittee on Emerging Threats and Capabilities, (202) 224-3871.
  Subcommittee on Personnel, (202) 224-3871.
  Subcommittee on Readiness and Management Support, (202) 224-3871.
  Subcommittee on Seapower, (202) 224-3871.
  Subcommittee on Strategic Forces, (202) 224-3871.
Senate Banking, Housing, and Urban Affairs Committee, (202) 224-7391.
Web, banking.senate.gov
  Subcommittee on National Security and International Trade and Finance, (202) 224-2023.

  Subcommittee on Securities, Insurance, and Investment, (202) 224-4642.
Senate Commerce, Science, and Transportation Committee, (202) 224-0411.
Web, commerce.senate.gov
Senate Environment and Public Works Committee, (202) 224-8832.
Web, epw.senate.gov
  Subcommittee on Clean Air and Nuclear Safety, (202) 224-8832.
  Subcommittee on Transportation and Infrastructure, (202) 224-8832.
Senate Foreign Relations Committee, (202) 224-4651.
Web, foreign.senate.gov
  Subcommittee on International Operations and Organizations, Human Rights, Democracy, and Global Women's Issues, (202) 224-4651.
Senate Health, Education, Labor, and Pensions Committee, (202) 224-5375.
Web, help.senate.gov
Senate Homeland Security and Governmental Affairs Committee, (202) 224-2627.
Web, hsgac.senate.gov
  Permanent Subcommittee on Investigations, (202) 224-9505.
  Subcommittee on Efficiency and Effectiveness of Federal Programs and the Federal Workforce, (202) 224-4551.
  Subcommittee on Emergency Management, Intergovernmental Relations, and the District of Columbia, (202) 224-4462.
  Subcommittee on Financial and Contracting Oversight, (202) 224-4462.
Senate Judiciary Committee, (202) 224-7703.
Web, judiciary.senate.gov
  Subcommittee on Crime and Terrorism, (202) 228-3740.
  Subcommittee on Immigration, Refugees, and Border Security, (202) 224-6498.
  Subcommittee on the Constitution, Civil Rights, and Human Rights, (202) 224-1158.
Senate Select Committee on Intelligence, (202) 224-1700.
Web, intelligence.senate.gov

entities to detect, prepare for, protect against, respond to, and recover from terrorist attacks and other emergencies in the United States.

Homeland Security Dept. (DHS), *Science and Technology Directorate, 245 Murray Lane 20528; (202) 254-6006. Fax, (202) 254-5704. Daniel M. Gerstein, Under Secretary,*

Acting. Press, (202) 282-8010.
Web, www.dhs.gov/st-directorate

Responsible for oversight and coordination of the development and augmentation of homeland security technology.

Marine Corps *(Defense Dept.), Commandant, Marine Corps Headquarters, 3000 Marine Corps Pentagon, #4E734*

20350-3000; (703) 614-2500. Fax, (703) 697-7246. Gen. James F. Amos, Commandant. Information, (703) 614-8010.
Web, www.hqmc.marines.mil/cmc/home.aspx

Military office that develops and directs Marine Corps national security policies in conjunction with the secretary of defense and the secretary of the Navy.

National Security Council (NSC) *(Executive Office of the President),* The White House 20504; (202) 456-9491. Fax, (202) 456-9490. Susan Rice, National Security Adviser. Press, (202) 456-9271.
Web, www.whitehouse.gov/administration/eop/nsc

Advises the president on domestic, foreign, and military policies relating to national security.

Navy Dept. *(Defense Dept.),* 1000 Navy Pentagon, #4E686 20350-1000; (703) 695-3131. Fax, (703) 693-9545. Raymond E. (Ray) Mabus Jr., Secretary; Thomas W. Hicks, Under Secretary, Acting.
Web, www.navy.mil

Civilian office that develops and reviews Navy and Marine Corps national security policies in conjunction with the chief of naval operations, the commandant of the Marine Corps, and the secretary of defense.

Navy Dept. *(Defense Dept.), Naval Operations,* 2000 Navy Pentagon, #4E658 20350-2000; (703) 695-5664. Fax, (703) 693-9408. Adm. Jonathan W. Greenert, Chief.
Web, www.navy.mil

Military office that develops Navy national security policies in conjunction with the secretary of defense and the secretary of the Navy and in cooperation with the commandant of the Marine Corps.

State Dept., *Conflict and Stabilization Operations,* 2121 Virginia Ave. N.W., 7th Floor 20037; (202) 663-0323. Fax, (202) 663-0327. Amb. Rick Barton, Assistant Secretary.
General email, csopublic@state.gov
Web, www.state.gov/j/cso/

Advances U.S. national security by working with partners in select countries to mitigate and prevent violent conflict. Conducts conflict analysis to identify factors contributing to mass violence or instability; develops prioritized strategies to address these factors; provides experienced leadership and technical experts to operationalize U.S. government and host-nation plans. Provides funding and training.

State Dept., *Foreign Missions,* 2201 C St. N.W., #2236 20520; (202) 647-3417. Fax, (202) 736-4145. Frederick Ketchem, Deputy Assistant Secretary, Acting.
General email, ofminfo@state.gov
Web, www.state.gov/ofm

Authorized to control the numbers, locations, and travel privileges of foreign diplomats and diplomatic staff in the United States.

State Dept., *International Organization Affairs,* 2201 C St. N.W., #6323 20520-6319; (202) 647-9600. Fax, (202) 736-4116. H. Dean Pittman, Assistant Secretary, Acting. Press, (202) 647-6899.
General email, io-bureau@state.gov
Web, www.state.gov

Coordinates and develops policy guidelines for U.S. participation in the United Nations and in other international organizations and conferences.

State Dept., *Political-Military Affairs,* 2201 C St. N.W., #6212 20520; (202) 647-9022. Fax, (202) 736-4779. Puneet Talwar, Assistant Secretary.
Web, www.state.gov

Responsible for security affairs policy; acts as a liaison between the Defense Dept. and the State Dept.

U.S. Coast Guard (USCG) *(Homeland Security Dept.),* 2703 Martin Luther King Jr. Ave. S.E., MS 7000 20593-7000; (202) 372-4411. Fax, (202) 372-8302. Adm. Robert J. Papp Jr., Commandant. Public Affairs, (202) 372-4600.
Web, www.uscg.mil

Provides homeland security for U.S. harbors, ports, and coastlines. Implements heightened security measures for commercial, tanker, passenger, and merchant vessels. Enforces federal laws on the high seas and navigable waters of the United States and its possessions; maintains a state of military readiness to assist the Navy in time of war or when directed by the president.

▶CONGRESS

For a listing of relevant congressional committees and subcommittees, please see pages 548–549 or the Appendix.

Government Printing Office, *Security and Intelligent Documents Unit,* 732 N. Capitol St. N.W., C566 20401; (202) 512-2285. Jim Bradley, Assistant Public Printer.
Web, www.gpo.gov/customers/sid.htm

Works with other federal agencies to ensure the safe and secure design, production, and distribution of security and intelligence documents such as U.S. passports, social security cards, travel documents, birth certificates, driver's licenses, and immigration forms. Develops electronic and other fraud and counterfeit protection features. Helps establish domestic and international standards for security and other sensitive documents.

▶NONGOVERNMENTAL

Air Force Assn., 1501 Lee Hwy., Arlington, VA 22209-1198; (703) 247-5800. Fax, (703) 247-5853. Gen. Craig R. Mckinley, (USAF, Ret.), President. Toll-free, (800) 727-3337. Press, (703) 247-5850.
General email, membership@afa.org
Web, www.afa.org

Membership: civilians and active duty, reserve, retired, and cadet personnel of the Air Force. Informs members and the public of developments in the aerospace field. Monitors legislation and Defense Dept. policies. Library on aviation history open to the public by appointment.

American Assn. for the Advancement of Science (AAAS), *Center for Science, Technology, and Security Policy, 1200 New York Ave. N.W. 20005; (202) 326-6493. Fax, (202) 289-1846. Norman P. Neureiter, Director, Acting. Press, (202) 326-6431.*
General email, cstspinfo@aaas.org

Web, http://aaas.org/program/center-science-technology-and-security-policy

Encourages the integration of science and public policy to enhance national and international security. Facilitates communication among academic centers, policy institutions, and policymakers. (Supported by the Science, Technology, and Security Initiative of the MacArthur Foundation.)

American Conservative Union (ACU), *1331 H St. N.W., #500 20005; (202) 347-9388. Fax, (202) 347-9389. Dan Schneider, Executive Director.*
General email, acu@conservative.org

Web, www.conservative.org

Legislative interest organization concerned with national defense policy, legislation related to nuclear weapons, U.S. strategic position vis-à-vis the former Soviet Union, missile defense programs, U.S. troops under U.N. command, and U.S. strategic alliance commitments.

American Enterprise Institute (AEI), *Foreign and Defense Policy Studies, 1150 17th St. N.W., #1100 20036; (202) 862-5800. Fax, (202) 862-7177. Danielle Pletka, Vice President.*
Web, www.aei.org

Research and educational organization that conducts conferences, seminars, and debates and sponsors research on national security, defense policy, and arms control.

American Security Council Foundation, *1250 24th St. N.W., #300 20037; (202) 263-3661. Fax, (202) 263-3662. Gary James, Director of Operations.*
General email, info@ascfusa.org

Web, www.ascfusa.org

Bipartisan organization that promotes developing and maintaining military, economic, and diplomatic strength to preserve national security. Monitors legislation and conducts educational activities.

Aspen Institute, *1 Dupont Circle N.W., #700 20036-7133; (202) 736-5800. Fax, (202) 467-0790. Walter Isaacson, President. Press, (202) 736-3849.*
General email, info@aspeninstitute.org

Web, www.aspeninstitute.org

Educational and policy studies organization. Promotes consideration of the public good in a wide variety of policy areas, including international relations homeland security. Working with international partners, offers educational seminars, nonpartisan policy forums, public conferences and events, and leadership development initiatives.

Assn. of the United States Army, *2425 Wilson Blvd., Arlington, VA 22201; (703) 841-4300. Fax, (703) 525-9039. Gordon R. Sullivan, President. Information, (800) 336-4570.*
Web, www.ausa.org

Membership: civilians and active duty and retired members of the armed forces. Conducts symposia on defense issues and researches topics that affect the military.

Atlantic Council, *1030 15th St. N.W., 12th Floor 20005; (202) 463-7226. Fax, (202) 463-4590. Frederick Kempe, President.*
General email, info@atlanticcouncil.org

Web, www.atlanticcouncil.org

Conducts studies and makes policy recommendations on U.S. foreign security and international economic policies in the Atlantic and Pacific communities; sponsors conferences and educational exchanges.

The Brookings Institution, *Foreign Policy Studies, 1775 Massachusetts Ave. N.W. 20036; (202) 797-6000. Fax, (202) 797-6004. Ted Piccone, Director. Press, (202) 797-6105.*
Web, www.brookings.edu/foreign-policy.aspx

Research and educational organization that focuses on major national security topics, including U.S. armed forces, weapons decisions, terrorism threats, employment policies, and the security aspects of U.S. foreign relations.

Business Executives for National Security (BENS), *1030 15th St. N.W., #200 East 20005; (202) 296-2125. Fax, (202) 296-2490. Norty Schwartz, Chief Executive Officer.*
General email, bensdc@bens.org

Web, www.bens.org

Monitors legislation on national security issues from a business perspective; holds conferences, congressional forums, and other meetings on national security issues; works with other organizations on defense policy issues.

Center for Naval Analyses (CNA), *4825 Mark Center Dr., Alexandria, VA 22311-1850; (703) 824-2000. Fax, (703) 824-2942. Robert J. Murray, President.*
General email, inquiries@cna.org

Web, www.cna.org

Conducts research on weapons acquisitions, tactical problems, and naval operations. Parent organization is CNA, which also operates CNA Institute for Public Research

Center for Security Policy, *1901 Pennsylvania Ave. N.W., #201 20006-3439; (202) 835-9077. Fax, (202) 835-9066. Frank J. Gaffney, President, (202) 835-9077, ext. 1006.*
General email, info@securefreedom.org

Web, www.centerforsecuritypolicy.org

Educational institution concerned with U.S. defense and foreign policy. Interests include arms control compliance and verification policy, and technology transfer policy.

Committee on the Present Danger, *P.O. Box 33249 20033-3249; (202) 207-0190. Fax, (202) 207-0191. George P. Shultz, Co-Chair; R. James Woolsey, Co-Chair.*
General email, commpresdanger@aol.com

Web, www.committeeonthepresentdanger.org

International, nonpartisan educational organization concerned with militant Islamist regimes, movements, and organizations around the world. Supports policies that use

Defense Department

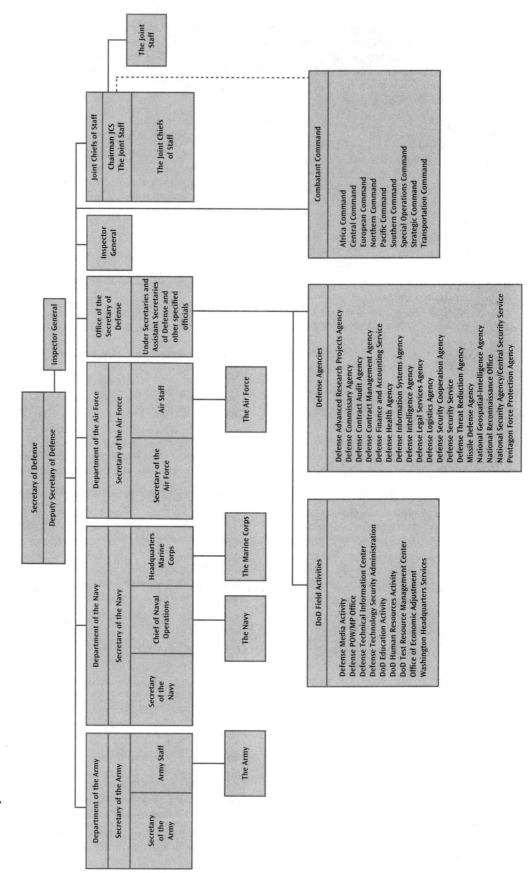

Secretary of Defense
Deputy Secretary of Defense

Inspector General

Department of the Army
Secretary of the Army
Army Staff
Secretary of the Army
The Army

Department of the Navy
Secretary of the Navy
Secretary of the Navy
Chief of Naval Operations
Headquarters Marine Corps
The Navy
The Marine Corps

Department of the Air Force
Secretary of the Air Force
Secretary of the Air Force
Air Staff
The Air Force

Office of the Secretary of Defense
Under Secretaries and Assistant Secretaries of Defense and other specified officials

Inspector General

Joint Chiefs of Staff
Chairman JCS
The Joint Staff
The Joint Chiefs of Staff

The Joint Staff

Combatant Command
Africa Command
Central Command
European Command
Northern Command
Pacific Command
Southern Command
Special Operations Command
Strategic Command
Transportation Command

DoD Field Activities
Defense Media Activity
Defense POW/MP Office
Defense Technical Information Center
Defense Technology Security Administration
DoD Education Activity
DoD Human Resources Activity
DoD Test Resource Management Center
Office of Economic Adjustment
Washington Headquarters Services

Defense Agencies
Defense Advanced Research Projects Agency
Defense Commissary Agency
Defense Contract Audit Agency
Defense Contract Management Agency
Defense Finance and Accounting Service
Defense Health Agency
Defense Information Systems Agency
Defense Intelligence Agency
Defense Legal Services Agency
Defense Logistics Agency
Defense Security Cooperation Agency
Defense Security Service
Defense Threat Reduction Agency
Missile Defense Agency
National Geospatial-Intelligence Agency
National Reconnaissance Office
National Security Agency/Central Security Service
Pentagon Force Protection Agency

---------- Indicates a support or advisory relationship with the unit rather than a direct reporting relationship

various means–military, economic, political, social–to address this threat. Members include former government officials, academics, writers, and other experts.

The Conservative Caucus (TCC), *92 Main St., #202-8, Warrenton, VA 20816; (540) 219-4536. Peter J. Thomas, Chair.*
General email, info@conservativeusa.org
Web, www.conservativeusa.org

Legislative interest organization that promotes grassroots activity on national defense and foreign policy.

Defense Orientation Conference Assn. (DOCA), *9271 Old Keene Mill Rd., #200, Burke, VA 22015-4202; (703) 451-1200. Fax, (703) 451-1201. Robert Currie, President.*
General email, doca@erolls.org
Web, www.doca.org

Membership: citizens interested in national defense. Under the auspices of the Defense Dept., promotes continuing education of members on national security issues through visits to embassies and tours of defense installations in the United States and abroad.

Ethics and Public Policy Center, *1730 M St. N.W., #910 20036; (202) 682-1200. Fax, (202) 408-0632. M. Edward Whelan III, President.*
General email, ethics@eppc.org
Web, www.eppc.org

Considers implications of Judeo-Christian moral tradition for domestic and foreign policy making. Conducts research and holds conferences on foreign policy, including the role of the U.S. military abroad.

Henry L. Stimson Center, *1111 19th St. N.W., 12th Floor 20036; (202) 223-5956. Fax, (202) 238-9604. Ellen Laipson, President.*
General email, info@stimson.org
Web, www.stimson.org

Research organization that studies arms control and international security, focusing on policy, technology, and politics.

Homeland Security Studies and Analysis Institute, *5275 Leesburg Pike, #N-500, Falls Church, VA 22041; (703) 416-2000. Fax, (703) 416-3530. Philip Anderson, Director. Toll-free, (800) 368-4173.*
General email, homelandsecurity@hsi.dhs.gov
Web, www.homelandsecurity.org

Federally Funded Research Development Center (FFRDC) sponsored by the Department of Homeland Security and chartered to examine the homeland security challenges faced by the United States in the twenty-first century. Explores issues, conducts research, works to promote dialogue, and provides executive education through workshops, conferences, publications, and outreach programs.

Hudson Institute, *National Security Studies, 1015 15th St. N.W., 6th Floor 20005; (202) 974-2400. Fax, (202) 974-2410. Kenneth R. Weinstein, Chief Executive Officer. Press, (202) 974-2417.*

General email, info@hudson.org
Web, www.hudson.org

Public policy research organization that conducts studies on U.S. overseas bases, U.S.-NATO relations, and missile defense programs. Focuses on long-range implications for U.S. national security.

Institute for Foreign Policy Analysis, *1725 DeSales St. N.W., #402 20036; (202) 463-7942. Fax, (202) 785-2785. Robert L. Pfaltzgraff Jr., President.*
General email, dcmail@ifpa.org
Web, www.ifpa.org

Trains policy analysts in the fields of foreign policy and national security. Sponsors research and workshops.

Institute of International Education, *National Security Education Program, 1400 K St. N.W., 7th Floor 20005-2403 (mailing address: P.O. Box 20010, Arlington, VA 22209); (703) 696-1991. Fax, (703) 696-5667. Michael Nugent, Director. Information, (800) 618-6737.*
General email, nsep@nsep.gov
Web, www.nsep.gov

Administers Boren Awards and Language Flagship programs; provides scholarships, fellowships, and institutional grants to students and academics with an interest in foreign affairs and national security.

Jewish Institute for National Security Affairs (JINSA), *1307 New York Ave. N.W., #200 20005; (202) 667-3900. Fax, (202) 667-0601. Michael Makovsky, Executive Director.*
General email, info@jinsa.org
Web, www.jinsa.org

Seeks to educate the public about the importance of effective U.S. defense capability and inform the U.S. defense and foreign affairs community about Israel's role in Mediterranean and Middle Eastern affairs. Sponsors lectures and conferences; facilitates dialogue between security policymakers, military officials, diplomats, and the general public.

Marine Corps League, *8626 Lee Hwy., #201, Fairfax, VA 22031-3070 (mailing address: P.O. Box 3070, Merrifield, VA 22116); (703) 207-9588. Fax, (703) 207-0047. Michael A. Blum, Executive Director. Toll-free, (800) 625-1775.*
Web, www.mcleague.org

Membership: active duty, retired, and reserve Marine Corps groups. Promotes the interests of the Marine Corps and works to preserve its traditions; assists veterans and their survivors. Monitors legislation and regulations.

National Institute for Public Policy, *9302 Lee Hwy., #750, Fairfax, VA 22031-6053; (703) 293-9181. Fax, (703) 293-9198. Keith B. Payne, President.*
Web, www.nipp.org

Studies public policy and its relation to national security. Interests include arms control, strategic weapons systems and planning, and foreign policy.

Homeland Security Department

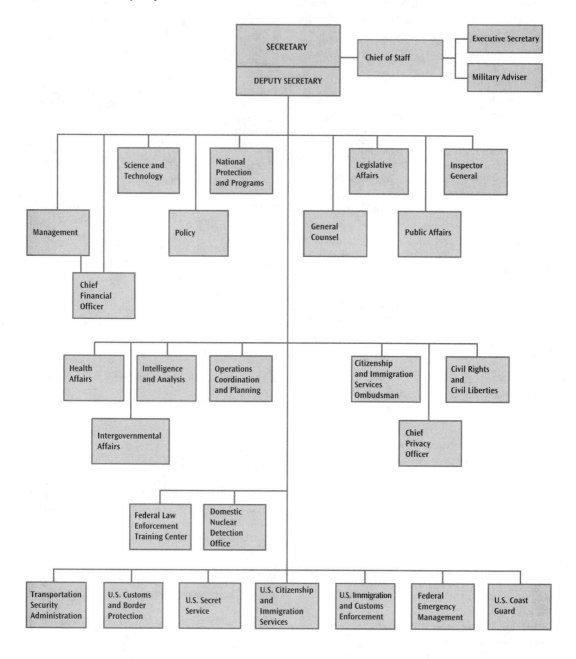

Navy League of the United States, *2300 Wilson Blvd., #200, Arlington, VA 22201-5424; (703) 528-1775. Fax, (703) 528-2333. Bruce K. Butler, National Executive Director, ext. 1550. Toll-free, (800) 356-5760. General email, service@navyleague.org*

Web, www.navyleague.org

Membership: retired and reserve military personnel and civilians interested in the U.S. Navy, Marine Corps, Coast Guard, and Merchant Marine. Distributes literature, provides speakers, and conducts seminars to promote interests of the sea services. Monitors legislation.

RAND Corporation, *Washington Office, 1200 S. Hayes St., Arlington, VA 22202-5050; (703) 413-1100. Fax, (703) 413-8111. Lynn E. Davis, Director, ext. 5399; Debra Knopman, Director, Justice, Infrastructure, and Environment.*

Web, www.rand.org

Conducts research on national security issues, including political/military affairs of the former Soviet Union and U.S. strategic policy. Research focuses on citizen preparedness, defense strategy, and military force planning. (Headquarters in Santa Monica, Calif.)

Civil Rights and Liberties

▶ **AGENCIES**

Homeland Security Dept. (DHS), *Civil Rights and Civil Liberties,* 245 Murray Lane S.W., Bldg. 410, MS 0190 20528-0190; (202) 401-1474. Fax, (202) 401-4708. Megan H. Mack, Civil Rights and Civil Liberties Officer. Toll-free, (866) 644-8360. Toll-free TTY, (866) 644-8361. General email, crcl@dhs.gov

Web, www.dhs.gov/about-office-civil-rights-and-civil-liberties

Provides legal and policy advice to the secretary and senior officers of the department on civil rights and civil liberties issues; maintains dialogue with minority communities; investigates and resolves complaints filed by members of the public.

Homeland Security Dept. (DHS), *Privacy Office,* 245 Murray Lane, Bldg. 110 20528-0800; (202) 282-8000. Fax, (202) 343-4010. Megan H. Mack, Officer for Civil Rights and Civil Liberties; Karen Neuman, Chief Privacy Officer. DHS Switchboard, (202) 282-8000. General email, privacy@dhs.gov

Web, www.dhs.gov/privacy

Responsible for ensuring that department policies and use of technology sustain individual privacy. Makes annual report to Congress and enforces the provisions of the 1974 Privacy Act and evaluates legislative and regulatory proposals involving collection, use, and disclosure of personal information by the federal government.

Justice Dept. (DOJ), *Information Policy,* 1425 New York Ave. N.W., #11050 20530; (202) 514-3642. Fax, (202) 514-1009. Melanie Ann Pustay, Director. Information, (202) 514-2000. General email, doj.oip.foia@usdoj.gov

Web, www.justice.gov/oip/index.html

Provides federal agencies with advice and policy guidance on matters related to implementing and interpreting the Freedom of Information Act (FOIA). Litigates selected FOIA and Privacy Act cases; adjudicates administrative appeals from Justice Dept. denials of public requests for access to documents; conducts FOIA training for government agencies.

Office of Management and Budget (OMB) *(Executive Office of the President), Information and Regulatory Affairs,* New Executive Office Bldg., #10236 20503; (202) 395-3785. Fax, (202) 395-5167. Boris Bershteyn, Administrator, Acting. Web, www.whitehouse.gov/omb/inforeg_infopoltech

Oversees development of federal regulatory programs. Supervises agency information management activities in accordance with the Paperwork Reduction Act of 1995, as amended; reviews agency analyses of the effect of government regulatory activities on the U.S. economy.

▶ **CONGRESS**

For a listing of relevant congressional committees and subcommittees, please see pages 548–549 or the Appendix.

▶ **NONGOVERNMENTAL**

American Civil Liberties Union (ACLU), *Washington Legislative Office,* 915 15th St. N.W. 20005; (202) 544-1681. Fax, (202) 546-0738. Laura W. Murphy, Director. Press, (202) 417-7547. General email, media@dcaclu.org

Web, www.aclu.org/legiupdate

Advocates for legislation to guarantee constitutional rights and civil liberties. Monitors agency compliance with the Privacy Act and other access statutes. Produces publications. (Headquarters in New York maintains docket of cases.)

American Society of Access Professionals, 1444 Eye St. N.W., #700 20005; (202) 712-9054. Fax, (202) 216-9646. Claire Shanley, Executive Director. General email, asap@bostrom.com

Web, www.accesspro.org

Membership: federal employees, attorneys, journalists, and others working with or interested in access-to-information laws. Seeks to improve the administration of the Freedom of Information Act, the Privacy Act, and other access statutes.

Center for Democracy and Technology, 1634 Eye St. N.W., #1100 20006; (202) 637-9800. Fax, (202) 637-0968. Nuala O'Connor, President. General email, info@cdt.org

Web, www.cdt.org

Promotes civil liberties and democratic values in computer and communications media, both in the United States and abroad. Interests include free speech, privacy, and open access to the Internet. Monitors legislation and regulations.

Center for National Security Studies, 1730 Pennsylvania Ave. N.W., 7th Floor 20006; (202) 721-5650. Fax, (202) 530-0128. Kate A. Martin, Director. General email, cnss@cnss.org

Web, www.cnss.org

Human rights and civil liberties organization specializing in national security, access to government information, government secrecy, government surveillance, intelligence oversight, and detentions.

Electronic Privacy Information Center (EPIC), 1718 Connecticut Ave. N.W., #200 20009; (202) 483-1140. Fax, (202) 483-1248. Marc Rotenberg, Executive Director. General email, info@epic.org

Web, www.epic.org

Public interest research center. Conducts research and conferences on domestic and international civil liberties issues, including privacy, free speech, information access, computer security, and encryption; litigates cases. Monitors legislation and regulations.

Radio Television Digital News Assn., 529 14th St. N.W., #1240 20045; (202) 659-6510. Fax, (202) 223-4007. Mike Cavender, Executive Director, (770) 622-7011.

General email, rtdna@rtdna.org

Web, www.rtdna.org

Membership: electronic journalists in radio, television, and all digital media. Sponsors and promotes education and advocacy concerning First Amendment issues, freedom of information, and government secrecy issues; ethics in reporting; improving coverage; implementing technology; and other news industry issues. Radio and Television News Directors Foundation (RTNDF) is the educational arm of the association.

Reporters Committee for Freedom of the Press, *1101 Wilson Blvd., #1100, Arlington, VA 22209; (703) 807-2100. Fax, (703) 807-2109. Bruce D. Brown, Executive Director. Legal defense hotline, (800) 336-4243.*

General email, info@rcfp.org

Web, www.rcfp.org

Membership: reporters, news editors, publishers, and lawyers from the print and broadcast media. Maintains a legal defense and research fund for members of the news media involved in freedom of the press court cases; interests include access to information and privacy issues faced by journalists covering antiterrorism initiatives and military actions abroad.

Defense and Homeland Security Budgets

▶AGENCIES

Defense Contract Audit Agency (DCAA) *(Defense Dept.), 8725 John Jay Kingman Rd., #2135, Fort Belvoir, VA 22060-6219; (703) 767-3200. Fax, (703) 767-3267. Patrick J. Fitzgerald, Director. Media, (703) 693-6858. Web, www.dcaa.mil*

Performs all contract audits for the Defense Dept. Provides Defense Dept. personnel responsible for procurement and contract administration with accounting and financial advisory services regarding the negotiation, administration, and settlement of contracts and subcontracts.

Defense Dept. (DoD), *Comptroller, 1100 Defense Pentagon, #3E770 20301-1100; (703) 695-3237. Fax, (703) 693-0582. Robert F. Hale, Comptroller. Press, (703) 693-8287.*

Web, http://comptroller.defense.gov

Supervises and reviews the preparation and implementation of the defense budget. Advises the secretary of defense on fiscal matters. Collects and distributes information on the department's management of resources.

Homeland Security Dept. (DHS), *Chief Financial Officer, 7th and D Sts. S.W. 20528; (202) 447-5751. Fax, (202) 447-5172. Chip Fulghum, Chief Financial Officer. Web, www.dhs.gov/office-chief-financial-officer*

Responsible for the Homeland Security Dept.'s budget, budget justifications, supplemental spending bill figures, and five-year financial blueprint.

Homeland Security Dept. (DHS), *Management Directorate, 3801 Nebraska Ave. N.W. 20528; 245 Murray Lane 20528; (202) 447-3400. Fax, (202) 447-3713. Rafael Borras, Under Secretary. Web, www.dhs.gov/about-directorate-management*

Responsible for Homeland Security Dept. budget, operations, appropriations, expenditure of funds, accounting and finance, procurement, human resources and personnel, information technology systems, facilities, property, equipment and all material resources, and performance measurement.

Office of Management and Budget (OMB) *(Executive Office of the President), Homeland Security, 725 17th St. N.W., New Executive Office Bldg., #9208 20503; (202) 395-4892. Fax, (202) 395-0850. James Holm, Chief. Web, www.whitehouse.gov/omb*

Assists and advises the OMB director on budget preparation, proposed legislation, and evaluations of Homeland Security Dept. programs, policies, and activities.

Office of Management and Budget (OMB) *(Executive Office of the President), National Security, 725 17th St. N.W., New Executive Office Bldg., #10001 20503; (202) 395-3884. Fax, (202) 395-3307. Mark Sandy, Deputy Associate Director. Web, www.whitehouse.gov/omb*

Supervises preparation of the Defense Dept., intelligence community, and veterans affairs portions of the federal budget.

▶CONGRESS

For a listing of relevant congressional committees and subcommittees, please see pages 548–549 or the Appendix.

Government Accountability Office (GAO), *Defense Capabilities and Management, 441 G St. N.W., #4440B 20548; (202) 512-4300. Cathleen Berrick, Managing Director.*

Web, www.gao.gov

Independent, nonpartisan agency in the legislative branch. Audits, analyzes, and evaluates defense spending programs; makes unclassified reports available to the public.

Government Accountability Office (GAO), *Homeland Security and Justice, 441 G St. N.W., #6834 20548; (202) 512-8777. George A. Scott, Managing Director.*

Web, www.gao.gov

Independent, nonpartisan agency in the legislative branch. Audits, analyzes, and evaluates federal administration of homeland security programs and initiatives related to national preparedness. Makes some reports available to the public.

▶NONGOVERNMENTAL

Center for Strategic and Budgetary Assessments (CSBA), *1667 K St. N.W., #900 20006-1659; (202) 331-7990. Fax, (202) 331-8019. Andrew F. Krepinevich, President.*

General email, info@csbaonline.org

Web, www.csbaonline.org

Think tank that promotes deliberation of national security strategy, the future of the U.S. military, and defense investment options. Conducts analyses of defense budget and programmatic analysis. Compares the relative strengths and weaknesses of the United States and potential military competitors. Conducts seminar-style wargames to analyze the operational and strategic levels of conflict, as well as strategy and investment alternatives. Anticipates future military trends, based on analysis of historical trends.

Institute for Policy Studies, *Foreign Policy in Focus,* 1112 16th St., #600 20036; (202) 234-9382. Fax, (202) 387-7915. John Feffer, Co-Director; Emira Woods, Co-Director.

General email, fpif@ips-dc.org

Web, www.fpif.org

Think tank that provides analysis of U.S. foreign policy and international affairs and recommends progressive policy alternatives. Publishes reports; organizes briefings for the public, media, and policymakers. Interests include climate change, global poverty, nuclear weapons, terrorism, and military conflict.

National Campaign for a Peace Tax Fund, 2121 Decatur Pl. N.W. 20008-1923; (202) 483-3751. Jack Payden-Travers, Executive Director. Toll-free, (888) 732-2382.

General email, info@peacetaxfund.org

Web, www.peacetaxfund.org

Supports legislation permitting taxpayers who are conscientiously opposed to military expenditures to have the military portion of their income tax money placed in a separate, nonmilitary fund.

Women's Action for New Directions (WAND), **Washington Office,** 322 4th St. N.E. 20002; (202) 544-5055. Fax, (202) 544-7612. Maureen Campbell, WAND Senior Associate; Kathy Crandall Robinson, Director, Public Policy.

General email, peace@wand.org

Web, www.wand.org

Seeks to redirect federal spending priorities from military spending toward domestic needs; works to develop citizen expertise through education and political involvement; provides educational programs and material about nuclear and conventional weapons; monitors defense legislation, budget policy legislation, and legislation affecting women. (Headquarters in Arlington, Mass.)

Military Aid and Peacekeeping

▶**AGENCIES**

Commission on Security and Cooperation in Europe (Helsinki Commission), 234 FHOB 20515; (202) 225-1901. Fax, (202) 226-4199. Sen. Benjamin L. Cardin, Chair; Rep. Christopher H. Smith, Co-Chair; Fred Turner, Chief of Staff.

General email, info@csce.gov

Web, www.csce.gov

Independent agency created by Congress. Membership includes individuals from the executive and legislative branches. Studies and evaluates international peacekeeping and peace enforcement operations, particularly as they relate to the Helsinki Accords.

Defense Dept. (DoD), *Defense Security Cooperation Agency,* 201 12th St. South, #203, Arlington, VA 22202-5408; (703) 604-6604. Fax, (703) 602-5403. Vice Adm. Joseph W. Rixey, Director. Public Affairs, (703) 604-6617.

General email, lpa-web@dsca.mil

Web, www.dsca.mil

Administers programs providing defense articles and services, military training and education, humanitarian assistance, and landmine removal to international partners in furtherance of U.S. policies and strategic objectives.

Defense Dept. (DoD), *European and NATO Policy,* The Pentagon, #5B652 20301-2400; (703) 695-5553. Fax, (703) 571-9637. Jim Townsend, Deputy Assistant Secretary.

Web, www.defense.gov

Advises the assistant secretary for international security affairs on matters dealing with Europe and NATO.

Defense Dept. (DoD), *International Security Affairs,* The Pentagon, #3C889 20301-2400; (703) 697-2788. Fax, (703) 697-3279. Derek H. Chollet, Assistant Secretary.

Web, www.defense.gov

Advises the secretary of defense and recommends policies on regional security issues in the Middle East, Africa, Russia/Eurasia, and Europe/NATO.

State Dept., *Arms Control and International Security,* 2201 C St. N.W., #7208 20520-7512; (202) 647-1049. Fax, (202) 736-4397. Rose Gottemoeller, Under Secretary.

Web, www.state.gov

Works with the secretary of state to develop policy on foreign security assistance programs, technology transfer, and arms control.

State Dept., *European Security and Political Affairs,* 2201 C St. N.W., #6511 20520; (202) 647-1358. Fax, (202) 647-1369. Richard Holtzapple, Director.

Web, www.state.gov

Coordinates and advises, with the Defense Dept. and other agencies, the U.S. mission to NATO and the U.S. delegation to the Organization for Security and Cooperation in Europe regarding political, military, and arms control matters.

State Dept., *Policy Planning Staff,* 2201 C St. N.W., #7311 20520; (202) 647-2972. Fax, (202) 647-0844. David McKean, Director.

Web, www.state.gov

Advises the secretary and other State Dept. officials on foreign policy matters, including international peacekeeping and peace enforcement operations.

State Dept., *Political-Military Affairs, 2201 C St. N.W., #6212 20520; (202) 647-9022. Fax, (202) 736-4779. Puneet Talwar, Assistant Secretary.*
Web, www.state.gov

Responsible for security affairs policy and operations for the non-European area.

State Dept., *United Nations Political Affairs, 2201 C St. N.W., #1828 20520-6319; (202) 647-2392. Fax, (202) 647-0039. Tom Duffy, Director.*
Web, www.state.gov

Deals with United Nations political and institutional matters and international security affairs.

U.S. Institute of Peace, *2301 Constitution Ave. N.W. 20037; (202) 457-1700. Fax, (202) 429-6063. Stephen J. Hadley, Chair; Kristin Lord, President, Acting. Press, (202) 429-4725. General email, info@usip.org*
Web, www.usip.org

Independent, nonpartisan institution established by Congress. Aims to prevent and resolve violent international conflicts, promote post-conflict stability, and increase peace-building capacity, tools, and intellectual capital worldwide.

► **CONGRESS**

For a listing of relevant congressional committees and sub-committees, please see pages 548–549 or the Appendix.

Government Accountability Office (GAO), *Defense Capabilities and Management, 441 G St. N.W., #4440B 20548; (202) 512-4300. Cathleen Berrick, Managing Director.*
Web, www.gao.gov

Independent, nonpartisan agency in the legislative branch. Audits, analyzes, and evaluates international programs, including U.S. participation in international peacekeeping and peace enforcement operations; makes unclassified reports available to the public.

► **INTERNATIONAL ORGANIZATIONS**

Inter-American Defense Board, *2600 16th St. N.W. 20441-0002; (202) 939-6041. Fax, (202) 319-2791. Lt. Gen. Werther Victor Araya Menghini, Chair (in Chile). Inter-American Defense College, (202) 646-1337.*
Web, http://iadb.jid.org

Membership: military officers from twenty-six countries of the Western Hemisphere. Plans for the collective self-defense of the American continents. Develops procedures for standardizing military organization and operations; operates the Inter-American Defense Board and Inter-American Defense College. Advises the Organization of American States on military and defense matters.

► **NONGOVERNMENTAL**

International Stability Operations Assn. (ISOA), *8221 Old Courthouse Rd., #200, Tysons Corner, VA 22182; (703) 596-7417. Fax, (571) 282-4800. Ado Machida, President.*

General email, isoa@stability-operations.org
Web, www.stability-operations.org

Membership: private-sector service companies involved in all sectors of peace and stability operations around the world, including mine clearance, logistics, security, training, and emergency humanitarian aid. Works to institute standards and codes of conduct. Monitors legislation.

ARMS CONTROL, DISARMAMENT, AND THREAT REDUCTION

General

► **AGENCIES**

Arms Control and Nonproliferation *(Executive Office of the President), Dwight D. Eisenhower Executive Office Bldg., #379 20506; (202) 456-9181. Fax, (202) 456-9180. Elizabeth Sherwood Randall, Coordinator for Arms Control and Nonproliferation, National Security Council.*

Responsible for policies concerning arms proliferation and control in the context of homeland security.

Defense Dept. (DoD), *Chemical and Biological Defense Program, 3050 Defense Pentagon, #5B1064 20301-3050; (703) 693-9410. Fax, (703) 695-0476. James B. Petio, Deputy Assistant, Acting.*
Web, www.acq.osd.mil/cp

Coordinates, integrates, and provides oversight for the Joint Services Chemical and Biological Defense Program.

Defense Dept. (DoD), *Global Strategic Affairs, 2900 Defense Pentagon, #3C852A 20301-2900; (703) 697-7728. Fax, (703) 614-2259. Madelyn R. Creedon, Assistant Secretary; Eric B. Rosenbach, Principal Deputy Assistant Secretary, Acting.*
Web, www.defense.gov

Advises the secretary on reducing and countering nuclear, biological, chemical, and missile threats to the United States and its forces and allies; arms control negotiations, implementation, and verification policy; nuclear weapons policy, denuclearization, threat reduction, and nuclear safety and security; and technology transfer and cyber security.

Defense Dept. (DoD), *Plans, 2000 Defense Pentagon, #5E384 20032; (703) 614-0462. Fax, (703) 695-7230. Robert M. Scher, Deputy Assistant Secretary. Press, (703) 697-5131.*
Web, www.defense.gov

Formulates national policies to prevent and counter the proliferation of nuclear, chemical, and biological weapons; missiles; and conventional technologies. Devises arms control agreements, export controls, technology transfer policies, and military planning policies.

Defense Threat Reduction Agency *(Defense Dept.), 8725 John Jay Kingman Rd., MS 6201, Fort Belvoir, VA*

22060-6201; (703) 767-4883. Kenneth A. Myers III, Director. Press, (703) 767-5870.
General email, dtra.publicaffairs@dtra.mil
Web, www.dtra.mil

Seeks to reduce, eliminate, and counter the threat to the United States and its allies from weapons of mass destruction; conducts technology security activities, cooperative threat reduction programs, arms control treaty monitoring, and on-site inspection; provides technical support on weapons of mass destruction matters to the Defense Dept. components.

State Dept., *Bureau of International Security and Nonproliferation (ISN),* 2201 C St. N.W., #3932 20520; (202) 647-9612. Fax, (202) 736-4863. Thomas M. Countryman, Assistant Secretary; Vann H. Van Diepen, Principal Deputy Assistant Secretary.
Web, www.state.gov/t/isn

Leads U.S. efforts to prevent the spread of weapons of mass destruction (WMD, including nuclear, chemical, and biological weapons) and their delivery systems; spearheads efforts to promote international consensus on WMD proliferation; supports efforts of foreign partners to prevent, protect against, and respond to the threat or use of WMD by terrorists.

State Dept., *Plans and Initiatives,* 2201 C St. N.W., #2811 20520; (202) 647-7775. Fax, (202) 647-8998. Michael Hauser, Director.
Web, www.state.gov/t/pm/pi

Facilitates training and equipping of international peacekeepers; addresses counterpiracy; provides diplomatic perspectives to Defense Dept. strategic planning.

State Dept., *Security Assistance,* 2201 C St. N.W., #2811 20520; (202) 647-7775. Fax, (202) 647-8998. Kevin O'Keefe, Director.
Web, www.state.gov/t/pm/sa

Administers funding for security assistance and capacity-building programs in foreign countries.

State Dept., *Threat Finance Countermeasures,* 2210 C St. N.W., #4657 20520; (202) 647-5763. Fax, (202) 647-7407. Andrew J. Weinschenk, Director.
Web, www.state.gov

Seeks to minimize the funding available to groups and individuals that prove a threat to domestic, international, and regional security.

▶ CONGRESS

For a listing of relevant congressional committees and subcommittees, please see pages 548–549 or the Appendix.

▶ NONGOVERNMENTAL

Arms Control Assn., 1313 L St. N.W., #130 20005; (202) 463-8270. Fax, (202) 463-8273. Daryl G. Kimball, Executive Director.
General email, aca@armscontrol.org
Web, www.armscontrol.org

Nonpartisan organization that seeks to broaden public understanding and support for effective arms control and disarmament in national security policy through education and media programs. Publishes *Arms Control Today.*

Council for a Livable World, 322 4th St. N.E. 20002-5824; (202) 543-4100. John D. Isaacs, Executive Director.
General email, livableworld.org/contact/
Web, http://livableworld.org

Citizens' interest group that supports nuclear arms control treaties, strengthened biological and chemical weapons conventions, reduced military spending, peacekeeping, and tight restrictions on international arms sales.

Federation of American Scientists (FAS), 1725 DeSales St. N.W., 6th Floor 20036; (202) 546-3300. Fax, (202) 675-1010. Charles D. Ferguson, President.
General email, fas@fas.org
Web, www.fas.org

Opposes the global arms race and supports nuclear disarmament and limits on government secrecy. Promotes learning technologies and conducts studies and monitors legislation on U.S. weapons policy; provides the public with information on arms control and related issues.

Friends Committee on National Legislation (FCNL), 245 2nd St. N.E. 20002-5795; (202) 547-6000. Fax, (202) 547-6019. Diane Randall, Executive Secretary. Toll-free, (800) 630-1330. Recorded information, (202) 547-4343.
General email, fcnl@fcnl.org
Web, www.fcnl.org

Supports world disarmament; international cooperation; domestic, economic, peace, and social justice issues; and improvement in relations between the United States and the former Soviet Union. Opposes conscription. Affiliated with the Religious Society of Friends (Quakers).

GlobalSecurity.org, 300 N. Washington St., #B-100, Alexandria, VA 22314-2540; (703) 548-2700. Fax, (703) 548-2424. John E. Pike, Director.
General email, info@globalsecurity.org
Web, www.globalsecurity.org

Provides background information and covers developing news stories on the military, weapons proliferation, space, homeland security, and intelligence. Offers profiles of agencies, systems, facilities, and current operations as well as a library of primary documentation.

High Frontier, 500 N. Washington St., Alexandria, VA 22314-2314; (703) 535-8774. Henry (Hank) Cooper, Director.
General email, info@highfrontier.org
Web, www.highfrontier.org

Educational organization that provides information on missile defense programs and proliferation. Advocates development of a single-stage-to-orbit space vehicle, a moon base program, and a layered missile defense system. Operates speakers bureau; monitors defense legislation.

Nonproliferation Policy Education Center (NPEC), *1601 North Kent St., #802, Arlington, VA 22209; (571) 970-3187. Henry D. Sokolski, Executive Director.*
General email, info@npolicy.org
Web, www.npolicy.org

Conducts and publishes research on strategic weapons proliferation issues and makes it available to the press, congressional and executive branch staff, foreign officials, and international organizations.

Nuclear Threat Initiative (NTI), *1747 Pennsylvania Ave. N.W., 7th Floor 20006; (202) 296-4810. Fax, (202) 296-4811. Joan Rohlfing, President.*
General email, contact@nti.org
Web, www.nti.org

Works to reduce threats from nuclear, biological, and chemical weapons; publishes a daily e-newsletter.

Peace Action, *8630 Fenton St., #524, Silver Spring, MD 20910-5642; (301) 565-4050. Fax, (301) 565-0850. Kevin Martin, Executive Director. Press, (951) 217-7285.*
Web, www.peace-action.org

Grassroots organization that supports a negotiated comprehensive test ban treaty. Seeks a reduction in the military budget and a transfer of those funds to nonmilitary programs. Works for an end to international arms trade. (Merger of Sane and The Nuclear Freeze.)

Physicians for Social Responsibility (PSR), *1111 14th St. N.W., #700 20005; (202) 667-4260. Fax, (202) 667-4201. Dr. Catherine Thomasson, Executive Director.*
General email, psrnatl@psr.org
Web, www.psr.org

Membership: doctors, nurses, health scientists, and concerned citizens. Works toward the elimination of nuclear weapons and to slow, stop, and reverse global warming and degradation of the environment. Conducts public education programs, monitors policy, and serves as a liaison with other concerned groups.

Union of Concerned Scientists, *Global Security, Washington Office, 1825 K St., N.W., #800 20006-1232; (202) 223-6133. Fax, (202) 223-6162. Stephen Young, Senior Washington Representative; Vacant, Nuclear Energy and Climate Change Project Manager.*
General email, ucs@ucsusa.org
Web, www.ucsusa.org

Combines technical analysis, education and advocacy, and engagement with the public and scientific community to promote policies that enhance national and international security. Focuses on technical issues, including verified reductions of nuclear arsenals, fissile material controls, missile defense, and space security. Plays a role in increasing the number of independent scientists and technical analysts working professionally on security issues worldwide. (Headquarters in Cambridge, Mass.)

Nuclear Weapons and Power

▶AGENCIES

Defense Nuclear Facilities Safety Board, *625 Indiana Ave. N.W., #700 20004-2901; (202) 694-7080. Fax, (202) 208-6518. Peter S. Winokur, Chair. Information, (202) 694-7000.*
General email, mailbox@dnfsb.gov
Web, www.dnfsb.gov

Independent board created by Congress and appointed by the president to provide external oversight of Energy Dept. defense nuclear weapons production facilities and make recommendations to the secretary of energy regarding public health and safety.

Energy Dept. (DOE), *National Nuclear Security Administration, Defense Programs, 1000 Independence Ave. S.W., #4A019 20585; (202) 586-2179. Fax, (202) 586-5670. Donald L. Cook, Deputy Administrator.*
Web, www.nnsa.energy.gov/aboutus/ourprograms/defenseprograms

Responsible for nuclear weapons research, development, and engineering; performs laser fusion research and development.

Energy Dept. (DOE), *National Nuclear Security Administration, Nuclear Nonproliferation and International Security, 1000 Independence Ave. S.W., #7A175 20585; (202) 586-0645. Fax, (202) 586-0862. Anne M. Harrington, Deputy Administrator.*
Web, www.nnsa.energy.gov/aboutus/ourprograms/dnn

Provides U.S. government agencies and departments with technical and operational expertise on foreign nuclear and energy issues. Oversees programs to prevent the spread of nuclear, chemical, and biological weapons and missiles for their delivery. Partners with Russia and other former Soviet states to secure weapons of mass destruction materials and expertise; works to strengthen legal and institutional nonproliferation norms; builds technologies to detect proliferation activities; and promotes the safe use of nuclear power.

Energy Dept. (DOE), *Under Secretary for Nuclear Security, 1000 Independence Ave. S.W., #7A049 20585; (202) 586-5555. Fax, (202) 586-4892. Edward Bruce Held, Under Secretary for Nuclear Security, Acting. Toll-free, (800) 342-5363.*
Web, http://nnsa.energy.gov

Maintains the safety, security, and effectiveness of the U.S. nuclear weapons stockpile without nuclear testing; provides the U.S. Navy with safe and effective nuclear propulsion; provides the nation with nuclear counterterrorism and incident response capability.

Homeland Security Dept. (DHS), *Domestic Nuclear Detection, Nebraska Ave. Complex, 3801 Nebraska Ave. N.W. 20528; (202) 254-7000. Huban Gowadia, Director, Acting.*

General email, dndo.info@dhs.gov

Web, www.dhs.gov/DNDO

Seeks to improve the nation's capability to detect and report unauthorized attempts to import, possess, store, develop, or transport nuclear or radiological material for use against the nation, and to further enhance this capability over time. Oversees the development of an integrated global and domestic nuclear detection program and the deployment of a nuclear detection system.

National Security Staff (NSS) *(Executive Office of the President), Defense Policy and Strategy,* The White House 20504; (202) 456-9191. Fax, (202) 456-9190. *Ronald J. Clark, Senior Director.*

Web, www.whitehouse.gov/administration/eop/nsc

Advises the assistant to the president for national security affairs on matters concerning defense policy.

Navy Dept. *(Defense Dept.), Naval Reactors, Naval Nuclear Propulsion,* 1240 Isaac Hull Ave. S.E. 20376-8010; (202) 781-6174. Fax, (202) 781-6403. *Adm. John Richardson, Director.*

Web, www.navy.mil

Responsible for naval nuclear propulsion.

State Dept., *Nuclear Energy, Safety, and Security Affairs,* 2201 C St. N.W., #3320 20520; (202) 647-4413. Fax, (202) 647-0775. *Richard J. K. Stratford, Director.*

Web, www.state.gov

Negotiates bilateral and multilateral agreements pertaining to nuclear trade, safety, and physical protection.

▶**CONGRESS**

For a listing of relevant congressional committees and subcommittees, please see pages 548–549 or the Appendix.

▶**NONGOVERNMENTAL**

Fourth Freedom Forum, *Washington Office,* 1101 14th St. N.W., #900 20036; (202) 464-6009. Fax, (202) 238-9604. *Alistair Millar, President.*

General email, amillar@fourthfreedom.org

Web, www.fourthfreedom.org

Conducts research and training to advance global cooperation to address transnational threats, including terrorism, nuclear proliferation, and drug trafficking. (Headquarters in Goshen, Ind.)

Institute for Science and International Security, 236 Massachusetts Ave. N.E., #305 20002; (202) 547-3633. Fax, (202) 547-3634. *David Albright, President.*

General email, isis@isis-online.org

Web, www.isis-online.org

Conducts research and analysis on nuclear weapons production and nonproliferation issues.

BORDERS, CUSTOMS, AND IMMIGRATION

General

▶**AGENCIES**

Federal Law Enforcement Training Center *(Homeland Security Dept.), Washington Operations,* 9000 Commo Rd., #32, Chelterham, MD 20623-5000; (202) 233-0260. Fax, (202) 233-0258. *Connie Patrick, Director, (912) 267-2070.*

General email, FLETC-WashingtonOffice@dhs.gov

Web, www.fletc.gov

Trains law enforcement personnel. Provides services to state, local, tribal, and international law enforcement agencies. (Headquarters in Glynco, Ga.)

Homeland Security Dept. (DHS), *Citizenship and Immigration Services Ombudsman,* Dept. of Homeland Security, MS 0180 20528-0180; (202) 357-8100. Fax, (202) 357-0042. *Maria Odom, Ombudsman.*

General email, cisombudsman@hq.dhs.gov

Web, www.dhs.gov/cisombudsman

Assists individuals and employers in resolving problems with the U.S. Citizenship and Immigration Services (USCIS); proposes changes in the administrative practices of USCIS in an effort to mitigate identified problems.

Interior Dept. (DOI), *Law Enforcement and Security: Drug Enforcement Coordination,* 1849 C St. N.W., MS 3409 MIB 20240; (202) 208-3759. Fax, (202) 219-1185. *Howard Huey Jr., National Drug Enforcement Coordinator.*

Web, www.doi.gov/pmb/oles/law-enforcement.cfm

Provides technical direction and assistance in the development of border practices, as well as supervision of field coordinators for the southwest, southeast, and northern borders. Coordinates with DHS's Border and Transportation Security, Customs and Border Protection, U.S. Border Patrol, and other external entities.

U.S. Citizenship and Immigration Services (USCIS) *(Homeland Security Dept.),* 20 Massachusetts Ave. N.W. 20529; (800) 375-5283. *Lori L. Scialabba, Director, Acting.* Press, (202) 272-1200.

Web, www.uscis.gov

Responsible for the delivery of immigration and citizenship services. Priorities include the promotion of national security and the implementation of measures to improve service delivery.

U.S. Customs and Border Protection *(Homeland Security Dept.), Agricultural Program and Trade Liaison Office,* 1300 Pennsylvania Ave. N.W., #2.5B 20229; (202) 344-3298. Fax, (202) 344-1442. *Kevin Harriger, Executive Director.*

Web, www.cbp.gov

Immigration Reform and Advocacy Resources

The following agencies, organizations, blogs, and hotlines offer information pertaining to immigrant and refugee advocacy and immigration reform.

ADVOCACY

American Immigration Lawyers Assn., (202) 507-7600; www.aila.org

Amnesty International, (202) 544-0200; www.amnestyusa.org

Ayuda, (202) 387-4848; www.ayudainc.org

Break the Chain Campaign (Institute for Policy Studies), (202) 234-9382; www.ips-dc.org/BTCC

Capital Area Immigrants' Rights (CAIR) Coalition, (202) 331-3320; www.caircoalition.org

Catholic Legal Immigration Network, Inc., (301) 565-4800; http://cliniclegal.org

Center for Community Change, (202) 339-9300; www.communitychange.org

Commission on Immigration at the American Bar Assn., (202) 662-1000; www.americanbar.org/groups/public_services/immigration.html

Detention Watch Network, (202) 350-9055; www.detentionwatchnetwork.org

United Nations High Commissioner for Refugees Regional Office, (800) 770-1100; www.unrefugees.org

U.S. Committee for Refugees and Immigrants, (703) 310-1130; www.refugees.org

U.S. Conference of Catholic Bishops, Migration, and Refugee Services, (202) 541-3000; www.usccb.org/mrs

Young Professionals in Foreign Policy Refugee Assistance Program, https://ypfp.org/content/refugee-assistance-program-rap or www.facebook.com/pages/YPFP-Refugee-Assistance-Program/137596365525

REFORM

America's Voice, (202) 463-8602; www.americasvoiceonline.org

Center for Immigration Studies, (202) 466-8185; www.cis.org

Federation for American Immigration Reform (FAIR), (202) 328-7004; www.fairus.org

Immigration Equality Action Fund, Press (202) 347-0002; http://immigrationequalityactionfund.org

Immigration Policy Center at the American Immigration Council, (202) 507-7500; www.immigrationpolicy.org

Immigration Reform Law Institute, (202) 232-5590; www.irli.org

Immigration Solutions Group, PLLC, (202) 234-0899; www.immigrationsolutions.com

ImmigrationWorks USA, (202) 506-4541; www.immigrationworksusa.org

Migration Policy Institute, (202) 266-1940; www.migrationpolicy.org

National Council of La Raza, (202) 785-1670; www.nclr.org

National Immigration Forum, (202) 347-0040; www.immigrationforum.org

SOCIAL MEDIA AND BLOGS

Borderlines Blog, Transborder Project, CIP Senior Analyst, Tom Barry (575) 313-4544; http://borderlinesblog.blogspot.com

Center for Immigration Studies Blog, http://cis.org/ImmigrationBlog

DC Immigration Blog, Kimberley Schaefer (202) 642-4529; www.dc-immigration-blog.com

Immigration Equality Action Fund Blog, http://immigrationequality.org/updates/

Progressives for Immigration Reform Blog, www.progressivesforimmigrationreform.org/blog/

Reform Immigration for America Blog, http://reformimmigrationforamerica.org/blog

HOTLINES

Asylee Information and Hotline, (800) 354-0365

Office of Special Counsel for Immigration-Related Unfair Employment Practices, U.S. Department of Justice, Civil Rights Division, Worker Hotline, (800) 255-7688; Employer hotline: (800) 255-8155, TTY (202) 616-5525 and (800) 237-2515

U.S. Immigration and Customs Enforcement (ICE), Detainees' Hotline, (855) 448-6903

U.S. Citizenship and Immigration Services National Customer Service Center, (800) 375-5283

Responsible for safeguarding the nation's animal and natural resources from pests and disease through inspections at ports of entry and beyond.

U.S. Customs and Border Protection (Homeland Security Dept.), Border Patrol, 1300 Pennsylvania Ave. N.W., #6.5E 20229; (202) 344-2050. Fax, (202) 344-3140. Michael J. Fisher, Chief.
Web, www.cbp.gov/xp/cgov/border_security/border_patrol

Mobile uniformed law enforcement arm of the Homeland Security Dept. Primary mission is to detect and prevent the illegal trafficking of people and contraband across U.S. borders.

U.S. Immigration and Customs Enforcement (ICE) (Homeland Security Dept.), 500 12th St. S.W. 20536; (202) 732-3000. Fax, (202) 732-3080. Vacant, Director. Press, (202) 732-4242. Hotline to report suspicious activity, (866) 347-2423.
Web, www.ice.gov

Enforces immigration and customs laws within the United States. Focuses on the protection of specified federal buildings and on air and marine enforcement. Undertakes investigations and conducts interdictions.

▶CONGRESS

For a listing of relevant congressional committees and subcommittees, please see pages 548–549 or the Appendix.

DEFENSE TRADE AND TECHNOLOGY

General

▶AGENCIES

Bureau of Industry and Security (Commerce Dept.), 14th St. and Constitution Ave. N.W., #3898 20230; (202) 482-1455. Fax, (202) 482-6216. Eric L. Hirschhorn, Under Secretary. Press, (202) 482-2721. Export licensing information, (202) 482-4811.
Web, www.bis.doc.gov

Administers Export Administration Act; maintains control lists and performs export licensing for the purposes of national security, foreign policy, and prevention of short supply.

Bureau of Industry and Security (Commerce Dept.), Export Enforcement, 14th St. and Constitution Ave. N.W., #3723 20230; (202) 482-3618. Fax, (202) 482-4173. David W. Mills, Assistant Secretary; Richard R. Majaukas, Deputy Assistant Secretary; Douglas Hassebrock, Director, (202) 482-1208. Export Enforcement Hotline, (800) 424-2980.
Web, www.bis.doc.gov

Enforces dual-use export controls on exports of U.S. goods and technology for purposes of national security, nonproliferation, counterterrorism, foreign policy, and

short supply. Enforces the antiboycott provisions of the Export Administration Regulations.

Defense Dept. (DoD), Defense Technology Security Administration, 4800 Mark Center Dr., #03D08, Alexandria, VA 22350-1600; (571) 372-2304. Fax, (571) 372-2433. Beth M. McCormick, Director.
Web, www.dtsa.mil

Develops and implements technology security policy for international transfers of defense-related goods, services, and technologies. Participates in interagency and international activities and regimes that monitor, control, and prevent transfers that could threaten U.S. national security interests.

Defense Dept. (DoD), International Cooperation, 3070 Defense Pentagon, #5A1062B 20301-3070; (703) 697-4172. Fax, (703) 693-2026. Keith Webster, Director.
Web, www.acq.osd.mil/ic

Advises the under secretary of defense for Acquisitions, Technology, and Logistics on cooperative research and development, production, procurement, and follow-up support programs with foreign nations; monitors the transfer of secure technologies to foreign nations.

Energy Dept. (DOE), National Nuclear Security Administration, Nuclear Nonproliferation and International Security, 1000 Independence Ave. S.W., #7A175 20585; (202) 586-0645. Fax, (202) 586-0862. Anne M. Harrington, Deputy Administrator.
Web, www.nnsa.energy.gov/aboutus/ourprograms/dnn

Provides U.S. government agencies and departments with technical and operational expertise on foreign nuclear and energy issues. Oversees programs to prevent the spread of nuclear, chemical, and biological weapons and missiles for their delivery. Partners with Russia and other former Soviet states to secure weapons of mass destruction materials and expertise; works to strengthen legal and institutional nonproliferation norms; builds technologies to detect proliferation activities; and promotes the safe use of nuclear power.

National Security Staff (NSS) (Executive Office of the President), International Economic Affairs, The White House 20504; (202) 456-9281. Fax, (202) 456-9280. Caroline Atkinson, Deputy National Security Adviser.
Web, www.whitehouse.gov/administration/eop/nsc

Advises the president, the National Security Council, and the National Economic Council on all aspects of U.S. foreign policy dealing with U.S. international economic policies.

Nuclear Regulatory Commission, International Programs, 11555 Rockville Pike, MS04E21, Rockville, MD 20852; (301) 415-2344. Fax, (301) 415-2400. Nader Mamesh, Director, (301) 415-1780.
Web, www.nrc.gov/about-nrc/organization/oipfuncdesc.html

Coordinates application review process for exports and imports of nuclear materials, facilities, and components. Makes recommendations on export-import

Air Force Department

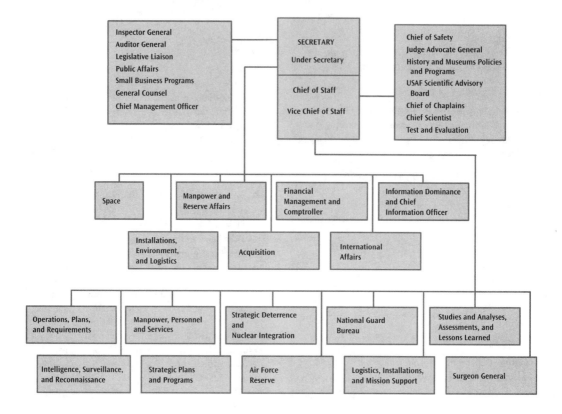

licensing upon completion of review process. Conducts related policy reviews.

State Dept., *Bureau of International Security and Nonproliferation (ISN)*, 2201 C St. N.W., #3932 20520; (202) 647-9612. Fax, (202) 736-4863. Thomas M. Countryman, Assistant Secretary; Vann H. Van Diepen, Principal Deputy Assistant Secretary.
Web, www.state.gov/t/isn

Leads U.S. efforts to prevent the spread of weapons of mass destruction (WMD, including nuclear, chemical, and biological weapons) and their delivery systems; spearheads efforts to promote international consensus on WMD proliferation; supports efforts of foreign partners to prevent, protect against, and respond to the threat or use of WMD by terrorists.

State Dept., *Defense Trade Controls*, 2401 E St. N.W., SA-1, #H1200 20037 (mailing address: PM/DDTC, SA-1, 12th Floor, Bureau of Political Military Affairs, Washington, DC 20522-0112); (202) 663-2861. Fax, (202) 261-8199. Kenneth B. Handelman, Deputy Assistant Secretary for Defense Trade Controls.
Web, www.pmddtc.state.gov

Controls the commercial export of defense articles, services, and related technical data; authorizes the permanent export and temporary import of such items.

State Dept., *Sanctions Policy and Implementation*, 2201 C St. N.W., #4657 20520; (202) 647-7489. Fax, (202) 647-4064. Darnall Steuart, Director, (202) 647-7677.
Web, www.state.gov

Develops and implements U.S. economic sanctions of embargoed countries. Coordinates U.S. participation in multilateral strategic trade control and revisions related to the export of strategically critical high-technology goods. Cooperates with the Commerce, Defense, and Treasury Depts. regarding export controls.

Treasury Dept., *Foreign Assets Control*, 1500 Pennsylvania Ave. N.W., OFAC 20220; (202) 622-2510. Fax, (202) 622-1657. Adam Szubin, Director. Fax-on-demand, (202) 622-0077. Hotline, (800) 540-6322. General email, ofac_feedback@do.treas.gov
Web, www.ustreas.gov/offices/enforcement/ofac

Authorized under the Enemy Act, the International Emergency Economic Powers Act, and United Nations Participation Act, and other relevant statutory authorities to control financial and commercial dealings with certain countries and their foreign nationals in times of war or emergencies. Regulations involving foreign assets control, narcotics, nonproliferation, and commercial transactions currently apply in varying degrees to the Balkans, Belarus, Burma, Côte d'Ivoire, Cuba, Iran, Iraq, Lebanon, Libya, North Korea, Somalia, Sudan, Syria, Yemen, and Zimbabwe, as well as terrorists wherever located and transnational criminal organizations.

► CONGRESS

For a listing of relevant congressional committees and sub-committees, please see pages 548–549 or the Appendix.

Research and Development

► AGENCIES

Air Force Dept. *(Defense Dept.), Acquisition,* 1060 Air Force Pentagon, #4E962 20330-1060; (703) 697-6361. Fax, (703) 693-6400. Lt. Gen. William LaPlante, Air Force Service Acquisition Executive.
Web, ww3.safaq.hq.af.mil

Air Force office that directs and reviews Air Force research, development, and acquisition of weapons systems.

Air Force Dept. *(Defense Dept.), Scientific Research,* 875 N. Randolph St., #3112, Arlington, VA 22203-1768; (703) 696-7551. Fax, (703) 696-9556. Vacant, Director.
Web, www.afosr.af.mil

Sponsors and sustains basic research; assists in the transfer of research results to the war fighter; supports Air Force goals of control and maximum utilization of air and space.

Army Corps of Engineers *(Defense Dept.), Research and Development,* 441 G St. N.W., #3Z10 20314-1000; (202) 761-1839. Fax, (202) 761-0907. Jeffery P. Holland, Chief Scientist, (601) 634-2000.
Web, www.usace.army.mil

Supports the research and development efforts of the corps by providing strategic planning and strategic direction and oversight, developing policy and doctrine, developing national program integration, and advising the chief of engineers on science and technology issues.

Army Dept. *(Defense Dept.), Acquisition, Logistics, and Technology,* 103 Army Pentagon, #2E532 20310-0103; (703) 695-6153. Fax, (703) 697-4003. Heidi Shyu, Assistant Secretary. Press, (703) 697-7592.
Web, www.alt.army.mil

Civilian office that directs Army acquisition research and development of weapons systems and missiles.

Army Dept. *(Defense Dept.), Research and Technology,* 103 Army Pentagon, #2E533 20310-0103; (703) 692-1837. Mary Miller, Director.
Web, www.army.mil

Sponsors and supports basic research at Army laboratories, universities, and other public and private organizations; assists in the transfer of research and technology to the field.

Defense Advanced Research Projects Agency *(Defense Dept.),* 675 N. Randolph St., Arlington, VA 22203-2114; (703) 696-2400. Fax, (703) 696-2209. Arati Prabhakar, Director; Eric Mazzacone, External Relations, (703) 526-4758.
Web, www.darpa.mil

Sponsors basic and applied research to maintain U.S. technological superiority and prevent strategic surprise by adversaries.

Defense Dept. (DoD), *Missile Defense Agency,* 5700 18th St., Bldg. 245, Fort Belvoir, VA 22060-5573; (571) 231-8006. Fax, (571) 231-8090. Vice Adm. James D. Syring, (USN), Director; Maj. Gen. Samuel A. Greaves, (USAF), Deputy Director. Fraud, Waste, and Abuse Hotline, (800) 424-9098. General email, mda.info@mda.mil
Web, www.mda.mil

Manages and directs the ballistic missile defense acquisition and research and development programs. Seeks to deploy improved theater missile defense systems and to develop options for effective national missile defenses while increasing the contribution of defensive systems to U.S. and allied security.

Defense Dept. (DoD), *Research and Engineering,* 3040 Defense Pentagon, #3C85A 20301-3040; (703) 695-9604. Fax, (703) 695-4277. Alan R. Shaffer, Principal Deputy Director; Alan R. Shaffer, Director, Acting.
Web, www.acq.osd.mil/chieftechnologist

Civilian office responsible for policy, guidance, and oversight for the Defense Dept.'s Science and Technology Program. Serves as focal point for in-house laboratories, university research, and other science and technology matters.

Defense Technical Information Center *(Defense Dept.),* 8725 John Jay Kingman Rd., #1948, Fort Belvoir, VA 22060-6218; (703) 767-9100. Fax, (703) 767-9183. Christopher Thomas, Administrator. Registration, (703) 767-8273. Toll-free, (800) 225-3842.
Web, www.dtic.mil

Acts as a central repository for the Defense Dept.'s collection of current and completed research and development efforts in all fields of science and technology. Disseminates research and development information to contractors, grantees, and registered organizations working on government research and development projects, particularly for the Defense Dept. Users must register with the center.

Marine Corps *(Defense Dept.), Systems Command,* 2200 Lester St., Quantico, VA 22134-6050; (703) 432-1800. Fax, (703) 432-3535. Brig. Gen. Frank Kelley, Commanding General.
Web, www.marcorsyscom.usmc.mil

Military office that directs Marine Corps research, development, and acquisition.

National Communications System *(Homeland Security Dept.), President's National Security Telecommunications Advisory Committee,* NCS, 245 Murray Lane, MS 0615, Arlington, VA 20598-0615; (202) 282-8000. Fax, (703) 235-4981. Helen Jackson, Program Manager. DHS switchboard, (202) 282-8000. Press, (202) 282-8010.
General email, nstac1@dhs.gov
Web, www.ncs.gov/nstac

Army Department

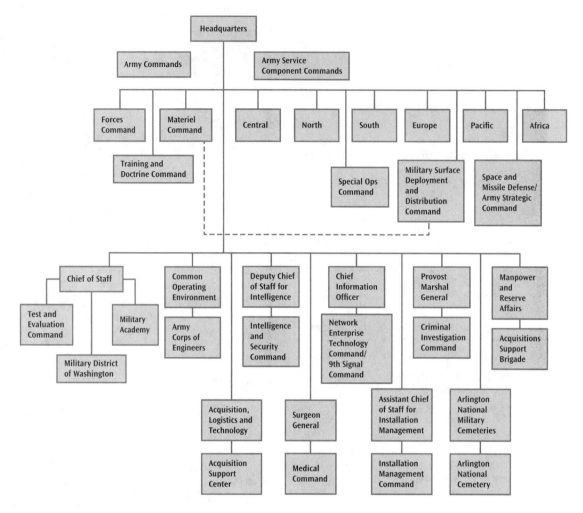

- - - - - - - - Designates a major subordinate command

Advises the president, the National Security Council, the Office of Science and Technology Policy, and the Office of Management and Budget on specific measures to improve telecommunications for the federal government. Areas of major focus include strengthening national security, enhancing cybersecurity, maintaining the global communications infrastructure, assuring communications for disaster response, and addressing infrastructure interdependencies and dependencies.

Naval Research Laboratory *(Defense Dept.), Research,* *4555 Overlook Ave. S.W. 20375-5320; (202) 767-3301.* *Fax, (202) 767-6991. Capt. Anthony Ferrari, Commanding* *Officer; John A. Montgomery, Director. Press, (202) 767-* *2541. Personnel locator, (202) 767-3200.* *General email, nrl1030@ccs.hrl.navy.mil*

Web, www.nrl.navy.mil

Conducts scientific research and develops advanced technology for the Navy. Areas of research include radar systems, radiation technology, tactical electronic warfare, and weapons guidance systems.

Navy Dept. *(Defense Dept.), Office of Naval Research,* *875 N. Randolph St., #1425, Arlington, VA 22203-1995;* *(703) 696-5031. Fax, (703) 696-5940. Rear* *Adm. Matthew L. Klunder, Chief.* *Web, www.onr.navy.mil*

Oversees the offices of Naval Research, Naval Technology, and Advanced Technology; works to ensure transition of research and technology to the fleet; sponsors and supports basic research at Navy laboratories, universities, and other public and private organizations.

Navy Dept. *(Defense Dept.), Research, Development, and* *Acquisition, 1000 Navy Pentagon, #4E665 20350-1000;* *(703) 695-6315. Fax, (703) 697-0172. Sean J. Stackley,* *Assistant Secretary.* *Web, www.acquisition.navy.mil*

Navy Department

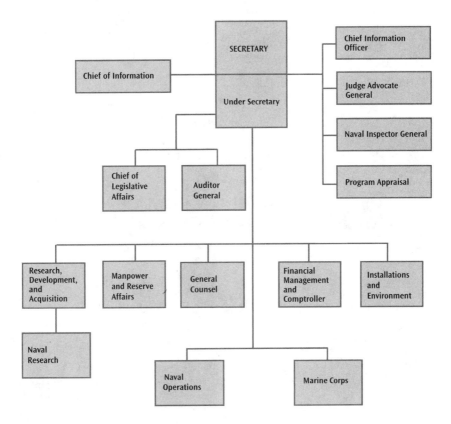

Civilian office that directs and reviews Navy and Marine Corps research and development of weapons systems.

Office of Science and Technology Policy (OSTP)
(Executive Office of the President), Eisenhower Executive Office Bldg., 1650 Pennsylvania Ave. N.W. 20504; (202) 456-7116. Fax, (202) 456-6021. John P. Holdren, Director. Press, (202) 456-6124.
General email, info@ostp.gov

Web, www.ostp.gov

Advises the president on science and technology matters as they affect national security; coordinates science and technology initiatives at the interagency level. Interests include nuclear materials, security, nuclear arms reduction, and counterterrorism.

State Dept., *Intelligence and Research, 2201 C St. N.W., #6468 20520-6531; (202) 647-9177. Fax, (202) 736-4688. Philip S. Goldberg, Assistant Secretary.*
Web, www.state.gov

Coordinates foreign policy–related research, analysis, and intelligence programs for the State Dept. and other federal agencies.

U.S. Coast Guard (USCG) *(Homeland Security Dept.), Engineering and Logistics, CG4, 2703 Martin Luther King Jr. Ave. S.E., MS 7714 20593; (202) 475-5554. Fax, (202)*

475-5957. Rear Adm. Ronald J. Rábago, Assistant Commandant; Albert Curry Jr., Deputy Assistant Commandant.
Web, www.uscg.mil/hq/cg4

Develops and maintains engineering standards for the building of ships, aircraft, shore infrastructure, and Coast Guard facilities. Publishes Engineering, Electronics and Logistics Quarterly, available on the Web site.

►CONGRESS

For a listing of relevant congressional committees and subcommittees, please see pages 548–549 or the Appendix.

►NONGOVERNMENTAL

American Society of Naval Engineers (ASNE), *1452 Duke St., Alexandria, VA 22314-3458; (703) 836-6727. Fax, (703) 836-7491. Dennis K. Kruse, Executive Director.*
General email, asnehq@navalengineers.org

Web, www.navalengineers.org

Membership: civilian, active duty, and retired naval engineers. Provides forum for an exchange of information between industry and government involving all phases of naval engineering.

U.S. Coast Guard

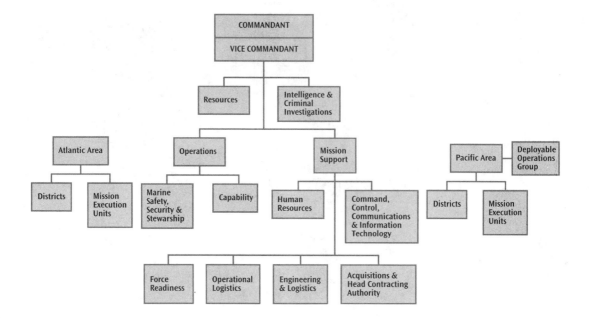

Analytic Services Inc., *2900 S. Quincy St., #800, Arlington, VA 22206-2233; (703) 416-2000. Fax, (703) 416-8408. Ruth David, President. Toll-free, (800) 368-4173.*
Web, www.anser.org

Systems analysis organization funded by government contracts. Conducts weapons systems analysis.

Armed Forces Communications and Electronics Assn. (AFCEA), *4400 Fair Lakes Court, Fairfax, VA 22033-3899; (703) 631-6100. Fax, (703) 631-6169. Kent Schneider, President. Toll-free, (800) 336-4583.*
General email, info@afcea.org
Web, www.afcea.org

Membership: industrial organizations, scientists, and military and government personnel in the fields of communications, electronics, computers, and electrical engineering. Consults with the Defense Dept. and other federal agencies on design and maintenance of command, control, communications, computer, and intelligence systems; holds shows displaying latest communications products.

Institute for Defense Analyses (IDA), *4850 Mark Center Dr., Alexandria, VA 22311-1882; (703) 845-2000. Fax, (703) 845-2588. David Chu, President. Library, (703) 845-2087.*
Web, www.ida.org

Federally funded research and development center that focuses on national security and defense. Conducts research, systems evaluation, and policy analysis for Defense Dept. and other agencies.

Johns Hopkins University Applied Physics Laboratory, *11100 Johns Hopkins Rd., Laurel, MD 20723-6099; (240) 228-5000. Fax, (240) 228-5995. Ralph D. Semmel, Director.*
Public Affairs, (443) 778-7536.
Web, www.jhuapl.edu

Research and development organization that conducts research for the Defense Dept. and other federal agencies. Interests include defense, national security, and space technologies.

LMI, *2000 Corporate Ridge, McLean, VA 22102-7805; (703) 917-9800. Fax, (703) 917-7591. Nelson M. Ford, President. Toll-free, (800) 213-4817.*
Web, www.lmi.org

Conducts research on military and nonmilitary logistics, including transportation, supply and maintenance, force management, weapons support, acquisition, health systems, international programs, energy and environment, mathematical modeling, installations, operations, and information systems. (Formerly Logistics Management Institute.)

Military Operations Research Society (MORS), *2111 Wilson Blvd., #700, Alexandria, VA 22201; (703) 933-9070. Fax, (703) 933-9066. Susan Reardon, Chief Executive Officer.*
General email, morsoffice@mors.org
Web, www.mors.org

Membership: professional analysts of military operations. Fosters information exchange; promotes professional development and high ethical standards; educates members on emerging issues, analytical techniques, and applications of research.

The Society of American Military Engineers, *607 Prince St., Alexandria, VA 22314-3117; (703) 549-3800. Fax, (703) 684-0231. Robert D. Wolff, Executive Director. Press, (703) 549-3800, 140.*

General email, editor@same.org

Web, www.same.org

Membership: military and civilian engineers, architects, and construction professionals. Conducts workshops and conferences on subjects related to military engineering.

SRI International, *Washington Office,* 1100 Wilson Blvd., #2800, Arlington, VA 22209; (703) 524-2053. Fax, (703) 247-8569. Jerry Harrison, Vice President, Government Business Development, (703) 247-8569.
Web, www.sri.com

Research organization supported by government and private contracts. Conducts research on military technology, including lasers and computers. Other interests include strategic planning and armed forces interdisciplinary research. (Headquarters in Menlo Park, Calif.)

EMERGENCY PREPAREDNESS AND RESPONSE

General

▶**AGENCIES**

Army Corps of Engineers *(Defense Dept.),* **Contingency Operations and Office of Homeland Security,** 441 G St. N.W. 20314-1000; (202) 761-4601. Fax, (202) 761-5096. Karen L. Durham-Aguilera, Chief.
Web, www.usace.army.mil

Assists military combatant commands, as well as federal, state, and local emergency management and emergency response organizations, with mitigation, planning, training, and exercises to build and sustain capabilities to protect from and respond to any emergency or disaster, including natural disasters and terrorist attacks involving weapons of mass destruction.

Civil Air Patrol National Capital Wing, 200 McChord St. S.W., #111, Joint Base Anacostia-Bolling 20032; (202) 767-4405. Bruce Heinlein, Wing Commander.
General email, pa@natcapwg.cap.gov

Web, www.natcapwg.cap.gov and www.natcapwing.org

Official auxiliary of the U.S. Air Force. Conducts search-and-rescue missions for the Air Force; participates in emergency airlift and disaster relief missions. (Headquarters at Maxwell Air Force Base, Ala.)

Energy Dept. (DOE), *National Nuclear Security Administration, Emergency Operations,* 1000 Independence Ave. S.W., #GH060 20585; (202) 586-9892. Fax, (202) 586-3904. Joseph J. Krol Jr., Associate Administrator.
Web, www.nnsa.energy.gov/aboutus/ourprograms/emergencyoperationscounterterrorism

Works to ensure coordinated Energy Dept. responses to energy-related emergencies. Recommends policies to mitigate the effects of energy supply crises on the United States; recommends government responses to energy emergencies.

Federal Emergency Management Agency (FEMA) *(Homeland Security Dept.),* 500 C St. S.W. 20472; (202) 646-3900. Fax, (202) 646-3930. W. Craig Fugate, Administrator. Press, (202) 646-3272. Locator, (202) 646-2500. Disaster assistance, (800) 621-3362. Toll-free, 800-621-FEMA.
General email, femaopa@dhs.gov

Web, www.fema.gov

Manages federal response and recovery efforts following natural disasters, terrorist attacks, and all other kinds of national emergencies. Initiates mitigation activities; works with state and local emergency managers; manages the National Flood Insurance Program.

Federal Emergency Management Agency (FEMA) *(Homeland Security Dept.), Disaster Assistance Recovery,* 500 C St. S.W. 20472; (202) 646-3642. Fax, (202) 646-2730. Deborah Ingram, Assistant Administrator.
Web, www.fema.gov

Responsible for coordination of the president's disaster relief program.

Federal Emergency Management Agency (FEMA) *(Homeland Security Dept.), Federal Insurance and Mitigation Administration,* 1800 S. Bell St., MS 3020, Arlington, VA 22202; (202) 646-2781. Fax, (202) 646-7970. David L. Miller, Associate Administrator.
Web, www.fema.gov/what-mitigation/federal-insurance-mitigation-administration

Administers federal flood insurance programs, including the National Flood Insurance Program. Makes low-cost flood insurance available to eligible homeowners.

Federal Emergency Management Agency (FEMA) *(Homeland Security Dept.), Grant Programs,* 500 C St. S.W. 20472; (800) 368-6498. Brian E. Kamoie, Assistant Administrator.
General email, askcsid@fema.dhs.gov

Web, www.fema.gov/government/grants

Administers and manages grants to states, local communities, regional authorities, and tribal jurisdictions to prevent, deter, and respond to terrorists and other threats to national security.

Federal Emergency Management Agency (FEMA) *(Homeland Security Dept.), National Continuity Programs,* 500 C St. S.W., #524 20472; (202) 646-4145. Fax, (202) 646-3921. Damon C. Penn, Assistant Administrator.
Web, www.fema.gov/protection-and-national-preparedness

Responsible for the coordination of all Federal Emergency Management Agency national security programs.

Federal Emergency Management Agency (FEMA) *(Homeland Security Dept.), National Integration Center,* 999 E St. N.W., 3rd Floor 20463; (202) 646-3850. Fax, (202) 646-3061. Carla Boyce, Director. Disaster Assistance, (800) 621-FEMA.
General email, FEMA-NIMS@dhs.gov

Web, www.fema.gov/national-incident-management-system

Oversees the National Incident Management System (NIMS). Integrates federal, state, local, and tribal emergency response and preparedness practices into a national framework. Seeks to enable all responders to work together effectively through such means as standardized structures and procedures and interoperable communications systems. Operates ten regional offices.

Federal Emergency Management Agency (FEMA) (Homeland Security Dept.), National Preparedness, Technological Hazards, *1800 S. Bell St., MS 3025, Arlington, VA 22202; (202) 646-3158. Fax, (703) 308-0324. Andrew Mitchell, Director, (202) 646-2618.*
Web, www.fema.gov/technological-hazards-division

Helps FEMA prepare to respond to disasters and incidents of all kinds. Coordinates and develops plans, resources, assessments, and national standards for emergency response operations. Oversees standards for emergency response operations. Oversees community response plans for chemical and nuclear hazards. Develops and delivers grant opportunities and education and training programs for the emergency management and first responder communities.

Health and Human Services Dept. (HHS), National Disaster Medical System, *200 Independence Ave. S.W, #638G 20201; (202) 205-7978. Dr. Andrew Garrett, Director. Public Affairs, (202) 205-8114.*
Web, http://phe.gov/ndms

Provides local, state, and tribal governments with medical response, patient movement, and the definitive care of victims of major emergencies and presidentially declared disasters, including those resulting from natural, technological, and human-caused hazards, such as transportation accidents and acts of terrorism involving chemical, biological, radiological, nuclear, and explosive weapons. Maintains a national capability to provide medical, veterinary, and mortuary teams, supplies, and equipment at the sites of disasters, and in transit from the impacted area into participating definitive care facilities.

Homeland Security Dept. (DHS), Cyber and Security Communications, *1110 N. Glebe Rd., Arlington, VA 22201; (202) 282-8000. Fax, (202) 447-3237. Roberta (Bobbie) Stempfley, Assistant Secretary, Acting. DHS Switchboard, (202) 282-8000.*
General email, soc@us-cert.gov
Web, www.dhs.gov/office-cybersecurity-and-communications

Works with other federal agencies in developing comprehensive plans to prevent and mitigate cyber-based attacks.

Homeland Security Dept. (DHS), Infrastructure Protection, *1310 N. Courthouse Rd., Arlington, VA 22201; (703) 235-2522. Fax, (202) 235-9757. Caitlin Durkovich, Assistant Secretary.*
Web, www.dhs.gov/about-office-infrastructure-protection

Identifies and assesses threats to the nation's physical and informational structure from acts of terrorism or natural disasters. Coordinates programs to respond to and quickly recover from attacks or other emergencies.

Homeland Security Dept. (DHS), National Protection and Programs Directorate, *3801 Nebraska Ave., Bldg. 5 20528; (202) 282-8000. Fax, (202) 295-0870. Suzanne Spaulding, Under Secretary, Acting. DHS Switchboard, (202) 282-8000.*
Web, www.dhs.gov/about-national-protection-and-programs-directorate

Identifies and assesses threats to the nation's physical and informational infrastructure; issues warnings to prevent damage.

Interior Dept. (DOI), Emergency Management, *1849 C St. N.W. 20240; (202) 208-4679. Fax, (202) 219-1185. Laurence Broun, Director. Watch Office (24/7), (202) 208-4108. Toll-free, (877) 246-1373.*
General email, DOI_Watch_Office@ios.doi.gov
Web, www.doi.gov/emergency/index.cfm

Establishes and disseminates policy and coordinates the development of Interior Dept. programs for emergency prevention, planning, response, and recovery that affects federal and tribal lands, facilities, infrastructure, and resources. Provides assistance to other units of government under federal laws, executive orders, interagency emergency response plans such as the National Response Framework, and other agreements.

National Response Center (Homeland Security Dept.), *2100 2nd St. S.W., #2111B 20593-0001; (202) 267-2180. Fax, (202) 267-1322. Syed M. Qadir, Director, (202) 372-2440. TTY, (202) 267-4477. Hotline, (800) 424-8802. local, (202) 267-2675.*
General email, hqs-dg-lst-nrcinfo@comdt.uscg.mil
Web, www.nrc.uscg.mil

Maintains twenty-four-hour hotline for reporting oil spills, hazardous materials accidents, and chemical releases. Notifies appropriate federal officials to reduce the effects of accidents.

Nuclear Regulatory Commission, Nuclear Material Safety and Safeguards, *11601 Landsdown St., N. Bethesda, MD 20852; (301) 287-9243. Fax, (301) 287-0500. Catherine Haney, Director.*
Web, www.nrc.gov/about-nrc/organization/nmssfuncdesc .html

Develops and implements safeguards programs; directs licensing and regulation activities for the management and disposal of nuclear waste.

Small Business Administration (SBA), Disaster Assistance, *409 3rd St. S.W., #6050 20416; (202) 205-6734. Fax, (202) 205-7728. James Rivera, Associate Administrator. Call center, (800) 659-2955.*
Web, www.sba.gov/about-offices-content/1/2462

Provides victims of physical disasters with disaster and economic injury loans for homes, businesses, and personal property. Lends funds for uncompensated losses incurred from any disaster declared by the president of the United States or the administrator of the SBA. Lends funds to individual homeowners, business concerns of all sizes, and nonprofit institutions to repair or replace damaged structures and furnishings, business machinery, equipment, and inventory. Provides economic injury loans to small businesses for losses to meet necessary operating expenses, provided the business could have paid these expenses prior to the disaster.

Transportation Dept. (DOT), *Intelligence, Security, and Emergency Response, 1200 New Jersey Ave. S.E., #56125 20590; (202) 366-6525. Fax, (202) 366-7261. Michael Lowder, Director, (202) 366-6530. Web, www.dot.gov/mission/administration/intelligence-security-emergency-response*

Advises the secretary on transportation intelligence and security policy. Acts as liaison with the intelligence community, federal agencies, corporations, and interest groups; administers counterterrorism strategic planning processes. Develops, coordinates, and reviews transportation emergency preparedness programs for use in emergencies affecting national defense and in emergencies caused by natural and man-made disasters and crisis situations.

U.S. Coast Guard (USCG) *(Homeland Security Dept.), Counterterrorism and Defense Operations, CG-532, 2703 Martin Luther King Jr. Ave. S.E. 20593; (202) 372-1015. Fax, (202) 372-2911. Robert Irvine, Chief. Web, www.uscg.mil/hq/cg5/cg532*

Ensures that the Coast Guard can mobilize effectively during national emergencies, including those resulting from enemy military attack.

U.S. Coast Guard (USCG) *(Homeland Security Dept.), Response Policy, CG-5R, 2703 Martin Luther King Jr. Ave. S.E., MS 7516 20593-7516; (202) 372-2010. Rear Adm. Peter Brown, Director. Web, www.uscg.mil*

Conducts search-and-rescue and polar and domestic ice-breaking operations. Regulates waterways under U.S. jurisdiction. Operates the Coast Guard National Response Center; participates in defense operations and homeland security; assists with law enforcement/drug interdictions.

U.S. Fire Administration *(Homeland Security Dept.), 16825 S. Seton Ave., Emmitsburg, MD 21727; (301) 447-1000. Fax, (301) 447-1270. Ernest Mitchell Jr., Administrator, (202) 646-4223. Web, www.usfa.fema.gov*

Provides public education, first responder training, technology, and data initiatives in an effort to prevent losses due to fire and related emergencies. Administers the Emergency Management Institute and the National Fire Academy for firefighters and emergency management personnel.

▶ **CONGRESS**

For a listing of relevant congressional committees and subcommittees, please see pages 548–549 or the Appendix.

▶ **NONGOVERNMENTAL**

American Red Cross, *Disaster Preparedness and Response, 2025 E St. N.W. 20006-5009; (202) 303-5000, ext. 1. Gail J. McGovern, President. Press, (202) 303-5551. Donations, (800) RED-CROSS. Toll-free, (800) 733-2767. Web, www.redcross.org* and *Disaster Preparedness, www.redcross.org/training*

Chartered by Congress to administer disaster relief. Provides disaster victims with food, shelter, first aid, medical care, and access to other available resources. Feeds emergency workers; handles inquiries from concerned family members outside the disaster area; helps promote disaster preparedness and prevention through training.

International Assn. of Chiefs of Police, *Advisory Committee for Patrol and Tactical Operations, 44 Canal Center Plaza, #200, Alexandria, VA 22314; (703) 836-6767. Fax, (703) 836-4543. Nancy Kolb, Staff Liaison, ext. 813. Toll-free, (800) 843-7227. General email, kollon@theiacp.org Web, www.theiacp.org*

Membership: foreign and U.S. police executives and administrators. Maintains liaison with civil defense and emergency service agencies in the United States and other nations; prepares guidelines for police cooperation with emergency and disaster relief agencies during emergencies.

National Assn. of State EMS Officials (NASEMSO), *201 Park Washington Ct., Falls Church, VA 22046-4527; (703) 538-1799. Fax, (703) 241-5603. Elizabeth B. Armstrong, Executive Vice President. General email, info@nasemso.org Web, www.nasemso.org*

Supports development of effective emergency medical services (EMS) systems at the local, state, and regional levels. Works to formulate national EMS policy and foster communication and sharing among state EMS officials.

National Emergency Management Assn., *Washington Office, 444 N. Capitol St. N.W., #401 20001-1557; (202) 624-5460. Fax, (202) 624-5875. Matt Cowles, Government Relations Director. Web, www.nemaweb.org*

Professional association of state emergency managers. Promotes improvement of emergency management through strategic partnerships and innovative programs. (Headquarters in Lexington, Ky.; member of the Council of State Governments)

National Voluntary Organizations Active in Disaster (NVOAD), *1501 Lee Hwy., #200, Arlington, VA 22209-1109; (703) 778-5088. Fax, (703) 778-5091. Daniel L. Stoecker, Executive Director. General email, info@nvoad.org Web, www.nvoad.org*

Seeks to promote communication, cooperation, coordination, and collaboration among voluntary agencies that participate in disaster response, relief, and recovery nationally.

The Salvation Army Disaster Service, *2626 Pennsylvania Ave. N.W. 20037-1618; (202) 756-2600. Fax, (202) 464-7203. Maj. Andrew Wiley, Divisional Secretary. Web, www.salvationarmyusa.org*

Provides U.S. and international disaster victims and rescuers with emergency support, including food, clothing, and counseling services.

Coordination and Partnerships

▶**AGENCIES**

Federal Bureau of Investigation (FBI) *(Justice Dept.), National Joint Terrorism Task Force (National JTTF), 935 Pennsylvania Ave. N.W. 20535-0001; (571) 280-5688. Fax, (571) 280-6922. William Callahan, Unit Chief. Web, www.fbi.gov/washingtondc/about-us/our-partnerships/partners*

Group of more than forty agencies from the fields of intelligence, public safety, and federal, state, and local law enforcement that collects terrorism information and intelligence and funnels it to the more than one hundred JTTFs (teams of local, state, and federal agents based at FBI field offices), various terrorism units within the FBI, and partner agencies. Helps the FBI with terrorism investigations.

Federal Emergency Management Agency (FEMA) *(Homeland Security Dept.), Emergency Management Institute, 16825 S. Seton Ave., Emmitsburg, MD 21727; (301) 447-1000. Fax, (301) 447-1658. Tony Russell, Superintendent, (301) 447-1286. Web, www.training.fema.gov/EMI*

Provides federal, state, tribal, and local government personnel and some private organizations engaged in emergency management with technical, professional, and vocational training. Educational programs include hazard mitigation, emergency preparedness, and disaster response.

Federal Emergency Management Agency (FEMA) *(Homeland Security Dept.), Grant Programs, 500 C St. S.W. 20472; (800) 368-6498. Brian E. Kamoie, Assistant Administrator. General email, askcsid@fema.dhs.gov Web, www.fema.gov/government/grants*

Administers and manages grants to states, local communities, regional authorities, and tribal jurisdictions to prevent, deter, and respond to terrorists and other threats to national security.

Federal Emergency Management Agency (FEMA) *(Homeland Security Dept.), Individual and Community Preparedness (ICPD), Techworld Bldg., 800 K St. N.W., #5127 20472-3630; (202) 786-9557. Karen Marsh, Director, Acting. General email, citizencorps@dhs.gov Web, www.citizencorps.gov and www.ready.gov/research*

Conducts research on individual, business, and community preparedness. Administers Citizen Corps, a national network of state, territory, tribal, and local councils that coordinate with local first responders to develop community-specific public education, outreach, training, and volunteer opportunities that address community preparedness and resiliency.

Federal Emergency Management Agency (FEMA) *(Homeland Security Dept.), Office of National Capital Region Coordination (ONCRC), 500 C St. S.W., #202 20472; (202) 212-1500. Fax, (202) 212-1515. Kim R. Kadesch, Deputy Director. Web, www.fema.gov/protection-and-national-preparedness*

Oversees and coordinates federal programs and domestic preparedness initiatives for state, local, and regional authorities in the District of Columbia, Maryland, and Virginia.

Homeland Security Dept. (DHS), *Bombing Prevention, Nebraska Ave. Complex, 3801 Nebraska Ave. N.W. 20528; (703) 235-9382. Fax, (703) 235-9711. Patrick Starke, Director. General email, obp@dhs.gov Web, www.dhs.gov/obp*

Coordinates national efforts to detect, prevent, and respond to terrorist improvised explosive device (IED) threats. Works with federal agencies, state and local governments, and the private sector to promote information sharing and IED awareness. Maintains database on equipment, training, and assets required for effective response to IED threats. Sponsors Technical Resource for Incident Prevention (TRIPwire), an online information-sharing network for bomb technicians and other law enforcement officials.

Homeland Security Dept. (DHS), *Office of Policy, Private Sector, Nebraska Ave. Complex, 3801 Nebraska Ave. N.W., Bldg. 1, 3rd Floor 20528; (202) 282-8484. Fax, (202) 282-9207. Michael Stroud, Assistant Secretary, Acting. Press, (202) 282-8010. Web, www.dhs.gov*

Works to facilitate outreach to industry and flow of information between industry and the department on security topics ranging from protecting critical infrastructure from sabotage to securing computer networks from hackers.

Homeland Security Dept. (DHS), *Operations Coordination and Planning, 3801 Nebraska Ave. N.W., Bldg. 3, #01107 20528; (202) 282-9580. Fax, (202) 282-8191. Richard Chavez, Director. Web, www.dhs.gov/about-office-operations-coordination-and-planning*

Collects and fuses intelligence and enforcement activities information that may have a terrorist nexus from a variety of federal, state, territorial, tribal, local, and private sector partners to continually monitor the nation's threat environment. Coordinates incident management activities within the department and with state governors, homeland security advisors, law enforcement partners, and

Federal Emergency Management Agency

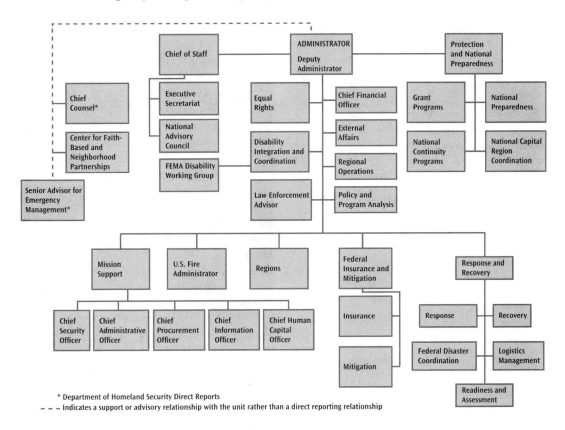

* Department of Homeland Security Direct Reports
– – – Indicates a support or advisory relationship with the unit rather than a direct reporting relationship

critical infrastructure operators in all states and major urban areas nationwide.

► CONGRESS

For a listing of relevant congressional committees and sub-committees, please see pages 548–549 or the Appendix.

► INFORMATION SHARING AND ANALYSIS CENTERS

A 1998 decision directive issued by President Bill Clinton defined various infrastructure industries critical to the national economy and public well-being. The directive proposed the creation of Information Sharing and Analysis Centers (ISACs), which would be established by each critical infrastructure industry to communicate with its members, its government partners, and other ISACs about threat indications, vulnerabilities, and protection strategies. Each ISAC is led by a government agency or private entity. ISACs led by Washington-area agencies or companies are listed below.

Communications ISAC *(Homeland Security Dept.), c/o* **National Coordinating Center for Communications,** *245 Murray Lane, MS0615 20520; (703) 235-5080.*
John O'Connor, Manager, National Coordinating Center for Communications; Rear Adm. Ronald T. Hewitt, Director, Office of Emergency Communications.

General email, ncc@hq.dhs.gov

Web, www.dhs.gov/national-coordinating.center-telecommunications

Communications network that links federal civilian, military, diplomatic, and intelligence agencies with private sector cyber and telecommunications providers to protect the nation's telecommunications infrastructure and restore it from disruptions caused by attacks or natural disasters. Includes the National Cybersecurity and Communications Integration Center, a 24/7 center for protection of computer end communications across federal, state, and local governments; intelligence and law enforcement agencies; and the private sector.

Emergency Management and Response-ISAC, *16825 S. Seton Ave., Emmitsburg, MD 21727-8920; (301) 447-1325. Fax, (301) 447-1346. Rick Ziebart, Emergency Response Support Branch Chief, USFA, (301) 447-1821; Dennis O'Neal, U.S. Fire Administrator, (202) 646-4223. General email, emr-isac@fema.dhs.gov*

Web, www.usfa.fema.gov/fireservice/emr-isac/index.shtm

Collects, analyzes, and disseminates information to support the critical infrastructure protection and resilience efforts of the nation's emergency services sector. Researches current physical and cyber protection issues, operates an information center, issues alerts and messages,

Domestic Disaster Relief Organizations

Adventist Development & Relief Agency International, (800) 424-2372; www.adra.org

American Red Cross, (800) 733-2767 or (202) 303-5214; www.redcross.org

AmeriCares, (800) 486-4357; www.americares.org

Ananda Marga Universal Relief Team, Inc., (301) 738-7122; www.amurt.net

Catholic Charities USA, (703) 549-1390; www.catholiccharitiesusa.org

Catholic Relief Services, (888) 277-7575; www.crs.org

Children's Miracle Network (Osmond Foundation for the Children of the World), (801) 214-7400; www.cmn.org

Children's Network International, (888) 818-4483; www.helpthechildren.org

Church World Service, (800) 297-1516 or (574) 264-3102; www.cwsglobal.org

Direct Relief International, (805) 964-4767; www.directrelief.org

Episcopal Relief & Development, (855) 312-4325; www.er-d.org

Federal Employee Education and Assistance Fund (FEEA), (303) 933-7580; www.feea.org

Feeding America, (800) 771-2303; www.feedingamerica.org

Feed the Children, (800) 627-4556; www.feedthechildren.org

Habitat for Humanity International, (800) 422-4828; www.habitat.org

Health Right International, (212) 226-9890; www.healthright.org

InterAction, (202) 667-8227; www.interaction.org

International Federation of Red Cross/Red Crescent, (212) 338-0161; www.ifrc.org

International Rescue Committee, (212) 551-3000; www.rescue.org

Islamic Relief USA, (855) 447-1001 or (703) 370-7202; www.irusa.org

Medical Teams International, (800) 959-4325 or (503) 624-1000; www.medicalteams.org

Mercy Corps, (888) 747-7440; www.mercycorps.org

Operation Blessing International Relief and Development Corporation, (800) 730-2537; www.ob.org

Operation USA, (800) 678-7255; www.opusa.org

Oxfam America, (800) 776-9326 or (202) 496-1180; www.oxfamamerica.org

Rebuilding Together, Inc., (800) 473-4229 or (202) 483-9083; www.rebuilingtogether.org

Save the Children, (800) 728-3843; www.savethechildren.org

United Methodist Committee on Relief, (202) 548-4002; www.umcor.org

United Way Worldwide, (703) 836-7112; www.unitedway.org

World Health Organization (Pan American Health Organization), (202) 974-3000; www.who.int/en or www.paho.org

World Vision, (888) 511-6548; www.worldvision.org

---

and prepares instructional materials relevant to the emergency services community.

Financial Services ISAC (FS-ISAC), *12020 Sunrise Valley Dr., #230, Reston, VA 20191; (877) 612-2622. Fax, (301) 579-6106. Bill Nelson, President. Toll-free, (888) 732-2812.*
General email, admin@fsisac.com
Web, www.fsisac.com

Provides a confidential venue for sharing security vulnerabilities and solutions, including data obtained from such sources as other ISACs, law enforcement agencies, technology providers, and security associations. Works to facilitate trust, cooperation, and information sharing among its participants and assesses proactive means of mitigating cybersecurity risks.

Surface Transportation Information Sharing and Analysis Center (ISAC), *c/o EWA Information and Infrastructure Technologies, Inc., 13873 Park Center Rd., #200, Herndon, VA 20171-5406; (866) 784-7221. Fax, (703) 478-7647. Paul G. Wolfe, Director.*

General email, st-isac@surfacetransportationisac.org
Web, www.surfacetransportationisac.org

Protects physical and electronic infrastructure of surface transportation and public transit carriers. Collects, analyzes, and distributes critical security and threat information from worldwide resources; shares best security practices and provides 24/7 immediate physical and cyber-threat warnings.

WaterISAC, *1620 Eye St. N.W., #500 20006-4027; (202) 331-0479. Diane VanDe Hei, Executive Director. Toll-free, (866) 426-4722.*
General email, info@waterisac.org
Web, www.waterisac.org

Gathers, analyzes, and disseminates threat information concerning the water community from utilities' security incident reports and agencies of the federal government. Provides the water community with access to sensitive information and resources about cyber, physical, and contamination threats.

▶ NONGOVERNMENTAL

International Assn. of Chiefs of Police, *Advisory Committee for Patrol and Tactical Operations, 44 Canal Center Plaza, #200, Alexandria, VA 22314; (703) 836-6767. Fax, (703) 836-4543. Nancy Kolb, Staff Liaison, ext. 813. Toll-free, (800) 843-7227.*
General email, kollon@theiacp.org

Web, www.theiacp.org

Membership: foreign and U.S. police executives and administrators. Maintains liaison with civil defense and emergency service agencies in the United States and other nations; prepares guidelines for police cooperation with emergency and disaster relief agencies during emergencies.

National Governors Assn. (NGA), *Center for Best Practices, Homeland Security and Public Safety Division, 444 N. Capitol St. N.W., #267 20001-1512; (202) 624-5300. Fax, (202) 624-5313. Thomas MacLellan, Division Director.*
Web, www.nga.org/cms/center/nsps

Provides support to governors in responding to the challenges of homeland security through technical assistance and policy research, and by facilitating their participation in national discussion and initiatives.

National Voluntary Organizations Active in Disaster (NVOAD), *1501 Lee Hwy., #200, Arlington, VA 22209-1109; (703) 778-5088. Fax, (703) 778-5091. Daniel L. Stoecker, Executive Director.*
General email, info@nvoad.org

Web, www.nvoad.org

Seeks to promote communication, cooperation, coordination, and collaboration among voluntary agencies that participate in disaster response, relief, and recovery nationally.

Emergency Communications

▶ AGENCIES

Air Force Dept. *(Defense Dept.), Office of Information Dominance and Chief Information Officer, 1800 Air Force Pentagon, #4E1050 20330-1800; (703) 695-6829. Fax, (703) 692-7512. Lt. Gen. Michael J. Basla, Chief Warfighting Integration and Information Officer. Press, (703) 695-0640.*
General email, safxc.workflow@pentagon.af.mil

Web, www.safxc.af.mil

Responsible for policy making, planning, programming, and evaluating performance of the Air Force's command, control, communications, and computer (C-4) system.

Army Dept. *(Defense Dept.), Chief Information Officer IG-6, 107 Army Pentagon, #3E608 20310-0107; (703) 695-4366. Fax, (703) 695-3091. Lt. Gen. Robert S. Ferrell, Chief Information Officer.*
Web, www.army.mil

Oversees policy and budget for the Army's information systems and programs.

Defense Dept. (DoD), *Chief Information Officer, 6000 Defense Pentagon, #3E1030 20301-6000; (703) 695-0348. Fax, (703) 614-8060. Teresa M. (Teri) Takai, Chief Information Officer.*
Web, http://dodcio.defense.gov

Civilian office with policy oversight for all command, control, and communications matters.

Defense Dept. (DoD), *Command, Control, Communications, and Computers, 8000 Joint Staff Pentagon, #1E1044 20318-6000; (703) 695-3562. Fax, (703) 614-2945. Lt. Gen. Mark S. Bowman, Deputy Director; Martin Westphal, Vice Deputy Director, C-4 Cyber.*
Web, www.defense.gov

Advises the secretary of defense on policy for command, control, communications, and computer/cyber matters throughout the Defense Dept.

Defense Dept. (DoD), *White House Communications Agency, U.S. Naval Station–Anacostia Annex, 2743 Defense Blvd. S.W., #220 20373-5815; (202) 757-5530. Fax, (202) 757-5529. Col. Donovan Routsis, Director.*
Web, www.disa.mil/whca

Responsible for presidential communications.

Federal Communications Commission (FCC), *Emergency Alert System, 445 12th St. S.W., #7-A807 20554; (202) 418-1228. Fax, (202) 418-2790. Bonnie Gay, EAS Coordinator. FCC 24/7 Operations Center, (202) 418-1122.*
General email, eas@fcc.gov

Web, www.fcc.gov/pshs/services/eas and www.fcc.gov/guides/emergency-alert-system-eas

Develops rules and regulations for the Emergency Alert System, which is the national warning system the president would use to communicate with the public during a national emergency in the event that access to normal media outlets becomes unavailable. It is also used by state and local officials for weather-related and manmade emergencies.

Federal Communications Commission (FCC), *Public Safety and Homeland Security, 445 12th St. S.W., #7C732 20554; (202) 418-0761. Fax, (202) 418-2817. David G. Simpson, Chief; Robert Pavlak, Director of ERIC. Press, (202) 418-0503.*
General email, pshsbinfo@fcc.gov

Web, www.fcc.gov/public-safety-homeland-security-bureau

Develops, recommends, and administers the FCC's policies pertaining to public safety communications issues, including 911 and E911. Responsible for the operability and interoperability of public safety communications, communications infrastructure protection and disaster response, and network security and reliability. Administers the Emergency Response Interoperability Network (ERIC), establishing and maintaining a broadband public safety wireless network, including authentication and encryption.

National Communications System *(Homeland Security Dept.), President's National Security Telecommunications Advisory Committee, NCS, 245 Murray Lane, MS 0615, Arlington, VA 20598-0615; (202) 282-8000. Fax, (703) 235-4981. Helen Jackson, Program Manager. DHS switchboard, (202) 282-8000. Press, (202) 282-8010.*
General email, nstac1@dhs.gov
Web, www.ncs.gov/nstac

Advises the president, the National Security Council, the Office of Science and Technology Policy, and the Office of Management and Budget on specific measures to improve telecommunications for the federal government. Areas of major focus include strengthening national security, enhancing cybersecurity, maintaining the global communications infrastructure, assuring communications for disaster response, and addressing infrastructure interdependencies and dependencies.

National Response Center *(Homeland Security Dept.), 2100 2nd St. S.W., #2111B 20593-0001; (202) 267-2180. Fax, (202) 267-1322. Syed M. Qadir, Director, (202) 372-2440. TTY, (202) 267-4477. Hotline, (800) 424-8802. local, (202) 267-2675.*
General email, hqs-dg-lst-nrcinfo@comdt.uscg.mil
Web, www.nrc.uscg.mil

Maintains twenty-four-hour hotline for reporting oil spills, hazardous materials accidents, and chemical releases. Notifies appropriate federal officials to reduce the effects of accidents.

Office of Emergency Communications *(Homeland Security Dept.), 245 Murray Lane, MS 0615, Arlington, VA 20528-0615; (703) 235-3660. Fax, (703) 235-4981. Jeremiah Jones, Information Officer. Press, (703) 235-4965.*
General email, oec@dhs.gov
Web, www.dhs.gov/about-office-emergency-communications

Ensures that the federal government has the necessary communications capabilities to permit its continued operation during a national emergency, including war; provides the Federal Emergency Management Agency with communications support as it directs the nation's recovery from a major disaster.

Industrial and Military Planning and Mobilization

►**AGENCIES**

Bureau of Industry and Security *(Commerce Dept.), Strategic Industries and Economic Security, 14th St. and Constitution Ave. N.W., #3876 20230; (202) 482-4506. Fax, (202) 482-5650. Michael Vaccaro, Director, (202) 482-8232.*
General email, petrina.bean@bis.doc.gov
Web, www.bis.doc.gov

Administers the Defense Production Act and provides industry with information on the allocation of resources falling under the jurisdiction of the act.

Defense Logistics Agency *(Defense Dept.), Logistics Operations, 8725 John Jay Kingman Rd., Fort Belvoir, VA 22060-6221; (703) 767-1600. Fax, (703) 767-1588. Maj. Gen. Kenneth S. Dowd, Director. Press, (703) 767-6200.*
Web, www.dla.mil

Oversees management, storage, and distribution of items used to support logistics for the military services and federal agencies. Synchronizes the Defense Logistics Agency's capabilities with the combatant commands, military services, the joint staff, other combat support defense agencies, and designated federal agencies. Provides logistics policy, with an emphasis on modernizing business systems and maximizing readiness and combat logistics support.

Maritime Administration *(Transportation Dept.), Emergency Preparedness, West Bldg., 1200 New Jersey Ave. S.E., #W23-304 20590; (202) 366-5900. Fax, (202) 366-5904. Thomas M. P. Christensen, Director.*
Web, www.marad.dot.gov/ports_landing_page/port_emergency/maritime_emergency_paredennessandresponse.htm

Plans for the transition of merchant shipping from peacetime to wartime operations under the direction of the National Shipping Authority. Participates in interagency planning and policy development for maritime security–related directives. Coordinates port personnel and the military for deployments through the commercial strategic seaports. Represents the United States at the NATO Planning Board for Ocean Shipping. (The National Shipping Authority is a stand-by organization that is activated upon the declaration of a war or other national emergency.)

Maritime Administration *(Transportation Dept.), National Security, West Bldg., 1200 New Jersey Ave. S.E., MAR-600, MS1, W25 20590; (202) 366-5400. Fax, (202) 366-5904. Kevin M. Tokarski, Associate Administrator.*
Web, www.marad.dot.gov/ships_shipping_landing_page/national_security/national_security.htm

Ensures that merchant shipping is available in times of war or national emergency.

Maritime Administration *(Transportation Dept.), Ship Operations, 1200 New Jersey Ave. S.E., MAR-610, MS2-W25-336 20590; (202) 366-1875. Fax, (202) 366-3954. William H. Cahill, Director.*
Web, http://marad.dot.gov

Maintains the National Defense Reserve Fleet, a fleet of older vessels traded in by U.S. flag operators that are called into operation during emergencies; manages and administers the Ready Reserve Force, a fleet of ships available for operation within four to twenty days, to meet the nation's sealift readiness requirements.

►**CONGRESS**

For a listing of relevant congressional committees and subcommittees, please see pages 548–549 or the Appendix.

►NONGOVERNMENTAL

National Defense Industrial Assn. (NDIA), *2111 Wilson Blvd., #400, Arlington, VA 22201-3061; (703) 522-1820. Fax, (703) 522-1885. Lt. Gen. Lawrence Farrell (USAF, Ret.), President.*
Web, www.ndia.org

Membership: U.S. citizens and businesses interested in national security. Also open to individuals and businesses in nations that have defense agreements with the United States. Provides information and expertise on defense preparedness issues; works to increase public awareness of national defense preparedness through education programs; serves as a forum for dialogue between the defense industry and the government.

NDTA (The Assn. for Global Logistics and Transportation), *50 S. Pickett St., #220, Alexandria, VA 22304-7296; (703) 751-5011. Fax, (703) 823-8761. Lt. Gen. Kenneth Wykle (USA, Ret.), President.*
Web, http://ndtahq.com

Membership: transportation service companies. Maintains liaison with the Defense Dept., the Transportation Dept., and the Transportation Security Administration to prepare emergency transportation plans.

Shipbuilders Council of America, *655 15th St. N.W., #225 20005; (202) 772-5577. Fax, (202) 347-5464. Matt Paxton, President.*
Web, http://shipbuilders.org

Membership: U.S. shipyards that repair and build commercial ships and naval and other government vessels; and allied industries and associations. Monitors legislation and regulations.

Infrastructure Protection

►AGENCIES

Cybersecurity and Communications *(Homeland Security Dept.), 245 Murray Lane S.W., Bldg. 410, MS 8570 20528-8570; (202) 282-8000, DHS switchboard. Fax, (703) 235-5150. Roberta (Bobbie) Stempfley, Assistant Secretary, Acting. Press, (202) 282-8010.*

Works with the public and private sectors as well as international partners to enhance the security of the nation's cyber and communications infrastructure. Identifies security vulnerabilities and coordinates warning and response procedures.

Energy Dept. (DOE), *Electricity Delivery and Energy Reliability, 1000 Independence Ave. S.W., #8H033 20585; (202) 586-1411. Fax, (202) 586-1472. Patricia Hoffman, Assistant Secretary.*
Web, www.oe.energy.gov

Leads the federal response to energy emergencies, guides technology research and development on the security and reliability of the nation's energy systems, provides training and support for stakeholders, and works to assess and mitigate energy system vulnerabilities. Works in conjunction with the Homeland Security Dept. and other DOE programs, federal groups, state and local governments, and private industry.

Federal Bureau of Investigation (FBI) *(Justice Dept.), Cyber Division, 935 Pennsylvania Ave. N.W., #5835 20535; (202) 324-7770. Fax, (202) 324-2840. Joseph M. Demarest Jr., Assistant Director.*
Web, www.fbi.gov/about-us/investigate/cyber

Coordinates the investigations of federal violations in which the Internet or computer networks are exploited for terrorist, foreign government–sponsored intelligence, or criminal activities, including copyright violations, fraud, pornography, child exploitation, and malicious computer intrusions.

Federal Protective Service (FPS) *(Homeland Security Dept.), 800 N. Capitol St., 5th Floor 20002; (202) 282-8000. Fax, (202) 732-8109. L. Eric Patterson, Director. Switchboard, (202) 282-8000. National hotline, (866) 347-2423.*
Web, www.dhs.gov/about-federal-protective-service

Works to ensure that appropriate levels of security are in place in General Services Administration–managed facilities throughout the United States. Conducts assessments on all GSA-controlled facilities to evaluate threats and tailor appropriate security countermeasures. Has enforcement capability to detain and arrest people, seize goods or conveyances, obtain arrest and search warrants, respond to incidents and emergency situations, provide protection during demonstrations or civil unrest, and to be deputized for law enforcement response in special situations.

Homeland Security Dept. (DHS), *Infrastructure Protection, 1310 N. Courthouse Rd., Arlington, VA 22201; (703) 235-2522. Fax, (202) 235-9757. Caitlin Durkovich, Assistant Secretary.*
Web, www.dhs.gov/about-office-infrastructure-protection

Assigned the lead responsibility for coordinating the collection and analysis of intelligence and information pertaining to threats against U.S. infrastructure. Handles the merging of capabilities to identify and assess current and future threats to homeland infrastructure; identifies and assesses vulnerabilities, takes preventive action, and issues timely warnings. Develops partnerships and communication lines with state and local governments and the private sector. Administers the Homeland Security Advisory System, which conveys threat information.

National Aeronautics and Space Administration (NASA), *Protective Services, 300 E St. S.W., #6T39 20546; (202) 358-2010. Fax, (202) 358-3238. Joseph Mahaley, Assistant Administrator; Charles Lombard, Deputy Assistant Administrator.*
Web, www.hq.nasa.gov/office/ospp

Serves as the focal point for policy formulation, oversight, coordination, and management of NASA's security, counterintelligence, counterterrorism, emergency preparedness and response, and continuity of operations programs.

National Institute of Standards and Technology (NIST)
(Commerce Dept.), Computer Security, 100 Bureau Dr., MS 8930, Gaithersburg, MD 20899-8930; (301) 975-8443. Fax, (301) 975-8670. Donna Dodson, Chief.
General email, inquiries@nist.gov
Web, www.csrc.nist.gov

Works to improve information systems security by raising awareness of information technology risks, vulnerabilities, and protection requirements; researches and advises government agencies of risks; devises measures for cost-effective security and privacy of sensitive federal systems.

Transportation Security Administration (TSA)
(Homeland Security Dept.), TSA-1, 601 S. 12th St., 7th Floor, Arlington, VA 20598-6001; (571) 227-2801. Fax, (571) 227-1398. John S. Pistole, Administrator. Press, (571) 227-2829. Questions and concerns regarding travel can be submitted to the TSA Contact Center, toll-free, (866) 289-9673.
General email, TSA-ContactCenter@dhs.gov
Web, www.tsa.gov/public

Responsible for aviation, rail, land, and maritime transportation security. Programs and interests include the stationing of federal security directors and federal passenger screeners at airports, the Federal Air Marshal Program, improved detection of explosives, and enhanced port security.

Transportation Security Administration (TSA)
(Homeland Security Dept.), Freedom Center, 13555 EDS Dr., Herndon, VA 20171 (mailing address: TSOC Annex, 601 S. 12th St., Arlington, VA 22202); (866) 655-7023. Robert S. Bray, Director.
Web, www.tsa.gov

Operations center that provides continual federal, state, and local coordination, communications, and domain awareness for all of the Homeland Security Dept.'s transportation-related security activities worldwide. Transportation domains include highway, rail, shipping, and aviation.

Treasury Dept., *Domestic Finance, Critical Infrastructure Protection and Compliance Policy, 1500 Pennsylvania Ave. N.W. 20220; (202) 622-3965. Fax, (202) 622-2310. Leigh Williams, Director, Acting.*
General email, OCIP@do.treas.gov
Web, www.treasury.gov/offices/about/organizational-structure/offices/Pages/–Offices-of-Critical-Infrastructure-Protection-and-Compliance-Policy.aspx

Works with the private sector to protect the nation's financial infrastructure. Maintains privacy protections for personal financial information. Develops regulations against money laundering and terrorism financing. Serves as the department's principal liaison with the Homeland Security Dept. on infrastructure protection issues.

U.S. Coast Guard (USCG) *(Homeland Security Dept.), Deputy for Operations Policy and Capabilities, Commandant, CG-DCO-D, MS 7318, 2703 Martin Luther King Jr. Ave. S.E. 20593; (202) 372-1001. Fax, (202) 372-2900. Rear Adm. William (Dean) Lee, Deputy Assistant Commandant.*
Web, www.uscg.mil/hq/cg5

Establishes and enforces regulations for port safety; environmental protection; vessel safety, inspection, design, documentation, and investigation; licensing of merchant vessel personnel; and shipment of hazardous materials.

U.S. Computer Emergency Readiness Team (US-CERT)
(Homeland Security Dept.), 245 Murray Lane S.W., Bldg. 410 20598; (888) 282-0870. Fax, (703) 235-5110. Ann Barron-DiCamillo, Director. Press, (202) 282-8010.
General email, info@us-cert.gov
Web, www.us-cert.gov

Leads and coordinates efforts to improve the nation's cybersecurity capabilities; promotes cyber information sharing; and manages cyber risks to the nation through detection, analysis, communication, coordination, and response activities.

U.S. Secret Service *(Homeland Security Dept.), Criminal Investigative Division, 950 H St. N.W., #5000 20223; (202) 406-9330. Fax, (202) 406-5016. Edward Lowery, Special Agent in Charge.*
Web, www.secretservice.gov/criminal.shtml

Investigates crimes associated with financial institutions. Jurisdiction includes bank fraud, access device fraud involving credit and debit cards, telecommunications and computer crimes, fraudulent identification, fraudulent government and commercial securities, and electronic funds transfer fraud.

▶CONGRESS

For a listing of relevant congressional committees and subcommittees, please see pages 548–549 or the Appendix.

▶NONGOVERNMENTAL

SANS Institute, *8120 Woodmont Ave., #205, Bethesda, MD 20814-2784; (301) 951-0102. Fax, (301) 951-0140. Alan Paller, Director. Customer sales and support, (301) 654-7267.*
General email, info@sans.org
Web, www.sans.org

Develops, maintains, and makes available at no cost the largest collection of research documents about information security. Operates Internet Storm Center, the Internet's early warning system. (Also known as SysAdmin, Audit, Network, Security Institute.)

StaySafeOnline.org/National Cyber Security Alliance,
1010 Vermont Ave. N.W., #821 20005; (202) 570-7431. Michael Kaiser, Executive Director.
General email, info@staysafeonline.org
Web, www.staysafeonline.org

Public-private partnership that promotes computer safety and responsible online behavior. Designated by the Homeland Security Dept. to provide tools and resources to help home users, small businesses, and schools stay safe online. Online resources include tips, a self-guided cyber security test and checklist, and educational materials.

Public Health and Environment

▶**AGENCIES**

Centers for Disease Control and Prevention (CDC)
(Health and Human Services Dept.), Washington Office,
395 E St. S.W., #9100 20201; (202) 245-0600. Fax, (202)
245-0602. Dr. Thomas R. Frieden, Director;
Edward Hunter, Director of Washington Office
(Congressional Affairs). Public inquiries, (800) 232-4636.
General email, cdinfo@cdc.gov
Web, www.cdc.gov/washington

Supports the CDC's Bioterrorism and Preparedness
and Response Program, which develops federal, state, and
local capacity to respond to bioterrorism. (Headquarters
in Atlanta, Ga.: 1600 Clifton Rd. N.E. 30333.)

Environmental Protection Agency (EPA), *Emergency*
Management, 1200 Pennsylvania Ave. N.W., #1448, MC
5104A 20460; (202) 564-8600. Fax, (202) 564-8222.
Lawrence M. Stanton, Director; Dana S. Tulis, Deputy
Director. Toll-free call center, (800) 424-9346.
Web, www.epa.gov/aboutepa/osweroe1

Responsible for planning for and responding to the
harmful effects of the release or dissemination of toxic
chemicals. Areas of responsibility include helping state
and local responders plan for emergencies; coordinating
with key federal partners; training first responders; and
providing resources in the event of a terrorist incident.

Health and Human Services Dept. (HHS), *National*
Disaster Medical System, 200 Independence Ave. S.W,
#638G 20201; (202) 205-7978. Dr. Andrew Garrett,
Director. Public Affairs, (202) 205-8114.
Web, http://phe.gov/ndms

Federally coordinated program that collaborates with
other federal agencies; tribal, states, and local governments;
private businesses; and civilian volunteers to ensure the
delivery of medical resources following a disaster.

Health and Human Services Dept. (HHS), *Preparedness*
and Response (ASPR), 200 Independence Ave. S.W., #638-
G 20201; (202) 205-2882. Nicole Lurie, Assistant Secretary.
Web, www.phe.gov

Responsible for coordinating U.S. medical and public
health preparedness and response to emergencies, including natural disasters, pandemic and emerging infectious
disease, and acts of biological, chemical, and nuclear terrorism. Manages advanced research and development of
medical countermeasures. Oversees the hospital preparedness grant program, which provides funding to state governments.

National Institute of Allergy and Infectious Diseases
(National Institutes of Health), 6610 Rockledge Dr.,
#2400, MSC 6612, Bethesda, MD 20892-6612; (301) 496-
5717. Fax, (301) 402-3573. Dr. Anthony S. Fauci, Director.
Toll-free, health and research information, (866) 284-4107.
TTY, health and research information, (800) 877-8339.
Press, (301) 402-1663.
Web, www.niaid.nih.gov

Responsible for coordinating and administering a medical program to counter radiological and nuclear threats.
Works with the National Cancer Institute and other federal agencies, academia, and industry to develop medical
measures to assess, diagnose, and care for civilians exposed
to radiation.

▶**CONGRESS**

For a listing of relevant congressional committees and sub-
committees, please see pages 548–549 or the Appendix.

▶**NONGOVERNMENTAL**

American Red Cross, *Disaster Preparedness and*
Response, 2025 E St. N.W. 20006-5009; (202) 303-5000,
ext. 1. Gail J. McGovern, President. Press, (202) 303-5551.
Donations, (800) RED-CROSS. Toll-free, (800) 733-2767.
Web, www.redcross.org and
Disaster Preparedness, www.redcross.org/training

Chartered by Congress to administer disaster relief.
Provides disaster victims with food, shelter, first aid, medical care, and access to other available resources. Feeds
emergency workers; handles inquiries from concerned
family members outside the disaster area; helps promote
disaster preparedness and prevention through training.

National Assn. of State EMS Officials (NASEMSO), *201*
Park Washington Ct., Falls Church, VA 22046-4527; (703)
538-1799. Fax, (703) 241-5603. Elizabeth B. Armstrong,
Executive Vice President.
General email, info@nasemso.org
Web, www.nasemso.org

Supports development of effective emergency medical
services (EMS) systems at the local, state, and regional
levels. Works to formulate national EMS policy and foster
communication and sharing among state EMS officials.

National Center for Biodefense and Infectious Diseases
(George Mason University), 10650 Pyramid Pl.,
Manassas, VA 20110; (703) 993-4271. Fax, (703) 993-4280.
Charles Bailey, Executive Director.
General email, cbailey@gmu.edu
Web, http://ncbid.gmu.edu and http://cos.gmu.edu

Researches and develops diagnostics and treatments
for emerging infectious diseases as well as those pathogens
that could be used as terrorist weapons that require special
containment. Manages a graduate education program.

National Vaccine Information Center, *21525 Ridgetop*
Circle, #100, Sterling, VA 20166; (703) 938-0342. Fax, (571)
313-1268. Barbara Loe Fisher, President, (703) 938-0342.
General email, contactnvic@gmail.com
Web, www.nvic.org

Educates the public and provides research on vaccination safety procedures and effectiveness; supports reform
of the vaccination system; publishes information on diseases and vaccines; and monitors legislation and regulations.

Selective Service

▶AGENCIES

Selective Service System, *1515 Wilson Blvd., Arlington, VA 22209-2425; (703) 605-4100. Fax, (703) 605-4106. Lawrence G. Romo, Director. Locator, (703) 605-4000. Toll-free, (888) 655-1825. TTY Espanol, (800) 845-6136. General email, information@sss.gov*

Web, www.sss.gov

Supplies the armed forces with manpower when authorized; registers male citizens of the United States ages eighteen to twenty-five. In an emergency, would institute a draft and would provide alternative service assignments to men classified as conscientious objectors.

▶CONGRESS

For a listing of relevant congressional committees and subcommittees, please see pages 548–549 or the Appendix.

Strategic Stockpiles

▶AGENCIES

Defense Dept. (DoD), *Manufacturing and Industrial Base Policy, 3330 Defense Pentagon, #3B854 20301-3300; (703) 697-0051. Fax, (703) 695-4885. Brett B. Lambert, Deputy Assistant Secretary, Acting. General email, MIBT@osd.mil*

Web, www.acq.osd.mil/mibp

Develops and oversees strategic, industrial, and critical materials policies, including oversight of the National Defense Stockpile.

Defense Logistics Agency *(Defense Dept.), Strategic Materials, 8725 John Jay Kingman Rd., #3229, Fort Belvoir, VA 22060-6223; (703) 767-5500. Fax, (703) 767-3316. Ronnie Favors, Administrator; Paula Stead, Deputy Administrator. Press, (703) 767-4430.*

Web, https://www.dnsc.dla.mil

Manages the national defense stockpile of strategic and critical materials. Purchases strategic materials, including beryllium and newly developed high-tech alloys. Disposes of excess materials, including tin, silver, industrial diamond stones, tungsten, and vegetable tannin.

Fossil Energy *(Energy Dept.), Petroleum Reserves, Forrestal Bldg., 1000 Independence Ave. S.W., FE-40 20585; (202) 586-4733. Robert Corbin, Deputy Assistant Secretary.*

Web, www.fossil.energy.gov

Manages programs that provide the United States with strategic and economic protection against disruptions in oil supplies, including the Strategic Petroleum Reserves, the Northeast Home Heating Oil Reserve, and the Naval Petroleum and Oil Shale Reserves.

▶CONGRESS

For a listing of relevant congressional committees and subcommittees, please see pages 548–549 or the Appendix.

INTELLIGENCE AND COUNTERTERRORISM

General

▶AGENCIES

Air Force Dept. *(Defense Dept.), Intelligence, Surveillance, and Reconnaissance (ISR), 1700 Air Force Pentagon, #4E1070 20330-1700; (703) 695-5613. Fax, (703) 697-4903. Lt. Gen. Larry D. James, Deputy Chief of Staff. General email, afxoi.workflow@pentagon.af.mil*

Web, www.afisr.af.mil

Responsible for policy formulation, planning, evaluation, oversight, and leadership of Air Force intelligence, surveillance, and reconnaissance capabilities.

Army Dept. *(Defense Dept.), Intelligence, 1000 Army Pentagon, #2E408 20310-1000; (703) 695-3033. Fax, (703) 697-7605. Lt. Gen. Mary A. Legere, Deputy Chief of Staff. Web, www.army.mil*

Military office that directs Army intelligence activities and coordinates activities with other intelligence agencies.

Central Intelligence Agency (CIA), *CIA Headquarters, 930 Dolley Madison Blvd., McLean, VA 20505 (mailing address: change to CIA Headquarters, Washington, DC 20505); (703) 482-0623. Fax, (703) 482-1739. John O. Brennan, Director; Avril D. Haines, Deputy Director. Web, www.cia.gov*

Gathers and evaluates foreign intelligence to assist the president and senior U.S. government policymakers in making foreign policy and national security decisions. Reports directly to the Office of National Intelligence, which coordinates intelligence functions of all government agencies involved with homeland security.

Defense Dept. (DoD), *Chief Information Officer, 6000 Defense Pentagon, #3E1030 20301-6000; (703) 695-0348. Fax, (703) 614-8060. Teresa M. (Teri) Takai, Chief Information Officer.*

Web, http://dodcio.defense.gov

Civilian office with policy oversight for all command, control, and communications matters.

Defense Dept. (DoD), *Intelligence, 5000 Defense Pentagon, #3E834 20301-5000; (703) 695-0971. Fax, (703) 693-5706. Michael G. Vickers, Under Secretary. Web, www.defense.gov*

Responsible for ensuring the secretary of defense's access to intelligence information.

Defense Dept. (DoD), *Intelligence Oversight, 7200 Defense Pentagon, #2E1052 20301-7200; (571) 372-6363.*

Counterterrorism Resources and Contacts

The following agencies, organizations, and hotlines offer information pertaining to terrorism and counterterrorism issues.

AGENCIES

Bureau of Industry and Security, Eric L. Hirschhorn, Under Secretary (202) 482-1455; toll free, (800) 424-2980, (Commerce Department)

Central Intelligence Agency, John O. Brennan, Director, (703) 482-1100, (Justice Department)

Defence Intelligence Agency, Lt. Gen. Michael T. Flynn, Director, (202) 231-5554, (Defense Department)

FBI Counterterrorism Division, Andrew McCabe, Asst. Director, (202) 324-3691, (Justice Department)

Homeland Security Council, Lisa Monaco, Assistant to the President for Counterterrorism and Homeland Security, (202) 456-6317, (Executive Office of the President)

Homeland Security Dept., Janet Napolitano, Secretary, (202) 282-8010

INTERPOL, United States Central Bureau, Shawn A. Bray, Director, (202) 616-9000, (Justice Department)

National Counterterrorism Center, Matthew G. Olsen, Director,

National Nuclear Security Administration, Michael K. Lempke, (202) 586-5555, (Energy Department)

National Security Agency/Central Security Service, Gen. Keith B. Alexander, Director, (301) 688-6524, (Defense Department)

National Security Council, Susan Rice, Assistant to the President for National Security Affairs, (202) 456-9491, (Executive Office of the President)

National Security Division, Counterterrorism and Espionage, John Carlin, Asst. Attorney General, (202) 514-1057, (Justice Department)

Office of Counterterrorism and Emergency Coordination (FDA), Rosemary Roberts, Director, (301) 796-2210, (Health and Human Services Department)

Office of Foreign Assets Control, Adam J. Szubin, Director, (202) 622-2510, (Treasury Department)

Office of Nuclear Security and Incident Response, James Wiggins, Director, (301) 415-8003

Office of Terrorism and Financial Intelligence, David S. Cohen, Under Secretary, (202) 622-8260, (Treasury Department)

Office of the Coordinator for Counterterrorism, Tina S. Kaidanow, Coordinator and Ambassador at Large, (202) 647-9892, (State Department)

Office of the Director of National Intelligence, James R. Clapper Jr., Director, (703) 733-8600

Transportation Security Administration, John S. Pistole, Administrator, (866) 289-9673, (Homeland Security Department)

U.S. Immigration and Customs Enforcement, Daniel Ragsdale, Deputy Director, (202) 732-4200

U.S. Secret Service, Julia Pierson, Director, (202) 406-8000, (Homeland Security Department)

ORGANIZATIONS

Foundation for Defense of Democracies, Mark Dubowitz, Director, (202) 207-0190

International Center for Terrorism Studies, Yonah Alexander, Director, (703) 525-0770

Memorial Institute for the Prevention of Terrorism, David Cid, Executive Director, (405) 278-6300

RAND Homeland Security and Defense Center, Michael D. Rich, President, (310) 393-0411 ext. 6934

HOTLINES

Federal Bureau of Investigation, (310) 477-6565

Office of Foreign Assets Control, (800) 540-6322

Transportation Security Administration, (866) 289-9673

U.S. Immigration and Customs Enforcement, (866) 347-2423

Fax, (703) 697-2974. Michael H. Decker, Assistant to the Secretary.
Web, http://atsdio.defense.gov

Responsible for the independent oversight of all Defense Dept. intelligence, counterintelligence, and related activities, and for the formulation of intelligence oversight policy; reviews intelligence operations and investigates and reports on possible violations of federal law or regulations.

Defense Dept. (DoD), *Special Operations and Low-Intelligence Conflict, 2500 Defense Pentagon, #3C852A 20301-2500; (703) 695-9667. Fax, (703) 693-6335. Michael D. Lumpkin, Assistant Secretary.*
Web, www.defense.gov

Serves as special staff assistant and civilian adviser to the secretary of defense on matters related to special operations and international terrorism.

Defense Information Systems Agency (DISA) *(Defense Dept.), 6910 Cooper Ave., Fort Meade, MD 20755; (703) 607-6001. Fax, (301) 225-0535. Lt. Gen. Ronnie D. Hawkins Jr., Director.*
General email, cosa@disa.mil
Web, www.disa.mil

The Defense Dept. agency responsible for information technology and the central manager for major portions of the defense information infrastructure. Units include the White House Communications Agency.

Defense Intelligence Agency *(Defense Dept.), 200 MacDill Blvd. 20340; (202) 231-5554. Fax, (202) 231-0851. Lt. Gen. Michael T. Flynn, Director. General email, DIA-PAO@dia.mil*

Web, www.dia.mil

Collects and evaluates foreign military-related intelligence information to satisfy the requirements of the secretary of defense, Joint Chiefs of Staff, selected components of the Defense Dept., Office of National Intelligence, and other authorized agencies.

Energy Dept. (DOE), *Intelligence and Counterintelligence, 1000 Independence Ave. S.W., #8F-089 20585; (202) 586-2610. Fax, (202) 287-5999. Steven K. Black, Director; Charles Durant, Deputy Director of Counterintelligence; Steven K. Black, Deputy Director of Intelligence.*

Web, www.energy.gov/office-intelligence-and-counterintelligence

Identifies and deters intelligence threats directed at Energy Dept. facilities, personnel, information, and technology. Protects nuclear weapons secrets and other sensitive scientific projects.

Federal Bureau of Investigation (FBI) *(Justice Dept.), Counterterrorism, 935 Pennsylvania Ave. N.W., #4204 20535; (202) 324-2770. Fax, (202) 324-7050. Joshua Skule, Assistant Director, Acting. Press, (202) 324-3691.*

Web, www.fbi.gov/about-us/investigate/counterterrorism

Collects, analyzes, and shares information and intelligence with authorities to combat international terrorism operations within the United States and in support of extraterritorial investigations, domestic terrorism operations, and counterterrorism. Maintains the Joint Terrorism Task Force, which includes representatives from the Defense Dept., Energy Dept., Federal Emergency Management Agency, CIA, U.S. Customs and Border Protection, U.S. Secret Service, and Immigration and Customs Enforcement.

Federal Bureau of Investigation (FBI) *(Justice Dept.), Critical Incident Response Group, Strategic Information and Operations Center, 935 Pennsylvania Ave. N.W., #5712 20535; (202) 323-3300. Fax, (202) 323-2212. Christopher Combs, Section Chief, (202) 323-2015. Press, (202) 324-3691. Toll-free, (877) 324-6324. Secure line, (202) 323-2214. General email, sioc@ic.fbi.gov*

Web, www.fbi.gov/about-us/cirg/sioc

Serves as a twenty-four-hour crisis management and information-processing center. Coordinates initial and crisis response investigations of violations of federal law relating to terrorism, sabotage, espionage, treason, sedition, and other matters affecting national security.

Federal Bureau of Investigation (FBI) *(Justice Dept.), National Joint Terrorism Task Force (National JTTF), 935 Pennsylvania Ave. N.W. 20535-0001; (571) 280-5688. Fax, (571) 280-6922. William Callahan, Unit Chief.*

Web, www.fbi.gov/washingtondc/about-us/our-partnerships/partners

Group of more than forty agencies from the fields of intelligence, public safety, and federal, state, and local law enforcement that collects terrorism information and intelligence and funnels it to the more than one hundred JTTFs (teams of local, state, and federal agents based at FBI field offices), various terrorism units within the FBI, and partner agencies. Helps the FBI with terrorism investigations.

Federal Bureau of Investigation (FBI) *(Justice Dept.), Terrorist Screening Center, 935 Pennsylvania Ave. N.W. 20535; (866) 872-5678. Fax, (703) 418-9563. Christopher M. Piehota, Director. General email, tsc@tsc.gov*

Web, www.fbi.gov/about-us/nsb/tsc

Coordinates access to terrorist watch lists from multiple agencies. Provides operational support to federal screeners and state and local law enforcement officials.

Homeland Security Council *(Executive Office of the President), The White House 20500; (202) 456-6317. Lisa O. Monaco, Assistant to the President for Homeland Security and Counterterrorism.*

Web, www.whitehouse.gov/infocus/homeland

Advises the president on combating global terrorism and homeland security policy.

Homeland Security Dept. (DHS), *Nebraska Ave. Complex, 3801 Nebraska Ave. N.W. 20528; (202) 282-8000. Fax, (202) 282-8401. Jeh Johnson, Secretary; Alejandro Mayorkas, Deputy Secretary. Press, (202) 282-8010. Comments, (202) 282-8495.*

Web, www.dhs.gov

Responsible for the development and coordination of a comprehensive national strategy to protect the United States against terrorist attacks and other threats and hazards. Coordinates the strategy of the executive branch with those of state and local governments and private entities to detect, prepare for, protect against, respond to, and recover from terrorist attacks and other emergencies in the United States.

Homeland Security Dept. (DHS), *Intelligence and Analysis, 3801 Nebraska Ave. N.W., Bldg. 19 20528; (202) 447-4154. Vacant, Under Secretary.*

Web, www.dhs.gov/about-office-intelligence-and-analysis

Uses intelligence from multiple sources to identify and assess current and future threats to the United States; provides guidance to the secretary on homeland security issues.

Marine Corps *(Defense Dept.), Intelligence, 3000 Marine Corps Pentagon, #1A262B 20350-3000; (703) 614-2522. Fax, (703) 614-5888. Brig. Gen. Michael S. Groen, Director.*

Web, www.hqmc.marines.mil/intelligence/unithome/aspx

Military office that directs Marine Corps intelligence policy and coordinates activities with other intelligence agencies.

National Aeronautics and Space Administration (NASA), *Protective Services, 300 E St. S.W., #6T39 20546; (202) 358-2010. Fax, (202) 358-3238. Joseph Mahaley, Assistant*

Office of the Director of National Intelligence

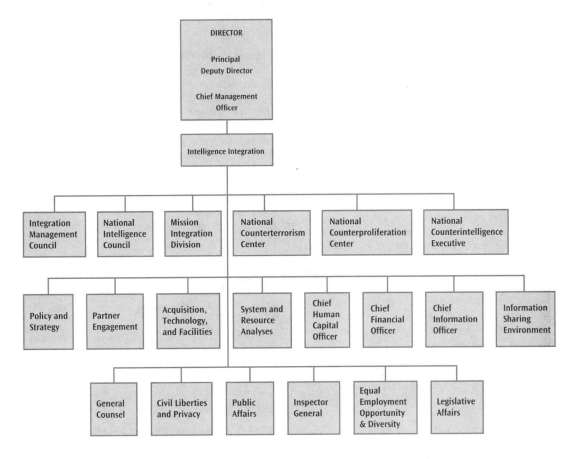

Administrator; Charles Lombard, Deputy Assistant Administrator.

Web, www.hq.nasa.gov/office/ospp

Serves as the focal point for policy formulation, oversight, coordination, and management of NASA's security, counterintelligence, counterterrorism, emergency preparedness and response, and continuity of operations programs.

National Geospatial-Intelligence Agency *(Defense Dept.), 7500 Geoint Dr., Springfield, VA 22150-7500; 4600 Sangamore Rd., Bethesda, MD 20816-5003; (571) 557-5400. Fax, (571) 558-3169. Letitia A. Long, Director. Maps and imagery products, (800) 455-0899.*
General email, medialist@nga.mil

Web, www.nga.mil

Combat support agency that develops imagery and map-based intelligence in support of national defense objectives.

National Reconnaissance Office *(Defense Dept.), 14675 Lee Rd., Chantilly, VA 20151-1715; (703) 808-1198. Fax, (703) 808-1171. Betty J. Sapp, Director.*
Web, www.nro.gov

Researches, develops, and operates intelligence satellites. Gathers intelligence for various purposes, including

indications and warnings, monitoring of arms control agreements, military operations and exercises, and monitoring of natural disasters and other environmental issues.

National Security Agency (NSA) *(Defense Dept.), 9800 Savage Rd., #6272, Fort Meade, MD 20755-6000; (301) 688-6524. Fax, (301) 688-6198. Gen. Keith B. Alexander (USA), Director; Richard H. Ledgett Jr., Deputy Director. FOIA Public Liaison Office, (301) 688-6527.*
General email, nsapao@nsa.gov

Web, www.nsa.gov

Provides technology, products, and services to secure information and information infrastructure critical to U.S. national security interests. Organizes and controls all foreign signals collection and processing activities of the United States in accordance with requirements established by the Defense Dept., the Office of the Director of National Intelligence, and by national policies with the advice of the National Foreign Intelligence Board.

National Security Division *(Justice Dept.), 950 Pennsylvania Ave. N.W., #7339 20530; (202) 514-1057. Fax, (202) 514-8714. John P. Carlin, Assistant Attorney General, Acting. Press, (202) 514-2007.*
General email, nsd.public@usdoj.gov

Web, www.justice.gov/nsd

Coordinates the Justice Dept.'s intelligence, counterterrorism, counterespionage, and other national security activities. Offers support for victims of overseas terrorism; provides legal assistance and advice, in coordination with the Office of Legal Counsel as appropriate, to all branches of government on matters of national security law and policy.

National Security Division *(Justice Dept.),*
Counterespionage, 950 Pennsylvania Ave. N.W. 20530;
(202) 514-1057. Fax, (202) 514-8714. John P. Carlin,
Assistant Attorney General, Acting.
General email, nsd.public@usdoj.gov
Web, www.justice.gov/nsd

Supervises the investigation and prosecution of cases affecting national security, foreign relations, and the export of military and strategic commodities and technology. Has executive responsibility for authorizing the prosecution of cases under criminal statutes relating to espionage, sabotage, neutrality, and atomic energy. Provides legal advice to U.S. Attorney's offices and investigates agencies on federal statutes concerning national security. Coordinates criminal cases involving the application of the Classified Information Procedures Act. Administers and enforces the Foreign Agents Registration Act of 1938 and related disclosure statutes.

National Security Division *(Justice Dept.),*
Counterterrorism, 950 Pennsylvania Ave. N.W. 20530;
(202) 514-1057. Fax, (202) 514-8714. Michael J. Mullaney,
Chief.
General email, nsd.public@usdoj.gov
Web, www.justice.gov/nsd

Responsible for the design, implementation, and support of law enforcement efforts, legislative initiatives, policies, and strategies related to combating international and domestic terrorism. Seeks to assist, through investigation and prosecution, in preventing and disrupting acts of terrorism anywhere in the world that impact significant U.S. interests and persons.

National Security Division *(Justice Dept.), Intelligence,*
950 Pennsylvania Ave. N.W. 20530; (202) 514-1057.
Fax, (202) 514-8714. Tashina Gauhar, Deputy Assistant
Attorney General.
General email, nsd.public@usdoj.gov
Web, www.justice.gov/nsd

Seeks to ensure that Intelligence Community agencies have the legal authorities necessary to conduct intelligence operations, particularly operations involving the Foreign Intelligence Surveillance Act (FISA). Oversees various national security activities of Intelligence Community agencies; participates in FISA-related litigation.

National Security Division *(Justice Dept.), Law and*
Policy, 950 Pennsylvania Ave. N.W. 20530; (202) 514-
1057. Brad Wiegmann, Deputy Assistant Attorney General.
General email, nsd.justice@usdoj.gov
Web, www.justice.gov/nsd

Develops and implements Justice Dept. policies with regard to intelligence, counterterrorism, and other national security matters. Provides legal assistance and advice on matters of national security law.

Office of the Director of National Intelligence (DNI),
20511; (703) 275-2012. James R. Clapper Jr., Director of
National Intelligence; Stephanie L. O'Sullivan, Principal
Deputy Director. Press, (202) 275-3700. DNIW Watch
24/7, (703) 733-8600.
Web, www.dni.gov

Leads a unified intelligence community and serves as the principal adviser to the president on intelligence matters. Orders the collection of new intelligence to ensure the sharing of information among agencies and to establish common standards for the intelligence community's personnel. Responsible for determining the annual budgets for all national intelligence agencies and for directing how these funds are spent.

Office of the Director of National Intelligence (DNI),
National Counterintelligence Executive (NCIX), ONCIX,
LX/ICC-B 20511; (301) 227-8529. Fax, (301) 227-8586.
Frank Montoya, National Counterintelligence Executive.
Web, www.ncix.gov

Conducts foreign intelligence threat assessments; promotes collaboration and information sharing throughout the U.S. counterintelligence community through conferences and other outreach and training activities; makes recommendations to decision makers concerning national counterintelligence strategy.

Office of the Director of National Intelligence (DNI),
National Counterterrorism Center (NCTC), Liberty
Crossing 20505; (571) 280-6160. Fax, (571) 280-5551.
Hon. Matthew G. Olsen, Director. Public Affairs, (571) 280-
6153.
Web, www.nctc.gov

Serves as a hub for terrorism threat–related information collected domestically and abroad. Responsible for assessing, integrating, and disseminating terrorist threat information and all-source analysis; maintains U.S. government's central database on known and suspected terrorists; and identifies collection requirements related to the terrorist threat. Participates in strategic planning for counterterrorism activities.

Office of the Director of National Intelligence (DNI),
National Intelligence Council, CIA Headquarters,
Langley, VA 20505; (703) 482-6724. Fax, (703) 482-8632.
Christopher Kojm, Chair.
Web, www.dni.gov/nic

Supports the director of national intelligence and serves as the intelligence community's center for mid- and long-term strategic thinking. Provides a focal point for policymakers' inquiries and needs. Establishes contacts with private sector and academic experts in the intelligence field.

President's Foreign Intelligence Advisory Board
(Executive Office of the President), New Executive Office
Bldg., #5020 20502; (202) 456-2352. Fax, (202) 395-3403.

Chuck Hagel, Chair; Stefanie R. Osburn, Executive Director.
Web, www.whitehouse.gov/administration/eop/piab

Members appointed by the president. Assesses the quality, quantity, and adequacy of foreign intelligence collection and of counterintelligence activities by all government agencies; advises the president on matters concerning intelligence and national security.

State Dept., *Counterterrorism,* 2201 C St. N.W., #2509 20520; (202) 647-9892. Fax, (202) 647-9256. Jerry P. Lanier, Coordinator, Acting. Press, (202) 647-1845.
Web, www.state.gov/s/ct

Implements U.S. counterterrorism policy and coordinates activities with foreign governments; responds to terrorist acts; works to promote a stronger counterterrorism stance worldwide.

State Dept., *Diplomatic Security Bureau,* 2201 C St. N.W., #6316 20520; (202) 647-1493. Fax, (202) 647-0953. Gregory B. Starr, Assistant Secretary.
General email, DSPublicAffairs@state.gov
Web, www.state.gov

Conducts the Antiterrorism Assistance Program, which provides training to foreign governments fighting terrorism.

State Dept., *Intelligence and Research,* 2201 C St. N.W., #6468 20520-6531; (202) 647-9177. Fax, (202) 736-4688. Philip S. Goldberg, Assistant Secretary.
Web, www.state.gov

Coordinates foreign policy–related research, analysis, and intelligence programs for the State Dept. and other federal agencies.

Transportation Dept. (DOT), *Intelligence, Security, and Emergency Response,* 1200 New Jersey Ave. S.E., #56125 20590; (202) 366-6525. Fax, (202) 366-7261. Michael Lowder, Director, (202) 366-6530.
Web, www.dot.gov/mission/administration/intelligence-security-emergency-response

Advises the secretary on transportation intelligence and security policy. Acts as liaison with the intelligence community, federal agencies, corporations, and interest groups; administers counterterrorism strategic planning processes. Develops, coordinates, and reviews transportation emergency preparedness programs for use in emergencies affecting national defense and in emergencies caused by natural and man-made disasters and crisis situations.

Transportation Security Administration (TSA) (Homeland Security Dept.), *Intelligence and Analysis,* TSA-10, 601 S. 12th St., 6th Floor, Arlington, VA 22202-4220; (703) 601-3100. Fax, (703) 601-3290. Stephen Sadler, Assistant Administrator.
Web, www.tsa.gov

Oversees TSA's intelligence gathering and information sharing as they pertain to national security and the safety of the nation's transportation systems.

Treasury Dept., *Terrorism and Financial Intelligence,* 1500 Pennsylvania Ave. N.W., #4316 20220; (202) 622-8260. Fax, (202) 622-1914. David S. Cohen, Under Secretary. Press, (202) 622-2960.
Web, www.treasury.gov/about/organizational-structure/offices/Pages/Office-of-Terrorism-and-Financial-Intelligence.aspx

Manages the Treasury Dept.'s efforts against financial networks supporting global terrorism and other national security threats.

Treasury Dept., *Terrorism and Financial Intelligence, Terrorist Financing and Financial Crime,* 1500 Pennsylvania Ave. N.W. 20220; (202) 622-1655. Fax, (202) 622-3915. Daniel L. Glaser, Assistant Secretary. Press, (202) 622-2960.
Web, www.treasury.gov/about/organizational-structure/offices/Pages/Office-of-Terrorist-Financing-and-Financial-Crime.aspx

Sets strategy and policy for combating the financing of terrorism both domestically and abroad.

U.S. Coast Guard (USCG) *(Homeland Security Dept.), Intelligence and Criminal Investigations,* 2703 Martin Luther King Jr. Ave. S.E. 20593; (202) 372-2700. Fax, (202) 372-2956. Rear Adm. Christopher J. Tomney, Assistant Commandant.
Web, www.uscg.mil

Manages all Coast Guard intelligence activities and programs. Conducts internal and external criminal investigations.

U.S. Customs and Border Protection *(Homeland Security Dept.), Intelligence and Investigative Liaison,* 1300 Pennsylvania Ave. N.W., #7.3D 20229; (202) 344-1150. Fax, (202) 344-3830. Donna A. Bucella, Assistant Commissioner.
Web, www.cbp.gov/xp/cgov/about/organization/assist_comm_off/intelligence_investigative_liaison.xml

Coordinates the effort to prevent the introduction of weapons of mass destruction into the United States and to prevent international terrorists from obtaining weapons of mass destruction materials, technologies, arms, funds, and other support.

►CONGRESS

For a listing of relevant congressional committees and subcommittees, please see pages 548–549 or the Appendix.

►INTERNATIONAL ORGANIZATIONS

INTERPOL, *Washington Office, U.S. National Central Bureau,* 145 N St. N.E. 20002 (mailing address: INTERPOL Washington, U.S. Dept. of Justice, Washington, DC 20530-0001); (202) 616-9000. Fax, (202) 616-8400. Shawn A. Bray, Director.
Web, www.justice.gov/usncb

U.S. representative to INTERPOL; interacts in international investigations of terrorism on behalf of U.S. police. Serves as liaison between foreign and U.S. law enforcement agencies. Headquarters office sponsors forums enabling foreign governments to discuss counterterrorism policy. (Headquarters in Lyons, France.)

Center for National Security Studies, *1730 Pennsylvania Ave. N.W., 7th Floor 20006; (202) 721-5650. Fax, (202) 530-0128. Kate A. Martin, Director.*
General email, cnss@cnss.org
Web, www.cnss.org

Monitors and conducts research on civil liberties and intelligence and national security, including activities of the Central Intelligence Agency and the Federal Bureau of Investigation.

Foundation for Defense of Democracies (FDD), *P.O. Box 33249 20033-0249; (202) 207-0190. Fax, (202) 207-0191. Clifford D. May, President; Mark Dubowitz, Executive Director.*
General email, info@defenddemocracy.org
Web, www.defenddemocracy.org

Conducts research and education related to the war on terrorism and the promotion of democracy.

Fourth Freedom Forum, *Washington Office, 1101 14th St. N.W., #900 20036; (202) 464-6009. Fax, (202) 238-9604. Alistair Millar, President.*
General email, amillar@fourthfreedom.org
Web, www.fourthfreedom.org

Conducts research and training to advance global cooperation to address transnational threats, including terrorism, nuclear proliferation, and drug trafficking. (Headquarters in Goshen, Ind.)

National Security Archive, *Gelman Library, George Washington University, 2130 H St. N.W., #701 20037; (202) 994-7000. Fax, (202) 994-7005. Thomas Blanton, Director.*
General email, nsarchiv@gwu.edu
Web, www.nsarchive.org

Research institute and library that provides information on U.S. foreign and economic policy and national security affairs. Maintains and publishes collection of declassified and unclassified documents obtained through the Freedom of Information Act. Archive open to the public by appointment.

Potomac Institute for Policy Studies, *International Center for Terrorism Studies (ICTS), 901 N. Stuart St., #200, Arlington, VA 22203-1821; (703) 525-0770. Fax, (703) 525-0299. Michael S. Swetnam, Chief Executive Officer.*
General email, webmaster@potomacinstitute.org
Web, www.potomacinstitute.org

Public policy research institute that conducts studies on key science and technology issues. The ICTS focuses on all forms of terrorism and the potential for terrorism, including biological, chemical, or nuclear violence, as well as information warfare and cyberterrorism.

Internal (Agency) Security

Air Force Dept. *(Defense Dept.), Special Investigations, 27130 Telegraph Rd., Quantico, VA 22134; (571) 305-8028. Brig. Gen. Kevin J. Jacobsen, Commander.*
Web, www.osi.andrews.af.mil

Develops and implements policy on investigations of foreign intelligence, terrorism, and other crimes as they relate to Air Force security.

Army Dept. *(Defense Dept.), Counterintelligence, Foreign Disclosure, and Security, 1000 Army Pentagon, #2D350 20310-1000; (703) 695-1007. Fax, (703) 695-3149. Gerry B. Turnbow, Director.*
Web, www.army.mil

Responsible for foreign disclosure, policy formation, planning, programming, oversight, and representation for counterintelligence, human intelligence, and security countermeasures of the Army.

Defense Dept. (DoD), *Counterintelligence, 5000 Defense Pentagon, #3C1088 20301-5000; (703) 697-5216. Fax, (703) 695-8217. Toby Sullivan, Director.*
Web, www.defense.gov

Oversees counterintelligence policy and oversight to protect against espionage and other foreign intelligence activities, sabotage, international terrorist activities, and assassination efforts of foreign powers, organizations, or persons directed against the Defense Dept.

Defense Security Service *(Defense Dept.), 27130 Telegraph Rd., Quantico, VA 22134; (571) 305-6083. Fax, (571) 305-6869. Col. Stanley L. Sims, Director. Press, (571) 305-6751.*
Web, www.dss.mil

Administers programs to protect classified government information and resources, including the National Industrial Security Program (NISP). Serves the Defense Dept. and other executive departments and agencies. Operates the Center for Development and Security Excellence to educate, train, and enhance awareness of security matters.

Energy Dept. (DOE), *Intelligence and Counterintelligence, 1000 Independence Ave. S.W., #8F-089 20585; (202) 586-2610. Fax, (202) 287-5999. Steven K. Black, Director; Charles Durant, Deputy Director of Counterintelligence; Steven K. Black, Deputy Director of Intelligence.*
Web, www.energy.gov/office-intelligence-and-counterintelligence

Identifies and deters intelligence threats directed at Energy Dept. facilities, personnel, information, and technology. Protects nuclear weapons secrets and other sensitive scientific projects.

National Archives and Records Administration (NARA), *Information Security Oversight (ISOO), 700 Pennsylvania Ave. N.W., #100 20408-0001; (202) 357-5250.*

Fax, (202) 357-5907. John P. Fitzpatrick, Director, (202) 357-5205.

General email, isoo@nara.gov

Web, www.archives.gov/isoo

Receiving guidance from the National Security Council, administers governmentwide security classification program under which information is classified, declassified, and safeguarded for national security purposes. Develops policies and procedures for sensitive unclassified information.

National Security Agency (NSA) (Defense Dept.), 9800 Savage Rd., #6272, Fort Meade, MD 20755-6000; (301) 688-6524. Fax, (301) 688-6198. Gen. Keith B. Alexander (USA), Director; Richard H. Ledgett Jr., Deputy Director. FOIA Public Liaison Office, (301) 688-6527.

General email, nsapao@nsa.gov

Web, www.nsa.gov

Maintains and operates the Defense Dept.'s Computer Security Center; ensures communications and computer security within the government.

Navy Dept. (Defense Dept.), Naval Criminal Investigative Service, 27130 Telegraph Rd., Quantico, VA 22134; (571) 305-9000. Andrew Traver, Director, Acting. Hotline, (877) 579-3648.

Web, www.ncis.navy.mil

Handles felony criminal investigations, counterintelligence, counterterrorism, and security for the Navy Dept., working with federal, state, local, and foreign agencies to investigate crimes; processes security clearances for the Navy Dept.

State Dept., Countermeasures, 1801 N. Lynn St., Rosslyn, VA 22209; (571) 345-3835. Gentry O. Smith, Director.

Web, www.state.gov

Oversees Physical Security, Security Technology, and Diplomatic Courier programs for the State Dept.

State Dept., Diplomatic Security Service, DS Public Affairs, 20522-2008; (202) 647-1493. Fax, (202) 647-0122. Gregory B. Starr, Assistant Secretary. Diplomatic Service Command Center, (571) 345-3146.

Web, www.state.gov

Oversees the safety and security of all U.S. government employees at U.S. embassies and consulates abroad. Responsible for the safety of the secretary of state and all foreign dignitaries below head of state level who are visiting the United States. Conducts background investigations of potential government employees, investigates passport and visa fraud, and warns government employees of any counterintelligence dangers they might encounter.

State Dept., Security Infrastructure, 1801 N. Lynn St., Rosslyn, VA 22209; (571) 345-3788. Fax, (571) 345-3792. Donald R. Reid, Senior Coordinator.

Web, www.state.gov

Manages matters relating to security infrastructure in the functional areas of information security, computer security, and personnel security and suitability.

MILITARY INSTALLATIONS

General

▶**AGENCIES**

Army Dept. (Defense Dept.), Installations, Housing, and Environment, 110 Army Pentagon, #3E464 20310-0110; (703) 697-8161. Fax, (703) 614-7394. Col J. Randell Robinson, Deputy Assistant Secretary, (703) 692-9800.

General email, asaie.webmaster@hqda.army.mil

Web, www.asaie.army.mil

Civilian office that manages all Army installations.

Defense Dept. (DoD), Installations and Environment, 3400 Defense Pentagon, #3B856A 20301-3400; (703) 695-2880. Fax, (703) 693-7011. John Conger, Deputy Under Secretary, Acting.

Web, www.acq.osd.mil/ie

Oversees and offers policy guidance for all Defense Dept. installations and environmental programs.

Defense Dept. (DoD), International Security Affairs, The Pentagon, #3C889 20301-2400; (703) 697-2788. Fax, (703) 697-3279. Derek H. Chollet, Assistant Secretary.

Web, www.defense.gov

Advises the secretary of defense and recommends policies on regional security issues in the Middle East, Africa, Russia/Eurasia, and Europe/NATO.

▶**CONGRESS**

For a listing of relevant congressional committees and subcommittees, please see pages 548–549 or the Appendix.

Base Closings, Economic Impact

▶**AGENCIES**

Air Force Dept. (Defense Dept.), Base Realignment and Closure, 1665 Air Force Pentagon, #4B941 20330-1665; (703) 697-6492. Col. Joe Morganti, Director.

Web, www.safie.hq.af.mil/library

Military office that provides management oversight for implementing base closings and base realignment under the Base Realignment Act (BRAC).

Air Force Dept. (Defense Dept.), Installations, 1665 Air Force Pentagon, #4B941, SAF/IEI 20330-1665; (703) 695-3592. Fax, (703) 693-7568. Timothy K. Bridges, Deputy Assistant Secretary.

General email, safiei.workflow@pentagon.af.mil

Web, www.safie.hq.af.mil

Civilian office that plans and reviews the building, repairing, renovating, and closing of Air Force bases.

Army Dept. (Defense Dept.), Employment Policy, 6010 6th St., #200, Bldg. 1465, Ft. Belvoir, VA 22060-5595; (703)

806-3846. *Fax, (703) 806-2345. Anna Miller, Chief, (703) 806-3202.*
Web, www.army.mil

Military office responsible for employment policies to assist civilian personnel in cases of Defense Dept. program changes, including base closings.

Defense Dept. (DoD), *Office of Economic Adjustment,* 2231 Crystal Dr., #520, Arlington, VA 22202-4704; (703) 697-2130. Fax, (703) 607-0170. Patrick J. O'Brien, Director. *Web, www.oea.gov*

Civilian office that helps community officials develop strategies and coordinate plans to alleviate the economic effect of major defense program changes, including base closings (BRAC) and contract cutbacks. Assists communities where defense activities are being expanded. Serves as the staff for the Economic Adjustment Committee, an interagency group that coordinates federal technical and financial transition assistance to localities.

Defense Dept. (DoD), *Staffing and Civilian Transition Programs,* 4800 Mark Center Dr., #05F16, SCTP Division, Alexandria, VA 22350-1100; (571) 372-1528. Fax, (571) 372-1704. William Mann, Chief of Staff. *Web, www.cpms.osd.mil/care*

Manages workforce restructuring programs for Defense Dept. civilians, including downsizing, placement, voluntary early retirement, and transition assistance programs.

Marine Corps *(Defense Dept.), Installations Command, Facilities Directorate,* 3000 Marine Corps Pentagon, #2D153A 20350-3000; (703) 695-8202. Fax, (703) 695-8550. Capt. Patrick Garin, Assistant Chief of Staff. *Web, www.mcicom.marines.mil/units/gffacilities.aspx*

Military office that reviews studies on base closings under the Base Realignment Act (BRAC).

Commissaries, PXs, and Service Clubs

►AGENCIES

Defense Dept. (DoD), *Army and Air Force Exchange, Washington Office,* 2530 Crystal Dr., #4158, Arlington, VA 22202; (703) 602-8975. Fax, (703) 604-7523. Gregg Cox, Director. *Web, www.shopmyexchange.com/aboutexchange*

Delivers goods and services to the military community at competitively low prices. Returns earnings to Army and Air Force to support morale, welfare, and recreation programs. (Headquarters in Dallas, Texas.)

Defense Dept. (DoD), *Defense Commissary Agency,* 1300 E Ave., Fort Lee, VA 23801-1800; (703) 571-7185. Fax, (703) 571-9297. Thomas C. Owens, Director, Washington Office. *General email, kevin.robinson@deca.mil*
Web, www.commissaries.com

Serves as a representative for the Defense Commissary Agency in the Pentagon and the Washington, D.C., area. Monitors legislation and regulations. (Headquarters in Fort Lee, Va.)

Navy Dept. *(Defense Dept.), Manpower and Reserve Affairs,* 1000 Navy Pentagon, #4E590 20350-1000; (703) 695-4333. Fax, (703) 614-4103. Juan M. Garcia III, Assistant Secretary. *Web, www.navy.mil/local/oasnmra*

Civilian office that develops policies for Navy and Marine Corps commissaries, exchanges, and service clubs and reviews their operations.

Navy Dept. *(Defense Dept.), Navy Exchange Service Command,* 701 S. Courthouse Rd., Arlington, VA 22204; (757) 631-4170. Gerald Outar, Director. Navy Exchange, (757) 631-4170. *Web, www.mynavyexchange.com*

Civilian office that serves as a liaison among the Navy Exchange Service Command, the Navy Supply Systems Command, Congress, and the Defense Dept. (Headquarters in Virginia Beach, Va.)

►CONGRESS

For a listing of relevant congressional committees and subcommittees, please see pages 548–549 or the Appendix.

►NONGOVERNMENTAL

American Logistics Assn., 1101 Vermont Ave. N.W., #1002 20005; (202) 466-2520. Fax, (202) 296-4419. Patrick B. Nixon, President. *General email, info@ala-national.org*
Web, www.ala-national.org

Membership: suppliers of military commissaries and exchanges. Acts as liaison between the Defense Dept. and service contractors; monitors legislation and testifies on issues of interest to members.

United Service Organizations (USO), 2111 Wilson Blvd., #1200, Arlington, VA 22201 (mailing address: P.O. Box 96322, Washington, DC 20090-6322); (703) 908-6400. Fax, (703) 908-6402. John I. Pray Jr., President. Toll-free, (888) 484-3876. *Web, www.uso.org*

Voluntary civilian organization chartered by Congress. Provides military personnel and their families in the United States and overseas with social, educational, and recreational programs.

Construction, Housing, and Real Estate

►AGENCIES

Air Force Dept. *(Defense Dept.), Civil Engineering,* 1260 Air Force Pentagon 20330; (703) 693-4301. Fax, (703) 693-4893. Maj. Gen. Theresa C. Carter, Director. *Web, www.afcec.af.mil*

Military office that plans and directs construction of Air Force facilities in the United States and overseas.

Air Force Dept. *(Defense Dept.), Housing Operations and Management,* 1260 Air Force Pentagon, #4C1057 20330-1260; (703) 693-4193. Sheila Schwartz, Branch Chief.
Web, www.housing.af.mil

Military office that manages the operation of Air Force housing on military installations in the United States and overseas.

Air Force Dept. *(Defense Dept.), Installations,* 1665 Air Force Pentagon, #4B941, SAF/IEI 20330-1665; (703) 695-3592. Fax, (703) 693-7568. Timothy K. Bridges, Deputy Assistant Secretary.
General email, safiei.workflow@pentagon.af.mil
Web, www.safie.hq.af.mil

Civilian office that plans and reviews construction policies and programs of Air Force military facilities (including the Military Construction Program), basing of major weapons systems and units, housing programs, and real estate buying, selling, and leasing in the United States.

Army Corps of Engineers *(Defense Dept.),* 441 G St. N.W., #3K05 20314-1000; (202) 761-0001. Fax, (202) 761-4463. Lt. Gen. Thomas Bostick, Chief of Engineers.
General email, hq-publicaffairs@usace.army.mil
Web, www.usace.army.mil

Military office that establishes policy and designs, directs, and manages civil works and military construction projects of the Army Corps of Engineers; directs the Army's real estate leasing and buying for military installations and civil works projects.

Army Dept. *(Defense Dept.), Installations, Housing, and Environment,* 110 Army Pentagon, #3E464 20310-0110; (703) 697-8161. Fax, (703) 614-7394. Col J. Randell Robinson, Deputy Assistant Secretary, (703) 692-9800.
General email, asaie.webmaster@hqda.army.mil
Web, www.asaie.army.mil

Civilian office that reviews housing programs, the construction of Army military facilities, and the buying and leasing of real estate in the United States and overseas.

Defense Dept. (DoD), *Facilities Investment and Management,* 3400 Defense Pentagon, #5C646 20301-3400; (703) 697-6195. Fax, (703) 693-2659. Michael McAndrew, Director.
Web, www.acq.osd.mil/ie/fim/index.shtml

Responsible for military construction and facility-related legislative proposals and policies to manage worldwide defense installations and to acquire, construct, maintain, modernize, and dispose of defense facilities. Prepares the department's annual military construction budget; manages military construction, real property maintenance, and base operations; oversees host nation programs for facilities; and develops procedures for measuring the effect of defense facilities on military readiness.

Marine Corps *(Defense Dept.), Facilities,* 3250 Catlin Ave., #235, Quantico, VA 22134-5001; (703) 784-2331. Fax, (703) 784-2332. Kirk Nelson, Director, (703) 784-2557.
Web, www.iandl.marines.mil/divisions/logisticsFacilities (LF).aspx

Control point for the Marine Corps divisions of public works, family housing, and natural resources and environmental affairs.

Marine Corps *(Defense Dept.), Installations Command, Facilities Directorate,* 3000 Marine Corps Pentagon, #2D153A 20350-3000; (703) 695-8202. Fax, (703) 695-8550. Capt. Patrick Garin, Assistant Chief of Staff.
Web, www.mcicom.marines.mil/units/gffacilities.aspx

Military office responsible for military construction and the acquisition, management, and disposal of Marine Corps real property.

Navy Dept. *(Defense Dept.), Energy, Installations, and Environment,* 1000 Navy Pentagon, #4E731 20350-1000; (703) 693-4527. Fax, (703) 693-1165.
Capt. Roger Natsuhara, USN (Ret.), Principal Deputy Assistant Secretary.
Web, www.navy.mil

Civilian office that monitors and reviews construction of Navy military facilities and housing and the buying and leasing of real estate in the United States and overseas.

Navy Dept. *(Defense Dept.), Naval Facilities Engineering Command,* 1322 Patterson Ave. S.E., #100 20374-5065; (202) 685-9499. Fax, (202) 685-1463. Rear
Adm. Katherine L. Gregory, Commander. Press, (202) 685-1423.
Web, www.navfac.navy.mil

Military command that plans, designs, and constructs facilities for Navy and other Defense Dept. activities around the world and manages Navy public works, utilities, environmental programs, and real estate.

Navy Dept. *(Defense Dept.), Real Estate,* 1000 Navy Pentagon, #4A674 20350; (703) 614-5848. Fax, (703) 614-1149. Jim Omans, Director.
Web, www.navfac.navy.mil

Military office that directs the Navy's real estate leasing, buying, and disposition for military installations.

U.S. Coast Guard (USCG) *(Homeland Security Dept.), Housing Programs,* CG-1333, 2703 Martin Luther King Jr. Ave. S.E., MS 7097 20593-7097; (202) 475-5407. Fax, (202) 475-5927. Melissa Fredrickson, Chief.
Web, http://uscg.mil/hr/cg133/housing

Provides housing and management for uniformed Coast Guard personnel.

▶ **CONGRESS**

For a listing of relevant congressional committees and subcommittees, please see pages 548–549 or the Appendix.

PROCUREMENT, ACQUISITION, AND LOGISTICS

General

Air Force Dept. *(Defense Dept.),* **Acquisition,** *1060 Air Force Pentagon, #4E962 20330-1060; (703) 697-6361. Fax, (703) 693-6400. Lt. Gen. William LaPlante, Air Force Service Acquisition Executive.*
Web, ww3.safaq.hq.af.mil

Air Force office that directs and reviews Air Force procurement policies and programs.

Air Force Dept. *(Defense Dept.),* **Contracting,** *1060 Air Force Pentagon, #700 20330-1060; (571) 256-2397. Maj. Gen. Wendy M. Masiello, Deputy Assistant Secretary.*
Web, ww3.safaq.hq.af.mil/contracting

Develops, implements, and enforces contracting policies on Air Force acquisitions worldwide, including research and development services, weapons systems, logistics services, and operational contracts.

Air Force Dept. *(Defense Dept.),* **Global Power Programs,** *1060 Air Force Pentagon, #4A122 20330; (571) 256-0196. Fax, (571) 256-0280. Maj. Gen. Timothy M. Ray, Director.*
Web, www.af.mil/publicwebsites/sitecmd

Military office that directs Air Force acquisition and development programs within the tactical arena.

Army Dept. *(Defense Dept.),* **Procurement,** *103 Army Pentagon, #2D528 20310-0103; (703) 695-2488. Harry Hallock, Deputy Assistant Secretary.*
Web, www.army.mil

Directs and reviews Army procurement policies.

Defense Acquisition University *(Defense Dept.), 9820 Belvoir Rd., Fort Belvoir, VA 22060-5565; (703) 805-3360. Fax, (703) 805-2639. James P. Woolsey, President. Toll-free, (866) 568-6924. Registrar, (703) 805-5142.*
Web, www.dau.mil

Academic institution that offers courses to military and civilian personnel who specialize in acquisition and procurement. Conducts research to support and improve management of defense systems acquisition programs.

Defense Contract Audit Agency (DCAA) *(Defense Dept.), 8725 John Jay Kingman Rd., #2135, Fort Belvoir, VA 22060-6219; (703) 767-3200. Fax, (703) 767-3267. Patrick J. Fitzgerald, Director. Media, (703) 693-6858.*
Web, www.dcaa.mil

Performs all contract audits for the Defense Dept. Provides Defense Dept. personnel responsible for procurement and contract administration with accounting and financial advisory services regarding the negotiation, administration, and settlement of contracts and subcontracts.

Defense Dept. (DoD), *Acquisition, Technology, and Logistics, 3010 Defense Pentagon, #3E1010 20301-3010; (703) 697-7021. Fax, (703) 697-5471. Frank Kendall III, Under Secretary.*
Web, www.acq.osd.mil

Formulates and directs policy relating to the department's purchasing system, research and development, logistics, advanced technology, international programs, environmental security, industrial base, and nuclear, biological, and chemical programs. Oversees all defense procurement and acquisition programs.

Defense Dept. (DoD), *Armed Services Board of Contract Appeals, Skyline 6, 7th Floor, 5109 Leesburg Pike, Falls Church, VA 22041-3208; (703) 681-8500. Fax, (703) 681-8535. Paul Williams, Chair.*
General email, asbca.recorder@mail.mil
Web, www.asbca.mil

Adjudicates disputes arising under Defense Dept. contracts.

Defense Dept. (DoD), *Defense Acquisition Regulations System (DARS) Directorate and DARS Council, 3060 Defense Pentagon, #3C152 20301-3060; (571) 372-6113. Fax, (571) 372-6101. Linda Neilson, Director.*
Web, www.acq.osd.mil/dpap

Develops procurement regulations and manages changes to procurement regulations for the Defense Dept.

Defense Dept. (DoD), *Defense Procurement and Acquisition Policy, 3060 Defense Pentagon, #3C152 20301-3060; (571) 256-7003. Fax, (571) 256-7004. Richard T. Ginman, Director.*
Web, www.acq.osd.mil/dpap

Responsible for all acquisition and procurement policy matters for the Defense Dept. Serves as principal adviser to the under secretary of defense for acquisition, technology, and logistics on strategies relating to all major weapon systems programs, major automated information systems programs, and services acquisitions.

Defense Dept. (DoD), *Logistics and Materiel Readiness, 3500 Defense Pentagon, #1E518 20301-3500; (703) 697-1369. Fax, (703) 693-0555. Paul D. Peters, Assistant Secretary, Acting.*
Web, www.acq.osd.mil/log

Formulates and implements department policies and programs for the conduct of logistics, maintenance, materiel readiness, strategic mobility, and sustainable support.

Defense Dept. (DoD), *Operational Test and Evaluation, 1700 Defense Pentagon, #3E1088 20301-1700; (703) 697-3655. Fax, (703) 693-5248. J. Michael (Mike) Gilmore, Director. Press, (703) 697-5331.*
Web, www.dote.osd.mil

Ensures that major acquisitions, including weapons systems, are operationally effective and suitable prior to full-scale investment. Provides the secretary of defense and Congress with independent assessment of these programs.

Defense Logistics Agency *(Defense Dept.)*, 8725 John Jay Kingman Rd., #2533, Fort Belvoir, VA 22060-6221; (703) 767-5200. Fax, (703) 767-5207. Vice Adm. Mark D. Harnitchek, Director. Press, (703) 767-6200.
Web, www.dla.mil

Administers defense contracts; acquires, stores, and distributes food, clothing, medical, and other supplies used by the military services and other federal agencies; administers programs related to logistical support for the military services; and assists military services with developing, acquiring, and using technical information and defense materiel and disposing of materiel no longer needed.

Marine Corps *(Defense Dept.)*, **Contracts**, 701 S. Courthouse Rd., #2000, Arlington, VA 22204; (703) 604-3580. Fax, (703) 604-6675. Frances Sullivan, Assistant Deputy Commandant.
Web, www.iandl.marines.mil/divisions/contracts(LB).aspx

Military office that directs Marine Corps procurement programs.

Navy Dept. *(Defense Dept.)*, **Acquisition and Procurement**, 1000 Navy Pentagon, #BF992A 20350-1000; (703) 614-9445. Fax, (703) 614-9394. Elliott Branch, Deputy Assistant Secretary.
Web, www.acquisition.navy.mil

Directs and reviews Navy acquisition and procurement policy.

Navy Dept. *(Defense Dept.)*, **Military Sealift Command**, Bldg. 210 20398-5540; (202) 685-5007. Fax, (202) 685-5020. Rear Adm. Thomas K. Shannon, Commander. Press, (202) 685-5055.
Web, www.msc.navy.mil

Provides sea transportation of equipment, fuel, supplies, and ammunition to sustain U.S. forces.

U.S. Coast Guard (USCG) *(Homeland Security Dept.)*, **Acquisition**, 2703 Martin Luther King Jr. Ave. S.E., 8th Floor 20593; (202) 475-3000. Fax, (202) 372-8432. Rear Adm. Bruce Baffer, Assistant Commandant.
General email, acquisitionweb@uscg.mil
Web, www.uscg.mil/acquisition

Administers all procurement made through the Acquisition Contract Support Division.

U.S. Coast Guard (USCG) *(Homeland Security Dept.)*, **Logistics Management**, 2703 Martin Luther King Jr. Ave. S.E., MS 7714 20593; (202) 475-5554. Fax, (202) 475-5951. Capt. Brenda Kerr, Director.
Web, www.uscg.mil/hq/cg5/cg533.asp

Sets policy and procedures for the procurement, distribution, maintenance, and replacement of materiel and personnel for the Coast Guard.

► **CONGRESS**

For a listing of relevant congressional committees and subcommittees, please see pages 548–549 or the Appendix.

Government Accountability Office (GAO), *Defense Capabilities and Management*, 441 G St. N.W., #4440B 20548; (202) 512-4300. Cathleen Berrick, Managing Director.
Web, www.gao.gov

Independent, nonpartisan agency in the legislative branch. Audits, analyzes, and evaluates Defense Dept. acquisition programs; makes unclassified reports available to the public.

► **NONGOVERNMENTAL**

NDTA (The Assn. for Global Logistics and Transportation), 50 S. Pickett St., #220, Alexandria, VA 22304-7296; (703) 751-5011. Fax, (703) 823-8761. Lt. Gen. Kenneth Wykle (USA, Ret.), President.
Web, http://ndtahq.com

Membership: transportation users, manufacturers, and mode carriers; information technology firms; and related military, government, and civil interests worldwide. Promotes a strong U.S. transportation capability through coordination of private industry, government, and the military.

TechAmerica, *Public Sector Group*, 601 Pennsylvania Ave. N.W., North Bldg., #600 20004; (202) 682-9110. Fax, (202) 682-9111. Shawn Osborne, Chief Executive Officer; Michael (Mike) Hettinger, Senior Vice President, Public Sector and Federal Government Affairs.
General email, csc@techamerica.org
Web, www.techamerica.org

Membership: companies providing information technology and electronics products and services to government organizations at the federal, state, and local levels. Provides information on governmental affairs, business intelligence, industry trends, and forecasts. Monitors legislation and regulations on federal procurement of technology products and services.

16 Science and Technology

GENERAL POLICY AND ANALYSIS

Basic Resources

▶**AGENCIES**

National Digital Information Infrastructure and Preservation Program (NDIIPP) *(Library of Congress),* *Office of Strategic Initiatives,* 101 Independence Ave. S.E. 20540-1300; (202) 707-3300. Fax, (202) 707-0815. *Vacant, Associate Librarian.*
Web, www.digitalpreservation.gov

Oversees development of a national strategy to collect, archive, and preserve digital content, and directs the activities of the Information Technology Directorate.

National Institutes of Health (NIH) *(Health and Human Services Dept.), Office of Intramural Training and Education,* 2 Center Dr., Bldg. 2, #2E04, MSC 0230, Bethesda, MD 20892-0240; (301) 496-2427. Fax, (301) 594-9606. *Sharon Milgram, Director.*
General email, trainingwww@mail.nih.gov
Web, www.training.nih.gov

Administers programs and initiatives to recruit and develop individuals who participate in research training activities on the NIH's campuses. Maintains an interactive Web site for the various research training programs. Supports the training mission of the NIH Intramural Research Program through placement, retention, support, and tracking of trainees at all levels, as well as program delivery and evaluation. Administers the NIH Academy, the Summer Internship Program, the Undergraduate Scholarship Program, the Graduate Partnerships Program, and the Postbac and Technical Intramural Research Training Award programs.

National Institutes of Health (NIH) *(Health and Human Services Dept.), Science Policy,* 6705 Rockledge Dr., MSC-7985, Bethesda, MD 20892-7985; (301) 496-9838. Fax, (301) 402-1759. *Dr. Amy Patterson, Associate Director.*
General email, osp@od.nih.gov
Web, http://osp.od.nih.gov

Advises the NIH director on science policy issues affecting the medical research community. Participates in the development of new policy and program initiatives. Monitors and coordinates agency planning and evaluation activities. Plans and implements a comprehensive science education program. Develops and implements NIH policies and procedures for the safe conduct of recombinant DNA and other biotechnology activities.

National Museum of Natural History *(Smithsonian Institution),* 10th St. and Constitution Ave. N.W. 20560-0106 (mailing address: P.O. Box 37012, MRC106, Washington, DC 20013-7012); (202) 633-2664. Fax, (202) 633-0181. *Kirk Johnson, Director.* Library, (202) 633-1680. General Smithsonian Information, (202) 633-1000. Press, (202) 633-2950.
General email, naturalexperience@si.edu
Web, www.mnh.si.edu and Twitter, @NMNH

Conducts research and maintains exhibitions and collections relating to the natural sciences. Collections are organized into seven research and curatorial departments: anthropology, botany, entomology, invertebrate zoology, mineral sciences, paleobiology, and vertebrate zoology.

National Science Board *(National Science Foundation),* 4201 Wilson Blvd., #1225N, Arlington, VA 22230; (703) 292-7000. Fax, (703) 292-9008. *Michael L. Van Woert, Director.*
General email, NSBoffice@nsf.gov
Web, www.nsf.gov/nsb

Formulates policy for the National Science Foundation; advises the president on national science policy.

National Science Foundation (NSF), 4201 Wilson Blvd., #1205N, Arlington, VA 22230; (703) 292-8000. Fax, (703) 292-9232. *Cora B. Marrett, Director, Acting,* (703) 292-8001. Library, (703) 292-7830. Publications, (703) 292-7827. Government Affairs, (703) 292-8070.
General email, info@nsf.gov
Web, www.nsf.gov

Sponsors scientific and engineering research; develops and helps implement science and engineering education programs; fosters dissemination of scientific information; promotes international cooperation within the scientific community; and assists with national science policy planning.

National Science Foundation (NSF), *Human Resource Development,* 4201 Wilson Blvd., #815N, Arlington, VA 22230; (703) 292-8640. Fax, (703) 292-9018. *Sylvia James, Division Director.*
Web, www.nsf.gov/div/index.jsp?div=hrd

Supports and encourages participation in scientific and engineering research by women, minorities, and people with disabilities. Awards grants and scholarships.

National Science Foundation (NSF), *National Center for Science and Engineering Statistics,* 4201 Wilson Blvd., #965S, Arlington, VA 22230; (703) 292-8780. Fax, (703) 292-9092. *John R. Gawalt, Director* (703) 292-7776.
Web, www.nsf.gov/statistics

Compiles, analyzes, and disseminates quantitative information about domestic and international resources devoted to science, engineering, and technology. Provides information to other federal agencies for policy formulation.

Office of Management and Budget (OMB) *(Executive Office of the President), Energy, Science, and Water,* New Executive Office Bldg., #8002 20503; (202) 395-3404. Fax, (202) 395-3049. *John Pasquantino, Deputy Associate Director.* Press, (202) 395-7254.
Web, www.whitehouse.gov/omb

Assists and advises the OMB director in budget preparation; analyzes and evaluates programs in space and science, including the activities of the National Science Foundation and the National Aeronautics and Space Administration; coordinates OMB science, energy, and space policies and programs.

SCIENCE AND TECHNOLOGY RESOURCES IN CONGRESS

For a complete listing of Congress committees, including their full contact information, leadership, membership, and jurisdictions, please refer to the Appendix on pages 724–842.

HOUSE:

House Administration Committee, (202) 225-8281. Web, cha.house.gov or democrats.cha.house.gov

House Agriculture Committee, (202) 225-2171. Web, agriculture.house.gov or democrats.agriculture.house.gov

   Subcommittee on Conservation, Energy, and Forestry, (202) 225-2171.

   Subcommittee on Horticulture, Research, Biotechnology, and Foreign Agriculture, (202) 225-2171.

House Appropriations Committee, (202) 225-2771. Web, appropriations.house.gov or democrats.appropriations.house.gov

   Subcommittee on Commerce, Justice, Science, and Related Agencies, (202) 225-3351.

   Subcommittee on Interior, Environment, and Related Agencies, (202) 225-3081.

   Subcommittee on Labor, Health and Human Services, Education, and Related Agencies, (202) 225-3508.

House Armed Services Committee, (202) 225-4151. Web, armedservices.house.gov or democrats.armedservices.house.gov

   Subcommittee on Intelligence, Emerging Threats, and Capabilities, (202) 226-2843.

House Education and the Workforce Committee, (202) 225-4527. Web, edworkforce.house.gov or democrats.edworkforce.house.gov

   Subcommittee on Early Childhood, Elementary, and Secondary Education, (202) 225-4527.

   Subcommittee on Higher Education, and Workforce Training, (202) 225-4527.

House Energy and Commerce Committee, (202) 225-2927. Web, energycommerce.house.gov or democrats.energycommerce.house.gov

   Subcommittee on Communications and Technology, (202) 225-2927.

House Homeland Security Committee, (202) 226-8417. Web, homeland.house.gov or chsdemocrats.house.gov

   Subcommittee on Cybersecurity, Infrastructure Protection, and Security Technologies, (202) 226-8417.

House Judiciary Committee, (202) 225-3951. Web, judiciary.house.gov or democrats.judiciary.house.gov

   Subcommittee on Courts, Intellectual Property, and the Internet, (202) 225-5741.

House Natural Resources Committee, (202) 225-2761. Web, naturalresources.house.gov or democrats.naturalresources.house.gov

   Subcommittee on Energy and Mineral Resources, (202) 225-9297.

   Subcommittee on Fisheries, Wildlife, Oceans, and Insular Affairs, (202) 226-0200.

   Subcommittee on Public Lands and Environmental Regulation, (202) 226-7736.

   Subcommittee on Water and Power, (202) 225-8331.

House Oversight and Government Reform Committee, (202) 225-5074. Web, oversight.house.gov or democrats.oversight.house.gov

   Subcommittee on Energy Policy, Health Care, and Entitlements, (202) 225-5074.

House Science, Space, and Technology Committee, (202) 225-6371. Web, science.house.gov or democrats.science.house.gov

   Subcommittee on Energy, (202) 225-6371.

   Subcommittee on Oversight, (202) 225-6371.

   Subcommittee on Research and Technology, (202) 225-6371.

   Subcommittee on Space, (202) 225-6371.

Office of Science *(Energy Dept.), 1000 Independence Ave. S.W., #7B058 20585; (202) 586-5430. Fax, (202) 586-4120. Patricia M. Dehmer, Director, Acting; Patricia Dehmer, Deputy Director of Science Programs.*
Web, www.science.energy.gov

Advises the secretary on the department's physical science and energy research and development programs; the management of the nonweapons multipurpose laboratories; and education and training activities required for basic and applied research. Manages the department's high-energy physics, nuclear physics, fusion energy sciences, basic energy sciences, health and environmental research, and computational and technology research. Provides and operates the large-scale facilities required for research in the physical and life sciences.

Office of Science and Technology Policy (OSTP) *(Executive Office of the President), Science, Eisenhower Executive Office Bldg., 1650 Pennsylvania Ave. N.W. 20504; (202) 456-4444. Fax, (202) 456-6027. Vacant, Associate Director; Philip Rubin, Principal Assistant Director for Science. General email, info@ostp.gov*
Web, www.ostp.gov

Analyzes policies and advises the president and others within the EOP on biological, physical, social, and behavioral sciences and on engineering; coordinates executive

House Small Business Committee, (202) 225-5821.
Web, smallbusiness.house.gov or
democrats.smallbusiness.house.gov
   Subcommittee on Health and Technology,
      (202) 225-5821.

SENATE:

Senate Agriculture, Nutrition, and Forestry
   Committee, (202) 224-2035.
Web, ag.senate.gov
   Subcommittee on Nutrition, Specialty Crops,
      Food, and Agricultural Research,
      (202) 224-2035.
Senate Appropriations Committee,
   (202) 224-7363.
Web, appropriations.senate.gov
   Subcommittee on Commerce, Justice, Science,
      and Related Agencies, (202) 224-5202.
   Subcommittee on Interior, Environment, and
      Related Agencies, (202) 228-0774.
   Subcommittee on Labor, Health and Human
      Services, Education, and Related Agencies,
      (202) 224-9145.
Senate Armed Services Committee,
   (202) 224-3871.
Web, armed-services.senate.gov
   Subcommittee on Emerging Threats and
      Capabilities, (202) 224-3871.
   Subcommittee on Strategic Forces,
      (202) 224-3871.
Senate Commerce, Science, and Transportation
   Committee, (202) 224-0411.
Web, commerce.senate.gov
   Subcommittee on Aviation Operations, Safety,
      and Security, (202) 224-9000.
   Subcommittee on Communications, Technology,
      and the Internet, (202) 224-9340.
   Subcommittee on Consumer Protection, Product
      Safety, and Insurance, (202) 224-1270.

   Subcommittee on Oceans, Atmosphere,
      Fisheries and the Coast Guard,
      (202) 224-4912.
   Subcommittee on Science and Space,
      (202) 224-0415.
   Subcommittee on Surface Transportation and
      Merchant Marine Infastructure, Safety, and
      Security, (202) 224-9000.
Senate Energy and Natural Resources Committee,
   (202) 224-4971.
Web, energy.senate.gov
   Subcommittee on Energy, (202) 224-4971.
   Subcommittee on Public Lands, Forests, and
      Mining, (202) 224-4971.
   Subcommittee on Water and Power,
      (202) 224-4971.
Senate Environment and Public Works Committee,
   (202) 224-8832.
Web, epw.senate.gov
   Subcommittee on Clean Air and Nuclear Safety,
      (202) 224-8832.
   Subcommittee on Water and Wildlife,
      (202) 224-8832.
Senate Health, Education, Labor, and Pensions
   Committee, (202) 224-5375.
Web, help.senate.gov
Senate Judiciary Committee, (202) 224-7703.
Web, judiciary.senate.gov
   Subcommittee on Crime and Terrorism,
      (202) 224-6791.
Senate Rules and Administration Committee,
   (202) 224-6352.
Web, rules.senate.gov
Senate Small Business and Entrepreneurship
   Committee, (202) 224-5175.
Web, sbc.senate.gov
Senate Special Committee on Aging,
   (202) 224-5364.
Web, aging.senate.gov

office and federal agency actions related to these issues.
Evaluates the effectiveness of government science programs.

Office of Science and Technology Policy (OSTP)
(Executive Office of the President), Technology,
Eisenhower Executive Office Bldg., 1650 Pennsylvania Ave.
N.W. 20504; (202) 456-4444. Fax, (202) 456-6021.
Todd Park, Associate Director and Chief Technology
Officer of the President.
General email, info@ostp.gov

Web, www.ostp.gov

   Analyzes policies and advices the president on technology and related issues of physical, computational, and

space sciences; coordinates executive office and federal
agency actions related to these issues.

▶ **CONGRESS**

For a listing of relevant congressional committees and sub-
committees, please see pages 594–595 or the Appendix.

▶ **NONGOVERNMENTAL**

American Assn. for Laboratory Accreditation (A2LA),
5301 Buckeystown Pike, #350, Frederick, MD 21704; (301)
644-3248. Fax, (240) 454-9449. Peter S. Unger, President,
(301) 644-3212.

General email, info@a2la.org

Web, www.a2la.org

Monitors and accredits laboratories that test construction materials and perform acoustics and vibration, biological, calibration, chemical, electrical, environmental, geotechnical, mechanical, nondestructive, and thermal testing. Offers laboratory-related training and programs for accreditation of inspection bodies, proficiency testing providers, and reference material producers.

American Assn. for the Advancement of Science (AAAS), *1200 New York Ave. N.W., 12th Floor 20005; (202) 326-6400. Fax, (202) 371-9526. Alan I. Leshner, Chief Executive Officer, (202) 326-6640. Press, (202) 326-6440.*

General email, ehr@aaas.org

Web, www.aaas.org

Membership: scientists, affiliated scientific organizations, and individuals interested in science. Promotes science education; the increased participation of women, minorities, and the disabled in the science and technology workforce; the responsible use of science in public policy; international cooperation in science; and the increased public engagement with science and technology. Sponsors national and international symposia, workshops, and meetings; publishes *Science* magazine.

American Assn. for the Advancement of Science (AAAS), *Scientific Responsibility, Human Rights, and Law Program, 1200 New York Ave. N.W., 8th Floor 20005; (202) 326-6600. Fax, (202) 289-4950. Mark S. Frankel, Director.*

Web, http://aaas.org/srhrl

Engages policymakers and the general public on the ethical, legal, and human rights issues related to the conduct and application of science and technology. Defends the freedom to engage in scientific inquiry; promotes responsible research practices; advances the application of science and technology to document human rights violations.

American Council of Independent Laboratories (ACIL), *1875 Eye St. N.W., #500 20006; (202) 887-5872. Fax, (202) 887-0021. Milton Bush, Chief Executive Officer.*

General email, info@acil.org

Web, www.acil.org

Membership: independent commercial scientific and engineering firms. Promotes professional and ethical business practices in providing analysis, testing, and research in engineering, food sciences, analytical chemistry, and environmental geosciences.

Assn. for Women in Science, *1321 Duke St., #210, Alexandria, VA 22314; (703) 894-4490. Fax, (703) 894-4489. Janet Bandows Koster, Executive Director.*

General email, awis@awis.org

Web, www.awis.org

Promotes equal opportunity for women in scientific professions; provides career and funding information. Provides educational scholarships for women in science. Interests include international development.

Federation of American Scientists (FAS), *1725 DeSales St. N.W., 6th Floor 20036; (202) 546-3300. Fax, (202) 675-1010. Charles D. Ferguson, President.*

General email, fas@fas.org

Web, www.fas.org

Conducts studies and monitors legislation on issues and problems related to science and technology, especially U.S. nuclear arms policy, energy, arms transfer, and civil aerospace issues.

George C. Marshall Institute, *1601 N. Kent St., #802, Arlington, VA 22209; (571) 970-3180. William O'Keefe, Chief Executive Officer.*

General email, info@marshall.org

Web, www.marshall.org

Analyzes the technical and scientific aspects of public policy issues; produces publications on environmental science, space, national security, cyberthreats, and technology policy.

Government-University-Industry Research Roundtable (GUIRR), *500 5th St. N.W., Keck 549 20001; (202) 334-3486. Fax, (202) 334-1369. Susan Sauer Sloan, Director.*

General email, guirr@nas.edu

Web, www.nationalacademies.org/guirr

Forum sponsored by the National Academy of Sciences, National Academy of Engineering, and Institute of Medicine. Provides scientists, engineers, and members of government, academia, and industry with an opportunity to discuss ways to catalyze productive cross-sector collaboration, take action on scientific matters of national importance, and improve the infrastructure for science and technology research.

Knowledge Ecology International (KEI), *1621 Connecticut Ave. N.W., #500 20009; (202) 332-2670. Fax, (202) 332-2673. James Love, Director.*

Web, www.keionline.org

Advocates consumer access to health care, electronic commerce, competition policy, and information regarding intellectual property rights. (Formerly the Consumer Project on Technology.)

Laboratory Products Assn., *5618 Ox Rd., Suite C, Fairfax, VA 22039 (mailing address: P.O. Box 428, Fairfax, VA 22038); (703) 836-1360. Fax, (703) 836-6644. Clark Mulligan, President.*

General email, aerrera@lpanet.org

Web, www.lpanet.org

Membership: manufacturers and distributors of laboratory products and optical instruments. (Affiliated with the Optical Imaging Assn.)

National Academy of Sciences (NAS), *2101 Constitution Ave. N.W. 20418; (202) 334-2000. Fax, (202) 334-2419. Ralph J. Cicerone, President; Bruce Darling, Executive Officer. Library, (202) 334-2125. Press, (202) 238-2138. Publications, (888) 624-8373.*

General email, news@nas.edu

Web, www.nasonline.org

Congressionally chartered independent organization that advises the federal government on questions of science, technology, and health. Library open to the public by appointment. (Affiliated with the National Academy of Engineering, the Institute of Medicine, and the National Research Council.)

National Geographic Society, *Committee for Research and Exploration,* *1145 17th St. N.W. 20036-4688; (202) 857-7444. Fax, (202) 429-5729. Peter H. Raven, Chair; John Francis, Vice President for Research, Conservation, and Exploration.*
General email, cre@ngs.org

Web, www.nationalgeographic.com/research

Sponsors basic research grants in the sciences, including anthropology, archaeology, astronomy, biology, botany, ecology, physical and human geography, geology, oceanography, paleontology, and zoology. To apply for grants, see Web site.

National Research Council (NRC), *500 5th St. N.W. 20001; (202) 334-2000. Fax, (202) 334-2158. Ralph J. Cicerone, Chair. Library, (202) 334-2125. Press, (202) 334-2138. Publications, (800) 624-6242.*
General email, news@nas.edu

Web, www.nationalacademies.org

Serves as the principal operating agency of the National Academy of Sciences, National Academy of Engineering, and Institute of Medicine. Program units focus on physical, social, and life sciences; applications of science, including medicine, transportation, and education; international affairs; and U.S. government policy. Library open to the public by appointment.

Society for Science & the Public, *1719 N Street, N.W. 20036; (202) 785-2255. Fax, (202) 785-3751. Rick Bates, Chief Executive Officer, Interim.*
Web, www.societyforscience.org/

Promotes understanding and appreciation of science and the role it plays in human advancement. Sponsors science competitions and other science education programs in schools; awards scholarships. Publishes *Science News* and *Science News for Kids.* Provides funds and training to select U.S. science and math teachers who serve under-resourced students.

Society of Research Administrators International *(SRA International)*, *500 N. Washington St., #300, Falls Church, VA 22046; (703) 741-0140. Fax, (703) 741-0142. Elliott Kulakowski, Executive Director, ext. 215.*
General email, info@srainternational.org

Web, www.srainternational.org

Membership: scientific and medical research administrators in the United States and other countries. Educates the public about the profession; offers professional development services; sponsors mentoring and awards programs.

Union of Concerned Scientists, *Strategy and Policy, Washington Office,* *1825 K St., N.W., #800 20006-1232;*
(202) 223-6133. Fax, (202) 223-6162. Kathleen M. Rest, Executive Director.
General email, ucs@ucsusa.org
Web, www.ucsusa.org

Data, Statistics, and References

▶**AGENCIES**

Dibner Library of the History of Science and Technology *(Smithsonian Institution),* *14th St. and Constitution Ave. N.W., NMAH 1041/MRC 672 20560 (mailing address: P.O. Box 37012, MRC 154, Washington, D.C. 20013-7012); (202) 633-3872. Lilla Vekerdy, Head of Special Collections. Press, (202) 633-1522.*
General email, Dibnerlibrary@si.edu

Web, www.library.si.edu/libraries/dibner

Collection includes major holdings in the history of science and technology dating from the fifteenth century to the nineteenth century. Extensive collections in engineering, transportation, chemistry, mathematics, physics, electricity, and astronomy. Open to the public by appointment.

National Aeronautics and Space Administration (NASA), *Science Proposal Support Office,* *Goddard Space Flight Center, Code 605, Greenbelt, MD 20771; (301) 286-0807. Fax, (301) 286-1772. David Leisawitz, Chief.*
General email, spso.gsfc@nasa.gov
Web, www.nasa.gov/centers/goddard

Supports the writing of proposals for NASA, within the Goddard Space Flight Center.

National Aeronautics and Space Administration (NASA), *Solar System Exploration Data Services,* *Goddard Space Flight Center, Code 690.1, Greenbelt, MD 20771; (301) 286-1743. Fax, (301) 286-1635. Thomas (Tom) Morgan, Program Manager, Planetary Data System.*
General email, request@nssdc.gsfc.nasa.gov
Web, http://ssedso.gsfc.nasa.gov

Coordinates data management and archiving plans within NASA's Science Mission. Operates the National Space Science Data Center (NSSDC) as a permanent archive for data associated with NASA's missions; the Crustal Dynamics Data Information System (CDDIS); and the Planetary Data System (PDS).

National Institute of Standards and Technology (NIST) *(Commerce Dept.), Information Services, Research Library,* *100 Bureau Dr., MS 2500, Gaithersburg, MD 20899-2500; (301) 975-3052. Fax, (301) 869-8071. Mary-Deirdre Coraggio, Director.*
General email, library@nist.gov
Web, www.nist.gov/nvl

Creates and maintains a knowledge base that supports research and administrative needs for the institute. Includes material on engineering, chemistry, physics, mathematics, materials science, and computer science. Home to NIST museum and history program.

National Institute of Standards and Technology (NIST)
(Commerce Dept.), Material Measurement Laboratory,
100 Bureau Dr., Bldg. 227, #A311, MS 8300, Gaithersburg,
MD 20899-8300; (301) 975-8300. Fax, (301) 975-3845.
Laurie E. Locascio, Director.
General email, mmlinfo@nist.gov

Web, www.nist.gov/mml

Serves as the national reference laboratory for measurements in the chemical, biological, and material sciences. Researches industrial, biological, and environmental materials and processes to support development in manufacturing, nanotechnology, electronics, energy, health care, law enforcement, food safety, and other areas. Disseminates reference measurement procedures, certified reference materials, and best-practice guides.

National Institute of Standards and Technology (NIST)
(Commerce Dept.), Physical Measurement Laboratory,
100 Bureau Dr., Bldg. 221, #B160, MS8400, Gaithersburg,
MD 20899-8400; (301) 975-4200. Fax, (301) 975-3038.
Joseph L. Dehmer, Director.
Web, www.nist.gov/pml

Develops and disseminates national standards of measurement for length, mass, force, acceleration, time, wavelength, frequency, humidity, and radiation. Conducts molecular and atomic research and research on physics, electromagnetics, and the properties of solids, liquids, and radio waves. Collaborates with industries, universities, and professional and standards-setting organizations.

National Institute of Standards and Technology (NIST)
(Commerce Dept.), Statistical Engineering, 100 Bureau
Dr., Bldg. 222, #A247, MS 8980, Gaithersburg, MD 20899-
8980; (301) 975-2853. Fax, (301) 975-3144.
Antonio Possolo, Chief.
Web, www.nist.gov/itl/sed

Promotes the use of effective statistical techniques for planning analysis of experiments in the physical sciences within industry and government; interprets experiments and data collection programs.

National Museum of American History *(Smithsonian Institution), Library, 14th St. and Constitution Ave. N.W., R5016, MRC 630 20560-0630 (mailing address: #5016 Smithsonian Institution, P.O. Box 37012, MRC 360, Washington, DC 20013-7012); (202) 633-3865. Fax, (202) 633-3427. William Baxter, Head Librarian.*
General email, askalibrarian@si.edu

Web, www.library.si.edu/libraries/national-museum-american-history-library

Collection includes materials on the history of science and technology, with concentrations in engineering, transportation, and applied science. Maintains collection of trade catalogs and materials about expositions and world fairs. Open to the public by appointment. All library holdings are listed in the online catalog at http://siris-libraries.si.edu/ipac20/ipac.jsp?profile=liball

National Oceanic and Atmospheric Administration
(NOAA) (Commerce Dept.), Central Library, Library and Information Services, 1315 East-West Hwy., SSMC3,

2nd Floor, Silver Spring, MD 20910; (301) 713-2600. Fax, (301) 713-4598. Neal Kaske, Director. Reference service, (301) 713-2600, ext. 157.
General email, library.reference@noaa.gov

Web, www.lib.noaa.gov

Collection includes electronic NOAA documents, reports, and videos; electronic and print journals; the NOAA Photo Library; bibliographic database of other NOAA libraries; and climate data. Makes interlibrary loans; library open to the public, with two forms of photo ID, Monday through Friday, from 9:00 a.m. to 4:00 p.m.

National Oceanic and Atmospheric Administration
(NOAA) (Commerce Dept.), National Environmental Satellite, Data, and Information Service, 1335 East-West Hwy., SSMC1, 8th Floor, Silver Spring, MD 20910; (301) 713-3578. Fax, (301) 713-1249. Mary E. Kicza, Assistant Administrator.
Web, www.nesdis.noaa.gov

Acquires and disseminates global environmental (marine, atmospheric, solid earth, and solar-terrestrial) data. Operates the following data facilities: National Climatic Data Center, Asheville, N.C.; National Geophysical Data Center, Boulder, Colo.; and National Oceanographic Data Center, Washington, D.C. Maintains comprehensive data and information referral service.

National Oceanic and Atmospheric Administration
(NOAA) (Commerce Dept.), National Oceanographic Data Center, 1315 East-West Hwy., SSMC3, 4th Floor, Silver Spring, MD 20910-3282; (301) 713-3277. Fax, (301) 713-3302. Margarita Gregg, Director, (301) 713-3270.
General email, nodc.services@noaa.gov

Web, www.nodc.noaa.gov

Offers a wide range of oceanographic data on the Web, on disk, and on CD-ROM; provides research scientists with data processing services; prepares statistical summaries and graphical data products. (Fee charged for some services.)

National Technical Information Service (NTIS)
(Commerce Dept.), 5301 Shawnee Rd., Alexandria, VA 22312; (703) 605-6000. Fax, (703) 605-6900. Bruce Borzino, Director, (703) 605-6400. Toll-free, (800) 553-6847. Bookstore, (703) 605-6040. Customer support, (703) 605-6050. Toll-free customer support, (888) 584-8332.
General email, info@ntis.gov

Web, www.ntis.gov

Collects and organizes technical, scientific, engineering, and business-related information generated by U.S. and foreign governments and makes it available for commercial use in the private sector. Makes available approximately 3 million works covering research and development, current events, business and management studies, translations of foreign open source reports, foreign and domestic trade, general statistics, environment and energy, health and social sciences, and hundreds of other areas. Provides computer software and computerized data files in a variety of formats, including Internet downloads. Houses the Homeland Security Information

Center, a centralized source on major security concerns for health and medicine, food and agriculture, and bio-chemical war.

Smithsonian Institution, *Office of the Director,* **Libraries,** *10th St. and Constitution Ave. N.W., National Museum of Natural History 20560 (mailing address: P.O. Box 37012, MRC 154, Washington, DC 20013-7012); (202) 633-2240. Fax, (202) 633-4315. Nancy E. Gwinn, Director. Web, http://library.si.edu*

Maintains collection of general reference, biographical, and interdisciplinary materials; serves as an information resource on institution libraries, a number of which have collections in scientific subjects, including horticulture, botany, science and technology, and anthropology.

U.S. Geological Survey (USGS) *(Interior Dept.),* **Library Services,** *950 National Center, Reston, VA 20192 (mailing address: 12201 Sunrise Valley Dr., #1D100, MS 950, Reston, VA 20192); (703) 648-4301. Fax, (703) 648-6373. Lisa Adamo, Branch Manager, (703) 648-6207; Mike McDermott, Director, Interim, (703) 648-5771. General email, library@usgs.gov*

Web, http://library.usgs.gov

Maintains collection of books, periodicals, serials, maps, and technical reports on geology, mineral and water resources, mineralogy, paleontology, petrology, soil and environmental sciences, biology, and physics and chemistry as they relate to natural sciences. Open to the public; makes interlibrary loans.

► **CONGRESS**

For a listing of relevant congressional committees and sub-committees, please see pages 594–595 or the Appendix.

Government Accountability Office (GAO), *Publications and Dissemination,* *441 G St. N.W., #1T61B 20548; (202) 512-3992. Leo Barbour, Director. General email, info@gao.gov*

Web, www.gao.gov

Provides information to the public on federal programs, reports, and testimonies. GAO publications and information about GAO publications are available upon request in print or online.

Library of Congress, *Science, Technology, and Business,* *101 Independence Ave. S.E., #LA508 20540; (202) 707-1212. Fax, (202) 707-1925. Ron Bluestone, Chief. Business Reference Services, (202) 707-3156. Science and Business reading room, (202) 707-5639. Technical reports, (202) 707-5655. Web, www.loc.gov/rr/scitech*

Offers reference service by telephone, by correspondence, and in person. Maintains a collection of more than 3 million reports on science, technology, business management, and economics.

► **NONGOVERNMENTAL**

American Statistical Assn., *732 N. Washington St., Alexandria, VA 22314-1943; (703) 684-1221. Fax, (703) 684-2037. Ronald Wasserstein, Executive Director. Toll-free, (888) 231-3473. General email, asainfo@amstat.org*

Web, www.amstat.org

Membership: statistical practitioners in industry, government, and academia. Supports excellence in the development, application, and dissemination of statistical science through meetings, publications, membership services, education, accreditation, and advocacy.

International Programs

► **AGENCIES**

International Trade Administration (ITA) *(Commerce Dept.), Industry and Analysis, Manufacturing,* *1401 Constitution Ave. N.W., #2800A 20230; (202) 482-1872. Fax, (202) 482-0856. Chandra Brown, Deputy Assistant Secretary, Acting. Web, www.trade.gov/td/manufacturing and www.manufacturing.gov*

Conducts analyses and competitive assessments of high-tech industries, including aerospace, automotive, and industrial machinery. Develops trade policies for these industries, negotiates market access for U.S. companies, assists in promoting exports through trade missions, shows, and fairs in major overseas markets.

National Oceanic and Atmospheric Administration (NOAA) *(Commerce Dept.), National Environmental Satellite, Data, and Information Service,* *1335 East-West Hwy., SSMC1, 8th Floor, Silver Spring, MD 20910; (301) 713-3578. Fax, (301) 713-1249. Mary E. Kicza, Assistant Administrator. Web, www.nesdis.noaa.gov*

Acquires and disseminates global environmental data: marine, atmospheric, solid earth, and solar-terrestrial. Participates, with the National Meteorological Center, in the United Nations World Weather Watch Programme developed by the World Meteorological Organization. Manages U.S. civil earth-observing satellite systems and atmospheric, oceanographic, geophysical, and solar data centers. Provides the public, businesses, and government agencies with environmental data and information products and services.

National Science Foundation (NSF), *International Science and Engineering,* *4201 Wilson Blvd., #11-1155, Arlington, VA 22230; (703) 292-8710. Fax, (703) 292-9067. Graham Harrison, Office Head, (703) 292-7252. Web, www.nsf.gov/oise*

Serves as the foundation's focal point for international scientific and engineering activities; promotes new partnerships between U.S. scientists and engineers and their foreign colleagues; provides support for U.S. participation in international scientific organizations.

National Weather Service *(National Oceanic and Atmospheric Administration), National Centers for Environmental Prediction, 5830 University Research Court, College Park, MD 20740; (301) 683-1315. Bill Lapenta, Director.*
Web, www.ncep.noaa.gov

The National Center for Environmental Prediction and the National Environmental Satellite, Data, and Information Service are part of the World Weather Watch Programme developed by the United Nations World Meteorological Organization. Collects and exchanges data with other nations; provides other national weather service offices, private meteorologists, and government agencies with products, including forecast guidance products.

Smithsonian Institution, *International Relations, 1100 Jefferson Dr. S.W., #3123 20560 (mailing address: P.O. Box 37012, Quad MRC 705, Washington, DC 20013-7012); (202) 633-4795. Fax, (202) 786-2557. Molly Fannon, Director.*
General email, global@si.edu

Web, www.si.edu/intrel

Fosters the development and coordinates the international aspects of Smithsonian scientific activities; facilitates basic research in the natural sciences and encourages international collaboration among individuals and institutions.

State Dept., *Global Systems, 2201 C St. N.W., #5333 20520; (202) 647-3049. Fax, (202) 647-8902. Robert J. Faucher, Director.*
Web, www.state.gov

Oversees U.S. participation in international specialized and technical organizations, including the International Atomic Energy Agency; the United Nations Environment Programme; and the Commission on Sustainable Development. Works to ensure that United Nations agencies follow United Nations Conference on Environment and Development recommendations on sustainable growth.

State Dept., *Oceans and International Environmental Scientific Affairs, 2201 C St. N.W., #3880 20520-7818; (202) 647-1554. Fax, (202) 647-0217. Kerri-Ann Jones, Assistant Secretary. Press, (202) 647-3486.*
Web, www.state.gov/e/oes

Formulates and implements policies and proposals for U.S. international scientific, technological, environmental, oceanic and marine, Arctic and Antarctic, and space programs; coordinates international science and technology policy with other federal agencies.

▶**INTERNATIONAL ORGANIZATIONS**

InterAcademy Panel on International Issues,
Washington Office, 500 5th St. N.W., #528 20001; (202) 334-2804. Fax, (202) 334-2139. John Boright, U.S. Contact, (202) 334-3847.
General email, jboright@nas.edu

Web, www.interacademies.net

Membership: academies of science in countries worldwide. Promotes communication among leading authorities in the natural and social sciences; establishes regional networks of academies to identify critical issues, thereby building capacity for advice to governments and international organizations. Interests include science education and sustainable management of water, energy, and other resources. (National Academy of Sciences is U.S. member. Headquarters in Trieste, Italy.)

▶**NONGOVERNMENTAL**

American Assn. for the Advancement of Science (AAAS), *International Office, 1200 New York Ave. N.W., 11th Floor 20005; (202) 326-6650. Fax, (202) 289-4958. Vaughan Turekian, Chief International Officer.*
Web, www.aaas.org

Promotes international cooperation among scientists. Helps build scientific infrastructure in developing countries. Works to improve the quality of scientific input in international discourse.

National Research Council (NRC), *Policy and Global Affairs, International Affairs, 500 5th St. N.W., Keck 528 20001; (202) 334-3847. Fax, (202) 334-2139. John Boright, Executive Director.*
General email, pga@nas.edu

Web, www.nationalacademies.org/nrc

Serves the international interests of the National Research Council, National Academy of Sciences, National Academy of Engineering, and Institute of Medicine. Promotes effective application of science and technology to the economic and social problems of industrialized and developing countries, and advises U.S. government agencies.

Research Applications

▶**AGENCIES**

Defense Technical Information Center *(Defense Dept.), 8725 John Jay Kingman Rd., #1948, Fort Belvoir, VA 22060-6218; (703) 767-9100. Fax, (703) 767-9183. Christopher Thomas, Administrator. Registration, (703) 767-8273. Toll-free, (800) 225-3842.*
Web, www.dtic.mil

Acts as a central repository for the Defense Dept.'s collection of current and completed research and development efforts in all fields of science and technology. Disseminates research and development information to contractors, grantees, and registered organizations working on government research and development projects, particularly for the Defense Dept. Users must register with the center.

National Aeronautics and Space Administration (NASA), *Science Mission Directorate, 300 E St. S.W., #3C26 20546; (202) 358-3889. Fax, (202) 358-3092. John Grunsfeld, Associate Administrator.*

General email, science@hq.nasa.gov

Web, http://science.nasa.gov/about-us/organization-and-leadership

Seeks to understand the origins, evolution, and structure of the solar system and the universe; to understand the integrated functioning of the earth and the sun; and to ascertain the potential for life elsewhere. Administers space mission programs and mission-enabling programs, including suborbital missions. Sponsors scientific research and analysis. Exchanges information with the international science community. Primary areas of study are astronomy and astrophysics, earth sciences, heliophysics, and planetary science.

National Institute of Standards and Technology (NIST) (Commerce Dept.), 100 Bureau Dr., Bldg. 101, #A1134, Gaithersburg, MD 20899-1000 (mailing address: 100 Bureau Dr., MS 1000, Gaithersburg, MD 20899); (301) 975-2300. Fax, (301) 869-8972. Patrick Gallagher, Director.
General email, director@nist.gov

Web, www.nist.gov/director/index.cfm

Nonregulatory agency that serves as national reference and measurement laboratory for the physical and engineering sciences. Works with industry, government agencies, and academia; promotes U.S. innovation and industrial competitiveness. Research interests include advanced manufacturing, information technology and cybersecurity, energy, health care, environment and consumer safety, and physical infrastructure.

National Institutes of Health (NIH) (Health and Human Services Dept.), Technology Transfer, 6011 Executive Blvd., #325, MSC-7660, Rockville, MD 20852-3804; (301) 496-7057. Fax, (301) 402-0220. Mark L. Rohrbaugh, Director.
General email, nihott@mail.nih.gov

Web, http://ott.od.nih.gov

Evaluates, protects, monitors, and manages the NIH invention portfolio. Oversees patent prosecution, negotiates and monitors licensing agreements, and provides oversight and central policy review of cooperative research and development agreements. Also manages the patent and licensing activities for the Food and Drug Administration (FDA). Responsible for the central development and implementation of technology transfer policies for three research components of the Public Health Service—the NIH, the FDA, and the Centers for Disease Control and Prevention.

National Science Foundation (NSF), Nanotechnology, 4201 Wilson Blvd., #505N, Arlington, VA 22230; (703) 292-8300. Fax, (703) 292-9013. Mihail C. Roco, Senior Adviser, (703) 292-7032.
General email, info@nnco.nano.gov

Web, www.nsf.gov/div/index.jsp?org=eng

Coordinates multiagency efforts in understanding nanoscale phenomena and furthering nanotechnology research and development.

▶NONGOVERNMENTAL

American National Standards Institute (ANSI), 1899 L St. N.W., 11th Floor 20036; (202) 293-8020. Fax, (202) 293-9287. Joe Bhatia, President.
Web, www.ansi.org

Administers and coordinates the voluntary U.S. private sector–led voluntary consensus standards and conformity assessment system. Serves as the official U.S. representative to the International Organization of Standardization (ISO) and, via the U.S. National Committee, the International Electrotechnical Commission (IEC); and is a U.S. representative to the International Accreditation Forum (IAF).

Institute for Alternative Futures (IAF), 100 N. Pitt St., #307, Alexandria, VA 22314-3134; (703) 684-5880. Fax, (703) 684-0640. Jonathan Peck, President.
General email, futurist@altfutures.org

Web, www.altfutures.org

Research and educational organization that explores the implications of future developments in various fields and facilitates planning efforts. Works with state and local governments, Congress, international organizations, federal government, and regional associations; conducts seminars. Interests include pharmaceutical research, health care, telecommunications, artificial intelligence, energy, the environment, and sustainability.

National Center for Advanced Technologies (NCAT), 1000 Wilson Blvd., #1700, Arlington, VA 22209-3901; (703) 358-1004. Fax, (703) 358-1012. Don Forest, President.
General email, ncat@ncat.com

Web, www.ncat.com

Encourages U.S. competition in the world market by uniting government, industry, and university efforts to develop advanced technologies. (Affiliated with the Aerospace Industries Assn. of America.)

Public Technology Institute (PTI), 1420 Prince St., #200, Alexandria, VA 22314-2815; (202) 626-2400. Alan R. Shark, Executive Director. Press, (202) 626-2432.
General email, info@pti.org

Web, www.pti.org

Cooperative research, development, and technology-transfer organization of cities and counties in North America. Applies available technological innovations and develops other methods to improve public services.

RAND Corporation, Washington Office, 1200 S. Hayes St., Arlington, VA 22202-5050; (703) 413-1100. Fax, (703) 413-8111. Lynn E. Davis, Director, ext. 5399; Debra Knopman, Director, Justice, Infrastructure, and Environment.
Web, www.rand.org

Research organization. Interests include energy, emerging technologies and critical systems, space and transportation, technology policies, international cooperative research, water resources, ocean and atmospheric sciences, and other technologies in defense and nondefense areas. (Headquarters in Santa Monica, Calif.)

SRI International, *Washington Office,* 1100 Wilson Blvd., #2800, Arlington, VA 22209; (703) 524-2053. Fax, (703) 247-8569. Jerry Harrison, Vice President, Government Business Development, (703) 247-8569.
Web, www.sri.com

Research and consulting organization that conducts basic and applied research for government, industry, and business. Interests include engineering, physical and life sciences, and international research. (Headquarters in Menlo Park, Calif.)

Scientific Research Practices

▶AGENCIES

Education Dept., *Office of the Chief Financial Officer, Financial Management Operations,* 550 12th St. S.W., 6th Floor 20005; (202) 245-8118. Fax, (202) 205-0765. Gary Wood, Director.
General email, gary.wood@ed.gov

Web, www2.ed.gov/about/offices/list/ocfo/humansub.html

Advises grantees and applicants for department-supported research on regulations for protecting human subjects. Provides guidance to the Education Dept. on the requirements for complying with the regulations. Serves as the primary Education Dept. contact for matters concerning the protection of human subjects in research.

Energy Dept. (DOE), *Biological Systems Science Division, Human Subjects Protection Program,* 19901 Germantown Rd., #SC-23, Germantown, MD 20874-1290 (mailing address: 1000 Independence Ave. S.W., Washington, DC 20585-1290); (301) 903-7693. Fax, (301) 903-0567. Sharlene Weatherwax, Associate Director; Elizabeth White, Program Manager.
General email, humansubjects@science.doe.gov

Web, http://humansubjects.energy.gov

Works to protect the rights and welfare of human subject research volunteers by establishing guidelines and enforcing regulations on scientific research that uses human subjects, including research that involves identifiable or high-risk data, worker populations or subgroups; humans testing devices, products, or materials; and bodily materials. Acts as an educational and technical resource to investigators, administrators, and institutional research boards.

Health and Human Services Dept. (HHS), *Human Research Protections,* 1101 Wootton Pkwy., The Tower Bldg., #200, Rockville, MD 20852; (240) 453-6900. Fax, (240) 453-6909. Dr. Jerry Menikoff, Director.
General email, ohrp@hhs.gov

Web, www.hhs.gov/ohrp

Promotes the rights, welfare, and well-being of subjects involved in research conducted or supported by the Health and Human Services Dept.; helps to ensure that research is carried out in accordance with federal regulations by providing clarification and guidance, developing educational programs and materials, and maintaining regulatory oversight.

Health and Human Services Dept. (HHS), *President's Commission for the Study of Bioethical Issues,* 1425 New York Ave. N.W., #C100 20005; (202) 233-3960. Fax, (202) 233-3990. Amy Gutmann, Chair; Lisa M. Lee, Executive Director.
General email, info@bioethics.gov

Web, www.bioethics.gov

Advises the president on ethical issues related to advances in biomedical science and technology, including stem cell research, assisted reproduction, cloning, end of life care, and the protection of human subjects in research.

Health and Human Services Dept. (HHS), *Research Integrity,* 1101 Wootton Pkwy., The Tower Bldg., #750, Rockville, MD 20852; (240) 453-8200. Fax, (240) 276-9574. David E. Wright, Director.
General email, askori@hhs.gov

Web, www.ori.hhs.gov

Seeks to promote the quality of Public Health Service extramural and intramural research programs. (Extramural programs provide funding to research institutions that are not part of the federal government. Intramural programs provide funding for research conducted within federal government facilities.) Develops policies and regulations that protect from retaliation individuals who disclose information about scientific misconduct; administers assurance program; provides technical assistance to institutions during inquiries and investigations of scientific misconduct; reviews institutional findings and recommends administrative actions to the assistant secretary of Health and Human Services; sponsors educational programs and activities for professionals interested in research integrity.

National Aeronautics and Space Administration (NASA), *Chief Health and Medical Officer,* 300 E St. S.W. 20546; (202) 358-2390. Fax, (202) 358-3349. Dr. Richard S. Williams, Chief Health and Medical Officer.
Web, www.hq.nasa.gov/office/chmo

Monitors human and animal research and clinical practice to ensure that NASA adheres to appropriate medical and ethical standards and satisfies all regulatory and statutory requirements.

National Institutes of Health (NIH) *(Health and Human Services Dept.),* **Animal Care and Use,** 31 Center Dr., Bldg. 31, #B1C37, MSC-2252, Bethesda, MD 20892-2252; (301) 496-5424. Fax, (301) 480-8298. Terri Clark, Director.
General email, secoacu@od.nih.gov

Web, http://oacu.od.nih.gov

Provides guidance for the humane care and use of animals in the intramural research program at NIH.

National Institutes of Health (NIH) *(Health and Human Services Dept.),* **Human Subjects Research,** 9000 Rockville Pike, Clinical Center, Bldg. 10, #2C146, MSC-1154, Bethesda, MD 20892-1154; (301) 402-3444. Fax, (301) 402-3443. Lynnette Nieman, Director.
Web, http://ohsr.od.nih.gov

Helps NIH investigators understand and comply with ethical principles and regulatory requirements involved in human subjects research. Assists NIH components in administering and regulating human subjects research activities.

National Institutes of Health (NIH) *(Health and Human Services Dept.), Laboratory Animal Welfare, 6705 Rockledge Dr., RLK1, #360, MSC 7982, Bethesda, MD 20892-7982; (301) 496-7163. Fax, (301) 402-7065. Patricia Brown, Director.*
General email, olaw@od.nih.gov
Web, http://grants.nih.gov/grants/olaw/olaw.htm

Develops and monitors policy on the humane care and use of animals in research conducted by any public health service entity.

National Institutes of Health (NIH) *(Health and Human Services Dept.), Stem Cell Task Force, 9000 Rockville Pike, 31 Center Dr., Bldg. 31, #8A52, MSC2540, Bethesda, MD 20892-2540; (301) 496-9746. Fax, (301) 496-0296. Dr. Story Landis, Chair.*
General email, stemcell@mail.nih.gov
Web, http://stemcells.nih.gov

The federal government's primary source for stem cell research, policy, and funding. Enables and speeds the pace of stem cell research by identifying resources and developing measures to enhance such resources. Seeks the advice of scientific leaders in stem cell research about the challenges to advancing the stem cell research agenda and strategies to overcome them.

▶NONGOVERNMENTAL

American Assn. for the Advancement of Science (AAAS), *Scientific Responsibility, Human Rights, and Law Program, 1200 New York Ave. N.W., 8th Floor 20005; (202) 326-6600. Fax, (202) 289-4950. Mark S. Frankel, Director.*
Web, http://aaas.org/srhrl

Engages policymakers and the general public on the ethical, legal, and human rights issues related to the conduct and application of science and technology. Defends the freedom to engage in scientific inquiry; promotes responsible research practices; advances the application of science and technology to document human rights violations.

Humane Society of the United States, *Animal Research Issues, 700 Professional Dr., Gaithersburg, MD 20879; (301) 721-6439. Fax, (301) 258-7760. Katy Conlee, Vice President.*
General email, ari@humanesociety.org
Web, www.humanesociety.org/animalsinlaboratories

Seeks to end the suffering of animals in research. Promotes the use of alternatives that replace, refine, or reduce the use of animals in scientific research, education, and consumer product testing. Conducts outreach programs aimed toward the public and the scientific community.

BIOLOGY AND LIFE SCIENCES

General

▶AGENCIES

Armed Forces Radiobiology Research Institute *(Defense Dept.), 8901 Wisconsin Ave., Bldg. 42, Bethesda, MD 20889-5603; (301) 295-1210. Fax, (301) 295-4967. Col. Lester Huff USAF, MC, Director. Public Affairs, (301) 295-1214.*
Web, www.afrri.usuhs.mil

Serves as the principal ionizing radiation radiobiology research laboratory under the jurisdiction of the Uniformed Services of the Health Sciences. Participates in international conferences and projects.

National Aeronautics and Space Administration (NASA), *Human Space Flight Capability Division, 300 E St. S.W., #7V20 20546; (202) 358-2320. Fax, (202) 358-3091. Benjamin J. Neumann, Program Executive.*
Web, www.hq.nasa.gov

Conducts NASA's life sciences research.

National Institute of General Medical Sciences *(National Institutes of Health), 45 Center Dr., #3AN32, MSC-6200, Bethesda, MD 20892-6200; (301) 496-7301. Fax, (301) 402-0224. Jon Lorsch, Director.*
General email, info@nigms.nih.gov
Web, www.nigms.nih.gov

Primarily supports basic biomedical research and training that lays the foundation for advances in disease diagnosis, treatment, and prevention. Areas of special interest include bioinformatics, cell biology, developmental biology, physiology, biological chemistry genetics, and computational biology. Major initiatives include the Pharmacogenetics Research Network, the Protein Structure Initiative, and the Models of Infectious Diseases Study.

National Museum of Natural History *(Smithsonian Institution), Library, 10th St. and Constitution Ave. N.W., East Court, 1st Floor 20560-0154 (mailing address: P.O. Box 37012, MRC 154, Washington, DC 20013-7012); (202) 633-1680. Gil Taylor, Head, (202) 633-1679.*
General email, askalibrarian@si.edu
Web, www.sil.si.edu

Maintains reference collections covering anthropology, biodiversity, biology, botany, ecology, entomology, ethnology, mineral sciences, paleobiology, and zoology; permits on-site use of the collections. Open to the public by appointment; makes interlibrary loans.

National Oceanic and Atmospheric Administration (NOAA) *(Commerce Dept.), National Marine Fisheries Service, 1315 East-West Hwy., SSMC3, Silver Spring, MD 20910; (301) 427-8000. Fax, (301) 713-1940. Eileen Sobeck, Assistant Administrator. Press, (301) 427-8003.*
Web, www.nmfs.noaa.gov

Conducts research and collects data on marine ecology and biology; collects, analyzes, and provides information through the Marine Resources Monitoring, Assessment, and Prediction Program. Administers the Magnuson-Stevens Fishery Conservation and Management Act and marine mammals and endangered species protection programs. Works with the Army Corps of Engineers on research into habitat restoration and conservation.

Naval Medical Research Center *(Defense Dept.), 503 Robert Grant Ave., #1W28, Silver Spring, MD 20910-7500; (301) 319-9646. Fax, (301) 319-7410. Capt. John W. Sanders, Commanding Officer.*
General email, svc.pao.nmrc@med.navy.mil
Web, www.med.navy.mil/sites/nmrc

Performs basic and applied biomedical research in areas of military importance, including infectious diseases, hyperbaric medicine, wound repair enhancement, environmental stress, and immunobiology. Provides support to field laboratories and naval hospitals; monitors research internationally.

U.S. Geological Survey (USGS) *(Interior Dept.),* **Ecosystems,** *12201 Sunrise Valley Dr., MS 300, Reston, VA 20192; (703) 648-4050. Fax, (703) 648-7031. Anne E. Kinsinger, Associate Director, (703) 648-4051.*
Web, www.usgs.gov/ecosystems

▶**NONGOVERNMENTAL**

American Institute of Biological Sciences, *1900 Campus Commons Dr., #200, Reston, VA 20191; (703) 674-2500, ext. 100. Fax, (703) 674-2509. Richard O'Grady, Executive Director, ext. 258.*
Web, www.aibs.org

Membership: biologists, biology educators, and biological associations. Promotes interdisciplinary cooperation among members engaged in biological research and education; conducts educational programs for members; reviews projects supported by government grants. Monitors legislation and regulations.

American Society for Biochemistry and Molecular Biology, *11200 Rockville Pike, #302, Bethesda, MD 20852-3110; (240) 283-6600. Fax, (301) 881-2080. Barbara A. Gordon, Executive Director.*
General email, asbmb@asbmb.org
Web, www.asbmb.org

Professional society of biological chemists. Participates in International Union of Biochemistry and Molecular Biology. Monitors legislation and regulations.

American Society for Cell Biology, *8120 Woodmont Ave., #750, Bethesda, MD 20814-2762; (301) 347-9300. Fax, (301) 347-9310. Stefano Bertuzzi, Executive Director.*
General email, ascbinfo@ascb.org
Web, www.ascb.org

Membership: scientists who have education or research experience in cell biology or an allied field. Promotes scientific exchange worldwide; organizes courses, workshops, and symposia. Monitors legislation and regulations.

American Society for Microbiology, *1752 N St. N.W. 20036-2904; (202) 737-3600. Fax, (202) 942-9333. Michael I. Goldberg, Executive Director. Press, (202) 942-9297.*
General email, oed@asmusa.org
Web, www.asm.org

Membership: microbiologists. Encourages education, training, scientific investigation, and application of research results in microbiology and related subjects; participates in international research.

American Type Culture Collection, *10801 University Blvd., Manassas, VA 20110-2209 (mailing address: P.O. Box 1549, Manassas, VA 20108); (703) 365-2700. Fax, (703) 365-2750. Raymond H. Cypress, Chief Executive Officer. Toll-free, (800) 638-6597.*
General email, sales@atcc.org
Web, www.atcc.org

Provides research and development tools and reagents and related biological material management services to government agencies, academic institutions, and private industry worldwide. Serves as a bio-resource center of live cultures and genetic material.

AOAC International, *481 N. Frederick Ave., #500, Gaithersburg, MD 20877-2417; (301) 924-7077. Fax, (301) 924-7089. E. James Bradford, Executive Director. Information, (800) 379-2622.*
General email, aoac@aoac.org
Web, www.aoac.org

International association of analytical science professionals, companies, government agencies, nongovernmental organizations, and institutions. Promotes methods validation and quality measurements in the analytical sciences. Supports the development, testing, validation, and publication of reliable chemical and biological methods of analyzing foods, drugs, feed, fertilizers, pesticides, water, and other substances.

Biophysical Society, *11400 Rockville Pike, #800, Rockville, MD 20852; (240) 290-5600. Fax, (240) 290-5555. Rosalba Kampman, Executive Officer.*
General email, society@biophysics.org
Web, www.biophysics.org

Membership: scientists, professors, and researchers engaged in biophysics or related fields. Encourages development and dissemination of knowledge in biophysics through meetings, publications, and outreach activities.

Carnegie Institution for Science of Washington, *1530 P St. N.W. 20005-1910; (202) 387-6400. Fax, (202) 387-8092. Richard A. Meserve, President, (202) 387-6404.*
Web, www.carnegiescience.edu

Conducts research in plant biology, developmental biology, earth and planetary sciences, astronomy, and global ecology at the Carnegie Institution's six research departments: Dept. of Embryology (Baltimore, Md.); Geophysical Laboratory (Washington, D.C.); Dept. of Global Ecology (Stanford, Calif.); Dept. of Plant Biology (Stanford, Calif.); Dept. of Terrestrial Magnetism (Washington,

D.C.); and The Observatories (Pasadena, Calif., and Las Campanas, Chile).

Ecological Society of America, *1990 M St. N.W., #700 20036; (202) 833-8773. Fax, (202) 833-8775. Katherine S. McCarter, Executive Director.*
General email, esahq@esa.org
Web, www.esa.org

Promotes research in ecology and the scientific study of the relationship between organisms and their past, present, and future environments. Interests include biotechnology; management of natural resources, habitats, and ecosystems to protect biological diversity; and ecologically sound public policies.

Federation of American Societies for Experimental Biology (FASEB), *9650 Rockville Pike, Bethesda, MD 20814-3998; (301) 634-7000. Fax, (301) 634-7001. Guy C. Fogleman, Executive Director.*
Web, www.faseb.org

Advances biological science through collaborative advocacy for research policies that promote scientific progress and education and lead to improvements in human health. Provides educational meetings and publications to disseminate biological research results. Represents 26 scientific societies and more than 115,000 biomedical researchers around the world.

National Ecological Observatory Network (NEON, Inc.), *Washington Office, 1100 Jefferson Dr. S.W., #3123, MRC 705 20560-0001; (202) 370-7891. Fax, (202) 204-0128. Brian Wee, Chief of External Affairs; Russell Lea, Chief Executive Officer (in Boulder). Press, (720) 746-4936.*
General email, bwee@neoninc.org
Web, www.neoninc.org

Collects data across the United States on the impact of climate change, land-use change, and invasive species on natural resources and biodiversity, with the goal of detecting and forecasting ecological change on a continental scale over multiple decades. Working with various government agencies to develop standards for environmental observations and data interooperability; expected to become fully operational by 2016. Funded by the National Science Foundation in partnership with Neon, Inc. (Visitors note: Co-located in the Smithsonian's S. Dillon Ripley Center.) (Headquarters in Boulder, Colo.)

Biotechnology

▶AGENCIES

Environmental Protection Agency (EPA), *Chemical Safety and Pollution Prevention (OCSPP), 1201 Constitution Ave. N.W., #3130 EPA-E, MS 7101M 20460-7101; (202) 564-2902. Fax, (202) 564-0801. James J. Jones, Assistant Administrator. Pollution prevention and toxic substances, (202) 564-3810. Pesticide programs, (703) 305-7090.*

Web, www.epa.gov/aboutepa/about-office-chemical-safety-and-pollution-prevention-ocspp

Studies and makes recommendations for regulating chemical substances under the Toxic Substances Control Act; compiles list of chemical substances subject to the act; registers, controls, and regulates use of pesticides and toxic substances; manages the Endocrine Disruptor Screening Program.

National Institutes of Health (NIH) *(Health and Human Services Dept.), Biotechnology Activities, 6705 Rockledge Dr., #750, MSC-7985, Bethesda, MD 20892-7985; (301) 496-9838. Fax, (301) 402-1759. Dr. Jacqueline Corrigan-Curay, Director, Acting.*
General email, oba-osp@od.nih.gov
Web, http://oba.od.nih.gov/oba

Reviews requests submitted to the NIH involving genetic testing, recombinant DNA technology, xenotransplantation, and biosecurity; develops and implements research guidelines for safe conduct of DNA-related research. Monitors scientific progress in human genetics.

National Library of Medicine *(National Institutes of Health), National Center for Biotechnology Information, 8600 Rockville Pike, Bldg. 38A, 8th Floor, Bethesda, MD 20892; (301) 496-2475. Fax, (301) 480-4559. Dr. David J. Lipman, Director.*
General email, info@ncbi.nlm.nih.gov
Web, www.ncbi.nlm.nih.gov and *www.pubmedcentral.nih.gov*

Creates automated systems for storing and analyzing knowledge of molecular biology and genetics. Develops new information technologies to aid in understanding the molecular processes that control human health and disease. Conducts basic research in computational molecular biology. Sponsors PubMed Central, a publicly accessible digital archive of life sciences journal literature.

National Science Foundation (NSF), *Biological Sciences, 4201 Wilson Blvd., #605N, Arlington, VA 22230; (703) 292-8400. Fax, (703) 292-9154. John C. Wingfield, Assistant Director.*
Web, www.nsf.gov/div/index.jsp?org=bio

Serves as a forum for addressing biotechnology research issues, sharing information, identifying gaps in scientific knowledge, and developing consensus among concerned federal agencies. Facilitates continuing cooperation among federal agencies on topical issues.

▶NONGOVERNMENTAL

Biotechnology Industry Organization, *1201 Maryland Ave. S.W., #900 20024; (202) 962-9200. Fax, (202) 488-6301. James Greenwood, President.*
General email, info@bio.org
Web, www.bio.org

Membership: U.S. and international companies engaged in biotechnology. Monitors government activities at all levels; promotes educational activities; conducts workshops.

Friends of the Earth (FOE), *Washington Office,* *1100 15th St. N.W., 11th Floor 20005; (202) 783-7400. Fax, (202) 783-0444. Erich Pica, President. Toll-free, (877) 843-8687.*
General email, foe@foe.org
Web, www.foe.org

Monitors legislation and regulations on issues related to seed industry consolidation and patenting laws and on business developments in genetic engineering and synthetic biology and their effect on farming, food production, genetic resources, and the environment.

Genetic Alliance, *4301 Connecticut Ave. N.W., #404 20008-2369; (202) 966-5557. Fax, (202) 966-8553. Sharon Terry, President.*
General email, info@geneticalliance.org
Web, www.geneticalliance.org

Coalition of government, industry, advocacy organizations, and private groups that seeks to advance genetic research and its applications. Promotes increased funding for research, improved access to services, and greater support for emerging technologies, tests, and treatments. Advocates on behalf of individuals and families living with genetic conditions.

The J. Craig Venter Institute, *9704 Medical Center Dr., Rockville, MD 20850; (301) 795-7000. J. Craig Venter, Chief Executive Officer.*
Web, www.jcvi.org

Research institute that analyzes genomes and gene products for medical, nutritional, and agricultural uses; studies genomic sciences and their ethical, legal, and economic implications for society. Produces reports; offers courses, workshops, and internships.

Kennedy Institute of Ethics *(Georgetown University), Healy Hall, 37th and O Sts. N.W., 4th Floor 20057; (202) 687-8099. Fax, (202) 687-8089. Margaret Little, Director. Library, (202) 687-3885. Toll-free, United States and Canada, (888) 246-3849 and (888) 633-3849.*
General email, kennedyinstitute@georgetown.edu
Web, http://kennedyinstitute.georgetown.edu

Carries out teaching and research on medical ethics, including legal and ethical definitions of death, allocation of health resources, and recombinant DNA and human gene therapy. Sponsors the annual Intensive Bioethics Course. Conducts international programs. Serves as the home of the Bioethics Research Library at Georgetown University (http://bioethics.georgetown.edu) and the National Information Resource on Ethics and Human Genetics (http://genthx.georgetown.edu). Provides free reference assistance and bibliographic databases covering all ethical issues in health care, genetics, and biomedical research. Library open to the public.

Botany

▶**AGENCIES**

National Arboretum *(Agriculture Dept.), 3501 New York Ave. N.E. 20002-1958; (202) 245-2726. Fax, (202) 245-4575. Colien Hefferan, Director.*
Web, www.usna.usda.gov

Maintains public display of plants on 446 acres; provides information and makes referrals concerning cultivated plants (exclusive of field crops and fruits); conducts plant breeding and research; maintains herbarium.

National Museum of Natural History *(Smithsonian Institution), Botany, 10th St. and Constitution Ave. N.W. 20560-0166 (mailing address: P.O. Box 37012, MRC 166, Washington, DC 20013-7012); (202) 633-0920. Fax, (202) 786-2563. Warren L. Wagner, Chair. Library, (202) 633-2146.*
Web, www.botany.si.edu

Seeks to discover and describe the diversity of plant life in terrestrial and marine environments, interpret the origins of diversity, and explain the processes responsible for diversity. Research includes systematics, phylogenetics, anatomy, morphology, biogeography, and ecology. Studies how humans are affected by, and have altered, plant diversity. Works to manage, grow, and conserve the collection in the United States National Herbarium (more than 5 million specimens) as a global plant resource. Library open to the public Monday through Friday, 10:00 a.m.–4:00 p.m., by appointment only.

Smithsonian Institution, *Botany and Horticulture Library, 10th St. and Constitution Ave. N.W., #W422 20560-0166 (mailing address: P.O. Box 37012, MRC 154, Washington, DC 20013-7012); (202) 633-1685. Robin Everly, Branch Librarian.*
General email, askalibrarian@si.edu
Web, www.library.si.edu/libraries/botany

Collections include taxonomic botany, plant morphology, general botany, history of botany, grasses, and algae. Permits on-site use of collections (10:00 a.m.–4:00 p.m; appointment necessary); makes interlibrary loans. (Housed at the National Museum of Natural History.)

▶**CONGRESS**

For a listing of relevant congressional committees and subcommittees, please see pages 594–595 or the Appendix.

U.S. Botanic Garden *100 Maryland Ave. S.W. 20001 (mailing address: 245 1st St. S.W., Washington, DC 20024); (202) 225-8333. Fax, (202) 225-1561. Holly H. Shimizu, Executive Director; Ari Novy, Horticulture hotline, (202) 226-4785. Program registration information, (202) 225-1116. Special events, (202) 226-7674. Tour line, (202) 226-2055.*
General email, usbg@aoc.gov
Web, www.usbg.gov

►NONGOVERNMENTAL

American Society for Horticultural Science (ASHS), *1018 Duke St., Alexandria, VA 22314; (703) 836-4606. Fax, (703) 836-2024. Michael W. Neff, Executive Director, ext. 106.*
General email, webmaster@ashs.org
Web, www.ashs.org

Membership: educators, government workers, firms, associations, and individuals interested in horticultural science. Promotes scientific research and education in horticulture, including international exchange of information.

American Society of Plant Biologists, *15501 Monona Dr., Rockville, MD 20855-2768; (301) 251-0560. Fax, (301) 279-2996. Crispin Taylor, Executive Director.*
General email, info@aspb.org
Web, www.aspb.org

Membership: plant physiologists, plant biochemists, and molecular biologists. Seeks to educate and promote public interest in the plant sciences. Publishes journals; provides job listings for members; sponsors awards, annual conference, meetings, courses, and seminars.

National Assn. of Plant Patent Owners, *1200 G St. N.W., #800 20005; (202) 789-2900. Fax, (202) 789-1893. Craig Regelbrugge, Administrator.*
Web, www.americanhort.org

Membership: owners of patents on newly propagated horticultural plants. Informs members of plant patents issued, provisions of patent laws, and changes in practice. Promotes the development, protection, production, and distribution of new varieties of horticultural plants. Works with international organizations of plant breeders on matters of common interest. (Affiliated with AmericanHort, formerly the American Nursery and Landscape Assn.)

Zoology

►AGENCIES

National Museum of Natural History *(Smithsonian Institution), Entomology, 10th St. and Constitution Ave. N.W. 20560-0105 (mailing address: P.O. Box 37012, MRC 187, #CE-723, Washington, DC 20013-7012); (202) 633-1033. Fax, (202) 786-3141. Sean G. Brady, Chair, (202) 633-0997. Library, (202) 633-1680.*
Web, http://entomology.si.edu

Conducts worldwide research in entomology. Maintains the national collection of insects; lends insect specimens to specialists for research and classification; conducts scholarly training and lectures; publishes research; and maintains databases. Library open to the public by appointment.

National Museum of Natural History *(Smithsonian Institution), Invertebrate Zoology, 10th St. and Constitution Ave. N.W. 20560-0163 (mailing address: P.O.*

Box 37012, MRC 163, Washington, DC 20013-7012); (202) 633-1740. Fax, (202) 633-0182. Jon Norenburg, Chair. Library, (202) 633-1680.
Web, http://invertebrates.si.edu

Conducts research on the identity, morphology, histology, life history, distribution, classification, and ecology of marine, terrestrial, and freshwater invertebrate animals (except insects); maintains the national collection of invertebrate animals; aids exhibit and educational programs; conducts pre- and postdoctoral fellowship programs; provides facilities for visiting scientists in the profession.

National Museum of Natural History *(Smithsonian Institution), Vertebrate Zoology, 10th St. and Constitution Ave. N.W. 20560-0159 (mailing address: P.O. Box 37012, MRC 163, Washington, DC 20013-7012); (202) 633-1740. Fax, (202) 633-0182. Richard P. Vari, Chair. Library, (202) 633-1680.*
General email, gravelya@si.edu
Web, http://vertebrates.si.edu

Conducts research worldwide on the systematics, ecology, evolution, zoogeography, and behavior of mammals, birds, reptiles, amphibians, and fish; maintains the national collection of specimens.

►NONGOVERNMENTAL

Assn. of Zoos and Aquariums, *8403 Colesville Rd., #710, Silver Spring, MD 20910-3314; (301) 562-0777. Fax, (301) 562-0888. Jim Maddy, President.*
General email, generalinquiry@aza.org
Web, www.aza.org

Membership: interested individuals and professionally run zoos and aquariums in North America. Administers professional accreditation program; participates in worldwide conservation, education, and research activities.

Entomological Society of America, *3 Park Pl., #307, Annapolis, MD 21401-3722; (301) 731-4535. Fax, (301) 731-4538. C. David Gammel, Executive Director.*
General email, esa@entsoc.org
Web, www.entsoc.org

Membership: entomology researchers, teachers, extension service personnel, administrators, marketing representatives, research technicians, consultants, students, and hobbyists. Sponsors symposia, conferences, journals, and continuing education seminars.

Jane Goodall Institute, *1595 Spring Hill Rd., #550, Vienna, VA 22182; (703) 682-9220. Fax, (703) 682-9312. Mary Humphrey, Chief Operating Officer.*
Web, www.janegoodall.org

Seeks to increase primate habitat conservation, expand noninvasive primate research, and promote activities that ensure the well-being of primates. (Affiliated with Jane Goodall Institutes in Canada, Europe, Asia, and Africa.)

ENGINEERING

General

►AGENCIES

National Institute of Standards and Technology (NIST) *(Commerce Dept.), Center for Nanoscale Science and Technology,* 100 Bureau Dr., MS 6200, Gaithersburg, MD 20899-6200; (301) 975-8001. Fax, (301) 975-8026. Robert J. Celotta, Director.
General email, cnst@nist.gov
Web, www.nist.gov/cnst/index.cfm

Provides nanoscale measurement and fabrication methods and access to nanoscale construction technologies to NIST labs, universities, and industries. Offers researchers training and use of in-house nanotechnology tools. Researches nanoscale measurement instruments and methods, and promotes collaboration and shared use.

National Institute of Standards and Technology (NIST) *(Commerce Dept.), Engineering Laboratory,* 100 Bureau Dr., MS 8600, Gaithersburg, MD 20899-8600; (301) 975-5900. Fax, (301) 975-4032. Howard H. Harary, Director, Acting.
General email, el@nist.gov
Web, www.nist.gov/el

Develops measurement techniques, test methods, and mathematical models to encourage energy conservation in large buildings. Interests include refrigeration, lighting, infiltration and ventilation, heating and air conditioning, indoor air quality, and heat transfer in the building envelope.

National Science Foundation (NSF), *Engineering,* 4201 Wilson Blvd., #505N, Arlington, VA 22230; (703) 292-8300. Fax, (703) 292-9013. Pramid Khargonekar, Assistant Director.
Web, www.nsf.gov/div/index.jsp?org=eng

Directorate that supports fundamental research and education in engineering through grants and special equipment awards. Programs are designed to enhance international competitiveness and to improve the quality of engineering in the United States.

►NONGOVERNMENTAL

American Assn. of Engineering Societies, 1801 Alexander Bell Dr., Reston, VA 20191; (202) 296-2237. Fax, (202) 296-1151. Wendy B. Cowan, Executive Director. Toll-free, (888) 400-2237.
Web, www.aaes.org

Federation of engineering societies; member associations are in industry, construction, government, academia, and private practice. Advances the knowledge, understanding, and practice of engineering. Serves as delegate to the World Federation of Engineering Organizations.

American Council of Engineering Companies, 1015 15th St. N.W., 8th Floor 20005-2605; (202) 347-7474. Fax, (202) 898-0068. David A. Raymond, President.
General email, acec@acec.org
Web, www.acec.org

Membership: practicing consulting engineering firms and state, local, and regional consulting engineers councils. Serves as an information clearinghouse for member companies in such areas as legislation, legal cases, marketing, management, professional liability, business practices, and insurance. Monitors legislation and regulations.

American Society for Engineering Education, 1818 N St. N.W., #600 20036-2479; (202) 331-3500. Fax, (202) 265-8504. Norman L. Fortenberry, Executive Director. Press, (202) 331-3537.
Web, www.asee.org

Membership: engineering faculty and administrators, professional engineers, government agencies, and engineering colleges, corporations, and professional societies. Conducts research, conferences, and workshops on engineering education. Monitors legislation and regulations.

American Society of Civil Engineers (ASCE), *Washington Office,* 1801 Alexander Bell Dr., Reston, VA 20191-4400; 101 Constitution Ave., #375E 20001; (202) 789-7850. Fax, (202) 789-7859. Patrick Natale, Executive Director. Toll-free, (800) 548-2723. Government Relations, (202) 789-7850. Press, (703) 295-6406.
Web, www.asce.org

Membership: professionals and students in civil engineering. Develops standards by consensus for construction documents and building codes, and standards for civil engineering education, licensure, and ethics. Organizes international conferences; maintains technical and professional reference materials; hosts e-learning sites. Advocates for improvements in public infrastructure; monitors legislation and regulations.

ASFE / The Geoprofessional Business Assn., 8811 Colesville Rd., #G106, Silver Spring, MD 20910; (301) 565-2733. Fax, (301) 589-2017. John P. Bachner, Executive Vice President; Kurt R. Fraese, President.
General email, info@asfe.org
Web, www.asfe.org

Membership: geoprofessional service firms, including firms that perform geotechnical and infrastructure engineering, environmental services, and construction materials engineering and testing. Conducts seminars and a peer review program on quality control policies and procedures in geoprofessional service firms. (Formerly the Assn. of Soil and Foundation Engineers.)

ASME (American Society of Mechanical Engineers), *Government Relations,* 1828 L St. N.W., #810 20036-5104; (202) 785-3756. Fax, (202) 429-9417. Kathryn Holmes, Director, Government Relations, (202) 785-7390.
General email, grdept@asme.org
Web, www.asme.org

Serves as a clearinghouse for sharing of information between the federal government and the engineering profession. Monitors legislation and regulations. (Headquarters in New York.)

Institute of Electrical and Electronics Engineers–USA (IEEE-USA), *Washington Office, 2001 L St. N.W., #700 20036; (202) 785-0017. Fax, (202) 785-0835. Chris Brantley, Managing Director. General email, ieeeusa@ieee.org*

Web, www.ieeeusa.org

U.S. arm of an international technological and professional organization concerned with all areas of electrotechnology policy, including aerospace, computers, communications, biomedicine, electric power, and consumer electronics. (Headquarters in New York.)

International Test and Evaluation Assn., *4400 Fair Lakes Court, #104, Fairfax, VA 22033-3801; (703) 631-6220. Fax, (703) 631-6221. James M. Gaidry, Executive Director, ext. 204. General email, info@itea.org*

Web, www.itea.org

Membership: engineers, scientists, managers, and other industry, government, and academic professionals interested in testing and evaluating products and complex systems. Provides a forum for information exchange; monitors international research.

National Academy of Engineering, *500 5th St. N.W. 20001; (202) 334-3200. Fax, (202) 334-2290. C. D. Mote Jr., President. Web, www.nae.edu*

Society whose members are elected in recognition of important contributions to the field of engineering and technology. Shares responsibility with the National Academy of Sciences for examining questions of science and technology at the request of the federal government; promotes international cooperation. (Affiliated with the National Academy of Sciences.)

National Society of Black Engineers, *205 Daingerfield Rd., Alexandria, VA 22314; (703) 549-2207. Fax, (703) 683-5312. Virginia Womack, Executive Director, Acting. General email, info@nsbe.org*

Web, www.nsbe.org

Membership: college students studying engineering. Offers academic excellence programs, scholarships, leadership training, and professional and career development opportunities. Activities include tutorial programs, group study sessions, high school/junior high outreach programs, technical seminars and workshops, career fairs, and an annual convention.

National Society of Professional Engineers (NSPE), *1420 King St., Alexandria, VA 22314-2794; (703) 684-2800. Fax, (703) 836-4875. Mark Golden, Executive Director. Member services, (888) 285-6773. General email, memserv@nspe.org*

Web, www.nspe.org

Membership: U.S.-licensed professional engineers from all disciplines. Holds engineering seminars; operates an information center.

ENVIRONMENTAL AND EARTH SCIENCES

General

▶**AGENCIES**

National Aeronautics and Space Administration (NASA), *Science Mission Directorate, 300 E St. S.W., #3C26 20546; (202) 358-3889. Fax, (202) 358-3092. John Grunsfeld, Associate Administrator. General email, science@hq.nasa.gov*

Web, http://science.nasa.gov/about-us/organization-and-leadership

Seeks to understand the integrated functioning of the earth and the sun. Administers space mission programs and mission-enabling programs, including suborbital missions. Sponsors scientific research and analysis. Exchanges information with the international science community. Interests include earth climate and environmental change.

National Oceanic and Atmospheric Administration (NOAA) *(Commerce Dept.), 1401 Constitution Ave. N.W., #5128 20230; (202) 482-3436. Fax, (202) 408-9674. Kathryn D. Sullivan, Under Secretary. Library, (301) 713-2600. Press, (202) 482-6090. Web, www.noaa.gov*

Conducts research in marine and atmospheric sciences; issues weather forecasts and warnings vital to public safety and the national economy; surveys resources of the sea; analyzes economic aspects of fisheries operations; develops and implements policies on international fisheries; provides states with grants to conserve coastal zone areas; protects marine mammals; maintains a national environmental center with data from satellite observations and other sources, including meteorological, oceanic, geodetic, and seismological data centers; provides colleges and universities with grants for research, education, and marine advisory services; prepares and provides nautical and aeronautical charts and maps.

National Oceanic and Atmospheric Administration (NOAA) *(Commerce Dept.), Central Library, Library and Information Services, 1315 East-West Hwy., SSMC3, 2nd Floor, Silver Spring, MD 20910; (301) 713-2600. Fax, (301) 713-4598. Neal Kaske, Director. Reference service, (301) 713-2600, ext. 157. General email, library.reference@noaa.gov*

Web, www.lib.noaa.gov

Collection includes electronic NOAA documents, reports, and videos; electronic and print journals; the NOAA Photo Library; bibliographic database of other NOAA libraries; and climate data. Makes interlibrary loans; library open to the public, with two forms of photo ID, Monday through Friday, from 9:00 a.m. to 4:00 p.m.

National Science Foundation (NSF), *Geosciences, 4201 Wilson Blvd., #705N, Arlington, VA 22230; (703) 292-8500. Fax, (703) 292-9042. Roger Wakimoto, Assistant Director. Web, www.nsf.gov/div/index.jsp?org=geo*

Directorate that supports research about the earth, including its atmosphere, continents, oceans, and interior. Works to improve the education and human resource base for the geosciences; participates in international and multidisciplinary activities, especially to study changes in the global climate.

National Science Foundation (NSF), *Polar Programs, 4201 Wilson Blvd., #755S, Arlington, VA 22230; (703) 292-8030. Fax, (703) 292-9081. Kelly K. Falkner, Director. Web, www.nsf.gov/div/index.jsp?div=plr*

Funds and manages U.S. activity in Antarctica; provides grants for arctic programs in polar biology and medicine, earth sciences, atmospheric sciences, meteorology, ocean sciences, and glaciology. The Polar Information Program serves as a clearinghouse for polar data and makes referrals on specific questions.

Smithsonian Environmental Research Center *(Smithsonian Institution), 647 Contees Wharf Rd., Edgewater, MD 21037 (mailing address: P.O. Box 28, Edgewater, MD 21037-0028); (443) 482-2200. Fax, (443) 482-2380. Anson H. Hines, Director. Press, (443) 482-2325. Web, www.serc.si.edu*

Performs laboratory and field research that measures physical, chemical, and biological interactions to determine the mechanisms of environmental responses to humans' use of air, land, and water. Evaluates properties of the environment that affect the functions of living organisms. Maintains research laboratories, public education program, facilities for controlled environments, and estuarine and terrestrial lands. Wildlife sanctuary open to the public Monday through Saturday, 9:00 a.m.–4:30 p.m except federal holidays.

United States Arctic Research Commission, *4350 N. Fairfax Dr., #510, Arlington, VA 22203; (703) 525-0111. Fax, (703) 525-0114. John W. Farrell, Executive Director, (703) 525-0113. General email, info@arctic.gov Web, www.arctic.gov*

Presidential advisory commission that develops policy for arctic research; assists the interagency Arctic Research Policy Committee in implementing a national plan of arctic research; recommends improvements in logistics, data management, and dissemination of arctic information.

U.S. Geological Survey (USGS) *(Interior Dept.), 12201 Sunrise Valley Dr., MS 100, Reston, VA 20192-0002; (703) 648-4000. Fax, (703) 648-4454. Suzette M. Kimball, Director, Acting, (703) 648-7412. Information, 888-ASK-USGS. Library, (703) 648-4301. Press, (703) 648-4460. General email, suzette_kimball@usgs.gov Web, www.usgs.gov*

Provides reports, maps, and databases that describe and analyze water, energy, biological, and mineral resources; the land surface; and the underlying geological structure and dynamic processes of the Earth.

U.S. Geological Survey (USGS) *(Interior Dept.), Climate and Land Use Change, 12201 Sunrise Valley Dr., MS 409, Reston, VA 20192; (703) 648-5215. Fax, (703) 648-7031. Matthew C. Larsen, Associate Director for Climate and Land Use Change. Web, www.usgs.gov/climate_landuse*

Researches the effects of climate and land use change on natural resources. Methods include monitoring, modeling, and forecasting. Operates the Landsat satellites. Provides coordination, technical support, and funding for existing research programs. Provides research products to policymakers, natural resources managers, and the general public.

U.S. Geological Survey (USGS) *(Interior Dept.), Library Services, 950 National Center, Reston, VA 20192 (mailing address: 12201 Sunrise Valley Dr., #1D100, MS 950, Reston, VA 20192); (703) 648-4301. Fax, (703) 648-6373. Lisa Adamo, Branch Manager, (703) 648-6207; Mike McDermott, Director, Interim, (703) 648-5771. General email, library@usgs.gov Web, http://library.usgs.gov*

Maintains collection of books, periodicals, serials, maps, and technical reports on geology, mineral and water resources, mineralogy, paleontology, petrology, soil and environmental sciences, biology, and physics and chemistry as they relate to natural sciences. Open to the public; makes interlibrary loans.

▶**CONGRESS**

For a listing of relevant congressional committees and subcommittees, please see pages 594–595 or the Appendix.

▶**NONGOVERNMENTAL**

American Geophysical Union, *2000 Florida Ave. N.W. 20009-1277; (202) 462-6900. Fax, (202) 328-0566. Christine McEntee, Executive Director; Carol A. Finn, President. Information, (800) 966-2481. General email, service@agu.org Web, www.agu.org*

Membership: scientists and technologists who study the environments and components of the earth, sun, and solar system. Promotes international cooperation; disseminates information.

Atmospheric Sciences

▶**AGENCIES**

National Science Foundation (NSF), *Atmospheric and GeoSpace Sciences, 4201 Wilson Blvd., #775S, Arlington, VA 22230; (703) 292-8520. Fax, (703) 292-9022. Michael C.*

Morgan, Division Director, (703) 292-2662.
Web, www.nsf.gov/div/index.jsp?div=ags

Supports research on the earth's atmosphere and the sun's effect on it, including studies of the physics, chemistry, and dynamics of the earth's upper and lower atmospheres and its space environment; climate processes and variations; and the natural global cycles of gases and particles in the earth's atmosphere.

National Weather Service *(National Oceanic and Atmospheric Administration), 1325 East-West Hwy., #18150, Silver Spring, MD 20910; (301) 713-9095. Fax, (301) 713-0610. Louis W. Uccellini, Assistant Administrator. Library, (301) 683-1307.*
Web, www.weather.gov

Issues warnings of hurricanes, severe storms, and floods; provides weather forecasts and services for the general public and for aviation and marine interests. National Weather Service forecast office, (703) 260-0107.

National Weather Service *(National Oceanic and Atmospheric Administration), Climate Prediction Center, 5830 University Research Court, College Park, MD 20740; (301) 683-3427. Mike Halpert, Deputy Director.*
Web, www.cpc.ncep.noaa.gov

Provides climate forecasts, assesses the impact of short-term climate variability, and warns of potentially extreme climate-related events.

National Weather Service *(National Oceanic and Atmospheric Administration), National Centers for Environmental Prediction, 5830 University Research Court, College Park, MD 20740; (301) 683-1315. Bill Lapenta, Director.*
Web, www.ncep.noaa.gov

The National Center for Environmental Prediction and the National Environmental Satellite, Data, and Information Service are part of the World Weather Watch Programme developed by the United Nations World Meteorological Organization. Collects and exchanges data with other nations; provides other national weather service offices, private meteorologists, and government agencies with products, including forecast guidance products.

▶ **NONGOVERNMENTAL**

Alliance for Responsible Atmospheric Policy, *2111 Wilson Blvd., #850, Arlington, VA 22201; (703) 243-0344. Fax, (703) 243-2874. Stephen Van Maren, Executive Director.*
General email, info@arap.org
Web, www.arap.org

Coalition of users and producers of chlorofluorocarbons (CFCs). Seeks further study of the ozone depletion theory.

Center for Climate and Energy Solutions, *2101 Wilson Blvd., #550, Arlington, VA 22201; (703) 516-4146. Fax, (703) 516-9551. Eileen Claussen, President.*
Web, www.c2es.org

Independent organization that issues information and promotes discussion by policymakers on the science, economics, and policy of climate change. (Formerly Pew Center on Global Climate Change.)

Climate Institute, *900 17th St. N.W., #700 20006; (202) 552-4723. Fax, (202) 737-6410. John C. Topping, President.*
General email, info@climate.org
Web, www.climate.org

Educates the public and policymakers on climate change (greenhouse effect, or global warming) and on the depletion of the ozone layer. Assesses climate change risks and develops strategies on mitigating climate change in developing countries and in North America.

Geology and Earth Sciences

▶ **AGENCIES**

National Museum of Natural History *(Smithsonian Institution), Mineral Sciences, 10th St. and Constitution Ave. N.W., 4th Floor, East Wing 20560 (mailing address: P.O. Box 37012, MRC 119, Washington, DC 20013-7012); (202) 633-1860. Fax, (202) 357-2476. Timothy McCoy, Chair. Library, (202) 633-1680.*
Web, www.mineralsciences.si.edu

Conducts research on gems, minerals, meteorites, rocks, and ores. Interests include mineralogy, petrology, volcanology, and geochemistry. Maintains the Global Volcanism Network, which reports worldwide volcanic and seismic activity. Library open to the public by appointment.

National Museum of Natural History *(Smithsonian Institution), Paleobiology, 10th St. and Constitution Ave. N.W. 20560-0121 (mailing address: P.O. Box 37012, MRC 121, Washington, DC 20013-7012); (202) 633-1312. Fax, (202) 786-2832. Brian Huber, Chair.*
General email, paleovisits@si.edu
Web, http://paleobiology.si.edu

Conducts research worldwide on invertebrate paleontology, paleobotany, sedimentology, and vertebrate paleontology; provides information on paleontology, paleoclimatology, paleoceanography, ecosystem dynamics, and processes of evolution and extinction. Maintains national collection of fossil organisms and sediment samples.

National Science Foundation (NSF), *Earth Sciences, 4201 Wilson Blvd., #785, Arlington, VA 22230; (703) 292-8550. Fax, (703) 292-9025. Paul Cutler, Division Director, Acting.*
Web, www.nsf.gov/div/index.jsp?div=ear

Provides grants for research in geology, geophysics, geochemistry, and related fields, including tectonics, hydrologic sciences, and continental dynamics.

U.S. Geological Survey (USGS) *(Interior Dept.), Earthquake Hazards, 12201 Sunrise Valley Dr., MS905, Reston, VA 20192 (mailing address: 905 National Center, Reston, VA 20192); (703) 648-6714. Fax, (703) 648-6717. William Leith, Senior Science Advisor.*
Web, http://earthquake.usgs.gov

Manages geologic, geophysical, and engineering investigations, including assessments of hazards from earthquakes; conducts research on the mechanisms and occurrences of earthquakes worldwide and their relationship to the behavior of the crust and upper mantle; develops methods for predicting the time, place, and magnitude of earthquakes; conducts engineering and geologic studies on ground failures.

U.S. Geological Survey (USGS) *(Interior Dept.),* *Geological Mapping, 12201 Sunrise Valley Dr., MS 908, Reston, VA 20192; (703) 648-6943. Fax, (703) 648-3937. Peter T. Lyttle, Program Coordinator.* *Web, http://ncgmp.usgs.gov*

Funds the production of geologic maps in the United States. Provides geologic mapping data from across North America to public and private organizations.

U.S. Geological Survey (USGS) *(Interior Dept.),* *Global Seismographic Network, 12201 Sunrise Valley Dr., MS 905, Reston, VA 20192; (703) 648-6786. Fax, (703) 648-6717. Cecily Wolfe, Advanced National Seismic System Coordinator.* *Web, http://earthquake.usgs.gov/monitoring/gsn*

Monitors and researches seismic activity globally through a network of seismological and geophysical sensors.

U.S. Geological Survey (USGS) *(Interior Dept.), Landslide Hazards, 12201 Sunrise Valley Dr., MS 908, Reston, VA 20192; (703) 648-6943. Fax, (703) 648-6937. Peter T. Lyttle, Program Coordinator. National Landslide Information Center, (800) 654-4966.* *Web, http://landslides.usgs.gov*

Researches the causes of ground failure. Produces scientific reports for specific communities on landslide hazards and mitigation strategies. Oversees the National Landslide Information Center (NLIC).

U.S. Geological Survey (USGS) *(Interior Dept.), Volcano Hazards, 12201 Sunrise Valley Dr., MS904, Reston, VA 20192 (mailing address: 904 National Center, Reston, VA 20192); (703) 648-6711. Fax, (703) 648-5483. Charles W. Mandeville, Program Coordinator.* *General email, vhpweb@usgs.gov* *Web, http://volcanoes.usgs.gov*

Manages geologic, geophysical, and engineering investigations, including assessments of hazards from volcanoes; conducts research worldwide on the mechanisms of volcanoes and on igneous and geothermal systems. Issues warnings of potential volcanic hazards.

▶**NONGOVERNMENTAL**

American Geosciences Institute, *4220 King St., Alexandria, VA 22302-1502; (703) 379-2480. Fax, (703) 379-7563. P. Patrick Leahy, Executive Director.* *General email, agi@agiweb.org* *Web, www.agiweb.org*

Membership: earth science societies and associations. Maintains a computerized database with worldwide information on geology, engineering and environmental geology, oceanography, and other geological fields (available to the public for a fee).

Oceanography

▶**AGENCIES**

National Museum of Natural History *(Smithsonian Institution), Botany, 10th St. and Constitution Ave. N.W. 20560-0166 (mailing address: P.O. Box 37012, MRC 166, Washington, DC 20013-7012); (202) 633-0920. Fax, (202) 786-2563. Warren L. Wagner, Chair. Library, (202) 633-2146.* *Web, www.botany.si.edu*

Investigates the biology, evolution, and classification of tropical and subtropical marine algae and seagrasses. Acts as curator of the national collection in this field. Develops and participates in scholarly programs. Library open to the public Monday through Friday, 10:00 a.m.–4:00 p.m., by appointment only.

National Museum of Natural History *(Smithsonian Institution), Invertebrate Zoology, 10th St. and Constitution Ave. N.W. 20560-0163 (mailing address: P.O. Box 37012, MRC 163, Washington, DC 20013-7012); (202) 633-1740. Fax, (202) 633-0182. Jon Norenburg, Chair. Library, (202) 633-1680.* *Web, http://invertebrates.si.edu*

Conducts research on the identity, morphology, histology, life history, distribution, classification, and ecology of marine, terrestrial, and freshwater invertebrate animals (except insects); maintains the national collection of invertebrate animals; aids exhibit and educational programs; conducts pre- and postdoctoral fellowship programs; provides facilities for visiting scientists in the profession.

National Museum of Natural History *(Smithsonian Institution), Library, 10th St. and Constitution Ave. N.W., East Court, 1st Floor 20560-0154 (mailing address: P.O. Box 37012, MRC 154, Washington, DC 20013-7012); (202) 633-1680. Gil Taylor, Head, (202) 633-1679.* *General email, askalibrarian@si.edu* *Web, www.sil.si.edu*

Maintains reference collections covering anthropology, biodiversity, biology, botany, ecology, entomology, ethnology, mineral sciences, paleobiology, and zoology; permits on-site use of the collections. Open to the public by appointment; makes interlibrary loans.

National Museum of Natural History *(Smithsonian Institution), Vertebrate Zoology, 10th St. and Constitution Ave. N.W. 20560-0159 (mailing address: P.O. Box 37012, MRC 163, Washington, DC 20013-7012); (202) 633-1740. Fax, (202) 633-0182. Richard P. Vari, Chair. Library, (202) 633-1680.* *General email, gravelya@si.edu* *Web, http://vertebrates.si.edu*

Processes, sorts, and distributes to scientists specimens of marine vertebrates; engages in taxonomic sorting, community analysis, and specimen and sample data management.

National Oceanic and Atmospheric Administration (NOAA) *(Commerce Dept.), Marine and Aviation Operations,* 8403 Colesville Rd., #500, Silver Spring, MD 20910-3282; (301) 713-1045. Fax, (301) 713-1541. Rear Adm. David A. Score, Director. Press, (301) 713-7671.
Web, www.omao.noaa.gov

Uniformed service of the Commerce Dept. that operates and manages NOAA's fleet of atmospheric, hydrographic, oceanographic, and fisheries research ships and aircraft. Supports NOAA's scientific programs.

National Oceanic and Atmospheric Administration (NOAA) *(Commerce Dept.), National Oceanographic Data Center,* 1315 East-West Hwy., SSMC3, 4th Floor, Silver Spring, MD 20910-3282; (301) 713-3277. Fax, (301) 713-3302. Margarita Gregg, Director, (301) 713-3270.
General email, nodc.services@noaa.gov
Web, www.nodc.noaa.gov

Offers a wide range of oceanographic data on the Web, on disk, and on CD-ROM; provides research scientists with data processing services; prepares statistical summaries and graphical data products. (Fee charged for some services.)

National Oceanic and Atmospheric Administration (NOAA) *(Commerce Dept.), National Ocean Service,* 1305 East-West Hwy., SSMC4, #13632, Silver Spring, MD 20910; (301) 713-3074. Fax, (301) 713-4269. Holly Ann Bamford, Assistant Administrator. Press, (301) 713-3066.
General email, nos.info@noaa.gov
Web, www.oceanservice.noaa.gov

Manages charting and geodetic services, oceanography and marine services, coastal resource coordination, and marine survey operations; conducts environmental cleanup of coastal pollution.

National Science Foundation (NSF), *Ocean Sciences,* 4201 Wilson Blvd., #725N, Arlington, VA 22230; (703) 292-8580. Fax, (703) 292-9085. Deborah Bronk, Director.
Web, www.nsf.gov/div/index.jsp?div=oce

Awards grants and contracts for acquiring, upgrading, and operating oceanographic research facilities that lend themselves to shared usage. Facilities supported include ships, submersibles, and shipboard and shorebased data logging and processing equipment. Supports development of new drilling techniques and systems.

U.S. Geological Survey (USGS) *(Interior Dept.), Coastal and Marine Geology Program,* 12201 Sunrise Valley Dr., Reston, VA 20192 (mailing address: USGS National Center, MS 915, Reston, VA 20192); (703) 648-6422. Fax, (703) 648-5464. John W. Haines, Program Coordinator.
Web, http://marine.usgs.gov

Surveys the continental margins and the ocean floor to provide information on the mineral resources potential of submerged lands.

► **NONGOVERNMENTAL**

Marine Technology Society, 1100 H St. N.W., #LL-100 20005; (202) 717-8705. Fax, (202) 347-4302. Richard Lawson, Executive Director.
General email, membership@mtsociety.org
Web, www.mtsociety.org

Membership: scientists, engineers, technologists, and others interested in marine science and technology. Provides information on marine science, technology, and education.

National Ocean Industries Assn., 1120 G St. N.W., #900 20005; (202) 347-6900. Fax, (202) 347-8650. Randall Luthi, President.
General email, noia@noia.org
Web, www.noia.org

Membership: manufacturers, producers, suppliers, and support and service companies involved in marine, offshore, and ocean work. Interests include offshore oil and gas supply and production, deep-sea mining, ocean thermal energy, and new energy sources.

MATHEMATICAL, COMPUTER, AND PHYSICAL SCIENCES

General

► **AGENCIES**

National Institute of Standards and Technology (NIST) *(Commerce Dept.),* 100 Bureau Dr., Bldg. 101, #A1134, Gaithersburg, MD 20899-1000 (mailing address: 100 Bureau Dr., MS 1000, Gaithersburg, MD 20899); (301) 975-2300. Fax, (301) 869-8972. Patrick Gallagher, Director.
General email, director@nist.gov
Web, www.nist.gov/director/index.cfm

Nonregulatory agency that serves as national reference and measurement laboratory for the physical and engineering sciences. Works with industry, government agencies, and academia; promotes U.S. innovation and industrial competitiveness. Research interests include advanced manufacturing, information technology and cybersecurity, energy, health care, environment and consumer safety, and physical infrastructure.

National Institute of Standards and Technology (NIST) *(Commerce Dept.), Information Technology Laboratory,* 100 Bureau Dr., Bldg. 225, #B264, MS 8900, Gaithersburg, MD 20899-8900; (301) 975-2900. Fax, (301) 975-2378. Charles H. (Chuck) Romine, Director.
Web, www.nist.gov/itl

Collaborates in mathematical, statistical, and computer sciences with other institute laboratories, other federal agencies, the U.S. private sector, standards development organizations, and other national and international stakeholders; provides consultations, methods, and research supporting the institute's scientific and engineering projects.

National Science Foundation (NSF), *Mathematical and Physical Sciences,* 4201 Wilson Blvd., #1005N, Arlington, VA 22230; (703) 292-8800. Fax, (703) 292-9151. F. Fleming Crim, Assistant Director.
Web, www.nsf.gov/div/index.jsp?org=mps

Directorate that supports research in the mathematical and physical sciences; divisions focus on physics, chemistry, materials research, mathematical sciences, and astronomical sciences. Works to improve the education and human resource base for these fields; participates in international and multidisciplinary activities.

▶**NONGOVERNMENTAL**

Carnegie Institution for Science of Washington,
1530 P St. N.W. 20005-1910; (202) 387-6400. Fax, (202) 387-8092. Richard A. Meserve, President, (202) 387-6404.
Web, www.carnegiescience.edu

Conducts research in plant biology, developmental biology, earth and planetary sciences, astronomy, and global ecology at the Carnegie Institution's six research departments: Dept. of Embryology (Baltimore, Md.); Geophysical Laboratory (Washington, D.C.); Dept. of Global Ecology (Stanford, Calif.); Dept. of Plant Biology (Stanford, Calif.); Dept. of Terrestrial Magnetism (Washington, D.C.); and The Observatories (Pasadena, Calif., and Las Campanas, Chile).

Chemistry

▶**AGENCIES**

National Institute of Standards and Technology (NIST)
(Commerce Dept.), *Center for Neutron Research,* 100 Bureau Dr., Bldg. 235, MS6100, Gaithersburg, MD 20899-8100; (301) 975-6210. Fax, (301) 869-4770. Robert Dimeo, Director.
General email, ncnr@nist.gov
Web, www.nist.gov/ncnr/index.cfm

Provides neutron measurement capabilities to the U.S. research community, universities, and industry.

National Science Foundation (NSF), *Chemistry,* 4201 Wilson Blvd., #1055, Arlington, VA 22230; (703) 292-8840. Fax, (703) 292-9037. Jacquelyn Gervay-Haque, Director, (703) 292-2665.
Web, www.nsf.gov/div/index.jsp?div=che

Awards grants to research programs in organic and macromolecular chemistry, experimental and theoretical physical chemistry, analytical and surface chemistry, and inorganic, bioinorganic, and organometallic chemistry; provides funds for instruments needed in chemistry research; coordinates interdisciplinary programs. Monitors international research.

National Science Foundation (NSF), *Materials Research,* 4201 Wilson Blvd., #1065N, Arlington, VA 22230; (703) 292-8810. Fax, (703) 292-9035. Mary Galvin, Director,

(703) 292-8562.
Web, www.nsf.gov/div/index.jsp?div=dmr

Provides grants for research in condensed matter physics; solid-state and materials, chemistry, polymers, metallic materials and nanostructures, ceramics, electronic and photonic materials and condensed matter and materials theory. Supports multidisciplinary research in these areas through Materials Research Science and Engineering Centers (MRSEC) and national facilities such as the National High Magnetic Field Laboratory (NHMFL) and Synchrotron Radiation Center (SRC); funds major instrumentation projects as well as the acquisition and development of instrumentation for research to create new or advance current capabilities; and encourages international collaboration to positively impact the global advancement of materials research.

▶**NONGOVERNMENTAL**

American Assn. for Clinical Chemistry, 1850 K St. N.W., #625 20006-2215; (202) 857-0717. Fax, (202) 887-5093. Janet Kreizman, Chief Executive Officer. Toll-free, (800) 892-1400.
General email, info@aacc.org
Web, www.aacc.org

International society of chemists, physicians, and other scientists specializing in clinical chemistry. Provides educational and professional development services; presents awards for outstanding achievement. Monitors legislation and regulations.

American Chemical Society, 1155 16th St. N.W. 20036; (202) 872-4600. Fax, (202) 872-4615. Madeleine Jacobs, Executive Director. Information, (800) 227-5558. Library, (202) 872-4513. Press, (202) 872-6042.
General email, help@acs.org
Web, www.acs.org

Membership: professional chemists and chemical engineers. Maintains educational programs, including those that evaluate college chemistry departments and high school chemistry curricula. Administers grants and fellowships for basic research; sponsors international exchanges; presents achievement awards. Library open to the public by appointment.

American Chemical Society, *Petroleum Research Fund,* 1155 16th St. N.W. 20036; (202) 872-4481. Fax, (202) 872-6319. Ronald E. Siatkowski, Director, Acting.
General email, prfinfo@acs.org
Web, www.acsprf.org

Makes grants to nonprofit institutions for advanced scientific education and fundamental research related to the petroleum industry in chemistry, geology, and engineering.

AOAC International, 481 N. Frederick Ave., #500, Gaithersburg, MD 20877-2417; (301) 924-7077. Fax, (301) 924-7089. E. James Bradford, Executive Director. Information, (800) 379-2622.

General email, aoac@aoac.org

Web, www.aoac.org

International association of analytical science professionals, companies, government agencies, nongovernmental organizations, and institutions. Promotes methods validation and quality measurements in the analytical sciences. Supports the development, testing, validation, and publication of reliable chemical and biological methods of analyzing foods, drugs, feed, fertilizers, pesticides, water, and other substances.

Society of Chemical Manufacturers and Affiliates (SOCMA), *1850 M St. N.W., #700 20036-5810; (202) 721-4100. Fax, (202) 296-8120. Lawrence D. (Larry) Sloan, President.*

General email, info@socma.com

Web, www.socma.com

Membership: companies that manufacture, distribute, and market organic chemicals; producers of chemical components; and providers of custom chemical services. Interests include international trade, environmental and occupational safety, chemical security, and health issues; conducts workshops and seminars. Promotes commercial opportunities for members. Monitors legislation and regulations. (Formerly Synthetic Organic Chemical Manufacturers.)

Society of the Plastics Industry (SPI), *1667 K St. N.W., #1000 20006; (202) 974-5200. Fax, (202) 296-7005. William R. (Bill) Carteaux, President.*

General email, feedback@plasticsindustry.org

Web, www.plasticsindustry.org

Promotes the plastics industry and its processes, raw materials suppliers, and machinery manufacturers. Monitors legislation and regulations.

Computer Sciences

►AGENCIES

National Coordination Office for Networking and Information Technology Research and Development, *4201 Wilson Blvd., Bldg. II-405, Arlington, VA 22230; (703) 292-4873. Fax, (703) 292-9097. George O. Strawn, Director.*

General email, nco@nitrd.gov

Web, www.nitrd.gov

Coordinates multiagency research and development projects that involve computing, communications, and technology research and development. Reports to the National Science and Technology Council; provides information to Congress, U.S. and foreign organizations, and the public.

National Institute of Standards and Technology (NIST) (Commerce Dept.), Information Technology Laboratory, *100 Bureau Dr., Bldg. 225, #B264, MS 8900, Gaithersburg, MD 20899-8900; (301) 975-2900. Fax, (301) 975-2378. Charles H. (Chuck) Romine, Director.*

Web, www.nist.gov/itl

Collaborates with other institute laboratories, other federal agencies, the U.S. private sector, standards development organizations, and other national and international stakeholders in the development and application of new information technologies to help meet national priorities; develops and deploys standards, tests, and metrics to assure secure, reliable, and interoperable information systems; collaborates to develop cybersecurity standards, guidelines, and techniques for federal agencies and U.S. industry; conducts research in computer science and technology.

National Science Foundation (NSF), *Advanced Cyberinfrastructure, 4201 Wilson Blvd., #1145S, Arlington, VA 22230; (703) 292-8970. Fax, (703) 292-9060. Irene Qualters, Director.*

Web, www.nsf.gov/div/index.jsp?div=aci

Supports the development of computing and information infrastructure and helps advance all science and engineering domains. Infrastructure is made accessible to researchers and educators nationwide.

National Science Foundation (NSF), *Computer and Information Science and Engineering (CISE), 4201 Wilson Blvd., #1105N, Arlington, VA 22230; (703) 292-8900. Fax, (703) 292-9074. Farnam Jahanian, Assistant Director.*

Web, www.nsf.gov/div/index.jsp?org=cise

Supports investigator-initiated research in computer science and engineering. Promotes the use of advanced computing, communications, and information systems. Provides grants for research and education.

National Science Foundation (NSF), *Computer and Network Systems, 4201 Wilson Blvd., #1175N, Arlington, VA 22230; (703) 292-8950. Fax, (703) 292-9010. Keith Marzullo, Director.*

Web, www.nsf.gov/div/index.jsp?div=CNS

Supports research and education activities that strive to create new computing and networking technologies and that explore new ways to utilize existing technologies. Seeks to foster the creation of better abstractions and tools for designing, building, analyzing, and measuring future systems. Supports the computing infrastructure that is required for experimental computer science and coordinates cross-divisional activities that foster integration of research and education and broadening of participation in the computer, information science, and engineering (CISE) workforce. Awards grants.

National Science Foundation (NSF), *Computing and Communication Foundations, 4201 Wilson Blvd., #1115N, Arlington, VA 22230; (703) 292-8910. Fax, (703) 292-9059. S. Rao Kosaraju, Division Director, (703) 292-7357.*

Web, www.nsf.gov/div/index.jsp?div=ccf

Supports research and educational activities exploring the foundations of computing and communication devices and their usage. Seeks advances in computing and communication theory, algorithms for computer and computational sciences, and architecture and design of computers and software. Awards grants.

National Science Foundation (NSF), *Information and Intelligent Systems,* 4201 Wilson Blvd., #1125S, Arlington, VA 22230; (703) 292-8930. Fax, (703) 292-9073. *Howard Wactlar, Director.*
Web, www.nsf.gov/div/index.jsp?div=iis

Supports research and education that develops new knowledge about the role people play in the design and use of information technology; advances the ability to represent, collect, store, organize, visualize, and communicate about data and information; and advances knowledge about how computational systems can perform tasks autonomously, robustly, and with flexibility. Awards grants.

▶ **NONGOVERNMENTAL**

American Council for Technology and Industry Advisory Council (ACT/IAC), 3040 Williams Dr., #500, Fairfax, VA 22031; (703) 208-4800. Fax, (703) 208-4805. *Kenneth Allen, Executive Director.*
General email, act-iac@actgov.org
Web, www.actgov.org

Brings government and industry IT executives together to enhance government's ability to use information technologies. Activities include conferences, white papers, professional development programs, and other events to foster education, the exchange of information, and collaboration.

Center for Strategic and International Studies, *Strategic Technologies Program,* 1616 Rhode Island Ave. N.W., 20036; (202) 775-3175. Fax, (202) 775-3199. *James A. Lewis, Director.*
General email, techpolicy@csis.org
Web, www.csis.org/program/technology-and-public-policy

Conducts and publishes research on emerging technologies, intelligence reform, and space and globalization programs.

Computer and Communications Industry Assn. (CCIA), 900 17th St. N.W., #1100 20006; (202) 783-0070. Fax, (202) 783-0534. *Edward J. Black, President; Heather Greenfield, Director of Communications.*
General email, hgreenfield@ccianet.org
Web, www.ccianet.org

Membership: Internet service providers, software providers, and manufacturers and suppliers of computer data processing and communications–related products and services. Interests include Internet freedom, privacy and neutrality, government electronic surveillance, telecommunications policy, tax policy, federal procurement policy, communications and computer industry standards, intellectual property policies, encryption, international trade, and antitrust reform.

Information Technology Industry Council (ITI), 1101 K St. N.W., #610 20005; (202) 737-8888. Fax, (202) 638-4922. *Dean C. Garfield, President. Press, (202) 626-5725.*
General email, info@itic.org
Web, www.itic.org

Membership: providers of information and communications technology products and services. Advocates for member companies in three main areas: environment and sustainability, global policy, and government relations. Interests include international tax reform, telecommunications, STEM education, trade, accessibility, voluntary standards, and sustainability.

Institute of Electrical and Electronics Engineers–USA (IEEE-USA), *Washington Office,* 2001 L St. N.W., #700 20036; (202) 785-0017. Fax, (202) 785-0835. *Chris Brantley, Managing Director.*
General email, ieeeusa@ieee.org
Web, www.ieeeusa.org

U.S. arm of an international technological and professional organization. Interests include computing and information technology and promoting career and technology policy interests of members. (Headquarters in New York.)

Software and Information Industry Assn. (SIIA), 1090 Vermont Ave. N.W., 6th Floor 20005; (202) 289-7442. Fax, (202) 289-7097. *Kenneth (Ken) Wasch, President, (202) 789-4440.*
Web, www.siia.net

Membership: software and digital content companies. Promotes the industry worldwide; conducts antipiracy program and other intellectual property initiatives; sponsors conferences, seminars, and other events. Monitors legislation and regulations.

TechAmerica, *Government Affairs Office,* 601 Pennsylvania Ave. N.W., North Bldg., #600 20004; (202) 682-9110. Fax, (202) 682-9111. *Shawn Osborne, President; Michael (Mike) Hettinger, Senior Vice President, Public Sector and Federal Government Affairs; Shawn Osborne, Chief Executive Officer. Press, (202) 682-4443.*
General email, csc@techamerica.org
Web, www.techamerica.org/government-affairs

Trade association for technology companies offering hardware, software, electronics, telecommunications, and information technology products and services. Offers business services and networking programs to members. Monitors legislation and regulations.

Mathematics

▶ **AGENCIES**

National Institute of Standards and Technology (NIST) *(Commerce Dept.), Information Technology Laboratory,* 100 Bureau Dr., Bldg. 225, #B264, MS 8900, Gaithersburg, MD 20899-8900; (301) 975-2900. Fax, (301) 975-2378. *Charles H. (Chuck) Romine, Director.*
Web, www.nist.gov/itl

Seeks to develop applied and computational mathematics to solve problems arising in measurement science and engineering applications; collaborates with NIST and external scientists; disseminates related reference data and software; develops and applies statistical and probabilistic methods and techniques supporting research in measurement science, technology, and the production of standard reference materials.

National Science Foundation (NSF), *Mathematical and Physical Sciences, 4201 Wilson Blvd., #1005N, Arlington, VA 22230; (703) 292-8800. Fax, (703) 292-9151. F. Fleming Crim, Assistant Director.*
Web, www.nsf.gov/div/index.jsp?org=mps

Provides grants for research in the mathematical sciences in the following areas: classical and modern analysis, geometric analysis, topology and foundations, algebra and number theory, applied and computational mathematics, and statistics and probability. Maintains special projects program, which supports scientific computing equipment for mathematics research and several research institutes. Sponsors conferences, workshops, and postdoctoral research fellowships. Monitors international research.

▶**NONGOVERNMENTAL**

American Statistical Assn., *732 N. Washington St., Alexandria, VA 22314-1943; (703) 684-1221. Fax, (703) 684-2037. Ronald Wasserstein, Executive Director. Toll-free, (888) 231-3473.*
General email, asainfo@amstat.org
Web, www.amstat.org

Membership: statistical practitioners in industry, government, and academia. Supports excellence in the development, application, and dissemination of statistical science through meetings, publications, membership services, education, accreditation, and advocacy.

Conference Board of the Mathematical Sciences, *1529 18th St. N.W. 20036; (202) 293-1170. Fax, (202) 293-3412. Ronald C. Rosier, Director.*
Web, www.cbmsweb.org

Membership: presidents of sixteen mathematical sciences professional societies. Serves as a forum for discussion of issues of concern to the mathematical sciences community.

Mathematical Assn. of America, *1529 18th St. N.W. 20036-1358; (202) 387-5200. Fax, (202) 265-2384. Michael Pearson, Executive Director. Information, (800) 741-9415.*
General email, maahq@maa.org
Web, www.maa.org

Membership: mathematics professors and individuals worldwide with a professional interest in mathematics. Seeks to improve the teaching of collegiate mathematics. Conducts professional development programs.

Physics

▶**AGENCIES**

National Science Foundation (NSF), *Materials Research, 4201 Wilson Blvd., #1065N, Arlington, VA 22230; (703) 292-8810. Fax, (703) 292-9035. Mary Galvin, Director,*

(703) 292-8562.
Web, www.nsf.gov/div/index.jsp?div=dmr

Provides grants for research in condensed matter physics; solid-state and materials, chemistry, polymers, metallic materials and nanostructures, ceramics, electronic and photonic materials and condensed matter and materials theory. Supports multidisciplinary research in these areas through Materials Research Science and Engineering Centers (MRSEC) and national facilities such as the National High Magnetic Field Laboratory (NHMFL) and Synchrotron Radiation Center (SRC); funds major instrumentation projects as well as the acquisition and development of instrumentation for research to create new or advance current capabilities; and encourages international collaboration to positively impact the global advancement of materials research.

National Science Foundation (NSF), *Physics, 4201 Wilson Blvd., #1015N, Arlington, VA 22230; (703) 292-8890. Fax, (703) 292-9078. Denise Caldwell, Director, (703) 292-7371.*
Web, www.nsf.gov/div/index.jsp?div=phy

Awards grants for research and special programs in atomic, molecular, and optical physics; elementary particle physics; and nuclear, theoretical, and gravitational physics.

Science *(Energy Dept.),* **High Energy Physics,** *19901 Germantown Rd., Germantown, MD 20874-1290 (mailing address: SC-25/Germantown Bldg., U.S. DOE, 1000 Independence Ave. S.W., Washington, DC 20585-1290); (301) 903-3624. Fax, (301) 903-2597. James L. Siegrist, Associate Director.*
Web, http://science.energy.gov/hep

Provides grants and facilities for research in high energy (or particle) physics. Constructs, operates, and maintains particle accelerators used in high energy research.

Science *(Energy Dept.),* **Nuclear Physics,** *19901 Germantown Rd., Germantown, MD 20874-1290 (mailing address: SC-26/Germantown Bldg., U.S. DOE, 1000 Independence Ave. S.W., Washington, DC 20585-1290); (301) 903-3613. Fax, (301) 903-3833. Timothy J. Hallman, Associate Director.*
General email, sc.np@science.doe.gov
Web, http://science.energy.gov/np

Provides grants and facilities for research in nuclear physics. Manages the nuclear data program. Develops, constructs, and operates accelerator facilities and detectors used in nuclear physics research.

▶**NONGOVERNMENTAL**

American Institute of Physics, *One Physics Ellipse, College Park, MD 20740-3843; (301) 209-3100. Fax, (301) 209-3133. H. Frederick Dylla, Executive Director.*
Web, www.aip.org

Fosters cooperation within the physics community; improves public understanding of science; disseminates information on scientific research.

American Institute of Physics, *Center for History of Physics,* One Physics Ellipse, College Park, MD 20740-3843; (301) 209-3100. Fax, (301) 209-0882. Joe Anderson, Director. Library, (301) 209-3177.
General email, chp@aip.org

Web, www.aip.org/history

Records and preserves the history of modern physics and allied fields, including astronomy, geophysics, and optics. Maintains a documentation program containing interviews, unpublished data, and historical records. Manages the Niels Bohr Library, which is open to the public.

American Physical Society, *Washington Office,* 529 14th St. N.W., #1050 20045-2065; (202) 662-8700. Fax, (202) 662-8711. Michael Lubell, Director, Public Affairs. Press Secretary, (202) 662-8702.
General email, opa@aps.org

Web, www.aps.org

Scientific and educational society of educators, students, citizens, and scientists, including industrial scientists. Sponsors studies on issues of public concern related to physics, such as reactor safety and energy use. Informs members of national and international developments. (Headquarters in College Park, Md.)

Optical Society, *2010 Massachusetts Ave. N.W. 20036;* (202) 223-8130. Fax, (202) 223-1096. Elizabeth Rogan, Chief Executive Officer.
General email, info@osa.org

Web, www.osa.org

Membership: global optics and photonic scientists, engineers, educators, students, technicians, business professionals, and others interested in optics and photonics worldwide. Promotes research and information exchange; conducts conferences; publishes a scientific journal; sponsors technical groups and programming, and outreach and educational activities.

Weights and Measures, Metric System

►AGENCIES

National Institute of Standards and Technology (NIST) *(Commerce Dept.), Material Measurement Laboratory,* 100 Bureau Dr., Bldg. 227, #A311, MS 8300, Gaithersburg, MD 20899-8300; (301) 975-8300. Fax, (301) 975-3845. Laurie E. Locasio, Director.
General email, mmlinfo@nist.gov

Web, www.nist.gov/mml

Serves as the national reference laboratory for measurements in the chemical, biological, and material sciences. Researches industrial, biological, and environmental materials and processes to support development in manufacturing, nanotechnology, electronics, energy, health care, law enforcement, food safety, and other areas. Disseminates reference measurement procedures, certified reference materials, and best-practice guides.

National Institute of Standards and Technology (NIST) *(Commerce Dept.), Physical Measurement Laboratory,* 100 Bureau Dr., Bldg. 221, #B160, MS8400, Gaithersburg, MD 20899-8400; (301) 975-4200. Fax, (301) 975-3038. Joseph L. Dehmer, Director.
Web, www.nist.gov/pml

National Institute of Standards and Technology (NIST) *(Commerce Dept.), Weights and Measures,* 100 Bureau Dr., MS 2600, Gaithersburg, MD 20899-2600; (301) 975-4004. Fax, (301) 975-8091. Carol Hockert, Chief.
General email, owm@nist.gov

Web, www.nist.gov/pml/wmd

Promotes uniformity in weights and measures law and enforcement. Provides weights and measures agencies with training and technical assistance; assists state and local agencies in adapting their weights and measures to meet national standards; conducts research; sets uniform standards and regulations. As the U.S. representative to the International Organization of Legal Metrology, works to harmonize international standards and regulatory practices.

National Institute of Standards and Technology (NIST) *(Commerce Dept.), Weights and Measures, Laws and Metric Group,* 100 Bureau Dr., MS 2600, Gaithersburg, MD 20899-2600; (301) 975-4004. Fax, (301) 975-8091. Kenneth S. Butcher, Group Leader.
General email, owm@nist.gov

Web, www.nist.gov/metric

Coordinates federal metric conversion transition to ensure consistency in the interpretation and enforcement of packaging, labeling, net content, and other laws; provides the public with technical and general information about the metric system; assists state and local governments, businesses, and educators with metric conversion activities.

►CONGRESS

For a listing of relevant congressional committees and subcommittees, please see pages 594–595 or the Appendix.

SOCIAL SCIENCES

General

►AGENCIES

National Institutes of Health (NIH) *(Health and Human Services Dept.), Behavioral and Social Sciences Research,* 31 Center Dr., Bldg. 31, #B1C19, Bethesda, MD 20892-0183; (301) 402-1146. Fax, (301) 402-1150. Robert M. Kaplan, Director.
Web, http://obssr.od.nih.gov

Works to advance behavioral and social sciences training, to integrate a biobehavioral perspective across the NIH, and to improve communication among scientists and with the public. Develops funding initiatives for research and training. Sets priorities for research. Provides training and career development opportunities for behavioral and social scientists. Links minority students with mentors. Organizes cultural workshops and lectures.

National Museum of Natural History *(Smithsonian Institution), Anthropology, 10th St. and Constitution Ave. N.W. 20560-0112 (mailing address: P.O. Box 37012, MRC 112, Washington, DC 20013-7012); (202) 633-1920. Fax, (202) 357-2208. Mary Jo Arnoldi, Chair. Library, (202) 633-1640. General Smithsonian Information, (202) 633-1000.*
Web, http://anthropology.si.edu

Studies humanity, past and present. Research tools include human-environmental interactions, population migrations, origins of domestication and agriculture, endangered languages and knowledge, and physical and forensic anthropology. Maintains archaeological, ethnographic, and skeletal biology collections; the National Anthropological Archive; the Human Studies Film Archives; and public exhibitions of human cultures.

National Museum of Natural History *(Smithsonian Institution), Library, 10th St. and Constitution Ave. N.W., East Court, 1st Floor 20560-0154 (mailing address: P.O. Box 37012, MRC 154, Washington, DC 20013-7012); (202) 633-1680. Gil Taylor, Head, (202) 633-1679.*
General email, askalibrarian@si.edu
Web, www.sil.si.edu

Maintains reference collections covering anthropology, biodiversity, biology, botany, ecology, entomology, ethnology, mineral sciences, paleobiology, and zoology; permits on-site use of the collections. Open to the public by appointment; makes interlibrary loans.

National Science Foundation (NSF), *Social, Behavioral, and Economic Sciences, 4201 Wilson Blvd., #905N, Arlington, VA 22230; (703) 292-8700. Fax, (703) 292-9083. Joanne S. Tornow, Assistant Director.*
Web, www.nsf.gov/dir/index.jsp?org=SBE

Directorate that awards grants for research in behavioral and cognitive sciences, social and economic sciences, science resources studies, and international programs. Provides support for workshops, symposia, and conferences.

▶ **NONGOVERNMENTAL**

American Anthropological Assn., *2200 Wilson Blvd., #600, Arlington, VA 22201; (703) 528-1902. Fax, (703) 528-3546. Edward Liebow, Executive Director.*
Web, www.aaanet.org

Membership: anthropologists, educators, students, and others interested in anthropological studies. Publishes research studies of member organizations, sponsors workshops, and disseminates to members information concerning developments in anthropology worldwide.

American Institutes for Research, *1000 Thomas Jefferson St. N.W. 20007; (202) 403-5000. Fax, (202) 403-5001. David Myers, President.*
General email, inquiry@air.org
Web, www.air.org

Conducts behavioral and social science research and provides technical assistance both domestically and internationally in the areas of education, health, and workforce productivity.

American Psychological Assn., *750 1st St. N.E. 20002-4242; (202) 336-5500. Fax, (202) 336-5502. Norman B. Anderson, Chief Executive Officer. Library, (202) 336-5640. Toll-free, (800) 374-2721.*
Web, www.apa.org

Membership: professional psychologists, educators, and behavioral research scientists. Supports research, training, and professional services; works toward improving the qualifications, competence, and training programs of psychologists. Monitors international research and U.S. legislation on mental health.

American Sociological Assn., *1430 K St. N.W., #600 20005; (202) 383-9005. Fax, (202) 638-0882. Sally T. Hillsman, Executive Officer.*
General email, executive.office@asanet.org
Web, www.asanet.org

Membership: sociologists, social scientists, and others interested in research, teaching, and application of sociology in the United States and internationally. Sponsors professional development program, teaching resources center, and education programs; offers congressional fellowships for sociologists with a PhD or substantial work experience, and predoctoral sociology fellowships for minorities.

Consortium of Social Science Assns., *1701 K St. N.W., #1150 20006; (202) 842-3525. Fax, (202) 842-2788. Wendy A. Naus, Executive Director.*
General email, cossa@cossa.org
Web, www.cossa.org

Consortium of more than 100 associations, scientific societies, universities, research centers, and institutions in the fields of criminology, economics, history, political science, psychology, sociology, statistics, geography, linguistics, law, and social science. Advocates support for research and monitors federal funding in the social and behavioral sciences; conducts seminars; publishes a biweekly electronic newsletter.

Human Resources Research Organization (HumRRO), *66 Canal Center Plaza, #700, Alexandria, VA 22314; (703) 549-3611. Fax, (703) 549-9025. William J. Strickland, President.*
Web, www.humrro.org

Studies, designs, develops, surveys, and evaluates personnel systems, chiefly in the workplace. Interests include personnel selection and promotion, career progression, performance appraisal, training, program evaluation, leadership assessment, and human capital analytics.

Institute for the Study of Man, *1133 13th St. N.W., #C2 20005-4297; (202) 371-2700. Fax, (202) 371-1523. Roger Pearson, Executive Director.*
General email, iejournal@aol.com
Web, www.jies.org

Publishes the *Journal of Indo-European Studies* and other academic journals, books, and monographs in areas related to Indo-European anthropology, archaeology, linguistics, cultural history, and mythology. Sponsors seminars.

Pew Research Center Social and Demographic Trends Project, *1615 L St. N.W., #700 20036; (202) 419-4374. Fax, (202) 419-4349. Kim Parker, Director of Social Trends Research. Media inquiries, (202) 419-4372.*
General email, info@socialtrends.org
Web, www.pewsocialtrends.org

Studies behaviors and attitudes of Americans in key realms of their daily lives, using original survey research and analysis of government data. Topics of study include the racial wealth gap, the millennial generation, population geography, demographics, immigration, and marriage and family needs.

Geography and Mapping

► **AGENCIES**

Census Bureau *(Commerce Dept.), Geography, 4600 Silver Hill Rd., #4H174, Suitland, MD 20746 (mailing address: Washington, DC 20233-7400); (301) 763-2131. Fax, (301) 763-4710. Timothy F. Trainor, Chief.*
Web, www.census.gov/geo

Manages the MAF TIGER system, a nationwide geographic and address database; prepares maps for use in conducting censuses and surveys and for showing their results geographically; determines names and current boundaries of legal geographic units; defines names and boundaries of selected statistical areas; develops geographic code schemes; maintains computer files of area measurements, geographic boundaries, and map features with address ranges.

National Archives and Records Administration (NARA), *Cartographic and Architectural Unit, 8601 Adelphi Rd., #3320, College Park, MD 20740-6001; (301) 837-3200. Fax, (301) 837-3622. Deborah Lelansky, Cartographic Supervisor, (301) 837-1911.*
General email, carto@nara.gov
Web, www.archives.gov/dc-metro/college-park/researcher-info.html#cartographic

Makes information available on federal government cartographic records, architectural drawings, and aerial mapping films; prepares descriptive guides and inventories of records. Research room open to the public. Records may be reproduced for a fee.

National Geospatial-Intelligence Agency *(Defense Dept.), 7500 Geoint Dr., Springfield, VA 22150-7500; 4600 Sangamore Rd., Bethesda, MD 20816-5003; (571) 557-5400. Fax, (571) 558-3169. Letitia A. Long, Director. Maps and imagery products, (800) 455-0899.*
General email, medialist@nga.mil
Web, www.nga.mil

Combat support agency that develops imagery and map-based intelligence in support of national defense objectives.

National Oceanic and Atmospheric Administration (NOAA) *(Commerce Dept.), National Geodetic Survey, 1315 East-West Hwy., SSMC-3, #9202, Silver Spring, MD 20910-3282; (301) 713-3242. Fax, (301) 713-4172. Juliana P. Blackwell, Director.*
Web, http://geodesy.noaa.gov

Develops and maintains the National Spatial Reference System, a national geodetic reference system that serves as a common reference for latitude, longitude, height, scale, orientation, and gravity measurements. Maps the nation's coastal zone and waterways; conducts research and development programs to improve the collection, distribution, and use of spatial data; coordinates the development and application of new surveying instrumentation and procedures.

State Dept., *Office of the Geographer and Global Issues, 2201 C St. N.W., #6722 20520; (202) 647-2021. Fax, (202) 647-0504. Lee R. Schwartz, Director.*
Web, www.state.gov

Advises the State Dept. and other federal agencies on geographic and cartographic matters. Furnishes technical and analytical research and advice in the field of geography.

U.S. Board on Geographic Names, *12201 Sunrise Valley Dr., MS523, Reston, VA 20192-0523 (mailing address: 523 National Center, Reston, VA 20192); (703) 648-4552. Fax, (703) 648-4549. Louis (Lou) Yost, Executive Secretary, U.S. Board on Geographic Names.*
General email, bgnexec@usgs.gov
Web, http://geonames.usgs.gov

Interagency organization established by Congress to standardize geographic names used by the U.S. government. Board members are representatives from the departments of Agriculture, Commerce, Defense, Homeland Security, Interior, and State; the Central Intelligence Agency; the Government Printing Office; the Library of Congress; and the U.S. Postal Service. Sets policy governing the use of both domestic and foreign geographic names as well as underseas feature names and Antarctic feature names. (Affiliated with the U.S. Geological Survey.)

U.S. Geological Survey (USGS) *(Interior Dept.), Geological Mapping, 12201 Sunrise Valley Dr., MS 908, Reston, VA 20192; (703) 648-6943. Fax, (703) 648-3937. Peter T. Lyttle, Program Coordinator.*
Web, http://ncgmp.usgs.gov

Funds the production of geologic maps in the United States. Provides geologic mapping data from across North America to public and private organizations.

U.S. Geological Survey (USGS) *(Interior Dept.),* **Landchange Science Program,** *12201 Sunrise Valley Dr., MS519, Reston, VA 20192 (mailing address: 519 National Center, Reston, VA 20192); (703) 648-4516. Fax, (703) 648-5542. Jonathan H. Smith, Program Coordinator. Web, http://gam.usgs.gov*

Collects, analyzes, and disseminates information about natural and human-induced changes to the Earth's surface to better understand the causes and consequences of land cover change. Develops methods and processes for the use of land-surface science in public policy.

U.S. Geological Survey (USGS) *(Interior Dept.),* **National Geospatial Program,** *12201 Sunrise Valley Dr., Reston, VA 20192 (mailing address: 511 National Center, Reston, VA 20192); (703) 648-5569. Fax, (703) 648-6821. Mark L. DeMulder, Chief. Web, www.usgs.gov/ngpo*

Plans and coordinates information dissemination activities.

▶ **CONGRESS**

For a listing of relevant congressional committees and subcommittees, please see pages 594–595 or the Appendix.

Library of Congress, *Geography and Map Division, Madison Bldg., 101 Independence Ave. S.E., #LMB01 20540; (202) 707-8530. Fax, (202) 707-8531. Ralph Ehrenberg, Chief. Reading room, (202) 707-6277. Web, www.loc.gov/rr/geogmap*

Maintains cartographic collection of maps, atlases, globes, and reference books. Reference service provided; reading room open to the public. Interlibrary loans available through the library's loan division; photocopies, when not limited by copyright or other restriction, available through the library's photoduplication service.

▶ **NONGOVERNMENTAL**

Assn. of American Geographers, *1710 16th St. N.W. 20009-3198; (202) 234-1450. Fax, (202) 234-2744. Douglas Richardson, Executive Director. General email, gaia@aag.org Web, www.aag.org*

Membership: educators, students, business executives, government employees, and scientists in the field of geography. Seeks to advance professional studies in geography and encourages the application of geographic research in education, government, and business.

National Geographic Maps, *1145 17th St. N.W. 20036-4688; (202) 775-6190. Fax, (202) 429-5704. Juan Valdés, Director, Editorial and Research. Toll-free and map orders, (800) 962-1643. Toll-free fax, (800) 626-8676. Web, www.natgeomaps.com*

Produces and sells to the public political, physical, and thematic maps, atlases, and globes. (Affiliated with the National Geographic Society.)

National Society of Professional Surveyors, *5119 Pegasus Ct., Suite Q, Frederick, MD 21704; (240) 439-4615. Fax, (240) 439-4952. Curtis W. Sumner, Executive Director. General email, info@nsps.org Web, www.nsps.us.com*

Membership: professionals working worldwide in surveying, cartography, geodesy, and geographic/land information systems (computerized mapping systems used in urban, regional, and environmental planning). Sponsors workshops and seminars for surveyors and mapping professionals; participates in accreditation of college and university surveying and related degree programs; grants scholarships; develops and administers certification programs for hydrographers and survey technicians. Monitors legislation and regulations.

SPACE SCIENCES

General

▶ **AGENCIES**

Air Force Dept. *(Defense Dept.),* **Space,** *1670 Air Force Pentagon, 4C855 20330-1640; (703) 693-5799. Fax, (703) 695-4028. Troy Menk, Under Secretary. Web, www.afspc.af.mil*

Manages the planning, programming, and acquisition of space systems for the Air Force and other military services.

Federal Aviation Administration (FAA) *(Transportation Dept.),* **Commercial Space Transportation,** *800 Independence Ave. S.W., #331, AST-1 20591; (202) 267-7793. Fax, (202) 267-5450. George Nield, Associate Administrator. Web, www.faa.gov/about/office_org/headquarters_offices/ast/about*

Promotes and facilitates the operation of commercial expendable space launch vehicles by the private sector; licenses and regulates these activities.

National Aeronautics and Space Administration (NASA), *300 E St. S.W. 20024-3210 (mailing address: 300 E St. S.W., Washington, DC 20546-0001); (202) 358-1010. Fax, (202) 358-2810. Charles F. Bolden Jr., Administrator. Information, (202) 358-0000. Library, (202) 358-0168. General email, public_inquiries@hq.nasa.gov Web, www.nasa.gov and Library, www.hq.nasa.gov/office/hqlibrary*

Develops, manages, and has oversight of the agency's programs and missions. Interacts with Congress and state officials and responds to national and international inquiries. Serves as the administrative office for the agency.

Library open to the public Monday through Friday, 7:30 a.m. –5:00 p.m.

National Aeronautics and Space Administration (NASA),
Aeronautics Research Mission Directorate, 300 E St. S.W., #6A70 20546 (mailing address: NASA Headquarters, Mail Code 6J39A, Washington, DC 20546); (202) 358-4600. Fax, (202) 358-2920. Jaiwon Shin, Associate Administrator.
Web, www.aeronautics.nasa.gov

Conducts research in aerodynamics, materials, structures, avionics, propulsion, high-performance computing, human factors, aviation safety, and space transportation in support of national space and aeronautical research and technology goals. Manages the following NASA research centers: Ames (Moffett Field, Calif.); Dryden (Edwards, Calif.); Langley (Hampton, Va.); and Glenn (Cleveland, Ohio).

National Aeronautics and Space Administration (NASA),
Chief Engineer, 300 E St. S.W., #6N19 20546; (202) 358-1823. Fax, (202) 358-3296. Ralph R. Roe Jr., Chief Engineer, (757) 864-2400.
Web, http://oce.nasa.gov

Serves as the agency's principal adviser on matters pertaining to the technical readiness and execution of programs and projects.

National Aeronautics and Space Administration (NASA),
Chief Health and Medical Officer, 300 E St. S.W. 20546; (202) 358-2390. Fax, (202) 358-3349. Dr. Richard S. Williams, Chief Health and Medical Officer.
Web, www.hq.nasa.gov/office/chmo

Ensures the health and safety of NASA employees in space and on the ground. Develops health and medical policy, establishes guidelines for health and medical practices, oversees health care delivery, and monitors human and animal research standards within the agency.

National Aeronautics and Space Administration (NASA),
Education, 300 E St. S.W., #5G15 20546; (202) 358-0103. Fax, (202) 358-7097. Roosevelt Johnson, Associate Administrator, Acting.
General email, education@nasa.gov
Web, http://education.nasa.gov

Coordinates NASA's education programs and activities to meet national educational needs and ensure a sufficient talent pool to preserve U.S. leadership in aeronautical technology and space science.

National Aeronautics and Space Administration (NASA),
Goddard Space Flight Center, 8800 Greenbelt Rd., Code 100, Greenbelt, MD 20771; (301) 286-5121. Fax, (301) 286-1714. Christopher J. Scolese, Director. Information, (301) 286-2000. Visitor Center, (301) 286-8981.
Web, www.nasa.gov/centers/goddard

Conducts space and earth science research; develops and operates flight missions; maintains spaceflight tracking and data acquisition networks; develops technology and instruments; develops and maintains advanced information systems for the display, analysis, archiving, and distribution of space and earth science data; and

develops National Oceanic and Atmospheric Administration (NOAA) satellite systems that provide environmental data for forecasting and research.

National Aeronautics and Space Administration (NASA),
Heliophysics Science Division, Goddard Space Flight Center, Code 670, Greenbelt, MD 20771; (301) 286-6418. Fax, (301) 286-5348. Michael Hesse, Director.
Web, http://hsd.gsfc.nasa.gov

Provides scientific expertise necessary to achieve NASA's strategic science goals in solar physics, heliospheric physics, geospace physics, and space weather. Houses the Solar Physics Laboratory, the Heliospheric Physics Laboratory, the Geospace Physics Laboratory, and the Space Weather Laboratory.

National Aeronautics and Space Administration (NASA),
Human Exploration and Operations Directorate, 300 E St. S.W., #7K39 20546 (mailing address: NASA Headquarters, #7L18, Washington, DC 20546); (202) 358-2015. Fax, (202) 358-2838. William H. Gerstenmaier, Associate Administrator. Information, (202) 358-0000.
Web, www.nasa.gov/directorates/heo

Responsible for space operations related to human and robotic exploration, including launch, transport, and communications. Manages the International Space Station, commercial space transportation, and research and development in space life sciences.

National Aeronautics and Space Administration (NASA),
NASA Advisory Council, 300 E St. S.W., #2V79 20546; (202) 358-4510. Fax, (202) 358-3030. Steven W. Squyres, Chair; P. Diane Rausch, Executive Director.
Web, www.nasa.gov/offices/nac

Advises the administrator on programs and issues of importance to NASA. The council consists of nine committees: Aeronautics; Audit, Finance, and Analysis; Commercial Space; Education and Public Outreach; Exploration; Information Technology Infrastructure; Science; Space Operations; and Technology and Innovation.

National Aeronautics and Space Administration (NASA),
National Space Science Data Center, Goddard Space Flight Center, Code 690.1, Greenbelt, MD 20771; (301) 286-6695. Fax, (301) 286-1635. Edwin Grayzeck, Head.
General email, nssdc-request@lists.nasa.gov
Web, http://nssdc.gsfc.nasa.gov

Permanent archive for NASA space science mission data. Acquires, catalogs, and distributes NASA mission data to the international space science community, including research organizations and scientists, universities, and other interested organizations worldwide. Teams with NASA's discipline-specific space science "active archives," which provide researchers and, in some cases, the general public with access to data. Provides software tools and network access, including online information databases about NASA and non-NASA data, to promote collaborative data analysis. (Mail data requests to above address, attention: NSSDC Code 690.1/Request Coordination Office.)

National Aeronautics and Space Administration (NASA), *Protective Services, 300 E St. S.W., #6T39 20546; (202) 358-2010. Fax, (202) 358-3238. Joseph Mahaley, Assistant Administrator; Charles Lombard, Deputy Assistant Administrator.*

Web, www.hq.nasa.gov/office/ospp

Serves as the focal point for policy formulation, oversight, coordination, and management of NASA's security, counterintelligence, counterterrorism, emergency preparedness and response, and continuity of operations programs.

National Aeronautics and Space Administration (NASA), *Safety and Mission Assurance, 300 E St. S.W., #5A42 20546; (202) 358-2406. Fax, (202) 358-2699. Terrence W. Wilcutt, Chief.*

Web, www.hq.nasa.gov/office/codeq

Evaluates the safety and reliability of NASA systems and programs. Alerts officials to technical execution and physical readiness of NASA projects.

National Aeronautics and Space Administration (NASA), *Science Mission Directorate, 300 E St. S.W., #3C26 20546; (202) 358-3889. Fax, (202) 358-3092. John Grunsfeld, Associate Administrator.*

General email, science@hq.nasa.gov

Web, http://science.nasa.gov/about-us/organization-and-leadership

Seeks to understand the origins, evolution, and structure of the solar system and the universe; to understand the integrated functioning of the earth and the sun; and to ascertain the potential for life elsewhere. Administers space mission programs and mission-enabling programs, including suborbital missions. Sponsors scientific research and analysis.

National Aeronautics and Space Administration (NASA), *Sciences and Exploration Directorate, Goddard Space Flight Center, 8800 Greenbelt Rd., Code 600, Greenbelt, MD 20771; (301) 286-6066. Fax, (301) 286-1772. Colleen Hartman, Director, Acting.*

Web, http://science.gsfc.nasa.gov

Plans, organizes, implements, and evaluates a broad system of theoretical and experimental scientific research in the study of the earth-sun system, the solar system and the origins of life, and the birth and evolution of the universe. Activities include modeling and basic research, flight experiment development, and data analysis.

National Aeronautics and Space Administration (NASA), *Solar System Exploration Data Services, Goddard Space Flight Center, Code 690.1, Greenbelt, MD 20771; (301) 286-1743. Fax, (301) 286-1635. Thomas (Tom) Morgan, Program Manager, Planetary Data System.*

General email, request@nssdc.gsfc.nasa.gov

Web, http://ssedso.gsfc.nasa.gov

Coordinates data management and archiving plans within NASA's Science Mission. Operates the National Space Science Data Center (NSSDC) as a permanent archive for data associated with NASA's missions; the Crustal

Dynamics Data Information System (CDDIS); and the Planetary Data System (PDS).

National Air and Space Museum *(Smithsonian Institution), 6th St. and Independence Ave. S.W. 20560; (202) 633-2214. Fax, (202) 633-8174. Gen. J. R. (Jack) Dailey, Director. Library, (202) 633-2320. Education office, (202) 633-2540. Tours, (202) 633-2563.*

General email, info@si.edu

Web, www.airandspace.si.edu

Collects, preserves, and exhibits astronautical objects and equipment of historical interest, including aircraft, spacecraft, and communications and weather satellites. Library open to the public by appointment.

National Oceanic and Atmospheric Administration (NOAA) *(Commerce Dept.), Space Commercialization, 1401 Constitution Ave. N.W., #2518 20230; (202) 482-6125. Fax, (202) 482-4429. Mark Paese, Director, Acting.*

General email, space.commerce@noaa.gov

Web, www.space.commerce.gov

The principal unit for space commerce within NOAA and the Commerce Dept. Promotes economic growth and technological advancement of U.S. commercial space industry focusing on sectors including satellite navigation, satellite imagery, space transportation, and entrepreneurial space business. Participates in discussions of national space policy.

Steven F. Udvar-Hazy Center *(Smithsonian Institution), National Air and Space Museum, 14390 Air and Space Museum Pkwy., Chantilly, VA 20151; (703) 572-4118. Gen. John R. Dailey (USMC, Ret.), Director. Public Affairs, (703) 572-4040.*

General email, nasm-visitorservices@si.edu

Web, www.airandspace.si.edu/visit/udvar-hazy-center

Displays and preserves a collection of historical aviation and space artifacts, including the B-29 Superfortress, *Enola Gay*, the Lockheed SR-71 Blackbird, the prototype of the Boeing 707, the space shuttle *Discovery*, and the Concord. Provides a center for research into the history, science, and technology of aviation and space flight. Open to the public daily 10:00 a.m.–5:30 p.m., except December 25.

►CONGRESS

For a listing of relevant congressional committees and subcommittees, please see pages 594–595 or the Appendix.

►INTERNATIONAL ORGANIZATIONS

European Space Agency (ESA), *Washington Office, 955 L'Enfant Plaza S.W., #7800 20024; (202) 488-4158. Fax, (202) 488-4930. Micheline Tabache, Head.*

Web, www.esa.int

Intergovernmental agency that promotes international collaboration in space research and development and the use of space technology for peaceful purposes. Members include Austria, Belgium, Czech Republic, Denmark, Finland, France, Germany, Greece, Ireland, Italy, Luxembourg,

National Aeronautics and Space Administration

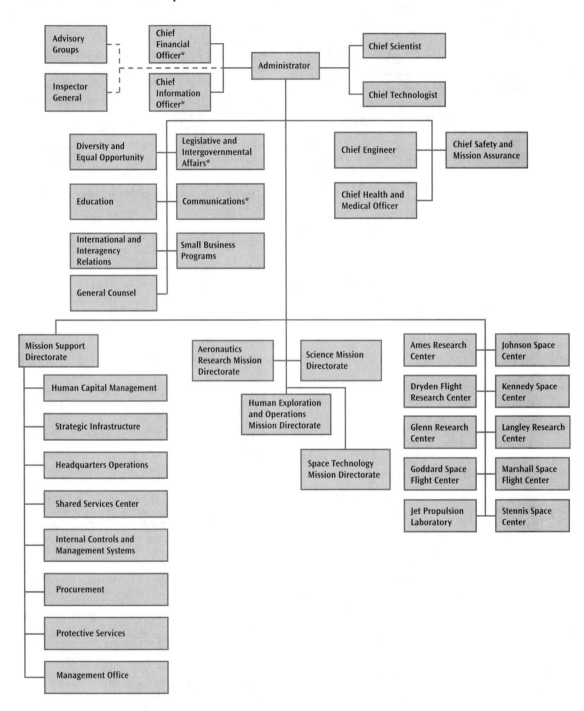

* Center functional office directors report to Agency Associate Administrator. Deputy and below report to center leadership.

– – – – Operate Independently

the Netherlands, Norway, Poland, Portugal, Romania, Spain, Sweden, Switzerland, and the United Kingdom; Canada participates in some programs; Hungary, Estonia, Latvia, and Slovenia are European Cooperating States. (Headquarters in Paris.)

▶ **NONGOVERNMENTAL**

Aerospace Industries Assn. (AIA), *1000 Wilson Blvd., #1700, Arlington, VA 22209-3928; (703) 358-1009. Fax, (703) 358-1012. Marion C. Blakey, President. Press, (703) 358-1076.*
General email, aia@aia-aerospace.org
Web, www.aia-aerospace.org

Represents manufacturers of commercial, military, and business aircraft; helicopters; aircraft engines; missiles; spacecraft; and related components and equipment. Interests include international standards and trade.

American Astronautical Society, *6352 Rolling Mill Pl., #102, Springfield, VA 22152-2370; (703) 866-0020. Fax, (703) 866-3526. James R. Kirkpatrick, Executive Director.*
General email, aas@astronautical.org
Web, www.astronautical.org

Scientific and technological society of researchers, scientists, astronauts, and other professionals in the field of astronautics and spaceflight engineering. Organizes national and local meetings and symposia; promotes international cooperation.

American Institute of Aeronautics and Astronautics (AIAA), *1801 Alexander Bell Dr., #500, Reston, VA 20191-4344; (703) 264-7500. Fax, (703) 264-7551. Sandy Magnus, Executive Director. Information, (800) 639-2422.*
General email, custserv@aiaa.org
Web, www.aiaa.org

Membership: engineers, scientists, and students in the fields of aeronautics and astronautics. Holds workshops on aerospace technical issues for congressional subcommittees; sponsors international conferences. Offers computerized database through its Technical Information Service.

National Research Council (NRC), *Aeronautics and Space Engineering Board, 500 5th St. N.W., Keck W932, 9th Floor 20001; (202) 334-2858. Fax, (202) 334-2482. Michael Moloney, Director.*
General email, aseb@nas.edu
Web, www.nationalacademies.org/aseb

Membership: aeronautics and space experts. Advises government agencies on aeronautics and space engineering research, technology, experiments, international programs, and policy. Library open to the public by appointment.

National Research Council (NRC), *Space Studies Board, Keck Center, 500 5th St. N.W., 9th Floor 20001; (202) 334-3477. Fax, (202) 334-3701. Michael Moloney, Director; Charles F. Kennel, Chair.*
General email, ssb@nas.edu
Web, www.nationalacademies.org/ssb

Provides advice to the government on space policy issues and issues concerning space science activities, including space-based astrophysics, heliophysics, solar system exploration, earth science, and microgravity life and physical sciences. Produces discipline-based "Decadal Surveys," which set priorities for government investments over ten-year time periods.

National Space Society, *1155 15th St. N.W., #500 20005; (202) 429-1600. Fax, (202) 530-0659. Paul Werbos, Executive Vice President; Dale Skran, Deputy Chair, National Space Society Policy Committee.*
General email, nsshq@nss.org
Web, www.nss.org

Membership: individuals interested in space programs and applications of space technology. Provides information on NASA, commercial space activities, and international cooperation; promotes public education on space exploration and development; conducts conferences and workshops; publishes quarterly magazine. Monitors legislation and regulations.

Resources for the Future, *1616 P St. N.W. 20036-1400; (202) 328-5000. Fax, (202) 939-3460. Philip R. Sharp, President, (202) 328-5077. Library, (202) 328-5089. Press, (202) 328-5019.*
General email, info@rff.org
Web, www.rff.org

Examines the economic aspects of U.S. space policy, including policy on the space shuttle, unmanned rockets, communications satellites, and the space station. Focuses on the role of private business versus that of government.

Space Policy Institute *(George Washington University), (Elliott School of International Affairs), 1957 E St. N.W., #403 20052; (202) 994-7292. Fax, (202) 994-1639. Scott Pace, Director.*
General email, spi@gwu.edu
Web, www.gwu.edu/~spi

Conducts research on space policy issues; organizes seminars, symposia, and conferences. Focuses on civilian space activities, including competitive and cooperative interactions on space between the United States and other countries.

Astronomy

▶ **AGENCIES**

National Aeronautics and Space Administration (NASA), *Science Mission Directorate, 300 E St. S.W., #3C26 20546; (202) 358-3889. Fax, (202) 358-3092. John Grunsfeld, Associate Administrator.*
General email, science@hq.nasa.gov
Web, http://science.nasa.gov/about-us/organization-and-leadership

Seeks to understand the origins, evolution, and structure of the solar system and the universe; to understand the integrated functioning of the earth and the sun; and to ascertain the potential for life elsewhere. Administers space mission programs and mission-enabling programs, including suborbital missions. Sponsors scientific research and analysis.

National Science Foundation (NSF), *Astronomical Sciences, 4201 Wilson Blvd., #1045S, Arlington, VA 22230; (703) 292-8820. Fax, (703) 292-9034. James S. Ulvestad, Division Director.*
Web, www.nsf.gov/div/index.jsp?div=ast

Provides grants for ground-based astronomy and astronomical research on planetary astronomy, stellar astronomy and astrophysics, galactic astronomy, extragalactic astronomy and cosmology, and advanced technologies and instrumentation. Maintains astronomical facilities; participates in international projects.

U.S. Naval Observatory *(Defense Dept.), 3450 Massachusetts Ave. N.W. 20392-5420; (202) 762-1467. Fax, (202) 762-1489. Capt. Brian Connon, Superintendent. Public Affairs, (202) 762-1438.*
General email, USNO_PAO@navy.mil
Web, www.usno.navy.mil/USNO

Determines the precise positions and motions of celestial bodies. Operates the U.S. master clock. Provides the U.S. Navy and Defense Dept. with astronomical and timing data for navigation, precise positioning, and command, control, and communications. Maintains a library, with the catalog available on the web site.

▶**NONGOVERNMENTAL**

American Astronomical Society, *2000 Florida Ave. N.W., #300 20009-1231; (202) 328-2010. Fax, (202) 234-2560. Joel Parriott, Director, Public Policy.*
General email, aas@aas.org
Web, www.aas.org

Membership: astronomers and other professionals interested in the advancement of astronomy in North America and worldwide. Publishes technical journals; holds scientific meetings; participates in international organizations; awards prizes for outstanding scientific achievements.

American Geophysical Union, *2000 Florida Ave. N.W. 20009-1277; (202) 462-6900. Fax, (202) 328-0566. Christine McEntee, Executive Director; Carol A. Finn, President. Information, (800) 966-2481.*
General email, service@agu.org
Web, www.agu.org

Membership: scientists and technologists who study the environments and components of the earth, sun, and solar system. Promotes international cooperation; disseminates information.

Assn. of Universities for Research in Astronomy (AURA), *1212 New York Ave. N.W., #450 20005; (202) 483-2101. Fax, (202) 483-2106. William S. Smith, President.*
Web, www.aura-astronomy.org

Consortium of universities. Manages three ground-based observatories and the international Gemini Project for the National Science Foundation and manages the Space Telescope Science Institute for the National Aeronautics and Space Administration.

17 ⚖

Social Services and Disabilities

GENERAL POLICY AND ANALYSIS

Basic Resources

►AGENCIES

Administration for Children and Families (ACF) *(Health and Human Services Dept.)*, 901 D St. S.W., #600 20447 *(mailing address: 370 L'Enfant Promenade S.W., Washington, DC 20447); (202) 401-2337. Fax, (202) 401-4678. Mark Greenberg, Assistant Secretary, Acting. Public Affairs, (202) 401-9215.*
Web, www.acf.hhs.gov

Administers and funds programs for Native Americans, low-income families and individuals, and persons with disabilities. Responsible for Social Services Block Grants to the states; coordinates Health and Human Services Dept. policy and regulations on child protection, day care, foster care, adoption services, child abuse and neglect, and special services for those with disabilities. Administers the Head Start program and funds the National Runaway Switchboard, (800) 621-4000, and the Domestic Violence Hotline, (800) 799-7233; TTY, (800) 787-3224.

Administration for Children and Families (ACF) *(Health and Human Services Dept.)*, *Office of Community Services, 370 L'Enfant Promenade S.W., 5th Floor 20447; (202) 401-9333. Fax, (202) 401-4694. Jeannie Chaffin, Director.*
Web, www.acf.hhs.gov

Administers the Community Services Block Grant and Discretionary Grant programs and the Low-Income Home Energy Assistance Block Grant Program for heating, cooling, and weatherizing low-income households.

Administration for Community Living (ACL) *(Health and Human Services Dept.)*, 1 Massachusetts Ave. N.W. 20001; (202) 401-4541. Kathy Greenlee, Administrator. Information, (202) 619-0724.*
General email, info@acl.hhs.gov
Web, www.acl.gov

Oversees programs that provide assistance to older adults, persons with disabilities, and family caregivers. Represents and advocates for individuals with disabilities and older adults throughout the federal government, seeking to ensure that these individuals are as involved as appropriate in the development and implementation of policies, programs, and regulations related to community living.

Administration for Native Americans *(Health and Human Services Dept.)*, 370 L'Enfant Promenade S.W., 2nd Floor, West Aerospace Center 20447-0002; (202) 690-7776. Fax, (202) 690-7441. Lillian A. Sparks, Commissioner. Toll-free, (877) 922-9262.*
General email, ana@acf.hhs.gov
Web, www.acf.hhs.gov/programs/ana

Awards grants for locally determined social and economic development strategies; promotes Native American economic and social self-sufficiency; funds tribes and Native American and Native Hawaiian organizations. Commissioner chairs the Intradepartmental Council on Indian Affairs, which coordinates Native American–related programs.

AmeriCorps *(Corporation for National and Community Service), Volunteers in Service to America (VISTA)*, 1201 New York Ave. N.W. 20525; (202) 606-5000. Fax, (202) 565-2789. Mary Strasser, Director, (202) 606-6943. Volunteer recruiting information, (800) 942-2677. TTY, (800) 833-3722.*
General email, questions@americorps.gov
Web, www.americorps.gov/programs/americorps/americorps-vista

Assigns full-time volunteers to public and private nonprofit organizations for one year to alleviate poverty in local communities. Volunteers receive a living allowance, health care, and other benefits and their choice of a postservice stipend or education award.

Bureau of Indian Affairs (BIA) *(Interior Dept.), Indian Services*, 1849 C St. N.W., MS 4513-MIB 20240; (202) 513-7640. Fax, (202) 208-5113. Hankie Ortiz, Deputy Bureau Director. Public Affairs, (202) 208-3710.*
Web, www.bia.gov/WhoWeAre/bia.ois/index.htm

Gives assistance, in accordance with state payment standards, to American Indians and Alaska Natives of federally recognized tribes living on or near reservations and in tribal service areas, and provides family and individual counseling and child welfare services. Assists tribal and Indian landowners with managing natural and energy trust resources; builds and maintains housing, transportation, energy, and irrigation infrastructure; and provides law enforcement protection, corrections, and administration of justice services on federal Indian lands.

Corporation for National and Community Service, 1201 New York Ave. N.W. 20525; (202) 606-5000. Fax, (202) 606-3460. Wendy M. Spencer, Chief Executive Officer, (202) 606-5000, ext. 6735. Press, (202) 606-6944. Volunteer recruiting information, (800) 942-2677.*
General email, info@cns.gov
Web, www.nationalservice.gov

Independent corporation that administers federally sponsored domestic volunteer programs that provide disadvantaged citizens with services, including AmeriCorps, AmeriCorps-VISTA (Volunteers in Service to America), AmeriCorps-NCCC (National Civilian Community Corps), Learn and Serve America, and the National Senior Service Corps.

Food and Nutrition Service *(Agriculture Dept.)*, 3101 Park Center Dr., #906, Alexandria, VA 22302-1500; (703) 305-2060. Fax, (703) 305-2908. Audrey Rowe, Administrator. Information, (703) 305-2286.*
Web, www.fns.usda.gov

Administers all Agriculture Dept. domestic food assistance, including the distribution of funds and food for school breakfast and lunch programs (preschool through secondary) to public and nonprofit private schools; the

SOCIAL SERVICES AND DISABILITIES RESOURCES IN CONGRESS

For a complete listing of Congress committees, including their full contact information, leadership, membership, and jurisdictions, please refer to the Appendix on pages 724–842.

HOUSE:

House Agriculture Committee, (202) 225-2171.
Web, agriculture.house.gov or
democrats.agriculture.house.gov
  Subcommittee on Department Operations,
    Oversight, and Nutrition, (202) 225-2171.
House Appropriations Committee, (202) 225-2771.
Web, appropriations.house.gov or
democrats.appropriations.house.gov
  Subcommittee on Agriculture, Rural
    Development, FDA, and Related Agencies,
    (202) 225-2638.
  Subcommittee on Financial Services and General
    Government, (202) 225-7245.
  Subcommittee on Labor, Health and Human
    Services, Education, and Related Agencies,
    (202) 225-3508.
  Subcommittee on Military Construction,
    Veterans Affairs, and Related Agencies,
    (202) 225-3047.
  Subcommittee on Transportation, HUD, and
    Related Agencies, (202) 225-2141.
House Education and the Workforce Committee,
  (202) 225-4527.
Web, edworkforce.house.gov or
democrats.edworkforce.house.gov
  Subcommittee on Early Childhood, Elementary,
    and Secondary Education, (202) 225-4527.
  Subcommittee on Health, Employment, Labor,
    and Pensions, (202) 225-4527.
  Subcommittee on Higher Education, and
    Workforce Training, (202) 225-4527.
House Energy and Commerce Committee,
  (202) 225-2927.
Web, energycommerce.house.gov or
democrats.energycommerce.house.gov
  Subcommittee on Health, (202) 225-2927.
House Small Business Committee, (202) 225-5821.
Web, smallbusiness.house.gov or
democrats.smallbusiness.house.gov
  Subcommittee on Health and Technology,
    (202) 225-5821.
House Veterans' Affairs Committee, (202) 225-3527.

Web, veterans.house.gov or
democrats.veterans.house.gov
  Subcommittee on Disability Assistance and
    Memorial Affairs, (202) 225-9164.
House Ways and Means Committee, (202) 225-3625.
Web, waysandmeans.house.gov or
democrats.waysandmeans.house.gov
  Subcommittee on Health, (202) 225-3943.
  Subcommittee on Social Security, (202) 225-9263.

SENATE:

Senate Agriculture, Nutrition, and Forestry
  Committee, (202) 224-2035.
Web, ag.senate.gov
  Subcommittee on Nutrition, Specialty Crops,
    Food, and Agricultural Research,
    (202) 224-2035.
Senate Appropriations Committee, (202) 224-7363.
Web, appropriations.senate.gov
  Subcommittee on Agriculture, Rural
    Development, FDA, and Related Agencies,
    (202) 224-8090.
  Subcommittee on Labor, Health and Human
    Services, Education, and Related Agencies,
    (202) 224-9145.
  Subcommittee on Transportation, HUD, and
    Related Agencies, (202) 224-7281.
Senate Finance Committee, (202) 224-4515.
Web, finance.senate.gov
  Subcommittee on Health Care, (202) 224-4515.
  Subcommittee on Social Security, Pensions and
    Family Policy, (202) 224-4515.
Senate Health, Education, Labor, and Pensions
  Committee, (202) 224-5375.
Web, help.senate.gov
  Subcommittee on Children and Families,
    (202) 224-5375.
  Subcommittee on Primary Health and Aging,
    (202) 224-5480.
Senate Special Committee on Aging, (202) 224-5364.
Web, aging.senate.gov
Senate Veterans' Affairs Committee, (202) 224-9126.
Web, veterans.senate.gov

Supplemental Nutrition Assistance Program (SNAP, formerly the food stamp program); and a supplemental nutrition program for women, infants, and children (WIC).

Food and Nutrition Service *(Agriculture Dept.), Food Distribution, 3101 Park Center Dr., #504, Alexandria, VA 22302-1500; (703) 305-2680. Fax, (703) 305-2964. Laura Castro, Director.*

General email, fdd-pst@fns.usda.gov
Web, www.fns.usda.gov/fdd

Administers the purchasing and distribution of food to state agencies for child care centers, public and private schools, public and nonprofit charitable institutions, and summer camps. Coordinates the distribution of special commodities, including surplus cheese and butter. Administers the National Commodity Processing Program, which facilitates distribution, at reduced prices, of processed foods to state agencies.

Food and Nutrition Service *(Agriculture Dept.),* *Supplemental Nutrition Assistance Program (SNAP),* *3101 Park Center Dr., #808, Alexandria, VA 22302-1500; (703) 305-2026. Fax, (703) 305-2454. Jessica Shahin, Associate Administrator, (703) 305-2022.* *Web, www.fns.usda.gov*

Administers SNAP through state welfare agencies to provide needy persons with Electronic Benefit Transfer cards to increase food purchasing power. Provides matching funds to cover half the cost of EBT card issuance.

Health and Human Services Dept. (HHS), *200 Independence Ave. S.W. 20201; (202) 690-7000. Fax, (202) 690-7203. Vacant, Secretary; William V. Corr, Deputy Secretary, (202) 690-6133. Press, (202) 690-6343. Press, (202) 690-6139. Toll-free, (877) 696-6775.* *Web, www.hhs.gov*

Acts as principal adviser to the president on health and welfare plans, policies, and programs of the federal government. Encompasses the Centers for Medicare and Medicaid Services, the Administration for Children and Families, the Public Health Service, and the Centers for Disease Control and Prevention.

Health and Human Services Dept. (HHS), *Disability, Aging, and Long-Term Care Policy, 200 Independence Ave. S.W., #424E 20201; (202) 690-6443. Fax, (202) 401-7733. Vacant, Deputy Assistant Secretary.* *Web, http://aspe.hhs.gov/office_specific/daltcp.cfm*

Responsible for developing, evaluating, and coordinating HHS policies and programs that support the independence, productivity, health, and long-term care needs of children, working-age adults, and older persons with disabilities. Operates regionally within ten HHS offices.

Health and Human Services Dept. (HHS), *Planning and Evaluation, Human Services Policy, Economic Support for Families, 200 Independence Ave. S.W., #404E.5 20201; (202) 690-7409. Fax, (202) 690-6562. John Tambornino, Director.* *Web, www.aspe.hhs.gov/office_specific/hsp.cfm*

Collects and disseminates information on human services programs that provide nonelderly populations, including families with children, with cash, employment, training, and related assistance.

White House Office of Faith-Based and Neighborhood Partnerships *(Executive Office of the President), The White House 20502; (202) 456-3394. Vacant, Director.* *General email, whpartnerships@who.eop.gov* *Web, www.whitehouse.gov*

Strengthens and expands the role of faith-based organizations in addressing social needs. Centers in eleven cabinet departments and agencies work with the office in the White House to help organizations gain access to federal funding. Targeted populations include at-risk youth, ex-offenders, homeless, hungry, substance abusers, HIV/AIDS sufferers, and welfare-to-work families.

►**CONGRESS**

For a listing of relevant congressional committees and subcommittees, please see page 629 or the Appendix.

Government Accountability Office (GAO), *Education, Workforce, and Income Security, 441 G St. N.W., #5928 20548; (202) 512-7215. Barbara D. Bovbjerg, Managing Director.* *Web, www.gao.gov*

Independent, nonpartisan agency in the legislative branch. Audits, analyzes, and evaluates Health and Human Services Dept. and Corporation for National and Community Service programs; makes reports available to the public.

►**NONGOVERNMENTAL**

American Public Human Services Assn., *1133 19th St. N.W., #400 20036; (202) 682-0100. Fax, (202) 289-6555. Tracy Wareing, Executive Director, ext. 231.* *General email, memberservice@aphsa.org* *Web, www.aphsa.org*

Membership: state and local human services administrators. Works toward an integrated human services system to improve the health and well-being of individuals and communities. Exchanges knowledge and best practices through conferences and publications; implements policies in partnership with government, businesses, and community organizations; monitors legislation and regulations.

Catholic Charities USA, *2050 Ballenger Ave., Alexandria, VA 22314; (703) 549-1390. Fax, (703) 549-1656. Rev. Larry Snyder, President, (703) 236-2600.* *General email, info@catholiccharitiesusa.org* *Web, www.catholiccharitiesusa.org*

Member agencies and institutions provide assistance to persons of all backgrounds; community-based services include day care, counseling, food, and housing. National office provides members with advocacy and professional support, including networking, training and consulting, program development, and financial benefits. Represents the Catholic community in times of domestic disaster.

Center for Community Change, *1536 U St. N.W. 20009; (202) 339-9300. Fax, (202) 387-4892. Deepak Bhargava, Executive Director.* *General email, info@communitychange.org* *Web, www.communitychange.org*

Works to strengthen grassroots organizations that help low-income people, working-class people, and minorities develop skills and resources to improve their communities and change the policies and institutions that affect their lives. Monitors legislation and regulations.

Center for Law and Social Policy, *1200 18th St. N.W., #200 20036; (202) 906-8000. Fax, (202) 842-2885. Olivia Golden, Executive Director.*

General email, info@clasp.org

Web, www.clasp.org

Public policy organization with expertise in national, state, and local policy affecting low-income Americans. Seeks to improve the economic security and educational and workforce prospects of low-income children, youth, adults, and families.

Center for the Study of Social Policy, *1575 Eye St. N.W., #500 20005-3922; (202) 371-1565. Fax, (202) 371-1472. Frank Farrow, Director.*

General email, info@cssp.org

Web, www.cssp.org

Assists states and communities in organizing, financing, and delivering human services, with a focus on children and families. Helps build capacity for local decision making; helps communities use informal supports in the protection of children; promotes nonadversarial approach to class action litigation on behalf of dependent children.

Christian Relief Services, *8301 Richmond Hwy., Alexandria, VA 22309; (703) 317-9086. Fax, (703) 317-9690. Paul Krizek, Executive Director. Information, 800-33-RELIEF.*

General email, info@christianrelief.org

Web, www.christianrelief.org

Promotes economic development and the alleviation of poverty in urban areas of the United States, Appalachia, Native American reservations, Haiti, Mexico, Honduras, Lithuania, the Czech Republic, and Africa. Donates medical supplies and food; administers housing, hospital, and school construction programs; provides affordable housing for low-income individuals and families.

Coalition on Human Needs, *1120 Connecticut Ave. N.W., #312 20036; (202) 223-2532. Fax, (202) 223-2538. Deborah Weinstein, Executive Director.*

General email, mtudor@chn.org

Web, www.chn.org

Promotes public policies that address the needs of low-income Americans. Members include civil rights, religious, labor, and professional organizations and service providers concerned with the well-being of children, women, the elderly, and people with disabilities.

Community Action Partnership, *1140 Connecticut Ave. N.W., #1210 20036; (202) 265-7546. Fax, (202) 265-5048. Donald W. Mathis, President, (202) 449-9774.*

General email, info@communityactionpartnership.com

Web, www.communityactionpartnership.com

Provides community action agencies with information, training, and technical assistance; advocates, at all levels of government, for low-income people.

Council on Social Work Education, *1701 Duke St., #200, Alexandria, VA 22314-3457; (703) 683-8080. Fax, (703) 683-8099. Darla Spence Coffey, Executive Director.*

General email, info@cswe.org

Web, www.cswe.org

Membership: educational and professional institutions, social welfare agencies, and private citizens. Promotes high-quality education in social work. Accredits social work programs.

Food Research and Action Center (FRAC), *1200 18th St. N.W., #400 20036; (202) 986-2200. Fax, (202) 986-2525. James D. Weill, President.*

General email, comments@frac.org

Web, www.frac.org

Public interest advocacy center that works to end hunger and undernutrition in the United States. Offers organizational aid, training, and information to groups seeking to improve or expand federal food programs, including food stamp, child nutrition, and WIC (women, infants, and children) programs; conducts studies relating to hunger and poverty; coordinates network of antihunger organizations. Monitors legislation and regulations.

Foundation for International Community Assistance (FINCA), *1101 14th St. N.W., 11th Floor 20005; (202) 682-1510. Fax, (202) 682-1535. Rupert Scofield, President.*

General email, info@finca.org

Web, www.finca.org

Provides financial services to low-income entrepreneurs outside the United States in order to create jobs, build assets, and improve standards of living. Delivers microfinance products and services through a network of wholly-owned programs in Africa, Eurasia, the Middle East, and Latin America, operating on commercial principals of performance and sustainability. Focuses efforts on those living on less than $2/day, with a loan portfolio of approximately $500 million estimated to reach about one million people worldwide.

Goodwill Industries International, *15810 Indianola Dr., Rockville, MD 20855; (301) 530-6500. Fax, (301) 530-1516. Jim Gibbons, President. Toll-free, (800) 466-3945.*

General email, contactus@goodwill.org

Web, www.goodwill.org

Serves people with disabilities, low-wage workers, and others by providing education and career services, as well as job placement opportunities and postemployment support. Helps people become independent, tax-paying members of their communities.

Grameen Foundation, *1101 15th St. N.W., 3rd Floor 20005; (202) 628-3560. Fax, (202) 628-3880. Alex Counts, President.*

Web, www.grameenfoundation.org

Seeks to eliminate poverty by providing microfinance and technology products and services in sub-Saharan Africa, Asia, the Middle East and North Africa (MENA) region, Latin America, and the Caribbean. Develops mobile phone–based solutions that address "information poverty" among the poor, providing tools, information, and services in the fields of health, agriculture, financial services, and livelihood creation. Focuses on assistance to women seeking to start or expand their own businesses.

Hudson Institute, *National Security Studies, 1015 15th St. N.W., 6th Floor 20005; (202) 974-2400. Fax, (202) 974-2410. Kenneth R. Weinstein, Chief Executive Officer. Press, (202) 974-2417.*
General email, info@hudson.org
Web, www.hudson.org

Studies welfare and health care policy; helps states create welfare reform programs.

Institute for Women's Policy Research (IWPR), *1200 18th St. N.W., #301 20036; (202) 785-5100. Fax, (202) 833-4362. Heidi Hartmann, President.*
General email, iwpr@iwpr.org
Web, www.iwpr.org

Public policy research organization that focuses on women's issues, including welfare reform, family and work policies, employment and wages, and discrimination based on gender, race, or ethnicity.

Jewish Federations of North America, *Washington Office, 1720 Eye St. N.W., #800 20006; (202) 785-5900. Fax, (202) 785-4937. William Daroff, Director.*
General email, dc@JewishFederations.org
Web, www.jewishfederations.org

Advocates for the 153 Jewish federations across the United States on issues of concern, including long-term care, families at risk, and naturally occurring retirement communities. Offers marketing, communications, and public relations support; coordinates a speakers bureau. (Formerly United Jewish Communities [UJC]. Headquarters in New York.)

National Assn. for the Advancement of Colored People (NAACP), *Washington Bureau, 1156 15th St. N.W., #915 20005; (202) 463-2940. Fax, (202) 463-2953. Hilary O. Shelton, Director.*
General email, washingtonbureau@naacpnet.org
Web, www.naacp.org

Membership: persons interested in civil rights for all minorities. Interests include welfare reform and related social welfare matters. Administers programs that create employment and affordable housing opportunities and that improve health care. Monitors legislation and regulations. (Headquarters in Baltimore, Md.)

National Assn. of Social Workers, *750 1st St. N.E., #700 20002-4241; (202) 408-8600. Fax, (202) 336-8313. Angelo McClain, Chief Executive Officer; Jeane Anastas, President. Press, (202) 336-8212.*
General email, membership@naswdc.org
Web, www.socialworkers.org

Membership: graduates of accredited social work education programs and students in accredited programs. Promotes the interests of social workers and their clients; promotes professional standards; offers professional development opportunities; certifies members of the Academy of Certified Social Workers; conducts research. Monitors legislation and regulations.

National Community Action Foundation (NCAF), *1 Massachusetts Ave. N.W., #680 20001; (202) 842-2092. Fax, (202) 842-2095. David A. Bradley, Executive Director.*
General email, info@ncaf.org
Web, www.ncaf.org

Organization for community action agencies concerned with issues that affect the poor. Provides information on Community Services Block Grants, low-income energy assistance, employment and training, weatherization of low-income housing, nutrition, and the Head Start program.

National Human Services Assembly, *1101 14th St. N.W., #600 20005; (202) 347-2080. Fax, (202) 393-4517. Irv Katz, President.*
General email, nassembly@nassembly.org
Web, www.nassembly.org

Membership: national voluntary health and human service organizations. Provides collective leadership in the areas of health and human service. Provides members' professional staff and volunteers with a forum to share information. Supports public policies, programs, and resources that advance the effectiveness of health and human service organizations and their service delivery. (Formerly the National Assembly of Health and Human Services Organizations.)

National Urban League, *Washington Bureau, 1805 7th St. N.W., #520 20001; (202) 898-1604. Chanelle Hardy, Executive Director.*
Web, www.nulwb.iamempowered.com

Federal advocacy division of social service organization concerned with the social welfare of African Americans and other minorities. (Headquarters in New York.)

Poverty and Race Research Action Council, *1200 18th St. N.W., #200 20036; (202) 906-8023. Fax, (202) 842-2885. Philip Tegeler, Executive Director.*
General email, info@prrac.org
Web, www.prrac.org

Facilitates cooperative links between researchers and activists who work on race and poverty issues. Publishes bimonthly *Poverty and Race* and a civil rights history curriculum guide. Policy research areas include housing, education, and health disparities.

Public Welfare Foundation, *1200 U St. N.W. 20009-4443; (202) 965-1800. Fax, (202) 265-8851. Mary E. McClymont, President. Media, ext. 242.*
General email, info@publicwelfare.org
Web, www.publicwelfare.org

Seeks to assist disadvantaged populations overcome barriers to full participation in society. Works to end over-incarceration of adults and juveniles. Awards grants to nonprofits in the following areas: criminal and juvenile justice and workers' rights.

Salvation Army, *Washington Office, 615 Slaters Lane, Alexandria, VA 22314 (mailing address: P.O. Box 269, Alexandria, VA 22313-0269); (703) 684-5500. Fax, (703)*

684-3478. *David Jeffrey, National Commander. Press, (703) 519-5890.*

General email, usn_national_commander@ usn.salvationarmy.org

Web, www.salvationarmyusa.org

International Christian social welfare organization that provides food, clothing, shelter, and social services to the homeless, the elderly, children, and persons with illness or disabilities. (International headquarters in London.)

Share Our Strength, *1030 15th St. N.W., #1100W 20005; (202) 393-2925. Fax, (202) 347-5868. Bill Shore, Executive Director. Toll-free, (800) 969-4767.*

General email, info@strength.org

Web, www.nokidhungry.org

Works to alleviate and prevent hunger and poverty for children in the United States. Provides food assistance; treats malnutrition; seeks long-term solutions to hunger and poverty through fundraising, partnerships with corporations and nonprofit organizations, grants, and educational programs.

Stalking Resource Center, *2000 M St. N.W., #480 20036; (202) 467-8700. Fax, (202) 467-8701. Michelle Garcia, Director.*

General email, src@ncvc.org

Web, www.ncvc.org/src

Acts as an information clearinghouse on stalking. Works to raise public awareness of the dangers of stalking. Encourages the development and implementation of multidisciplinary responses to stalking in local communities. Offers practitioner training and technical assistance. (Affiliated with the National Center for Victims of Crime.)

Urban Institute, *2100 M St. N.W. 20037; (202) 833-7200. Fax, (202) 467-5775. Sarah Rosen Wartell, President. Public Affairs, (202) 261-5709.*

General email, publicaffairs@urban.org

Web, www.urban.org

Nonpartisan public policy research and education organization. Interests include states' use of federal funds; delivery of social services to specific groups, including children of mothers in welfare reform programs; retirement policy, income, and community-based services for the elderly; job placement and training programs for welfare recipients; health care cost containment and access; food stamps; child nutrition; the homeless; housing; immigration; justice policy and prisoner reentry; federal, state, and local tax policy; and education policy.

Urban Institute, *Center on Labor, Human Services, and Population, 2100 M St. N.W. 20037; (202) 833-7200. Fax, (202) 463-8522. Elizabeth Peters, Director.*

Web, www.urban.org/center/lhp/index.cfm

Analyzes employment and income trends, studies how the U.S. population is growing, and evaluates programs dealing with homelessness, child welfare, and job training. Other areas of interest include immigration, mortality, sexual and reproductive health, adolescent risk behavior, child care, domestic violence, and youth development.

Urban Institute, *The Income and Benefits Policy Center, 2100 M St. N.W. 20037; (202) 833-7200. Fax, (202) 833-4388. Gregory Acf, Director.*

Web, www.urban.org/center/ibp and Retirement policy, http://urban.org/retirement_policy/index.cfm

Studies how public policy influences behavior and the economic well-being of families, particularly the disabled, the elderly, and those with low incomes.

U.S. Conference of City Human Services Officials, *1620 Eye St. N.W., 4th Floor 20006; (202) 293-7330. Fax, (202) 293-2352. Crystal D. Swann, Assistant Executive Director for Children, Health, and Human Services, (202) 293-6707.*

General email, info@usmayors.org

Web, www.usmayors.org/humanservices

Promotes improved social services for specific urban populations through meetings, technical assistance, and training programs for members; fosters information exchange among federal, state, and local governments, human services experts, and other groups concerned with human services issues. (Affiliate of the U.S. Conference of Mayors.)

CHILDREN AND FAMILIES

General

▶**AGENCIES**

Administration for Children and Families (ACF) *(Health and Human Services Dept.), 901 D St. S.W., #600 20447 (mailing address: 370 L'Enfant Promenade S.W., Washington, DC 20447); (202) 401-2337. Fax, (202) 401-4678. Mark Greenberg, Assistant Secretary, Acting. Public Affairs, (202) 401-9215.*

Web, www.acf.hhs.gov

Plans, manages, and coordinates national assistance programs that promote stability, economic security, responsibility, and self-support for families; supervises programs and the use of funds to provide the most needy with aid and to increase alternatives to public assistance. Programs include Temporary Assistance to Needy Families, Child Welfare, Head Start, Child Support Enforcement, Low-Income Home Energy Assistance, Community Services Block Grant, and Refugee Resettlement Assistance.

Administration for Children and Families (ACF) *(Health and Human Services Dept.), Child Support Enforcement, 901 D St. S.W. 20447 (mailing address: 370 L'Enfant Promenade S.W., Washington, DC 20447); (202) 401-9369. Fax, (202) 401-5655. Vicki Turetsky, Commissioner. Information, (202) 401-9373.*

Web, www.acf.hhs.gov/programs/cse

Helps states develop, manage, and operate child support programs. Maintains the Federal Parent Locator Service, which provides state and local child support agencies with information for locating absent parents. State enforcement agencies locate absent parents, establish paternity, establish and enforce support orders, and collect child support payments.

Administration for Children and Families (ACF) *(Health and Human Services Dept.), Children's Bureau,* 1250 Maryland Ave. S.W., 8th Floor 20024; (202) 205-8618. Fax, (202) 205-9721. JooYeun Chang, Deputy Associate Commissioner.
Web, www.acf.hhs.gov/programs/cb

Works with state and local agencies to develop programs that focus on preventing the abuse of children in troubled families, protecting children from further abuse, and finding permanent placements for those who cannot safely return to their homes. Administers grants.

Administration for Children and Families (ACF) *(Health and Human Services Dept.), Family and Youth Services,* 1250 Maryland Ave. S.W., 8th Floor 20024; (202) 205-8347. Fax, (202) 205-9721. Debbie Powell, Associate Commissioner, Acting.
Web, www.acf.hhs.gov/programs/fysb

Administers federal discretionary grant programs for projects serving runaway and homeless youth and for projects that deter youth involvement in gangs. Provides youth service agencies with training and technical assistance. Monitors federal policies, programs, and legislation. Supports research on youth development issues, including gangs, runaways, and homeless youth. Operates national clearinghouse on families and youth. Issues grants and monitors abstinence education programs.

Administration for Children and Families (ACF) *(Health and Human Services Dept.), Family Assistance,* 370 L'Enfant Promenade S.W., 5th Floor 20447; (202) 401-9275. Fax, (202) 205-5887. Earl Johnson, Director.
Web, www.acf.hhs.gov/programs/ofa

Provides leadership, direction, and technical guidance to the states and territories on administration of the TANF (Temporary Assistance to Needy Families) Block Grant. Focuses efforts to increase economic independence and productivity for families. Provides direction and guidance in collection and dissemination of performance and other data for these programs.

Eunice Kennedy Shriver National Institute of Child Health and Human Development *(National Institutes of Health),* 31 Center Dr., Bldg. 31, #2A32, MSC-2425, Bethesda, MD 20892-2425 (mailing address: NICHD Information Resource Center, P.O. Box 3006, Rockville, MD 20847); (301) 496-3454. Fax, (301) 402-1104. Alan E. Guttmacher, Director. Toll-free, (800) 370-2943. Toll-free fax, (866) 760-5947. Information, (301) 496-5133. General email, nichdinformationresourcescenter@mail.nih.gov
Web, www.nichd.nih.gov

Supports and conducts clinical and translational research in biomedical, behavioral, and social sciences related to child and maternal health; in medical rehabilitation; and in the reproductive sciences. Interests include health education, sudden infant death syndrome (SIDS), media and how it impacts decisions on nutrition and physical activity, and environmental effects on child health

and development. Information available in both English and Spanish.

Food and Nutrition Service *(Agriculture Dept.), Child Nutrition,* 3101 Park Center Dr., #640, Alexandria, VA 22302-1500; (703) 305-2590. Fax, (703) 305-2879. Cindy Long, Director, (703) 305-2054. Press, (703) 305-2281.
General email, cndinternet@fns.usda.gov
Web, www.fns.usda.gov/cnd

Administers the transfer of funds to state agencies for the National School Lunch Program; the School Breakfast Program; the Special Milk Program, which helps schools and institutions provide children who do not have access to full meals under other child nutrition programs with fluid milk; the Child and Adult Care Food Program, which provides children in nonresidential child-care centers and family day-care homes with year-round meal service; and the Summer Food Service Program, which provides children from low-income areas with meals during the summer months.

Food and Nutrition Service *(Agriculture Dept.), Research and Analysis,* 3101 Park Center Dr., #1014, Alexandria, VA 22302-1500; (703) 305-2017. Fax, (703) 305-2576. Richard (Rich) Lucas, Associate Administrator, Acting.
General email, oaneweb@fns.usda.gov
Web, www.fns.usda.gov/ora

Evaluates federal nutrition assistance programs; provides results to policymakers and program administrators. Funds demonstration grants for state and local nutrition assistance projects.

Food and Nutrition Service *(Agriculture Dept.), Supplemental Food Programs,* 3101 Park Center Dr., #528, Alexandria, VA 22302-1594; (703) 305-2746. Fax, (703) 305-2196. Debra Whitford, Director.
Web, www.fns.usda.gov/wic

Provides health departments and agencies with federal funding for food supplements and administrative expenses to make food, nutrition education, and health services available to infants, young children, and pregnant, nursing, and postpartum women.

Health and Human Services Dept. (HHS), *Head Start,* 1250 Maryland Ave. S.W., 8th Floor 20024; (202) 205-8573. Fax, (202) 205-9721. Ann M. Linehan, Director, Acting.
Web, http://transition.acf.hhs.gov/programs/ohs

Awards grants to nonprofit and for-profit organizations and local governments for operating community Head Start programs (comprehensive development programs for children, ages three to five, of low-income families); manages a limited number of parent and child centers for families with children up to age five. Conducts research and manages demonstration programs, including those under the Comprehensive Child Care Development Act of 1988; administers the Child Development Associate scholarship program, which trains individuals for careers in child development, often as Head Start teachers.

Health and Human Services Dept. (HHS), *Planning and Evaluation, Human Services Policy, Children and Youth Policy,* 200 Independence Ave. S.W., #405F 20201; (202) 690-7409. Fax, (202) 690-6562. Martha Moorehouse, Director.
Web, www.aspe.hhs.gov/office_specific/hsp.cfm

Develops policies and procedures for programs that benefit children, youth, and families. Interests include child protection, domestic violence, family support, gang violence, child care and development, and care for drug-exposed, runaway, and homeless children and their families.

Justice Dept. (DOJ), *Violence Against Women,* 145 N St. N.E., #10W.121 20530; (202) 307-6026. Fax, (202) 305-2589. Beatrice A. Hanson, Director, Acting, (202) 307-0728. National Domestic Violence Hotline, (800) 799-SAFE.
General email, ovwdirector@usdoj.gov
Web, www.ovw.usdoj.gov

Seeks more effective policies and services to combat domestic violence, sexual assault, stalking, and other crimes against women. Helps administer grants to states to fund shelters, crisis centers, and hotlines, and to hire law enforcement officers, prosecutors, and counselors specializing in cases of sexual violence and other violent crimes against women.

National Institute of Food and Agriculture (NIFA) *(Agriculture Dept.), Institute of Youth, Family, and Community,* 800 9th St. S.W., #4330, MS2250 20024 (mailing address: 1400 Independence Ave. S.W., #2225, Washington, DC 20250-2225); (202) 720-5305. Fax, (202) 720-9366. Muquarrab Qureshi, Assistant Director.
Web, www.nifa.usda.gov/about/pdfs/fact_sheets/inst_fs_iyfc.pdf

Provides grants and programmatic training to support youth and family development; partners with county governments, the private sector, and state land-grant universities. Program areas include food and agricultural science education, particularly in minority-serving institutions; childhood nutrition; community food projects; and community service. Includes divisions of Community Education, Family and Consumer Sciences, and Youth and 4-H.

Office of Justice Programs (OJP) *(Justice Dept.), Juvenile Justice and Delinquency Prevention,* 810 7th St. N.W. 20531; (202) 307-5911. Fax, (202) 514-7805. Robert L. Listenbee Jr., Administrator, Acting. Clearinghouse, (800) 851-3420.
Web, www.ojgdp.gov

Administers federal programs related to prevention and treatment of juvenile delinquency; missing and exploited children; child victimization; and training, technical assistance, and research and evaluation in these areas. Coordinates with youth programs of the departments of Agriculture, Education, Housing and Urban Development, Interior, and Labor, and the Health and Human Services Administration, including the Center for Studies of Crime and Delinquency. Operates the Juvenile Justice Clearinghouse.

► CONGRESS

For a listing of relevant congressional committees and subcommittees, please see page 629 or the Appendix.

► NONGOVERNMENTAL

Alliance for Children and Families, *Public Policy and Civil Engagement Office,* 1001 Connecticut Ave. N.W., #601 20036; (202) 429-0400. Fax, (202) 429-0178. Katherine Astrich, Vice President, Public Policy, (202) 429-0270. Toll-free, (800) 220-1016.
General email, policy@alliance1.org
Web, www.alliance1.org

Provides resources and leadership to more than 300 nonprofit child- and family-serving organizations in the United States and Canada. Works to strengthen community-based programs and services to families, children, and communities. Monitors legislation. (Headquarters in Milwaukee, Wis. Affiliated with United Neighborhood Centers of America.)

American Assn. for Marriage and Family Therapy, 112 S. Alfred St., Alexandria, VA 22314-3061; (703) 838-9808. Fax, (703) 838-9805. Tracy Todd, Executive Director.
General email, central@aamft.org
Web, www.aamft.org

Membership: professional marriage and family therapists. Promotes professional standards in marriage and family therapy through training programs; provides the public with educational material and online referral service for marriage and family therapy.

American Bar Assn. (ABA), *Center on Children and the Law,* 1050 Connecticut Ave. N.W., #400 20036; (202) 662-1720. Fax, (202) 662-1755. Howard Davidson, Director. Toll-free, (800) 285-2221.
General email, ctrchildlaw@americanbar.org
Web, www.americanbar.org/child

Works to increase lawyer representation of children; sponsors speakers and conferences; monitors legislation. Interests include child sexual abuse and exploitation, missing and runaway children, parental kidnapping, child support, foster care, and adoption of children with special needs.

American Humane Assn., 1400 16th St. N.W., #360 20036; (202) 841-6080. Fax, (202) 450-2335. Mark Stubis, Chief Communications Officer. Toll-free, (800) 227-4645.
General email, info@americanhumane.org
Web, www.americanhumane.org

Membership: animal shelters, humane organizations, child protection agencies, government agencies, and individuals. Prepares model state legislation on child abuse and its prevention; publishes surveys on child and animal abuse and state abuse laws.

America's Promise Alliance, 1110 Vermont Ave. N.W., #900 20005; (202) 657-0600. Fax, (202) 657-0601. Alma Johnson Powell, Chair; John Gomperts, President.
Web, www.americaspromise.org

Works with national and local organizations to support America's youth. Interests include adult mentoring, safe environments, physical and psychological health, effective education, and opportunities to help others. Seeks to reduce the high school dropout rate.

Boys and Girls Clubs of America, *Government Relations,* 1707 L St. N.W., #670 20036; (202) 507-6670. Kevin McCartney, Senior Vice President, (202) 507-6671. General email, info@bgca.org

Web, www.bgca.org

National network of neighborhood-based facilities that provide programs for underserved children six to eighteen years old, conducted by professional staff. Programs emphasize leadership development, education and career exploration, financial literacy, health and life skills, the arts, sports, fitness and recreation, and family outreach. (Headquarters in Atlanta, Ga.)

Boy Scouts of America, *National Capitol Area Council,* Marriott Scout Service Center, 9190 Rockville Pike, Bethesda, MD 20814-3897; (301) 530-9360. Fax, (301) 564-9513. Les Baron, Scout Executive.

Web, www.boyscouts-ncac.org

Educational service organization for youth that supports more than 1,700 local units that provide quality youth programs, including cub scouting, boy scouting, venturing, and exploring. (Headquarters in Irving, Texas.)

Caregiver Action Network, 2000 M St. N.W., #400 20036; (202) 772-5050. John Schall, Chief Executive Officer. General email, info@caregiveraction.org

Web, www.caregiveraction.org

Seeks to increase the quality of life of family caregivers by providing support and information; works to raise public awareness of caregiving through educational activities. (Formerly National Family Caregivers Assn.)

Child Welfare League of America, 1726 M St. N.W., #500 20036-4522; (202) 688-4200. Fax, (202) 833-1689. Christine L. James-Brown, President.

Web, www.cwla.org

Membership: public and private child welfare agencies. Develops standards for the field; provides information on adoption, day care, foster care, group home services, child protection, residential care for children and youth, services to pregnant adolescents and young parents, and other child welfare issues. Monitors legislation.

ChildFund International, *Washington Office,* 1413 K St. N.W., #1200 20005; (202) 682-3482. Fax, (202) 682-3481. Anne Lynam Goddard, Director; Sarah Bouchie, Vice President of Program Development. Toll-free, (800) 776-6767.

General email, washington@childfund.org

Web, www.childfund.org

Works internationally to ensure the survival, protection, and development of children. Promotes the improvement in quality of life of children within the context of family, community, and culture. Helps children in unstable situations brought on by war, natural disasters, and other high-risk circumstances. (Headquarters in Richmond, Va.)

Children's Defense Fund, 25 E St. N.W. 20001; (202) 628-8787. Fax, (202) 662-3510. Marian Wright Edelman, President. Toll-free, (800) 233-1200. General email, cdfinfo@childrensdefense.org

Web, www.childrensdefense.org

Advocacy group concerned with programs and policies for children and youth, particularly poor and minority children. Interests include health care, child welfare and mental health, early childhood development, education and youth development, child care, job training and employment, and family support. Works to ensure educational and job opportunities for youth.

Children's Home Society and Family Services, *Washington Office,* 8555 16th St., #600, Silver Spring, MD 20910; (301) 562-6500. Fax, (301) 587-3869. Jodi Harpstead, Director. Toll-free, (888) 904-2229. General email, welcome@chsfs.org

Web, www.chsfs.org

Provides information on international adoption; sponsors seminars and workshops for adoptive and prospective adoptive parents. (Headquarters in St. Paul, Minn.)

Children's Rights Council (CRC), 1296 Cronson Blvd., #3086, Crofton, MD 21114; (301) 459-1220. Fax, (301) 459-1227. Sal Frasca, Chief Executive Officer. General email, crdc@erols.com

Web, www.crckids.org

Membership: parents and professionals. Works to strengthen families through education and advocacy. Supports family formation and preservation. Conducts conferences and serves as an information clearinghouse. Interests include children whose parents are separated, unwed, or divorced.

Council for Professional Recognition, *Child Development Associate National Credentialing Program,* 2460 16th St. N.W. 20009-3575; (202) 265-9090. Fax, (202) 265-9161. Valora Washington, Chief Executive Officer. Toll-free, (800) 424-4310. General email, feedback@cdacouncil.org

Web, www.cdacouncil.org

Promotes high standards for early childhood teachers. Awards credentials to family day care, preschool, home visitor, and infant-toddler caregivers.

Cradle of Hope, 8630 Fenton St., #310, Silver Spring, MD 20910; (301) 587-4400. Fax, (301) 588-3091. Linda Perilstein, Executive Director. General email, cradle@cradlehope.org

Web, www.cradlehope.org

International adoption center specializing in the placement of children from the former Soviet Union, Eastern Europe, China, and Latin America. Offers pre- and post-adoption support services. Sponsors the Bridge of Hope program, a summer camp where older Russian children meet and spend time with potential host families, in several U.S. locations, including the Washington, D.C., metro region.

Every Child Matters, *1023 15th St. N.W., #401 20005; (202) 223-8177. Fax, (202) 223-8499. Michael Petit, President.*
General email, info@everychildmatters.org
Web, www.everychildmatters.org

Works to make children's needs a political priority through public education activities. Interests include prevention of child abuse and neglect, improvement of the health of low-income children, solutions in child care, early childhood education, and after-school programs.

Family and Home Network, *P.O. Box 492, Merrifield, VA 22116; (703) 698-8383. Catherine Myers, Executive Director.*
General email, cmyers@familyandhome.org
Web, www.familyandhome.org

Provides information and support for parents who stay home, or who would like to stay home (full or part time), to raise their children, in the United States and abroad. Monitors legislation and regulations relating to family issues.

Foster Care to Success, *21351 Gentry Dr., #130, Sterling, VA 20166; (571) 203-0270. Fax, (571) 203-0273. Eileen McCaffrey, Executive Director; Tina Raheem, Director, Scholarships and Grants.*
General email, tinar@fc2success.org
Web, www.fc2success.org

Advocates for orphaned, abandoned, and homeless teenage youths. Provides scholarships, research, information, emergency cash grants, volunteer programs, guidance, and support. Interests include the rights of orphaned children, transition from youth foster care to young adult independence, and breaking the welfare cycle. Learning center provides training and educational materials. (Formerly Orphan Foundation of America.)

Generations United, *1331 H St. N.W., #900 20005; (202) 289-3979. Fax, (202) 289-3952. Donna M. Butts, Executive Director.*
General email, gu@gu.org
Web, www.gu.org

Membership organization that promotes intergenerational programs and public policies. Focuses on the economic, social, and personal benefits of intergenerational cooperation. Encourages collaboration between organizations that represent different age groups.

Girl Scouts of the U.S.A., *Public Policy and Advocacy, 816 Connecticut Ave. N.W., 3rd Floor 20006; (202) 659-3780. Fax, (202) 331-8065. Anna Maria Chavez, Chief Executive Officer.*
General email, advocacy@girlscouts.org
Web, www.girlscouts.org

Educational service organization for girls ages five to seventeen that promotes personal development through social action, leadership, and other projects. Areas of advocacy include girls' healthy living, increasing girls' participation in STEM (science, technology, engineering, and math) fields, financial literacy, career education, and supporting girls in underserved communities. (Headquarters in New York.)

International Youth Advocate Foundation, *4000 Albermarle St. N.W., #500 20016; (202) 244-6410. Fax, (202) 244-6396. Mubarak E. Awad, President.*
General email, mawad@iyaf.org
Web, www.iyaf.org

Supports the development and operation of community-based services for at-risk youth and their families. (Formerly the National Youth Advocate Program. Affiliated with Youth Advocate Program International.)

Kidsave, *Washington Office, 5185 MacArthur Blvd. N.W., #108 20016; (202) 503-3100. Fax, (202) 503-3131. Terry Baugh, President.*
General email, info@kidsave.org
Web, www.kidsave.org

Maintains programs that provide children age eight and older in orphanages and foster care the opportunity for weekend visits and short stays with families in the community with the goal of permanent adoption or long-term mentoring. Monitors child welfare legislation and regulations worldwide.

National Assn. for the Education of Young Children, *1313 L St. N.W., #500 20005; (202) 232-8777. Fax, (202) 328-1846. Rhian Allvin, Executive Director. Information, (800) 424-2460.*
General email, naeyc@naeyc.org
Web, www.naeyc.org

Membership: early childhood teachers, administrators, college faculty, and directors of early childhood programs at the state and local levels. Works to improve the quality of early childhood care and education. Administers national accreditation system for early childhood programs. Maintains information service.

National Black Child Development Institute, *1313 L St. N.W., #110 20005-4110; (202) 833-2220. Fax, (202) 833-8222. Cindra Taylor, President, Acting. Toll-free, (800) 556-2234.*
General email, moreinfo@nbcdi.org
Web, www.nbcdi.org and Twitter, @NBDCI

Advocacy group for African American children, youth, and families. Interests include child care, adoption, and health, and early childhood education. Provides information on government policies that affect African American children, youth, and families.

National Campaign to Prevent Teen and Unplanned Pregnancy, *1776 Massachusetts Ave. N.W., #200 20036; (202) 478-8500. Fax, (202) 478-8588. Sarah S. Brown, Chief Executive Officer.*
General email, campaign@thenc.org
Web, www.thenationalcampaign.org and Twitter, @TheNC

Nonpartisan initiative that seeks to reduce the U.S. teen and unplanned pregnancy rates. Provides education and information regarding contraception.

National Center for Missing and Exploited Children, *Charles B. Wang International Children's Building, 699 Prince St., Alexandria, VA 22314-3175; (703) 224-2150. Fax, (703) 224-2122. John Ryan, Chief Executive Officer. Toll-free hotline, (800) 843-5678.*
Web, www.missingkids.com

Private organization that assists parents and citizens' groups in locating and safely returning missing children; offers technical assistance to law enforcement agencies; coordinates public and private missing children programs; maintains database that coordinates information on missing children.

National Child Support Enforcement Assn., *1760 Old Meadow Rd., #500, McLean, VA 22102; (703) 506-2880. Fax, (703) 506-3266. Colleen Delaney Eubanks, Executive Director.*
General email, customerservice@ncsea.org
Web, www.ncsea.org

Promotes enforcement of child support obligations and educates social workers, attorneys, judges, and other professionals on child support issues. Fosters exchange of ideas among child support professionals. Monitors legislation and regulations.

National Coalition Against Domestic Violence, *Public Policy, Washington Office, 1100 H St. N.W., #300 20005; (202) 745-1211, ext. 143. Fax, (202) 785-8576. Rita Smith, Executive Director, (303) 839-1852; Tralonne R. Shorter, Director, Public Policy Advisor, (202) 744-8455. Toll-free Helpline, (800) 799-7233 (SAFE).*
General email, publicpolicy@ncadv.org
Web, www.ncadv.org

Monitors legislation and public policy initiatives concerning violence against women and family safety. Work includes empowering victims, promoting and coordinating direct services, and educating the public about domestic violence. (Headquarters in Denver, Colo.)

National Collaboration for Youth, *1101 14th St. N.W., #600 20005; (202) 347-2080. Fax, (202) 393-4517. Irv Katz, President.*
General email, irv@nassembly.org
Web, www.collab4youth.org

Membership: national youth-serving organizations. Works to improve members' youth development programs through information exchange and other support. Raises public awareness of youth issues. Monitors legislation and regulations. (Affiliate of the National Human Services Assembly.)

National Council for Adoption, *225 N. Washington St., Alexandria, VA 22314-2561; (703) 299-6633. Fax, (703) 299-6004. Charles (Chuck) Johnson, Chief Executive Officer. Press, (301) 751-3750.*
General email, ncfa@adoptioncouncil.org
Web, www.adoptioncouncil.org

Organization of individuals, national and international agencies, and corporations interested in adoption. Supports adoption through legal, ethical agencies; advocates the right to confidentiality in adoption. Conducts research and holds conferences; provides information; supports pregnancy counseling, maternity services, and counseling for infertile couples. Monitors legislation and regulations.

National Fatherhood Initiative, *20410 Observation Dr., #107, Germantown, MD 20876; (301) 948-0599. Fax, (301) 948-4325. Chris Brown, President.*
General email, info@fatherhood.org
Web, www.fatherhood.org

Works to improve the well-being of children by increasing the proportion of children growing up with involved, responsible, and committed fathers. Provides curricula, training, and assistance to state and community fatherhood initiatives. Conducts public awareness campaigns and research. Monitors legislation.

National 4-H Council, *7100 Connecticut Ave., Chevy Chase, MD 20815-4999; (301) 961-2800. Fax, (301) 961-2894. Jennifer L. Sirangelo, President, (301) 961-2820. Press, (301) 961-2972.*
Web, www.4-h.org

4-H membership: young people across the United States engaged in hands-on learning activities in leadership, citizenship, life skills, science, healthy living, and food security. National 4-H Council is a national, private-sector partner of the 4-H Youth Development Program and its parent, the Cooperative Extension System of the United States Department of Agriculture. In the United States, 4-H programs are implemented by 109 land-grant universities and more than 3,000 cooperative extension offices. Outside the United States, 4-H programs operate through independent, country-led organizations in more than 50 countries.

National Head Start Assn., *1651 Prince St., Alexandria, VA 22314; (703) 739-0875. Fax, (703) 739-0878. Yasmina Vinci, Executive Director; Vanessa Rich, Chair. Toll-free, (866) 677-8724.*
Web, www.nhsa.org

Membership: organizations that represent Head Start children, families, and staff. Recommends strategies on issues affecting Head Start programs; provides training and professional development opportunities. Monitors legislation and regulations.

National Network for Youth (NN4Y), *741 8th St. S.E. 20003; (202) 783-7949. Fax, (202) 783-7955. Darla Bardine, Policy Director.*
General email, info@nn4youth.org
Web, www.nn4youth.org

Membership: providers of services related to runaway and homeless youth. Offers technical assistance to new and existing youth projects. Monitors legislation and regulations.

National Network to End Domestic Violence, *1400 16th St. N.W., #330 20036; (202) 543-5566. Fax, (202) 543-5626.*

Kim Grandy, President. National Domestic Violence Hotline, (800) 799-7233.
Web, www.nnedv.org

Represents state domestic violence coalitions at the federal level. Advocates for stronger legislation against domestic violence.

National PTA, 1250 N. Pitt St., Alexandria, VA 22314; (703) 518-1200. Fax, (703) 836-0942. Joanne Dunne, Executive Director, Acting. Toll-free, (800) 307-4782.
General email, info@pta.org
Web, www.pta.org

Membership: parent-teacher associations at the pre-school, elementary, and secondary levels. Supports school breakfast and lunch programs; works as an active member of the Child Nutrition Forum, which supports federally funded nutrition programs for children. (Formerly the National Congress of Parents and Teachers.)

National Urban League, *Washington Bureau,* 1805 7th St. N.W., #520 20001; (202) 898-1604. Chanelle Hardy, Executive Director.
Web, www.nulwb.iamempowered.com

Federal advocacy division of social service organization concerned with the social welfare of African Americans and other minorities. Youth Development division provides local leagues with technical assistance for youth programs and seeks training opportunities for youth within Urban League programs. (Headquarters in New York.)

Rape, Abuse, and Incest National Network (RAINN), 1220 L St. N.W., #505 20005; (202) 544-1034. Fax, (202) 544-3556. Scott Berkowitz, President. National Sexual Assault Hotline, (800) 656-4673.
General email, info@rainn.org
Web, www.rainn.org

Links sexual assault victims to confidential local services through national sexual assault hotline. Operates the Defense Dept.'s sexual assault helpline. Provides extensive public outreach and education programs nationwide on sexual assault prevention, prosecution, and recovery. Promotes national policy efforts to improve services to victims.

Stop Child Predators, 5185 MacArthur Blvd. 20006; (202) 248-7052. Fax, (202) 248-4427. Stacie D. Rumenap, President.
General email, srumenap@stopchildpredators.org
Web, www.stopchildpredators.org

Advocacy organization that seeks to protect children from crime and hold their victimizers accountable. Works with victims' families, law enforcement, and decision makers to develop effective policies and solutions. Goals include establishing penalty enhancements for those who commit sexual offenses against children and creating an integrated nationwide sex offender registry.

Urban Institute, *The Low-Income Working Families Project,* 2100 M St. N.W. 20037; (202) 833-7200. Fax, (202) 833-4388. Elizabeth Peters, Director.
Web, www.urban.org/center/lwf/index.cfm

Studies low-income families, identifies factors that contribute to poor outcomes, and develops public policy solutions. Interests include economic security, the public programs safety net, better life chances for children, and racial and ethnic disparities.

Older Adults

► **AGENCIES**

Administration for Community Living (ACL) *(Health and Human Services Dept.),* **Administration on Aging (AoA),** 1 Massachusetts Ave. N.W. 20201; (202) 619-0724. Fax, (202) 357-3555. Edwin L. Walker, Deputy Assistant Secretary, (202) 401-4634. Press, (202) 357-3507. Eldercare Locator, (800) 677-1116.
General email, aclinfo@acl.hhs.gov
Web, www.aoa.hhs.gov

Advocacy agency for older Americans and their concerns. Collaborates with tribal organizations, community and national organizations, and state and area agencies to implement grant programs and services designed to improve the quality of life for older Americans, such as information and referral, adult day care, elder abuse prevention, home-delivered meals, in-home care, transportation, and services for caregivers.

Senior Corps *(Corporation for National and Community Service),* **Retired and Senior Volunteer Program, Foster Grandparent Program, and Senior Companion Program,** 1201 New York Ave. N.W. 20525; (202) 606-5000. Erwin Tan, Director, (202) 606-3237. National service information hotline, (800) 942-2677. TTY, (800) 833-3722.
General email, info@cns.gov
Web, www.seniorcorps.gov

Network of programs that help older Americans find service opportunities in their communities, including the Retired and Senior Volunteer Program, which encourages older citizens to use their talents and experience in community service; the Foster Grandparent Program, which gives older citizens opportunities to work with exceptional children and children with special needs; and the Senior Companion Program, which recruits older citizens to help homebound adults, especially seniors, with special needs.

► **CONGRESS**

For a listing of relevant congressional committees and subcommittees, please see page 629 or the Appendix.

► **NONGOVERNMENTAL**

AARP, 601 E St. N.W. 20049; (202) 434-2277. Fax, (202) 434-2320. A. Barry Rand, Chief Executive Officer. Press, (202) 434-2560. Library, (202) 434-6233. Toll-free, (888) 687-2277. Membership, (202) 434-3525.
General email, member@aarp.org
Web, www.aarp.org

Selected Resources for Older Adults

ADVOCACY

AARP, (888) OUR-AARP or (202) 434-2277 (Spanish); www.aarp.org

AARP, Legal Services Network, (886) 330-0753

Alliance for Retired Americans, (888) 373-6497 or (202) 637-5399; www.retiredamericans.org

Gray Panthers, (800) 280-5362 or (202) 737-6637; www.graypanthers.org

National Caucus and Center on Black Aged, Inc., (202) 637-8400; www.ncba-aged.org

National Committee to Preserve Social Security and Medicare, (800) 966-1935 or (202) 216-0420; www.ncpssm.org

National Consumers League, (202) 835-3323; www.nclnet.org or www.sosrx.org

National Hispanic Council on Aging, (202) 347-9733; www.nhcoa.org

Seniors Coalition, 202) 261-3594; www.senior.org

60 Plus, (703) 807-2070; www.60plus.org

AGENCIES

Administration on Aging (AoA), (202) 619-0724; www.aoa.gov

Centers for Medicare and Medicaid Services (CMS), (877) 267-2323; www.cms.gov

Employment and Training Administration, Older Worker Program, (877) 872-5627; www.doleta.gov/seniors

National Assn. of Area Agencies on Aging, Eldercare Locator, (202) 872-0888; www.n4a.org

National Institute on Aging (NIA), (301) 496-1752; www.nia.nih.gov

National Institutes of Health (NIH), Senior Health, nihseniorhealth.gov

Social Security Administration (SSA), (800) 772-1213; www.ssa.gov

Veterans Affairs Dept., (800) 827-1000; www.va.gov

HEALTH

Alliance for Aging Research, (202) 293-2856; www.agingresearch.org

Alzheimer's Assn., (800) 272-3900; www.alz.org

American Assn. for Geriatric Psychiatry, (301) 654-7850; www.aagpgpa.org or www.gmhfonline.org

Families USA, (202) 628-3030; www.familiesusa.org

National Osteoporosis Foundation, (800) 231-4222 or (202) 223-2226; www.nof.org

HOUSING, NURSING HOMES, ASSISTED LIVING

Armed Forces Retirement Home–Washington, (202) 541-7501; www.afrh.gov

Army Distaff Foundation, (800) 541-4255 or (202) 541-0149; www.armydistaff.org

B'nai B'rith International, Center for Senior Services, (202) 857-2785; www.bnaibrith.org/senior-services–housing.html

Consumer Consortium on Assisted Living, (703) 533-8121; www.ccal.org

National Consumer Voice for Quality Long-term Care, (202) 332-2275; www.theconsumervoice.org

SERVICES, COMMUNITY SERVICE

American Veterans (AMVETS), (877) 726-8387 or (301) 459-9600; www.amvets.org

Jewish Council for the Aging of Greater Washington, (301) 255-4200; www.accessjca.org

National Council on the Aging, (202) 479-1200; www.ncoa.org

National Senior Service Corps, (800) 424-8867 or (202) 606-5000; www.seniorcorps.org

Senior Community Service Employment Program, (877) 872-5677; www.doleta.gov/seniors

---

Membership: people fifty years of age and older. Conducts educational and counseling programs in areas concerning older adults, such as widowed persons services, health promotion, housing, and consumer protection.

Alliance for Retired Americans, *815 16th St. N.W., 4th Floor North 20006-4104; (202) 637-5399. Fax, (202) 637-5398. Barbara J. Esterling, President. Membership, (800) 333-7212.*
Web, www.retiredamericans.org

Seeks to strengthen benefits to the elderly, including improved Social Security payments, increased employment, and education and health programs. (Affiliate of the AFL-CIO.)

Experience Works, Inc., *4401 Wilson Blvd., #1100, Arlington, VA 22203; (703) 522-7272. Fax, (703) 522-0141. Sarah Biggery, Executive Director. Toll-free, (866) 397-9757. Web, www.experienceworks.org*

Trains and places older adults in the workforce. Seeks to increase awareness of issues affecting older workers and build support for policies and legislation benefiting older adults. Maintains a help line for those unemployed who are 55 and older.

Families USA, *1201 New York Ave. N.W., #1100 20005; (202) 628-3030. Fax, (202) 347-2417. Ron Pollack, Executive Director.*
General email, info@familiesusa.org
Web, www.familiesusa.org

Interests include health care, the Affordable Care Act, Social Security, Medicare, and Medicaid. Offers Enrollment Assistant Resource Centers to help consumers and businesses obtain high-quality, affordable health care. Monitors legislation and regulations affecting the elderly. Focuses on communities of color.

Jewish Council for the Aging of Greater Washington, *12320 Parklawn Dr., Rockville, MD 20852-1726; (301) 255-4200. Fax, (301) 231-9360. David N. Gamse, Chief Executive Officer.*
General email, seniorhelpline@accessjca.org
Web, www.accessjca.org

Nonsectarian organization that provides programs and services throughout the metropolitan D.C. area to help older people continue living independent lives. Offers employment services, computer training, adult day care, social day care, transportation, information services and referrals for transportation and in-home services, and volunteer opportunities.

National Assn. of Area Agencies on Aging, *1730 Rhode Island Ave. N.W., #1200 20036; (202) 872-0888. Fax, (202) 872-0057. Sandy Markwood, Chief Executive Officer.*
General email, receptionist@n4a.org
Web, www.n4a.org

Works to establish an effective national policy on aging; provides local agencies on aging and Native American aging programs with training and technical assistance; disseminates information to these agencies and the public. Monitors legislation and regulations.

National Assn. of Area Agencies on Aging, *Eldercare Locator, 1730 Rhode Island Ave. N.W., #1200 20036; (202) 872-0888. Fax, (202) 872-0057. Mary Osborne, Program Manager. Toll-free, (800) 677-1116.*
General email, eldercarelocator@n4a.org
Web, www.eldercare.gov

National toll-free directory assistance service that connects older people and caregivers with local support resources, including meal services, home care, transportation, housing alternatives, home repair, recreation, social activities, and legal services. Language interpretation service for 150 languages available 9:00 a.m.–8:00 p.m. at the toll-free number. (Provided by the U.S. Administration on Aging and administered by the National Assn. of Area Agencies on Aging.)

National Assn. of States United for Aging and Disabilities, *1201 15th St. N.W., #350 20005-2842; (202) 898-2578. Fax, (202) 898-2583. Martha Roherty, Executive Director.*
General email, info@nasuad.org
Web, www.nasuad.org

Membership: state and territorial governmental units that deal with older adults, people with disabilities, and their caregivers. Provides members with information, technical assistance, and professional training. Monitors legislation and regulations.

National Caucus and Center for the Black Aged, Inc., *1220 L St. N.W., #800 20005-2407; (202) 637-8400. Fax, (202) 347-0895. Karyne Jones, President.*
General email, support@ncba-aged.org
Web, www.ncba-aged.org

Concerned with issues that affect older African Americans and other minorities. Sponsors employment and housing programs for older adults and education and training for professionals in gerontology. Monitors legislation and regulations.

National Council on the Aging, *1901 L St. N.W., 4th Floor 20036; (202) 479-1200. Fax, (202) 479-0735. James P. Firman, President. Press, (202) 600-3131. Eldercare Locator, (800) 677-1116.*
General email, info@ncoa.org
Web, www.ncoa.org

Serves as an information clearinghouse on training, technical assistance, advocacy, and research on every aspect of aging. Provides information on social services for older persons. Monitors legislation and regulations.

National Hispanic Council on Aging, *734 15th St. N.W., #1050 20005; (202) 347-9733. Fax, (202) 347-9735. Yanira Cruz, President.*
General email, nhcoa@nhcoa.org
Web, www.nhcoa.org

Membership: senior citizens, health care workers, professionals in the field of aging, and others in the United States and Puerto Rico who are interested in topics related to Hispanics and aging. Provides research training, policy analysis, consulting, and technical assistance; sponsors seminars, workshops, and management internships.

DISABILITIES

General

▶**AGENCIES**

Access Board, *1331 F St. N.W., #1000 20004-1111; (202) 272-0080. Fax, (202) 272-0081. David M. Capozzi, Executive Director, (202) 272-0010. TTY toll-free, (800) 993-2822. Toll-free technical assistance, (800) 872-2253.*
General email, info@access-board.gov
Web, www.access-board.gov

Develops and maintains accessibility requirements for buildings, transit vehicles, telecommunications equipment, medical diagnostic equipment, and electronic and information technology. Provides technical assistance and training on these guidelines and standards. Enforces access standards for federally funded facilities through the Architectural Barriers Act.

Administration for Community Living (ACL) *(Health and Human Services Dept.), Administration on Intellectual and Developmental Disabilities, 1 Massachusetts Ave. N.W. 20201; (202) 401-4541. Fax, (202) 205-8037. Aaron Bishop, Commissioner, Acting.*

General email, info@acl.gov

Web, www.acl.gov

Administers the Intellectual and Developmental Disabilities Assistance and Bill of Rights Act of 2000, providing grants for state protection and advocacy systems for people with intellectual and developmental disabilities; state councils on intellectual and developmental disabilities; university centers for intellectual and developmental disabilities education, research, and services; and projects of national significance that must be addressed on a local level affecting people with intellectual and developmental disabilities and their families. Also administers the disability provisions in the Help America Vote Act.

Education Dept., *Special Education and Rehabilitative Services,* 550 12th St. S.W., 5th Floor 20202 (mailing address: 400 Maryland Ave. S.W., Washington, DC 20202-7000); (202) 245-6496. Fax, (202) 245-7638. Michael Yudin, Assistant Secretary, Acting.
Web, www2.ed.gov/about/offices/list/osers

Provides information on federal legislation and programs and national organizations concerning individuals with disabilities.

Education Dept., *Special Education and Rehabilitation Services, National Institute on Disability and Rehabilitation Research,* 550 12th St. S.W. 20202-7100 (mailing address: 400 Maryland Ave. S.W., MS 2700, Washington, DC 20202-7100); (202) 245-7640. Fax, (202) 245-7323. K. Charlie Lakin, Director. Main number is TTY enabled.
General email, nidrr-mailbox@ed.gov

Web, www3.ed.gov/about/offices/list/osers/nidrr/index .html

Supports applied research, training, and development to improve the lives of individuals with disabilities. Generates new knowledge and promotes its effective use to improve the abilities of people with disabilities to perform activities of their choice in the community, and also to expand society's capacity to provide full opportunities and accommodations for its citizens with disabilities.

Education Dept., *Special Education and Rehabilitative Services, Rehabilitation Services Administration,* 400 Maryland Ave. S.W. 20202-7100; (202) 245-7468. Janet L. Labreck, Commissioner.
Web, www2.ed.gov/about/offices/list/osers/rsa/index.html

Provides leadership and fiscal resources to state and other agencies to provide vocational rehabilitation, independent living, and other services to individuals with disabilities.

Equal Employment Opportunity Commission (EEOC), *Legal Counsel, Americans with Disabilities Act Policy Division,* 131 M St. N.E. 20507; (202) 663-4691. Fax, (202) 663-4679. Christopher J. Kuczynski, Assistant Legal Counsel, (202) 663-4665.
Web, www.eeoc.gov

Provides interpretations, opinions, and technical assistance on the ADA provisions relating to employment.

Eunice Kennedy Shriver National Institute of Child Health and Human Development *(National Institutes of Health), National Center for Medical Rehabilitation Research,* 6100 Executive Blvd., Bldg. 6100, #2A-03, MSC 7510, Bethesda, MD 20892; (301) 402-2242. Fax, (301) 402-0832. Ralph Nitkin, Director, (301) 402-4201.
General email, RN21E@nih.gov

Web, www.nichd.nih.gov/about/org/ncmrr

Fosters the development of scientific knowledge needed to enhance the health, productivity, independence, and quality of life of persons with disabilities. Supports a program of basic and applied research promoting tissue plasticity, assistive technology and devices, improved outcomes, and increased patient participation.

John F. Kennedy Center for the Performing Arts, *Dept. of VSA and Accessibility,* 2700 F St. N.W. 20566 (mailing address: P.O. Box 10150, Arlington, VA 22210); (202) 416-8898. Fax, (202) 416-8802. Betty Siegel, Director.
General email, access@kennedy-center.org

Web, www.vsarts.org

Initiates and supports research and program development providing arts training and programming for persons with disabilities to make classrooms and communities more inclusive. Provides technical assistance and training to VSA Arts state organizations; acts as an information clearinghouse for arts and persons with disabilities.

Justice Dept. (DOJ), *Civil Rights Division, Disability Rights,* 1425 New York Ave. N.W., #4055 20004; (202) 307-0663. Fax, (202) 307-1197. Rebecca Bond, Chief. Information and ADA specialist, (800) 514-0301.
Web, www.justice.gov/crt/about/drs

Litigates cases under Titles I, II, and III of the Americans with Disabilities Act, which prohibits discrimination on the basis of disability in places of public accommodation and in all activities of state and local government. Provides technical assistance to businesses and individuals affected by the law.

National Council on Disability, 1331 F St. N.W., #850 20004-1107; (202) 272-2004. Fax, (202) 272-2022. Jeffrey T. Rosen, Chair.
General email, ncd@ncd.gov

Web, www.ncd.gov

Independent federal agency providing advice to the president, Congress, and executive branch agencies to promote policies and programs that ensure equal opportunity for individuals with disabilities and enable individuals with disabilities to achieve self-sufficiency and full integration into society.

National Institute on Disability and Rehabilitation Research *(Education Dept.),* 550 12th St. S.W., #5148 20024-6122 (mailing address: 400 Maryland Ave. S.W., Bldg. PCP5118-1, MS 2700, Washington, DC 20202-2700); (202) 245-7640. Fax, (202) 245-7323. John Tschida, Director. Press, (202) 245-6721.
General email, nidrr_mailbox@ed.gov

Web, www2.ed.gov/about/offices/list/osers/nidrr/index.html

Awards grants for research programs in rehabilitating people with disabilities from birth to adulthood; provides information on developments in the field; awards grants and contracts for scientific, technical, and methodological research; coordinates federal research programs on rehabilitation; offers fellowships to individuals conducting research in the field.

Office of Disability Employment Policy *(Labor Dept.),* 200 Constitution Ave. N.W., #S1303 20210; (202) 693-7880. Fax, (202) 693-7888. Kathleen Martinez, Assistant Secretary. Toll-free, 866-ODEP-DOL (633-7365).
General email, odep@dol.gov
Web, www.dol.gov/odep

Seeks to eliminate physical and psychological barriers to the disabled through education and information programs; promotes education, training, rehabilitation, and employment opportunities for people with disabilities.

Rehabilitation Services Administration *(Education Dept.),* 400 Maryland Ave. S.W. 20202-7100; (202) 245-7468. Fax, (202) 245-7591. Janet L. Labreck, Commissioner.
Web, www2.ed.gov/about/offices/list/osers/rsa/index.html

Coordinates and directs major federal programs for eligible physically and mentally disabled persons. Administers distribution of grants for training and employment programs and for establishing supported-employment and independent-living programs. Provides vocational training and job placement.

Smithsonian Institution, *Accessibility Program,* 14th St. and Constitution Ave. N.W., #1050, NMAH, MRC 607 20013-7012; (202) 633-2921. Fax, (202) 633-4352. Elizabeth Ziebarth, Director. Information, (888) 783-0001.
General email, ziebarth@si.edu
Web, www.si.edu/accessibility

Coordinates the Smithsonian's efforts to improve accessibility of its programs and facilities to visitors and staff with disabilities. Serves as a resource for museums and individuals nationwide.

Social Security Administration (SSA), *Disability Determinations,* 3570 Annex Bldg., 6401 Security Blvd., Baltimore, MD 21235; (410) 965-1170. Fax, (410) 965-6503. Ann Roberts, Associate Commissioner, Acting. Information, (800) 772-1213.
Web, www.ssa.gov/disability

Administers and regulates the disability insurance program and disability provisions of the Supplemental Security Income (SSI) program.

U.S. AbilityOne Commission, 1401 S. Clark St., Arlington, VA 22202; 1421 Jefferson Davis Hwy., #10800, Arlington, VA 22202-3259; (703) 603-7740. Fax, (703) 603-0655. Tina Ballard, Executive Director.
General email, info@abilityone.gov
Web, www.abilityone.gov

Presidentially appointed committee. Determines which products and services are suitable for federal procurement from qualified nonprofit agencies that employ people who are blind or have other significant disabilities; seeks to increase employment opportunities for these individuals. (Formerly Committee for Purchase from People Who Are Blind or Severely Disabled.)

Workers Compensation (OWCP) *(Labor Dept.),* **Coal Mine Workers' Compensation,** 200 Constitution Ave. N.W., #C3524 20210; (202) 693-0036. Fax, (202) 693-1378. Michael A. Chance, Director, Acting, (202) 693-0046. Toll-free, (800) 638-7072.
Web, www.dol.gov/owcp/dcmwc/index.htm

Provides direction for administration of the black lung benefits program. Adjudicates all black lung claims; certifies benefit payments and maintains black lung beneficiary rolls.

▶ **CONGRESS**

For a listing of relevant congressional committees and subcommittees, please see page 629 or the Appendix.

Library of Congress, *National Library Service for the Blind and Physically Handicapped,* 1291 Taylor St. N.W. 20542 (mailing address: Library of Congress, Washington, DC 20542); (202) 707-5100. Fax, (202) 707-0712. Karen Keninger, Director. Toll-free, (800) 424-8567.
General email, nls@loc.gov
Web, www.loc.gov/nls

Administers a national program of free library services for persons with physical disabilities in cooperation with regional and subregional libraries. Produces and distributes full-length books and magazines in recorded form and in Braille. Reference section answers questions relating to blindness and physical disabilities and on library services available to persons with disabilities.

▶ **NONGOVERNMENTAL**

American Assn. of People with Disabilities (AAPD), 2013 H St. N.W., 5th Floor 20006; (202) 457-0046. Mark Perriello, President. Toll-free, (800) 840-8844.
General email, communications@aapd.com
Web, www.aapd.com

Works to organize the disability community to effect political, economic, and social change through programs on employment, independent living, and assistive technology. Seeks to educate the public and policymakers on issues affecting persons with disabilities. Works in coalition with other organizations toward full enforcement of disability and antidiscrimination laws.

American Bar Assn. (ABA), *Commission on Disability Rights,* 1050 Connecticut Ave. N.W., #400 20036; (202) 662-1570. Fax, (202) 442-3439. Amy Allbright, Director.
General email, cdr@americanbar.org
Web, www.americanbar.org/disability

Promotes the rule of law for persons with mental, physical, and sensory disabilities and their full and equal participation in the legal profession. Offers online resources, publications, and continuing education opportunities on disability law topics and engages in national initiatives to remove barriers to the education, employment, and advancement of lawyers with disabilities.

American Counseling Assn., *Rehabilitation, 5999 Stevenson Ave., Alexandria, VA 22304-3300; (703) 823-9800. Fax, (703) 823-0252. Richard Yep, Executive Director. Toll-free, (800) 347-6647.*
General email, ryep@counseling.org
Web, www.counseling.org

Membership: counselors, counselor educators, and graduate students in the rehabilitation field, and other interested persons. Establishes counseling and research standards; encourages establishment of rehabilitation facilities; conducts leadership training and continuing education programs; serves as a liaison between counselors and clients. Monitors legislation and regulations.

American Medical Rehabilitation Providers Assn. (AMRPA), *1710 N St. N.W. 20036; (202) 223-1920. Fax, (202) 223-1925. Carolyn Zollar, Vice President, Government Relations. Information, (888) 346-4624.*
Web, www.amrpa.org

Membership: freestanding rehabilitation hospitals and rehabilitation units of general hospitals, outpatient rehabilitation facilities, skilled nursing facilities, and others. Provides leadership, advocacy, and resources to develop medical rehabilitation services and supports for persons with disabilities and others in need of services. Acts as a clearinghouse for information to members on the nature and availability of services. Monitors legislation and regulations.

American Network of Community Options and Resources (ANCOR), *1101 King St., #380, Alexandria, VA 22314; (703) 535-7850. Fax, (703) 535-7860. Renee Pietrangelo, Chief Executive Officer.*
General email, ancor@ancor.org
Web, www.ancor.org

Membership: privately operated agencies and corporations that provide support and services to people with disabilities. Advises and works with regulatory and consumer agencies that serve people with disabilities; provides information and sponsors seminars and workshops. Monitors legislation and regulations.

American Occupational Therapy Assn., *4720 Montgomery Lane, Bethesda, MD 20814; (301) 652-2682. Fax, (301) 652-7711. Fred Somers, Executive Director.*
Web, www.aota.org

Membership: registered occupational therapists, certified occupational therapy assistants, and students. Associate members include businesses and organizations supportive of occupational therapy. Accredits educational programs and credentials occupational therapists. Supports research and sponsors scholarships, grants, and fellowships. Library is open to the public by appointment.

American Orthotic and Prosthetic Assn., *330 John Carlyle St., #200, Alexandria, VA 22314-5760; (571) 431-0876.*

Fax, (571) 431-0899. Tom Fise, Executive Director.
Web, www.aopanet.org

Membership: companies that manufacture or supply artificial limbs and braces, and patient care professionals who fit and supervise their use.

American Physical Therapy Assn., *1111 N. Fairfax St., Alexandria, VA 22314-1488; (703) 684-2782. Fax, (703) 684-7343. Michael Bowers, Chief Executive Officer. Information, (800) 999-2782.*
General email, memberservices@apta.org
Web, www.apta.org

Membership: physical therapists, assistants, and students. Establishes professional standards and accredits physical therapy programs; seeks to improve physical therapy education, practice, and research.

American Speech-Language-Hearing Assn. (ASHA), *2200 Research Blvd., Rockville, MD 20850-3289; (301) 296-5700. Fax, (301) 296-8580. Arlene Pietranton, Executive Director. Press, (301) 296-8732. Toll-free hotline (except Alaska, Hawaii, and Maryland), (800) 638-8255 (voice and TTY accessible).*
General email, actioncenter@asha.org
Web, www.asha.org

Membership: specialists in speech-language pathology and audiology. Sponsors professional education programs; acts as accrediting agent for graduate programs; certifies audiologists and speech-language pathologists. Advocates the rights of the communicatively disabled; provides information on speech, hearing, and language problems. Provides referrals to speech-language pathologists and audiologists. Interests include national and international standards for bioacoustics and noise.

Assn. of University Centers on Disabilities (AUCD), *1100 Wayne Ave., #1000, Silver Spring, MD 20910; (301) 588-8252. Fax, (301) 588-2842. Andrew J. Imparato, Executive Director.*
General email, aucdinfo@aucd.org
Web, www.aucd.org

Network of facilities that diagnose and treat the developmentally disabled. Trains graduate students and professionals in the field; helps state and local agencies develop services. Interests include interdisciplinary training and services, early screening to prevent developmental disabilities, and development of equipment and programs to serve persons with disabilities.

Brain Injury Assn. of America, *1608 Spring Hill Rd., #110, Vienna, VA 22182; (703) 761-0750. Fax, (703) 761-0755. Susan H. Connors, President. Information, (800) 444-6443.*
General email, info@biausa.org
Web, www.biausa.org

Works to improve the quality of life for persons with traumatic brain injuries and for their families. Promotes the prevention of head injuries through public awareness and education programs. Offers state-level support services for individuals and their families. Monitors legislation and regulations.

Consortium for Citizens with Disabilities (CCD), *1825 K St. N.W., #1200 20006; (202) 783-2229. Fax, (202) 783-8250. Kathy Bea Neas, Chair.*
General email, info@c-c-d.org
Web, www.c-c-d.org

Coalition of national disability organizations. Advocates for a national public policy that ensures the self-determination, independence, empowerment, and integration in all aspects of society for children and adults with disabilities.

Disabled American Veterans, *National Service and Legislative Headquarters, 807 Maine Ave. S.W. 20024-2410; (202) 554-3501. Fax, (202) 554-3581. J. Marc Burgess, National Adjutant; Joseph W. Johnston, National Commander.*
Web, www.dav.org

Chartered by Congress to assist veterans with claims for benefits; represents veterans seeking to correct alleged errors in military records. Assists families of veterans with disabilities. (Headquarters in Cold Spring, Ky.)

Disabled Sports USA, *451 Hungerford Dr., #100, Rockville, MD 20850; (301) 217-0960. Fax, (301) 217-0968. Kirk M. Bauer, Executive Director, (301) 217-9838.*
General email, info@dsusa.org
Web, www.dsusa.org and www.disabledsportsusa.org

Offers nationwide sports rehabilitation programs in more than forty summer and winter sports; promotes independence, confidence, and fitness through programs for people with permanent disabilities, including wounded service personnel; conducts workshops and competitions through community-based chapters; participates in world championships.

Easter Seals, *Greater Washington–Baltimore Region Office, 1420 Spring Street, Silver Spring, MD 20910; (301) 588-8700. Fax, (301) 920-9770. Lisa Reeves, Executive Officer. Toll-free, (800) 886-3771.*
Web, www.gwbr.easterseals.com

Promotes equal opportunity for people with disabilities or special needs. Interests include child development, early childhood education, adult day services, and services aimed to aid military veterans and their families as they reenter their communities. (Headquarters in Chicago, Ill.)

Epilepsy Foundation, *8301 Professional Pl. East, #200, Landover, MD 20785-7223; (301) 459-3700. Fax, (301) 577-2684. Phillip Gattone, Chief Executive Officer. Information, (800) 332-1000. Library, (800) 332-4050. Spanish language, (866) 748-8008.*
General email, contactus@efa.org
Web, www.epilepsyfoundation.org

Promotes research and treatment of epilepsy; makes research grants; disseminates information and educational materials. Affiliates provide direct services for people with epilepsy and make referrals when necessary. Library open to the public by appointment.

Girl Scouts of the U.S.A., *Public Policy and Advocacy, 816 Connecticut Ave. N.W., 3rd Floor 20006; (202) 659-3780. Fax, (202) 331-8065. Anna Maria Chavez, Chief Executive Officer.*
General email, advocacy@girlscouts.org
Web, www.girlscouts.org

Educational service organization for girls ages five to seventeen. Promotes personal development through social action, leadership, and such programs as Girl Scouting for Handicapped Girls. (Headquarters in New York.)

Goodwill Industries International, *15810 Indianola Dr., Rockville, MD 20855; (301) 530-6500. Fax, (301) 530-1516. Jim Gibbons, President. Toll-free, (800) 466-3945.*
General email, contactus@goodwill.org
Web, www.goodwill.org

Serves people with disabilities, low-wage workers, and others by providing education and career services, as well as job placement opportunities and postemployment support. Helps people become independent, tax-paying members of their communities.

Helen A. Kellar Institute for Human Disabilities, *George Mason University, 4400 University Dr., MS 1F2, Fairfax, VA 22030; (703) 993-3670. Fax, (703) 993-3681. Michael M. Behrmann, Director.*
Web, http://kihd.gmu.edu

Combines resources from local, state, national, public, and private affiliations to develop products, services, and programs for persons with disabilities.

International Code Council, *500 New Jersey Ave. N.W., 6th Floor 20001-2070; (202) 370-1800. Fax, (202) 783-2348. Dominic Sims, Chief Executive Officer. Toll-free, (888) 422-7233.*
Web, www.iccsafe.org

Provides review board for the American National Standards Institute accessibility standards, which ensure that buildings are accessible to persons with physical disabilities.

National Assn. of Councils on Developmental Disabilities, *1825 K St. N.W., #600 20006; (202) 506-5813. Fax, (202) 506-5846. Donna A. Meltzer, Chief Executive Officer.*
General email, info@nacdd.org
Web, www.nacdd.org

Membership: state and territorial councils authorized by the Developmental Disabilities Act. Promotes the interests of people with developmental disabilities. Interests include services, supports, and equal opportunity. Monitors legislation and regulations.

National Assn. of States United for Aging and Disabilities, *1201 15th St. N.W., #350 20005-2842; (202) 898-2578. Fax, (202) 898-2583. Martha Roherty, Executive Director.*
General email, info@nasuad.org
Web, www.nasuad.org

Membership: state and territorial governmental units that deal with older adults, people with disabilities, and their caregivers. Provides members with information, technical assistance, and professional training. Monitors legislation and regulations.

National Council on Independent Living, *2013 H St. N.W., 6th Floor 20006; (202) 207-0334. Fax, (202) 207-0341. Kelly Buckland, Executive Director. Toll-free, (877) 525-3400.*
General email, ncil@ncil.org
Web, www.ncil.org

Membership: independent living centers, their staff and volunteers, and individuals with disabilities. Seeks to strengthen independent living centers; facilitates the integration of people with disabilities into society; provides training and technical assistance; sponsors referral service and speakers bureau.

National Multiple Sclerosis Society, *Washington Chapter, 1800 M St. N.W., #750 South 20036; (202) 296-5363. Fax, (202) 296-3425. Christopher Broullire, Chapter President. Toll-free, (800) 344-4867.*
General email, information@msandyou.org
Web, www.msandyou.org

Seeks to advance medical knowledge of multiple sclerosis, a disease of the central nervous system; disseminates information worldwide. Patient services include individual and family counseling, exercise programs, equipment loans, medical and social service referrals, transportation assistance, back-to-work training programs, and in-service training seminars for nurses, homemakers, and physical and occupational therapists. (Headquarters in New York.)

National Rehabilitation Assn., *P.O. Box 150235, Alexandria, VA 22315; (703) 836-0850. Fax, (703) 836-0848. Patricia Leahy, Executive Director, Interim. Toll-free, (888) 258-4295.*
General email, info@nationalrehab.org
Web, www.nationalrehab.org

Membership: administrators, counselors, therapists, disability examiners, vocational evaluators, instructors, job placement specialists, disability managers in the corporate sector, and others interested in rehabilitation of the physically and mentally disabled. Sponsors conferences and workshops. Monitors legislation and regulations.

National Rehabilitation Information Center (NARIC), *8400 Corporate Dr., #500, Landover, MD 20785; (301) 459-5900. Fax, (301) 459-4263. Mark Odum, Director. Information, (800) 346-2742.*
General email, naricinfo@heitechservices.com
Web, http://naric.com

Provides information on disability and rehabilitation research. Acts as referral agency for disability and rehabilitation facilities and programs.

Paralyzed Veterans of America, *801 18th St. N.W. 20006-3517; (202) 872-1300. Fax, (202) 416-7662. Homer Townsend, Executive Director. Information, (800) 424-8200.*
General email, info@pva.org
Web, www.pva.org

Congressionally chartered veterans service organization that assists veterans with claims for benefits. Distributes information on special education for paralyzed veterans; advocates for high-quality care and supports and raises funds for medical research.

RESNA, *1700 N. Moore St., #1540, Arlington, VA 22209-1903; (703) 524-6686. Fax, (703) 524-6630. Michael Birogioli, Executive Director; Alex Mihailidis, President.*
General email, info@resna.org
Web, www.resna.org

Membership: engineers, health professionals, assistive technologists, persons with disabilities, and others. Promotes and supports developments in rehabilitation engineering and technology; acts as an information clearinghouse. (RESNA stands for Rehabilitation Engineering and Assistive Technology Society of North America.)

Special Olympics International Inc., *1133 19th St. N.W. 20036-3604; (202) 628-3630. Fax, (202) 824-0200. Janet Froetscher, Chief Executive Officer; Timothy P. Shriver, Chair. Toll-free, (800) 700-8585.*
General email, info@specialolympics.org
Web, www.specialolympics.org

Offers individuals with intellectual disabilities opportunities for year-round sports training; sponsors athletic competition for 4 million athletes worldwide in twenty-two individual and team sports.

Spina Bifida Assn., *1600 Wilson Blvd., #800, Arlington, VA 22209 (mailing address: P.O. Box 17427, Arlington, VA 22216); (202) 944-3285. Fax, (202) 944-3295. Sara Struwe, Chief Executive Officer, Interim. Information, (800) 621-3141.*
General email, sbaa@sbaa.org
Web, www.spinabifidaassociation.org

Membership: individuals with spina bifida, their supporters, and concerned professionals. Offers educational programs, scholarships, and support services; acts as a clearinghouse; provides referrals and information about treatment and prevention. Serves as U.S. member of the International Federation for Hydrocephalus and Spina Bifida, which is headquartered in Geneva. Monitors legislation and regulations.

United Cerebral Palsy Assns., *1825 K St. N.W., #600 20006; (202) 776-0406. Fax, (202) 776-0414. Stephen Bennett, President. Information, (800) 872-5827.*
General email, info@ucp.org
Web, www.ucp.org

National network of state and local affiliates that assists individuals with cerebral palsy and other developmental disabilities and their families. Provides parent education, early intervention, employment services, family support and respite programs, therapy, assistive technology, and vocational training. Promotes research on cerebral palsy; supports the use of assistive technology and community-based living arrangements for persons with cerebral palsy and other developmental disabilities.

Blind and Visually Impaired

►AGENCIES

U.S. AbilityOne Commission, *1401 S. Clark St., Arlington, VA 22202; 1421 Jefferson Davis Hwy., #10800, Arlington, VA 22202-3259; (703) 603-7740. Fax, (703) 603-0655. Tina Ballard, Executive Director.*
General email, info@abilityone.gov

Web, www.abilityone.gov

Presidentially appointed committee. Determines which products and services are suitable for federal procurement from qualified nonprofit agencies that employ people who are blind or have other significant disabilities; seeks to increase employment opportunities for these individuals. (Formerly Committee for Purchase from People Who Are Blind or Severely Disabled.)

►CONGRESS

For a listing of relevant congressional committees and sub-committees, please see page 629 or the Appendix.

Library of Congress, *National Library Service for the Blind and Physically Handicapped, 1291 Taylor St. N.W. 20542 (mailing address: Library of Congress, Washington, DC 20542); (202) 707-5100. Fax, (202) 707-0712. Karen Keninger, Director. Toll-free, (800) 424-8567.*
General email, nls@loc.gov

Web, www.loc.gov/nls

Administers a national program of free library services for persons with physical disabilities in cooperation with regional and subregional libraries. Produces and distributes full-length books and magazines in recorded form and in Braille. Reference section answers questions relating to blindness and physical disabilities and on library services available to persons with disabilities.

►NONGOVERNMENTAL

American Assn. of Visually Impaired Attorneys, *2200 Wilson Blvd., #650, Arlington, VA 22201; (202) 467-5081. Fax, (703) 465-5085. Chris Prentice, President. Toll-free, (800) 424-8666.*
General email, info@acb.org

Web, www.visuallyimpairedattorneys.org

Membership: visually impaired lawyers and law students. Provides members with legal information; acts as an information clearinghouse on legal materials available in Braille, in large print, on computer disc, and on tape. (Formerly the American Blind Lawyers Assn. Affiliated with American Council of the Blind.)

American Council of the Blind (ACB), *2200 Wilson Blvd., #650, Arlington, VA 22201; (202) 467-5081. Fax, (703) 465-5085. Melanie Brunson, Executive Director. Toll-free, (800) 424-8666.*
General email, info@acb.org

Web, www.acb.org

Membership organization serving blind and visually impaired individuals. Interests include telecommunications, rehabilitation services, and transportation. Provides blind individuals with information and referral services; advises state organizations and agencies serving the blind; sponsors scholarships for the blind and visually impaired. Provides information to the public.

American Foundation for the Blind, *Public Policy Center, 1660 L St. N.W., #513 20036; (202) 469-6831. Fax, (646) 478-9260. Paul W. Schroeder, Vice President, Programs and Policy.*
General email, afbgov@afb.net

Web, www.afb.org

Advocates equality of access and opportunity for the blind and visually impaired. Conducts research and provides consulting; develops and implements public policy and legislation. Maintains the Helen Keller Archives and M.C. Migel Memorial Library at its headquarters in New York.

Assn. for Education and Rehabilitation of the Blind and Visually Impaired, *1703 N. Beauregard St., #440, Alexandria, VA 22311; (703) 671-4500. Fax, (703) 671-6391. Louis M. Tutt, Executive Director. Toll-free, (877) 492-2708.*
General email, aer@aerbvi.org

Web, www.aerbvi.org

Membership: professionals who work in all phases of education and rehabilitation of children and adults who are blind and visually impaired. Provides support and professional development opportunities through conferences, continuing education, and publications. Issues professional recognition awards and student scholarships. Monitors legislation and regulations.

Blinded Veterans Assn., *477 H St. N.W. 20001-2694; (202) 371-8880. Fax, (202) 371-8258. Al Avina, Executive Director. Toll-free, (800) 669-7079.*
General email, bva@bva.org

Web, www.bva.org

Chartered by Congress to assist veterans with claims for benefits. Seeks out blinded veterans to make them aware of benefits and services available to them.

National Industries for the Blind (NIB), *1310 Braddock Pl., Alexandria, VA 22314-1691; (703) 310-0500. Kevin Lynch, Chief Executive Officer.*
General email, communications@nib.org

Web, www.nib.org

Works to develop and improve opportunities for evaluating, training, employing, and advancing people who are blind and visually disabled. Develops business opportunities in the federal, state, and commercial marketplaces for organizations employing people who are blind or visually impaired.

Prevention of Blindness Society of Metropolitan Washington, *1775 Church St. N.W. 20036; (202) 234-1010. Fax, (202) 234-1020. Michele Hartlove, Executive Director.*

General email, mail@youreyes.org

Web, www.youreyes.org

Conducts preschool and elementary school screening program and glaucoma screening; provides information and referral service on eye health care; assists low-income persons in obtaining eye care and provides eyeglasses for a nominal fee to persons experiencing financial stress; conducts macular degeneration support group.

Deaf and Hard of Hearing

►AGENCIES

General Services Administration (GSA), *Federal Relay Service (FedRelay), 10304 Eaton Pl., Fairfax, VA 22030; (703) 306-6308. Vacant, Program Manager. Customer service, (800) 877-0996 (Voice/TTY, ASCII, Spanish). Toll-free, (800) 877-8339 (TTY/ASCII). VCO (Voice Carry Over), (877) 877-6280. Speech-to-Speech, (877) 877-8982. Voice, (866) 377-8642. TeleBraille, (866) 893-8340.*

General email, ed.smith@gsa.gov

Web, www.gsa.gov/fedrelay and http://ITCSC@gsa.gov

Provides telecommunications services for conducting official business with and within the federal government to individuals who are deaf, hard of hearing, or have speech disabilities. Federal Relay Service features are: Voice, TTY, HCO, Speech-to-Speech, Spanish, Telebraille, Captioned Telephone Service (CTS), IP Relay, Video Relay Service (VRS), Internet Relay (FRSO), and Relay Conference Captioning (RCC). For those with limited English proficiency, contact fas.car@gsa.gov, as services are available in Spanish, Vietnamese, Russian, Portuguese, Polish, Haitian, Creole, and Arabic.

National Institute on Deafness and Other Communication Disorders *(National Institutes of Health), 31 Center Dr., #3C02, MSC-2320, Bethesda, MD 20892-2320; (301) 402-0900. Fax, (301) 402-1590. Dr. James F. Battey Jr., Director. Information Toll-free, (800) 241-1044.*

General email, nidcdinfo@nidcd.nih.gov

Web, www.nidcd.nih.gov

Conducts and supports research and research training and disseminates information on hearing disorders and other communication processes, including diseases that affect hearing, balance, smell, taste, voice, speech, and language. Monitors international research.

►NONGOVERNMENTAL

Alexander Graham Bell Assn. for the Deaf and Hard of Hearing, *3417 Volta Pl. N.W. 20007-2778; (202) 337-5220. Fax, (202) 337-8314. Alexander T. Graham, Executive Director, (202) 204-4671, ext. 107.*

General email, info@agbell.org

Web, nc.agbell.org

Provides hearing-impaired children in the United States and abroad with information and special education programs; works to improve employment opportunities for deaf persons; acts as a support group for parents of deaf persons.

American Academy of Audiology, *11480 Commerce Park Dr., #220, Reston, VA 20191; (703) 790-8466. Fax, (703) 790-8631. Ed Sullivan, Interim Director. Toll-free, (800) 222-2336.*

General email, infoaud@audiology.org

Web, www.audiology.org

Membership: more than 11,000 audiologists. Provides consumer information on testing and treatment for hearing loss and balance care; sponsors research and continuing education for audiologists. Monitors legislation and regulations.

American Speech-Language-Hearing Assn. (ASHA), *2200 Research Blvd., Rockville, MD 20850-3289; (301) 296-5700. Fax, (301) 296-8580. Arlene Pietranton, Executive Director. Press, (301) 296-8732. Toll-free hotline (except Alaska, Hawaii, and Maryland), (800) 638-8255 (voice and TTY accessible).*

General email, actioncenter@asha.org

Web, www.asha.org

Membership: specialists in speech-language pathology and audiology. Sponsors professional education programs; acts as accrediting agent for graduate programs; certifies audiologists and speech-language pathologists. Advocates the rights of the communicatively disabled; provides information on speech, hearing, and language problems. Provides referrals to speech-language pathologists and audiologists. Interests include national and international standards for bioacoustics and noise.

Better Hearing Institute, *1444 Eye St. N.W., #700 20005; (202) 449-1100. Fax, (202) 216-9646. Carole M. Rogin, President. Hearing helpline, (800) 327-9355.*

General email, mail@betterhearing.org

Web, www.betterhearing.org

Educational organization that conducts national public information programs on hearing loss, hearing aids, and other treatments. (Affiliated with the Hearing Loss Assn. of America.)

Gallaudet University, *800 Florida Ave. N.E. 20002-3695; (202) 651-5000. Fax, (202) 651-5508. T. Alan Horowitz, President, (202) 651-5005. Video phone, (202) 651-5866 (or IP address, 134.231.18.170). Toll-free, (866) 563-8896.*

Web, www.gallaudet.edu

Offers undergraduate, graduate, and doctoral degree programs for deaf, hard of hearing, and hearing students. Conducts research; maintains the Laurent Clerc National Deaf Education Center and demonstration preschool, elementary (Kendall Demonstration Elementary School), and secondary (Model Secondary School for the Deaf) programs. Sponsors the Center for Global Education, National Deaf Education Network and Clearinghouse, and the Cochlear Implant Education Center.

Hearing Industries Assn., *1444 Eye St. N.W., #700 20005; (202) 449-1090. Fax, (202) 216-9646. Andy Bopp, Executive Director.*

General email, mjones@bostrom.com

Web, www.hearing.org

Membership: hearing aid manufacturers and companies that supply hearing aid components.

Hearing Loss Assn. of America, *7910 Woodmont Ave., #1200, Bethesda, MD 20814; (301) 657-2248. Fax, (301) 913-9413. Anna Gilmore Hall, Executive Director.*
Web, www.hearingloss.org

Promotes understanding of the nature, causes, and remedies of hearing loss. Provides hearing-impaired people with support and information. Seeks to educate the public about hearing loss and the problems of the hard of hearing. Provides travelers with information on assistive listening devices in museums, theaters, and places of worship. (Formerly Self Help for Hard of Hearing People.)

Laurent Clerc National Deaf Education Center,
Planning, Development, and Dissemination, *800 Florida Ave. N.E. 20002-3695; (202) 651-5340, Voice and TTY. Fax, (202) 651-5708. Edward Bosso, Vice President. Toll-free, (800) 526-9105. Cochlear Implant Education Center, (202) 651-5638.*
Web, http://clerccenter.gallaudet.edu

Provides information on topics dealing with hearing loss and deafness for children and young adults up to age twenty-one, and operates elementary and secondary demonstration schools. Houses the Cochlear Implant Education Center and serves as a clearinghouse for information on questions related to deafness. (Affiliated with Gallaudet University.)

National Assn. of the Deaf, *8630 Fenton St., #820, Silver Spring, MD 20910-3819; (301) 587-1788. Fax, (301) 587-1791. Howard Rosenblum, Chief Executive Officer.*
Web, www.nad.org and Twitter, @NADtweets

Membership: state associations, affiliate organizations, and individuals that promote, protect, and preserve the civil, human, and linguistic rights of deaf and hard of hearing individuals in the United States. Provides advocacy and legal expertise in the areas of early intervention, education, employment, health care, technology and telecommunications. Provides youth leadership training. Represents the United States to the World Federation of the Deaf (WFD).

Registry of Interpreters for the Deaf, *333 Commerce St., Alexandria, VA 22314; (703) 838-0030. Fax, (703) 838-0454. Shane Feldman, Executive Director.*
General email, info@rid.org
Web, www.rid.org

Trains, tests, and certifies interpreters; maintains registry of certified interpreters; establishes certification standards. Sponsors training workshops and conferences; publishes professional development literature.

TDI, *8630 Fenton St., #121, Silver Spring, MD 20910-3803; (301) 563-9112. Claude L. Stout, Executive Director. Phone (voice/video), (301) 563-9112.*
General email, info@TDIforaccess.org
Web, www.TDIforaccess.org

Membership: individuals, organizations, and businesses that advocate for equal access to telecommunications, media, and information technologies for Americans who are deaf and hard of hearing. Interests include closed captioning for television, movies, DVDs, and online videos; emergency access (911); and TTY and Telecommunications Relays Services. Publishes a quarterly magazine and an annual resource directory. Monitors legislation and regulations. (Formerly Telecommunications for the Deaf and Hard of Hearing.)

Intellectual and Developmental Disabilities

►**AGENCIES**

Administration for Community Living (ACL) *(Health and Human Services Dept.),* **Administration on Intellectual and Developmental Disabilities,** *1 Massachusetts Ave. N.W. 20201; (202) 401-4541. Fax, (202) 205-8037. Aaron Bishop, Commissioner, Acting.*
General email, info@acl.gov
Web, www.acl.gov

Administers the Intellectual and Developmental Disabilities Assistance and Bill of Rights Act of 2000, providing grants for state protection and advocacy systems for people with intellectual and developmental disabilities; state councils on intellectual and developmental disabilities; university centers for intellectual and developmental disabilities education, research, and services; and projects of national significance that must be addressed on a local level affecting people with intellectual and developmental disabilities and their families. Also administers the disability provisions in the Help America Vote Act.

►**NONGOVERNMENTAL**

AAIDD (American Assn. on Intellectual and Developmental Disabilities), *501 3rd St. N.W., #200 20001-2760; (202) 387-1968. Fax, (202) 387-2193. Margaret Nygren, Executive Director.*
Web, www.aaidd.org

Association for professionals who work in the field of intellectual and developmental disabilities. Promotes progressive policy, sound research, effective practices, and human rights for people with intellectual and developmental disabilities. Sponsors conferences and training workshops. Monitors legislation and regulations.

The Arc, *1825 K St. N.W., #1200 20006; (202) 534-3700. Fax, (202) 534-3731. Peter V. Berns, Chief Executive Officer. Information, (800) 433-5255.*
General email, info@thearc.org
Web, www.thearc.org

Membership: individuals assisting people with intellectual and developmental disability. Provides oversight and technical assistance for local groups that provide services and support.

The Arc, *Governmental Affairs, 1825 K St. N.W., #1200 20006; (202) 783-2229. Fax, (202) 534-3731. Marty Ford, Director.*
General email, info@thearc.org
Web, www.thearc.org/what-we-do/public-policy

Membership: people with intellectual and developmental disabilities and their service providers. Provides services and support for individuals with disabilities, their families, and The Arc's state and local chapters nationwide. Monitors federal legislation, regulations, and legal decisions.

Autism Society of America, *4340 East-West Hwy., #350, Bethesda, MD 20814; (301) 657-0881. Fax, (301) 657-0869. Scott Badesch, President. Information, (800) 328-8476.*
General email, info@autism-society.org
Web, www.autism-society.org

Monitors legislation and regulations affecting support, education, training, research, and other services for individuals with autism. Offers referral service and information to the public.

Best Buddies International, *Washington Office, 1020 19th St., #500 20036; (202) 568-8000. Fax, (202) 568-8050. Lisa Derx, Vice President. Information, (800) 892-8339.*
Web, www.bestbuddies.org

Volunteer organization that provides companionship and jobs to people with intellectual disabilities worldwide. (Headquarters in Miami, Fla.)

Joseph P. Kennedy Jr. Foundation, *1133 19th St. N.W., 12th Floor 20036-3604; (202) 393-1250. Fax, (202) 824-0351. Steve Eidelman, Executive Director.*
General email, eidelman@jpkf.org
Web, www.jpkf.org

Seeks to enhance the quality of life of persons with intellectual disabilities and their families through public policy advocacy. Provides information and training on the policy-making process.

National Assn. of State Directors of Developmental Disabilities Services (NASDDDS), *113 Oronoco St., Alexandria, VA 22314; (703) 683-4202. Fax, (703) 684-1395. Nancy Thaler, Executive Director.*
Web, www.nasddds.org

Membership: chief administrators of state intellectual and developmental disability programs. Coordinates exchange of information on intellectual and developmental disability programs among the states; provides technical assistance to members and information on state programs.

National Children's Center, *6200 2nd St. N.W. 20011; (202) 722-2300. Fax, (202) 722-2383. Scott Filer, President.*
Web, www.nccinc.org

Provides educational, social, and clinical services to infants, children, and adults with intellectual and other developmental disabilities. Services provided through a 24-hour intensive treatment program, group homes and independent living programs, educational services, adult treatment programs, and early intervention programs for infants with disabilities or infants at high risk. Operates a child development center for children with and without disabilities.

National Disability Rights Network, *900 2nd St. N.E., #211 20002; (202) 408-9514. Fax, (202) 408-9520. Curtis L. Decker, Executive Director, ext. 107.*
General email, info@ndrn.org
Web, www.ndrn.org

Membership: agencies working for people with disabilities. Provides state agencies with training and technical assistance; maintains an electronic mail network. Monitors legislation and regulations. (Formerly the National Assn. of Protection and Advocacy Systems.)

Psychiatric Rehabilitation Assn., *1760 Old Meadow Rd., #500, McLean, VA 22102; (703) 442-2075. Fax, (703) 506-3266. Tom Gibson, Chief Executive Officer, Interim.*
General email, info@uspra.org
Web, www.uspra.org

Membership: agencies, mental health practitioners, researchers, policymakers, family groups, and consumer organizations. Supports the community adjustment of persons with psychiatric disabilities. Promotes the role of rehabilitation in mental health systems; opposes discrimination based on mental disability. Certifies psychosocial rehabilitation practitioners.

HOMELESSNESS

General

▶**AGENCIES**

Education Dept., *Office of Vocational and Adult Education (OVAE), Adult Education and Literacy, 550 12th St. S.W., 11th Floor 20202-7100 (mailing address: 400 Maryland Ave. S.W., P-OVAE, DAEL, Washington, DC 20202); (202) 245-7700. Fax, (202) 245-7838. Cheryl L. Keenan, Director.*
Web, www2.ed.gov/about/offices/list/ovae/pi/AdultEd/index.html

Provides state and local agencies and community-based organizations with assistance in establishing education programs for homeless adults.

Education Dept., *Title I Office, Education for Homeless Children and Youth Program, 400 Maryland Ave. S.W., #3C130, FB-6 20202-6132; (202) 401-0962. Fax, (202) 260-7764. John McLaughlin, Program Specialist.*
Web, www2.ed.gov/programs/homeless

Provides formula grants to education agencies in the states, Puerto Rico, and through the Bureau of Indian Affairs to Native Americans to educate homeless children and youth and to establish an office of coordinator of education for homeless children and youth in each jurisdiction.

Emergency Food and Shelter National Board Program, *701 N. Fairfax St., #310, Alexandria, VA 22314-2064; (703) 706-9660. Sharon Bailey, Vice President.*
Web, www.efsp.unitedway.org

Public/private partnership that administers the Emergency Food and Shelter Program under the McKinney-Vento Act. Gives supplemental assistance to more than 14,000 human service agencies. Does not provide direct assistance to the public.

Housing and Urban Development Dept. (HUD), *Community Planning and Development, 451 7th St. S.W., #7100 20410; (202) 708-2690. Fax, (202) 708-3336. Mark Johnston, Assistant Secretary, Acting; Clifford Taffet, General Deputy Assistant Secretary.*
Web, www.hud.gov/offices/cpd

Gives supplemental assistance to facilities that aid the homeless; awards grants for innovative programs that address the needs of homeless families with children.

Housing and Urban Development Dept. (HUD), *Special Needs Assistance Programs, Community Assistance, 451 7th St. S.W., #7262 20410; (202) 708-1234. Fax, (202) 401-0053. Robin Raseur, Deputy Director.*
Web, www.hud.gov

Advises and represents the secretary on homelessness matters; promotes cooperation among federal agencies on homelessness issues; coordinates assistance programs for the homeless under the McKinney Act. Trains HUD field staff in administering homelessness programs. Distributes funds to eligible nonprofit organizations, cities, counties, tribes, and territories for shelter, care, transitional housing, and permanent housing for the disabled homeless. Programs provide for acquisition and rehabilitation of buildings, prevention of homelessness, counseling, and medical care. Administers the Federal Surplus Property Program and spearheads the initiative to lease HUD-held homes to the homeless.

▶ **NONGOVERNMENTAL**

Housing Assistance Council, *1025 Vermont Ave. N.W., #606 20005-3516; (202) 842-8600. Fax, (202) 347-3441. Moises Loza, Executive Director.*
General email, hac@ruralhome.org
Web, www.ruralhome.org

Provides low-income housing development groups in rural areas with seed money loans and technical assistance; assesses programs designed to respond to rural housing needs; makes recommendations for federal and state involvement; publishes technical guides and reports on rural housing issues.

National Alliance to End Homelessness, *1518 K St. N.W., #410 20005; (202) 638-1526. Fax, (202) 638-4664. Nan Roman, President.*
General email, naeh@naeh.org
Web, www.endhomelessness.org

Policy, research, and capacity-building organization that works to prevent, alleviate, and end problems of the homeless. Provides data and research to policymakers and the public; encourages public-private collaboration for stronger programs to reduce the homeless population, and works with communities to improve assistance programs for the homeless.

National Coalition for Homeless Veterans, *333 1/2 Pennsylvania Ave. S.E. 20003-1148; (202) 546-1969. Fax, (202) 546-2063. John Driscoll, President. Toll-free, (800) VET-HELP. Toll-free fax, (888) 233-8582.*
General email, info@nchv.org
Web, www.nchv.org

Provides technical assistance to service providers; advocates on behalf of homeless veterans.

National Coalition for the Homeless, *2201 P St. N.W. 20037-1033; (202) 462-4822. Jerry Jones, Executive Director.*
General email, info@nationalhomeless.org
Web, www.nationalhomeless.org

Advocacy network of persons who are or have been homeless, state and local coalitions, other activists, service providers, housing developers, and others. Seeks to create the systemic and attitudinal changes necessary to end homelessness. Works to meet the needs of persons who are homeless or at risk of becoming homeless.

National Law Center on Homelessness and Poverty, *2000 M St. N.W., #210 20036; (202) 638-2535. Fax, (202) 628-2737. Maria Foscarinis, Executive Director.*
General email, nlchp@nlchp.org
Web, www.nlchp.org

Legal advocacy group that works to prevent and end homelessness through impact litigation, legislation, and education. Conducts research on homelessness issues. Acts as a clearinghouse for legal information and technical assistance. Monitors legislation and regulations.

Salvation Army, *Washington Office, 615 Slaters Lane, Alexandria, VA 22314 (mailing address: P.O. Box 269, Alexandria, VA 22313-0269); (703) 684-5500. Fax, (703) 684-3478. David Jeffrey, National Commander. Press, (703) 519-5890.*
General email, usn_national_commander@ usn.salvationarmy.org
Web, www.salvationarmyusa.org

International religious social welfare organization that provides the homeless with residences and social services, including counseling, emergency help, and employment services. (International headquarters in London.)

U.S. Conference of Mayors, *Task Force on Hunger and Homelessness, 1620 Eye St. N.W., #400 20006; (202) 293-7330. Fax, (202) 293-2352. Eugene T. Lowe, Assistant Executive Director for Community Development and Housing, (202) 861-6710.*
Web, www.usmayors.org

Tracks trends in hunger, homelessness, and community programs that address homelessness and hunger in U.S. cities; issues reports. Monitors legislation and regulations.

Social Security Administration

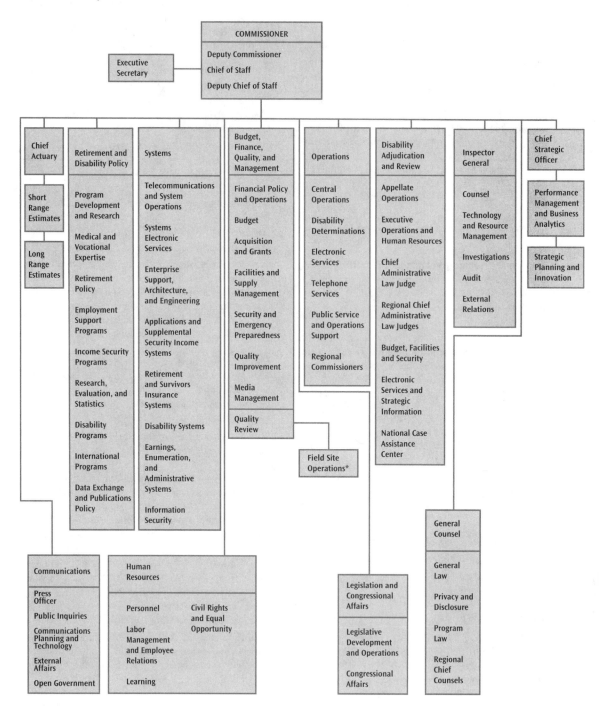

COMMISSIONER

Deputy Commissioner
Chief of Staff
Deputy Chief of Staff

Executive Secretary

Chief Actuary
- Short Range Estimates
- Long Range Estimates

Retirement and Disability Policy
- Program Development and Research
- Medical and Vocational Expertise
- Retirement Policy
- Employment Support Programs
- Income Security Programs
- Research, Evaluation, and Statistics
- Disability Programs
- International Programs
- Data Exchange and Publications Policy

Systems
- Telecommunications and System Operations
- Systems Electronic Services
- Enterprise Support, Architecture, and Engineering
- Applications and Supplemental Security Income Systems
- Retirement and Survivors Insurance Systems
- Disability Systems
- Earnings, Enumeration, and Administrative Systems
- Information Security

Budget, Finance, Quality, and Management
- Financial Policy and Operations
- Budget
- Acquisition and Grants
- Facilities and Supply Management
- Security and Emergency Preparedness
- Quality Improvement
- Media Management
- Quality Review

Operations
- Central Operations
- Disability Determinations
- Electronic Services
- Telephone Services
- Public Service and Operations Support
- Regional Commissioners

Field Site Operations*

Disability Adjudication and Review
- Appellate Operations
- Executive Operations and Human Resources
- Chief Administrative Law Judge
- Regional Chief Administrative Law Judges
- Budget, Facilities and Security
- Electronic Services and Strategic Information
- National Case Assistance Center

Inspector General
- Counsel
- Technology and Resource Management
- Investigations
- Audit
- External Relations

Chief Strategic Officer
- Performance Management and Business Analytics
- Strategic Planning and Innovation

Communications
- Press Officer
- Public Inquiries
- Communications Planning and Technology
- External Affairs
- Open Government

Human Resources
- Personnel
- Labor Management and Employee Relations
- Learning
- Civil Rights and Equal Opportunity

Legislation and Congressional Affairs
- Legislative Development and Operations
- Congressional Affairs

General Counsel
- General Law
- Privacy and Disclosure
- Program Law
- Regional Chief Counsels

*Field Site Operations reports to Quality Review

SOCIAL SECURITY

General

▶AGENCIES

Social Security Administration (SSA), *6401 Security Blvd., Baltimore, MD 21235; (410) 965-3120. Fax, (410) 966-1463. Carolyn Colvin, Commissioner, Acting; Carolyn Colvin, Deputy Commissioner. Information, (800) 772-1213. Press, (410) 965-8904.*
Web, www.ssa.gov

Administers national Social Security programs and the Supplemental Security Income program.

Social Security Administration (SSA), *Central Operations, 1500 Woodlawn Dr., Baltimore, MD 21241; (410) 966-7000. Fax, (410) 966-6005. Van T. Nguyen, Associate Commissioner. Information, (800) 772-1213.*

Reviews and authorizes claims for benefits under the disability insurance program and all claims for beneficiaries living abroad; certifies benefits payments; maintains beneficiary rolls.

Social Security Administration (SSA), *Disability Adjudication and Review, 5107 Leesburg Pike, #1600, Falls Church, VA 22041-3255; (703) 605-8200. Fax, (703) 605-8201. Glenn E. Sklar, Deputy Commissioner.*
Web, www.ssa.gov/disability/index.htm

Administers a nationwide system of administrative law judges who conduct hearings and decide appealed cases concerning benefits provisions. Reviews decisions for appeals council action, if necessary, and renders the secretary's final decision. Reviews benefits cases on disability, retirement and survivors' benefits, and supplemental security income.

Social Security Administration (SSA), *Disability Determinations, 3570 Annex Bldg., 6401 Security Blvd., Baltimore, MD 21235; (410) 965-1170. Fax, (410) 965-6503. Ann Roberts, Associate Commissioner, Acting. Information, (800) 772-1213.*
Web, www.ssa.gov/disability

Provides direction for administration of the disability insurance program, which is paid out of the Social Security Trust Fund. Administers disability and blindness provisions of the Supplemental Security Income (SSI) program. Responsible for claims filed under black lung benefits program before July 1, 1973.

Social Security Administration (SSA), *Income Security Programs, 6401 Security Blvd., #252, Altmeyer Bldg., Baltimore, MD 21235; (410) 966-0607. Fax, (410) 965-8582. Nancy J. Martinez, Associate Commissioner.*
Web, www.ssa.gov

Develops policies and procedures for administering the Retirement and Survivors' Insurance (RSI) programs and the Supplemental Security Income (SSI) program for the elderly, blind, and disabled. Develops agreements with the states and other agencies that govern state supplementation programs, Medicaid eligibility, food stamps, and fiscal reporting processes.

Social Security Administration (SSA), *Operations, 6401 Security Blvd., West High Rise, #1204, Baltimore, MD 21235; (410) 965-3145. Fax, (410) 966-7941. Nancy A. Berryhill, Deputy Commissioner. Information, (800) 772-1213.*
Web, www.ssa.gov

Issues Social Security numbers, maintains earnings and beneficiary records, authorizes claims, certifies benefits, and makes postadjudicative changes in beneficiary records for retirement, survivors', and disability insurance and black lung claims. Maintains toll-free number for workers who want information on future Social Security benefits.

Social Security Administration (SSA), *Research, Evaluation, and Statistics, 500 E St. S.W., #922 20254; (202) 358-6020. Fax, (202) 358-6187. Theodore M. Horan, Associate Commissioner, Acting. Publications, (202) 358-6263.*
Web, www.socialsecurity.gov/policy/about/ores.html

Compiles statistics on beneficiaries; conducts research on the economic status of beneficiaries and the relationship between Social Security, the American people, and the economy; analyzes the effects of proposed Social Security legislation, especially on lower- and middle-income individuals and families; disseminates results of research and statistical programs through publications.

Workers Compensation (OWCP) *(Labor Dept.),* **Coal Mine Workers' Compensation,** *200 Constitution Ave. N.W., #C3524 20210; (202) 693-0036. Fax, (202) 693-1378. Michael A. Chance, Director, Acting, (202) 693-0046. Toll-free, (800) 638-7072.*
Web, www.dol.gov/owcp/dcmwc/index.htm

Provides direction for administration of the black lung benefits program. Adjudicates all black lung claims; certifies benefit payments and maintains black lung beneficiary rolls.

▶CONGRESS

For a listing of relevant congressional committees and subcommittees, please see page 629 or the Appendix.

Government Accountability Office (GAO), *Education, Workforce, and Income Security, 441 G St. N.W., #5928 20548; (202) 512-7215. Barbara D. Bovbjerg, Managing Director.*
Web, www.gao.gov

Independent, nonpartisan agency in the legislative branch that audits, analyzes, and evaluates programs within the Dept. of Health and Human Services, including Social Security; makes reports available to the public.

▶**NONGOVERNMENTAL**

AARP, *601 E St. N.W. 20049; (202) 434-2277. Fax, (202) 434-2320. A. Barry Rand, Chief Executive Officer. Press, (202) 434-2560. Library, (202) 434-6233. Toll-free, (888) 687-2277. Membership, (202) 434-3525.*
General email, member@aarp.org
Web, www.aarp.org

Membership: persons fifty and older. Works to address members' needs and interests through education, advocacy, and service. Monitors legislation and regulations and disseminates information on issues affecting older Americans, including issues related to Social Security. (Formerly the American Assn. of Retired Persons.)

National Academy of Social Insurance, *1776 Massachusetts Ave. N.W., #400 20036-1904; (202) 452-8097. Fax, (202) 452-8111. Pamela J. Larson, Executive Vice President.*
General email, nasi@nasi.org
Web, www.nasi.org

Promotes research and education on Social Security, Medicare, health care financing, and related public and private programs; assesses social insurance programs and their relationship to other programs; supports research and leadership development. Acts as a clearinghouse for social insurance information.

National Committee to Preserve Social Security and Medicare, *10 G St. N.E., #600 20002-4215; (202) 216-0420. Fax, (202) 216-0446. May Richtman, President. Press, (202) 216-8378. Senior hotline/Legislative updates, (800) 998-0180.*
Web, www.ncpssm.org

Educational and advocacy organization that focuses on Social Security and Medicare programs and on related income security and health issues. Interests include retirement income protection, health care reform, and the quality of life of seniors. Monitors legislation and regulations.

18 Transportation

GENERAL POLICY AND ANALYSIS

Basic Resources

▶ **AGENCIES**

Access Board, *1331 F St. N.W., #1000 20004-1111; (202) 272-0080. Fax, (202) 272-0081. David M. Capozzi, Executive Director, (202) 272-0010. TTY toll-free, (800) 993-2822. Toll-free technical assistance, (800) 872-2253. General email, info@access-board.gov*

Web, www.access-board.gov

Develops and maintains accessibility requirements for buildings, transit vehicles, telecommunications equipment, medical diagnostic equipment, and electronic and information technology. Provides technical assistance and training on these guidelines and standards. Enforces access standards for federally funded facilities through the Architectural Barriers Act.

National Transportation Safety Board, *490 L'Enfant Plaza East S.W. 20594-2000; (202) 314-6000. Fax, (202) 314-6018. Deborah A. P. Hersman, Chair. Information, (202) 314-6000. Press, (202) 314-6100.*

Web, www.ntsb.gov

Promotes transportation safety through independent investigations of accidents and other safety problems. Makes recommendations for safety improvement.

National Transportation Safety Board, *Research and Engineering, 490 L'Enfant Plaza East S.W. 20594-2000; (202) 314-6000. Fax, (202) 314-6599. Joseph M. Kolly, Director.*

Web, www.ntsb.gov

Evaluates effectiveness of federal, state, and local safety programs. Identifies transportation safety issues not being addressed by government or industry. Conducts studies on specific safety problems.

National Transportation Safety Board, *Safety Recommendations and Advocacy, 490 L'Enfant Plaza East S.W. 20594-2000; (202) 314-6000. Fax, (202) 314-6178. Paula Sind Prunier, Director.*

Web, www.ntsb.gov

Makes transportation safety recommendations to federal and state agencies on all modes of transportation. Produces the annual "Most Wanted" list of critical transportation safety projects.

Office of Management and Budget (OMB) *(Executive Office of the President), Transportation and Security, New Executive Office Bldg., 725 17th St. N.W., #9002 20503; (202) 395-5704. Fax, (202) 395-4797. Andrew Abrams, Chief. Press, (202) 395-7316.*

Web, www.whitehouse.gov/omb

Assists and advises the OMB director on budget preparation, proposed legislation, and evaluations of Transportation Dept. programs, policies, and activities.

Pipeline and Hazardous Materials Safety Administration *(Transportation Dept.), 1200 New Jersey Ave. S.E., #E27-300 20590; (202) 366-4433. Fax, (202) 366-3666. Cynthia L. Quarterman, Administrator. Hazardous Materials Information Center, (800) 467-4922. To report an incident, (800) 424-8802.*

Web, www.phmsa.dot.gov and Twitter, PHMSA@PHMSA_DOT

Oversees the safe and secure movement of hazardous materials to industry and consumers by all modes of transportation, including pipelines. Works to eliminate transportation-related deaths and injuries. Promotes transportation solutions to protect communities and the environment.

Pipeline and Hazardous Materials Safety Administration *(Transportation Dept.), Hazardous Materials Safety, 1200 New Jersey Ave. S.E., E21-317 20590; (202) 366-0656. Fax, (202) 366-5713. Magdy A. El-Sibaie, Associate Administrator. Hazardous Materials Information Center, (800) 467-4922.*

General email, phmsa.hmhazmatsafety@dot.gov

Web, http://hazmat.dot.gov

Federal safety authority for the transportation of hazardous materials by air, rail, highway, and water. Works to reduce dangers of hazardous materials transportation. Issues regulations for classifications, communications, shipper and carrier operations, training and security requirements, and packaging and container specifications.

Pipeline and Hazardous Materials Safety Administration *(Transportation Dept.), Pipeline Safety, 1200 New Jersey Ave. S.E., E22-321 20590; (202) 366-4595. Fax, (202) 493-2311. Jeffery D. Wiese, Associate Administrator.*

General email, phmsa.pipelinesafety@dot.gov

Web, http://phmsa.dot.gov

Issues and enforces federal regulations for oil, natural gas, and petroleum products pipeline safety. Inspects pipelines and oversees risk management by pipeline operators.

Research and Innovative Technology Administration *(Transportation Dept.), Bureau of Transportation Statistics, 1200 New Jersery Ave. S.E., #E34-314 20590; (202) 366-1270. Fax, (202) 366-3640. Patricia S. Hu, Director. Information, (800) 853-1351. Media, (202) 366-5568.*

General email, ritainfo@dot.gov

Web, www.rita.dot.gov/bts

Works to improve public awareness of the nation's transportation systems. Collects, analyzes, and publishes a comprehensive, cross-modal set of transportation statistics.

Research and Innovative Technology Administration *(Transportation Dept.), Research, Development, and Technology, 1200 New Jersey Ave. S.E., #E33-304 20590-0001; (202) 366-5447. Fax, (202) 366-3671. Kevin Womack, Associate Administrator.*

Web, www.rita.dot.gov/rdt

TRANSPORTATION RESOURCES IN CONGRESS

For a complete listing of Congress committees, including their full contact information, leadership, membership, and jurisdictions, please refer to the Appendix on pages 724–842.

HOUSE:

House Appropriations Committee, (202) 225-2771. Web, appropriations.house.gov or democrats.appropriations.house.gov
  Subcommittee on Energy and Water Development, and Related Agencies, (202) 225-3421.
  Subcommittee on Financial Services and General Government, (202) 225-7245.
  Subcommittee on Homeland Security, (202) 225-5834.
  Subcommittee on Transportation, HUD, and Related Agencies, (202) 225-2141.
House Energy and Commerce Committee, (202) 225-2927. Web, energycommerce.house.gov or democrats.energycommerce.house.gov
  Subcommittee on Commerce, Manufacturing, and Trade, (202) 225-2927.
House Homeland Security Committee, (202) 226-8417. Web, homeland.house.gov or chsdemocrats.house.gov
  Subcommittee on Border and Maritime Security, (202) 226-8417.
  Subcommittee on Transportation Security, (202) 226-8417.
House Natural Resources Committee, (202) 225-2761. Web, naturalresources.house.gov or democrats.naturalresources.house.gov
  Subcommittee on Water and Power, (202) 225-8331.
House Science, Space, and Technology Committee, (202) 225-6371. Web, science.house.gov or democrats.science.house.gov
  Subcommittee on Research and Technology, (202) 225-6371.
  Subcommittee on Space, (202) 225-6371.
House Transportation and Infrastructure Committee, (202) 225-9446. Web, transportation.house.gov or democrats.transportation.house.gov
  Subcommittee on Aviation, (202) 226-3220.
  Subcommittee on Coast Guard and Maritime Transportation, (202) 226-3552.
  Subcommittee on Economic Development, Public Buildings, and Emergency Management, (202) 225-3014.
  Subcommittee on Highways and Transit, (202) 225-6715.
  Subcommittee on Railroads, Pipelines, and Hazardous Materials, (202) 226-0727.
  Subcommittee on Water Resources and Environment, (202) 225-4360.

SENATE:

Senate Appropriations Committee, (202) 224-7363. Web, appropriations.senate.gov
  Subcommittee on Energy and Water Development, (202) 224-8119.
  Subcommittee on Homeland Security, (202) 224-8244.
  Subcommittee on Transportation, HUD, and Related Agencies, (202) 224-7281.
Senate Banking, Housing, and Urban Affairs Committee, (202) 224-7391. Web, banking.senate.gov
  Subcommittee on Housing, Transportation and Community Development, (202) 224-4744.
Senate Commerce, Science, and Transportation Committee, (202) 224-0411. Web, commerce.senate.gov
  Subcommittee on Aviation Operations, Safety, and Security, (202) 224-9000.
  Subcommittee on Competitiveness, Innovation, and Export Promotion, (202) 224-1270.
  Subcommittee on Consumer Protection, Product Safety, and Insurance, (202) 224-1270.
  Subcommittee on Oceans, Atmosphere, Fisheries and the Coast Guard, (202) 224-4912.
  Subcommittee on Science and Space, (202) 224-0415.
  Subcommittee on Surface Transportation and Merchant Marine Infastructure, Safety, and Security, (202) 224-9000.
Senate Energy and Natural Resources Committee, (202) 224-4971. Web, energy.senate.gov
  Subcommittee on Water and Power, (202) 224-4971.
Senate Environment and Public Works Committee, (202) 224-8832. Web, epw.senate.gov
  Subcommittee on Transportation and Infrastructure, (202) 224-8832.
Senate Finance Committee, (202) 224-4515. Web, finance.senate.gov
  Subcommittee on Energy, Natural Resources, and Infrastructure, (202) 224-4515.
Senate Health, Education, Labor, and Pensions Committee, (202) 224-5375. Web, help.senate.gov
Senate Homeland Security and Governmental Affairs Committee, (202) 224-2627. Web, hsgac.senate.gov
Senate Special Committee on Aging, (202) 224-5364. Web, aging.senate.gov

Transportation Department

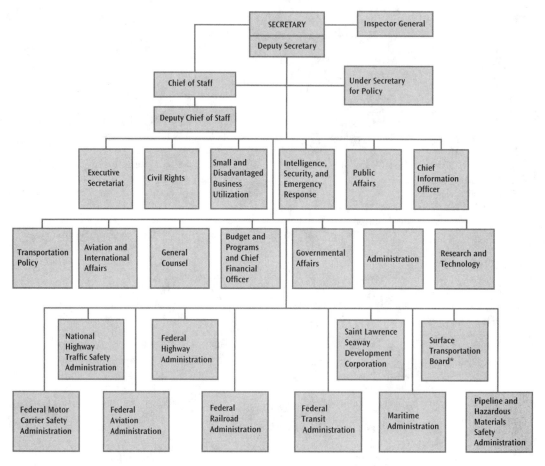

*The Surface Transportation Board is decisionally independent, although it is administratively affiliated with the Department of Transportation.

Supports transportation innovation research, engineering, education, and safety training. Focus includes intermodal transportation; partnerships among government, universities, and industry; and economic growth and competitiveness through use of new technologies. Monitors international research.

Transportation Dept. (DOT), *1200 New Jersey Ave. S.E. 20590; (202) 366-4000. Anthony Foxx, Secretary; Victor M. Mendez, Deputy Secretary, Acting. Press, (202) 366-4570. Web, www.dot.gov*

Responsible for shaping and administering policies and programs to protect and enhance the transportation system and services. Includes the Federal Aviation Administration, Federal Highway Administration, Federal Motor Carrier Safety Administration, Federal Railroad Administration, Maritime Administration, National Highway Traffic Safety Administration, Pipeline and Hazardous Materials Safety Administration, Federal Transit Administration, and the Saint Lawrence Seaway Development Corp. The Surface Transportation Board is also administratively affiliated, but decisionally independent.

Transportation Dept. (DOT), *Aviation and International Affairs, 1200 New Jersey Ave. S.E., #W88-322 20590; (202) 366-8822. Fax, (202) 493-2005. Susan Kurland, Assistant Secretary. Press, (202) 366-4570. Web, www.dot.gov/policy/assistant-secretary-aviation-international-affairs*

Develops and implements public policy related to the airline industry and international civil aviation. Administers laws and regulations over a range of aviation trade issues, including U.S. and foreign carrier economic authority to engage in air transportation, small community transportation, the establishment of mail rates within Alaska and in the international market, and access at U.S. airports.

Transportation Dept. (DOT), *Aviation Consumer Protection, 1200 New Jersey Ave. S.E. 20590; (202) 366-2220. Norman Strickman, Director, (202) 366-5960. Disability-Related Problems, (800) 778-4838. TTY, (202) 366-0511. Web, www.dot.gov/airconsumer*

Processes consumer complaints; advises the secretary on consumer issues; investigates air travel consumer rule violations; educates the public about air travel via reports and Web site.

Transportation Dept. (DOT), *Intelligence, Security, and Emergency Response,* 1200 New Jersey Ave. S.E., #56125 20590; (202) 366-6525. Fax, (202) 366-7261. Michael Lowder, Director, (202) 366-6530.
Web, www.dot.gov/mission/administration/intelligence-security-emergency-response

Advises the secretary on transportation intelligence and security policy. Acts as liaison with the intelligence community, federal agencies, corporations, and interest groups; administers counterterrorism strategic planning processes. Develops, coordinates, and reviews transportation emergency preparedness programs for use in emergencies affecting national defense and in emergencies caused by natural and man-made disasters and crisis situations.

Transportation Dept. (DOT), *Safety, Energy, and Environment,* 1200 New Jersey Ave. S.E., #W84-310 20590; (202) 366-4416. Fax, (202) 366-0263. Barbara McCann, Director.
Web, www.dot.gov/policy/office-safety-energy-environment

Develops, coordinates, and evaluates public policy with respect to safety, environmental, energy, and accessibility issues affecting all aspects of transportation. Assesses the economic and institutional implications of domestic transportation matters. Oversees legislative and regulatory proposals affecting transportation. Provides advice on research and development requirements. Develops policy proposals to improve the performance, safety, and efficiency of the transportation system.

Transportation Security Administration (TSA) *(Homeland Security Dept.),* TSA-1, 601 S. 12th St., 7th Floor, Arlington, VA 20598-6001; (571) 227-2801. Fax, (571) 227-1398. John S. Pistole, Administrator. Press, (571) 227-2829. Questions and concerns regarding travel can be submitted to the TSA Contact Center, toll-free, (866) 289-9673.
General email, TSA-ContactCenter@dhs.gov
Web, www.tsa.gov/public

Protects the nation's transportation systems to ensure freedom of movement for people and commerce.

Transportation Security Administration (TSA) *(Homeland Security Dept.),* *Acquisition,* TSA-25, 601 S. 12th St., Arlington, VA 20598-6025; (571) 227-2161. Fax, (571) 227-2911. Latetia Anderson, Assistant Administrator.
Web, www.tsa.gov

Administers contract grants, cooperative agreements, and other transactions in support of TSA's mission. Develops acquisitions strategies, policies, programs, and processes.

Transportation Security Administration (TSA) *(Homeland Security Dept.),* *Intelligence and Analysis,* TSA-10, 601 S. 12th St., 6th Floor, Arlington, VA

22202-4220; (703) 601-3100. Fax, (703) 601-3290. Stephen Sadler, Assistant Administrator.
Web, www.tsa.gov

Oversees TSA's intelligence gathering and information sharing as they pertain to national security and the safety of the nation's transportation systems. Conducts a range of programs designed to ensure that known or suspected terrorists do not gain access to sensitive areas of the nation's transportation system, including the Alien Flight, Registered Traveler, Secure Flight, and Transportation Worker Identification Credential programs and Hazmat Materials Truck Drivers Background Checks.

Transportation Security Administration (TSA) *(Homeland Security Dept.),* *Legislative Affairs,* TSA-5, 601 S. 12th St., Arlington, VA 20598-6001; (571) 227-2717. Sarah Dietch, Assistant Administrator.
Web, www.tsa.gov

Serves as the TSA's primary point of contact for Congress. Coordinates responses to congressional inquiries, verifies hearings and witnesses, and delivers testimony related to the nation's transportation security.

Transportation Security Administration (TSA) *(Homeland Security Dept.),* *Security Policy and Industry Engagement,* TSA-28, 601 S. 12th St., Arlington, VA 20598-6028; (571) 227-1417. Fax, (571) 227-2932. John P. Sammon, Assistant Administrator.
Web, www.tsa.gov

Formulates policy and shares information related to security in various segments of the transportation industry, including commercial airports, commercial airlines, general aviation, mass transit and passenger rail, freight rail, maritime, highway and motor carrier, pipeline and air cargo. Coordinates with the U.S. Coast Guard.

Transportation Security Administration (TSA) *(Homeland Security Dept.),* *Strategic Communications and Public Affairs,* TSA-4, 601 S. 12th St., Arlington, VA 20598-6028; (571) 227-2829. Fax, (571) 227-2552. LuAnn Canipe, Assistant Administrator.
General email, tsamedia@tsa.dhs.gov
Web, www.tsa.gov/press

Responsible for TSA's communications and public information outreach, both externally and internally.

▶ **CONGRESS**

For a listing of relevant congressional committees and subcommittees, please see page 657 or the Appendix.

Government Accountability Office (GAO), *Physical Infrastructure,* 441 G St. N.W., #2063 20548 (mailing address: 441 G St. N.W., #2T23B, Washington, DC 20548); (202) 512-2834. Phil Herr, Managing Director.
Web, www.gao.gov

Independent, nonpartisan agency in the legislative branch. Audits, analyzes, and evaluates performance of the Transportation Dept. and its component agencies; makes reports available to the public.

Transportation Security Administration

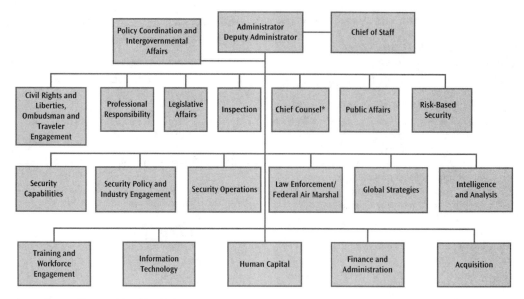

*General Counsel has oversight of the Chief Counsel.

American Concrete Pavement Assn. (ACPA), *Washington Office,* *500 New Jersey Ave. N.W., 7th Floor 20001; (202) 638-2272. Fax, (202) 638-2688. Gerald F. Voigt, President. Web, www.acpa.org*

Represents the concrete pavement industry. Promotes use of concrete for airport, highway, street, and local road pavements. Provides members with project assistance, educational workshops, and training programs. Researches concrete pavement design, construction, and rehabilitation. (Headquarters in Rosemont, Ill.)

American Public Works Assn., *Washington Office, 1275 K St. N.W., #750 20005; (202) 408-9541. Fax, (202) 408-9542. Peter B. King, Executive Director. General email, apwa.dc@apwa.net Web, www.apwa.net*

Membership: engineers, architects, and others who maintain and manage public works facilities and services. Conducts research and education and promotes exchange of information on transportation and infrastructure-related issues. (Headquarters in Kansas City, Mo.)

Americans for Transportation Mobility Coalition, *U.S. Chamber of Commerce, 430 1st St. S.E. 20003; 1615 H St. N.W. 20016; (202) 463-5871. Fax, (202) 887-3430. Janet F. Kavinoky, Vice President. General email, mobility@uschamber.com Web, www.fasterbettersafer.org*

Advocates increased dedicated federal and private sector funding for roads, bridges, and public transportation systems. Members include associations involved in designing, building, or maintaining transportation infrastructure.

Monitors legislation. (Affiliated with the U.S. Chamber of Commerce.)

Assn. for Safe International Road Travel, *12320 Parklawn Dr., Rockville, MD 20852; (240) 249-0100. Fax, (301) 230-0411. Cathy Silberman, Executive Director. General email, asirt@asirt.org Web, www.asirt.org*

Promotes road safety through education and advocacy with governments in the United States and abroad. Serves as information resource for governments, study abroad programs, travel organizations, nongovernmental organizations, and individual travelers.

Assn. of Metropolitan Planning Organizations, *Transportation, 444 N. Capitol St., #345 20001; (202) 624-3680. Fax, (202) 624-3685. DeLania Hardy, Executive Director. Web, www.ampo.org*

Membership: more than 385 metropolitan councils of elected officials and transportation professionals responsible for planning local transportation systems. Provides a forum for professional and organizational development; sponsors conferences and training programs.

Assn. of Transportation Law Professionals, *P.O. Box 5407, Annapolis, MD 21403; (410) 268-1311. Fax, (410) 268-1322. Lauren Michalski, Executive Director. General email, atlp@keyassnmgt.com Web, www.atlp.org*

Provides members with continuing educational development in transportation law and practice. Interests include railroad, motor, energy, pipeline, antitrust, labor, logistics, safety, environmental, air, and maritime matters.

(Formerly the Assn. for Transportation Law, Logistics, and Policy.)

Diesel Technology Forum, *5291 Corporate Drive, #102, Frederick, MD 21703-2875; (301) 668-7230. Fax, (301) 668-7234. Allen Schaeffer, Executive Director.*
General email, dtf@dieselforum.org
Web, www.dieselforum.org

Membership: vehicle and engine manufacturers, component suppliers, petroleum refineries, and emissions control device makers. Advocates use of diesel engines. Provides information on diesel power technology use and efforts to improve fuel efficiency and emissions control. Monitors legislation and regulations.

Eno Center for Transportation, *1710 Rhode Island Ave. N.W., #500 20005; (202) 879-4700. Fax, (202) 879-4719. Joshua L. Schank, President, (202) 879-4711.*
Web, www.enotrans.org

Seeks continuous improvement in transportation and its public and private leadership in order to increase the system's mobility, safety, and sustainability. Offers professional development programs, policy forums, and publications.

Institute of Navigation, *8551 Rixlew Lane, #360, Manassas, VA 20109; (703) 366-2723. Fax, (703) 366-2724. Lisa Beaty, Executive Director.*
General email, membership@ion.org
Web, www.ion.org

Membership: individuals and organizations interested in navigation and position-determining systems. Encourages research in navigation and establishment of uniform practices in navigation operations and education; conducts symposia on air, space, marine, and land navigation, as well as position determination.

Institute of Transportation Engineers (ITE), *1627 Eye St. N.W., #600 20006; (202) 785-0060. Fax, (202) 785-0609. Philip J. Caruso, Deputy Executive Director, ext. 126.*
General email, ite_staff@ite.org
Web, www.ite.org

Membership: international professional transportation engineers. Conducts research, seminars, and training sessions; provides professional and scientific information on transportation standards and recommended practices.

International Brotherhood of Teamsters, *25 Louisiana Ave. N.W. 20001-2198; (202) 624-6800. Fax, (202) 624-6918. James P. Hoffa, General President; Fred McLuckie, Director, Federal Legislation and Regulation, (202) 624-8741. Press, (202) 624-6911.*
General email, feedback@teamster.org
Web, www.teamster.org

Membership: more than 1.4 million workers in the transportation and construction industries, factories, offices, hospitals, warehouses, and other workplaces. Helps members negotiate pay, benefits, and better working conditions; conducts training programs and workshops. Monitors legislation and regulations.

National Research Council (NRC), *Transportation Research Board, 500 5th St. N.W., 7th Floor 20001; (202) 334-2934. Fax, (202) 334-2003. Robert E. Skinner Jr., Executive Director. Library, (202) 334-2989. Press, (202) 334-2138.*
Web, www.trb.org

Promotes research in transportation systems planning and administration and in the design, construction, maintenance, and operation of transportation facilities. Provides information to state and national highway and transportation departments; operates research information services; conducts studies, conferences, and workshops; publishes technical reports. Library open to the public by appointment.

National Research Council (NRC), *Transportation Research Board Library, 500 5th St. N.W., Keck 439 20001; (202) 334-2989. Fax, (202) 334-2527. Lisa Loyo, Information Services Manager, (202) 334-2990. Press, (202) 334-3252.*
General email, TRBlibrary@nas.edu
Web, www.trb.org/library

Primary archive for the Transportation Research Board, Highway Research Board, Strategic Highway Research Program, and Marine Board. Subject areas include transportation, aviation, engineering, rail, roads, and transit.

NDTA (The Assn. for Global Logistics and Transportation), *50 S. Pickett St., #220, Alexandria, VA 22304-7296; (703) 751-5011. Fax, (703) 823-8761. Lt. Gen. Kenneth Wykle (USA, Ret.), President.*
Web, http://ndtahq.com

Membership: transportation users, manufacturers, and mode carriers; information technology firms; and related military, government, and civil interests worldwide. Promotes a strong U.S. transportation capability through coordination of private industry, government, and the military.

Sheet Metal Workers International Assn., *1750 New York Ave. N.W., 6th Floor 20006; (202) 783-5880. Fax, (202) 662-0880. Joseph J. Nigro, General President.*
Web, www.smwia.org

Membership: U.S., Puerto Rican, and Canadian workers in the building and construction trades, manufacturing, and the railroad and shipyard industries. Assists members with contract negotiation and grievances; conducts training programs and workshops. Monitors legislation and regulations. (Affiliated with the Sheet Metal and Air Conditioning Contractors' Assn., the AFL-CIO, and the Canadian Labour Congress.)

Surface Transportation Information Sharing and Analysis Center (ISAC), *c/o EWA Information and Infrastructure Technologies, Inc., 13873 Park Center Rd., #200, Herndon, VA 20171-5406; (866) 784-7221. Fax, (703) 478-7647. Paul G. Wolfe, Director.*
General email, st-isac@surfacetransportationisac.org
Web, www.surfacetransportationisac.org

Protects physical and electronic infrastructure of surface transportation and public transit carriers. Collects, analyzes, and distributes critical security and threat information from worldwide resources; shares best security practices and provides 24/7 immediate physical and cyber-threat warnings.

United Transportation Union, *Washington Office,* *304 Pennsylvania Ave. S.E. 20003; (202) 543-7714. Fax, (202) 544-3024. James A. Stem Jr., National Legislative Director; John J. Risch III, Alternate National Legislative Director.*
General email, jstem@smart-union.org
Web, www.utu.org

Membership: approximately 150,000 workers in the transportation industry. Helps members negotiate pay, benefits, and better working conditions; conducts training programs and workshops. Monitors legislation and regulations. (Headquarters in Cleveland, Ohio.)

Freight and Intermodalism

▶AGENCIES

Federal Railroad Administration *(Transportation Dept.), Public Engagement,* West Bldg., 1200 New Jersey Ave. S.E., MS 10 20590; (202) 493-6405. Fax, (202) 493-6009. Timothy Barkley, Director.*
General email, yvonne.white@dot.gov
Web, www.fra.dot.gov/page/p0030

Maritime Administration *(Transportation Dept.), Infrastructure Development and Congestion Mitigation,* West Bldg., 1200 New Jersey Ave. S.E. 20590; (202) 366-5076. Fax, (202) 366-6988. Robert Bouchard, Director.*
Web, www.marad.dot.gov

Provides coordination and management of port infrastructure projects; provides leadership in national congestion mitigation efforts that involve waterway and port issues; promotes the development and improved utilization of ports and port facilities, including intermodal connections, terminals, and distribution networks; and provides technical information and advice to other agencies and organizations concerned with intermodal development. Information and advice include the analysis of intermodal economics, the development of applicable information systems, investigation of institutional and regulatory impediments, and the application of appropriate transportation management systems.

Surface Transportation Board *(Transportation Dept.),* *395 E St. S.W., #1220 20423-0001 (mailing address: 395 E St. S.W., Washington, DC 20024); (202) 245-0245. Fax, (202) 245-0458. Daniel R. Elliott III, Chair, (202) 245-0220. Library, (202) 245-0406. TTY, (800) 877-8339. Press, (202) 245-0234.*
Web, www.stb.dot.gov

Regulates rates for water transportation and intermodal connections in noncontiguous domestic trade (between the mainland and Alaska, Hawaii, or U.S. territories). Library open to the public.

▶NONGOVERNMENTAL

American Moving and Storage Assn. (AMSA), *1611 Duke St., Alexandria, VA 22314-3406; (703) 683-7410. Fax, (703) 683-7527. Linda Bauer Darr, President. Information, (888) 849-2672.*
General email, info@moving.org
Web, www.promover.org

Represents members' views before the Transportation Dept. and other government agencies. Conducts certification and training programs. Provides financial support for research on the moving and storage industry.

Intermodal Assn. of North America, *11785 Beltsville Dr., #1100, Calverton, MD 20705-4048; (301) 982-3400. Fax, (301) 982-4815. Joanne F. (Joni) Casey, President, ext. 349.*
General email, info@intermodal.org
Web, www.intermodal.org

Membership: railroads, stacktrain operators, water carriers, motor carriers, marketing companies, and suppliers to the intermodal industry. Promotes intermodal transportation of freight. Monitors legislation and regulations.

National Assn. of Chemical Distributors (NACD), *1560 Wilson Blvd., #1100, Arlington, VA 22209; (703) 527-6223. Fax, (703) 527-7747. Eric Byer, President.*
General email, nacdpublicaffairs@nacd.com
Web, www.nacd.com

Membership: firms involved in purchasing, processing, blending, storing, transporting, and marketing of chemical products. Provides members with information on such topics as training, safe handling and transport of chemicals, liability insurance, and environmental issues. Manages the NACD Chemical Educational Foundation. Monitors legislation and regulations.

National Customs Brokers and Forwarders Assn. of America, *1200 18th St. N.W., #901 20036; (202) 466-0222. Fax, (202) 466-0226. Barbara Reilly, Executive Vice President.*
General email, staff@ncbfaa.org
Web, www.ncbfaa.org

Membership: customs brokers and freight forwarders in the United States. Fosters information exchange within the industry. Monitors legislation and regulations.

National Industrial Transportation League, *1700 N. Moore St., #1900, Arlington, VA 22209-1904; (703) 524-5011. Fax, (703) 524-5017. Bruce J. Carlton, President.*
General email, info@nitl.org
Web, www.nitl.org

Membership: air, water, and surface shippers and receivers, including industries, corporations, chambers of commerce, and trade associations. Monitors legislation and regulations.

Federal Aviation Administration

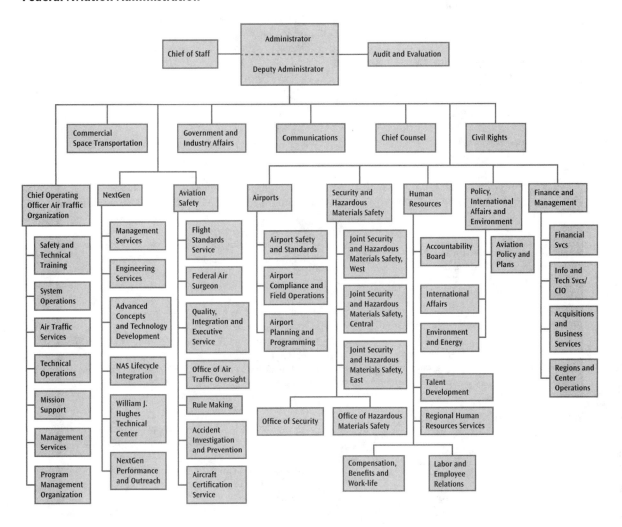

AIR TRANSPORTATION

General

Civil Air Patrol National Capital Wing, *200 McChord St. S.W., #111, Joint Base Anacostia-Bolling 20032; (202) 767-4405. Bruce Heinlein, Wing Commander.*
General email, pa@natcapwg.cap.gov
Web, www.natcapwg.cap.gov and www.natcapwing.org

Official civilian auxiliary of the U.S. Air Force. Primary function is to conduct search-and-rescue missions for the Air Force. Maintains an aerospace education program for adults and a cadet program for junior and senior high school students. (Headquarters at Maxwell Air Force Base, Ala.)

Federal Aviation Administration (FAA) *(Transportation Dept.), 800 Independence Ave. S.W. 20591; (202) 267-3111. Fax, (202) 267-5047. Michael P. Huerta, Administrator. Press, (202) 267-3883. Toll-free, (866) 835-5322.*
Web, www.faa.gov

Regulates air commerce to improve aviation safety; promotes development of a national system of airports; develops and operates a common system of air traffic control and air navigation for both civilian and military aircraft; prepares the annual National Aviation System Plan.

Federal Aviation Administration (FAA) *(Transportation Dept.), Airport Planning and Environment, 800 Independence Ave. S.W., #619, APP-400 20591-0001; (202) 267-3263. Lori Pagnanelli, Manager, Acting.*
Web, www.faa.gov/about/office_org/headquarters_offices/apl

Leads the FAA's strategic policy and planning efforts, coordinates the agency's reauthorization before Congress, and is responsible for national aviation policies and strategies in the environment and energy arenas, including aviation activity forecasts, economic analyses, aircraft noise and emissions research and policy, environmental policy, and aviation insurance.

Federal Aviation Administration (FAA) *(Transportation Dept.), Environment and Energy, 800 Independence Ave. S.W., #900W 20591; (202) 267-3576. Fax, (202) 267-5594. Lourdes Maurice, Director.*
Web, www.faa.gov/about/office_org/headquarters_offices/apl/research

Responsible for environmental affairs and energy conservation for aviation, including implementation and administration of various aviation-related environmental acts.

Federal Aviation Administration (FAA) *(Transportation Dept.), Finance, Acquisition, and Business Services, 800 Independence Ave. S.W., #1002 West, AJA-O 20591; (202) 267-7222. Fax, (202) 267-5738. Patricia A. McNall, Deputy Assistant Administrator.*
Web, www.faa.gov/about/office_org/headquarters_offices/afn

Advises and assists in developing concepts for applying new technologies to meet long-range national airspace system requirements and for system acquisition, engineering, and management activities.

Federal Aviation Administration (FAA) *(Transportation Dept.), International Affairs, 600 Independence Ave. S.W., #10B, 6th Floor East, API-1 20591; (202) 385-8900. Fax, (202) 267-7198. Carey Fagan, Executive Director.*
Web, www.faa.gov/about/office_org/headquarters_offices/apl/international_affairs

Coordinates all activities of the FAA that involve foreign relations; acts as liaison with the State Dept. and other agencies concerning international aviation; provides other countries with technical assistance on civil aviation problems; formulates international civil aviation policy for the United States.

Federal Aviation Administration (FAA) *(Transportation Dept.), Operations, Systems Engineering and Safety, 1250 Maryland Ave. S.W., 3rd Floor 20024; (202) 385-7100. Fax, (202) 385-7105. Michele Merkel, Director.*
Web, www.faa.gov

Designs and maintains the National Airspace System (NAS) Enterprise Architecture and provides systems engineering and safety expertise to bridge the gap between today's NAS and the Next Generation Air Transportation System (NextGen).

International Trade Administration (ITA) *(Commerce Dept.), Industry and Analysis, Transportation and Machinery, 1401 Constitution Ave. N.W., #4036 20230-0001; (202) 482-0554. Fax, (202) 482-0674. Scott Kennedy, Director, Acting.*
Web, http://trade.gov/mas/index.asp

Promotes the export of U.S. aerospace, automotive, and machinery products; compiles and analyzes industry data; seeks to secure a favorable position for the U.S. aerospace, auto, and machinery industries in global markets through policy and trade agreements.

Justice Dept. (DOJ), *Civil Division, Torts Branch, Aviation and Admiralty Litigation, 1425 New York Ave. N.W., #10100 20005 (mailing address: P.O. Box 14271, Washington, DC 20044-4271); (202) 616-4100. Fax, (202) 616-4002. Peter F. Frost, Director.*
Web, www.justice.gov/civil/torts/aa/t-aa.html

Represents the federal government in civil suits arising from aviation and admiralty incidents and accidents. In aviation, handles tort litigation for the government's activities in the operation of the air traffic control system, regulation of air commerce, weather services, aeronautical charting, and operation of its own civil and military aircraft. In admiralty, defends the government's placement and maintenance of maritime navigational aids, its nautical charting and dredging activities, and its operation and maintenance of U.S. and contract-operated vessels. Brings cases for government cargo damage, pollution cleanups, and damage to U.S. locks, dams, and navaids.

National Aeronautics and Space Administration (NASA), *Aeronautics Research Mission Directorate, 300 E St. S.W., #6A70 20546 (mailing address: NASA Headquarters, Mail Code 6J39A, Washington, DC 20546); (202) 358-4600. Fax, (202) 358-2920. Jaiwon Shin, Associate Administrator.*
Web, www.aeronautics.nasa.gov

Conducts research in aerodynamics, materials, structures, avionics, propulsion, high-performance computing, human factors, aviation safety, and space transportation in support of national space and aeronautical research and technology goals. Manages the following NASA research centers: Ames (Moffett Field, Calif.); Dryden (Edwards, Calif.); Langley (Hampton, Va.); and Glenn (Cleveland, Ohio).

National Air and Space Museum *(Smithsonian Institution), 6th St. and Independence Ave. S.W. 20560; (202) 633-2214. Fax, (202) 633-8174. Gen. J.R. (Jack) Dailey, Director. Library, (202) 633-2320. Education office, (202) 633-2540. Tours, (202) 633-2563.*
General email, info@si.edu
Web, www.airandspace.si.edu

Maintains exhibits and collections on aeronautics, pioneers of flight, and early aircraft through modern air technology. Library open to the public by appointment.

Research and Innovative Technology Administration *(Transportation Dept.), Bureau of Transportation Statistics, Airline Information, 1200 New Jersey Ave. S.E., #E-34, RTS-42 20590; (202) 366-4373. Fax, (202) 366-3383. William Chadwick, Director.*
Web, www.rita.dot.gov/bts/sites/rita.gov/bts/Files/subject_area/airline_information/sources/index.html

Develops, interprets, and enforces accounting and reporting regulations for all areas of the aviation industry;

issues air carrier reporting instructions, waivers, and due-date extensions.

Steven F. Udvar-Hazy Center *(Smithsonian Institution)*, *National Air and Space Museum*, *14390 Air and Space Museum Pkwy., Chantilly, VA 20151; (703) 572-4118. Gen. John R. Dailey (USMC, Ret.), Director. Public Affairs, (703) 572-4040.*
General email, nasm-visitorservices@si.edu
Web, www.airandspace.si.edu/visit/udvar-hazy-center

Displays and preserves a collection of historical aviation and space artifacts, including the B-29 Superfortress, *Enola Gay*, the Lockheed SR-71 Blackbird, the prototype of the Boeing 707, the space shuttle *Discovery*, and the Concord. Provides a center for research into the history, science, and technology of aviation and space flight. Open to the public daily 10:00 a.m.–5:30 p.m., except December 25.

Transportation Dept. (DOT), *Aviation Analysis*, *1200 New Jersey Ave. S.E., #W86-481 20590; (202) 366-5903. Fax, (202) 366-7638. Todd M. Homan, Director. Press, (202) 366-4570.*
Web, www.dot.gov/policy/aviation-policy/office-aviation-analysis

Analyzes essential air service needs of communities; directs subsidy policy and programs; guarantees air service to small communities; conducts research for the department on airline mergers, international route awards, and employee protection programs; administers the air carrier fitness provisions of the Federal Aviation Act; registers domestic air carriers; enforces charter regulations for tour operators.

Transportation Dept. (DOT), *Aviation Consumer Protection*, *1200 New Jersey Ave. S.E. 20590; (202) 366-2220. Norman Strickman, Director, (202) 366-5960. Disability-Related Problems, (800) 778-4838. TTY, (202) 366-0511.*
Web, www.dot.gov/airconsumer

Addresses complaints about airline service and consumer-protection matters. Conducts investigations, provides assistance, and reviews regulations affecting air carriers.

► CONGRESS

For a listing of relevant congressional committees and subcommittees, please see page 657 or the Appendix.

► NONGOVERNMENTAL

Aeronautical Repair Station Assn., *121 N. Henry St., Alexandria, VA 22314-2903; (703) 739-9543. Fax, (703) 739-9488. Sarah MacLeod, Executive Director.*
General email, arsa@arsa.org
Web, www.arsa.org

Membership: repair stations that have Federal Aviation Administration certificates or comparable non-U.S. certification; associate members are suppliers and distributors of components and parts. Works to improve relations between repair stations and manufacturers. Interests include establishing uniformity in the application, interpretation, and enforcement of FAA regulations. Monitors legislation and regulations.

Aerospace Industries Assn. (AIA), *1000 Wilson Blvd., #1700, Arlington, VA 22209-3928; (703) 358-1009. Fax, (703) 358-1012. Marion C. Blakey, President. Press, (703) 358-1076.*
General email, aia@aia-aerospace.org
Web, www.aia-aerospace.org

Represents manufacturers of commercial, military, and business aircraft; helicopters; aircraft engines; missiles; spacecraft; and related components and equipment. Interests include international standards and trade.

Aircraft Owners and Pilots Assn. (AOPA), *Legislative Affairs, 50 F St. N.W., #750 20001; (202) 737-7950. Fax, (202) 737-7951. Jim Coon, Vice President. Toll-free for members, (800) 872-2672.*
Web, www.aopa.org

Membership: owners and pilots of general aviation aircraft. Washington office monitors legislation and regulations. Headquarters office provides members with a variety of aviation-related services; issues airport directory and handbook for pilots; sponsors the Air Safety Foundation. (Headquarters in Frederick, Md.)

Air Line Pilots Assn. International, *1625 Massachusetts Ave. N.W. 20036; (202) 797-4033. Fax, (202) 797-4030. W. Randolph Helling, Treasurer. Press, (703) 481-4440. Toll-free, (888) 359-2572.*
General email, alpaemail@alpa.org
Web, www.alpa.org

Membership: airline pilots in the United States and Canada. Promotes air travel safety; assists investigations of aviation accidents. Monitors legislation and regulations. (Affiliated with the AFL-CIO and the Canadian Labour Conference.)

Airlines for America, *1301 Pennsylvania Ave. N.W., #1100 20004-1707; (202) 626-4000. Fax, (202) 626-4166. Nicholas Calio, President. Press, (202) 626-4173.*
General email, a4a@airlines.org
Web, www.airlines.org

Membership: U.S. scheduled air carriers. Promotes aviation safety and the facilitation of air transportation for passengers and cargo. Collects data on trends in airline operations. Monitors legislation and regulations.

American Helicopter Society *(AHS International)*, *217 N. Washington St., Alexandria, VA 22314-2538; (703) 684-6777. Fax, (703) 739-9279. Michael Hirschberg, Executive Director.*
General email, staff@vtol.org
Web, www.vtol.org

Membership: individuals and organizations interested in vertical flight. Acts as an information clearinghouse for technical data on helicopter design improvement, aerodynamics, and safety. Awards the Vertical Flight Foundation Scholarship to college students interested in helicopter technology.

American Institute of Aeronautics and Astronautics (AIAA), *1801 Alexander Bell Dr., #500, Reston, VA 20191-4344; (703) 264-7500. Fax, (703) 264-7551. Sandy Magnus, Executive Director. Information, (800) 639-2422.*

General email, custserv@aiaa.org

Web, www.aiaa.org

Membership: engineers, scientists, and students in the fields of aeronautics and astronautics. Holds workshops on aerospace technical issues for congressional subcommittees; sponsors international conferences. Offers computerized database through its Technical Information Service.

Assn. of Flight Attendants–CWA, *501 3rd St. N.W. 20001-2797; (202) 434-1300. Fax, (202) 434-1319. Veda Shook, President. Press, (202) 434-0586. Toll-free, (800) 424-2401.*

General email, info@afacwa.org

Web, www.afanet.org

Membership: approximately 60,000 flight attendants. Helps members negotiate pay, benefits, and better working conditions; conducts training programs and workshops. Monitors legislation and regulations. (Affiliated with the AFL-CIO.)

Cargo Airline Assn., *1620 L St. N.W., #610 20036-2438; (202) 293-1030. Fax, (202) 293-4377. Stephen A. Alterman, President.*

General email, info@cargoair.org

Web, www.cargoair.org

Membership: cargo airlines and other firms interested in the development and promotion of air freight.

Coalition of Airline Pilots Assns. (CAPA), *444 N. Capitol St., #532 20001; (202) 624-3535. Fax, (202) 624-3536. Maryann DeMarco, Executive Director.*

General email, capapilots@capapilots.org

Web, www.capapilots.org

Trade association of more than 28,000 professional pilots. Addresses safety, security, legislative, and regulatory issues affecting flight deck crews.

General Aviation Manufacturers Assn. (GAMA), *1400 K St. N.W., #801 20005-2485; (202) 393-1500. Fax, (202) 842-4063. Peter J. Bunce, President.*

General email, bforan@gama.aero

Web, www.gama.aero

Membership: manufacturers of business, commuter, and personal aircraft and manufacturers of engines, avionics, and related equipment. Monitors legislation and regulations; sponsors safety and public information programs.

Helicopter Assn. International, *1920 Ballanger Ave., Alexandria, VA 22314-2898; (703) 683-4646. Fax, (703) 683-4745. Matthew Zuccaro, President.*

General email, questions@rotor.com

Web, www.rotor.com

Membership: owners, manufacturers, and operators of helicopters and affiliated companies in the civil helicopter industry. Provides information on use and operation of helicopters; offers business management and aviation

safety courses; sponsors annual industry exposition. Monitors legislation and regulations.

International Assn. of Machinists and Aerospace Workers, *9000 Machinists Pl., Upper Marlboro, MD 20772-2687; (301) 967-4500. Fax, (301) 967-4588. R. Thomas Buffenbarger, International President. Information, (301) 967-4520.*

General email, websteward@iamaw.org

Web, www.goiam.org

Membership: machinists in more than 200 industries. Helps members negotiate pay, benefits, and better working conditions; conducts training programs and workshops. Monitors legislation and regulations. (Affiliated with the AFL-CIO, the Canadian Labour Congress, the International Metalworkers Federation, the International Transport Workers' Federation, and the Railway Labor Executives Assn.)

National Aeronautic Assn., *Reagan National Airport, Hangar 7, #202 20001-6015; (703) 416-4888. Fax, (703) 416-4877. Jonathan Gaffney, President.*

General email, naa@naa.aero

Web, www.naa.aero

Membership: persons interested in development of general and sporting aviation, including skydiving, commercial and military aircraft, and spaceflight. Supervises sporting aviation competitions; administers awards in aviation; oversees and approves official U.S. aircraft, aeronautics, and space records. Serves as U.S. representative to the International Aeronautical Federation in Lausanne, Switzerland.

National Agricultural Aviation Assn., *1440 Duke St., Alexandria, VA 22314; (202) 546-5722. Fax, (202) 546-5726. Andrew D. Moore, Executive Director.*

General email, information@agaviation.org

Web, www.agaviation.org

Membership: agricultural pilots; operating companies that seed, fertilize, and spray land by air; and allied industries. Monitors legislation and regulations. (Affiliated with National Agricultural Aviation Research and Education Foundation.)

National Air Carrier Assn., *1000 Wilson Blvd., #1700, Arlington, VA 22209-3901; (703) 358-8060. Fax, (703) 358-8070. A. Oakley Brooks, President.*

Web, www.naca.cc

Membership: U.S. air carriers certified for nonscheduled and scheduled operations for passengers and cargo in the United States and abroad. Monitors legislation and regulations.

National Air Transportation Assn., *4226 King St., Alexandria, VA 22302; (703) 845-9000. Fax, (703) 845-8176. Thomas L. Hendricks, President. Information, (800) 808-6282.*

Web, www.nata.aero

Membership: companies that provide on-demand air charter, flight training, maintenance and repair, avionics, and other services. Manages an education foundation;

compiles statistics; provides business assistance programs. Monitors legislation and regulations. (Affiliated with the National Air Transportation Foundation.)

National Assn. of State Aviation Officials, *Washington National Airport, Hangar 7, #218 20001; (703) 417-1880. Fax, (703) 417-1885. Kim Stevens, President, Acting. General email, info@nasao.org*

Web, www.nasao.org

Membership: state and territorial aeronautics agencies that deal with aviation issues, including regulation. Seeks uniform aviation laws; manages an aviation research and education foundation.

National Business Aviation Assn. (NBAA), *1200 G St. N.W., #1100 20005; (202) 783-9000. Fax, (202) 331-8364. Ed Bolen, President. Toll-free, (800) 394-6222. General email, info@nbaa.org*

Web, www.nbaa.org

Membership: companies owning and operating aircraft for business use, suppliers, and maintenance and air fleet service companies. Conducts seminars and workshops in business aviation management. Sponsors annual civilian aviation exposition. Monitors legislation and regulations.

Regional Airline Assn., *2025 M St. N.W., #800 20036-3309; (202) 367-1170. Fax, (202) 367-2170. Roger Cohen, President. General email, raa@raa.org*

Web, www.raa.org

Membership: regional airlines that provide passenger, scheduled cargo, and mail service. Issues annual report on the industry.

RTCA, *1150 18th St., #910 20036; (202) 833-9339. Fax, (202) 833-9434. Margaret T. Jenny, President. General email, info@rtca.org*

Web, www.rtca.org

Membership: federal agencies, aviation organizations, and commercial firms interested in aeronautical systems. Develops and publishes standards for aviation, including minimum operational performance standards for equipment; conducts research, makes recommendations to FAA, and issues reports on the field of aviation electronics and telecommunications. (Formerly the Radio Technical Commission for Aeronautics.)

Airports

▶AGENCIES

Animal and Plant Health Inspection Service (APHIS) *(Agriculture Dept.), Wildlife Services, 1400 Independence Ave. S.W., #1624S 20250-3402; 4700 River Road, Riverdale, MD 20737; (202) 799-7095. Fax, (202) 690-0053. William H. Clay, Deputy Administrator. Hotline, (866) 487-3297.*

Web, www.aphis.usda.gov/wildlife_damage

Works to minimize damage caused by wildlife to human health and safety. Interests include aviation safety; works with airport managers to reduce the risk of bird strikes. Oversees the National Wildlife Research Center in Ft. Collins, Colo.

Bureau of Land Management (BLM) *(Interior Dept.), Lands, Realty, and Cadastral Survey, 20 M St. S.E. 20003 (mailing address: 1849 C St. N.W., Washington, DC 20240); (202) 912-7300. Fax, (202) 912-7199. Robyn Shoop, Division Chief, Acting.*

Web, www.blm.gov/wo/st/en/info/directory/WO-350_dir.html

Operates the Airport Lease Program, which leases public lands for use as public airports.

Federal Aviation Administration (FAA) *(Transportation Dept.), Airports, 800 Independence Ave. S.W., #600E, ARP-1 20591; (202) 267-8738. Fax, (202) 267-5301. Benito DeLeon, Associate Administrator, Acting.*

Web, www.faa.gov/about/office_org/headquarters_offices/arp/offices

Makes grants for development and improvement of publicly operated and owned airports and some privately owned airports; certifies safety design standards for airports; administers the congressional Airport Improvement Program; oversees construction and accessibility standards for people with disabilities. Questions about local airports are usually referred to a local FAA field office.

Maryland Aviation Administration, *P.O. Box 8766, BWI Airport, Terminal Bldg., 3rd Floor, MD 21240-0766; (410) 859-7100. Fax, (410) 850-4729. Paul J. Wiedefeld, Executive Director. Information, (800) 435-9294. Press, (410) 859-7027. General email, maa@mdot.state.md.us*

Web, www.marylandaviation.com and www.bwiairport.com

Responsible for aviation operations, planning, instruction, and safety in Maryland; operates Baltimore/Washington International Thurgood Marshall Airport (BWI) and Martin State Airport.

Metropolitan Washington Airports Authority, *1 Aviation Circle 20001-6000; (703) 417-8610. Fax, (703) 417-8949. John E. Potter, President. Information, (703) 417-8600. Press, (703) 417-8370.*

Web, www.mwaa.com

Independent interstate agency created by Virginia and the District of Columbia with the consent of Congress; operates Washington Dulles International Airport and Ronald Reagan Washington National Airport.

▶NONGOVERNMENTAL

Airports Council International (ACI), *1615 L St. N.W., #300 20036; (202) 293-8500. Fax, (202) 331-1362. Kevin Burke, President. General email, postmaster@aci-na.org*

Web, www.aci-na.org

Membership: authorities, boards, commissions, and municipal departments operating public airports. Serves as liaison with government agencies and other aviation organizations; works to improve passenger and freight facilitation; acts as clearinghouse on engineering and operational aspects of airport development. Monitors legislation and regulations.

American Assn. of Airport Executives, *601 Madison St., #400, Alexandria, VA 22314; (703) 824-0504. Fax, (703) 820-1395. Charles M. Barclay, President, (703) 824-0504, ext. 129.*
Web, www.aaae.org

Membership: airport managers, superintendents, consultants, government officials, authorities and commissioners, and others interested in the construction, management, and operation of airports. Conducts examination for and awards the professional designation of Accredited Airport Executive.

Aviation Safety and Security

▶**AGENCIES**

Federal Aviation Administration (FAA) *(Transportation Dept.), Accident Investigation and Prevention, 800 Independence Ave. S.W., #840, AVP-1 20591; (202) 267-9612. Fax, (202) 267-5043. Anthony F. Fazio, Director.*
Web, www.faa.gov/about/office_org/headquarters_offices/avs/offices/avp

Investigates aviation accidents and incidents to detect unsafe conditions and trends in the national airspace system and to coordinate corrective action.

Federal Aviation Administration (FAA) *(Transportation Dept.), Air Traffic Organization, 800 Independence Ave. S.W., #1018A, AJA-O 20591; (202) 493-5602. Fax, (202) 267-5085. Teri O. Bristle, Chief Operating Officer, Acting. Press, (202) 267-3883.*
Web, www.faa.gov/about/office_org/headquarters_offices/ato

Operates the national air traffic control system; employs air traffic controllers at airport towers, en route air traffic control centers, and flight service stations; maintains the William J. Hughes Technical Center for aviation research, testing, and evaluation.

Federal Aviation Administration (FAA) *(Transportation Dept.), Air Traffic Organization, Technical Operations, 800 Independence Ave. S.W., #700E, ATO 20591; (202) 267-3366. Fax, (202) 267-6060. Vaughn Turner, Vice President.*
Web, www.faa.gov/about/office_org/headquarters_offices/ato/service_units/techops

Conducts research and development programs aimed at providing procedures, facilities, and devices needed for a safe and efficient system of air navigation and air traffic control.

Federal Aviation Administration (FAA) *(Transportation Dept.), Aviation Safety, Aerospace Medicine, 800 Independence Ave. S.W., #800W, AAM-1 20591; (202) 267-3535. Fax, (202) 267-5399. Dr. Frederick E. Tilton, Federal Air Surgeon.*
Web, www.faa.gov/about/office_org/headquarters_offices/avs/offices/aam

Responsible for the medical activities and policies of the FAA; designates, through regional offices, aviation medical examiners who conduct periodic medical examinations of all air personnel; regulates and oversees drug and alcohol testing programs for pilots, air traffic controllers, and others who hold safety-sensitive positions; maintains a Civil Aerospace Medical Institute in Oklahoma City.

Federal Aviation Administration (FAA) *(Transportation Dept.), Aviation Safety, Aircraft Certification Service, 800 Independence Ave. S.W., #800E, AIR-1 20591-0004; (202) 267-8235. Fax, (202) 267-5364. Dorenda Baker, Director.*
Web, www.faa.gov/about/office_org/field_offices/aco

Certifies all aircraft for airworthiness; approves designs and specifications for new aircraft, aircraft engines, propellers, and appliances; supervises aircraft manufacturing and testing.

Federal Aviation Administration (FAA) *(Transportation Dept.), Aviation Safety, Flight Standards Service, 800 Independence Ave. S.W., #821, AFS-1 20591; (202) 267-8237. Fax, (202) 267-5230. John Duncan, Director. Press, (202) 267-3883.*
Web, www.faa.gov/about/office_org/headquarters_offices/avs/offices/afs

Sets certification standards for air carriers, commercial operators, air agencies, and air personnel (except air traffic control tower operators); directs and executes certification and inspection of flight procedures, operating methods, air personnel qualification and proficiency, and maintenance aspects of airworthiness programs; manages the registry of civil aircraft and all official air personnel records; supports law enforcement agencies responsible for drug interdiction.

Federal Aviation Administration (FAA) *(Transportation Dept.), En Route and Oceanic Services, 600 Independence Ave. S.W., #FOB 10-B, #3E 1500 20591; (202) 385-8501. Fax, (202) 493-4306. Gregory D. Burke, Vice President.*
Web, www.faa.gov/about/office_org/headquarters_offices/ato/service_units/enroute

Directs 20 air route traffic control centers, which provide satellite-based capability for en route navigation and a color display for en route controllers. Improves the safety of hazardous weather avoidance. Increases operations efficiency through the use of cockpit surveillance and other means. Resolves support issues.

Federal Bureau of Investigation (FBI) *(Justice Dept.), Criminal Investigative Division, 935 Pennsylvania Ave. N.W., #3012 20535; (202) 324-4260. Fax, (202) 324-0027. Ronald Hosko, Assistant Director.*
Web, www.fbi.gov

Investigates cases of aircraft hijacking, destruction of aircraft, and air piracy. Works with TSA and FAA to ensure security of national air carrier systems in areas of violent crime, organized crime, civil rights, corruption, and financial crimes.

Federal Communications Commission (FCC),
Enforcement Bureau, 445 12th St. S.W., 3rd Floor, #7C723 20554; (202) 418-7450. P. Michele Ellison, Chief, Enforcement Bureau. Toll-free fax, (888) 418-0232. Media Relations, (202) 418-0500.
Web, www.fcc.gov/enforcement-bureau

Provides technical services to aid the Federal Aviation Administration in locating aircraft in distress; provides interference resolution for air traffic control radio frequencies.

National Transportation Safety Board, *Aviation Safety, 490 L'Enfant Plaza East S.W., #5400 20594-0001; (202) 314-6300. Fax, (202) 314-6309. John Delisi, Director. Information, (202) 314-6540. Press, (202) 314-6100.*
Web, www.ntsb.gov

Responsible for management, policies, and programs in aviation safety and for aviation accident investigations. Manages programs on special investigations, safety issues, and safety objectives. Acts as U.S. representative in international investigations.

Transportation Security Administration (TSA)
(Homeland Security Dept.), TSA-1, 601 S. 12th St., 7th Floor, Arlington, VA 20598-6001; (571) 227-2801. Fax, (571) 227-1398. John S. Pistole, Administrator. Press, (571) 227-2829. Questions and concerns regarding travel can be submitted to the TSA Contact Center, toll-free, (866) 289-9673.
General email, TSA-ContactCenter@dhs.gov
Web, www.tsa.gov/public

Protects the nation's transportation system. Performs and oversees airport security, including passenger and baggage screeners, airport federal security directors, and air marshals.

Transportation Security Administration (TSA)
(Homeland Security Dept.), Office of Law Enforcement, Federal Air Marshal Service, TSA-18, 601 S. 12th St., Arlington, VA 20598-6018; (703) 487-3400. Fax, (703) 487-3405. Robert S. Bray, Director.
Web, www.tsa.gov/about-tsa/office-law-enforcement

Protects air security in the United States. Promotes public confidence in the U.S. civil aviation system. Deploys marshals on flights around the world to detect and deter hostile acts targeting U.S. air carriers, airports, passengers, and crews.

▶**NONGOVERNMENTAL**

Aerospace Medical Assn., *320 S. Henry St., Alexandria, VA 22314-3579; (703) 739-2240. Fax, (703) 739-9652. Jeffery Sventek, Executive Director.*
General email, inquiries@asma.org
Web, www.asma.org

Membership: physicians, flight surgeons, aviation medical examiners, flight nurses, scientists, technicians, and specialists in clinical, operational, and research fields of aerospace medicine. Promotes programs to improve aerospace medicine and maintain safety in aviation by examining and monitoring the health of aviation personnel; members may consult in aircraft investigation and cockpit design.

Air Traffic Control Assn., *1101 King St., #300, Alexandria, VA 22314-2963; (703) 299-2430. Fax, (703) 299-2437. Peter F. Dumont, President.*
General email, info@atca.org
Web, www.atca.org

Membership: air traffic controllers, flight service station specialists, pilots, aviation engineers and manufacturers, and others interested in air traffic control systems. Compiles and publishes information and data concerning air traffic control; provides information to members, Congress, and federal agencies.

American Assn. of Airport Executives, *601 Madison St., #400, Alexandria, VA 22314; (703) 824-0504. Fax, (703) 820-1395. Charles M. Barclay, President, (703) 824-0504, ext. 129.*
Web, www.aaae.org

Maintains the Transportation Security Clearinghouse, which matches fingerprints and other personal information from airport and airline employees against FBI databases.

Flight Safety Foundation, *801 N. Fairfax St., #400, Alexandria, VA 22314-1774; (703) 739-6700. Fax, (703) 739-6708. David McMillan, Chair; Ken Hylander, Chief Executive Officer, Acting. Press, (703) 739-6700, ext. 126.*
General email, info@flightsafety.org
Web, www.flightsafety.org

Membership: aerospace manufacturers, domestic and foreign airlines, energy and insurance companies, educational institutions, and organizations and corporations interested in flight safety. Sponsors seminars, publishes literature, and conducts studies and safety audits on air safety for governments and industries. Administers award programs that recognize achievements in air safety.

International Society of Air Safety Investigators (ISASI),
107 E. Holly Ave., #11, Sterling, VA 20164-5405; (703) 430-9668. Fax, (703) 430-4970. Frank S. Del Gandio, President; Ann Schull, International Office Manager.
General email, isasi@erols.com
Web, www.isasi.org

Membership: specialists who investigate and seek to define the causes of aircraft accidents. Encourages improvement of air safety and investigative procedures through information exchange and educational seminars.

National Air Traffic Controllers Assn., *1325 Massachusetts Ave. N.W. 20005; (202) 628-5451. Fax, (202) 628-5767. Paul Rinaldi, President. Toll-free, (800) 266-0895.*
Web, www.natca.org

National Transportation Safety Board

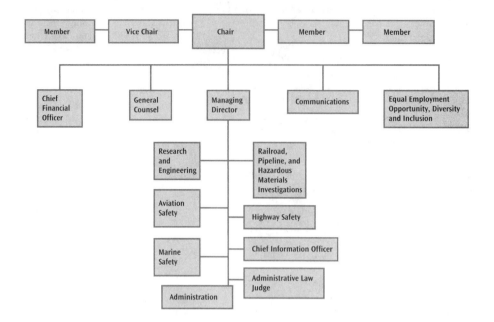

Seeks to increase air traffic controller staffing levels, improve working conditions, and encourage procurement of more modern, reliable equipment. Concerned with airport safety worldwide.

MARITIME TRANSPORTATION

General

▶AGENCIES

Army Corps of Engineers *(Defense Dept.),* 441 G St. N.W., #3K05 20314-1000; (202) 761-0001. Fax, (202) 761-4463. Lt. Gen. Thomas Bostick, Chief of Engineers.
General email, hq-publicaffairs@usace.army.mil

Web, www.usace.army.mil

Provides local governments with navigation, flood control, disaster relief, and hydroelectric power services.

Federal Maritime Commission (FMC), 800 N. Capitol St. N.W. 20573-0001; (202) 523-5725. Fax, (202) 523-0014. Vern W. Hill, Managing Director; Mario Cordero, Chair. Library, (202) 523-5762.
General email, inquiries@fmc.gov

Web, www.fmc.gov

Regulates the foreign ocean shipping of the United States; enforces maritime shipping laws and regulations regarding rates and charges, freight forwarding, passengers, and port authorities. Library open to the public.

Federal Maritime Commission (FMC), *Certification and Licensing,* 800 N. Capitol St. N.W., #970 20573-0001; (202) 523-5787. Fax, (202) 566-0011. Sandra L. Kusumoto, Director.

General email, blc@fmc.gov

Web, www.fmc.gov/bureaus_offices/bureau_of_certification_and_licensing.aspx

Licenses ocean freight forwarders and non-vessel-operating common carriers. Issues certificates of financial responsibility to ensure that cruise lines refund fares and meet their liability in case of death, injury, or nonperformance.

Federal Maritime Commission (FMC), *Trade Analysis,* 800 N. Capitol St. N.W., #940 20573-0001; (202) 523-5796. Fax, (202) 523-4372. Sandra L. Kusumoto, Director. Library, (202) 523-5762.
General email, tradeanalysis@fmc.gov

Web, www.fmc.gov/bureaus_offices/bureau_of_trade_analysis.aspx

Analyzes and monitors agreements between terminal operators and shipping companies and agreements among ocean common carriers. Reviews and analyzes service contracts, monitors rates of government-owned controlled carriers, reviews carrier-published tariff systems under the accessibility and accuracy standards, and responds to inquiries or issues that arise concerning service contracts or tariffs. Conducts competition and market analysis to detect activity that is substantially anticompetitive. Library open to the public.

Justice Dept. (DOJ), *Civil Division, Torts Branch, Aviation and Admiralty Litigation,* 1425 New York Ave. N.W., #10100 20005 (mailing address: P.O. Box 14271, Washington, DC 20044-4271); (202) 616-4100. Fax, (202) 616-4002. Peter F. Frost, Director.
Web, www.justice.gov/civil/torts/aa/t-aa.html

Represents the federal government in civil suits concerning the maritime industry, including ships, shipping, and merchant marine personnel. Handles civil cases arising from admiralty incidents and accidents, including oil spills.

Maritime Administration *(Transportation Dept.)*, *West Bldg., 1200 New Jersey Ave. S.E., #W22-300 20590; (202) 366-1719. Fax, (202) 366-3890. Capt. Paul N. Jaenichen Sr., Deputy Maritime Administrator, Acting. Press, (202) 366-5807.*
General email, pao_marad@dot.gov

Web, www.marad.dot.gov

Conducts research on shipbuilding and operations; provides financing guarantees and a tax-deferred fund for shipbuilding; promotes the maritime industry; operates the U.S. Merchant Marine Academy in Kings Point, New York.

Maritime Administration *(Transportation Dept.)*, *Business and Workforce Development, West Bldg., 1200 New Jersey Ave. S.E., MAR-700 20590; (202) 366-1883. Fax, (202) 366-3890. Owen Doherty, Associate Administrator, Acting.*
Web, http://marad.dot.gov

Works with private industry to develop standardized ship designs and improved shipbuilding techniques and materials; offices dealing with cargo preference, Title XI, war risk insurance, and workforce development.

Maritime Administration *(Transportation Dept.)*, *Cargo Preference and Domestic Trade, West Bldg., 1200 New Jersey Ave. S.E., MAR-730/MS2, 2nd Floor 20590; (202) 366-4610. Fax, (202) 366-5522. Dennis J. Brennan, Director.*
General email, cargo.marad@dot.gov

Web, www.marad.dot.gov/ships_shipping_landing_page/ cargo_preference/cargo_preference_landing_page.htm

Enforces cargo preference laws and regulations. Promotes and monitors the use of U.S. flag vessels in the movement of cargo on international waters.

Maritime Administration *(Transportation Dept.)*, *Environment and Compliance, West Bldg., 1200 New Jersey Ave. S.E., W28-342 20590; (202) 366-1931. Fax, (202) 366-6988. John P. Quinn, Associate Administrator.*
General email, john.quinn@dot.gov

Web, www.marad.dot.gov/environment_safety_landing_ page/environment_and_safety_landing_page.htm

Focuses on environmental stewardship, maritime safety, and maritime security; maritime research and development; and maritime international and domestic rules, regulations, and standards.

Maritime Administration *(Transportation Dept.)*, *International Activities, West Bldg., 1200 New Jersey Ave. S.E., W28-314 20590; (202) 366-2765. Fax, (202) 366-3746. Lonnie Kishiyama, Director.*
Web, http://marad.dot.gov

Formulates the agency's position on international issues affecting the U.S. maritime industry with the goal of reducing or eliminating international barriers to trade and improving market access.

Maritime Administration *(Transportation Dept.)*, *Marine Financing, West Bldg., 1200 New Jersey Ave. S.E., 2nd Floor 20590; (202) 366-5744. Fax, (202) 366-7901. Kevin Feury, Director, Acting.*
Web, www.marad.dot.gov/ships_shipping_landing_page/ title_xi_home/title_xi_home.htm

Provides ship financing guarantees for ship construction and shipyard modernization; administers the Capital Construction Fund Program.

Maritime Administration *(Transportation Dept.)*, *Maritime Workforce Development, West Bldg., 1200 New Jersey Ave. S.E., 2nd Floor 20590; (202) 366-5469. Fax, (202) 366-7901. Anne Wehde, Director.*
Web, www.marad.dot.gov/mariners_landing_page/ mariner_landing_page.htm

Administers programs for the U.S. Merchant Marine Academy and State Academies. Promotes maritime workforce development.

Maritime Administration *(Transportation Dept.)*, *National Security, West Bldg., 1200 New Jersey Ave. S.E., MAR-600, MS1, W25 20590; (202) 366-5400. Fax, (202) 366-5904. Kevin M. Tokarski, Associate Administrator.*
Web, www.marad.dot.gov/ships_shipping_landing_page/ national_security/national_security.htm

Ensures that merchant shipping is available in times of war or national emergency.

Maritime Administration *(Transportation Dept.)*, *Policy and Plans, West Bldg., 1200 New Jersey Ave. S.E., MAR-232 20590; (202) 366-4894. Fax, (202) 366-3890. Eric Gabler, Director, Acting.*
Web, http://marad.dot.gov/library_landing_page/data_ and_statistics/data_and_statistics.htm

Supports the agency's policy development process with research, analysis, and documentation. Assesses the effects of legislative and regulatory proposals on maritime programs and maritime industries. Investigates the effects of national and global events on maritime policy and operations.

National Oceanic and Atmospheric Administration (NOAA) *(Commerce Dept.)*, *National Ocean Service, 1305 East-West Hwy., SSMC4, #13632, Silver Spring, MD 20910; (301) 713-3074. Fax, (301) 713-4269. Holly Ann Bamford, Assistant Administrator. Press, (301) 713-3066.*
General email, nos.info@noaa.gov

Web, www.oceanservice.noaa.gov

Manages charting and geodetic services, oceanography and marine services, coastal resource coordination, and marine survey operations; conducts environmental cleanup of coastal pollution.

Navy Dept. *(Defense Dept.)*, *Military Sealift Command, Bldg. 210 20398-5540; (202) 685-5007. Fax, (202) 685-5020. Rear Adm. Thomas K. Shannon, Commander. Press, (202) 685-5055.*
Web, www.msc.navy.mil

Provides sea transportation of equipment, fuel, supplies, and ammunition to sustain U.S. forces.

Surface Transportation Board *(Transportation Dept.)*, *395 E St. S.W., #1220 20423-0001 (mailing address: 395 E St. S.W., Washington, DC 20024); (202) 245-0245. Fax, (202) 245-0458. Daniel R. Elliott III, Chair, (202) 245-0220. Library, (202) 245-0406. TTY, (800) 877-8339. Press, (202) 245-0234.* *Web, www.stb.dot.gov*

U.S. Coast Guard (USCG) *(Homeland Security Dept.)*, *2703 Martin Luther King Jr. Ave. S.E., MS 7000 20593-7000; (202) 372-4411. Fax, (202) 372-8302. Adm. Robert J. Papp Jr., Commandant. Public Affairs, (202) 372-4600.* *Web, www.uscg.mil*

Carries out search-and-rescue missions in and around navigable waters and on the high seas; enforces federal laws on the high seas and navigable waters of the United States and its possessions; conducts marine environmental protection programs; administers boating safety programs; inspects and regulates construction, safety, and equipment of merchant marine vessels; establishes and maintains a system of navigation aids; carries out domestic ice-breaking activities; maintains a state of military readiness to assist the Navy in time of war or when directed by the president.

U.S. Coast Guard (USCG) *(Homeland Security Dept.)*, *Investigations and Casualty Analysis, CG-545, 2703 Martin Luther King Jr. Ave. S.E. 20593-7581; (202) 372-1015. Fax, (202) 372-1907. Capt. David Fish, Chief.* *Web, www.uscg.mil/marinesafetyprogram/org.asp*

Handles disciplinary proceedings for merchant marine personnel. Compiles and analyzes records of marine casualties. Focuses on marine safety and environmental protection through marine inspection activities, including investigation of spills and drug and alcohol testing.

U.S. Coast Guard (USCG) *(Homeland Security Dept.)*, *Strategic Analysis, CG095, 2703 Martin Luther King Jr. Ave. S.E., MS 7104 20593-7104; (202) 372-3011. Fax, (202) 372-4976. Capt. Robert L. (Rob) Gandolfo, Chief.* *Web, www.uscg.mil/strategy/documents.asp*

Identifies and analyzes emerging geopolitical, economic, and environmental issues and trends; develops specific recommendations to improve the strategic and operational posture of the U.S. Coast Guard.

▶CONGRESS

For a listing of relevant congressional committees and subcommittees, please see page 657 or the Appendix.

▶NONGOVERNMENTAL

American Maritime Congress, *444 N. Capitol St. N.W., #800 20001-1570; (202) 347-8020. Fax, (202) 347-1550. Lee Kincaid, President.* *General email, diannelauer@americanmaritime.org* *Web, www.americanmaritime.org*

Organization of U.S.-flag carriers engaged in oceanborne transportation. Conducts research, education, and advocacy on behalf of the U.S.-flag merchant marine.

Boat Owners Assn. of the United States (Boat U.S.), *880 S. Pickett St., Alexandria, VA 22304-4695; (703) 461-2864. Fax, (703) 461-2847. Margaret Podlich, President.* *General email, govtaffairs@boatus.com* *Web, www.boatus.com*

Membership: owners of recreational boats. Represents boat-owner interests before the federal, state, and local governments.

Chamber of Shipping of America, *1730 Rhode Island Ave. N.W., #702 20036-4517; (202) 775-4399. Fax, (202) 659-3795. Joseph J. Cox, President.* *Web, www.knowships.org*

Represents U.S.-based companies that own, operate, or charter oceangoing tankers, container ships, and other merchant vessels engaged in domestic and international trade.

Marine Engineers' Beneficial Assn. (MEBA), *444 N. Capitol St. N.W., #800 20001-1570; (202) 638-5355. Fax, (202) 638-5369. Marshall Ainley, President.* *Web, www.mebaunion.org*

Maritime labor union. Represents engineers and deck officers, domestically and internationally. Monitors legislation and regulation.

Maritime Institute for Research and Industrial Development, *1025 Connecticut Ave. N.W., #507 20036-5412; (202) 463-6505. Fax, (202) 223-9093. C. James (Jim) Patti, President.* *General email, jpatti@miraid.org*

Membership: U.S.-flag ship operators. Promotes the development of the U.S. merchant marine. Interests include the use of private commercial merchant vessels by the Defense Dept., enforcement of cargo preference (Jones Act) laws for U.S.-flag ships, and maintenance of cabotage laws.

National Marine Manufacturers Assn., *Government Relations, 650 Massachusetts Ave. N.W., #520 20001; (202) 737-9750. Fax, (202) 628-4716. John McKnight, Vice President.* *Web, www.nmma.org*

Membership: recreational marine equipment manufacturers. Promotes boating safety and the development of boating facilities. Serves as liaison with Congress and regulatory agencies. Monitors legislation and regulations. (Headquarters in Chicago, Ill.)

Shipbuilders Council of America, *655 15th St. N.W., #225 20005; (202) 772-5577. Fax, (202) 347-5464. Matt Paxton, President.* *Web, http://shipbuilders.org*

Membership: U.S. shipyards that repair and build commercial ships and naval and other government vessels; and allied industries and associations. Monitors legislation and regulations.

Transportation Institute, *5201 Auth Way, Camp Springs, MD 20746-4211; (301) 423-3335. Fax, (301) 423-0634. James L. Henry, President.*
General email, info@trans-inst.org
Web, www.trans-inst.org

Membership: U.S.-flag maritime shipping companies. Conducts research on freight regulation and rates, government subsidies and assistance, domestic and international maritime matters, maritime safety, ports, Saint Lawrence Seaway, shipbuilding, and regulation of shipping.

World Shipping Council, *1156 15th St. N.W., #300 20005; (202) 589-1230. Fax, (202) 589-1231. Christopher L. Koch, President.*
General email, info@worldshipping.org
Web, www.worldshipping.org

Membership association representing the liner shipping industry. Works with policymakers and other industry groups interested in international transportation issues, including maritime security, regulatory policy, tax issues, safety, the environment, harbor dredging, and trade infrastructure. Monitors legislation and regulations.

Maritime Safety

▶**AGENCIES**

National Oceanic and Atmospheric Administration (NOAA) *(Commerce Dept.), National Ocean Service, Office of Coast Survey, 1315 East-West Hwy., #6147, SSMC3, Silver Spring, MD 20910-3282; (301) 713-2770. Fax, (301) 713-4019. Rear Adm. Gerd F. Glang, Director.*
Web, www.nauticalcharts.noaa.gov and Twitter, @NOAAcharts

Directs programs and conducts research to support fundamental scientific and engineering activities and resource development for safe navigation of the nation's waterways and territorial seas. Prints on demand and distributes nautical charts.

National Response Center *(Homeland Security Dept.), 2100 2nd St. S.W., #2111B 20593-0001; (202) 267-2180. Fax, (202) 267-1322. Syed M. Qadir, Director, (202) 372-2440. TTY, (202) 267-4477. Hotline, (800) 424-8802; local, (202) 267-2675.*
General email, hqs-dg-lst-nrcinfo@comdt.uscg.mil
Web, www.nrc.uscg.mil

Maintains twenty-four-hour hotline for reporting oil spills, hazardous materials accidents, and chemical releases. Notifies appropriate federal officials to reduce the effects of accidents.

National Transportation Safety Board, *Marine Safety, 490 L'Enfant Plaza East S.W., #6300 20594-0001; (202) 314-6450. Fax, (202) 314-6454. Tracy Murrell, Director.*
Web, www.ntsb.gov

Investigates selected marine transportation accidents, including major marine accidents that involve U.S. Coast Guard operations or functions. Determines the facts upon which the board establishes probable cause; makes recommendations on matters pertaining to marine transportation safety and accident prevention.

Occupational Safety and Health Administration (OSHA) *(Labor Dept.), Maritime, 200 Constitution Ave. N.W., #N3609 20210-0001; (202) 693-2086. Fax, (202) 693-1663. Amy Wangdahl, Office Director.*
Web, www.osha.gov/dts/maritime/index.html

Writes occupational safety and health standards and guidance products for the maritime industry.

Occupational Safety and Health Administration (OSHA) *(Labor Dept.), Maritime Enforcement, 200 Constitution Ave. N.W., #N3610 20210-0001; (202) 693-2399. Fax, (202) 693-2369. Stephen Butler, Director.*
Web, www.osha.gov/dts/maritime/dir_maritime.html

Administers occupational safety and health enforcement program for the maritime industries. Provides comprehensive program guidelines, policies, procedures, technical assistance, and information dissemination.

U.S. Coast Guard (USCG) *(Homeland Security Dept.), Boating Safety, CG-BSX-2, 2703 Martin Luther King Jr. Ave. S.E., MS 7501 20593; (202) 372-1062. Fax, (202) 372-1908. Jeffrey Hoedt, Chief.*
Web, www.uscgboating.org

Tracks and analyzes boating accidents; writes and enforces safety regulations for recreational boats and associated equipment; sets boater education standards; coordinates public awareness and information programs; awards grants to states and nongovernmental organizations to improve safety.

U.S. Coast Guard (USCG) *(Homeland Security Dept.), Deputy for Operations Policy and Capabilities, Commandant, CG-DCO-D, MS 7318, 2703 Martin Luther King Ave. S.E. 20593; (202) 372-1001. Fax, (202) 372-2900. Rear Adm. William (Dean) Lee, Deputy Assistant Commandant.*
Web, www.uscg.mil/hq/cg5

Establishes and enforces regulations for port safety; environmental protection; vessel safety, inspection, design, documentation, and investigation; licensing of merchant vessel personnel; and shipment of hazardous materials.

U.S. Coast Guard (USCG) *(Homeland Security Dept.), Design and Engineering Standards, CG-521, 2703 Martin Luther King Jr. Ave. S.E., MS 7509 20593; (202) 372-1352. Fax, (202) 372-1925. Capt. John W. Mauger, Chief.*
Web, www.uscg.mil/hq/cg5/cg521

Develops standards; responsible for general vessel arrangements, naval architecture, vessel design and construction, and transport of bulk dangerous cargoes. Supports national advisory committees and national professional organizations to achieve industry standards.

U.S. Coast Guard (USCG) *(Homeland Security Dept.), Investigations and Casualty Analysis, CG-545, 2703 Martin Luther King Jr. Ave. S.E. 20593-7581; (202) 372-1015. Fax, (202) 372-1907. Capt. David Fish, Chief.*
Web, www.uscg.mil/marinesafetyprogram/org.asp

Compiles and analyzes records of accidents involving commercial vessels that result in loss of life, serious injury, or substantial damage.

U.S. Coast Guard (USCG) *(Homeland Security Dept.),* *Marine Safety Center, MS 7410 420 Wilson Blvd., #400, Arlington, VA 20598-7410; (703) 872-6729. Fax, (703) 872-6801. Capt. John Nadeau, Commanding Officer.*
General email, msc@uscg.mil
Web, www.uscg.mil/hq/msc

Reviews and approves commercial vessel plans and specifications to ensure technical compliance with federal safety and pollution abatement standards.

U.S. Coast Guard (USCG) *(Homeland Security Dept.),* *Response Policy, CG-5R, 2703 Martin Luther King Jr. Ave. S.E., MS 7516 20593-7516; (202) 372-2010. Rear Adm. Peter Brown, Director.*
Web, www.uscg.mil

Conducts search-and-rescue and polar and domestic ice-breaking operations. Regulates waterways under U.S. jurisdiction. Operates the Coast Guard National Response Center; participates in defense operations and homeland security; assists with law enforcement/drug interdictions.

▶**NONGOVERNMENTAL**

Cruise Lines International Assn., *2111 Wilson Blvd., 8th Floor, Arlington, VA 22201; (703) 522-8463. Fax, (703) 522-3811. Christine Duffy, President.*
General email, info@cruising.org
Web, www.cruising.org

Membership: chief executives of twenty-six cruise lines and other cruise industry professionals. Advises domestic and international regulatory organizations on shipping policy. Works with U.S. and international agencies to promote safety, public health, security, medical facilities, environmental awareness, and passenger protection. Monitors legislation and regulations. (Formerly the International Council of Cruise Lines.)

National Maritime Safety Assn., *919 18th St. N.W., #901 20006; (202) 587-4830. Fax, (202) 587-4888. Charles T. (Chuck) Carroll Jr., Executive Director, (202) 587-4801.*
General email, mto@nmsa.us
Web, www.nmsa.us

Represents the marine cargo handling industry in safety and health matters arising under various statutes, including the Occupational Safety and Health Act. Serves as a clearinghouse on information to help reduce injuries and illnesses in the marine cargo handling workplace. Monitors legislation and regulations.

U.S. Coast Guard Office of Auxiliary and Boating Safety, *2100 2nd St. S.W., #3501, MS 7581 20593-7581; (202) 372-1260. Fax, (202) 372-1920. Jeffrey Hoedt, Division Chief.*
Web, www.uscgboating.org

Seeks to minimize the loss of life, personal injury, property damage, and environmental impact associated

with the use of recreational boats in order to maximize safe use and enjoyment of U.S. waterways by the public. Offers public education programs and free vessel safety inspections. Works with the U.S. Coast Guard and others involved in waterways activities to maintain marine safety.

Ports and Waterways

▶**AGENCIES**

Army Corps of Engineers *(Defense Dept.), Civil Works, 441 G St. N.W. 20314-1000; (202) 761-0099. Fax, (202) 761-8992. Steven L. Stockton, Director; Maj. Gen. John W. Peabody, Deputy Commanding General for Civil and Emergency Operations.*
Web, www.usace.army.mil

Coordinates field offices that oversee harbors, dams, levees, waterways, locks, reservoirs, and other construction projects designed to facilitate transportation, flood control, and environmental restoration projects. Major projects include the Mississippi, Missouri, and Ohio Rivers; Bay Delta in California; the Great Lakes; the Chesapeake Bay; the Everglades in Florida; and the Gulf of Mexico.

Federal Maritime Commission (FMC), *Agreements, 800 N. Capitol St. N.W., #940 20573-0001; (202) 523-5793. Fax, (202) 523-4372. Tanga S. FitzGibbon, Office Director.*
Web, www.fmc.gov

Analyzes agreements between terminal operators and shipping companies for docking facilities and agreements among ocean common carriers.

Maritime Administration *(Transportation Dept.), Intermodal System Development, West Bldg., 1200 New Jersey Ave. S.E., MAR-500, W21-320 20590; (202) 366-1624. Fax, (202) 366-6988. H. Keith Lesnick, Associate Administrator.*
Web, www.marad.dot.gov/ports_landing_page/ports_landing_page.htm

Responsible for direction and administration of port and intermodal transportation development and port readiness for national defense.

Saint Lawrence Seaway Development Corp. *(Transportation Dept.), 1200 New Jersey Ave. S.E., #W32-300 20590; (202) 366-0091. Fax, (202) 366-7147. Betty Sutton, Administrator. Toll-free, (800) 785-2779.*
Web, www.greatlakes-seaway.com

Operates and maintains the Saint Lawrence Seaway within U.S. territorial limits; conducts development programs and coordinates activities with its Canadian counterpart.

Tennessee Valley Authority, *Government Affairs, 1 Massachusetts Ave. N.W., #300 20444; (202) 898-2999. Fax, (202) 898-2998. Nick Pearson, Director.*
General email, latootle@tva.gov
Web, www.tva.gov

Coordinates resource conservation, development, and land-use programs in the Tennessee River Valley. Operates the river control system; projects include flood control, navigation development, and multiple-use reservoirs.

U.S. Coast Guard (USCG) *(Homeland Security Dept.),* *2703 Martin Luther King Jr. Ave. S.E., MS 7000 20593-7000; (202) 372-4411. Fax, (202) 372-8302. Adm. Robert J. Papp Jr., Commandant. Public Affairs, (202) 372-4600.* *Web, www.uscg.mil*

Enforces rules and regulations governing the safety and security of ports and anchorages and the movement of vessels in U.S. waters. Supervises cargo transfer operations, storage, and stowage; conducts harbor patrols and waterfront facility inspections; establishes security zones and monitors vessel movement.

▶ **NONGOVERNMENTAL**

American Assn. of Port Authorities (AAPA), *1010 Duke St., Alexandria, VA 22314-3589; (703) 684-5700. Fax, (703) 684-6321. Kurt J. Nagle, President.* *General email, info@aapa-ports.org* *Web, www.aapa-ports.org*

Membership: public port authorities in the Western Hemisphere. Provides technical and economic information on port finance, environmental issues, construction, operation, and security.

American Waterways Operators, *801 N. Quincy St., #200, Arlington, VA 22203-1708; (703) 841-9300. Fax, (703) 841-0389. Thomas A. Allegretti, President.* *Web, www.americanwaterways.com*

Membership: operators of barges, tugboats, and towboats on navigable coastal and inland waterways. Acts as liaison with Congress, the U.S. Coast Guard, the Army Corps of Engineers, and other federal agencies. Establishes safety standards and conducts training for efficient, environmentally responsible transportation. Monitors legislation and regulations.

International Longshore and Warehouse Union (ILWU), *Washington Office, 1025 Connecticut Ave. N.W., #507 20036; (202) 463-6265. Fax, (202) 467-4875. Lindsay McLaughlin, Legislative Director.* *General email, washdc@ilwu.org* *Web, www.ilwu.org*

Membership: approximately 60,000 longshore and warehouse personnel. Helps members negotiate pay, benefits, and better working conditions; conducts training programs and workshops. Monitors legislation and regulations. (Headquarters in San Francisco, Calif.; affiliated with the AFL-CIO.)

International Longshoremen's Assn., *Washington Office, 1101 17th St. N.W., #400 20036-4704; (202) 955-*

6304. Fax, (202) 955-6048. John Bowers Jr., Executive Director. General email, iladc@aol.com* *Web, www.ilaunion.org*

Membership: approximately 65,000 longshore personnel. Helps members negotiate pay, benefits, and better working conditions; conducts training programs and workshops. Monitors legislation and regulations. (Headquarters in New Jersey; affiliated with the AFL-CIO.)

National Assn. of Waterfront Employers, *919 18th St. N.W., #901 20006; (202) 587-4800. Fax, (202) 587-4888. John Crowley, Executive Director.* *General email, mto@nawe.us* *Web, www.nawe.us*

Membership: private sector stevedore companies and marine terminal operators, their subsidiaries, and other waterfront-related employers. Legislative interests include trade, shipping, antitrust issues, insurance, port security, and user-fee issues. Monitors legislation and regulations.

National Waterways Conference, *1100 N. Glebe Rd., #1010, Arlington, VA 22201; (703) 224-8007. Fax, (866) 371-1390. Amy W. Larson, President, (703) 462-4210.* *General email, info@waterways.org* *Web, www.waterways.org*

Membership: petroleum, coal, chemical, electric power, building materials, iron and steel, and grain companies; port authorities; water carriers; and others interested or involved in waterways. Sponsors educational programs on waterways. Monitors legislation and regulations.

Passenger Vessel Assn., *103 Oronoco St., #200, Alexandria, VA 22314; (703) 518-5005. Fax, (703) 518-5151. John R. Groundwater, Executive Director. Toll-free, (800) 807-8360.* *General email, pvainfo@passengervessel.com* *Web, www.passengervessel.com*

Membership: owners, operators, and suppliers for U.S. and Canadian passenger vessels and international vessel companies. Interests include insurance, safety and security, and U.S. congressional impact upon dinner and excursion boats, car and passenger ferries, overnight cruise ships, and riverboat casinos. Monitors legislation and regulations.

Waterways Council, Inc., *801 N. Quincy St., #200, Arlington, VA 22203; (703) 373-2261. Fax, (703) 373-2037. Michael Toohey, President. Press, dcolbert@vesselalliance .com.* *Web, www.waterwayscouncil.org*

Membership: port authorities, waterways carriers, shippers, shipping associations, and waterways advocacy groups. Advocates for a modern and well-maintained system of inland waterways and port infrastructure. Monitors legislation and regulations.

MOTOR VEHICLES

General

▶AGENCIES

Federal Highway Administration (FHWA)
(Transportation Dept.), 1200 New Jersey Ave. S.E. 20590-0001; (202) 366-4000. Fax, (202) 366-3244. Jeffrey F. Paniati, Executive Director. Press, (202) 366-0660. Web, www.fhwa.dot.gov

Administers federal-aid highway programs with money from the Highway Trust Fund; works to improve highway and motor vehicle safety; coordinates research and development programs on highway and traffic safety, construction costs, and the environmental impact of highway transportation; administers regional and territorial highway building programs and the highway beautification program.

Federal Motor Carrier Safety Administration
(Transportation Dept.), Bus and Truck Standards and Operations, 1200 New Jersey Ave. S.E., #N64-330 20590; (202) 366-5370. Fax, (202) 366-8842. Chuck Horan, Director, (202) 366-2362. Web, www.fmcsa.dot.gov/safety-security/pcs/index.aspx

Regulates motor vehicle size and weight on federally aided highways; conducts studies on issues relating to motor carrier transportation; promotes uniformity in state and federal motor carrier laws and regulations.

Transportation Security Administration (TSA)
(Homeland Security Dept.), Freedom Center, 13555 EDS Dr., Herndon, VA 20171 (mailing address: TSOC Annex, 601 S. 12th St., Arlington, VA 22202); (866) 655-7023. Robert S. Bray, Director. Web, www.tsa.gov

Operations center that provides continual federal, state, and local coordination, communications, and domain awareness for all of the Homeland Security Dept.'s transportation-related security activities worldwide. Transportation domains include highway, rail, shipping, and aviation.

▶CONGRESS

For a listing of relevant congressional committees and subcommittees, please see page 657 or the Appendix.

▶NONGOVERNMENTAL

American Assn. of Motor Vehicle Administrators (AAMVA), *4301 Wilson Blvd., #400, Arlington, VA 22203-1753; (703) 522-4200. Fax, (703) 522-1553. Neil Schuster, President. Press, (703) 908-5891. General email, info@aamva.org Web, www.aamva.org*

Membership: officials responsible for administering and enforcing motor vehicle and traffic laws in the United States and Canada. Promotes uniform laws and regulations

for vehicle registration, driver's licenses, and motor carrier services.

American Automobile Assn. (AAA), *Washington Office, 607 14th St. N.W., #200 20005-4798; (202) 942-2050. Fax, (202) 783-4788. Jill Ingrassia, Managing Director of Government Relations and Traffic Safety Advocacy; Kathleen Bower, Vice President. General email, jingrassia@national.AAA.com Web, www.aaa.com*

Membership: state and local automobile associations. Conducts public outreach and offers publications through the AAA Foundation for Traffic Safety. Interests include all aspects of highway transportation, travel and tourism, safety, drunk driving, and legislation that affects motorists. (Headquarters in Heathrow, Fla.)

American Bus Assn., *111 K St. N.E., 9th Floor 20002; (202) 842-1645. Fax, (202) 842-0850. Peter J. Pantuso, President, (202) 218-7229. Toll-free, (800) 283-2877. General email, abainfo@buses.org Web, www.buses.org*

Membership: privately owned intercity bus companies, state associations, travel/tourism businesses, bus manufacturers, and those interested in the bus industry. Monitors legislation and regulations.

American Trucking Assns., *950 N. Glebe Rd., #210, Arlington, VA 22203-4181; (703) 838-1700. Fax, (703) 838-1936. William P. Graves, President. Press, (703) 838-1873. General email, media@trucking.org Web, www.trucking.org*

Membership: state trucking associations, individual trucking and motor carrier organizations, and related supply companies. Maintains departments on industrial relations, law, management systems, research, safety, traffic, state laws, taxation, communications, legislation, economics, and engineering.

Electric Drive Transportation Assn. (EDTA), *1250 Eye St., #902 20005; (202) 408-0774. Fax, (202) 408-7610. Brian P. Wynne, President. Press, (202) 408-0774, ext. 312. General email, info@electricdrive.org Web, www.electricdrive.org*

Membership: automotive and other equipment manufacturers, utilities, technology developers, component suppliers, and government agencies. Conducts public policy advocacy, education, industry networking, and international conferences in the areas of battery, hybrid, and fuel cell electric drive technologies and infrastructures.

Highway Loss Data Institute, *1005 N. Glebe Rd., #700, Arlington, VA 22201; (703) 247-1600. Fax, (703) 247-1588. Adrian Lund, President. Web, www.iihs.org*

Research organization that gathers, processes, and publishes data on the ways in which insurance losses vary among different kinds of vehicles. (Affiliated with Insurance Institute for Highway Safety.)

International Parking Institute, *1330 Braddock Pl., #350, Alexandria, VA 22314; (571) 699-3011. Fax, (571) 371-8022. Shawn D. Conrad, Executive Director.*
General email, ipi@parking.org
Web, www.parking.org

Membership: operators, designers, and builders of parking lots and structures. Provides leadership to the parking industry; supports professional development; works with transportation and related fields.

Motorcycle Industry Council, *Government Relations, 1235 South Clark St., #600, Arlington, VA 22202; (703) 416-0444. Fax, (703) 416-2269. Kathy Van Kleeck, Senior Vice President.*
Web, www.mic.org

Membership: manufacturers and distributors of motorcycles, mopeds, and related parts, accessories, and equipment. Monitors legislation and regulations. (Headquarters in Irvine, Calif.)

National Assn. of Regulatory Utility Commissioners, *1101 Vermont Ave. N.W., #200 20005-3521; (202) 898-2200. Fax, (202) 898-2213. Charles D. Gray, Executive Director.*
General email, admin@naruc.org
Web, www.naruc.org

Membership: members of federal, state, municipal, and international regulatory commissions that have jurisdiction over motor and common carriers. Interests include motor carriers.

National Institute for Automotive Service Excellence, *101 Blue Seal Dr. S.E., #101, Leesburg, VA 20175; (703) 669-6600. Fax, (703) 669-6122. Timothy Zilke, President. Toll-free, (800) 390-6789, ext. 3.*
General email, asehelp@ase.com
Web, www.ase.com

Administers program for testing and certifying automotive technicians; researches methods to improve technician training.

National Motor Freight Traffic Assn., *1001 N. Fairfax St., #600, Alexandria, VA 22314; (703) 838-1810. Fax, (703) 683-6296. Paul Levine, General Manager. Toll-free, (866) 411-6632.*
General email, customerservice@nmfta.org
Web, www.nmfta.org

Membership: motor carriers of general goods in interstate and intrastate commerce. Publishes *National Motor Freight Classification.*

National Parking Assn., *1112 16th St. N.W., #840 20036-4880; (202) 296-4336. Fax, (202) 296-3102. Christine Banning, President. Toll-free, (800)-647-7275.*
General email, info@npapark.org
Web, www.npapark.org

Membership: parking garage operators, parking consultants, universities, municipalities, medical centers, and vendors. Offers information and research services; sponsors

seminars and educational programs on garage design and equipment. Monitors legislation and regulations.

National Private Truck Council, *950 N. Glebe Rd., #530, Arlington, VA 22203-4183; (703) 683-1300. Fax, (703) 683-1217. Gary F. Petty, President, (703) 838-8876.*
General email, memberservice@nptc.org
Web, www.nptc.org

Membership: manufacturers, retailers, distributors, wholesalers, and suppliers that operate their own private truck fleets in conjunction with their nontransportation businesses. Interests include standards, best practices, benchmarking, federal regulatory compliance, peer-to-peer networking, and business economics. Supports economic deregulation of the trucking industry and uniformity in state taxation of the industry. NPTC Institute supports continuing education and certification programs.

National Tank Truck Carriers (NTTC), *950 N. Glebe Rd., #520, Arlington, VA 22203-4183; (703) 838-1960. Fax, (703) 838-8860. Dan Furth, President.*
General email, nttcstaff@tanktruck.org
Web, www.tanktruck.org

Focuses on issues of the tank truck industry and represents the industry before Congress and federal agencies.

NATSO, Inc., *1300 Braddock Rd., #501, Alexandria, VA 22314; (703) 549-2100. Fax, (703) 684-4525. Lisa J. Mullings, President. Toll-free, (888) 275-6287.*
Web, www.natso.com

Membership: travel plaza and truck stop operators and suppliers to the truck stop industry. Provides credit information and educational training programs. Monitors legislation and regulations. Operates the NATSO Foundation, which promotes highway safety.

NGVAmerica (Natural Gas Vehicles for America), *400 N. Capitol St. N.W. 20001; (202) 824-7366. Fax, (202) 824-9160. Richard R. Kolodziej, President; Paul Kerkhoven, Director, Government Affairs, (202) 824-7363.*
General email, pkerkhoven@ngvamerica.org
Web, www.ngvamerica.org

Membership: natural gas distributors and producers; automobile and engine manufacturers; natural gas vehicle product and service suppliers; research and development organizations; and state and local government agencies. Advocates installation of natural gas and biomethane fuel stations and development of industry standards. Helps market new products and equipment related to natural gas– and biomethane-powered vehicles. (Formerly known as the Natural Gas Vehicle Coalition.)

Truckload Carriers Assn., *555 E. Braddock Rd., Alexandria, VA 22314; (703) 838-1950. Fax, (703) 836-6610. Chris Burruss, President.*
General email, tca@truckload.org
Web, www.truckload.org

Membership: truckload carriers and industry suppliers. Provides information and educational programs to members. Represents intercity common and contract trucking companies before Congress, federal agencies, courts, and the media.

Union of Concerned Scientists, *Clean Vehicles Program,* *Washington Office,* 1825 K St. N.W., #800 20006-1232; *(202) 223-6133. Fax, (202) 223-6162. Michelle Robinson, Director.*
General email, ucs@ucsusa.org
Web, www.ucsusa.org

Develops and promotes strategies to reduce U.S. consumption of oil, including increasing fuel efficiency of cars and trucks, as well as promoting advanced vehicle technology like battery-electric, hybrid-electric, and fuel cell vehicles, and next-generation biofuels. (Headquarters in Cambridge, Mass.)

Highways

▶ **AGENCIES**

Federal Highway Administration (FHWA)
(Transportation Dept.), Infrastructure, 1200 New Jersey Ave. S.E., #E75-312 20590; (202) 366-0371. Fax, (202) 493-0099. Walter C. (Butch) Waidelich Jr., Associate Administrator.
Web, www.fhwa.dot.gov/infrastructure

Provides guidance and oversight for planning, design, construction, and maintenance operations relating to federal aid, direct federal construction, and other highway programs; establishes design guidelines and specifications for highways built with federal funds.

Federal Highway Administration (FHWA)
(Transportation Dept.), National Highway Institute, 1310 N. Courthouse Rd., Arlington, VA 22201-1555; (703) 235-0520. Fax, (703) 235-0593. Vacant, Director. Toll-free, (877) 558-6873.
Web, www.nhi.fhwa.dot.gov

Develops and administers, in cooperation with state highway departments, technical training programs for agency, state, and local highway department employees.

Federal Highway Administration (FHWA)
(Transportation Dept.), Planning, Environment, and Realty, 1200 New Jersey Ave. S.E., #E76-306 20590; (202) 366-0116. Fax, (202) 366-3713. Gloria M. Shepherd, Associate Administrator.
Web, www.fhwa.dot.gov/realestate

Works with developers and municipalities to ensure conformity with the National Environmental Policy Act (NEPA) project development process.

Federal Highway Administration (FHWA)
(Transportation Dept.), Policy and Governmental Affairs, 1200 New Jersey Ave. S.E., 8th Floor 20590-0001; (202) 366-8169. Fax, (202) 366-3590. David Kim, Associate Administrator.
Web, www.fhwa.dot.gov/policy

Develops policy and administers the Federal Highway Administration's international programs. Conducts policy studies and analyzes legislation; makes recommendations; compiles and reviews highway-related data. Represents the administration at international conferences; administers foreign assistance programs.

Federal Highway Administration (FHWA)
(Transportation Dept.), Research, Development, and Technology, 6300 Georgetown Pike, #T306, McLean, VA 22101-2296; (202) 493-3259. Fax, (202) 493-3170. Michael Trentacoste, Associate Administrator.
General email, execsecretariat.fhwa@dot.gov
Web, www.fhwa.dot.gov/research

Conducts highway research and development programs; studies safety, location, design, construction, operation, and maintenance of highways; cooperates with state and local highway departments in utilizing results of research.

U.S. Coast Guard (USCG) *(Homeland Security Dept.),* 2703 Martin Luther King Jr. Ave. S.E., MS 7000 20593-7000; (202) 372-4411. Fax, (202) 372-8302. Adm. Robert J. Papp Jr., Commandant. Public Affairs, (202) 372-4600.
Web, www.uscg.mil

Regulates the construction, maintenance, and operation of bridges across U.S. navigable waters.

▶ **NONGOVERNMENTAL**

American Assn. of State Highway and Transportation Officials (AASHTO), 444 N. Capitol St. N.W., #249 20001-1512; (202) 624-5800. Fax, (202) 624-5806. Frederick G. (Bud) Wright, Executive Director, (202) 624-5811.
General email, info@aashto.org
Web, www.transportation.org

Membership: the transportation departments of the 50 states, the District of Columbia, and Puerto Rico, and affiliated agencies, including the U.S. Department of Transportation as a nonvoting ex officio member. Maintains committees on all modes of transportation and departmental affairs.

American Road and Transportation Builders Assn. (ARTBA), 1219 28th St. N.W. 20007-3389; (202) 289-4434. Fax, (202) 289-4435. T. Peter Ruane, President.
General email, general@artba.org
Web, www.artba.org

Membership: highway and transportation contractors; federal, state, and local engineers and officials; construction equipment manufacturers and distributors; and others interested in the transportation construction industry. Serves as liaison with government; provides information on highway engineering and construction developments.

Intelligent Transportation Society of America, 1100 New Jersey Ave. S.E., #850 20003; (202) 484-4847. Fax, (202) 484-3483. Scott Belcher, President; Quentin Kelly, Legislative Affairs, (202) 721-4212. Press, (202) 721-4204. Toll-free, (800) 374-8472.
General email, info@itsa.org
Web, www.itsa.org

Advocates application of electronic, computer, and communications technology to make surface transportation more efficient and to improve safety, security, and environmental sustainability. Coordinates research, development, and implementation of intelligent transportation systems by government, academia, and industry.

International Bridge, *Tunnel and Turnpike Assn.,* *1146 19th St. N.W., #600 20036-3725; (202) 659-4620. Fax, (202) 659-0500. Patrick D. Jones, Executive Director, ext. 21; Neil Gray, Government Affairs, ext. 14.*
General email, ibtta@ibtta.org
Web, www.ibtta.org

Membership: public and private operators of toll facilities and associated industries. Conducts research; compiles statistics.

International Road Federation (IRF), *Madison Pl., 500 Montgomery St., 5th Floor, Alexandria, VA 22314; (703) 535-1001. Fax, (703) 535-1007. C. Patrick Sankey, President.*
General email, info@irfnews.org
Web, www.irfnews.org

Membership: contractors, consultants, equipment manufacturers, researchers, and others involved in the road-building industry. Administers fellowship program that allows foreign engineering students to study at U.S. graduate schools. Maintains interest in roads and highways worldwide.

The Road Information Program (TRIP), *3000 Connecticut Ave. N.W., #208 20008; (202) 466-6706. William M. Wilkins, Executive Director.*
Web, www.tripnet.org

Organization of transportation specialists; conducts research on economic and technical transportation issues; promotes consumer awareness of the condition of the national road and bridge system.

Manufacturing and Sales

▶**AGENCIES**

Energy Efficiency and Renewable Energy *(Energy Dept.),* *Vehicle Technologies, 1000 Independence Ave. S.W., #5G030 20585; (202) 586-8055. Fax, (202) 586-7409. Patrick Davis, Program Manager.*
Web, www1.eere.energy.gov/vehiclesandfuels

Works with the motor vehicle industry to develop technologies for improved vehicle fuel efficiency and cleaner fuels.

International Trade Administration (ITA) *(Commerce Dept.),* *Industry and Analysis, Transportation and Machinery, 1401 Constitution Ave. N.W., #4036 20230-0001; (202) 482-0554. Fax, (202) 482-0674. Scott Kennedy, Director, Acting.*
Web, http://trade.gov/mas/index.asp

Promotes the export of U.S. aerospace, automotive, and machinery products; compiles and analyzes industry data; seeks to secure a favorable position for the U.S.

aerospace, auto, and machinery industries in global markets through policy and trade agreements.

▶**NONGOVERNMENTAL**

Alliance of Automobile Manufacturers, *803 7th St. N.W. 20001; (202) 326-5500. Fax, (202) 326-5598. Mitch Bainwol, President.*
Web, www.autoalliance.org

Trade association of thirteen major automakers. Provides advocacy on automotive issues focusing primarily on environment, energy, and safety. Seeks to harmonize global automotive standards.

American Automotive Leasing Assn., *675 N. Washington St., #410, Alexandria, VA 22314-1939; (703) 548-0777. Fax, (703) 548-1925. Pamela Sederholm, Executive Director.*
General email, sederholm@aalafleet.com
Web, www.aalafleet.com

Membership: automotive commercial fleet leasing and management companies. Monitors legislation and regulations.

American International Automobile Dealers Assn., *211 N. Union St., #300, Alexandria, VA 22314; (703) 519-7800. Fax, (703) 519-7810. Cody Lusk, President. Toll-free, (800) 462-4232.*
General email, goaiada@aiada.org
Web, www.aiada.org

Promotes a favorable market for international nameplate automobiles in the United States through education of policymakers and the general public. Monitors legislation and regulations concerning tariffs, quotas, taxes, fuel economy, and clean air initiatives.

Assn. of Global Automakers, *1050 K St. N.W., #650 20001; (202) 650-5555. Michael J. Stanton, President.*
General email, info@globalautomakers.org
Web, www.globalautomakers.org

Membership: automobile manufacturers and parts suppliers. Monitors legislation and regulations.

Automotive Aftermarket Industry Assn. (AAIA), *7101 Wisconsin Ave., #1300, Bethesda, MD 20814; (301) 654-6664. Fax, (301) 654-3299. Kathleen Schmatz, President.*
General email, aaia@aftermarket.org
Web, www.aftermarket.org

Membership: domestic and international manufacturers, manufacturers' representatives, retailers, and distributors in the automotive aftermarket industry, which involves service of a vehicle after it leaves the dealership. Offers educational programs, conducts research, and provides members with technical and international trade services; acts as liaison with government; sponsors annual marketing conference and trade shows.

Automotive Parts Remanufacturers Assn., *4460 Brookfield Corporate Dr., Suite H, Chantilly, VA 20151-1671; (703) 968-2772. Fax, (703) 968-2878. Joe Kripli, President.*

General email, mail@apra.org

Web, www.apra.org

Membership: rebuilders and remanufacturers of automotive parts. Conducts educational programs on transmission, brake, clutch, water pump, air conditioning, electrical parts, heavy-duty brake, and carburetor rebuilding.

Automotive Recyclers Assn. (ARA), *9113 Church St., Manassas, VA 20110-5456; (571) 208-0428. Fax, (571) 208-0430. Michael E. Wilson, Chief Executive Officer. Toll-free, (888) 385-1005.*

General email, staff@a-r-a.org

Web, www.a-r-a.org

Membership: retail and wholesale firms involved in the dismantling and sale of used motor vehicle parts. Works to increase the efficiency of businesses in the automotive recycling industry. Cooperates with public and private agencies to encourage further automotive recycling efforts.

Coalition for Auto Repair Equality, *105 Oronoco St., #115, Alexandria, VA 22314-2015; (703) 519-7555. Fax, (703) 519-7747. Sandy Bass-Cors, Executive Director. Toll-free, (800) 229-5380.*

General email, sandy@careauto.org; care@careauto.org

Web, www.careauto.org

Works to promote greater competition in the automotive aftermarket repair industry in order to protect consumers. Monitors state and federal legislation that impacts motorists and the automotive aftermarket repair industry.

Japan Automobile Manufacturers Assn. (JAMA), *Washington Office, 1050 17th St. N.W., #410 20036; (202) 296-8537. Fax, (202) 872-1212. Ronald Bookbinder, General Director.*

General email, info@jama.org

Web, www.jama.org

Membership: Japanese motor vehicle manufacturers. Interests include energy, market, trade, and environmental issues. (Headquarters in Tokyo.)

National Automobile Dealers Assn. (NADA), *8400 Westpark Dr., McLean, VA 22102-3591; (703) 821-7000. Fax, (703) 821-7075. Peter K. Welch, President; David W. Regan, Vice President, Legislative Affairs; David Hyatt, Vice President, Public Affairs. Press, (703) 821-7121. Toll-free, (800) 252-6232.*

General email, help@nada.org

Web, www.nada.org

Membership: domestic and imported franchised new car and truck dealers. Publishes the *National Automobile Dealers Used Car Guide* (Blue Book).

Recreation Vehicle Dealers Assn. of North America (RVDA), *3930 University Dr., Fairfax, VA 22030-2515; (703) 591-7130. Fax, (703) 359-0152. Phil Ingrassia, President.*

General email, info@rvda.org

Web, www.rvda.org

Membership: recreation vehicle dealers. Interests include government regulation of safety, trade, warranty,

and franchising; provides members with educational services, certification programs, and conventions; works to improve service standards for consumers.

Recreation Vehicle Industry Assn. (RVIA), *1896 Preston White Dr., Reston, VA 20191-4363 (mailing address: P.O. Box 2999, Reston, VA 20195-0999); (703) 620-6003. Fax, (703) 620-5071. Richard Coon, President.*

Web, www.rvia.org

Membership: manufacturers of recreation vehicles and their suppliers. Compiles shipment statistics and other technical data; provides consumers and the media with information on the industry. Assists members' compliance with American National Standards Institute requirements for recreation vehicles. Monitors legislation and regulations.

Tire Industry Assn., *1532 Pointer Ridge Pl., Suite G, Bowie, MD 20716-1883; (301) 430-7280. Fax, (301) 430-7283. Ken Brown, President. Toll-free, (800) 876-8372.*

General email, info@tireindustry.org

Web, www.tireindustry.org

Membership: all segments of the tire industry, including those that manufacture, repair, recycle, sell, service, or use new or retreaded tires and also suppliers that furnish equipment or services to the industry. Interests include environmental and small-business issues. Monitors legislation and regulations.

Truck Renting and Leasing Assn., *675 N. Washington St., #410, Alexandria, VA 22314-1939; (703) 299-9120. Fax, (703) 299-9115. Thomas James, President.*

Web, www.trala.org

Membership: vehicle renting and leasing companies and suppliers to the industry. Acts as liaison with state and federal legislative bodies and regulatory agencies. Interests include truck security and safety, tort reform, operating taxes and registration fees, insurance, and environmental issues. Monitors state and federal legislation and regulations.

Truck Trailer Manufacturers Assn. (TTMA), *7001 Heritage Village Plaze, #220, Gainsville, VA 20155; (703) 549-3010. Jeff Sims, President.*

General email, ttma@erols.com

Web, www.ttmanet.org

Membership: trailer manufacturing and supply companies. Serves as liaison between its members and government agencies. Publishes technical and industry news reports.

UNITE HERE, *Washington Office, 1775 K St. N.W., #620 20006-1530; (202) 393-4373. Fax, (202) 223-6213. Tom Snyder, Political Director; John W. Wilhelm, President.*

Web, www.unitehere.org

Membership: more than 270,000 workers in the United States and Canada who work in the hospitality, gaming, food service, manufacturing, textile, laundry, and airport industries. Assists members with contract negotiation and grievances; conducts training programs and workshops.

Monitors legislation and regulations. (Headquarters in New York. Formed by the merger of the former Union of Needletrades, Textiles and Industrial Employees and the Hotel Employees and Restaurant Employees International Union.)

United Auto Workers, Washington Office, *1757 N St. N.W. 20036; (202) 828-8500. Fax, (202) 293-3457. Josh Nassar, Legislative Director. Web, www.uaw.org*

Membership: approximately 750,000 active and 600,000 retired North American workers in aerospace, automotive, defense, manufacturing, steel, technical, and other industries. Assists members with contract negotiations and grievances; conducts training programs and workshops. Monitors legislation and regulations. (Headquarters in Detroit, Mich.)

Traffic Safety

▶**AGENCIES**

Federal Highway Administration (FHWA)
(Transportation Dept.), Operations, 1200 New Jersey Ave. S.E., #E86-205 20590-0001; (202) 366-8753. Fax, (202) 366-3225. Jeffrey A. Lindley, Associate Administrator. Toll-free helpline, (866) 367-7487. Press, (202) 366-4650. Web, www.ops.fhwa.dot.gov

Fosters the efficient management and operation of the highway system. Responsible for congestion management, pricing, ITS deployment, traffic operations, emergency management, and freight management. Includes offices of Transportation Management, Freight Management and Operations, and Transportation Operations.

Federal Motor Carrier Safety Administration
(Transportation Dept.), 1200 New Jersey Ave. S.E., #W60-300 20590; (202) 366-8773. Fax, (202) 366-3224. Anne S. Ferro, Administrator. Toll-free information, (800) 832-5660. Toll-free hotline, (888) 327-4236. Consumer complaints, (888) 368-7238. Web, www.fmcsa.dot.gov

Partners with federal, state, and local enforcement agencies, the motor carrier industry, safety groups, and organized labor in efforts to reduce bus- and truck-related crashes.

Federal Motor Carrier Safety Administration
(Transportation Dept.), Bus and Truck Standards and Operations, 1200 New Jersey Ave. S.E., #N64-330 20590; (202) 366-5370. Fax, (202) 366-8842. Chuck Horan, Director, (202) 366-2362. Web, www.fmcsa.dot.gov/safety-security/pcs/index.aspx

Interprets and disseminates national safety regulations regarding commercial drivers' qualifications, maximum hours of service, accident reporting, and transportation of hazardous materials. Sets minimum levels of financial liability for trucks and buses. Responsible for Commercial Driver's License Information Program.

National Highway Traffic Safety Administration
(Transportation Dept.), West Bldg., 1200 New Jersey Ave. S.E. 20590; (202) 366-1836. Fax, (202) 366-2106. David J. Friedman, Administrator, Acting. Press, (202) 366-9550. Toll-free 24-hour hotline, (888) 327-4236. Web, www.nhtsa.gov and www.safercar.gov

Implements motor vehicle safety programs; issues federal motor vehicle safety standards; conducts testing programs to determine compliance with these standards; rates vehicles under the 5-star government rating program for crashworthiness and antirollover stability; maintains the Web site www.safercar.gov, a consumer auto safety information site; funds local and state motor vehicle and driver safety programs; conducts research on motor vehicle safety and equipment, and human factors relating to auto and traffic safety. The Auto Safety Hotline and the Web site provide safety information and handle consumer problems and complaints involving safety-related defects and noncompliance matters.

National Highway Traffic Safety Administration
(Transportation Dept.), National Driver Register, 1200 New Jersey Ave. S.E., #W55-123 20590-0001; (202) 366-4800. Fax, (202) 366-2746. Sean H. McLaurin, Chief. Toll-free, (888) 851-0436. Web, www.nhtsa.gov/Data/National+Driver+Register+%28NDR%29

Maintains and operates the National Driver Register, a program in which states exchange information on motor vehicle driving records to ensure that drivers with suspended licenses in one state cannot obtain licenses in any other state.

National Transportation Safety Board, *490 L'Enfant Plaza East S.W. 20594-2000; (202) 314-6000. Fax, (202) 314-6018. Deborah A. P. Hersman, Chair. Information, (202) 314-6000. Press, (202) 314-6100. Web, www.ntsb.gov*

Promotes transportation safety through independent investigations of accidents and other safety problems. Makes recommendations for safety improvement.

▶**NONGOVERNMENTAL**

AAA Foundation for Traffic Safety, *607 14th St. N.W., #201 20005; (202) 638-5944. Fax, (202) 638-5943. J. Peter Kissinger, President. To order educational materials, (800) 305-7233. General email, info@aaafoundation.org Web, www.aaafoundation.org*

Sponsors "human factor" research on traffic safety issues, including bicycle, pedestrian, and road safety; supplies traffic safety educational materials to elementary and secondary schools, commercial driving schools, law enforcement agencies, motor vehicle administrations, and programs for older drivers.

Advocates for Highway and Auto Safety, *750 1st St. N.E., #901 20002-8007; (202) 408-1711. Fax, (202) 408-1699. Jacqueline Gillan, President.*

General email, advocates@saferoads.org

Web, www.saferoads.org

Coalition of insurers, citizens' groups, and public health and safety organizations. Advocates public policy designed to reduce deaths, injuries, and economic costs associated with motor vehicle crashes and fraud and theft involving motor vehicles. Interests include safety belts and child safety seats, drunk driving abuse, motorcycle helmets, vehicle crashworthiness, and speed limits. Monitors legislation and regulations.

American Highway Users Alliance, *1101 14th St. N.W., #750 20005; (202) 857-1200. Fax, (202) 857-1220. Gregory M. Cohen, President.*

General email, info@highways.org

Web, www.highways.org

Membership: companies and associations representing major industry and highway user groups. Develops information, analyzes public policy, and advocates legislation to improve roadway safety and efficiency and to increase the mobility of the American public. (Affiliated with the Roadway Safety Foundation.)

American Trucking Assns., *Policy and Regulatory Affairs, 950 N. Glebe Rd., #210, Arlington, VA 22203; (703) 838-1996. Fax, (703) 838-1748. David J. Osiecki, Senior Vice President. Press, (703) 838-1873.*

Web, www.trucking.org

Membership: state trucking associations, individual trucking and motor carrier organizations, and related supply companies. Provides information on safety for the trucking industry. Monitors legislation and regulations.

Center for Auto Safety, *1825 Connecticut Ave. N.W., #330 20009-5708; (202) 328-7700. Fax, (202) 387-0140. Clarence Ditlow, Executive Director.*

General email, accounts@autosafety.org

Web, www.autosafety.org

Public interest organization that receives written consumer complaints against auto manufacturers; monitors federal agencies responsible for regulating and enforcing auto and highway safety rules.

Commercial Vehicle Safety Alliance (CVSA), *6303 Ivy Lane, #310, Greenbelt, MD 20770-6319 (mailing address: Policy and Government Affairs: 444 N. Capitol St. N.W., #722, Washington, DC 20001-1534); (301) 830-6143. Fax, (301) 830-6144. Adrienne L. Gildea, Policy and Government Affairs; Stephen A. Keppler, Executive Director.*

General email, cvsahq@cvsa.org

Web, www.cvsa.org

Membership: local, state, provincial, territorial, and federal motor carrier safety officials and industry representatives from the United States, Canada, and Mexico. Promotes improved methods of highway and terminal inspection of commercial vehicles, drivers, and cargo; and uniformity and reciprocity of inspection criteria and enforcement across jurisdictions.

Governors Highway Safety Assn., *444 N. Capitol St. N.W., #722 20001-1534; (202) 789-0942. Fax, (202) 789-0946. Jonathan Adkins, Executive Director.*

General email, headquarters@ghsa.org

Web, www.ghsa.org

Membership: state officials who manage highway safety programs. Interprets technical data concerning highway safety. Represents the states in policy debates on national highway safety issues.

Institute of Transportation Engineers (ITE), *1627 Eye St. N.W., #600 20006; (202) 785-0060. Fax, (202) 785-0609. Philip J. Caruso, Deputy Executive Director, ext. 126.*

General email, ite_staff@ite.org

Web, www.ite.org

Membership: international professional transportation engineers. Interests include safe and efficient surface transportation; provides professional and scientific information on transportation standards and recommended practices.

Insurance Institute for Highway Safety, *1005 N. Glebe Rd., #800, Arlington, VA 22201; (703) 247-1500. Fax, (703) 247-1588. Adrian Lund, President. Highway Loss Data Institute, (703) 247-1600. Vehicle Research Center, (434) 985-4600.*

Web, www.iihs.org

Membership: property and casualty insurance associations and individual insurance companies. Conducts research and provides data on highway safety; seeks ways to reduce losses from vehicle crashes. (Operates with Highway Loss Data Institute and the Vehicle Research Center.)

Mothers Against Drunk Driving (MADD), *Public Policy Office, 1025 Connecticut Ave. N.W., #1210 20036-5415; (202) 688-1193. Fax, (972) 869-2206. J. T. Griffin, Chief; Frank Harris, State Legislative Affairs Manager, (202) 688-1194. Toll-free, (877) 275-6233. 24-hr Helpline, 877-MADD-HELP.*

General email, madd@madd.org

Web, www.madd.org

Advocacy group that seeks to stop drunk driving and prevent underage drinking. Monitors legislation and regulations. (Headquarters in Irving, Texas.)

National Crash Analysis Center *(George Washington University), 45085 University Dr., #3015, Ashburn, VA 20147; (703) 726-3600. Fax, (703) 726-3530. Azim Es Kandarian, Director. Library, (703) 726-8226.*

General email, library@ncac.gwu.edu

Web, www.ncac.gwu.edu

Conducts advanced crash research on transportation safety and security issues; applies research for the development and evaluation of vehicle safety systems, road features and hardware, and infrastructure systems. Interests include improving crash and precrash analysis methods, computer simulation, modeling, and methods in crash avoidance studies. Collaborates with the Federal Highway Administration and the National Highway Traffic Safety Administration.

National School Transportation Assn. (NSTA), *122 Royal St., Alexandria, VA 22314; (703) 684-3200. Fax, (703) 684-3212. Donna Weber, Executive Director; Travis Pryor, Coordinator of Marketing.*
General email, info@yellowbuses.org
Web, www.yellowbuses.org

Membership: private owners who operate school buses on contract, bus manufacturers, and allied companies. Primary area of interest and research is school bus safety.

Network of Employers for Traffic Safety, *344 Maple Ave. West, #357, Vienna, VA 22180; (703) 273-6005. Fax, (703) 273-7122. Jack Hanley, Executive Director. Toll-free, (888) 221-0045.*
General email, sgillies@trafficsafety.org
Web, www.trafficsafety.org

Dedicated to reducing the human and economic cost associated with automobile and highway crashes. Helps employers develop and implement workplace traffic and highway safety programs. Provides technical assistance.

Roadway Safety Foundation, *1101 14th St. N.W., #750 20005; (202) 857-1200. Fax, (202) 857-1220. Gregory M. Cohen, Executive Director.*
General email, info@roadwaysafety.org
Web, www.roadwaysafety.org

Conducts highway safety programs to reduce automobile-related crashes and deaths. (Affiliated with American Highway Users Alliance.)

Rubber Manufacturers Assn., *1400 K St. N.W., #900 20005; (202) 682-4800. Fax, (202) 682-4854. Charles A. (Charlie) Cannon, President.*
General email, info@rma.org
Web, www.rma.org

Membership: American tire manufacturers. Provides consumers with information on tire care and safety.

United Motorcoach Assn. (UMA), *113 S. West St., 4th Floor, Alexandria, VA 22314-2824; (703) 838-2929. Fax, (703) 838-2950. Victor S. Parra, Chief Executive Officer. Toll-free, (800) 424-8262.*
General email, info@uma.org
Web, www.uma.org

Membership: professional bus and motorcoach companies and suppliers and manufacturers in the industry. Provides information, offers technical assistance, conducts research, and monitors legislation. Interests include insurance, safety programs, and credit.

RAIL TRANSPORTATION

General

▶**AGENCIES**

Federal Railroad Administration *(Transportation Dept.), 1200 New Jersey Ave. S.E., 3rd Floor 20590; (202) 493-6014. Fax, (202) 493-6008. Joseph C. Szabo, Deputy*

Administrator. Public Affairs, (202) 493-6024.
General email, frapa@dot.gov
Web, www.fra.dot.gov

Develops national rail policies; enforces rail safety laws; administers financial assistance programs available to states and the rail industry; conducts research and development on improved rail safety. Operates eight regional offices

Federal Railroad Administration *(Transportation Dept.), Public Engagement, West Bldg., 1200 New Jersey Ave. S.E., MS 10 20590; (202) 493-6405. Fax, (202) 493-6009. Timothy Barkley, Director.*
General email, yvonne.white@dot.gov
Web, www.fra.dot.gov/page/p0030

Plans, coordinates, and administers activities related to railroad economics, finance, traffic and network analysis, labor management, and transportation planning, as well as intermodal, environmental, emergency response, and international programs.

Federal Railroad Administration *(Transportation Dept.), Railroad Policy and Development, 1200 New Jersey Ave. S.E., 3rd Floor 20590; (202) 493-6381. Fax, (202) 493-6330. Paul W. Nissenbaum, Associate Administrator.*
General email, OfficeofRPD@dot.gov
Web, www.fra.dot.gov/page/p0031

Administers federal assistance programs for national, regional, and local rail services, including freight service assistance, service continuation, and passenger service. Conducts research on and development of new rail technologies.

Federal Railroad Administration *(Transportation Dept.), Railroad Safety, 1200 New Jersey Ave. S.E., 3rd Floor 20590; (202) 493-6300. Fax, (202) 493-6216. Robert C. Lauby, Associate Administrator.*
Web, www.fra.dot.gov

Administers and enforces federal laws and regulations that promote railroad safety, including track maintenance, inspection and equipment standards, operating practices, and transportation of explosives and other hazardous materials. Conducts inspections and reports on railroad equipment facilities and accidents. All safety and/or security issues, such as bomb threats or biochemical threats, are managed by security specialists.

National Mediation Board, *1301 K St. N.W., #250E 20005; (202) 692-5000. Fax, (202) 692-5080. Harry R. Hoglander, Chair. Information, (202) 692-5050.*
General email, infoline@nmb.gov
Web, www.nmb.gov

Mediates labor disputes in the airline and railroad industries; determines and certifies labor representatives for the industry.

National Railroad Passenger Corp. (Amtrak), *60 Massachusetts Ave. N.E. 20002; (202) 906-3000. Joseph H. Boardman, President. Press, (202) 906-3860.*

Travel and ticket information, consumer relations and complaints (800) 872-7245.
Web, www.amtrak.com

Quasi-public corporation created by the Rail Passenger Service Act of 1970 to improve and develop intercity passenger rail service.

Railroad Retirement Board, *Legislative Affairs, 1310 G St. N.W., #500 20005-3004; (202) 272-7742. Fax, (202) 272-7728. Margaret S. Lindsley, Director. Toll-free, (877) 772-5772.*
General email, ola@rrb.gov/org/ogc/ola.asp
Web, www.rrb.gov

Assists congressional offices with inquiries on retirement, spouse, survivor, unemployment, and sickness benefits for railroad employees and retirees. Assists with legislation. (Headquarters in Chicago, Ill.)

Surface Transportation Board *(Transportation Dept.), 395 E St. S.W., #1220 20423-0001 (mailing address: 395 E St. S.W., Washington, DC 20024); (202) 245-0245. Fax, (202) 245-0458. Daniel R. Elliott III, Chair, (202) 245-0220. Library, (202) 245-0406. TTY, (800) 877-8339. Press, (202) 245-0234.*
Web, www.stb.dot.gov

Regulates rail rate disputes, railroad consolidations, rail line construction proposals, line abandonments, and rail car service. Library open to the public.

Surface Transportation Board *(Transportation Dept.), Public Assistance, Governmental Affairs, and Compliance, 395 E St. S.W., #1202 20423-0001; (202) 245-0238. Fax, (202) 245-0461. Lucille L. Marvin, Director. Press, (202) 245-0234. Toll-free, (866) 254-1792.*
General email, stbhelp@stb.dot.gov
Web, www.stb.dot.gov/stb/about/office_ocps.html

Informs members of Congress, the public, and the media of board actions. Prepares testimony for hearings; comments on proposed legislation; assists the public in matters involving transportation regulations.

U.S. Coast Guard (USCG) *(Homeland Security Dept.), 2703 Martin Luther King Jr. Ave. S.E., MS 7000 20593-7000; (202) 372-4411. Fax, (202) 372-8302. Adm. Robert J. Papp Jr., Commandant. Public Affairs, (202) 372-4600.*
Web, www.uscg.mil

Regulates the construction, maintenance, and operation of bridges across U.S. navigable waters, including railway bridges.

▶CONGRESS

For a listing of relevant congressional committees and subcommittees, please see page 657 or the Appendix.

▶NONGOVERNMENTAL

American Short Line and Regional Railroad Assn. (ASLRRA), *50 F St. N.W., #7020 20001-1564; (202) 628-4500. Richard F. Timmons, President.*
General email, aslrra@aslrra.org
Web, www.aslrra.org

Membership: independently owned short line and regional railroad systems. Assists members with technical and legal questions; compiles information on laws, regulations, and other matters affecting the industry.

Assn. of American Railroads, *425 3rd St. S.W., #1000 20024; (202) 639-2100. Fax, (202) 639-2886. Edward R. Hamberger, President. Press, (202) 639-2345.*
General email, info@aar.org
Web, www.aar.org

Membership: major freight railroads in the United States, Canada, and Mexico, as well as Amtrak. Provides information on freight railroad operations, safety and maintenance, economics and finance, management, and law and legislation; conducts research; issues statistical reports.

Brotherhood of Maintenance of Way Employees, *International Brotherhood of Teamsters, National Legislation, 25 Louisiana Ave. N.W., 7th Floor 20001; (202) 508-6445. Fax, (202) 508-6450. Freddie N. Simpson, President.*
General email, bmwe-dc@bmwewash.org
Web, www.bmwe.org

Membership: rail industry workers and others. Assists members with contract negotiation and grievances; conducts training programs and workshops. Monitors legislation and regulations. (Headquarters in Novi, Mich.)

International Assn. of Machinists and Aerospace Workers, *Transportation Communications Union, 3 Research Pl., Rockville, MD 20850-3279; (301) 948-4910. Fax, (301) 948-1369. Robert A. Scardelletti, President.*
General email, websteward@tcunion.org
Web, www.goiam.org/index.php/tcunion

Membership: approximately 46,000 railway workers. Assists members with contract negotiation and grievances; conducts training programs and workshops. Monitors legislation and regulations. (Affiliated with the AFL-CIO and Canadian Labour Congress.)

National Assn. of Railroad Passengers, *505 Capital Court N.E., #300 20002-7706; (202) 408-8362. Fax, (202) 408-8287. Ross B. Capon, Chief Executive Officer.*
General email, narp@narprail.org
Web, www.narprail.org

Education and advocacy organization. Works to expand and improve U.S. intercity and commuter rail passenger service, increase federal funds for mass transit, and address environmental concerns pertaining to mass transit. Works with Amtrak on scheduling, new services, fares, and advertising.

National Assn. of Regulatory Utility Commissioners, *1101 Vermont Ave. N.W., #200 20005-3521; (202) 898-2200. Fax, (202) 898-2213. Charles D. Gray, Executive Director.*

General email, admin@naruc.org

Web, www.naruc.org

Membership: members of federal, state, municipal, and international regulatory commissions that have jurisdiction over motor and common carriers. Interests include railroads.

National Railway Labor Conference, *1901 L St. N.W., #500 20036-3506; (202) 862-7200. Ken Gradia, Chair.*

Web, www.nrlc.ws

Assists member railroad lines with labor matters; negotiates with railroad labor representatives.

Railway Supply Institute (RSI), *425 3rd St. S.W., #920 20024; (202) 347-4664. Fax, (202) 347-0047. Thomas D. Simpson, President.*

General email, rsi@railwaysupply.org

Web, www.rsiweb.org

Membership: railroad and rail rapid transit suppliers. Conducts research on safety and new technology; monitors legislation.

TRANSIT SYSTEMS

General

▶**AGENCIES**

Federal Transit Administration *(Transportation Dept.), 1200 New Jersey Ave. S.E., #E57-310 20590; (202) 366-4040. Fax, (202) 366-9854. Peter M. Rogoff, Administrator; Therese W. McMillan, Deputy Administrator. Information and Press, (202) 366-4043.*

Web, www.fta.dot.gov

Responsible for developing improved public transportation facilities, equipment, techniques, and methods; assists state and local governments in financing public transportation systems; oversees the safety of U.S. public transit.

Federal Transit Administration *(Transportation Dept.), Budget and Policy, 1200 New Jersey Ave. S.E., #E52-323 20590; (202) 366-4050. Fax, (202) 366-7989. Robert Tuccillo, Associate Administrator. Press, (202) 366-4043.*

Web, www.fta.dot.gov

Develops budgets, programs, legislative proposals, and policies for the federal transit program; evaluates program proposals and their potential impact on local communities; coordinates private sector initiatives of the agency.

Federal Transit Administration *(Transportation Dept.), Program Management, 1200 New Jersey Ave. S.E., 4th Floor 20590; (202) 366-4020. Fax, (202) 366-7951. Henrika Buchanan-Smith, Associate Administrator. Information and Press, (202) 366-4043.*

Web, www.fta.dot.gov/office/program

Administers capital planning and operating assistance grants and loan activities; monitors transit projects in such areas as environmental impact, special provisions for the elderly and people with disabilities, efficiency, and investment.

Federal Transit Administration *(Transportation Dept.), Research, Demonstration, and Innovation, 1200 New Jersey Ave. S.E., #E43-314 20590; (202) 366-4052. Fax, (202) 366-3765. Vincent Valdes, Associate Administrator. Information and Press, (202) 366-4043.*

Web, www.fta.dot.gov/office/research

Provides industry and state and local governments with contracts, cooperative agreements, and grants for testing, developing, and demonstrating methods of improved mass transportation service and technology.

Maryland Transit Administration, *6 St. Paul St., Baltimore, MD 21202-1614; (410) 539-5000. Fax, (410) 333-0893. Robert L. Smith, Administrator. Information, 866-RIDE-MTA. Press, (410) 767-3936. Mobility/ Paratransit, (410) 764-8181.*

Web, http://mta.maryland.gov

Responsible for mass transit programs in Maryland; provides MARC commuter rail service for Baltimore, Washington, and suburbs in Maryland and West Virginia.

Surface Transportation Board *(Transportation Dept.), 395 E St. S.W., #1220 20423-0001 (mailing address: 395 E St. S.W., Washington, DC 20024); (202) 245-0245. Fax, (202) 245-0458. Daniel R. Elliott III, Chair, (202) 245-0220. Library, (202) 245-0406. TTY, (800) 877-8339. Press, (202) 245-0234.*

Web, www.stb.dot.gov

Regulates mergers and through-route requirements for the intercity bus industry. Library open to the public.

Virginia Railway Express (VRE), *1500 King St., #202, Alexandria, VA 22314; (703) 684-1001. Fax, (703) 684-1313. Doug Allen, Chief Executive Officer. Press, (703) 838-5416. Toll-free, (800) 743-3873.*

General email, gotrains@vre.org

Web, www.vre.org

Regional transportation partnership that provides commuter rail service from Fredericksburg and Manassas, Va., to Washington, D.C.

Washington Metropolitan Area Transit Authority (Metro), *600 5th St. N.W. 20001; (202) 962-1234. Fax, (202) 962-1133. Richard Sarles, General Manager. Information, (202) 637-7000. Metro Access (for those with disabilities), (800) 523-7009. Lost and Found, (202) 962-1195.*

Web, www.wmata.com

Provides bus and rail transit service to Washington, D.C., and neighboring Maryland and Virginia communities; assesses and plans for transportation needs. Provides fare, schedule, and route information; promotes accessibility for persons with disabilities and the elderly.

▶ CONGRESS

For a listing of relevant congressional committees and sub-committees, please see page 657 or the Appendix.

▶ NONGOVERNMENTAL

Amalgamated Transit Union (ATU), *5025 Wisconsin Ave. N.W. 20016-4139; (202) 537-1645. Fax, (202) 244-7824. Lawrence J. Hanley, President. Toll-free, (888) 240-1196. General email, mreza@atu.org*

Web, www.atu.org

Membership: transit workers in the United States and Canada, including bus, van, ambulance, subway, and light rail operators; clerks, baggage handlers, and maintenance employees in urban transit, over-the-road, and school bus industries; and municipal workers. Assists members with contract negotiations and grievances; conducts training programs and seminars. Monitors legislation and regulations. (Affiliated with the AFL-CIO.)

American Bus Assn., *111 K St. N.E., 9th Floor 20002; (202) 842-1645. Fax, (202) 842-0850. Peter J. Pantuso, President, (202) 218-7229. Toll-free, (800) 283-2877. General email, abainfo@buses.org*

Web, www.buses.org

Membership: privately owned intercity bus companies, state associations, travel/tourism businesses, bus manufacturers, and those interested in the bus industry. Monitors legislation and regulations.

American Public Transportation Assn. (APTA), *1666 K St. N.W., 11th Floor 20006-1215; (202) 496-4800. Fax, (202) 496-4324. Michael Melaniphy, President. Press, (202) 496-4816. General email, apta@apta.com*

Web, www.apta.com

Membership: rapid rail and motor bus systems and manufacturers, suppliers, and consulting firms. Compiles data on the industry; promotes research. Monitors legislation and regulations.

Community Transportation Assn. of America, *1341 G St. N.W., 10th Floor 20005; (800) 891-0590. Fax, (202) 737-9197. Barbara Cline, Board President; Dale J. Marsico, Executive Director. Toll-free, (800) 891-0590. Press, (202) 247-1921. Web, www.ctaa.org*

Works to improve mobility for the elderly, the poor, and persons with disabilities; concerns include rural, small-city, and specialized transportation.

National Assn. of Railroad Passengers, *505 Capital Court N.E., #300 20002-7706; (202) 408-8362. Fax, (202) 408-8287. Ross B. Capon, Chief Executive Officer. General email, narp@narprail.org*

Web, www.narprail.org

Education and advocacy organization. Works to expand and improve U.S. intercity and commuter rail passenger service, increase federal funds for mass transit, and address environmental concerns pertaining to mass transit. Works with Amtrak on scheduling, new services, fares, and advertising.

United Motorcoach Assn. (UMA), *113 S. West St., 4th Floor, Alexandria, VA 22314-2824; (703) 838-2929. Fax, (703) 838-2950. Victor S. Parra, Chief Executive Officer. Toll-free, (800) 424-8262. General email, info@uma.org*

Web, www.uma.org

Membership: professional bus and motorcoach companies and suppliers and manufacturers in the industry. Provides information, offers technical assistance, conducts research, and monitors legislation. Interests include insurance, safety programs, and credit.

19 🏛

U.S. Congress and Politics

ACCESS TO CONGRESSIONAL INFORMATION

Basic Resources

▶AGENCIES

National Archives and Records Administration (NARA), *Federal Register, 800 N. Capitol St. N.W., #700 20001 (mailing address: FP, 8601 Adelphi Rd., College Park, MD 20740-6001); (202) 741-6000. Fax, (202) 741-6012. Charley Barth, Director. Public Laws Update Service (PLUS), (202) 741-6043.*
General email, fedreg.info@nara.gov
Web, www.archives.gov/federal_register

Assigns public law numbers to enacted legislation, executive orders, and proclamations. Responds to inquiries on public law numbers. Assists inquirers in finding presidential signing or veto messages in the Daily Compilation of Presidential Documents and the Public Papers of the Presidents. Compiles slip laws and annual United States Statutes at Large; compiles indexes for finding statutory provisions. Operates Public Law Electronic Notification System (PENS), which provides information by email on new legislation. Coordinates the functions of the Electoral College and the constitutional amendment process. Publications available from the U.S. Government Printing Office.

▶CONGRESS

For a listing of relevant congressional committees and subcommittees, please see page 689 or the Appendix.

Clerk of the House of Representatives, *H154 CAP 20515-6601; (202) 225-7000. Karen L. Haas, Clerk. Publication Services, (202) 225-1908.*
General email, info.clerkweb@mail.house.gov
Web, http://clerk.house.gov

Maintains and distributes House bills, reports, public laws, and documents to members' offices, committee staffs, and the general public. Provides daily schedules, when the House is in session, on web site. Provides legislative history of all measures reported by House and Senate committees. Provides additional materials in the *Congressional Record* (also available from the Contact Center, Government Printing Office, Washington, D.C., (202) 512-1800 or in electronic format at www.gpoaccess .gov). Provides video coverage of House floor proceedings through http://houselive.gov.

Government Printing Office (GPO), *Contact Center, 732 N. Capitol St. N.W. 20401; (202) 512-1800. Fax, (202) 512-2104. Esther Edmonds, Director. Toll-free, (866) 512-1800.*
General email, contactcenter@gpo.gov
Web, www.gpo.gov

Prints and distributes federal and congressional documents, prints, public laws, reports, and House calendars.

Documents may be obtained electronically through GPO's federal digital system (www.fdsys.gov) or purchased from GPO's online bookstore (http://bookstore.gpo.gov). Information about government documents and agencies at all levels is available from government information librarians at http://govtinfo.org. Information about how to locate the *Congressional Record* and other documents in the 1,400 federal depository libraries is also available at www.fdsys.gov.

Office of Art and Archives, *Office of the Clerk, House of Representatives, B53 CHOB 20515; (202) 226-1300. Fax, (202) 226-4635. Farar P. Elliott, Chief, Art and Archives.*
Web, http://clerk.house.gov

Works with the Office of the Historian to provide access to published documents and historical records of the House. Advises members on the disposition of their records and papers; maintains information on manuscript collections of former members; maintains biographical files on former members; houses photographs and artifacts of former members. Produces publications on Congress and its members.

Office of the Historian, *Office of the Clerk, U.S. House of Representatives, B56 CHOB 20515; (202) 226-5525. Fax, (202) 226-2931. Matthew A. Wasniewski, House Historian.*
Web, http://clerk.house.gov

Works with the Office of Art and Archives to provide access to published documents and historical records of the House. Conducts historical research. Advises members on the disposition of their records and papers; maintains information on manuscript collections of former members; maintains biographical files on former members. Produces publications on Congress and its members.

Senate Executive Clerk, *S138 CAP 20510; (202) 224-4341. Jennifer Gorham, Executive Clerk.*

Maintains and distributes copies of treaties submitted to the Senate for ratification; provides information on submitted treaties and nominations. (Shares distribution responsibility with Senate Printing and Document Services, [202] 224-7701.)

Senate Historical Office, *SH-201 20510; (202) 224-6900. Donald A. Ritchie, Historian.*
General email, historian@sec.senate.gov
Web, www.senate.gov

Serves as an information clearinghouse on Senate history, traditions, and members. Collects, organizes, and distributes to the public unpublished Senate documents; collects and preserves photographs and pictures related to Senate history; conducts an oral history program; advises senators and Senate committees on the disposition of their noncurrent papers and records. Produces publications on the history of the Senate.

Senate Office of Conservation and Preservation, *S416 CAP 20510; (202) 224-4550. Vacant, Director.*

Develops and coordinates programs related to the conservation and preservation of Senate records and materials for the secretary of the Senate.

U.S. CONGRESS AND POLITICS RESOURCES IN CONGRESS

For a complete listing of Congress committees, including their full contact information, leadership, membership, and jurisdictions, please refer to the Appendix on pages 724–842.

HOUSE:

House Administration Committee, (202) 225-8281.
Web, cha.house.gov or democrats.cha.house.gov
    Subcommittee on Elections, (202) 225-8281.
    Subcommittee on Oversight, (202) 225-8281.
House Appropriations Committee, (202) 225-2771.
Web, appropriations.house.gov or
    democrats.appropriations.house.gov
    Subcommittee on Financial Services and General
        Government, (202) 225-7245.
    Subcommittee on Legislative Branch,
        (202) 226-7252.
House Ethics Committee, (202) 225-7103.
Web, ethics.house.gov
House Judiciary Committee, (202) 225-3951.
Web, judiciary.house.gov or
    democrats.judiciary.house.gov
    Subcommittee on the Constitution and Civil
        Justice, (202) 225-2825.
House Oversight and Government Reform
    Committee, (202) 225-5074.
Web, oversight.house.gov or
    democrats.oversight.house.gov
    Subcommittee on Federal Workforce, U.S. Postal
        Service, and the Census, (202) 225-5074.
    Subcommittee on Government Operations,
        (202) 225-5074.
House Rules Committee, (202) 225-9191.
Web, rules.house.gov or democrats.rules.house.gov
    Subcommittee on the Legislative and Budget
        Process, (202) 225-2231.
    Subcommittee on Rules and Organization of the
        House, (202) 225-1002.
House Transportation and Infrastructure
    Committee, (202) 225-9446.
Web, transportation.house.gov or
    democrats.transportation.house.gov
    Subcommittee on Economic Development,
        Public Buildings, and Emergency
        Management, (202) 225-3014.

House Ways and Means Committee, (202) 225-3625.
Web, waysandmeans.house.gov or
    democrats.waysandmeans.house.gov

JOINT:

Joint Committee on Printing, (202) 225-8281.
Web, cha.house.gov/jointcommittees/joint-committee-
    on-printing
Joint Committee on the Library of Congress,
    (202) 225-8281.
Web, cha.house.gov/jointcommittees/joint-committee-
    library

SENATE:

Senate Appropriations Committee,
    (202) 224-7363.
Web, appropriations.senate.gov
    Subcommittee on Financial Services and General
        Government, (202) 224-1133.
    Subcommittee on Legislative Branch,
        (202) 224-7256.
Senate Finance Committee, (202) 224-4515.
Web, finance.senate.gov
Senate Homeland Security and Governmental Affairs
    Committee, (202) 224-2627.
Web, hsgac.senate.gov
    Permanent Subcommittee on Investigations,
        (202) 224-9505.
    Subcommittee on Emergency Management,
        Intergovernmental Relations, and the District
        of Columbia, (202) 224-4462.
Senate Judiciary Committee, (202) 224-7703.
Web, judiciary.senate.gov
    Subcommittee on the Constitution, Civil Rights,
        and Human Rights, (202) 224-1158.
Senate Rules and Administration Committee,
    (202) 224-6352.
Web, rules.senate.gov
Senate Select Committee on Ethics, (202) 224-2981.
Web, ethics.senate.gov

Senate Printing and Document Services, *SH-B04*
20510-7106; (202) 224-0205. Fax, (202) 228-2815.
Karen Moore, Director.
General email, orders@sec.senate.gov

*Web, www.senate.gov/legislative/common/generic/Doc_*
Room.htm

Maintains and distributes Senate bills, reports, public laws, and documents. To obtain material send a self-addressed mailing label or fax with request. Documents and information may be accessed on the Web site.

▶**NEWS SERVICES**

CQ Press, *2300 N St. N.W., #800 20037; (202) 729-1900.*
Fax, (805) 375-5291. Blaise R. Simqu, President. Toll-free,
(866) 818-7243.
General email, customerservice@cqpress.com

Web, www.cqpress.com

Publishes books, directories, periodicals, and Web products on U.S. government, history, and politics. Products include the *CQ Weekly, CQ Press Encyclopedia of American*

Government, and *CQ Researcher.* (An imprint of SAGE Publications.)

Washington Post, *1150 15th St. N.W. 20071; (202) 334-6000. Katharine Weymouth, Publisher; Marty Baron, Executive Editor. Toll-free, (800) 627-1150.*
General email, national@washpost.com
Web, www.washingtonpost.com

Provides news and analysis of congressional activities.

▶**NONGOVERNMENTAL**

White House Correspondents' Assn., *600 New Hampshire Ave., #800 20037; (202) 266-7453. Fax, (202) 266-7454. Julia Whiston, Executive Director.*
General email, whca@starpower.net
Web, www.whca.net

Membership: reporters with permanent White House press credentials. Acts as a liaison between reporters and White House staff. Sponsors annual WHCA Journalism Awards and Scholarships fundraising dinner.

Congressional Record

The Congressional Record, *published daily when Congress is in session, is a printed account of proceedings on the floor of the House and Senate. A Daily Digest section summarizes the day's action on the floor and in committees and lists committee meetings scheduled for the following day. An index is published biweekly and at the close of sessions of Congress. Since January 1995, House members have not been allowed to edit their remarks before they appear in the Record, but senators retain this privilege. Material not spoken on the floor may be inserted through unanimous consent to revise or extend a speech and is published in a distinctive typeface. Grammatical, typographical, and technical corrections are also permitted.*

▶**CONGRESS**

For a listing of relevant congressional committees and subcommittees, please see page 689 or the Appendix.

Government Printing Office, Main Bookstore (GPO), Congressional Order Desk, *732 N. Capitol St. N.W. 20401; (202) 512-1800. Fax, (202) 512-2104. Esther Edmonds, Director, (202) 512-1694. Bookstore Contact Center, (866) 512-1800; in DC area, (202) 512-1800.*
General email, ContactCenter@gpo.gov
Web, http://bookstore.gpo.gov

Sells copies of and subscriptions to the *Congressional Record.* Expert help from government information librarians is available at http://govtinfo.org. Orders may be placed on Web site. The *Congressional Record* from 1994 to the present is available online at www.fdsys.gov.

Library of Congress, *Law Library, Madison Bldg., 101 Independence Ave. S.E., #LM240 20540;*

(202) 707-5065. Fax, (202) 707-1820. David S. Mao, Law Librarian. Reading room, (202) 707-5080. Reference information, (202) 707-5079.
Web, www.loc.gov/law

Copies of the *Congressional Record* are available for reading. Terminals in the reading room provide access to a computer system containing bill digests from the 93rd Congress to date. The Congressional Record can also be accessed online at thomas.loc.gov.

▶**NONGOVERNMENTAL**

Martin Luther King Jr. Memorial Library, *901 G St. N.W. 20001-4599; (202) 727-0321. Fax, (202) 727-1129. Richard Reyes-Gavilan, Director. Circulation, (202) 727-1579.*
General email, mlkjrlibrary@dc.gov
Web, www.dclibrary.org/mlk

Maintains collection of *Congressional Record* from 1879 to the present, available in various formats (bound volumes, microfilm, microfiche, and electronic).

Schedules, Status of Legislation

Information can also be obtained from the Congressional Record *(Daily Digest) and from individual congressional committees (see 113th Congress, p. 724).*

▶**CONGRESS**

For a listing of relevant congressional committees and subcommittees, please see page 689 or the Appendix.

Clerk of the House of Representatives, *H154 CAP 20515-6601; (202) 225-7000. Karen L. Haas, Clerk. Publication Services, (202) 225-1908.*
General email, info.clerkweb@mail.house.gov
Web, http://clerk.house.gov

Maintains and distributes House bills, reports, public laws, and documents to members' offices, committee staffs, and the general public. Provides daily schedules, when the House is in session, on web site. Provides legislative history of all measures reported by House and Senate committees. Provides additional materials in the *Congressional Record* (also available from the Contact Center, Government Printing Office, Washington, DC, (202) 512-1800 or in electronic format at www.gpoaccess.gov). Provides video coverage of House floor proceedings through http://houselive.gov.

House Democratic Cloakroom, *H222 CAP 20515; (202) 225-7330. Robert Fischer, Manager. House floor action, (202) 225-7400. Legislative program, (202) 225-1600.*
Provides information about House floor proceedings.

House Republican Cloakroom, *H223 CAP 20515; (202) 225-7350. Fax, (202) 225-8247. Tim Harroun, Manager. Legislative Program Recording, (202) 225-2020.*
Web, http://repcloakroom.house.gov and
Twitter, @repcloakroom
Provides information about House floor proceedings.

Legislative Resource Center, *Office of the Clerk, House of Representatives,* B106 CHOB 20515; (202) 226-5200. Fax, (202) 226-5208. Ronald (Dale) Thomas, Chief. Bill status, (202) 225-1772.
General email, info.clerkweb@mail.house.gov
Web, http://clerk.house.gov/about/offices_lrc.aspx

Senate Democratic Cloakroom, *S225 CAP 20510; (202) 224-4691. Tequia Delgado, Assistant; Stephanie Paone, Assistant; Daniel Tinsley, Assistant; Brad Watt, Assistant. Senate floor action, (202) 224-8541.*

Provides information about Senate floor proceedings.

Senate Republican Cloakroom, *S226 CAP 20510; (202) 224-6191. Fax, (202) 224-2860. Laura Dove, Secretary. Senate floor action, (202) 224-8601.*

Provides information about Senate floor proceedings.

▶ NEWS SERVICES

Associated Press, *Washington Office,* 1100 13th St. N.W., #700 20005-4076; (202) 641-9000. Fax, (202) 263-8800. Sally Buzbee, Bureau Chief.
General email, info@ap.org
Web, www.ap.org

Publishes daybook that lists congressional committee meetings and hearings and their location and subject matter. Fee for services. (Headquarters in New York.)

CQ Roll Call, 77 K St. N.E. 20002-4681; (202) 650-6500.
Web, www.cqrollcall.com

Provides online congressional news and analysis, including legislative summaries, votes, testimony, and archival and reference materials. Provides hearing and markup schedules, including time and location, meeting agendas, and full witness listings. Fee for services. (Merger of Congressional Quarterly, Roll Call, and Capitol Advantage; subsidiary of the Economist Group.)

United Press International (UPI), 1133 19th Street, N.W. 20036; (202) 898-8000. Fax, (202) 898-8048. Seyla Seng, Chief Digital Officer.
Web, www.upi.com

Wire service that lists congressional committee meetings and hearings, locations, and subject matter. Fee for services.

CAMPAIGNS AND ELECTIONS

General

▶ AGENCIES

Election Assistance Commission, 1335 East-West Hwy., #4300, Silver Spring, MD 20910; (301) 563-3919. Fax, (202) 566-3127. Alice P. Miller, Executive Director, Acting. Toll-free, (866) 747-1471.
General email, HAVAinfo@eac.gov
Web, www.eac.gov

Serves as national information clearinghouse on the administration of federal elections. Responsible for adopting voting system guidelines. Tests and certifies voting system hardware and software. Studies election technology and voting accessibility. Reports data from the states for each federal election and maintains the National Mail Voter registration from.

Federal Communications Commission (FCC), *Media Bureau, Policy Division,* 445 12th St. S.W. 20554; (202) 418-2120. Fax, (202) 418-1069. Mary Beth Murphy, Chief. Web, www.fcc.gov/encyclopedia/policy-division-media-bureau

Handles complaints and inquiries concerning the equal time rule, which requires equal broadcast opportunities for all legally qualified candidates for the same office, and other political broadcast, cable, and satellite rules. Interprets and enforces related Communications Act provisions, including the requirement for sponsorship identification of all paid political broadcast, cable, and satellite announcements and the requirement for broadcasters to furnish federal candidates with reasonable access to broadcast time for political advertising. Administers Equal Employment Opportunity (EEO) matters.

Federal Election Commission (FEC), 999 E St. N.W. 20463; (202) 694-1000. Lee E. Goodman, Chair. Press, (202) 694-1220. Toll-free information, (800) 424-9530.
General email, info@fec.gov
Web, www.fec.gov

Formulates, administers, and enforces policy with respect to the Federal Election Campaign Act of 1971 as amended, including campaign disclosure requirements, contribution and expenditure limitations, and public financing of presidential nominating conventions and campaigns. Receives campaign finance reports; makes rules and regulations; conducts audits and investigations. Makes copies of campaign finance reports available for inspection.

Federal Election Commission (FEC), *Public Disclosure,* 999 E St. N.W. 20463; (202) 694-1120. Fax, (202) 501-0693. Patricia Young, Director. Information, (800) 424-9530.
General email, pubrec@fec.gov
Web, www.fec.gov

Makes available for public inspection and copying the detailed campaign finance reports on contributions and expenditures filed by candidates for federal office, their supporting political committees, and individuals and committees making expenditures on behalf of a candidate. Maintains copies of all reports and statements filed since 1972.

Justice Dept. (DOJ), *Election Crimes,* 1400 New York Ave. N.W., #12100 20005; (202) 514-1412. Fax, (202) 514-3003. Richard Pilger, Director, (202) 514-1178. Press, (202) 514-2007.
Web, www.justice.gov

Supervises enforcement of federal criminal laws related to campaigns and elections. Oversees investigation of deprivation of voting rights; intimidation and coercion

Federal Election Commission

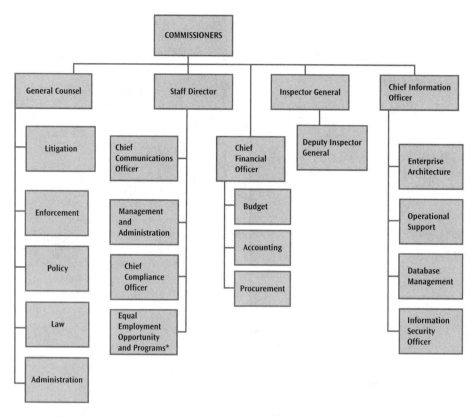

*Reports to the Staff Director for management and administrative purposes; however, has direct reporting authority to the Commission on all EEO matters.

of voters; denial or promise of federal employment or other benefits; illegal political contributions, expenditures, and solicitations; and all other election violations referred to the division.

► CONGRESS

For a listing of relevant congressional committees and subcommittees, please see page 689 or the Appendix.

House Commission on Congressional Mailing Standards (Franking Commission), *1313 LHOB 20515-6328; (202) 225-8281. Rep. Candice S. Miller, Chair; Richard Cappetto, Majority Staff Director, (202) 226-0647; Kyle Anderson, Minority Staff Director.*
Web, http://cha.house.gov/franking-commission

Issues regulations governing mass mailings by members' offices. Receives complaints, conducts investigations, and issues decisions on disputes arising from the alleged abuse of franked mail by House members.

Legislative Resource Center, *Records and Registration, Office of the Clerk, House of Representatives, B106 CHOB 20515-6612; (202) 226-5200. Fax, (202) 226-4874.*

Steve Pingeton, Manager.
Web, http://clerk.house.gov

Receives personal financial disclosure reports for members of the House, candidates for the House, and certain employees. Open for public inspection.

► NONGOVERNMENTAL

American Assn. of Political Consultants, *8400 Westpark Dr., 2nd Floor, McLean, VA 22102; (703) 245-8020. Fax, (703) 995-0628. Alana Joyce, Executive Director.*
General email, info@theaapc.org
Web, www.theaapc.org

Membership: political consultants, media specialists, campaign managers, corporate public affairs officers, pollsters, public officials, academicians, fundraisers, lobbyists, college students, and congressional staffers. Focuses on ethics of the profession; provides members with opportunities to meet industry leaders and learn new techniques and emerging technologies.

American Bar Assn. (ABA), *Standing Committee on Election Law, 1050 Connecticut Ave. N.W. 20036; (202) 662-1691. Fax, (202) 638-3844. Elizabeth M. Young, Director.*

General email, election@abanet.org

Web, www.americanbar.org/groups/public_services/ election_law.html

Studies ways to improve the U.S. election and campaign process.

Campaign Finance Institute, *1425 K St. N.W., #350 20005; (202) 969-8890. Michael J. Malbin, Executive Director.*

General email, info@CFInst.org

Web, www.cfinst.org

Conducts objective research and educates about campaign financing. Makes recommendations for policy changes in campaign financing.

Campaign Legal Center, *215 E St. N.E. 20002; (202) 736-2200. Fax, (202) 736-2222. J. Gerald Hebert, Executive Director.*

General email, info@campaignlegalcenter.org

Web, www.campaignlegalcenter.org

Dedicated to improving the elections process by promoting voluntary, realistic standards of campaign conduct.

Commission on Presidential Debates, *1200 New Hampshire Ave. N.W., #445 20036; (202) 872-1020. Fax, (202) 783-5923. Frank J. Fahrenkopf Jr., Co-Chair; Michael McCurry, Co-Chair; Janet H. Brown, Executive Director.*

General email, comments@debates.org

Web, www.debates.org

Independent, nonpartisan organization established to sponsor general election presidential and vice presidential debates and to undertake educational and research activities related to the debates.

Common Cause, *1133 19th St. N.W., 9th Floor 20036; (202) 833-1200. Fax, (202) 659-3716. Miles Rapoport, President, (202) 736-5740. Press, (202) 736-5770.*

General email, mrapoport@commoncause.org

Web, www.commoncause.org

Nonpartisan citizens' legislative interest group. Records and analyzes campaign contributions to congressional candidates and campaign committees, particularly those from political action committees, and soft money contributions to national political parties.

CQ Political MoneyLine, *77 K St. N.E. 20002-4681; (202) 650-6599. Kent Cooper, Editor; Tony Raymond, Editor.*

General email, questions@cq.com

Web, www.politicalmoneyline.com

Monitors and reports on money as it is used in campaigns, political action committees, 527s, political parties, and by lobbyists. (Affiliated with CQ-Roll Call.)

Electionline.org, *2630 Adams Mill Rd. N.W., #208 20009; (202) 588-7332. Mindy Moretti, Editor.*

General email, info@electionline.org

Web, www.electionline.org

Online resource providing news and analysis on election reform. (Receives support from Hewlett Fund and Democracy Fund.)

OpenSecrets.org/Center for Responsive Politics, *1101 14th St. N.W., #1030 20005-5635; (202) 857-0044. Fax, (202) 857-7809. Sheila Krumholz, Executive Director; Viveca Novak, Editorial and Communications Director. Press, (202) 354-0111.*

General email, info@crp.org; press@crp.org

Web, www.opensecrets.org

Conducts research on federal campaign finance and lobbying in connection with congressional and presidential elections.

Public Campaign, *1133 19th St. N.W., 9th Floor 20036; (202) 640-5600. Fax, (202) 640-5601. Nick Nyhart, President.*

General email, info@publiccampaign.org

Web, www.publiccampaign.org

National grassroots organization interested in campaign finance reform. Supports the Fair Election model of campaign finance under which candidates who accept only small donations receive additional money from a public fund sufficient to run a competitive campaign.

Election Statistics and Apportionment

▶AGENCIES

Census Bureau *(Commerce Dept.), Census Redistricting Data, 4600 Silver Hill Rd., #8H019, Suitland, MD 20746 (mailing address: Washington, DC 20233-0100); (301) 763-4039. Fax, (301) 763-4348. Catherine C. McCully, Chief.*

Web, www.census.gov/rdo

Provides state legislatures with population figures for use in legislative redistricting.

Census Bureau *(Commerce Dept.), Customer Services Center, 4600 Silver Hill Rd., North Bldg., 8th Floor, Suitland, MD 20746 (mailing address: Customer Service, Bureau of the Census, MS-0801, Washington, DC 20233-0500); (301) 763-4636. Fax, (301) 763-3842. Kendall B. Johnson, Chief. Press, (301) 763-3030. Orders, (800) 923-8282.*

General email, clmso@census.gov

Web, www.census.gov

Main contact for information about the Census Bureau's products and services. Census data and maps on counties, municipalities, and other small areas are available on the Web site and in libraries.

Census Bureau *(Commerce Dept.), Population, 4600 Silver Hill Rd., #5H174, Suitland, MD 20746 (mailing address: change city, state, and zip code to Washington, DC 20233-8800); (301) 763-2071. Fax, (301) 763-2516. Victoria A. Velkoff, Division Chief.*

General email, pop@census.gov

Web, www.census.gov/popest

Computes every ten years the population figures that determine the number of representatives each state may have in the House of Representatives.

►CONGRESS

For a listing of relevant congressional committees and sub-committees, please see page 689 or the Appendix.

Clerk of the House of Representatives, *H154 CAP 20515-6601; (202) 225-7000. Karen L. Haas, Clerk. Publication Services, (202) 225-1908.*
General email, info.clerkweb@mail.house.gov

Web, http://clerk.house.gov

Publishes biennial compilation of statistics on congressional and presidential elections.

►NONGOVERNMENTAL

Common Cause, *State Organization, 1133 19th St. N.W., 9th Floor 20036; (202) 833-1200. Fax, (202) 659-3716. Jenny Rose Flanagan, Vice President for State Operations, (303) 842-1515; Jenny Rose Flanagan, Director of Voting and Election Reform, Acting. Press, (202) 736-5770.*
Web, www.commoncause.org

Nonpartisan citizens' interest group. Seeks to alter procedures governing redistricting by the establishment of independent redistricting commissions. Serves as an information clearinghouse; provides research and support for regional field offices.

Voting, Political Participation

►NONGOVERNMENTAL

America Votes, *1155 Connecticut Ave. N.W., #600 20036; (202) 962-7240. Fax, (202) 962-7241. Greg Speed, Executive Director; Greg Speed, President.*
Web, www.americavotes.org

Coalition that seeks to increase voter registration, education, and participation in electoral politics.

Arab American Institute, *1600 K St. N.W., #601 20006; (202) 429-9210. Fax, (202) 429-9214. James J. Zogby, President.*
General email, webmaster@aaiusa.org

Web, www.aaiusa.org

Fosters civic and political empowerment of Americans of Arab descent through research, policy formation, and political activism.

Center for Progressive Leadership, *1133 19th St. N.W., 9th Floor 20036; (202) 775-2003. Fax, (202) 318-0485. Ng'ethe Maina, President.*
General email, office@progressiveleaders.org

Web, www.progressiveleaders.org

Provides training and development for youths interested in progressive political leadership and activism. Seeks to increase progressive influence in key states and connect aspiring leaders with established ones through networking events, mentorship programs, online forums, and fellowship programs.

Clare Booth Luce Policy Institute, *112 Elden St., Suite P, Herndon, VA 20170; (703) 318-0730. Fax, (703) 318-8867. Michelle Easton, President. Toll-free, (888) 891-4288.*
General email, info@cblpi.org

Web, www.cblpi.org

Seeks to engage young women through student programs promoting conservative values and leadership. Offers mentoring, internship, and networking opportunities for young women.

Coalition of Black Trade Unionists, *1150 17th St. N.W., #300 20036 (mailing address: P.O. Box 66268, Washington, DC 20035); (202) 778-3318. Fax, (202) 293-5308. Terrence L. Melvin, President.*
General email, cbtul@hotmail.com

Web, www.cbtu.org

Monitors legislation affecting African American and other minority trade unionists. Focuses on equal employment opportunity, unemployment, and voter education and registration.

Democracy 21, *2000 Massachusetts Ave. N.W. 20036; (202) 355-9600. Fax, (202) 355-9606. Fred Wertheimer, President.*
General email, info@Democracy21.org

Web, www.democracy21.org

Focuses on using the communications revolution to strengthen democracy and on eliminating the influence of big money in American politics.

Democratic National Committee (DNC), *Campaign Division, 430 S. Capitol St. S.E. 20003-4024; (202) 863-8000. Fax, (202) 863-8174. Rep. Debbie Wasserman Schultz, Chair. Press, (202) 863-8148.*
General email, info@democrats.org

Web, www.democrats.org

Responsible for electoral activities at the federal, state, and local levels; sponsors workshops to recruit Democratic candidates and to provide instruction in campaign techniques; conducts party constituency outreach programs; coordinates voter registration; plans the party's quadrennial presidential nominating convention.

FairVote, *6930 Carroll Ave., #610, Takoma Park, MD 20912; (301) 270-4616. Fax, (301) 270-4133. Robert Richie, Executive Director.*
General email, info@fairvote.org

Web, www.fairvote.org

Studies how voting systems affect participation, representation, and governance both domestically and internationally. Advocates for a national popular vote for president, American forms of proportional representation, instant runoff voting, a constitutionally protected right to

Resources for Political Participation

NATIONWIDE CAMPAIGNS

Democratic Congressional Campaign Committee,
(202) 863-1500; www.dccc.org

Democratic Governors Assn., (202) 772-5600;
www.democraticgovernors.org

Democratic National Committee (DNC), (202) 863-8000;
www.democrats.org

Democratic Senatorial Campaign Committee,
(202) 224-2447; www.dscc.org

FairVote-The Center for Voting and Democracy,
(301) 270-4616; www.fairvote.org

Fieldworks, (202) 667-4400; www.fieldworks.com

Green Party of the United States, (202) 319-7191;
www.gp.org

League of Women Voters (LWV), (202) 429-1965;
www.lwv.org

Libertarian Party, (202) 333-0008; www.lp.org

Mobilize, (202) 642-4320; www.mobilize.org

National Republican Congressional Committee,
(202) 479-7000; www.nrcc.org

National Republican Senatorial Committee,
(202) 675-6000; www.nrsc.org

Republican Governors Assn., (202) 662-4140;
www.rga.org

Republican National Committee (RNC), (202) 863-8500;
www.gop.org

Rock the Vote, (202) 719-9910; www.rockthevote.com

IN MARYLAND, VIRGINIA, AND WASHINGTON, D.C.

District of Columbia Board of Elections and Ethics,
(202) 727-2525; www.dcboee.org

DC Vote, (202) 462-6000; www.dcvote.org

Maryland State Board of Elections, (800) 222-8683;
www.elections.state.md.us

Volunteer on Election Day in Maryland,
www.elections.state.md.us/get_involved

Virginia State Board of Elections, (800) 552-9745;
www.sbe.virginia.gov

Volunteer on Election Day in Virginia,
www.sbe.virginia.gov/cms/Voter_Information/
Local_Voter_Registration_Offices/Index.asp

---

vote, and universal voter registration. (Formerly the Center for Voting and Democracy.)

Internet Education Foundation, *1634 Eye St. N.W., #1100 20006; (202) 638-4370. Fax, (202) 637-0968. Tim Lordan, Executive Director.*
General email, info@neted.org

Web, www.neted.org

Sponsors educational initiatives promoting the Internet as a valuable medium for democratic participation, communications, and commerce. Funds the Congressional Internet Caucus Advisory Committee, which works to inform Congress of important Internet-related policy issues. Monitors legislation and regulations.

Joint Center for Political and Economic Studies, *805 15th St. N.W., 2nd Floor 20005-4928; (202) 789-3500. Fax, (202) 789-6390. Spencer Overton, President, Acting.*
General email, general@jointcenter.org

Web, www.jointcenter.org

Documents and analyzes the political and economic status of African Americans and other minority populations, focusing on political participation, economic advancement, and health policy. Publishes an annual profile of African American elected officials in federal, state, and local government; disseminates information through forums, conferences, publications, and the Internet.

Labor Council for Latin American Advancement,
815 16th St. N.W., 3rd Floor 20006; (202) 508-6919. Fax, (202) 508-6922. Hector Sanchez, Executive Director.

General email, headquarters@lclaa.org

Web, www.lclaa.org

Membership: Hispanic trade unionists. Encourages equal employment opportunity, voter registration, and participation in the political process. (Affiliated with the AFL-CIO and the Change to Win Federation.)

League of Women Voters (LWV), *1730 M St. N.W., #1000 20036-4508; (202) 429-1965. Fax, (202) 429-4343. Elisabeth MacNamara, President; Nancy E. Tate, Executive Director.*
General email, lwv@lwv.org

Web, www.lwv.org

Membership: women and men interested in nonpartisan political action and study. Works to increase participation in government; provides information on voter registration and balloting. Interests include social policy, natural resources, international relations, and representative government.

Mobilize.org, *1029 Vermont Ave. N.W., #501 20005; (202) 400-3848. Scott Stein, Director.*
General email, info@mobilize.org

Web, www.mobilize.org and Twitter, @mob_org

Encourages young people, ages sixteen through thirty, to become active participants in the democratic process at local, state, and national levels. Conducts outreach on college campuses and through social networking sites. Provides information about effective political advocacy.

National Assn. of Latino Elected and Appointed Officials Educational Fund, *Washington Office, 600 Pennsylvania Ave. S.E., #230 20003; (202) 546-2536. Fax, (202) 546-4121. Arturo Vargas, Executive Director. General email, dparfaiteclaude@naleo.org*

Web, www.naleo.org

Research and advocacy group that provides civic affairs information and assistance on legislation affecting Latinos. Encourages Latino participation in local, state, and national politics. Interests include health care and social, economic, and educational issues. (Headquarters in Los Angeles, Calif.)

National Black Caucus of Local Elected Officials (NBC/LEO), *c/o National League of Cities, 1301 Pennsylvania Ave. N.W. 20004-1763; (202) 626-3169. Adam McFadden, President. Press, (202) 626-3015. General email, constituencygroup@nlc.org*

Web, www.nlc.org

Membership: African American elected officials at the local level and other interested individuals. Seeks to increase African American participation on the National League of Cities' steering and policy committees. Informs members on issues, and plans strategies to achieve objectives through legislation and direct action. Interests include cultural diversity, local government and community participation, housing, economics, job training, the family, and human rights.

National Black Caucus of State Legislators, *444 N. Capitol St. N.W., #622 20001; (202) 624-5457. Fax, (202) 508-3826. LaKimba DeSadier, Executive Director.*

Web, www.nbcsl.org

Membership: African American state legislators. Promotes effective leadership among African American state legislators through education, research, and training; serves as an information network and clearinghouse for members.

National Coalition on Black Civic Participation, *1050 Connecticut Ave. N.W., 10th Floor, #1000 20036; (202) 659-4929. Fax, (202) 659-5025. Melanie L. Campbell, President. General email, ncbcp@ncbcp.org*

Web, www.ncbcp.org

Seeks to increase black voter civic participation to eliminate barriers to political participation for African Americans. Sponsors a variety of voter education, registration, and get-out-the-vote and protect-the-vote activities, including Operation Big Vote, Black Youth Vote, Black Women's Roundtable, the Information Resource Center, Civic Engagement, Voices of the Electorate, and the Unity Black Voter Empowerment Campaign. Monitors legislation and regulations.

National Congress of Black Women, *1250 4th St. S.W., #WG1 20024; (202) 678-6788. E. Faye Williams, Chair. General email, info@nationalcongressbw.org*

Web, www.nationalcongressbw.org

Nonpartisan political organization that encourages African American women to participate in the political process. Advocates nonpartisan voter registration and encourages African American women to engage in other political activities. Develops positions and participates in platform development and strategies that address the needs of communities at every level of government.

National Women's Political Caucus, *110 H St. N.W., #300 20005 (mailing address: P.O. Box 50476, Washington, DC 20091); (202) 785-1100. Fax, (202) 370-6306. Linda Young, President; Bettina M. Hager, Program Director. General email, info@nwpc.org*

Web, www.nwpc.org

Advocacy group that seeks greater involvement of women in politics. Seeks to identify, recruit, and train women for elective and appointive political office, regardless of party affiliation; serves as an information clearinghouse on women in politics, particularly during election campaigns; publishes directory of women holding federal and state offices.

Republican National Committee (RNC), *Political, 310 1st St. S.E. 20003; (202) 863-8500. Fax, (202) 863-8773. Christopher McNulty, Political Director; Reince Priebus, Chair. Press, (202) 863-8614. General email, info@gop.org*

Web, www.gop.com

Responsible for electoral activities at the federal, state, and local levels; operates party constituency outreach programs; coordinates voter registration.

USAction, *1825 K St. N.W., #210 20006; (202) 263-4520. Fax, (202) 262-4530. Fred Azcarate, Executive Director. Press, (202) 263-4567.*

Web, www.usaction.org

Provides funding and training to register, educate, and mobilize voters to influence federal and state issues, based on progressive priorities. Has affiliates in 22 states.

Voter Participation Center, *1707 L St. N.W., #300 20036; (202) 659-9570. Fax, (202) 659-9585. Page S. Gardner, Founder; Gail Leftwich Kitch, Chief Operating Officer. General email, info@voterparticipation.org*

Web, www.voterparticipation.org

Nonpartisan organization that seeks to increase voter participation, especially of unmarried women (single, widowed, divorced, or separated), people of color, and 18 to 29-year-old citizens. (Formerly Women's Voices, Women Vote.)

Younger Women's Task Force, *1111 16th St. N.W. 20036; (202) 785-7700. Fax, (202) 833-1112. LaToya Millet, Executive Director, (202) 785-7713. Toll-free, (800) 326-2289. General email, ywtf@aauw.org*

Web, www.ywtf.org

Grassroots organization that encourages young women to engage in political activism on issues directly affecting them. Provides leadership training and a local and national network for peer mentoring; runs financial literacy programs. (Sponsored by the American Assn. of University Women.)

CAPITOL

Capitol switchboard, (202) 224-3121; Federal Relay Service (TTY), (800) 877-8339, and, in DC area, (202) 885-1000. See also 113th Congress (p. 724) for each member's office.

General

▶ CONGRESS

Architect of the Capitol, *SB15 CAP 20515; (202) 228-1793. Fax, (202) 228-1893. Stephen T. Ayers, Architect. Flag Office, (202) 228-4239.*
Web, www.aoc.gov

Maintains the Capitol and its grounds, the House and Senate office buildings, Capitol power plant, Robert A. Taft Memorial, Thurgood Marshall Federal Judiciary Building, Capitol Police headquarters, and buildings and grounds of the Supreme Court and the Library of Congress; operates the Botanic Garden and Senate restaurants. Acquires property and plans and constructs buildings for Congress, the Supreme Court, and the Library of Congress. Assists in deciding which artwork, historical objects, and exhibits are to be accepted for display in the Capitol and is responsible for their care and repair, as well as the maintenance and restoration of murals and architectural elements throughout the Capitol complex. Arranges inaugural ceremonies and other ceremonies held in the buildings or on the grass. Flag office flies American flags over the Capitol at legislators' request.

Architect of the Capitol, *Office of the Curator, S411 CAP 20515; (202) 224-2955. Melinda K. Smith, Curator.*
General email, curator@sec.senate.gov
Web, www.aoc.gov

Preserves artwork; maintains collection of drawings, photographs, and manuscripts on and about the Capitol and the House and Senate office buildings. Maintains records of the Architect of the Capitol. Library open to the public.

Capitol Police, *119 D St. N.E. 20510; (202) 224-9806. Fax, (202) 228-2592. Kim C. Dine, Chief. Public information, (202) 224-1677.*
General email, ASKUSCP@uscp.gov
Web, www.uscapitolpolice.gov

Responsible for security for the Capitol, House and Senate office buildings, and Botanic Garden; approves demonstration permits.

Senate Commission on Art, *S-411 CAP 20510; (202) 224-2955. Melinda K. Smith, Curator of the Senate.*
General email, curator@sec.senate.gov
Web, www.senate.gov/pagelayout/art/one_item_and_teasers/Explore_Senate_Art.htm

Accepts artwork and historical objects for display in Senate office buildings and the Senate wing of the Capitol. Maintains and exhibits Senate collections (paintings, sculptures, furniture, and manuscripts); oversees and maintains old Senate and Supreme Court chambers.

Superintendent of the House Office Buildings, *B341 RHOB 20515; (202) 225-7012. William M. Weidemeyer, Superintendent.*
Web, www.aoc.gov

Oversees construction, maintenance, and operation of House office buildings; assigns office space to House members under rules of procedure established by the Speaker's office and the House Office Building Commission.

Superintendent of the Senate Office Buildings, *SD-G-245 20510; (202) 224-5023. Takis Tzamaras, Superintendent.*
Web, www.aoc.gov

Oversees construction, maintenance, and operation of Senate office buildings.

U.S. Botanic Garden, *100 Maryland Ave. S.W. 20001 (mailing address: 245 1st St. S.W., Washington, DC 20024); (202) 225-8333. Fax, (202) 225-1561. Holly H. Shimizu, Executive Director; Ari Novy, Horticulture hotline, (202) 226-4785. Program registration information, (202) 225-1116. Special events, (202) 226-7674. Tour line, (202) 226-2055.*
General email, usbg@aoc.gov
Web, www.usbg.gov

Collects, cultivates, and grows various plants for public display and study.

▶ NONGOVERNMENTAL

U.S. Capitol Historical Society, *200 Maryland Ave. N.E. 20002; (202) 543-8919. Fax, (202) 544-8244. Ronald A. Sarasin, President; Donald R. Kennon, Vice President for Scholarship and Education (historian). Information, (800) 887-9318.*
General email, uschs@uschs.org
Web, www.uschs.org

Membership: members of Congress, individuals, and organizations interested in the preservation of the history and traditions of the U.S. Capitol. Conducts historical research; offers tours, lectures, workshops, and films; holds events involving members of Congress; publishes an annual historical calendar.

Tours and Events

▶CONGRESS

The House and Senate public galleries are open when Congress is in session. The House galleries are also open when the House is not in session. Free gallery passes are available from any congressional office.

Congressional Accessibility Services, *Crypt of The Capitol 20510; (202) 224-4048. Fax, (202) 228-4679. David Hauck, Director.*
Web, www.visitthecapitol.gov and www.aoc.gov

Office works to make the Capitol and its grounds and buildings accessible to members of Congress and the public.

Sergeant at Arms and Doorkeeper of the Senate, *S151 CAP 20510-7200; (202) 224-2341. Terrance W. Gainer, Sergeant at Arms and Doorkeeper.*
Web, www.senate.gov/reference/office/sergeant_at_arms .htm

Enforces rules and regulations of the Senate public gallery. Responsible for security of the Capitol and Senate buildings. Approves visiting band performances on the Senate steps. (To arrange for performances, contact your senator.)

Sergeant at Arms of the House of Representatives, *H124 CAP 20515-6611; (202) 225-2456. Fax, (202) 225-3233. Paul D. Irving, Sergeant at Arms.*
Web, www.clerk.house.gov/art_history/house_history/ sergeants_at_arms.html

Enforces rules and regulations of the House public gallery. Responsible for the security of the Capitol and House buildings. Approves visiting band performances on the House steps. (To arrange for performances, contact your representative.)

U.S. Capitol Visitor Center, *The Capitol 20510; (202) 593-1816. Fax, (202) 593-1832. Beth Plemmons, Chief Executive Officer for Visitor Services, (202) 593-1816. Press, (202) 593-1833. Visitor information, (202) 225-6827; (202) 226-8000.*
Web, www.visitthecapitol.gov

Offers the general public free guided tours of the interior of the U.S. Capitol. Provides accommodations for visitors with special needs.

▶NONGOVERNMENTAL

U.S. Capitol Historical Society, *200 Maryland Ave. N.E. 20002; (202) 543-8919. Fax, (202) 544-8244. Ronald A. Sarasin, President; Donald R. Kennon, Vice President for Scholarship and Education (historian). Information, (800) 887-9318.*
General email, uschs@uschs.org
Web, www.uschs.org

Offers tours, lectures, films, publications, and merchandise; maintains information centers in the Capitol.

CAUCUSES: ORGANIZATIONS OF MEMBERS

General

▶HOUSE AND SENATE

California Democratic Congressional Delegation, *1401 LHOB 20515; (202) 225-3072. Fax, (202) 225-3336. Rep. Zoe Lofgren, Chair; Martin Radosevich, Policy Adviser.*

Pursues a common legislative agenda. Seeks to educate Congress on California's various contributions to the United States.

Commission on Security and Cooperation in Europe (Helsinki Commission), *234 FHOB 20515; (202) 225-1901. Fax, (202) 226-4199. Sen. Benjamin L. Cardin, Chair; Rep. Christopher H. Smith, Co-Chair; Fred Turner, Chief of Staff.*
General email, info@csce.gov
Web, www.csce.gov

Independent agency created by Congress. Membership includes individuals from the executive and legislative branches. Monitors and encourages compliance with the Helsinki Accords, a series of agreements with provisions on security, economic, environmental, human rights, and humanitarian issues; conducts hearings; serves as an information clearinghouse for issues in eastern and western Europe, Canada, and the United States relating to the Helsinki Accords.

Congressional Arts Caucus, *2469 RHOB 20515; (202) 225-3615. Rep. Louise M. Slaughter, Co-Chair; Rep. Leonard Lance, Co-Chair; Stefanie Winzeler, Staff Contact.*
Web, http://congressionalartscaucus-slaughter.house.gov

Works to secure adequate funding for federal initiatives concerning art, including the National Endowment for the Arts (NEA).

Congressional Asian Pacific American Caucus, *1520 LHOB 20515; (202) 225-5464. Rep. Judy Chu, Chair; Del. Madeleine Z. Bordallo, Vice Chair; Rep. Mark Takano, Whip; Krystal Ka'ai, Executive Director. Toll-free, (800) 643-4715.*
Web, http://house.gov

Establishes policies and educates Congress about issues relating to persons of Asian and Pacific Islands ancestry who are citizens, nationals, or residents of the United States.

Congressional Black Caucus, *2344 RHOB 20515; (202) 226-9776. Fax, (202) 225-1336. Rep. Marcia Fudge, Chair; Rep. G. K. Butterfield, First Vice Chair; Rep. Yvette Clark, Second Vice Chair; Rep. Andre Carson, Secretary; Rep. Karen Bass, Whip; LaDavia Drane, Executive Director.*
General email, congressionalblackcaucus@mail.house.gov
Web, www.thecongressionalblackcaucus.com

Promotes the legislative concerns of black and minority citizens.

Congressional Caucus on HIV/AIDS, *2267 RHOB 20515; (202) 225-2661. Fax, (202) 225-9817. Rep. Barbara Lee, Co-Chair; Rep. Jim McDermott, Co-Chair; Rep. Ileana Ros-Lehtinen, Co-Chair; Jirair Ratevosian, Staff Contact. Web, www.congressionalhivaidscaucus_lee.house.gov*

Studies the spread of HIV/AIDS in the developing world; helps plan the U.S. government's response.

Congressional Caucus on Wild Salmon, *2314 RHOB 20515; (202) 225-5765. Fax, (202) 225-0425. Rep. Mike Thompson, Vice Chair; Sen. Ron Wyden, Co-Chair; Rep. Don Young, Co-Chair; Rep. Lisa Murkowski, Co-Chair; Erik Elam, Legislative Director.*

Addresses wild salmon conservation and management issues.

Congressional Fire Services Caucus, *1127 LHOB 20510; (202) 225-7761. Rep. Robert E. Andrews, Co-Chair; Rep. Steny H. Hoyer, Co-Chair; Rep. Peter T. King, Co-Chair; Rep. Dave Reichert, Co-Chair; Sen. Thomas R. Carper, Co-Chair; Sen. Susan M. Collins, Co-Chair; Sen. Jon Tester, Co-Chair; Sen. John McCain, Co-Chair.*

Seeks to increase awareness of fire and emergency services issues. Largest bipartisan caucus in Congress.

Congressional Fire Services Institute, *900 2nd St. N.E., #303 20002-3557; (202) 371-1277. Fax, (202) 682-3473. William M. Webb, Executive Director. General email, update@cfsi.org Web, www.cfsi.org*

Seeks to educate Congress on fire and emergency services issues through various programs for members and their staffs.

Congressional Hispanic Caucus, *2262 RHOB 20515; (202) 225-2531. Fax, (202) 226-5688. Rep. Rubén Hinojosa, Chair; Rep. Ben Ray Luján, 1st Vice Chair; Rep. Linda Sánchez, 2nd Vice Chair; Rep. Michelle Lujan-Grisham, Whip; Lesley J. Lopez, Communications Director. Web, www.chci.org*

Seeks to promote and advance, through the legislative process, issues facing Hispanic Americans.

Congressional Internet Caucus, *2309 RHOB 20515; (202) 225-3951. Rep. Anna G. Eshoo, Co-Chair; Rep. Bob Goodlatte, Co-Chair; Sen. Patrick Leahy, Co-Chair; Sen. John Thune, Co-Chair; Jason Cervenak, Staff Contact. Web, www.netcaucus.org*

Promotes growth of the Internet, including government participation; educates members and congressional staff about the potential of the Internet.

Congressional Long Island Sound Caucus, *2457 RHOB 20515; (202) 225-3335. Rep. Steve Israel, Co-Chair; Rep. Rosa L. DeLauro, Co-Chair; Mark Snyder, Staff Contact.*

Works to improve the health of Long Island Sound and facilitates cross-sound dialogue between New York and Connecticut members to build better regional politics.

Congressional Privacy Caucus, *2107 RHOB 20510; (202) 225-2002. Fax, (202) 225-3052. Rep. Joe Barton, Co-Chair; Rep. Diana L. DeGette, Co-Chair; Emmanual Guillory, Legislative Assistant.*

Explores matters relating to individual data privacy and security on issues coming before Congress.

Senate-House Steering Committee on Retirement Security, *1501-LHOB 20510; (202) 225-2611. Sen. Jeff Bingaman, Co-Chair; Rep. Earl Pomeroy, Co-Chair; Vacant, Staff Contact.*

Seeks to raise awareness about pension and retirement issues and pursues policies that will improve retirement security for all Americans.

U.S. Assn. of Former Members of Congress, *1401 K St. N.W., #503 20005-3417; (202) 222-0972. Fax, (202) 222-0977. Constance A. Morella, President; Peter M. Weichlein, Chief Executive Officer. General email, admin@usafmc.org Web, www.usafmc.org*

Bipartisan group of almost 600 former senators and representatives. Promotes public service and seeks to strengthen democracy via domestic and international programs, such as election monitoring abroad, civic education for high school and university students, and the support of severely wounded veterans upon their return from Iraq and Afghanistan.

▶ HOUSE

Ad Hoc Congressional Committee for Irish Affairs, *339 CHOB 20515; (202) 225-7896. Rep. Richard E. Neal, Co-Chair; Rep. Peter T. King, Co-Chair; Kevin Fogarty, Chief of Staff.*

Aims to bring peace, justice, and an end to violence in Northern Ireland by sponsoring legislation and hearings in support of the Irish people.

Bi-Partisan Congressional Pro-Life Caucus, *2373 RHOB 20515; (202) 225-3765. Rep. Christopher H. Smith, Co-Chair; Rep. Daniel Lipinski, Co-Chair; Autumn Fredericks, Staff Coordinator.*

Provides information and advances legislation related to antiabortion concerns.

Blue Dog Coalition, *CHOB 108 20515; (202) 225-5711. Rep. John Barrow, Co-Chair for Administration; Rep. Kurt Schrader, Co-Chair for Communications; Rep. Jim Cooper, Co-Chair for Policy; Paul Gage, Staff Contact. General email, BlueDog@mail.house.gov Web, http://bluedog.schrader.house.gov*

Works to find bipartisan solutions to major issues that promote financial stability and national security.

Congressional Aerospace Caucus, *312 CHOB 20515; (202) 225-5951. Rep. Pete Olson, Co-Chair;*

Rep. Donna Edwards, Co-Chair; Thomas Divine, Staff Contact.

Seeks to revitalize the U.S. aeronautics and space program by providing legislative support and acting as an information clearinghouse.

Congressional Automotive Caucus, *1609 LHOB 20515; (202) 225-5802. Rep. John Campbell, Co-Chair; Rep. Gary Peters, Co-Chair; David H. Malech, Legislative Director; Jordan Wells, Legislative Assistant.*

Seeks to solve the various problems and answer the needs of the U.S. automotive industry.

Congressional Balanced Budget Amendment Caucus, *2443 RHOB 20515; (202) 225-7882. Fax, (202) 226-4623. Rep. Mike Coffman, Chair; Mike Cosio, Legislative Director.*
Web, www.coffman.house.gov

Supports the passage of an amendment that would require the president of the United States to submit to Congress a balanced budget each fiscal year.

Congressional Career and Technical Education Caucus, *109 CHOB 20515; (202) 225-2735. Fax, (202) 225-5976. Rep. Glenn Thompson, Co-Chair, (202) 225-5121; Rep. Jim Langevin, Co-Chair; Sam Morgante, Legislative Assistant.*

Works to enhance awareness in Congress of the importance of career and technical education in preparing a well-educated and skilled U.S. workforce.

Congressional Caucus for Women's Issues *(Women's Policy Inc.), 1130 LHOB 20515; (202) 225-3536. Rep. Donna Edwards, Co-Chair; Rep. Jaime Herrera Beutler, Co-Chair; Jessica Wixson, Legislative Assistant.*
General email, webmaster@womenspolicy.org
Web, www.womenspolicy.org

Works to set the policy agenda for women and families through introduction of various bills.

Congressional Caucus on HIV/AIDS, *2267 RHOB 20515; (202) 225-2661. Fax, (202) 225-9817. Rep. Barbara Lee, Co-Chair; Rep. Jim McDermott, Co-Chair; Rep. Ileana Ros-Lehtinen, Co-Chair; Jirair Ratevosian, Staff Contact.*
Web, www.congressionalhivaidscaucus_lee.house.gov

Studies the spread of HIV/AIDS in the developing world; helps plan the U.S. government's response.

Congressional Caucus on Innovation and Entrepreneurship, *2104 RHOB 20515; (202) 225-5015. Fax, (202) 226-0828. Rep. Jared Polis, Co-Chair, (202) 225-2161; Rep. Vern Buchanan, Co-Chair.*

Works to accelerate innovation by reducing barriers to U.S. entrepreneurship.

Congressional Caucus on Intellectual Property Promotion and Piracy Prevention, *2188 RHOB 20515; (202) 225-3065. Fax, (202) 225-8611. Rep. Howard Coble, Co-Chair; Rep. Adam Smith, Co-Chair; Meredith Preloh, Legislative Assistant.*

Consults experts in order to foresee legislation needed on intellectual property protection and domestic and international piracy issues.

Congressional Caucus on Korea, *151 LHOB 20515-0533; (202) 225-5406. Fax, (202) 225-3103. Rep. Gerald E. Connolly, Co-Chair; Rep. Peter Roskam, Co-Chair; Rep. Mike Kelly, Co-Chair; Rep. Loretta Sanchez, Co-Chair; Isaac Fong, Legislative Counsel.*

Coordinates Congress's efforts to strengthen democracy throughout the Korean Peninsula. Monitors the North Korean refugee situation.

Congressional Children's Caucus, *2160 RHOB 20515; (202) 225-3816. Fax, (202) 225-3317. Rep. Sheila Jackson Lee, Chair; Shashrina Thomas, Deputy Chief of Staff.*

Formulates the national agenda on all matters relating to children, including health care and adoption.

Congressional Coast Guard Caucus, *2188 RHOB 20515; (202) 225-3065. Fax, (202) 225-8611. Rep. Howard Coble, Co-Chair; Rep. Joe Courtney, Co-Chair; Rep. Larsen Rick, Co-Chair; Rep. Frank A. LoBiondo, Co-Chair; Kirk Bell, Legislative Assistant.*

Works to advance the needs of the U.S. Coast Guard in Congress and seeks adequate funding for its mission.

Congressional Hispanic Caucus Institute, *300 M St. S.E. 20003; (202) 543-1771. Fax, (202) 546-2143. Rep. Rubén Hinojosa, Chair, (202) 225-2531; Esther Aguilera, President.*
General email, chci@chci.org
Web, www.chci.org

Develops educational and leadership programs to familiarize Hispanic students with policy-related careers and to encourage their professional development. Aids in the developing of future Latino leaders. Provides scholarship, internship, and fellowship opportunities.

Congressional Immigration Reform Caucus, *2412 RHOB 20515; (202) 225-6565. Rep. Ted Poe, Chair; Tim Tarpley, Deputy Chief of Staff.*
General email, tim.tarpley@mail.house.gov
Web, http://irc.bilbray/house.gov

Initiates new immigration policy designed to protect America's borders, including a visa tracking system and reform of the U.S. Immigration and Naturalization Service.

Congressional Marcellus Shale Caucus, *1504 LHOB 20515; (202) 225-3161. Rep. Gene Green, Co-Chair; Rep. Tom Reed, Co-Chair; Drew Wayne, Staff Contact.*
Web, http://congressionalmarcellusshalecaucus-reed.house .gov

Provides a platform for discussion of issues surrounding the Marcellus Shale. Holds meetings with advocacy groups, industry, and educational institutions.

Congressional Native American Caucus, *2458 RHOB 20515; (202) 225-6165. Rep. Tom Cole, Co-Chair; Rep. Betty McCollum, Co-Chair; Stratton Edwards, Legislative Counsel.*

Educates Congress about issues affecting Native Americans and allows for dialogue between the caucus and Native American leaders.

Congressional Nepal Caucus, *440 CHOB 20515; (202) 225-2501. Rep. Ander Crenshaw, Co-Chair; Rep. Jared Polis, Co-Chair; Cate Sadler, Legislative Assistant. Web, www.crenshaw.house.gov*

Seeks to educate the American public and policymakers on U.S. policy objectives toward Nepal, including supporting democratic institutions and economic liberalization, promoting peace and stability in South Asia, supporting Nepalese territorial integrity, alleviating poverty, and promoting development.

Congressional Northern Border Caucus, *405 CHOB 20515; (202) 225-4611. Fax, (202) 226-0621. Rep. Bill Owens, Co-Chair; Rep. Kevin Cramer, Co-Chair; Andrew Fitzpatrick, Legislative Assistant.*

Conveys to Congress the concerns of constituents who reside near the northern U.S. border with Canada.

Congressional Pro-Choice Caucus, *2469 RHOB 20515; (202) 225-3615. Rep. Diana L. DeGette, Co-Chair; Rep. Louise M. Slaughter, Co-Chair; Cheri Hoffman, Legislative Director.*

Promotes the right to choose and is concerned with all issues surrounding family planning and sexuality education.

Congressional Steel Caucus, *2332 RHOB 20515; (202) 225-2301. Rep. Tim Murphy, Co-Chair; Rep. Peter J. Visclosky, Co-Chair; Brad Grantz, Legislative Director. Web, www.visclosky.house.gov/legislation/fighting-for-the-northwest-indiana-steel-industry.shtml*

Works to preserve American jobs in the steel industry and to advance the interests of steel workers.

Congressional Technology Transfer Caucus, *2446 RHOB 20515; (202) 225-6190. Fax, (202) 225-1528. Rep. Ben Ray Luján, Co-Chair; Rep. Gus M. Bilirakis, Co-Chair, (202) 225-5755; Brian Crone, Congressional Fellow; Ian Martorana, Legislative Assistant.*

Brings together members who share the goal of helping move technological innovations that are occurring at national labs and universities into the marketplace.

Congressional Urban Caucus, *2301 RHOB 20515; (202) 225-4001. Rep. Chaka Fattah, Co-Chair; Rep. Michael R. Turner, Co-Chair; Jared Bass, Staff Contact.*

Promotes America's metropolitan centers and addresses the unique challenges that face urban communities.

Congressional Western Caucus, *2432 RHOB 20515; (202) 225-2365. Rep. Steve Pearce, Co-Chair; Rep. Cynthia Lummis, Co-Chair; Jonathan Shuffield, Executive Director. Web, http://westerncaucus.pearce.house.gov*

Works to better the quality of western and rural life through environmental and natural resource policies.

Congressional Wine Caucus, *231 CHOB 20515; (202) 225-3311. Rep. Mike Thompson, Co-Chair; Rep. Duncan Hunter, Co-Chair; Jesse Haladay, Legislative Assistant. Web, http://mikethompson.house.gov/WineCaucus/*

Protects the interests of the wine industry and works to understand the industry's economic impact.

Crohns and Colitis Caucus, *440 CHOB 20515; (202) 225-2501. Fax, (202) 225-2504. Rep. Ander Crenshaw, Co-Chair; Rep. Jim Moran, Co-Chair; Cate Sadler, Legislative Assistant. Web, http://crenshaw.house.gov/*

Works toward expanding research and providing insurance and disability coverage for people with Crohn's disease and colitis.

House Army Caucus, *2369 CHOB 20515; (202) 225-3864. Rep. John Carter, Co-Chair; Rep. C.A. "Dutch" Ruppersberger, Co-Chair; Efrain Reyna, Legislative Director.*

Seeks to advance the Army's needs as well as assist the Army in presenting programs to Congress.

House Republican Israel Caucus, *512 CHOB 20515; (202) 225-3371. Fax, (202) 226-1272. Rep. Michael Grimm, Co-Chair; Rep. Doug Lamborn, Co-Chair; Rep. Leonard Lance, Co-Chair; Rep. Peter Roskam, Co-Chair, (202) 225-4561; Nick Iacono, Staff Contact.*

Connects members and staff with leading Middle East policy analysts to deepen their understanding of the issues Israel faces. Collaborates with policy experts, academics, the Israel and Jewish communities, and members to host events that open dialogue on issues in the Middle East.

House Rural Health Care Coalition, *1502 LHOB 20515; (202) 225-5506. Fax, (202) 225-5739. Rep. Ron Kind, Chair; Travis Robey, Legislative Assistant.*

Promotes concerns about urban biases in federal health policy.

Kurdish-American Caucus, *2229 RHOB 20515; (202) 225-2452. Fax, (202) 225-2455. Rep. Jared Polis, Co-Chair; Rep. Joe Wilson, Co-Chair; Baker Elmore, Staff Contact.*

Promotes understanding of Kurdish interests, provides information about issues affecting the Kurdish people, and recommends initiatives to promote American-Kurdish cooperation on issues of mutual interest to the executive branch, the U.S. Congress, and the general public.

Medical Technology Caucus, *244 CHOB 20515-2303; (202) 225-8104. Rep. Anna G. Eshoo, Co-Chair; Rep. Erik Paulsen, Co-Chair; Erin Katzelnick-Wise, Staff Contact (Eshoo); Matt Gallivan, Staff Contact (Paulsen).*

Provides a forum on medical technology issues but does not take a position on any matter.

Military Veterans Caucus, *231 CHOB 20575; (202) 225-3311. Rep. Gus M. Bilirakis, Co-Chair; Rep. Collin C. Peterson, Co-Chair; Rep. Jon Runyan, Co-Chair; Rep. Mike Thompson, Co-Chair; Jesse Haladay, Staff Contact.*

Seeks to advance the issues of American military personnel, active and retired.

National Parks Caucus, *1127 LHOB 20515; (202) 225-7761. Rep. Dave Reichert, Co-Chair; Rep. Ron Kind, Co-Chair; Ashley Johnson, Legislative Assistant.*

Seeks to preserve the National Parks and raise awareness of the problems facing the parks.

Northeast-Midwest Congressional Coalition, *1519 LHOB 20515-2308; (202) 226-6106. Rep. Mike Kelly, Co-Chair; Rep. James P. McGovern, Co-Chair; Samuel Breene, Legislative Director.*

Develops public policies emphasizing regional equity, manufacturing efficiency, and sustainable development; looks into such issues as manufacturing, energy, transportation, and the environment.

Republican New Media Caucus, *1323 LHOB 20515; (202) 225-6405. Fax, (202) 225-1985. Rep. John Culberson, Co-Chair, (202) 225-2571; Rep. Bob Latta, Co-Chair; Rep. Cathy Ann McMorris Rodgers, Co-Chair, (202) 225-2006; Rep. Robert J. Wittman, Co-Chair, (202) 225-4382; Sarah Criser, Staff Contact.*
Web, http://rnmc.latta.house.gov

Educates members on evolving new media technology.

Republican Study Committee, *2338 RHOB 20515; (202) 226-9718. Fax, (202) 226-0386. Rep. Steve Scalise, Chair; Will Durham, Executive Director.*
General email, RSC@mail.house.gov
Web, www.rsc.scalise.house.gov

Works to advance a conservative social and economic agenda.

Tom Lantos Human Rights Commission, *233 CHOB 20515; (202) 225-5136. Rep. James P. McGovern, Co-Chair; Rep. Frank R. Wolf, Co-Chair; Elyse Anderson, Staff Contact (Wolf); Katya Misachleva, Staff Contact (McGovern).*
Web, http://tlhrc.house.gov

Seeks to protect human rights through legislation and various forums.

U.S.-Lebanon Friendship Caucus, *2374 RHOB 20515; (202) 225-3906. Fax, (202) 225-3303. Rep. Darrell Issa, Chair; Michael O'Neill, Staff Contact.*

Seeks to inform other members of Congress on Lebanese issues.

U.S.-Mexico Friendship Caucus, *1013 LHOB 20515; (202) 225-2523. Rep. Devin Nunes, Co-Chair; Rep. Jared Polis, Co-Chair; Jack Langer, Staff Contact.*

Promotes dialogue between the United States and Mexico regarding issues arising from integration of both economies.

▶SENATE

Senate Auto Caucus, *SR-269 20510; (202) 224-6221. Sen. Carl Levin, Co-Chair; Sen. Rob Portman, Co-Chair; Alison Pascale, Staff Contact (Levin); Eric Toy, Staff Contact (Portman), (202) 224-3353.*

Discusses issues affecting the automotive industry, including transportation, safety, and the environment.

Senate Cancer Coalition, *SH-331 20510; (202) 224-3841. Sen. Johnny Isakson, Co-Chair; Sen. Dianne Feinstein, Co-Chair; Megan Thompson, Staff Contact.*

Seeks to educate the Senate and the public about cancer and to promote the nation's commitment to cancer research.

Senate Steel Caucus, *SR-326 20510; (202) 224-4124. Sen. John D. Rockefeller IV, Co-Chair; Sen. Jeff Sessions, Co-Chair; Mark Lidell, Legislative Director (Rockefeller); Christopher Jackson, Legislative Assistant (Sessions).*

Advocates the interests of the steel industry and works to preserve American jobs in the industry.

Senate Western Caucus, *D-307 20510; (202) 224-6441. Fax, (202) 224-1724. Sen. John Barrasso, Chair; Brian Clifford, Staff Contact.*

Coordinates legislation addressing the special needs of citizens in the Western states.

CONGRESS AT WORK

See 113th Congress (p. 724) for members' offices and committee assignments and for rosters of congressional committees and subcommittees.

General

▶CONGRESS

For a listing of relevant congressional committees and subcommittees, please see page 689 or the Appendix.

Emergency Management, *192 FHOB 20515-6462; (202) 226-0950. Fax, (202) 226-6598. J. Curtis Coughlin, Senior Assistant Sergeant at Arms.*

Liaises between the House and the Homeland Security Dept., the U.S. Capitol Police, and other responders in the coordination of response to emergency situations.

House Recording Studio, *B310 RHOB 20515; (202) 225-3941. Fax, (202) 225-0707. Patrick Hirsch, Director.*

Assists House members in making tape recordings. Provides daily gavel-to-gavel television coverage of House floor proceedings.

Interparliamentary Affairs, *HC4 CAP 20510; (202) 226-1766. Janice Robinson, Director.*

Assists the House Speaker with international travel and the reception of foreign legislators.

Interparliamentary Services, *SH-808 20510; (202) 224-3047. Sally Walsh, Director.*

Provides support to senators participating in interparliamentary conferences and other international travel. Responsible for financial, administrative, and protocol functions.

U.S. House of Representatives

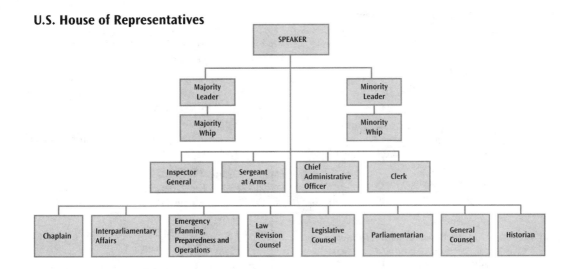

Office of Photography, *B302 RHOB 20515; (202) 225-2840. Fax, (202) 225-5896. Tina Agee, Director.*

Provides House members with photographic assistance.

Parliamentarian of the House of Representatives, *H223CAP and H209 CAP 20515; (202) 225-7373. Thomas J. Wickham, Parliamentarian.*

Advises presiding officers on parliamentary procedures and committee jurisdiction over legislation; prepares and maintains a compilation of the precedents of the House.

Parliamentarian of the Senate, *S133 CAP 20510; (202) 224-6128. Elizabeth C. MacDonough, Parliamentarian.*

Advises presiding officers on parliamentary procedures and committee jurisdiction over legislation; prepares and maintains a compilation of the precedents of the Senate.

Senate Democratic Policy and Communications Center, *S318 CAP 20510; (202) 224-2939. Fax, (202) 228-5576. Sen. Charles E. Schumer, Chair; Matthew House, Chief Spokesperson, (202) 224-2939.*
Web, http://democrats.senate.gov

Offers radio, television, and Internet services to Senate Democrats and their staffs to more effectively disseminate information to constituents at home.

Sergeant at Arms and Doorkeeper of the Senate, *Senate Photo Studio, SD-G85 20510; (202) 224-6000. Bill Allen, Manager.*

Provides Senate members with photographic assistance.

Leadership

▶ **HOUSE**

See House Leadership and Partisan Committees (p. 748).

House Democratic Caucus, *1420 LHOB 20515; (202) 225-1400. Rep. Xavier Becerra, Chair; Rep. Joseph Crowley, Vice Chair; Fabiola Rodriguez-Ciampoli, Executive Director.*

General email, democratic.caucus@mail.house.gov
Web, www.dems.gov

Membership: House Democrats. Selects Democratic leadership; formulates party rules and floor strategy; considers caucus members' recommendations on major issues; votes on the Democratic Steering and Policy Committee's recommendations for Democratic committee assignments.

House Democratic Steering and Policy Committee, *235 CHOB 20515-6527; (202) 225-4965. Fax, (202) 225-4188. Rep. Nancy Pelosi, Chair; Rep. Rosa L. DeLauro, Co-Chair; Rep. Robert E. Andrews, Co-Chair; Jonathan Stivers, Staff Contact.*

Makes recommendations to the Democratic leadership on party policy and priorities and participates in decision making with the leadership.

House Republican Conference, *202A CHOB 20515; (202) 225-5107. Fax, (202) 226-0154. Rep. Cathy Ann McMorris Rodgers, Chair; Rep. Lynn Jenkins, Vice Chair; Jeren Deutsch, Staff Contact.*
Web, www.gop.gov

Membership: House Republicans. Selects Republican leadership; formulates party rules and floor strategy, and considers party positions on major legislation; votes on the Republican Committee on Committees' recommendations for House committee chairs and Republican committee assignments; publishes *Weekly Floor Briefing* and *Daily Floor Briefing*, which analyze pending legislation.

House Republican Policy Committee, *228 CHOB 20515-6549; (202) 225-2132. Fax, (202) 226-1463. Rep. James Lankford, Chair; Randy Swanson, Staff Contact.*
General email, policycommittee@mail.house.gov
Web, http://policy.house.gov

Studies legislation and makes recommendations on House Republican policies and positions on proposed legislation.

Majority Leader of the House of Representatives,
H329 CAP 20515; (202) 225-4000. Fax, (202) 226-1115.
Rep. Eric Cantor, Majority Leader; Steven C. Stombres,
Chief of Staff.
Web, www.majorityleader.gov

Serves as chief strategist and floor spokesperson for the
majority party in the House.

Majority Whip of the House of Representatives,
H107 CAP 20515-6503; (202) 225-0197. Fax, (202)
226-0781. Rep. Kevin McCarthy, Majority Whip;
Timothy J. Berry, Chief of Staff.
Web, http://majoritywhip.house.gov

Serves as assistant majority leader in the House; helps
marshal majority forces in support of party strategy.

Minority Leader of the House of Representatives,
H204 CAP 20515-6537; (202) 225-0100. Fax, (202) 225-
4188. Rep. Nancy Pelosi, Minority Leader;
Nadeam Elshami, Chief of Staff.
Web, http://democraticleader.gov

Serves as chief strategist and floor spokesperson for the
minority party in the House.

Minority Whip of the House of Representatives,
H148 CAP 20515; (202) 225-3130. Fax, (202) 226-0663.
Rep. Steny H. Hoyer, Minority Whip; Alexis Covey-Brandt,
Chief of Staff.
Web, http://democraticwhip.gov

Serves as assistant minority leader in the House; helps
marshal minority forces in support of party strategy.

**Speaker of the House of Representatives, Speaker's
Office,** H232 CAP 20515; (202) 225-0600. Fax, (202) 225-
5117. Rep. John A. Boehner, Speaker; Michael J. Sommers,
Chief of Staff.
Web, http://speaker.house.gov

Presides over the House while in session; preserves
decorum and order; announces vote results; recognizes
members for debate and introduction of bills, amendments,
and motions; refers bills and resolutions to committees;
decides points of order; appoints House members to conference committees; votes at own discretion.

▶SENATE

See Senate Leadership and Partisan Committees (p. 822).

Democratic Policy Committee, SH-419 20510; (202) 224-
3232. Fax, (202) 228-3432. Sen. Charles E. Schumer, Chair.
Web, http://dpc.senate.gov

Studies and makes recommendations to the Democratic leadership on legislation for consideration by the
Senate; prepares policy papers and develops Democratic
policy initiatives.

Democratic Steering and Outreach Committee, SH-712
20510; (202) 224-9048. Fax, (202) 224-5476.
Sen. Mark Begich, Chair.
Web, www.democrats.senate.gov/steering

Makes Democratic committee assignments subject to
approval by the Senate Democratic Conference. Develops
and maintains relationships with leaders and organizations outside of Congress.

Majority Leader of the Senate, S221 CAP 20510-7010;
(202) 224-2158. Fax, (202) 224-7327. Sen. Harry M. Reid,
Majority Leader; David B. Krone, Chief of Staff.
Web, www.reid.senate.gov

Serves as chief strategist and floor spokesperson for the
majority party in the Senate.

Majority Whip of the Senate, S321 CAP 20510-7012;
(202) 224-9447. Fax, (202) 228-0400. Sen. Richard J.
Durbin, Majority Whip; Patrick J. Souders, Chief of Staff.
Web, www.durbin.senate.gov

Serves as assistant majority leader in the Senate; helps
marshal majority forces in support of party strategy.

Minority Leader of the Senate, S230 CAP 20510; (202)
224-3135. Sen. Mitch McConnell, Minority Leader;
Sharon Soderstrom, Chief of Staff.
Web, www.mcconnell.senate.gov

Serves as chief strategist and floor spokesperson for the
minority party in the Senate.

Minority Whip of the Senate, S208 CAP 20510-7022;
(202) 224-2708. Sen. John Cornyn, Minority Whip;
Russ Thomasson, Chief of Staff.

Serves as assistant minority leader in the Senate; helps
marshal minority forces in support of party strategy.

President Pro Tempore of the Senate, 437 SROB 20510;
(202) 224-4242. Fax, (202) 224-3479. Sen. Patrick Leahy,
President Pro Tempore.

Presides over the Senate in the absence of the vice president.

Senate Democratic Conference, S309 CAP 20510; (202)
224-3735. Sen. Harry M. Reid, Chair; Sen. Charles E.
Schumer, Vice Chair; Sen. Patty Murray, Secretary.
Web, www.democrats.senate.gov

Membership: Democratic senators. Selects Democratic
leadership; formulates party rules and floor strategy and
considers party positions on major legislation; votes on the
Democratic Steering Committee's recommendations for
Democratic committee assignments.

Senate Republican Conference, SH-405 20510; (202)
224-2764. Fax, (202) 224-6984. Sen. John Thune, Chair;
Rep. Roy Blunt, Vice Chair.
Web, http://republican.senate.gov

Membership: Republican senators. Serves as caucus
and central coordinating body of the party. Organizes and
elects Senate Republican leadership; votes on Republican
Committee on Committees' recommendations for Senate
committee chairs and Republican committee assignments.
Staff provides various support and media services for
Republican members.

Senate Republican Policy Committee, SR-347 20510;
(202) 224-2946. Sen. John Barrasso, Chair.
Web, http://rpc.senate.gov

U.S. Senate

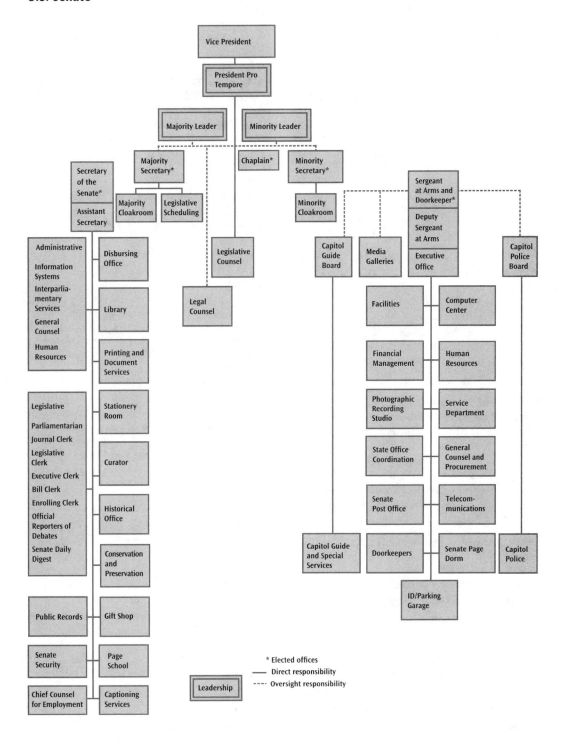

Studies and makes recommendations to the Republican leader on the priorities and scheduling of legislation on the Senate floor; prepares policy papers and develops Republican policy initiatives.

Vice President of the United States, *President of the Senate,* *The White House 20500; (202) 224-2424. Joseph R. Biden Jr., President of the Senate; Lorea Stallard, Assistant, Special Legislative Affairs.*
General email, vice.president@whitehouse.gov

Web, www.whitehouse.gov/vicepresident

Presides over the Senate while in session; preserves decorum and order; announces vote results; recognizes members for debate and introduction of bills, amendments, and motions; decides points of order; votes only in the case of a tie. (President pro tempore of the Senate presides in the absence of the vice president.)

Officers

▶ HOUSE

Chaplain of the House of Representatives, *HB25 CAP 20515; (202) 225-2509. Fax, (202) 226-4928. Patrick J. Conroy S.J., Chaplain.*
General email, chaplainoffice@mail.house.gov

Web, http://chaplain.house.gov

Opens each day's House session with a prayer and offers other religious services to House members, their families, and staffs. (Prayer sometimes offered by visiting chaplain.)

Chief Administrative Officer of the House of Representatives, *HB28 CAP 20515; (202) 225-8000. Ed Cassidy, Chief Administrative Officer.*
Web, www.cao.house.gov

Responsible for House member and staff payrolls; computer system; internal mail, office furnishings and supplies; telecommunications; tour guides; nonlegislative functions of the House printing services, recording studio, and records office; and other administrative areas.

Clerk of the House of Representatives, *H154 CAP 20515-6601; (202) 225-7000. Karen L. Haas, Clerk. Publication Services, (202) 225-1908.*
General email, info.clerkweb@mail.house.gov

Web, http://clerk.house.gov

Responsible for direction of duties of House employees; receives lobby registrations and reports of campaign expenditures and receipts of House candidates; disburses funds appropriated for House expenditures; responsible for other activities necessary for the continuing operation of the House.

Floor Assistant to the Speaker of the House of Representatives, *H223CAP and H209 CAP 20515; (202) 225-0600. Annie Minkler, Floor Assistant; Alex Becker, Floor Assistant.*

Assists the majority leadership and members on legislative matters.

General Counsel of the House of Representatives, *219 CHOB 20515; (202) 225-9700. Kerry W. Kircher, General Counsel.*
General email, www.ogc.house.gov

Advises House members and committees on legal matters.

House Legislative Counsel, *136 CHOB 20515-6721; (202) 225-6060. Fax, (202) 225-3437. Sandra Strokoff, Legislative Counsel.*
General email, legooun@mail.house.gov

Web, www.house.gov/legcoun/index.shtml

Assists House members and committees in drafting legislation.

Inspector General of the House of Representatives, *386 FHOB 20515; (202) 226-1250. Fax, (202) 225-4240. Theresa M. Grafenstine, Inspector General; Debbie B. Hunter, Deputy Inspector General; Michael Ptasienski, Deputy Inspector General.*
General email, HouseIG@mail.house.gov

Web, www.house.gov/IG

Conducts periodic audits of the financial and administrative functions of the House and joint entities.

Sergeant at Arms of the House of Representatives, *H124 CAP 20515-6611; (202) 225-2456. Fax, (202) 225-3233. Paul D. Irving, Sergeant at Arms.*
Web, www.clerk.house.gov/art_history/house_history/sergeants_at_arms.html

Maintains order on the House floor; executes orders from the Speaker of the House. Serves on the Capitol Police Board and Capitol Guide Board; oversees Capitol security (with Senate Sergeant at Arms) and protocol.

▶ SENATE

Chaplain of the Senate, *S332 CAP 20510-7002; (202) 224-2510. Fax, (202) 224-9686. Barry C. Black, Chaplain.*
Web, www.senate.gov/reference/office/chaplain.htm

Opens each day's Senate session with a prayer and offers other religious services to Senate members, their families, and staffs. (Prayer sometimes offered by visiting chaplain.)

Legislative Counsel of the Senate, *SD-668 20510-7250; (202) 224-6461. Fax, (202) 224-0567. James W. Fransen, Legislative Counsel.*

Assists Senate members and committees in drafting legislation.

Majority Secretary of the Senate, *S118 CAP 20510-7024; (202) 224-3735. Gary Myrick, Secretary; Tim Mitchell, Assistant Secretary, (202) 224-5551.*

Assists the majority leader and majority party in the Senate.

Minority Secretary of the Senate, *S337 CAP 20510-7014; (202) 224-3835. Fax, (202) 224-2860. Laura Dove, Secretary; Robert Doncan, Assistant Secretary.*

Assists the minority leader and the minority party in the Senate.

Secretary of the Senate, *S312 CAP 20510; (202) 224-3622. Nancy Erickson, Secretary of the Senate; Robert Paxton, Chief of Staff.*
Web, www.senate.gov/reference/office/secretary_of_senate .htm

Chief legislative, financial, and administrative officer of the Senate. Responsible for direction of duties of Senate employees and administration of oaths; receives lobby registrations and reports of campaign expenditures and receipts of Senate candidates; responsible for other day-to-day Senate activities.

Senate Legal Counsel, *SH-642 20510-7250; (202) 224-4435. Fax, (202) 224-3391. Morgan J. Frankel, Legal Counsel.*

Advises Senate members and committees on legal matters.

Sergeant at Arms and Doorkeeper of the Senate, *S151 CAP 20510-7200; (202) 224-2341. Terrance W. Gainer, Sergeant at Arms and Doorkeeper.*
Web, www.senate.gov/reference/office/sergeant_at_arms. htm

Oversees the Senate wing of the Capitol; doormen; Senate pages; and telecommunication, photographic, supply, and janitorial services. Maintains order on the Senate floor and galleries; oversees Capitol security (with House Sergeant at Arms); sits on the Capitol Police Board and Capitol Guide Board.

Pay and Perquisites

▶CONGRESS

For a listing of relevant congressional committees and subcommittees, please see page 689 or the Appendix.

Attending Physician, *H166 CAP 20515-8907; (202) 225-5421. Dr. Brian Monahan, Attending Physician; Christopher R. Picaut, Chief of Staff.*

Provides members with primary care, first aid, emergency care, and environmental/occupational health services; provides House and Senate employees, visiting dignitaries, and tourists with first-aid and emergency care.

Clerk of the House of Representatives, *H154 CAP 20515-6601; (202) 225-7000. Karen L. Haas, Clerk. Publication Services, (202) 225-1908.*
General email, info.clerkweb@mail.house.gov
Web, http://clerk.house.gov

Prepares and submits quarterly reports covering the receipts and expenditures of the House, including disbursements by each committee and each member's office and staff. Reports available from the Legislative Resource Center.

House Commission on Congressional Mailing Standards (Franking Commission), *1313 LHOB 20515-6328; (202) 225-8281. Rep. Candice S. Miller, Chair; Richard Cappetto, Majority Staff Director, (202) 226-0647; Kyle Anderson, Minority Staff Director.*
Web, http://cha.house.gov/franking-commission

Oversight of the use of franked mail by House members.

Secretary of the Senate, *S312 CAP 20510; (202) 224-3622. Nancy Erickson, Secretary of the Senate; Robert Paxton, Chief of Staff.*
Web, www.senate.gov/reference/office/secretary_of_senate. htm

Prepares and submits semiannual reports covering the receipts and expenditures of the Senate, including data on each committee and each member's office and staff. Reports available from the Government Printing Office.

▶NONGOVERNMENTAL

National Taxpayers Union, *Communications, 108 N. Alfred St., Alexandria, VA 22314; (703) 683-5700. Fax, (703) 683-5722. Peter Sepp, Executive Vice President; Duane Parde, President.*
General email, ntu@ntu.org
Web, www.ntu.org

Citizens' interest group that publishes reports on congressional pay and perquisites, including pensions and the franking privilege.

Standards of Conduct

▶AGENCIES

Justice Dept. (DOJ), *Public Integrity, 1400 New York Ave. N.W., #12100 20005; (202) 514-1412. Fax, (202) 514-3003. Jack Smith, Chief.*
Web, www.justice.gov/criminal/pin

Conducts investigations of wrongdoing in selected cases that involve alleged corruption of public office or violations of election law by public officials, including members of Congress.

▶CONGRESS

For a listing of relevant congressional committees and subcommittees, please see page 689 or the Appendix.

Legislative Resource Center, *Records and Registration, Office of the Clerk, House of Representatives, B106 CHOB 20515-6612; (202) 226-5200. Fax, (202) 226-4874. Steve Pingeton, Manager.*
Web, http://clerk.house.gov

Receives and maintains the financial disclosure records of House members, officers, employees, candidates, and certain legislative organizations. Receives reports from committee chairs on foreign travel by members and staff. Records open for public inspection.

Secretary of the Senate, *Public Records, Ethics,* SH-232 20510; (202) 224-0758. Dana K. McCallum, *Superintendent of Public Records.*
Web, www.senate.gov/lobby

Receives and maintains the financial disclosure records of Senate members, officers, employees, candidates, and legislative organizations. Receives reports from committee chairs on foreign travel by senators and staff. Records open for public inspection, 9:00 a.m.–5:30 p.m.

CONGRESSIONAL SUPPORT GROUPS

General

▶**CONGRESS**

For a listing of relevant congressional committees and subcommittees, please see page 689 or the Appendix.

Congressional Budget Office, 402 FHOB 20515; (202) 226-2700. Fax, (202) 225-7509. Douglas W. Elmendorf, *Director. Information, (202) 226-2600. Publications, (202) 226-2809.*
Web, www.cbo.gov

Nonpartisan office that provides the House and Senate with analyses needed for economic and budget decisions, and with the information and estimates required for the congressional budget process.

Government Accountability Office (GAO), 441 G St. N.W. 20548; (202) 512-5500. Fax, (202) 512-5507. Gene L. Dodaro, *Comptroller General. Information, (202) 512-3000. Publications and Documents, (202) 512-6000. Congressional Relations, (202) 512-4400.*
Web, www.gao.gov

Independent, nonpartisan agency in the legislative branch. Serves as the investigating agency for Congress; carries out legal, accounting, auditing, and claims settlement functions; makes recommendations for more effective government operations; publishes monthly lists of reports available to the public.

House Legislative Counsel, 136 CHOB 20515-6721; (202) 225-6060. Fax, (202) 225-3437. Sandra Strokoff, *Legislative Counsel.*
General email, legooun@mail.house.gov
Web, www.house.gov/legcoun/index.shtml

Assists House members and committees in drafting legislation.

Law Revision Counsel, H2-308 FHOB 20515-6711; (202) 226-2411. Fax, (202) 225-0010. Ralph V. Seep, *Law Revision Counsel.*
Web, http://uscode.house.gov

Develops and updates an official classification of U.S. laws. Codifies, cites, and publishes the U.S. Code.

Library of Congress, *Congressional Research Service,* 101 Independence Ave. S.E., #LM 203 20540; (202) 707-5775. Fax, (202) 707-2615. Mary B. Mazanec, *Director. Information, (202) 707-5700. Inquiry, (202) 707-5770.*
Web, www.loc.gov/crsinfo

Provides confidential policy and legal research and analysis exclusively to committees and members of the House and Senate, regardless of party affiliation. Using multiple disciplines and research methodologies, assists at every stage of the legislative process, from early considerations that precede bill drafting, through committee hearings and floor debate, to the oversight of enacted laws and various agency activities.

Senate Legal Counsel, SH-642 20510-7250; (202) 224-4435. Fax, (202) 224-3391. Morgan J. Frankel, *Legal Counsel.*

Advises Senate members and committees on legal matters.

Liaison Offices

▶**CONGRESS**

For a listing of relevant congressional committees and subcommittees, please see page 689 or the Appendix.

Office of Personnel Management (OPM), *Congressional Legislative, and Intergovernmental Affairs,* 1900 E St. N.W., #6316G 20415 (mailing address: Constituent Services, B332 RHOB, Washington, DC 20515); (202) 606-1300. Fax, (202) 606-2526. Angela Kouters, *Director, Acting. Constituent Services, (202) 225-4955.*
Web, www.opm.gov

Provides House and Senate members with information on federal civil service matters, especially those pertaining to federal employment, retirement, and health benefits programs. Offices include Congressional Relations, Legislative Analysis, Intergovernmental Affairs, and Constituent Services.

▶**HOUSE**

Air Force Liaison, B322 RHOB 20515-0001; (202) 225-6656. Fax, (202) 685-2592. Col. Patrick McKenzie, *Chief. Alternate phone, (202) 685-4531.*
General email, usaf@mail.house.gov

Provides House members with services and information on all matters related to the U.S. Air Force.

Army Liaison, *B325 RHOB 20515; (202) 225-3853. Fax, (202) 685-2674. Col. La'Tonya Lynn, Chief. Web, www.army.mil*

Provides House members with services and information on all matters related to the U.S. Army.

Navy–Marine Corps Liaison, *B324 RHOB 20515; (202) 225-7126. Fax, (202) 685-6077. Capt. Paul Gronemeyer, Navy Director, House; Col. Daniel Greenwood, Marine Corps Director, House. Navy (House), (202) 225-7126. Marine Corps (House), (202) 225-7124.*

Provides House members with services and information on all matters related to the U.S. Navy and the U.S. Marine Corps.

U.S. Coast Guard Liaison, *B320 RHOB 20515; (202) 225-4775. Fax, (202) 426-6081. Cmdr. Bion Stewart, Chief.*

Provides House members with services and information on all matters related to the U.S. Coast Guard.

Veterans Affairs Dept., *Congressional Liaison Service, B328 RHOB 20515; (202) 225-2280. Fax, (202) 453-5225. Ron Maurer, Director, House and Senate. General email, ocia-cls@va.gov Web, www.va.gov*

Provides House members with services and information on all matters related to veterans' benefits and services.

White House Legislative Affairs, *White House 20502; (202) 456-2230. Fax, (202) 456-3343. Katie Beirne Fallon, Assistant to the President for Legislative Affairs; Jonathan Samuels, Deputy Director, House Liaison; Anne Wall, Deputy Director, Senate Liaison.*

Serves as a liaison between the president and the House of Representatives.

Air Force Liaison, *SR-182 20510; (202) 224-2481. Fax, (202) 685-2575. Col. Billy Thompson, Director. General email, SAFLLS@pentagon.af.mil*

Provides senators with services and information on all matters related to the U.S. Air Force.

Army Liaison, *SR-183 20510; (202) 224-2881. Fax, (202) 693-4754. Col. Robert McAleer, Chief.*

Provides senators with services and information on all matters related to the U.S. Army.

Navy–Marine Corps Liaison, *SR-182 20510; (202) 224-4682. Fax, (202) 685-6005. Capt. Cedric Pringle, Navy Director, Senate; Col. Robert Jones, Marine Corps Director, Senate. Navy (Senate), (202) 224-4682. Marine Corps (Senate), (202) 224-4681.*

Provides senators with services and information on all matters related to the U.S. Navy and the U.S. Marine Corps.

U.S. Coast Guard Liaison, *SR-183 20510; (202) 224-2913. Fax, (202) 755-1695. Cmdr. Daniel P. Walsh, Chief.*

Provides senators with services and information on all matters related to the U.S. Coast Guard.

Veterans Affairs Dept., *Congressional Liaison Service, SR-189 20510; (202) 224-5351. Fax, (202) 453-5218. Ron Maurer, Director, House and Senate. General email, ocia-cls@va.gov*

Provides senators with services and information on all matters related to veterans' benefits and services.

White House Legislative Affairs, *White House 20502; (202) 456-2230. Fax, (202) 456-3343. Katie Beirne Fallon, Assistant to the President for Legislative Affairs; Jonathan Samuels, Deputy Director, House Liaison; Anne Wall, Deputy Director, Senate Liaison.*

Serves as a liaison between the Senate and the president.

Libraries

▶**CONGRESS**

For a listing of relevant congressional committees and sub-committees, please see page 689 or the Appendix.

Legislative Resource Center, *Library Services, Office of the Clerk, House of Representatives, B106 CHOB 20515; (202) 225-9000. Fax, (202) 226-4874. Rae Ellen Best, House Librarian. Web, http://library.clerk.house.gov*

Serves as the statutory and official depository of House reports, hearings, prints, and documents for the clerk of the House. Includes the divisions of Library Services, Public Information, Records and Registration, and the House Document Room.

Library of Congress, *Congressional Research Service, 101 Independence Ave. S.E., #LM 203 20540; (202) 707-5775. Fax, (202) 707-2615. Mary B. Mazanec, Director. Information, (202) 707-5700. Inquiry, (202) 707-5770. Web, www.loc.gov/crsinfo*

Provides members of Congress and committees with research and reference assistance.

Library of Congress, *Law Library, Madison Bldg., 101 Independence Ave. S.E., #LM240 20540; (202) 707-5065. Fax, (202) 707-1820. David S. Mao, Law Librarian. Reading room, (202) 707-5080. Reference information, (202) 707-5079. Web, www.loc.gov/law*

Maintains collections of foreign, international, and comparative law texts organized jurisdictionally by country; covers all legal systems–common, civil, Roman, canon, religious, and ancient and medieval law. Services include a public reading room; a microtext facility, with readers and printers for microfilm and microfiche; and foreign law/rare book reading areas. Staff of legal specialists is competent in approximately forty languages; does not provide advice on legal matters.

Congressional Liaisons at Federal Departments and Agencies

DEPARTMENTS

Agriculture, Ann Wright (Acting), (202) 720-4031

Commerce, Jim Stowers, (202) 482-5631

Defense, Elizabeth King, (703) 697-6210

  Air Force, Maj. Gen. Thomas Bergeson, (703) 697-8153

  Army, Maj. Gen. William Rapp, (703) 697-6767

  Navy, Rear Adm. Michael A. Franken, (703) 697-7146

Education, Gabriella Gomez, (202) 401-0020

Energy, Brad Crowell, (202) 586-5450

Health and Human Services, Jim Esquea, (202) 690-7627

Homeland Security, Brian de Vallance, (202) 447-5890

Housing and Urban Development, Bernard Fulton, (202) 708-0005

Interior, Sarah Neimeyer, (202) 208-7693

Justice, Peter J. Kadzik, (202) 514-2141

Labor, Brian Kennedy, (202) 693-4600

State, Julia Frifield, (202) 228-1603

Transportation, Dana Gresham, (202) 366-4573

Treasury, Alastair M. Fitzpayne, (202) 622-1900

Veterans Affairs, Joan Mooney, (202) 461-6490

AGENCIES

Agency for International Development, Barbara Larkin, (202) 712-4300

Commission on Civil Rights, Lenore Ostrowsky (Acting), (202) 376-7700

Commodity Futures Trading Commission, John Riley, (202) 418-5075

Consumer Product Safety Commission, Jenilee Keefe Singer, (301) 504-7488

Corporation for National and Community Service, Kim Allman (Acting), (202) 606-6731

Environmental Protection Agency, Laura Vaught, (202) 564-5200

Equal Employment Opportunity Commission, Patricia Crawford, (202) 663-4191

Export-Import Bank, Scott P. Schloegel, (202) 565-3230

Farm Credit Administration, Michael Stokke, (703) 883-4067

Federal Communications Commission, Sara Morris, (202) 418-1900

Federal Deposit Insurance Corporation, Eric Spitler, (877) 275-3342

Federal Election Commission, J. Duane Pugh, (202) 694-1006

Federal Emergency Management Agency, Aaron Davis, (202) 212-1890

Federal Labor Relations Authority, Sarah Whittle Spooner, (202) 218-7791

Federal Maritime Commission, Stacey M. Evans, (202) 523-5740

Federal Mediation and Conciliation Service, Dawn E. Starr, (202) 606-5444

Federal Reserve System, Linda Robertson, (202) 974-7008

Library of the Senate, *SR-B15 20510; (202) 224-7106. Fax, (202) 229-0879. Leona Faust, Librarian.*

Maintains special collection for Senate private use of primary source legislative materials, including reports, hearing transcripts, prints, documents, and debate proceedings. (Not open to the public.)

Pages

►CONGRESS

For a listing of relevant congressional committees and subcommittees, please see page 689 or the Appendix.

Senate Page School, *U.S. Senate 20510-7248; (202) 224-3927. Kathryn S. Weeden, Principal.*

Provides education for pages of the Senate.

Sergeant at Arms and Doorkeeper of the Senate, *Senate Page Program, Webster Hall, #11 20510; (202) 228-1291. Elizabeth Roach, Director.*

Oversees and enforces rules and regulations concerning Senate pages after they have been appointed.

Staff

►CONGRESS

Human Resources, *House Vacancy Announcement and Placement Service, H2-102 FHOB 20515-6201; (202) 225-2926. Fax, (202) 226-7514. Jason Hite, Chief Human Resources Officer.*

Holds résumés and provides as requested by House committees.

Senate Placement Office, *SH-116 20510; (202) 224-9167. Brian Bean, Administrator. General email, placementofficeinfo@saa.senate.gov Web, www.senate.gov/employment*

Provides members, committees, and administrative offices of the Senate with placement and referral services. Compiles *Senate Employment Bulletin,* an online listing of available jobs.

Federal Trade Commission, Jeanne Bumpus, (202) 326-2946

General Services Administration, Lisa Austin, (202) 501-0563

Legal Services Corporation, Carol Bergman, (202) 295-1611

Merit Systems Protection Board, Rosalyn Coates, (202) 653-6772, ext. 4485

National Aeronautics and Space Administration, Seth Statler, (202) 358-1055

National Archives and Records Administration, John Hamilton, (202) 357-5100

National Credit Union Administration, Todd M. Harper, (703) 518-6330

National Endowment for the Arts, Michael Griffin, (202) 682-5773

National Endowment for the Humanities, Courtney Chapin, (202) 606-8298

National Labor Relations Board, Lester A. Heltzer, (202) 273-1940

National Mediation Board, Mary L. Johnson, (202) 692-5040

National Science Foundation, Judith Gan, (703) 292-8070

National Transportation Safety Board, Jane Terry, (202) 314-6218

Nuclear Regulatory Commission, Rebecca L. Schmidt, (301) 415-1776

Occupational Safety and Health Review Commission, Richard Huberman, (202) 606-5723

Office of Personnel Management, Tania A. Shand, (202) 606-1300

Office of Special Counsel, Adam Miles, (202) 254-3607

Pension Benefit Guaranty Corporation, Jioni Palmer (Acting), (202) 326-4010

Postal Regulatory Commission, Ann Fisher, (202) 789-6803

Securities and Exchange Commission, Timothy Henseler (Acting), (202) 551-2010

Selective Service System, Richard S. Flahaven, (703) 605-4017

Small Business Administration, Nicholas Coutsos, (202) 205-6700

Smithsonian Institution, Nell Payne, (202) 633-5125

Social Security Administration, Sharon A. Wilson, (410) 965-3930

Surface Transportation Board, Lucille Marvin, (202) 245-0238

Tennessee Valley Authority, Justin C. Maierhofer, (865) 632-4315

U.S. International Trade Commission, Joshua Levy, (202) 205-3151

U.S. Postal Service, Patricia Licata, (202) 268-2783

▶NONGOVERNMENTAL

Congressional Management Foundation, *710 E St. S.E. 20003; (202) 546-0100. Fax, (202) 547-0936. Brad Fitch, President.*
General email, cmf@congressfoundation.org
Web, www.congressfoundation.org

Nonpartisan organization that provides members of Congress and their staffs with management information and services through seminars, consultation, research, and publications.

Federal Bar Assn., *1220 N. Fillmore St., #444, Arlington, VA 22201; (571) 481-9100. Fax, (571) 481-9090. Karen Silberman, Executive Director.*
General email, fba@fedbar.org
Web, www.fedbar.org

Organization of bar members who are present or former staff members of the House, Senate, Library of Congress, Supreme Court, Government Accountability Office, or Government Printing Office, or attorneys in legislative practice before federal courts or agencies.

House Chiefs of Staff Assn., *2455 RHOB 20515; (202) 225-6411. Fax, (202) 226-0778. Drew Kent, Chief of Staff.*

Sponsors professional development programs and social activities for current chiefs of staff and staff directors. Promotes bipartisanship.

POLITICAL ADVOCACY

General

▶AGENCIES

Justice Dept. (DOJ), *Foreign Agents Registration Unit, 600 E St. N.W., #1301 20004; (202) 233-0776. Fax, (202) 233-2147. Heather H. Hunt, Chief.*
General email, fara.public@usdoj.gov
Web, www.fara.gov

Receives and maintains the registration of agents representing foreign countries, companies, organizations, and individuals. Compiles semiannual report on foreign agent registrations. Foreign agent registration files are open for public inspection.

For a listing of relevant congressional committees and subcommittees, please see page 689 or the Appendix.

Legislative Resource Center, *Records and Registration, Office of the Clerk, House of Representatives, B106 CHOB 20515-6612; (202) 226-5200. Fax, (202) 226-4874. Steve Pingeton, Manager.*
Web, http://clerk.house.gov

Receives and maintains lobby registrations and quarterly financial reports of lobbyists. Administers the statutes of the Federal Regulation of Lobbying Act of 1995 and counsels lobbyists. Receives and maintains agency filings made under the requirements of Section 319 of the Interior Dept. and Related Agencies Appropriations Act for fiscal 1990 (known as the Byrd Amendment). Open for public inspection.

Assn. of Government Relations Professionals,
300 N. Washington St., #205, Alexandria, VA 22314; (703) 960-3011. Danielle R. Staudt, Executive Director.
General email, info@grp.org
Web, www.grp.org

Membership: lobbyists and government relations and public affairs professionals. Works to improve the skills, ethics, and public image of lobbyists. Monitors lobby legislation; conducts educational programs on public issues, lobbying techniques, and other topics of interest to membership.

Citizens United, *1006 Pennsylvania Ave. S.E. 20003-2142; (202) 547-5420. Fax, (202) 547-5421. David N. Bossie, President.*
General email, info@citizensunited.org
Web, www.citizensunited.org

Advocates for key elements of the conservative legislative and policy agenda.

Political Action Committees and 527s

The following are some key political action committees (PACs) based in Washington.

Active Ballot Club *(United Food and Commercial Workers International Union, AFL-CIO), 1775 K St. N.W. 20006; (202) 223-3111. Fax, (202) 728-1830. Joseph T. Hansen, President; Anthony M. (Marc) Perrone, Treasurer.*
Web, www.ufcw.org

Air Line Pilots Assn. PAC *1625 Massachusetts Ave. N.W., 8th Floor 20036; (703) 689-2270. Fax, (202) 797-4030. Capt. Don Lee Moak, President; Sean Cassidy, Treasurer.*
Web, www.alpa.org

Amalgamated Transit Union—COPE (Committee on Political Education) *5025 Wisconsin Ave. N.W. 20016; (202) 537-1645. Fax, (202) 244-7824. Oscar Owens, Treasurer.*
Web, www.atu.org

American Federation of State, County, and Municipal Employees (AFSCME) *1625 L St. N.W. 20036-5687; (202) 429-1000. Fax, (202) 429-1293. Lee A. Saunders, President. Press, (202) 429-1145.*
Web, www.afscme.org

American Federation of Teachers (AFT), *Political Dept., 555 New Jersey Ave. N.W. 20001; (202) 879-4436. Fax, (202) 393-6375. John Ost, Political Director; Lorretta Johnson, Secretary-Treasurer, (202) 879-4400. Press, (202) 879-4458.*
Web, www.aft.org

Committee on Letter Carriers Political Education *(National Assn. of Letter Carriers, AFL-CIO), 100 Indiana Ave. N.W. 20001-2144; (202) 393-4695. Fax, (202) 756-7400. Fredric V. Rolando, President; Jeremy Goldberg, Director.*
General email, nalcinf@nalc.org
Web, www.nalc.org

Committee on Political Action of the American Postal Workers Union, AFL-CIO *1300 L St. N.W. 20005; (202) 842-4210. Fax, (202) 682-2528. John L. Marcotte, Director.*
Web, www.apwu.org

CWA-COPE Political Contributions Committee *(Communications Workers of America, AFL-CIO), 501 3rd St. N.W. 20001-2797; (202) 434-1100. Fax, (202) 434-1279. Larry Cohen, President.*
Web, www.cwa-union.org

International Brotherhood of Electrical Workers Political Action Committee *900 7th St. N.W. 20001; (202) 728-6046. Fax, (202) 728-6144. Sherilyn Wright, Director, Political and Legislative Affairs. Press, (202) 728-6014. General email, ibewpoliticaldept@ibew.org*
Web, www.ibew.org

The International Brotherhood of Teamsters, *Federal Legislation and Regulation, 25 Louisiana Ave. N.W. 20001-2194; (202) 624-8741. Fax, (202) 624-8973. Fred McLuckie, Director; Ken Hall, General Secretary–Treasurer. Press, (202) 624-6911.*
General email, drive@teamster.org
Web, www.teamster.org

Ironworkers Political Action League *1750 New York Ave. N.W., #400 20006; (202) 383-4800. Fax, (202) 638-4856. Dave Kolbe, Political and Legislative Representative; Ron Piksa, General Treasurer.*

Ratings of Members

The following organizations either publish voting records on selected issues or regularly rate members of Congress.

AFL-CIO, 815 16th St. N.W., 20006; (202) 637-5018; Web, www.aflcio.org

American Conservative Union, 1331 H St. N.W. #500, 20005; (202) 347-9388, Fax: (202) 347-9389; Web, www.conservative.org

American Farm Bureau Federation, 600 Maryland Ave. S.W. #1000W, 20024; (202) 406-3600; Web, www.fb.org

Americans for Democratic Action, 1629 K St. N.W. #300, 20006; (202) 600-7762, Fax: (202) 204-8637; Web, www.adaction.org

Americans for Tax Reform, 722 12th St. N.W. #400, 20005; (202) 785-0266, Fax: (202) 785-0261; Web, www.atr.org

Citizens Against Government Waste, 1301 Pennsylvania Ave. N.W. #1075, 20004; (202) 467-5300, Fax: (202) 467-4253; Web, www.cagw.org

Citizens for Responsibility and Ethics in Washington, 1400 Eye St. N.W. #450, 20005; (202) 408-5565. Web, www.citizensforethics.org

The Club for Growth, 2001 L Street N.W. #600, 20036; (202) 955-5500, Fax: (202) 955-9466; Web, www.clubforgrowth.org

Drum Major Institute for Public Policy, 122 C St. N.W. #505, 20001; Web, www.drummajorinstitute.org

Human Rights Campaign, 1640 Rhode Island Ave. N.W., 20036-3278; (800) 777-4723 or (202) 628-4160, Fax: (202) 347-5323, TTY: (202) 216-1572; Web, www.hrc.org

Leadership Conference on Civil Rights, 1629 K St. N.W., 10th Floor 20006; (202) 466-3311; Web, www.civilrights.org

League of Conservation Voters, 1920 L St. N.W. #800, 20036; (202) 785-8683 Fax:(202) 835-0491; Web, www.lcv.org

NAACP (National Assn. for the Advancement of Colored People), 4805 Mt. Hope Drive Baltimore, MD 21215; (410) 580-5777; Web, www.naacp.org

NARAL Pro-Choice America, 1156 15th St. N.W. #700, 20005; (202) 973-3000, Fax: (202) 973-3000; Web, www.prochoiceamerica.org

National Assn. of Social Workers-PACE (Political Action for Candidate Election), 750 1st St. N.E. #700, 20002; (202) 408-8600; Web, www.socialworkers.org/pace

National Education Assn., 1201 16th St. N.W., 20036-3290; (202) 833-4000, Fax: (202) 822-7974; Web, www.nea.org

National Federation of Independent Business, 1201 F St. N.W., #200 20004-1221; (202) 554-9000; Web, www.nfib.com

National Right to Life Committee, 512 10th St. N.W., 20004; (202) 626-8800; Web, www.nrlc.org

National Taxpayers Union, 108 N. Alfred St., Alexandria, VA 22314; (703) 683-5700; Web, www.ntu.org

Population Connection, 2120 L St. N.W. #500, 20037; (202) 332-2200, Fax: (202) 332-2302; Web, www.populationconnection.org

Public Citizen, Congress Watch, 215 Pennsylvania Ave. S.E., 20003; (202) 546-4996; Web, www.citizen.org

U.S. Chamber of Commerce, Congressional Affairs, 1615 H St. N.W., 20062; (202) 659-6000; Web, www.uschamber.com

U.S. Student Assn., 1211 Connecticut Ave. N.W. #406, 20036; (202) 640-6570, Fax: (202) 223-4005; Web, www.usstudents.org

---

General email, dkolb@iwintl.org

Web, www.ironworkers.org

Laborers' Political League of Laborers' International Union of North America *905 16th St. N.W. 20006-1765; (202) 942-2234. Fax, (202) 942-2307. Bevin Albertani, Legislative and Political Director; Armand E. Sabitoni, General Secretary-Treasurer.*
General email, political@liuna.org
Web, www.liuna.org

Machinists Non-Partisan Political League *(International Assn. of Machinists and Aerospace Workers, AFL-CIO), 9000 Machinists Pl., Upper Marlboro, MD 20772-2687; (301) 967-4575. Fax, (301)*

967-4595. Rick de la Fuente, Political Action Director; Hasan Solomon, Legislative Director; Robert Roach, General Secretary–Treasurer.
Web, www.goiam.org/index.php/mnpl

National Education Assn., *Government Relations, 1201 16th St. N.W., #510 20036-3290; (202) 822-7300. Fax, (202) 822-7309. Mary Kusler, Director.*
Web, www.nea.org

Seafarers International Union of North America, *5201 Auth Way, Camp Springs, MD 20746-4275; (301) 899-0675. Fax, (301) 899-7355. Michael Sacco, President; Kermett Mangram, Vice President, Government Services; David W. Heindel, Secretary-Treasurer.*

Press, (301) 899-0675, ext. 4300.
Web, www.seafarers.org

Represents U.S. merchant mariners.

**Sheet Metal Workers International Assn. Political
Action League** *1750 New York Ave. N.W., 6th Floor
20006-5386; (202) 662-0865. Fax, (202) 662-0880.
Jay Potesta, Political Director; Joseph J. Nigro, President.
Press, (202) 662-0874.*
General email, info@smwia.org
Web, www.smwia.org

United Mine Workers of America, *Coal Miners PAC,
18354 Quantico Gateway Dr., #200, Triangle, VA 22172;
(703) 291-2400. Daniel J. Kane, Secretary-Treasurer.*
Web, www.umwa.org

▶ **NONCONNECTED**

American Sugarbeet Growers Assn. PAC *1156 15th St.
N.W., #1101 20005; (202) 833-2398. Fax, (240) 235-4291.
Ruth Ann Geib, Vice President.*
Web, www.americansugarbeet.org

America Votes, *1155 Connecticut Ave. N.W., #600 20036;
(202) 962-7240. Fax, (202) 962-7241. Greg Speed, Executive
Director; Greg Speed, President.*
Web, www.americavotes.org

Seeks to mobilize Americans to register and vote around
critical issues.

Automotive Free International Trade PAC *1625 Prince
St., #225, Alexandria, VA 22314-2889; (703) 684-8880.
Fax, (703) 684-8920. Mary Drape Hanagan, Executive
Director. Toll-free, (800) 234-8748.*
General email, information@afitpac.com
Web, www.afitpac.com

Black America's PAC *1325 G. St. N.W., #500 20005; (202)
552-7422. Fax, (202) 552-7421. Alvin Williams, President.*
General email, www.bampac.org/bampac_contact form.org
Web, www.bampac.org

Club for Growth, *2001 L St. N.W., #600 20036; (202) 955-
5500. Fax, (202) 955-9466. Chris Chocola, President.*
General email, www.clubforgrowth.org/contact
Web, www.clubforgrowth.org

Promotes mainly Republican candidates with conservative economic policies and voting records.

Council for a Livable World, *322 4th St. N.E. 20002-5824;
(202) 543-4100. John D. Isaacs, Executive Director.*
General email, livableworld.org/contact/
Web, http://livableworld.org

Supports congressional candidates who advocate arms
control and progressive national security policy.

Deloitte and Touche LLP Federal PAC *701 Pennsylvania
Ave. N.W., #530 20004; (202) 734-3205. Cindy M. Stevens,
Treasurer; Chris Patriquin, Manager.*
Web, www.deloittepac.com

EMILY's List, *1800 M St., #375N 20036; (202) 326-1400.
Fax, (202) 326-1415. Stephanie Schriock, President.*
Web, www.emilyslist.org

Raises money to support pro-choice Democratic women
candidates for political office.

Gay & Lesbian Victory Fund and Leadership Institute,
*1133 15th St. N.W., #350 20005; (202) 842-8679. Fax, (202)
289-3863. Chuck Wolfe, President.*
General email, victory@victoryfund.org
Web, www.victoryfund.org

Identifies, trains, and supports open lesbian, gay, bisexual, and transgender candidates and officials at the local,
state, and federal levels of government. Raises funds for
endorsed candidates.

GOPAC, *1101 16th St. N.W., #400 20036; (202) 464-5170.
Fax, (202) 464-5177. Frank J. Donatelli, National Chair;
David Avella, President.*
General email, info@gopac.org
Web, www.gopac.org

Recruits and trains conservative Republican candidates for local and state office.

KPMG PAC, *1801 K St. N.W. 20006 (mailing address: P.O.
Box 18254, Washington, DC 20036-9998); (202) 533-5816.
Fax, (202) 533-8516. Stephen E. Allis, Treasurer.*
Web, www.kpmg.com

KPMG is a global network of firms providing audit,
tax, and advisory services to businesses.

NDN (New Democrat Network), *729 15th St. N.W.,
2nd Floor 20005; (202) 544-9200. Fax, (202) 547-2929.
Simon Rosenberg, President.*
General email, info@ndn.org
Web, www.ndn.org

Studies progressive politics as it relates to the rise in
conservatism, changing voter trends, and new media strategies for campaigns. (Formerly New Politics Institute.)

PricewaterhouseCoopers PAC *1301 K St. N.W., #800
West 20005-3333; (202) 414-1000. Fax, (202) 414-1301.
Laura Cox Kaplan, Principal-in-Charge of U.S. Govern-
ment Regulatory Affairs and Public Policy; Gary Price,
Chief Administrative Officer.*
Web, http://pwc.com

Progressive Majority, *1825 K St. N.W., #450 20006; (202)
408-8603. Fax, (202) 429-0755. Gloria A. Totten, President.*
Web, www.progressivemajority.org

Identifies, trains, and supports progressive candidates
for public office at the state and local levels. Prioritizes
recruitment of candidates of color and people new to the
political process.

▶ **TRADE, MEMBERSHIP, AND HEALTH**

Action Committee for Rural Electrification *(National
Rural Electric Cooperative Assn.),* *4301 Wilson Blvd.,
Arlington, VA 22203-1860; (703) 907-5500. Fax, (703)
907-5516. Michael Whelan, Director.*

General email, nreca@nreca.coop

Web, www.nreca.coop

Represents national interests of cooperative electric utility companies and their consumers.

American Assn. for Justice PAC, *777 6th St. N.W., #200 20001; (202) 965-3500. Fax, (202) 338-8709. Tara Pinto, Associate Director. Toll-free, (800) 424-2725.*

General email, outreach@justice.org

Web, www.justice.org

(Formerly the Assn. of Trial Lawyers of America.)

American Bankers Assn. BankPAC *1120 Connecticut Ave. N.W., 8th Floor 20036; (202) 663-5113. Fax, (202) 663-7544. Gary W. Fields, Treasurer.*

General email, gfields@aba.com

Web, www.aba.com

American Health Care Assn. Political Action Committee (AHCA-PAC) *1201 L St. N.W. 20005-4015; (202) 898-2856. Fax, (202) 842-3860. Jennifer Knorr Hahs, Political Action Director.*

Web, www.ahcancal.org

American Medical Assn. Political Action Committee (AMPAC) *25 Massachusetts Ave. N.W., #600 20001; (202) 789-7400. Fax, (202) 789-7469. Kevin Walker, Executive Director.*

Web, www.ampaconline.org

BUILD PAC of the National Assn. of Home Builders, *1201 15th St. N.W. 20005-2800; (202) 266-5242. Fax, (202) 266-8400. Meghan Everngam, Director.*

Web, www.nahb.org/generic.aspx? genericContentID=45262&fromGSA=1

Membership: includes building contractors, remodelers, and others who support candidates and issues affecting the home-building industry.

Credit Union Legislative Action Council

601 Pennsylvania Ave. N.W., #600, South Bldg. 20004-2601; (202) 638-5777. Fax, (202) 638-7734. Trey Hawkins, Political Affairs Director. Toll-free, (800) 356-9655, ext. 4077.

General email, thawkins@cuna.coop

Web, www.cuna.org/pol_affairs/culac.html

Dealers Election Action Committee of the National Automobile Dealers Assn. *412 1st St. S.E., 1st Floor 20003; (202) 627-6755. Fax, (703) 556-8571. Peter K. Welch, President. Toll-free, (877) 501-3322.*

General email, deac@nada.org

Web, www.nada.org

Human Rights Campaign PAC (HRC), *1640 Rhode Island Ave. N.W. 20036; (202) 216-1545. Fax, (202) 347-5323. Mike Mings, Director.*

General email, hrc@hrc.org

Web, www.hrc.org/issues/pages/federal-pac

Supports candidates for state and federal office who favor lesbian, gay, bisexual, and transgender rights.

Independent Insurance Agents and Brokers of America Political Action Committee (InsurPac) *412 1st St. S.E., #300 20003-1804; (202) 863-7000. Fax, (202) 863-7015. Nathan Riedel, Vice President of Political Affairs.*

General email, InsurPac@iiaba.net

Web, www.independentagent.com/governmentaffairs/insurPac

Insurance and Financial Advisors PAC *2901 Telestar Ct., Falls Church, VA 22042-1205; (703) 770-8100. Fax, (703) 770-8151. Magenta Ishak, Assistant Vice President for Political Affairs.*

General email, mishak@naifa.org

Web, www.naifa.org/advocacy/ifapac

National Active and Retired Federal Employees PAC (NARFE) *606 N. Washington St., Alexandria, VA 22314; (703) 838-7760. Fax, (703) 838-7785. John Hatton, Deputy Legislative Director. Member relations, (800) 456-8410.*

General email, leg@narfe.org

Web, www.narfe.org/legislation/articles.cfm?ID=1778

National Assn. of Broadcasters Television and Radio Political Action Committee *1771 N St. N.W. 20036; (202) 429-5314. Fax, (202) 429-7422. Jennifer Stong, Director.*

General email, pac@nab.org

Web, www.nabpac.org

National Assn. of Social Workers Political Action for Candidate Election *750 1st St. N.E., #700 20002-4241; (202) 408-8600. Fax, (202) 336-8311. Brian Dautch, Senior Political Affairs Associate.*

General email, info@naswdc.org

Web, www.naswdc.org/pace

National Beer Wholesalers Assn. PAC *1101 King St., #600, Alexandria, VA 22314-2965; (703) 683-4300. Fax, (703) 683-8965. Linda Auglis, Director.*

General email, info@nbwa.org

Web, www.nbwa.org

National Committee to Preserve Social Security and Medicare PAC *10 G St. N.E., #600 20002-4215; (202) 216-0420. Fax, (202) 216-0445. Phillip Rotondi, Administrator. Press, (202) 216-8378.*

Web, www.ncpssm.org

Physical Therapy Political Action Committee (PT-PAC) *1111 N. Fairfax St., Alexandria, VA 22314-1488; (703) 706-3163. Fax, (703) 706-3246. Paul Rockar Jr., President; Michael Matlack, Director.*

Web, www.ptpac.org

Planned Parenthood Action Fund, *1110 Vermont Ave. N.W., #300 20005; (202) 973-4800. Fax, (202) 296-3242. Cecile Richards, President.*

General email, actionfund@ppfa.org

Web, www.ppaction.org

Nonpartisan organization that supports candidates who advocate for reproductive health care, including sex education, health care reform for women, birth control, and legal abortion access in the United States. Seeks to influence voters through grassroots organization and education. Monitors legislation and regulations.

Solar Energy Industries Assn. PAC, *505 9th St. N.W., #800 20004; (202) 682-0556. Fax, (202) 682-0559. Suzanne Farish, Director.*
General email, pac@seia.org
Web, www.seia.org/cs/solarPAC

Seeks to raise awareness of solar energy and supports congressional candidates who promote solar technologies in the global marketplace.

Women's Campaign Forum, *1900 L St. N.W., #500 20036; (202) 393-8164. Fax, (202) 393-0649. Georgia Berner, President, Acting.*
General email, info@wcfonline.org
Web, www.wcfonline.org

Nonpartisan organization that seeks to increase the number of women in elected office who support reproductive health choices.

▶NONCONNECTED

Independent expenditure-only committees, commonly known as SuperPACs, are organizations registered with the Federal Election Commission that may raise unlimited funds from individuals, corporations, businesses, and others to advocate for or against specific candidates for public office. Direct contributions to candidates' campaigns are prohibited.

American Crossroads, *P.O. Box 34413 20043; (202) 559-6428. Jo Ann Davidson, Director.*
General email, info@americancrossroads.org
Web, www.americancrossroads.org

Promotes Republican candidates who support strong defense, free enterprise, and limited government. Targets voters through television ads, mailings, and phone campaigns.

American Dental Assn. PAC, *1111 14th St. N.W., #1100 20005; (202) 898-2400. Fax, (202) 898-2437. Sarah Milligan, Director of Political Affairs.*
General email, govtpol@ada.org
Web, www.ada.org

Nonpartisan organization that promotes congressional candidates who advocate for dentists, oral health, and oral health's connection to overall health. Provides educational resources to dentists interested in seeking public office at local, state, or national levels.

Club for Growth Action, *2001 L St. N.W., #600 20036; (202) 955-5500. Fax, (202) 955-9466. Chris Chocola, President.*
Web, www.clubforgrowth.org

Promotes fiscally conservative congressional candidates during Republican primary and general campaigns. Interests include limited government, low taxes, estate tax repeal, social security reform, free trade, tax code reform, school choice, and deregulation.

National Realtors Assn. Political Action Committee, *Washington Office, 500 New Jersey Ave. N.W. 20001-2020; (202) 383-1000. William J. Armstrong III, Treasurer. Toll-free, (800) 874-6500.*
Web, www.realtor.org/rpac

Nonpartisan organization that promotes federal, state, and local candidates who advocate for private property rights and free enterprise. (Headquarters in Chicago.)

NEA Fund for Children and Public Education, *1201 16th St. N.W. 20036; (202) 833-4000. Fax, (202) 822-7974. Dennis Van Roekel, President.*
General email, neafund@nea.org
Web, www.neafund.org and www.nea.org

Provides direct financial support to recommended candidates for president and the U.S. Congress who will fight to improve public education and support students, teachers, and staff.

United Mine Workers of America Power PAC, *18354 Quantico Gateway Dr., #200, Triangle, VA 22172-1779; (703) 291-2401. Daniel J. Kane, Treasurer.*
General email, mdelbalzo@umwa.org
Web, www.umwa.org

Promotes candidates who advocate for coal miners, clean coal technicians, health care workers, truck drivers, manufacturing workers, and public employees. Interests include workplace safety, wages and benefits, and workplace representation.

Women Vote! – EMILY's List, *1800 M St. N.W., #375N 20036; (202) 326-1400. Denise Feriozzi, Political Director.*
Web, http://emilyslist.org/what/reaching_women_voters

Seeks to influence women to vote for pro-choice Democratic women candidates and other Democratic candidates. Targets candidates opposed to these positions.

Working for Us PAC, *888 16th St. N.W., #650 20006; (202) 499-7420. Steve Rosenthal, President.*
General email, info@workingforuspac.org
Web, www.workingforuspac.org

Promotes candidates focused on job creation, health care reform, and expanding public services. Campaigns against candidates opposed to these principles. (Affiliated with The Organizing Group.)

Political Interest Groups

▶NONGOVERNMENTAL

American Conservative Union (ACU), *1331 H St. N.W., #500 20005; (202) 347-9388. Fax, (202) 347-9389. Dan Schneider, Executive Director.*

General email, acu@conservative.org

Web, www.conservative.org

Legislative interest organization that focuses on defense, foreign policy, economics, the national budget, taxes, and legal and social issues. Monitors legislation and regulations.

American Family Voices, *1250 Eye St. N.W., #250 20005; (202) 393-4352. Fax, (202) 331-0131. Michael Lux, President.*
General email, admin@americanfamilyvoices.org

Web, www.americanfamilyvoices.org

Advocates on behalf of middle-class and low-income families dealing with economic, health care, and consumer issues.

Americans for Democratic Action, *1629 K St. N.W., #300 20006; (202) 600-7762. Fax, (202) 204-8637. Don Kusler, Executive Director.*
General email, info@adaction.org

Web, www.adaction.org

Legislative interest organization that seeks to strengthen civil, constitutional, women's, family, workers', and human rights, and promotes grassroots activism. Interests include education, health care, immigration, peace, tax reform, and voter access.

Americans for Prosperity, *2111 Wilson Blvd., #350, Arlington, VA 22201; (703) 224-3200. Fax, (703) 224-3201. Tim Phillips, President. Toll-free, (866) 730-0150.*
General email, info@AFPhq.org

Web, www.americansforprosperity.org

Grassroots organization that seeks to educate citizens about economic policy and encourage their participation in the public policy process. Supports limited government and free markets on the local, state, and federal levels. Specific interests include Social Security, trade, and taxes. Monitors legislation and regulations.

Americans United For Change, *1250 Eye St. N.W., #250 20005 (mailing address: P.O. Box 34606, Washington, DC 20043); (202) 470-6954. Fax, (202) 331-0131. Caren Benjamin, Executive Director. Press, (202) 470-5878.*
Web, http://americansunitedforchange.org

Conducts national campaigns that utilize grassroots organizing, polling, and message development; earned and paid media; online organizing; and paid and volunteer phonework to advance the progressive agenda. Interests include Medicare, Medicaid, Social Security, health care reform, gun violence prevention, clean energy, and economic fairness and security.

B'nai B'rith International, *2020 K St. N.W., 7th Floor 20006; (202) 857-6600. Fax, (202) 857-2700. Allan J. Jacobs, President; Daniel S. Mariaschin, Executive Vice President. Toll-free, (888) 388-4224.*
General email, info@bnaibrith.org

Web, www.bnaibrith.org

International Jewish organization that promotes the security and continuity of the Jewish people and the State

of Israel; defends human rights; combats anti-Semitism; and promotes Jewish identity through cultural activities. Interests include strengthening family life and the education and training of youth, providing broad-based services for the benefit of senior citizens, and advocacy on behalf of Jews throughout the world.

The Brookings Institution, *1775 Massachusetts Ave. N.W. 20036; (202) 797-6000. Fax, (202) 797-6004. Strobe Talbott, President. Press, (202) 797-6105.*
General email, communications@brookings.edu

Web, www.brookings.edu

Public policy research organization that seeks to improve the performance of American institutions, the effectiveness of government programs, and the quality of public policy through research and analysis. Sponsors lectures, debates, and policy forums.

Campaign for America's Future, *1825 K St. N.W., #400 20006; (202) 955-5665. Fax, (202) 955-5606. Robert L. Borosage, Co-Director; Roger Hickey, Co-Director.*
Web, www.ourfuture.org

Operates the Campaign for America's Future and the Institute for America's Future. Advocates policies to help working people. Supports improved employee benefits, including health care, child care, and paid family leave; promotes lifelong education and training of workers. Seeks full employment, higher wages, and increased productivity. Monitors legislation and regulations.

Cato Institute, *1000 Massachusetts Ave. N.W. 20001-5403; (202) 842-0200. Fax, (202) 842-3490. John Allison, President. Press, (202) 842-0200, ext. 800.*
General email, pr@cato.org

Web, www.cato.org

Public policy research organization that advocates limited government and individual liberty. Interests include privatization and deregulation, low and simple taxes, and reduced government spending. Encourages voluntary solutions to social and economic problems.

Center for American Progress, *1333 H St. N.W., 10th Floor 20005; (202) 682-1611. Fax, (202) 682-1867. Neera Tanden, President.*
General email, progress@americanprogress.org

Web, www.americanprogress.org

Nonpartisan research and educational institute that strives to ensure opportunity for all Americans. Advocates policies to create sustained economic growth and new opportunities. Supports fiscal discipline, shared prosperity, and investments in people through education, health care, and workforce training.

Center for National Policy, *1250 Eye St., #500 20005; (202) 682-1800. Fax, (202) 682-1818. Scott Bates, President.*
General email, info@cnponline.org

Web, www.cnponline.org

Public policy research and educational organization that serves as a forum for development of national policy alternatives. Governed by a board of directors experienced in government and private sectors. Studies issues of national and international concern, focusing on national security; sponsors conferences and symposia.

Christian Coalition of America, *P.O. Box 37030 20013-7030; (202) 479-6900. Fax, (202) 479-4262. Roberta Combs, President. Press, (202) 549-6257. General email, coalition@cc.org*

Web, www.cc.org

Membership: individuals who support traditional, conservative Christian values. Represents members' views to all levels of government and to the media.

Committee for a Responsible Federal Budget, *1899 L St. N.W., #400 20036; (202) 596-3597. Fax, (202) 986-3696. Maya MacGuineas, President. General email, crfb@crfb.org*

Web, www.crfb.org

Bipartisan, nonprofit organization that educates the public about issues that have significant fiscal policy impact. Monitors legislation and regulation. (Affiliated with the New America Foundation.)

Common Cause, *1133 19th St. N.W., 9th Floor 20036; (202) 833-1200. Fax, (202) 659-3716. Miles Rapoport, President, (202) 736-5740. Press, (202) 736-5770. General email, mrapoport@commoncause.org*

Web, www.commoncause.org

Nonpartisan citizens' legislative interest group that works for institutional reform in federal and state government. Advocates partial public financing of congressional election campaigns, ethics in government, nuclear arms control, oversight of defense spending, tax reform, and a reduction of political action committee influence in Congress.

Concerned Women for America, *1015 15th St. N.W., #1100 20005; (202) 488-7000. Fax, (202) 488-0806. Penny Young Nance, Chief Executive Officer.*

Web, www.cwfa.org

Educational organization that seeks to protect the rights of the family and preserve Judeo-Christian values. Monitors legislation affecting family and religious issues.

Concord Coalition, *1011 Arlington Blvd., #300, Arlington, VA 22209; (703) 894-6222. Fax, (703) 894-6231. Robert L. Bixby, Executive Director. General email, concordcoalition@concordcoalition.org*

Web, www.concordcoalition.org

Nonpartisan grassroots organization advocating fiscal responsibility and ensuring Social Security, Medicare, and Medicaid are secure for all generations.

The Conservative Caucus (TCC), *92 Main St., #202-8, Warrenton, VA 20816; (540) 219-4536. Peter J. Thomas, Chair. General email, info@conservativeusa.org*

Web, www.conservativeusa.org

Legislative interest organization that promotes grassroots activity on issues such as national defense and economic and tax policy. The Conservative Caucus Research, Analysis, and Education Foundation studies public issues

including Central American affairs, defense policy, and federal funding of political advocacy groups.

Eagle Forum, *Washington Office, 316 Pennsylvania Ave. S.E., #203 20003; (202) 544-0353. Fax, (202) 547-6996. Glyn Wright, Executive Director. General email, glyn@eagleforum.org*

Web, www.eagleforum.org

Supports conservative, pro-family policies at all levels of government. Promotes traditional marriage, pro-life policies, limited government, and American sovereignty. Other concerns include education, national defense, and taxes. (Headquarters in Alton, Ill.)

English First, *8001 Forbes Pl., #102, Springfield, VA 22151-2205; (703) 321-8818. Fax, (703) 321-7636. Frank McGlynn, Executive Director. Web, www.englishfirst.org*

Seeks to make English the official language of the United States. Advocates policies that make English education available to all children. Monitors legislation and regulations. Opposes multilingual education and governmental policies, including Clinton Executive Order 13166.

Family Research Council, *801 G St. N.W. 20001-3729; (202) 393-2100. Fax, (202) 393-2134. Tony Perkins, President. Toll-free, (800) 225-4008. Web, www.frc.org*

Legislative interest organization that analyzes issues affecting the family and seeks to ensure that the interests of the family are considered in the formulation of public policy.

Feminist Majority, *1600 Wilson Blvd., #801, Arlington, VA 22209-2505; (703) 522-2214. Fax, (703) 522-2219. Eleanor Smeal, President; Norma Gattsek, Director, Government Relations. General email, feedback@feminist.org*

Web, www.feministmajority.org

Legislative interest group that seeks to increase the number of feminists running for public office; promotes a national feminist agenda.

Free Congress Research and Education Foundation
(FCF), *901 N. Washington, #206, Alexandria, VA 22314; (703) 837-0030. Fax, (703) 837-0031. James Gilmore, President. General email, contact@freecongress.org*

Web, www.freecongress.org

Conservative political think tank that promotes traditional values. Studies economic and transportation policy. Trains citizens to participate in a democracy.

FreedomWorks, *400 N. Capitol St. N.W., #765 20001; (202) 783-3870. Fax, (202) 942-7649. Matt Kibbe, President. Toll-free, (888) 564-6273. Web, www.freedomworks.org*

Recruits, educates, trains, and mobilizes citizens to promote lower taxes, less government, and greater economic freedom. Maintains scorecards on members of the Senate and House based on adherence to FreedomWorks positions.

Frontiers of Freedom, *4094 Majestic Lane, #380, Fairfax, VA 22033; (703) 246-0110. Fax, (703) 246-0129. George C. Landrith, President.*
General email, info@ff.org
Web, www.ff.org

Seeks to increase personal freedom through a reduction in the size of government. Interests include property rights, regulatory and tax reform, global warming, national missile defense, Internet regulation, school vouchers, and Second Amendment rights. Monitors legislation and regulations.

The Heritage Foundation, *214 Massachusetts Ave. N.E. 20002-4999; (202) 546-4400. Fax, (202) 546-8328. Jim DeMint, President. Press, (202) 675-1761.*
General email, info@heritage.org
Web, www.heritage.org

Conservative public policy research organization that conducts research and analysis and sponsors lectures, debates, and policy forums advocating individual freedom, limited government, the free market system, and a strong national defense.

Interfaith Alliance, *1250 24th St. N.W., #300 20037; (202) 466-0567. Fax, (202) 466-0502. Rev. Dr. C. Welton Gaddy, President.*
General email, info@interfaithalliance.org
Web, www.interfaithalliance.org

Membership: seventy-five faith traditions, including Protestant, Catholic, Jewish, and Muslim clergy, laity, and others who favor a positive, nonpartisan role for religious faith in public life. Advocates mainstream religious values; promotes tolerance and social opportunity; opposes the use of religion to promote political extremism at national, state, and local levels. Monitors legislation and regulations.

Log Cabin Republicans, *1090 Vermont Ave. N.W., #850 20005; (202) 420-7873. Gregory T. Angelo, Executive Director.*
General email, info@logcabin.org
Web, www.logcabin.org

Membership: lesbian, gay, bisexual, transgender and allied Republicans. Educates conservative politicians and voters on LGBT issues; disseminates information; conducts seminars for members. Promotes conservative values among members of the gay community. Raises campaign funds. Monitors legislation and regulations.

Millennium Institute, *1634 Eye St. N.W., #300 20006; (202) 383-6200. Fax, (202) 383-6209. Hans R. Herren, President.*
General email, info@millennium-institute.org
Web, www.millennium-institute.org

Research and development organization that provides computer modeling services for planning and building a sustainable economic and ecological future.

National Center for Policy Analysis, *Washington Office, 601 Pennsylvania Ave. N.W., #900 South Bldg. 20004-3615; (202) 220-3082. Fax, (202) 220-3096. John C. Goodman, President; Brian Williams, Legislative Director.*
General email, ncpa@ncpa.org
Web, www.ncpa.org

Nonpartisan public policy research organization. Disseminates research on health care, taxes, retirement, small business, and the environment. Develops policies that promote private, free-market alternatives to government regulation and control. (Headquarters in Dallas, Texas.)

National Jewish Democratic Council, *P.O. Box 65683 20035; (202) 216-9060. Fax, (202) 216-9061. Jack Moline, Executive Director.*
General email, njdc@njdc.org
Web, www.njdc.org

Encourages Jewish involvement in the Democratic party and its political campaigns. Monitors and analyzes domestic and foreign policy issues that concern the American Jewish community.

National Organization for Marriage, *2029 K St. N.W., #300 20006; (888) 894-3604. Brian S. Brown, President.*
General email, contact@nationformarriage.org
Web, www.nationformarriage.org

Supports marriage-related initiatives at state and local levels, with an emphais on the Northeast and West Coast. Opposes same-sex marriage. Monitors legislation.

National Organization for Women (NOW), *1100 H St. N.W., #300 20005; (202) 628-8669. Fax, (202) 785-8576. Terry O'Neill, President.*
General email, now@now.org
Web, www.now.org

Advocacy organization that works for women's civil rights. Acts through demonstrations, court cases, and legislative efforts to improve the status of all women. Interests include increasing the number of women in elected and appointed office, improving women's economic status and health coverage, ending violence against women, preserving abortion rights, and abolishing discrimination based on gender, race, age, and sexual orientation.

National Taxpayers Union, *Communications, 108 N. Alfred St., Alexandria, VA 22314; (703) 683-5700. Fax, (703) 683-5722. Peter Sepp, Executive Vice President; Duane Parde, President.*
General email, ntu@ntu.org
Web, www.ntu.org

Citizens' interest group that promotes tax and spending reduction at all levels of government. Supports constitutional amendments to balance the federal budget and limit taxes.

New America Foundation, *1899 L St. N.W., #400 20036; (202) 986-2700. Fax, (202) 986-3696. Steve Coll, President; Eric Schmidt, Chair.*
Web, www.newamerica.org

Ideologically diverse public policy institute that seeks to bring innovative policy ideas to the fore and nurture the next generation of public policy intellectuals. Sponsors research, writing, conferences, and events. Funds studies of government programs. Seeks to stimulate more informed reporting and analyses of government activities.

People for the American Way (PFAW), *1101 15th St. N.W., #600 20005-5002; (202) 467-4999. Fax, (202) 293-2672. Michael B. Keegan, President. Toll-free, (800) 326-7329.*
General email, pfaw@pfaw.org
Web, www.pfaw.org

Nonpartisan organization that promotes public policies that reflect the values of freedom, fairness, and equal opportunity; advocates for constitutional protections and civil rights, and for strong democratic institutions, including a federal judiciary that upholds individual rights. Conducts leadership development programs for college students, African American religious leaders, and young elected officials.

Public Affairs Council, *2121 K St. N.W., #900 20037; (202) 787-5950. Fax, (202) 787-5942. Douglas G. Pinkham, President.*
General email, pac@pac.org
Web, www.pac.org

Membership: public affairs professionals. Informs and counsels members on public affairs programs. Sponsors conferences on election issues, government relations, and political trends. Sponsors the Foundation for Public Affairs.

Public Citizen, *Congress Watch, 215 Pennsylvania Ave. S.E., 3rd Floor 20003; (202) 546-4996. Fax, (202) 546-5562. Lisa Gilbert, Director.*
General email, congress@citizen.org
Web, www.citizen.org/congress

Citizens' interest group engaged in public education, research, media outreach, and citizen activism. Interests include campaign finance reform, consumer protection, financial services, public health and safety, government reform, trade, and the environment.

Rainbow PUSH Coalition, *Public Policy Institute, Government Relations and Telecommunications Project, 727 15th St. N.W., #1200 20005; (202) 393-7874. Fax, (202) 393-1495. Steve Smith, Executive Director, Government Relations; Jesse L. Jackson Sr., President. Press, (773) 373-3366.*
General email, info@rainbowpush.org
Web, http://rainbowpush.org

Independent civil rights organization concerned with U.S. domestic and foreign policy. Interests include D.C. statehood, defense policy, agriculture, HIV/AIDS, poverty, the economy, energy, the environment, hate crimes, and social justice. (Headquarters in Chicago, Ill.)

Republican Jewish Coalition, *50 F St. N.W., #100 20001; (202) 638-6688. Fax, (202) 638-6694. Matthew Brooks, Executive Director; David Flaum, National Chair.*

General email, rjc@rjchq.org
Web, www.rjchq.org

Legislative interest group that works to build support among Republican party decision makers on issues of concern to the Jewish community; studies domestic and foreign policy issues affecting the Jewish community; supports a strong relationship between the United States and Israel.

Taxpayers for Common Sense, *651 Pennsylvania Ave. S.E. 20003; (202) 546-8500. Ryan Alexander, President.*
General email, info@taxpayer.net
Web, www.taxpayer.net

Nonpartisan organization that works with Congress, the media, and grassroots organizations to reduce government waste and increase accountability for federal expenditures. Disseminates research results to the public via media and Web outreach.

Third Way, *1025 Connecticut Ave. N.W., #501 20036; (202) 384-1700. Fax, (202) 775-0430. Jonathan Cowan, President.*
General email, contact@thirdway.org
Web, www.thirdway.org

Think tank that works with moderate and progressive legislators to develop modern solutions to economic, cultural, and national security issues. Conducts studies and polls; develops policy papers and strategy documents.

Traditional Values Coalition, *Washington Office, 139 C St. S.E. 20003; (202) 547-8570. Fax, (202) 546-6403. Andrea S. Lafferty, President.*
General email, mail@traditionalvalues.org
Web, www.traditionalvalues.org

Legislative interest group that supports religious liberties and traditional, conservative Judeo-Christian values. Interests include antiabortion issues, pornography, decreased federal funding for the arts, parental rights, and the promotion of school prayer. Opposes gay rights legislation. (Headquarters in Anaheim, Calif.)

Urban Institute, *2100 M St. N.W. 20037; (202) 833-7200. Fax, (202) 467-5775. Sarah Rosen Wartell, President. Public Affairs, (202) 261-5709.*
General email, publicaffairs@urban.org
Web, www.urban.org

Nonpartisan research and education organization. Investigates U.S. social and economic problems; encourages discussion on solving society's problems, improving and implementing government decisions, and increasing citizens' awareness of public choices.

U.S. Chamber of Commerce, *Political Affairs and Federation Relations, 1615 H St. N.W. 20062-2000; (202) 463-5560. Robert Engstrom, Senior Vice President.*
General email, federation@uschamber.com
Web, www.uschamber.com/political-affairs-and-federation-relations

Federation that works to enact pro-business legislation; tracks election law legislation; coordinates the chamber's candidate endorsement program and its grass-roots lobbying activities.

Women Legislators' Lobby (WiLL), *Policy and Programs,* *322 4th St. N.E. 20002; (202) 544-5055, ext. 2603.* *Fax, (202) 544-7612. Maureen Campbell, Senior WiLL Associate.* *General email, will@wand.org* *Web, www.wand.org*

Bipartisan group of women state legislators. Sponsors conferences, training workshops, issue briefings, and seminars; provides information and action alerts on ways federal policies affect states. Interests include federal budget priorities, national security, and arms control. Monitors related legislation and regulations. (National office in Arlington, Mass. Affiliated with Women's Action for New Directions.)

Women's Policy, Inc., *409 12th St. S.W., #310 20024; (202) 554-2323. Fax, (202) 554-2346. Cynthia A. Hall, President.* *General email, webmaster@womenspolicy.org* *Web, www.womenspolicy.org*

Nonpartisan organization that provides legislative analysis and information services on congressional actions affecting women and their families. Works with congressional women's caucus leaders at federal, state, and local levels, as well as other groups, to provide information pertaining to women's issues.

POLITICAL PARTY ORGANIZATIONS

Democratic

Democratic Congressional Campaign Committee, *430 S. Capitol St. S.E. 20003-4024; (202) 863-1500.* *Fax, (202) 485-3412. Rep. Steve Israel, Chair.* *General email, dccc@dccc.org* *Web, www.dccc.org*

Provides Democratic House candidates with financial and other campaign services.

Democratic Governors Assn., *1401 K St. N.W., #200 20005; (202) 772-5600. Fax, (202) 772-5602. Gov. Peter Shumlin, Chair; Colm O'Comartun, Executive Director.* *General email, dga@dga.net* *Web, www.democraticgovernors.org*

Serves as a liaison between governors' offices and Democratic Party organizations; assists Democratic gubernatorial candidates.

Democratic National Committee (DNC), *430 S. Capitol St. S.E. 20003-4024; (202) 863-8000. Fax, (202) 863-8063. Rep. Debbie Wasserman Schultz, Chair. Press, (202) 863-8148.* *General email, info@democrats.org* *Web, www.democrats.org*

Formulates and promotes Democratic Party policies and positions; assists Democratic candidates for state and national office; organizes national political activities; works with state and local officials and organizations.

Democratic National Committee (DNC), *Assn. of State Democratic Chairs, 430 S. Capitol St. S.E. 20003-4024; (202) 863-8000. John Bisograno, Executive Director. Press, (202) 863-8148.* *General email, info@democrats.org* *Web, www.democrats.org*

Acts as a liaison between state parties and the DNC; works to strengthen state parties for national, state, and local elections; conducts fundraising activities for state parties.

Democratic National Committee (DNC), *Communications, 430 S. Capitol St. S.E. 20003-4024; (202) 863-8148. Mo Elleithee, Director.* *General email, DNCPress@dnc.org* *Web, www.democrats.org*

Assists federal, state, and local Democratic candidates and officials in delivering a coordinated message on current issues; works to improve and expand relations with the press and to increase the visibility of Democratic officials and the Democratic Party.

Democratic National Committee (DNC), *Finance, 430 S. Capitol St. S.E. 20003-4024; (202) 863-8000. Fax, (202) 863-8082. Jordan Kaplan, Director. Press, (202) 863-8148.* *General email, info@democrats.org* *Web, www.democrats.org*

Responsible for developing the Democratic Party's financial base. Coordinates fundraising efforts for and gives financial support to Democratic candidates in national, state, and local campaigns.

Democratic National Committee (DNC), *Research, 430 S. Capitol St. S.E. 20003-4024; (202) 863-8000. Lauren Dillon, Director. Press, (202) 863-8148.* *General email, info@democrats.org* *Web, www.democrats.org*

Provides Democratic elected officials, candidates, state party organizations, and the general public with information on Democratic Party policy and programs.

Democratic Senatorial Campaign Committee, *120 Maryland Ave. N.E. 20002-5610; (202) 224-2447. Fax, (202) 969-0354. Sen. Michael F. Bennet, Chair; Guy Cecil, Executive Director.* *General email, info@dscc.org* *Web, www.dscc.org*

Provides Democratic senatorial candidates with financial, research, and consulting services.

Woman's National Democratic Club, *Committee on Public Policy, 1526 New Hampshire Ave. N.W. 20036; (202) 232-7363. Fax, (202) 986-2791. Elizabeth Spiro Clark, Vice President for Public Policy.* *General email, info@democraticwoman.org* *Web, www.democraticwoman.org*

Studies issues and presents views to congressional committees, the Democratic Party Platform Committee, Democratic leadership groups, elected officials, and other interested groups.

Republican

College Republican National Committee, *1500 K St. N.W., #325 20005; (202) 608-1411. Fax, (202) 608-1429. Alex Smith, National Chair; Matthew Donnellan, Executive Director. Information, (888) 765-3564.*
General email, info@crnc.org

Web, www.crnc.org

Membership: Republican college students. Promotes grassroots support for the Republican Party and provides campaign assistance.

National Federation of Republican Women,
124 N. Alfred St., Alexandria, VA 22314; (703) 548-9688. Fax, (703) 548-9836. Kathy Brugger, President.
General email, mail@nfrw.org

Web, www.nfrw.org

Organizes volunteers for support of Republican candidates for national, state, and local offices; encourages candidacy of Republican women; sponsors campaign management schools. Recruits Republican women candidates for office.

National Republican Congressional Committee,
320 1st St. S.E. 20003-1838; (202) 479-7000. Fax, (202) 863-0693. Rep. Greg Walden, Chair; Rep. Lynn Westmoreland, Deputy Chair; Liesl Hickey, Executive Director.
General email, website@nrcc.org

Web, www.nrcc.org

Provides Republican House candidates with campaign assistance, including financial, public relations, media, and direct mail services.

National Republican Senatorial Committee (NRSC),
425 2nd St. N.E. 20002-4914; (202) 675-6000. Rep. Jerry Moran, Chair; Rob W. Collins, Executive Director.
General email, info@nrsc.org

Web, www.nrsc.org

Provides Republican senatorial candidates with financial and public relations services.

Republican Governors Assn., *1747 Pennsylvania Ave. N.W., #250 20006; (202) 662-4140. Fax, (202) 662-4924. Gov. Chris Christie, Chair; Phil Cox, Executive Director. Press, (202) 662-4147.*
General email, info@rga.org

Web, www.rga.org

Serves as a liaison between governors' offices and Republican Party organizations; assists Republican candidates for governor.

Republican Main Street Partnership, *325 7th St. N.W., #610 20004; (202) 393-4353. Fax, (202) 393-4354. Rep. Steven C. LaTourette, President; Amory Houghton, Chair.*
General email, news@rmsp.org

Web, www.republicanmainstreet.org

Membership: centrist Republican Party members and public officials. Develops and promotes moderate Republican policies.

Republican National Committee (RNC), *310 1st St. S.E. 20003; (202) 863-8500. Fax, (202) 863-8820. Reince Priebus, Chair; John Ryder, General Counsel. Press, (202) 863-8614.*
General email, info@gop.com

Web, www.gop.com

Develops and promotes Republican Party policies and positions; assists Republican candidates for state and national office; sponsors workshops to recruit Republican candidates and provide instruction in campaign techniques; organizes national political activities; works with state and local officials and organizations.

Republican National Committee (RNC), *Communications, 310 1st St. S.E. 20003; (202) 863-8614. Fax, (202) 863-8773. Sean M. Spicer, Director; Ryan Mahoney, Press Secretary.*
General email, RNcommunications@gop.com

Web, www.gop.com

Assists federal, state, and local Republican candidates and officials in delivering a coordinated message on current issues; works to improve and expand relations with the press and to increase the visibility of Republican officials and the Republican message.

Republican National Committee (RNC), *Counsel, 310 1st St. S.E. 20003; (202) 863-8638. Fax, (202) 863-8654. John Phillippe, Chief Counsel; John Ryder, General Counsel. Press, (202) 863-8614.*
General email, counsel@gop.com

Web, www.gop.com

Responsible for legal affairs of the RNC, including equal time and fairness cases before the Federal Communications Commission. Advises the RNC and state parties on redistricting and campaign finance law compliance.

Republican National Committee (RNC), *Finance, 310 1st St. S.E. 20003; (202) 863-8720. Fax, (202) 863-8690. Katie Walsh, Director.*
General email, finance@gop.com

Web, www.rnc.org

Responsible for developing the Republican Party's financial base. Coordinates fundraising efforts for and gives financial support to Republican candidates in national, state, and local campaigns.

Ripon Society, *1155 15th St. N.W., #550 20005; (202) 216-1008. James K. Conzelman, Chief Executive Officer.*

General email, info@riponsoc.org

Web, www.riponsociety.org

Membership: moderate Republicans. Works for the adoption of moderate policies within the Republican party.

Other Political Parties

Green Party of the United States, 7059 Blair Rd. N.W., #104 20012 (mailing address: P.O. Box 75075, Washington, DC 20013); (202) 319-7191. Brian Bittner, Office Manager. Press, (202) 518-5624.

General email, office@gp.org

Web, www.gp.org

Committed to environmentalism, nonviolence, social justice, and grassroots organizing.

Libertarian Party, 2600 Virginia Ave. N.W., #200 20037; (202) 333-0008. Fax, (202) 333-0072. Carla Howell, Executive Director. Press, (202) 333-0008, ext. 225. Toll-free, (800) 353-2887.

General email, info@hq.lp.org

Web, www.lp.org

Nationally organized political party. Seeks to bring libertarian ideas into the national political debate. Believes in the primacy of the individual over government; supports property rights, free trade, and eventual elimination of taxes.

113th Congress

Delegations to the 113th Congress

Following are the senators and representatives of state delegations for the 113th Congress. This information is current as of March 28, 2014. Senators are presented first and listed according to seniority. Representatives follow, listed by district. Freshman members appear in italics and "AL" indicates at-large members. # indicates new senators who served in the House of Representatives in the 112th Congress. $ indicates members of the House of Representatives who were elected on Nov. 6, 2012 both to finish the 112th Congress and for a full term in the 113th Congress; they are italicized with the true freshmen members.

ALABAMA

Richard Shelby (R)
Jeff A. Sessions (R)
1. *Bradley Byrne (R)*
2. Martha Roby (R)
3. Mike Rogers (R)
4. Robert B. Aderholt (R)
5. Mo Brooks (R)
6. Spencer Bachus (R)
7. Terri A. Sewell (D)

ALASKA

Lisa Murkowski (R)
Mark Begich (D)
AL Don A. Young (R)

AMERICAN SAMOA (NON-VOTING DELEGATE)

AL Eni F. H. Faleomavaega (D)

ARIZONA

John McCain (R)
Jeff Flake (R) #
1. *Ann Kirkpatrick (D)*
2. Ron Barber (D)
3. Raúl M. Grijalva (D)
4. Paul Gosar (R)
5. *Matt Salmon (R)*
6. David Schweikert (R)
7. Ed Pastor (D)
8. Trent Franks (R)
9. *Krysten Sinema (D)*

ARKANSAS

Mark Pryor (D)
John Boozman (R)
1. Rick Crawford (R)
2. Tim Griffin (R)
3. Steve Womack (R)
4. *Tom Cotton (R)*

CALIFORNIA

Dianne Feinstein (D)
Barbara Boxer (D)
1. *Doug LaMalfa (R)*
2. *Jared Huffman (D)*
3. John Garamendi (D)
4. Tom McClintock (R)
5. Mike Thompson (D)
6. Doris Matsui (D)
7. *Ami Bera (D)*
8. *Paul Cook (R)*
9. Jerry McNerney (D)
10. Jeff Denham (R)
11. George Miller (D)
12. Nancy Pelosi (D)
13. Barbara Lee (D)
14. Jackie Speier (D)
15. *Eric Swalwell (D)*
16. Jim Costa (D)
17. Mike Honda (D)
18. Anna G. Eshoo (D)
19. Zoe Lofgren (D)
20. Sam Farr (D)
21. *David Valadao (R)*
22. Devin Nunes (R)
23. Kevin McCarthy (R)
24. Lois Capps (D)
25. Buck McKeon (R)
26. *Julia Brownley (D)*
27. Judy Chu (D)
28. Adam Schiff (D)
29. *Tony Cárdenas (D)*
30. Brad Sherman (D)
31. Gary Miller (R)
32. Grace F. Napolitano (D)
33. Henry A. Waxman (D)
34. Xavier Becerra (D)
35. *Gloria Negrete McLeod (D)*
36. *Raul Ruiz (D)*
37. Karen Bass (D)
38. Linda Sanchez (D)
39. Ed Royce (R)
40. Lucille Roybal-Allard (D)
41. *Mark Takano (D)*
42. Ken Calvert (R)
43. Maxine Waters (D)
44. Janice Hahn (D)
45. John Campbell (R)
46. Loretta Sanchez (D)
47. *Alan Lowenthal (D)*
48. Dana Rohrabacher (R)
49. Darrell Issa (R)
50. Duncan Hunter (R)
51. *Juan Vargas (D)*
52. *Scott H. Peters (D)*
53. Susan Davis (D)

COLORADO

Mark Udall (D)
Michael F. Bennet (D)
1. Diana DeGette (D)
2. Jared Polis (D)
3. Scott Tipton (R)
4. Cory Gardner (R)
5. Doug Lamborn (R)
6. Mike Coffman (R)
7. Ed Perlmutter (D)

CONNECTICUT

Richard Blumenthal (D)
Chris Murphy (D) #
1. John B. Larson (D)
2. Joe Courtney (D)
3. Rosa L. DeLauro (D)
4. Jim Himes (D)
5. *Elizabeth Esty (D)*

DELAWARE

Tom Carper (D)
Christopher Coons (D)
AL John Carney (D)

DISTRICT OF COLUMBIA (NON-VOTING DELEGATE)

AL Eleanor Holmes Norton (D)

FLORIDA

Bill J. Nelson (D)
Marco Rubio (R)
1. Jeff Miller (R)
2. Steve Southerland (R)
3. *Ted Yoho (R)*
4. Ander Crenshaw (R)
5. Corrine Brown (D)
6. *Ron DeSantis (R)*
7. John Mica (R)
8. Bill Posey (R)
9. *Alan Grayson (D)*
10. Daniel Webster (R)
11. Richard Nugent (R)
12. Gus Bilirakis (R)
13. David Jolly (R)
14. Kathy Castor (D)
15. Dennis Ross (R)
16. Vern Buchanan (R)
17. Thomas J. Rooney (R)
18. *Patrick Murphy (D)*
19. Vacant
20. Alcee L. Hastings (D)
21. Ted Deutch (D)
22. *Lois Frankel (D)*
23. Debbie Wasserman Schultz (D)
24. Frederica Wilson (D)
25. Mario Diaz-Balart (R)
26. *Joe Garcia (D)*
27. Ileana Ros-Lehtinen (R)

GEORGIA

Saxby Chambliss (R)
Johnny Isakson (R)
1. Jack Kingston (R)
2. Sanford D. Bishop Jr. (D)
3. Lynn A. Westmoreland (R)
4. Hank Johnson (D)
5. John Lewis (D)
6. Tom Price (R)
7. Rob Woodall (R)
8. Austin Scott (R)
9. *Doug Collins (R)*
10. Paul C. Broun Jr. (R)
11. Phil Gingrey (R)
12. John Barrow (D)
13. David Scott (D)
14. Tom Graves (R)

GUAM (NON-VOTING DELEGATE)

AL Madeleine Bordallo (D)

HAWAII

Brian Schatz (D)
Mazie K. Hirono (D) #
1. Colleen Hanabusa (D)
2. *Tulsi Gabbard (D)*

IDAHO

Mike Crapo (R)
James E. Risch (R)
1. Raul Labrador (R)
2. Mike Simpson (R)

ILLINOIS

Richard J. Durbin (D)
Mark Kirk (R)
1. Bobby L. Rush (D)
2. *Robin Kelly (D)*
3. Daniel Lipinski (D)
4. Luis V. Gutierrez (D)
5. Mike Quigley (D)
6. Peter Roskam (R)
7. Danny K. Davis (D)
8. *Tammy Duckworth (D)*
9. Jan Schakowsky (D)
10. *Brad Schneider (D)*
11. *Bill Foster (D)*
12. *William Enyart (D)*
13. *Rodney L. Davis (R)*
14. Randy Hultgren (R)
15. John Shimkus (R)
16. Adam Kinzinger (R)
17. *Cheri Bustos (D)*
18. Aaron Schock (R)

INDIANA

Dan Coats (R)
Joe Donnelly (D) #
1. Peter Visclosky (D)
2. *Jackie Walorski (R)*
3. Marlin Stutzman (R)
4. Todd Rokita (R)
5. *Susan Brooks (R)*
6. *Luke Messer (R)*
7. André Carson (D)
8. Larry Bucshon (R)
9. Todd Young (R)

IOWA

Chuck Grassley (R)
Tom R. Harkin (D)
1. Bruce Braley (D)
2. Dave Loebsack (D)
3. Tom Latham (R)
4. Steve King (R)

KANSAS

Pat Roberts (R)
Jerry Moran (R)
1. Tim Huelskamp (R)
2. Lynn Jenkins (R)
3. Kevin Yoder (R)
4. Mike Pompeo (R)

KENTUCKY

Mitch McConnell (R)
Rand Paul (R)
1. Ed Whitfield (R)
2. Brett Guthrie (R)
3. John Yarmuth (D)
4. *Thomas Massie (R) $*
5. Hal Rogers (R)
6. *Andy Barr (R)*

LOUISIANA

Mary Landrieu (D)
David Vitter (R)
1. Steve Scalise (R)
2. Cedric Richmond (D)
3. Charles W. Boustany Jr. (R)
4. John Fleming (R)
5. *Vance McAllister (R)*
6. William Cassidy (R)

MAINE

Susan Collins (R)
Angus King (I)
1. Chellie Pingree (D)
2. Mike Michaud (D)

MARYLAND

Barbara Mikulski (D)
Benjamin L. Cardin (D)
1. *Andy Harris (R)*
2. C. A. (Dutch) Ruppersberger (D)
3. John Sarbanes (D)
4. Donna F. Edwards (D)
5. Steny Hoyer (D)
6. *John Delaney (D)*
7. Elijah E. Cummings (D)
8. Chris Van Hollen Jr. (D)

MASSACHUSETTS

Elizabeth Warren (D)
Edward J. Markey (D) #
1. Richard Neal (D)
2. Jim McGovern (D)
3. Niki Tsongas (D)
4. *Joe Kennedy III (D)*

5. *Katherine Clark (D)*
6. John F. Tierney (D)
7. Michael E. Capuano (D)
8. Stephen F. Lynch (D)
9. William Keating (D)

MICHIGAN

Carl S. Levin (D)
Debbie A. Stabenow (D)
1. *Dan Benishek (R)*
2. Bill Huizenga (R)
3. Justin Amash (R)
4. Dave Camp (R)
5. *Dan E. Kildee (D)*
6. Fred Upton (R)
7. Tim Walberg (R)
8. Mike Rogers (R)
9. Sander Levin (D)
10. Candice Miller (R)
11. *Kerry Bentivolio (R)*
12. John D. Dingell (D)
13. John Conyers Jr. (D)
14. Gary Peters (D)

MINNESOTA

Amy Klobuchar (D)
Al Franken (D)
1. Tim Walz (D)
2. John Kline (R)
3. Erik Paulsen (R)
4. Betty McCollum (D)
5. Keith Ellison (D)
6. Michele Bachmann (R)
7. Collin Peterson (D)
8. *Rick Nolan (D)*

MISSISSIPPI

Thad A. Cochran (R)
Roger Wicker (R)
1. Alan Nunnelee (R)
2. Bennie Thompson (D)
3. Gregg Harper (R)
4. Steven Palazzo (R)

MISSOURI

Claire McCaskill (D)
Roy Blunt (R)
1. William Lacy Clay Jr. (D)
2. *Ann Wagner (R)*
3. Blaine Luetkemeyer (R)
4. Vicky Hartzler (R)
5. Emanuel Cleaver II (D)
6. Sam Graves (R)
7. Billy Long (R)
8. *Jason Smith (R)*

MONTANA

John Walsh (D)
Jon Tester (D)
AL *Steve Daines (R)*

NEBRASKA

Mike Johanns (R)
Deb Fischer (R)
1. Jeff Fortenberry (R)
2. Lee Terry (R)
3. Adrian Smith (R)

NEVADA

Harry Reid (D)
Dean Heller (R)
1. *Dina Titus (D)*
2. Mark Amodei (R)
3. Joe Heck (R)
4. *Steven Horsford (D)*

NEW HAMPSHIRE

Jeanne Shaheen (D)
Kelly Ayotte (R)
1. *Carol Shea-Porter (D)*
2. *Ann McLane Kuster (D)*

NEW JERSEY

Bob Menéndez (D)
Cory Booker (D)
1. Vacant
2. Frank A. LoBiondo (R)
3. Jon Runyan (R)
4. Chris Smith (R)
5. Scott Garrett (R)
6. Frank Pallone Jr. (D)
7. Leonard Lance (R)
8. Albio Sires (D)
9. Bill Pascrell Jr. (D)
10. *Donald M. Payne Jr. (D)*
11. Rodney Frelinghuysen (R)
12. Rush Holt (D)

NEW MEXICO

Tom Udall (D)
Martin Heinrich (D) #
1. *Michelle Lujan Grisham (D)*
2. Steve Pearce (R)
3. Ben Ray Luján (D)

NEW YORK

Charles E. Schumer (D)
Kirsten Gillibrand (D)
1. Tim Bishop (D)
2. Pete King (R)
3. Steve Israel (D)
4. Carolyn McCarthy (D)
5. Gregory W. Meeks (D)
6. *Grace Meng (D)*
7. Nydia M. Velázquez (D)
8. *Hakeem Jeffries (D)*
9. Yvette D. Clarke (D)
10. Jerrold Nadler (D)
11. Michael Grimm (R)
12. Carolyn B. Maloney (D)
13. Charles B. Rangel (D)
14. Joseph Crowley (D)
15. José E. Serrano (D)
16. Eliot L. Engel (D)
17. Nita Lowey (D)
18. *Sean Patrick Maloney (D)*
19. Chris Gibson (R)
20. Paul D. Tonko (D)
21. Bill Owens (D)
22. Richard Hanna (R)
23. Tom Reed II (R)
24. *Dan Maffei (D)*
25. Louise M. Slaughter (D)
26. Brian Higgins (D)
27. *Chris Collins (R)*

NORTH CAROLINA

Richard Burr (R)
Kay Hagan (D)
1. G. K. Butterfield Jr. (D)
2. *Renee Ellmers (R)*
3. Walter B. Jones (R)
4. David Price (D)
5. Virginia Foxx (R)
6. Howard Coble (R)
7. Mike McIntyre (D)
8. *Richard Hudson (R)*
9. *Robert Pittenger (R)*
10. Patrick McHenry (R)
11. *Mark Meadows (R)*
12. Vacant
13. *George Holding (R)*

NORTH DAKOTA

John Hoeven (R)
Heidi Heitkamp (D)
AL *Kevin Cramer (R)*

NORTHERN MARIANA ISLANDS (NON-VOTING DELEGATE)

AL Gregorio Sablan (D)

OHIO

Sherrod Brown (D)
Rob Portman (R)
1. Steve Chabot (R)
2. *Brad Wenstrup (R)*
3. *Joyce Beatty (D)*
4. Jim Jordan (R)
5. Bob Latta (R)
6. Bill Johnson (R)
7. Bob Gibbs (R)
8. John Boehner (R)
9. Marcy Kaptur (D)
10. Michael Turner (R)
11. Marcia L. Fudge (D)
12. Patrick J. Tiberi (R)
13. Tim Ryan (D)
14. *David Joyce (R)*
15. Steve Stivers (R)
16. Jim Renacci (R)

OKLAHOMA

James M. Inhofe (R)
Tom Coburn (R)
1. *Jim Bridenstine (R)*
2. *Markwayne Mullin (R)*
3. Frank Lucas (R)
4. Tom Cole (R)
5. James Lankford (R)

OREGON

Ron Wyden (D)
Jeff Merkley (D)
1. Suzanne Bonamici (D)
2. Greg Walden (R)
3. Earl Blumenauer (D)
4. Peter DeFazio (D)
5. Kurt Schrader (D)

PENNSYLVANIA

Robert P. Casey Jr. (D)
Pat Toomey (R)
1. Robert Brady (D)
2. Chaka Fattah (D)
3. Mike Kelly (R)
4. *Scott Perry (R)*
5. Glenn W. Thompson (R)
6. Jim Gerlach (R)
7. Pat Meehan (R)
8. Mike Fitzpatrick (R)
9. Bill Shuster (R)
10. Tom Marino (R)
11. Lou Barletta (R)
12. *Keith Rothfus (R)*
13. Allyson Y. Schwartz (D)
14. Mike Doyle Jr. (D)
15. Charlie Dent (R)
16. Joe Pitts (R)
17. *Matthew Cartwright (D)*
18. Tim Murphy (R)

PUERTO RICO (NON-VOTING DELEGATE)

AL Pedro Pierluisi (D)

RHODE ISLAND

Jack D. Reed (D)
Sheldon Whitehouse (D)
1. David Cicilline (D)
2. Jim Langevin (D)

SOUTH CAROLINA

Lindsey Graham (R)
Tim Scott (R) #
1. Mark Sanford (R)
2. Joe Wilson (R)
3. Jeff Duncan (R)
4. Trey Gowdy (R)
5. Mick Mulvaney (R)
6. James E. Clyburn (D)
7. *Tom Rice (R)*

SOUTH DAKOTA

Tim Johnson (D)
John P. Thune (R)
AL Kristi Noem (R)

TENNESSEE

Lamar Alexander (R)
Bob Corker (R)
1. Phil Roe (R)
2. John J. Duncan Jr. (R)
3. Chuck Fleischmann (R)
4. Scott DesJarlais (R)
5. Jim Cooper (D)
6. Diane Black (R)
7. Marsha Blackburn (R)
8. Stephen Fincher (R)
9. Steve Cohen (D)

TEXAS

John Cornyn (R)
Ted Cruz (R)
1. Louie Gohmert (R)
2. Ted Poe (R)
3. Sam Johnson (R)
4. Ralph Hall (R)
5. Jeb Hensarling (R)
6. Joe Barton (R)
7. John Culberson (R)
8. Kevin Brady (R)
9. Al Green (D)
10. Michael McCaul (R)
11. Mike Conaway (R)
12. Kay Granger (R)
13. Mac Thornberry (R)
14. *Randy Weber (R)*
15. Rubén Hinojosa (D)
16. *Beto O'Rourke (D)*
17. Bill Flores (R)
18. Sheila Jackson Lee (D)
19. Randy Neugebauer (R)
20. *Joaquin Castro (D)*
21. Lamar Smith (R)
22. Pete Olson (R)
23. *Pete Gallego (D)*
24. Kenny Marchant (R)
25. *Roger Williams (R)*
26. Michael C. Burgess (R)
27. Blake Farenthold (R)
28. Henry Cuellar (D)
29. Gene Green (D)
30. Eddie Bernice Johnson (D)
31. John Carter (R)
32. Pete Sessions (R)
33. *Marc Veasey (D)*
34. *Filemon Vela (D)*
35. *Lloyd Doggett (D)*
36. *Steve Stockman (R)*

UTAH

Orrin G. Hatch (R)
Mike Lee (R)
1. Rob Bishop (R)
2. *Chris Stewart (R)*
3. Jason Chaffetz (R)
4. Jim Matheson (D)

VERMONT

Patrick P. Leahy (D)
Bernie Sanders (I)
AL Peter Welch (D)

VIRGINIA

Mark R. Warner (D)
Tim Kaine (D)
1. Rob Wittman (R)
2. Scott Rigell (R)
3. Bobby Scott (D)
4. J. Randy Forbes (R)
5. Robert Hurt (R)
6. Bob Goodlatte (R)
7. Eric Cantor (R)
8. Jim Moran (D)
9. H. Morgan Griffith (R)
10. Frank R. Wolf (R)
11. Gerald E. Connolly (D)

VIRGIN ISLANDS (NON-VOTING DELEGATE)

AL Donna M. Christensen (D)

WASHINGTON

Patty Murray (D)
Maria Cantwell (D)
    1. *Suzan DelBene (D) $*
    2. Rick Larsen (D)
    3. Jaime Herrera Beutler (R)
    4. Doc Hastings (R)
    5. Cathy McMorris
       Rodgers (R)
    6. *Derek Kilmer (D)*
    7. Jim McDermott (D)
    8. Dave Reichert (R)

    9. Adam Smith (D)
   10. *Dennis Heck (D)*

WEST VIRGINIA

Jay Rockefeller IV (D)
Joe Manchin III (D)
    1. David R. McKinley (R)
    2. Shelley Moore Capito (R)
    3. Nick Rahall II (D)

WISCONSIN

Ron Johnson (R)
Tammy Baldwin (D) #
    1. Paul Ryan (R)
    2. *Mark Pocan (D)*

    3. Ron Kind (D)
    4. Gwen Moore (D)
    5. Jim Sensenbrenner Jr. (R)
    6. Tom Petri (R)
    7. Sean Duffy (R)
    8. Reid Ribble (R)

WYOMING

Mike Enzi (R)
John Dan Barrasso (R)
AL Cynthia Lummis (R)

House Committees

The standing and select committees of the U.S. House of Representatives follow. Each listing includes the room number, office building, zip code, telephone and fax numbers, Web address, minority Web address if available, key majority and minority staff members, jurisdiction for each full committee, and party ratio. Subcommittees are listed under the full committees. Members are listed in order of seniority on the committee or subcommittee. Many committees and subcommittees may be contacted via Web-based email forms found on their Web sites.

Republicans, the current majority, are shown in roman type; Democrats, in the minority, appear in italic. The top name in the italicized list is the Ranking Minority Member. Vacancy indicates that a committee or subcommittee seat had not been filled as of March 28, 2014. The partisan committees of the House are listed on pages 748–749. The area code for all phone and fax numbers is (202). A phone number and/or office number next to either the Majority or Minority Staff Director indicates a change from the full committee's office number and/or phone number. If no numbers are listed, the individual's office number and phone number are the same as for the full committee.

AGRICULTURE

Office: 1301 LHOB 20515-6001
Phone: 225-2171   **Fax:** 225-0917
Web: agriculture.house.gov
Minority Web: democrats.agriculture.house.gov
Majority Staff Director: Nicole Scott
Minority Staff Director: Rob Larew 225-0317 1305 LHOB
   Jurisdiction: (1) adulteration of seeds, insect pests, and protection of birds and animals in forest reserves; (2) agriculture generally; (3) agricultural and industrial chemistry; (4) agricultural colleges and experiment stations; (5) agricultural economics and research; (6) agricultural education extension services; (7) agricultural production and marketing, and stabilization of prices of agricultural products and commodities (not including distribution outside of the United States); (8) animal industry and diseases of animals; (9) commodities exchanges; (10) crop insurance and soil conservation; (11) dairy industry; (12) entomology and plant quarantine; (13) extension of farm credit and farm security; (14) livestock inspection, poultry inspection, meat and meat products inspection, and seafood and seafood products inspection; (15) forestry in general, and forest reserves other than those created from the public domain; (16) human nutrition and home economics; (17) plant industry, soils, and agricultural engineering; (18) rural electrification; (19) rural development; (20) water conservation related to activities of the Department of Agriculture.
Party Ratio: R 25-D 21

Frank Lucas, Okla., Chair	*Collin Peterson, Minn.*
Bob Goodlatte, Va.	*Mike McIntyre, N.C.*
Steve King, Iowa	*David Scott, Ga.*
Randy Neugebauer, Tex.	*Jim Costa, Calif.*
Mike Rogers, Ala.	*Tim Walz, Minn.*
Mike Conaway, Tex.	*Kurt Schrader, Ore.*
Glenn Thompson, Pa.	*Marcia L. Fudge, Ohio*
Bob Gibbs, Ohio	*Jim McGovern, Mass.*
Austin Scott, Ga.	*Suzan DelBene, Wash.*
Scott R. Tipton, Colo.	*Gloria Negrete McLeod,*
Rick Crawford, Ark.	*Calif.*
Scott DesJarlais, Tenn.	*Filemon Vela, Tex.*
Chris Gibson, N.Y.	*Michelle Lujan Grisham,*
Vicky Hartzler, Mo.	*N.M.*
Reid Ribble, Wisc.	*Ann Kuster, N.H.*
Kristi Noem, S.D.	*Richard Nolan, Minn.*
Dan Benishek, Mich.	*Pete Gallego, Tex.*
Jeff Denham, Calif.	*William Enyart, Ill.*
Stephen Lee Fincher, Tenn.	*Juan Vargas, Calif.*
Doug LaMalfa, Calif.	*Cheri Bustos, Ill.*
Richard Hudson, N.C.	*Sean Patrick Maloney, N.Y.*
Rodney Davis, Ill.	*Joe Courtney, Conn.*
Chris Collins, N.Y.	*John Garamendi, Calif.*
Ted Yoho, Fla.	
Vance McAllister, La.	

Subcommittees

Conservation, Energy, and Forestry
Office: 1301 LHOB 20515   **Phone:** 225-2171
   Glenn Thompson (Chair), Mike Rogers, Bob Gibbs, Scott Tipton, Rick Crawford, Reid Ribble, Kristi Noem, Dan Benishek, Vance McAllister
   Tim Walz (Ranking Minority Member), Gloria Negrete McLeod, Ann Kuster, Richard Nolan, Mike McIntyre, Kurt Schrader, Suzan DelBene

Department Operations, Oversight, and Nutrition
Office: 1301 LHOB 20515   **Phone:** 225-2171
   Steve King (Chair), Bob Goodlatte, Bob Gibbs, Austin Scott, Stephen Lee Fincher, Vance McAllister
   Marcia L. Fudge (Ranking Minority Member), Jim McGovern, Michelle Lujan Grisham, Gloria Negrete McLeod

General Farm Commodities and Risk Management
Office: 1301 LHOB 20515   **Phone:** 225-2171
   Mike Conaway (Chair), Randy Neugebauer, Mike Rogers, Bob Gibbs, Austin Scott, Rick Crawford, Chris Gibson, Vicky Hartzler, Kristi Noem, Dan Benishek, Doug LaMalfa, Richard Hudson, Rodney Davis, Chris Collins, Vance McAllister
   David Scott (Ranking Minority Member), Filemon Vela, Pete Gallego, William Enyart, Juan Vargas, Cheri Bustos, Sean Patrick Maloney, Tim Walz, Gloria Negrete McLeod, Jim Costa, John Garamendi

Horticulture, Research, Biotechnology, and Foreign Agriculture

Office: 1301 LHOB 20515   **Phone:** 225-2171

Austin Scott (Chair), Vicky Hartzler, Jeff Denham, Stephen Lee Fincher, Doug LaMalfa, Rodney Davis, Chris Collins, Ted Yoho

Kurt Schrader (Ranking Minority Member), Suzan DelBene, Jim Costa, Marcia Fudge, Ann Kuster, Juan Vargas, Sean Patrick Maloney

Livestock, Rural Development, and Credit

Office: 1301 LHOB 20515   **Phone:** 225-2171

Rick Crawford (Chair), Bob Goodlatte, Steve King, Randy Neugebauer, Mike Rogers, Mike Conaway, Glenn Thompson, Scott DesJarlais, Chris Gibson, Reid Ribble, Jeff Denham, Richard Hudson, Ted Yoho

Jim Costa (Ranking Minority Member), Mike McIntyre, David Scott, Filemon Vela, Michelle Lujan Grisham, Pete Gallego, William Enyart, Cheri Bustos, Kurt Schrader, Richard Nolan, Joe Courtney

APPROPRIATIONS

Office: H-305 CAP 20515-6015

Phone: 225-2771   **Fax:** 225-5078

Web: appropriations.house.gov

Minority Web: democrats.appropriations.house.gov

Majority Staff Director: Will Smith

Minority Staff Director: David Pomerantz, 225-3481, 1016 LHOB

Jurisdiction: (1) appropriation of the revenue for the support of the Government; (2) rescissions of appropriations contained in appropriations acts; (3) transfers of unexpected balances; (4) Bills and Joint Resolutions reported by other Committees that provide new entitlement authority as defined in Section 3(9) of the Congressional Budget Act of 1974 and referred to the Committee under Clause 4(a)(2).

Party Ratio: R 29-D 22

Hal Rogers, Ky., Chair	*Nita Lowey, N.Y.*
Frank R. Wolf, Va.	*Marcy Kaptur, Ohio*
Jack Kingston, Ga.	*Pete Visclosky, Ind.*
Rodney Frelinghuysen, N.J.	*José E. Serrano, N.Y.*
Tom Latham, Iowa	*Rosa L. DeLauro, Conn.*
Robert B. Aderholt, Ala.	*Jim Moran, Va.*
Kay Granger, Tex.	*Ed Pastor, Ariz.*
Mike Simpson, Idaho	*David Price, N.C.*
John Culberson, Tex.	*Lucille Roybal-Allard, Calif.*
Ander Crenshaw, Fla.	*Sam Farr, Calif.*
John Carter, Tex.	*Chaka Fattah, Pa.*
Ken Calvert, Calif.	*Sanford D. Bishop Jr., Ga.*
Tom Cole, Okla.	*Barbara Lee, Calif.*
Mario Diaz-Balart, Fla.	*Adam Schiff, Calif.*
Charlie Dent, Pa.	*Mike Honda, Calif.*
Tom Graves, Ga.	*Betty McCollum, Minn.*
Kevin Yoder, Kans.	*Tim Ryan, Ohio*
Steve Womack, Ark.	*Debbie Wasserman Schultz, Fla.*
Alan Nunnelee, Miss.	

Jeff Fortenberry, Neb.	*Henry Cuellar, Tex.*
Thomas J. Rooney, Fla.	*Chellie Pingree, Maine*
Chuck Fleischmann, Tenn.	*Mike Quigley, Ill.*
Jaime Herrera Beutler, Wash.	*Bill Owens, N.Y.*
David Joyce, Ohio	
David Valadao, Calif.	
Andy Harris, Md.	
Martha Roby, Ala.	
Mark Amodei, Nev.	
Chris Stewart, Utah	

Subcommittees

Agriculture, Rural Development, Food and Drug Administration, and Related Agencies

Office: 2362A RHOB 20515   **Phone:** 225-2638

Robert B. Aderholt (Chair), Tom Latham, Alan Nunnelee, Kevin Yoder, Jeff Fortenberry, Thomas J. Rooney, David Valadao

Sam Farr (Ranking Minority Member), Rosa L. DeLauro, Sanford D. Bishop Jr., Chellie Pingree

Commerce, Justice, Science, and Related Agencies

Office: H-309 CAP 20515   **Phone:** 225-3351

Frank R. Wolf (Chair), John Culberson, Robert B. Aderholt, Andy Harris, John Carter, Mario Diaz-Balart, Mark Amodei

Chaka Fattah (Ranking Minority Member), Adam Schiff, Mike Honda, Jose E. Serrano

Defense

Office: H-405 CAP 20515   **Phone:** 225-2847

Rodney Frelinghuysen (Chair), Jack Kingston, Kay Granger, Ander Crenshaw, Ken Calvert, Tom Cole, Steve Womack, Robert Aderholt, John Carter

Pete Visclosky (Ranking Minority Member), Jim Moran, Betty McCollum, Tim Ryan, Bill Owens, Marcy Kaptur

Energy and Water Development, and Related Agencies

Office: 2362B RHOB 20515   **Phone:** 225-3421

Mike Simpson (Chair), Rodney Frelinghuysen, Alan Nunnelee, Ken Calvert, Chuck Fleischmann, Tom Graves, Jeff Fortenberry

Marcy Kaptur (Ranking Minority Member), Pete Visclosky, Ed Pastor, Chaka Fattah

Financial Services and General Government

Office: B300 RHOB 20515   **Phone:** 225-7245

Ander Crenshaw (Chair), Mario Diaz-Balart, Tom Graves, Kevin Yoder, Steve Womack, Jaime Herrera Beutler, Mark Amodei

Jose E. Serrano (Ranking Minority Member), Mike Quigley, Marcy Kaptur, Ed Pastor

Homeland Security

Office: B307 RHOB 20515   **Phone:** 225-5834

John Carter (Chair), John Culberson, Rodney Frelinghuysen, Tom Latham, Charlie Dent, Chuck Fleischmann, Jack Kingston

David Price (Ranking Minority Member), Lucille Roybal-Allard, Henry Cuellar, Bill Owens

APPROPRIATIONS (continued)

Interior, Environment, and Related Agencies
Office: B308 RHOB 20515   **Phone:** 225-3081

Ken Calvert (Chair), Mike Simpson, Tom Cole, Jaime Herrera Beutler, David Joyce, David Valadao, Chris Stewart

Jim Moran (Ranking Minority Member), Betty McCollum, Chellie Pingree, Jose E. Serrano

Labor, Health and Human Services, Education, and Related Agencies
Office: 2358B RHOB 20515   **Phone:** 225-3508

Jack Kingston (Chair), Steve Womack, Chuck Fleischmann, David Joyce, Andy Harris, Martha Roby, Chris Stewart

Rosa L. DeLauro (Ranking Minority Member), Nita Lowey, Lucille Roybal-Allard, Barbara Lee, Mike Honda

Legislative Branch
Office: HT-2 CAP 20515   **Phone:** 226-7252

Tom Cole (Chair), Andy Harris, Martha Roby, Mark Amodei, Chris Stewart

Debbie Wasserman Schultz (Ranking Minority Member), James Moran, Sanford D. Bishop Jr.

Military Construction, Veterans Affairs, and Related Agencies
Office: HVC-227 CAP 20515   **Phone:** 225-3047

John Culberson (Chair), Alan Nunnelee, Jeff Fortenberry, Thomas J. Rooney, Tom Graves, David Valadao, Martha Roby

Sanford D. Bishop Jr. (Ranking Minority Member), Sam Farr, David E. Price, Chaka Fattah

State, Foreign Operations, and Related Programs
Office: HT-2 CAP 20515   **Phone:** 225-2041

Kay Granger (Chair), Frank R. Wolf, Mario Diaz-Balart, Charlie Dent, Ander Crenshaw, Kevin Yoder, Tom Rooney

Nita Lowey (Ranking Minority Member), Adam Schiff, Barbara Lee, Debbie Wasserman Schultz, Henry Cuellar

Transportation, Housing and Urban Development, and Related Agencies
Office: 2358A RHOB 20515   **Phone:** 225-2141

Tom Latham (Chair), Frank R. Wolf, Charlie Dent, Kay Granger, Jaime Herrera Beutler, David Joyce, Mike Simpson

Ed Pastor (Ranking Minority Member), David Price, Mike Quigley, Tim Ryan

ARMED SERVICES

Office: 2120 RHOB 20515-6035
Phone: 225-4151   **Fax:** 225-9077
Web: armedservices.house.gov
Minority Web: democrats.armedservices.house.gov
Majority Staff Director: Robert L. Simmons
Minority Staff Director: Paul Arcangeli

Jurisdiction: (1) ammunition depots, forts, arsenals, Army, Navy and Air Force reservations and establishments; (2) common defense generally; (3) conservation, development, and use of naval petroleum reserves and oil shale reserves; (4) the Department of Defense generally, including the Departments of the Army, Navy, and Air Force generally; (5) interoceanic canals generally, including measures relating to the maintenance, operation, and administration of interoceanic canals; (6) Merchant Marine Academy and State Merchant Marine Academies; (7) military applications of nuclear energy; (8) tactical intelligence and intelligence-related activities of the Department of Defense; (9) national security aspects of the merchant marine, including financial assistance for the construction and operation of vessels, the maintenance of the United States shipbuilding and ship repair industrial base, cabotage (trade or transport in coastal waters or air space, or between two points within a country), cargo preference and merchant marine personnel as these matters relate to the national security; (10) pay, promotion, retirement, and other benefits and privileges of members of the armed services; (11) scientific research and development in support of the armed services; (12) selective service; (13) size and composition of the Army, Navy, Marine Corps, and Air Force; (14) soldiers' and sailors' homes; (15) strategic and critical materials necessary for the common defense. In addition to its legislative jurisdiction under the preceding provisions (and its general oversight functions under clause 2(b)(1)), the committee has special oversight functions provided for in clause 3(a) with respect to international arms control and disarmament; and education of military dependents in school pursuant to clause 3(g) of Rule X of the Rules of the House of Representatives.
Party Ratio: R 34-D 28

Buck McKeon, Calif., Chair	*Adam Smith, Wash.*
Mac Thornberry, Tex.	*Loretta Sanchez, Calif.*
Walter B. Jones, N.C.	*Mike McIntyre, N.C.*
J. Randy Forbes, Va.	*Robert Brady, Pa.*
Jeff Miller, Fla.	*Susan Davis, Calif.*
Joe Wilson, S.C.	*Jim Langevin, R.I.*
Frank A. LoBiondo, N.J.	*Rick Larsen, Wash.*
Rob Bishop, Utah	*Jim Cooper, Tenn.*
Michael Turner, Ohio	*Madeleine Z. Bordallo,*
John Kline, Minn.	*Guam*
Mike Rogers, Ala.	*Joe Courtney, Conn.*
Trent Franks, Ariz.	*Dave Loebsack, Iowa*
Bill Shuster, Pa.	*Niki Tsongas, Mass.*
Mike Conaway, Tex.	*John Garamendi, Calif.*
Doug Lamborn, Colo.	*Hank Johnson, Ga.*
Rob Wittman, Va.	*Colleen Hanabusa, Hawaii*
Duncan Hunter, Calif.	*Jackie Speier, Calif.*
John Fleming, La.	*Ron Barber, Ariz.*
Mike Coffman, Colo.	*André Carson, Ind.*
Scott Rigell, Va.	*Carol Shea-Porter, N.H.*
Chris Gibson, N.Y.	*Daniel Maffei, N.Y.*
Vicky Hartzler, Mo.	*Derek Kilmer, Wash.*
Joe Heck, Nev.	*Joaquin Castro, Tex.*
Jon Runyan, N.J.	*Tammy Duckworth, Ill.*

Austin Scott, Ga.
Steven Palazzo, Miss.
Mo Brooks, Ala.
Richard Nugent, Fla.
Kristi Noem, S.D.
Paul Cook, Calif.
Jim Bridenstine, Okla.
Brad Wenstrup, Ohio
Jackie Walorski, Ind.
Bradley Byrne, Ala.

Scott Peters, Calif.
William Enyart, Ill.
Pete Gallego, Tex.
Marc Veasey, Tex.
Vacant

Subcommittees

Intelligence, Emerging Threats and Capabilities
Office: 2120 RHOB 20515   **Phone:** 225-4151
Mac Thornberry (Chair), Jeff Miller, John Kline, Bill Shuster, Richard Nugent, Trent Franks, Duncan Hunter, Chris Gibson, Vicky Hartzler, Joe Heck
Jim Langevin (Ranking Minority Member), Susan Davis, Hank Johnson, André Carson, Daniel Maffei, Derek Kilmer, Joaquin Castro, Scott Peters

Military Personnel
Office: 2120 RHOB 20515   **Phone:** 225-4151
Joe Wilson (Chair), Walter B. Jones, Joe Heck, Austin Scott, Brad Wenstrup, Jackie Walorski, Chris Gibson, Kristi Noem
Susan Davis (Ranking Minority Member), Robert Brady, Madeleine Z. Bordallo, Dave Loebsack, Niki Tsongas, Carol Shea-Porter

Oversight and Investigations
Office: 2120 RHOB 20515   **Phone:** 225-4151
Joe Heck (Chair), Mike Conaway, Mo Brooks, Walter B. Jones, Austin Scott, Jim Bridenstine
Niki Tsongas (Ranking Minority Member), Jackie Speier, Tammy Duckworth

Readiness
Office: 2120 RHOB 20515   **Phone:** 225-4151
Rob Wittman (Chair), Rob Bishop, Vicky Hartzler, Austin Scott, Kristi Noem, J. Randy Forbes, Frank A. LoBiondo, Mike Rogers, Doug Lamborn, Scott Rigell, Steven Palazzo
Madeleine Z. Bordallo (Ranking Minority Member), Joe Courtney, Dave Loebsack, Colleen Hanabusa, Jackie Speier, Ron Barber, Carol Shea-Porter, William Enyart, Pete Gallego

Seapower and Projection Forces
Office: 2120 RHOB 20515   **Phone:** 225-4151
J. Randy Forbes (Chair), Mike Conaway, Duncan Hunter, Scott Rigell, Steven Palazzo, Rob Wittman, Mike Coffman, Jon Runyan, Kristi Noem, Paul Cook, Bradley Byrne
Mike McIntyre (Ranking Minority Member), Joe Courtney, James Langevin, Rick Larsen, Hank Johnson, Colleen Hanabusa, Derek Kilmer, Scott Peters

Strategic Forces
Office: 2120 RHOB 20515   **Phone:** 225-4151

Mike Rogers (Chair), Trent Franks, Doug Lamborn, Mike Coffman, Mo Brooks, Joe Wilson, Mike Turner, John Fleming, Richard Nugent, Jim Bridenstine
Jim Cooper (Ranking Minority Member), Loretta Sanchez, James Langevin, Rick Larsen, John Garamendi, Hank Johnson, Andre Carson, Marc Veasey

Tactical Air and Land Forces
Office: 2120 RHOB 20515   **Phone:** 225-4151
Mike Turner (Chair), Frank A. LoBiondo, John Fleming, Chris Gibson, Jon Runyan, Paul Cook, Jim Bridenstine, Brad Wenstrup, Jackie Walorski, Mac Thornberry, Walter Jones, Rob Bishop, Bradley Byrne
Loretta Sanchez (Ranking Minority Member), Mike McIntyre, Jim Cooper, John Garamendi, Ron Barber, Daniel Maffei, Joaquin Castro, Tammy Duckworth, William Enyart, Pete Gallego, Marc Veasey

BUDGET

Office: 207 CHOB 20515-6065
Phone: 226-7270   **Fax:** 226-7174
Web: budget.house.gov
Minority Web: democrats.budget.house.gov
Majority Staff Director: Austin Smythe
Minority Staff Director: Thomas S. Kahn, 226-7200, Fax: 225-9905, B-71 CHOB
Jurisdiction: (1) concurrent resolutions on the budget (as defined in Section 3(4) of the Congressional Budget Act of 1974), other matters required to be referred to the committee under Titles III and IV of that Act, and other measures setting forth appropriate levels of budget totals for the United States Government; (2) budget process generally; (3) establishment, extension, and enforcement of special controls over the federal budget, including the budgetary treatment of off-budget federal agencies and measures providing exemption from reduction under any order issued under Part C of the Balanced Budget and Emergency Deficit Control Act of 1985; (4) the Committee shall have the duty: (A) to make continuing studies of the effect on budget outlays of relevant existing and proposed legislation and to report the results of such studies to the House on a recurring basis; (B) review on a continuing basis the conduct by the Congressional Budget Office of its functions and duties; (C) hold hearings and receive testimony from Members, Senators, Delegates, the Resident Commissioner, and such appropriate representatives of Federal departments and agencies, the general public, and national organizations as it considers desirable in developing concurrent resolutions on the budget for each fiscal year; (D) make all reports required of it by the Congressional Budget Act of 1974; (E) study on a continuing basis those provisions of law that exempt Federal agencies or any of their activities or outlays from inclusion in the Budget of the United States Government, and report to the House from time to time its recommendations for terminating or modifying such provisions; (F) study on a continuing basis proposals designed to improve and facilitate the congressional budget process, and report to the House from time to time the results of such studies, together with its

BUDGET (continued)

recommendations; (G) request and evaluate continuing studies of tax expenditures, devise methods of coordinating tax expenditures, policies, and programs with direct budget outlays, and report the results of such studies to the House on a recurring basis and (H) to review, on a continuing basis, the conduct by the Congressional Budget Office of its functions and duties. Membership: The Committee on the Budget shall consist of the following Members: (A) Members who are members of other standing committees, including five Members who are members of the Committee on Appropriations, five Members who are members of the Committee on Ways and Means, and one Member who is a member of the Rules Committee; (B) one Member from the leadership of the majority party; and (C) one Member from the leadership of the minority party. No Member other than a representative from the leadership of a party may serve as a member of the Committee on the Budget during more than four Congresses in any period of six successive Congresses (The Democratic Caucus further limits Democrats, other than the Member designated by leadership, from serving more than three out of five successive congresses). The House elects a new chair at the beginning of each Congress.

Party Ratio: R 22-D 17

Paul Ryan, Wisc., Chair	*Chris Van Hollen Jr., Md.*
Tom Price, Ga.	*John Yarmuth, Ky.*
Scott Garrett, N.J.	*Bill Pascrell Jr., N.J.*
John Campbell, Calif.	*Tim Ryan, Ohio*
Ken Calvert, Calif.	*Gwen Moore, Wisc.*
Tom Cole, Okla.	*Kathy Castor, Via.*
Tom McClintock, Calif.	*Jim McDermott, Wash.*
James Lankford, Okla.	*Barbara Lee, Calif.*
Diane Black, Tenn.	*Hakeem Jeffries, N.Y.*
Reid Ribble, Wisc.	*Mark Pocan, Wisc.*
Bill Flores, Tex.	*Michelle Lujan Grisham,*
Todd Rokita, Ind.	*N.M.*
Rob Woodall, Ga.	*Jared Huffman, Calif.*
Marsha Blackburn,	*Tony Cárdenas, Calif.*
Tenn.	*Earl Blumenauer, Ore.*
Alan Nunnelee, Miss.	*Kurt Schrader, Ore.*
Scott Rigell, Va.	
Vicky Hartzler, Mo.	
Jackie Walorski, Ind.	
Luke Messer, Ind.	
Tom Rice, S.C.	
Roger Williams, Tex.	
Sean Duffy, Wisc.	

EDUCATION AND THE WORKFORCE

Office: 2181 RHOB 20515-6100
Phone: 225-4527   **Fax:** 225-9571
Web: edworkforce.house.gov
Minority Web: democrats.edworkforce.house.gov
Majority Staff Director: Juliane Sullivan
Minority Staff Director: Jody Calemine, 225-3725, 2101 RHOB

Jurisdiction: (1) elementary and secondary education initiatives including the No Child Left Behind Act, school choice for low-income families, special education (the Individuals with Disabilities Education Act), and teacher quality and training; (2) higher education programs, including the Higher Education Act, which supports college access for low- and middle-income students and helps families pay for college; (3) job training, adult education, and workforce development initiatives, including those under the Workforce Investment Act (WIA), which help local communities train and retrain workers; (4) early childhood care and preschool education programs, including Head Start and the Child Care and Development Block Grant; (5) career and technical education programs; (6) school lunch and child nutrition programs; (7) programs for the care and treatment of at-risk youth, child abuse prevention, and adoption; (8) programs for older Americans; (9) educational research and improvement; (10) work requirements under the Temporary Assistance for Needy Families (TANF) program created in the 1996 welfare reform law; (11) anti-poverty programs, including the Community Services Block Grant Act and the Low Income Home Energy Assistance Program (LIHEAP); (12) pensions, health care, and other employer-sponsored benefits covered by the Employee Retirement Income Security Act (ERISA); (13) application of the National Labor Relations Act (NLRA) to collective bargaining and union representation; (14) occupational safety and health and mine safety; (15) unpaid, job-protected leave as outlined in the Family Medical Leave Act (FMLA), as well as "comp time" or family friendly work schedules; (16) equal employment opportunity and civil rights in employment, including the Americans with Disabilities Act (ADA); (17) various temporary worker programs under the Immigration and Nationality Act; (18) wage and hour requirements under the Fair Labor Standards Act (FLSA); (19) prevailing wage requirements for federal contractors under the Davis-Bacon Act and the Service Contract Act; (20) workers' compensation for federal employees, energy employees, longshore and harbor employees, and individuals affected by black lung disease; (21) matters dealing with employer and employee relations, as well as union transparency (the Labor-Management Reporting and Disclosure Act). In addition to its legislative jurisdiction under the preceding provisions (and its general oversight function under clause 2 (b)(1)), the Committee has the special oversight function provided for in clause 3 (c) with respect to domestic educational programs and institutions, and programs of student assistance, which are within the jurisdiction of other committees.

Party Ratio: R 22-D 18

John Kline, Minn.,	*George Miller, Calif.*
Chair	*Bobby Scott, Va.*
Tom Petri, Wisc.	*Ruben Hinojosa, Tex.*
Buck McKeon, Calif.	*Carolyn McCarthy, N.Y.*
Joe Wilson, S.C.	*John F. Tierney, Mass.*
Virginia Foxx, N.C.	*Rush Holt, N.J.*
Tom Price, Ga.	*Susan Davis, Calif.*

Kenny Marchant, Tex.
Duncan Hunter, Calif.
David Roe, Tenn.
Glenn Thompson, Pa.
Tim Walberg, Mich.
Matt Salmon, Ariz.
Brett Guthrie, Ky.
Scott DesJarlais, Tenn.
Todd Rokita, Ind.
Larry Bucshon, Ind.
Trey Gowdy, S.C.
Lou Barletta, Penn.
Joe Heck, Nev.
Susan Brooks, Ind.
Richard Hudson, N.C.
Luke Messer, Ind.
Vacant

Raul M. Grijalva, Ariz.
Tim Bishop, N.Y.
Dave Loebsack, Iowa
Joe Courtney, Conn.
Marcia L. Fudge, Ohio
Jared Polis, Colo.
Gregorio Sablan, Northern
* Mariana Islands*
Frederica Wilson, Fla.
Suzanne Bonamici, Ore.
Mark Pocan, Wisc.
Vacant

Subcommittees

Early Childhood, Elementary, and Secondary Education

Office: 2181 RHOB 20515   **Phone:** 225-4527

Todd Rokita (Chair), John Kline, Tom Petri, Virginia Foxx, Kenny Marchant, Duncan Hunter, David Roe, Glenn Thompson, Susan Brooks

Carolyn McCarthy (Ranking Minority Member), Bobby Scott, Susan Davis, Raul M. Grijalva, Marcia Fudge, Jared Polis, Gregorio Sablan, Mark Pocan

Health, Employment, Labor, and Pensions

Office: 2181 RHOB 20515   **Phone:** 225-4527

David Roe (Chair), Joe Wilson, Tom Price, Kenny Marchant, Matt Salmon, Brett Guthrie, Scott DesJarlais, Larry Bucshon, Trey Gowdy, Lou Barletta, Joe Heck, Susan Brooks, Luke Messer

Vacant (Ranking Minority Member), Rush Holt, Dave Loebsack, Bobby Scott, Rubén Hinojosa, John Tierney, Raul M. Grijalva, Joe Courtney, Jared Polis, Frederica Wilson, Suzanne Bonamici

Higher Education and Workforce Training

Office: 2181 RHOB 20515   **Phone:** 225-4527

Virginia Foxx (Chair), Tom Petri, Buck McKeon, Glenn Thompson, Tim Walberg, Matt Salmon, Brett Guthrie, Lou Barletta, Joe Heck, Susan Brooks, Richard Hudson, Luke Messer

Ruben Hinojosa (Ranking Minority Member), John F. Tierney, Tim Bishop, Suzanne Bonamici, Carolyn McCarthy, Rush Holt, Susan Davis, David Loebsack, Frederica Wilson

Workforce Protections

Office: 2181 RHOB 20515   **Phone:** 225-4527

Tim Walberg (Chair), John Kline, Tom Price, Duncan Hunter, Scott DesJarlais, Todd Rokita, Larry Bucshon, Richard Hudson

Joe Courtney (Ranking Minority Member), Tim Bishop, Marcia Fudge, Gregorio Sablan, Mark Pocan

ENERGY AND COMMERCE

Office: 2125 RHOB 20515-6115
Phone: 225-2927   **Fax:** 225-1919
Web: energycommerce.house.gov
Minority Web: democrats.energycommerce.house.gov
Majority Staff Director: Gary Andres
Minority Staff Director: Phil Barnett, 225-3641, 2322-A RHOB

Jurisdiction: (1) biomedical research and development; (2) consumer affairs and consumer protection; (3) health and health facilities (except health care supported by payroll deductions); (4) interstate energy compacts; (5) interstate and foreign commerce generally; (6) measures relating to the exploration, production, storage, supply, marketing, pricing, and regulation of energy resources, including all fossil fuels, solar energy, and other unconventional or renewable energy resources; (7) conservation of energy resources; (8) energy information generally; (9) the generation and marketing of power (except by federally chartered or Federal regional power marketing authorities); the reliability and interstate transmission of, and rate-making for, all power, and siting of generation facilities, except the installation of inter-connections between Government water power projects; (10) measures relating to general management of the Department of Energy, and the management and all functions of the Federal Energy Regulatory Commission; (11) national energy policy generally; (12) public health and quarantine; (13) regulation of the domestic nuclear energy industry, including regulation of research and development reactors and nuclear regulatory research; (14) regulation of interstate and foreign communications; (15) travel and tourism. The Committee has the same jurisdiction with respect to regulation of nuclear facilities and of use of nuclear energy as it has with respect to regulation of non-nuclear facilities and of use of non-nuclear energy. In addition to its legislative jurisdiction under the preceding provisions (and its general oversight functions under clause 2(b)(1)), the Committee has the special oversight function provided for in clause 3(e) with respect to all laws, programs, and government activities affecting nuclear and other energy, and non-military nuclear energy and research and development, including the disposal of nuclear waste.

Party Ratio: R 30-D 24

Fred Upton, Mich., Chair
Ralph Hall, Tex.
Joe Barton, Tex.
Ed Whitfield, Ky.
John Shimkus, Ill.
Joe Pitts, Pa.
Greg Walden, Ore.
Lee Terry, Neb.
Mike Rogers, Mich.
Tim Murphy, Pa.
Michael C. Burgess, Tex.
Marsha Blackburn, Tenn.
Phil Gingrey, Ga.
Steve Scalise, La.

Henry A. Waxman, Calif.
John D. Dingell, Mich.
Frank Pallone Jr., N.J.
Bobby L. Rush, Ill.
Anna G. Eshoo, Calif.
Eliot L. Engel, N.Y.
Gene Green, Tex.
Diana DeGette, Colo.
Lois Capps, Calif.
Mike Doyle Jr., Pa.
Jan Schakowsky, Ill.
Jim Matheson, Utah
G. K. Butterfield Jr., N.C.
John Barrow, Ga.

ENERGY AND COMMERCE (continued)

Bob Latta, Ohio
Cathy McMorris Rodgers, Wash.
Gregg Harper, Miss.
Leonard Lance, N.J.
Bill Cassidy, La.
Brett Guthrie, Ky.
Pete Olson, Tex.
David McKinley, W. Va.
Cory Gardner, Colo.
Mike Pompeo, Kans.
Adam Kinzinger, Ill.
H. Morgan Griffith, Va.
Gus Bilirakis, Fla.
Bill Johnson, Ohio
Billy Long, Mo.
Renee Ellmers, N.C.

Doris Matsui, Calif.
Donna M. Christensen, Virgin Is.
Kathy Castor, Fla.
John Sarbanes, Md.
Jerry McNerney, Calif.
Bruce Braley, Iowa
Peter Welch, Vt.
Ben Ray Lujan, N.M.
Paul Tonko, N.Y.
John Yarmuth, Ky.

Subcommittees

Commerce, Manufacturing and Trade
Office: 2125 RHOB 20515   **Phone:** 225-2927
Lee Terry (Chair), Leonard Lance, Marsha Blackburn, Gregg Harper, Brett Guthrie, Pete Olson, David McKinley, Mike Pompeo, Adam Kinzinger, Gus Bilirakis, Bill Johnson, Billy Long, Joe Barton, Fred Upton *(ex officio)*
Jan Schakowsky (Ranking Minority Member), John Sarbanes, Jerry McNerney, Peter Welch, John Yarmuth, John D. Dingell, Bobby L. Rush, Jim Matheson, John Barrow, Donna M. Christensen, Henry Waxman (ex officio)

Communications and Technology
Office: 2125 RHOB 20515   **Phone:** 225-2927
Greg Walden (Chair), Bob Latta, John Shimkus, Lee Terry, Mike Rogers, Marsha Blackburn, Steve Scalise, Leonard Lance, Brett Guthrie, Cory Gardner, Mike Pompeo, Adam Kinzinger, Billy Long, Renee Ellmers, Joe Barton, Fred Upton (ex officio)
Anna G. Eshoo (Ranking Minority Member), Mike Doyle Jr., Doris Matsui, Bruce Braley, Peter Welch, Ben Ray Lujan, John D. Dingell, Frank Pallone Jr., Bobby L. Rush, Diana DeGette, Jim Matheson, G. K. Butterfield Jr., Henry Waxman (ex officio)

Energy and Power
Office: 2125 RHOB 20515   **Phone:** 225-2927
Ed Whitfield (Chair), Steve Scalise, Ralph Hall, John Shimkus, Joe Pitts, Lee Terry, Michael C. Burgess, Bob Latta, Bill Cassidy, Pete Olson, David McKinley, Cory Gardner, Mike Pompeo, Adam Kinzinger, H. Morgan Griffith, Joe Barton, Fred Upton (ex officio)
Bobby L. Rush (Ranking Minority Member), Jerry McNerney, Paul Tonko, John Yarmuth, Eliot L. Engel, Gene Green, Lois Capps, Mike Doyle Jr., John Barrow, Doris Matsui, Donna M. Christensen, Kathy Castor, John D. Dingell (ex officio), Henry Waxman (ex officio)

Environment and the Economy
Office: 2125 RHOB 20515   **Phone:** 225-2927
John Shimkus (Chair), Phil Gingrey, Ralph Hall, Ed Whitfield, Joe Pitts, Tim Murphy, Bob Latta, Gregg Harper, Bill Cassidy, David McKinley, Gus Bilirakis, Bill Johnson, Joe Barton, Fred Upton (ex officio)
Paul Tonko (Ranking Minority Member), Frank Pallone Jr., Gene Green, Diana DeGette, Lois Capps, Jerry McNerney, John D. Dingell, Jan Schakowsky, John Barrow, Doris Matsui, Henry Waxman (ex officio)

Health
Office: 2125 RHOB 20515   **Phone:** 225-2927
Joe Pitts (Chair), Michael C. Burgess, Ed Whitfield, John Shimkus, Mike Rogers, Tim Murphy, Marsha Blackburn, Phil Gingrey, Cathy McMorris Rodgers, Leonard Lance, Bill Cassidy, Brett Guthrie, H. Morgan Griffith, Gus Bilirakis, Renee Ellmers, Joe Barton, Fred Upton (ex officio)
Frank Pallone Jr. (Ranking Minority Member), John D. Dingell, Eliot L. Engel, Lois Capps, Jan Schakowsky, Jim Matheson, Gene Green, G.K. Butterfield Jr., John Barrow, Donna M. Christensen, Kathy Castor, John Sarbanes, Henry Waxman (ex officio)

Oversight and Investigations
Office: 2125 RHOB 20515   **Phone:** 225-2927
Tim Murphy (Chair), Michael C. Burgess, Marsha Blackburn, Phil Gingrey, Steve Scalise, Gregg Harper, Pete Olson, Cory Gardner, H. Morgan Griffith, Bill Johnson, Billy Long, Renee Ellmers, Joe Barton, Fred Upton (ex officio)
Diana DeGette (Ranking Minority Member), Bruce Braley, Ben Ray Lujan, Jan Schakowsky, G.K. Butterfield Jr., Kathy Castor, Peter Welch, Paul Tonko, John Yarmuth, Gene Green, John D. Dingell (ex officio), Henry Waxman (ex officio)

ETHICS

Office: 1015 LHOB 20515-6328
Phone: 225-7103   **Fax:** 225-7392
Web: ethics.house.gov
Majority Staff Director: Tom Rust
Counsel to the Ranking Member: Dan Taylor
Jurisdiction: all bills, resolutions and other matters relating to the Code of Official Conduct adopted under House Rule XXIII (Code of Official Conduct); with respect to Members, officers and employees of the U.S. House of Representatives, the Committee is the supervising ethics office for the U.S. House of Representatives, and is authorized to: (1) recommend administrative actions to establish or enforce standards of official conduct; (2) investigate violations of the Code of Official Conduct or of any applicable rules, laws, or regulations governing the performance of official duties or the discharge of official responsibilities; (3) report to appropriate federal or state authorities substantial evidence of a violation of any law applicable to the performance of official duties that may have been disclosed in a Committee investigation (such reports must be approved by the House or by an affirmative vote of two-thirds of the Committee); (4) render advisory opinions regarding the propriety of any current or proposed conduct of a Member, officer or employee, and issue general guidance on such

matters as necessary; and (5) consider requests for written waivers of the gift rule (clause 5 of House Rule XXV).
Party Ratio: R 5-D 5

Mike Conaway, Tex., Chair	*Linda Sánchez, Calif.*
Charlie Dent, Penn.	*Pedro Pierluisi, P.R.*
Patrick Meehan, Penn.	*Michael E. Capuano, Mass.*
Trey Gowdy, S.C.	*Yvette D. Clark, N.Y.*
Susan Brooks, Ind.	*Ted Deutch, Fla.*

FINANCIAL SERVICES

Office: 2129 RHOB 20515-6050
Phone: 225-7502   **Fax:** 226-0682
Web: financialservices.house.gov
Minority Web: democrats.financialservices.house.gov
Majority Staff Director: Shannon McGahn
Minority Deputy Staff Director: Kelly Larkin, 225-4247, B301C RHOB
   Jurisdiction: (1) banks and banking, including deposit insurance and federal monetary policy; ((2) economic stabilization, defense production, renegotiation, and control of the price of commodities, rents, and services; (3) financial aid to commerce and industry (other than transportation); (4) insurance generally; (5) international finance; (6) international financial and monetary organizations; (7) money and credit, including currency and the issuance of notes and redemption thereof; gold and silver, including the coinage thereof; valuation and revaluation of the dollar; (8) public and private housing; (9) securities and exchanges; (10) urban development.
Party Ratio: R 33-D 27

Jeb Hensarling, Tex., Chair	*Maxine Waters, Calif.*
Gary Miller, Calif.	*Carolyn B. Maloney, N.Y.*
Spencer Bachus, Ala.	*Nydia M. Velázquez, N.Y.*
Pete King, N.Y.	*Brad Sherman, Calif.*
Ed Royce, Calif.	*Gregory W. Meeks, N.Y.*
Frank Lucas, Okla.	*Michael E. Capuano, Mass.*
Shelley Moore Capito, W. Va.	*Rubén Hinojosa, Tex.*
	William Lacy Clay Jr., Mo.
Scott Garrett, N.J.	*Carolyn McCarthy, N.Y.*
Randy Neugebauer, Tex.	*Stephen F. Lynch, Mass.*
Patrick McHenry, N.C.	*David Scott, Ga.*
John Campbell, Calif.	*Al Green, Tex.*
Michele Bachmann, Minn.	*Emanuel Cleaver, Mo.*
Kevin McCarthy, Calif.	*Gwen Moore, Wisc.*
Steve Pearce, N.M.	*Keith Ellison, Minn.*
Bill Posey, Fla.	*Ed Perlmutter, Colo.*
Mike Fitzpatrick, Pa.	*Jim Himes, Conn.*
Lynn A. Westmoreland, Ga.	*Gary Peters, Mich.*
	John Carney, Del.
Blaine Luetkemeyer, Mo.	*Terri Sewell, Ala.*
Bill Huizenga, Mich.	*Bill Foster, Ill.*
Sean Duffy, Wisc.	*Daniel Kildee, Mich.*
Robert Hurt, Va.	*Patrick Murphy, Fla.*
Michael Grimm, N.Y.	*John Delaney, Md.*
Steve Stivers, Ohio	*Krysten Sinema, Ariz.*
Stephen Fincher, Tenn.	*Joyce Beatty, Ohio*
Marlin Stutzman, Ind.	*Denny Heck, Wash.*

Mick Mulvaney, S.C.	*Vacant*
Randy Hultgren, Ill.	
Dennis Ross, Fla.	
Robert Pittenger, N.C.	
Ann Wagner, Mo.	
Andy Barr, Ky.	
Tom Cotton, Ark.	
Keith Rothfus, Penn.	

Subcommittees

Capital Markets and Government Sponsored Enterprises
Office: 2129 RHOB 20515   **Phone:** 225-7502
   Scott Garrett (Chair), Robert Hurt, Spencer Bachus, Pete King, Ed Royce, Frank Lucas, Randy Neugebauer, Michele Bachmann, Kevin McCarthy, Lynn Westmoreland, Bill Huizenga, Michael Grimm, Steve Stivers, Stephen Lee Fincher, Mick Mulvaney, Randy Hultgren, Dennis Ross, Ann Wagner, Jeb Hensarling (ex officio)
   Carolyn Maloney (Ranking Minority Member), Brad Sherman, Rubén Hinojosa, Stephen F. Lynch, Gwen Moore, Ed Perlmutter, David Scott, Jim Himes, Gary Peters, Keith Ellison, Bill Foster, John Carney, Terri Sewell, Daniel Kildee, Maxine Waters (ex officio), Vacant

Financial Institutions and Consumer Credit
Office: 2129 RHOB 20515   **Phone:** 225-7502
   Shelley Moore Capito (Chair), Sean Duffy, Spencer Bachus, Gary Miller, Patrick McHenry, John Campbell, Kevin McCarthy, Steve Pearce, Bill Posey, Michael Fitzpatrick, Lynn Westmoreland, Blaine Luetkemeyer, Marlin Stutzman, Robert Pittenger, Andy Barr, Tom Cotton, Keith Rothfus, Jeb Hensarling (ex officio)
   Gregory W. Meeks (Ranking Minority Member), Carolyn B. Maloney, Rubén Hinojosa, Carolyn McCarthy, David Scott, Al Green, Keith Ellison, Nydia M. Velázquez, Stephen F. Lynch, Michael E. Capuano, Patrick Murphy, John K. Delaney, Denny Heck, Maxine Waters (ex officio), Vacant

Housing and Insurance
Office: 2129 RHOB 20515   **Phone:** 225-7502
   Randy Neugebauer (Chair), Blaine Luetkemeyer, Ed Royce, Gary Miller, Shelley Moore Capito, Scott Garrett, Lynn A. Westmoreland, Sean Duffy, Robert Hurt, Steve Stivers, Dennis Ross, Jeb Hensarling (ex officio), Spencer Bachus (emeritus)
   Michael E. Capuano (Ranking Minority Member), Nydia M. Velázquez, Emanuel Cleaver, William Lacy Clay Jr., Brad Sherman, Jim Himes, Carolyn McCarthy, Krysten Sinema, Joyce Beatty, Maxine Waters (ex officio)

Monetary Policy and Trade
Office: 2129 RHOB 20515   **Phone:** 225-7502
   John Campbell (Chair), Bill Huizenga, Frank Lucas, Steve Pearce, Bill Posey, Michael Grimm, Stephen Lee Fincher, Marlin Stutzman, Mick Mulvaney, Robert Pittenger, Tom Cotton, Jeb Hensarling (ex officio), Spencer Bachus (emeritus)

FINANCIAL SERVICES (continued)

William Lacy Clay Jr. (Ranking Minority Member), Gwen Moore, Gary Peters, Ed Perlmutter, Bill Foster, John Carney, Terri Sewell, Daniel Kildee, Patrick Murphy, Maxine Waters (ex officio)

Oversight and Investigations

Office: 2129 RHOB 20515   **Phone:** 225-7502

Patrick McHenry (Chair), Mike Fitzpatrick, Pete King, Michele Bachmann, Sean Duffy, Michael Grimm, Stephen Lee Fincher, Randy Hultgren, Ann Wagner, Andy Barr, Keith Rothfus, Jeb Hensarling (ex officio), Spencer Bachus (emeritus)

Al Green (Ranking Minority Member), Emanuel Cleaver, Keith Ellison, Ed Perlmutter, Carolyn B. Maloney, John K. Delaney, Kyrsten Sinema, Joyce Beatty, Denny Heck, Maxine Waters (ex officio)

FOREIGN AFFAIRS

Office: 2170 RHOB 20515-6050
Phone: 225-5021   **Fax:** 226-7269
Web: foreignaffairs.house.gov
Minority Web: democrats.foreignaffairs.house.gov
Majority Chief of Staff: Amy Porter
Minority Staff Director: Jason Steinbaum, 226-8467, B360 RHOB

Jurisdiction: oversight and legislation relating to: (1) foreign assistance (including development assistance, Millennium Challenge Corporation, the Millennium Challenge Account, HIV/AIDS in foreign countries, security assistance, and Public Law 480 programs abroad); (2) the Peace Corps; (3) national security developments affecting foreign policy; (4) strategic planning and agreements; (5) war powers, treaties, executive agreements, and the deployment and use of United States Armed Forces; (5) peacekeeping, peace enforcement, and enforcement of United Nations or other international sanctions; (6) arms control and disarmament issues; (7) the United States Agency for International Development; (8) activities and policies of the State, Commerce and Defense Departments and other agencies related to the Arms Export Control Act, and the Foreign Assistance Act including export and licensing policy for munitions items and technology and dual-use equipment and technology; (9) international law; (10) promotion of democracy; (11) international law enforcement issues, including narcotics control programs and activities; (12) Broadcasting Board of Governors; (13) embassy security; (14) international broadcasting; (15) public diplomacy, including international communication, information policy, international education, and cultural programs; and all other matters not specifically assigned to a subcommittee; jurisdiction over legislation with respect to the administration of the Export Administration Act, including the export and licensing of dual-use equipment and technology and other matters related to international economic policy and trade not otherwise assigned to a subcommittee, and with respect to the United Nations, its affiliated agencies and other international organizations, including assessed and voluntary contributions to such organizations.
Party Ratio: R 25-D 21

Ed Royce, Calif., Chair	Eliot L. Engel, N.Y.
Chris Smith, N.J.	Eni F. H. Faleomavaega,
Ileana Ros-Lehtinen, Fla.	Am. Samoa
Dana Rohrabacher, Calif.	Brad Sherman, Calif.
Steve Chabot, Ohio	Gregory W. Meeks, N.Y.
Joe Wilson, S.C.	Albio Sires, N.J.
Michael McCaul, Tex.	Gerald E. Connolly, Va.
Ted Poe, Tex.	Ted Deutch, Fla.
Matt Salmon, Ariz.	Brian Higgins, N.Y.
Tom Marino, Penn.	Karen Bass, Calif.
Jeff Duncan, S.C.	William Keating, Mass.
Adam Kinzinger, Ill.	David Cicilline, R.I.
Mo Brooks, Ala.	Alan Grayson, Fla.
Tom Cotton, Ark.	Juan Vargas, Calif.
Paul Cook, Calif.	Bradley Schneider, Ill.
George Holding, N.C.	Joseph Kennedy, Mass.
Randy K. Weber, Tex.	Ami Bera, Calif.
Scott Perry, Penn.	Alan Lowenthal, Calif.
Steve Stockman, Tex.	Grace Meng, N. Y.
Ron DeSantis, Fla.	Lois Frankel, Fla.
Doug Collins, Ga.	Tulsi Gabbard, Hawaii
Mark Meadows, N.C.	Joaquin Castro, Tex.
Ted Yoho, Fla.	
Luke Messer, Ind.	

Subcommittees

Tom Lantos Human Rights Commission

Office: 2170 RHOB 20515   **Phone:** 225-3599

Frank R. Wolf (Co-Chair)
James P. McGovern (Co-Chair)

Africa, Global Health, Global Human Rights, and International Organizations

Office: 259A CHOB 20515   **Phone:** 226-7812

Chris Smith (Chair), Tom Marino, Randy K. Weber, Steve Stockman, Mark Meadows

Karen Bass (Ranking Minority Member), David Cicilline, Ami Bera

Asia and the Pacific

Office: 255 FHOB 20515   **Phone:** 226-7825

Steve Chabot (Chair), Dana Rohrabacher, Matt Salmon, Mo Brooks, George Holding, Scott Perry, Doug Collins, Luke Messer

Eni F. H. Faleomavaega (Ranking Minority Member), Ami Bera, Tulsi Gabbard, Brad Sherman, Gerald Connolly, William Keating

Europe and Eurasia, and Emerging Threats

Office: 256 FHOB 20515   **Phone:** 226-6434

Dana Rohrabacher (Chair), Ted Poe, Tom Marino, Jeff Duncan, Paul Cook, George Holding, Steve Stockman

William Keating (Ranking Minority Member), Gregory W. Meeks, Albio Sires, Brian Higgins, Alan Lowenthal

Middle East and North Africa

Office: B358 RHOB 20515   **Phone:** 225-3345

Ileana Ros-Lehtinen (Chair), Steve Chabot, Joe Wilson, Adam Kinzinger, Tom Cotton, Randy K. Weber, Ron DeSantis, Doug Collins, Mark Meadows, Ted Yoho, Luke Messer

Ted Deutch (Ranking Minority Member), Gerald E. Connolly, Brian Higgins, David Cicilline, Alan Grayson, Juan Vargas, Bradley Schneider, Joseph Kennedy, Grace Meng, Lois Frankel

Terrorism, Nonproliferation, and Trade
Office: 340 FHOB 20515   **Phone:** 226-1500

Ted Poe (Chair), Joe Wilson, Adam Kinzinger, Mo Brooks, Tom Cotton, Paul Cook, Scott Perry, Ted Yoho

Brad Sherman (Ranking Minority Member), Alan Lowenthal, Joaquin Castro, Juan Vargas, Bradley Schneider, Joseph Kennedy

Western Hemisphere
Office: 257 FHOB 20515   **Phone:** 226-9980

Matt Salmon (Chair), Chris Smith, Ileana Ros-Lehtinen, Michael McCaul, Jeff Duncan, Ron DeSantis

Albio Sires (Ranking Minority Member), Gregory W. Meeks, Eni F. H. Faleomavaega. Ted Deutch, Alan Grayson

HOMELAND SECURITY

Office: H2-176 FHOB 20515-6480
Phone: 226-8417   **Fax:** 226-3399
Web: homeland.house.gov
Minority Web: chsdemocrats.house.gov
Majority Staff Director: Greg Hill
Minority Staff Director: I. Lanier Avant, 226-2616, H2-117 FHOB

Jurisdiction: (1) Overall homeland security policy; (2) Organization and administration of the Department of Homeland Security; (3) Functions of the Department of Homeland Security relating to the following: (a) Border security (except immigration policy and non-border enforcement); (b) Customs (except customs revenue); (c) Integration, analysis, and dissemination of homeland security information; (d) Domestic preparedness for and collective response to terrorism; (e) Research and development; (f) Transportation security, including cargo screening and port security. The Committee shall review and study on a continuing basis all Government activities relating to homeland security, including the interaction of all departments and agencies with the Department of Homeland Security.
Party Ratio: R 17-D 14

Michael McCaul, N.Y., Chair	*Bennie Thompson, Miss.*
Lamar Smith, Tex.	*Loretta Sanchez, Calif.*
Pete King, Calif.	*Sheila Jackson Lee, Tex.*
Mike Rogers, Ala.	*Yvette D. Clarke, N.Y.*
Paul C. Broun Jr., Ga.	*Brian Higgins, N. Y.*
Candice Miller, Mich.	*Cedric Richmond, La.*
Pat Meehan, Penn.	*William Keating, Mass.*
Jeff Duncan, S.C.	*Ron Barber, Ariz.*
Tom Marino, Penn.	*Donald M. Payne Jr., N.J.*
	Beta O'Rourke, Tex.

Jason Chaffetz, Utah
Steven Palazzo, Miss.
Lou Barletta, Penn.
Richard Hudson, N.C.
Steve Daines, Mont.
Susan Brooks, Ind.
Scott Perry, Penn.
Mark Sanford, S.C.

Tulsi Gabbard, Hawaii
Filemon Vela, Tex.
Steven Horsford, Nev.
Eric Swalwell, Calif.

Subcommittees

Border and Maritime Security
Office: H2-176 FHOB 20515   **Phone:** 226-8417

Candice Miller (Chair), Jeff Duncan, Tom Marino, Steven Palazzo, Lou Barletta

Sheila Jackson Lee (Ranking Minority Member), Loretta Sanchez, Beta O'Rourke, Tulsi Gabbard

Counterterrorism and Intelligence
Office: H2-176 FHOB 20515   **Phone:** 226-8417

Pete King (Chair), Paul C. Broun Jr., Pat Meehan, Jason Chaffetz,

Brian Higgins (Ranking Minority Member), Loretta Sanchez, William Keating

Cybersecurity, Infrastructure Protection, and Security Technologies
Office: H2-176 FHOB 20515   **Phone:** 226-8417

Pat Meehan (Chair), Mike Rogers, Tom Marino, Jason Chaffetz, Steve Daines, Scott Perry

Yvette D. Clarke (Ranking Minority Member), William Keating, Filemon Vela, Steven Horsford

Emergency Preparedness, Response, and Communications
Office: H2-176 FHOB 20515   **Phone:** 226-8417

Susan Brooks (Chair), Pete King, Steven Palazzo, Scott Perry, Mark Sanford

Donald M. Payne Jr. (Ranking Minority Member), Yvette D. Clarke, Brian Higgins

Oversight and Management Efficiency
Office: H2-176 FHOB 20515   **Phone:** 226-8417

Jeff Duncan (Chair), Paul C. Broun Jr., Lou Barletta, Richard Hudson, Steve Daines

Ron Barber (Ranking Minority Member), Donald M. Payne Jr., Beta O'Rourke

Transportation Security
Office: H2-176 FHOB 20515   **Phone:** 226-8417

Richard Hudson (Chair), Mike Rogers, Candice Miller, Susan Brooks, Mark Sanford

Cedric Richmond (Ranking Minority Member), Sheila Jackson Lee, Eric Swalwell

HOUSE ADMINISTRATION

Office: 1309 LHOB 20515-6157
Phone: 225-8281   **Fax:** 225-9957
Web: cha.house.gov
Minority Web: democrats.cha.house.gov
Majority Staff Director: Sean Moran

HOUSE ADMINISTRATION (continued)

Minority Staff Director: Kyle Anderson, 225-2061, 1307 LHOB

Jurisdiction: (1) appropriations from accounts for committee salaries and expenses (except for the Committee on Appropriations), House Information Resources, and allowances and expenses of Members, House Officers and administrative offices of the House; (2) auditing and settling of all accounts described in (1), above; (3) employment of persons by the House, including clerks for Members and committees, and reporters of debates; (4) except as provided in clause 1(q)(11), matters relating to the Library of Congress and the House Library, statuary and pictures in the United States Capitol and House office buildings, acceptance or purchase of works of art for the United States Capitol and House office buildings, the United States Botanic Garden, management of the Library of Congress, purchase of books and manuscripts; (5) except as provided in clause 1(q)(11), matters relating to the Smithsonian Institution and the incorporation of similar institutions; (6) expenditure of accounts described in (1), above; (7) Franking Commission; (8) matters relating to printing and correction of the Congressional Record; (9) measures relating to accounts of the House generally; (10) measures relating to assignment of office space for Members, Delegates, the Resident Commissioner, and committees; (11) measures relating to the disposition of useless executive papers; (12) measures relating to the election of the President, Vice President, and Members of the House of Representatives, Senators, Delegates, or the Resident Commissioner; corrupt practices, contested elections, credentials and qualifications, and federal elections generally; (13) measures relating to services to the House, including the House Restaurant, parking facilities and administration of the House Office Buildings and of the House wing of the United States Capitol; (14) measures relating to the travel of Members of the House of Representatives, Delegates, and the Resident Commissioner; (15) measures relating to the raising, reporting and use of campaign contributions for candidates for office of Representative in the House of Representatives, Delegate to the House of Representatives, and of Resident Commissioner; (16) Measures relating to the compensation, retirement and other benefits of the Members, Delegates, the Resident Commissioner, officers, and employees of the Congress. In addition to its legislative jurisdiction under the preceding provisions (and its general oversight function under clause 2(b)(1), the committee has the function of performing the duties which are provided for in clause 4(d).

Party Ratio: R 6-D 3

Candice Miller, Calif., Chair	*Robert Brady, Pa.*
	Zoe Lofgren, Calif.
Gregg Harper, Miss.	*Juan Vargas, Calif.*
Phil Gingrey, Ga.	
Aaron Schock, Ill.	
Todd Rokita, Ind.	
Richard Nugent, Fla.	

JUDICIARY

Office: 2138 RHOB 20515-6216
Phone: 225-3951   **Fax:** 225-7682
Web: judiciary.house.gov
Minority Web: democrats.judiciary.house.gov
Majority Chief of Staff: Shelly Husband
Minority Staff Director: Perry H. Apelbaum, 225-6906, B351 RHOB

Jurisdiction: (1) the judiciary and judicial proceedings, civil and criminal; (2) administrative practice and procedure; (3) apportionment of Representatives; (4) bankruptcy, mutiny, espionage, and counterfeiting; (5) civil liberties; (6) constitutional amendments; (7) criminal law enforcement; (8) federal courts and judges, and local courts in United States territories and possessions; (9) immigration policy and non-border enforcement; (10) interstate compacts generally; (11) measures relating to claims against the United States; (12) Members of Congress, attendance of members, Delegates, and the Resident Commissioner; and their acceptance of incompatible offices; (13) national penitentiaries; (14) patents, the Patent and Trademark Office, copyrights, and trademarks; (15) presidential succession; (16) protection of trade and commerce against unlawful restraints and monopolies; (17) revision and codification of the Statutes of the United States; (18) state and territorial boundaries; (19) subversive activities affecting the internal security of the United States.

Party Ratio: R 22-D 17

Bob Goodlatte, Va., Chair	*John Conyers Jr., Mich.*
Jim Sensenbrenner Jr., Wisc.	*Jerrold Nadler, NY.*
Howard Coble, N.C.	*Bobby Scott, Va.*
Lamar Smith, Tex.	*Zoe Lofgren, Calif.*
Steve Chabot, Ohio	*Sheila Jackson Lee, Tex.*
Spencer Bachus, Ala.	*Steve Cohen, Tenn.*
Darrell Issa, Calif.	*Hank Johnson, Ga.*
J. Randy Forbes, Va.	*Pedro Pierluisi, P.R.*
Steve King, Iowa	*Judy Chu, Calif.*
Trent Franks, Ariz.	*Ted Deutch, Fla.*
Louie Gohmert, Tex.	*Luis Gutierrez, Ill.*
Jim Jordan, Ohio	*Karen Bass, Calif.*
Ted Poe, Tex.	*Cedric Richmond, La.*
Jason Chaffetz, Utah	*Suzan DelBene, Wash.*
Tom Marino, Pa.	*Joe Garcia, Fla.*
Trey Gowdy, S.C.	*Hakeem Jeffries, N.Y.*
Rául Labrador, Idaho	*David Cicilline, R.I.*
Blake Farenthold, Tex.	
George Holding, N.C.	
Doug Collins, Ga.	
Ron DeSantis, Fla.	
Jason Smith, Mo.	

Subcommittees

The Constitution and Civil Justice
Office: H2-362 FHOB 20515   **Phone:** 225-2825
Trent Franks (Chair), Jim Jordan, Steve Chabot, J. Randy Forbes, Steve King, Louie Gohmert, Ron DeSantis, Jason Smith

Steve Cohen (Ranking Minority Member), Jerrold Nadler, Bobby Scott, Hank Johnson, Ted Deutch

Courts, Intellectual Property, and the Internet
Office: 517 CHOB 20515   **Phone:** 226-7680
Howard Coble (Chair), Tom Marino, Jim Sensenbrenner Jr., Lamar Smith, Steve Chabot, Darrell Issa, Ted Poe, Jason Chaffetz, Blake Farenthold, George Holding, Doug Collins, Ron DeSantis, Jason Smith, Vacant
Jerrold Nadler (Ranking Minority Member), John Conyers Jr., Judy Chu, Ted Deutch, Karen Bass, Cedric Richmond, Suzan DelBene, Hakeem Jeffries, David Cicilline, Zoe Lofgren, Sheila Jackson Lee, Steve Cohen

Crime, Terrorism, Homeland Security, and Investigations
Office: B370 RHOB 20515   **Phone:** 225-5727
Jim Sensenbrenner Jr. (Chair), Louie Gohmert, Howard Coble, Spencer Bachus, J. Randy Forbes, Trent Franks, Jason Chaffetz, Trey Gowdy, Raúl Labrador
Bobby Scott (Ranking Minority Member), Pedro Pierluisi, Judy Chu, Luis Gutierrez, Karen Bass, Cedric Richmond

Immigration and Border Security
Office: B353 RHOB 20515   **Phone:** 225-3926
Trey Gowdy (Chair), Ted Poe, Lamar Smith, Steve King, Jim Jordan, Raúl Labrador, George Holding, Vacant
Zoe Lofgren (Ranking Minority Member), Sheila Jackson Lee, Luis Gutierrez, Joe Garcia, Pedro Pierluisi

Regulatory Reform, Commercial and Antitrust Law
Office: B352 RHOB 20515   **Phone:** 225-5741
Spencer Bachus (Chair), Blake Farenthold, Darrell Issa, Tom Marino, George Holding, Doug Collins, Jason Smith
Hank Johnson (Ranking Minority Member), Suzan DelBene, Joe Garcia, Hakeem Jeffries, David Cicilline

NATURAL RESOURCES

Office: 1324 LHOB 20515-6201
Phone: 225-2761   **Fax:** 225-5929
Web: naturalresources.house.gov
Minority Web: democrats.naturalresources.house.gov
Majority Staff Director: Todd Young
Minority Staff Director: Penny Dodge, 225-6065, 1329 LHOB
Jurisdiction: (1) fisheries and wildlife, including research, restoration, refuges, and conservation; (2) forest reserves and national parks created from the public domain; (3) forfeiture of land grants and alien ownership, including alien ownership of mineral lands; (4) Geological Survey; (5) international fishing agreements; (6) interstate compacts relating to apportionment of waters for irrigation purposes; (7) irrigation and reclamation, including water supply for reclamation projects and easements of public lands for irrigation projects; and acquisition of private lands when necessary to complete irrigation projects; (8) Native Americans generally, including the care and allotment of Native American lands and general and special measures relating to claims that are paid out of Native

American funds; (9) insular possessions of the United States generally (except those affecting the revenue and appropriations); (10) military parks and battlefields, national cemeteries administered by the Secretary of the Interior, parks within the District of Columbia, and the erection of monuments to the memory of individuals; (11) mineral land laws and claims and entries thereunder; (12) mineral resources of public lands; (13) mining interests generally; (14) mining schools and experimental stations; (15) marine affairs, including coastal zone management (except for measures relating to oil and other pollution of navigable waters); (16) oceanography; (17) petroleum conservation on public lands and conservation of the radium supply in the United States; (18) preservation of prehistoric ruins and objects of interest on the public domain; (19) public lands generally, including entry, easements, and grazing thereon; (20) relations of the United States with Native Americans and Native American tribes. (21) Trans-Alaska Oil Pipeline (except ratemaking).
Party Ratio: R 26-D 21

Doc Hastings, Wash., Chair	Peter DeFazio, Ore.
Don Young, Alaska	Eni F. H. Faleomavaega, Am. Samoa
Louie Gohmert, Tex.	Frank Pallone Jr., N.J.
Rob Bishop, Utah	Grace F. Napolitano, Calif.
Doug Lamborn, Colo.	Rush Holt, N.J.
Rob Wittman, Va.	Raul M. Grijalva, Ariz.
Paul C. Broun Jr., Ga.	Madeleine Z. Bordallo, Guam
John Fleming, La.	Jim Costa, Calif.
Tom McClintock, Calif.	Gregorio Sablan, Northern Mariana Islands
Glenn Thompson, Pa.	Niki Tsongas, Mass.
Cynthia Lummis, Wyo.	Pedro Pierluisi, P.R.
Dan Benishek, Mich.	Colleen Hanabusa, Hawaii
Jeff Duncan, S.C.	Tony Cárdenas, Calif.
Scott Tipton, Colo.	Steven Horsford, Nev.
Paul Gosar, Ariz.	Jared Huffman, Calif.
Raúl Labrador, Idaho	Raúl Ruiz, Calif.
Steve Southerland, Fla.	Carol Shea-Porter, N.H.
Bill Flores, Tex.	Alan Lowenthal, Calif.
Jon Runyan, N.J.	Joe Garcia, Fla.
Markwayne Mullin, Okla.	Matt Cartwright, Penn.
Steve Daines, Mont.	Katherine Clark, Mass.
Kevin Cramer, N.D.	
Doug LaMalfa, Calif.	
Jason Smith, Mo.	
Vance McAllister, La.	
Bradley Byrne, Ala.	

Subcommittees

Energy and Mineral Resources
Office: 1333 LHOB 20515   **Phone:** 225-9297
Doug Lamborn (Chair), Louie Gohmert, Rob Bishop, Robert Wittman, Paul C. Broun Jr., John Fleming, Glenn Thompson, Cynthia Lummis, Dan Benishek, Jeff Duncan, Paul Gosar, Bill Flores, Markwayne Mullin, Steve Daines, Kevin Cramer, Vacant, Doc Hastings (ex officio)
Rush Holt (Ranking Minority Member), Steven Horsford, Matt Cartwright, Jim Costa, Niki Tsongas, Jared

NATURAL RESOURCES (continued)

Huffman, Alan Lowenthal, Tony Cárdenas, Raúl M. Grijalva, Colleen Hanabusa, Joe Garcia, Katherine Clark, Vacant, Vacant, Peter DeFazio (ex officio)

Fisheries, Wildlife, Oceans, and Insular Affairs
Office: 140 CHOB 20515 **Phone:** 226-0200
John Fleming (Chair), Don Young, Rob Wittman, Glenn Thompson, Jeff Duncan, Steve Southerland, Bill Flores, Jon Runyan, Vance McAllister, Bradley Byrne, Doc Hastings
Gregorio Kilili Camacho Sablan (Ranking Minority Member), Eni F. H. Faleomavaega, Frank Pallone Jr., Madeleine Z. Bordallo, Pedro Pierluisi, Carol Shea-Porter, Alan Lowenthal, Joe Garcia, Peter DeFazio (ex officio)

Indian and Alaska Native Affairs
Office: 1337 LHOB 20515 **Phone:** 226-9725
Don Young (Chair), Dan Benishek, Paul Gosar, Markwayne Mullin, Steve Daines, Kevin Cramer, Doug LaMalfa, Doc Hastings (ex officio)
Colleen Hanabusa (Ranking Minority Member), Tony Cárdenas, Raul Ruiz, Eni F.H. Faleomavaega, Raúl M. Grijalva, Peter DeFazio (ex officio)

Public Lands and Environmental Regulation
Office: 1017 LHOB 20515 **Phone:** 226-7736
Rob Bishop (Chair), Don Young, Louie Gohmert, Doug Lamborn, Paul C. Broun Jr., Tom McClintock, Cynthia Lummis, Scott Tipton, Raúl Labrador, Steve Daines, Kevin Cramer, Doug LaMalfa, Jason Smith, Vance McAllister, Doc Hastings (ex officio)
Raúl M. Grijalva (Ranking Minority Member), Niki Tsongas, Rush Holt, Madeleine Z. Bordallo, Gregorio Kilili, Camacho Sablan, Pedro Pierluisi, Colleen Hanabusa, Steven Horsford, Carol Shea-Porter, Joe Garcia, Matt Cartwright, Jared Huffman, Peter DeFazio (ex officio)

Water and Power
Office: 1522 LHOB 20515 **Phone:** 225-8331
Tom McClintock (Chair), Cynthia Lummis, Scott Tipton, Paul Gosar, Raúl Labrador, Doug LaMalfa, Jason Smith, Bradley Byrne, Doc Hastings (ex officio)
Grace F. Napolitano (Ranking Minority Member), Jim Costa, Jared Huffman, Tony Cárdenas, Raul Ruiz, Alan Lowenthal, Peter DeFazio (ex officio)

OVERSIGHT AND GOVERNMENT REFORM

Office: 2157 FHOB 20515-6143
Phone: 225-5074 **Fax:** 225-3974
Web: oversight.house.gov
Minority Web: democrats.oversight.house.gov
Majority Staff Director: Lawrence Brady
Minority Staff Director: David Rapallo, 225-5051, 2471 RHOB
Jurisdiction: The legislative jurisdiction of the Committee includes the following areas, as set forth in House Rule X, clause 1: (1) Federal civil service, including intergovernmental personnel; and the status of officers and employees of the United States, including their compensation,

classification, and retirement; (2) Municipal affairs of the District of Columbia in general (other than appropriations); (3) Federal paperwork reduction; (4) Government management and accounting measures generally; (5) Holidays and celebrations; (6) Overall economy, efficiency, and management of government operations and activities, including federal procurement; (7) National archives; (8) Population and demography generally, including the Census; (9) Postal service generally, including transportation of the mails; (10) Public information and records; (11) Relationship of the federal government to the states and municipalities generally; and (12) Reorganizations in the executive branch of the government.
Party Ratio: R 23-D 17

Darrell Issa, Calif., Chair	Elijah E. Cummings, Md.
John Mica, Fla.	Carolyn B. Maloney, N.Y.
Michael Turner, Ohio	Eleanor Holmes Norton,
John J. Duncan Jr., Tenn.	D.C.
Patrick McHenry, N.C.	John F. Tierney, Mass.
Jim Jordan, Ohio	William Lacy Clay Jr., Mo.
Jason Chaffetz, Utah	Stephen F. Lynch, Mass.
Tim Walberg, Mich.	Jim Cooper, Tenn.
James Lankford, Okla.	Gerald E. Connolly, Va.
Justin Amash, Mich.	Jackie Speier, Calif.
Paul Gosar, Ariz.	Matt Cartwright, Venn.
Pat Meehan, Pa.	Tammy Duckworth, Ill.
Scott DesJarlais, Tenn.	Danny K. Davis, Ill.
Trey Gowdy, S.C.	Robin Kelly, Ill.
Blake Farenthold, Tex.	Peter Welch, Vt.
Doc Hastings, Wash.	Tony Cárdenas, Calif.
Cynthia Lummis, Wyo.	Steven Horsford, Nev.
Rob Woodall, Ga.	Michelle Lujan Grisham,
Thomas Massie, Ky.	N.M.
Doug Collins, Ga.	
Mark Meadows, N.C.	
Kerry Bentivolio, Mich.	
Ron DeSantis, Fla.	

Subcommittees

Economic Growth, Job Creation and Regulatory Affairs
Office: B349B RHOB 20515 **Phone:** 225-5074
Jim Jordan (Chair), John J. Duncan Jr., Patrick McHenry, Paul Gosar, Patrick Meehan, Scott DesJarlais, Doc Hastings, Cynthia Lummis, Doug Collins, Mark Meadows, Kerry Bentivolio, Ron DeSantis
Matt Cartwright (Ranking Minority Member), Tammy Duckworth, Gerald Connolly, Danny Davis, Steven Horsford, Robin Kelly

Energy Policy, Health Care, and Entitlements
Office: B349C RHOB 20515 **Phone:** 225-5074
James Lankford (Chair), Paul Gosar, Patrick McHenry, Jim Jordan, Jason Chaffetz, Tim Walberg, Pat Meehan, Scott DesJarlais, Blake Farenthold, Doc Hastings, Rob Woodall, Thomas Massie
Jackie Speier (Ranking Minority Member), Eleanor Holmes Norton, Jim Cooper, Matt Cartwright, Tammy Duckworth, Tony Cárdenas, Michelle Lujan Grisham, Danny Davis, Steven Horsford

Federal Workforce, U.S. Postal Service, and the Census
Office: B349A RHOB 20515   **Phone:** 225-5074

Blake Farenthold (Chair), Tim Walberg, Trey Gowdy, Doug Collins, Ron DeSantis

Stephen F. Lynch (Ranking Minority Member), Eleanor Holmes Norton, William Lacy Clay Jr.

Government Operations
Office: B349A RHOB 20515   **Phone:** 225-5074

John Mica (Chair), Michael Turner, Justin Amash, Thomas Massie, Mark Meadows

Gerald Connolly (Ranking Minority Member), Jim Cooper

National Security
Office: B371C RHOB 20515   **Phone:** 225-5074

Jason Chaffetz (Chair), John Mica, John J. Duncan Jr., Justin Amash, Paul Gosar, Trey Gowdy, Cynthia Lummis, Rob Woodall, Kerry Bentivolio

John F. Tierney (Ranking Minority Member), Carolyn B. Maloney, Stephen F. Lynch, Jackie Speier, Robin Kelly, Peter Welch, Michelle Lujan Grishman

Rules
Office: H-312 CAP 20515-6269
Phone: 225-9191   **Fax:** 225-6763
Web: rules.house.gov
Minority Web: democrats.rules.house.gov
Majority Staff Director: Hugh Halpern
Minority Staff Director: Miles M. Lackey, 225-9091, 1627 LHOB

Jurisdiction: (1) the rules and joint rules (other than rules or joint rules relating to the Code of Official Conduct), and order of business of the House; (2) recesses and final adjournments of Congress.

Party Ratio: R 9-D 4

Pete Sessions, Tex., Chair	*Louise M. Slaughter, N.Y.*
Virginia Foxx, N.C.	*Jim McGovern, Mass.*
Rob Bishop, Utah	*Alcee L. Hastings, Fla.*
Tom Cole, Okla.	*Jared Polis, Colo.*
Rob Woodall, Ga.	
Richard Nugent, Fla.	
Daniel Webster, Fla.	
Ileana Ros-Lehtinen, Fla.	
Michael C. Burgess, Tex.	

Subcommittees

Legislative and Budget Process
Office: H-312 CAP 20515   **Phone:** 225-9191

Rob Woodall (Chair), Virginia Foxx, Richard Nugent, Daniel Webster, Michael C. Burgess

Alcee L. Hastings (Ranking Minority Member), Jared Polis

Rules and Organization of the House
Office: H-312 CAP 20515   **Phone:** 225-9191

Richard Nugent (Chair), Rob Bishop, Daniel Webster, Ileana Ros-Lehtinen, Pete Sessions

Jim McGovern (Ranking Minority Member), Louise M. Slaughter

SCIENCE, SPACE, AND TECHNOLOGY
Office: 2321 RHOB 20515-6301
Phone: 225-6371   **Fax:** 226-0113
Web: science.house.gov
Minority Web: democrats.science.house.gov
Majority Chief of Staff: Jennifer Brown
Minority Chief of Staff: Dick Obermann, 225-6375, 394 FHOB

Jurisdiction: (1) all energy research, development, and demonstration, and projects therefor, and all federally owned or operated non-military energy laboratories; (2) astronautical research and development, including resources, personnel, equipment, and facilities; (3) civil aviation research and development; (4) environmental research and development; (5) marine research; (6) measures relating to the commercial application of energy technology; (7) National Institute of Standards and Technology, standardization of weights and measures and the metric system; (8) the research and development programs of the Department of Energy, Environmental Protection Agency, Federal Aviation Administration, Federal Emergency Management Agency, National Aeronautics and Space Administration, National Institute of Standards and Technology, National Oceanic and Atmospheric Administration, National Science Foundation, National Space Council, National Weather Service, and United States Fire Administration; (9) outer space, including exploration and control thereof; (10) science scholarships; (11) scientific research, development, and demonstration, and projects therefor. In addition to its legislative jurisdiction under the preceding provisions (and its general oversight function under clause 2(b)(1)), the Committee has the special oversight function provided for in clause 3(f) with respect to all non-military research and development.

Party Ratio: R 22-D 18

Lamar Smith, Tex., Chair	*Eddie Bernice Johnson, Tex.*
Dana Rohrabacher, Calif.	*Zoe Lofgren, Calif.*
Ralph Hall, Tex.	*Daniel Lipinski, Ill.*
Jim Sensenbrenner Jr., Wisc.	*Donna F. Edwards, Md.*
Frank Lucas, Okla.	*Frederica Wilson, Fla.*
Randy Neugebauer, Tex.	*Suzanne Bonamici, Ore.*
Michael McCaul, Tex.	*Eric Swalwell, Calif.*
Paul C. Broun Jr., Ga.	*Daniel Maffei, N.Y.*
Steven Palazzo, Miss.	*Alan Grayson, Fla.*
Mo Brooks, Ala.	*Joseph Kennedy, Mass.*
Randy Hultgren, Ill.	*Scott Peters, Calif.*
Larry Bucshon, Ind.	*Derek Kilmer, Wash.*
Steve Stockman, Tex.	*Ami Bera, Calif.*
Bill Posey, Fla.	*Elizabeth Esty, Conn.*
Cynthia Lummis, Wyo.	*Marc Veasey, Tex.*
David Schweikert, Ariz.	*Julia Brownley, Calif.*
Thomas Massie, Ky.	*Mark Takano, Calif.*
Kevin Cramer, N.D.	*Robin Kelly, Ill.*
Jim Bridenstine, Okla.	
Randy K. Weber, Tex.	
Chris Collins, N.Y.	
Vacant	

SCIENCE, SPACE, AND TECHNOLOGY
(continued)

Subcommittees

Energy
Office: 2321 RHOB 20515   **Phone:** 225-6371
Cynthia Lummis (Chair), Ralph Hall, Frank Lucas, Randy Neugebauer, Michael McCaul, Randy Hultgren, Thomas Massie, Kevin Cramer, Randy K. Weber
Eric Swalwell (Ranking Minority Member), Alan Grayson, Joseph Kennedy, Marc Veasey, Mark Takano, Zoe Lofgren, Daniel Lipinski

Environment
Office: 2321 RHOB 20515   **Phone:** 225-6371
David Schweikert (Chair), Jim Sensenbrenner Jr., Dana Rohrabacher, Randy Neugebauer, Paul C. Broun Jr., Jim Bridenstine, Randy K. Weber
Suzanne Bonamici (Ranking Minority Member), Julia Brownley, Donna F. Edwards, Mark Takano, Alan Grayson

Oversight
Office: 2321 RHOB 20515   **Phone:** 225-6371
Paul C. Broun Jr. (Chair), Jim Sensenbrenner Jr., Bill Posey, Kevin Cramer, Vacant
Daniel Maffei (Ranking Minority Member), Eric Swalwell, Scott Peters

Research and Technology
Office: 2321 RHOB 20515   **Phone:** 225-6371
Larry Buchson (Chair), Steven Palazzo, Mo Brooks, Randy Hultgren, Steve Stockman, Cynthia Lummis, David Schweikert, Thomas Massie, Jim Bridenstine, Chris Collins
Daniel Lipinski (Ranking Minority Member), Frederica Wilson, Zoe Lofgren, Scott Peters, Ami Bera, Derek Kilmer, Elizabeth Esty, Robin Kelly

Space
Office: 2321 RHOB 20515   **Phone:** 225-6371
Steven Palazzo (Chair), Ralph Hall, Dana Rohrabacher, Frank Lucas, Michael McCaul, Mo Brooks, Larry Bucshon, Steve Stockman, Bill Posey, David Schweikert, Jim Bridenstine, Chris Collins
Donna F. Edwards (Ranking Minority Member), Suzanne Bonamici, Daniel Maffei, Joseph Kennedy, Derek Kilmer, Ami Bera, Marc Veasey, Julia Brownley, Frederica Wilson

SMALL BUSINESS

Office: 2361 RHOB 20515-6315
Phone: 225-5821   **Fax:** 226-5276
Web: smallbusiness.house.gov
Minority Web: democrats.smallbusiness.house.gov
Majority Staff Director: Lori Salley Ring
Minority Staff Director: Michael Day, 225-4038, B-343C RHOB
Jurisdiction: (1) assistance to and protection of small business, including financial aid, regulatory flexibility and paperwork reduction; (2) participation of small business enterprises in federal procurement and government contracts. In addition to its legislative jurisdiction under the preceding provisions (and its general oversight function under clause 2(b)(1)), the committee has the special oversight function provided for in clause 3(g) with respect to the problems of small business.
Party Ratio: R 14-D 11

Sam Graves, Mo., Chair	*Nydia M. Velázquez, N.Y.*
Steve Chabot, Ohio	*Kurt Schrader, Ore.*
Steve King, Iowa	*Yvette D. Clarke, N.Y.*
Mike Coffman, Colo.	*Judy Chu, Calif.*
Blaine Luetkemeyer, Mo.	*Janice Hahn, Calif.*
Mick Mulvaney, S.C.	*Donald M. Payne Jr., N.J.*
Scott Tipton, Colo.	*Grace Meng, N.Y.*
Jaime Herrera Beutler, Wash.	*Bradley Schneider, Calif.*
Richard Hanna, N.Y.	*Ron Barber, Ariz.*
Tim Huelskamp, Kans.	*Ann McLane Kuster, N.H.*
David Schweikert, Ariz.	*Patrick Murphy, Fla.*
Kerry Bentivolio, Mich.	
Chris Collins, N.Y.	
Tom Rice, S.C.	

Subcommittees

Agriculture, Energy and Trade
Office: 2361 RHOB 20515   **Phone:** 225-5821
Scott Tipton (Chair), Steve King, Blaine Luetkemeyer, Mick Mulvaney, Richard Hanna, Tim Huelskamp
Patrick Murphy (Ranking Minority Member), Kurt Schrader, Grace Meng, Ron Barber

Contracting and Workforce
Office: 2361 RHOB 20515
Phone: 225-5821
Richard Hanna (Chair), Steve King, Mick Mulvaney, Scott Tipton, Tim Huelskamp, Kerry Bentivolio
Grace Meng (Ranking Minority Member), Yvette D. Clarke, Judy Chu

Economic Growth, Tax, and Capital Access
Office: 2361 RHOB 20515
Phone: 225-5821
Tom Rice (Chair), Steve Chabot, Steve King, Mike Coffman, Mick Mulvaney, David Schweikert
Judy Chu (Ranking Minority Member), Donald M. Payne Jr., Bradley Schneider, Ron Barber

Health and Technology
Office: 2361 RHOB 20515
Phone: 225-5821
Chris Collins (Chair), Steve King, Mike Coffman, Blaine Luetkemeyer, Jaime Herrera Beutler, Tim Huelskamp
Janice Hahn (Ranking Minority Member), Kurt Schrader, Bradley Schneider

Investigations, Oversight, and Regulations
Office: 2361 RHOB 20515
Phone: 225-5821
Vacant (Chair), Steve Chabot, Jaime Herrera Beutler, Kerry Bentivolio, Chris Collins, Tom Rice
Yvette D. Clarke (Ranking Minority Member), Judy Chu, Ann Kuster

TRANSPORTATION AND INFRASTRUCTURE

Office: 2165 RHOB 20515-6256
Phone: 225-9446 **Fax:** 225-6782
Web: transportation.house.gov
Minority Web: democrats.transportation.house.gov
Majority Chief of Staff: Chris Bertram
Minority Staff Director: Jim Zoia, 225-4472, 2163 RHOB
Jurisdiction: (1) Coast Guard, including lifesaving service, lighthouses, lightships, ocean derelicts, and the United States Coast Guard Academy (New London, Conn.); (2) federal management of emergencies and natural disasters; (3) flood control and improvement of rivers and harbors; (4) inland waterways; (5) inspection of merchant marine vessels, lights and signals, lifesaving equipment, and fire protection on such vessels; (6) navigation and the laws relating thereto, including pilotage; (7) registering and licensing of vessels and small boats; (8) rules and international arrangements to prevent collisions at sea; (9) measures relating to the United States Capitol building and the Senate and House office buildings; (10) measures relating to the construction or maintenance of roads and post roads, other than appropriations therefor; but it shall not be in order for any bill providing general legislation in relation to roads to contain any provision for any specific road, nor for any bill in relation to a specific road to embrace a provision in relation to any other specific road; (11) measures relating to the construction or reconstruction, maintenance, and care of the buildings and grounds of the United States Botanic Garden, the Library of Congress, and the Smithsonian Institution; (12) measures relating to merchant marine, except for national security aspects of merchant marine; (13) measures relating to the purchase of sites and construction of post offices, customhouses, federal courthouses, and government buildings within the District of Columbia; (14) oil pollution and other pollution of navigable waters, including inland waters, coastal waters, and ocean waters; (15) marine affairs (including coastal zone management) as they relate to oil and other pollution of navigable waters; (16) public buildings and grounds of the United States generally; (17) public works for the benefit of navigation, including bridges and dams (other than international bridges and dams); (18) related transportation regulatory agencies (except the Transportation Security Administration); (19) roads and the safety thereof; (20) transportation, including civil aviation, railroads, water transportation, transportation safety (except automobile safety and transportation security functions of the Department of Homeland Security), transportation infrastructure, transportation labor, and railroad retirement and railroad unemployment (except revenue measures related thereto); (21) water power.
Party Ratio: R 33-D 27

Bill Shuster, Penn., Chair	*Nick Rahall II, W. Va.*
Don Young, Alaska	*Peter DeFazio, Ore.*
Tom Petri, Wisc.	*Eleanor Holmes Norton,*
Howard Coble, N.C.	*D.C.*
John J. Duncan Jr., Tenn.	*Jerrold Nadler, N.Y.*
John Mica, Fla.	*Corrine Brown, Fla.*
Frank A. LoBiondo, N.J.	*Eddie Bernice Johnson, Tex.*
Gary Miller, Calif.	*Elijah E. Cummings, Md.*
Sam Graves, Mo.	*Rick Larsen, Wash.*
Shelley Moore Capito,	*Michael E. Capuano, Mass.*
W. Va.	*Tim Bishop, N.Y.*
Candice Miller, Mich.	*Mike Michaud, Maine*
Duncan Hunter, Calif.	*Grace F. Napolitano, Calif.*
Rick Crawford, Ark.	*Daniel Lipinski, Ill.*
Lou Barletta, Pa.	*Tim Walz, Minn.*
Blake Farenthold, Tex.	*Steve Cohen, Tenn.*
Larry Bucshon, Ind.	*Albio Sires, N.J.*
Bob Gibbs, Ohio	*Donna F. Edwards, Md.*
Pat Meehan, Pa.	*John Garamendi, Calif.*
Richard Hanna, N.Y.	*André Carson, Ind.*
Daniel Webster, Fla.	*Janice Hahn, Calif.*
Steve Southerland II, Fla.	*Richard Nolan, Minn.*
Jeff Denham, Calif.	*Ann Kirkpatrick, Ariz.*
Reid Ribble, Wisc.	*Dina Titus, Nev.*
Thomas Massie, Ky.	*Sean Patrick Maloney, N.Y.*
Steve Daines, Mont.	*Elizabeth Esty, Conn.*
Tom Rice, S.C.	*Lois Frankel, Fla.*
Markwayne Mullin, Okla.	*Cheri Bustos, Ill.*
Roger Williams, Tex.	
Mark Meadows, N.C.	
Scott Perry, Penn.	
Rodney Davis, Ill.	
Mark Sanford, S.C.	
David Jolly, Fla.	

Subcommittees

Aviation
Office: 2251 RHOB 20515 **Phone:** 226-3220
Frank A. LoBiondo (Chair), Tom Petri, Howard Coble, John J. Duncan Jr., Sam Graves, Blake Farenthold, Larry Bucshon, Pat Meehan, Richard Hanna, Daniel Webster, Jeff Denham, Reid Ribble, Thomas Massie, Steve Daines, Roger Williams, Mark Meadows, Rodney Davis, Bill Shuster (ex officio)
Rick Larsen (Ranking Minority Member), Peter DeFazio, Eddie Bernice Johnson, Michael E. Capuano, Daniel Lipinski, Steve Cohen, André Carson, Richard Nolan, Dina Titus, Sean Patrick Maloney, Cheri Bustos, Corrine Brown, Elizabeth Esty, Nick Rahall II (ex officio)

Coast Guard and Maritime Transportation
Office: 507 FHOB 20515 **Phone:** 226-3552
Duncan Hunter (Chair), Don Young, Howard Coble, Frank LoBiondo, Pat Meehan, Steve Southerland II, Tom Rice, Mark Sanford, David Jolly, Bill Shuster (ex officio)
John Garamendi (Ranking Minority Member), Elijah E. Cummings, Rick Larsen, Timothy Bishop, Lois Frankel, Corrine Brown, Janice Hahn, Nick Rahill II (ex officio)

Economic Development, Public Buildings, and Emergency Management
Office: 585 FHOB 20515 **Phone:** 225-3014
Lou Barletta (Chair), Tom Petri, John Mica, Rick Crawford, Blake Farenthold, Markwayne Mullin, Mark Meadows, Scott Perry, Mark Sanford, Bill Shuster (ex officio)
André Carson (Ranking Minority Member), Eleanor Holmes Norton, Mike Michaud, Tim Walz, Donna

TRANSPORTATION AND INFRASTRUCTURE
(continued)

F. Edwards, Richard Nolan, Dina Titus, Nick Rahill II (ex officio)

Highways and Transit
Office: B376 RHOB 20515   **Phone:** 225-6715

Tom Petri (Chair), Don Young, Howard Coble, John J. Duncan Jr., John Mica, Frank A. LoBiondo, Gary Miller, Sam Graves, Shelley Moore Capito, Duncan Hunter, Rick Crawford, Lou Barletta, Blake Farenthold, Larry Bucshon, Bob Gibbs, Richard Hanna, Steve Southerland, Reid Ribble, Steve Daines, Tom Rice, Markwayne Mullin, Roger Williams, Scott Perry, Rodney Davis, Bill Shuster (ex officio)

Eleanor Holmes Norton (Ranking Minority Member), Peter DeFazio, Jerrold Nadler, Eddie Bernice Johnson, Michael E. Capuano, Mike Michaud, Grace F. Napolitano, Tim Walz, Steve Cohen, Albio Sires, Donna F. Edwards, Janice Hahn, Richard Nolan, Ann Kirkpatrick, Dina Titus, Sean Patrick Maloney, Elizabeth Esty, Lois Frankel, Cheri Bustos, Nick Rahill II (ex officio)

Railroads, Pipelines, and Hazardous Materials
Office: B376 RHOB 20515   **Phone:** 226-0727

Jeff Denham (Chair), John J. Duncan Jr., John Mica, Gary Miller, Sam Graves, Shelley Moore Capito, Candice Miller, Lou Barletta, Larry Bucshon, Bob Gibbs, Pat Meehan, Richard Hanna, Daniel Webster, Thomas Massie, Roger Williams, Scott Perry, Bill Shuster (ex officio)

Corrine Brown (Ranking Minority Member), Daniel Lipinski, Jerrold Nadler, Elijah Cummings, Mike Michaud, Grace F. Napolitano, Tim Walz, Albio Sires, Janice Hahn, Ann Kirkpatrick, Elizabeth Esty, Peter DeFazio, Michael E. Capuano, Nick Rahill II (ex officio)

Water Resources and Environment
Office: B370A RHOB 20515   **Phone:** 225-4360

Bob Gibbs (Chair), Don Young, Gary Miller, Shelley Moore Capito, Candice Miller, Rick Crawford, Richard Hanna, Daniel Webster, Jeff Denham, Reid Ribble, Thomas Massie, Steve Daines, Tom Rice, Markwayne Mullin, Mark Meadows, Rodney Davis, Mark Sanford, David Jolly, Bill Shuster (ex officio)

Tim Bishop (Ranking Minority Member), Donna F. Edwards, John Garamendi, Lois Frankel, Eleanor Holmes Norton, Eddie Bernice Johnson, Grace F. Napolitano, Steve Cohen, Janice Hahn, Richard Nolan, Ann Kirkpatrick, Dina Titus, Sean Patrick Maloney, Nick Rahill II (ex officio)

VETERANS' AFFAIRS

Office: 335 CHOB 20515-6335
Phone: 225-3527   **Fax:** 225-5486
Web: veterans.house.gov
Minority Web: democrats.veterans.house.gov
Majority Staff Director: Jon Towers
Minority Staff Director: Nancy Dolan, 225-9756, 333 CHOB
Jurisdiction: (1) veterans measures generally; (2) National Cemeteries; (3) compensation, vocational rehabilitation,

and education of veterans; (4) life insurance issued by the government on account of service in the Armed Forces; (5) pensions of all the wars of the United States, general and special; (6) readjustment of service personnel to civil life; (7) Soldiers' and Sailors' Civil Relief; (8) veterans hospitals, medical care and treatment of veterans.
Party Ratio: R 14-D 11

Jeff Miller, Fla., Chair.	*Mike Michaud, Maine.*
Doug Lamborn, Colo.	*Corrine Brown, Fla.*
Gus Bilirakis, Fla.	*Mark Takano, Calif.*
David Roe, Tenn.	*Julia Brownley, Calif.*
Bill Flores, Tex.	*Dina Titus, Nev.*
Jeff Denham, Calif.	*Ann Kirkpatrick, Ariz.*
Jon Runyan, N.J.	*Raul Ruiz, Calif.*
Dan Benishek, Mich.	*Gloria Negrete McLeod,*
Tim Huelskamp, Kans.	*Calif.*
Mark Amodei, Nev.	*Ann Kuster, N.H.*
Mike Coffman, Colo.	*Beto O'Rourke, Tex.*
Brad Wenstrup, Ohio	*Tim Walz, Minn.*
Paul Cook, Calif.	
Jackie Walorski, Ind.	
David Jolly, Fla.	

Subcommittees

Disability Assistance and Memorial Affairs
Office: 337 CHOB 20515   **Phone:** 225-9164

Jon Runyan (Chair), Doug Lamborn, Gus Bilirakis, Mark Amodei, Paul Cook

Dina Titus (Ranking Minority Member), Beto O'Rourke, Raul Ruiz, Gloria Negrete McLeod

Economic Opportunity
Office: 335 CHOB 20515   **Phone:** 226-5491

Bill Flores (Chair), Jon Runyan, Mike Coffman, Paul Cook, Brad Wenstrup

Mark Takano (Ranking Minority Member), Julia Brownley, Dina Titus, Ann Kirkpatrick

Health
Office: 338 CHOB 20515   **Phone:** 225-9154

Dan Benishek (Chair), David Roe, Jeff Dunham, Tim Huelskamp, Jackie Walorski, Brad Wenstrup, Vacant

Julia Brownley (Ranking Minority Member), Corrine Brown, Raul Ruiz, Gloria Negrete McLeod, Ann Kuster

Oversight and Investigations
Office: 337A CHOB 20515   **Phone:** 225-3569

Mike Coffman (Chair), Doug Lamborn, David Roe, Tim Huelskamp, Dan Benishek, Jackie Walorski

Ann Kirkpatrick (Ranking Minority Member), Mark Takano, Ann Kuster, Beto O'Rourke, Tim Walz

WAYS AND MEANS

Office: 1102 LHOB 20515-6348
Phone: 225-3625   **Fax:** 225-2610
Web: waysandmeans.house.gov
Minority Web: democrats.waysandmeans.house.gov
Majority Staff Director: Jennifer M. Safavian
Minority Chief Counsel: Janice A. Mays, 225-4021, 1106 LHOB

Jurisdiction: (1) customs revenue, collection districts, and ports of entry and delivery; (2) reciprocal trade agreements; (3) revenue measures generally; (4) revenue measures relating to the insular possessions; (5) the bonded debt of the United States (subject to the last sentence of clause 4(f) of Rule X); (6) the deposit of public monies; (7) transportation of dutiable goods; (8) tax exempt foundations and charitable trusts; (9) National Social Security, except (A) health care and facilities programs that are supported from general revenues as opposed to payroll deductions and (B) work incentive programs.

Party Ratio: R 23-D 16

Dave Camp, Mich., Chair	Sander Levin, Mich.
Sam Johnson, Tex.	Charles B. Rangel, N.Y.
Kevin Brady, Tex.	Jim McDermott, Wash.
Paul Ryan, Wisc.	John Lewis, Ga.
Devin Nunes, Calif.	Richard Neal, Mass.
Patrick J. Tiberi, Ohio	Xavier Becerra, Calif.
Dave Reichert, Wash.	Lloyd Doggett, Tex.
Charles W. Boustany Jr., La.	Mike Thompson, Calif.
Peter Roskam, Ill.	John B. Larson, Conn.
Jim Gerlach, Penn.	Earl Blumenauer, Ore.
Tom Price, Ga.	Ron Kind, Wisc.
Vern Buchanan, Fla.	Bill Pascrell Jr., N.J.
Adrian Smith, Neb.	Joseph Crowley, N.Y.
Aaron Schock, Ill.	Allyson Schwartz, Penn.
Lynn Jenkins, Kans.	Danny Davis, Ill.
Erik Paulsen, Minn.	Linda Sánchez, Calif.
Kenny Marchant, Tex.	
Diane Black, Tenn.	
Tom Reed, N.Y.	
Todd Young, Ind.	
Mike Kelly, Penn.	
Tim Griffin, Ark.	
James Renacci, Ohio	

Subcommittees

Health

Office: 1135 LHOB 20515   **Phone:** 225-3943

Kevin Brady (Chair), Sam Johnson, Paul Ryan, Devin Nunes, Peter Roskam, Jim Gerlach, Tom Price, Vern Buchanan, Adrian Smith

Jim McDermott (Ranking Minority Member), Mike Thompson, Ron Kind, Earl Blumenauer, Bill Pascrell Jr.

Human Resources

Office: 1129 LHOB 20515   **Phone:** 225-1025

David Reichert (Chair), Todd Young, Mike Kelly, Tim Griffin, James Renacci, Tom Reed, Charles W. Boustany Jr.

Lloyd Doggett (Ranking Minority Member), John Lewis, Joseph Crowley, Danny Davis

Oversight

Office: 1136 LHOB 20515   **Phone:** 225-5522

Charles W. Boustany Jr. (Chair), Diane Black, Lynn Jenkins, Kenny Marchant, Tom Reed, Erik Paulsen, Mike Kelly

John Lewis (Ranking Minority Member), Joseph Crowley, Danny Davis, Linda Sánchez

Select Revenue Measures

Office: 1136 LHOB 20515   **Phone:** 225-5522

Patrick J. Tiberi (Chair), Erik Paulsen, Kenny Marchant, Jim Gerlach, Aaron Schock, Tom Reed, Todd Young

Richard Neal (Ranking Minority Member), John B. Larson, Allyson Schwartz, Linda Sánchez

Social Security

Office: B317 RHOB 20515   **Phone:** 225-9263

Sam Johnson (Chair), Patrick J. Tiberi, Tim Griffin, James Renacci, Aaron Schock, Mike Kelly, Kevin Brady

Xavier Becerra (Ranking Minority Member), Lloyd Doggett, Mike Thompson, Allyson Schwartz

Trade

Office: 1104 LHOB 20515   **Phone:** 225-6649

Devin Nunes (Chair), Kevin Brady, David Reichert, Vern Buchanan, Adrian Smith, Aaron Schock, Lynn Jenkins, Charles W. Boustany Jr., Peter Roskam

Charles B. Rangel (Ranking Minority Member), Richard Neal, John B. Larson, Earl Blumenauer, Ron Kind

PERMANENT SELECT INTELLIGENCE

Office: HVC-304 CAP 20515-6415
Phone: 225-4121   **Fax:** 225-1991
Web: intelligence.house.gov
Minority Web: democrats.intelligence.house.gov
Majority Staff Director: Darren Dick
Minority Staff Director: Heather Molino, 225-7690, HVC-304 CAP

Jurisdiction: (a)(1) There is established a Permanent Select Committee on Intelligence (hereafter in this clause referred to as the "select committee"). The select committee shall be composed of not more than 20 Members, Delegates, or the Resident Commissioner, of whom not more than 12 may be from the same party. The select committee shall include at least one Member, Delegate, or the Resident Commissioner from each of the following committees: (A) the Committee on Appropriations; (B) the Committee on Armed Services; (C) the Committee on Foreign Affairs; and (D) the Committee on the Judiciary. (2) The Speaker and the Minority Leader shall be ex officio members of the select committee but shall have no vote in the select committee and may not be counted for purposes of determining a quorum thereof. (3) The Speaker and Minority Leader each may designate a respective leadership staff member to assist in the capacity of the Speaker or Minority Leader as ex officio member, with the same access to committee meetings, hearings, briefings, and materials as employees of the select committee and subject to the same security clearance and confidentiality requirements as employees of the select committee under this clause. (4)(A) Except as permitted by subdivision (B), a Member, Delegate, or Resident Commissioner, other than the Speaker or the Minority Leader, may not serve as a member of the select committee during more than four Congresses in a period of six successive Congresses (disregarding for this purpose any service for less than a full session in a Congress). (B) In the case of a Member, Delegate, or Resident Commissioner appointed to serve as the chair or the

PERMANENT SELECT INTELLIGENCE
(continued)

ranking minority member of the select committee, tenure on the select committee shall not be limited. (b)(1) There shall be referred to the select committee proposed legislation, messages, petitions, memorials, and other matters relating to the following: (A) The Central Intelligence Agency, the Director of National Intelligence, and the National Intelligence Program as defined in section 3(6) of the National Security Act of 1947. (B) Intelligence and intelligence-related activities of all other departments and agencies of the Government, including the tactical intelligence and intelligence-related activities of the Department of Defense. (C) The organization or reorganization of a department or agency of the Government to the extent that the organization or reorganization relates to a function or activity involving intelligence or intelligence-related activities. (D) Authorizations for appropriations, both direct and indirect, for the following: (i) The Central Intelligence Agency, the Director of National Intelligence, and the National Intelligence Program as defined in section 3 (6) of the National Security Act of 1947. (ii) Intelligence and intelligence related activities of all other departments and agencies of the Government, including the tactical intelligence and intelligence-related activities of the Department of Defense. (iii) A department, agency, subdivision, or program that is a successor to an agency or program named or referred to in (i) or (ii).

Party Ratio: R 12-D 9

Mike Rogers, Mich., Chair	*C. A. Ruppersberger, Md.*
Mac Thornberry, Tex.	*Mike Thompson, Calif.*
Jeff Miller, Fla.	*Jan Schakowsky, Ill.*
Mike Conaway, Tex.	*Jim Langevin, R.I.*
Pete King, N.Y.	*Adam Schiff, Calif.*
Frank A. LoBiondo, N.J.	*Luis V. Gutierrez, Ill.*
Devin Nunes, Calif.	*Ed Pastor, Ariz.*
Lynn A. Westmoreland, Ga.	*Jim Himes, Conn.*
Michele Bachmann, Minn.	*Terri Sewell, Ala.*
Thomas J. Rooney, Fla.	
Joe Heck, Nev.	
Mike Pompeo, Kans.	

Subcommittees

Oversight and Investigations
Office: HVC-304 CAP 20515   **Phone:** 225-4121
Lynn A. Westmoreland (Chair), Jeff Miller, Michele Bachmann, Thomas J. Rooney, Mike Pompeo
Jan Schakowsky (Ranking Minority Member), Ed Pastor, Jim Himes

Technical and Tactical Intelligence
Office: HVC-304 CAP 20515   **Phone:** 225-4121
Joe Heck (Chair), Mac Thornberry, Frank A. LoBiondo, Michele Bachmann, Mike Pompeo
Adam Schiff (Ranking Minority Member), Jim Langevin, Terri Sewell

Terrorism, Human Intelligence, Analysis, and Counterintelligence
Office: HVC-304 CAP 20515   **Phone:** 225-4121
Mike Conaway (Chair), Pete King, Frank A. LoBiondo, Devin Nunes, Thomas J. Rooney
Mike Thompson (Ranking Minority Member), Luis V. Gutierrez, Jim Himes

HOUSE LEADERSHIP AND PARTISAN COMMITTEES

REPUBLICAN LEADERS

Speaker of the House: John Boehner, Ohio
Majority Leader: Eric Cantor, Va.
Majority Whip: Kevin McCarthy, Calif.
Chief Deputy Majority Whip: Peter Roskam, Ill.

REPUBLICAN PARTISAN COMMITTEES

National Republican Congressional Committee
Office: 320 1st St. S.E. 20003-1838
Phone: 479-7000   **Fax:** 863-0693
Web: www.nrcc.org
Email: website@nrcc.org
Greg Walden, Ore., Chair
Other Leadership (in alphabetical order)
Jaime Herrera Beutler, Wash., Coalitions Vice Chair
Jason Chaffetz, Utah, Digitial Vice Chair
Cory Gardner, Colo., Patriot Program Vice Chair
Tom Graves, Ga., Coalitions Vice Chair
Tim Griffin, Ark., Communications and Strategy Vice Chair
Tom Price, Ga., Policy Vice Chair
Reid Ribble, Wisc., Patriot Program Vice Chair
Steve Stivers, Ohio, Finance Vice Chair

Republican Conference
Office: 202A CHOB 20515
Phone: 225-5107   **Fax:** 226-0154
Web: www.gop.gov
Email: GOP@mail.house.gov
Cathy McMorris Rodgers, Wash., Chair
Lynn Jenkins, Kans., Vice Chair
Virginia Foxx, N.C., Secretary

Republican Policy Committee
Office: 228 CHOB 20515-6549
Phone: 225-2132   **Fax:** 225-4656
Web: policy.house.gov
James Lankford, Okla., Chair

Republican Steering Committee
Office: 1011 LHOB 20515-3508
Phone: 225-6205   **Fax:** 225-0704
Web: speaker.house.gov
John A. Boehner, Ohio, Speaker of the House
Eric Cantor, Va., Majority Leader

DEMOCRATIC LEADERS

Minority Leader: *Nancy Pelosi, Calif.*
Minority Whip: *Steny Hoyer, Md.*
Assistant to the Democratic Leader: *James E. Clyburn, S.C.*

DEMOCRATIC PARTISAN COMMITTEES

Democratic Congressional Campaign Committee
Office: 430 S. Capitol St. S.E. 20003-4024
Phone: 863-1500 **Fax:** 485-3412
Web: www.dccc.org
Email: dccc@dccc.org
Steve Israel, N.Y., Chair
Other Leadership (in alphabetical order)
James E. Clyburn, S.C., National Mobilization Chair
Joe Crowley, N.Y., D.C. Finance Chair
Donna Edwards, Recruitment Chair
Jim Himes, Conn., National Finance Chair, Business Council Co-Chair

Richard Neal, Mass., Business Council Co-Chair
Gary Peters, Mich., Recruitment Vice Chair
Jared Polis, Colo., Candidate Services National Chair
Terri Sewell, Ala., Business Council Co-Chair
Tim Walz, Minn., Frontline Program Chair

Democratic Caucus
Office: 1420 LHOB 20515
Phone: 225-1400 **Fax:** 226-4412
Web: www.dems.gov
Email: democratic.caucus@mail.house.gov
Xavier Becerra, Calif., Chair
Joe Crowley, N.Y., Vice Chair

Democratic Steering and Policy Committee
Office: 235 CHOB 20515
Phone: 225-4965 **Fax:** 224-4188
Rosa L. DeLauro, Conn., Co-Chair
Rob Andrews, N.J., Co-Chair
Karen Bass, Calif., Chair of Organization, Study, and Review

House Members' Offices

Listed below are House members and their party, state, and district affiliation, followed by the address and telephone number for their Washington office. The area code for all Washington, D.C., numbers is 202. The top administrative aide, Web address, Facebook page, and Twitter account for each member are also provided, when available. Most members may be contacted via the Web-based email forms found on their Web sites. These are followed by the address, telephone and fax numbers, and name of a key aide in the member's district office(s). Each listing concludes with the representative's committee assignments. For partisan committee assignments, see page 748–749.

As of March 28, 2014, there were 233 Republicans, 199 Democrats, 0 Independents, 3 vacancies (Florida District 19, North Carolina District 12, and New Jersey District 1), and 5 non-voting members in the House of Representatives.

Aderholt, Robert B., R-Ala. (4)

Capitol Hill Office: 2369 RHOB 20515; 225-4876;
Fax: 225-5587; *Chief of Staff:* Brian Rell
Web: http://aderholt.house.gov/
Facebook: http://facebook.com/RobertAderholt
Twitter: http://twitter.com/robert_aderholt
District Offices: 205 4th Ave., N.E., #104, Cullman, AL 35055-1965; 256-734-6043; Fax: 256-737-0885;
Director of Constituent Services: Jennifer Butler-Taylor
Federal Bldg., 600 Broad St., #107, Gadsden, AL 35901-3745; 256-546-0201; Fax: 256-546-8778; *Field Rep.:* Joseph Morgan
Carl Elliott Federal Bldg., 1710 Alabama Ave., #247, Jasper, AL 35501-5400; 205-221-2310; Fax: 205-221-9035; *District Field Director:* Paul Housel
1011 George Wallace Blvd., #146, Tuscumbia, AL 35674; 256-381-3450; Fax: 256-381-7659; *Field Rep.:* Kreg Kennedy
Committee Assignments: Commission on Security and Cooperation in Europe (Helsinki Commission); Appropriations

Amash, Justin, R-Mich. (3)

Capitol Hill Office: 114 CHOB 20515-2203; 225-3831;
Fax: 225-5144; *Chief of Staff:* Will Adams
Web: http://amash.house.gov/
Facebook: http://facebook.com/repjustinamash
Twitter: http://twitter.com/repjustinamash
District Office: 110 Michigan St., N.W., #460, Grand Rapids, MI 49503-2313; 616-451-8383; Fax: 616-454-5630; *District Director:* Jordan Bush
70 W. Michigan Ave., #212, Battle Creek, MI 49017; 269-205-3823
Committee Assignments: Oversight and Government Reform, Joint Economic

Amodei, Mark, R-Nev. (2)

Capitol Hill Office: 222 CHOB 20515; 225-6155;
Fax: 225-5679; *Chief of Staff:* Richard B. Goddard
Web: http://amodei.house.gov/
Facebook: http://facebook.com/MarkAmodeiNV2
Twitter: https://twitter.com/markamodeinv2

District Offices: 905 Railroad St., #104 D, Elko, NV 89801; 775-777-7705; Fax: 775-753-9984; *Rural Rep.:* Meghan Brown
5310 Kietzke Lane, #103, Reno, NV 89511; 775-686-5760; Fax: 775-686-5711; *District Director:* Stacy Parobek
Committee Assignments: Judiciary; Natural Resources; Veterans' Affairs, Appropriations

Bachmann, Michele, R-Minn. (6)

Capitol Hill Office: 2417 RHOB 20515; 225-2331;
Fax: 225-6475; *Chief of Staff:* Robert Boland
Web: http://bachmann.house.gov/
Facebook: http://facebook.com/RepMicheleBachmann
Twitter: http://twitter.com/MicheleBachmann
District Office: 2850 Cutters Grove Ave., #205, Anoka, MN 55303; 763-323-8922; Fax: 763-323-6585; *District Director:* Deb Steiskal
Committee Assignments: Financial Services; Permanent Select Intelligence

Bachus, Spencer, R-Ala. (6)

Capitol Hill Office: 2246 RHOB 20515-0106; 225-4921;
Fax: 225-2082; *Chief of Staff:* Michael Staley
Web: http://bachus.house.gov/
Facebook: http://facebook.com/SpencerBachus
Twitter: http://twitter.com/BachusAL06
District Offices: 1900 International Park Dr., #107, Birmingham, AL 35243-4217; 205-969-2296; Fax: 205-969-3958; *Field Rep.; Grant Coord.:* Ethan Vice
703 2nd Ave. N., P. O. Box 502, Clanton, AL 35243; 205-280-0704; Fax: 205-280-3060;
Committee Assignments: Financial Services, Chair; Judiciary

Barber, Ron, D-Ariz. (2)

Capitol Hill Office: 1029 LHOB 20515; 225-2542;
Fax: 225-0378; *Chief of Staff:* Jennifer Cox
Web: http://barber.house.gov/
Facebook: http://facebook.com/RepRonBarber
Twitter: http://twitter.com/RepRonBarber
District Office: 3945 E. Fort Lowell Rd., #211, Tucson, AZ 85712-1036; 520-881-3588; Fax: 520-322-9490; *Office Manager:* Taj Sultan

77 Calle Portal, Suite B-160, Sierra Vista, AZ 85635; 520-459-3115; Fax: 520-459-5419
Committee Assignments: Armed Services; Homeland Security; Small Business

Barletta, Lou, R-Pa. (11)

Capitol Hill Office: 115 CHOB 20515; 225-6511; Fax: 226-6250; *Chief of Staff:* Andrea Waldock
Web: http://barletta.house.gov/
Facebook: http://facebook.com/CongressmanLouBarletta
Twitter: http://twitter.com/reploubarletta
District Offices: 59 W. Louther St., Carlisle, PA 17013; 717-249-0190; Fax: 717-218-0190; *Field Rep.:* Leah Kithcart
4813 Jonestown Rd., #101, Harrisburg, PA 17109; 717-525-7002; Fax: 717-695-6794; *Director of Constituent Services:* Bruce Krell
1 S. Church St., #100, Hazleton, PA 18201-6200; 570-751-0050; Fax: 570-751-0054; *District Director:* Joe Gerdes
106 Arch St., Sunbury, PA 17801; 570-988-7801; Fax: 570-988-7805; *Field Rep.:* Vincent Kundrick
Committee Assignments: Education and the Workforce; Homeland Security; Transportation and Infrastructure

Barr, Andy, R-Ky. (6)

Capitol Hill Office: 1432 LHOB 20515; 225-4706; Fax: 225-2122; *Chief of Staff:* Betsy Hawkings
Web: http://barr.house.gov/
Facebook: http://facebook.com/RepAndyBarr
Twitter: http://twitter.com/RepAndyBarr
District Office: 2709 Old Rosebud Rd., Lexington, KY 40509; 859-219-1366; Fax: 859-219-3437; *District Director:* Colleen Cheney
Committee Assignment: Financial Services, Republican Study

Barrow, John, D-Ga. (12)

Capitol Hill Office: 2202 RHOB 20515-1012; 225-2823; Fax: 225-3377; *Chief of Staff:* Ashley Jones
Web: http://barrow.house.gov/
Facebook: http://facebook.com/CongressmanJohnBarrow
Twitter: https://twitter.com/repjohnbarrow
District Offices: 1450 Greene St., #550, Augusta, GA 30901; 706-722-4494; Fax: 706-722-4496; *District Director:* Lynthia Ross
107 Old Airport Rd., Suite A, Vidalia, GA 30474; 912-537-9301; Fax: 912-537-9266; *Director of Constituent Services:* Kristen Fulford
50 E. Main St., Statesboro, GA 30458; 912-489-4494
211 S. Gaskin Ave., Douglas, GA 31533
100 S. Church Street, Dublin, GA 31021; 478-272-7088
Committee Assignment: Energy and Commerce

Barton, Joe, R-Tex. (6)

Capitol Hill Office: 2107 RHOB 20515; 225-2002; Fax: 225-3052; *Chief of Staff:* Ryan Thompson
Web: http://joebarton.house.gov/
Facebook: http://facebook.com/RepJoeBarton
Twitter: http://twitter.com/RepJoeBarton

District Offices: 6001 W. I-20, #200, Arlington, TX 76017; 817-543-1000; Fax: 817-548-7029; *Deputy District Director:* Michael Taylor
2106-A W. Ennis Ave., Ennis, TX 75119-3624; 972-875-8488; Fax: 972-875-1907; *Deputy District Director:* Dub Maines
Committee Assignment: Energy and Commerce

Bass, Karen, D-Calif. (37)

Capitol Hill Office: 408 CHOB 20515-0533; 225-7084; Fax: 225-2422; *Chief of Staff:* Carrie Kohns
Web: http://karenbass.house.gov/
Facebook: http://facebook.com/RepKarenBass
Twitter: http://twitter.com/RepKarenBass
District Office: 4929 Wilshire Blvd., #650, Los Angeles, CA 90010-3820; 323-965-1422; Fax: 323-965-1113; *Deputy Chief of Staff:* Solomon Rivera
Committee Assignments: Foreign Affairs; Judiciary

Beatty, Joyce, D-Ohio (3)

Capitol Hill Office: 417 CHOB 20515; 225-4324; Fax: 225-1984; Chief of Staff: Kimberly Ross
Web: http://beatty.house.gov/
Twitter: http://twitter.com/RepBeatty
District Office: 471 E. Broad St., #1100, Columbus, OH 43215; 614-220-0003; Fax: 614-220-5640; *Deputy District Director:* Ron McGuire
Committee Assignment: Financial Services

Becerra, Xavier, D-Calif. (34)

Capitol Hill Office: 1226 LHOB 20515-0531; 225-6235; Fax: 225-2202; *Chief of Staff:* Debra Dixon
Web: http://becerra.house.gov/
Facebook: http://facebook.com/XavierBecerra
Twitter: http://twitter.com/repbecerra
District Office: 350 S. Bixel St., #120, Los Angeles, CA 90017; 213-481-1425; Fax: 213-481-1427; *District Director:* Liz Saldivar
Committee Assignment: Ways and Means

Benishek, Dan, R-Mich. (1)

Capitol Hill Office: 514 CHOB 20515-2201; 225-4735; Fax: 225-4710; *Chief of Staff:* John Billings
Web: http://benishek.house.gov/
Facebook: http://facebook.com/CongressmanDan
Twitter: http://twitter.com/congressmandan
District Offices: 1349 S. Otsego Ave., #7A, Gaylord, MI 49735; 877-376-5613; Fax: 877-504-0291; Deputy *District Director:* Jesse Osmer
500 S. Stephenson Ave., #500, Iron Mountain, MI 49801-3420; 906-828-1581; Fax: 906-828-1583; *District Director:* Traci Jahnke
307 S. Front St., #120, Marquette, MI 49855-4613; 906-273-1661; Fax: 906-273-1663; *Special Asst.:* Jennifer VanDeuren, Tom Hatfield
3301 Veterans Dr., #106, Traverse City, MI 49684; 877-376-5613; Fax: 877-504-0291; *Constituent Services Rep.:* Matthew Lee, Sam Campillo

Committee Assignments: Agriculture; Natural Resources; Veterans' Affairs

Bentivolio, Kerry, R-Mich. (11)

Capitol Hill Office: 226 CHOB 20515; 225-8171; Fax: 225-2667; *Chief of Staff:* Rob Wasinger
Web: http://bentivolio.house.gov/
Facebook: http://facebook.com/repkerryb
Twitter: http://twitter.com/repkerryb
District Office: 800 Welch Rd., Commerce, MI 48390; 248-859-2982; Fax: 248-859-2989; *District Director:* Tony Lis
Committee Assignments: Oversight and Government Reform; Small Business

Bera, Ami, D-Calif. (7)

Capitol Hill Office: 1408 LHOB 20515; 225-5716; Fax: 226-1298; *Chief of Staff:* Mini Timmaraju
Web: http://bera.house.gov/
Facebook: http://facebook.com/RepAmiBera
Twitter: http://twitter.com/RepBera
District Office: 11070 White Rock Rd., #195, Rancho Cordova, CA 95670; 916-635-0505; Fax: 916-635-0514; *District Director:* Faith Whitmore
Committee Assignments: Foreign Affairs; Science, Space, and Technology

Bilirakis, Gus, R-Fla. (12)

Capitol Hill Office: 2313 RHOB 20515-0909; 225-5755; Fax: 225-4085; *Chief of Staff:* Elizabeth Hittos
Web: http://bilirakis.house.gov/
Facebook: http://facebook.com/GusBilirakis
Twitter: http://twitter.com/RepGusBilirakis
District Offices: 36739 State Rd. 52, #212, Dade City, FL 33525
7132 Little Rd., New Port Richey, FL 34654; 727-232-2921; Fax: 727-232-2923; *District Director:* Summer Robertson
600 Klosterman Rd., Room BB-038, Tarpon Springs, FL 34689-1299; 727-940-5860; Fax: 727-940-5861
5901 Argerian Dr., #102, Wesley Chapel, FL 33545-4220; 813-501-4942; Fax: 813-501-4944
Committee Assignments: Energy and Commerce; Veteran's Affairs

Bishop, Rob, R-Utah (1)

Capitol Hill Office: 123 CHOB 20515-4401; 225-0453; Fax: 225-5857; *Chief of Staff:* Scott B. Parker
Web: http://robbishop.house.gov/
Facebook: http://facebook.com/RepRobBishop
Twitter: http://twitter.com/RepRobBishop
District Offices: 6 N. Main St., Brigham City, UT 84302-2116; 435-734-2270; Fax: 435-734-2290
Federal Bldg., 324 25th St., #1017, Ogden UT 84401; 801-625-0107; Fax: 801-625-0124; *District Director:* Peter Jenks
Committee Assignments: Armed Services; Natural Resources; Rules

Bishop, Sanford D. Jr., D-Ga. (2)

Capitol Hill Office: 2429 RHOB 20515-1002; 225-3631; Fax: 225-2203; *Chief of Staff:* Tracey Thornton
Web: http://bishop.house.gov/
Facebook: http://facebook.com/sanfordbishop
Twitter: http://twitter.com/sanfordbishop
District Offices: Albany Towers, 235 Roosevelt Ave., #114, Albany, GA 31701-2662; 229-439-8067; Fax: 229-436-2099; *District Director:* Kenneth Cutts
18 Ninth St., #201, Columbus, GA 31901-2778; 706-320-9477; Fax: 706-320-9479; *Field Rep.:* Elaine Gillespie
Committee Assignment: Appropriations

Bishop, Tim, D-N.Y. (1)

Capitol Hill Office: 306 CHOB 20515-3201; 225-3826; Fax: 225-3143; *Chief of Staff:* Pete Spiro
Web: http://timbishop.house.gov/
Facebook: https://facebook.com/RepTimBishop
Twitter: http://twitter.com/TimBishopNY
District Offices: 31 Oak St., #20, Patchogue, NY 11772-2841; 631-289-6500; Fax: 631-289-3181; *District Director:* Adam Santiago
137 Hampton Rd., Southampton, NY 11968-4923; 631-259-8450; Fax: 631-259-8451; *Special Projects Director:* Jane Finalborgo
Committee Assignments: Education and Workforce; Transportation and Infrastructure

Black, Diane, R-Tenn. (6)

Capitol Hill Office: 1531 LHOB 20515-4206; 225-4231; Fax: 225-6887; *Chief of Staff:* Teresa Koeberlein
Web: http://black.house.gov/
Facebook: http://facebook.com/DianeBlackTN06
Twitter: https://twitter.com/RepDianeBlack
District Offices: 321 E. Spring St., #301, Cookeville, TN 38501-4168; 931-854-0069; Fax: 615-206-8980; *Caseworker:* Bonny Warren
29 Taylor Ave., #201, Crossville, TN 38555; 931-854-0069; Fax: 615-206-8980; *Caseworker:* Kenna Balch
355 N. Belvedere Dr., #308, Gallatin, TN 37066-5410; 615-206-8204; Fax: 615-206-8980; *District Director:* Charles Schneider
Committee Assignments: Budget; Ways and Means

Blackburn, Marsha, R-Tenn. (7)

Capitol Hill Office: 217 CHOB 20515-4207; 225-2811; Fax: 225-3004; *Chief of Staff:* Michael R. Platt
Web: http://blackburn.house.gov/
Facebook: http://facebook.com/marshablackburn
Twitter: http://twitter.com/MarshaBlackburn
District Offices: 128 N. 2nd St., #202, Clarksville, TN 37040; 931-503-0391; Fax: 931-503-0393; *Sr. Case Manager:* Stephanie Scott
305 Public Square, #212, Franklin, TN 37062; 615-591-5161; Fax: 615-599-2916; *District Director:* Darcy Anderson
Committee Assignments: Budget; Energy and Commerce

Blumenauer, Earl, D-Ore. (3)

Capitol Hill Office: 1111 LHOB 20515; 225-4811; Fax: 225-8941; *Deputy Chief of Staff:* David Gillman
Web: http://blumenauer.house.gov/
Facebook: https://facebook.com/blumenauer
Twitter: http://twitter.com/repblumenauer
District Office: 729 N.E. Oregon St., #115, Portland, OR 97232-2184; 503-231-2300; Fax: 503-230-5413; *Chief of Staff:* Julia Pomeroy
Committee Assignments: Budget; Ways and Means

Boehner, John, R-Ohio (8)

Capitol Hill Office: 1011 LHOB 20515-3508; 225-6205; Fax: 225-0704; *Chief of Staff:* Ryan Day
Web: http://johnboehner.house.gov/
Facebook: http://facebook.com/OfficeofSpeakerBoehner
Twitter: http://twitter.com/SpeakerBoehner
District Offices: 12 S. Plum St., Troy, OH 45373-3282; 937-339-1524; Fax: 937-339-1878; *Field Rep.:* Frank DeBrosse
76 E. High St., 3rd Floor, Springfield, OH 45502; 937-322-1120; *Field Rep.:* Austin Bingham
7969 Cincinnati-Dayton Rd., Suite B, West Chester, OH 45069-6637; 513-779-5400; Fax: 513-779-5315; *District Chief of Staff:* Ryan Day
Speaker of the House

Bonamici, Suzanne, D-Ore. (1)

Capitol Hill Office: 439 CHOB 20515; 225-0855; Fax: 225-9497; *Chief of Staff:* Rachael Bornstein
Web: http://bonamici.house.gov/
Facebook: http://facebook.com/CongresswomanBonamici
Twitter: http://twitter.com/RepBonamici
District Office: 12725 S.W. Millikan Way, #220, Beaverton, OR 97005; 503-469-6010; Fax: 503-469-6018; *District Director:* Abby Tibbs
Committee Assignments: Education and the Workforce; Science, Space, and Technology

Bordallo, Madeleine Z., D-Guam (At Large)

Capitol Hill Office: 2441 RHOB 20515-5301; 225-1188; Fax: 226-0341; *Chief of Staff:* John Whitt
Web: http://house.gov/bordallo/
Facebook: http://facebook.com/madeleine.bordallo
District Office: 120 Father Duenas Ave., #107, Hagatna, GU 96910-5058; 671-477-4272; Fax: 671-477-2587; *District Director:* Jon Junior Calvo
Committee Assignments: Armed Services; Natural Resources

Boustany, Charles W., R-La. (3)

Capitol Hill Office: 1431 LHOB 20515-1807; 225-2031; Fax: 225-5724; *Chief of Staff:* Jeff Dobrozsi
Web: http://boustany.house.gov/
Facebook: http://facebook.com/RepBoustany
Twitter: http://twitter.com/Repboustany

District Offices: 800 Lafayette St., #1400, Lafayette, LA 70501-6800; 337-235-6322; Fax: 337-235-6072; *District Director:* Joan Finley
Capital One Tower, One Lakeshore Dr., #1775, Lake Charles, LA 70629-0114; 337-433-1747; Fax: 337-433-0974; *Constituent Services Rep.:* Theresa Martin
Committee Assignment: Ways and Means

Brady, Kevin, R-Tex. (8)

Capitol Hill Office: 301 CHOB 20515-4308; 225-4901; Fax: 225-5524; *Chief of Staff:* Doug Centilli
Web: http://kevinbrady.house.gov/
Facebook: http://facebook.com/kevinbrady
Twitter: http://twitter.com/RepKevinBrady
District Offices: Conroe District Office, 200 River Pointe Dr., #304, Conroe, TX 77304-2817; 936-441-5700; Fax: 936-441-5757; *District Director:* Todd Stephens
1300 11th St., #400, Huntsville, TX 77340; 936-439-9532; Fax: 936-439-9546; *Field Rep.:* Payton Roberts
Committee Assignment: Ways and Means, Joint Economic (Chair)

Brady, Robert, D-Pa. (1)

Capitol Hill Office: 102 CHOB 20515-3801; 225-4731; Fax: 225-0088; *Chief of Staff:* Stanley V. White
Web: http://brady.house.gov/
Facebook: http://facebook.com/RepRobertBrady
Twitter: http://twitter.com/RepBrady
District Offices: 1350 Edgmont Ave., #2575, Chester, PA 19013; 610-874-7094; Fax: 484-816-0029; *Office Manager:* Susie Kirkland
2637 E. Clearfield St., Philadelphia, PA 19134-5023; 267-519-2252; Fax: 267-519-2262; *Community Liaison:* Tom Johnson
2630 Memphis St., Philadelphia, PA 19125-2344; 215-426-4616; Fax: 215-426-7741; *Community Liaison:* Peg Rzepski
1907-09 S. Broad St., Philadelphia, PA 19148-2216; 215-389-4627; Fax: 215-389-4636; *District Director:* Shirley Gregory
Committee Assignments: Armed Services; House Administration, Ranking Minority Member; Joint Printing; Joint Library of Congress

Braley, Bruce, D-Iowa (1)

Capitol Hill Office: 2263 RHOB 20515; 225-2911; Fax: 225-6666; *Chief of Staff:* John Davis
Web: http://braley.house.gov/
Facebook: http://facebook.com/RepBruceBraley
Twitter: https://twitter.com/BruceBraley
District Offices: 310 3rd St. S.E., Cedar Rapids, IA 52401; 319-364-2288; Fax: 319-364-2994; *Deputy District Director:* Will McIntee
1050 Main St., Dubuque, IA 52001-4723; 563-557-7789; Fax: 563-557-1324; *District Director:* John Murphy
219 E. 4th St., Waterloo, IA 50703-4701; 319-287-3233; Fax: 319-287-5104; *Caseworker:* Ardie Blakeney
Committee Assignment: Energy and Commerce

Bridenstine, Jim, R-Okla. (1)

Capitol Hill Office: 216 CHOB 20515-3601; 225-2211; Fax: 225-9187; *Chief of Staff:* Joseph Kaufman
Web: http://bridenstine.house.gov/
Facebook:http://facebook.com/ CongressmanJimBridenstine
Twitter: http://twitter.com/RepJBridenstine
District Office: 2448 E. 81st St., #5150, Tulsa, OK 74137; 918-935-3222; Fax: 918-935-2716; *District Director:* Gabe Sherman
Committee Assignments: Armed Services; Science, Space, and Technology

Brooks, Mo, R-Ala. (5)

Capitol Hill Office: 1230 LHOB 20515; 225-4801; Fax: 225-4392; *Chief of Staff Legis. Director:* Mark Pettitt
Web: http://brooks.house.gov/
Facebook: http://facebook.com/pages/Congressman-Mo-Brooks/155220881193244
Twitter: http://twitter.com/RepMoBrooks
District Offices: 302 Lee St., Room 86, Decatur, AL 35601-1926; 256-355-9400; Fax: 256-355-9406; *Field Rep.:* Johnny Turner
102 S. Court St., #310, Florence, AL 35630; 256-718-5155; Fax: 256-718-5156; *Field Rep.:* Laura Smith
2101 W. Clinton Ave., #302, Huntsville, AL 35805-3109; 256-551-0190; Fax: 256-551-0194; *District Director:* Tiffany Noel
Committee Assignments: Armed Services; Foreign Affairs; Science, Space, and Technology

Brooks, Susan W., R-Ind. (5)

Capitol Hill Office: 1505 LHOB 20515; 225-2276; Fax: 225-0016; *Chief of Staff:* Mel Raines
Web: http://susanwbrooks.house.gov/
Facebook: http://facebook.com/ CongresswomanSusanWBrooks
Twitter: http://twitter.com/@SusanWBrooks
District Office: 11611 N. Meridian St., Carmel, IN 46032; 317-848-0201; Fax: 317-846-7306; *District Director:* Karen Glaser
120 E. 8th St., #101, Anderson, IN 46016; 765-640-5115; Fax: 765-640-5116; *Deputy District Director:* Kevin Sulc
Committee Assignments: Education and Workforce; Ethics; Homeland Security

Broun, Paul C, R-Ga. (10)

Capitol Hill Office: 2437 RHOB 20515; 225-4101; Fax: 226-0776; *Chief of Staff:* David Bowser
Web: http://broun.house.gov/
Facebook: http://facebook.com/RepPaulBroun
Twitter: http://twitter.com/RepPaulBrounMD
District Offices: 3706 Atlanta Hwy., #2, Athens, GA 30606-7202; 706-549-9588; Fax: 706-549-9590; *District Director:* Jessica Hayes
Committee Assignments: Homeland Security; Natural Resources; Science, Space, and Technology

Brown, Corrine, D-Fla. (5)

Capitol Hill Office: 2111 RHOB 20515; 225-0123; Fax: 225-2256; *Chief of Staff:* Ronnie Simmons
Web: http://corrinebrown.house.gov/
Facebook: http://facebook.com/congresswomanbrown
Twitter: http://twitter.com/RepCorrineBrown
District Offices: 101 Union St. East, #202, Jacksonville, FL 32202-6002; 904-354-1652; Fax: 904-354-2721; *District Director:* Glenel Bowden
455 N. Garland Ave., #414, Orlando FL 32801; 407-872-2208; Fax: 407-872-5763; *Area Director:* Ronita Sanders
Committee Assignments: Transportation and Infrastructure; Veterans' Affairs

Brownley, Julia, D-Calif. (26)

Capitol Hill Office: 1019 LHOB 20515; 225-5811; Fax: 225-1100; *Chief of Staff:* Lenny Young
Web: http://juliabrownley.house.gov/
Facebook http://facebook.com/RepJuliaBrownley
Twitter: http://twitter.com/JuliaBrownley26
District Offices: 300 E. Esplanade Dr., #470, Oxnard, CA 93036; 805-379-1779; Fax: 805-379-1799; *District Director:* Carina Armenta
223 E. Thousand Oaks Blvd., #411, Thousand Oaks, CA 91360; 805-379-1779; Fax: 805-379-1799; *Field Rep.:* Sheri Orgel
Committee Assignments: Science, Space, and Technology; Veteran's Affairs

Buchanan, Vern, R-Fla. (16)

Capitol Hill Office: 2104 RHOB 20515; 225-5015; Fax: 226-0828; *Chief of Staff:* Dave Karvelas
Web: http://buchanan.house.gov/
Facebook: http://facebook.com/CongressmanBuchanan
Twitter: http://twitter.com/vernbuchanan
District Offices: 1051 Manatee Ave. West, #305, Bradenton, FL 34205-4954; 941-747-9081; Fax: 941-748-1564; *Field Rep.:* Gary Tibbetts
111 S. Orange Ave., Floor 2R #202W, Sarasota, FL 34236-5806; 941-951-6643; Fax: 941-951-2972; *District Director:* Sally Tibbetts
Committee Assignment: Ways and Means

Bucshon, Larry, R-Ind. (8)

Capitol Hill Office: 1005 LHOB 20515; 225-4636; Fax: 225-3284; *Chief of Staff:* Jonathan Causey
Web: http://bucshon.house.gov/
Facebook: http://facebook.com/RepLarryBucshon
Twitter: http://twitter.com/RepLarryBucshon
District Offices: 101 N.W. Martin Luther King, Jr. Blvd., Room 124, Evansville, IN 47708-1951; 812-465-6482; Fax: 812-422-4761
610 Main St., 2nd Floor, Jasper, IN 47547; 812-482-4255; Fax: 812-422-4761; *Field Rep.:* Kyi Kessler
901 Wabash Ave., #140, Terre Haute, IN 47807-3232; 812-232-0523; Fax: 812-232-0526; *Intern District Director:* Matthew Huckleby
1500 N. Chestnut St., Vincennes, IN 47591; 855-519-1629

Committee Assignments: Education and the Workforce; Science, Space, and Technology; Transportation and Infrastructure

Burgess, Michael C, R-Tex. (26)

Capitol Hill Office: 2336 RHOB 20515; 225-7772; Fax: 225-2919; *Chief of Staff:* Kelle Strickland
Web: http://burgess.house.gov/
Facebook: http://facebook.com/michaelcburgess
Twitter: http://twitter.com/michaelcburgess
District Office: 1660 S. Stemmons Freeway, #230, Lewisville, TX 75067-0600; 972-434-9700; Fax: 972-434-9705; *District Director:* Erik With
Committee Assignments: Commission on Security and Cooperation in Europe (Helsinki Commission); Energy and Commerce; Rules

Bustos, Cheri, D-Ill. (17)

Capitol Hill Office: 1009 LHOB 20515; 225-5905; Fax: 225-5396; *Chief of Staff:* Allison Jaslow
Web: http://bustos.house.gov/
Facebook: http://facebook.com/RepCheri
Twitter: http://twitter.com/RepCheri
District Offices: 3100 N. Knoxville Ave., #205, Peoria, IL 61603; 309-966-1813; *Constituent Advocate:* Andy Colgan
119 N. Church St., #207-208, Rockford, IL 61101; 815-968-8011; *Constituent Advocate:* Catherine Gray
2401 4th Ave., Rock Island, IL 61201; 309-786-3406; Fax: 309-786-3720; *District Director:* Heidi Schultz
Committee Assignments: Agriculture; Transportation and Infrastructure

Butterfield, G. K., D-N.C. (1)

Capitol Hill Office: 2305 RHOB 20515-3301; 225-3101; Fax: 225-3354; *Chief of Staff:* Troy G. Clair
Web: http://butterfield.house.gov/
Twitter: http://twitter.com/GKButterfield
District Offices: 411 W. Chapel Hill St., #905, Durham, NC 27701; 919-908-0164; Fax: 919-908-0169; *Field Rep.:* Dollie Burwell; *Director of Constituent Affairs/Northwest District Outreach:* Dollie Burwell
216 N.E. Nash St., Suite B, Wilson, NC 27893-3802; 252-237-9816; Fax: 252-291-0356; *District Director:* Ray Rogers
Committee Assignment: Energy and Commerce

Byrne, Bradley, R-Ala. (1)

Capitol Hill Office: 2236 RHOB 20515-0101; 225-4931; Fax: 225-0562; *Chief of Staff:* Alex Schriver
Web: http://byrne.house.gov/
Facebook: http://facebook.com/RepByrne
Twitter: http://twitter.com/RepByrne
District Offices: 201 E. Section Ave., Foley, AL 36535; 251-972-8545; Fax: 251-972-8546; *Field Rep.:* Daniel Catlin
11 N. Water St., #15290, Mobile, AL 36602; 251-690-2811; Fax: 251-690-2815; *District Director:* Elizabeth Roney
Committee Assignment: Armed Services; Natural Resources

Calvert, Ken, R-Calif. (42)

Capitol Hill Office: 2269 RHOB 20515-0544; 225-1986; Fax: 225-2004; *Chief of Staff:* Dave Ramey
Web: http://calvert.house.gov/
Facebook: http://facebook.com/RepKenCalvert
Twitter: http://twitter.com/KenCalvert
District Office: 4160 Temescal Canyon Rd., #214, Corona, CA 92883-4624; 951-277-0042; Fax: 951-277-0420; *District Director:* Jolyn Murphy
Committee Assignments: Appropriations; Budget

Camp, Dave, R-Mich. (4)

Capitol Hill Office: 341 CHOB 20515-2204; 225-3561; Fax: 225-9679; *Chief of Staff:* Jim Brandell
Web: http://camp.house.gov/
Facebook: http://facebook.com/repdavecamp
Twitter: http://twitter.com/RepDaveCamp
District Offices: 112 Spruce St., Suite A, Cadillac, MI 49601; 231-876-9205; Fax: 231-876-9252; *District Director:* Ryan Tarrant
135 Ashman St., Midland, MI 48640-5103; 989-631-2552; Fax: 989-631-6271; *Communications Director:* Allie Walker
Committee Assignment: Ways and Means, Chair

Campbell, John, R-Calif. (45)

Capitol Hill Office: 2331 RHOB 20515; 225-5611; Fax: 225-9177; *Chief of Staff:* Muffy Day
Web: http://campbell.house.gov/
Facebook: http://facebook.com/JohnCampbell
Twitter: http://twitter.com/RepJohnCampbell
District Office: 20 Pacifica, #660, Irvine, CA 92618; 949-756-2244; Fax: 949-251-9309
Committee Assignments: Budget; Financial Services, Joint Economic

Cantor, Eric, R-Va. (7)

Capitol Hill Office: 303 CHOB 20515-4607; 225-2815; Fax: 225-0011; *Chief of Staff:* Kristi Way
Web: http://cantor.house.gov/
Facebook: http://facebook.com/ericcantor
Twitter: http://twitter.com/EricCantor
District Offices: 763 Madison Rd., #207, Culpeper, VA 22701; 540-825-8960; Fax: 540-825-8964; *District Rep.:* Chris Snider
4201 Dominion Blvd., #110, Glen Allen, VA 23060-6149; 804-747-4073; Fax: 804-747-5308; *District Director:* Jennifer Nolen
Majority Leader

Capito, Shelley Moore, R-W. Va. (2)

Capitol Hill Office: 2366 RHOB 20515; 225-2711; Fax: 225-7856; *Chief of Staff:* Joel Brubaker
Web: http://capito.house.gov/
Facebook: http://facebook.com/pages/Shelley-Moore-Capito/8057864757
Twitter: https://twitter.com/RepShelley

District Offices: 4815 MacCorkle Ave., S.E., Charleston, WV 25304-1948; 304-925-5964; Fax: 304-926-8912; *District Director:* Mary Eckerson

300 Foxcroft Ave., #102, Martinsburg, WV 25401-5341; 304-264-8810; Fax: 304-264-8815; *Constituent Services Rep.:* Ashley Paxson

Committee Assignments: Financial Services; Transportation and Infrastructure

Capps, Lois, D-Calif. (24)

Capitol Hill Office: 2231 RHOB 20515-0523; 225-3601; Fax: 225-5632; *Chief of Staff:* Sarah Rubinfield

Web: http://capps.house.gov/

Facebook: http://facebook.com/loiscapps

Twitter: https://twitter.com/RepLoisCapps

District Offices: 1411 Marsh St., #205, San Luis Obispo, CA 93401-2923; 805-546-8348; Fax: 805-546-8368; *District Rep.:* Greg Haas

301 E. Carrillo St., Suite A, Santa Barbara, CA 93101-1410; 805-730-1710; Fax: 805-730-9153; *District Director:* Mollie Culver

1101 S. Broadway St., Suite A, Santa Maria, CA 93454; 805-349-3832; *Field Rep:* Blanca Figueroa

Committee Assignment: Energy and Commerce

Capuano, Michael E., D-Mass. (7)

Capitol Hill Office: 1414 LHOB 20515-2108; 225-5111; Fax: 225-9322; *Chief of Staff Admin. Asst.:* Robert E. Primus

Web: http://house.gov/capuano/

Facebook: https://facebook.com/RepMichaelCapuano

Twitter: https://twitter.com/mikecapuano

District Offices: 110 First St., Cambridge, MA 02141-2109; 617-621-6208; Fax: 617-621-8628; *District Director:* Jon Lenicheck

Roxbury Community College, Campus Library, Room 211, Boston, MA 02120; 617-621-6208; Fax: 617-621-8628; *District Rep.:* Kate Chang

Stetson Hall, Rm. 124, 6 S. Main St., Randolph, MA 02368; 617-621-6208; Fax: 617-621-8628; *District Rep.:* Kate Auspitz, Kate Chang

Committee Assignments: Ethics; Financial Services; Transportation and Infrastructure

Cardenas, Tony, D-Calif. (29)

Capitol Hill Office: 1508 LHOB 20515; 225-6131; Fax: 225-0819; *Chief of Staff:* Sam Jammal

Web: http://cardenas.house.gov/

Facebook: http://facebook.com/repcardenas

Twitter: http://twitter.com/@repcardenas

District Office: 9300 Laurel Canyon Blvd., 2nd Floor, Arleta, CA 91331; 818-504-0090; Fax: 818-504-0280; *Sr. Field Rep.:* Gabriela Marquez

Committee Assignments: Budget; Natural Resources; Oversight and Government Reform

Carney, John, D-Del. (At Large)

Capitol Hill Office: 1406 LHOB 20515; 225-4165; Fax: 225-2291; *Chief of Staff:* Elizabeth Hart

Web: http://johncarney.house.gov/

Facebook: http://facebook.com/JohnCarneyDE

Twitter: http://twitter.com/johncarneyde

District Offices: 33 The Circle, Georgetown, DE 19947; 302-854-0667; Fax: 302-854-0669; *Kent and Sussex County Coord.:* Drew Slater

233 N. King St., #200, Wilmington, DE 19801-2521; 302-691-7333; Fax: 302-428-1950; *State Director:* Doug Gramiak

Committee Assignment: Financial Services

Carson, André, D-Ind. (7)

Capitol Hill Office: 2453 RHOB 20515-1407; 225-4011; Fax: 225-5633; *Chief of Staff:* Kim Rudolph

Web: http://carson.house.gov/

Facebook: http://facebook.com/CongressmanAndreCarson

Twitter: http://twitter.com/repandrecarson

District Office: Julia M. Carson Government Center, #300, E. Fall Creek Pkwy. N. Dr., Indianapolis, IN 46205-4258; 317-283-6516; Fax: 317-283-6567; *District Director:* Megan Sims

Committee Assignments: Armed Services; Transportation and Infrastructure

Carter, John, R-Tex. (31)

Capitol Hill Office: 409 CHOB 20515-4331; 225-3864; Fax: 225-5886; *Chief of Staff:* Jonas Miller

Web: http://carter.house.gov/

Facebook: http://facebook.com/judgecarter

Twitter: http://twitter.com/JudgeCarter

District Offices: One Financial Centre, 1717 N. Hwy. 35, #303, Round Rock, TX 78664; 512-246-1600; Fax: 512-246-1620; *Texas Chief of Staff:* Jonas Miller

6544 S. General Bruce Dr., Suite B, Temple, TX 76502-5811; 254-933-1392; Fax: 254-933-1650; *Constituent Liaison:* Cheryl Hassmann

Committee Assignment: Appropriations

Cartwright, Matthew, D-Pa. (17)

Capitol Hill Office: 1419 LHOB 20515; 225-5546; Fax: 226-0996; *Chief of Staff:* Hunter Ridgway

Web: http://cartwright.house.gov/

Facebook: https://facebook.com/CongressmanMattCartwright

Twitter: https://twitter.com/RepCartwright

District Offices: 121 Progress Ave., #310, Pottsville, PA 17901; 570-624-0140; *Caseworker:* Sabrina McLaughlin

226 Wyoming Ave., Scranton, PA 18503; 570-341-1050; Fax: 570-341-1055; *District Director:* Bob Morgan

1 S. 3rd St., 9th floor, Easton, PA 18042; 484-546-0776; *Field Rep.:* Anne Lauritzen

20 N. Pennsylvania Avenue, #201, Wilkes-Barre, PA 18711; 570-371-0317; *Caseworker:* Christa Mecadon

Committee Assignments: Natural Resources; Oversight and Government Reform

Cassidy, Bill, R-La. (6)

Capitol Hill Office: 1131 LHOB 20515; 225-3901;
Fax: 225-7313; *Chief of Staff:* James Quinn
Web: http://cassidy.house.gov/
Facebook: https://facebook.com/billcassidy
Twitter: https://twitter.com/BillCassidy
District Offices: 5555 Hilton Ave., #100, Baton Rouge, LA
70808-2597; 225-929-7711; Fax: 225-929-7688; *District
Director:* Brian McNabb
29261Frost Rd., Livingston, LA 70754; 225-686-4413;
Fax: 225-929-7688; *Outreach Coord.:* Brian McNabb
200 W. 1st St., Thibodaux, LA 70301; 985-447-1662 *Office
Director:* David Cabell
Committee Assignment: Energy and Commerce

Castor, Kathy, D-Fla. (14)

Capitol Hill Office: 205 CHOB 20515-0911; 225-3376;
Fax: 225-5652; *Chief of Staff:* Clay Phillips
Web: http://castor.house.gov/
Facebook: http://facebook.com/USRepKathyCastor
District Office: 4144 N. Armenia Ave., #300, Tampa, FL
33607-6435; 813-871-2817; Fax: 813-871-2864; *Press
Secy.:* Marcia Mejia
University of South Florida-St. Pete Williams House; 511
Second St., S. St. Petersburg, FL 33701; 727-873-2817
Field Rep.: Marcia Mejia
Committee Assignments: Budget; Energy and Commerce

Castro, Joaquin, D-Tex. (20)

Capitol Hill Office: 212 CHOB 20515; 225-3236;
Fax: 225-1915; *Chief of Staff:* Carlos Sanchez
Web: http://castro.house.gov/
Facebook: hhtp://facebook.com/JoaquinCastroTX
Twitter: http://twitter.com/JoaquinCastrotx
District Office: 4715 Fredericksburg Rd., #512, San
Antonio, TX 78229; 210-348-8216; Fax: 210-979-0737;
District Director: Cary Clack
Committee Assignments: Armed Services; Foreign Affairs

Chabot, Steve, R-Ohio (1)

Capitol Hill Office: 2371 RHOB 20515; 225-2216;
Fax: 225-3012; *Chief of Staff:* Mark S. Wellman
Web: http://chabot.house.gov/
Facebook: http://facebook.com/RepSteveChabot
Twitter: http://twitter.com/repstevechabot
District Office: 441 Vine St., Rm.3003, Cincinnati, OH
45202-3003; 513-684-2723; Fax: 513-421-8722; *District
Director:* Michael Cantwell
11 S. Broadway, Lebanon, OH 45036; 513-421-8704; *Field
Rep.:* David McCandless
Committee Assignments: Foreign Affairs; Judiciary; Small
Business

Chaffetz, Jason, R-Utah (3)

Capitol Hill Office: 2464 RHOB 20515; 225-7751;
Fax: 225-5629; *Chief of Staff:* Justin Harding
Web: http://chaffetz.house.gov/

Facebook: http://facebook.com/
CongressmanJasonChaffetz
Twitter: http://twitter.com/jasoninthehouse
District Office: 51 S. University Ave., #318, Provo, UT
84601-4491; 801-851-2500; Fax: 801-851-2509; *District
Director:* Wade Garrett
Committee Assignments: Homeland Security; Judiciary;
Oversight and Government Reform

Christensen, Donna M., D-Virgin Is. (At Large)

Capitol Hill Office: 1510 LHOB 20515-5501; 225-1790;
Fax: 225-5517; *Chief of Staff:* Monique Clendinen
Watson
Web: http://donnachristensen.house.gov/
Facebook: http://facebook.com/pages/Congresswoman-
Donna-M-Christensen/138013351189
Twitter: http://twitter.com/DelegateDonna
District Offices: Sunshine Mall Space #204 and #205,
#1 Estate Cane, Frederiksted, St. Croix, VI 00840;
340-778-5900; Fax: 340-778-5111; *District Director:*
Ullmont James
St.John, VI 00831; 202-664-36638000 Nisky Shopping
Center, #207, St. Thomas, VI 00802-5844; 340-774-
4408; Fax: 340-774-8033; *St. Thomas Office Manager:*
Joyce Jackson
Committee Assignment: Energy and Commerce

Chu, Judy, D-Calif. (27)

Capitol Hill Office: 1520 LHOB 20515-0532; 225-5464;
Fax: 225-5467; *Chief of Staff:* Amelia Wang
Web: http://chu.house.gov/
Facebook: http://facebook.com/RepJudyChu
Twitter: http://twitter.com/RepJudyChu
District Office: 527 S. Lake Ave., #106, Pasadena, CA
91101; 626-304-0110; Fax: 626-304-0132; *Asst. District
Director:* Becky Cheng
415 W. Foothill Blvd., #122, Claremont, CA 91711;
909-625-5394; Fax: 909-399-0198; *Field Rep.:* Enrique
Robles
Committee Assignments: Judiciary; Small Business

Cicilline, David, D-R.I. (1)

Capitol Hill Office: 128 CHOB 20515-3901; 225-4911;
Fax: 225-3290; *Chief of Staff:* Peter Karafotas
Web: http://cicilline.house.gov/
Facebook: http://facebook.com/
CongressmanDavidCicilline
Twitter: http://twitter.com/repcicilline
District Office: 1070 Main St., #300, Pawtucket,
RI 02860-2134; 401-729-5600; Fax: 401-729-5608;
District Director: Dianne Mederos
Committee Assignments: Foreign Affairs; Judiciary

Clark, Katherine, D-Mass. (5)

Capitol Hill Office: 2108 RHOB 20515-2107; 225-2836;
Fax: 226-0092; *Chief of Staff:* Brooke Scannell
Web: http://katherineclark.house.gov/
Facebook: http://facebook.com/CongresswomanClark
Twitter: http://twitter.com/KatherineClark

District Offices: 5 High St., #101, Medford, Massachusetts 02155; 781-396-2900; *District Director:* Christian Lobue

Committee Assignments: Natural Resources

Clarke, Yvette D., D-N.Y. (9)

Capitol Hill Office: 2351 RHOB 20515; 225-6231; Fax: 226-0112; *Chief of Staff:* Shelley Davis

Web: http://clarke.house.gov/

Facebook: http://facebook.com/repyvettedclarke

Twitter: http://twitter.com/YvetteClarke

District Office: 123 Linden Blvd., 4th Floor, Brooklyn, NY 11226-3302; 718-287-1142; Fax: 718-287-1223; *District Director:* Anita Taylor

Committee Assignments: Ethics; Homeland Security; Small Business

Clay, Wm. Lacy, D-Mo. (1)

Capitol Hill Office: 2418 RHOB 20515-2501; 225-2406; Fax: 226-3717; *Chief of Staff:* Darryl A. Piggee

Web: http://lacyclay.house.gov/

Facebook: http://facebook.com/pages/Congressman-Wm-Lacy-Clay/109135405838588

Twitter: https://twitter.com/LacyClayMO1

District Offices: 111 S. 10th St., #24.334, St. Louis, MO 63102; 314-367-1970; Fax: 314-367-1341; *Community Outreach Coord.:* Jasmina Hadzic

6830 Gravois, St. Louis MO 63116; 314-669-9393; 314-669-9398; *Communications Director; Press Secy.:* Steve Engelhardt

Committee Assignments: Financial Services; Oversight and Government Reform

Cleaver, Emanuel, D-Mo. (5)

Capitol Hill Office: 2335 RHOB 20515; 225-4535; Fax: 225-4403; *Chief of Staff:* Geoff Jolley

Web: http://cleaver.house.gov/

Facebook: http://facebook.com/emanuelcleaverii

Twitter: http://twitter.com/repcleaver

District Offices: 211 W. Maple Ave., Independence, MO 64050-2815; 816-833-4545; Fax: 816-833-2991; *Community Affairs Liaison:* Nicki Cardwell

101 W. 31st St., Kansas City, MO 64108-3318; 816-842-4545; Fax: 816-471-5215; *District Director:* Geoff Jolley

1923 Main St., Higginsville, MO 64037; 660-584-7373; Fax: 660-584-7227; *Field Rep.:* Kyle Wilkens

Committee Assignment: Financial Services

Clyburn, James E., D-S.C. (6)

Capitol Hill Office: 242 CHOB 20515; 225-3315; Fax: 225-2313; *Chief of Staff Ethics; Telecommunications:* Yelberton R. Watkins

Web: http://clyburn.house.gov/

Facebook: http://facebook.com/jameseclyburn

Twitter: http://twitter.com/clyburn

District Offices: 1225 Lady St., #200, Columbia, SC 29201-3210; 803-799-1100; Fax: 803-799-9060; *District Director:* Robert Nance

130 W. Main St., Kingstree, SC 29556; 843-355-1211; Fax: 843-355-1232; *Caseworker:* Kenneth Barnes

176 Brooks Blvd., Santee, SC 29142; 803-854-4700; Fax: 803-854-4900; *District Director:* Robert Nance

Assistant to the Democratic Leader

Coble, Howard, R-N.C. (6)

Capitol Hill Office: 2188 RHOB 20515-3306; 225-3065; Fax: 225-8611; *Chief of Staff; Press Secy.:* Ed McDonald

Web: http://coble.house.gov/

Facebook: http://facebook.com/HowardCoble6

Twitter: http://twitter.com/HowardCoble

District Offices: P.O. Box 812, 124 W. Elm St., Graham, NC 27253-2802; 336-229-0159; Fax: 336-228-7974; *District Rep.:* Janine Osborne

2102 N. Elm St., Suite B, Greensboro, NC 27408-5100; 336-333-5005; Fax: 336-333-5048; *District Rep.:* Brad Langston

1634 N. Main St., #101, High Point, NC 27262-2644; 336-886-5106; Fax: 336-886-8740; *District Rep.:* Nancy Mazza

107 Midtown Commons, Madison, NC 27025; 336-427-0044; Fax: 336-427-0480; *District Rep.:* Lindsay Morris

Committee Assignments: Judiciary; Transportation and Infrastructure

Coffman, Mike, R-Colo. (6)

Capitol Hill Office: 2443 RHOB 20515; 225-7882; Fax: 226-4623; *Communications Director:* Clay Sutton

Web: http://coffman.house.gov/

Facebook: http://facebook.com/repmikecoffman

Twitter: http://twitter.com/RepMikeCoffman

District Office: Cherry Creek PL IV, #305, 3300 S. Parker Rd., Aurora, CO 80014; 720-748-7514; Fax: 720-748-7680; *Chief of Staff:* Jacque Ponder

Committee Assignments: Armed Services; Small Business; Veterans' Affairs

Cohen, Steve, D-Tenn. (9)

Capitol Hill Office: 2404 RHOB 20515; 225-3265; Fax: 225-5663; *Chief of Staff:* Marilyn Dillihay

Web: http://cohen.house.gov/

Facebook: http://facebook.com/CongressmanSteveCohen

Twitter: http://twitter.com/repcohen

District Office: Clifford Davis/Odell Horton Federal Bldg., 167 N. Main St., #369, Memphis, TN 38103-1822; 901-544-4131; Fax: 901-544-4329; *District Director:* Marzie Thomas

Committee Assignments: Commission on Security and Cooperation in Europe (Helsinki Commission); Judiciary; Transportation and Infrastructure

Cole, Tom, R-Okla. (4)

Capitol Hill Office: 2458 RHOB 20515-3604; 225-6165; Fax: 225-3512; *Chief of Staff:* Sean P. Murphy

Web: http://cole.house.gov/

Facebook: http://facebook.com/TomColeOK04

Twitter: http://twitter.com/tomcoleok04

District Offices: 100 E. 13th St., #213, Ada, OK 74820-6548; 580-436-5375; Fax: 580-436-5451; *Field Rep.:* Amber Savage

711 S.W. D Ave., #201, Lawton, OK 73501-4561; 580-357-2131; Fax: 580-357-7477; *Field Rep.:* Will Roberts

2424 Springer Dr., #201, Norman, OK 73069-3965; 405-329-6500; Fax: 405-321-7369; *District Director:* Joshua Grogis

Committee Assignments: Appropriations; Budget; Rules

Collins, Chris, R-N.Y. (27)

Capitol Hill Office: 1117 LHOB 20515; 225-5265; Fax: 225-5910; *Chief of Staff:* Chris Grant
Web: http://chriscollins.house.gov/
Facebook: http://facebook.com/RepChrisCollins
Twitter: http://twitter.com/RepChrisCollins
District Offices: 128 Main St., Unit 2, Geneseo, NY 14454; 585-519-4002; Fax: 585-519-4009; *Field Rep.:* Emily Knight

2813 Wehrle Dr., #13, Williamsville, NY 14221; 716-634-2324; Fax: 716-631-7610; *District Director:* Michael Kracker

Committee Assignments: Agriculture; Small Business; Science, Space, and Technology

Collins, Doug, R-Ga. (9)

Capitol Hill Office: 513 CHOB 20515; 225-9893; Fax: 226-1224; *Chief of Staff:* Brendan Belair
Web: http://dougcollins.house.gov/
Facebook: http://facebook.com/RepresentativeDougCollins
Twitter: http://twitter.com/RepDougCollins
District Office: 111 Green St., S.E., Gainesville, GA 30501; 770-297-3388; Fax: 770-297-3390; *District Director:* Darren Kendall
Committee Assignments: Foreign Affairs; Judiciary; Oversight and Government Reform

Conaway, Mike, R-Tex. (11)

Capitol Hill Office: 2430 RHOB 20515-4311; 225-3605; Fax: 225-1783; *Chief of Staff:* Scott Graves
Web: http://conaway.house.gov/
Facebook: http://facebook.com/mike.conaway
Twitter: http://twitter.com/ConawayTX11
District Offices: Brownwood City Hall, 501 Center Ave., Brownwood, TX 76801-2809; 325-646-1950; Fax: 325-646-2979; *Field Rep.:* Hilary Stegemoller

County Annex, 104 W. Sandstone St., Llano, TX 78643-2319; 325-247-2826; Fax: 325-247-2676; *Field Rep.:* Nancy Watson

6 Desta Dr., #2000, Midland, TX 79705-5520; 432-687-2390; Fax: 432-687-0277; *District Director:* Evan Thomas

City Hall, 411 W. 8th St., 5th Floor, Odessa, TX 79761-4422; 432-331-9667; Fax: 432-332-6538; *Field Rep.:* Evan Thomas

O.C. Fisher Federal Bldg., 33 E. Twohig Ave., #307, San Angelo, TX 76903-6451; 325-659-4010; Fax: 325-659-4014; *Regional Director:* Joanne Powell

Committee Assignments: Agriculture; Armed Services; Ethics, Chair; Permanent Select Intelligence

Connolly, Gerald E., D-Va. (11)

Capitol Hill Office: 424 CHOB 20515-4611; 225-1492; Fax: 225-3071; *Chief of Staff:* James Walkinshaw
Web: http://connolly.house.gov/
Facebook: http://facebook.com/CongressmanGerryConnolly
Twitter: http://twitter.com/gerryconnolly
District Offices: 4115 Annandale Rd., #103, Annandale, VA 22003-2500; 703-256-3071; Fax: 703-354-1284; *District Director:* Sharon Stark

4308 Ridgewood Center Dr., Woodbridge, VA 22192-5307; 703-670-4989; Fax: 703-670-6042; *Prince William County Director:* Collin Davenport

Committee Assignments: Foreign Affairs; Oversight and Government Reform

Conyers, John, D-Mich. (13)

Capitol Hill Office: 2426 RHOB 20515-2214; 225-5126; Fax: 225-0072; *Chief of Staff; Legis. Counsel, Black Caucus, Korean Caucus:* Cynthia Martin
Web: http://conyers.house.gov/
Facebook: http://facebook.com/CongressmanConyers
Twitter: http://twitter.com/repjohnconyers
District Offices: Theodore Levin U.S. Courthouse, 231 W. Lafayette Blvd., Room 669, Detroit, MI 48226-2766; 313-961-5670; Fax: 313-226-2085; *District Director:* Yolonda Lipsey

33300 Warren Rd., #13, Westland, MI 48185-9620; 734-675-4084; Fax: 734-675-4218; *Caseworker:* Jane Mackey

Committee Assignment: Judiciary, Ranking Member

Cook, Paul, R-Calif. (8)

Capitol Hill Office: 1222 LHOB 20515; 225-5861; Fax: 225-6498; *Chief of Staff:* John Sobel
Web: http://cook.house.gov/
Facebook: http://facebook.com/RepPaulCook
Twitter: http://twitter.com/RepPaulCook
District Office: Apple Valley Town Hall, 14955 Dale Evans Pkwy., Apple Valley, CA 92307; 760-247-1815; Fax: 760-247-8073; *District Director:* Matt Knox

34932 Yucaipa Blvd., Yucaipa, CA 92399; 909-797-4900; Fax: 909-797-4997; *District Director:* Matt Knox

Committee Assignments: Armed Services; Foreign Affairs; Veterans' Affairs

Cooper, Jim, D-Tenn. (5)

Capitol Hill Office: 1536 LHOB 20515-4205; 225-4311; Fax: 226-1035; *Chief of Staff:* Lisa Quigley
Web: http://cooper.house.gov/
Facebook: http://facebook.com/JimCooper
Twitter: http://twitter.com/repjimcooper
District Office: 605 Church St., Nashville, TN 37219-2314; 615-736-5295; Fax: 615-736-7479; *Chief of Staff:* Lisa Quigley
Committee Assignments: Armed Services; Oversight and Government Reform

Costa, Jim, D-Calif. (16)

Capitol Hill Office: 1314 LHOB 20515-0520; 225-3341;
Fax: 225-9308; *Chief of Staff; Ethics:* Juan Lopez
Web: http://costa.house.gov/
Facebook: http://facebook.com/RepJimCosta
Twitter: http://twitter.com/RepJimCosta
District Office: 855 M St., #940, Fresno, CA 93721-2757;
559-495-1620; Fax: 559-495-1027; *District Director:*
Ian LeMay
2222 M St., #305, Merced, CA 95340; 209-384-1620; *Field
Rep.:* Daniel Martinez, Matthew Wainwright
Committee Assignments: Agriculture; Natural Resources

Cotton, Tom, R-Ark. (4)

Capitol Hill Office: 415 CHOB 20515; 225-3772;
Fax: 225-1314; *Chief of Staff:* Doug Coutts
Web: http://cotton.house.gov/
Facebook: http://facebook.com/RepTomCotton
Twitter: http://twitter.com/RepTomCotton
District Offices: Johnson County Courthouse, 215 W.
Main St., Room 300, Clarksville, AR 72830; 479-
754-2120; *Field Rep.:* Lisa Harst
Union County Courthouse, 101 N. Washington Ave., #406,
El Dorado, AR 71730-5669; 870-881-0681; Fax: 870-
881-0683; *Constituent Advocate:* Patricia Herring
Federal Bldg., 100 Reserve St., #307, Hot Springs, AR
71901-4144; 501-520-5892; Fax: 501-520-5873; *District
Director:* Lesley Nelms
George Howard Jr. Federal Bldg., 100 E. 8th Ave.,
Room 2521, Pine Bluff, AR 71601-5070; 870-536-3376;
Fax: 870-536-4058; *Field Rep.:* Vannessa Moody
Committee Assignments: Financial Services; Foreign
Affairs

Courtney, Joe, D-Conn. (2)

Capitol Hill Office: 2348 RHOB 20515; 225-2076;
Fax: 225-4977; *Chief of Staff:* Jason J. Gross
Web: http://courtney.house.gov/
Facebook: http://facebook.com/joecourtney
Twitter: http://twitter.com/repjoecourtney
District Offices: 77 Hazard Ave., Unit J, Enfield, CT
06082-3890; 860-741-6011; Fax: 860-741-6036; *Field
Rep.:* Dorothy Grady
55 Main St., #250, Norwich, CT 06360; 860-886-0139;
Fax: 860-886-2974; *District Director:* Jenny Contois
Committee Assignments: Agriculture; Armed Services;
Education and Workforce

Cramer, Kevin, R-N.D. (At Large)

Capitol Hill Office: 1032 LHOB 20515; 225-2611;
Fax: 226-0893; *Chief of Staff:* Mark Gruman
Web: http://cramer.house.gov/
Facebook: http://facebook.com/
CongressmanKevinCramer
Twitter: http://twitter.com/RepKevinCramer
District Offices: Federal Bldg., 220 E. Rosser Ave., Room
328, Bismarck, ND 58501-3869; 701-224-0355;
Fax: 701-224-0431; *Deputy State Director:* Larry
Jahnke
3217 Fiechtner Dr., Suite D, Fargo, ND 58103; 701-356-
2216; Fax: 701-356-2217; *State Director:* Lisa Gibbens
4200 James Ray Dr., #600, Grand Forks, ND 58202;
701-738-4880; *Field Rep.:* Randy Richards
315 Main St., #203, Minot, ND 58701; 701-839-0255;
Field Rep.: Daryl Lies
Committee Assignments: Natural Resources; Science,
Space, and Technology

Crawford, Rick, R-Ark. (1)

Capitol Hill Office: 1711 LHOB 20515; 225-4076;
Fax: 225-5602; *Chief of Staff:* Jonah Shumate
Web: http://crawford.house.gov/
Facebook: http://facebook.com/RepRickCrawford
Twitter: http://twitter.com/reprickcrawford
District Offices: 112 S. 1st St., Cabot, AR 72023-3007; 501-
843-3043; Fax: 501-843-4955; *Field Rep.:* Jay Sherrod
2400 E. Highland Dr., #300, Jonesboro, AR 72401-6229;
870-203-0540; Fax: 870-203-0542; *District Director:*
Andrea Allen
1001 Hwy. 62 E., #9, Mountain Home, AR 72653; 870-424-
2075; Fax: 870-424-3149; *Field Rep.:* Joseph Didden
Committee Assignments: Agriculture; Transportation
and Infrastructure

Crenshaw, Ander, R-Fla. (4)

Capitol Hill Office: 440 CHOB 20515-0904; 225-2501;
Fax: 225-2504; *Chief of Staff:* Erica Striebel
Web: http://crenshaw.house.gov/
Facebook: http://facebook.com/pages/Congressman-
Ander-Crenshaw/200388204657
Twitter: http://twitter.com/AnderCrenshaw
District Office: 1061 Riverside Ave., #100, Jacksonville, FL
32204-4151; 904-598-0481; Fax: 904-598-0486; *District
Director:* Jacquelyn Smith
Committee Assignment: Appropriations

Crowley, Joseph, D-N.Y. (14)

Capitol Hill Office: 1436 LHOB 20515; 225-3965;
Fax: 225-1909; *Chief of Staff:* Kate Winkler
Web: http://crowley.house.gov/
Facebook: https://facebook.com/repjoecrowley
Twitter: https://twitter.com/repjoecrowley
District Offices: 2800 Bruckner Blvd., #201, Bronx, NY
10465-1907; 718-931-1400; Fax: 718-931-1340; *District
Chief of Staff:* Anne Marie Anzalone
82-11 37th Ave., #402, Queens, NY 11372; 718-779-1400;
Fax: 718-505-0156; *Field Rep.:* Anne Marie Anzalone
Committee Assignment: Ways and Means

Cuellar, Henry, D-Tex. (28)

Capitol Hill Office: 2431 RHOB 20515; 225-1640;
Fax: 225-1641; *Chief of Staff:* Cynthia Gaona
Web: http://cuellar.house.gov/
Facebook: http://.facebook.com/pages/USCongressman-
Henry-Cuellar-TX-28/152569121550
Twitter: http://twitter.com/RepCuellar

District Offices: 602 E. Calton Rd., #2, Laredo, TX 78041-3693; 956-725-0639; Fax: 956-725-2647; *Grants Coord.:* Juan Sanchez

117 E. Tom Landry St., Mission, TX 78572-4160; 956-424-3942; Fax: 956-424-3936; *Area I Outreach Coord.:* Alexis Gallegos

100 N. F.M. 3167, Rio Grande City, TX 78582; 956-487-5603; Fax: 956-488-0952; *Constituent Services Rep. / Outreach:* Nicole Hernandez

615 E. Houston St., #563, San Antonio, TX 78205-2048; 210-271-2851; Fax: 210-277-6671; *Outreach Coord.:* Gilbert La Fuente

Committee Assignment: Appropriations

Culberson, John, R-Tex. (7)

Capitol Hill Office: 2352 RHOB 20515-4307; 225-2571; Fax: 225-4381; *Chief of Staff:* Jamie Gahun

Web: http://culberson.house.gov/

Facebook: http://facebook.com/CongressmanCulberson

Twitter: http://twitter.com/congculberson

District Office: 10000 Memorial Dr., #620, Houston, TX 77024; 713-682-8828; Fax: 713-680-8070; *District Director:* Brittany Seabury

Committee Assignment: Appropriations

Cummings, Elijah E., D-Md. (7)

Capitol Hill Office: 2235 RHOB 20515-2007; 225-4741; Fax: 225-3178; *Chief of Staff:* Vernon Simms

Web: http://cummings.house.gov/

Facebook: http://facebook.com/elijahcummings

Twitter: http://twitter.com/RepCummings

District Offices: 1010 Park Ave., #105 Baltimore, MD 21201-5600; 410-685-9199; Fax: 410-685-9399; *District Director:* Francine Allen

754 Frederick Rd., Catonsville, MD 21228-4504; 410-719-8777; Fax: 410-455-0110; *Special Asst. Military Immigration:* Katie Malone

8267 Main St., Room 102, Ellicott City, MD 21043-9903; 410-465-8259; Fax: 410-465-8740; *Special Asst.:* Amy Stratton

Committee Assignments: Oversight and Government Reform, Ranking Member; Transportation and Infrastructure

Daines, Steve, R-Mont. (At Large)

Capitol Hill Office: 206 CHOB 20515; 225-3211; Fax: 225-5687; *Chief of Staff:* Jason Thielman

Web: http://daines.house.gov/

Facebook: http://facebook.com/SteveDainesMT

Twitter: http://twitter.com/stevedaines

District Offices: 222 N. 32nd St., #900, Billings, MT 59101; 406-969-1736; Fax: 406-702-1182; *Casework Manager:* Sheila Rath

104 2nd St. South, #103, Great Falls, MT 59401; 406-315-3860; Fax: 406-315-3862; *Regional Director:* Cari Kent

910 N. Last Chance Gulch, Suite B., Helena, MT 59601-3858; 406-502-1435; Fax: 406-502-1436; *State Director:* Charles Robinson

110 W. Front St., Missoula, MT 59802; 406-926-2122; Fax: 406-926-2125; *Regional Director:* Dan Stusek

Committee Assignments: Homeland Security; Natural Resources; Transportation and Infrastructure

Davis, Danny K., D-Ill. (7)

Capitol Hill Office: 2159 RHOB 20515-1307; 225-5006; Fax: 225-5641; *Chief of Staff:* Yul Edwards

Web: http://davis.house.gov/

Facebook: http://facebook.com/CongressmanDKDavis

Twitter: http://twitter.com/DannyKDavis

District Office: 2746 W. Madison St., Chicago, IL 60612-2040; 773-533-7520; Fax: 773-533-7530; *District Director:* Cherita Logan

Committee Assignments: Oversight and Government Reform; Ways and Means

Davis, Rodney L, R-Ill. (13)

Capitol Hill Office: 1740 LHOB 20515; 225-2371; Fax: 226-0791; *Chief of Staff:* Jen Daulby

Web: http://rodneydavis.house.gov/

Facebook: http://facebook.com/RepRodneyDavis

Twitter: https://twitter.com/RodneyDavis

District Office: 2004 Fox Dr., Champaign, IL 61820; 217-403-4690; Fax: 217-403-4691; *District Director:* Tim Butler

243 S. Water St., #100, Decatur, IL 62523; 217-791-6224; Fax: 217-791-6168; *Chief of Staff:* Tim Butler

9 Junction Dr., #9, Glen Carbon, IL 62034; 618-205-8660; Fax: 618-205-8662; *Grants and Projects Coord.:* Phillip Lasseigne

104 W. North Street, Normal, IL 61761; 309-252-8834; *Casework Director:* Jennifer White

108 E. Market, Taylorville, IL 62568; 217-824-5117; Fax: 217-824-5121; *Constituent Services Rep.:* Margaret Kettelkamp

Committee Assignments: Agriculture; Transportation and Infrastructure

Davis, Susan, D-Calif. (53)

Capitol Hill Office: 1526 LHOB 20515-0553; 225-2040; Fax: 225-2948; *Chief of Staff:* Lisa Sherman

Web: http://house.gov/susandavis/

Facebook: http://facebook.com/RepSusanDavis

Twitter: http://twitter.com/RepSusanDavis

District Office: 2700 Adams Ave., #102, San Diego, CA 92116; 619-280-5353; Fax: 619-280-5311; *District Director:* Jessica Poole

Committee Assignments: Armed Services; Education and the Workforce

DeFazio, Peter, D-Ore. (4)

Capitol Hill Office: 2134 RHOB 20515-3704; 225-6416; Fax: 226-3493; *Chief of Staff Homeland Security; Gun Control:* Kathy Dedrick

Web: http://defazio.house.gov/

Facebook: http://facebook.com/RepPeterDeFazio

Twitter: http://twitter.com/RepPeterDeFazio

District Offices: 125 Central Ave., #350, Coos Bay, OR 97420-2342; 541-269-2609; Fax: 541-269-5760; *Coastal Field Rep.; Projects Director:* Kathy Erickson

405 E. 8th Ave., #2030, Eugene, OR 97401-2706; 541-465-6732; Fax: 541-465-6458; *District Director:* Nick Batz

612 S.E. Jackson St., Room 9, Roseburg, OR 97470-4956; 541-440-3523; Fax: 541-440-3525; *Field Rep.:* Christine Conroy

Committee Assignments: Natural Resources; Transportation and Infrastructure

DeGette, Diana, D-Colo. (1)

Capitol Hill Office: 2368 RHOB 20515; 225-4431; Fax: 225-5657; *Chief of Staff:* Lisa B. Cohen

Web: http://degette.house.gov/

Facebook: http://facebook.com/DianaDeGette

Twitter: http://twitter.com/RepDianaDeGette

District Office: 600 Grant St., #202, Denver, CO 80203-3525; 303-844-4988; Fax: 303-844-4996; *District Director:* Morris Price

Committee Assignment: Energy and Commerce

Delaney, John, D-Md. (6)

Capitol Hill Office: 1632 LHOB 20515; 225-2721; Fax: 225-2193; *Chief of Staff:* Lisa Bianco

Web: http://delaney.house.gov/

Facebook: http://facebook.com/congressmanjohndelaney

Twitter: http://twitter.com/RepJohnDelaney

District Offices: 9801 Washingtonian Blvd., #330, Gaithersburg, MD 20878; 301-926-0300; *District Director:* Lisa Bianco

6 W. Washington St., #210, Hagerstown, MD 21740; 301-733-2900; *Field Rep.:* Sonny Holding

Committee Assignment: Financial Services; Joint Economic

DeLauro, Rosa L, D-Conn. (3)

Capitol Hill Office: 2413 RHOB 20515-0703; 225-3661; Fax: 225-4890; *Chief of Staff:* Beverly Aimaro Pheto

Web: http://delauro.house.gov/

Facebook: http://facebook.com/CongresswomanRosaDeLauro

Twitter: http://twitter.com/rosadelauro

District Offices: Valley Regional Planning Agency, Conference Room, 12 Main St., Derby, CT 06418-1931; 203-735-5005; *District Director:* Jennifer Lamb

Municipal Bldg., 245 DeKoven Dr., Room B-20, Middletown, CT 06457-3460; 860-344-1159; *District Director:* Jennifer Lamb

Municipal Bldg., 229 Church St., Mayors Conference Room, 4th Floor, Naugatuck, CT 06770-4145; 203-729-0204; *District Director:* Jennifer Lamb

59 Elm St., #205, New Haven, CT 06510-2036; 203-562-3718; Fax: 203-772-2260; *District Director:* Jennifer Lamb

Committee Assignment: Appropriations

DelBene, Suzan, D-Wash. (1)

Capitol Hill Office: 318 CHOB 20515; 225-6311; Fax: 226-1606; *Chief of Staff:* Aaron Schmidt

Web: http://delbene.house.gov/

Facebook: http://facebook.com/RepDelBene

Twitter: http://twitter.com/@RepDelBene

District Office: 22121 17th Ave. S.E., Bldg. E, #220, Bothell, WA 98021; 425-485- 0085; Fax: 425-0083; *District Director:* Julien Loh

Committee Assignments: Agriculture; Judiciary

Denham, Jeff, R-Calif. (10)

Capitol Hill Office: 1730 LHOB 20515; 225-4540; Fax: 225-3402; *Chief of Staff:* Jason G. Larrabee

Web: http://denham.house.gov/

Facebook: http://facebook.com/RepJeffDenham

Twitter: http://twitter.com/RepJeffDenham

District Offices: 4701 Sisk Rd., #202, Modesto, CA 95356; 209-579-5458; Fax: 209-579-5028; *District Director:* Bob Rucker

Committee Assignments: Agriculture; Transportation and Infrastructure; Veterans' Affairs

Dent, Charlie, R-Pa. (15)

Capitol Hill Office: 2455 RHOB 20515; 225-6411; Fax: 226-0778; *Chief of Staff:* Drew Kent

Web: http://dent.house.gov/

Facebook: http://facebook.com/congressmandent

Twitter: http://twitter.com/DentPressShop

District Offices: 3900 Hamilton Blvd., #207, Allentown, PA 18103-6122; 610-770-3490; Fax: 610-770-3498; *District Director:* Vincent O'Domski

250 W. Chocolate Ave., #2, Hershey, PA 17033; 717-533-3959; Fax: 717-533-3979 *Community Outreach Director; Constituent Services Rep.:* Victoria Wood

61 N. 3rd St., Hamburg, PA 19526; 610-562-4281; Fax: 610-562-4352; *Berks County Coordinator:* Jason Lane

342 W. Main St., Annville, PA 17003; 717-867-1026; Fax: 717-867-1540; *Lebanon County Coordinator:* Brian Craig

Committee Assignments: Appropriations; Ethics

DeSantis, Ron, R-Fla. (6)

Capitol Hill Office: 427 CHOB 20515; 225-2706; Fax: 226-6299; *Chief of Staff:* Justin Roth

Web: http://desantis.house.gov/

Facebook: http://facebook.com/RepDeSantis

Twitter: http://twitter.com/RepDeSantis

District Offices: 1000 City Center Circle, Port Orange, FL 32129; 386-756-9798; Fax: 386-756-9903; *District Rep.:* Naomi Weiss

3940 Lewis Speedway, #2104, St. Augustine, FL 32084; 904-827-1101; Fax: 904-827-1114; *District Rep.:* Roy Alaimo

Committee Assignments: Foreign Affairs; Judiciary; Oversight and Government Reform

DesJarlais, Scott, R-Tenn. (4)

Capitol Hill Office: 413 CHOB 20515-4204; 225-6831; Fax: 226-5172; *Chief of Staff:* Richard Vaughn
Web: http://desJarlais.house.gov/
Facebook: http://facebook.com/ScottDesJarlaisTN04
Twitter: http://twitter.com/DesJarlaisTN04
District Offices: 301 Keith St., #212, Cleveland, TN 37311; 423-472-7500; Fax: 423-472-7800; *Field Rep.:* Shirley Pond
807 S. Garden St., Columbia, TN 38401-3262; 931-381-9920; Fax: 931-381-9945; *Constituent Services Coord.:* Becky Moon
305 W. Main St., Murfreesboro, TN 37130; 615-896-1986; Fax: 615-896-8218; *Field Rep.:* Tina Jones
Federal Bldg., 200 S. Jefferson St., #311, Winchester, TN 37398; 931-962-3180; Fax: 931-962-3435; *District Rep.:* Isiah Robinson
Committee Assignments: Agriculture; Education and the Workforce; Oversight and Government Reform

Deutch, Ted, D-Fla. (21)

Capitol Hill Office: 1024 LHOB 20515-0919; 225-3001; Fax: 225-5974; *Chief of Staff:* Joshua Rogin
Web: http://deutch.house.gov/
Facebook: http://facebook.com/CongressmanTedDeutch
Twitter: http://twitter.com/repteddeutch
District Offices: 8177 Glades Rd., #211, Boca Raton, FL 33434; 561-470-5440; Fax: 561-470-5446; *District Director:* Wendi Lipsich
Margate City Hall, 5790 Margate Blvd., Margate, FL 33063-3614; 954-972-6454; Fax: 954-974-3191; *District Rep.:* Theresa Brier
1300 Coral Springs Dr., Coral Springs, FL 33071; 954-255-8336; *District Rep.:* Theresa Brier
Committee Assignments: Ethics; Foreign Affairs; Judiciary

Diaz-Balart, Mario, R-Fla. (25)

Capitol Hill Office: 436 CHOB 20515-0921; 225-4211; Fax: 225-8576; *Chief of Staff:* Cesar A. Gonzalez
Web: http://mariodiazbalart.house.gov/
Facebook: http://facebook.com/mdiazbalart
Twitter: http://twitter.com/mariodb
District Offices: 8669 N.W. 36th St., #100, Doral, FL 33166-6640; 305-470-8555; Fax: 305-470-8575; *District Director:* Miguel Otero
4715 Golden Gate Pkwy., #1, Naples, FL 34116; 239-348-1620; Fax: 239-348-3569; *Field Rep.:* Monica Maziarz
Committee Assignment: Appropriations

Dingell, John D., D-Mich. (12)

Capitol Hill Office: 2328 RHOB 20515-2215; 225-4071; Fax: 226-0371; *Chief of Staff:* Katie Murtha
Web: http://dingell.house.gov/
Facebook: http://facebook.com/johndingell
Twitter: http://twitter.com/john_dingell
District Offices: 19855 W. Outer Dr., #103-E, Dearborn, MI 48124-2028; 313-278-2936; Fax: 313-278-3914; *District Director:* Derek Dobies

301 W. Michigan Ave., #400, Ypsilanti, MI 48197; 734-481-1100; *Field Rep.:* Jelani McGadney
Committee Assignment: Energy and Commerce

Doggett, Lloyd, D-Tex. (35)

Capitol Hill Office: 201 CHOB 20515-4325; 225-4865; Fax: 225-3073; *Chief of Staff:* Michael J. Mucchetti
Web: http://doggett.house.gov/
Facebook: http://facebook.com/lloyddoggett
Twitter: http://twitter.com/replloyddoggett
District Offices: Federal Bldg., 300 E. 8th St., #763, Austin, TX 78701-3224; 512-916-5921; Fax: 512-916-5108; *Deputy District Director:* Lee Ann Calaway
217 W. Travis St., San Antonio, TX 78205; 210-704-1080; Fax: 210-299-1442; *District Director:* Andrew Solano
Committee Assignment: Ways and Means

Doyle, Mike, D-Pa. (14)

Capitol Hill Office: 239 CHOB 20515; 225-2135; Fax: 225-3084; *Chief of Staff:* David G. Lucas
Web: http://doyle.house.gov/
Facebook: http://facebook.com/usrepmikedoyle
Twitter: http://twitter.com/usrepmikedoyle
District Offices: 1350 5th Ave., Coraopolis, PA 15108-2024; 412-264-3460; *Caseworker:* Joseph Heffley
627 Lysle Blvd., McKeesport, PA 15132; 412-664-4049; Fax: 412-664-4053; *Economic Development Rep.:* Jeffrey Schaffer
11 Duff Rd., Penn Hills, PA 15235; 412-241-6055; Fax: 412-241-6820; *Caseworker:* John Jones
2637 E. Carson St., Pittsburgh, PA 15203-5109; 412-390-1499; Fax: 412-390-2118; *District Director:* Paul D'Alesandro
Committee Assignment: Energy and Commerce

Duckworth, Tammy, D-Ill. (8)

Capitol Hill Office: 104 CHOB 20515; 225-3711; Fax: 225-7830; *Chief of Staff:* Kaitlin Fahey
Web: http://duckworth.house.gov/
Facebook: http://facebook.com/CongresswomanTammyDuckworth
Twitter: http://twitter.com/repduckworth
District Office: 1701 E. Woodfield Rd., #900, Schaumburg, IL 60173; 847-413-1959; *District Director:* Sendy Soto
Committee Assignments: Armed Services; Oversight and Government Reform

Duffy, Sean, R-Wisc. (7)

Capitol Hill Office: 1208 LHOB 20515-4907; 225-3365; Fax: 225-3240; *Chief of Staff:* Pete Meachum
Web: http://duffy.house.gov/
Facebook: http://facebook.com/RepSeanDuffy
Twitter: http://twitter.com/RepSeanDuffy
District Offices: 823 Belknap St., #225, Superior, WI 54880-2974; 715-392-3984; Fax: 715-392-3999; *Regional Rep.:* Craig Rossand
208 Grand Ave., Wausau, WI 54403-6217; 715-298-9344; Fax: 715-298-9348; *District Director:* Jesse Garza

502 2nd St., #202, Hudson, WI 54016; 715-808-8160;
District Director: Jesse Garzaf
Committee Assignments: Budget; Financial Services, Joint
Economic

Duncan, Jeff, R-S.C. (3)

Capitol Hill Office: 116 CHOB 20515-4003; 225-5301;
Fax: 225-3216; *Chief of Staff:* Lance Williams
Web: http://jeffduncan.house.gov/
Facebook: http://facebook.com/RepJeffDuncan
Twitter: http://twitter.com/RepJeffDuncan
District Offices: 303 W. Beltline Blvd., Anderson, SC
29625-1505; 864-224-7401; Fax: 864-225-7049; *District
Director:* Rick Adkins
200 Courthouse Public Square, P.O. Box 471, Laurens, SC
29360; 864-681-1028; Fax: 864-681-1030; *Field Rep.:*
Tasha Hart
Committee Assignments: Foreign Affairs; Homeland
Security; Natural Resources

Duncan, John J., Jr., R-Tenn. (2)

Capitol Hill Office: 2207 RHOB 20515-4202; 225-5435;
Fax: 225-6440; *Deputy Chief of Staff; Transportation
and Infrastructure Committee:* Don Walker
Web: http://duncan.house.gov/
Facebook: http://facebook.com/CongressmanDuncan
Twitter: http://twitter.com/RepJohnDuncanJr
District Offices: Howard H. Baker, Jr. U.S. Courthouse,
800 Market St., #110, Knoxville, TN 37902-2303;
865-523-3772; Fax: 865-544-0728; *Chief of Staff:* Bob
Griffitts
Blount County Courthouse, 331 Court St., Maryville, TN
37804; 865-984-5464; Fax: 865-984-0521; *Office
Manager:* Vickie Flynn
Committee Assignments: Oversight and Government
Reform; Transportation and Infrastructure

Edwards, Donna F., D-Md. (4)

Capitol Hill Office: 2445 RHOB 20515; 225-8699;
Fax: 225-8714; *Chief of Staff:* Adrienne Christian
Web: http://donnaedwards.house.gov/
Facebook: http://facebook.com/
CongresswomanDonnaFEdwards
Twitter: http://twitter.com/repdonnaedwards
District Offices: 5001 Silver Hill Rd., #106, Suitland, MD
20746-5208; 301-516-7601; Fax: 301-516-7608;
*Director of Community Outreach and Constiuent
Services:* Betty Horton-Hodge
877 Baltimore Annapolis Blvd., Ritchie Court Office Bldg.,
#101, Severna Park, MD 21146; 410-421-8061;
301-516-7608 *Field Rep.:* Betty Horton-Hodge
Committee Assignments: Science, Space, and Technology;
Transportation and Infrastructure

Ellison, Keith, D-Minn. (5)

Capitol Hill Office: 2244 RHOB 20515; 225-4755;
Fax: 225-4886; *Chief of Staff:* Kari Moe
Web: http://ellison.house.gov/
Facebook: http://facebook.com/Keith.Ellison

Twitter: http://twitter.com/keithellison
District Office: 2100 Plymouth Ave. N., Minneapolis, MN
55411-3675; 612-522-1212; Fax: 612-522-9915; *District
Director:* Jamie Long
Committee Assignment: Financial Services

Ellmers, Renee, R-N.C. (2)

Capitol Hill Office: 426 CHOB 20515; 225-4531;
Fax: 225-5662; *Chief of Staff:* Al Lytton
Web:http://ellmers.house.gov/
Facebook: http://facebook.com/reneeellmers
Twitter: http://twitter.com/RepReneeEllmers
District Offices: 222 Sunset Ave., #101, Asheboro, NC
27203; 336-626-3060; Fax: 336-629-7819; *Field Rep.:*
Cindy Wilkins; *Constituent Services Director:* Rebecca
Briles
406 W. Broad St., Dunn, NC 28334-4808; 910-230-1910;
Fax: 910-230-1940; *District Director:* Pat Fitzgerald
Committee Assignment: Energy and Commerce

Engel, Eliot L, D-N.Y. (16)

Capitol Hill Office: 2161 RHOB 20515-3217; 225-2464;
Fax: 225-5513; *Admin. Asst.; Appropriations:* Ned
Michalek
Web: http://engel.house.gov/
Facebook: http://facebook.com/RepEliotEngel
Twitter: https://twitter.com/RepEliotEngel
District Offices: 3655 Johnson Ave., Bronx, NY 10463-
1671; 718-796-9700; Fax: 718-796-5134; *Chief of Staff:*
William Weitz
6 Gramatan Ave., #205, Mount Vernon, NY 10550-3208;
914-699-4100; Fax: 914-699-3646; *Staff Asst.:* Cynthia
Miller
177 Dreiser Loop, Rm. 3, Bronx, NY 10475; 718-320-2314;
Fax: 718-320-2047 *Staff Asst.:* Maxine Sullivan
Committee Assignments: Energy and Commerce; Foreign
Affairs, Ranking Member

Enyart, William, D-Ill. (12)

Capitol Hill Office: 1722 LHOB 20515; 225-5661;
Fax: 225-0285; *Chief of Staff:* Kevin Kern
Web: http://enyart.house.gov/
Facebook: http://facebook.com/CongressmanBillEnyart
Twitter: http://twitter.com/repbillenyart
District Offices: 23 Public Square, #404, Belleville, IL
62220; 618-233-8026; Fax: 618-233-8765; *District
Director:* Renysha Brown
250 W. Cherry St., Carbondale, IL 62901-2856; 618-529-
3791; Fax: 618-549-3768; *Staff Asst.:* Brandi Bradley
1330 Swanwick St., Chester, IL 62233-1314; 618-826-3043;
Fax: 618-826-1923; *Staff Asst.:* Lynne Mueth
2060 Delmar Ave., Suite B, Granite City, IL 62040-4511;
618-451-7065; Fax: 618-451-2126; *Staff Asst.:* David
Cueto
201 E. Nolen St., West Frankfort, IL 62896-2437; 618-937-
6402; Fax: 618-937-3307; *Staff Asst.:* Karl Maple
SIUE East. St. Louis Center, Building A, Rm. 1051, 601
James R. Thompson Blvd., East St. Louis, IL 62201l;
618-233-8026; *Field Rep.:* Kim Clark

1100 Main St., Mt. Vernon, IL 62864; 618-316-9035; *Field Rep.*: Karl Maple

Committee Assignments: Agriculture; Armed Services

Eshoo, Anna G., D-Calif. (18)

Capitol Hill Office: 241 CHOB 20515; 225-8104; Fax: 225-8890; *Exec. Asst; Scheduler:* Jena Gross
Web: http://eshoo.house.gov/
Facebook: http://facebook.com/RepAnnaEshoo
Twitter: http://twitter.com/RepAnnaEshoo
District Office: 698 Emerson St., Palo Alto, CA 94301-1609; 650-323-2984; Fax: 650-323-3498; *District Chief of Staff:* Karen Chapman

Committee Assignment: Energy and Commerce

Esty, Elizabeth, D-Conn. (5)

Capitol Hill Office: 509 CHOB 20515; 225-4476; Fax: 225-5933; *Chief of Staff:* Tony Baker
Web: http://esty.house.gov/
Facebook: http://facebook.com/RepEsty
Twitter: http://twitter.com/RepEsty
District Offices: 114 W. Main St., Old Post Office Plaza, LLC, New Britain, CT 06051-4223; 860-223-8412; Fax: 860-225-7289; *Director of Operations:* Russell Griffin

Committee Assignments: Science, Space, and Technology; Transportation and Infrastructure

Faleomavaega, Eni F. H., D-Am. Samoa (At Large)

Capitol Hill Office: 2422 RHOB 20515-5201; 225-8577; Fax: 225-8757; *D.C. Chief of Staff; Staff Director Subcommittee on Asia, the Pacific and the Global Environment, Appropriations, International Relations:* Lisa Williams
Web: http://house.gov/faleomavaega/
District Office: P.O. Drawer X, Pago Pago, AS 96799; 684-699-8577; Fax: 684-699-8582; *Chief of Staff:* Alexander Godinet

Committee Assignments: Foreign Affairs; Natural Resources

Farenthold, Blake, R-Tex. (27)

Capitol Hill Office: 117 CHOB 20515; 225-7742; Fax: 226-1134; *Chief of Staff:* Bob Haueter
Web: http://farenthold.house.gov/
Facebook: http://facebook.com/BlakeFarenthold
Twitter: http://twitter.com/farenthold
District Offices: 101 N. Shoreline Blvd., #300, Corpus Christi, TX 78401-2837; 361-884-2222; Fax: 361-884-2223; *District Director:* Bob Haueter
5606 N. Navarro St., #203, Victoria, TX 77904; 361-894-6446; Fax: 361-894-6460; *Constituent Liaison:* Michelle Gloor

Committee Assignments: Judiciary; Oversight and Government Reform; Transportation and Infrastructure

Farr, Sam, D-Calif. (20)

Capitol Hill Office: 1126 LHOB 20515-0517; 225-2861; Fax: 225-6791; *Chief of Staff:* Rochelle S. Dornatt
Web: http://farr.house.gov/
Facebook: http://facebook.com/RepSamFarr
Twitter: https://twitter.com/repsamfarr
District Offices: 100 W. Alisal St., Salinas, CA 93901; 831-424-2229; Fax: 831-424-7099; *District Director:* Alec Arago
701 Ocean St., Room 318C, Santa Cruz, CA 95060-4027; 831-429-1976; Fax: 831-429-1458; *Congressional Aide:* Sonja Arndt

Committee Assignment: Appropriations

Fattah, Chaka, D-Pa. (2)

Capitol Hill Office: 2301 RHOB 20515-3802; 225-4001; Fax: 225-5392; *Chief of Staff:* Maisha C. Leek
Web: http://fattah.house.gov/
Facebook: http://facebook.com/repfattah
Twitter: http://twitter.com/chakafattah
District Office: 2401 N. 54th St., Philadelphia, PA 19131; 215-871-4455; Fax: 215-871-4456; *District Chief of Staff:* Bonnie Bowser

Committee Assignment: Appropriations

Fincher, Stephen, R-Tenn. (8)

Capitol Hill Office: 1118 LHOB 20515-4208; 225-4714; Fax: 225-1765; *Chief of Staff:* Jessica Carter
Web: http://fincher.house.gov/
Facebook: http://facebook.com/RepFincherTN08
Twitter: http://twitter.com/repfinchertn08
District Offices: 100 S. Main St., #1, Dyersburg, TN 38024-4662; 731-285-0910; Fax: 731-285-5008; *Field Rep.:* Ivy Fultz
117 N. Liberty St., Jackson, TN 38301-6205; 731-423-4848; Fax: 731-427-1537; *Deputy Chief of Staff:* Scott Golden
406 Lindell St. South, Suite C, Martin, TN 38237-2481; 731-588-5190; *Field Rep.:* Heather Waggoner
12015 Walker St., Arlington, TN 38002; 901-581-4718; *Field Rep.:* Marianne Dunavant
5384 Poplar Ave., #410, Memphis, TN 38119; 901-682-4422; *Field Rep.:* Chris Connolly

Committee Assignments: Agriculture; Financial Services

Fitzpatrick, Mike, R-Pa. (8)

Capitol Hill Office: 2400 RHOB 20515; 225-4276; Fax: 225-9511; *Chief of Staff:* Athan Koutsiouroumbas
Web: http://fitzpatrick.house.gov/
Facebook: http://facebook.com/RepFitzpatrick
Twitter: http://twitter.com/RepFitzpatrick
District Office: 1717 Langhorne Newtown Rd., #400, Langhorne, PA 19047-1086; 215-579-8102; Fax: 215-579-8109; *District Director:* Stacey Mulholland

Committee Assignment: Financial Services

Fleischmann, Chuck, R-Tenn. (3)

Capitol Hill Office: 230 CHOB 20515; 225-3271; Fax: 225-3494; *Chief of Staff:* Jim Hippe

Web: http://fleischmann.house.gov/
Facebook: http://facebook.com/repchuck
Twitter: http://twitter.com/repchuck
District Offices: 6 E. Madison Ave., Athens, TN 37303;
423-745-4671; Fax: 423-745-6025; *Field Rep.:* Maxine
O'Dell-Gernert
900 Georgia Ave., #126, Chattanooga, TN 37402-2282; 423-
756-2342; Fax: 423-756-6613; *District Director:* Bob White
200 Administration Rd., #100, Oak Ridge, TN 37830-8823;
865-576-1976; Fax: 865-576-3221; *Policy Advisor:*
Helen Hardin
Committee Assignment: Appropriations

Fleming, John, R-La. (4)

Capitol Hill Office: 416 CHOB 20515-1804; 225-2777;
Fax: 225-8039; *Chief of Staff:* Dana G. Gartzke
Web: http://fleming.house.gov/
Facebook: http://facebook.com/RepJohnFleming
Twitter: http://twitter.com/RepFleming
District Offices: 700 Benton Rd., Bossier City, LA 71111-
3705; 318-549-1712; *Field Rep.:* Stephanie McKenzie
103 N. 3rd St., Leesville, LA 71446-4013; 337-238-0778;
Fax: 337-238-0566; *District Director, Southern Region:*
Lee Turner
6425 Youree Dr., #350, Shreveport, LA 71105-4634;
318-798-2254; Fax: 318-798-2063; *District Director:*
Stephanie McKenzie
Committee Assignments: Armed Services; Natural
Resources

Flores, Bill, R-Tex. (17)

Capitol Hill Office: 1030 LHOB 20515; 225-6105;
Fax: 225-0350; *Chief of Staff:* Jeff Morhouse
Web: http://flores.house.gov/
Facebook: http://facebook.com/RepBillFlores
Twitter: http://twitter.com/RepBillFlores
District Offices: 14205 Burnet Rd., #230, Austin, TX
78728; 512-373-3378; Fax: 512-373-3511; *Field Rep.:*
Brandon Simon
3000 Briarcrest Dr., #406, Bryan, TX 77802; 979-703-4037;
Fax: 979-703-8845; *Deputy District Director:* James
Edge
400 Austin Ave., #302, Waco, TX 76701-2139; 254-732-
0748; Fax: 254-732-1755; *District Director:* Tim Head
Committee Assignments: Budget; Natural Resources;
Veterans' Affairs

Forbes, J. Randy, R-Va. (4)

Capitol Hill Office: 2135 RHOB 20515; 225-6365;
Fax: 226-1170; *Chief of Staff:* Dee Gilmore
Web: http://forbes.house.gov/
Facebook: http://facebook.com/randyforbes
Twitter: http://twitter.com/randy_forbes
District Offices: 505 Independence Pkwy., #104,
Chesapeake, VA 23320-5178; 757-382-0080;
Fax: 757-382-0780; *District Rep.:* Curtis Byrd
9401 Courthouse Rd., # 202, Chesterfield, VA 23832; 804-
318-1363; Fax: 804-318-1013; *District Rep.:* Ron White
Committee Assignments: Armed Services; Judiciary

Fortenberry, Jeff, R-Neb. (1)

Capitol Hill Office: 1514 LHOB 20515-2701; 225-4806;
Fax: 225-5686; *Chief of Staff:* Margo Matter
Web: http://fortenberry.house.gov/
Facebook: http://facebook.com/jefffortenberry
Twitter: http://twitter.com/JeffFortenberry
District Offices: 629 Broad St., P.O. Box 377, Fremont,
NE 68026-4932; 402-727-0888; Fax: 402-727-9130;
Field Rep.: Louis Pofahl
301 S. 13th St., #100, Lincoln, NE 68508-2532; 402-438-
1598; Fax: 402-438-1604; *Field Rep.:* Nate Blum
125 S. 4th St., #101, Norfolk, NE 68701-5200; 402-379-
2064; Fax: 402-379-2101; *District Director:* Josh
Moenning
Committee Assignment: Appropriations

Foster, Bill, D-Ill. (11)

Capitol Hill Office: 1224 LHOB 20515; 225-3515;
Fax: 225-9420; *Chief of Staff:* Elizabeth Glidden
Web: http://foster.house.gov/
Facebook: http://facebook.com/CongressmanBillFoster
Twitter: http://twitter.com/RepBillFoster
District Office: 2711 E. New York St., #204, Aurora, IL
60502; 630-585-7672; *District Director:* Carole Cheney
195 Springfield Ave., #102, Joliet, IL 60435; 815-280-5876;
Constituent Services Director: Chastity Wells-Armstrong
Committee Assignment: Financial Services

Foxx, Virginia, R-N.C. (5)

Capitol Hill Office: 2350 RHOB 20515; 225-2071;
Fax: 225-2995; *Chief of Staff:* Brandon Renz
Web: http://foxx.house.gov/
Facebook: http://facebook.com/RepVirginiaFoxx
Twitter: http://twitter.com/virginiafoxx
District Offices: 240 Hwy. 105 Extension, #200, Boone, NC
28607-4291; 828-265-0240; Fax: 828-265-0390; *District
Director:* Aaron Whitener
3540 Clemmons Rd., #125, Clemmons, NC 27012-8775;
336-778-0211; Fax: 336-778-2290; *District Director:*
Aaron Whitener
Committee Assignments: Education and the Workforce;
Rules

Frankel, Lois, D-Fla. (22)

Capitol Hill Office: 1037 LHOB 20515; 225-9890;
Fax: 226-3944; *Chief of Staff:* Jonathon Bray
Web: http://frankel.house.gov/
Facebook: http://facebook.com/RepLoisFrankel
Twitter: http://twitter.com/RepLoisFrankel
District Office: 2500 N. Military Trail, #490, Boca Raton,
FL 33431; 561-998-9045; Fax: 561-998-9048; *District
Director:* Felicia Goldstein
Committee Assignments: Foreign Affairs; Transportation
and Infrastructure

Franks, Trent, R-Ariz. (8)

Capitol Hill Office: 2435 RHOB 20515-0302; 225-4576;
Fax: 225-6328; *Chief of Staff:* Randy M. Kutz

Web: http://franks.house.gov/
Facebook: http://facebook.com/TrentFranks
Twitter: http://twitter.com/RepTrentFranks
District Office: 7121 W. Bell Rd., #200, Glendale, AZ 85308-8549; 623-776-7911; Fax: 623-776-7832; *District Director:* Dan Hay
Committee Assignments: Armed Services; Judiciary

Frelinghuysen, Rodney, R-N.J. (11)

Capitol Hill Office: 2306 RHOB 20515-3011; 225-5034; Fax: 225-3186; *Chief of Staff:* Nancy Fox
Web: http://frelinghuysen.house.gov/
Twitter: http://twitter.com/USRepRodney
District Office: 30 Schuyler Pl., 2nd Floor, Morristown, NJ 07960-5128; 973-984-0711; Fax: 973-292-1569; *District Director:* Pam Thievon
Committee Assignment: Appropriations

Fudge, Marcia L., D-Ohio (11)

Capitol Hill Office: 2344 RHOB 20515; 225-7032; Fax: 225-1339; *Chief of Staff:* Veleter Mazyck
Web: http://fudge.house.gov/
Facebook: http://facebook.com/RepMarciaLFudge
Twitter: http://twitter.com/RepMarciaFudge
District Office: 4834 Richmond Rd., #150, Warrensville Heights, OH 44128-5922; 216-522-4900; Fax: 216-522-4908; *Communications Director:* Belinda Prinz
1225 Lawton St., Akron, OH 44320; 330-835-4758; Fax: 330-835-4863; *Communications Director:* Belinda Prinz
Committee Assignments: Agriculture; Education and the Workforce

Gabbard, Tulsi, D-Hawaii (2)

Capitol Hill Office: 502 CHOB 20515; 225-4906; Fax: 225-4987; *Chief of Staff:* Jessica Vandenberg
Web: http://gabbard.house.gov/
Facebook: http://facebook.com/RepTulsiGabbard
Twitter: http://twitter.com/tulsipress
District Office: 5-104 Prince Kuhio Federal Bldg., 300 Ala Moana Blvd., Honolulu, HI 96850-0001; 808-541-1986; Fax: 808-538-0233; *District Director:* Walt Kaneakua
Committee Assignments: Foreign Affairs; Homeland Security

Gallego, Pete, D-Tex. (23)

Capitol Hill Office: 431 CHOB 20515; 225-4511; Fax: 225-2237; *Chief of Staff:* Rene Munoz
Web: http://gallego.house.gov/
Facebook: http://facebook.com/CongressmanPeteGallego
Twitter: http://twitter.com/RepPeteGallego
District Offices: 1915 Veterans Blvd., Del Rio Civic Center, Del Rio, TX 78840; 830-488-6600; *Field Rep.:* Cynthia Martinez
100 S. Monroe St., Eagle Pass, TX 78852-4830; 830-488-6600; *Field Rep.:* Cynthia Martinez
1714 S.W. Military Dr., #110, San Antonio TX 78221; 210-927-4592; Fax: 210-927-4903; *District Director:* Irma Gutierrez

124 S. Horizon Blvd., Socorro, TX 79927; 915-872-1066; *Field Rep.:* Nancy Beh
Committee Assignments: Agriculture; Armed Services

Garamendi, John, D-Calif. (3)

Capitol Hill Office: 2438 RHOB 20515; 225-1880; Fax: 225-5914; *Acting Chief of Staff:* Chris Austin
Web: http://garamendi.house.gov/
Facebook: http://facebook.com/repgaramendi
Twitter: http://twitter.com/RepGaramendi
District Offices: 412 G. St., Davis, CA 95616; 530-753-5301; Fax: 530-753-5614; *District Director:* Elly Fairclough
609 Jefferson St., Fairfield, CA 94533-6293; 707-438-1822; Fax: 707-438-0523; *District Rep.:* Brandon Thompson
990 Klamath Lane, #4, Yuba City, CA 95993; 530-329-8865; Fax: 530-763-4248; *Field Rep.:* Jeannie Klever
Committee Assignments: Agriculture; Armed Services; Transportation and Infrastructure

Garcia, Joe, D-Fla. (26)

Capitol Hill Office: 1440 LHOB 20515; 225-2778; Fax: 226-2346; *Chief of Staff:* Caitlin Fishman
Web: http://garcia.house.gov/
Facebook: https://facebook.com/joegarciaforcongress
Twitter: http://twitter.com/JoeGarcia
District Offices: 1100 Simonton St., #1-213, Key West, FL 33040; 305-292-4485; Fax: 305-292-4486; *Constituent Services:* Rita Cotter
12851 S.W. 42nd St., #131, Miami, FL 33175; 305-222-0160; 305-228-9397; *District Director:* Raul Martinez
Committee Assignments: Judiciary; Natural Resources

Gardner, Cory, R-Colo. (4)

Capitol Hill Office: 213 CHOB 20515-0604; 225-4676; Fax: 225-5870; *Chief of Staff:* Natalie Farr
Web: http://gardner.house.gov/
Facebook: http://facebook.com/CongressmanGardner
Twitter: http://twitter.com/repcorygardner
District Offices: 7505 Village Square Dr., #207, Castle Rock, CO 80108; 720-508-3937; Fax: 720-583-0873; *District Director:* Chuck Poplstein
2425 35th Ave., #202, Greeley, CO 80634-3930; 970-351-6007; Fax: 970-351-6068; *Field Rep.:* Maria Secrest
408 N. Main St., Suite F, P.O. Box 104, Rocky Ford, CO 81067; 719-316-1101; Fax: 719-316-1103; *Field Rep.:* Doris Morgan
529 N. Albany, #1220, Yuma, CO 80759; 970-848-2845; Fax: 970-848-2835; *Field Rep.:* Alan Soutz
Committee Assignment: Energy and Commerce

Garrett, Scott, R-N.J. (5)

Capitol Hill Office: 2232 RHOB 20515-3005; 225-4465; Fax: 225-9048; *Chief of Staff:* Amy Smith
Web: http://garrett.house.gov/
Facebook: http://facebook.com/repscottgarrett
Twitter: http://twitter.com/RepGarrett

District Offices: 266 Harristown Rd., #104, Glen Rock, NJ 07452-3321; 201-444-5454; Fax: 201-444-5488; *District Director:* Rob Pettet

83 Spring St., #302A, Newton, NJ 07860-2080; 973-300-2000; Fax: 973-300-1051; *Constituent Services Rep.:* Amy Nittolo

Committee Assignments: Budget; Financial Services

Gerlach, Jim, R-Pa. (6)

Capitol Hill Office: 2442 RHOB 20515-3806; 225-4315; Fax: 225-8440; *Chief of Staff:* Lauryn Schothorst

Web: http://gerlach.house.gov/

Facebook: http://facebook.com/repjimgerlach

Twitter: http://twitter.com/JimGerlach

District Offices: 111 E. Uwchlan Ave., Exton, PA 19341-1206; 610-594-1415; Fax: 610-594-1419; *District Director; Press Secy.:* Kori Walter

580 Main St., #4, Trappe, PA 19426; 610-409-2780; Fax: 610-409-7988; *Director of Constituent Services:* Jason Carver

840 N. Park Rd., Wyomissing, PA 19610-2919; 610-376-7630; Fax: 610-376-7633; *District Rep.:* Wes Stesanik

Lebanon Municipal Building, Rm. 110, 400 S. Eighth St., Lebanon, PA 17042; 717-454-0462; *District Director:* Kori Walter

Committee Assignment: Ways and Means

Gibbs, Bob, R-Ohio (7)

Capitol Hill Office: 329 CHOB 20515-3518; 225-6265; Fax: 225-3394; *Chief of Staff:* Ryan Stenger

Web: http://gibbs.house.gov/

Facebook: http://facebook.com/RepBobGibbs

Twitter: http://twitter.com/repbobgibbs

District Office: 110 Cottage St., Ashland, OH 44805; 419-207-0650; Fax: 419-207-0655; *District Director:* Daryl Gerber

110 Central Plaza, South Canton, OH 44702; 330-730-1631; *Field Rep.:* Jason Wise

Committee Assignments: Agriculture; Transportation and Infrastructure

Gibson, Chris, R-N.Y. (19)

Capitol Hill Office: 1708 LHOB 20515; 225-5614; Fax: 225-1168; *Chief of Staff:* Steve J. Stallmer

Web: http://gibson.house.gov/

Facebook: http://facebook.com/RepChrisGibson

Twitter: http://twitter.com/repchrisgibson

District Offices: 25 Chestnut St., Cooperstown, NY 13326; 607-282-4002; *Field Rep.:* Carol Waller

111 Main St., Delhi, NY 13753-1233; 607-746-9537; *Field Rep.:* Paula Brown

4328 Albany Post Rd., Route 9, Hyde Park, NY 12538; 845-698-0132; *Field Rep.:* Patty Hohmann

2 Hudson St., PO Box 775, Kinderhook, NY 12106; 518-610-8133; *Office Manager:* Ann Mueller; *District Director:* Steve Bulger

721 Broadway, Kingston, NY 12401; 845-514-2322; *Field Rep.:* George Christian

92 Sullivan Ave., P.O. Box 578, Ferndale, NY 12754; 845-747-9261; *Field Rep.:* Christine Schiff

Committee Assignments: Agriculture; Armed Services

Gingrey, Phil, R-Ga. (11)

Capitol Hill Office: 442 CHOB 20515-1011; 225-2931; Fax: 225-2944; *Chief of Staff:* David Sours

Web: http://gingrey.house.gov/

Facebook: http://facebook.com/RepPhilGingrey

Twitter: http://twitter.com/RepPhilGingrey

District Offices: 135 W. Cherokee Ave., Cartersville, GA 30120; 678-721-2509; Fax: 678-721-7995; *District Director:* Janet Byington

100 North St., #150, Canton, GA 30114; 770-345-2931; Fax: 770-345-2930; *Field Rep.:* John Wallace

219 Roswell St., Marietta, GA 30060-2063; 770-429-1776; Fax: 770-795-9551; *Deputy District Director; Special Projects Manager:* John O'Keefe

Committee Assignments: Commission on Security and Cooperation in Europe (Helsinki Commission); Energy and Commerce; House Administration

Gohmert, Louie, R-Tex. (1)

Capitol Hill Office: 2443 RHOB 20515-4301; 225-3035; Fax: 226-1230; *Chief of Staff:* Connie Hair

Web: http://gohmert.house.gov/

Facebook: http://facebook.com/pages/Louie-Gohmert/50375006903

Twitter: https://twitter.com/replouiegohmert

District Offices: Gregg County Courthouse, 101 E. Methvin St., #302, Longview, TX 75601-7277; 903-236-8597; Fax: 903-561-7110; *Caseworker:* Shannon Crisp

300 E. Shepherd Ave., #210, Lufkin, TX 75901-3252; 936-632-3180; Fax: 903-561-7110; *District Director:* Jonna Fitzgerald

102 W. Houston St., Marshall, TX 75670-4038; 903-938-8386; Fax: 903-561-7110; *District Director:* Jonna Fitzgerald

101 W. Main St., #160, Nacogdoches, TX 75961-4830; 936-715-9514; Fax: 903-561-7110; *Caseworker:* Melinda Kartye

1121 E.S.E. Loop 323, #206, Tyler, TX 75701-9637; 903-561-6349; Fax: 903-561-7110; *Caseworker:* Lisa Blackman

Committee Assignments: Judiciary; Natural Resources

Goodlatte, Bob, R-Va. (6)

Capitol Hill Office: 2309 RHOB 20515-4606; 225-5431; Fax: 225-9681; *Chief of Staff Internet Caucus; International Anti-Piracy Caucus:* Peter Larkin

Web: http://house.gov/goodlatte/

Facebook: http://facebook.com/BobGoodlatte

Twitter: http://twitter.com/RepGoodlatte

District Offices: 70 N. Mason St., Harrisonburg, VA 22802; 540-432-2391; Fax: 540-432-6593; *District Rep.:* Eric Bagwell, Matt Homer

916 Main St., #300, Lynchburg, VA 24504; 434-845-8306; Fax: 434-845-8245; *District Rep.:* Aaron Van Allen

10 Franklin Rd., S.E., #540, Roanoke, VA 24011; 540-857-2672; Fax: 540-857-2675; *District Director:* Debbie Garrett

117 S. Lewis St., #215, Staunton, VA 24401; 540-885-3861; Fax: 540-885-3930; *District Rep.:* Debbie Garrett

Committee Assignments: Agriculture; Judiciary, Chair

Gosar, Paul, R-Ariz. (4)

Capitol Hill Office: 504 CHOB 20515-0301; 225-2315; Fax: 226-9739; *Chief of Staff:* Tom Van Flein

Web: http://gosar.house.gov/

Facebook: http://facebook.com/repgosar

Twitter: http://twitter.com/repgosar

District Offices: 220 N. 4th St., Kingman, AZ 86401; *District Director:* Penny Pew

122 N. Cortez St., #104, Prescott, AZ 86301; 928-445-1683; Fax: 928-445-3414; *Office Manager:* Julie Schriener

270 E. Hunt Hwy., #12, San Tan Valley, AZ 85143; 480-882-2697; Fax: 480-882-2698; *District Director:* Penny Pew

Committee Assignments: Natural Resources; Oversight and Government Reform

Gowdy, Trey, R-S.C. (4)

Capitol Hill Office: 1404 LHOB 20515; 225-6030; Fax: 226-1177; *Chief of Staff:* Matthew Van Patton

Web: http://gowdy.house.gov/

Facebook: http://facebook.com/RepTreyGowdy

Twitter: http://twitter.com/tgowdysc

District Offices: 104 S. Main St., Greenville, SC 29601-2742; 864-241-0175; Fax: 864-241-0982; *District Director:* Cindy Crick

Spartan Centre, 101 W. St. John St., Spartanburg, SC 29306-5179; 864-583-3264; Fax: 864-583-3926; *Office Manager:* Missy House

Committee Assignments: Education and the Workforce; Ethics; Judiciary; Oversight and Government Reform

Granger, Kay, R-Tex. (12)

Capitol Hill Office: 1026 LHOB 20515; 225-5071; Fax: 225-5683; *Chief of Staff:* Matt Leffingwell

Web: http://kaygranger.house.gov/

Facebook: http://facebook.com/RepKayGranger

Twitter: http://twitter.com/RepKayGranger

District Office: River Plaza, 1701 River Run Rd., #407, Fort Worth, TX 76107-6548; 817-338-0909; Fax: 817-335-5852; *District Director:* Mattie Parker

Committee Assignment: Appropriations

Graves, Sam, R-Mo. (6)

Capitol Hill Office: 1415 LHOB 20515-2506; 225-7041; Fax: 225-8221; *Chief of Staff:* Tom Brown

Web: http://graves.house.gov/

Facebook: http://facebook.com/pages/Sam-Graves/118514606128

District Offices: 11724 N.W. Plaza Circle, #900, Kansas City, MO 64153; 816-792-3976; Fax: 816-792-0694; *District Director:* Melissa Roe

411 Jules St., Room 111, St. Joseph, MO 64501-2275; 816-749-0800; Fax: 816-749-0801; *Field Rep.:* Matt Barry

906 Broadway, PO Box 364, Hannibal, MO 63401; 573-221-3400; *District Director:* Melissa Roe

Committee Assignments: Small Business, Chair; Transportation and Infrastructure

Graves, Tom, R-Ga. (14)

Capitol Hill Office: 432 CHOB 20515; 225-5211; Fax: 225-8272; *Chief of Staff:* Timothy R. Baker

Web: http://tomgraves.house.gov/

Facebook: http://facebook.com/reptomgraves

Twitter: http://twitter.com/reptomgraves

District Offices: 702 S. Thornton Ave., Dalton, GA 30720-8211; 706-226-5320; Fax: 706-278-0840; *District Director:* Ericka Pertierra

600 E. 1st St., #301, Rome, GA 30161; 706-290-1776; Fax: 706-232-7864; *Field Rep.:* Drew Ferguson

Committee Assignment: Appropriations

Grayson, Alan, D-Fla. (9)

Capitol Hill Office: 430 CHOB 20515; 225-9889; Fax: 225-9742; *Chief of Staff:* Julie Tagen

Web: http://grayson.house.gov/

Facebook: http://facebook.com/alangrayson

Twitter: http://twitter.com/AlanGrayson

District Offices: 101 N. Church St., #550, Kissimme, FL 34741; 407-518-4983; Fax: 407-846-2087; *Field Rep.:* Viviana Rodriguez

5842 S. Semoran Blvd., Orlando, FL 32822; 407-615-8889; Fax: 407-615-8890; *District Director:* Susannah Randolph

Committee Assignments: Foreign Affairs; Science, Space, and Technology

Green, Al, D-Tex. (9)

Capitol Hill Office: 2201 RHOB 20515-4309; 225-7508; Fax: 225-2947; *Chief of Staff:* Jacqueline A. Ellis

Web: http://algreen.house.gov/

Facebook: http://facebook.com/repalgreen

Twitter: http://twitter.com/RepAlGreen

District Office: 3003 S. Loop W., #460, Houston, TX 77054-1301; 713-383-9234; Fax: 713-383-9202; *District Manager of Administration:* Crystal Webster

Committee Assignment: Financial Services

Green, Gene, D-Tex. (29)

Capitol Hill Office: 2470 RHOB 20515-4329; 225-1688; Fax: 225-9903; *Chief of Staff; Ethics; Election Reform; Campaign Reform:* Rhonda Jackson

Web: http://green.house.gov/

Facebook: http://facebook.com/RepGeneGreen

Twitter: http://twitter.com/RepGeneGreen

District Offices: 11811 I-10 E., #430, Houston, TX 77029-1974; 713-330-0761; Fax: 713-330-0807; *District Scheduler:* Sophia Gutierrez

256 N. Sam Houston Pkwy. E., #29, Houston, TX 77060-2028; 281-999-5879; Fax: 281-999-5716; *Chief of Staff, Office Manager:* Rhonda Jackson

Committee Assignment: Energy and Commerce

Griffin, Tim, R-Ark. (2)

Capitol Hill Office: 1232 LHOB 20515-0402; 225-2506;
Fax: 225-5903; *Chief of Staff:* D. Clayton Hall
Web: http://griffin.house.gov/
Facebook: http://facebook.com/reptimgriffin
Twitter: http://twitter.com/reptimgriffin
District Offices: 1105 Deer St., #12, Conway, AR 72032;
501-358-3481; Fax: 501-358-3494; *Field Rep.:* Thomas
McNabb, Peter Davidson
1501 N. University Ave., #150, Little Rock, AR 72207-5230;
501-324-5941; Fax: 501-324-6029; *District Director:*
Carl Vogelpohl
Committee Assignment: Ways and Means

Griffith, H. Morgan, R-Va. (9)

Capitol Hill Office: 1108 LHOB 20515-4609; 225-3861;
Fax: 225-0076; *Chief of Staff:* Kelly Lungren McCollum
Web: http://morangriffith.house.gov/
Facebook: http://facebook.com/RepMorganGriffith
Twitter: http://twitter.com/RepMGriffith
District Offices: 323 W. Main St., Abingdon, VA 24210-
2605; 276-525-1405; Fax: 276-525-1444; *District
Director:* K. Jenkins
17 W. Main St., Christiansburg, VA 24073-3055; 540-381-
5671; Fax: 540-381-5675; *Constituent Rep.:* Barbara
Stafford
Committee Assignment: Energy and Commerce

Grijalva, Raul M., D-Ariz. (3)

Capitol Hill Office: 1511 LHOB 20515-0307; 225-2435;
Fax: 225-1541; *Chief of Staff:* Amy Emerick
Web: http://grijalva.house.gov/
Facebook: http://facebook.com/Rep.Grijalva
Twitter: http://twitter.com/RepRaulGrijalva
District Offices: Rancho Santa Fe Center, 13065 W.
McDowell Rd., #C-123, Avondale, AZ 85392; 623-536-
3388; Fax: 623-748-0451; *District Rep.:* Jose Miranda
146 N. State Ave., P.O. Box 4105, Somerton, AZ 85350;
928-343-7933; Fax: 928-343-7949; *District Aide*;
Caseworker: Martha Garcia
738 N. 5th Ave., #110, Tucson, AZ 85705-8485; 520-622-
6788; Fax: 520-622-0198; *District Director:* Rubén
Reyes
Committee Assignments: Education and the Workforce;
Natural Resources

Grimm, Michael, R-N.Y. (11)

Capitol Hill Office: 512 CHOB 20515-3213; 225-3371;
Fax: 226-1272; *Chief of Staff:* Chris Berardini
Web: http://grimm.house.gov/
Facebook: http://facebook.com/repmichaelgrimm
Twitter: http://twitter.com/repmichaelgrimm
District Offices: 7308 13th Ave., Brooklyn, NY 11228-
2011; 718-630-5277; Fax: 718-630-5388; *Brooklyn Staff
Director:* Fran Vella-Marrone
265 New Dorp Lane, 2nd Floor, Staten Island, NY 10306-
3005; 718-351-1062; Fax: 718-980-0768; *District
Director:* Nick Curran
Committee Assignment: Financial Services

Guthrie, Brett, R-Ky. (2)

Capitol Hill Office: 308 CHOB 20515-1702; 225-3501;
Fax: 226-2019; *Chief of Staff:* Eric Bergren
Web: http://guthrie.house.gov/
Facebook: http://facebook.com/CongressmanGuthrie
Twitter: http://twitter.com/RepGuthrie
District Offices: 1001 Center St., #300, Bowling Green, KY
42101-2192; 270-842-9896; Fax: 270-842-9081; *District
Director:* Mark Lord
411 W. Lincoln Trail Blvd., Radcliff, KY 40160; *Field Rep.:*
Brian Smith
2200 Airport Rd., Owensboro, KY 42301; *District
Director, Field Rep*: Mark Lord
Committee Assignment: Education and the Workforce;
Energy and Commerce

Gutierrez, Luis V., D-Ill. (4)

Capitol Hill Office: 2408 RHOB 20515; 225-8203;
Fax: 225-7810; *Chief of Staff; Oversight of Committees
Appropriations Oversight House Administration
Standards of Official Conduct Transportation*: Susan
Collins
Web: http://gutierrez.house.gov/
Facebook: http://facebook.com/RepGutierrez
Twitter: http://twitter.com/LuisGutierrez
District Offices: 3210 W. North Ave., Chicago, IL 60647-
5429; 773-342-0774; Fax: 773-342-0776; *District
Scheduler:* Theresa Paucar
5531 W. Cermak Rd., Cicero, IL 60804; 708-652-5180;
Fax: 708-652-5118; *Field Rep.:* Theresa Paucar
Committee Assignments: Judiciary; Permanent Select
Intelligence

Hahn, Janice, D-Calif. (44)

Capitol Hill Office: 404 CHOB 20515; 225-8220; Fax: 226-
7290; *Chief of Staff, Legis. Director:* Laurie Saroff
Web: http://hahn.house.gov/
Facebook: http://facebook.com/RepJaniceHahn
Twitter: http://twitter.com/Rep_JaniceHahn
District Offices: 205 S. Willowbrook Ave., Compton, CA
90220; 310-605-5520; Fax: 310-761-1457; *Field
Deputy:* Michelle Chambers
140 W. 6th St., San Pedro, CA 90731; 310-831-1799;
Fax: 310-831-1885; *District Director:* Elise Swanson
544 N. Avalon Blvd., #307, Wilmington, CA 90744-5806;
310-549-8282; Fax: 310-549-8250; *Field Rep.:* Michelle
Chambers
8650 California Ave., South Gate, CA 90280; 323-563-
9562; *Field Rep.:* Michelle Chambers, Elise Swanson
Committee Assignments: Small Business; Transportation
and Infrastructure

Hall, Ralph, R-Tex. (4)

Capitol Hill Office: 2405 RHOB 20515-4304; 225-6673;
Fax: 225-3332; *Chief of Staff and Science Committee
Republican Chief of Staff:* Janet Poppleton
Web: http://ralphhall.house.gov/
Facebook: http://facebook.com/pages/Ralph-Hall/
6311458773

Twitter: http://twitter.com/RalphHallPress
District Offices:
104 N. San Jacinto St., Rockwall, TX 75087-2508; 972-771-9118; Fax: 972-722-0907; *District Director:* Thomas Hughes
4303 Texas Blvd., #2, Texarkana, TX 75503-3094; 903-794-4445; Fax: 903-794-5577; *District Asst.:* Marjorie Chandler
Grayson County Courthouse, 100 W. Houston St., 2nd Floor, Sherman, TX 75090-6019; 903-813-4281; Fax: 903-868-8613; *District Asst.:* Jennyne Reeves
123 Kaufman St., Room 102, Linden, TX 75563-0449; 903-306-0540; Fax: 855-858-3630; *District Asst.:* Eric Cain District
Committee Assignments: Energy, and Commerce; Science, Space, and Technology

Hanabusa, Colleen, D-Hawaii (1)

Capitol Hill Office: 238 CHOB 20515-1101; 225-2726; Fax: 225-0688; *Chief of Staff:* Rod Tanonaka
Web: http://hanabusa.house.gov/
Facebook: http://facebook.com/pages/Congresswoman-Colleen-Hanabusa/169979129710178
Twitter: http://twitter.com/RepHanabusa
District Office: 300 Ala Moana Blvd., Room 4-104, Honolulu, HI 96850-4104; 808-541-2570; Fax: 808-533-0133; *Chief of Staff:* Rod Tanonaka
Committee Assignments: Armed Services; Natural Resources

Hanna, Richard, R-N.Y. (22)

Capitol Hill Office: 319 CHOB 20515-3224; 225-3665; Fax: 225-1891; *Chief of Staff:* Justin Stokes
Web: http://hanna.house.gov/
Facebook: http://facebook.com/reprichardhanna
Twitter: http://twitter.com/reprichardhanna
District Offices: 49 Court St., #230, Binghamton, NY 13901; 607-723-0212; Fax: 607-723-0215; *Regional Director:* Terre Dennis
258 Genesee St., 1st Floor, Utica, NY 13502; 315-724-9740; Fax: 315-724-9746; *District Director:* Patricia Dellonte
Committee Assignments: Small Business; Transportation and Infrastructure; Joint Economic

Harper, Gregg, R-Miss. (3)

Capitol Hill Office: 307 CHOB 20515-2403; 225-5031; Fax: 225-5797; *Chief of Staff:* Michael J. Cravens
Web: http://harper.house.gov/
Facebook: https://facebook.com/GreggHarper
Twitter: http://twitter.com/GreggHarper
District Offices: 230 S. Whitworth St., Brookhaven, MS 39601-3343; 601-823-3400; Fax: 601-823-5512; *Field Director:* Evan Gardner
1901 Front St., Suite A, Meridian, MS 39301-5206; 601-693-6681; Fax: 601-693-1801; *Special Asst. Constituent Services:* Francis White
2507-A Old Brandon Rd., Pearl, MS 39208; 601-932-2410; Fax: 601-932-4647; *District Director:* Chip Reynolds

1 Research Blvd., #206, Starkville, MS 39759-8749; 662-324-0007; Fax: 662-324-0033; *Special Asst. Constituent Services:* Kyle Jordan
Committee Assignments: Energy and Commerce; House Administration; Joint Printing, Chair; Joint Library of Congress, Vice Chair

Harris, Andy, R-Md. (1)

Capitol Hill Office: 1533 LHOB 20515; 225-5311; Fax: 225-0254; *Chief of Staff:* Kevin C. Reigrut
Web: http://harris.house.gov/
Facebook: http://facebook.com/AndyHarrisMD
Twitter: http://twitter.com/repandyharrismd
District Offices: 15 E. Churchville Rd., #102B, Bel Air, MD 21014-3837; 410-588-5670; Fax: 410-588-5673; *Community Liaison:* Mary O'Keefe
100 Olde Point Village, #101, Chester, MD 21619; 410-643-5425; Fax: 410-643-5429; *Community Liaison:* Denise Lovelady
212 W. Main St., #204B, Salisbury, MD 21801-5026; 443-944-8624; Fax: 443-944-8625; *Constituent Liaison:* Bill Redish
Committee Assignments: Appropriations

Hartzler, Vicky, R-Mo. (4)

Capitol Hill Office: 1023 LHOB 20515-2504; 225-2876; Fax: 225-0148; *Chief of Staff:* Eric Bohl
Web: http://hartzler.house.gov/
Facebook: http://facebook.com/Congresswoman.Hartzler
Twitter: http://twitter.com/rephartzler
District Offices: 2415 Carter Lane, #4, Columbia, MO 65201; 573-442-9311; Fax: 573-442-9309; *District Director:* Donna Spickert
1909 N. Commercial St., Harrisonville, MO 64701-1252; 816-884-3411; Fax: 816-884-3163; *Field Rep.:* Zack Brown
219 N. Adams Ave., Lebanon, MO 65536-3029; 417-532-5582; Fax: 417-532-3886; *Field Rep.:* Levi Mitchell
415 S. Ohio Ave., #212B, Sedalia, MO 65301-4445; 573-634-4884; *District Director:* Donna Spickert
Committee Assignments: Agriculture; Armed Services; Budget

Hastings, Alcee L., D-Fla. (20)

Capitol Hill Office: 2353 RHOB 20515-0923; 225-1313; Fax: 225-1171; *Chief of Staff:* Lale M. Mamaux
Web: http://alceehastings.house.gov/
Facebook: http://facebook.com/pages/Congressman-Alcee-L-Hastings/95696782238
District Office: 2701 W. Oakland Park Blvd., #200, Fort Lauderdale, FL 33311; 954-733-2800; Fax: 954-735-9444; *Florida Chief of Staff:* Art Kennedy
Town of Mangonia Park Municipal Center; 1755 E. Tiffany Dr., Mangonia Park, FL 33407; 561-676-7911; *Staff Asst.:* Dan Liftman
Committee Assignments: Commission on Security and Cooperation in Europe (Helsinki Commission); Rules

Hastings, Doc, R-Wash. (4)

Capitol Hill Office: 1203 LHOB 20515-4704; 225-5816; Fax: 225-3251; *Chief of Staff:* Jenny Gorski
Web: http://hastings.house.gov/
Facebook: http://facebook.com/RepDocHastings
Twitter: http://twitter.com/DocHastings
District Offices: 2715 St. Andrews Loop, Suite D, Pasco, WA 99301-3386; 509-543-9396; Fax: 509-545-1972; *District Director:* Barbara Lisk
402 E. Yakima Ave., #760, Yakima, WA 98901-5410; 509-452-3243; Fax: 509-452-3438; *Field Rep.:* Peter Godlewski
Committee Assignments: Natural Resources, Chair; Oversight and Government Reform

Heck, Dennis, D-Wash. (10)

Capitol Hill Office: 425 CHOB 20515; 225-9740; Fax: 225-0129; *Chief of Staff:* Hart Edmonson
Web: http://dennyheck.house.gov/
Facebook: http://facebook.com/CongressmanDennyHeck
Twitter: http://twitter.com/RepDennyHeck
District Offices: 420 College St., S.E., #3000, Lacey, WA 98503; 360-459-8514; Fax: 360-459-8581; *District Director:* LaTasha Wortham6000 Main St. S.W., #3B, Lakewood, WA 98499; 253-208 6172; *Field Rep:* Lauren Adler
Committee Assignment: Financial Services

Heck, Joe, R-Nev. (3)

Capitol Hill Office: 132 CHOB 20515-2803; 225-3252; Fax: 225-2185; *Chief of Staff:* Greg Facchiano
Web: http://heck.house.gov/
Facebook: http://facebook.com/RepJoeHeck
Twitter: http://twitter.com/RepJoeHeck
District Office: 8872 S. Eastern Ave., #220, Las Vegas, NV 89123; 702-387-4941; Fax: 702-837-0728; *District Director:* Keith Hughes
Committee Assignments: Armed Services; Education and the Workforce; Permanent Select Intelligence

Hensarling, Jeb, R-Tex. (5)

Capitol Hill Office: 2228 RHOB 20515; 225-3484; Fax: 226-4888; *Chief of Staff:* Andrew Duke
Web: http://hensarling.house.gov/
Facebook: http://facebook.com/RepHensarling
Twitter: http://twitter.com/RepHensarling
District Offices: 810 E. Corsicana St., Suite C, Athens, TX 75751-2629; 903-675-8288; Fax: 903-675-8351; *Regional Director:* Phillip Smith
6510 Abrams Rd., #243, Dallas, TX 75231-7278; 214-349-9996; Fax: 214-349-0738; *District Director:* Mike Garcia
Committee Assignment: Financial Services, Chair

Holding, George, R-N.C. (13)

Capitol Hill Office: 507 CHOB 20515; 225-3032; Fax: 225-0181; *Chief of Staff:* Tucker Knott
Web: http://holding.house.gov/
Facebook: http://facebook.com/CongressmanGeorgeHolding
Twitter: http://twitter.com/RepHolding
District Office: 3725 National Dr., #101, Raleigh, NC 27612; 919-782-4400; Fax: 919-782-4490; *District Director:* Alice McCall
120 Main St., Fremont, NC 27830; 919-440-5247; *Field Rep.:* Debra Marm
Committee Assignments: Foreign Affairs; Judiciary

Hudson, Richard, R-N.C. (8)

Capitol Hill Office: 429 CHOB 20515; 225-3715; Fax: 225-4036; *Chief of Staff:* Pepper Natonski
Web: http://hudson.house.gov/
Facebook: http://facebook.com/RepRichHudson
Twitter: http://twitter.com/@RepRichHudson
District Office: 325 McGill Ave., #500, Concord, NC 28027-6194; 704-786-1612; Fax: 704-782-1004; *District Director:* Chris Carter
1015 Fayetteville Rd., Rockingham, NC 28379; 910-997-2070; *Constituent Liaison:* Chris Maples
Committee Assignments: Agriculture; Education and Workforce; Homeland Security

Huffman, Jared, D-Calif. (2)

Capitol Hill Office: 1630 LHOB 20515; 225-5161; Fax: 225-5163; *Chief of Staff:* Ben Miller
Web: http://huffman.house.gov/
Facebook: http://facebook.com/RepHuffman
Twitter: http://twitter.com/RepHuffman
District Offices: 317 Third St., #1, Eureka, CA 95501; 707-407-3585; Fax: 707-407-3559; *District Director:* Jenny Callaway
430 N. Franklin St., P.O. Box 2208, Fort Bragg, CA 95437; 707-962-0933; Fax: 707-962-0905; *District Rep.:* Heidi Dickerson
999 Fifth Ave., #290, San Rafael, CA 94901; 415-258-9657; Fax: 415-258-9913; *Field Rep.:* Val Cartwright
206 G St., Petaluma, CA 94952; 707-981-8967; *Field Rep.:* Kelly Meeker
559 Low Gap Rd., Ukiah, CA 95482; 707-671-7449; *District Rep.:* Heidi Dickerson
Committee Assignments: Budget; Natural Resources

Herrera Beutler, Jaime, R-Wash. (3)

Capitol Hill Office: 1130 LHOB 20515-4703; 225-3536; Fax: 225-3478; *Chief of Staff:* Casy Bowman
Web: http://herrerabeutler.house.gov/
Facebook: http://facebook.com/herrerabeutler
Twitter: http://twitter.com/herrerabeutler
District Offices: Chehalis City Hall Bldg., 350 N. Market Blvd., Chehalis, WA 98532; *Staff Asst.:* Terassa Wren
O.O. Howard House, 750 Anderson St., Suite B, Vancouver, WA 98661-3853; 360-695-6292; Fax: 360-695-6197; *District Director:* Ryan Hart
Committee Assignments: Appropriations; Small Business

Higgins, Brian, D-N.Y. (26)

Capitol Hill Office: 2459 RHOB 20515-3227; 225-3306; Fax: 226-0347; *Chief of Staff; Legis. Director:* Andrew Tantillo
Web: http://higgins.house.gov/
Facebook: http://facebook.com/RepBrianHiggins
Twitter: http://twitter.com/RepBrianHiggins
District Offices: Larkin Bldg., 726 Exchange St., #601, Buffalo, NY 14210-1484; 716-852-3501; Fax: 716-852-3929; *District Chief of Staff:* Chuck Eaton
640 Park PL, Niagara Falls, NY 14301; 716-282-1274; Fax: 716-282-2479; *Field Rep.:* Donna Coughlin
Committee Assignments: Foreign Affairs; Homeland Security

Himes, Jim, D-Conn. (4)

Capitol Hill Office: 119 CHOB 20515-0704; 225-5541; Fax: 225-9629; *Chief of Staff:* Mark Henson
Web: http://himes.house.gov/
Facebook: http://facebook.com/CongressmanJimHimes
Twitter: http://twitter.com/jahimes
District Offices: Court Exchange, 211 State St., 2nd Floor, Bridgeport, CT 06604-4808; 866-453-0028; Fax: 203-333-6655; *District Director:* Tyrone McClain
888 Washington Blvd., 10th Floor, Stamford, CT 06901-2902; 203-353-9400; Fax: 203-333-6655; *Constituent Services Rep.:* Gloria DePina
Committee Assignments: Financial Services; Permanent Select Intelligence

Hinojosa, Ruben, D-Tex. (15)

Capitol Hill Office: 2262 RHOB 20515-4315; 225-2531; Fax: 225-5688; *Chief of Staff:* Connie J. Humphrey
Web: http://hinojosa.house.gov/
Facebook: http://facebook.com/CongressmanRubenHinojosa
Twitter: http://twitter.com/USRepRHinojosa
District Offices: 2864 W. Trenton Rd., Edinburg, TX 78539-9232; 956-682-5545; Fax: 956-682-0141; *District Director:* Cynthia Garza
100 S. Austin St., #1, Seguin, TX 78155; 830-401-0457; Fax: 830-379-0984; *District Director:* Mark Gonzales
Committee Assignments: Education and the Workforce; Financial Services

Holt, Rush, D-N.J. (12)

Capitol Hill Office: 1214 LHOB 20515-3012; 225-5801; Fax: 225-6025; *Chief of Staff:* Chris Gaston
Web: http://holt.house.gov/
Facebook: http://facebook.com/RushHolt
Twitter: http://twitter.com/RushHolt
District Office: 50 Washington Rd., West Windsor, NJ 08550-1012; 609-750-9365; Fax: 609-750-0618; *District Director:* Sarah Steward
Committee Assignments: Education and the Workforce; Natural Resources

Honda, Mike, D-Calif. (17)

Capitol Hill Office: 1713 LHOB 20515-0515; 225-2631; Fax: 225-2699; *Chief of Staff:* Jennifer Van der Heide
Web: http://honda.house.gov/
Facebook: http://facebook.com/RepMikeHonda
Twitter: http://twitter.com/RepMikeHonda
District Office: 2001 Gateway Pl., #670W, San Jose, CA 95110; 408-436-2720; Fax: 408-436-2721; *District Director:* Meri Maben
Main Library, 2400 Stevenson Blvd., Fremont, CA 94538; 855-680-3759; *District Director:* Meri Maben
Committee Assignment: Appropriations

Horsford, Steven, D-Nev. (4)

Capitol Hill Office: 1330 LHOB 20515; 225-9894; Fax: 225-9783; *Scheduling Director:* Lewis Myers
Web: http://horsford.house.gov/
Facebook: http://facebook.com/RepHorsford
Twitter: http://twitter.com/@RepHorsford
District Office: 2250 N. Las Vegas Blvd, #500, North Las Vegas, NV 89030; 702-802-4500; *Deputy District Director:* Detrick Sanford
Committee Assignments: Homeland Security; Natural Resources; Oversight and Government Reform

Hoyer, Steny, D-Md. (5)

Capitol Hill Office: 1705 LHOB 20515-2005; 225-4131; Fax: 225-4300; *Chief of Staff:* Alexis Covey-Brandt
Web: http://hoyer.house.gov/
Facebook: http://facebook.com/WhipHoyer
Twitter: http://twitter.com/WhipHoyer
District Offices: U.S. District Courthouse, 6500 Cherrywood Lane, #310, Greenbelt, MD 20770-1287; 301-474-0119; Fax: 301-474-4697; *Deputy District Director:* Terrance Taylor
401 Post Office Rd., #202, Waldorf, MD 20602-2738; 301-843-1577; Fax: 301-843-1331; *District Director:* Betsy Bossart
Minority Whip

Huelskamp, Tim, R-Kans. (1)

Capitol Hill Office: 129 CHOB 20515-1601; 225-2715; Fax: 225-5124; *Chief of Staff:* Jim Pfaff
Web: http://huelskamp.house.gov/
Facebook: http://facebook.com/congressmanhuelskamp
Twitter: http://twitter.com/conghuelskamp
District Offices: 100 Military Ave., #205, Dodge City, KS 67801-4945; 620-225-0172; Fax: 620-225-0297; *Constituent Services Rep.:* Lynn Ballinger
1 N. Main St., #525, Hutchinson, KS 67501-5228; 620-665-6138; Fax: 620-665-6360; *Constituent Services Rep.:* Nathan Cox
727 Poyntz Ave., #10, Manhattan, KS 66502; 785-309-0572; Fax: 785-827-6957; *Constituent Services Rep.:* Ashley Howe
119 W. Iron Ave., 4th Floor, Suite A, Salina, KS 67402; 785-309-0572; Fax: 785-827-6957; *Deputy District Director:* Steven Howe
Committee Assignments: Small Business; Veterans' Affairs

Huizenga, Bill, R-Mich. (2)

Capitol Hill Office: 1217 LHOB 20515-2202; 225-4401;
    Fax: 226-0779; *Chief of Staff:* Jon DeWitte
Web: http://huizenga.house.gov/
Facebook: http://facebook.com/rephuizenga
Twitter: http://twitter.com/rephuizenga
District Offices: 1 S. Harbor Ave., #6B, Grand Haven, MI
    49417; 616-414-5516; Fax: 616-414-5521; *District*
    Director: Greg Van Woerkom
4555 Wilson Ave. S.W., #3, Grandville, MI 49418;
    616-570-0917; Fax: 616-570-0934; *District Director:*
    Greg Van Woerkom
Committee Assignment: Financial Services

Hultgren, Randy, R-Ill. (14)

Capitol Hill Office: 332 CHOB 20515; 225-2976;
    Fax: 225-0697; *Chief of Staff:* Katherine McGuire
Web: http://hultgren.house.gov/
Facebook: http://facebook.com/RepHultgren
Twitter: http://twitter.com/rephultgren
District Office: 1797 W. State St., Suite A, Geneva, IL
    60134-4710; 630-232-7104; Fax: 630-232-7174;
    District Director: Sean McCarthy
Committee Assignments: Financial Services; Science,
    Space, and Technology

Hunter, Duncan, R-Calif. (50)

Capitol Hill Office: 223 CHOB 20515-0552; 225-5672;
    Fax: 225-0235; *Chief of Staff:* Victoria J. Middleton
Web: http://hunter.house.gov/
Facebook: http://facebook.com/DuncanHunter
District Offices: 1611 N. Magnolia Ave., #310, El Cajon,
    CA 92020; 619-448-5201; Fax: 619-449-2251;
    District Chief of Staff: Rick Terrazas
333 S. Juniper St., #110, Escondido, CA 92025; 760-743-
    3260; *District Chief of Staff:* Rick Terrazas
41000 Main St., Temecula, CA 92590; 951-695-5108;
    District Chief of Staff: Rick Terrazas
Committee Assignments: Armed Services; Education and
    the Workforce; Transportation and Infrastructure

Hurt, Robert, R-Va. (5)

Capitol Hill Office: 125 CHOB 20515; 225-4711;
    Fax: 225-5681; *Chief of Staff:* Kelly Simpsom
Web: http://hurt.house.gov/
Facebook: http://facebook.com/RepRobertHurt
Twitter: http://twitter.com/reproberthurt
District Offices: 686 Berkmar Circle, Charlottesville, VA
    22901-1464; 434-973-9631; Fax: 434-973-9635;
    Outreach and Coalitions Director: Scott Leake
308 Craghead St., #102-D, Danville, VA 24541-1470;
    434-791-2596; Fax: 434-791-4619; *District Director:*
    Linda Green
515 S. Main St., P.O. Box 0, Farmville, VA 23901; 434-395-
    0120; Fax: 434-395-1248; *District Director; Field Rep.:*
    Linda Green
Committee Assignment: Financial Services

Israel, Steve, D-N.Y. (3)

Capitol Hill Office: 2457 RHOB 20515-3202; 225-3335;
    Fax: 225-4669; *Chief of Staff:* Patricia Russell
Web: http://israel.house.gov/
Facebook: http://facebook.com/RepSteveIsrael
Twitter: http://twitter.com/repSteveIsrael
District Office: 534 Broad Hollow Rd., #302, Melville, NY
    11747; 631-777-7391; Fax: 631-777-7610; *District*
    Director: Katie Horst
Democratic Congressional Campaign Committee, Chair

Issa, Darrell, R-Calif. (49)

Capitol Hill Office: 2347 RHOB 20515-0549; 225-3906;
    Fax: 225-3303; *Chief of Staff:* Dale Neugebauer
Web: http://issa.house.gov/
Facebook: http://facebook.com/darrellissa
Twitter: http://twitter.com/DarrellIssa
District Office: 1800 Thibodo Rd., #310, Vista, CA 92081-
    7515; 760-599-5000; Fax: 760-599-1178; *District*
    Director: Bill Christiansen
33282 Golden Lantern, #102, Dana Point, CA 92629;
    949-281-2449; *Field Rep.:* Amy Walker
Committee Assignments: Judiciary; Oversight and
    Government Reform, Chair

Jackson Lee, Sheila, D-Tex. (18)

Capitol Hill Office: 2160 RHOB 20515-4318; 225-3816;
    Fax: 225-3317; *Chief of Staff:* Glenn Rushing
Web: http://jacksonlee.house.gov/
Facebook: http://facebook.com/
    CongresswomanSheilaJacksonLee
Twitter: http://twitter.com/JacksonLeeTX18
District Offices: 1919 Smith St., #1180, Houston, TX
    77002-8098; 713-655-0050; Fax: 713-655-1612;
    Caseworker/Field Rep.: Michael Halpin
6719 W. Montgomery Rd., #204, Houston, TX 77091-
    3105; 713-691-4882; Fax: 713-699-8292; *Caseworker/*
    Field Rep.: Ivan Sanchez
420 W. 19th St., Houston, TX 77008-3914; 713-861-4070;
    Fax: 713-861-4323; *Caseworker/Field Rep.:* Tonya
    Williams
4300 Lyons Ave., Houston, TX 77020; 713-227-7740;
    Fax: 713-227-7707; *Caseworker/Field Rep.:* Purnell
    Davis
Committee Assignments: Homeland Security; Judiciary

Jeffries, Hakeem, D-N.Y. (8)

Capitol Hill Office: 1339 LHOB 20515; 225-5936;
    Fax: 225-1018; *Chief of Staff:* Cedric Grant
Web: http://jeffries.house.gov/
Facebook: http://facebook.com/RepHakeemJeffries
Twitter: http://twitter.com/RepJeffries
District Offices: 445 Neptune Ave., 1st Floor, Brooklyn,
    NY 11224; 718-373-0033; Fax: 718-373-1333;
    Community Rep.: Larry Savinkin
55 Hanson Pl., #603, Brooklyn, NY 11217; 718-237-2211;
    Fax: 718-237-2273; *District Director:* Stina Skewes-Cox
Committee Assignments: Budget; Judiciary

Jenkins, Lynn, R-Kans. (2)

Capitol Hill Office: 1027 LHOB 20515; 225-6601;
Fax: 225-7986; *Chief of Staff:* Pat Leopold
Web: http://lynnjenkins.house.gov/
Facebook: http://facebook.com/replynnjenkins
Twitter: http://twitter.com/replynnjenkins
District Offices: 1001 N. Broadway St., Suite C, Pittsburg,
KS 66762-3944; 620-231-5966; Fax: 620-231-5972;
District Director: Bill Roe
3550 S.W. 5th St., Topeka, KS 66606-1998; 785-234-5966;
Fax: 785-234-5967; *District Director:* Bill Roe
120 N. 6th St., Independence, KS 67301; 620-231-5966,
Fax: 620-231-5972
Committee Assignment: Ways and Means

Johnson, Bill, R-Ohio (6)

Capitol Hill Office: 1710 LHOB 20515; 225-5705;
Fax: 225-5907; *Chief of Staff:* Mike Smullen
Web: http://billjohnson.house.gov/
Facebook: http://facebook.com/RepBillJohnson
Twitter: http://twitter.com/repbilljohnson
District Offices: 116 Southgate Pkwy., Cambridge, OH
43725; 740-432-2366; Fax: 740-432-2587; *Field Rep.:*
Anthony Adornetto
202 Park Ave., Suite C, Ironton, OH 45638-1595; 740-534-
9431; Fax: 740-534-9482; *Field Rep.:* Alexander
Scharfetter
246 Front St., Marietta, OH 45750-2908; 740-376-0868;
Fax: 740-376-0886; *Field Rep:* Dan Halliburton
192 E. State St., Salem, OH 44460-2843; 330-337-6951;
Fax: 330-337-7125; *District Director:* Jacquelyn
Stewart
Committee Assignment: Energy and Commerce

Johnson, Eddie Bernice, D-Tex. (30)

Capitol Hill Office: 2468 RHOB 20515-4330; 225-8885;
Fax: 226-1477; *Chief of Staff Texas Democratic
Delegation:* Murat T. Gokcigdem
Web: http://ebjohnson.house.gov/
Facebook: http://facebook.com/CongresswomanEBJtx30
Twitter: http://twitter.com/RepEBJ
District Office: 3102 Maple Ave., #600, Dallas, TX 75201-
1236; 214-922-8885; Fax: 214-922-7028; *District
Director:* Rod Givens
Committee Assignments: Science, Space, and Technology,
Ranking Minority Member; Transportation and
Infrastructure

Johnson, Hank, D-Ga. (4)

Capitol Hill Office: 2240 RHOB 20515; 225-1605;
Fax: 226-0691; *Chief of Staff:* Arthur D. Sidney
Web: http://hankjohnson.house.gov/
Facebook: http://facebook.com/pages/Congressman-
Hank-Johnson/115356957005
Twitter: http://twitter.com/rephankjohnson
District Offices: 1184 Scott St., S.E., Conyers, GA 30012-
5436; 770-987-2291; Fax: 770-987-8721;
Communications Director: Andy Phelan

5700 Hillandale Dr., #120, Lithonia, GA 30058-4104;
770-987-2291; Fax: 770-987-8721; *District Director:*
Kathy Register
Committee Assignments: Armed Services; Judiciary

Johnson, Sam, R-Tex. (3)

Capitol Hill Office: 1211 LHOB 20515-4303; 225-4201;
Fax: 225-1485; *Chief of Staff:* David J. Heil
Web: http://samjohnson.house.gov/
Facebook: http://facebook.com/RepSamJohnson
Twitter: http://twitter.com/SamsPressShop
District Office: 1255 W. 15th St., #170, Plano, TX 75075;
469-304-0382; Fax: 469-304-0392; *District Director:*
Lori McMahon
Committee Assignment: Ways and Means, Joint on
Taxation

Jolly, David, R-Fla. (13)

Capitol Hill Office: 2407 RHOB 20515; 225-5961;
Fax: 225-9764; *Chief of Staff:* John David (J.D.) White
Web: http://jolly.house.gov/
Facebook: http://facebook.com/DavidJollyCD13
Twitter: https://twitter.com/DavidJollyCD13
District Office: 9210 113th St., Seminole, FL 33772;
727-392-4100; *Chief of Staff:* John David (J.D.) White
Committee Assignments: Transportation and
Infrastructure; Veterans' Affairs

Jones, Walter B., R-N.C. (3)

Capitol Hill Office: 2333 RHOB 20515-3303; 225-3415;
Fax: 225-3286; *Chief of Staff:* Glen Downs
Web: http://jones.house.gov/
Facebook: http://facebook.com/pages/Walter-Jones/
15083070102
Twitter: http://twitter.com/RepWalterJones
District Office: 1105-C Corporate Dr., Greenville, NC
27858-5968; 252-931-1003; Fax: 252-931-1002;
Director of Outreach: Catherine Jordan
Committee Assignment: Armed Services

Jordan, Jim, R-Ohio (4)

Capitol Hill Office: 1524 LHOB 20515-3504; 225-2676;
Fax: 226-0577; *Chief of Staff:* Ray Yonkura
Web: http://jordan.house.gov/
Facebook: http://facebook.com/repjimjordan
Twitter: http://twitter.com/Jim_Jordan
District Offices: 3121 W. Elm Plaza, Lima, OH 45805-
2516; 419-999-6455; Fax: 419-999-4238; *Deputy
District Director:* Neil Lynch
13 B E. Main St., Norwalk, OH 44857; 419-663-1426;
Fax: 419-668-3015; *District Director:* Cameron
Warner
Committee Assignments: Judiciary; Oversight and
Government Reform

Joyce, David, R-Ohio (14)

Capitol Hill Office: 1535 LHOB 20515; 225-5731;
Fax: 225-3307; *Chief of Staff:* Dino DiSanto

Web: http://joyce.house.gov/
Facebook: http://facebook.com/RepDaveJoyce
Twitter: http://twitter.com/RepDaveJoyce
District Offices: 1 Victoria PL, Room 320, Painesville, OH 44077; 440-352-3939; Fax: 440-352-3622; *District Director:* Nick Ciofani
10075 Ravenna Rd., Twinsburg, OH 44087-1718; 330-425-9291; Fax: 330-425-7071; *District Director:* Nick Ciofani
Committee Assignment: Appropriations

Kaptur, Marcy, D-Ohio (9)

Capitol Hill Office: 2186 RHOB 20515-3509; 225-4146; Fax: 225-7711; *Senior Legislative Asst.:* John Latini
Web: http://kaptur.house.gov/
Facebook: http://facebook.com/RepresentativeMarcyKaptur
Twitter: http://twitter.com/@RepMarcyKaptur
District Office: 1 Maritime Plaza, Room 600, Toledo, OH 43604-1853; 419-259-7500; Fax: 419-255-9623; *Chief of Staff:* Steve Katich
200 W. Erie, Room 310, Lorain, OH 44052; 440-288-1500; *Constituent Services Director:* Susan Rowe
16024 Madison St., #3, Lakewood, OH 44107; 216-767-5933; *Constituent Services Director:* Susan Rowe
5592 Broadview Rd., Room 101, Parma, OH 44134; 440-799-8499; *Constituent Services Director:* Susan Rowe
Committee Assignment: Appropriations

Keating, William, D-Mass. (9)

Capitol Hill Office: 315 CHOB 20515-2110; 225-3111; Fax: 225-5658; *Chief of Staff:* Garrett Donovan
Web: http://keating.house.gov/
Facebook: http://facebook.com/Congressman.Keating
Twitter: http://twitter.com/USRepKeating
District Offices: 297 North St., #312, Hyannis, MA 02601-5134; 508-771-0666; Fax: 508-790-1959; *District Rep.:* Anthony Morse
558 Pleasant St., #309, New Bedford, MA 02740; 508-999-6462; Fax: 508-999-6468; *Regional Director:* Ines Goncalves-Drolet
2 Court St., Plymouth, MA 02360; 508-746-9000; Fax: 508-732-0072; *District Director:* Michael Jackman
Committee Assignments: Foreign Affairs; Homeland Security

Kelly, Mike, R-Pa. (3)

Capitol Hill Office: 1519 LHOB 20515; 225-5406; Fax: 225-3103; *Chief of Staff:* Matthew Stroia
Web: http://kelly.house.gov/
Facebook: http://facebook.com/pages/Representative-Mike-Kelly/191056827594903
Twitter: http://twitter.com/MikeKellyPA
District Offices: 101 E. Diamond St., #218, Butler, PA 16001; 724-282-2557; Fax: 724-282-3682; *Office Manager:* Marci Mustello
208 E. Bayfront Pkwy., #102, Erie, PA 16507-2405; 814-454-8190; Fax: 814-454-8197; *District Director:* Brad Moore

33 Chestnut Ave., Sharon, PA 16146; 724-342-7170; Fax: 724-342-7242; *Senior Constituent Service Rep.:* Jill Burke
908 Diamond Pk., Meadville, PA 16335; 814-454-8190; *Caseworker:* Kristi Kujawa
300 S. McKean St., Kittanning, PA 16201; *Caseworker:* Jill Burke
Lawrence County Courthouse, 430 Court St., New Castle, PA 16101; *Caseworker:* Jill Burke
Committee Assignment: Ways and Means

Kelly, Robin, D-Ill. (2)

Capitol Hill Office: 2419 RHOB 20515; 225-0773; Fax: 225-4583; *Chief of Staff:* Brandon Garrett
Web: http://robinkelly.house.gov/
Facebook: http://facebook.com/RobinKellyforCongress
Twitter: http://twitter.com/Robin42CD
District Office: 600 Holiday Plaza Dr., #505, Matteson, IL 60443; 708-679-0078; *District Director:* Aubrey Wilson
1000 E. 111th St., 11th Floor, Chicago, IL 60628; 773-568-2623; *Director of Constituent Services:* Cynthia DeWitt
Committee Assignments: Oversight and Government Reform; Science, Space, and Technology

Kennedy, Joe, D-Mass. (4)

Capitol Hill Office: 1218 LHOB 20515; 225-5931; Fax: 225-0182; *Chief of Staff:* Craig Mecher
Web: http://kennedy.house.gov/
Facebook: http://facebook.com/pages/Congressman-Joe-Kennedy-III/301936109927957
Twitter: http://twitter.com/RepJoeKennedy
District Offices: 8 N. Main St., #200, Attleboro, MA 02703; 508-431-1110; Fax: 508-431-1101; *Field Rep.:* Lisa Nelson
City Hall, 1 Government Center, Fall River, MA 02772; 617-332-3333; *Outreach Director:* Stephanie Noguera
29 Crafts St., #375, Newton, MA 02458-1275; 617-332-3333; Fax: 617-332- 3308; *District Director:* Nick Clemons
Committee Assignments: Foreign Affairs; Science, Space, and Technology

Kildee, Dan, D-Mich. (5)

Capitol Hill Office: 327 CHOB 20515; 225-3611; Fax: 225-6393; *Chief of Staff:* Andy Lavitt
Web: http://dankildee.house.gov/
Facebook: http://facebook.com/RepDanKildee
Twitter: http://twitter.com/RepDanKildee
District Offices: 801 S. Saginaw St., Plaza Level, Flint, MI 48502; 810-238-8627; Fax: 810-238-8658; *District Chief of Staff:* Amy Hovey
Committee Assignment: Financial Services

Kilmer, Derek, D-Wash (6)

Capitol Hill Office: 1429 LHOB 20515; 225-5916; Fax: 226-3575; *Chief of Staff:* Jonathon Smith
Web: http://kilmer.house.gov/

Facebook: http://facebook.com/derek.kilmer
Twitter: http://twitter.com/@RepDerekKilmer
District Offices: 345 6th St., #500, Bremerton, WA 98337;
360-373-9725; *Deputy District Director:* Joe Dacca
950 Pacific Ave., #1230, Tacoma, WA 98402; 253-272-
3515; *District Director:* Meadow Johnson
332 E. 5th St., Port Angeles, WA 98632; 360-797-3623;
Constituent Services Rep.: Brad Forbes
Committee Assignments: Armed Services; Science, Space,
and Technology

Kind, Ron, D-Wisc. (3)

Capitol Hill Office: 1502 LHOB 20515; 225-5506;
Fax: 225-5739; *Chief of Staff:* Travis Robey
Web: http://kind.house.gov/
Facebook: http://facebook.com/repronkind
Twitter: http://twitter.com/repronkind
District Offices: 131 S. Barstow St., #301, Eau Claire, WI
54701-2625; 715-831-9214; Fax: 715-831-9272;
Congressional Aide: Mark Aumann
205 5th Ave. South, #400, La Crosse, WI 54601-4059;
608-782-2558; Fax: 608-782-4588; *District Chief of
Staff:* Loren Kannenberg
Committee Assignment: Ways and Means

King, Pete, R-N.Y. (2)

Capitol Hill Office: 339 CHOB 20515-3203; 225-7896;
Fax: 226-2279; *Chief of Staff Press Secy.:* Kevin C.
Fogarty
Web: http://peteking.house.gov/
Facebook: http://facebook.com/reppeteking
Twitter: http://twitter.com/reppeteking
District Office: 1003 Park Blvd., Massapequa Park, NY
11762-2758; 516-541-4225; Fax: 516-541-6602; *District
Director:* Anne Rosenfeld
Committee Assignments: Financial Services; Homeland
Security; Permanent Select Intelligence

King, Steve, R-Iowa (4)

Capitol Hill Office: 2210 RHOB 20515; 225-4426;
Fax: 225-3193; *Chief of Staff:* Tracie Gibler
Web: http://steveking.house.gov/
Facebook: http://facebook.com/SteveKingIA
Twitter: http://twitter.com/SteveKingIA
District Offices: 1421 S. Bell Ave., #102, Ames, Iowa
50010; 515-232-2885; Fax: 515-232-2844; *District Rep.:*
Jeremy Davis
723 Central Ave., Fort Dodge, Iowa 50501; 515-573-2738;
Fax: 515-576-7141; *District Rep.:* Jim Oberhelman
202-lst St. S.E., #126, Mason City, Iowa, 50401; 641-201-
1624; Fax: 641-201-1523; *District Rep.:* Merlin Bartz
526 Nebraska St., Sioux City, IA 51101-1313; 712-224-
4692; Fax: 712-224-4693; *District Director:* Wayne
Brincks
306 N. Grand Ave., P.O. Box 650, Spencer, IA 51301-4141;
712-580-7754; Fax: 712-580-3354; *District Rep.:*
Andrea Easter
Committee Assignments: Agriculture; Judiciary; Small
Business

Kingston, Jack, R-Ga. (1)

Capitol Hill Office: 2372 RHOB 20515-1001; 225-5831;
Fax: 226-2269; *Chief of Staff:* Adam Sullivan
Web: http://kingston.house.gov/
Facebook: http://facebook.com/JackKingston
Twitter: http://twitter.com/JackKingston
District Offices: 1510 Newcastle St., #200, Brunswick, GA
31520-6826; 912-265-9010; Fax: 912-265-9013;
Caseworker; Field Rep.: Charles Wilson
1 Diamond Causeway, #7, Savannah, GA 31406-7434;
912-352-0101; Fax: 912-352-0105; *Deputy District
Director; Scheduler:* Brianna Foran
Committee Assignment: Appropriations

Kinzinger, Adam, R-Ill. (16)

Capitol Hill Office: 1221 LHOB 20515-1311; 225-3635;
Fax: 225-3521; *Chief of Staff:* Austin Weatherford
Web: http://kinzinger.house.gov/
Facebook: http://facebook.com/RepKinzinger
Twitter: http://twitter.com/repkinzinger
District Office: 628 Columbus St., #507, Ottawa, IL 61350;
815-431-9271; Fax: 815-431-9383; *District Director:*
Bonnie Walsh
342 W. Walnut, Watseka, IL 60970; 815-432-0580; *District
Director/Field Rep.:* Bonnie Walsh
401 Whitney Blvd., Belvidere, IL 61008; 815-547-8226;
Field Rep.: Casey Gorham
Committee Assignments: Energy and Commerce; Foreign
Affairs

Kirkpatrick, Ann, D-Ariz. (1)

Capitol Hill Office: 330 CHOB 20515; 225-3361;
Fax: 225-3462; *Chief of Staff:* Carmen Gallus
Web: http://kirkpatrick.house.gov/
Facebook: http://facebook.com/RepKirkpatrick
Twitter: http://twitter.com/RepKirkpatrick
District Offices: 211 N. Florence St., #1, Casa Grande, AZ
85122; 520-316-0839; Fax: 520-316-0842; *Community
Outreach Rep.:* Blanca Rubio-Varela
405 N. Beaver St., #6, Flagstaff, AZ 86001; 928-213-9977;
Fax: 928-213-9981; *District Director:* Ron Lee
1400 E. Ash, Globe, AZ 85501; 928-425-3231; Fax: 928-
402-4363; *Community Outreach Rep.:* Cathy Melvin
11555 W. Civic Center Dr., #104A, Marana, AZ 85653;
520-382-2663; Fax: 520-382-2664; *Caseworker:* Zak
Royse
550 N. 9th PL, Show Low, AZ 85901; 928-537-5657;
Fax: 928-537-5657; *Community Outreach Rep.:* Bruce
Sitko
Committee Assignments: Transportation and
Infrastructure; Veterans' Affairs

Kline, John, R-Minn. (2)

Capitol Hill Office: 2439 RHOB 20515-2302; 225-2271;
Fax: 225-2595; *Chief of Staff:* Jean Hinz
Web: http://kline.house.gov/
Facebook: http://facebook.com/repjohnkline
Twitter: http://twitter.com/RepJohnKline

District Office: 350 W. Burnsville Pkwy., #135, Burnsville, MN 55337-2572; 952-808-1213; Fax: 952-808-1261; *District Director:* Brooke Dorobiala
Committee Assignments: Armed Services; Education and the Workforce, Chair

Kuster, Ann McLane, D-N.H. (2)

Capitol Hill Office: 137 CHOB 20515; 225-5206; Fax: 225-2946; *Chief of Staff:* Abby Curran
Web: http://kuster.house.gov/
Facebook: http://facebook.com/ CongresswomanAnnieKuster
Twitter: http://twitter.com/@RepAnnieKuster
District Offices: 18 N. Main St., 4th Floor, Concord, NH 03301; 603-226-1002; Fax: 603-226-1010; *District Director:* Sean Downey
70 E. Pearl St., Nashua, NH 03060; 603-595-2006; Fax: 603-595-2016; *Constituent Services Coord.:* Collin Lever
107 Glessner Rd., Bethlehem, NH 03561; 603-444-7700; *Service Coordinator:* Brian Bresnahan
Committee Assignments: Agriculture; Small Business; Veterans' Affairs

Labrador, Raul, R-Idaho (1)

Capitol Hill Office: 1523 LHOB 20515-1201; 225-6611; Fax: 225-3029; *Chief of Staff:* Mike Hunnington
Web: http://labrador.house.gov/
Facebook: http://facebook.com/raul.r.labrador
Twitter: http://twitter.com/Raul_Labrador
District Offices: 1250 W. Ironwood Dr., #243, Coeur d'Alene, ID 83814-2682; 208-667-0127; Fax: 208-667-0310; *Regional Director:* Aaron Calkins
313 D St., #107, Lewiston, ID 83501-1894; 208-743-1388; Fax: 208-888-0894; *Regional Director:* Scott Carlton
33 E. Broadway Ave., #251, Meridian, ID 83642-2619; 208-888-3188; Fax: 208-888-0894; *District Director:* Doug Taylor
Committee Assignments: Judiciary; Natural Resources

LaMalfa, Doug, R-Calif. (1)

Capitol Hill Office: 506 CHOB 20515; 225-3076; Fax: 226-0852; *Chief of Staff:* Mark Spannagel
Web: http://lamalfa.house.gov/
Twitter: http://twitter.com/RepLaMalfa
District Offices: 1453 Downer St., Suite A, Oroville, CA 95965; 530-534-7100; Fax: 530-534-7800; *District Director:* Lisa Buescher
2885 Churn Creek Rd., Suite C, Redding, CA 96002; 530-223-5898; Fax: 530-223-5897; *District Rep.:* Stephanie White
13626 New Airport Rd., #106, Auburn, CA 95602; 530-878-5035; Fax: 530-878-5037; *Caseworker:* Leslie Schuessler
Committee Assignments: Agriculture; Natural Resources

Lamborn, Doug, R-Colo. (5)

Capitol Hill Office: 2402 RHOB 20515; 225-4422; Fax: 226-2638; *Chief of Staff:* Adam Magary

Web: http://lamborn.house.gov/
Facebook: http://facebook.com/ CongressmanDougLamborn
Twitter: http://twitter.com/RepDLamborn
District Offices: 415 Main St., Buena Vista, CO 81211; 719-520-0055; Fax: 719-520-0840; *Field Director:* Robin Coran
1125 Kelly Johnson Blvd., #330, Colorado Springs, CO 80920-3965; 719-520-0055; Fax: 719-520-0840; *District Director:* Neal Schuerer
Committee Assignments: Armed Services; Natural Resources; Veterans' Affairs

Lance, Leonard, R-N.J. (7)

Capitol Hill Office: 133 CHOB 20515; 225-5361; Fax: 225-9460; *Chief of Staff:* Todd Mitchell
Web: http://lance.house.gov/
Facebook: http://facebook.com/CongressmanLance
Twitter: http://twitter.com/RepLanceNJ7
District Offices: 361 Route 31, #1400, Flemington, NJ 08822; 908-788-6900; Fax: 908-788-2869; *Community Relations Manager:* Nick Bahnsen
425 North Ave. East, Westfield, NJ 07090-1443; 908-518-7733; Fax: 908-518-7751; *District Director:* Amanda Woloshen
Committee Assignment: Energy and Commerce

Langevin, Jim, D-R.I. (2)

Capitol Hill Office: 109 CHOB 20515-3902; 225-2735; Fax: 225-5976; *Chief of Staff:* Kristin E. Nicholson
Web: http://langevin.house.gov/
Facebook: http://facebook.com/ CongressmanJimLangevin
Twitter: http://twitter.com/jimlangevin
District Office: 300 Centerville Rd., #200 S., Warwick, RI 02886-0200; 401-732-9400; Fax: 401-737-2982; *District Director:* Seth Klaiman
Committee Assignments: Armed Services; Permanent Select Intelligence

Lankford, James, R-Okla. (5)

Capitol Hill Office: 228 CHOB 20515; 225-2132; Fax: 226-1463; *Chief of Staff:* Randy Swanson
Web: http://lankford.house.gov/
Facebook: http://facebook.com/RepLankford
Twitter: http://twitter.com/replankford
District Office: 1015 N. Broadway Ave., #310, Oklahoma City, OK 73102-5849; 405-234-9900; Fax: 405-234-9909; *District Director:* Mona Taylor
Committee Assignments: Budget; Oversight and Government Reform

Larsen, Rick, D-Wash. (2)

Capitol Hill Office: 2113 RHOB 20515; 225-2605; Fax: 225-4420; *Chief of Staff:* Kimberly Johnston
Web: http://larsen.house.gov/
Facebook: http://facebook.com/RepRickLarsen
Twitter: http://twitter.com/RepRickLarsen

District Offices: 119 N. Commercial St., #1350, Bellingham, WA 98225-4452; 360-733-4500; Fax: 360-733-5144; *Community Liaison:* Thomas Boucher
Wall Street Bldg., 2930 Wetmore Ave., #9F, Everett, WA 98201-4070; 425-252-3188; Fax: 425-252-6606; *District Director:* Jill McKinnie
Committee Assignments: Armed Services; Transportation and Infrastructure

Larson, John B., D-Conn. (1)

Capitol Hill Office: 1501 LHOB 20515-0701; 225-2265; Fax: 225-1031; *Chief of Staff:* Lee Slater
Web: http://larson.house.gov/
Facebook: http://facebook.com/RepJohnLarson
Twitter: http://twitter.com/repjohnlarson
District Office: 221 Main St., 2nd Floor, Hartford, CT 06106-1890; 860-278-8888; Fax: 860-278-2111; *District Chief of Staff:* John Rossi
Committee Assignment: Ways and Means

Latham, Tom, R-Iowa (3)

Capitol Hill Office: 2217 RHOB 20515-1504; 225-5476; Fax: 225-3301; *Chief of Staff:* James D. Carstensen
Web: http://latham.house.gov/
Facebook: http://facebook.com/tom.latham.733
Twitter: http://twitter.com/TomLatham
District Offices: 116 W. Broadway St., Council Bluffs, IA 51503; 712-325-1404; Fax: 712-325-1405; *Regional Rep.:* Emily Clark
208 W. Taylor St., Creston, Iowa 50801; 641-782-2495; Fax: 641-782-249; *Regional Rep.:* Laura Hartman
2700 Grand Ave., #109, Des Moines, IA 50312; 515-282-1909; Fax: 515-0282-1785; *District Director:* Clarke Scanlon
Committee Assignment: Appropriations

Latta, Bob, R-Ohio (5)

Capitol Hill Office: 2448 RHOB 20515; 225-6405; Fax: 225-1985; *Chief of Staff:* Ryan Walker
Web: http://latta.house.gov/
Facebook: http://facebook.com/boblatta?ref=name
Twitter: http://twitter.com/boblatta
District Offices: 1045 N. Main St., #6, Bowling Green, OH 43402-1361; 419-354-8700; Fax: 419-354-8702; *District Director:* Andrew Lorenz
101 Clinton St., #1200, Defiance, OH 43512-2165; 419-782-1996; Fax: 419-784-9808; *Sr. District Rep.:* Kathy Shaver
318 Dorney Plaza, Room 302, Findlay, OH 45840; 419-422-7791; *District Rep.:* LuAnne Cooke
Committee Assignment: Energy and Commerce

Lee, Barbara, D-Calif. (13)

Capitol Hill Office: 2267 RHOB 20515-0509; 225-2661; Fax: 225-9817; *Chief of Staff:* Julie Nickson
Web: http://lee.house.gov/
Facebook: http://facebook.com/RepBarbaraLee
Twitter: http://twitter.com/RepBarbaraLee

District Office: 1301 Clay St., #1000-N, Oakland, CA 94612-5233; 510-763-0370; Fax: 510-763-6538; *District Director:* Katherine Jolly
300 Estudillo Ave., Room C 1st and 3rd, San Leandro, CA 94577; *Casework Manager/Congressional Aide:* Jonathan Gast
1550 Oak St., Floor 2, Staff Room, Alameda, CA 94501; *Congressional Aide:* Katherine Kwong
Citizens Foundation, 1470 Fruitvale Ave., Oakland, CA 94601; *Congressional Aide:* Jose Hernandez
Committee Assignment: Appropriations; Budget

Levin, Sander, D-Mich. (9)

Capitol Hill Office: 1236 LHOB 20515-2212; 225-4961; Fax: 226-1033; *Chief of Staff:* Hilarie Chambers
Web: http://levin.house.gov/
Facebook: http://facebook.com/RepSandyLevin
Twitter: http://twitter.com/repsandylevin
District Office: 27085 Gratiot Ave., Roseville, MI 48066-2947; 586-498-7122; Fax: 586-498-7123; *District Director:* Walt Herzig
Committee Assignments: Ways and Means, Ranking Minority Member

Lewis, John, D-Ga. (5)

Capitol Hill Office: 343 CHOB 20515-1005; 225-3801; Fax: 225-0351; *Chief of Staff; Floor Asst.:* Michael Collins
Web: http://johnlewis.house.gov/
Facebook: http://facebook.com/RepJohnLewis
Twitter: http://twitter.com/repjohnlewis
District Office: Equitable Bldg., 100 Peachtree St., N.W., #1920, Atlanta, GA 30303-1906; 404-659-0116; Fax: 404-331-0947; *District Director:* Aaron Ward
Committee Assignment: Ways and Means

Lipinski, Daniel, D-Ill. (3)

Capitol Hill Office: 1717 LHOB 20515-1303; 225-5701; Fax: 225-1012; *Chief of Staff:* Eric L. Lausten
Web: http://lipinski.house.gov/
Facebook: http://facebook.com/repdanlipinski
Twitter: http://twitter.com/RepLipinski
District Offices: 6245 S. Archer Ave., Chicago, IL 60638-2609; 312-886-0481; Fax: 773-767-9395; *District Director:* Jerry Hurckes
Central Square Bldg., 222 E. 9th St., #109, Lockport, IL 60441; 815-838-1990; Fax: 815-838-1993; *Communications Director:* Guy Tridgell
5309 W. 95th St., Oak Lawn, IL 60453-2444; 708-424-0853; Fax: 708-424-1855; *Congressional Aide:* Jerry Mulvihill
Orland Park Village Hall, 14700 S. Ravinia Ave., Orland Park, IL 60462; 708-403-4379; Fax: 708-403-5963; *Congressional Aide:* Marianne Chmela
Committee Assignments: Science, Space, and Technology; Transportation and Infrastructure

LoBiondo, Frank A., R-N.J. (2)

Capitol Hill Office: 2427 RHOB 20515-3002; 225-6572; Fax: 225-3318; *Chief of Staff:* Mary Annie Harper

Web: http://lobiondo.house.gov/
Facebook: http://facebook.com/FrankLoBiondo
Twitter: http://twitter.com/RepLoBiondo
District Office: 5914 Main St., #103, Mays Landing, NJ 08330-1746; 609-625-5008; Fax: 609-625-5071; *Director of Constituent Services:* Joan Dermanoski
Committee Assignments: Armed Services; Transportation and Infrastructure; Permanent Select Intelligence

Loebsack, Dave, D-Iowa (2)

Capitol Hill Office: 1527 LHOB 20515-1502; 225-6576; Fax: 226-0757; *Chief of Staff:* Eric Witte
Web: http://loebsack.house.gov/
Facebook: http://facebook.com/DaveLoebsack
Twitter: https://twitter.com/daveloebsack
District Offices: 209 W. 4th St., #104, Davenport, IA 52801; 563-323-5988; Fax: 563-323-5231; *District Director:* Robert Sueppel
125 S. Dubuque St., Iowa City, IA 52240-4000; 319-351-0789; Fax: 319-351-5789; *District Rep.:* David Leshtz
Committee Assignments: Armed Services; Education and the Workforce

Lofgren, Zoe, D-Calif. (19)

Capitol Hill Office: 1401 LHOB 20515-0516; 225-3072; Fax: 225-3336; *Chief of Staff:* Stacey Leavandosky
Web: http://lofgren.house.gov/
Facebook: http://facebook.com/zoelofgren
Twitter: http://twitter.com/RepZoeLofgren
District Office: 635 N. First St., Suite B, San Jose, CA 95112-5110; 408-271-8700; Fax: 408-271-8714; *District Chief of Staff:* Sandra Soto
Committee Assignments: House Administration; Judiciary; Science, Space, and Technology; Joint Library of Congress

Long, Billy, R-Mo. (7)

Capitol Hill Office: 1541 LHOB 20515-2507; 225-6536; Fax: 225-5604; *Chief of Staff:* Joe Lillis
Web: http://long.house.gov/
Facebook: http://facebook.com/Rep.Billy.Long
Twitter: http://twitter.com/UsRepLong
District Offices: 2727 E. 32nd St., #2, Joplin, MO 64804-3155; 417-781-1041; Fax: 417-781-2832; *Field Rep.:* Jacob Heisten
3232 E. Ridgeview St., Springfield, MO 65804-4076; 417-889-1800; Fax: 417-889-4915; *District Director:* Royce Reding
Committee Assignment: Energy and Commerce

Lowenthal, Alan, D-Calif. (47)

Capitol Hill Office: 515 CHOB 20515; 225-7924; Fax: 225-7926; *Chief of Staff:* Tim Hysom
Web: http://lowenthal.house.gov/
Facebook: http://facebook.com/RepLowenthal
Twitter: http://twitter.com/RepLowenthal
District Office: West Tower, 100 W. Broadway, #600, Long Beach, CA 90802; 562-436-3828; Fax: 562-437-6434; *District Director:* Mark Pulido
Committee Assignments: Foreign Affairs; Natural Resources

Lowey, Nita, D-N.Y. (17)

Capitol Hill Office: 2365 RHOB 20515-3218; 225-6506; Fax: 225-0546; *Chief of Staff:* Elizabeth Stanley
Web: http://lowey.house.gov/
Facebook: http://facebook.com/RepLowey
Twitter: http://twitter.com/NitaLowey
District Offices: 67 N. Main St., #101, New City, NY 10956; 845-639-3485; Fax: 845-634-4079; *District Rep.:* Sarah Levine
222 Mamaroneck Ave., #312, White Plains, NY 10605; 914-428-1707; Fax: 914-328-1505; *District Director:* Patricia Keegan
Committee Assignment: Appropriations, Ranking Minority Member

Lucas, Frank, R-Okla. (3)

Capitol Hill Office: 2311 RHOB 20515-3603; 225-5565; Fax: 225-8698; *Communications Director:* Laramie Adams
Web: http://lucas.house.gov/
Facebook: http://facebook.com/pages/Frank-Lucas/7872057395
Twitter: http://twitter.com/FrankDLucas
District Office: 10952 N.W. Expressway, Suite B, Yukon, OK 73099-8214; 405-373-1958; Fax: 405-373-2046; *Chief of Staff:* Stacey Glasscock
Committee Assignments: Agriculture, Chair; Financial Services; Science, Space, and Technology

Luetkemeyer, Blaine, R-Mo. (3)

Capitol Hill Office: 2440 RHOB 20515; 225-2956; Fax: 225-5712; *Chief of Staff; Legis. Director:* Seth Appleton
Web: http://luetkemeyer.house.gov/
Facebook: http://facebook.com/BlaineLuetkemeyer
Twitter: http://twitter.com/RepBlainePress
District Offices: 2117 Missouri Blvd., Jefferson City, MO 65109; 573-635-7232; Fax: 573-635-8347; *Deputy District Director:* Jeremy Ketterer
113 E. Pearce Blvd., Wentzville, MO 63385; 636-327-7055; Fax: 636-327-3254; *Deputy District Director:* Tanner Smith
516 Jefferson St., Washington, MO 63090-2706; 636-239-2276; Fax: 636-239-0478; *Deputy District Director:* Dan Engemann
Committee Assignments: Financial Services; Small Business

Luján, Ben Ray, D-N.M. (3)

Capitol Hill Office: 2446 RHOB 20515; 225-6190; Fax: 226-1528; *Chief of Staff:* Angela K. Ramirez
Web: http://lujan.house.gov/
Facebook: http://facebook.com/RepBenRayLujan
Twitter: http://twitter.com/repbenraylujan
District Offices: 800 Municipal Dr., Farmington, NM 87401-2663; 505-324-1005; Fax: 505-324-1026; *Field Rep.:* Pete Valencia

110 W. Aztec Ave., Gallup, NM 87301-6202; 505-863-0582; Fax: 505-863-0678; Field Rep.; *Navajo Nation Advisor:* Brian Lee

903 University Ave., Las Vegas, NM 87701; 505-454-3038; Fax: 505-454-3265; *Constituent Liaison:* Pam Garcia

3200 Civic Center Circle N.E., #330, Rio Rancho, NM 87144-4503; 505-994-0499; Fax: 505-994-0550; *Constituent Liaison:* Joseph Casados

1611 Calle Lorca, Suite A, Santa Fe, NM 87505-7640; 505-984-8950; Fax: 505-986-5047; *District Director:* Jennifer Conn-Catechis

404 W. Route 66 Blvd., Tucumcari, NM 88401-3279; 575-461-3029; Fax: 575-461-3192; *Field Rep.:* Ron Wilmot

Committee Assignment: Energy and Commerce

Lujan Grisham, Michelle, D-N.M. (1)

Capitol Hill Office: 214 CHOB 20515; 225-6316; Fax: 225-4975; *Chief of Staff:* Dominic Gabello

Web: http://lujangrisham.house.gov/

Facebook: http://facebook.com/RepLujanGrisham

Twitter: http://twitter.com/@replujangrisham

District Offices: 505 Marquette Ave., N.W., #1605, Albuquerque, NM 87102; 505-346-6781; Fax: 505-346-6723; *District Director:* Marianna Padilla

Committee Assignments: Agriculture; Budget; Oversight and Government Reform

Lummis, Cynthia, R-Wyo. (At Large)

Capitol Hill Office: 113 CHOB 20515-5001; 225-2311; Fax: 225-3057; *Chief of Staff:* Tom Wiblemo

Web: http://lummis.house.gov/

Facebook: http://facebook.com/cynthia.lummis

Twitter: http://twitter.com/CynthiaLummis

District Offices: 100 E. B St., #4003, Casper, WY 82602-1969; 307-261-6595; Fax: 307-261-6597; *Field Rep.:* Jackie King

2120 Capitol Ave., #8005, Cheyenne, WY 82001-3631; 307-772-2595; Fax: 307-772-2597; *Chief of Staff:* Tucker Fagan

404 N St., #204, Rock Springs, WY 82901-5474; 307-362-4095; Fax: 307-362-4097; *Field Rep.:* Pat Aullman

45 E. Loucks St., #300F, Sheridan, WY 82801-6331; 307-673-4608; Fax: 307-673-4982; *Field Rep.:* Matt Jones

Committee Assignments: Natural Resources; Oversight and Government Reform; Science, Space, and Technology

Lynch, Stephen F., D-Mass. (8)

Capitol Hill Office: 2133 RHOB 20515; 225-8273; Fax: 225-3984; *Chief of Staff:* Kevin Ryan

Web: http://lynch.house.gov/

Facebook: http://facebook.com/repstephenlynch

Twitter: https://twitter.com/RepStephenLynch

District Offices: 88 Black Falcon Ave., #340, Boston, MA 02210-2433; 617-428-2000; Fax: 617-428-2011; *District Director:* Bob Fowkes

Plymouth County Registry of Deeds, 155 W. Elm St., #200, Brockton, MA 02301-4326; 508-586-5555; Fax: 508-580-4692; *District Rep.:* Shaynah Barnes

1245 Hancock St., #16, Quincy, MA 02169; 617-657-6305; Fax: 617-773-0955; *District Rep.:* Catherine Shea

Committee Assignments: Financial Services; Oversight and Government Reform

Maffei, Dan, D-N.Y. (24)

Capitol Hill Office: 422 CHOB 20515; 225-3701; Fax: 225-4042; *Chief of Staff:* Charles Kelly

Web: http://maffei.house.gov/

Facebook: http://facebook.com/repmaffei

Twitter: http://twitter.com/RepDanMaffei

District Offices: 30 Dill St., Auburn NY 13021; 315-253-4176; Fax: 315-253-4939; *Field Manager:* Ian Phillips

100 N. Salina St., 1 Clinton Square, Syracuse, NY 13202; 315-423-5657; Fax: 315-423-5604; *District Director:* Corinne Driscoll

13 W. Oneida St., 2nd Floor, Oswego, NY 13126; 315-342-2192; Fax: 315-342-2528; *Caseworker:* Meave Gillen

Committee Assignments: Armed Services; Science, Space, and Technology

Maloney, Carolyn B., D-N.Y. (12)

Capitol Hill Office: 2308 RHOB 20515; 225-7944; Fax: 225-4709; *Chief of Staff:* Michael Iger

Web: http://maloney.house.gov/

Facebook: https://facebook.com/CarolynMaloney

Twitter: http://twitter.com/RepMaloney

District Offices: 31-19 Newtown Ave., Astoria, NY 11102; 718-932-1804; Fax: 718-932-1805; *District Rep.:* Edward Babor

1651 3rd Ave., #311, New York, NY 10128-3679; 212-860-0606; Fax: 212-860-0704; *New York Chief of Staff:* Minna Elias

619 Lorimer St., Brooklyn, NY 11211; 718-349-5972; Fax: 718-349-5973; *District Rep.:* Mary Odomirok

Committee Assignments: Financial Services; Oversight and Government Reform; Joint Economic

Maloney, Sean Patrick, D-N.Y. (18)

Capitol Hill Office: 1529 LHOB 20515; 225-5441; Fax: 225-3289; *Chief of Staff:* Timothy Persico

Web: http://seanmaloney.house.gov/

Facebook: http://facebook.com/repseanmaloney

Twitter: http://twitter.com/@RepSeanMaloney

District Office: 123 Grand St., 2nd Floor, Newburgh, NY 12550; 845-561-1259; Fax: 845-561-2890; *District Director:* Ed Brancati

Committee Assignments: Agriculture; Transportation and Infrastructure

Marchant, Kenny, R-Tex. (24)

Capitol Hill Office: 1110 LHOB 20515-4324; 225-6605; Fax: 225-0074; *Chief of Staff:* Brian Thomas

Web: http://marchant.house.gov/

Facebook: http://facebook.com/RepKennyMarchant

Twitter: http://twitter.com/repkenmarchant

District Office: 9901 E. Valley Ranch Pkwy., #3035, Irving, TX 75063-7186; 972-556-0162; Fax: 972-409-9704; *District Director:* Susie Miller

Committee Assignment: Education and the Workforce; Ways and Means

Marino, Tom, R-Pa. (10)

Capitol Hill Office: 410 CHOB 20515-3810; 225-3731; Fax: 225-9594; *Chief of Staff:* William Tighe
Web: http://marino.house.gov/
Facebook: http://facebook.com/CongressmanMarino
Twitter: http://twitter.com/RepTomMarino
District Offices: 543 Easton Tunpike, #101, Lake Ariel, PA 18436, 570-689-6024; Fax: 570-689-6028; *District Director:* David Weber
30 S. Market St., #1A, Selinsgrove, PA 17870; 570-374-9469; Fax: 570-374-9589; *District Rep.:* Aimee Snyder
1020 Commerce Park Dr., #1A, Williamsport, PA 17701-5434; 570-322-3961; Fax: 570-322-3965; *Constituent Services Rep.:* Jacque Bell
Committee Assignments: Foreign Affairs; Homeland Security; Judiciary

Massie, Thomas, R-Ky. (4)

Capitol Hill Office: 314 CHOB 20515; 225-3465; Fax: 225-0003; *Chief of Staff:* Hans Hoge
Web: http://massie.house.gov/
Facebook: http://facebook.com/RepThomasMassie
Twitter: http://twitter.com/RepThomasMassie
District Offices: 1700 Greenup Ave., R-505, Ashland, KY 41101-7573; 606-324-9898; Fax: 606-325-9866; *Field Rep.:* J.R. Reed
541Buttermilk Pike, #208, Crescent Springs, KY 41017-3924; 859-426-0080; Fax: 859-426-0061; *District Director:* Chris McCane
108 W. Jefferson St., LaGrange, KY 40031; 502-265-9119; Fax: 502-265-9126; *Western District Field Rep.:* Stacey Rockaway
Committee Assignments: Oversight and Government Reform; Science, Space, and Technology; Transportation and Infrastructure

Matheson, Jim, D-Utah (4)

Capitol Hill Office: 2211 RHOB 20515; 225-3011; Fax: 225-5638; *Chief of Staff:* Meg Joseph
Web: http://matheson.house.gov/
Facebook: http://facebook.com/RepJimMatheson
Twitter: http://twitter.com/RepJimMatheson
District Office: 9067 S. 1300 West, #101, West Jordan, UT 84008; 801-486-1236; Fax: 801-486-1417; *Field Rep.:* Pam Juliano
Committee Assignment: Energy and Commerce

Matsui, Doris, D-Calif. (6)

Capitol Hill Office: 2434 RHOB 20515-0506; 225-7163; Fax: 225-0566; *Chief of Staff:* Julie Eddy
Web: http://matsui.house.gov/
Facebook: http://facebook.com/doris.matsui
Twitter: http://twitter.com/dorismatsui
District Office: Robert T. Matsui U.S. Courthouse, 501 I St.,#12-600, Sacramento, CA 95814-4778; 916-498-5600; Fax: 916-444-6117; *District Director:* Nathan Dietrich
Committee Assignment: Energy and Commerce

McAllister, Vance, R-La. (5)

Capitol Hill Office: 316 CHOB 20515-1805; 225-8490; Fax: 225-5639; *Chief of Staff:* Adam Terry
Web: http://mcallister.house.gov/
Facebook: http://facebook.com/Rep McAllister
Twitter: http://twitter.com/RepMcAllister
District Offices: 1434 Dorchester Drive, Suite E, Alexandria, LA 71301-3449; 318-445-0818; Fax: 318-445-3776; *District Director:* Tommie Seaton
1900 Stubbs Ave., Suite B, Monroe, LA 71201-5751; 318-322-3500; Fax: 318-322-3577
Committee Assignments: Appropriations

McCarthy, Carolyn, D-N.Y. (4)

Capitol Hill Office: 2346 RHOB 20515-3204; 225-5516; Fax: 225-5758; *Chief of Staff:* Georgette Sierra
Web: http://carolynmccarthy.house.gov/
Twitter: https://twitter.com/RepMcCarthyNY
District Office: 300 Garden City Plaza, #200, Garden City, NY 11530-3338; 516-739-3008; Fax: 516-739-2973; *District Director:* Chris Chaffee
Committee Assignments: Education and the Workforce; Financial Services

McCarthy, Kevin, R-Calif. (23)

Capitol Hill Office: 2421 RHOB 20515; 225-2915; Fax: 225-2908; *Chief of Staff:* James B. Min
Web: http://kevinmccarthy.house.gov/
Facebook: http://facebook.com/ CongressmanKevinMcCarthy
Twitter: http://twitter.com/GOPWhip
District Offices: 4100 Empire Dr., #150, Bakersfield, CA 93309-0409; 661-327-3611; Fax: 661-637-0867; *District Director:* Vincent Fong
Committee Assignment: Financial Services

McCaul, Michael, R-Tex. (10)

Capitol Hill Office: 131 CHOB 20515-4310; 225-2401; Fax: 225-5955; *Chief of Staff:* Hans Klingler
Web: http://mccaul.house.gov/
Facebook: http://facebook.com/michaeltmccaul
Twitter: http://twitter.com/McCaulPressShop
District Offices: 9009 Mountain Ridge Dr., Austin Bldg., #230, Austin, TX 78759; 512-473-2357; Fax: 512-473-0514; *District Director:* Mary Elen Williams
2000 S. Market St., #303, Brenham, TX 77833-5800; 979-830-8497; Fax: 979-830-1984; *Caseworker:* Marita Mikeska
Rosewood Professional Bldg., 990 Village Square Dr., Suite B, Tomball, TX 77375-4269; 281-255-8372; Fax: 281-255-0034; *Constituent Liaison/Caseworker:* Sherrie Meicher
Katy Commerce Center, 1773 Westborough Dr., #223, Katy, TX 77449; 281-398-1247; *Constituent Liaison/ Caseworker:* Sherrie Meicher
Committee Assignments: Foreign Affairs; Homeland Security, Chair; Science, Space, and Technology

McClintock, Tom, R-Calif. (4)

Capitol Hill Office: 434 CHOB 20515-0504; 225-2511; Fax: 225-5444; *Chief of Staff:* Igor Birman; *Deputy Chief of Staff:* Kristen Glen
Web: http://mcclintock.house.gov/
Facebook: http://facebook.com/pages/Congressman-Tom-McClintock/81125319109
Twitter: http://twitter.com/RepMcClintock
District Office: 8700 Auburn Folsom Rd., #100, Granite Bay, CA 95746-8501; 916-786-5560; Fax: 916-786-6364; *District Director:* Rocklun Deal
Committee Assignments: Budget; Natural Resources

McCollum, Betty, D-Minn. (4)

Capitol Hill Office: 1714 LHOB 20515-2304; 225-6631; Fax: 225-1968; *Chief of Staff:* Bill Harper
Web: http://mccollum.house.gov/
Facebook: http://facebook.com/repbettymccollum
Twitter: https://twitter.com/BettyMcCollum04
District Office: 165 Western Ave. N., #17, St. Paul, MN 55102-4613; 651-224-9191; Fax: 651-224-3056; *District Director:* Joshua Straka
Committee Assignment: Appropriations

McDermott, Jim, D-Wash. (7)

Capitol Hill Office: 1035 LHOB 20515-4707; 225-3106; Fax: 225-6197; *Chief of Staff:* Diane M. Shust
Web: http://mcdermott.house.gov/
Facebook: http://facebook.com/CongressmanJimMcDermott
Twitter: http://twitter.com/RepJimMcDermott
District Office: 1809 7th Ave., #1212, Seattle, WA 98101-1399; 206-553-7170; Fax: 206-553-7175; *District Director:* Olivia Robinson
Committee Assignments: Budget; Ways and Means

McGovern, Jim, D-Mass. (2)

Capitol Hill Office: 438 CHOB 20515-2103; 225-6101; Fax: 225-5759; *Deputy Chief of Staff:* Michael Merson
Web: http://mcgovern.house.gov/
Facebook: http://facebook.com/RepJimMcGovern
Twitter: http://twitter.com/RepMcGovern
District Offices: 24 Church St., Room 29, Leominster, MA 01453; 978-466-3552; Fax: 978-466-3973; *District Rep.:* Eladia Romero
94 Pleasant St., Northhampton, MA 01060; 413-341-8700; Fax: 413-584-1216; *District Rep.:* Keith Barnacle
12 E. Worcester St., #1, Worcester, MA 01604; 508-831-7356; Fax: 508-754-0982; *District Director:* Kathleen Polanowicz
Committee Assignments: Agriculture; Rules

McHenry, Patrick, R-N.C. (10)

Capitol Hill Office: 2334 RHOB 20515; 225-2576; Fax: 225-0316; *Chief of Staff:* Parker Poling
Web: http://mchenry.house.gov/
Facebook: http://facebook.com/CongressmanMcHenry
Twitter: http://twitter.com/PatrickMcHenry

District Offices: 160 Midland Ave., Black Mountain, NC 28711; 828-669-0600; *Regional Director:* Roger Kumpf
128 W. Main Ave., Gaston County Administrative Bldg., #115, , Gastonia, NC 28053; 704-833-0096; Fax: 704-833-0887; *Regional Director.:* Brett Keeter
87 4th St., N.W., Suite A, P.O. Box 1830, Hickory, NC 28603; 828-327-6100; Fax: 828-327-8311; *District Director:* Mark Fleming
Committee Assignments: Financial Services; Oversight and Government Reform

McIntyre, Mike, D-N.C. (7)

Capitol Hill Office: 2428 RHOB 20515; 225-2731; Fax: 225-5773; *Chief of Staff:* Marie Thompson
Web: http://mcintyre.house.gov/
Facebook: http://facebook.com/mikemcintyre
Twitter: http://twitter.com/RepMikeMcIntyre
District Offices: Benson Town Hall, 303 E. Church St., Benson, NC 27504; 919-894-3553; *Field Rep.:* Billy Barker
Clayton Town Hall, 111 E. 2nd St., Clayton, NC 27520; 910-977-7792; Fax: 910-316-6552; *Field Rep.:* Billy Barker
497 Olde Waterford Way, #206, Leland, NC 28451; 910-399-1134; Fax: 910-399-4172; *Director of Veteran Services:* Rosalie Calarco
119 Courthouse Dr., P.O. Box 2107, Elizabethtown, NC 28337; 910-862-1437; Fax: 910-862-2286; *Office Manager:* Lillian Hunt
Smithfield Town Hall, 350 E. Market St., P.O. Box 761, Smithfield, NC 27577; 919-934-2116; *Constituent Services Asst.:* Emily Farnell
Committee Assignments: Commission on Security and Cooperation in Europe (Helsinki Commission); Agriculture; Armed Services

McKeon, Buck, R-Calif. (25)

Capitol Hill Office: 2310 RHOB 20515; 225-1956; Fax: 226-0683; *Chief of Staff:* Alan Tennille
Web: http://mckeon.house.gov/
Facebook: http://facebook.com/BuckMcKeon
Twitter: http://twitter.com/BuckMcKeon
District Offices: 1008 W. Ave. M-14, Suite E, Palmdale, CA 93551-1441; 661-274-9688; Fax: 661-274-8744; *Field Rep.:* J. D. Kennedy
26650 The Old Road, #203, Santa Clarita, CA 91381-0750; 661-254-2111; Fax: 661-254-2380; *District Director:* Morris Thomas
Committee Assignments: Armed Services, Chair; Education and the Workforce

McKinley, David, R-W. Va. (1)

Capitol Hill Office: 412 CHOB 20515; 225-4172; Fax: 225-7564; *Chief of Staff:* Mike Hamilton
Web: http://mckinley.house.gov/
Facebook: http://facebook.com/RepMcKinley
Twitter: http://twitter.com/RepMcKinley

District Offices: 709 Beechurst Ave., #14B, Morgantown, WV 26505-4689; 304-284-8506; *District Director*: Richie Parsons

425 Juliana St., #1004, Parkersburg, WV 26101-5323; 304-422-5972; *Constituent Services Rep.*: Robert Villers

Horne Bldg., 1100 Main St., #101, Wheeling, WV 26003; 304-232-3801; Fax: 304-232-3813; *Constituent Services Rep.*: Chelsea Wright-Saus

Committee Assignment: Energy and Commerce

McLeod, Gloria Negrete, D-Calif. (35)

Capitol Hill Office: 1641 LHOB 20515; 225-6161; Fax: 225-8671; *Chief of Staff:* Alfonso Sanchez
Web: http://negretemcleod.house.gov/
Facebook: http://facebook.com/NegreteMcLeod
Twitter: http://twitter.com/@RepMcLeod
District Office: 4959 Palo Verde St., #110B, Montclair, CA 91763; 909-626-2054; Fax: 909-626-2678; *District Director:* Marti Rodriguez
Committee Assignments: Agriculture; Veteran's Affairs

McMorris Rodgers, Cathy, R-Wash. (5)

Capitol Hill Office: 203 CHOB 20515; 225-2006; Fax: 225-3392; *Chief of Staff:* Jeremy Deutsch
Web: http://mcmorris.house.gov/
Facebook: http://facebook.com/mcmorrisrodgers
Twitter: http://twitter.com/cathymcmorris
District Offices: 555 S. Main St., Colville, WA 99114-2503; 509-684-3481; Fax: 202-225-3392; *Deputy District Director:* Sheila Stalp
10 N. Post St., #625, Spokane, WA 99201-0706; 509-353-2374; Fax: 202-225-3392; *District Director:* Louise Sendrich
29 S. Palouse St., Walla Walla, WA 99362-1925; 509-529-9358; Fax: 202-225-3392; *Constituent Relations Liaison:* Karen Dodson
Committee Assignment: Energy and Commerce

McNerney, Jerry, D-Calif. (9)

Capitol Hill Office: 1210 LHOB 20515-0511; 225-1947; Fax: 225-4060; *Chief of Staff:* Nicole Alioto
Web: http://mcnerney.house.gov/
Facebook: http://facebook.com/jerrymcnerney
Twitter: http://twitter.com/RepMcNerney
District Offices: Antioch Community Center, 4703 Lone Tree Way, Antioch, CA 94531; 925-754-0716; Fax: 925-754-0728; *District Director:* Alisa Alva
2222 Grand Canal Blvd., #7, Stockton, CA 95207-6671; 209-476-8552; Fax: 209-476-8587; *District Scheduler:* Jaclyn Smith
Committee Assignment: Energy and Commerce

Meadows, Mark, R-N.C. (11)

Capitol Hill Office: 1516 LHOB 20515; 225-6401; Fax: 226-6422; *Chief of Staff:* Kenneth West
Web: http://meadows.house.gov/
Facebook: http://facebook.com/Repmarkmeadows
Twitter: http://twitter.com/RepMarkMeadows

District Offices: 200 N. Grove St., #90, Hendersonville, NC 28792; 828-693-5660; Fax: 828-693-5603; *District Director; Office Manager:* Pamela Ward

2345 Morganton Blvd., Lenoir, NC 28645; 828-426-8701; *Field Rep.:* Doug Crosby

11 Crystal St., Spruce Pine, NC 28777; 828-765-0573; *Field Rep.:* Martha Peterson

285 N. Main St., #1300, Waynesville, NC 28786; 828-452-6022; *Field Rep.:* Beverly Elliott

Committee Assignments: Foreign Affairs; Oversight and Government Reform; Transportation and Infrastructure

Meehan, Pat, R-Pa. (7)

Capitol Hill Office: 204 CHOB 20515; 225-2011; Fax: 226-0820; *Chief of Staff:* Brian Schubert
Web: http://meehan.house.gov/
Facebook: http://facebook.com/CongressmanPatrickMeehan
Twitter: http://twitter.com/repmeehan
District Office: 940 W. Sproul Rd., Springfield, PA 19064-1255; 610-690-7323; Fax: 610-690-7329; *District Director:* Caitlin Ganley
Committee Assignments: Ethics; Homeland Security; Oversight and Government Reform; Transportation and Infrastructure

Meeks, Gregory W., D-N.Y. (5)

Capitol Hill Office: 2234 RHOB 20515; 225-3461; Fax: 226-4169; *Chief of Staff:* Sofia Lafargue
Web: http://meeks.house.gov/
Facebook: http://facebook.com/gregorymeeksny05
Twitter: http://twitter.com/GregoryMeeks
District Offices: 67-12 Rockaway Beach Blvd., Arverne, NY 11692; 347-230-4032; Fax: 347-230-4045; *District Chief of Staff:* Robert Simmons
153-01 Jamaica Ave., 2nd Floor, Jamaica, NY 11432; 718-725-6000; Fax: 718-725-9868; *Executive Director*: Joe Edwards
Committee Assignments: Financial Services; Foreign Affairs

Meng, Grace, D-N.Y. (6)

Capitol Hill Office: 1317 LHOB 20515; 225-2601; Fax: 225-1589; *Chief of Staff:* Jedd Moskowitz
Web: http://meng.house.gov/
Facebook: http://facebook.com/repgracemeng
Twitter: http://twitter.com/RepGraceMeng
District Office: 32-26 Union St., #1B, Flushing, NY 11354; 718-445-7860; Fax: 718-445-7868; *Deputy District Director:* Anthony Lemma
118-35 Queens Blvd., #1610, Forest Hills, NY 11375; 718-445-7861; *District Director:* Greg Lavine
Committee Assignments: Foreign Affairs; Small Business

Messer, Luke, R-Ind. (6)

Capitol Hill Office: 508 CHOB 20515; 225-3021; Fax: 225-3382; *Chief of Staff:* Doug Menorca
Web: http://messer.house.gov/

Facebook: http://facebook.com/RepLukeMesser
Twitter: http://twitter.com/RepLukeMesser
District Offices: 107 W. Charles St., Munice, IN 47305-2420; 765-747-5566; Fax: 765-747-5586; *District Director:* Mike Lynch
50 N. 5th St., Richmond, IN 47374-4247; 765-962-2883; Fax: 765-962-3225; *Caseworker:* Debbie Berry
2 Public Sq., Shelbyville, IN 46176; 317-421-0704; Fax: 317-421-0739; *Field Rep.:* Tim Hawkins
Committee Assignments: Budget; Education and the Workforce; Foreign Affairs

Mica, John, R-Fla. (7)

Capitol Hill Office: 2187 RHOB 20515; 225-4035; Fax: 226-0821; *Chief of Staff:* Wiley Deck
Web: http://mica.house.gov/
Facebook: http://facebook.com/JohnMica
District Offices: 840 Deltona Blvd., Suite G, Deltona, FL 32725; 386-860-1499; Fax: 386-860-5730; *District Rep.:* John Booker
100 E. Sybelia Ave., #340, Maitland, FL 32751-4495; 407-657-8080; Fax: 407-657-5353; *District Rep.:* Dick Harkey
95 E. Mitchell Hammock Rd., #202, Oviedo, FL 32765; 407-366-0833; Fax: 407-366-0839; *District Rep.:* Patrick Kelly
Committee Assignments: Oversight and Government Reform; Transportation and Infrastructure

Michaud, Mike, D-Maine (2)

Capitol Hill Office: 1724 LHOB 20515-1902; 225-6306; Fax: 225-2943; *Chief of Staff:* Peter H. Chandler
Web: http://michaud.house.gov/
Facebook: http://facebook.com/RepMikeMichaud
Twitter: http://twitter.com/RepMikeMichaud
District Offices: 6 State St., #101, Bangor, ME 04401-5124; 207-942-6935; Fax: 207-942-5907; *Caseworker:* Chris Winstead
179 Lisbon St., Lewiston, ME 04240-7248; 207-782-3704; Fax: 207-782-5330; *Deputy Chief of Staff:* John Graham
445 Main St., Presque Isle, ME 04769-2651; 207-764-1036; Fax: 207-764-1060; *Caseworker:* Rachel Smith
Committee Assignments: Transportation and Infrastructure; Veterans' Affairs, Ranking Minority Member

Miller, Candice, R-Mich. (10)

Capitol Hill Office: 320 CHOB 20515; 225-2106; Fax: 226-1169; *Chief of Staff:* Jamie Roe
Web: http://candicemiller.house.gov/
Facebook: http://facebook.com/CongresswomanCandiceMiller
Twitter: http://twitter.com/CandiceMiller
District Office: 48701 Van Dyke Ave., Shelby Township, MI 48317-2562; 586-997-5010; Fax: 586-997-5013; *District Director:* Karen Czernel
Committee Assignments: House Administration, Chair; Homeland Security; Transportation and Infrastructure; Joint Library of Congress; Joint Printing

Miller, Gary, R-Calif. (31)

Capitol Hill Office: 2467 RHOB 20515; 225-3201; Fax: 226-6962; *Chief of Staff:* John Rothrock
Web: http://garymiller.house.gov/
Facebook: http://facebook.com/RepGaryMiller
Twitter: http://twitter.com/repgarymiller
District Office: 8300 Utica Ave., #105, Rancho Cucamonga, CA 91730; 909-980-1492; Fax: 909-980-1651; *District Director:* Chris Marsh
Committee Assignments: Financial Services; Transportation and Infrastructure

Miller, George, D-Calif. (11)

Capitol Hill Office: 2205 RHOB 20515-0507; 225-2095; Fax: 225-5609; *Chief of Staff:* Daniel Weiss
Web: http://georgemiller.house.gov/
Facebook: http://facebook.com/repgeorgemiller
Twitter: http://twitter.com/askgeorge
District Offices: 1333 Willow Pass Rd., #203, Concord, CA 94520-7931; 925-602-1880; Fax: 925-674-0983; *District Director:* Barbara Johnson
3220 Blume Dr., #160, Richmond, CA 94806-5741; 510-262-6500; Fax: 510-222-1306; *Field Rep.; Caseworker:* Damian Alarcon
Committee Assignment: Education and the Workforce, Ranking Minority Member

Miller, Jeff, R-Fla. (1)

Capitol Hill Office: 336 CHOB 20515; 225-4136; Fax: 225-3414; *Chief of Staff:* Daniel F. McFaul
Web: http://jeffmiller.house.gov/
Facebook: https://facebook.com/RepJeffMiller
District Offices: 348 Miracle Strip Pkwy. S.W., #24, Fort Walton Beach, FL 32548-5263; 850-664-1266; Fax: 850-664-0851; *Field Rep.:* Bob Black
4300 Bayou Blvd., #13, Pensacola, FL 32503-2671; 850-479-1183; Fax: 850-479-9394; *District Director:* Sheilah Bowman
Committee Assignments: Armed Services; Veterans' Affairs, Chair; Permanent Select Intelligence

Moore, Gwen, D-Wisc. (4)

Capitol Hill Office: 2245 RHOB 20515-4904; 225-4572; Fax: 225-8135; *Chief of Staff:* Minh Ta
Web: http://gwenmoore.house.gov/
Facebook: http://facebook.com/GwenSMoore
Twitter: http://twitter.com/RepGwenMoore
District Office: 219 N. Milwaukee St., #3A, Milwaukee, WI 53202-5818; 414-297-1140; Fax: 414-297-1086; *District Director:* Lois O'Keefe
Committee Assignments: Budget; Financial Services

Moran, Jim, D-Va. (8)

Capitol Hill Office: 2252 RHOB 20515-4608; 225-4376; Fax: 225-0017; *Chief of Staff:* Austin Durrer
Web: http://moran.house.gov/
Facebook: http://facebook.com/RepJimMoran
Twitter: http://twitter.com/Jim_Moran

District Office: 333 N. Fairfax St., #201, Alexandria, VA 22314-2632; 703-971-4700; Fax: 703-922-9436; *District Director:* Susie Warner
Committee Assignment: Appropriations

Mullin, Markwayne, R-Okla. (2)

Capitol Hill Office: 1113 LHOB 20515; 225-2701; Fax: 225-3038; *Chief of Staff:* Karl Ahlgren
Web: http://mullin.house.gov/
Facebook: http://facebook.com/ CongressmanMarkwayneMullin
Twitter: http://twitter.com/RepMullin
District Offices: Claremore, OK 74017; 918-341-9336; Fax: 918-342-4806; *Field Rep.:* Debbie Dooley
Durant, OK 74701-4718; 580-931-0333; Fax: 580-920-0041; *Field Rep.:* Eddie Dempsey
1 E. Choctaw, #175, McAlester, OK 74501; 918-423-5951; Fax: 918-423-1940; *Field Rep.:* Betty Ford
431 W. Broadway St., Muskogee, OK 74401-6614; 918-687-2533; Fax: 918-686-0128; *Field Rep.:* Dwane Thompson
Committee Assignments: Natural Resources; Transportation and Infrastructure

Mulvaney, Mick, R-S.C. (5)

Capitol Hill Office: 1207 LHOB 20515-4005; 225-5501; Fax: 225-0464; *Chief of Staff:* Al Simpson
Web: http://mulvaney.house.gov/
Facebook: http://facebook.com/MulvaneySC5
Twitter: http://twitter.com/RepMickMulvaney
District Offices: 110 Railroad Ave., Gaffney, SC 29340; 864-206-6004; Fax: 864-206-6005; *Constituent Services Director:* Park Gillespie
1456 Ebenezer Rd., Rock Hill, SC 29732-2339; 803-327-1114; Fax: 803-327-4330; *District Director:* Jeffery Sligh
531-A Oxford Dr., Sumter, SC 29150; 803-774-0186; Fax: 803-774-0188; *Field Rep.:* Bobbie Williams
Committee Assignments: Financial Services; Small Business

Murphy, Patrick, D-Fla. (18)

Capitol Hill Office: 1517 LHOB 20515; 225-3026; Fax: 225-8398; *Chief of Staff:* Tiffany Muller
Web: http://patrickmurphy.house.gov/
Facebook: http://facebook.com/ CongressmanPatrickMurphy
Twitter: http://twitter.com/RepMurphyFL
District Offices: 2000 PGA Blvd., #A3220, Palm Beach Gardens, FL 33408; 561-253-8433; Fax: 561-253-8436; *District Director:* Michael Kenny
121 S.W. Port St. Lucie Blvd., Room 187, Port St. Lucie, FL 34984; 772-336-2877; Fax: 772-336-2899; *Constituent Services Rep.:* Candance Walls
171 S.W. Flagler Ave., Stuart, FL 34994 772-781-3266; Fax: 772-781-3267; *Constituent Services Rep.:* Kalene Rowley
2300 Virginia Ave., Room 200A, Fort Pierce, FL 34982; 772-489-0736; Fax: 772-464-8392; *Constituent Services Rep.:* Charity Lewis
Committee Assignments: Financial Services; Small Business

Murphy, Tim, R-Pa. (18)

Capitol Hill Office: 2332 RHOB 20515; 225-2301; Fax: 225-1844; *Chief of Staff:* Susan Mosychuk
Web: http://murphy.house.gov/
Facebook: http://facebook.com/reptimmurphy
Twitter: http://twitter.com/RepTimMurphy
District Offices: 2040 Frederickson Pl., Greensburg, PA 15601-9688; 724-850-7312; Fax: 724-850-7315; *Deputy Chief of Staff:* Lou Lazzaro
504 Washington Rd., Pittsburgh, PA 15228-2817; 412-344-5583; Fax: 412-429-5092; *Field Director:* Nate Nevala
Committee Assignment: Energy and Commerce

Nadler, Jerrold, D-N.Y. (10)

Capitol Hill Office: 2110 RHOB 20515; 225-5635; Fax: 225-6923; *Washington Director; Administrative Asst.:* John Doty
Web: http://nadler.house.gov/
Facebook: http://facebook.com/CongressmanNadler
Twitter: http://twitter.com/RepJerryNadler
District Offices: 6605 Fort Hamilton Pkwy., Brooklyn, NY 11219; 718-373-3198; Fax: 718-996-0039; *Brooklyn Director:* Maya Kremen
201 Varick St., #669, New York, NY 10014-7069; 212-367-7350; Fax: 212-367-7356; *Chief of Staff:* Amy Rutkin
Committee Assignments: Judiciary; Transportation and Infrastructure

Napolitano, Grace F., D-Calif. (32)

Capitol Hill Office: 1610 LHOB 20515-0538; 225-5256; Fax: 225-0027; *Chief of Staff:* Daniel S. Chao
Web: http://napolitano.house.gov/
Facebook: http://facebook.com/RepGraceNapolitano
Twitter: http://twitter.com/gracenapolitano
District Office: 4401 Santa Anita Ave., #201, El Monte, CA 91731; 626-350-0150; Fax: 626-350-0450; *District Director:* Benjamin Cardenas
Committee Assignments: Natural Resources; Transportation and Infrastructure

Neal, Richard, D-Mass. (1)

Capitol Hill Office: 2208 RHOB 20515-2102; 225-5601; Fax: 225-8112; *Chief of Staff:* Ann M. Jablon
Web: http://neal.house.gov/
Facebook: http://facebook.com/pages/Congressman-Richard-Neal/325642654132598
Twitter: https://twitter.com/RepRichardNeal
District Offices: 78 Center St., Pittsfield, MA 01201; 413-442-0946; Fax: 413-443-2792; *Staff Asst.:* Cynthia Clark
300 State St., #200, Springfield, MA 01105-1711; 413-785-0325; Fax: 413-747-0604; *Scheduler:* Elizabeth Quigley
Committee Assignment: Ways and Means

Neugebauer, Randy, R-Tex. (19)

Capitol Hill Office: 1424 LHOB 20515-4319; 225-4005; Fax: 225-9615; *Chief of Staff:* Jeanette Whitener
Web: http://randy.house.gov/

Facebook: http://facebook.com/rep.randy.neugebauer
Twitter: http://twitter.com/RandyNeugebauer
District Offices: 500 Chestnut St., #819, Abilene, TX 79602-1453; 325-675-9779; Fax: 325-675-5038; *District Rep.:* Marci Braden
1510 Scurry St., Suite B, Big Spring, TX 79720-4441; 432-264-0722; Fax: 432-264-1838; *District Rep.:* Lisa Brooks
611 University Ave., #220, Lubbock, TX 79401-2206; 806-763-1611; Fax: 806-767-9168; *District Director:* Mitch Barnett
Committee Assignments: Agriculture; Financial Services; Science, Space, and Technology

Noem, Kristi, R-S.D. (At Large)

Capitol Hill Office: 1323 LHOB 20515; 225-2801; Fax: 225-5823; *Chief of Staff:* Jordan Stoick
Web: http://noem.house.gov/
Facebook: http://facebook.com/kristiforcongress
Twitter: http://twitter.com/RepKristiNoem
District Offices: 415 S. Main St., #203, Aberdeen, SD 57401; 605-262-2862; Fax: 605-262-2869; *Northeast Director, Aberdeen:* Mary Beth Hollatz
343 Quincy St., Rapid City, SD 57701-3797; 605-791-4673; Fax: 605-791-4679; *West River Director:* Brad Otten
2310 W. 41st St., #101, Sioux Falls, SD 57105-6139; 605-275-2868; Fax: 605-275-2875; *Constituent Services Rep.:* Andrew Curley
505 12th St., S.E., Watertown, SD 57201-4973; 605-878-2868; Fax: 605-878-2871; *Northeast Director, Watertown:* Mary Beth Hollatz
Committee Assignments: Agriculture; Armed Services

Nolan, Rick, D-Minn. (8)

Capitol Hill Office: 2447 RHOB 20515; 225-6211; Fax: 225-0699; *Chief of Staff:* Jodi Torkelson
Web: http://nolan.house.gov/
Facebook: http://facebook.com/UsRepRickNolan
Twitter: http://twitter.com/usrepricknolan
District Offices: Brainerd City Hall, 501 Laurel St., Brainerd, MN 56401-3595; 218-454-4078; Fax: 218-454-4096; *Field Rep.:* Mark Privratsky
Chisago County Government Center, 313 N. Main St., Room 174, Center City, MN 55012; 218-491-3131; *Field Rep.:* Rick Olseen
Duluth Technology Village, 11 E. Superior St., #125, Duluth, MN 55802; 218-464-5095; Fax: 218-464-5098; *District Director:* Jeff Anderson
316 W. Lake St., Room 7, Chisholm, MN 55719; 218-491-3114; *Field Rep.:* Jordan Metsa, Tom Rukavina
Committee Assignments: Agriculture; Transportation and Infrastructure

Norton, Eleanor Holmes, D-D.C. (At Large)

Capitol Hill Office: 2136 RHOB 20515-5101; 225-8050; Fax: 225-3002; *Chief of Staff:* Gwen Benson-Walker
Web: http://norton.house.gov/
Facebook: http://facebook.com/CongresswomanNorton
Twitter: http://twitter.com/eleanornorton

District Offices: 2041 Martin Luther King, Jr. Ave., S.E., #238, Washington, DC 20020-7005; 202-678-8900; Fax: 202-678-8844; *District Director:* Raven Reeder
90 K St., N.E., #100, Washington, DC 20001; 202-408-9041; Fax: 202-408-9048; *District Director:* Raven Reeder
Committee Assignments: Oversight and Government Reform; Transportation and Infrastructure

Nugent, Richard, R-Fla. (11)

Capitol Hill Office: 1727 LHOB 20515; 225-1002; Fax: 226-6559; *Chief of Staff:* Justin Grabelle
Web: http://nugent.house.gov/
Facebook: http://facebook.com/RepRichNugent
Twitter: http://twitter.com/RepRichNugent
District Offices: 212 W. Main St., #204, Inverness, FL 34450; 352-341-2354; Fax: 352-341-2316; *Outreach Coord.:* Jeanne McInTosh
115 S.E. 25th Ave., Ocala, FL 34471; 352-351-1670; Fax: 352-689-4621; *Constituent Services Rep.:* Nick Catroppo
11035 Spring Hill Dr., Spring Hill, FL 34608; 352-684-4446; Fax: 352-684-4484; *Constituent Services Rep.:* Kathy Mansfield
8015 E. CR-466, The Villages, FL 32162; 352-689-4684; Fax: 352-689-4621 *Constituent Services Rep.:* Al Harrison
Committee Assignments: Armed Services; House Administration; Rules; Joint Printing

Nunes, Devin, R-Calif. (22)

Capitol Hill Office: 1013 LHOB 20515-0521; 225-2523; Fax: 225-3404; *Chief of Staff:* Johnny Amaral
Web: http://nunes.house.gov/
Facebook: http://facebook.com/pages/Devin-Nunes/376470350795
Twitter: https://twitter.com/DevinNunes
District Offices: 264 Clovis Ave., #206, Clovis, CA 93612-1115; 559-323-5235; Fax: 559-323-5528; *Field Rep.:* Jose Avilas
113 N. Church St., #208, Visalia, CA 93291-6300; 559-733-3861; Fax: 559-733-3865; *Constituent Liaison:* Melissa Mederos
Committee Assignments: Ways and Means; Permanent Select Intelligence

Nunnelee, Alan, R-Miss. (1)

Capitol Hill Office: 1427 LHOB 20515-2401; 225-4306; Fax: 225-3549; *Chief of Staff:* Ted Maness
Web: http://nunnelee.house.gov/
Facebook: http://facebook.com/CongressmanNunnelee
Twitter: http://twitter.com/RepAlanNunnelee
District Offices: 318 N. 7th St., Columbus, MS 30701; 662-327-0748; Fax: 662-328-5982; *Field Rep.; Caseworker:* Kelli Russell
133 E. Commerce St., P.O. Box 218, Hernando, MS 38632-2343; 662-449-3090; Fax: 662-449-4836; *Field Rep.; Caseworker:* Walt Starr

431 W. Main St., #450, Tupelo, MS 38804-4025; 662-841-8808; Fax: 662-841-8845; *District Director:* Mabel Murphree

Committee Assignments: Appropriations; Budget

Olson, Pete, R-Tex. (22)

Capitol Hill Office: 312 CHOB 20515-4322; 225-5951; Fax: 225-5241; *Chief of Staff:* Tyler Nelson
Web: http://olson.house.gov/
Facebook: http://facebook.com/pages/Pete-Olson/20718168936
District Offices: 6302 W. Broadway St., #220, Pearland, TX 77581; 281-485-4855; Fax: 281-485-4850; *Field Rep.:* Brock Gillespie
1650 Hwy. 6, #150, Sugar Land, TX 77478-4921; 281-494-2690; Fax: 281-494-2649; *District Director:* Robert Quarles

Committee Assignment: Energy and Commerce

O'Rourke, Beto, D-Tex. (16)

Capitol Hill Office: 1721 LHOB 20515; 225-4831; Fax: 225-2016; *Chief of Staff:* David Wysong
Web: http://orourke.house.gov/
Facebook: http://facebook.com/BetoORourkeTX16
Twitter: http://twitter.com/RepBetoORourke
District Office: 303 N. Oregon St., #210, El Paso, TX 79901-1301; 915-541-1400; Fax: 915-541-1407; *District Director:* Cynthia Cano

Committee Assignments: Homeland Security; Veterans' Affairs

Owens, Bill, D-N.Y. (21)

Capitol Hill Office: 405 CHOB 20515; 225-4611; Fax: 226-0621; *Chief of Staff:* Bradley Katz
Web: http://owens.house.gov/
Facebook: http://facebook.com/repbillowens
Twitter: http://twitter.com/BillOwensNY
District Offices: 136 Glen St., Glen Falls, NY 12801; 518-743-0964; Fax: 518-743-1391; *Constituent Liaison:* Mark Luciano
3 Frontage Rd., Gloversville, NY 12078; 518-773-4568; *Constituent Liaison:* Matthew Scollin
14 Durkee St., #320, Plattsburgh, NY 12901-2998; 518-563-1406; Fax: 518-561-9723; *Constituent Liaison:* Chance St. Germain
120 Washington St., #200, Watertown, NY 13601-3370; 315-782-3150; Fax: 315-782-1291; *District Director:* Steve Hunt

Committee Assignment: Appropriations

Palazzo, Steven, R-Miss. (4)

Capitol Hill Office: 331 CHOB 20515-2404; 225-5772; Fax: 225-7074; *Chief of Staff:* Casey Street
Web: http://palazzo.house.gov/
Facebook: http://facebook.com/stevenpalazzo
Twitter: http://twitter.com/congpalazzo
District Offices: 1325 25th Ave., Gulfport, MS 39501; 228-864-7670; Fax: 228-864-3099; *Deputy Chief of Staff; District Director:* Hunter Lipscomb

641 Main St., #142, Hattiesburg, MS 39401-3478; 601-582-3246; Office Manager: Anita Bourn
3118 Pascagoula St., #181, Pascagoula, MS 39567-4215; 228-202-8104; Fax: 228-202-8105; *Constituent Liaison:* Debora Nelson
72 Technology Blvd., #216, Ellisville, MS 39437; 601-428-9711; *Constituent Liaison:* Stella Hall

Committee Assignments: Armed Services; Homeland Security; Science, Space, and Technology

Pallone, Frank, D-N.J. (6)

Capitol Hill Office: 237 CHOB 20515-3006; 225-4671; Fax: 225-9665; *Chief of Staff:* Jeffrey C. Carroll
Web: http://pallone.house.gov/
Facebook: https://facebook.com/RepFrankPallone
Twitter: http://twitter.com/FrankPallone
District Offices: 504 Broadway, Long Branch, NJ 07740-5951; 732-571-1140; Fax: 732-870-3890; *District Director:* Janice Fuller
Kilmer Square, 67-69 Church St., New Brunswick, NJ 08901; 732-249-8892; Fax: 732-249-1335; *Constituent Services Director:* Alexandra Maldonado

Committee Assignments: Energy and Commerce; Natural Resources

Pascrell, Bill, D-N.J. (9)

Capitol Hill Office: 2370 RHOB 20515-3008; 225-5751; Fax: 225-5782; *Chief of Staff:* Benjamin Rich
Web: http://pascrell.house.gov/
Facebook: http://facebook.com/pascrell
Twitter: https://twitter.com/BillPascrell
District Offices: Passaic City Hall, 330 Passaic St., 1st Floor, Passaic, NJ 07055-5815; 973-472-4510; Fax: 973-472-0852; *Field Rep.:* Orville Morales
Robert A. Roe Federal Bldg., 200 Federal Plaza, #500, Paterson, NJ 07505-1999; 973-523-5152; Fax: 973-523-0637; *Deputy Chief of Staff:* Assad Akhter
367 Valley Brook Ave., Lyndhurst, NJ 07071; 201-935-2248; *Caseworker:* Shannon Mcgee
2-10 N. Van Brunt St., Englewood, NJ 07631; 201-935-2248; *Caseworker:* Shannon Mcgee

Committee Assignments: Budget; Ways and Means

Pastor, Ed, D-Ariz. (7)

Capitol Hill Office: 2465 RHOB 20515-0304; 225-4065; Fax: 225-1655; *Exec. Asst., Scheduler, Office Manager:* Laura Campos
Web: http://pastor.house.gov/
Facebook: http://facebook.com/edpastor04
Twitter: http://twitter.com/PastorForAZ
District Office: 411 N. Central Ave., #150, Phoenix, AZ 85004-2120; 602-256-0551; Fax: 602-257-9103; *District Director:* Elisa de la Vara

Committee Assignments: Appropriations; Permanent Select Intelligence

Paulsen, Erik, R-Minn. (3)

Capitol Hill Office: 127 CHOB 20515-2303; 225-2871; Fax: 225-6351; *Chief of Staff:* Laurie Esau

Web: http://paulsen.house.gov/
Facebook: http://facebook.com/CongressmanErikPaulsen
Twitter: http://twitter.com/RepErikPaulsen
District Office: 250 Prairie Center Dr., #230, Eden Prairie, MN 55344-7909; 952-405-8510; Fax: 952-405-8514; *District Director:* Kelli Commers
Committee Assignment: Ways and Means, Joint Economic

Payne, Donald Jr., D-N.J. (10)

Capitol Hill Office: 103 CHOB 20515; 225-3436; Fax: 225-4160; *Chief of Staff:* LaVerne Alexander
Web: http://payne.house.gov/
Facebook: http://facebook.com/DonaldPayneJr
Twitter: http://twitter.com/RepDonaldPayne
District Offices: 253 Martin Luther King, Jr. Dr., Jersey City, NJ 07305-3427; 201-369-0392; Fax: 201-369-0395; *Constituent Service Asst.:* Yvonne Hatchett, Patricia Campbell
60 Nelson Pl., 14th Floor, Newark, NJ 07102; 973-645-3213; Fax: 973-645-5902; *District Director:* Sarah Jones
Committee Assignments: Homeland Security; Small Business

Pearce, Steve, R-N.M. (2)

Capitol Hill Office: 2432 RHOB 20515-3102; 225-2365; Fax: 225-9599; *Chief of Staff:* Todd D. Willens
Web: http://pearce.house.gov/
Facebook: http://facebook.com/RepStevePearce
Twitter: http://twitter.com/repstevepearce
District Offices: 1101 New York Ave., Room 115, Alamogordo, NM 88310-6923; 855-473-2723
200 E. Broadway St., #200, Hobbs, NM 88240-8425; 855-473-2723; *Communications Director:* Eric Layer
570 N. Telshor Blvd., Las Cruces, NM 88011-8223; 855-473-2723; *Field Rep.:* Joe Martinez
3445 Lambros Loop, N.E., Los Lunas, NM 87031-6472; 855-473-2723; *Field Rep.:* Joe Martinez
1717 W. 2nd St., #110, Roswell, NM 88201-2029; 855-473-2723; *District Director:* Barbara Romero
111 School of Mines Rd., Socorro, NM 87801-4533; 855-473-2723; Deputy *District Director:* Barbara Romero
Committee Assignment: Financial Services

Pelosi, Nancy, D-Calif. (12)

Capitol Hill Office: 235 CHOB 20515-0508; 225-4965; Fax: 225-8259; *Chief of Staff:* Robert Edmonson
Web: http://pelosi.house.gov/
Facebook: http://facebook.com/NancyPelosi
Twitter: http://twitter.com/NancyPelosi
District Office: 90 7th St., #2-800, San Francisco, CA 94103-6723; 415-556-4862; Fax: 415-861-1670; *Chief of Staff, San Francisco:* Dan Bernal
Democratic Minority Leader

Perlmutter, Ed, D-Colo. (7)

Capitol Hill Office: 1410 LHOB 20515; 225-2645; Fax: 225-5278; *Chief of Operations:* Alison Inderfurth
Web: http://perlmutter.house.gov/
Facebook: https://facebook.com/RepPerlmutter

Twitter: http://twitter.com/repperlmutter
District Office: 12600 W. Colfax Ave., #B400, Lakewood, CO 80215-3779; 303-274-7944; Fax: 303-274-6455; *Chief of Staff:* Danielle Piper
Committee Assignment: Financial Services

Perry, Scott, R-Pa. (4)

Capitol Hill Office: 126 CHOB 20515; 225-5836; Fax: 226-1000; *Chief of Staff:* Lauren Muglia
Web: http://perry.house.gov/
Facebook: http://facebook.com/repscottperry
Twitter: http://twitter.com/RepScottPerry
District Offices: 22 Chambersburg St., Gettysburg, PA 17325; 717-338-1919; Fax: 717-334-6314; *Field Rep.:* Holly Sutthin
730 N. Front St., Wormleysburg, PA 17043; 717-635-9504; Fax: 717-635-9861; *Deputy Chief of Staff:* Bob Reilly
2209 E. Market St., York, PA 17402; 717-600-1919; Fax: 717-757-5001; *District Rep., Deputy Chief of Staff:* Bob Reilly
Committee Assignments: Foreign Affairs; Homeland Security; Transportation and Infrastructure

Peters, Gary, D-Mich. (14)

Capitol Hill Office: 1609 LHOB 20515-2209; 225-5802; Fax: 226-2356; *Chief of Staff:* Eric Feldman
Web: http://peters.house.gov/
Facebook: http://facebook.com/RepGaryPeters
Twitter: http://twitter.com/RepGaryPeters
District Office: 400 Monroe St., #290, Detroit, MI 48226-2960; 313-964-9960; Fax: 313-964-9959; *Congressional Liaison:* Bethany Mindlin
Committee Assignment: Financial Services

Peters, Scott H., D-Calif. (52)

Capitol Hill Office: 2410 RHOB 20515-0550; 225-0508; Fax: 225-2558; *Chief of Staff:* Michelle Dorothy
Web: http://scottpeters.house.gov/
Facebook: http://facebook.com/CongressmanScottPeters
Twitter: http://twitter.com/RepScottPeters
District Office: 4350 Executive Dr., #105, San Diego, CA 92121; 858-455-5550; Fax: 858-455-5516; *District Director:* Marianne Pintar
Committee Assignments: Armed Services; Science, Space, and Technology

Peterson, Collin, D-Minn. (7)

Capitol Hill Office: 2109 RHOB 20515-2307; 225-2165; Fax: 225-1593; *Chief of Staff:* Cherie Slayton
Web: http://collinpeterson.house.gov/
Facebook: http://facebook.com/pages/Collin-Peterson/6595227967
District Offices: 714 Lake Ave., #107, Detroit Lakes, MN 56501-3057; 218-847-5056; Fax: 218-847-5109; *Communications Director:* Allison Myhre
1420 E. College Dr. S.W. / WC, Marshall, MN 56258-2065; 507-537-2299; Fax: 507-537-2298; *Staff Asst.:* Meg Louwagie

100 N. 1st St., Montevideo, MN 56265, Montevideo, MN 56265; 320-235-1061; *Staff Asst.:* Tom Meium

2603 Wheat Dr., Red Lake Falls, MN 56750-4800; 218-253-4356; Fax: 218-253-4373; *Staff Asst.:* Wally Sparby

230 E. 3rd St., Redwood Falls, MN 56283; 507-637-2270; *Staff Asst.:* Meg Louwagie

324 3rd St., S.W., #4, Willmar, MN 56201-3696; 320-235-1061; Fax: 320-235-2651; *Staff Asst.:* Mary Bertram

Committee Assignment: Agriculture, Ranking Minority Member

Petri, Tom, R-Wisc. (6)

Capitol Hill Office: 2462 RHOB 20515-4906; 225-2476; Fax: 225-2356; *Chief of Staff; Legis. Director:* Debra Gebhardt

Web: http://petri.house.gov/

Facebook: http://facebook.com/ThomasPetri

District Offices: 490 W. Rolling Meadows Dr., Suite B, Fond du Lac, WI 54937; 920-922-1180; Fax: 920-922-4498; *District Director:* Tyler Vorpagel

2390 State Rd. 44, Suite B, Oshkosh, WI 54904-6438; 920-231-6333; Fax: 920-231-0464; *Field Rep., Senior Citizen Liaison:* Gregg Underheim

Committee Assignments: Education and the Workforce; Transportation and Infrastructure

Pierluisi, Pedro, D-P.R. (At Large)

Capitol Hill Office: 1213 LHOB 20515-5401; 225-2615; Fax: 225-2154; *Chief of Staff Puerto Rico Federal Affairs Administration Liaison Municipalities /Puerto Rico Legislature Appropriations Overview:* Carmen M. Feliciano

Web: http://pierluisi.house.gov/

Facebook: https://facebook.com/pedropierluisi

Twitter: http://twitter.com/pedropierluisi

District Office:, Edificio de Medicina Tropical; Avenida Juan Ponce De León, San Juan, Puerto Rico, 00901; 787-723-6333; Fax: 787-729-7738; *District Director:* Rosemarie Vizcarrondo

Committee Assignments: Ethics; Judiciary; Natural Resources

Pingree, Chellie, D-Maine (1)

Capitol Hill Office: 1318 LHOB 20515-1901; 225-6116; Fax: 225-5590; *Chief of Staff:* Jesse Connolly

Web: http://pingree.house.gov/

Facebook: http://facebook.com/ChelliePingree

Twitter: http://twitter.com/chelliepingree

District Office: 2 Portland Fish Pier, #304, Portland, ME 04101; 207-774-5019; Fax: 207-871-0720; *Communications Coordinator:* Andrew Colvin

108 Main St., Waterville, ME 04901; 207-774-5019; *Field Rep.:* Pamela Trinward

Committee Assignments: Appropriations

Pittenger, Robert, R-N.C. (9)

Capitol Hill Office: 224 CHOB 20515; 225-1976; Fax: 225-3389; *Chief of Staff:* Brad Jones

Web: http://pittenger.house.gov/

Facebook: http://facebook.com/congressmanpittenger

Twitter: http://twitter.com/@RepPittenger

District Offices: 2701 Coltsgate Rd., #105, Charlotte, NC 28211; 704-362-1060; Fax: 704-365-6384; *District Director:* Robert Becker

116 Morlake Dr., #101A, Mooresville, NC 28117; 704-696-8188; Fax: 704-696-8190; *Regional Constituent Rep.:* Preston Curtis

Committee Assignment: Financial Services

Pitts, Joe, R-Pa. (16)

Capitol Hill Office: 420 CHOB 20515-3816; 225-2411; Fax: 225-2013; *D.C. Chief of Staff:* Gabe Neville

Web: http://pitts.house.gov/

Facebook: http://facebook.com/CongressmanJoePitts

Twitter: http://twitter.com/RepJoePitts

District Offices: 150 N. Queen St., #716, Lancaster, PA 17603-3562; 717-393-0667; Fax: 717-393-0924; *District Chief of Staff:* Thomas Tillett

Reading City Hall, 815 Washington St., Room 2-36, Reading, PA 19601; 610-374-3637; Fax: 610-444-5750; *Outreach Coord.:* Nicholas Cammaus

P.O. Box 837, Unionville, PA 19375; 610-444-4581; Fax: 610-444-5750; *District Chief of Staff:* Thomas Tillett

Committee Assignments: Commission on Security and Cooperation in Europe (Helsinki Commission); Energy and Commerce

Pocan, Mark, D-Wisc. (2)

Capitol Hill Office: 313 CHOB 20515; 225-2906; Fax: 225-6942; *Chief of Staff:* Glenn Wavrunek

Web: http://pocan.house.gov/

Facebook: http://facebook.com/repmarkpocan

Twitter: http://twitter.com/repmarkpocan

District Office: 10 E. Doty St., #405, Madison, WI 53703-5103; 608-258-9800; Fax: 608-258-0377; *District Director:* Janet Piraino

100 State St., 3rd Floor, Beloit, WI 53511; 608-365-8001; *District Director:* Janet Piraino

Committee Assignments: Budget; Education and the Workforce

Poe, Ted, R-Tex. (2)

Capitol Hill Office: 2412 RHOB 20515; 225-6565; Fax: 225-5547; *Chief of Staff:* Gina Santucci

Web: http://poe.house.gov/

Facebook: http://facebook.com/pages/Ted-Poe/106631626049851

Twitter: http://twitter.com/JudgeTedPoe

District Offices: 710 N. Post Oak Rd., #510, Houston, TX 77024; 713-681-8763; Fax: 713-681-1150; *Executive Asst.:* Heather Ramsey-Cook

1801 Kingwood Dr., #240, Kingwood, TX 77339-3058; 281-446-0242; Fax: 281-446-0252; *Caseworker:* Amy Harrison

Committee Assignments: Foreign Affairs; Judiciary

Polis, Jared, D-Colo. (2)

Capitol Hill Office: 1433 LHOB 20515; 225-2161; Fax: 226-7840; *Chief of Staff:* Dan Turentine
Web: http://polis.house.gov/
Facebook: http://facebook.com/jaredpolis
Twitter: http://twitter.com/jaredpolis
District Offices: 4770 Baseline Rd., #220, Boulder, CO 80303-2668; 303-484-9596; Fax: 303-568-9007; *District Director:*
101 W. Main St., #101G, P.O. Box 1453, Frisco, CO 80443; 970-668-3240; Fax: 970-668-9679; *Constituent Advocate:* Nissa Erickson
300 E. Horsetooth Rd., #103, Fort Collins, CO 80525; 970-226-1239; Fax: 970-226-8597; *Constituent Advocate:* Mara Brosy-Wiwecher
Committee Assignments: Education and the Workforce; Rules

Pompeo, Mike, R-Kans. (4)

Capitol Hill Office: 107 CHOB 20515-1604; 225-6216; Fax: 225-3489; *Chief of Staff:* Jim Richardson
Web: http://pompeo.house.gov/
Facebook: http://facebook.com/CongressmanPompeo
Twitter: http://twitter.com/repmikepompeo
District Office: 7701 E. Kellogg Dr., #510, Wichita, KS 67207-1722; 316-262-8992; Fax: 316-262-5309; *District Director:* Tony Porter
Committee Assignments: Energy and Commerce; Permanent Select Intelligence

Posey, Bill, R-Fla. (8)

Capitol Hill Office: 120 CHOB 20515-0915; 225-3671; Fax: 225-3516; *Chief of Staff:* Stuart Burns
Web: http://posey.house.gov/
Facebook: http://facebook.com/bill.posey15
Twitter: http://twitter.com/CongBillPosey
District Office: 2725 Judge Fran Jamieson Way, Bldg. C, Melbourne, FL 32940-6605; 321-632-1776; Fax: 321-639-8595; *Scheduler; Community Relations Director:* Patrick Gavin
Committee Assignments: Financial Services; Science, Space, and Technology

Price, David, D-N.C. (4)

Capitol Hill Office: 2162 RHOB 20515-3304; 225-1784; Fax: 225-2014; *Chief of Staff:* Jean-Louise Beard
Web: http://price.house.gov/
Facebook: http://facebook.com/pages/David-Price/8338225975
Twitter: http://twitter.com/RepDavidEPrice
District Offices: 1777 Fordham Blvd., #204, Chapel Hill, NC 27514; 919-967-7924; Fax: 919-967-8324; *Constituent Services Liaison:* Robyn Winneberger
301 Green St., #315, Fayetteville, NC 28301; 910-323-0260; Fax: 910-339-0159; *Constituent Services Liaison:* William Munn
436 N. Harrington St., #100, Raleigh, NC 27603; 919-859-5999; Fax: 919-859-5998; *District Director:* Beau Mills
Committee Assignment: Appropriations

Price, Tom, R-Ga. (6)

Capitol Hill Office: 100 CHOB 20515; 225-4501; Fax: 225-4656; *Chief of Staff:* Kris Skrzycki
Web: http://tomprice.house.gov/
Facebook: http://facebook.com/reptomprice
Twitter: http://twitter.com/RepTomPrice
District Office: 85-C Mill St., #300, Roswell, GA 30075; 770-998-0049; Fax: 770-998-0500; *District Director:* Kyle McGowan
Committee Assignments: Budget; Education and the Workforce; Ways and Means

Quigley, Mike, D-Ill. (5)

Capitol Hill Office: 1124 LHOB 20515-1305; 225-4061; Fax: 225-5603; *Chief of Staff:* Juan Hinojosa
Web: http://quigley.house.gov/
Facebook: http://facebook.com/repmikequigley
Twitter: http://twitter.com/RepMikeQuigley
District Office: 3742 W. Irving Park Rd., Chicago, IL 60618-3116; 773-267-5926; Fax: 773-267-6583; *District Director:* Mary Ann Levar
3223 N. Sheffield Ave., Chicago, IL 60657; *District Director:* Mary Ann Levar
Committee Assignment: Appropriations

Rahall, Nick, D-W. Va. (3)

Capitol Hill Office: 2307 RHOB 20515-4803; 225-3452; Fax: 225-9061; *Chief of Staff:* David McMaster
Web: http://rahall.house.gov/
Facebook: http://facebook.com/NickRahall
Twitter: http://twitter.com/HouseTransInf
District Offices: 109 Main St., Beckley, WV 25801-4610; 304-252-5000; Fax: 304-252-9803; *District Director:* Kelly Dyke
Federal Bldg., 601 Federal St., Room 1005, Bluefield, WV 24701-3033; 304-325-6222; Fax: 304-325-0552; *Community Relations Asst.:* Deborah Stevens
845 Fifth Ave., Huntington, WV 25701-2031; 304-522-6425; Fax: 304-529-5716; *Community Relation Asst.:* Teri Booth
220 Dingess St., Logan, WV 25601-3626; 304-752-4934; Fax: 304-752-8797; *Community Relations Asst.:* Debrina Workman
Committee Assignment: Transportation and Infrastructure, Ranking Minority Member

Rangel, Charles B., D-N.Y. (13)

Capitol Hill Office: 2354 RHOB 20515-3215; 225-4365; Fax: 225-0816; *Chief of Staff:* George Henry
Web: http://rangel.house.gov/
Facebook: http://facebook.com/CBRangel
Twitter: http://twitter.com/cbrangel
District Office: 163 W. 125th St., #737, New York, NY 10027-4404; 212-663-3900; Fax: 212-663-4277; *Deputy Chief of Staff:* Geoffrey Eaton
Committee Assignment: Ways and Means; Taxation

Reed, Tom, R-N.Y. (23)

Capitol Hill Office: 1504 LHOB 20515; 225-3161;
   Fax: 226-6599; *Chief of Staff:* Tim Kolpien
Web: http://reed.house.gov/
Facebook: http://facebook.com/RepTomReed
Twitter: http://twitter.com/RepTomReed
District Offices: 89 W. Market St., Corning, NY 14830-
   2526; 607-654-7566; Fax: 607-654-7568; *District
   Director:* Joe Sempolinski
433 Exchange St., Geneva, NY 14456; 315-759-5229;
   Fax: 315-325-4045; *Regional Director:* James Smith
2 E. 2nd St., #300, Jamestown, NY 14701; 716-708-6369;
   Fax: 716-708-6058; *Regional Director:* Jacqueline
   Chiarot
One Bluebird Square, Olean, NY 14760-2500; 716-379-
   8434; Fax: 716-806-1069; *Constituent Services
   Specialist:* Lee James
Committee Assignment: Ways and Means

Reichert, Dave, R-Wash. (8)

Capitol Hill Office: 1127 LHOB 20515; 225-7761;
   Fax: 225-4282; *Chief of Staff:* Jeff Harvey
Web: http://reichert.house.gov/
Facebook: http://facebook.com/repdavereichert
Twitter: http://twitter.com/davereichert
District Offices: 2 1st St. S.E., Auburn, WA 98001; 206-
   498-8103; *Sr. Outreach Coord.:* Zach Guill
22605 S.E. 56th St., #130, Issaquah, WA 98029-5297;
   425-677-7414; Fax: 425-270-3589; *District Director:*
   Sue Foy
200 Palouse St., #201-1, Wenatchee, WA 98801; 509-885-
   6615; *Constituent Services Liaison:* Tyler McKay
Committee Assignment: Ways and Means

Renacci, Jim, R-Ohio (16)

Capitol Hill Office: 130 CHOB 20515-3516; 225-3876;
   Fax: 225-3059; *Chief of Staff:* James Slepian
Web: http://renacci.house.gov/
Facebook: http://facebook.com/repjimrenacci
Twitter: http://twitter.com/repjimrenacci
District Office: 1 Park Center Dr., #302, Wadsworth, OH
   44281; 330-334-0040; Fax: 330-334-0061; *Community
   and Media Relations Rep.:* Thomas Queen
Committee Assignment: Ways and Means

Ribble, Reid, R-Wisc. (8)

Capitol Hill Office: 1513 LHOB 20515-4908; 225-5665;
   Fax: 225-5729; *Chief of Staff:* McKay Daniels
Web: http://ribble.house.gov/
Facebook: http://facebook.com/CongressmanReidRibble
Twitter: http://twitter.com/RepRibble/
District Offices: 333 W. College Ave., Appleton, WI
   54911-5898; 920-380-0061; Fax: 920-380-0051; *District
   Chief of Staff:* Rick Sense
550 N. Military Ave., #4B, Green Bay, WI 54303-4569; 920-
   471-1950; *Constituent Services Rep.:* Kerry Niemcek
Committee Assignments: Agriculture; Budget;
   Transportation and Infrastructure

Rice, Tom, R-S.C. (7)

Capitol Hill Office: 325 CHOB 20515; 225-9895;
   Fax: 225-9690; *Chief of Staff:* Tyler Grassmeyer
Web: http://rice.house.gov/
Facebook: http://facebook.com/reptomrice
Twitter: http://twitter.com/RepTomRice
District Offices: 1831 W. Evans St., #300, Florence, SC
   29501; 843-679-9781; Fax: 843-679-9783; *Regional
   Director:* Stefanie Rawlingson
2411 N. Oak St., #405, Myrtle Beach, SC 29577; 843-445-
   6459; 843-445-6418; *District Director:* Jennifer Watson
Committee Assignments: Budget; Small Business;
   Transportation and Infrastructure

Richmond, Cedric, D-La. (2)

Capitol Hill Office: 240 CHOB 20515; 225-6636;
   Fax: 225-1988; *Chief of Staff:* Virgil A. Miller
Web: http://richmond.house.gov/
Facebook: http://facebook.com/RepRichmond
Twitter: http://twitter.com/reprichmond
District Offices: 200 Derbigny St., #3200, Gretna, LA
   70053-5876; 504-365-0390; *Deputy District Director:*
   DeShannon Cobb-Russell
2021 Lakeshore Dr., #309, New Orleans, LA 70122-3501;
   504-288-3777; Fax: 504-288-4090; *District Director:*
   Enix Smith
1520 Thomas H. Delpit Dr., #126, Baton Rouge, LA 70802;
   225-636-5600; Fax: 225-636-5680; *Deputy District
   Director:* Darlene Fields
Committee Assignments: Homeland Security; Judiciary

Rigell, Scott, R-Va. (2)

Capitol Hill Office: 418 CHOB 20515; 225-4215;
   Fax: 225-4218; *Chief of Staff:* Chris Connelly
Web: http://rigell.house.gov/
Facebook: http://facebook.com/RepScottRigell
Twitter: http://twitter.com/RepScottRigell
District Offices: 23386 Front St., PO Box 447, Accomac,
   VA 23301; 757-789-5172; Fax: 757-789-5175; *Eastern
   Shore Caseworker:* Deborah Christie
4772 Euclid Rd., Suite E, Virginia Beach, VA 23462-3800;
   757-687-8290; Fax: 757-687-8298; *District Director:*
   Shannon Kendrick
1100 Exploration Way, #302R. Hampton, VA 23666;
   757-687-8290; Fax: 757-687-8298; *District Director:*
   Shannon Kendrick
Committee Assignments: Armed Services; Budget

Roby, Martha, R-Ala. (2)

Capitol Hill Office: 428 CHOB 20515-0102; 225-2901;
   Fax: 225-8913; *Chief of Staff:* Stephen Boyd
Web: http://roby.house.gov/
Facebook: http://facebook.com/Representative.Martha.
   Roby
Twitter: http://twitter.com/RepMarthaRoby
District Offices: 505 E. Three Notch St., No. #322,
   Andalusia, AL 36420-3129; 334-428-1129;
   Fax: 334-222-3342; *Constituent Services Rep.:* Amelia
   McMahon

217 Graceland Dr., #5, Dothan, AL 36305-7376; 334-794-9680; Fax: 334-671-1480; *District Director:* Joe Williams

401 Adams Ave., #160, Montgomery, AL 36104-4340; 334-277-9113; Fax: 334-277-8534; *Constituent Services Rep.:* Charlotte Bent

Committee Assignments: Appropriations

Roe, Phil, R-Tenn. (1)

Capitol Hill Office: 407 CHOB 20515-4201; 225-6356; Fax: 225-5714; *Chief of Staff:* Matthew Meyer

Web: http://roe.house.gov/

Facebook: http://facebook.com/DrPhilRoe

Twitter: http://twitter.com/drphilroe

District Offices: P.O. Box 1728, Kingsport, TN 37662; 423-247-8161; Fax: 423-247-0119; *District Director:* Bill Snodgrass

1609 College Park Dr., #4, Morristown, TN 37813-1659; 423-254-1400; Fax: 423-254-1403; *Caseworker:* Cheryl Bennett

Committee Assignments: Education and the Workforce; Veterans' Affairs

Rogers, Hal, R-Ky. (5)

Capitol Hill Office: 2406 RHOB 20515-1705; 225-4601; Fax: 225-0940; *Chief of Staff:* David Thomas

Web: http://halrogers.house.gov/

Facebook: http://facebook.com/CongressmanHalRogers

Twitter: http://twitter.com/RepHalRogers

District Offices: 48 S. KY Hwy. 15, Hazard, KY 41701; 606-439-0794; Fax: 606-439-4647; *Field Rep.:* Nana Estep

110 Resource Court, Suite A, Prestonsburg, KY 41653-7851; 606-886-0844; Fax: 606-889-0371; *Field Rep.:* Adam Rice

551 Clifty St., Somerset, KY 42503; 800-632-8588; Fax: 606-678-4856; *District Director:* Karen Kelly

Committee Assignment: Appropriations, Chair

Rogers, Mike, R-Ala. (3)

Capitol Hill Office: 324 CHOB 20515-0103; 225-3261; Fax: 226-8485; *Chief of Staff:* Marshall C. Macomber

Web: http://mike-rogers.house.gov/

Facebook: http://facebook.com/CongressmanMikeDRogers

Twitter: http://twitter.com/RepMikeRogersAL

District Offices: Federal Bldg., 1129 Noble St., #104, Anniston, AL 36201-4674; 256-236-5655; Fax: 256-237-9203; *District Director:* Sheri Rollins

1819 Pepperell Pkwy., #203, Opelika, AL 36801-5476; 334-745-6221; Fax: 334-742-0109; *Field Rep.:* Cheryl Cunningham

Committee Assignments: Agriculture; Armed Services; Homeland Security

Rogers, Mike, R-Mich. (8)

Capitol Hill Office: 2112 RHOB 20515; 225-4872; Fax: 225-5820; *Chief of Staff:* Andrew Hawkins

Web: http://mikerogers.house.gov/

Facebook: http://facebook.com/pages/Mike-JRogers/168209963203416

Twitter: http://twitter.com/RepMikeRogers

District Office: 1000 W. St. Joseph, #300, Lansing, MI 48915-2552; 517-702-8000; Fax: 517-702-8642; *Deputy Chief of Staff:* Allan Filip

Committee Assignments: Energy and Commerce; Permanent Select Intelligence, Chair

Rohrabacher, Dana, R-Calif. (48)

Capitol Hill Office: 2300 RHOB 20515-0546; 225-2415; Fax: 225-0145; *Chief of Staff:* Richard T. Dykema

Web: http://rohrabacher.house.gov/

Facebook: http://facebook.com/danarohrabacher

Twitter: http://twitter.com/DanaRohrabacher

District Office: 101 Main St., #380, Huntington Beach, CA 92648-8149; 714-960-6483; Fax: 714-960-7806; *District Director:* Kathleen Staunton

12 Journey, Aliso Viejo, CA 92656; 714-960-6483; *District Director:* Kathleen Staunton

Committee Assignments: Foreign Affairs; Science, Space, and Technology

Rokita, Todd, R-Ind. (4)

Capitol Hill Office: 236 CHOB 20515-1404; 225-5037; Fax: 226-0544; *Chief of Staff:* Michael J. Ward

Web: http://rokita.house.gov/

Facebook: http://facebook.com/RepToddRokita

Twitter: http://twitter.com/toddrokita

District Offices: 355 S. Washington St., 2nd Floor, Danville, IN 46122-1779; 317-718-0404; Fax: 317-718-0405; District Director; *Deputy Chief of Staff:* Tim Edson

337 Columbia St., Lafayette, IN 47901-1315; 765-838-3930; Fax: 765-838-3931; *Field Rep.:* Penny Titus

Committee Assignments: Budget; Education and the Workforce; House Administration

Rooney, Thomas J., R-Fla. (17)

Capitol Hill Office: 221 CHOB 20515; 225-5792; Fax: 225-3132; *Chief of Staff:* Pete Giambastiani

Web: http://rooney.house.gov/

Facebook: http://facebook.com/reptomrooney

Twitter: http://twitter.com/TomRooney

District Offices: 226 Taylor St., #230, Punta Gorda, FL 33950-4422; 941-575-9101; Fax: 941-575-9103 *District Director:* Leah Valenti

Summerfield Shoppes, 11345 Big Bend Rd., Riverview, FL 33579; 813-677-8646; Fax: 813-677-8698; *Constituent Services Rep.:* Courtney Burgess

4507 George Blvd., Sebring, FL 33875; 863-402-9082; Fax: 863-402-9084; *Constituent Services Rep.:* Sherry Mccorle

Committee Assignments: Appropriations; Permanent Select Intelligence

Roskam, Peter, R-Ill. (6)

Capitol Hill Office: 227 CHOB 20515-1306; 225-4561; Fax: 225-1166; *Chief of Staff:* David Mork

Web: http://roskam.house.gov/

Facebook: http://facebook.com/RepRoskam

Twitter: http://twitter.com/PeterRoskam
District Office: 2700 International Dr., #304, West Chicago, IL 60185; 630-232-0006; Fax: 630-232-7393; *District Director:* Brian McCarthy
200 S. Hough St., 2nd Floor, Barrington, IL 60010; 847-656-6354; *District Director:* Brian McCarthy
Committee Assignment: Ways and Means

Ros-Lehtinen, Ileana, R-Fla. (27)

Capitol Hill Office: 2206 RHOB 20515-0918; 225-3931; Fax: 225-5620; *Chief of Staff:* Arthur A. Estopiñán
Web: http://ros-lehtinen.house.gov/
Facebook: http://facebook.com/voteileana
Twitter: http://twitter.com/RosLehtinen
District Office: 4960 S.W. 72nd Ave., #208, Miami, FL 33155; 305-668-2285; Fax: 305-668-5970; *District Chief of Staff:* Maytee Sanz
10720 Caribbean Blvd., Cutler Bay, FL 33189; *Caseworker:* Lourdes Ruiz
201 Westward Dr., Miami Springs, FL 33166; *Caseworker:* Lourdes Ruiz
Committee Assignments: Foreign Affairs; Rules

Ross, Dennis, R-Fla. (15)

Capitol Hill Office: 229 CHOB 20515; 225-1252; Fax: 226-0585; *Chief of Staff:* Anthony Foti
Web: http://dennisross.house.gov/
Facebook: http://facebook.com/dennis.ross.376
Twitter: http://twitter.com/RepDennisRoss
District Office: 170 Fitzgerald Rd., #1, Lakeland, FL 33813-2607; 863-644-8215; Fax: 863-648-0749; *District Director:* Blaine Gravitt
Committee Assignment: Financial Services

Rothfus, Keith, R-Pa. (12)

Capitol Hill Office: 503 CHOB 20515; 225-2065; Fax: 225-5709; *Chief of Staff:* Armstrong Robinson
Web: http://rothfus.house.gov/
Facebook: http://facebook.com/keithrothfus
Twitter: http://twitter.com/@KeithRothfus
District Offices: 250 Insurance St., #203, Beaver, PA 15009; 724-359-1626; Fax: 412-593-2022; *Field Rep.:* Jeremy Honhold
Cambria County Complex, 110 Franklin St., #150, Johnstown, PA 15901; 814-619-3659; Fax: 412-593-2022; *Field Rep.:* Seth Mckinley
6000 Babcock Blvd., #104, Pittsburgh, PA 15237; 412-837-1361; Fax: 412-593-2022; *District Director:* Jonathon Raso
Committee Assignments: Financial Services

Roybal-Allard, Lucille, D-Calif. (40)

Capitol Hill Office: 2330 RHOB 20515-0534; 225-1766; Fax: 226-0350; *Chief of Staff:* Victor Castillo
Web: http://roybal-allard.house.gov/
Facebook: http://facebook.com/RepRoybalAllard
Twitter: http://twitter.com/RepRoybalAllard

District Office: 500 Citadel Dr., #320, Commerce, CA 90040; 323-721-8790; Fax: 323-721-8789; *District Chief of Staff:* Ana Figueroa
Committee Assignment: Appropriations

Royce, Ed, R-Calif. (39)

Capitol Hill Office: 2185 RHOB 20515-0540; 225-4111; Fax: 226-0335; *Chief of Staff:* Amy Porter
Web: http://royce.house.gov/
Facebook: http://facebook.com/EdRoyce
Twitter: http://twitter.com/RepEdRoyce
District Offices: 210 W. Birch St., #201, Brea, CA 92821; 714-255-0101; Fax: 714-255-0109; *District Director:* Sara Catalan
1380 S. Fullerton Rd., #205, Rowland Heights, CA 91748; 626-964-5123; Fax: 626-810-3891; *Caseworker:* Stephanie Hu
Committee Assignments: Financial Services; Foreign Affairs, Chair

Ruiz, Raul, D-Calif. (36)

Capitol Hill Office: 1319 LHOB 20515; 225-5330; Fax: 225-1238; *Chief of Staff:* Kyle Layman
Web: http://ruiz.house.gov/
Facebook: http://facebook.com/CongressmanRaulRuizMD
Twitter: http://twitter.com/CongressmanRuiz
District Office: 777 E. Tahquitz Canyon Way, #338, Palm Springs, CA 92262; 760-424-8888; Fax: 760-424-8993; *District Director:* Greg Rodriguez
445 E. Florida Ave., 2nd Floor, Hemet, CA 92543; 951-765-2304; Fax: 951-765-3784; *Constituent Services Rep.:* Shelley Martin
45691 Monroe St., #3, Indio, CA 92201; 760-989-4111; Fax: 760-289-7234; *Constituent Services Rep.:* Gina Chapa
Committee Assignments: Natural Resources; Veterans' Affairs

Runyan, Jon, R-N.J. (3)

Capitol Hill Office: 1239 LHOB 20515-3003; 225-4765; Fax: 225-0778; *Chief of Staff:* Stacy Palmer-Barton
Web: http://runyan.house.gov/
Facebook: http://facebook.com/CongressmanJonRunyan
Twitter: http://twitter.com/RepJonRunyan
District Offices: 4167 Church Rd., Mount Laurel, NJ 08054-2220; 856-780-6436; Fax: 856-780-6440; *District Director:* Kristin Antonello
600 Mule Rd., Unit 6, Toms River, NJ 08757; 732-279-6013; Fax: 732-279-6062; *Constituent Services Liaison:* Mariella Kuchenbrod
Committee Assignments: Armed Services; Natural Resources; Veterans' Affairs

Ruppersberger, C. A., D-Md. (2)

Capitol Hill Office: 2416 RHOB 20515-2002; 225-3061; Fax: 225-3094; *Chief of Staff:* Tara Oursler
Web: http://dutch.house.gov/
Facebook: http://facebook.com/DutchForCongress

Twitter: http://twitter.com/Call_Me_Dutch
District Office: 375 W. Padonia Rd., #200, Timonium, MD 21093-2130; 410-628-2701; Fax: 410-628-2708; *District Director:* Jennifer Riggs
Committee Assignment: Permanent Select Intelligence, Ranking Minority Member

Rush, Bobby L., D-Ill. (1)

Capitol Hill Office: 2268 RHOB 20515-1301; 225-4372; Fax: 226-0333; *Chief of Staff Appropriations Budget Census Transportation Housing:* Stanley Watkins
Web: http://rush.house.gov/
Facebook: http://facebook.com/congressmanbobbyrush
Twitter: http://twitter.com/RepBobbyRush
District Offices: 700 E. 79th St., Chicago, IL 60619-3102; 773-224-6500; Fax: 773-224-9624; *District Director Appropriations Commerce Manufacturing Trade District Outreach Energy and Power Subcommittee Grants Labor Minimum Wage:* Robyn Grange
3235 147th St., Midlothian, IL 60445-3656; 708-385-9550; Fax: 708-385-3860; *Deputy District Director Contracts Procurement Immigration Passports Customs Tourism Trade Visas:* Younus Suleman
Committee Assignment: Energy and Commerce

Ryan, Paul, R-Wisc. (1)

Capitol Hill Office: 1233 LHOB 20515-4901; 225-3031; Fax: 225-3393; *Washington, D.C. Chief of Staff; Admin. Asst.:* Joyce Yamat Meyer
Web: http://paulryan.house.gov/
Facebook: http://facebook.com/paulryanwi
Twitter: http://twitter.com/reppaulryan
District Offices: 20 S. Main St., #10, Janesville, WI 53545-3959; 608-752-4050; Fax: 608-752-4711; *Chief of Staff:* Andy Speth
5031 7th Ave., Kenosha, WI 53140-4129; 262-654-1901; Fax: 262-654-2156; *Field Rep.:* Vacant
216 6th St., Racine, WI 53403; 262-637-0510; Fax: 262-637-5689; *Field Rep.:* Teresa Mora
Committee Assignments: Budget, Chair; Ways and Means

Ryan, Tim, D-Ohio (13)

Capitol Hill Office: 1421 LHOB 20515-3517; 225-5261; Fax: 225-3719; *Chief of Staff:* Ron Grimes
Web: http://timryan.house.gov/
Facebook: http://facebook.com/timryan
Twitter: http://twitter.com/RepTimRyan
District Offices: 1030 E. Tallmadge Ave., Akron, OH 44310-3563; 330-630-7311; Fax: 330-630-7314; *Economic Development Coord.:* Chris Cupples
197 W. Market St., Warren, OH 44481-1024; 800-856-4152; Fax: 330-373-0098; *District Director:* Rick Leonard
241 W. Federal St., Youngstown, OH 44503-1207; 330-740-0193; Fax: 330-740-0182; *Constituent Liaison:* Matthew Vadas
Committee Assignments: Appropriations; Budget

Sablan, Gregorio Kilili Camacho, D-M.P. (At Large)

Capitol Hill Office: 423 CHOB 20515-5601; 225-2646; Fax: 226-4249; *Chief of Staff:* Robert J. Schwalbach
Web: http://sablan.house.gov/
Facebook: http://facebook.com/pages/Gregorio-Kilili-Camacho-Sablan/153423912663
District Offices: P.O. Box 1361, Rota, MP 96951; 670-532-2647; Fax: 670-532-2649; *Staff Asst.:* Harry Masga
P.O. Box 504879, Saipan, MP 96950; 670-323-2647; Fax: 670-323-2649; *District Director:* Peter Tenorio
General Delivery, Tinian, MP 96952; 670-433-2647; Fax: 670-433-2648; *Staff Asst.:* Jose Kiyoshi
Committee Assignments: Education and the Workforce; Natural Resources

Salmon, Matt, R-Ariz. (5)

Capitol Hill Office: 2349 RHOB 20515; 225-2635; 226-4386; *Chief of Staff:* Adam Deguire
Web: http://salmon.house.gov/
Facebook: http://facebook.com/RepMattSalmon
Twitter: http://twitter.com/RepMattSalmon
District Office: 207 N. Gilbert Rd., #209, Gilbert, AZ 85234; 480-699-8239; Fax: 480-699-4730; *District Director:* Chuck Gray
Committee Assignments: Education and the Workforce; Natural Resources

Sánchez, Linda, D-Calif. (38)

Capitol Hill Office: 2423 RHOB 20515-0539; 225-6676; Fax: 226-1012; *Chief of Staff:* Adam Brand
Web: http://lindasanchez.house.gov/
Facebook: http://facebook.com/CongresswomanLindaSanchez
Twitter: http://twitter.com/RepLindaSanchez
District Office: 17906 Crusader Ave., #100, Cerritos, CA 90703-2694; 562-860-5050; Fax: 562-924-2914; *District Director:* Jóse Delgado
Committee Assignments: Ethics, Ranking Minority Member; Ways and Means

Sanchez, Loretta, D-Calif. (46)

Capitol Hill Office: 1114 LHOB 20515-0547; 225-2965; Fax: 225-5859; *Chief of Staff:* Jennifer Warburton
Web: http://lorettasanchez.house.gov/
Facebook: http://facebook.com/LorettaSanchez
Twitter: http://twitter.com/LorettaSanchez
District Office: 12397 Lewis St., #101, Garden Grove, CA 92840-4695; 714-621-0102; Fax: 714-621-0401; *District Director:* Gus Castellanos
Committee Assignments: Armed Services; Homeland Security; Joint Economic

Sarbanes, John, D-Md. (3)

Capitol Hill Office: 2444 RHOB 20515-2003; 225-4016; Fax: 225-9219; *Chief of Staff:* Jason Gleason
Web: http://sarbanes.house.gov/

Facebook: http://facebook.com/JSarbanes
Twitter: http://twitter.com/JohnSarbanes
District Offices: Arundel Center, 44 Calvert St., #349, Annapolis, MD 21401-1930; 410-295-1679; Fax: 410-295-1682; *Community Relations Specialist:* Robert Beans

600 Baltimore Ave., #303, Towson, MD 21204-4022; 410-832-8890; Fax: 410-832-8898; *Office Administrator:* Cyndy Clausen

3901 National Dr., #220, Burtonsville, MD 20866; 301-421-4078; Fax: 301-421-4079; *Community Outreach Specialist:* Alexis Reed
Committee Assignment: Energy and Commerce

Scalise, Steve, R-La. (1)

Capitol Hill Office: 2338 RHOB 20515; 225-3015; Fax: 226-0386; *Chief of Staff:* Lynnel Ruckert
Web: http://scalise.house.gov/
Facebook http://facebook.com/RepSteveScalise
Twitter: http://twitter.com/SteveScalise
District Offices: 1514 Martens Dr., #10, Hammond, LA 70401; 985-340-2185; Fax: 985-340-3122; *Regional Director:* Justin Crossie

8026 Main St., #700, Houma, LA 70360; 985-879-2300; Fax: 985-879-2306; *Field Rep.:* Matthew Jewell

21454 Koop Rd., #1-E, Mandeville, LA 70471-7513; 985-893-9064; Fax: 985-893-9707; *Field Rep.:* Danielle Evans

110 Veterans Memorial Blvd., #500, Metairie, LA 70005-4970; 504-837-1259; Fax: 504-837-4239; *Deputy Chief of Staff:* Charles Henry
Committee Assignment: Energy and Commerce

Schakowsky, Jan, D-Ill. (9)

Capitol Hill Office: 2367 RHOB 20515-1309; 225-2111; Fax: 226-6890; *Chief of Staff Labor Legis. Asst.:* Cathy Hurwit
Web: http://schakowsky.house.gov/
Facebook: http://facebook.com/janschakowsky
Twitter: http://twitter.com/janschakowsky
District Offices: 5533 N. Broadway St., Chicago, IL 60640-1405; 773-506-7100; Fax: 773-506-9202; *District Director; Scheduler:* Leslie Combs

820 Davis St., #105, Evanston, IL 60201-4400; 847-328-3409; Fax: 847-328-3425; *Grants Coord.; Constituent Advocate:* James Yoo

1852 Johns Dr., Glenview, IL 60025; 847-328-3409; Fax: 847-328-3425; *Constituent Advocate:* Abbey Eusebio
Committee Assignments: Energy and Commerce; Permanent Select Intelligence

Schiff, Adam, D-Calif. (28)

Capitol Hill Office: 2411 RHOB 20515-0529; 225-4176; Fax: 225-5828; *Chief of Staff:* Timothy S. Bergreen
Web: http://schiff.house.gov/
Facebook: http://facebook.com/RepAdamSchiff
Twitter: http://twitter.com/RepAdamSchiff

District Office: 245 E. Olive Ave., #200, Burbank, CA 91502; 818-450-2900; 323-315-5555; Fax: 818-450-2928; *District Director:* Ann Peifer
Committee Assignments: Appropriations; Permanent Select Intelligence

Schneider, Brad, D-Ill. (10)

Capitol Hill Office: 317 CHOB 20515; 225-4835; Fax: 225-0837; *Chief of Staff:* Reed Adamson
Web: http://schneider.house.gov
Facebook: http://facebook.com/CongressmanBradSchneider
Twitter: http://twitter.com/RepSchneider
District Office: 111 Barclay Blvd., #200, Lincolnshire, IL 60069; 847-793-0625; Fax: 847-793-0677; *District Director:* Barbara Cornew
Committee Assignments: Foreign Affairs; Small Business

Schock, Aaron, R-Ill. (18)

Capitol Hill Office: 328 CHOB 20515-1318; 225-6201; Fax: 225-9249; *Chief of Staff:* Mark Rowman
Web: http://schock.house.gov/
Facebook: http://facebook.com/RepAaronSchock
Twitter: http://twitter.com/repaaronschock
District Offices: 201 W. Morgan, Jacksonville, IL 62650-2001; 217-245-1431; Fax: 217-243-6852; *Constituent Services Specialist:* Barbara Baker

100 N.E. Monroe St., Room 100, Peoria, IL 61602-1047; 309-671-7027; Fax: 309-671-7309; *District Chief of Staff:* Carol Merna

235 S. 6th St., Springfield, IL 62701-1502; 217-670-1653; Fax: 217-670-1806
Committee Assignments: House Administration; Ways and Means

Schrader, Kurt, D-Ore. (5)

Capitol Hill Office: 108 CHOB 20515; 225-5711; Fax: 225-5699; *Chief of Staff:* Paul Gage
Web: http://schrader.house.gov/
Facebook: http://facebook.com/repschrader
Twitter: http://twitter.com/repschrader
District Offices: 621 High St., Oregon City, OR 97045-2240; 503-557-1324; Fax: 503-557-1981; *District Director:* Suzanne Kunse

544 Ferry St. S.E., #2, Salem, OR 97301-3830; 503-588-9100; Fax: 503-588-5517; *District Aide:* Dana Baugher
Committee Assignments: Agriculture; Budget; Small Business

Schwartz, Allyson Y., D-Pa. (13)

Capitol Hill Office: 1227 LHOB 20515-3813; 225-6111; Fax: 226-0611; *Chief of Staff:* Craig Kwiecinski
Web: http://schwartz.house.gov/
Facebook: http://facebook.com/RepAllysonSchwartz
District Offices: 801 Old York Rd., #212, Jenkintown, PA 19046-2710; 215-517-6572; Fax: 215-517-6575; *Deputy Chief of Staff:* Charlene Macdonald

7712 Castor Ave., Philadelphia, PA 19152; 215-335-3355; Fax: 215-333-4508; *Sr. Constituent Services Rep.:* Annamarie Feeney

Committee Assignments: Budget; Ways and Means

Schweikert, David, R-Ariz. (6)

Capitol Hill Office: 1205 LHOB 20515-0305; 225-2190; Fax: 225-0096; *Chief of Staff:* Oliver Schwab

Web: http://schweikert.house.gov/

Facebook: http://facebook.com/repdavidschweikert

Twitter: http://twitter.com/RepDavid

District Office: 10603 N. Hayden Rd., #108, Scottsdale, AZ 85260-5571; 480-946-2411; Fax: 480-946-2446; *District Director:* Kevin Knight

Committee Assignment: Science, Space, and Technology; Small Business

Scott, Austin, R-Ga. (8)

Capitol Hill Office: 516 CHOB 20515-1008; 225-6531; Fax: 225-3013; *Chief of Staff:* Joby Young

Web: http://austinscott.house.gov/

Facebook: http://facebook.com/RepAustinScott

Twitter: http://twitter.com/AustinScottGA08

District Offices: 127-B N. Central Ave., Tifton, GA 31794-4087; 229-396-5175; Fax: 229-396-5179; *District Director:* Alice Johnson

230 Margie Dr., #500, Warner Robins, GA 31088; 478-971-1776; Fax: 478-971-1778; *Constituent Services Rep.:* Phyllis Chalkley

Committee Assignments: Agriculture; Armed Services

Scott, Bobby, D-Va. (3)

Capitol Hill Office: 1201 LHOB 20515-4603; 225-8351; Fax: 225-8354; *Chief of Staff:* Joni L. Ivey

Web: http://bobbyscott.house.gov/

Facebook: http://facebook.com/CongressmanBobbyScott

Twitter: http://twitter.com/repbobbyscott

District Offices: 2600 Washington Ave., #1010, Newport News, VA 23607-4333; 757-380-1000; Fax: 757-928-6694; *District Manager:* Gisele Russell

400 N. 8th St., #430, Richmond, VA 23219-4815; 804-644-4845; Fax: 804-648-6026; *Legis. Asst.; District Scheduler:* Nkechi Winkler

Committee Assignments: Education and the Workforce; Judiciary

Scott, David, D-Ga. (13)

Capitol Hill Office: 225 CHOB 20515-1013; 225-2939; Fax: 225-4628; *Chief of Staff; Press Secy.:* Michael Andel

Web: http://davidscott.house.gov/

Facebook: http://facebook.com/RepDavidScott

Twitter: http://twitter.com/RepDavidScott

District Offices: 173 N. Main St., Jonesboro, GA 30236-3567; 770-210-5073; Fax: 770-210-5673; *District Director:* Chandra Harris

888 Concord Rd., #100, Smyrna, GA 30080-4202; 770-432-5405; Fax: 770-432-5813; *Deputy District Director:* Isaac Dodoo

Committee Assignments: Agriculture; Financial Services

Sensenbrenner, Jim, R-Wisc. (5)

Capitol Hill Office: 2449 RHOB 20515-4905; 225-5101; Fax: 225-3190; *Chief of Staff:* Bart Forsyth

Web: http://sensenbrenner.house.gov/

Facebook: http://facebook.com/RepSensenbrenner

Twitter: http://twitter.com/JimPressOffice

District Office: 120 Bishops Way, #154, Brookfield, WI 53005-6249; 262-784-1111; Fax: 262-784-9437; *District Director:* Loni Hagerup

Committee Assignments: Judiciary; Science, Space, and Technology

Serrano, José E., D-N.Y. (15)

Capitol Hill Office: 2227 RHOB 20515-3216; 225-4361; Fax: 225-6001; *DC Office Deputy Chief of Staff:* Philip Schmidt, Matthew Alpert

Web: http://serrano.house.gov/

Facebook: http://facebook.com/RepJoseSerrano

Twitter: http://twitter.com/RepJoseSerrano

District Office: 1231 Lafayette Ave., 4th Floor, Bronx, NY 10474-5331; 718-620-0084; Fax: 718-620-0658; *District Director:* Javier Lopez

Committee Assignment: Appropriations

Sessions, Pete, R-Tex. (32)

Capitol Hill Office: 2233 RHOB 20515-4332; 225-2231; Fax: 225-5878; *Chief of Staff:* Lee Padilla

Web: http://sessions.house.gov/

Facebook: http://facebook.com/petesessions

Twitter: http://twitter.com/petesessions

District Office: Park Central VII, 12750 Merit Dr., #1434, Dallas, TX 75251-1229; 972-392-0505; Fax: 972-392-0615; *District Director:* Taylor Bledsoe

Committee Assignment: Rules, Chair

Sewell, Terri A., D-Ala. (7)

Capitol Hill Office: 1133 LHOB 20515-0107; 225-2665; Fax: 226-9567; *Chief of Staff:* Nichole Francis Reynolds

Web: http://sewell.house.gov/

Facebook: http://facebook.com/RepSewell

Twitter: http://twitter.com/RepTerriSewell

District Offices: Two 20th St. N., #1130, Birmingham, AL 35203-4014; 205-254-1960; Fax: 205-254-1974; *District Director:* Chasseny Lewis

186 Field of Dreams Dr., Demopolis, AL 36732; 334-287-0860; Fax: 334-877-4489; *Constituent Services Rep./ Grants Coordinator:* Carolyn Powell

205 N. Washington St., University of West Alabama, Station 40, Webb Hall 236-237, Livingston, AL 35470-2099; 205-652-5834; Fax: 205-652-5935; *Constituent Services Rep.:* Reba Love

Perry County Courthouse, 300 Washington St., Marion, AL 36756-2336; 334-683-2157; Fax: 334-683-2201; *Constituent Services Rep.:* Dianna Johnson

101 S. Lawrence St., Montgomery, AL 36104; 334-262-1919; Fax: 334-262-1921; *Constituent Services Manager/Outreach Coordinator:* Melinda Williams

908 Alabama Ave., Federal Bldg., #112, Selma, AL 36701-4660; 334-877-4414; Fax: 334-877-4489; *Constituent Services Rep.:* Dianna Johnson
Committee Assignments: Financial Services; Permanent Select Intelligence

Shea-Porter, Carol, D-N.H. (1)

Capitol Hill Office: 1530 LHOB 20515; 225-5456; Fax: 225-5822; *Chief of Staff:* Naomi Andrews
Web: http://shea-porter.house.gov/
Facebook: https://facebook.com/RepSheaPorter
Twitter: http://twitter.com/RepSheaPorter
District Office: 33 Lowell St., Manchester, NH 03101-1641; 603-641-9536; Fax: 603-641-9561; *District Director:* Chuck Gilboy
20 N. Main St., Rochester, NH 03867; 603-335-7700; Fax: 603-335-7702; *Caseworker:* Olga Clough
Committee Assignments: Armed Services; Natural Resources

Sherman, Brad, D-Calif. (30)

Capitol Hill Office: 2242 RHOB 20515-0527; 225-5911; Fax: 225-5879; *Chief of Staff:* Don MacDonald
Web: http://bradsherman.house.gov/
Facebook: http://facebook.com/pages/Congressman-Brad-Sherman/63158229861
Twitter: http://twitter.com/bradsherman
District Office: 5000 Van Nuys Blvd., #420, Sherman Oaks, CA 91403-6126; 818-501-9200; Fax: 818-501-1554; *District Director:* Matt Dababneh
Committee Assignments: Financial Services; Foreign Affairs

Shimkus, John, R-Ill. (15)

Capitol Hill Office: 2452 RHOB 20515; 225-5271; Fax: 225-5880; *Chief of Staff:* Craig A. Roberts
Web: http://shimkus.house.gov/
Facebook: http://facebook.com/repshimkus
Twitter: http://twitter.com/RepShimkus
District Offices: 201 N. Vermilion St., #218, Danville, IL 61832; 217-446-0664; Fax: 217-446-0670; *District Aide:* Kate Holloway
101 N. 4th St., #303, Effingham, IL 62401; 217-347-7947; Fax: 217-342-1219; *District Aide:* Michael Hall
110 E. Locust St., Room 12, Harrisburg, IL 62946-1557; 618-252-8271; Fax: 618-252-8317; *District Aide:* Holly Healy
15 Professional Park Dr., Maryville, IL 62062; 618-288-7190; Fax: 618-288-7219; *District Director:* Deb Detmers
Committee Assignment: Energy and Commerce

Shuster, Bill, R-Pa. (9)

Capitol Hill Office: 2209 RHOB 20515; 225-2431; Fax: 225-2486; *Chief of Staff:* Eric Burgeson
Web: http://shuster.house.gov/
Facebook: http://facebook.com/Rep.Shuster
Twitter: http://twitter.com/repbillshuster

District Offices: 100 Lincoln Way E., Suite B, Chambersburg, PA 17201-2274; 717-264-8308; Fax: 717-264-0269; *Constituent Services Rep.:* Nancy Bull
310 Penn St., #200, Hollidaysburg, PA 16648-2044; 814-696-6318; Fax: 814-696-6726; *District Director:* Jim Frank
827 Water St., #3, Indiana, PA 15701; 724-463-0516; Fax: 724-463-0518; *Constituent Services Rep.:* Ron Nocco
Committee Assignments: Armed Services; Transportation and Infrastructure, Chair

Simpson, Mike, R-Idaho (2)

Capitol Hill Office: 2312 RHOB 20515-1202; 225-5531; Fax: 225-8216; *Chief of Staff:* Lindsay J. Slater
Web: http://simpson.house.gov/
Facebook: http://facebook.com/pages/Mike-Simpson/96007744606
Twitter: http://twitter.com/CongMikeSimpson
District Offices: 802 W. Bannock St., #600, Boise, ID 83702-5843; 208-334-1953; Fax: 208-334-9533; *Deputy Chief of Staff:* John Revier
410 Memorial Dr., #203, Idaho Falls, ID 83402-3600; 208-523-6701; Fax: 208-523-2384; *Regional Director:* Ethan Huffman
275 S. 5th Ave., #275, Pocatello, ID 83201-6400; 208-233-2222; Fax: 208-233-2095; *Regional Director:* Steve Brown
1341 Filmore St., #202, Twin Falls, ID 83301-3392; 208-734-7219; Fax: 208-734-7244; *Regional Director:* Linda Culver
Committee Assignment: Appropriations

Sinema, Kyrsten, D-Ariz. (9)

Capitol Hill Office: 1237 LHOB 20515; 225-9888; Fax: 225-9731; *Chief of Staff:* JoDee Winterhof
Web: http://sinema.house.gov/
Facebook: http://facebook.com/CongresswomanSinema
Twitter: http://twitter.com/RepSinema
District Offices: 2944 N. 44th St., #150, Phoenix, AZ 85018; 602-956-2285; Fax: 602-956-2468; *District Director:* Michelle Davidson
Committee Assignment: Financial Services

Sires, Albio, D-N.J. (8)

Capitol Hill Office: 2342 RHOB 20515-3013; 225-7919; Fax: 226-0792; *Chief of Staff:* Gene Martorony
Web: http://sires.house.gov/
Facebook: http://facebook.com/pages/Albio-Sires/81058818750
Twitter: http://twitter.com/RepSires
District Offices: 630 Ave. C, Room Nine, Bayonne, NJ 07002-3878; 201-823-2900; Fax: 201-858-7139; *Congressional Aide:* Janis Demellier
800 Anna St., Elizabeth, NJ 07201; 908-820-0692; Fax: 908-820-0694; *Congressional Aide:* Ada Morell

121 Newark Ave., #200, Jersey City, NJ 07302; 201-309-0301; Fax: 201-309-0384; *District Director:* Richard Turner

5500 Palisade Ave., Suite A, West New York, NJ 07093-2124; 201-558-0800; Fax: 201-617-2809; *Constituent Services Director:* Danita Torres

Committee Assignments: Foreign Affairs; Transportation and Infrastructure

Slaughter, Louise M., D-N.Y. (25)

Capitol Hill Office: 2469 RHOB 20515-3228; 225-3615; Fax: 225-7822; *Chief of Staff:* Liam Fitzsimmons
Web: http://louise.house.gov/
Facebook: http://facebook.com/RepLouiseSlaughter
Twitter: http://twitter.com/louiseslaughter
District Office: 3120 Federal Bldg., 100 State St., Rochester, NY 14614-1309; 585-232-4850; Fax: 585-232-1954; *District Director:* Patricia Larke
Committee Assignments: Commission on Security and Cooperation in Europe (Helsinki Commission); Rules, Ranking Minority Member

Smith, Adam, D-Wash. (9)

Capitol Hill Office: 2264 RHOB 20515-4709; 225-8901; Fax: 225-5893; *Chief of Staff:* Shana M. Chandler
Web: http://adamsmith.house.gov/
Facebook: http://facebook.com/RepAdamSmith
Twitter: http://twitter.com/RepAdamSmith
District Office: 101 Evergreen Bldg., 15 S. Grady Way, Renton, WA 98057; 425-793-5180; Fax: 425-793-5181; *District Director:* Matt Perry
Committee Assignment: Armed Services, Ranking Minority Member

Smith, Adrian, R-Neb. (3)

Capitol Hill Office: 2241 RHOB 20515; 225-6435; Fax: 225-0207; *Chief of Staff:* Monica Jirik
Web: http://adriansmith.house.gov/
Facebook: http://facebook.com/AdrianSmithNE
Twitter: https://twitter.com/RepAdrianSmith
District Offices: 1811 W. 2nd St., #275, Grand Island, NE 68803-5400; 308-384-3900; Fax: 308-384-3902; *Director of Constituent Services:* Todd Crawford
416 Valley View Dr., #600, Scottsbluff, NE 69361-1486; 308-633-6333; Fax: 308-633-6335; *Office Coord.:* Lenora Brotzman
Committee Assignment: Ways and Means

Smith, Chris, R-N.J. (4)

Capitol Hill Office: 2373 RHOB 20515-3004; 225-3765; Fax: 225-7768; *Chief of Staff:* Mary McDermott Noonan
Web: http://chrissmith.house.gov/
Twitter: http://twitter.com/RepChrisSmith
District Offices: 4573 S. Broad St., First Floor, Hamilton, NJ 08619-3828; 609-585-7878; Fax: 609-581-9155; *District Director for Casework:* Jeff Sagnip

Whiting Shopping Center, 108 Lacey Rd., #38-A, Whiting, NJ 08759-1331; 732-350-2300; Fax: 732-350-6260; *District Director for Public Policy:* Joan Schloeder

Raintree Shopping Center, 112 Village Center Dr., Second Floor, Freehold, NJ 07728; 732-780-3035; Fax: 732-780-3079; *District Director for Casework:* Jeff Sagnip

Committee Assignments: Commission on Security and Cooperation in Europe (Helsinki Commission), Co-Chair; Foreign Affairs

Smith, Lamar, R-Tex. (21)

Capitol Hill Office: 2409 RHOB 20515-4321; 225-4236; Fax: 225-8628; *Chief of Staff:* Jennifer Young Brown
Web: http://lamarsmith.house.gov/
Facebook: http://facebook.com/LamarSmithTX21
Twitter: http://twitter.com/LamarSmithTX21
District Offices: 2211 S. IH-35, #106, Austin, TX 78741; 512-912-7508; Fax: 512-912-7519; *Constituent Services Liaison:* Morgan McFall
301 Junction Hwy., #346C, Kerrville, TX 78028-4247; 830-896-0154; Fax: 830-896-0168; *Constituent Services Liaison; Service Academy Liaison:* Anne Overby
Guaranty Federal Bldg., 1100 N.E. Loop 410, #640, San Antonio, TX 78209; 210-821-5024; Fax: 210-821-5947; *District Director:* Mike Asmus
Committee Assignments: Homeland Security; Judiciary; Science, Space, and Technology, Chair

Southerland, Steve, R-Fla. (2)

Capitol Hill Office: 1229 LHOB 20515-0902; 225-5235; Fax: 225-5615; *Chief of Staff:* Jonathan Hayes
Web: http://southerland.house.gov/
Facebook: http://facebook.com/RepSteveSoutherland
Twitter: http://twitter.com/Rep_Southerland
District Offices: 840 W. 11th St., #2250, Panama City, FL 32401-2336; 850-785-0812; Fax: 850-763-3764; *Deputy District Director:* Melissa Thompson
3116 Capital Circle N.E., #9, Tallahassee, FL 32308-7791; 850-561-3979; Fax: 850-681-2902; *Deputy District Director:* Lori Hutto
Committee Assignments: Natural Resources; Transportation and Infrastructure

Speier, Jackie, D-Calif. (14)

Capitol Hill Office: 211 CHOB 20515-0512; 225-3531; Fax: 226-4183; *Chief of Staff:* Cookab Hashemi
Web: http://speier.house.gov/
Facebook: http://facebook.com/JackieSpeier
Twitter: http://twitter.com/RepSpeier
District Office: 155 Bovet Rd., 780, San Mateo, CA 94402; 415-566-5257; Fax: 650-375-8270; *District Director:* Brian Perkins
Committee Assignments: Armed Services; Oversight and Government Reform

Stewart, Chris, R-Utah (2)

Capitol Hill Office: 323 CHOB 20515; 225-9730; Fax: 225-9627; *Chief of Staff:* Brian Steed
Web: http://stewart.house.gov/

Facebook: http://facebook.com/RepChrisStewart
Twitter: http://twitter.com/repchrisstewart
District Offices: 136 E. South Temple St., #900, Salt Lake City, UT 84111; 801-364-5550; Fax: 801-364-5551; *District Director:* Dell Smith

253 W. St. George Blvd., #100, St. George, UT 84770; 435-627-1500; Fax: 435-627-1911; *Deputy Director:* Gary Webster
Committee Assignments: Appropriations

Stivers, Steve, R-Ohio (15)

Capitol Hill Office: 1022 LHOB 20515-3515; 225-2015; Fax: 225-3529; *Chief of Staff:* Adam Kuhn
Web: http://stivers.house.gov/
Facebook: http://facebook.com/RepSteveStivers
Twitter: http://twitter.com/RepSteveStivers
District Office: 3790 Municipal Way, Hilliard, OH 43026-1620; 614-771-4968; Fax: 614-771-3990; *District Director:* Grant Shaffer

123 S. Broad St., #235, Lancaster, OH 43130; 740-654-2654; Fax: 740-654-2482; *Field Rep.:* Emily Schmidbauer

69 N. South St., Wilmington, OH 45177; 937-283-7049; Fax: 937-283-7052; *Field Rep.:* Sherry Stuckert
Committee Assignment: Financial Services

Stockman, Steve, R-Tex. (36)

Capitol Hill Office: 326 CHOB 20515; 225-1555; Fax: 226-0396; *Chief of Staff:* Kirk Clinkenbeard
Web: http://stockman.house.gov/
Facebook: http://facebook.com/congressmanstockman
Twitter: http://twitter.com/SteveWorks4You
District Offices: 420 Green Ave., Orange, TX 77630; 409-883-8075; Fax: 409-886-9918; *District Rep.:* David Covey

8060 Spencer Hwy., San Jacinto College, Bldg. 1, Room 108, Pasadena, TX 77505; 281-478-2799; *District Director:* Bonnie Norman

907 E. Houston St., Cleveland City Hall, Cleveland, TX 77327; 409-886-9918; *Caseworker:* Jonathan Covey
Committee Assignments: Foreign Affairs; Science, Space, and Technology

Stutzman, Marlin, R-Ind. (3)

Capitol Hill Office: 1728 LHOB 20515-1403; 225-4436; Fax: 226-9870; *Deputy Chief of Staff; Legis. Director:* John Hammond
Web: http://stutzman.house.gov/
Facebook: http://facebook.com/CongressmanMarlinStutzman
Twitter: http://twitter.com/RepStutzman
District Offices: 1300 S. Harrison St., #3105, Fort Wayne, IN 46802-3492; 260-424-3041; Fax: 260-424-4042; *Chief of Staff:* Matt Lloyd

700 Park Ave., Suite D, Winona Lake, IN 46590-1066; 574-269-1940; Fax: 574-269-3112; *Deputy District Director:* Allison McSherry
Committee Assignment: Financial Services

Swalwell, Eric, D-Calif. (15)

Capitol Hill Office: 501 CHOB 20515; 225-5065; Fax: 226-3805; *Chief of Staff:* Ricky Le
Web: http://swalwell.house.gov/
Facebook: http://facebook.com/CongressmanEricSwalwell
Twitter: http://twitter.com/repswalwell
District Office: 5075 Hopyard Rd., #220, Pleasanton, CA 94588; 925-460-5100; *Sr. Field Rep.:* Josh Huber

1260 B St., #150, Hayward, CA 94541; 510-370-3322; *District Rep.:* Gabriel Arteaga
Committee Assignments: Homeland Security; Science, Space, and Technology

Takano, Mark, D-Calif. (41)

Capitol Hill Office: 1507 LHOB 20515; 225-2305; Fax: 225-7018; *Chief of Staff:* Richard McPike
Web: http://takano.house.gov/
Facebook: http://facebook.com/RepMarkTakano
Twitter: http://twitter.com/RepMarkTakano
District Office: 3403 10th St., #610, Riverside, CA 92501; *District Director:* Rafael Elizalde
Committee Assignments: Science, Space, and Technology; Veterans' Affairs

Terry, Lee, R-Neb. (2)

Capitol Hill Office: 2266 RHOB 20515-2702; 225-4155; Fax: 226-5452; *Chief of Staff:* Mark J. Anderson
Web: http://leeterry.house.gov/
Facebook: http://facebook.com/leeterry
Twitter: http://twitter.com/leeterryne
District Office: 11717 Burt St., #106, Omaha, NE 68154-1500; 402-397-9944; Fax: 402-397-8787; *District Director:* Felicia Rogers
Committee Assignment: Energy and Commerce

Thompson, Bennie, D-Miss. (2)

Capitol Hill Office: 2466 RHOB 20515-2402; 225-5876; Fax: 225-5898; *Chief of Staff:* I. Lanier Avant
Web: http://benniethompson.house.gov/
Facebook: http://facebook.com/pages/BennieGThompson/7259193379
Twitter: http://twitter.com/BennieGThompson
District Offices: 107 W. Madison St., Bolton, MS 39041; 601-866-9003; Fax: 601-866-9036; *District Rep.:* Brenda Funches

910 Courthouse Lane, Greenville, MS 38701-3764; 662-335-9003; Fax: 662-334-1304; *Community Development Coord.:* Timla Washington

509 Hwy. 82 W., Greenwood, MS 38930-5030; 662-455-9003; Fax: 662-453-0118; *Caseworker:* Ashley Beale

3607 Medgar Evers Blvd., Jackson, MS 39213-6364; 601-946-9003; Fax: 601-982-5337; *Caseworker; Field Rep.:* Steven Gavin

263 E. Main St., P.O. Box 356, Marks, MS 38646; 662-326-9003; *Caseworker:* Sandra Jamison

106 Green Ave., #106, Mound Bayou, MS 38762-9594; 662-741-9003; Fax: 662-741-9002; *Caseworker:* Geri Adams
Committee Assignment: Homeland Security, Ranking Minority Member

Thompson, Glenn, R-Pa. (5)

Capitol Hill Office: 124 CHOB 20515-3805; 225-5121; Fax: 225-5796; *Chief of Staff:* Jordan Clark
Web: http://thompson.house.gov/
Facebook: http://facebook.com/CongressmanGT
Twitter: http://twitter.com/CongressmanGT
District Offices: 3555 Benner Pike, #101, Bellefonte, PA 16823-8474; 814-353-0215; Fax: 814-353-0218; *Field Rep.:* Mike Glazer
127 W. Spring St., Suite C, Titusville, PA 16354-1727; 814-827-3985; Fax: 814-827-7307; *District Director:* Peter Winkler
Committee Assignments: Agriculture; Education and the Workforce; Natural Resources

Thompson, Mike, D-Calif. (5)

Capitol Hill Office: 231 CHOB 20515-0501; 225-3311; Fax: 225-4335; *Chief of Staff:* Melanie Rhinehart Van Tassell
Web: http://mikethompson.house.gov/
Facebook: http://facebook.com/RepMikeThompson
Twitter: http://twitter.com/RepThompson
District Offices: 1040 Main St., #101, Napa, CA 94559-2605; 707-226-9898; Fax: 707-251-9800; *District Rep.:* Brad Onorato
2300 County Center Dr., #A100, Santa Rosa, CA 95403; 707-542-7182; Fax: 707-542-2745; *District Rep.:* Cheryl Diehm
985 Walnut Ave., Vallejo, CA 94592; 707-645-1888; Fax: 707-645-1870; *District Rep.:* Mel Orpilla
Committee Assignments: Ways and Means; Permanent Select Intelligence

Thornberry, Mac, R-Tex. (13)

Capitol Hill Office: 2329 RHOB 20515-4313; 225-3706; Fax: 225-3486; *Chief of Staff:* Josh Martin
Web: http://thornberry.house.gov/
Facebook: http://facebook.com/repmacthornberry
Twitter: https://twitter.com/MacTXPress
District Offices: 905 S. Fillmore St., #520, Amarillo, TX 79101-3541; 806-371-8844; Fax: 806-371-7044; *District Director:* Sandra Ross
2525 Kell Blvd., #406, Wichita Falls, TX 76308; 940-692-1700; Fax: 940-692-0539; *Deputy District Director:* Paul Simpson
Committee Assignments: Armed Services, Vice Chair; Permanent Select Intelligence

Tiberi, Patrick J., R-Ohio (12)

Capitol Hill Office: 106 CHOB 20515-3512; 225-5355; Fax: 226-4523; *Chief of Staff:* Mark Bell
Web: http://tiberi.house.gov/
Facebook: http://facebook.com/RepPatTiberi
Twitter: http://twitter.com/tiberipress
District Office: 3000 Corporate Exchange Dr., #310, Columbus, OH 43231-7689; 614-523-2555; Fax: 614-818-0887; *District Director:* Walter Taylor
Committee Assignment: Ways and Means

Tierney, John F., D-Mass. (6)

Capitol Hill Office: 2238 RHOB 20515-2106; 225-8020; Fax: 225-5915; *Chief of Staff:* Betsy Arnold Marr
Web: http://tierney.house.gov/
Facebook: http://facebook.com/CongressmanJohnTierney
Twitter: http://twitter.com/RepTierney
District Offices: Lynn City Hall, Room 412, Lynn, MA 01902; 781-595-7375; Fax: 781-595-7492; *Outreach Coord.:* Drew Russo
17 Peabody Square, Peabody, MA 01960-5646; 978-531-1669; Fax: 978-531-1996; *District Scheduler:* Sarah Jackson
Committee Assignments: Education and the Workforce; Oversight and Government Reform

Tipton, Scott, R-Colo. (3)

Capitol Hill Office: 218 CHOB 20515-0603; 225-4761; Fax: 226-9669; *Chief of Staff:* Nicholas Zupancic
Web: http://tipton.house.gov/
Facebook: http://facebook.com/CongressmanScottTipton
Twitter: http://twitter.com/reptipton
District Offices: 609 Main St., #105 Box 11, Alamosa, CO 81101-2557; 719-587-5105; Fax: 719-587-5137; *Field Rep.:* Brenda Felmlee
835 E. 2nd Ave., #230, Durango, CO 81301-5474; 970-259-1490; Fax: 970-259-1563; *Field Rep.:* Darlene Marcus
225 N. 5th St., #702, Grand Junction, CO 81501-2658; 970-241-2499; Fax: 970-241-3053; *District Director:* Joshua Green
503 N. Main St., #658, Pueblo, CO 81003-3132; 719-542-1073; Fax: 719-542-1127; *Regional Director:* Brian McCain
PO Box 774932, Steamboat Springs, CO 80477; 970-640-9718;
Committee Assignments: Agriculture; Natural Resources; Small Business

Titus, Dina, D-Nev. (1)

Capitol Hill Office: 401 CHOB 20515; 225-5965; Fax: 225-3119; *Chief of Staff:* Jay Gertsema
Web: http://titus.house.gov/
Facebook: http://facebook.com/CongresswomanTitus
Twitter: http://twitter.com/repdinatitus
District Office: 550 E. Charleston Blvd., Suite B, Las Vegas, NV 89104; 702-220-9823; Fax: 702-220-9841; *District Director:* Mike Naft
Committee Assignments: Transportation and Infrastructure; Veterans' Affairs

Tonko, Paul D., D-N.Y. (20)

Capitol Hill Office: 2463 RHOB 20515; 225-5076; Fax: 225-5077; *Chief of Staff:* Clinton Britt
Web: http://tonko.house.gov/
Facebook: http://facebook.com/reppaultonko
Twitter: http://twitter.com/RepPaulTonko
District Offices: 61 Columbia St., 4th Floor, Albany, NY 12210; 518-465-0700; Fax: 518-427-5107; *District Director:* Sean Shortell

61 Church St., Room 309, Amsterdam, NY 12010-4424; 518-843-3400; Fax: 518-843-8874; *Constituent Rep.:* Kelly Quist-Demars

105 Jay St., Room 15, Schenectady, NY 12305-1970; 518-374-4547; Fax: 518-374-7908; *Constituent Rep.:* Cora Schroeter

Committee Assignments: Energy and Commerce

Tsongas, Niki, D-Mass. (3)

Capitol Hill Office: 1607 LHOB 20515-2105; 225-3411; Fax: 226-0771; *Communications Director:* Michael Hartigan

Web: http://tsongas.house.gov/

Facebook: http://facebook.com/RepTsongas

Twitter: http://twitter.com/nikiinthehouse

District Offices: 15 Union St., #401, Lawrence, MA 01840; 978-681-6200; Fax: 978-682-6070; *Regional Coord.; Constituent Services Director:* June Black

11 Kearney Square, 4thFloor, Lowell, MA 01852; 978-459-0101; Fax: 978-459-1907; *Chief of Staff:* Katie Enos

Haverhill Citizens Center, 10 Welcome St., Room 4, Haverhill, MA 01830; 978-459-0101; *Constituent Services Rep.:* Denise Johnson

Frank D. Walker Bldg., 255 Main St., Room 106, Marlborough, MA 01752; 978-459-0101; *Constituent Services Rep.:* Denise Johnson

Fitchburg State University, Center for Professional Studies Office, 150 Main St., Fitchburg, MA 01420; 978-459-0101; *Constituent Services Rep.:* Denise Johnson

Committee Assignments: Armed Services; Natural Resources

Turner, Michael, R-Ohio (10)

Capitol Hill Office: 2239 RHOB 20515-3503; 225-6465; Fax: 225-6754; *Chief of Staff:* Adam Howard

Web: http://turner.house.gov/

Facebook: http://facebook.com/RepMikeTurner

Twitter: https://twitter.com/RepMikeTurner

District Office: 120 W. 3rd St., #305, Dayton, OH 45402-1819; 937-225-2843; Fax: 937-225-2752; *District Director:* Kelly Geers

Committee Assignments: Armed Services; Oversight and Government Reform

Upton, Fred, R-Mich. (6)

Capitol Hill Office: 2183 RHOB 20515-2206; 225-3761; Fax: 225-4986; *Chief of Staff; Press Secretary:* Joan Hillebrands

Web: http://upton.house.gov/

Facebook: http://facebook.com/RepFredUpton

Twitter: http://twitter.com/RepFredUpton

District Offices: 157 S. Kalamazoo Mall, #180, Kalamazoo, MI 49007-4861; 269-385-0039; Fax: 269-385-2888; *District Director:* Clay McCausland

800 Centre, #106, 800 Ship St., St. Joseph, MI 49085-2182; 269-982-1986; Fax: 269-982-0237; *Sr. Constituent Services Rep.:* Janet Zielke

Committee Assignment: Energy and Commerce, Chair

Valadao, David, R-Calif. (21)

Capitol Hill Office: 1004 LHOB 20515; 225-4695; Fax: 225-3196; *Chief of Staff:* Tal Eslick

Web: http://valadao.house.gov/

Facebook: http://facebook.com/CongressmanDavidValadao

Twitter: http://twitter.com/RepDavidValadao

District Offices: 2700 M St., #250B, Bakersfield, CA 93301; 661-864-7736; *Field Rep.:* Michael Bowers

101 N. Irwin St., #110B, Hanford, CA 93230; 559-582-5526; Fax: 559-582-5527; *District Director:* George Andrews

Committee Assignment: Appropriations

Van Hollen, Chris, D-Md. (8)

Capitol Hill Office: 1707 LHOB 20515-2008; 225-5341; Fax: 225-0375; *Chief of Staff:* William Parsons

Web: http://vanhollen.house.gov/

Facebook: http://facebook.com/chrisvanhollen

Twitter: http://twitter.com/chrisvanhollen

District Office: 51 Monroe St., #507, Rockville, MD 20850-2406; 301-424-3501; Fax: 301-424-5992; *District Director:* Joan Kleinman

205 Center St., #206, Mount Airy, MD 21771; 301-829-2181; *Field Rep.:* Melissa Joseph

Committee Assignment: Budget, Ranking Minority Member

Vargas, Juan, D-Calif. (51)

Capitol Hill Office: 1605 LHOB 20515; 225-8045; Fax: 225-9073; *Chief of Staff:* Tim Walsh

Web: http://vargas.house.gov/

Facebook: http://facebook.com/RepJuanVargas

Twitter: http://twitter.com/RepJuanVargas

District Office: 333 F St., Suite A, Chula Vista, CA 91910-2624; 619-422-5963; Fax: 619-422-7290; *Sr. Field Rep.:* Eddie Meyer

380 N. 8th St., #14, El Centro, CA 92243; 760-355-8800; Fax: 760-312-9664; *Field Director:* Rebecca Terrazas-Baxter

Committee Assignments: Agriculture; Foreign Affairs; House Administration; Joint Printing

Veasey, Marc, D-Tex. (33)

Capitol Hill Office: 414 CHOB 20515; 225-9897; Fax: 225-9702; *Chief of Staff:* Jane Hamilton

Web: http://veasey.house.gov/

Facebook: http://facebook.com/CongressmanMarcVeasey

Twitter: http://twitter.com/RepVeasey

District Offices: JP Morgan Chase Bldg., 1881 Sylvan Ave., #108, Dallas, TX 75208; 214-741-1387; Fax: 214-741-2026; *District Director:* Anne Hagan

La Gran Plaza Office Tower, 4200 S. Freeway, #412, Fort Worth, TX 76115; 817-920-9086; Fax: 817-920-9324; *Director of Constituent Services:* Jennifer Wood

Committee Assignments: Armed Services; Science, Space, and Technology

Vela, Filemon, D-Tex. (34)

Capitol Hill Office: 437 CHOB 20515; 225-9901;
Fax: 225-9770; *Chief of Staff:* Perry Brody
Web: http://vela.house.gov/
Facebook: http://facebook.com/
UsCongressmanFilemonVela
Twitter: http://twitter.com/RepFilemonVela
District Offices: 500 E. Main, Alice, TX 78332; 956-544-
8352; *District Director:* Trey Lewis
333 Ebony Ave., Brownsville, TX 78520; 956-544-8352;
Cameron County District Director: Marisela Cortez
1390 W. Expressway 83, San Benito, TX 78586; 956-544-
8352; *Hidalgo County District Director:* Humberto Garza
Committee Assignments: Agriculture; Homeland Security

Velázquez, Nydia M., D-N.Y. (7)

Capitol Hill Office: 2302 RHOB 20515-3212; 225-2361;
Fax: 226-0327; *Chief of Staff:* Michael Day
Web: http://velazquez.house.gov/index.shtml
Facebook: http://facebook.com/pages/Nydia-Velazquez/
8037068318
Twitter: http://twitter.com/NydiaVelazquez
District Offices: 266 Broadway, #201, Brooklyn, NY
11211-6215; 718-599-3658; Fax: 718-599-4537;
Exec. Asst.: Lucy Morcelo
16 Court St., #1006, Brooklyn, NY 11241-1010; 718-222-
5819; Fax: 718-222-5830; *Community Coord.:* Daniel
Wiley
500 Pearl St., #973, New York, NY 10007; *Community
Liaison:* Iris Quiñones
Committee Assignments: Financial Services; Small
Business, Ranking Minority Member

Visclosky, Pete, D-Ind. (1)

Capitol Hill Office: 2256 RHOB 20515-1401; 225-2461;
Fax: 225-2493; *Chief of Staff:* Mark Lopez
Web: http://visclosky.house.gov/
Facebook: http://facebook.com/repvisclosky
Twitter: http://twitter.com/repvisclosky
District Office: 7895 Broadway, Suite A, Merrillville,
IN 46410-5529; 219-795-1844; Fax: 219-795-1850;
Chief of Casework: Greg Gulvas
Committee Assignment: Appropriations

Wagner, Ann, R-Mo. (2)

Capitol Hill Office: 435 CHOB 20515; 225-1621;
Fax: 225-2563; *Chief of Staff:* Christian Morgan
Web: http://wagner.house.gov/
Facebook: http://facebook.com/RepAnnWagner
Twitter: http://twitter.com/@RepAnnWagner
District Offices: 301 Sovereign Court, #201, Ballwin, MO
63011-4442; 636-779-5449; *District Director:* Miriam
Stonebreaker
Committee Assignment: Financial Services

Walberg, Tim, R-Mich. (7)

Capitol Hill Office: 2436 RHOB 20515; 225-6276;
Fax: 225-6281; *Chief of Staff:* R.J. Laukitis

Web: http://walberg.house.gov/
Facebook: http://facebook.com/RepWalberg
Twitter: http://twitter.com/RepWalberg
District Office: 110 1st Street, #2, Jackson, MI 49202-4203;
517-780-9075; Fax: 517-780-9081; *District Director:*
Ryan Boeskool
Committee Assignments: Education and the Workforce;
Oversight and Government Reform

Walden, Greg, R-Ore. (2)

Capitol Hill Office: 2182 RHOB 20515-3702; 225-6730;
Fax: 225-5774; *Chief of Staff:* Brian C. MacDonald
Web: http://walden.house.gov/
Facebook: http://facebook.com/repgregwalden
Twitter: http://twitter.com/repgregwalden
District Offices: 1051 N.W. Bond St., #400, Bend, OR
97701-2061; 541-389-4408; Fax: 541-389-4452;
Director, Central Oregon Office: Nick Strader
1211 Washington Ave., La Grande, OR 97850-2535; 541-
624-2400; Fax: 541-624-6402; *Field Rep.:* Kirby Garrett
14 N. Central Ave., #112, Medford, OR 97501-5912; 541-
776-4646; Fax: 541-779-0204; *Field Rep.:* Riley Bushue
Committee Assignment: Energy and Commerce

Walorski, Jackie, R-Ind. (2)

Capitol Hill Office: 419 CHOB 20515; 225-3915;
Fax: 225-6798; *Chief of Staff:* Brendon DelToro
Web: http://walorski.house.gov/
Facebook: http://facebook.com/RepJackieWalorski
Twitter: http://twitter.com/RepWalorski
District Office: 202 Lincolnway E., #101, Mishawaka, IN
46544; 574-204-2645; Fax: 574-217-8735; *District
Director:* Ben Falkowski
709 Main St., Rochester, IN 46975; 574-780-1330;
Field Rep.: Brian Spaulding
Committee Assignments: Armed Services; Budget;
Veterans' Affairs

Walz, Tim, D-Minn. (1)

Capitol Hill Office: 1034 LHOB 20515; 225-2472;
Fax: 225-3433; *Deputy Chief of Staff Legis. Director:*
Sara Severs
Web: http://walz.house.gov/
Facebook: http://facebook.com/TimWalz4Congress
Twitter: http://twitter.com/Tim_Walz
District Offices: 227 E. Main St., #220, Mankato,
MN 56001-3573; 507-388-2149; *Chief of Staff:* Josh
Syrjamaki
1130 1/2 7th St., N.W., #208, Rochester, MN 55901-1732;
507-206-0643; *District Director:* Marcus Schmit
Committee Assignments: Agriculture; Transportation
and Infrastructure; Veterans' Affairs

Wasserman Schultz, Debbie, D-Fla. (23)

Capitol Hill Office: 118 CHOB 20515-0920; 225-7931;
Fax: 226-2052; *Chief of Staff:* Tracie Pough
Web: http://wassermanschultz.house.gov/
Facebook: http://facebook.com/RepDWS
Twitter: http://twitter.com/DWStweets

District Offices: 19200 W. Country Club Dr., Aventura, FL 33180-2403; 305-936-5724; Fax: 305-932-9664; *Deputy District Director:* Laurie Flink

10100 Pines Blvd., Pembroke Pines, FL 33026-6040; 954-437-3936; Fax: 954-437-4776; *District Director:* Jodi Davidson

Committee Assignment: Appropriations

Waters, Maxine, D-Calif. (43)

Capitol Hill Office: 2221 RHOB 20515-0535; 225-2201; Fax: 225-7854; *Chief of Staff:* Mikael Moore
Web: http://waters.house.gov/
Facebook: http://facebook.com/MaxineWaters
Twitter: http://twitter.com/MaxineWaters
District Office: 10124 S. Broadway, #1, Los Angeles, CA 90003-4535; 323-757-8900; Fax: 323-757-9506; *District Director:* Blanca Jimenez
Committee Assignment: Financial Services, Ranking Minority Member

Waxman, Henry A., D-Calif. (33)

Capitol Hill Office: 2204 RHOB 20515-0530; 225-3976; Fax: 225-4099; *Chief of Staff:* Pat Delgado
Web: http://waxman.house.gov/
Facebook: http://facebook.com/Rep.HenryWaxman
Twitter: http://twitter.com/WaxmanClimate/
District Office: 5055 Wilshire Blvd., #310, Los Angeles, CA 90036; 310-652-3095; Fax: 323-655-0502; *District Director:* Lisa Pinto

1600 Rosebrans Ave., 4th Floor, Manhattan Beach, CA 90266; 310-321-7664; Fax: 323-655-0502; *Field Rep., Caseworker:* Erika Braxton-White

Committee Assignment: Energy and Commerce, Ranking Minority Member

Weber, Randy, R-Tex. (14)

Capitol Hill Office: 510 CHOB 20515; 225-2831; Fax: 225-0271; *Chief of Staff:* Chara McMichael
Web: http://weber.house.gov/
Facebook: http://facebook.com/TXRandy14
Twitter: http://twitter.com/TXRandy14
District Offices: 505 Orleans St., #103, Beaumont, TX 77701; 409-835-0108; Fax: 409-835-0578; *Deputy District Director:* Blake Hopper

122 W. Way, #301, Lake Jackson, TX 77566-5245; 979-285-0231; Fax: 979-285-0271; *District Director:* Dianna Kile

174 Calder Rd., League City, TX 77573; 281-316-0231; Fax: 281-316-0271; *District Director:* Dianna Kile

Committee Assignments: Foreign Affairs; Science, Space, and Technology

Webster, Daniel, R-Fla. (10)

Capitol Hill Office: 1039 LHOB 20515-0908; 225-2176; Fax: 225-0999; *Chief of Staff:* Frank Walker
Web: http://webster.house.gov/
Facebook: http://facebook.com/RepWebster
Twitter: http://twitter.com/RepWebster

District Offices: 685 W. Montrose St., Clermont, FL 34711; 352-383-3552; Fax: 407-654-5814; *Constituent Services Rep.:* Ann Drawdy

122 E. Main St., Tavares, FL 32778-3806; 352-383-3552; Fax: 407-654-5814; *Constituent Services Rep.:* Ann Drawdy

451 3rd St. N.W., Winter Haven, FL 33881; 863-453-0273; Fax: 407-654-5814; *Constituent Services Rep.:* Natali Knight

300 W. Plant St., Winter Garden, FL 34787-3009; 407-654-5705; Fax: 407-654-5814; *Constituent Services Director:* Abigail Tyrrell

Committee Assignments: Rules; Transportation and Infrastructure

Welch, Peter, D-Vt. (At Large)

Capitol Hill Office: 2303 RHOB 20515; 225-4115; Fax: 225-6790; *Chief of Staff:* Bob Rogan
Web: http://welch.house.gov/
Facebook: http://facebook.com/PeterWelch
Twitter: http://twitter.com/PeterWelch
District Office: 128 Lakeside Ave., #235, Burlington, VT 05401; 802-652-2450; Fax: 802-652-2497; *State Director:* Patricia Coates
Committee Assignments: Energy and Commerce; Oversight and Government Reform

Wenstrup, Brad, R-Ohio (2)

Capitol Hill Office: 1223 LHOB 20515; 225-3164; Fax: 225-1992; *Chief of Staff:* Derek Harley
Web: http://wenstrup.house.gov/
Facebook: http://facebook.com/RepBradWenstrup
Twitter: http://twitter.com/@RepBradWenstrup
District Offices: 7954 Beechmont Ave., #200, Cincinnati, OH 45255; 513-474-7777; Fax: 513-605-1377; *District Director:* John Stanton

170 N. Main St., Peebles, OH 45660; 513-605-1380; *Field Rep.:* Annie Wilkerson, Kaci Compton, Jeff Uckotter

4350 Alcholtz Rd., Cincinnati, OH 45255; *Field Rep.:* Annie Wilkerson, Kaci Compton, Jeff Uckotter

Committee Assignments: Armed Services; Veteran's Affairs

Westmoreland, Lynn A., R-Ga. (3)

Capitol Hill Office: 2433 RHOB 20515-1003; 225-5901; Fax: 225-2515; *Chief of Staff:* Brad Bohannon
Web: http://westmoreland.house.gov/
Facebook: http://facebook.com/pages/Congressman-Lynn-Westmoreland/71389451419
Twitter: http://twitter.com/RepWestmoreland
District Office: 1601-B E. Hwy. 34, Newnan, GA 30265-1325; 770-683-2033; Fax: 770-683-2042; *District Director:* Andy Bush
Committee Assignments: Financial Services; Permanent Select Intelligence

Whitfield, Ed, R-Ky. (1)

Capitol Hill Office: 2184 RHOB 20515; 225-3115; Fax: 225-3547; *Chief of Staff:* Cory Hicks
Web: http://whitfield.house.gov/

Facebook: http://facebook.com/RepEdWhitfield
Twitter: http://twitter.com/repedwhitfield
District Offices: 222 1st St., #224, Henderson, KY 42420-3181; 270-826-4180; Fax: 270-826-6783; *Field Rep.:* Ed West

1403 S. Main St., Hopkinsville, KY 42240-2017; 270-885-8079; Fax: 270-885-8598; *District Director:* Michael Pape

100 Fountain Ave., #104, Paducah, KY 42001-2771; 270-442-6901; Fax: 270-442-6805; *Field Rep.:* Janece Everett

200 N. Main St., Suite F, Tompkinsville, KY 42167; 270-487-9509; Fax: 270-487-0019; *Field Rep.:* Sandy Simpson
Committee Assignment: Energy and Commerce

Williams, Roger, R-Tex. (25)

Capitol Hill Office: 1122 LHOB 20515; 225-9896; Fax: 225-9692; *Chief of Staff:* Colby Hale
Web: http://williams.house.gov/
Facebook: http://facebook.com/RepRogerWilliams
Twitter: http://twitter.com/@RepRWilliams
District Offices: 1005 Congress Ave., #925, Austin, TX 78701; 512-473-8910; Fax: 512-473-8946; *District Director:* John Etue

1 Walnut St., #145, Cleburne, TX 76033; 817-774-2575; Fax: 817-774-2576; *District Rep.:* Robert Camacho
Committee Assignments: Budget; Transportation and Infrastructure

Wilson, Frederica, D-Fla. (24)

Capitol Hill Office: 208 CHOB 20515-0917; 225-4506; Fax: 226-0777; *Chief of Staff:* Kim Bowman
Web: http://wilson.house.gov/
Facebook: http://facebook.com/RepWilson
Twitter: http://twitter.com/RepWilson
District Offices: 18425 N.W. 2nd Ave., Miami Gardens, FL 33169-4534; 305-690-5905; Fax: 305-690-5951; *District Chief of Staff:* Alexis Snyder

Pembroke Pine City Hall, 10100 Pines Blvd., Bldg. B, 3rd Floor, Pembroke Pines, FL 33025; 954-450-6767; *District Chief of Staff:* Alexis Snyder

West Park City Hall, 1965 S. State Rd. 7, West Park, FL 33023; 954-989-2688; *District Chief of Staff:* Alexis Snyder
Committee Assignments: Education and the Workforce; Science, Space, and Technology

Wilson, Joe, R-S.C. (2)

Capitol Hill Office: 2229 RHOB 20515-4002; 225-2452; Fax: 225-2455; *Chief of Staff:* Jonathan Day
Web: http://joewilson.house.gov/
Facebook: http://facebook.com/JoeWilson
Twitter: http://twitter.com/CongJoeWilson
District Offices: 828 Richland Ave. West, #300, P.O. Box 104, Aiken, SC 29801; 803-642-6416; 803-642-6418; *Field Rep.:* Ted Felder

1700 Sunset Blvd. (U.S. 378), #1, West Columbia, SC 29169; 803-939-0041; Fax: 803-939-0078; *District Director:* Butch Wallace
Committee Assignments: Armed Services; Education and the Workforce; Foreign Affairs

Wittman, Rob, R-Va. (1)

Capitol Hill Office: 2454 RHOB 20515; 225-4261; Fax: 225-4382; *Chief of Staff:* Jamie Miller
Web: http://wittman.house.gov/
Facebook: http://facebook.com/RepRobWittman
Twitter: http://twitter.com/RobWittman
District Offices: 2777 Jefferson Davis Hwy., #105, Stafford, VA 22554; 540-659-2734, Fax: 540-659-2737; *District Rep.:* Kristin Baroody

508 Church Lane, P.O. Box 3106, Tappahannock, VA 22560; 804-443-0668; Fax: 804-443-0671; *District Rep.:* Chris Jones

401 Main St., P.O. Box 494, Yorktown, VA 23690; 757-874-6687; Fax: 757-874-7164; *District Director:* Joe Schumacher
Committee Assignments: Armed Services; Natural Resources

Wolf, Frank R., R-Va. (10)

Capitol Hill Office: 233 CHOB 20515-4610; 225-5136; Fax: 225-0437; *Chief of Staff Press Secy.:* Daniel F. Scandling
Web: http://wolf.house.gov/
Facebook: http://facebook.com/RepFrankWolf
Twitter: https://twitter.com/RepWOLFPress
District Offices: 13873 Park Center Rd., #130, Herndon, VA 20171-3248; 703-709-5800; Fax: 703-709-5802; *Director of Constituent Services:* Lucy Norment

110 N. Cameron St., Winchester, VA 22601-4730; 540-667-0990; Fax: 540-678-0402; *Director of Constituent Services:* Lucy Norment
Committee Assignment: Appropriations

Womack, Steve, R-Ark. (3)

Capitol Hill Office: 1119 LHOB 20515; 225-4301; Fax: 225-5713; *Chief of Staff:* Beau T. Walker
Web: http://womack.house.gov/
Facebook: http://facebook.com/RepSteveWomack
Twitter: http://twitter.com/rep_stevewomack
District Offices: 423 N. 6th St., Ft. Smith, AR 72902; 479-424-1146; Fax: 479-424-2737; *Field Rep.:* Bob Moody

303 N. Main St., #102, Harrison, AR 72601-3508; 870-741-6900; Fax: 870-741-7741; *Field Rep.:* Teri Garrett

3333 Pinnacle Hills Pkwy., #120, Rogers, AR 72758-9100; 479-464-0446; Fax: 479-464-0063; *District Director:* Bootsie Ackerman
Committee Assignment: Appropriations

Woodall, Rob, R-Ga. (7)

Capitol Hill Office: 1725 LHOB 20515-1007; 225-4272; Fax: 225-4696; *Chief of Staff District Director:* Derick Corbett
Web: http://woodall.house.gov/
Facebook: http://facebook.com/RepRobWoodall
Twitter: http://twitter.com/votewoodall
District Office: 770-232-3005; Fax: 770-232-2909; *Chief of Staff; District Director:* Derick Corbett
Committee Assignments: Budget; Oversight and Government Reform; Rules

Yarmuth, John, D-Ky. (3)

Capitol Hill Office: 403 CHOB 20515-1703; 225-5401; Fax: 225-5776; *Chief of Staff:* Julie Carr
Web: http://yarmuth.house.gov/
Facebook: http://facebook.com/pages/Congressman-John-Yarmuth-KY-3/214258646163
Twitter: http://twitter.com/RepJohnYarmuth
District Offices: Romano L. Mazzoli Federal Bldg., 600 Martin Luther King, Jr. Pl., #216, Louisville, KY 40202; 502-582-5129; Fax: 502-582-5897; *District Director:* Carolyn Whitaker-Tandy
Southwest Government Center, 7219 Dixie Hwy., Louisville, KY 40258-3756; 502-933-5863; Fax: 502-935-6934; *Congressional Aide:* Shelley Spratt
Committee Assignments: Budget; Education and the Workforce

Yoder, Kevin, R-Kans. (3)

Capitol Hill Office: 215 CHOB 20515-1603; 225-2865; Fax: 225-2807; *Chief of Staff Press Secy.:* Travis Smith
Web: http://yoder.house.gov/
Facebook: http://facebook.com/CongressmanKevinYoder
Twitter: http://twitter.com/RepKevinYoder
District Office: 7325 W. 79th St., Overland Park, KS 66204-2908; 913-621-0832; Fax: 913-621-1533; *District Director:* Molly Haase
Committee Assignment: Appropriations

Yoho, Ted, R-Fla. (3)

Capitol Hill Office: 511 CHOB 20515; 225-5744; Fax: 225-3973; *Chief of Staff:* Kat Cammack
Web: http://yoho.house.gov/
Facebook: http://facebook.com/CongressmanTedYoho
Twitter: http://twitter.com/RepTedYoho
District Offices: 5000 N.W. 27th Court, Suite E, Gainesville, FL 32606; 352-505-0838; Fax: 352-505-3511; *Deputy District Director:* Clay Martin
1213 Blanding Blvd., Orange Park, FL 32065; 904-276-9626; Fax: 904-276-9336; *Deputy District Director:* Greg Rawson
Committee Assignments: Agriculture; Foreign Affairs

Young, Don A., R-Alaska (At Large)

Capitol Hill Office: 2314 RHOB 20515-0201; 225-5765; Fax: 225-0425; *Chief of Staff:* Pamela A. Day
Web: http://donyoung.house.gov/
Facebook: http://facebook.com/RepDonYoung
Twitter: http://twitter.com/RepDonYoung
District Offices: 4241 B St., #203, Anchorage, AK 99503-5920; 907-271-5978; Fax: 907-271-5950; *State Director:* Chad Padgett
100 Cushman St., #307, Key Bank Bldg., Fairbanks, AK 99701-4673; 907-456-0210; Fax: 907-456-0279; *State Director:* Chad Padgett
612 W. Willoughby Ave., Suite B, P.O. Box 21247, Juneau, AK 99802-1732; 907-586-7400; Fax: 907-586-8922; *Special Asst.:* Rhonda Boyle
Committee Assignments: Natural Resources; Transportation and Infrastructure

Young, Todd, R-Ind. (9)

Capitol Hill Office: 1007 LHOB 20515; 225-5315; Fax: 226-6866; *Chief of Staff:* John Connell
Web: http://toddyoung.house.gov/
Facebook: http://facebook.com/RepToddYoung
Twitter: http://twitter.com/ToddYoungIN
District Offices: 320 W. 8th St., #114, Bloomington, IN 47404-3700; 812-336-3000; Fax: 812-336-3355; *Office Manager:* Harold Turner
2 N. Madison Ave., Greenwood, IN 46142; 317-661-0696; *Office Manager:* Ben Bauer
279 Quartermaster Court, Jeffersonville, IN 47130-3669; 812-288-3999; Fax: 812-288-3873; *District Director:* Deb Johannes
Committee Assignment: Ways and Means

Vacant-Fla. (19)

Capitol Hill: 1123 LHOB 20515; 225-2536; Fax: 226-0439; *Chief of Staff:* Karen L. Haas (Clerk of the House of Representatives)
District Offices: 804 Nicholas Parkway E., #1, Cape Coral, FL 33990; 239-573-5837; Fax: 239-573-9125;
3299 E. Tamiami Trail, #105, Naples, FL 34112; 239-252-6225

Vacant-N.C. (12)

Capitol Hill: 2304 RHOB 20515-3312; 225-1510; Fax: 225-1512; *Chief of Staff:* Karen L. Haas (Clerk of the House of Representatives)
District Offices: 1230 W. Morehead St., #306, Charlotte, NC 28208-5214; 704-344-9950; Fax: 704-344-9971;
301 S. Greene St., #203, Greensboro, NC 27401-2615; 336-275-9950; Fax: 336-379-9951

Vacant-N.J. (1)

Capitol Hill: 2265 RHOB 20515; 225-6501; *Chief of Staff:* Karen L. Haas (Clerk of the House of Representatives)
District Offices: 515 Grove St., #3C, Haddon Heights, NJ 08035; 856-546-5100

Joint Committees of Congress

The joint committees of Congress follow. Each listing includes room number, office building, zip code, telephone number, Web address(es), key staffers, committee jurisdiction, and membership (in order of seniority) for each committee. Members are drawn from the Senate and House and from both parties. As of March 28, 2014, there is one vacancy.

Senate Democrats, the current majority in that chamber, are shown in roman type; Republicans, in the minority, appear in italic. On the other hand, House Republicans are shown in roman type due to their majority in that chamber; while House Democrats appear in italics. When a senator serves as chair, the vice chair usually is a representative, and vice versa. The location of the chair usually rotates from one chamber to the other at the beginning of each Congress. The area code for all phone and fax numbers is (202). A phone number and/or office number next to either the Majority or Minority Staff Director indicates a change from the full committee's office number and/or phone number. If no numbers are listed, the individual's office number and phone number are the same as for the full committee.

JOINT ECONOMIC COMMITTEE

Office: 433 CHOB 20515-6432
Phone: 224-5171
Web: jec.senate.gov/republicans
Minority Web: jec.senate.gov/republicans
Majority Staff Director: Robert O'Quinn
Minority Staff Director: Niles Godes, 224-5171, G-01 DSOB
Jurisdiction: (1) make a continuing study of matters relating to the Economic Report of the President; (2) study means of coordinating programs in order to further the policy of this Act; and (3) as a guide to the several committees of the Congress dealing with legislation relating to the Economic Report, not later than March 1 of each year (beginning with the year 1947) to file a report with the Senate and the House of Representatives containing its findings and recommendations with respect to each of the main recommendations made by the President in the Economic Report, and from time to time to make other reports and recommendations to the Senate and the House of Representatives as it deems advisable.

Senate Members

Amy Klobuchar, Minn., Vice Chair
Robert P. Casey Jr., Pa.
Mark Pryor, Ark.
Bernie Sanders, Vt. (I)
Chris Murphy, Conn.
Martin Heinrich, N.M.

Dan Coats, Ind.
Mike Lee, Utah
Roger Wicker, Miss.
Pat Toomey, Pa.

House Members

Kevin Brady, Tex., Chair
John Cambell, Calif.
Sean Duffy, Wisc.
Justin Amash, Mich.
Erik Paulsen, Minn.
Richard Hanna, N.Y.

Carolyn B. Maloney, N.Y.
Loretta Sanchez, Calif.
Elijah E. Cummings, Md.
John Delaney, Md.

JOINT COMMITTEE ON THE LIBRARY

Office: 1309 LHOB 20515
Phone: 225-8281   **Fax:** 225-9957
Web: cha.house.gov/jointcommittees/joint-committee-library
Majority Staff Director: Sean Ryan
Minority Staff Director: Jamie Fleet
Jurisdiction: considers proposals concerning the management and expansion of the Library of Congress, the development and maintenance of the United States Botanic Garden, the receipt of gifts for the benefit of the Library, and certain matters relating to placing of statues and other works of art in the United States Capitol.

Senate Members

Charles E. Schumer, N.Y., Vice Chair
Richard J. Durbin, Ill.
Patrick Leahy, Vt.

Pat Roberts, Kans.
Roy Blunt, Mo.

House Members

Gregg Harper, Miss., Chair
Candice Miller, Mich.
Tom Cole, Okla.

Robert Brady, Pa.
Zoe Lofgren, Calif.

JOINT COMMITTEE ON PRINTING

Office: 1309 LHOB 20515
Phone: 225-8281   **Fax:** 225-9957
Web: cha.house.gov/jointcommittees/joint-committee-on-printing
Majority Professional Staff Member: Dominic A. Storelli
Minority Professional Staff Member: Michael L. Harrison, 225-2061, 1307 LHOB
Jurisdiction: oversight of (1) the functions of the Government Printing Office and general printing procedures of the federal government; and (2) compliance by federal entities with Title 44 of the U.S. Code, and the Government Printing and Binding Regulations.

Senate Members

Charles E. Schumer, N.Y., Chair
Tom Udall, N.M.
Mark Warner, Va.

Pat Roberts, Kans.
Saxby Chambliss, Ga.

Senate Members

Gregg Harper, Miss., Vice Chair
Candice Miller, Mich.
Richard Nugent, Fla.

Robert Brady, Pa.
Juan Vargas, Calif.

JOINT COMMITTEE ON TAXATION

Office: 1625 LHOB 20515-6453
Phone: 225-3621   **Fax:** 225-0832
Web: jct.gov
Chief of Staff: Thomas A. Barthold
   Jurisdiction: involved with every aspect of the tax legislative process, including: (1) assisting Congressional tax-writing committees and Members of Congress with development and analysis of legislative proposals; (2) preparing official revenue estimates of all tax legislation considered by the Congress; (3) drafting legislative histories for tax-related bills; (4) investigating various aspects of the Federal tax system.

Senate Members

Vacant, Chair
Jay Rockefeller IV, W. Va.
Ron Wyden, Ore.

Orrin G. Hatch, Utah
Chuck Grassley, Iowa

House Members

Dave Camp, Mich., Vice Chair
Sam Johnson, Tex.
Kevin Brady, Tex.

Sander Levin, Mich.
Charles B. Rangel, N.Y.

COMMISSION ON SECURITY AND COOPERATION IN EUROPE (HELSINKI COMMISSION)

Office: 234 FHOB 20515-6460
Phone: 225-1901   **Fax:** 226-4199
Web: csce.gov
Chief of Staff: Fred Turner
Counsel for International Law: Erika B. Schlager
   Jurisdiction: Established in 1976 to monitor and encourage compliance with the Final Act of the Organization for Security and Cooperation in Europe (OSCE), concluded at Helsinki, Finland on August 1, 1975. The Commission responds to the changing nature of the Helsinki process by: convening public hearings with expert witnesses to discuss issues affecting the OSCE community; organizing official delegations to OSCE states to assess political, economic and human rights developments; providing accurate and relevant information on the OSCE to the Congress and the public; furnishing Congress and the public with reports on the current diplomatic initiatives in the OSCE; participating in training seminars and conferences on human rights and the rule of law for official and non-governmental representatives; bringing the OSCE-related concerns of private citizens and groups to the attention of U.S. Government officials,
the U.S. Congress, and other OSCE participating States; and providing an important base of technical and political analysis for policy-makers at home and abroad.

Senate Members

Benjamin L. Cardin, Md., Chair
Sheldon Whitehouse, R.I.
Tom Udall, N.M.
Jeanne Shaheen, N.H.
Richard Blumenthal, Conn.

Roger Wicker, Miss.
Saxby Chambliss, Ga.
John Boozman, Ark.

House Members

Chris Smith, N.J., Co-Chair
Joe Pitts, Pa.
Robert B. Aderholt, Ala.
Phil Gingrey, Ga.
Michael C. Burgess, Tex.

Alcee L. Hastings, Fla.
Louise M. Slaughter, N.Y.
Mike McIntyre, N.C.
Steve Cohen, Tenn.

CONGRESSIONAL-EXECUTIVE COMMISSION ON CHINA

Office: 243 FHOB 20515-0001
Phone: 226-3766   **Fax:** 226-3804
Web: cecc.gov
CECC Political Prisoner Database: cecc.gov/resources/political-prisoner-database
International Human Rights Materials: cecc.gov/resources/international-human-rights-materials
Staff Director: Lawrence Liu
   Jurisdiction: Monitor China's compliance with international human rights standards, encourage the development of the rule of law in the People's Republic of China, and establish and maintain a list of victims of human rights abuses in China. The Commission's professional staff is made up of U.S. experts on China specializing in religious freedom, labor affairs, Tibet and ethnic minorities, the Internet and free-flow of broadcast and print information, and law and legal reform, including commercial law reform. The Commission submits an annual report to the Congressional leadership and the President. To gather information for the report, the Commission holds formal hearings and informal issues roundtables that bring together academics, activists, government officials, business representatives, and other experts on issues related to the Commission's mandate. Staff members also make frequent trips to China to gather information, meet Chinese officials, scholars, and analysts, and consult about the human rights situation and the development of the rule of law in China with U.S. diplomats and others.

Senate Members

Sherrod Brown, Ohio, Chair
Dianne Feinstein, Calif.
Carl Levin, Mich.
Jeff Merkley, Ore.

House Members

Chris Smith, N.J., Co-Chair
Frank R. Wolf, Va.
Mark Meadows, N.C.
Robert Pittenger, N.C.

Tim Walz, Minn.
Marcy Kaptur, Ohio
Mike Honda, Calif.

Senate Committees

The standing and select committees of the U.S. Senate follow. This information is current as of March 28, 2014. Each listing includes room number, office building, zip code, telephone and fax numbers, Web address, minority Web address if available, key majority and minority staff members, jurisdiction for the full committee, and party ratio. Subcommittees are listed under the full committees. Members are listed in order of seniority on the committee or subcommittee. Many committees and subcommittees may be contacted via Web-based email forms found on their Web sites. A phone number and/or office number next to either the Majority or Minority Staff Director indicates a change from the full committee's office number and/or phone number. If no numbers are listed, the individual's office number and phone number are the same as for the full committee.

Democrats, the current majority, are shown in roman type; Republicans, in the minority, appear in italic. The top name in the italicized list is the Ranking Minority Member. Bernard Sanders, I-Vt., caucuses with Democrats and accrues committee seniority with Democrats; thus, he is counted with the Democrats in the party ratio, although (I) appears after his name. The partisan committees of the Senate are listed on page 821. The area code for all phone and fax numbers is (202).

AGRICULTURE, NUTRITION, AND FORESTRY

Office: 328A SROB 20510-6000
Phone: 224-2035 **Fax:** 228-2125
Web: ag.senate.gov
Minority Web: ag.senate.gov/newsroom/minority-news
Majority Staff Director: Chris Adamo
Minority Staff Director: Bruce Evans, 224-5054
Jurisdiction: (1) agricultural economics and agricultural research; (2) agricultural extension services and agricultural experiment stations; (3) agricultural production, agricultural marketing, and stabilization of prices; (4) agriculture and agricultural commodities; (5) animal industry and animal diseases; (6) crop insurance and soil conservation; (7) farm credit and farm security; (8) food from fresh waters; (9) food stamp programs; (10) forestry and forest reserves and wilderness areas other than those created from the public domain; (11) home economics; (12) human nutrition; (13) inspection of livestock, meat, and agricultural products; (14) pests and pesticides; (15) plant industry, soils, and agricultural engineering; (16) rural development, rural electrification, and watersheds; (17) school nutrition programs. The committee shall also study and review, on a comprehensive basis, matters relating to food, nutrition, and hunger, both in the United States and in foreign countries, and rural affairs.
Party Ratio: D 11-R 9

Debbie Stabenow, Mich., Chair
Patrick Leahy, Vt.
Tom Harkin, Iowa
Sherrod Brown, Ohio
Amy Klobuchar, Minn.
Michael F. Bennet, Colo.
Kirsten Gillibrand, N.Y.
Joe Donnelly, Ind.
Heidi Heitkamp, N.D.
Robert P. Casey Jr., Pa.
John Walsh, Mont.

Thad Cochran, Miss.
Mitch McConnell, Ky.
Pat Roberts, Kans.
Saxby Chambliss, Ga.
John Boozman, Ark.
John Hoeven, N.D.
Mike Johanns, Neb.
Chuck Grassley, Iowa
John Thune, S.D.

Subcommittees

Commodities, Markets, Trade and Risk Management
Office: 328A SROB 20510 **Phone:** 224-2035
Joe Donnelly (Chair), Heidi Heitkamp, Tom Harkin, Sherrod Brown, Kirsten Gillibrand, John Walsh
Saxby Chambliss (Ranking Minority Member), Pat Roberts, John Boozman, John Hoeven, Mike Johanns

Conservation, Forestry and Natural Resources
Office: 328A SROB 20510 **Phone:** 224-2035
Michael F. Bennet (Chair), Tom Harkin, Amy Klobuchar, Patrick Leahy, Heidi Heitkamp, John Walsh
John Boozman (Ranking Minority Member), Mitch McConnell, Saxby Chambliss, John Thune, Pat Roberts

Jobs, Rural Economic Growth and Energy Innovation
Office: 328A SROB 20510 **Phone:** 224-2035
Heidi Heitkamp (Chair), Sherrod Brown, Amy Klobuchar, Michael F. Bennet, Joe Donnelly, Robert P. Casey Jr.
Mike Johanns (Ranking Minority Member), John Hoeven, Charles Grassley, John Thune, John Boozman

Livestock, Dairy, Poultry, Marketing and Agriculture Security
Office: 328A SROB 20510 **Phone:** 224-2035
Kirsten Gillibrand (Chair), Patrick Leahy, Amy Klobuchar, Joe Donnelly, Robert P. Casey Jr., John Walsh
Pat Roberts (Ranking Minority Member), Mitch McConnell, John Boozman, Mike Johanns, Chuck Grassley

Nutrition, Specialty Crops, Food and Agricultural Research
Office: 328A SROB 20510 **Phone:** 224-2035
Robert P. Casey Jr. (Chair), Patrick Leahy, Tom Harkin, Sherrod Brown, Kirsten Gillibrand, Michael F. Bennet
John Hoeven (Ranking Minority Member), Mitch McConnell, Saxby Chambliss, Chuck Grassley, John Thune

APPROPRIATIONS

Office: S-128 CAP 20510-6025
Phone: 224-7363   **Fax:** 224-2100
Web: appropriations.senate.gov
Minority Web: appropriations.senate.gov/republican.cfm
Majority Staff Director: Charles Kieffer
Minority Staff Director: William D. Duhnke, 224-7257, S-146A CAP

Jurisdiction: (1) appropriation of the revenue for the support of the government, except as provided in subparagraph (e); (2) rescission of appropriations contained in appropriation acts (referred to in section 105 of title 1, United States Code); (3) the amount of new spending authority described in section 401 (c) (2) (A) and (B) of the Congressional Budget and Impoundment Control Act of 1974 which is to be effective for a fiscal year; (4) new spending authority described in section 401 (c) (2) (C) of the Congressional Budget and Impoundment Control Act of 1974 provided in bills and resolutions referred to the committee under section 401 (b) (2) of that Act.
Party Ratio: D 16-R 14

Barbara Mikulski, Md., Chair	Richard Shelby, Ala.
Patrick Leahy, Vt.	Thad Cochran, Miss.
Tom Harkin, Iowa	Mitch McConnell, Ky.
Patty Murray, Wash.	Lamar Alexander, Tenn.
Dianne Feinstein, Calif.	Susan Collins, Maine
Richard J. Durbin, Ill.	Lisa Murkowski, Alaska
Tim Johnson, S.D.	Lindsey Graham, S.C.
Mary Landrieu, La.	Mark Kirk, Ill.
Jack Reed, R.I.	Dan Coats, Ind.
Mark Pryor, Ark.	Roy Blunt, Mo.
Jon Tester, Mont.	Jerry Moran, Kans.
Tom Udall, N.M.	John Hoeven, N.D.
Jeanne Shaheen, N.H.	Mike Johanns, Neb.
Jeff Merkley, Ore.	John Boozman, Ark.
Mark Begich, Alaska	
Chris Coons, Del.	

Subcommittees

Agriculture, Rural Development, Food and Drug Administration, and Related Agencies
Office: 129 SDOB 20510   **Phone:** 224-8090
Mark Pryor (Chair), Tom Harkin, Dianne Feinstein, Tim Johnson, John Tester, Tom Udall, Jeff Merkley
Roy Blunt (Ranking Minority Member), Thad Cochran, Mitch McConnell, Susan Collins, Jerry Moran, John Hoeven

Commerce, Justice, Science, and Related Agencies
Office: 142 SDOB 20510   **Phone:** 224-5202
Barbara Mikulski (Chair), Patrick Leahy, Dianne Feinstein, Jack Reed, Mark Pryor, Mary Landrieu, Jeanne Shaheen, Jeff Merkley, Chris Coons
Richard Shelby, Mitch McConnell, Lamar Alexander, Susan Collins, Lisa Murkowski, Lindsey Graham, Mark Kirk, John Boozman

Defense
Office: 122 SDOB 20510   **Phone:** 224-6688
Dick Durbin (Chair), Patrick Leahy, Tom Harkin, Dianne Feinstein, Barbara Mikulski, Patty Murray, Tim Johnson, Jack Reed, Mary Landrieu, Mark Pryor
Thad Cochran (Ranking Minority Member), Mitch McConnell, Richard Shelby, Lamar Alexander, Susan Collins, Lisa Murkowski, Lindsey Graham, Dan Coats, Roy Blunt

Energy and Water Development
Office: 184 SDOB 20510   **Phone:** 224-8119
Dianne Feinstein (Chair), Patty Murray, Tim Johnson, Mary Landrieu, Tom Harkin, Jon Tester, Richard J. Durbin, Tom Udall, Jeanne Shaheen
Lamar Alexander (Ranking Minority Member), Thad Cochran, Mitch McConnell, Richard Shelby, Susan Collins, Lisa Murkowski, Lindsey Graham, John Hoeven

Financial Services and General Government
Office: 133 SDOB 20510   **Phone:** 224-1133
Tom Udall (Chair), Richard J. Durbin, Chris Coons
Mike Johanns (Ranking Minority Member), Jerry Moran

Homeland Security
Office: 135 SDOB 20510   **Phone:** 224-8244
Mary Landrieu (Chair), Patrick Leahy, Patty Murray, Jon Tester, Mark Begich, Chris Coons
Dan Coats (Ranking Minority Member), Thad Cochran, Richard Shelby, Lisa Murkowski, Jerry Moran

Interior, Environment, and Related Agencies
Office: 131 SDOB 20510   **Phone:** 228-0774
Jack Reed (Chair), Dianne Feinstein, Patrick Leahy, Tim Johnson, Jon Tester, Tom Udall, Jeff Merkley, Mark Begich
Lisa Murkowski (Ranking Minority Member), Thad Cochran, Lamar Alexander, Roy Blunt, John Hoeven, Mike Johanns

Labor, Health and Human Services, Education, and Related Agencies
Office: 131 SDOB 20510   **Phone:** 224-9145
Tom Harkin (Chair), Patty Murray, Mary Landrieu, Richard J. Durbin, Jack Reed, Mark Pryor, Barbara Mikulski, Jon Tester, Jeanne Shaheen, Jeff Merkley
Jerry Moran (Ranking Minority Member), Thad Cochran, Richard Shelby, Lamar Alexander, Lindsey Graham, Mark Kirk, Mike Johanns, John Boozman

Legislative Branch
Office: S-128 CAP 20510   **Phone:** 224-7256
Jeanne Shaheen (Chair), Mark Begich, Chris Coons
John Hoeven (Ranking Minority Member), John Boozman

Military Construction, Veterans Affairs, and Related Agencies
Office: 125 SDOB 20510   **Phone:** 224-8224
Tim Johnson (Chair), Patty Murray, Jack Reed, Mark Pryor, Jon Tester, Tom Udall, Mark Begich, Jeff Merkley
Mark Kirk (Ranking Minority Member), Mitch McConnell, Susan Collins, Lisa Murkowski, Dan Coats, John Hoeven, Mike Johanns

State, Foreign Operations, and Related Programs
Office: 127 SDOB 20510   **Phone:** 224-7284

Patrick Leahy (Chair), Tom Harkin, Barbara Mikulski, Richard J. Durbin, Mary Landrieu, Jeanne Shaheen, Mark Begich, Chris Coons
Lindsey Graham (Ranking Minority Member), Mitch McConnell, Mark Kirk, Dan Coats, Roy Blunt, Mike Johanns, John Boozman

Transportation, Housing and Urban Development, and Related Agencies
Office: 142 SDOB 20510   **Phone:** 224-7281

Patty Murray (Chair), Barbara Mikulski, Richard J. Durbin, Patrick Leahy, Tom Harkin, Dianne Feinstein, Tim Johnson, Mark Pryor, Jack Reed, Tom Udall
Susan Collins (Ranking Minority Member), Richard Shelby, Lamar Alexander, Lindsey Graham, Mark Kirk, Dan Coats, Roy Blunt, Jerry Moran, John Boozman

ARMED SERVICES

Office: 228 SROB 20510-6050
Phone: 224-3871 **Fax:** 228-0036
Web: armed-services.senate.gov
Majority Staff Director: Peter Levine
Minority Staff Director: John Bonsell, 224-4928, 228 SROB

Jurisdiction: (1) aeronautical and space activities peculiar to or primarily associated with the development of weapons systems or military operations; (2) common defense; (3) Department of Defense, the Department of the Army, the Department of the Navy, and the Department of the Air Force, generally; (4) maintenance and operation of the Panama Canal, including administration, sanitation, and government of the Canal Zone; (5) military research and development; (6) national security aspects of nuclear energy; (7) naval petroleum reserves, except those in Alaska; (8) pay, promotion, retirement, and other benefits and privileges of members of the armed forces, including overseas education of civilian and military dependents; (9) Selective service system; (10) strategic and critical materials necessary for the common defense. The committee shall also study and review, on a comprehensive basis, matters relating to the common defense policy of the United States.
Party Ratio: D 14-R 12

Carl Levin, Mich., Chair	*James M. Inhofe, Okla.*
Jack Reed, R.I.	*John McCain, Ariz.*
Bill Nelson, Fla.	*Jeff Sessions, Ala.*
Claire McCaskill, Mo.	*Saxby Chambliss, Ga.*
Mark Udall, Colo.	*Roger Wicker, Miss.*
Kay Hagan, N.C.	*Kelly Ayotte, N.H.*
Joe Manchin III, W. Va.	*Deb Fischer, Neb.*
Jeanne Shaheen, N.H.	*Lindsey Graham, S.C.*
Kirsten Gillibrand, N.Y.	*David Vitter, La.*
Richard Blumenthal, Conn.	*Roy Blunt, Mo.*
Joe Donnelly, Ind.	*Mike Lee, Utah*
Mazie K. Hirono, Hawaii	*Ted Cruz, Tex.*
Tim Kaine, Va.	
Angus King, Maine (I)	

Subcommittees

Airland
Office: 228 SROB 20510   **Phone:** 224-3871

Joe Manchin III (Chair), Bill Nelson, Claire McCaskill, Kirsten Gillibrand, Richard Blumenthal, Joe Donnelly
Roger Wicker (Ranking Minority Member), John McCain, Jeff Sessions, Saxby Chambliss, Roy Blunt

Emerging Threats and Capabilities
Office: 228 SROB 20510   **Phone:** 224-3871

Kay Hagan (Chair), Jack Reed, Ben Nelson, Mark Udall, Joe Manchin III, Jeanne Shaheen, Kirsten Gillibrand
Deb Fischer (Ranking Minority Member), John McCain, Roger Wicker, Lindsey Graham, David Vitter, Ted Cruz

Personnel
Office: 228 SROB 20510   **Phone:** 224-3871

Kirsten Gillibrand (Chair), Kay Hagan, Richard Blumenthal, Mazie K. Hirono, Tim Kaine, Angus King
Lindsey Graham (Ranking Minority Member), Saxby Chambliss, Kelly Ayotte, Roy Blunt, Mike Lee

Readiness and Management Support
Office: 228 SROB 20510   **Phone:** 224-3871

Jeanne Shaheen (Chair), Claire McCaskill, Mark Udall, Joe Manchin III, Joe Donnelly, Mazie K. Hirono, Tim Kaine
Kelly Ayotte (Ranking Minority Member), Saxby Chambliss, Deb Fischer, Roy Blunt, Mike Lee, Ted Cruz

Seapower
Office: 228 SROB 20510   **Phone:** 224-3871

Jack Reed (Chair), Bill Nelson, Kay Hagan, Jeanne Shaheen, Richard Blumenthal, Mazie K. Hirono, Tim Kaine, Angus King
John McCain (Ranking Minority Member), Jeff Sessions, Roger Wicker, Kelly Ayotte, Lindsey Graham, David Vitter, Ted Cruz

Strategic Forces
Office: 228 SROB 20510   **Phone:** 224-3871

Mark Udall (Chair), Jack Reed, Claire McCaskill, Joe Donnelly, Angus King
Jeff Sessions (Ranking Minority Member), Deb Fischer, David Vitter, Mike Lee

BANKING, HOUSING, AND URBAN AFFAIRS

Office: 534 SDOB 20510-6075
Phone: 224-7391 **Fax:** 224-5137
Web: banking.senate.gov
Majority Staff Director: Charles Yi
Minority Staff Director: Gregg Richard

Jurisdiction: (1) banks, banking, and financial institutions; (2) financial aid to commerce and industry; (3) deposit insurance; (4) public and private housing (including veterans housing); (5) federal monetary policy (including the Federal Reserve System); (6) money and credit, including currency and coinage; (7) issuance and redemption of notes; (8) Control of prices of commodities, rents and services; (9) financial aid to commerce and industry; (10) urban development and urban mass transit; (11) economic

BANKING, HOUSING, AND URBAN AFFAIRS
(continued)

stabilization and defense production; (12) export controls; (13) export and foreign trade promotion; (14) nursing home construction; (15) renegotiation of government contracts. In addition, the committee is mandated to study and review all matters relating to international economic policy as it affects U.S. monetary affairs, credit, and financial institutions, economic growth, and urban affairs.
Party Ratio: D 12-R 10

Tim Johnson, S.D., Chair	*Mike Crapo, Idaho*
Jack Reed, R.I.	*Richard Shelby, Ala.*
Charles E. Schumer, N.Y.	*Bob Corker, Tenn.*
Robert Menendez, N.J.	*David Vitter, La.*
Sherrod Brown, Ohio	*Mike Johanns, Neb.*
Jon Tester, Mont.	*Pat Toomey, Pa.*
Mark R. Warner, Va.	*Mark Kirk, Ill.*
Jeff Merkley, Ore.	*Jerry Moran, Kans.*
Kay Hagan, N.C.	*Tom Coburn, Okla.*
Joe Manchin III, W. Va.	*Dean Heller, Nev.*
Elizabeth Warren, Mass.	
Heidi Heitkamp, N.D.	

Subcommittees

Economic Policy
Office: 713 SROB 20510   **Phone:** 224-2315
Jeff Merkley (Chair), Jon Tester, Mark R. Warner, Kay Hagan, Joe Manchin III, Heidi Heitkamp, Tim Johnson (ex officio)
Dean Heller (Ranking Minority Member), Tom Coburn, David Vitter, Mike Johanns, Mike Crapo (ex officio)

Financial Institutions and Consumer Protection
Office: 713 SHOB 20510 **Phone:** 224-2315
Sherrod Brown (Chair), Jack Reed, Charles E. Schumer, Robert Menendez, Jon Tester, Jeff Merkley, Kay Hagan, Elizabeth Warren, Tim Johnson (ex officio)
Pat Toomey (Ranking Minority Member), Richard Shelby, David Vitter, Mike Johanns, Jerry Moran, Dean Heller, Bob Corker, Mike Crapo (ex officio)

Housing, Transportation, and Community Development
Office: 528 SHOB 20510   **Phone:** 224-4744
Robert Menendez (Chair), Jack Reed, Charles E. Schumer, Sherrod Brown, Jeff Merkley, Joe Manchin III, Elizabeth Warren, Heidi Heitkamp, Tim Johnson (ex officio)
Jerry Moran (Ranking Minority Member), Bob Corker, Pat Toomey, Mark Kirk, Tom Coburn, Dean Heller, Richard Shelby, Mike Crapo (ex officio)

National Security and International Trade and Finance
Office: 459A SROB 20510   **Phone:** 224-2023
Joe Manchin III (Chair), Sherrod Brown, Mark Warner, Tim Johnson (ex officio)
Mark Kirk (Ranking Minority Member), Jerry Moran, Mike Crapo (ex officio)

Securities, Insurance, and Investment
Office: 728 SHOB 20510   **Phone:** 224-4642
Mark Warner (Chair), Jack Reed, Charles E. Schumer, Robert Menendez, Jon Tester , Kay Hagan, Elizabeth Warren, Heidi Heitkamp, Tim Johnson (ex officio)
Mike Johanns (Ranking Minority Member), Bob Corker, Richard Shelby, David Vitter, Pat Toomey, Mark Kirk, Tom Coburn, Mike Crapo (ex officio)

BUDGET
Office: 624 SDOB 20510-6100
Phone: 224-0642   **Fax:** 228-2007
   Web: budget.senate.gov/democratic
Minority Web: budget.senate.gov/republican
Majority Staff Director: Evan Schatz
Minority Staff Director: Eric Ueland
   Jurisdiction: (1) all concurrent resolutions on the budget (as defined in Section 3 (a) (4) of the Congressional Budget Act of 1974) and all other matters required to be referred to that committee under Titles III and IV of that Act, and messages, petitions, memorials, and other matters relating thereto. (2) The committee shall have the duty (A) to report the matters required to be reported by it under Titles III and IV of the Congressional Budget and Impoundment Control Act of 1974; (B) to make continuing studies of the effect on budget outlays of relevant existing and proposed legislation and to report the results of such studies to the Senate on a recurring basis; (C) to request and evaluate continuing studies of tax expenditures, policies, and programs with direct budget outlays, and to report the results of such studies to the Senate on a recurring basis; and (D) to review, on a continuing basis, the conduct by the Congressional Budget Office of its functions and duties.
Party Ratio: D 12-R 10

Patty Murray, Wash., Chair	*Jeff Sessions, Ala.*
Ron Wyden, Ore.	*Chuck Grassley, Iowa*
Bill Nelson, Fla.	*Mike Enzi, Wyo.*
Debbie Stabenow, Mich.	*Mike Crapo, Idaho*
Bernie Sanders, Vt. (I)	*Lindsey Graham, S.C.*
Sheldon Whitehouse, R.I.	*Rob Portman, Ohio*
Mark R. Warner, Va.	*Pat Toomey, Pa.*
Jeff Merkley, Ore.	*Ron Johnson, Wisc.*
Christopher Coons, Del.	*Kelly Ayotte, N.H.*
Tammy Baldwin, Wisc.	*Roger Wicker, Miss.*
Tim Kaine, Va.	
Angus King, Maine (I)	

COMMERCE, SCIENCE, AND TRANSPORTATION
Office: 254 SDOB 20510-6125
Phone: 224-0411   **Fax:** 228-0303
Web: commerce.senate.gov
Minority Web: commerce.senate.gov/public/index.cfm?p= Minority
Majority Staff Director: Ellen Doneski
Minority Staff Director: David Schwietert, 224-1251, 560 SDOB

Jurisdiction: (1) United States Coast Guard (Homeland Security); (2) coastal zone management; (3) communications; (4) highway safety; (5) inland waterways, except construction; (6) interstate commerce; (7) marine and ocean navigation, marine and ocean safety, and marine and ocean transportation, including navigational aspects of deepwater ports; (8) marine fisheries; (9) United States Merchant Marine and navigation; (10) non-military aeronautical and space sciences; (11) oceans, weather, and atmospheric activities; (12) Panama Canal and interoceanic canals generally, except as provided in subparagraph (c); (13) regulation of consumer products and services, including testing related to toxic substances, other than pesticides, and except for credit, financial services, and housing; (14) regulation of interstate common carriers, including railroads, buses, trucks, vessels, pipelines, and civil aviation; (15) science engineering, and technology research, development, and policy; (16) sports; (17) standards and measurement; (18) transportation; (19) transportation and commerce aspects of Outer Continental Shelf land. The committee shall also study and review, on a comprehensive basis, all matters relating to science and technology, oceans policy, transportation, communications, and consumer affairs.

Party Ratio: D 13-R 11

Jay Rockefeller IV, W. Va., Chair
Barbara Boxer, Calif.
Bill Nelson, Fla.
Maria Cantwell, Wash.
Mark Pryor, Ark.
Claire McCaskill, Mo.
Amy Klobuchar, Minn.
Mark Begich, Alaska
Richard Blumenthal, Conn.
Brian Schatz, Hawaii
Ed Markey, Mass.
Cory Booker, N.J.
John Walsh, Mont.

John Thune, S.D.
Roger Wicker, Miss.
Roy Blunt, Mo.
Marco Rubio, Fla.
Kelly Ayotte, N.H.
Dean Heller, Nev.
Dan Coats, Ind.
Tim Scott, S.C.
Ted Cruz, Tex.
Deb Fischer, Neb.
Ron Johnson, Wisc.

Subcommittees

Aviation Operations, Safety and Security
Office: 427 SHOB 20510   **Phone:** 224-9000
Maria Cantwell (Chair), Barbara Boxer, Bill Nelson, Mark Pryor, Amy Klobuchar, Mark Begich, Brian Schatz, Cory Booker
Kelly Ayotte (Ranking Minority Member), Roger Wicker, Roy Blunt, Marco Rubio, Dean Heller, Tim Scott, Ted Cruz, Deb Fischer, Ron Johnson

Communications, Technology, and the Internet
Office: 428 SHOB 20510   **Phone:** 224-9340
Mark Pryor (Chair), Barbara Boxer, Bill Nelson, Maria Cantwell, Claire McCaskill, Amy Klobuchar, Mark Begich, Richard Blumenthal, Brian Schatz, Ed Markey, Cory Booker
Roger Wicker (Ranking Minority Member), Roy Blunt, Marco Rubio, Kelly Ayotte, Dean Heller, Dan Coats, Tim Scott, Ted Cruz, Deb Fischer, Ron Johnson

Competitiveness, Innovation, and Export Promotion
Office: 428 SHOB 20510   **Phone:** 224-1270
Amy Klobuchar (Chair), Mark Pryor, Mark R. Warner, Mark Begich, Richard Blumenthal, Ed Markey
Tim Scott (Ranking Minority Member), Roy Blunt, Dan Coats, Deb Fischer, Ron Johnson

Tourism, Competitiveness, and Innovation
Office: 428 SHOB 20510   **Phone:** 224-1270
Brian Schatz (Chair), Mark Pryor, Amy Klobuchar, Mark Begich, Ed Markey
Tim Scott (Ranking Minority Member), Roy Blunt, Dan Coats, Deb Fischer, Ron Johnson

Oceans, Atmosphere, Fisheries, and Coast Guard
Office: 425 SHOB 20510   **Phone:** 224-4912
Mark Begich (Chair), Bill Nelson, Maria Cantwell, Richard Blumenthal, Brian Schatz, Ed Markey, Cory Booker
Marco Rubio (Ranking Minority Member), Roger Wicker, Kelly Ayotte, Dan Coats, Tim Scott, Ted Cruz

Science and Space
Office: 427 SHOB 20510   **Phone:** 224-0415
Bill Nelson (Chair), Barbara Boxer, Mark Pryor, Amy Klobuchar, Richard Blumenthal, Ed Markey
Ted Cruz (Ranking Minority Member), Roger Wicker, Marco Rubio, Dean Heller, Dan Coats, Ron Johnson

Surface Transportation and Merchant Marine Infrastructure, Safety, and Security
Office: 427 SHOB 20510   **Phone:** 224-9000
Richard Blumenthal (Chair), Barbara Boxer, Maria Cantwell, Mark Pryor, Claire McCaskill, Amy Klobuchar, Mark Begich, Brian Schatz, Ed Markey, Cory Booker
Roy Blunt (Ranking Minority Member), Roger Wicker, Marco Rubio, Kelly Ayotte, Dean Heller, Dan Coats, Tim Scott, Ted Cruz, Deb Fischer, Ron Johnson

ENERGY AND NATURAL RESOURCES

Office: 304 SDOB 20510-6150
Phone: 224-4971   **Fax:** 224-6163
Web: energy.senate.gov
Majority Staff Director: Elizabeth Leoty Craddock
Minority Staff Director: Karen Billups
Jurisdiction: (1) coal production, distribution, and utilization; (2) energy policy; (3) energy regulation and energy conservation; (4) energy related aspects of deepwater ports; (5) energy research and development; (6) extraction of minerals from oceans and Outer Continental Shelf lands; (7) hydroelectric power, irrigation, and reclamation; (8) mining education and research; (9) mining, mineral lands, mining claims, and mineral conservation; (10) national parks, recreation areas, wilderness areas, wild and scenic rivers, historic sites, military parks and battlefields, and on the public domain, preservation of prehistoric ruins and objects of interest; (11) naval petroleum reserves in Alaska; (12) non-military development of nuclear energy; (13) oil and gas production and distribution; (14) public lands and forests, including farming and grazing thereon, and mineral extraction therefrom; (15) solar energy systems;

ENERGY AND NATURAL RESOURCES
(continued)

(16) territorial possessions of the United States, including trusteeships; international energy affairs and emergency preparedness; nuclear waste policy; privatization of federal assets; Trans-Alaska Pipeline System and other oil or gas pipeline transportation systems within Alaska; Alaska Native Claims Settlement Act of 1971; Alaska National Interest Lands Conservation Act of 1980; Antarctic research and energy development; Arctic research and energy development; Native Hawaiian matters. The Committee shall also study and review, on a comprehensive basis, matters relating to energy and resources development.
Party Ratio: D 12-R 10

Mary L. Landrieu, La., Chair	*Lisa Murkowski, Alaska*
Ron Wyden, Ore.	*John Barrasso, Wyo.*
Tim Johnson, S.D.	*James E. Risch, Idaho*
Maria Cantwell, Wash.	*Mike Lee, Utah*
Bernie Sanders, Vt. (I)	*Dean Heller, Nev.*
Debbie Stabenow, Mich.	*Jeff Flake, Ariz.*
Mark Udall, Colo.	*Tim Scott, S.C.*
Al Franken, Minn.	*Lamar Alexander, Tenn.*
Joe Manchin III, W. Va.	*Rob Portman, Ohio*
Brian Schatz, Hawaii	*John Hoeven, N.D.*
Martin Heinrich, N.M.	
Tammy Baldwin, Wisc.	

Subcommittees

Energy
Office: 304 SDOB 20510   **Phone:** 224-4971
Al Franken (Chair), Tim Johnson, Maria Cantwell, Bernie Sanders, Debbie Stabenow, Mark Udall, Joe Manchin III, Martin Heinrich, Tammy Baldwin, Mary Landrieu (ex officio)
James E. Risch (Ranking Minority Member), Dean Heller, Jeff Flake, Lamar Alexander, Rob Portman, John Hoeven, Lisa Murkowski (ex officio)

National Parks
Office: 304 SDOB 20510   **Phone:** 224-4971
Mark Udall (Chair), Bernie Sanders, Debbie Stabenow, Brian Schatz, Martin Heinrich, Tammy Baldwin, Mary Landrieu (ex officio)
Rob Portman (Ranking Minority Member), John Barrasso, Mike Lee, Lamar Alexander, John Hoeven, Lisa Murkowski (ex officio)

Public Lands, Forests, and Mining
Office: 304 SDOB 20510   **Phone:** 224-4971
Joe Manchin III (Chair), Tim Johnson, Maria Cantwell, Mark Udall, Al Franken, Brian Schatz, Martin Heinrich, Tammy Baldwin, Mary Landrieu (ex officio)
John Barrasso (Ranking Minority Member), James E. Risch, Mike Lee, Dean Heller, Jeff Flake, Tim Scott, Lamar Alexander, John Hoeven, Lisa Murkowski (ex officio)

Water and Power
Office: 304 SDOB 20510   **Phone:** 224-4971

Brian Schatz (Chair), Tim Johnson, Maria Cantwell, Bernie Sanders, Debbie Stabenow, Joe Manchin III, Al Franken, Mary Landrieu (ex officio)
Mike Lee (Ranking Minority Member), John Barrasso, James E. Risch, Dean Heller, Jeff Flake, Tim Scott, Lisa Murkowski (ex officio)

ENVIRONMENT AND PUBLIC WORKS
Office: 410 SDOB 20510-6175
Phone: 224-8832   **Fax:** 224-1273
Web: epw.senate.gov
Minority Web: epw.senate.gov/public/index.cfm?
FuseAction=Minority.WelcomeMessage
Majority Staff Director: Bettina M. Poirier
Minority Staff Director: Zak Baig, 224-6176, 456 SDOB
Jurisdiction: (1) air pollution; (2) construction and maintenance of highways; (3) environmental aspects of Outer Continental Shelf lands; (4) environmental effects of toxic substances, other than pesticides; (5) environmental policy; (6) environmental research and development; (7) fisheries and wildlife; (8) flood control and improvements of rivers and harbors, including environmental aspects of deepwater ports; (9) noise pollution; (10) nonmilitary environmental regulation and control of nuclear energy; (11) ocean dumping; (12) public buildings and improved grounds of the United States generally, including Federal buildings in the District of Columbia; (13) public works, bridges, and dams; (14) regional economic development; (15) solid waste disposal and recycling; (16) water pollution; (17) water resources. The committee shall also study and review, on a comprehensive basis, matters relating to environmental protection and resource utilization and conservation.
Party Ratio: D 10-R 8

Barbara Boxer, Calif., Chair	*David Vitter, La.*
Tom Carper, Del.	*James M. Inhofe, Okla.*
Benjamin L. Cardin, Md.	*John Barrasso, Wyo.*
Bernie Sanders, Vt. (I)	*Jeff Sessions, Ala.*
Sheldon Whitehouse, R.I.	*Mike Crapo, Idaho*
Tom Udall, N.M.	*Roger Wicker, Miss.*
Jeff Merkley, Ore.	*John Boozman, Ark.*
Kirsten Gillibrand, N.Y.	*Deb Fischer, Neb.*
Cory A. Booker, N.J.	
Edward Markey, Mass.	

Subcommittees

Clean Air and Nuclear Safety
Office: 410 SDOB 20510   **Phone:** 224-8832
Sheldon Whitehouse (Chair), Thomas Carper, Benjamin L. Cardin, Bernie Sanders, Tom Udall, Edward Markey
Jeff Sessions (Ranking Minority Member), John Barrasso, Mike Crapo, Roger Wicker, John Boozman

Green Jobs and the New Economy
Office: 410 SDOB 20510   **Phone:** 224-8832
Jeff Merkley (Chair), Tom Carper, Bernie Sanders
Roger Wicker (Ranking Minority Member), Jeff Sessions

Oversight
Office: 410 SDOB 20510   **Phone:** 224-8832
Cory A. Booker (Chair), Sheldon Whitehouse, Edward Markey
James M. Inhofe (Ranking Minority Member), John Boozman

Superfund, Toxics and Environmental Health
Office: 410 SDOB 20510   **Phone:** 224-8832
Tom Udall (Chair), Jeff Merkley, Kirsten Gillibrand, Cory A. Booker, Edward Markey
Mike Crapo (Ranking Minority Member), James M. Inhofe, Roger Wicker, Deb Fischer

Transportation and Infrastructure
Office: 410 SDOB 20510   **Phone:** 224-8832
Tom Carper (Chair), Benjamin L. Cardin, Bernie Sanders, Tom Udall, Kirsten Gillibrand, Cory A. Booker, Edward Markey
John Barrasso (Ranking Minority Member), James M. Inhofe, Jeff Sessions, Mike Crapo, Roger Wicker, Deb Fischer

Water and Wildlife
Office: 410 SDOB 20510   **Phone:** 224-8832
Benjamin L. Cardin (Chair), Tom Carper, Sheldon Whitehouse, Jeff Merkley, Kirsten Gillibrand, Cory A. Booker
John Boozman (Ranking Minority Member), James M. Inhofe, John Barrasso, Jeff Sessions, Deb Fischer

FINANCE

Office: 219 SDOB 20510-6200
Phone: 224-4515 **Fax:** 228-0554
Web: finance.senate.gov
Majority Staff Director: Joshua Sheinkman
Minority Staff Director: Christopher Campbell
Jurisdiction: (1) bonded debt of the United States, except as provided in the Congressional Budget and Impoundment Control Act of 1974; (2) customs, collection districts, and ports of entry and delivery; (3) deposit of public moneys; (4) general revenue sharing; (5) health programs under the Social Security Act and health programs financed by a specific tax or trust fund; (6) national social security; (7) reciprocal trade agreements; (8) revenue measures generally, except as provided in the Congressional Budget and Impoundment Control Act of 1974; (9) revenue measures relating to the insular possessions; (10) tariffs and import quotas, and matters related thereto; (11) transportation of dutiable goods.
Party Ratio: D 13-R 11

Ron Wyden, Ore., Chair	*Orrin G. Hatch, Utah*
Jay Rockefeller IV, W. Va.	*Chuck Grassley, Iowa*
Charles E. Schumer, N.Y.	*Mike Crapo, Idaho*
Debbie Stabenow, Mich.	*Pat Roberts, Kans.*
Maria Cantwell, Wash.	*Mike Enzi, Wyo.*
Bill Nelson, Fla.	*John Cornyn, Tex.*
Robert Menendez, N.J.	*John Thune, S.D.*
Tom Carper, Del.	*Richard Burr, N.C.*
Benjamin L. Cardin, Md.	*Johnny Isakson, Ga.*
Sherrod Brown, Ohio	*Rob Portman, Ohio*
Michael Bennet, Colo.	*Pat Toomey, Penn.*
Robert P. Casey Jr., Penn.	
Mark R. Warner, Va.	

Subcommittees

Energy, Natural Resources, and Infrastructure
Office: 219 SDOB 20510   **Phone:** 224-4515
Debbie Stabenow (Chair), Jay Rockefeller IV, Ron Wyden, Maria Cantwell, Bill Nelson, Tom Carper, Michael F. Bennet,
John Cornyn (Ranking Minority Member), Chuck Grassley, Mike Crapo, Mike Enzi, John Thune, Richard Burr, Johnny Isakson

Fiscal Responsibility and Economic Growth
Office: 219 SDOB 20510   **Phone:** 224-4515
Robert P. Casey Jr. (Chair), Sherrod Brown,
Rob Portman (Ranking Minority Member), Richard Burr

Health Care
Office: 219 SDOB 20510   **Phone:** 224-4515
Jay Rockefeller IV (Chair), Debbie Stabenow, Maria Cantwell, Bill Nelson, Robert Menendez, Tom Carper, Benjamin L. Cardin, Robert P. Casey Jr.
Pat Roberts (Ranking Minority Member), Orrin G. Hatch, Chuck Grassley, Mike Enzi, John Cornyn, Richard Burr, Pat Toomey

International Trade, Customs, and Global Competitiveness
Office: 219 SDOB 20510   **Phone:** 224-4515
Ron Wyden (Chair), Jay Rockefeller IV, Charles E. Schumer, Debbie Stabenow, Maria Cantwell, Robert Menendez, Sherrod Brown, Michael F. Bennet
Johnny Isakson (Ranking Minority Member), Orrin G. Hatch, Chuck Grassley, Pat Robert, John Thune, Rob Portman

Social Security, Pensions, and Family Policy
Office: 219 SDOB 20510   **Phone:** 224-4515
Sherrod Brown (Chair), Jay Rockefeller IV, Charles E. Schumer, Bill Nelson, Benjamin L. Cardin
Pat Toomey (Ranking Minority Member), Mike Crapo, Johnny Isakson, Rob Portman

Taxation and IRS Oversight
Office: 219 SDOB 20510   **Phone:** 224-4515
Michael F. Bennet (Chair), Ron Wyden, Charles E. Schumer, Robert Menendez, Tom Carper, Benjamin L. Cardin, Robert P. Casey Jr.
Mike Enzi (Ranking Minority Member), Orrin G. Hatch, Mike Crapo, Pat Roberts, John Cornyn, John Thune, Pat Toomey

FOREIGN RELATIONS

Office: 444 SDOB 20510-6225
Phone: 224-4651 **Fax:** 228-3612
Web: foreign.senate.gov
Minority Web: foreign.senate.gov/press/ranking

FOREIGN RELATIONS (continued)

Acting Majority Staff Director: Daniel O'Brien
Minority Staff Director: Lester Munster, 224-6797, 446 SDOB

Jurisdiction: (1) acquisition of land and buildings for embassies and legations in foreign countries; (2) boundaries of the United States; (3) diplomatic service; (4) foreign economic, military, technical, and humanitarian assistance; (5) foreign loans; (6) international activities of the American National Red Cross, and the International Committee of the Red Cross; (7) international aspects of nuclear energy, including nuclear transfer policy; (8) international conferences and congresses; (9) international law as it relates to foreign policy; (10) International Monetary Fund and other international organizations established primarily for international monetary purposes (except that, at the request of the Committee on Banking, Housing, and Urban Affairs, any proposed legislation relating to such subjects reported by the Committee on Foreign Relations shall be referred to the Committee on Banking, Housing, and Urban Affairs); (11) intervention abroad and declarations of war; (12) measures to foster commercial intercourse with foreign nations and to safeguard United States business interests abroad; (13) national security and international aspects of trusteeships of the United States; (14) oceans and international environmental and scientific affairs as they relate to foreign policy; (15) protection of United States citizens abroad and expatriation; (16) relations of the United States with foreign nations generally; (17) treaties, conventions, and international agreements, and executive agreements, except reciprocal trade agreements; (18) the United Nations and its affiliated organizations; (19) World Bank group, the regional development banks, and other international organizations established primarily for development assistance purposes. The committee shall also study and review, on a comprehensive basis, matters relating to national security policy, foreign policy, and international economic policy as they relate to the foreign policy of the United States, and matters relating to food, hunger and nutrition in foreign countries.
Party Ratio: D 10-R 8

Robert Menendez, N.J., Chair / Bob Corker, Tenn.
Barbara Boxer, Calif. / James E. Risch, Idaho
Benjamin L. Cardin, Md. / Marco Rubio, Fla.
Jeanne Shaheen, N.H. / Ron Johnson, Wisc.
Christopher Coons, Del. / Jeff Flake, Ariz.
Richard J. Durbin, Ill. / John McCain, Ariz.
Tom Udall, N.M. / John Barrasso, Wyo.
Chris Murphy, Conn. / Rand Paul, Ky.
Tim Kaine, Va.
Ed Markey, Mass.

Subcommittees

African Affairs
Office: 444 SDOB 20510 **Phone:** 224-4651
Christopher Coons (Chair), Richard J. Durbin, Benjamin L. Cardin, Jeanne Shaheen, Tom Udall
Jeff Flake (Ranking Minority Member), John McCain, John Barrasso, Rand Paul

East Asian and Pacific Affairs
Office: 444 SDOB 20510 **Phone:** 224-4651
Benjamin L. Cardin (Chair), Christopher Murphy, Barbara Boxer, Tom Udall, Ed Markey
Marco Rubio (Ranking Minority Member), Ron Johnson, Jeff Flake, John McCain

European Affairs
Office: 444 SDOB 20510 **Phone:** 224-4651
Chris Murphy (Chair), Jeanne Shaheen, Ed Markey, Benjamin L. Cardin, Richard J. Durbin
Ron Johnson (Ranking Minority Member), James E. Risch, Jeff Flake, John Barrasso

International Development and Foreign Assistance, Economic Affairs, International Environmental Protection, and Peace Corps
Office: 444 SDOB 20510 **Phone:** 224-4651
Ed Markey (Chair), Tom Udall, Christopher Coons, Chris Murphy, Tim Kaine
John Barrasso (Ranking Minority Member), James E. Risch, Jeff Flake, Rand Paul

International Operations and Organizations, Human Rights, Democracy, and Global Women's Issues
Office: 444 SDOB 20510 **Phone:** 224-4651
Barbara Boxer (Chair), Jeanne Shaheen, Richard J. Durbin, Christopher Coons, Tim Kaine
Rand Paul (Ranking Minority Member), James E. Risch, Marco Rubio, Ron Johnson

Near Eastern and South and Central Asian Affairs
Office: 444 SDOB 20510 **Phone:** 224-4651
Tim Kaine (Chair), Barbara Boxer, Benjamin L. Cardin, Christopher Coons, Richard J. Durbin
James E. Risch (Ranking Minority Member), Marco Rubio, Ron Johnson, John McCain

Western Hemisphere and Global Narcotics Affairs
Office: 444 SDOB 20510 **Phone:** 224-4651
Tom Udall (Chair), Tim Kaine, Barbara Boxer, Jeanne Shaheen, Chris Murphy,
John McCain (Ranking Minority Member), Marco Rubio, John Barrasso, Rand Paul

HEALTH, EDUCATION, LABOR, AND PENSIONS

Office: 428 SDOB 20510-6300
Phone: 224-5375 **Fax:** 228-5044
Web: help.senate.gov
Majority Staff Director: Derek Miller
Minority Staff Director: David Cleary, 224-6770, 833 SHOB

Jurisdiction: (1) measures relating to education, labor, health, and public welfare; (2) aging; (3) agricultural colleges; (4) arts and humanities; (5) biomedical research and development, including cloning and stem cell research; (6) child labor; (7) convict labor and the entry of goods made by convicts into interstate commerce; (8) domestic activities of the American National Red Cross; (9) equal employment opportunity; (10) Gallaudet University (Washington, D.C.), Howard University (Washington, D.C.), and St.

Elizabeth's Hospital (Washington, D.C.); (11) individuals with disabilities; (12) labor standards and labor statistics; (13) mediation and arbitration of labor disputes; (14) occupational safety and health, including the welfare of miners; (15) private pension plans; (16) public health; (17) railway labor and railway retirement; (18) regulation of foreign laborers; (19) student loans; (20) wages and hours of labor. The committee shall also study and review, on a comprehensive basis, matters relating to health, education, and training, and public welfare.

Party Ratio: D 12-R 10

Tom Harkin, Iowa, Chair	*Lamar Alexander, Tenn.*
Barbara Mikulski, Md.	*Mike Enzi, Wyo.*
Patty Murray, Wash.	*Richard Burr, N.C.*
Bernie Sanders, Vt. (I)	*Johnny Isakson, Ga.*
Robert P. Casey Jr., Pa.	*Rand Paul, Ky.*
Kay Hagan, N.C.	*Orrin G. Hatch, Utah*
Al Franken, Minn.	*Pat Roberts, Kans.*
Michael F. Bennet, Colo.	*Lisa Murkowski, Alaska*
Sheldon Whitehouse, R.I.	*Mark Kirk, Ill.*
Tammy Baldwin, Wisc.	*Tim Scott, S.C.*
Chris Murphy, Conn.	
Elizabeth Warren, Mass.	

Subcommittees

Children and Families
Office: 428 SDOB 20510   **Phone:** 224-9243

Kay Hagan (Chair), Barbara Mikulski, Patty Murray, Bernie Sanders, Robert P. Casey Jr., Al Franken, Michael F. Bennet, Chris Murphy, Elizabeth Warren, Tom Harkin (ex officio)

Mike Enzi (Ranking Minority Member), Mark Kirk, Richard Burr, Johnny Isakson, Rand Paul, Orrin G. Hatch, Pat Roberts, Lamar Alexander (ex officio)

Employment and Workplace Safety
Office: 113 SHOB 20510   **Phone:** 228-1455

Robert P. Casey Jr. (Chair), Patty Murray, Al Franken, Michael F. Bennet, Sheldon Whitehouse, Tammy Baldwin, Tom Harkin (ex officio)

Johnny Isakson (Ranking Minority Member), Rand Paul, Orrin G. Hatch, Tim Scott, Lamar Alexander (ex officio)

Primary Health and Aging
Office: 648 SDOB 20510   **Phone:** 224-5480

Bernie Sanders (Chair), Barbara Mikulski, Kay Hagan, Sheldon Whitehouse, Tammy Baldwin, Chris Murphy, Elizabeth Warren, Tom Harkin (ex officio)

Richard Burr (Ranking Minority Member), Pat Roberts, Lisa Murkowski, Mike Enzi, Mark Kirk, Lamar Alexander (ex officio)

HOMELAND SECURITY AND GOVERNMENTAL AFFAIRS

Office: 340 SDOB 20510-6250
Phone: 224-2627 **Fax:** 228-3792
Web: hsgac.senate.gov
Minority Web: hsgac.senate.gov/media/minority-media
Majority Staff Director: Richard Kessler

Minority Staff Director: Keith Ashdown, 224-4751, 344 SDOB

Jurisdiction: (1) Department of Homeland Security, except matters relating to: the Coast Guard, the Transportation Security Administration, the Federal Law Enforcement Training Center, or the Secret Service; and the United States Citizenship and Immigration Service; or the immigration functions of the United States Customs and Border Protection or the United States Immigration and Custom Enforcement or the Directorate of Border and Transportation Security; and the following functions performed by any employee of the Department of Homeland Security: any customs revenue function, including any function provided for in Section 415 of the Homeland Security Act of 2002; any commercial function or commercial operation of the Bureau of Customs and Border Protection or Bureau of Immigration and Customs Enforcement, including matters relating to trade facilitation and trade regulation; or any other function related to the above items that was exercised by the United States Customs Service on the day before the effective date of the Homeland Security Act of 2002; (2) archives of the United States; (3) budget and accounting measures, other than appropriations, except as provided in the Congressional Budget and Impoundment Control Act of 1974; (4) census and collection of statistics, including economic and social statistics; (5) congressional organization, except for any part of the matter that amends the rules or orders of the Senate; (6) federal civil service; (7) government information; (8) intergovernmental relations; (9) municipal affairs of the District of Columbia, except appropriations therefore; (10) organization and management of United States nuclear export policy; (11) organization and reorganization of the executive branch of the Government; (12) United States Postal Service; (13) status of officers and employees of the United States, including their classification, compensation, and benefits. The committee shall have the duty of (A) receiving and examining reports of the Comptroller General of the United States and of submitting such recommendations to the Senate as it deems necessary or desirable in connection with the subject matter of such reports; (B) studying the efficiency, economy, and effectiveness of all agencies and departments of the Government; (C) evaluating laws enacted to effect the reorganization of the legislative and executive branches of the Government; and (D) studying the intergovernmental relationships between the United States and the states and municipalities, and between the United States and international organizations of which the United States is a member.

Party Ratio: D 9-R 7

Tom Carper, Del., Chair	*Tom Coburn, Okla.*
Carl Levin, Mich.	*John McCain, Ariz.*
Mark Pryor, Ark.	*Ron Johnson, Wisc.*
Mary Landrieu, La.	*Rob Portman, Ohio*
Claire McCaskill, Mo.	*Rand Paul, Ky.*
Jon Tester, Mont.	*Mike Enzi, Wyo.*
Mark Begich, Alaska	*Kelly Ayotte, N.H.*
Tammy Baldwin, Wisc.	
Heidi Heitkamp, N.D.	

HOMELAND SECURITY AND GOVERNMENTAL AFFAIRS (continued)

Subcommittees

Efficiency and Effectiveness of Federal Programs and the Federal Workforce
Office: 601 SHOB 20510   **Phone:** 224-4551
Jon Tester (Chair), Mark Pryor, Claire McCaskill, Mark Begich, Tammy Baldwin, Heidi Heitkamp, Tom Carper
Rob Portman (Ranking Minority Member), Ron Johnson, Rand Paul, Mike Enzi, Tom Coburn

Emergency Management, Intergovernmental Relations, and the District of Columbia
Office: 601 SHOB 20510   **Phone:** 224-4462
Mark Begich (Chair), Carl Levin, Mark Pryor, Mary Landrieu, Jon Tester, Heidi Heitkamp, Tom Carper
Rand Paul (Ranking Minority Member), John McCain, Rob Portman, Mike Enzi, Tom Coburn

Permanent Investigations
Office: 601 SHOB 20510   **Phone:** 224-4462
Carl Levin (Chair), Mark Pryor, Mary Landrieu, Claire McCaskill, Jon Tester, Tammy Baldwin, Heidi Heitkamp, Tom Carper
John McCain (Ranking Minority Member), Ron Johnson, Rob Portman, Rand Paul, Kelly Ayotte, Tom Coburn

Financial and Contracting Oversight
Office: 432 SROB 20510   **Phone:** 224-7155
Claire McCaskill (Chair), Carl Levin, Mark Pryor, Mary Landrieu, Mark Begich, Tammy Baldwin, Tom Carper
Ron Johnson (Ranking Minority Member), John McCain, Mike Enzi, Kelly Ayotte, Tom Coburn

INDIAN AFFAIRS

Office: 838 SHOB 20510-6450
Phone: 224-2251 **Fax:** 228-2589
Web: indian.senate.gov
Majority Staff Director: Mary Pavel
Minority Deputy Chief Counsel: Rhonda Harjo
Jurisdiction: (1) all proposed legislation, messages, petitions, memorials, and other matters relating to Indian affairs shall be referred to the committee; (2) study any and all matters pertaining to problems and opportunities of Indians, including but not limited to, Indian land management and trust responsibilities, Indian education, Indian health, special services, and Indian loan programs, the National Indian Gaming Regulatory Act of 1988, the National Indian Gaming Commission, and Indian claims against the United States.
Party Ratio: D 8-R 6

Jon Tester, Mont., Chair	*John Barrasso, Wyo.*
Maria Cantwell, Wash.	*John McCain, Ariz.*
Tim Johnson, S.D.	*Lisa Murkowski, Alaska*
Tom Udall, N.M.	*John Hoeven, N.D.*
Al Franken, Minn.	*Mike Crapo, Idaho*
Mark Begich, Alaska	*Deb Fischer, Neb.*

Brian Schatz, Hawaii
Heidi Heitkamp, N.D.

JUDICIARY

Office: 224 SDOB 20510-6275
Phone: 224-7703 **Fax:** 224-9516
Web: judiciary.senate.gov
Majority Staff Director: Christine Lucius
Minority Staff Director: Kolan L. Davis, 224-5225, 152 SDOB
Jurisdiction: (1) apportionment of Representatives; (2) bankruptcy, mutiny, espionage, and counterfeiting; (3) civil liberties; (4) constitutional amendments; (5) federal courts and federal judges; (6) government information; (7) holidays and celebrations; (8) immigration and naturalization; (9) interstate compacts generally; (10) judicial proceedings, civil and criminal, generally; (11) local courts in United States territories and possessions; (12) measures relating to claims against the United States; (13) national penitentiaries; (14) United States Patent and Trademark Office (Commerce); (15) patents, copyrights, and trademarks; (16) protection of trade and commerce against unlawful restraints and monopolies; (17) revision and codification of the statutes of the United States; (18) state and territorial boundary lines.
Party Ratio: D 10-R 8

Patrick Leahy, Vt., Chair	*Chuck Grassley, Iowa*
Dianne Feinstein, Calif.	*Orrin G. Hatch, Utah*
Charles E. Schumer, N.Y.	*Jeff Sessions, Ala.*
Richard J. Durbin, Ill.	*Lindsey Graham, S.C.*
Sheldon Whitehouse, R.I.	*John Cornyn, Tex.*
Amy Klobuchar, Minn.	*Mike Lee, Utah*
Al Franken, Minn.	*Ted Cruz, Tex.*
Christopher Coons, Del.	*Jeff Flake, Ariz.*
Richard Blumenthal, Conn.	
Mazie Hirono, Hawaii	

Subcommittees

Antitrust, Competition Policy and Consumer Rights
Office: 224 SDOB 20510   **Phone:** 224-7703
Amy Klobuchar (Chair), Charles E. Schumer, Al Franken, Christopher Coons, Richard Blumenthal
Mike Lee (Ranking Minority Member), Lindsey Graham, Chuck Grassley, Jeff Flake

Bankruptcy and the Courts
Office: 224 SDOB 20510   **Phone:** 224-7703
Christopher Coons (Chair), Richard J. Durbin, Sheldon Whitehouse, Amy Klobuchar, Al Franken
Jeff Sessions (Ranking Minority Member), Chuck Grassley, Jeff Flake, Ted Cruz

The Constitution, Civil Rights and Human Rights
Office: 224 SDOB 20510   **Phone:** 224-1158
Richard J. Durbin (Chair), Al Franken, Christopher Coons, Richard Blumenthal, Mazie Hirono
Ted Cruz (Ranking Minority Member), Lindsey Graham, John Cornyn, Orrin G. Hatch

Crime and Terrorism
Office: 224 SDOB 20510   **Phone:** 228-3740
Sheldon Whitehouse (Chair), Dianne Feinstein, Charles E. Schumer, Richard J. Durbin, Amy Klobuchar
Lindsey Graham (Ranking Minority Member), Ted Cruz, Jeff Sessions, Mike Lee

Immigration, Refugees and Border Security
Office: 224 SDOB 20510   **Phone:** 224-6498
Charles E. Schumer (Chair), Patrick Leahy, Dianne Feinstein, Richard J. Durbin, Amy Klobuchar, Richard Blumenthal, Mazie Hirono
John Cornyn (Ranking Minority Member), Chuck Grassley, Orrin G. Hatch, Jeff Sessions, Jeff Flake, Ted Cruz

Oversight, Federal Rights, and Agency Actions
Office: 224 SDOB 20510   **Phone:** 224-7703
Richard Blumenthal (Chair), Patrick Leahy, Amy Klobuchar
Orrin G. Hatch (Ranking Minority Member), Jeff Flake

Privacy, Technology and the Law
Office: 224 SDOB 20510   **Phone:** 228-3177
Al Franken (Chair), Dianne Feinstein, Charles E. Schumer, Sheldon Whitehouse, Christopher Coons, Mazie Hirono
Jeff Flake (Ranking Minority Member), Orrin G. Hatch, Mike Lee, John Cornyn, Lindsey Graham

RULES AND ADMINISTRATION

Office: 305 SROB 20510-6325
Phone: 224-6352 **Fax:** 224-1912
Web: rules.senate.gov
Majority Staff Director: Jean Bordewich
Minority Staff Director: Mary Suit Jones, 224-6352, 479 SROB
Jurisdiction: (1) administration of the Senate office buildings and the Senate wing of the United States Capitol, including the assignment of office space for Senators and Senate Committees; (2) Senate organization relative to rules and procedures, and Senate rules and regulations, including Senate floor rules and Senate gallery rules; (3) corrupt practices; (4) credentials and qualifications of Members of the Senate, contested elections, and acceptance of incompatible offices; (5) federal elections generally, including the election of the President, Vice President, and Members of the Senate; (6) Government Printing Office, and the printing and correction of the Congressional Record, as well as those matters provided for under Rule XI; (7) meetings of the Congress and attendance of Members; (8) payment of money out of the contingent fund of the Senate or creating a charge upon the same (except that any resolution relating to substantive matter within the jurisdiction of any other standing committee of the Senate shall be first referred to such committee); (9) Presidential Succession Act of 1947; (10) purchase of books and manuscripts and erection of monuments to the memory of individuals; (11) Senate Library and statuary, art, and pictures in the United States Capitol and Senate office buildings; (12) services to the Senate, including the Senate restaurant; (13) United States

Capitol and Senate office buildings, the Library of Congress, the Smithsonian Institution (and the incorporation of similar institutions), and the United States Botanic Garden. The committee shall also (A) make a continuing study of the organization and operation of the Congress of the United States and shall recommend improvements in such organization and operation with a view toward strengthening the Congress, simplifying its operations, improving its relationships with other branches of the United States Government, and enabling it better to meet its responsibilities under the Constitution of the United States; (B) identify any court proceeding or action which, in the opinion of the Committee, is of vital interest to the Congress as a constitutionally established institution of the Federal Government and call such proceeding or action to the attention of the Senate; (C) develop, implement, and update as necessary a strategic planning process and a strategic plan for the functional and technical infrastructure support of the Senate and provide oversight over plans developed by Senate officers and others in accordance with the strategic planning process.
Party Ratio: D 10-R 8

Charles E. Schumer, N.Y., Chair	*Pat Roberts, Kans.*
Dianne Feinstein, Calif.	*Mitch McConnell, Ky.*
Richard J. Durbin, Ill.	*Thad Cochran, Miss.*
Mark Pryor, Ark.	*Saxby Chambliss, Ga.*
Tom Udall, N.M.	*Lamar Alexander, Tenn.*
Mark R. Warner, Va.	*Richard Shelby, Ala.*
Patrick Leahy, Vt.	*Roy Blunt, Mo.*
Amy Klobuchar, Minn.	*Ted Cruz, Tex.*
Angus King, Maine	
John Walsh, Mont.	

SMALL BUSINESS AND ENTREPRENEURSHIP

Office: 428A SROB 20510-6350
Phone: 224-5175 **Fax:** 224-5619
Web: sbc.senate.gov
Minority Web: sbc.senate.gov/republican
Majority Staff Director: Jane Campbell
Minority Staff Director: Skiffington Holderness
Jurisdiction: (1) all proposed legislation, messages, petitions, memorials and other matters relating to the Small Business Administration; (2) any proposed legislation reported by such committee which relates to matters other than the functions of the Small Business Administration shall, at the request of the chair of any standing committee having jurisdiction over the subject matter extraneous to the functions of the Small Business Administration, be considered and reported by such standing committee prior to its consideration by the Senate; and likewise measures reported by other committees directly relating to the Small Business Administration shall, at the request of the chair of the Committee on Small Business and Entrepreneurship, be referred to the Committee on Small Business and Entrepreneurship for its consideration of any portions of the measure dealing with the Small Business Administration, and be reported by this Committee prior to its consideration by the Senate; (3) study and survey by means of

SMALL BUSINESS AND ENTREPRENEURSHIP

(continued)

research and investigation all problems of small business enterprises.

Party Ratio: D 10-R 8

Maria Cantwell, Wash., Chair	*James E. Risch, Idaho*
Carl Levin, Mich.	*David Vitter, La.*
Mary Landrieu, La.	*Marco Rubio, Fla.*
Mark Pryor, Ark.	*Rand Paul, Ky.*
Benjamin L. Cardin, Md.	*Tim Scott, S.C.*
Jeanne Shaheen, N.H.	*Deb Fischer, Neb.*
Kay Hagan, N.C.	*Mike Enzi, Wyo.*
Heidi Heitkamp, N.D.	*Ron Johnson, Wisc.*
Edward Markey, Mass.	
Cory A. Booker, N.J.	

VETERANS' AFFAIRS

Office: 412 SROB 20510-6375
Phone: 224-9126 **Fax:** 224-9575
Web: veterans.senate.gov
Minority Web: veterans.senate.gov/newsroom/minority-news
Majority Staff Director: Steve Robertson
Minority Staff Director: Marie Guadalupe Wissel, 224-2074, 825A SHOB
   Jurisdiction: (1) compensation of veterans; (2) life insurance issued by the government on account of service in the Armed Forces; (3) national cemeteries; (4) pensions of all the wars of the United States; (5) readjustment of service personnel to civil life; (6) soldiers' and sailors' civil relief, including oversight of and appropriate modifications to the Soldiers' and Sailors' Civil Relief Act of 1940; (7) veterans' hospitals, medical care and treatment of veterans; (8) veterans' measures generally; (9) vocational rehabilitation and education of veterans.
Party Ratio: D 8-R 6

Bernie Sanders, Vt. (I), Chair	*Richard Burr, N.C.*
	Johnny Isakson, Ga.
Jay Rockefeller IV, W. Va.	*Mike Johanns, Neb.*
Patty Murray, Wash.	*Jerry Moran, Kans.*
Sherrod Brown, Ohio	*John Boozman, Ark.*
Jon Tester, Mont.	*Dean Heller, Nev.*
Mark Begich, Alaska	
Richard Blumenthal, Conn.	
Mazie Hirono, Hawaii	

SELECT ETHICS

Office: 220 SHOB 20510-6425
Phone: 224-2981 **Fax:** 224-7416
Web: ethics.senate.gov
Staff Director: John C. Sassaman
Deputy Staff Director: Annette Gillis
   Jurisdiction: (1) receive complaints and investigate allegations of improper conduct which may reflect upon the Senate, violations of law, violations of the Senate Code of Official Conduct, and violations of rules and regulations of the Senate, relating to the conduct of individuals in the performance of their duties as Members of the Senate, or as officers or employees of the Senate, and to make appropriate findings of fact and conclusions with respect thereto; (2) recommend, when appropriate, disciplinary action against Members and staff; (3) recommend rules or regulations necessary to insure appropriate Senate standards of conduct; (4) report violations of any law to the proper Federal and State authorities; (5) regulate the use of the franking privilege in the Senate; (6) investigate unauthorized disclosures of intelligence information; (7) implement the Senate public financial disclosure requirements of the Ethics in Government Act of 1978; (8) regulate the receipt and disposition of gifts from foreign governments received by Members, officers, and employees of the Senate; and (9) render advisory opinions on the application of Senate rules and laws to Members, officers, and employees.
Party Ratio: D 3-R 3

Barbara Boxer, Calif., Chair	*Johnny Isakson, Ga.*
Mark Pryor, Ark.	*Pat Roberts, Kans.*
Sherrod Brown, Ohio	*James E. Risch, Idaho*

SELECT INTELLIGENCE

Office: 211 SHOB 20510-6475
Phone: 224-1700 **Fax:** 224-1772
Web: intelligence.senate.gov
Majority Staff Director: David Grannis
Minority Staff Director: Martha Scott Poindexter
   Jurisdiction: (1) oversee and make continuing studies of the intelligence activities and programs of the United States Government, including, but not limited to, the Central Intelligence Agency Act of 1949, Classified Information Procedures Act of 1980, classified national security information, foreign intelligence electronic surveillance, Foreign Intelligence Surveillance Act of 1978, National Security Act of 1947, National Security Agency Act of 1959, national security information, President's Foreign Intelligence Advisory Board (Executive Office of the President), Provide Appropriate Tools Required to Intercept and Obstruct Terrorism (PATRIOT) Act of 2001, security requirements for government employment; (2) submit to the Senate appropriate proposals for legislation; (3) report to the Senate concerning such intelligence activities and programs.
Party Ratio: D 8-R 7

Dianne Feinstein, Calif., Chair	*Saxby Chambliss, Ga.*
	Richard Burr, N.C.
Jay Rockefeller IV, W. Va.	*James E. Risch, Idaho*
Ron Wyden, Ore.	*Dan Coats, Ind.*
Barbara Mikulski, Md.	*Marco Rubio, Via.*
Mark Udall, Colo.	*Susan Collins, Maine*
Mark R Warner, Va.	*Tom Coburn, Okla.*
Martin Heinrich, N.M.	
Angus King, Maine.	

   Note: Party ratio does not include ex. officio members: Harry Reid, D-Nev.; Sen. Mitch McConnell, R-Ky.; Carl Levin, D-Mich.; and James Inhofe, R-Okla.

SPECIAL AGING

Office: G-31 SDOB 20510-6400
Phone: 224-5364 **Fax:** 224-9926
Web: aging.senate.gov/
Majority Staff Director: Kin Lipsky
Minority Staff Director: Priscilla Hanley, 224-5364, 628 SHOB

Jurisdiction: (1) conduct a continuing study of any and all matters pertaining to problems and opportunities of older people, including, but not limited to, assisted living, elder abuse, health care, identity theft, long-term care, Medicare, Older Americans Act, prescription drugs, retirement income security, retirement pensions, rural health care, Social Security, telemedicine, problems and opportunities of maintaining health, of assuring adequate income, of finding employment, of engaging in productive and rewarding activity, of securing proper housing, and when necessary, of obtaining care or assistance. No proposed legislation shall be referred to such committee, and such committee shall not have power to report by bill, or otherwise have legislative jurisdiction. (2) The special committee shall, from time to time (but not less often than once each year), report to the Senate the results of the study conducted pursuant to paragraph (1), together with such recommendation as it considers appropriate.
Party Ratio: D 11-R9

Bill Nelson, Fla., Chair	*Susan Collins, Maine*
Robert P. Casey Jr., Pa.	*Bob Corker, Tenn.*
Claire McCaskill, Mo.	*Orrin G. Hatch, Utah*
Sheldon Whitehouse, R.I.	*Mark Kirk, Ill.*
Kirsten Gillibrand, N.Y.	*Dean Heller, Nev.*
Joe Manchin III, W. Va.	*Jeff Flake, Ariz.*
Richard Blumenthal, Conn.	*Kelly Ayotte, N.H.*
Tammy Baldwin, Wisc.	*Tim Scott, S.C.*
Joe Donnelly, Ind.	*Ted Cruz, Tex.*
Elizabeth Warren, Mass.	
John Walsh, Mont.	

SENATE LEADERSHIP AND PARTISAN COMMITTEES

DEMOCRATIC LEADERS

Majority Floor Leader: Harry M. Reid, Nev.
Assistant Floor Leader: Richard J. Durbin, Ill.
Chief Deputy Whip: Barbara Boxer, Calif.

DEMOCRATIC PARTISAN COMMITTEES

Democratic Policy and Communications Center
Office: S-318 CAP 20510
Phone: 224-2939
Fax: 228-5576
Web: dppc.senate.gov
Charles E. Schumer, N.Y., Chair
Debbie Stabenow, Mich., Vice Chair

Regional Chairs (in alphabetical order)
Mary L. Landrieu, La.
Patty Murray, Wash.
Jack Reed, N.H.

Democratic Senatorial Campaign Committee
Office: 120 Maryland Ave. N.E. 20002-5610
Phone: 224-2447
Fax: 969-0354
Web: www.dscc.org
Email: info@dscc.org
Michael Bennet, Colo., Chair

Democratic Steering and Outreach Committee
Office: 712 SHOB 20510
Phone: 224-9048

Fax: 224-5476
Web: dsoc.senate.gov
Mark Begich, Ark., Chair
Jeanne Shaheen, N.H., Vice Chair

REPUBLICAN LEADERS

Minority Floor Leader: *Mitch McConnell, Ky.*
Minority Whip: *John Cornyn, Tex.*

REPUBLICAN PARTISAN COMMITTEES

National Republican Senatorial Committee
Office: 425 2nd St. N.E. 20002-4914
Phone: 675-6000
Fax: 675-4730
Web: nrsc.org
Jerry Moran, Kans., Chair
Ted Cruz, Tex., Vice Chair for Grassroots Outreach
Rob Portman, Ohio, Vice Chair for Finance

Republican Conference
Office: 405 SHOB 20510-7060
Phone: 224-2764
Fax: 228-4276
Web: src.senate.gov
John Thune, S.D., Chair
Roy Blunt, Mo., Vice Chair

Republican Policy Committee
Office: 347 SROB 20510-7064
Phone: 224-2946
Fax: 228-2628
Web: rpc.senate.gov
John Barrasso, Wyo., Chair

Senate Members' Offices

The following list gives Senate members and their party and state affiliation, followed by the address and telephone and fax numbers for their Washington office. The area code for all Washington, D.C., numbers is 202. A top administrative aide, a Web address, a Facebook page, and a Twitter account for each senator are also provided, when available. Most members may be contacted via the Web-based email forms found on their Web sites. These are followed by the address, telephone and fax numbers, and name of a key aide for the senator's district office(s). Each listing concludes with the senator's Committee Assignments. For partisan Committee Assignments, see page 821.

As of March 28, 2014, there were 53 Democrats, 45 Republicans, and 2 Independents who caucus with the Democrats in the Senate.

Alexander, Lamar, R-Tenn.

Capitol Hill Office: 455 SDOB 20510-4206; 224-4944; Fax: 228-3398; *Chief of Staff:* David Cleary
Web: http://alexander.senate.gov/
Facebook: http://facebook.com/lamaralexander
Twitter: http://twitter.com/senalexander
District Offices: Tri-Cities Regional Airport, 2525 Hwy. 75, #101, Blountville, TN 37617-6366; 423-325-6240; Fax: 423-325-6236; *Field Rep.:* Lana Moore
Joel E. Soloman Federal Bldg., 900 Georgia Ave., #260, Chattanooga, TN 37402-2240; 423-752-5337; Fax: 423-752-5342; *Field Rep.:* Evann Freeman
Federal Bldg., 109 S. Highland St., Room #B-9, Jackson, TN 38301-6149; 731-423-9344; Fax: 731-423-8918; *Field Rep.:* Matt Varino
Howard H. Baker, Jr. U.S. Courthouse, 800 Market St., #112, Knoxville, TN 37902-2303; 865-545-4253; Fax: 865-545-4252; *State Director:* Patrick Jaynes
Clifford Davis and Odell Horton Federal Bldg., 167 N. Main St., #1068, Memphis, TN 38103-1858; 901-544-4224; Fax: 901-544-4227; *Field Rep.:* Lora Jobe
3322 West End Ave., #120, Nashville, TN 37203-6821; 615-736-5129; Fax: 615-269-4803; *State Scheduler and Office Manager:* Faye Head
Committee Assignments: Appropriations; Health, Education, Labor, and Pensions; Rules and Administration; Energy and Natural Resources

Ayotte, Kelly, R-N.H.

Capitol Hill Office: 144 SROB 20510-2907; 224-3324; Fax: 224-4952; *Chief of Staff:* John R. Easton
Web: http://ayotte.senate.gov/
Facebook: http://facebook.com/kellyayottenh
Twitter: http://twitter.com/KellyAyotte
District Offices: 19 Pleasant St., #13B, Berlin, NH 03570-1917; 603-752-7702; Fax: 603-752-7704; *Special Asst. for Casework and Projects:* Michael Scala
1200 Elm St. #2, Manchester, NH 03101-2503; 603-622-7979; Fax: 603-622-0422; *State Director:* Orville Fitch
144 Main St., Nashua, NH 03060-2702; 603-880-3335; *Outreach Manager:* Andy Leach
14 Manchester Square, #140, Portsmouth, NH 03801-7866; 603-436-7161; *Caseworker:* Kate Pyle

Committee Assignments: Armed Services; Budget; Commerce, Science, and Transportation; Homeland Security and Government Affairs; Special Aging; Commission on Security and Cooperation in Europe (Helsinki Commission)

Baldwin, Tammy, D-Wisc.

Capitol Hill Office: 717 SHOB 20510; 202-224-5653; Fax: 224-9787; *Chief of Staff:* Bill Murat
Web: http://baldwin.senate.gov/
Facebook: http://facebook.com/TammyBaldwin
Twitter: http://twitter.com/tammybaldwin
District Offices: 205 5th Ave. South, Room 216, La Crosse, WI 54601; 608-796-0045; Fax: 608-796-0089; *Regional Coord.:* John Medinger
30 W. Mifflin St., #700, Madison, WI 53703-2568; 608-264-5338; Fax: 608-264-5473; *State Director:* Doug Hill
633 W. Wisconsin Ave., #1920, Milwaukee, WI 53203-2205; 414-297-4451; Fax: 414-297-4455; *Field Rep.:* Benjamin Juarez
402 Graham St., #206, Eau Claire, WI 54701-2633; 715-832-8424; *Field Rep.:* Kristin Dexter
Committee Assignments: Budget; Health, Education, Labor, and Pensions; Homeland Security and Governmental Affairs; Special Aging; Energy and Natural Resources

Barrasso, John Dan, R-Wyo.

Capitol Hill Office: 307 SDOB 20510-5005; 224-6441; Fax: 224-1724; *Chief of Staff:* J. Dan Kunsman
Web: http://barrasso.senate.gov/
Facebook: http://facebook.com/johnbarrasso
Twitter: http://twitter.com/senjohnbarrasso
District Offices: 100 E. B St., #2201, Casper, WY 82601-7021; 307-261-6413; Fax: 307-265-6706; *Field Rep.:* Jinx Clark
2120 Capitol Ave., #2013, Cheyenne, WY 82001-3631; 307-772-2451; Fax: 307-638-3512; *State Director:* Kristi Wallin
324 E. Washington Ave., Riverton, WY 82501-4342; 307-856-6642; Fax: 307-856-5901; *Field Rep.:* Pam Buline
1575 Dewar Dr., #218, Rock Springs, WY 82901-5972; 307-362-5012; Fax: 307-362-5129; *Field Rep.:* Sandy DaRif

2 N. Main St., #206, Sheridan, WY 82801-6322; 307-672-6456; Fax: 307-672-6456; *Field Rep.:* Denise Ebzery

Committee Assignments: Energy and Natural Resources; Environment and Public Works; Foreign Relations; Indian Affairs, Vice Chair,

Begich, Mark, D-Alaska

Capitol Hill Office: 111 SROB 20510-0204; 224-3004; Fax: 224-2354; *Chief of Staff; Foreign Affairs:* David S. Ramseur

Web: http://begich.senate.gov/

Facebook: http://facebook.com/Begich

Twitter: http://twitter.com/SenatorBegich

District Offices: Peterson Tower, 510 L St., #750, Anchorage, AK 99501-1959; 907-271-5915; Fax: 907-258-9305; *State Director:* Susanne Fleek-Green

Federal Bldg., 101 12th Ave., Room 328, Fairbanks, AK 99701-6237; 907-456-0261; Fax: 907-451-7290; *Regional Director:* Tom Moyer

One Sealaska Plaza, #308, Juneau, AK 99801-1245; 907-586-7700; Fax: 907-586-7702; *Field Rep., Juneau:* Sally Smith

Benco Bldg., 805 Frontage Rd., #101, Kenai, AK 99611-9104; 907-283-4000; Fax: 907-283-4401; *Field Rep., Kenai:* Kim Howard

Whitecliff Bldg., 1900 1st Ave., #230, Ketchikan, AK 99901-6059; 907-225-3000; Fax: 907-247-3000; *Field Rep., Ketchikan:* Bob Weinstein

851 E. Westpoint Dr., #309, Wasilla, AK 99654-7183; 907-357-9956; Fax: 907-357-9964; *Field Rep., Mat-Su:* Casey Estinau

Committee Assignments: Appropriations; Commerce, Science, and Transportation; Homeland Security and Governmental Affairs; Indian Affairs; Veterans' Affairs

Bennet, Michael F., D-Colo.

Capitol Hill Office: 458 SROB 20510-0608; 224-5852; Fax: 228-5097; *Chief of Staff:* Jonathan Davidson

Web: http://bennet.senate.gov/

Facebook: http://facebook.com/senatorbennet

Twitter: http://twitter.com/senbennetco

District Offices: 609 Main St., #110, Alamosa, CO 81101-2557; 719-587-0096; Fax: 719-587-0098; *Regional Rep.:* Charlotte Bobicki

409 N. Tejon St., #107, Colorado Springs, CO 80903-1163; 719-328-1100; Fax: 719-328-1129; *Regional Director:* Annie Oatman-Gardner

1127 Sherman St., #150, Denver, CO 80203-2398; 303-455-7600; Fax: 303-455-8851; *Deputy Chief of Staff:* Sarah Hughes

835 E. 2nd Ave., #203, Durango, CO 81301-5475; 970-259-1710; Fax: 970-259-9789; *Regional Director:* John Whitney

1200 S. College Ave., #211, Fort Collins, CO 80524-3746; 970-224-2200; Fax: 970-224-2205; *Regional Director:* James Thompson

225 N. 5th St., #511, Grand Junction, CO 81501-2656; 970-241-6631; Fax: 970-241-8313; *Regional Rep.:* Aaron Torres

129 W. B St., Pueblo, CO 81003-3400; 719-542-7550; Fax: 719-542-7555; *Regional Director:* Dwight Gardner

Committee Assignments: Agriculture, Nutrition, and Forestry; Finance; Health, Education, Labor, and Pensions

Blumenthal, Richard, D-Conn.

Capitol Hill Office: 724 SHOB 20510-0704; 224-2823; Fax: 224-9673; *Chief of Staff:* Laurie Rubiner

Web: http://blumenthal.senate.gov/

Facebook: http://facebook.com/SenBlumenthal

Twitter: http://twitter.com/SenBlumenthal

District Offices: 90 State House Square, 10th Floor, Hartford, CT 06103; 860-258-6940; Fax: 860-258-6958; *State Director:* Rich Kehoe

915 Lafayette Blvd., Rm. 230, Bridgeport, CT 06604; 203-330-0598; Fax: 203-330-0608; *State Director:* Rich Kehoe

Committee Assignments: Armed Services; Commerce, Science, and Transportation; Commission on Security and Cooperation in Europe (Helsinki Commission); Judiciary; Special Aging; Veterans' Affairs

Blunt, Roy, R-Mo.

Capitol Hill Office: 260 SROB 20510-2508; 224-5721; Fax: 224-8149; *Chief of Staff:* Glen R. Chambers

Web: http://blunt.senate.gov/

Facebook: http://facebook.com/SenatorBlunt

Twitter: http://twitter.com/RoyBlunt

District Offices: 2502 Tanner Dr., #208, Cape Girardeau, MO 63703; 573-334-7044; Fax: 573-334-7352; *Office Director:* Tom Schulte

7700 Bonhomme Ave., #315, Clayton, MO 63105; 314-725-4484; Fax: 314-727-3548; *Office Director:* Mary Wolf

1001 Cherry St., #104, Columbia, MO 65201-7931; 573-442-8151; Fax: 573-442-8162; *State Director:* Derek Coats

308 E. High St., #202, Jefferson City, MO 65101-3237; 573-634-2488; Fax: 573-634-6005; *Constituent Services Director:* Liz Behrouz

911 Main St., #2224, Kansas City, MO 64105-5321; 816-471-7141; Fax: 816-471-7338; *Office Director:* Matt Haase

2740 B E. Sunshine St., Springfield, MO 65804-2016; 417-877-7814; Fax: 417-823-9662; *District Office Director:* Sue Ball

Committee Assignments: Appropriations; Armed Services; Commerce, Science, and Transportation; Rules and Administration; Joint Library of Congress

Booker, Cory, D-N.J.

Capitol Hill Office: 140 SHOB 20510; 224-3224; Fax: 224-7981; *Chief of Staff:* Louisa Terrell

Web: http://booker.senate.gov/

Facebook: http://facebook.com/corybooker

Twitter: http://twitter.com/corybooker

District Offices: One Port Center, 2 Riverside Dr., #505, Camden, NJ 08101; 856-338-8922; *South Jersey Director:* Bill Moen

Gateway One, 11-43 Raymond Plaza W., #2300, Newark, NJ 07102; 973-639-8700; Fax: 973-639-8723; *State Director:* Mo Butler

Committee Assignments: Commerce, Science, and Transportation; Environment and Public Works; Small Business and Entrepreneurship

Boozman, John, R-Ark.

Capitol Hill Office: 320 SHOB 20510-0406; 224-4843; Fax: 228-1371; *Chief of Staff:* Helen Tolar

Web: http://boozman.senate.gov/

Facebook: https://facebook.com/JohnBoozman

Twitter: http://twitter.com/JohnBoozman

District Offices: 106 W. Main St., #104, El Dorado, AR 71730-5634; 870-863-4641; Fax: 870-863-4105; *Constituent Services Rep.:* Callie Travis

1120 Garrison Ave., Suite B, Fort Smith, AR 72901-2617; 479-573-0189; Fax: 479-573-0553; *Casework Coord.:* Kathy Watson

300 S. Church St., #400, Jonesboro, AR 72401-2911; 870-268-6925; Fax: 870-268-6887; *Caseworker:* Diane Holm

1401 W. Capitol Ave., Plaza F, Little Rock, AR 72201-2942; 501-372-7153; Fax: 501-372-7163; *Grants Coord.:* Tim Riley

213 W. Monroe Ave., Suite N, Lowell, AR 72745-9451; 479-725-0400; Fax: 479-725-0408; *State Director:* Stacey McClure

1001 Hwy 62 E., #11, Mountain Home, AR 72653-3215; 870-424-0129; Fax: 870-424-0141; *Caseworker, Social Security Medicare:* Sarah Hartley

620 E. 22nd St., #204, Stuttgart, AR 72160-9007; 870-672-6941; Fax: 870-672-6962; *Field Rep.:* Ty Davis

Committee Assignments: Agriculture, Nutrition, and Forestry; Appropriations; Environment and Public Works; Veterans' Affairs; Commission on Security and Cooperation in Europe (Helsinki Commission)

Boxer, Barbara, D-Calif.

Capitol Hill Office: 112 SHOB 20510-0505; 224-3553; Fax: 224-0454; *Chief of Staff:* Laura Schiller

Web: http://boxer.senate.gov/

Facebook: http://facebook.com/senatorboxer

Twitter: http://twitter.com/senatorboxer

District Offices: 2500 Tulare St., #5290, Fresno, CA 93721-1318; 559-497-5109; Fax: 202-228-3864; *State Director:* Thomas Bohigian

312 N. Spring St., #1748, Los Angeles, CA 90012-4719; 213-894-5000; Fax: 202-224-0357; *Deputy State Director; Sr. Advisor:* Yvette Martinez

70 Washington St., #203, Oakland, CA 94607-3705; 510-286-8537; Fax: 202-224-0454; *Director of State Operations:* Nicole Kaneko

3403 10th St., #704, Riverside, CA 92501-3641; 951-684-4849; Fax: 202-228-3868; *Senior Advisor:* Alton Garrett

501 I St., #7-600, Sacramento, CA 95814-7308; 916-448-2787; Fax: 202-228-3865; *Deputy State Director; State Press Liaison:* Stacey Smith

600 B St., #2240, San Diego, CA 92101-4508; 619-239-3884; Fax: 202-228-3863; *San Diego County and Imperial County Director:* Caridad Sanchez

Committee Assignments: Commerce, Science, and Transportation; Environment and Public Works, Chair; Foreign Relations; Select Ethics, Chair

Brown, Sherrod, D-Ohio

Capitol Hill Office: 713 SHOB 20510-3505; 224-2315; Fax: 228-6321; *Chief of Staff:* Mark E. Powden

Web: http://brown.senate.gov/

Facebook: http://facebook.com/sherrod

Twitter: http://twitter.com/sensherrodbrown

District Offices: 425 Walnut St., #2310, Cincinnati, OH 45202-3915; 513-684-1021; Fax: 513-684-1029; *Southwest Regional Director:* Brooke Hill

1301 E. 9th St., #1710, Cleveland, OH 44114-1869; 216-522-7272; Fax: 216-522-2239; *State Director:* John Ryan

200 N. High St., Room 614, Columbus, OH 43215-2408; 614-469-2083; Fax: 614-469-2171; *Central Ohio Regional Director:* Joe Gilligan

200 W. Erie Ave., #312, Lorain, OH 44052; 440-242-4100; Fax: 440-242-4108; *Constituent Service Liaison:* Margaret Molnar

Committee Assignments: Finance; Select Ethics; Veterans' Affairs; Banking, Housing, and Urban Affairs; Agriculture, Nutrition, and Forestry

Burr, Richard, R-N.C.

Capitol Hill Office: 217 SROB 20510-3308; 224-3154; Fax: 228-2981; *Chief of Staff:* Christopher A. Joyner

Web: http://burr.senate.gov/

Facebook: http://facebook.com/SenatorRichardBurr

Twitter: http://twitter.com/senatorburr

District Offices: Federal Bldg., 151 Patton Ave., #204, Asheville, NC 28801-2689; 828-350-2437; Fax: 828-350-2439; *State Director:* L. Myers

City Hall, 181 South St., Room 222, Gastonia, NC 28052-4126; 704-833-0854; Fax: 704-833-1467; *Field Rep.:* Josh Ward

100 Coast Line St., Rm. 210, Rocky Mount, NC 27804-5849; 252-977-9522; Fax: 252-977-7902; *Constituent Advocate:* Esther Clark

201 N. Front St., #809, Wilmington, NC 28401-5089; 910-251-1058; Fax: 910-251-7975; *Constituent Advocate:* Rebecca Anderson

2000 W. 1st St., #508, Winston-Salem, NC 27104-4225; 336-631-5125; Fax: 336-725-4493; *State Director:* L. Myers

Committee Assignments: Finance; Health, Education, Labor, and Pensions; Veterans' Affairs, Ranking Minority Member; Select Intelligence

Cantwell, Maria, D-Wash.

Capitol Hill Office: 311 SHOB 20510-4705; 224-3441; Fax: 228-0514; *Chief of Staff:* Jennifer Griffith

Web: http://cantwell.senate.gov/
Twitter: http://twitter.com/CantwellPress
District Offices: 2930 Wetmore Ave., #9B, Everett, WA98201-4044; 425-303-0114; Fax: 425-303-8351; *Northwest Washington Director:* Sally Hintz

825 Jadwin Ave., #206, Richland, WA 99352-3562; 509-946-8106; Fax: 509-946-6937; *Central Washington Director:* David Reeploeg

915 2nd Ave., #3206, Seattle, WA 98174-1011; 206-220-6400; Fax: 206-220-6404; *Staff Director:* Jennifer Griffith

920 W. Riverside Ave., #697, Spokane, WA 99201-1008; 509-353-2507; Fax: 509-353-2547; *Eastern Outreach Director:* Tanya Riordan

950 Pacific Ave., #615, Tacoma, WA 98402-4431; 253-572-2281; Fax: 253-572-5859; *Olympic Peninsula and Pierce County Director:* Tommy Bauer

1313 Officers Row, Vancouver, WA 98661-3856; 360-696-7838; Fax: 360-696-7844; *Southwest Outreach Director:* Dena Horton

Committee Assignments: Commerce, Science, and Transportation; Energy and Natural Resources; Finance; Indian Affairs, Chair; Small Business and Entrepreneurship

Cardin, Benjamin L., D-Md.

Capitol Hill Office: 509 SHOB 20510-2004; 224-4524; Fax: 224-1651; *Chief of Staff:* Christopher W. Lynch
Web: http://cardin.senate.gov/
Facebook: http://facebook.com/senatorbencardin
Twitter: http://twitter.com/SenatorCardin
District Offices: 100 S. Charles St., Tower 1, #1710, Baltimore, MD 21201-2788; 410-962-4436; Fax: 410-962-4156; *State Director:* Carlton Atkinson

10201 Martin Luther King, Jr. Hwy, #210, Bowie, MD 20720-4000; 301-860-0414; Fax: 301-860-0416; *Field Rep.:* Angel C. Rivera

Western Maryland Railway Station, 13 Canal St., Room 305, Cumberland, MD 21502-3054; 301-777-2957; Fax: 301-777-2959; *Field Rep.:* Robin Summerfield

451 Hungerford Dr., #230, Rockville, MD 20850-4187; 301-762-2974; Fax: 301-762-2976; *Field Rep.:* Ken Reichard

212 W. Main St., #301C, Salisbury, MD 21801-4920; 410-546-4250; Fax: 410-546-4252; *Field Rep.:* Kim Kratovil

Committee Assignments: Commission on Security and Cooperation in Europe (Helsinki Commission), Chair; Environment and Public Works; Finance; Foreign Relations; Small Business and Entrepreneurship

Carper, Tom, D-Del.

Capitol Hill Office: 513 SHOB 20510-0803; 224-2441; Fax: 228-2190; *Chief of Staff:* James D. Reilly
Web: http://carper.senate.gov/
Facebook: http://facebook.com/tomcarper
Twitter: http://twitter.com/senatorcarper
District Offices: 500 W. Loockerman St., #470, Dover, DE 19904-3298; 302-674-3308; Fax: 302-674-5464; *State Director:* Lori James

12 The Circle, Georgetown, DE 19947-1501; 302-856-7690; Fax: 302-856-3001; *Sussex County Regional Director:* Karen McGrath

301 N. Walnut St., #102L-1, Wilmington, DE 19801-3974; 302-573-6291; Fax: 302-573-6434; *New Castle County Regional Director:* Bonnie Wu

Committee Assignments: Environment and Public Works; Finance; Homeland Security and Governmental Affairs, Chair

Casey, Robert P., Jr., D-Pa.

Capitol Hill Office: 393 SROB 20510-3805; 224-6324; Fax: 228-0604; *Chief of Staff:* James W. Brown
Web: http://casey.senate.gov/
Facebook: http://facebook.com/SenatorBobCasey
Twitter: http://twitter.com/SenBobCasey
District Offices: 840 Hamilton St., #301, Allentown, PA 18101-2456; 610-782-9470; Fax: 610-782-9474; *Regional Manager:* Carol Obando-Derstine

817 E. Bishop St., Suite C, Bellefonte, PA 16823-2321; 814-357-0314; Fax: 814-357-0318; *Regional Manager:* Kim Bierly

17 S. Park Row, #B-150, Erie, PA 16501-1162; 814-874-5080; Fax: 814-874-5084; *Field Rep.:* Kyle Hannon

22 S. 3rd St., #6A, Harrisburg, PA 17101-2105; 717-231-7540; Fax: 717-231-7542; *Director of Constituent Services:* Bonnie Seaman

2000 Market St., #1870, Philadelphia, PA 19103-3231; 215-405-9660; Fax: 215-405-9669; *State Director; Sr. Counsel:* Ed Williams

Grant Bldg., 310 Grant St., #2415, Pittsburgh, PA 15219; 412-803-7370; Fax: 412-803-7379; *Southwestern PA Regional Director:* Jackie Erickson

417 Lackawanna Ave., #303, Scranton, PA 18503-2013; 570-941-0930; Fax: 570-941-0937; *State Scheduler:* Maurya Morris

Committee Assignments: Finance; Health, Education, Labor, and Pensions; Joint Economic Committee, Vice Chair; Special Aging; Agriculture, Nutrition, and Forestry

Chambliss, Saxby, R-Ga.

Capitol Hill Office: 416 SROB 20510-1007; 224-3521; Fax: 224-0103; *Chief of Staff:* Camila Knowles
Web: http://chambliss.senate.gov/
Facebook: http://facebook.com/SaxbyChambliss
Twitter: http://twitter.com/SaxbyChambliss
District Offices: 100 Galleria Pkwy, #1340, Atlanta, GA 30339-3179; 770-763-9090; Fax: 770-226-8633; *State Director:* Marisa Simpson

3633 Wheeler Rd., #270, Augusta, GA 30909-6655; 706-650-1555; Fax: 706-650-7985; *Regional Rep.:* Jim Hussey

300 Mulberry St., #502, Macon, GA 31201-5102; 478-741-1417; Fax: 478-741-1437; *Regional Rep.:* Bill Stembridge

585 S. Main St., P.O. Box 3217, Moultrie, GA 31776-3217; 229-985-2112; Fax: 229-985-2123; *Regional Rep.:* Debbie Cannon

Committee Assignments: Commission on Security and Cooperation in Europe (Helsinki Commission); Agriculture, Nutrition, and Forestry; Armed Services; Rules and Administration; Joint Printing; Select Intelligence, Vice Chair

Coats, Dan, R-Ind.

Capitol Hill Office: 493 SROB 20510-1405; 224-5623; Fax: 228-1820; *Chief of Staff:* Dean Hingson
Web: http://coats.senate.gov/
Facebook: http://facebook.com/pages/Senator-Dan-Coats/180671148633644
Twitter: http://twitter.com/SenDanCoats
District Offices: 11035 Broadway, Suite A, Crown Point, IN 46307; 219-663-2595; Fax: 663-4586; *Regional Director:* Dave Murtough
101 Martin Luther King, Jr. Blvd., Evansville, IN, 47708; 812-465-6500; Fax: 812-465-6503; *Regional Director:* Brenda Goff
1300 S. Harrison St., #3161, Fort Wayne, IN 46802; 260-426-3151; Fax: 260-420-0060; *Regional Director:* Paul Lagenann
1650 Market Tower, 10 W. Market St., Indianapolis, IN 46204-2934; 317-554-0750; Fax: 317-554-0760; *State Director:* Eric Holcomb
2 E. McClain Ave., #2-A, Scottsburg, IN, 47170; 812-754-0520; Fax: 812-754-0539; *Regional Director:* Aaron Erinhouchin
Committee Assignments: Appropriations; Joint Economic Committee; Select Intelligence; Commerce, Science, and Transportation

Coburn, Tom, R-Okla.

Capitol Hill Office: 172 SROB 20510-3604; 224-5754; Fax: 224-6008; *Chief of Staff:* Brian Treat
Web: http://coburn.senate.gov/
Facebook: http://facebook.com/teamcoburn
Twitter: http://twitter.com/TomCoburn
District Offices: 100 N. Broadway Ave., #1820, Oklahoma City, OK 73102-8800; 405-231-4941; Fax: 405-231-5051; *Central Field Rep.:* Craig Smith
1800 S. Baltimore Ave., #800, Tulsa, OK 74119-5238; 918-581-7651; Fax: 918-581-7195; *State Director, Northwest Field Rep.:* Jerry Morris
Committee Assignments: Banking, Housing, and Urban Affairs; Homeland Security and Governmental Affairs, Ranking Member; Select Intelligence

Cochran, Thad A., R-Miss.

Capitol Hill Office: 113 SDOB 20510-2402; 224-5054; Fax: 224-9450; *Chief of Staff:* Bruce Evans
Web: http://cochran.senate.gov/
Twitter: http://twitter.com/SenThadCochran
District Offices: 2012 15th St., #451, Gulfport, MS 39501-2036; 228-867-9710; Fax: 228-867-9789; *Southern District Director:* Myrtis Franke
190 E. Capitol St., #550, Jackson, MS 39201-2137; 601-965-4459; Fax: 601-965-4919; *Central District Director:* Brad Davis

Federal Bldg. and U.S. Courthouse, 911 E. Jackson Ave., #249, Oxford, MS 38655-3652; 662-236-1018; Fax: 662-236-7618; *Northern District Director:* Mindy Maxwell
Committee Assignments: Agriculture, Nutrition, and Forestry, Ranking Minority Member; Appropriations; Rules and Administration

Collins, Susan, R-Maine

Capitol Hill Office: 413 SDOB 20510-1904; 224-2523; Fax: 224-2693; *Chief of Staff:* Steve Abbott
Web: http://collins.senate.gov/
Facebook: http://facebook.com/susancollins
Twitter: http://twitter.com/senatorcollins
District Offices: 68 Sewall St., Room 507, Augusta, ME 04330-6354; 207-622-8414; Fax: 207-622-5884; *State Office Rep.:* Bobby Reynolds
202 Harlow St., Room 204, Bangor, ME 04402-4919; 207-945-0417; Fax: 207-990-4604; *State Office Rep.:* Carol Woodcock
160 Main St., Biddeford, ME 04005-2580; 207-283-1101; Fax: 207-283-4054; *State Office Rep.:* Cathy Goodwin
25 Sweden St., Suite A, Caribou, ME 04736-2149; 207-493-7873; Fax: 207-493-7810; *State Office Rep.:* Phil Bosse
55 Lisbon St., Lewiston, ME 04240-7117; 207-784-6969; Fax: 207-782-6475; *State Office Rep.:* Carlene Tremblay
One Canal Plaza, #802, Portland, ME 04101-4083; 207-780-3575; Fax: 207-828-0380; *State Office Rep.:* Sara Holmbom-Lund
Committee Assignments: Appropriations; Special Aging, Ranking Minority Member; Select Intelligence

Coons, Christopher, D-Del.

Capitol Hill Office: 127A SROB 20510-0805; 224-5042; Fax: 228-3075; *Chief of Staff:* Todd Webster
Web: http://coons.senate.gov/
Facebook: http://facebook.com/senatorchriscoons
Twitter: http://twitter.com/ChrisCoons
District Offices: 500 W. Loockerman St., #450, Dover, DE 19904-3298; 302-736-5601; Fax: 302-736-5609; *Kent/Sussex Coord.:* Kate Rorher
1105 N. Market St., Wilmington, DE 19801-1233; 302-573-6345; Fax: 302-573-6351; *State Director:* Jim Paoli
Committee Assignments: Budget; Foreign Relations; Judiciary; Appropriations

Corker, Bob, R-Tenn.

Capitol Hill Office: SD-425 SDOB; 224-3344; Fax: 228-0566; *Chief of Staff:* Todd Womack
Web: http://corker.senate.gov/
Facebook: http://facebook.com/bobcorker
Twitter: http://twitter.com/senbobcorker
District Offices: 10 W. Martin Luther King Blvd., 6th Floor, Chattanooga, TN 37402-1813; 423-756-2757; Fax: 423-756-5313; *State Director:* Betsy Ranalli
800 Market St., #121, Knoxville, TN 37902-2349; 865-637-4180; Fax: 865-637-9886; *Field Director:* Jane Jolley

100 Peabody PL, #1125, Memphis, TN 38103-3654; 901-683-1910; Fax: 901-575-3528; *Sr. Field Director:* Nick Kistenmacher

3322 W. End Ave., #610, Nashville, TN 37203-1096; 615-279-8125; Fax: 615-279-9488; *Field Director:* Katie Davis

91 Stonebridge Blvd., #103, Jackson, TN 38305; 731-664-2294; Fax: 731-664-4670; *Sr. Field Director:* Jennifer Weems

1105 E. Jackson Blvd., #4, Jonesborough, TN 37659; 423-753-2263; Fax: 423-753-3679; *Field Director:* Jill Salyers

Committee Assignments: Banking, Housing, and Urban Affairs; Foreign Relations, Ranking Minority Member; Special Aging

Cornyn, John, R-Tex.

Capitol Hill Office: 517 SHOB 20510-4305; 224-2934; Fax: 228-2856; *Chief of Staff:* Beth Jafari

Web: http://cornyn.senate.gov/

Facebook: http://facebook.com/Sen.JohnCornyn

Twitter: http://twitter.com/JohnCornyn

District Offices: Chase Tower, 221 W. 6th St., #1530, Austin, TX 78701-3403; 512-469-6034; Fax: 512-469-6020; *State Field Director:* David James

5001 Spring Valley Rd., #1125E, Dallas, TX 75244-3916; 972-239-1310; Fax: 972-239-2110; *Regional Director:* John Wood

222 E. Van Buren, #404, Harlingen, TX 78550-6804; 956-423-0162; Fax: 956-423-0193; *Regional Director:* Ana Garcia

5300 Memorial Dr., #980, Houston, TX 77007; 713-572-3337; Fax: 713-572-3777; *Regional Director:* Jay Guerrero

Wells Fargo Center, 1500 Broadway, #1230, Lubbock, TX 79401-3114; 806-472-7533; Fax: 806-472-7536; *Regional Director:* Brent Oden

600 Navarro St., #210, San Antonio, TX 78205-2455; 210-224-7485; Fax: 210-224-8569; *Regional Director:* Daniel Mezza

100 E. Ferguson St., #1004, Tyler, TX 75702-5706; 903-593-0902; Fax: 903-593-0920; *Regional Director:* Luellen Lowe

Committee Assignments: Finance; Judiciary

Crapo, Mike, R-Idaho

Capitol Hill Office: 239 SDOB 20510-1205; 224-6142; Fax: 228-1375; *Chief of Staff:* Susan Wheeler

Web: http://crapo.senate.gov/

Facebook: http://www.facebook.com/mikecrapo

Twitter: http://twitter.com/mikecrapo

District Offices: 251 E. Front St., #205, Boise, ID 83702-7312; 208-334-1776; Fax: 208-334-9044; *Chief of Staff:* John Hoehne

610 W. Hubbard St., #209, Coeur D'Alene, ID 83814-2287; 208-664-5490; Fax: 208-664-0889; *Regional Director:* Karen Roetter

410 Memorial Dr., #204, Idaho Falls, ID 83402-3600; 208-522-9779; Fax: 208-529-8367; *Regional Director:* Leslie Huddleston

313 D St., #105, Lewiston, ID 83501-1894; 208-743-1492; Fax: 208-743-6484; *State Director for Intergovernmental Affairs and Environment:* Mitch Silvers

275 S. 5th Ave., #225, Pocatello, ID 83201; 208-236-6775; Fax: 208-236-6935; *Regional Director:* Farhana Hibbert

202 Falls Ave., #2, Twin Falls, ID 83301-3372; 208-734-2515; Fax: 208-733-0414; *Regional Director:* A.J. Church

Committee Assignments: Banking, Housing, and Urban Affairs; Ranking Minority Member; Budget; Environment and Public Works; Finance; Indian Affairs

Cruz, Ted, R-Tex.

Capitol Hill Office: 185 SDOB 20510; 224-5922; Fax: 224-0776; *Chief of Staff:* Chip Roy

Web: http://cruz.senate.gov/

Facebook: http://facebook.com/SenatorTedCruz

Twitter: http://twitter.com/SenTedCruz

District Offices: 300 E. 8th St., #961, Austin, TX 78701-3226; 512-916-5834; Fax: 512-916-5839; *State Director:* John Drogin

Lee Park Tower II, 3626 N. Hall St., #410, Dallas, TX 75219; 214-599-8749; *Regional Director:* Bruce Redden

808 Travis St., #1420, Houston, TX 77002; 713-718-3057; *Regional Director:* David Sawyer

9901 IH-10W, #950, San Antonio, TX 78230; 210-340-2885; *Regional Director:* Michael Korner

305 S. Broadway, #501, Tyler, TX 75702; 903-593-5130; *Regional Director:* Bruce Redden

200 S. 10th St., #1603, McAllen, TX 78501; 956-686-7339; *Regional Director:* Michael Korner

Committee Assignments: Armed Services; Commerce, Science, and Transportation; Judiciary; Rules and Administration; Special Aging

Donnelly, Joe, D-Ind.

Capitol Hill Office: 720 SHOB 20510; 224-4814; Fax: 224-5011; *Chief of Staff:* Joel Elliott

Web: http://donnelly.senate.gov/

Facebook: http://facebook.com/senatordonnelly

Twitter: http://twitter.com/SenDonnelly

District Offices: Ten W. Market St., Room 1180, Indianapolis, IN 46204-2964; 317-226-5555; Fax: 855-772-7518; *State Director:* Hodge Patel

11 E. St., South Bend, IN 46501, 505-988-6647; Fax: 505-992-8435; *Regional Director:* Meredith Perks

119 E. Marcy St., #101, Jeffersonville, IN 46204; 505-988-6647; Fax: 505-992-8435; *Regional Director:* Kent Yeager

505 S. Main St., #148, Hammond, IN 46204; 575-523-6561; Fax: 575-523-6584; *Regional Director:* Justin Mount

7450 E. Main St., Ste. A, Fort Wayne, IN 46204; 505-325-5030; Fax: 505-325-6035; *Regional Director:* Jorge Ortiz

10 W. Market St., #1180, Evansville, IN 46204; 317-226-5555; Fax: 855-772-7518; *Regional Director:* Sarah Helming

Committee Assignments: Agriculture, Nutrition, and Forestry; Armed Services; Special Aging

Durbin, Richard J., D-Ill.

Capitol Hill Office: 711 SHOB 20510-1304; 224-2152; Fax: 228-0400; *Chief of Staff:* Patrick J. Souders

Web: http://durbin.senate.gov/

Facebook: http://facebook.com/SenatorDurbin

Twitter: http://twitter.com/SenatorDurbin

District Offices: 250 W. Cherry St., #115-D, Carbondale, IL 62901-2856; 618-351-1122; Fax: 618-351-1124; *Staff Asst.:* Melissa O'Dell

230 S. Dearborn St., #3892, Chicago, IL 60604-1505; 312-353-4952; Fax: 312-353-0150; *Sr. Advisor:* Michael Daly

1504 3rd Ave., #227, Rock Island, IL 61201-8612; 618-351-1122; Fax: 618-351-1124 *Western Illinois Outreach Coord.:* Brad Middleton

525 S. 8th St., Springfield, IL 62703-1606; 217-492-4062; Fax: 217-492-4382; *State Director:* Bill Houlihan

Committee Assignments: Appropriations; Foreign Relations; Judiciary; Rules and Administration; Joint Library of Congress

Enzi, Mike, R-Wyo.

Capitol Hill Office: 379A SROB 20510-5004; 224-3424; Fax: 228-0359; *Chief of Staff:* Flip McConnaughey

Web: http://enzi.senate.gov/

Facebook: http://facebook.com/mikeenzi

Twitter: https://twitter.com/SenatorEnzi

District Offices: 100 E. B St., Room 3201, P.O. Box 33201, Casper, WY 82602; 307-261-6572; Fax: 307-261-6574; *Field Rep.:* Kelly Carpenter

2120 Capitol Ave., #2007, Cheyenne, WY 82001-3631; 307-772-2477; Fax: 307-772-2480; *Field Rep.:* Debbie McCann

1285 Sheridan Ave., #210, Cody, WY 82414-3653; 307-527-9444; Fax: 307-527-9476; *Field Rep.:* Karen McCreery

400 S. Kendrick Ave., #303, Gillette, WY 82716-3803; 307-682-6268; Fax: 307-682-6501; *State Director:* Robin Bailey

1110 Maple Way, Suite G, P.O. Box 12470, Jackson, WY 83002-2470; 307-739-9507; Fax: 307-739-9520; *Field Rep.:* Reagen Green

Committee Assignments: Budget; Finance; Homeland Security and Governmental Affairs; Health, Education, Labor, and Pensions; Business and Entrepreneurship

Feinstein, Dianne, D-Calif.

Capitol Hill Office: 331 SHOB 20510-0504; 224-3841; Fax: 228-3954; *Chief of Staff:* Jennifer Duck

Web: http://feinstein.senate.gov/

Facebook: http://facebook.com/SenatorFeinstein

Twitter: http://twitter.com/senfeinstein

District Offices: 2500 Tulare St., #4290, Fresno, CA 93721-1331; 559-485-7430; Fax: 559-485-9689; *District Director:* Shelly Abajian

11111 Santa Monica Blvd., #915, Los Angeles, CA 90025-3343; 310-914-7300; Fax: 310-914-7318; *State Director:* Trevor Daley

880 Front St., #3296, San Diego, CA 92101-; 619-231-9712; Fax: 619-231-1108; *District Director:* Catherine Field

1 Post St., #2450, San Francisco, CA 94104-5240; 415-393-0707; Fax: 415-393-0710; *Deputy State Director:* Shawn Elsbernd

Committee Assignments: Appropriations; Judiciary; Rules and Administration; Select Intelligence, Chair

Fischer, Deb, R-Neb.

Capitol Hill Office: 383 SROB 20510; 224-6551; Fax: 228-1325; *Chief of Staff:* Mike Hybl

Web: http://fischer.senate.gov/public/

Facebook: http://facebook.com/senatordebfischer

Twitter: http://twitter.com/SenatorFischer

District Offices: 440 N. 8th St., #120, Lincoln, NE 68508; 402-441-4600; Fax: 402-476-8753; *State Director:* Dusty Vaughan

11819 Miracle Hills Dr., #205, Omaha, NE 68154; 402-391-3411; Fax: 402-391-4724; *Outreach Coord.:* Tiffany Settles

1110 Circle Dr., Ste. F2, Scottsbluff, NE 69361; 308-630-2329; Fax: 308-630-2321; *Constituent Services Director:* Brandy McCaslin

Committee Assignments: Armed Services; Commerce, Science, and Transportation; Environment and Public Works; Indian Affairs; Small Business and Entrepreneurship

Flake, Jeff, R-Ariz.

Capitol Hill Office: 368 SROB 20510; 224-4521; Fax: 228-0515; *Chief of Staff:* Steve Voeller

Web: http://flake.senate.gov/

Facebook: http://facebook.com/senatorjeffflake

Twitter: http://twitter.com/jeffflake

District Offices: 2200 E. Camelback Rd., #120, Phoenix, AZ 85016-9021; 602-840-1891; Fax: 602-840-4092; *State Director:* Matthew Specht

6840 N. Oracle Rd., #150, Tucson, AZ 85704-4252; 520-575-8633; Fax: 520-797-3232; *Regional Director:* Julie Katsel

Committee Assignments: Energy and Natural Resources; Foreign Relations; Judiciary; Special Aging

Franken, Al, D-Minn.

Capitol Hill Office: 309 SHOB 20510-2308; 224-5641; Fax: 224-0044; *Chief of Staff:* Casey Aden-Wansbury

Web: http://franken.senate.gov/

Facebook: http://facebook.com/Sen.Franken

Twitter: http://twitter.com/alfranken

District Offices: 515 W. 1st St., #104, Duluth, MN 55802-1302; 218-722-2390; Fax: 218-722-4131; *Constituent Services Rep.:* Janet Nelson

916 W. Saint Germain St., #110, St. Cloud, MN 56301-4097; 320-251-2721; Fax: 320-251-4164 *Constituent Services Rep.:* Diane Gerten

60 E. Plato Blvd., #220, St. Paul, MN 55107-1827; 651-221-1016; Fax: 651-221-1078; *State Director:* Alana Petersen

208 S. Minnesota Ave., #6, St. Peter, MN 56082-2546; 507-931-5813; Fax: 507-931-7345; *Field Rep.:* Bruce Barnum

Committee Assignments: Energy and Natural Resources; Health, Education, Labor, and Pensions; Indian Affairs; Judiciary

Gillibrand, Kirsten, D-N.Y.

Capitol Hill Office: 478 SROB 20510-3205; 224-4451; Fax: 228-0282; *Chief of Staff:* Jess C. Fassler

Web: http://gillibrand.senate.gov/

Facebook: http://facebook.com/KirstenGillibrand

Twitter: http://twitter.com/SenGillibrand/

District Offices: Leo W. O'Brien Federal Office Bldg., 11A Clinton Ave., Room 821, Albany, NY 12207-2202; 518-431-0120; Fax: 518-431-0128; *Regional Director:* David Connors

Larkin At Exchange, 726 Exchange St., #511, Buffalo, NY 14210-1485; 716-854-9725; Fax: 716-854-9731; *Regional Director:* James Kennedy

P.O. Box 273, Lowville, NY 13367; 315-376-6118; Fax: 315-376-6118; *Regional Director:* Susan Merrell

P.O. Box 893, Mahopac, NY 10541; 845-875-4585; Fax: 845-875-9099; *Regional Director:* Susan Spear

155 Pinelawn Rd., #250 N., Melville, NY 11747-3247; 631-249-2825; Fax: 631-249-2847; *Regional Director:* Kristen Walsh

780 3rd Ave., #2601, New York, NY 10017-2177; 212-688-6262; Fax: 866-824-6340; *State Director:* Emily Arsenault

Kenneth B. Keating Federal Office Bldg., 100 State St., Room 4195, Rochester, NY 14614-1318; 585-263-6250; Fax: 585-263-6247; *Deputy State Director:* Sarah Clark

James M. Hanley Federal Bldg., 100 S. Clinton St., Room 1470, P.O. Box 7378, Syracuse, NY 13261; 315-448-0470; Fax: 315-448-0476; *Regional Director:* Colleen Deacon

Committee Assignments: Agriculture, Nutrition, and Forestry; Armed Services; Environment and Public Works; Special Aging

Graham, Lindsey, R-S.C.

Capitol Hill Office: 290 SROB 20510-4003; 224-5972; Fax: 224-3808; *Chief of Staff:* Richard S. Perry

Web: http://lgraham.senate.gov/

Facebook: http://facebook.com/USSenatorLindseyGraham

Twitter: http://twitter.com/GrahamBlog

District Offices: 508 Hampton St., #202, Columbia, SC 29201-2718; 803-933-0112; Fax: 803-933-0957; *Midlands Regional Director:* Yvette Rowland

McMillan Federal Bldg., 401 W. Evans St., #111, Florence, SC 29501-3460; 843-669-1505; Fax: 843-669-9015; *Pee Dee Regional Director:* Celia Urquhart

130 S. Main St., #700, Greenville, SC 29601-4870; 864-250-1417; Fax: 864-250-4322; *State Director:* Van Cato

530 Johnnie Dodds Blvd., #202, Mt. Pleasant, SC 29464-3029; 843-849-3887; Fax: 843-971-3669; *Low Country Regional Director:* Bill Tuten

124 Exchange St., Suite A, Pendleton, SC 29670-1312; 864-646-4090; Fax: 864-646-8609; *Sr. Advisor:* Denise Bauld

235 E. Main St., #100, Rock Hill, SC 29730-4891; 803-366-2828; Fax: 803-366-5353; *Piedmont Regional Director:* Philip Land

Committee Assignments: Appropriations; Armed Services; Budget; Judiciary

Grassley, Chuck, R-Iowa

Capitol Hill Office: 135 SHOB 20510-1501; 224-3744; Fax: 224-6020; *Chief of Staff:* Jill Kozeny

Web: http://grassley.senate.gov/

Facebook: http://facebook.com/grassley

Twitter: http://twitter.com/chuckgrassley

District Offices: 111 7th Ave. S.E., Box 13, #6800, Cedar Rapids, IA 52401; 319-363-6832; Fax: 319-363-7179; *Regional Director:* Fred Schuster

307 Federal Bldg., 8 S. 6th St., Council Bluffs, IA 51501; 712-322-7103; Fax: 712-322-7196; *Regional Director; Constituent Services Specialist:* Donna Barry

201 W. 2nd St., #720, Davenport, IA 52801-1419; 563-322-4331; Fax: 563-322-8552; *Regional Director:* Penny Vacek

721 Federal Bldg., 210 Walnut St., Des Moines, IA 50309-2140; 515-288-1145; Fax: 515-288-5097; *State Director:* Robert Renaud

120 Federal Bldg., 320 6th St., , Sioux City, IA 51101-1244; 712-233-1860; Fax: 712-233-1634; *Regional Director:* Jacob Bossman

210 Waterloo Bldg., 531 Commercial St., Waterloo, IA 50701-5497; 319-232-6657; Fax: 319-232-9965; *Regional Director:* Valerie Nehl

Committee Assignments: Agriculture, Nutrition, and Forestry; Budget; Finance; Judiciary, Ranking Minority Member; Joint Taxation

Hagan, Kay, D-N.C.

Capitol Hill Office: 521 SDOB 20510-3309; 224-6342; Fax: 228-2563; *Chief of Staff:* Mike Harney

Web: http://hagan.senate.gov/

Facebook: http://facebook.com/SenatorHagan

Twitter: http://twitter.com/SenatorHagan

District Offices: 82 Patton Ave., #635, Asheville, NC 28801-3339; 828-257-6510; Fax: 828-257-6514; *Western Regional Liaison:* Freddie Harrill

1520 S. Blvd., #205, Charlotte, NC 28203-3711; 704-334-2448; Fax: 704-334-2405; *Regional Liaison:* Carrie Cook

701 Green Valley Rd., #201, Greensboro, NC 27408-7096; 336-333-5311; Fax: 336-333-5331; *State Director:* Melissa Midgett

301 S. Evans St., #102, Greenville, NC 27858-1831; 252-754-0707; Fax: 252-754-0766; *Community Outreach Director:* Joyce Mitchell

310 New Bern Ave., Raleigh, NC 27601-1441; 919-856-4630; Fax: 919-856-4053; *Sr. Constituent Services Rep.:* Jean Reaves

Committee Assignments: Armed Services; Banking, Housing, and Urban Affairs; Health, Education, Labor, and Pensions; Small Business and Entrepreneurship

Harkin, Tom R., D-Iowa

Capitol Hill Office: 731 SHOB 20510-1502; 224-3254; Fax: 224-9369; *Chief of Staff:* Brian R. Ahlberg
Web: http://harkin.senate.gov/
Facebook: http://facebook.com/tomharkin
Twitter: http://twitter.com/SenatorHarkin
District Offices: 111 7th Ave. S.E., Box 16, #480, Cedar Rapids, IA 52401-2101; 319-365-4504; Fax: 319-365-4683; *Regional Director:* Tom Larkin
1606 Brady St., #323, Davenport, IA 52803-4709; 563-322-1338; Fax: 563-322-0417; *Regional Director:* Alison Hart
Federal Bldg., 210 Walnut St., Room 733, Des Moines, IA 50309-2106; 515-284-4574; Fax: 515-284-4937; *State Director:* Rob Barron
315 Federal Bldg., 350 W. 6th St., Dubuque, IA 52001-4648; 563-582-2130; Fax: 563-582-2342; *Staff Asst:* Sue-Ellen Flynn
110 Federal Bldg., 320 6th St., Sioux City, IA 51101-1244; 712-252-1550; Fax: 712-252-7104; *Regional Director:* Amanda Nelson
Committee Assignments: Agriculture, Nutrition, and Forestry; Appropriations; Health, Education, Labor, and Pensions, Chair

Hatch, Orrin G., R-Utah

Capitol Hill Office: 104 SHOB 20510-4402; 224-5251; Fax: 224-6331; *Chief of Staff:* Michael J. Kennedy
Web: http://hatch.senate.gov/
Twitter: http://twitter.com/OrrinHatch
District Offices: 77 N. Main St, #112, Cedar City, UT 84720-2648; 435-586-8435; Fax: 435-586-2147; *Southern Utah Director:* William Swadley
1006 Federal Bldg., 324 25th St., Ogden, UT 84401-2341; 801-625-5672; Fax: 801-394-4503; *Northern Area Director:* Sandra Kester
51 S. University Ave., #320, Provo, UT 84601-4491; 801-375-7881; Fax: 801-374-5005; *Regional Director:* Ron Dean
8402 Federal Bldg., 125 S. State St., Salt Lake City, UT 84138-1191; 801-524-4380; Fax: 801-524-4379; *State Director:* Melanie Bowen
196 E. Tabernacle St., Room 14, St. George, UT 84770-3474; 435-634-1795; Fax: 435-634-1796; *Southern Utah Director:* William Swadley
Committee Assignments: Finance, Ranking Minority Member; Health, Education, Labor, and Pensions; Judiciary; Joint Taxation; Special Aging

Heinrich, Martin, D-N.M.

Capitol Hill Office: 702 SHOB 20510; 224-5521; Fax: 228-2841; *Chief of Staff:* Steven Haro
Web: http://heinrich.senate.gov/

Facebook: http://facebook.com/MartinHeinrich
Twitter: http://twitter.com/martinheinrich
District Offices: 625 Silver Ave., S.W., #130, Albuquerque, NM 87102-3185; 505-346-6601; Fax: 505-346-6780; *Deputy District Director:* Miguel Negrete
7450 E. Main St., Ste. A, Farmington, NM 87402; 505-325-5030; Fax: 505-325-6035; *Field Rep.:* Jim Dumont
Loretto Towne Center, 505 S. Main St., #148, Las Cruces, NM 88001-1200; 575-523-6561; Fax: 575-523-6584; *Field Rep.:* Dara Parker
200 E. 4th St., #300, Roswell, NM 88201; 575-622-7113; Fax: 575-622-3538; *Constituent Services Rep.:* Iris Chavez
119 E. Marcy St., #101, Santa Fe, NM 87501-2046; 505-988-6647; Fax: 505-992-8435; *Field Rep.:* Patricia Dominguez
Committee Assignments: Energy and Natural Resources; Select Intelligence; Joint Economic

Heitkamp, Heidi, D-N.D.

Capitol Hill Office: SH-502 SHOB 20510; 224-2043; Fax: 224-7776; *Chief of Staff:* Tessa Gould
Web: http://heitkamp.senate.gov/
Facebook: http://facebook.com/SenatorHeidiHeitkamp
Twitter: http://twitter.com/SenatorHeitkamp
District Offices: 228 Federal Bldg., 220 E. Rosser Ave., Bismarck, ND 58501-3869; 701-258-4648; Fax: 701-258-1254; *State Director:* Ross Keys
306 Federal Bldg., 657 2nd Ave. N., Fargo, ND 58102-4727; 701-232-8030; Fax: 701-232-6449; *State Director:* Ryan Nagle
33 S. 3rd St., Suite B, Grand Forks, ND 58201; 701-775-9601; Fax: 701-746-1990; *State Rep.:* Gail Hand
105 Federal Bldg., 100 1st St., S.W., Minot, ND 58701-3846; 701-852-0703; Fax: 701-838-8196; *State Rep.:* Norman McCloud
40 1st Ave. W., #202, Dickinson, ND 58601; 701-225-0974; Fax: 701-225-3287; *Southwest Area Director:* Shirley Meyer
Committee Assignments: Agriculture, Nutrition, and Forestry; Banking, Housing, and Urban Development; Homeland Security and Government Affairs; Indian Affairs; Small Business and Entrepreneurship

Heller, Dean, R-Nev.

Capitol Hill Office: 324 SHOB 20510-2806; 224-6244; Fax: 228-6753; *Chief of Staff:* Edgar M. Abrams
Web: http://heller.senate.gov/
Facebook: http://facebook.com/SenDeanHeller
Twitter: http://twitter.com/SenDeanHeller
District Offices: 8930 W. Sunset Rd., #230, Las Vegas, NV 89148; 702-388-6605; Fax: 702-388-6501; *Southern Nevada Director:* Jack Finn
Bruce Thompson Federal Bldg., 400 S. Virginia St., #738, Reno, NV 89501-2125; 775-686-5770; Fax: 775-686-5729; *State Director:* Ashley Carrigan
Committee Assignments: Banking Housing, and Urban Affairs; Commerce, Science, and Transportation; Energy and Natural Resources; Veterans' Affairs; Special Aging

Hirono, Mazie K., D-Hawaii

Capitol Hill Office: 330 SHOB 20510; 224-6361; Fax: 224-2126; *Chief of Staff:* Betsy Lin
Web: http://hirono.senate.gov/
Facebook: http://facebook.com/mazie.hirono
Twitter: http://twitter.com/maziehirono
District Offices: 300 Ala Moana Blvd., Room 3-106, Honolulu, HI 96850; 808-522-8970; Fax: 808-545-4683; *State Director:* Alan Yamamoto
Committee Assignments: Armed Services; Judiciary; Veterans' Affairs

Hoeven, John, R-N.D.

Capitol Hill Office: 338 RSOB 20510-3406; 224-2551; Fax: 224-7999; *Chief of Staff:* Ryan Bernstein
Web: http://hoeven.senate.gov/
Facebook: http://facebook.com/SenatorJohnHoeven
Twitter: http://twitter.com/SenJohnHoeven
District Offices: U.S. Federal Bldg., 220 E. Rosser Ave., Room 312, Bismarck, ND 58501-3869; 701-250-4618; Fax: 701-250-4484; *State Director:* Don Larson
1802 32nd Ave. South, Room B, Fargo, ND 58103-6747; 701-239-5389; Fax: 701-293-5112; *Constituent Services Rep.:* Sally Johnson
Federal Bldg., 102 N. 4th St., Room 108, Grand Forks, ND 58203-3738; 701-746-8972; Fax: 701-746-5613; *Field Rep.:* Tom Brusegaard
315 Main St. South, #204, Minot, ND 58701-3956; 701-838-1361; Fax: 701-838-1381; *Field Rep.:* Jackie Velk
Committee Assignments: Agriculture, Nutrition, and Forestry; Appropriations; Energy and Natural Resources; Indian Affairs

Inhofe, James M., R-Okla.

Capitol Hill Office: 205 SROB 20510-3603; 224-4721; Fax: 228-0380; *Chief of Staff:* Ryan Jackson
Web: http://inhofe.senate.gov/
Facebook: http://facebook.com/jiminhofe
Twitter: http://twitter.com/jiminhofe
District Offices: 302 N. Independence St., #104, Enid, OK 73701-4025; 580-234-5105; Fax: 580-234-5094; *Field Rep.:* Cale Walker
215 E. Choctaw Ave., #106, McAlester, OK 74501-5069; 918-426-0933; Fax: 918-426-0935; *Field Rep.:* Rusty Appleton
1900 N.W. Expressway St., #1210, Oklahoma City, OK 73118; 405-608-4381; Fax: 405-608-4120; *State Director:* Michael Lee
1924 S. Utica Ave., #530, Tulsa, OK 74104; 918-748-5111; Fax: 918-748-5119; *Exec. Asst:* Kathie Lopp
Committee Assignments: Armed Services, Ranking Minority Member; Environment and Public Works; Select Intelligence

Isakson, Johnny, R-Ga.

Capitol Hill Office: 131 SROB 20510-1008; 224-3643; Fax: 228-0724; *Chief of Staff:* Joan Kirchner
Web: http://isakson.senate.gov/
Facebook: http://facebook.com/isakson

Twitter: http://twitter.com/SenatorIsakson
District Offices: One Overton Park, 3625 Cumberland Blvd., #970, Atlanta, GA 30339-6406; 770-661-0999; Fax: 770-661-0768; *State Director:* Edward Tate
Committee Assignments: Finance; Health, Education, Labor, and Pensions; Veterans' Affairs; Select Ethics, Vice Chair

Johanns, Mike, R-Neb.

Capitol Hill Office: 404 SROB 20510-2707; 224-4224; Fax: 228-0436; *Chief of Staff:* Terri Moore
Web: http://johanns.senate.gov/public/
Facebook: http://facebook.com/MikeJohanns
Twitter: http://twitter.com/Mike_Johanns
District Offices: 4111 4th Ave., #26, Kearney, NE 68845-2884; 308-236-7602; Fax: 308-236-7473; *Central Nebraska Director of Constituent Services:* Sallie Atkins
287 Federal Bldg., 100 Centennial Mall North, Lincoln, NE 68508-3812; 402-476-1400; Fax: 402-476-0605; *State Director:* Nancy Johner
9900 Nicholas St., #325, Omaha, NE 68114-2214; 402-758-8981; Fax: 402-758-9165; *Omaha Director of Constituent Services:* Holly Baker
115 Railway St., #C102, Scottsbluff, NE 69361-3185; 308-632-6032; Fax: 308-632-6295; *Outreach Coord.; Constituent Services Rep.:* Cassie Nichols
Committee Assignments: Agriculture, Nutrition, and Forestry; Appropriations; Banking, Housing, and Urban Affairs; Veterans' Affairs

Johnson, Ron, R-Wisc.

Capitol Hill Office: 328 SHOB 20510-4905; 224-5323; Fax: 228-6965; *Chief of Staff:* Tony Blando
Web: http://ronjohnson.senate.gov/
Facebook: http://facebook.com/senronjohnson
Twitter: http://twitter.com/SenRonJohnson

District Offices: 517 E. Wisconsin Ave., Room 408, Milwaukee, WI 53202-4510; 414-276-7282; Fax: 414-276-7284; *Regional Director:* Terry Spannbauer
219 Washington Ave., Oshkosh, WI 54901-5029; 920-230-7250; Fax: 920-230-7262; *State Director:* Julie Leschke
Committee Assignments: Budget; Commerce, Science, and Transportation; Foreign Relations; Homeland Security and Governmental Affairs; Small Business and Entrepreneurship

Johnson, Tim, D-S.D.

Capitol Hill Office: 136 SHOB 20510-4104; 224-5842; Fax: 228-5765; *Chief of Staff:* Drey Samuelson
Web: http://johnson.senate.gov/
Facebook: http://facebook.com/SenatorTimJohnson
Twitter: http://twitter.com/SenJohnsonSD
District Offices: 320 S. 1st St., #103, Aberdeen, SD 57401-4168; 605-226-3440; Fax: 605-226-2439; *Northeast Area Director:* Sharon Stroschein
405 E. Omaha St., Suite B, Rapid City, SD 57701-2975; 605-341-3990,; Fax: 605-341-2207; *West River Area Director:* Darrell Shoemaker

5015 S. Bur Oak Pl., Sioux Falls, SD 57108-2228; 605-332-8896; Fax: 605-332-2824; *State Director:* Sharon Boysen

Committee Assignments: Appropriations; Banking, Housing, and Urban Affairs, Chair; Energy and Natural Resources; Indian Affairs

Kaine, Tim, D-Va.

Capitol Hill Office: 338 SROB 20510; 224-4024; Fax: 228-6363; *Chief of Staff:* Mike Henry
Web: http://kaine.senate.gov/
Facebook: http://facebook.com/timkaine
Twitter: https://twitter.com/timkaine
District Offices: 756 Park Ave., N.W., P.O. Box 1300, Norton, VA 24273-1923; 276-679-4925; Fax: 276-679-4929; *Regional Rep.:* Laura Blevins
919 E. Main St., #970, Richmond, VA 23219; 804-771-2221; Fax: 804-771-8313; *State Director:* John Knapp
222 Central Park Dr., #120, Virginia Beach, VA 23462-3023; 757-518-1674; Fax: 757-518-1679; *Regional Rep.:* Andrea Trotter
308 Craghead St., #102A, Danville, VA 24541; 434-792-0976; Fax: 434-792-0978; *Regional Rep.:* Chris Collins
611 S. Jefferson St., #5B, Roanoke, VA 24011; 540-682-5693; Fax: 540-682-5697; *Regional Rep.:* Gwen Mason
9408 Grant Ave., #202, Manassas, VA 20110; 703-361-3192; Fax: 703-361-3198; *Regional Rep.:* Joe Montano
Committee Assignments: Armed Services, Budget, Foreign Relations

King, Angus, I-Maine

Capitol Hill Office: 359 SDOB 20510; 224-5344; Fax: 224-1946; *Chief of Staff:* Kay Rand
Web: http://king.senate.gov/
Facebook: http://facebook.com/SenatorAngusSKingJr
Twitter: http://twitter.com/SenAngusKing
District Offices: 4 Gabriel Dr., #3, Augusta, ME 04330; 207-622-8292; *Regional Rep.:* Chris Rector
169 Academy St., Ste. A, Presque Isle, ME 04769; 207-764-5124; *Regional Rep.:* Sharon Campbell
383 US Route 1, #1C, Scarborough, ME 04074; 207-883-1588; *Regional Rep.:* Travis Kennedy
Committee Assignments: Armed Services; Budget; Rules and Administration; Select Intelligence

Kirk, Mark, R-Ill.

Capitol Hill Office: 524 SHOB 20510-1308; 224-2854; Fax: 228-4611; *Chief of Staff:* Kate Dickens
Web: http://kirk.senate.gov/
Facebook: http://facebook.com/SenatorKirk
Twitter: http://twitter.com/SenatorKirk
District Offices: 230 S. Dearborn St., #3900, Chicago, IL 60604-1480; 312-886-3506; Fax: 312-886-2117; *Chicago Chief of Staff:* Eric Elk
607 E. Adams St., #1520, Springfield, IL 62701-1635; 217-492-5089; Fax: 217-492-5099; *Outreach Coord.:* Michael Rasmussen

Committee Assignments: Appropriations; Banking, Housing, and Urban Affairs; Health, Education, Labor, and Pensions; Special Aging

Klobuchar, Amy, D-Minn.

Capitol Hill Office: 302 SHOB 20510-2307; 224-3244; Fax: 228-2186; *Chief of Staff:* Jonathan Becker
Web: http://klobuchar.senate.gov/
Facebook: http://facebook.com/amyklobuchar
Twitter: http://twitter.com/amyklobuchar
District Offices: 1200 Washington Ave. South, #250, Minneapolis, MN 55415-1588; 612-727-5220; Fax: 612-727-5223; *State Director:* Sammy Clark
121 4th St. South, Moorhead, MN 56560-2613; 218-287-2219; Fax: 218-287-2930; *Regional Outreach Director:* Andy Martin
1130 1/2 7th St., N.W., #208, Rochester, MN 55901-2995; 507-288-5321; Fax: 507-288-2922; *Regional Outreach Director:* Chuck Ackman
Olcott Plaza, 820 9th St. N., #105, Virginia, MN 55792-2300; 218-741-9690; Fax: 218-741-3692; *Regional Outreach Director:* Jerry Fallos
Committee Assignments: Agriculture, Nutrition, and Forestry; Commerce, Science, and Transportation; Judiciary; Joint Economic Committee, Vice Chair; Rules and Administration

Landrieu, Mary, D-La.

Capitol Hill Office: 703 SHOB 20510; 224-5824; Fax: 224-9735; *Chief of Staff:* Donald Cravins
Web: http://landrieu.senate.gov/
Facebook: http://facebook.com/senatormarylandrieu
Twitter: http://twitter.com/SenLandrieu
District Offices: Federal Bldg., 707 Florida St., Room 326, Baton Rouge, LA 70801-1713; 225-389-0395; Fax: 225-389-0660; *State Director:* T. Bradley Keith
Capital One Tower, One Lakeshore Dr., #1260, Lake Charles, LA 70629-0104; 337-436-6650; Fax: 337-439-3762; *Regional Manager:* Mark Herbert
Hale Boggs Federal Bldg., 500 Poydras St., #1005, New Orleans, LA 70130-3309; 504-589-2427; Fax: 504-589-4023; *Regional Manager:* LaVerne Saulny
U.S. Courthouse, 300 Fannin St., #2240, Shreveport, LA 71101-3123; 318-676-3085; Fax: 318-676-3100; *Deputy State Director:* Tari Bradford
Committee Assignments: Appropriations; Energy and Natural Resources; Homeland Security and Governmental Affairs; Small Business and Entrepreneurship, Chair

Leahy, Patrick P., D-VT.

Capitol Hill Office: 437 SROB 20510-4502; 224-4242; Fax: 224-3479; *Chief of Staff:* John P. Dowd
Web: http://leahy.senate.gov/
Facebook: http://facebook.com/SenatorPatrickLeahy
Twitter: http://twitter.com/SenatorLeahy
District Offices: 199 Main St., 4th Floor, Burlington, VT 05401-8309; 802-863-2525; Fax: 802-658-1009; *Vermont Office Director:* John Tracy

87 State St., Room 338, Montpelier, VT 05602-9505; 802-229-0569; Fax: 802-229-1915; *Field Rep.*: Tom Berry

Committee Assignments: Agriculture, Nutrition, and Forestry; Appropriations; Judiciary, Chair; Rules and Administration; Joint Library of Congress

Lee, Mike, R-Utah

Capitol Hill Office: 316 SHOB 20510-4404; 224-5444; Fax: 228-1168; *Chief of Staff:* Boyd Matheson

Web: http://lee.senate.gov/

Facebook: http://facebook.com/senatormikelee

Twitter: http://twitter.com/SenMikeLee

District Offices: Wallace F. Bennett Federal Bldg., 125 S. State St., #4225, Salt Lake City, UT 84138-1188; 801-524-5933; Fax: 801-524-5730; *Deputy State Director:* Alison Bell

285 W. Tabernacle St., #200, St. George, UT 84770-3474; 435-628-5514; Fax: 435-628-4160; *Southern Utah Director:* Ellen Schunk

Committee Assignments: Armed Services; Energy and Natural Resources; Judiciary; Joint Economic Committee

Levin, Carl S., D-Mich.

Capitol Hill Office: 269 SROB 20510-2202; 224-6221; Fax: 224-1388; *Chief of Staff:* Jack Danielson

Web: http://levin.senate.gov/

Facebook: http://facebook.com/carllevin

Twitter: http://twitter.com/sencarllevin

District Offices: Patrick V. McNamara Federal Bldg., 477 Michigan Ave., #1860, Detroit, MI 48226-2576; 313-226-6020; Fax: 313-226-6948; *Regional Rep.:* Gale Govaere

524 Ludington St., #LL-103, Escanaba, MI 49829-3949; 906-789-0052; Fax: 906-789-0015; *Regional Rep.:* Amy Berglund

Gerald R. Ford Federal Bldg., 110 Michigan Ave., N.W., #720, Grand Rapids, MI 49503-2313; 616-456-2531; Fax: 616-456-5147; *Regional Rep.:* Paul Troost

124 W. Allegan St., #1810, Lansing, MI 48933-1716; 517-377-1508; Fax: 517-377-1506; *Regional Rep.; State Systems Admin.:* Melissa Horste

515 N. Washington Ave., #402, Saginaw, MI 48607-1370; 989-754-2494; Fax: 989-754-2920; *Regional Rep.:* Derrick Matthis

107 Cass St., Suite E, Traverse City, MI 49684-2602; 231-947-9569; Fax: 231-947-9518; *Regional Rep.:* Gabe Schwarz-Schneider

30500 Van Dyke Ave., #206, Warren, MI 48093-2109; 586-573-9145; Fax: 586-573-8260; *Regional Rep.:* Steve Nelson

Committee Assignments: Armed Services, Chair; Homeland Security and Governmental Affairs; Small Business and Entrepreneurship; Select Intelligence

Manchin, Joe, D-W.Va.

Capitol Hill Office: 306 SHOB 20510-4803; 224-3954; Fax: 228-0002; *Chief of Staff:* Hayden Rogers

Web: http://manchin.senate.gov/

Facebook: http://facebook.com/JoeManchinIII

Twitter: http://twitter.com/Sen_JoeManchin

District Offices: 900 Pennsylvania Ave., #629, Charleston, WV 25302; 304-342-5855; Fax: 304-343-7144; *State Director:* Mara Boss

217 W. King St., Room 238, Martinsburg, WV 25401-3377; 304-264-4626; Fax: 304-262-3039; *Admin. Manager:* Missy Phalyn

48 Donley St., #504, Morgantown, WV 26501-5900; 304-284-8663; Fax: 304-284-8681; *Regional Coord.:* Todd Anderson

Committee Assignments: Armed Services; Banking, Housing, and Urban Development; Energy and Natural Resources; Special Aging

Markey, Ed, D-Mass.

Capitol Hill Office: 218 SROB 20510; 202-224-2742; *Chief of Staff:* Mark Bayer

Web: http://markey.senate.gov/

Facebook: http://facebook.com/EdJMarkey

Twitter: http://twitter.com/markeymemo

District Offices: 975 JFK Federal Bldg., 15 New Sudbury St., Boston, MA 02203; 617-565-8519; *State Director:* Mark Gallagher

222 Milliken Blvd., #312, Fall River, MA 02721; 508-677-0523; 1550 Main St., 4th Floor, Springfield, MA 01101; 413-785-4610;

Committee Assignments: Foreign Relations; Commerce, Science, and Transportation; Small Business and Entrepreneurship

McCain, John, R-Ariz.

Capitol Hill Office: 241 SROB 20510-0303; 224-2235; Fax: 228-2862; *Chief of Staff:* Pablo Carillo

Web: http://mccain.senate.gov/

Facebook: http://facebook.com/johnmccain

Twitter: http://twitter.com/senjohnmccain

District Offices: 2201 E. Camelback Rd., #115, Phoenix, AZ 85016-3446; 602-952-2410; Fax: 602-952-8702; *State Director:* Gina Gormley

122 N. Cortez St., #108, Prescott, AZ 86301-3022; 928-445-0833; Fax: 928-445-8594; *Staff Asst.:* Naomi King/ Cheryl Bennett

407 W. Congress St., #103, Tucson, AZ 85701-1349; 520-670-6334; Fax: 520-670-6637; *Office Manager:* Rosemary Alexander

Committee Assignments: Armed Services; Foreign Relations; Homeland Security and Governmental Affairs, Ranking Minority Member; Indian Affairs

McCaskill, Claire, D-Mo.

Capitol Hill Office: 506 SHOB 20510-2507; 224-6154; Fax: 228-6326; *Chief of Staff:* Julie Dwyer

Web: http://mccaskill.senate.gov/

Facebook: http://facebook.com/senatormccaskill

Twitter: http://twitter.com/clairecmc

District Offices: 555 Independence St., Room 1600, Cape Girardeau, MO 63703-6235; 573-651-0964; Fax: 573-334-4278; *District Director:* Christy Mercer

915 E. Ash St., Columbia, MO 65201-4853; 573-442-7130; Fax: 573-442-7140; *Constituent Services Rep.:* Samantha Brewer

4141 Pennsylvania Ave., #101, Kansas City, MO 64111-3064; 816-421-1639; Fax: 816-421-2562; *Regional Director:* Corey Dillon

324 Park Central W., #101, Springfield, MO 65806-1218; 417-868-8745; Fax: 417-831-1349; *District Director:* David Rauch

5850 Delmar Blvd., Suite A, St. Louis, MO 63112-2346; 314-367-1364; Fax: 314-361-8649; *Deputy Chief of Staff:* Tod Martin

Committee Assignments: Armed Services; Commerce, Science, and Transportation; Homeland Security and Governmental Affairs; Special Aging

McConnell, Mitch, R-Ky.

Capitol Hill Office: 317 SROB 20510-1702; 224-2541; Fax: 224-2499; *Chief of Staff:* Reb Brownell
Web: http://mcconnell.senate.gov/
Facebook: http://facebook.com/mitchmcconnell
Twitter: http://twitter.com/McConnellPress
District Offices: Federal Bldg., 241 E. Main St., Room 102, Bowling Green, KY 42101-2175; 270-781-1673; Fax: 270-782-1884; *Field Rep.:* Holly Lewis

1885 Dixie Hwy., #345, Fort Wright, KY 41011-2679; 859-578-0188; Fax: 859-578-0488; *Field Rep.:* Chase Crigler

771 Corporate Dr., #108, Lexington, KY 40503-5439; 859-224-8286; Fax: 859-224-9673; *Field Rep.:* Regina Crawford Stivers

300 S. Main St., #310, London, KY 40741-2415; 606-864-2026; Fax: 606-864-2035; *Field Rep.:* Donna McClure

601 W. Broadway, Room 630, Louisville, KY 40202-2228; 502-582-6304; Fax: 502-582-5326; *State Director:* Terry Carmack

Professional Arts Bldg., 2320 Broadway, #100, Paducah, KY 42001-7146; 270-442-4554; Fax: 270-443-3102; *Field Rep.:* Martie Wiles

Committee Assignments: Agriculture, Nutrition, and Forestry; Appropriations; Rules and Administration; Select Intelligence

Menéndez, Robert, D-N.J.

Capitol Hill Office: 528 SHOB 20510-3006; 224-4744; Fax: 224-2197; *Chief of Staff:* Danny O'Brien
Web: http://menendez.senate.gov/
Facebook: http://facebook.com/senatormenendez
Twitter: http://twitter.com/SenatorMenendez
District Offices: 208 White Horse Pike, #18, Barrington, NJ 08007-1322; 856-757-5353; Fax: 856-546-1526; *Deputy State Director:* Karin Elkis

One Gateway Center, #1100, Newark, NJ 07102-5323; 973-645-3030; Fax: 973-645-0502; *Deputy Chief of Staff:* Kellie Drakeford

Committee Assignments: Banking, Housing, and Urban Affairs; Finance; Foreign Relations, Chair

Merkley, Jeff, D-Ore.

Capitol Hill Office: 313 SHOB 20510-3705; 224-3753; Fax: 228-3997; *Chief of Staff:* Michael S. Zamore
Web: http://merkley.senate.gov/
Facebook: http://facebook.com/jeffmerkley
Twitter: http://twitter.com/SenJeffMerkley
District Offices: 131 N.W. Hawthorne Ave., #208, Bend, OR 97701-2958; 541-318-1298; *Field Rep.:* Susana Julber

405 E. 8th Ave., #2010, Eugene, OR 97401-2730; 541-465-6750; *Field Rep.:* Dan Whelan

10 S. Bartlett St., #201, Medford, OR 97501-7204; 541-608-9102; *Field Rep.:* Amy Amrhein

310 S.E. 2nd St., #105, Pendleton, OR 97801-2263; 541-278-1129; *Field Rep.:* Elizabeth Scheeler

121 S.W. Salmon St., #1400, Portland, OR 97204-2948; 503-326-3386; Fax: 503-326-2900; *State Director:* Jeanne Atkins

495 State St., #330, Salem, OR 97301-4384; 503-362-8102; *Field Rep.:* Katie Gauthier

Committee Assignments: Appropriations; Banking, Housing, and Urban Affairs; Budget; Environment and Public Works

Mikulski, Barbara, D-Md.

Capitol Hill Office: 503 SHOB 20510-2003; 224-4654; Fax: 224-8858; *Chief of Staff:* Shannon Kula
Web: http://mikulski.senate.gov/
Facebook: http://facebook.com/SenatorMikulski
Twitter: http://twitter.com/SenatorBarb
District Offices: 60 West St., #202, Annapolis, MD 21401-2448; 410-263-1805; Fax: 410-263-5949; *Asst. to Senator:* Rachel Jones/Molly Martin

901 S. Bond St., #310, Baltimore, MD 21231-3358; 410-962-4510; Fax: 410-962-4760; *State Director:* Lori Albin

6404 Ivy Lane, #406, Greenbelt, MD 20770-1407; 301-345-5517; Fax: 301-345-7573; *Asst. to the Senator:* Nichelle Schoultz

32 W. Washington St., Room 203, Hagerstown, MD 21740-4804; 301-797-2826; Fax: 301-797-2241; *Outreach Rep.:* Juliana Albowicz

The Gallery Plaza Bldg., 212 W. Main St., #200, Salisbury, MD 21801-5106; 410-546-7711; Fax: 410-546-9324; *Special Asst. to the Senator:* Linda Prochaska

Committee Assignments: Appropriations, Chair; Health, Education, Labor, and Pensions; Select Intelligence

Moran, Jerry, R-Kans.

Capitol Hill Office: 361A SROB 20510-1606; 224-6521; Fax: 228-6966; *Chief of Staff:* Todd Novascone
Web: http://moran.senate.gov/public/
Facebook: http://facebook.com/jerrymoran
Twitter: http://twitter.com/jerrymoran
District Offices: P.O. Box 249, 1200 Main St., #402, Hays, KS 67601-3649; 785-628-6401; Fax: 785-628-3791; *Field Rep.:* Chelsey Gillogly

923 Westport Pl., #210, P.O. Box 067, Manhattan, KS 66502; 785-539-8973; Fax: 785-587-0789; *State Rep.:* Brennen Britton

P.O. Box 1154, 23600 College Blvd., #201, Olathe, KS 66061-8709; 913-393-0711; Fax: 913-768-1366; *Kansas Scheduler:* Lisa Dethloff

P.O. Box 1372, 306 N. Broadway St., #125, Pittsburg, KS 66762-4836; 620-232-2286; Fax: 620-232-2284; *District Rep.:* Pam Henderson

P.O. Box 781753, 3450 N. Rock Rd., Bldg. 200, #209, Wichita, KS 67226-1352; 316-631-1410; Fax: 316-631-1297; *Deputy State Director:* Mike Zamrzla

Committee Assignments: Appropriations; Banking, Housing, and Urban Affairs; Veterans' Affairs

Murkowski, Lisa, R-Alaska

Capitol Hill Office: 709 SHOB 20510-0203; 224-6665; Fax: 224-5301; *Chief of Staff:* Edward G. Hild

Web: http://murkowski.senate.gov/

Facebook: http://facebook.com/SenLisaMurkowski

Twitter: http://twitter.com/lisamurkowski

District Offices: 510 L St., #600, Anchorage, AK 99501-1956; 907-271-3735; Fax: 877-857-0322; *State Director:* Kevin Sweeney

101 12th Ave., #329, Fairbanks, AK 99701-6237; 907-456-0233; Fax: 907-451-7146; *Special Asst.:* Althea St. Martin

800 Glacier Ave., #101, Juneau, AK 99801-1852; 907-586-7277; Fax: 907-586-7201; *Special Asst.:* Sonia Henrick

805 Frontage Rd., #105, Kenai, AK 99611-9104; 907-283-5808; Fax: 907-283-4363; *Special Asst.:* Michelle Blackwell

4079 Tongass Ave., #204, Ketchikan, AK 99901-5526; 907-225-6880; Fax: 907-225-0390; *Special Asst.:* Sonia Henrick

851 E. Westpoint Dr., #307, Wasilla, AK 99654-7183; 907-376-7665; Fax: 907-376-8526; *Special Asst.:* Gerri Sumpter

Committee Assignments: Appropriations; Energy and Natural Resources, Ranking Minority Member; Health, Education, Labor, and Pensions; Indian Affairs

Murphy, Chris, D-Conn.

Capitol Hill Office: 303 SHOB 20510; 224-4041; Fax: 224-9750; *Chief of Staff:* Francis Creighton

Web: http://murphy.senate.gov/

Facebook: http://facebook.com/ChrisMurphyCT

Twitter: http://twitter.com/ChrisMurphyCT

District Offices: One Constitution Plaza, 7th Floor, Hartford, CT 06103; 860-549-8463; Fax: 860-524-5091; *State Director:* Kenny Curran

Committee Assignments: Foreign Relations; Health, Education, Labor, and Pensions; Joint Economic

Murray, Patty, D-Wash.

Capitol Hill Office: 154 SROB 20510; 224-2621; Fax: 224-0238; *Chief of Staff:* Mike Spahn

Web: http://murray.senate.gov/

Facebook: http://facebook.com/pattymurray

Twitter: http://twitter.com/pattymurray

District Offices: 2930 Wetmore Ave., #903, Everett, WA 98201-4067; 425-259-6515; Fax: 425-259-7152; *Regional Director:* Max Brown

2988 Jackson Federal Bldg., 915 2nd Ave., Seattle, WA 98174-1003; 206-553-5545; Fax: 206-553-0891; *State Director:* Brian Kristjansson

10 N. Post St., #600, Spokane, WA 99201-0712; 509-624-9515; Fax: 509-624-9561; *Eastern Washington Director:* John Culton

950 Pacific Ave., #650, Tacoma, WA 98402-4450; 253-572-3636; Fax: 253-572-9488; *South Sound Director:* Kristiné Reeves (Temporary Field Rep.: Katie Whittier)

Marshall House, 1323 Officers Row, Vancouver, WA 98661-3856; 360-696-7797; Fax: 360-696-7798; *Southwest Washington Regional Rep.:* David Hodges

402 E. Yakima Ave., #420, Yakima, WA 98901-2760; 509-453-7462; Fax: 509-453-7731; *Central Washington Director:* Rebecca Thornton

Committee Assignments: Appropriations; Budget, Chair; Health, Education, Labor, and Pensions; Rules and Administration; Veterans' Affairs

Nelson, Bill, D-Fla.

Capitol Hill Office: 716 SHOB 20510-0905; 224-5274; Fax: 228-2183; *Chief of Staff:* Peter J. Mitchell

Web: http://billnelson.senate.gov/

Facebook: http://facebook.com/billnelson

Twitter: http://twitter.com/senbillnelson

District Offices: 2925 Salzedo St., Coral Gables, FL 33134-6611; 305-536-5999; Fax: 305-536-5991; *Regional Director:* Pedro Villa

3416 S. University Dr., Ft. Lauderdale, FL 33328-2022; 954-693-4851; Fax: 954-693-4862; *Regional Director*: Willowstine Lawson

Justice Center Annex Bldg., 2000 Main St., #801, Ft. Myers, FL 33901-5503; 239-334-7760; Fax: 239-334-7710; *Regional Director:* Diana McGee

1301 Riverplace Blvd., #2010, Jacksonville, FL 32207-9021; 904-346-4500; Fax: 904-346-4506; *Regional Director:* Katie Ross

Landmark Two, 225 E. Robinson St., #410, Orlando, FL 32801-4326; 407-872-7161; Fax: 407-872-7165; *Director of Constituent Services:* Sherry Davich

U.S. Courthouse Annex, 111 N. Adams St., Tallahassee, FL 32301-7736; 850-942-8415; Fax: 850-942-8450; *Director of Outreach:* Mary-Louise Hester

Sam M. Gibbons Federal Courthouse, 801 N. Florida Ave., 4th Floor, Tampa, FL 33602-3849; 813-225-7040; Fax: 813-225-7050; *Regional Director:* Digna Alvarez

413 Clematis St., #210, West Palm Beach, FL 33401-5319; 561-514-0189; Fax: 561-514-4078; *Regional Director:* Michelle McGovern

Committee Assignments: Armed Services; Budget; Commerce, Science, and Transportation; Finance; Special Aging, Chair

Paul, Rand, R-Ky.

Capitol Hill Office: 124 SROB 20510-1704; 224-4343; Fax: 228-6917; *Chief of Staff:* William Henderson

Web: http://paul.senate.gov/
Facebook: http://facebook.com/SenatorRandPaul
Twitter: http://twitter.com/SenRandPaul
District Offices: 1029 State St., Bowling Green, KY 42101-2652; 270-782-8303; Fax: 270-782-8315; *Casework Supervisor:* Bobette Franklin
541 Buttermilk Pike, #102, Crescent Springs, KY 41017-1689; 859-426-0165; *Field Rep.:* Vacant
William D. Gorman Education Center, 601 Main St., #2, Hazard, KY 41701-1382; 606-435-2390; Fax: 606-435-1761; *Field Rep.:* Bryan Mills
1100 S. Main St., #12, Hopkinsville, KY 42240-2079; 270-885-1212; *Deputy State Director:* Rachel McCubbin
771 Corporate Dr., #105, Lexington, KY 40503; 859-219-2239; *Field Rep.:* Dan Bayens
600 Dr. Martin Luther King, Jr. Pl., Room 1072B, Louisville, KY 40202-2230; 502-582-5341; *State Director:* Jim Milliman
423 Frederica St., #305, Owensboro, KY 42301-3013; 270-689-9085; *Field Rep.:* Jason Hastert
Committee Assignments: Foreign Relations; Health, Education, Labor, and Pensions; Homeland Security and Governmental Affairs; Small Business and Entrepreneurship

Portman, Rob, R-Ohio

Capitol Hill Office: 338 SROB 20510-3506; 224-3353; Fax: 224-9075; *Chief of Staff:* Robert D. Lehman
Web: http://portman.senate.gov/
Facebook: http://facebook.com/robportman
Twitter: http://twitter.com/robportman
District Offices: 312 Walnut St., #3075, Cincinnati, OH 45202; 513-684-3265; *Southwest Ohio District Director:* Connie Laug
1240 E. 9th St., Room 3061, Cleveland, OH 44199-2001; 216-522-7095; *Northeast Ohio District Director:* Caryn Candisky
37 W. Broad St., Room 300, Columbus, OH 43215-4180; 614-469-6774; *State Director:* Teri Geiger
420 Madison Ave., Room 1210, Toledo, OH 43604-1221; 419-259-3895; *Grant Coord.:* Linda Greenwood
Committee Assignments: Budget; Energy and Natural Resources; Finance; Homeland Security and Governmental Affairs

Pryor, Mark, D-Ark.

Capitol Hill Office: 255 SDOB 20510-0405; 224-2353; Fax: 228-0908; *Chief of Staff:* Andy York
Web: http://pryor.senate.gov/
Facebook: http://facebook.com/MarkPryor
Twitter: https://twitter.com/senmarkpryor
District Offices: The River Market, 500 Clinton Ave., #401, Little Rock, AR 72201-1745; 501-324-6336; Fax: 501-324-5320; *State Director:* Randy Massanelli
Committee Assignments: Appropriations; Commerce, Science, and Transportation; Homeland Security and Governmental Affairs; Rules and Administration; Small Business and Entrepreneurship; Select Ethics

Reed, Jack D., D-R.I.

Capitol Hill Office: 728 SHOB 20510-3903; 224-4642; Fax: 224-4680; *Chief of Staff:* Neil D. Campbell
Web: http://reed.senate.gov/
Facebook: http://facebook.com/SenJackReed
Twitter: http://twitter.com/SenJackReed
District Offices: 1000 Chapel View Blvd., #290, Cranston, RI 02920-5602; 401-943-3100; Fax: 401-464-6837; *Rhode Island Chief of Staff:* Raymond Simone
U.S. Courthouse, One Exchange Terrace, #408, Providence, RI 02903-1773; 401-528-5200; Fax: 202-224-4680; *Policy Director:* Aaron Donovan
Committee Assignments: Appropriations; Armed Services; Banking, Housing, and Urban Affairs

Reid, Harry, D-Nev.

Capitol Hill Office: 522 SHOB 20510-2803; 224-3542; Fax: 224-7327; *Chief of Staff:* David B. Krone
Web: http://reid.senate.gov/
Facebook: http://facebook.com/HarryReid
Twitter: http://twitter.com/SenatorReid
District Offices: 600 E. William St., #302, Carson City, NV 89701-4052; 775-882-7343; Fax: 775-883-1980; *Regional Rep.:* Yolanda Garcia/Jared Perkins
Lloyd D. George, 333 Las Vegas Blvd. South, #8016, Las Vegas, NV 89101-7075; 702-388-5020; Fax: 702-388-5030; *Southern Nevada Director:* Shannon Raborn
Courthouse and Federal Bldg., 400 S. Virginia St., #902, Reno, NV 89501-2109; 775-686-5750; Fax: 775-686-5757; *State Director:* Mary Conelly
Committee Assignments: Select Intelligence

Risch, James E., R-Idaho

Capitol Hill Office: 483 SROB 20510-1206; 224-2752; Fax: 224-2573; *Chief of Staff:* John A. Sandy
Web: http://risch.senate.gov/
Twitter: http://twitter.com/SenatorRisch
District Offices: 350 N. 9th St., #302, Boise, ID 83702-5409; 208-342-7985; Fax: 208-343-2458; *Regional Director:* Melinda Smyser
Harbor Plaza, 610 W. Hubbard St., #213, Coeur D'Alene, ID 83814-2288; 208-667-6130; Fax: 208-765-1743; *Regional Director:* Sid Smith
901 Pier View Dr., #202A, Idaho Falls, ID 83402-5070; 208-523-5541; Fax: 208-523-9373; *Regional Director:* Amy Taylor
313 D St., #106, Lewiston, ID 83501-1894; 208-743-0792; Fax: 208-746-7275; *Regional Director:* Mike Hanna
275 S. 5th Ave., #290, Pocatello, ID 83201-6410; 208-236-6817; Fax: 208-236-6820; *Regional Director:* Jeremy Field
1411 Falls Ave. East, #201, Twin Falls, ID 83301-3455; 208-734-6780; Fax: 208-734-3905; *Regional Director:* Mike Matthews
Committee Assignments: Energy and Natural Resources; Foreign Relations; Small Business and Entrepreneurship, Ranking Minority Member; Select Ethics; Select Intelligence

Roberts, Pat, R-Kans.

Capitol Hill Office: 109 SHOB 20510-1605; 224-4774; Fax: 224-3514; *Chief of Staff Ethics:* Jackie Cottrell
Web: http://roberts.senate.gov/
Facebook: http://facebook.com/SenPatRoberts
Twitter: http://twitter.com/senpatroberts
District Offices: 100 Military Plaza, P.O. Box 550 , Dodge City, KS 67801-4990; 620-227-2244; Fax: 620-227-2264; *District Director:* Debbie Pugh
11900 College Blvd., #203, Overland Park, KS 66210-3939; 913-451-9343; Fax: 913-451-9446; *State Director:* Chad Tenpenny
Frank Carlson Federal Bldg., 444 S.E. Quincy St., #392, Topeka, KS 66683-3599; 785-295-2745; Fax: 785-235-3665; *District Director:* Gilda Lintz
155 N. Market St., #120, Wichita, KS 67202-1802; 316-263-0416; Fax: 316-263-0273; *District Director:* Karin Wisdom
Committee Assignments: Agriculture, Nutrition, and Forestry; Finance; Health, Education, Labor, and Pensions; Rules and Administration, Ranking Minority Member; Select Ethics; Joint Printing; Joint Library of Congress

Rockefeller, Jay, D-W.Va.

Capitol Hill Office: 531 SHOB 20510-4802; 224-6472; Fax: 224-7665; *Chief of Staff:* James Reid
Web: http://rockefeller.senate.gov/
Facebook: http://facebook.com/SenRockefeller
Twitter: http://twitter.com/senrockefeller
District Offices: 220 N. Kanawha St., #1, Beckley, WV 25801-4514; 304-253-9704; Fax: 304-253-2578; *Area Coord.:* Jennifer Pennington
405 Capitol St., #508, Charleston, WV 25301-1749; 304-347-5372; Fax: 304-347-5371; *State Director:* Rochelle Goodwin
118 Adams St., #301, Fairmont, WV 26554-2841; 304-367-0122; Fax: 304-367-0822; *Staff Asst.:* Patty Hawkins
217 W. King St., #307, Martinsburg, WV 25401-3211; 304-262-9285; Fax: 304-262-9288; *Director, Eastern West Virginia Satellite Office:* Penny Porter
Committee Assignments: Commerce, Science, and Transportation, Chair; Finance; Veterans' Affairs; Joint Taxation

Rubio, Marco, R-Fla.

Capitol Hill Office: 284 SROB 20510; 224-3041; Fax: 228-0285; *Chief of Staff:* Cesar V. Conda
Web: http://rubio.senate.gov/
Facebook: http://facebook.com/SenatorMarcoRubio
Twitter: http://twitter.com/SenRubioPress
District Offices: 1650 Prudential Dr., #220, Jacksonville, FL 32207-8149; 904-398-8586; *Regional Director:* Adele Griffin
8669 N.W. 36th St., #110, Doral, FL 33166-6640; 305-418-8553; *Regional Director:* Alyn Fernandez
3229 E. Tamiami Trail, #106, Naples, FL 34112; 239-213-1521; *Regional Director:* Zachary Zampella
201 S. Orange Ave., #350, Orlando, FL 32801-3499; 407-254-2573; *State Director:* Todd Reid
1 N. Palafox St., #159, Pensacola, FL 32502-5658; 850-433-2603; *Regional Director:* Kris Tande
402 S. Monroe St., #2105E, Tallahassee, FL 32399-6526; 850-599-9100; *Regional Director:* Janelle Pepe
3802 Spectrum Blvd., #106, Tampa, FL 33612-9220; 813-977-6450; *Regional Director:* Ryan Patmintra
4580 PGA Blvd., #201, Palm Beach Gardens, FL 33418; 561-775-3360; *Regional Director:* Greg Longowski
Committee Assignments: Commerce, Science, and Transportation; Foreign Relations; Small Business and Entrepreneurship; Select Intelligence

Sanders, Bernie, I-Vt.

Capitol Hill Office: 332 SDOB 20510-4504; 224-5141; Fax: 228-0776; *Chief of Staff:* Michaeleen Crowell
Web: http://sanders.senate.gov/
Facebook: http://facebook.com/senatorsanders
Twitter: http://twitter.com/SenatorSanders
District Offices: 1 Church St., 3rd Floor, Burlington, VT 05401-4451; 802-862-0697; Fax: 802-860-6370; *Outreach Director:* Phil Fiermonte
357 Western Ave., #1B, St. Johnsbury, VT 05819; 802-748-0191; Fax: 802-748-0302; *Agriculture Policy Advisor; Legis. Liaison:* Jenny Nelson
Committee Assignments: Budget; Energy and Natural Resources; Environment and Public Works; Health, Education, Labor, and Pensions; Veterans' Affairs, Chair; Joint Economic Committee

Schatz, Brian, D-Hawaii

Capitol Hill Office: 722 SHOB 20510; 224-3934; Fax: 228-1153; *Chief of Staff:* Andrew Winer
Web: http://schatz.senate.gov/
Facebook: http://facebook.com/BrianSchatz
Twitter: http://twitter.com/brianschatz
District Offices: 300 Ala Moana Blvd., Room 7-212, Honolulu, HI 96850; 808-523-2061; Fax: 808-523-206; *Political Director:* Kimberley Yoshimoto
Committee Assignments: Commerce, Science, and Transportation; Energy and Natural Resources, Indian Affairs

Schumer, Charles E., D-N.Y.

Capitol Hill Office: 322 SHOB 20510-3203; 224-6542; Fax: 228-3027; *Chief of Staff:* Mike Lynch
Web: http://schumer.senate.gov/
Facebook: http://facebook.com/chuckschumer
Twitter: http://twitter.com/chuckschumer
District Offices: Leo O'Brien Bldg., Room 420, Albany, NY 12207; 518-431-4070; Fax: 518-431-4076; *Deputy State Director:* Steve Mann
15 Henry St., Room 100 A-F , Binghamton, NY 13901; 607-772-6792; Fax: 607-772-8124; *Regional Rep.:* Amanda Spellicy
130 S. Elmwood Ave., #660, Buffalo, NY 14202-2371; 716-846-4111; Fax: 716-846-4113; *Regional Rep.:* Nick Dhimitri

145 Pine Lawn Rd., #300, Melville, NY 11747; 631-753-0978; Fax: 631-753-0997; *Regional Rep.:* Kyle Strober

780 3rd Ave., #2301, New York, NY 10017-2110; 212-486-4430; Fax: 202-228-2838; *State Director:* Martin Brennan

One Park Pl., #100, Peekskill, NY 10566; 914-734-1532; Fax: 914-734-1673; *Regional Rep.:* Cody Peluso

100 State St., Room 3040, Rochester, NY 14614-1317; 585-263-5866; Fax: 585-263-3173; *Regional Rep.:* Christopher Zeltmann

100 S. Clinton St., Room 841, Syracuse, NY 13261-7318; 315-423-5471; Fax: 315-423-5185; *Regional Rep.:* Angelo Roefaro

Committee Assignments: Banking, Housing, and Urban Affairs; Finance; Judiciary; Rules and Administration, Chair; Joint Printing, Chair; Joint Library of Congress, Vice Chair

Scott, Tim, R-S.C.

Capitol Hill Office: 167 SROB 20510-4004; 224-6121; Fax: 228-5143; *Chief of Staff:* Mike Bennett
Web: http://scott.senate.gov/
Facebook: http://facebook.com/SenatorTimScott
Twitter: http://twitter.com/SenatorTimScott
District Offices: 1301 Gervais St., #825, Columbia, SC 29201-2435; 803-771-6112; Fax: 855-802-9355; *State Director:* Matt Moore

40 W. Broad St., #320, Greenville, SC 29601; 864-233-5366; Fax: 855-802-9355; *Constituent Services Director:* Deb Blickenstaff

2500 City Hall Lane, 3rd Floor, North Charleston, SC 29406; 843-727-4525; Fax: 855-802-9355; *Executive Director:* Joe McKeown

Committee Assignments: Commerce, Science, and Transportation; Energy and Natural Resources; Health, Education, Labor, and Pensions; Small Business and Entrepreneurship, Special Aging

Sessions, Jeff A., R-Ala.

Capitol Hill Office: 326 SROB 20510-0104; 224-4124; Fax: 224-3149; *Chief of Staff:* Rick A. Dearborn
Web: http://sessions.senate.gov/
Facebook: http://facebook.com/jeffsessions
Twitter: http://twitter.com/senatorsessions
District Offices: 341 Vance Federal Bldg., 1800 5th Ave., N., Birmingham, AL 35203-2171; 205-731-1500; Fax: 205-731-0221; *Field Rep.:* Virginia Amason

100 W. Troy St., #302, Dothan, AL 36303-4574; 334-792-4924; Fax: 334-792-4928; *Caseworker:* Lindsay Grubbs

200 Clinton Ave., N.W., #802, Huntsville, AL 35801-4932; 256-533-0979; Fax: 256-533-0745; *Caseworker:* Shan McMillan

41 W. I-65 Service Rd. N., #2003-A, Mobile, AL 36608; 251-414-3083; Fax: 251-414-5845; *Caseworker:* Susan Thompson

7550 Halcyon Summit Dr., #150, Montgomery, AL 36117-7012; 334-244-7017; Fax: 334-244-7091; *Field Rep.:* Cecelia Meeks

Committee Assignments: Armed Services; Budget, Ranking Minority Member; Environment and Public Works; Judiciary

Shaheen, Jeanne, D-N.H.

Capitol Hill Office: 520 SHOB 20510-2906; 224-2841; Fax: 228-3194; *Chief of Staff:* Maura Keefe
Web: http://shaheen.senate.gov/
Facebook: http://facebook.com/SenatorShaheen
Twitter: http://twitter.com/SenatorShaheen
District Offices: 961 Main St., Berlin, NH 03570-3031; 603-752-6300; Fax: 603-752-6305; *Special Asst. for Constituent Services/Outreach:* Chuck Henderson

50 Opera House Square, Claremont, NH 03743-5407; 603-542-4872; Fax: 603-542-6582; *Special Asst. for Constituent Services/Outreach:* Bethany Yeurek

340 Central Ave., #205, Dover, NH 03820-3770; 603-750-3004; *Special Asst. for Constituent Services / Outreach:* Cara Osborn

1589 Elm St., #3, Manchester, NH 03101-1261; 603-647-7500; *Acting State Director:* Sarah Holmes

60 Main St., Nashua, NH 03060-2720; 603-883-0196; *Special Asst. for Constituent Services/Outreach:* Letizia Ortiz

12 Gilbo Ave., Ste. C, Keene, NH 03431; 603-358-6604; *Special Asst. for Constituent Services/Outreach:* Pam Slack

Committee Assignments: Commission on Security and Cooperation in Europe (Helsinki Commission); Appropriations; Armed Services; Foreign Relations; Small Business and Entrepreneurship

Shelby, Richard, R-Ala.

Capitol Hill Office: 304 SROB 20510-0103; 224-5744; Fax: 224-3416; *Chief of Staff:* Alan R. Hanson
Web: http://shelby.senate.gov/
Facebook: http://facebook.com/RichardShelby
Twitter: http://twitter.com/SenShelby
District Offices: 321 Federal Bldg., 1800 5th Ave. N., #321, Birmingham, AL 35203-2113; 205-731-1384; Fax: 205-731-1386; *State Rep.:* Heather Adams

1000 Glenn Hearn Blvd., #20127, Huntsville, AL 35824-2107; 256-772-0460; Fax: 256-772-8387; *State Rep.:* Carrie Suggs

445 Federal Courthouse, 113 St. Joseph St., Mobile, AL 36602-3606; 251-694-4164; Fax: 251-694-4166; *State Rep.:* Tera Johnson

Frank M. Johnson, Jr. Federal Courthouse, 15 Lee St., #208, Montgomery, AL 36104-4054; 334-223-7303; Fax: 334-223-7317; *State Rep.:* Vera Jordan

2005 University Blvd., #2100, Tuscaloosa, AL 35401; 205-759-5047; Fax: 205-759-5067; *State Rep.:* Kay Presley

Committee Assignments: Appropriations, Ranking Minority Member; Banking, Housing, and Urban Affairs; Rules and Administration

Stabenow, Debbie A., D-Mich.

Capitol Hill Office: 133 SHOB 20510-2204; 224-4822; Fax: 228-0325; *Chief of Staff:* Bill Sweeney
Web: http://stabenow.senate.gov/
Facebook: https://facebook.com/stabenow
Twitter: http://twitter.com/StabenowPress
District Offices: 243 W. Congress St., #550, Detroit, MI 48226-3248; 313-961-4330; Fax: 313-961-7566; *Regional Manager:* Korey Hall, Barbara McCalahan, Matt Williams

221 W. Lake Lansing Rd., #100, East Lansing, MI 48823-8661; 517-203-1760; Fax: 517-203-1778; *State Director:* Teresa Plachetka; *Regional Manager:* Kali Fox

432 Saginaw St., #301, Flint, MI 48502; 810-720-4172; Fax: 810-720-4178; *Regional Manager:* Adrian Walker

3280 Beltline Court, N.E., #400, Grand Rapids, MI 49525-9494; 616-975-0052; Fax: 616-975-5764; *Regional Manager:* Mary Judnich

1901 W. Ridge St., #7, Marquette, MI 49855-3198; 906-228-8756; Fax: 906-228-9162; *Regional Manager:* Jeremy Hosking

3335 S. Airport Rd. W., #6B, Traverse City, MI 49684-7928; 231-929-1031; Fax: 231-929-1250; *Regional Manager:* Brandon Fewins

Committee Assignments: Agriculture, Nutrition, and Forestry, Chair; Budget; Energy and Natural Resources; Finance

Tester, Jon, D-Mont.

Capitol Hill Office: 724 SHOB 20510-2604; 224-2644; Fax: 224-8594; *Chief of Staff:* Tom Lopach
Web: http://tester.senate.gov/
Facebook: http://facebook.com/senatortester
Twitter: http://twitter.com/jontester
District Offices: 2900 4th Ave. N., #201, Billings, MT 59101; 406-252-0550; Fax: 406-252-7768; *Scheduler:* Jeanne Forrester

1 E. Main St., #202, Bozeman, MT 59715-6248; 406-586-4450; Fax: 406-586-7647; *Regional Director:* Jennifer Madgic

Silver Bow Center, 125 W. Granite St., #200, Butte, MT 59701-9215; 406-723-3277; Fax: 406-782-4717; *Regional Director:* Erik Nylund

122 W. Towne St., Glendive, MT 59330-1735; 406-365-2391; Fax: 406-365-8836; *Regional Director:* Penny Zimmerman

119 1st Ave. N., #102, Great Falls, MT 59401-2568; 406-452-9585; Fax: 406-452-9586; *Regional Director:* Cheryl Ulmer

Capital One Center, 208 N. Montana Ave., #202, Helena, MT 59601-3837; 406-449-5401; Fax: 406-449-5462; *Veteran Liaison:* Bruce Knutson

14 3rd St. East, #230, Kalispell, MT 59901-4588; 406-257-3360; Fax: 406-257-3974; *Regional Director:* Virginia Sloan

130 W. Front St., Missoula, MT 59802-4304; 406-728-3003; Fax: 406-728-2193; *State Director:* Dayna Swanson, *Regional Director:* Deborah Frandsen

Committee Assignments: Appropriations; Banking, Housing, and Urban Affairs; Homeland Security and Governmental Affairs; Indian Affairs; Veterans' Affairs

Thune, John, R-S.D.

Capitol Hill Office: 511 SDOB 20510-4105; 224-2321; Fax: 228-5429; *Chief of Staff:* Ryan P. Nelson
Web: http://thune.senate.gov/
Facebook: http://facebook.com/johnthune
Twitter: http://twitter.com/johnthune
District Offices: 320 S. 1st St., #101, Aberdeen, SD 57401-4168; 605-225-8823; Fax: 605-225-8468; *Northeast Regional Director:* Judy Vrchota

1313 W. Main St., Rapid City, SD 57701-2540; 605-348-7551; Fax: 605-348-7208; *West River Regional Director:* Qusi Al-Haj

320 N. Main Ave., Suite B, Sioux Falls, SD 57104-6056; 605-334-9596; Fax: 605-334-2591; *Chief of Staff; State Director:* Ryan Nelson

Committee Assignments: Agriculture, Nutrition, and Forestry; Commerce, Science, and Transportation, Ranking Minority Member; Finance

Toomey, Pat, R-Pa.

Capitol Hill Office: 248 SROB 20510-3806; 224-4254; Fax: 228-0284; *Chief of Staff:* Christopher T. Gahan
Web: http://toomey.senate.gov/
Facebook: http://facebook.com/senatortoomey
Twitter: http://twitter.com/sentoomey
District Offices: 1150 S. Cedar Crest Blvd., #101, Allentown, PA 18103-7937; 610-434-1444; Fax: 610-434-1844; *Deputy State Director:* Sue Zimskind

Federal Bldg., 17 S. Park Row, #B-120, Erie, PA 16501-1156; 814-453-3010; Fax: 814-455-9925; *Northwest Pennsylvania Regional Manager:* Sheila Sterrett

Federal Bldg., 228 Walnut St., #1104, Harrisburg, PA 17101-1722; 717-782-3951; Fax: 717-782-4920; *State Director:* Bob DeSousa

Richland Square III, 1397 Eisenhower Blvd., #302, Johnstown, PA 15904-3267; 814-266-5970; Fax: 814-266-5973; *Greater Johnstown Regional Manager:* John Frick

1628 JFK Blvd., 8 Penn Center, #1702, Philadelphia, PA 19103-2136; 215-241-1090; Fax: 215-241-1095; *Southeast Pennsylvania Director:* Mitch Vidovitch

100 W. Station Square Dr., #225, Pittsburgh, PA 15219-1180; 412-803-3501; Fax: 412-803-3504; *Western Pennsylvania Director:* Matthew Blackburn

538 Spruce St., #302, Scranton, PA 18503-1816; 570-941-3540; Fax: 570-941-3544; *Northeast Pennsylvania Regional Manager:* Brian Langan

Committee Assignments: Banking, Housing, and Urban Affairs; Budget; Finance; Joint Economic Committee

Udall, Mark, D-Colo.

Capitol Hill Office: 730 SHOB 20510-0607; 224-5941; Fax: 224-6471; *Chief of Staff:* Michael L. Sozan
Web: http://markudall.senate.gov/
Facebook: http://facebook.com/markudall

Twitter: http://twitter.com/MarkUdall

District Offices: 609 Main St., #205, Alamosa, CO 81101-2557; 719-589-2101; *Regional Director:* Erin Minks

P.O. Box 866, Clark, CO 80428; 303-650-7820; *Regional Director:* Jay Fetcher

2880 International Circle, #107, Colorado Springs, CO 80910; 719-471-3993; *Regional Director:* Angela Joslyn

999 18th St., North Tower, #1525, Denver, CO 80202-2499; 303-650-7820; Fax: 303-650-7827; *State Director:* Jennifer Rokala

954 E. 2nd Ave., #106, Durango, CO 81301-5109; 970-247-1047; *Regional Director:* Wanda Cason

400 Rood Ave., #220, Grand Junction, CO 81501-2520; 970-245-9553; Fax: 970-245-9523; *Regional Director:* Jerry Otero

801 8th St., #140A, Greeley, CO 80631-3900; 970-356-5586; *Regional Director:* Pamela Shaddock

107 W. B St., Pueblo, CO 81003-3400; 719-542-1701; *Regional Director:* Gloria Gutierrez

Committee Assignments: Armed Services; Energy and Natural Resources; Select Intelligence

Udall, Tom, D-N.M.

Capitol Hill Office: 110 SHOB 20510-3103; 224-6621; Fax: 228-3261; *Chief of Staff:* Michael Collins

Web: http://tomudall.senate.gov/

Facebook: http://facebook.com/senatortomudall

Twitter: http://twitter.com/SenatorTomUdall

District Offices: 219 Central Ave. N.W., #210, Albuquerque, NM 87102; 505-346-6791; Fax: 505-346-6720; *State Director:* Bianca Wertheim

102 W. Hagerman St., Suite A, Carlsbad, NM 88220; 575-234-0366; Fax: 575-234-1507; *Field Rep.:* Beverly Allen-Ananins

201 N. Church St., #201B, Las Cruces, NM 88001; 575-526-5475; Fax: 575-523-6589; *Field Rep.:* Elizabeth Driggers

120 S. Federal Pl., #302, Santa Fe, NM 87501-1966; 505-988-6511; Fax: 505-988-6514; *Field Rep.:* Michele Jacquez-Ortiz

100 S. Ave. A, #113, Portales, NM 88130; 575-356-6811; *Field Rep.:* Jack Carpenter

Committee Assignments: Commission on Security and Cooperation in Europe (Helsinki Commission); Appropriations; Environment and Public Works; Foreign Relations; Indian Affairs; Rules and Administration; Joint Printing

Vitter, David, R-La.

Capitol Hill Office: 516 SHOB 20510-1805; 224-4623; Fax: 228-5061; *Chief of Staff:* Kyle Ruckert

Web: http://vitter.senate.gov/

Facebook: http://facebook.com/DavidVitter

Twitter: http://twitter.com/DavidVitter

District Offices: Plaza 28, 6501 Coliseum Blvd., #700-A, Alexandria, LA 71303; 318-448-0169; Fax: 318-448-0189; *Regional Rep.:* Quint Carriere

858 Convention St., Baton Rouge, LA 70802-5626; 225-383-0331; Fax: 225-383-0952; *State Director:* David Doss

2201 Kaliste Saloom Rd., #201 Lafayette, LA 70508; 337-993-9502; Fax: 337-993-9567; *Deputy State Director:* Nicole Hebert

1424 Ryan St., Ste. A, Lake Charles, LA 70601; 337-436-0453; Fax: 337-436-3163; *Regional Rep.:* Brooke David

2800 Veterans Blvd., #201, Metairie, LA 70002; 504-589-2753; Fax: 504-589-2607; *State Director:* David Doss

1651 Louisville Ave., Monroe, LA 71201-5435; 318-325-8120; Fax: 318-325-9165; *Regional Rep.:* Hayden Haines

920 Pierremont Rd., #113, Shreveport, LA 71106-2079; 318-861-0437; Fax: 318-861-4865; *Regional Director:* Chip Layton

Committee Assignments: Armed Services; Banking, Housing, and Urban Affairs; Environment and Public Works, Ranking Minority Member; Small Business and Entrepreneurship

Walsh, John, D-Mont.

Capitol Hill Office: 2 Russell Courtyard SROB 20510; 224-2651; *Chief of Staff:* Elizabeth Kelley

Web: http://johnwalsh2014.com/

Facebook: http://facebook.com/WalshforMontana

Twitter: https://twitter.com/JohnWalsh

District Offices: 30 W. 14th St., #206, Helena, MT 59601; 406-449-5480; Fax: 406-449-5484; *State Scheduler:* Holly Luck

222 N. 32nd St., #100, Billings, MT 59101; 406-657-6790; Fax: 406-657-6793; *Regional Director:* James Corson

280 E. Front St., #100, Missoula, MT 59802; 406-329-3123; Fax: 406-728-7610; *Field Rep.:* Maureen Porter

8 Third St. E., Kalispell, MT 59901; 406-756-1150; Fax: 406-756-1152

220 W. Lamme St., #1D, Bozeman, MT 59715; 406-586-6104; Fax: 406-587-9177; *State Director:* Brianne Dugan

245 E. Park St., Lower Level East, Butte, MT 59701; 406-782-8700; Fax: 406-782-6553; *Regional Director:* Kim Kreuger

113 3rd St. N., Great Falls, MT 59401; 406-761-1574; Fax: 406-452-1117; *Regional Director:* Bonnie Keller

122 W. Towne St., Glendive, MT 59330; 406-365-7002; Fax: 406-365-7040; *Field Director:* Cathy Kirkpatrick

Committee Assignments: Special Aging; Agriculture, Nutrition, and Forestry; Commerce, Science, and Transportation; Rules and Administration

Warner, Mark R., D-Va.

Capitol Hill Office: 475 SROB 20510-4606; 224-2023; Fax: 224-6295; *Chief of Staff:* Luke S. Albee

Web: http://warner.senate.gov/

Facebook: http://facebook.com/MarkRWarner

Twitter: http://twitter.com/MarkWarner

District Offices: 180 W. Main St., Abingdon, VA 24210-2844; 276-628-8158; Fax: 276-628-1036; *Outreach Rep.:* Drew Lumpkin

101 W. Main St., #4900, Norfolk, VA 23510-1690; 757-441-3079; Fax: 757-441-6250; *Constituent Services Director:* Denise Goode

919 E. Main St., #630, Richmond, VA 23219-4600; 804-775-2314; Fax: 804-775-2319; *State Director:* Dietra Trent

129B Salem Ave., S.W., Roanoke, VA 24011-1203; 540-857-2676; Fax: 540-857-2800; *Constituent Services Director:* Lou Kadiri

8000 Towers Crescent Dr., #200, Vienna, VA 22182-6203; 703-442-0670; Fax: 703-442-0408; *State Services Director:* Ann Rust

Committee Assignments: Banking, Housing, and Urban Affairs; Budget; Commerce, Science, and Transportation; Rules and Administration; Joint Economic Committee; Select Intelligence; Joint Printing

Warren, Elizabeth, D-Mass.

Capitol Hill Office: 2 Russell Courtyard SROB 20510; 224-4543; Fax: 228-2072; *Chief of Staff:* Mindy Myers
Web: http://warren.senate.gov/
Facebook: http://facebook.com/senatorelizabethwarren
Twitter: http://twitter.com/senwarren
District Offices: 2400 John F. Kennedy Federal Bldg., 15 New Sudbury St., Boston, MA 02203; 617-565-3170; Fax: 617-723-7325; *State Director:* Roger Lau

1550 Main St., #406, Springfield, MA 01103-1429; 413-788-2690; *Regional Rep.:* Jeremiah Thompson
Committee Assignments: Banking, Housing, and Urban Affairs; Health, Education, Labor, and Pensions; Special Aging

Whitehouse, Sheldon, D-R.I.

Capitol Hill Office: 717 SHOB 20510-3905; 224-2921; Fax: 228-6362; *Chief of Staff:* Sam Goodstein
Web: http://whitehouse.senate.gov/
Facebook: http://facebook.com/SenatorWhitehouse
Twitter: http://twitter.com/SenWhitehouse
District Offices: 170 Westminster St., #1100, Providence, RI 02903-2109; 401-453-5294; Fax: 401-453-5085; *State Director:* George Carvalho
Committee Assignments: Commission on Security and Cooperation in Europe (Helsinki Commission); Budget; Environment and Public Works; Health, Education, Labor, and Pensions; Judiciary; Special Aging

Wicker, Roger, R-Miss.

Capitol Hill Office: 555 SDOB 20510-2404; 224-6253; Fax: 228-0378; *Chief of Staff:* Michelle Barlow Richardson
Web: http://wicker.senate.gov/
Facebook: http://facebook.com/wicker
Twitter: http://twitter.com/rogerwicker
District Offices: 2909 13th St., 3rd Floor, #303, Gulfport, MS 39501; 228-871-2017; Fax: 228-871-7196; *Southern Regional Director:* Jennifer Schmidt

321 Losher St., P.O. Box 385, Hernando, MS 38632-2124; 662-429-1002; Fax: 662-429-6002; *Constituent Liaison:* Kim Chamberlin

501 E. Court St., #3-500, Jackson, MS 39201-5037; 601-965-4644; Fax: 601-965-4007; *State Field Director:* Ryan Annison

330 W. Jefferson St., Ste. B, Tupelo, MS 38804, Tupelo, MS 38803; 662-844-5010; Fax: 662-844-5030; *North Regional Director:* Drew Robertson

Committee Assignments: Commission on Security and Cooperation in Europe (Helsinki Commission); Armed Services; Budget; Commerce, Science, and Transportation; Environment and Public Works; Joint Economic Committee

Wyden, Ron, D-Ore.

Capitol Hill Office: 221 SDOB 20510-3703; 224-5244; Fax: 228-2717; *Chief of Staff:* Jeff Michels
Web: http://wyden.senate.gov/
Facebook: http://facebook.com/wyden
Twitter: http://twitter.com/ronwyden
District Offices: The Jamison Bldg., 131 N.W. Hawthorne Ave., #107, Bend, OR 97701-2957; 541-330-9142; *Field Rep.:* Wayne Kinney

405 E. 8th Ave., #2020, Eugene, OR 97401-2733; 541-431-0229; *Field Rep.:* Juine Chada

SAC Annex Bldg., 105 Fir St., #201, La Grande, OR 97850-2661; 541-962-7691; *Field Rep.:* Kathleen Cathey

Federal Courthouse, 310 W. 6th St., #118, Medford, OR 97501-2700; 541-858-5122; *Field Rep.:* Molly McCarthy

911 N.E. 11th Ave., #630, Portland, OR 97232-4107; 503-326-7525; *State Director:* Lisa Rockower

707 13th St., S.E., #285, Salem, OR 97301-4087; 503-589-4555; *Field Rep.:* Fritz Graham

Committee Assignments: Budget; Energy and Natural Resources, Chair; Finance; Select Intelligence; Special Aging; Joint Taxation

Ready Reference

Government Hotlines

DEPARTMENTS

Agriculture,
Fraud, waste, and abuse hotline, (800) 424-9121
Meat and poultry safety inquiries, (800) 674-6854

Commerce,
Export enforcement hotline, (800) 424-2980
Fraud, waste, and abuse hotline, (800) 424-5197
Trade Information Center, (800) 872-8723

Defense,
Army Department's Casualty and Mortuary Affairs
Information Center, (800) 626-3317
Fraud, waste, and abuse hotline, (800) 424-9098
Military OneSource, (800) 342-9647

Education,
Fraud, waste, and abuse hotline, (800) 647-8733
Student financial aid information, (800) 433-3243

Energy,
Energy Efficiency and Renewable Energy Information
Center, (877) 337-3463
Fraud, waste, mismanagement, and abuse, hotline,
(800) 541-1625

Health and Human Services,
Child Welfare Information Gateway, (800) 394-3366
Fraud hotline, (800) 447-8477
General health information, (800) 336-4797
HIV/AIDS, STDs, and immunization information,
including pandemic flu, (800) 232-4636
Medicare hotline (including prescription drug discounts),
(800) 633-4227
National Adoption Center, (800) 862-3678
National Cancer Institute cancer information,
(800) 422-6237
National Runaway Safeline, (800) 786-2929
Traveler's health information, (800) 232-4636

Homeland Security,
Disaster assistance, (800) 621-3362
Fraud, abuse, and mismanagement, (800) 323-8603
Investigations Tip Line, (866) 347-2423
National Emergency Training Center, (800) 238-3358
Security breaches, hazardous material, chemical, and oil
spills, (202) 267-2675
U.S. Immigration and Customs Enforcement suspicious
activity (866) 347-2423, detainees' rights, (855) 448-6903

Housing and Urban Development,
Fair Housing Complaints, (800) 669-9777

Justice,
Americans With Disabilities Act information,
(800) 514-0301, TTY: (800) 514-0383
Arson hotline, (888) 283-3473
Bomb information hotline (ATF), (888) 283-2662
Fraud, abuse, or misconduct hotline, (800) 869-4499
Illegal firearms activity hotline, (800) 283-4867
National Criminal Justice Reference Service, (800) 851-3420
National Institute for Corrections Information Center,
(800) 877-1461
Stolen firearms hotline, (888) 930-9275
Unfair employment practices hotline (immigration
related), (800) 255-7688

Transportation,
Auto safety hotline, (800) 424-9393
Aviation safety hotline, (800) 255-1111
Federal Aviation Administration consumer hotline,
(866) 835-5322

Treasury,
Comptroller of the Currency customer assistance hotline,
(800) 613-6743
Fraud, waste, mismanagement, and abuse; Hotline (IRS
programs), (800) 366-4484
Identity Theft; Hotline, (800) 908-4490
Tax forms, tax refund information, and general
information, (800) 829-3676
Tax refund status, (800) 829-1954
Taxpayer Advocate Service, (877) 777-4778
Taxpayer assistance, (800) 829-1040

Veterans Affairs,
Benefits hotline, (800) 827-1000
Debt Management Center, (800) 827-0648
Fraud, waste, abuse, and mismanagement hotline,
(800) 488-8244
Insurance policy information, (800) 669-8477

AGENCIES

Consumer Product Safety Commission,
Product safety information, (800) 638-2772

Environmental Protection Agency,
Asbestos and small business hotline, (800) 368-5888
Endangered species hotline, (800) 447-3813
National Lead Information Center, (800) 424-5323
National Pesticides Information Center, (800) 858-7378
National radon hotline, (800) 767-7236
Ozone Protection hotline, (800) 296-1996
Safe drinking water hotline, (800) 426-4791
Superfund hotline, (800) 424-9346, (703) 412-9810
in Washington; Wetlands information hotline,
(800) 832-7828

Export-Import Bank,
Export finance hotline, (800) 565-3946;
(202) 565-3946 in Washington

Federal Deposit Insurance Corporation,
Banking complaints and inquiries, (877) 275-3342

Federal Election Commission,
Campaign finance law information, (202) 694-1100

General Services Administration,
Federal Citizen Information Center, (800) 333-4636

Office of Special Counsel,
Prohibited personnel practices information,
(800) 872-9855

Small Business Administration,
Fraud, waste, abuse, and mismanagement hotline,
(800) 767-0385
Small business assistance, (800) 827-5722

Social Security Administration,
Fraud and abuse hotline, (800) 269-0271
Social Security benefits (including Medicare) information,
(800) 772-1213

Directory of Government Information on the Internet

Listed below are Web addresses that lead to executive, legislative, and judicial information on the Internet. These links were active as of March 28, 2014. Government information can also be explored online through the www.usa.gov, which is the U.S. government's official Internet portal to Web pages for federal and state governments, the District of Columbia, and U.S. territories.

EXECUTIVE BRANCH

The White House

Main: www.whitehouse.gov
Twitter: @whitehouse
Facebook: www.facebook.com/WhiteHouse
News: www.whitehouse.gov/briefing-room
President's Bio: www.whitehouse.gov/administration/president-obama
Vice President's Bio: www.whitehouse.gov/administration/vice-president-biden
First Lady's Bio: www.whitehouse.gov/administration/first-lady-michelle-obama
Contacting the White House: www.whitehouse.gov/contact/
Blog: www.whitehouse.gov/blog

Agriculture Dept.

Main: www.usda.gov
Twitter: @usda
Facebook: www.facebook.com/USDA
About the Agriculture Dept.: www.usda.gov/about_usda
News: www.usda.gov/newsroom/
Secretary's Bio: www.usda.gov/wps/portal/usda/usdahome?contentid=bios_vilsack.xml&contentidonly=true
Employee Directory: http://dc-directory.hqnet.usda.gov/DLSNew/phone.aspx
Link to Regional Offices: www.usda.gov/wps/portal/usda/usdahome?navtype=MA&navid=AGENCIES_OFFICES_C
Department Budget: www.usda.gov/wps/portal/usda/usdahome?navid=BUDGET
Blog: http://blogs.usda.gov

Commerce Dept.

Main: www.commerce.gov
Twitter: @CommerceGov
Facebook: www.facebook.com/Commercegov
About the Commerce Dept.: www.commerce.gov/about-department-commerce
News: www.commerce.gov/news; www.youtube.com/commercenews
Secretary's Bio: www.commerce.gov/about-commerce/commerce-leadership/secretary-gary-locke
Employee Directory: http://dir.commerce.gov
Links to State and Regional Offices:
  Census Bureau: www.census.gov/regions/
  Commerce Dept.: www.commerce.gov/about-commerce/services
  Economic Development Administration: www.eda.gov/contacts.htm
Department Budget: www.osec.doc.gov/bmi/budget
Photos: www.flickr.com/photos/commercegov

Defense Dept.

Main: www.defense.gov/
Twitter: @deptofdefense
Facebook: www.facebook.com/DeptofDefense
About the Defense Dept.: www.defense.gov/about
News: www.defense.gov/news/
Secretary's Bio: www.defense.gov/bios/biographydetail.aspx?biographyid=365
Directory of Senior Defense Officials: www.defense.gov/home/top-leaders/
Department Budget: http://comptroller.defense.gov/
Live Blog: www.dodlive.mil
The Pentagon Channel: www.youtube.com/thepentagonchannel

Education Dept.

Main: www.ed.gov
Twitter: @usedgov
Facebook: www.facebook.com/ED.gov
About the Education Dept.: www2.ed.gov/about/landing.jhtml
News: www2.ed.gov/news
Secretary's Bio: www2.ed.gov/news/staff/bios/duncan.html
Employee Directory: http://wdcrobcolp01.ed.gov/CFAPPS/employee_locator/index.cfm
State Contacts and Information: www2.ed.gov/about/contacts/state/index.html
Department Budget: www2.ed.gov/about/overview/budget/index.html
Blog: www.ed.gov/blog/
Video: www.youtube.com/usedgov

Energy Dept.

Main: www.energy.gov
Twitter: @energy
Facebook: www.facebook.com/energygov
About the Energy Dept.: www.energy.gov/about
News: www.energy.gov/news
Secretary's Bio: http://energy.gov/contributors/dr-ernest-moniz
Employee Directory: http://phonebook.doe.gov/callup.html
Link to Regional Offices: www.energy.gov/organization/index.htm
Department Budget: http://energy.gov/budget-performance

Health and Human Services Dept.

Main: www.hhs.gov
Twitter: @HHSGov
Facebook: www.hhs.gov/facebook
About the Health and Human Services Dept.: www.hhs.gov/about
News: www.hhs.gov/news
Secretary's Bio: www.hhs.gov/secretary
Employee Directory: http://directory.psc.gov/employee.htm
Link to Regional Offices: www.hhs.gov/about/regionmap.html
Department Budget: www.hhs.gov/budget

Homeland Security Dept.

Main: www.dhs.gov
Twitter: @DHSgov
Facebook: www.facebook.com/homelandsecurity
About the Homeland Security Dept.: www.dhs.gov/about-dhs
News: www.dhs.gov/news
Secretary's Bio: www.dhs.gov/secretary-jeh-johnson
Leadership Directory: www.dhs.gov/leadership
Links to Regional Offices:
  Federal Emergency Management Agency: www.fema.gov/
  U.S. Citizenship and Immigration Services: www.uscis.gov
  U.S. Secret Service: www.secretservice.gov/field_offices.shtml
Department Budget: www.dhs.gov/dhs-budget
Video: www.youtube.com/ushomelandsecurity

Housing and Urban Development Dept.

Main: www.hud.gov
Twitter: @HUDNews
Facebook: www.facebook.com/HUD
About the Housing and Urban Development Dept.: www.hud.gov/about
News: www.hud.gov/news
Interactive Self-Assessment Tool: http://makinghomeaffordable.gov/
Secretary's Bio: http://portal.hud.gov/hudportal/HUD?src=/about/principal_staff/secretary_donovan

Employee Directory: www5.hud.gov:63001/po/i/netlocator/
Link to Regional Offices: http://portal.hud.gov/hudportal/HUD?src=/states
Department Budget: http://portal.hud.gov/hudportal/HUD?src=/program_offices/cfo/budget
Video: www.youtube.com/hudchannel

Interior Dept.

Main: www.doi.gov
Twitter: @Interior
Facebook: www.facebook.com/USInterior
About the Interior Dept.: www.doi.gov/whoweare/index.cfm
News: www.doi.gov/news/index.cfm
Secretary's Bio: www.doi.gov/whoweare/secretaryjewell.cfm
Employee Directory: www.doi.gov/employees
Links to Regional Offices:
  Bureau of Indian Affairs: www.bia.gov/
  Bureau of Land Management: www.blm.gov
  Bureau of Ocean Energy Management: www.boem.gov
  Bureau of Reclamation: www.usbr.gov
  National Park Service: www.nps.gov
  Office of Surface Mining: www.osmre.gov
  U.S. Fish and Wildlife Service: www.fws.gov
  U.S. Geological Survey: www.usgs.gov
Department Budget: www.doi.gov/budget
Video: www.youtube.com/USInterior

Justice Dept.

Main: www.justice.gov
Twitter: @TheJusticeDept
Facebook: www.facebook.com/DOJ
About the Justice Dept.: www.justice.gov/about/about.html
News: www.justice.gov/briefing-room.html
Attorney General's Bio: www.justice.gov/ag
Links to Regional Offices:
  Drug Enforcement Administration: www.justice.gov/dea/contactinfo.htm
  Federal Bureau of Investigation: www.fbi.gov/contact-us/contact-us
  Federal Bureau of Prisons: www.bop.gov/about/contactus.jsp
Department Budget: www.justice.gov/about/bpp.htm
Video: www.youtube.com/thejusticedepartment

Labor Dept.

Main: www.dol.gov
Twitter: @USDOL
Facebook: www.facebook.com/departmentoflabor
About the Labor Dept.: www.dol.gov/dol/aboutdol/main.htm
News: www.dol.gov/dol/media
Secretary's Bio: www.dol.gov/_sec/welcome.htm
Employee Directory: www.dol.gov/dol/contact/contact-phonekeypersonnel.htm

Links to Regional Offices:
    Bureau of Labor Statistics: www.bls.gov/bls/
      regnhome.htm
    Employment and Training Administration:
      http://wdr.doleta.gov/contacts
    Occupational Safety and Health Administration:
      www.osha.gov/dcsp/osp/index.html
Department Budget: www.dol.gov/dol/aboutdol/#budget
Video: www.youtube.com/usdepartmentoflabor

State Dept.

Main: www.state.gov
Twitter: @StateDept
Facebook: www.facebook.com/usdos
Mobile: http://rn.state.gov/
About the State Dept.: www.state.gov/aboutstate
News: www.state.gov/media/
Secretary's Bio: www.state.gov/secretary
Employee Directory: www.state.gov/m/a/gps/directory
Link to Regional Offices:
    Passport Services: http://iafdb.travel.state.gov
Department Budget: www.state.gov/s/d/rm/rls/
Video: www.youtube.com/statevideo

Transportation Dept.

Main: www.dot.gov
Twitter: @usdot
Facebook: www.facebook.com/USDOT
About the Transportation Dept.: www.dot.gov/
  about.html
News: www.dot.gov/briefing-room.html
Secretary's Bio: www.dot.gov/secretary
Links to Regional Offices:
    Federal Aviation Administration: www.faa.gov/about/
      office_org/
    Federal Highway Administration: www.fhwa.dot.gov/
      field.html
    Federal Railroad Administration: www.fra.dot.gov/
      Page/P0001
    Federal Transit Administration: www.fta.dot.gov/
      12926.html
    Maritime Administration: www.marad.dot.gov/
    National Highway Traffic Safety Administration:
      www.nhtsa.gov/nhtsa/whatis/regions/
Department Budget: www.dot.gov/budget
Video: www.youtube.com/user/usdotgov

Treasury Dept.

Main: www.treasury.gov/
Twitter: @USTreasury
Facebook: www.facebook.com/ustreasury
About the Treasury Dept.: www.treasury.gov/about/
  Pages/default.aspx
News: www.treasury.gov/press-center/Pages/default
  .aspx
Interactive Self-Assessment Tool: www
  .makinghomeaffordable.gov/
Secretary's Bio: www.treasury.gov/about/Pages/
  Secretary.aspx

Directory of Treasury Officials: www.treasury.gov/about/
  organizational-structure/Pages/officials.aspx
Links to Regional Offices:
  http://benefits.va.gov/benefits/offices.asp
    Comptroller of the Currency: www.occ.treas.gov/
      about/organization/index-organization.html
    Financial Management Service: http://fms.treas.gov/
      aboutfms/locations.html
    Internal Revenue Service: www.irs.gov/uac/Contact-
      Your-Local-IRS-Office-1
Department Budget: www.treasury.gov/about/budget-
  performance/Pages/index.aspx
Video: www.youtube.com/USTreasGov

Veterans Affairs Dept.

Main: www.va.gov
Twitter: @DeptVetAffairs
Facebook: www.facebook.com/VeteransAffairs
About the Veterans Affairs Dept.: www.va.gov/about_va/
News: www.va.gov/opa/pressrel/
Secretary's Bio: www.va.gov/opa/bios/secretary.asp
Link to Regional Offices: www2.va.gov/directory/guide/
  home.asp?isFlash=1
Department Budget: www.va.gov/budget/products.asp
Video: www.youtube.com/deptvetaffairs
Blog: www.blogs.va.gov/VAntage

LEGISLATIVE BRANCH

Congress

U.S. Constitution: www.archives.gov/exhibits/charters/
  constitution_transcript.html
Legislative Process: www.rules.house.gov; http://thomas
  .loc.gov
How Laws Are Made: http://thomas.loc.gov/home/
  lawsmade.toc.html
Biographical Directory of the U.S. Congress: http://
  bioguide.congress.gov/biosearch/biosearch.asp
Election Statistics (1920-present): http://clerk.house.gov/
  member_info/electionInfo

House

Main: www.house.gov
Twitter: @HouseFloor
Annual Calendar: www.majorityleader.gov/Calendar
Daily Business: www.clerk.house.gov/floorsummary.floor
  .aspx
Committees: http://clerk.house.gov/committee_info/
  commact.aspx
Committee Hearing Schedules: http://docs.house.gov/
  Committee/Calendar/ByWeek.aspx
Pending Business: http://clerk.house.gov/floorsummary/
  floor.aspx
Link to Roll Call Votes: http://clerk.house.gov/legislative/
  legvotes.aspx
Leadership: www.house.gov/leadership
Media Galleries: www.house.gov/content/media

Government of the United States

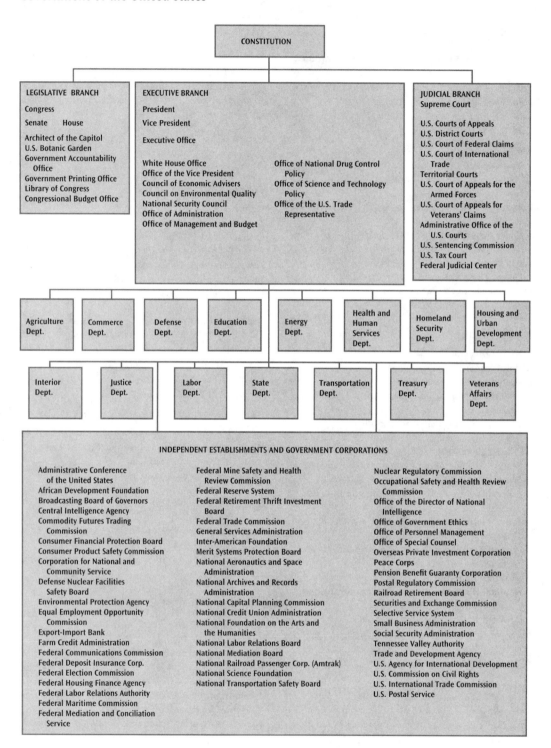

CONSTITUTION

LEGISLATIVE BRANCH

Congress

Senate   House

Architect of the Capitol
U.S. Botanic Garden
Government Accountability
  Office
Government Printing Office
Library of Congress
Congressional Budget Office

EXECUTIVE BRANCH

President

Vice President

Executive Office

White House Office
Office of the Vice President
Council of Economic Advisers
Council on Environmental Quality
National Security Council
Office of Administration
Office of Management and Budget

Office of National Drug Control
  Policy
Office of Science and Technology
  Policy
Office of the U.S. Trade
  Representative

JUDICIAL BRANCH
Supreme Court

U.S. Courts of Appeals
U.S. District Courts
U.S. Court of Federal Claims
U.S. Court of International
  Trade
Territorial Courts
U.S. Court of Appeals for the
  Armed Forces
U.S. Court of Appeals for
  Veterans' Claims
Administrative Office of the
  U.S. Courts
U.S. Sentencing Commission
U.S. Tax Court
Federal Judicial Center

Agriculture Dept.

Commerce Dept.

Defense Dept.

Education Dept.

Energy Dept.

Health and Human Services Dept.

Homeland Security Dept.

Housing and Urban Development Dept.

Interior Dept.

Justice Dept.

Labor Dept.

State Dept.

Transportation Dept.

Treasury Dept.

Veterans Affairs Dept.

INDEPENDENT ESTABLISHMENTS AND GOVERNMENT CORPORATIONS

Administrative Conference
  of the United States
African Development Foundation
Broadcasting Board of Governors
Central Intelligence Agency
Commodity Futures Trading
  Commission
Consumer Financial Protection Board
Consumer Product Safety Commission
Corporation for National and
  Community Service
Defense Nuclear Facilities
  Safety Board
Environmental Protection Agency
Equal Employment Opportunity
  Commission
Export-Import Bank
Farm Credit Administration
Federal Communications Commission
Federal Deposit Insurance Corp.
Federal Election Commission
Federal Housing Finance Agency
Federal Labor Relations Authority
Federal Maritime Commission
Federal Mediation and Conciliation
  Service

Federal Mine Safety and Health
  Review Commission
Federal Reserve System
Federal Retirement Thrift Investment
  Board
Federal Trade Commission
General Services Administration
Inter-American Foundation
Merit Systems Protection Board
National Aeronautics and Space
  Administration
National Archives and Records
  Administration
National Capital Planning Commission
National Credit Union Administration
National Foundation on the Arts and
  the Humanities
National Labor Relations Board
National Mediation Board
National Railroad Passenger Corp. (Amtrak)
National Science Foundation
National Transportation Safety Board

Nuclear Regulatory Commission
Occupational Safety and Health Review
  Commission
Office of the Director of National
  Intelligence
Office of Government Ethics
Office of Personnel Management
Office of Special Counsel
Overseas Private Investment Corporation
Peace Corps
Pension Benefit Guaranty Corporation
Postal Regulatory Commission
Railroad Retirement Board
Securities and Exchange Commission
Selective Service System
Small Business Administration
Social Security Administration
Tennessee Valley Authority
Trade and Development Agency
U.S. Agency for International Development
U.S. Commission on Civil Rights
U.S. International Trade Commission
U.S. Postal Service

Senate

Main: www.senate.gov
Twitter: @SenateFloor
Annual Calendar: www.republican.senate.gov/public/
index.cfm/senate-calendar
Daily Calendar: www.senate.gov/legislative/LIS/executive_
calendar/xcalv.pdf
Committees: www.senate.gov/pagelayout/committees/d_
three_sections_with_teasers/committees_home.htm
Committee Hearing Schedules: www.senate.gov/
pagelayout/committees/b_three_sections_with_
teasers/committee_hearings.htm
Link to Roll Call Votes: www.senate.gov/pagelayout/
legislative/a_three_sections_with_teasers/votes.htm
Leadership: www.senate.gov/pagelayout/senators/a_
three_sections_with_teasers/leadership.htm
Media Galleries: www.senate.gov/galleries
Executive Nominations: http://judiciary.senate.gov/
nominations/executive.cfm

Government Accountability Office

Main: www.gao.gov
Twitter: @usgao
About the Government Accountability Office: www.gao
.gov/about/index.html
Comptroller General's Bio: www.gao.gov/cghome/
gdbiog.html
GAO Reports: www.gao.gov/docsearch/repandtest
.html
Media: www.gao.gov/multimedia/video

Government Printing Office

Main: www.gpo.gov; www.gpoaccess.gov
Facebook: www.facebook.com/USGPO
Twitter: @usgpo
About the Government Printing Office: www.gpo
.gov/about/
Video: www.youtube.com/gpoprinter

Library of Congress

Main: www.loc.gov/index.html
Twitter: @librarycongress
Facebook: www.facebook.com/libraryofcongress
Online Catalog: http://catalog.loc.gov
Thomas (Legislative Information on the Internet):
http://thomas.loc.gov
Copyright Office: www.copyright.gov
Video: www.youtube.com/libraryofcongress

JUDICIAL BRANCH

The Supreme Court

Main: www.supremecourt.gov/
Twitter: @USSupremeCourt
About the Supreme Court: www.supremecourt.gov/
about/about.aspx
News: www.supremecourt.gov/opinions/slipopinions.aspx
Biographies of the Justices: www.supremecourt
.gov/about/biographies.aspx
Supreme Court Docket: www.supremecourt.gov/docket/
docket.aspx
Visiting the Supreme Court: www.supremecourt
.gov/visiting/visiting.aspx

Federal Judicial Center

Main: www.fjc.gov
History: www.fjc.gov/history/home.nsf

U.S. Federal Courts

Main: www.uscourts.gov
About the U.S. Federal Courts: www.uscourts
.gov/FederalCourts.aspx
News: http://news.uscourts.gov/
Publications: www.uscourts.gov/FederalCourts/
PublicationsAndReports.aspx

Governors and Other State Officials

Political affiliations, when available, are indicated by (D) for Democrat, (R) for Republican, and (I) for Independent. For key officials of the District of Columbia and other Washington-area localities, see page 314.

Alabama   Web, www.alabama.gov

Gov. Robert Bentley (R), State Capitol, 600 Dexter Ave., #N-104, Montgomery 36130; (334) 242-7100; Fax, (334) 353-0004; Press: Jennifer Ardis, (334) 242-7150; Twitter: @governorbentley; www.facebook.com/bentley2010

Lt. Gov. Kay Ivey (R), Alabama State House, 11 S. Union St., #725, Montgomery 36130-6050; (334) 242-7900; Fax, (334) 242-4661; Twitter: @LtGovIvey; Email: kay.ivey@ltgov.alabama.gov

Secy. of State Jim Bennett(R), State Capitol Bldg., 600 Dexter Ave., #S-105, Montgomery 36130, P.O. Box 5616, Montgomery 36103-5616; (334) 242-7200; Fax, (334) 242-4993; Email: JimBennett@sos.alabama.gov; Twitter: @alasecofstate

Atty. Gen. Luther Strange (R), Alabama State House, 501 Washington Ave., Montgomery 36130; P.O. Box 300152, Montgomery, AL 36130-0152; (334) 242-7300; Fax, (334) 242-4891; Twitter: @lutherstrange

Treasurer Young Boozer (R), State Capitol, 600 Dexter Ave., #S-106, Montgomery 36104; (334) 242-7500; Fax, (334) 242-7592; Email: alatreas@treasury.alabama.gov; or young.boozer@treasury.alabama.gov

In Washington, DC: Jill Boxler, Director, Washington Office of the Governor, State of Georgia, 444 N. Capitol St. N.W., #382A, 20001; (202) 220-1379

Alaska   Web, www.alaska.gov

Gov. Sean Parnell (R), State Capitol, 3rd Floor, P.O. Box 110001, Juneau 99811-0001; (907) 465-3500; Fax, (907) 465-3532; Twitter: @AKGovParnell; www.facebook.com/Alaska.Governor

Lt. Gov. Mead Treadwell (R), State Capitol, 3rd Floor, Juneau 99811-0015; (907) 465-3520; Fax, (907) 465-5400; Twitter: @LGMeadTreadwell; www.facebook.com/Alaska.Lt.Governor

(No office of Secretary of State)

Atty. Gen. Michael Geraghty (R), P.O. Box 110300, Juneau, 99811-0300; (907) 465-2133; Fax, (907) 465-2075; Email: attorney.general@alaska.gov

In Washington, DC: Kip Knudson, Director, Washington, Office of the Governor, State of Alaska, 444 N. Capitol St. N.W., #336, 20001-1512, (202) 624-5858; Fax, (202) 624-5857

Arizona   Web, www.az.gov

Gov. Janice K. (Jan) Brewer (R), State Capitol, 1700 W. Washington St., 9th Floor, Phoenix 85007; Press: Ann Dockendorff, (602) 542-4331; Fax, (602) 5421381; Toll-free (in-state only), (800) 253-0883; Twitter: @GovBrewer; www.facebook.com/GovJanBrewer

(No office of Lieutenant Governor)

Secy. of State Ken Bennett (R), State Capitol, 1700 W. Washington St., 7th Floor, Phoenix 85007-2888; (602) 542-4285; Fax, (602) 542-1575; TTY, (602) 255-8683; Twitter: @therealAZsos; www.facebook.com/AZSOS

Atty. Gen. Tom Horne (R), 1275 W. Washington St., Phoenix 85007-2926; (602) 542-5025 or 5763; Fax, (602) 542-4085; Toll-free (in-state only), (800) 352-8431; Twitter: @arizonaago; www.facebook.com/AZSOS

Treasurer Doug Ducey (R), 1700 W. Washington St., 1st Floor, Phoenix 85007; (602) 604-7800; Fax, (602) 542-7176; Toll-free, (877) 365-8310; Email: info@aztreasury.gov; Twitter: @dougducey

In Washington, DC: Ryan Serote, Director, Washington Office of the Governor, State of Arizona, 444 N. Capitol St. N.W., #428, 20001; (202) 220-1396; Fax, (202) 624-1475

Arkansas   Web, www.arkansas.gov

Gov. Mike Beebe (D), State Capitol, #250, Little Rock 72201; (501) 682-2345; Press: Matt DeCample, (501) 683-6414; Fax, (501) 682-3597; Toll-free, (877) 727-3468; TTY, (501) 682-7515; Twitter: @GovBeebeMedia; www.facebook.com/pages/Office-of-Arkansas-Governor-Mike-Beebe/177813702279256?sk=wall

Lt. Gov. Mark A. Darr (D), State Capitol, #270, Little Rock 72201-1061; (501) 682-2144; Fax, (501) 682-2894; Email: mark.darr@arkansas.gov

Secy. of State Mark Martin (R), State Capitol, #256, Little Rock 72201-1094; (501) 682-1010; Fax, (501) 682-3510; Email: generalinfo@sos.arkansas.gov

Atty. Gen. Dustin McDaniel (D), Tower Bldg., 323 Center St., #200, Little Rock 72201-2610; (501) 682-2007; Fax, (501) 682-8084; Toll-free, (800) 482-8982; Twitter: @AttyGenMcDaniel; www.facebook.com/ pages/Arkansas-Attorney-General/204193772950925

Treasurer Charles L. Robinson (D), State Capitol, #220, Little Rock 72201; (501) 682-5888/3835; Fax, (501) 682-3842; Email: crobinson@artreasury.gov

Washington, DC Representative: Haley Keenan-Gray, Office of the Governor State Capitol Bldg., Little Rock 72201; (501) 682-2345

California   Web, www.ca.gov

Gov. Edmund G. (Jerry) Brown Jr. (D), State Capitol, #1173, Sacramento 95814; Press: Gil Duran, (916) 445-2841; Fax, (916) 558-3160; TTY (916) 464-1580; Email: stateinformation@state.ca.gov

Lt. Gov. Gavin Newsom (D), State Capitol, #1114, Sacramento 95814; (916) 445-8994; Fax, (916) 3234998; Twitter: @GavinNewsom; www.facebook.com/GavinNewsom

Secy. of State Debra Bowen (D), 1500 11th St., #600, Sacramento 95814; (916) 653-6814; Fax, (916) 653-4795; Email: secretary.bowen@sos.ca.gov

Atty. Gen. Kamala D. Harris (D), 1300 T St., Sacramento 95814-2929 P.O. Box 944255, Sacramento 94244-2550, (916) 445-9555; Toll-free, (800) 952-5225; TTY, (800) 735-2929; TTY Spanish, (800) 855-3000; Twitter: @CalAGHarris; www.facebook.com/pages/CaliforniaAttorney-General/149799031764167

Treasurer Bill Lockyer (D), 915 Capitol Mall, #110, C-15, Sacramento 95814; (916) 653-2995; Fax, (916) 6533125; Twitter:@STONewsroom; www.facebook.com/ pages/Bill-Lockyer/108042709216400

In Washington, DC: Katie Mathews, Deputy Director, Washington Office of the Governor, State of California, 444 N. Capitol St. N.W., #134, 20001; (202) 624-5270; Fax, (202) 624-5280

Colorado   Web, www.colorado.gov

Gov. John Hickenlooper (D), 136 State Capitol, Denver 80203-1792; Press: Tanuj Deora, (303) 866-2471; Fax, (303) 866-2003; Twitter: @hickforco www.facebook.com/JohnHickenlooper

Lt. Gov. Joseph Garcia (D), 130 State Capitol, Denver 80203-1793; (303) 866-2087; Fax, (303) 866-5469; www.facebook.com/pages/Lt-Governor-Joe-Garcia/154673694591317

Secy. of State Scott Gessler (R), 1700 Broadway, #250, Denver 80202; (303) 894-2200; Fax, (303) 869-4860; TTY, (303) 869-4867; Twitter: @ColoSecofState; www.facebook.com/ColoradoSoS

Atty. Gen. John W. Suthers (R), 1525 Sherman St., 5th Floor, Denver 80203; (303) 866-4500; Fax, (303) 866-5691; www.facebook.com/ColoradoAttorneyGeneral

Treasurer Walker Stapleton (R), 140 State Capitol, Denver 80203; (303) 866-2441; Fax, (303) 866-2123: Twitter: @WalkerStapleton; www.facebook.com/Walker.R.Stapleton

In Washington, DC: Jena Griswold, Washington Director, Office of the Governor State of Colorado, 444 N. Capitol St. #314 20001; (202) 624-5278

Connecticut   Web, www.ct.gov

Gov. Dannel Malloy (D), State Capitol, 210 Capitol Ave., #202, Hartford 06106; (860) 566-4840; Press: Juliet Manalan; Fax, (860) 524-7395; Toll-free, (800) 406-1527; TTY, (860) 524-7397; Twitter: @GovMalloyOffice www.facebook.com/GovMalloyOffice

Lt. Gov. Nancy Wyman (D), State Capitol, 210 Capitol Ave., #304, Hartford 06106; (860) 524-7384; Fax, (860) 524-7304; Toll-free, (866) 712-6998; TTY, (860) 524-7397; Email: ltgovernor.wyman@ct.gov

Secy. of State Denise Merrill (D), 30 Trinity St., P.O. Box 150470, Hartford 06115-0470; (860) 509-6200; Fax, (860) 509-6209; Twitter: @sotsmerrill; www.facebook.com/pages/Office-of-Secretary-of-theState-Denise-Merrill/171809006194936

Atty. Gen. George C. Jepsen (D), 55 Elm St., Hartford 06106; (860) 808-5318; Fax, (860) 808-5387; Twitter: @AGJepsen; www.facebook.com/AGGeorgeJepsen

Treasurer Denise L. Nappier (D), 55 Elm St., Hartford 06106-1773; (860) 702-3010; Fax, (860) 702-3043; Info: (860) 702-3000; Toll-free, (800) 618-3404; www.facebook.com/pages/Office-of-State-Treasurer-Denise-L-Nappier/ 155790827915958

In Washington, DC: Dan DeSimone, Director, Washington Office of the Governor, State of Connecticut, 444 N. Capitol St. N.W., #317, 20001; (202) 347-4535; Fax, (202) 347-7151

Delaware   Web, http://delaware.gov

Gov. Jack A. Markell (D), 150 Martin Luther King Jr. Blvd. South, 2nd Floor, William Penn St., Dover 19901; Press: Catherine Rossi, (302) 744-4101; Fax, (302) 739-2775; Twitter: @GovernorMarkell; www.facebook.com/GovernorMarkell

Lt. Gov. Matt Denn (D), Tatnall Bldg. 3rd Floor, Dover 19901; (302) 744-4333; Fax, (302) 739-6965; Email: matthew.denn@state.de.us

Secy. of State Jeffrey W. Bullock (D), 401 Federal St., #3, Dover 19901; (302) 739-4111; Fax, (302) 739-3811; www.facebook.com/DEDepartmentofState

Atty. Gen. Joseph R. (Beau) Biden III (D), Carvel State Office Bldg., 820 N. French St., Wilmington 19801; (302) 577-8400; Fax, (302) 5776630; TTY (302) 577-5783; Email: Attorney.General@state.de.us

Treasurer Chip Flowers Jr. (D), 820 Silver Lake Blvd., #100, Dover 19904; (302) 672-6700; Fax, (302) 739-5635; Email: statetreasurer@state.de.us

In Washington, DC: Emily Kuiken, Director, Washington Office of the Governor, State of Delaware, 444 N. Capitol St. N.W., #230, 20001; (202) 624-7724; Fax, (202) 624-5495

Florida   Web, www.flgov.com

Gov. Rick Scott (R), The Capitol, 400 S. Monroe St., Tallahassee 32399-0001; Press: Brian Burgess, (850) 488-7146; Fax, (850) 488-4042; TTY, (850) 922-7795; Twitter: @flgovscott; www.facebook.com/scottforflorida

Lt. Gov. Carlos Lopez-Cantera (R), The Capitol, 400 S. Monroe St., PL-05, Tallahassee 32399-0001; (850) 717-9331; Fax, (850) 487-0830

Secy. of State Kenneth Detzner (R), R.A. Gray Bldg., 500 S. Bronough, #15, Tallahassee 32399-0250; (850) 245-6500; Fax, (850) 245-6125 Email: SecretaryofState@DOS.MyFlorida.com

Atty. Gen. Pam Bondi (R), The Capitol, PL-01, 500 S. Bronough St., Tallahassee 32399-1050; (850) 414-3300; Fax, (850) 410-1630; Twitter: @PamBondi; www.facebook.com/pambondi

Chief Financial Officer Jeff Atwater (R), 200 E. Gaines St., Tallahassee 32399-0300; (850) 413-3100; Fax, (850) 413-4993; Twitter: @JeffAtwater; www.facebook.com/ JeffAtwater

In Washington, DC: Doug Callaway, Director, Washington Office, State of Florida, 444 N. Capitol St. N.W., #349, 20001; (202) 624-5885; Fax, (202) 624-5886

Georgia   Web, www.georgia.gov

Gov. Nathan Deal (R), 203 State Capitol, Atlanta, 30334; Press: Brian Robinson, (404) 656-1776; Fax, (404) 6577332; Twitter: @GovernorDeal; www.facebook .com/GovernorDeal

Lt. Gov. Casey Cagle (R), 240 State Capitol, Atlanta, 30334; (404) 656-5030; Fax, (404) 656-6739; Twitter: @caseycagle; www.facebook.com/CaseyCaglePage

Secy. of State Brian Kemp (R), 2 MLK Jr. Dr. #313 Floyd West Tower Atlanta, 30334; (404) 656-2817; Fax, (404) 656-0513; Twitter: @GASOSKemp; www.facebook .com/GASOSKemp

Atty. Gen. Sam Olens (R), 40 Capitol Square S.W., Atlanta 30334-1300; (404) 656-3300; Fax, (404) 657-8733; Email: AGOlens@law.ga.gov

Treasurer Steve McCoy (R), 200 Piedmont Ave., West Tower, #1204, Atlanta 30334; (404) 656-2168; Fax, (404) 656-9048; Email: ostweb@treasury.ga.gov

In Washington, DC: Todd Smith, Washington Office of the Governor, State of Georgia, 1455 Pennsylvania Ave. N.W., #400, 20004; (202) 652-2299; Fax, (202) 347-1142

Hawaii   Web, www.hawaii.gov

Gov. Neil Abercrombie (D), State Capitol, 415 S. Beretania St., Honolulu 96813; Press: Laurie Au, (808) 586-0034; Fax, (808) 586-0006; Twitter: @neilabercrombie; www.facebook.com/GovernorAbercrombie

Lt. Gov. Shan S. Tsutsui (D), State Capitol, 415 S. Beretania St., Honolulu 96813; (808) 586-0255; Fax, (808) 586-0231

(No office of Secretary of State)

Atty. Gen. David M. Louie (D), 425 Queen St., Honolulu 96813; (808) 586-1282; Fax, (808) 586-1239; Email: hawaiiag@hawaii.gov

Budget and Finance Director Kalbert K. Young (D), 1 Capitol District Bldg., 250 S. Hotel St., Honolulu 96813; P.O. Box 150, Honolulu 96810; (808) 586-1518; Fax, (808) 586-1976; Email: HI .BudgetandFinance@hawaii.gov

Washington, DC Representative: Bruce Coppa, Chief of Staff, (808) 223-7971

Idaho   Web, www.state.id.us

Gov. C. L. (Butch) Otter (R), State Capitol, West Wing., 2nd Floor, Boise 83720-0034; Press: Jon Hanian, (208) 3342100; Fax, (208) 334-3454; Twitter: @ButchOtter;

www.facebook.com/pages/Governor-C-L-Butch-Otter/ 292986829831

Lt. Gov. Brad Little (R), State Capitol, #225, Boise 83720-0057; (208) 334-2200; Fax, (208) 334-3259; Twitter: @LTGovBradLittle; www.facebook.com/ LtGovBradLittle

Secy. of State Ben Ysursa (R), 700 W. Jefferson, #E205, Boise, P.O. Box 83720, Boise 83720-0080; (208) 334-2300; Fax, (208) 334-2282

Atty. Gen. Lawrence G. Wasden (R), 700 W. Jefferson St., #210, P.O. Box 83720, Boise 83720-0010, (208) 334-2400; Fax, (208) 854-8071

Treasurer Ron G. Crane (R), 700 W.Jefferson St., #126, P.O. Box 83720, Boise 83720; (208) 334-3200; Fax, (208) 332-2959; Twitter:@RonGCrane

Washington, DC Representative: David Hensley, Chief of Staff, (208) 854-3005

Illinois   Web, www.illinois.gov

Gov. Pat Quinn (D), 207 State House, Springfield 62706; Press: Mia Mastoff, (217) 782-0244; TTY, (888) 261-3336; Twitter: @GovernorQuinn; www.facebook.com/ GovernorQuinn

Lt. Gov. Sheila Simon (D), 214 State House, Springfield 62706; (217) 558-3085; Fax, (217) 558-3094; Twitter: @LTGovSimon; www.facebook.com/SheilaSimonIL

Secy. of State Jesse White (D), 213 State Capitol Springfield 62756; (217) 782-2201; Fax, (217) 785-0358; Outside of Illinois, (217) 785-3000

Atty. Gen. Lisa Madigan (D), 500 S. 2nd St., Springfield 62706-1771; (217) 782-1090; TTY, (877) 844-5461; Twitter: @LisaforIL; www.facebook.com/lisamadigan

Treasurer Dan Rutherford (R), Capitol Bldg., 219, Springfield 62706-1000; (217) 782-2211; Fax, (217) 785-2777; Twitter: @RutherfordDan; www.facebook .com/RutherfordDan

In Washington, DC: Shayna Cherry, Director (Acting), Washington Office of the Governor, State of Illinois, 444 N. Capitol St. N.W., #400, 20001; (202) 624-7760; Fax, (202) 724-0689

Indiana   Web, www.in.gov

Gov. Mike Pence (R), 206 State House, 200 W. Washington St., Indianapolis 46204-2790; Press: Jane Jankowski, (317) 232-4567; Twitter: @GovPenceIN; www.facebook.com/GovernorMikePence

Lt. Gov. Sue Ellspermann (R), 333 State House, 200 W. Washington St., Indianapolis 46204-2790; (317) 2324545; Fax, (317) 232-4788; Twitter: @SueEllsnermann; www.facebook.com/sue. ellspermann

Secy. of State Connie Lawson (R), 200 W. Washington St., #201 Indianapolis 46204-2790; (317) 232-6531; Fax, (317) 233-3283; Email: constituent@sos.IN.gov

Atty. Gen. Greg Zoeller (R), Indiana Government Center South, 302 W. Washington St., 5th Floor, Indianapolis 46204-2770; (317) 232-6201; Fax, (317) 232-7979; Email: Constituent@atg.in.gov

Treasurer Richard Mourdock (R), 242 State House, 200 W. Washington St., Indianapolis 46204; (317) 232-6386; Fax, (317) 233-1780; Email: tosstaff@tos.state .in.us

In Washington, DC: Josh Pitcock, Federal Representative, Washington Office of the Governor, State of Indiana, 444 N. Capitol St. N.W., #400, 20001; (202) 624-1474; Fax, (202) 833-1587

Iowa   Web, www.iowa.gov

Gov. Terry Branstad (R), State Capitol, 1007 E. Grand Ave., Des Moines 50319; Press: Tim Albrecht, (515) 281-5211; Fax, (515) 281-6611; Twitter: @TerryBranstad; www.facebook.com/TerryBranstad

Lt. Gov. Kim Reynolds (R), State Capitol, 1007 E. Grand Ave., Des Moines 50319; (515) 281-5211; Fax, (515) 725-3527; Twitter: @KimReynoldsia; www.facebook .com/KimReynoldsIA

Secy. of State Matt Schultz (R), 1st Floor, Lucas Bldg., 321 E. 12th St., Des Moines 50319; (515) 281-5204; Fax, (515) 242-5952; Email: sos@sos.iowa.gov

Atty. Gen. Tom Miller (D), Hoover Bldg., 2nd Floor, 1305 E. Walnut St., Des Moines 50319; (515) 281-5164; Fax, (515) 281-4209; Email: webteam@ag.state.ia.us

Treasurer Michael L. Fitzgerald (D), Capitol Bldg., 1007 E. Grand Ave., Des Moines 50319; (515) 281-5368; Fax, (515) 281-7562; Email: treasurer@iowa.gov

In Washington, DC: Doug Hoelscher, Director, Washington Office of the Governor, State of Iowa, 400 N. Capitol St. N.W., #359, 20001; (202) 624-5479; Fax, (202) 624-8189

Kansas   Web, www.kansas.gov

Gov. Sam Brownback (R), Capitol, 300 S.W. 10th Ave., #241S, Topeka 66612-1590; Press: Sherriene Jones-Sontag, (785) 296-3232; Fax, (785) 368-8500; Toll-Free, (877) 579-6757; Twitter: @govsambrownback; www.facebook.com/govsambrownback

Lt. Gov. Jeff Colyer, MD (R), State Capitol, 2nd Floor, 300 S.W. 10th Ave., Topeka 66612-1590; (785) 296-2214; Fax, (785) 296-5669; TTY, (800) 766-3777

Secy. of State Kris Kobach (R), Memorial Hall, 1st Floor, 120 S.W. 10th Ave., Topeka 66612-1594; (785) 296-4564; Fax, (785) 296-4570; Twitter: @kansassos; www.facebook.com/pages/Kansas-Secretary-of-State/110068102381195

Atty. Gen. Derek Schmidt (R), Memorial Hall, 120 S.W. 10th Ave., 2nd Floor, Topeka 66612-1594; (785) 296-2215; Fax, (785) 296-6296; Toll-free, (888) 428-8436; Twitter: @KSAGOffice; www.facebook.com/DerekSchmidt

Treasurer Ron Estes (R), Landon State Office Bldg., 900 S.W. Jackson St., #201, Topeka 66612-1235; (785) 296-3171; Fax, (785) 296-7950; Email: ron@treasurer.ks.gov

In Washington, DC: Adam Nordstrom, Washington Representative, Washington Office of the Governor, State of Kansas, 500 New Jersey Ave. N.W., #400, 20001; (202) 715-2923; Fax, (202) 638-1045

Kentucky   Web, www.kentucky.gov

Gov. Steve Beshear (D), The Capitol Bldg., 700 Capitol Ave., #100, Frankfort 40601; Press: Allison Gardner Martin, (502) 564-2611; Fax, (502) 564-2517; TTY, (502) 564-9551; Twitter: @GovSteveBeshear; www.facebook.com/govstevebeshear

Lt. Gov. Jerry Abramson (D), The Capitol Bldg., 700 Capitol Ave., #142, Frankfort 40601; (502) 564-2611; Fax, (502) 564-2849; Twitter: @ltgovabramson; www.facebook.com/ltgovjerryabramson

Secy. of State Alison Lundergan Grimes (D), The Capitol Bldg., 700 Capitol Ave., #152, Frankfort 40601-3493; (502) 564-3490; Fax, (502) 564-5687; Twitter: @KySecofState; www.facebook.com/kysecretaryofstate

Atty. Gen. Jack Conway (D), State Capitol, 700 Capitol Ave., #118, Frankfort 40601-3449; (502) 696-5300; Fax, (502) 564-2894; Twitter: @kyoag; www.facebook .com/pages/Jack-Conway-forKentucky/93023971130

Treasurer Todd Hollenbach (D), 1050 U.S. Hwy 127 S., #100, Frankfort 40601; (502) 564-4722; Fax, (502) 564-6545; Email: treasury.web@ky.gov

In Washington, DC: Rebecca Byers, Director, Washington Office of the Governor, State of Kentucky, 444 N. Capitol St. N.W., #380, 20001; (202) 220-1350; Fax, (202) 220-1359

Louisiana   Web, www.louisiana.gov

Gov. Bobby Jindal (R), State Capitol, 900 N. 3rd St., 4th Floor, Baton Rouge 70802-9004; P.O. Box 94004, Baton Rouge 70804-9004; Press: Kyle Plotkin, (225) 342-7015; Fax, (225) 342-7099; Toll-free, (866) 366-1121; Twitter: @bobbyjindal; www.facebook.com/bobbyjindal

Lt. Gov. Jay Dardenne (R), Capitol Annex, Bldg. 1051 N. 3rd St., Baton Rouge 70802; P.O. Box 44243, Baton Rouge, 70804-4242; (225) 342-7009; Fax, (225) 342-1949; Email: ltgov@crt.la.gov: Twitter: @JayDardenne; www.facebook.com/JayDardenne

Secy. of State Tom Schedler (R), 8585 Archives Ave., Baton Rouge 70809; P.O. Box 94125, Baton Rouge 70804-9125; (225) 922-2880; Fax, (225) 922-2003; Twitter: @Louisiana_SOS; www.facebook.com/ILikeTom

Atty. Gen. James D. (Buddy) Caldwell (R), 1885 N. 3rd St., Baton Rouge 70802, P.O. Box 94005, Baton Rouge 70804; (225) 326-6079; Fax, (225) 326-6793; Twitter: @LouisianaAGO; www.facebook.com/pages/Buddy-Caldwell/202447313126698

Treasurer John Neely Kennedy (R), 900 N. 3rd St., 3rd Floor, State Capitol, Baton Rouge 70802; P.O. Box 44154, Baton Rouge 70804; (225) 342-0010; Fax, (225) 342-0046; Twitter: @latreasury; www.facebook.com/LouisianaTreasury

Washington, DC Representative: Paul Rainwater, Chief of Staff, (225) 342-7188

Maine   Web, www.maine.gov

Gov. Paul R. LePage (R), 1 State House Station, Augusta 04333-0001; Press: Adrienne A. Bennett, (207) 287-3531; Fax, (207) 287-1034; TTY, (207) 287-6548; Email: governor@maine.gov

Secy. of State Mathew Dunlap (D), Nash School Bldg., 103 Sewall St., 2nd Floor, Augusta 04333; Mailing: 148 State House Station, Augusta 04333-0148; (207) 626-8400; Fax, (207) 287-8598; Email: sos.office@state.me.us

Atty. Gen. Janet T. Mills (D), Burton M. Cross Bldg., 3rd Floor, 111 Sewall St., Augusta 04333; Mailing: 6 State House Station, Augusta 04333-0006; (207) 626-8800; TTY, (207) 626-8865

Treasure Neria Douglass (D), Burton M. Cross Bldg., 3rd Floor, 111 Sewall St., Augusta 04333; Mailing: 39 State House Station, Augusta 04333-0039; (207) 624-7477; Fax: (207) 287-2367; Email: state.treasurer@state.me.us

Washington, DC Representative: Lance Libby, Legislative Policy Coordinator, (207) 287-3533

Maryland   Web, www.maryland.gov

Gov. Martin O'Malley (D), State House, 100 State Circle, Annapolis 21401-1925; Press: Shaun Adamec, (410) 974-3901; Toll-free, (800) 811-8336; TTY, (800) 2017165; Twitter: @governoromalley; www.facebook .com/MDGov

Lt. Gov. Anthony G. Brown (D), State House, 100 State Circle, Annapolis 21401-1925; (410) 974-2804; Twitter: @ltgovbrown; www.facebook.com/AnthonyBrown .Maryland

Secy. of State John P. McDonough (D), Fred L. Wineland Bldg., 16 Francis St., Annapolis 2140; (410) 974-5521; Fax, (410) 974-5190

Atty. Gen. Douglas F. Gansler (D), 200 St. Paul Pl., Baltimore 21202; (410) 576-6300; TTY, (410) 576-6372; www.facebook.com/MarylandAttorneyGeneral; Email: oag@oag.state.md.us

Treasurer Nancy K. Kopp (D), Treasury Bldg. #109, 80 Calvert St., Annapolis 21401; (410) 260-7160; Fax, (410) 974-3530; Toll-free, (800) 974-0468

In Washington, DC: Dana Thompson, Director, Washington Office of the Governor, State of Maryland, 444 N. Capitol St. N.W., #311, 20001; (202) 624-1430; Fax, (202) 783-3061

Massachusetts   Web, www.mass.gov

Gov. Deval Patrick (D), Executive Office, State House, #105, Boston 02133; Press: Kim Haberlin, (617) 725-4005; Fax, (617) 727-9725; Toll-free (in-state only), (888) 870-7770; TTY, (617) 727-3666; Twitter: @massgovernor; www.facebook.com/GovernorPatrick

Lt. Gov. Timothy (Tim) P. Murray (D), State House, #360, Boston 02133; (617) 725-4005; Fax, (617) 727-9725; Twitter: @MassLtGov; www.facebook.com/ timmurray2010

Secy. of the Commonwealth William Francis Galvin (D), One Ashburton Pl., #1611, Boston 02108-1512; (617) 727-7030; Fax, (617) 742-4528; Toll-free (in-state only), (800) 392-6090; TTY, (617) 878-3889; Email: cis@sec.state.ma.us

Atty. Gen. Martha Coakley (D), McCormack Bldg., One Ashburton Pl., #2010, Boston 02108-1518; (617) 727-2200; TTY, (617) 727-4765; Twitter: @MassAGO; www.facebook.com/MarthaCoakley

Treasurer Steven Grossman (D), State House, #227, Boston, 02133; (617) 367-6900; Fax, (617) 248-0372; Twitter: @MASSTreasury; www.facebook.com/pages/ Massachusetts-State-Treasury-Steven-GrossmanTreasurer/335356276509711

In Washington, DC: Valerie Young, Director of State and Federal Relations, Washington Office of the Governor, Commonwealth of Massachusetts, 444 N. Capitol St. N.W., #208, 20001; (202) 624-7713; Fax, (202) 6247714

Michigan   Web, www.michigan.gov

Gov. Rick Snyder (R), Romney Bldg., 111 S. Capitol Ave., P.O. Box 30013, Lansing 48909; Press: Sara Wurfel, (517) 373-3400; Fax, (517) 335-6863; Twitter: @onetoughnerd; www.facebook.com/RickForMichigan

Lt. Gov. Brian Calley (R), Romney Bldg., 111 S. Capitol Ave., 5th Floor, Lansing 48909; (517) 373-6800; Fax, (517) 241-3956; Twitter: @briancalley; www.facebook.com/briancalley

Secy. of State Ruth Johnson (R), Treasury Bldg., 430 W. Allegan St., 1st Floor, Lansing 48918-9900; (517) 3221460; Fax, (517) 373-0727; Toll-free, (888) 767-6424; Twitter: @MichSOS; www.facebook.com/ MichiganSoS

Atty. Gen. Bill Schuette (R), G. Mennen Williams Bldg., 525 W. Ottawa St., 7th Floor, P.O. Box 30212 Lansing 48909; (517) 373-1110; Fax, (517) 373-3042; Toll-free, (877) 765-8388; Twitter: @SchuetteOnDuty; www .facebook.com/BillSchuette; Email: miag@michigan.gov

Treasurer Kevin Clinton (D), Treasury Bldg., 430 W. Allegan St., Lansing 48922; (517) 373-3200; Fax, (517) 373-4968; TTY, (517) 636-4999

In Washington, DC: Bill McBride, Washington Representative, Washington Office of the Governor, State of Michigan, 444 N. Capitol St. N.W., #411, 20001; (202) 624-5840; Fax, (202) 624-5841

Minnesota   Web, www.state.mn.us

Gov. Mark Dayton (D), 130 State Capitol, 75 Rev. Dr. Martin Luther King Jr. Blvd., St. Paul 55155; Press: Pat Turgeon, (651) 201-3400; Fax, (651) 797-1850; Toll-free, (800) 657-3717; Twitter: @GovMarkDayton; www.facebook.com/GovMarkDayton

Lt. Gov. Yvonne Prettner Solon (D), 130 State Capitol, 75 Rev. Dr. Martin Luther King Jr. Blvd., St. Paul 55155; (651) 201-3400; Fax, (651) 797-1850; www.facebook .com/yvonne.p.solon

Secy. of State Mark Ritchie (D), 180 State Capitol, 100 Rev. Dr. Martin Luther King Jr. Blvd., St. Paul 55155; (651) 201-1324; Fax, (651) 296-9073; Toll-free, (877) 5516767; Email: secretary.state@state.mn.us

Atty. Gen. Lori Swanson (D), 1400 Bremer Tower, 445 Minnesota St., St. Paul 55101-2131; (651) 296-3353; Toll-free, (800) 657-3787; TTY, (800) 366-4812

Commissioner of Minnesota Management and Budget (MMB) Jim Schowalter, 400 Centennial Bldg., 658 Cedar St., St. Paul, 55155; (651) 201-8000; Fax, (651) 296-8685; TTY, (800) 627-3529; Twitter: @MMBCommissioner

In Washington, DC: Bill Richard, Director, Washington Office of the Governor, State of Minnesota, 1017 8th St. N.E., #380, 20002, (202) 236-3717

Mississippi   Web, www.ms.gov

Gov. Phil Bryant (R), P.O. Box 139, Jackson 39215; Press: Mick Bullock, (601) 359-3150; Fax, (601) 359-3741; Toll-free, (877) 405-0733; Email: governor@governor .state.ms.us; Twitter: @PhilBryantMS; www.facebook .com/im4phil

Lt. Gov. Tate Reeves (R), New Capitol Bldg., #315, 400 High St., P.O. Box 1018, Jackson 39215-1018; (601) 359-3200; Fax, (601) 359-4054; Twitter: @tatereeves; Email: ltgov@ms.gov

Secy. of State Delbert Hosemann (R), 401 Mississippi St., Jackson 39201, (601) 359-1350; Fax, (601) 359-1499; Twitter: @DelbertHosemann Email: administrator@sos.ms.gov

Atty. Gen. Jim Hood (D), Walter Sillers Bldg., 550 High St., #1200, Jackson 39201, P.O. Box 220, Jackson 39205; (601) 359-3680; Fax, (601) 359-3796; Twitter: @AGJimHood; Email: msag05@ago.sate.ms.us

Treasurer Lynn Fitch (R), 1101-A Woolfolk Bldg., 501 N. West St., Jackson 39201, P.O. Box 138, Jackson 39205; (601) 359-3600; Fax, (601) 359-2001; Twitter: @lynnfitch; Email: mmitchell@treasury.state.ms.gov

Missouri   Web, www.mo.gov

Gov. Jeremiah W. (Jay) Nixon (D), State Capitol, #216, Jefferson City 65101; Mailing, P.O. Box 720, Jefferson City 65102; Press: Scott Holste, (573) 751-3222; Twitter: @GovJayNixon; www.facebook.com/pages/ Jay-Nixon/6517667731

Lt. Gov. Peter Kinder (R), State Capitol, #224, Jefferson City 65101; (573) 751-4727; Fax, (573) 751-9422; Email: ltgovinfo@ltgov.mo.gov

Secy. of State Jason Kander (D), 600 W. Main St., Jefferson City 65101; (573) 751-4936; Fax, (573) 751-2490; Email: Info@sos.mo.gov

Atty. Gen. Chris Koster (D), Supreme Court Bldg., 207 W. High St., P.O. Box 899, Jefferson City 65102; (573) 751-3321; Fax, (573) 751-0774; Email: attorney .general@ago.mo.gov

Treasurer Clint Zweifel (D), P.O. Box 210, Jefferson City 65102, (573) 751-8533; Fax, (573) 751-0343; Twitter: @ClintZweifel; Email: angie.robyn@treasurer.mo.gov

Washington, DC Representative: Dustin Allison, Deputy Chief of Staff, (573) 751-3222

Montana   Web, http://mt.gov/

Gov. Steve Bullock (D), State Capitol, #204, P.O. Box 200801, Helena 59620-0801; Press: Sarah Elliot, (406) 444-3111; Fax, (406) 444-5529; Twitter: @GovSteveBullock; www.facebook.com/ GovSteveBullock

Lt. Gov. Angela McLean (D), State Capitol, #207, P.O. Box 201901, Helena 59620-1901; (406) 444-5665; Fax, (406) 444-4648

Secy. of State Linda McCulloch (D), State Capitol, Bldg. 1301 6th Ave., #260, Helena 59601; P.O. Box 202801, Helena, 59620; (406) 444-4195 Fax, (406) 444-3976; Twitter: @SOSMcCulloch; Email: secretary@mt.gov

Atty. Gen. Tim Fox (R), Justice Bldg., 215 N. Sanders St., P.O. Box 201401, Helena 59620-1401; (406) 444-2026; Fax, (406) 444-3549; Email: contact doj@mt.gov

Director of Dept. of Administration Sheila Hogan, 125 N. Roberts St., P.O. Box 200101, Helena 59620-0101; (406) 444-2032 or 444-2023; Fax (406) 444-6194

Washington, DC Representative: Kevin O'Brien, Deputy Chief of Staff, (406) 444-3111

Nebraska   Web, www.nebraska.gov

Gov. Dave Heineman (R), State Capitol, 1445 K St., #2316, P.O. Box 96843, Lincoln 68509; Press: Jen Hein, (402) 471-2244; Fax, (402) 471-6031; Twitter: @Gov_ Heineman; www.facebook.com/negovernor

Lt. Gov. Lavon Heidemann (I), State Capitol, #2315, Lincoln, P.O. Box 94863, 68509; (402) 471-2256; Fax, (402) 471-6031; Email: sarah.schoen@nebraska .gov

Secy. of State John A. Gale (R), State Capitol, 1445 K St., #2300, Lincoln; P.O. Box 94608, Lincoln 68509; (402) 471-2554; Fax, (402) 471-3237; Twitter: @NESecJGale; www.facebook.com/pages/John-Gale-Nebraska-Secretary-of-State/101674183249332?sk=wall

Atty. Gen. Jon Bruning (R), 2115 State Capitol, Lincoln 68509; (402) 471-2682; Fax, (402) 471-3297; Twitter: @JoeBruning

Treasurer Don Stenberg (R), State Capitol, #2005, P.O. Box 94788, Lincoln 68509; (402) 471-2455; Fax, (402) 471-4390

Washington, DC Representative: Lauren Kintner, Policy Director and General Counsel, (402) 471-2244

Nevada   Web, www.nv.gov

Gov. Brian Sandoval (R), State Capitol Bldg., 101 N. Carson St., Carson City 89701; Press, Mary-Sarah Kinner, (775) 684-5670; Fax, (775) 684-5683; Twitter: @GovSandoval

Lt. Gov. Brian Krolicki (R), State Capitol Bldg., 101 N. Carson St., #2, Carson City 89701; (775) 684-7111; Fax, (775) 684-7110

Secy. of State Ross Miller (D), State Capitol Bldg., 101 N. Carson St., #3, Carson City 89701-4786; (775) 684-5708; Fax, (775) 684-5725; Twitter: @rossjmiller; www.facebook.com/electrossmiller

Atty. Gen. Catherine Cortez Masto (D), Capitol Complex, 100 N. Carson St., Carson City 89701-4717; (775) 684-1100; Fax, (775) 684-1108; Twitter: @NevadaAG; Email: aginfo@ag.nv.gov

Treasurer Kate Marshall (D), Capitol Bldg., 101 N. Carson St., #4, Carson City 89701-4786; (775) 684-5600; Fax, (775) 684-5781; Twitter: @KateMarshallNV; Email: statetreasurer@nevadatreasurer.gov

In Washington, DC: Ryan McGinness, Director, Washington Office of the Governor, State of Nevada, 444 N. Capitol St. N.W., #209, 20001; (202) 624-5405

New Hampshire   Web, www.nh.gov

Gov. Maggie Hassan (D), State House, 107 North Main St., Concord 03301; Press: Colin Manning, (603) 271-2121; Fax, (603) 271-7640; Twitter: @GovernorHassan; www.facebook.com/GovernorHassan

(No office of Lieutenant Governor)

Secy. of State William M. Gardner (D), State House, #204, 107 North Main St., Concord 03301; (603) 271-3242; Fax, (603) 271-6316; Email: elections@sos.state.nh.us

Atty. Gen. Joseph Foster (D), 33 Capitol St., Concord 03301; (603) 271-3658; Fax, (603) 271-2110; TTY, (800) 735-2964; Email: attorneygeneral@doj.nh.gov

Treasurer Catherine A. Provencher (D), State House Annex, 25 Capitol St., #121, Concord 03301; (603) 271-2621; Fax, (603) 271-3922; Email: treasury@treasury.state.nh.us

New Jersey   Web, www.newjersey.gov

Gov. Chris Christie (R), State House, 125 W. State St., P.O. Box 001, Trenton 08625; Press: Michael Drewniak, (609) 292-6000; Twitter: @GovChristie; www.facebook.com/GovChrisChristie

Lt. Gov. & Secy. of State Kim Guadagno (R), 225 W. State St., P.O. Box 300, Trenton 08625; (609) 984-1900; Fax, (609) 777-1764; Twitter: @sheriffkim; Email: Feedback@sos.state.nj.us

Atty. Gen. John Jay Hoffman (acting) (R), 25 Market St., 8th Floor, West Wing, P.O. Box 080, Trenton 08625-0080; (609) 292-4925; Fax, (609) 292-3508

Treasurer Andrew P. Sidamon-Eristoff (R), State House, 125 W. State St., Trenton 08625; Mailing, P.O. Box 002, Trenton 08625; (609) 292-6748

In Washington, DC: Dona De Leon, Director, Washington Office of the Governor, State of New Jersey, 444 N. Capitol St. N.W., #201, 20001; (202) 638-0631; Fax, (202) 638-2296

New Mexico   Web, www.newmexico.gov

Gov. Susana Martinez (R), State Capitol Bldg., 490 Old Santa Fe Trail, #400, Santa Fe 87501; Press: Phil Sisneros, (505) 476-2200; Fax, (505) 476-2226; Twitter: @Gov_Martinez; www.facebook.com/SusanaMartinezFan

Lt. Gov. John A. Sanchez (R), State Capitol Bldg., 490 Old Santa Fe Trail, #417, Santa Fe 87501, (505) 476-2250; Fax, (505) 476-2257; Twitter: @LtGovSanchez

Secy. of State Dianna J. Duran (R), State Capitol North Annex, 325 Don Gaspar Ave., #300, Santa Fe 87501; (505) 827-3614; Fax, (505) 827-8081; Toll-free, (800) 477-3632

Atty. Gen. Gary King (D), Villagra Bldg., 408 Galisteo St., Santa Fe 87501; P.O. Drawer 1508, Santa Fe 87504-1508; (505) 827-6000; Fax, (505) 827-5826; Twitter: @New MexicoAGO; www.facebook.com/NMAttorneyGeneral

Treasurer James B. Lewis (D), State Treasurer's Office, 2055 S. Pacheco St., #100 & 200, Santa Fe 87505-5135; (505) 955-1120; Fax, (505) 955-1195

Washington, DC Representative: James Ross, Cabinet Director, (505) 476-2200

New York   Web, www.state.ny.us

Gov. Andrew Cuomo (D), NYS State Capitol Bldg., Albany 12224; Press: Josh Vlasto, (518) 474-8390; Twitter: @NYGovCuomo; www.facebook.com/GovernorAndrewCuomo

Lt. Gov. Robert Duffy (D), Executive Chamber, State Capitol, Albany 12224-0341; (518) 474-8390; Fax, (518) 474-1513

Secy. of State Cesar A. Perales (D), One Commerce Plaza, 99 Washington Ave., Albany 12231-0001; (518) 486-9844; Fax, (518) 474-4769; Twitter: @NYSDOS

Atty. Gen. Eric T. Schneiderman (D), State Capitol, Albany 12224-0341; (518) 474-7330; Toll-free, (800) 771-7755; Twitter: @AGSchneiderman; www.facebook.com/eric.schneiderman

Treasurer Aida Brewer (R), 110 State St., 2nd Floor, Albany 12207; P.O. Box 22119, Albany 12201-2119; (518) 474-4250; Fax, (518) 402-4118

In Washington, DC: Alexander Cochran, Director, Washington Office of the Governor, State of New York, 444 N. Capitol St. N.W., #301, 20001; (202) 434-7112; Fax, (202) 434-7110

North Carolina   Web, www.nc.gov

Gov. Pat McCrory (R), State Capitol, Raleigh 27699; Mailing: 20301 Mail Service Center, Raleigh 27699; (919) 814-2000; Fax, (919) 733-2120; Twitter: @PatMcCoryNC; www.facebook.com/GovernorPat

Lt. Gov. Dan Forest (R), 310 N. Blount St., Raleigh 27601; 20401 Mail Service Center, Raleigh, 27699-0401; (919) 733-7350; Fax, (919) 733-6595; Twitter: @DanForestNC; www.facebook.com/DanForestNC

Secy. of State Elaine F. Marshall (D), 2 S. Salisbury St., Raleigh, 27601; P.O. Box 29622, Raleigh 27626; (919) 807-2005; Fax, (919) 807-2039; Twitter: @Elaine4NC; www.facebook.com/Elaine4NC

Atty. Gen. Roy Cooper (D), 9001 Mail Service Ctr., Raleigh 27699-9001; (919) 716-6400; Fax, (919) 716-6750; Twitter: NCAGO; www.facebook.com/pages/NCAttorney-Generals-Office/157759274279900

Treasurer Janet Cowell (D), 325 N. Salisbury St., Raleigh 27603-1385; (919) 508-5176; Fax, (919) 508-5167; Twitter: @JanetCowell; www.facebook.com/janetcowell

In Washington, DC: Chloe Gossage, Policy Director, (919) 733-4240

North Dakota   Web, www.nd.gov

Gov. Jack Dalrymple (R), State Capitol, 600 E. Boulevard Ave., Bismarck 58505-0100; Press: Jeff Zent, (701) 328-2200; Fax, (701) 328-2205; Twitter: @DalrympleforGov; www.facebook.com/NDGovDalrymple

Lt. Gov. Drew Wrigley (R), State Capitol, 600 E. Boulevard Ave., Dept. 101, Bismarck 58505-0100; (701) 328-2200; Fax, (701) 328-2205; Twitter: @DrewWrigley

Secy. of State Al Jaeger (R), State Capitol, 600 E. Boulevard Ave., Dept. 108, Bismarck 58505-0500; (701) 328-2900; Fax, (701) 328-2992; Toll-free, (800) 3520867; TTY, (800) 366-6888; Email: sos@nd.gov

Atty. Gen. Wayne Stenehjem (R), State Capitol, 600 E. Boulevard Ave., Dept. 125, Bismarck 58505; (701) 328-2210; Fax, (701) 328-2226; TTY, (800) 366-6888; Email: ndag@nd.gov

Treasurer Kelly L. Schmidt (R), State Capitol, 3rd Floor, 600 E. Boulevard Ave., Dept. 120, Bismarck 58505-0660; (701) 328-2643; Fax, (701) 328-3002; Email: treasurer@nd.gov

In Washington, DC: Krista Carman, Washington Representative, Washington Office of the Governor, State of North Dakota, 211 North Union St., #100, Alexandria, VA 22314; (703) 519-1207; Fax, (202) 478-0811

Ohio   Web, www.ohio.gov

Gov. John R. Kasich (R), Vern Riffe Center, 30th Floor, 77 South High St., Columbus 43215-6117; Press: Rob Nichols, (614) 466-3555; Fax, (614) 466-9354; Twitter: @OHPressSec; www.facebook.com/JohnRKasich

Lt. Gov. Mary Taylor (R), Vern Riffe Center, 30th Floor, 77 S. High St., Columbus 43215-6117; (614) 644-3379; Fax, (614) 644-9345; Twitter: @marytayloroh; www.facebook.com/MaryTaylorOH

Secy. of State Jon Husted (R), 180 E. Broad St., 16th Floor, Columbus 43215; (614) 466-2655; Fax, (614) 466-3899; TTY, (614) 466-0562;Twitter: @OhioSOSHusted; www.facebook.com/ohiososhusted

Atty. Gen. Mike DeWine (R), 30 E. Broad St., 14th Floor, Columbus 43215-3428; (614) 466-4320; Help line, (614) 466-4986; Twitter: @OhioAG; www.facebook.com/OhioAttorneyGeneral

Treasurer Josh Mandel (R), 30 E. Broad St., 9th Floor, Columbus 43215; (614) 466-2160; Fax, (614) 644-7313; TTY, (800) 228-1102; Twitter: @Ohiotreasurer; Email: constituentaffairs@tos.ohio.gov

Washington, DC Representative: Erik L. Johnson, Director, (614) 995-1813

Oklahoma   Web, www.ok.gov

Gov. Mary Fallin (R), State Capitol, 2300 N. Lincoln Blvd., #212, Oklahoma City 73105; Press: Aaron Cooper, (405) 521-2342; Fax, (405) 521-3353; Twitter: @GovMaryFallin; www.facebook.com/GovernorMaryFallin

Lt. Gov. Todd Lamb (R), State Capitol, 2300 N. Lincoln Blvd., #211, Oklahoma City 73105; (405) 521-2161; Fax, (405) 522-8694; Twitter:@LtGovToddLamb; www.facebook.com/LtGovernorToddLamb

Secy. of State Chris Benge (R), 2300 N. Lincoln Blvd., #101 Oklahoma City 73105; (405) 521-3912

Atty. Gen. E. Scott Pruitt (R), 1313 N.E. 21st St., Oklahoma City 73105; (405) 521-3921; Twitter: @OklaAG; www.facebook.com/AttorneyGeneralPruitt

Treasurer Ken Miller (R), State Capitol, 2300 N. Lincoln Blvd., #217, Oklahoma City 73105; (405) 521-3191; Twitter: @OKTreasurer

In Washington, DC: Chelsea Barnett, Washington Office of the Governor State of Oklahoma, 444 North Capitol St., #200 20001; (202) 624-5945

Oregon   Web, www.oregon.gov

Gov. John Kitzhaber (D), 160 State Capitol, 900 Court St. N.E., Salem 97301-4047; Press: Tim Raphael, (503) 378-4582; Fax, (503) 378-6827; Twitter: @govkitz; www.facebook.com/johnkitzhaber

(No office of Lieutenant Governor)

Secy. of State Kate Brown (D), 136 State Capitol, Salem 97301-0722; (503) 986-1523; Fax, (503) 986-1616; Twitter: @OregonSOS; Email: oregon.sos@state.or.us

Atty. Gen. Ellen F. Rosenblum (D), Justice Bldg., 1162 Court St. N.E., Salem 97301-4096; (503) 378-4400; Fax, (503) 378-4017; Twitter: @ EllenRosenblum

Treasurer Ted Wheeler (D), 900 Court St. N.E., Salem 97301-4043; (503) 378-4329; Fax, (503) 373-7051; Twitter: @tedwheeler; Email: oregon.treasurer@state.or.us

In Washington, DC: Dan Carol, Washington Office of the Governor State of Oregon, 444 North Capitol St., # 134 20001; (503) 373-1027

Pennsylvania   Web, www.state.pa.us

Gov. Tom Corbett (R), 225 Capitol Bldg., 501 N. 3rd St., Harrisburg 17120; Press: Kevin Harley, (717) 787-2500; Fax, (717) 772-8284; Twitter: @GovernorCorbett; www.facebook.com/Gov.TomCorbett

Lt. Gov. Jim Cawley (R), 200 Capitol Bldg., 501 N. 3rd St., Harrisburg 17120-0002; (717) 787-3300; Fax, (717) 783-0150; www.facebook.com/LGJimCawley

Secy. of the Commonwealth Carol Aichele (R), 302 North Office Bldg., Harrisburg 17120; (717) 787-6458; Fax, (717) 787-1734

Atty. Gen. Kathleen G. Kane (D), 11 N. 3rd St., Strawberry Square, 16th Floor, Harrisburg 17120; (717) 787-3391; Fax, (717) 783-1107

Treasurer Rob McCord (D), 613 North St., Finance Bldg., Harrisburg 17120; (717) 787-2465; Fax, (717) 783-9760

Washington, DC Representative: Chris Gray, Special Assistant to Director of Policy and Planning, (717) 787-2500

Rhode Island   Web, www.ri.gov

Gov. Lincoln Chafee (I), State House, 82 Smith St., Providence 02903-1196; Press: Christine Hunsinger, (401) 222-2080; Email: governor@governor.ri.gov; Twitter: @Lincoln Chafee;

Lt. Gov. Elizabeth Roberts (D), State House, #116, 82 Smith St., Providence 02903; (401) 222-2371; Fax, (401) 222-2012; Email: info@ltgov.state.ri.us; Twitter: @LtGovRoberts;

Secy. of State A. Ralph Mollis (D), 82 Smith St., State House, #217, Providence 02903-1105; (401) 222-2357; Fax, (401) 222-1356; TTY, 711 (in-state); Email: aralphmollis@sos.ri.gov Twitter: @RalphMollis

Atty. Gen. Peter Kilmartin (D), 150 S. Main St., Providence 02903-2856; (401) 274-4400; Fax, (401) 222-1302; Twitter: @AGKilmartin

Treasurer Gina Raimondo (D), State House, #102, 82 Smith St., Providence 02903; (401) 222-2397;

Fax, (401) 222-6140; Twitter: @GinaRaimondo;
www.facebook.com/GinaMRaimondo

In Washington, DC: Sam Reid, Director, Washington
Office of the Governor, State of Rhode Island, 444 N.
Capitol St. N.W., #619, 20001; (202) 257-8431;
Fax, (202) 965-5789

South Carolina   Web, www.sc.gov

Gov. Nikki Haley (R), Office of the Governor, 1205
Pendleton St., Columbia 29201; Press: Rob Godfrey,
(803) 734-2100; Fax: (803) 734-5167; Twitter:
@SCGOVOFFICE; www.facebook.com/NikkiHaley

Lt. Gov. Glenn McConnell (R), State House, 1st Floor,
Columbia 29202; Mailing, P.O. Box 142, Columbia
29202; (803) 734-2080; Fax, (803) 734-2082; Email:
LtGovernor@scstatehouse.gov

Secy. of State Mark Hammond (R), 1205 Pendleton St.,
#525, Columbia 29201; Mailing, P.O. Box 11350,
Columbia 29211; (803) 734-2170; Fax, (803) 734-1661

Atty. Gen. Alan Wilson (R), Rembert Dennis Bldg., 1000
Assembly St., #519, Columbia 29201; P.O. Box 11549,
Columbia, 29201; (803) 734-3970; Fax: (803) 253-6283;
@SCAttyGenOffice; www.facebook.com/pages/
Attorney-General-Alan-Wilson/197896563584053

Treasurer Curtis M. Loftis Jr. (R), Wade Hampton Office
Bldg., 1200 Senate St., #118, Columbia 29201; P.O. Box
11778, Columbia, 29211; (803) 734-2016; Fax, (803)
734-2690; Email: treasurer@sto.sc.gov Twitter:
@TreasurerLoftis; www.facebook.com/curtis.loftis

Washington, DC Representative: Josh Baker, Budget
Director, (803) 734-2100

South Dakota   Web, www.state.sd.us

Gov. Dennis Daugaard (R), Capitol Bldg., 500 E. Capitol
Ave., Pierre 57501; Press: Joe Kafka, (605) 773-3212;
Fax, (605) 773-4711; Twitter: @SDGovDaugaard;
www.facebook.com/SDGovDaugaard

Lt. Gov. Matt Michels (R), Capitol Bldg., 500 E. Capitol
Ave., Pierre 57501-5070; (605) 773-3212; Fax, (605)
773-4711

Secy. of State Jason Gant (R), Capitol Bldg, 500 E. Capitol
Ave., #204, Pierre 57501-5070; (605) 773-3537;
Fax, (605) 773-6580; Email: sdsos@state.sd.us Twitter:
@SOSGantl; www.facebook.com/SOSGant

Atty. Gen. Marty Jackley (R), 1302 E. Hwy. 14, #1, Pierre
57501-8501; (605) 773-3215; Fax, (605) 773-4106;
TTY, (605) 773-6585; Twitter: @sdattorneygen;
www.facebook.com/SDATG

Treasurer Richard L. Sattgast (R), State Capitol, 500 E.
Capitol Ave., #212, Pierre 57501-5070; (605) 773-3378;
Fax, (605) 773-3115

Washington, DC Representative: Jim Soyer, Legislative
Director, (605) 773-3212

Tennessee   Web, www.tn.gov

Gov. Bill Haslam (R), State Capitol, 1st Floor, Nashville
37243-0001; Press: Blake Fortenay, (615) 741-2001;
Fax, (615) 532-9711; Twitter: @billhaslam;
www.facebook.com/TeamHaslam

Lt. Gov. Ron Ramsey (R), 1 Legislative Plaza, 301 6th Ave.,
North Nashville 37243-0202; (615) 741-4524;
Fax, (615) 253-0197; Email: lt.gov.ron.ramsey@capitol
.tn.gov; Twitter: @RonRamsey;

Secy. of State Tre Hargett (R), State Capitol, 312 Rosa L.
Parks Ave., Nashville 37243-1102; (615) 741-2819/
2078; Fax, (615) 741-5962; Email: administrative
.procedures@tn.gov; Twitter: @SecTreHargett

Atty. Gen. Robert E. Cooper Jr. (D), 425 5th Ave. North,
Cordell Hull Bldg., Nashville 37243-0485; Mailing, P.O.
Box 20207, Nashville 37202-0207; (615) 741-3491;
Fax, (615) 741-2009; Twitter: @TNattygen

Treasurer David H. Lillard Jr. (R), Tennessee State Capitol,
1st Floor, 600 Charlotte Ave., Nashville 37243-0225;
(615) 741-2956

Washington, DC Representative: Beth Tipps, Deputy
Director of Policy and Research, (615) 741-2001

Texas   Web, www.tx.gov

Gov. Rick Perry (R), State Insurance Bldg., 1100 San
Jacinto Blvd., # 151B, Austin 78701; P.O. Box 12428,
Austin 78711; (512) 463-2000; www.facebook.com/
GovernorPerry

Lt. Gov. David Dewhurst (R), Capitol Station, P.O. Box
12068, Austin 78711-2068; (512) 463-0001; Fax, (512)
463-0677; Twitter: @DavidHDewhurst; www.facebook
.com/dewhurstfortexas

Secy. of State Nandita Berry (R), 1100 Congress Capitol
Bldg., #1E.8, Austin 78701; P.O. Box 12887, Austin
78701; (512) 475-4578; Fax, (512) 475-2761; Twitter:
@TXsecofstate

Atty. Gen. Greg Abbott (R), 300 W. 15th St., 8th Floor,
Austin 78701; (512) 463-2100; Fax, (512) 463-2063;
Email: public.information@oag.state.tx.us; Twitter:
@GregAbbott_TX; www.facebook.com/
TexasAttorneyGeneral

Comptroller Susan Combs (R), Lyndon B. Johnson Bldg.,
111 E. 17th St., 1st St., Austin 78774-0100; P.O. Box
13528 Capitol Station, Austin 78711-3528; (512)
463-4000; Fax, (512) 475-0352; Email: texas
.comptroller@cpa.state.tx.us; Twitter: @txcomptroller

In Washington, DC: Dan Wilmot, Director, Office of State-
Federal Relations, State of Texas, 10 G St. N.E., #650,
20001; (202) 638-3927; Fax, (202) 628-1943

Utah   Web, www.utah.gov

Gov. Gary Herbert (R), Utah State Capitol Complex,
350 N. State St., #200, P.O. Box 142220, Salt Lake City
84114-2220; (801) 538-1000; Fax, (801) 538-1528;
Toll-free, (800) 705-2464; (801) 538-1509; Twitter:
@governorherbert; www.facebook.com/pages/Gary-R-
Herbert/211722425515547

Lt. Gov. Spencer J. Cox (R), Utah State Capitol Complex,
#220, P.O. Box 142325, Salt Lake City 84114-2220; (801)
538-1041; Fax, (801) 538-1133; Toll-free, (800) 995-8683

(No office of Secretary of State)

Atty. Gen. Sean D. Reyes (R), State Capitol Complex,
350 N. State St., #230, P.O. Box 142320, Salt Lake City
84114-2320; (801) 366-0260; Fax, (801) 538-1121;
Email: uag@utah.gov

Treasurer Richard K. Ellis (R), State Capitol Complex, 350 N. State St., #180, P.O. Box 142315, Salt Lake City 84114-2315; (801) 538-1042; Fax, (801) 538-1465

In Washington, DC: Wesley Smith, Washington Officer of the Governor, Director State and Federal Regulations, (801) 538-1000

Vermont   Web, www.vermont.gov

Gov. Peter Shumlin (D), 109 State St., Pavilion, Montpelier 05609-0101; Press: Susan Allen, (802) 828-3333; Fax, (802) 828-3339; TTY, (800) 649-6825; Twitter: @GovPeterShumlin;

Lt. Gov. Phil Scott (R), 115 State St., Montpelier 05633-5401; (802) 828-2226; Fax, (802) 828-3198; www.facebook.com/pages/Phil-Scott/171004602919914

Secy. of State Jim Condos (D), 128 State St., Montpelier 05633-1101; (802) 828-2148; Info, (802) 828-2363; Fax, (802) 828-2496; Email: jim.condos@sec.state.vt.us

Atty. Gen. William H. Sorrell (D), Pavilion Office Bldg., 109 State St., Montpelier 05609-1001; (802) 828-3171; TTY, (802) 828-3665; Email: atginfo@atg.state.vt.us

Treasurer Elizabeth (Beth) Pearce (D), Pavilion Office Bldg., 109 State St., 4th Floor, Montpelier 05609-6200; (802) 828-2301; Fax, (802) 828-2772; TTY, (800) 253-0191; Email: Treasurers.Office@state.vt.us

Washington, DC Representative: Alyson Richards, Policy Advisor, Washington Officer of the Governor, (802) 371-9750

Virginia   Web, www.virginia.gov

Gov. Terence (Terry) R. McAuliffe (D), Patrick Henry Bldg., 3rd Floor, 1111 E. Broad St., Richmond 23219; (804) 786-2211; Fax, (804) 371-6351; TTY, (800) 828-1120; Twitter: @GovernorVA; www.facebook.com/pages/Governor-of-Virginia/61634046094

Lt. Gov. Ralph S. Northam (D), 102 Governor St., Richmond 23219; P.O. Box 1195, Richmond 23218; (804) 786-2078; Fax, (804) 786-7514; Email: ltgov@ltgov.virginia.gov

Secy. of the Commonwealth Levar Stoney(D), 1111 E. Broad St., 4th Floor, Richmond 23219; Mailing: P.O. Box 2454, Richmond 23218, (804) 786-2441; Fax, (804) 371-0017

Atty. Gen. Mark R. Herring (D), 900 E. Main St., Richmond 23219; (804) 786-2071

Treasurer Manju Ganeriwala (D), James Monroe Bldg., 3rd Floor, 101 N. 14th St., Richmond 23219; (804) 371-6011; Fax, (804) 225-3187

In Washington, DC: Maribel Ramos, Director, Virginia Office of Intergovernmental Affairs, Commonwealth of Virginia, 444 N. Capitol St. N.W., #214, 20001; (202) 783-1769; Fax, (202) 783-7687

Washington   Web, www.access.wa.gov

Gov. Jay Inslee (D), Legislative Bldg., 2nd Floor, 1143 Capitol Way South, P.O. Box 40002, Olympia 98504-0002; (360) 902-4111; Fax, (360) 753-4110; TTY [WA. Only] (800) 833-6388; Twitter: @GovInslee

Lt. Gov. Brad Owen (D), Legislative Bldg., #220, 416 Sid Snyder Ave. S.W., P.O. Box 40400, Olympia 98504-0400; (360) 786-7700; Fax, (360) 786-7749; Email: ltgov@leg.wa.gov

Secy. of State Kim Wyman (R), Legislative Bldg., 2nd Floor, 416 Sid Snyder Ave. S.W., P.O. Box 40220 Olympia 98504-0220; (360) 902-4151; Fax, (360) 586-5629; TTY, (800) 422-8683; Email: mail@sos.wa.gov; Twitter: @secstatewa; www.facebook.com/WaSecretaryOfState

Atty. Gen. Bob Ferguson (D), 1125 Washington St. S.E., P.O. Box 40100, Olympia 98504-0100; (360) 753-6200; Fax, (360) 664-0228; Twitter: @AGOWA; www.facebook.com/WAStateAttorneyGeneral

Treasurer James L McIntire (D), Legislative Bldg., #230, 416 Sid Synder Ave., S.W. P.O. Box 40200, Olympia 98504; (360) 902-9001; Fax, (360) 902-9037 TTY, (360) 902-8963 Email: watreas@tre.wa.gov

In Washington, DC: Sam Ricketts, Director, Washington Office of the Governor, State of Washington, 444 N. Capitol St. N.W., #411, 20001; (202) 624-3691; Fax, (202) 624-5841

West Virginia   Web, www.wv.gov

Gov. Earl Ray Tomblin (D), State Capitol, 1900 Kanawha Blvd. East, Charleston 25305-0370; Press: Amy Shuler Goodwin, (304) 558-2000; Toll-free, (888) 438-2731

Lt. Gov. Jeffrey Kessler (D), Capitol Complex, Bldg. 1, #227M, Charleston 25305; (304) 357-7801; Fax, (304) 357-7839; Email: jeff.kessler@wvsenate.gov

Secy. of State Natalie E. Tennant (D), Capitol Complex, Bldg. 1, #157-K, 1900 Kanawha Blvd. East, Charleston 25305-0770; (304) 558-6000; Fax, (304) 558-0900; Twitter: @natalietennant; www.facebook.com/wvsos

Atty. Gen. Patrick Morrisey (R), Capitol Complex, Bldg. 1, #26-E, 1900 Kanawha Blvd. East, Charleston 25305; (304) 558-2021; Fax, (304) 558-0140; Twitter: @WestVirginiaAG; www.facebook.com/agwestv

Treasurer John D. Perdue (D), Capitol Complex, Bldg. 1, #E-145, 1900 Kanawha Blvd., Charleston 25305; (304) 558-5000; Toll-free, (800) 422-7498; TTY, (304) 3401598; Twitter: @WV_Treasurer; www.facebook.com/WVTreasury

Washington, DC Representative: Chris Weikle, Policy Advisor, Washington Officer of the Governor, (304) 624-3961

Wisconsin   Web, www.wisconsin.gov

Gov. Scott Walker (R), State Capitol, #115-E, P.O. Box 2043, Madison 53702-7863; (608) 266-1212; Fax, (608) 267-8983; TTY, (608) 267-6790; Email: govgeneral@wisconsin.gov; Twitter: @GovWalker;

Lt. Gov. Rebecca Kleefisch (R), State Capitol, #19-E, P.O. Box 2043, Madison 53702; (608) 266-3516; Fax, (608) 267-3571; Email: ltgov@wisconsin.gov Twitter: @LTGovKleefisch

Secy. of State Douglas La Follette (D), 30 W. Mifflin St., 10th Floor, Madison 53703; P.O. Box 7848, 53707;

(608) 266-8888; X3 Fax, (608) 266-3159; Email: statesec@sos.state.wi.us; Twitter: @DougLaFollette

Atty. Gen. J. B. Van Hollen (R), 17 W. Main St., Madison 53702, P.O. Box 7857, Madison 53707-7857; (608) 266-1221; Fax, (608) 267-2779; Twitter: @WisDOJ; www.facebook.com/AGVanHollen

Treasurer Kurt Schuller (R), 1 S. Pinckney, #360, Madison 53703; Mailing: P.O. Box 2114, Madison 53701; (855) 375-2274; Fax, (608) 261-6799; Twitter: @WIStateTreasury

In Washington, DC: Wendy Riemann, Director, Washington Office of the Governor, State of Wisconsin, 444 N. Capitol St. N.W., #613, 20001; (202) 624-5870; Fax, (202) 624-5871

Wyoming   Web, www.wy.gov

Gov. Matt Mead (R), State Capitol, 200 W. 24th St., Cheyenne 82002-0010; (307) 777-7434; Fax, (307) 632-3909

(No office of Lieutenant Governor)

Secy. of State Max Maxfield (R), State Capitol Bldg., 200 W. 24th St., Cheyenne 82002-0020; (307) 777-7378; Fax, (307) 777-6217; Email: secofstate@wyo.gov

Atty. Gen. Gregory A. Phillips (D), 123 State Capitol, 200 W. 24th St., Cheyenne 82002; (307) 777-7841; Fax, (307) 777-6869; TTY, (307) 777-5351; Email: attorneygeneral.state.wy.us

Treasurer Mark Gordon (R), 200 W. 24th St., Cheyenne 82002; (307) 777-7408; Fax, (307) 777-5411; Twitter: @Mark_Gordon_WY

Washington, DC Representative: Tony Young, Washington Officer of the Governor, Deputy Chief of Staff, (307) 777-7434

U.S. TERRITORIES

American Samoa   Web, www.americansamoa.gov

Gov. HTC Lolo Matalasi Moliga (I), P. Lutali Executive Office Bldg., Pago Pago, American Samoa 96799; (684) 633-4116; Fax: (684) 633-2269

Lt. Gov. HC Lemanu Peleti Mauga (I)

In Washington, DC: Minnie Tuia, 1101 Vermont Ave. N.W., #403, 20005; (202) 408-4998; Fax: (202) 408-4997; (011) 684-633-4116

Guam   Web www.guam.gov

Gov. Eddie Baza Calvo (R), Ricardo J. Bordallo Governor's Complex, Adelup, Guam 96910; (671) 472-8931 or 8936; Fax: (671) 472-4826; Twitter: @eddiebazacalvo; www.facebook.com/eddiebazacalvo

Lt. Gov. Ray Tenorio (R), Ricardo J. Bordallo Governor's Complex's P.O. BOX 2950, Hagåtña, Guam 96932; (671) 475-9380/3; Fax, (671) 477-2007

In Washington, DC: Jay Rojas, Director, Washington Office, Governor of Guam, 444 North Capitol St. N.W., #619, 20001; (202) 434-4855; Fax (202) 434-4856

Northern Mariana Islands   Web, www.gov.mp

Gov. Eloy S. Inos (Covenant Party), Memorial Bldg., Capitol Hill, Caller Box 10007, Saipan, MP 96950; (670) 664-2280

Lt. Gov. Jude U. Hofschneider (R), www.facebook.com/pages/Lt-Governor-Jude-U-Hofschneider/152085438278987?ref=stream

Washington, DC Representative: Esther Fleming, Washington Office of the Governor, Chief of Staff, (670) 664-2212

Puerto Rico   Web, www.pr.gov; www.2.pr.gov and www.fortaleza.gobierno.pr/en/

Gov. Alejandro Garcia Padilla (Popular Democratic Party), Calle Fortaleza #63, Viejo San Juan, P.O. Box 9020082, San Juan, PR 00902-0082; (787) 721-7000; Fax (787) 723-3287; www.facebook.com/agarciapadilla

Lt. Gov. and Secretary of State David Bernier (PDP)

In Washington, DC: Juan Eugenio Hernandez, Executive Director Puerto Rico Federal Affairs Administration 1100 17th St., N.W., #800, 20036; (202) 778-0710; Fax, (202) 822-0916

Virgin Islands   Web, VI.gov

Gov. John P. de Jongh Jr. (D), St. Thomas and Water Island, 21-22 Kongens Gade, Charlotte Amalie, St. Thomas, VI 00802; (340) 774-0001; Fax: (340) 774-1361; www.facebook.com/governordejongh

Lt. Gov. Gregory R. Francis (D), #18 Kongens Gade, St. Thomas, VI.00802; (340) 774-2991; Fax, (340) 774-6953; Email: Gregory.francis@lgo-vi.gov

In Washington, DC: Steven Steele, Director, Washington Office of the Governor of the U.S. Virgin Islands, 444 North Capitol St. N.W., #305, 20001; (202) 624-3560; Fax: (202) 624-3594

Foreign Embassies, U.S. Ambassadors, and Country Desk Offices

Following are key foreign diplomats in the United States, U.S. ambassadors or ranking diplomatic officials abroad, and country offices of the State Department that follow political, cultural, and economic developments. This information is current as of March 28, 2014.

For information on investing or doing business abroad, contact the Commerce Department's Trade Information Center at (800) USA-TRAD(E) (800-872-8723) or visit www.export.gov. The Office of the United States Trade Representative also offers trade information by region at www.ustr.gov/countries-regions.

Afghanistan   Web, www.embassyofafghanistan.org

Ambassador: Eklil Ahmad Hakimi
Chancery: 2341 Wyoming Ave. N.W. 20008; (202) 483-6410; Fax, (202) 483-6488; Email: info@embassyofafghanistan.org
U.S. Ambassador in Kabul: James B. Cunningham
State Dept. Country Office: (202) 647-5175

Albania   Web, www.embassyofalbania.org

Ambassador: Gilbert Galanxhi
Chancery: 1312 18th St. N.W., 4th Floor 20036; (202) 223-4942; Fax, (202) 628-7342; Email: embassy.washington@mfa.gov.al
U.S. Ambassador in Tirana: Alexander A. Arvizu
State Dept. Country Office: (202) 647-3747

Algeria   Web, www.algeria-us.org

Ambassador: Abdallah Baali
Chancery: 2118 Kalorama Rd. N.W. 20008; (202) 265-2800; Fax, (202) 986-5906; Email: mail@algeria-us.org
U.S. Ambassador in Algiers: Henry S. Ensher
State Dept. Country Office: (202) 647-4371

Andorra

Ambassador: Narcis Casal de Fondeviela (in New York)
Chancery: 2 UN Plaza, 25th Floor, New York, NY 10017; (212) 750-8064; Fax, (212) 750-6630
U.S. Ambassador: James Costos (resident in Madrid, Spain)
State Dept. Country Office: (202) 647-1412

Angola   Web, www.angola.org

Ambassador: Alberto do Carmo Bento Ribeiro
Chancery: 2100-2108 16th St. N.W. 20009; (202) 785-1156; Fax, (202) 785-1268
U.S. Ambassador in Luanda: Christopher J. McMullen
State Dept. Country Office: (202) 647-9858

Antigua and Barbuda

Ambassador: Deborah-Mae Lovell
Chancery: 3216 New Mexico Ave. N.W. 20016; (202) 362-5122; Fax, (202) 362-5225

U.S. Ambassador: Larry Palmer (resident in Bridgetown, Barbados)
State Dept. Country Office: (202) 647-4384

Aruba   (See The Netherlands)

Argentina   Web, http://embassyofargentina.us

Ambassador: Cecilia Nahon
Chancery: 1600 New Hampshire Ave. N.W. 20009; (202) 238-6400; Fax, (202) 332-3171
U.S. Ambassador in Buenos Aires: Kevin Sullivan
State Dept. Country Office: (202) 647-2401

Armenia   Web, www.usa.mfa.am

Ambassador: Tatoul Markarian
Chancery: 2225 R St. N.W. 20008; (202) 319-1976; Fax, (202) 319-2982
U.S. Ambassador in Yerevan: John A. Heffern
State Dept. Country Office: (202) 647-6576

Australia   Web, www.usa.embassy.gov.au

Ambassador: Kim Christian Beazley
Chancery: 1601 Massachusetts Ave. N.W. 20036; (202) 797-3000; Fax, (202) 797-3168
U.S. Ambassador in Canberra: John Berry
State Dept. Country Office: (202) 647-7828

Austria   Web, www.austria.org

Ambassador: Hans Peter Manz
Chancery: 3524 International Court N.W. 20008; (202) 895-6700; Fax, (202) 895-6750; Email: austro@austria.org
U.S. Ambassador in Vienna: Alexa L. Wesner
State Dept. Country Office: (202) 647-4782

Azerbaijan   Web, www.azembassy.us

Ambassador: Elin Suleymanoy
Chancery: 2741 34th St. N.W. 20008; (202) 337-3500; Fax, (202) 337-5911; Email: azerbaijan@azembassy.us
U.S. Ambassador: Richard L. Morningstar
State Dept. Country Office: (202) 647-9677

Bahamas   Web, www.bahamas.gov.bs

Ambassador: Vacant
Chancery: 2220 Massachusetts Ave. N.W. 20008; (202) 319-2660; Fax, (202) 319-2668
U.S. Chargé d'Affaires in Nassau: John Dinkelman
State Dept. Country Office: (202) 736-4322

Bahrain   Web, www.bahrainembassy.org

Ambassador: Shaikh Abdullah bin Mohammed bin Rashid Al Khalifa
Chancery: 3502 International Dr. N.W. 20008; (202) 342-1111; Fax, (202) 362-2192; Email: ambsecretary@bahrainembassy.org
U.S. Ambassador in Manama: Thomas C. Krajeski
State Dept. Country Office: (202) 647-6571

Bangladesh   Web, www.bdembassyusa.org

Ambassador: Akramul Qader
Chancery: 3510 International Dr. N.W. 20008; (202) 244-0183; Fax, (202) 244-7830
U.S. Ambassador in Dhaka: Dan W. Mozena
State Dept. Country Office: (202) 647-9515

Barbados

Ambassador: John Ernest Beale
Chancery: 2144 Wyoming Ave. N.W. 20008; (202) 939-9200; Fax, (202) 332-7467
U.S. Ambassador in Bridgetown: Larry L. Palmer
State Dept. Country Office: (202) 647-4384

Belarus   Web, www.usamfa.gov.by

Chargé d'Affaires: Oleg I. Kravchenko
Chancery: 1619 New Hampshire Ave. N.W. 20009; (202) 986-1604; Fax, (202) 986-1805; Email: usa@mfa.gov.by
U.S. Chargé d'Affaires in Minsk: Ethan A. Goldrich
State Dept. Country Office: (202) 736-4443

Belgium   Web, www.diplobel.us

Ambassador: Johan Verbeke
Chancery: 3330 Garfield St. N.W. 20008; (202) 333-6900; Fax, (202) 333-4960; Email: washington@diplobel.fed.be
U.S. Ambassador in Brussels: Howard W. Gutman
State Dept. Country Office: (202) 647-6555

Belize   Web, www.embassyofbelize.org

Ambassador: Nestor Mendez
Chancery: 2535 Massachusetts Ave. N.W. 20008; (202) 332-9636; Fax, (202) 332-6888
Chargé d' Affaires: Margaret Hawthorne
State Dept. Country Office: (202) 647-3519

Benin   Web, www.beninembassy.us

Ambassador: Segbe Cyrille Oguin
Chancery: 2124 Kalorama Rd. N.W. 20008; (202) 232-6656; Fax, (202) 265-1996; Email: info@beinembassy.us
U.S. Ambassador in Cotonou: Michael A. Raynor
State Dept. Country Office: (202) 647-1658

Bhutan

The United States and Bhutan do not maintain formal diplomatic relations. Informal contact is made between the U.S. embassy and the Bhutanese embassy in New Delhi, India.
State Dept. Country Office: (202) 647-2941

Bolivia   Web, www.bolivia-usa.org

Chief of Mission: General Freddy Bersatti
Chancery: 3014 Massachusetts Ave. N.W., #2, 20008; (202) 232-4827; Fax, (202) 328-3712; Email: assistant@bolivia-usa.org
U.S. Chargé d'Affaires in La Paz: Larry L. Memmott
State Dept. Country Office: (202) 647-4193

Bosnia and Herzegovina   Web, www.bhembassy.org

Ambassador: Jadranka Negodic
Chancery: 2109 E St. N.W. 20037; (202) 337-1500; Fax, (202) 337-1502; Email: info@bhembassy.org
U.S. Ambassador in Sarajevo: Vacant
State Dept. Country Office: (202) 647-4277

Botswana   Web, www.botswanaembassy.org

Ambassador: Tebelelo Mazile Seretse
Chancery: 1531-1533 New Hampshire Ave. N.W. 20036; (202) 244-4990; Fax, (202) 244-4164. Email: matengu@botswanaembassy.org
U.S. Ambassador in Gaborone: Michelle D. Gavin
State Dept. Country Office: (202) 647-9852

Brazil   Web, www.brasilemb.org

Ambassador: Mauro Vieira
Chancery: 3006 Massachusetts Ave. N.W. 20008; (202) 238-2700; Fax, (202) 238-2827
U.S. Ambassador in Brasilia: Liliana Ayalde
State Dept. Country Office: (202) 647-2407

Brunei   Web, www.bruneiembassy.org

Ambassador: Dato Paduka Haji Yusoff Haji Abdul Hamid
Chancery: 3520 International Court N.W. 20008; (202) 237-1838; Fax, (202) 885-0560; Email: info@bruneiembassy.org
Acting U.S. Ambassador in Bandar Seri Begawan: Daniel L. Shields
State Dept. Country Office: (202) 647-2769

Bulgaria   Web, www.bulgaria-embassy.org

Ambassador: Elena Poptodorova
Chancery: 1621 22nd St. N.W. 20008; (202) 387-0174; Fax, (202) 234-7973; Email: office@bulgaria-embassy.org
U.S. Ambassador in Sofia: Marcie B. Ries
State Dept. Country Office: (202) 736-7152

Burkina Faso   Web, http://burkina-usa.org

Ambassador: Seydou Bouda
Chancery: 2340 Massachusetts Ave. N.W. 20008; (202) 332-5577; Fax, (202) 667-1882; Email: contact@burkina-usa.org

U.S. Ambassador in Ouagadougou: Tulinabo Mushingi
State Dept. Country Office: (202) 647-1755

Burma   (See Myanmar)

Burundi   Web, www.burundiembassydc-usa.org

Ambassador: Angele Niyuhire
Chancery: 2233 Wisconsin Ave. N.W., #408, 20007; (202) 342-2574; Fax, (202) 342-2578; Email: burundiembassy@erols.com
U.S. Ambassador in Bujumbura: Dawn Liberi
State Dept. Country Office: (202) 647-4965

Cambodia   Web, www.embassyofcambodia.org

Ambassador: Hem Heng
Chancery: 4530 16th St. N.W. 20011; (202) 726-7742; Fax, (202) 726-8381; Email: camemb.usa@mfa.gov.kh
U.S. Ambassador in Phnom Penh: William E. Todd
State Dept. Country Office: (202) 647-3095

Cameroon   Web, www.cameroonembassyusa.org

Ambassador: Joseph Bienvenu Charles Foe-Atangana
Chancery: 3400 International Dr. N.W. 20008; (202) 265-8790; Fax, (202) 387-3826; Email: mail@cameroonembassyusa.org
U.S. Ambassador in Yaounde: Vacant
State Dept. Country Office: (202) 647-4514

Canada

Web, www.canadainternational.gc.ca/washington

Ambassador: Gary Albert Doer
Chancery: 501 Pennsylvania Ave. N.W. 20001; (202) 682-1740; Fax, (202) 682-7726
U.S. Ambassador in Ottawa: Richard M. Sanders (Interim)
State Dept. Country Office: (202) 647-2170

Cape Verde   Web, www.embcv-usa.gov.cv

Ambassador: Maria de Fatima Lima da Veiga
Chancery: 3415 Massachusetts Ave. N.W. 20007; (202) 965-6820; Fax, (202) 965-1207; Email: admin@caboverdeus.net
U.S. Ambassador in Praia: Adrienne S. O'Neal
State Dept. Country Office: (202) 647-0252

Central African Republic

Web, www.centrafricaine.info

Ambassador: Stanislas Moussa-Kembe
Chancery: 1618 22nd St. N.W. 20008 (202) 483-7800; Fax, (202) 332-9893
U.S. Ambassador in Bangui: Vacant
State Dept. Country Office: (202) 647-2973

Chad   Web, http://embassyofchad.info/index.php/en

Ambassado: Mahamat Nasser Hassan

Chancery: 2401 Massachusetts Ave. N.W. 20906; (202) 652-1312; Fax, (202) 758-0431; Email: info@chadembassy.info
U.S. Ambassador in N'Djamena: James Knight
State Dept. Country Office: (202) 647-2973

Chile   Web, www.chile-usa.org

Ambassador: Felipe Bulnes
Chancery: 1732 Massachusetts Ave. N.W. 20036; (202) 785-1746; Fax, (202) 887-5579; Email: echile.eeuu@minrel.gov.cl
U.S. Ambassador in Santiago: Michael Hammer (Interim)
State Dept. Country Office: (202) 647-2575

China   Web, www.china-embassy.org/eng

Ambassador: Cui Tiankai
Chancery: 3505 International Pl. N.W. 20008; (202) 495-2266; Fax, (202) 495-2138
U.S. Ambassador in Beijing: Gary Locke
State Dept. Country Office: (202) 647-9141

Colombia   Web, www.colombiaemb.org

Ambassador: Luis Carlos Villegas
Chancery: 2118 Leroy Pl. N.W. 20008; (202) 387-8338; Fax, (202) 232-8643; Email: embassyofcolumbia@columbiaemb.org
U.S. Ambassador in Bogota: Kevin Whitaker
State Dept. Country Office: (202) 647-3142

Comoros   Web, www.comorosembassy.org

Ambassador: Kaambi Roubani (in New York)
Chancery: 866 UN Plaza, #418, New York, NY 10017; Email: comoros@un.in

Chargé d'Affaires: Eric Wong (Interim) (resident in Antananarivo, Madagascar)
State Dept. Country Office: (202) 736-5922

Congo, Democratic Republic of the (DRC)

Web, www.ambardcusa.org

Ambassador: Faida M. Mitifu
Chancery: 1726 M St. N.W., #601, 20036; (202) 234-7690; Fax, (202) 234-2609; Email: ambassade@ambardcusa.org
U.S. Ambassador in Kinshasa: James Swan
State Dept. Country Office: (202) 647-2216

Congo, Republic of the

Web, http://ambacongo-us.org

Ambassador: Serge Mombouli
Chancery: 1720 16th St. N.W. 20009; (202) 726-5500; Fax, (202) 726-1860; Email: info@ambacongo-us.org
U.S. Ambassador in Brazzaville: Stephanie S. Sullivan
State Dept. Country Office: (202) 647-1637

Costa Rica   Web, www.costarica-embassy.org

Ambassador: Muni Figueres
Chancery: 2114 S St. N.W. 20008; (202) 499-2991; Fax, (202)
    265-4795; Email: consulate@costarica-embassy.org
U.S. Ambassador in San Jose: Gonzalo Gallegos (Interim)
State Dept. Country Office: (202) 647-3519

Côte d'Ivoire   Web, www.ambaciusa.org/en

Ambassador: Daouda Diabate
Chancery: 2424 Massachusetts Ave. N.W. 20008; (202)
    797-0317; Fax, (202) 204-3967
U.S. Ambassador in Abidjan: Terence P. McCulley
State Dept. Country Office: (202) 647-2791

Croatia
    Web, http://us.mvp.hr (Croatian);
    http://us.mfa.hr (English)

Ambassador: Josip Josko Paro
Chancery: 2343 Massachusetts Ave. N.W. 20008; (202)
    588-5899; Fax, (202) 588-8936; Email:
    Washington@mvep.hr
U.S. Ambassador in Zagreb: Kenneth Merten
State Dept. Country Office: (202) 647-4987

Cuba   Web, www.cubadiplomatica.cu/sicw/EN

The United States severed diplomatic relations with Cuba
in January 1961. Cuba's interests in the United States are
represented by the Swiss embassy.
Cuban Interests Section: 2630 16th St. N.W. 20009; (202)
    797-8518; Fax, (202) 797-8521; Email:
    recepcion@slcuw.org
**U.S. interests in Cuba are represented by the U.S. Interests
    Section in Havana:** John Caulfield, Chief of Mission
State Dept. Country Office: (202) 647-9272

Curacao   (See The Netherlands)
State Dept. Country Office: (202) 647-4719

Cyprus   Web, www.cyprusembassy.net

Ambassador: George Chacalli
Chancery: 2211 R St. N.W. 20008; (202) 462-5772;
    Fax, (202) 483-6710; Email: info@cyprusembassy.net
U.S. Chargé d'Affaires in Nicosia: John M. Koenig
State Dept. Country Office: (202) 647-6112

Czech Republic   Web, www.mzv.cz/washington

Ambassador: Petr Gandalovic
Chancery: 3900 Spring of Freedom St. N.W. 20008; (202)
    274-9100; Fax, (202) 966-8540; Email:
    Washington@embassy.mzv.cz
U.S. Ambassador in Prague: Norman L. Eisen
State Dept. Country Office: (202) 647-3191

Denmark   Web, www.usa.um.dk

Ambassador: Peter Taksøe-Jensen
Chancery: 3200 Whitehaven St. N.W. 20008; (202) 234-
    4300; Fax, (202) 328-1470; Email: mwasamb@um.dk

U.S. Ambassador in Copenhagen: Rufus Gifford
State Dept. Country Office: (202) 647-8431

Djibouti   Web, www.embassy.org/embassies/dj.html

Ambassador: Roble Olhaye
Chancery: 1156 15th St. N.W., #515, 20005; (202) 331-
    0270; Fax, (202) 331-0302
U.S. Ambassador in Djibouti: Geeta Pasi
State Dept. Country Office: (202) 647-6453

Dominica   Web, www.embassy.org/embassies/dm.html

Ambassador: Hubert John Charles
Chancery: 3216 New Mexico Ave. N.W. 20016; (202) 364-
    6781 Fax, (202) 364-6791; Email: Embdomdc@aol.com
U.S. Ambassador: Larry L. Palmer (resident in
    Bridgetown, Barbados)
State Dept. Country Office: (202) 647-4384

Dominican Republic   Web, www.domrep.org

Ambassador: Aníbal de Castro
Chancery: 1715 22nd St. N.W. 20008; (202) 332-6280;
    Fax, (202) 265-8057; Email: embassy@us.serex.gov.do
U.S. Ambassador in Santo Domingo: Daniel Foote
    (Interim)
State Dept. Country Office: (202) 647-5088

East Timor   (See Timor-Leste)

Ecuador   Web, www.ecuador.org

Ambassador: Nathalie Cely Suárez
Chancery: 2535 15th St. N.W. 20009; (202) 234-7200;
    Fax, (202) 333-2893; Email: embassy@ecudor.org
U.S. Ambassador in Quito: Adam E. Namm
State Dept. Country Office: (202) 647-2807

Egypt   Web, www.egyptembassy.net

Ambassador: Mohamed M. Tawfik
Chancery: 3521 International Court N.W. 20008; (202)
    895-5400; Fax, (202) 244-5131
Chargé d'Affaires in Cairo: David M. Satterfield
State Dept. Country Office: (202) 647-4680

El Salvador   Web, www.elsalvador.org

Ambassador: Rubin Zamora
Chancery: 1400 16th St. N.W., #100, 20036; (202) 595-
    7500; Fax, (202) 232-3763; Email: correo@elsalvador.org
U.S. Ambassador in San Salvador: Mari Carmen Aponte
State Dept. Country Office: (202) 647-4161

Equatorial Guinea   Web, http://egembassydc.com

Ambassador: Ruben Maye Nsue Mangue
Chancery: 2020 16th St. N.W. 20009; (202) 518-5700;
    Fax, (202) 518-5252; Email: eg_africa@yahoo.com
U.S. Ambassador in Malabo: Mark L. Asquino
State Dept. Country Office: (202) 647-4514

Eritrea   Web, www.embassyeritrea.org

Ambassador: Girma Asmerom
Chancery: 1708 New Hampshire Ave. N.W. 20009; (202) 319-1991; Fax, (202) 319-1304; Email: embassyeritrea@embassyeritrea.org
U.S. Chargé d'Affaires in Asmara: Sue Bremner
State Dept. Country Office: (202) 647-6453

Estonia   Web, www.estemb.org

Ambassador: Marina Kaljurand
Chancery: 2131 Massachusetts Ave. N.W. 20008; (202) 588-0101; Fax, (202) 588-0108; Email: Embassy .Washington@mfa.ee
U.S. Ambassador in Tallinn: Jeffrey D. Levine
State Dept. Country Office: (202) 647-6582

Ethiopia   Web, www.ethiopianembassy.org

Ambassador: Girma Birru
Chancery: 3506 International Dr. N.W. 20008; (202) 364-1200; Fax, (202) 587-0195; Email: ethiopia@ethiopianembassy.org
U.S. Ambassador in Addis Ababa: Pat Haslach
State Dept. Country Office: (202) 647-6473

Fiji   Web, www.fijiembassydc.com

Ambassador: Winston Thompson
Chancery: 2000 M St. N.W. #710, 20036; (202) 466-8320; Fax: (202) 466-8325; Email: info@fijiembassydc.com
U.S. Ambassador in Suva: Frankie A. Reed
State Dept. Country Office: (202) 647-5156

Finland   Web, http://finland.org

Ambassador: Ritva Koukku-Ronde.
Chancery: 3301 Massachusetts Ave. N.W. 20008; (202) 298-5800; Fax, (202) 298-6030; Email: sanomat .was@formin.fi
U.S. Ambassador in Helsinki: Bruce J. Oreck
State Dept. Country Office: (202) 647-6582

France   Web, http://franceintheus.org

Ambassador: François Delattre
Chancery: 4101 Reservoir Rd. N.W. 20007; (202) 944-6000; Fax, (202) 944-6166; Email: info@ambafrance-us.org
U.S. Ambassador in Paris: Vacant
State Dept. Country Office: (202) 647-3072

Gabon   Web, www.gabonembassyusa.org

Ambassador: Michael Moussa-Adamo
Chancery: 2034 20th St. N.W., #200, 20009; (202) 797-1000; Fax, (202) 332-0668; Email: info@gabonembassy .org
U.S. Ambassador in Libreville: Vacant
State Dept. Country Office: (202) 647-3138

The Gambia   Web, http://gambiaembassy.us

Ambassador: Alieu Momodou Ngum
Chancery: 2233 Wisconsin Ave. N.W., Georgetown Plaza, #240, 20007; (202) 785-1399; Fax, (202) 342-0240; Email: info@gambiaembassy.us
U.S. Ambassador in Banjul: Vacant
State Dept. Country Office: (202) 647-1596

Georgia   Web, usa.mfa.gov.ge

Ambassador: Archil Gegeshidze
Chancery: 2209 Massachusetts Ave. N.W. 20008; (202) 387-2390; Fax, (202) 387-0864
U.S. Ambassador in Tbilisi: Richard B. Norland
State Dept. Country Office: (202) 647-6048

Germany   Web, www.germany.info

Ambassador: Peter Ammon
Chancery: (temporary) 2300 M St. N.W., 20037, (permanent) 4645 Reservoir Rd. N.W. 20007; (202) 298-4000; Fax, (202) 298-4249. The German embassy is at M St. until its permanent building has completed renovations.
U.S. Ambassador in Berlin: Vacant
State Dept. Country Office: (202) 647-3746

Ghana   Web, www.ghanaembassy.org

Ambassador: Daniel Ohene Agyekum
Chancery: 3512 International Dr. N.W. 20008; (202) 686-4520; Fax, (202) 686-4527
U.S. Ambassador in Accra: Gene A. Cretz
State Dept. Country Office: (202) 647-1540

Greece   Web, www.mfa.gr/washington

Ambassador: Christos P. Panagopoulos
Chancery: 2217 Massachusetts Ave. N.W. 20008; (202) 939-1300; Fax, (202) 939-1324; Email: gremb.was@mfa.gr
U.S. Ambassador in Athens: David D. Pearce
State Dept. Country Office: (202) 647-6113

Greenland   (See Denmark)

Grenada   Web, www.grenadaembassyusa.org

Ambassador: E. Angus Friday
Chancery: 1701 New Hampshire Ave. N.W. 20009-2501; (202) 265-2561; Fax, (202) 265-2468; Email: embassy@grenadaembassyusa.org
U.S. Ambassador: Larry L. Palmer (resident in Bridgetown, Barbados)
State Dept. Country Office: (202) 647-4384

Guatemala   Web, www.guatemala-embassy.org

Ambassador: Julio Ligorria
Chancery: 2220 R St. N.W. 20008; (202) 745-4953; Fax, (202) 745-1908; Email: info@guatemala-embassy .org
U.S. Ambassador in Guatemala City: Arnold A. Chacon
State Dept. Country Office: (202) 647-3727

Guinea   Web, http://guineaembassyusa.com

Ambassador: Blaise Cherif
Chancery: 2112 Leroy Pl. N.W. 20008; (202) 986-4300;
    Fax, (202) 986-3800
U.S. Ambassador in Conakry: Alexander Mark Laskaris
State Dept. Country Office: (202) 647-1540

Guinea-Bissau

Ambassador: Vacant
Contact: P.O. Box 33813, 20033
The U.S. embassy in Bissau suspended operations in June
1998. The U.S. ambassador to Senegal, Lewis Lukens,
covers matters pertaining to Guinea-Bissau.
State Dept. Country Office: (202) 647-0252

Guyana

    Web, www.guyana.org/govt/ foreign_missions.html

Ambassador: Bayney Ram Karran
Chancery: 2490 Tracy Pl. N.W. 20008; (202) 265-6900;
    Fax, (202) 232-1297; Email:
    guyanaembassydc@verizon.net
U.S. Ambassador in Georgetown: D. Brent Hardt
State Dept. Country Office: (202) 647-4719

Haiti   Web, www.haiti.org

Ambassador: Paul Altidor
Chancery: 2311 Massachusetts Ave. N.W. 20008; (202)
    332-4090; Fax, (202) 745-7215; Email: amb
    .washington@diplomatie.ht
U.S. Ambassador in Port-au-Prince: Pamela A. White
State Dept. Country Office: (202) 647-9510

The Holy See

Ambassador: Carlo Maria Viganò, Apostolic Nuncio
Office: 3339 Massachusetts Ave. N.W. 20008; (202) 333-
    7121; Fax, (202) 337-4036
U.S. Ambassador in Vatican City: Kenneth F. Hackett
State Dept. Country Office: (202) 647-3746

Honduras   Web, www.hondurasemb.org

Ambassador: Jorge Ramón Hernández Alcerro
Chancery: 3007 Tilden St. N.W. 20008; (202) 966-7702;
    Fax, (202) 966-9751
U.S. Ambassador in Tegucigalpa: Lisa Kubiske
State Dept. Country Office: (202) 647-3482

Hong   Kong (See China)

State Dept. Country Office: (202) 647-6300

Hungary   Web, www.washington.kormany.hu

Ambassador: György Szapáry
Chancery: 3910 Shoemaker St. N.W. 20008; (202) 362-
    6730; Fax, (202) 966-8135; Email: Ambassador.
    was@mfa.gov.hu
U.S. Ambassador in Budapest: Vacant
State Dept. Country Office: (202) 647-3238

Iceland   Web, www.iceland.org/us

Ambassador: Gudmundur Arni Stefansson
Chancery: House of Sweden, 2900 K St. N.W., #509,
    20007-1704, (202) 265-6653; Fax, (202) 265-6656;
    Email: icemb.wash@utn.stjr.is
U.S. Ambassador in Reykjavik: Vacant
State Dept. Country Office: (202) 647-8431

India   Web, www.indianembassy.org

Ambassador: S. Jaishankar
Chancery: 2107 Massachusetts Ave. N.W. 20008; (202)
    939-7000; Fax, (202) 265-4351
U.S. Ambassador in New Delhi: Vacant
State Dept. Country Office: (202) 647-1112

Indonesia   Web, www.embassyofindonesia.org

Ambassador: Dino Patti Djalal
Chancery: 2020 Massachusetts Ave. N.W. 20036; (202)
    775-5200; Fax, (202) 775-5365
U.S. Ambassador in Jakarta: Robert O. Blake Jr.
State Dept. Country Office: (202) 647-2301

Iran   Web, www.daftar.org

The United States severed diplomatic relations with Iran in
April 1980. Iran's interests in the United States are repre-
sented by the Pakistani embassy.
Iranian Interests Section: 2209 Wisconsin Ave. N.W.
    20007; (202) 965-4990; Fax, (202) 965-1073
U.S. interests in Iran are represented by the Swiss embassy
in Tehran, Deputy Asst. Secretary Brett H. McGurk
State Dept. Country Office: (202) 647-2520

Iraq   Web, www.iraqiembassy.us

The United States and Iraq resumed diplomatic relations
in June 2004.
Ambassador: Lukman Faily
Chancery: 3421 Massachusetts Ave. N.W. 20007; (202)
    742-1600, ext. 136
Consulate: 1801 P St. N.W. 20036; (202) 483-7500;
    Fax, (202) 462-5066
U.S. Ambassador to Baghdad: Robert Stephen Beecroft
State Dept. Country Office: (202) 647-5692

Ireland   Web, www.embassyofireland.org

Ambassador: Anne Anderson
Chancery: 2234 Massachusetts Ave. N.W. 20008; (202)
    462-3939; Fax, (202) 232-5993
U.S. Chargé d'Affaires in Dublin: Stuart Dwyer
State Dept. Country Office: (202) 647-6591

Israel   Web, www.israelemb.org

Ambassador: Ron Dermer
Chancery: 3514 International Dr. N.W. 20008; (202) 364-
    5500; Fax, (202) 364-5423
U.S. Ambassador in Tel Aviv: Daniel B. Shapiro
State Dept. Country Office: (202) 647-3672

Italy   Web, www.ambwashingtondc.esteri.it

Ambassador: Claudio Bisogniero
Chancery: 3000 Whitehaven St. N.W. 20008; (202) 612-4400; Fax, (202) 518-2154
U.S. Ambassador in Rome: John R. Phillips
State Dept. Country Office: (202) 647-3746

Jamaica   Web, http://embassyofjamaica.org

Ambassador: Stephen C. Vasciannie
Chancery: 1520 New Hampshire Ave. N.W. 20036; (202) 452-0660; Fax, (202) 452-0036; Email: firstsec@jamaicaembassy.org
U.S. Ambassador in Kingston: Pamela Bridgewater
State Dept. Country Office: (202) 736-4322

Japan   Web, www.us.emb-japan.go.jp/english/html/

Ambassador: Kenichiro Sasae
Chancery: 2520 Massachusetts Ave. N.W. 20008; (202) 238-6700; Fax, (202) 328-2187
U.S. Ambassador in Tokyo: Caroline Kennedy
State Dept. Country Office: (202) 647-3152

Jordan   Web, www.jordanembassyus.org

Ambassador: Alia Hatoug-Bouran
Chancery: 3504 International Dr. N.W. 20008; (202) 966-2664; Fax, (202) 966-3110; Email: hkjembassydc@jordanembassyus.org
U.S. Ambassador in Amman: Stuart E. Jones
State Dept. Country Office: (202) 647-1091

Kazakhstan   Web, www.kazakhembus.com

Ambassador: Kairat Umarov
Chancery: 1401 16th St. N.W. 20036; (202) 232-5488; Fax, (202) 232-5845; Email: washington@mfa.kz
U.S. Chargé d'Affaires: John Ordway
State Dept. Country Office: (202) 647-6859

Kenya   Web, www.kenyaembassy.com

Ambassador: Elkanah Odembo
Chancery: 2249 R St. N.W. 20008; (202) 387-6101; Fax, (202) 462-3829; Email: information@kenyaembassy.com
U.S. Ambassador in Nairobi: Robert F. Godec
State Dept. Country Office: (202) 647-8913

Kiribati

U.S. Ambassador: Frankie A. Reed (resident in Suva, Fiji)
State Dept. Country Office: (202) 647-5156

Korea, Democratic People's Republic of (North)

The United States does not maintain diplomatic relations with North Korea.
North Korea maintains a Permanent Mission to the United Nations: 515 E. 72nd St., #38F, New York, NY, 10021; (212) 772-0712; Fax, (212) 772-0735
State Dept. Country Office: (202) 647-7717

Korea, Republic of (South)

Web, http://usa.mofat.go.Kr/english

Ambassador: Ahn Ho-young
Chancery: 2450 Massachusetts Ave. N.W. 20008; (202) 939-5600; Fax, (202) 797–0595; Email: consular_usa@mofa.go.kr
U.S. Ambassador in Seoul: Sung Kim
State Dept. Country Office: (202) 647-7717

Kosovo   Web, www.ambasada-ks.net/us

Ambassador: Akan Ismaili
Chancery: 1011 30th St. N.W., #330, 20007; (202) 380-3581; Fax, (202) 380-3628; Email: embassy.usa@rks-gov.net
U.S. Ambassador in Pristina: Tracey Ann Jacobson
State Dept. Country Office: (202) 647-0608

Kuwait   Web, www.kuwaitembassy.us

Ambassador: Salem Abdullah Al-Jaber Al-Sabah
Chancery: 2940 Tilden St. N.W. 20008; (202) 966-0702; Fax, (202) 364-2868
U.S. Ambassador in Kuwait City: Matthew H. Tueller
State Dept. Country Office: (202) 647-6571

Kyrgyz, Republic of   Web, www.kgembassy.org

Ambassador: Muktar Djumaliev
Chancery: 2360 Massachusetts Ave. N.W. 20008; (202) 449-9822; Fax, (202) 386-7550; Email: kgembassyusa@gmail.com
U.S. Ambassador in Bishkek: Pamela L. Spratlen
State Dept. Country Office: (202) 647-9119

Laos   Web, www.laoembassy.com

Ambassador: Seng Soukhathivong
Chancery: 2222 S St. N.W. 20008; (202) 332–6416; Fax, (202) 332-4923; Email: embasslao@gmail.com
U.S. Ambassador in Vientiane: Daniel A. Clune
State Dept. Country Office: (202) 647-2459

Latvia   Web, www.latvia-usa.org

Ambassador: Andris Razans
Chancery: 2306 Massachusetts Ave. N.W. 20008; (202) 328-2840; Fax, (202) 328-2860; Email: embassy.usa@mfa.gov.lv
U.S. Ambassador in Riga: Mark A. Pekala
State Dept. Country Office: (202) 647-8378

Lebanon   Web, www.lebanonembassyus.org

Ambassador: Antoine Chedid
Chancery: 2560 28th St. N.W. 20008; (202) 939-6300; Fax, (202) 939-6324
U.S. Ambassador in Beirut: Maura Connelly
State Dept. Country Office: (202) 647-1030

Lesotho   Web, www.lesothoemb-usa.gov.ls

Ambassador: Eliachim Molapi Sebatane
Chancery: 2511 Massachusetts Ave. N.W. 20008; (202) 797-5533; Fax, (202) 234-6815; Email: lesothoembassy@verizon.net

U.S. Chargé d'Affaires in Maseru: Carl B. Fox
State Dept. Country Office: (202) 647-9838

Liberia   Web, www.liberianembassyus.org
Ambassador: Jeremiah C. Sulunteh
Chancery: 5201 16th St. N.W. 20011; (202) 723-0437;
   Fax, (202) 723-0436
U.S. Ambassador in Monrovia: Deborah R. Malac
State Dept. Country Office: (202) 647-3469

Libya   Web, www.libyausaembassy.com
Ambassador: Ali Suleiman Aujali
Chancery: 2600 Virginia Ave. N.W., #705, 20037; (202)
   944-9601; Fax, (202) 944-9606; Email:
   info@embassyoflibyadc.org
U.S. Ambassador in Tripoli: Deborah K. Jones
The U.S. Embassy in Libya resumed operations on
September 22, 2011. However, services available to U.S.
citizens in Libya are limited to emergency services.
State Dept. Country Office: (202) 647-4674

Liechtenstein   Web, http://liechtensteinusa.org
Ambassador: Claudia Fritsche
Chancery: 2900 K St. N.W., #602B, 20007; (202) 331-0590;
   Fax, (202) 331-3221
U.S. Chargé d'Affaires: Jeffrey Cellars (resident in Bern,
   Switzerland)
State Dept. Country Office: (202) 647-0425

Lithuania   Web, http://usa.mfa.lt
Ambassador: Zygimantas Pavilionis
Chancery: 2622 16th St. N.W. 20009; (202) 234-5860;
   Fax, (202) 328-0466; Email: info@usa.mfa.lt
U.S. Ambassador in Vilnius: Deborah A. McCarthy
State Dept. Country Office: (202) 647-8378

Luxembourg   Web, http://washington.mae.lu/en
Ambassador: Jean-Louis Wolzfeld
Chancery: 2200 Massachusetts Ave. N.W. 20008; (202)
   265-4171; Fax, (202) 328-8270; Email: luxembassy
   .was@mae.etat.lu
U.S. Ambassador in Luxembourg: Robert A. Mandell
State Dept. Country Office: (202) 647-5674

Macau   (See China)
State Dept. Country Office: (202) 647-6300

Macedonia, Former Yugoslav Republic of
   Web, www.macedonianembassy.org
Ambassador: Zoran Jolevski
Chancery: 2129 Wyoming Ave. N.W. 20008; (202) 667-
   0501; Fax, (202) 667-2131; Email:
   usoffice@macedonianembassy.org
U.S. Ambassador in Skopje: Paul D. Wohlers
State Dept. Country Office: (202) 647-3747

Madagascar   Web, www.madagascar-embassy.org
Ambassador: Jocelyn B. Radifera
Chancery: 2374 Massachusetts Ave. N.W. 20008; (202)
   265-5525; Fax, (202) 265-3034; Email: Malagasy
   .Embassy@verizon.net
U.S. Chargé d'Affaires in Antananarivo: Eric M. Wong
State Dept. Country Office: (202) 647-5922

Malawi   Web, www.malawiembassy-dc.org
Ambassador: Steve Matenje
Chancery: 2408 Massachusetts Ave. N.W., 20008; (202)
   721-0270; Fax, (202) 721-0288
U.S. Ambassador in Lilongwe: Jeanine Jackson
State Dept. Country Office: (202) 647-9857

Malaysia
   Web, www.kln.gov.my/web/usa_washington/home
Ambassador: Vacant
Chargé d'Affaires: Shahril Effendi Bin Abd Ghany
   (Interim)
Chancery: 3516 International Court N.W. 20008; (202)
   572-9700; Fax, (202) 572-9882; Email: malwashdc@kln
   .gov.my
U.S. Ambassador in Kuala Lumpur: Joseph Y. Yun
State Dept. Country Office: (202) 647-4932

Maldives   Web, www.maldivesmission.com
Ambassador: Ahmed Sareer (in New York)
Chancery: 800 2nd Ave., #400E, New York, NY 10017;
   (212) 599-6194; Fax, (212) 661-6405
U.S. Ambassador: Michele J. Sison (resident in Colombo,
   Sri Lanka)
State Dept. Country Office: (202) 647-1078

Mali   Web, www.maliembassy.us
Ambassador: Al Maamoun Baba Lamine Keita
Chancery: 2130 R St. N.W. 20008; (202) 332-2249;
   Fax, (202) 332-6603
U.S. Ambassador in Bamako: Mary Beth Leonard
State Dept. Country Office: (202) 647-1596

Malta   Web, www.foreign.gov.mt/
Ambassador: Marisa Micallef
Chancery: 2017 Connecticut Ave. N.W. 20008; (202) 462-
   3611; Fax, (202) 387-5470; Email: maltaembassy
   .washington@gov.mt
U.S. Ambassador in Valletta: Gina Abercrombie-
   Winstanley
State Dept. Country Office: (202) 647-6555

Marshall Islands   Web, www.rmiembassyus.org
Ambassador: Charles R. Paul
Chancery: 2433 Massachusetts Ave. N.W. 20008; (202)
   234-5414; Fax, (202) 232-3236; Email:
   info@rmiembassyus.org
U.S. Ambassador in Majuro: Thomas H. Armbruster
State Dept. Country Office: (202) 736-4683

Mauritania

Ambassador: Mohamed Lemine El Haycen
Chancery: 2129 Leroy Pl. N.W. 20008; (202) 232-5700;
Fax, (202) 232-5701
U.S. Ambassador in Nouakchott: Jo Ellen Powell
State Dept. Country Office: (202) 647-2637

Mauritius

Web, www.maurinet.com/tourist_information/
mauritius_embassies
Ambassador: Somduth Soburun
Chancery: 1709 N St. N.W. 20036; (202) 244-1491;
Fax, (202) 966-0983; Email: Mauritius
.embassy@verizon.net
U.S Ambassador in Port Louis: Shari Villarosa
State Dept. Country Office: (202) 736-5922

Mexico   Web, www.embassyofmexico.org

Ambassador: Eduardo Medina Mora
Chancery: 1911 Pennsylvania Ave. N.W. 20006; (202) 728-
1600; Fax, (202) 728-1698
U.S. Ambassador in Mexico City: E. Anthony (Tony)
Wayne
State Dept. Country Office: (202) 647-8113

Micronesia   Web, www.fsmembassydc.org

Ambassador: Asterio Takesy
Chancery: 1725 N St. N.W. 20036; (202) 223-4383;
Fax, (202) 223-4391
U.S. Ambassador in Kolonia: Dorothea-Maria (Doria)
Rosen
State Dept. Country Office: (202) 736-4683

Moldova   Web, www.sua.mfa.md/about-embassy-en

Ambassador: Igor Munteanu
Chancery: 2101 S St. N.W. 20008; (202) 667-1130;
Fax, (202) 667-2624
U.S. Ambassador in Chisinau: William H. Moser
State Dept. Country Office: (202) 647-6733

Monaco   Web, www.monacodc.org

Ambassador: Maguy Maccario
Chancery: 4000 Connecticut Ave. N.W.; 20008-3306;
Mailing, 3400 International Dr. N.W., #2K–100 20008;
(202) 234-1530; Fax: (202) 244-7656; Email:
info@monacodc.org
U.S. Consulate General: Vacant (resident in Marseille,
France)
State Dept. Country Office: (202) 647-3072

Mongolia   Web, www.mongolianembassy.us

Ambassador: Bugaa Attangerel
Chancery: 2833 M St. N.W. 20007; (202) 333-7117;
Fax, (202) 298-9227
U.S. Ambassador in Ulaanbaatar: Piper Anne Wind
Campbell
State Dept. Country Office: (202) 647-7628

Montenegro

Ambassador: Srdan Darmanovic
Chancery: 1610 New Hampshire Ave. N.W. 20009; (202)
234-6108; Fax, (202) 234-6109
U.S. Ambassador in Podgorica: Sue K. Brown
State Dept. Country Office: (202) 647-7660

Morocco   Web, www.embassyofmorocco.us

Ambassador: Mohammed Rachad Bouhlal
Chancery: 1601 21st St. N.W. 20009; (202) 462-7979;
Fax, (202)265-0161
U.S. Ambassador in Rabat: Samuel L. Kaplan
State Dept. Country Office: (202) 647-1724

Mozambique   Web, www.embamoc-usa.org

Ambassador: Amelia Matos Sumbana
Chancery: 1525 New Hampshire Ave. N.W. 20036;
(202) 293-7146; Fax, (202) 835-0245; Email:
embamoc@aol.com
U.S. Ambassador in Maputo: Douglas M. Griffiths
State Dept. Country Office: (202) 647-9857

Myanmar (Burma)

Web, www.mewashingtondc.com
Chargé d'Affaires: U Kyaw Tin
Chancery: 2300 S St. N.W. 20008; (202) 332-3344;
Fax, (202) 332-4351; Email: info@mewashingtondc
.com
U.S. Ambassador in Rangoon: Derek J. Mitchell
State Dept. Country Office: (202) 647-0056

Namibia   Web, www.namibianembassyusa.org

Ambassador: Martin Andjaba
Chancery: 1605 New Hampshire Ave. N.W. 20009; (202)
986-0540; Fax, (202) 986-0443; Email:
info@namibianembassyusa.org
U.S. Chargé d'Affaires in Windhoek: Mary Grace
McGeehan
State Dept. Country Office: (202) 647-9858

Nauru   Web, un.int/nauru/mission.html

Ambassador: Marlene I. Moses (in New York)
Chancery: 800 Second Ave., #400A, New York NY 10017;
(212) 937-0074; Fax, (212) 937-0079; Email:
nauru@un.int
U.S. Ambassador: Frankie A. Reed (resident in Suva, Fiji)
State Dept. Country Office: (202) 647-5156

Nepal   Web, www.nepalembassyusa.org

Ambassador: Shankar Prasad Sharma
Chancery: 2131 Leroy Pl. N.W. 20008; (202) 667-4550;
Fax, (202) 667-5534; Email: info@nepalembassyusa.org
U.S. Ambassador in Kathmandu: Peter W. Bodde
State Dept. Country Office: (202) 647-2941

The Netherlands

Web, http://dc.the-netherlands.org

Ambassador: Rudolf Bekink
Chancery: 4200 Linnean Ave. N.W. 20008; (202) 244-5300; 877-DUTCHHELP (1-877-388-2443); Fax, (202) 362-3430; Email: info@dutchhelp.com
U.S. Ambassador at The Hague: Timothy M. Broas
State Dept. Country Office: (202) 647-5674

New Zealand
Web, www.nzembassy.com/usa

Ambassador: Mike Moore
Chancery: 37 Observatory Circle N.W. 20008; (202) 328-4800; Fax, (202) 667-5227; Email: wshinfo@mfat.govt.nz
U.S. Ambassador in Wellington: David Huebner
State Dept. Country Office: (202) 736-4745

Nicaragua
Web, http://consuladodenicaragua.com

Ambassador: Francisco Obadiah Campbell Hooker
Chancery: 1627 New Hampshire Ave. N.W. 20009; (202) 939-6570; Fax, (202) 939-6542
U.S. Chargé d'Affaires in Managua: Phyllis M. Powers
State Dept. Country Office: (202) 647-1510

Niger
Web, www.embassyofniger.org

Ambassador: Maman S. Sidikou
Chancery: 2204 R St. N.W. 20008; (202) 483-4224; Fax, (202) 483-3169; Email: communication@embassyofniger.org
U.S. Chargé d'Affaires in Niamey: Richard Bell
State Dept. Country Office: (202) 647-3469

Nigeria
Web, www.nigeriaembassyusa.org

Ambassador: Adebowale Ibidapo Adefuye
Chancery: 3519 International Court N.W. 20008; (202) 986-8400; Fax, (202) 362-6541; Email: info@nigeriaembassyusa.org
U.S. Ambassador in Abuja: James F. Entwhistle
State Dept. Country Office: (202) 647-2791

Norway
Web, www.norway.org

Ambassador: Kare R. Aas
Chancery: 2720 34th St. N.W. 20008; (202) 333-6000; Fax, (202) 469-3990; Email: emb.washington@mfa.no
U.S. Ambassador in Oslo: Barry B. White
State Dept. Country Office: (202) 647-8178

Oman
Web, www.omanembassy.net

Ambassador: Hunaina Sultan Ahmed Al-Mughairy
Chancery: 2535 Belmont Rd. N.W. 20008; (202) 387-1980
U.S. Ambassador in Muscat: Greta C. Holtz
State Dept. Country Office: (202) 647-6558

Pakistan
Web, www.embassyofpakistanusa.org

Ambassador: Jalani Abbas Jilani
Chancery: 3517 International Court N.W. 20008; (202) 243-6500; Fax, (202) 686-1534; Email: info@embassyofpakistanusa.org
U.S. Ambassador in Islamabad: Richard Olson
State Dept. Country Office: (202) 647-9823

Palau
Web, www.palauembassy.com

Ambassador: Hersey Kyota
Chancery: 1701 Pennsylvania Ave. N.W., #300, 20006; (202) 452-6814; Fax, (202) 452-6281; Email: info@palauembassy.com
U.S. Ambassador in Koror: Helen Reed-Rowe
State Dept. Country Office: (202) 736-4683

Panama
Web, www.embassyofpanama.org

Ambassador: Mario E. Jaramillo
Chancery: 2862 McGill Terrace N.W. 20008; (202) 483-1407; Fax, (202) 483-8413; Email: info@embassyofpanama.org
U.S. Ambassador in Panama City: Jonathan D. Farrar
State Dept. Country Office: (202) 647-3505

Papua New Guinea
Web, www.pngembassy.org

Ambassador: Evan J. Paki
Chancery: 1779 Massachusetts Ave. N.W., #805, 20036; (202) 745-3680; Fax, (202) 745-3679; Email: info@pngembassy.org
U.S. Ambassador in Port Moresby: Walter E. North
State Dept. Country Office: (202) 647-5156

Paraguay
Web, www.embaparusa.gov.py

Chargé d'Affaires: Fernando A. Pfanni Caballero
Chancery: 2400 Massachusetts Ave. N.W. 20008; (202) 483-6960; Fax, (202) 234-4508
U.S. Ambassador in Asunción: James H. Thessin
State Dept. Country Office: (202) 647-1551

Peru
Web, www.embassyofperu.org

Ambassador: Harold W. Forsyth
Chancery: 1700 Massachusetts Ave. N.W. 20036; (202) 833-9860; Fax, (202) 659-8124
U.S. Chargé d'Affaires in Lima: Michael J. Fitzpatrick (Interim)
State Dept. Country Office: (202) 647-4177

Philippines
Web, www.philippineembassy-usa.org

Ambassador: Jose L. Cuisia Jr.
Chancery: 1600 Massachusetts Ave. N.W. 20036; (202) 467-9300; Fax, (202) 467-9417
U.S. Ambassador in Manila: Phillip S. Goldberg
State Dept. Country Office: (202) 647-2927

Poland
Web, www.polandembassy.org

Ambassador: Ryszard Schnepf

Chancery: 2640 16th St. N.W. 20009; (202) 499-1700; Fax, (202) 328-6271; Email: washington.amb@msz.gov.pl
U.S. Ambassador in Warsaw: Stephen Mull
State Dept. Country Office: (202) 647-4139

Portugal   Web, www.embassyportugal-us.org

Ambassador: Nuno Brito
Chancery: 2012 Massachusetts Ave. N.W. 20036; (202) 350-5400; Fax, (202) 462-3726; Email: info@embassyportugal-us.org
U.S. Chargé d'Affaires in Lisbon: John Olson (Interim)
State Dept. Country Office: (202) 647-3746

Qatar   Web, www.qatarembassy.net

Ambassador: Mohamed Bin Adbulla Al-Rumaihi
Chancery: 2555 M St. N.W. 20037; (202) 274-1600; Fax, (202) 237-0061; Email: info@quatembassy.net
U.S. Ambassador in Doha: Susan L. Ziadeh
State Dept. Country Office: (202) 647-4709

Romania   Web, http://washington.mae.ro/en

Ambassador: Lulian Buga
Chancery: 1607 23rd St. N.W. 20008; (202) 332-4848; Fax, (202) 232-4748; Email: office@roembus.org
U.S. Chargé d'Affaires in Bucharest: Duane C. Butcher (Interim)
State Dept. Country Office: (202) 647-1457

Russia   Web, www.russianembassy.org

Ambassador: Sergei I. Kislyak
Chancery: 2650 Wisconsin Ave. N.W. 20007; (202) 298-5700; Fax, (202) 298-5735
U.S. Ambassador in Moscow: Michael A. McFaul
State Dept. Country Office: (202) 647-9806

Rwanda   Web, www.rwandaembassy.org

Ambassador: Mathilde Mukantabana
Chancery: 1875 Connecticut Ave N.W. 20009; (202) 232-2882; Fax, (202) 232-4544
U.S. Ambassador in Kigali: Donald W. Koran
State Dept. Country Office: (202) 647-4965

Saint Kitts and Nevis   Web, www.embassy.gov.kn

Ambassador: Jacinth Lorna Henry-Martin
Chancery: 3216 New Mexico Ave. N.W. 20016-2745; (202) 686-2636; Fax, (202) 686-5740; Email: stkittsnevis@embskn.com
U.S. Ambassador: Larry L. Palmer (resident in Bridgetown, Barbados)
State Dept. Country Office: (202) 647-4384

Saint Lucia   Web, www.govt.lc

Ambassador: Sonia M. Johnny
Chancery: 3216 New Mexico Ave. N.W. 20016; (202) 364-6792; Fax, (202) 364-672; Email: EOSaintlu@aol.com

U.S. Ambassador: Larry L. Palmer (resident in Bridgetown, Barbados)
State Dept. Country Office: (202) 647-4384

Saint Vincent and the Grenadines

Web, www.embsvg.com

Ambassador: La Celia Aritha Prince
Chancery: 3216 New Mexico Ave. N.W. 20016; (202) 364-6730; Fax, (202) 364-6736; Email: info@embsvg.com
U.S. Ambassador: Larry L. Palmer (resident in Bridgetown, Barbados)
State Dept. Country Office: (202) 647-4384

Samoa   Web, www.mfat.govt.ws

Ambassador: Aliîoaiga Feturi Elisaia (in New York)
Chancery: (212) 599-6196; Fax, (212) 599-0797; Email: samoa@un.int
U.S. Chargé d'Affaires to Apia: David Huebner (resident in Wellington, New Zealand)
State Dept. Country Office: (202) 736-4745

San Marino

Ambassador: Paolo Rondelli
Chancery: 1711 N St. N.W., 2nd Floor 20036; (202) 250-1535
U.S. Consul General: John R. Phillips (resident in Florence, Italy)
State Dept. Country Office: (202) 647-3072

São Tomé and Principe

Web, http://embstpusa.com

Ambassador: Ovido Manuel Barbosa Pequeno
Chancery: 1211 Connecticut Ave. N.W., #300, 20036; (202) 775-2076; Fax, (202) 775-2077; Email: embstpusa@verizon.net
U.S. Ambassador in Libreville: Eric D. Benjaminson
State Dept. Country Office: (202) 647-3138

Saudi Arabia   Web, www.saudiembassy.net

Ambassador: Adel A. Al-Jubeir
Chancery: 601 New Hampshire Ave. N.W. 20037; (202) 342-3800; Fax, (202) 944-5983; Email: info@saudiembassy.net
U.S. Ambassador in Riyadh: Joseph William Westphal
State Dept. Country Office: (202) 647-7550

Senegal   Web, www.ambasenegal-us.org

Ambassador: Cheikh Niang
Chancery: 2031 Florida Ave. N.W. 20009; (202) 234-0540; Fax, (202) 629-2961; Email: contact@ambasenegal-us.org
U.S. Ambassador in Dakar: Lewis A. Lukens
State Dept. Country Office: (202) 647-0252

Serbia   Web, www.serbiaembusa.org

Chargé d'Affaires: Vladimir Jovicic

Chancery: 2134 Kalorama Rd. N.W. 20008; (202) 332-0333; Fax, (202) 332-3933; Email: info@serbiaembusa.org
U.S. Ambassador in Belgrade: Michael D. Kirby
State Dept. Country Office: (202) 647-0310

Seychelles

Ambassador: Ronald (Ronny) Jean Jumeau (in New York)
Chancery: (212) 972-1785, Fax, (212) 972-1786; Email: Seychelles@un.int
U.S. Ambassador: Shari Villarosa (resident in Port Louis, Mauritius)
State Dept. Country Office: (202) 647-6453

Sierra Leone   Web, www.embassyofsierraleone.net

Chief of Mission: Bockari Kortu Stevens
Chancery: 1701 19th St. N.W. 20009-1605; (202) 939-9261; Fax, (202) 483-1798; Email: info@embassyofsierraleone.net
U.S. Ambassador in Freetown: Vacant
State Dept. Country Office: (202) 647-0252

Singapore   Web, www.mfa.gov.sg/washington

Ambassador: Ashok Kumar Mirpuri
Chancery: 3501 International Pl. N.W. 20008; (202) 537-3100; Fax, (202) 537-0876; Email: singemb_was@sgmfa.gov.sg
U.S. Ambassador in Singapore: Kirk Wagar
State Dept. Country Office: (202) 647-2769

Slovakia   Web, www.mzv.sk/washington

Ambassador: Peter Kmec
Chancery: 3523 International Court N.W. 20008; (202) 237-1054; Fax, (202) 237-6438; Email: emb.washington@mzv.sk
U.S. Ambassador in Bratislava: Theodore Sedgwick
State Dept. Country Office: (202) 647-3238

Slovenia   Web, http://washington.embassy.si/

Ambassador: Bozo Cerar
Chancery: 2410 California St. N.W., 20008; (202) 386-6601; Fax, (202) 386-6633; Email: vwa@gov.si
U.S. Ambassador in Ljubljana: Joseph A. Mussomeli
State Dept. Country Office: (202) 647-4782

Solomon Islands

Web, www.un.int/wcm/content/site/solomonislands/pid/3603

Ambassador: Collin David Beck (in New York)
Chancery: (212) 599-6192; Fax, (212) 661-8925; Email: simun@foreignaffairs-solomons.org
U.S. Ambassador in Honiara: Walter E. North (resident in Port Moresby, Papua New Guinea)
State Dept. Country Office: (202) 647-5156

Somalia   Web, http://somalia.usvpp.gov

The Washington embassy ceased operations May 1991. The U.S. embassy in Mogadishu is unstaffed. Diplomatic relations are handled out of the U.S. embassy in Nairobi, Kenya.
U.S. Special Representative on Somalia: James Swan
State Dept. Country Office: (202) 647-8284

South Africa   Web, www.saembassy.org

Ambassador: Ebrahim Rasool
Chancery: 3400 International Dr. N.W. 20008; (202) 232-4400; Fax, (202) 265-1607
U.S. Chargé d'Affaires in Pretoria: Patrick H. Gaspard
State Dept. Country Office: (202) 647-9862

South Sudan

Web, www.southsudanembassydc.org

Ambassador: Akek Khoc.Aciew
Chancery: 1015 31st St. N.W., #300, 20007; (202) 293-7940; Fax, (202) 293-7941; Email: info@southsudanembassydc.com
U.S. Ambassador: Susan D. Page
State Dept. Country Office: (202) 647-4531

Spain

Web, www.spanish-embassy.com/washington.html

Ambassador: D. Ramón Gil-Casares Satrustegui
Chancery: 2375 Pennsylvania Ave. N.W. 20037; (202) 452-0100; Fax, (202) 833-5670; Email: emb.washington@maec.es
U.S. Ambassador in Madrid: James Costos
State Dept. Country Office: (202) 647-3151

Sri Lanka   Web, http://slembassyusa.org

Ambassador: Jaliya Wickramasuriya
Chancery: 2148 Wyoming Ave. N.W. 20008; (202) 483-4025; Fax, (202) 232-7181; Email: slembassy@slembassyusa.org
U.S. Ambassador in Colombo: Michele J. Sison
State Dept. Country Office: (202) 647-1078

Sudan   Web, www.sudanembassy.org

Chargé d'Affaires: Emad Mirghani Altohamy
Chancery: 2210 Massachusetts Ave. N.W. 20008; (202) 338-8565; Fax, (202) 667-2406
U.S. Chargé d'Affaires in Khartoum: Joseph D. Stafford III
State Dept. Country Office: (202) 647-4531

Suriname   Web, www.surinameembassy.org

Ambassador: Subhas-Chandra Munga
Chancery: 4301 Connecticut Ave. N.W., #460, 20008; (202) 244-7488; Fax, (202) 244-5878
U.S. Ambassador in Paramaribo: Jay N. Anania
State Dept. Country Office: (202) 647-4719

Swaziland

Ambassador: Abednigo Mandla Ntshangase
Chancery: 1712 New Hampshire Ave. N.W. 20009; (202) 234-5002; Fax, (202) 234-8254; Email: info@swazilandembassyus.com
U.S. Ambassador in Mbabane: Makila James
State Dept. Country Office: (202) 647-9852

Sweden

Web, www.swedenabroad.com/en-GB/Embassies/ Washington

Ambassador: Bjorn Lyrvall
Chancery: 2900 K St. N.W. 20007; (202) 467-2600; Fax, (202) 467-2699; Email: ambassaden.washington@gov.se
U.S. Ambassador in Stockholm: Mark Francis Brzezinski
State Dept. Country Office: (202) 647-8178

Switzerland   Web, www.swissemb.org

Ambassador: Manuel Sager
Chancery: 2900 Cathedral Ave. N.W. 20008; (202) 745-7900; Fax, (202) 387-2564; Email: was.vertretung@eda.admin.ch
U.S. Chargé d'Affaires in Bern: Jeffrey Cellars
State Dept. Country Office: (202) 647-0425

Syria   Web, www.syrianembassy.us

Chargé d'Affaires: Mounir Koudmani
Chancery: 2215 Wyoming Ave. N.W. 20008; (202) 232-6316; Fax, (202) 265-4585; Email: info@syrembassy.net
U.S. Ambassador in Damascus: Robert Stephen Ford
State Dept. Country Office: (202) 647-1131

Taiwan

Web, www.taiwanembassy.org/US/mp.asp?mp=12

Representation is maintained by the Taipei Economic and Cultural Representatives Office in the United States: 4201 Wisconsin Ave. N.W. 20016; (202) 895-1800; Email: tecroinfodc@tecro.us; Pu-tsung King, Representative of the Republic of China (Taiwan)
The United States maintains unofficial relations with Taiwan through the American Institute in Taiwan: 1700 N. Moore St., Arlington, VA 22209-1996; (703) 525-8474; Christopher J. Marut, Director
State Dept. Country Office: (202) 647-7711

Tajikistan   Web, www.tjus.org

Ambassador: Nuriddin Shamsov
Chancery: 1005 New Hampshire Ave. N.W. 20037; (202) 223-6090; Fax, (202) 223-6091; Email: tajikistan@verizon.net
U.S. Ambassador in Dushanbe: Susan Elliott
State Dept. Country Office: (202) 647-6757

Tanzania   Web, www.tanzaniaembassy-us.org

Ambassador: Liberata Mulamula

Chancery: 1232 22nd St. N.W., Washington D.C. 20037; (202) 884-1080; Fax, (202) 797-7408; Email: ubalozi@tanzaniaembassy-us.org
U.S. Deputy Chief of Mission in Dar es Salaam: Virginia Blaser
State Dept. Country Office: (202) 647-8295

Thailand   Web, www.thaiembdc.org

Ambassador: Vijavat Isarabhakdi
Chancery: 1024 Wisconsin Ave. N.W. 20007; (202) 944-3600; Fax, (202) 944-3611; Email: information@thaiembdc.org
U.S. Ambassador in Bangkok: Kristie A. Kenney
State Dept. Country Office: (202) 647-0036

Timor-Leste   Web, www.timorlesteembassy.org

Ambassador: Constancio da Conceicao Pinto
Chancery: 4201 Connecticut Ave. N.W., #504, 20008; (202) 966-3202; Fax, (202) 966-3205; Email: info@timorlesteembassy.org
U.S. Ambassador in Dili: Scott Tickner
State Dept. Country Office: (202) 647-1823

Togo   Web, www.togoleseembassy.com

Ambassador: Limbiyè Edawe Kadangha Bariki
Chancery: 2208 Massachusetts Ave. N.W. 20008; (202) 234-4212; Fax, (202) 232-3190; Email: info@togoembassy.us
U.S. Ambassador in Lomé: Robert E. Whitehead
State Dept. Country Office: (202) 647-1540

Tonga   Web, www.tongaconsul.com

Consul General: Sela Tukia (Acting)
Chancery: 360 Post St., #604, San Francisco, CA 94108; (415) 781-0365; Fax, (414) 781-3964; Email: consulategeneraloftonga@gmail.com
U.S. Ambassador: Frankie A. Reed (resident in Suva, Fiji)
State Dept. Country Office: (202) 647-5156

Trinidad and Tobago   Web, www.ttembassy.org

Ambassador: Neil Parsan
Chancery: 1708 Massachusetts Ave. N.W. 20036; (202) 467-6490; Fax, (202) 785-3130
U.S. Chargé d'Affaires in Port-of-Spain: Margaret Diop
State Dept. Country Office: (202) 647-4384

Tunisia   Web, www.tunconsusa.org

Ambassador: Mokhtar Chaouachi
Chancery: 1515 Massachusetts Ave. N.W. 20005; (202) 862-1850; Fax, (202) 862-1858; Email: info@tunconsusa.org
U.S. Ambassador in Tunis: Jacob Walles
State Dept. Country Office: (202) 647-4676

Turkey   Web, www.turkishembassy.org

Ambassador: Namik Tan

Chancery: 2525 Massachusetts Ave. N.W. 20008; (202) 612-6701; Fax, (202) 612-6744; Email: embassy.washingtondc@mfa.gov.tr
U.S. Ambassador in Ankara: Francis J. Ricciardone, Jr.
State Dept. Country Office: (202) 647-6113

Turkmenistan   Web, http://turkmenistanembassy.org

Ambassador: Meret B. Orazov
Chancery: 2207 Massachusetts Ave. N.W. 20008; (202) 588-1500; Fax, (202) 280-1003; Email: turkmenembassyus@verizon.net
U.S. Ambassador in Ashgabat: Robert Patterson
State Dept. Country Office: (202) 647-9031

Tuvalu

Ambassador: Aunese Makoi Simati
U.S. Ambassador: Frankie A. Reed
State Dept. Country Office: (202) 647-5156

Uganda   Web, www.ugandaembassy.com

Ambassador: Oliver Wonekha
Chancery: 5911 16th St. N.W. 20011; (202) 726-7100; Fax, (202) 726-1727
U.S. Ambassador in Kampala: Scott DeLisl
State Dept. Country Office: (202) 647-5924

Ukraine   Web, www.mfa.gov.ua/usa/en

Ambassador: Olexander Motsyk
Chancery: 3350 M St. N.W. 20007; (202) 349-2920; Fax, (202) 333-0817; Email: owonekha@ugandaembassyus.org
U.S. Ambassador in Kiev: Geoffrey R. Pyatt
State Dept. Country Office: (202) 647-8671

United Arab Emirates   Web, www.uae-embassy.org

Ambassador: Yousef Al Otaiba
Chancery: 3522 International Court N.W., #400, 20008; (202) 243-2400; Fax, (202) 243-2432
U.S. Ambassador in Abu Dhabi: Michael H. Corbin
State Dept. Country Office: (202) 647-4709

United Kingdom   Web, ukinusa.fco.gov.uk/en

Ambassador: Sir Peter Westmacott
Chancery: 3100 Massachusetts Ave. N.W. 20008; (202) 588-6500; Fax, (202) 588-7870; Email: britishembassyenquiries@gmail.com
U.S. Ambassador to London: Mathew Barzun
State Dept. Country Office: (202) 647-6557

Uruguay   Web, www.uruwashi.org

Ambassador: Carlos Pita Alvariza
Chancery: 1913 Eye St. N.W. 20006; (202) 331-1313; Fax, (202) 331-8142; Email: uruwashi@uruwashi.org
U.S. Chargé d'Affaires in Montevideo: Julissa Reynoso
State Dept. Country Office: (202) 647-1551

Uzbekistan   Web, www.uzbekistan.org

Ambassador: Bakhtiyar Gulyamov
Chancery: 1746 Massachusetts Ave. N.W. 20036; (202) 887-5300; Fax, (202) 293-6804; Email: info@uzbekistan.org
U.S. Ambassador in Tashkent: George A. Krol
State Dept. Country Office: (202) 647-6765

Vanuatu   Web, www.vanuatuun.us

Email: info@vanuatuun.us
U.S. Ambassador: Walter E. North (resident in Port Moresby, Papua New Guinea)
State Dept. Country Office: (202) 647-5156

Vatican   City (See The Holy See)

Venezuela   Web, http://venezuela-us.org

Chargé d'Affaires: Angelo Rivero Santos
Chancery: 1099 30th St. N.W. 20007; (202) 342-2214; Fax, (202) 342-6820
U.S. Chargé d'Affaires in Caracas: Philip C. Laidlaw
State Dept. Country Office: (202) 647-4984

Vietnam   Web, http://vietnamembassy-usa.org

Ambassador: Nguyen Quoc Cuong
Chancery: 1233 20th St. N.W., #400, 20036; (202) 861-0737; Fax, (202) 861-0917; Email: info@vietnamembassy.us
U.S. Ambassador in Hanoi: David B. Shear
State Dept. Country Office: (202) 647-4023

Western Samoa   (See Samoa)

Yemen   Web, www.yemenembassy.org

Chargé d'Affaires: Adel Alsunaini
Chancery: 2319 Wyoming Ave. N.W. 20008; (202) 965-4760; Fax, (202) 337-2017; Email: Ambassador@YemenEmbassy.org
U.S. Ambassador in Sanaa: Gerald Michael Feierstein
State Dept. Country Office: (202) 647-6558

Zambia   Web, www.zambiaembassy.org

Ambassador: Palan Mulonda
Chancery: 2419 Massachusetts Ave. N.W. 20008; (202) 265-9717; Fax, (202) 332-0826; Email: geninfo@zambiaembassy.org
U.S. Chargé d'Affaires in Lusaka: David J. Young (Interim)
State Dept. Country Office: (202) 647-9857

Zimbabwe   Web, www.zimbabwe-embassy.us

Ambassador: Machivenyika T. Mapuranga
Chancery: 1608 New Hampshire Ave. N.W. 20009; (202) 332-7100; Fax, (202) 483-9326; Email: info33@zimbabwe-embassy.us
U.S. Ambassador in Harare: David Bruce Wharton
State Dept. Country Office: (202) 647-9852

Freedom of Information Act

Access to government information remains a key issue in Washington. In 1966, Congress passed legislation to broaden access: the Freedom of Information Act, or FOIA (PL 89-487; codified in 1967 by PL 90-23). Amendments to expand access even further were passed into law over President Gerald Ford's veto in 1974 (PL 93-502).

Several organizations in Washington specialize in access to government information. See the "Freedom of Information" section in the Communications and the Media chapter for details (p. 98). The Justice Department electronically publishes a clearinghouse of FOIA information at http://www.justice.gov/oip/foia-resources.html.

1966 Act

The 1966 act requires executive branch agencies and independent commissions of the federal government to make records, reports, policy statements, and staff manuals available to citizens who request them, unless the materials fall into one of nine exempted categories:

- secret national security or foreign policy information
- internal personnel practices
- information exempted by law (e.g., income tax returns)
- trade secrets, other confidential commercial or financial information
- inter-agency or intra-agency memos
- personal information, personnel or medical files
- law enforcement investigatory information
- information related to reports on financial institutions
- geological and geophysical information

1974 Amendments

Further clarification of the rights of citizens to gain access to government information came in late 1974, when Congress enacted legislation to remove some of the obstacles that the bureaucracy had erected since 1966. Included in the amendments are provisions that:

- Require federal agencies to publish their indexes of final opinions on settlements of internal cases, policy statements, and administrative staff manuals. If, under special circumstances, the indexes are not published, they are to be furnished to any person requesting them for the cost of duplication. The 1966 law simply required agencies to make such indexes available for public inspection and copying.
- Require agencies to release unlisted documents to someone requesting them with a reasonable description (a change designed to ensure that an agency could not refuse to provide material simply because the applicant could not give its precise title).
- Direct each agency to publish a uniform set of fees for providing documents at the cost of finding and copying them. The amendment allows waiver or reduction of those fees when in the public interest.
- Set time limits for agency responses to requests: ten working days for an initial request; twenty working days for an appeal from an initial refusal to produce documents; a possible ten-working-day extension that can be granted only once in a single case.
- Set a thirty-day time limit for an agency response to a complaint filed in court under the act; provide that the courts give such cases priority attention at the appeal, as well as the trial, level.
- Empower federal district courts to order agencies to produce withheld documents and to examine the contested materials privately *(in camera)* to determine if they are properly exempted.
- Require annual agency reports to Congress, including a list of all agency decisions to withhold information requested under the act; the reasons; the appeals; the results; all relevant rules; the fee schedule; and the names of officials responsible for each denial of information.
- Allow courts to order the government to pay attorneys' fees and court costs for persons winning suits against them under the act.
- Authorize a court to find that an agency employee has acted capriciously or arbitrarily in withholding information; stipulate that disciplinary action is determined by Civil Service Commission proceedings.
- Amend and clarify the wording of the national defense and national security exemption to make clear that it applies only to *properly* classified information.
- Amend the wording of the law enforcement exemption to allow withholding of information that, if disclosed, would interfere with enforcement proceedings, deprive someone of a fair trial or hearing, invade personal privacy in an unwarranted way, disclose the identity of a confidential source, disclose investigative techniques, or endanger law enforcement personnel; protect from disclosure all information from a confidential source obtained by a criminal law enforcement agency or a lawful national security investigation.
- Provide that separable non-exempt portions of requested material be released after deletion of the exempt portions.
- Require an annual report from the attorney general to Congress.

1984 Amendments

In 1984 Congress enacted legislation that clarified the requirements of the Central Intelligence Agency (CIA) to respond to citizen requests for information. Included in the amendments are provisions that:

• Authorize the CIA to close from FOIA review certain operational files that contain information on the identities of sources and methods. The measure removed the requirement that officials search the files for material that might be subject to disclosure.

• Reverse a ruling by the Justice Department and the Office of Management and Budget that invoked the Privacy Act to deny individuals FOIA access to information about themselves in CIA records. HR 5164 required the CIA to search files in response to FOIA requests by individuals for information about themselves.

• Require the CIA to respond to FOIA requests for information regarding covert actions or suspected CIA improprieties.

All agencies of the executive branch have issued regulations to implement the Freedom of Information Act. To locate a specific agency's regulations, consult the general index of the *Code of Federal Regulations* under "Information availability" or search in http://www.USA.gov, "FOIA Regulations."

Electronic Freedom of Information Act of 1996

In 1996 Congress enacted legislation clarifying that electronic documents are subject to the same FOIA disclosure rules as are printed documents. The 1996 law also requires federal agencies to make records available to the public in various electronic formats, such as email, compact disc, and files accessible via the Internet. An additional measure seeks to improve the government's response time on FOIA requests by requiring agencies to report annually on the number of pending requests and how long it will take to respond.

Homeland Security Act of 2002

In 2002 Congress passed legislation that established the Homeland Security Department and exempted from FOIA disclosure rules certain information about national defense systems. Included in the act are provisions that:

• Grant broad exemption from FOIA requirements to information that private companies share with the government about vulnerabilities in the nation's critical infrastructure.

• Exempt from FOIA rules and other federal and state disclosure requirements any information about the critical infrastructure that is submitted voluntarily to a covered federal agency to ensure the security of this infrastructure and protected systems; require accompanying statement that such information is being submitted voluntarily in expectation of nondisclosure protection.

• Require the secretary of homeland security to establish procedures for federal agencies to follow in receiving, caring for, and storing critical infrastructure information

that has been submitted voluntarily; provide criminal penalties for the unauthorized disclosure of such information.

Executive Order 13392: Improving Agency Disclosure of Information

On December 14, 2005, President George W. Bush issued Executive Order 13392: Improving Agency Disclosure of Information. The order sought to streamline the effectiveness of government agencies in responding to FOIA requests and to reduce backlogs of FOIA requests. The order did not expand the information available under FOIA. The executive order provided:

• A chief FOIA officer (at the assistant secretary or equivalent level) of each government agency to monitor FOIA compliance throughout the agency. The chief FOIA officer must inform agency heads and the attorney general of the agency's FOIA compliance performance.

• A FOIA Requester Service Center that would serve as the first point of contact for a person seeking information concerning the status of a FOIA request and appropriate information about the agency's FOIA response.

• FOIA public liaisons, supervisory officials who would facilitate further action if a requester had concerns regarding how an initial request was handled by the center staff.

• Requirement that the chief FOIA officer review and evaluate the agency's implementation and administration of FOIA pursuant to the executive order. The agency head was mandated to report the findings to the attorney general and to the director of the Office of Management and Budget. The report also must be published on the agency's Web site or in the *Federal Register*. Initial reports were submitted in June 2006, with follow-up plans included in each agency's annual FOIA reports for fiscal years 2006 and 2007 and continuing thereafter.

• The attorney general shall review the agency-specific plans and submit to the president a report on government-wide FOIA implementation. The initial report was submitted in October 2006. The Justice Department publishes annual reports of federal agency compliance on its Web site.

Open Government Act of 2007

On December 31, 2007, President George W. Bush signed the "Openness Promotes Effectiveness in our National (OPEN) Government Act of 2007." The OPEN Government Act amends the Freedom of Information Act (FOIA) by:

• defining "a representative of the news media";

• directing that required attorney fees be paid from an agency's appropriation rather than from the U.S. Treasury's Claims and Judgment Fund;

• prohibiting an agency from assessing search and duplication fees if it fails to comply with FOIA deadlines; and establishing an Office of Government Information Services within the National Archives and Records Administration to review agency compliance with FOIA.

Executive Order 13526: Classified National Security Information

On December 29, 2009, an Executive Order on Classified National Security Information was issued. The Executive Order contains two parts:

● The government may classify certain types of information pertaining to the National Security interests of the United States, even after a FOIA request has been submitted. They may do so if they believe that keeping the information secret is necessary for National Security.

● Additionally, the order sets a timeline for automatic declassification of old information that has not been specifically tagged as needing to remain secret.

H.R. 4173: The Dodd – Frank Wall Street Reform and Consumer Protection Act

H.R. 4173 was passed in both the House and Senate and signed by President Barack Obama on July 21, 2010. The law has specific implications for the FOIA, and they are as follows:

● Section 9291 of the statute shields the Securities and Exchange Commission (SEC) from FOIA requests, because of the worry that FOIA requests could potentially hinder SEC investigations.

S. 3717, a Bill to Amend the Securities Exchange Act of 1934, the Investment Company Act of 1940, and the Investment Advisers Act of 1940 to Provide for Certain Disclosures Under Section 552 of Title 5, United States Code, (Commonly Referred to as the Freedom of Information Act), and for Other Purposes

This legislation passed both the House and Senate in late September 2010, and it was signed by President Obama on October 5, 2010. The laws FOIA applications are as follows:

● The provision in S. 3717 essentially rolls back the shielding of the SEC from FOIA requests, as previously mandated by Section 9291 of H.R. 4173.

FOIA Oversight and Implementation Act of 2014

A bill introduced on March 15, 2013 to amend the Freedom of Information Act to make it easier to request and receive information. Under the amendment, the Office of Management and Budget would be required to operate a free Web site where users could submit requests for records and receive information on the status of said request. The bill would also:

● Require agencies to determine whether the release of agency records would contribute significantly to public understanding of the operations or activities of government

● Require agencies to document additional search or duplication fees

● Require agencies to submit annual FOIA reports to the Director of the Office of Government Information Services, in addition to the Attorney General

● Expand the duties of the Chief FOIA Officer of each agency to require an annual compliance review of FOIA requirements

● Establish the Chief FOIA Officers Council to develop recommendations for increasing compliance with FOIA requirements

● Require each agency to update its FOIA regulations within 180 days of the enactment of this Act

● Requires the Inspector General of each federal agency to:

　● Periodically review compliance with FOIA disclosure requirements, including the timely processing of requests, assessment of fees and fee waivers, and the use of disclosure exemptions; and

　● Make recommendations to the head of an agency, including recommendations for disciplinary action. Makes the improper withholding of information under FOIA a basis for disciplinary action

Privacy Legislation

Privacy Act

To protect citizens from invasions of privacy by the federal government, Congress passed the Privacy Act of 1974 (PL 93-579). The act permitted individuals for the first time to inspect information about themselves contained in federal agency files and to challenge, correct, or amend the material. The major provisions of the act:

• Permit an individual to have access to personal information in federal agency files and to correct or amend that information.

• Prevent an agency maintaining a file on an individual from making it available to another agency without the individual's consent.

• Require federal agencies to keep records that are necessary, lawful, accurate, and current, and to disclose the existence of all databanks and files containing information on individuals.

• Bar the transfer of personal information to other federal agencies for nonroutine use without the individual's prior consent or written request.

• Require agencies to keep accurate accountings of transfers of records and make them available to the individual.

• Prohibit agencies from keeping records on an individual's exercise of First Amendment rights unless the records are authorized by statute, approved by the individual, or within the scope of an official law enforcement activity.

• Permit an individual to seek injunctive relief to correct or amend a record maintained by an agency and permit the individual to recover actual damages when an agency acts in a negligent manner that is "willful or intentional."

• Exempt from disclosure records maintained by the Central Intelligence Agency; records maintained by law enforcement agencies; Secret Service records; statistical information; names of persons providing material used for determining the qualification of an individual for federal government service; federal testing material; and National Archives historical records.

• Provide that an officer or employee of an agency who violates provisions of the act be fined no more than $5,000.

• Prohibit an agency from selling or renting an individual's name or address for mailing list use.

• Require agencies to submit to Congress and to the Office of Management and Budget any plan to establish or alter records. Virtually all agencies of the executive branch have issued regulations to implement the Privacy Act.

To locate a specific agency's regulations, consult the general index of the Code of Federal Regulations under "Privacy Act" or search in www.USA.gov, "Privacy Act."

USA PATRIOT Act

Following the terrorist attacks of September 11, 2001, Congress passed the USA PATRIOT Act (Uniting and Strengthening America by Providing Appropriate Tools Required to Intercept and Obstruct Terrorism; PL 107-56). Included in the USA PATRIOT Act are provisions that:

• Amend the federal criminal code to authorize the interception of wire, oral, and electronic communications to produce evidence of chemical weapons, terrorism, and computer fraud and abuse.

• Amend the Foreign Intelligence Surveillance Act of 1978 (FISA) to require an application for an electronic surveillance order or search warrant certifying that a significant purpose (formerly, the sole or main purpose) of the surveillance is to obtain foreign intelligence information. The administration of President George W. Bush aggressively defended its use of wiretaps approved by the Foreign Intelligence Surveillance Court, which handles intelligence requests involving suspected spies, terrorists, and foreign agents. Established under FISA, this court operates secretly within the Justice Department.

USA PATRIOT Improvement and Reauthorization Act of 2005 and USA PATRIOT Act Additional Reauthorizing Amendments Act of 2006

Some provisions of the USA PATRIOT Act were set to expire at the end of 2005. After a lengthy battle Congress voted to reauthorize the act with some of the more controversial provisions intact, including the FISA amendments and the electronic wiretap provisions. Civil libertarians were concerned with issues regarding four provisions: sections 206 (roving wiretaps), 213 (delayed notice warrants), 215 (business records), and 505 (national security letters). The Senate addressed some of these concerns in a separate bill, S. 2271, USA PATRIOT Act Additional Reauthorizing Amendments Act of 2006.

On March 9, 2006, the president signed into law the USA PATRIOT Improvement and Reauthorization Act of 2005 as well as the USA PATRIOT Act Additional Reauthorizing Amendments Act of 2006.

The reauthorized USA PATRIOT Act allows for greater congressional oversight and judicial review of section 215 orders, section 206 roving wiretaps, and national security letters. In addition, the act included requirements for high-level approval for section 215 FISA orders for library, bookstore, firearm sale, medical, tax return, and educational records. The act also provided for greater judicial review for delayed notice ("sneak and peek") search warrants. Fourteen of sixteen USA PATRIOT Act provisions were made permanent, and a new sunset date of December 31, 2009, was enacted for sections 206 and 215.

On February 27, 2010, President Barack Obama signed a one-year extension of sections 206 and 215 of the USA PATRIOT Act.

On May 26, 2011, President Barack Obama signed three expiring provisions of the USA PATRIOT Act into law for four more years. These expiring provisions included sections 215, 206, and 6001.

Homeland Security Act of 2002

The Homeland Security Act of 2002 was also passed in the aftermath of the September 11, 2001, terrorist attacks. It contains provisions that:

• Establish the Homeland Security Department.

• Exempt from criminal penalties any disclosure made by an electronic communication service to a federal, state, or local government. In making the disclosure, the service must believe that an emergency involving risk of death or serious physical injury requires disclosure without delay. Any government agency receiving such disclosure must report it to the attorney general.

• Direct the secretary of homeland security to appoint a senior department official to take primary responsibility for information privacy policy.

Protect America Act and Subsequent Follow-up Legislation

On August 5, 2007, President George W. Bush signed the Protect America Act, which amended the Foreign Intelligence Surveillance Act of 1978 (FISA), declaring that nothing under its definition of "electronic surveillance" shall be construed to encompass surveillance directed at a person reasonably believed to be located outside the United States. Prior to this act, no court permission was obtained for surveillance of parties located outside the United States, though a warrant was required for electronic surveillance of targets within the United States. The Protect America Act allowed the Attorney General or the Director of National Intelligence to direct a third party (i.e., telecommunications provider) to assist with intelligence gathering about individuals located outside the United States and shields such parties from liability without a warrant from the FISA Court. The act did provide FISA Court oversight via requiring the Attorney General to submit to the FISA Court the procedures by which the government determines that such acquisitions do not constitute electronic surveillance. The Attorney General was required to report to the congressional intelligence and judiciary committees semiannually concerning acquisitions made during the previous six-month period.

The Protect America Act was designed as a temporary act to allow intelligence policy officials six months to establish a permanent law. The act expired 180 days later in January; it was briefly reauthorized and expired in February 2008. The Senate passed the FISA Amendments Act of 2007 (S. 2248) in February, which would make many of the provisions of the Protect America Act permanent. However, House leadership objected to many of the provisions. Instead, the House supported its version, the Respected Electronic Surveillance That is Overseen, Reviewed and Effective (RESTORE) Act (H. 3773). This act authorizes the Attorney General and the Director of National Intelligence to conduct electronic surveillance of persons outside the United States in order to acquire foreign intelligence, but places limitations, including: the methods must be conducted in a manner consistent with the Fourth Amendment to the U.S. Constitution and it prohibits targeting of persons reasonably believed to be in the United States (with exceptions). As amended, the bill allowed for limited retroactive immunity for telecommunications service providers. It provides for greater court oversight for targeting procedures, minimization procedures, and guidelines for obtaining warrants. The act expired December 31, 2009, when certain provisions of the PATRIOT Act expired.

2013–2014 Supreme Court Cases Affecting Privacy

Fernandez v. California
Holding: The Court's decision in *Georgia v. Randolph*, holding that the consent of one occupant is insufficient to authorize police to search a premises if another occupant is present and objects to the search, does not apply when an occupant provides consent well after the objecting occupant has been removed from the premises.
Judgment: Affirmed, 6-3, in an opinion by Justice Alito on February 25, 2014. Justice Scalia and Justice Thomas filed concurring opinions. Justice Ginsburg filed a dissenting opinion in which Justice Sotomayor and Justice Kagan joined.

Navarette v. California
Issue: Whether the Fourth Amendment requires an officer who receives an anonymous tip regarding a drunken or reckless driver to corroborate dangerous driving before stopping the vehicle. *(Still circulating as of 3/11/14)*

Riley v. California
Issue: Whether evidence admitted at petitioner's trial was obtained in a search of petitioner's cell phone that violated petitioner's Fourth Amendment rights. (Riley's petition had posed a general question about whether the Fourth Amendment allowed police without a warrant to search "the digital contents of an individual's cellphone seized from the person at the time of arrest." In granting review, the Court said it would only rule on this issue: "Whether evidence admitted at [his] trial was obtained in a search of [his] cellphone that violated [his] Fourth Amendment rights.") *(Still circulating as of 3/11/14)*

United States v. Wurie
Issue: Whether the Fourth Amendment permits the police, without obtaining a warrant, to review the call log of a cellphone found on a person who has been lawfully arrested. *(Still circulating as of 3/11/14)*

Name Index

Barton, Joe (R–Texas), 699, 728, 735, 736, 751
Barton, Rick, 423, 550
Bartz, Merlin, 777
Barutta, Daniel, 486
Bascetta, Cynthia A., 320
Basheerud-Deen, Hakeem, 179, 206, 209, 298, 302, 541
Bashista, John, 307
Basile, Julie, 307
Baskerville, Lezli, 182
Basla, Michael J., 575
Basla, Michael, 91
Basnight, Elisa, 538
Bassani, Antonella, 445
Bass-Cors, Sandy, 680
Bass, Jared, 701
Bass, Karen (D–Calif.), 698, 725, 738, 740, 741, 749, 751
Basta, Daniel J., 282
Bates, Rick, 189, 597
Bates, Scott, 717
Battey, James F., Jr., 347, 648
Batz, Nick, 762
Bauer, Ben, 806
Bauer, Kirk M., 142, 645
Bauer, Tommy, 826
Baugher, Dana, 796
Baugh, Terry, 637
Baukol, Andrew, 231
Bauld, Denise, 830
Bauman, Barry, 473
Baumgarten, Alexander, 146
Baxter, William, 598
Bayens, Dan, 837
Bayer, Mark, 834
Bayer, Thomas A., 91
Beale, Ashley, 800
Beal, Robert E., 263
Bealle, Michael, 12, 39, 388, 410
Beall, Robert J., 364, 369
Bean, Brian, 710
Bean, Chuck, 315
Beans, Robert, 796
Beard, Jean-Louise, 791
Beard, Michael K., 502
Beat, Jerry, 208
Beatty, Joyce (D–Ohio), 728, 737, 738, 751
Beaty, Lisa, 661
Beauchemin, Patricia, 374
Beaudoin, Joseph, 304
Beaudreau, Tommy P., 223, 279, 280
Becerra, Xavier (D–Calif.), 703, 725, 747, 749, 751
Becker, Alex, 706
Becker, Bill, 269
Becker, Jonathan, 833
Becker, Mike, 71
Becker, Robert, 790
Becker, Scott, 340
Becker, Sylvia, 434
Beck, Roy, 197, 431
Beckmann, David, 27
Bedford, Paula E., 208
Beebe-Center, William Horton, 465
Beede, Christopher, 453
Begich, Mark (D–Ala.), 704, 725, 810, 811, 813, 817, 818, 820, 822, 824
Beh, Nancy, 767
Behrmann, Michael M., 645
Behrouz, Liz, 824
Belair, Brendan, 759
Belcher, Scott, 678
Belkind, Myron, 105

Bellaman, Michael, 392
Bell, Alison, 834
Bell, Ford W., 123
Bell, Hubert T., 301
Bell, Jacque, 782
Bell, Kirk, 700
Bell, Mark, 801
Bell, Michael, 98
Bell, Peter H., 401, 409
Bell, Phil, 69
Benard, Barb, 544
BenAvram, Debra, 21
Benda, Leigh, 298
Benishek, Dan (R–Mich.), 727, 730, 741, 742, 746, 751
Benjamin, Caren, 717
Benjamin, Georges, 321, 356
Benjamin, Maynard H., 65
Bennet, Michael F. (D–Colo.), 721, 725, 809, 815, 817, 822, 824
Bennett, Cheryl, 793
Bennett, Craig A., 275
Bennett, Mike, 839
Bennett, Naomi King/Cheryl, 834
Bennett, Shannon, 438
Bennett, Stephen, 372, 646
Bennett, Tim, 457
Benson, David, 299
Benson, Martha, 295
Benson-Walker, Gwen, 787
Bent, Charlotte, 793
Bent, Rodney, 418, 445
Bentivolio, Kerry (R–Mich.), 727, 742, 743, 744, 752
Bentsen, Kenneth, Jr., 63
Bera, Ami (D–Calif.), 725, 738, 743, 744, 752
Berardi, Dana, 204
Berardini, Chris, 770
Bercaw, Sarah, 531
Berenbach, Shari, 452
Berger, Dan, 60
Berger, Thomas J. (Tom), 544
Bergeson, Thomas, 710
Bergey, Barry, 129
Bergin, Christopher, 46
Berglund, Amy, 834
Bergman, Carol, 711
Bergo, Sandy, 103
Bergreen, Timothy S., 796
Bergren, Eric, 770
Berkowitz, Barry, 307
Berkowitz, Scott, 500, 639
Berlase, George, 47, 399
Berman, Alan, 377
Berman, Ellen, 225
Berman, Henry L., 138
Berman, Richard, 50, 194, 213
Bernal, Dan, 789
Bernal, Janet, 208
Bernal, Les, 144
Bernanke, Ben S., 31, 40, 57, 61
Berner, Georgia, 716
Bernier-Toth, Michelle, 435
Berning, Judy, 298
Berns, Peter V., 649
Bernstein, Edward, 66
Bernstein, Robert, 378, 512
Bernstein, Ryan, 832
Berrick, Cathleen, 556, 558, 591
Berrien, Jacqueline A., 206, 207, 208, 481
Berrigan, Michael, 281
Berry, Debbie, 785
Berry, Timothy J., 704

Berry, Tom, 834
Berryhill, Nancy A., 653
Bershteyn, Boris, 96, 290, 495, 555
Bertram, Chris, 745
Bertram, Mary, 790
Bertuzzi, Stefano, 604
Best, Rae Ellen, 709
Best-Wong, Benita, 285
Beswick, Paul, 299
Betancourt, Edward A., 435
BetGeorge, Alex, 204
Betts, Maura, 520
Beutler, Jaime Herrera (R–Wash.), 700, 729, 731, 732, 744
Bevacqua, Frank, 259, 435
Beychok, Bradley, 83
Beyerhelm, Chris, 17, 388
Bhargava, Anurima, 181
Bhargava, Deepak, 386, 403, 630
Bhatia, Joe, 65, 601
Bianchi, Dominic, 475
Bianco, Lisa, 762
Bibby, Douglas, 410
Biddick, Dennis, 537
Biden, Jill, 292
Biden, Joseph R., Jr., 292, 293, 706
Bierly, Kim, 826
Biggery, Sarah, 205, 640
Biggs, Jeffrey C., 159
Bilheimer, Linda, 324
Bilirakis, Gus M., 701
Bilirakis, Gus (R–Fla.), 726, 736, 746, 752
Billings, John, 751
Billings, Paul, 268, 369
Billington, James H., 166
Billy, Carrie L., 181
Bimonte, Robert, 178
Bingaman, Bob, 229, 256
Bingaman, Jeff, 699
Bingham, Austin, 753
Bingham, Tony, 186, 202
Bingham, Austin, 753
Birdsall, Nancy, 445
Birks, Heather, 107
Birman, Igor, 783
Birnbaum, Linda S., 251
Birns, Larry R., 459
Birns, Larry, 204
Birogioli, Michael, 646
Birx, Deborah L., 366
Bisacquino, Thomas J., 410
Bishop, Aaron, 641, 649
Bishop, David J., 524
Bishop, Rob (R–Utah), 728, 732, 733, 741, 742, 743, 752
Bishop, Sanford D., Jr. (D–Ga.), 726, 731, 732, 752
Bishop, Tim (D–N.Y.), 727, 735, 745, 746, 752
Bishop, Timothy, 745
Bisograno, John, 721
Bissell, Mary Sue, 455
Biswal, Nisha Desai, 460
Bittner, Brian, 723
Bittner, Mamie, 97
Bixby, Robert L., 42, 718
Blackburn, Marsha (R–Tenn.), 728, 734, 735, 736, 752
Blackburn, Matthew, 840
Black, Andrew J., 240
Black, Barry C., 706
Black, Bob, 785
Black, David F., 475
Black, Diane (R–Tenn.), 728, 734, 747, 752
Black, Edward J., 83, 100, 616

Levin, Carl S. (D–Mich.), 702, 727, 808, 811, 817, 818, 820, 834
Levin, Mark B., 149, 465
Levin, Rachel F., 10, 265
Levin, Sander (D–Mich.), 727, 747, 779, 808
Levin, Saul, 343, 377
Levinson, Daniel, 301
Levy, Joshua, 711
Lew, Jack, 293
Lew, Jacob J., 35, 40
Lewis, Allison L., 337
Lewis, Anisha N., 378
Lewis, Charity, 786
Lewis, Chasseny, 797
Lewis, Craig M., 44, 58, 62, 78
Lewis, Holly, 835
Lewis, James A., 616
Lewis, John (D–Ga.), 726, 747, 779
Lewis, Lorna, 208
Lewis, Lorraine, 217
Lewis, Madeline H., 208
Lewis, Teresa, 77
Lewis, Trey, 803
Lewis, Vicky J., 98
Lhamon, Catherine, 180, 481
Liang, J. Nellie, 31
Licata, Patricia, 711
Lichtenstein, Mark, 273
Lichter, S. Robert, 83, 105
Lidell, Mark, 702
Liebow, Edward, 619
Lies, Daryl, 760
Liftman, Dan, 771
Lightbourne, James H., 158
Light, Malia, 400
Lighthizer, James, 130
Lillis, Joe, 780
Limaye, Satu P., 454, 455
Limón, Lavinia, 426, 432
Lincoln, Paula, 144
Lincoln, Walt, 523, 544
Lindberg, Donald A. B., 354
Lindborg, Nancy E., 423
Lindley, Jeffrey A., 681
Lindquist, Peter, 535
Lindsley, Margaret S., 684
Lindsley, Tom, 168
Linehan, Ann M., 175, 634
Lin, Betsy, 832
Linick, Steve, 301
Lintz, Gilda, 838
Lion, Margo, 112
Liotta, Lance, 356
Lipinski, Daniel (D–Ill.), 699, 726, 743, 744, 745, 746, 779
Lipman, David J., 355, 605
Lippincott, John, 157
Lipscomb, Hunter, 788
Lipscomb, Sara D., 475
Lipsen, Linda, 70, 469
Lipsey, Yolonda, 759
Lipsich, Wendi, 763
Lisack, John, Jr., 333
Lis, Tony, 752
Liske, Jim, 507
Lisk, Barbara, 772
Liss, Cathy, 262, 266
Listenbee, Robert L., Jr., 503, 635
Littlefield, Elizabeth L., 442
Little, Caroline, 109
Little, George E., 96
Little, Margaret, 365, 606
Liu, Amy, 390
Liu, Lawrence T., 436

Liu, Simon Y., 6, 22
Livornese, John, 98
Lloyd, Matt, 800
Loar, Peggy, 123
LoBiondo, Frank A. (R–N.J.), 700, 727, 732, 733, 745, 746, 748, 779
LoBiondo, Frank, 745
Lobue, Christian, 758
Locasio, Laurie E., 598, 618
Loebsack, Dave (D–Iowa), 726, 732, 733, 735, 780
Loebsack, David, 735
Lofgren, Zoe (D–Calif.), 698, 725, 740, 741, 743, 744, 780, 807
Logan, Cherita, 761
Logan, Linda, 521
LoGrande, Michael F., 530
Loh, Julien, 762
Loh, Wallace D., 170
Lohman, Walter, 454
Lohnes, Robin C., 262
Loiko, Patricia, 119
Lomax, Michael L., 183
Lombard, Charles, 577, 583, 623
Lomellin, Carmen, 458
LoMonte, Frank, 108
Long, Billy (R–Mo.), 727, 736, 780
Long, Cindy, 19, 634
Long, Edward L., Jr., 314
Long, Gregory T., 215
Long, Jamie, 764
Long, Letitia A., 583, 620
Longowski, Greg, 838
Longwell, Sarah, 23
Lonsway, Peter, 135
Loosle, Byron, 128, 283
Loosli, Michelle, 370
Lopach, Tom, 840
Lopez-Buck, Anna, 104
Lopez, Arthur A., 98
Lopez, Javier, 797
Lopez, Juan, 760
Lopez, Lesley J., 699
Lopez, Mark, 432, 803
Lopez, P. David, 474
Lopp, Kathie, 832
Lordan, Tim, 101, 695
Lord, Kristin, 416, 429, 558
Lord, Mark, 770
Lorentzen, Ronald K., 441
Lorenz, Andrew, 779
Lorsch, Jon, 353, 603
Lott, Alfred, 174
Louwagie, Meg, 789, 790
Love, James, 596
Love, Jean, 526
Love, Reba, 797
Lovelady, Denise, 771
Lowder, Michael, 571, 585, 659
Lowe, Eugene T., 651
Lowe, Luellen, 828
Lowe, Mary Frances, 20, 434
Lowenthal, Alan (D–Calif.), 725, 738, 739, 741, 742, 780
Lowery, Edward, 89, 578
Lowey, Nita (D–N.Y.), 727, 731, 732, 780
Loyo, Lisa, 661
Loza, Moises, 388, 401, 651
Lu, Christopher P., 195
Lubell, Michael, 241, 618
Lucas, David G., 763
Lucas, Frank (R–Okla.), 728, 730, 737, 743, 744, 780
Lucas, Richard (Rich), 19, 634

Luciano, Mark, 788
Luck, Holly, 841
Ludwig, Terry L., 401
Luebke, Thomas, 112
Luetkemeyer, Blaine (R–Mo.), 727, 737, 744, 780
Luévano, Mary, 257
Lu, Christopher, 292
Lu, Michael, 363
Luft, Gal, 246
Lugar, Katherine, 151
Luján, Ben Ray (D–N.M.), 699, 701, 727, 736, 780
Lujan Grisham, Michelle (D–N.M.), 699, 734, 781
Lukken, Walter L., 62
Lukow, Gregory, 116, 126
Lukowski, Gary A., 298
Luksenburg, Harvey, 364
Lummis, Cynthia (R–Wyo.), 701, 729, 741, 742, 743, 744, 781
Lumpkin, Drew, 842
Lumpkin, Michael D., 547, 581
Lund, Adrian, 676, 682
Lundsager, Meg, 418, 451
Lunzer, Bernard J., 105
Luparaello, Stephen, 62
Lupis, Jeffery, 307
Lurie, Nicole, 320, 579
Lushniak, Boris D., 317
Lusk, Cody, 679
Lussier, Thomas, 216
Luthi, Randall, 239, 248, 283, 613
Lutschaunig, Mark, 261
Luttrell, Edward L., 4
Lux, Michael, 717
Luzier, Michael, 396
Lybarger, Stephen A., 57
Lyles, Loctifa, 211
Lyles, Sylvia, 174
Lyman, John, 232
Lynch, Christopher W., 826
Lynch, Clifford A., 100
Lynch, John, 94, 507
Lynch, Kevin, 647
Lynch, Mike, 785, 838
Lynch, Neil, 775
Lynch, Robert L., 112
Lynch, Stephen F. (D–Mass.), 727, 737, 742, 743, 781
Lynn, Barry W., 145, 177, 496
Lynn, La'Tonya, 709
Lyons, Chris, 105
Lyons, James E., 170
Lyons, Judd, 536
Lyons, Peter B., 243
Lytle, Laura, 105
Lyttle, Peter T., 612, 620
Lytton, Al, 764

Maben, Meri, 773
Mabus, Raymond E. (Ray) Jr., 550
Maccabe, Andrew T., 261
MacDonald, Brian C., 803
Macdonald, Charlene, 796
MacDonald, Don, 798
MacDonough, Elizabeth C., 703
Macey, Scott, 70, 217
MacGuineas, Maya, 718
Machida, Ado, 429, 558
MacIntyre, Douglas M., 238, 246
Mackabee, William, 450
Mackay, Trent, 362, 375
Mackey, James G., 298

Organization Index

CQ Roll Call, 691
CQ Weekly, 104
Cradle of Hope, 636
Credit Union Legislative Action Council, 715
Credit Union National Assn., 59
Criminal Division, 497
 Asset Forfeiture and Money Laundering, 503
 Child Exploitation and Obscenity, 499
 Computer Crime and Intellectual Property, 94, 507
 Enforcement Operations, 497
  International Prisoner Transfer Unit, 497
 Fraud, 504
 Narcotic and Dangerous Drugs, 500, 503
 Organized Crime and Gang Section, 211, 215, 497, 503
Critical Incident Response Group, Strategic Information and
 Operations Center, 582
Crohns and Colitis Caucus, 701
Croplife America, 8
Cruise Lines International Assn., 151, 674
C-SPAN, 104
 internships, 204
CTAM, 86
CTIA—The Wireless Assn., 89
Cultural Diversity in the Church, Office of Hispanic Affairs, 485
Current Employment Statistics
 National, 198
 State and Area, 198
CWA-COPE Political Contributions Committee, 712
Cyber Crimes Center (C3), 95
Cyber Security Policy and Research Institute, 100
Cybersecurity and Communications, 577
Cystic Fibrosis Foundation, 364, 369

Dance/USA, 127
Dangerous Goods Advisory Council, 271
Data Interchange Standards Assn. (DISA), 100
Daughters of the American Revolution, National Society,
 130, 133
Daughters of the American Revolution (DAR) Museum,
 museum education programs, 120
David S. Wyman Institute for Holocaust Studies, 130, 419
DC Immigration Blog, 562
DC Vote, 695
Dealers Election Action Committee of the National Automobile
 Dealers Assn., 715
Death Penalty Information Center, 472
DECA Inc., 157
Decatur House, museum education programs, 120
Defence Intelligence Agency, counterterrorism resources and
 contacts, 581
Defenders of Wildlife, 266
Defense Acquisition University, 528, 590
Defense Advanced Research Projects Agency, 95, 565
Defense Contract Audit Agency (DCAA), 556, 590
Defense Credit Union Council, 523
Defense Department (DoD), 547, 208
 Accession Policy, 526, 528
 Accounting and Finance Policy Analysis, 523
 Acquisition, Technology, and Logistics, 590
 Air Force Department. *See that heading*
 Armed Forces Chaplains Board, 518
 Armed Forces Radiobiology Research Institute, 272
 Armed Services Board of Contract Appeals, 590
 Army and Air Force Exchange, 588
 Army Corps of Engineers. *See that heading*
 Army Department. *See that heading*
 Asian and Pacific Security Affairs, 453
 Cabinet member, 293
 Chemical and Biological Defense Program, 558
 Chief Information Officer, 91, 575, 580
 Command, Control, Communications, and Computers, 575
 Community and Public Outreach, 515, 535
 Comptroller, 556
 Congressional Liaisons, 710

Counterintelligence, 586
Counternarcotics and Global Threats, 439, 500
Court of Appeals for the Armed Forces, 531
Defense Acquisition Regulations System (DARS) Directorate
 and DARS Council, 590
Defense Acquisition University, 528, 590
Defense Advanced Research Projects Agency, 95, 565
Defense Commissary Agency, 588
Defense Contract Audit Agency (DCAA), 556, 590
Defense Department Advisory Committee on Women in the
 Services, 520
Defense Health Agency (DHA). *See that heading*
Defense Information Systems Agency (DISA), 581
Defense Intelligence Agency, 582
Defense Logistics Agency. *See that heading*
Defense Prisoners of War/Missing Personnel, 525
Defense Procurement and Acquisition Policy, 590
Defense Security Cooperation Agency, 557
Defense Security Service, 586
Defense Technical Information Center, 565
Defense Technology Security Administration, 563
Defense Threat Reduction Agency, 558
Diversity Management and Equal Opportunity, 520, 530
Dwight D. Eisenhower School for National Security and
 Resource Strategy. *See that heading*
Education Activity, 521
European and NATO Policy, 455, 557
Facilities Investment and Management, 589
Financial Officer, 298
Force Health Protection and Readiness, 542
freedom of information contact, 98
General Counsel, 474
Global Strategic Affairs, 547, 558
Health Affairs, 524
 Clinical Program Policy, 524
Historical Office, 532
Homeland Defense and America's Security Affairs, 547
Inspectors General, 301
Installations and Environment, 269, 547, 587
Intelligence, 580
Intelligence Oversight, 580
International Cooperation, 563
International Security Affairs, 413, 452, 455, 460, 464,
 557, 587
Joint Chiefs of Staff, 547
Joint History Office, 532
Legal Policy, 530–531, 541
Library, 165
Logistics and Materiel Readiness, 590
Manufacturing and Industrial Base Policy, 580
Marine Corps. *See that heading*
Military Compensation, 526–527
Military Personnel Policy, 515
Missile Defense Agency, 565
National Committee for Employer Support of the Guard and
 Reserve (ESGR), 212
National Defense University, 528
National Geospatial-Intelligence Agency. *See that heading*
National Guard Bureau. *See that heading*
National Intrepid Center of Excellence, 524
National Museum of Health and Medicine, 532
National Reconnaissance Office, 583
National Security Agency (NSA). *See that heading*
National War College, 528
Naval Medical Research Center, 524
Naval Research Laboratory, 566
Navy Department. *See that heading*
Office of Economic Adjustment, 385, 588
Operational Test and Evaluation, 590
Personnel and Readiness, 515
Plans, 558
Policy, 547
Procurement Officer, 307
Public Affairs, 106, 515, 525

Subject Index

Entries in **CAPITALS** are chapters.